PEARSON

ALWAYS LEARNING

Reece • Urry • Cain • Wasserman • Minorsky • Jackson

Biology 93

Fifth Custom Edition for University of California, Irvine

Taken from:
Campbell Biology, Tenth Edition
by Jane B. Reece, Lisa A. Urry, Michael L. Cain, Steven A. Wasserman,
Peter V. Minorsky, Robert B. Jackson.

Cover Art: Courtesy of Lenart Nilsson/AlbertBonniersForlag/BoehringerIngelheim/Scanpix

Taken from:

Campbell Biology, Tenth Edition
by Jane B. Reece, Lisa A. Urry, Michael L. Cain, Steven A. Wasserman, Peter V. Minorsky, Robert B. Jackson
Copyright © 2014, 2011, 2008 by Pearson Education, Inc.
Upper Saddle River, New Jersey 07458

This special edition published in cooperation with Pearson Learning Solutions.

Pearson Learning Solutions, 501 Boylston Street, Suite 900, Boston, MA 02116
A Pearson Education Company
www.pearsoned.com

Printed in the United States of America

1 2 3 4 5 6 7 8 9 10 V3N4 17 16 15 14

000200010271886517

AL/JL

ISBN 10: 1-269-92302-1
ISBN 13: 978-1-269-92302-6

1 Evolution, the Themes of Biology, and Scientific Inquiry 1

THE CHEMISTRY OF LIFE 27

2 The Chemical Context of Life 28
3 Water and Life 44
4 Carbon and the Molecular Diversity of Life 56
5 The Structure and Function of Large Biological Molecules 66

THE CELL 92

6 A Tour of the Cell 93
7 Membrane Structure and Function 124
8 An Introduction to Metabolism 141
9 Cellular Respiration and Fermentation 162
10 Photosynthesis 185
11 Cell Communication 210
12 The Cell Cycle 232

GENETICS 251

13 Meiosis and Sexual Life Cycles 252
14 Mendel and the Gene Idea 267
15 The Chromosomal Basis of Inheritance 292

16 The Molecular Basis of Inheritance 312
17 Gene Expression: From Gene to Protein 333
18 Regulation of Gene Expression 360
19 Viruses 392
20 DNA Tools and Biotechnology 408
21 Genomes and Their Evolution 436

ANIMAL FORM AND FUNCTION 866

40 Basic Principles of Animal Form and Function 867
41 Animal Nutrition 892
42 Circulation and Gas Exchange 915
43 The Immune System 946
44 Osmoregulation and Excretion 971
45 Hormones and the Endocrine System 993
46 Animal Reproduction 1013
47 Animal Development 1037
48 Neurons, Synapses, and Signaling 1061
49 Nervous Systems 1079
50 Sensory and Motor Mechanisms 1101
51 Animal Behavior 1133

The Tenth Edition author team's contributions reflect their biological expertise as researchers and their teaching sensibilities gained from years of experience as instructors at diverse institutions. The team's highly collaborative style continues to be evident in the cohesiveness and consistency of the Tenth Edition.

Jane B. Reece

Jane Reece was Neil Campbell's longtime collaborator, and she has participated in every edition of *CAMPBELL BIOLOGY*. Earlier, Jane taught biology at Middlesex County College and Queensborough Community College. She holds an A.B. in biology from Harvard University, an M.S. in microbiology from Rutgers University, and a Ph.D. in bacteriology from the University of California, Berkeley. Jane's research as a doctoral student at UC Berkeley and post-doctoral fellow at Stanford University focused on genetic recombination in bacteria. Besides her work on *CAMPBELL BIOLOGY*, she has been a coauthor on *Campbell Biology in Focus, Campbell Biology: Concepts & Connections, Campbell Essential Biology*, and *The World of the Cell*.

Lisa A. Urry

Lisa Urry is Professor of Biology and Chair of the Biology Department at Mills College in Oakland, California, and a Visiting Scholar at the University of California, Berkeley. After graduating from Tufts University with a double major in biology and French, Lisa completed her Ph.D. in molecular and developmental biology at the Massachusetts Institute of Technology (MIT) in the MIT/Woods Hole Oceanographic Institution Joint Program. She has published a number of research papers, most of them focused on gene expression during embryonic and larval development in sea urchins. Lisa has taught a variety of courses, from introductory biology to developmental biology and senior seminar. As a part of her mission to increase understanding of evolution, Lisa also teaches a nonmajors course called Evolution for Future Presidents and is on the Teacher Advisory Board for the Understanding Evolution website developed by the University of California Museum of Paleontology. Lisa is also deeply committed to promoting opportunities in science for women and underrepresented minorities. Lisa is also a coauthor of *Campbell Biology in Focus*.

Michael L. Cain

Michael Cain is an ecologist and evolutionary biologist who is now writing full-time. Michael earned a joint degree in biology and math at Bowdoin College, an M.Sc. from Brown University, and a Ph.D. in ecology and evolutionary biology from Cornell University. As a faculty member at New Mexico State University and Rose-Hulman Institute of Technology, he taught a wide range of courses, including introductory biology, ecology, evolution, botany, and conservation biology. Michael is the author of dozens of scientific papers on topics that include foraging behavior in insects and plants, long-distance seed dispersal, and speciation in crickets. In addition to his work on *CAMPBELL BIOLOGY* and *Campbell Biology in Focus*, Michael is the lead author of an ecology textbook.

Steven A. Wasserman

Steve Wasserman is Professor of Biology at the University of California, San Diego (UCSD). He earned his A.B. in biology from Harvard University and his Ph.D. in biological sciences from MIT. Through his research on regulatory pathway mechanisms in the fruit fly *Drosophila*, Steve has contributed to the fields of developmental biology, reproduction, and immunity. As a faculty member at the University of Texas Southwestern Medical Center and UCSD, he has taught genetics, development, and physiology to undergraduate, graduate, and medical students. He currently focuses on teaching introductory biology. He has also served as the research mentor for more than a dozen doctoral students and more than 50 aspiring scientists at the undergraduate and high school levels. Steve has been the recipient of distinguished scholar awards from both the Markey Charitable Trust and the David and Lucile Packard Foundation. In 2007, he received UCSD's Distinguished Teaching Award for undergraduate teaching. Steve is also a coauthor of *Campbell Biology in Focus*.

Peter V. Minorsky

Peter Minorsky is Professor of Biology at Mercy College in New York, where he teaches introductory biology, evolution, ecology, and botany. He received his A.B. in biology from Vassar College and his Ph.D. in plant physiology from Cornell University. He is also the science writer for the journal *Plant Physiology*. After a postdoctoral fellowship at the University of Wisconsin at Madison, Peter taught at Kenyon College, Union College, Western Connecticut State University, and Vassar College. His research interests concern how plants sense environmental change. Peter received the 2008 Award for Teaching Excellence at Mercy College. Peter is also a coauthor of *Campbell Biology in Focus*.

Robert B. Jackson

Rob Jackson is the Douglas Professor of Environment and Energy in the Department of Environmental Earth System Science at Stanford University. Rob holds a B.S. in chemical engineering from Rice University, as well as M.S. degrees in ecology and statistics and a Ph.D. in ecology from Utah State University. While a biology professor at Duke University, Rob directed the university's Program in Ecology and was Vice President of Science for the Ecological Society of America. He has received numerous awards, including a Presidential Early Career Award in Science and Engineering from the National Science Foundation. Rob is a Fellow of both the Ecological Society of America and the American Geophysical Union. He also enjoys popular writing, having published a trade book about the environment, *The Earth Remains Forever*, and two books of poetry for children, *Animal Mischief* and *Weekend Mischief*. Rob is also a coauthor of *Campbell Biology in Focus*.

Neil A. Campbell

Neil Campbell (1946–2004) combined the investigative nature of a research scientist with the soul of an experienced and caring teacher. He earned his M.A. in zoology from the University of California, Los Angeles, and his Ph.D. in plant biology from the University of California, Riverside, where he received the Distinguished Alumnus Award in 2001. Neil published numerous research articles on desert and coastal plants and how the sensitive plant (*Mimosa*) and other legumes move their leaves. His 30 years of teaching in diverse environments included introductory biology courses at Cornell University, Pomona College, and San Bernardino Valley College, where he received the college's first Outstanding Professor Award in 1986. Neil was a visiting scholar in the Department of Botany and Plant Sciences at the University of California, Riverside.

We are honored to present the Tenth Edition of *CAMPBELL BIOLOGY*. For the last quarter century, *CAMPBELL BIOLOGY* has been the leading college text in the biological sciences. It has been translated into more than a dozen languages and has provided millions of students with a solid foundation in college-level biology. This success is a testament not only to Neil Campbell's original vision but also to the dedication of thousands of reviewers, who, together with editors, artists, and contributors, have shaped and inspired this work. Although this Tenth Edition represents a milestone, science and pedagogy are not static—as they evolve, so does *CAMPBELL BIOLOGY*.

Our goals for the Tenth Edition include:

- helping students **make connections visually** across the diverse topics of biology
- giving students a strong foundation in **scientific thinking and quantitative reasoning skills**
- inspiring students with the excitement and relevance of modern biology, particularly in the realm of **genomics**

Our starting point, as always, is our commitment to crafting text and visuals that are accurate, are current, and reflect our passion for teaching and learning about biology.

New to This Edition

Here we provide an overview of the new features that we have developed for the Tenth Edition; we invite you to explore pages x–xxvi for more information and examples.

- **Make Connections Figures** draw together topics from different chapters to show how they are all related in the "big picture." By reinforcing fundamental conceptual connections throughout biology, these figures help overcome students' tendencies to compartmentalize information.
- **Scientific Skills Exercises** in every chapter use real data and guide students in learning and practicing data interpretation, graphing, experimental design, and math skills. All 56 Scientific Skills Exercises have assignable, automatically graded versions in **MasteringBiology**®.

- **Interpret the Data Questions** throughout the text engage students in scientific inquiry by asking them to interpret data presented in a graph, figure, or table. The Interpret the Data Questions can be assigned and automatically graded in **MasteringBiology**.
- The impact of genomics across biology is explored throughout the Tenth Edition with examples that reveal how our ability to rapidly sequence DNA and proteins is transforming all areas of biology, from molecular and cell biology to phylogenetics, physiology, and ecology. Chapter 5 provides a launching point for this feature in a new Key Concept, "Genomics and proteomics have transformed biological inquiry and applications." Illustrative examples are distributed throughout later chapters.
- **Synthesize Your Knowledge Questions** at the end of each chapter ask students to synthesize the material in the chapter and demonstrate their big-picture understanding. A striking photograph with a thought-provoking question helps students see how material they learned in the chapter connects to their world and provides insight into natural phenomena.
- The Tenth Edition provides a range of new practice and assessment opportunities in **MasteringBiology.** Besides the Scientific Skills Exercises and Interpret the Data Questions, **Solve It Tutorials** in MasteringBiology engage students in a multistep investigation of a "mystery" or open question. Acting as scientists, students must analyze real data and work through a simulated investigation.

In addition, **Adaptive Follow-Up Assignments** provide coaching and practice that continually adapt to each student's needs, making efficient use of study time. Students can use the **Dynamic Study Modules** to study anytime and anywhere with their smartphones, tablets, or computers.

- **Learning Catalytics**™ allows students to use their smartphones, tablets, or laptops to respond to questions in class.
- As in each new edition of *CAMPBELL BIOLOGY*, the Tenth Edition incorporates **new content** and **organizational improvements**. These are summarized on pp. viii–ix, following this Preface.

Our Hallmark Features

Teachers of general biology face a daunting challenge: to help students acquire a conceptual framework for organizing an ever-expanding amount of information. The hallmark features of CAMPBELL BIOLOGY provide such a framework, while promoting a deeper understanding of biology and the process of science.

To help students distinguish the "forest from the trees," each chapter is organized around a framework of three to seven carefully chosen **Key Concepts**. The text, Concept Check Questions, Summary of Key Concepts, and MasteringBiology all reinforce these main ideas and essential facts.

CAMPBELL BIOLOGY also helps students organize and make sense of what they learn by emphasizing **evolution and other unifying themes** that pervade biology. These themes are introduced in Chapter 1 and are integrated throughout the book. Each chapter includes at least one Evolution section that explicitly focuses on evolutionary aspects of the chapter material, and each chapter ends with an Evolution Connection Question and a Write About a Theme Question.

Because text and illustrations are equally important for learning biology, **integration of text and figures** has been a hallmark of this text since the First Edition. In addition to the new Make Connections Figures, our popular Exploring Figures on selected topics epitomize this approach: Each is a learning unit of core content that brings together related illustrations and text. Another example is our Guided Tour Figures, which use descriptions in blue type to walk students through complex figures as an instructor would. Visual Organizer Figures highlight the main parts of a figure, helping students see key categories at a glance. And Summary Figures visually recap information from the chapter.

To encourage **active reading** of the text, CAMPBELL BIOLOGY includes numerous opportunities for students to stop and think about what they are reading, often by putting pencil to paper to draw a sketch, annotate a figure, or graph data. Active learning questions include Make Connections Questions, What If? Questions, Figure Legend Questions, Draw It Questions, Summary Questions, and the new Synthesize Your Knowledge and Interpret the Data Questions.

Finally, CAMPBELL BIOLOGY has always featured **scientific inquiry**, an essential component of any biology course. Complementing stories of scientific discovery in the text narrative and the unit-opening interviews, our standard-setting Inquiry Figures deepen the ability of students to understand how we know what we know. Scientific Inquiry Questions give students opportunities to practice scientific thinking, along with the new Scientific Skills Exercises and Interpret the Data Questions.

MasteringBiology®

MasteringBiology, the most widely used online assessment and tutorial program for biology, provides an extensive library of homework assignments that are graded automatically. In addition to the new Scientific Skills Exercises, Interpret the Data Questions, Solve It Tutorials, Adaptive Follow-Up Assignments, and Dynamic Study Modules, MasteringBiology offers BioFlix® Tutorials with 3-D Animations, Experimental Inquiry Tutorials, Interpreting Data Tutorials, BLAST Tutorials, Make Connections Tutorials, Video Tutor Sessions, Get Ready for Biology, Activities, Reading Quiz Questions, Student Misconception Questions, 4,500 Test Bank Questions, and MasteringBiology Virtual Labs. MasteringBiology also includes the CAMPBELL BIOLOGY eText, Study Area, and Instructor Resources. See pages xviii–xxi and www.masteringbiology.com for more details.

Our Partnership with Instructors and Students

A core value underlying our work is our belief in the importance of a partnership with instructors and students. One primary way of serving instructors and students, of course, is providing a text that teaches biology well. In addition, Pearson Education offers a rich variety of instructor and student resources, in both print and electronic form (see pp. xviii–xxiii). In our continuing efforts to improve the book and its supplements, we benefit tremendously from instructor and student feedback, not only in formal reviews from hundreds of scientists, but also via e-mail and other avenues of informal communication.

The real test of any textbook is how well it helps instructors teach and students learn. We welcome comments from both students and instructors. Please address your suggestions to any of us:

Jane Reece
    janereece@cal.berkeley.edu
Lisa Urry (Chapter 1 and Units 1–3)
    lurry@mills.edu
Michael Cain (Units 4 and 5)
    mcain@bowdoin.edu
Peter Minorsky (Unit 6)
    pminorsky@mercy.edu
Steven Wasserman (Unit 7)
    stevenw@ucsd.edu
Rob Jackson (Unit 8)
    rob.jackson@stanford.edu

This section highlights selected new content and organizational changes in CAMPBELL BIOLOGY, Tenth Edition.

CHAPTER 1 ## Evolution, the Themes of Biology, and Scientific Inquiry

To help students focus on the big ideas of biology, we now emphasize five themes: Organization, Information, Energy and Matter, Interactions, and the core theme of Evolution. The new Figure 1.8 on gene expression equips students from the outset with an understanding of how gene sequences determine an organism's characteristics. Concept 1.3 has been reframed to more realistically reflect the scientific process, including a new figure on the complexity of the practice of science (Figure 1.23). A new case study in scientific inquiry (Figures 1.24 and 1.25) deals with evolution of coloration in mice.

 ## 1 The Chemistry of Life

New chapter-opening photos and introductory stories engage students in learning this foundational material. Chapter 2 has a new Evolution section on radiometric dating. In Chapter 5, there is a new Key Concept section, "Genomics and proteomics have transformed biological inquiry and applications" (Concept 5.6), and a new Make Connections Figure, "Contributions of Genomics and Proteomics to Biology" (Figure 5.26).

2 The Cell

Our main goal for this unit was to make the material more accessible to students. We have streamlined coverage of the cytoskeleton in Chapter 6 and historical aspects of the membrane model in Chapter 7. We have revised the photosynthesis summary figure (Figure 10.22) to incorporate a big-picture view of photosynthesis. The new Make Connections Figure 10.23 integrates the cellular activities covered in Chapters 5–10 in the context of a single plant cell. Concept 12.3 has been streamlined, with a new Figure 12.17 that covers the M checkpoint as well as the G_1 checkpoint.

 ## 3 Genetics

In Chapters 13–17, we have incorporated changes that help students make connections between the more abstract concepts of genetics and their molecular underpinnings. For example, Chapter 13 includes a new figure (Figure 13.9) detailing the events of crossing over during prophase. Figure 14.4, showing alleles on chromosomes, has been enhanced to show the DNA sequences of both alleles, along with their biochemical and phenotypic consequences. A new figure on sickle-cell disease also connects these levels (Figure 14.17). In Chapter 17, material on coupled transcription and translation in bacteria has been united with coverage of polyribosomes.

Chapters 18–21 are extensively updated, driven by exciting new discoveries based on high-throughput sequencing. Chapter 18 includes a new figure (Figure 18.15) on the role of siRNAs in chromatin remodeling. A new Make Connections Figure (Figure 18.27) describes four subtypes of breast cancer that have recently been proposed, based on gene expression in tumor cells. In Chapter 20, techniques that are less commonly used have been pruned, and the chapter has been reorganized to emphasize the important role of sequencing. A new figure (Figure 20.4) illustrates next-generation sequencing. Chapter 21 has been updated to reflect new research, including the ENCODE project, the Cancer Genome Atlas, and the genome sequences of the gorilla and bonobo. A new figure (Figure 21.15) compares the 3-D structures of lysozyme and α-lactalbumin and their amino acid sequences, providing support for their common evolutionary origin.

 ## 4 Mechanisms of Evolution

One goal of this revision was to highlight connections among fundamental evolutionary concepts. Helping meet this goal, new material connects Darwin's ideas to what can be learned from phylogenetic trees, and a new figure (Figure 25.13) and text illustrate how the combined effects of speciation and extinction determine the number of species in different groups of organisms. The unit also features new material on nucleotide variability within genetic loci, including a new figure (Figure 23.4) that shows variability within coding and noncoding regions of a gene. Other changes enhance the storyline of the unit. For instance, Chapter 25 includes new text on how the rise of large eukaryotes in the Ediacaran period represented a monumental transition in the history of life—the end of a microbe-only world. Updates include revised discussions of the events and underlying causes of the Cambrian explosion and the Permian mass extinction, as well as new figures providing fossil evidence of key evolutionary events, such as the formation of plant-fungi symbioses (Figure 25.12). A new Make Connections Figure (Figure 23.17) explores the sickle-cell allele and its impact from the molecular and cellular levels to organisms to the evolutionary explanation for the allele's global distribution in the human population.

5 The Evolutionary History of Biological Diversity

In keeping with our Tenth Edition goals, we have expanded the coverage of genomic and other molecular studies and how they inform our understanding of phylogeny. Examples include a new Inquiry Figure (Figure 34.49) on the Neanderthal genome and presentation of new evidence that mutualistic interactions between plants and fungi are ancient. In addition, many phylogenies have been revised to reflect recent miRNA and genomic data. The unit also contains new material on tree-thinking, such as a new figure (Figure 26.11) that distinguishes between paraphyletic and polyphyletic taxa. We continue to emphasize evolutionary events that underlie the diversity of life on Earth. For example, a new section in Chapter 32 discusses the origin of multicellularity in animal ancestors. A new Make Connections Figure (Figure 33.9) explores the diverse structural solutions for maximizing surface area that have evolved across different kingdoms.

6 Plant Form and Function

In developing the Tenth Edition, we have continued to provide students with a basic understanding of plant anatomy and function while highlighting dynamic areas of plant research and the many important connections between plants and other organisms. To underscore the relevance of plant biology to society, there is now expanded coverage of plant biotechnology and the development of biofuels in Chapter 38. Other updates include expanded coverage of bacterial components of the rhizosphere (Figure 37.9), plant mineral deficiency symptoms (Table 37.1), evolutionary trends in floral morphology (Chapter 38), and chemical communication between plants (Chapter 39). The discussion of plant defenses against pathogens and herbivores has been extensively revised and now includes a Make Connections Figure that examines how plants deter herbivores at numerous levels of biological organization, ranging from the molecular level to the community level (Figure 39.27).

7 Animal Form and Function

In revising this unit, we strove to enhance student appreciation of the core concepts and ideas that apply across diverse organisms and varied organ systems. For example, a new Make Connections Figure (Figure 40.22) highlights challenges common to plant and animal physiology and presents both shared and divergent solutions to those challenges; this figure provides both a useful summary of plant physiology and an introduction to animal physiology. To help students recognize the central concept of homeostasis, figures have been revised across six chapters to provide a consistent organization that facilitates interpretation of individual hormone pathways as well as the comparison of pathways for different hormones. Homeostasis and endocrine regulation are highlighted by new and engaging chapter-opening photos and stories on the desert ant (Chapter 40) and on sexual dimorphism (Chapter 45), a revised presentation of the variation in target cell responses to a hormone (Figure 45.8), and a new figure integrating art and text on human endocrine glands and hormones (Figure 45.9). Many figures have been reconceived to emphasize key information, including new figures introducing the classes of essential nutrients (Figure 41.2) and showing oxygen and carbon dioxide partial pressures throughout the circulatory system (Figure 42.29). A new Make Connections Figure (Figure 44.17) demonstrates the importance of concentration gradients in animals as well as all other organisms. Throughout the unit, new state-of-the-art images and material on current and compelling topics—such as the human stomach microbiome (Figure 41.18) and the identification of the complete set of human taste receptors (Chapter 50)—will help engage students and encourage them to make connections beyond the text.

8 Ecology

For the Tenth Edition, the ecology unit engages students with new ideas and examples. Chapter 52 highlights the discovery of the world's smallest vertebrate species. New text and a figure use the saguaro cactus to illustrate how abiotic and biotic factors limit the distribution of species (Figure 52.15). Greater emphasis is placed on the importance of disturbances, such as the effects of Hurricane Katrina on forest mortality. Chapter 53 features the loggerhead turtle in the chapter opener, Concept 53.1 (reproduction), and Concept 53.4 (evolution and life history traits). The chapter also includes new molecular coverage: how ecologists use genetic profiles to estimate the number of breeding loggerhead turtles (Figure 53.7) and how a single gene influences dispersal in the Glanville fritillary. In Chapter 54, new text and a figure highlight the mimic octopus, a recently discovered species that illustrates how predators use mimicry (Figure 54.6). A new Make Connections Figure ties together population, community, and ecosystem processes in the arctic tundra (Figure 55.13). Chapter 55 also has a new opening story on habitat transformation in the tundra. Chapter 56 highlights the emerging fields of urban ecology and conservation biology, including the technical and ethical challenges of resurrecting extinct species. It also examines the threat posed by pharmaceuticals in the environment. The book ends on a hopeful note, charging students to use biological knowledge to help solve problems and improve life on Earth.

KEY CONCEPTS

Each chapter is organized around a framework of 3 to 7 **Key Concepts** that focus on the big picture and provide a context for the supporting details.

41
Animal Nutrition

KEY CONCEPTS

41.1 An animal's diet must supply chemical energy, organic molecules, and essential nutrients

41.2 The main stages of food processing are ingestion, digestion, absorption, and elimination

41.3 Organs specialized for sequential stages of food processing form the mammalian digestive system

41.4 Evolutionary adaptations of vertebrate digestive systems correlate with diet

41.5 Feedback circuits regulate digestion, energy storage, and appetite

▲ Figure 41.1 **How does a crab help an otter make fur?**

The Need to Feed

Dinnertime has arrived for the sea otter in **Figure 41.1** (and for the crab, though in quite a different sense). The muscles and other organs of the crab will be chewed into pieces, broken down by acid and enzymes in the otter's digestive system, and finally absorbed as small molecules into the body of the otter. Such a process is what is meant by animal **nutrition**: food being taken in, taken apart, and taken up.

Although dining on fish, crabs, urchins, and abalone is the sea otter's specialty, all animals eat other organisms—dead or alive, piecemeal or whole. Unlike plants, animals must consume food for both energy and the organic molecules used to assemble new molecules, cells, and tissues. Despite this shared need, animals have diverse diets. **Herbivores**, such as cattle, sea slugs, and caterpillars, dine mainly on plants or algae. **Carnivores**, such as sea otters, hawks, and spiders, mostly eat other animals. Rats and other **omnivores** (from the Latin *omnis*, all) don't in fact eat everything, but they do regularly consume animals as well as plants or algae. We humans are typically omnivores, as are cockroaches and crows.

The terms *herbivore, carnivore,* and *omnivore* represent the kinds of food an animal usually eats. Keep in mind, however, that most animals are opportunistic feeders, eating foods outside their standard diet when their usual foods aren't available.

◄ Every chapter opens with a visually dynamic **photo** accompanied by an **intriguing question** that invites students into the chapter.

▲ The **List of Key Concepts** introduces the big ideas covered in the chapter.

After reading a Key Concept section, students can check their understanding using the **Concept Check Questions.**

◄ Questions throughout the chapter encourage students to **read the text actively.**

Make Connections Questions ► ask students to relate content in the chapter to material presented earlier in the course.

What if? Questions ask students ► to apply what they've learned.

CONCEPT CHECK 41.1

1. All 20 amino acids are needed to make animal proteins. Why aren't they all essential to animal diets?

2. **MAKE CONNECTIONS** Considering the role of enzymes in metabolic reactions (see Concept 8.4), explain why vitamins are required in very small amounts in the diet.

3. **WHAT IF?** If a zoo animal eating ample food shows signs of malnutrition, how might a researcher determine which nutrient is lacking in its diet?

The **Summary of Key Concepts** refocuses students on the main points of the chapter.

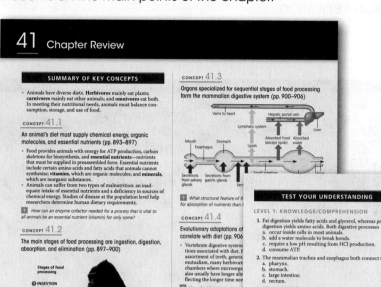

41 Chapter Review

SUMMARY OF KEY CONCEPTS

- Animals have diverse diets. **Herbivores** mainly eat plants; **carnivores** mainly eat other animals; and **omnivores** eat both. In meeting their nutritional needs, animals must balance consumption, storage, and use of food.

CONCEPT 41.1

An animal's diet must supply chemical energy, organic molecules, and essential nutrients (pp. 893–897)

- Food provides animals with energy for ATP production, carbon skeletons for biosynthesis, and **essential nutrients**—nutrients that must be supplied in preassembled form. Essential nutrients include certain amino acids and fatty acids that animals cannot synthesize; **vitamins**, which are organic molecules; and **minerals**, which are inorganic substances.
- Animals can suffer from two types of malnutrition: an inadequate intake of essential nutrients and a deficiency in sources of chemical energy. Studies of disease at the population level help researchers determine human dietary requirements.

? How can an enzyme cofactor needed for a process that is vital to all animals be an essential nutrient (vitamin) for only some?

CONCEPT 41.2

The main stages of food processing are ingestion, digestion, absorption, and elimination (pp. 897–900)

Stages of food processing
1. **INGESTION** (eating)
2. **DIGESTION** (enzymatic breakdown of large molecules)
3. **ABSORPTION** (uptake of nutrients by cells)
4. **ELIMINATION** (passage of undigested materials out of the body in feces)
Undigested material

- Animals differ in the ways they obtain and ingest food. Many animals are **bulk feeders**, eating large pieces of food. Other strategies include filter feeding, suspension feeding, and fluid feeding.
- Compartmentalization is necessary to avoid self-digestion. In intracellular digestion, food particles are engulfed by endocytosis and digested within food vacuoles that have fused with lysosomes. In extracellular digestion, which is used by most animals, enzymatic hydrolysis occurs outside cells in a **gastrovascular cavity** or **alimentary canal**.

? Propose an artificial diet that would eliminate the need for one of the first three steps in food processing.

CONCEPT 41.3

Organs specialized for sequential stages of food processing form the mammalian digestive system (pp. 900–906)

? What structural feature of the [...] for absorption of nutrients than [...]

CONCEPT 41.4

Evolutionary adaptations of [...] correlate with diet (pp. 906 [...])

- Vertebrate digestive system [...] tions associated with diet. F[...] assortment of teeth, genera[...] mutualism, many herbivore [...] chambers where microorga[...] also usually have longer ali[...] flecting the longer time nee[...]

? How does human anatomy [...] were not strict vegetarians?

CONCEPT 41.5

Feedback circuits regulate [...] appetite (pp. 908–912)

- **Nutrition** is regulated at m[...] canal triggers nervous and [...] secretion of digestive juices[...] ingested material through t[...] for energy production is reg[...] and **glucagon**, which contr[...] glycogen.
- Vertebrates store excess cal[...] cells) and in fat (in adipose [...] tapped when an animal exp[...] If, however, an animal cons[...] normal metabolism, the res[...] the serious health problem [...]
- Several hormones, includin[...] by affecting the brain's satie[...]

? Explain why your stomach m[...] skip a meal.

TEST YOUR UNDERSTANDING

LEVEL 1: KNOWLEDGE/COMPREHENSION

1. Fat digestion yields fatty acids and glycerol, whereas protein digestion yields amino acids. Both digestive processes
   a. occur inside cells in most animals.
   b. add a water molecule to break bonds.
   c. require a low pH resulting from HCl production.
   d. consume ATP.

2. The mammalian trachea and esophagus both connect to the
   a. pharynx.
   b. stomach.
   c. large intestine.
   d. rectum.

3. Which of the following organs is *incorrectly* paired with its function?
   a. stomach—protein digestion
   b. large intestine—bile production
   c. small intestine—nutrient absorption
   d. pancreas—enzyme production

4. Which of the following is *not* a major activity of the stomach?
   a. mechanical digestion
   b. HCl production
   c. nutrient absorption
   d. enzyme secretion

LEVEL 2: APPLICATION/ANALYSIS

5. After surgical removal of an infected gallbladder, a person must be especially careful to restrict dietary intake of
   a. starch.
   b. protein.
   c. sugar.
   d. fat.

6. If you were to jog 1 km a few hours after lunch, which stored fuel would you probably tap?
   a. muscle proteins
   b. muscle and liver glycogen
   c. fat in the liver
   d. fat in adipose tissue

LEVEL 3: SYNTHESIS/EVALUATION

7. **DRAW IT** Make a flowchart of the events that occur after partially digested food leaves the stomach. Use the following terms: bicarbonate secretion, circulation, decrease in acidity, increase in acidity, secretin secretion, signal detection. Next to each term, indicate the compartment(s) involved. You may use terms more than once.

8. **EVOLUTION CONNECTION**
   The human esophagus and trachea share a passage leading from the mouth and nasal passages, which can cause problems. After reviewing vertebrate evolution (see Chapter 34), explain how the evolutionary concept of descent with modification explains this "imperfect" anatomy.

9. **SCIENTIFIC INQUIRY**
   In human populations of northern European origin, the disorder called hemochromatosis causes excess iron uptake from food and affects one in 200 adults. Among adults, men are ten times as likely as women to suffer from iron overload. Taking into account the existence of a menstrual cycle in humans, devise a hypothesis that explains this difference.

10. **WRITE ABOUT A THEME: ORGANIZATION**
    Hair is largely made up of the protein keratin. In a short essay (100–150 words), explain why a shampoo containing protein is not effective in replacing the protein in damaged hair.

11. **SYNTHESIZE YOUR KNOWLEDGE**

Hummingbirds are well adapted to obtain sugary nectar from flowers, but they use some of the energy obtained from nectar when they forage for insects and spiders. Explain why this foraging is necessary.

For selected answers, see Appendix A.

MasteringBiology®

Students Go to **MasteringBiology** for assignments, the eText, and the Study Area with practice tests, animations, and activities.
Instructors Go to **MasteringBiology** for automatically graded tutorials and questions that you can assign to your students, plus Instructor Resources.

▼ **Test Your Understanding Questions** at the end of each chapter are organized into three levels based on **Bloom's Taxonomy**:

- Level 1: Knowledge/Comprehension
- Level 2: Application/Analysis
- Level 3: Synthesis/Evaluation

Test Bank questions and multiple-choice questions in MasteringBiology® are also categorized by Bloom's Taxonomy.

◄ **NEW! Synthesize Your Knowledge Questions** ask students to apply their understanding of the chapter content to explain an intriguing photo.

▲ **Summary Figures** recap key information in a visual way. **Summary of Key Concepts Questions** check students' understanding of a key idea from each concept.

▲ To reinforce the themes, every chapter ends with an **Evolution Connection Question** and a **Write About a Theme Question**.

THEMES

To help students focus on the big ideas of biology, five **themes** are introduced in Chapter 1 and woven throughout the text:

- Evolution
- Organization
- Information
- Energy and Matter
- Interactions

Every chapter has a section ▶ explicitly relating the chapter content to evolution, the fundamental theme of biology.

The Evolutionary Origins of Mitochondria and Chloroplasts

EVOLUTION Mitochondria and chloroplasts display similarities with bacteria that led to the **endosymbiont theory**, illustrated in **Figure 6.16**. This theory states that an early ancestor of eukaryotic cells engulfed an oxygen-using nonphotosynthetic prokaryotic cell. Eventually, the engulfed

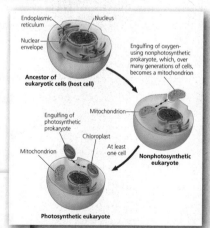

Endoplasmic reticulum
Nucleus
Nuclear envelope
Ancestor of eukaryotic cells (host cell)
Engulfing of oxygen-using nonphotosynthetic prokaryote, which, over many generations of cells, becomes a mitochondrion
Mitochondrion
Engulfing of photosynthetic prokaryote
Chloroplast
At least one cell
Mitochondrion
Nonphotosynthetic eukaryote
Photosynthetic eukaryote

Make Connections Visually

Make Connections Figures include:

Figure 5.26 Contributions of Genomics and Proteomics to Biology, p. 88

Figure 10.23 The Working Cell, shown at right and on pp. 206–207

Figure 18.27 Genomics, Cell-Signaling, and Cancer, p. 387

Figure 23.17 The Sickle-Cell Allele, pp. 496–497

Figure 33.9 Maximizing Surface Area, p. 689

Figure 39.27 Levels of Plant Defenses Against Herbivores, pp. 862–863

Figure 40.22 Life Challenges and Solutions in Plants and Animals, pp. 888–889

Figure 44.17 Ion Movement and Gradients, p. 987

Figure 55.13 The Working Ecosystem, pp. 1242–1243

▼ Figure 10.23

MAKE CONNECTIONS

The Working Cell

This figure illustrates how a generalized plant cell functions, integrating the cellular activities you learned about in Chapters 5–10.

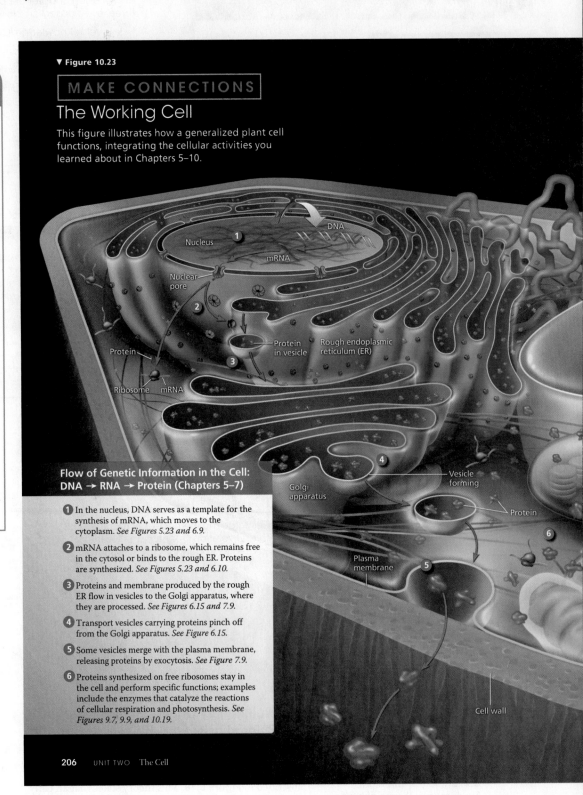

Flow of Genetic Information in the Cell:
DNA → RNA → Protein (Chapters 5–7)

❶ In the nucleus, DNA serves as a template for the synthesis of mRNA, which moves to the cytoplasm. *See Figures 5.23 and 6.9.*

❷ mRNA attaches to a ribosome, which remains free in the cytosol or binds to the rough ER. Proteins are synthesized. *See Figures 5.23 and 6.10.*

❸ Proteins and membrane produced by the rough ER flow in vesicles to the Golgi apparatus, where they are processed. *See Figures 6.15 and 7.9.*

❹ Transport vesicles carrying proteins pinch off from the Golgi apparatus. *See Figure 6.15.*

❺ Some vesicles merge with the plasma membrane, releasing proteins by exocytosis. *See Figure 7.9.*

❻ Proteins synthesized on free ribosomes stay in the cell and perform specific functions; examples include the enzymes that catalyze the reactions of cellular respiration and photosynthesis. *See Figures 9.7, 9.9, and 10.19.*

206 UNIT TWO   The Cell

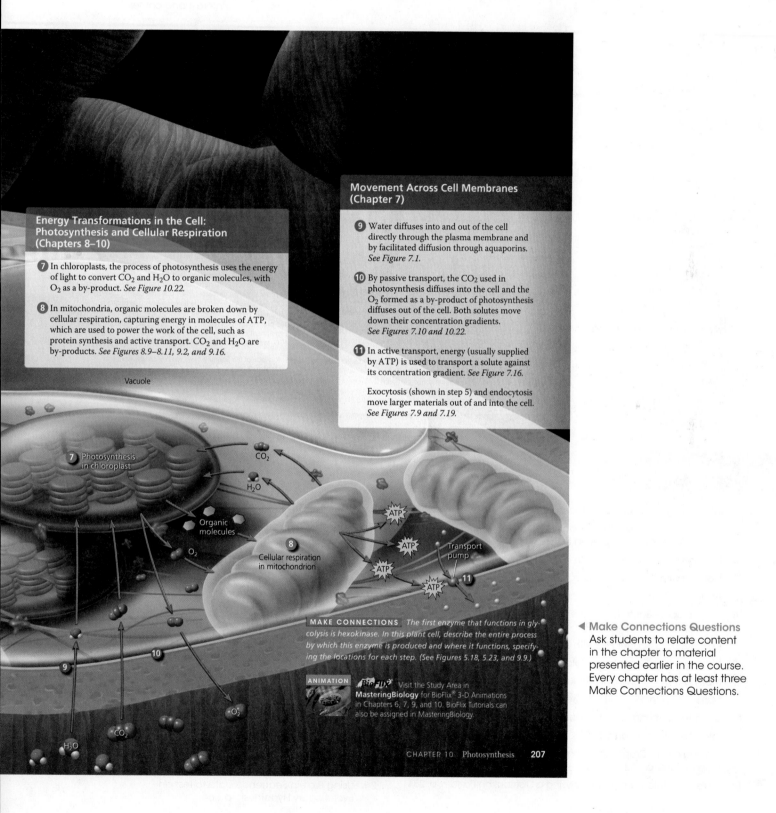

Energy Transformations in the Cell: Photosynthesis and Cellular Respiration (Chapters 8–10)

7 In chloroplasts, the process of photosynthesis uses the energy of light to convert CO_2 and H_2O to organic molecules, with O_2 as a by-product. *See Figure 10.22.*

8 In mitochondria, organic molecules are broken down by cellular respiration, capturing energy in molecules of ATP, which are used to power the work of the cell, such as protein synthesis and active transport. CO_2 and H_2O are by-products. *See Figures 8.9–8.11, 9.2, and 9.16.*

Vacuole

Movement Across Cell Membranes (Chapter 7)

9 Water diffuses into and out of the cell directly through the plasma membrane and by facilitated diffusion through aquaporins. *See Figure 7.1.*

10 By passive transport, the CO_2 used in photosynthesis diffuses into the cell and the O_2 formed as a by-product of photosynthesis diffuses out of the cell. Both solutes move down their concentration gradients. *See Figures 7.10 and 10.22.*

11 In active transport, energy (usually supplied by ATP) is used to transport a solute against its concentration gradient. *See Figure 7.16.*

Exocytosis (shown in step 5) and endocytosis move larger materials out of and into the cell. *See Figures 7.9 and 7.19.*

7 Photosynthesis in chloroplast

CO_2

H_2O

Organic molecules

O_2

8 Cellular respiration in mitochondrion

ATP

ATP

ATP

ATP

Transport pump

11

10

9

O_2

H_2O

CO_2

MAKE CONNECTIONS *The first enzyme that functions in glycolysis is hexokinase. In this plant cell, describe the entire process by which this enzyme is produced and where it functions, specifying the locations for each step. (See Figures 5.18, 5.23, and 9.9.)*

ANIMATION *Bio Flix* Visit the Study Area in **MasteringBiology** for BioFlix® 3-D Animations in Chapters 6, 7, 9, and 10. BioFlix Tutorials can also be assigned in MasteringBiology.

◀ **Make Connections Questions**
Ask students to relate content in the chapter to material presented earlier in the course. Every chapter has at least three Make Connections Questions.

Make Connections Visually   **xiii**

Practice Scientific Skills

NEW! Scientific Skills Exercises in every chapter use real data to build key skills needed for biology, including data interpretation, graphing, experimental design, and math skills.

▼ **Photos** provide visual interest and context.

◀ Each Scientific Skills Exercise is based on an **experiment related to the chapter content.**

SCIENTIFIC SKILLS EXERCISE

Interpreting a Scatter Plot with a Regression Line

How Does the Carbonate Ion Concentration of Seawater Affect the Calcification Rate of a Coral Reef? Scientists predict that acidification of the ocean due to higher levels of atmospheric CO_2 will lower the concentration of dissolved carbonate ions, which living corals use to build calcium carbonate reef structures. In this exercise, you will analyze data from a controlled experiment that examined the effect of carbonate ion concentration ($[CO_3^{2-}]$) on calcium carbonate deposition, a process called calcification.

How the Experiment Was Done The Biosphere 2 aquarium in Arizona contains a large coral reef system that behaves like a natural reef. For several years, a group of researchers measured the rate of calcification by the reef organisms and examined how the calcification rate changed with differing amounts of dissolved carbonate ions in the seawater.

Data from the Experiment The black data points in the graph form a scatter plot. The red line, known as a linear regression line, is the best-fitting straight line for these points.

Interpret the Data

1. When presented with a graph of experimental data, the first step in analysis is to determine what each axis represents. (a) In words, explain what is being shown on the *x*-axis. Be sure to include the units. (b) What is being shown on the *y*-axis (including units)? (c) Which variable is the independent variable—the variable that was *manipulated* by the researchers? (d) Which variable is the dependent variable—the variable that responded to or depended on the treatment, which was *measured* by the researchers? (For additional information about graphs, see the Scientific Skills Review in Appendix F and in the Study Area in MasteringBiology.)

2. Based on the data shown in the graph, describe in words the relationship between carbonate ion concentration and calcification rate.

3. (a) If the seawater carbonate ion concentration is 270 µmol/kg, what is the approximate rate of calcification, and approximately how many days would it take 1 square meter of reef to accumulate 30 mmol of calcium carbonate ($CaCO_3$)? (b) If the seawater carbonate ion concentration is 250 µmol/kg, what is the approximate rate of calcification, and approximately how many days would it take 1 square meter of reef to accumulate 30 mmol of calcium carbonate? (c) If carbonate ion concentration decreases, how does the calcification rate change, and how does that affect the time it takes coral to grow?

4. (a) Referring to the equations in Figure 3.11, determine which step of the process is measured in this experiment. (b) Are the results of this experiment consistent with the hypothesis that increased atmospheric $[CO_2]$ will slow the growth of coral reefs? Why or why not?

MB A version of this Scientific Skills Exercise can be assigned in MasteringBiology.

Data from C. Langdon et al., Effect of calcium carbonate saturation state on the calcification rate of an experimental coral reef, *Global Biogeochemical Cycles* 14:639–654 (2000).

◀ Most Scientific Skills Exercises use **data from published research.**

◀ **Questions build in difficulty,** walking students through new skills step by step and providing opportunities for higher-level critical thinking.

▲ Each Scientific Skills Exercise cites **the published research.**

Every chapter has a Scientific Skills Exercise

1. Interpreting a Pair of Bar Graphs, p. 22

2. Calibrating a Standard Radioactive Isotope Decay Curve and Interpreting Data, p. 33

3. Interpreting a Scatter Plot with a Regression Line, p. 54

4. Working with Moles and Molar Ratios, p. 58

5. Analyzing Polypeptide Sequence Data, p. 89

6. Using a Scale Bar to Calculate Volume and Surface Area of a Cell, p. 99

7. Interpreting a Scatter Plot with Two Sets of Data, p. 134

8. Making a Line Graph and Calculating a Slope, p. 155

9. Making a Bar Graph and Evaluating a Hypothesis, p. 177

10. Making Scatter Plots with Regression Lines, p. 203

11. Using Experiments to Test a Model, p. 226

12. Interpreting Histograms, p. 248

13. Making a Line Graph and Converting Between Units of Data, p. 262

14. Making a Histogram and Analyzing a Distribution Pattern, p. 281

15. Using the Chi-Square (χ^2) Test, p. 302

16. Working with Data in a Table, p. 316

17. Interpreting a Sequence Logo, p. 349

18. Analyzing DNA Deletion Experiments, p. 370

19. Analyzing a Sequence-Based Phylogenetic Tree to Understand Viral Evolution, p. 404

20. Analyzing Quantitative and Spatial Gene Expression Data, p. 420

21. Reading an Amino Acid Sequence Identity Table, p. 452

22. Making and Testing Predictions, p. 477

23. Using the Hardy-Weinberg Equation to Interpret Data and Make Predictions, p. 487

24. Identifying Independent and Dependent Variables, Making a Scatter Plot, and Interpreting Data, p. 507

25. Estimating Quantitative Data from a Graph and Developing Hypotheses, p. 532

26. Using Protein Sequence Data to Test an Evolutionary Hypothesis, p. 564

NEW! All **56 Scientific Skills Exercises** from the text have assignable, interactive versions in MasteringBiology® that are automatically graded.

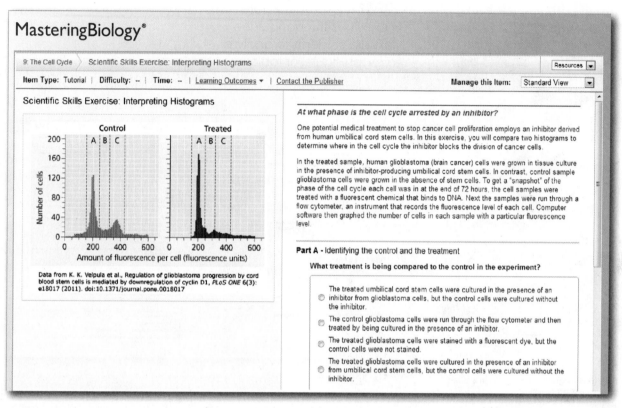

MasteringBiology®

To learn more, visit www.masteringbiology.com

27. Making a Bar Graph and Interpreting Data, p. 584
28. Interpreting Comparisons of Genetic Sequences, p. 589
29. Making Bar Graphs and Interpreting Data, p. 623
30. Using Natural Logarithms to Interpret Data, p. 633
31. Interpreting Genomic Data and Generating Hypotheses, p. 651
32. Calculating and Interpreting Correlation Coefficients, p. 672
33. Understanding Experimental Design and Interpreting Data, p. 694
34. Determining the Equation of a Regression Line, p. 745
35. Using Bar Graphs to Interpret Data, p. 756
36. Calculating and Interpreting Temperature Coefficients, p. 784
37. Making Observations, p. 806
38. Using Positive and Negative Correlations to Interpret Data, p. 828
39. Interpreting Experimental Results from a Bar Graph, p. 858
40. Interpreting Pie Charts, p. 886
41. Interpreting Data from Experiments with Genetic Mutants, p. 912

42. Making and Interpreting Histograms, p. 932
43. Comparing Two Variables on a Common x-Axis, p. 967
44. Describing and Interpreting Quantitative Data, p. 975
45. Designing a Controlled Experiment, p. 1008
46. Making Inferences and Designing an Experiment, p. 1025
47. Interpreting a Change in Slope, p. 1043
48. Interpreting Data Values Expressed in Scientific Notation, p. 1076
49. Designing an Experiment Using Genetic Mutants, p. 1089
50. Interpreting a Graph with Log Scales, p. 1130
51. Testing a Hypothesis with a Quantitative Model, p. 1144
52. Making a Bar Graph and a Line Graph to Interpret Data, p. 1181
53. Using the Logistic Equation to Model Population Growth, p. 1194
54. Making a Bar Graph and a Scatter Plot, p. 1211
55. Interpreting Quantitative Data in a Table, p. 1240
56. Graphing Cyclic Data, p. 1273

Interpret Data

CAMPBELL *BIOLOGY*, Tenth Edition, and MasteringBiology®
offer a wide variety of ways for students to move beyond
memorization and **think like a scientist.**

◀ **NEW!** Interpret the Data
Questions throughout the
text ask students to analyze
a graph, figure, or table.

▲ **Figure 56.25 Biological magnification of PCBs in a Great
Lakes food web.** (ppm = parts per million)

INTERPRET THE DATA *If a typical smelt weighs 225 g, what is the
total mass of PCBs in a smelt in the Great Lakes? If an average lake trout
weighs 4,500 g, what is the total mass of PCBs in a trout in the Great
Lakes? Assume that a lake trout from an unpolluted source is introduced
into the Great Lakes and smelt are the only source of PCBs in the trout's
diet. The new trout would have the same level of PCBs as the existing
trout after eating how many smelt? (Assume that the trout retains 100%
of the PCBs it consumes.)*

▲ **NEW!** Every Interpret the
Data Question from the text is
assignable in MasteringBiology.

MasteringBiology®

Learn more at
www.masteringbiology.com

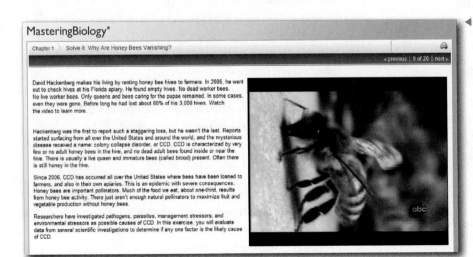

◀ **NEW!** Solve It Tutorials engage
students in a multi-step investigation of
a "mystery" or open question in which
they must analyze real data. These are
assignable in MasteringBiology.

Topics include:

- Is It Possible to Treat Bacterial Infections Without
  Traditional Antibiotics?
- Are You Getting the Fish You Paid For?
- Why Are Honey Bees Vanishing?
- Which Biofuel Has the Most Potential to Reduce
  our Dependence on Fossil Fuels?
- Which Insulin Mutations May Result in Disease?
- What is Causing Episodes of Muscle Weakness
  in a Patient?

NEW! Throughout the Tenth Edition, new examples show students how our ability to **sequence DNA and proteins rapidly and inexpensively** is transforming every subfield of biology, from cell biology to physiology to ecology.

◀ Figure 5.26

MAKE CONNECTIONS

Contributions of Genomics and Proteomics to Biology

Nucleotide sequencing and the analysis of large sets of genes and proteins can be done rapidly and inexpensively due to advances in technology and information processing. Taken together, genomics and proteomics have advanced our understanding of biology across many different fields.

Paleontology

New DNA sequencing techniques have allowed decoding of minute quantities of DNA found in ancient tissues from our extinct relatives, the Neanderthals (*Homo neanderthalensis*). Sequencing the Neanderthal genome has informed our understanding of their physical appearance as well as their relationship with modern humans. *See Figure 34.49.*

Medical Science

Identifying the genetic basis for human diseases like cancer helps researchers focus their search for potential future treatments. Currently, sequencing the sets of genes expressed in an individual's tumor can allow a more targeted approach to treating the cancer, a type of "personalized medicine." *See Figures 12.20 and 18.27.*

Evolution

A major aim of evolutionary biology is to understand the relationships among species, both living and extinct. For example, genome sequence comparisons have identified the hippopotamus as the land mammal sharing the most recent common ancestor with whales. *See Figure 22.20.*

Hippopotamus

Short-finned pilot whale

Conservation Biology

The tools of molecular genetics and genomics are increasingly used by ecologists to identify which species of animals and plants are killed illegally. In one case, genomic sequences of DNA from illegal shipments of elephant tusks were used to track down poachers and pinpoint the territory where they were operating. *See Figure 56.9.*

Species Interactions

Over 90% of all plant species exist in a mutually beneficial partnership with fungi that are associated with

88   UNIT ONE   The Chemistry of Life

◀ This new **Make Connections Figure** in Chapter 5 previews some examples of how genomics and proteomics have helped shed light on diverse biological questions. These examples are explored in greater depth later in the text.

SCIENTIFIC SKILLS EXERCISE

Analyzing Polypeptide Sequence Data

▶ Human   ▶ Rhesus monkey   ▶ Gibbon

Are Rhesus Monkeys or Gibbons More Closely Related to Humans? DNA and polypeptide sequences from closely related species are more similar to each other than are sequences from more distantly related species. In this exercise, you will look at amino acid sequence data for the β polypeptide chain of hemoglobin, often called β-globin. You will then interpret the data to hypothesize whether the monkey or the gibbon is more closely related to humans.

How Such Experiments Are Done Researchers can isolate the polypeptide of interest from an organism and then determine the amino acid sequence. More frequently, the DNA of the relevant gene is sequenced, and the amino acid sequence of the polypeptide is deduced from the DNA sequence of its gene.

Data from the Experiments In the data below, the letters give the sequence of the 146 amino acids in β-globin from humans, rhesus

monkeys, and gibbons. Because a complete sequence would not fit on one line here, the sequences are broken into three segments. The sequences for the three different species are aligned so that you can compare them easily. For example, you can see that for all three species, the first amino acid is V (valine) and the 146th amino acid is H (histidine).

Interpret the Data

1. Scan the monkey and gibbon sequences, letter by letter, circling any amino acids that do not match the human sequence. (a) How many amino acids differ between the monkey and the human sequences? (b) Between the gibbon and human?

2. For each nonhuman species, what percent of its amino acids are identical to the human sequence of β-globin?

3. Based on these data alone, state a hypothesis for which of these two species is more closely related to humans. What is your reasoning?

4. What other evidence could you use to support your hypothesis?

A version of this Scientific Skills Exercise can be assigned in MasteringBiology.

Data from Human: http://www.ncbi.nlm.nih.gov/protein/AAA21113.1; rhesus monkey: http://www.ncbi.nlm.nih.gov/protein/122634; gibbon: http://www.ncbi.nlm.nih.gov/protein/122616

Species	Alignment of Amino Acid Sequences of β-globin
Human	1 VHLTPEEKSA VTALWGKVNV DEVGGEALGR LLVVYPWTQR FFESFGDLST
Monkey	1 VHLTPEEKNA VTTLWGKVNV DEVGGEALGR LLLVYPWTQR FFESFGDLSS
Gibbon	1 VHLTPEEKSA VTALWGKVNV DEVGGEALGR LLVVYPWTQR FFESFGDLST
Human	51 PDAVMGNPKV KAHGKKVLGA FSDGLAHLDN LKGTFATLSE LHCDKLHVDP
Monkey	51 PDAVMGNPKV KAHGKKVLGA FSDGLNHLDN LKGTFAQLSE LHCDKLHVDP
Gibbon	51 PDAVMGNPKV KAHGKKVLGA FSDGLAHLDN LKGTFAQLSE LHCDKLHVDP
Human	101 ENFRLLGNVL VCVLAHHFGK EFTPPVQAAY QKVVAGVANA LAHKYH
Monkey	101 ENFKLLGNVL VCVLAHHFGK EFTPQVQAAY QKVVAGVANA LAHKYH
Gibbon	101 ENFRLLGNVL VCVLAHHFGK EFTPQVQAAY QKVVAGVANA LAHKYH

Selected Scientific Skills Exercises involve **working with DNA or protein sequences**. ▶

MasteringBiology®

eTEXT

Access the complete textbook online!

▲ The **Pearson eText** gives students access to the text whenever and wherever they can access the Internet. The eText can be viewed on PCs, Macs, and tablets, including iPad® and Android.® The eText includes powerful interactive and customization functions:

- Write notes
- Highlight text
- Bookmark pages
- Zoom

- Click hyperlinked words to view definitions
- Search
- Link to media activities and quizzes

Instructors can even write notes for the class and highlight important materials using a tool that works like an electronic pen on a whiteboard.

STUDY AREA

Students can access the **Study Area** for use on their own or in a study group.

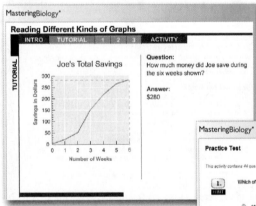

BioFlix® 3-D Animations ▶ explore the most difficult biology topics, reinforced with tutorials, quizzes, and more.

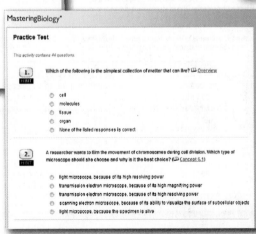

▲ **Get Ready for Biology** helps students get up to speed for their course by covering study skills, basic math, terminology, chemistry, and biology basics.

◀ **Practice Tests** help students assess their understanding of each chapter, providing feedback for right and wrong answers.

The **Study Area** also includes: Cumulative Test, MP3 Tutor Sessions, Videos, Activities, Investigations, Lab Media, Audio Glossary, Word Roots, Key Terms, Flashcards, and Art.

DYNAMIC STUDY MODULES

NEW! Dynamic Study Modules, designed to enable students to study effectively on their own, help students quickly access and learn the information they need to be more successful on quizzes and exams.

How it works:

1. Students receive an initial **set of questions**.

◀ A unique answer format asks students to indicate how **confident** they are about their answer.

2. After answering each set of questions, students **review their answers**.

3. Each answer has an **explanation** using material that is taken directly **from the textbook**.

◀ These modules can be accessed on smartphones, tablets, and computers. Results can be tracked in the MasteringBiology Gradebook.

4. Once students review the explanations from the textbook, they are presented with a new set of questions. Students cycle through this **dynamic process of test–learn–retest** until they achieve mastery of the textbook material.

Learn more at www.masteringbiology.com

Instructors can assign **self-paced MasteringBiology® tutorials** that provide students with individualized coaching with specific hints and feedback on the toughest topics in the course.

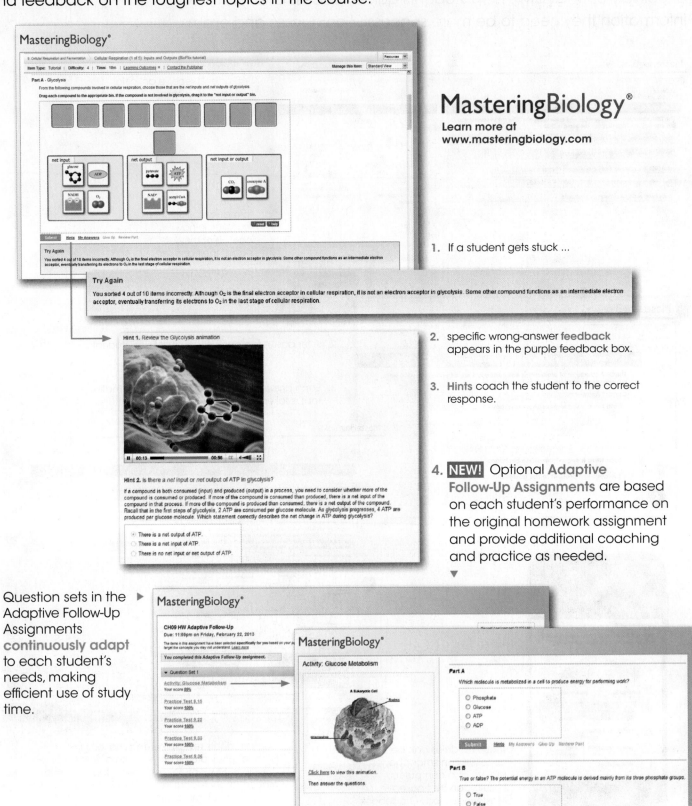

MasteringBiology®

Learn more at
www.masteringbiology.com

1. If a student gets stuck ...

2. specific wrong-answer **feedback** appears in the purple feedback box.

3. **Hints** coach the student to the correct response.

4. **NEW!** Optional **Adaptive Follow-Up Assignments** are based on each student's performance on the original homework assignment and provide additional coaching and practice as needed.

Question sets in the Adaptive Follow-Up Assignments **continuously adapt** to each student's needs, making efficient use of study time.

The MasteringBiology® Gradebook provides instructors with quick results and easy-to-interpret insights into student performance. Every assignment is automatically graded. Shades of red highlight vulnerable students and challenging assignments.

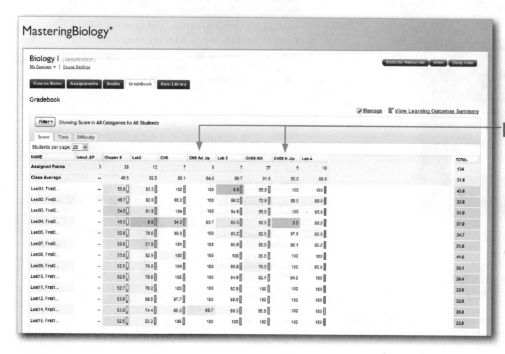

NEW! Student scores on the optional **Adaptive Follow-Up Assignments** are recorded in the gradebook and offer additional diagnostic information for instructors to monitor learning outcomes and more.

MasteringBiology offers a wide variety of tutorials that can be assigned as homework. For example, **BioFlix Tutorials** use 3-D, movie-quality **Animations** and coaching exercises to help students master tough topics outside of class. Animations can also be shown in class.

BioFlix Tutorials and 3-D Animations include:

- A Tour of the Animal Cell
- A Tour of the Plant Cell
- Membrane Transport
- Cellular Respiration
- Photosynthesis
- Mitosis

- Meiosis
- DNA Replication
- Protein Synthesis
- Mechanisms of Evolution
- Water Transport in Plants
- Homeostasis: Regulating Blood Sugar

- Gas Exchange
- How Neurons Work
- How Synapses Work
- Muscle Contraction
- Population Ecology
- The Carbon Cycle

Supplements

FOR INSTRUCTORS

NEW! Learning Catalytics™ allows students to use their smartphone, tablet, or laptop to respond to questions in class. Visit www.learningcatalytics.com.

Instructor's Resource DVD (IRDVD) Package
978-0-321-83494-2 / 0-321-83494-1

The instructor resources for *CAMPBELL BIOLOGY,* **Tenth Edition,** are combined into one chapter-by-chapter resource that includes DVDs of all chapter visual resources. Assets include:

- Editable figures (art and photos) and tables from the text in PowerPoint®
- Prepared PowerPoint Lecture Presentations for each chapter, with lecture notes, editable figures, tables, and links to animations and videos
- 250+ Instructor Animations and Videos, including BioFlix® 3-D Animations and *ABC News* Videos

- JPEG Images, including labeled and unlabeled art, photos from the text, and extra photos
- Digital Transparencies
- Clicker Questions in PowerPoint
- Quick Reference Guide
- Test Bank questions in TestGen® software and Microsoft® Word

Instructor Resources Area in MasteringBiology®

This area includes:

- Art and Photos in PowerPoint
- PowerPoint Lecture Presentations
- Videos and Animations, including BioFlix®
- JPEG Images
- Digital Transparencies
- Clicker Questions
- Test Bank Files
- Lecture Outlines
- Learning Objectives

- Pre-Tests, Post-Tests, and Strategies for Overcoming Common Student Misconceptions
- Instructor Guides for Supplements
- Rubric and Tips for Grading Short-Answer Essays
- Suggested Answers for Scientific Skills Exercises and Short-Answer Essay Questions
- Lab Media

Experiments: Data Interpretation

Water snakes on islands in Lake Erie vary in coloration from banded to unbanded. Researchers hypothesized that unbanded snakes escape predation from hawks at higher rates than do banded snakes. Imagine that you tested survival rates on four different islands by measuring recapture rates of banded and unbanded snakes and collected the data shown below. Which of the following conclusions best derive from the data shown?

a) Lack of bands helps snakes escape predation by hawks.

b) Lack of bands improves snake survival but the mechanism is unknown.

c) Lack of bands decreases snake survival rate.

d) The two groups do not differ in survival rate.

e) Survival rates of banded snakes differ among islands.

Energy Transfer

Like jackrabbits, elephants have many blood vessels in their ears that help them cool their bodies by radiating heat. Which of the following statements about this radiated energy would be accurate?

a) The original source of the energy was the sun.

b) The energy will be recycled through the ecosystem.

c) The radiated energy will be trapped by predators of the elephants.

d) More energy is radiated in cold conditions than in hot conditions.

e) More energy is radiated at night than during the day.

▲ **Clicker Questions** can be used to stimulate effective classroom discussions (for use with or without clickers).

Instructor Resources for Flipped Classrooms

- Lecture videos can be posted on MasteringBiology for students to view before class.
- Homework can be assigned in MasteringBiology so students come to class prepared.
- In-class resources: Learning Catalytics, Clicker Questions, Student Misconception Questions, end-of-chapter essay questions, and activities and case studies from the student supplements.

Chloroplasts: The Sites of Photosynthesis in Plants

- **Leaves are the major locations of photosynthesis**
- Their green color is from **chlorophyll**, the green pigment within chloroplasts
- Light energy absorbed by chlorophyll drives the synthesis of organic molecules in the chloroplast
- CO_2 enters and O_2 exits the leaf through microscopic pores called **stomata**

▲ **Customizable PowerPoints** provide a jumpstart for each lecture.

▲ All of the art, graphs, and photos from the book are provided with customizable labels. More than 1,600 photos from the text and other sources are included.

Printed Test Bank
978-0-321-82371-7 / 0-321-82371-0

This invaluable resource contains more than 4,500 questions, including scenario-based questions and art, graph, and data interpretation questions. In addition to a print version, the Test Bank is available electronically in MasteringBiology, on the Instructor's Resource DVD Package, within the Blackboard course management system, and at www.pearsonhighered.com.

Course Management Systems
Content is available in **Blackboard**. Also, **MasteringBiology New Design** offers the usual Mastering features plus:

- Blackboard integration with single sign-on
- Temporary access (grace period)
- Discussion boards

- Email
- Chat and class live (synchronous whiteboard presentation)
- Submissions (Dropbox)

FOR STUDENTS

Study Guide, Tenth Edition
by Martha R. Taylor, *Ithaca, New York*
978-0-321-83392-1 / 0-321-83392-9
This popular study aid provides concept maps, chapter summaries, word roots, and a variety of interactive activities including multiple-choice, short-answer essay, art labeling, and graph-interpretation questions.

Inquiry in Action: Interpreting Scientific Papers, Third Edition*
by Ruth Buskirk, *University of Texas at Austin*,
and Christopher M. Gillen, *Kenyon College*
978-0-321-83417-1 / 0-321-83417-8
This guide helps students learn how to read and understand primary research articles. Part A presents complete articles accompanied by questions that help students analyze the article. Related Inquiry Figures are included in the supplement. Part B covers every part of a research paper, explaining the aim of the sections and how the paper works as a whole.

Practicing Biology: A Student Workbook, Fifth Edition*
by Jean Heitz and Cynthia Giffen, *University of Wisconsin, Madison*
978-0-321-87705-5 / 0-321-87705-5
This workbook offers a variety of activities to suit different learning styles. Activities such as modeling and concept mapping allow students to visualize and understand biological processes. Other activities focus on basic skills, such as reading and drawing graphs.

Biological Inquiry: A Workbook of Investigative Cases, Fourth Edition*
by Margaret Waterman, *Southeast Missouri State University*, and Ethel Stanley, *BioQUEST Curriculum Consortium and Beloit College*
978-0-321-83391-4 / 0-321-83391-0
This workbook offers ten investigative cases. Each case study requires students to synthesize information from multiple chapters of the text and apply that knowledge to a real-world scenario as they pose hypotheses, gather new information, analyze evidence, graph data, and draw conclusions. A link to a student website is in the Study Area in MasteringBiology.

Study Card, Tenth Edition
978-0-321-83415-7 / 0-321-83415-1
This quick-reference card provides students with an overview of the entire field of biology, helping them see the connections among topics.

Spanish Glossary, Tenth Edition
by Laura P. Zanello, *University of California, Riverside*
978-0-321-83498-0 / 0-321-83498-4
This resource provides definitions in Spanish for glossary terms.

Into the Jungle: Great Adventures in the Search for Evolution
by Sean B. Carroll, *University of Wisconsin, Madison*
978-0-321-55671-4 / 0-321-55671-2
These nine short tales vividly depict key discoveries in evolutionary biology and the excitement of the scientific process. Online resources available at www.aw-bc.com/carroll.

Get Ready for Biology
978-0-321-50057-1 / 0-321-50057-1
This engaging workbook helps students brush up on important math and study skills and get up to speed on biological terminology and the basics of chemistry and cell biology.

A Short Guide to Writing About Biology, Eighth Edition
by Jan A. Pechenik, *Tufts University*
978-0-321-83386-0 / 0-321-83386-4
This best-selling writing guide teaches students to think as biologists and to express ideas clearly and concisely through their writing.

An Introduction to Chemistry for Biology Students, Ninth Edition
by George I. Sackheim, *University of Illinois, Chicago*
978-0-8053-9571-6 / 0-8053-9571-7
This text/workbook helps students review and master all the basic facts, concepts, and terminology of chemistry that they need for their life science course.

FOR LAB

Investigating Biology Laboratory Manual, Eighth Edition
by Judith Giles Morgan, *Emory University*, and M. Eloise Brown Carter, *Oxford College of Emory University*
978-0-321-83899-5 / 0-321-83899-8
Now in full color! With its distinctive investigative approach to learning, this best-selling laboratory manual is now more engaging than ever, with full-color art and photos throughout. As always, the lab manual encourages students to participate in the process of science and develop creative and critical-reasoning skills.

The Eighth Edition includes major revisions that reflect new molecular evidence and the current understanding of phylogenetic relationships for plants, invertebrates, protists, and fungi. A new lab topic, "Fungi," has been added, providing expanded coverage of the major fungi groups. The "Protists" lab topic has been revised and expanded with additional examples of all the major clades. In the new edition, population genetics is covered in one lab topic with new problems and examples that connect ecology, evolution, and genetics.

Annotated Instructor Edition for Investigating Biology Laboratory Manual, Eighth Edition
by Judith Giles Morgan, *Emory University*, and M. Eloise Brown Carter, *Oxford College of Emory University*
978-0-321-83497-3 / 0-321-83497-6

Preparation Guide for Investigating Biology Laboratory Manual, Eighth Edition
by Judith Giles Morgan, *Emory University*, and M. Eloise Brown Carter, *Oxford College of Emory University*
978-0-321-83445-4 / 0-321-83445-3

Symbiosis: The Pearson Custom Laboratory Program for the Biological Sciences
www.pearsoncustom.com/database/symbiosis/bc.html

MasteringBiology® Virtual Labs
www.masteringbiology.com
This online environment promotes critical thinking skills using virtual experiments and explorations that may be difficult to perform in a wet lab environment due to time, cost, or safety concerns. Designed to supplement or substitute for existing wet labs, this product offers students unique learning experiences and critical thinking exercises in the areas of microscopy, molecular biology, genetics, ecology, and systematics.

*An Instructor Guide is available for download in the Instructor Resources Area in MasteringBiology.

Make Connections Figures

5.26 Contributions of Genomics and Proteomics to Biology *88*

10.23 The Working Cell *206*

18.27 Genomics, Cell Signaling, and Cancer *387*

23.17 The Sickle-Cell Allele *496*

33.9 Maximizing Surface Area *689*

39.27 Levels of Plant Defenses Against Herbivores *862*

40.22 Life Challenges and Solutions in Plants and Animals *888*

44.17 Ion Movement and Gradients *987*

55.13 The Working Ecosystem *1242*

Exploring Figures

1.3 Levels of Biological Organization *2*

5.18 Levels of Protein Structure *80*

6.3 Microscopy *95*

6.8 Eukaryotic Cells *100*

6.30 Cell Junctions in Animal Tissues *120*

7.19 Endocytosis in Animal Cells *138*

11.8 Cell-Surface Transmembrane Receptors *215*

12.7 Mitosis in an Animal Cell *236*

13.8 Meiosis in an Animal Cell *258*

16.22 Chromatin Packing in a Eukaryotic Chromosome *328*

24.3 Reproductive Barriers *502*

25.7 The Origin of Mammals *525*

27.16 Selected Major Groups of Bacteria *578*

28.2 Protistan Diversity *590*

29.3 Derived Traits of Land Plants *614*

29.7 Bryophyte Diversity *620*

29.13 Seedless Vascular Plant Diversity *626*

30.7 Gymnosperm Diversity *636*

30.17 Angiosperm Diversity *644*

31.10 Fungal Diversity *655*

33.3 Invertebrate Diversity *681*

33.41 Insect Diversity *706*

34.40 Mammalian Diversity *738*

35.10 Examples of Differentiated Plant Cells *758*

37.14 Unusual Nutritional Adaptations in Plants *812*

38.3 Trends in the Evolution of Flowers *817*

38.5 Flower Pollination *820*

38.12 Fruit and Seed Dispersal *826*

40.5 Structure and Function in Animal Tissues *871*

41.6 Four Main Feeding Mechanisms of Animals *898*

44.12 The Mammalian Excretory System *980*

46.11 Human Gametogenesis *1022*

49.11 The Organization of the Human Brain *1086*

50.10 The Structure of the Human Ear *1107*

50.17 The Structure of the Human Eye *1112*

50.30 The Regulation of Skeletal Muscle Contraction *1123*

52.2 The Scope of Ecological Research *1159*

52.3 Global Climate Patterns *1160*

52.11 Terrestrial Biomes *1167*

52.14 Aquatic Biomes *1173*

53.18 Mechanisms of Density-Dependent Regulation *1198*

55.14 Water and Nutrient Cycling *1244*

55.19 Restoration Ecology Worldwide *1250*

Inquiry Figures

1.25 Does camouflage affect predation rates on two populations of mice? *20*

4.2 Can organic molecules form under conditions estimated to simulate those on the early Earth? *57*

5.22 What can the 3-D shape of the enzyme RNA polymerase II tell us about its function? *84*

7.4 Do membrane proteins move? *126*

†10.10 Which wavelengths of light are most effective in driving photosynthesis? *192*

12.9 At which end do kinetochore microtubules shorten during anaphase? *239*

12.14 Do molecular signals in the cytoplasm regulate the cell cycle? *243*

14.3 When F_1 hybrid pea plants self- or cross-pollinate, which traits appear in the F_2 generation? *269*

14.8 Do the alleles for one character assort into gametes dependently or independently of the alleles for a different character? *274*

†15.4 In a cross between a wild-type female fruit fly and a mutant white-eyed male, what color eyes will the F_1 and F_2 offspring have? *295*

15.9 How does linkage between two genes affect inheritance of characters? *299*

16.2 Can a genetic trait be transferred between different bacterial strains? *313*

16.4 Is protein or DNA the genetic material of phage T2? *314*

*†16.11 Does DNA replication follow the conservative, semiconservative, or dispersive model? *320*

17.2 Do individual genes specify the enzymes that function in a biochemical pathway? *335*

18.22 Could Bicoid be a morphogen that determines the anterior end of a fruit fly? *382*

19.2 What causes tobacco mosaic disease? *393*

20.16 Can the nucleus from a differentiated animal cell direct development of an organism? *423*

20.21 Can a fully differentiated human cell be "deprogrammed" to become a stem cell? *427*

21.18 What is the function of a gene (*FOXP2*) that is rapidly evolving in the human lineage? *455*

22.13 Can a change in a population's food source result in evolution by natural selection? *471*

*23.16 Do females select mates based on traits indicative of "good genes"? *494*

24.7 Can divergence of allopatric populations lead to reproductive isolation? *506*

24.11 Does sexual selection in cichlids result in reproductive isolation? *509*

24.18 How does hybridization lead to speciation in sunflowers? *515*

25.26 What causes the loss of spines in lake stickleback fish? *540*

26.6 What is the species identity of food being sold as whale meat? *551*

27.10 Can prokaryotes evolve rapidly in response to environmental change? *572*

28.24 What is the root of the eukaryotic tree? *605*

29.8 Can bryophytes reduce the rate at which key nutrients are lost from soils? *621*

31.20 Do fungal endophytes benefit a woody plant? *661*

33.29 Did the arthropod body plan result from new *Hox* genes? *700*

34.49 Did gene flow occur between Neanderthals and humans? *747*

36.17 Does phloem sap contain more sugar near sources than near sinks? *795*

37.9 How variable are the compositions of bacterial communities inside and outside of roots? *807*

39.5 What part of a grass coleoptile senses light, and how is the signal transmitted? *841*

39.6 What causes polar movement of auxin from shoot tip to base? *842*

39.16 How does the order of red and far-red illumination affect seed germination? *851*

40.16 How does a Burmese python generate heat while incubating eggs? *882*

40.21 What happens to the circadian clock during hibernation? *887*

41.4 Can diet influence the frequency of birth defects? *896*

42.25 What causes respiratory distress syndrome? *938*

43.5 Can a single antimicrobial peptide protect fruit flies against infection? *949*

44.20 Can aquaporin mutations cause diabetes? *989*

46.8 Why is sperm usage biased when female fruit flies mate twice? *1018*

†47.4 Does the distribution of Ca^{2+} in an egg correlate with formation of the fertilization envelope? *1040*

47.23 How does distribution of the gray crescent affect the developmental potential of the first two daughter cells? *1055*

47.24 Can the dorsal lip of the blastopore induce cells in another part of the amphibian embryo to change their developmental fate? *1056*

47.26 What role does the zone of polarizing activity (ZPA) play in limb pattern formation in vertebrates? *1057*

50.23 How do mammals detect different tastes? *1117*

51.8 Does a digger wasp use landmarks to find her nest? *1140*

51.24 Are differences in migratory orientation within a species genetically determined? *1151*

52.18 Does feeding by sea urchins limit seaweed distribution? *1179*

53.14 How does caring for offspring affect parental survival in kestrels? *1196*

†54.3 Can a species' niche be influenced by interspecific competition? *1210*

54.18 Is *Pisaster ochraceus* a keystone predator? *1220*

54.26 How does species richness relate to area? *1227*

55.8 Which nutrient limits phytoplankton production along the coast of Long Island? *1237*

55.15 How does temperature affect litter decomposition in an ecosystem? *1247*

*56.14 What caused the drastic decline of the Illinois greater prairie chicken population? *1262*

Research Method Figures

6.4 Cell Fractionation *96*

10.9 Determining an Absorption Spectrum *191*

13.3 Preparing a Karyotype *254*

14.2 Crossing Pea Plants *268*

14.7 The Testcross *273*

15.11 Constructing a Linkage Map *303*

20.3 Dideoxy Chain Termination Method for Sequencing DNA *410*

20.4 Next-Generation Sequencing *411*

20.8 The Polymerase Chain Reaction (PCR) *415*

20.12 RT-PCR Analysis of the Expression of Single Genes *419*

20.17 Reproductive Cloning of a Mammal by Nuclear Transplantation *424*

26.15 Applying Parsimony to a Problem in Molecular Systematics *557*

35.21 Using Dendrochronology to Study Climate *767*

35.25 Using the Ti Plasmid to Produce Transgenic Plants *770*

37.7 Hydroponic Culture *804*

48.8 Intracellular Recording *1066*

53.2 Determining Population Size Using the Mark-Recapture Method *1185*

54.12 Determining Microbial Diversity Using Molecular Tools *1217*

55.5 Determining Primary Production with Satellites *1236*

*The Inquiry Figure, original research paper, and a worksheet to guide you through the paper are provided in *Inquiry in Action: Interpreting Scientific Papers*, Third Edition.
†A related Experimental Inquiry Tutorial can be assigned in MasteringBiology.®

Interviews

 UNIT 1

THE CHEMISTRY OF LIFE 27

Venki Ramakrishnan

MRC Laboratory of Molecular Biology
Cambridge, England

 UNIT 2

THE CELL 92

Haifan Lin

Yale Stem Cell Center
Yale University

 UNIT 3

GENETICS 251

Charles Rotimi

Center for Research on
Genomics and Global Health,
National Institutes of Health

 UNIT 4

MECHANISMS OF EVOLUTION 461

Hopi Hoekstra

Harvard University

 UNIT 5

THE EVOLUTIONARY HISTORY OF BIOLOGICAL DIVERSITY 546

Nicole King

University of California,
Berkeley

 UNIT 6

PLANT FORM AND FUNCTION 751

Jeffery Dangl

University of North Carolina,
Chapel Hill

 UNIT 7

ANIMAL FORM AND FUNCTION 866

Ulrike Heberlein

HHMI Janelia Farm Research
Campus

 UNIT 8

ECOLOGY 1157

Monica Turner

University of Wisconsin,
Madison

Acknowledgments

The authors wish to express their gratitude to the global community of instructors, researchers, students, and publishing professionals who have contributed to the Tenth Edition of CAMPBELL BIOLOGY.

As authors of this text, we are mindful of the daunting challenge of keeping up to date in all areas of our rapidly expanding subject. We are grateful to the many scientists who helped shape this text by discussing their research fields with us, answering specific questions in their areas of expertise, and sharing their ideas about biology education. We are especially grateful to the following, listed alphabetically: Monika Abedin, John Archibald, Chris Austin, Kristian Axelsen, Jamie Bascom, Ethan Bier, Barbara Bowman, Daniel Boyce, Jean DeSaix, Amy Dobberteen, Ira Greenbaum, Ken Halanych, Robert Hebbel, Erin Irish, Duncan Irschick, Azarias Karamanlidis, Patrick Keeling, Nikos Kyrpides, Teri Liegler, Gene Likens, Tom Owens, Kevin Peterson, Michael Pollock, Amy Rappaport, Andrew Roger, Andrew Roth, Andrew Schaffner, Thomas Schneider, Alastair Simpson, Doug Soltis, Pamela Soltis, Anna Thanukos, Elisabeth Wade, Phillip Zamore, and Christine Zardecki. In addition, the biologists listed on pages xxviii–xxxi provided detailed reviews, helping us ensure the text's scientific accuracy and improve its pedagogical effectiveness. We thank Marty Taylor, author of the Study Guide, for her many contributions to the accuracy, clarity, and consistency of the text; and we thank Carolyn Wetzel, Ruth Buskirk, Joan Sharp, Jennifer Yeh, and Charlene D'Avanzo for their contributions to the Scientific Skills Exercises.

Thanks also to the other professors and students, from all over the world, who contacted the authors directly with useful suggestions. We alone bear the responsibility for any errors that remain, but the dedication of our consultants, reviewers, and other correspondents makes us confident in the accuracy and effectiveness of this text.

Interviews with prominent scientists have been a hallmark of CAMPBELL BIOLOGY since its inception, and conducting these interviews was again one of the great pleasures of revising the book. To open the eight units of this edition, we are proud to include interviews with Venki Ramakrishnan, Haifan Lin, Charles Rotimi, Hopi Hoekstra, Nicole King, Jeffery Dangl, Ulrike Heberlein, and Monica Turner.

The value of CAMPBELL BIOLOGY as a learning tool is greatly enhanced by the supplementary materials that have been created for instructors and students. We recognize that the dedicated authors of these materials are essentially writing mini (and not so mini) books. We appreciate the hard work and creativity of all the authors listed, with their creations, on page xxiii. We are also grateful to Kathleen Fitzpatrick and Nicole Tunbridge (PowerPoint® Lecture Presentations); Scott Meissner, Roberta Batorsky, Tara Turley Stoulig, Lisa Flick, and Bryan Jennings (Clicker Questions); Ed Zalisko, Melissa Fierke, Rebecca Orr, and Diane Jokinen (Test Bank); Natalie Bronstein, Linda Logdberg, Matt McArdle, Ria Murphy, Chris Romero, and Andy Stull (Dynamic Study Modules); and Eileen Gregory, Rebecca Orr, and Elena Pravosudova (Adaptive Follow-up Assignments).

MasteringBiology® and the other electronic accompaniments for this text are invaluable teaching and learning aids. We thank the hardworking, industrious instructors who worked on the revised and new media: Beverly Brown, Erica Cline, Willy Cushwa, Tom Kennedy, Tom Owens, Michael Pollock, Frieda Reichsman, Rick Spinney, Dennis Venema, Carolyn Wetzel, Heather Wilson-Ashworth, and Jennifer Yeh. We are also grateful to the many other people—biology instructors, editors, and production experts—who are listed in the credits for these and other elements of the electronic media that accompany the text.

CAMPBELL BIOLOGY results from an unusually strong synergy between a team of scientists and a team of publishing professionals.

Our editorial team at Pearson Education again demonstrated unmatched talents, commitment, and pedagogical insights. Our Senior Acquisitions Editor, Josh Frost, brought publishing savvy, intelligence, and a much appreciated level head to leading the whole team. The clarity and effectiveness of every page owe much to our extraordinary Supervising Editors Pat Burner and Beth Winickoff, who worked with a top-notch team of Developmental Editors in Mary Ann Murray, John Burner, Matt Lee, Hilair Chism, and Andrew Recher (Precision Graphics). Our unsurpassed Executive Editorial Manager Ginnie Simione Jutson, Executive Director of Development Deborah Gale, Assistant Editor Katherine Harrison-Adcock, and Editor-in-Chief Beth Wilbur were indispensable in moving the project in the right direction. We also want to thank Robin Heyden for organizing the annual Biology Leadership Conferences and keeping us in touch with the world of AP Biology.

You would not have this beautiful text if not for the work of the production team: Director of Production Erin Gregg; Managing Editor Michael Early; Project Manager Shannon Tozier; Senior Photo Editor Donna Kalal; Photo Researcher Maureen Spuhler; Copy Editor Joanna Dinsmore; Proofreader Pete Shanks; Text Permissions Project Managers Alison Bruckner and Joe Croscup; Text Permissions Manager Tim Nicholls; Senior Project Editor Emily Bush, Paging Specialist Donna Healy, and the rest of the staff at S4Carlisle; Art Production Manager Kristina Seymour, Artist Andrew Recher, and the rest of the staff at Precision Graphics; Design Manager Marilyn Perry; Art/Design Specialist Kelly Murphy; Text Designer tani hasegawa; Cover Designer Yvo Riezebos; and Manufacturing Buyer Jeffery Sargent. We also thank those who worked on the text's supplements: Susan Berge, Brady Golden, Jane Brundage, Phil Minnitte, Katherine Harrison-Adcock, Katie Cook, Melanie Field, Kris Langan, Pete Shanks, and John Hammett. And for creating the wonderful package of electronic media that accompanies the text, we are grateful to Tania Mlawer (Director of Content Development for MasteringBiology), Sarah Jensen, J. Zane Barlow, Lee Ann Doctor, Caroline Ross, Taylor Merck, and Brienn Buchanan, as well as Director of Media Development Lauren Fogel and Director of Media Strategy Stacy Treco.

For their important roles in marketing the text and media, we thank Christy Lesko, Lauren Harp, Scott Dustan, Chris Hess, Jane Campbell, Jessica Perry, and Jennifer Aumiller. For her market development support, we thank Michelle Cadden. We are grateful to Paul Corey, President of Pearson Science, for his enthusiasm, encouragement, and support.

The Pearson sales team, which represents CAMPBELL BIOLOGY on campus, is an essential link to the users of the text. They tell us what you like and don't like about the text, communicate the features of the text, and provide prompt service. We thank them for their hard work and professionalism. David Theisen, national director for Key Markets, tirelessly visits countless instructors every year, providing us with meaningful editorial guidance. For representing our text to our international audience, we thank our sales and marketing partners throughout the world. They are all strong allies in biology education.

Finally, we wish to thank our families and friends for their encouragement and patience throughout this long project. Our special thanks to Paul, Dan, Maria, Armelle, and Sean (J.B.R.); Lillian Alibertini Urry and Ross, Lily, and Alex (L.A.U.); Debra and Hannah (M.L.C.); Harry, Elga, Aaron, Sophie, Noah, and Gabriele (S.A.W.); Natalie (P.V.M.); and Sally, Will, David, and Robert (R.B.J.). And, as always, thanks to Rochelle, Allison, Jason, McKay, and Gus.

Jane B. Reece, Lisa A. Urry, Michael L. Cain,
Steven A. Wasserman, Peter V. Minorsky, and Robert B. Jackson

Tenth Edition Reviewers

John Alcock, *Arizona State University*
Rodney Allrich, *Purdue University*
Teri Balser, *University of Wisconsin, Madison*
David Bos, *Purdue University*
Scott Bowling, *Auburn University*
Beverly Brown, *Nazareth College*
Warren Burggren, *University of North Texas*
Dale Burnside, *Lenoir-Rhyne University*
Mickael Cariveau, *Mount Olive College*
Jung Choi, *Georgia Institute of Technology*
Steve Christensen, *Brigham Young University*
Reggie Cobb, *Nashville Community College*
Sean Coleman, *University of the Ozarks*
Deborah Dardis, *Southeastern Louisiana University*
Melissa Deadmond, *Truckee Meadows Community College*
Jean DeSaix, *University of North Carolina, Chapel Hill*
Jason Douglas, *Angelina College*
Anna Edlund, *Lafayette College*
Kurt Elliott, *North West Vista College*
Rob Erdman, *Florida Gulf Coast College*
Dale Erskine, *Lebanon Valley College*
Margaret Folsom, *Methodist College*
Robert Fowler, *San Jose State University*
Kim Fredericks, *Viterbo University*
Craig Gatto, *Illinois State University*
Kristen Genet, *Anoka Ramsey Community College*
Phil Gibson, *University of Oklahoma*
Eric Gillock, *Fort Hayes State University*
Edwin Ginés-Candelaria, *Miami Dade College*
Eileen Gregory, *Rollins College*
Bradley Griggs, *Piedmont Technical College*
Edward Gruberg, *Temple University*
Carla Guthridge, *Cameron University*
Carla Haas, *Pennsylvania State University*
Pryce Pete Haddix, *Auburn University*
Heather Hallen-Adams, *University of Nebraska, Lincoln*
Monica Hall-Woods, *St. Charles Community College*
Bill Hamilton, *Washington & Lee University*
Dennis Haney, *Furman University*
Jean Hardwick, *Ithaca College*
Luke Harmon, *University of Idaho*
Chris Haynes, *Shelton State Community College*
Jean Heitz, *University of Wisconsin, Madison*
Albert Herrera, *University of Southern California*
Chris Hess, *Butler University*
Kendra Hill, *San Diego State University*
Laura Houston, *Northeast Lakeview College*
Harry Itagaki, *Kenyon College*
Kathy Jacobson, *Grinnell College*
Roishene Johnson, *Bossier Parish Community College*
The-Hui Kao, *Pennsylvania State University*
Judy Kaufman, *Monroe Community College*
Thomas Keller, *Florida State University*
Janice Knepper, *Villanova University*
Charles Knight, *California Polytechnic State University*
Jacob Krans, *Western New England University*
Barb Kuemerle, *Case Western Reserve University*
Jani Lewis, *State University of New York*
Nancy Magill, *Indiana University*
Charles Mallery, *University of Miami*
Mark Maloney, *University of South Mississippi*
Darcy Medica, *Pennsylvania State University*
Mike Meighan, *University of California, Berkeley*
Jan Mikesell, *Gettysburg College*
Sarah Milton, *Florida Atlantic University*
Linda Moore, *Georgia Military College*
Karen Neal, *Reynolds University*
Ross Nehm, *Ohio State University*
Eric Nielsen, *University of Michigan*
Gretchen North, *Occidental College*
Margaret Olney, *St. Martin's College*
Rebecca Orr, *Spring Creek College*

Matt Palmtag, *Florida Gulf Coast University*
Eric Peters, *Chicago State University*
Larry Peterson, *University of Guelph*
Deb Pires, *University of California, Los Angeles*
Crima Pogge, *San Francisco Community College*
Michael Pollock, *Mount Royal University*
Jason Porter, *University of the Sciences, Philadelphia*
Elena Pravosudova, *University of Nevada, Reno*
Eileen Preston, *Tarrant Community College Northwest*
Pushpa Ramakrishna, *Chandler-Gilbert Community College*
David Randall, *City University Hong Kong*
Robert Reavis, *Glendale Community College*
Todd Rimkus, *Marymount University*
John Rinehart, *Eastern Oregon University*
Diane Robins, *University of Michigan*
Deb Roess, *Colorado State University*
Suzanne Rogers, *Seton Hill University*
Glenn-Peter Saetre, *University of Oslo*
Sanga Saha, *Harold Washington College*
Kathleen Sandman, *Ohio State University*
Andrew Schaffner, *Cal Poly San Luis Obispo*
Duane Sears, *University of California, Santa Barbara*
Joan Sharp, *Simon Fraser University*
Eric Shows, *Jones County Junior College*
John Skillman, *California State University, San Bernardino*
Doug Soltis, *University of Florida, Gainesville*
Mike Toliver, *Eureka College*
Victoria Turgeon, *Furman University*
Amy Volmer, *Swarthmore College*
James Wandersee, *Louisiana State University*
James Wee, *Loyola University*
Murray Wiegand, *University of Winnipeg*
Kimberly Williams, *Kansas State University*
Shuhai Xiao, *Virginia Polytechnic Institute*

Reviewers of Previous Editions

Kenneth Able, *State University of New York, Albany*; Thomas Adams, *Michigan State University*; Martin Adamson, *University of British Columbia*; Dominique Adriaens, *Ghent University*; Ann Aguanno, *Marymount Manhattan College*; Shylaja Akkaraju, *Bronx Community College of CUNY*; Marc Albrecht, *University of Nebraska*; John Alcock, *Arizona State University*; Eric Alcorn, *Acadia University*; George R. Aliaga, *Tarrant County College*; Richard Almon, *State University of New York, Buffalo*; Bonnie Amos, *Angelo State University*; Katherine Anderson, *University of California, Berkeley*; Richard J. Andren, *Montgomery County Community College*; Estry Ang, *University of Pittsburgh, Greensburg*; Jeff Appling, *Clemson University*; J. David Archibald, *San Diego State University*; David Armstrong, *University of Colorado, Boulder*; Howard J. Arnott, *University of Texas, Arlington*; Mary Ashley, *University of Illinois, Chicago*; Angela S. Aspbury, *Texas State University*; Robert Atherton, *University of Wyoming*; Karl Aufderheide, *Texas A&M University*; Leigh Auleb, *San Francisco State University*; Terry Austin, *Temple College*; P. Stephen Baenziger, *University of Nebraska*; Brian Bagatto, *University of Akron*; Ellen Baker, *Santa Monica College*; Katherine Baker, *Millersville University*; Virginia Baker, *Chipola College*; William Barklow, *Framingham State College*; Susan Barman, *Michigan State University*; Steven Barnhart, *Santa Rosa Junior College*; Andrew Barton, *University of Maine Farmington*; Rebecca A. Bartow, *Western Kentucky University*; Ron Basmajian, *Merced College*; David Bass, *University of Central Oklahoma*; Bonnie Baxter, *Westminster College*; Tim Beagley, *Salt Lake Community College*; Margaret E. Beard, *College of the Holy Cross*; Tom Beatty, *University of British Columbia*; Chris Beck, *Emory University*; Wayne Becker, *University of Wisconsin, Madison*; Patricia Bedinger, *Colorado State University*; Jane Beiswenger, *University of Wyoming*; Anne Bekoff, *University of Colorado, Boulder*; Marc Bekoff, *University of Colorado, Boulder*; Tania Beliz, *College of San Mateo*; Adrianne Bendich, *Hoffman-La Roche, Inc.*; Marilee Benore, *University of Michigan, Dearborn*; Barbara Bentley, *State University of New York, Stony Brook*; Darwin Berg, *University of California, San Diego*; Werner Bergen, *Michigan State University*; Gerald Bergstrom, *University of Wisconsin, Milwaukee*; Anna W. Berkovitz, *Purdue University*; Dorothy Berner, *Temple University*; Annalisa Berta, *San Diego State University*; Paulette Bierzychudek, *Pomona College*; Charles Biggers, *Memphis State University*; Kenneth Birnbaum, *New York University*; Catherine Black, *Idaho State University*; Michael W. Black, *California Polytechnic State University, San Luis Obispo*; William Blaker, *Furman University*; Robert Blanchard, *University of New Hampshire*; Andrew R. Blaustein, *Oregon State University*; Judy Bluemer, *Morton*

College; Edward Blumenthal, *Marquette University*; Robert Blystone, *Trinity University*; Robert Boley, *University of Texas, Arlington*; Jason E. Bond, *East Carolina University*; Eric Bonde, *University of Colorado, Boulder*; Cornelius Bondzi, *Hampton University*; Richard Boohar, *University of Nebraska, Omaha*; Carey L. Booth, *Reed College*; Allan Bornstein, *Southeast Missouri State University*; David Bos, *Purdue University*; Oliver Bossdorf, *State University of New York, Stony Book*; James L. Botsford, *New Mexico State University*; Lisa Boucher, *University of Nebraska, Omaha*; J. Michael Bowes, *Humboldt State University*; Richard Bowker, *Alma College*; Robert Bowker, *Glendale Community College, Arizona*; Scott Bowling, *Auburn University*; Barbara Bowman, *Mills College*; Barry Bowman, *University of California, Santa Cruz*; Deric Bownds, *University of Wisconsin, Madison*; Robert Boyd, *Auburn University*; Sunny Boyd, *University of Notre Dame*; Jerry Brand, *University of Texas, Austin*; Edward Braun, *Iowa State University*; Theodore A. Bremner, *Howard University*; James Brenneman, *University of Evansville*; Charles H. Brenner, *Berkeley, California*; Lawrence Brewer, *University of Kentucky*; Donald P. Briskin, *University of Illinois, Urbana*; Paul Broady, *University of Canterbury*; Chad Brommer, *Emory University*; Judith L. Bronstein, *University of Arizona*; Danny Brower, *University of Arizona*; Carole Browne, *Wake Forest University*; Mark Browning, *Purdue University*; David Bruck, *San Jose State University*; Robb T. Brumfield, *Louisiana State University*; Herbert Bruneau, *Oklahoma State University*; Gary Brusca, *Humboldt State University*; Richard C. Brusca, *University of Arizona, Arizona-Sonora Desert Museum*; Alan H. Brush, *University of Connecticut, Storrs*; Howard Buhse, *University of Illinois, Chicago*; Arthur Buikema, *Virginia Tech*; Beth Burch, *Huntington University*; Al Burchsted, *College of Staten Island*; Meg Burke, *University of North Dakota*; Edwin Burling, *De Anza College*; William Busa, *Johns Hopkins University*; Jorge Busciglio, *University of California, Irvine*; John Bushnell, *University of Colorado*; Linda Butler, *University of Texas, Austin*; David Byrnes, *Florida Community College, Jacksonville*; Guy A. Caldwell, *University of Alabama*; Jane Caldwell, *West Virginia University*; Kim A. Caldwell, *University of Alabama*; Ragan Callaway, *The University of Montana*; Kenneth M. Cameron, *University of Wisconsin, Madison*; R. Andrew Cameron, *California Institute of Technology*; Alison Campbell, *University of Waikato*; Iain Campbell, *University of Pittsburgh*; Patrick Canary, *Northland Pioneer College*; W. Zacheus Cande, *University of California, Berkeley*; Deborah Canington, *University of California, Davis*; Robert E. Cannon, *University of North Carolina, Greensboro*; Frank Cantelmo, *St. John's University*; John Capeheart, *University of Houston, Downtown*; Gregory Capelli, *College of William and Mary*; Cheryl Keller Capone, *Pennsylvania State University*; Richard Cardullo, *University of California, Riverside*; Nina Caris, *Texas A&M University*; Jeffrey Carmichael, *University of North Dakota*; Robert Carroll, *East Carolina University*; Laura L. Carruth, *Georgia State University*; J. Aaron Cassill, *University of Texas, San Antonio*; Karen I. Champ, *Central Florida Community College*; David Champlin, *University of Southern Maine*; Brad Chandler, *Palo Alto College*; Wei-Jen Chang, *Hamilton College*; Bruce Chase, *University of Nebraska, Omaha*; P. Bryant Chase, *Florida State University*; Doug Cheeseman, *De Anza College*; Shepley Chen, *University of Illinois, Chicago*; Giovina Chinchar, *Tougaloo College*; Joseph P. Chinnici, *Virginia Commonwealth University*; Jung H. Choi, *Georgia Institute of Technology*; Steve Christensen, *Brigham Young University, Idaho*; Geoffrey Church, *Fairfield University*; Henry Claman, *University of Colorado Health Science Center*; Anne Clark, *Binghamton University*; Greg Clark, *University of Texas*; Patricia J. Clark, *Indiana University-Purdue University, Indianapolis*; Ross C. Clark, *Eastern Kentucky University*; Lynwood Clemens, *Michigan State University*; Janice J. Clymer, *San Diego Mesa College*; William P. Coffman, *University of Pittsburgh*; Austin Randy Cohen, *California State University, Northridge*; J. John Cohen, *University of Colorado Health Science Center*; James T. Colbert, *Iowa State University*; John Colpaert, *Hasselt University*; Robert Colvin, *Ohio University*; Jay Comeaux, *McNeese State University*; David Cone, *Saint Mary's University*; Elizabeth Connor, *University of Massachusetts*; Joanne Conover, *University of Connecticut*; Gregory Copenhaver, *University of North Carolina, Chapel Hill*; John Corliss, *University of Maryland*; James T. Costa, *Western Carolina University*; Stuart J. Coward, *University of Georgia*; Charles Creutz, *University of Toledo*; Bruce Criley, *Illinois Wesleyan University*; Norma Criley, *Illinois Wesleyan University*; Joe W. Crim, *University of Georgia*; Greg Crowther, *University of Washington*; Karen Curto, *University of Pittsburgh*; William Cushwa, *Clark College*; Anne Cusic, *University of Alabama, Birmingham*; Richard Cyr, *Pennsylvania State University*; Marymegan Daly, *The Ohio State University*; W. Marshall Darley, *University of Georgia*; Cynthia Dassler, *The Ohio State University*; Shannon Datwyler, *California State University, Sacramento*; Marianne Dauwalder, *University of Texas, Austin*; Larry Davenport, *Samford University*; Bonnie J. Davis, *San Francisco State University*; Jerry Davis, *University of Wisconsin, La Crosse*; Michael A. Davis, *Central Connecticut State University*; Thomas Davis, *University of New Hampshire*; John Dearn, *University of Canberra*; Maria E. de Bellard, *California State University, Northridge*; Teresa DeGolier, *Bethel College*; James Dekloe, *University of California, Santa Cruz*; Eugene Delay, *University of Vermont*; Patricia A. DeLeon, *University of Delaware*; Veronique Delesalle, *Gettysburg College*; T. Delevoryas, *University of Texas, Austin*; Roger Del Moral, *University of Washington*; Charles F. Delwiche, *University of Maryland*; Diane C. DeNagel, *Northwestern University*; William L. Dentler, *University of Kansas*; Daniel DerVartanian, *University of Georgia*; Jean DeSaix, *University of North Carolina, Chapel Hill*; Janet De Souza-Hart, *Massachusetts College of Pharmacy & Health Sciences*; Biao Ding, *Ohio State University*; Michael Dini, *Texas Tech University*; Andrew Dobson, *Princeton University*; Stanley Dodson, *University of Wisconsin, Madison*; Mark Drapeau, *University of California, Irvine*; John Drees, *Temple University School of Medicine*; Charles Drewes, *Iowa State University*; Marvin Druger, *Syracuse University*; Gary Dudley, *University of Georgia*; Susan Dunford, *University of Cincinnati*; Kathryn A. Durham, *Lorain Community College*; Betsey Dyer, *Wheaton College*; Robert Eaton, *University of Colorado*; Robert S. Edgar, *University of California, Santa Cruz*; Douglas J. Eernisse, *California State University, Fullerton*; Betty J. Eidemiller, *Lamar University*; Brad Elder, *Doane College*; Curt Elderkin, *College of New Jersey*; William D. Eldred, *Boston University*; Michelle Elekonich, *University of Nevada, Las Vegas*; George Ellmore, *Tufts University*; Mary Ellard-Ivey, *Pacific Lutheran University*; Norman Ellstrand, *University of California, Riverside*; Johnny El-Rady, *University of South Florida*; Dennis Emery, *Iowa State University*; John Endler, *University of California, Santa Barbara*; Margaret T. Erskine, *Lansing Community College*; Gerald Esch, *Wake Forest University*; Frederick B. Essig, *University of South Florida*; Mary Eubanks, *Duke University*; David Evans, *University of Florida*; Robert C. Evans, *Rutgers University, Camden*; Sharon Eversman, *Montana State University*; Olukemi Fadayomi, *Ferris State University*; Lincoln Fairchild, *Ohio State University*; Peter Fajer, *Florida State University*; Bruce Fall, *University of Minnesota*; Sam Fan, *Bradley University*; Lynn Fancher, *College of DuPage*; Ellen H. Fanning, *Vanderbilt University*; Paul Farnsworth, *University of New Mexico*; Larry Farrell, *Idaho State University*; Jerry F. Feldman, *University of California, Santa Cruz*; Lewis Feldman, *University of California, Berkeley*; Myriam Alhadeff Feldman, *Cascadia Community College*; Eugene Fenster, *Longview Community College*; Russell Fernald, *University of Oregon*; Rebecca Ferrell, *Metropolitan State College of Denver*; Kim Finer, *Kent State University*; Milton Fingerman, *Tulane University*; Barbara Finney, *Regis College*; Teresa Fischer, *Indian River Community College*; Frank Fish, *West Chester University*; David Fisher, *University of Hawaii, Manoa*; Jonathan S. Fisher, *St. Louis University*; Steven Fisher, *University of California, Santa Barbara*; David Fitch, *New York University*; Kirk Fitzhugh, *Natural History Museum of Los Angeles County*; Lloyd Fitzpatrick, *University of North Texas*; William Fixsen, *Harvard University*; T. Fleming, *Bradley University*; Abraham Flexer, *Manuscript Consultant, Boulder, Colorado*; Kerry Foresman, *University of Montana*; Norma Fowler, *University of Texas, Austin*; Robert G. Fowler, *San Jose State University*; David Fox, *University of Tennessee, Knoxville*; Carl Frankel, *Pennsylvania State University, Hazleton*; Robert Franklin, *College of Charleston*; James Franzen, *University of Pittsburgh*; Art Fredeen, *University of Northern British Columbia*; Bill Freedman, *Dalhousie University*; Matt Friedman, *University of Chicago*; Otto Friesen, *University of Virginia*; Frank Frisch, *Chapman University*; Virginia Fry, *Monterey Peninsula College*; Bernard Frye, *University of Texas, Arlington*; Jed Fuhrman, *University of Southern California*; Alice Fulton, *University of Iowa*; Chandler Fulton, *Brandeis University*; Sara Fultz, *Stanford University*; Berdell Funke, *North Dakota State University*; Anne Funkhouser, *University of the Pacific*; Zofia E. Gagnon, *Marist College*; Michael Gaines, *University of Miami*; Cynthia M. Galloway, *Texas A&M University, Kingsville*; Arthur W. Galston, *Yale University*; Stephen Gammie, *University of Wisconsin, Madison*; Carl Gans, *University of Michigan*; John Gapter, *University of Northern Colorado*; Andrea Gargas, *University of Wisconsin, Madison*; Lauren Garner, *California Polytechnic State University, San Luis Obispo*; Reginald Garrett, *University of Virginia*; Patricia Gensel, *University of North Carolina*; Chris George, *California Polytechnic State University, San Luis Obispo*; Robert George, *University of Wyoming*; J. Whitfield Gibbons, *University of Georgia*; J. Phil Gibson, *Agnes Scott College*; Frank Gilliam, *Marshall University*; Simon Gilroy, *University of Wisconsin, Madison*; Alan D. Gishlick, *Gustavus Adolphus College*; Todd Gleeson, *University of Colorado*; Jessica Gleffe, *University of California, Irvine*; John Glendinning, *Barnard College*; David Glenn-Lewin, *Wichita State University*; William Glider, *University of Nebraska*; Tricia Glidewell, *Marist School*; Elizabeth A. Godrick, *Boston University*; Jim Goetze, *Laredo Community College*; Lynda Goff, *University of California, Santa Cruz*; Elliott Goldstein, *Arizona State University*; Paul Goldstein, *University of Texas, El Paso*; Sandra Gollnick, *State University of New York, Buffalo*; Roy Golsteyn, *University of Lethbridge*; Anne Good, *University of California, Berkeley*; Judith Goodenough, *University of Massachusetts, Amherst*; Wayne Goodey, *University of British Columbia*; Barbara E. Goodman, *University of South Dakota*; Robert Goodman, *University of Wisconsin, Madison*; Ester Goudsmit, *Oakland University*; Linda Graham, *University of Wisconsin, Madison*; Robert Grammer, *Belmont University*; Joseph Graves, *Arizona State University*; Phyllis Griffard, *University of Houston, Downtown*; A. J. F. Griffiths, *University of British Columbia*; William Grimes, *University of Arizona*; David Grise, *Texas A&M University, Corpus Christi*; Mark Gromko, *Bowling Green State University*; Serine Gropper, *Auburn University*; Katherine L. Gross, *Ohio State University*; Gary Gussin, *University of Iowa*; Mark Guyer, *National Human Genome Research Institute*; Ruth Levy Guyer, *Bethesda, Maryland*; R. Wayne Habermehl, *Montgomery County Community College*; Mac Hadley, *University of Arizona*; Joel Hagen, *Radford University*; Jack P. Hailman, *University of Wisconsin*; Leah Haimo, *University of California, Riverside*; Ken Halanych, *Auburn University*; Jody Hall, *Brown University*; Douglas Hallett, *Northern Arizona University*; Rebecca Halyard, *Clayton State College*; Devney Hamilton, *Stanford University (student)*; E. William Hamilton, *Washington and Lee University*; Matthew B. Hamilton, *Georgetown University*; Sam Hammer, *Boston University*; Penny Hanchey-Bauer, *Colorado State University*; William F. Hanna, *Massasoit Community College*; Laszlo Hanzely, *Northern Illinois University*; Jeff Hardin, *University of Wisconsin, Madison*; Lisa Harper, *University of California, Berkeley*; Jeanne M. Harris, *University of Vermont*; Richard Harrison, *Cornell University*; Stephanie Harvey, *Georgia Southwestern State University*; Carla Hass, *Pennsylvania State University*; Chris Haufler, *University of Kansas*; Bernard A. Hauser, *University of Florida*; Chris Haynes,

Shelton State Community College; Evan B. Hazard, *Bemidji State University*, (emeritus); H. D. Heath, *California State University, East Bay*; George Hechtel, *State University of New York, Stony Brook*; S. Blair Hedges, *Pennsylvania State University*; Brian Hedlund, *University of Nevada, Las Vegas*; David Heins, *Tulane University*; Jean Heitz, *University of Wisconsin, Madison*; Andreas Hejnol, *Sars International Centre for Marine Molecular Biology*; John D. Helmann, *Cornell University*; Colin Henderson, *University of Montana*; Susan Hengeveld, *Indiana University*; Michelle Henricks, *University of California, Los Angeles*; Caroll Henry, *Chicago State University*; Frank Heppner, *University of Rhode Island*; Albert Herrera, *University of Southern California*; Scott Herrick, *Missouri Western State College*; Ira Herskowitz, *University of California, San Francisco*; Paul E. Hertz, *Barnard College*; David Hibbett, *Clark University*; R. James Hickey, *Miami University*; William Hillenius, *College of Charleston*; Kenneth Hillers, *California Polytechnic State University, San Luis Obispo*; Ralph Hinegardner, *University of California, Santa Cruz*; William Hines, *Foothill College*; Robert Hinrichsen, *Indiana University of Pennsylvania*; Helmut Hirsch, *State University of New York, Albany*; Tuan-hua David Ho, *Washington University*; Carl Hoagstrom, *Ohio Northern University*; Jason Hodin, *Stanford University*; James Hoffman, *University of Vermont*; A. Scott Holaday, *Texas Tech University*; N. Michele Holbrook, *Harvard University*; James Holland, *Indiana State University, Bloomington*; Charles Holliday, *Lafayette College*; Lubbock Karl Holte, *Idaho State University*; Alan R. Holyoak, *Brigham Young University, Idaho*; Laura Hoopes, *Occidental College*; Nancy Hopkins, *Massachusetts Institute of Technology*; Sandra Horikami, *Daytona Beach Community College*; Kathy Hornberger, *Widener University*; Pius F. Horner, *San Bernardino Valley College*; Becky Houck, *University of Portland*; Margaret Houk, *Ripon College*; Daniel J. Howard, *New Mexico State University*; Ronald R. Hoy, *Cornell University*; Sandra Hsu, *Skyline College*; Sara Huang, *Los Angeles Valley College*; Cristin Hulslander, *University of Oregon*; Donald Humphrey, *Emory University School of Medicine*; Catherine Hurlbut, *Florida State College, Jacksonville*; Diane Husic, *Moravian College*; Robert J. Huskey, *University of Virginia*; Steven Hutcheson, *University of Maryland, College Park*; Linda L. Hyde, *Gordon College*; Bradley Hyman, *University of California, Riverside*; Jeffrey Ihara, *Mira Costa College*; Mark Iked, *San Bernardino Valley College*; Cheryl Ingram-Smith, *Clemson University*; Alice Jacklet, *State University of New York, Albany*; John Jackson, *North Hennepin Community College*; Thomas Jacobs, *University of Illinois*; Mark Jaffe, *Nova Southeastern University*; John C. Jahoda, *Bridgewater State College*; Douglas Jensen, *Converse College*; Dan Johnson, *East Tennessee State University*; Lance Johnson, *Midland Lutheran College*; Lee Johnson, *The Ohio State University*; Randall Johnson, *University of California, San Diego*; Stephen Johnson, *William Penn University*; Wayne Johnson, *Ohio State University*; Kenneth C. Jones, *California State University, Northridge*; Russell Jones, *University of California, Berkeley*; Cheryl Jorcyk, *Boise State University*; Chad Jordan, *North Carolina State University*; Alan Journet, *Southeast Missouri State University*; Walter Judd, *University of Florida*; Thomas W. Jurik, *Iowa State University*; Caroline M. Kane, *University of California, Berkeley*; Thomas C. Kane, *University of Cincinnati*; Tamos Kapros, *University of Missouri*; E. L. Karlstrom, *University of Puget Sound*; Jennifer Katcher, *Pima Community College*; Laura A. Katz, *Smith College*; Maureen Kearney, *Field Museum of Natural History*; Eric G. Keeling, *Cary Institute of Ecosystem Studies*; Patrick Keeling, *University of British Columbia*; Elizabeth A. Kellogg, *University of Missouri, St. Louis*; Norm Kenkel, *University of Manitoba*; Chris Kennedy, *Simon Fraser University*; George Khoury, *National Cancer Institute*; Rebecca T. Kimball, *University of Florida*; Mark Kirk, *University of Missouri, Columbia*; Robert Kitchin, *University of Wyoming*; Hillar Klandorf, *West Virginia University*; Attila O. Klein, *Brandeis University*; Daniel Klionsky, *University of Michigan*; Mark Knauss, *Georgia Highlands College*; Jennifer Knight, *University of Colorado*; Ned Knight, *Linfield College*; Roger Koeppe, *University of Arkansas*; David Kohl, *University of California, Santa Barbara*; Greg Kopf, *University of Pennsylvania School of Medicine*; Thomas Koppenheffer, *Trinity University*; Peter Kourtev, *Central Michigan University*; Margareta Krabbe, *Uppsala University*; Anselm Kratochwil, *Universität Osnabrück*; Eliot Krause, *Seton Hall University*; Deborah M. Kristan, *California State University, San Marcos*; Steven Kristoff, *Ivy Tech Community College*; William Kroll, *Loyola University, Chicago*; Janis Kuby, *San Francisco State University*; Justin P. Kumar, *Indiana University*; Rukmani Kuppuswami, *Laredo Community College*; David Kurijaka, *Ohio University*; Lee Kurtz, *Georgia Gwinnett College*; Michael P. Labare, *United States Military Academy, West Point*; Marc-André Lachance, *University of Western Ontario*; J. A. Lackey, *State University of New York, Oswego*; Elaine Lai, *Brandeis University*; Mohamed Lakrim, *Kingsborough Community College*; Ellen Lamb, *University of North Carolina, Greensboro*; William Lamberts, *College of St Benedict and St John's University*; William L'Amoreaux, *College of Staten Island*; Lynn Lamoreux, *Texas A&M University*; Carmine A. Lanciani, *University of Florida*; Kenneth Lang, *Humboldt State University*; Dominic Lannutti, *El Paso Community College*; Allan Larson, *Washington University*; John Latto, *University of California, Santa Barbara*; Diane K. Lavett, *State University of New York, Cortland, and Emory University*; Charles Leavell, *Fullerton College*; C. S. Lee, *University of Texas*; Daewoo Lee, *Ohio University*; Tali D. Lee, *University of Wisconsin, Eau Claire*; Hugh Lefcort, *Gonzaga University*; Robert Leonard, *University of California, Riverside*; Michael R. Leonardo, *Coe College*; John Lepri, *University of North Carolina, Greensboro*; Donald Levin, *University of Texas, Austin*; Joseph Levine, *Boston College*; Mike Levine, *University of California, Berkeley*; Alcinda Lewis, *University of Colorado, Boulder*; Bill Lewis, *Shoreline Community College*; John Lewis, *Loma Linda University*; Lorraine Lica, *California State University, East Bay*; Harvey Liftin,

Broward Community College; Harvey Lillywhite, *University of Florida, Gainesville*; Graeme Lindbeck, *Valencia Community College*; Clark Lindgren, *Grinnell College*; Diana Lipscomb, *George Washington University*; Christopher Little, *The University of Texas, Pan American*; Kevin D. Livingstone, *Trinity University*; Andrea Lloyd, *Middlebury College*; Sam Loker, *University of New Mexico*; Christopher A. Loretz, *State University of New York, Buffalo*; Jane Lubchenco, *Oregon State University*; Douglas B. Luckie, *Michigan State University*; Hannah Lui, *University of California, Irvine*; Margaret A. Lynch, *Tufts University*; Steven Lynch, *Louisiana State University, Shreveport*; Richard Machemer Jr., *St. John Fisher College*; Elizabeth Machunis-Masuoka, *University of Virginia*; James MacMahon, *Utah State University*; Christine R. Maher, *University of Southern Maine*; Linda Maier, *University of Alabama, Huntsville*; Jose Maldonado, *El Paso Community College*; Richard Malkin, *University of California, Berkeley*; Charles Mallery, *University of Miami*; Keith Malmos, *Valencia Community College, East Campus*; Cindy Malone, *California State University, Northridge*; Carol Mapes, *Kutztown University of Pennsylvania*; William Margolin, *University of Texas Medical School*; Lynn Margulis, *Boston University*; Julia Marrs, *Barnard College* (student); Kathleen A. Marrs, *Indiana University-Purdue University, Indianapolis*; Edith Marsh, *Angelo State University*; Diane L. Marshall, *University of New Mexico*; Karl Mattox, *Miami University of Ohio*; Joyce Maxwell, *California State University, Northridge*; Jeffrey D. May, *Marshall University*; Mike Mayfield, *Ball State University*; Kamau Mbuthia, *Bowling Green State University*; Lee McClenaghan, *San Diego State University*; Richard McCracken, *Purdue University*; Andrew McCubbin, *Washington State University*; Kerry McDonald, *University of Missouri, Columbia*; Tanya McGhee, *Craven Community College*; Jacqueline McLaughlin, *Pennsylvania State University, Lehigh Valley*; Neal McReynolds, *Texas A&M International*; Darcy Medica, *Pennsylvania State University*; Lisa Marie Meffert, *Rice University*; Susan Meiers, *Western Illinois University*; Michael Meighan, *University of California, Berkeley*; Scott Meissner, *Cornell University*; Paul Melchior, *North Hennepin Community College*; Phillip Meneely, *Haverford College*; John Merrill, *Michigan State University*; Brian Metscher, *University of California, Irvine*; Ralph Meyer, *University of Cincinnati*; James Mickle, *North Carolina State University*; Roger Milkman, *University of Iowa*; Helen Miller, *Oklahoma State University*; John Miller, *University of California, Berkeley*; Kenneth R. Miller, *Brown University*; Alex Mills, *University of Windsor*; Eli Minkoff, *Bates College*; John E. Minnich, *University of Wisconsin, Milwaukee*; Subhash Minocha, *University of New Hampshire*; Michael J. Misamore, *Texas Christian University*; Kenneth Mitchell, *Tulane University School of Medicine*; Ivona Mladenovic, *Simon Fraser University*; Alan Molumby, *University of Illinois, Chicago*; Nicholas Money, *Miami University*; Russell Monson, *University of Colorado, Boulder*; Joseph P. Montoya, *Georgia Institute of Technology*; Frank Moore, *Oregon State University*; Janice Moore, *Colorado State University*; Randy Moore, *Wright State University*; William Moore, *Wayne State University*; Carl Moos, *Veterans Administration Hospital, Albany, New York*; Linda Martin Morris, *University of Washington*; Michael Mote, *Temple University*; Alex Motten, *Duke University*; Jeanette Mowery, *Madison Area Technical College*; Deborah Mowshowitz, *Columbia University*; Rita Moyes, *Texas A&M College Station*; Darrel L. Murray, *University of Illinois, Chicago*; Courtney Murren, *College of Charleston*; John Mutchmor, *Iowa State University*; Elliot Myerowitz, *California Institute of Technology*; Gavin Naylor, *Iowa State University*; John Neess, *University of Wisconsin, Madison*; Tom Neils, *Grand Rapids Community College*; Kimberlyn Nelson, *Pennsylvania State University*; Raymond Neubauer, *University of Texas, Austin*; Todd Newbury, *University of California, Santa Cruz*; James Newcomb, *New England College*; Jacalyn Newman, *University of Pittsburgh*; Harvey Nichols, *University of Colorado, Boulder*; Deborah Nickerson, *University of South Florida*; Bette Nicotri, *University of Washington*; Caroline Niederman, *Tomball College*; Maria Nieto, *California State University, East Bay*; Anders Nilsson, *University of Umeå*; Greg Nishiyama, *College of the Canyons*; Charles R. Noback, *College of Physicians and Surgeons, Columbia University*; Jane Noble-Harvey, *Delaware University*; Mary C. Nolan, *Irvine Valley College*; Kathleen Nolta, *University of Michigan*; Peter Nonacs, *University of California, Los Angeles*; Mohamed A. F. Noor, *Duke University*; Shawn Nordell, *St. Louis University*; Richard S. Norman, *University of Michigan, Dearborn* (emeritus); David O. Norris, *University of Colorado, Boulder*; Steven Norris, *California State University, Channel Islands*; Gretchen North, *Occidental College*; Cynthia Norton, *University of Maine, Augusta*; Steve Norton, *East Carolina University*; Steve Nowicki, *Duke University*; Bette H. Nybakken, *Hartnell College*; Brian O'Conner, *University of Massachusetts, Amherst*; Gerard O'Donovan, *University of North Texas*; Eugene Odum, *University of Georgia*; Mark P. Oemke, *Alma College*; Linda Ogren, *University of California, Santa Cruz*; Patricia O'Hern, *Emory University*; Nathan O. Okia, *Auburn University, Montgomery*; Jeanette Oliver, *St. Louis Community College, Florissant Valley*; Gary P. Olivetti, *University of Vermont*; John Olsen, *Rhodes College*; Laura J. Olsen, *University of Michigan*; Sharman O'Neill, *University of California, Davis*; Wan Ooi, *Houston Community College*; Aharon Oren, *The Hebrew University*; John Oross, *University of California, Riverside*; Catherine Ortega, *Fort Lewis College*; Charissa Osborne, *Butler University*; Gay Ostarello, *Diablo Valley College*; Henry R. Owen, *Eastern Illinois University*; Thomas G. Owens, *Cornell University*; Penny Padgett, *University of North Carolina, Chapel Hill*; Kevin Padian, *University of California, Berkeley*; Dianna Padilla, *State University of New York, Stony Brook*; Anthony T. Paganini, *Michigan State University*; Barry Palevitz, *University of Georgia*; Michael A. Palladino, *Monmouth University*; Stephanie Pandolfi, *Michigan State University*; Daniel Papaj, *University of Arizona*; Peter Pappas, *County College of Morris*; Nathalie Pardigon, *Institut Pasteur*; Bulah Parker, *North Carolina State University*; Stanton

Parmeter, *Chemeketa Community College*; Cindy Paszkowski, *University of Alberta*; Robert Patterson, *San Francisco State University*; Ronald Patterson, *Michigan State University*; Crellin Pauling, *San Francisco State University*; Kay Pauling, *Foothill Community College*; Daniel Pavuk, *Bowling Green State University*; Debra Pearce, *Northern Kentucky University*; Patricia Pearson, *Western Kentucky University*; Andrew Pease, *Stevenson University*; Nancy Pelaez, *Purdue University*; Shelley Penrod, *North Harris College*; Imara Y. Perera, *North Carolina State University*; Beverly Perry, *Houston Community College*; Irene Perry, *University of Texas of the Permian Basin*; Roger Persell, *Hunter College*; David Pfennig, *University of North Carolina, Chapel Hill*; Mark Pilgrim, *College of Coastal Georgia*; David S. Pilliod, *California Polytechnic State University, San Luis Obispo*; Vera M. Piper, *Shenandoah University*; J. Chris Pires, *University of Missouri, Columbia*; Bob Pittman, *Michigan State University*; James Platt, *University of Denver*; Martin Poenie, *University of Texas, Austin*; Scott Poethig, *University of Pennsylvania*; Crima Pogge, *City College of San Francisco*; Michael Pollock, *Mount Royal University*; Roberta Pollock, *Occidental College*; Jeffrey Pommerville, *Texas A&M University*; Therese M. Poole, *Georgia State University*; Angela R. Porta, *Kean University*; Warren Porter, *University of Wisconsin*; Daniel Potter, *University of California, Davis*; Donald Potts, *University of California, Santa Cruz*; Robert Powell, *Avila University*; Andy Pratt, *University of Canterbury*; David Pratt, *University of California, Davis*; Elena Pravosudova, *University of Nevada, Reno*; Halina Presley, *University of Illinois, Chicago*; Mary V. Price, *University of California, Riverside*; Mitch Price, *Pennsylvania State University*; Terrell Pritts, *University of Arkansas, Little Rock*; Rong Sun Pu, *Kean University*; Rebecca Pyles, *East Tennessee State University*; Scott Quackenbush, *Florida International University*; Ralph Quatrano, *Oregon State University*; Peter Quinby, *University of Pittsburgh*; Val Raghavan, *Ohio State University*; Deanna Raineri, *University of Illinois, Champaign-Urbana*; Talitha Rajah, *Indiana University Southeast*; Charles Ralph, *Colorado State University*; Thomas Rand, *Saint Mary's University*; Monica Ranes-Goldberg, *University of California, Berkeley*; Robert S. Rawding, *Gannon University*; Robert H. Reavis, *Glendale Community College*; Kurt Redborg, *Coe College*; Ahnya Redman, *Pennsylvania State University*; Brian Reeder, *Morehead State University*; Bruce Reid, *Kean University*; David Reid, *Blackburn College*; C. Gary Reiness, *Lewis & Clark College*; Charles Remington, *Yale University*; Erin Rempala, *San Diego Mesa College*; David Reznick, *University of California, Riverside*; Fred Rhoades, *Western Washington State University*; Douglas Rhoads, *University of Arkansas*; Eric Ribbens, *Western Illinois University*; Christina Richards, *New York University*; Sarah Richart, *Azusa Pacific University*; Christopher Riegle, *Irvine Valley College*; Loren Rieseberg, *University of British Columbia*; Bruce B. Riley, *Texas A&M University*; Donna Ritch, *Pennsylvania State University*; Carol Rivin, *Oregon State University East*; Laurel Roberts, *University of Pittsburgh*; Kenneth Robinson, *Purdue University*; Thomas Rodella, *Merced College*; Heather Roffey, *Marianopolis College*; Rodney Rogers, *Drake University*; William Roosenburg, *Ohio University*; Mike Rosenzweig, *Virginia Polytechnic Institute and State University*; Wayne Rosing, *Middle Tennessee State University*; Thomas Rost, *University of California, Davis*; Stephen I. Rothstein, *University of California, Santa Barbara*; John Ruben, *Oregon State University*; Albert Ruesink, *Indiana University*; Patricia Rugaber, *College of Coastal Georgia*; Scott Russell, *University of Oklahoma*; Neil Sabine, *Indiana University*; Tyson Sacco, *Cornell University*; Rowan F. Sage, *University of Toronto*; Tammy Lynn Sage, *University of Toronto*; Don Sakaguchi, *Iowa State University*; Walter Sakai, *Santa Monica College*; Mark F. Sanders, *University of California, Davis*; Louis Santiago, *University of California, Riverside*; Ted Sargent, *University of Massachusetts, Amherst*; K. Sathasivan, *University of Texas, Austin*; Gary Saunders, *University of New Brunswick*; Thomas R. Sawicki, *Spartanburg Community College*; Inder Saxena, *University of Texas, Austin*; Carl Schaefer, *University of Connecticut*; Maynard H. Schaus, *Virginia Wesleyan College*; Renate Scheibe, *University of Osnabrück*; David Schimpf, *University of Minnesota, Duluth*; William H. Schlesinger, *Duke University*; Mark Schlissel, *University of California, Berkeley*; Christopher J. Schneider, *Boston University*; Thomas W. Schoener, *University of California, Davis*; Robert Schorr, *Colorado State University*; Patricia M. Schulte, *University of British Columbia*; Karen S. Schumaker, *University of Arizona*; Brenda Schumpert, *Valencia Community College*; David J. Schwartz, *Houston Community College*; Christa Schwintzer, *University of Maine*; Erik P. Scully, *Towson State University*; Robert W. Seagull, *Hofstra University*; Edna Seaman, *Northeastern University*; Duane Sears, *University of California, Santa Barbara*; Brent Selinger, *University of Lethbridge*; Orono Shukdeb Sen, *Bethune-Cookman College*; Wendy Sera, *Seton Hill University*; Alison M. Shakarian, *Salve Regina University*; Timothy E. Shannon, *Francis Marion University*; Joan Sharp, *Simon Fraser University*; Victoria C. Sharpe, *Blinn College*; Elaine Shea, *Loyola College, Maryland*; Stephen Sheckler, *Virginia Polytechnic Institute and State University*; Robin L. Sherman, *Nova Southeastern University*; Richard Sherwin, *University of Pittsburgh*; Lisa Shimeld, *Crafton Hills College*; James Shinkle, *Trinity University*; Barbara Shipes, *Hampton University*; Richard M. Showman, *University of South Carolina*; Peter Shugarman, *University of Southern California*; Alice Shuttey, *DeKalb Community College*; James Sidie, *Ursinus College*; Daniel Simberloff, *Florida State University*; Rebecca Simmons, *University of North Dakota*; Anne Simon, *University of Maryland, College Park*; Robert Simons, *University of California, Los Angeles*; Alastair Simpson, *Dalhousie University*; Susan Singer, *Carleton College*; Sedonia Sipes, *Southern Illinois University, Carbondale*; Roger Sloboda, *Dartmouth University*; John Smarrelli, *Le Moyne College*; Andrew T. Smith, *Arizona State University*; Kelly Smith, *University of North Florida*; Nancy Smith-Huerta, *Miami Ohio University*; John Smol, *Queen's University*; Andrew J. Snope, *Essex Community College*; Mitchell Sogin, *Woods Hole Marine Biological Laboratory*; Julio G. Soto, *San Jose State University*; Susan Sovonick-Dunford, *University of Cincinnati*; Frederick W. Spiegel, *University of Arkansas*; John Stachowicz, *University of California, Davis*; Joel Stafstrom, *Northern Illinois University*; Alam Stam, *Capital University*; Amanda Starnes, *Emory University*; Karen Steudel, *University of Wisconsin*; Barbara Stewart, *Swarthmore College*; Gail A. Stewart, *Camden County College*; Cecil Still, *Rutgers University, New Brunswick*; Margery Stinson, *Southwestern College*; James Stockand, *University of Texas Health Science Center, San Antonio*; John Stolz, *California Institute of Technology*; Judy Stone, *Colby College*; Richard D. Storey, *Colorado College*; Stephen Strand, *University of California, Los Angeles*; Eric Strauss, *University of Massachusetts, Boston*; Antony Stretton, *University of Wisconsin, Madison*; Russell Stullken, *Augusta College*; Mark Sturtevant, *University of Michigan, Flint*; John Sullivan, *Southern Oregon State University*; Gerald Summers, *University of Missouri*; Judith Sumner, *Assumption College*; Marshall D. Sundberg, *Emporia State University*; Cynthia Surmacz, *Bloomsburg University*; Lucinda Swatzell, *Southeast Missouri State University*; Daryl Sweeney, *University of Illinois, Champaign-Urbana*; Samuel S. Sweet, *University of California, Santa Barbara*; Janice Swenson, *University of North Florida*; Michael A. Sypes, *Pennsylvania State University*; Lincoln Taiz, *University of California, Santa Cruz*; David Tam, *University of North Texas*; Yves Tan, *Cabrillo College*; Samuel Tarsitano, *Southwest Texas State University*; David Tauck, *Santa Clara University*; Emily Taylor, *California Polytechnic State University, San Luis Obispo*; James Taylor, *University of New Hampshire*; John W. Taylor, *University of California, Berkeley*; Martha R. Taylor, *Cornell University*; Franklyn Tan Te, *Miami Dade College*; Thomas Terry, *University of Connecticut*; Roger Thibault, *Bowling Green State University*; Kent Thomas, *Wichita State University*; William Thomas, *Colby-Sawyer College*; Cyril Thong, *Simon Fraser University*; John Thornton, *Oklahoma State University*; Robert Thornton, *University of California, Davis*; William Thwaites, *Tillamook Bay Community College*; Stephen Timme, *Pittsburg State University*; Eric Toolson, *University of New Mexico*; Leslie Towill, *Arizona State University*; James Traniello, *Boston University*; Paul Q. Trombley, *Florida State University*; Nancy J. Trun, *Duquesne University*; Constantine Tsoukas, *San Diego State University*; Marsha Turell, *Houston Community College*; Robert Tuveson, *University of Illinois, Urbana*; Maura G. Tyrrell, *Stonehill College*; Catherine Uekert, *Northern Arizona University*; Claudia Uhde-Stone, *California State University, East Bay*; Gordon Uno, *University of Oklahoma*; Lisa A. Urry, *Mills College*; Saba Valadkhan, *Center for RNA Molecular Biology*; James W. Valentine, *University of California, Santa Barbara*; Joseph Vanable, *Purdue University*; Theodore Van Bruggen, *University of South Dakota*; Kathryn VandenBosch, *Texas A&M University*; Gerald Van Dyke, *North Carolina State University*; Brandi Van Roo, *Framingham State College*; Moira Van Staaden, *Bowling Green State University*; Sarah VanVickle-Chavez, *Washington University, St. Louis*; William Velhagen, *New York University*; Steven D. Verhey, *Central Washington University*; Kathleen Verville, *Washington College*; Sara Via, *University of Maryland*; Frank Visco, *Orange Coast College*; Laurie Vitt, *University of California, Los Angeles*; Neal Voelz, *St. Cloud State University*; Thomas J. Volk, *University of Wisconsin, La Crosse*; Leif Asbjørn Vøllestad, *University of Oslo*; Janice Voltzow, *University of Scranton*; Margaret Voss, *Penn State Erie*; Susan D. Waaland, *University of Washington*; Charles Wade, *C.S. Mott Community College*; William Wade, *Dartmouth Medical College*; John Waggoner, *Loyola Marymount University*; Jyoti Wagle, *Houston Community College*; Edward Wagner, *University of California, Irvine*; D. Alexander Wait, *Southwest Missouri State University*; Claire Walczak, *Indiana University*; Jerry Waldvogel, *Clemson University*; Dan Walker, *San Jose State University*; Robert Lee Wallace, *Ripon College*; Jeffrey Walters, *North Carolina State University*; Linda Walters, *University of Central Florida*; Nickolas M. Waser, *University of California, Riverside*; Fred Wasserman, *Boston University*; Margaret Waterman, *University of Pittsburgh*; Charles Webber, *Loyola University of Chicago*; Peter Webster, *University of Massachusetts, Amherst*; Terry Webster, *University of Connecticut, Storrs*; Beth Wee, *Tulane University*; Andrea Weeks, *George Mason University*; John Weishampel, *University of Central Florida*; Peter Wejksnora, *University of Wisconsin, Milwaukee*; Kentwood Wells, *University of Connecticut*; David J. Westenberg, *University of Missouri, Rolla*; Richard Wetts, *University of California, Irvine*; Matt White, *Ohio University*; Susan Whittemore, *Keene State College*; Ernest H. Williams, *Hamilton College*; Kathy Williams, *San Diego State University*; Stephen Williams, *Glendale Community College*; Elizabeth Willott, *University of Arizona*; Christopher Wills, *University of California, San Diego*; Paul Wilson, *California State University, Northridge*; Fred Wilt, *University of California, Berkeley*; Peter Wimberger, *University of Puget Sound*; Robert Winning, *Eastern Michigan University*; E. William Wischusen, *Louisiana State University*; Clarence Wolfe, *Northern Virginia Community College*; Vickie L. Wolfe, *Marshall University*; Janet Wolkenstein, *Hudson Valley Community College*; Robert T. Woodland, *University of Massachusetts Medical School*; Joseph Woodring, *Louisiana State University*; Denise Woodward, *Pennsylvania State University*; Patrick Woolley, *East Central College*; Sarah E. Wyatt, *Ohio University*; Grace Wyngaard, *James Madison University*; Ramin Yadegari, *University of Arizona*; Paul Yancey, *Whitman College*; Philip Yant, *University of Michigan*; Linda Yasui, *Northern Illinois University*; Anne D. Yoder, *Duke University*; Hideo Yonenaka, *San Francisco State University*; Gina M. Zainelli, *Loyola University, Chicago*; Edward Zalisko, *Blackburn College*; Nina Zanetti, *Siena College*; Sam Zeveloff, *Weber State University*; Zai Ming Zhao, *University of Texas, Austin*; John Zimmerman, *Kansas State University*; Miriam Zolan, *Indiana University*; Theresa Zucchero, *Methodist University*; Uko Zylstra, *Calvin College*

Detailed Contents

1 Evolution, the Themes of Biology, and Scientific Inquiry 1

Inquiring About Life 1
CONCEPT 1.1 The study of life reveals common themes 2
    Theme: New Properties Emerge at Successive Levels of Biological Organization 3
    Theme: Life's Processes Involve the Expression and Transmission of Genetic Information 5
    Theme: Life Requires the Transfer and Transformation of Energy and Matter 7
    Theme: From Ecosystems to Molecules, Interactions Are Important in Biological Systems 8
    Evolution, the Core Theme of Biology 9
CONCEPT 1.2 The Core Theme: Evolution accounts for the unity and diversity of life 10
    Classifying the Diversity of Life 10
    Charles Darwin and the Theory of Natural Selection 12
    The Tree of Life 14
CONCEPT 1.3 In studying nature, scientists make observations and form and test hypotheses 16
    Making Observations 16
    Forming and Testing Hypotheses 16
    The Flexibility of the Scientific Process 18
    A Case Study in Scientific Inquiry: Investigating Coat Coloration in Mouse Populations 19
    Experimental Variables and Controls 20
    Theories in Science 21
CONCEPT 1.4 Science benefits from a cooperative approach and diverse viewpoints 21
    Building on the Work of Others 21
    Science, Technology, and Society 23
    The Value of Diverse Viewpoints in Science 23

UNIT 1 THE CHEMISTRY OF LIFE 27

2 The Chemical Context of Life 28

A Chemical Connection to Biology 28
CONCEPT 2.1 Matter consists of chemical elements in pure form and in combinations called compounds 29
    Elements and Compounds 29
    The Elements of Life 29
    Case Study: Evolution of Tolerance to Toxic Elements 30

CONCEPT 2.2 An element's properties depend on the structure of its atoms 30
    Subatomic Particles 30
    Atomic Number and Atomic Mass 31
    Isotopes 31
    The Energy Levels of Electrons 32
    Electron Distribution and Chemical Properties 34
    Electron Orbitals 35
CONCEPT 2.3 The formation and function of molecules depend on chemical bonding between atoms 36
    Covalent Bonds 36
    Ionic Bonds 37
    Weak Chemical Bonds 38
    Molecular Shape and Function 39
CONCEPT 2.4 Chemical reactions make and break chemical bonds 40

3 Water and Life 44

The Molecule That Supports All of Life 44
CONCEPT 3.1 Polar covalent bonds in water molecules result in hydrogen bonding 45
CONCEPT 3.2 Four emergent properties of water contribute to Earth's suitability for life 45
    Cohesion of Water Molecules 45
    Moderation of Temperature by Water 46
    Floating of Ice on Liquid Water 48
    Water: The Solvent of Life 48
    Possible Evolution of Life on Other Planets 50
CONCEPT 3.3 Acidic and basic conditions affect living organisms 51
    Acids and Bases 51
    The pH Scale 51
    Buffers 52
    Acidification: A Threat to Water Quality 53

4 Carbon and the Molecular Diversity of Life 56

Carbon: The Backbone of Life 56
CONCEPT 4.1 Organic chemistry is the study of carbon compounds 57
    Organic Molecules and the Origin of Life on Earth 57
CONCEPT 4.2 Carbon atoms can form diverse molecules by bonding to four other atoms 58
    The Formation of Bonds with Carbon 59
    Molecular Diversity Arising from Variation in Carbon Skeletons 60
CONCEPT 4.3 A few chemical groups are key to molecular function 62
    The Chemical Groups Most Important in the Processes of Life 62
    ATP: An Important Source of Energy for Cellular Processes 64
    The Chemical Elements of Life: A Review 64

5 The Structure and Function of Large Biological Molecules 66

The Molecules of Life 66

CONCEPT 5.1 Macromolecules are polymers, built from monomers 67
    The Synthesis and Breakdown of Polymers 67
    The Diversity of Polymers 67

CONCEPT 5.2 Carbohydrates serve as fuel and building material 68
    Sugars 68
    Polysaccharides 70

CONCEPT 5.3 Lipids are a diverse group of hydrophobic molecules 72
    Fats 72
    Phospholipids 74
    Steroids 75

CONCEPT 5.4 Proteins include a diversity of structures, resulting in a wide range of functions 75
    Amino Acid Monomers 75
    Polypeptides (Amino Acid Polymers) 78
    Protein Structure and Function 78

CONCEPT 5.5 Nucleic acids store, transmit, and help express hereditary information 84
    The Roles of Nucleic Acids 84
    The Components of Nucleic Acids 85
    Nucleotide Polymers 86
    The Structures of DNA and RNA Molecules 86

CONCEPT 5.6 Genomics and proteomics have transformed biological inquiry and applications 87
    DNA and Proteins as Tape Measures of Evolution 89

UNIT 2 THE CELL 92

6 A Tour of the Cell 93

The Fundamental Units of Life 93

CONCEPT 6.1 Biologists use microscopes and the tools of biochemistry to study cells 94
    Microscopy 94
    Cell Fractionation 96

CONCEPT 6.2 Eukaryotic cells have internal membranes that compartmentalize their functions 97
    Comparing Prokaryotic and Eukaryotic Cells 97
    A Panoramic View of the Eukaryotic Cell 99

CONCEPT 6.3 The eukaryotic cell's genetic instructions are housed in the nucleus and carried out by the ribosomes 102
    The Nucleus: Information Central 102
    Ribosomes: Protein Factories 102

CONCEPT 6.4 The endomembrane system regulates protein traffic and performs metabolic functions in the cell 104
    The Endoplasmic Reticulum: Biosynthetic Factory 104
    The Golgi Apparatus: Shipping and Receiving Center 105
    Lysosomes: Digestive Compartments 107
    Vacuoles: Diverse Maintenance Compartments 108
    The Endomembrane System: *A Review* 108

CONCEPT 6.5 Mitochondria and chloroplasts change energy from one form to another 109
    The Evolutionary Origins of Mitochondria and Chloroplasts 109
    Mitochondria: Chemical Energy Conversion 110
    Chloroplasts: Capture of Light Energy 110
    Peroxisomes: Oxidation 112

CONCEPT 6.6 The cytoskeleton is a network of fibers that organizes structures and activities in the cell 112
    Roles of the Cytoskeleton: Support and Motility 112
    Components of the Cytoskeleton 113

CONCEPT 6.7 Extracellular components and connections between cells help coordinate cellular activities 118
    Cell Walls of Plants 118
    The Extracellular Matrix (ECM) of Animal Cells 118
    Cell Junctions 119
    The Cell: A Living Unit Greater Than the Sum of Its Parts 121

7 Membrane Structure and Function 124

Life at the Edge 124

CONCEPT 7.1 Cellular membranes are fluid mosaics of lipids and proteins 125
    The Fluidity of Membranes 126
    Evolution of Differences in Membrane Lipid Composition 127
    Membrane Proteins and Their Functions 127
    The Role of Membrane Carbohydrates in Cell-Cell Recognition 128
    Synthesis and Sidedness of Membranes 129

CONCEPT 7.2 Membrane structure results in selective permeability 129
    The Permeability of the Lipid Bilayer 130
    Transport Proteins 130

CONCEPT 7.3 Passive transport is diffusion of a substance across a membrane with no energy investment 130
    Effects of Osmosis on Water Balance 131
    Facilitated Diffusion: Passive Transport Aided by Proteins 133

CONCEPT 7.4 Active transport uses energy to move solutes against their gradients 134
    The Need for Energy in Active Transport 134
    How Ion Pumps Maintain Membrane Potential 135
    Cotransport: Coupled Transport by a Membrane Protein 136

CONCEPT 7.5 Bulk transport across the plasma membrane occurs by exocytosis and endocytosis 137
    Exocytosis 137
    Endocytosis 137

8   An Introduction to Metabolism 141

The Energy of Life 141

CONCEPT 8.1 An organism's metabolism transforms matter and energy, subject to the laws of thermodynamics 142
Organization of the Chemistry of Life into Metabolic Pathways 142
Forms of Energy 142
The Laws of Energy Transformation 143

CONCEPT 8.2 The free-energy change of a reaction tells us whether or not the reaction occurs spontaneously 145
Free-Energy Change, ΔG 145
Free Energy, Stability, and Equilibrium 145
Free Energy and Metabolism 146

CONCEPT 8.3 ATP powers cellular work by coupling exergonic reactions to endergonic reactions 148
The Structure and Hydrolysis of ATP 149
How the Hydrolysis of ATP Performs Work 149
The Regeneration of ATP 151

CONCEPT 8.4 Enzymes speed up metabolic reactions by lowering energy barriers 151
The Activation Energy Barrier 151
How Enzymes Speed Up Reactions 152
Substrate Specificity of Enzymes 153
Catalysis in the Enzyme's Active Site 154
Effects of Local Conditions on Enzyme Activity 155
The Evolution of Enzymes 157

CONCEPT 8.5 Regulation of enzyme activity helps control metabolism 157
Allosteric Regulation of Enzymes 157
Localization of Enzymes Within the Cell 159

9   Cellular Respiration and Fermentation 162

Life Is Work 162

CONCEPT 9.1 Catabolic pathways yield energy by oxidizing organic fuels 163
Catabolic Pathways and Production of ATP 163
Redox Reactions: Oxidation and Reduction 163
The Stages of Cellular Respiration: *A Preview* 166

CONCEPT 9.2 Glycolysis harvests chemical energy by oxidizing glucose to pyruvate 168

CONCEPT 9.3 After pyruvate is oxidized, the citric acid cycle completes the energy-yielding oxidation of organic molecules 169
Oxidation of Pyruvate to Acetyl CoA 169
The Citric Acid Cycle 170

CONCEPT 9.4 During oxidative phosphorylation, chemiosmosis couples electron transport to ATP synthesis 172
The Pathway of Electron Transport 172
Chemiosmosis: The Energy-Coupling Mechanism 173
An Accounting of ATP Production by Cellular Respiration 175

CONCEPT 9.5 Fermentation and anaerobic respiration enable cells to produce ATP without the use of oxygen 177
Types of Fermentation 178
Comparing Fermentation with Anaerobic and Aerobic Respiration 179
The Evolutionary Significance of Glycolysis 179

CONCEPT 9.6 Glycolysis and the citric acid cycle connect to many other metabolic pathways 180
The Versatility of Catabolism 180
Biosynthesis (Anabolic Pathways) 181
Regulation of Cellular Respiration via Feedback Mechanisms 181

10   Photosynthesis 185

The Process That Feeds the Biosphere 185

CONCEPT 10.1 Photosynthesis converts light energy to the chemical energy of food 187
Chloroplasts: The Sites of Photosynthesis in Plants 187
Tracking Atoms Through Photosynthesis: *Scientific Inquiry* 188
The Two Stages of Photosynthesis: *A Preview* 189

CONCEPT 10.2 The light reactions convert solar energy to the chemical energy of ATP and NADPH 190
The Nature of Sunlight 190
Photosynthetic Pigments: The Light Receptors 191
Excitation of Chlorophyll by Light 193
A Photosystem: A Reaction-Center Complex Associated with Light-Harvesting Complexes 193
Linear Electron Flow 195
Cyclic Electron Flow 196
A Comparison of Chemiosmosis in Chloroplasts and Mitochondria 197

CONCEPT 10.3 The Calvin cycle uses the chemical energy of ATP and NADPH to reduce CO_2 to sugar 199

CONCEPT 10.4 Alternative mechanisms of carbon fixation have evolved in hot, arid climates 201
Photorespiration: An Evolutionary Relic? 201
C_4 Plants 201
CAM Plants 203
The Importance of Photosynthesis: *A Review* 204

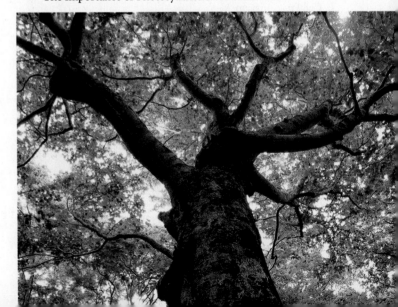

11 Cell Communication 210

Cellular Messaging 210

CONCEPT 11.1 External signals are converted to responses within the cell 211
Evolution of Cell Signaling 211
Local and Long-Distance Signaling 212
The Three Stages of Cell Signaling: *A Preview* 212

CONCEPT 11.2 Reception: A signaling molecule binds to a receptor protein, causing it to change shape 214
Receptors in the Plasma Membrane 214
Intracellular Receptors 217

CONCEPT 11.3 Transduction: Cascades of molecular interactions relay signals from receptors to target molecules in the cell 218
Signal Transduction Pathways 218
Protein Phosphorylation and Dephosphorylation 219
Small Molecules and Ions as Second Messengers 220

CONCEPT 11.4 Response: Cell signaling leads to regulation of transcription or cytoplasmic activities 223
Nuclear and Cytoplasmic Responses 223
Regulation of the Response 223

CONCEPT 11.5 Apoptosis integrates multiple cell-signaling pathways 227
Apoptosis in the Soil Worm *Caenorhabditis elegans* 228
Apoptotic Pathways and the Signals That Trigger Them 228

12 The Cell Cycle 232

The Key Roles of Cell Division 232

CONCEPT 12.1 Most cell division results in genetically identical daughter cells 233
Cellular Organization of the Genetic Material 233
Distribution of Chromosomes During Eukaryotic Cell Division 234

CONCEPT 12.2 The mitotic phase alternates with interphase in the cell cycle 235
Phases of the Cell Cycle 235
The Mitotic Spindle: *A Closer Look* 235
Cytokinesis: *A Closer Look* 239
Binary Fission in Bacteria 240
The Evolution of Mitosis 241

CONCEPT 12.3 The eukaryotic cell cycle is regulated by a molecular control system 242
The Cell Cycle Control System 242
Loss of Cell Cycle Controls in Cancer Cells 246

3 GENETICS 251

13 Meiosis and Sexual Life Cycles 252

Variations on a Theme 252

CONCEPT 13.1 Offspring acquire genes from parents by inheriting chromosomes 253
Inheritance of Genes 253
Comparison of Asexual and Sexual Reproduction 253

CONCEPT 13.2 Fertilization and meiosis alternate in sexual life cycles 254
Sets of Chromosomes in Human Cells 254
Behavior of Chromosome Sets in the Human Life Cycle 255
The Variety of Sexual Life Cycles 256

CONCEPT 13.3 Meiosis reduces the number of chromosome sets from diploid to haploid 257
The Stages of Meiosis 257
Crossing Over and Synapsis During Prophase I 260
A Comparison of Mitosis and Meiosis 260

CONCEPT 13.4 Genetic variation produced in sexual life cycles contributes to evolution 263
Origins of Genetic Variation Among Offspring 263
The Evolutionary Significance of Genetic Variation Within Populations 264

14 Mendel and the Gene Idea 267

Drawing from the Deck of Genes 267

CONCEPT 14.1 Mendel used the scientific approach to identify two laws of inheritance 268
Mendel's Experimental, Quantitative Approach 268
The Law of Segregation 269
The Law of Independent Assortment 272

CONCEPT 14.2 Probability laws govern Mendelian inheritance 274
The Multiplication and Addition Rules Applied to Monohybrid Crosses 275
Solving Complex Genetics Problems with the Rules of Probability 275

CONCEPT 14.3 Inheritance patterns are often more complex than predicted by simple Mendelian genetics 276
Extending Mendelian Genetics for a Single Gene 277
Extending Mendelian Genetics for Two or More Genes 279
Nature and Nurture: The Environmental Impact on Phenotype 280
A Mendelian View of Heredity and Variation 280

CONCEPT 14.4 Many human traits follow Mendelian patterns of inheritance 282
Pedigree Analysis 282
Recessively Inherited Disorders 283
Dominantly Inherited Disorders 285
Multifactorial Disorders 285
Genetic Testing and Counseling 285

15 The Chromosomal Basis of Inheritance 292

Locating Genes Along Chromosomes 292
CONCEPT 15.1 Morgan showed that Mendelian inheritance has its physical basis in the behavior of chromosomes: *Scientific inquiry* 294
  Morgan's Choice of Experimental Organism 294
  Correlating Behavior of a Gene's Alleles with Behavior of a Chromosome Pair 295
CONCEPT 15.2 Sex-linked genes exhibit unique patterns of inheritance 296
  The Chromosomal Basis of Sex 296
  Inheritance of X-Linked Genes 297
  X Inactivation in Female Mammals 298
CONCEPT 15.3 Linked genes tend to be inherited together because they are located near each other on the same chromosome 299
  How Linkage Affects Inheritance 299
  Genetic Recombination and Linkage 300
  Mapping the Distance Between Genes Using Recombination Data: *Scientific Inquiry* 303
CONCEPT 15.4 Alterations of chromosome number or structure cause some genetic disorders 304
  Abnormal Chromosome Number 305
  Alterations of Chromosome Structure 305
  Human Disorders Due to Chromosomal Alterations 306
CONCEPT 15.5 Some inheritance patterns are exceptions to standard Mendelian inheritance 308
  Genomic Imprinting 308
  Inheritance of Organelle Genes 309

16 The Molecular Basis of Inheritance 312

Life's Operating Instructions 312
CONCEPT 16.1 DNA is the genetic material 313
  The Search for the Genetic Material: *Scientific Inquiry* 313
  Building a Structural Model of DNA: *Scientific Inquiry* 316
CONCEPT 16.2 Many proteins work together in DNA replication and repair 318
  The Basic Principle: Base Pairing to a Template Strand 318
  DNA Replication: *A Closer Look* 320
  Proofreading and Repairing DNA 325
  Evolutionary Significance of Altered DNA Nucleotides 326
  Replicating the Ends of DNA Molecules 326
CONCEPT 16.3 A chromosome consists of a DNA molecule packed together with proteins 328

17 Gene Expression: From Gene to Protein 333

The Flow of Genetic Information 333
CONCEPT 17.1 Genes specify proteins via transcription and translation 334
  Evidence from the Study of Metabolic Defects 334
  Basic Principles of Transcription and Translation 336
  The Genetic Code 337
CONCEPT 17.2 Transcription is the DNA-directed synthesis of RNA: *A closer look* 340
  Molecular Components of Transcription 340
  Synthesis of an RNA Transcript 341
CONCEPT 17.3 Eukaryotic cells modify RNA after transcription 342
  Alteration of mRNA Ends 342
  Split Genes and RNA Splicing 343
CONCEPT 17.4 Translation is the RNA-directed synthesis of a polypeptide: *A closer look* 345
  Molecular Components of Translation 345
  Building a Polypeptide 348
  Completing and Targeting the Functional Protein 351
  Making Multiple Polypeptides in Bacteria and Eukaryotes 352
CONCEPT 17.5 Mutations of one or a few nucleotides can affect protein structure and function 355
  Types of Small-Scale Mutations 355
  New Mutations and Mutagens 357
  What Is a Gene? *Revisiting the Question* 357

18 Regulation of Gene Expression 360

Differential Expression of Genes 360
CONCEPT 18.1 Bacteria often respond to environmental change by regulating transcription 361
  Operons: The Basic Concept 361
  Repressible and Inducible Operons: Two Types of Negative Gene Regulation 363
  Positive Gene Regulation 364
CONCEPT 18.2 Eukaryotic gene expression is regulated at many stages 365
  Differential Gene Expression 365
  Regulation of Chromatin Structure 366
  Regulation of Transcription Initiation 367
  Mechanisms of Post-Transcriptional Regulation 372
CONCEPT 18.3 Noncoding RNAs play multiple roles in controlling gene expression 374
  Effects on mRNAs by MicroRNAs and Small Interfering RNAs 374
  Chromatin Remodeling by ncRNAs 375
  The Evolutionary Significance of Small ncRNAs 376
CONCEPT 18.4 A program of differential gene expression leads to the different cell types in a multicellular organism 376
  A Genetic Program for Embryonic Development 376
  Cytoplasmic Determinants and Inductive Signals 377
  Sequential Regulation of Gene Expression During Cellular Differentiation 378
  Pattern Formation: Setting Up the Body Plan 379

CONCEPT 18.5 Cancer results from genetic changes that affect cell cycle control 383

Types of Genes Associated with Cancer 383
Interference with Normal Cell-Signaling Pathways 384
The Multistep Model of Cancer Development 386
Inherited Predisposition and Environmental Factors
    Contributing to Cancer 388
The Role of Viruses in Cancer 388

19 Viruses 392

A Borrowed Life 392
CONCEPT 19.1 A virus consists of a nucleic acid surrounded by a protein coat 393

The Discovery of Viruses: *Scientific Inquiry* 393
Structure of Viruses 394
CONCEPT 19.2 Viruses replicate only in host cells 395

General Features of Viral Replicative Cycles 395
Replicative Cycles of Phages 396
Replicative Cycles of Animal Viruses 398
Evolution of Viruses 400
CONCEPT 19.3 Viruses, viroids, and prions are formidable pathogens in animals and plants 402

Viral Diseases in Animals 402
Emerging Viruses 402
Viral Diseases in Plants 405
Viroids and Prions: The Simplest Infectious Agents 405

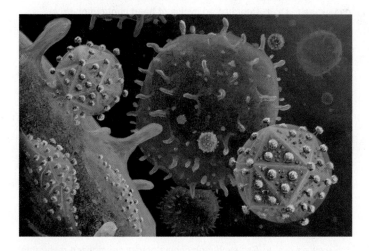

20 DNA Tools and Biotechnology 408

The DNA Toolbox 408
CONCEPT 20.1 DNA sequencing and DNA cloning are valuable tools for genetic engineering and biological inquiry 409

DNA Sequencing 409
Making Multiple Copies of a Gene or Other DNA Segment 412
Using Restriction Enzymes to Make a Recombinant DNA
    Plasmid 413
Amplifying DNA: The Polymerase Chain Reaction (PCR)
    and Its Use in Cloning 414
Expressing Cloned Eukaryotic Genes 416
CONCEPT 20.2 Biologists use DNA technology to study gene expression and function 417

Analyzing Gene Expression 417
Determining Gene Function 421

CONCEPT 20.3 Cloned organisms and stem cells are useful for basic research and other applications 422

Cloning Plants: Single-Cell Cultures 423
Cloning Animals: Nuclear Transplantation 423
Stem Cells of Animals 425
CONCEPT 20.4 The practical applications of DNA-based biotechnology affect our lives in many ways 428

Medical Applications 428
Forensic Evidence and Genetic Profiles 430
Environmental Cleanup 432
Agricultural Applications 432
Safety and Ethical Questions Raised by DNA Technology 432

21 Genomes and Their Evolution 436

Reading the Leaves from the Tree of Life 436
CONCEPT 21.1 The Human Genome Project fostered development of faster, less expensive sequencing techniques 437
CONCEPT 21.2 Scientists use bioinformatics to analyze genomes and their functions 438

Centralized Resources for Analyzing Genome Sequences 438
Identifying Protein-Coding Genes and Understanding Their
    Functions 439
Understanding Genes and Gene Expression at the Systems
    Level 440
CONCEPT 21.3 Genomes vary in size, number of genes, and gene density 442

Genome Size 442
Number of Genes 443
Gene Density and Noncoding DNA 443
CONCEPT 21.4 Multicellular eukaryotes have much noncoding DNA and many multigene families 444

Transposable Elements and Related Sequences 444
Other Repetitive DNA, Including Simple Sequence DNA 446
Genes and Multigene Families 446
CONCEPT 21.5 Duplication, rearrangement, and mutation of DNA contribute to genome evolution 448

Duplication of Entire Chromosome Sets 448
Alterations of Chromosome Structure 448
Duplication and Divergence of Gene-Sized Regions of
    DNA 449
Rearrangements of Parts of Genes: Exon Duplication and Exon
    Shuffling 450
How Transposable Elements Contribute to Genome
    Evolution 453
CONCEPT 21.6 Comparing genome sequences provides clues to evolution and development 453

Comparing Genomes 453
Widespread Conservation of Developmental Genes Among
    Animals 457

7 ANIMAL FORM AND FUNCTION 866

40 Basic Principles of Animal Form and Function 867

Diverse Forms, Common Challenges 867

CONCEPT 40.1 Animal form and function are correlated at all levels of organization 868

Evolution of Animal Size and Shape 868
Exchange with the Environment 868
Hierarchical Organization of Body Plans 870
Coordination and Control 874

CONCEPT 40.2 Feedback control maintains the internal environment in many animals 875

Regulating and Conforming 875
Homeostasis 875

CONCEPT 40.3 Homeostatic processes for thermoregulation involve form, function, and behavior 878

Endothermy and Ectothermy 878
Variation in Body Temperature 878
Balancing Heat Loss and Gain 879
Acclimatization in Thermoregulation 882
Physiological Thermostats and Fever 882

CONCEPT 40.4 Energy requirements are related to animal size, activity, and environment 883

Energy Allocation and Use 883
Quantifying Energy Use 884
Minimum Metabolic Rate and Thermoregulation 884
Influences on Metabolic Rate 885
Torpor and Energy Conservation 886

41 Animal Nutrition 892

The Need to Feed 892

CONCEPT 41.1 An animal's diet must supply chemical energy, organic molecules, and essential nutrients 893

Essential Nutrients 893
Dietary Deficiencies 895
Assessing Nutritional Needs 896

CONCEPT 41.2 The main stages of food processing are ingestion, digestion, absorption, and elimination 897

Digestive Compartments 897

CONCEPT 41.3 Organs specialized for sequential stages of food processing form the mammalian digestive system 900

The Oral Cavity, Pharynx, and Esophagus 900
Digestion in the Stomach 901
Digestion in the Small Intestine 902
Absorption in the Small Intestine 904
Processing in the Large Intestine 905

CONCEPT 41.4 Evolutionary adaptations of vertebrate digestive systems correlate with diet 906

Dental Adaptations 906
Stomach and Intestinal Adaptations 906
Mutualistic Adaptations 907

CONCEPT 41.5 Feedback circuits regulate digestion, energy storage, and appetite 908

Regulation of Digestion 908
Regulation of Energy Storage 909
Regulation of Appetite and Consumption 911

42 Circulation and Gas Exchange 915

Trading Places 915

CONCEPT 42.1 Circulatory systems link exchange surfaces with cells throughout the body 916

Gastrovascular Cavities 916
Open and Closed Circulatory Systems 917
Organization of Vertebrate Circulatory Systems 918

CONCEPT 42.2 Coordinated cycles of heart contraction drive double circulation in mammals 920

Mammalian Circulation 920
The Mammalian Heart: *A Closer Look* 920
Maintaining the Heart's Rhythmic Beat 922

CONCEPT 42.3 Patterns of blood pressure and flow reflect the structure and arrangement of blood vessels 923

Blood Vessel Structure and Function 923
Blood Flow Velocity 924
Blood Pressure 924
Capillary Function 926
Fluid Return by the Lymphatic System 927

CONCEPT 42.4 Blood components function in exchange, transport, and defense 928

Blood Composition and Function 928
Cardiovascular Disease 931

CONCEPT 42.5 Gas exchange occurs across specialized respiratory surfaces 933

Partial Pressure Gradients in Gas Exchange 933
Respiratory Media 933
Respiratory Surfaces 933
Gills in Aquatic Animals 934
Tracheal Systems in Insects 935
Lungs 936

CONCEPT 42.6 Breathing ventilates the lungs 938

How an Amphibian Breathes 938
How a Bird Breathes 938
How a Mammal Breathes 939
Control of Breathing in Humans 940

CONCEPT 42.7 Adaptations for gas exchange include pigments that bind and transport gases 941

Coordination of Circulation and Gas Exchange 941
Respiratory Pigments 941
Respiratory Adaptations of Diving Mammals 943

43 The Immune System 946

Recognition and Response 946

CONCEPT 43.1 In innate immunity, recognition and response rely on traits common to groups of pathogens 947
Innate Immunity of Invertebrates 947
Innate Immunity of Vertebrates 948
Evasion of Innate Immunity by Pathogens 952

CONCEPT 43.2 In adaptive immunity, receptors provide pathogen-specific recognition 952
Antigen Recognition by B Cells and Antibodies 953
Antigen Recognition by T Cells 954
B Cell and T Cell Development 954

CONCEPT 43.3 Adaptive immunity defends against infection of body fluids and body cells 958
Helper T Cells: A Response to Nearly All Antigens 958
Cytotoxic T Cells: A Response to Infected Cells 959
B Cells and Antibodies: A Response to Extracellular Pathogens 960
Summary of the Humoral and Cell-Mediated Immune Responses 961
Active and Passive Immunity 962
Antibodies as Tools 963
Immune Rejection 963

CONCEPT 43.4 Disruptions in immune system function can elicit or exacerbate disease 964
Exaggerated, Self-Directed, and Diminished Immune Responses 964
Evolutionary Adaptations of Pathogens That Underlie Immune System Avoidance 966
Cancer and Immunity 968

44 Osmoregulation and Excretion 971

A Balancing Act 971

CONCEPT 44.1 Osmoregulation balances the uptake and loss of water and solutes 972
Osmosis and Osmolarity 972
Osmoregulatory Challenges and Mechanisms 972
Energetics of Osmoregulation 974
Transport Epithelia in Osmoregulation 975

CONCEPT 44.2 An animal's nitrogenous wastes reflect its phylogeny and habitat 976
Forms of Nitrogenous Waste 976
The Influence of Evolution and Environment on Nitrogenous Wastes 977

CONCEPT 44.3 Diverse excretory systems are variations on a tubular theme 978
Excretory Processes 978
Survey of Excretory Systems 978

CONCEPT 44.4 The nephron is organized for stepwise processing of blood filtrate 981
From Blood Filtrate to Urine: *A Closer Look* 982
Solute Gradients and Water Conservation 983
Adaptations of the Vertebrate Kidney to Diverse Environments 985

CONCEPT 44.5 Hormonal circuits link kidney function, water balance, and blood pressure 988
Homeostatic Regulation of the Kidney 988

45 Hormones and the Endocrine System 993

The Body's Long-Distance Regulators 993

CONCEPT 45.1 Hormones and other signaling molecules bind to target receptors, triggering specific response pathways 994
Intercellular Communication 994
Chemical Classes of Local Regulators and Hormones 995
Cellular Response Pathways 996
Multiple Effects of Hormones 998
Endocrine Tissues and Organs 998

CONCEPT 45.2 Feedback regulation and coordination with the nervous system are common in endocrine signaling 1000
Simple Hormone Pathways 1000
Feedback Regulation 1001
Coordination of Endocrine and Nervous Systems 1001
Thyroid Regulation: A Hormone Cascade Pathway 1004
Hormonal Regulation of Growth 1005

CONCEPT 45.3 Endocrine glands respond to diverse stimuli in regulating homeostasis, development, and behavior 1006
Parathyroid Hormone and Vitamin D: Control of Blood Calcium 1006
Adrenal Hormones: Response to Stress 1006
Sex Hormones 1008
Hormones and Biological Rhythms 1009
Evolution of Hormone Function 1010

46 Animal Reproduction 1013

Pairing Up for Sexual Reproduction 1013
CONCEPT 46.1 Both asexual and sexual reproduction occur in the animal kingdom 1014
    Mechanisms of Asexual Reproduction 1014
    Sexual Reproduction: An Evolutionary Enigma 1014
    Reproductive Cycles 1015
    Variation in Patterns of Sexual Reproduction 1016
CONCEPT 46.2 Fertilization depends on mechanisms that bring together sperm and eggs of the same species 1016
    Ensuring the Survival of Offspring 1017
    Gamete Production and Delivery 1017
CONCEPT 46.3 Reproductive organs produce and transport gametes 1019
    Human Male Reproductive Anatomy 1019
    Human Female Reproductive Anatomy 1020
    Gametogenesis 1021
CONCEPT 46.4 The interplay of tropic and sex hormones regulates mammalian reproduction 1024
    Hormonal Control of the Male Reproductive System 1024
    Hormonal Control of Female Reproductive Cycles 1025
    Human Sexual Response 1027
CONCEPT 46.5 In placental mammals, an embryo develops fully within the mother's uterus 1028
    Conception, Embryonic Development, and Birth 1028
    Maternal Immune Tolerance of the Embryo and Fetus 1031
    Contraception and Abortion 1032
    Modern Reproductive Technologies 1033

47 Animal Development 1037

A Body-Building Plan 1037
CONCEPT 47.1 Fertilization and cleavage initiate embryonic development 1038
    Fertilization 1038
    Cleavage 1041
CONCEPT 47.2 Morphogenesis in animals involves specific changes in cell shape, position, and survival 1044
    Gastrulation 1044
    Developmental Adaptations of Amniotes 1047
    Organogenesis 1048
    Mechanisms of Morphogenesis 1050
CONCEPT 47.3 Cytoplasmic determinants and inductive signals contribute to cell fate specification 1051
    Fate Mapping 1051
    Cell Fate Determination and Pattern Formation by Inductive Signals 1055
    Cilia and Cell Fate 1058

48 Neurons, Synapses, and Signaling 1061

Lines of Communication 1061
CONCEPT 48.1 Neuron structure and organization reflect function in information transfer 1062
    Neuron Structure and Function 1062
    Introduction to Information Processing 1063
CONCEPT 48.2 Ion pumps and ion channels establish the resting potential of a neuron 1064
    Formation of the Resting Potential 1064
    Modeling the Resting Potential 1065
CONCEPT 48.3 Action potentials are the signals conducted by axons 1066
    Hyperpolarization and Depolarization 1066
    Graded Potentials and Action Potentials 1067
    Generation of Action Potentials: *A Closer Look* 1068
    Conduction of Action Potentials 1069
CONCEPT 48.4 Neurons communicate with other cells at synapses 1071
    Generation of Postsynaptic Potentials 1072
    Summation of Postsynaptic Potentials 1073
    Modulated Signaling at Synapses 1073
    Neurotransmitters 1074

49 Nervous Systems 1079

Command and Control Center 1079
CONCEPT 49.1 Nervous systems consist of circuits of neurons and supporting cells 1080
    Glia 1081
    Organization of the Vertebrate Nervous System 1082
    The Peripheral Nervous System 1083
CONCEPT 49.2 The vertebrate brain is regionally specialized 1085
    Arousal and Sleep 1088
    Biological Clock Regulation 1088
    Emotions 1089
    Functional Imaging of the Brain 1090
CONCEPT 49.3 The cerebral cortex controls voluntary movement and cognitive functions 1090
    Information Processing 1090
    Language and Speech 1092
    Lateralization of Cortical Function 1092
    Frontal Lobe Function 1092
    Evolution of Cognition in Vertebrates 1093
CONCEPT 49.4 Changes in synaptic connections underlie memory and learning 1093
    Neuronal Plasticity 1094
    Memory and Learning 1094
    Long-Term Potentiation 1095
CONCEPT 49.5 Many nervous system disorders can be explained in molecular terms 1096
    Schizophrenia 1096
    Depression 1097
    The Brain's Reward System and Drug Addiction 1097
    Alzheimer's Disease 1097
    Parkinson's Disease 1098

50 Sensory and Motor Mechanisms 1101

Sense and Sensibility 1101

CONCEPT 50.1 Sensory receptors transduce stimulus energy and transmit signals to the central nervous system 1102
Sensory Reception and Transduction 1102
Transmission 1103
Perception 1103
Amplification and Adaptation 1103
Types of Sensory Receptors 1104

CONCEPT 50.2 The mechanoreceptors responsible for hearing and equilibrium detect moving fluid or settling particles 1106
Sensing of Gravity and Sound in Invertebrates 1106
Hearing and Equilibrium in Mammals 1106
Hearing and Equilibrium in Other Vertebrates 1110

CONCEPT 50.3 The diverse visual receptors of animals depend on light-absorbing pigments 1111
Evolution of Visual Perception 1111
The Vertebrate Visual System 1113

CONCEPT 50.4 The senses of taste and smell rely on similar sets of sensory receptors 1117
Taste in Mammals 1117
Smell in Humans 1118

CONCEPT 50.5 The physical interaction of protein filaments is required for muscle function 1119
Vertebrate Skeletal Muscle 1120
Other Types of Muscle 1125

CONCEPT 50.6 Skeletal systems transform muscle contraction into locomotion 1126
Types of Skeletal Systems 1126
Types of Locomotion 1129

51 Animal Behavior 1133

The How and Why of Animal Activity 1133

CONCEPT 51.1 Discrete sensory inputs can stimulate both simple and complex behaviors 1134
Fixed Action Patterns 1134
Migration 1135
Behavioral Rhythms 1135
Animal Signals and Communication 1136

CONCEPT 51.2 Learning establishes specific links between experience and behavior 1138
Experience and Behavior 1138
Learning 1138

CONCEPT 51.3 Selection for individual survival and reproductive success can explain diverse behaviors 1143
Evolution of Foraging Behavior 1143
Mating Behavior and Mate Choice 1145

CONCEPT 51.4 Genetic analyses and the concept of inclusive fitness provide a basis for studying the evolution of behavior 1149
Genetic Basis of Behavior 1149
Genetic Variation and the Evolution of Behavior 1150
Altruism 1151
Inclusive Fitness 1152
Evolution and Human Culture 1153

APPENDIX A Answers A-1
APPENDIX B Periodic Table of the Elements B-1
APPENDIX C The Metric System C-1
APPENDIX D A Comparison of the Light Microscope and the Electron Microscope D-1
APPENDIX E Classification of Life E-1
APPENDIX F Scientific Skills Review F-1

CREDITS CR-1
GLOSSARY G-1
INDEX I-1

1

Evolution, the Themes of Biology, and Scientific Inquiry

KEY CONCEPTS

1.1 The study of life reveals common themes

1.2 The Core Theme: Evolution accounts for the unity and diversity of life

1.3 In studying nature, scientists make observations and form and test hypotheses

1.4 Science benefits from a cooperative approach and diverse viewpoints

▲ **Figure 1.1** How is the dandelion adapted to its environment?

Inquiring About Life

The dandelions shown in **Figure 1.1** send their seeds aloft for dispersal. A seed is an embryo surrounded by a store of food and a protective coat. The dandelion's seeds, shown at the lower left, are borne on the wind by parachute-like structures made from modified flower parts. The parachutes harness the wind, which carries such seeds to new locations where conditions may favor sprouting and growth. Dandelions are very successful plants, found in temperate regions worldwide.

An organism's adaptations to its environment, such as the dandelion seed's parachute, are the result of evolution. **Evolution** is the process of change that has transformed life on Earth from its earliest beginnings to the diversity of organisms living today. Because evolution is the fundamental organizing principle of biology, it is the core theme of this book.

Although biologists know a great deal about life on Earth, many mysteries remain. For instance, what processes led to the origin of flowering among plants such as the ones pictured above? Posing questions about the living world and seeking answers through scientific inquiry are the central activities of **biology**, the scientific study of life. Biologists' questions can be ambitious. They may ask how a single tiny cell becomes a tree or a dog, how the human mind works, or how the different

Order. This close-up of a sunflower illustrates the highly ordered structure that characterizes life.

Evolutionary adaptation. The appearance of this pygmy sea horse camouflages the animal in its environment. Such adaptations evolve over many generations by the reproductive success of those individuals with heritable traits that are best suited to their environments.

Regulation. The regulation of blood flow through the blood vessels of this jackrabbit's ears helps maintain a constant body temperature by adjusting heat exchange with the surrounding air.

Energy processing. This butterfly obtains fuel in the form of nectar from flowers. The butterfly will use chemical energy stored in its food to power flight and other work.

Growth and development. Inherited information carried by genes controls the pattern of growth and development of organisms, such as this oak seedling.

Response to the environment. This Venus flytrap closed its trap rapidly in response to the environmental stimulus of a damselfly landing on the open trap.

Reproduction. Organisms (living things) reproduce their own kind.

▲ **Figure 1.2**
Some properties of life.

forms of life in a forest interact. Many interesting questions probably occur to you when you are out-of-doors, surrounded by the natural world. When they do, you are already thinking like a biologist. More than anything else, biology is a quest, an ongoing inquiry about the nature of life.

At the most fundamental level, we may ask: What is life? Even a child realizes that a dog or a plant is alive, while a rock or a car is not. Yet the phenomenon we call life defies a simple, one-sentence definition. We recognize life by what living things do. **Figure 1.2** highlights some of the properties and processes we associate with life.

While limited to a handful of images, Figure 1.2 reminds us that the living world is wondrously varied. How do biologists make sense of this diversity and complexity? This opening chapter sets up a framework for answering this question. The first part of the chapter provides a panoramic view of the biological "landscape," organized around some unifying themes. We then focus on biology's core theme, evolution, which accounts for life's unity and diversity. Next, we look at scientific inquiry—how scientists ask and attempt to answer questions about the natural world. Finally, we address the culture of science and its effects on society.

The study of life reveals common themes

Biology is a subject of enormous scope, and exciting new biological discoveries are being made every day. How can you organize into a comprehensible framework all the information you'll encounter as you study the broad range of topics included in biology? Focusing on a few big ideas will

help. Here, we'll list five unifying themes—ways of thinking about life that will still hold true decades from now. These unifying themes are described in greater detail in the next few pages. We hope they will serve as touchstones as you proceed through this text:

- Organization
- Information
- Energy and Matter
- Interactions
- Evolution

▼ Figure 1.3
Exploring Levels of Biological Organization

◄ 1 The Biosphere

Even from space, we can see signs of Earth's life—in the green mosaic of the forests, for example. We can also see the scale of the entire biosphere, which consists of all life on Earth and all the places where life exists: most regions of land, most bodies of water, the atmosphere to an altitude of several kilometers, and even sediments far below the ocean floor.

◄ 2 Ecosystems

Our first scale change brings us to a North American forest with many deciduous trees (trees that lose their leaves and grow new ones each year). A deciduous forest is an example of an ecosystem, as are grasslands, deserts, and coral reefs. An ecosystem consists of all the living things in a particular area, along with all the nonliving components of the environment with which life interacts, such as soil, water, atmospheric gases, and light.

▶ 3 Communities

The array of organisms inhabiting a particular ecosystem is called a biological community. The community in our forest ecosystem includes many kinds of trees and other plants, various animals, mushrooms and other fungi, and enormous numbers of diverse microorganisms, which are living forms, such as bacteria, that are too small to see without a microscope. Each of these forms of life is called a *species*.

▶ 4 Populations

A population consists of all the individuals of a species living within the bounds of a specified area. For example, our forest includes a population of sugar maple trees and a population of white-tailed deer. A community is therefore the set of populations that inhabit a particular area.

▲ 5 Organisms

Individual living things are called organisms. Each of the maple trees and other plants in the forest is an organism, and so is each deer, frog, beetle, and other forest animals. The soil teems with microorganisms such as bacteria.

Theme: New Properties Emerge at Successive Levels of Biological Organization

ORGANIZATION In **Figure 1.3**, we zoom in from space to take a closer and closer look at life in a deciduous forest in Ontario, Canada. This journey shows the different levels of organization recognized by biologists: The study of life extends from the global scale of the entire living planet to the microscopic scale of cells and molecules. The numbers in the figure guide you through the hierarchy of biological organization.

Zooming in at ever-finer resolution illustrates an approach called *reductionism*, which reduces complex systems to simpler components that are more manageable to study. Reductionism is a powerful strategy in biology. For example, by studying the molecular structure of DNA that had been extracted from cells, James Watson and Francis Crick inferred the chemical basis of biological inheritance. However, although it has propelled many major discoveries, reductionism provides a necessarily incomplete view of life on Earth, as we'll discuss next.

▼ 6 Organs and Organ Systems

The structural hierarchy of life continues to unfold as we explore the architecture of more complex organisms. A maple leaf is an example of an organ, a body part that carries out a particular function in the body. Stems and roots are the other major organs of plants. The organs of complex animals and plants are organized into organ systems, each a team of organs that cooperate in a larger function. Organs consist of multiple tissues.

◄ 7 Tissues

Viewing the tissues of a leaf requires a microscope. Each tissue is a group of cells that work together, performing a specialized function. The leaf shown here has been cut on an angle. The honeycombed tissue in the interior of the leaf (left side of photo) is the main location of photosynthesis, the process that converts light energy to the chemical energy of sugar. The jigsaw puzzle–like "skin" on the surface of the leaf is a tissue called epidermis (right side of photo). The pores through the epidermis allow entry of the gas CO_2, a raw material for sugar production.

50 μm

Cell   10 μm

▶ 10 Molecules

Our last scale change drops us into a chloroplast for a view of life at the molecular level. A molecule is a chemical structure consisting of two or more units called atoms, represented as balls in this computer graphic of a chlorophyll molecule. Chlorophyll is the pigment molecule that makes a maple leaf green, and it absorbs sunlight during photosynthesis. Within each chloroplast, millions of chlorophyll molecules are organized into systems that convert light energy to the chemical energy of food.

Atoms

Chlorophyll molecule

▲ 8 Cells

The cell is life's fundamental unit of structure and function. Some organisms are single cells, while others are multicellular. A single cell performs all the functions of life, while a multicellular organism has a division of labor among specialized cells. Here we see a magnified view of cells in a leaf tissue. One cell is about 40 micrometers (μm) across—about 500 of them would reach across a small coin. As tiny as these cells are, you can see that each contains numerous green structures called chloroplasts, which are responsible for photosynthesis.

▶ 9 Organelles

Chloroplasts are examples of organelles, the various functional components present in cells. This image, taken by a powerful microscope, shows a single chloroplast.

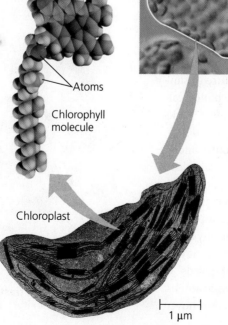

Chloroplast

1 μm

Emergent Properties

Let's reexamine Figure 1.3, beginning this time at the molecular level and then zooming out. This approach allows us to see novel properties emerge at each level that are absent from the preceding level. These **emergent properties** are due to the arrangement and interactions of parts as complexity increases. For example, although photosynthesis occurs in an intact chloroplast, it will not take place in a disorganized test-tube mixture of chlorophyll and other chloroplast molecules. The coordinated processes of photosynthesis require a specific organization of these molecules in the chloroplast. Isolated components of living systems, serving as the objects of study in a reductionist approach to biology, lack a number of significant properties that emerge at higher levels of organization.

Emergent properties are not unique to life. A box of bicycle parts won't transport you anywhere, but if they are arranged in a certain way, you can pedal to your chosen destination. Compared with such nonliving examples, however, biological systems are far more complex, making the emergent properties of life especially challenging to study.

To explore emergent properties more fully, biologists today complement reductionism with **systems biology**, the exploration of a biological system by analyzing the interactions among its parts. In this context, a single leaf cell can be considered a system, as can a frog, an ant colony, or a desert ecosystem. By examining and modeling the dynamic behavior of an integrated network of components, systems biology enables us to pose new kinds of questions. For example, we can ask how a drug that lowers blood pressure affects the functioning of organs throughout the human body. At a larger scale, how does a gradual increase in atmospheric carbon dioxide alter ecosystems and the entire biosphere? Systems biology can be used to study life at all levels.

Structure and Function

At each level of the biological hierarchy, we find a correlation of structure and function. Consider the leaf shown in Figure 1.3: Its thin, flat shape maximizes the capture of sunlight by chloroplasts. More generally, analyzing a biological structure gives us clues about what it does and how it works. Conversely, knowing the function of something provides insight into its structure and organization. Many examples from the animal kingdom show a correlation between structure and function. For example, the hummingbird's anatomy allows the wings to rotate at the shoulder, so hummingbirds have the ability, unique among birds, to fly backward or hover

in place. While hovering, the birds can extend their long, slender beaks into flowers and feed on nectar. The elegant match of form and function in the structures of life is explained by natural selection, which we'll explore shortly.

The Cell: An Organism's Basic Unit of Structure and Function

In life's structural hierarchy, the cell is the smallest unit of organization that can perform all activities required for life. In fact, the actions of organisms are all based on the functioning of cells. For instance, the movement of your eyes as you read this sentence results from the activities of muscle and nerve cells. Even a process that occurs on a global scale, such as the recycling of carbon atoms, is the product of cellular functions, including the photosynthetic activity of chloroplasts in leaf cells.

All cells share certain characteristics. For instance, every cell is enclosed by a membrane that regulates the passage of materials between the cell and its surroundings. Nevertheless, we recognize two main forms of cells: prokaryotic and eukaryotic. The cells of two groups of single-celled microorganisms—bacteria (singular, *bacterium*) and archaea (singular, *archaean*)—are prokaryotic. All other forms of life, including plants and animals, are composed of eukaryotic cells.

A **eukaryotic cell** contains membrane-enclosed organelles **(Figure 1.4)**. Some organelles, such as the DNA-containing nucleus, are found in the cells of all eukaryotes; other organelles are specific to particular cell types. For example, the chloroplast in Figure 1.3 is an organelle found

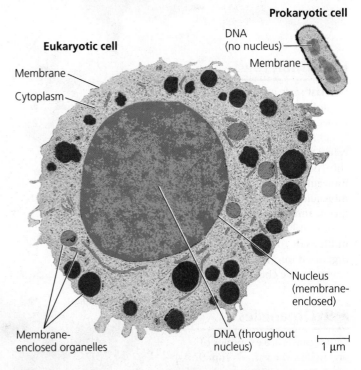

Prokaryotic cell

DNA (no nucleus)

Membrane

Eukaryotic cell

Membrane

Cytoplasm

Nucleus (membrane-enclosed)

Membrane-enclosed organelles

DNA (throughout nucleus)

1 μm

▲ **Figure 1.4 Contrasting eukaryotic and prokaryotic cells in size and complexity.**

only in eukaryotic cells that carry out photosynthesis. In contrast to eukaryotic cells, a **prokaryotic cell** lacks a nucleus or other membrane-enclosed organelles. Another distinction is that prokaryotic cells are generally smaller than eukaryotic cells, as shown in Figure 1.4.

Theme: Life's Processes Involve the Expression and Transmission of Genetic Information

INFORMATION Within cells, structures called chromosomes contain genetic material in the form of **DNA (deoxyribonucleic acid)**. In cells that are preparing to divide, the chromosomes may be made visible using a dye that appears blue when bound to the DNA **(Figure 1.5)**.

25 µm

▲ **Figure 1.5 A lung cell from a newt divides into two smaller cells that will grow and divide again.**

DNA, the Genetic Material

Each time a cell divides, the DNA is first replicated, or copied, and each of the two cellular offspring inherits a complete set of chromosomes, identical to that of the parent cell. Each chromosome contains one very long DNA molecule with hundreds or thousands of **genes**, each a section of the DNA of the chromosome. Transmitted from parents to offspring, genes are the units of inheritance. They encode the information necessary to build all of the molecules synthesized within a cell, which in turn establish that cell's identity and function. Each of us began as a single cell stocked with DNA inherited from our parents. The replication of that DNA during each round of cell division transmitted copies of the DNA to what eventually became the trillions of cells of our body. As the cells grew and divided, the genetic information encoded by the DNA directed our development **(Figure 1.6)**.

The molecular structure of DNA accounts for its ability to store information. A DNA molecule is made up of two long chains, called strands, arranged in a double helix. Each chain is made up of four kinds of chemical building blocks called nucleotides, abbreviated A, T, C, and G **(Figure 1.7)**.

▲ **Figure 1.6 Inherited DNA directs development of an organism.**

(a) DNA double helix. This model shows the atoms in a segment of DNA. Made up of two long chains (strands) of building blocks called nucleotides, a DNA molecule takes the three-dimensional form of a double helix.

(b) Single strand of DNA. These geometric shapes and letters are simple symbols for the nucleotides in a small section of one strand of a DNA molecule. Genetic information is encoded in specific sequences of the four types of nucleotides. Their names are abbreviated A, T, C, and G.

▲ **Figure 1.7 DNA: The genetic material.**

The way DNA encodes information is analogous to how we arrange the letters of the alphabet into words and phrases with specific meanings. The word *rat*, for example, evokes a rodent; the words *tar* and *art*, which contain the same letters, mean very different things. We can think of nucleotides as a four-letter alphabet. Specific sequences of these four nucleotides encode the information in genes.

Many genes provide the blueprints for making proteins, which are the major players in building and maintaining the cell and carrying out its activities. For instance, a given bacterial gene may specify a particular protein (an enzyme) required to break down a certain sugar molecule, while a human gene may denote a different protein (an antibody) that helps fight off infection.

Genes control protein production indirectly, using a related molecule called RNA as an intermediary (**Figure 1.8**). The sequence of nucleotides along a gene is transcribed into RNA, which is then translated into a linked series of protein building blocks called amino acids. These two stages result in a specific protein with a unique shape and function. The entire process, by which the information in a gene directs the manufacture of a cellular product, is called **gene expression**.

In translating genes into proteins, all forms of life employ essentially the same genetic code: A particular sequence of nucleotides says the same thing in one organism as it does in another. Differences between organisms reflect differences between their nucleotide sequences rather than between their genetic codes. Comparing the sequences in several species for a gene that codes for a particular protein can provide valuable information both about the protein and about the relationship of the species to each other, as you will see.

In addition to RNA molecules (called mRNAs) that are translated into proteins, some RNAs in the cell carry out other important tasks. For example, we have known for decades that some types of RNA are actually components of the cellular machinery that manufactures proteins. Recently, scientists have discovered whole new classes of RNA that play other roles in the cell, such as regulating the functioning of protein-coding genes. All of these RNAs are specified by genes, and the production of these RNAs is also referred to as gene expression. By carrying the instructions for making proteins and RNAs and by replicating with each cell division, DNA ensures faithful inheritance of genetic information from generation to generation.

Genomics: Large-Scale Analysis of DNA Sequences

The entire "library" of genetic instructions that an organism inherits is called its **genome**. A typical human cell has two similar sets of chromosomes, and each set has approximately 3 billion nucleotide pairs of DNA. If the one-letter abbreviations for the nucleotides of a set were written in letters the size of those you are now reading, the genetic text would fill about 700 biology textbooks.

(a) The lens of the eye (behind the pupil) is able to focus light because lens cells are tightly packed with transparent proteins called crystallin.

Lens cell

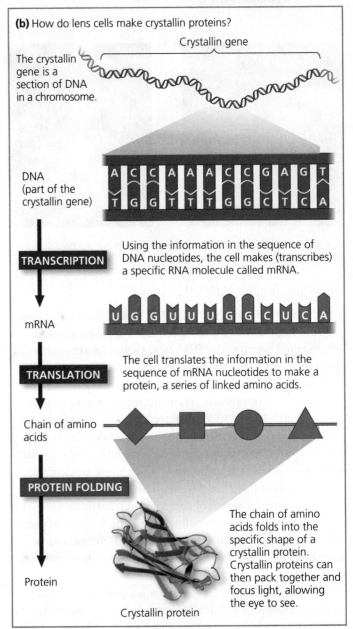

(b) How do lens cells make crystallin proteins?

Crystallin gene

The crystallin gene is a section of DNA in a chromosome.

DNA (part of the crystallin gene)

A C C A A A C C G A G T
T G G T T T G G C T C A

TRANSCRIPTION

Using the information in the sequence of DNA nucleotides, the cell makes (transcribes) a specific RNA molecule called mRNA.

mRNA

U G G U U U G G C U C A

TRANSLATION

The cell translates the information in the sequence of mRNA nucleotides to make a protein, a series of linked amino acids.

Chain of amino acids

PROTEIN FOLDING

The chain of amino acids folds into the specific shape of a crystallin protein. Crystallin proteins can then pack together and focus light, allowing the eye to see.

Protein

Crystallin protein

▲ **Figure 1.8 Gene expression: The transfer of information from a gene results in a functional protein.**

Since the early 1990s, the pace at which researchers can determine the sequence of a genome has accelerated at an astounding rate, enabled by a revolution in technology. The entire sequence of nucleotides in the human genome is now known, along with the genome sequences of many other organisms, including other animals and numerous plants, fungi, bacteria, and archaea. To make sense of the deluge of data from genome-sequencing projects and the growing catalog of known gene functions, scientists are applying a systems biology approach at the cellular and molecular levels. Rather than investigating a single gene at a time, researchers study whole sets of genes (or other DNA) in one or more species—an approach called **genomics**. Likewise, the term **proteomics** refers to the study of sets of proteins and their properties. (The entire set of proteins expressed by a given cell or group of cells is called a **proteome**).

Three important research developments have made the genomic and proteomic approaches possible. One is "high-throughput" technology, tools that can analyze many biological samples very rapidly. The second major development is **bioinformatics**, the use of computational tools to store, organize, and analyze the huge volume of data that results from high-throughput methods. The third development is the formation of interdisciplinary research teams—groups of diverse specialists that may include computer scientists, mathematicians, engineers, chemists, physicists, and, of course, biologists from a variety of fields. Researchers in such teams aim to learn how the activities of all the proteins and non-translated RNAs encoded by the DNA are coordinated in cells and in whole organisms.

Theme: Life Requires the Transfer and Transformation of Energy and Matter

ENERGY AND MATTER A fundamental characteristic of living organisms is their use of energy to carry out life's activities. Moving, growing, reproducing, and the various cellular activities of life are work, and work requires energy. The input of energy, primarily from the sun, and the transformation of energy from one form to another make life possible. A plant's leaves absorb sunlight, and molecules within the leaves convert the energy of sunlight to the chemical energy of food, such as sugars, produced during photosynthesis. The chemical energy in the food molecules is then passed along by plants and other photosynthetic organisms (**producers**) to consumers. **Consumers** are organisms, such as animals, that feed on producers and other consumers.

When an organism uses chemical energy to perform work, such as muscle contraction or cell division, some of that energy is lost to the surroundings as heat. As a result, energy flows one way *through* an ecosystem, usually entering as light and exiting as heat. In contrast, chemicals are recycled *within* an ecosystem **(Figure 1.9)**. Chemicals that a plant absorbs from the air or soil may be incorporated into the plant's body and then passed to an animal that eats the plant. Eventually, these chemicals will be returned to the environment by decomposers, such as bacteria and fungi, that break down waste products, leaf litter, and the bodies of dead organisms. The chemicals are then available to be taken up by plants again, thereby completing the cycle.

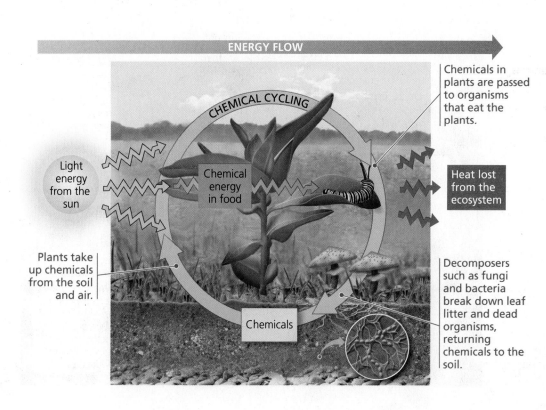

ENERGY FLOW

CHEMICAL CYCLING

Light energy from the sun

Chemical energy in food

Chemicals in plants are passed to organisms that eat the plants.

Heat lost from the ecosystem

Plants take up chemicals from the soil and air.

Chemicals

Decomposers such as fungi and bacteria break down leaf litter and dead organisms, returning chemicals to the soil.

◀ **Figure 1.9 Energy flow and chemical cycling.** There is a one-way flow of energy in an ecosystem: During photosynthesis, plants convert energy from sunlight to chemical energy (stored in food molecules such as sugars), which is used by plants and other organisms to do work and is eventually lost from the ecosystem as heat. In contrast, chemicals cycle between organisms and the physical environment.

Theme: From Ecosystems to Molecules, Interactions Are Important in Biological Systems

INTERACTIONS At any level of the biological hierarchy, interactions between the components of the system ensure smooth integration of all the parts, such that they function as a whole. This holds true equally well for the components of an ecosystem and the molecules in a cell; we'll discuss both as examples.

Ecosystems: An Organism's Interactions with Other Organisms and the Physical Environment

At the ecosystem level, each organism interacts with other organisms. For instance, an acacia tree interacts with soil microorganisms associated with its roots, insects that live on it, and animals that eat its leaves and fruit (Figure 1.10). In some cases, interactions between organisms are mutually beneficial. An example is the association between a sea turtle and the so-called "cleaner fish" that hover around it. The fish feed on parasites that would otherwise harm the turtle, while gaining a meal and protection from predators. Sometimes, one species benefits and the other is harmed, as when a lion kills and eats a zebra. In yet other cases, both species are harmed—for example, when two plants compete for a soil resource that is in short supply. Interactions among organisms help regulate the functioning of the ecosystem as a whole.

Organisms also interact continuously with physical factors in their environment. The leaves of a tree, for example, absorb light from the sun, take in carbon dioxide from the air, and release oxygen to the air (see Figure 1.10). The environment is also affected by the organisms living there. For instance, in addition to taking up water and minerals from the soil, the roots of a plant break up rocks as they grow, thereby contributing to the formation of soil. On a global scale, plants and other photosynthetic organisms have generated all the oxygen in the atmosphere.

Molecules: Interactions Within Organisms

At lower levels of organization, the interactions between components that make up living organisms—organs, tissues, cells, and molecules—are crucial to their smooth operation. Consider the sugar in your blood, for instance. After a meal, the level of the sugar glucose in your blood rises (Figure 1.11). The increase in blood glucose stimulates the pancreas to release insulin into the blood. Once it reaches liver or muscle cells, insulin causes excess glucose to be stored in the form of a very large carbohydrate called glycogen, reducing blood glucose level to a range that is optimal for bodily functioning. The lower blood glucose level that results no longer stimulates insulin secretion by pancreas cells. Some sugar is also used by cells for energy: When you exercise, your muscle cells increase their consumption of sugar molecules.

Interactions among the body's molecules are responsible for most of the steps in this process. For instance, like most chemical activities in the cell, those that either decompose or store sugar are accelerated at the molecular level (catalyzed) by proteins called enzymes. Each type of enzyme

▶ Figure 1.10 Interactions of an African acacia tree with other organisms and the physical environment.

Sunlight

Leaves absorb light energy from the sun.

Leaves take in carbon dioxide from the air and release oxygen.

CO_2

O_2

Leaves fall to the ground and are decomposed by organisms that return minerals to the soil.

Water and minerals in the soil are taken up by the tree through its roots.

Animals eat leaves and fruit from the tree, returning nutrients and minerals to the soil in their waste products.

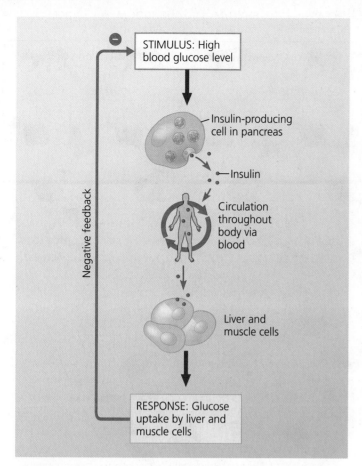

STIMULUS: High blood glucose level

Negative feedback

Insulin-producing cell in pancreas

Insulin

Circulation throughout body via blood

Liver and muscle cells

RESPONSE: Glucose uptake by liver and muscle cells

▲ **Figure 1.11 Feedback regulation.** The human body regulates the use and storage of glucose, a major cellular fuel derived from food. This figure shows negative feedback: The response (glucose uptake by cells) decreases the high glucose levels that provide the stimulus for insulin secretion, thus negatively regulating the process.

catalyzes a specific chemical reaction. In many cases, these reactions are linked into chemical pathways, each step with its own enzyme. How does the cell coordinate its various chemical pathways? In our example of sugar management, how does the cell match fuel supply to demand, regulating its opposing pathways of sugar consumption and storage? The key is the ability of many biological processes to self-regulate by a mechanism called feedback.

In **feedback regulation**, the output, or product, of a process regulates that very process. The most common form of regulation in living systems is *negative feedback*, a loop in which the response reduces the initial stimulus. As seen in the example of insulin signaling (see Figure 1.11), the uptake of glucose by cells (the response) decreases blood glucose levels, eliminating the stimulus for insulin secretion and thereby shutting off the pathway. Thus, the output of the process negatively regulates that process.

Though less common than processes regulated by negative feedback, there are also many biological processes regulated by *positive feedback*, in which an end product *speeds up* its own production. The clotting of your blood in response to injury is an example. When a blood vessel is damaged, structures in the blood called platelets begin to aggregate at the site. Positive feedback occurs as chemicals released by the platelets attract *more* platelets. The platelet pileup then initiates a complex process that seals the wound with a clot.

Feedback is a regulatory motif common to life at all levels, from the molecular level through ecosystems and the biosphere. Interactions between organisms can affect system-wide processes like the growth of a population. And as we'll see, interactions between individuals not only affect the participants, but also affect how populations evolve over time.

Evolution, the Core Theme of Biology

Having considered four of the unifying themes that run through this text (organization, information, energy and matter, and interactions), let's now turn to biology's core theme—evolution. Evolution is the one idea that makes logical sense of everything we know about living organisms. As we will see in Units 4 and 5 of this text, the fossil record documents the fact that life has been evolving on Earth for billions of years, resulting in a vast diversity of past and present organisms. But along with the diversity are many shared features. For example, while sea horses, jackrabbits, hummingbirds, and giraffes all look very different, their skeletons are organized in the same basic way. The scientific explanation for this unity and diversity—as well as for the adaptation of organisms to their environments—is evolution: the concept that the organisms living on Earth today are the modified descendants of common ancestors. In other words, we can explain the sharing of traits by two organisms with the premise that the organisms have descended from a common ancestor, and we can account for differences with the idea that heritable changes have occurred along the way. Many kinds of evidence support the occurrence of evolution and the theory that describes how it takes place. In the next section, we'll consider the fundamental concept of evolution in greater detail.

CONCEPT CHECK 1.1

1. Starting with the molecular level in Figure 1.3, write a sentence that includes components from the previous (lower) level of biological organization, for example: "A molecule consists of *atoms* bonded together." Continue with organelles, moving up the biological hierarchy.

2. Identify the theme or themes exemplified by (a) the sharp quills of a porcupine, (b) the development of a multicellular organism from a single fertilized egg, and (c) a hummingbird using sugar to power its flight.

3. **WHAT IF?** For each theme discussed in this section, give an example not mentioned in the text.

For suggested answers, see Appendix A.

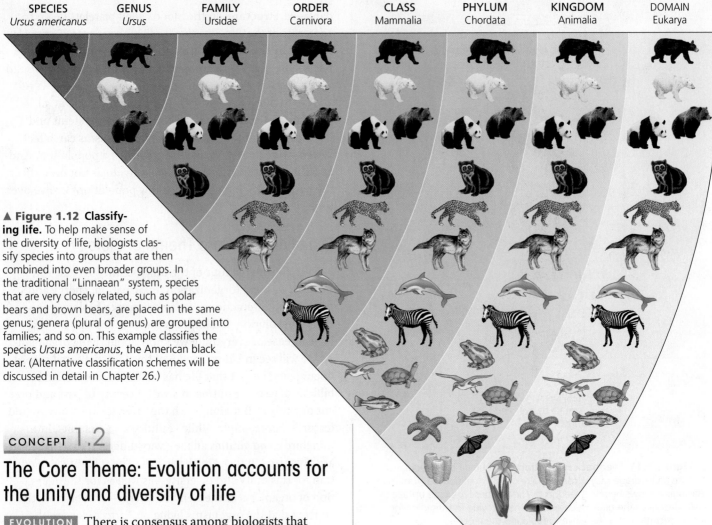

SPECIES	GENUS	FAMILY	ORDER	CLASS	PHYLUM	KINGDOM	DOMAIN
Ursus americanus	*Ursus*	Ursidae	Carnivora	Mammalia	Chordata	Animalia	Eukarya

▲ **Figure 1.12 Classifying life.** To help make sense of the diversity of life, biologists classify species into groups that are then combined into even broader groups. In the traditional "Linnaean" system, species that are very closely related, such as polar bears and brown bears, are placed in the same genus; genera (plural of genus) are grouped into families; and so on. This example classifies the species *Ursus americanus*, the American black bear. (Alternative classification schemes will be discussed in detail in Chapter 26.)

CONCEPT 1.2

The Core Theme: Evolution accounts for the unity and diversity of life

EVOLUTION There is consensus among biologists that evolution is the core theme of biology. The evolutionary changes seen in the fossil record are observable facts. Furthermore, as we'll describe, evolutionary mechanisms account for the unity and diversity of all species on Earth. To quote one of the founders of modern evolutionary theory, Theodosius Dobzhansky, "Nothing in biology makes sense except in the light of evolution."

In addition to encompassing a hierarchy of size scales from molecules to the biosphere, biology explores the great diversity of species that have ever lived on Earth. To understand Dobzhansky's statement, we need to discuss how biologists think about this vast diversity.

Classifying the Diversity of Life

Diversity is a hallmark of life. Biologists have so far identified and named about 1.8 million species. To date, this diversity of life is known to include at least 100,000 species of fungi, 290,000 plant species, 57,000 vertebrate species (animals with backbones), and 1 million insect species (more than half of all known forms of life)—not to mention the myriad types of single-celled organisms. Researchers identify thousands of additional species each year. Estimates of the total number of species range from about 10 million

to over 100 million. Whatever the actual number, the enormous variety of life gives biology a very broad scope. Biologists face a major challenge in attempting to make sense of this variety.

Grouping Species: The Basic Idea

There is a human tendency to group diverse items according to their similarities and their relationships to each other. For instance, we may speak of "squirrels" and "butterflies," though we recognize that many different species belong to each group. We may even sort groups into broader categories, such as rodents (which include squirrels) and insects (which include butterflies). Taxonomy, the branch of biology that names and classifies species, formalizes this ordering of species into groups of increasing breadth, based on the degree to which they share characteristics **(Figure 1.12)**. You will learn more about the details of this taxonomic scheme in Chapter 26. Here, we will focus on the big picture by considering the broadest units of classification, kingdoms and domains.

The Three Domains of Life

Historically, scientists have classified the diversity of life-forms into species and broader groupings by careful comparisons of structure, function, and other obvious features. In the last few decades, new methods of assessing species relationships, such as comparisons of DNA sequences, have led to an ongoing reevaluation of the number and boundaries of kingdoms. Researchers have proposed anywhere from six kingdoms to dozens of kingdoms. While debate continues at the kingdom level, biologists agree that the kingdoms of life can be grouped into three even higher levels of classification called domains. The three domains are named Bacteria, Archaea, and Eukarya **(Figure 1.13)**.

As you read earlier, the organisms making up two of the three domains—**Bacteria** and **Archaea**—are prokaryotic.

All the eukaryotes (organisms with eukaryotic cells) are now grouped in domain **Eukarya**. This domain includes three kingdoms of multicellular eukaryotes: kingdoms Plantae, Fungi, and Animalia. These three kingdoms are distinguished partly by their modes of nutrition. Plants produce their own sugars and other food molecules by photosynthesis, fungi absorb dissolved nutrients from their surroundings, and animals obtain food by eating and digesting other organisms. Animalia is, of course, the kingdom to which we belong. But neither plants, nor fungi, nor animals are as numerous or diverse as the single-celled eukaryotes we call protists. Although protists were once placed in a single kingdom, recent evidence shows that some protists are more closely related to plants, animals, or fungi than they are to other protists. Thus, the recent taxonomic trend has been to split the protists into several kingdoms.

▼ **Figure 1.13 The three domains of life.**

(a) Domain Bacteria

Bacteria are the most diverse and widespread prokaryotes and are now classified into multiple kingdoms. Each rod-shaped structure in this photo is a bacterial cell.

(b) Domain Archaea

Some of the prokaryotes known as **archaea** live in Earth's extreme environments, such as salty lakes and boiling hot springs. Domain Archaea includes multiple kingdoms. Each round structure in this photo is an archaeal cell.

(c) Domain Eukarya

◀ **Kingdom Animalia** consists of multicellular eukaryotes that ingest other organisms.

▲ **Kingdom Plantae** consists of terrestrial multicellular eukaryotes (land plants) that carry out photosynthesis, the conversion of light energy to the chemical energy in food.

▶ **Kingdom Fungi** is defined in part by the nutritional mode of its members (such as this mushroom), which absorb nutrients from outside their bodies.

▶ **Protists** are mostly unicellular eukaryotes and some relatively simple multicellular relatives. Pictured here is an assortment of protists inhabiting pond water. Scientists are currently debating how to classify protists in a way that accurately reflects their evolutionary relationships.

Cross section of a cillum, as viewed with an electron microscope

Cilia of *Paramecium*.
The cilia of the single-celled *Paramecium* propel the organism through pond water.

15 μm

5 μm

Cilia of windpipe cells.
The cells that line the human windpipe are equipped with cilia that help keep the lungs clean by sweeping a film of debris-trapping mucus upward.

0.1 μm

▲ **Figure 1.14 An example of unity underlying the diversity of life: the architecture of cilia in eukaryotes.** Cilia (singular, *cilium*) are extensions of cells that function in locomotion. They occur in eukaryotes as diverse as *Paramecium* (found in pond water) and humans. Even organisms so different share a common architecture for their cilia, which have an elaborate system of tubules that is striking in cross-sectional views.

Unity in the Diversity of Life

As diverse as life is, it also displays remarkable unity. Earlier we mentioned both the similar skeletons of different vertebrate animals and the universal genetic language of DNA (the genetic code). In fact, similarities between organisms are evident at all levels of the biological hierarchy. For example, unity is obvious in many features of cell structure, even among distantly related organisms **(Figure 1.14)**.

How can we account for life's dual nature of unity and diversity? The process of evolution, explained next, illuminates both the similarities and differences in the world of life. It also introduces another important dimension of biology: historical time.

Charles Darwin and the Theory of Natural Selection

The history of life, as documented by fossils and other evidence, is the saga of a changing Earth billions of years old, inhabited by an evolving cast of living forms **(Figure 1.15)**. This evolutionary view of life came into sharp focus in November 1859, when Charles Robert Darwin published one of the most important and influential books ever written.

▼ **Figure 1.15 Digging into the past.** Paleontologists carefully excavate the hind leg of a long-necked dinosaur (*Rapetosaurus krausei*) from rocks in Madagascar.

▲ **Figure 1.16 Charles Darwin as a young man.** His revolutionary book *On the Origin of Species* was first published in 1859.

Entitled *On the Origin of Species by Means of Natural Selection,* Darwin's book was an immediate bestseller and soon made "Darwinism," as it was dubbed at the time, almost synonymous with the concept of evolution (**Figure 1.16**).

On the Origin of Species articulated two main points. The first point was that contemporary species arose from a succession of ancestors that differed from them. Darwin called this process "descent with modification." This insightful phrase captured the duality of life's unity and diversity—unity in the kinship among species that descended from common ancestors and diversity in the modifications that evolved as species branched from their common ancestors (**Figure 1.17**).

Darwin's second main point was his proposal that "natural selection" is an evolutionary mechanism for descent with modification.

Darwin developed his theory of natural selection from observations that by themselves were neither new nor profound. Others had described the pieces of the puzzle, but Darwin saw how they fit together. He started with the following three observations from nature: First, individuals in a population vary in their traits, many of which seem to be heritable (passed on from parents to offspring). Second, a population can produce far more offspring than can survive to produce offspring of their own. With more individuals than the environment is able to support, competition is inevitable. Third, species generally suit their environments—in other words, they are adapted to their environments. For instance, a common adaptation among birds that eat tough seeds as their major food source is that they have especially thick, strong beaks.

Making inferences from these three observations, Darwin arrived at his theory of evolution. He reasoned that individuals with inherited traits that are better suited to the local environment are more likely to survive and reproduce than less well-suited individuals. Over many generations, a higher and higher proportion of individuals in a population will have the advantageous traits. Evolution occurs as the unequal reproductive success of individuals ultimately leads to adaptation to their environment, as long as the environment remains the same.

Darwin called this mechanism of evolutionary adaptation **natural selection** because the natural environment "selects" for the propagation of certain traits among naturally occurring variant traits in the population. The example

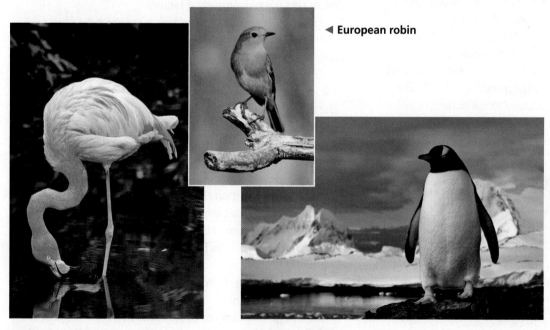

◄ **European robin**

▲ **American flamingo**

▲ **Gentoo penguin**

◄ **Figure 1.17 Unity and diversity among birds.** These three birds are variations on a common body plan. For example, each has feathers, a beak, and wings—although these features are highly specialized for the birds' diverse lifestyles.

① Population with varied inherited traits
② Elimination of individuals with certain traits
③ Reproduction of survivors
④ Increasing frequency of traits that enhance survival and reproductive success

▲ **Figure 1.18 Natural selection.** This imaginary beetle population has colonized a locale where the soil has been blackened by a recent brush fire. Initially, the population varies extensively in the inherited coloration of the individuals, from very light gray to charcoal. For hungry birds that prey on the beetles, it is easiest to spot the beetles that are lightest in color.

in **Figure 1.18** illustrates the ability of natural selection to "edit" a population's heritable variations in color. We see the products of natural selection in the exquisite adaptations of various organisms to the special circumstances of their way of life and their environment. The wings of the bat shown in **Figure 1.19** are an excellent example of adaptation.

The Tree of Life

Take another look at the skeletal architecture of the bat's wings in Figure 1.19. These wings are not like those of feathered birds; the bat is a mammal. The bat's forelimbs, though adapted for flight, actually have all the same bones, joints, nerves, and blood vessels found in other limbs as diverse as the human arm, the foreleg of a horse, and the flipper of a whale. Indeed, all mammalian forelimbs are anatomical variations of a common architecture, much as the birds in Figure 1.17 are variations on an underlying "avian" theme. Such examples of kinship connect life's unity in diversity to the Darwinian concept of descent with modification. In this view, the unity of mammalian limb anatomy reflects inheritance of that structure from a common

ancestor—the "prototype" mammal from which all other mammals descended. The diversity of mammalian forelimbs results from modification by natural selection operating over millions of generations in different environmental contexts. Fossils and other evidence corroborate anatomical unity in supporting this view of mammalian descent from a common ancestor.

Darwin proposed that natural selection, by its cumulative effects over long periods of time, could cause an ancestral species to give rise to two or more descendant species. This could occur, for example, if one population fragmented into several subpopulations isolated in different environments. In these separate arenas of natural selection, one species could gradually radiate into multiple species as the geographically isolated populations adapted over many generations to different sets of environmental factors.

The "family tree" of 14 finches in **Figure 1.20** illustrates a famous example of adaptive radiation of new species from a common ancestor. Darwin collected specimens of these birds during his 1835 visit to the remote Galápagos Islands, 900 kilometers (km) off the Pacific coast of South America. These relatively young, volcanic islands are home to many species of plants and animals found nowhere else in the world, though many Galápagos organisms are clearly related to species on the South American mainland. After volcanoes built up the Galápagos several million years ago, finches probably diversified on the various islands from an ancestral finch species that by chance reached the archipelago from elsewhere. Years after Darwin collected the Galapagos finches, researchers began to sort out the relationships among these finch species, first from anatomical and geographic data and more recently with the help of DNA sequence comparisons.

Biologists' diagrams of evolutionary relationships generally take treelike forms, though the trees are often turned

▲ **Figure 1.19 Evolutionary adaptation.** Bats, the only mammals capable of active flight, have wings with webbing between extended "fingers." Darwin proposed that such adaptations are refined over time by natural selection.

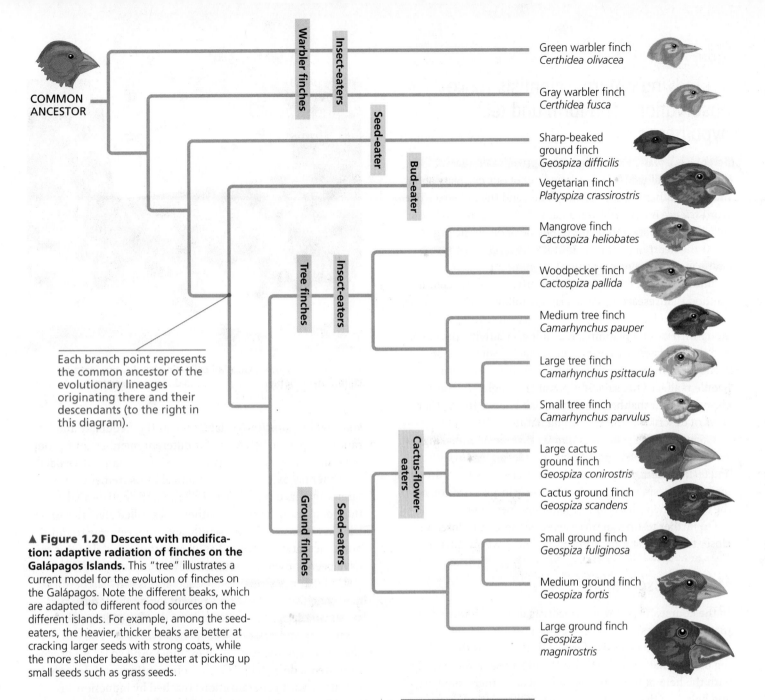

COMMON ANCESTOR

Warbler finches
Insect-eaters

Seed-eater

Bud-eater

Tree finches
Insect-eaters

Ground finches
Seed-eaters

Cactus-flower-eaters

Green warbler finch
Certhidea olivacea

Gray warbler finch
Certhidea fusca

Sharp-beaked ground finch
Geospiza difficilis

Vegetarian finch
Platyspiza crassirostris

Mangrove finch
Cactospiza heliobates

Woodpecker finch
Cactospiza pallida

Medium tree finch
Camarhynchus pauper

Large tree finch
Camarhynchus psittacula

Small tree finch
Camarhynchus parvulus

Large cactus ground finch
Geospiza conirostris

Cactus ground finch
Geospiza scandens

Small ground finch
Geospiza fuliginosa

Medium ground finch
Geospiza fortis

Large ground finch
Geospiza magnirostris

Each branch point represents the common ancestor of the evolutionary lineages originating there and their descendants (to the right in this diagram).

▲ **Figure 1.20 Descent with modification: adaptive radiation of finches on the Galápagos Islands.** This "tree" illustrates a current model for the evolution of finches on the Galápagos. Note the different beaks, which are adapted to different food sources on the different islands. For example, among the seed-eaters, the heavier, thicker beaks are better at cracking larger seeds with strong coats, while the more slender beaks are better at picking up small seeds such as grass seeds.

sideways as in Figure 1.20. Tree diagrams make sense: Just as an individual has a genealogy that can be diagrammed as a family tree, each species is one twig of a branching tree of life extending back in time through ancestral species more and more remote. Species that are very similar, such as the Galápagos finches, share a common ancestor at a relatively recent branch point on the tree of life. But through an ancestor that lived much farther back in time, finches are related to sparrows, hawks, penguins, and all other birds. And birds, mammals, and all other vertebrates share a common ancestor even more ancient. Trace life back far enough, and we reach the early prokaryotes that inhabited Earth over 3.5 billion years ago. We can recognize their vestiges in our own cells—in the universal genetic code, for example. Indeed, all of life is connected through its long evolutionary history.

CONCEPT CHECK 1.2

1. How is a mailing address analogous to biology's hierarchical taxonomic system?

2. Explain why "editing" is an appropriate metaphor for how natural selection acts on a population's heritable variation.

3. **WHAT IF?** The three domains you learned about in Concept 1.2 can be represented in the tree of life as the three main branches, with three subbranches on the eukaryotic branch being the kingdoms Plantae, Fungi, and Animalia. What if fungi and animals are more closely related to each other than either of these kingdoms is to plants—as recent evidence strongly suggests? Draw a simple branching pattern that symbolizes the proposed relationship between these three eukaryotic kingdoms.

For suggested answers, see Appendix A.

In studying nature, scientists make observations and form and test hypotheses

Science is a way of knowing—an approach to understanding the natural world. It developed out of our curiosity about ourselves, other life-forms, our planet, and the universe. The word *science* is derived from a Latin verb meaning "to know." Striving to understand seems to be one of our basic urges.

At the heart of science is **inquiry**, a search for information and explanations of natural phenomena. There is no formula for successful scientific inquiry, no single scientific method that researchers must rigidly follow. As in all quests, science includes elements of challenge, adventure, and luck, along with careful planning, reasoning, creativity, patience, and the persistence to overcome setbacks. Such diverse elements of inquiry make science far less structured than most people realize. That said, it is possible to highlight certain characteristics that help to distinguish science from other ways of describing and explaining nature.

Scientists use a process of inquiry that includes making observations, forming logical, testable explanations (*hypotheses*), and testing them. The process is necessarily repetitive: In testing a hypothesis, more observations may inspire revision of the original hypothesis or formation of a new one, thus leading to further testing. In this way, scientists circle closer and closer to their best estimation of the laws governing nature.

Making Observations

In the course of their work, scientists describe natural structures and processes as accurately as possible through careful observation and analysis of data. Observation is the gathering of information, either through direct use of the senses or with the help of tools such as microscopes, thermometers, and balances that extend our senses. Observations can reveal valuable information about the natural world. For example, a series of detailed observations have shaped our understanding of cell structure, and another set of observations is currently expanding our databases of genomes of diverse species and of genes whose expression is altered in cancer and other diseases.

Recorded observations are called **data**. Put another way, data are items of information on which scientific inquiry is based. The term *data* implies numbers to many people. But some data are *qualitative*, often in the form of recorded descriptions rather than numerical measurements. For example, Jane Goodall spent decades recording her observations of chimpanzee behavior during field research in a Tanzanian jungle **(Figure 1.21)**. Along with these qualitative data, Goodall also enriched the field of animal behavior with

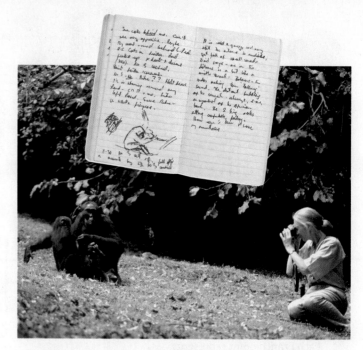

▲ **Figure 1.21 Jane Goodall collecting qualitative data on chimpanzee behavior.** Goodall recorded her observations in field notebooks, often with sketches of the animals' behavior.

volumes of *quantitative* data, such as the frequency and duration of specific behaviors for different members of a group of chimpanzees in a variety of situations. Quantitative data are generally expressed as numerical measurements and often organized into tables and graphs. Scientists analyze their data using a type of mathematics called statistics to test whether their results are significant or merely due to random fluctuations. (Note that all results presented in this text have been shown to be statistically significant.)

Collecting and analyzing observations can lead to important conclusions based on a type of logic called **inductive reasoning**. Through induction, we derive generalizations from a large number of specific observations. "The sun always rises in the east" is an example. And so is "All organisms are made of cells." Careful observations and data analyses, along with generalizations reached by induction, are fundamental to our understanding of nature.

Forming and Testing Hypotheses

Our innate curiosity often stimulates us to pose questions about the natural basis for the phenomena we observe in the world. What *caused* the different chimpanzee behaviors that Goodall observed in different situations? What *causes* the roots of a plant seedling to grow downward? In science, such inquiry usually involves the forming and testing of hypothetical explanations—that is, hypotheses.

In science, a **hypothesis** is a tentative answer to a well-framed question—an explanation on trial. It is usually a rational account for a set of observations, based on the available data and guided by inductive reasoning. A scientific hypothesis must lead to predictions that can be tested by

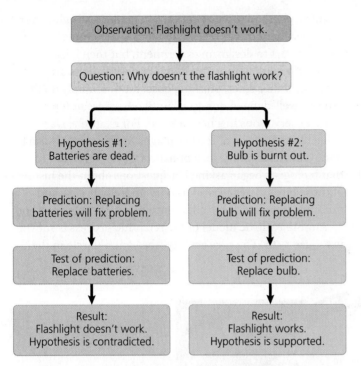

Observation: Flashlight doesn't work.

↓

Question: Why doesn't the flashlight work?

Hypothesis #1:
Batteries are dead.

Hypothesis #2:
Bulb is burnt out.

Prediction: Replacing
batteries will fix problem.

Prediction: Replacing
bulb will fix problem.

Test of prediction:
Replace batteries.

Test of prediction:
Replace bulb.

Result:
Flashlight doesn't work.
Hypothesis is contradicted.

Result:
Flashlight works.
Hypothesis is supported.

▲ **Figure 1.22 A simplified view of the scientific process.** The idealized process sometimes called the "scientific method" is shown in this flow chart, using a campground example of hypothesis testing.

making additional observations or by performing experiments. An *experiment* is a scientific test, carried out under controlled conditions.

We all use observations and develop questions and hypotheses in solving everyday problems. Let's say, for example, that your flashlight fails while you are camping. That's an observation. The question is obvious: Why doesn't the flashlight work? Two reasonable hypotheses based on your experience are that (1) the batteries in the flashlight are dead or (2) the bulb is burnt out. Each of these alternative hypotheses leads to predictions you can test with informal experiments. For example, the dead-battery hypothesis predicts that replacing the batteries will fix the problem. **Figure 1.22** diagrams this campground inquiry. Figuring things out like this, by systematic trial and error, is a hypothesis-based approach.

Sometimes we can't carry out an experiment but can test a hypothesis using observations. Let's say you don't have a spare bulb or spare batteries. How could you figure out which hypothesis is more likely? You could examine the bulb and see if it looks burnt out. You could also check the expiration date on the battery. Experiments are great ways to test hypotheses, but when experiments aren't possible, we can often test a hypothesis in other ways.

Deductive Reasoning

A type of logic called deduction is also built into the use of hypotheses in science. While induction entails reasoning from a set of specific observations to reach a general

conclusion, **deductive reasoning** involves logic that flows in the opposite direction, from the general to the specific. From general premises, we extrapolate to the specific results we should expect if the premises are true. In the scientific process, deductions usually take the form of predictions of results that will be found if a particular hypothesis (premise) is correct. We then test the hypothesis by carrying out experiments or observations to see whether or not the results are as predicted. This deductive testing takes the form of "*If . . . then*" logic. In the case of the flashlight example: *If* the dead-battery hypothesis is correct, *then* the flashlight should work if you replace the batteries with new ones.

The flashlight inquiry demonstrates two other key points about the use of hypotheses in science. First, the initial observations may give rise to multiple hypotheses. The ideal plan is to design experiments to test all these candidate explanations. For instance, another of the many possible alternative hypotheses to explain our dead flashlight is that *both* the batteries *and* the bulb are bad, and you could design an experiment to test this.

Second, we can never *prove* that a hypothesis is true. Based on the experiments shown in Figure 1.22, the burnt-out bulb hypothesis stands out as the most likely explanation. The results support that hypothesis but do not absolutely prove it is correct. Perhaps the first bulb was simply loose, so it wasn't making electrical contact, and the new bulb was inserted correctly. We could attempt to test the burnt-out bulb hypothesis again by trying another experiment—removing the original bulb and carefully reinstalling it. If the flashlight still doesn't work, the burnt-out bulb hypothesis is supported by another line of evidence—but still not proven. For example, the bulb may have another defect not related to being burnt out. Testing a hypothesis in various ways, producing different sorts of data, can increase our confidence in it tremendously, but no amount of experimental testing can *prove* a hypothesis beyond a shadow of doubt.

Questions That Can and Cannot Be Addressed by Science

Scientific inquiry is a powerful way to learn about nature, but there are limitations to the kinds of questions it can answer. A scientific hypothesis must be *testable*; there must be some observation or experiment that could reveal if such an idea is likely to be true or false. The hypothesis that dead batteries are the sole cause of the broken flashlight could be (and was) tested by replacing the old batteries with new ones.

Not all hypotheses meet the criteria of science: You wouldn't be able to test the hypothesis that invisible campground ghosts are fooling with your flashlight! Because science only deals with natural, testable explanations for natural phenomena, it can neither support nor contradict the invisible ghost hypothesis, nor whether spirits, elves, or fairies, either benevolent or evil, cause storms, rainbows, illnesses, and cures. Such supernatural explanations, because they cannot be tested, are simply outside the bounds of science. For the same reason, science does not deal with religious matters, which are issues of personal faith. Science and religion are not mutually exclusive or contradictory, they are simply concerned with different issues.

The Flexibility of the Scientific Process

The flashlight example of Figure 1.22 traces an idealized process of inquiry sometimes called *the scientific method*. We can recognize the elements of this process in most of the research articles published by scientists, but rarely in such structured form. Very few scientific inquiries adhere rigidly to the sequence of steps prescribed by the "textbook"

scientific method, which is often applied in hindsight, after the experiment or study is completed. For example, a scientist may start to design an experiment, but then backtrack after realizing that more preliminary observations are necessary. In other cases, puzzling observations simply don't prompt well-defined questions until other research places those observations in a new context. For example, Darwin collected specimens of the Galápagos finches, but it wasn't until years later, as the idea of natural selection began to gel, that biologists began asking key questions about the history of those birds. Science is a lot more unpredictable—and exciting—than lock-step adherence to any five-step method.

A more realistic model of the scientific process is shown in **Figure 1.23**. The core activity (the central circle in the

▶ **Figure 1.23 The process of science: A more realistic model.** In reality, the process of science is not linear, but is more circular, involving backtracking, repetitions, and interactions of different parts of the process. This illustration is based on a model (How Science Works) from the website Understanding Science (www.understandingscience.org).

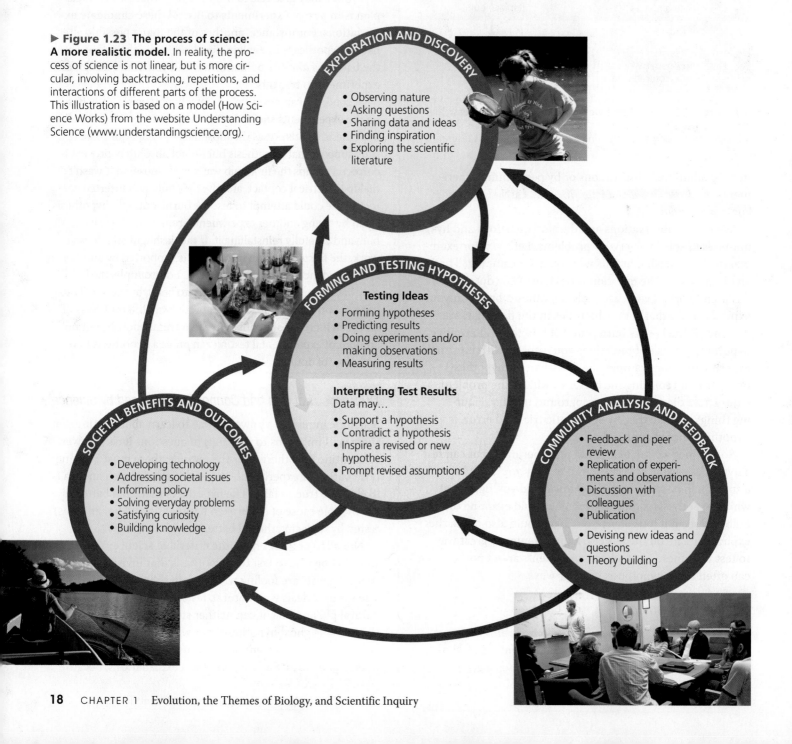

EXPLORATION AND DISCOVERY
- Observing nature
- Asking questions
- Sharing data and ideas
- Finding inspiration
- Exploring the scientific literature

FORMING AND TESTING HYPOTHESES

Testing Ideas
- Forming hypotheses
- Predicting results
- Doing experiments and/or making observations
- Measuring results

Interpreting Test Results
Data may...
- Support a hypothesis
- Contradict a hypothesis
- Inspire a revised or new hypothesis
- Prompt revised assumptions

SOCIETAL BENEFITS AND OUTCOMES
- Developing technology
- Addressing societal issues
- Informing policy
- Solving everyday problems
- Satisfying curiosity
- Building knowledge

COMMUNITY ANALYSIS AND FEEDBACK
- Feedback and peer review
- Replication of experiments and observations
- Discussion with colleagues
- Publication
- Devising new ideas and questions
- Theory building

figure) is the forming and testing of hypotheses. This is the most fundamental aspect of science and is the reason that science does such a reliable job of explaining phenomena in the natural world. However, there is much more to the scientific process than just testing. The choice of ideas to test, the interpretation and evaluation of results, and the decision about which ideas to pursue for further study are influenced by three other arenas as well.

First, well-framed questions, new hypotheses, and good study designs do not spring to life out of thin air; they are inspired and nurtured by the sorts of endeavors associated with exploration and discovery (the upper circle in Figure 1.23). Second, testing is not performed in a social vacuum; community analysis and feedback play an important role (lower right circle). Interactions within the scientific community influence which hypotheses are tested and how, provoke reinterpretations of test results, provide independent assessments of the validity of study designs, and much more. Finally, the process of science is interwoven with the fabric of society (lower left circle). A societal need—for example, to understand the process of climate change—may inspire a flurry of hypotheses and studies. Similarly, well-supported hypotheses may wind up enabling an important technological innovation or encouraging a particular policy, which may, in turn, inspire new scientific questions. Though

testing hypotheses and interpreting data are at the heart of science, these pursuits represent only part of the picture.

A Case Study in Scientific Inquiry: Investigating Coat Coloration in Mouse Populations

Now that we have highlighted the key features of scientific inquiry—making observations and forming and testing hypotheses—you should be able to recognize these features in a case study of actual scientific research.

The story begins with a set of observations and inductive generalizations. Color patterns of animals vary widely in nature, sometimes even among members of the same species. What accounts for such variation? An illustrative example is found in two populations of mice that belong to the same species (*Peromyscus polionotus*) but have different color patterns and reside in different environments (**Figure 1.24**). The beach mouse lives along the Florida seashore, a habitat of brilliant white sand dunes with sparse clumps of beach grass. The inland mouse lives on darker, more fertile soil farther inland. Even a brief glance at the photographs in Figure 1.24 reveals a striking match of mouse coloration to its habitat. The natural predators of these mice, including hawks, owls, foxes, and coyotes, are all visual hunters (they use their

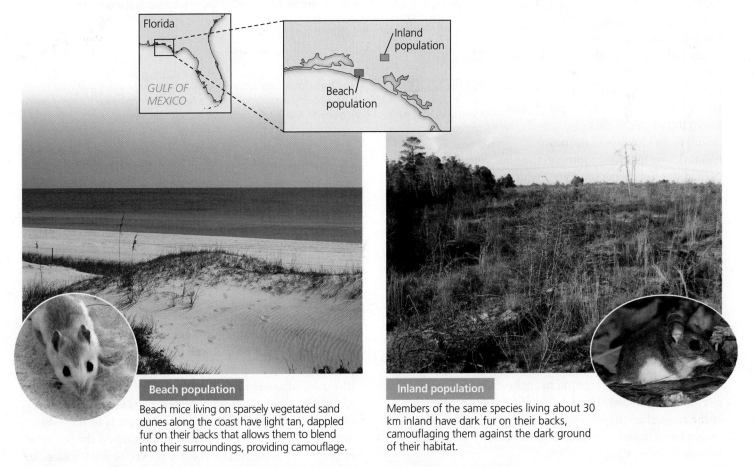

Beach population

Beach mice living on sparsely vegetated sand dunes along the coast have light tan, dappled fur on their backs that allows them to blend into their surroundings, providing camouflage.

Inland population

Members of the same species living about 30 km inland have dark fur on their backs, camouflaging them against the dark ground of their habitat.

▲ **Figure 1.24 Different coloration in beach and inland populations of *Peromyscus polionotus*.**

eyes to look for prey). It was logical, therefore, for Francis Bertody Sumner, a naturalist studying populations of these mice in the 1920s, to form the hypothesis that their coloration patterns had evolved as adaptations that camouflage the mice in their native environments, protecting them from predation.

As obvious as the camouflage hypothesis may seem, it still required testing. In 2010, biologist Hopi Hoekstra of Harvard University and a group of her students headed to Florida to test the prediction that mice with coloration that did not match their habitat would be preyed on more heavily than the native, well-matched mice. **Figure 1.25** summarizes this field experiment.

The researchers built hundreds of plasticine models of mice and spray-painted them to resemble either beach mice (light colored) or inland mice (darker colored), so that the models differed only in their color patterns. The researchers placed equal numbers of these model mice randomly in both habitats and left them overnight. The mouse models resembling the native mice in the habitat were the *control* group (for instance, light-colored beach mouse models in the beach habitat), while the mouse models with the non-native coloration were the *experimental* group (for example, darker-colored inland mouse models in the beach habitat). The following morning, the team counted and recorded signs of predation events, which ranged from bites and gouge marks on some models to the outright disappearance of others. Judging by the shape of the predator's bites and the tracks surrounding the experimental sites, the predators appeared to be split fairly evenly between mammals (such as foxes and coyotes) and birds (such as owls, herons, and hawks).

For each environment, the researchers then calculated the percentage of predation events that targeted camouflaged mouse models. The results were clear: Camouflaged models experienced much less predation than those lacking camouflage in both the beach habitat (where light mice were less vulnerable) and the inland habitat (where dark mice were less vulnerable). The data thus fit the key prediction of the camouflage hypothesis. For more information about Hopi Hoekstra and her research with beach mice, see the interview before Chapter 22.

▼ **Figure 1.25**   Inquiry

Does camouflage affect predation rates on two populations of mice?

Experiment Hopi Hoekstra and colleagues wanted to test the hypothesis that coloration of beach and inland mice (*Peromyscus polionotus*) provides camouflage that protects them from predation in their respective habitats. The researchers spray-painted mouse models with either light or dark color patterns that matched those of the beach and inland mice and then placed models with both patterns in each of the habitats. The next morning, they counted damaged or missing models.

Results For each habitat, the researchers calculated the percentage of attacked models that were camouflaged or non-camouflaged. In both habitats, the models whose pattern did not match their surroundings suffered much higher "predation" than did the camouflaged models.

Conclusion The results are consistent with the researchers' prediction: that mouse models with camouflage coloration would be preyed on less often than non-camouflaged mouse models. Thus, the experiment supports the camouflage hypothesis.

Source: S. N. Vignieri, J. G. Larson, and H. E. Hoekstra, The selective advantage of crypsis in mice, *Evolution* 64:2153–2158 (2010).

INTERPRET THE DATA *The bars indicate the percentage of the attacked models that were either light or dark. Assume 100 mouse models were attacked in each habitat. For the beach habitat, how many were light models? Dark models? Answer the same questions for the inland habitat.*

Experimental Variables and Controls

Earlier in this section, we described an experiment as a scientific test carried out under controlled conditions. More specifically, an **experiment** involves manipulation of one factor in a system in order to see the effects of changing it. Both the factor that is manipulated and the effects that are measured are types of experimental **variables**—factors that vary in an experiment.

The mouse camouflage experiment described in Figure 1.25 is an example of a **controlled experiment**, one that is designed to compare an experimental group (the non-camouflaged mice, in this case) with a control group (the camouflaged mice normally resident in the area). Ideally, the experimental and control groups are designed to differ only in the one factor the experiment is testing—in our example, the effect of mouse coloration on the behavior of predators. Here, mouse color is the factor manipulated by the researchers; it is called the the **independent variable**. The amount of predation is the **dependent variable**, a factor that is measured in the experiment. Without the control group, the researchers would not have been able to rule out other factors as causes of the more frequent attacks on the non-camouflaged mice—such as different numbers of predators or different temperatures in the different test areas. The clever experimental design left coloration as the only factor that could account for the low predation rate on the camouflaged mice placed in their normal environment.

A common misconception is that the term *controlled experiment* means that scientists control the experimental environment to keep everything strictly constant except the one variable being tested. But that's impossible in field research and not realistic even in highly regulated laboratory environments. Researchers usually "control" unwanted variables not by *eliminating* them through environmental regulation, but by *canceling out* their effects by using control groups.

Theories in Science

Our everyday use of the term *theory* often implies an untested speculation: "It's just a theory!" But the term *theory* has a different meaning in science. What is a scientific theory, and how is it different from a hypothesis or from mere speculation?

First, a scientific **theory** is much broader in scope than a hypothesis. This is a hypothesis: "Fur coloration well-matched to their habitat is an adaptation that protects mice from predators." But *this* is a theory: "Evolutionary adaptations arise by natural selection." This theory proposes that natural selection is the evolutionary mechanism that accounts for an enormous variety of adaptations, of which coat color in mice is but one example.

Second, a theory is general enough to spin off many new, specific hypotheses that can be tested. For example, two researchers at Princeton University, Peter and Rosemary Grant, were motivated by the theory of natural selection to test the specific hypothesis that the beaks of Galápagos finches evolve in response to changes in the types of available food. (Their results supported their hypothesis; see the Chapter 23 overview.)

And third, compared with any hypothesis, a theory is generally supported by a much greater body of evidence. The theory of natural selection has been supported by a vast quantity of evidence, with more being found every day, and has not been contradicted by any scientific data. Other similarly supported theories include the theory of gravity and the theory that the Earth revolves around the sun. Those theories that become widely adopted in science explain a great range of observations and are supported by a vast accumulation of evidence. In fact, scrutiny of theories

continues through testing of the specific hypotheses they generate.

In spite of the body of evidence supporting a widely accepted theory, scientists will modify or even reject theories when new research produces results that don't fit. For example, the theory of biological diversity that lumped bacteria and archaea together as a kingdom of prokaryotes began to erode when new methods for comparing cells and molecules made it possible to test some of the hypothetical relationships between organisms that were based on the theory. If there is "truth" in science, it is at best conditional, based on the preponderance of available evidence.

CONCEPT CHECK 1.3

1. Contrast inductive reasoning with deductive reasoning.
2. In the mouse camouflage experiment, what is the independent variable? The dependent variable? Explain.
3. Why is natural selection called a theory?
4. **WHAT IF?** In the deserts of the southwestern United States, the soils are mostly sandy, with occasional large regions of black rock derived from lava flows that occurred 1.7 million years ago. Mice are found in both sandy and rocky areas, and owls are known predators. What might you expect about coat color in these two mouse populations? Explain. How would you use this ecosystem to further test the camouflage hypothesis?

For suggested answers, see Appendix A.

CONCEPT 1.4

Science benefits from a cooperative approach and diverse viewpoints

Movies and cartoons sometimes portray scientists as loners working in isolated labs. In reality, science is an intensely social activity. Most scientists work in teams, which often include both graduate and undergraduate students. And to succeed in science, it helps to be a good communicator. Research results have no impact until shared with a community of peers through seminars, publications, and websites.

Building on the Work of Others

The great scientist Isaac Newton once said: "To explain all nature is too difficult a task for any one man or even for any one age. 'Tis much better to do a little with certainty, and leave the rest for others that come after you. . . ." Anyone who becomes a scientist, driven by curiosity about how nature works, is sure to benefit greatly from the rich storehouse of discoveries by others who have come before. In fact, Hopi Hoekstra's experiment benefited from the work of another researcher, D. W. Kaufman, 40 years earlier. You

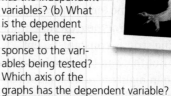

SCIENTIFIC SKILLS EXERCISE

Interpreting a Pair of Bar Graphs

How Much Does Camouflage Affect Predation on Mice by Owls with and without Moonlight? D. W. Kaufman investigated the effect of prey camouflage on predation. Kaufman tested the hypothesis that the amount of contrast between the coat color of a mouse and the color of its surroundings would affect the rate of nighttime predation by owls. He also hypothesized that the color contrast would be affected by the amount of moonlight. In this exercise, you will analyze data from his owl-mouse predation studies.

How the Experiment Was Done Pairs of mice (*Peromyscus poliono-tus*) with different coat colors, one light brown and one dark brown, were released simultaneously into an enclosure that contained a hungry owl. The researcher recorded the color of the mouse that was first caught by the owl. If the owl did not catch either mouse within 15 minutes, the test was recorded as a zero. The release trials were repeated multiple times in enclosures with either a dark-colored soil surface or a light-colored soil surface. The presence or absence of moonlight during each assay was recorded.

Data from the Experiment

Interpret the Data

1. First, make sure you understand how the graphs are set up. Graph A shows data from the light-colored soil enclosure and graph B from the dark-colored enclosure, but in all other respects the graphs are the same. (a) There is more than one independent variable in these graphs. What are the independent variables, the variables that were tested by the researcher? Which axis of the graphs has the independent variables? (b) What is the dependent variable, the response to the variables being tested? Which axis of the graphs has the dependent variable?

2. (a) How many dark brown mice were caught in the light-colored soil enclosure on a moonlit night? (b) How many dark brown mice were caught in the dark-colored soil enclosure on a moonlit night? (c) On a moonlit night, would a dark brown mouse be more likely to escape predation by owls on dark- or light-colored soil? Explain your answer.

3. (a) Is a dark brown mouse on dark-colored soil more likely to escape predation under a full moon or with no moon? (b) A light brown mouse on light-colored soil? Explain.

4. (a) Under which conditions would a dark brown mouse be most likely to escape predation at night? (b) A light brown mouse?

5. (a) What combination of independent variables led to the highest predation level in enclosures with light-colored soil? (b) What combination of independent variables led to the highest predation level in enclosures with dark-colored soil? (c) What relationship, if any, do you see in your answers to parts (a) and (b)?

6. What conditions are most deadly for both light brown and dark brown mice?

7. Combining the data shown in both graphs, estimate the total number of mice caught in moonlight versus no-moonlight conditions. Which condition is optimal for predation by the owl on mice? Explain your answer.

MB A version of this Scientific Skills Exercise can be assigned in MasteringBiology.

Data from D. W. Kaufman, Adaptive coloration in *Peromyscus polionotus*: Experimental selection by owls, *Journal of Mammalogy* 55:271–283 (1974).

---

can study the design of Kaufman's experiment and interpret the results in the Scientific Skills Exercise.

Scientific results are continually vetted through the repetition of observations and experiments. Scientists working in the same research field often check one another's claims by attempting to confirm observations or repeat experiments. If experimental results cannot be repeated by scientific colleagues, this failure may reflect some underlying weakness in the original claim, which will then have to be revised. In this sense, science polices itself. Integrity and adherence to high professional standards in reporting results are central to the scientific endeavor. After all, the validity of experimental data is key to designing further lines of inquiry.

It is not unusual for several scientists to converge on the same research question. Some scientists enjoy the challenge of being first with an important discovery or key experiment, while others derive more satisfaction from cooperating with fellow scientists working on the same problem.

Cooperation is facilitated when scientists use the same organism. Often it is a widely used **model organism**—a species that is easy to grow in the lab and lends itself particularly well to the questions being investigated. Because all species are evolutionarily related, such an organism may be viewed as a model for understanding the biology of other species and their diseases. For example, genetic studies of the fruit fly *Drosophila melanogaster* have taught us a lot about how genes work in other species, even humans. Some other popular model organisms are the mustard plant *Arabidopsis thaliana*, the soil worm *Caenorhabditis elegans*, the zebrafish *Danio rerio*, the mouse *Mus musculus*, and the bacterium *Escherichia coli*. As you read through this book, note the many contributions that these and other model organisms have made to the study of life.

Biologists may approach interesting questions from different angles. Some biologists focus on ecosystems, while others study natural phenomena at the level of organisms or cells. This text is divided into units that look at biology at different levels. Yet any given problem can be addressed from many perspectives, which in fact complement each other. For example, Hoekstra's work uncovered at least one genetic mutation that underlies the differences between beach and inland mouse coloration. Her lab includes biologists specializing at different biological levels, allowing links to be made between the evolutionary adaptations she focuses on and their molecular basis in DNA sequences.

As a biology student, you can benefit from making connections between the different levels of biology. You can develop this skill by noticing when certain topics crop up again and again in different units. One such topic is sickle-cell disease, a well-understood genetic condition that is prevalent among native inhabitants of Africa and other warm regions and their descendants. Sickle-cell disease will appear in several units of the text, each time addressed at a new level. In addition, we have designed a number of figures that make connections between the content in different chapters, as well as questions that ask you to make the connections yourselves. We hope these features will help you integrate the material you're learning and enhance your enjoyment of biology by encouraging you to keep the big picture in mind.

Science, Technology, and Society

The research community is part of society at large, and the relationship of science to society becomes clearer when we add technology to the picture (see Figure 1.23). Though science and technology sometimes employ similar inquiry patterns, their basic goals differ. The goal of science is to understand natural phenomena, while that of **technology** is to *apply* scientific knowledge for some specific purpose. Biologists and other scientists usually speak of "discoveries," while engineers and other technologists more often speak of "inventions." Because scientists put new technology to work in their research, science and technology are interdependent.

The potent combination of science and technology can have dramatic effects on society. Sometimes, the applications of basic research that turn out to be the most beneficial come out of the blue, from completely unanticipated observations in the course of scientific exploration. For example, discovery of the structure of DNA by Watson and Crick 60 years ago and subsequent achievements in DNA science led to the technologies of DNA manipulation that are transforming applied fields such as medicine, agriculture, and forensics **(Figure 1.26)**. Perhaps Watson and Crick

▲ **Figure 1.26 DNA technology and crime scene investigation.** In 2011, forensic analysis of DNA samples from a crime scene led to the release of Michael Morton from prison after he had served nearly 25 years for a crime he didn't commit, the brutal murder of his wife. The DNA analysis linked another man, also charged in a second murder, to the crime. The photo shows Mr. Morton hugging his parents after his conviction was overturned. The details of forensic analysis of DNA will be described in Chapter 20.

envisioned that their discovery would someday lead to important applications, but it is unlikely that they could have predicted exactly what all those applications would be.

The directions that technology takes depend less on the curiosity that drives basic science than on the current needs and wants of people and on the social environment of the times. Debates about technology center more on "*should* we do it" than "*can* we do it." With advances in technology come difficult choices. For example, under what circumstances is it acceptable to use DNA technology to find out if particular people have genes for hereditary diseases? Should such tests always be voluntary, or are there circumstances when genetic testing should be mandatory? Should insurance companies or employers have access to the information, as they do for many other types of personal health data? These questions are becoming much more urgent as the sequencing of individual genomes becomes quicker and cheaper.

Ethical issues raised by such questions have as much to do with politics, economics, and cultural values as with science and technology. All citizens—not only professional scientists—have a responsibility to be informed about how science works and about the potential benefits and risks of technology. The relationship between science, technology, and society increases the significance and value of any biology course.

The Value of Diverse Viewpoints in Science

Many of the technological innovations with the most profound impact on human society originated in settlements along trade routes, where a rich mix of different cultures ignited new ideas. For example, the printing press, which helped spread knowledge to all social classes and ultimately led to the book in your hands, was invented by the German

Johannes Gutenberg around 1440. This invention relied on several innovations from China, including paper and ink. Paper traveled along trade routes from China to Baghdad, where technology was developed for its mass production. This technology then migrated to Europe, as did water-based ink from China, which was modified by Gutenberg to become oil-based ink. We have the cross-fertilization of diverse cultures to thank for the printing press, and the same can be said for other important inventions.

Along similar lines, science stands to gain much from embracing a diversity of backgrounds and viewpoints among its practitioners. But just how diverse a population are scientists in relation to gender, race, ethnicity, and other attributes?

The scientific community reflects the cultural standards and behaviors of the society around it. It is therefore not surprising that until recently, women and certain minorities have faced huge obstacles in their pursuit to become professional scientists in many countries around the world. Over the past 50 years, changing attitudes about career choices have increased the proportion of women in biology and some other sciences, so that now women constitute roughly half of undergraduate biology majors and biology Ph.D. students. The pace has been slow at higher levels in the profession, however, and women and many racial and ethnic groups are still significantly underrepresented in many branches of science. This lack of diversity hampers the progress of science. The more voices that are heard at the table, the more robust, valuable, and productive the scientific interchange will be. The authors of this text welcome all students to the community of biologists, wishing you the joys and satisfactions of this exciting field of science.

1 Chapter Review

SUMMARY OF KEY CONCEPTS

CONCEPT 1.1

The study of life reveals common themes (pp. 2–9)

Organization Theme: New Properties Emerge at Successive Levels of Biological Organization

- The hierarchy of life unfolds as follows: biosphere > ecosystem > community > population > organism > organ system > organ > tissue > cell > organelle > molecule > atom. With each step upward from atoms, new **emergent properties** result from interactions among components at the lower levels. In an approach called reductionism, complex systems are broken down to simpler components that are more manageable to study. In **systems biology**, scientists attempt to model the dynamic behavior of whole biological systems by studying the interactions among the system's parts.
- The structure and function of biological components are interrelated. The cell, an organism's basic unit of structure and function, is the lowest level of organization that can perform all activities required for life. Cells are either prokaryotic or eukaryotic. **Eukaryotic cells** contain membrane-enclosed organelles, including a DNA-containing nucleus. **Prokaryotic cells** lack membrane-enclosed organelles.

Information Theme: Life's Processes Involve the Expression and Transmission of Genetic Information

- Genetic information is encoded in the nucleotide sequences of **DNA**. It is DNA that transmits heritable information from parents to offspring. DNA sequences called **genes** program a cell's protein production by being transcribed into mRNAs and then translated into specific proteins, a process called **gene expression**. Gene expression also results in RNAs that are not translated into protein but serve other important functions. **Genomics** is the large-scale analysis of the DNA sequences of a species (its **genome**) as well as the comparison of genomes between species. **Bioinformatics** uses computational tools to deal with huge volumes of sequence data.

Energy and Matter Theme: Life Requires the Transfer and Transformation of Energy and Matter

- Energy flows through an ecosystem. All organisms must perform work, which requires energy. Producers convert energy from sunlight to chemical energy, some of which is then passed on to consumers. (The rest is lost as heat energy.) Chemicals cycle between organisms and the environment.

ENERGY FLOW

CHEMICAL CYCLING

Interactions Theme: From Ecosystems to Molecules, Interactions Are Important in Biological Systems
- Organisms interact continuously with physical factors. Plants take up nutrients from the soil and chemicals from the air and use energy from the sun. Interactions among plants, animals, and other organisms affect the participants in various ways.

- In **feedback regulation,** a process is regulated by its output or end product. In negative feedback, accumulation of the end product slows its production. In positive feedback, an end product speeds up its own production. Feedback is a type of regulation common to life at all levels, from molecules to ecosystems.

Evolution, the Core Theme of Biology
- **Evolution**, the process of change that has transformed life on Earth, accounts for the unity and diversity of life. It also explains evolutionary adaptation— the match of organisms to their environments.

? *Why is evolution considered the core theme of biology?*

CONCEPT 1.2

The Core Theme: Evolution accounts for the unity and diversity of life (pp. 10–15)

- Biologists classify species according to a system of broader and broader groups. Domain **Bacteria** and domain **Archaea** consist of prokaryotes. Domain **Eukarya**, the eukaryotes, includes various groups of protists and the kingdoms Plantae, Fungi, and Animalia. As diverse as life is, there is also evidence of remarkable unity, which is revealed in the similarities between different kinds of organisms.
- Darwin proposed **natural selection** as the mechanism for evolutionary adaptation of populations to their environments.

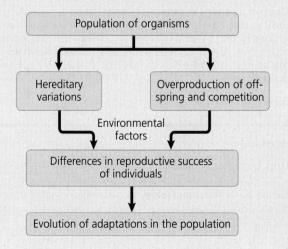

- Each species is one twig of a branching tree of life extending back in time through ancestral species more and more remote. All of life is connected through its long evolutionary history.

? *How could natural selection have led to the evolution of adaptations such as the parachute-like structure carrying a seed shown on the first page of this chapter?*

CONCEPT 1.3

In studying nature, scientists make observations and form and test hypotheses (pp. 16–21)

- In scientific **inquiry**, scientists make observations (collect **data**) and use **inductive reasoning** to draw a general conclusion, which can be developed into a testable **hypothesis**. **Deductive reasoning** makes predictions that can be used to test hypotheses. Hypotheses must be testable; science can address neither the possibility of supernatural phenomena nor the validity of religious beliefs. Hypotheses can be tested by experimentation or, when that is not possible, by making observations. In the process of science, the core activity is testing ideas. This endeavor is influenced by three arenas: exploration and discovery, community analysis and feedback, and societal benefits and outcomes. Testing ideas, in turn, affects each of these three pursuits as well.
- **Controlled experiments**, such as the study investigating coat coloration in mouse populations, are designed to demonstrate the effect of one variable by testing control groups and experimental groups that differ in only that one variable.
- A scientific **theory** is broad in scope, generates new hypotheses, and is supported by a large body of evidence.

? *What are the roles of gathering and interpreting data in the process of scientific inquiry?*

CONCEPT 1.4

Science benefits from a cooperative approach and diverse viewpoints (pp. 21–24)

- Science is a social activity. The work of each scientist builds on the work of others that have come before. Scientists must be able to repeat each other's results, so integrity is key. Biologists approach questions at different levels; their approaches complement each other.
- **Technology** consists of any method or device that applies scientific knowledge for some specific purpose that affects society. The ultimate impact of basic research is not always immediately obvious.
- Diversity among scientists promotes progress in science.

? *Explain why different approaches and diverse backgrounds among scientists are important.*

TEST YOUR UNDERSTANDING

LEVEL 1: KNOWLEDGE/COMPREHENSION

1. All the organisms on your campus make up
   a. an ecosystem.
   b. a community.
   c. a population.
   d. a taxonomic domain.

2. Which of the following is a correct sequence of levels in life's hierarchy, proceeding downward from an individual animal?
   a. organism, brain, organ system, nerve cell
   b. organ system, nervous tissue, brain, nerve cell
   c. organism, organ system, tissue, cell, organ
   d. nervous system, brain, nervous tissue, nerve cell

3. Which of the following is *not* an observation or inference on which Darwin's theory of natural selection is based?
   a. Poorly adapted individuals never produce offspring.
   b. There is heritable variation among individuals.
   c. Because of overproduction of offspring, there is competition for limited resources.
   d. A population can become adapted to its environment over time.

4. Systems biology is mainly an attempt to
   a. analyze genomes from different species.
   b. simplify complex problems by reducing the system into smaller, less complex units.
   c. understand the behavior of entire biological systems by studying interactions among its component parts.
   d. build high-throughput machines for the rapid acquisition of biological data.

5. Protists and bacteria are grouped into different domains because
   a. protists eat bacteria.
   b. bacteria are not made of cells.
   c. protists have a membrane-bounded nucleus.
   d. protists are photosynthetic.

6. Which of the following best demonstrates the unity among all organisms?
   a. emergent properties
   b. descent with modification
   c. the structure and function of DNA
   d. natural selection

7. A controlled experiment is one that
   a. proceeds slowly enough that a scientist can make careful records of the results.
   b. tests experimental and control groups in parallel.
   c. is repeated many times to make sure the results are accurate.
   d. keeps all variables constant.

8. Which of the following statements best distinguishes hypotheses from theories in science?
   a. Theories are hypotheses that have been proved.
   b. Hypotheses are guesses; theories are correct answers.
   c. Hypotheses usually are relatively narrow in scope; theories have broad explanatory power.
   d. Theories are proved true; hypotheses are often contradicted by experimental results.

LEVEL 2: APPLICATION/ANALYSIS

9. Which of the following is an example of qualitative data?
   a. The fish swam in a zigzag motion.
   b. The contents of the stomach are mixed every 20 seconds.
   c. The temperature decreased from 20°C to 15°C.
   d. The six pairs of robins hatched an average of three chicks each.

10. Which of the following best describes the logic of scientific inquiry?
    a. If I generate a testable hypothesis, tests and observations will support it.
    b. If my prediction is correct, it will lead to a testable hypothesis.
    c. If my observations are accurate, they will support my hypothesis.
    d. If my hypothesis is correct, I can expect certain test results.

11. **DRAW IT** With rough sketches, draw a biological hierarchy similar to the one in Figure 1.3 but using a coral reef as the ecosystem, a fish as the organism, its stomach as the organ, and DNA as the molecule. Include all levels in the hierarchy.

LEVEL 3: SYNTHESIS/EVALUATION

12. **EVOLUTION CONNECTION**
    A typical prokaryotic cell has about 3,000 genes in its DNA, while a human cell has almost 21,000 genes. About 1,000 of these genes are present in both types of cells. Based on your understanding of evolution, explain how such different organisms could have this same subset of 1,000 genes. What sorts of functions might these shared genes have?

13. **SCIENTIFIC INQUIRY**
    Based on the results of the mouse coloration case study, suggest another hypothesis researchers might use to further study the role of predators in the natural selection process.

14. **WRITE ABOUT A THEME: EVOLUTION**
    In a short essay (100–150 words), discuss Darwin's view of how natural selection resulted in both unity and diversity of life on Earth. Include in your discussion some of his evidence. (See a suggested grading rubric and tips for writing good essays in the Study Area of MasteringBiology under "Write About a Theme.")

15. **SYNTHESIZE YOUR KNOWLEDGE**

Can you pick out the mossy leaf-tailed gecko lying against the tree trunk in this photo? How is the appearance of the gecko a benefit in terms of survival? Given what you learned about evolution, natural selection, and genetic information in this chapter, describe how the gecko's coloration might have evolved.

For selected answers, see Appendix A.

MasteringBiology®

Students Go to **MasteringBiology** for assignments, the eText, and the Study Area with practice tests, animations, and activities.

Instructors Go to **MasteringBiology** for automatically graded tutorials and questions that you can assign to your students, plus Instructor Resources.

THE CHEMISTRY OF LIFE

AN INTERVIEW WITH

Venki Ramakrishnan

Born in India, Venkatraman (Venki) Ramakrishnan received his B.Sc. from Baroda University and a Ph.D. in physics from Ohio University. Changing to biology, he then spent two years as a graduate student at the University of California, San Diego, followed by postdoctoral work at Yale University, where he began to study ribosomes. He spent 12 years at the Brookhaven National Laboratory and four more years at the University of Utah before moving to the MRC Laboratory of Molecular Biology in Cambridge, England in 1999. In 2009, he shared the Nobel Prize in Chemistry for research on ribosomal structure and function.

Tell us about your switch from physics to biology.

While at graduate school in physics, I found that my work did not engage me, and I became distracted. Among other things, I spent time reading *Scientific American*, and I was fascinated by the explosive growth of biology. Every month, there'd be some big new discovery! So I thought I'd go into biology, and I wrote to a few universities asking if I could join their graduate program in biology. The reason was I didn't know any biology. This led to my going to UC San Diego as a biology graduate student. But towards the end of my second year, I realized that I'd learned quite a bit of biology and didn't actually need a second Ph.D. So at that point I went to Yale, to work on ribosomes.

> "We could never understand how a ribosome functions if we didn't know its molecular structure."

▶ Computer model of a ribosome.

What is a ribosome?

A ribosome (see below) is one of the most fundamental structures in all of biology. It is an assembly of many different proteins and large pieces of RNA, which make up two-thirds of its mass and actually play the key roles in its functioning. The ribosome takes the information in RNA transcribed from a gene and then stitches together a specific sequence of amino acids to make a protein. Everything made by the cell is made either by ribosomes or by proteins called enzymes, which are made by ribosomes.

The ribosome is the interface between genetic information and how things actually appear. It's at the crossroads of biology, in a way. So people worldwide have devoted decades to trying to understand how the ribosome works.

How do you study ribosome structure?

There are many ribosomes in every cell—many thousands in cells that make lots of protein, such as liver cells or actively growing bacteria. To date, nearly all the work we've done is on bacterial ribosomes. We grow bacteria in a large fermenter, break them open, and purify the ribosomes. To determine their structure, we crystallize them and then use a technique called X-ray crystallography. After crystallization, the scattering pattern produced when X-rays are passed through a crystal can be converted into a detailed image by computer analysis.

Why is the structure of a ribosome useful in understanding its function?

I can give you an analogy. Suppose some Martians come to visit Earth. They hover around, and they see all these machines going up and down the streets—cars. Now if they don't know the details of car structure, the only thing they can tell is that gasoline goes in and carbon dioxide and water come out (along with some pollutants). The thing moves as a result, but they wouldn't be able to tell how it worked. To tell how it worked, they would need to look at it in detail: They would need to open up the hood, look at the engine, see how all the parts are connected, and so on.

The ribosome can be thought of as a molecular machine. We could never understand how a ribosome functions if we didn't know its molecular structure. Knowing the structure in detail means we can do experiments to find out in detail how it works.

(MB) For an extended interview and video clip, go to the Study Area in MasteringBiology.

2

The Chemical Context of Life

KEY CONCEPTS

2.1 Matter consists of chemical elements in pure form and in combinations called compounds

2.2 An element's properties depend on the structure of its atoms

2.3 The formation and function of molecules depend on chemical bonding between atoms

2.4 Chemical reactions make and break chemical bonds

▲ **Figure 2.1 What weapon are these wood ants shooting into the air?**

A Chemical Connection to Biology

Like other animals, ants have structures and mechanisms that defend them from attack. Wood ants live in colonies of hundreds or thousands, and the colony as a whole has a particularly effective mechanism for dealing with enemies. When threatened, the ants shoot volleys of formic acid into the air from their abdomens, and the acid rains down upon the potential invaders **(Figure 2.1)**. This substance is produced by many species of ants and in fact got its name from the Latin word for ant, *formica*. For quite a few ant species, the formic acid isn't shot out, but probably serves as a disinfectant that protects the ants against microbial parasites. Scientists have long known that chemicals play a major role in insect communication, the attraction of mates, and defense against predators.

Research on ants and other insects is a good example of how relevant chemistry is to the study of life. Unlike college courses, nature is not neatly packaged into individual sciences—biology, chemistry, physics, and so forth. Biologists specialize in the study of life, but organisms and their environments are natural systems to which the concepts of chemistry and physics apply. Biology is multidisciplinary.

This unit of chapters introduces some basic concepts of chemistry that apply to the study of life. Somewhere in the transition from molecules to cells, we will cross the blurry boundary between nonlife and life. This chapter focuses on the chemical components that make up all matter.

Matter consists of chemical elements in pure form and in combinations called compounds

Organisms are composed of **matter**, which is anything that takes up space and has mass.* Matter exists in many forms. Rocks, metals, oils, gases, and living organisms are a few examples of what seems to be an endless assortment of matter.

Elements and Compounds

Matter is made up of elements. An **element** is a substance that cannot be broken down to other substances by chemical reactions. Today, chemists recognize 92 elements occurring in nature; gold, copper, carbon, and oxygen are examples. Each element has a symbol, usually the first letter or two of its name. Some symbols are derived from Latin or German; for instance, the symbol for sodium is Na, from the Latin word *natrium*.

A **compound** is a substance consisting of two or more different elements combined in a fixed ratio. Table salt, for example, is sodium chloride (NaCl), a compound composed of the elements sodium (Na) and chlorine (Cl) in a 1:1 ratio. Pure sodium is a metal, and pure chlorine is a poisonous gas. When chemically combined, however, sodium and chlorine form an edible compound. Water (H_2O), another compound, consists of the elements hydrogen (H) and oxygen (O) in a 2:1 ratio. These are simple examples of organized matter having emergent properties: A compound has characteristics different from those of its elements **(Figure 2.2)**.

Sodium   **Chlorine**   **Sodium chloride**

▲ **Figure 2.2 The emergent properties of a compound.** The metal sodium combines with the poisonous gas chlorine, forming the edible compound sodium chloride, or table salt.

---

*In everyday language we tend to substitute the term weight for mass, although the two are not identical. Mass is the amount of matter in an object, whereas the weight of an object is how strongly that mass is pulled by gravity. The weight of an astronaut walking on the moon is approximately ⅙ the astronaut's weight on Earth, but his or her mass is the same. However, as long as we are earthbound, the weight of an object is a measure of its mass; in everyday language, therefore, we tend to use the terms interchangeably.

The Elements of Life

Of the 92 natural elements, about 20–25% are **essential elements** that an organism needs to live a healthy life and reproduce. The essential elements are similar among organisms, but there is some variation—for example, humans need 25 elements, but plants need only 17.

Just four elements—oxygen (O), carbon (C), hydrogen (H), and nitrogen (N)—make up 96% of living matter. Calcium (Ca), phosphorus (P), potassium (K), sulfur (S), and a few other elements account for most of the remaining 4% of an organism's mass. **Trace elements** are required by an organism in only minute quantities. Some trace elements, such as iron (Fe), are needed by all forms of life; others are required only by certain species. For example, in vertebrates (animals with backbones), the element iodine (I) is an essential ingredient of a hormone produced by the thyroid gland. A daily intake of only 0.15 milligram (mg) of iodine is adequate for normal activity of the human thyroid. An iodine deficiency in the diet causes the thyroid gland to grow to abnormal size, a condition called goiter. Where it is available, eating seafood or iodized salt reduces the incidence of goiter. All the elements needed by the human body are listed in **Table 2.1**.

Some naturally occurring elements are toxic to organisms. In humans, for instance, the element arsenic has been linked to numerous diseases and can be lethal. In some areas of the world, arsenic occurs naturally and can make its way into the groundwater. As a result of using water from drilled

Table 2.1	Elements in the Human Body	
Element	**Symbol**	**Percentage of Body Mass (including water)**
Oxygen	O	65.0%
Carbon	C	18.5%
Hydrogen	H	9.5%
Nitrogen	N	3.3%
Calcium	Ca	1.5%
Phosphorus	P	1.0%
Potassium	K	0.4%
Sulfur	S	0.3%
Sodium	Na	0.2%
Chlorine	Cl	0.2%
Magnesium	Mg	0.1%

Oxygen, Carbon, Hydrogen, Nitrogen: 96.3%
Calcium through Magnesium: 3.7%

Trace elements (less than 0.01% of mass): Boron (B), chromium (Cr), cobalt (Co), copper (Cu), fluorine (F), iodine (I), iron (Fe), manganese (Mn), molybdenum (Mo), selenium (Se), silicon (Si), tin (Sn), vanadium (V), zinc (Zn)

INTERPRET THE DATA *Given what you know about the human body, what do you think could account for the high percentage of oxygen (65.0%)?*

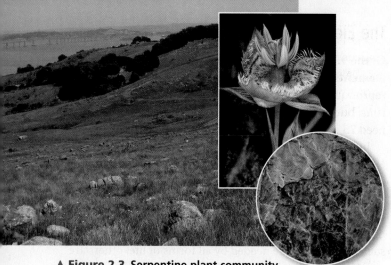

▲ **Figure 2.3 Serpentine plant community.**
These plants are growing on serpentine soil, which contains elements that are usually toxic to plants. The insets show a close-up of serpentine rock and one of the plants, a Tiburon Mariposa lily.

wells in southern Asia, millions of people have been inadvertently exposed to arsenic-laden water. Efforts are under way to reduce arsenic levels in their water supply.

Case Study: Evolution of Tolerance to Toxic Elements

EVOLUTION Some species have become adapted to environments containing elements that are usually toxic; an example is serpentine plant communities. Serpentine is a jade-like mineral that contains elevated concentrations of elements such as chromium, nickel, and cobalt. Although most plants cannot survive in soil that forms from serpentine rock, a small number of plant species have adaptations that allow them to do so **(Figure 2.3)**. Presumably, variants of ancestral, nonserpentine species arose that could survive in serpentine soils, and subsequent natural selection resulted in the distinctive array of species we see in these areas today. Researchers are studying whether serpentine-adapted plants could take up toxic heavy metals in contaminated areas, concentrating them for safer disposal.

CONCEPT CHECK 2.1

1. MAKE CONNECTIONS Explain how table salt has emergent properties. (See Concept 1.1.)

2. Is a trace element an essential element? Explain.

3. WHAT IF? In humans, iron is a trace element required for the proper functioning of hemoglobin, the molecule that carries oxygen in red blood cells. What might be the effects of an iron deficiency?

4. MAKE CONNECTIONS Explain how natural selection might have played a role in the evolution of species that are tolerant of serpentine soils. (Review Concept 1.2.)

For suggested answers, see Appendix A.

An element's properties depend on the structure of its atoms

Each element consists of a certain type of atom that is different from the atoms of any other element. An **atom** is the smallest unit of matter that still retains the properties of an element. Atoms are so small that it would take about a million of them to stretch across the period printed at the end of this sentence. We symbolize atoms with the same abbreviation used for the element that is made up of those atoms. For example, the symbol C stands for both the element carbon and a single carbon atom.

Subatomic Particles

Although the atom is the smallest unit having the properties of an element, these tiny bits of matter are composed of even smaller parts, called *subatomic particles*. Using high-energy collisions, physicists have produced more than a hundred types of particles from the atom, but only three kinds of particles are relevant here: **neutrons**, **protons**, and **electrons**. Protons and electrons are electrically charged. Each proton has one unit of positive charge, and each electron has one unit of negative charge. A neutron, as its name implies, is electrically neutral.

Protons and neutrons are packed together tightly in a dense core, or **atomic nucleus**, at the center of an atom; protons give the nucleus a positive charge. The rapidly moving electrons form a "cloud" of negative charge around the nucleus, and it is the attraction between opposite charges that keeps the electrons in the vicinity of the nucleus. **Figure 2.4**

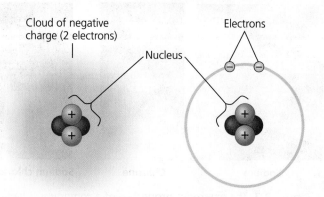

(a) This model represents the two electrons as a cloud of negative charge.

(b) In this more simplified model, the electrons are shown as two small yellow spheres on a circle around the nucleus.

▲ **Figure 2.4 Simplified models of a helium (He) atom.** The helium nucleus consists of 2 neutrons (brown) and 2 protons (pink). Two electrons (yellow) exist outside the nucleus. These models are not to scale; they greatly overestimate the size of the nucleus in relation to the electron cloud.

shows two commonly used models of the structure of the helium atom as an example.

The neutron and proton are almost identical in mass, each about 1.7×10^{-24} gram (g). Grams and other conventional units are not very useful for describing the mass of objects that are so minuscule. Thus, for atoms and subatomic particles (and for molecules, too), we use a unit of measurement called the **dalton**, in honor of John Dalton, the British scientist who helped develop atomic theory around 1800. (The dalton is the same as the *atomic mass unit*, or *amu*, a unit you may have encountered elsewhere.) Neutrons and protons have masses close to 1 dalton. Because the mass of an electron is only about 1/2,000 that of a neutron or proton, we can ignore electrons when computing the total mass of an atom.

Atomic Number and Atomic Mass

Atoms of the various elements differ in their number of subatomic particles. All atoms of a particular element have the same number of protons in their nuclei. This number of protons, which is unique to that element, is called the **atomic number** and is written as a subscript to the left of the symbol for the element. The abbreviation $_2$He, for example, tells us that an atom of the element helium has 2 protons in its nucleus. Unless otherwise indicated, an atom is neutral in electrical charge, which means that its protons must be balanced by an equal number of electrons. Therefore, the atomic number tells us the number of protons and also the number of electrons in an electrically neutral atom.

We can deduce the number of neutrons from a second quantity, the **mass number**, which is the sum of protons plus neutrons in the nucleus of an atom. The mass number is written as a superscript to the left of an element's symbol. For example, we can use this shorthand to write an atom of helium as $_2^4$He. Because the atomic number indicates how many protons there are, we can determine the number of neutrons by subtracting the atomic number from the mass number. Accordingly, the helium atom $_2^4$He has 2 neutrons. For sodium (Na):

Mass number = number of protons + neutrons
= 23 for sodium

$_{11}^{23}$Na

Atomic number = number of protons
= number of electrons in a neutral atom
= 11 for sodium

Number of neutrons = mass number − atomic number
= 23 − 11 = 12 for sodium

The simplest atom is hydrogen $_1^1$H, which has no neutrons; it consists of a single proton with a single electron.

Because the contribution of electrons to mass is negligible, almost all of an atom's mass is concentrated in its nucleus. And since neutrons and protons each have a mass very close to 1 dalton, the mass number is an approximation of the total mass of an atom, called its **atomic mass**. So we might say that the atomic mass of sodium ($_{11}^{23}$Na) is 23 daltons, although more precisely it is 22.9898 daltons.

Isotopes

All atoms of a given element have the same number of protons, but some atoms have more neutrons than other atoms of the same element and therefore have greater mass. These different atomic forms of the same element are called **isotopes** of the element. In nature, an element occurs as a mixture of its isotopes. As an explanatory example, let's consider the three naturally occurring isotopes of the element carbon, which has the atomic number 6. The most common isotope is carbon-12, $_6^{12}$C, which accounts for about 99% of the carbon in nature. The isotope $_6^{12}$C has 6 neutrons. Most of the remaining 1% of carbon consists of atoms of the isotope $_6^{13}$C, with 7 neutrons. A third, even rarer isotope, $_6^{14}$C, has 8 neutrons. Notice that all three isotopes of carbon have 6 protons; otherwise, they would not be carbon. Although the isotopes of an element have slightly different masses, they behave identically in chemical reactions. (The number usually given as the atomic mass of an element, such as 12.01 daltons for carbon, is actually an average of the atomic masses of all the element's naturally occurring isotopes, weighted according to the abundance of each.)

Both ^{12}C and ^{13}C are stable isotopes, meaning that their nuclei do not have a tendency to lose subatomic particles, a process called decay. The isotope ^{14}C, however, is unstable, or radioactive. A **radioactive isotope** is one in which the nucleus decays spontaneously, giving off particles and energy. When the radioactive decay leads to a change in the number of protons, it transforms the atom to an atom of a different element. For example, when an atom of carbon-14 (^{14}C) decays, it becomes an atom of nitrogen (^{14}N). Radioactive isotopes have many useful applications in biology.

Radioactive Tracers

Radioactive isotopes are often used as diagnostic tools in medicine. Cells can use radioactive atoms just as they would use nonradioactive isotopes of the same element. The radioactive isotopes are incorporated into biologically active molecules, which are then used as tracers to track atoms during metabolism, the chemical processes of an organism. For example, certain kidney disorders are diagnosed by injecting small doses of radioactively-labeled substances into the blood and then analyzing the tracer molecules excreted in the urine. Radioactive tracers are also used in combination with sophisticated imaging instruments, such as PET

◀ **Figure 2.5 A PET scan, a medical use for radioactive isotopes.** PET, an acronym for positron-emission tomography, detects locations of intense chemical activity in the body. The bright yellow spot marks an area with an elevated level of radioactively labeled glucose, which in turn indicates high metabolic activity, a hallmark of cancerous tissue.

Cancerous throat tissue

scanners that can monitor growth and metabolism of cancers in the body (**Figure 2.5**).

Although radioactive isotopes are very useful in biological research and medicine, radiation from decaying isotopes also poses a hazard to life by damaging cellular molecules. The severity of this damage depends on the type and amount of radiation an organism absorbs. One of the most serious environmental threats is radioactive fallout from nuclear accidents. The doses of most isotopes used in medical diagnosis, however, are relatively safe.

Radiometric Dating

EVOLUTION Researchers measure radioactive decay in fossils to date these relics of past life. Fossils provide a large body of evidence for evolution, documenting differences between organisms from the past and those living at present and giving us insight into species that have disappeared over time. While the layering of fossil beds establishes that deeper fossils are older than more shallow ones, the actual age (in years) of the fossils in each layer cannot be determined by position alone. This is where radioactive isotopes come in.

A "parent" isotope decays into its "daughter" isotope at a fixed rate, expressed as the **half-life** of the isotope—the time it takes for 50% of the parent isotope to decay. Each radioactive isotope has a characteristic half-life that is not affected by temperature, pressure, or any other environmental variable. Using a process called **radiometric dating**, scientists measure the ratio of different isotopes and calculate how many half-lives (in years) have passed since an organism was fossilized or a rock was formed. Half-life values range from very short for some isotopes, measured in seconds or days, to extremely long—uranium-238 has a half-life of 4.5 billion years! Each isotope can best "measure" a particular range of years: Uranium 238 was used to determine that moon rocks are approximately 4.5 billion years old, similar to the estimated age of Earth. In the Scientific Skills Exercise, you can work with data from an experiment that used carbon-14 to determine the age of an important fossil. (You'll learn more about radiometric dating of fossils in Chapter 25.)

The Energy Levels of Electrons

The simplified models of the atom in Figure 2.4 greatly exaggerate the size of the nucleus relative to that of the whole atom. If an atom of helium were the size of a typical football stadium, the nucleus would be the size of a pencil eraser in the center of the field. Moreover, the electrons would be like two tiny gnats buzzing around the stadium. Atoms are mostly empty space. When two atoms approach each other during a chemical reaction, their nuclei do not come close enough to interact. Of the three subatomic particles we have discussed, only electrons are directly involved in chemical reactions.

An atom's electrons vary in the amount of energy they possess. **Energy** is defined as the capacity to cause change—for instance, by doing work. **Potential energy** is the energy that matter possesses because of its location or structure. For example, water in a reservoir on a hill has potential energy because of its altitude. When the gates of the reservoir's dam are opened and the water runs downhill, the energy can be used to do work, such as moving the blades of turbines to generate electricity. Because energy has been expended, the water has less energy at the bottom of the hill than it did in the reservoir. Matter has a natural tendency to move toward the lowest possible state of potential energy; in our example, the water runs downhill. To restore the potential energy of a reservoir, work must be done to elevate the water against gravity.

The electrons of an atom have potential energy due to their distance from the nucleus (**Figure 2.6**). The negatively

(a) A ball bouncing down a flight of stairs provides an analogy for energy levels of electrons, because the ball can come to rest only on each step, not between steps.

Third shell (highest energy level in this model)

Second shell (next highest energy level)

First shell (lowest energy level)

Energy absorbed

Energy lost

Atomic nucleus

(b) An electron can move from one shell to another only if the energy it gains or loses is exactly equal to the difference in energy between the energy levels of the two shells. Arrows in this model indicate some of the stepwise changes in potential energy that are possible.

▲ **Figure 2.6 Energy levels of an atom's electrons.** Electrons exist only at fixed levels of potential energy called electron shells.

Calibrating a Standard Radioactive Isotope Decay Curve and Interpreting Data

When Did Neanderthals Become Extinct? Neanderthals (*Homo neanderthalensis*) were living in Europe by 350,000 years ago, perhaps coexisting with early *Homo sapiens* in parts of Eurasia for hundreds or thousands of years. Researchers sought to more accurately determine the extent of their overlap by pinning down when Neanderthals became extinct. They used carbon-14 dating to determine the age of a Neanderthal fossil from the most recent (uppermost) archeological layer containing Neanderthal bones. In this exercise you will calibrate a standard carbon-14 decay curve and use it to determine the age of this Neanderthal fossil. The age will help you approximate the last time the two species may have coexisted at the site where this fossil was collected.

How the Experiment Was Done Carbon-14 (^{14}C) is a radioactive isotope of carbon that decays to ^{14}N at a constant rate. ^{14}C is present in the atmosphere in small amounts at a constant ratio with both ^{13}C and ^{12}C, two other isotopes of carbon. When carbon is taken up from the atmosphere by a plant during photosynthesis, ^{12}C, ^{13}C, and ^{14}C isotopes are incorporated into the plant in the same proportions in which they were present in the atmosphere. These proportions remain the same in the tissues of an animal that eats the plant. While an organism is alive, the ^{14}C in its body constantly decays to ^{14}N but is constantly replaced by new carbon from the environment. Once an organism dies, it stops taking in new ^{14}C but the ^{14}C in its tissues continues to decay, while the ^{12}C in its tissues remains the same because it is not radioactive and does not decay. Thus, scientists can calculate how long the pool of original ^{14}C has been decaying in a fossil by measuring the ratio of ^{14}C to ^{12}C and comparing it to the ratio of ^{14}C to ^{12}C present originally in the atmosphere. The fraction of ^{14}C in a fossil compared to the original fraction of ^{14}C can be converted to years because we know that the half-life of ^{14}C is 5,730 years—in other words, half of the ^{14}C in a fossil decays every 5,730 years.

Data from the Experiment The researchers found that the Neanderthal fossil had approximately 0.0078 (or, in scientific notation, 7.8×10^{-3}) as much ^{14}C as the atmosphere. The questions will guide you through translating this fraction into the age of the fossil.

Interpret the Data

1. A standard graph of radioactive isotope decay is shown at the top of the right column. The graph line shows the fraction of the radioactive isotope over time (before present) in units of half-lives. Recall that a half-life is the amount of time it takes for half of the radioactive isotope to decay. Labeling each data point with the corresponding fractions will help orient you to this graph. Draw an arrow to the data point for half-life = 1 and write the fraction of ^{14}C that will remain after one half-life. Calculate the fraction of ^{14}C remaining at each half-life and write the fractions on the graph near arrows pointing to the data points. Convert each fraction to a decimal number and round off to a maximum of three significant digits (zeros at the

► Neanderthal fossils

beginning of the number do not count as significant digits). Also write each decimal number in scientific notation.

2. Recall that ^{14}C has a half-life of 5,730 years. To calibrate the x-axis for ^{14}C decay, write the time before present in years below each half-life.

3. The researchers found that the Neanderthal fossil had approximately 0.0078 as much ^{14}C as found originally in the atmosphere. (a) Using the numbers on your graph, determine how many half-lives have passed since the Neanderthal died. (b) Using your ^{14}C calibration on the x-axis, what is the approximate age of the Neanderthal fossil in years (round off to the nearest thousand)? (c) Approximately when did Neanderthals become extinct according to this study? (d) The researchers cite evidence that modern humans (*H. sapiens*) became established in the same region as the last Neanderthals approximately 39,000–42,000 years ago. What does this suggest about the overlap of Neanderthals and modern humans?

4. Carbon-14 dating works for fossils up to about 75,000 years old; fossils older than that contain too little ^{14}C to be detected. Most dinosaurs went extinct 65.5 million years ago. (a) Can ^{14}C be used to date dinosaur bones? Explain. (b) Radioactive uranium-235 has a half-life of 704 million years. If it was incorporated into dinosaur bones, could it be used to date the dinosaur fossils? Explain.

(MB) A version of this Scientific Skills Exercise can be assigned in MasteringBiology.

Data from R. Pinhasi et al., Revised age of late Neanderthal occupation and the end of the Middle Paleolithic in the northern Caucasus, *Proceedings of the National Academy of Sciences USA* 147:8611–8616 (2011). doi 10.1073/pnas.1018938108

---

charged electrons are attracted to the positively charged nucleus. It takes work to move a given electron farther away from the nucleus, so the more distant an electron is from the nucleus, the greater its potential energy. Unlike the continuous flow of water downhill, changes in the potential energy of electrons can occur only in steps of fixed amounts. An electron having a certain amount of energy is something like a ball on a staircase **(Figure 2.6a)**. The ball can have different amounts of potential energy, depending on which step it is on, but it cannot spend much time between the steps.

Similarly, an electron's potential energy is determined by its energy level. An electron can exist only at certain energy levels, not between them.

An electron's energy level is correlated with its average distance from the nucleus. Electrons are found in different **electron shells**, each with a characteristic average distance and energy level. In diagrams, shells can be represented by concentric circles **(Figure 2.6b)**. The first shell is closest to the nucleus, and electrons in this shell have the lowest potential energy. Electrons in the second shell have more energy, and electrons in the third shell even more energy. An electron can move from one shell to another, but only by absorbing or losing an amount of energy equal to the difference in potential energy between its position in the old shell and that in the new shell. When an electron absorbs energy, it moves to a shell farther out from the nucleus. For example, light energy can excite an electron to a higher energy level. (Indeed, this is the first step taken when plants harness the energy of sunlight for photosynthesis, the process that produces food from carbon dioxide and water. You'll learn more about photosynthesis in Chapter 10.) When an electron loses energy, it "falls back" to a shell closer to the nucleus, and the lost energy is usually released to the environment as heat. For example, sunlight excites electrons in the surface of a car to higher energy levels. When the electrons fall back to their original levels, the car's surface heats up. This thermal energy can be transferred to the air or to your hand if you touch the car.

Electron Distribution and Chemical Properties

The chemical behavior of an atom is determined by the distribution of electrons in the atom's electron shells. Beginning with hydrogen, the simplest atom, we can imagine building the atoms of the other elements by adding 1 proton and 1 electron at a time (along with an appropriate number of neutrons). **Figure 2.7**, an abbreviated version of what is called the *periodic table of the elements*, shows this distribution of electrons for the first 18 elements, from hydrogen ($_1H$) to argon ($_{18}Ar$). The elements are arranged in three rows, or *periods*, corresponding to the number of electron shells in their atoms. The left-to-right sequence of elements in each row corresponds to the sequential addition of electrons and protons. (See Appendix B for the complete periodic table.)

Hydrogen's 1 electron and helium's 2 electrons are located in the first shell. Electrons, like all matter, tend to exist in the lowest available state of potential energy. In an atom, this state is in the first shell. However, the first shell can hold no more than 2 electrons; thus, hydrogen and helium are the only elements in the first row of the table. In an atom with more than 2 electrons, the additional electrons must occupy higher shells because the first shell is full. The next element, lithium, has 3 electrons. Two of these electrons fill the first shell, while the third electron occupies the second shell. The second shell holds a maximum of 8 electrons. Neon, at the

▲ **Figure 2.7 Electron distribution diagrams for the first 18 elements in the periodic table.** In a standard periodic table (see Appendix B), information for each element is presented as shown for helium in the inset. In the diagrams in this table, electrons are represented as yellow dots and electron shells as concentric circles. These diagrams are a convenient way to picture the distribution of an atom's electrons among its electron shells, but these simplified models do not accurately represent the shape of the atom or the location of its electrons. The elements are arranged in rows, each representing the filling of an electron shell. As electrons are added, they occupy the lowest available shell.

? *What is the atomic number of magnesium? How many protons and electrons does it have? How many electron shells? How many valence electrons?*

end of the second row, has 8 electrons in the second shell, giving it a total of 10 electrons.

The chemical behavior of an atom depends mostly on the number of electrons in its *outermost* shell. We call those outer electrons **valence electrons** and the outermost electron shell the **valence shell**. In the case of lithium, there is only 1 valence electron, and the second shell is the valence shell. Atoms with the same number of electrons in their valence shells exhibit similar chemical behavior. For example, fluorine (F) and chlorine (Cl) both have 7 valence electrons, and both form compounds when combined with the element sodium (Na): Sodium fluoride (NaF) is commonly added to toothpaste to prevent tooth decay, and, as described earlier, NaCl is table salt (see Figure 2.2). An atom with a completed valence shell is unreactive; that is, it will not interact readily with other atoms. At the far right of the periodic table are helium, neon, and argon, the only three elements shown in Figure 2.7 that have full valence shells. These elements are said to be *inert*, meaning chemically unreactive. All the other atoms in Figure 2.7 are chemically reactive because they have incomplete valence shells.

Electron Orbitals

In the early 1900s, the electron shells of an atom were visualized as concentric paths of electrons orbiting the nucleus, somewhat like planets orbiting the sun. It is still convenient to use two-dimensional concentric-circle diagrams, as in Figure 2.7, to symbolize three-dimensional electron shells. However, you need to remember that each concentric circle represents only the *average* distance between an electron in that shell and the nucleus. Accordingly, the concentric-circle diagrams do not give a real picture of an atom. In reality, we can never know the exact location of an electron. What we can do instead is describe the space in which an electron spends most of its time. The three-dimensional space where an electron is found 90% of the time is called an **orbital**.

Each electron shell contains electrons at a particular energy level, distributed among a specific number of orbitals of distinctive shapes and orientations. **Figure 2.8** shows the orbitals of neon as an example, with its electron distribution diagram for reference. You can think of an orbital as a component of an electron shell. The first electron shell has only one spherical *s* orbital (called 1*s*), but the second shell has four orbitals: one large spherical *s* orbital (called 2*s*) and three dumbbell-shaped *p* orbitals (called 2*p* orbitals). (The third shell and other higher electron shells also have *s* and *p* orbitals, as well as orbitals of more complex shapes.)

No more than 2 electrons can occupy a single orbital. The first electron shell can therefore accommodate up to 2 electrons in its *s* orbital. The lone electron of a hydrogen atom occupies the 1*s* orbital, as do the 2 electrons of a helium atom. The four orbitals of the second electron shell can hold

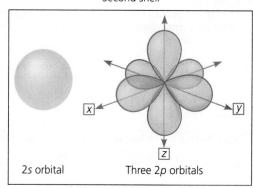

(a) Electron distribution diagram. An electron distribution diagram is shown here for a neon atom, which has a total of 10 electrons. Each concentric circle represents an electron shell, which can be subdivided into electron orbitals.

First shell   Second shell

1*s* orbital   2*s* orbital   Three 2*p* orbitals

(b) Separate electron orbitals. The three-dimensional shapes represent electron orbitals—the volumes of space where the electrons of an atom are most likely to be found. Each orbital holds a maximum of 2 electrons. The first electron shell, on the left, has one spherical (*s*) orbital, designated 1*s*. The second shell, on the right, has one larger *s* orbital (designated 2*s* for the second shell) plus three dumbbell-shaped orbitals called *p* orbitals (2*p* for the second shell). The three 2*p* orbitals lie at right angles to one another along imaginary *x*-, *y*-, and *z*-axes of the atom. Each 2*p* orbital is outlined here in a different color.

1*s*, 2*s*, and 2*p* orbitals

(c) Superimposed electron orbitals. To reveal the complete picture of the electron orbitals of neon, we superimpose the 1*s* orbital of the first shell and the 2*s* and three 2*p* orbitals of the second shell.

▲ **Figure 2.8 Electron orbitals.**

up to 8 electrons, 2 in each orbital. Electrons in each of the four orbitals have nearly the same energy, but they move in different volumes of space.

The reactivity of an atom arises from the presence of unpaired electrons in one or more orbitals of its valence shell. As you will see in the next section, atoms interact in a way that completes their valence shells. When they do so, it is the *unpaired* electrons that are involved.

1. A lithium atom has 3 protons and 4 neutrons. What is its mass number?

2. A nitrogen atom has 7 protons, and the most common isotope of nitrogen has 7 neutrons. A radioactive isotope of nitrogen has 8 neutrons. Write the atomic number and mass number of this radioactive nitrogen as a chemical symbol with a subscript and superscript.

3. How many electrons does fluorine have? How many electron shells? Name the orbitals that are occupied. How many electrons are needed to fill the valence shell?

4. **WHAT IF?** In Figure 2.7, if two or more elements are in the same row, what do they have in common? If two or more elements are in the same column, what do they have in common?

For suggested answers, see Appendix A.

CONCEPT 2.3

The formation and function of molecules depend on chemical bonding between atoms

Now that we have looked at the structure of atoms, we can move up the hierarchy of organization and see how atoms combine to form molecules and ionic compounds. Atoms with incomplete valence shells can interact with certain other atoms in such a way that each partner completes its valence shell: The atoms either share or transfer valence electrons. These interactions usually result in atoms staying close together, held by attractions called **chemical bonds**. The strongest kinds of chemical bonds are covalent bonds and ionic bonds (when in dry ionic compounds).

Covalent Bonds

A **covalent bond** is the sharing of a pair of valence electrons by two atoms. For example, let's consider what happens when two hydrogen atoms approach each other. Recall that hydrogen has 1 valence electron in the first shell, but the shell's capacity is 2 electrons. When the two hydrogen atoms come close enough for their $1s$ orbitals to overlap, they can share their electrons **(Figure 2.9)**. Each hydrogen atom is now associated with 2 electrons in what amounts to a completed valence shell. Two or more atoms held together by covalent bonds constitute a **molecule**, in this case a hydrogen molecule.

Figure 2.10a shows several ways of representing a hydrogen molecule. Its *molecular formula*, H_2, simply indicates that the molecule consists of two atoms of hydrogen. Electron sharing can be depicted by an electron distribution diagram or by a *Lewis dot structure*, in which element symbols are surrounded by dots that represent the valence electrons (H:H). We can also use a *structural formula*, H—H, where

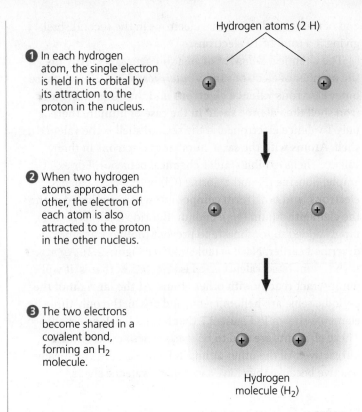

Hydrogen atoms (2 H)

1. In each hydrogen atom, the single electron is held in its orbital by its attraction to the proton in the nucleus.

2. When two hydrogen atoms approach each other, the electron of each atom is also attracted to the proton in the other nucleus.

3. The two electrons become shared in a covalent bond, forming an H_2 molecule.

Hydrogen molecule (H_2)

▲ **Figure 2.9 Formation of a covalent bond.**

the line represents a **single bond**, a pair of shared electrons. A space-filling model comes closest to representing the actual shape of the molecule. You may also be familiar with ball-and-stick models, which are shown in Figure 2.15.

Oxygen has 6 electrons in its second electron shell and therefore needs 2 more electrons to complete its valence shell. Two oxygen atoms form a molecule by sharing *two* pairs of valence electrons **(Figure 2.10b)**. The atoms are thus joined by what is called a **double bond** (O=O).

Each atom that can share valence electrons has a bonding capacity corresponding to the number of covalent bonds the atom can form. When the bonds form, they give the atom a full complement of electrons in the valence shell. The bonding capacity of oxygen, for example, is 2. This bonding capacity is called the atom's **valence** and usually equals the number of unpaired electrons required to complete the atom's outermost (valence) shell. See if you can determine the valences of hydrogen, oxygen, nitrogen, and carbon by studying the electron distribution diagrams in Figure 2.7. You can see that the valence of hydrogen is 1; oxygen, 2; nitrogen, 3; and carbon, 4. However, the situation is more complicated for elements in the third row of the periodic table. Phosphorus, for example, can have a valence of 3, as we would predict from the presence of 3 unpaired electrons in its valence shell. In some molecules that are biologically important, however, phosphorus can form three single bonds and one double bond. Therefore, it can also have a valence of 5.

Name and Molecular Formula	Electron Distribution Diagram	Lewis Dot Structure and Structural Formula	Space-Filling Model
(a) Hydrogen (H_2). Two hydrogen atoms share one pair of electrons, forming a single bond.		H:H H—H	
(b) Oxygen (O_2). Two oxygen atoms share two pairs of electrons, forming a double bond.		:Ö::Ö: O=O	
(c) Water (H_2O). Two hydrogen atoms and one oxygen atom are joined by single bonds, forming a molecule of water.		:Ö:H H O—H | H	
(d) Methane (CH_4). Four hydrogen atoms can satisfy the valence of one carbon atom, forming methane.		H H:C:H H H | H—C—H | H	

▲ **Figure 2.10 Covalent bonding in four molecules.** The number of electrons required to complete an atom's valence shell generally determines how many covalent bonds that atom will form. This figure shows several ways of indicating covalent bonds.

The molecules H_2 and O_2 are pure elements rather than compounds because a compound is a combination of two or more *different* elements. Water, with the molecular formula H_2O, is a compound. Two atoms of hydrogen are needed to satisfy the valence of one oxygen atom. **Figure 2.10c** shows the structure of a water molecule. (Water is so important to life that Chapter 3 is devoted entirely to its structure and behavior.)

Methane, the main component of natural gas, is a compound with the molecular formula CH_4. It takes four hydrogen atoms, each with a valence of 1, to complement one atom of carbon, with its valence of 4 **(Figure 2.10d)**. (We will look at many other compounds of carbon in Chapter 4.)

Atoms in a molecule attract shared bonding electrons to varying degrees, depending on the element. The attraction of a particular atom for the electrons of a covalent bond is called its **electronegativity**. The more electronegative an atom is, the more strongly it pulls shared electrons toward

Because oxygen (O) is more electronegative than hydrogen (H), shared electrons are pulled more toward oxygen.

This results in a partial negative charge on the oxygen and a partial positive charge on the hydrogens.

▲ **Figure 2.11 Polar covalent bonds in a water molecule.**

itself. In a covalent bond between two atoms of the same element, the electrons are shared equally because the two atoms have the same electronegativity—the tug-of-war is at a standoff. Such a bond is called a **nonpolar covalent bond**. For example, the single bond of H_2 is nonpolar, as is the double bond of O_2. However, when an atom is bonded to a more electronegative atom, the electrons of the bond are not shared equally. This type of bond is called a **polar covalent bond**. Such bonds vary in their polarity, depending on the relative electronegativity of the two atoms. For example, the bonds between the oxygen and hydrogen atoms of a water molecule are quite polar **(Figure 2.11)**.

Oxygen is one of the most electronegative elements, attracting shared electrons much more strongly than hydrogen does. In a covalent bond between oxygen and hydrogen, the electrons spend more time near the oxygen nucleus than they do near the hydrogen nucleus. Because electrons have a negative charge and are pulled toward oxygen in a water molecule, the oxygen atom has a partial negative charge (indicated by the Greek letter δ with a minus sign, δ−, or "delta minus"), and each hydrogen atom has a partial positive charge (δ+, or "delta plus"). In contrast, the individual bonds of methane (CH_4) are much less polar because the electronegativities of carbon and hydrogen are similar.

Ionic Bonds

In some cases, two atoms are so unequal in their attraction for valence electrons that the more electronegative atom strips an electron completely away from its partner. The two resulting oppositely charged atoms (or molecules) are called **ions**. A positively charged ion is called a **cation**, while a negatively charged ion is called an **anion**. Because of their opposite charges, cations and anions attract each other; this attraction is called an ionic bond. Note that the transfer of an electron is not, by itself, the formation of a bond; rather, it allows a bond to form because it results in two ions of opposite charge. Any two ions of opposite charge can form an **ionic bond**. The ions do not need to have acquired their charge by an electron transfer with each other.

① The lone valence electron of a sodium atom is transferred to join the 7 valence electrons of a chlorine atom.

② Each resulting ion has a completed valence shell. An ionic bond can form between the oppositely charged ions.

Na
Sodium atom

Cl
Chlorine atom

Na⁺
Sodium ion
(a cation)

Cl⁻
Chloride ion
(an anion)

Sodium chloride (NaCl)

▲ **Figure 2.12 Electron transfer and ionic bonding.** The attraction between oppositely charged atoms, or ions, is an ionic bond. An ionic bond can form between any two oppositely charged ions, even if they have not been formed by transfer of an electron from one to the other.

This is what happens when an atom of sodium ($_{11}$Na) encounters an atom of chlorine ($_{17}$Cl) **(Figure 2.12)**. A sodium atom has a total of 11 electrons, with its single valence electron in the third electron shell. A chlorine atom has a total of 17 electrons, with 7 electrons in its valence shell. When these two atoms meet, the lone valence electron of sodium is transferred to the chlorine atom, and both atoms end up with their valence shells complete. (Because sodium no longer has an electron in the third shell, the second shell is now the valence shell.) The electron transfer between the two atoms moves one unit of negative charge from sodium to chlorine. Sodium, now with 11 protons but only 10 electrons, has a net electrical charge of 1+; the sodium atom has become a cation. Conversely, the chlorine atom, having gained an extra electron, now has 17 protons and 18 electrons, giving it a net electrical charge of 1−; it has become a chloride ion—an anion.

Compounds formed by ionic bonds are called **ionic compounds**, or **salts**. We know the ionic compound sodium chloride (NaCl) as table salt **(Figure 2.13)**. Salts are often found in nature as crystals of various sizes and shapes. Each salt crystal is an aggregate of vast numbers of cations and anions bonded by their electrical attraction and arranged in

▲ **Figure 2.13 A sodium chloride (NaCl) crystal.** The sodium ions (Na⁺) and chloride ions (Cl⁻) are held together by ionic bonds. The formula NaCl tells us that the ratio of Na⁺ to Cl⁻ is 1:1.

Na⁺
Cl⁻

a three-dimensional lattice. Unlike a covalent compound, which consists of molecules having a definite size and number of atoms, an ionic compound does not consist of molecules. The formula for an ionic compound, such as NaCl, indicates only the ratio of elements in a crystal of the salt. "NaCl" by itself is not a molecule.

Not all salts have equal numbers of cations and anions. For example, the ionic compound magnesium chloride ($MgCl_2$) has two chloride ions for each magnesium ion. Magnesium ($_{12}$Mg) must lose 2 outer electrons if the atom is to have a complete valence shell, so it has a tendency to become a cation with a net charge of 2+ (Mg^{2+}). One magnesium cation can therefore form ionic bonds with two chloride anions (Cl⁻).

The term *ion* also applies to entire molecules that are electrically charged. In the salt ammonium chloride (NH_4Cl), for instance, the anion is a single chloride ion (Cl⁻), but the cation is ammonium (NH_4^+), a nitrogen atom covalently bonded to four hydrogen atoms. The whole ammonium ion has an electrical charge of 1+ because it has given up 1 electron and thus is 1 electron short.

Environment affects the strength of ionic bonds. In a dry salt crystal, the bonds are so strong that it takes a hammer and chisel to break enough of them to crack the crystal in two. If the same salt crystal is dissolved in water, however, the ionic bonds are much weaker because each ion is partially shielded by its interactions with water molecules. Most drugs are manufactured as salts because they are quite stable when dry but can dissociate (come apart) easily in water. (In the next chapter, you will learn how water dissolves salts.)

Weak Chemical Bonds

In organisms, most of the strongest chemical bonds are covalent bonds, which link atoms to form a cell's molecules. But weaker bonding within and between molecules is also indispensable, contributing greatly to the emergent properties of life. Many large biological molecules are held in their functional form by weak bonds. In addition, when two molecules in the cell make contact, they may adhere temporarily by weak bonds. The reversibility of weak bonding can be an advantage: Two molecules can come together, respond to one another in some way, and then separate.

Several types of weak chemical bonds are important in organisms. One is the ionic bond as it exists between ions dissociated in water, which we just discussed. Hydrogen bonds and van der Waals interactions are also crucial to life.

Water (H₂O)

Ammonia (NH₃)

This hydrogen bond results from the attraction between the partial positive charge on the hydrogen atom of water and the partial negative charge on the nitrogen atom of ammonia.

▲ **Figure 2.14**
A hydrogen bond.

DRAW IT *Draw five water molecules. (Use structural formulas; show partial charges.) Show how they make hydrogen bonds with each other.*

Hydrogen Bonds

Among weak chemical bonds, hydrogen bonds are so central to the chemistry of life that they deserve special attention. When a hydrogen atom is covalently bonded to an electronegative atom, the hydrogen atom has a partial positive charge that allows it to be attracted to a different electronegative atom nearby. This attraction between a hydrogen and an electronegative atom is called a **hydrogen bond**. In living cells, the electronegative partners are usually oxygen or nitrogen atoms. Refer to **Figure 2.14** to examine the simple case of hydrogen bonding between water (H_2O) and ammonia (NH_3).

Van der Waals Interactions

Even a molecule with nonpolar covalent bonds may have positively and negatively charged regions. Electrons are not always evenly distributed; at any instant, they may accumulate by chance in one part of a molecule or another. The results are ever-changing regions of positive and negative charge that enable all atoms and molecules to stick to one another. These **van der Waals interactions** are individually weak and occur only when atoms and molecules are very close together. When many such interactions occur simultaneously, however, they can be powerful: Van der Waals interactions allow a gecko lizard (below) to walk straight up a wall! The anatomy of the gecko's foot—including many minuscule hairlike projections from the toes and strong tendons underlying the skin—strikes a balance between maximum surface contact with the wall and necessary stiffness of the foot. The van der Waals interactions between the foot molecules and the molecules of the wall's surface are so numerous that despite their individual weakness, together they can support the

gecko's body weight. This discovery has inspired development of an artificial adhesive called Geckskin™: A patch the size of an index card can hold a 700 pound weight to a wall!

Van der Waals interactions, hydrogen bonds, ionic bonds in water, and other weak bonds may form not only between molecules but also between parts of a large molecule, such as a protein. The cumulative effect of weak bonds is to reinforce the three-dimensional shape of the molecule. (You will learn more about the very important biological roles of weak bonds in Chapter 5.)

Molecular Shape and Function

A molecule has a characteristic size and precise shape, which are crucial to its function in the living cell. A molecule consisting of two atoms, such as H_2 or O_2, is always linear, but most molecules with more than two atoms have more complicated shapes. These shapes are determined by the positions of the atoms' orbitals **(Figure 2.15)**. When an

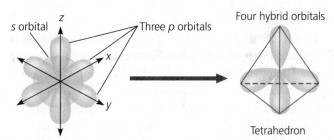

(a) Hybridization of orbitals. The single *s* and three *p* orbitals of a valence shell involved in covalent bonding combine to form four teardrop-shaped hybrid orbitals. These orbitals extend to the four corners of an imaginary tetrahedron (outlined in pink).

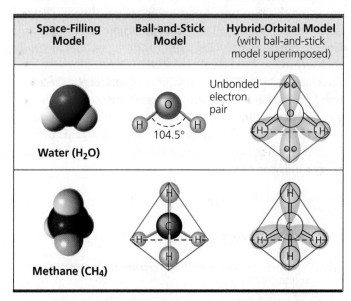

Space-Filling Model	Ball-and-Stick Model	Hybrid-Orbital Model (with ball-and-stick model superimposed)

(b) Molecular-shape models. Three models representing molecular shape are shown for water and methane. The positions of the hybrid orbitals determine the shapes of the molecules.

▲ **Figure 2.15 Molecular shapes due to hybrid orbitals.**

atom forms covalent bonds, the orbitals in its valence shell undergo rearrangement. For atoms with valence electrons in both *s* and *p* orbitals (review Figure 2.8), the single *s* and three *p* orbitals form four new hybrid orbitals shaped like identical teardrops extending from the region of the atomic nucleus **(Figure 2.15a)**. If we connect the larger ends of the teardrops with lines, we have the outline of a geometric shape called a tetrahedron, a pyramid with a triangular base.

For water molecules (H_2O), two of the hybrid orbitals in the oxygen's valence shell are shared with hydrogens **(Figure 2.15b)**. The result is a molecule shaped roughly like a V, with its two covalent bonds at an angle of 104.5°.

The methane molecule (CH_4) has the shape of a completed tetrahedron because all four hybrid orbitals of the carbon atom are shared with hydrogen atoms (see Figure 2.15b). The carbon nucleus is at the center, with its four covalent bonds radiating to hydrogen nuclei at the corners of the tetrahedron. Larger molecules containing multiple carbon atoms, including many of the molecules that make up living matter, have more complex overall shapes. However, the tetrahedral shape of a carbon atom bonded to four other atoms is often a repeating motif within such molecules.

Molecular shape is crucial: It determines how biological molecules recognize and respond to one another with specificity. Biological molecules often bind temporarily to each other by forming weak bonds, but only if their shapes are complementary. Consider the effects of opiates, drugs such as morphine and heroin derived from opium. Opiates relieve pain and alter mood by weakly binding to specific receptor molecules on the surfaces of brain cells. Why would brain cells carry receptors for opiates, compounds that are not made by the body? In 1975, the discovery of endorphins answered this question. Endorphins are signaling molecules made by the pituitary gland that bind to the receptors, relieving pain and producing euphoria durisng times of stress, such as intense exercise. Opiates have shapes similar to endorphins and mimic them by binding to endorphin receptors in the brain. That is why opiates and endorphins have similar effects **(Figure 2.16)**. The role of molecular shape in brain chemistry illustrates how biological organization leads to a match between structure and function, one of biology's unifying themes.

Key

■ Carbon   ■ Nitrogen
■ Hydrogen   ■ Sulfur
     ■ Oxygen

Natural endorphin

Morphine

(a) Structures of endorphin and morphine. The boxed portion of the endorphin molecule (left) binds to receptor molecules on target cells in the brain. The boxed portion of the morphine molecule (right) is a close match.

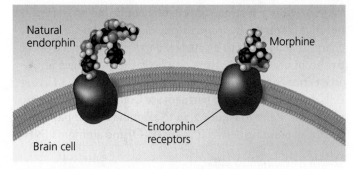

(b) Binding to endorphin receptors. Both endorphin and morphine can bind to endorphin receptors on the surface of a brain cell.

▲ **Figure 2.16 A molecular mimic.** Morphine affects pain perception and emotional state by mimicking the brain's natural endorphins.

CONCEPT 2.4

Chemical reactions make and break chemical bonds

The making and breaking of chemical bonds, leading to changes in the composition of matter, are called **chemical reactions**. An example is the reaction between hydrogen and oxygen molecules that forms water:

$2 H_2$ + O_2 ⟶ $2 H_2O$

Reactants   **Reaction**   **Products**

This reaction breaks the covalent bonds of H_2 and O_2 and forms the new bonds of H_2O. When we write a chemical reaction, we use an arrow to indicate the conversion of the starting materials, called the **reactants**, to the **products**. The coefficients indicate the number of molecules involved; for example, the coefficient 2 in front of the H_2 means that the reaction starts with two molecules of hydrogen. Notice that all atoms of the reactants must be accounted for in the products. Matter is conserved in a chemical reaction: Reactions cannot create or destroy atoms but can only rearrange (redistribute) the electrons among them.

Photosynthesis, which takes place within the cells of green plant tissues, is an important biological example of how chemical reactions rearrange matter. Humans and other animals ultimately depend on photosynthesis for food and oxygen, and this process is at the foundation of almost all ecosystems. The following chemical shorthand summarizes the process of photosynthesis:

$$6\ CO_2 + 6\ H_2O \rightarrow C_6H_{12}O_6 + 6\ O_2$$

The raw materials of photosynthesis are carbon dioxide (CO_2), which is taken from the air, and water (H_2O), which is absorbed from the soil. Within the plant cells, sunlight powers the conversion of these ingredients to a sugar called glucose ($C_6H_{12}O_6$) and oxygen molecules (O_2), a by-product that the plant releases into the surroundings **(Figure 2.17)**. Although photosynthesis is actually a sequence of many chemical reactions, we still end up with the same number and types of atoms that we had when we started. Matter has simply been rearranged, with an input of energy provided by sunlight.

All chemical reactions are reversible, with the products of the forward reaction becoming the reactants for the reverse reaction. For example, hydrogen and nitrogen molecules can combine to form ammonia, but ammonia can also decompose to regenerate hydrogen and nitrogen:

$$3\ H_2 + N_2 \rightleftharpoons 2\ NH_3$$

The two opposite-headed arrows indicate that the reaction is reversible.

One of the factors affecting the rate of a reaction is the concentration of reactants. The greater the concentration of reactant molecules, the more frequently they collide with one another and have an opportunity to react and form products. The same holds true for products. As products accumulate, collisions resulting in the reverse reaction become more frequent. Eventually, the forward and reverse reactions occur at the same rate, and the relative concentrations of products and reactants stop changing. The point at which the reactions offset one another exactly is called **chemical equilibrium**. This is a dynamic equilibrium; reactions are still going on, but with no net effect on the concentrations of reactants and products. Equilibrium does *not* mean that the

▲ **Figure 2.17 Photosynthesis: a solar-powered rearrangement of matter.** *Elodea,* a freshwater plant, produces sugar by rearranging the atoms of carbon dioxide and water in the chemical process known as photosynthesis, which is powered by sunlight. Much of the sugar is then converted to other food molecules. Oxygen gas (O_2) is a by-product of photosynthesis; notice the bubbles of O_2-containing gas escaping from the leaves submerged in water.

? *Explain how this photo relates to the reactants and products in the equation for photosynthesis given in the text. (You will learn more about photosynthesis in Chapter 10.)*

reactants and products are equal in concentration, but only that their concentrations have stabilized at a particular ratio. The reaction involving ammonia reaches equilibrium when ammonia decomposes as rapidly as it forms. In some chemical reactions, the equilibrium point may lie so far to the right that these reactions go essentially to completion; that is, virtually all the reactants are converted to products.

We will return to the subject of chemical reactions after more detailed study of the various types of molecules that are important to life. In the next chapter, we focus on water, the substance in which all the chemical processes of organisms occur.

CONCEPT CHECK 2.4

1. **MAKE CONNECTIONS** Consider the reaction between hydrogen and oxygen that forms water, shown with ball-and-stick models at the beginning of Concept 2.4. Study Figure 2.10 and draw the Lewis dot structures representing this reaction.

2. Which type of chemical reaction occurs faster at equilibrium, the formation of products from reactants or reactants from products?

3. Write an equation that uses the products of photosynthesis as reactants and the reactants of photosynthesis as products. Add energy as another product. This new equation describes a process that occurs in your cells. Describe this equation in words. How does this equation relate to breathing?

For suggested answers, see Appendix A.

CONCEPT 2.1

Matter consists of chemical elements in pure form and in combinations called compounds (pp. 29–30)

- **Elements** cannot be broken down chemically to other substances. A **compound** contains two or more different elements in a fixed ratio. Oxygen, carbon, hydrogen, and nitrogen make up approximately 96% of living matter.

? *In what way does the need for iodine or iron in your diet differ from your need for calcium or phosphorus?*

CONCEPT 2.2

An element's properties depend on the structure of its atoms (pp. 30–36)

- An **atom**, the smallest unit of an element, has the following components:

- An electrically neutral atom has equal numbers of electrons and protons; the number of protons determines the **atomic number**. The **atomic mass** is measured in **daltons** and is roughly equal to the **mass number**, the sum of protons plus neutrons. **Isotopes** of an element differ from each other in neutron number and therefore mass. Unstable isotopes give off particles and energy as radioactivity.
- In an atom, electrons occupy specific **electron shells**; the electrons in a shell have a characteristic energy level. Electron distribution in shells determines the chemical behavior of an atom. An atom that has an incomplete outer shell, the **valence shell**, is reactive.
- Electrons exist in **orbitals**, three-dimensional spaces with specific shapes that are components of electron shells.

DRAW IT *Draw the electron distribution diagrams for neon ($_{10}$Ne) and argon ($_{18}$Ar). Use these diagrams to explain why these elements are chemically unreactive.*

CONCEPT 2.3

The formation and function of molecules depend on chemical bonding between atoms (pp. 36–40)

- **Chemical bonds** form when atoms interact and complete their valence shells. **Covalent bonds** form when pairs of electrons are shared.

$$H\cdot + H\cdot \longrightarrow H{:}H \qquad {:}\ddot{O}{\cdot} + {\cdot}\ddot{O}{:} \longrightarrow \ddot{O}{::}\ddot{O}$$

Single covalent bond   **Double covalent bond**

- **Molecules** consist of two or more covalently bonded atoms. The attraction of an atom for the electrons of a covalent bond is its **electronegativity**. If both atoms are the same, they have the same electronegativity and share a **nonpolar covalent bond**. Electrons of a **polar covalent bond** are pulled closer to the more electronegative atom.
- An **ion** forms when an atom or molecule gains or loses an electron and becomes charged. An **ionic bond** is the attraction between two oppositely charged ions.

Na   **Cl**   **Na⁺**   **Cl⁻**
Sodium atom   Chlorine atom   Sodium ion   Chloride ion
                              (a cation)   (an anion)

- Weak bonds reinforce the shapes of large molecules and help molecules adhere to each other. A **hydrogen bond** is an attraction between a hydrogen atom carrying a partial positive charge ($\delta+$) and an electronegative atom ($\delta-$). **Van der Waals interactions** occur between transiently positive and negative regions of molecules.
- A molecule's shape is determined by the positions of its atoms' valence orbitals. Covalent bonds result in hybrid orbitals, which are responsible for the shapes of H_2O, CH_4, and many more complex biological molecules. Shape is usually the basis for the recognition of one biological molecule by another.

? *In terms of electron sharing between atoms, compare nonpolar covalent bonds, polar covalent bonds, and the formation of ions.*

CONCEPT 2.4

Chemical reactions make and break chemical bonds (pp. 40–41)

- **Chemical reactions** change **reactants** into **products** while conserving matter. All chemical reactions are theoretically reversible. **Chemical equilibrium** is reached when the forward and reverse reaction rates are equal.

? *What would happen to the concentration of products if more reactants were added to a reaction that was in chemical equilibrium? How would this addition affect the equilibrium?*

LEVEL 1: KNOWLEDGE/COMPREHENSION

1. In the term *trace element*, the adjective *trace* means that
   a. the element is required in very small amounts.
   b. the element can be used as a label to trace atoms through an organism's metabolism.
   c. the element is very rare on Earth.
   d. the element enhances health but is not essential for the organism's long-term survival.

2. Compared with ^{31}P, the radioactive isotope ^{32}P has
   a. a different atomic number.
   b. one more proton.
   c. one more electron.
   d. one more neutron.

3. The reactivity of an atom arises from
   a. the average distance of the outermost electron shell from the nucleus.
   b. the existence of unpaired electrons in the valence shell.
   c. the sum of the potential energies of all the electron shells.
   d. the potential energy of the valence shell.

4. Which statement is true of all atoms that are anions?
   a. The atom has more electrons than protons.
   b. The atom has more protons than electrons.
   c. The atom has fewer protons than does a neutral atom of the same element.
   d. The atom has more neutrons than protons.

5. Which of the following statements correctly describes any chemical reaction that has reached equilibrium?
   a. The concentrations of products and reactants are equal.
   b. The reaction is now irreversible.
   c. Both forward and reverse reactions have halted.
   d. The rates of the forward and reverse reactions are equal.

LEVEL 2: APPLICATION/ANALYSIS

6. We can represent atoms by listing the number of protons, neutrons, and electrons—for example, $2p^+$, $2n^0$, $2e^-$ for helium. Which of the following represents the ^{18}O isotope of oxygen?
   a. $7p^+$, $2n^0$, $9e^-$
   b. $8p^+$, $10n^0$, $8e^-$
   c. $9p^+$, $9n^0$, $9e^-$
   d. $10p^+$, $8n^0$, $9e^-$

7. The atomic number of sulfur is 16. Sulfur combines with hydrogen by covalent bonding to form a compound, hydrogen sulfide. Based on the number of valence electrons in a sulfur atom, predict the molecular formula of the compound.
   a. HS   c. H_2S
   b. HS_2 d. H_4S

8. What coefficients must be placed in the following blanks so that all atoms are accounted for in the products?

$$C_6H_{12}O_6 \rightarrow \underline{\quad} C_2H_6O + \underline{\quad} CO_2$$

   a. 2; 1   c. 1; 3
   b. 3; 1   d. 2; 2

9. **DRAW IT** Draw Lewis dot structures for each hypothetical molecule shown below, using the correct number of valence electrons for each atom. Determine which molecule makes sense because each atom has a complete valence shell and each bond has the correct number of electrons. Explain what makes the other molecules nonsensical, considering the number of bonds each type of atom can make.

```
        H   H                    H         H
        |   |                    |         |
   H — O — C — C = O        H — C — H — C = O
            |                    |
   (a)      H          (b)       H
```

LEVEL 3: SYNTHESIS/EVALUATION

10. **EVOLUTION CONNECTION**
    The percentages of naturally occurring elements making up the human body (see Table 2.1) are similar to the percentages of these elements found in other organisms. How could you account for this similarity among organisms?

11. **SCIENTIFIC INQUIRY**
    Female silkworm moths (*Bombyx mori*) attract males by emitting chemical signals that spread through the air. A male hundreds of meters away can detect these molecules and fly toward their source. The sensory organs responsible for this behavior are the comblike antennae visible in the photograph shown here. Each filament of an antenna is equipped with thousands of receptor cells that detect the sex attractant. Based on what you learned in this chapter, propose a hypothesis to account for the ability of the male moth to detect a specific molecule in the presence of many other molecules in the air. What predictions does your hypothesis make? Design an experiment to test one of these predictions.

12. **WRITE ABOUT A THEME: ORGANIZATION**
    While waiting at an airport, Neil Campbell once overheard this claim: "It's paranoid and ignorant to worry about industry or agriculture contaminating the environment with their chemical wastes. After all, this stuff is just made of the same atoms that were already present in our environment." Drawing on your knowledge of electron distribution, bonding, and emergent properties (see Concept 1.1), write a short essay (100–150 words) countering this argument.

13. **SYNTHESIZE YOUR KNOWLEDGE**

This bombardier beetle is spraying a boiling hot liquid that contains irritating chemicals, used as a defense mechanism against its enemies. The beetle stores two sets of chemicals separately in its glands. Using what you learned about chemistry in this chapter, propose a possible explanation for why the beetle is not harmed by the chemicals it stores and what causes the explosive discharge.

For selected answers, see Appendix A.

MasteringBiology®

Students Go to **MasteringBiology** for assignments, the eText, and the Study Area with practice tests, animations, and activities.

Instructors Go to **MasteringBiology** for automatically graded tutorials and questions that you can assign to your students, plus Instructor Resources.

3

Water and Life

KEY CONCEPTS

3.1 Polar covalent bonds in water molecules result in hydrogen bonding

3.2 Four emergent properties of water contribute to Earth's suitability for life

3.3 Acidic and basic conditions affect living organisms

▲ Figure 3.1 **How does the habitat of a whooper swan depend on the chemistry of water?**

The Molecule That Supports All of Life

Life on Earth began in water and evolved there for 3 billion years before spreading onto land. Water is the substance that makes possible life as we know it here on Earth. All organisms familiar to us are made mostly of water and live in an environment dominated by water. Water is the biological medium here on Earth, and possibly on other planets as well.

Three-quarters of Earth's surface is covered by water. Although most of this water is in liquid form, water is also present on Earth as a solid (ice) and a gas (water vapor). Water is the only common substance to exist in the natural environment in all three physical states of matter. Furthermore, the solid state of water floats on the liquid, a rare property emerging from the chemistry of the water molecule. All three states of water can be seen in **Figure 3.1**, which shows water vapor rising from hot springs that feed into a partially frozen lake in Hokkaido, Japan. The lake is a migratory stop for the elegant whooper swan (*Cygnus cygnus*). The growing young require a watery habitat because their legs can't support their body weight on land for long periods of time.

In this chapter, you will learn how the structure of a water molecule allows it to interact with other molecules, including other water molecules. This ability leads to water's unique emergent properties that help make Earth suitable for life.

▲ A young whooper swan paddles after its parent.

CONCEPT 3.1

Polar covalent bonds in water molecules result in hydrogen bonding

Water is so familiar to us that it is easy to overlook its many extraordinary qualities. Following the theme of emergent properties, we can trace water's unique behavior to the structure and interactions of its molecules.

Studied on its own, the water molecule is deceptively simple. It is shaped like a wide V, with its two hydrogen atoms joined to the oxygen atom by single covalent bonds. Oxygen is more electronegative than hydrogen, so the electrons of the covalent bonds spend more time closer to oxygen than to hydrogen; these are **polar covalent bonds** (see Figure 2.11). This unequal sharing of electrons and water's V-like shape make it a **polar molecule**, meaning that its overall charge is unevenly distributed. In water, the oxygen region of the molecule has a partial negative charge ($\delta-$), and each hydrogen has a partial positive charge ($\delta+$).

The properties of water arise from attractions between oppositely charged atoms of different water molecules: The slightly positive hydrogen of one molecule is attracted to the slightly negative oxygen of a nearby molecule. The two molecules are thus held together by a hydrogen bond **(Figure 3.2)**. When water is in its liquid form, its hydrogen bonds are very fragile, each only about 1/20 as strong as a covalent bond. The hydrogen bonds form, break, and re-form with great

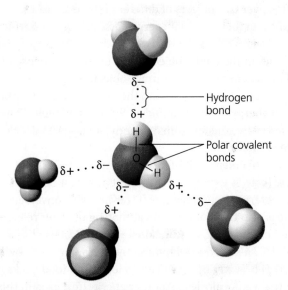

▲ **Figure 3.2 Hydrogen bonds between water molecules.** The charged regions in a water molecule are due to its polar covalent bonds. Oppositely charged regions of neighboring water molecules are attracted to each other, forming hydrogen bonds. Each molecule can hydrogen-bond to multiple partners, and these associations are constantly changing.

DRAW IT *Draw partial charges on the water molecule at the far left, and draw two more water molecules hydrogen-bonded to it.*

frequency. Each lasts only a few trillionths of a second, but the molecules are constantly forming new hydrogen bonds with a succession of partners. Therefore, at any instant, most of the water molecules are hydrogen-bonded to their neighbors. The extraordinary properties of water emerge from this hydrogen bonding, which organizes water molecules into a higher level of structural order.

CONCEPT CHECK 3.1

1. **MAKE CONNECTIONS** What is electronegativity, and how does it affect interactions between water molecules? (Review Figure 2.11.)

2. Why is it unlikely that two neighboring water molecules would be arranged like this?

$$O \overset{H\,H}{\diagdown} O \overset{H\,H}{\diagup}$$

3. **WHAT IF?** What would be the effect on the properties of the water molecule if oxygen and hydrogen had equal electronegativity?

For suggested answers, see Appendix A.

CONCEPT 3.2

Four emergent properties of water contribute to Earth's suitability for life

We will examine four emergent properties of water that contribute to Earth's suitability as an environment for life: cohesive behavior, ability to moderate temperature, expansion upon freezing, and versatility as a solvent.

Cohesion of Water Molecules

Water molecules stay close to each other as a result of hydrogen bonding. Although the arrangement of molecules in a sample of liquid water is constantly changing, at any given moment many of the molecules are linked by multiple hydrogen bonds. These linkages make water more structured than most other liquids. Collectively, the hydrogen bonds hold the substance together, a phenomenon called **cohesion**.

Cohesion due to hydrogen bonding contributes to the transport of water and dissolved nutrients against gravity in plants. Water from the roots reaches the leaves through a network of water-conducting cells **(Figure 3.3)**. As water evaporates from a leaf, hydrogen bonds cause water molecules leaving the veins to tug on molecules farther down, and the upward pull is transmitted through the water-conducting cells all the way to the roots. **Adhesion**, the clinging of one substance to another, also plays a role. Adhesion of

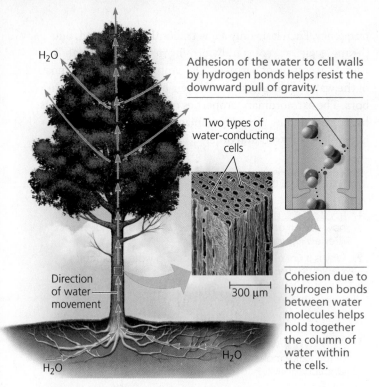

H$_2$O

Adhesion of the water to cell walls by hydrogen bonds helps resist the downward pull of gravity.

Two types of water-conducting cells

Direction of water movement

300 μm

Cohesion due to hydrogen bonds between water molecules helps hold together the column of water within the cells.

H$_2$O

H$_2$O

▲ **Figure 3.3 Water transport in plants.** Evaporation from leaves pulls water upward from the roots through water-conducting cells. Because of the properties of cohesion and adhesion, the tallest trees can transport water more than 100 m upward—approximately one-quarter the height of the Empire State Building in New York City.

ANIMATION **BioFlix** Visit the Study Area in **MasteringBiology** for the BioFlix ® 3-D Animation on Water Transport in Plants.

water by hydrogen bonds to the molecules of cell walls helps counter the downward pull of gravity (see Figure 3.3).

Related to cohesion is **surface tension**, a measure of how difficult it is to stretch or break the surface of a liquid. At the interface between water and air is an ordered arrangement of water molecules, hydrogen-bonded to one another and to the water below. This gives water an unusually high surface tension, making it behave as though it were coated with an invisible film. You can observe the surface tension of water by slightly overfilling a drinking glass; the water will stand above the rim. The spider in **Figure 3.4** takes advantage of the surface tension of water to walk across a pond without breaking the surface.

▼ **Figure 3.4 Walking on water.** The high surface tension of water, resulting from the collective strength of its hydrogen bonds, allows this raft spider to walk on the surface of a pond.

Moderation of Temperature by Water

Water moderates air temperature by absorbing heat from air that is warmer and releasing the stored heat to air that is cooler. Water is effective as a heat bank because it can absorb or release a relatively large amount of heat with only a slight change in its own temperature. To understand this capability of water, let's first look at temperature and heat.

Temperature and Heat

Anything that moves has **kinetic energy**, the energy of motion. Atoms and molecules have kinetic energy because they are always moving, although not necessarily in any particular direction. The faster a molecule moves, the greater its kinetic energy. The kinetic energy associated with the random movement of atoms or molecules is called **thermal energy**. Thermal energy is related to temperature, but they are not the same thing. **Temperature** is a measure of energy that represents the *average* kinetic energy of the molecules in a body of matter, regardless of volume, whereas the *total* thermal energy depends in part on the matter's volume. When water is heated in a coffeemaker, the average speed of the molecules increases, and the thermometer records this as a rise in temperature of the liquid. The total amount of thermal energy also increases in this case. Note, however, that although the pot of coffee has a much higher temperature than, say, the water in a swimming pool, the swimming pool contains more thermal energy because of its much greater volume.

Whenever two objects of different temperature are brought together, thermal energy passes from the warmer to the cooler object until the two are the same temperature. Molecules in the cooler object speed up at the expense of the thermal energy of the warmer object. An ice cube cools a drink not by adding coldness to the liquid, but by absorbing thermal energy from the liquid as the ice itself melts. Thermal energy in transfer from one body of matter to another is defined as **heat**.

One convenient unit of heat used in this book is the **calorie (cal)**. A calorie is the amount of heat it takes to raise the temperature of 1 g of water by 1°C. Conversely, a calorie is also the amount of heat that 1 g of water releases when it cools by 1°C. A **kilocalorie (kcal)**, 1,000 cal, is the quantity of heat required to raise the temperature of 1 kilogram (kg) of water by 1°C. (The "calories" on food packages are actually kilocalories.) Another energy unit used in this book is the **joule (J)**. One joule equals 0.239 cal; one calorie equals 4.184 J.

Water's High Specific Heat

The ability of water to stabilize temperature stems from its relatively high specific heat. The **specific heat** of a substance is defined as the amount of heat that must be absorbed or lost for 1 g of that substance to change its temperature by 1°C. We already know water's specific heat because we have defined a calorie as the amount of heat that causes 1 g of water to change its temperature by 1°C. Therefore, the specific heat of water is 1 calorie per gram and per degree Celsius, abbreviated as 1 cal/g · °C. Compared with most other substances, water has an unusually high specific heat. For example, ethyl alcohol, the type of alcohol in alcoholic beverages, has a specific heat of 0.6 cal/g · °C; that is, only 0.6 cal is required to raise the temperature of 1 g of ethyl alcohol by 1°C.

Because of the high specific heat of water relative to other materials, water will change its temperature less than other liquids when it absorbs or loses a given amount of heat. The reason you can burn your fingers by touching the side of an iron pot on the stove when the water in the pot is still lukewarm is that the specific heat of water is ten times greater than that of iron. In other words, the same amount of heat will raise the temperature of 1 g of the iron much faster than it will raise the temperature of 1 g of the water. Specific heat can be thought of as a measure of how well a substance resists changing its temperature when it absorbs or releases heat. Water resists changing its temperature; when it does change its temperature, it absorbs or loses a relatively large quantity of heat for each degree of change.

We can trace water's high specific heat, like many of its other properties, to hydrogen bonding. Heat must be absorbed in order to break hydrogen bonds; by the same token, heat is released when hydrogen bonds form. A calorie of heat causes a relatively small change in the temperature of water because much of the heat is used to disrupt hydrogen bonds before the water molecules can begin moving faster. And when the temperature of water drops slightly, many additional hydrogen bonds form, releasing a considerable amount of energy in the form of heat.

What is the relevance of water's high specific heat to life on Earth? A large body of water can absorb and store a huge amount of heat from the sun in the daytime and during summer while warming up only a few degrees. At night and during winter, the gradually cooling water can warm the air. This capability of water serves to moderate air temperatures in coastal areas **(Figure 3.5)**. The high specific heat of water also tends to stabilize ocean temperatures, creating a favorable environment for marine life. Thus, because of its high specific heat, the water that covers most of Earth keeps temperature fluctuations on land and in water within limits that permit life. Also, because organisms are made primarily of water, they are better able to resist changes in their own temperature than if they were made of a liquid with a lower specific heat.

Evaporative Cooling

Molecules of any liquid stay close together because they are attracted to one another. Molecules moving fast enough to overcome these attractions can depart the liquid and enter the air as a gas (vapor). This transformation from a liquid to a gas is called vaporization, or evaporation. Recall that the speed of molecular movement varies and that temperature is the *average* kinetic energy of molecules. Even at low temperatures, the speediest molecules can escape into the air. Some evaporation occurs at any temperature; a glass of water at room temperature, for example, will eventually evaporate completely. If a liquid is heated, the average kinetic energy of molecules increases and the liquid evaporates more rapidly.

Heat of vaporization is the quantity of heat a liquid must absorb for 1 g of it to be converted from the liquid to the gaseous state. For the same reason that water has a high specific heat, it also has a high heat of vaporization relative to most other liquids. To evaporate 1 g of water at 25°C, about 580 cal of heat is needed—nearly double the amount needed to vaporize a gram of alcohol or ammonia. Water's high heat of vaporization is another emergent property resulting from the strength of its hydrogen bonds, which must be broken before the molecules can exit from the liquid in the form of water vapor (see Figure 3.1).

The high amount of energy required to vaporize water has a wide range of effects. On a global scale, for example, it helps moderate Earth's climate. A considerable amount of solar heat absorbed by tropical seas is consumed during the evaporation of surface water. Then, as moist tropical air circulates poleward, it releases heat as it condenses and forms rain. On an organismal level, water's high heat of vaporization accounts for the severity of steam burns. These burns are caused by the heat energy released when steam condenses into liquid on the skin.

As a liquid evaporates, the surface of the liquid that remains behind cools down (its temperature decreases). This **evaporative cooling** occurs because the "hottest" molecules, those with the greatest kinetic energy, are the most likely to leave as gas. It is as if the hundred fastest runners at a college transferred to another school; the average speed of the remaining students would decline.

Evaporative cooling of water contributes to the stability of temperature in lakes and ponds and also provides a mechanism that prevents terrestrial organisms from overheating. For example, evaporation of water from the leaves of a plant

▲ **Figure 3.5 Temperatures for the Pacific Ocean and Southern California on an August day.**

INTERPRET THE DATA *Explain the pattern of temperatures shown in this diagram.*

helps keep the tissues in the leaves from becoming too warm in the sunlight. Evaporation of sweat from human skin dissipates body heat and helps prevent overheating on a hot day or when excess heat is generated by strenuous activity. High humidity on a hot day increases discomfort because the high concentration of water vapor in the air inhibits the evaporation of sweat from the body.

Floating of Ice on Liquid Water

Water is one of the few substances that are less dense as a solid than as a liquid. In other words, ice floats on liquid water. While other materials contract and become denser when they solidify, water expands. The cause of this exotic behavior is, once again, hydrogen bonding. At temperatures above 4°C, water behaves like other liquids, expanding as it warms and contracting as it cools. As the temperature falls from 4°C to 0°C, water begins to freeze because more and more of its molecules are moving too slowly to break hydrogen bonds. At 0°C, the molecules become locked into a crystalline lattice, each water molecule hydrogen-bonded to four partners **(Figure 3.6)**. The hydrogen bonds keep the molecules at "arm's length," far enough apart to make ice about 10% less dense (10% fewer molecules for the same volume) than liquid water at 4°C. When ice absorbs enough heat for its temperature to rise above 0°C, hydrogen bonds between molecules are disrupted. As the crystal collapses, the ice melts, and molecules are free to slip closer together. Water reaches its greatest density at 4°C and then begins to expand as the molecules move faster. Even in liquid water, many of the molecules are connected by hydrogen bonds, though only transiently: The hydrogen bonds are constantly breaking and re-forming.

The ability of ice to float due to its lower density is an important factor in the suitability of the environment for life. If ice sank, then eventually all ponds, lakes, and even oceans would freeze solid, making life as we know it impossible on Earth. During

summer, only the upper few inches of the ocean would thaw. Instead, when a deep body of water cools, the floating ice insulates the liquid water below, preventing it from freezing and allowing life to exist under the frozen surface, as shown in the photo in Figure 3.6. Besides insulating the water below, ice also provides a solid habitat for some animals, such as polar bears and seals.

Many scientists are worried that these bodies of ice are at risk of disappearing. Global warming, which is caused by carbon dioxide and other "greenhouse" gases in the atmosphere, is having a profound effect on icy environments around the globe. In the Arctic, the average air temperature has risen 1.4°C just since 1961. This temperature increase has affected the seasonal balance between Arctic sea ice and liquid water, causing ice to form later in the year, to melt earlier, and to cover a smaller area. The rate at which glaciers and Arctic sea ice are disappearing is posing an extreme challenge to animals that depend on ice for their survival.

Water: The Solvent of Life

A sugar cube placed in a glass of water will dissolve with a little stirring. The glass will then contain a uniform mixture of sugar and water; the concentration of dissolved sugar will be the same everywhere in the mixture. A liquid that is a completely homogeneous mixture of two or more substances is called a **solution**. The dissolving agent of a solution is the **solvent**, and the substance that is dissolved is the **solute**. In this case, water is the solvent and sugar is the solute. An **aqueous solution** is one in which the solute is dissolved in water; water is the solvent.

Water is a very versatile solvent, a quality we can trace to the polarity of the water molecule. Suppose, for example, that a spoonful of table salt, the ionic compound sodium chloride (NaCl), is placed in water **(Figure 3.7)**. At the surface of each grain, or crystal, of salt, the sodium and chloride ions are exposed to the solvent. These ions and regions of the water molecules are attracted to each other due to their opposite

▶ **Figure 3.6 Ice: crystalline structure and floating barrier.** In ice, each molecule is hydrogen-bonded to four neighbors in a three-dimensional crystal. Because the crystal is spacious, ice has fewer molecules than an equal volume of liquid water. In other words, ice is less dense than liquid water. Floating ice becomes a barrier that insulates the liquid water below from the colder air. The marine organism shown here is a type of shrimp called krill; it was photographed beneath floating ice in the Southern Ocean near Antarctica.

Hydrogen bond

Ice:
Hydrogen bonds
are stable

Liquid water:
Hydrogen bonds
break and re-form

WHAT IF? *If water did not form hydrogen bonds, what would happen to the shrimp's habitat, shown here?*

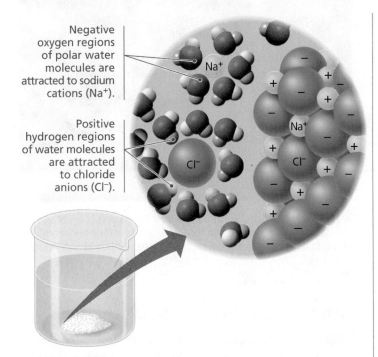

Negative oxygen regions of polar water molecules are attracted to sodium cations (Na⁺).

Positive hydrogen regions of water molecules are attracted to chloride anions (Cl⁻).

▲ **Figure 3.7 Table salt dissolving in water.** A sphere of water molecules, called a hydration shell, surrounds each solute ion.

WHAT IF? *What would happen if you heated this solution for a long time?*

charges. The oxygen regions of the water molecules are negatively charged and are attracted to sodium cations. The hydrogen regions are positively charged and are attracted to chloride anions. As a result, water molecules surround the individual sodium and chloride ions, separating and shielding them from one another. The sphere of water molecules around each dissolved ion is called a **hydration shell**. Working inward from the surface of each salt crystal, water eventually dissolves all the ions. The result is a solution of two solutes, sodium cations and chloride anions, homogeneously mixed with water, the solvent. Other ionic compounds also dissolve in water. Seawater, for instance, contains a great variety of dissolved ions, as do living cells.

A compound does not need to be ionic to dissolve in water; many compounds made up of nonionic polar molecules, such as the sugar in the sugar cube mentioned earlier, are also water-soluble. Such compounds dissolve when water molecules surround each of the solute molecules, forming hydrogen bonds with them. Even molecules as large as proteins can dissolve in water if they have ionic and polar regions on their surface (**Figure 3.8**). Many different kinds of polar

compounds are dissolved (along with ions) in the water of such biological fluids as blood, the sap of plants, and the liquid within all cells. Water is the solvent of life.

Hydrophilic and Hydrophobic Substances

Any substance that has an affinity for water is said to be **hydrophilic** (from the Greek *hydro*, water, and *philos*, loving). In some cases, substances can be hydrophilic without actually dissolving. For example, some molecules in cells are so large that they do not dissolve. Another example of a hydrophilic substance that does not dissolve is cotton, a plant product. Cotton consists of giant molecules of cellulose, a compound with numerous regions of partial positive and partial negative charges that can form hydrogen bonds with water. Water adheres to the cellulose fibers. Thus, a cotton towel does a great job of drying the body, yet it does not dissolve in the washing machine. Cellulose is also present in the walls of water-conducting cells in a plant; you read earlier how the adhesion of water to these hydrophilic walls helps water move up the plant against gravity.

There are, of course, substances that do not have an affinity for water. Substances that are nonionic and nonpolar (or otherwise cannot form hydrogen bonds) actually seem to repel water; these substances are said to be **hydrophobic** (from the Greek *phobos*, fearing). An example from the kitchen is vegetable oil, which, as you know, does not mix stably with water-based substances such as vinegar. The hydrophobic behavior of the oil molecules results from a prevalence of relatively nonpolar covalent bonds, in this case bonds between carbon and hydrogen, which share electrons almost equally. Hydrophobic molecules related to oils are major ingredients of cell membranes. (Imagine what would happen to a cell if its membrane dissolved!)

This oxygen is attracted to a slight positive charge on the lysozyme molecule.

This hydrogen is attracted to a slight negative charge on the lysozyme molecule.

▶ **Figure 3.8 A water-soluble protein.** Human lysozyme is a protein found in tears and saliva that has antibacterial action. This model shows the lysozyme molecule (purple) in an aqueous environment. Ionic and polar regions on the protein's surface attract water molecules.

Solute Concentration in Aqueous Solutions

Most of the chemical reactions in organisms involve solutes dissolved in water. To understand such reactions, we must know how many atoms and molecules are involved and calculate the concentration of solutes in an aqueous solution (the number of solute molecules in a volume of solution).

When carrying out experiments, we use mass to calculate the number of molecules. We must first calculate the **molecular mass**, which is the sum of the masses of all the atoms in a molecule. As an example, let's calculate the molecular mass of table sugar (sucrose), $C_{12}H_{22}O_{11}$. In round numbers of daltons, the mass of a carbon atom is 12, the mass of a hydrogen atom is 1, and the mass of an oxygen atom is 16. Thus, sucrose has a molecular mass of (12×12) + (22×1) + (11×16) = 342 daltons. Because we can't weigh out small numbers of molecules, we usually measure substances in units called moles. Just as a dozen always means 12 objects, a **mole (mol)** represents an exact number of objects: 6.02×10^{23}, which is called Avogadro's number. Because of the way in which Avogadro's number and the unit *dalton* were originally defined, there are 6.02×10^{23} daltons in 1 g. Once we determine the molecular mass of a molecule such as sucrose, we can use the same number (342), but with the unit *gram*, to represent the mass of 6.02×10^{23} molecules of sucrose, or 1 mol of sucrose (this is sometimes called the *molar mass*). To obtain 1 mol of sucrose in the lab, therefore, we weigh out 342 g.

The practical advantage of measuring a quantity of chemicals in moles is that a mole of one substance has exactly the same number of molecules as a mole of any other substance. If the molecular mass of substance A is 342 daltons and that of substance B is 10 daltons, then 342 g of A will have the same number of molecules as 10 g of B. A mole of ethyl alcohol (C_2H_6O) also contains 6.02×10^{23} molecules, but its mass is only 46 g because the mass of a molecule of ethyl alcohol is less than that of a molecule of sucrose. Measuring in moles makes it convenient for scientists working in the laboratory to combine substances in fixed ratios of molecules.

How would we make a liter (L) of solution consisting of 1 mol of sucrose dissolved in water? We would measure out 342 g of sucrose and then gradually add water, while stirring, until the sugar was completely dissolved. We would then add enough water to bring the total volume of the solution up to 1 L. At that point, we would have a 1-molar ($1\ M$) solution of sucrose. **Molarity**—the number of moles of solute per liter of solution—is the unit of concentration most often used by biologists for aqueous solutions.

Water's capacity as a versatile solvent complements the other properties discussed in this chapter. Since these remarkable properties allow water to support life on Earth so well, scientists who seek life elsewhere in the universe look for water as a sign that a planet might sustain life.

▲ **Figure 3.9 Evidence for subsurface liquid water on Mars.** The dark streaks running down the lower portion of the photo are proposed to be streams of subsurface flowing water because they appear only during the warm season. The gullies in the middle of the photo could have been formed by flowing water.

Possible Evolution of Life on Other Planets

EVOLUTION Biologists who look for life elsewhere in the universe (known as *astrobiologists*) have concentrated their search on planets that might have water. More than 800 planets have been found outside our solar system, and there is evidence for the presence of water vapor on a few of them. In our own solar system, Mars has been a focus of study. Like Earth, Mars has an ice cap at both poles. Images from spacecraft sent to Mars show that ice is present just under the surface of Mars and enough water vapor exists in its atmosphere for frost to form. **Figure 3.9** shows streaks that form along steep slopes during the Mars spring and summer, features that vanish during the winter. Some scientists have proposed that these are seasonal streams of flowing water occurring when subsurface ice melts during the warm season, while others think they are the result of CO_2 rather than water. Drilling below the surface may be the next step in the search for signs of life on Mars. If any life-forms or fossils are found, their study will shed light on the process of evolution from an entirely new perspective.

CONCEPT CHECK 3.2

1. Describe how properties of water contribute to the upward movement of water in a tree.
2. Explain the saying "It's not the heat; it's the humidity."
3. How can the freezing of water crack boulders?
4. **WHAT IF?** A water strider (which can walk on water) has legs that are coated with a hydrophobic substance. What might be the benefit? What would happen if the substance were hydrophilic?
5. **INTERPRET THE DATA** The concentration of the appetite-regulating hormone ghrelin is about $1.3 \times 10^{-10}\ M$ in the blood of a fasting person. How many molecules of ghrelin are in 1 L of blood?

For suggested answers, see Appendix A.

Acidic and basic conditions affect living organisms

Occasionally, a hydrogen atom participating in a hydrogen bond between two water molecules shifts from one molecule to the other. When this happens, the hydrogen atom leaves its electron behind, and what is actually transferred is a **hydrogen ion** (H^+), a single proton with a charge of 1+. The water molecule that lost a proton is now a **hydroxide ion** (OH^-), which has a charge of 1−. The proton binds to the other water molecule, making that molecule a **hydronium ion** (H_3O^+). We can picture the chemical reaction as follows:

2 H_2O Hydronium ion (H_3O^+)   Hydroxide ion (OH^-)

By convention, H^+ (the hydrogen ion) is used to represent H_3O^+ (the hydronium ion), and we follow that practice in this book. Keep in mind, though, that H^+ does not exist on its own in an aqueous solution. It is always associated with a water molecule in the form of H_3O^+.

As indicated by the double arrows, this is a reversible reaction that reaches a state of dynamic equilibrium when water molecules dissociate at the same rate that they are being reformed from H^+ and OH^-. At this equilibrium point, the concentration of water molecules greatly exceeds the concentrations of H^+ and OH^-. In pure water, only one water molecule in every 554 million is dissociated; the concentration of each ion in pure water is 10^{-7} M (at 25°C). This means there is only one ten-millionth of a mole of hydrogen ions per liter of pure water and an equal number of hydroxide ions. (Even so, this is a huge number—over 60,000 *trillion*—of each ion.)

Although the dissociation of water is reversible and statistically rare, it is exceedingly important in the chemistry of life. H^+ and OH^- are very reactive. Changes in their concentrations can drastically affect a cell's proteins and other complex molecules. As we have seen, the concentrations of H^+ and OH^- are equal in pure water, but adding certain kinds of solutes, called acids and bases, disrupts this balance. Biologists use something called the pH scale to describe how acidic or basic (the opposite of acidic) a solution is. In the remainder of this chapter, you will learn about acids, bases, and pH and why changes in pH can adversely affect organisms.

Acids and Bases

What would cause an aqueous solution to have an imbalance in H^+ and OH^- concentrations? When acids dissolve in water, they donate additional H^+ to the solution. An **acid** is a substance that increases the hydrogen ion concentration of a solution. For example, when hydrochloric acid (HCl) is added to water, hydrogen ions dissociate from chloride ions:

$$HCl \rightarrow H^+ + Cl^-$$

This source of H^+ (dissociation of water is the other source) results in an acidic solution—one having more H^+ than OH^-.

A substance that reduces the hydrogen ion concentration of a solution is called a **base**. Some bases reduce the H^+ concentration directly by accepting hydrogen ions. Ammonia (NH_3), for instance, acts as a base when the unshared electron pair in nitrogen's valence shell attracts a hydrogen ion from the solution, resulting in an ammonium ion (NH_4^+):

$$NH_3 + H^+ \rightleftharpoons NH_4^+$$

Other bases reduce the H^+ concentration indirectly by dissociating to form hydroxide ions, which combine with hydrogen ions and form water. One such base is sodium hydroxide (NaOH), which in water dissociates into its ions:

$$NaOH \rightarrow Na^+ + OH^-$$

In either case, the base reduces the H^+ concentration. Solutions with a higher concentration of OH^- than H^+ are known as basic solutions. A solution in which the H^+ and OH^- concentrations are equal is said to be neutral.

Notice that single arrows were used in the reactions for HCl and NaOH. These compounds dissociate completely when mixed with water, so hydrochloric acid is called a strong acid and sodium hydroxide a strong base. In contrast, ammonia is a weak base. The double arrows in the reaction for ammonia indicate that the binding and release of hydrogen ions are reversible reactions, although at equilibrium there will be a fixed ratio of NH_4^+ to NH_3.

Weak acids are acids that reversibly release and accept back hydrogen ions. An example is carbonic acid:

$$\underset{\text{Carbonic acid}}{H_2CO_3} \rightleftharpoons \underset{\text{Bicarbonate ion}}{HCO_3^-} + \underset{\text{Hydrogen ion}}{H^+}$$

Here the equilibrium so favors the reaction in the left direction that when carbonic acid is added to pure water, only 1% of the molecules are dissociated at any particular time. Still, that is enough to shift the balance of H^+ and OH^- from neutrality.

The pH Scale

In any aqueous solution at 25°C, the *product* of the H^+ and OH^- concentrations is constant at 10^{-14}. This can be written

$$[H^+][OH^-] = 10^{-14}$$

In such an equation, brackets indicate molar concentration. In a neutral solution at 25°C (close to room temperature), $[H^+] = 10^{-7}$ and $[OH^-] = 10^{-7}$, so in this case, 10^{-14} is the product of 10^{-7} and 10^{-7}. If enough acid is added to a solution to increase [H⁺] to 10^{-5} *M*, then [OH⁻] will decline by an equivalent factor to 10^{-9} *M* (note that $10^{-5} \times 10^{-9} = 10^{-14}$). This constant relationship expresses the behavior of acids and bases in an aqueous solution. An acid not only adds hydrogen ions to a solution, but also removes hydroxide ions because of the tendency for H⁺ to combine with OH⁻, forming water. A base has the opposite effect, increasing OH⁻ concentration but also reducing H⁺ concentration by the formation of water. If enough of a base is added to raise the OH⁻ concentration to 10^{-4} *M*, it will cause the H⁺ concentration to drop to 10^{-10} *M*. Whenever we know the concentration of either H⁺ or OH⁻ in an aqueous solution, we can deduce the concentration of the other ion.

Because the H⁺ and OH⁻ concentrations of solutions can vary by a factor of 100 trillion or more, scientists have developed a way to express this variation more conveniently than in moles per liter. The pH scale (**Figure 3.10**) compresses the range of H⁺ and OH⁻ concentrations by employing

logarithms. The **pH** of a solution is defined as the negative logarithm (base 10) of the hydrogen ion concentration:

$$pH = -\log [H^+]$$

For a neutral aqueous solution, [H⁺] is 10^{-7} *M*, giving us

$$-\log 10^{-7} = -(-7) = 7$$

Notice that pH *declines* as H⁺ concentration *increases*. Notice, too, that although the pH scale is based on H⁺ concentration, it also implies OH⁻ concentration. A solution of pH 10 has a hydrogen ion concentration of 10^{-10} *M* and a hydroxide ion concentration of 10^{-4} *M*.

The pH of a neutral aqueous solution at 25°C is 7, the midpoint of the pH scale. A pH value less than 7 denotes an acidic solution; the lower the number, the more acidic the solution. The pH for basic solutions is above 7. Most biological fluids, such as blood and saliva, are within the range of pH 6–8. There are a few exceptions, however, including the strongly acidic digestive juice of the human stomach, which has a pH of about 2.

Remember that each pH unit represents a tenfold difference in H⁺ and OH⁻ concentrations. It is this mathematical feature that makes the pH scale so compact. A solution of pH 3 is not twice as acidic as a solution of pH 6, but a thousand times $(10 \times 10 \times 10)$ more acidic. When the pH of a solution changes slightly, the actual concentrations of H⁺ and OH⁻ in the solution change substantially.

Buffers

The internal pH of most living cells is close to 7. Even a slight change in pH can be harmful, because the chemical processes of the cell are very sensitive to the concentrations of hydrogen and hydroxide ions. The pH of human blood is very close to 7.4, which is slightly basic. A person cannot survive for more than a few minutes if the blood pH drops to 7 or rises to 7.8, and a chemical system exists in the blood that maintains a stable pH. If 0.01 mol of a strong acid is added to a liter of pure water, the pH drops from 7.0 to 2.0. If the same amount of acid is added to a liter of blood, however, the pH decrease is only from 7.4 to 7.3. Why does the addition of acid have so much less of an effect on the pH of blood than it does on the pH of water?

The presence of substances called buffers allows biological fluids to maintain a relatively constant pH despite the addition of acids or bases. A **buffer** is a substance that minimizes changes in the concentrations of H⁺ and OH⁻ in a solution. It does so by accepting hydrogen ions from the solution when they are in excess and donating hydrogen ions to the solution when they have been depleted. Most buffer solutions contain a weak acid and its corresponding base, which combine reversibly with hydrogen ions.

Several buffers contribute to pH stability in human blood and many other biological solutions. One of these is

pH Scale

Increasingly Acidic [H⁺] > [OH⁻]

Acidic solution

Neutral [H⁺] = [OH⁻]

Neutral solution

Increasingly Basic [H⁺] < [OH⁻]

Basic solution

- 0
- 1   Battery acid
- 2   Gastric juice, lemon juice
- 3   Vinegar, wine, cola
- 4   Tomato juice
       Beer
- 5   Black coffee
       Rainwater
- 6   Urine
       Saliva
- 7   **Pure water**
       Human blood, tears
- 8   Seawater
       Inside of small intestine
- 9
- 10
       Milk of magnesia
- 11
       Household ammonia
- 12
       Household bleach
- 13
       Oven cleaner
- 14

▲ **Figure 3.10 The pH scale and pH values of some aqueous solutions.**

carbonic acid (H_2CO_3), which is formed when CO_2 reacts with water in blood plasma. As mentioned earlier, carbonic acid dissociates to yield a bicarbonate ion (HCO_3^-) and a hydrogen ion (H^+):

$$\underset{\substack{\text{H}^+ \text{ donor} \\ \text{(acid)}}}{H_2CO_3} \underset{\substack{\text{Response to} \\ \text{a drop in pH}}}{\overset{\substack{\text{Response to} \\ \text{a rise in pH}}}{\rightleftharpoons}} \underset{\substack{\text{H}^+ \text{ acceptor} \\ \text{(base)}}}{HCO_3^-} + \underset{\substack{\text{Hydrogen} \\ \text{ion}}}{H^+}$$

The chemical equilibrium between carbonic acid and bicarbonate acts as a pH regulator, the reaction shifting left or right as other processes in the solution add or remove hydrogen ions. If the H^+ concentration in blood begins to fall (that is, if pH rises), the reaction proceeds to the right and more carbonic acid dissociates, replenishing hydrogen ions. But when the H^+ concentration in blood begins to rise (when pH drops), the reaction proceeds to the left, with HCO_3^- (the base) removing the hydrogen ions from the solution and forming H_2CO_3. Thus, the carbonic acid–bicarbonate buffering system consists of an acid and a base in equilibrium with each other. Most other buffers are also acid-base pairs.

Acidification: A Threat to Water Quality

Among the many threats to water quality posed by human activities is the burning of fossil fuels, which releases gaseous compounds into the atmosphere. When certain of these compounds react with water, the water becomes more acidic, altering the delicate balance of conditions for life on Earth. Carbon dioxide is the main product of fossil fuel combustion. About 25% of human-generated CO_2 is absorbed by the oceans. In spite of the huge volume of water in the oceans, scientists worry that the absorption of so much CO_2 will harm marine ecosystems.

Recent data have shown that such fears are well founded. When CO_2 dissolves in seawater, it reacts with water to form carbonic acid, which lowers ocean pH, a process known as **ocean acidification.** Based on measurements of CO_2 levels in air bubbles trapped in ice over thousands of years, scientists calculate that the pH of the oceans is 0.1 pH unit lower now than at any time in the past 420,000 years. Recent studies predict that it will drop another 0.3–0.5 pH unit by the end of this century.

As seawater acidifies, the extra hydrogen ions combine with carbonate ions (CO_3^{2-}) to form bicarbonate ions (HCO_3^-), thereby reducing the carbonate ion concentration **(Figure 3.11)**. Scientists predict that ocean acidification will cause the carbonate ion concentration to decrease by 40% by the year 2100. This is of great concern because carbonate ions are required for calcification, the production of calcium carbonate ($CaCO_3$) by many marine organisms, including reef-building corals and animals that build shells. The **Scientific Skills Exercise** allows you to work with data

▲ **Figure 3.11 Atmospheric CO_2 from human activities and its fate in the ocean.**

Some carbon dioxide (CO_2) in the atmosphere dissolves in the ocean, where it reacts with water to form carbonic acid (H_2CO_3).

$$CO_2 + H_2O \rightarrow H_2CO_3$$

Carbonic acid dissociates into hydrogen ions (H^+) and bicarbonate ions (HCO_3^-).

$$H_2CO_3 \rightarrow H^+ + HCO_3^-$$

The added H^+ combines with carbonate ions (CO_3^{2-}), forming more HCO_3^-.

$$H^+ + CO_3^{2-} \rightarrow HCO_3^-$$

Less CO_3^{2-} is available for calcification—the formation of calcium carbonate ($CaCO_3$)—by marine organisms such as corals.

$$CO_3^{2-} + Ca^{2+} \rightarrow CaCO_3$$

from an experiment examining the effect of carbonate ion concentration on coral reefs. Coral reefs are sensitive ecosystems that act as havens for a great diversity of marine life. The disappearance of coral reef ecosystems would be a tragic loss of biological diversity.

If there is any reason for optimism about the future quality of water resources on our planet, it is that we have made progress in learning about the delicate chemical balances in oceans, lakes, and rivers. Continued progress can come only from the actions of informed individuals, like yourselves, who are concerned about environmental quality. This requires understanding the crucial role that water plays in the suitability of the environment for continued life on Earth.

CONCEPT CHECK 3.3

1. Compared with a basic solution at pH 9, the same volume of an acidic solution at pH 4 has _____ times as many hydrogen ions (H^+).

2. HCl is a strong acid that dissociates in water: HCl → H^+ + Cl^-. What is the pH of 0.01 M HCl?

3. Acetic acid (CH_3COOH) can be a buffer, similar to carbonic acid. Write the dissociation reaction, identifying the acid, base, H^+ acceptor, and H^+ donor.

4. **WHAT IF?** Given a liter of pure water and a liter solution of acetic acid, what would happen to the pH if you added 0.01 mol of a strong acid to each? Use the reaction equation from question 3 to explain the result.

For suggested answers, see Appendix A.

Interpreting a Scatter Plot with a Regression Line

How Does the Carbonate Ion Concentration of Seawater Affect the Calcification Rate of a Coral Reef? Scientists predict that acidification of the ocean due to higher levels of atmospheric CO_2 will lower the concentration of dissolved carbonate ions, which living corals use to build calcium carbonate reef structures. In this exercise, you will analyze data from a controlled experiment that examined the effect of carbonate ion concentration ($[CO_3^{2-}]$) on calcium carbonate deposition, a process called calcification.

How the Experiment Was Done The Biosphere 2 aquarium in Arizona contains a large coral reef system that behaves like a natural reef. For several years, a group of researchers measured the rate of calcification by the reef organisms and examined how the calcification rate changed with differing amounts of dissolved carbonate ions in the seawater.

Data from the Experiment The black data points in the graph form a scatter plot. The red line, known as a linear regression line, is the best-fitting straight line for these points.

Interpret the Data

1. When presented with a graph of experimental data, the first step in analysis is to determine what each axis represents. (a) In words, explain what is being shown on the *x*-axis. Be sure to include the units. (b) What is being shown on the *y*-axis (including units)? (c) Which variable is the independent variable—the variable that was *manipulated* by the researchers? (d) Which variable is the dependent variable—the variable that responded to or depended on the treatment, which was *measured* by the researchers? (For additional information about graphs, see the Scientific Skills Review in Appendix F and in the Study Area in MasteringBiology.)

2. Based on the data shown in the graph, describe in words the relationship between carbonate ion concentration and calcification rate.

3. (a) If the seawater carbonate ion concentration is 270 µmol/kg, what is the approximate rate of calcification, and approximately how many days would it take 1 square meter of reef to accumulate 30 mmol of

calcium carbonate ($CaCO_3$)? (b) If the seawater carbonate ion concentration is 250 µmol/kg, what is the approximate rate of calcification, and approximately how many days would it take 1 square meter of reef to accumulate 30 mmol of calcium carbonate? (c) If carbonate ion concentration decreases, how does the calcification rate change, and how does that affect the time it takes coral to grow?

4. (a) Referring to the equations in Figure 3.11, determine which step of the process is measured in this experiment. (b) Are the results of this experiment consistent with the hypothesis that increased atmospheric $[CO_2]$ will slow the growth of coral reefs? Why or why not?

(MB) A version of this Scientific Skills Exercise can be assigned in MasteringBiology.

Data from C. Langdon et al., Effect of calcium carbonate saturation state on the calcification rate of an experimental coral reef, *Global Biogeochemical Cycles* 14:639–654 (2000).

---

3 Chapter Review

SUMMARY OF KEY CONCEPTS

CONCEPT 3.1

Polar covalent bonds in water molecules result in hydrogen bonding (p. 45)

- Water is a **polar molecule**. A hydrogen bond forms when the slightly negatively charged oxygen of one water molecule is attracted to the slightly positively charged hydrogen of a nearby water molecule. Hydrogen bonding between water molecules is the basis for water's properties.

DRAW IT *Label a hydrogen bond and a polar covalent bond in this figure. Is a hydrogen bond a covalent bond? Explain.*

CONCEPT 3.2

Four emergent properties of water contribute to Earth's suitability for life (pp. 45–50)

- Hydrogen bonding keeps water molecules close to each other, and this **cohesion** helps pull water upward in the microscopic water-conducting cells of plants. Hydrogen bonding is also responsible for water's **surface tension**.
- Water has a high **specific heat**: Heat is absorbed when hydrogen bonds break and is released when hydrogen bonds form. This helps keep temperatures relatively steady, within limits that permit life. **Evaporative cooling** is based on water's high **heat of vaporization**. The evaporative loss of the most energetic water molecules cools a surface.
- Ice floats because it is less dense than liquid water. This property allows life to exist under the frozen surfaces of lakes and polar seas.
- Water is an unusually versatile **solvent** because its polar molecules are attracted to ions and polar substances that can form

hydrogen bonds. **Hydrophilic** substances have an affinity for water; **hydrophobic** substances do not. **Molarity**, the number of moles of **solute** per liter of **solution**, is used as a measure of solute concentration in solutions. A **mole** is a certain number of molecules of a substance. The mass of a mole of a substance in grams is the same as the **molecular mass** in daltons.

- The emergent properties of water support life on Earth and may contribute to the potential for life to have evolved on other planets.

? *Describe how different types of solutes dissolve in water. Explain what a solution is.*

CONCEPT 3.3

Acidic and basic conditions affect living organisms (pp. 51–54)

- A water molecule can transfer an H^+ to another water molecule to form H_3O^+ (represented simply by H^+) and OH^-.
- The concentration of H^+ is expressed as **pH**; $pH = -\log [H^+]$. A **buffer** consists of an acid-base pair that combines reversibly with hydrogen ions, allowing it to resist pH changes.

Acidic
$[H^+] > [OH^-]$

Acids donate H^+ in aqueous solutions.

Neutral
$[H^+] = [OH^-]$

Bases donate OH^- or accept H^+ in aqueous solutions.

Basic
$[H^+] < [OH^-]$

0

7

14

- The burning of fossil fuels increases the amount of CO_2 in the atmosphere. Some CO_2 dissolves in the oceans, causing **ocean acidification**, which has potentially grave consequences for coral reefs.

? *Explain how increasing amounts of CO_2 dissolving in the ocean leads to ocean acidification. How does this change in pH affect carbonate ion concentration and the rate of calcification?*

TEST YOUR UNDERSTANDING

LEVEL 1: KNOWLEDGE/COMPREHENSION

1. Which of the following is a hydrophobic material?
   a. paper
   b. table salt
   c. wax
   d. sugar

2. We can be sure that a mole of table sugar and a mole of vitamin C are equal in their
   a. mass.
   b. volume.
   c. number of atoms.
   d. number of molecules.

3. Measurements show that the pH of a particular lake is 4.0. What is the hydrogen ion concentration of the lake?
   a. $4.0\ M$
   b. $10^{-10}\ M$
   c. $10^{-4}\ M$
   d. $10^4\ M$

4. What is the *hydroxide* ion concentration of the lake described in question 3?
   a. $10^{-10}\ M$
   b. $10^{-4}\ M$
   c. $10^{-7}\ M$
   d. $10.0\ M$

LEVEL 2: APPLICATION/ANALYSIS

5. A slice of pizza has 500 kcal. If we could burn the pizza and use all the heat to warm a 50-L container of cold water, what would be the approximate increase in the temperature of the water? (*Note*: A liter of cold water weighs about 1 kg.)
   a. 50°C
   b. 5°C
   c. 100°C
   d. 10°C

6. **DRAW IT** Draw the hydration shells that form around a potassium ion and a chloride ion when potassium chloride (KCl) dissolves in water. Label the positive, negative, and partial charges on the atoms.

LEVEL 3: SYNTHESIS/EVALUATION

7. In agricultural areas, farmers pay close attention to the weather forecast. Right before a predicted overnight freeze, farmers spray water on crops to protect the plants. Use the properties of water to explain how this method works. Be sure to mention why hydrogen bonds are responsible for this phenomenon.

8. **EVOLUTION CONNECTION**
   This chapter explains how the emergent properties of water contribute to the suitability of the environment for life. Until fairly recently, scientists assumed that other physical requirements for life included a moderate range of temperature, pH, atmospheric pressure, and salinity, as well as low levels of toxic chemicals. That view has changed with the discovery of organisms known as extremophiles, which have been found flourishing in hot, acidic sulfur springs, around hydrothermal vents deep in the ocean, and in soils with high levels of toxic metals. Why would astrobiologists be interested in studying extremophiles? What does the existence of life in such extreme environments say about the possibility of life on other planets?

9. **SCIENTIFIC INQUIRY**
   Design a controlled experiment to test the hypothesis that water acidification caused by acidic rain would inhibit the growth of *Elodea*, a freshwater plant (see Figure 2.17).

10. **WRITE ABOUT A THEME: ORGANIZATION**
    Several emergent properties of water contribute to the suitability of the environment for life. In a short essay (100–150 words), describe how the ability of water to function as a versatile solvent arises from the structure of water molecules.

11. **SYNTHESIZE YOUR KNOWLEDGE**

How do cats drink? While dogs form their tongues into spoons and scoop water into their mouths, scientists using high-speed video have shown that cats use a different technique to drink aqueous substances like water and milk. Four times a second, the cat touches the tip of its tongue to the water and draws a column of water up into its mouth (as you can see in the photo), which then shuts before gravity can pull the water back down. Describe how the properties of water allow cats to drink in this fashion, including how water's molecular structure contributes to the process.

For selected answers, see Appendix A.

MasteringBiology®

Students Go to **MasteringBiology** for assignments, the eText, and the Study Area with practice tests, animations, and activities.

Instructors Go to **MasteringBiology** for automatically graded tutorials and questions that you can assign to your students, plus Instructor Resources.

4

Carbon and the Molecular Diversity of Life

KEY CONCEPTS

4.1 Organic chemistry is the study of carbon compounds

4.2 Carbon atoms can form diverse molecules by bonding to four other atoms

4.3 A few chemical groups are key to molecular function

▲ **Figure 4.1 What properties make carbon the basis of all life?**

▲ Carbon can bond to four other atoms or groups of atoms, making a large variety of molecules possible.

Carbon: The Backbone of Life

Living organisms, such as the plants and the Qinling golden snub-nosed monkeys shown in **Figure 4.1**, are made up of chemicals based mostly on the element carbon. Carbon enters the biosphere through the action of plants and other photosynthetic organisms. Plants use solar energy to transform atmospheric CO_2 into the molecules of life, which are then taken in by plant-eating animals.

Of all the chemical elements, carbon is unparalleled in its ability to form molecules that are large, complex, and varied, making possible the diversity of organisms that have evolved on Earth. Proteins, DNA, carbohydrates, and other molecules that distinguish living matter from inanimate material are all composed of carbon atoms bonded to one another and to atoms of other elements. Hydrogen (H), oxygen (O), nitrogen (N), sulfur (S), and phosphorus (P) are other common ingredients of these compounds, but it is the element carbon (C) that accounts for the enormous variety of biological molecules.

Large biological molecules, such as proteins, are the main focus of Chapter 5. In this chapter, we investigate the properties of smaller molecules. We will use these small molecules to illustrate concepts of molecular architecture that will help explain why carbon is so important to life, at the same time highlighting the theme that emergent properties arise from the organization of matter in living organisms.

CONCEPT 4.1

Organic chemistry is the study of carbon compounds

For historical reasons, compounds containing carbon are said to be organic, and their study is called **organic chemistry**. By the early 1800s, chemists had learned to make simple compounds in the laboratory by combining elements under the right conditions. Artificial synthesis of the complex molecules extracted from living matter seemed impossible, however. Organic compounds were thought to arise only in living organisms, which were believed to contain a life force beyond the jurisdiction of physical and chemical laws.

Chemists began to chip away at this notion when they learned to synthesize organic compounds in the laboratory. In 1828, Friedrich Wöhler, a German chemist, tried to make an "inorganic" salt, ammonium cyanate, by mixing solutions of ammonium ions (NH_4^+) and cyanate ions (CNO^-). Wöhler was astonished to find that instead he had made urea, an organic compound present in the urine of animals.

The next few decades saw laboratory synthesis of increasingly complex organic compounds, supporting the view that physical and chemical laws govern the processes of life. Organic chemistry was redefined as the study of carbon compounds, regardless of origin. Organic compounds range from simple molecules, such as methane (CH_4), to colossal ones, such as proteins, with thousands of atoms.

Organic Molecules and the Origin of Life on Earth

EVOLUTION In 1953, Stanley Miller, a graduate student of Harold Urey's at the University of Chicago, helped bring the abiotic (nonliving) synthesis of organic compounds into the context of evolution. Study **Figure 4.2** to learn about his classic experiment. From his results, Miller concluded that complex organic molecules could arise spontaneously under conditions thought at that time to have existed on the early Earth. You can work with the data from a related experiment in the Scientific Skills Exercise. These experiments support the idea that abiotic synthesis of organic compounds, perhaps near volcanoes, could have been an early stage in the origin of life (see Chapter 25).

The overall percentages of the major elements of life—C, H, O, N, S, and P—are quite uniform from one organism to another, reflecting the common evolutionary origin of all life. Because of carbon's ability to form four bonds, however, this limited assortment of atomic building blocks can be used to build an inexhaustible variety of organic molecules. Different species of organisms, and different individuals within a species, are distinguished by variations in the types

▼ **Figure 4.2** | Inquiry

Can organic molecules form under conditions estimated to simulate those on the early Earth?

Experiment In 1953, Stanley Miller set up a closed system to mimic conditions thought at that time to have existed on the early Earth. A flask of water simulated the primeval sea. The water was heated so that some vaporized and moved into a second, higher flask containing the "atmosphere"—a mixture of gases. Sparks were discharged in the synthetic atmosphere to mimic lightning.

❷ The "atmosphere" contained a mixture of hydrogen gas (H_2), methane (CH_4), ammonia (NH_3), and water vapor.

❸ Sparks were discharged to mimic lightning.

❶ The water mixture in the "sea" flask was heated; vapor entered the "atmosphere" flask.

"Atmosphere"

Electrode

Water vapor

CH_4

NH_3 H_2

Condenser

Cooled "rain" containing organic molecules

Cold water

H_2O "sea"

Sample for chemical analysis

❺ As material cycled through the apparatus, Miller periodically collected samples for analysis.

❹ A condenser cooled the atmosphere, raining water and dissolved molecules into the sea flask.

Results Miller identified a variety of organic molecules that are common in organisms. These included simple compounds, such as formaldehyde (CH_2O) and hydrogen cyanide (HCN), and more complex molecules, such as amino acids and long chains of carbon and hydrogen known as hydrocarbons.

Conclusion Organic molecules, a first step in the origin of life, may have been synthesized abiotically on the early Earth. Although new evidence indicates that the early Earth's atmosphere was different from the "atmosphere" used by Miller in this experiment, recent experiments using the revised list of chemicals also produced organic molecules. (We will explore this hypothesis in more detail in Chapter 25.)

Source: S. L. Miller, A production of amino acids under possible primitive Earth conditions, *Science* 117:528–529 (1953).

WHAT IF? *If Miller had increased the concentration of NH_3 in his experiment, how might the relative amounts of the products HCN and CH_2O have differed?*

Working with Moles and Molar Ratios

Could the First Biological Molecules Have Formed Near Volcanoes on Early Earth? In 2007, Jeffrey Bada, a former graduate student of Stanley Miller's, discovered some vials of samples that had never been analyzed from an experiment performed by Miller in 1958. In this experiment, Miller used hydrogen sulfide gas (H_2S) as one of the gases in the reactant mixture. Since H_2S is released by volcanoes, the H_2S experiment was designed to mimic conditions near volcanoes on early Earth. In 2011, Bada and colleagues published the results of their analysis of these "lost" samples. In this exercise, you will make calculations using the molar ratios of reactants and products from the H_2S experiment.

How the Experiment Was Done According to his laboratory notebook, Miller used the same apparatus as in his original experiment (see Figure 4.2), but the mixture of gaseous reactants included methane (CH_4), carbon dioxide (CO_2), hydrogen sulfide (H_2S), and ammonia (NH_3). After three days of simulated volcanic activity, he collected samples of the liquid, partially purified the chemicals, and sealed the samples in sterile vials. In 2011, Bada's research team used modern analytical methods to analyze the products in the vials for the presence of amino acids, the building blocks of proteins.

Data from the Experiment The table below shows 4 of the 23 amino acids detected in the samples from Miller's 1958 H_2S experiment.

Product Compound	Molecular Formula	Molar Ratio (Relative to Glycine)
Glycine	$C_2H_5NO_2$	1.0
Serine	$C_3H_7NO_3$	3.0×10^{-2}
Methionine	$C_5H_{11}NO_2S$	1.8×10^{-3}
Alanine	$C_3H_7NO_2$	1.1

Interpret the Data

1. A *mole* is the number of grams of a substance that equals its molecular (or atomic) mass in daltons. There are 6.02×10^{23} molecules (or atoms) in 1.0 mole (Avogadro's number; see Concept 3.2). The data table shows the "molar ratios" of some of the products from the Miller H_2S experiment. In a molar ratio, each unitless value is expressed relative to a standard for that experiment. Here, the standard is the number of moles of the amino acid glycine, which is set to a value of 1.0. For instance, serine has a molar ratio of 3.0×10^{-2}, meaning that for every mole of glycine, there is 3.0×10^{-2} mole of serine. (a) Give the molar ratio of methionine to glycine and explain what it means. (b) How many molecules of glycine are present in 1.0 mole? (c) For every 1.0 mole of glycine in the sample, how many molecules of methionine are present? (Recall that to multiply two

▲ Some of Stanley Miller's notes from his 1958 hydrogen sulfide (H_2S) experiment along with his original vials.

numbers with exponents, you add their exponents; to divide them, you subtract the exponent in the denominator from that in the numerator.)

2. (a) Which amino acid is present in higher amounts than glycine? (b) How many more molecules of that amino acid are present than the number of molecules in 1.0 mole of glycine?

3. The synthesis of products is limited by the amount of reactants. (a) If one mole each of CH_4, NH_3, H_2S, and CO_2 is added to 1 liter of water (= 55.5 moles of H_2O) in a flask, how many moles of hydrogen, carbon, oxygen, nitrogen, and sulfur are in the flask? (b) Looking at the molecular formula in the table, how many moles of each element would be needed to make 1.0 mole of glycine? (c) What is the maximum number of moles of glycine that could be made in that flask, with the specified ingredients, if no other molecules were made? Explain. (d) If serine or methionine were made individually, which element(s) would be used up first for each? How much of each product could be made?

4. The earlier published experiment carried out by Miller did not include H_2S in the reactants (see Figure 4.2). Which of the compounds shown in the data table can be made in the H_2S experiment but could not be made in the earlier experiment?

(MB) A version of this Scientific Skills Exercise can be assigned in MasteringBiology.

Data from E. T. Parker et al., Primordial synthesis of amines and amino acids in a 1958 Miller H_2S-rich spark discharge experiment, *Proceedings of the National Academy of Sciences USA* 108:5526-5531 (2011). www.pnas.org/cgi/doi/10.1073/pnas.1019191108.

of organic molecules they make. In a sense, the great diversity of living organisms we see on the planet (and in fossil remains) is made possible by the unique chemical versatility of the element carbon.

CONCEPT CHECK 4.1

1. Why was Wöhler astonished to find he had made urea?
2. **WHAT IF?** Miller carried out a control experiment without the electrical discharge and found no organic compounds. What might explain this result?

For suggested answers, see Appendix A.

CONCEPT 4.2

Carbon atoms can form diverse molecules by bonding to four other atoms

The key to an atom's chemical characteristics is its electron configuration. This configuration determines the kinds and number of bonds an atom will form with other atoms. Recall that it is the valence electrons, those in the outermost shell, that are available to form bonds with other atoms.

Molecule and Molecular Shape	Molecular Formula	Structural Formula	Ball-and-Stick Model (molecular shape in pink)	Space-Filling Model
(a) Methane. When a carbon atom has four single bonds to other atoms, the molecule is tetrahedral.	CH_4	H–C–H with H above and H below		
(b) Ethane. A molecule may have more than one tetrahedral group of single-bonded atoms. (Ethane consists of two such groups.)	C_2H_6	H–C–C–H with H above and below each C		
(c) Ethene (ethylene). When two carbon atoms are joined by a double bond, all atoms attached to those carbons are in the same plane, and the molecule is flat.	C_2H_4	H₂C=CH₂ structure		

▲ **Figure 4.3** The shapes of three simple organic molecules.

The Formation of Bonds with Carbon

Carbon has 6 electrons, with 2 in the first electron shell and 4 in the second shell; thus, it has 4 valence electrons in a shell that can hold up to 8 electrons. A carbon atom usually completes its valence shell by sharing its 4 electrons with other atoms so that 8 electrons are present. Each pair of shared electrons constitutes a covalent bond (see Figure 2.10d). In organic molecules, carbon usually forms single or double covalent bonds. Each carbon atom acts as an intersection point from which a molecule can branch off in as many as four directions. This enables carbon to form large, complex molecules.

When a carbon atom forms four single covalent bonds, the arrangement of its four hybrid orbitals causes the bonds to angle toward the corners of an imaginary tetrahedron. The bond angles in methane (CH_4) are 109.5° **(Figure 4.3a)**, and they are roughly the same in any group of atoms where carbon has four single bonds. For example, ethane (C_2H_6) is shaped like two overlapping tetrahedrons **(Figure 4.3b)**. In molecules with more carbons, every grouping of a carbon bonded to four other atoms has a tetrahedral shape. But when two carbon atoms are joined by a double bond, as in ethene (C_2H_4), the bonds from both carbons are all in the same plane, so the atoms joined to those carbons are in the same plane as well **(Figure 4.3c)**. We find it convenient to write molecules as structural formulas, as if the molecules being represented are two-dimensional, but keep in mind that molecules are three-dimensional and that the shape of a molecule is central to its function.

▲ **Figure 4.4** **Valences of the major elements of organic molecules.** Valence is the number of covalent bonds an atom can form. It is generally equal to the number of electrons required to complete the valence (outermost) shell (see Figure 2.7). All the electrons are shown for each atom in the electron distribution diagrams (top). Only the valence shell electrons are shown in the Lewis dot structures (bottom). Note that carbon can form four bonds.

MAKE CONNECTIONS *Draw the Lewis dot structures for sodium, phosphorus, sulfur, and chlorine. (Refer to Figure 2.7.)*

The electron configuration of carbon gives it covalent compatibility with many different elements. **Figure 4.4** shows the valences of carbon and its most frequent bonding partners—hydrogen, oxygen, and nitrogen. These are the four major atomic components of organic molecules. These valences are the basis for the rules of covalent bonding in organic chemistry—the building code for the architecture of organic molecules.

How do the rules of covalent bonding apply to carbon atoms with partners other than hydrogen? We'll look at two examples, the simple molecules carbon dioxide and urea.

In the carbon dioxide molecule (CO_2), a single carbon atom is joined to two atoms of oxygen by double covalent bonds. The structural formula for CO_2 is shown here:

$$O=C=O$$

Each line in a structural formula represents a pair of shared electrons. Thus, the two double bonds in CO_2 have the same number of shared electrons as four single bonds. The arrangement completes the valence shells of all atoms in the molecule. Because CO_2 is a very simple molecule and lacks hydrogen, it is often considered inorganic, even though it contains carbon. Whether we call CO_2 organic or inorganic, however, it is clearly important to the living world as the source of carbon for all organic molecules in organisms.

Urea, $CO(NH_2)_2$, is the organic compound found in urine that Wöhler synthesized in the early 1800s. Again, each atom has the required number of covalent bonds. In this case, one carbon atom participates in both single and double bonds.

Urea and carbon dioxide are molecules with only one carbon atom. But as Figure 4.3 shows, a carbon atom can also use one or more valence electrons to form covalent bonds to other carbon atoms, each of which can also form four bonds. Thus, the atoms can be linked into chains of seemingly infinite variety.

Molecular Diversity Arising from Variation in Carbon Skeletons

Carbon chains form the skeletons of most organic molecules. The skeletons vary in length and may be straight, branched, or arranged in closed rings (**Figure 4.5**). Some carbon skeletons have double bonds, which vary in number and location. Such variation in carbon skeletons is one important source of the molecular complexity and diversity that characterize living matter. In addition, atoms of other elements can be bonded to the skeletons at available sites.

Hydrocarbons

All of the molecules that are shown in Figures 4.3 and 4.5 are **hydrocarbons**, organic molecules consisting of only carbon and hydrogen. Atoms of hydrogen are attached to the carbon skeleton wherever electrons are available for covalent bonding. Hydrocarbons are the major components of petroleum, which is called a fossil fuel because it consists of the partially decomposed remains of organisms that lived millions of years ago.

Although hydrocarbons are not prevalent in most living organisms, many of a cell's organic molecules have regions consisting of only carbon and hydrogen. For example, the

▼ **Figure 4.5** Four ways that carbon skeletons can vary.

(a) Length

Ethane   Propane

Carbon skeletons vary in length.

(b) Branching

Butane   2-Methylpropane (commonly called isobutane)

Skeletons may be unbranched or branched.

(c) Double bond position

1-Butene   2-Butene

The skeleton may have double bonds, which can vary in location.

(d) Presence of rings

Cyclohexane   Benzene

Some carbon skeletons are arranged in rings. In the abbreviated structural formula for each compound (at the right), each corner represents a carbon and its attached hydrogens.

molecules known as fats have long hydrocarbon tails attached to a nonhydrocarbon component (**Figure 4.6**). Neither petroleum nor fat dissolves in water; both are hydrophobic compounds because the great majority of their bonds are relatively nonpolar carbon-to-hydrogen linkages. Another characteristic of hydrocarbons is that they can undergo reactions that release a relatively large amount of energy. The gasoline that fuels a car consists of hydrocarbons, and the hydrocarbon tails of fats serve as stored fuel for plant embryos (seeds) and animals.

— Nucleus

— Fat droplets

10 μm

(a) Part of a human adipose cell **(b) A fat molecule**

▲ **Figure 4.6 The role of hydrocarbons in fats. (a)** Mammalian adipose cells stockpile fat molecules as a fuel reserve. This colorized micrograph shows part of a human adipose cell with many fat droplets, each containing a large number of fat molecules. **(b)** A fat molecule consists of a small, nonhydrocarbon component joined to three hydrocarbon tails that account for the hydrophobic behavior of fats. The tails can be broken down to provide energy. (Black = carbon; gray = hydrogen; red = oxygen.)

MAKE CONNECTIONS *How do the tails account for the hydrophobic nature of fats? (See Concept 3.2.)*

Isomers

Variation in the architecture of organic molecules can be seen in **isomers**, compounds that have the same numbers of atoms of the same elements but different structures and hence different properties. We will examine three types of isomers: structural isomers, *cis-trans* isomers, and enantiomers.

Structural isomers differ in the covalent arrangements of their atoms. Compare, for example, the two five-carbon compounds in **Figure 4.7a**. Both have the molecular formula C_5H_{12}, but they differ in the covalent arrangement of their carbon skeletons. The skeleton is straight in one compound but branched in the other. The number of possible isomers increases tremendously as carbon skeletons increase in size. There are only three forms of C_5H_{12} (two of which are shown in Figure 4.7a), but there are 18 variations of C_8H_{18} and 366,319 possible structural isomers of $C_{20}H_{42}$. Structural isomers may also differ in the location of double bonds.

In *cis-trans* isomers (formerly called *geometric isomers*), carbons have covalent bonds to the same atoms, but these atoms differ in their spatial arrangements due to the inflexibility of double bonds. Single bonds allow the atoms they join to rotate freely about the bond axis without changing the compound. In contrast, double bonds do not permit such rotation. If a double bond joins two carbon atoms, and each C also has two different atoms (or groups of atoms) attached to it, then two distinct *cis-trans* isomers are possible. Consider a simple molecule with two double-bonded carbons, each of which has an H and an X attached to it **(Figure 4.7b)**. The arrangement with both Xs on the same side of the double bond is called a *cis isomer*, and that with the Xs on opposite sides is

© Pearson Education, Inc.

▼ **Figure 4.7 Three types of isomers, compounds with the same molecular formula but different structures.**

(a) Structural isomers

Pentane   2-methyl butane

Structural isomers differ in covalent partners, as shown in this example of two isomers of C_5H_{12}.

(b) *Cis-trans* isomers

cis isomer: The two Xs are on the same side.   *trans* isomer: The two Xs are on opposite sides.

Cis-trans isomers differ in arrangement about a double bond. In these diagrams, X represents an atom or group of atoms attached to a double-bonded carbon.

(c) Enantiomers

CO_2H CO_2H

H NH_2 NH_2 H

CH_3 CH_3

L isomer   D isomer

Enantiomers differ in spatial arrangement around an asymmetric carbon, resulting in molecules that are mirror images, like left and right hands. The two isomers here are designated the L and D isomers from the Latin for "left" and "right" (*levo* and *dextro*). Enantiomers cannot be superimposed on each other.

© Pearson Education, Inc.

DRAW IT *There are three structural isomers of C_5H_{12}; draw the one not shown in (a).*

called a *trans isomer.* The subtle difference in shape between such isomers can dramatically affect the biological activities of organic molecules. For example, the biochemistry of vision involves a light-induced change of retinal, a chemical compound in the eye, from the *cis* isomer to the *trans* isomer (see Figure 50.17). Another example involves *trans* fats, which are discussed in Chapter 5.

Enantiomers are isomers that are mirror images of each other and that differ in shape due to the presence of an *asymmetric carbon*, one that is attached to four different atoms or groups of atoms. (See the middle carbon in

Drug	Effects	Effective Enantiomer	Ineffective Enantiomer
Ibuprofen	Reduces inflammation and pain	S-Ibuprofen	R-Ibuprofen
Albuterol	Relaxes bronchial (airway) muscles, improving airflow in asthma patients	R-Albuterol	S-Albuterol

▲ **Figure 4.8 The pharmacological importance of enantiomers.** Ibuprofen and albuterol are drugs whose enantiomers have different effects. (*S* and *R* are used here to distinguish between enantiomers.) Ibuprofen is commonly sold as a mixture of the two enantiomers; the *S* enantiomer is 100 times more effective than the *R* form. Albuterol is synthesized and sold only as the *R* form of the drug; the *S* form counteracts the active *R* form.

the ball-and-stick models shown in **Figure 4.7c**.) The four groups can be arranged in space around the asymmetric carbon in two different ways that are mirror images. Enantiomers are, in a way, left-handed and right-handed versions of the molecule. Just as your right hand won't fit into a left-handed glove, a "right-handed" molecule won't fit into the same space as the "left-handed" version. Usually, only one isomer is biologically active because only that form can bind to specific molecules in an organism.

The concept of enantiomers is important in the pharmaceutical industry because the two enantiomers of a drug may not be equally effective, as is the case for both ibuprofen and the asthma medication albuterol **(Figure 4.8)**. Methamphetamine also occurs in two enantiomers that have very different effects. One enantiomer is the highly addictive stimulant drug known as "crank," sold illegally in the street drug trade. The other has a much weaker effect and is the active ingredient in an over-the-counter vapor inhaler for treatment of nasal congestion. The differing effects of enantiomers in the body demonstrate that organisms are sensitive to even the most subtle variations in molecular architecture. Once again, we see that molecules have emergent properties that depend on the specific arrangement of their atoms.

CONCEPT CHECK 4.2

1. **DRAW IT** (a) Draw a structural formula for C_2H_4. (b) Draw the *trans* isomer of $C_2H_2Cl_2$.
2. Which molecules in Figure 4.5 are isomers? For each pair, identify the type of isomer.
3. How are gasoline and fat chemically similar?
4. Can propane (C_3H_8) form isomers? Explain.

For suggested answers, see Appendix A.

CONCEPT 4.3

A few chemical groups are key to molecular function

The properties of an organic molecule depend not only on the arrangement of its carbon skeleton but also on the chemical groups attached to that skeleton. We can think of hydrocarbons, the simplest organic molecules, as the underlying framework for more complex organic molecules. A number of chemical groups can replace one or more hydrogens of the hydrocarbon. These groups may participate in chemical reactions or may contribute to function indirectly by their effects on molecular shape; they help give each molecule its unique properties.

The Chemical Groups Most Important in the Processes of Life

Consider the differences between estradiol (a type of estrogen) and testosterone. These compounds are female and male sex hormones, respectively, in humans and other vertebrates. Both are steroids, organic molecules with a common carbon skeleton in the form of four fused rings. They differ only in the chemical groups attached to the rings (shown here in abbreviated form); the distinctions in molecular architecture are shaded in blue:

The different actions of these two molecules on many targets throughout the body are the basis of gender, producing the contrasting features of male and female vertebrates. In this case, the chemical groups are important because they affect molecular shape, contributing to function.

In other cases, chemical groups are directly involved in chemical reactions; such groups are known as **functional groups**. Each has certain properties, such as shape and charge, that cause it to participate in chemical reactions in a characteristic way.

The seven chemical groups most important in biological processes are the hydroxyl, carbonyl, carboxyl, amino, sulfhydryl, phosphate, and methyl groups. The first six groups can be chemically reactive; of these, all except the sulfhydryl group are also hydrophilic and thus increase the solubility of organic compounds in water. The methyl group is not reactive, but instead often serves as a recognizable tag on biological molecules. Study **Figure 4.9** to become familiar with these biologically important chemical groups.

▼ Figure 4.9 Some biologically important chemical groups.

Chemical Group	Group Properties and Compound Name	Examples
Hydroxyl group (—OH) —OH (may be written HO—)	Is polar due to electronegative oxygen. Forms hydrogen bonds with water, helping dissolve compounds such as sugars. Compound name: Alcohol (specific name usually ends in *-ol*)	$H-\overset{H}{\underset{H}{C}}-\overset{H}{\underset{H}{C}}-OH$ **Ethanol**, the alcohol present in alcoholic beverages
Carbonyl group ($>$C$=$O) $-\overset{\|\overset{O}{}}{C}-$	Sugars with ketone groups are called ketoses; those with aldehydes are called aldoses. Compound name: Ketone (carbonyl group is within a carbon skeleton) or aldehyde (carbonyl group is at the end of a carbon skeleton)	**Acetone**, the simplest ketone **Propanal**, an aldehyde
Carboxyl group (—COOH) $-\overset{\overset{O}{\|\|}}{\underset{OH}{C}}$	Acts as an acid (can donate H⁺) because the covalent bond between oxygen and hydrogen is so polar. Compound name: Carboxylic acid, or organic acid	**Acetic acid**, which gives vinegar its sour taste $\rightleftharpoons$ Ionized form of —COOH (carboxylate ion), found in cells
Amino group (—NH$_2$) $-N\overset{H}{\underset{H}{}}$	Acts as a base; can pick up an H⁺ from the surrounding solution (water, in living organisms). Compound name: Amine	**Glycine**, an amino acid (note its carboxyl group) $\rightleftharpoons$ Ionized form of —NH$_2$, found in cells
Sulfhydryl group (—SH) —SH (may be written HS —)	Two —SH groups can react, forming a "cross-link" that helps stabilize protein structure. Hair protein cross-links maintain the straightness or curliness of hair; in hair salons, permanent treatments break cross-links, then re-form them while the hair is in the desired shape. Compound name: Thiol	**Cysteine**, a sulfur-containing amino acid
Phosphate group (—OPO$_3{}^{2-}$) $-O-\overset{\overset{O}{\|\|}}{\underset{O^-}{P}}-O^-$	Contributes negative charge (1– when positioned inside a chain of phosphates; 2– when at the end). When attached, confers on a molecule the ability to react with water, releasing energy. Compound name: Organic phosphate	**Glycerol phosphate**, which takes part in many important chemical reactions in cells
Methyl group (—CH$_3$) $-\overset{H}{\underset{H}{C}}-H$	Affects the expression of genes when on DNA or on proteins bound to DNA. Affects the shape and function of male and female sex hormones. Compound name: Methylated compound	**5-Methyl cytosine**, a component of DNA that has been modified by addition of a methyl group

ATP: An Important Source of Energy for Cellular Processes

The "Phosphate group" row in Figure 4.9 shows a simple example of an organic phosphate molecule. A more complicated organic phosphate, **adenosine triphosphate**, or **ATP**, is worth mentioning here because its function in the cell is so important. ATP consists of an organic molecule called adenosine attached to a string of three phosphate groups:

Where three phosphates are present in series, as in ATP, one phosphate may be split off as a result of a reaction with water. This inorganic phosphate ion, $HOPO_3^{2-}$, is often abbreviated P_i in this book, and a phosphate group in an organic molecule is often written as P. Having lost one phosphate, ATP becomes adenosine *di*phosphate, or ADP. Although ATP is sometimes said to store energy, it is more accurate to think of it as storing the potential to react with water. This reaction releases energy that can be used by the cell. You will learn about this in more detail in Chapter 8.

$$P\text{-}P\text{-}P\text{-}\boxed{\text{Adenosine}} \xrightarrow[\text{with } H_2O]{\text{Reacts}} P_i + P\text{-}P\text{-}\boxed{\text{Adenosine}} + \text{Energy}$$

ATP   Inorganic   ADP
               phosphate

CONCEPT CHECK 4.3

1. What does the term *amino acid* signify about the structure of such a molecule?
2. What chemical change occurs to ATP when it reacts with water and releases energy?
3. **WHAT IF?** Suppose you had an organic molecule such as cysteine (see Figure 4.9, sulfhydryl group example), and you chemically removed the —NH_2 group and replaced it with —COOH. Draw the structural formula for this molecule and speculate about its chemical properties. Is the central carbon asymmetric before the change? After?

For suggested answers, see Appendix A.

The Chemical Elements of Life: *A Review*

Living matter, as you have learned, consists mainly of carbon, oxygen, hydrogen, and nitrogen, with smaller amounts of sulfur and phosphorus. These elements all form strong covalent bonds, an essential characteristic in the architecture of complex organic molecules. Of all these elements, carbon is the virtuoso of the covalent bond. The versatility of carbon makes possible the great diversity of organic molecules, each with particular properties that emerge from the unique arrangement of its carbon skeleton and the chemical groups appended to that skeleton. This variation at the molecular level provides the foundation for the rich biological diversity found on our planet.

4 Chapter Review

SUMMARY OF KEY CONCEPTS

CONCEPT 4.1

Organic chemistry is the study of carbon compounds (pp. 57–58)

- Organic compounds, once thought to arise only within living organisms, were finally synthesized in the laboratory.
- Living matter is made mostly of carbon, oxygen, hydrogen, and nitrogen. Biological diversity results from carbon's ability to form a huge number of molecules with particular shapes and properties.

? *How did Stanley Miller's experiments support the idea that, even at life's origins, physical and chemical laws govern the processes of life?*

CONCEPT 4.2

Carbon atoms can form diverse molecules by bonding to four other atoms (pp. 58–62)

- Carbon, with a valence of 4, can bond to various other atoms, including O, H, and N. Carbon can also bond to other carbon atoms, forming the carbon skeletons of organic compounds. These skeletons vary in length and shape and have bonding sites for atoms of other elements.
- **Hydrocarbons** consist of carbon and hydrogen.
- **Isomers** are compounds that have the same molecular formula but different structures and therefore different properties. Three types of isomers are **structural isomers**, *cis-trans* **isomers**, and **enantiomers**.

? *Refer back to Figure 4.9. What type of isomers are acetone and propanal? How many asymmetric carbons are present in acetic acid, glycine, and glycerol phosphate? Can these three molecules exist as forms that are enantiomers?*

CONCEPT 4.3

A few chemical groups are key to molecular function (pp. 62–64)

- Chemical groups attached to the carbon skeletons of organic molecules participate in chemical reactions (**functional groups**) or contribute to function by affecting molecular shape (see Figure 4.9).
- **ATP (adenosine triphosphate)** consists of adenosine attached to three phosphate groups. ATP can react with water, forming

inorganic phosphate and ADP (adenosine diphosphate). This reaction releases energy that can be used by the cell.

Ⓟ–Ⓟ–Ⓟ–[Adenosine] —Reacts with H_2O→ Ⓟᵢ + Ⓟ–Ⓟ–[Adenosine] + Energy

ATP   Inorganic   ADP
             phosphate

? *In what ways does a methyl group differ chemically from the other six important chemical groups shown in Figure 4.9?*

TEST YOUR UNDERSTANDING

LEVEL 1: KNOWLEDGE/COMPREHENSION

1. Organic chemistry is currently defined as
   a. the study of compounds made only by living cells.
   b. the study of carbon compounds.
   c. the study of natural (as opposed to synthetic) compounds.
   d. the study of hydrocarbons.

2. Which functional group is *not* present in this molecule?
   a. carboxyl
   b. sulfhydryl
   c. hydroxyl
   d. amino

3. **MAKE CONNECTIONS** Which chemical group is most likely to be responsible for an organic molecule behaving as a base (see Concept 3.3)?
   a. hydroxyl
   b. carbonyl
   c. amino
   d. phosphate

LEVEL 2: APPLICATION/ANALYSIS

4. Which of the following hydrocarbons has a double bond in its carbon skeleton?
   a. C_3H_8 c. C_2H_4
   b. C_2H_6 d. C_2H_2

5. Choose the term that correctly describes the relationship between these two sugar molecules:
   a. structural isomers
   b. *cis-trans* isomers
   c. enantiomers
   d. isotopes

6. Identify the asymmetric carbon in this molecule:

7. Which action could produce a carbonyl group?
   a. the replacement of the —OH of a carboxyl group with hydrogen
   b. the addition of a thiol to a hydroxyl
   c. the addition of a hydroxyl to a phosphate
   d. the replacement of the nitrogen of an amine with oxygen

8. Which of the molecules shown in question 5 has an asymmetric carbon? Which carbon is asymmetric?

LEVEL 3: SYNTHESIS/EVALUATION

9. **EVOLUTION CONNECTION**
   DRAW IT Some scientists think that life elsewhere in the universe might be based on the element silicon, rather than on carbon, as on Earth. Look at the electron distribution diagram for silicon in Figure 2.7 and draw the Lewis dot structure for silicon. What properties does silicon share with carbon that would make silicon-based life more likely than, say, neon-based life or aluminum-based life?

10. **SCIENTIFIC INQUIRY**
    50 years ago, pregnant women who were prescribed thalidomide for morning sickness gave birth to children with birth defects. Thalidomide is a mixture of two enantiomers; one reduces morning sickness, but the other causes severe birth defects. Today, the FDA has approved this drug for non-pregnant individuals with Hansen's disease (leprosy) or newly diagnosed multiple myeloma, a blood and bone marrow cancer. The beneficial enantiomer can be synthesized and given to patients, but over time, both the beneficial *and* the harmful enantiomer can be detected in the body. Propose a possible explanation for the presence of the harmful enantiomer.

11. **WRITE ABOUT A THEME: ORGANIZATION**
    In 1918, an epidemic of sleeping sickness caused an unusual rigid paralysis in some survivors, similar to symptoms of advanced Parkinson's disease. Years later, L-dopa (below, left), a chemical used to treat Parkinson's disease, was given to some of these patients. L-dopa was remarkably effective at eliminating the paralysis, at least temporarily. However, its enantiomer, D-dopa (right), was subsequently shown to have no effect at all, as is the case for Parkinson's disease. In a short essay (100–150 words), discuss how the effectiveness of one enantiomer and not the other illustrates the theme of structure and function.

L-dopa   **D-dopa**

12. **SYNTHESIZE YOUR KNOWLEDGE**

Explain how the chemical structure of the carbon atom accounts for the differences between the male and female lions seen in the photo.

For selected answers, see Appendix A.

MasteringBiology®

Students Go to **MasteringBiology** for assignments, the eText, and the Study Area with practice tests, animations, and activities.

Instructors Go to **MasteringBiology** for automatically graded tutorials and questions that you can assign to your students, plus Instructor Resources.

5

The Structure and Function of Large Biological Molecules

KEY CONCEPTS

5.1 Macromolecules are polymers, built from monomers

5.2 Carbohydrates serve as fuel and building material

5.3 Lipids are a diverse group of hydrophobic molecules

5.4 Proteins include a diversity of structures, resulting in a wide range of functions

5.5 Nucleic acids store, transmit, and help express hereditary information

5.6 Genomics and proteomics have transformed biological inquiry and applications

▲ Figure 5.1 Why is the structure of a protein important for its function?

The Molecules of Life

Given the rich complexity of life on Earth, it might surprise you that the most important large molecules found in all living things—from bacteria to elephants—can be sorted into just four main classes: carbohydrates, lipids, proteins, and nucleic acids. On the molecular scale, members of three of these classes—carbohydrates, proteins, and nucleic acids—are huge and are therefore called **macromolecules**. For example, a protein may consist of thousands of atoms that form a molecular colossus with a mass well over 100,000 daltons. Considering the size and complexity of macromolecules, it is noteworthy that biochemists have determined the detailed structure of so many of them. The image in **Figure 5.1** is a molecular model of a protein called alcohol dehydrogenase, which breaks down alcohol in the body.

The architecture of a large biological molecule plays an essential role in its function. Like water and simple organic molecules, large biological molecules exhibit unique emergent properties arising from the orderly arrangement of their atoms. In this chapter, we'll first consider how macromolecules are built. Then we'll examine the structure and function of all four classes of large biological molecules: carbohydrates, lipids, proteins, and nucleic acids.

Macromolecules are polymers, built from monomers

The macromolecules in three of the four classes of life's organic compounds—carbohydrates, proteins, and nucleic acids, all except lipids—are chain-like molecules called polymers (from the Greek *polys*, many, and *meros*, part). A **polymer** is a long molecule consisting of many similar or identical building blocks linked by covalent bonds, much as a train consists of a chain of cars. The repeating units that serve as the building blocks of a polymer are smaller molecules called **monomers** (from the Greek *monos*, single). Some monomers also have other functions of their own.

The Synthesis and Breakdown of Polymers

Although each class of polymer is made up of a different type of monomer, the chemical mechanisms by which cells make and break down polymers are basically the same in all cases. In cells, these processes are facilitated by **enzymes**, specialized macromolecules that speed up chemical reactions. Monomers are connected by a reaction in which two molecules are covalently bonded to each other, with the loss of a water molecule; this is known as a **dehydration reaction** (**Figure 5.2a**). When a bond forms between two monomers, each monomer contributes part of the water molecule that is released during the reaction: One monomer provides a hydroxyl group (—OH), while the other provides a hydrogen (—H). This reaction is repeated as monomers are added to the chain one by one, making a polymer.

Polymers are disassembled to monomers by **hydrolysis**, a process that is essentially the reverse of the dehydration reaction (**Figure 5.2b**). Hydrolysis means water breakage (from the Greek *hydro*, water, and *lysis*, break). The bond between monomers is broken by the addition of a water molecule, with a hydrogen from water attaching to one monomer and the hydroxyl group attaching to the other. An example of hydrolysis within our bodies is the process of digestion. The bulk of the organic material in our food is in the form of polymers that are much too large to enter our cells. Within the digestive tract, various enzymes attack the polymers, speeding up hydrolysis. Released monomers are then absorbed into the bloodstream for distribution to all body cells. Those cells can then use dehydration reactions to assemble the monomers into new, different polymers that can perform specific functions required by the cell.

The Diversity of Polymers

A cell has thousands of different macromolecules; the collection varies from one type of cell to another. The inherited

▼ Figure 5.2 The synthesis and breakdown of polymers.

(a) Dehydration reaction: synthesizing a polymer

Short polymer | Unlinked monomer

Dehydration removes a water molecule, forming a new bond.

H_2O

Longer polymer

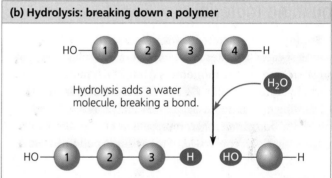

(b) Hydrolysis: breaking down a polymer

Hydrolysis adds a water molecule, breaking a bond.

H_2O

differences between close relatives such as human siblings reflect small variations in polymers, particularly DNA and proteins. Molecular differences between unrelated individuals are more extensive, and those between species greater still. The diversity of macromolecules in the living world is vast, and the possible variety is effectively limitless.

What is the basis for such diversity in life's polymers? These molecules are constructed from only 40 to 50 common monomers and some others that occur rarely. Building a huge variety of polymers from such a limited number of monomers is analogous to constructing hundreds of thousands of words from only 26 letters of the alphabet. The key is arrangement—the particular linear sequence that the units follow. However, this analogy falls far short of describing the great diversity of macromolecules because most biological polymers have many more monomers than the number of letters a word, even the longest ones. Proteins, for example, are built from 20 kinds of amino acids arranged in chains that are typically hundreds of amino acids long. The molecular logic of life is simple but elegant: Small molecules common to all organisms are ordered into unique macromolecules.

Despite this immense diversity, molecular structure and function can still be grouped roughly by class. Let's examine each of the four major classes of large biological molecules. For each class, the large molecules have emergent properties not found in their individual building blocks.

1. What are the four main classes of large biological molecules? Which class does not consist of polymers?

2. How many molecules of water are needed to completely hydrolyze a polymer that is ten monomers long?

3. **WHAT IF?** If you eat a piece of fish, what reactions must occur for the amino acid monomers in the protein of the fish to be converted to new proteins in your body?

For suggested answers, see Appendix A.

CONCEPT 5.2

Carbohydrates serve as fuel and building material

Carbohydrates include sugars and polymers of sugars. The simplest carbohydrates are the monosaccharides, or simple sugars; these are the monomers from which more complex carbohydrates are built. Disaccharides are double sugars, consisting of two monosaccharides joined by a covalent bond. Carbohydrate macromolecules are polymers called polysaccharides, composed of many sugar building blocks.

Sugars

Monosaccharides (from the Greek *monos*, single, and *sacchar*, sugar) generally have molecular formulas that are some multiple of the unit CH_2O. Glucose ($C_6H_{12}O_6$), the most common monosaccharide, is of central importance in the chemistry of life. In the structure of glucose, we can see the trademarks of a sugar: The molecule has a carbonyl group (CO) and multiple hydroxyl groups (—OH) **(Figure 5.3)**. Depending on the location of the carbonyl group, a sugar is either an aldose (aldehyde sugar) or a ketose (ketone sugar). Glucose, for example, is an aldose; fructose, an isomer of glucose, is a ketose. (Most names for sugars end in *-ose*.) Another criterion for classifying sugars is the size of the carbon skeleton, which ranges from three to seven carbons long. Glucose, fructose, and other sugars that have six carbons are called hexoses. Trioses (three-carbon sugars) and pentoses (five-carbon sugars) are also common.

Still another source of diversity for simple sugars is in the spatial arrangement of their parts around asymmetric carbons. (Recall that an asymmetric carbon is a carbon attached to four different atoms or groups of atoms.) Glucose and galactose, for example, differ only in the placement of parts around one asymmetric carbon (see the purple boxes in Figure 5.3). What seems like a small difference is significant enough to give the two sugars distinctive shapes and binding activities, thus different behaviors.

Although it is convenient to draw glucose with a linear carbon skeleton, this representation is not completely accurate.

▲ **Figure 5.3 The structure and classification of some monosaccharides.** Sugars vary in the location of their carbonyl groups (orange), the length of their carbon skeletons, and the spatial arrangement around asymmetric carbons (compare, for example, the purple portions of glucose and galactose).

MAKE CONNECTIONS *In the 1970s, a process was developed that converts the glucose in corn syrup to its sweeter-tasting isomer, fructose. High-fructose corn syrup, a common ingredient in soft drinks and processed food, is a mixture of glucose and fructose. What type of isomers are glucose and fructose? (See Figure 4.7.)*

(a) Linear and ring forms. Chemical equilibrium between the linear and ring structures greatly favors the formation of rings. The carbons of the sugar are numbered 1 to 6, as shown. To form the glucose ring, carbon 1 (magenta) bonds to the oxygen (blue) attached to carbon 5.

(b) Abbreviated ring structure. Each unlabeled corner represents a carbon. The ring's thicker edge indicates that you are looking at the ring edge-on; the components attached to the ring lie above or below the plane of the ring.

▲ **Figure 5.4 Linear and ring forms of glucose.**

DRAW IT *Start with the linear form of fructose (see Figure 5.3) and draw the formation of the fructose ring in two steps. First, number the carbons starting at the top of the linear structure. Then draw the molecule in the same orientation as the glucose in the middle of (a) above, attaching carbon 5 via its oxygen to carbon 2. Compare the number of carbons in the fructose and glucose rings.*

In aqueous solutions, glucose molecules, as well as most other five- and six-carbon sugars, form rings **(Figure 5.4)**.

Monosaccharides, particularly glucose, are major nutrients for cells. In the process known as cellular respiration, cells extract energy from glucose molecules by breaking them down in a series of reactions. Not only are simple-sugar molecules a major fuel for cellular work, but their carbon skeletons also serve as raw material for the synthesis of other types of small organic molecules, such as amino acids and fatty acids. Sugar molecules that are not immediately used in these ways are generally incorporated as monomers into disaccharides or polysaccharides.

A **disaccharide** consists of two monosaccharides joined by a **glycosidic linkage**, a covalent bond formed between two monosaccharides by a dehydration reaction. For example, maltose is a disaccharide formed by the linking of two molecules of glucose **(Figure 5.5a)**. Also known as malt sugar, maltose is an ingredient used in brewing beer. The most prevalent disaccharide is sucrose, which is table sugar. Its two monomers are glucose and fructose **(Figure 5.5b)**. Plants generally transport carbohydrates from leaves to roots and other nonphotosynthetic organs in the form of sucrose. Lactose, the sugar present in milk, is another disaccharide, in this case a glucose molecule joined to a galactose molecule.

(a) Dehydration reaction in the synthesis of maltose. The bonding of two glucose units forms maltose. The 1–4 glycosidic linkage joins the number 1 carbon of one glucose to the number 4 carbon of the second glucose. Joining the glucose monomers in a different way would result in a different disaccharide.

Glucose   Glucose   Maltose

(b) Dehydration reaction in the synthesis of sucrose. Sucrose is a disaccharide formed from glucose and fructose. Notice that fructose forms a five-sided ring, though it is a hexose like glucose.

Glucose   Fructose   Sucrose

▲ **Figure 5.5 Examples of disaccharide synthesis.**

DRAW IT *Referring to Figures 5.3 and 5.4, number the carbons in each sugar in this figure. Insert arrows linking the carbons to show how the numbering is consistent with the name of each glycosidic linkage.*

Polysaccharides

Polysaccharides are macromolecules, polymers with a few hundred to a few thousand monosaccharides joined by glycosidic linkages. Some polysaccharides serve as storage material, hydrolyzed as needed to provide sugar for cells. Other polysaccharides serve as building material for structures that protect the cell or the whole organism. The architecture and function of a polysaccharide are determined by its sugar monomers and by the positions of its glycosidic linkages.

Storage Polysaccharides

Both plants and animals store sugars for later use in the form of storage polysaccharides **(Figure 5.6)**. Plants store **starch**, a polymer of glucose monomers, as granules within cellular structures known as plastids, which include chloroplasts. Synthesizing starch enables the plant to stockpile surplus glucose. Because glucose is a major cellular fuel, starch represents stored energy. The sugar can later be withdrawn from this carbohydrate "bank" by hydrolysis, which breaks the bonds between the glucose monomers. Most animals, including humans, also have enzymes that can hydrolyze plant starch, making glucose available as a nutrient for cells. Potato tubers and grains are the major sources of starch in the human diet.

Most of the glucose monomers in starch are joined by 1–4 linkages (number 1 carbon to number 4 carbon), like the glucose units in maltose (see Figure 5.5a). The simplest form of starch, amylose, is unbranched. Amylopectin, a more complex starch, is a branched polymer with 1–6 linkages at the branch points. Both of these starches are shown in **Figure 5.6a**.

▲ **Figure 5.6 Polysaccharides of plants and animals. (a)** Starch stored in plant cells, **(b)** glycogen stored in muscle cells, and **(c)** structural cellulose fibers in plant cell walls are all polysaccharides composed entirely of glucose monomers (green hexagons). In starch and glycogen, the polymer chains tend to form helices in unbranched regions because of the angle of the linkages between glucose molecules. There are two kinds of starch: amylose and amylopectin. Cellulose, with a different kind of glucose linkage, is always unbranched.

Animals store a polysaccharide called **glycogen**, a polymer of glucose that is like amylopectin but more extensively branched **(Figure 5.6b)**. Vertebrates store glycogen mainly in liver and muscle cells. Hydrolysis of glycogen in these cells releases glucose when the demand for sugar increases. This stored fuel cannot sustain an animal for long, however. In humans, for example, glycogen stores are depleted in about a day unless they are replenished by consumption of food. This is an issue of concern in low-carbohydrate diets, which can result in weakness and fatigue.

Structural Polysaccharides

Organisms build strong materials from structural polysaccharides. For example, the polysaccharide called **cellulose** is a major component of the tough walls that enclose plant cells **(Figure 5.6c)**. On a global scale, plants produce almost 10^{14} kg (100 billion tons) of cellulose per year; it is the most abundant organic compound on Earth.

Like starch, cellulose is a polymer of glucose, but the glycosidic linkages in these two polymers differ. The difference is based on the fact that there are actually two slightly different ring structures for glucose **(Figure 5.7a)**. When glucose forms a ring, the hydroxyl group attached to the number 1 carbon is positioned either below or above the plane of the ring. These two ring forms for glucose are called alpha (α) and beta (β), respectively. (Greek letters are often used as a "numbering" system for different versions of biological structures, much as we use the letters a, b, c, and so on for the parts of a question or a figure.) In starch, all the glucose monomers are in the α configuration **(Figure 5.7b)**, the

arrangement we saw in Figures 5.4 and 5.5. In contrast, the glucose monomers of cellulose are all in the β configuration, making every glucose monomer "upside down" with respect to its neighbors **(Figure 5.7c;** see also Figure 5.6c).

The differing glycosidic linkages in starch and cellulose give the two molecules distinct three-dimensional shapes. Whereas certain starch molecules are largely helical, a cellulose molecule is straight. Cellulose is never branched, and some hydroxyl groups on its glucose monomers are free to hydrogen-bond with the hydroxyls of other cellulose molecules lying parallel to it. In plant cell walls, parallel cellulose molecules held together in this way are grouped into units called microfibrils (see Figure 5.6c). These cable-like microfibrils are a strong building material for plants and an important substance for humans because cellulose is the major constituent of paper and the only component of cotton.

Enzymes that digest starch by hydrolyzing its α linkages are unable to hydrolyze the β linkages of cellulose due to the different shapes of these two molecules. In fact, few organisms possess enzymes that can digest cellulose. Almost all animals, including humans, do not; the cellulose in our food passes through the digestive tract and is eliminated with the feces. Along the way, the cellulose abrades the wall of the digestive tract and stimulates the lining to secrete mucus, which aids in the smooth passage of food through the tract. Thus, although cellulose is not a nutrient for humans, it is an important part of a healthful diet. Most fruits, vegetables, and whole grains are rich in cellulose. On food packages, "insoluble fiber" refers mainly to cellulose.

Some microorganisms can digest cellulose, breaking it down into glucose monomers. A cow harbors

(a) α and β glucose ring structures. These two interconvertible forms of glucose differ in the placement of the hydroxyl group (highlighted in blue) attached to the number 1 carbon.

α Glucose

β Glucose

(b) Starch: 1–4 linkage of α glucose monomers. All monomers are in the same orientation. Compare the positions of the —OH groups highlighted in yellow with those in cellulose (c).

(c) Cellulose: 1–4 linkage of β glucose monomers. In cellulose, every β glucose monomer is upside down with respect to its neighbors. (See the highlighted —OH groups.)

▲ **Figure 5.7 Starch and cellulose structures.**

The structure of the chitin monomer

CH_2OH

◀ Chitin, embedded in proteins, forms the exoskeleton of arthropods. This cicada is molting—shedding its old exoskeleton and emerging in adult form.

▶ Chitin is used to make a strong and flexible surgical thread that decomposes after the wound or incision heals.

▲ **Figure 5.8 Chitin, a structural polysaccharide.**

cellulose-digesting prokaryotes and protists in its gut. These microbes hydrolyze the cellulose of hay and grass and convert the glucose to other compounds that nourish the cow. Similarly, a termite, which is unable to digest cellulose by itself, has prokaryotes or protists living in its gut that can make a meal of wood. Some fungi can also digest cellulose in soil and elsewhere, thereby helping recycle chemical elements within Earth's ecosystems.

Another important structural polysaccharide is **chitin**, the carbohydrate used by arthropods (insects, spiders, crustaceans, and related animals) to build their exoskeletons **(Figure 5.8)**. An exoskeleton is a hard case that surrounds the soft parts of an animal. Made up of chitin embedded in a layer of proteins, the case is leathery and flexible at first, but becomes hardened when the proteins are chemically linked to each other (as in insects) or encrusted with calcium carbonate (as in crabs). Chitin is also found in fungi, which use this polysaccharide rather than cellulose as the building material for their cell walls. Chitin is similar to cellulose, with β linkages, except that the glucose monomer of chitin has a nitrogen-containing appendage (see Figure 5.8, top right).

1. Write the formula for a monosaccharide that has three carbons.

2. A dehydration reaction joins two glucose molecules to form maltose. The formula for glucose is $C_6H_{12}O_6$. What is the formula for maltose?

3. **WHAT IF?** After a cow is given antibiotics to treat an infection, a vet gives the animal a drink of "gut culture" containing various prokaryotes. Why is this necessary?

For suggested answers, see Appendix A.

CONCEPT 5.3

Lipids are a diverse group of hydrophobic molecules

Lipids are the one class of large biological molecules that does not include true polymers, and they are generally not big enough to be considered macromolecules. The compounds called **lipids** are grouped with each other because they share one important trait: They mix poorly, if at all, with water. The hydrophobic behavior of lipids is based on their molecular structure. Although they may have some polar bonds associated with oxygen, lipids consist mostly of hydrocarbon regions. Lipids are varied in form and function. They include waxes and certain pigments, but we will focus on the types of lipids that are most biologically important: fats, phospholipids, and steroids.

Fats

Although fats are not polymers, they are large molecules assembled from smaller molecules by dehydration reactions. A **fat** is constructed from two kinds of smaller molecules: glycerol and fatty acids **(Figure 5.9a)**. Glycerol is an alcohol; each of its three carbons bears a hydroxyl group. A **fatty acid** has a long carbon skeleton, usually 16 or 18 carbon atoms in length. The carbon at one end of the skeleton is part of a carboxyl group, the functional group that gives these molecules the name fatty *acid*. The rest of the skeleton consists of a hydrocarbon chain. The relatively nonpolar C—H bonds in the hydrocarbon chains of fatty acids are the reason fats are hydrophobic. Fats separate from water because the water molecules hydrogen-bond to one another and exclude the fats. This is the reason that vegetable oil (a liquid fat) separates from the aqueous vinegar solution in a bottle of salad dressing.

In making a fat, three fatty acid molecules are each joined to glycerol by an ester linkage, a bond formed by a dehydration reaction between a hydroxyl group and a carboxyl group. The resulting fat, also called a **triacylglycerol**, thus consists of three fatty acids linked to one glycerol molecule.

Glycerol

(a) One of three dehydration reactions in the synthesis of a fat

Ester linkage

(b) Fat molecule (triacylglycerol)

▲ **Figure 5.9 The synthesis and structure of a fat, or triacylglycerol.** The molecular building blocks of a fat are one molecule of glycerol and three molecules of fatty acids. **(a)** One water molecule is removed for each fatty acid joined to the glycerol. **(b)** A fat molecule with three fatty acid units, two of them identical. The carbons of the fatty acids are arranged zigzag to suggest the actual orientations of the four single bonds extending from each carbon (see Figure 4.3a).

(Still another name for a fat is *triglyceride*, a word often found in the list of ingredients on packaged foods.) The fatty acids in a fat can all be the same, or they can be of two or three different kinds, as in **Figure 5.9b.**

The terms *saturated* fats and *unsaturated* fats are commonly used in the context of nutrition (**Figure 5.10**). These terms refer to the structure of the hydrocarbon chains of the fatty acids. If there are no double bonds between carbon atoms composing a chain, then as many hydrogen atoms as possible are bonded to the carbon skeleton. Such a structure is said to be *saturated* with hydrogen, and the resulting fatty acid is therefore called a **saturated fatty acid** (**Figure 5.10a**). An **unsaturated fatty acid** has one or more double bonds, with one fewer hydrogen atom on each double-bonded carbon. Nearly all double bonds in naturally occurring fatty acids are *cis* double bonds, which cause a kink in the hydrocarbon chain wherever they occur (**Figure 5.10b**). (See Figure 4.7b to remind yourself about *cis* and *trans* double bonds.)

A fat made from saturated fatty acids is called a saturated fat. Most animal fats are saturated: The hydrocarbon chains of their fatty acids—the "tails" of the fat molecules—lack double bonds, and their flexibility allows the fat molecules to pack together tightly. Saturated animal fats—such as lard

▼ **Figure 5.10 Saturated and unsaturated fats and fatty acids.**

(a) Saturated fat

At room temperature, the molecules of a saturated fat, such as the fat in butter, are packed closely together, forming a solid.

Structural formula of a saturated fat molecule (Each hydrocarbon chain is represented as a zigzag line, where each bend represents a carbon atom and hydrogens are not shown.)

Space-filling model of stearic acid, a saturated fatty acid (red = oxygen, black = carbon, gray = hydrogen)

(b) Unsaturated fat

At room temperature, the molecules of an unsaturated fat such as olive oil cannot pack together closely enough to solidify because of the kinks in some of their fatty acid hydrocarbon chains.

Structural formula of an unsaturated fat molecule

Space-filling model of oleic acid, an unsaturated fatty acid

Cis double bond causes bending.

and butter—are solid at room temperature. In contrast, the fats of plants and fishes are generally unsaturated, meaning that they are built of one or more types of unsaturated fatty acids. Usually liquid at room temperature, plant and fish fats are referred to as oils—olive oil and cod liver oil are examples. The kinks where the *cis* double bonds are located prevent the molecules from packing together closely enough to solidify at room temperature. The phrase "hydrogenated vegetable oils" on food labels means that unsaturated fats have been synthetically converted to saturated fats by adding hydrogen. Peanut butter, margarine, and many other products are hydrogenated to prevent lipids from separating out in liquid (oil) form.

A diet rich in saturated fats is one of several factors that may contribute to the cardiovascular disease known as atherosclerosis. In this condition, deposits called plaques develop within the walls of blood vessels, causing inward bulges that impede blood flow and reduce the resilience of the vessels. Recent studies have shown that the process of hydrogenating vegetable oils produces not only saturated fats but also unsaturated fats with *trans* double bonds. These **trans fats** may contribute more than saturated fats to atherosclerosis (see Chapter 42) and other problems. Because trans fats are especially common in baked goods and processed foods, the U.S. Department of Agriculture requires nutritional labels to include information on trans fat content. Some U.S. cities and at least two countries—Denmark and Switzerland—have even banned the use of trans fats in restaurants.

The major function of fats is energy storage. The hydrocarbon chains of fats are similar to gasoline molecules and just as rich in energy. A gram of fat stores more than twice as much energy as a gram of a polysaccharide, such as starch. Because plants are relatively immobile, they can function with bulky energy storage in the form of starch. (Vegetable oils are generally obtained from seeds, where more compact storage is an asset to the plant.) Animals, however, must carry their energy stores with them, so there is an advantage to having a more compact reservoir

of fuel—fat. Humans and other mammals stock their long-term food reserves in adipose cells (see Figure 4.6a), which swell and shrink as fat is deposited and withdrawn from storage. In addition to storing energy, adipose tissue also cushions such vital organs as the kidneys, and a layer of fat beneath the skin insulates the body. This subcutaneous layer is especially thick in whales, seals, and most other marine mammals, protecting them from cold ocean water.

Phospholipids

Cells as we know them could not exist without another type of lipid—phospholipids. Phospholipids are essential for cells because they are major constituents of cell membranes. Their structure provides a classic example of how form fits function at the molecular level. As shown in **Figure 5.11**, a **phospholipid** is similar to a fat molecule but has only two fatty acids attached to glycerol rather than three. The third hydroxyl group of glycerol is joined to a phosphate group, which has a negative electrical charge in the cell. Typically, an additional small charged or polar molecule is also linked to the phosphate group. Choline is one such molecule (see Figure 5.11), but there are many others as well, allowing formation of a variety of phospholipids that differ from each other.

The two ends of phospholipids show different behavior toward water. The hydrocarbon tails are hydrophobic and are excluded from water. However, the phosphate group and its attachments form a hydrophilic head that has an affinity for water. When phospholipids are added to water, they self-assemble into double-layered structures called

◀ **Figure 5.11 The structure of a phospholipid.** A phospholipid has a hydrophilic (polar) head and two hydrophobic (nonpolar) tails. This particular phospholipid, called a phosphatidylcholine, has a choline attached to a phosphate group. Shown here are **(a)** the structural formula, **(b)** the space-filling model (yellow = phosphorus, blue = nitrogen), **(c)** the symbol for a phospholipid that will appear throughout this book, and **(d)** the bilayer structure formed by self-assembly of phospholipids in an aqueous environment.

DRAW IT *Draw an oval around the hydrophilic head of the space-filling model.*

© Pearson Education, Inc.

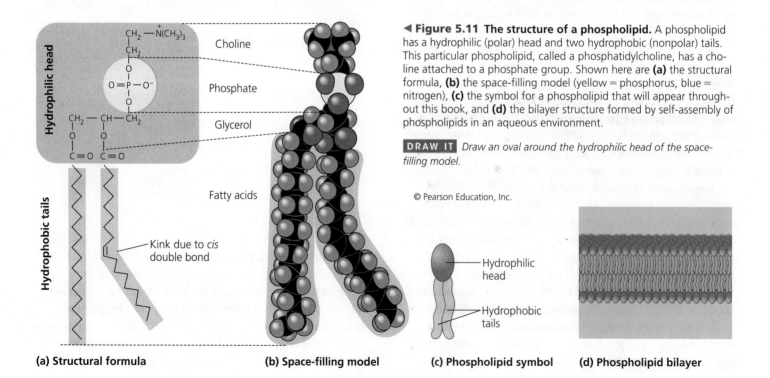

(a) **Structural formula**   (b) **Space-filling model**   (c) **Phospholipid symbol**   (d) **Phospholipid bilayer** "bilayers," shielding their hydrophobic portions from water (Figure 5.11d).

At the surface of a cell, phospholipids are arranged in a similar bilayer. The hydrophilic heads of the molecules are on the outside of the bilayer, in contact with the aqueous solutions inside and outside of the cell. The hydrophobic tails point toward the interior of the bilayer, away from the water. The phospholipid bilayer forms a boundary between the cell and its external environment; in fact, the existence of cells depends on the properties of phospholipids.

Steroids

Steroids are lipids characterized by a carbon skeleton consisting of four fused rings. Different steroids are distinguished by the particular chemical groups attached to this ensemble of rings. **Cholesterol**, a type of steroid, is a crucial molecule in animals **(Figure 5.12)**. It is a common component of animal cell membranes and is also the precursor from which other steroids, such as the vertebrate sex hormones, are synthesized. In vertebrates, cholesterol is synthesized in the liver and is also obtained from the diet. A high level of cholesterol in the blood may contribute to atherosclerosis. In fact, both saturated fats and trans fats exert their negative impact on health by affecting cholesterol levels.

▲ **Figure 5.12 Cholesterol, a steroid.** Cholesterol is the molecule from which other steroids, including the sex hormones, are synthesized. Steroids vary in the chemical groups attached to their four interconnected rings (shown in gold).

MAKE CONNECTIONS *Compare cholesterol with the sex hormones shown in the figure at the beginning of Concept 4.3. Circle the chemical groups that cholesterol has in common with estradiol; put a square around the chemical groups that cholesterol has in common with testosterone.*

CONCEPT CHECK 5.3

1. Compare the structure of a fat (triglyceride) with that of a phospholipid.
2. Why are human sex hormones considered lipids?
3. **WHAT IF?** Suppose a membrane surrounded an oil droplet, as it does in the cells of plant seeds and in some animal cells. Describe and explain the form it might take.

For suggested answers, see Appendix A.

Proteins include a diversity of structures, resulting in a wide range of functions

Nearly every dynamic function of a living being depends on proteins. In fact, the importance of proteins is underscored by their name, which comes from the Greek word *proteios*, meaning "first," or "primary." Proteins account for more than 50% of the dry mass of most cells, and they are instrumental in almost everything organisms do. Some proteins speed up chemical reactions, while others play a role in defense, storage, transport, cellular communication, movement, or structural support. **Figure 5.13** shows examples of proteins with these functions, which you'll learn more about in later chapters.

Life would not be possible without enzymes, most of which are proteins. Enzymatic proteins regulate metabolism by acting as **catalysts**, chemical agents that selectively speed up chemical reactions without being consumed by the reaction. Because an enzyme can perform its function over and over again, these molecules can be thought of as workhorses that keep cells running by carrying out the processes of life.

A human has tens of thousands of different proteins, each with a specific structure and function; proteins, in fact, are the most structurally sophisticated molecules known. Consistent with their diverse functions, they vary extensively in structure, each type of protein having a unique three-dimensional shape.

Diverse as proteins are, they are all constructed from the same set of 20 amino acids, linked in unbranched polymers. The bond between amino acids is called a peptide bond, so a polymer of amino acids is called a **polypeptide**. A **protein** is a biologically functional molecule made up of one or more polypeptides, each folded and coiled into a specific three-dimensional structure.

Amino Acid Monomers

All amino acids share a common structure. An **amino acid** is an organic molecule with both an amino group and a carboxyl group (see Figure 4.9). The figure at the right shows the general formula for an amino acid. At the center of the amino acid is an asymmetric carbon atom called the *alpha* (α) *carbon*. Its four different partners are an amino group, a carboxyl group, a hydrogen atom, and a variable group symbolized by R. The R group, also called the side chain, differs with each amino acid.

Side chain (R group)

α carbon

Amino group

Carboxyl group

Enzymatic proteins

Function: Selective acceleration of chemical reactions

Example: Digestive enzymes catalyze the hydrolysis of bonds in food molecules.

Defensive proteins

Function: Protection against disease

Example: Antibodies inactivate and help destroy viruses and bacteria.

Storage proteins

Function: Storage of amino acids

Examples: Casein, the protein of milk, is the major source of amino acids for baby mammals. Plants have storage proteins in their seeds. Ovalbumin is the protein of egg white, used as an amino acid source for the developing embryo.

Transport proteins

Function: Transport of substances

Examples: Hemoglobin, the iron-containing protein of vertebrate blood, transports oxygen from the lungs to other parts of the body. Other proteins transport molecules across membranes, as shown here.

Hormonal proteins

Function: Coordination of an organism's activities

Example: Insulin, a hormone secreted by the pancreas, causes other tissues to take up glucose, thus regulating blood sugar concentration.

Receptor proteins

Function: Response of cell to chemical stimuli

Example: Receptors built into the membrane of a nerve cell detect signaling molecules released by other nerve cells.

Contractile and motor proteins

Function: Movement

Examples: Motor proteins are responsible for the undulations of cilia and flagella. Actin and myosin proteins are responsible for the contraction of muscles.

Structural proteins

Function: Support

Examples: Keratin is the protein of hair, horns, feathers, and other skin appendages. Insects and spiders use silk fibers to make their cocoons and webs, respectively. Collagen and elastin proteins provide a fibrous framework in animal connective tissues.

Figure 5.14 shows the 20 amino acids that cells use to build their thousands of proteins. Here the amino groups and carboxyl groups are all depicted in ionized form, the way they usually exist at the pH found in a cell.

The physical and chemical properties of the side chain determine the unique characteristics of a particular amino acid, thus affecting its functional role in a polypeptide. In Figure 5.14, the amino acids are grouped according to the properties of their side chains. One group consists of amino acids with nonpolar side chains, which are hydrophobic.

Another group consists of amino acids with polar side chains, which are hydrophilic. Acidic amino acids are those with side chains that are generally negative in charge due to the presence of a carboxyl group, which is usually dissociated (ionized) at cellular pH. Basic amino acids have amino groups in their side chains that are generally positive in charge. (Notice that *all* amino acids have carboxyl groups and amino groups; the terms *acidic* and *basic* in this context refer only to groups in the side chains.) Because they are charged, acidic and basic side chains are also hydrophilic.

▼ **Figure 5.14 The 20 amino acids of proteins.** The amino acids are grouped here according to the properties of their side chains (R groups) and shown in their prevailing ionic forms at pH 7.2, the pH within a cell. The three-letter and one-letter abbreviations for the amino acids are in parentheses. All of the amino acids used in proteins are L enantiomers (see Figure 4.7c).

Nonpolar side chains; hydrophobic

Polar side chains; hydrophilic

Since cysteine is only weakly polar, it is sometimes classified as a nonpolar amino acid.

Electrically charged side chains; hydrophilic

Polypeptides (Amino Acid Polymers)

Now that we have examined amino acids, let's see how they are linked to form polymers (**Figure 5.15**). When two amino acids are positioned so that the carboxyl group of one is adjacent to the amino group of the other, they can become joined by a dehydration reaction, with the removal of a water molecule. The resulting covalent bond is called a **peptide bond**. Repeated over and over, this process yields a polypeptide, a polymer of many amino acids linked by peptide bonds.

The repeating sequence of atoms highlighted in purple in Figure 5.15 is called the *polypeptide backbone*. Extending from this backbone are the different side chains (R groups) of the amino acids. Polypeptides range in length from a few amino acids to a thousand or more. Each specific polypeptide has a unique linear sequence of amino acids. Note that one end of the polypeptide chain has a free amino group, while

Side chains

Back-bone

Peptide bond

New peptide bond forming

H_2O

Amino end
(N-terminus)

Peptide bond

Carboxyl end
(C-terminus)

▲ **Figure 5.15 Making a polypeptide chain.** Peptide bonds are formed by dehydration reactions, which link the carboxyl group of one amino acid to the amino group of the next. The peptide bonds are formed one at a time, starting with the amino acid at the amino end (N-terminus). The polypeptide has a repetitive backbone (purple) to which the amino acid side chains (yellow and green) are attached.

DRAW IT *Label the three amino acids in the upper part of the figure using three-letter and one-letter codes. Circle and label the carboxyl and amino groups that will form the new peptide bond.*

the opposite end has a free carboxyl group. Thus, a polypeptide of any length has a single amino end (N-terminus) and a single carboxyl end (C-terminus). In a polypeptide of any significant size, the side chains far outnumber the terminal groups, so the chemical nature of the molecule as a whole is determined by the kind and sequence of the side chains. The immense variety of polypeptides in nature illustrates an important concept introduced earlier—that cells can make many different polymers by linking a limited set of monomers into diverse sequences.

Protein Structure and Function

The specific activities of proteins result from their intricate three-dimensional architecture, the simplest level of which is the sequence of their amino acids. The pioneer in determining the amino acid sequence of proteins was Frederick Sanger, who, with his colleagues at Cambridge University in England, worked on the hormone insulin in the late 1940s and early 1950s. He used agents that break polypeptides at specific places, followed by chemical methods to determine the amino acid sequence in these small fragments. Sanger and his co-workers were able, after years of effort, to reconstruct the complete amino acid sequence of insulin. Since then, the steps involved in sequencing a polypeptide have been automated.

Once we have learned the amino acid sequence of a polypeptide, what can it tell us about the three-dimensional structure (commonly referred to simply as the "structure") of the protein and its function? The term *polypeptide* is not synonymous with the term *protein*. Even for a protein consisting of a single polypeptide, the relationship is somewhat analogous to that between a long strand of yarn and a sweater of particular size and shape that can be knit from the yarn. A functional protein is not *just* a polypeptide chain, but one or more polypeptides precisely twisted, folded, and coiled into a molecule of unique shape, which can be shown in several different types of models (**Figure 5.16**). And it is the amino acid sequence of each polypeptide that determines what three-dimensional structure the protein will have under normal cellular conditions.

When a cell synthesizes a polypeptide, the chain may fold spontaneously, assuming the functional structure for that protein. This folding is driven and reinforced by the formation of various bonds between parts of the chain, which in turn depends on the sequence of amino acids. Many proteins are roughly spherical (*globular proteins*), while others are shaped like long fibers (*fibrous proteins*). Even within these broad categories, countless variations exist.

A protein's specific structure determines how it works. In almost every case, the function of a protein depends on its ability to recognize and bind to some other molecule. In an especially striking example of the marriage of form and

Groove

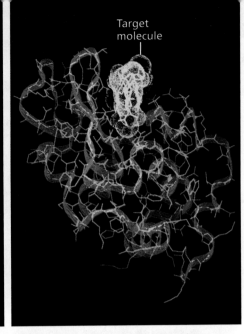

Groove

Target molecule

(a) A **ribbon model** shows how the single polypeptide chain folds and coils to form the functional protein. (The yellow lines represent disulfide bridges that stabilize the protein's shape.)

(b) A **space-filling model** shows more clearly the globular shape seen in many proteins, as well as the specific three-dimensional structure unique to lysozyme.

(c) In this view, a ribbon model is superimposed on a **wireframe model**, which shows the backbone with the side chains extending from it. The yellow structure is the target molecule.

▲ **Figure 5.16 Structure of a protein, the enzyme lysozyme.** Present in our sweat, tears, and saliva, lysozyme is an enzyme that helps prevent infection by binding to and catalyzing the destruction of specific molecules on the surface of many kinds of bacteria. The groove is the part of the protein that recognizes and binds to the target molecules on bacterial walls.

function, **Figure 5.17** shows the exact match of shape between an antibody (a protein in the body) and the particular foreign substance on a flu virus that the antibody binds to and marks for destruction. In Chapter 43, you'll learn more about how the immune system generates antibodies that match the shapes of specific foreign molecules so well. Also, you may recall from Chapter 2 that natural signaling molecules called endorphins bind to specific receptor proteins on the surface of brain cells in humans, producing euphoria and relieving pain. Morphine, heroin, and other opiate drugs are able to mimic endorphins because they all share a similar shape with endorphins and can thus fit into and bind to endorphin receptors in the brain. This fit is very specific, something like a lock and key (see Figure 2.16). Thus, the function of a protein—for instance, the ability of a receptor protein to bind to a particular pain-relieving signaling molecule—is an emergent property resulting from exquisite molecular order.

Four Levels of Protein Structure

With the goal of understanding the function of a protein, learning about its structure is often productive. In spite of their great diversity, all proteins share three superimposed levels of structure, known as primary, secondary, and tertiary structure. A fourth level, quaternary structure, arises

Antibody protein

Protein from flu virus

▲ **Figure 5.17 An antibody binding to a protein from a flu virus.** A technique called X-ray crystallography was used to generate a computer model of an antibody protein (blue and orange, left) bound to a flu virus protein (green and yellow, right). Computer software was then used to back the images away from each other, revealing the exact complementarity of shape between the two protein surfaces.

when a protein consists of two or more polypeptide chains. **Figure 5.18** describes these four levels of protein structure. Be sure to study this figure thoroughly before going on to the next section.

Exploring Levels of Protein Structure

Primary Structure

Linear chain of amino acids

Primary structure of transthyretin

Secondary Structure

Regions stabilized by hydrogen bonds between atoms of the polypeptide backbone

α helix

Hydrogen bond

β pleated sheet

β strand, often shown as a flat arrow pointing toward the carboxyl end (here, shown folded)

Hydrogen bond

Most proteins have segments of their polypeptide chains repeatedly coiled or folded in patterns that contribute to the protein's overall shape. These coils and folds, collectively referred to as **secondary structure**, are the result of hydrogen bonds between the repeating constituents of the polypeptide backbone (not the amino acid side chains). Within the backbone, the oxygen atoms have a partial negative charge, and the hydrogen atoms attached to the nitrogens have a partial positive charge (see Figure 2.14); therefore, hydrogen bonds can form between these atoms. Individually, these hydrogen bonds are weak, but because there are so many of them over a relatively long region of the polypeptide chain, they can support a particular shape for that part of the protein.

One such secondary structure is the **α helix**, a delicate coil held together by hydrogen bonding between every fourth amino acid, as shown above. Although each transthyretin polypeptide has only one α helix region (see tertiary structure), other globular proteins have multiple stretches of α helix separated by nonhelical regions (see hemoglobin on the next page). Some fibrous proteins, such as α-keratin, the structural protein of hair, have the α helix structure over most of their length.

The other main type of secondary structure is the **β pleated sheet**. As shown above, in this structure two or more segments of the polypeptide chain lying side by side (called β strands) are connected by hydrogen bonds between parts of the two parallel segments of the polypeptide backbone. β pleated sheets make up the core of many globular proteins, as is the case for transthyretin (see tertiary structure), and dominate some fibrous proteins, including the silk protein of a spider's web. The teamwork of so many hydrogen bonds makes each spider silk fiber stronger than a steel strand of the same weight.

The **primary structure** of a protein is its sequence of amino acids. As an example, let's consider transthyretin, a globular blood protein that transports vitamin A and one of the thyroid hormones throughout the body. Transthyretin is made up of four identical polypeptide chains, each composed of 127 amino acids. Shown here is one of these chains unraveled for a closer look at its primary structure. Each of the 127 positions along the chain is occupied by one of the 20 amino acids, indicated here by its three-letter abbreviation.

The primary structure is like the order of letters in a very long word. If left to chance, there would be 20^{127} different ways of making a polypeptide chain 127 amino acids long. However, the precise primary structure of a protein is determined not by the random linking of amino acids, but by inherited genetic information. The primary structure in turn dictates secondary and tertiary structure, due to the chemical nature of the backbone and the side chains (R groups) of the amino acids along the polypeptide.

▼ Spiders secrete silk fibers made of a structural protein containing β pleated sheets, which allow the spider web to stretch and recoil.

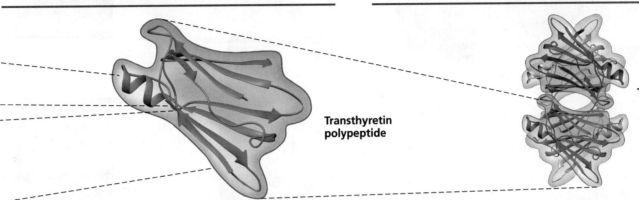

Tertiary Structure

Three-dimensional shape stabilized by interactions between side chains

Transthyretin
polypeptide

Quaternary Structure

Association of two or more polypeptides (some proteins only)

Transthyretin
protein
(four identical
polypeptides)

Superimposed on the patterns of secondary structure is a protein's tertiary structure, shown above in a ribbon model of the transthyretin polypeptide. While secondary structure involves interactions between backbone constituents, **tertiary structure** is the overall shape of a polypeptide resulting from interactions between the side chains (R groups) of the various amino acids. One type of interaction that contributes to tertiary structure is called—somewhat misleadingly— a **hydrophobic interaction**. As a polypeptide folds into its functional shape, amino acids with hydrophobic (nonpolar) side chains usually end up in clusters at the core of the protein, out of contact with water. Thus, a "hydrophobic interaction" is actually caused by the exclusion of nonpolar substances by water molecules. Once nonpolar amino acid side chains are close together, van der Waals interactions help hold them together. Meanwhile, hydrogen bonds between polar side chains and ionic bonds between positively and negatively charged side chains also help stabilize tertiary structure. These are all weak interactions in the aqueous cellular environment, but their cumulative effect helps give the protein a unique shape.

Covalent bonds called **disulfide bridges** may further reinforce the shape of a protein. Disulfide bridges form where two cysteine monomers, which have sulfhydryl groups (—SH) on their side chains (see Figure 4.9), are brought close together by the folding of the protein. The sulfur of one cysteine bonds to the sulfur of the second, and the disulfide bridge (—S—S—) rivets parts of the protein together (see the yellow lines in Figure 5.16a). All of these different kinds of interactions can contribute to the tertiary structure of a protein, as shown here in a small part of a hypothetical protein:

Some proteins consist of two or more polypeptide chains aggregated into one functional macromolecule. **Quaternary structure** is the overall protein structure that results from the aggregation of these polypeptide subunits. For example, shown above is the complete globular transthyretin protein, made up of its four polypeptides.

Another example is collagen, shown below, which is a fibrous protein that has three identical helical polypeptides intertwined into a larger triple helix, giving the long fibers great strength. This suits collagen fibers to their function as the girders of connective tissue in skin, bone, tendons, ligaments, and other body parts. (Collagen accounts for 40% of the protein in a human body.)

Collagen

Hemoglobin, the oxygen-binding protein of red blood cells shown below, is another example of a globular protein with quaternary structure. It consists of four polypeptide subunits, two of one kind (α) and two of another kind (β). Both α and β subunits consist primarily of α-helical secondary structure. Each subunit has a nonpolypeptide component, called heme, with an iron atom that binds oxygen.

Heme
Iron
β subunit
α subunit
α subunit
β subunit
Hemoglobin

CH₂
OH
Hydrogen bond
NH₂
CH₂
CH CH₃ CH₃ CH₃ CH₃ CH
Hydrophobic interactions and van der Waals interactions
CH₂
C O O⁻
NH₃⁺
Disulfide bridge
CH₂ S S CH₂
Ionic bond
CH₂ CH₂ CH₂ CH₂
Polypeptide backbone

	Primary Structure	Secondary and Tertiary Structures	Quaternary Structure	Function	Red Blood Cell Shape
Normal hemoglobin	1 Val 2 His 3 Leu 4 Thr 5 Pro 6 Glu 7 Glu	Normal β subunit	Normal hemoglobin β β α α	Normal hemoglobin proteins do not associate with one another; each carries oxygen.	Normal red blood cells are full of individual hemoglobin proteins. ⊢ 5 μm ⊣
Sickle-cell hemoglobin	1 Val 2 His 3 Leu 4 Thr 5 Pro 6 Val 7 Glu	Sickle-cell β subunit	Sickle-cell hemoglobin β β α α	Hydrophobic interactions between sickle-cell hemoglobin proteins lead to their aggregation into a fiber; capacity to carry oxygen is greatly reduced.	Fibers of abnormal hemoglobin deform red blood cell into sickle shape. ⊢ 5 μm ⊣

▲ **Figure 5.19 A single amino acid substitution in a protein causes sickle-cell disease.**

MAKE CONNECTIONS *Considering the chemical characteristics of the amino acids valine and glutamic acid (see Figure 5.14), propose a possible explanation for the dramatic effect on protein function that occurs when valine is substituted for glutamic acid.*

Sickle-Cell Disease: A Change in Primary Structure

Even a slight change in primary structure can affect a protein's shape and ability to function. For instance, **sickle-cell disease**, an inherited blood disorder, is caused by the substitution of one amino acid (valine) for the normal one (glutamic acid) at a particular position in the primary structure of hemoglobin, the protein that carries oxygen in red blood cells. Normal red blood cells are disk-shaped, but in sickle-cell disease, the abnormal hemoglobin molecules tend to aggregate into chains, deforming some of the cells into a sickle shape **(Figure 5.19)**. A person with the disease has periodic "sickle-cell crises" when the angular cells clog tiny blood vessels, impeding blood flow. The toll taken on such patients is a dramatic example of how a simple change in protein structure can have devastating effects on protein function.

What Determines Protein Structure?

You've learned that a unique shape endows each protein with a specific function. But what are the key factors determining protein structure? You already know most of the answer: A polypeptide chain of a given amino acid sequence can be arranged into a three-dimensional shape determined by the interactions responsible for secondary and tertiary structure. This folding normally occurs as the protein is being synthesized in the crowded environment within a cell, aided by other proteins. However, protein structure also depends on

the physical and chemical conditions of the protein's environment. If the pH, salt concentration, temperature, or other aspects of its environment are altered, the weak chemical bonds and interactions within a protein may be destroyed, causing the protein to unravel and lose its native shape, a change called **denaturation (Figure 5.20)**. Because it is misshapen, the denatured protein is biologically inactive.

Most proteins become denatured if they are transferred from an aqueous environment to a nonpolar solvent, such as ether or chloroform; the polypeptide chain refolds so that its hydrophobic regions face outward toward the solvent. Other denaturation agents include chemicals that disrupt

▲ **Figure 5.20 Denaturation and renaturation of a protein.** High temperatures or various chemical treatments will denature a protein, causing it to lose its shape and hence its ability to function. If the denatured protein remains dissolved, it may renature when the chemical and physical aspects of its environment are restored to normal.

the hydrogen bonds, ionic bonds, and disulfide bridges that maintain a protein's shape. Denaturation can also result from excessive heat, which agitates the polypeptide chain enough to overpower the weak interactions that stabilize the structure. The white of an egg becomes opaque during cooking because the denatured proteins are insoluble and solidify. This also explains why excessively high fevers can be fatal: Proteins in the blood tend to denature at very high body temperatures.

When a protein in a test-tube solution has been denatured by heat or chemicals, it can sometimes return to its functional shape when the denaturing agent is removed. (Sometimes this is not possible: For example, a fried egg will not become liquefied when placed back into the refrigerator!) We can conclude that the information for building specific shape is intrinsic to the protein's primary structure. The sequence of amino acids determines the protein's shape—where an α helix can form, where β pleated sheets can exist, where disulfide bridges are located, where ionic bonds can form, and so on. But how does protein folding occur in the cell?

Protein Folding in the Cell

Biochemists now know the amino acid sequence for more than 24 million proteins, with about 1 million added each month, and the three-dimensional shape for more than 25,000. Researchers have tried to correlate the primary structure of many proteins with their three-dimensional structure to discover the rules of protein folding. Unfortunately, however, the protein-folding process is not that simple. Most proteins probably go through several intermediate structures on their way to a stable shape, and looking at the mature structure does not reveal the stages of folding required to achieve that form. However, biochemists have developed methods for tracking a protein through such stages.

Crucial to the folding process are **chaperonins** (also called chaperone proteins), protein molecules that assist in the proper folding of other proteins **(Figure 5.21)**. Chaperonins do not specify the final structure of a polypeptide.

Instead, they keep the new polypeptide segregated from disruptive chemical conditions in the cytoplasmic environment while it folds spontaneously. The chaperonin shown in Figure 5.21, from the bacterium *E. coli*, is a giant multiprotein complex shaped like a hollow cylinder. The cavity provides a shelter for folding polypeptides, and recent research suggests that minute amounts of water are present, ensuring a hydrophilic environment that aids the folding process. Molecular systems have been identified that interact with chaperonins and check whether proper folding has occurred. Such systems either refold the misfolded proteins correctly or mark them for destruction.

Misfolding of polypeptides is a serious problem in cells that has come under increasing scrutiny by medical researchers. Many diseases—such as cystic fibrosis, Alzheimer's, Parkinson's, and mad cow disease—are associated with an accumulation of misfolded proteins. In fact, misfolded versions of the transthyretin protein featured in Figure 5.18 have been implicated in several diseases, including one form of senile dementia.

Even when scientists have a correctly folded protein in hand, determining its exact three-dimensional structure is not simple, for a single protein molecule has thousands of atoms. The first 3-D structures were worked out in the late 1950s for hemoglobin and a related protein called myoglobin. The method that made these feats possible was **X-ray crystallography**, which has since been used to determine the 3-D structure of many other proteins. In a recent example, Roger Kornberg and his colleagues at Stanford University used this method to elucidate the structure of RNA polymerase, an enzyme that plays a crucial role in the expression of genes **(Figure 5.22)**. Another method for analyzing protein structure is nuclear magnetic resonance (NMR) spectroscopy, which does not require protein crystallization. A still newer approach employs bioinformatics (see Concept 5.6) to predict the 3-D structure of polypeptides from their amino acid sequence. X-ray crystallography, NMR spectroscopy, and bioinformatics are complementary approaches to understanding protein structure and function.

▶ **Figure 5.21 A chaperonin in action.** The computer graphic (left) shows a large chaperonin protein complex from the bacterium *E. coli*. It has an interior space that provides a shelter for the proper folding of newly made polypeptides. The complex consists of two proteins: One is a hollow cylinder; the other is a cap that can fit on either end. The steps of chaperonin activity are shown at the right.

Cap
Hollow cylinder

Chaperonin
(fully assembled)

Polypeptide

❶ An unfolded polypeptide enters the cylinder from one end.

❷ Cap attachment causes the cylinder to change shape, creating a hydrophilic environment for polypeptide folding.

Correctly folded protein

❸ The cap comes off, and the properly folded protein is released.

What can the 3-D shape of the enzyme RNA polymerase II tell us about its function?

Experiment In 2006, Roger Kornberg was awarded the Nobel Prize in Chemistry for using X-ray crystallography to determine the 3-D shape of RNA polymerase II, which binds to the DNA double helix and synthesizes RNA. After crystallizing a complex of all three components, Kornberg and his colleagues aimed an X-ray beam through the crystal. The atoms of the crystal diffracted (bent) the X-rays into an orderly array that a digital detector recorded as a pattern of spots called an X-ray diffraction pattern.

Results Using data from X-ray diffraction patterns, as well as the amino acid sequence determined by chemical methods, the researchers built a 3-D model of the complex with the help of computer software.

Conclusion Analysis of the model led to a hypothesis about the functions of different regions of RNA polymerase II. For example, the region above the DNA may act as a clamp that holds the nucleic acids in place. (You'll learn more about this enzyme in Chapter 17.)

Source: A. L. Gnatt et al., Structural basis of transcription: an RNA polymerase II elongation complex at 3.3Å, *Science* 292:1876–1882 (2001). Computer graphic copyright © 2001 by AAAS. Reprinted with permission.

WHAT IF? *Looking at the model, can you identify any elements of secondary structure?*

CONCEPT CHECK 5.4

1. What parts of a polypeptide participate in the bonds that hold together secondary structure? Tertiary structure?

2. Thus far in the chapter, the Greek letters α and β have been used to specify at least three different pairs of structures. Name and briefly describe them.

3. **WHAT IF?** Where would you expect a polypeptide region rich in the amino acids valine, leucine, and isoleucine to be located in a folded polypeptide? Explain.

For suggested answers, see Appendix A.

Nucleic acids store, transmit, and help express hereditary information

If the primary structure of polypeptides determines a protein's shape, what determines primary structure? The amino acid sequence of a polypeptide is programmed by a discrete unit of inheritance known as a **gene**. Genes consist of DNA, which belongs to the class of compounds called nucleic acids. **Nucleic acids** are polymers made of monomers called nucleotides.

The Roles of Nucleic Acids

The two types of nucleic acids, **deoxyribonucleic acid (DNA)** and **ribonucleic acid (RNA)**, enable living organisms to reproduce their complex components from one generation to the next. Unique among molecules, DNA provides directions for its own replication. DNA also directs RNA synthesis and, through RNA, controls protein synthesis; this entire process is called **gene expression (Figure 5.23)**.

DNA is the genetic material that organisms inherit from their parents. Each chromosome contains one long DNA molecule, usually carrying several hundred or more genes. When a cell reproduces itself by dividing, its DNA molecules are copied and passed along from one generation of

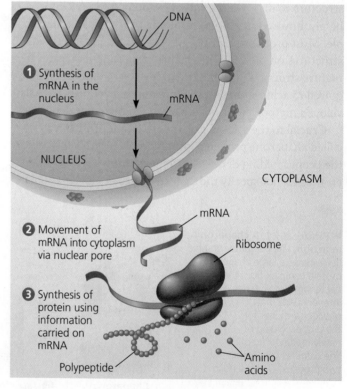

▲ **Figure 5.23 Gene expression: DNA → RNA → protein.** In a eukaryotic cell, DNA in the nucleus programs protein production in the cytoplasm by dictating synthesis of messenger RNA (mRNA).

cells to the next. Encoded in the structure of DNA is the information that programs all the cell's activities. The DNA, however, is not directly involved in running the operations of the cell, any more than computer software by itself can read the bar code on a box of cereal. Just as a scanner is needed to read a bar code, proteins are required to implement genetic programs. The molecular hardware of the cell—the tools for biological functions—consists mostly of proteins. For example, the oxygen carrier in red blood cells is the protein hemoglobin that you saw earlier (see Figure 5.17), not the DNA that specifies its structure.

How does RNA, the other type of nucleic acid, fit into gene expression, the flow of genetic information from DNA to proteins? Each gene along a DNA molecule directs synthesis of a type of RNA called *messenger RNA (mRNA)*. The mRNA molecule interacts with the cell's protein-synthesizing machinery to direct production of a polypeptide, which folds into all or part of a protein. We can summarize the flow of genetic information as DNA → RNA → protein (see Figure 5.23). The sites of protein synthesis are cellular structures called ribosomes. (In the Unit 1 interview before Chapter 2, Venki Ramakrishnan describes how the structure of ribosomes was determined by X-ray crystallography.) In a eukaryotic cell, ribosomes are in the region between the nucleus and the plasma membrane (the cytoplasm), but DNA resides in the nucleus. Messenger RNA conveys genetic instructions for building proteins from the nucleus to the cytoplasm. Prokaryotic cells lack nuclei but still use mRNA to convey a message from the DNA to ribosomes and other cellular equipment that translate the coded information into amino acid sequences. In Chapter 18, you'll read about other functions of some recently discovered RNA molecules.

The Components of Nucleic Acids

Nucleic acids are macromolecules that exist as polymers called **polynucleotides (Figure 5.24a)**. As indicated by the name, each polynucleotide consists of monomers called **nucleotides**. A nucleotide, in general, is composed of three parts: a five-carbon sugar (a pentose), a nitrogen-containing (nitrogenous) base, and one or more phosphate groups **(Figure 5.24b)**. In a polynucleotide, each monomer has only one phosphate group. The portion of a nucleotide without any phosphate groups is called a *nucleoside*.

To build a nucleotide, let's first consider the nitrogenous bases **(Figure 5.24c)**. Each nitrogenous base has one or two rings that include nitrogen atoms. (They are called nitrogenous *bases* because the nitrogen atoms tend to take up

▼ **Figure 5.24 Components of nucleic acids. (a)** A polynucleotide has a sugar-phosphate backbone with variable appendages, the nitrogenous bases. **(b)** A nucleotide monomer includes a nitrogenous base, a sugar, and a phosphate group. Note that carbon numbers in the sugar include primes ('). **(c)** A nucleoside includes a nitrogenous base (purine or pyrimidine) and a five-carbon sugar (deoxyribose or ribose).

5′ end

Sugar-phosphate backbone (on blue background)

5′C
3′C
5′C
3′C
OH

3′ end

(a) Polynucleotide, or nucleic acid

Nucleoside

Nitrogenous base

Phosphate group

5′C
CH₂
3′C
1′C
Sugar (pentose)

(b) Nucleotide

NITROGENOUS BASES

Pyrimidines

Cytosine (C)   Thymine (T, in DNA)   Uracil (U, in RNA)

Purines

Adenine (A)   Guanine (G)

SUGARS

Deoxyribose (in DNA)   Ribose (in RNA)

(c) Nucleoside components

H$^+$ from solution, thus acting as bases.) There are two families of nitrogenous bases: pyrimidines and purines. A **pyrimidine** has one six-membered ring of carbon and nitrogen atoms. The members of the pyrimidine family are cytosine (C), thymine (T), and uracil (U). **Purines** are larger, with a six-membered ring fused to a five-membered ring. The purines are adenine (A) and guanine (G). The specific pyrimidines and purines differ in the chemical groups attached to the rings. Adenine, guanine, and cytosine are found in both DNA and RNA; thymine is found only in DNA and uracil only in RNA.

Now let's add the sugar to which the nitrogenous base is attached. In DNA the sugar is **deoxyribose**; in RNA it is **ribose** (see Figure 5.24c). The only difference between these two sugars is that deoxyribose lacks an oxygen atom on the second carbon in the ring; hence the name *deoxy*ribose.

So far, we have built a nucleoside (nitrogenous base plus sugar). To complete the construction of a nucleotide, we attach a phosphate group to the 5′ carbon of the sugar (see Figure 5.24b). The molecule is now a nucleoside monophosphate, more often called a nucleotide.

Nucleotide Polymers

The linkage of nucleotides into a polynucleotide involves a dehydration reaction. (You will learn the details in Chapter 16). In the polynucleotide, adjacent nucleotides are joined by a phosphodiester linkage, which consists of a phosphate group that links the sugars of two nucleotides. This bonding results in a repeating pattern of sugar-phosphate units called the *sugar-phosphate backbone* (see Figure 5.24a). (Note that the nitrogenous bases are not part of the backbone.) The two free ends of the polymer are distinctly different from each other. One end has a phosphate attached to a 5′ carbon, and the other end has a hydroxyl group on a 3′ carbon; we refer to these as the *5′ end* and the *3′ end*, respectively. We can say that a polynucleotide has a built-in directionality along its sugar-phosphate backbone, from 5′ to 3′, somewhat like a one-way street. All along this sugar-phosphate backbone are appendages consisting of the nitrogenous bases.

The sequence of bases along a DNA (or mRNA) polymer is unique for each gene and provides very specific information to the cell. Because genes are hundreds to thousands of nucleotides long, the number of possible base sequences is effectively limitless. A gene's meaning to the cell is encoded in its specific sequence of the four DNA bases. For example, the sequence 5′-AGGTAACTT-3′ means one thing, whereas the sequence 5′-CGCTTTAAC-3′ has a different meaning. (Entire genes, of course, are much longer.) The linear order of bases in a gene specifies the amino acid sequence—the primary structure—of a protein, which in turn specifies that protein's three-dimensional structure and its function in the cell.

The Structures of DNA and RNA Molecules

DNA molecules have two polynucleotides, or "strands," that wind around an imaginary axis, forming a **double helix (Figure 5.25a)**. The two sugar-phosphate backbones run in opposite 5′ → 3′ directions from each other; this arrangement is referred to as **antiparallel**, somewhat like a divided highway. The sugar-phosphate backbones are on the outside of the helix, and the nitrogenous bases are paired in the interior of the helix. The two strands are held together by hydrogen bonds between the paired bases (see Figure 5.25a). Most DNA molecules are very long, with thousands or even millions of base pairs. For example, the one long DNA double helix in a eukaryotic chromosome includes many genes, each one a particular segment of the molecule.

In base pairing, only certain bases in the double helix are compatible with each other. Adenine (A) in one strand always pairs with thymine (T) in the other, and guanine (G) always pairs with cytosine (C). Reading the sequence of bases along one strand of the double helix would tell us the sequence of bases along the other strand. If a stretch of one strand has the base sequence 5′-AGGTCCG-3′, then the base-pairing rules tell us that the same stretch of the other strand must have the sequence 3′-TCCAGGC-5′. The two strands of the double helix are *complementary*, each the predictable counterpart of the other. It is this feature of DNA that makes it possible to generate two identical copies of each DNA molecule in a cell that is preparing to divide. When the cell divides, the copies are distributed to the daughter cells, making them genetically identical to the parent cell. Thus, the structure of DNA accounts for its function of transmitting genetic information whenever a cell reproduces.

RNA molecules, by contrast, exist as single strands. Complementary base pairing can occur, however, between regions of two RNA molecules or even between two stretches of nucleotides in the *same* RNA molecule. In fact, base pairing within an RNA molecule allows it to take on the particular three-dimensional shape necessary for its function. Consider, for example, the type of RNA called *transfer RNA (tRNA)*, which brings amino acids to the ribosome during the synthesis of a polypeptide. A tRNA molecule is about 80 nucleotides in length. Its functional shape results from base pairing between nucleotides where complementary stretches of the molecule can run antiparallel to each other **(Figure 5.25b)**.

Note that in RNA, adenine (A) pairs with uracil (U); thymine (T) is not present in RNA. Another difference between RNA and DNA is that DNA almost always exists as a double helix, whereas RNA molecules are more variable in shape. RNAs are very versatile molecules, and many biologists believe RNA may have preceded DNA as the carrier of genetic information in early forms of life (see Concept 25.1).

▶ **Figure 5.25 The structures of DNA and tRNA molecules. (a)** The DNA molecule is usually a double helix, with the sugar-phosphate backbones of the antiparallel polynucleotide strands (symbolized here by blue ribbons) on the outside of the helix. Hydrogen bonds between pairs of nitrogenous bases hold the two strands together. As illustrated here with symbolic shapes for the bases, adenine (A) can pair only with thymine (T), and guanine (G) can pair only with cytosine (C). Each DNA strand in this figure is the structural equivalent of the polynucleotide diagrammed in Figure 5.24a. **(b)** A tRNA molecule has a roughly L-shaped structure, with complementary base pairing of antiparallel stretches of RNA. In RNA, A pairs with U.

Sugar-phosphate backbones

Hydrogen bonds

Base pair joined by hydrogen bonding

Base pair joined by hydrogen bonding

(a) DNA

(b) Transfer RNA

CONCEPT CHECK 5.5

1. **DRAW IT** Go to Figure 5.24a and, for the top three nucleotides, number all the carbons in the sugars, circle the nitrogenous bases, and star the phosphates.

2. **DRAW IT** In a DNA double helix, a region along one DNA strand has this sequence of nitrogenous bases: 5'-TAGGCCT-3'. Copy this sequence, and write down its complementary strand, clearly indicating the 5' and 3' ends of the complementary strand.

For suggested answers, see Appendix A.

CONCEPT 5.6

Genomics and proteomics have transformed biological inquiry and applications

Experimental work in the first half of the 20th century established the role of DNA as the bearer of genetic information, passed from generation to generation, that specified the functioning of living cells and organisms. Once the structure of the DNA molecule was described in 1953, and the linear sequence of nucleotide bases was understood to specify the amino acid sequence of proteins, biologists sought to "decode" genes by learning their base sequences.

The first chemical techniques for *DNA sequencing*, or determining the sequence of nucleotides along a DNA strand, one by one, were developed in the 1970s. Researchers began to study gene sequences, gene by gene, and the more they learned, the more questions they had: How was expression of genes regulated? Genes and their protein products clearly interacted with each other, but how? What was the function, if any, of the DNA that is not part of genes? To fully understand the genetic functioning of a living organism, the entire sequence of the full complement of DNA, the organism's

genome, would be most enlightening. In spite of the apparent impracticality of this idea, in the late 1980s several prominent biologists put forth an audacious proposal to launch a project that would sequence the entire human genome—all 3 billion bases of it! This endeavor began in 1990 and was effectively completed in the early 2000s.

An unplanned but profound side benefit of this project—the Human Genome Project—was the rapid development of faster and less expensive methods of sequencing. This trend has continued apace: The cost for sequencing 1 million bases in 2001, well over $5,000, has decreased to less than $0.10 in 2012. And a human genome, the first of which took over 10 years to sequence, could be completed at today's pace in just a few days. The number of genomes that have been fully sequenced has burgeoned, generating reams of data and prompting development of *bioinformatics*, the use of computer software and other computational tools that can handle and analyze these large data sets.

The reverberations of these developments have transformed the study of biology and related fields. Biologists often look at problems by analyzing large sets of genes or even comparing whole genomes of different species, an approach called **genomics**. A similar analysis of large sets of proteins, including their sequences, is called **proteomics**. (Protein sequences can be determined either by using biochemical techniques or by translating the DNA sequences that code for them.) These approaches permeate all fields of biology, some examples of which are shown in **Figure 5.26**.

Perhaps the most significant impact of genomics and proteomics on the field of biology as a whole has been their contributions to our understanding of evolution. In addition to confirming evidence for evolution from the study of fossils and characteristics of currently existing species, genomics has helped us tease out relationships among different groups of organisms that had not been resolved by previous types of evidence, and thus infer evolutionary history.

Contributions of Genomics and Proteomics to Biology

Nucleotide sequencing and the analysis of large sets of genes and proteins can be done rapidly and inexpensively due to advances in technology and information processing. Taken together, genomics and proteomics have advanced our understanding of biology across many different fields.

Paleontology

New DNA sequencing techniques have allowed decoding of minute quantities of DNA found in ancient tissues from our extinct relatives, the Neanderthals (*Homo neanderthalensis*). Sequencing the Neanderthal genome has informed our understanding of their physical appearance as well as their relationship with modern humans. *See Figure 34.49.*

Medical Science

Identifying the genetic basis for human diseases like cancer helps researchers focus their search for potential future treatments. Currently, sequencing the sets of genes expressed in an individual's tumor can allow a more targeted approach to treating the cancer, a type of "personalized medicine." *See Figures 12.20 and 18.27.*

Evolution

A major aim of evolutionary biology is to understand the relationships among species, both living and extinct. For example, genome sequence comparisons have identified the hippopotamus as the land mammal sharing the most recent common ancestor with whales. *See Figure 22.20.*

Hippopotamus

Short-finned pilot whale

Conservation Biology

The tools of molecular genetics and genomics are increasingly used by ecologists to identify which species of animals and plants are killed illegally. In one case, genomic sequences of DNA from illegal shipments of elephant tusks were used to track down poachers and pinpoint the territory where they were operating. *See Figure 56.9.*

Species Interactions

Over 90% of all plant species exist in a mutually beneficial partnership with fungi that are associated with the plants' roots. Genome sequencing and analysis of gene expression in several plant-fungal pairs promise major advances in our understanding of such interactions and may have implications for agricultural practices. *(See the Scientific Skills Exercise in Chapter 31.)*

MAKE CONNECTIONS *Considering the examples provided here, describe how the approaches of genomics and proteomics help us to address a variety of biological questions.*

DNA and Proteins as Tape Measures of Evolution

EVOLUTION We are accustomed to thinking of shared traits, such as hair and milk production in mammals, as evidence of shared ancestry. Because DNA carries heritable information in the form of genes, sequences of genes and their protein products document the hereditary background of an organism. The linear sequences of nucleotides in DNA molecules are passed from parents to offspring; these sequences determine the amino acid sequences of proteins. As a result, siblings have greater similarity in their DNA and proteins than do unrelated individuals of the same species.

Given our evolutionary view of life, we can extend this concept of "molecular genealogy" to relationships between species: We would expect two species that appear to be closely related based on anatomical evidence (and possibly fossil evidence) to also share a greater proportion of their DNA and protein sequences than do less closely related species. In fact, that is the case. An example is the comparison of the β polypeptide chain of human hemoglobin with the corresponding hemoglobin polypeptide in other vertebrates. In this chain of 146 amino acids, humans and gorillas differ in just 1 amino acid, while humans and frogs, more distantly related, differ in 67 amino acids. In the **Scientific Skills Exercise**, you can apply this sort of reasoning to additional species. And this conclusion holds true as well when comparing whole genomes: The human genome is 95–98% identical to that of the chimpanzee, but only roughly 85% identical to that of the mouse, a more distant evolutionary relative. Molecular biology has added a new tape measure to the toolkit biologists use to assess evolutionary kinship.

CONCEPT CHECK 5.6

1. How would sequencing the entire genome of an organism help scientists to understand how that organism functioned?

2. Given the function of DNA, why would you expect two species with very similar traits to also have very similar genomes?

For suggested answers, see Appendix A.

SCIENTIFIC SKILLS EXERCISE

Analyzing Polypeptide Sequence Data

► Human ► Rhesus monkey ► Gibbon

Are Rhesus Monkeys or Gibbons More Closely Related to Humans? DNA and polypeptide sequences from closely related species are more similar to each other than are sequences from more distantly related species. In this exercise, you will look at amino acid sequence data for the β polypeptide chain of hemoglobin, often called β-globin. You will then interpret the data to hypothesize whether the monkey or the gibbon is more closely related to humans.

How Such Experiments Are Done Researchers can isolate the polypeptide of interest from an organism and then determine the amino acid sequence. More frequently, the DNA of the relevant gene is sequenced, and the amino acid sequence of the polypeptide is deduced from the DNA sequence of its gene.

Data from the Experiments In the data below, the letters give the sequence of the 146 amino acids in β-globin from humans, rhesus monkeys, and gibbons. Because a complete sequence would not fit on one line here, the sequences are broken into three segments. The sequences for the three different species are aligned so that you can compare them easily. For example, you can see that for all three species, the first amino acid is V (valine) and the 146th amino acid is H (histidine).

Interpret the Data

1. Scan the monkey and gibbon sequences, letter by letter, circling any amino acids that do not match the human sequence. (a) How many amino acids differ between the monkey and the human sequences? (b) Between the gibbon and human?

2. For each nonhuman species, what percent of its amino acids are identical to the human sequence of β-globin?

3. Based on these data alone, state a hypothesis for which of these two species is more closely related to humans. What is your reasoning?

4. What other evidence could you use to support your hypothesis?

MB A version of this Scientific Skills Exercise can be assigned in MasteringBiology.

Data from Human: http://www.ncbi.nlm.nih.gov/protein/AAA21113.1; rhesus monkey: http://www.ncbi.nlm.nih.gov/protein/122634; gibbon: http://www.ncbi.nlm.nih.gov/protein/122616

Species	Alignment of Amino Acid Sequences of β-globin
Human	1 VHLTPEEKSA VTALWGKVNV DEVGGEALGR LLVVYPWTQR FFESFGDLST
Monkey	1 VHLTPEEKNA VTTLWGKVNV DEVGGEALGR LLLVYPWTQR FFESFGDLSS
Gibbon	1 VHLTPEEKSA VTALWGKVNV DEVGGEALGR LLVVYPWTQR FFESFGDLST
Human	51 PDAVMGNPKV KAHGKKVLGA FSDGLAHLDN LKGTFATLSE LHCDKLHVDP
Monkey	51 PDAVMGNPKV KAHGKKVLGA FSDGLNHLDN LKGTFAQLSE LHCDKLHVDP
Gibbon	51 PDAVMGNPKV KAHGKKVLGA FSDGLAHLDN LKGTFAQLSE LHCDKLHVDP
Human	101 ENFRLLGNVL VCVLAHHFGK EFTPPVQAAY QKVVAGVANA LAHKYH
Monkey	101 ENFKLLGNVL VCVLAHHFGK EFTPQVQAAY QKVVAGVANA LAHKYH
Gibbon	101 ENFRLLGNVL VCVLAHHFGK EFTPQVQAAY QKVVAGVANA LAHKYH

CONCEPT 5.1

Macromolecules are polymers, built from monomers (pp. 67–68)

- Large carbohydrates (polysaccharides), proteins, and nucleic acids are **polymers**, which are chains of **monomers**. The components of lipids vary. Monomers form larger molecules by **dehydration reactions**, in which water molecules are released. Polymers can disassemble by the reverse process, **hydrolysis**. An immense variety of polymers can be built from a small set of monomers.

? *What is the fundamental basis for the differences between large carbohydrates, proteins, and nucleic acids?*

Large Biological Molecules	Components	Examples	Functions
CONCEPT 5.2 **Carbohydrates serve as fuel and building material (pp. 68–72)** **?** *Compare the composition, structure, and function of starch and cellulose. What role do starch and cellulose play in the human body?*	 Monosaccharide monomer	**Monosaccharides:** glucose, fructose	Fuel; carbon sources that can be converted to other molecules or combined into polymers
		Disaccharides: lactose, sucrose	
		Polysaccharides: • Cellulose (plants) • Starch (plants) • Glycogen (animals) • Chitin (animals and fungi)	• Strengthens plant cell walls • Stores glucose for energy • Stores glucose for energy • Strengthens exoskeletons and fungal cell walls
CONCEPT 5.3 **Lipids are a diverse group of hydrophobic molecules (pp. 72–75)** **?** *Why are lipids not considered to be polymers or macromolecules?*	 Glycerol, 3 fatty acids	**Triacylglycerols** (fats or oils): glycerol + 3 fatty acids	Important energy source
	 Head with P, 2 fatty acids	**Phospholipids:** glycerol + phosphate group + 2 fatty acids	Lipid bilayers of membranes Hydrophobic tails Hydrophilic heads
	 Steroid backbone	**Steroids:** four fused rings with attached chemical groups	• Component of cell membranes (cholesterol) • Signaling molecules that travel through the body (hormones)
CONCEPT 5.4 **Proteins include a diversity of structures, resulting in a wide range of functions (pp. 75–84)** **?** *Explain the basis for the great diversity of proteins.*	 Amino acid monomer (20 types)	• Enzymes • Structural proteins • Hormones • Receptor proteins • Motor proteins • Defensive proteins	• Catalyze chemical reactions • Provide structural support • Coordinate organismal responses • Receive signals from outside cell • Function in cell movement • Protect against disease
CONCEPT 5.5 **Nucleic acids store, transmit, and help express hereditary information (pp. 84–87)** **?** *What role does complementary base pairing play in the functions of nucleic acids?*	 Nitrogenous base, Phosphate group, Sugar Nucleotide monomer	**DNA:** • Sugar = deoxyribose • Nitrogenous bases = C, G, A, T • Usually double-stranded	Stores hereditary information
		RNA: • Sugar = ribose • Nitrogenous bases = C, G, A, U • Usually single-stranded	Various functions in gene expression, including carrying instructions from DNA to ribosomes

Genomics and proteomics have transformed biological inquiry and applications (pp. 87–89)

- Recent technological advances in DNA sequencing have given rise to **genomics**, an approach that analyzes large sets of genes or whole genomes, and **proteomics**, a similar approach for large sets of proteins. Bioinformatics is the use of computational tools and computer software to analyze these large data sets.
- The more closely two species are related evolutionarily, the more similar their DNA sequences are. DNA sequence data confirms models of evolution based on fossils and anatomical evidence.

? *Given the sequences of a particular gene in fruit flies, fish, mice, and humans, predict the relative similarity of the human sequence to that of each of the other species.*

TEST YOUR UNDERSTANDING

LEVEL 1: KNOWLEDGE/COMPREHENSION

1. Which of the following categories includes all others in the list?
   a. monosaccharide
   b. polysaccharide
   c. starch
   d. carbohydrate

2. The enzyme amylase can break glycosidic linkages between glucose monomers only if the monomers are in the α form. Which of the following could amylase break down?
   a. glycogen, starch, and amylopectin
   b. glycogen and cellulose
   c. cellulose and chitin
   d. starch, chitin, and cellulose

3. Which of the following is true of *unsaturated* fats?
   a. They are more common in animals than in plants.
   b. They have double bonds in the carbon chains of their fatty acids.
   c. They generally solidify at room temperature.
   d. They contain more hydrogen than do saturated fats having the same number of carbon atoms.

4. The structural level of a protein *least* affected by a disruption in hydrogen bonding is the
   a. primary level.
   b. secondary level.
   c. tertiary level.
   d. quaternary level.

5. Enzymes that break down DNA catalyze the hydrolysis of the covalent bonds that join nucleotides together. What would happen to DNA molecules treated with these enzymes?
   a. The two strands of the double helix would separate.
   b. The phosphodiester linkages of the polynucleotide backbone would be broken.
   c. The pyrimidines would be separated from the deoxyribose sugars.
   d. All bases would be separated from the deoxyribose sugars.

LEVEL 2: APPLICATION/ANALYSIS

6. The molecular formula for glucose is $C_6H_{12}O_6$. What would be the molecular formula for a polymer made by linking ten glucose molecules together by dehydration reactions?
   a. $C_{60}H_{120}O_{60}$
   b. $C_{60}H_{102}O_{51}$
   c. $C_{60}H_{100}O_{50}$
   d. $C_{60}H_{111}O_{51}$

7. Which of the following pairs of base sequences could form a short stretch of a normal double helix of DNA?
   a. 5′-AGCT-3′ with 5′-TCGA-3′
   b. 5′-GCGC-3′ with 5′-TATA-3′
   c. 5′-ATGC-3′ with 5′-GCAT-3′
   d. All of these pairs are correct.

8. Construct a table that organizes the following terms, and label the columns and rows.

Monosaccharides	Polypeptides	Phosphodiester linkages
Fatty acids	Triacylglycerols	Peptide bonds
Amino acids	Polynucleotides	Glycosidic linkages
Nucleotides	Polysaccharides	Ester linkages

9. **DRAW IT** Copy the polynucleotide strand in Figure 5.24a and label the bases G, T, C, and T, starting from the 5′ end. Assuming this is a DNA polynucleotide, now draw the complementary strand, using the same symbols for phosphates (circles), sugars (pentagons), and bases. Label the bases. Draw arrows showing the 5′ → 3′ direction of each strand. Use the arrows to make sure the second strand is antiparallel to the first. *Hint*: After you draw the first strand vertically, turn the paper upside down; it is easier to draw the second strand from the 5′ toward the 3′ direction as you go from top to bottom.

LEVEL 3: SYNTHESIS/EVALUATION

10. **EVOLUTION CONNECTION**
    Comparisons of amino acid sequences can shed light on the evolutionary divergence of related species. If you were comparing two living species, would you expect all proteins to show the same degree of divergence? Why or why not?

11. **SCIENTIFIC INQUIRY**
    Suppose you are a research assistant in a lab studying DNA-binding proteins. You have been given the amino acid sequences of all the proteins encoded by the genome of a certain species and have been asked to find candidate proteins that could bind DNA. What type of amino acids would you expect to see in the DNA-binding regions of such proteins? Why?

12. **WRITE ABOUT A THEME: ORGANIZATION**
    Proteins, which have diverse functions in a cell, are all polymers of the same kinds of monomers—amino acids. Write a short essay (100–150 words) that discusses how the structure of amino acids allows this one type of polymer to perform so many functions.

13. **SYNTHESIZE YOUR KNOWLEDGE**

Given that the function of egg yolk is to nourish and support the developing chick, explain why egg yolks are so high in fat, protein, and cholesterol.

For selected answers, see Appendix A.

MasteringBiology®

Students Go to **MasteringBiology** for assignments, the eText, and the Study Area with practice tests, animations, and activities.

Instructors Go to **MasteringBiology** for automatically graded tutorials and questions that you can assign to your students, plus Instructor Resources.

2 THE CELL

AN INTERVIEW WITH

Haifan Lin

Born in China, Haifan Lin majored in biochemistry at Fudan University in Shanghai. He then earned a Ph.D. in genetics and development from Cornell University and was a postdoctoral fellow at the Carnegie Institution of Washington (now the Carnegie Institution for Science). There, he started using the fruit fly (*Drosophila melanogaster*) as a model to explore fundamental questions in stem cells. Dr. Lin then spent 12 years as a faculty member at Duke University, broadening his study of stem cells by working on mammalian models and clinical applications. He is one of the discoverers of Piwi-interacting RNAs, a finding that was heralded by *Science* magazine as a Discovery of the Year in 2006. That same year, Dr. Lin moved to Yale University, where he founded and now directs the Yale Stem Cell Center.

"If we hadn't started by working on basic cell biology in *Drosophila*, I don't think we could have found this connection to cancer so quickly."

How did you get interested in science?

As a child I liked to build things, so I imagined myself a ship builder or an architect, something like that. I didn't get attracted to biology until high school. Genetic engineering had become a very fashionable term in China, and I thought, "That's cool. That's the engineering of life." I was more attracted by the word "engineering" than "genetics." However, people told me it was important to have a solid biochemistry foundation in order to become a genetic engineer, so I became a biochemistry major in college. And the more I learned about biology, the more I loved it.

◀ Cross section of a tubule in the testis of a mouse, showing the Piwi protein (red-orange in this fluorescence micrograph).

What did you study in graduate school and as a postdoc?

At Cornell, I thought about the very first cell division of the embryo. To me, it's literally the first step of life—the division of a fertilized egg. Working on a cell division process with developmental significance was really intellectually rewarding. For my postdoc, I felt that I should continue to study cell division with developmental consequences but expand to a different cell type, so I turned to stem cells.

What is a stem cell?

Stem cells are really the mother of all cells. Embryonic stem cells lead to the development of all tissues—the entire adult body. Tissue stem cells are responsible for the generation and/or maintenance of a specific tissue. All stem cells share a unique property—they can self-renew (reproduce) as well as give rise to more specialized cells. In theory, stem cells are immortal; they are like a fountain of youth that goes on and on.

How do you study stem cells?

To study stem cells, you have to identify the cell unambiguously, so cell biology is the first step. Cell biology defines a problem, describes the phenomenon, and provides the biological context for further mechanistic studies. It's crucially important. Then we move on to genetics, and, in my style of research, biochemistry usually comes as a third component.

What is the most interesting thing you have discovered about stem cells?

Using the genetic approach, we found a fruit fly (*Drosophila*) gene that encodes a protein called Piwi. The Piwi protein is also required in mammalian stem cells that make the testis (see micrograph). Piwi proteins bind to a kind of small RNA we and others independently discovered and called Piwi-interacting RNAs (or piRNAs). One of the wonderful things about working with fruit flies is that as soon as you identify new genes in flies and confirm that they function in stem cells, you can immediately look in humans to see whether these same genes become overactivated in cancer. It turns out the human Piwi gene is expressed at least sixfold more in a common kind of testicular cancer. We published the Piwi gene family in 1998, and amazingly, in 2002, we already had the results on this human cancer. If we hadn't started by working on basic cell biology in *Drosophila*, I don't think we could have found this connection to cancer so quickly.

(MB) For an extended interview and video clip, go to the Study Area in MasteringBiology.

6

A Tour of the Cell

KEY CONCEPTS

6.1 Biologists use microscopes and the tools of biochemistry to study cells

6.2 Eukaryotic cells have internal membranes that compartmentalize their functions

6.3 The eukaryotic cell's genetic instructions are housed in the nucleus and carried out by the ribosomes

6.4 The endomembrane system regulates protein traffic and performs metabolic functions in the cell

6.5 Mitochondria and chloroplasts change energy from one form to another

6.6 The cytoskeleton is a network of fibers that organizes structures and activities in the cell

6.7 Extracellular components and connections between cells help coordinate cellular activities

▲ Figure 6.1 How do your cells help you learn about biology?

The Fundamental Units of Life

Cells are as fundamental to the living systems of biology as the atom is to chemistry. Many different types of cells are working for you right now. The contraction of muscle cells moves your eyes as you read this sentence. **Figure 6.1** shows extensions from a nerve cell (orange) making contact with muscle cells (red). The words on the page are translated into signals that nerve cells carry to your brain, where they are passed on to other nerve cells. As you study, you are making cell connections like these that solidify memories and permit learning to occur.

All organisms are made of cells. In the hierarchy of biological organization, the cell is the simplest collection of matter that can be alive. Indeed, many forms of life exist as single-celled organisms. Larger, more complex organisms, including plants and animals, are multicellular; their bodies are cooperatives of many kinds of specialized cells that could not survive for long on their own. Even when cells are arranged into higher levels of organization, such as tissues and organs, the cell remains the organism's basic unit of structure and function.

All cells are related by their descent from earlier cells. During the long evolutionary history of life on Earth, cells have been modified in many different ways. But although cells can differ substantially from one another, they share common features. In this chapter, we'll first examine the tools and techniques that allow us to understand cells, then tour the cell and become acquainted with its components.

93

CONCEPT 6.1

Biologists use microscopes and the tools of biochemistry to study cells

Dr. Haifan Lin, featured in the interview before this chapter, points out that studying the inner workings of cells is often the first step in making exciting biological discoveries. But how do we study cells, usually too small to be seen by the unaided eye?

Microscopy

The development of instruments that extend the human senses allowed the discovery and early study of cells. Microscopes were invented in 1590 and further refined during the 1600s. Cell walls were first seen by Robert Hooke in 1665 as he looked through a microscope at dead cells from the bark of an oak tree. But it took the wonderfully crafted lenses of Antoni van Leeuwenhoek to visualize living cells. Imagine Hooke's awe when he visited van Leeuwenhoek in 1674 and the world of microorganisms—what his host called "very little animalcules"—was revealed to him.

The microscopes first used by Renaissance scientists, as well as the microscopes you are likely to use in the laboratory, are all light microscopes. In a **light microscope (LM)**, visible light is passed through the specimen and then through glass lenses. The lenses refract (bend) the light in such a way that the image of the specimen is magnified as it is projected into the eye or into a camera (see Appendix D).

Three important parameters in microscopy are magnification, resolution, and contrast. *Magnification* is the ratio of an object's image size to its real size. Light microscopes can magnify effectively to about 1,000 times the actual size of the specimen; at greater magnifications, additional details cannot be seen clearly. *Resolution* is a measure of the clarity of the image; it is the minimum distance two points can be separated and still be distinguished as separate points. For example, what appears to the unaided eye as one star in the sky may be resolved as twin stars with a telescope, which has a higher resolving ability than the eye. Similarly, using standard techniques, the light microscope cannot resolve detail finer than about 0.2 micrometer (μm), or 200 nanometers (nm), regardless of the magnification **(Figure 6.2)**. The third parameter, *contrast*, is the difference in brightness between the light and dark areas of an image. Methods for enhancing contrast include staining or labeling cell components to stand out visually. **Figure 6.3** shows some different types of microscopy; study this figure as you read this section.

Until recently, the resolution barrier prevented cell biologists from using standard light microscopy when studying **organelles**, the membrane-enclosed structures within eukaryotic cells. To see these structures in any detail required the development of a new instrument. In the 1950s, the electron microscope was introduced to biology. Rather than

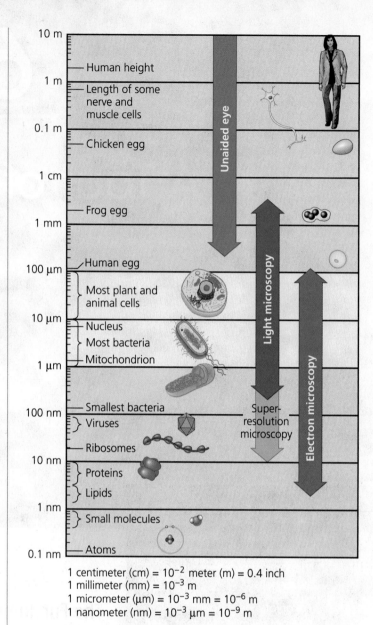

1 centimeter (cm) = 10^{-2} meter (m) = 0.4 inch
1 millimeter (mm) = 10^{-3} m
1 micrometer (μm) = 10^{-3} mm = 10^{-6} m
1 nanometer (nm) = 10^{-3} μm = 10^{-9} m

▲ **Figure 6.2 The size range of cells.** Most cells are between 1 and 100 μm in diameter (yellow region of chart) and their components are even smaller, as are viruses. Notice that the scale along the left side is logarithmic, to accommodate the range of sizes shown. Starting at the top of the scale with 10 m and going down, each reference measurement marks a tenfold decrease in diameter or length. For a complete table of the metric system, see Appendix C.

focusing light, the **electron microscope (EM)** focuses a beam of electrons through the specimen or onto its surface (see Appendix D). Resolution is inversely related to the wavelength of the light (or electrons) a microscope uses for imaging, and electron beams have much shorter wavelengths than visible light. Modern electron microscopes can theoretically achieve a resolution of about 0.002 nm, though in practice they usually cannot resolve structures smaller than about 2 nm across. Still, this is a 100-fold improvement over the standard light microscope.

The **scanning electron microscope (SEM)** is especially useful for detailed study of the topography of a specimen

Light Microscopy (LM)

Brightfield (unstained specimen). Light passes directly through the specimen. Unless the cell is naturally pigmented or artificially stained, the image has little contrast. (The first four light micrographs show human cheek epithelial cells; the scale bar pertains to all four micrographs.)

Brightfield (stained specimen). Staining with various dyes enhances contrast. Most staining procedures require that cells be fixed (preserved), thereby killing them.

Phase-contrast. Variations in density within the specimen are amplified to enhance contrast in unstained cells; this is especially useful for examining living, unpigmented cells.

Differential-interference-contrast (Nomarski). As in phase-contrast microscopy, optical modifications are used to exaggerate differences in density; the image appears almost 3-D.

Fluorescence. The locations of specific molecules in the cell can be revealed by labeling the molecules with fluorescent dyes or antibodies; some cells have molecules that fluoresce on their own. Fluorescent substances absorb ultraviolet radiation and emit visible light. In this fluorescently labeled uterine cell, nuclear material is blue, organelles called mitochondria are orange, and the cell's "skeleton" is green.

Confocal. The top image is a standard fluorescence micrograph of fluorescently labeled nervous tissue (nerve cells are green, support cells are orange, and regions of overlap are yellow); below it is a confocal image of the same tissue. Using a laser, this "optical sectioning" technique eliminates out-of-focus light from a thick sample, creating a single plane of fluorescence in the image. By capturing sharp images at many different planes, a 3-D reconstruction can be created. The standard image is blurry because out-of-focus light is not excluded.

Deconvolution. The top of this split image is a compilation of standard fluorescence micrographs through the depth of a white blood cell. Below is an image of the same cell reconstructed from many blurry images at different planes, each of which was processed using deconvolution software. This process digitally removes out-of-focus light and reassigns it to its source, creating a much sharper 3-D image.

Super-resolution. On the top is a confocal image of part of a nerve cell, using a fluorescent label that binds to a molecule clustered in small sacs in the cell (vesicles) that are 40 nm in diameter. The greenish-yellow spots are blurry because 40 nm is below the 200-nm limit of resolution for standard light microscopy. Below is an image of the same part of the cell, seen using a new super-resolution technique. Sophisticated equipment is used to light up individual fluorescent molecules and record their position. Combining information from many molecules in different places "breaks" the limit of resolution, resulting in the sharp greenish-yellow dots seen here. (Each dot is a 40-nm vesicle.)

Electron Microscopy (EM)

Scanning electron microscopy (SEM). Micrographs taken with a scanning electron microscope show a 3-D image of the surface of a specimen. This SEM shows the surface of a cell from a trachea (windpipe) covered with cilia. Beating of the cilia helps move inhaled debris upward toward the throat. Electron micrographs are black and white, but are often artificially colorized to highlight particular structures, as has been done with both micrographs (SEM and TEM) shown here.

Abbreviations used in figure legends in this book:
LM = Light Micrograph
SEM = Scanning Electron Micrograph
TEM = Transmission Electron Micrograph

Cilia

Longitudinal section of cilium   Cross section of cilium

Transmission electron microscopy (TEM). A transmission electron microscope profiles a thin section of a specimen. Here we see a section through a tracheal cell, revealing its internal structure. In preparing the specimen, some cilia were cut along their lengths, creating longitudinal sections, while other cilia were cut straight across, creating cross sections.

(see Figure 6.3). The electron beam scans the surface of the sample, usually coated with a thin film of gold. The beam excites electrons on the surface, and these secondary electrons are detected by a device that translates the pattern of electrons into an electronic signal sent to a video screen. The result is an image of the specimen's surface that appears three-dimensional.

The **transmission electron microscope (TEM)** is used to study the internal structure of cells (see Figure 6.3). The TEM aims an electron beam through a very thin section of the specimen, much as a light microscope aims light through a sample on a slide. For the TEM, the specimen has been stained with atoms of heavy metals, which attach to certain cellular structures, thus enhancing the electron density of some parts of the cell more than others. The electrons passing through the specimen are scattered more in the denser regions, so fewer are transmitted. The image displays the pattern of transmitted electrons. Instead of using glass lenses, both the SEM and TEM use electromagnets as lenses to bend the paths of the electrons, ultimately focusing the image onto a monitor for viewing.

Electron microscopes have revealed many subcellular structures that were impossible to resolve with the light microscope. But the light microscope offers advantages, especially in studying living cells. A disadvantage of electron microscopy is that the methods used to prepare the specimen kill the cells. Specimen preparation for any type of microscopy can introduce artifacts, structural features seen in micrographs that do not exist in the living cell.

In the past several decades, light microscopy has been revitalized by major technical advances (see Figure 6.3). Labeling individual cellular molecules or structures with fluorescent markers has made it possible to see such structures with increasing detail. In addition, both confocal and deconvolution microscopy have produced sharper images of three-dimensional tissues and cells. Finally, a group of new techniques and labeling molecules developed in recent years have allowed researchers to "break" the resolution barrier and distinguish subcellular structures as small as 10–20 nm across. As this *super-resolution microscopy* becomes more widespread, the images we see of living cells are proving as awe-inspiring to us as van Leeuwenhoek's were to Robert Hooke 350 years ago.

Microscopes are the most important tools of *cytology*, the study of cell structure. Understanding the function of each structure, however, required the integration of cytology and *biochemistry*, the study of the chemical processes (metabolism) of cells.

Cell Fractionation

A useful technique for studying cell structure and function is **cell fractionation (Figure 6.4)**, which takes cells apart

▼ **Figure 6.4** **Research Method**

Cell Fractionation

Application Cell fractionation is used to isolate (fractionate) cell components based on size and density.

Technique Cells are homogenized in a blender to break them up. The resulting mixture (homogenate) is centrifuged. The supernatant (liquid) is poured into another tube and centrifuged at a higher speed for a longer period. This process is repeated several times. This "differential centrifugation" results in a series of pellets, each containing different cell components.

Tissue cells

Homogenization

Homogenate

Centrifugation

Centrifuged at 1,000 *g* (1,000 times the force of gravity) for 10 min

Supernatant poured into next tube

Differential centrifugation

20,000 *g* 20 min

80,000 *g* 60 min

150,000 *g* 3 hr

Pellet rich in nuclei and cellular debris

Pellet rich in mitochondria (and chloroplasts if cells are from a plant)

Pellet rich in "microsomes" (pieces of plasma membranes and cells' internal membranes)

Pellet rich in ribosomes

Results In early experiments, researchers used microscopy to identify the organelles in each pellet and biochemical methods to determine their metabolic functions. These identifications established a baseline for this method, enabling today's researchers to know which cell fraction they should collect in order to isolate and study particular organelles.

and separates major organelles and other subcellular structures from one another. The piece of equipment that is used for this task is the centrifuge, which spins test tubes holding mixtures of disrupted cells at a series of increasing speeds. At each speed, the resulting force causes a subset of the cell components to settle to the bottom of the tube, forming a pellet. At lower speeds, the pellet consists of larger components, and higher speeds result in a pellet with smaller components.

Cell fractionation enables researchers to prepare specific cell components in bulk and identify their functions, a task not usually possible with intact cells. For example, on one of the cell fractions, biochemical tests showed the presence of enzymes involved in cellular respiration, while electron microscopy revealed large numbers of the organelles called mitochondria. Together, these data helped biologists determine that mitochondria are the sites of cellular respiration. Biochemistry and cytology thus complement each other in correlating cell function with structure.

CONCEPT CHECK 6.1

1. How do stains used for light microscopy compare with those used for electron microscopy?
2. **WHAT IF?** Which type of microscope would you use to study (a) the changes in shape of a living white blood cell and (b) the details of surface texture of a hair?

For suggested answers, see Appendix A.

CONCEPT 6.2

Eukaryotic cells have internal membranes that compartmentalize their functions

Cells—the basic structural and functional units of every organism—are of two distinct types: prokaryotic and eukaryotic. Organisms of the domains Bacteria and Archaea consist of prokaryotic cells. Protists, fungi, animals, and plants all consist of eukaryotic cells. ("Protist" is an informal term referring to a group of mostly unicellular eukaryotes.)

Comparing Prokaryotic and Eukaryotic Cells

All cells share certain basic features: They are all bounded by a selective barrier, called the *plasma membrane*. Inside all cells is a semifluid, jellylike substance called **cytosol**, in which subcellular components are suspended. All cells contain *chromosomes*, which carry genes in the form of DNA. And all cells have *ribosomes*, tiny complexes that make proteins according to instructions from the genes.

A major difference between prokaryotic and eukaryotic cells is the location of their DNA. In a **eukaryotic cell**, most of the DNA is in an organelle called the *nucleus*, which is bounded by a double membrane (see Figure 6.8). In a **prokaryotic cell**, the DNA is concentrated in a region that is not membrane-enclosed, called the **nucleoid (Figure 6.5)**.

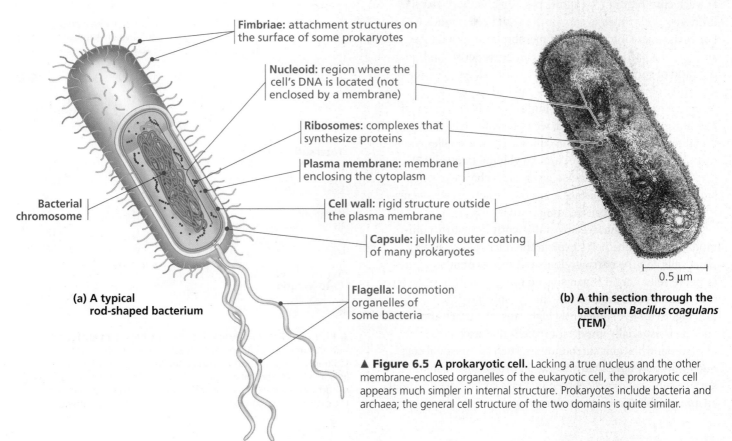

Fimbriae: attachment structures on the surface of some prokaryotes

Nucleoid: region where the cell's DNA is located (not enclosed by a membrane)

Ribosomes: complexes that synthesize proteins

Plasma membrane: membrane enclosing the cytoplasm

Cell wall: rigid structure outside the plasma membrane

Capsule: jellylike outer coating of many prokaryotes

Bacterial chromosome

Flagella: locomotion organelles of some bacteria

(a) A typical rod-shaped bacterium

0.5 μm

(b) A thin section through the bacterium *Bacillus coagulans* (TEM)

▲ **Figure 6.5 A prokaryotic cell.** Lacking a true nucleus and the other membrane-enclosed organelles of the eukaryotic cell, the prokaryotic cell appears much simpler in internal structure. Prokaryotes include bacteria and archaea; the general cell structure of the two domains is quite similar.

Eukaryotic means "true nucleus" (from the Greek *eu*, true, and *karyon*, kernel, referring to the nucleus), and *prokaryotic* means "before nucleus" (from the Greek *pro*, before), reflecting the earlier evolution of prokaryotic cells.

The interior of either type of cell is called the **cytoplasm**; in eukaryotic cells, this term refers only to the region between the nucleus and the plasma membrane. Within the cytoplasm of a eukaryotic cell, suspended in cytosol, are a variety of organelles of specialized form and function. These membrane-bounded structures are absent in prokaryotic cells, another distinction between prokaryotic and eukaryotic cells. However, in spite of the absence of organelles, the prokaryotic cytoplasm is not a formless soup of cytoplasm, but appears to be organized into different regions.

Eukaryotic cells are generally much larger than prokaryotic cells (see Figure 6.2). Size is a general feature of cell structure that relates to function. The logistics of carrying out cellular metabolism sets limits on cell size. At the lower limit, the smallest cells known are bacteria called mycoplasmas, which have diameters between 0.1 and 1.0 μm. These are perhaps the smallest packages with enough DNA to program metabolism and enough enzymes and other cellular equipment to carry out the activities necessary for a cell to sustain itself and reproduce. Typical bacteria are 1–5 μm in diameter, about ten times the size of mycoplasmas. Eukaryotic cells are typically 10–100 μm in diameter.

Metabolic requirements also impose theoretical upper limits on the size that is practical for a single cell. At the boundary of every cell, the **plasma membrane** functions as a selective barrier that allows passage of enough oxygen, nutrients, and wastes to service the entire cell **(Figure 6.6)**. For each square micrometer of membrane, only a limited amount of a particular substance can cross per second, so the ratio of surface area to volume is critical. As a cell (or any other object) increases in size, its surface area grows proportionately less than its volume. (Area is proportional to a linear dimension squared, whereas volume is proportional to the linear dimension cubed.) Thus, a smaller object has a greater ratio of surface area to volume **(Figure 6.7)**. The Scientific Skills Exercise gives you a chance to calculate the volumes and surface areas of two actual cells—a mature yeast cell and a cell budding from it.

The need for a surface area sufficiently large to accommodate the volume helps explain the microscopic size of most cells and the narrow, elongated shapes of others, such as nerve cells. Larger organisms do not generally have *larger* cells than smaller organisms—they simply have *more* cells (see Figure 6.7). A sufficiently high ratio of surface area to volume is especially important in cells that exchange a lot of material with their surroundings, such as intestinal cells. Such cells may have many long, thin projections from their surface called *microvilli*, which increase surface area without an appreciable increase in volume.

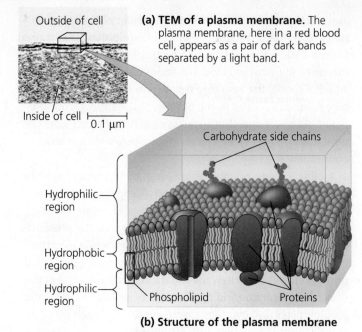

(a) **TEM of a plasma membrane.** The plasma membrane, here in a red blood cell, appears as a pair of dark bands separated by a light band.

Outside of cell

Inside of cell

Carbohydrate side chains

Hydrophilic region

Hydrophobic region

Hydrophilic region

Phospholipid

Proteins

(b) **Structure of the plasma membrane**

© Pearson Education, Inc.

▲ **Figure 6.6 The plasma membrane.** The plasma membrane and the membranes of organelles consist of a double layer (bilayer) of phospholipids with various proteins attached to or embedded in it. The hydrophobic parts of phospholipids and membrane proteins are found in the interior of the membrane, while the hydrophilic parts are in contact with aqueous solutions on either side. Carbohydrate side chains may be attached to proteins or lipids on the outer surface of the plasma membrane.

MAKE CONNECTIONS *Review Figure 5.11 and describe the characteristics of phospholipids that allow them to function as the major components of the plasma membrane.*

Surface area increases while total volume remains constant

Total surface area [sum of the surface areas (height × width) of all box sides × number of boxes]	6	150	750
Total volume [height × width × length × number of boxes]	1	125	125
Surface-to-volume (S-to-V) ratio [surface area ÷ volume]	6	1.2	6

▲ **Figure 6.7 Geometric relationships between surface area and volume.** In this diagram, cells are represented as boxes. Using arbitrary units of length, we can calculate the cell's surface area (in square units, or units^2), volume (in cubic units, or units^3), and ratio of surface area to volume. A high surface-to-volume ratio facilitates the exchange of materials between a cell and its environment.

Using a Scale Bar to Calculate Volume and Surface Area of a Cell

How Much New Cytoplasm and Plasma Membrane Are Made by a Growing Yeast Cell? The unicellular yeast *Saccharomyces cerevisiae* divides by budding off a small new cell that then grows to full size (see the yeast cells at the bottom of Figure 6.8). During its growth, the new cell synthesizes new cytoplasm, which increases its volume, and new plasma membrane, which increases its surface area. In this exercise, you will use a scale bar to determine the sizes of a mature parent yeast cell and a cell budding from it. You will then calculate the volume and surface area of each cell. You will use your calculations to determine how much cytoplasm and plasma membrane the new cell needs to synthesize to grow to full size.

How the Experiment Was Done Yeast cells were grown under conditions that promoted division by budding. The cells were then viewed with a differential interference contrast light microscope and photographed.

Data from the Experiment This light micrograph shows a budding yeast cell about to be released from the mature parent cell:

Mature parent cell

Budding cell

1 µm

Interpret the Data

1. Examine the micrograph of the yeast cells. The scale bar under the photo is labeled 1 µm. The scale bar works in the same way as a scale on a map, where, for example, 1 inch equals 1 mile. In this case the bar represents one thousandth of a millimeter. Using the scale bar as a basic unit, determine the diameter of the mature parent cell and the

new cell. Start by measuring the scale bar and then the diameter of each cell. The units you use are irrelevant, but working in millimeters is convenient. Divide each diameter by the length of the scale bar and then multiply by the scale bar's length value to give you the diameter in micrometers.

2. The shape of a yeast cell can be approximated by a sphere. (a) Calculate the volume of each cell using the formula for the volume of a sphere:

$$V = \frac{4}{3} \pi r^3$$

Note that π (the Greek letter pi) is a constant with an approximate value of 3.14, *d* stands for diameter, and *r* stands for radius, which is half the diameter. (b) How much new cytoplasm will the new cell have to synthesize as it matures? To determine this, calculate the difference between the volume of the full-sized cell and the volume of the new cell.

3. As the new cell grows, its plasma membrane needs to expand to contain the increased volume of the cell. (a) Calculate the surface area of each cell using the formula for the surface area of a sphere: $A = 4\pi r^2$. (b) How much area of new plasma membrane will the new cell have to synthesize as it matures?

4. When the new cell matures, it will be approximately how many times greater in volume and how many times greater in surface area than its current size?

Micrograph from Kelly Tatchell, using yeast cells grown for experiments described in L. Kozubowski et al., Role of the septin ring in the asymmetric localization of proteins at the mother-bud neck in *Saccharomyces cerevisiae*, *Molecular Biology of the Cell* 16:3455–3466 (2005).

(MB) A version of this Scientific Skills Exercise can be assigned in MasteringBiology.

The evolutionary relationships between prokaryotic and eukaryotic cells will be discussed later in this chapter, and prokaryotic cells will be described in detail in Chapter 27. Most of the discussion of cell structure that follows in this chapter applies to eukaryotic cells.

A Panoramic View of the Eukaryotic Cell

In addition to the plasma membrane at its outer surface, a eukaryotic cell has extensive, elaborately arranged internal membranes that divide the cell into compartments—the organelles mentioned earlier. The cell's compartments provide different local environments that support specific metabolic functions, so incompatible processes can occur simultaneously in a single cell. The plasma membrane and organelle membranes also participate directly in the cell's metabolism, because many enzymes are built right into the membranes.

The basic fabric of most biological membranes is a double layer of phospholipids and other lipids. Embedded in this lipid bilayer or attached to its surfaces are diverse proteins (see Figure 6.6). However, each type of membrane has a unique composition of lipids and proteins suited to that membrane's specific functions. For example, enzymes embedded in the membranes of the organelles called mitochondria function in cellular respiration. Because membranes are so fundamental to the organization of the cell, Chapter 7 will discuss them in detail.

Before continuing with this chapter, examine the eukaryotic cells in **Figure 6.8**, on the next two pages. The generalized diagrams of an animal cell and a plant cell introduce the various organelles and show the key differences between animal and plant cells. The micrographs at the bottom of the figure give you a glimpse of cells from different types of eukaryotic organisms.

Exploring Eukaryotic Cells

Animal Cell (cutaway view of generalized cell)

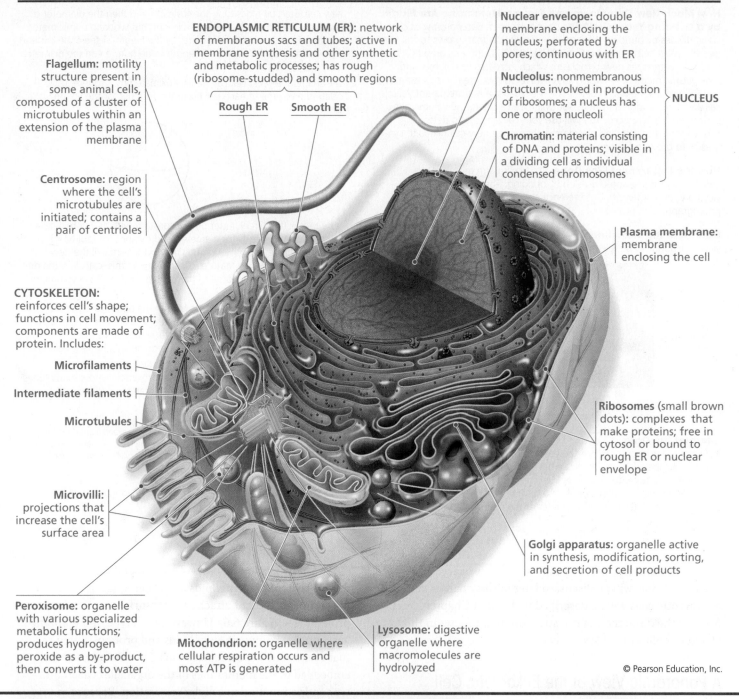

Flagellum: motility structure present in some animal cells, composed of a cluster of microtubules within an extension of the plasma membrane

ENDOPLASMIC RETICULUM (ER): network of membranous sacs and tubes; active in membrane synthesis and other synthetic and metabolic processes; has rough (ribosome-studded) and smooth regions

Rough ER   Smooth ER

Nuclear envelope: double membrane enclosing the nucleus; perforated by pores; continuous with ER

Nucleolus: nonmembranous structure involved in production of ribosomes; a nucleus has one or more nucleoli

NUCLEUS

Chromatin: material consisting of DNA and proteins; visible in a dividing cell as individual condensed chromosomes

Centrosome: region where the cell's microtubules are initiated; contains a pair of centrioles

Plasma membrane: membrane enclosing the cell

CYTOSKELETON: reinforces cell's shape; functions in cell movement; components are made of protein. Includes:

Microfilaments

Intermediate filaments

Microtubules

Ribosomes (small brown dots): complexes that make proteins; free in cytosol or bound to rough ER or nuclear envelope

Microvilli: projections that increase the cell's surface area

Golgi apparatus: organelle active in synthesis, modification, sorting, and secretion of cell products

Peroxisome: organelle with various specialized metabolic functions; produces hydrogen peroxide as a by-product, then converts it to water

Mitochondrion: organelle where cellular respiration occurs and most ATP is generated

Lysosome: digestive organelle where macromolecules are hydrolyzed

© Pearson Education, Inc.

Animal Cells

Cell

Nucleus

Nucleolus

Human cells from lining of uterus (colorized TEM)

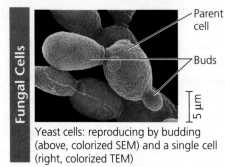

Fungal Cells

Parent cell

Buds

Yeast cells: reproducing by budding (above, colorized SEM) and a single cell (right, colorized TEM)

1 μm

Cell wall

Vacuole

Nucleus

Mitochondrion

Plant Cell (cutaway view of generalized cell)

NUCLEUS
- Nuclear envelope
- Nucleolus
- Chromatin

Rough endoplasmic reticulum

Smooth endoplasmic reticulum

ANIMATION

BioFlix Visit the Study Area in **MasteringBiology** for the BioFlix® 3-D Animations Tour of an Animal Cell and Tour of a Plant Cell. BioFlix Tutorials can also be assigned in MasteringBiology.

Ribosomes (small brown dots)

Central vacuole: prominent organelle in older plant cells; functions include storage, breakdown of waste products, and hydrolysis of macromolecules; enlargement of the vacuole is a major mechanism of plant growth

Golgi apparatus

Microfilaments
Microtubules } **CYTOSKELETON**

Mitochondrion

Peroxisome

Plasma membrane

Cell wall: outer layer that maintains cell's shape and protects cell from mechanical damage; made of cellulose, other polysaccharides, and protein

Wall of adjacent cell

Chloroplast: photosynthetic organelle; converts energy of sunlight to chemical energy stored in sugar molecules

Plasmodesmata: cytoplasmic channels through cell walls that connect the cytoplasms of adjacent cells

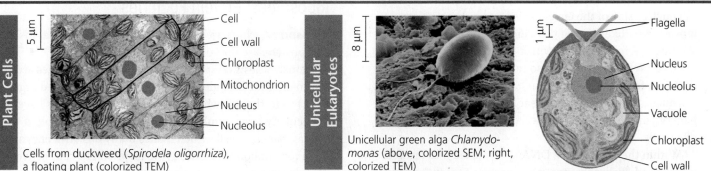

Plant Cells

5 μm

- Cell
- Cell wall
- Chloroplast
- Mitochondrion
- Nucleus
- Nucleolus

Cells from duckweed (*Spirodela oligorrhiza*), a floating plant (colorized TEM)

Unicellular Eukaryotes

8 μm

Unicellular green alga *Chlamydomonas* (above, colorized SEM; right, colorized TEM)

1 μm

- Flagella
- Nucleus
- Nucleolus
- Vacuole
- Chloroplast
- Cell wall

1. Briefly describe the structure and function of the nucleus, the mitochondrion, the chloroplast, and the endoplasmic reticulum.

2. **WHAT IF?** Imagine an elongated cell (such as a nerve cell) that measures 125 × 1 × 1 arbitrary units. Predict how its surface-to-volume ratio would compare with those in Figure 6.7. Then calculate the ratio and check your prediction.

For suggested answers, see Appendix A.

CONCEPT 6.3

The eukaryotic cell's genetic instructions are housed in the nucleus and carried out by the ribosomes

On the first stop of our detailed tour of the eukaryotic cell, let's look at two cellular components involved in the genetic control of the cell: the nucleus, which houses most of the cell's DNA, and the ribosomes, which use information from the DNA to make proteins.

The Nucleus: Information Central

The **nucleus** contains most of the genes in the eukaryotic cell. (Some genes are located in mitochondria and chloroplasts.) It is generally the most conspicuous organelle (see blue structure in cell on right), averaging about 5 μm in diameter. The **nuclear envelope** encloses the nucleus **(Figure 6.9)**, separating its contents from the cytoplasm.

The nuclear envelope is a *double* membrane. The two membranes, each a lipid bilayer with associated proteins, are separated by a space of 20–40 nm. The envelope is perforated by pore structures that are about 100 nm in diameter. At the lip of each pore, the inner and outer membranes of the nuclear envelope are continuous. An intricate protein structure called a *pore complex* lines each pore and plays an important role in the cell by regulating the entry and exit of proteins and RNAs, as well as large complexes of macromolecules. Except at the pores, the nuclear side of the envelope is lined by the **nuclear lamina**, a netlike array of protein filaments that maintains the shape of the nucleus by mechanically supporting the nuclear envelope. There is also much evidence for a *nuclear matrix*, a framework of protein fibers extending throughout the nuclear interior. The nuclear lamina and matrix may help organize the genetic material so it functions efficiently.

Within the nucleus, the DNA is organized into discrete units called **chromosomes**, structures that carry the genetic

Nucleus

5 μm

information. Each chromosome contains one long DNA molecule associated with many proteins. Some of the proteins help coil the DNA molecule of each chromosome, reducing its length and allowing it to fit into the nucleus. The complex of DNA and proteins making up chromosomes is called **chromatin**. When a cell is not dividing, stained chromatin appears as a diffuse mass in micrographs, and the chromosomes cannot be distinguished from one another, even though discrete chromosomes are present. As a cell prepares to divide, however, the chromosomes coil (condense) further, becoming thick enough to be distinguished under a microscope as separate structures. Each eukaryotic species has a characteristic number of chromosomes. For example, a typical human cell has 46 chromosomes in its nucleus; the exceptions are the sex cells (eggs and sperm), which have only 23 chromosomes in humans. A fruit fly cell has 8 chromosomes in most cells and 4 in the sex cells.

A prominent structure within the nondividing nucleus is the **nucleolus** (plural, *nucleoli*), which appears through the electron microscope as a mass of densely stained granules and fibers adjoining part of the chromatin. Here a type of RNA called *ribosomal RNA* (rRNA) is synthesized from instructions in the DNA. Also in the nucleolus, proteins imported from the cytoplasm are assembled with rRNA into large and small subunits of ribosomes. These subunits then exit the nucleus through the nuclear pores to the cytoplasm, where a large and a small subunit can assemble into a ribosome. Sometimes there are two or more nucleoli; the number depends on the species and the stage in the cell's reproductive cycle.

As we saw in Figure 5.23, the nucleus directs protein synthesis by synthesizing messenger RNA (mRNA) according to instructions provided by the DNA. The mRNA is then transported to the cytoplasm via the nuclear pores. Once an mRNA molecule reaches the cytoplasm, ribosomes translate the mRNA's genetic message into the primary structure of a specific polypeptide. (This process of transcribing and translating genetic information is described in detail in Chapter 17.)

Ribosomes: Protein Factories

Ribosomes, which are complexes made of ribosomal RNA and protein, are the cellular components that carry out protein synthesis **(Figure 6.10)**. (Note that ribosomes are not membrane bounded and thus are not considered organelles.) Cells that have high rates of protein synthesis have particularly large numbers of ribosomes. For example, a human pancreas cell, which makes many digestive enzymes, has a few million ribosomes. Not surprisingly, cells active in protein synthesis also have prominent nucleoli.

1 μm

Nucleus

Nucleus

Nucleolus

Chromatin

Nuclear envelope:
Inner membrane
Outer membrane

Nuclear pore

Rough ER

▲ **Surface of nuclear envelope (TEM).** This specimen was prepared by a technique known as freeze-fracture.

Pore complex

Ribosome

◄ **Close-up of nuclear envelope**

▲ **Chromatin.** This segment of a chromosome from a non-dividing cell shows two states of coiling of the DNA (blue) and protein (purple) complex. The thicker form is sometimes also organized into long loops.

0.25 μm

▲ **Pore complexes (TEM).** Each pore is ringed by protein particles.

0.5 μm

◄ **Nuclear lamina (TEM).** The netlike lamina lines the inner surface of the nuclear envelope.

© Pearson Education, Inc.

▲ **Figure 6.9 The nucleus and its envelope.** Within the nucleus are the chromosomes, which appear as a mass of chromatin (DNA and associated proteins) and one or more nucleoli (singular, *nucleolus*), which function in ribosome synthesis. The nuclear envelope, which consists of two membranes separated by a narrow space, is perforated with pores and lined by the nuclear lamina.

MAKE CONNECTIONS *Since the chromosomes contain the genetic material and reside in the nucleus, how does the rest of the cell get access to the information they carry? (See Figure 5.23.)*

0.25 μm

Ribosomes

ER

Free ribosomes in cytosol

Endoplasmic reticulum (ER)

Ribosomes bound to ER

Large subunit

Small subunit

TEM showing ER and ribosomes

Diagram of a ribosome

Computer model of a ribosome

▲ **Figure 6.10 Ribosomes.** This electron micrograph of a pancreas cell shows both free and bound ribosomes. The simplified diagram and computer model show the two subunits of a ribosome.

Ribosomes build proteins in two cytoplasmic locales. At any given time, *free ribosomes* are suspended in the cytosol, while *bound ribosomes* are attached to the outside of the endoplasmic reticulum or nuclear envelope (see Figure 6.10). Bound and free ribosomes are structurally identical, and ribosomes can alternate between the two roles. Most of the proteins made on free ribosomes function within the cytosol; examples are enzymes that catalyze the first steps of sugar breakdown. Bound ribosomes generally make proteins that are destined for insertion into membranes, for packaging within certain organelles such as lysosomes (see Figure 6.8), or for export from the cell (secretion). Cells that specialize in protein secretion—for instance, the cells of the pancreas that secrete digestive enzymes—frequently have a high proportion of bound ribosomes. (You will learn more about ribosome structure and function in Chapter 17.)

CONCEPT CHECK 6.3

1. What role do ribosomes play in carrying out genetic instructions?
2. Describe the molecular composition of nucleoli and explain their function.
3. **WHAT IF?** As a cell begins the process of dividing, its chromosomes become shorter, thicker, and individually visible in an LM. Explain what is happening at the molecular level.

For suggested answers, see Appendix A.

CONCEPT 6.4

The endomembrane system regulates protein traffic and performs metabolic functions in the cell

Many of the different membranes of the eukaryotic cell are part of the **endomembrane system**, which includes the nuclear envelope, the endoplasmic reticulum, the Golgi apparatus, lysosomes, various kinds of vesicles and vacuoles, and the plasma membrane. This system carries out a variety of tasks in the cell, including synthesis of proteins, transport of proteins into membranes and organelles or out of the cell, metabolism and movement of lipids, and detoxification of poisons. The membranes of this system are related either through direct physical continuity or by the transfer of membrane segments as tiny **vesicles** (sacs made of membrane). Despite these relationships, the various membranes are not identical in structure and function. Moreover, the thickness, molecular composition, and types of chemical reactions carried out in a given membrane are not fixed, but may be modified several times during the membrane's life. Having already discussed the nuclear envelope, we will now focus on the endoplasmic reticulum and the other endomembranes to which the endoplasmic reticulum gives rise.

The Endoplasmic Reticulum: Biosynthetic Factory

The **endoplasmic reticulum (ER)** is such an extensive network of membranes that it accounts for more than half the total membrane in many eukaryotic cells. (The word *endoplasmic* means "within the cytoplasm," and *reticulum* is Latin for "little net.") The ER consists of a network of membranous tubules and sacs called cisternae (from the Latin *cisterna*, a reservoir for a liquid). The ER membrane separates the internal compartment of the ER, called the *ER lumen* (cavity) or cisternal space, from the cytosol. And because the ER membrane is continuous with the nuclear envelope, the space between the two membranes of the envelope is continuous with the lumen of the ER **(Figure 6.11)**.

There are two distinct, though connected, regions of the ER that differ in structure and function: smooth ER and rough ER. **Smooth ER** is so named because its outer surface lacks ribosomes. **Rough ER** is studded with ribosomes on the outer surface of the membrane and thus appears rough through the electron microscope. As already mentioned, ribosomes are also attached to the cytoplasmic side of the nuclear envelope's outer membrane, which is continuous with rough ER.

Functions of Smooth ER

The smooth ER functions in diverse metabolic processes, which vary with cell type. These processes include synthesis of lipids, metabolism of carbohydrates, detoxification of drugs and poisons, and storage of calcium ions.

Enzymes of the smooth ER are important in the synthesis of lipids, including oils, steroids, and new membrane phospholipids. Among the steroids produced by the smooth ER in animal cells are the sex hormones of vertebrates and the various steroid hormones secreted by the adrenal glands. The cells that synthesize and secrete these hormones—in the testes and ovaries, for example—are rich in smooth ER, a structural feature that fits the function of these cells.

Other enzymes of the smooth ER help detoxify drugs and poisons, especially in liver cells. Detoxification usually involves adding hydroxyl groups to drug molecules, making them more soluble and easier to flush from the body. The sedative phenobarbital and other barbiturates are examples of drugs metabolized in this manner by smooth ER in liver cells. In fact, barbiturates, alcohol, and many other drugs induce the proliferation of smooth ER and its associated detoxification enzymes, thus increasing the rate of detoxification. This, in turn, increases tolerance to the drugs, meaning that higher doses are required to achieve a particular effect, such as sedation. Also, because some of the detoxification enzymes have relatively broad action, the proliferation of smooth ER in response to one drug can increase the need for higher dosages of other drugs as well. Barbiturate abuse, for example, can decrease the effectiveness of certain antibiotics and other useful drugs.

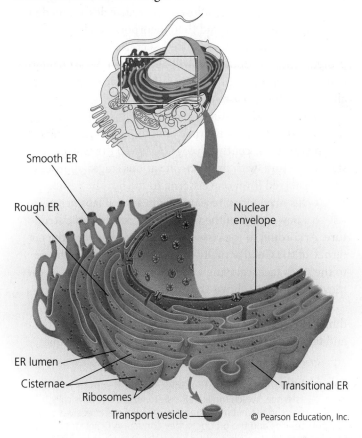

Smooth ER

Rough ER

Nuclear envelope

ER lumen

Cisternae

Ribosomes

Transitional ER

Transport vesicle

© Pearson Education, Inc.

Smooth ER

Rough ER

0.20 μm

▲ **Figure 6.11 Endoplasmic reticulum (ER).** A membranous system of interconnected tubules and flattened sacs called cisternae, the ER is also continuous with the nuclear envelope, as shown in the cutaway diagram at the top. The membrane of the ER encloses a continuous compartment called the ER lumen (or cisternal space). Rough ER, which is studded on its outer surface with ribosomes, can be distinguished from smooth ER in the electron micrograph (TEM). Transport vesicles bud off from a region of the rough ER called transitional ER and travel to the Golgi apparatus and other destinations.

The smooth ER also stores calcium ions. In muscle cells, for example, the smooth ER membrane pumps calcium ions from the cytosol into the ER lumen. When a muscle cell is stimulated by a nerve impulse, calcium ions rush back across the ER membrane into the cytosol and trigger contraction of the muscle cell. In other cell types, calcium ion release from the smooth ER triggers different responses, such as secretion of vesicles carrying newly synthesized proteins.

Functions of Rough ER

Many cells secrete proteins that are produced by ribosomes attached to rough ER. For example, certain pancreatic cells synthesize the protein insulin in the ER and secrete this hormone into the bloodstream. As a polypeptide chain grows from a bound ribosome, the chain is threaded into the ER lumen through a pore formed by a protein complex in the ER membrane. The new polypeptide folds into its functional shape as it enters the ER lumen. Most secretory proteins are **glycoproteins**, proteins with carbohydrates covalently bonded to them. The carbohydrates are attached to the proteins in the ER lumen by enzymes built into the ER membrane.

After secretory proteins are formed, the ER membrane keeps them separate from proteins that are produced by free ribosomes and that will remain in the cytosol. Secretory proteins depart from the ER wrapped in the membranes of vesicles that bud like bubbles from a specialized region called transitional ER (see Figure 6.11). Vesicles in transit from one part of the cell to another are called **transport vesicles**; we will discuss their fate shortly.

In addition to making secretory proteins, rough ER is a membrane factory for the cell; it grows in place by adding membrane proteins and phospholipids to its own membrane. As polypeptides destined to be membrane proteins grow from the ribosomes, they are inserted into the ER membrane itself and anchored there by their hydrophobic portions. Like the smooth ER, the rough ER also makes membrane phospholipids; enzymes built into the ER membrane assemble phospholipids from precursors in the cytosol. The ER membrane expands, and portions of it are transferred in the form of transport vesicles to other components of the endomembrane system.

The Golgi Apparatus: Shipping and Receiving Center

After leaving the ER, many transport vesicles travel to the **Golgi apparatus**. We can think of the Golgi as a warehouse for receiving, sorting, shipping, and even some manufacturing. Here, products of the ER, such as proteins, are modified and stored and then sent to other destinations. Not surprisingly, the Golgi apparatus is especially extensive in cells specialized for secretion.

The Golgi apparatus consists of flattened membranous sacs—cisternae—looking like a stack of pita bread **(Figure 6.12)**. A cell may have many, even hundreds, of these stacks. The membrane of each cisterna in a stack separates its internal space from the cytosol. Vesicles concentrated in the vicinity of the Golgi apparatus are engaged in the transfer of material between parts of the Golgi and other structures.

A Golgi stack has a distinct structural directionality, with the membranes of cisternae on opposite sides of the stack differing in thickness and molecular composition. The two sides of a Golgi stack are referred to as the *cis* face and the *trans* face; these act, respectively, as the receiving and shipping departments of the Golgi apparatus. The term *cis* means "on the same side," and the *cis* face is usually located near the ER. Transport vesicles move material from the ER to the Golgi apparatus. A vesicle that buds from the ER can add its membrane and the contents of its lumen to the *cis* face by fusing with a Golgi membrane. The *trans* face ("on the opposite side") gives rise to vesicles that pinch off and travel to other sites.

Products of the endoplasmic reticulum are usually modified during their transit from the *cis* region to the *trans* region of the Golgi apparatus. For example, glycoproteins formed in the ER have their carbohydrates modified, first in the ER itself, then as they pass through the Golgi. The Golgi removes some sugar monomers and substitutes others, producing a large variety of carbohydrates. Membrane phospholipids may also be altered in the Golgi.

In addition to its finishing work, the Golgi apparatus also manufactures some macromolecules. Many polysaccharides secreted by cells are Golgi products. For example, pectins and certain other noncellulose polysaccharides are made in the Golgi of plant cells and then incorporated along with cellulose into their cell walls. Like secretory proteins, nonprotein Golgi products that will be secreted depart from the *trans* face of the Golgi inside transport vesicles that eventually fuse with the plasma membrane.

The Golgi manufactures and refines its products in stages, with different cisternae containing unique teams of enzymes. Until recently, biologists viewed the Golgi as a static structure, with products in various stages of processing transferred from one cisterna to the next by vesicles. While this may occur, research from several labs has given rise to a new model of the Golgi as a more dynamic structure. According to the *cisternal maturation model*, the cisternae of the Golgi actually progress forward from the *cis* to the *trans* face, carrying and modifying their cargo as they move. Figure 6.12 shows the details of this model.

Before a Golgi stack dispatches its products by budding vesicles from the *trans* face, it sorts these products and targets them for various parts of the cell. Molecular

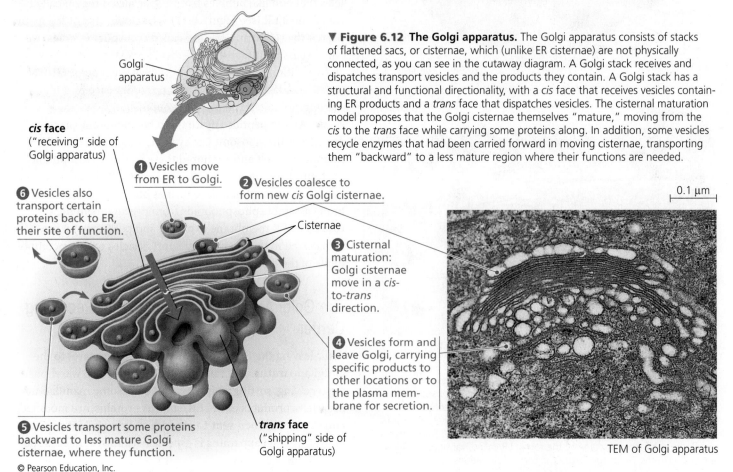

Golgi apparatus

▼ **Figure 6.12 The Golgi apparatus.** The Golgi apparatus consists of stacks of flattened sacs, or cisternae, which (unlike ER cisternae) are not physically connected, as you can see in the cutaway diagram. A Golgi stack receives and dispatches transport vesicles and the products they contain. A Golgi stack has a structural and functional directionality, with a *cis* face that receives vesicles containing ER products and a *trans* face that dispatches vesicles. The cisternal maturation model proposes that the Golgi cisternae themselves "mature," moving from the *cis* to the *trans* face while carrying some proteins along. In addition, some vesicles recycle enzymes that had been carried forward in moving cisternae, transporting them "backward" to a less mature region where their functions are needed.

cis face
("receiving" side of Golgi apparatus)

❶ Vesicles move from ER to Golgi.

❻ Vesicles also transport certain proteins back to ER, their site of function.

❷ Vesicles coalesce to form new *cis* Golgi cisternae.

Cisternae

❸ Cisternal maturation: Golgi cisternae move in a *cis*-to-*trans* direction.

❹ Vesicles form and leave Golgi, carrying specific products to other locations or to the plasma membrane for secretion.

0.1 μm

❺ Vesicles transport some proteins backward to less mature Golgi cisternae, where they function.

trans face
("shipping" side of Golgi apparatus)

TEM of Golgi apparatus

© Pearson Education, Inc.

identification tags, such as phosphate groups added to the Golgi products, aid in sorting by acting like zip codes on mailing labels. Finally, transport vesicles budded from the Golgi may have external molecules on their membranes that recognize "docking sites" on the surface of specific organelles or on the plasma membrane, thus targeting the vesicles appropriately.

Lysosomes: Digestive Compartments

A **lysosome** is a membranous sac of hydrolytic enzymes that many eukaryotic cells use to digest (hydrolyze) macromolecules. Lysosomal enzymes work best in the acidic environment found in lysosomes. If a lysosome breaks open or leaks its contents, the released enzymes are not very active because the cytosol has a near-neutral pH. However, excessive leakage from a large number of lysosomes can destroy a cell by self-digestion.

Hydrolytic enzymes and lysosomal membrane are made by rough ER and then transferred to the Golgi apparatus for further processing. At least some lysosomes probably arise by budding from the *trans* face of the Golgi apparatus (see Figure 6.12). How are the proteins of the inner surface of the lysosomal membrane and the digestive enzymes themselves spared from destruction? Apparently, the three-dimensional shapes of these proteins protect vulnerable bonds from enzymatic attack.

Lysosomes carry out intracellular digestion in a variety of circumstances. Amoebas and many other unicellular eukaryotes eat by engulfing smaller organisms or food particles, a process called **phagocytosis** (from the Greek *phagein*, to eat, and *kytos*, vessel, referring here to the cell). The *food vacuole* formed in this way then fuses with a lysosome, whose enzymes digest the food **(Figure 6.13a**, bottom). Digestion products, including simple sugars, amino acids, and other monomers, pass into the cytosol and become nutrients for the cell. Some human cells also carry out phagocytosis. Among them are macrophages, a type of white blood cell that helps defend the body by engulfing and destroying bacteria and other invaders (see Figure 6.13a, top, and Figure 6.31).

1 Lysosome contains active hydrolytic enzymes.

2 Lysosome fuses with food vacuole.

3 Hydrolytic enzymes digest food particles.

Digestive enzymes

Lysosome

Plasma membrane

Food vacuole

Digestion

(a) Phagocytosis: lysosome digesting food

Vesicle containing two damaged organelles

Mitochondrion fragment

Peroxisome fragment

1 Lysosome fuses with vesicle containing damaged organelles.

2 Hydrolytic enzymes digest organelle components.

Lysosome

Peroxisome

Vesicle

Mitochondrion

Digestion

(b) Autophagy: lysosome breaking down damaged organelles

▲ **Figure 6.13 Lysosomes.** Lysosomes digest (hydrolyze) materials taken into the cell and recycle intracellular materials. **(a)** *Top*: In this macrophage (a type of white blood cell) from a rat, the lysosomes are very dark because of a stain that reacts with one of the products of digestion inside the lysosome (TEM).

Macrophages ingest bacteria and viruses and destroy them using lysosomes. *Bottom*: This diagram shows a lysosome fusing with a food vacuole during the process of phagocytosis by a unicellular eukaryote. **(b)** *Top*: In the cytoplasm of this rat liver cell is a vesicle containing two disabled organelles (TEM). The vesicle will fuse

with a lysosome in the process of autophagy. *Bottom*: This diagram shows fusion of such a vesicle with a lysosome. This type of vesicle has a double membrane of unknown origin. The outer membrane fuses with the lysosome, and the inner membrane is degraded along with the damaged organelles.

Lysosomes also use their hydrolytic enzymes to recycle the cell's own organic material, a process called *autophagy*. During autophagy, a damaged organelle or small amount of cytosol becomes surrounded by a double membrane (of unknown origin), and a lysosome fuses with the outer membrane of this vesicle (**Figure 6.13b**). The lysosomal enzymes dismantle the enclosed material, and the resulting small organic compounds are released to the cytosol for reuse. With the help of lysosomes, the cell continually renews itself. A human liver cell, for example, recycles half of its macromolecules each week.

The cells of people with inherited lysosomal storage diseases lack a functioning hydrolytic enzyme normally present in lysosomes. The lysosomes become engorged with indigestible material, which begins to interfere with other cellular activities. In Tay-Sachs disease, for example, a lipid-digesting enzyme is missing or inactive, and the brain becomes impaired by an accumulation of lipids in the cells. Fortunately, lysosomal storage diseases are rare in the general population.

Vacuoles: Diverse Maintenance Compartments

Vacuoles are large vesicles derived from the endoplasmic reticulum and Golgi apparatus. Thus, vacuoles are an integral part of a cell's endomembrane system. Like all cellular membranes, the vacuolar membrane is selective in transporting solutes; as a result, the solution inside a vacuole differs in composition from the cytosol.

Vacuoles perform a variety of functions in different kinds of cells. **Food vacuoles**, formed by phagocytosis, have already been mentioned (see Figure 6.13a). Many unicellular eukaryotes living in fresh water have **contractile vacuoles** that pump excess water out of the cell, thereby maintaining a suitable concentration of ions and molecules inside the cell (see Figure 7.13). In plants and fungi, certain vacuoles carry out enzymatic hydrolysis, a function shared by lysosomes in animal cells. (In fact, some biologists consider these hydrolytic vacuoles to be a type of lysosome.) In plants, small vacuoles can hold reserves of important organic compounds, such as the proteins stockpiled in the storage cells in seeds. Vacuoles may also help protect the plant against herbivores by storing compounds that are poisonous or unpalatable to animals. Some plant vacuoles contain pigments, such as the red and blue pigments of petals that help attract pollinating insects to flowers.

Mature plant cells generally contain a large **central vacuole (Figure 6.14)**, which develops by the coalescence of smaller vacuoles. The solution inside the central vacuole, called cell sap, is the plant cell's main repository of inorganic ions, including potassium and chloride. The central vacuole plays a major role in the growth of plant cells, which enlarge

▲ **Figure 6.14 The plant cell vacuole.** The central vacuole is usually the largest compartment in a plant cell; the rest of the cytoplasm is often confined to a narrow zone between the vacuolar membrane and the plasma membrane (TEM).

as the vacuole absorbs water, enabling the cell to become larger with a minimal investment in new cytoplasm. The cytosol often occupies only a thin layer between the central vacuole and the plasma membrane, so the ratio of plasma membrane surface to cytosolic volume is sufficient, even for a large plant cell.

The Endomembrane System: *A Review*

Figure 6.15 reviews the endomembrane system, showing the flow of membrane lipids and proteins through the various organelles. As the membrane moves from the ER to the Golgi and then elsewhere, its molecular composition and metabolic functions are modified, along with those of its contents. The endomembrane system is a complex and dynamic player in the cell's compartmental organization.

We'll continue our tour of the cell with some organelles that are not closely related to the endomembrane system but play crucial roles in the energy transformations carried out by cells.

CONCEPT CHECK 6.4

1. Describe the structural and functional distinctions between rough and smooth ER.

2. Describe how transport vesicles integrate the endomembrane system.

3. **WHAT IF?** Imagine a protein that functions in the ER but requires modification in the Golgi apparatus before it can achieve that function. Describe the protein's path through the cell, starting with the mRNA molecule that specifies the protein.

For suggested answers, see Appendix A.

① Nuclear envelope is connected to rough ER, which is also continuous with smooth ER.

Smooth ER

Nucleus

Rough ER

② Membranes and proteins produced by the ER flow in the form of transport vesicles to the Golgi.

cis Golgi

③ Golgi pinches off transport vesicles and other vesicles that give rise to lysosomes, other types of specialized vesicles, and vacuoles.

trans Golgi

Plasma membrane

④ Lysosome is available for fusion with another vesicle for digestion.

⑤ Transport vesicle carries proteins to plasma membrane for secretion.

⑥ Plasma membrane expands by fusion of vesicles; proteins are secreted from cell.

© Pearson Education, Inc.

▲ **Figure 6.15 Review: relationships among organelles of the endomembrane system.**
The red arrows show some of the migration pathways for membranes and the materials they enclose.

CONCEPT 6.5

Mitochondria and chloroplasts change energy from one form to another

Organisms transform the energy they acquire from their surroundings. In eukaryotic cells, mitochondria and chloroplasts are the organelles that convert energy to forms that cells can use for work. **Mitochondria** (singular, *mitochondrion*) are the sites of cellular respiration, the metabolic process that uses oxygen to drive the generation of ATP by extracting energy from sugars, fats, and other fuels. **Chloroplasts**, found in plants and algae, are the sites of photosynthesis. This process in chloroplasts converts solar energy to chemical energy by absorbing sunlight and using it to drive the synthesis of organic compounds such as sugars from carbon dioxide and water.

In addition to having related functions, mitochondria and chloroplasts share similar evolutionary origins, which we'll discuss briefly before describing their structures. In this section, we will also consider the peroxisome, an oxidative organelle. The evolutionary origin of the peroxisome, as well as its relation to other organelles, is still a matter of some debate.

The Evolutionary Origins of Mitochondria and Chloroplasts

EVOLUTION Mitochondria and chloroplasts display similarities with bacteria that led to the **endosymbiont theory**, illustrated in **Figure 6.16**. This theory states that an early ancestor of eukaryotic cells engulfed an oxygen-using nonphotosynthetic prokaryotic cell. Eventually, the engulfed cell formed a relationship with the host cell in which it was enclosed, becoming an *endosymbiont* (a cell living within another cell). Indeed, over the course of evolution, the host cell and its endosymbiont merged into a single organism, a eukaryotic cell with a mitochondrion. At least one of these cells may have then taken up a photosynthetic prokaryote, becoming the ancestor of eukaryotic cells that contain chloroplasts.

This is a widely accepted theory, which we will discuss in more detail in Chapter 25. This theory is consistent with many structural features of mitochondria and chloroplasts. First, rather than being bounded by a single membrane like organelles of the endomembrane system, mitochondria and typical chloroplasts have two membranes surrounding them. (Chloroplasts also have an internal system of membranous sacs.) There is evidence that the ancestral engulfed

Endoplasmic reticulum

Nucleus

Nuclear envelope

Ancestor of eukaryotic cells (host cell)

Engulfing of oxygen-using nonphotosynthetic prokaryote, which, over many generations of cells, becomes a mitochondrion

Engulfing of photosynthetic prokaryote

Mitochondrion

Chloroplast

Mitochondrion

At least one cell

Nonphotosynthetic eukaryote

Photosynthetic eukaryote

▲ **Figure 6.16 The endosymbiont theory of the origins of mitochondria and chloroplasts in eukaryotic cells.** According to this theory, the proposed ancestors of mitochondria were oxygen-using nonphotosynthetic prokaryotes, while the proposed ancestors of chloroplasts were photosynthetic prokaryotes. The large arrows represent change over evolutionary time; the small arrows inside the cells show the process of the endosymbiont becoming an organelle, also over long periods of time.

prokaryotes had two outer membranes, which became the double membranes of mitochondria and chloroplasts. Second, like prokaryotes, mitochondria and chloroplasts contain ribosomes, as well as multiple circular DNA molecules associated with their inner membranes. The DNA in these organelles programs the synthesis of some organelle proteins on ribosomes that have been synthesized and assembled there as well. Third, also consistent with their probable evolutionary origins as cells, mitochondria and chloroplasts are autonomous (somewhat independent) organelles that grow and reproduce within the cell.

Next, we focus on the structures of mitochondria and chloroplasts, while providing an overview of their structures and functions. (In Chapters 9 and 10, we will examine their roles as energy transformers.)

Mitochondria: Chemical Energy Conversion

Mitochondria are found in nearly all eukaryotic cells, including those of plants, animals, fungi, and most unicellular eukaryotes. Some cells have a single large mitochondrion,

but more often a cell has hundreds or even thousands of mitochondria; the number correlates with the cell's level of metabolic activity. For example, cells that move or contract have proportionally more mitochondria per volume than less active cells.

Each of the two membranes enclosing the mitochondrion is a phospholipid bilayer with a unique collection of embedded proteins (**Figure 6.17**). The outer membrane is smooth, but the inner membrane is convoluted, with infoldings called **cristae**. The inner membrane divides the mitochondrion into two internal compartments. The first is the intermembrane space, the narrow region between the inner and outer membranes. The second compartment, the **mitochondrial matrix**, is enclosed by the inner membrane. The matrix contains many different enzymes as well as the mitochondrial DNA and ribosomes. Enzymes in the matrix catalyze some of the steps of cellular respiration. Other proteins that function in respiration, including the enzyme that makes ATP, are built into the inner membrane. As highly folded surfaces, the cristae give the inner mitochondrial membrane a large surface area, thus enhancing the productivity of cellular respiration. This is another example of structure fitting function.

Mitochondria are generally in the range of 1–10 μm long. Time-lapse films of living cells reveal mitochondria moving around, changing their shapes, and fusing or dividing in two, unlike the static structures seen in electron micrographs of dead cells. These observations helped cell biologists understand that mitochondria in a living cell form a branched tubular network, seen in a whole cell in Figure 6.17b, that is in a dynamic state of flux.

Chloroplasts: Capture of Light Energy

Chloroplasts contain the green pigment chlorophyll, along with enzymes and other molecules that function in the photosynthetic production of sugar. These lens-shaped organelles, about 3–6 μm in length, are found in leaves and other green organs of plants and in algae (**Figure 6.18**; see also Figure 6.26c).

The contents of a chloroplast are partitioned from the cytosol by an envelope consisting of two membranes separated by a very narrow intermembrane space. Inside the chloroplast is another membranous system in the form of flattened, interconnected sacs called **thylakoids**. In some regions, thylakoids are stacked like poker chips; each stack is called a **granum** (plural, *grana*). The fluid outside the thylakoids is the **stroma**, which contains the chloroplast DNA and ribosomes as well as many enzymes. The membranes of the chloroplast divide the chloroplast space into three compartments: the intermembrane space, the stroma, and the thylakoid space. This compartmental organization enables the chloroplast to convert light energy to chemical energy

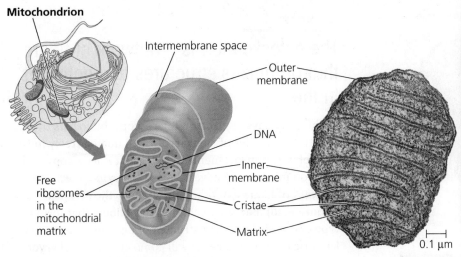

Mitochondrion

Intermembrane space

Outer membrane

DNA

Inner membrane

Cristae

Matrix

Free ribosomes in the mitochondrial matrix

0.1 μm

(a) Diagram and TEM of mitochondrion

10 μm

Mitochondria

Mitochondrial DNA

Nuclear DNA

(b) Network of mitochondria in *Euglena* (LM)

▲ **Figure 6.17 The mitochondrion, site of cellular respiration. (a)** The inner and outer membranes of the mitochondrion are evident in the drawing and electron micrograph (TEM). The cristae are infoldings of the inner membrane, which increase its surface area. The cutaway drawing shows the two compartments bounded by the membranes: the intermembrane space and the mitochondrial matrix. Many respiratory enzymes are found in the inner membrane and the matrix. Free ribosomes are also present in the matrix. The DNA molecules are usually circular and they are associated with the inner mitochondrial membrane. **(b)** The light micrograph shows an entire unicellular eukaryote (*Euglena gracilis*) at a much lower magnification than the TEM. The mitochondrial matrix has been stained green. The mitochondria form a branched tubular network. The nuclear DNA is stained red; molecules of mitochondrial DNA appear as bright yellow spots.

during photosynthesis. (You will learn more about photosynthesis in Chapter 10.)

As with mitochondria, the static and rigid appearance of chloroplasts in micrographs or schematic diagrams is not true to their dynamic behavior in the living cell. Their shape is changeable, and they grow and occasionally pinch in two, reproducing themselves. They are mobile and, with mitochondria and other organelles, move around the cell along tracks of the cytoskeleton, a structural network we will consider later in this chapter.

The chloroplast is a specialized member of a family of closely related plant organelles called **plastids**. One type of plastid, the *amyloplast*, is a colorless organelle that stores starch (amylose), particularly in roots and tubers. Another is the *chromoplast*, which has pigments that give fruits and flowers their orange and yellow hues.

▼ **Figure 6.18 The chloroplast, site of photosynthesis. (a)** Many plants have lens-shaped chloroplasts, as shown here. A typical chloroplast has three compartments: the intermembrane space, the stroma, and the thylakoid space. Free ribosomes are present in the stroma, as are copies of chloroplast DNA molecules. **(b)** This fluorescence micrograph shows a whole cell of the green alga *Spirogyra crassa*, which is named for its spiral chloroplasts. Under natural light the chloroplasts appear green, but under ultraviolet light they naturally fluoresce red, as shown here.

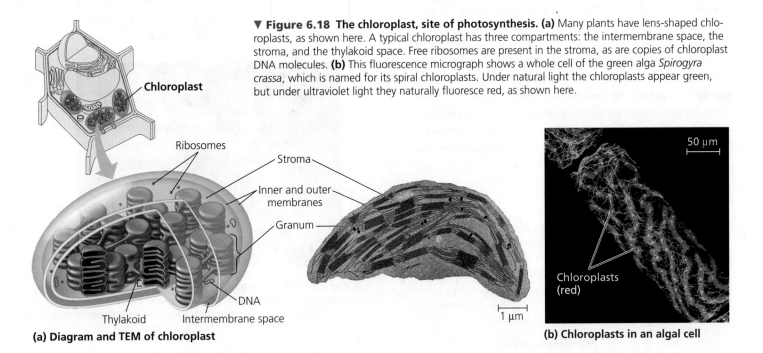

Chloroplast

Ribosomes

Stroma

Inner and outer membranes

Granum

DNA

Thylakoid

Intermembrane space

(a) Diagram and TEM of chloroplast

1 μm

50 μm

Chloroplasts (red)

(b) Chloroplasts in an algal cell

▶ Figure 6.19
A peroxisome. Peroxisomes are roughly spherical and often have a granular or crystalline core that is thought to be a dense collection of enzyme molecules. Chloroplasts and mitochondria cooperate with peroxisomes in certain metabolic functions (TEM).

Peroxisome

Mitochondrion

Chloroplasts

1 µm

Peroxisomes: Oxidation

The **peroxisome** is a specialized metabolic compartment bounded by a single membrane **(Figure 6.19)**. Peroxisomes contain enzymes that remove hydrogen atoms from various substrates and transfer them to oxygen (O_2), producing hydrogen peroxide (H_2O_2) as a by-product (from which the organelle derives its name). These reactions have many different functions. Some peroxisomes use oxygen to break fatty acids down into smaller molecules that are transported to mitochondria and used as fuel for cellular respiration. Peroxisomes in the liver detoxify alcohol and other harmful compounds by transferring hydrogen from the poisons to oxygen. The H_2O_2 formed by peroxisomes is itself toxic, but the organelle also contains an enzyme that converts H_2O_2 to water. This is an excellent example of how the cell's compartmental structure is crucial to its functions: The enzymes that produce H_2O_2 and those that dispose of this toxic compound are sequestered away from other cellular components that could be damaged.

Specialized peroxisomes called *glyoxysomes* are found in the fat-storing tissues of plant seeds. These organelles contain enzymes that initiate the conversion of fatty acids to sugar, which the emerging seedling uses as a source of energy and carbon until it can produce its own sugar by photosynthesis.

How peroxisomes are related to other organelles is still an open question. They grow larger by incorporating proteins made in the cytosol and ER, as well as lipids made in the ER and within the peroxisome itself. Peroxisomes may increase in number by splitting in two when they reach a certain size, sparking the suggestion of an endosymbiotic evolutionary origin, but others argue against this scenario. Discussion of this issue is ongoing.

CONCEPT CHECK 6.5

1. Describe two common characteristics of chloroplasts and mitochondria. Consider both function and membrane structure.
2. Do plant cells have mitochondria? Explain.
3. **WHAT IF?** A classmate proposes that mitochondria and chloroplasts should be classified in the endomembrane system. Argue against the proposal.

For suggested answers, see Appendix A.

The cytoskeleton is a network of fibers that organizes structures and activities in the cell

In the early days of electron microscopy, biologists thought that the organelles of a eukaryotic cell floated freely in the cytosol. But improvements in both light microscopy and electron microscopy have revealed the **cytoskeleton**, a network of fibers extending throughout the cytoplasm **(Figure 6.20)**. Bacterial cells also have fibers that form a type of cytoskeleton, constructed of proteins similar to eukaryotic ones, but here we will concentrate on eukaryotes. The eukaryotic cytoskeleton, which plays a major role in organizing the structures and activities of the cell, is composed of three types of molecular structures: microtubules, microfilaments, and intermediate filaments.

Roles of the Cytoskeleton: Support and Motility

The most obvious function of the cytoskeleton is to give mechanical support to the cell and maintain its shape. This is especially important for animal cells, which lack walls. The remarkable strength and resilience of the cytoskeleton as a whole are based on its architecture. Like a dome tent, the cytoskeleton is stabilized by a balance between opposing forces exerted by its elements. And just as the skeleton of an animal helps fix the positions of other body parts, the cytoskeleton provides anchorage for many organelles and even cytosolic enzyme molecules. The cytoskeleton is more dynamic than an animal skeleton, however. It can be quickly dismantled in one part of the cell and reassembled in a new location, changing the shape of the cell.

10 µm

▲ Figure 6.20 The cytoskeleton. As shown in this fluorescence micrograph, the cytoskeleton extends throughout the cell. The cytoskeletal elements have been tagged with different fluorescent molecules: green for microtubules and reddish orange for microfilaments. A third component of the cytoskeleton, intermediate filaments, is not evident here. (The blue color tags the DNA in the nucleus.)

Some types of cell motility (movement) also involve the cytoskeleton. The term *cell motility* includes both changes in cell location and movements of cell parts. Cell motility generally requires interaction of the cytoskeleton with **motor proteins**. There are many such examples: Cytoskeletal elements and motor proteins work together with plasma membrane molecules to allow whole cells to move along fibers outside the cell. Inside the cell, vesicles and other organelles often use motor protein "feet" to "walk" to their destinations along a track provided by the cytoskeleton. For example, this is how vesicles containing neurotransmitter molecules migrate to the tips of axons, the long extensions of nerve cells that release these molecules as chemical signals to adjacent nerve cells **(Figure 6.21)**. The cytoskeleton also manipulates the plasma membrane, bending it inward to form food vacuoles or other phagocytic vesicles.

Components of the Cytoskeleton

Now let's look more closely at the three main types of fibers that make up the cytoskeleton: *Microtubules* are the thickest of the three types; *microfilaments* (also called actin filaments) are the thinnest; and *intermediate filaments* are fibers with diameters in a middle range **(Table 6.1)**.

(a) Motor proteins that attach to receptors on vesicles can "walk" the vesicles along microtubules or, in some cases, along microfilaments.

(b) In this SEM of a squid giant axon (a nerve cell extension), two vesicles containing neurotransmitters move toward the axon's tip.

▲ **Figure 6.21 Motor proteins and the cytoskeleton.**

Table 6.1	The Structure and Function of the Cytoskeleton		
Property	**Microtubules (Tubulin Polymers)**	**Microfilaments (Actin Filaments)**	**Intermediate Filaments**
Structure	Hollow tubes	Two intertwined strands of actin	Fibrous proteins coiled into cables
Diameter	25 nm with 15-nm lumen	7 nm	8–12 nm
Protein subunits	Tubulin, a dimer consisting of α-tubulin and β-tubulin	Actin	One of several different proteins (such as keratins)
Main functions	Maintenance of cell shape (compression-resisting "girders"); cell motility (as in cilia or flagella); chromosome movements in cell division; organelle movements	Maintenance of cell shape (tension-bearing elements); changes in cell shape; muscle contraction; cytoplasmic streaming in plant cells; cell motility (as in amoeboid movement); division of animal cells	Maintenance of cell shape (tension-bearing elements); anchorage of nucleus and certain other organelles; formation of nuclear lamina
Fluorescence micrographs of fibroblasts. Fibroblasts are a favorite cell type for cell biology studies. In each, the structure of interest has been tagged with fluorescent molecules. The DNA in the nucleus has also been tagged in the first micrograph (blue) and third micrograph (orange).	10 µm. Column of tubulin dimers. 25 nm. α β Tubulin dimer	10 µm. Actin subunit. 7 nm	5 µm. Keratin proteins. Fibrous subunit (keratins coiled together). 8–12 nm

Microtubules

All eukaryotic cells have **microtubules**, hollow rods constructed from a globular protein called tubulin. Each tubulin protein is a *dimer*, a molecule made up of two subunits. A tubulin dimer consists of two slightly different polypeptides, α-tubulin and β-tubulin. Microtubules grow in length by adding tubulin dimers; they can also be disassembled and their tubulin used to build microtubules elsewhere in the cell. Because of the orientation of tubulin dimers, the two ends of a microtubule are slightly different. One end can accumulate or release tubulin dimers at a much higher rate than the other, thus growing and shrinking significantly during cellular activities. (This is called the "plus end," not because it can only add tubulin proteins but because it's the end where both "on" and "off" rates are much higher.)

Microtubules shape and support the cell and also serve as tracks along which organelles equipped with motor proteins can move. In addition to the example in Figure 6.21, microtubules guide vesicles from the ER to the Golgi apparatus and from the Golgi to the plasma membrane. Microtubules are also involved in the separation of chromosomes during cell division, which will be discussed in Chapter 12.

Centrosomes and Centrioles In animal cells, microtubules grow out from a **centrosome**, a region that is often located near the nucleus. These microtubules function as compression-resisting girders of the cytoskeleton. Within the centrosome is a pair of **centrioles**, each composed of nine sets of triplet microtubules arranged in a ring **(Figure 6.22)**. Although centrosomes with centrioles may help organize microtubule assembly in animal cells, many other eukaryotic cells lack centrosomes with centrioles and instead organize microtubules by other means.

Cilia and Flagella In eukaryotes, a specialized arrangement of microtubules is responsible for the beating of **flagella** (singular, *flagellum*) and **cilia** (singular, *cilium*), microtubule-containing extensions that project from some cells. (The bacterial flagellum, shown in Figure 6.5, has a completely different structure.) Many unicellular eukaryotes are propelled through water by cilia or flagella that act as locomotor appendages, and the sperm of animals, algae, and some plants have flagella. When cilia or flagella extend from cells that are held in place as part of a tissue layer, they can move fluid over the surface of the tissue. For example, the ciliated lining of the trachea (windpipe) sweeps mucus containing trapped debris out of the lungs (see the EMs in Figure 6.3). In a woman's reproductive tract, the cilia lining the oviducts help move an egg toward the uterus.

Motile cilia usually occur in large numbers on the cell surface. Flagella are usually limited to just one or a few per cell, and they are longer than cilia. Flagella and cilia differ in their beating patterns **(Figure 6.23)**. A flagellum has an

Centrosome

Microtubule

Centrioles

0.25 µm

Longitudinal section of one centriole   Microtubules   Cross section of the other centriole

▲ **Figure 6.22 Centrosome containing a pair of centrioles.** Most animal cells have a centrosome, a region near the nucleus where the cell's microtubules are initiated. Within the centrosome is a pair of centrioles, each about 250 nm (0.25 µm) in diameter. The two centrioles are at right angles to each other, and each is made up of nine sets of three microtubules. The blue portions of the drawing represent nontubulin proteins that connect the microtubule triplets.

? *How many microtubules are in a centrosome? In the drawing, circle and label one microtubule and describe its structure. Circle and label a triplet.*

undulating motion like the tail of a fish. In contrast, cilia work more like oars, with alternating power and recovery strokes, much like the oars of a racing crew boat.

A cilium may also act as a signal-receiving "antenna" for the cell. Cilia that have this function are generally nonmotile, and there is only one per cell. (In fact, in vertebrate animals, it appears that almost all cells have such a cilium, which is called a *primary cilium*.) Membrane proteins on this kind of cilium transmit molecular signals from the cell's environment to its interior, triggering signaling pathways that may lead to changes in the cell's activities. Cilium-based

(a) Motion of flagella. A flagellum usually undulates, its snakelike motion driving a cell in the same direction as the axis of the flagellum. Propulsion of a human sperm cell is an example of flagellate locomotion (LM).

Direction of swimming

5 μm

(b) Motion of cilia. Cilia have a back-and-forth motion. The rapid power stroke moves the cell in a direction perpendicular to the axis of the cilium. Then, during the slower recovery stroke, the cilium bends and sweeps sideways, closer to the cell surface. A dense nap of cilia, beating at a rate of about 40 to 60 strokes a second, covers this *Colpidium*, a freshwater protist (colorized SEM).

Direction of organism's movement

Power stroke   Recovery stroke

15 μm

▲ **Figure 6.23 A comparison of the beating of flagella and motile cilia.**

signaling appears to be crucial to brain function and to embryonic development.

Though different in length, number per cell, and beating pattern, motile cilia and flagella share a common structure. Each motile cilium or flagellum has a group of microtubules sheathed in an extension of the plasma membrane **(Figure 6.24a)**. Nine doublets of microtubules are arranged in a ring, with two single microtubules in its center **(Figure 6.24b)**. This arrangement, referred to as the "9 + 2" pattern, is found in nearly all eukaryotic flagella and motile cilia. (Nonmotile primary cilia have a "9 + 0" pattern, lacking the central pair of microtubules.) The microtubule assembly of a cilium or flagellum is anchored in the cell by a **basal body**, which is structurally very similar to a centriole, with microtubule triplets in a "9 + 0" pattern **(Figure 6.24c)**. In fact, in many animals (including humans), the basal body of the fertilizing sperm's flagellum enters the egg and becomes a centriole.

How does the microtubule assembly produce the bending movements of flagella and motile cilia? Bending involves large motor proteins called **dyneins** (red in the diagram in Figure 6.24) that are attached along each outer microtubule doublet. A typical dynein protein has two "feet" that "walk" along the microtubule of the adjacent doublet, using ATP

for energy. One foot maintains contact, while the other releases and reattaches one step farther along the microtubule (see Figure 6.21). The outer doublets and two central microtubules are held together by flexible cross-linking proteins (blue in the diagram in Figure 6.24), and the walking movement is coordinated so that it happens on one side of the circle at a time. If the doublets were not held in place, the walking action would make them slide past each other. Instead, the movements of the dynein feet cause the microtubules—and the organelle as a whole—to bend.

Microfilaments (Actin Filaments)

Microfilaments are thin solid rods. They are also called actin filaments because they are built from molecules of **actin**, a globular protein. A microfilament is a twisted double chain of actin subunits (see Table 6.1). Besides occurring as linear filaments, microfilaments can form structural networks when certain proteins bind along the side of such a filament and allow a new filament to extend as a branch. Like microtubules, microfilaments seem to be present in all eukaryotic cells.

In contrast to the compression-resisting role of microtubules, the structural role of microfilaments in the cytoskeleton is to bear tension (pulling forces). A three-dimensional

0.1 µm

Outer microtubule doublet

Motor proteins (dyneins)

Central microtubule

Radial spoke

Cross-linking proteins between outer doublets

Plasma membrane

Microtubules

Plasma membrane

Basal body

0.5 µm

(a) A longitudinal section of a motile cilium shows microtubules running the length of the membrane-sheathed structure (TEM).

(b) A cross section through a motile cilium shows the "9 + 2" arrangement of microtubules (TEM). The outer microtubule doublets are held together with the two central microtubules by flexible cross-linking proteins (blue in art), including the radial spokes. The doublets also have attached motor proteins called dyneins (red in art).

(c) Basal body: The nine outer doublets of a cilium or flagellum extend into the basal body, where each doublet joins another microtubule to form a ring of nine triplets. Each triplet is connected to the next by nontubulin proteins (thinner blue lines in diagram). This is a "9 + 0" arrangement: The two central microtubules are not present because they terminate above the basal body (TEM).

0.1 µm

Triplet

Cross section of basal body

▲ **Figure 6.24 Structure of a flagellum or motile cilium.**

DRAW IT *In (a) and (b), circle the central pair of microtubules. In (a), show where they terminate, and explain why they aren't seen in the cross section of the basal body in (c).*

network formed by microfilaments just inside the plasma membrane (*cortical microfilaments*) helps support the cell's shape (see Figure 6.8). This network gives the outer cytoplasmic layer of a cell, called the **cortex**, the semisolid consistency of a gel, in contrast with the more fluid state of the interior cytoplasm. In some kinds of animal cells, such as nutrient-absorbing intestinal cells, bundles of microfilaments make up the core of microvilli, delicate projections that increase the cell's surface area **(Figure 6.25)**.

Microfilaments are well known for their role in cell motility. Thousands of actin filaments and thicker filaments made of a protein called **myosin** interact to cause

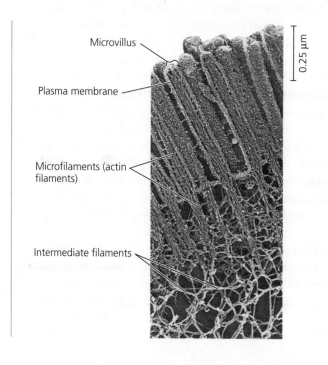

Microvillus

0.25 µm

Plasma membrane

Microfilaments (actin filaments)

Intermediate filaments

▶ **Figure 6.25 A structural role of microfilaments.** The surface area of this nutrient-absorbing intestinal cell is increased by its many microvilli (singular, *microvillus*), cellular extensions reinforced by bundles of microfilaments. These actin filaments are anchored to a network of intermediate filaments (TEM).

contraction of muscle cells (**Figure 6.26a**); muscle contraction is described in detail in Chapter 50. In the unicellular eukaryote *Amoeba* and some of our white blood cells, localized contractions brought about by actin and myosin are involved in the amoeboid (crawling) movement of the cells (**Figure 6.26b**). The cell crawls along a surface by extending cellular extensions called **pseudopodia** (from the Greek *pseudes*, false, and *pod*, foot) and moving toward them. In plant cells, both actin-myosin interactions contribute to **cytoplasmic streaming**, a circular flow of cytoplasm within cells (**Figure 6.26c**). This movement, which is especially common in large plant cells, speeds the distribution of materials within the cell.

Intermediate Filaments

Intermediate filaments are named for their diameter, which is larger than the diameter of microfilaments but smaller than that of microtubules (see Table 6.1). Unlike microtubules and microfilaments, which are found in all eukaryotic cells, intermediate filaments are only found in the cells of some animals, including vertebrates. Specialized for bearing tension (like microfilaments), intermediate filaments are a diverse class of cytoskeletal elements. Each type is constructed from a particular molecular subunit belonging to a family of proteins whose members include the keratins. Microtubules and microfilaments, in contrast, are consistent in diameter and composition in all eukaryotic cells.

Intermediate filaments are more permanent fixtures of cells than are microfilaments and microtubules, which are often disassembled and reassembled in various parts of a cell. Even after cells die, intermediate filament networks often persist; for example, the outer layer of our skin consists of dead skin cells full of keratin filaments. Chemical treatments that remove microfilaments and microtubules from the cytoplasm of living cells leave a web of intermediate filaments that retains its original shape. Such experiments suggest that intermediate filaments are especially sturdy and that they play an important role in reinforcing the shape of a cell and fixing the position of certain organelles. For instance, the nucleus typically sits within a cage made of intermediate filaments, fixed in location by branches of the filaments that extend into the cytoplasm. Other intermediate filaments make up the nuclear lamina, which lines the interior of the nuclear envelope (see Figure 6.9). By supporting a cell's shape, intermediate filaments help the cell carry out its specific function. For example, the network of intermediate filaments shown in Figure 6.25 anchor the microfilaments supporting the intestinal microvilli. Thus, the various kinds of intermediate filaments may function together as the permanent framework of the entire cell.

(a) Myosin motors in muscle cell contraction. The "walking" of myosin projections (the so-called heads) drives the parallel myosin and actin filaments past each other so that the actin filaments approach each other in the middle (red arrows). This shortens the muscle cell. Muscle contraction involves the shortening of many muscle cells at the same time (TEM).

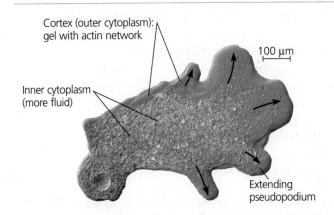

(b) Amoeboid movement. Interaction of actin filaments with myosin causes contraction of the cell, pulling the cell's trailing end (at left) forward (to the right) (LM).

(c) Cytoplasmic streaming in plant cells. A layer of cytoplasm cycles around the cell, moving over a carpet of parallel actin filaments. Myosin motors attached to organelles in the fluid cytosol may drive the streaming by interacting with the actin (LM).

▲ **Figure 6.26 Microfilaments and motility.** In these three examples, interactions between actin filaments and motor proteins bring about cell movement.

CONCEPT CHECK 6.6

1. Describe shared features of microtubule-based motion of flagella and microfilament-based muscle contraction.

2. **WHAT IF?** Males afflicted with Kartagener's syndrome are sterile because of immotile sperm, and they tend to suffer from lung infections. This disorder has a genetic basis. Suggest what the underlying defect might be.

For suggested answers, see Appendix A.

CONCEPT 6.7

Extracellular components and connections between cells help coordinate cellular activities

Having crisscrossed the cell to explore its interior components, we complete our tour of the cell by returning to the surface of this microscopic world, where there are additional structures with important functions. The plasma membrane is usually regarded as the boundary of the living cell, but most cells synthesize and secrete materials that are then extracellular, or external to the plasma membrane. Although these materials and the structures they form are outside the cell, their study is important to cell biology because they are involved in a great many important cellular functions.

Cell Walls of Plants

The **cell wall** is an extracellular structure of plant cells that distinguishes them from animal cells (see Figure 6.8). The wall protects the plant cell, maintains its shape, and prevents excessive uptake of water. On the level of the whole plant, the strong walls of specialized cells hold the plant up against the force of gravity. Prokaryotes, fungi, and some unicellular eukaryotes also have cell walls, as you saw in Figures 6.5 and 6.8, but we will postpone discussion of them until Unit Five.

Plant cell walls are much thicker than the plasma membrane, ranging from 0.1 μm to several micrometers. The exact chemical composition of the wall varies from species to species and even from one cell type to another in the same plant, but the basic design of the wall is consistent. Microfibrils made of the polysaccharide cellulose (see Figure 5.6) are synthesized by an enzyme called cellulose synthase and secreted to the extracellular space, where they become embedded in a matrix of other polysaccharides and proteins. This combination of materials, strong fibers in a "ground substance" (matrix), is the same basic architectural design found in steel-reinforced concrete and in fiberglass.

A young plant cell first secretes a relatively thin and flexible wall called the **primary cell wall** (**Figure 6.27**). Between primary walls of adjacent cells is the **middle lamella**, a thin layer rich in sticky polysaccharides called pectins. The

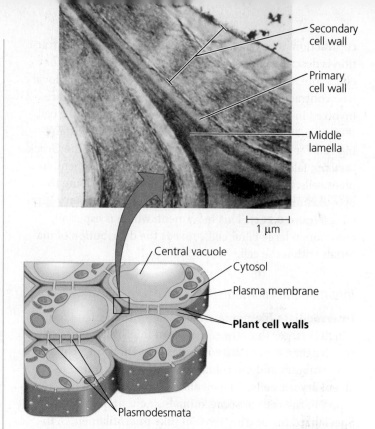

▲ **Figure 6.27 Plant cell walls.** The drawing shows several cells, each with a large vacuole, a nucleus, and several chloroplasts and mitochondria. The transmission electron micrograph shows the cell walls where two cells come together. The multilayered partition between plant cells consists of adjoining walls individually secreted by the cells.

middle lamella glues adjacent cells together. (Pectin is used in cooking as a thickening agent in jams and jellies.) When the cell matures and stops growing, it strengthens its wall. Some plant cells do this simply by secreting hardening substances into the primary wall. Other cells add a **secondary cell wall** between the plasma membrane and the primary wall. The secondary wall, often deposited in several laminated layers, has a strong and durable matrix that affords the cell protection and support. Wood, for example, consists mainly of secondary walls. Plant cell walls are usually perforated by channels between adjacent cells called plasmodesmata (see Figure 6.27), which will be discussed shortly.

The Extracellular Matrix (ECM) of Animal Cells

Although animal cells lack walls akin to those of plant cells, they do have an elaborate **extracellular matrix (ECM)**. The main ingredients of the ECM are glycoproteins and other carbohydrate-containing molecules secreted by the cells. (Recall that glycoproteins are proteins with covalently bonded carbohydrates, usually short chains of sugars.) The most abundant glycoprotein in the ECM of most animal cells is **collagen**, which forms strong fibers outside the cells (see Figure 5.18). In fact, collagen accounts for about 40% of the total protein in the human body. The collagen fibers are embedded in a network woven out of **proteoglycans**

Collagen fibers are embedded in a web of proteoglycan complexes.

Fibronectin attaches the ECM to integrins embedded in the plasma membrane.

Plasma membrane

EXTRACELLULAR FLUID

Microfilaments

CYTOPLASM

A **proteoglycan complex** consists of hundreds of proteoglycan molecules attached noncovalently to a single long polysaccharide molecule.

Integrins, membrane proteins with two subunits, bind to the ECM on the outside and to associated proteins attached to microfilaments on the inside. This linkage can transmit signals between the cell's external environment and its interior and can result in changes in cell behavior.

Polysaccharide molecule

Carbohydrates

Core protein

Proteoglycan molecule

Proteoglycan complex

▲ **Figure 6.28 Extracellular matrix (ECM) of an animal cell.** The molecular composition and structure of the ECM vary from one cell type to another. In this example, three different types of ECM molecules are present: proteoglycans, collagen, and fibronectin.

secreted by cells **(Figure 6.28)**. A proteoglycan molecule consists of a small core protein with many carbohydrate chains covalently attached, so that it may be up to 95% carbohydrate. Large proteoglycan complexes can form when hundreds of proteoglycan molecules become noncovalently attached to a single long polysaccharide molecule, as shown in Figure 6.28. Some cells are attached to the ECM by ECM glycoproteins such as **fibronectin**. Fibronectin and other ECM proteins bind to cell-surface receptor proteins called **integrins** that are built into the plasma membrane. Integrins span the membrane and bind on their cytoplasmic side to associated proteins attached to microfilaments of the cytoskeleton. The name *integrin* is based on the word *integrate*: Integrins are in a position to transmit signals between the ECM and the cytoskeleton and thus to integrate changes occurring outside and inside the cell.

Current research on fibronectin, other ECM molecules, and integrins is revealing the influential role of the ECM in the lives of cells. By communicating with a cell through integrins, the ECM can regulate a cell's behavior. For example, some cells in a developing embryo migrate along specific pathways by matching the orientation of their microfilaments to the "grain" of fibers in the extracellular matrix. Researchers have also learned that the extracellular matrix around a cell can influence the activity of genes in the nucleus. Information about the ECM probably reaches the nucleus by a combination of mechanical and chemical signaling pathways. Mechanical signaling involves fibronectin, integrins, and microfilaments of the cytoskeleton. Changes in the cytoskeleton may in turn trigger chemical signaling pathways inside the cell, leading to changes in the

set of proteins being made by the cell and therefore changes in the cell's function. In this way, the extracellular matrix of a particular tissue may help coordinate the behavior of all the cells of that tissue. Direct connections between cells also function in this coordination, as we discuss next.

Cell Junctions

Cells in an animal or plant are organized into tissues, organs, and organ systems. Neighboring cells often adhere, interact, and communicate via sites of direct physical contact.

Plasmodesmata in Plant Cells

It might seem that the nonliving cell walls of plants would isolate plant cells from one another. But in fact, as shown in **Figure 6.29**, cell walls are perforated with **plasmodesmata** (singular, *plasmodesma*; from the Greek *desma*, bond), channels that connect cells. Cytosol passing

Cell walls

Interior of cell

Interior of cell

0.5 μm

Plasmodesmata   Plasma membranes

▲ **Figure 6.29 Plasmodesmata between plant cells.** The cytoplasm of one plant cell is continuous with the cytoplasm of its neighbors via plasmodesmata, cytoplasmic channels through the cell walls (TEM).

through the plasmodesmata joins the internal chemical environments of adjacent cells. These connections unify most of the plant into one living continuum. The plasma membranes of adjacent cells line the channel of each plasmodesma and thus are continuous. Water and small solutes can pass freely from cell to cell, and several experiments have shown that in some circumstances, certain proteins and RNA molecules can do this as well (see Concept 36.6). The macromolecules transported to neighboring cells appear to reach the plasmodesmata by moving along fibers of the cytoskeleton.

Tight Junctions, Desmosomes, and Gap Junctions in Animal Cells

In animals, there are three main types of cell junctions: *tight junctions*, *desmosomes*, and *gap junctions*. (Gap junctions are most like the plasmodesmata of plants, although gap junction pores are not lined with membrane.) All three types of cell junctions are especially common in epithelial tissue, which lines the external and internal surfaces of the body. **Figure 6.30** uses epithelial cells of the intestinal lining to illustrate these junctions.

▼ **Figure 6.30**
Exploring Cell Junctions in Animal Tissues

Tight junctions prevent fluid from moving across a layer of cells.

Tight junction

Tight junction

Intermediate filaments

Tight junction

Desmosome

Gap junction

Ions or small molecules

Plasma membranes of adjacent cells

Space between cells

Extracellular matrix

TEM   0.5 μm

TEM   1 μm

TEM   0.1 μm

Tight Junctions

At **tight junctions**, the plasma membranes of neighboring cells are very tightly pressed against each other, bound together by specific proteins (purple). Forming continuous seals around the cells, tight junctions establish a barrier that prevents leakage of extracellular fluid across a layer of epithelial cells (see red dashed arrow). For example, tight junctions between skin cells make us watertight.

Desmosomes

Desmosomes (also called *anchoring junctions*) function like rivets, fastening cells together into strong sheets. Intermediate filaments made of sturdy keratin proteins anchor desmosomes in the cytoplasm. Desmosomes attach muscle cells to each other in a muscle. Some "muscle tears" involve the rupture of desmosomes.

Gap Junctions

Gap junctions (also called *communicating junctions*) provide cytoplasmic channels from one cell to an adjacent cell and in this way similar in their function to the plasmodesmata in plants. Gap junctions consist of membrane proteins that surround a pore through which ions, sugars, amino acids, and other small molecules may pass. Gap junctions are necessary for communication between cells in many types of tissues, such as heart muscle, and in animal embryos.

1. In what way are the cells of plants and animals structurally different from single-celled eukaryotes?
2. **WHAT IF?** If the plant cell wall or the animal extracellular matrix were impermeable, what effect would this have on cell function?
3. **MAKE CONNECTIONS** The polypeptide chain that makes up a tight junction weaves back and forth through the membrane four times, with two extracellular loops, and one loop plus short C-terminal and N-terminal tails in the cytoplasm. Looking at Figure 5.14, what would you predict about the amino acid sequence of the tight-junction protein?

For suggested answers, see Appendix A.

The Cell: A Living Unit Greater Than the Sum of Its Parts

From our panoramic view of the cell's compartmental organization to our close-up inspection of each organelle's architecture, this tour of the cell has provided many opportunities to correlate structure with function. (This would be a good time to review cell structure by returning to Figure 6.8.) But even as we dissect the cell, remember that none of its components works alone. As an example of cellular integration, consider the microscopic scene in **Figure 6.31**. The large cell is a macrophage (see Figure 6.13a). It helps defend the mammalian body against infections by ingesting bacteria (the smaller cells) into phagocytic vesicles. The macrophage crawls along a surface and reaches out to the bacteria with thin pseudopodia

▲ **Figure 6.31 The emergence of cellular functions.** The ability of this macrophage (brown) to recognize, apprehend, and destroy bacteria (yellow) is a coordinated activity of the whole cell. Its cytoskeleton, lysosomes, and plasma membrane are among the components that function in phagocytosis (colorized SEM).

(specifically, filopodia). Actin filaments interact with other elements of the cytoskeleton in these movements. After the macrophage engulfs the bacteria, they are destroyed by lysosomes. The elaborate endomembrane system produces the lysosomes. The digestive enzymes of the lysosomes and the proteins of the cytoskeleton are all made by ribosomes. And the synthesis of these proteins is programmed by genetic messages dispatched from the DNA in the nucleus. All these processes require energy, which mitochondria supply in the form of ATP. Cellular functions arise from cellular order: The cell is a living unit greater than the sum of its parts.

6 Chapter Review

SUMMARY OF KEY CONCEPTS

CONCEPT 6.1

Biologists use microscopes and the tools of biochemistry to study cells (pp. 94–97)

- Improvements in microscopy that affect the parameters of magnification, resolution, and contrast have catalyzed progress in the study of cell structure. **Light microscopy** (LM) and **electron microscopy** (EM), as well as other types, remain important tools.
- Cell biologists can obtain pellets enriched in particular cellular components by centrifuging disrupted cells at sequential speeds, a process known as **cell fractionation**. Larger cellular components are in the pellet after lower-speed centrifugation, and smaller components are in the pellet after higher-speed centrifugation.

? *How do microscopy and biochemistry complement each other to reveal cell structure and function?*

CONCEPT 6.2

Eukaryotic cells have internal membranes that compartmentalize their functions (pp. 97–102)

- All cells are bounded by a **plasma membrane**.
- **Prokaryotic cells** lack nuclei and other membrane-enclosed **organelles**, while **eukaryotic cells** have internal membranes that compartmentalize cellular functions.
- The surface-to-volume ratio is an important parameter affecting cell size and shape.
- Plant and animal cells have most of the same organelles: a nucleus, endoplasmic reticulum, Golgi apparatus, and mitochondria. Chloroplasts are present only in cells of photosynthetic eukaryotes.

? *Explain how the compartmental organization of a eukaryotic cell contributes to its biochemical functioning.*

	Cell Component	Structure	Function
CONCEPT 6.3 The eukaryotic cell's genetic instructions are housed in the nucleus and carried out by the ribosomes (pp. 102–104) **?** *Describe the relationship between the nucleus and ribosomes.*	**Nucleus** (ER)	Surrounded by nuclear envelope (double membrane) perforated by nuclear pores; nuclear envelope continuous with endoplasmic reticulum (ER)	Houses chromosomes, which are made of chromatin (DNA and proteins); contains nucleoli, where ribosomal subunits are made; pores regulate entry and exit of materials
	Ribosome	Two subunits made of ribosomal RNA and proteins; can be free in cytosol or bound to ER	Protein synthesis
CONCEPT 6.4 The endomembrane system regulates protein traffic and performs metabolic functions in the cell (pp. 104–109) **?** *Describe the key role played by transport vesicles in the endomembrane system.*	**Endoplasmic reticulum** (Nuclear envelope)	Extensive network of membrane-bounded tubules and sacs; membrane separates lumen from cytosol; continuous with nuclear envelope	Smooth ER: synthesis of lipids, metabolism of carbohydrates, Ca^{2+} storage, detoxification of drugs and poisons Rough ER: aids in synthesis of secretory and other proteins from bound ribosomes; adds carbohydrates to proteins to make glycoproteins; produces new membrane
	Golgi apparatus	Stacks of flattened membranous sacs; has polarity (*cis* and *trans* faces)	Modification of proteins, carbohydrates on proteins, and phospholipids; synthesis of many polysaccharides; sorting of Golgi products, which are then released in vesicles
	Lysosome	Membranous sac of hydrolytic enzymes (in animal cells)	Breakdown of ingested substances, cell macromolecules, and damaged organelles for recycling
	Vacuole	Large membrane-bounded vesicle	Digestion, storage, waste disposal, water balance, cell growth, and protection
CONCEPT 6.5 Mitochondria and chloroplasts change energy from one form to another (pp. 109–112) **?** *What is the endosymbiont theory?*	**Mitochondrion**	Bounded by double membrane; inner membrane has infoldings (cristae)	Cellular respiration
	Chloroplast	Typically two membranes around fluid stroma, which contains thylakoids stacked into grana (in cells of photosynthetic eukaryotes, including plants)	Photosynthesis
	Peroxisome	Specialized metabolic compartment bounded by a single membrane	Contains enzymes that transfer hydrogen atoms from substrates to oxygen, producing hydrogen peroxide (H_2O_2) as a by-product; H_2O_2 is converted to water by another enzyme

CONCEPT 6.6

The cytoskeleton is a network of fibers that organizes structures and activities in the cell (pp. 112–118)

- The **cytoskeleton** functions in structural support for the cell and in motility and signal transmission.
- **Microtubules** shape the cell, guide organelle movement, and separate chromosomes in dividing cells. **Cilia** and **flagella** are motile appendages containing microtubules. Primary cilia also play sensory and signaling roles. **Microfilaments** are thin rods that function in muscle contraction, amoeboid movement, **cytoplasmic streaming**, and support of microvilli. **Intermediate filaments** support cell shape and fix organelles in place.

? *Describe the role of motor proteins inside the eukaryotic cell and in whole-cell movement.*

CONCEPT 6.7

Extracellular components and connections between cells help coordinate cellular activities (pp. 118–121)

- Plant **cell walls** are made of cellulose fibers embedded in other polysaccharides and proteins.
- Animal cells secrete glycoproteins and proteoglycans that form the **extracellular matrix (ECM)**, which functions in support, adhesion, movement, and regulation.
- Cell junctions connect neighboring cells. Plants have **plasmodesmata** that pass through adjoining cell walls. Animal cells have **tight junctions**, **desmosomes**, and **gap junctions**.

? *Compare the structure and functions of a plant cell wall and the extracellular matrix of an animal cell.*

TEST YOUR UNDERSTANDING

LEVEL 1: KNOWLEDGE/COMPREHENSION

1. Which structure is *not* part of the endomembrane system?
   a. nuclear envelope
   b. chloroplast
   c. Golgi apparatus
   d. plasma membrane

2. Which structure is common to plant *and* animal cells?
   a. chloroplast
   b. central vacuole
   c. mitochondrion
   d. centriole

3. Which of the following is present in a prokaryotic cell?
   a. mitochondrion
   b. ribosome
   c. nuclear envelope
   d. chloroplast

4. Which structure-function pair is *mismatched*?
   a. microtubule; muscle contraction
   b. ribosome; protein synthesis
   c. Golgi; protein trafficking
   d. nucleolus; production of ribosomal subunits

LEVEL 2: APPLICATION/ANALYSIS

5. Cyanide binds to at least one molecule involved in producing ATP. If a cell is exposed to cyanide, most of the cyanide will be found within the
   a. mitochondria.
   b. ribosomes.
   c. peroxisomes.
   d. lysosomes.

6. What is the most likely pathway taken by a newly synthesized protein that will be secreted by a cell?
   a. Golgi → ER → lysosome
   b. nucleus → ER → Golgi
   c. ER → Golgi → vesicles that fuse with plasma membrane
   d. ER → lysosomes → vesicles that fuse with plasma membrane

7. Which cell would be best for studying lysosomes?
   a. muscle cell
   b. nerve cell
   c. phagocytic white blood cell
   d. bacterial cell

8. **DRAW IT** From memory, draw two eukaryotic cells, labeling the structures listed here and showing any physical connections between the internal structures of each cell: nucleus, rough ER, smooth ER, mitochondrion, centrosome, chloroplast, vacuole, lysosome, microtubule, cell wall, ECM, microfilament, Golgi apparatus, intermediate filament, plasma membrane, peroxisome, ribosome, nucleolus, nuclear pore, vesicle, flagellum, microvilli, plasmodesma.

LEVEL 3: SYNTHESIS/EVALUATION

9. **EVOLUTION CONNECTION**
   Which aspects of cell structure best reveal evolutionary unity? What are some examples of specialized modifications?

10. **SCIENTIFIC INQUIRY**
    Imagine protein X, destined to span the plasma membrane. Assume that the mRNA carrying the genetic message for protein X has already been translated by ribosomes in a cell culture. If you fractionate the cells (see Figure 6.4), in which fraction would you find protein X? Explain by describing its transit through the cell.

11. **WRITE ABOUT A THEME: ORGANIZATION**
    Considering some of the characteristics that define life and drawing on your knowledge of cellular structures and functions, write a short essay (100–150 words) that discusses this statement: Life is an emergent property that appears at the level of the cell. (See Concept 1.1.)

12. **SYNTHESIZE YOUR KNOWLEDGE**

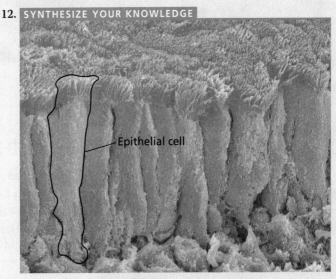

Epithelial cell

The cells in the SEM are epithelial cells from the small intestine. Discuss how aspects of their structure contribute to their specialized functions of nutrient absorption and as a barrier between the intestinal contents and the blood supply on the other side of the sheet of epithelial cells.

For selected answers, see Appendix A.

MasteringBiology®

Students Go to **MasteringBiology** for assignments, the eText, and the Study Area with practice tests, animations, and activities.

Instructors Go to **MasteringBiology** for automatically graded tutorials and questions that you can assign to your students, plus Instructor Resources.

7

Membrane Structure and Function

KEY CONCEPTS

7.1   Cellular membranes are fluid mosaics of lipids and proteins

7.2   Membrane structure results in selective permeability

7.3   Passive transport is diffusion of a substance across a membrane with no energy investment

7.4   Active transport uses energy to move solutes against their gradients

7.5   Bulk transport across the plasma membrane occurs by exocytosis and endocytosis

▲ **Figure 7.1 How do cell membrane proteins help regulate chemical traffic?**

Life at the Edge

The plasma membrane is the edge of life, the boundary that separates the living cell from its surroundings and controls traffic into and out of the cell it surrounds. Like all biological membranes, the plasma membrane exhibits **selective permeability**; that is, it allows some substances to cross it more easily than others. The ability of the cell to discriminate in its chemical exchanges with its environment is fundamental to life, and it is the plasma membrane and its component molecules that make this selectivity possible.

In this chapter, you will learn how cellular membranes control the passage of substances. The image in **Figure 7.1** shows a computer model of water molecules (red and gray) passing through a short section of membrane. The blue ribbons within the lipid bilayer (green) represent helical regions of a membrane protein called an aquaporin. One molecule of this protein enables billions of water molecules to pass through the membrane every second, many more than could cross on their own. Found in many cells, aquaporins are but one example of how the plasma membrane and its proteins enable cells to survive and function. To understand how membranes work, we'll begin by examining their structure. Then, in the rest of the chapter, we'll describe in some detail how plasma membranes control transport into and out of cells, sometimes through proteins like the ion channel to the left.

CONCEPT 7.1

Cellular membranes are fluid mosaics of lipids and proteins

Lipids and proteins are the staple ingredients of membranes, although carbohydrates are also important. The most abundant lipids in most membranes are phospholipids. The ability of phospholipids to form membranes is inherent in their molecular structure. A phospholipid is an **amphipathic** molecule, meaning it has both a hydrophilic region and a hydrophobic region (see Figure 5.11). Other types of membrane lipids are also amphipathic. A phospholipid bilayer can exist as a stable boundary between two aqueous compartments because the molecular arrangement shelters the hydrophobic tails of the phospholipids from water while exposing the hydrophilic heads to water **(Figure 7.2)**.

Like membrane lipids, most membrane proteins are amphipathic. Such proteins can reside in the phospholipid bilayer with their hydrophilic regions protruding. This molecular orientation maximizes contact of hydrophilic regions of proteins with water in the cytosol and extracellular fluid, while providing their hydrophobic

▼ **Figure 7.2 Phospholipid bilayer (cross section).**

Hydrophilic head

Hydrophobic tail

WATER

WATER

MAKE CONNECTIONS *Consulting Figure 5.11, circle the hydrophilic and hydrophobic portions of the enlarged phospholipids on the right. Explain what each portion contacts when the phospholipids are in the plasma membrane.*

parts with a nonaqueous environment. **Figure 7.3** shows the currently accepted model of the arrangement of molecules in the plasma membrane. In this **fluid mosaic model**, the membrane is a mosaic of protein molecules bobbing in a fluid bilayer of phospholipids.

▲ **Figure 7.3 Updated model of an animal cell's plasma membrane (cutaway view).**

Fibers of extra-cellular matrix (ECM)

Glyco-protein

Carbohydrate

Glycolipid

EXTRACELLULAR SIDE OF MEMBRANE

Cholesterol

Microfilaments of cytoskeleton

Peripheral proteins

Integral protein

CYTOPLASMIC SIDE OF MEMBRANE

The proteins are not randomly distributed in the membrane, however. Groups of proteins are often associated in long-lasting, specialized patches, where they carry out common functions. The lipids themselves appear to form defined regions as well. Also, in some regions the membrane may be much more packed with proteins than shown in Figure 7.3. Like all models, the fluid mosaic model is continually being refined as new research reveals more about membrane structure.

The Fluidity of Membranes

Membranes are not static sheets of molecules locked rigidly in place. A membrane is held together primarily by hydrophobic interactions, which are much weaker than covalent bonds (see Figure 5.18). Most of the lipids and some of the proteins can shift about laterally—that is, in the plane of the membrane, like partygoers elbowing their way through a crowded room. Very rarely, also, a lipid may flip-flop across the membrane, switching from one phospholipid layer to the other.

The lateral movement of phospholipids within the membrane is rapid. Adjacent phospholipids switch positions about 10^7 times per second, which means that a phospholipid can travel about 2 μm—the length of many bacterial cells—in 1 second. Proteins are much larger than lipids and move more slowly, but some membrane proteins do drift, as shown in a classic experiment described in **Figure 7.4**. Some membrane proteins seem to move in a highly directed

manner, perhaps driven along cytoskeletal fibers in the cell by motor proteins connected to the membrane proteins' cytoplasmic regions. However, many other membrane proteins seem to be held immobile by their attachment to the cytoskeleton or to the extracellular matrix (see Figure 7.3).

A membrane remains fluid as temperature decreases until the phospholipids settle into a closely packed arrangement and the membrane solidifies, much as bacon grease forms lard when it cools. The temperature at which a membrane solidifies depends on the types of lipids it is made of. The membrane remains fluid to a lower temperature if it is rich in phospholipids with unsaturated hydrocarbon tails (see Figures 5.10 and 5.11). Because of kinks in the tails where double bonds are located, unsaturated hydrocarbon tails cannot pack together as closely as saturated hydrocarbon tails, making the membrane more fluid (**Figure 7.5a**).

The steroid cholesterol, which is wedged between phospholipid molecules in the plasma membranes of animal cells, has different effects on membrane fluidity at different temperatures (**Figure 7.5b**). At relatively high temperatures—at 37°C, the body temperature of humans, for example—cholesterol makes the membrane less fluid by restraining phospholipid movement. However, because cholesterol also hinders the close packing of phospholipids, it lowers the temperature required for the membrane to solidify. Thus, cholesterol can be thought of as a "fluidity buffer" for the membrane, resisting changes in membrane fluidity that can be caused by changes in temperature.

▼ Figure 7.4 | Inquiry

Do membrane proteins move?

Experiment Larry Frye and Michael Edidin, at Johns Hopkins University, labeled the plasma membrane proteins of a mouse cell and a human cell with two different markers and fused the cells. Using a microscope, they observed the markers on the hybrid cell.

Results

Conclusion The mixing of the mouse and human membrane proteins indicates that at least some membrane proteins move sideways within the plane of the plasma membrane.

Source: L. D. Frye and M. Edidin, The rapid intermixing of cell surface antigens after formation of mouse-human heterokaryons, *Journal of Cell Science* 7:319 (1970).

WHAT IF? *Suppose the proteins did not mix in the hybrid cell, even many hours after fusion. Would you be able to conclude that proteins don't move within the membrane? What other explanation could there be?*

▼ Figure 7.5 **Factors that affect membrane fluidity.**

(a) Unsaturated versus saturated hydrocarbon tails.

Fluid | Viscous

Unsaturated hydrocarbon tails (kinked) prevent packing, enhancing membrane fluidity.

Saturated hydrocarbon tails pack together, increasing membrane viscosity.

(b) Cholesterol within the animal cell membrane.

Cholesterol

Cholesterol reduces membrane fluidity at moderate temperatures by reducing phospholipid movement, but at low temperatures it hinders solidification by disrupting the regular packing of phospholipids.

Membranes must be fluid to work properly; the fluidity of a membrane affects both its permeability and the ability of membrane proteins to move to where their function is needed. Usually, membranes are about as fluid as salad oil. When a membrane solidifies, its permeability changes, and enzymatic proteins in the membrane may become inactive if their activity requires movement within the membrane. However, membranes that are too fluid cannot support protein function either. Therefore, extreme environments pose a challenge for life, resulting in evolutionary adaptations that include differences in membrane lipid composition.

Evolution of Differences in Membrane Lipid Composition

EVOLUTION Variations in the cell membrane lipid compositions of many species appear to be evolutionary adaptations that maintain the appropriate membrane fluidity under specific environmental conditions. For instance, fishes that live in extreme cold have membranes with a high proportion of unsaturated hydrocarbon tails, enabling their membranes to remain fluid (see Figure 7.5a). At the other extreme, some bacteria and archaea thrive at temperatures greater than 90°C (194°F) in thermal hot springs and geysers. Their membranes include unusual lipids that may prevent excessive fluidity at such high temperatures.

The ability to change the lipid composition of cell membranes in response to changing temperatures has evolved in organisms that live where temperatures vary. In many plants that tolerate extreme cold, such as winter wheat, the percentage of unsaturated phospholipids increases in autumn, an adjustment that keeps the membranes from solidifying during winter. Certain bacteria and archaea can also change the proportion of unsaturated phospholipids in their cell membranes, depending on the temperature at which they are growing. Overall, natural selection has apparently favored organisms whose mix of membrane lipids ensures an appropriate level of membrane fluidity for their environment.

Membrane Proteins and Their Functions

Now we come to the *mosaic* aspect of the fluid mosaic model. Somewhat like a tile mosaic, a membrane is a collage of different proteins, often clustered together in groups, embedded in the fluid matrix of the lipid bilayer (see Figure 7.3). In the plasma membrane of red blood cells alone, for example, more than 50 kinds of proteins have been found so far. Phospholipids form the main fabric of the membrane, but proteins determine most of the membrane's functions. Different types of cells contain different sets of membrane proteins, and the various membranes within a cell each have a unique collection of proteins.

▶ **Figure 7.6 The structure of a transmembrane protein.** Bacteriorhodopsin (a bacterial transport protein) has a distinct orientation in the membrane, with its N-terminus outside the cell and its C-terminus inside. This ribbon model highlights the α-helical secondary structure of the hydrophobic parts, which lie mostly within the hydrophobic interior of the membrane. The protein includes seven transmembrane helices. The nonhelical hydrophilic segments are in contact with the aqueous solutions on the extracellular and cytoplasmic sides of the membrane. Although shown as simple purple shapes in many figures in this book, each protein has its own unique structure.

Notice in Figure 7.3 that there are two major populations of membrane proteins: integral proteins and peripheral proteins. **Integral proteins** penetrate the hydrophobic interior of the lipid bilayer. The majority are *transmembrane proteins*, which span the membrane; other integral proteins extend only partway into the hydrophobic interior. The hydrophobic regions of an integral protein consist of one or more stretches of nonpolar amino acids (see Figure 5.14), usually coiled into α helices **(Figure 7.6)**. The hydrophilic parts of the molecule are exposed to the aqueous solutions on either side of the membrane. Some proteins also have one or more hydrophilic channels that allow passage through the membrane of hydrophilic substances (even of water itself; see Figure 7.1). **Peripheral proteins** are not embedded in the lipid bilayer at all; they are appendages loosely bound to the surface of the membrane, often to exposed parts of integral proteins (see Figure 7.3).

On the cytoplasmic side of the plasma membrane, some membrane proteins are held in place by attachment to the cytoskeleton. And on the extracellular side, certain membrane proteins are attached to fibers of the extracellular matrix (see Figure 6.28; *integrins* are one type of integral, transmembrane protein). These attachments combine to give animal cells a stronger framework than the plasma membrane alone could provide.

A single cell may have cell surface membrane proteins that carry out several different functions, such as transport through the cell membrane, enzymatic activity, or attaching a cell to either a neighboring cell or the extracellular matrix. Furthermore, a single membrane protein may itself carry out multiple functions. Thus, the membrane is not only a structural mosaic, but also a functional mosaic. **Figure 7.7** illustrates six major functions performed by proteins of the plasma membrane.

(a) Transport. *Left:* A protein that spans the membrane may provide a hydrophilic channel across the membrane that is selective for a particular solute. *Right:* Other transport proteins shuttle a substance from one side to the other by changing shape (see Figure 7.14b). Some of these proteins hydrolyze ATP as an energy source to actively pump substances across the membrane.

(b) Enzymatic activity. A protein built into the membrane may be an enzyme with its active site exposed to substances in the adjacent solution. In some cases, several enzymes in a membrane are organized as a team that carries out sequential steps of a metabolic pathway.

(c) Signal transduction. A membrane protein (receptor) may have a binding site with a specific shape that fits the shape of a chemical messenger, such as a hormone. The external messenger (signaling molecule) may cause the protein to change shape, allowing it to relay the message to the inside of the cell, usually by binding to a cytoplasmic protein (see Figure 11.6).

(d) Cell-cell recognition. Some glycoproteins serve as identification tags that are specifically recognized by membrane proteins of other cells. This type of cell-cell binding is usually short-lived compared to that shown in (e).

(e) Intercellular joining. Membrane proteins of adjacent cells may hook together in various kinds of junctions, such as gap junctions or tight junctions (see Figure 6.30). This type of binding is more long-lasting than that shown in (d).

(f) Attachment to the cytoskeleton and extracellular matrix (ECM). Microfilaments or other elements of the cytoskeleton may be noncovalently bound to membrane proteins, a function that helps maintain cell shape and stabilizes the location of certain membrane proteins. Proteins that can bind to ECM molecules can coordinate extracellular and intracellular changes (see Figure 6.28).

▲ **Figure 7.7 Some functions of membrane proteins.** In many cases, a single protein performs multiple tasks.

 Some transmembrane proteins can bind to a particular ECM molecule and, when bound, transmit a signal into the cell. Use the proteins shown in (c) and (f) to explain how this might occur.

Proteins on a cell's surface are important in the medical field. For example, a protein called CD4 on the surface of immune cells helps the human immunodeficiency virus (HIV) infect these cells, leading to acquired immune deficiency syndrome (AIDS). Despite multiple exposures to HIV, however, a small number of people do not develop AIDS and show no evidence of HIV-infected cells. Comparing their genes with the genes of infected individuals, researchers learned that resistant people have an unusual form of a gene that codes for an immune cell-surface protein called CCR5. Further work showed although CD4 is the main HIV receptor, HIV must also bind to CCR5 as a "co-receptor" to infect most cells **(Figure 7.8a).** An absence of CCR5 on the cells of resistant individuals, due to the gene alteration, prevents the virus from entering the cells **(Figure 7.8b).**

This information has been key to developing a treatment for HIV infection. Interfering with CD4 could cause dangerous side effects because it performs many important functions in cells. Discovery of the CCR5 co-receptor provided a safer target for development of drugs that mask this protein and block HIV entry. One such drug, maraviroc (brand name Selzentry), was approved for treatment of HIV in 2007 and is still being used today. A clinical trial began in 2012 to test whether this drug might also work to prevent HIV infection in uninfected, at-risk patients.

The Role of Membrane Carbohydrates in Cell-Cell Recognition

Cell-cell recognition, a cell's ability to distinguish one type of neighboring cell from another, is crucial to the functioning of an organism. It is important, for example, in the sorting of cells into tissues and organs in an animal embryo. It is also the basis for the rejection of foreign cells by the immune

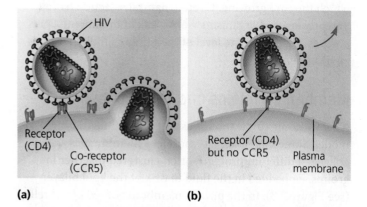

▲ **Figure 7.8 The genetic basis for HIV resistance. (a)** HIV can infect a cell with CCR5 on its surface, as in most people. **(b)** HIV cannot infect a cell lacking CCR5 on its surface, as in resistant individuals.

MAKE CONNECTIONS *Study Figures 2.16 and 5.17, both of which show pairs of molecules binding to each other. What would you predict about CCR5 that would allow HIV to bind to it? How could a drug molecule interfere with this binding?*

system, an important line of defense in vertebrate animals (see Chapter 43). Cells recognize other cells by binding to molecules, often containing carbohydrates, on the extracellular surface of the plasma membrane (see Figure 7.7d).

Membrane carbohydrates are usually short, branched chains of fewer than 15 sugar units. Some are covalently bonded to lipids, forming molecules called **glycolipids**. (Recall that *glyco* refers to the presence of carbohydrate.) However, most are covalently bonded to proteins, which are thereby **glycoproteins** (see Figure 7.3).

The carbohydrates on the extracellular side of the plasma membrane vary from species to species, among individuals of the same species, and even from one cell type to another in a single individual. The diversity of the molecules and their location on the cell's surface enable membrane carbohydrates to function as markers that distinguish one cell from another. For example, the four human blood types designated A, B, AB, and O reflect variation in the carbohydrate part of glycoproteins on the surface of red blood cells.

Synthesis and Sidedness of Membranes

Membranes have distinct inside and outside faces. The two lipid layers may differ in lipid composition, and each protein has directional orientation in the membrane (see Figure 7.6). **Figure 7.9** shows how membrane sidedness arises: The asymmetrical arrangement of proteins, lipids, and their

associated carbohydrates in the plasma membrane is determined as the membrane is being built by the endoplasmic reticulum (ER) and Golgi apparatus, components of the endomembrane system (see Figure 6.15).

CONCEPT 7.2

Membrane structure results in selective permeability

The biological membrane is an exquisite example of a supramolecular structure—many molecules ordered into a higher level of organization—with emergent properties beyond those of the individual molecules. The remainder of this chapter focuses on one of those properties: the ability to regulate transport across cellular boundaries, a function

▼ **Figure 7.9 Synthesis of membrane components and their orientation in the membrane.** The cytoplasmic (orange) face of the plasma membrane differs from the extracellular (aqua) face. The latter arises from the inside face of ER, Golgi, and vesicle membranes.

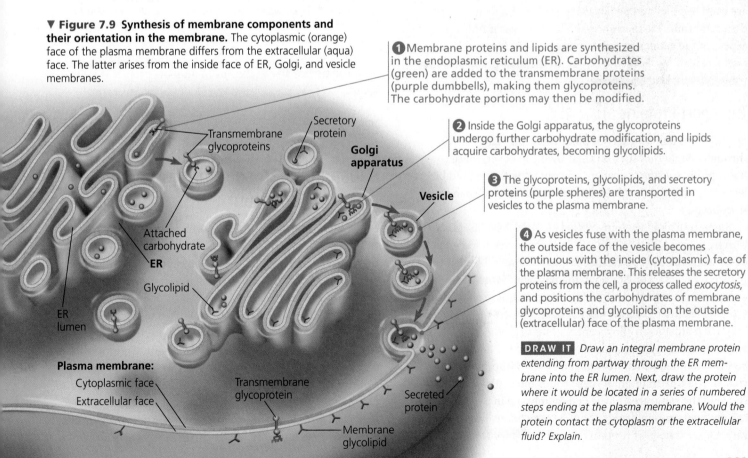

❶ Membrane proteins and lipids are synthesized in the endoplasmic reticulum (ER). Carbohydrates (green) are added to the transmembrane proteins (purple dumbbells), making them glycoproteins. The carbohydrate portions may then be modified.

❷ Inside the Golgi apparatus, the glycoproteins undergo further carbohydrate modification, and lipids acquire carbohydrates, becoming glycolipids.

❸ The glycoproteins, glycolipids, and secretory proteins (purple spheres) are transported in vesicles to the plasma membrane.

❹ As vesicles fuse with the plasma membrane, the outside face of the vesicle becomes continuous with the inside (cytoplasmic) face of the plasma membrane. This releases the secretory proteins from the cell, a process called *exocytosis*, and positions the carbohydrates of membrane glycoproteins and glycolipids on the outside (extracellular) face of the plasma membrane.

DRAW IT *Draw an integral membrane protein extending from partway through the ER membrane into the ER lumen. Next, draw the protein where it would be located in a series of numbered steps ending at the plasma membrane. Would the protein contact the cytoplasm or the extracellular fluid? Explain.*

essential to the cell's existence. We will see once again that form fits function: The fluid mosaic model helps explain how membranes regulate the cell's molecular traffic.

A steady traffic of small molecules and ions moves across the plasma membrane in both directions. Consider the chemical exchanges between a muscle cell and the extracellular fluid that bathes it. Sugars, amino acids, and other nutrients enter the cell, and metabolic waste products leave it. The cell takes in O_2 for use in cellular respiration and expels CO_2. Also, the cell regulates its concentrations of inorganic ions, such as Na^+, K^+, Ca^{2+}, and Cl^-, by shuttling them one way or the other across the plasma membrane. Although the heavy traffic through them may seem to suggest otherwise, cell membranes are selectively permeable, and substances do not cross the barrier indiscriminately. The cell is able to take up some small molecules and ions and exclude others.

The Permeability of the Lipid Bilayer

Nonpolar molecules, such as hydrocarbons, CO_2, and O_2, are hydrophobic. They can therefore dissolve in the lipid bilayer of the membrane and cross it easily, without the aid of membrane proteins. However, the hydrophobic interior of the membrane impedes direct passage through the membrane of ions and polar molecules, which are hydrophilic. Polar molecules such as glucose and other sugars pass only slowly through a lipid bilayer, and even water, a very small polar molecule, does not cross rapidly. A charged atom or molecule and its surrounding shell of water (see Figure 3.7) are even less likely to penetrate the hydrophobic interior of the membrane. Furthermore, the lipid bilayer is only one aspect of the gatekeeper system responsible for a cell's selective permeability. Proteins built into the membrane play key roles in regulating transport.

Transport Proteins

Specific ions and a variety of polar molecules can't move through cell membranes on their own. However, these hydrophilic substances can avoid contact with the lipid bilayer by passing through **transport proteins** that span the membrane.

Some transport proteins, called *channel proteins*, function by having a hydrophilic channel that certain molecules or atomic ions use as a tunnel through the membrane (see Figure 7.7a, left). For example, the passage of water molecules through the membrane in certain cells is greatly facilitated by channel proteins known as **aquaporins** (see Figure 7.1). Each aquaporin allows entry of up to *3 billion* (3×10^9) water molecules per second, passing single file through its central channel, which fits ten at a time. Without aquaporins, only a tiny fraction of these water molecules would pass through the same area of the cell membrane in a second, so the channel protein brings about a tremendous increase in rate. Other transport proteins, called *carrier proteins*, hold

onto their passengers and change shape in a way that shuttles them across the membrane (see Figure 7.7a, right).

A transport protein is specific for the substance it translocates (moves), allowing only a certain substance (or a small group of related substances) to cross the membrane. For example, a specific carrier protein in the plasma membrane of red blood cells transports glucose across the membrane 50,000 times faster than glucose can pass through on its own. This "glucose transporter" is so selective that it even rejects fructose, a structural isomer of glucose.

Thus, the selective permeability of a membrane depends on both the discriminating barrier of the lipid bilayer and the specific transport proteins built into the membrane. But what establishes the *direction* of traffic across a membrane? At a given time, what determines whether a particular substance will enter the cell or leave the cell? And what mechanisms actually drive molecules across membranes? We will address these questions next as we explore two modes of membrane traffic: passive transport and active transport.

CONCEPT CHECK 7.2

1. What property allows O_2 and CO_2 to cross a lipid bilayer without the help of membrane proteins?

2. Why is a transport protein needed to move many water molecules rapidly across a membrane?

3. **MAKE CONNECTIONS** Aquaporins exclude passage of hydronium ions (H_3O^+), but some aquaporins allow passage of glycerol, a three-carbon alcohol (see Figure 5.9), as well as H_2O. Since H_3O^+ is closer in size to water than glycerol is, yet cannot pass through, what might be the basis of this selectivity?

For suggested answers, see Appendix A.

CONCEPT 7.3

Passive transport is diffusion of a substance across a membrane with no energy investment

Molecules have a type of energy called thermal energy, due to their constant motion (see Concept 3.2). One result of this motion is **diffusion**, the movement of particles of any substance so that they spread out into the available space. Each molecule moves randomly, yet diffusion of a *population* of molecules may be directional. To understand this process, let's imagine a synthetic membrane separating pure water from a solution of a dye in water. Study **Figure 7.10a** carefully to appreciate how diffusion would result in both solutions having equal concentrations of the dye molecules. Once that point is reached, there will be a dynamic equilibrium, with roughly as many dye molecules crossing the membrane each second in one direction as in the other.

Molecules of dye ─── Membrane (cross section)

WATER

Net diffusion | Net diffusion | Equilibrium

(a) Diffusion of one solute. The membrane has pores large enough for molecules of dye to pass through. Random movement of dye molecules will cause some to pass through the pores; this will happen more often on the side with more dye molecules. The dye diffuses from where it is more concentrated to where it is less concentrated (called diffusing down a concentration gradient). This leads to a dynamic equilibrium: The solute molecules continue to cross the membrane, but at roughly equal rates in both directions.

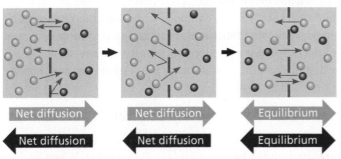

Net diffusion | Net diffusion | Equilibrium
Net diffusion | Net diffusion | Equilibrium

(b) Diffusion of two solutes. Solutions of two different dyes are separated by a membrane that is permeable to both. Each dye diffuses down its own concentration gradient. There will be a net diffusion of the purple dye toward the left, even though the *total* solute concentration was initially greater on the left side.

▲ **Figure 7.10 The diffusion of solutes across a synthetic membrane.** Each of the large arrows under the diagrams shows the net diffusion of the dye molecules of that color.

We can now state a simple rule of diffusion: In the absence of other forces, a substance will diffuse from where it is more concentrated to where it is less concentrated. Put another way, any substance will diffuse down its **concentration gradient**, the region along which the density of a chemical substance increases or decreases (in this case, decreases). No work must be done to make this happen; diffusion is a spontaneous process, needing no input of energy. Note that each substance diffuses down its *own* concentration gradient, unaffected by the concentration gradients of other substances **(Figure 7.10b)**.

Much of the traffic across cell membranes occurs by diffusion. When a substance is more concentrated on one side of a membrane than on the other, there is a tendency for the substance to diffuse across the membrane down its concentration gradient (assuming that the membrane is permeable to that substance). One important example is the uptake of oxygen by a cell performing cellular respiration. Dissolved oxygen diffuses into the cell across the plasma membrane. As long as cellular respiration consumes the O_2 as it enters, diffusion into the cell will continue because the concentration gradient favors movement in that direction.

The diffusion of a substance across a biological membrane is called **passive transport** because the cell does not have to expend energy to make it happen. The concentration gradient itself represents potential energy (see Concept 2.2 and Figure 8.5b) and drives diffusion. Remember, however, that membranes are selectively permeable and therefore have different effects on the rates of diffusion of various molecules. In the case of water, aquaporins allow water to diffuse very rapidly across the membranes of certain cells. As we'll see next, the movement of water across the plasma membrane has important consequences for cells.

Effects of Osmosis on Water Balance

To see how two solutions with different solute concentrations interact, picture a U-shaped glass tube with a selectively permeable artificial membrane separating two sugar solutions **(Figure 7.11)**. Pores in this synthetic membrane

Lower concentration of solute (sugar) | Higher concentration of solute | More similar concentrations of solute

Sugar molecule

H_2O

Selectively permeable membrane

Water molecules can pass through pores, but sugar molecules cannot. | Water molecules cluster around sugar molecules.

This side has fewer solute molecules, more free water molecules. | This side has more solute molecules, fewer free water molecules.

Osmosis

Water moves from an area of higher to lower free water concentration (lower to higher solute concentration).

▲ **Figure 7.11 Osmosis.** Two sugar solutions of different concentrations are separated by a membrane that the solvent (water) can pass through but the solute (sugar) cannot. Water molecules move randomly and may cross in either direction, but overall, water diffuses from the solution with less concentrated solute to that with more concentrated solute. This passive transport of water, or osmosis, makes the sugar concentrations on both sides more nearly equal. (The concentrations are prevented from being exactly equal due to the effect of water pressure on the higher side, which is not discussed here for simplicity.)

WHAT IF? *If an orange dye capable of passing through the membrane was added to the left side of the tube above, how would it be distributed at the end of the experiment? (See Figure 7.10.) Would the final solution levels in the tube be affected?*

are too small for sugar molecules to pass through but large enough for water molecules. However, tight clustering of water molecules around the hydrophilic solute molecules makes some of the water unavailable to cross the membrane. As a result, the solution with a higher solute concentration has a lower *free* water concentration. Water diffuses across the membrane from the region of higher free water concentration (lower solute concentration) to that of lower free water concentration (higher solute concentration) until the solute concentrations on both sides of the membrane are more nearly equal. The diffusion of free water across a selectively permeable membrane, whether artificial or cellular, is called **osmosis**. The movement of water across cell membranes and the balance of water between the cell and its environment are crucial to organisms. Let's now apply what we've learned in this system to living cells.

Water Balance of Cells Without Cell Walls

To explain the behavior of a cell in a solution, we must consider both solute concentration and membrane permeability. Both factors are taken into account in the concept of **tonicity**, the ability of a surrounding solution to cause a cell to gain or lose water. The tonicity of a solution depends in part on its concentration of solutes that cannot cross the membrane (nonpenetrating solutes) relative to that inside the cell. If there is a higher concentration of nonpenetrating solutes in the surrounding solution, water will tend to leave the cell, and vice versa.

If a cell without a cell wall, such as an animal cell, is immersed in an environment that is **isotonic** to the cell (*iso* means "same"), there will be no *net* movement of water across the plasma membrane. Water diffuses across the membrane, but at the same rate in both directions. In an isotonic environment, the volume of an animal cell is stable **(Figure 7.12a)**.

Let's transfer the cell to a solution that is **hypertonic** to the cell (*hyper* means "more," in this case referring to nonpenetrating solutes). The cell will lose water, shrivel, and probably die. This is why an increase in the salinity (saltiness) of a lake can kill the animals there; if the lake water becomes hypertonic to the animals' cells, they might shrivel and die. However, taking up too much water can be just as hazardous as losing water. If we place the cell in a solution that is **hypotonic** to the cell (*hypo* means "less"), water will enter the cell faster than it leaves, and the cell will swell and lyse (burst) like an overfilled water balloon.

A cell without rigid cell walls can tolerate neither excessive uptake nor excessive loss of water. This problem of water balance is automatically solved if such a cell lives in isotonic surroundings. Seawater is isotonic to many marine invertebrates. The cells of most terrestrial (land-dwelling) animals are bathed in an extracellular fluid that is isotonic to the cells. In hypertonic or hypotonic environments, however, organisms that lack rigid cell walls must have other adaptations for **osmoregulation**, the control of solute concentrations and water balance. For example, the unicellular protist *Paramecium caudatum* lives in pond water, which is hypotonic to the cell. *P. caudatum* has a plasma membrane that is much less permeable to water than the membranes of most other cells, but this only slows the uptake of water, which continually enters the cell. The *P. caudatum* cell doesn't burst because it is also equipped with a contractile vacuole, an organelle that functions as a bilge pump to force water out of the cell as fast as it enters by osmosis **(Figure 7.13)**. We will examine other evolutionary adaptations for osmoregulation in Chapter 44.

Water Balance of Cells with Cell Walls

The cells of plants, prokaryotes, fungi, and some protists are surrounded by cell walls (see Figure 6.27). When such a cell is immersed in a hypotonic solution—bathed in rainwater, for example—the cell wall helps maintain the cell's water balance. Consider a plant cell. Like an animal cell, the plant cell swells as water enters by osmosis **(Figure 7.12b)**. However, the relatively inelastic cell wall will expand only so much before it exerts a back pressure on the cell, called *turgor pressure*, that opposes further water uptake. At this

(a) Animal cell. An animal cell fares best in an isotonic environment unless it has special adaptations that offset the osmotic uptake or loss of water.

(b) Plant cell. Plant cells are turgid (firm) and generally healthiest in a hypotonic environment, where the uptake of water is eventually balanced by the wall pushing back on the cell.

Hypotonic solution   Isotonic solution   Hypertonic solution

Lysed   Normal   Shriveled

Turgid (normal)   Flaccid   Plasmolyzed

▲ **Figure 7.12 The water balance of living cells.** How living cells react to changes in the solute concentration of their environment depends on whether or not they have cell walls. **(a)** Animal cells, such as this red blood cell, do not have cell walls. **(b)** Plant cells do. (Arrows indicate net water movement after the cells were first placed in these solutions.)

50 μm

Contractile vacuole

▲ **Figure 7.13 The contractile vacuole of *Paramecium caudatum*.** The vacuole collects fluid from a system of canals in the cytoplasm. When full, the vacuole and canals contract, expelling fluid from the cell (LM).

point, the cell is **turgid** (very firm), which is the healthy state for most plant cells. Plants that are not woody, such as most houseplants, depend for mechanical support on cells kept turgid by a surrounding hypotonic solution. If a plant's cells and their surroundings are isotonic, there is no net tendency for water to enter, and the cells become **flaccid** (limp).

However, a cell wall is of no advantage if the cell is immersed in a hypertonic environment. In this case, a plant cell, like an animal cell, will lose water to its surroundings and shrink. As the plant cell shrivels, its plasma membrane pulls away from the cell wall at multiple places. This phenomenon, called **plasmolysis**, causes the plant to wilt and can lead to plant death. The walled cells of bacteria and fungi also plasmolyze in hypertonic environments.

Facilitated Diffusion: Passive Transport Aided by Proteins

Let's look more closely at how water and certain hydrophilic solutes cross a membrane. As mentioned earlier, many polar molecules and ions impeded by the lipid bilayer of the membrane diffuse passively with the help of transport proteins that span the membrane. This phenomenon is called **facilitated diffusion**. Cell biologists are still trying to learn exactly how various transport proteins facilitate diffusion. Most transport proteins are very specific: They transport some substances but not others.

As mentioned earlier, the two types of transport proteins are channel proteins and carrier proteins. Channel proteins simply provide corridors that allow specific molecules or ions to cross the membrane **(Figure 7.14a)**. The hydrophilic passageways provided by these proteins can allow water molecules or small ions to diffuse very quickly from one side of the membrane to the other. Aquaporins, the water channel proteins, facilitate the massive amounts of diffusion that occur in plant cells and in animal cells such as red blood cells (see Figure 7.12). Certain kidney cells also have a high number of aquaporins, allowing them to reclaim water from

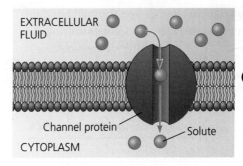

EXTRACELLULAR FLUID

Channel protein

Solute

CYTOPLASM

(a) A channel protein (purple) has a channel through which water molecules or a specific solute can pass.

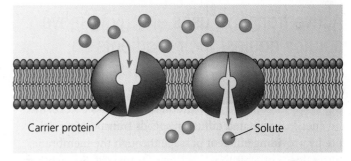

Carrier protein

Solute

(b) A carrier protein alternates between two shapes, moving a solute across the membrane during the shape change.

▲ **Figure 7.14 Two types of transport proteins that carry out facilitated diffusion.** In both cases, the protein can transport the solute in either direction, but the net movement is down the concentration gradient of the solute.

urine before it is excreted. If the kidneys did not perform this function, you would excrete about 180 L of urine per day—and have to drink an equal volume of water!

Channel proteins that transport ions are called **ion channels**. Many ion channels function as **gated channels**, which open or close in response to a stimulus. For some gated channels, the stimulus is electrical. In a nerve cell, for example, an ion channel opens in response to an electrical stimulus, allowing a stream of potassium ions to leave the cell. (See the orange ion in the center of the ion channel shown at the bottom left of the chapter-opening page.) This restores the cell's ability to fire again. Other gated channels open or close when a specific substance other than the one to be transported binds to the channel. These are also important in the functioning of the nervous system, as you'll learn in Chapter 48.

Carrier proteins, such as the glucose transporter mentioned earlier, seem to undergo a subtle change in shape that somehow translocates the solute-binding site across the membrane **(Figure 7.14b)**. Such a change in shape may be triggered by the binding and release of the transported molecule. Like ion channels, carrier proteins involved in facilitated diffusion result in the net movement of a substance down its concentration gradient. No energy input is thus required: This is passive transport. The Scientific Skills Exercise gives you an opportunity to work with data from an experiment related to glucose transport.

1. How do you think a cell performing cellular respiration rids itself of the resulting CO_2?

2. **WHAT IF?** If a *Paramecium caudatum* swims from a hypotonic to an isotonic environment, will its contractile vacuole become more active or less? Why?

For suggested answers, see Appendix A.

CONCEPT 7.4

Active transport uses energy to move solutes against their gradients

Despite the help of transport proteins, facilitated diffusion is considered passive transport because the solute is moving down its concentration gradient, a process that requires no energy. Facilitated diffusion speeds transport of a solute by providing efficient passage through the membrane, but it does not alter the direction of transport. Some other transport proteins, however, can move solutes against their concentration gradients, across the plasma membrane from the side where they are less concentrated (whether inside or outside) to the side where they are more concentrated.

The Need for Energy in Active Transport

To pump a solute across a membrane against its gradient requires work; the cell must expend energy. Therefore, this type of membrane traffic is called **active transport**. The transport proteins that move solutes against their concentration gradients are all carrier proteins rather than channel proteins. This makes sense because when channel proteins are open, they merely allow solutes to diffuse down their concentration gradients rather than picking them up and transporting them against their gradients.

Active transport enables a cell to maintain internal concentrations of small solutes that differ from concentrations in its environment. For example, compared with its surroundings, an animal cell has a much higher concentration of potassium ions (K^+) and a much lower concentration of sodium ions (Na^+). The plasma membrane helps maintain these steep gradients by pumping Na^+ out of the cell and K^+ into the cell.

As in other types of cellular work, ATP supplies the energy for most active transport. One way ATP can power active transport is by transferring its terminal phosphate group directly to the transport protein. This can induce the protein to change its shape in a manner that translocates a solute

---

SCIENTIFIC SKILLS EXERCISE

Interpreting a Scatter Plot with Two Sets of Data

Is Glucose Uptake into Cells Affected by Age? Glucose, an important energy source for animals, is transported into cells by facilitated diffusion using protein carriers. In this exercise, you will interpret a graph with two sets of data from an experiment that examined glucose uptake over time in red blood cells from guinea pigs of different ages. You will determine if the age of the guinea pigs affected their cells' rate of glucose uptake.

How the Experiment Was Done Researchers incubated guinea pig red blood cells in a 300 mM (millimolar) radioactive glucose solution at pH 7.4 at 25°C. Every 10 or 15 minutes, they removed a sample of cells and measured the concentration of radioactive glucose inside those cells. The cells came from either a 15-day-old or 1-month-old guinea pig.

Data from the Experiment When you have multiple sets of data, it can be useful to plot them on the same graph for comparison. In the graph here, each set of dots (of the same color) forms a *scatter plot*, in which every data point represents two numerical values, one for each variable. For each data set, a curve that best fits the points has been drawn to make it easier to see the trends. (For additional information about graphs, see the Scientific Skills Review in Appendix F and in the Study Area in MasteringBiology.)

Interpret the Data

1. First make sure you understand the parts of the graph. (a) Which variable is the independent variable—the variable controlled by the researchers? (b) Which variable is the dependent variable—the variable that depended on the treatment and was measured by the researchers? (c) What do the red dots represent? (d) the blue dots?

2. From the data points on the graph, construct a table of the data. Put "Incubation Time (min)" in the left column of the table.

Glucose Uptake Over Time in Guinea Pig Red Blood Cells

3. What does the graph show? Compare and contrast glucose uptake in red blood cells from 15-day-old and 1-month-old guinea pigs.

4. Develop a hypothesis to explain the difference between glucose uptake in red blood cells from 15-day-old and 1-month-old guinea pigs. (Think about how glucose gets into cells.)

5. Design an experiment to test your hypothesis.

(MB) A version of this Scientific Skills Exercise can be assigned in MasteringBiology.

Data from T. Kondo and E. Beutler, Developmental changes in glucose transport of guinea pig erythrocytes, *Journal of Clinical Investigation* 65:1–4 (1980).

▶ **Figure 7.15 The sodium-potassium pump: a specific case of active transport.**
This transport system pumps ions against steep concentration gradients: Sodium ion concentration ([Na$^+$]) is high outside the cell and low inside, while potassium ion concentration ([K$^+$]) is low outside the cell and high inside. The pump oscillates between two shapes in a cycle that moves 3 Na$^+$ out of the cell for every 2 K$^+$ pumped into the cell. The two shapes have different affinities for Na$^+$ and K$^+$. ATP powers the shape change by transferring a phosphate group to the transport protein (phosphorylating the protein).

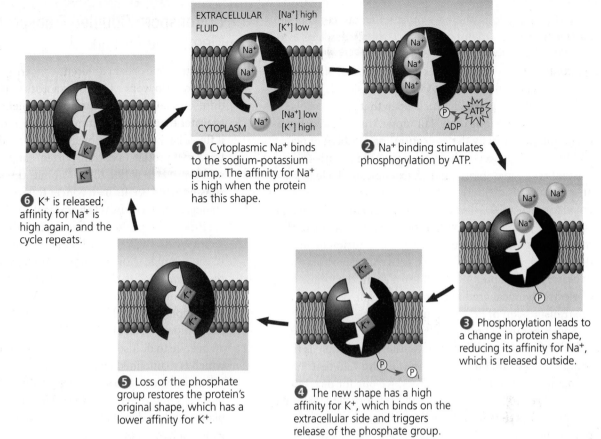

6 K$^+$ is released; affinity for Na$^+$ is high again, and the cycle repeats.

EXTRACELLULAR FLUID   [Na$^+$] high   [K$^+$] low

CYTOPLASM   [Na$^+$] low   [K$^+$] high

1 Cytoplasmic Na$^+$ binds to the sodium-potassium pump. The affinity for Na$^+$ is high when the protein has this shape.

2 Na$^+$ binding stimulates phosphorylation by ATP.

3 Phosphorylation leads to a change in protein shape, reducing its affinity for Na$^+$, which is released outside.

5 Loss of the phosphate group restores the protein's original shape, which has a lower affinity for K$^+$.

4 The new shape has a high affinity for K$^+$, which binds on the extracellular side and triggers release of the phosphate group.

bound to the protein across the membrane. One transport system that works this way is the **sodium-potassium pump**, which exchanges Na$^+$ for K$^+$ across the plasma membrane of animal cells **(Figure 7.15)**. The distinction between passive transport and active transport is reviewed in **Figure 7.16**.

How Ion Pumps Maintain Membrane Potential

All cells have voltages across their plasma membranes. Voltage is electrical potential energy—a separation of opposite charges. The cytoplasmic side of the membrane is negative in charge relative to the extracellular side because of an unequal distribution of anions and cations on the two sides. The voltage across a membrane, called a **membrane potential**, ranges from about −50 to −200 millivolts (mV). (The minus sign indicates that the inside of the cell is negative relative to the outside.)

The membrane potential acts like a battery, an energy source that affects the traffic of all charged substances across the membrane. Because the inside of the cell is negative compared with the outside, the membrane potential favors the passive transport of cations into the cell and anions out of the cell. Thus, *two* forces drive the diffusion of ions across a membrane: a chemical force (the ion's concentration gradient) and an electrical force (the effect of the membrane potential on the ion's movement). This combination of forces acting on an ion is called the **electrochemical gradient**.

▼ **Figure 7.16 Review: passive and active transport.**

Passive transport. Substances diffuse spontaneously down their concentration gradients, crossing a membrane with no expenditure of energy by the cell. The rate of diffusion can be greatly increased by transport proteins in the membrane.

Active transport. Some transport proteins act as pumps, moving substances across a membrane against their concentration (or electrochemical) gradients. Energy for this work is usually supplied by ATP.

Diffusion. Hydrophobic molecules and (at a slow rate) very small uncharged polar molecules can diffuse through the lipid bilayer.

Facilitated diffusion. Many hydrophilic substances diffuse through membranes with the assistance of transport proteins, either channel proteins (left) or carrier proteins (right).

? *For each solute in the right panel, describe its direction of movement, and state whether it is going with or against its concentration gradient.*

In the case of ions, then, we must refine our concept of passive transport: An ion diffuses not simply down its *concentration* gradient but, more exactly, down its *electrochemical* gradient. For example, the concentration of Na^+ inside a resting nerve cell is much lower than outside it. When the cell is stimulated, gated channels open that facilitate Na^+ diffusion. Sodium ions then "fall" down their electrochemical gradient, driven by the concentration gradient of Na^+ and by the attraction of these cations to the negative side (inside) of the membrane. In this example, both electrical and chemical contributions to the electrochemical gradient act in the same direction across the membrane, but this is not always so. In cases where electrical forces due to the membrane potential oppose the simple diffusion of an ion down its concentration gradient, active transport may be necessary. In Chapter 48, you'll learn about the importance of electrochemical gradients and membrane potentials in the transmission of nerve impulses.

Some membrane proteins that actively transport ions contribute to the membrane potential. An example is the sodium-potassium pump. Notice in Figure 7.15 that the pump does not translocate Na^+ and K^+ one for one, but pumps three sodium ions out of the cell for every two potassium ions it pumps into the cell. With each "crank" of the pump, there is a net transfer of one positive charge from the cytoplasm to the extracellular fluid, a process that stores energy as voltage. A transport protein that generates voltage across a membrane is called an **electrogenic pump**. The sodium-potassium pump appears to be the major electrogenic pump of animal cells. The main electrogenic pump of plants, fungi, and bacteria is a **proton pump**, which actively transports protons (hydrogen ions, H^+) out of the cell. The pumping of H^+ transfers positive charge from the cytoplasm to the extracellular solution **(Figure 7.17)**. By generating voltage across membranes, electrogenic pumps help store energy that can be tapped for cellular work. One important use of proton gradients in the cell is for ATP synthesis during cellular respiration, as you will see in Chapter 9. Another is a type of membrane traffic called cotransport.

Cotransport: Coupled Transport by a Membrane Protein

A solute that exists in different concentrations across a membrane can do work as it moves across that membrane by diffusion down its concentration gradient. This is analogous to water that has been pumped uphill and performs work as it flows back down. In a mechanism called **cotransport**, a transport protein (a cotransporter) can couple the "downhill" diffusion of the solute to the "uphill" transport of a second substance against its own concentration gradient. For instance, a plant cell uses the gradient of H^+ generated by its ATP-powered proton pumps to drive the active transport of amino acids, sugars, and several other nutrients into the cell. In the example shown in **Figure 7.18**, a cotransporter couples the return of H^+ to the transport of sucrose into the cell. This protein can translocate sucrose into the cell against its concentration gradient, but only if the sucrose molecule travels in the company of an H^+. The H^+ uses the transport protein as an avenue to diffuse down its own electrochemical gradient, which is maintained by the proton pump. Plants use sucrose-H^+ cotransport to load sucrose produced by photosynthesis into cells in the veins of leaves. The vascular tissue of the plant can then distribute the sugar to nonphotosynthetic organs, such as roots.

What we know about cotransport proteins in animal cells has helped us find more effective treatments for diarrhea, a serious problem in developing countries. Normally, sodium in waste is reabsorbed in the colon, maintaining constant levels in the body, but diarrhea expels waste so rapidly that

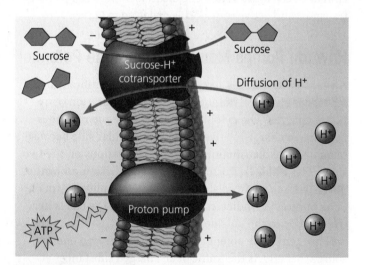

▲ **Figure 7.18 Cotransport: active transport driven by a concentration gradient.** A carrier protein, such as this sucrose-H^+ cotransporter in a plant cell (top), is able to use the diffusion of H^+ down its electrochemical gradient into the cell to drive the uptake of sucrose. (The cell wall is not shown.) Although not technically part of the cotransport process, an ATP-driven proton pump is shown here (bottom), which concentrates H^+ outside the cell. The resulting H^+ gradient represents potential energy that can be used for active transport—of sucrose, in this case. Thus, ATP indirectly provides the energy necessary for cotransport.

▲ **Figure 7.17 A proton pump.** Proton pumps are electrogenic pumps that store energy by generating voltage (charge separation) across membranes. A proton pump translocates positive charge in the form of hydrogen ions. The voltage and H^+ concentration gradient represent a dual energy source that can drive other processes, such as the uptake of nutrients. Most proton pumps are powered by ATP.

reabsorption is not possible, and sodium levels fall precipitously. To treat this life-threatening condition, patients are given a solution to drink containing high concentrations of salt (NaCl) and glucose. The solutes are taken up by sodium-glucose cotransporters on the surface of intestinal cells and passed through the cells into the blood. This simple treatment has lowered infant mortality worldwide.

CONCEPT CHECK 7.4

1. Sodium-potassium pumps help nerve cells establish a voltage across their plasma membranes. Do these pumps use ATP or produce ATP? Explain.
2. Explain why the sodium-potassium pump in Figure 7.15 would not be considered a cotransporter.
3. MAKE CONNECTIONS Review the characteristics of the lysosome in Concept 6.4. Given the internal environment of a lysosome, what transport protein might you expect to see in its membrane?

For suggested answers, see Appendix A.

CONCEPT 7.5

Bulk transport across the plasma membrane occurs by exocytosis and endocytosis

Water and small solutes enter and leave the cell by diffusing through the lipid bilayer of the plasma membrane or by being pumped or moved across the membrane by transport proteins. However, large molecules—such as proteins and polysaccharides, as well as larger particles—generally cross the membrane in bulk, packaged in vesicles. Like active transport, these processes require energy.

Exocytosis

As seen in Chapter 6, the cell secretes certain molecules by the fusion of vesicles with the plasma membrane; this process is called **exocytosis**. A transport vesicle that has budded from the Golgi apparatus moves along microtubules of the cytoskeleton to the plasma membrane. When the vesicle membrane and plasma membrane come into contact, specific proteins rearrange the lipid molecules of the two bilayers so that the two membranes fuse. The contents of the vesicle spill out of the cell, and the vesicle membrane becomes part of the plasma membrane (see Figure 7.9, step 4).

Many secretory cells use exocytosis to export products. For example, cells in the pancreas that make insulin secrete it into the extracellular fluid by exocytosis. In another example, nerve cells use exocytosis to release neurotransmitters that signal other neurons or muscle cells. When plant cells are making cell walls, exocytosis delivers proteins and carbohydrates from Golgi vesicles to the outside of the cell.

Endocytosis

In **endocytosis**, the cell takes in molecules and particulate matter by forming new vesicles from the plasma membrane. Although the proteins involved in the processes are different, the events of endocytosis look like the reverse of exocytosis. First, a small area of the plasma membrane sinks inward to form a pocket. Then, as the pocket deepens, it pinches in, forming a vesicle containing material that had been outside the cell. Study **Figure 7.19** carefully to understand the three types of endocytosis: phagocytosis ("cellular eating"), pinocytosis ("cellular drinking"), and receptor-mediated endocytosis (which is considered a form of pinocytosis).

Human cells use receptor-mediated endocytosis to take in cholesterol for membrane synthesis and the synthesis of other steroids. Cholesterol travels in the blood in particles called low-density lipoproteins (LDLs), each a complex of lipids and a protein. LDLs bind to LDL receptors on plasma membranes and then enter the cells by endocytosis. (LDLs thus act as **ligands**, a term for any molecule that binds specifically to a receptor site on another molecule.) In the inherited disease familial hypercholesterolemia, characterized by a very high level of cholesterol in the blood, LDLs cannot enter cells because the LDL receptor proteins are defective or missing. Consequently, cholesterol accumulates in the blood, where it contributes to early atherosclerosis, the buildup of lipid deposits within the walls of blood vessels. This buildup narrows the space in the vessels and impedes blood flow, and can result in heart damage and stroke.

Vesicles not only transport substances to be released from the cell but also provide a mechanism for rejuvenating or remodeling the plasma membrane. Endocytosis and exocytosis occur continually in most eukaryotic cells, yet the amount of plasma membrane in a nongrowing cell remains fairly constant. The addition of membrane by one process appears to offset the loss of membrane by the other.

Energy and cellular work have figured prominently in our study of membranes. We have seen, for example, that active transport is powered by ATP. In the next three chapters, you will learn more about how cells acquire chemical energy to do the work of life.

CONCEPT CHECK 7.5

1. As a cell grows, its plasma membrane expands. Does this involve endocytosis or exocytosis? Explain.
2. DRAW IT Return to Figure 7.9, and circle a patch of plasma membrane that is coming from a vesicle involved in exocytosis.
3. MAKE CONNECTIONS In Concept 6.7, you learned that animal cells make an extracellular matrix (ECM). Describe the cellular pathway of synthesis and deposition of an ECM glycoprotein.

For suggested answers, see Appendix A.

Exploring Endocytosis in Animal Cells

Phagocytosis

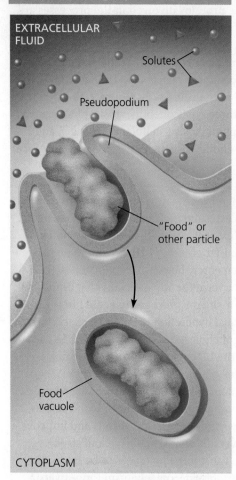

EXTRACELLULAR
FLUID

Solutes

Pseudopodium

"Food" or
other particle

Food
vacuole

CYTOPLASM

In **phagocytosis**, a cell engulfs a particle by extending pseudopodia (singular, *pseudopodium*) around it and packaging it within a membranous sac called a food vacuole. The particle will be digested after the food vacuole fuses with a lysosome (see Figure 6.13a).

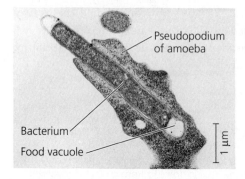

Pseudopodium
of amoeba

Bacterium

Food vacuole

1 μm

An amoeba engulfing a bacterium via phago-cytosis (TEM).

 ANIMATION **BioFlix** Visit the Study Area in **MasteringBiology** for the BioFlix® 3-D Animation on Membrane Transport. BioFlix Tutorials can also be assigned in MasteringBiology.

Pinocytosis

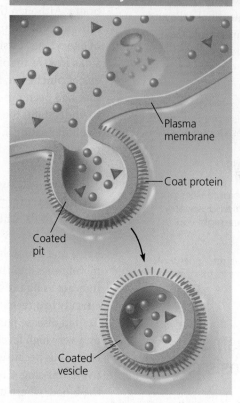

Plasma
membrane

Coat protein

Coated
pit

Coated
vesicle

In **pinocytosis**, a cell continually "gulps" droplets of extracellular fluid into tiny vesicles, formed by infoldings of the plasma membrane. In this way, the cell obtains molecules dissolved in the droplets. Because any and all solutes are taken into the cell, pinocytosis as shown here is nonspecific for the substances it transports. In many cases, as above, the parts of the plasma membrane that form vesicles are lined on their cytoplasmic side by a fuzzy layer of coat protein; the "pits" and resulting vesicles are said to be "coated."

0.25 μm

Pinocytotic vesicles forming (TEMs).

Receptor-Mediated Endocytosis

Receptor

Receptor-mediated endocytosis is a specialized type of pinocytosis that enables the cell to acquire bulk quantities of specific substances, even though those substances may not be very concentrated in the extracellular fluid. Embedded in the plasma membrane are proteins with receptor sites exposed to the extracellular fluid. Specific solutes bind to the sites. The receptor proteins then cluster in coated pits, and each coated pit forms a vesicle containing the bound molecules. Notice that there are relatively more bound molecules (purple triangles) inside the vesicle, but other molecules (green balls) are also present. After the ingested material is liberated from the vesicle, the emptied receptors are recycled to the plasma membrane by the same vesicle (not shown).

Plasma
membrane

Coat
protein

0.25 μm

Top: A coated pit. *Bottom*: A coated vesicle forming during receptor-mediated endocytosis (TEMs).

A diver has more potential energy on the platform than in the water.

Diving converts potential energy to kinetic energy.

Climbing up converts the kinetic energy of muscle movement to potential energy.

A diver has less potential energy in the water than on the platform.

▲ **Figure 8.2 Transformations between potential and kinetic energy.**

How is energy converted from one form to another? Consider **Figure 8.2**. The young woman climbing the ladder to the diving platform is releasing chemical energy from the food she ate for lunch and using some of that energy to perform the work of climbing. The kinetic energy of muscle movement is thus being transformed into potential energy due to her increasing height above the water. The young man diving is converting his potential energy to kinetic energy, which is then transferred to the water as he enters it. A small amount of energy is lost as heat due to friction.

Now let's consider the original source of the organic food molecules that provided the necessary chemical energy for the diver to climb the steps. This chemical energy was itself derived from light energy by plants during photosynthesis. Organisms are energy transformers.

The Laws of Energy Transformation

The study of the energy transformations that occur in a collection of matter is called **thermodynamics**. Scientists use the word *system* to denote the matter under study; they refer to the rest of the universe—everything outside the system—as the *surroundings*. An *isolated system*, such as that approximated by liquid in a thermos bottle, is unable to exchange either energy or matter with its surroundings outside the thermos. In an *open system*, energy and matter can be transferred between the system and its surroundings. Organisms are open systems. They absorb energy—for instance, light energy or chemical energy in the form of organic molecules—and release heat and metabolic waste products, such as carbon dioxide, to the surroundings. Two laws of thermodynamics govern energy transformations in organisms and all other collections of matter.

The First Law of Thermodynamics

According to the **first law of thermodynamics**, the energy of the universe is constant: *Energy can be transferred and transformed, but it cannot be created or destroyed.* The first law is also known as the *principle of conservation of energy*. The electric company does not make energy, but merely converts it to a form that is convenient for us to use. By converting sunlight to chemical energy, a plant acts as an energy transformer, not an energy producer.

The brown bear in **Figure 8.3a** will convert the chemical energy of the organic molecules in its food to kinetic and other forms of energy as it carries out biological processes.

Heat

CO_2 + H_2O

Chemical energy

(a) First law of thermodynamics: Energy can be transferred or transformed but neither created nor destroyed. For example, chemical reactions in this brown bear will convert the chemical (potential) energy in the fish into the kinetic energy of running.

(b) Second law of thermodynamics: Every energy transfer or transformation increases the disorder (entropy) of the universe. For example, as it runs, disorder is increased around the bear by the release of heat and small molecules that are the by-products of metabolism. A brown bear can run at speeds up to 35 miles per hour (56 km/hr)—as fast as a racehorse.

▲ **Figure 8.3 The two laws of thermodynamics.**

What happens to this energy after it has performed work? The second law of thermodynamics helps to answer this question.

The Second Law of Thermodynamics

If energy cannot be destroyed, why can't organisms simply recycle their energy over and over again? It turns out that during every energy transfer or transformation, some energy becomes unavailable to do work. In most energy transformations, more usable forms of energy are at least partly converted to thermal energy and released as heat. Only a small fraction of the chemical energy from the food in Figure 8.3a is transformed into the motion of the brown bear shown in **Figure 8.3b**; most is lost as heat, which dissipates rapidly through the surroundings.

In the process of carrying out chemical reactions that perform various kinds of work, living cells unavoidably convert other forms of energy to heat. A system can put this energy to work only when there is a temperature difference that results in thermal energy flowing as heat from a warmer location to a cooler one. If temperature is uniform, as it is in a living cell, then the heat generated during a chemical reaction will simply warm a body of matter, such as the organism. (This can make a room crowded with people uncomfortably warm, as each person is carrying out a multitude of chemical reactions!)

A logical consequence of the loss of usable energy as heat to the surroundings is that each energy transfer or transformation makes the universe more disordered. Scientists use a quantity called **entropy** as a measure of disorder, or randomness. The more randomly arranged a collection of matter is, the greater its entropy. We can now state the **second law of thermodynamics**: *Every energy transfer or transformation increases the entropy of the universe.* Although order can increase locally, there is an unstoppable trend toward randomization of the universe as a whole.

In many cases, increased entropy is evident in the physical disintegration of a system's organized structure. For example, you can observe increasing entropy in the gradual decay of an unmaintained building. Much of the increasing entropy of the universe is less obvious, however, because it takes the form of increasing amounts of heat and less ordered forms of matter. As the bear in Figure 8.3b converts chemical energy to kinetic energy, it is also increasing the disorder of its surroundings by producing heat and small molecules, such as the CO_2 it exhales, that are the breakdown products of food.

The concept of entropy helps us understand why certain processes are energetically favorable and occur on their own. It turns out that if a given process, by itself, leads to an increase in entropy, that process can proceed without requiring an input of energy. Such a process is called a **spontaneous process**. Note that as we're using it here, the word *spontaneous* does not imply that the process would occur quickly; rather, the word signifies that it is energetically favorable. (In fact, it may be helpful for you to think of the phrase "energetically favorable" when you read the formal term "spontaneous.") Some spontaneous processes, such as an explosion, may be virtually instantaneous, while others, such as the rusting of an old car over time, are much slower.

A process that, considered on its own, leads to a decrease in entropy is said to be nonspontaneous: It will happen only if energy is supplied. We know from experience that certain events occur spontaneously and others do not. For instance, we know that water flows downhill spontaneously but moves uphill only with an input of energy, such as when a machine pumps the water against gravity. Some energy is inevitably lost as heat, increasing entropy in the surroundings, so usage of energy ensures that a nonspontaneous process also leads to an increase in the entropy of the universe as a whole.

Biological Order and Disorder

Living systems increase the entropy of their surroundings, as predicted by thermodynamic law. It is true that cells create ordered structures from less organized starting materials. For example, simpler molecules are ordered into the more complex structure of an amino acid, and amino acids are ordered into polypeptide chains. At the organismal level as well, complex and beautifully ordered structures result from biological processes that use simpler starting materials **(Figure 8.4)**. However, an organism also takes in organized forms of matter and energy from the surroundings and replaces them with less ordered forms. For example, an animal obtains starch, proteins, and other complex molecules from the food it eats. As catabolic pathways break these molecules down, the animal releases carbon

▲ **Figure 8.4 Order as a characteristic of life.** Order is evident in the detailed structures of the sea urchin skeleton and the succulent plant shown here. As open systems, organisms can increase their order as long as the order of their surroundings decreases.

dioxide and water—small molecules that possess less chemical energy than the food did (see Figure 8.3b). The depletion of chemical energy is accounted for by heat generated during metabolism. On a larger scale, energy flows into most ecosystems in the form of light and exits in the form of heat (see Figure 1.10).

During the early history of life, complex organisms evolved from simpler ancestors. For instance, we can trace the ancestry of the plant kingdom from much simpler organisms called green algae to more complex flowering plants. However, this increase in organization over time in no way violates the second law. The entropy of a particular system, such as an organism, may actually decrease as long as the total entropy of the *universe*—the system plus its surroundings—increases. Thus, organisms are islands of low entropy in an increasingly random universe. The evolution of biological order is perfectly consistent with the laws of thermodynamics.

CONCEPT 8.2

The free-energy change of a reaction tells us whether or not the reaction occurs spontaneously

The laws of thermodynamics that we've just discussed apply to the universe as a whole. As biologists, we want to understand the chemical reactions of life—for example, which reactions occur spontaneously and which ones require some input of energy from outside. But how can we know this without assessing the energy and entropy changes in the entire universe for each separate reaction?

Free-Energy Change, ΔG

Recall that the universe is really equivalent to "the system" plus "the surroundings." In 1878, J. Willard Gibbs, a professor at Yale, defined a very useful function called the Gibbs free energy of a system (without considering its surroundings), symbolized by the letter G. We'll refer to the Gibbs free energy simply as free energy. **Free energy** is the portion of a system's energy that can perform work when temperature and pressure are uniform throughout the system, as in a living cell. Let's consider how we determine the free-energy change that occurs when a system changes—for example, during a chemical reaction.

The change in free energy, ΔG, can be calculated for a chemical reaction by applying the following equation:

$$\Delta G = \Delta H - T\Delta S$$

This equation uses only properties of the system (the reaction) itself: ΔH symbolizes the change in the system's *enthalpy* (in biological systems, equivalent to total energy); ΔS is the change in the system's entropy; and T is the absolute temperature in Kelvin (K) units (K = °C + 273; see Appendix C).

Once we know the value of ΔG for a process, we can use it to predict whether the process will be spontaneous (that is, whether it is energetically favorable and will occur without an input of energy). More than a century of experiments has shown that only processes with a negative ΔG are spontaneous. For ΔG to be negative, ΔH must be negative (the system gives up enthalpy and H decreases) or $T\Delta S$ must be positive (the system gives up order and S increases), or both: When ΔH and $T\Delta S$ are tallied, ΔG has a negative value ($\Delta G < 0$) for all spontaneous processes. In other words, every spontaneous process decreases the system's free energy, and processes that have a positive or zero ΔG are never spontaneous.

This information is immensely interesting to biologists, for it gives us the power to predict which kinds of change can happen without an input of energy. Such spontaneous changes can be harnessed to perform work. This principle is very important in the study of metabolism, where a major goal is to determine which reactions can supply energy for cellular work.

Free Energy, Stability, and Equilibrium

As we saw in the previous section, when a process occurs spontaneously in a system, we can be sure that ΔG is negative. Another way to think of ΔG is to realize that it represents the difference between the free energy of the final state and the free energy of the initial state:

$$\Delta G = G_{\text{final state}} - G_{\text{initial state}}$$

Thus, ΔG can be negative only when the process involves a loss of free energy during the change from initial state to final state. Because it has less free energy, the system in its final state is less likely to change and is therefore more stable than it was previously.

We can think of free energy as a measure of a system's instability—its tendency to change to a more stable state. Unstable systems (higher G) tend to change in such a way that they become more stable (lower G). For example, a diver on top of a platform is less stable (more likely to fall) than when floating in the water; a drop of concentrated dye is less stable (more likely to disperse) than when the dye is spread randomly through the liquid; and a glucose molecule is less stable (more likely to break down) than the simpler molecules into which it can be split **(Figure 8.5)**. Unless something prevents it, each of these systems will move toward greater stability: The diver falls, the solution becomes uniformly colored, and the glucose molecule is broken down into smaller molecules.

Another term that describes a state of maximum stability is *equilibrium*, which you learned about in Chapter 2 in connection with chemical reactions. There is an important relationship between free energy and equilibrium, including chemical equilibrium. Recall that most chemical reactions are reversible and proceed to a point at which the forward and backward reactions occur at the same rate. The reaction is then said to be at chemical equilibrium, and there is no further net change in the relative concentration of products and reactants.

As a reaction proceeds toward equilibrium, the free energy of the mixture of reactants and products decreases. Free energy increases when a reaction is somehow pushed away from equilibrium, perhaps by removing some of the products (and thus changing their concentration relative to that of the reactants). For a system at equilibrium, G is at its lowest possible value in that system. We can think of the equilibrium state as a free-energy valley. Any change from the equilibrium position will have a positive ΔG and will not be spontaneous. For this reason, systems never spontaneously move away from equilibrium. Because a system at equilibrium cannot spontaneously change, it can do no work. *A process is spontaneous and can perform work only when it is moving toward equilibrium.*

Free Energy and Metabolism

We can now apply the free-energy concept more specifically to the chemistry of life's processes.

Exergonic and Endergonic Reactions in Metabolism

Based on their free-energy changes, chemical reactions can be classified as either exergonic ("energy outward") or endergonic ("energy inward"). An **exergonic reaction** proceeds

- More free energy (higher G)
- Less stable
- Greater work capacity

In a **spontaneous change**
- The free energy of the system decreases ($\Delta G < 0$)
- The system becomes more stable
- The released free energy can be harnessed to do work

- Less free energy (lower G)
- More stable
- Less work capacity

(a) Gravitational motion. Objects move spontaneously from a higher altitude to a lower one.

(b) Diffusion. Molecules in a drop of dye diffuse until they are randomly dispersed.

(c) Chemical reaction. In a cell, a glucose molecule is broken down into simpler molecules.

▲ **Figure 8.5 The relationship of free energy to stability, work capacity, and spontaneous change.** Unstable systems (top) are rich in free energy, G. They have a tendency to change spontaneously to a more stable state (bottom), and it is possible to harness this "downhill" change to perform work.

MAKE CONNECTIONS *Compare the redistribution of molecules shown in (b) to the transport of hydrogen ions (H^+) across a membrane by a proton pump, creating a concentration gradient, as shown in Figure 7.17. Which process(es) result(s) in higher free energy? Which system(s) can do work?*

▼ **Figure 8.6** Free energy changes (ΔG) in exergonic and endergonic reactions.

(a) Exergonic reaction: energy released, spontaneous

Free energy →

Reactants

Energy

Products

Amount of energy released ($\Delta G < 0$)

Progress of the reaction →

(b) Endergonic reaction: energy required, nonspontaneous

Free energy →

Products

Energy

Reactants

Amount of energy required ($\Delta G > 0$)

Progress of the reaction →

with a net release of free energy **(Figure 8.6a)**. Because the chemical mixture loses free energy (G decreases), ΔG is negative for an exergonic reaction. Using ΔG as a standard for spontaneity, exergonic reactions are those that occur spontaneously. (Remember, the word *spontaneous* implies that it is energetically favorable, not that it will occur rapidly.) The magnitude of ΔG for an exergonic reaction represents the maximum amount of work the reaction can perform.* The greater the decrease in free energy, the greater the amount of work that can be done.

We can use the overall reaction for cellular respiration as an example:

$$C_6H_{12}O_6 + 6\ O_2 \rightarrow 6\ CO_2 + 6\ H_2O$$
$$\Delta G = -686\ \text{kcal/mol}\ (-2{,}870\ \text{kJ/mol})$$

For each mole (180 g) of glucose broken down by respiration under what are called "standard conditions" (1 M of each

---

*The word *maximum* qualifies this statement, because some of the free energy is released as heat and cannot do work. Therefore, ΔG represents a theoretical upper limit of available energy.

reactant and product, 25°C, pH 7), 686 kcal (2,870 kJ) of energy are made available for work. Because energy must be conserved, the chemical products of respiration store 686 kcal less free energy per mole than the reactants. The products are, in a sense, the spent exhaust of a process that tapped the free energy stored in the bonds of the sugar molecules.

It is important to realize that the breaking of bonds does not release energy; on the contrary, as you will soon see, it requires energy. The phrase "energy stored in bonds" is shorthand for the potential energy that can be released when new bonds are formed after the original bonds break, as long as the products are of lower free energy than the reactants.

An **endergonic reaction** is one that absorbs free energy from its surroundings **(Figure 8.6b)**. Because this kind of reaction essentially *stores* free energy in molecules (G increases), ΔG is positive. Such reactions are nonspontaneous, and the magnitude of ΔG is the quantity of energy required to drive the reaction. If a chemical process is exergonic (downhill), releasing energy in one direction, then the reverse process must be endergonic (uphill), using energy. A reversible process cannot be downhill in both directions. If $\Delta G = -686$ kcal/mol for respiration, which converts glucose and oxygen to carbon dioxide and water, then the reverse process—the conversion of carbon dioxide and water to glucose and oxygen—must be strongly endergonic, with $\Delta G = +686$ kcal/mol. Such a reaction would never happen by itself.

How, then, do plants make the sugar that organisms use for energy? Plants get the required energy—686 kcal to make a mole of glucose—from the environment by capturing light and converting its energy to chemical energy. Next, in a long series of exergonic steps, they gradually spend that chemical energy to assemble glucose molecules.

Equilibrium and Metabolism

Reactions in an isolated system eventually reach equilibrium and can then do no work, as illustrated by the isolated hydroelectric system in **Figure 8.7**. The chemical reactions of metabolism are reversible, and they, too, would reach

▲ **Figure 8.7 Equilibrium and work in an isolated hydroelectric system.** Water flowing downhill turns a turbine that drives a generator providing electricity to a lightbulb, but only until the system reaches equilibrium.

equilibrium if they occurred in the isolation of a test tube. Because systems at equilibrium are at a minimum of *G* and can do no work, a cell that has reached metabolic equilibrium is dead! The fact that metabolism as a whole is never at equilibrium is one of the defining features of life.

Like most systems, a living cell is not in equilibrium. The constant flow of materials in and out of the cell keeps the metabolic pathways from ever reaching equilibrium, and the cell continues to do work throughout its life. This principle is illustrated by the open (and more realistic) hydroelectric system in **Figure 8.8a**. However, unlike this simple system in which water flowing downhill turns a single turbine, a catabolic pathway in a cell releases free energy in a series of reactions. An example is cellular respiration, illustrated by analogy in **Figure 8.8b**. Some of the reversible reactions of respiration are constantly "pulled" in one direction—that is, they are kept out of equilibrium. The key to maintaining this lack of equilibrium is that the product of a reaction does not accumulate but instead becomes a reactant in the next step; finally, waste products are expelled from the cell. The overall sequence of reactions is kept going by the huge free-energy difference between glucose and oxygen at the top of the energy "hill" and carbon dioxide and water at the "downhill" end. As long as our cells have a steady supply of glucose or other fuels and oxygen and are able to expel waste products to the surroundings,

their metabolic pathways never reach equilibrium and can continue to do the work of life.

Stepping back to look at the big picture, we can see once again how important it is to think of organisms as open systems. Sunlight provides a daily source of free energy for an ecosystem's plants and other photosynthetic organisms. Animals and other nonphotosynthetic organisms in an ecosystem must have a source of free energy in the form of the organic products of photosynthesis. Now that we have applied the free-energy concept to metabolism, we are ready to see how a cell actually performs the work of life.

CONCEPT CHECK 8.2

1. Cellular respiration uses glucose and oxygen, which have high levels of free energy, and releases CO_2 and water, which have low levels of free energy. Is cellular respiration spontaneous or not? Is it exergonic or endergonic? What happens to the energy released from glucose?

2. How would the processes of catabolism and anabolism relate to Figure 8.5c?

3. **WHAT IF?** Some nighttime partygoers wear glow-in-the-dark necklaces. The necklaces start glowing once they are "activated" by snapping the necklace in a way that allows two chemicals to react and emit light in the form of chemiluminescence. Is the chemical reaction exergonic or endergonic? Explain your answer.

For suggested answers, see Appendix A.

(a) **An open hydroelectric system.** Water flowing through a turbine keeps driving the generator because intake and outflow of water keep the system from reaching equilibrium.

$\Delta G < 0$

$\Delta G < 0$

$\Delta G < 0$

$\Delta G < 0$

(b) **A multistep open hydroelectric system.** Cellular respiration is analogous to this system: Glucose is broken down in a series of exergonic reactions that power the work of the cell. The product of each reaction is used as the reactant for the next, so no reaction reaches equilibrium.

▲ **Figure 8.8 Equilibrium and work in open systems.**

CONCEPT 8.3

ATP powers cellular work by coupling exergonic reactions to endergonic reactions

A cell does three main kinds of work:

- *Chemical work*, the pushing of endergonic reactions that would not occur spontaneously, such as the synthesis of polymers from monomers (chemical work will be discussed further here and in Chapters 9 and 10)
- *Transport work*, the pumping of substances across membranes against the direction of spontaneous movement (see Chapter 7)
- *Mechanical work*, such as the beating of cilia (see Chapter 6), the contraction of muscle cells, and the movement of chromosomes during cellular reproduction

A key feature in the way cells manage their energy resources to do this work is **energy coupling**, the use of an exergonic process to drive an endergonic one. ATP is responsible for mediating most energy coupling in cells, and in most cases it acts as the immediate source of energy that powers cellular work.

The Structure and Hydrolysis of ATP

ATP (adenosine triphosphate) was introduced when we discussed the phosphate group as a functional group (see Concept 4.3). ATP contains the sugar ribose, with the nitrogenous base adenine and a chain of three phosphate groups (the triphosphate group) bonded to it **(Figure 8.9a)**. In addition to its role in energy coupling, ATP is also one of the nucleoside triphosphates used to make RNA (see Figure 5.24).

The bonds between the phosphate groups of ATP can be broken by hydrolysis. When the terminal phosphate bond is broken by addition of a water molecule, a molecule of inorganic phosphate ($HOPO_3^{2-}$, abbreviated Ⓟ$_i$ throughout this book) leaves the ATP, which becomes adenosine diphosphate, or ADP **(Figure 8.9b)**. The reaction is exergonic and releases 7.3 kcal of energy per mole of ATP hydrolyzed:

$$ATP + H_2O \rightarrow ADP + Ⓟ_i$$
$$\Delta G = -7.3 \text{ kcal/mol} \ (-30.5 \text{ kJ/mol})$$

This is the free-energy change measured under standard conditions. In the cell, conditions do not conform to standard conditions, primarily because reactant and product concentrations differ from 1 M. For example, when ATP hydrolysis occurs under cellular conditions, the actual ΔG is about −13 kcal/mol, 78% greater than the energy released by ATP hydrolysis under standard conditions.

Because their hydrolysis releases energy, the phosphate bonds of ATP are sometimes referred to as high-energy phosphate bonds, but the term is misleading. The phosphate bonds of ATP are not unusually strong bonds, as "high-energy" may imply; rather, the reactants (ATP and water) themselves have high energy relative to the energy of the products (ADP and Ⓟ$_i$). The release of energy during the hydrolysis of ATP comes from the chemical change of the system to a state of lower free energy, not from the phosphate bonds themselves.

ATP is useful to the cell because the energy it releases on losing a phosphate group is somewhat greater than the energy most other molecules could deliver. But why does this hydrolysis release so much energy? If we reexamine the ATP molecule in Figure 8.9a, we can see that all three phosphate groups are negatively charged. These like charges are crowded together, and their mutual repulsion contributes to the instability of this region of the ATP molecule. The triphosphate tail of ATP is the chemical equivalent of a compressed spring.

How the Hydrolysis of ATP Performs Work

When ATP is hydrolyzed in a test tube, the release of free energy merely heats the surrounding water. In an organism, this same generation of heat can sometimes be beneficial. For instance, the process of shivering uses ATP hydrolysis during muscle contraction to warm the body. In most cases

(a) The structure of ATP. In the cell, most hydroxyl groups of phosphates are ionized (—O⁻).

Adenosine triphosphate (ATP)

H₂O

Inorganic phosphate

Adenosine diphosphate (ADP)

Energy

(b) The hydrolysis of ATP. The reaction of ATP and water yields inorganic phosphate ((Ⓟ$_i$)) and ADP and releases energy.

▲ **Figure 8.9 The structure and hydrolysis of adenosine triphosphate (ATP).** Throughout this book, the chemical structure of the triphosphate group seen in (a) will be represented by the three joined yellow circles shown in (b).

in the cell, however, the generation of heat alone would be an inefficient (and potentially dangerous) use of a valuable energy resource. Instead, the cell's proteins harness the energy released during ATP hydrolysis in several ways to perform the three types of cellular work—chemical, transport, and mechanical.

For example, with the help of specific enzymes, the cell is able to use the energy released by ATP hydrolysis directly to drive chemical reactions that, by themselves, are endergonic. If the ΔG of an endergonic reaction is less than the amount of energy released by ATP hydrolysis, then the two reactions can be coupled so that, overall, the coupled reactions are exergonic. This usually involves phosphorylation, the transfer of a phosphate group from ATP to some other molecule, such as the reactant. The recipient molecule with the phosphate group covalently bonded to it is then called a **phosphorylated intermediate**. The key to coupling exergonic and endergonic reactions is the formation of this phosphorylated intermediate, which is more reactive

(a) Glutamic acid conversion to glutamine. Glutamine synthesis from glutamic acid (Glu) by itself is endergonic (ΔG is positive), so it is not spontaneous.

$\Delta G_{Glu} = +3.4$ kcal/mol

Glutamic acid   Ammonia   Glutamine

(b) Conversion reaction coupled with ATP hydrolysis. In the cell, glutamine synthesis occurs in two steps, coupled by a phosphorylated intermediate. ❶ ATP phosphorylates glutamic acid, making it less stable. ❷ Ammonia displaces the phosphate group, forming glutamine.

Glutamic acid   + ADP   Phosphorylated intermediate   Glutamine   + ADP + Ⓟᵢ

(c) Free-energy change for coupled reaction. ΔG for the glutamic acid conversion to glutamine (+3.4 kcal/mol) plus ΔG for ATP hydrolysis (−7.3 kcal/mol) gives the free-energy change for the overall reaction (−3.9 kcal/mol). Because the overall process is exergonic (net ΔG is negative), it occurs spontaneously.

$\Delta G_{Glu} = +3.4$ kcal/mol

$\Delta G_{ATP} = -7.3$ kcal/mol

$\Delta G_{Glu} = +3.4$ kcal/mol
$+ \Delta G_{ATP} = \underline{-7.3\ \text{kcal/mol}}$

Net $\Delta G = -3.9$ kcal/mol

▲ **Figure 8.10 How ATP drives chemical work: Energy coupling using ATP hydrolysis.** In this example, the exergonic process of ATP hydrolysis is used to drive an endergonic process— the cellular synthesis of the amino acid glutamine from glutamic acid and ammonia.

MAKE CONNECTIONS *Referring to Figure 5.14, explain why glutamine (Gln) is diagrammed as a glutamic acid (Glu) with an amino group attached.*

(less stable) than the original unphosphorylated molecule (**Figure 8.10**).

Transport and mechanical work in the cell are also nearly always powered by the hydrolysis of ATP. In these cases, ATP hydrolysis leads to a change in a protein's shape and often its ability to bind another molecule. Sometimes this occurs via a phosphorylated intermediate, as seen for the transport protein in **Figure 8.11a**. In most instances of mechanical work involving motor proteins "walking" along

cytoskeletal elements (**Figure 8.11b**), a cycle occurs in which ATP is first bound noncovalently to the motor protein. Next, ATP is hydrolyzed, releasing ADP and Ⓟᵢ. Another ATP molecule can then bind. At each stage, the motor protein changes its shape and ability to bind the cytoskeleton, resulting in movement of the protein along the cytoskeletal track. Phosphorylation and dephosphorylation promote crucial protein shape changes during many other important cellular processes as well.

(a) Transport work: ATP phosphorylates transport proteins.

(b) Mechanical work: ATP binds noncovalently to motor proteins and then is hydrolyzed.

▲ **Figure 8.11 How ATP drives transport and mechanical work.** ATP hydrolysis causes changes in the shapes and binding affinities of proteins. This can occur either **(a)** directly, by phosphorylation, as shown for a membrane protein carrying out active transport of a solute (see also Figure 7.15), or **(b)** indirectly, via noncovalent binding of ATP and its hydrolytic products, as is the case for motor proteins that move vesicles (and other organelles) along cytoskeletal "tracks" in the cell (see also Figure 6.21).

ATP synthesis from ADP + P_i requires energy.

ATP hydrolysis to ADP + P_i yields energy.

Energy from catabolism (exergonic, energy-releasing processes)

Energy for cellular work (endergonic, energy-consuming processes)

▲ **Figure 8.12 The ATP cycle.** Energy released by breakdown reactions (catabolism) in the cell is used to phosphorylate ADP, regenerating ATP. Chemical potential energy stored in ATP drives most cellular work.

The Regeneration of ATP

An organism at work uses ATP continuously, but ATP is a renewable resource that can be regenerated by the addition of phosphate to ADP **(Figure 8.12)**. The free energy required to phosphorylate ADP comes from exergonic breakdown reactions (catabolism) in the cell. This shuttling of inorganic phosphate and energy is called the ATP cycle, and it couples the cell's energy-yielding (exergonic) processes to the energy-consuming (endergonic) ones. The ATP cycle proceeds at an astonishing pace. For example, a working muscle cell recycles its entire pool of ATP in less than a minute. That turnover represents 10 million molecules of ATP consumed and regenerated per second per cell. If ATP could not be regenerated by the phosphorylation of ADP, humans would use up nearly their body weight in ATP each day.

Because both directions of a reversible process cannot be downhill, the regeneration of ATP is necessarily endergonic:

$$ADP + P_i \rightarrow ATP + H_2O$$
$$\Delta G = +7.3 \text{ kcal/mol } (+30.5 \text{ kJ/mol}) \text{ (standard conditions)}$$

Since ATP formation from ADP and P_i is not spontaneous, free energy must be spent to make it occur. Catabolic (exergonic) pathways, especially cellular respiration, provide the energy for the endergonic process of making ATP. Plants also use light energy to produce ATP. Thus, the ATP cycle is a revolving door through which energy passes during its transfer from catabolic to anabolic pathways.

CONCEPT CHECK 8.3

1. How does ATP typically transfer energy from exergonic to endergonic reactions in the cell?

2. Which of the following has more free energy: glutamic acid + ammonia + ATP OR glutamine + ADP + P_i? Explain your answer.

3. **MAKE CONNECTIONS** Does Figure 8.11a show passive or active transport? Explain. (See Concepts 7.3 and 7.4.)

For suggested answers, see Appendix A.

Enzymes speed up metabolic reactions by lowering energy barriers

The laws of thermodynamics tell us what will and will not happen under given conditions but say nothing about the rate of these processes. A spontaneous chemical reaction occurs without any requirement for outside energy, but it may occur so slowly that it is imperceptible. For example, even though the hydrolysis of sucrose (table sugar) to glucose and fructose is exergonic, occurring spontaneously with a release of free energy ($\Delta G = -7$ kcal/mol), a solution of sucrose dissolved in sterile water will sit for years at room temperature with no appreciable hydrolysis. However, if we add a small amount of the enzyme sucrase to the solution, then all the sucrose may be hydrolyzed within seconds, as shown below:

Sucrose ($C_{12}H_{22}O_{11}$) + H_2O → Sucrase → Glucose ($C_6H_{12}O_6$) + Fructose ($C_6H_{12}O_6$)

How does the enzyme do this?

An **enzyme** is a macromolecule that acts as a **catalyst**, a chemical agent that speeds up a reaction without being consumed by the reaction. In this chapter, we are focusing on enzymes that are proteins. (Some RNA molecules, called ribozymes, can function as enzymes; these will be discussed in Chapters 17 and 25.) Without regulation by enzymes, chemical traffic through the pathways of metabolism would become terribly congested because many chemical reactions would take such a long time. In the next two sections, we will see why spontaneous reactions can be slow and how an enzyme changes the situation.

The Activation Energy Barrier

Every chemical reaction between molecules involves both bond breaking and bond forming. For example, the hydrolysis of sucrose involves breaking the bond between glucose and fructose and one of the bonds of a water molecule and then forming two new bonds, as shown above. Changing one molecule into another generally involves contorting the starting molecule into a highly unstable state before the reaction can proceed. This contortion can be compared to the bending of a metal key ring when you pry it open to add a new key. The key ring is highly unstable in its opened form but returns to a stable state once the key is threaded all the way onto the ring. To reach the contorted state where bonds can change, reactant molecules must absorb energy from their surroundings. When the new bonds of the product molecules form, energy is released as heat, and the molecules return to stable shapes with lower energy than the contorted state.

The initial investment of energy for starting a reaction—the energy required to contort the reactant molecules so the bonds can break—is known as the *free energy of activation*, or **activation energy**, abbreviated E_A in this book. We can think of activation energy as the amount of energy needed to push the reactants to the top of an energy barrier, or uphill, so that the "downhill" part of the reaction can begin. Activation energy is often supplied by heat in the form of thermal energy that the reactant molecules absorb from the surroundings. The absorption of thermal energy accelerates the reactant molecules, so they collide more often and more forcefully. It also agitates the atoms within the molecules, making the breakage of bonds more likely. When the molecules have absorbed enough energy for the bonds to break, the reactants are in an unstable condition known as the *transition state*.

Figure 8.13 graphs the energy changes for a hypothetical exergonic reaction that swaps portions of two reactant molecules:

$$AB + CD \rightarrow AC + BD$$
$$\text{Reactants} \qquad \text{Products}$$

The reactants AB and CD must absorb enough energy from the surroundings to reach the unstable transition state, where bonds can break.

After bonds have broken, new bonds form, releasing energy to the surroundings.

▲ **Figure 8.13 Energy profile of an exergonic reaction.** The "molecules" are hypothetical, with A, B, C, and D representing portions of the molecules. Thermodynamically, this is an exergonic reaction, with a negative ΔG, and the reaction occurs spontaneously. However, the activation energy (E_A) provides a barrier that determines the rate of the reaction.

DRAW IT *Graph the progress of an endergonic reaction in which EF and GH form products EG and FH, assuming that the reactants must pass through a transition state.*

The activation of the reactants is represented by the uphill portion of the graph, in which the free-energy content of the reactant molecules is increasing. At the summit, when energy equivalent to E_A has been absorbed, the reactants are in the transition state: They are activated, and their bonds can be broken. As the atoms then settle into their new, more stable bonding arrangements, energy is released to the surroundings. This corresponds to the downhill part of the curve, which shows the loss of free energy by the molecules. The overall decrease in free energy means that E_A is repaid with dividends, as the formation of new bonds releases more energy than was invested in the breaking of old bonds.

The reaction shown in Figure 8.13 is exergonic and occurs spontaneously ($\Delta G < 0$). However, the activation energy provides a barrier that determines the rate of the reaction. The reactants must absorb enough energy to reach the top of the activation energy barrier before the reaction can occur. For some reactions, E_A is modest enough that even at room temperature there is sufficient thermal energy for many of the reactant molecules to reach the transition state in a short time. In most cases, however, E_A is so high and the transition state is reached so rarely that the reaction will hardly proceed at all. In these cases, the reaction will occur at a noticeable rate only if energy is provided, usually by heat. For example, the reaction of gasoline and oxygen is exergonic and will occur spontaneously, but energy is required for the molecules to reach the transition state and react. Only when the spark plugs fire in an automobile engine can there be the explosive release of energy that pushes the pistons. Without a spark, a mixture of gasoline hydrocarbons and oxygen will not react because the E_A barrier is too high.

How Enzymes Speed Up Reactions

Proteins, DNA, and other complex cellular molecules are rich in free energy and have the potential to decompose spontaneously; that is, the laws of thermodynamics favor their breakdown. These molecules persist only because at temperatures typical for cells, few molecules can make it over the hump of activation energy. The barriers for selected reactions must occasionally be surmounted, however, for cells to carry out the processes needed for life. Heat can increase the rate of a reaction by allowing reactants to attain the transition state more often, but this would not work well in biological systems. First, high temperature denatures proteins and kills cells. Second, heat would speed up *all* reactions, not just those that are needed. Instead of heat, organisms use catalysis to speed up reactions.

An enzyme catalyzes a reaction by lowering the E_A barrier **(Figure 8.14)**, enabling the reactant molecules to absorb enough energy to reach the transition state even at moderate temperatures, as we'll discuss shortly. An enzyme cannot change the ΔG for a reaction; it cannot make an endergonic

▲ **Figure 8.14 The effect of an enzyme on activation energy.** Without affecting the free-energy change (ΔG) for a reaction, an enzyme speeds the reaction by reducing its activation energy (E_A).

reaction exergonic. Enzymes can only hasten reactions that would eventually occur anyway, but this enables the cell to have a dynamic metabolism, routing chemicals smoothly through metabolic pathways. Also, enzymes are very specific for the reactions they catalyze, so they determine which chemical processes will be going on in the cell at any given time.

Substrate Specificity of Enzymes

The reactant an enzyme acts on is referred to as the enzyme's **substrate**. The enzyme binds to its substrate (or substrates, when there are two or more reactants), forming an **enzyme-substrate complex**. While enzyme and substrate are joined, the catalytic action of the enzyme converts the

substrate to the product (or products) of the reaction. The overall process can be summarized as follows:

$$\text{Enzyme} + \text{Substrate(s)} \rightleftharpoons \text{Enzyme-substrate complex} \rightleftharpoons \text{Enzyme} + \text{Product(s)}$$

For example, the enzyme sucrase (most enzyme names end in *-ase*) catalyzes the hydrolysis of the disaccharide sucrose into its two monosaccharides, glucose and fructose (see p. 151):

$$\text{Sucrase} + \text{Sucrose} + H_2O \rightleftharpoons \text{Sucrase-sucrose-}H_2O \text{ complex} \rightleftharpoons \text{Sucrase} + \text{Glucose} + \text{Fructose}$$

The reaction catalyzed by each enzyme is very specific; an enzyme can recognize its specific substrate even among closely related compounds. For instance, sucrase will act only on sucrose and will not bind to other disaccharides, such as maltose. What accounts for this molecular recognition? Recall that most enzymes are proteins, and proteins are macromolecules with unique three-dimensional configurations. The specificity of an enzyme results from its shape, which is a consequence of its amino acid sequence.

Only a restricted region of the enzyme molecule actually binds to the substrate. This region, called the **active site**, is typically a pocket or groove on the surface of the enzyme where catalysis occurs **(Figure 8.15a)**. Usually, the active site is formed by only a few of the enzyme's amino acids, with the rest of the protein molecule providing a framework that determines the shape of the active site. The specificity of an enzyme is attributed to a complementary fit between the shape of its active site and the shape of the substrate.

An enzyme is not a stiff structure locked into a given shape. In fact, recent work by biochemists has shown clearly that enzymes (and other proteins as well) seem to "dance" between subtly different shapes in a dynamic equilibrium, with slight differences in free energy for each "pose." The shape that best fits the substrate isn't necessarily the one with the lowest energy, but during the very short time the enzyme takes on this shape, its active site can bind to the substrate. It has been known for more than 50 years that the active site itself is also not a rigid receptacle for the substrate. As the substrate enters the active site, the enzyme changes shape slightly due to interactions between the substrate's chemical groups and chemical groups on the side chains of the amino acids that form the active site. This shape change makes the active site fit even more snugly around the substrate **(Figure 8.15b)**. The process is like

(a) In this space-filling model of the enzyme hexokinase (blue), the active site forms a groove on the surface. The enzyme's substrate is glucose (red).

(b) When the substrate enters the active site, it forms weak bonds with the enzyme, inducing a change in the shape of the protein. This change allows additional weak bonds to form, causing the active site to enfold the substrate and hold it in place.

▲ **Figure 8.15 Induced fit between an enzyme and its substrate.**

a clasping handshake, with binding between enzyme and substrate becoming tighter after the initial contact. This so-called **induced fit** brings chemical groups of the active site into positions that enhance their ability to catalyze the chemical reaction.

Catalysis in the Enzyme's Active Site

In most enzymatic reactions, the substrate is held in the active site by so-called weak interactions, such as hydrogen bonds and ionic bonds. R groups of a few of the amino acids that make up the active site catalyze the conversion of substrate to product, and the product departs from the active site. The enzyme is then free to take another substrate molecule into its active site. The entire cycle happens so fast that a single enzyme molecule typically acts on about a thousand substrate molecules per second, and some enzymes are even faster. Enzymes, like other catalysts, emerge from the reaction in their original form. Therefore, very small amounts of enzyme can have a huge metabolic impact by functioning over and over again in catalytic cycles. **Figure 8.16** shows a catalytic cycle involving two substrates and two products.

Most metabolic reactions are reversible, and an enzyme can catalyze either the forward or the reverse reaction, depending on which direction has a negative ΔG. This in turn depends mainly on the relative concentrations of reactants and products. The net effect is always in the direction of equilibrium.

Enzymes use a variety of mechanisms that lower activation energy and speed up a reaction (see Figure 8.16, step ❸):

- When there are two or more reactants, the active site provides a template on which the substrates can come together in the proper orientation for a reaction to occur between them.
- As the active site of an enzyme clutches the bound substrates, the enzyme may stretch the substrate molecules toward their transition-state form, stressing and bending critical chemical bonds that must be broken during the reaction. Because E_A is proportional to the difficulty of breaking the bonds, distorting the substrate helps it approach the transition state and thus reduces the amount of free energy that must be absorbed to achieve that state.
- The active site may also provide a microenvironment that is more conducive to a particular type of reaction than the solution itself would be without the enzyme. For example, if the active site has amino acids with acidic R groups, the active site may be a pocket of low pH in an otherwise neutral cell. In such cases, an acidic amino acid may facilitate H^+ transfer to the substrate as a key step in catalyzing the reaction.
- Amino acids in the active site directly participate in the chemical reaction. Sometimes this process even involves

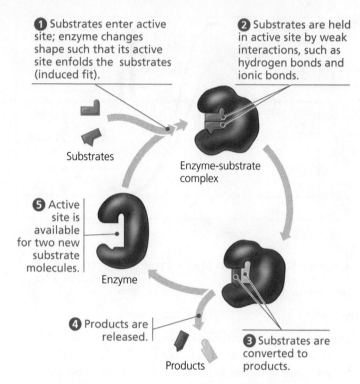

① Substrates enter active site; enzyme changes shape such that its active site enfolds the substrates (induced fit).

② Substrates are held in active site by weak interactions, such as hydrogen bonds and ionic bonds.

Substrates

Enzyme-substrate complex

⑤ Active site is available for two new substrate molecules.

Enzyme

④ Products are released.

Products

③ Substrates are converted to products.

▲ **Figure 8.16 The active site and catalytic cycle of an enzyme.** An enzyme can convert one or more reactant molecules to one or more product molecules. The enzyme shown here converts two substrate molecules to two product molecules.

DRAW IT *The enzyme-substrate complex passes through a transition state (see Figure 8.13). Label the part of the cycle where the transition state occurs.*

brief covalent bonding between the substrate and the side chain of an amino acid of the enzyme. Subsequent steps of the reaction restore the side chains to their original states, so that the active site is the same after the reaction as it was before.

The rate at which a particular amount of enzyme converts substrate to product is partly a function of the initial concentration of the substrate: The more substrate molecules that are available, the more frequently they access the active sites of the enzyme molecules. However, there is a limit to how fast the reaction can be pushed by adding more substrate to a fixed concentration of enzyme. At some point, the concentration of substrate will be high enough that all enzyme molecules have their active sites engaged. As soon as the product exits an active site, another substrate molecule enters. At this substrate concentration, the enzyme is said to be *saturated*, and the rate of the reaction is determined by the speed at which the active site converts substrate to product. When an enzyme population is saturated, the only way to increase the rate of product formation is to add more enzyme. Cells often increase the rate of a reaction by producing more enzyme molecules. You can graph the overall progress of an enzymatic reaction in the **Scientific Skills Exercise.**

Making a Line Graph and Calculating a Slope

Does the Rate of Glucose 6-Phosphatase Activity Change over Time in Isolated Liver Cells? Glucose 6-phosphatase, which is found in mammalian liver cells, is a key enzyme in control of blood glucose levels. The enzyme catalyzes the breakdown of glucose 6-phosphate into glucose and inorganic phosphate (Ⓟ$_i$). These products are transported out of liver cells into the blood, increasing blood glucose levels. In this exercise, you will graph data from a time-course experiment that measured Ⓟ$_i$ concentration in the buffer outside isolated liver cells, thus indirectly measuring glucose 6-phosphatase activity inside the cells.

How the Experiment Was Done Isolated rat liver cells were placed in a dish with buffer at physiological conditions (pH 7.4, 37°C). Glucose 6-phosphate (the substrate) was added to the dish, where it was taken up by the cells. Then a sample of buffer was removed every 5 minutes and the concentration of Ⓟ$_i$ determined.

Data from the Experiment

Time (min)	Concentration of Ⓟ$_i$ (µmol/mL)
0	0
5	10
10	90
15	180
20	270
25	330
30	355
35	355
40	355

Interpret the Data

1. To see patterns in the data from a time-course experiment like this, it is helpful to graph the data. First, determine which set of data goes on each axis. (a) What did the researchers intentionally vary in the experiment? This is the independent variable, which goes on the x-axis. (b) What are the units (abbreviated) for the independent variable? Explain in words what the abbreviation stands for. (c) What was measured by the researchers? This is the dependent variable, which goes

on the y-axis. (d) What does the units abbreviation stand for? Label each axis, including the units.

2. Next, you'll want to mark off the axes with just enough evenly spaced tick marks to accommodate the full set of data. Determine the range of data values for each axis. (a) What is the largest value to go on the x-axis? What is a reasonable spacing for the tick marks, and what should be the highest one? (b) What is the largest value to go on the y-axis? What is a reasonable spacing for the tick marks, and what should be the highest one?

3. Plot the data points on your graph. Match each x-value with its partner y-value and place a point on the graph at that coordinate. Draw a line that connects the points. (For additional information about graphs, see the Scientific Skills Review in Appendix F and in the Study Area in MasteringBiology.)

4. Examine your graph and look for patterns in the data. (a) Does the concentration of Ⓟ$_i$ increase evenly through the course of the experiment? To answer this question, describe the pattern you see in the graph. (b) What part of the graph shows the highest rate of enzyme activity? Consider that the rate of enzyme activity is related to the slope of the line, $\Delta y/\Delta x$ (the "rise" over the "run"), in µmol/mL · min, with the steepest slope indicating the highest rate of enzyme activity. Calculate the rate of enzyme activity (slope) where the graph is steepest. (c) Can you think of a biological explanation for the pattern you see?

5. If your blood sugar level is low from skipping lunch, what reaction (discussed in this exercise) will occur in your liver cells? Write out the reaction and put the name of the enzyme over the reaction arrow. How will this reaction affect your blood sugar level?

(MB) A version of this Scientific Skills Exercise can be assigned in MasteringBiology.

Data from S. R. Commerford et al., Diets enriched in sucrose or fat increase gluconeogenesis and G-6-Pase but not basal glucose production in rats, *American Journal of Physiology—Endocrinology and Metabolism* 283:E545–E555 (2002).

Effects of Local Conditions on Enzyme Activity

The activity of an enzyme—how efficiently the enzyme functions—is affected by general environmental factors, such as temperature and pH. It can also be affected by chemicals that specifically influence that enzyme. In fact, researchers have learned much about enzyme function by employing such chemicals.

Effects of Temperature and pH

Recall from Chapter 5 that the three-dimensional structures of proteins are sensitive to their environment. As a consequence, each enzyme works better under some conditions than under other conditions, because these *optimal conditions* favor the most active shape for the enzyme.

Temperature and pH are environmental factors important in the activity of an enzyme. Up to a point, the

rate of an enzymatic reaction increases with increasing temperature, partly because substrates collide with active sites more frequently when the molecules move rapidly. Above that temperature, however, the speed of the enzymatic reaction drops sharply. The thermal agitation of the enzyme molecule disrupts the hydrogen bonds, ionic bonds, and other weak interactions that stabilize the active shape of the enzyme, and the protein molecule eventually denatures. Each enzyme has an optimal temperature at which its reaction rate is greatest. Without denaturing the enzyme, this temperature allows the greatest number of molecular collisions and the fastest conversion of the reactants to product molecules. Most human enzymes have optimal temperatures of about 35–40°C (close to human body temperature). The thermophilic bacteria that live in hot springs contain enzymes with optimal temperatures of 70°C or higher **(Figure 8.17a)**.

(a) Optimal temperature for two enzymes

(b) Optimal pH for two enzymes

▲ **Figure 8.17 Environmental factors affecting enzyme activity.** Each enzyme has an optimal **(a)** temperature and **(b)** pH that favor the most active shape of the protein molecule.

DRAW IT *Given that a mature lysosome has an internal pH of around 4.5, draw a curve in (b) showing what you would predict for a lysosomal enzyme, labeling its optimal pH.*

Just as each enzyme has an optimal temperature, it also has a pH at which it is most active. The optimal pH values for most enzymes fall in the range of pH 6–8, but there are exceptions. For example, pepsin, a digestive enzyme in the human stomach, works best at pH 2. Such an acidic environment denatures most enzymes, but pepsin is adapted to maintain its functional three-dimensional structure in the acidic environment of the stomach. In contrast, trypsin, a digestive enzyme residing in the alkaline environment of the human intestine, has an optimal pH of 8 and would be denatured in the stomach **(Figure 8.17b)**.

Cofactors

Many enzymes require nonprotein helpers for catalytic activity. These adjuncts, called **cofactors**, may be bound tightly to the enzyme as permanent residents, or they may bind loosely and reversibly along with the substrate. The cofactors of some enzymes are inorganic, such as the metal atoms zinc, iron, and copper in ionic form. If the cofactor is an organic molecule, it is referred to, more specifically, as a **coenzyme**. Most vitamins are important in nutrition because they act as coenzymes or raw materials from which coenzymes are made.

Enzyme Inhibitors

Certain chemicals selectively inhibit the action of specific enzymes. Sometimes, the inhibitor attaches to the enzyme by covalent bonds, in which case the inhibition is usually irreversible. Many enzyme inhibitors, however, bind to the enzyme by weak interactions, and when this occurs the inhibition is reversible. Some reversible inhibitors resemble the normal substrate molecule and compete for admission into the active site **(Figure 8.18a** and **b)**. These mimics, called **competitive inhibitors**, reduce the productivity of enzymes by blocking substrates from entering active sites. This kind of inhibition can be overcome by increasing the concentration of substrate so that as active sites become available, more substrate molecules than inhibitor molecules are around to gain entry to the sites.

In contrast, **noncompetitive inhibitors** do not directly compete with the substrate to bind to the enzyme at the active site **(Figure 8.18c)**. Instead, they impede enzymatic reactions by binding to another part of the enzyme. This interaction causes the enzyme molecule to change its shape

▼ **Figure 8.18 Inhibition of enzyme activity.**

(a) Normal binding

A substrate can bind normally to the active site of an enzyme.

Substrate
Active site
Enzyme

(b) Competitive inhibition

A competitive inhibitor mimics the substrate, competing for the active site.

Competitive inhibitor

(c) Noncompetitive inhibition

A noncompetitive inhibitor binds to the enzyme away from the active site, altering the shape of the enzyme so that even if the substrate can bind, the active site functions less effectively, if it all.

Noncompetitive inhibitor

in such a way that the active site becomes less effective at catalyzing the conversion of substrate to product.

Toxins and poisons are often irreversible enzyme inhibitors. An example is sarin, a nerve gas. Sarin was released by terrorists in the Tokyo subway in 1995, causing the death of several people and injury to many others. This small molecule binds covalently to the R group on the amino acid serine, which is found in the active site of acetylcholinesterase, an enzyme important in the nervous system. Other examples include the pesticides DDT and parathion, inhibitors of key enzymes in the nervous system. Finally, many antibiotics are inhibitors of specific enzymes in bacteria. For instance, penicillin blocks the active site of an enzyme that many bacteria use to make their cell walls.

The Evolution of Enzymes

EVOLUTION   Thus far, biochemists have discovered and named more than 4,000 different enzymes in various species, most likely a very small fraction of all enzymes. How did this grand profusion of enzymes arise? Recall that most enzymes are proteins, and proteins are encoded by genes. A permanent change in a gene, known as a *mutation*, can result in a protein with one or more changed amino acids. In the case of an enzyme, if the changed amino acids are in the active site or some other crucial region, the altered enzyme might have a novel activity or might bind to a different substrate. Under environmental conditions where the new function benefits the organism, natural selection would tend to favor the mutated form of the gene, causing it to persist in the population. This simplified model is generally accepted as the main way in which the multitude of different enzymes arose over the past few billion years of life's history.

Data supporting this model have been collected by researchers using a lab procedure that mimics evolution in natural populations. One group tested whether the function of an enzyme called β-galactosidase could change over time in populations of the bacterium *Escherichia coli* (*E. coli*). β-galactosidase breaks down the disaccharide lactose into the simple sugars glucose and galactose. Using molecular techniques, the researchers introduced random mutations into *E. coli* genes and then tested the bacteria for their ability to break down a slightly different disaccharide (one that has the sugar fucose in place of galactose). At the end of the experiment, the "evolved" enzyme bound the new substrate several hundred times more strongly, and broke it down 10 to 20 times more quickly, than did the original enzyme.

The researchers found that six amino acids had changed in the enzyme altered in this experiment. Two of these changed amino acids were in the active site, two were nearby, and two were on the surface of the protein **(Figure 8.19)**. This experiment and others like it strengthen the notion that a few changes can indeed alter enzyme function.

Two changed amino acids were found near the active site.

Active site

Two changed amino acids were found in the active site.

Two changed amino acids were found on the surface.

▲ **Figure 8.19 Mimicking evolution of an enzyme with a new function.** After seven rounds of mutation and selection in a lab, the enzyme β-galactosidase evolved into an enzyme specialized for breaking down a sugar different from lactose. This ribbon model shows one subunit of the altered enzyme; six amino acids were different.

CONCEPT CHECK 8.4

1. Many spontaneous reactions occur very slowly. Why don't all spontaneous reactions occur instantly?

2. Why do enzymes act only on very specific substrates?

3. **WHAT IF?** Malonate is an inhibitor of the enzyme succinate dehydrogenase. How would you determine whether malonate is a competitive or noncompetitive inhibitor?

4. **MAKE CONNECTIONS** In nature, what conditions could lead to natural selection favoring bacteria with enzymes that could break down the fucose-containing disaccharide discussed above? See the discussion of natural selection in Concept 1.2.

For suggested answers, see Appendix A.

CONCEPT 8.5

Regulation of enzyme activity helps control metabolism

Chemical chaos would result if all of a cell's metabolic pathways were operating simultaneously. Intrinsic to life's processes is a cell's ability to tightly regulate its metabolic pathways by controlling when and where its various enzymes are active. It does this either by switching on and off the genes that encode specific enzymes (as we will discuss in Unit Three) or, as we discuss here, by regulating the activity of enzymes once they are made.

Allosteric Regulation of Enzymes

In many cases, the molecules that naturally regulate enzyme activity in a cell behave something like reversible noncompetitive inhibitors (see Figure 8.18c): These regulatory molecules change an enzyme's shape and the functioning of its active site by binding to a site elsewhere on the molecule, via noncovalent interactions. **Allosteric regulation** is the term used to describe any case in which a protein's function at one site is affected by the binding of a regulatory molecule to a separate site. It may result in either inhibition or stimulation of an enzyme's activity.

Allosteric Activation and Inhibition

Most enzymes known to be allosterically regulated are constructed from two or more subunits, each composed of a polypeptide chain with its own active site. The entire complex oscillates between two different shapes, one catalytically active and the other inactive (**Figure 8.20a**). In the simplest kind of allosteric regulation, an activating or inhibiting regulatory molecule binds to a regulatory site (sometimes called an allosteric site), often located where subunits join. The binding of an *activator* to a regulatory site stabilizes the shape that has functional active sites, whereas the binding of an *inhibitor* stabilizes the inactive form of the enzyme. The subunits of an allosteric enzyme fit together in such a way that a shape change in one subunit is transmitted to all others. Through this interaction of subunits, a single activator or inhibitor molecule that binds to one regulatory site will affect the active sites of all subunits.

Fluctuating concentrations of regulators can cause a sophisticated pattern of response in the activity of cellular enzymes. The products of ATP hydrolysis (ADP and (P_i)), for example, play a complex role in balancing the flow of traffic between anabolic and catabolic pathways by their effects on key enzymes. ATP binds to several catabolic enzymes allosterically, lowering their affinity for substrate and thus inhibiting their activity. ADP, however, functions as an activator of the same enzymes. This is logical because catabolism functions in regenerating ATP. If ATP production lags behind its use, ADP accumulates and activates the enzymes that speed up catabolism, producing more ATP. If the supply of ATP exceeds demand, then catabolism slows down as ATP molecules accumulate and bind to the same enzymes, inhibiting them. (You'll see specific examples of this type of regulation when you learn about cellular respiration in the next chapter.) ATP, ADP, and other related molecules also affect key enzymes in anabolic pathways. In this way, allosteric enzymes control the rates of important reactions in both sorts of metabolic pathways.

In another kind of allosteric activation, a *substrate* molecule binding to one active site in a multisubunit enzyme triggers a shape change in all the subunits, thereby increasing catalytic activity at the other active sites (**Figure 8.20b**). Called **cooperativity**, this mechanism amplifies the response of enzymes to substrates: One substrate molecule primes an enzyme to act on additional substrate molecules more readily. Cooperativity is considered "allosteric" regulation

▼ **Figure 8.20 Allosteric regulation of enzyme activity.**

(a) Allosteric activators and inhibitors

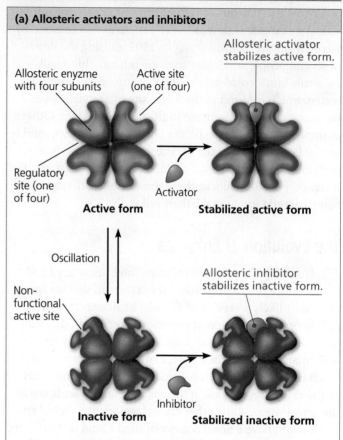

At low concentrations, activators and inhibitors dissociate from the enzyme. The enzyme can then oscillate again.

(b) Cooperativity: another type of allosteric activation

The inactive form shown on the left oscillates with the active form when the active form is not stabilized by substrate.

because binding of the substrate to one active site affects catalysis in another active site.

Although hemoglobin is not an enzyme (it carries O_2), classic studies on hemoglobin have elucidated the principle of cooperativity. Hemoglobin is made up of four subunits, each with an oxygen-binding site (see Figure 5.18). The binding of an oxygen molecule to one binding site increases the affinity for oxygen of the remaining binding sites. Thus, where oxygen is at high levels, such as in the lungs or gills, hemoglobin's affinity for oxygen increases as more binding sites are filled. In oxygen-deprived tissues, however, the release of each oxygen molecule decreases the oxygen affinity of the other binding sites, resulting in the release of oxygen where it is most needed. Cooperativity works similarly in multisubunit enzymes that have been studied.

Feedback Inhibition

When ATP allosterically inhibits an enzyme in an ATP-generating pathway, the result is feedback inhibition, a common mode of metabolic control. In **feedback inhibition**, a metabolic pathway is halted by the inhibitory binding of its end product to an enzyme that acts early in the pathway. **Figure 8.21** shows an example of feedback inhibition operating on an anabolic pathway. Some cells use this five-step pathway to synthesize the amino acid isoleucine from threonine, another amino acid. As isoleucine accumulates, it slows down its own synthesis by allosterically inhibiting the enzyme for the first step of the pathway. Feedback inhibition thereby prevents the cell from making more isoleucine than is necessary and thus wasting chemical resources.

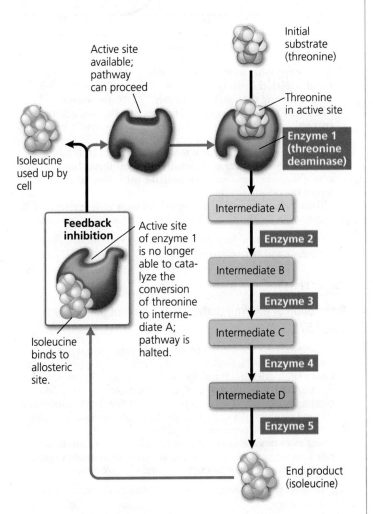

▲ **Figure 8.21 Feedback inhibition in isoleucine synthesis.**

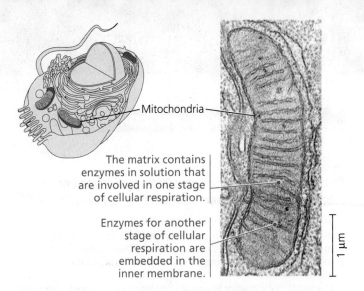

▲ **Figure 8.22 Organelles and structural order in metabolism.** Organelles such as the mitochondrion (TEM) contain enzymes that carry out specific functions, in this case cellular respiration.

Localization of Enzymes Within the Cell

The cell is not just a bag of chemicals with thousands of different kinds of enzymes and substrates in a random mix. The cell is compartmentalized, and cellular structures help bring order to metabolic pathways. In some cases, a team of enzymes for several steps of a metabolic pathway are assembled into a multienzyme complex. The arrangement facilitates the sequence of reactions, with the product from the first enzyme becoming the substrate for an adjacent enzyme in the complex, and so on, until the end product is released. Some enzymes and enzyme complexes have fixed locations within the cell and act as structural components of particular membranes. Others are in solution within particular membrane-enclosed eukaryotic organelles, each with its own internal chemical environment. For example, in eukaryotic cells, the enzymes for cellular respiration reside in specific locations within mitochondria (**Figure 8.22**).

In this chapter, you have learned that metabolism, the intersecting set of chemical pathways characteristic of life, is a choreographed interplay of thousands of different kinds of cellular molecules. In the next chapter, we will explore cellular respiration, the major catabolic pathway that breaks down organic molecules, releasing energy that can be used for the crucial processes of life.

CONCEPT CHECK 8.5

1. How do an activator and an inhibitor have different effects on an allosterically regulated enzyme?

2. Regulation of isoleucine synthesis is an example of feedback inhibition of an anabolic pathway. With that in mind, explain how ATP might be involved in feedback inhibition of a catabolic pathway.

For suggested answers, see Appendix A.

SUMMARY OF KEY CONCEPTS

CONCEPT 8.1

An organism's metabolism transforms matter and energy, subject to the laws of thermodynamics (pp. 142–145)

- **Metabolism** is the collection of chemical reactions that occur in an organism. Enzymes catalyze reactions in intersecting **metabolic pathways**, which may be **catabolic** (breaking down molecules, releasing energy) or **anabolic** (building molecules, consuming energy).
- **Energy** is the capacity to cause change; some forms of energy do work by moving matter. **Kinetic energy** is associated with motion and includes **thermal energy** associated with random motion of atoms or molecules. **Heat** is thermal energy in transfer from one object to another. **Potential energy** is related to the location or structure of matter and includes **chemical energy** possessed by a molecule due to its structure.
- **The first law of thermodynamics**, conservation of energy, states that energy cannot be created or destroyed, only transferred or transformed. The **second law of thermodynamics** states that **spontaneous processes**, those requiring no outside input of energy, increase the **entropy** (disorder) of the universe.

? *Explain how the highly ordered structure of a cell does not conflict with the second law of thermodynamics.*

CONCEPT 8.2

The free-energy change of a reaction tells us whether or not the reaction occurs spontaneously (pp. 145–148)

- A living system's **free energy** is energy that can do work under cellular conditions. The change in free energy (ΔG) during a biological process is related directly to enthalpy change (ΔH) and to the change in entropy (ΔS): $\Delta G = \Delta H - T\Delta S$. Organisms live at the expense of free energy. A spontaneous process occurs with no energy input; during such a process, free energy decreases and the stability of a system increases. At maximum stability, the system is at equilibrium and can do no work.
- In an **exergonic** (spontaneous) chemical reaction, the products have less free energy than the reactants ($-\Delta G$). **Endergonic** (nonspontaneous) reactions require an input of energy ($+\Delta G$). The addition of starting materials and the removal of end products prevent metabolism from reaching equilibrium.

? *Explain the meaning of each component in the equation for the change in free energy of a spontaneous chemical reaction. Why are spontaneous reactions important in the metabolism of a cell?*

CONCEPT 8.3

ATP powers cellular work by coupling exergonic reactions to endergonic reactions (pp. 148–151)

- **ATP** is the cell's energy shuttle. Hydrolysis of its terminal phosphate yields ADP and $\text{\textcircled{P}}_i$ and releases free energy.
- Through **energy coupling**, the exergonic process of ATP hydrolysis drives endergonic reactions by transfer of a phosphate group to specific reactants, forming a **phosphorylated intermediate** that is more reactive. ATP hydrolysis (sometimes with

protein phosphorylation) also causes changes in the shape and binding affinities of transport and motor proteins.
- Catabolic pathways drive regeneration of ATP from ADP + $\text{\textcircled{P}}_i$.

? *Describe the ATP cycle: How is ATP used and regenerated in a cell?*

CONCEPT 8.4

Enzymes speed up metabolic reactions by lowering energy barriers (pp. 151–157)

- In a chemical reaction, the energy necessary to break the bonds of the reactants is the **activation energy**, E_A.
- **Enzymes** lower the E_A barrier:

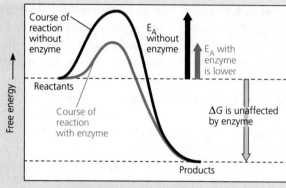

- Each enzyme has a unique **active site** that binds one or more **substrate(s)**, the reactants on which it acts. It then changes shape, binding the substrate(s) more tightly (**induced fit**).
- The active site can lower an E_A barrier by orienting substrates correctly, straining their bonds, providing a favorable microenvironment, or even covalently bonding with the substrate.
- Each enzyme has an optimal temperature and pH. Inhibitors reduce enzyme function. A **competitive inhibitor** binds to the active site, whereas a **noncompetitive inhibitor** binds to a different site on the enzyme.
- Natural selection, acting on organisms with variant enzymes, is responsible for the diversity of enzymes found in organisms.

? *How do both activation energy barriers and enzymes help maintain the structural and metabolic order of life?*

CONCEPT 8.5

Regulation of enzyme activity helps control metabolism (pp. 157–159)

- Many enzymes are subject to **allosteric regulation**: Regulatory molecules, either activators or inhibitors, bind to specific regulatory sites, affecting the shape and function of the enzyme. In **cooperativity**, binding of one substrate molecule can stimulate binding or activity at other active sites. In **feedback inhibition**, the end product of a metabolic pathway allosterically inhibits the enzyme for a previous step in the pathway.
- Some enzymes are grouped into complexes, some are incorporated into membranes, and some are contained inside organelles, increasing the efficiency of metabolic processes.

? *What roles do allosteric regulation and feedback inhibition play in the metabolism of a cell?*

TEST YOUR UNDERSTANDING

LEVEL 1: KNOWLEDGE/COMPREHENSION

1. Choose the pair of terms that correctly completes this sentence: Catabolism is to anabolism as _____ is to _____.
   a. exergonic; spontaneous
   b. exergonic; endergonic
   c. free energy; entropy
   d. work; energy

2. Most cells cannot harness heat to perform work because
   a. heat does not involve a transfer of energy.
   b. cells do not have much thermal energy; they are relatively cool.
   c. temperature is usually uniform throughout a cell.
   d. heat can never be used to do work.

3. Which of the following metabolic processes can occur without a net influx of energy from some other process?
   a. $ADP + P_i \rightarrow ATP + H_2O$
   b. $C_6H_{12}O_6 + 6\,O_2 \rightarrow 6\,CO_2 + 6\,H_2O$
   c. $6\,CO_2 + 6\,H_2O \rightarrow C_6H_{12}O_6 + 6\,O_2$
   d. Amino acids $\rightarrow$ Protein

4. If an enzyme in solution is saturated with substrate, the most effective way to obtain a faster yield of products is to
   a. add more of the enzyme.
   b. heat the solution to 90°C.
   c. add more substrate.
   d. add a noncompetitive inhibitor.

5. Some bacteria are metabolically active in hot springs because
   a. they are able to maintain a lower internal temperature.
   b. high temperatures make catalysis unnecessary.
   c. their enzymes have high optimal temperatures.
   d. their enzymes are completely insensitive to temperature.

LEVEL 2: APPLICATION/ANALYSIS

6. If an enzyme is added to a solution where its substrate and product are in equilibrium, what will occur?
   a. Additional substrate will be formed.
   b. The reaction will change from endergonic to exergonic.
   c. The free energy of the system will change.
   d. Nothing; the reaction will stay at equilibrium.

LEVEL 3: SYNTHESIS/EVALUATION

7. **DRAW IT** Using a series of arrows, draw the branched metabolic reaction pathway described by the following statements, and then answer the question at the end. Use red arrows and minus signs to indicate inhibition.

   L can form either M or N.

   M can form O.

   O can form either P or R.

   P can form Q.

   R can form S.

   O inhibits the reaction of L to form M.

   Q inhibits the reaction of O to form P.

   S inhibits the reaction of O to form R.

   Which reaction would prevail if both Q and S were present in the cell in high concentrations?
   a. $L \rightarrow M$
   b. $M \rightarrow O$
   c. $L \rightarrow N$
   d. $O \rightarrow P$

8. **EVOLUTION CONNECTION** A recent revival of the antievolutionary "intelligent design" argument holds that biochemical pathways are too complex to have evolved, because all intermediate steps in a given pathway must be present to produce the final product. Critique this argument. How could you use the diversity of metabolic pathways that produce the same or similar products to support your case?

9. **SCIENTIFIC INQUIRY**
   DRAW IT A researcher has developed an assay to measure the activity of an important enzyme present in liver cells growing in culture. She adds the enzyme's substrate to a dish of cells and then measures the appearance of reaction products. The results are graphed as the amount of product on the y-axis versus time on the x-axis. The researcher notes four sections of the graph. For a short period of time, no products appear (section A). Then (section B) the reaction rate is quite high (the slope of the line is steep). Next, the reaction gradually slows down (section C). Finally, the graph line becomes flat (section D). Draw and label the graph, and propose a model to explain the molecular events occurring at each stage of this reaction profile.

10. **WRITE ABOUT A THEME: ENERGY AND MATTER** Life requires energy. In a short essay (100–150 words), describe the basic principles of bioenergetics in an animal cell. How is the flow and transformation of energy different in a photosynthesizing cell? Include the role of ATP and enzymes in your discussion.

11. **SYNTHESIZE YOUR KNOWLEDGE**

Explain what is happening in this photo in terms of kinetic energy and potential energy. Include the energy conversions that occur when the penguins eat fish and climb back up on the glacier. Describe the role of ATP and enzymes in the underlying molecular processes, including what happens to the free energy of some of the molecules involved.

For selected answers, see Appendix A.

MasteringBiology®

Students Go to **MasteringBiology** for assignments, the eText, and the Study Area with practice tests, animations, and activities.

Instructors Go to **MasteringBiology** for automatically graded tutorials and questions that you can assign to your students, plus Instructor Resources.

9

Cellular Respiration and Fermentation

KEY CONCEPTS

9.1 Catabolic pathways yield energy by oxidizing organic fuels

9.2 Glycolysis harvests chemical energy by oxidizing glucose to pyruvate

9.3 After pyruvate is oxidized, the citric acid cycle completes the energy-yielding oxidation of organic molecules

9.4 During oxidative phosphorylation, chemiosmosis couples electron transport to ATP synthesis

9.5 Fermentation and anaerobic respiration enable cells to produce ATP without the use of oxygen

9.6 Glycolysis and the citric acid cycle connect to many other metabolic pathways

▲ **Figure 9.1** How do these leaves power the work of life for this giraffe?

Life Is Work

Living cells require transfusions of energy from outside sources to perform their many tasks—for example, assembling polymers, pumping substances across membranes, moving, and reproducing. The giraffe in **Figure 9.1** is obtaining energy for its cells by eating the leaves of plants; some other animals obtain energy by feeding on other organisms that eat plants.

The energy stored in the organic molecules of food ultimately comes from the sun. Energy flows into an ecosystem as sunlight and exits as heat; in contrast, the chemical elements essential to life are recycled (**Figure 9.2**). Photosynthesis generates oxygen and organic molecules that are used by the mitochondria of eukaryotes (including plants and algae) as fuel for cellular respiration. Respiration breaks this fuel down, generating ATP. The waste products of this type of respiration, carbon dioxide and water, are the raw materials for photosynthesis.

In this chapter, we consider how cells harvest the chemical energy stored in organic molecules and use it to generate ATP, the molecule that drives most cellular work. After presenting some basics about respiration, we'll focus on three key pathways of respiration: glycolysis, the citric acid cycle, and oxidative phosphorylation. We'll also consider fermentation, a somewhat simpler pathway coupled to glycolysis that has deep evolutionary roots.

▲ **Figure 9.2 Energy flow and chemical recycling in ecosystems.** Energy flows into an ecosystem as sunlight and ultimately leaves as heat, while the chemical elements essential to life are recycled.

Catabolic pathways yield energy by oxidizing organic fuels

Metabolic pathways that release stored energy by breaking down complex molecules are called catabolic pathways (see Chapter 8). Electron transfer plays a major role in these pathways. In this section, we consider these processes, which are central to cellular respiration.

Catabolic Pathways and Production of ATP

Organic compounds possess potential energy as a result of the arrangement of electrons in the bonds between their atoms. Compounds that can participate in exergonic reactions can act as fuels. Through the activity of enzymes, a cell systematically degrades complex organic molecules that are rich in potential energy to simpler waste products that have less energy. Some of the energy taken out of chemical storage can be used to do work; the rest is dissipated as heat.

One catabolic process, **fermentation**, is a partial degradation of sugars or other organic fuel that occurs without the use of oxygen. However, the most efficient catabolic pathway is **aerobic respiration**, in which oxygen is consumed as a reactant along with the organic fuel (*aerobic* is from the Greek *aer*, air, and *bios*, life). The cells of most eukaryotic and many prokaryotic organisms can carry out aerobic respiration. Some prokaryotes use substances other than oxygen as reactants in a similar process that harvests chemical energy without oxygen; this process is called

anaerobic respiration (the prefix *an-* means "without"). Technically, the term **cellular respiration** includes both aerobic and anaerobic processes. However, it originated as a synonym for aerobic respiration because of the relationship of that process to organismal respiration, in which an animal breathes in oxygen. Thus, *cellular respiration* is often used to refer to the aerobic process, a practice we follow in most of this chapter.

Although very different in mechanism, aerobic respiration is in principle similar to the combustion of gasoline in an automobile engine after oxygen is mixed with the fuel (hydrocarbons). Food provides the fuel for respiration, and the exhaust is carbon dioxide and water. The overall process can be summarized as follows:

$$\text{Organic compounds} + \text{Oxygen} \rightarrow \text{Carbon dioxide} + \text{Water} + \text{Energy}$$

Carbohydrates, fats, and protein molecules from food can all be processed and consumed as fuel, as we will discuss later in the chapter. In animal diets, a major source of carbohydrates is starch, a storage polysaccharide that can be broken down into glucose ($C_6H_{12}O_6$) subunits. Here, we will learn the steps of cellular respiration by tracking the degradation of the sugar glucose:

$$C_6H_{12}O_6 + 6\,O_2 \rightarrow 6\,CO_2 + 6\,H_2O + \text{Energy (ATP + heat)}$$

This breakdown of glucose is exergonic, having a free-energy change of −686 kcal (2,870 kJ) per mole of glucose decomposed ($\Delta G = -686$ kcal/mol). Recall that a negative ΔG indicates that the products of the chemical process store less energy than the reactants and that the reaction can happen spontaneously—in other words, without an input of energy.

Catabolic pathways do not directly move flagella, pump solutes across membranes, polymerize monomers, or perform other cellular work. Catabolism is linked to work by a chemical drive shaft—ATP (see Chapter 8). To keep working, the cell must regenerate its supply of ATP from ADP and ⓟᵢ (see Figure 8.12). To understand how cellular respiration accomplishes this, let's examine the fundamental chemical processes known as oxidation and reduction.

Redox Reactions: Oxidation and Reduction

How do the catabolic pathways that decompose glucose and other organic fuels yield energy? The answer is based on the transfer of electrons during the chemical reactions. The relocation of electrons releases energy stored in organic molecules, and this energy ultimately is used to synthesize ATP.

The Principle of Redox

In many chemical reactions, there is a transfer of one or more electrons (e^-) from one reactant to another. These electron transfers are called oxidation-reduction reactions, or **redox reactions** for short. In a redox reaction, the loss of electrons from one substance is called **oxidation**, and the addition of electrons to another substance is known as **reduction**. (Note that *adding* electrons is called *reduction*; adding negatively charged electrons to an atom *reduces* the amount of positive charge of that atom.) To take a simple, nonbiological example, consider the reaction between the elements sodium (Na) and chlorine (Cl) that forms table salt:

$$\text{Na} + \text{Cl} \longrightarrow \text{Na}^+ + \text{Cl}^-$$

becomes oxidized (loses electron)
becomes reduced (gains electron)

We could generalize a redox reaction this way:

$$\text{X}e^- + \text{Y} \longrightarrow \text{X} + \text{Y}e^-$$

becomes oxidized
becomes reduced

In the generalized reaction, substance Xe^-, the electron donor, is called the **reducing agent**; it reduces Y, which accepts the donated electron. Substance Y, the electron acceptor, is the **oxidizing agent**; it oxidizes Xe^- by removing its electron. Because an electron transfer requires both an electron donor and an acceptor, oxidation and reduction always go hand in hand.

Not all redox reactions involve the complete transfer of electrons from one substance to another; some change the degree of electron sharing in covalent bonds. Methane combustion, shown in **Figure 9.3**, is an example. The covalent electrons in methane are shared nearly equally between the bonded atoms because carbon and hydrogen have about the same affinity for valence electrons; they are about equally electronegative (see Chapter 2). But when methane reacts with oxygen, forming carbon dioxide, electrons end up shared less equally between the carbon atom and its new covalent partners, the oxygen atoms, which are very electronegative. In effect, the carbon atom has partially "lost" its shared electrons; thus, methane has been oxidized.

Now let's examine the fate of the reactant O_2. The two atoms of the oxygen molecule (O_2) share their electrons equally. But when oxygen reacts with the hydrogen from methane, forming water, the electrons of the covalent bonds spend more time near the oxygen (see Figure 9.3). In effect, each oxygen atom has partially "gained" electrons, so the oxygen molecule has been reduced. Because oxygen is so electronegative, it is one of the most potent of all oxidizing agents.

Energy must be added to pull an electron away from an atom, just as energy is required to push a ball uphill. The more electronegative the atom (the stronger its pull on electrons), the more energy is required to take an electron away from it. An electron loses potential energy when it shifts from a less electronegative atom toward a more electronegative one, just as a ball loses potential energy when it rolls

▲ **Figure 9.3 Methane combustion as an energy-yielding redox reaction.** The reaction releases energy to the surroundings because the electrons lose potential energy when they end up being shared unequally, spending more time near electronegative atoms such as oxygen.

downhill. A redox reaction that moves electrons closer to oxygen, such as the burning (oxidation) of methane, therefore releases chemical energy that can be put to work.

Oxidation of Organic Fuel Molecules During Cellular Respiration

The oxidation of methane by oxygen is the main combustion reaction that occurs at the burner of a gas stove. The combustion of gasoline in an automobile engine is also a redox reaction; the energy released pushes the pistons. But the energy-yielding redox process of greatest interest to biologists is respiration: the oxidation of glucose and other molecules in food. Examine again the summary equation for cellular respiration, but this time think of it as a redox process:

$$\text{C}_6\text{H}_{12}\text{O}_6 + 6\,\text{O}_2 \longrightarrow 6\,\text{CO}_2 + 6\,\text{H}_2\text{O} + \text{Energy}$$

becomes oxidized
becomes reduced

As in the combustion of methane or gasoline, the fuel (glucose) is oxidized and oxygen is reduced. The electrons lose potential energy along the way, and energy is released.

In general, organic molecules that have an abundance of hydrogen are excellent fuels because their bonds are a source of "hilltop" electrons, whose energy may be released as these electrons "fall" down an energy gradient when they are transferred to oxygen. The summary equation for respiration indicates that hydrogen is transferred from glucose to oxygen. But the important point, not visible in the summary equation, is that the energy state of the electron changes as hydrogen (with its electron) is transferred to oxygen. In respiration, the oxidation of glucose transfers electrons to a lower energy state, liberating energy that becomes available for ATP synthesis.

The main energy-yielding foods—carbohydrates and fats—are reservoirs of electrons associated with hydrogen.

Only the barrier of activation energy holds back the flood of electrons to a lower energy state (see Figure 8.13). Without this barrier, a food substance like glucose would combine almost instantaneously with O_2. If we supply the activation energy by igniting glucose, it burns in air, releasing 686 kcal (2,870 kJ) of heat per mole of glucose (about 180 g). Body temperature is not high enough to initiate burning, of course. Instead, if you swallow some glucose, enzymes in your cells will lower the barrier of activation energy, allowing the sugar to be oxidized in a series of steps.

Stepwise Energy Harvest via NAD$^+$ and the Electron Transport Chain

If energy is released from a fuel all at once, it cannot be harnessed efficiently for constructive work. For example, if a gasoline tank explodes, it cannot drive a car very far. Cellular respiration does not oxidize glucose (or any other organic fuel) in a single explosive step either. Rather, glucose is broken down in a series of steps, each one catalyzed by an enzyme. At key steps, electrons are stripped from the glucose. As is often the case in oxidation reactions, each electron travels with a proton—thus, as a hydrogen atom. The hydrogen atoms are not transferred directly to oxygen, but instead are usually passed first to an electron carrier, a coenzyme called **NAD$^+$** (nicotinamide adenine dinucleotide, a derivative of the vitamin niacin). NAD$^+$ is well suited as an electron carrier because it can cycle easily between oxidized (NAD$^+$) and reduced (NADH) states. As an electron acceptor, NAD$^+$ functions as an oxidizing agent during respiration.

How does NAD$^+$ trap electrons from glucose and the other organic molecules in food? Enzymes called dehydrogenases remove a pair of hydrogen atoms (2 electrons and 2 protons) from the substrate (glucose, in the above example),

thereby oxidizing it. The enzyme delivers the 2 electrons along with 1 proton to its coenzyme, NAD$^+$ **(Figure 9.4)**. The other proton is released as a hydrogen ion (H$^+$) into the surrounding solution:

$$\text{H}-\overset{|}{\underset{|}{\text{C}}}-\text{OH} + \text{NAD}^+ \xrightarrow{\text{Dehydrogenase}} \overset{|}{\text{C}}=\text{O} + \text{NADH} + \text{H}^+$$

By receiving 2 negatively charged electrons but only 1 positively charged proton, the nicotinamide portion of NAD$^+$ has its charge neutralized when NAD$^+$ is reduced to NADH. The name NADH shows the hydrogen that has been received in the reaction. NAD$^+$ is the most versatile electron acceptor in cellular respiration and functions in several of the redox steps during the breakdown of glucose.

Electrons lose very little of their potential energy when they are transferred from glucose to NAD$^+$. Each NADH molecule formed during respiration represents stored energy. This energy can be tapped to make ATP when the electrons complete their "fall" in a series of steps down an energy gradient from NADH to oxygen.

How do electrons that are extracted from glucose and stored as potential energy in NADH finally reach oxygen? It will help to compare the redox chemistry of cellular respiration to a much simpler reaction: the reaction between hydrogen and oxygen to form water **(Figure 9.5a)**. Mix H_2 and O_2, provide a spark for activation energy, and the gases combine explosively. In fact, combustion of liquid H_2 and O_2 was harnessed to help power the main engines of the Space Shuttle, boosting it into orbit. The explosion represents a release of energy as the electrons of hydrogen "fall" closer to the electronegative oxygen atoms. Cellular respiration also brings hydrogen and oxygen together to form water, but there are two important differences. First, in cellular respiration, the hydrogen that reacts with oxygen is derived from

▲ **Figure 9.4 NAD$^+$ as an electron shuttle.** The full name for NAD$^+$, nicotinamide adenine dinucleotide, describes its structure—the molecule consists of two nucleotides joined together at their phosphate groups (shown in yellow). (Nicotinamide is a nitrogenous base, although not one that is present in DNA or RNA; see Figure 5.24.) The enzymatic transfer of 2 electrons and 1 proton (H$^+$) from an organic molecule in food to NAD$^+$ reduces the NAD$^+$ to NADH: Most of the electrons removed from food are transferred initially to NAD$^+$, forming NADH.

? *Describe the structural differences between the oxidized form and the reduced form of nicotinamide.*

organic molecules rather than H_2. Second, instead of occurring in one explosive reaction, respiration uses an electron transport chain to break the fall of electrons to oxygen into several energy-releasing steps (**Figure 9.5b**). An **electron transport chain** consists of a number of molecules, mostly proteins, built into the inner membrane of the mitochondria of eukaryotic cells (and the plasma membrane of respiring prokaryotes). Electrons removed from glucose are shuttled by NADH to the "top," higher-energy end of the chain. At the "bottom," lower-energy end, O_2 captures these electrons along with hydrogen nuclei (H^+), forming water. (Anaerobically respiring prokaryotes have an electron acceptor at the end of the chain that is different from O_2.)

Electron transfer from NADH to oxygen is an exergonic reaction with a free-energy change of −53 kcal/mol (−222 kJ/mol). Instead of this energy being released and wasted in a single explosive step, electrons cascade down the chain from one carrier molecule to the next in a series of redox reactions, losing a small amount of energy with each step until they finally reach oxygen, the terminal electron acceptor, which has a very great affinity for electrons. Each "downhill" carrier is more electronegative than, and thus capable of oxidizing, its "uphill" neighbor, with oxygen at the bottom of the chain. Therefore, the electrons transferred from glucose to NAD^+, which is thus reduced to NADH, fall down an energy gradient in the electron transport chain to a far more stable location in the electronegative oxygen atom. Put another way, oxygen pulls electrons down the chain in

an energy-yielding tumble analogous to gravity pulling objects downhill.

In summary, during cellular respiration, most electrons travel the following "downhill" route: glucose → NADH → electron transport chain → oxygen. Later in this chapter, you will learn more about how the cell uses the energy released from this exergonic electron fall to regenerate its supply of ATP. For now, having covered the basic redox mechanisms of cellular respiration, let's look at the entire process by which energy is harvested from organic fuels.

The Stages of Cellular Respiration: *A Preview*

The harvesting of energy from glucose by cellular respiration is a cumulative function of three metabolic stages. We list them here along with a color-coding scheme we will use throughout the chapter to help you keep track of the big picture:

1. GLYCOLYSIS (color-coded blue throughout the chapter)
2. PYRUVATE OXIDATION and the CITRIC ACID CYCLE (color-coded orange)
3. OXIDATIVE PHOSPHORYLATION: Electron transport and chemiosmosis (color-coded purple)

Biochemists usually reserve the term *cellular respiration* for stages 2 and 3 together. In this text, however, we include glycolysis as a part of cellular respiration because most respiring cells deriving energy from glucose use glycolysis to produce the starting material for the citric acid cycle.

As diagrammed in **Figure 9.6**, glycolysis and pyruvate oxidation followed by the citric acid cycle are the catabolic pathways that break down glucose and other organic fuels. **Glycolysis**, which occurs in the cytosol, begins the degradation process by breaking glucose into two molecules of a compound called pyruvate. In eukaryotes, pyruvate enters the mitochondrion and is oxidized to a compound called acetyl CoA, which enters the **citric acid cycle**. There, the breakdown of glucose to carbon dioxide is completed. (In prokaryotes, these processes take place in the cytosol.) Thus, the carbon dioxide produced by respiration represents fragments of oxidized organic molecules.

Some of the steps of glycolysis and the citric acid cycle are redox reactions in which dehydrogenases transfer electrons from substrates to NAD^+, forming NADH. In the third stage of respiration, the electron transport chain accepts electrons (most often via

▲ **Figure 9.5 An introduction to electron transport chains. (a)** The one-step exergonic reaction of hydrogen with oxygen to form water releases a large amount of energy in the form of heat and light: an explosion. **(b)** In cellular respiration, the same reaction occurs in stages: An electron transport chain breaks the "fall" of electrons in this reaction into a series of smaller steps and stores some of the released energy in a form that can be used to make ATP. (The rest of the energy is released as heat.)

▶ **Figure 9.6 An overview of cellular respiration.** During glycolysis, each glucose molecule is broken down into two molecules of the compound pyruvate. In eukaryotic cells, as shown here, the pyruvate enters the mitochondrion. There it is oxidized to acetyl CoA, which is further oxidized to CO_2 in the citric acid cycle. NADH and a similar electron carrier, a coenzyme called $FADH_2$, transfer electrons derived from glucose to electron transport chains, which are built into the inner mitochondrial membrane. (In prokaryotes, the electron transport chains are located in the plasma membrane.) During oxidative phosphorylation, electron transport chains convert the chemical energy to a form used for ATP synthesis in the process called chemiosmosis.

 BioFlix Visit the Study Area in **MasteringBiology** for the BioFlix® 3-D Animation on Cellular Respiration. BioFlix Tutorials can also be assigned in MasteringBiology.

NADH) from the breakdown products of the first two stages and passes these electrons from one molecule to another. At the end of the chain, the electrons are combined with molecular oxygen and hydrogen ions (H^+), forming water (see Figure 9.5b). The energy released at each step of the chain is stored in a form the mitochondrion (or prokaryotic cell) can use to make ATP from ADP. This mode of ATP synthesis is called **oxidative phosphorylation** because it is powered by the redox reactions of the electron transport chain.

In eukaryotic cells, the inner membrane of the mitochondrion is the site of electron transport and chemiosmosis, the processes that together constitute oxidative phosphorylation. (In prokaryotes, these processes take place in the plasma membrane.) Oxidative phosphorylation accounts for almost 90% of the ATP generated by respiration. A smaller amount of ATP is formed directly in a few reactions of glycolysis and the citric acid cycle by a mechanism called **substrate-level phosphorylation (Figure 9.7)**. This

mode of ATP synthesis occurs when an enzyme transfers a phosphate group from a substrate molecule to ADP, rather than adding an inorganic phosphate to ADP as in oxidative phosphorylation. "Substrate molecule" here refers to an organic molecule generated as an intermediate during the catabolism of glucose. You'll see examples of substrate-level phosphorylation later in the chapter, in both glycolysis and the citric acid cycle.

When you withdraw a relatively large sum of money from an ATM machine, it is not delivered to you in a single bill of larger denomination. Instead, a number of smaller denomination bills are dispensed that you can spend more easily. This is analogous to ATP production during cellular respiration. For each molecule of glucose degraded to carbon dioxide and water by respiration, the cell makes up to about 32 molecules of ATP, each with 7.3 kcal/mol of free energy. Respiration cashes in the large denomination of energy banked in a single molecule of glucose (686 kcal/mol) for the small change of many molecules of ATP, which is more practical for the cell to spend on its work.

This preview has introduced you to how glycolysis, the citric acid cycle, and oxidative phosphorylation fit into the process of cellular respiration. We are now ready to take a closer look at each of these three stages of respiration.

▲ **Figure 9.7 Substrate-level phosphorylation.** Some ATP is made by direct transfer of a phosphate group from an organic substrate to ADP by an enzyme. (For examples in glycolysis, see Figure 9.9, steps 7 and 10.)

MAKE CONNECTIONS *Review Figure 8.9. Do you think the potential energy is higher for the reactants or the products in the reaction shown above? Explain.*

CONCEPT CHECK 9.1

1. Compare and contrast aerobic and anaerobic respiration.

2. **WHAT IF?** If the following redox reaction occurred, which compound would be oxidized? Reduced?

$$C_4H_6O_5 + NAD^+ \rightarrow C_4H_4O_5 + NADH + H^+$$

For suggested answers, see Appendix A.

CONCEPT 9.2

Glycolysis harvests chemical energy by oxidizing glucose to pyruvate

The word *glycolysis* means "sugar splitting," and that is exactly what happens during this pathway. Glucose, a six-carbon sugar, is split into two three-carbon sugars. These smaller sugars are then oxidized and their remaining atoms rearranged to form two molecules of pyruvate. (Pyruvate is the ionized form of pyruvic acid.)

As summarized in **Figure 9.8**, glycolysis can be divided into two phases: the energy investment phase and the energy payoff phase. During the energy investment phase, the cell actually spends ATP. This investment is repaid with interest during the energy payoff phase, when ATP is produced by substrate-level phosphorylation and NAD^+ is reduced to NADH by electrons released from the oxidation of glucose. The net energy yield from glycolysis, per glucose molecule, is 2 ATP plus 2 NADH. The ten steps of the glycolytic pathway are shown in **Figure 9.9**.

All of the carbon originally present in glucose is accounted for in the two molecules of pyruvate; no carbon is released as CO_2 during glycolysis. Glycolysis occurs whether or not O_2 is present. However, if O_2 *is* present, the chemical energy stored in pyruvate and NADH can be extracted by pyruvate oxidation, the citric acid cycle, and oxidative phosphorylation.

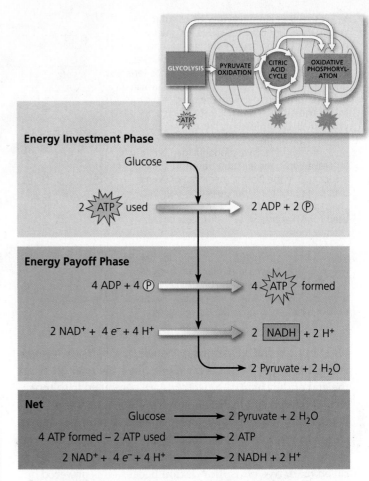

▲ **Figure 9.8** **The energy input and output of glycolysis.**

▼ **Figure 9.9** **A closer look at glycolysis.** Note that glycolysis is a source of ATP and NADH.

GLYCOLYSIS: Energy Investment Phase

WHAT IF? *What would happen if you removed the dihydroxyacetone phosphate generated in step 4 as fast as it was produced?*

1. During the redox reaction in glycolysis (step 6 in Figure 9.9), which molecule acts as the oxidizing agent? The reducing agent?

For suggested answers, see Appendix A.

CONCEPT 9.3

After pyruvate is oxidized, the citric acid cycle completes the energy-yielding oxidation of organic molecules

Glycolysis releases less than a quarter of the chemical energy in glucose that can be harvested by cells; most of the energy remains stockpiled in the two molecules of pyruvate. When O_2 is present, the pyruvate in eukaryotic cells enters a mitochondrion, where the oxidation of glucose is completed. In aerobically respiring prokaryotic cells, this process occurs in the cytosol. (Later in the chapter, we'll discuss what happens to pyruvate when O_2 is unavailable or in a prokaryote that is unable to use O_2.)

Oxidation of Pyruvate to Acetyl CoA

Upon entering the mitochondrion via active transport, pyruvate is first converted to a compound called acetyl coenzyme A, or **acetyl CoA (Figure 9.10)**. This step, linking glycolysis and the citric acid cycle, is carried out by a multienzyme

▲ **Figure 9.10 Oxidation of pyruvate to acetyl CoA, the step before the citric acid cycle.** Pyruvate is a charged molecule, so in eukaryotic cells it must enter the mitochondrion via active transport, with the help of a transport protein. Next, a complex of several enzymes (the pyruvate dehydrogenase complex) catalyzes the three numbered steps, which are described in the text. The acetyl group of acetyl CoA will enter the citric acid cycle. The CO_2 molecule will diffuse out of the cell. By convention, coenzyme A is abbreviated S-CoA when it is attached to a molecule, emphasizing the sulfur atom (S).

complex that catalyzes three reactions: ① Pyruvate's carboxyl group (—COO^-), which is already fully oxidized and thus has little chemical energy, is removed and given off as a molecule of CO_2. This is the first step in which CO_2 is

The energy payoff phase occurs after glucose is split into two three-carbon sugars. Thus, the coefficient 2 precedes all molecules in this phase.

GLYCOLYSIS: Energy Payoff Phase

Two sequential reactions: (1) The sugar is oxidized by the transfer of electrons to NAD^+, forming NADH. (2) Using energy from this exergonic redox reaction, a phosphate group is attached to the oxidized substrate, making a high-energy product.

1,3-Bisphosphoglycerate ⑥

The phosphate group is transferred to ADP (substrate-level phosphorylation) in an exergonic reaction. The carbonyl group of G3P has been oxidized to the carboxyl group (—COO^-) of an organic acid (3-phosphoglycerate). ⑦

3-Phosphoglycerate

This enzyme relocates the remaining phosphate group. ⑧

2-Phosphoglycerate

Enolase causes a double bond to form in the substrate by extracting a water molecule, yielding phosphoenolpyruvate (PEP), a compound with a very high potential energy. ⑨

Phosphoenolpyruvate (PEP)

The phosphate group is transferred from PEP to ADP (a second example of substrate-level phosphorylation), forming pyruvate. ⑩

Pyruvate

© Pearson Education, Inc.

released during respiration. ❷ The remaining two-carbon fragment is oxidized, forming acetate (CH_3COO^-, which is the ionized form of acetic acid). The extracted electrons are transferred to NAD^+, storing energy in the form of NADH. ❸ Finally, coenzyme A (CoA), a sulfur-containing compound derived from a B vitamin, is attached via its sulfur atom to the acetate, forming acetyl CoA, which has a high potential energy; in other words, the reaction of acetyl CoA to yield lower-energy products is highly exergonic. This molecule will now feed its acetyl group into the citric acid cycle for further oxidation.

The Citric Acid Cycle

The citric acid cycle functions as a metabolic furnace that oxidizes organic fuel derived from pyruvate. **Figure 9.11** summarizes the inputs and outputs as pyruvate is broken

▲ **Figure 9.11 An overview of pyruvate oxidation and the citric acid cycle.** The inputs and outputs per pyruvate molecule are shown. To calculate on a per-glucose basis, multiply by 2, because each glucose molecule is split during glycolysis into two pyruvate molecules.

down to three CO_2 molecules, including the molecule of CO_2 released during the conversion of pyruvate to acetyl CoA. The cycle generates 1 ATP per turn by substrate-level phosphorylation, but most of the chemical energy is transferred to NAD^+ and a related electron carrier, the coenzyme FAD (flavin adenine dinucleotide, derived from riboflavin, a B vitamin), during the redox reactions. The reduced coenzymes, NADH and $FADH_2$, shuttle their cargo of high-energy electrons into the electron transport chain. The citric acid cycle is also called the tricarboxylic acid cycle or the Krebs cycle, the latter honoring Hans Krebs, the German-British scientist who was largely responsible for working out the pathway in the 1930s.

Now let's look at the citric acid cycle in more detail. The cycle has eight steps, each catalyzed by a specific enzyme. You can see in **Figure 9.12** that for each turn of the citric acid cycle, two carbons (red) enter in the relatively reduced form of an acetyl group (step ❶), and two different carbons (blue) leave in the completely oxidized form of CO_2 molecules (steps ❸ and ❹). The acetyl group of acetyl CoA joins the cycle by combining with the compound oxaloacetate, forming citrate (step ❶). Citrate is the ionized form of citric acid, for which the cycle is named. The next seven steps decompose the citrate back to oxaloacetate. It is this regeneration of oxaloacetate that makes the process a *cycle*.

We can refer to Figure 9.12 in order to tally the energy-rich molecules produced by the citric acid cycle. For each acetyl group entering the cycle, 3 NAD^+ are reduced to NADH (steps ❸, ❹, and ❽). In step ❻, electrons are transferred not to NAD^+, but to FAD, which accepts 2 electrons and 2 protons to become $FADH_2$. In many animal tissue cells, the reaction in step ❺ produces a guanosine triphosphate (GTP) molecule by substrate-level phosphorylation. GTP is a molecule similar to ATP in its structure and cellular function. This GTP may be used to make an ATP molecule (as shown) or directly power work in the cell. In the cells of plants, bacteria, and some animal tissues, step ❺ forms an ATP molecule directly by substrate-level phosphorylation. The output from step ❺ represents the only ATP generated during the citric acid cycle. Recall that each glucose gives rise to two acetyl CoAs that enter the cycle. Because the numbers noted earlier are obtained from a single acetyl group entering the pathway, the total yield per glucose from the citric acid cycle turns out to be 6 NADHs, 2 $FADH_2$s, and the equivalent of 2 ATPs.

Most of the ATP produced by respiration results from oxidative phosphorylation, when the NADH and $FADH_2$ produced by the citric acid cycle relay the electrons extracted from food to the electron transport chain. In the process, they supply the necessary energy for the phosphorylation of ADP to ATP. We will explore this process in the next section.

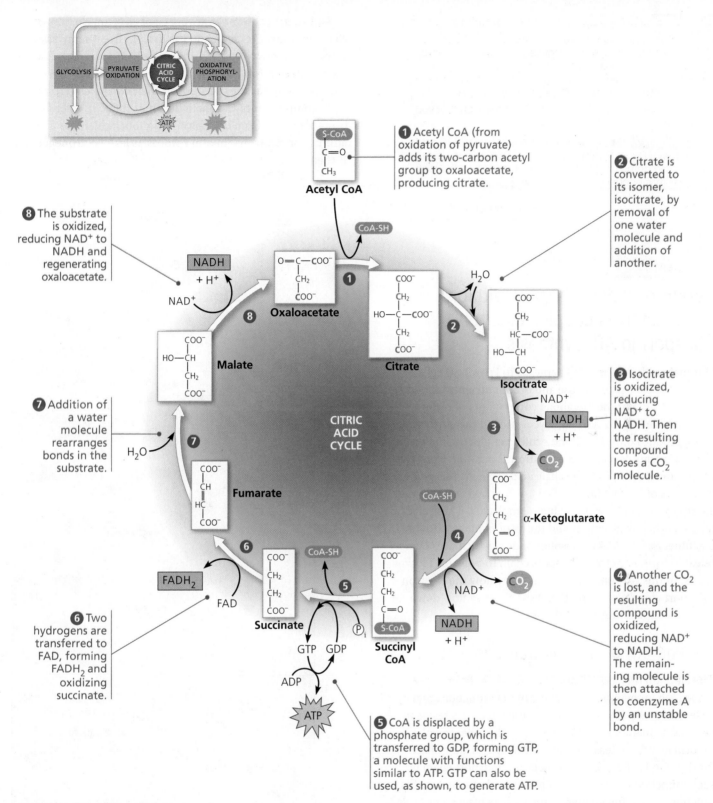

The diagram shows the citric acid cycle with the following components and annotations:

Acetyl CoA (with S-CoA, C=O, CH₃ structure)

① Acetyl CoA (from oxidation of pyruvate) adds its two-carbon acetyl group to oxaloacetate, producing citrate.

② Citrate is converted to its isomer, isocitrate, by removal of one water molecule and addition of another.

③ Isocitrate is oxidized, reducing NAD⁺ to NADH. Then the resulting compound loses a CO₂ molecule.

④ Another CO₂ is lost, and the resulting compound is oxidized, reducing NAD⁺ to NADH. The remaining molecule is then attached to coenzyme A by an unstable bond.

⑤ CoA is displaced by a phosphate group, which is transferred to GDP, forming GTP, a molecule with functions similar to ATP. GTP can also be used, as shown, to generate ATP.

⑥ Two hydrogens are transferred to FAD, forming FADH₂ and oxidizing succinate.

⑦ Addition of a water molecule rearranges bonds in the substrate.

⑧ The substrate is oxidized, reducing NAD⁺ to NADH and regenerating oxaloacetate.

Cycle intermediates labeled: Oxaloacetate, Citrate, Isocitrate, α-Ketoglutarate, Succinyl CoA, Succinate, Fumarate, Malate

Other labels: CoA-SH, H₂O, NAD⁺, NADH + H⁺, CO₂, FAD, FADH₂, GTP, GDP, ADP, ATP, Pᵢ

Top left inset diagram: GLYCOLYSIS → PYRUVATE OXIDATION → CITRIC ACID CYCLE → OXIDATIVE PHOSPHORYLATION, with ATP

▲ **Figure 9.12 A closer look at the citric acid cycle.** In the chemical structures, red type traces the fate of the two carbon atoms that enter the cycle via acetyl CoA (step 1), and blue type indicates the two carbons that exit the cycle as CO₂ in steps 3 and 4. (The red type goes only through step 5 because the succinate molecule is symmetrical; the two ends cannot be distinguished from each other.) Notice that the carbon atoms that enter the cycle from acetyl CoA do not leave the cycle in the same turn. They remain in the cycle, occupying a different location in the molecules on their next turn, after another acetyl group is added. Therefore, the oxaloacetate regenerated at step 8 is made up of different carbon atoms each time around. In eukaryotic cells, all the citric acid cycle enzymes are located in the mitochondrial matrix except for the enzyme that catalyzes step 6, which resides in the inner mitochondrial membrane. Carboxylic acids are represented in their ionized forms, as —COO⁻, because the ionized forms prevail at the pH within the mitochondrion.

1. Name the molecules that conserve most of the energy from the redox reactions of the citric acid cycle (see Figure 9.12). How is this energy converted to a form that can be used to make ATP?

2. What processes in your cells produce the CO_2 that you exhale?

3. **WHAT IF?** The conversions shown in Figure 9.10 and step 4 of Figure 9.12 are each catalyzed by a large multi-enzyme complex. What similarities are there in the reactions that occur in these two cases?

For suggested answers, see Appendix A.

CONCEPT 9.4

During oxidative phosphorylation, chemiosmosis couples electron transport to ATP synthesis

Our main objective in this chapter is to learn how cells harvest the energy of glucose and other nutrients in food to make ATP. But the metabolic components of respiration we have dissected so far, glycolysis and the citric acid cycle, produce only 4 ATP molecules per glucose molecule, all by substrate-level phosphorylation: 2 net ATP from glycolysis and 2 ATP from the citric acid cycle. At this point, molecules of NADH (and $FADH_2$) account for most of the energy extracted from each glucose molecule. These electron escorts link glycolysis and the citric acid cycle to the machinery of oxidative phosphorylation, which uses energy released by the electron transport chain to power ATP synthesis. In this section, you will learn first how the electron transport chain works and then how electron flow down the chain is coupled to ATP synthesis.

The Pathway of Electron Transport

The electron transport chain is a collection of molecules embedded in the inner membrane of the mitochondrion in eukaryotic cells. (In prokaryotes, these molecules reside in the plasma membrane.) The folding of the inner membrane to form cristae increases its surface area, providing space for thousands of copies of the electron transport chain in each mitochondrion. Once again, we see that structure fits function—the infolded membrane with its placement of electron carrier molecules in a row, one after the other, is well-suited for the series of sequential redox reactions that take place along the electron transport chain. Most components of the chain are proteins, which exist in multiprotein complexes numbered I through IV. Tightly bound to these proteins are *prosthetic groups*, nonprotein components essential for the catalytic functions of certain enzymes.

Figure 9.13 shows the sequence of electron carriers in the electron transport chain and the drop in free energy as electrons travel down the chain. During electron transport along the chain, electron carriers alternate between reduced and oxidized states as they accept and then donate electrons. Each component of the chain becomes reduced when it accepts electrons from its "uphill" neighbor, which has a lower affinity for electrons (in other words, is less electronegative). It then returns to its oxidized form as it passes electrons to its "downhill," more electronegative neighbor.

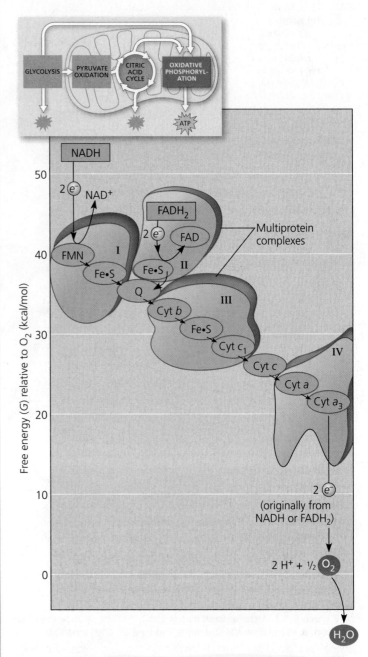

▲ **Figure 9.13 Free-energy change during electron transport.** The overall energy drop (ΔG) for electrons traveling from NADH to oxygen is 53 kcal/mol, but this "fall" is broken up into a series of smaller steps by the electron transport chain. (An oxygen atom is represented here as $^1/_2$ O_2 to emphasize that the electron transport chain reduces molecular oxygen, O_2, not individual oxygen atoms.)

Now let's take a closer look at the electron transport chain in Figure 9.13. We'll first describe the passage of electrons through complex I in some detail, as an illustration of the general principles involved in electron transport. Electrons acquired from glucose by NAD^+ during glycolysis and the citric acid cycle are transferred from NADH to the first molecule of the electron transport chain in complex I. This molecule is a flavoprotein, so named because it has a prosthetic group called flavin mononucleotide (FMN). In the next redox reaction, the flavoprotein returns to its oxidized form as it passes electrons to an iron-sulfur protein (Fe·S in complex I), one of a family of proteins with both iron and sulfur tightly bound. The iron-sulfur protein then passes the electrons to a compound called ubiquinone (Q in Figure 9.13). This electron carrier is a small hydrophobic molecule, the only member of the electron transport chain that is not a protein. Ubiquinone is individually mobile within the membrane rather than residing in a particular complex. (Another name for ubiquinone is coenzyme Q, or CoQ; you may have seen it sold as a nutritional supplement in health food stores.)

Most of the remaining electron carriers between ubiquinone and oxygen are proteins called **cytochromes**. Their prosthetic group, called a heme group, has an iron atom that accepts and donates electrons. (The heme group in the cytochromes is similar to the heme group in hemoglobin, the protein of red blood cells, except that the iron in hemoglobin carries oxygen, not electrons.) The electron transport chain has several types of cytochromes, each a different protein with a slightly different electron-carrying heme group. The last cytochrome of the chain, Cyt a_3, passes its electrons to oxygen, which is *very* electronegative. Each oxygen atom also picks up a pair of hydrogen ions (protons) from the aqueous solution, neutralizing the −2 charge of the added electrons and forming water.

Another source of electrons for the transport chain is $FADH_2$, the other reduced product of the citric acid cycle. Notice in Figure 9.13 that $FADH_2$ adds its electrons to the electron transport chain from within complex II, at a lower energy level than NADH does. Consequently, although NADH and $FADH_2$ each donate an equivalent number of electrons (2) for oxygen reduction, the electron transport chain provides about one-third less energy for ATP synthesis when the electron donor is $FADH_2$ rather than NADH. We'll see why in the next section.

The electron transport chain makes no ATP directly. Instead, it eases the fall of electrons from food to oxygen, breaking a large free-energy drop into a series of smaller steps that release energy in manageable amounts, step by step. How does the mitochondrion (or the plasma membrane, in the case of prokaryotes) couple this electron transport and energy release to ATP synthesis? The answer is a mechanism called chemiosmosis.

1 H^+ ions flowing down their gradient enter a channel in a **stator**, which is anchored in the membrane.

2 H^+ ions enter binding sites within a **rotor**, changing the shape of each subunit so that the rotor spins within the membrane.

3 Each H^+ ion makes one complete turn before leaving the rotor and passing through a second channel in the stator into the mitochondrial matrix.

4 Spinning of the rotor causes an internal **rod** to spin as well. This rod extends like a stalk into the **knob** below it, which is held stationary by part of the stator.

5 Turning of the rod activates catalytic sites in the knob that produce ATP from ADP and P_i.

INTERMEMBRANE SPACE

Rotor

H^+ Stator

Internal rod

Catalytic knob

ADP + P_i

ATP

MITOCHONDRIAL MATRIX

▲ **Figure 9.14 ATP synthase, a molecular mill.** The ATP synthase protein complex functions as a mill, powered by the flow of hydrogen ions. Multiple ATP synthases reside in eukaryotic mitochondrial and chloroplast membranes and in prokaryotic plasma membranes. Each part of the complex consists of a number of polypeptide subunits. ATP synthase is the smallest molecular rotary motor known in nature.

Chemiosmosis: The Energy-Coupling Mechanism

Populating the inner membrane of the mitochondrion or the prokaryotic plasma membrane are many copies of a protein complex called **ATP synthase**, the enzyme that makes ATP from ADP and inorganic phosphate **(Figure 9.14)**. ATP synthase works like an ion pump running in reverse. Ion pumps usually use ATP as an energy source to transport ions against their gradients. Enzymes can catalyze a reaction in either direction, depending on the ΔG for the reaction, which is affected by the local concentrations of reactants and products (see Chapter 8). Rather than hydrolyzing ATP to pump protons against their concentration gradient, under the conditions of cellular respiration ATP synthase uses the energy of an existing ion gradient to power ATP synthesis. The power source for ATP synthase is a difference in the concentration of H^+ on opposite sides of the inner mitochondrial membrane.

Inner mitochondrial membrane

Intermembrane space

Protein complex of electron carriers

Inner mitochondrial membrane

Mitochondrial matrix

Cyt c

ATP synthase

I
Q
II
III
IV

H⁺

FADH₂ → FAD

NADH → NAD⁺
(carrying electrons from food)

$2 H^+ + \frac{1}{2}O_2$ H_2O

$ADP + ℗_i$ ATP

H⁺

1 Electron transport chain
Electron transport and pumping of protons (H⁺), which create an H⁺ gradient across the membrane

2 Chemiosmosis
ATP synthesis powered by the flow of H⁺ back across the membrane

Oxidative phosphorylation

▲ **Figure 9.15 Chemiosmosis couples the electron transport chain to ATP synthesis.**
1 NADH and FADH₂ shuttle high-energy electrons extracted from food during glycolysis and the citric acid cycle into an electron transport chain built into the inner mitochondrial membrane. The gold arrows trace the transport of electrons, which are finally passed to a terminal acceptor (O_2, in the case of aerobic respiration) at the "downhill" end of the chain, forming water. Most of the electron carriers of the chain are grouped into four complexes (I–IV). Two mobile carriers, ubiquinone (Q) and cytochrome c (Cyt c), move rapidly, ferrying electrons between the large complexes. As the complexes shuttle electrons, they pump protons from the mitochondrial matrix into the intermembrane space. FADH₂ deposits its electrons via complex II—at a lower energy level than complex I, where NADH deposits its electrons—and so results in fewer protons being pumped into the intermembrane space than occurs with NADH. Chemical energy that was originally harvested from food is transformed into a proton-motive force, a gradient of H⁺ across the membrane.
2 During chemiosmosis, the protons flow back down their gradient via ATP synthase, which is built into the membrane nearby. The ATP synthase harnesses the proton-motive force to phosphorylate ADP, forming ATP. Together, electron transport and chemiosmosis make up oxidative phosphorylation.

WHAT IF? *If complex IV were nonfunctional, could chemiosmosis produce any ATP, and if so, how would the rate of synthesis differ?*

This process, in which energy stored in the form of a hydrogen ion gradient across a membrane is used to drive cellular work such as the synthesis of ATP, is called **chemiosmosis** (from the Greek *osmos*, push). We have previously used the word *osmosis* in discussing water transport, but here it refers to the flow of H⁺ across a membrane.

From studying the structure of ATP synthase, scientists have learned how the flow of H⁺ through this large enzyme powers ATP generation. ATP synthase is a multisubunit complex with four main parts, each made up of multiple polypeptides. Protons move one by one into binding sites on one of the parts (the rotor), causing it to spin in a way that catalyzes ATP production from ADP and inorganic phosphate. The flow of protons thus behaves somewhat like a rushing stream that turns a waterwheel.

How does the inner mitochondrial membrane or the prokaryotic plasma membrane generate and maintain the H⁺ gradient that drives ATP synthesis by the ATP synthase protein complex? Establishing the H⁺ gradient is a major function of the electron transport chain, which is shown in its mitochondrial location in **Figure 9.15**. The chain is an energy converter that uses the exergonic flow of electrons from NADH and FADH₂ to pump H⁺ across the membrane, from the mitochondrial matrix into the intermembrane space. The H⁺ has a tendency to move back across the membrane, diffusing down its gradient. And the ATP synthases are the only sites that provide a route through the membrane for H⁺. As we described previously, the passage of H⁺ through ATP synthase uses the exergonic flow of H⁺ to drive the phosphorylation of ADP. Thus, the energy stored in an

H^+ gradient across a membrane couples the redox reactions of the electron transport chain to ATP.

At this point, you may be wondering how the electron transport chain pumps hydrogen ions. Researchers have found that certain members of the electron transport chain accept and release protons (H^+) along with electrons. (The aqueous solutions inside and surrounding the cell are a ready source of H^+.) At certain steps along the chain, electron transfers cause H^+ to be taken up and released into the surrounding solution. In eukaryotic cells, the electron carriers are spatially arranged in the inner mitochondrial membrane in such a way that H^+ is accepted from the mitochondrial matrix and deposited in the intermembrane space (see Figure 9.15). The H^+ gradient that results is referred to as a **proton-motive force**, emphasizing the capacity of the gradient to perform work. The force drives H^+ back across the membrane through the H^+ channels provided by ATP synthases.

In general terms, *chemiosmosis is an energy-coupling mechanism that uses energy stored in the form of an H^+ gradient across a membrane to drive cellular work.* In mitochondria, the energy for gradient formation comes from exergonic redox reactions, and ATP synthesis is the work performed. But chemiosmosis also occurs elsewhere and in other variations. Chloroplasts use chemiosmosis to generate ATP during photosynthesis; in these organelles, light (rather than chemical energy) drives both electron flow down an electron transport chain and the resulting H^+ gradient

formation. Prokaryotes, as already mentioned, generate H^+ gradients across their plasma membranes. They then tap the proton-motive force not only to make ATP inside the cell but also to rotate their flagella and to pump nutrients and waste products across the membrane. Because of its central importance to energy conversions in prokaryotes and eukaryotes, chemiosmosis has helped unify the study of bioenergetics. Peter Mitchell was awarded the Nobel Prize in 1978 for originally proposing the chemiosmotic model.

An Accounting of ATP Production by Cellular Respiration

In the last few sections, we have looked rather closely at the key processes of cellular respiration. Now let's take a step back and remind ourselves of its overall function: harvesting the energy of glucose for ATP synthesis.

During respiration, most energy flows in this sequence: glucose → NADH → electron transport chain → proton-motive force → ATP. We can do some bookkeeping to calculate the ATP profit when cellular respiration oxidizes a molecule of glucose to six molecules of carbon dioxide. The three main departments of this metabolic enterprise are glycolysis, pyruvate oxidation and the citric acid cycle, and the electron transport chain, which drives oxidative phosphorylation. **Figure 9.16** gives a detailed accounting of the ATP yield for each glucose molecule that is oxidized. The tally adds the

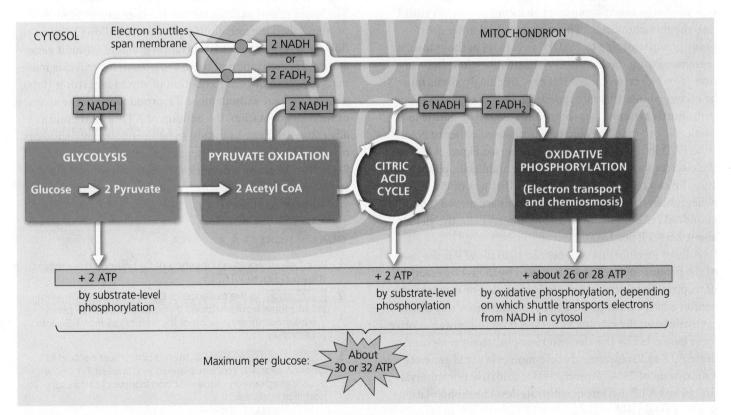

▲ **Figure 9.16 ATP yield per molecule of glucose at each stage of cellular respiration.**

[?] *Explain exactly how the total of 26 or 28 ATP (see the yellow bar in the figure) was calculated.*

4 ATP produced directly by substrate-level phosphorylation during glycolysis and the citric acid cycle to the many more molecules of ATP generated by oxidative phosphorylation. Each NADH that transfers a pair of electrons from glucose to the electron transport chain contributes enough to the proton-motive force to generate a maximum of about 3 ATP.

Why are the numbers in Figure 9.16 inexact? There are three reasons we cannot state an exact number of ATP molecules generated by the breakdown of one molecule of glucose. First, phosphorylation and the redox reactions are not directly coupled to each other, so the ratio of the number of NADH molecules to the number of ATP molecules is not a whole number. We know that 1 NADH results in 10 H^+ being transported out across the inner mitochondrial membrane, but the exact number of H^+ that must reenter the mitochondrial matrix via ATP synthase to generate 1 ATP has long been debated. Based on experimental data, however, most biochemists now agree that the most accurate number is 4 H^+. Therefore, a single molecule of NADH generates enough proton-motive force for the synthesis of 2.5 ATP. The citric acid cycle also supplies electrons to the electron transport chain via $FADH_2$, but since its electrons enter later in the chain, each molecule of this electron carrier is responsible for transport of only enough H^+ for the synthesis of 1.5 ATP. These numbers also take into account the slight energetic cost of moving the ATP formed in the mitochondrion out into the cytosol, where it will be used.

Second, the ATP yield varies slightly depending on the type of shuttle used to transport electrons from the cytosol into the mitochondrion. The mitochondrial inner membrane is impermeable to NADH, so NADH in the cytosol is segregated from the machinery of oxidative phosphorylation. The 2 electrons of NADH captured in glycolysis must be conveyed into the mitochondrion by one of several electron shuttle systems. Depending on the kind of shuttle in a particular cell type, the electrons are passed either to NAD^+ or to FAD in the mitochondrial matrix (see Figure 9.16). If the electrons are passed to FAD, as in brain cells, only about 1.5 ATP can result from each NADH that was originally generated in the cytosol. If the electrons are passed to mitochondrial NAD^+, as in liver cells and heart cells, the yield is about 2.5 ATP per NADH.

A third variable that reduces the yield of ATP is the use of the proton-motive force generated by the redox reactions of respiration to drive other kinds of work. For example, the proton-motive force powers the mitochondrion's uptake of pyruvate from the cytosol. However, if *all* the proton-motive force generated by the electron transport chain were used to drive ATP synthesis, one glucose molecule could generate a maximum of 28 ATP produced by oxidative phosphorylation plus 4 ATP (net) from substrate-level phosphorylation to give a total yield of about 32 ATP (or only about 30 ATP if the less efficient shuttle were functioning).

We can now roughly estimate the efficiency of respiration—that is, the percentage of chemical energy in glucose that has been transferred to ATP. Recall that the complete oxidation of a mole of glucose releases 686 kcal of energy under standard conditions ($\Delta G = -686$ kcal/mol). Phosphorylation of ADP to form ATP stores at least 7.3 kcal per mole of ATP. Therefore, the efficiency of respiration is 7.3 kcal per mole of ATP times 32 moles of ATP per mole of glucose divided by 686 kcal per mole of glucose, which equals 0.34. Thus, about 34% of the potential chemical energy in glucose has been transferred to ATP; the actual percentage is bound to vary as ΔG varies under different cellular conditions. Cellular respiration is remarkably efficient in its energy conversion. By comparison, even the most efficient automobile converts only about 25% of the energy stored in gasoline to energy that moves the car.

The rest of the energy stored in glucose is lost as heat. We humans use some of this heat to maintain our relatively high body temperature (37°C), and we dissipate the rest through sweating and other cooling mechanisms.

Surprisingly, perhaps, it may be beneficial under certain conditions to reduce the efficiency of cellular respiration. A remarkable adaptation is shown by hibernating mammals, which overwinter in a state of inactivity and lowered metabolism. Although their internal body temperature is lower than normal, it still must be kept significantly higher than the external air temperature. One type of tissue, called brown fat, is made up of cells packed full of mitochondria. The inner mitochondrial membrane contains a channel protein called the uncoupling protein that allows protons to flow back down their concentration gradient without generating ATP. Activation of these proteins in hibernating mammals results in ongoing oxidation of stored fuel stores (fats), generating heat without any ATP production. In the absence of such an adaptation, the buildup of ATP would eventually cause cellular respiration to be shut down by regulatory mechanisms that will be discussed later. In the Scientific Skills Exercise, you can work with data in a related but different case where a decrease in metabolic efficiency in cells is used to generate heat.

CONCEPT CHECK 9.4

1. What effect would an absence of O_2 have on the process shown in Figure 9.15?

2. **WHAT IF?** In the absence of O_2, as in question 1, what do you think would happen if you decreased the pH of the intermembrane space of the mitochondrion? Explain your answer.

3. **MAKE CONNECTIONS** Membranes must be fluid to function properly (as you learned in Concept 7.1). How does the operation of the electron transport chain support that assertion?

For suggested answers, see Appendix A.

Making a Bar Graph and Evaluating a Hypothesis

Does Thyroid Hormone Level Affect Oxygen Consumption in Cells? Some animals, such as mammals and birds, maintain a relatively constant body temperature, above that of their environment, by using heat produced as a by-product of metabolism. When the core temperature of these animals drops below an internal set point, their cells are triggered to reduce the efficiency of ATP production by the electron transport chains in mitochondria. At lower efficiency, extra fuel must be consumed to produce the same number of ATPs, generating additional heat. Because this response is moderated by the endocrine system, researchers hypothesized that thyroid hormone might trigger this cellular response. In this exercise, you will use a bar graph to visualize data from an experiment that compared the metabolic rate (by measuring oxygen consumption) in mitochondria of cells from animals with different levels of thyroid hormone.

How the Experiment Was Done Liver cells were isolated from sibling rats that had low, normal, or elevated thyroid hormone levels. The oxygen consumption rate due to activity of the mitochondrial electron transport chains of each type of cell was measured under controlled conditions.

Data from the Experiment

Thyroid Hormone Level	Oxygen Consumption Rate (nmol O_2/min · mg cells)
Low	4.3
Normal	4.8
Elevated	8.7

Interpret the Data

1. To visualize any differences in oxygen consumption between cell types, it will be useful to graph the data in a bar graph. First, set up the axes. (a) What is the independent variable (intentionally varied by the researchers), which goes on the x-axis? List the categories along the x-axis; because they are discrete rather than continuous, you can list them in any order. (b) What is the dependent variable (measured by the researchers), which goes on the y-axis? (c) What units (abbreviated) should go on the y-axis? Label the y-axis, including the units specified in the data table. Determine the range of values of the data that will need to go on the y-axis. What is the largest value? Draw evenly spaced tick marks and label them, starting with 0 at the bottom.

2. Graph the data for each sample. Match each x-value with its y-value and place a mark on the graph at that coordinate, then draw a bar from the x-axis up to the correct height for each sample. Why is a bar graph more appropriate than a scatter plot or line graph? (For additional information about graphs, see the Scientific Skills Review in Appendix F and in the Study Area in MasteringBiology.)

3. Examine your graph and look for a pattern in the data. (a) Which cell type had the highest rate of oxygen consumption, and which had the lowest? (b) Does this support the researchers' hypothesis? Explain. (c) Based on what you know about mitochondrial electron transport and heat production, predict which rats had the highest, and which had the lowest, body temperature.

(MB) A version of this Scientific Skills Exercise can be assigned in MasteringBiology.

Data from M. E. Harper and M. D. Brand, The quantitative contributions of mitochondrial proton leak and ATP turnover reactions to the changed respiration rates of hepatocytes from rats of different thyroid status, *Journal of Biological Chemistry* 268:14850–14860 (1993).

CONCEPT 9.5

Fermentation and anaerobic respiration enable cells to produce ATP without the use of oxygen

Because most of the ATP generated by cellular respiration is due to the work of oxidative phosphorylation, our estimate of ATP yield from aerobic respiration is contingent on an adequate supply of oxygen to the cell. Without the electronegative oxygen to pull electrons down the transport chain, oxidative phosphorylation eventually ceases. However, there are two general mechanisms by which certain cells can oxidize organic fuel and generate ATP *without* the use of oxygen: anaerobic respiration and fermentation. The distinction between these two is that an electron transport chain is used in anaerobic respiration but not in fermentation. (The electron transport chain is also called the respiratory chain because of its role in both types of cellular respiration.)

We have already mentioned anaerobic respiration, which takes place in certain prokaryotic organisms that live in environments without oxygen. These organisms have an electron transport chain but do not use oxygen as a final electron acceptor at the end of the chain. Oxygen performs this function very well because it is extremely electronegative, but other, less electronegative substances can also serve as final electron acceptors. Some "sulfate-reducing" marine bacteria, for instance, use the sulfate ion (SO_4^{2-}) at the end of their respiratory chain. Operation of the chain builds up a proton-motive force used to produce ATP, but H_2S (hydrogen sulfide) is made as a by-product rather than water. The rotten-egg odor you may have smelled while walking through a salt marsh or a mudflat signals the presence of sulfate-reducing bacteria.

Fermentation is a way of harvesting chemical energy without using either oxygen or any electron transport chain—in other words, without cellular respiration. How can food be oxidized without cellular respiration? Remember, oxidation simply refers to the loss of electrons to an electron acceptor, so it does not need to involve oxygen. Glycolysis oxidizes glucose to two molecules of pyruvate. The oxidizing agent of glycolysis is NAD^+, and neither oxygen nor any electron transfer chain is involved. Overall, glycolysis is exergonic, and some of the energy made available is used to produce 2 ATP (net) by substrate-level phosphorylation. If oxygen *is* present, then additional ATP is made by oxidative phosphorylation when NADH passes electrons removed from glucose to the electron transport chain. But glycolysis generates 2 ATP whether oxygen is present or not—that is, whether conditions are aerobic or anaerobic.

As an alternative to respiratory oxidation of organic nutrients, fermentation is an extension of glycolysis that allows continuous generation of ATP by the substrate-level phosphorylation of glycolysis. For this to occur, there must be a sufficient supply of NAD^+ to accept electrons during the oxidation step of glycolysis. Without some mechanism to recycle NAD^+ from NADH, glycolysis would soon deplete the cell's pool of NAD^+ by reducing it all to NADH and would shut itself down for lack of an oxidizing agent. Under aerobic conditions, NAD^+ is recycled from NADH by the transfer of electrons to the electron transport chain. An anaerobic alternative is to transfer electrons from NADH to pyruvate, the end product of glycolysis.

Types of Fermentation

Fermentation consists of glycolysis plus reactions that regenerate NAD^+ by transferring electrons from NADH to pyruvate or derivatives of pyruvate. The NAD^+ can then be reused to oxidize sugar by glycolysis, which nets two molecules of ATP by substrate-level phosphorylation. There are many types of fermentation, differing in the end products formed from pyruvate. Two types commonly harnessed by humans for food and industrial production are alcohol fermentation and lactic acid fermentation.

In **alcohol fermentation (Figure 9.17a)**, pyruvate is converted to ethanol (ethyl alcohol) in two steps. The first step releases carbon dioxide from the pyruvate, which is

▲ **Figure 9.17 Fermentation.** In the absence of oxygen, many cells use fermentation to produce ATP by substrate-level phosphorylation. Pyruvate, the end product of glycolysis, serves as an electron acceptor for oxidizing NADH back to NAD^+, which can then be reused in glycolysis. Two of the common end products formed from fermentation are **(a)** ethanol and **(b)** lactate, the ionized form of lactic acid.

converted to the two-carbon compound acetaldehyde. In the second step, acetaldehyde is reduced by NADH to ethanol. This regenerates the supply of NAD^+ needed for the continuation of glycolysis. Many bacteria carry out alcohol fermentation under anaerobic conditions. Yeast (a fungus) also carries out alcohol fermentation. For thousands of years, humans have used yeast in brewing, winemaking, and baking. The CO_2 bubbles generated by baker's yeast during alcohol fermentation allow bread to rise.

During **lactic acid fermentation (Figure 9.17b)**, pyruvate is reduced directly by NADH to form lactate as an end product, with no release of CO_2. (Lactate is the ionized form of lactic acid.) Lactic acid fermentation by certain fungi and bacteria is used in the dairy industry to make cheese and yogurt.

Human muscle cells make ATP by lactic acid fermentation when oxygen is scarce. This occurs during strenuous exercise, when sugar catabolism for ATP production outpaces the muscle's supply of oxygen from the blood. Under these conditions, the cells switch from aerobic respiration to fermentation. The lactate that accumulates was previously thought to cause muscle fatigue and pain, but recent research suggests instead that increased levels of potassium ions (K^+) may be to blame, while lactate appears to enhance muscle performance. In any case, the excess lactate is gradually carried away by the blood to the liver, where it is converted back to pyruvate by liver cells. Because oxygen is available, this pyruvate can then enter the mitochondria in liver cells and complete cellular respiration.

Comparing Fermentation with Anaerobic and Aerobic Respiration

Fermentation, anaerobic respiration, and aerobic respiration are three alternative cellular pathways for producing ATP by harvesting the chemical energy of food. All three use glycolysis to oxidize glucose and other organic fuels to pyruvate, with a net production of 2 ATP by substrate-level phosphorylation. And in all three pathways, NAD^+ is the oxidizing agent that accepts electrons from food during glycolysis.

A key difference is the contrasting mechanisms for oxidizing NADH back to NAD^+, which is required to sustain glycolysis. In fermentation, the final electron acceptor is an organic molecule such as pyruvate (lactic acid fermentation) or acetaldehyde (alcohol fermentation). In cellular respiration, by contrast, electrons carried by NADH are transferred to an electron transport chain, which regenerates the NAD^+ required for glycolysis.

Another major difference is the amount of ATP produced. Fermentation yields 2 molecules of ATP, produced by substrate-level phosphorylation. In the absence of an electron transport chain, the energy stored in pyruvate is unavailable. In cellular respiration, however, pyruvate is completely oxidized in the mitochondrion. Most of the chemical energy from this process is shuttled by NADH and $FADH_2$ in the form of electrons to the electron transport chain. There, the electrons move stepwise down a series of redox reactions to a final electron acceptor. (In aerobic respiration, the final electron acceptor is oxygen; in anaerobic respiration, the final acceptor is another molecule that is electronegative, although less so than oxygen.) Stepwise electron transport drives oxidative phosphorylation, yielding ATPs. Thus, cellular respiration harvests much more energy from each sugar molecule than fermentation can. In fact, aerobic respiration yields up to 32 molecules of ATP per glucose molecule—up to 16 times as much as does fermentation.

Some organisms, called **obligate anaerobes**, carry out only fermentation or anaerobic respiration. In fact, these

▲ **Figure 9.18 Pyruvate as a key juncture in catabolism.** Glycolysis is common to fermentation and cellular respiration. The end product of glycolysis, pyruvate, represents a fork in the catabolic pathways of glucose oxidation. In a facultative anaerobe or a muscle cell, which are capable of both aerobic cellular respiration and fermentation, pyruvate is committed to one of those two pathways, usually depending on whether or not oxygen is present.

organisms cannot survive in the presence of oxygen, some forms of which can actually be toxic if protective systems are not present in the cell. A few cell types, such as cells of the vertebrate brain, can carry out only aerobic oxidation of pyruvate, not fermentation. Other organisms, including yeasts and many bacteria, can make enough ATP to survive using either fermentation or respiration. Such species are called **facultative anaerobes**. On the cellular level, our muscle cells behave as facultative anaerobes. In such cells, pyruvate is a fork in the metabolic road that leads to two alternative catabolic routes **(Figure 9.18)**. Under aerobic conditions, pyruvate can be converted to acetyl CoA, and oxidation continues in the citric acid cycle via aerobic respiration. Under anaerobic conditions, lactic acid fermentation occurs: Pyruvate is diverted from the citric acid cycle, serving instead as an electron acceptor to recycle NAD^+. To make the same amount of ATP, a facultative anaerobe has to consume sugar at a much faster rate when fermenting than when respiring.

The Evolutionary Significance of Glycolysis

EVOLUTION The role of glycolysis in both fermentation and respiration has an evolutionary basis. Ancient prokaryotes are thought to have used glycolysis to make ATP long before oxygen was present in Earth's atmosphere. The oldest known fossils of bacteria date back 3.5 billion years, but appreciable quantities of oxygen probably did not begin to accumulate in the atmosphere until about 2.7 billion years ago. Cyanobacteria produced this O_2 as a by-product of photosynthesis. Therefore, early prokaryotes may have generated ATP exclusively from glycolysis. The fact that glycolysis is today the most widespread metabolic pathway among Earth's organisms suggests that it evolved very early in the history of life. The cytosolic location of glycolysis also implies great antiquity; the pathway does not require any of the membrane-enclosed organelles of the eukaryotic cell, which evolved approximately 1 billion years after the first prokaryotic cell. Glycolysis is a metabolic heirloom from early cells that continues to function in fermentation and as the first stage in the breakdown of organic molecules by respiration.

CONCEPT CHECK 9.5

1. Consider the NADH formed during glycolysis. What is the final acceptor for its electrons during fermentation? What is the final acceptor for its electrons during aerobic respiration?

2. **WHAT IF?** A glucose-fed yeast cell is moved from an aerobic environment to an anaerobic one. How would its rate of glucose consumption change if ATP were to be generated at the same rate?

For suggested answers, see Appendix A.

CONCEPT 9.6

Glycolysis and the citric acid cycle connect to many other metabolic pathways

So far, we have treated the oxidative breakdown of glucose in isolation from the cell's overall metabolic economy. In this section, you will learn that glycolysis and the citric acid cycle are major intersections of the cell's catabolic (breakdown) and anabolic (biosynthetic) pathways.

The Versatility of Catabolism

Throughout this chapter, we have used glucose as an example of a fuel for cellular respiration. But free glucose molecules are not common in the diets of humans and other animals. We obtain most of our calories in the form of fats, proteins, sucrose and other disaccharides, and starch, a polysaccharide. All these organic molecules in food can be used by cellular respiration to make ATP **(Figure 9.19)**.

Glycolysis can accept a wide range of carbohydrates for catabolism. In the digestive tract, starch is hydrolyzed to glucose, which can then be broken down in the cells by glycolysis and the citric acid cycle. Similarly, glycogen, the polysaccharide that humans and many other animals store

▲ **Figure 9.19 The catabolism of various molecules from food.** Carbohydrates, fats, and proteins can all be used as fuel for cellular respiration. Monomers of these molecules enter glycolysis or the citric acid cycle at various points. Glycolysis and the citric acid cycle are catabolic funnels through which electrons from all kinds of organic molecules flow on their exergonic fall to oxygen.

in their liver and muscle cells, can be hydrolyzed to glucose between meals as fuel for respiration. The digestion of disaccharides, including sucrose, provides glucose and other monosaccharides as fuel for respiration.

Proteins can also be used for fuel, but first they must be digested to their constituent amino acids. Many of the amino acids are used by the organism to build new proteins. Amino acids present in excess are converted by enzymes to intermediates of glycolysis and the citric acid cycle. Before amino acids can feed into glycolysis or the citric acid cycle, their amino groups must be removed, a process called *deamination*. The nitrogenous refuse is excreted from the animal in the form of ammonia (NH_3), urea, or other waste products.

Catabolism can also harvest energy stored in fats obtained either from food or from storage cells in the body. After fats are digested to glycerol and fatty acids, the glycerol is converted to glyceraldehyde 3-phosphate, an intermediate of glycolysis. Most of the energy of a fat is stored in the fatty acids. A metabolic sequence called **beta oxidation** breaks the fatty acids down to two-carbon fragments, which enter the citric acid cycle as acetyl CoA. NADH and $FADH_2$ are also generated during beta oxidation; they can enter the electron transport chain, leading to further ATP production. Fats make excellent fuels, in large part due to their chemical structure and the high energy level of their electrons (equally shared between carbon and hydrogen) compared to those of carbohydrates. A gram of fat oxidized by respiration produces more than twice as much ATP as a gram of carbohydrate. Unfortunately, this also means that a person trying to lose weight must work hard to use up fat stored in the body because so many calories are stockpiled in each gram of fat.

Biosynthesis (Anabolic Pathways)

Cells need substance as well as energy. Not all the organic molecules of food are destined to be oxidized as fuel to make ATP. In addition to calories, food must also provide the carbon skeletons that cells require to make their own molecules. Some organic monomers obtained from digestion can be used directly. For example, as previously mentioned, amino acids from the hydrolysis of proteins in food can be incorporated into the organism's own proteins. Often, however, the body needs specific molecules that are not present as such in food. Compounds formed as intermediates of glycolysis and the citric acid cycle can be diverted into anabolic pathways as precursors from which the cell can synthesize the molecules it requires. For example, humans can make about half of the 20 amino acids in proteins by modifying compounds siphoned away from the citric acid cycle; the rest are "essential amino acids" that must be obtained in the diet. Also, glucose can be made from pyruvate, and fatty acids can be synthesized from acetyl CoA. Of course, these anabolic, or biosynthetic, pathways do not generate ATP, but instead consume it.

In addition, glycolysis and the citric acid cycle function as metabolic interchanges that enable our cells to convert some kinds of molecules to others as we need them. For example, an intermediate compound generated during glycolysis, dihydroxyacetone phosphate (see Figure 9.9, step 5), can be converted to one of the major precursors of fats. If we eat more food than we need, we store fat even if our diet is fat-free. Metabolism is remarkably versatile and adaptable.

Regulation of Cellular Respiration via Feedback Mechanisms

Basic principles of supply and demand regulate the metabolic economy. The cell does not waste energy making more of a particular substance than it needs. If there is a glut of a

certain amino acid, for example, the anabolic pathway that synthesizes that amino acid from an intermediate of the citric acid cycle is switched off. The most common mechanism for this control is feedback inhibition: The end product of the anabolic pathway inhibits the enzyme that catalyzes an early step of the pathway (see Figure 8.21). This prevents the needless diversion of key metabolic intermediates from uses that are more urgent.

The cell also controls its catabolism. If the cell is working hard and its ATP concentration begins to drop, respiration speeds up. When there is plenty of ATP to meet demand, respiration slows down, sparing valuable organic molecules for other functions. Again, control is based mainly on regulating the activity of enzymes at strategic points in the catabolic pathway. As shown in **Figure 9.20**, one important

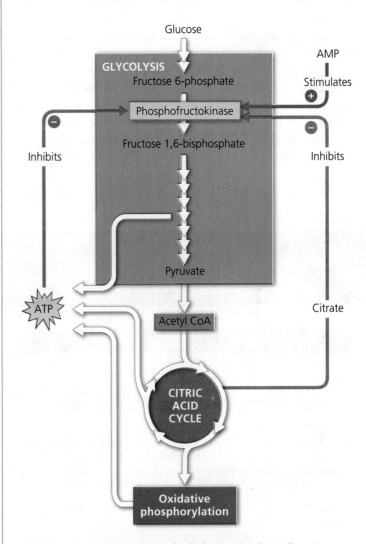

▲ **Figure 9.20 The control of cellular respiration.** Allosteric enzymes at certain points in the respiratory pathway respond to inhibitors and activators that help set the pace of glycolysis and the citric acid cycle. Phosphofructokinase, which catalyzes an early step in glycolysis (see Figure 9.9, step 3), is one such enzyme. It is stimulated by AMP (derived from ADP) but is inhibited by ATP and by citrate. This feedback regulation adjusts the rate of respiration as the cell's catabolic and anabolic demands change.

switch is phosphofructokinase, the enzyme that catalyzes step 3 of glycolysis (see Figure 9.9). That is the first step that commits the substrate irreversibly to the glycolytic pathway. By controlling the rate of this step, the cell can speed up or slow down the entire catabolic process. Phosphofructokinase can thus be considered the pacemaker of respiration.

Phosphofructokinase is an allosteric enzyme with receptor sites for specific inhibitors and activators. It is inhibited by ATP and stimulated by AMP (adenosine monophosphate), which the cell derives from ADP. As ATP accumulates, inhibition of the enzyme slows down glycolysis. The enzyme becomes active again as cellular work converts ATP to ADP (and AMP) faster than ATP is being regenerated. Phosphofructokinase is also sensitive to citrate, the first product of the citric acid cycle. If citrate accumulates in mitochondria, some of it passes into the cytosol and inhibits phosphofructokinase. This mechanism helps synchronize the rates of glycolysis and the citric acid cycle. As citrate accumulates, glycolysis slows down, and the supply of acetyl groups to the citric acid cycle decreases. If citrate consumption increases, either because of a demand for more ATP or because anabolic pathways are draining off intermediates of the citric acid cycle, glycolysis accelerates and meets the demand. Metabolic balance is augmented by the control of enzymes that catalyze other key steps of glycolysis and the citric acid cycle. Cells are thrifty, expedient, and responsive in their metabolism.

Cellular respiration and metabolic pathways play a role of central importance in organisms. Examine Figure 9.2 again to put cellular respiration into the broader context of energy flow and chemical cycling in ecosystems. The energy that keeps us alive is *released*, not *produced*, by cellular respiration. We are tapping energy that was stored in food by photosynthesis. In the next chapter, you will learn how photosynthesis captures light and converts it to chemical energy.

CONCEPT CHECK 9.6

1. **MAKE CONNECTIONS** Compare the structure of a fat (see Figure 5.9) with that of a carbohydrate (see Figure 5.3). What features of their structures make fat a much better fuel?

2. Under what circumstances might your body synthesize fat molecules?

3. **WHAT IF?** What will happen in a muscle cell that has used up its supply of oxygen and ATP? (Review Figures 9.18 and 9.20.)

4. **WHAT IF?** During intense exercise, can a muscle cell use fat as a concentrated source of chemical energy? Explain. (Review Figures 9.18 and 9.19.)

For suggested answers, see Appendix A.

9 Chapter Review

SUMMARY OF KEY CONCEPTS

CONCEPT 9.1

Catabolic pathways yield energy by oxidizing organic fuels (pp. 163–167)

- Cells break down glucose and other organic fuels to yield chemical energy in the form of ATP. **Fermentation** is a process that results in the partial degradation of glucose without the use of oxygen. **Cellular respiration** is a more complete breakdown of glucose; in **aerobic respiration**, oxygen is used as a reactant. The cell taps the energy stored in food molecules through **redox reactions**, in which one substance partially or totally shifts electrons to another. **Oxidation** is the loss of electrons from one substance, while **reduction** is the addition of electrons to the other.
- During aerobic respiration, glucose ($C_6H_{12}O_6$) is oxidized to CO_2, and O_2 is reduced to H_2O. Electrons lose potential energy during their transfer from glucose or other organic compounds to oxygen. Electrons are usually passed first to NAD^+, reducing it to NADH, and then from NADH to an **electron transport chain**, which conducts them to O_2 in energy-releasing steps. The energy is used to make ATP.

- Aerobic respiration occurs in three stages: (1) **glycolysis**, (2) pyruvate oxidation and the **citric acid cycle**, and (3) **oxidative phosphorylation** (electron transport and chemiosmosis).

? *Describe the difference between the two processes in cellular respiration that produce ATP: oxidative phosphorylation and substrate-level phosphorylation.*

CONCEPT 9.2

Glycolysis harvests chemical energy by oxidizing glucose to pyruvate (pp. 168–169)

- Glycolysis ("splitting of sugar") is a series of reactions that break down glucose into two pyruvate molecules, which may go on to enter the citric acid cycle, and nets 2 ATP and 2 NADH per glucose molecule.

Inputs		Outputs		
Glucose	GLYCOLYSIS →	2 Pyruvate	+ 2 ATP	+ 2 NADH

? *Which reactions in glycolysis are the source of energy for the formation of ATP and NADH?*

After pyruvate is oxidized, the citric acid cycle completes the energy-yielding oxidation of organic molecules (pp. 169–172)

- In eukaryotic cells, pyruvate enters the mitochondrion and is oxidized to **acetyl CoA**, which is further oxidized in the citric acid cycle.

? *What molecular products indicate the complete oxidation of glucose during cellular respiration?*

During oxidative phosphorylation, chemiosmosis couples electron transport to ATP synthesis (pp. 172–177)

- NADH and $FADH_2$ transfer electrons to the electron transport chain. Electrons move down the chain, losing energy in several energy-releasing steps. Finally, electrons are passed to O_2, reducing it to H_2O.

- At certain steps along the electron transport chain, electron transfer causes protein complexes to move H^+ from the mitochondrial matrix (in eukaryotes) to the intermembrane space, storing energy as a **proton-motive force** (H^+ gradient). As H^+ diffuses back into the matrix through **ATP synthase**, its passage drives the phosphorylation of ADP to form ATP, a process called **chemiosmosis**.

- About 34% of the energy stored in a glucose molecule is transferred to ATP during cellular respiration, producing a maximum of about 32 ATP.

? *Briefly explain the mechanism by which ATP synthase produces ATP. List three locations in which ATP synthases are found.*

Fermentation and anaerobic respiration enable cells to produce ATP without the use of oxygen (pp. 177–180)

- Glycolysis nets 2 ATP by substrate-level phosphorylation, whether oxygen is present or not. Under anaerobic conditions, either anaerobic respiration or fermentation can take place. In anaerobic respiration, an electron transport chain is present with a final electron acceptor other than oxygen. In fermentation, the electrons from NADH are passed to pyruvate or a derivative of pyruvate, regenerating the NAD^+ required to oxidize more glucose. Two common types of fermentation are **alcohol fermentation** and **lactic acid fermentation**.
- Fermentation and anaerobic or aerobic respiration all use glycolysis to oxidize glucose, but they differ in their final electron acceptor and whether an electron transport chain is used (respiration) or not (fermentation). Respiration yields more ATP; aerobic respiration, with O_2 as the final electron acceptor, yields about 16 times as much ATP as does fermentation.
- Glycolysis occurs in nearly all organisms and is thought to have evolved in ancient prokaryotes before there was O_2 in the atmosphere.

? *Which process yields more ATP, fermentation or anaerobic respiration? Explain.*

Glycolysis and the citric acid cycle connect to many other metabolic pathways (pp. 180–182)

- Catabolic pathways funnel electrons from many kinds of organic molecules into cellular respiration. Many carbohydrates can enter glycolysis, most often after conversion to glucose. Amino acids of proteins must be deaminated before being oxidized. The fatty acids of fats undergo **beta oxidation** to two-carbon fragments and then enter the citric acid cycle as acetyl CoA. Anabolic pathways can use small molecules from food directly or build other substances using intermediates of glycolysis or the citric acid cycle.
- Cellular respiration is controlled by allosteric enzymes at key points in glycolysis and the citric acid cycle.

? *Describe how the catabolic pathways of glycolysis and the citric acid cycle intersect with anabolic pathways in the metabolism of a cell.*

TEST YOUR UNDERSTANDING

LEVEL 1: KNOWLEDGE/COMPREHENSION

1. The *immediate* energy source that drives ATP synthesis by ATP synthase during oxidative phosphorylation is the
   a. oxidation of glucose and other organic compounds.
   b. flow of electrons down the electron transport chain.
   c. H^+ concentration gradient across the membrane holding ATP synthase.
   d. transfer of phosphate to ADP.

2. Which metabolic pathway is common to both fermentation and cellular respiration of a glucose molecule?
   a. the citric acid cycle
   b. the electron transport chain
   c. glycolysis
   d. reduction of pyruvate to lactate

3. The final electron acceptor of the electron transport chain that functions in aerobic oxidative phosphorylation is
   a. oxygen. b. water. c. NAD^+. d. pyruvate.

4. In mitochondria, exergonic redox reactions
   a. are the source of energy driving prokaryotic ATP synthesis.
   b. provide the energy that establishes the proton gradient.
   c. reduce carbon atoms to carbon dioxide.
   d. are coupled via phosphorylated intermediates to endergonic processes.

LEVEL 2: APPLICATION/ANALYSIS

5. What is the oxidizing agent in the following reaction?

$$\text{Pyruvate} + \text{NADH} + \text{H}^+ \rightarrow \text{Lactate} + \text{NAD}^+$$

   a. oxygen
   b. NADH
   c. lactate
   d. pyruvate

6. When electrons flow along the electron transport chains of mitochondria, which of the following changes occurs?
   a. The pH of the matrix increases.
   b. ATP synthase pumps protons by active transport.
   c. The electrons gain free energy.
   d. NAD^+ is oxidized.

7. Most CO_2 from catabolism is released during
   a. glycolysis.
   b. the citric acid cycle.
   c. lactate fermentation.
   d. electron transport.

8. **MAKE CONNECTIONS** Step 3 in Figure 9.9 is a major point of regulation of glycolysis. The enzyme phosphofructokinase is allosterically regulated by ATP and related molecules (see Concept 8.5). Considering the overall result of glycolysis, would you expect ATP to inhibit or stimulate activity of this enzyme? Explain. (*Hint:* Make sure you consider the role of ATP as an allosteric regulator, not as a substrate of the enzyme.)

9. **MAKE CONNECTIONS** The proton pump shown in Figure 7.17 is depicted as a simplified oval purple shape, but it is, in fact, an ATP synthase (see Figure 9.14). Compare the processes shown in the two figures, and say whether they are involved in active or passive transport (see Concepts 7.3 and 7.4).

LEVEL 3: SYNTHESIS/EVALUATION

10. **INTERPRET THE DATA**

Phosphofructokinase is an enzyme that acts on fructose 6-phosphate at an early step in glucose breakdown. Regulation of this enzyme controls whether the sugar will continue on in the glycolytic pathway. Considering this graph, under which condition is phosphofructokinase more active? Given what you know about glycolysis and regulation of metabolism by this enzyme, explain the mechanism by which phosphofructokinase activity differs depending on ATP concentration.

11. **DRAW IT** The graph here shows the pH difference across the inner mitochondrial membrane over time in an actively respiring cell. At the time indicated by the vertical arrow, a metabolic poison is added that specifically and completely inhibits all function of mitochondrial ATP synthase. Draw what you would expect to see for the rest of the graphed line, and explain your reasoning for drawing the line as you did.

12. **EVOLUTION CONNECTION**
ATP synthases are found in the prokaryotic plasma membrane and in mitochondria and chloroplasts. What does this suggest about the evolutionary relationship of these eukaryotic organelles to prokaryotes? How might the amino acid sequences of the ATP synthases from the different sources support or refute your hypothesis?

13. **SCIENTIFIC INQUIRY**
In the 1930s, some physicians prescribed low doses of a compound called dinitrophenol (DNP) to help patients lose weight. This unsafe method was abandoned after some patients died. DNP uncouples the chemiosmotic machinery by making the lipid bilayer of the inner mitochondrial membrane leaky to H^+. Explain how this could cause weight loss and death.

14. **WRITE ABOUT A THEME: ORGANIZATION**
In a short essay (100–150 words), explain how oxidative phosphorylation—production of ATP using energy from the redox reactions of a spatially organized electron transport chain followed by chemiosmosis—is an example of how new properties emerge at each level of the biological hierarchy.

15. **SYNTHESIZE YOUR KNOWLEDGE**

Coenzyme Q (CoQ) is sold as a nutritional supplement. One company uses this marketing slogan for CoQ: "Give your heart the fuel it craves most." Considering the role of coenzyme Q, how do you think this product might function as a nutritional supplement to benefit the heart? Is CoQ used as a "fuel" during cellular respiration?

For selected answers, see Appendix A.

MasteringBiology®

Students Go to **MasteringBiology** for assignments, the eText, and the Study Area with practice tests, animations, and activities.

Instructors Go to **MasteringBiology** for automatically graded tutorials and questions that you can assign to your students, plus Instructor Resources.

10
Photosynthesis

KEY CONCEPTS

10.1 Photosynthesis converts light energy to the chemical energy of food

10.2 The light reactions convert solar energy to the chemical energy of ATP and NADPH

10.3 The Calvin cycle uses the chemical energy of ATP and NADPH to reduce CO_2 to sugar

10.4 Alternative mechanisms of carbon fixation have evolved in hot, arid climates

▲ Other organisms also benefit from photosynthesis.

▲ Figure 10.1 How does sunlight help build the trunk, branches, and leaves of this broadleaf tree?

The Process That Feeds the Biosphere

Life on Earth is solar powered. The chloroplasts in plants and other photosynthetic organisms capture light energy that has traveled 150 million kilometers from the sun and convert it to chemical energy that is stored in sugar and other organic molecules. This conversion process is called **photosynthesis**. Let's begin by placing photosynthesis in its ecological context.

Photosynthesis nourishes almost the entire living world directly or indirectly. An organism acquires the organic compounds it uses for energy and carbon skeletons by one of two major modes: autotrophic nutrition or heterotrophic nutrition. **Autotrophs** are "self-feeders" (*auto-* means "self," and *trophos* means "feeder"); they sustain themselves without eating anything derived from other living beings. Autotrophs produce their organic molecules from CO_2 and other inorganic raw materials obtained from the environment. They are the ultimate sources of organic compounds for all nonautotrophic organisms, and for this reason, biologists refer to autotrophs as the *producers* of the biosphere.

Almost all plants are autotrophs; the only nutrients they require are water and minerals from the soil and carbon dioxide from the air. Specifically, plants are *photo*autotrophs, organisms that use light as a source of energy to synthesize organic substances **(Figure 10.1)**. Photosynthesis also occurs in algae, certain other unicellular eukaryotes, and some prokaryotes **(Figure 10.2)**. In this chapter, we will touch on these other groups in passing, but our emphasis will be on plants. Variations in autotrophic nutrition that occur in prokaryotes and algae will be described in Chapters 27 and 28.

(a) Plants

(b) Multicellular alga

(c) Unicellular eukaryotes

10 µm

(d) Cyanobacteria

40 µm

1 µm

(e) Purple sulfur bacteria

▲ **Figure 10.2 Photoautotrophs.** These organisms use light energy to drive the synthesis of organic molecules from carbon dioxide and (in most cases) water. They feed themselves and the entire living world. **(a)** On land, plants are the predominant producers of food. In aquatic environments, photoautotrophs include unicellular and **(b)** multicellular algae, such as this kelp; **(c)** some non-algal unicellular eukaryotes, such as *Euglena*; **(d)** the prokaryotes called cyanobacteria; and **(e)** other photosynthetic prokaryotes, such as these purple sulfur bacteria, which produce sulfur (the yellow globules within the cells) (c–e, LMs).

Heterotrophs obtain organic material by the second major mode of nutrition. Unable to make their own food, they live on compounds produced by other organisms (*hetero-* means "other"). Heterotrophs are the biosphere's *consumers*. The most obvious "other-feeding" occurs when an animal eats plants or other animals. But heterotrophic nutrition may be more subtle. Some heterotrophs consume the remains of dead organisms by decomposing and feeding on organic litter such as carcasses, feces, and fallen leaves; these types of organisms are known as decomposers. Most fungi and many types of prokaryotes get their nourishment this way. Almost all heterotrophs, including humans, are completely dependent, either directly or indirectly, on photoautotrophs for food—and also for oxygen, a by-product of photosynthesis.

The Earth's supply of fossil fuels was formed from remains of organisms that died hundreds of millions of years ago. In a sense, then, fossil fuels represent stores of the sun's energy from the distant past. Because these resources are being used at a much higher rate than they are replenished, researchers are exploring methods of capitalizing on the photosynthetic process to provide alternative fuels **(Figure 10.3)**.

In this chapter, you'll learn how photosynthesis works. After discussing general principles of photosynthesis, we'll consider the two stages of photosynthesis: the light reactions, which capture solar energy and transform it into chemical energy; and the Calvin cycle, which uses that chemical energy to make the organic molecules of food. Finally, we will consider some aspects of photosynthesis from an evolutionary perspective.

▲ **Figure 10.3 Alternative fuels from algae.** The power of sunlight can be tapped to generate a sustainable alternative to fossil fuels. Species of unicellular algae that are prolific producers of plant oils can be cultured in long, transparent tanks called photobioreactors, such as the one shown here at Arizona State University. A simple chemical process can yield "biodiesel," which can be mixed with gasoline or used alone to power vehicles.

WHAT IF? *The main product of fossil fuel combustion is CO_2, and this is the source of the increase in atmospheric CO_2 concentration. Scientists have proposed strategically situating containers of these algae near industrial plants or near highly congested city streets. Considering the process of photosynthesis, how does this arrangement make sense?*

Photosynthesis converts light energy to the chemical energy of food

The remarkable ability of an organism to harness light energy and use it to drive the synthesis of organic compounds emerges from structural organization in the cell: Photosynthetic enzymes and other molecules are grouped together in a biological membrane, enabling the necessary series of chemical reactions to be carried out efficiently. The process of photosynthesis most likely originated in a group of bacteria that had infolded regions of the plasma membrane containing clusters of such molecules. In existing photosynthetic bacteria, infolded photosynthetic membranes function similarly to the internal membranes of the chloroplast, a eukaryotic organelle. According to what has come to be known as the endosymbiont theory, the original chloroplast was a photosynthetic prokaryote that lived inside an ancestor of eukaryotic cells. (You learned about this theory in Chapter 6, and it will be described more fully in Chapter 25.) Chloroplasts are present in a variety of photosynthesizing organisms (see some examples in Figure 10.2), but here we focus on chloroplasts in plants.

Chloroplasts: The Sites of Photosynthesis in Plants

All green parts of a plant, including green stems and unripened fruit, have chloroplasts, but the leaves are the major sites of photosynthesis in most plants (**Figure 10.4**). There are about half a million chloroplasts in a chunk of leaf with a top surface area of 1 mm². Chloroplasts are found mainly in the cells of the **mesophyll**, the tissue in the interior of the leaf. Carbon dioxide enters the leaf, and oxygen exits, by way of microscopic pores called **stomata** (singular, *stoma*; from the Greek, meaning "mouth"). Water absorbed by the roots is delivered to the leaves in veins. Leaves also use veins to export sugar to roots and other nonphotosynthetic parts of the plant.

A typical mesophyll cell has about 30–40 chloroplasts, each measuring about 2–4 µm by 4–7 µm. A chloroplast has an envelope of two membranes surrounding a dense fluid called the **stroma**. Suspended within the stroma is a third membrane system, made up of sacs called **thylakoids**, which segregates the stroma from the *thylakoid space* inside these sacs. In some places, thylakoid sacs are stacked in columns called *grana* (singular, *granum*). **Chlorophyll**, the green pigment that gives leaves their color, resides in the thylakoid membranes of the chloroplast. (The internal photosynthetic membranes of some prokaryotes are also called thylakoid

▲ **Figure 10.4 Zooming in on the location of photosynthesis in a plant.** Leaves are the major organs of photosynthesis in plants. These pictures take you into a leaf, then into a cell, and finally into a chloroplast, the organelle where photosynthesis occurs (middle, LM; bottom, TEM).

membranes; see Figure 27.8b.) It is the light energy absorbed by chlorophyll that drives the synthesis of organic molecules in the chloroplast. Now that we have looked at the sites of photosynthesis in plants, we are ready to look more closely at the process of photosynthesis.

Tracking Atoms Through Photosynthesis: *Scientific Inquiry*

Scientists have tried for centuries to piece together the process by which plants make food. Although some of the steps are still not completely understood, the overall photosynthetic equation has been known since the 1800s: In the presence of light, the green parts of plants produce organic compounds and oxygen from carbon dioxide and water. Using molecular formulas, we can summarize the complex series of chemical reactions in photosynthesis with this chemical equation:

$$6 CO_2 + 12 H_2O + \text{Light energy} \rightarrow C_6H_{12}O_6 + 6 O_2 + 6 H_2O$$

We use glucose ($C_6H_{12}O_6$) here to simplify the relationship between photosynthesis and respiration, but the direct product of photosynthesis is actually a three-carbon sugar that can be used to make glucose. Water appears on both sides of the equation because 12 molecules are consumed and 6 molecules are newly formed during photosynthesis. We can simplify the equation by indicating only the net consumption of water:

$$6 CO_2 + 6 H_2O + \text{Light energy} \rightarrow C_6H_{12}O_6 + 6 O_2$$

Writing the equation in this form, we can see that the overall chemical change during photosynthesis is the reverse of the one that occurs during cellular respiration (see Concept 9.1). Both of these metabolic processes occur in plant cells. However, as you will soon learn, chloroplasts do not synthesize sugars by simply reversing the steps of respiration.

Now let's divide the photosynthetic equation by 6 to put it in its simplest possible form:

$$CO_2 + H_2O \rightarrow [CH_2O] + O_2$$

Here, the brackets indicate that CH_2O is not an actual sugar but represents the general formula for a carbohydrate (see Concept 5.2). In other words, we are imagining the synthesis of a sugar molecule one carbon at a time. Six repetitions would theoretically produce a glucose molecule ($C_6H_{12}O_6$). Let's now see how researchers tracked the elements C, H, and O from the reactants of photosynthesis to the products.

The Splitting of Water

One of the first clues to the mechanism of photosynthesis came from the discovery that the O_2 given off by plants is derived from H_2O and not from CO_2. The chloroplast splits water into hydrogen and oxygen. Before this discovery, the prevailing hypothesis was that photosynthesis split carbon dioxide ($CO_2 \rightarrow C + O_2$) and then added water to the carbon ($C + H_2O \rightarrow [CH_2O]$). This hypothesis predicted that the O_2 released during photosynthesis came from CO_2. This idea was challenged in the 1930s by C. B. van Niel, of Stanford University. Van Niel was investigating photosynthesis in bacteria that make their carbohydrate from CO_2 but do not release O_2. He concluded that, at least in these bacteria, CO_2 is not split into carbon and oxygen. One group of bacteria used hydrogen sulfide (H_2S) rather than water for photosynthesis, forming yellow globules of sulfur as a waste product (these globules are visible in Figure 10.2e). Here is the chemical equation for photosynthesis in these sulfur bacteria:

$$CO_2 + 2 H_2S \rightarrow [CH_2O] + H_2O + 2 S$$

Van Niel reasoned that the bacteria split H_2S and used the hydrogen atoms to make sugar. He then generalized that idea, proposing that all photosynthetic organisms require a hydrogen source but that the source varies:

Sulfur bacteria: $CO_2 + 2 H_2S \rightarrow [CH_2O] + H_2O + 2 S$
Plants: $CO_2 + 2 H_2O \rightarrow [CH_2O] + H_2O + O_2$
General: $CO_2 + 2 H_2X \rightarrow [CH_2O] + H_2O + 2 X$

Thus, van Niel hypothesized that plants split H_2O as a source of electrons from hydrogen atoms, releasing O_2 as a by-product.

Nearly 20 years later, scientists confirmed van Niel's hypothesis by using oxygen-18 (^{18}O), a heavy isotope, as a tracer to follow the fate of oxygen atoms during photosynthesis. The experiments showed that the O_2 from plants was labeled with ^{18}O *only* if water was the source of the tracer (experiment 1). If the ^{18}O was introduced to the plant in the form of CO_2, the label did not turn up in the released O_2 (experiment 2). In the following summary, red denotes labeled atoms of oxygen (^{18}O):

Experiment 1: $CO_2 + 2 H_2O \rightarrow [CH_2O] + H_2O + O_2$
Experiment 2: $CO_2 + 2 H_2O \rightarrow [CH_2O] + H_2O + O_2$

A significant result of the shuffling of atoms during photosynthesis is the extraction of hydrogen from water and its incorporation into sugar. The waste product of photosynthesis, O_2, is released to the atmosphere. **Figure 10.5** shows the fates of all atoms in photosynthesis.

▲ **Figure 10.5 Tracking atoms through photosynthesis.** The atoms from CO_2 are shown in magenta, and the atoms from H_2O are shown in blue.

Photosynthesis as a Redox Process

Let's briefly compare photosynthesis with cellular respiration. Both processes involve redox reactions. During cellular respiration, energy is released from sugar when electrons associated with hydrogen are transported by carriers to oxygen, forming water as a by-product. The electrons lose potential energy as they "fall" down the electron transport chain toward electronegative oxygen, and the mitochondrion harnesses that energy to synthesize ATP (see Figure 9.15). Photosynthesis reverses the direction of electron flow. Water is split, and electrons are transferred along with hydrogen ions from the water to carbon dioxide, reducing it to sugar.

$$\text{Energy} + 6\,CO_2 + 6\,H_2O \longrightarrow C_6H_{12}O_6 + 6\,O_2$$

becomes reduced

becomes oxidized

Because the electrons increase in potential energy as they move from water to sugar, this process requires energy—in other words is endergonic. This energy boost that occurs during photosynthesis is provided by light.

The Two Stages of Photosynthesis: *A Preview*

The equation for photosynthesis is a deceptively simple summary of a very complex process. Actually, photosynthesis is not a single process, but two processes, each with multiple steps. These two stages of photosynthesis are known as the **light reactions** (the *photo* part of photosynthesis) and the **Calvin cycle** (the *synthesis* part) **(Figure 10.6)**.

The light reactions are the steps of photosynthesis that convert solar energy to chemical energy. Water is split, providing a source of electrons and protons (hydrogen ions, H^+) and giving off O_2 as a by-product. Light absorbed by chlorophyll drives a transfer of the electrons and hydrogen ions from water to an acceptor called **NADP⁺** (nicotinamide adenine dinucleotide phosphate), where they are temporarily stored. The electron acceptor $NADP^+$ is first cousin to NAD^+, which functions as an electron carrier in cellular respiration; the two molecules differ only by the presence of an extra phosphate group in the $NADP^+$ molecule. The light reactions use solar energy to reduce $NADP^+$ to NADPH by adding a pair of electrons along with an H^+. The light reactions also generate ATP, using chemiosmosis to power the addition of a phosphate group to ADP, a process called **photophosphorylation**. Thus, light energy is initially converted to chemical energy in the form of two compounds: NADPH and ATP. NADPH, a source of electrons, acts as "reducing power" that can be passed along to an electron acceptor, reducing it, while ATP is the versatile energy currency of cells. Notice that the light reactions produce no sugar; that happens in the second stage of photosynthesis, the Calvin cycle.

The Calvin cycle is named for Melvin Calvin, who, along with his colleagues James Bassham and Andrew Benson, began to elucidate its steps in the late 1940s. The cycle begins by incorporating CO_2 from the air into organic molecules already present in the chloroplast. This initial incorporation of carbon into organic compounds is known as **carbon fixation**. The Calvin cycle then reduces the fixed carbon

▶ **Figure 10.6 An overview of photosynthesis: cooperation of the light reactions and the Calvin cycle.** In the chloroplast, the thylakoid membranes (green) are the sites of the light reactions, whereas the Calvin cycle occurs in the stroma (gray). The light reactions use solar energy to make ATP and NADPH, which supply chemical energy and reducing power, respectively, to the Calvin cycle. The Calvin cycle incorporates CO_2 into organic molecules, which are converted to sugar. (Recall that most simple sugars have formulas that are some multiple of CH_2O.)

BioFlix Visit the Study Area in **MasteringBiology** for the BioFlix® 3-D Animation on Photosynthesis. BioFlix Tutorials can also be assigned in MasteringBiology.

to carbohydrate by the addition of electrons. The reducing power is provided by NADPH, which acquired its cargo of electrons in the light reactions. To convert CO_2 to carbohydrate, the Calvin cycle also requires chemical energy in the form of ATP, which is also generated by the light reactions. Thus, it is the Calvin cycle that makes sugar, but it can do so only with the help of the NADPH and ATP produced by the light reactions. The metabolic steps of the Calvin cycle are sometimes referred to as the dark reactions, or light-independent reactions, because none of the steps requires light *directly*. Nevertheless, the Calvin cycle in most plants occurs during daylight, for only then can the light reactions provide the NADPH and ATP that the Calvin cycle requires. In essence, the chloroplast uses light energy to make sugar by coordinating the two stages of photosynthesis.

As Figure 10.6 indicates, the thylakoids of the chloroplast are the sites of the light reactions, while the Calvin cycle occurs in the stroma. On the outside of the thylakoids, molecules of $NADP^+$ and ADP pick up electrons and phosphate, respectively, and NADPH and ATP are then released to the stroma, where they play crucial roles in the Calvin cycle. The two stages of photosynthesis are treated in this figure as metabolic modules that take in ingredients and crank out products. In the next two sections, we'll look more closely at how the two stages work, beginning with the light reactions.

CONCEPT CHECK 10.1

1. How do the reactant molecules of photosynthesis reach the chloroplasts in leaves?
2. How did the use of an oxygen isotope help elucidate the chemistry of photosynthesis?
3. **WHAT IF?** The Calvin cycle requires ATP and NADPH, products of the light reactions. If a classmate asserted that the light reactions don't depend on the Calvin cycle and, with continual light, could just keep on producing ATP and NADPH, how would you respond?

For suggested answers, see Appendix A.

CONCEPT 10.2

The light reactions convert solar energy to the chemical energy of ATP and NADPH

Chloroplasts are chemical factories powered by the sun. Their thylakoids transform light energy into the chemical energy of ATP and NADPH, which will be used to synthesize glucose and other molecules that can be used as energy sources. To better understand the conversion of light to chemical energy, we need to know about some important properties of light.

The Nature of Sunlight

Light is a form of energy known as electromagnetic energy, also called electromagnetic radiation. Electromagnetic energy travels in rhythmic waves analogous to those created by dropping a pebble into a pond. Electromagnetic waves, however, are disturbances of electric and magnetic fields rather than disturbances of a material medium such as water.

The distance between the crests of electromagnetic waves is called the **wavelength**. Wavelengths range from less than a nanometer (for gamma rays) to more than a kilometer (for radio waves). This entire range of radiation is known as the **electromagnetic spectrum (Figure 10.7)**. The segment most important to life is the narrow band from about 380 nm to 750 nm in wavelength. This radiation is known as **visible light** because it can be detected as various colors by the human eye.

The model of light as waves explains many of light's properties, but in certain respects light behaves as though it consists of discrete particles, called **photons**. Photons are not tangible objects, but they act like objects in that each of them has a fixed quantity of energy. The amount of energy is inversely related to the wavelength of the light: the shorter the wavelength, the greater the energy of each photon of that light. Thus, a photon of violet light packs nearly twice as much energy as a photon of red light (see Figure 10.7).

Although the sun radiates the full spectrum of electromagnetic energy, the atmosphere acts like a selective window, allowing visible light to pass through while screening out a substantial fraction of other radiation. The part of the spectrum we can see—visible light—is also the radiation that drives photosynthesis.

▲ **Figure 10.7 The electromagnetic spectrum.** White light is a mixture of all wavelengths of visible light. A prism can sort white light into its component colors by bending light of different wavelengths at different angles. (Droplets of water in the atmosphere can act as prisms, causing a rainbow to form.) Visible light drives photosynthesis.

Photosynthetic Pigments: The Light Receptors

When light meets matter, it may be reflected, transmitted, or absorbed. Substances that absorb visible light are known as *pigments*. Different pigments absorb light of different wavelengths, and the wavelengths that are absorbed disappear. If a pigment is illuminated with white light, the color we see is the color most reflected or transmitted by the pigment. (If a pigment absorbs all wavelengths, it appears black.) We see green when we look at a leaf because chlorophyll absorbs violet-blue and red light while transmitting and reflecting green light (Figure 10.8). The ability of a pigment to absorb various wavelengths of light can be measured with an instrument called a **spectrophotometer**. This machine directs beams of light of different wavelengths through a solution of the pigment and measures the fraction of the light transmitted at each wavelength. A graph plotting a pigment's light absorption versus wavelength is called an **absorption spectrum (Figure 10.9)**.

The absorption spectra of chloroplast pigments provide clues to the relative effectiveness of different wavelengths for driving photosynthesis, since light can perform work in chloroplasts only if it is absorbed. **Figure 10.10a** shows the absorption spectra of three types of pigments in chloroplasts: **chlorophyll *a***, the key light-capturing pigment that participates directly in the light reactions; the accessory pigment **chlorophyll *b***; and a separate group of accessory pigments called carotenoids. The spectrum of chlorophyll

▲ **Figure 10.8 Why leaves are green: interaction of light with chloroplasts.** The chlorophyll molecules of chloroplasts absorb violet-blue and red light (the colors most effective in driving photosynthesis) and reflect or transmit green light. This is why leaves appear green.

Determining an Absorption Spectrum

Application An absorption spectrum is a visual representation of how well a particular pigment absorbs different wavelengths of visible light. Absorption spectra of various chloroplast pigments help scientists decipher the role of each pigment in a plant.

Technique A spectrophotometer measures the relative amounts of light of different wavelengths absorbed and transmitted by a pigment solution.

1 White light is separated into colors (wavelengths) by a prism.

2 One by one, the different colors of light are passed through the sample (chlorophyll in this example). Green light and blue light are shown here.

3 The transmitted light strikes a photoelectric tube, which converts the light energy to electricity.

4 The electric current is measured by a galvanometer. The meter indicates the fraction of light transmitted through the sample, from which we can determine the amount of light absorbed.

The high transmittance (low absorption) reading indicates that chlorophyll absorbs very little green light.

The low transmittance (high absorption) reading indicates that chlorophyll absorbs most blue light.

Results See Figure 10.10a for absorption spectra of three types of chloroplast pigments.

a suggests that violet-blue and red light work best for photosynthesis, since they are absorbed, while green is the least effective color. This is confirmed by an **action spectrum** for photosynthesis **(Figure 10.10b)**, which profiles the relative effectiveness of different wavelengths of radiation in driving the process. An action spectrum is prepared by illuminating chloroplasts with light of different colors and then plotting wavelength against some measure of photosynthetic rate,

▼ Figure 10.10   Inquiry

Which wavelengths of light are most effective in driving photosynthesis?

Experiment Absorption and action spectra, along with a classic experiment by Theodor W. Engelmann, reveal which wavelengths of light are photosynthetically important.

Results

(a) Absorption spectra. The three curves show the wavelengths of light best absorbed by three types of chloroplast pigments.

(b) Action spectrum. This graph plots the rate of photosynthesis versus wavelength. The resulting action spectrum resembles the absorption spectrum for chlorophyll *a* but does not match exactly (see part a). This is partly due to the absorption of light by accessory pigments such as chlorophyll *b* and carotenoids.

(c) Engelmann's experiment. In 1883, Theodor W. Engelmann illuminated a filamentous alga with light that had been passed through a prism, exposing different segments of the alga to different wavelengths. He used aerobic bacteria, which concentrate near an oxygen source, to determine which segments of the alga were releasing the most O₂ and thus photosynthesizing most. Bacteria congregated in greatest numbers around the parts of the alga illuminated with violet-blue or red light.

Conclusion Light in the violet-blue and red portions of the spectrum is most effective in driving photosynthesis.

Source: T. W. Engelmann, Bacterium photometricum. *Ein Beitrag zur vergleichenden Physiologie des Licht-und Farbensinnes,* Archiv. für Physiologie *30:95–124 (1883).*

(MB) An Experimental Inquiry Tutorial can be assigned in MasteringBiology.

INTERPRET THE DATA *What wavelengths of light drive the highest rates of photosynthesis?*

such as CO_2 consumption or O_2 release. The action spectrum for photosynthesis was first demonstrated by Theodor W. Engelmann, a German botanist, in 1883. Before equipment for measuring O_2 levels had even been invented, Engelmann performed a clever experiment in which he used bacteria to measure rates of photosynthesis in filamentous algae **(Figure 10.10c)**. His results are a striking match to the modern action spectrum shown in Figure 10.10b.

Notice by comparing Figures 10.10a and 10.10b that the action spectrum for photosynthesis is much broader than the absorption spectrum of chlorophyll *a*. The absorption spectrum of chlorophyll *a* alone underestimates the effectiveness of certain wavelengths in driving photosynthesis. This is partly because accessory pigments with different absorption spectra also present in chloroplasts—including chlorophyll *b* and carotenoids—broaden the spectrum of colors that can be used for photosynthesis. **Figure 10.11** shows the structure of chlorophyll *a* compared with that of chlorophyll *b*. A slight structural difference between them is enough to cause the two pigments to absorb at slightly different wavelengths in the red and blue parts of the spectrum (see Figure 10.10a). As a result, chlorophyll *a* appears blue green and chlorophyll *b* olive green under visible light.

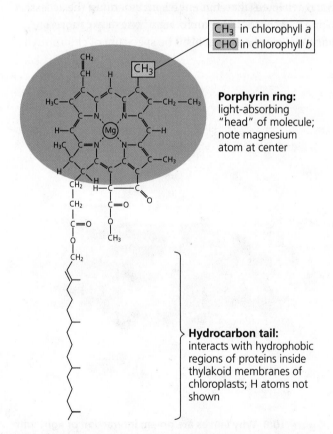

▲ Figure 10.11 Structure of chlorophyll molecules in chloroplasts of plants. Chlorophyll *a* and chlorophyll *b* differ only in one of the functional groups bonded to the porphyrin ring. (Also see the space-filling model of chlorophyll in Figure 1.3.)

Other accessory pigments include **carotenoids**, hydrocarbons that are various shades of yellow and orange because they absorb violet and blue-green light (see Figure 10.10a). Carotenoids may broaden the spectrum of colors that can drive photosynthesis. However, a more important function of at least some carotenoids seems to be *photoprotection*: These compounds absorb and dissipate excessive light energy that would otherwise damage chlorophyll or interact with oxygen, forming reactive oxidative molecules that are dangerous to the cell. Interestingly, carotenoids similar to the photoprotective ones in chloroplasts have a photoprotective role in the human eye. (Remember being told to eat your carrots for improved night vision?) These and related molecules are, of course, found naturally in many vegetables and fruits. They are also often advertised in health food products as "phytochemicals" (from the Greek *phyton*, plant), some of which have antioxidant properties. Plants can synthesize all the antioxidants they require, but humans and other animals must obtain some of them from their diets.

Excitation of Chlorophyll by Light

What exactly happens when chlorophyll and other pigments absorb light? The colors corresponding to the absorbed wavelengths disappear from the spectrum of the transmitted and reflected light, but energy cannot disappear. When a molecule absorbs a photon of light, one of the molecule's electrons is elevated to an orbital where it has more potential energy (see Figure 2.6b). When the electron is in its normal orbital, the pigment molecule is said to be in its ground state. Absorption of a photon boosts an electron to an orbital of higher energy, and the pigment molecule is then said to be in an excited state. The only photons absorbed are those whose energy is exactly equal to the energy difference between the ground state and an excited state, and this energy difference varies from one kind of molecule to another. Thus, a particular compound absorbs only photons corresponding to specific wavelengths, which is why each pigment has a unique absorption spectrum.

Once absorption of a photon raises an electron to an excited state, the electron cannot stay there long. The excited state, like all high-energy states, is unstable. Generally, when isolated pigment molecules absorb light, their excited electrons drop back down to the ground-state orbital in a billionth of a second, releasing their excess energy as heat. This conversion of light energy to heat is what makes the top of an automobile so hot on a sunny day. (White cars are coolest because their paint reflects all wavelengths of visible light.) In isolation, some pigments, including chlorophyll, emit light as well as heat after absorbing photons. As excited electrons fall back to the ground state, photons are given off, an afterglow called fluorescence. An illuminated solution of chlorophyll isolated from chloroplasts will fluoresce in the red part of the spectrum and also give off heat **(Figure 10.12)**. This is best seen by illuminating with ultraviolet light, which chlorophyll can also absorb (see Figures 10.7 and 10.10a). Viewed under visible light, the fluorescence would be harder to see against the green of the solution.

A Photosystem: A Reaction-Center Complex Associated with Light-Harvesting Complexes

Chlorophyll molecules excited by the absorption of light energy produce very different results in an intact chloroplast than they do in isolation (see Figure 10.12). In their native environment of the thylakoid membrane, chlorophyll molecules are organized along with other small organic molecules and proteins into complexes called photosystems.

▶ **Figure 10.12 Excitation of isolated chlorophyll by light. (a)** Absorption of a photon causes a transition of the chlorophyll molecule from its ground state to its excited state. The photon boosts an electron to an orbital where it has more potential energy. If the illuminated molecule exists in isolation, its excited electron immediately drops back down to the ground-state orbital, and its excess energy is given off as heat and fluorescence (light). **(b)** A chlorophyll solution excited with ultraviolet light fluoresces with a red-orange glow.

WHAT IF? *If a leaf containing a similar concentration of chlorophyll as the solution was exposed to the same ultraviolet light, no fluorescence would be seen. Propose an explanation for the difference in fluorescence emission between the solution and the leaf.*

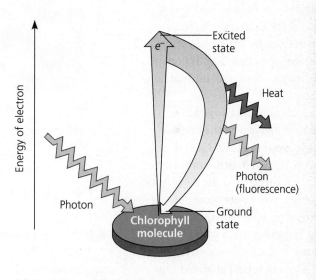

(a) Excitation of isolated chlorophyll molecule

(b) Fluorescence

A **photosystem** is composed of a **reaction-center complex** surrounded by several light-harvesting complexes (**Figure 10.13**). The reaction-center complex is an organized association of proteins holding a special pair of chlorophyll *a* molecules. Each **light-harvesting complex** consists of various pigment molecules (which may include chlorophyll *a*, chlorophyll *b*, and multiple carotenoids) bound to proteins. The number and variety of pigment molecules enable a photosystem to harvest light over a larger surface area and a larger portion of the spectrum than could any single pigment molecule alone. Together, these light-harvesting complexes act as an antenna for the reaction-center complex. When a pigment molecule absorbs a photon, the energy is transferred from pigment molecule to pigment molecule within a light-harvesting complex, somewhat like a human "wave" at a sports arena, until it is passed into the reaction-center complex. The reaction-center complex also contains a molecule capable of accepting electrons and becoming reduced; this is called the **primary electron acceptor**. The pair of chlorophyll *a* molecules in the reaction-center complex are special because their molecular environment—their location and the other molecules with which they are associated—enables them to use the energy from light not only to boost one of their electrons to a higher energy level, but also to transfer it to a different molecule—the primary electron acceptor.

The solar-powered transfer of an electron from the reaction-center chlorophyll *a* pair to the primary electron acceptor is the first step of the light reactions. As soon as the chlorophyll electron is excited to a higher energy level, the primary electron acceptor captures it; this is a redox reaction. In the flask shown in Figure 10.12b, isolated chlorophyll fluoresces because there is no electron acceptor, so electrons of photoexcited chlorophyll drop right back to the ground state. In the structured environment of a chloroplast, however, an electron acceptor is readily available, and the potential energy represented by the excited electron is not dissipated as light and heat. Thus, each photosystem—a reaction-center complex surrounded by light-harvesting complexes—functions in the chloroplast as a unit. It converts light energy to chemical energy, which will ultimately be used for the synthesis of sugar.

The thylakoid membrane is populated by two types of photosystems that cooperate in the light reactions of photosynthesis. They are called **photosystem II (PS II)** and **photosystem I (PS I)**. (They were named in order of their discovery, but photosystem II functions first in the light reactions.) Each has a characteristic reaction-center complex—a particular kind of primary electron acceptor next to a special pair of chlorophyll *a* molecules associated with specific proteins. The reaction-center chlorophyll *a* of photosystem II is known as P680 because this pigment is best at absorbing

(a) How a photosystem harvests light. When a photon strikes a pigment molecule in a light-harvesting complex, the energy is passed from molecule to molecule until it reaches the reaction-center complex. Here, an excited electron from the special pair of chlorophyll *a* molecules is transferred to the primary electron acceptor.

(b) Structure of a photosystem. This computer model, based on X-ray crystallography, shows two photosystem complexes side by side, oriented opposite to each other. Chlorophyll molecules (small green ball-and-stick models) are interspersed with protein subunits (cylinders and ribbons). For simplicity, this photosystem will be shown as a single complex in the rest of the chapter.

▲ **Figure 10.13 The structure and function of a photosystem.**

light having a wavelength of 680 nm (in the red part of the spectrum). The chlorophyll *a* at the reaction-center complex of photosystem I is called P700 because it most effectively absorbs light of wavelength 700 nm (in the far-red part of the spectrum). These two pigments, P680 and P700, are nearly identical chlorophyll *a* molecules. However, their association with different proteins in the thylakoid membrane affects the electron distribution in the two pigments and accounts for the slight differences in their light-absorbing properties. Now let's see how the two photosystems work together in using light energy to generate ATP and NADPH, the two main products of the light reactions.

Linear Electron Flow

Light drives the synthesis of ATP and NADPH by energizing the two photosystems embedded in the thylakoid membranes of chloroplasts. The key to this energy transformation is a flow of electrons through the photosystems and other molecular components built into the thylakoid membrane. This is called **linear electron flow**, and it occurs during the light reactions of photosynthesis, as shown in **Figure 10.14**. The numbered steps in the text correspond to the numbered steps in the figure.

❶ A photon of light strikes one of the pigment molecules in a light-harvesting complex of PS II, boosting one of its electrons to a higher energy level. As this electron falls back to its ground state, an electron in a nearby pigment molecule is simultaneously raised to an excited state. The process continues, with the energy being relayed to other pigment molecules until it reaches the P680 pair of chlorophyll *a* molecules in the PS II reaction-center complex. It excites an electron in this pair of chlorophylls to a higher energy state.

❷ This electron is transferred from the excited P680 to the primary electron acceptor. We can refer to the resulting form of P680, missing an electron, as P680$^+$.

❸ An enzyme catalyzes the splitting of a water molecule into two electrons, two hydrogen ions (H$^+$), and an oxygen atom. The electrons are supplied one by one to the P680$^+$ pair, each electron replacing one transferred to the primary electron acceptor. (P680$^+$ is the strongest biological oxidizing agent known; its electron "hole" must be filled. This greatly facilitates the transfer of electrons from the split water molecule.) The H$^+$ are released into

▼ **Figure 10.14 How linear electron flow during the light reactions generates ATP and NADPH.** The gold arrows trace the flow of light-driven electrons from water to NADPH. The black arrows trace the transfer of energy from pigment molecule to pigment molecule.

Photosystem II (PS II)

Photosystem I (PS I)

the thylakoid space. The oxygen atom immediately combines with an oxygen atom generated by the splitting of another water molecule, forming O_2.

4 Each photoexcited electron passes from the primary electron acceptor of PS II to PS I via an electron transport chain, the components of which are similar to those of the electron transport chain that functions in cellular respiration. The electron transport chain between PS II and PS I is made up of the electron carrier plastoquinone (Pq), a cytochrome complex, and a protein called plastocyanin (Pc).

5 The exergonic "fall" of electrons to a lower energy level provides energy for the synthesis of ATP. As electrons pass through the cytochrome complex, H^+ are pumped into the thylakoid space, contributing to the proton gradient that is subsequently used in chemiosmosis.

6 Meanwhile, light energy has been transferred via light-harvesting complex pigments to the PS I reaction-center complex, exciting an electron of the P700 pair of chlorophyll *a* molecules located there. The photoexcited electron is then transferred to PS I's primary electron acceptor, creating an electron "hole" in the P700—which we now can call $P700^+$. In other words, $P700^+$ can now act as an electron acceptor, accepting an electron that reaches the bottom of the electron transport chain from PS II.

7 Photoexcited electrons are passed in a series of redox reactions from the primary electron acceptor of PS I down a second electron transport chain through the protein ferredoxin (Fd). (This chain does not create a proton gradient and thus does not produce ATP.)

8 The enzyme $NADP^+$ reductase catalyzes the transfer of electrons from Fd to $NADP^+$. Two electrons are required for its reduction to NADPH. This molecule is at a higher energy level than water, so its electrons are more readily available for the reactions of the Calvin cycle. This process also removes an H^+ from the stroma.

▲ **Figure 10.15 A mechanical analogy for linear electron flow during the light reactions.**

The energy changes of electrons during their linear flow through the light reactions are shown in a mechanical analogy in **Figure 10.15**. Although the scheme shown in Figures 10.14 and 10.15 may seem complicated, do not lose track of the big picture: The light reactions use solar power to generate ATP and NADPH, which provide chemical energy and reducing power, respectively, to the carbohydrate-synthesizing reactions of the Calvin cycle.

Cyclic Electron Flow

In certain cases, photoexcited electrons can take an alternative path called **cyclic electron flow**, which uses photosystem I but not photosystem II. You can see in **Figure 10.16** that cyclic flow is a short circuit: The electrons cycle back from ferredoxin (Fd) to the cytochrome complex and from there continue on to a P700 chlorophyll in the PS I reaction-center

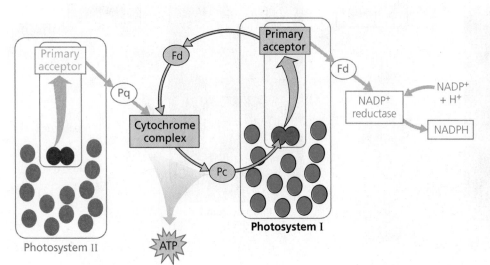

◄ **Figure 10.16 Cyclic electron flow.** Photoexcited electrons from PS I are occasionally shunted back from ferredoxin (Fd) to chlorophyll via the cytochrome complex and plastocyanin (Pc). This electron shunt supplements the supply of ATP (via chemiosmosis) but produces no NADPH. The "shadow" of linear electron flow is included in the diagram for comparison with the cyclic route. The two Fd molecules in this diagram are actually one and the same—the final electron carrier in the electron transport chain of PS I—although it is depicted twice to clearly show its role in two parts of the process.

? *Look at Figure 10.15, and explain how you would alter it to show a mechanical analogy for cyclic electron flow.*

complex. There is no production of NADPH and no release of oxygen that results from this process. On the other hand, cyclic flow does generate ATP.

Rather than having both PSII and PSI, several of the currently existing groups of photosynthetic bacteria are known to have a single photosystem related to either PSII or PSI. For these species, which include the purple sulfur bacteria (see Figure 10.2e) and the green sulfur bacteria, cyclic electron flow is the one and only means of generating ATP during the process of photosynthesis. Evolutionary biologists hypothesize that these bacterial groups are descendants of ancestral bacteria in which photosynthesis first evolved, in a form similar to cyclic electron flow.

Cyclic electron flow can also occur in photosynthetic species that possess both photosystems; this includes some prokaryotes, such as the cyanobacteria shown in Figure 10.2d, as well as the eukaryotic photosynthetic species that have been tested thus far. Although the process is probably in part an "evolutionary leftover," research suggests it plays at least one beneficial role for these organisms. Mutant plants that are not able to carry out cyclic electron flow are capable of growing well in low light, but do not grow well where light is intense. This is evidence for the idea that cyclic electron flow may be photoprotective. Later you'll learn more about cyclic electron flow as it relates to a particular adaptation of photosynthesis (C_4 plants; see Concept 10.4).

Whether ATP synthesis is driven by linear or cyclic electron flow, the actual mechanism is the same. Before we move on to consider the Calvin cycle, let's review chemiosmosis, the process that uses membranes to couple redox reactions to ATP production.

A Comparison of Chemiosmosis in Chloroplasts and Mitochondria

Chloroplasts and mitochondria generate ATP by the same basic mechanism: chemiosmosis. An electron transport chain pumps protons (H^+) across a membrane as electrons are passed through a series of carriers that are progressively more electronegative. Thus, electron transport chains transform redox energy to a proton-motive force, potential energy stored in the form of an H^+ gradient across a membrane. An ATP synthase complex in the same membrane couples the diffusion of hydrogen ions down their gradient to the phosphorylation of ADP, forming ATP.

Some of the electron carriers, including the iron-containing proteins called cytochromes, are very similar in chloroplasts and mitochondria. The ATP synthase complexes of the two organelles are also quite similar. But there are noteworthy differences between photophosphorylation in chloroplasts and oxidative phosphorylation in mitochondria. In chloroplasts, the high-energy electrons dropped down the transport chain come from water, while in mitochondria, they are extracted from organic molecules (which are thus oxidized). Chloroplasts do not need molecules from food to make ATP; their photosystems capture light energy and use it to drive the electrons from water to the top of the transport chain. In other words, mitochondria use chemiosmosis to transfer chemical energy from food molecules to ATP, whereas chloroplasts transform light energy into chemical energy in ATP.

Although the spatial organization of chemiosmosis differs slightly between chloroplasts and mitochondria, it is easy to see similarities in the two (**Figure 10.17**). The inner

▶ **Figure 10.17 Comparison of chemiosmosis in mitochondria and chloroplasts.** In both kinds of organelles, electron transport chains pump protons (H^+) across a membrane from a region of low H^+ concentration (light gray in this diagram) to one of high H^+ concentration (dark gray). The protons then diffuse back across the membrane through ATP synthase, driving the synthesis of ATP.

membrane of the mitochondrion pumps protons from the mitochondrial matrix out to the intermembrane space, which then serves as a reservoir of hydrogen ions. The thylakoid membrane of the chloroplast pumps protons from the stroma into the thylakoid space (interior of the thylakoid), which functions as the H^+ reservoir. If you imagine the cristae of mitochondria pinching off from the inner membrane, this may help you see how the thylakoid space and the intermembrane space are comparable spaces in the two organelles, while the mitochondrial matrix is analogous to the stroma of the chloroplast.

In the mitochondrion, protons diffuse down their concentration gradient from the intermembrane space through ATP synthase to the matrix, driving ATP synthesis. In the chloroplast, ATP is synthesized as the hydrogen ions diffuse from the thylakoid space back to the stroma through ATP synthase complexes, whose catalytic knobs are on the stroma side of the membrane (**Figure 10.18**). Thus, ATP forms in the stroma, where it is used to help drive sugar synthesis during the Calvin cycle.

The proton (H^+) gradient, or pH gradient, across the thylakoid membrane is substantial. When chloroplasts in an

▲ **Figure 10.18 The light reactions and chemiosmosis: Current model of the organization of the thylakoid membrane.**
The gold arrows track the linear electron flow outlined in Figure 10.14. At least three steps in the light reactions contribute to the H^+ gradient by increasing H^+ concentration in the thylakoid space: ❶ Water is split by photosystem II on the side of the membrane facing the thylakoid space; ❷ as plastoquinone (Pq) transfers electrons to the cytochrome complex, four protons are translocated across the membrane into the thylakoid space; and ❸ a hydrogen ion is removed from the stroma when it is taken up by $NADP^+$. Notice that in step 2, hydrogen ions are being pumped from the stroma into the thylakoid space, as in Figure 10.17. The diffusion of H^+ from the thylakoid space back to the stroma (along the H^+ concentration gradient) powers the ATP synthase. These light-driven reactions store chemical energy in NADPH and ATP, which shuttle the energy to the carbohydrate-producing Calvin cycle.

experimental setting are illuminated, the pH in the thylakoid space drops to about 5 (the H^+ concentration increases), and the pH in the stroma increases to about 8 (the H^+ concentration decreases). This gradient of three pH units corresponds to a thousandfold difference in H^+ concentration. If the lights are then turned off, the pH gradient is abolished, but it can quickly be restored by turning the lights back on. Experiments such as this provided strong evidence in support of the chemiosmotic model.

The currently-accepted model for the organization of the light-reaction "machinery" within the thylakoid membrane is based on several research studies. Each of the molecules and molecular complexes in the figure is present in numerous copies in each thylakoid. Notice that NADPH, like ATP, is produced on the side of the membrane facing the stroma, where the Calvin cycle reactions take place.

Let's summarize the light reactions. Electron flow pushes electrons from water, where they are at a low state of potential energy, ultimately to NADPH, where they are stored at a high state of potential energy. The light-driven electron flow also generates ATP. Thus, the equipment of the thylakoid membrane converts light energy to chemical energy stored in ATP and NADPH. (Oxygen is a by-product.) Let's now see how the Calvin cycle uses the products of the light reactions to synthesize sugar from CO_2.

CONCEPT CHECK 10.2

1. What color of light is *least* effective in driving photosynthesis? Explain.
2. In the light reactions, what is the initial electron donor? Where do the electrons finally end up?
3. **WHAT IF?** In an experiment, isolated chloroplasts placed in an illuminated solution with the appropriate chemicals can carry out ATP synthesis. Predict what would happen to the rate of synthesis if a compound is added to the solution that makes membranes freely permeable to hydrogen ions.

For suggested answers, see Appendix A.

CONCEPT 10.3

The Calvin cycle uses the chemical energy of ATP and NADPH to reduce CO_2 to sugar

The Calvin cycle is similar to the citric acid cycle in that a starting material is regenerated after some molecules enter the cycle and others exit the cycle. However, the citric acid cycle is catabolic, oxidizing acetyl CoA and using the energy to synthesize ATP. In contrast, the Calvin cycle is anabolic, building carbohydrates from smaller molecules

and consuming energy. Carbon enters the Calvin cycle in the form of CO_2 and leaves in the form of sugar. The cycle spends ATP as an energy source and consumes NADPH as reducing power for adding high-energy electrons to make the sugar.

As we mentioned previously (in Concept 10.1), the carbohydrate produced directly from the Calvin cycle is actually not glucose, but a three-carbon sugar; the name of this sugar is **glyceraldehyde 3-phosphate (G3P)**. For the net synthesis of *one* molecule of G3P, the cycle must take place three times, fixing *three* molecules of CO_2—one per turn of the cycle. (Recall that the term carbon fixation refers to the initial incorporation of CO_2 into organic material.) As we trace the steps of the cycle, it's important to keep in mind that we are following three molecules of CO_2 through the reactions. **Figure 10.19** divides the Calvin cycle into three phases: carbon fixation, reduction, and regeneration of the CO_2 acceptor.

Phase 1: Carbon fixation. The Calvin cycle incorporates each CO_2 molecule, one at a time, by attaching it to a five-carbon sugar named ribulose bisphosphate (abbreviated RuBP). The enzyme that catalyzes this first step is RuBP carboxylase-oxygenase, or **rubisco**. (This is the most abundant protein in chloroplasts and is also thought to be the most abundant protein on Earth.) The product of the reaction is a six-carbon intermediate that is short-lived because it is so energetically unstable that it immediately splits in half, forming two molecules of 3-phosphoglycerate (for each CO_2 fixed).

Phase 2: Reduction. Each molecule of 3-phosphoglycerate receives an additional phosphate group from ATP, becoming 1,3-bisphosphoglycerate. Next, a pair of electrons donated from NADPH reduces 1,3-bisphosphoglycerate, which also loses a phosphate group in the process, becoming glyceraldehyde 3-phosphate (G3P). Specifically, the electrons from NADPH reduce a carboyxl group on 1,3-bisphosphoglycerate to the aldehyde group of G3P, which stores more potential energy. G3P is a sugar—the same three-carbon sugar formed in glycolysis by the splitting of glucose (see Figure 9.9). Notice in Figure 10.19 that for every *three* molecules of CO_2 that enter the cycle, there are *six* molecules of G3P formed. But only one molecule of this three-carbon sugar can be counted as a net gain of carbohydrate because the rest are required to complete the cycle. The cycle began with 15 carbons' worth of carbohydrate in the form of three molecules of the five-carbon sugar RuBP. Now there are 18 carbons' worth of carbohydrate in the form of six molecules of G3P. One molecule exits the cycle to be used by the plant cell, but the other five molecules must be recycled to regenerate the three molecules of RuBP.

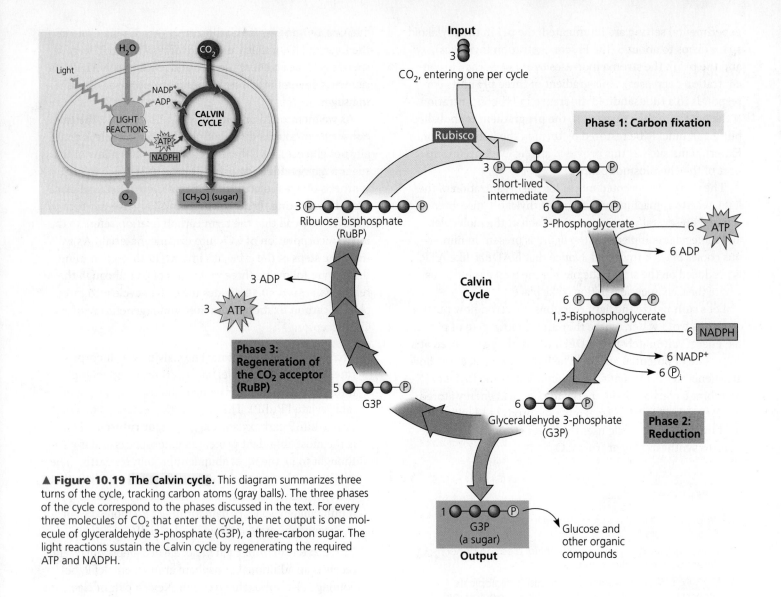

Input
3 ●●
CO_2, entering one per cycle

Phase 1: Carbon fixation

Rubisco

3 (P)●●●●●(P)
Short-lived
intermediate

6 ●●●(P)
3-Phosphoglycerate

6 ●●●(P)●●●(P)
Ribulose bisphosphate
(RuBP)

Calvin
Cycle

6 ATP
6 ADP

6 (P)●●●(P)
1,3-Bisphosphoglycerate

6 NADPH
6 NADP+
6 (P)ᵢ

3 ADP
3 ATP

**Phase 3:
Regeneration of
the CO_2 acceptor
(RuBP)**

5 ●●●(P)
G3P

6 ●●●(P)
Glyceraldehyde 3-phosphate
(G3P)

**Phase 2:
Reduction**

1 ●●●(P)
G3P
(a sugar)
Output

Glucose and
other organic
compounds

▲ **Figure 10.19 The Calvin cycle.** This diagram summarizes three turns of the cycle, tracking carbon atoms (gray balls). The three phases of the cycle correspond to the phases discussed in the text. For every three molecules of CO_2 that enter the cycle, the net output is one molecule of glyceraldehyde 3-phosphate (G3P), a three-carbon sugar. The light reactions sustain the Calvin cycle by regenerating the required ATP and NADPH.

Phase 3: Regeneration of the CO_2 acceptor (RuBP). In a complex series of reactions, the carbon skeletons of five molecules of G3P are rearranged by the last steps of the Calvin cycle into three molecules of RuBP. To accomplish this, the cycle spends three more molecules of ATP. The RuBP is now prepared to receive CO_2 again, and the cycle continues.

For the net synthesis of one G3P molecule, the Calvin cycle consumes a total of nine molecules of ATP and six molecules of NADPH. The light reactions regenerate the ATP and NADPH. The G3P spun off from the Calvin cycle becomes the starting material for metabolic pathways that synthesize other organic compounds, including glucose (formed by combining two molecules of G3P), the disaccharide sucrose, and other carbohydrates. Neither the light reactions nor the Calvin cycle alone can make sugar from CO_2. Photosynthesis is an emergent property of the intact chloroplast, which integrates the two stages of photosynthesis.

CONCEPT CHECK 10.3

1. To synthesize one glucose molecule, the Calvin cycle uses _____ molecules of CO_2, _____ molecules of ATP, and _____ molecules of NADPH.

2. How are the large numbers of ATP and NADPH molecules used during the Calvin cycle consistent with the high value of glucose as an energy source?

3. **WHAT IF?** Explain why a poison that inhibits an enzyme of the Calvin cycle will also inhibit the light reactions.

4. **DRAW IT** Redraw the cycle in Figure 10.19 using numerals to indicate the numbers of carbons instead of gray balls, multiplying at each step to ensure that you have accounted for all carbons. In what forms do the carbon atoms enter and leave the cycle?

5. **MAKE CONNECTIONS** Review Figures 9.9 and 10.19. Discuss the roles of intermediate and product played by glyceraldehyde 3-phosphate (G3P) in the two processes shown in these figures.

For suggested answers, see Appendix A.

CONCEPT 10.4

Alternative mechanisms of carbon fixation have evolved in hot, arid climates

EVOLUTION Ever since plants first moved onto land about 475 million years ago, they have been adapting to the problems of terrestrial life, particularly the problem of dehydration. In Chapters 29 and 36, we will consider anatomical adaptations that help plants conserve water, while in this chapter we are concerned with metabolic adaptations. The solutions often involve trade-offs. An important example is the compromise between photosynthesis and the prevention of excessive water loss from the plant. The CO_2 required for photosynthesis enters a leaf (and the resulting O_2 exits) via stomata, the pores on the leaf surface (see Figure 10.4). However, stomata are also the main avenues of transpiration, the evaporative loss of water from leaves. On a hot, dry day, most plants close their stomata, a response that conserves water. This response also reduces photosynthetic yield by limiting access to CO_2. With stomata even partially closed, CO_2 concentrations begin to decrease in the air spaces within the leaf, and the concentration of O_2 released from the light reactions begins to increase. These conditions within the leaf favor an apparently wasteful process called photorespiration.

Photorespiration: An Evolutionary Relic?

In most plants, initial fixation of carbon occurs via rubisco, the Calvin cycle enzyme that adds CO_2 to ribulose bisphosphate. Such plants are called **C_3 plants** because the first organic product of carbon fixation is a three-carbon compound, 3-phosphoglycerate (see Figure 10.19). Rice, wheat, and soybeans are C_3 plants that are important in agriculture. When their stomata partially close on hot, dry days, C_3 plants produce less sugar because the declining level of CO_2 in the leaf starves the Calvin cycle. In addition, rubisco is capable of binding O_2 in place of CO_2. As CO_2 becomes scarce within the air spaces of the leaf and O_2 builds up, rubisco adds O_2 to the Calvin cycle instead of CO_2. The product splits, and a two-carbon compound leaves the chloroplast. Peroxisomes and mitochondria within the plant cell rearrange and split this compound, releasing CO_2. The process is called **photorespiration** because it occurs in the light (*photo*) and consumes O_2 while producing CO_2 (*respiration*). However, unlike normal cellular respiration, photorespiration uses ATP rather than generating it. And unlike photosynthesis, photorespiration produces no sugar. In fact, photorespiration *decreases* photosynthetic output by siphoning organic material from the Calvin cycle and

releasing CO_2 that would otherwise be fixed. This CO_2 can eventually be fixed if it is still in the leaf once the CO_2 concentration is high enough. In the meantime, though, the process is energetically costly, much like a hamster running on its wheel.

How can we explain the existence of a metabolic process that seems to be counterproductive for the plant? According to one hypothesis, photorespiration is evolutionary baggage—a metabolic relic from a much earlier time when the atmosphere had less O_2 and more CO_2 than it does today. In the ancient atmosphere that prevailed when rubisco first evolved, the inability of the enzyme's active site to exclude O_2 would have made little difference. The hypothesis suggests that modern rubisco retains some of its chance affinity for O_2, which is now so concentrated in the atmosphere that a certain amount of photorespiration is inevitable.

We now know that, at least in some cases, photorespiration plays a protective role in plants. Plants that are impaired in their ability to carry out photorespiration (due to defective genes) are more susceptible to damage induced by excess light. Researchers consider this clear evidence that photorespiration acts to neutralize the otherwise damaging products of the light reactions, which build up when a low CO_2 concentration limits the progress of the Calvin cycle. Whether there are other benefits of photorespiration is still unknown. In many types of plants—including a significant number of crop plants—photorespiration drains away as much as 50% of the carbon fixed by the Calvin cycle. As heterotrophs that depend on carbon fixation in chloroplasts for our food, we naturally view photorespiration as wasteful. Indeed, if photorespiration could be reduced in certain plant species without otherwise affecting photosynthetic productivity, crop yields and food supplies might increase.

In some plant species, alternate modes of carbon fixation have evolved that minimize photorespiration and optimize the Calvin cycle—even in hot, arid climates. The two most important of these photosynthetic adaptations are C_4 photosynthesis and crassulacean acid metabolism (CAM).

C_4 Plants

The **C_4 plants** are so named because they preface the Calvin cycle with an alternate mode of carbon fixation that forms a four-carbon compound as its first product. The C_4 pathway is believed to have evolved independently at least 45 separate times and is used by several thousand species in at least 19 plant families. Among the C_4 plants important to agriculture are sugarcane and corn, members of the grass family.

The anatomy of a C_4 leaf is correlated with the mechanism of C_4 photosynthesis. In C_4 plants, there are two distinct types of photosynthetic cells: bundle-sheath cells and mesophyll cells. **Bundle-sheath cells** are arranged into tightly

Photosynthetic cells of C₄ plant leaf
- Mesophyll cell
- Bundle-sheath cell

Vein (vascular tissue)

C₄ leaf anatomy

Stoma

Mesophyll cell

PEP carboxylase

CO₂

The C₄ pathway

❶ In mesophyll cells, the enzyme PEP carboxylase adds carbon dioxide to PEP.

Oxaloacetate (4C)   PEP (3C)

ADP
ATP

Malate (4C)

Pyruvate (3C)

CO₂

Bundle-sheath cell

Calvin Cycle

Sugar

Vascular tissue

❷ A four-carbon compound (such as malate) conveys the atoms of the CO₂ into a bundle-sheath cell via plasmodesmata.

❸ In bundle-sheath cells, CO₂ is released and enters the Calvin cycle.

▲ **Figure 10.20 C₄ leaf anatomy and the C₄ pathway.** The structure and biochemical functions of the leaves of C₄ plants are an evolutionary adaptation to hot, dry climates. This adaptation maintains a CO₂ concentration in the bundle sheath that favors photosynthesis over photorespiration.

packed sheaths around the veins of the leaf (**Figure 10.20**). Between the bundle sheath and the leaf surface are the more loosely arranged mesophyll cells, which, in C₄ leaves, are closely associated and never more than two to three cells away from the bundle-sheath cells. The Calvin cycle is confined to the chloroplasts of the bundle-sheath cells. However, the Calvin cycle is preceded by incorporation of CO₂ into organic compounds in the mesophyll cells. See the numbered steps in Figure 10.20, which are also described here:

❶ The first step is carried out by an enzyme present only in mesophyll cells called **PEP carboxylase**. This enzyme adds CO₂ to phosphoenolpyruvate (PEP), forming the four-carbon product oxaloacetate. PEP carboxylase has a much higher affinity for CO₂ than does rubisco and no affinity for O₂. Therefore, PEP carboxylase can fix carbon efficiently when rubisco cannot—that is, when it is hot and dry and stomata are partially closed, causing CO₂ concentration in the leaf to be lower and O₂ concentration to be relatively higher.

❷ After the C₄ plant fixes carbon from CO₂, the mesophyll cells export their four-carbon products (malate in the example shown in Figure 10.20) to bundle-sheath cells through plasmodesmata (see Figure 6.29).

❸ Within the bundle-sheath cells, the four-carbon compounds release CO₂, which is reassimilated into organic material by rubisco and the Calvin cycle. The same reaction regenerates pyruvate, which is transported to mesophyll cells. There, ATP is used to convert pyruvate to PEP, allowing the reaction cycle to continue.

This ATP can be thought of, in a sense, as the "price" of concentrating CO₂ in the bundle-sheath cells. To generate this extra ATP, bundle-sheath cells carry out cyclic electron flow, the process described earlier in this chapter (see Figure 10.16). In fact, these cells contain PS I but no PS II, so cyclic electron flow is their only photosynthetic mode of generating ATP.

In effect, the mesophyll cells of a C₄ plant pump CO₂ into the bundle sheath, keeping the CO₂ concentration in the bundle-sheath cells high enough for rubisco to bind CO₂ rather than O₂. The cyclic series of reactions involving PEP carboxylase and the regeneration of PEP can be thought of as a CO₂-concentrating pump that is powered by ATP. In this way, C₄ photosynthesis spends ATP energy to minimize photorespiration and enhance sugar production. This adaptation is especially advantageous in hot regions with intense sunlight, where stomata partially close during the day, and it is in such environments that C₄ plants evolved and thrive today.

The concentration of CO₂ in the atmosphere has drastically increased since the Industrial Revolution began in the 1800s, and it continues to rise today due to human activities such as the burning of fossil fuels. The resulting global climate change, including an increase in average temperatures around the planet, may have far-reaching effects on plant species. Scientists are concerned that increasing CO₂ concentration and temperature may affect C₃ and C₄ plants differently, thus changing the relative abundance of these species in a given plant community.

Which type of plant would stand to gain more from increasing CO_2 levels? Recall that in C_3 plants, the binding of O_2 rather than CO_2 by rubisco leads to photorespiration, lowering the efficiency of photosynthesis. C_4 plants overcome this problem by concentrating CO_2 in the bundle-sheath cells at the cost of ATP. Rising CO_2 levels should benefit C_3 plants by lowering the amount of photorespiration that occurs. At the same time, rising temperatures have the opposite effect, increasing photorespiration. (Other factors such as water availability may also come into play.) In contrast, many C_4 plants could be largely unaffected by increasing CO_2 levels or temperature. Researchers have investigated aspects of this question in several studies; you can work with data from one such experiment in the **Scientific Skills Exercise**. In different regions, the particular combination of CO_2 concentration and temperature is likely to alter the balance of C_3 and C_4 plants in varying ways. The effects of such a widespread and variable change in community structure are unpredictable and thus a cause of legitimate concern.

CAM Plants

A second photosynthetic adaptation to arid conditions has evolved in many succulent (water-storing) plants, numerous cacti, pineapples, and representatives of several other plant families. These plants open their stomata during the night and close them during the day, just the reverse of how other plants behave. Closing stomata during the day helps desert plants conserve water, but it also prevents CO_2 from entering the leaves. During the night, when their stomata are open, these plants take up CO_2 and incorporate it into a variety of organic acids. This mode of carbon fixation is called **crassulacean acid metabolism**, or **CAM**, after the plant family Crassulaceae, the succulents in which the process was first discovered. The mesophyll cells of **CAM plants** store the organic acids they make during the night in their vacuoles until morning, when the stomata close. During the day, when the light reactions can supply ATP and NADPH for the Calvin cycle, CO_2 is released from the organic acids made the night before to become incorporated into sugar in the chloroplasts.

Notice in **Figure 10.21** that the CAM pathway is similar to the C_4 pathway in that carbon dioxide is first incorporated into organic intermediates before it enters the Calvin

Sugarcane

Pineapple

(a) Spatial separation of steps. In C_4 plants, carbon fixation and the Calvin cycle occur in different types of cells.

(b) Temporal separation of steps. In CAM plants, carbon fixation and the Calvin cycle occur in the same cell at different times.

▲ **Figure 10.21 C_4 and CAM photosynthesis compared.** Both adaptations are characterized by ❶ preliminary incorporation of CO_2 into organic acids, followed by ❷ transfer of CO_2 to the Calvin cycle. The C_4 and CAM pathways are two evolutionary solutions to the problem of maintaining photosynthesis with stomata partially or completely closed on hot, dry days.

cycle. The difference is that in C_4 plants, the initial steps of carbon fixation are separated structurally from the Calvin cycle, whereas in CAM plants, the two steps occur at separate times but within the same cell. (Keep in mind that CAM, C_4, and C_3 plants all eventually use the Calvin cycle to make sugar from carbon dioxide.)

CONCEPT CHECK 10.4

1. Describe how photorespiration lowers photosynthetic output for plants.
2. The presence of only PS I, not PS II, in the bundle-sheath cells of C_4 plants has an effect on O_2 concentration. What is that effect, and how might that benefit the plant?
3. **MAKE CONNECTIONS** Refer to the discussion of ocean acidification in Concept 3.3. Ocean acidification and changes in the distribution of C_3 and C_4 plants may seem to be two very different problems, but what do they have in common? Explain.
4. **WHAT IF?** How would you expect the relative abundance of C_3 versus C_4 and CAM species to change in a geographic region whose climate becomes much hotter and drier, with no change in CO_2 concentration?

For suggested answers, see Appendix A.

The Importance of Photosynthesis: *A Review*

In this chapter, we have followed photosynthesis from photons to food. The light reactions capture solar energy and use it to make ATP and transfer electrons from water to $NADP^+$, forming NADPH. The Calvin cycle uses the ATP and NADPH to produce sugar from carbon dioxide. The energy that enters the chloroplasts as sunlight becomes stored as chemical energy in organic compounds. The entire process is reviewed visually in **Figure 10.22**, where photosynthesis is also put in its natural context.

As for the fates of photosynthetic products, enzymes in the chloroplast and cytosol convert the G3P made in the Calvin cycle to many other organic compounds. In fact, the sugar made in the chloroplasts supplies the entire plant with chemical energy and carbon skeletons for the synthesis of all the major organic molecules of plant cells. About 50% of the organic material made by photosynthesis is consumed as fuel for cellular respiration in plant cell mitochondria.

Technically, green cells are the only autotrophic parts of the plant. The rest of the plant depends on organic molecules exported from leaves via veins (see Figure 10.22, top). In most plants, carbohydrate is transported out of the leaves to the rest of the plant in the form of sucrose, a disaccharide. After arriving at nonphotosynthetic cells, the sucrose provides raw material for cellular respiration and a multitude of anabolic pathways that synthesize proteins, lipids, and other products. A considerable amount of sugar in the form of glucose is linked together to make the polysaccharide cellulose (see Figure 5.6c), especially in plant cells that are still growing and maturing. Cellulose, the main ingredient of cell walls, is the most abundant organic molecule in the plant—and probably on the surface of the planet.

Most plants and other photosynthesizers make more organic material each day than they need to use as respiratory fuel and precursors for biosynthesis. They stockpile the extra sugar by synthesizing starch, storing some in the chloroplasts themselves and some in storage cells of roots, tubers, seeds, and fruits. In accounting for the consumption of the food molecules produced by photosynthesis, let's not forget that most plants lose leaves, roots, stems, fruits, and sometimes their entire bodies to heterotrophs, including humans.

On a global scale, photosynthesis is the process responsible for the presence of oxygen in our atmosphere.

Furthermore, while each chloroplast is minuscule, their collective productivity in terms of food production is prodigious: Photosynthesis makes an estimated 150 billion metric tons of carbohydrate per year (a metric ton is 1,000 kg, about 1.1 tons). That's organic matter equivalent in mass to a stack of about 60 trillion biology textbooks—17 stacks of books reaching from Earth to the sun! No chemical process is more important than photosynthesis to the welfare of life on Earth.

In Chapters 5 through 10, you have learned about many activities of cells. **Figure 10.23** integrates these processes in the context of a working plant cell. As you study the figure, reflect on how each process fits into the big picture: As the most basic unit of living organisms, a cell performs all functions characteristic of life.

▼ **Figure 10.22 A review of photosynthesis.** This diagram shows the main reactants and products of photosynthesis as they move through the tissues of a tree (left) and a chloroplast (right).

MAKE CONNECTIONS *Can plants use the sugar they produce during photosynthesis to directly power the work of the cell? Explain. (See Figures 8.10, 8.11, and 9.6.)*

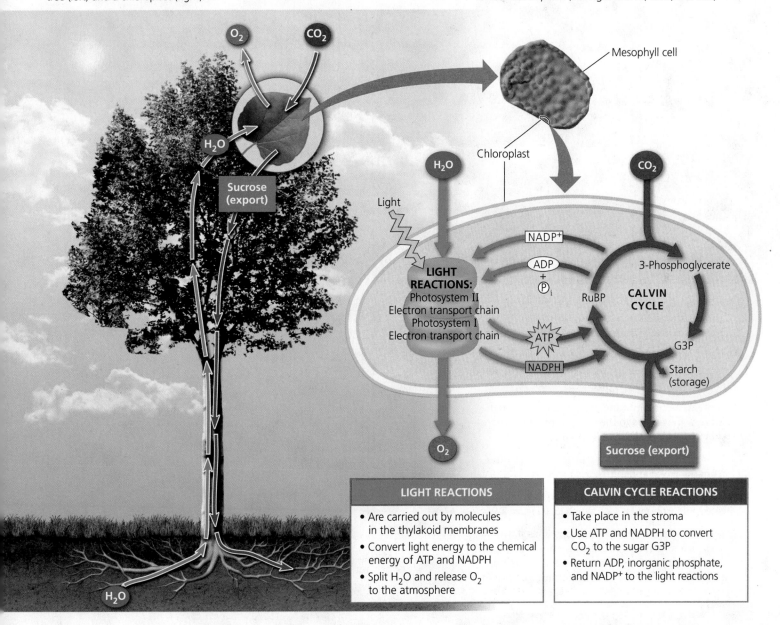

The Working Cell

This figure illustrates how a generalized plant cell functions, integrating the cellular activities you learned about in Chapters 5–10.

DNA

Nucleus ➊

mRNA

Nuclear pore

➋

Protein in vesicle

Rough endoplasmic reticulum (ER)

Protein

➌

Ribosome   mRNA

➍

Vesicle forming

Golgi apparatus

Protein

➏

Plasma membrane

➎

Cell wall

Flow of Genetic Information in the Cell: DNA → RNA → Protein (Chapters 5–7)

➊ In the nucleus, DNA serves as a template for the synthesis of mRNA, which moves to the cytoplasm. *See Figures 5.23 and 6.9.*

➋ mRNA attaches to a ribosome, which remains free in the cytosol or binds to the rough ER. Proteins are synthesized. *See Figures 5.23 and 6.10.*

➌ Proteins and membrane produced by the rough ER flow in vesicles to the Golgi apparatus, where they are processed. *See Figures 6.15 and 7.9.*

➍ Transport vesicles carrying proteins pinch off from the Golgi apparatus. *See Figure 6.15.*

➎ Some vesicles merge with the plasma membrane, releasing proteins by exocytosis. *See Figure 7.9.*

➏ Proteins synthesized on free ribosomes stay in the cell and perform specific functions; examples include the enzymes that catalyze the reactions of cellular respiration and photosynthesis. *See Figures 9.7, 9.9, and 10.19.*

Energy Transformations in the Cell: Photosynthesis and Cellular Respiration (Chapters 8–10)

7 In chloroplasts, the process of photosynthesis uses the energy of light to convert CO_2 and H_2O to organic molecules, with O_2 as a by-product. *See Figure 10.22.*

8 In mitochondria, organic molecules are broken down by cellular respiration, capturing energy in molecules of ATP, which are used to power the work of the cell, such as protein synthesis and active transport. CO_2 and H_2O are by-products. *See Figures 8.9–8.11, 9.2, and 9.16.*

Movement Across Cell Membranes (Chapter 7)

9 Water diffuses into and out of the cell directly through the plasma membrane and by facilitated diffusion through aquaporins. *See Figure 7.1.*

10 By passive transport, the CO_2 used in photosynthesis diffuses into the cell and the O_2 formed as a by-product of photosynthesis diffuses out of the cell. Both solutes move down their concentration gradients. *See Figures 7.10 and 10.22.*

11 In active transport, energy (usually supplied by ATP) is used to transport a solute against its concentration gradient. *See Figure 7.16.*

Exocytosis (shown in step 5) and endocytosis move larger materials out of and into the cell. *See Figures 7.9 and 7.19.*

Vacuole

7 Photosynthesis in chloroplast

CO_2

H_2O

ATP

Organic molecules

O_2

8 Cellular respiration in mitochondrion

ATP

ATP

Transport pump

ATP

11

O_2

10

CO_2

9

H_2O

MAKE CONNECTIONS *The first enzyme that functions in glycolysis is hexokinase. In this plant cell, describe the entire process by which this enzyme is produced and where it functions, specifying the locations for each step. (See Figures 5.18, 5.23, and 9.9.)*

ANIMATION **BioFlix** Visit the Study Area in **MasteringBiology** for BioFlix® 3-D Animations in Chapters 6, 7, 9, and 10. BioFlix Tutorials can also be assigned in MasteringBiology.

SUMMARY OF KEY CONCEPTS

CONCEPT 10.1

Photosynthesis converts light energy to the chemical energy of food (pp. 187–190)

- In **autotrophic** eukaryotes, photosynthesis occurs in chloroplasts, organelles containing **thylakoids**. Stacks of thylakoids form grana. **Photosynthesis** is summarized as

  $$6 \, CO_2 + 12 \, H_2O + \text{Light energy} \rightarrow C_6H_{12}O_6 + 6 \, O_2 + 6 \, H_2O.$$

  Chloroplasts split water into hydrogen and oxygen, incorporating the electrons of hydrogen into sugar molecules. Photosynthesis is a redox process: H_2O is oxidized, and CO_2 is reduced. The **light reactions** in the thylakoid membranes split water, releasing O_2, producing ATP, and forming **NADPH**. The **Calvin cycle** in the **stroma** forms sugar from CO_2, using ATP for energy and NADPH for reducing power.

  ? *Compare the roles of CO_2 and H_2O in respiration and photosynthesis.*

CONCEPT 10.2

The light reactions convert solar energy to the chemical energy of ATP and NADPH (pp. 190–199)

- Light is a form of electromagnetic energy. The colors we see as **visible light** include those **wavelengths** that drive photosynthesis. A pigment absorbs light of specific wavelengths; **chlorophyll *a*** is the main photosynthetic pigment in plants. Other accessory pigments absorb different wavelengths of light and pass the energy on to chlorophyll *a*.
- A pigment goes from a ground state to an excited state when a **photon** of light boosts one of the pigment's electrons to a higher-energy orbital. This excited state is unstable. Electrons from isolated pigments tend to fall back to the ground state, giving off heat and/or light.
- A **photosystem** is composed of a **reaction-center complex** surrounded by **light-harvesting complexes** that funnel the energy of photons to the reaction-center complex. When a special pair of reaction-center chlorophyll *a* molecules absorbs energy, one of its electrons is boosted to a higher energy level and transferred to the **primary electron acceptor**. **Photosystem II** contains P680 chlorophyll *a* molecules in the reaction-center complex; **photosystem I** contains P700 molecules.
- **Linear electron flow** during the light reactions uses both photosystems and produces NADPH, ATP, and oxygen:

- **Cyclic electron flow** employs only one photosystem, producing ATP but no NADPH or O_2.
- During chemiosmosis in both mitochondria and chloroplasts, electron transport chains generate an H^+ gradient across a membrane. ATP synthase uses this proton-motive force to make ATP.

  ? *The absorption spectrum of chlorophyll a differs from the action spectrum of photosynthesis. Explain this observation.*

CONCEPT 10.3

The Calvin cycle uses the chemical energy of ATP and NADPH to reduce CO_2 to sugar (pp. 199–200)

- The Calvin cycle occurs in the stroma, using electrons from NADPH and energy from ATP. One molecule of **G3P** exits the cycle per three CO_2 molecules fixed and is converted to glucose and other organic molecules.

DRAW IT *On the diagram above, draw where ATP and NADPH are used and where rubisco functions. Describe these steps.*

CONCEPT 10.4

Alternative mechanisms of carbon fixation have evolved in hot, arid climates (pp. 201–207)

- On dry, hot days, **C_3 plants** close their stomata, conserving water. Oxygen from the light reactions builds up. In **photorespiration**, O_2 substitutes for CO_2 in the active site of rubisco. This process consumes organic fuel and releases CO_2 without producing ATP or carbohydrate. Photorespiration may be an evolutionary relic, and it may play a photoprotective role.
- **C_4 plants** minimize the cost of photorespiration by incorporating CO_2 into four-carbon compounds in mesophyll cells. These compounds are exported to **bundle-sheath cells**, where they release carbon dioxide for use in the Calvin cycle.
- **CAM plants** open their stomata at night, incorporating CO_2 into organic acids, which are stored in mesophyll cells. During the day, the stomata close, and the CO_2 is released from the organic acids for use in the Calvin cycle.
- Organic compounds produced by photosynthesis provide the energy and building material for Earth's ecosystems.

  ? *Why are C_4 and CAM photosynthesis more energetically expensive than C_3 photosynthesis? What climate conditions would favor C_4 and CAM plants?*

TEST YOUR UNDERSTANDING

LEVEL 1: KNOWLEDGE/COMPREHENSION

1. The light reactions of photosynthesis supply the Calvin cycle with
   a. light energy.
   b. CO_2 and ATP.
   c. H_2O and NADPH.
   d. ATP and NADPH.

2. Which of the following sequences correctly represents the flow of electrons during photosynthesis?
   a. $NADPH \rightarrow O_2 \rightarrow CO_2$
   b. $H_2O \rightarrow NADPH \rightarrow$ Calvin cycle
   c. $H_2O \rightarrow$ photosystem I $\rightarrow$ photosystem II
   d. $NADPH \rightarrow$ electron transport chain $\rightarrow O_2$

3. How is photosynthesis similar in C_4 plants and CAM plants?
   a. In both cases, only photosystem I is used.
   b. Both types of plants make sugar without the Calvin cycle.
   c. In both cases, rubisco is not used to fix carbon initially.
   d. Both types of plants make most of their sugar in the dark.

4. Which of the following statements is a correct distinction between autotrophs and heterotrophs?
   a. Autotrophs, but not heterotrophs, can nourish themselves beginning with CO_2 and other nutrients that are inorganic.
   b. Only heterotrophs require chemical compounds from the environment.
   c. Cellular respiration is unique to heterotrophs.
   d. Only heterotrophs have mitochondria.

5. Which of the following does *not* occur during the Calvin cycle?
   a. carbon fixation
   b. oxidation of NADPH
   c. release of oxygen
   d. regeneration of the CO_2 acceptor

LEVEL 2: APPLICATION/ANALYSIS

6. In mechanism, photophosphorylation is most similar to
   a. substrate-level phosphorylation in glycolysis.
   b. oxidative phosphorylation in cellular respiration.
   c. carbon fixation.
   d. reduction of $NADP^+$.

7. Which process is most directly driven by light energy?
   a. creation of a pH gradient by pumping protons across the thylakoid membrane
   b. reduction of $NADP^+$ molecules
   c. removal of electrons from chlorophyll molecules
   d. ATP synthesis

LEVEL 3: SYNTHESIS/EVALUATION

8. **SCIENCE, TECHNOLOGY, AND SOCIETY**
   Scientific evidence indicates that the CO_2 added to the air by the burning of wood and fossil fuels is contributing to global warming, a rise in global temperature. Tropical rain forests are estimated to be responsible for approximately 20% of global photosynthesis, yet the consumption of large amounts of CO_2 by living trees is thought to make little or no *net* contribution to reduction of global warming. Why might this be? (*Hint*: What processes in both living and dead trees produce CO_2?)

9. **EVOLUTION CONNECTION**
   Photorespiration can decrease soybeans' photosynthetic output by about 50%. Would you expect this figure to be higher or lower in wild relatives of soybeans? Why?

10. **SCIENTIFIC INQUIRY**
    MAKE CONNECTIONS The following diagram represents an experiment with isolated thylakoids. The thylakoids were first made acidic by soaking them in a solution at pH 4. After the thylakoid space reached pH 4, the thylakoids were transferred to a basic solution at pH 8. The thylakoids then made ATP in the dark. (See Concept 3.3 to review pH.)

    Draw an enlargement of part of the thylakoid membrane in the beaker with the solution at pH 8. Draw ATP synthase. Label the areas of high H^+ concentration and low H^+ concentration. Show the direction protons flow through the enzyme, and show the reaction where ATP is synthesized. Would ATP end up in the thylakoid or outside of it? Explain why the thylakoids in the experiment were able to make ATP in the dark.

11. **WRITE ABOUT A THEME: ENERGY AND MATTER**
    Life is solar powered. Almost all the producers of the biosphere depend on energy from the sun to produce the organic molecules that supply the energy and carbon skeletons needed for life. In a short essay (100–150 words), describe how the process of photosynthesis in the chloroplasts of plants transforms the energy of sunlight into the chemical energy of sugar molecules.

12. **SYNTHESIZE YOUR KNOWLEDGE**

    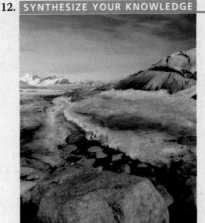

    The photo shows "watermelon snow" in Antarctica, caused by a species of photosynthetic green algae that thrives in subzero temperatures (*Chlamydomonas nivalis*). These algae are also found in high altitude year-round snowfields. In both locations, UV light levels tend to be high. Based on what you learned in this chapter, propose an explanation for why this photosynthetic alga appears reddish-pink.

For selected answers, see Appendix A.

MasteringBiology®

Students Go to **MasteringBiology** for assignments, the eText, and the Study Area with practice tests, animations, and activities.

Instructors Go to **MasteringBiology** for automatically graded tutorials and questions that you can assign to your students, plus Instructor Resources.

11
Cell Communication

KEY CONCEPTS

11.1 External signals are converted to responses within the cell

11.2 Reception: A signaling molecule binds to a receptor protein, causing it to change shape

11.3 Transduction: Cascades of molecular interactions relay signals from receptors to target molecules in the cell

11.4 Response: Cell signaling leads to regulation of transcription or cytoplasmic activities

11.5 Apoptosis integrates multiple cell-signaling pathways

▲ Figure 11.1 How does cell signaling trigger the desperate flight of this impala?

Cellular Messaging

The impala in **Figure 11.1** flees for its life, racing to escape the predatory cheetah nipping at its heels. The impala is breathing rapidly, its heart pounding and its legs pumping furiously. These physiological functions are all part of the impala's "fight-or-flight" response, driven by hormones released from its adrenal glands at times of stress—in this case, upon sensing the cheetah. What systems of cell-to-cell communication allow the trillions of cells in the impala to "talk" to each other, coordinating their activities?

Cells can signal to each other and interpret the signals they receive from other cells and the environment. The signals may include light and touch, but are most often chemicals. The flight response shown here is triggered by a signaling molecule called epinephrine (also called adrenaline; see the model to the left). Studying cell communication, biologists have discovered ample evidence for the evolutionary relatedness of all life. The same small set of cell-signaling mechanisms shows up again and again in diverse species, in processes ranging from bacterial signaling to embryonic development to cancer. In this chapter, we focus on the main mechanisms by which cells receive, process, and respond to chemical signals sent from other cells. We will also consider *apoptosis*, a type of programmed cell death that integrates input from multiple signaling pathways.

▶ Epinephrine

210

CONCEPT 11.1

External signals are converted to responses within the cell

What does a "talking" cell say to a "listening" cell, and how does the latter cell respond to the message? Let's approach these questions by first looking at communication among microorganisms.

Evolution of Cell Signaling

EVOLUTION One topic of cell "conversation" is sex. Cells of the yeast *Saccharomyces cerevisiae*—which are used to make bread, wine, and beer—identify their mates by chemical signaling. There are two sexes, or mating types, called **a** and **α** (Figure 11.2). Each type secretes a specific factor that binds to receptors only on the other type of cell. When exposed to each other's mating factors, a pair of cells of opposite type change shape, grow toward each other, and fuse (mate). The new **a/α** cell contains all the genes of both original cells, a combination of genetic resources that provides advantages to the cell's descendants, which arise by subsequent cell divisions.

Once received by the yeast cell surface receptor, a mating signal is changed, or *transduced*, into a form that brings

about the cellular response of mating. This occurs in a series of steps called a *signal transduction pathway*. Many such pathways exist in both yeast and animal cells. In fact, the molecular details of signal transduction in yeasts and mammals are strikingly similar, even though their last common ancestor lived over a billion years ago. This suggests that early versions of cell-signaling mechanisms evolved well before the first multicellular creatures appeared on Earth.

Scientists think that signaling mechanisms first evolved in ancient prokaryotes and single-celled eukaryotes and then were adopted for new uses by their multicellular descendants. Cell signaling is critical in the microbial world (Figure 11.3). Bacterial cells secrete molecules that can be detected by other bacterial cells. Sensing the concentration of such signaling molecules allows bacteria to monitor the local density of cells, a phenomenon called *quorum sensing*. Quorum sensing allows bacterial populations to coordinate their behaviors in activities that require a given number

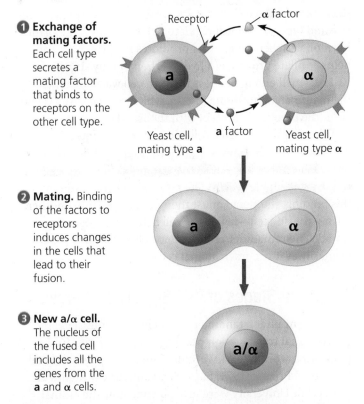

1 Exchange of mating factors. Each cell type secretes a mating factor that binds to receptors on the other cell type.

2 Mating. Binding of the factors to receptors induces changes in the cells that lead to their fusion.

3 New a/α cell. The nucleus of the fused cell includes all the genes from the **a** and **α** cells.

▲ **Figure 11.2 Communication between mating yeast cells.** *Saccharomyces cerevisiae* cells use chemical signaling to identify cells of opposite mating type and initiate the mating process. The two mating types and their corresponding chemical signaling molecules, or mating factors, are called **a** and **α**.

1 Individual rod-shaped cells

0.5 mm

2 Aggregation in progress

2.5 mm

3 Spore-forming structure (fruiting body)

Fruiting bodies

▲ **Figure 11.3 Communication among bacteria.** Soil-dwelling bacteria called myxobacteria ("slime bacteria") use chemical signals to share information about nutrient availability. When food is scarce, starving cells secrete a molecule that stimulates neighboring cells to aggregate. The cells form a structure, called a fruiting body, that produces thick-walled spores capable of surviving until the environment improves. The bacteria shown here are *Myxococcus xanthus* (steps 1–3, SEMs; lower photo, LM).

of cells acting synchronously. One example is formation of a *biofilm*, an aggregation of bacterial cells adhered to a surface. The cells in the biofilm generally derive nutrition from the surface they are on. You have probably encountered biofilms many times, perhaps without realizing it. The slimy coating on a fallen log or on leaves lying on a forest path, and even the film on your teeth each morning, are examples of bacterial biofilms. (In fact, tooth-brushing disrupts biofilms that would otherwise cause cavities.) The formation of biofilms requires a sophisticated communication system, the basis of which is cell signaling.

Local and Long-Distance Signaling

Like bacteria or yeast cells, cells in a multicellular organism usually communicate via signaling molecules targeted for cells that may or may not be immediately adjacent. As we saw in Chapters 6 and 7, eukaryotic cells may communicate by direct contact, one type of local signaling **(Figure 11.4)**. Both animals and plants have cell junctions that, where present, directly connect the cytoplasms of adjacent cells **(Figure 11.4a)**. In these cases, signaling substances dissolved in the cytosol can pass freely between adjacent cells. Moreover, animal cells may communicate via direct contact between membrane-bound cell-surface molecules in a process called cell-cell recognition **(Figure 11.4b)**. This sort of local signaling is especially important in embryonic development and the immune response.

In many other cases of local signaling, messenger molecules are secreted by the signaling cell. Some of these travel

only short distances; such local regulators influence cells in the vicinity. One class of local regulators in animals, *growth factors*, are compounds that stimulate nearby target cells to grow and divide. Numerous cells can simultaneously receive and respond to the molecules of growth factor produced by a single cell in their vicinity. This type of local signaling in animals is called *paracrine signaling* **(Figure 11.5a)**.

Another, more specialized type of local signaling called *synaptic signaling* occurs in the animal nervous system **(Figure 11.5b)**. An electrical signal along a nerve cell triggers the secretion of neurotransmitter molecules. These molecules act as chemical signals, diffusing across the synapse—the narrow space between the nerve cell and its target cell—triggering a response in the target cell.

Beyond communication through plasmodesmata (plant cell junctions), local signaling in plants is not as well understood. Because of their cell walls, plants use mechanisms different from those operating locally in animals.

Both animals and plants use chemicals called **hormones** for long-distance signaling. In hormonal signaling in animals, also known as *endocrine signaling*, specialized cells release hormone molecules, which travel via the circulatory system to other parts of the body, where they reach target cells that can recognize and respond to the hormones **(Figure 11.5c)**. Plant hormones (often called *plant growth regulators*) sometimes travel in vessels but more often reach their targets by moving through cells or by diffusing through the air as a gas (see Concept 39.2). Hormones vary widely in size and type, as do local regulators. For instance, the plant hormone ethylene, a gas that promotes fruit ripening and helps regulate growth, is a hydrocarbon of only six atoms (C_2H_4), small enough to pass through cell walls. In contrast, the mammalian hormone insulin, which regulates sugar levels in the blood, is a protein with thousands of atoms.

What happens when a cell encounters a secreted signaling molecule? The ability of a cell to respond is determined by whether it has a specific receptor molecule that can bind to the signaling molecule. The information conveyed by this binding, the signal, must then be changed into another form—transduced—inside the cell before the cell can respond. The remainder of the chapter discusses this process, primarily as it occurs in animal cells.

The Three Stages of Cell Signaling: *A Preview*

Our current understanding of how chemical messengers act via signal transduction pathways had its origins in the pioneering work of Earl W. Sutherland, whose research led to a Nobel Prize in 1971. Sutherland and his colleagues at Vanderbilt University were investigating how the animal hormone epinephrine (adrenaline) stimulates the breakdown of the storage polysaccharide glycogen within liver cells and skeletal muscle cells. Glycogen breakdown releases the sugar glucose 1-phosphate, which the cell converts

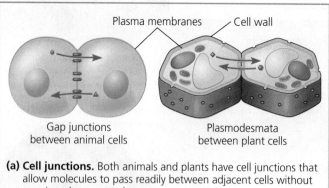

Plasma membranes   Cell wall

Gap junctions
between animal cells

Plasmodesmata
between plant cells

(a) Cell junctions. Both animals and plants have cell junctions that allow molecules to pass readily between adjacent cells without crossing plasma membranes.

(b) Cell-cell recognition. Two cells in an animal may communicate by interaction between molecules protruding from their surfaces.

▲ **Figure 11.4 Communication by direct contact between cells.**

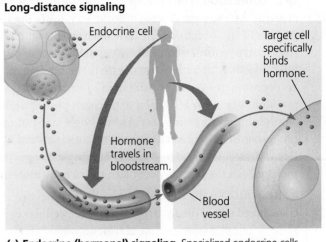

Local signaling

Target cells

Secreting cell

Secretory vesicles

Local regulator

(a) Paracrine signaling. A secreting cell acts on nearby target cells by secreting molecules of a local regulator (a growth factor, for example).

Electrical signal triggers release of neurotransmitter.

Neurotransmitter diffuses across synapse.

Target cell

(b) Synaptic signaling. A nerve cell releases neurotransmitter molecules into a synapse, stimulating the target cell, such as a muscle or nerve cell.

Long-distance signaling

Endocrine cell

Target cell specifically binds hormone.

Hormone travels in bloodstream.

Blood vessel

(c) Endocrine (hormonal) signaling. Specialized endocrine cells secrete hormones into body fluids, often blood. Hormones reach virtually all body cells, but are bound only by some cells.

▲ **Figure 11.5 Local and long-distance cell signaling by secreted molecules in animals.** In both local and long-distance signaling, only specific target cells that can recognize a given signaling molecule will respond to it.

to glucose 6-phosphate. The liver or muscle cell can then use this compound, an early intermediate in glycolysis, for energy production. Alternatively, the compound can be stripped of phosphate and released from the cell into the blood as glucose, which can fuel cells throughout the body. Thus, one effect of epinephrine is the mobilization of fuel reserves, which can be used by the animal to either defend itself (fight) or escape whatever elicited a scare (flight). (The impala in Figure 11.1 is obviously engaged in the latter.)

Sutherland's research team discovered that epinephrine stimulates glycogen breakdown by somehow activating a cytosolic enzyme, glycogen phosphorylase. However, when epinephrine was added to a test-tube mixture containing the enzyme and its substrate, glycogen, no breakdown occurred. Glycogen phosphorylase could be activated by epinephrine only when the hormone was added to *intact* cells

in a solution. This result told Sutherland two things. First, epinephrine does not interact directly with the enzyme responsible for glycogen breakdown; an intermediate step or series of steps must be occurring inside the cell. Second, the plasma membrane itself is necessary for transmission of the signal to take place.

Sutherland's early work suggested that the process going on at the receiving end of a cellular conversation can be dissected into three stages: reception, transduction, and response **(Figure 11.6):**

❶ Reception. Reception is the target cell's detection of a signaling molecule coming from outside the cell. A chemical signal is "detected" when the signaling molecule binds to a receptor protein located at the cell's surface (or inside the cell, to be discussed later).

▶ **Figure 11.6 Overview of cell signaling.** From the perspective of the cell receiving the message, cell signaling can be divided into three stages: signal reception, signal transduction, and cellular response. When reception occurs at the plasma membrane, as shown here, the transduction stage is usually a pathway of several steps, with each specific relay molecule in the pathway bringing about a change in the next molecule. The final molecule in the pathway triggers the cell's response.

❓ *How does the epinephrine in Sutherland's experiment fit into this diagram of cell signaling?*

EXTRACELLULAR FLUID

CYTOPLASM

Plasma membrane

❶ **Reception** ❷ **Transduction** ❸ **Response**

Receptor

Three relay molecules in a signal transduction pathway

Activation of cellular response

Signaling molecule

❷ Transduction. The binding of the signaling molecule changes the receptor protein in some way, initiating the process of transduction. The transduction stage converts the signal to a form that can bring about a specific cellular response. In Sutherland's system, the binding of epinephrine to a receptor protein in a liver cell's plasma membrane leads to activation of glycogen phosphorylase. Transduction sometimes occurs in a single step but more often requires a sequence of changes in a series of different molecules—a **signal transduction pathway**. The molecules in the pathway are often called relay molecules.

❸ Response. In the third stage of cell signaling, the transduced signal finally triggers a specific cellular response. The response may be almost any imaginable cellular activity—such as catalysis by an enzyme (for example, glycogen phosphorylase), rearrangement of the cytoskeleton, or activation of specific genes in the nucleus. The cell-signaling process helps ensure that crucial activities like these occur in the right cells, at the right time, and in proper coordination with the activities of other cells of the organism. We'll now explore the mechanisms of cell signaling in more detail, including a discussion of regulation and termination of the process.

CONCEPT CHECK 11.1

1. Explain how signaling is involved in ensuring that yeast cells fuse only with cells of the opposite mating type.

2. In liver cells, glycogen phosphorylase acts in which of the three stages of the signaling pathway associated with an epinephrine-initiated signal?

3. **WHAT IF?** When epinephrine is mixed with glycogen phosphorylase and glycogen in a test tube, is glucose 1-phosphate generated? Why or why not?

For suggested answers, see Appendix A.

CONCEPT 11.2

Reception: A signaling molecule binds to a receptor protein, causing it to change shape

A radio station broadcasts its signal indiscriminately, but it can be picked up only by radios tuned to the right frequency: Reception of the signal depends on the receiver. Similarly, the signals emitted by an **a** yeast cell are "heard" only by its prospective mates, **α** cells. In the case of the epinephrine circulating throughout the bloodstream of the impala in Figure 11.1, the hormone encounters many types of cells, but only certain target cells detect and react to the hormone molecule. A receptor protein on or in the target cell allows the cell to "hear" the signal and respond to it. The signaling

molecule is complementary in shape to a specific site on the receptor and attaches there, like a key in a lock. The signaling molecule acts as a **ligand**, the term for a molecule that specifically binds to another molecule, often a larger one. Ligand binding generally causes a receptor protein to undergo a change in shape. For many receptors, this shape change directly activates the receptor, enabling it to interact with other cellular molecules. For other kinds of receptors, the immediate effect of ligand binding is to cause the aggregation of two or more receptor molecules, which leads to further molecular events inside the cell. Most signal receptors are plasma membrane proteins, but others are located inside the cell. We discuss both of these types next.

Receptors in the Plasma Membrane

Cell-surface receptor proteins play crucial roles in the biological systems of animals. The largest family of human cell surface receptors are the nearly 1,000 G protein-coupled receptors (GPCRs); an example is shown in **(Figure 11.7)**.

Most water-soluble signaling molecules bind to specific sites on transmembrane receptor proteins that transmit information from the extracellular environment to the inside of the cell. We can see how cell-surface transmembrane receptors work by looking at three major types: G protein-coupled receptors (GPCRs), receptor tyrosine kinases, and ion channel receptors. These receptors are discussed and illustrated in **Figure 11.8**; study this figure before going on.

Given the many important functions of cell-surface receptors, it is not surprising that their malfunctions are associated with many human diseases, including cancer, heart disease, and asthma. To better understand and treat these conditions, a major focus of both university research teams and the pharmaceutical industry has been to analyze the structure of these receptors.

▲ **Figure 11.7 The structure of a G protein-coupled receptor (GPCR).** Shown here is a model of the human β₂-adrenergic receptor in the presence of a molecule mimicking the natural ligand (green in the model) and cholesterol (orange). Two receptor molecules (blue) are shown as ribbon models in a side view within the plasma membrane.

G Protein-Coupled Receptors

Signaling molecule binding site

Segment that interacts with G proteins

G protein-coupled receptor

A **G protein-coupled receptor** (GPCR) is a cell-surface transmembrane receptor that works with the help of a **G protein**, a protein that binds the energy-rich molecule GTP. Many different signaling molecules—including yeast mating factors, epinephrine (adrenaline) and many other hormones, as well as neurotransmitters—use GPCRs. These receptors vary in the binding sites for their signaling molecules (often referred to as their ligands) and also for different types of G proteins inside the cell. Nevertheless, GPCR proteins are all remarkably similar in structure. In fact, they make up a large family of eukaryotic receptor proteins with a secondary structure in which the single polypeptide, represented here in a ribbon model, has seven transmembrane α helices, outlined with cylinders and depicted in a row for clarity. Specific loops between the helices (here, the loops on the right) form binding sites for signaling molecules (outside the cell) and G proteins (on the cytoplasmic side).

GPCR-based signaling systems are extremely widespread and diverse in their functions, including roles in embryonic development and sensory reception. In humans, for example, vision, smell, and taste depend on GPCRs. Similarities in structure in G proteins and GPCRs in diverse organisms suggest that G proteins and their associated receptors evolved very early among eukaryotes.

Malfunctions of the associated G proteins themselves are involved in many human diseases, including bacterial infections. The bacteria that cause cholera, pertussis (whooping cough), and botulism, among others, make their victims ill by producing toxins that interfere with G protein function. Pharmacologists now realize that up to 60% of all medicines used today exert their effects by influencing G protein pathways.

G protein-coupled receptor — Plasma membrane — G protein (inactive) — GDP — Enzyme — CYTOPLASM

❶ Loosely attached to the cytoplasmic side of the membrane, the G protein functions as a molecular switch that is either on or off, depending on which of two guanine nucleotides is attached, GDP or GTP—hence the term *G protein*. (GTP, or guanosine triphosphate, is similar to ATP.) When GDP is bound to the G protein, as shown above, the G protein is inactive. The receptor and G protein work together with another protein, usually an enzyme.

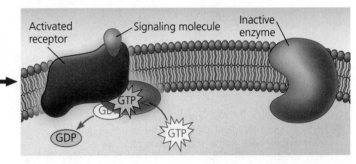

Activated receptor — Signaling molecule — Inactive enzyme — GTP — GDP — GDP — GTP

❷ When the appropriate signaling molecule binds to the extracellular side of the receptor, the receptor is activated and changes shape. Its cytoplasmic side then binds an inactive G protein, causing a GTP to displace the GDP. This activates the G protein.

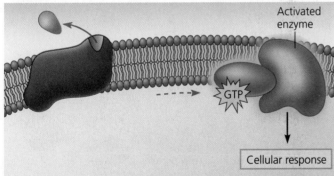

Activated enzyme — GTP — Cellular response

❸ The activated G protein dissociates from the receptor, diffuses along the membrane, and then binds to an enzyme, altering the enzyme's shape and activity. Once activated, the enzyme can trigger the next step leading to a cellular response. Binding of signaling molecules is reversible: Like other ligands, they bind and dissociate many times. The ligand concentration outside the cell determines how often a ligand is bound and causes signaling.

GDP — Pᵢ

❹ The changes in the enzyme and G protein are only temporary because the G protein also functions as a GTPase enzyme—in other words, it then hydrolyzes its bound GTP to GDP and P_i. Now inactive again, the G protein leaves the enzyme, which returns to its original state. The G protein is now available for reuse. The GTPase function of the G protein allows the pathway to shut down rapidly when the signaling molecule is no longer present.

Continued on next page

Exploring Cell-Surface Transmembrane Receptors

Receptor Tyrosine Kinases

Receptor tyrosine kinases (RTKs) belong to a major class of plasma membrane receptors characterized by having enzymatic activity. A kinase is any enzyme that catalyzes the transfer of phosphate groups. The part of the receptor protein extending into the cytoplasm functions more specifically as a tyrosine kinase, an enzyme that catalyzes the transfer of a phosphate group from ATP to the amino acid tyrosine on a substrate protein. Thus, RTKs are membrane receptors that attach phosphates to tyrosines.

One RTK may activate ten or more different transduction pathways and cellular responses. Often, more than one signal transduction pathway can be triggered at once, helping the cell regulate and coordinate many aspects of cell growth and cell reproduction. The ability of a single ligand-binding event to trigger so many pathways is a key difference between RTKs and GPCRs, which activate a single transduction pathway. Abnormal RTKs that function even in the absence of signaling molecules are associated with many kinds of cancer.

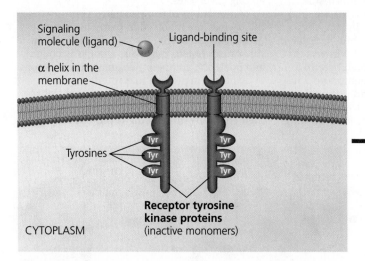

❶ Many receptor tyrosine kinases have the structure depicted schematically here. Before the signaling molecule binds, the receptors exist as individual units referred to as monomers. Notice that each has an extracellular ligand-binding site, an α helix spanning the membrane, and an intracellular tail containing multiple tyrosines.

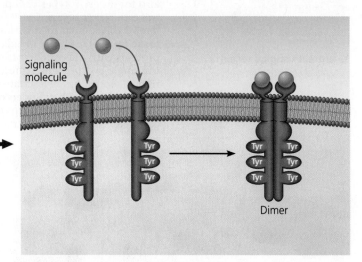

❷ The binding of a signaling molecule (such as a growth factor) causes two receptor monomers to associate closely with each other, forming a complex known as a dimer in a process called dimerization (In some cases, larger clusters form. The details of monomer association are a focus of current research.)

❸ Dimerization activates the tyrosine kinase region of each monomer; each tyrosine kinase adds a phosphate from an ATP molecule to a tyrosine on the tail of the other monomer.

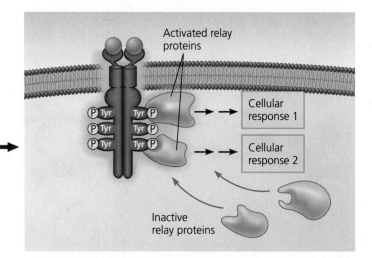

❹ Now that the receptor is fully activated, it is recognized by specific relay proteins inside the cell. Each such protein binds to a specific phosphorylated tyrosine, undergoing a resulting structural change that activates the bound protein. Each activated protein triggers a transduction pathway, leading to a cellular response.

Ion Channel Receptors

A **ligand-gated ion channel** is a type of membrane receptor containing a region that can act as a "gate" when the receptor changes shape. When a signaling molecule binds as a ligand to the receptor protein, the gate opens or closes, allowing or blocking the flow of specific ions, such as Na^+ or Ca^{2+}, through a channel in the receptor. Like the other receptors we have discussed, these proteins bind the ligand at a specific site on their extracellular sides.

1 Here we show a ligand-gated ion channel receptor in which the gate remains closed until a ligand binds to the receptor.

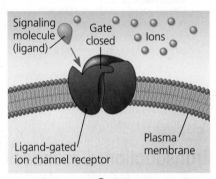

2 When the ligand binds to the receptor and the gate opens, specific ions can flow through the channel and rapidly change the concentration of that particular ion inside the cell. This change may directly affect the activity of the cell in some way.

3 When the ligand dissociates from this receptor, the gate closes and ions no longer enter the cell.

Ligand-gated ion channels are very important in the nervous system. For example, the neurotransmitter molecules released at a synapse between two nerve cells (see Figure 11.5b) bind as ligands to ion channels on the receiving cell, causing the channels to open. Ions flow in (or, in some cases, out), triggering an electrical signal that propagates down the length of the receiving cell. Some gated ion channels are controlled by electrical signals instead of ligands; these voltage-gated ion channels are also crucial to the functioning of the nervous system, as we will discuss in Chapter 48. Some ion channels are present on membranes of organelles, such as the ER.

MAKE CONNECTIONS | *Is the flow of ions through a ligand-gated channel an example of active or passive transport? (Review Concepts 7.3 and 7.4.)*

Although cell-surface receptors represent 30% of all human proteins, determining their structures has proved challenging: They make up only 1% of the proteins whose structures have been determined by X-ray crystallography (see Figure 5.22). For one thing, cell-surface receptors tend to be flexible and inherently unstable, thus difficult to crystallize. It took years of persistent efforts for researchers to determine the first few of these structures, such as the GPCR shown in Figure 11.7. In that case, the β-adrenergic receptor was stable enough to be crystallized while it was among membrane molecules, in the presence of its ligand.

Abnormal functioning of receptor tyrosine kinases (RTKs) is associated with many types of cancers. For example, breast cancer patients have a poor prognosis if their tumor cells harbor excessive levels of a receptor tyrosine kinase called HER2 (see Concept 12.3 and Figure 18.27). Using molecular biological techniques, researchers have developed a protein called Herceptin that binds to HER2 on cells and inhibits cell division, thus thwarting further tumor development. In some clinical studies, treatment with Herceptin improved patient survival rates by more than one-third. One goal of ongoing research into these cell-surface receptors and other cell-signaling proteins is development of additional successful treatments.

Intracellular Receptors

Intracellular receptor proteins are found in either the cytoplasm or nucleus of target cells. To reach such a receptor, a signaling molecule passes through the target cell's plasma membrane. A number of important signaling molecules can do this because they are either hydrophobic enough or small enough to cross the hydrophobic interior of the membrane. These hydrophobic chemical messengers include the steroid hormones and thyroid hormones of animals. Another chemical signaling molecule with an intracellular receptor is nitric oxide (NO), a gas; its very small molecules readily pass between the membrane phospholipids.

Once a hormone has entered a cell, it may bind to an intracellular receptor in the cytoplasm or the nucleus. The binding changes the receptor into a hormone-receptor complex that is able to cause a response—in many cases, the turning on or off of particular genes.

The behavior of aldosterone is a representative example of how steroid hormones work. This hormone is secreted by cells of the adrenal gland, a gland that sits above the kidney. Aldosterone then travels through the blood and enters cells all over the body. However, a response occurs only in kidney cells, which contain receptor molecules for this hormone. In these cells, the hormone binds to the receptor protein, activating it. With aldosterone attached, the active form of the receptor protein then enters the nucleus and turns on specific genes that control water and sodium flow in kidney cells, ultimately affecting blood volume (**Figure 11.9**).

How does the activated hormone-receptor complex turn on genes? Recall that the genes in a cell's DNA function by being transcribed and processed into messenger RNA (mRNA), which leaves the nucleus and is translated into a specific protein by ribosomes in the cytoplasm (see Figure 5.23). Special proteins called *transcription factors* control which genes are turned on—that is, which genes are transcribed into mRNA—in a particular cell at a particular time. When the aldosterone receptor is activated, it acts as a transcription factor that turns on specific genes. (You'll learn more about transcription factors in Chapters 17 and 18.)

By acting as a transcription factor, the aldosterone receptor itself carries out the transduction part of the signaling pathway. Most other intracellular receptors function in the same way, although many of them, such as the thyroid hormone receptor, are already in the nucleus before the signaling molecule reaches them. Interestingly, many of these intracellular receptor proteins are structurally similar, suggesting an evolutionary kinship.

▲ **Figure 11.9 Steroid hormone interacting with an intracellular receptor.**

❶ The steroid hormone aldosterone passes through the plasma membrane.

❷ Aldosterone binds to a receptor protein in the cytoplasm, activating it.

❸ The hormone-receptor complex enters the nucleus and binds to specific genes.

❹ The bound protein acts as a transcription factor, stimulating the transcription of the gene into mRNA.

❺ The mRNA is translated into a specific protein.

? *Why is a cell-surface receptor protein not required for this steroid hormone to enter the cell?*

CONCEPT CHECK 11.2

1. Nerve growth factor (NGF) is a water-soluble signaling molecule. Would you expect the receptor for NGF to be intracellular or in the plasma membrane? Why?

2. **WHAT IF?** What would the effect be if a cell made defective receptor tyrosine kinase proteins that were unable to dimerize?

3. **MAKE CONNECTIONS** How is ligand binding similar to the process of allosteric regulation of enzymes? See Figure 8.20.

4. **WHAT IF?** The model shown in Figure 11.7 represents the receptor in an inactive state, not bound to a G protein. Can you suggest an approach for crystallizing the protein that would reveal the structure of the receptor while it is actively signaling?

For suggested answers, see Appendix A.

CONCEPT 11.3

Transduction: Cascades of molecular interactions relay signals from receptors to target molecules in the cell

When receptors for signaling molecules are plasma membrane proteins, like most of those we have discussed, the transduction stage of cell signaling is usually a multistep pathway involving many molecules. Steps often include activation of proteins by addition or removal of phosphate groups or release of other small molecules or ions that act as messengers. One benefit of multiple steps is the possibility of greatly amplifying a signal. If each molecule in a pathway transmits the signal to numerous molecules at the next step in the series, the result is a geometric increase in the number of activated molecules by the end of the pathway. Moreover, multistep pathways provide more opportunities for coordination and control than do simpler systems. This allows regulation of the response, as we'll discuss later in the chapter.

Signal Transduction Pathways

The binding of a specific signaling molecule to a receptor in the plasma membrane triggers the first step in the chain of molecular interactions—the signal transduction pathway—that leads to a particular response within the cell. Like falling dominoes, the signal-activated receptor activates another molecule, which activates yet another molecule, and so on, until the protein that produces the final cellular response is activated. The molecules that relay a signal from receptor to response, which we call relay molecules in this book, are often proteins. The interaction of proteins is a major theme of cell signaling. Indeed, protein interaction is a unifying theme of all cellular activities.

Keep in mind that the original signaling molecule is not physically passed along a signaling pathway; in most cases, it never even enters the cell. When we say that the signal is relayed along a pathway, we mean that certain information is passed on. At each step, the signal is transduced into a different form, commonly a shape change in the next protein. Very often, the shape change is brought about by phosphorylation.

Protein Phosphorylation and Dephosphorylation

Previous chapters introduced the concept of activating a protein by adding one or more phosphate groups to it (see Figure 8.11a). In Figure 11.8, you have already seen how phosphorylation is involved in the activation of receptor tyrosine kinases. In fact, the phosphorylation and dephosphorylation of proteins is a widespread cellular mechanism

for regulating protein activity. An enzyme that transfers phosphate groups from ATP to a protein is generally known as a **protein kinase**. Recall that a receptor tyrosine kinase is a specific kind of protein kinase that phosphorylates tyrosines on the other receptor tyrosine kinase in a dimer. Most cytoplasmic protein kinases, however, act on proteins different from themselves. Another distinction is that most cytoplasmic protein kinases phosphorylate either of two other amino acids, serine or threonine, rather than tyrosine. Serine/threonine kinases are widely involved in signaling pathways in animals, plants, and fungi.

Many of the relay molecules in signal transduction pathways are protein kinases, and they often act on other protein kinases in the pathway. **Figure 11.10** depicts a hypothetical pathway containing three different protein kinases that create a **phosphorylation cascade**. The sequence of steps

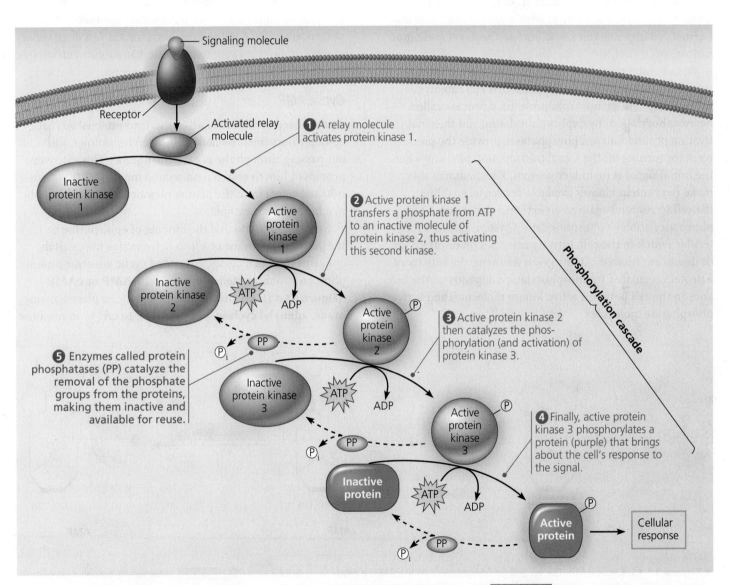

▲ **Figure 11.10 A phosphorylation cascade.** In a phosphorylation cascade, a series of different proteins in a pathway are phosphorylated in turn, each protein adding a phosphate group to the next one in line. Here, phosphorylation activates each protein, and dephosphorylation returns it to its inactive form. The active and inactive forms of each protein are represented by different shapes to remind you that activation is usually associated with a change in molecular shape.

WHAT IF? *What would happen if a mutation in protein kinase 3 made it incapable of being phosphorylated?*

shown in the figure is similar to many known pathways, including those triggered in yeast by mating factors and in animal cells by many growth factors. The signal is transmitted by a cascade of protein phosphorylations, each causing a shape change because of the interaction of the newly added phosphate groups with charged or polar amino acids on the protein being phosphorylated (see Figure 5.14). The change in shape alters the function of the protein, most often activating it. In some cases, though, phosphorylation *decreases* the activity of the protein.

The importance of protein kinases can hardly be overstated. About 2% of our own genes are thought to code for protein kinases. A single cell may have hundreds of different kinds, each specific for a different substrate protein. Together, they probably regulate the activity of a large proportion of the thousands of proteins in a cell. Among these are most of the proteins that, in turn, regulate cell division. Abnormal activity of such a kinase can cause abnormal cell division and contribute to the development of cancer.

Equally important in the phosphorylation cascade are the **protein phosphatases**, enzymes that can rapidly remove phosphate groups from proteins, a process called dephosphorylation. By dephosphorylating and thus inactivating protein kinases, phosphatases provide the mechanism for turning off the signal transduction pathway when the initial signal is no longer present. Phosphatases also make the protein kinases available for reuse, enabling the cell to respond again to an extracellular signal. The phosphorylation-dephosphorylation system acts as a molecular switch in the cell, turning activities on or off, or up or down, as required. At any given moment, the activity of a protein regulated by phosphorylation depends on the balance in the cell between active kinase molecules and active phosphatase molecules.

Small Molecules and Ions as Second Messengers

Not all components of signal transduction pathways are proteins. Many signaling pathways also involve small, nonprotein, water-soluble molecules or ions called **second messengers**. (This term is used because the pathway's "first messenger" is considered to be the extracellular signaling molecule—the ligand—that binds to the membrane receptor.) Because second messengers are small and also water-soluble, they can readily spread throughout the cell by diffusion. For example, as we'll see shortly, a second messenger called cyclic AMP carries the signal initiated by epinephrine from the plasma membrane of a liver or muscle cell into the cell's interior, where the signal eventually brings about glycogen breakdown. Second messengers participate in pathways that are initiated by both G protein-coupled receptors and receptor tyrosine kinases. The two most widely used second messengers are cyclic AMP and calcium ions, Ca^{2+}. A large variety of relay proteins are sensitive to the cytosolic concentration of one or the other of these second messengers.

Cyclic AMP

As discussed previously, Earl Sutherland established that epinephrine somehow causes glycogen breakdown without passing through the plasma membrane. This discovery prompted him to search for a second messenger that transmits the signal from the plasma membrane to the metabolic machinery in the cytoplasm.

Sutherland found that the binding of epinephrine to the plasma membrane of a liver cell elevates the cytosolic concentration of a compound called cyclic adenosine monophosphate, abbreviated as either **cyclic AMP** or **cAMP** (Figure 11.11). An enzyme embedded in the plasma membrane, **adenylyl cyclase**, converts ATP to cAMP in response

▲ **Figure 11.11 Cyclic AMP.** The second messenger cyclic AMP (cAMP) is made from ATP by adenylyl cyclase, an enzyme embedded in the plasma membrane. Note that the phosphate group in cAMP is attached to both the 5′ and the 3′ carbons; this cyclic arrangement is the basis for the molecule's name. Cyclic AMP is inactivated by phosphodiesterase, an enzyme that converts it to AMP.

WHAT IF? *What would happen if a molecule that inactivated phosphodiesterase were introduced into the cell?*

to an extracellular signal—in this case, provided by epinephrine. But epinephrine doesn't stimulate adenylyl cyclase directly. When epinephrine outside the cell binds to a specific receptor protein, the protein activates adenylyl cyclase, which in turn can catalyze the synthesis of many molecules of cAMP. In this way, the normal cellular concentration of cAMP can be boosted 20-fold in a matter of seconds. The cAMP broadcasts the signal to the cytoplasm. It does not persist for long in the absence of the hormone because another enzyme, called phosphodiesterase, converts cAMP to AMP. Another surge of epinephrine is needed to boost the cytosolic concentration of cAMP again.

Subsequent research has revealed that epinephrine is only one of many hormones and other signaling molecules that trigger the formation of cAMP. It has also brought to light the other components of cAMP pathways, including G proteins, G protein-coupled receptors, and protein kinases (**Figure 11.12**). The immediate effect of an elevation in cAMP levels is usually the activation of a serine/threonine kinase called *protein kinase A*. The activated protein kinase A then phosphorylates various other proteins, depending on the cell type. (The complete pathway for epinephrine's stimulation of glycogen breakdown is shown later, in Figure 11.16.)

Further regulation of cell metabolism is provided by other G protein systems that *inhibit* adenylyl cyclase. In these systems, a different signaling molecule activates a different receptor, which in turn activates an *inhibitory* G protein that blocks activation of adenylyl cyclase.

Now that we know about the role of cAMP in G protein signaling pathways, we can explain in molecular detail how certain microbes cause disease. Consider cholera, a disease that is frequently epidemic in places where the water supply is contaminated with human feces. People acquire the cholera bacterium, *Vibrio cholerae*, by drinking contaminated water. The bacteria form a biofilm on the lining of the small intestine and produce a toxin. The cholera toxin is an enzyme that chemically modifies a G protein involved in regulating salt and water secretion. Because the modified G protein is unable to hydrolyze GTP to GDP, it remains stuck in its active form, continuously stimulating adenylyl cyclase to make cAMP. The resulting high concentration of cAMP causes the intestinal cells to secrete large amounts of salts into the intestines, with water following by osmosis. An infected person quickly develops profuse diarrhea and if left untreated can soon die from the loss of water and salts.

Our understanding of signaling pathways involving cyclic AMP or related messengers has allowed us to develop treatments for certain conditions in humans. In one pathway, *cyclic GMP*, or *cGMP*, acts as a signaling molecule whose effects include relaxation of smooth muscle cells in artery walls. A compound that inhibits the hydrolysis of cGMP to GMP, thus prolonging the signal, was originally prescribed for chest pains because it increased blood flow to the heart muscle. Under the trade name Viagra, this compound is now widely used as a treatment for erectile dysfunction in human males. Because Viagra leads to dilation of blood vessels, it also allows increased blood flow to the penis, optimizing physiological conditions for penile erections.

Calcium Ions and Inositol Trisphosphate (IP₃)

Many of the signaling molecules that function in animals—including neurotransmitters, growth factors, and some hormones—induce responses in their target cells via signal transduction pathways that increase the cytosolic concentration of calcium ions (Ca^{2+}). Calcium is even more widely used than cAMP as a second messenger. Increasing the cytosolic concentration of Ca^{2+} causes many responses in animal cells, including muscle cell contraction, secretion of certain substances, and cell division. In plant cells, a wide range of hormonal and environmental stimuli can cause brief increases in cytosolic Ca^{2+} concentration, triggering various signaling pathways, such as the pathway for greening in response to light (see Figure 39.4). Cells use Ca^{2+} as a second messenger in pathways triggered by both G protein-coupled receptors and receptor tyrosine kinases.

Although cells always contain some Ca^{2+}, this ion can function as a second messenger because its concentration in the cytosol is normally much lower than the concentration

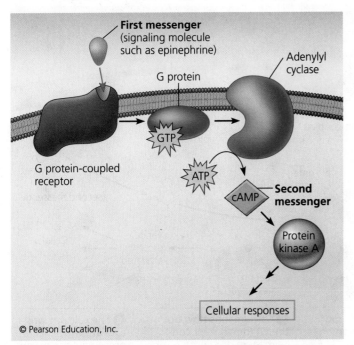

▲ **Figure 11.12 cAMP as a second messenger in a G protein signaling pathway.** The first messenger activates a G protein coupled receptor, which activates a specific G protein. In turn, the G protein activates adenylyl cyclase, which catalyzes the conversion of ATP to cAMP. The cAMP then acts as a second messenger and activates another protein, usually protein kinase A, leading to cellular responses.

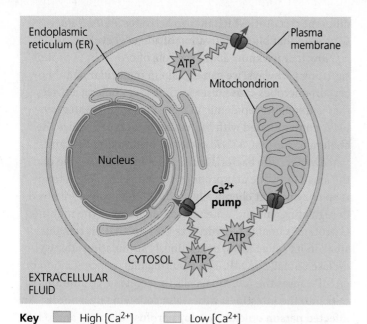

Key ▮ High [Ca^{2+}] ▯ Low [Ca^{2+}]

▲ **Figure 11.13 The maintenance of calcium ion concentrations in an animal cell.** The Ca^{2+} concentration in the cytosol is usually much lower (beige) than in the extracellular fluid and ER (blue). Protein pumps in the plasma membrane and the ER membrane, driven by ATP, move Ca^{2+} from the cytosol into the extracellular fluid and into the lumen of the ER. Mitochondrial pumps, driven by chemiosmosis (see Concept 9.4), move Ca^{2+} into mitochondria when the calcium level in the cytosol rises significantly.

messengers are produced by cleavage of a certain kind of phospholipid in the plasma membrane. **Figure 11.14** shows the complete picture of how a signal causes IP$_3$ to stimulate the release of calcium from the ER. Because IP$_3$ acts before calcium in these pathways, calcium could be considered a "*third* messenger." However, scientists use the term *second messenger* for all small, nonprotein components of signal transduction pathways.

CONCEPT CHECK 11.3

1. What is a protein kinase, and what is its role in a signal transduction pathway?

2. When a signal transduction pathway involves a phosphorylation cascade, how does the cell's response get turned off?

3. What is the actual "signal" that is being transduced in any signal transduction pathway, such as those shown in Figures 11.6 and 11.10? In what way is this information being passed from the exterior to the interior of the cell?

4. **WHAT IF?** Upon activation of phospholipase C by the binding of a ligand to a receptor, what effect does the IP$_3$-gated calcium channel have on Ca^{2+} concentration in the cytosol?

For suggested answers, see Appendix A.

outside the cell **(Figure 11.13)**. In fact, the level of Ca^{2+} in the blood and extracellular fluid of an animal is often more than 10,000 times higher than that in the cytosol. Calcium ions are actively transported out of the cell and are actively imported from the cytosol into the endoplasmic reticulum (and, under some conditions, into mitochondria and chloroplasts) by various protein pumps. As a result, the calcium concentration in the ER is usually much higher than that in the cytosol. Because the cytosolic calcium level is low, a small change in absolute numbers of ions represents a relatively large percentage change in calcium concentration.

In response to a signal relayed by a signal transduction pathway, the cytosolic calcium level may rise, usually by a mechanism that releases Ca^{2+} from the cell's ER. The pathways leading to calcium release involve two other second messengers, **inositol trisphosphate (IP$_3$)** and **diacylglycerol (DAG)**. These two

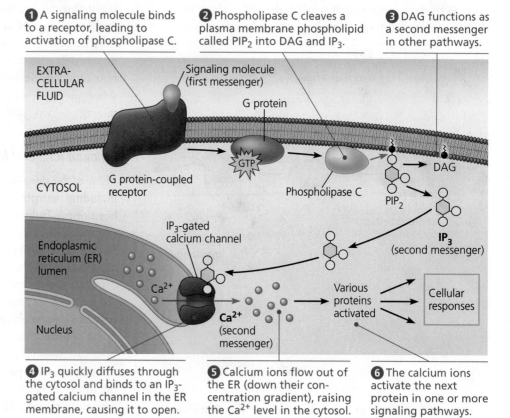

❶ A signaling molecule binds to a receptor, leading to activation of phospholipase C.

❷ Phospholipase C cleaves a plasma membrane phospholipid called PIP$_2$ into DAG and IP$_3$.

❸ DAG functions as a second messenger in other pathways.

❹ IP$_3$ quickly diffuses through the cytosol and binds to an IP$_3$-gated calcium channel in the ER membrane, causing it to open.

❺ Calcium ions flow out of the ER (down their concentration gradient), raising the Ca^{2+} level in the cytosol.

❻ The calcium ions activate the next protein in one or more signaling pathways.

▲ **Figure 11.14 Calcium and IP$_3$ in signaling pathways.** Calcium ions (Ca^{2+}) and inositol trisphosphate (IP$_3$) function as second messengers in many signal transduction pathways. In this figure, the process is initiated by the binding of a signaling molecule to a G protein-coupled receptor. A receptor tyrosine kinase could also initiate this pathway by activating phospholipase C.

Response: Cell signaling leads to regulation of transcription or cytoplasmic activities

We now take a closer look at the cell's subsequent response to an extracellular signal—what some researchers call the "output response." What is the nature of the final step in a signaling pathway?

Nuclear and Cytoplasmic Responses

Ultimately, a signal transduction pathway leads to the regulation of one or more cellular activities. The response at the end of the pathway may occur in the nucleus of the cell or in the cytoplasm.

Many signaling pathways ultimately regulate protein synthesis, usually by turning specific genes on or off in the nucleus. Like an activated steroid receptor (see Figure 11.9), the final activated molecule in a signaling pathway may function as a transcription factor. **Figure 11.15** shows an example in which a signaling pathway activates a transcription factor that turns a gene on: The response to this growth factor signal is transcription, the synthesis of one or more specific mRNAs, which will be translated in the cytoplasm into specific proteins. In other cases, the transcription factor might regulate a gene by turning it off. Often a transcription factor regulates several different genes.

Sometimes a signaling pathway may regulate the *activity* of proteins rather than causing their *synthesis* by activating gene expression. This directly affects proteins that function outside the nucleus. For example, a signal may cause the opening or closing of an ion channel in the plasma membrane or a change in cell metabolism. As we have seen, the response of liver cells to the hormone epinephrine helps regulate cellular energy metabolism by affecting the activity of an enzyme. The final step in the signaling pathway that begins with epinephrine binding activates the enzyme that catalyzes the breakdown of glycogen. **Figure 11.16** shows the complete pathway leading to the release of glucose 1-phosphate molecules from glycogen. Notice that as each molecule is activated, the response is amplified, a subject we'll return to shortly.

Signal receptors, relay molecules, and second messengers participate in a variety of pathways, leading to both nuclear and cytoplasmic responses. Some of these pathways lead to cell division. The molecular messengers that initiate cell division pathways include growth factors and certain plant and animal hormones. Malfunctioning of growth factor pathways like the one in Figure 11.15 can contribute to the development of cancer, as we'll see in Chapter 18.

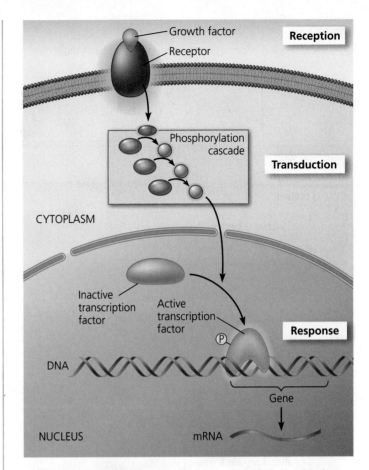

▲ **Figure 11.15 Nuclear responses to a signal: the activation of a specific gene by a growth factor.** This diagram is a simplified representation of a typical signaling pathway that leads to regulation of gene activity in the cell nucleus. The initial signaling molecule, a growth factor, triggers a phosphorylation cascade, as in Figure 11.10. (The ATP molecules and phosphate groups are not shown here.) Once phosphorylated, the last kinase in the sequence enters the nucleus and activates a gene-regulating protein, a transcription factor. This protein stimulates transcription of a specific gene (or genes). The resulting mRNAs then direct the synthesis of a particular protein in the cytoplasm.

Regulation of the Response

Whether the response occurs in the nucleus or in the cytoplasm, it is not simply turned "on" or "off." Rather, the extent and specificity of the response are regulated in multiple ways. Here we'll consider four aspects of this regulation. First, as mentioned earlier, signaling pathways generally amplify the cell's response to a single signaling event. The degree of amplification depends on the function of the specific molecules in the pathway. Second, the many steps in a multistep pathway provide control points at which the cell's response can be further regulated, contributing to the specificity of the response and allowing coordination with other signaling pathways. Third, the overall efficiency of the response is enhanced by the presence of proteins known as scaffolding proteins. Finally, a crucial point in regulating the response is the termination of the signal.

Reception

Binding of epinephrine to G protein-coupled receptor (1 molecule)

Transduction

Inactive
G protein

Active G protein (10^2 molecules)

Inactive
adenylyl cyclase

Active adenylyl cyclase (10^2)

ATP

Cyclic AMP (10^4)

Inactive
protein kinase A

Active protein kinase A (10^4)

Inactive
phosphorylase kinase

Active phosphorylase kinase (10^5)

Inactive
glycogen phosphorylase

Active glycogen phosphorylase (10^6)

Response

Glycogen

Glucose 1-phosphate
(10^8 molecules)

▲ **Figure 11.16 Cytoplasmic response to a signal: the stimulation of glycogen breakdown by epinephrine (adrenaline).** In this signaling system, the hormone epinephrine acts through a G protein-coupled receptor to activate a succession of relay molecules, including cAMP and two protein kinases (see also Figure 11.12). The final protein activated is the enzyme glycogen phosphorylase, which uses inorganic phosphate to release glucose monomers from glycogen in the form of glucose 1-phosphate molecules. This pathway amplifies the hormonal signal: One receptor protein can activate approximately 100 molecules of G protein, and each enzyme in the pathway, once activated, can act on many molecules of its substrate, the next molecule in the cascade. The number of activated molecules given for each step is approximate.

? *In the figure, how many glucose molecules are released in response to one signaling molecule? Calculate the factor by which the response is amplified in going from each step to the next.*

Signal Amplification

Elaborate enzyme cascades amplify the cell's response to a signal. At each catalytic step in the cascade, the number of activated products can be much greater than in the preceding step. For example, in the epinephrine-triggered pathway in Figure 11.16, each adenylyl cyclase molecule catalyzes the formation of 100 or so cAMP molecules, each molecule of protein kinase A phosphorylates about 10 molecules of the next kinase in the pathway, and so on. The amplification effect stems from the fact that these proteins persist in the active form long enough to process multiple molecules of substrate before they become inactive again. As a result of the signal's amplification, a small number of epinephrine molecules binding to receptors on the surface of a liver cell or muscle cell can lead to the release of hundreds of millions of glucose molecules from glycogen.

The Specificity of Cell Signaling and Coordination of the Response

Consider two different cells in your body—a liver cell and a heart muscle cell, for example. Both are in contact with your bloodstream and are therefore constantly exposed to many different hormone molecules, as well as to local regulators secreted by nearby cells. Yet the liver cell responds to some signals but ignores others, and the same is true for the heart cell. And some kinds of signals trigger responses in both cells—but different responses. For instance, epinephrine stimulates the liver cell to break down glycogen, but the main response of the heart cell to epinephrine is contraction, leading to a more rapid heartbeat. How do we account for this difference?

The explanation for the specificity exhibited in cellular responses to signals is the same as the basic explanation for virtually all differences between cells: Because different kinds of cells turn on different sets of genes, *different kinds of cells have different collections of proteins* **(Figure 11.17)**. The response of a particular cell to a signal depends on its particular collection of signal receptor proteins, relay proteins, and proteins needed to carry out the response. A liver cell, for example, is poised to respond appropriately to epinephrine by having the proteins listed in Figure 11.16 as well as those needed to manufacture glycogen.

Thus, two cells that respond differently to the same signal differ in one or more of the proteins that handle and respond to the signal. Notice in Figure 11.17 that different pathways may have some molecules in common. For example, cells A, B, and C all use the same receptor protein for the red signaling molecule; differences in other proteins account for their differing responses. In cell D, a different receptor protein is used for the same signaling molecule, leading to yet another response. In cell B, a pathway that is triggered by a single kind of signal diverges to produce two

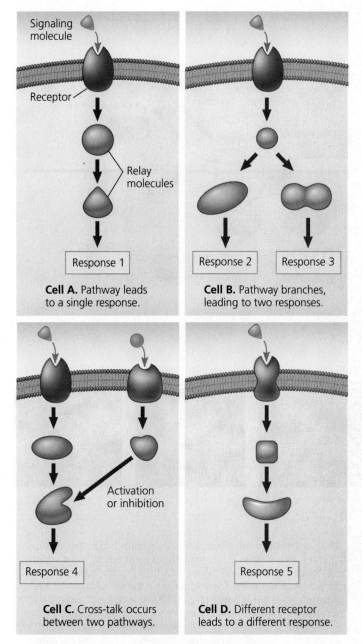

▲ **Figure 11.17 The specificity of cell signaling.** The particular proteins a cell possesses determine what signaling molecules it responds to and the nature of the response. The four cells in these diagrams respond to the same signaling molecule (red) in different ways because each has a different set of proteins (purple and teal). Note, however, that the same kinds of molecules can participate in more than one pathway.

MAKE CONNECTIONS *Study the signaling pathway shown in Figure 11.14, and explain how the situation pictured for cell B above could apply to that pathway.*

responses; such branched pathways often involve receptor tyrosine kinases (which can activate multiple relay proteins) or second messengers (which can regulate numerous proteins). In cell C, two pathways triggered by separate signals converge to modulate a single response. Branching of pathways and "cross-talk" (interaction) between pathways are

important in regulating and coordinating a cell's responses to information coming in from different sources in the body. (You'll learn more about this coordination in Concept 11.5.) Moreover, the use of some of the same proteins in more than one pathway allows the cell to economize on the number of different proteins it must make.

An example of a signal that leads to a complex, coordinated cellular response can be found in the processes leading to the mating of yeast cells described earlier (see Figure 11.2). In the Scientific Skills Exercise, you can work with data from experiments investigating the cellular response of a yeast cell to the signal initiated by a mating factor from a cell of the opposite mating type.

Signaling Efficiency: Scaffolding Proteins and Signaling Complexes

The illustrations of signaling pathways in Figure 11.17 (as well as diagrams of other pathways in this chapter) are greatly simplified. The diagrams show only a few relay molecules and, for clarity's sake, display these molecules spread out in the cytosol. If this were true in the cell, signaling pathways would operate very inefficiently because most relay molecules are proteins, and proteins are too large to diffuse quickly through the viscous cytosol. How does a particular protein kinase, for instance, find its substrate?

In many cases, the efficiency of signal transduction is apparently increased by the presence of **scaffolding proteins**, large relay proteins to which several other relay proteins are simultaneously attached. For example, one scaffolding protein isolated from mouse brain cells holds three protein kinases and carries these kinases with it when it binds to an appropriately activated membrane receptor; it thus facilitates a specific phosphorylation cascade **(Figure 11.18)**. Researchers have found scaffolding proteins in brain cells that *permanently* hold together networks of signaling pathway proteins at synapses. This hardwiring enhances the speed and accuracy of signal transfer between cells, because the

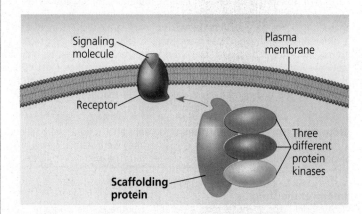

▲ **Figure 11.18 A scaffolding protein.** The scaffolding protein shown here simultaneously binds to a specific activated membrane receptor and three different protein kinases. This physical arrangement facilitates signal transduction by these molecules.

Using Experiments to Test a Model

Are Both Fus3 Kinase and Formin Required for Directional Cell Growth During Mating in Yeast? When a yeast cell binds mating factor molecules from a cell of the opposite mating type, a signaling pathway causes it to grow a projection toward the potential mate. The cell with the projection is called a "shmoo" (because it resembles a 1950s cartoon character by that name). Researchers sought to determine how mating factor signaling leads to growth of this cell projection on one side of the cell—in other words, to asymmetric cell growth. Previous work had shown that activation of Fus3, one of the kinases in the signaling cascade, caused it to move to the membrane near where the mating factor bound its receptor. The researchers' first experiment identified one of the phosphorylation targets of Fus3 kinase as formin, a protein directing microfilament construction. Based on this information, the researchers developed the working model shown here for the signaling pathway that leads to the formation of shmoo projections in yeast cells.

How the Experiment Was Done To determine if Fus3 and formin were required for shmoo formation, the researchers generated two mutant yeast strains: one that lacked the gene for making Fus3 kinase (a strain called ΔFus3) and one that lacked the gene for making formin (Δformin). To observe the effects of these mutations on schmoo formation after cells' exposure to mating factor, the symmetry of growth was investigated. First, the existing cell walls of each strain were stained with a green fluorescent dye. These green-stained cells were then exposed to mating factor and stained with a red fluorescent dye that labels only new cell wall growth. Growth of the cell on all sides (symmetric growth) is indicated by a uniform yellow color, resulting from merged green and red stains. (This occurs normally in wild-type cells that have not been exposed to mating factor, which are not shown.)

Data from the Experiment The micrographs above, right, were taken of wild-type, ΔFus3, and Δformin cells after they were stained green, exposed to mating factor, and then stained red. The wild-type cells expressed both Fus3 and formin.

Interpret the Data

1. A model helps scientists form a testable hypothesis. The diagram shows the working model of shmoo formation developed by the researchers. (a) What hypothesis from the model was being tested with the ΔFus3 strain? (b) With the Δformin strain? (c) What is the purpose of including wild-type yeast cells in the experiment?

Wild type   ΔFus3   Δformin

2. When designing an experiment, scientists make predictions about what results will occur if their hypothesis is correct. (a) If the hypothesis about the role of Fus3 kinase activity in shmoo production is correct, what result should be observed in the ΔFus3 strain? If it is incorrect, what result is expected? (b) If the hypothesis about the role of formin in shmoo production is correct, what result should be observed in the Δformin strain? If it is incorrect, what result is expected?

3. For each micrograph, describe the shape of the cells and the pattern of cell wall staining. Explain the significance of your observations. Which strain(s) of yeast cells formed shmoos?

4. (a) Do the data support the hypothesis about the role of Fus3 kinase in shmoo production? (b) Do the data support the hypothesis about the role of formin in shmoo production? (c) Do the data support the working model (the working hypothesis) in the diagram?

5. Fus3 kinase and formin proteins are generally distributed evenly throughout a yeast cell. Based on the model in the diagram, explain why the projection would emerge on the same side of the cell that bound the mating factor.

6. What do you predict would happen if the yeast had a mutation that prevented the G protein from binding GTP?

(MB) A version of this Scientific Skills Exercise can be assigned in MasteringBiology.

Data from D. Matheos et al., Pheromone-induced polarization is dependent on the Fus3p MAPK acting through the formin Bni1p, *Journal of Cell Biology* 165:99–109 (2004).

rate of protein-protein interaction is not limited by diffusion. Furthermore, in some cases the scaffolding proteins themselves may directly activate relay proteins.

When signaling pathways were first discovered, they were thought to be linear, independent pathways. Our understanding of cellular communication has benefited from the realization that signaling pathway components interact with each other in various ways. As seen in Figure 11.17, some proteins may participate in more than one pathway, either in different cell types or in the same cell at different times or under different conditions. These observations underscore the importance of transient—or, in some cases, permanent—protein complexes in the process of cell signaling.

The importance of the relay proteins that serve as points of branching or intersection in signaling pathways is highlighted by the problems arising when these proteins are defective or missing. For instance, in an inherited disorder called Wiskott-Aldrich syndrome (WAS), the absence of a single relay protein leads to such diverse effects as abnormal bleeding, eczema, and a predisposition to infections and leukemia. These symptoms are thought to arise primarily from the absence of the protein in cells of the immune system. By studying normal cells, scientists found that the WAS protein is located just beneath the immune cell surface. The protein interacts both with microfilaments of the cytoskeleton and with several different components of signaling pathways that relay information from the cell surface, including pathways regulating immune cell proliferation. This multifunctional relay protein is thus both a branch point and an important intersection point in a complex signal transduction network that controls immune cell behavior. When the WAS protein is absent, the cytoskeleton is not properly organized and signaling pathways are disrupted, leading to the WAS symptoms.

Termination of the Signal

To keep Figure 11.17 simple, we did not indicate the *inactivation* mechanisms that are an essential aspect of any cell-signaling pathway. For a cell of a multicellular organism to remain capable of responding to incoming signals, each molecular change in its signaling pathways must last only a short time. As we saw in the cholera example, if a signaling pathway component becomes locked into one state, whether active or inactive, consequences for the organism can be dire.

The ability of a cell to receive new signals depends on reversibility of the changes produced by prior signals. The binding of signaling molecules to receptors is reversible. As the external concentration of signaling molecules falls, fewer receptors are bound at any given moment, and the unbound receptors revert to their inactive form. The cellular response occurs only when the concentration of receptors with bound signaling molecules is above a certain threshold. When the number of active receptors falls below that threshold, the cellular response ceases. Then, by a variety of means, the

relay molecules return to their inactive forms: The GTPase activity intrinsic to a G protein hydrolyzes its bound GTP; the enzyme phosphodiesterase converts cAMP to AMP; protein phosphatases inactivate phosphorylated kinases and other proteins; and so forth. As a result, the cell is soon ready to respond to a fresh signal.

In this section, we explored the complexity of signaling initiation and termination in a single pathway, and we saw the potential for pathways to intersect with each other. In the next section, we'll consider one especially important network of interacting pathways in the cell.

CONCEPT 11.5

Apoptosis integrates multiple cell-signaling pathways

To be or not to be? One of the most elaborate networks of signaling pathways in the cell seems to ask and answer this question, originally posed by Hamlet. Cells that are infected, are damaged, or have reached the end of their functional life span often undergo "programmed cell death" **(Figure 11.19)**.

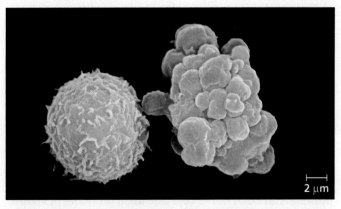

▲ **Figure 11.19 Apoptosis of a human white blood cell.** On the left is a normal white blood cell, while on the right is a white blood cell undergoing apoptosis. The apoptotic cell is shrinking and forming lobes ("blebs"), which eventually are shed as membrane-bounded cell fragments (colorized SEMs).

The best-understood type of this controlled cell suicide is **apoptosis** (from the Greek, meaning "falling off," and used in a classic Greek poem to refer to leaves falling from a tree). During this process, cellular agents chop up the DNA and fragment the organelles and other cytoplasmic components. The cell shrinks and becomes lobed (a change called "blebbing"), and the cell's parts are packaged up in vesicles that are engulfed and digested by specialized scavenger cells, leaving no trace. Apoptosis protects neighboring cells from damage that they would otherwise suffer if a dying cell merely leaked out all its contents, including its many digestive enzymes.

The signal that triggers apoptosis can come from either outside or inside the cell. Outside the cell, signaling molecules released from other cells can initiate a signal transduction pathway that activates the genes and proteins responsible for carrying out cell death. Within a cell whose DNA has been irretrievably damaged, a series of protein-protein interactions can pass along a signal that similarly triggers cell death. Considering some examples of apoptosis can help us to see how signaling pathways are integrated in cells.

Apoptosis in the Soil Worm *Caenorhabditis elegans*

The molecular mechanisms of apoptosis were worked out by researchers studying embryonic development of a small soil worm, a nematode called *Caenorhabditis elegans*. Because the adult worm has only about 1,000 cells, the researchers were able to work out the entire ancestry of each cell. The timely suicide of cells occurs exactly 131 times during normal development of *C. elegans*, at precisely the same points in the cell lineage of each worm. In worms and other species, apoptosis is triggered by signals that activate a cascade of "suicide" proteins in the cells destined to die.

Genetic research on *C. elegans* initially revealed two key apoptosis genes, called *ced-3* and *ced-4* (*ced* stands for "cell death"), which encode proteins essential for apoptosis. The proteins are called Ced-3 and Ced-4, respectively. These and most other proteins involved in apoptosis are continually present in cells, but in inactive form; thus, regulation in this case occurs at the level of protein activity rather than through gene activity and protein synthesis. In *C. elegans*, a protein in the outer mitochondrial membrane, called Ced-9 (the product of the *ced-9* gene), serves as a master regulator of apoptosis, acting as a brake in the absence of a signal promoting apoptosis **(Figure 11.20)**. When a death signal is received by the cell, signal transduction involves a change in Ced-9 that disables the brake, and the apoptotic pathway activates proteases and nucleases, enzymes that cut up the proteins and DNA of the cell. The main proteases of apoptosis are called *caspases*; in the nematode, the chief caspase is the Ced-3 protein.

(a) No death signal. As long as Ced-9, located in the outer mitochondrial membrane, is active, apoptosis is inhibited, and the cell remains alive.

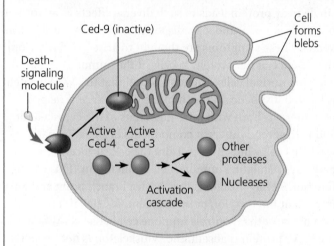

(b) Death signal. When a cell receives a death signal, Ced-9 is inactivated, relieving its inhibition of Ced-3 and Ced-4. Active Ced-3, a protease, triggers a cascade of reactions leading to activation of nucleases and other proteases. The action of these enzymes causes the changes seen in apoptotic cells and eventual cell death.

▲ **Figure 11.20 Molecular basis of apoptosis in *C. elegans*.** Three proteins, Ced-3, Ced-4, and Ced-9, are critical to apoptosis and its regulation in the nematode. Apoptosis is more complicated in mammals but involves proteins similar to those in the nematode.

Apoptotic Pathways and the Signals That Trigger Them

In humans and other mammals, several different pathways, involving about 15 different caspases, can carry out apoptosis. The pathway that is used depends on the type of cell and on the particular signal that initiates apoptosis. One major pathway involves certain mitochondrial proteins that are triggered to form molecular pores in the mitochondrial outer membrane, causing it to leak and release other proteins that promote apoptosis. Perhaps surprisingly, these latter include cytochrome *c*, which functions in mitochondrial electron transport in healthy cells (see Figure 9.15) but acts as a cell death factor when released from mitochondria. The process of mitochondrial apoptosis in mammals uses proteins similar to the nematode proteins Ced-3, Ced-4, and Ced-9. These can be thought of as relay proteins capable of transducing the apoptotic signal.

At key gateways into the apoptotic program, relay proteins integrate signals from several different sources and can send a cell down an apoptotic pathway. Often, the signal originates outside the cell, like the death-signaling molecule depicted in Figure 11.20b, which presumably was released by a neighboring cell. When a death-signaling ligand occupies a cell-surface receptor, this binding leads to activation of caspases and other enzymes that carry out apoptosis, without involving the mitochondrial pathway. This process of signal reception, transduction, and response is similar to what we have discussed throughout this chapter. In a twist on the classic scenario, two other types of alarm signals that can lead to apoptosis originate from *inside* the cell rather than from a cell-surface receptor. One signal comes from the nucleus, generated when the DNA has suffered irreparable damage, and a second comes from the endoplasmic reticulum when excessive protein misfolding occurs. Mammalian cells make life-or-death "decisions" by somehow integrating the death signals and life signals they receive from these external and internal sources.

A built-in cell suicide mechanism is essential to development and maintenance in all animals. The similarities between apoptosis genes in nematodes and those in mammals, as well as the observation that apoptosis occurs in multicellular fungi and even in single-celled yeasts, indicate that the basic mechanism evolved early in the evolution of eukaryotes. In vertebrates, apoptosis is essential for normal development of the nervous system, for normal operation of the immune system, and for normal morphogenesis of hands and feet in humans and paws in other mammals **(Figure 11.21)**. The level of apoptosis between the developing digits is lower in the webbed feet of ducks and other water birds than in the nonwebbed feet of land birds, such as chickens. In the case of humans, the failure of appropriate apoptosis can result in webbed fingers and toes.

Significant evidence points to the involvement of apoptosis in certain degenerative diseases of the nervous system, such as Parkinson's disease and Alzheimer's disease. In Alzheimer's disease, an accumulation of aggregated proteins in neuronal cells activates an enzyme that triggers apoptosis, resulting in the loss of brain function seen in these patients. Furthermore, cancer can result from a failure of cell suicide; some cases of human melanoma, for example, have been linked to faulty forms of the human version of the *C. elegans* Ced-4 protein. It is not surprising, therefore, that the signaling pathways feeding into apoptosis are quite elaborate. After all, the life-or-death question is the most fundamental one imaginable for a cell.

This chapter has introduced you to many of the general mechanisms of cell communication, such as ligand binding, protein-protein interactions and shape changes, cascades of interactions, and protein phosphorylation. Throughout your study of biology, you will encounter numerous examples of cell signaling.

CONCEPT CHECK 11.5

1. Give an example of apoptosis during embryonic development, and explain its function in the developing embryo.

2. **WHAT IF?** What types of protein defects could result in apoptosis occurring when it should not? What types could result in apoptosis not occurring when it should?

For suggested answers, see Appendix A.

Interdigital tissue

Cells undergoing apoptosis

|← 1 mm →|

Space between digits

▲ **Figure 11.21 Effect of apoptosis during paw development in the mouse.** In mice, humans, other mammals, and land birds, the embryonic region that develops into feet or hands initially has a solid, platelike structure.

Apoptosis eliminates the cells in the interdigital regions, thus forming the digits. The embryonic mouse paws shown in these fluorescence light micrographs are stained so that cells undergoing apoptosis appear a bright yellowish green.

Apoptosis of cells begins at the margin of each interdigital region (left), peaks as the tissue in these regions is reduced (middle), and is no longer visible when the interdigital tissue has been eliminated (right).

CONCEPT 11.1

External signals are converted to responses within the cell (pp. 211–214)

- **Signal transduction pathways** are crucial for many processes. Signaling during yeast cell mating has much in common with processes in multicellular organisms, suggesting an early evolutionary origin of signaling mechanisms. Bacterial cells can sense the local density of bacterial cells (quorum sensing).
- Local signaling by animal cells involves direct contact or the secretion of local regulators. For long-distance signaling, animal and plant cells use **hormones**; animals also pass signals electrically.
- Like other hormones that bind to membrane receptors, epinephrine triggers a three-stage cell-signaling pathway:

? *What determines whether a cell responds to a hormone such as epinephrine? What determines how a cell responds to such a hormone?*

CONCEPT 11.2

Reception: A signaling molecule binds to a receptor protein, causing it to change shape (pp. 214–218)

- The binding between signaling molecule (**ligand**) and receptor is highly specific. A specific shape change in a receptor is often the initial transduction of the signal.
- There are three major types of cell-surface transmembrane receptors: (1) **G protein-coupled receptors (GPCRs)** work with cytoplasmic **G proteins**. Ligand binding activates the receptor, which then activates a specific G protein, which activates yet another protein, thus propagating the signal. (2) **Receptor tyrosine kinases (RTKs)** react to the binding of signaling molecules by forming dimers and then adding phosphate groups to tyrosines on the cytoplasmic part of the other monomer making up the dimer. Relay proteins in the cell can then be activated by binding to different phosphorylated tyrosines, allowing this receptor to trigger several pathways at once. (3) **Ligand-gated ion channels** open or close in response to binding by specific signaling molecules, regulating the flow of specific ions across the membrane.
- The activity of all three types of receptors is crucial; abnormal GPCRs and RTKs are associated with many human diseases.
- Intracellular receptors are cytoplasmic or nuclear proteins. Signaling molecules that are hydrophobic or small enough to cross the plasma membrane bind to these receptors inside the cell.

? *How are the structures of a GPCR and an RTK similar? How does initiation of signal transduction differ for these two types of receptors?*

CONCEPT 11.3

Transduction: Cascades of molecular interactions relay signals from receptors to target molecules in the cell (pp. 218–222)

- At each step in a signal transduction pathway, the signal is transduced into a different form, which commonly involves a shape change in a protein. Many signal transduction pathways include **phosphorylation cascades**, in which a series of **protein kinases** each add a phosphate group to the next one in line, activating it. Enzymes called **protein phosphatases** remove the phosphate groups. The balance between phosphorylation and dephosphorylation regulates the activity of proteins involved in the sequential steps of a signal transduction pathway.
- **Second messengers**, such as the small molecule **cyclic AMP (cAMP)** and the ion Ca^{2+}, diffuse readily through the cytosol and thus help broadcast signals quickly. Many G proteins activate **adenylyl cyclase**, which makes cAMP from ATP. Cells use Ca^{2+} as a second messenger in both GPCR and RTK pathways. The tyrosine kinase pathways can also involve two other second messengers, **diacylglycerol (DAG)** and **inositol trisphosphate (IP₃)**. IP₃ can trigger a subsequent increase in Ca^{2+} levels.

? *What is the difference between a protein kinase and a second messenger? Can both operate in the same signal transduction pathway?*

CONCEPT 11.4

Response: Cell signaling leads to regulation of transcription or cytoplasmic activities (pp. 223–227)

- Some pathways lead to a nuclear response: Specific genes are turned on or off by activated transcription factors. In others, the response involves cytoplasmic regulation.
- Cellular responses are not simply on or off; they are regulated at many steps. Each protein in a signaling pathway amplifies the signal by activating multiple copies of the next component; for long pathways, the total amplification may be over a millionfold. The combination of proteins in a cell confers specificity in the signals it detects and the responses it carries out. **Scaffolding proteins** increase signaling efficiency. Pathway branching further helps the cell coordinate signals and responses. Signal response is terminated quickly by the reversal of ligand binding.

? *What mechanisms in the cell terminate its response to a signal and maintain its ability to respond to new signals?*

CONCEPT 11.5

Apoptosis integrates multiple cell-signaling pathways (pp. 227–229)

- **Apoptosis** is a type of programmed cell death in which cell components are disposed of in an orderly fashion. Studies of the soil worm *Caenorhabditis elegans* clarified molecular details of the relevant signaling pathways. A death signal leads to activation of caspases and nucleases, the main enzymes involved in apoptosis.
- Several apoptotic signaling pathways exist in the cells of humans and other mammals, triggered in different ways. Signals eliciting apoptosis can originate from outside or inside the cell.

? *What is an explanation for the similarities between genes in yeasts, nematodes, and mammals that control apoptosis?*

TEST YOUR UNDERSTANDING

LEVEL 1: KNOWLEDGE/COMPREHENSION

1. Binding of a signaling molecule to which type of receptor leads directly to a change in the distribution of ions on opposite sides of the membrane?
   a. intracellular receptor
   b. G protein-coupled receptor
   c. phosphorylated receptor tyrosine kinase dimer
   d. ligand-gated ion channel

2. The activation of receptor tyrosine kinases is characterized by
   a. dimerization and phosphorylation.
   b. dimerization and IP_3 binding.
   c. a phosphorylation cascade.
   d. GTP hydrolysis.

3. Lipid-soluble signaling molecules, such as aldosterone, cross the membranes of all cells but affect only target cells because
   a. only target cells retain the appropriate DNA segments.
   b. intracellular receptors are present only in target cells.
   c. only target cells have enzymes that break down aldosterone.
   d. only in target cells is aldosterone able to initiate the phosphorylation cascade that turns genes on.

4. Consider this pathway: epinephrine → G protein-coupled receptor → G protein → adenylyl cyclase → cAMP. Identify the second messenger.
   a. cAMP   c. GTP
   b. G protein   d. adenylyl cyclase

5. Apoptosis involves all but which of the following?
   a. fragmentation of the DNA
   b. cell-signaling pathways
   c. lysis of the cell
   d. digestion of cellular contents by scavenger cells

LEVEL 2: APPLICATION/ANALYSIS

6. Which observation suggested to Sutherland the involvement of a second messenger in epinephrine's effect on liver cells?
   a. Enzymatic activity was proportional to the amount of calcium added to a cell-free extract.
   b. Receptor studies indicated that epinephrine was a ligand.
   c. Glycogen breakdown was observed only when epinephrine was administered to intact cells.
   d. Glycogen breakdown was observed when epinephrine and glycogen phosphorylase were combined.

7. Protein phosphorylation is commonly involved with all of the following *except*
   a. activation of receptor tyrosine kinases.
   b. activation of protein kinase molecules.
   c. activation of G protein-coupled receptors.
   d. regulation of transcription by signaling molecules.

LEVEL 3: SYNTHESIS/EVALUATION

8. **DRAW IT** Draw the following apoptotic pathway, which operates in human immune cells. A death signal is received when a molecule called Fas binds its cell-surface receptor. The binding of many Fas molecules to receptors causes receptor clustering. The intracellular regions of the receptors, when together, bind proteins called adaptor proteins. These in turn bind to inactive molecules of caspase-8, which become activated and then activate caspase-3. Once activated, caspase-3 initiates apoptosis.

9. **EVOLUTION CONNECTION**
   What evolutionary mechanisms might account for the origin and persistence of cell-to-cell signaling systems in prokaryotes?

10. **SCIENTIFIC INQUIRY**
    Epinephrine initiates a signal transduction pathway that produces cyclic AMP (cAMP) and leads to the breakdown of glycogen to glucose, a major energy source for cells. But glycogen breakdown is only part of the fight-or-flight response that epinephrine brings about; the overall effect on the body includes an increase in heart rate and alertness, as well as a burst of energy. Given that caffeine blocks the activity of cAMP phosphodiesterase, propose a mechanism by which caffeine ingestion leads to heightened alertness and sleeplessness.

11. **SCIENCE, TECHNOLOGY, AND SOCIETY**
    The aging process is thought to be initiated at the cellular level. Among the changes that can occur after a certain number of cell divisions is the loss of a cell's ability to respond to growth factors and other signals. Much research into aging is aimed at understanding such losses, with the ultimate goal of extending the human life span. Not everyone, however, agrees that this is a desirable goal. If life expectancy were greatly increased, what might be the social and ecological consequences?

12. **WRITE ABOUT A THEME: ORGANIZATION**
    The properties of life emerge at the biological level of the cell. The highly regulated process of apoptosis is not simply the destruction of a cell; it is also an emergent property. Write a short essay (about 100–150 words) that briefly explains the role of apoptosis in the development and proper functioning of an animal, and describe how this form of programmed cell death is a process that emerges from the orderly integration of signaling pathways.

13. **SYNTHESIZE YOUR KNOWLEDGE**

There are five basic tastes—sour, salty, sweet, bitter, and "umami." Salt is detected when the concentration of salt outside of a taste bud cell is higher than that inside of it, and ion channels allow the passive leakage of Na^+ into the cell. The resulting change in membrane potential (see Concept 7.4) sends the "salty" signal to the brain. Umami is a savory taste generated by glutamate (glutamic acid, found in monosodium glutamate, or MSG), which is used as a flavor enhancer in foods such as taco-flavored tortilla chips. The glutamate receptor is a GPCR, which, when bound, initiates a signaling pathway that ends with a cellular response, perceived by you as "taste." If you eat a regular potato chip and then rinse your mouth, you will no longer taste salt. But if you eat a flavored tortilla chip and then rinse, the taste persists. (Try it!) Propose a possible explanation for this difference.

For selected answers, see Appendix A.

MasteringBiology®

Students Go to **MasteringBiology** for assignments, the eText, and the Study Area with practice tests, animations, and activities.

Instructors Go to **MasteringBiology** for automatically graded tutorials and questions that you can assign to your students, plus Instructor Resources.

12

The Cell Cycle

KEY CONCEPTS

12.1 Most cell division results in genetically identical daughter cells

12.2 The mitotic phase alternates with interphase in the cell cycle

12.3 The eukaryotic cell cycle is regulated by a molecular control system

▲ Chromosomes (blue) are moved by cell machinery (red) during division of a rat kangaroo cell.

▲ **Figure 12.1 How do dividing cells distribute chromosomes to daughter cells?**

The Key Roles of Cell Division

The ability of organisms to produce more of their own kind is the one characteristic that best distinguishes living things from nonliving matter. This unique capacity to procreate, like all biological functions, has a cellular basis. Rudolf Virchow, a German physician, put it this way in 1855: "Where a cell exists, there must have been a preexisting cell, just as the animal arises only from an animal and the plant only from a plant." He summarized this concept with the Latin axiom "*Omnis cellula e cellula*," meaning "Every cell from a cell." The continuity of life is based on the reproduction of cells, or **cell division**. The series of confocal fluorescence micrographs in **Figure 12.1**, starting at the upper left, follows the events of cell division as the cells of a two-celled embryo become four.

Cell division plays several important roles in life. When a prokaryotic cell divides, it is actually reproducing, since the process gives rise to a new organism (another cell). The same is true of any unicellular eukaryote, such as the amoeba shown in **Figure 12.2a**. As for multicellular eukaryotes, cell division enables each of these organisms to develop from a single cell—the fertilized egg. A two-celled embryo, the first stage in this process, is shown in **Figure 12.2b**. And cell division continues to function in renewal and repair in fully grown multicellular eukaryotes, replacing cells that die from normal wear and tear or accidents. For example, dividing cells in your bone marrow continuously make new blood cells **(Figure 12.2c)**.

◄ **(a) Reproduction.** An amoeba, a single-celled eukaryote, is dividing into two cells. Each new cell will be an individual organism (LM).

100 μm

► **(b) Growth and development.** This micrograph shows a sand dollar embryo shortly after the fertilized egg divided, forming two cells (LM).

50 μm

◄ **(c) Tissue renewal.** These dividing bone marrow cells will give rise to new blood cells (LM).

20 μm

▲ **Figure 12.2 The functions of cell division.**

The cell division process is an integral part of the **cell cycle**, the life of a cell from the time it is first formed during division of a parent cell until its own division into two daughter cells. (Our use of the words *daughter* or *sister* in relation to cells is not meant to imply gender.) Passing identical genetic material to cellular offspring is a crucial function of cell division. In this chapter, you will learn how this process occurs. After studying the cellular mechanics of cell division in eukaryotes and bacteria, you will learn about the molecular control system that regulates progress through the eukaryotic cell cycle and what happens when the control system malfunctions. Because a breakdown in cell cycle control plays a major role in cancer development, this aspect of cell biology is an active area of research.

CONCEPT 12.1

Most cell division results in genetically identical daughter cells

The reproduction of a cell, with all of its complexity, cannot occur by a mere pinching in half; a cell is not like a soap bubble that simply enlarges and splits in two. In both prokaryotes and eukaryotes, most cell division involves the distribution of identical genetic material—DNA—to two daughter cells. (The exception is meiosis, the special type of eukaryotic cell division that can produce sperm and eggs.) What is most remarkable about cell division is the fidelity with which the DNA is passed from one generation of cells to the next. A dividing cell replicates its DNA, allocates the two copies to opposite ends of the cell, and only then splits into daughter cells.

Cellular Organization of the Genetic Material

A cell's endowment of DNA, its genetic information, is called its **genome**. Although a prokaryotic genome is often a single DNA molecule, eukaryotic genomes usually consist of a number of DNA molecules. The overall length of DNA in a eukaryotic cell is enormous. A typical human cell, for example, has about 2 m of DNA—a length about 250,000 times greater than the cell's diameter. Before the cell can divide to form genetically identical daughter cells, all of this DNA must be copied, or replicated, and then the two copies must be separated so that each daughter cell ends up with a complete genome.

The replication and distribution of so much DNA is manageable because the DNA molecules are packaged into structures called **chromosomes**, so named because they take up certain dyes used in microscopy (from the Greek *chroma*, color, and *soma*, body; **Figure 12.3**). Each eukaryotic chromosome consists of one very long, linear DNA molecule associated with many proteins (see Figure 6.9). The DNA molecule carries several hundred to a few thousand genes, the units of information that specify an organism's inherited traits. The associated proteins maintain the structure of the chromosome and help control the activity of the genes. Together, the entire complex of DNA and proteins that is the building material of chromosomes is referred to as **chromatin**. As you will soon see, the chromatin of a chromosome varies in its degree of condensation during the process of cell division.

Every eukaryotic species has a characteristic number of chromosomes in each cell's nucleus. For example, the nuclei of human **somatic cells** (all body cells except the reproductive cells) each contain 46 chromosomes, made up of two sets of 23, one set inherited from each parent. Reproductive

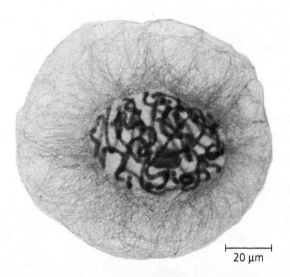

20 μm

▲ **Figure 12.3 Eukaryotic chromosomes.** Chromosomes (stained purple) are visible within the nucleus of this cell from an African blood lily. The thinner red threads in the surrounding cytoplasm are the cytoskeleton. The cell is preparing to divide (LM).

cells, or **gametes**—sperm and eggs—have one set, or half as many chromosomes as somatic cells; in our example, human gametes have one set of 23 chromosomes. The number of chromosomes in somatic cells varies widely among species: 18 in cabbage plants, 48 in chimpanzees, 56 in elephants, 90 in hedgehogs, and 148 in one species of alga. We'll now consider how these chromosomes behave during cell division.

Distribution of Chromosomes During Eukaryotic Cell Division

When a cell is not dividing, and even as it replicates its DNA in preparation for cell division, each chromosome is in the form of a long, thin chromatin fiber. After DNA replication, however, the chromosomes condense as a part of cell division: Each chromatin fiber becomes densely coiled and folded, making the chromosomes much shorter and so thick that we can see them with a light microscope.

Each duplicated chromosome has two **sister chromatids**, which are joined copies of the original chromosome **(Figure 12.4)**. The two chromatids, each containing an identical DNA molecule, are initially attached all along their lengths by protein complexes called *cohesins*; this attachment is known as *sister chromatid cohesion*. Each sister chromatid has a **centromere**, a region of the chromosomal DNA where the chromatid is attached most closely to its sister chromatid. This attachment is mediated by proteins bound to the centromeric DNA; other bound proteins condense the DNA, giving the duplicated chromosome a narrow "waist." The portion of a chromatid to either side of the centromere is referred to as an *arm* of the chromatid. (An unduplicated chromosome has a single centromere, distinguished by the proteins that bind there, and two arms.)

Later in the cell division process, the two sister chromatids of each duplicated chromosome separate and move into two new nuclei, one forming at each end of the cell. Once the sister chromatids separate, they are no longer called sister chromatids but are considered individual chromosomes; this step essentially doubles the number of chromosomes in the cell. Thus, each new nucleus receives a collection of chromosomes identical to that of the parent cell **(Figure 12.5)**. **Mitosis**, the

Sister chromatids

Centromere

0.5 µm

▲ **Figure 12.4** A highly condensed, duplicated human chromosome (SEM).

DRAW IT *Circle one sister chromatid of the chromosome in this micrograph.*

division of the genetic material in the nucleus, is usually followed immediately by **cytokinesis**, the division of the cytoplasm. One cell has become two, each the genetic equivalent of the parent cell.

From a fertilized egg, mitosis and cytokinesis produced the 200 trillion somatic cells that now make up your body, and the same processes continue to generate new cells to

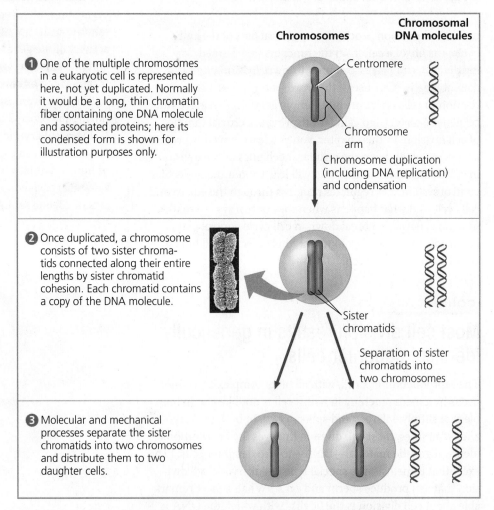

Chromosomes **Chromosomal DNA molecules**

❶ One of the multiple chromosomes in a eukaryotic cell is represented here, not yet duplicated. Normally it would be a long, thin chromatin fiber containing one DNA molecule and associated proteins; here its condensed form is shown for illustration purposes only.

Centromere

Chromosome arm

Chromosome duplication (including DNA replication) and condensation

❷ Once duplicated, a chromosome consists of two sister chromatids connected along their entire lengths by sister chromatid cohesion. Each chromatid contains a copy of the DNA molecule.

Sister chromatids

Separation of sister chromatids into two chromosomes

❸ Molecular and mechanical processes separate the sister chromatids into two chromosomes and distribute them to two daughter cells.

▲ **Figure 12.5** Chromosome duplication and distribution during cell division.

? *How many chromatid arms does the chromosome in ❷ have?*

replace dead and damaged ones. In contrast, you produce gametes—eggs or sperm—by a variation of cell division called *meiosis*, which yields daughter cells with only one set of chromosomes, half as many chromosomes as the parent cell. Meiosis in humans occurs only in special cells in the ovaries or testes (the gonads). Generating gametes, meiosis reduces the chromosome number from 46 (two sets) to 23 (one set). Fertilization fuses two gametes together and returns the chromosome number to 46 (two sets). Mitosis then conserves that number in every somatic cell nucleus of the new human individual. In Chapter 13, we will examine the role of meiosis in reproduction and inheritance in more detail. In the remainder of this chapter, we focus on mitosis and the rest of the cell cycle in eukaryotes.

▲ **Figure 12.6 The cell cycle.** In a dividing cell, the mitotic (M) phase alternates with interphase, a growth period. The first part of interphase (G_1) is followed by the S phase, when the chromosomes duplicate; G_2 is the last part of interphase. In the M phase, mitosis distributes the daughter chromosomes to daughter nuclei, and cytokinesis divides the cytoplasm, producing two daughter cells.

CONCEPT CHECK 12.1

1. How many chromosomes are drawn in each part of Figure 12.5? (Ignore the micrograph in part 2.)

2. **WHAT IF?** A chicken has 78 chromosomes in its somatic cells. How many chromosomes did the chicken inherit from each parent? How many chromosomes are in each of the chicken's gametes? How many chromosomes will be in each somatic cell of the chicken's offspring?

For suggested answers, see Appendix A.

CONCEPT 12.2

The mitotic phase alternates with interphase in the cell cycle

In 1882, a German anatomist named Walther Flemming developed dyes that allowed him to observe, for the first time, the behavior of chromosomes during mitosis and cytokinesis. (In fact, Flemming coined the terms *mitosis* and *chromatin*.) During the period between one cell division and the next, it appeared to Flemming that the cell was simply growing larger. But we now know that many critical events occur during this stage in the life of a cell.

Phases of the Cell Cycle

Mitosis is just one part of the cell cycle **(Figure 12.6)**. In fact, the **mitotic (M) phase**, which includes both mitosis and cytokinesis, is usually the shortest part of the cell cycle. The mitotic phase alternates with a much longer stage called **interphase**, which often accounts for about 90% of the cycle. Interphase can be divided into subphases: the **G_1 phase** ("first gap"), the **S phase** ("synthesis"), and the **G_2 phase** ("second gap"). The G phases were misnamed as "gaps" when they were first observed because the cells appeared inactive, but we now know that intense metabolic activity and growth occur throughout interphase. During all three subphases of interphase, in fact, a cell grows by producing proteins and cytoplasmic organelles such as mitochondria and endoplasmic reticulum. Duplication of the chromosomes, crucial for eventual division of the cell, occurs entirely during the S phase. (We will discuss synthesis of DNA in Chapter 16.) Thus, a cell grows (G_1), continues to grow as it copies its chromosomes (S), grows more as it completes preparations for cell division (G_2), and divides (M). The daughter cells may then repeat the cycle.

A particular human cell might undergo one division in 24 hours. Of this time, the M phase would occupy less than 1 hour, while the S phase might occupy about 10–12 hours, or about half the cycle. The rest of the time would be apportioned between the G_1 and G_2 phases. The G_2 phase usually takes 4–6 hours; in our example, G_1 would occupy about 5–6 hours. G_1 is the most variable in length in different types of cells. Some cells in a multicellular organism divide very infrequently or not at all. These cells spend their time in G_1 (or a related phase called G_0) doing their job in the organism—a nerve cell carries impulses, for example.

Mitosis is conventionally broken down into five stages: **prophase**, **prometaphase**, **metaphase**, **anaphase**, and **telophase**. Overlapping with the latter stages of mitosis, cytokinesis completes the mitotic phase. **Figure 12.7** describes these stages in an animal cell. Study this figure thoroughly before progressing to the next two sections, which examine mitosis and cytokinesis more closely.

The Mitotic Spindle: *A Closer Look*

Many of the events of mitosis depend on the **mitotic spindle**, which begins to form in the cytoplasm during prophase. This structure consists of fibers made of microtubules and

Exploring Mitosis in an Animal Cell

G_2 of Interphase	Prophase	Prometaphase

G_2 of Interphase

Centrosomes (with centriole pairs) — Chromosomes (duplicated, uncondensed)

Nucleolus — Nuclear envelope — Plasma membrane

Prophase

Early mitotic spindle — Aster — Centromere

Two sister chromatids of one chromosome

Prometaphase

Fragments of nuclear envelope — Nonkinetochore microtubules

Kinetochore — Kinetochore microtubule

G_2 of Interphase

- A nuclear envelope encloses the nucleus.
- The nucleus contains one or more nucleoli (singular, *nucleolus*).
- Two centrosomes have formed by duplication of a single centrosome. Centrosomes are regions in animal cells that organize the microtubules of the spindle. Each centrosome contains two centrioles.
- Chromosomes, duplicated during S phase, cannot be seen individually because they have not yet condensed.

The fluorescence micrographs show dividing lung cells from a newt; this species has 22 chromosomes. Chromosomes appear blue, microtubules green, and intermediate filaments red. For simplicity, the drawings show only 6 chromosomes.

Prophase

- The chromatin fibers become more tightly coiled, condensing into discrete chromosomes observable with a light microscope.
- The nucleoli disappear.
- Each duplicated chromosome appears as two identical sister chromatids joined at their centromeres and, in some species, all along their arms by cohesins (sister chromatid cohesion).
- The mitotic spindle (named for its shape) begins to form. It is composed of the centrosomes and the microtubules that extend from them. The radial arrays of shorter microtubules that extend from the centrosomes are called asters ("stars").
- The centrosomes move away from each other, propelled partly by the lengthening microtubules between them.

Prometaphase

- The nuclear envelope fragments.
- The microtubules extending from each centrosome can now invade the nuclear area.
- The chromosomes have become even more condensed.
- Each of the two chromatids of each chromosome now has a kinetochore, a specialized protein structure at the centromere.
- Some of the microtubules attach to the kinetochores, becoming "kinetochore microtubules," which jerk the chromosomes back and forth.
- Nonkinetochore microtubules interact with those from the opposite pole of the spindle.

? *How many molecules of DNA are in the prometaphase drawing? How many molecules per chromosome? How many double helices are there per chromosome? Per chromatid?*

10 μm

| Metaphase | Anaphase | Telophase and Cytokinesis |

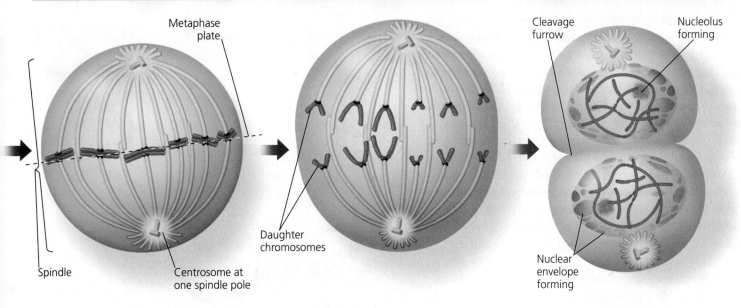

Metaphase plate

Spindle

Centrosome at one spindle pole

Daughter chromosomes

Cleavage furrow

Nucleolus forming

Nuclear envelope forming

Metaphase

- The centrosomes are now at opposite poles of the cell.
- The chromosomes have all arrived at the *metaphase plate*, a plane that is equidistant between the spindle's two poles. The chromosomes' centromeres lie at the metaphase plate.
- For each chromosome, the kinetochores of the sister chromatids are attached to kinetochore microtubules coming from opposite poles.

Anaphase

- Anaphase is the shortest stage of mitosis, often lasting only a few minutes.
- Anaphase begins when the cohesin proteins are cleaved. This allows the two sister chromatids of each pair to part suddenly. Each chromatid thus becomes a full-fledged chromosome.
- The two liberated daughter chromosomes begin moving toward opposite ends of the cell as their kinetochore microtubules shorten. Because these microtubules are attached at the centromere region, the chromosomes move centromere first (at about 1 μm/min).
- The cell elongates as the nonkinetochore microtubules lengthen.
- By the end of anaphase, the two ends of the cell have equivalent—and complete—collections of chromosomes.

Telophase

- Two daughter nuclei form in the cell. Nuclear envelopes arise from the fragments of the parent cell's nuclear envelope and other portions of the endomembrane system.
- Nucleoli reappear.
- The chromosomes become less condensed.
- Any remaining spindle microtubules are depolymerized.
- Mitosis, the division of one nucleus into two genetically identical nuclei, is now complete.

Cytokinesis

- The division of the cytoplasm is usually well under way by late telophase, so the two daughter cells appear shortly after the end of mitosis.
- In animal cells, cytokinesis involves the formation of a cleavage furrow, which pinches the cell in two.

ANIMATION

BioFlix Visit the Study Area in **MasteringBiology** for the BioFlix® 3-D Animation on Mitosis. BioFlix Tutorials can also be assigned in MasteringBiology.

associated proteins. While the mitotic spindle assembles, the other microtubules of the cytoskeleton partially disassemble, providing the material used to construct the spindle. The spindle microtubules elongate (polymerize) by incorporating more subunits of the protein tubulin (see Table 6.1) and shorten (depolymerize) by losing subunits.

In animal cells, the assembly of spindle microtubules starts at the **centrosome**, a subcellular region containing material that functions throughout the cell cycle to organize the cell's microtubules. (It is also a type of *microtubule-organizing center*.) A pair of centrioles is located at the center of the centrosome, but they are not essential for cell division: If the centrioles are destroyed with a laser microbeam, a spindle nevertheless forms during mitosis. In fact, centrioles are not even present in plant cells, which do form mitotic spindles.

During interphase in animal cells, the single centrosome duplicates, forming two centrosomes, which remain near the nucleus. The two centrosomes move apart during prophase and prometaphase of mitosis as spindle microtubules grow out from them. By the end of prometaphase, the two centrosomes, one at each pole of the spindle, are at opposite ends of the cell. An **aster**, a radial array of short microtubules, extends from each centrosome. The spindle includes the centrosomes, the spindle microtubules, and the asters.

Each of the two sister chromatids of a duplicated chromosome has a **kinetochore**, a structure made up of proteins that have assembled on specific sections of DNA at each centromere. The chromosome's two kinetochores face in opposite directions. During prometaphase, some of the spindle microtubules attach to the kinetochores; these are called kinetochore microtubules. (The number of microtubules attached to a kinetochore varies among species, from one microtubule in yeast cells to 40 or so in some mammalian cells.) When one of a chromosome's kinetochores is "captured" by microtubules, the chromosome begins to move toward the pole from which those microtubules extend. However, this movement is checked as soon as microtubules from the opposite pole attach to the kinetochore on the other chromatid. What happens next is like a tug-of-war that ends in a draw. The chromosome moves first in one direction, then in the other, back and forth, finally settling midway between the two ends of the cell. At metaphase, the centromeres of all the duplicated chromosomes are on a plane midway between the spindle's two poles. This plane is called the **metaphase plate**, which is an imaginary plate rather than an actual cellular structure **(Figure 12.8)**. Meanwhile, microtubules that do not attach to kinetochores have been elongating, and by metaphase they overlap and interact with other nonkinetochore microtubules from the opposite pole of the spindle. By metaphase, the microtubules of the asters have also grown and are in contact with the plasma membrane. The spindle is now complete.

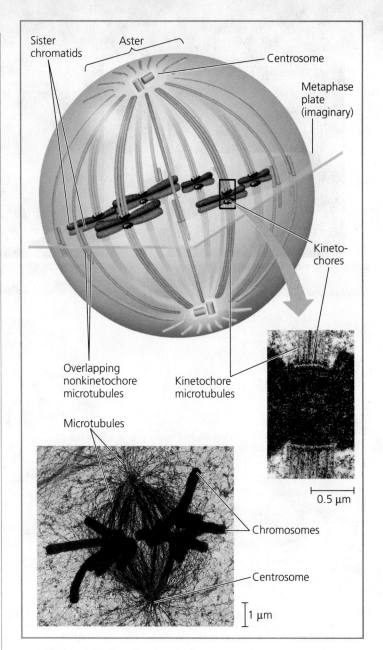

▲ **Figure 12.8 The mitotic spindle at metaphase.** The kinetochores of each chromosome's two sister chromatids face in opposite directions. Here, each kinetochore is attached to a cluster of kinetochore microtubules extending from the nearest centrosome. Non-kinetochore microtubules overlap at the metaphase plate (TEMs).

DRAW IT *On the lower micrograph, draw a line indicating the position of the metaphase plate. Circle an aster. Draw arrows indicating the directions of chromosome movement once anaphase begins.*

The structure of the spindle correlates well with its function during anaphase. Anaphase begins suddenly when the cohesins holding together the sister chromatids of each chromosome are cleaved by an enzyme called *separase*. Once separated, the chromatids become full-fledged chromosomes that move toward opposite ends of the cell.

How do the kinetochore microtubules function in this poleward movement of chromosomes? Apparently, two mechanisms are in play, both involving motor proteins. (To review how motor proteins move an object along a microtubule, see Figure 6.21.) Results of a cleverly designed experiment suggested that motor proteins on the kinetochores "walk" the chromosomes along the microtubules, which depolymerize at their kinetochore ends after the motor proteins have passed **(Figure 12.9)**. (This is referred to as the "Pac-man" mechanism because of its resemblance to the arcade game character that moves by eating all the dots in its path.) However, other researchers, working with different cell types or cells from other species, have shown that chromosomes are "reeled in" by motor proteins at the spindle poles and that the microtubules depolymerize after they pass by these motor proteins. The general consensus now is that both mechanisms are used and that their relative contributions vary among cell types.

In a dividing animal cell, the nonkinetochore microtubules are responsible for elongating the whole cell during anaphase. Nonkinetochore microtubules from opposite poles overlap each other extensively during metaphase (see Figure 12.8). During anaphase, the region of overlap is reduced as motor proteins attached to the microtubules walk them away from one another, using energy from ATP. As the microtubules push apart from each other, their spindle poles are pushed apart, elongating the cell. At the same time, the microtubules lengthen somewhat by the addition of tubulin subunits to their overlapping ends. As a result, the microtubules continue to overlap.

At the end of anaphase, duplicate groups of chromosomes have arrived at opposite ends of the elongated parent cell. Nuclei re-form during telophase. Cytokinesis generally begins during anaphase or telophase, and the spindle eventually disassembles by depolymerization of microtubules.

Cytokinesis: *A Closer Look*

In animal cells, cytokinesis occurs by a process known as **cleavage**. The first sign of cleavage is the appearance of a **cleavage furrow**, a shallow groove in the cell surface near the old metaphase plate **(Figure 12.10a)**. On the cytoplasmic side of the furrow is a contractile ring of actin microfilaments associated with molecules of the protein myosin. The actin microfilaments interact with the myosin molecules, causing the ring to contract. The contraction of the dividing cell's ring of microfilaments is like the pulling of a drawstring. The cleavage furrow deepens until the parent cell is pinched in two, producing two completely separated cells, each with its own nucleus and its own share of cytosol, organelles, and other subcellular structures.

Cytokinesis in plant cells, which have cell walls, is markedly different. There is no cleavage furrow. Instead, during telophase, vesicles derived from the Golgi apparatus move along microtubules to the middle of the cell, where they

▼ **Figure 12.9** | **Inquiry**

At which end do kinetochore microtubules shorten during anaphase?

Experiment Gary Borisy and colleagues at the University of Wisconsin wanted to determine whether kinetochore microtubules depolymerize at the kinetochore end or the pole end as chromosomes move toward the poles during mitosis. First they labeled the microtubules of a pig kidney cell in early anaphase with a yellow fluorescent dye.

Then they marked a region of the kinetochore microtubules between one spindle pole and the chromosomes by using a laser to eliminate the fluorescence from that region, while leaving the microtubules intact (see below). As anaphase proceeded, they monitored the changes in microtubule length on either side of the mark.

Results As the chromosomes moved poleward, the microtubule segments on the kinetochore side of the mark shortened, while those on the spindle pole side stayed the same length.

Conclusion During anaphase in this cell type, chromosome movement is correlated with kinetochore microtubules shortening at their kinetochore ends and not at their spindle pole ends. This experiment supports the hypothesis that during anaphase, a chromosome is walked along a microtubule as the microtubule depolymerizes at its kinetochore end, releasing tubulin subunits.

Source: G. J. Gorbsky, P. J. Sammak, and G. G. Borisy, Chromosomes move poleward in anaphase along stationary microtubules that coordinately disassemble from their kinetochore ends, *Journal of Cell Biology* 104:9–18 (1987).

WHAT IF? *If this experiment had been done on a cell type in which "reeling in" at the poles was the main cause of chromosome movement, how would the mark have moved relative to the poles? How would the microtubule lengths have changed?*

▼ **Figure 12.10** Cytokinesis in animal and plant cells.

(a) Cleavage of an animal cell (SEM)

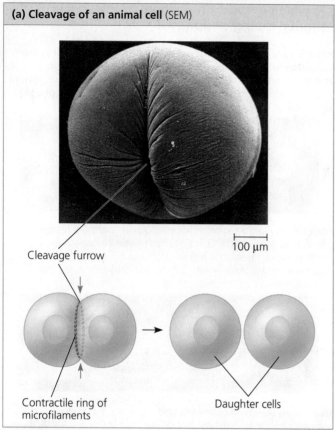

100 μm

Cleavage furrow

Contractile ring of microfilaments

Daughter cells

(b) Cell plate formation in a plant cell (TEM)

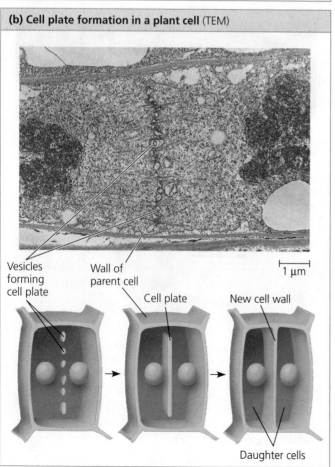

1 μm

Vesicles forming cell plate

Wall of parent cell

Cell plate

New cell wall

Daughter cells

coalesce, producing a **cell plate (Figure 12.10b)**. Cell wall materials carried in the vesicles collect inside the cell plate as it grows. The cell plate enlarges until its surrounding membrane fuses with the plasma membrane along the perimeter of the cell. Two daughter cells result, each with its own plasma membrane. Meanwhile, a new cell wall arising from the contents of the cell plate has formed between the daughter cells.

Figure 12.11 is a series of micrographs of a dividing plant cell. Examining this figure will help you review mitosis and cytokinesis.

Binary Fission in Bacteria

Prokaryotes (bacteria and archaea) can undergo a type of reproduction in which the cell grows to roughly double its size and then divides to form two cells. The term **binary fission**, meaning "division in half," refers to this process and to the asexual reproduction of single-celled eukaryotes, such as the amoeba in Figure 12.2a. However, the process in eukaryotes involves mitosis, while that in prokaryotes does not.

In bacteria, most genes are carried on a single bacterial chromosome that consists of a circular DNA molecule and associated proteins. Although bacteria are smaller and simpler than eukaryotic cells, the challenge of replicating their genomes in an orderly fashion and distributing the copies equally to two daughter cells is still formidable. The chromosome of the bacterium *Escherichia coli*, for example, when it is fully stretched out, is about 500 times as long as the cell. For such a long chromosome to fit within the cell requires that it be highly coiled and folded.

In *E. coli*, the process of cell division is initiated when the DNA of the bacterial chromosome begins to replicate at a specific place on the chromosome called the **origin of replication**, producing two origins. As the chromosome continues to replicate, one origin moves rapidly toward the opposite end of the cell **(Figure 12.12)**. While the chromosome is replicating, the cell elongates. When replication is complete and the bacterium has reached about twice its initial size, its plasma membrane pinches inward, dividing the parent *E. coli* cell into two daughter cells. In this way, each cell inherits a complete genome.

Using the techniques of modern DNA technology to tag the origins of replication with molecules that glow green in fluorescence microscopy (see Figure 6.3), researchers have directly observed the movement of bacterial chromosomes. This movement is reminiscent of the poleward movements of the centromere regions of eukaryotic chromosomes during anaphase of mitosis, but bacteria don't have visible mitotic spindles or even microtubules. In most bacterial species studied, the two origins of replication end up at opposite ends of the cell or in some other very specific location, possibly anchored there by one or more proteins. How bacterial chromosomes move and how their specific location is

10 µm

1 Prophase. The chromosomes are condensing and the nucleolus is beginning to disappear. Although not yet visible in the micrograph, the mitotic spindle is starting to form.

2 Prometaphase. Discrete chromosomes are now visible; each consists of two aligned, identical sister chromatids. Later in prometaphase, the nuclear envelope will fragment.

3 Metaphase. The spindle is complete, and the chromosomes, attached to microtubules at their kinetochores, are all at the metaphase plate.

4 Anaphase. The chromatids of each chromosome have separated, and the daughter chromosomes are moving to the ends of the cell as their kinetochore microtubules shorten.

5 Telophase. Daughter nuclei are forming. Meanwhile, cytokinesis has started: The cell plate, which will divide the cytoplasm in two, is growing toward the perimeter of the parent cell.

▲ **Figure 12.11 Mitosis in a plant cell.** These light micrographs show mitosis in cells of an onion root.

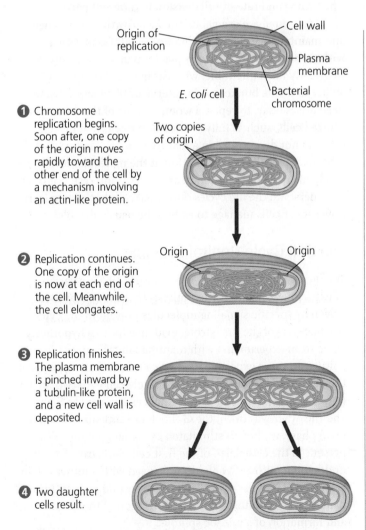

1 Chromosome replication begins. Soon after, one copy of the origin moves rapidly toward the other end of the cell by a mechanism involving an actin-like protein.

2 Replication continues. One copy of the origin is now at each end of the cell. Meanwhile, the cell elongates.

3 Replication finishes. The plasma membrane is pinched inward by a tubulin-like protein, and a new cell wall is deposited.

4 Two daughter cells result.

▲ **Figure 12.12 Bacterial cell division by binary fission.** The bacterium *E. coli*, shown here, has a single, circular chromosome.

established and maintained are active areas of research. Several proteins have been identified that play important roles. Polymerization of one protein resembling eukaryotic actin apparently functions in bacterial chromosome movement during cell division, and another protein that is related to tubulin helps pinch the plasma membrane inward, separating the two bacterial daughter cells.

The Evolution of Mitosis

EVOLUTION Given that prokaryotes preceded eukaryotes on Earth by more than a billion years, we might hypothesize that mitosis evolved from simpler prokaryotic mechanisms of cell reproduction. The fact that some of the proteins involved in bacterial binary fission are related to eukaryotic proteins that function in mitosis supports that hypothesis.

As eukaryotes with nuclear envelopes and larger genomes evolved, the ancestral process of binary fission, seen today in bacteria, somehow gave rise to mitosis. Variations on cell division exist in different groups of organisms. These variant processes may be similar to mechanisms used by ancestral species and thus may resemble steps in the evolution of mitosis from a binary fission-like process presumably carried out by very early bacteria. Possible intermediate stages are suggested by two unusual types of nuclear division found today in certain unicellular eukaryotes—dinoflagellates, diatoms, and some yeasts **(Figure 12.13)**. These two modes of nuclear division are thought to be cases where ancestral mechanisms have remained relatively unchanged over evolutionary time. In both types, the nuclear envelope remains intact, in contrast to what happens in most eukaryotic cells.

Bacterial chromosome

(a) Bacteria. During binary fission in bacteria, the origins of the daughter chromosomes move to opposite ends of the cell. The mechanism involves polymerization of actin-like molecules, and possibly proteins that may anchor the daughter chromosomes to specific sites on the plasma membrane.

Chromosomes

Microtubules

Intact nuclear envelope

(b) Dinoflagellates. In unicellular protists called dinoflagellates, the chromosomes attach to the nuclear envelope, which remains intact during cell division. Microtubules pass through the nucleus inside cytoplasmic tunnels, reinforcing the spatial orientation of the nucleus, which then divides in a process reminiscent of bacterial binary fission.

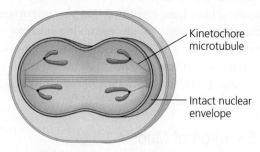

Kinetochore microtubule

Intact nuclear envelope

(c) Diatoms and some yeasts. In these two other groups of unicellular eukaryotes, the nuclear envelope also remains intact during cell division. In these organisms, the microtubules form a spindle *within* the nucleus. Microtubules separate the chromosomes, and the nucleus splits into two daughter nuclei.

Kinetochore microtubule

Fragments of nuclear envelope

(d) Most eukaryotes. In most other eukaryotes, including plants and animals, the spindle forms outside the nucleus, and the nuclear envelope breaks down during mitosis. Microtubules separate the chromosomes, and two nuclear envelopes then form.

▲ **Figure 12.13 Mechanisms of cell division in several groups of organisms.** Some unicellular eukaryotes existing today have mechanisms of cell division that may resemble intermediate steps in the evolution of mitosis. Except for (a), these schematic diagrams do not show cell walls.

1. How many chromosomes are drawn in Figure 12.8? Are they duplicated? How many chromatids are shown?

2. Compare cytokinesis in animal cells and plant cells.

3. During which stages of the cell cycle does a chromosome consist of two identical chromatids?

4. Compare the roles of tubulin and actin during eukaryotic cell division with the roles of tubulin-like and actin-like proteins during bacterial binary fission.

5. A kinetochore has been compared to a coupling device that connects a motor to the cargo that it moves. Explain.

6. **MAKE CONNECTIONS** What other functions do actin and tubulin carry out? Name the proteins they interact with to do so. (Review Figures 6.21a and 6.26a.)

For suggested answers, see Appendix A.

CONCEPT 12.3

The eukaryotic cell cycle is regulated by a molecular control system

The timing and rate of cell division in different parts of a plant or animal are crucial to normal growth, development, and maintenance. The frequency of cell division varies with the type of cell. For example, human skin cells divide frequently throughout life, whereas liver cells maintain the ability to divide but keep it in reserve until an appropriate need arises—say, to repair a wound. Some of the most specialized cells, such as fully formed nerve cells and muscle cells, do not divide at all in a mature human. These cell cycle differences result from regulation at the molecular level. The mechanisms of this regulation are of great interest, not only to understand the life cycles of normal cells but also to learn how cancer cells manage to escape the usual controls.

The Cell Cycle Control System

What controls the cell cycle? In the early 1970s, a variety of experiments led to the hypothesis that the cell cycle is driven by specific signaling molecules present in the cytoplasm. Some of the first strong evidence for this hypothesis came from experiments with mammalian cells grown in culture. In these experiments, two cells in different phases of the cell cycle were fused to form a single cell with two nuclei **(Figure 12.14).** If one of the original cells was in the S phase and the other was in G_1, the G_1 nucleus immediately entered the S phase, as though stimulated by signaling molecules present in the cytoplasm of the first cell. Similarly, if a cell undergoing mitosis (M phase) was fused with another cell in any stage of its cell cycle, even G_1, the second nucleus immediately entered mitosis, with condensation of the chromatin and formation of a mitotic spindle.

The experiment shown in Figure 12.14 and other experiments on animal cells and yeasts demonstrated that the

Inquiry

Do molecular signals in the cytoplasm regulate the cell cycle?

Experiment Researchers at the University of Colorado wondered whether a cell's progression through the cell cycle is controlled by cytoplasmic molecules. To investigate this, they selected cultured mammalian cells that were at different phases of the cell cycle and induced them to fuse. Two such experiments are shown here.

Experiment 1	Experiment 2

When a cell in the S phase was fused with a cell in G_1, the G_1 nucleus immediately entered the S phase—DNA was synthesized.

When a cell in the M phase was fused with a cell in G_1, the G_1 nucleus immediately began mitosis—a spindle formed and the chromosomes condensed, even though the chromosomes had not been duplicated.

Conclusion The results of fusing a G_1 cell with a cell in the S or M phase of the cell cycle suggest that molecules present in the cytoplasm during the S or M phase control the progression to those phases.

Source: R. T. Johnson and P. N. Rao, Mammalian cell fusion: Induction of premature chromosome condensation in interphase nuclei, *Nature* 226:717–722 (1970).

WHAT IF? *If the progression of phases did not depend on cytoplasmic molecules and, instead, each phase automatically began when the previous one was complete, how would the results have differed?*

sequential events of the cell cycle are directed by a distinct **cell cycle control system**, a cyclically operating set of molecules in the cell that both triggers and coordinates key events in the cell cycle. The cell cycle control system has been compared to the control device of an automatic washing machine **(Figure 12.15)**. Like the washer's timing device, the cell cycle control system proceeds on its own, according to a built-in clock. However, just as a washer's cycle is subject to both internal control (such as the sensor that detects when the tub is filled with water) and external adjustment (such as starting or stopping the machine), the cell cycle is regulated at certain checkpoints by both internal and external signals that stop or restart the machine. A **checkpoint** is a control point in the cell cycle where stop and go-ahead signals can regulate the cycle. Three important checkpoints are found in the G_1, G_2, and M phases (the red gates in Figure 12.15).

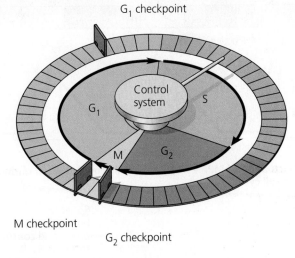

▲ **Figure 12.15 Mechanical analogy for the cell cycle control system.** In this diagram of the cell cycle, the flat "stepping stones" around the perimeter represent sequential events. Like the control device of an automatic washer, the cell cycle control system proceeds on its own, driven by a built-in clock. However, the system is subject to internal and external regulation at various checkpoints; three important checkpoints are shown (red).

To understand how cell cycle checkpoints work, we first need to see what kinds of molecules make up the cell cycle control system (the molecular basis for the cell cycle clock) and how a cell progresses through the cycle. Then we will consider the internal and external checkpoint signals that can make the clock either pause or continue.

The Cell Cycle Clock: Cyclins and Cyclin-Dependent Kinases

Rhythmic fluctuations in the abundance and activity of cell cycle control molecules pace the sequential events of the cell cycle. These regulatory molecules are mainly proteins of two types: protein kinases and cyclins. Protein kinases are enzymes that activate or inactivate other proteins by phosphorylating them (see Chapter 11).

Many of the kinases that drive the cell cycle are actually present at a constant concentration in the growing cell, but much of the time they are in an inactive form. To be active, such a kinase must be attached to a **cyclin**, a protein that gets its name from its cyclically fluctuating concentration in the cell. Because of this requirement, these kinases are called **cyclin-dependent kinases**, or **Cdks**. The activity of a Cdk rises and falls with changes in the concentration of its cyclin partner. **Figure 12.16a** shows the fluctuating activity of **MPF**, the cyclin-Cdk complex that was discovered first (in frog eggs). Note that the peaks of MPF activity correspond to the peaks of cyclin concentration. The cyclin level rises during the S and G_2 phases and then falls abruptly during M phase.

The initials MPF stand for "maturation-promoting factor," but we can think of MPF as "M-phase-promoting factor" because it triggers the cell's passage into the M phase,

(a) **Fluctuation of MPF activity and cyclin concentration during the cell cycle**

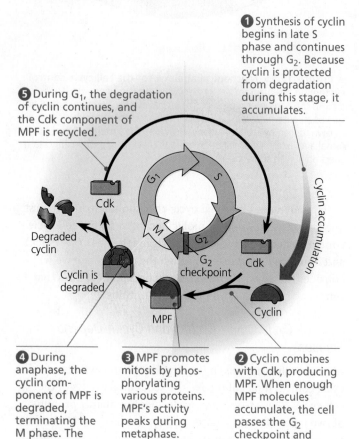

① Synthesis of cyclin begins in late S phase and continues through G₂. Because cyclin is protected from degradation during this stage, it accumulates.

⑤ During G₁, the degradation of cyclin continues, and the Cdk component of MPF is recycled.

④ During anaphase, the cyclin component of MPF is degraded, terminating the M phase. The cell enters the G₁ phase.

③ MPF promotes mitosis by phosphorylating various proteins. MPF's activity peaks during metaphase.

② Cyclin combines with Cdk, producing MPF. When enough MPF molecules accumulate, the cell passes the G₂ checkpoint and begins mitosis.

(b) **Molecular mechanisms that help regulate the cell cycle**

▲ **Figure 12.16 Molecular control of the cell cycle at the G₂ checkpoint.** The steps of the cell cycle are timed by rhythmic fluctuations in the activity of cyclin-dependent kinases (Cdks). Here we focus on a cyclin-Cdk complex in animal cells called MPF, which acts at the G₂ checkpoint as a go-ahead signal, triggering the events of mitosis.

❓ *Explain how the events in the diagram in (b) are related to the "Time" axis of the graph in (a), beginning at the left end.*

past the G₂ checkpoint **(Figure 12.16b)**. When cyclins that accumulate during G₂ associate with Cdk molecules, the resulting MPF complex phosphorylates a variety of proteins, initiating mitosis. MPF acts both directly as a kinase and indirectly by activating other kinases. For example, MPF causes phosphorylation of various proteins of the nuclear

lamina (see Figure 6.9), which promotes fragmentation of the nuclear envelope during prometaphase of mitosis. There is also evidence that MPF contributes to molecular events required for chromosome condensation and spindle formation during prophase.

During anaphase, MPF helps switch itself off by initiating a process that leads to the destruction of its own cyclin. The noncyclin part of MPF, the Cdk, persists in the cell, inactive until it becomes part of MPF again by associating with new cyclin molecules synthesized during the S and G₂ phases of the next round of the cycle.

The fluctuating activities of different cyclin-Cdk complexes are of major importance in controlling all the stages of the cell cycle and give the go-ahead signals at some checkpoints as well. As mentioned above, MPF controls the cell's passage through the G₂ checkpoint. Cell behavior at the G₁ checkpoint is also regulated by the activity of cyclin-Cdk protein complexes. Animal cells appear to have at least three Cdk proteins and several different cyclins that operate at this checkpoint. Next, let's consider checkpoints in more detail.

Stop and Go Signs: Internal and External Signals at the Checkpoints

Animal cells generally have built-in stop signals that halt the cell cycle at checkpoints until overridden by go-ahead signals. (The signals are transmitted within the cell by the kinds of signal transduction pathways discussed in Chapter 11.) Many signals registered at checkpoints come from cellular surveillance mechanisms inside the cell. These signals report whether crucial cellular processes that should have occurred by that point have in fact been completed correctly and thus whether or not the cell cycle should proceed. Checkpoints also register signals from outside the cell. Three important checkpoints are those in G₁, G₂, and M phases, shown in Figure 12.15.

For many cells, the G₁ checkpoint—dubbed the "restriction point" in mammalian cells—seems to be the most important. If a cell receives a go-ahead signal at the G₁ checkpoint, it will usually complete the G₁, S, G₂, and M phases and divide. If it does not receive a go-ahead signal at that point, it may exit the cycle, switching into a nondividing state called the **G₀ phase (Figure 12.17a)**. Most cells of the human body are actually in the G₀ phase. As mentioned earlier, mature nerve cells and muscle cells never divide. Other cells, such as liver cells, can be "called back" from the G₀ phase to the cell cycle by external cues, such as growth factors released during injury.

Biologists are currently working out the pathways that link signals originating inside and outside the cell with the responses by cyclin-dependent kinases and other proteins. An example of an internal signal occurs at the third important checkpoint, the M phase checkpoint **(Figure 12.17b)**.

▶ **Figure 12.17 Two important checkpoints.** At certain checkpoints in the cell cycle (red gates), cells do different things depending on the signals they receive. Events of the **(a)** G_1 and **(b)** M checkpoints are shown. In **(b)**, the G_2 checkpoint has already been passed by the cell.

WHAT IF? *What might be the result if the cell ignored either checkpoint and progressed through the cell cycle?*

G_1 checkpoint

G_0

G_1

In the absence of a go-ahead signal, a cell exits the cell cycle and enters G_0, a nondividing state.

(a) G_1 checkpoint

G_1

If a cell receives a go-ahead signal, the cell continues on in the cell cycle.

G_1

M G_2

M checkpoint

Prometaphase

A cell in mitosis receives a stop signal when any of its chromosomes are not attached to spindle fibers.

(b) M checkpoint

G_1

M G_2

Anaphase

G_2 checkpoint

Metaphase

When all chromosomes are attached to spindle fibers from both poles, a go-ahead signal allows the cell to proceed into anaphase.

Anaphase, the separation of sister chromatids, does not begin until all the chromosomes are properly attached to the spindle at the metaphase plate. Researchers have learned that as long as some kinetochores are unattached to spindle microtubules, the sister chromatids remain together, delaying anaphase. Only when the kinetochores of all the chromosomes are properly attached to the spindle does the appropriate regulatory protein complex become activated. (In this case, the regulatory molecule is not a cyclin-Cdk complex but, instead, a different complex made up of several proteins.) Once activated, the complex sets off a chain of molecular events that activates the enzyme separase, which cleaves the cohesins, allowing the sister chromatids to separate. This mechanism ensures that daughter cells do not end up with missing or extra chromosomes.

Studies using animal cells in culture have led to the identification of many external factors, both chemical and physical, that can influence cell division. For example, cells fail to divide if an essential nutrient is lacking in the culture medium. (This is analogous to trying to run a washing machine without the water supply hooked up; an internal sensor won't allow the machine to continue past the point where water is needed.) And even if all other conditions are favorable, most types of mammalian cells divide in culture only if the growth medium includes specific growth factors. As mentioned in Chapter 11, a **growth factor** is a protein released by certain cells that stimulates other cells to divide.

Different cell types respond specifically to different growth factors or combinations of growth factors.

Consider, for example, *platelet-derived growth factor (PDGF)*, which is made by blood cell fragments called platelets. The experiment illustrated in **Figure 12.18** demonstrates that PDGF is required for the division of cultured fibroblasts, a type of connective tissue cell. Fibroblasts have PDGF receptors on their plasma membranes. The binding of PDGF molecules to these receptors (which are receptor tyrosine kinases; see Figure 11.8) triggers a signal transduction pathway that allows the cells to pass the G_1 checkpoint and divide. PDGF stimulates fibroblast division not only in the artificial conditions of cell culture, but also in an animal's body. When an injury occurs, platelets release PDGF in the vicinity. The resulting proliferation of fibroblasts helps heal the wound.

The effect of an external physical factor on cell division is clearly seen in **density-dependent inhibition**, a phenomenon in which crowded cells stop dividing **(Figure 12.19a)**. As first observed many years ago, cultured cells normally divide until they form a single layer of cells on the inner surface of the culture flask, at which point the cells stop dividing. If some cells are removed, those bordering the open

1 A sample of human connective tissue is cut up into small pieces.

Scalpels

Petri dish

2 Enzymes are used to digest the extracellular matrix in the tissue pieces, resulting in a suspension of free fibroblasts.

3 Cells are transferred to culture vessels containing a basic growth medium consisting of glucose, amino acids, salts, and antibiotics (to prevent bacterial growth).

4 PDGF is added to half the vessels. The culture vessels are incubated at 37°C for 24 hours.

◀ **Figure 12.18 The effect of platelet-derived growth factor (PDGF) on cell division.**

Without PDGF

In the basic growth medium without PDGF (the control), the cells fail to divide.

With PDGF

In the basic growth medium plus PDGF, the cells proliferate. The SEM shows cultured fibroblasts.

MAKE CONNECTIONS

PDGF signals cells by binding to a cell-surface receptor tyrosine kinase. If you added a chemical that blocked phosphorylation, how would the results differ? (See Figure 11.8.)

10 μm

Cells anchor to dish surface and divide (anchorage dependence).

When cells have formed a complete single layer, they stop dividing (density-dependent inhibition).

If some cells are scraped away, the remaining cells divide to fill the gap and then stop once they contact each other (density-dependent inhibition).

20 μm

(a) Normal mammalian cells. Contact with neighboring cells and the availability of nutrients, growth factors, and a substratum for attachment limit cell density to a single layer.

20 μm

(b) Cancer cells. Cancer cells usually continue to divide well beyond a single layer, forming a clump of overlapping cells. They do not exhibit anchorage dependence or density-dependent inhibition.

▲ **Figure 12.19 Density-dependent inhibition and anchorage dependence of cell division.** Individual cells are shown disproportionately large in the drawings.

space begin dividing again and continue until the vacancy is filled. Follow-up studies revealed that the binding of a cell-surface protein to its counterpart on an adjoining cell sends a cell division-inhibiting signal forward in the cell cycle, even in the presence of growth factors.

Most animal cells also exhibit **anchorage dependence** (see Figure 12.19a). To divide, they must be attached to a substratum, such as the inside of a culture flask or the extracellular matrix of a tissue. Experiments suggest that like cell density, anchorage is signaled to the cell cycle control system via pathways involving plasma membrane proteins and elements of the cytoskeleton linked to them.

Density-dependent inhibition and anchorage dependence appear to function not only in cell culture but also in the body's tissues, checking the growth of cells at some optimal density and location during embryonic development and throughout an organism's life. Cancer cells, which we discuss next, exhibit neither density-dependent inhibition nor anchorage dependence **(Figure 12.19b)**.

Loss of Cell Cycle Controls in Cancer Cells

Cancer cells do not heed the normal signals that regulate the cell cycle. In culture, they do not stop dividing when growth factors are depleted. A logical hypothesis is that cancer cells do not need growth factors in their culture medium to grow and divide. They may make a required growth factor themselves, or they may have an abnormality in the signaling pathway that conveys the growth factor's signal to the cell cycle control system even in the absence of that factor. Another possibility is an abnormal cell cycle control system. In these scenarios, the underlying basis of the abnormality is almost always a change in one or more genes (for example, a mutation) that alters the function of their protein products, resulting in faulty cell cycle control.

There are other important differences between normal cells and cancer cells that reflect derangements of the cell cycle. If and when they stop dividing, cancer cells do so at random points in the cycle, rather than at the normal checkpoints. Moreover, cancer cells can go on dividing indefinitely in culture if they are given a continual supply of nutrients; in essence, they are "immortal." A striking example is a cell line that has been reproducing in culture since 1951. Cells of this line are called HeLa cells because their original source was a tumor removed from a woman named *Henrietta La*cks. Cells in culture that acquire the ability to divide indefinitely are said to have undergone **transformation**, the process that causes them to behave like cancer cells. By contrast, nearly all normal, nontransformed mammalian cells growing in culture divide only about 20 to 50 times before they stop dividing, age, and die. Finally, cancer cells evade the normal controls that trigger a cell to undergo apoptosis when something is wrong—for example, when an irreparable mistake has occurred during DNA replication preceding mitosis.

The abnormal behavior of cancer cells can be catastrophic when it occurs in the body. The problem begins when a single cell in a tissue undergoes the first changes of the multistep process that converts a normal cell to a cancer cell. Such a cell often has altered proteins on its surface, and the body's immune system normally recognizes the cell as "nonself"—an insurgent—and destroys it. However, if the cell evades destruction, it may proliferate and form a tumor, a mass of abnormal cells within otherwise normal tissue. The abnormal cells may remain at the original site if they have too few genetic and cellular changes to survive at another site. In that case, the tumor is called a **benign tumor**. Most benign tumors do not cause serious problems and can be removed by surgery. In contrast, a **malignant tumor** includes cells whose genetic and cellular changes enable them to spread to new tissues and impair the functions of one or more organs; these cells are also considered *transformed* cells. An individual with a malignant tumor is said to have cancer; **Figure 12.20** shows the development of breast cancer, as well as a typical breast cancer cell.

The changes that have occurred in cells of malignant tumors show up in many ways besides excessive proliferation. These cells may have unusual numbers of chromosomes, though whether this is a cause or an effect of transformation is a topic of debate. Their metabolism may be altered, and they may cease to function in any constructive way. Abnormal changes on the cell surface cause cancer cells to lose attachments to neighboring cells and the extracellular matrix, allowing them to spread into nearby tissues. Cancer cells may also secrete signaling molecules that cause blood vessels to grow toward the tumor. A few tumor cells may separate from the original tumor, enter blood vessels and lymph vessels, and travel to other parts of the body. There, they may proliferate and form a new tumor. This spread of cancer cells to locations distant from their original site is called **metastasis** (see Figure 12.20).

A tumor that appears to be localized may be treated with high-energy radiation, which damages DNA in cancer cells much more than it does in normal cells, apparently because the majority of cancer cells have lost the ability to repair such damage. To treat known or suspected metastatic tumors, chemotherapy is used, in which drugs that are toxic to actively dividing cells are administered through the circulatory system. As you might expect, chemotherapeutic drugs interfere with specific steps in the cell cycle. For example, the drug Taxol freezes the mitotic spindle by preventing microtubule depolymerization, which stops actively dividing cells from proceeding past metaphase and leads to their destruction. The side effects of chemotherapy are due to the effects of the drugs on normal cells that divide often, due to the function of that cell type in the organism. For example, nausea results from chemotherapy's effects on intestinal cells, hair loss from effects on hair follicle cells, and susceptibility to infection from effects on immune system cells. You'll work

▼ **Figure 12.20 The growth and metastasis of a malignant breast tumor.** A series of genetic and cellular changes contribute to a tumor becoming malignant (cancerous). The cells of malignant tumors grow in an uncontrolled way and can spread to neighboring tissues and, via lymph and blood vessels, to other parts of the body. The spread of cancer cells beyond their original site is called metastasis.

Breast cancer cell (colorized SEM)

1 A tumor grows from a single cancer cell.

2 Cancer cells invade neighboring tissue.

3 Cancer cells spread through lymph and blood vessels to other parts of the body.

4 A small percentage of cancer cells may metastasize to another part of the body.

with data from an experiment involving a potential chemo-therapeutic agent in the Scientific Skills Exercise.

Over the past several decades, researchers have produced a flood of valuable information about cell-signaling pathways and how their malfunction contributes to the development of cancer through effects on the cell cycle. Coupled with new molecular techniques, such as the ability to rapidly sequence the DNA of cells in a particular tumor, medical treatments for cancer are beginning to become more "personalized" to a particular patient's tumor (see Figure 18.27).

For example, the cells of roughly 20% of breast cancer tumors show abnormally high amounts of a cell-surface receptor tyrosine kinase called HER2, and many show an increase in the number of estrogen receptor (ER) molecules, intracellular receptors that can trigger cell division. Based on lab findings, a physician can prescribe chemotherapy with a molecule that blocks the function of the specific protein (Herceptin for HER2 and tamoxifen for ERs). Treatment using these agents, when appropriate, has led to increased survival rates and fewer cancer recurrences.

CONCEPT CHECK 12.3

1. In Figure 12.14, why do the nuclei resulting from experiment 2 contain different amounts of DNA?

2. How does MPF allow a cell to pass the G_2 phase checkpoint and enter mitosis? (See Figure 12.16.)

3. **MAKE CONNECTIONS** Explain in general how receptor tyrosine kinases and intracellular receptors might function in triggering cell division. (Review Figures 11.8 and 11.9 and Chapter 11.)

For suggested answers, see Appendix A.

SCIENTIFIC SKILLS EXERCISE

Interpreting Histograms

At What Phase Is the Cell Cycle Arrested by an Inhibitor?
Many medical treatments are aimed at stopping cancer cell proliferation by blocking the cell cycle of cancerous tumor cells. One potential treatment is a cell cycle inhibitor derived from human umbilical cord stem cells. In this exercise, you will compare two histograms to determine where in the cell cycle the inhibitor blocks the division of cancer cells.

How the Experiment Was Done In the treated sample, human glioblastoma (brain cancer) cells were grown in tissue culture in the presence of the inhibitor, while control sample cells were grown in its absence. After 72 hours of growth, the two cell samples were harvested. To get a "snapshot" of the phase of the cell cycle each cell was in at that time, the samples were treated with a fluorescent chemical that binds to DNA and then run through a flow cytometer, an instrument that records the fluorescence level of each cell. Computer software then graphed the number of cells in each sample with a particular fluorescence level, as shown below.

Data from the Experiment

The data are plotted in a type of graph called a histogram (above), which groups values for a numeric variable on the x-axis into intervals. A histogram allows you to see how all the experimental subjects (cells, in this case) are distributed along a continuous variable (amount of fluorescence). In these histograms, the bars are so narrow that the data appear to follow a curve for which you can detect peaks and dips. Each narrow bar represents the number of cells observed to have a level of fluorescence in the range of that interval. This in turn indicates the relative amount of DNA in those cells. Overall, comparing the two histograms allows you to see how the DNA content of this cell population is altered by the treatment.

Interpret the Data
1. Familiarize yourself with the data shown in the histograms. (a) Which axis indirectly shows the relative amount of DNA per cell? Explain your answer. (b) In the control sample, compare the first peak in the histogram (in region A) to the second peak (in region C). Which peak shows the population of cells with the higher amount of DNA per cell? Explain. (For additional information about graphs, see the Scientific Skills Review in Appendix F and in the Study Area in MasteringBiology.)

2. (a) In the control sample histogram, identify the phase of the cell cycle (G_1, S, or G_2) of the population of cells in each region delineated by vertical lines. Label the histogram with these phases and explain your answer. (b) Does the S phase population of cells show a distinct peak in the histogram? Why or why not?

3. The histogram representing the treated sample shows the effect of growing the cancer cells alongside human umbilical cord stem cells that produce the potential inhibitor. (a) Label the histogram with the cell cycle phases. Which phase of the cell cycle has the greatest number of cells in the treated sample? Explain. (b) Compare the distribution of cells among G_1, S, and G_2 phases in the control and treated samples. What does this tell you about the cells in the treated sample? (c) Based on what you learned in Concept 12.3, propose a mechanism by which the stem cell-derived inhibitor might arrest the cancer cell cycle at this stage. (More than one answer is possible.)

MB A version of this Scientific Skills Exercise can be assigned in MasteringBiology.

Data from K. K. Velpula et al., Regulation of glioblastoma progression by cord blood stem cells is mediated by downregulation of cyclin D1, *PLoS ONE* 6(3): e18017 (2011).

12 Chapter Review

SUMMARY OF KEY CONCEPTS

- Unicellular organisms reproduce by **cell division**; multicellular organisms depend on cell division for their development from a fertilized egg and for growth and repair. Cell division is part of the **cell cycle**, an ordered sequence of events in the life of a cell.

CONCEPT 12.1

Most cell division results in genetically identical daughter cells (pp. 233–235)

- The genetic material (DNA) of a cell—its **genome**—is partitioned among **chromosomes**. Each eukaryotic chromosome consists of one DNA molecule associated with many proteins. Together, the complex of DNA and associated proteins is called **chromatin**. The chromatin of a chromosome exists in different states of condensation at different times. In animals, **gametes** have one set of chromosomes and **somatic cells** have two sets.

- Cells replicate their genetic material before they divide, each daughter cell receiving a copy of the DNA. Prior to cell division, chromosomes are duplicated. Each one then consists of two identical **sister chromatids** joined along their lengths by sister chromatid cohesion and held most tightly together at a constricted region at the **centromeres**. When this cohesion is broken, the chromatids separate during cell division, becoming the chromosomes of the daughter cells. Eukaryotic cell division consists of **mitosis** (division of the nucleus) and **cytokinesis** (division of the cytoplasm).

> ? *Differentiate between these terms: chromosome, chromatin, and chromatid.*

CONCEPT 12.2

The mitotic phase alternates with interphase in the cell cycle (pp. 235–242)

- Between divisions, a cell is in **interphase**: the G_1, S, and G_2 phases. The cell grows throughout interphase, with DNA being replicated only during the synthesis (S) phase. Mitosis and cytokinesis make up the **mitotic (M) phase** of the cell cycle.

- The **mitotic spindle**, made up of microtubules, controls chromosome movement during mitosis. In animal cells, it arises from the **centrosomes** and includes spindle microtubules and **asters**. Some spindle microtubules attach to the **kinetochores** of chromosomes and move the chromosomes to the **metaphase plate**. After sister chromatids separate, motor proteins move them along kinetochore microtubules toward opposite ends of the cell. The cell elongates when motor proteins push nonkinetochore microtubules from opposite poles away from each other.

- Mitosis is usually followed by cytokinesis. Animal cells carry out cytokinesis by **cleavage**, and plant cells form a **cell plate**.

- During **binary fission** in bacteria, the chromosome replicates and the daughter chromosomes actively move apart. Some of the proteins involved in bacterial binary fission are related to eukaryotic actin and tubulin.

- Since prokaryotes preceded eukaryotes by more than a billion years, it is likely that mitosis evolved from prokaryotic cell division. Certain unicellular eukaryotes exhibit mechanisms of cell division that may be similar to those of ancestors of existing eukaryotes. Such mechanisms might represent intermediate steps in the evolution of mitosis.

> ? *In which of the three subphases of interphase and the stages of mitosis do chromosomes exist as single DNA molecules?*

CONCEPT 12.3

The eukaryotic cell cycle is regulated by a molecular control system (pp. 242–248)

- Signaling molecules present in the cytoplasm regulate progress through the cell cycle.

- The **cell cycle control system** is molecularly based. Cyclic changes in regulatory proteins work as a cell cycle clock. The key molecules are **cyclins** and **cyclin-dependent kinases (Cdks)**. The clock has specific **checkpoints** where the cell cycle stops until a go-ahead signal is received; important checkpoints occur in G_1, G_2, and M phases. Cell culture has enabled researchers to study the molecular details of cell division. Both internal signals and external signals control the cell cycle checkpoints via signal transduction pathways. Most cells exhibit **density-dependent inhibition** of cell division as well as **anchorage dependence**.

- Cancer cells elude normal cell cycle regulation and divide unchecked, forming tumors. **Malignant tumors** invade nearby tissues and can undergo **metastasis**, exporting cancer cells to other sites, where they may form secondary tumors. Recent cell cycle and cell signaling research, and new techniques for sequencing DNA, have led to improved cancer treatments.

> ? *Explain the significance of the G_1, G_2, and M checkpoints and the go-ahead signals involved in the cell cycle control system.*

TEST YOUR UNDERSTANDING

LEVEL 1: KNOWLEDGE/COMPREHENSION

1. Through a microscope, you can see a cell plate beginning to develop across the middle of a cell and nuclei forming on either side of the cell plate. This cell is most likely
   a. an animal cell in the process of cytokinesis.
   b. a plant cell in the process of cytokinesis.
   c. a bacterial cell dividing.
   d. a plant cell in metaphase.

2. Vinblastine is a standard chemotherapeutic drug used to treat cancer. Because it interferes with the assembly of microtubules, its effectiveness must be related to
   a. disruption of mitotic spindle formation.
   b. suppression of cyclin production.
   c. myosin denaturation and inhibition of cleavage furrow formation.
   d. inhibition of DNA synthesis.

3. One difference between cancer cells and normal cells is that cancer cells
   a. are unable to synthesize DNA.
   b. are arrested at the S phase of the cell cycle.
   c. continue to divide even when they are tightly packed together.
   d. cannot function properly because they are affected by density-dependent inhibition.

4. The decline of MPF activity at the end of mitosis is due to
   a. the destruction of the protein kinase Cdk.
   b. decreased synthesis of Cdk.
   c. the degradation of cyclin.
   d. the accumulation of cyclin.

5. In the cells of some organisms, mitosis occurs without cytokinesis. This will result in
   a. cells with more than one nucleus.
   b. cells that are unusually small.
   c. cells lacking nuclei.
   d. cell cycles lacking an S phase.

6. Which of the following does *not* occur during mitosis?
   a. condensation of the chromosomes
   b. replication of the DNA
   c. separation of sister chromatids
   d. spindle formation

LEVEL 2: APPLICATION/ANALYSIS

7. A particular cell has half as much DNA as some other cells in a mitotically active tissue. The cell in question is most likely in
   a. G_1.   c. prophase.
   b. G_2.   d. metaphase.

8. The drug cytochalasin B blocks the function of actin. Which of the following aspects of the animal cell cycle would be most disrupted by cytochalasin B?
   a. spindle formation
   b. spindle attachment to kinetochores
   c. cell elongation during anaphase
   d. cleavage furrow formation and cytokinesis

9. In the light micrograph below of dividing cells near the tip of an onion root, identify a cell in each of the following stages: prophase, prometaphase, metaphase, anaphase, and telophase. Describe the major events occurring at each stage.

10. **DRAW IT** Draw one eukaryotic chromosome as it would appear during interphase, during each of the stages of mitosis, and during cytokinesis. Also draw and label the nuclear envelope and any microtubules attached to the chromosome(s).

LEVEL 3: SYNTHESIS/EVALUATION

11. **EVOLUTION CONNECTION**
    The result of mitosis is that the daughter cells end up with the same number of chromosomes that the parent cell had. Another way to maintain the number of chromosomes would be to carry out cell division first and then duplicate the chromosomes in each daughter cell. Do you think this would be an equally good way of organizing the cell cycle? Why do you suppose that evolution has not led to this alternative?

12. **SCIENTIFIC INQUIRY**
    Although both ends of a microtubule can gain or lose subunits, one end (called the plus end) polymerizes and depolymerizes at a higher rate than the other end (the minus end). For spindle microtubules, the plus ends are in the center of the spindle, and the minus ends are at the poles. Motor proteins that move along microtubules specialize in walking either toward the plus end or toward the minus end; the two types are called plus end–directed and minus end–directed motor proteins, respectively. Given what you know about chromosome movement and spindle changes during anaphase, predict which type of motor proteins would be present on (a) kinetochore microtubules and (b) nonkinetochore microtubules.

13. **WRITE ABOUT A THEME: INFORMATION**
    Continuity of life is based on heritable information in the form of DNA. In a short essay (100–150 words), explain how the process of mitosis faithfully parcels out exact copies of this heritable information in the production of genetically identical daughter cells.

14. **SYNTHESIZE YOUR KNOWLEDGE**

Shown here are two HeLa cancer cells that are just completing cytokinesis. Explain how the cell division of cancer cells like these is misregulated. What genetic and other changes might have caused these cells to escape normal cell cycle regulation?

For selected answers, see Appendix A.

MasteringBiology®

Students Go to **MasteringBiology** for assignments, the eText, and the Study Area with practice tests, animations, and activities.

Instructors Go to **MasteringBiology** for automatically graded tutorials and questions that you can assign to your students, plus Instructor Resources.

3 GENETICS

AN INTERVIEW WITH

Charles Rotimi

Charles Rotimi was born in Nigeria and received a B.S. in biochemistry from the University of Benin. He also received advanced degrees in health care administration from the University of Mississippi and in public health from the University of Alabama. As a professor at the medical schools of Loyola University (Chicago) and Howard University, Dr. Rotimi focused his research on health disparities in populations of African ancestry. He is now the Director of the Center for Research on Genomics and Global Health at the National Institutes of Health.

How did you become interested in public health?

After arriving in Mississippi for graduate study in biochemistry, I learned that African-Americans in the local community were disproportionately affected by hypertension (high blood pressure), diabetes, and obesity. "Why was that?" I wondered. I started thinking I should go into public health, and I applied to study epidemiology at the University of Alabama. Epidemiology is the branch of medicine that studies diseases at the population level. Research in epidemiology can help determine the risk factors for various diseases and can influence public health policy. I realized I wanted to devote my career to investigating health disparities worldwide.

> " **Our ability to query the whole genome at once, for a large number of people, puts biology on a completely new scale.** "

My research career has been driven by a few fundamental questions: Why would a group of people be disproportionately affected by multiple conditions that cut across many metabolic pathways? For example, a person with diabetes tends to have hypertension, is often overweight, and may also have abnormal blood lipid levels and kidney function. Why is there such a clustering of metabolic disorders?

How did you get involved in genetics—and genomics?

One day I saw an exciting ad from Loyola University, seeking an assistant professor to study why we see different distributions of diseases across different populations of African ancestry. I said to myself, "This ad was written for me," and I got the position.

My mentor, Richard S. Cooper, had funding to look at the distribution of hypertension in selected populations in Africa, the Caribbean, and the United States. In the first study, we found that the prevalence of hypertension increases from rural West Africa to African urban centers to the black nations of the Caribbean to Maywood, Illinois. We were able to explain much of the observed increase by differences in factors like salt intake, physical activity, and weight. But we couldn't explain everything. We knew that our study subjects shared relatively recent ancestry but had varying genetic contributions from parental African and European populations. (For example, African-Americans have, on average, about 20% of their DNA from Europe.) These understandings led us to realize that we needed to incorporate genetics in our attempts to explain the residual variability.

Today, we use genomics on a routine basis. I can sequence all the genes of study participants. I feel like a kid in a candy store! Our ability to query the whole genome at once, for a large number of people, puts biology on a completely new scale.

What is the role of genetics in personalized medicine?

One of the things genomics is teaching us is that diseases such as hypertension or diabetes or cancer can be very different on the molecular level from person to person. Being able to use genetics to subclassify these diseases will enable us to treat individuals with specific drugs that will help them.

In my center here at NIH we are studying variation in important drug-metabolizing enzymes in people from various populations. Using a new chip that analyzes the genes for these enzymes, we have looked at 19 different populations across the world. We've found that people can belong to the same ethnic group yet have very different responses to a drug because of individual variation. These data really caution against using easy labels like "black," "African," or "European" for drug prescription at the individual level.

(MB) For an extended interview and video clip, go to the Study Area in MasteringBiology.

13

Meiosis and Sexual Life Cycles

KEY CONCEPTS

13.1 Offspring acquire genes from parents by inheriting chromosomes

13.2 Fertilization and meiosis alternate in sexual life cycles

13.3 Meiosis reduces the number of chromosome sets from diploid to haploid

13.4 Genetic variation produced in sexual life cycles contributes to evolution

▲ **Figure 13.1** What accounts for family resemblance?

Variations on a Theme

We all know that offspring resemble their parents more than they do unrelated individuals. If you examine the family members shown in **Figure 13.1**, you can pick out some similar features among them. The transmission of traits from one generation to the next is called inheritance, or **heredity** (from the Latin *heres*, heir). However, sons and daughters are not identical copies of either parent or of their siblings. Along with inherited similarity, there is also **variation**. What are the biological mechanisms leading to the "family resemblance" evident among the family members in the photo above? The answer to this question eluded biologists until the advance of genetics in the 20th century.

Genetics is the scientific study of heredity and hereditary variation. In this unit, you'll learn about genetics at multiple levels, from organisms to cells to molecules. We begin by examining how chromosomes pass from parents to offspring in sexually reproducing organisms. The processes of meiosis (a special type of cell division) and fertilization (the fusion of sperm and egg, as seen in the photo at the left) maintain a species' chromosome count during the sexual life cycle. We will describe the cellular mechanics of meiosis and explain how this process differs from mitosis. Finally, we will consider how both meiosis and fertilization contribute to genetic variation, such as that seen in Figure 13.1.

Offspring acquire genes from parents by inheriting chromosomes

Family friends may tell you that you have your mother's freckles or your father's eyes. Of course, parents do not, in any literal sense, give their children freckles, eyes, hair, or any other traits. What, then, *is* actually inherited?

Inheritance of Genes

Parents endow their offspring with coded information in the form of hereditary units called **genes**. The genes we inherit from our mothers and fathers are our genetic link to our parents, and they account for family resemblances such as shared eye color or freckles. Our genes program the specific traits that emerge as we develop from fertilized eggs into adults.

The genetic program is written in the language of DNA, the polymer of four different nucleotides you learned about in Concepts 1.1 and 5.5. Inherited information is passed on in the form of each gene's specific sequence of DNA nucleotides, much as printed information is communicated in the form of meaningful sequences of letters. In both cases, the language is symbolic. Just as your brain translates the word *apple* into a mental image of the fruit, cells translate genes into freckles and other features. Most genes program cells to synthesize specific enzymes and other proteins, whose cumulative action produces an organism's inherited traits. The programming of these traits in the form of DNA is one of the unifying themes of biology.

The transmission of hereditary traits has its molecular basis in the replication of DNA, which produces copies of genes that can be passed from parents to offspring. In animals and plants, reproductive cells called **gametes** are the vehicles that transmit genes from one generation to the next. During fertilization, male and female gametes (sperm and eggs) unite, passing on genes of both parents to their offspring.

Except for small amounts of DNA in mitochondria and chloroplasts, the DNA of a eukaryotic cell is packaged into chromosomes within the nucleus. Every species has a characteristic number of chromosomes. For example, humans have 46 chromosomes in their **somatic cells**—all cells of the body except the gametes and their precursors. Each chromosome consists of a single long DNA molecule elaborately coiled in association with various proteins. One chromosome includes several hundred to a few thousand genes, each of which is a specific sequence of nucleotides within the DNA molecule. A gene's specific location along the length of a chromosome is called the gene's **locus** (plural, *loci*; from the Latin, meaning "place"). Our genetic endowment (our genome) consists of the genes and other DNA that make up the chromosomes we inherited from our parents.

Comparison of Asexual and Sexual Reproduction

Only organisms that reproduce asexually have offspring that are exact genetic copies of themselves. In **asexual reproduction**, a single individual is the sole parent and passes copies of all its genes to its offspring without the fusion of gametes. For example, single-celled eukaryotic organisms can reproduce asexually by mitotic cell division, in which DNA is copied and allocated equally to two daughter cells. The genomes of the offspring are virtually exact copies of the parent's genome. Some multicellular organisms are also capable of reproducing asexually (**Figure 13.2**). Because the cells of the offspring are derived by mitosis in the parent, the "chip off the old block" is usually genetically identical to its parent. An individual that reproduces asexually gives rise to a **clone**, a group of genetically identical individuals. Genetic differences occasionally arise in asexually reproducing organisms as a result of changes in the DNA called mutations, which we will discuss in Chapter 17.

In **sexual reproduction**, two parents give rise to offspring that have unique combinations of genes inherited from the two parents. In contrast to a clone, offspring of sexual reproduction vary genetically from their siblings and both parents: They are variations on a common theme of family resemblance, not exact replicas. Genetic variation like that shown in Figure 13.1 is an important consequence of sexual reproduction. What mechanisms generate this genetic variation? The key is the behavior of chromosomes during the sexual life cycle.

0.5 mm

Parent

Bud

(a) Hydra

(b) Redwoods

▲ **Figure 13.2 Asexual reproduction in two multicellular organisms. (a)** This relatively simple animal, a hydra, reproduces by budding. The bud, a localized mass of mitotically dividing cells, develops into a small hydra, which detaches from the parent (LM). **(b)** All the trees in this circle of redwoods arose asexually from a single parent tree, whose stump is in the center of the circle.

MAKE CONNECTIONS Using what you know of gene expression in a cell, explain what causes the traits of parents (such as hair color) to show up in their offspring. (See Concept 5.5.)

2. How do asexually reproducing eukaryotic organisms produce offspring that are genetically identical to each other and to their parents?

3. **WHAT IF?** A horticulturalist breeds orchids, trying to obtain a plant with a unique combination of desirable traits. After many years, she finally succeeds. To produce more plants like this one, should she cross-breed it with another plant or clone it? Why?

For suggested answers, see Appendix A.

CONCEPT 13.2

Fertilization and meiosis alternate in sexual life cycles

A **life cycle** is the generation-to-generation sequence of stages in the reproductive history of an organism, from conception to production of its own offspring. In this section, we use humans as an example to track the behavior of chromosomes through the sexual life cycle. We begin by considering the chromosome count in human somatic cells and gametes. We will then explore how the behavior of chromosomes relates to the human life cycle and other types of sexual life cycles.

Sets of Chromosomes in Human Cells

In humans, each somatic cell has 46 chromosomes. During mitosis, the chromosomes become condensed enough to be visible under a light microscope. At this point, they can be distinguished from one another by their size, the positions of their centromeres, and the pattern of colored bands produced by certain chromatin-binding stains.

Careful examination of a micrograph of the 46 human chromosomes from a single cell in mitosis reveals that there are two chromosomes of each of 23 types. This becomes clear when images of the chromosomes are arranged in pairs, starting with the longest chromosomes. The resulting ordered display is called a **karyotype (Figure 13.3)**. The two chromosomes of a pair have the same length, centromere position, and staining pattern: These are called **homologous chromosomes**, or **homologs**. Both chromosomes of each pair carry genes controlling the same inherited characters. For example, if a gene for eye color is situated at a particular locus on a certain chromosome, then the homolog of that chromosome will also have a version of the same gene specifying eye color at the equivalent locus.

The two distinct chromosomes referred to as X and Y are an important exception to the general pattern of homologous chromosomes in human somatic cells. Human females

▼ **Figure 13.3** | Research Method

Preparing a Karyotype

Application A karyotype is a display of condensed chromosomes arranged in pairs. Karyotyping can be used to screen for defective chromosomes or abnormal numbers of chromosomes associated with certain congenital disorders, such as Down syndrome.

Technique Karyotypes are prepared from isolated somatic cells, which are treated with a drug to stimulate mitosis and then grown in culture for several days. Cells arrested in metaphase, when chromosomes are most highly condensed, are stained and then viewed with a microscope equipped with a digital camera. An image of the chromosomes is displayed on a computer monitor, and digital software is used to arrange them in pairs according to their appearance.

Results This karyotype shows the chromosomes from a normal human male, digitally colored to emphasize their banding patterns. The size of the chromosome, position of the centromere, and pattern of stained bands help identify specific chromosomes. Although difficult to discern in the karyotype, each metaphase chromosome consists of two closely attached sister chromatids (see the diagram of a pair of homologous duplicated chromosomes).

have a homologous pair of X chromosomes (XX), but males have one X and one Y chromosome (XY). Only small parts of the X and Y are homologous. Most of the genes carried on the X chromosome do not have counterparts on the tiny Y, and the Y chromosome has genes lacking on the X. Because they determine an individual's sex, the X and Y chromosomes are called **sex chromosomes**. The other chromosomes are called **autosomes**.

The pairs of homologous chromosomes in each human somatic cell is a consequence of our sexual origins. We inherit one chromosome of a pair from each parent. Thus, the 46 chromosomes in our somatic cells are actually two sets of 23 chromosomes—a maternal set (from our mother) and a paternal set (from our father). The number of chromosomes in a single set is represented by n. Any cell with two chromosome sets is called a **diploid cell** and has a diploid number of chromosomes, abbreviated $2n$. For humans, the diploid number is 46 ($2n = 46$), the number of chromosomes in our somatic cells. In a cell in which DNA synthesis has occurred, all the chromosomes are duplicated, and therefore each consists of two identical sister chromatids, associated closely at the centromere and along the arms. (Even though the chromosomes are duplicated, we still say the cell is diploid ($2n$) because it has only two sets of information.) **Figure 13.4** helps clarify the various terms that we use to describe duplicated chromosomes in a diploid cell.

Unlike somatic cells, gametes contain a single set of chromosomes. Such cells are called **haploid cells**, and each has a haploid number of chromosomes (n). For humans, the

haploid number is 23 ($n = 23$). The set of 23 consists of the 22 autosomes plus a single sex chromosome. An unfertilized egg contains an X chromosome, but a sperm may contain an X or a Y chromosome.

Each sexually reproducing species has a characteristic diploid and haploid number. For example, the fruit fly *Drosophila melanogaster* has a diploid number ($2n$) of 8 and a haploid number (n) of 4, while for dogs, $2n$ is 78 and n is 39. Now let's consider chromosome behavior during sexual life cycles. We'll use the human life cycle as an example.

Behavior of Chromosome Sets in the Human Life Cycle

The human life cycle begins when a haploid sperm from the father fuses with a haploid egg from the mother **(Figure 13.5)**. This union of gametes, culminating in fusion of their nuclei, is called **fertilization**. The resulting fertilized egg, or **zygote**, is diploid because it contains two haploid sets of chromosomes bearing genes representing the maternal and paternal family

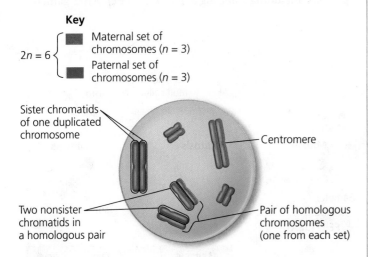

Key

$2n = 6$ {
  ▮ Maternal set of chromosomes ($n = 3$)
  ▮ Paternal set of chromosomes ($n = 3$)
}

Sister chromatids of one duplicated chromosome

Centromere

Two nonsister chromatids in a homologous pair

Pair of homologous chromosomes (one from each set)

▲ **Figure 13.4 Describing chromosomes.** A cell from an organism with a diploid number of 6 ($2n = 6$) is depicted here following chromosome duplication and condensation. Each of the six duplicated chromosomes consists of two sister chromatids associated closely along their lengths. Each homologous pair is composed of one chromosome from the maternal set (red) and one from the paternal set (blue). Each set is made up of three chromosomes in this example (long, medium, and short). Together, one maternal and one paternal chromatid in a pair of homologous chromosomes are called nonsister chromatids.

? *How many sets of chromosomes are present in this diagram? How many pairs of homologous chromosomes are present?*

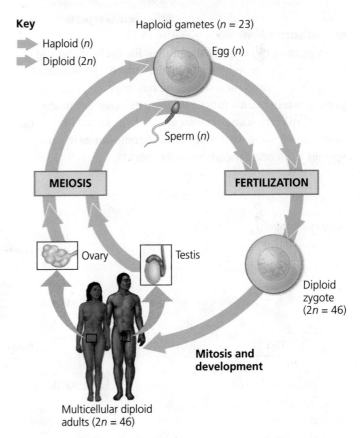

Key
➡ Haploid (n)
➡ Diploid ($2n$)

Haploid gametes ($n = 23$)

Egg (n)

Sperm (n)

MEIOSIS

FERTILIZATION

Ovary

Testis

Diploid zygote ($2n = 46$)

Mitosis and development

Multicellular diploid adults ($2n = 46$)

▲ **Figure 13.5 The human life cycle.** In each generation, the number of chromosome sets doubles at fertilization but is halved during meiosis. For humans, the number of chromosomes in a haploid cell is 23, consisting of one set ($n = 23$); the number of chromosomes in the diploid zygote and all somatic cells arising from it is 46, consisting of two sets ($2n = 46$).

This figure introduces a color code that will be used for other life cycles later in this book. The aqua arrows identify haploid stages of a life cycle, and the tan arrows identify diploid stages.

lines. As a human develops into a sexually mature adult, mitosis of the zygote and its descendant cells generates all the somatic cells of the body. Both chromosome sets in the zygote and all the genes they carry are passed with precision to the somatic cells.

The only cells of the human body not produced by mitosis are the gametes, which develop from specialized cells called *germ cells* in the gonads—ovaries in females and testes in males. Imagine what would happen if human gametes were made by mitosis: They would be diploid like the somatic cells. At the next round of fertilization, when two gametes fused, the normal chromosome number of 46 would double to 92, and each subsequent generation would double the number of chromosomes yet again. This does not happen, however, because in sexually reproducing organisms, gamete formation involves a type of cell division called **meiosis**. This type of cell division reduces the number of sets of chromosomes from two to one in the gametes, counterbalancing the doubling that occurs at fertilization. As a result of meiosis, each human sperm and egg is haploid ($n = 23$). Fertilization restores the diploid condition by combining two haploid sets of chromosomes, and the human life cycle is repeated, generation after generation (see Figure 13.5).

In general, the steps of the human life cycle are typical of many sexually reproducing animals. Indeed, the processes of fertilization and meiosis are the hallmarks of sexual reproduction in plants, fungi, and protists as well as in animals. Fertilization and meiosis alternate in sexual life cycles, maintaining a constant number of chromosomes in each species from one generation to the next.

The Variety of Sexual Life Cycles

Although the alternation of meiosis and fertilization is common to all organisms that reproduce sexually, the timing of these two events in the life cycle varies, depending on the species. These variations can be grouped into three main types of life cycles. In the type that occurs in humans and most other animals, gametes are the only haploid cells (**Figure 13.6a**). Meiosis occurs in germ cells during the production of gametes, which undergo no further cell division prior to fertilization. After fertilization, the diploid zygote divides by mitosis, producing a multicellular organism that is diploid.

Plants and some species of algae exhibit a second type of life cycle called **alternation of generations (Figure 13.6b)**. This type includes both diploid and haploid stages that are multicellular. The multicellular diploid stage is called the *sporophyte*. Meiosis in the sporophyte produces haploid cells called *spores*. Unlike a gamete, a haploid spore doesn't fuse with another cell but divides mitotically, generating a multicellular haploid stage called the *gametophyte*. Cells of the gametophyte give rise to gametes by mitosis. Fusion of two haploid gametes at fertilization results in a diploid zygote, which develops into the next sporophyte generation. Therefore, in this type of life cycle, the sporophyte generation produces a gametophyte as its offspring, and the gametophyte generation produces the next sporophyte generation (see Figure 13.6b). The term *alternation of generations* fits well as a name for this type of life cycle.

A third type of life cycle occurs in most fungi and some protists, including some algae (**Figure 13.6c**). After gametes

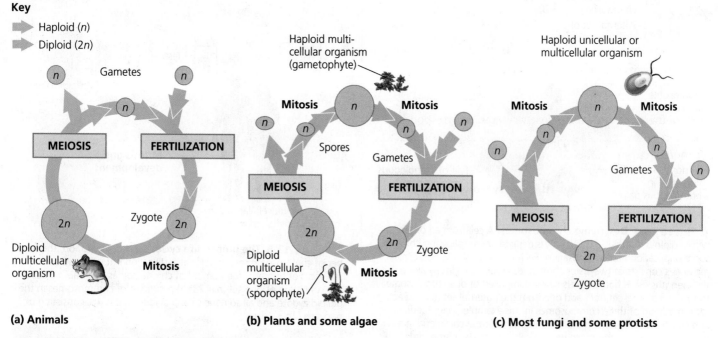

(a) Animals

(b) Plants and some algae

(c) Most fungi and some protists

▲ **Figure 13.6 Three types of sexual life cycles.** The common feature of all three cycles is the alternation of meiosis and fertilization, key events that contribute to genetic variation among offspring. The cycles differ in the timing of these two key events.

fuse and form a diploid zygote, meiosis occurs without a multicellular diploid offspring developing. Meiosis produces not gametes but haploid cells that then divide by mitosis and give rise to either unicellular descendants or a haploid multicellular adult organism. Subsequently, the haploid organism carries out further mitoses, producing the cells that develop into gametes. The only diploid stage found in these species is the single-celled zygote.

Note that *either* haploid or diploid cells can divide by mitosis, depending on the type of life cycle. Only diploid cells, however, can undergo meiosis because haploid cells have only a single set of chromosomes that cannot be further reduced. Though the three types of sexual life cycles differ in the timing of meiosis and fertilization, they share a fundamental result: genetic variation among offspring.

CONCEPT CHECK 13.2

1. **MAKE CONNECTIONS** In Figure 13.4, how many DNA molecules (double helices) are present (see Figure 12.5)? What is the haploid number of this cell? Is a set of chromosomes haploid or diploid?

2. In the karyotype shown in Figure 13.3, how many pairs of chromosomes are present? How many sets?

3. **WHAT IF?** A certain eukaryote lives as a unicellular organism, but during environmental stress, it produces gametes. The gametes fuse, and the resulting zygote undergoes meiosis, generating new single cells. What type of organism could this be?

For suggested answers, see Appendix A.

CONCEPT 13.3

Meiosis reduces the number of chromosome sets from diploid to haploid

Many of the steps of meiosis closely resemble corresponding steps in mitosis. Meiosis, like mitosis, is preceded by the duplication of chromosomes. However, this single duplication is followed by not one but two consecutive cell divisions, called **meiosis I** and **meiosis II**. These two divisions result in four daughter cells (rather than the two daughter cells of mitosis), each with only half as many chromosomes as the parent cell—one set, rather than two.

The Stages of Meiosis

The overview of meiosis in **Figure 13.7** shows, for a single pair of homologous chromosomes in a diploid cell, that both members of the pair are duplicated and the copies sorted into four haploid daughter cells. Recall that sister chromatids are two copies of *one* chromosome, closely associated all

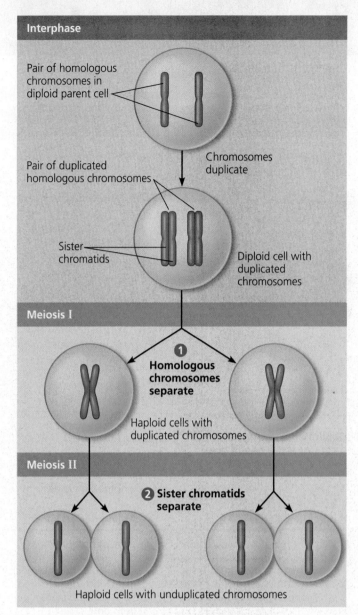

Interphase

Pair of homologous chromosomes in diploid parent cell

Chromosomes duplicate

Pair of duplicated homologous chromosomes

Sister chromatids

Diploid cell with duplicated chromosomes

Meiosis I

① Homologous chromosomes separate

Haploid cells with duplicated chromosomes

Meiosis II

② Sister chromatids separate

Haploid cells with unduplicated chromosomes

▲ **Figure 13.7 Overview of meiosis: how meiosis reduces chromosome number.** After the chromosomes duplicate in interphase, the diploid cell divides *twice*, yielding four haploid daughter cells. This overview tracks just one pair of homologous chromosomes, which for the sake of simplicity are drawn in the condensed state throughout.

DRAW IT *Redraw the cells in this figure using a simple double helix to represent each DNA molecule.*

along their lengths; this association is called *sister chromatid cohesion*. Together, the sister chromatids make up one duplicated chromosome (see Figure 13.4). In contrast, the two chromosomes of a homologous pair are individual chromosomes that were inherited from different parents. Homologs appear alike in the microscope, but they may have different versions of genes, each called an *allele*, at corresponding loci. Homologs are not associated with each other in any obvious way except during meiosis.

Figure 13.8 describes in detail the stages of the two divisions of meiosis for an animal cell whose diploid number is 6. Study this figure thoroughly before going on.

Exploring Meiosis in an Animal Cell

MEIOSIS I: Separates homologous chromosomes

Prophase I	Metaphase I	Anaphase I	Telophase I and Cytokinesis

Sister chromatids
Centrosome (with centriole pair)
Chiasmata
Spindle

Homologous chromosomes
Fragments of nuclear envelope

Duplicated homologous chromosomes (red and blue) pair and exchange segments; 2n = 6 in this example.

Centromere (with kinetochore)
Metaphase plate

Microtubules attached to kinetochore

Chromosomes line up by homologous pairs.

Sister chromatids remain attached

Homologous chromosomes separate

Each pair of homologous chromosomes separates.

Cleavage furrow

Two haploid cells form; each chromosome still consists of two sister chromatids.

Prophase I

- Centrosome movement, spindle formation, and nuclear envelope breakdown occur as in mitosis. Chromosomes condense progressively throughout prophase I.

- During early prophase I, before the stage shown above, each chromosome pairs with its homolog, aligned gene by gene, and **crossing over** occurs: The DNA molecules of non-sister chromatids are broken (by proteins) and are rejoined to each other.

- At the stage shown above, each homologous pair has one or more X-shaped regions called **chiasmata** (singular, *chiasma*), where crossovers have occurred.

- Later in prophase I, after the stage shown above, microtubules from one pole or the other will attach to the two kinetochores, one at the centromere of each homolog. (The two kinetochores of a homolog, not yet visible above, act as a single kinetochore.) The homologous pairs will then move toward the metaphase plate.

Metaphase I

- Pairs of homologous chromosomes are now arranged at the metaphase plate, with one chromosome in each pair facing each pole.

- Both chromatids of one homolog are attached to kinetochore microtubules from one pole; those of the other homolog are attached to microtubules from the opposite pole.

Anaphase I

- Breakdown of proteins that are responsible for sister chromatid cohesion along chromatid arms allows homologs to separate.

- The homologs move toward opposite poles, guided by the spindle apparatus.

- Sister chromatid cohesion persists at the centromere, causing chromatids to move as a unit toward the same pole.

Telophase I and Cytokinesis

- When telophase I begins, each half of the cell has a complete haploid set of duplicated chromosomes. Each chromosome is composed of two sister chromatids; one or both chromatids include regions of nonsister chromatid DNA.

- Cytokinesis (division of the cytoplasm) usually occurs simultaneously with telophase I, forming two haploid daughter cells.

- In animal cells like these, a cleavage furrow forms. (In plant cells, a cell plate forms.)

- In some species, chromosomes decondense and nuclear envelopes form.

- No chromosome duplication occurs between meiosis I and meiosis II.

MEIOSIS II: Separates sister chromatids

Prophase II	Metaphase II	Anaphase II	Telophase II and Cytokinesis

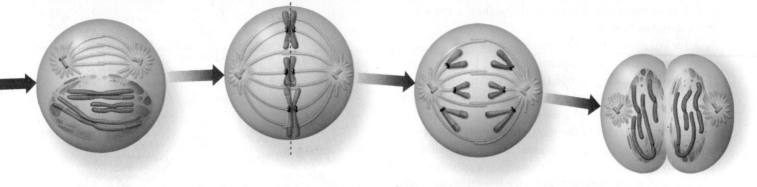

During another round of cell division, the sister chromatids finally separate; four haploid daughter cells result, containing unduplicated chromosomes.

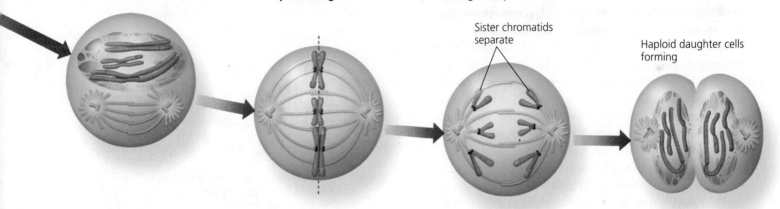

Sister chromatids separate

Haploid daughter cells forming

Prophase II

- A spindle apparatus forms.

- In late prophase II (not shown here), chromosomes, each still composed of two chromatids associated at the centromere, move toward the metaphase II plate.

Metaphase II

- The chromosomes are positioned at the metaphase plate as in mitosis.

- Because of crossing over in meiosis I, the two sister chromatids of each chromosome are *not* genetically identical.

- The kinetochores of sister chromatids are attached to microtubules extending from opposite poles.

Anaphase II

- Breakdown of proteins holding the sister chromatids together at the centromere allows the chromatids to separate. The chromatids move toward opposite poles as individual chromosomes.

Telophase II and Cytokinesis

- Nuclei form, the chromosomes begin decondensing, and cytokinesis occurs.

- The meiotic division of one parent cell produces four daughter cells, each with a haploid set of (unduplicated) chromosomes.

- The four daughter cells are genetically distinct from one another and from the parent cell.

MAKE CONNECTIONS *Look at Figure 12.7 and imagine the two daughter cells undergoing another round of mitosis, yielding four cells. Compare the number of chromosomes in each of those four cells, after mitosis, with the number in each cell in Figure 13.8, after meiosis. What is it about the process of meiosis that accounts for this difference, even though meiosis also includes two cell divisions?*

ANIMATION **BioFlix** Visit the Study Area in **MasteringBiology** for the BioFlix® 3-D Animation on Meiosis. BioFlix Tutorials can also be assigned in MasteringBiology.

Crossing Over and Synapsis During Prophase I

Prophase I of meiosis is a very busy time. The prophase I cell shown in Figure 13.8 is at a point fairly late in prophase I, when homologous pairing, crossing over, and chromosome condensation have already taken place. The sequence of events leading up to that point is shown in more detail in **Figure 13.9**.

After interphase, the chromosomes have been duplicated and the sister chromatids are held together by proteins called *cohesins*. Early in prophase I, the two members of a homologous pair associate loosely along their length. Each gene on one homolog is aligned precisely with the corresponding gene on the other homolog. The DNA of two nonsister chromatids—one maternal and one paternal—is broken by specific proteins at precisely corresponding points. Next, the formation of a zipper-like structure called the **synaptonemal complex** holds one homolog tightly to the other. During this association, called **synapsis**, the DNA breaks are closed up so that each broken end is joined to the corresponding segment of the *nonsister* chromatid. Thus, a paternal chromatid is joined to a piece of maternal chromatid beyond the crossover point, and vice versa.

These points of crossing over become visible as chiasmata (singular, *chiasma*) after the synaptonemal complex disassembles and the homologs move slightly apart from each other. The homologs remain attached because sister chromatids are still held together by sister chromatid cohesion, even though some of the DNA may no longer be attached to its original chromosome. At least one crossover per chromosome must occur in order for the homologous pair to stay together as it moves to the metaphase I plate.

A Comparison of Mitosis and Meiosis

Figure 13.10 summarizes the key differences between meiosis and mitosis in diploid cells. Basically, meiosis reduces the number of chromosome sets from two (diploid) to one (haploid), whereas mitosis conserves the number of chromosome sets. Therefore, meiosis produces cells that differ genetically from their parent cell and from each other, whereas mitosis produces daughter cells that are genetically identical to their parent cell and to each other.

Three events unique to meiosis occur during meiosis I:

1. **Synapsis and crossing over.** During prophase I, duplicated homologs pair up and crossing over occurs, as described above. Synapsis and crossing over normally do not occur during prophase of mitosis.

2. **Homologous pairs at the metaphase plate.** At metaphase I of meiosis, chromosomes are positioned at the metaphase plate as pairs of homologs, rather than individual chromosomes, as in metaphase of mitosis.

❶ After interphase, the chromosomes have been duplicated and sister chromatids are held together by proteins called cohesins (purple). Each pair of homologs associate along their length. The DNA molecules of two nonsister chromatids are broken at precisely corresponding points. The chromatin of the chromosomes is beginning to condense.

❷ A zipperlike protein complex, the synaptonemal complex (green), begins to form, attaching one homolog to the other. The chromatin continues to condense.

❸ The synaptonemal complex is fully formed; the two homologs are said to be in synapsis. During synapsis, the DNA breaks are closed up when each broken end is joined to the corresponding segment of the nonsister chromatid, producing crossovers.

❹ After the synaptonemal complex disassembles, the homologs move slightly apart from each other but remain attached because of sister chromatid cohesion, even though some of the DNA may no longer be attached to its original chromosome. The points of attachment where crossovers have occurred show up as chiasmata. The chromosomes continue to condense as they move toward the metaphase plate.

▲ **Figure 13.9 Crossing over and synapsis in prophase I: a closer look.** For simplicity, the four chromatids of the homologous pair shown here are depicted side by side, but in reality, the blue chromosome would be right on top of the red one (see the top cell in Figure 13.12).

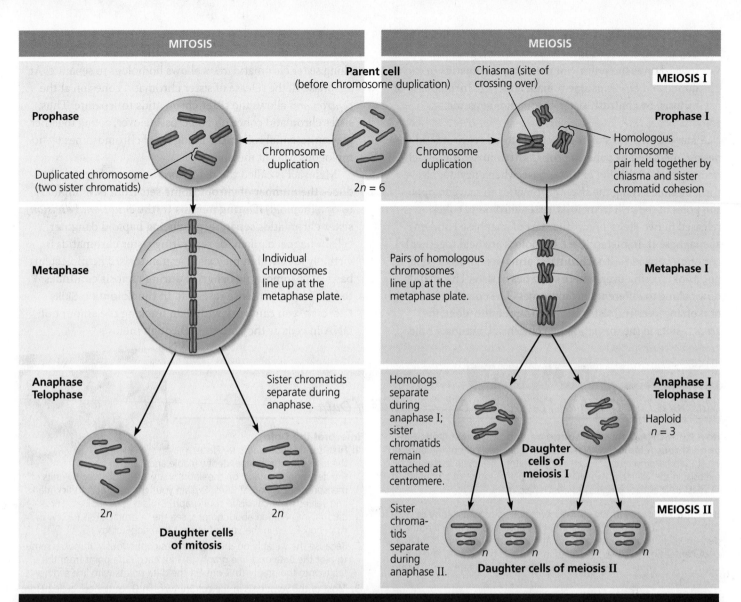

	MITOSIS	MEIOSIS

Parent cell
(before chromosome duplication)

Prophase

Duplicated chromosome
(two sister chromatids)

Chromosome
duplication

$2n = 6$

Chromosome
duplication

Chiasma (site of
crossing over)

MEIOSIS I

Prophase I

Homologous
chromosome
pair held together by
chiasma and sister
chromatid cohesion

Metaphase

Individual
chromosomes
line up at the
metaphase plate.

Pairs of homologous
chromosomes
line up at the
metaphase plate.

Metaphase I

Anaphase
Telophase

Sister chromatids
separate during
anaphase.

Homologs
separate
during
anaphase I;
sister
chromatids
remain
attached at
centromere.

**Daughter
cells of
meiosis I**

Anaphase I
Telophase I

Haploid
$n = 3$

$2n$ $2n$

**Daughter cells
of mitosis**

Sister
chroma-
tids
separate
during
anaphase II.

n n n n

MEIOSIS II

Daughter cells of meiosis II

SUMMARY

Property	Mitosis (occurs in both diploid and haploid cells)	Meiosis (can only occur in diploid cells)
DNA replication	Occurs during interphase before mitosis begins	Occurs during interphase before meiosis I begins
Number of divisions	One, including prophase, prometaphase, metaphase, anaphase, and telophase	Two, each including prophase, metaphase, anaphase, and telophase
Synapsis of homologous chromosomes	Does not occur	Occurs during prophase I along with crossing over between nonsister chromatids; resulting chiasmata hold pairs together due to sister chromatid cohesion
Number of daughter cells and genetic composition	Two, each genetically identical to the parent cell, with the same number of chromosomes	Four, each haploid (n); genetically different from the parent cell and from each other
Role in the animal or plant body	Enables multicellular animal or plant (gametophyte or sporophyte) to arise from a single cell; produces cells for growth, repair, and, in some species, asexual reproduction; produces gametes in the gametophyte plant	Produces gametes (in animals) or spores (in the sporophyte plant); reduces number of chromosome sets by half and introduces genetic variability among the gametes or spores

▲ **Figure 13.10 A comparison of mitosis and meiosis.**

DRAW IT *Could any other combinations of chromosomes be generated during meiosis II from the specific cells shown in telophase I? Explain. (Hint: Draw the cells as they would appear in metaphase II.)*

3. **Separation of homologs.** At anaphase I of meiosis, the duplicated chromosomes of each homologous pair move toward opposite poles, but the sister chromatids of each duplicated chromosome remain attached. In anaphase of mitosis, by contrast, sister chromatids separate.

Sister chromatids stay together due to sister chromatid cohesion, mediated by cohesin proteins. In mitosis, this attachment lasts until the end of metaphase, when enzymes cleave the cohesins, freeing the sister chromatids to move to opposite poles of the cell. In meiosis, sister chromatid cohesion is released in two steps, one at the start of anaphase I and one at anaphase II. In metaphase I, homologs are held together by cohesion between sister chromatid arms in regions beyond points of crossing over, where stretches of sister chromatids now belong to different chromosomes. The combination of crossing over and sister chromatid cohesion along the arms results in the formation of a chiasma. Chiasmata hold homologs together as the spindle forms for the first meiotic division. At the onset of anaphase I, the release of cohesion along sister chromatid *arms* allows homologs to separate. At anaphase II, the release of sister chromatid cohesion at the *centromeres* allows the sister chromatids to separate. Thus, sister chromatid cohesion and crossing over, acting together, play an essential role in the lining up of chromosomes by homologous pairs at metaphase I.

Meiosis I is called the *reductional division* because it reduces the number of chromosome sets from two (diploid) to one (haploid). During meiosis II (the *equational division*), sister chromatids separate, producing haploid daughter cells. The mechanism for separating sister chromatids is virtually identical in meiosis II and mitosis. The molecular basis of chromosome behavior during meiosis continues to be a focus of intense research. In the **Scientific Skills Exercise**, you can work with data tracking the amount of DNA in cells as they progress through meiosis.

Making a Line Graph and Converting Between Units of Data

How Does DNA Content Change as Budding Yeast Cells Proceed Through Meiosis? When nutrients are low, cells of the budding yeast (*Saccharomyces cerevisiae*) exit the mitotic cell cycle and enter meiosis. In this exercise, you will track the DNA content of a population of yeast cells as they progress through meiosis.

How the Experiment Was Done Researchers grew a culture of yeast cells in a nutrient-rich medium and then transferred them to a nutrient-poor medium to induce meiosis. At different times after induction, the DNA content per cell was measured in a sample of the cells, and the average DNA content per cell was recorded in femtograms (fg; 1 femtogram = 1×10^{-15} gram).

Data from the Experiment

Time After Induction (hours)	Average Amount of DNA per Cell (fg)
0.0	24.0
1.0	24.0
2.0	40.0
3.0	47.0
4.0	47.5
5.0	48.0
6.0	48.0
7.0	47.5
7.5	25.0
8.0	24.0
9.0	23.5
9.5	14.0
10.0	13.0
11.0	12.5
12.0	12.0
13.0	12.5
14.0	12.0

Interpret the Data

1. First, set up your graph. (a) Place the labels for the independent variable and the dependent variable on the appropriate axes, followed by units of measurement in parentheses. Explain your choices. (b) Add tick marks and values for each axis in your graph. Explain your choices. (For additional information about graphs, see the Scientific Skills Review in Appendix F and in the Study Area in MasteringBiology.)

2. Because the variable on the *x*-axis varies continuously, it makes sense to plot the data on a line graph. (a) Plot each data point from the table onto the graph. (b) Connect the data points with line segments.

3. Most of the yeast cells in the culture were in G_1 of the cell cycle before being moved to the nutrient-poor medium. (a) How many femtograms of DNA are there in each yeast cell in G_1? Estimate this value from the data in your graph. (b) How many femtograms of DNA should be present in each cell in G_2? (See Concept 12.2 and Figure 12.6.) At the end of meiosis I (MI)? At the end of meiosis II (MII)? (See Figure 13.7.) (c) Using these values as a guideline, distinguish the different phases by inserting vertical dashed lines in the graph between phases and label each phase (G_1, S, G_2, MI, MII). You can figure out where to put the dividing lines based on what you know about the DNA content of each phase (see Figure 13.7). (d) Think carefully about the point where the line at the highest value begins to slope downward. What specific point of meiosis does this "corner" represent? What stage(s) correspond to the downward sloping line?

4. Given the fact that 1 fg of DNA = 9.78×10^5 base pairs (on average), you can convert the amount of DNA per cell to the length of DNA in numbers of base pairs. (a) Calculate the number of base pairs of DNA in the haploid yeast genome. Express your answer in millions of base pairs (Mb), a standard unit for expressing genome size. Show your work. (b) How many base pairs per minute were synthesized during the S phase of these yeast cells?

(MB) A version of this Scientific Skills Exercise can be assigned in MasteringBiology.

Further Reading G. Simchen, Commitment to meiosis: what determines the mode of division in budding yeast? *BioEssays* 31:169–177 (2009).

1. **MAKE CONNECTIONS** Compare the chromosomes in a cell at metaphase of mitosis with those in a cell at metaphase II. (See Figures 12.7 and 13.8.)

2. **WHAT IF?** After the synaptonemal complex disappears, how would the two homologs be associated if crossing over did not occur? What effect might this ultimately have on gamete formation?

For suggested answers, see Appendix A.

CONCEPT 13.4

Genetic variation produced in sexual life cycles contributes to evolution

How do we account for the genetic variation of the family members in Figure 13.1? As you will learn in later chapters, mutations are the original source of genetic diversity. These changes in an organism's DNA create the different versions of genes known as alleles. Once these differences arise, re-shuffling of the alleles during sexual reproduction produces the variation that results in each member of a sexually reproducing population having a unique combination of traits.

Origins of Genetic Variation Among Offspring

In species that reproduce sexually, the behavior of chromosomes during meiosis and fertilization is responsible for most of the variation that arises in each generation. Three mechanisms contribute to the genetic variation arising from sexual reproduction: independent assortment of chromosomes, crossing over, and random fertilization.

Independent Assortment of Chromosomes

One aspect of sexual reproduction that generates genetic variation is the random orientation of pairs of homologous chromosomes at metaphase of meiosis I. At metaphase I, the homologous pairs, each consisting of one maternal and one paternal chromosome, are situated at the metaphase plate. (Note that the terms *maternal* and *paternal* refer, respectively, to the mother and father of the individual whose cells are undergoing meiosis.) Each pair may orient with either its maternal or paternal homolog closer to a given pole—its orientation is as random as the flip of a coin. Thus, there is a 50% chance that a particular daughter cell of meiosis I will get the maternal chromosome of a certain homologous pair and a 50% chance that it will get the paternal chromosome.

Because each pair of homologous chromosomes is positioned independently of the other pairs at metaphase I, the first meiotic division results in each pair sorting its maternal and paternal homologs into daughter cells independently of every other pair. This is called *independent assortment*. Each daughter cell represents one outcome of all possible combinations of maternal and paternal chromosomes. As shown in **Figure 13.11**, the number of combinations possible for daughter cells formed by meiosis of a diploid cell with two pairs of homologous chromosomes ($n = 2$) is four: two possible arrangements for the first pair times two possible arrangements for the second pair. Note that only two of the four combinations of daughter cells shown in the figure would result from meiosis of a *single* diploid cell, because a single parent cell would have one or the other possible chromosomal arrangement at metaphase I, but not both. However, the population of daughter cells resulting from meiosis of a large number of diploid cells contains all four types in approximately equal numbers. In the case of $n = 3$, eight combinations of chromosomes are possible for daughter cells. More generally, the number of possible combinations when chromosomes sort independently during meiosis is 2^n, where n is the haploid number of the organism.

In the case of humans ($n = 23$), the number of possible combinations of maternal and paternal chromosomes in the resulting gametes is 2^{23}, or about 8.4 million. Each gamete that you produce in your lifetime contains one of roughly 8.4 million possible combinations of chromosomes.

Crossing Over

As a consequence of the independent assortment of chromosomes during meiosis, each of us produces a collection of gametes differing greatly in their combinations of the chromosomes we inherited from our two parents. Figure 13.11

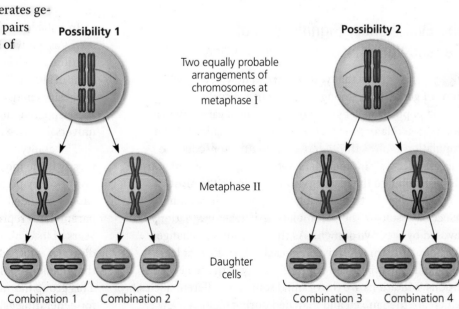

Possibility 1 **Possibility 2**

Two equally probable arrangements of chromosomes at metaphase I

Metaphase II

Daughter cells

Combination 1   Combination 2   Combination 3   Combination 4

▲ **Figure 13.11 The independent assortment of homologous chromosomes in meiosis.**

suggests that each chromosome in a gamete is exclusively maternal or paternal in origin. In fact, this is *not* the case, because crossing over produces **recombinant chromosomes**, individual chromosomes that carry genes (DNA) derived from two different parents **(Figure 13.12)**. In meiosis in humans, an average of one to three crossover events occur per chromosome pair, depending on the size of the chromosomes and the position of their centromeres.

As you learned in Figure 13.9, crossing over produces chromosomes with new combinations of maternal and paternal alleles. At metaphase II, chromosomes that contain one or more recombinant chromatids can be oriented in two alternative, nonequivalent ways with respect to other chromosomes, because their sister chromatids are no longer identical (see Figure 13.12). The different possible arrangements of nonidentical sister chromatids during meiosis II further increase the number of genetic types of daughter cells that can result from meiosis.

You will learn more about crossing over in Chapter 15. The important point for now is that crossing over, by combining DNA inherited from two parents into a single chromosome, is an important source of genetic variation in sexual life cycles.

Random Fertilization

The random nature of fertilization adds to the genetic variation arising from meiosis. In humans, each male and female gamete represents one of about 8.4 million (2^{23}) possible chromosome combinations due to independent assortment. The fusion of a male gamete with a female gamete during fertilization will produce a zygote with any of about 70 trillion ($2^{23} \times 2^{23}$) diploid combinations. If we factor in the variation brought about by crossing over, the number of possibilities is truly astronomical. It may sound trite, but you really *are* unique.

The Evolutionary Significance of Genetic Variation Within Populations

EVOLUTION Now that you've learned how new combinations of genes arise among offspring in a sexually reproducing population, let's see how the genetic variation in a population relates to evolution. Darwin recognized that a population evolves through the differential reproductive success of its variant members. On average, those individuals best suited to the local environment leave the most offspring, thereby transmitting their genes. Thus, natural selection results in the accumulation of genetic variations favored by the environment. As the environment changes, the population may survive if, in each generation, at least some of its members can cope effectively with the new conditions. Mutations are the original source of different alleles, which are then mixed and matched during meiosis. New

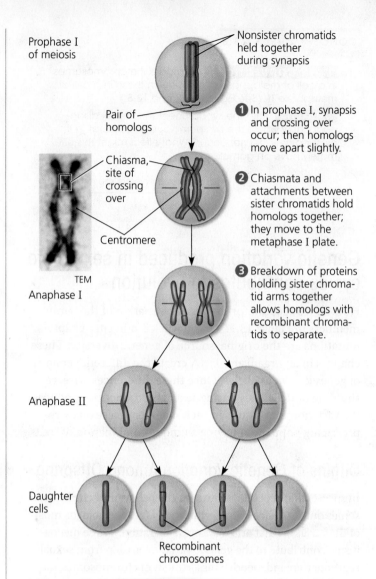

Prophase I of meiosis

Nonsister chromatids held together during synapsis

Pair of homologs

Chiasma, site of crossing over

Centromere

TEM

Anaphase I

Anaphase II

Daughter cells

Recombinant chromosomes

❶ In prophase I, synapsis and crossing over occur; then homologs move apart slightly.

❷ Chiasmata and attachments between sister chromatids hold homologs together; they move to the metaphase I plate.

❸ Breakdown of proteins holding sister chromatid arms together allows homologs with recombinant chromatids to separate.

▲ **Figure 13.12 The results of crossing over during meiosis.**

and different combinations of alleles may work better than those that previously prevailed.

In a stable environment, though, sexual reproduction seems as if it would be less advantageous than asexual reproduction, which ensures perpetuation of successful combinations of alleles. Furthermore, sexual reproduction is more expensive energetically than asexual reproduction. In spite of these apparent disadvantages, sexual reproduction is almost universal among animals. Why is this?

The ability of sexual reproduction to generate genetic diversity is the most commonly proposed explanation for the evolutionary persistence of this process. Consider the rare case of the bdelloid rotifer **Figure 13.13**. This group has apparently not reproduced sexually throughout the 40 million years of its evolutionary history. Does this mean that genetic diversity is not advantageous in this species? It turns out that bdelloid rotifers are an exception that proves the rule: This group has mechanisms other than sexual reproduction for generating genetic diversity. For example, they live in environments that can dry up for long periods of time, during which they can enter a state of suspended animation. In this state, their cell membranes may crack in places, allowing entry of DNA from other rotifers and even other species. Evidence suggests that this DNA can become incorporated into the genome of the rotifer, leading to increased genetic diversity. This supports the idea that genetic diversity is advantageous, and that sexual reproduction has persisted because it generates such diversity.

▲ **Figure 13.13 A bdelloid rotifer, an animal that reproduces only asexually.**

In this chapter, we have seen how sexual reproduction greatly increases the genetic variation present in a population. Although Darwin realized that heritable variation is what makes evolution possible, he could not explain why offspring resemble—but are not identical to—their parents. Ironically, Gregor Mendel, a contemporary of Darwin, published a theory of inheritance that helps explain genetic variation, but his discoveries had no impact on biologists until 1900, more than 15 years after Darwin (1809–1882) and Mendel (1822–1884) had died. In the next chapter, you'll learn how Mendel discovered the basic rules governing the inheritance of specific traits.

CONCEPT CHECK 13.4

1. What is the original source of variation among the different alleles of a gene?

2. The diploid number for fruit flies is 8, and the diploid number for grasshoppers is 46. If no crossing over took place, would the genetic variation among offspring from a given pair of parents be greater in fruit flies or grasshoppers? Explain.

3. **WHAT IF?** If maternal and paternal chromatids have the same two alleles for every gene, will crossing over lead to genetic variation?

For suggested answers, see Appendix A.

13 Chapter Review

SUMMARY OF KEY CONCEPTS

CONCEPT 13.1

Offspring acquire genes from parents by inheriting chromosomes (pp. 253–254)

- Each **gene** in an organism's DNA exists at a specific **locus** on a certain chromosome.
- In **asexual reproduction**, a single parent produces genetically identical offspring by mitosis. **Sexual reproduction** combines genes from two parents, leading to genetically diverse offspring.

? *Explain why human offspring resemble their parents but are not identical to them.*

CONCEPT 13.2

Fertilization and meiosis alternate in sexual life cycles (pp. 254–257)

- Normal human **somatic cells** are **diploid**. They have 46 chromosomes made up of two sets of 23, one set from each parent. Human diploid cells have 22 **homologous** pairs of **autosomes**, and one pair of **sex chromosomes**; the latter determines whether the person is female (XX) or male (XY).
- In humans, ovaries and testes produce **haploid gametes** by **meiosis**, each gamete containing a single set of 23 chromosomes (*n* = 23). During **fertilization**, an egg and sperm unite, forming a diploid (2*n* = 46) single-celled **zygote**, which develops into a multicellular organism by mitosis.

- Sexual life cycles differ in the timing of meiosis relative to fertilization and in the point(s) of the cycle at which a multicellular organism is produced by mitosis.

? *Compare the life cycles of animals and plants, mentioning their similarities and differences.*

CONCEPT 13.3

Meiosis reduces the number of chromosome sets from diploid to haploid (pp. 257–263)

- The two cell divisions of meiosis, **meiosis I** and **meiosis II**, produce four haploid daughter cells. The number of chromosome sets is reduced from two (diploid) to one (haploid) during meiosis I, the reductional division.
- Meiosis is distinguished from mitosis by three events of meiosis I:

Prophase I: Each homologous pair undergoes **synapsis** and **crossing over** between nonsister chromatids with the subsequent appearance of **chiasmata**.

Metaphase I: Chromosomes line up as homologous pairs on the metaphase plate.

Anaphase I: Homologs separate from each other; sister chromatids remain joined at the centromere.

Meiosis II separates the sister chromatids.

- Sister chromatid cohesion and crossing over allow chiasmata to hold homologs together until anaphase I. Cohesins are cleaved along the arms at anaphase I, allowing homologs to separate, and at the centromeres in anaphase II, releasing sister chromatids.

? *In prophase I, homologous chromosomes pair up and undergo synapsis and crossing over. Can this also occur during prophase II? Explain.*

CONCEPT 13.4

Genetic variation produced in sexual life cycles contributes to evolution (pp. 263–265)

- Three events in sexual reproduction contribute to genetic variation in a population: independent assortment of chromosomes during meiosis I, crossing over during meiosis I, and random fertilization of egg cells by sperm. During crossing over, DNA of nonsister chromatids in a homologous pair is broken and rejoined.
- Genetic variation is the raw material for evolution by natural selection. Mutations are the original source of this variation; recombination of variant genes generates additional genetic diversity.

? *Explain how three processes unique to meiosis generate a great deal of genetic variation.*

TEST YOUR UNDERSTANDING

LEVEL 1: KNOWLEDGE/COMPREHENSION

1. A human cell containing 22 autosomes and a Y chromosome is
   a. a sperm.
   b. an egg.
   c. a zygote.
   d. a somatic cell of a male.

2. Homologous chromosomes move toward opposite poles of a dividing cell during
   a. mitosis.
   b. meiosis I.
   c. meiosis II.
   d. fertilization.

LEVEL 2: APPLICATION/ANALYSIS

3. Meiosis II is similar to mitosis in that
   a. sister chromatids separate during anaphase.
   b. DNA replicates before the division.
   c. the daughter cells are diploid.
   d. homologous chromosomes synapse.

4. If the DNA content of a diploid cell in the G_1 phase of the cell cycle is x, then the DNA content of the same cell at metaphase of meiosis I would be
   a. $0.25x$. b. $0.5x$. c. x. d. $2x$.

5. If we continued to follow the cell lineage from question 4, then the DNA content of a single cell at metaphase of meiosis II would be
   a. $0.25x$. b. $0.5x$. c. x. d. $2x$.

6. **DRAW IT** The diagram at right shows a cell in meiosis.

   (a) Label the appropriate structures with these terms, drawing lines or brackets as needed: chromosome (label as duplicated or unduplicated), centromere, kinetochore, sister chromatids, nonsister chromatids, homologous pair, homologs, chiasma, sister chromatid cohesion, alleles (of the F and H genes).
   (b) Describe the makeup of a haploid set and a diploid set.
   (c) Identify the stage of meiosis shown.

LEVEL 3: SYNTHESIS/EVALUATION

7. How can you tell that the cell in question 6 is undergoing meiosis, not mitosis?

8. **EVOLUTION CONNECTION**
   Many species can reproduce either asexually or sexually. What might be the evolutionary significance of the switch from asexual to sexual reproduction that occurs in some organisms when the environment becomes unfavorable?

9. **SCIENTIFIC INQUIRY**
   The diagram in question 6 represents just a few of the chromosomes of a meiotic cell in a certain person. A previous study has shown that the freckles gene is located at the locus marked F, and the hair-color gene is located at the locus marked H, both on the long chromosome. The individual from whom this cell was taken has inherited different alleles for each gene ("freckles" and "black hair" from one parent, and "no freckles" and "blond hair" from the other). Predict allele combinations in the gametes resulting from this meiotic event. (It will help if you draw out the rest of meiosis, labeling alleles by name.) List other possible combinations of these alleles in this individual's gametes.

10. **WRITE ABOUT A THEME: INFORMATION**
    The continuity of life is based on heritable information in the form of DNA. In a short essay (100–150 words), explain how chromosome behavior during sexual reproduction in animals ensures perpetuation of parental traits in offspring and, at the same time, genetic variation among offspring.

11. **SYNTHESIZE YOUR KNOWLEDGE**

    The Cavendish banana is the most popular fruit in the world, but is currently threatened by extinction due to a fungal agent (see the photo). This banana variety is "triploid" ($3n$, with three sets of chromosomes) and can only reproduce through cloning by cultivators. Given what you know about meiosis, explain how the banana's triploid number accounts for its seedless condition. Considering genetic diversity, discuss how the absence of sexual reproduction might contribute to the vulnerability of this domesticated species to infectious agents.

For selected answers, see Appendix A.

MasteringBiology®

Students Go to **MasteringBiology** for assignments, the eText, and the Study Area with practice tests, animations, and activities.

Instructors Go to **MasteringBiology** for automatically graded tutorials and questions that you can assign to your students, plus Instructor Resources.

14

Mendel and the Gene Idea

KEY CONCEPTS

14.1 Mendel used the scientific approach to identify two laws of inheritance

14.2 Probability laws govern Mendelian inheritance

14.3 Inheritance patterns are often more complex than predicted by simple Mendelian genetics

14.4 Many human traits follow Mendelian patterns of inheritance

▲ **Figure 14.1 What principles of inheritance did Gregor Mendel discover by breeding pea plants?**

Drawing from the Deck of Genes

The crowd at a soccer match attests to the marvelous variety and diversity of humankind. Brown, blue, or gray eyes; black, brown, or blond hair—these are just a few examples of heritable variations that we may observe. What principles account for the transmission of such traits from parents to offspring?

The explanation of heredity most widely in favor during the 1800s was the "blending" hypothesis, the idea that genetic material contributed by the two parents mixes just as blue and yellow paints blend to make green. This hypothesis predicts that over many generations, a freely mating population will give rise to a uniform population of individuals, something we don't see. The blending hypothesis also fails to explain the reappearance of traits after they've skipped a generation.

An alternative to the blending model is a "particulate" hypothesis of inheritance: the gene idea. In this model, parents pass on discrete heritable units—genes—that retain their separate identities in offspring. An organism's collection of genes is more like a deck of cards than a pail of paint. Like playing cards, genes can be shuffled and passed along, generation after generation, in undiluted form.

Modern genetics had its genesis in an abbey garden, where a monk named Gregor Mendel documented a particulate mechanism for inheritance using pea plants (**Figure 14.1**). Mendel developed his theory of inheritance several

◄ **Mendel (third from right, holding a sprig of fuchsia) with his fellow monks.**

267

decades before chromosomes were observed under the microscope and the significance of their behavior was understood. In this chapter, we'll step into Mendel's garden to re-create his experiments and explain how he arrived at his theory of inheritance. We'll also explore inheritance patterns more complex than those observed by Mendel in garden peas. Finally, we will see how the Mendelian model applies to the inheritance of human variations, including hereditary disorders such as sickle-cell disease.

CONCEPT 14.1

Mendel used the scientific approach to identify two laws of inheritance

Mendel discovered the basic principles of heredity by breeding garden peas in carefully planned experiments. As we retrace his work, you will recognize the key elements of the scientific process that were introduced in Chapter 1.

Mendel's Experimental, Quantitative Approach

Mendel grew up on his parents' small farm in a region of Austria that is now part of the Czech Republic. In this agricultural area, Mendel and the other children received agricultural training in school along with their basic education. As an adolescent, Mendel overcame financial hardship and illness to excel in high school and, later, at the Olmutz Philosophical Institute.

In 1843, at the age of 21, Mendel entered an Augustinian monastery, a reasonable choice at that time for someone who valued the life of the mind. He considered becoming a teacher but failed the necessary examination. In 1851, he left the monastery to pursue two years of study in physics and chemistry at the University of Vienna. These were very important years for Mendel's development as a scientist, in large part due to the strong influence of two professors. One was the physicist Christian Doppler, who encouraged his students to learn science through experimentation and trained Mendel to use mathematics to help explain natural phenomena. The other was a botanist named Franz Unger, who aroused Mendel's interest in the causes of variation in plants.

After attending the university, Mendel returned to the monastery and was assigned to teach at a local school, where several other instructors were enthusiastic about scientific research. In addition, his fellow monks shared a long-standing fascination with the breeding of plants. Around 1857, Mendel began breeding garden peas in the abbey garden to study inheritance. Although the question of heredity had long been a focus of curiosity at the monastery, Mendel's fresh approach allowed him to deduce principles that had remained elusive to others.

One reason Mendel probably chose to work with peas is that there are many varieties. For example, one variety

has purple flowers, while another variety has white flowers. A heritable feature that varies among individuals, such as flower color, is called a **character**. Each variant for a character, such as purple or white color for flowers, is called a **trait**.

Other advantages of using peas are their short generation time and the large number of offspring from each mating. Furthermore, Mendel could strictly control mating between plants **(Figure 14.2)**. Each pea flower has both pollen-producing organs (stamens) and an egg-bearing organ (carpel). In nature, pea plants usually self-fertilize: Pollen grains from the stamens land on the carpel of the same flower, and sperm released from the pollen grains fertilize

---

▼ Figure 14.2 | **Research Method**

Crossing Pea Plants

Application By crossing (mating) two true-breeding varieties of an organism, scientists can study patterns of inheritance. In this example, Mendel crossed pea plants that varied in flower color.

Technique

① Removed stamens from purple flower

② Transferred sperm-bearing pollen from stamens of white flower to egg-bearing carpel of purple flower

Parental generation (P)

Carpel   Stamens

③ Waited for pollinated carpel to mature into pod

④ Planted seeds from pod

Results When pollen from a white flower was transferred to a purple flower, the first-generation hybrids all had purple flowers. The result was the same for the reciprocal cross, which involved the transfer of pollen from purple flowers to white flowers.

First filial generation offspring (F_1)

⑤ Examined offspring: all purple flowers

eggs present in the carpel.* To achieve cross-pollination of two plants, Mendel removed the immature stamens of a plant before they produced pollen and then dusted pollen from another plant onto the altered flowers (see Figure 14.2). Each resulting zygote then developed into a plant embryo encased in a seed (pea). Mendel could thus always be sure of the parentage of new seeds.

Mendel chose to track only those characters that occurred in two distinct, alternative forms, such as purple or white flower color. He also made sure that he started his experiments with varieties that, over many generations of self-pollination, had produced only the same variety as the parent plant. Such plants are said to be **true-breeding**. For example, a plant with purple flowers is true-breeding if the seeds produced by self-pollination in successive generations all give rise to plants that also have purple flowers.

In a typical breeding experiment, Mendel cross-pollinated two contrasting, true-breeding pea varieties—for example, purple-flowered plants and white-flowered plants (see Figure 14.2). This mating, or *crossing*, of two true-breeding varieties is called **hybridization**. The true-breeding parents are referred to as the **P generation** (parental generation), and their hybrid offspring are the F_1 **generation** (first filial generation, the word *filial* from the Latin word for "son"). Allowing these F_1 hybrids to self-pollinate (or to cross-pollinate with other F_1 hybrids) produces an F_2 **generation** (second filial generation). Mendel usually followed traits for at least the P, F_1, and F_2 generations. Had Mendel stopped his experiments with the F_1 generation, the basic patterns of inheritance would have eluded him. Mendel's quantitative analysis of the F_2 plants from thousands of genetic crosses like these allowed him to deduce two fundamental principles of heredity, which have come to be called the law of segregation and the law of independent assortment.

The Law of Segregation

If the blending model of inheritance were correct, the F_1 hybrids from a cross between purple-flowered and white-flowered pea plants would have pale purple flowers, a trait intermediate between those of the P generation. Notice in Figure 14.2 that the experiment produced a very different result: All the F_1 offspring had flowers just as purple as the purple-flowered parents.

What happened to the white-flowered plants' genetic contribution to the hybrids? If it were lost, then the F_1 plants could produce only purple-flowered offspring in the F_2 generation. But when Mendel allowed the F_1 plants to

self-pollinate and planted their seeds, the white-flower trait reappeared in the F_2 generation. Mendel used very large sample sizes and kept accurate records of his results: 705 of the F_2 plants had purple flowers, and 224 had white flowers. These data fit a ratio of approximately three purple to one white (**Figure 14.3**). Mendel reasoned that the heritable factor for white flowers did not disappear in the F_1 plants but was somehow hidden, or masked, when the purple-flower factor was present. In Mendel's terminology, purple flower color is a *dominant* trait, and white flower color is a *recessive* trait. The reappearance of white-flowered plants in the

▼ **Figure 14.3** | **Inquiry**

When F_1 hybrid pea plants self- or cross-pollinate, which traits appear in the F_2 generation?

Experiment Mendel crossed true-breeding purple-flowered plants and white-flowered plants (crosses are symbolized by ×). The resulting F_1 hybrids were allowed to self-pollinate or were cross-pollinated with other F_1 hybrids. The F_2 generation plants were then observed for flower color.

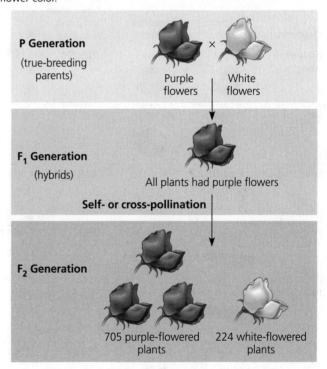

P Generation (true-breeding parents)

Purple flowers × White flowers

F_1 Generation (hybrids)

All plants had purple flowers

Self- or cross-pollination

F_2 Generation

705 purple-flowered plants   224 white-flowered plants

Results Both purple-flowered and white-flowered plants appeared in the F_2 generation, in a ratio of approximately 3:1.

Conclusion The "heritable factor" for the recessive trait (white flowers) had not been destroyed, deleted, or "blended" in the F_1 generation but was merely masked by the presence of the factor for purple flowers, which is the dominant trait.

Source: G. Mendel, Experiments in plant hybridization, *Proceedings of the Natural History Society of Brünn* 4:3–47 (1866).

WHAT IF? *If you mated two purple-flowered plants from the P generation, what ratio of traits would you expect to observe in the offspring? Explain.*

---

*As you learned in Figure 13.6b, meiosis in plants produces spores, not gametes. In flowering plants like the pea, each spore develops into a microscopic haploid gametophyte that contains only a few cells and is located on the parent plant. The gametophyte produces sperm, in pollen grains, and eggs, in the carpel. For simplicity, we will not include the gametophyte stage in our discussion of fertilization in plants.

F_2 generation was evidence that the heritable factor causing white flowers had not been diluted or destroyed by coexisting with the purple-flower factor in the F_1 hybrids. Instead, it had been hidden when in the presence of the purple flower factor.

Mendel observed the same pattern of inheritance in six other characters, each represented by two distinctly different traits **(Table 14.1)**. For example, when Mendel crossed a true-breeding variety that produced smooth, round pea seeds with one that produced wrinkled seeds, all the F_1 hybrids produced round seeds; this is the dominant trait for seed shape. In the F_2 generation, approximately 75% of the seeds were round and 25% were wrinkled—a 3:1 ratio, as in Figure 14.3. Now let's see how Mendel deduced the law of segregation from his experimental results. In the discussion that follows, we will use modern terms instead of some of the terms used by Mendel. (For example, we'll use "gene" instead of Mendel's "heritable factor.")

Table 14.1	The Results of Mendel's F_1 Crosses for Seven Characters in Pea Plants			
Character	Dominant Trait	× Recessive Trait	F_2 Generation Dominant: Recessive	Ratio
Flower color	Purple	× White	705:224	3.15:1
Seed color	Yellow	× Green	6,022:2,001	3.01:1
Seed shape	Round	× Wrinkled	5,474:1,850	2.96:1
Pod shape	Inflated	× Constricted	882:299	2.95:1
Pod color	Green	× Yellow	428:152	2.82:1
Flower position	Axial	× Terminal	651:207	3.14:1
Stem length	Tall	× Dwarf	787:277	2.84:1

Mendel's Model

Mendel developed a model to explain the 3:1 inheritance pattern that he consistently observed among the F_2 offspring in his pea experiments. We describe four related concepts making up this model, the fourth of which is the law of segregation.

First, *alternative versions of genes account for variations in inherited characters.* The gene for flower color in pea plants, for example, exists in two versions, one for purple flowers and the other for white flowers. These alternative versions of a gene are called **alleles**. Today, we can relate this concept to chromosomes and DNA. As shown in **Figure 14.4**, each gene is a sequence of nucleotides at a specific place, or locus, along a particular chromosome. The DNA at that locus, however, can vary slightly in its nucleotide sequence. This variation in information content can affect the function of the encoded protein and thus the phenotype of the organism. The purple-flower allele and the white-flower allele are two DNA sequence variations possible at the flower-color locus on one of a pea plant's chromosomes, one that allows synthesis of purple pigment and one that does not.

Second, *for each character, an organism inherits two copies (that is, two alleles) of a gene, one from each parent.* Remarkably, Mendel made this deduction without knowing about the role, or even the existence, of chromosomes. Each somatic cell in a diploid organism has two sets of chromosomes, one set inherited from each parent (see Concept 13.2). Thus, a genetic locus is actually represented twice in a diploid cell, once on each homolog of a specific pair of chromosomes. The two alleles at a particular locus may be identical, as in the true-breeding plants of Mendel's P generation. Or the alleles may differ, as in the F_1 hybrids (see Figure 14.4).

Third, *if the two alleles at a locus differ, then one, the **dominant allele**, determines the organism's appearance; the other, the **recessive allele**, has no noticeable effect on the organism's appearance.* Accordingly, Mendel's F_1 plants had purple flowers because the allele for that trait is dominant and the allele for white flowers is recessive.

The fourth and final part of Mendel's model, the **law of segregation**, states that *the two alleles for a heritable character segregate (separate from each other) during gamete formation and end up in different gametes.* Thus, an egg or a sperm gets only one of the two alleles that are present in the somatic cells of the organism making the gamete. In terms of chromosomes, this segregation corresponds to the distribution of the two members of a pair of homologous chromosomes to different gametes in meiosis (see Figure 13.7). Note that if an organism has identical alleles for a particular character—that is, the organism is true-breeding for that character—then that allele is present in all gametes. But if different alleles are present, as in the F_1 hybrids, then 50% of the gametes receive the dominant allele and 50% receive the recessive allele.

► **Figure 14.4 Alleles, alternative versions of a gene.** Shown is a pair of homologous chromosomes in an F_1 hybrid pea plant, with the DNA sequence from the flower color allele of each. The paternally inherited chromosome (blue) has an allele for purple flowers, which codes for a protein that indirectly controls synthesis of purple pigment. The maternally inherited chromosome (red) has an allele for white flowers, which results in no functional protein being made.

Allele for purple flowers

Locus for flower-color gene

Allele for white flowers

Pair of homologous chromosomes

DNA with nucleotide sequence CTAAATCGGT

Through a series of steps, this DNA sequence results in production of an enzyme that helps synthesize purple pigment.

Enzyme

One purple-flower allele results in sufficient pigment for purple flowers.

This DNA sequence results in the absence of the enzyme.

DNA with nucleotide sequence ATAAATCGGT

Does Mendel's segregation model account for the 3:1 ratio he observed in the F_2 generation of his numerous crosses? For the flower-color character, the model predicts that the two different alleles present in an F_1 individual will segregate into gametes such that half the gametes will have the purple-flower allele and half will have the white-flower allele. During self-pollination, gametes of each class unite randomly. An egg with a purple-flower allele has an equal chance of being fertilized by a sperm with a purple-flower allele or one with a white-flower allele. Since the same is true for an egg with a white-flower allele, there are four equally likely combinations of sperm and egg. **Figure 14.5** illustrates these combinations using a **Punnett square**, a handy diagrammatic device for predicting the allele composition of offspring from a cross between individuals of known genetic makeup. Notice that we use a capital letter to symbolize a dominant allele and a lowercase letter for a recessive allele. In our example, P is the purple-flower allele, and p is the white-flower allele; it is often useful as well to be able to refer to the gene itself as the P/p gene.

In the F_2 offspring, what color will the flowers be? One-fourth of the plants have inherited two purple-flower alleles; clearly, these plants will have purple flowers. One-half of the F_2 offspring

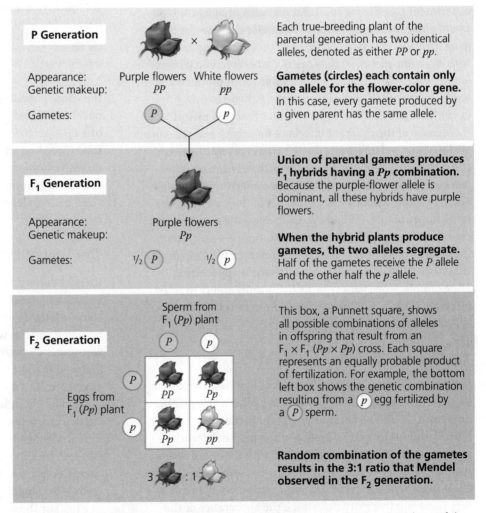

P Generation

Appearance: Purple flowers   White flowers
Genetic makeup: PP pp

Gametes: P p

Each true-breeding plant of the parental generation has two identical alleles, denoted as either PP or pp.

Gametes (circles) each contain only one allele for the flower-color gene. In this case, every gamete produced by a given parent has the same allele.

F_1 Generation

Appearance: Purple flowers
Genetic makeup: Pp

Gametes: $\frac{1}{2}$ P $\frac{1}{2}$ p

Union of parental gametes produces F_1 hybrids having a Pp combination. Because the purple-flower allele is dominant, all these hybrids have purple flowers.

When the hybrid plants produce gametes, the two alleles segregate. Half of the gametes receive the P allele and the other half the p allele.

F_2 Generation

Sperm from F_1 (Pp) plant

P p

Eggs from F_1 (Pp) plant

P PP Pp
p Pp pp

3 : 1

This box, a Punnett square, shows all possible combinations of alleles in offspring that result from an $F_1 \times F_1$ ($Pp \times Pp$) cross. Each square represents an equally probable product of fertilization. For example, the bottom left box shows the genetic combination resulting from a p egg fertilized by a P sperm.

Random combination of the gametes results in the 3:1 ratio that Mendel observed in the F_2 generation.

▲ **Figure 14.5 Mendel's law of segregation.** This diagram shows the genetic makeup of the generations in Figure 14.3. It illustrates Mendel's model for inheritance of the alleles of a single gene. Each plant has two alleles for the gene controlling flower color, one allele inherited from each of the plant's parents. To construct a Punnett square that predicts the F_2 generation offspring, we list all the possible gametes from one parent (here, the F_1 female) along the left side of the square and all the possible gametes from the other parent (here, the F_1 male) along the top. The boxes represent the offspring resulting from all the possible unions of male and female gametes.

have inherited one purple-flower allele and one white-flower allele; these plants will also have purple flowers, the dominant trait. Finally, one-fourth of the F₂ plants have inherited two white-flower alleles and will express the recessive trait. Thus, Mendel's model accounts for the 3:1 ratio of traits that he observed in the F₂ generation.

Useful Genetic Vocabulary

An organism that has a pair of identical alleles for a character is said to be **homozygous** for the gene controlling that character. In the parental generation in Figure 14.5, the purple pea plant is homozygous for the dominant allele (*PP*), while the white plant is homozygous for the recessive allele (*pp*). Homozygous plants "breed true" because all of their gametes contain the same allele—either *P* or *p* in this example. If we cross dominant homozygotes with recessive homozygotes, every offspring will have two different alleles—*Pp* in the case of the F₁ hybrids of our flower-color experiment (see Figure 14.5). An organism that has two different alleles for a gene is said to be **heterozygous** for that gene. Unlike homozygotes, heterozygotes produce gametes with different alleles, so they are not true-breeding. For example, *P*- and *p*-containing gametes are both produced by our F₁ hybrids. Self-pollination of the F₁ hybrids thus produces both purple-flowered and white-flowered offspring.

Because of the different effects of dominant and recessive alleles, an organism's traits do not always reveal its genetic composition. Therefore, we distinguish between an organism's appearance or observable traits, called its **phenotype**, and its genetic makeup, its **genotype**. In the case of flower color in pea plants, *PP* and *Pp* plants have the same phenotype (purple) but different genotypes. **Figure 14.6** reviews these terms. Note that "phenotype" refers to physiological traits as well as traits that relate directly to appearance. For example, a pea variety lacks the normal ability to self-pollinate. This physiological variation (non-self-pollination) is a phenotypic trait.

The Testcross

Suppose we have a "mystery" pea plant that has purple flowers. We cannot tell from its flower color if this plant is homozygous (*PP*) or heterozygous (*Pp*) because both genotypes result in the same purple phenotype. To determine the genotype, we can cross this plant with a white-flowered plant (*pp*), which will make only gametes with the recessive allele (*p*). The allele in the gamete contributed by the mystery plant will therefore determine the appearance of the offspring **(Figure 14.7)**. If all the offspring of the cross have purple flowers, then the purple-flowered mystery plant must be homozygous for the dominant allele, because a *PP* × *pp* cross produces all *Pp* offspring. But if both the purple and

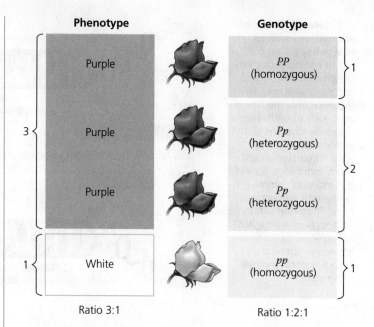

▲ **Figure 14.6 Phenotype versus genotype.** Grouping F₂ offspring from a cross for flower color according to phenotype results in the typical 3:1 phenotypic ratio. In terms of genotype, however, there are actually two categories of purple-flowered plants, *PP* (homozygous) and *Pp* (heterozygous), giving a 1:2:1 genotypic ratio.

the white phenotypes appear among the offspring, then the purple-flowered parent must be heterozygous. The offspring of a *Pp* × *pp* cross will be expected to have a 1:1 phenotypic ratio. Breeding an organism of unknown genotype with a recessive homozygote is called a **testcross** because it can reveal the genotype of that organism. The testcross was devised by Mendel and continues to be an important tool used by geneticists.

The Law of Independent Assortment

Mendel derived the law of segregation from experiments in which he followed only a *single* character, such as flower color. All the F₁ progeny produced in his crosses of true-breeding parents were **monohybrids**, meaning that they were heterozygous for the one particular character being followed in the cross. We refer to a cross between such heterozygotes as a **monohybrid cross**.

Mendel identified his second law of inheritance by following *two* characters at the same time, such as seed color and seed shape. Seeds (peas) may be either yellow or green. They also may be either round (smooth) or wrinkled. From single-character crosses, Mendel knew that the allele for yellow seeds is dominant (*Y*), and the allele for green seeds is recessive (*y*). For the seed-shape character, the allele for round is dominant (*R*), and the allele for wrinkled is recessive (*r*).

Imagine crossing two true-breeding pea varieties that differ in *both* of these characters—a cross between a plant with yellow-round seeds (*YYRR*) and a plant with green-wrinkled

Research Method

The Testcross

Application An organism that exhibits a dominant trait, such as purple flowers in pea plants, can be either homozygous for the dominant allele or heterozygous. To determine the organism's genotype, geneticists can perform a testcross.

Technique In a testcross, the individual with the unknown genotype is crossed with a homozygous individual expressing the recessive trait (white flowers in this example), and Punnett squares are used to predict the possible outcomes.

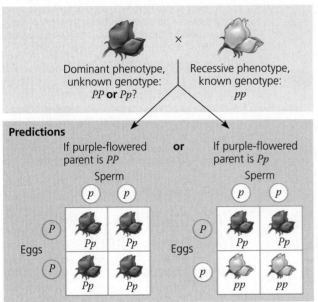

Results Matching the results to either prediction identifies the unknown parental genotype (either *PP* or *Pp* in this example). In this testcross, we transferred pollen from a white-flowered plant to the carpels of a purple-flowered plant; the opposite (reciprocal) cross would have led to the same results.

seeds (*yyrr*). The F$_1$ plants will be **dihybrids**, individuals heterozygous for the two characters being followed in the cross (*YyRr*). But are these two characters transmitted from parents to offspring as a package? That is, will the *Y* and *R* alleles always stay together, generation after generation? Or are seed color and seed shape inherited independently? **Figure 14.8** shows how a **dihybrid cross**, a cross between F$_1$ dihybrids, can determine which of these two hypotheses is correct.

The F$_1$ plants, of genotype *YyRr*, exhibit both dominant phenotypes, yellow seeds with round shapes, no matter which hypothesis is correct. The key step in the experiment is to see what happens when F$_1$ plants self-pollinate

and produce F$_2$ offspring. If the hybrids must transmit their alleles in the same combinations in which the alleles were inherited from the P generation, then the F$_1$ hybrids will produce only two classes of gametes: *YR* and *yr*. This "dependent assortment" hypothesis predicts that the phenotypic ratio of the F$_2$ generation will be 3:1, just as in a monohybrid cross (see Figure 14.8, left side).

The alternative hypothesis is that the two pairs of alleles segregate independently of each other. In other words, genes are packaged into gametes in all possible allelic combinations, as long as each gamete has one allele for each gene (see Figure 13.11). In our example, an F$_1$ plant will produce four classes of gametes in equal quantities: *YR*, *Yr*, *yR*, and *yr*. If sperm of the four classes fertilize eggs of the four classes, there will be 16 (4 × 4) equally probable ways in which the alleles can combine in the F$_2$ generation, as shown in Figure 14.8, right side. These combinations result in four phenotypic categories with a ratio of 9:3:3:1 (nine yellow-round to three green-round to three yellow-wrinkled to one green-wrinkled). When Mendel did the experiment and classified the F$_2$ offspring, his results were close to the predicted 9:3:3:1 phenotypic ratio, supporting the hypothesis that the alleles for one gene—controlling seed color or seed shape, in this example—are sorted into gametes independently of the alleles of other genes.

Mendel tested his seven pea characters in various dihybrid combinations and always observed a 9:3:3:1 phenotypic ratio in the F$_2$ generation. Is this consistent with the 3:1 phenotypic ratio seen for the monohybrid cross shown in Figure 14.5? To investigate this question, let's consider one of the two dihybrid characters by itself: Looking only at pea color, we see that there are 416 yellow and 140 green peas—a 2.97:1 ratio, or roughly 3:1. In the dihybrid cross, the pea color alleles segregate as if this were a monohybrid cross. The results of Mendel's dihybrid experiments are the basis for what we now call the **law of independent assortment**, which states that *two or more genes assort independently—that is, each pair of alleles segregates independently of each other pair of alleles—during gamete formation.*

This law applies only to genes (allele pairs) located on different chromosomes (that is to say, on chromosomes that are not homologous) or, alternatively, to genes that are very far apart on the same chromosome. (The latter case will be explained in Chapter 15, along with the more complex inheritance patterns of genes located near each other, which tend to be inherited together.) All the pea characters Mendel chose for analysis were controlled by genes on different chromosomes or were far apart on the same chromosome; this situation greatly simplified interpretation of his multicharacter pea crosses. All the examples we consider in the rest of this chapter involve genes located on different chromosomes.

Inquiry

Do the alleles for one character assort into gametes dependently or independently of the alleles for a different character?

Experiment To follow the characters of seed color and seed shape through the F_2 generation, Mendel crossed a true-breeding plant with yellow-round seeds with a true-breeding plant with green-wrinkled seeds, producing dihybrid F_1 plants. Self-pollination of the F_1 dihybrids produced the F_2 generation. The two hypotheses (dependent and independent assortment) predict different phenotypic ratios.

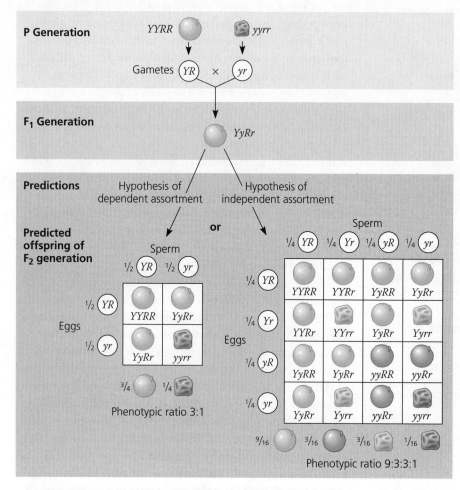

Results

| 315 🟡 | 108 🟡 | 101 🟢 | 32 🟢 | Phenotypic ratio approximately 9:3:3:1 |

Conclusion Only the hypothesis of independent assortment predicts two of the observed phenotypes: green-round seeds and yellow-wrinkled seeds (see the right-hand Punnett square). The alleles for each gene segregate independently of those of the other, and the two genes are said to assort independently.

Source: G. Mendel, Experiments in plant hybridization, *Proceedings of the Natural History Society of Brünn* 4:3–47 (1866).

WHAT IF? *Suppose Mendel had transferred pollen from an F_1 plant to the carpel of a plant that was homozygous recessive for both genes. Set up the cross and draw Punnett squares that predict the offspring for both hypotheses. Would this cross have supported the hypothesis of independent assortment equally well?*

CONCEPT CHECK 14.1

1. **DRAW IT** Pea plants heterozygous for flower position and stem length (*AaTt*) are allowed to self-pollinate, and 400 of the resulting seeds are planted. Draw a Punnett square for this cross. How many offspring would be predicted to have terminal flowers and be dwarf? (See Table 14.1.)

2. **WHAT IF?** List all gametes that could be made by a pea plant heterozygous for seed color, seed shape, and pod shape (*YyRrIi*; see Table 14.1). How large a Punnett square would you need to draw to predict the offspring of a self-pollination of this "trihybrid"?

3. **MAKE CONNECTIONS** In some pea plant crosses, the plants are self-pollinated. Explain whether self-pollination is considered asexual or sexual reproduction. (See Concept 13.1.)

For suggested answers, see Appendix A.

CONCEPT 14.2

Probability laws govern Mendelian inheritance

Mendel's laws of segregation and independent assortment reflect the same rules of probability that apply to tossing coins, rolling dice, and drawing cards from a deck. The probability scale ranges from 0 to 1. An event that is certain to occur has a probability of 1, while an event that is certain *not* to occur has a probability of 0. With a coin that has heads on both sides, the probability of tossing heads is 1, and the probability of tossing tails is 0. With a normal coin, the chance of tossing heads is $\frac{1}{2}$, and the chance of tossing tails is $\frac{1}{2}$. The probability of drawing the ace of spades from a 52-card deck is $\frac{1}{52}$. The probabilities of all possible outcomes for an event must add up to 1. With a deck of cards, the chance of picking a card other than the ace of spades is $\frac{51}{52}$.

Tossing a coin illustrates an important lesson about probability. For every toss, the probability of heads is $\frac{1}{2}$. The outcome of any particular toss is unaffected by what has happened on previous trials. We refer to phenomena such as coin tosses as independent events. Each toss of a coin, whether done sequentially with one coin or simultaneously with many, is independent of every other toss. And like two separate coin tosses, the alleles of one gene segregate into gametes independently of another gene's alleles (the law of independent assortment). Two basic rules of probability can help us predict the outcome of the fusion of such gametes in simple monohybrid crosses and more complicated crosses as well.

The Multiplication and Addition Rules Applied to Monohybrid Crosses

How do we determine the probability that two or more independent events will occur together in some specific combination? For example, what is the chance that two coins tossed simultaneously will both land heads up? The **multiplication rule** states that to determine this probability, we multiply the probability of one event (one coin coming up heads) by the probability of the other event (the other coin coming up heads). By the multiplication rule, then, the probability that both coins will land heads up is $\frac{1}{2} \times \frac{1}{2} = \frac{1}{4}$.

We can apply the same reasoning to an F_1 monohybrid cross. With seed shape in pea plants as the heritable character, the genotype of F_1 plants is *Rr*. Segregation in a heterozygous plant is like flipping a coin in terms of calculating the probability of each outcome: Each egg produced has a $\frac{1}{2}$ chance of carrying the dominant allele (*R*) and a $\frac{1}{2}$ chance of carrying the recessive allele (*r*). The same odds apply to each sperm cell produced. For a particular F_2 plant to have wrinkled seeds, the recessive trait, both the egg and the sperm that come together must carry the *r* allele. The probability that an *r* allele will be present in both gametes at fertilization is found by multiplying $\frac{1}{2}$ (the probability that the egg will have an *r*) $\times \frac{1}{2}$ (the probability that the sperm will have an *r*). Thus, the multiplication rule tells us that the probability of an F_2 plant having wrinkled seeds (*rr*) is $\frac{1}{4}$ **(Figure 14.9)**. Likewise, the probability of an F_2 plant carrying both dominant alleles for seed shape (*RR*) is $\frac{1}{4}$.

To figure out the probability that an F_2 plant from a monohybrid cross will be heterozygous rather than homozygous, we need to invoke a second rule. Notice in Figure 14.9 that the dominant allele can come from the egg and the recessive allele from the sperm, or vice versa. That is, F_1 gametes can combine to produce *Rr* offspring in two *mutually exclusive* ways: For any particular heterozygous F_2 plant, the dominant allele can come from the egg *or* the sperm, but not from both. According to the **addition rule**, the probability that any one of two or more mutually exclusive events will occur is calculated by adding their individual probabilities. As we have just seen, the multiplication rule gives us the individual probabilities that we will now add together. The probability for one possible way of obtaining an F_2 heterozygote—the dominant allele from the egg and the recessive allele from the sperm—

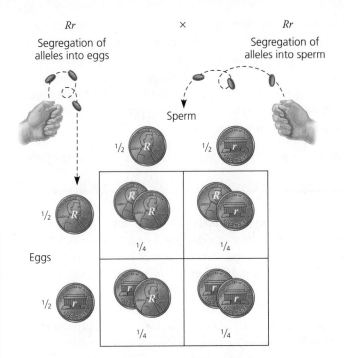

▲ **Figure 14.9 Segregation of alleles and fertilization as chance events.** When a heterozygote (*Rr*) forms gametes, whether a particular gamete ends up with an *R* or an *r* is like the toss of a coin. We can determine the probability for any genotype among the offspring of two heterozygotes by multiplying together the individual probabilities of an egg and sperm having a particular allele (*R* or *r* in this example).

is $\frac{1}{4}$. The probability for the other possible way—the recessive allele from the egg and the dominant allele from the sperm—is also $\frac{1}{4}$ (see Figure 14.9). Using the rule of addition, then, we can calculate the probability of an F_2 heterozygote as $\frac{1}{4} + \frac{1}{4} = \frac{1}{2}$.

Solving Complex Genetics Problems with the Rules of Probability

We can also apply the rules of probability to predict the outcome of crosses involving multiple characters. Recall that each allelic pair segregates independently during gamete formation (the law of independent assortment). Thus, a dihybrid or other multicharacter cross is equivalent to two or more independent monohybrid crosses occurring simultaneously. By applying what we have learned about monohybrid crosses, we can determine the probability of specific genotypes occurring in the F_2 generation without having to construct unwieldy Punnett squares.

Consider the dihybrid cross between *YyRr* heterozygotes shown in Figure 14.8. We will focus first on the seed-color character. For a monohybrid cross of *Yy* plants, we can use a simple Punnett square to determine that the probabilities of the offspring genotypes are $\frac{1}{4}$ for *YY*, $\frac{1}{2}$ for *Yy*, and $\frac{1}{4}$ for *yy*. We can draw a second Punnett square to determine that the same probabilities apply to the offspring genotypes for seed shape: $\frac{1}{4}$ *RR*, $\frac{1}{2}$ *Rr*, and $\frac{1}{4}$ *rr*. Knowing these probabilities, we can simply use the multiplication rule to determine the probability of each of the genotypes in the F$_2$ generation. To give two examples, the calculations for finding the probabilities of two of the possible F$_2$ genotypes (*YYRR* and *YyRR*) are shown below:

Probability of *YYRR* = $\frac{1}{4}$(probability of *YY*) $\times$ $\frac{1}{4}$(*RR*) = $\frac{1}{16}$

Probability of *YyRR* = $\frac{1}{2}$(*Yy*) $\times$ $\frac{1}{4}$(*RR*) = $\frac{1}{8}$

The *YYRR* genotype corresponds to the upper left box in the larger Punnett square in Figure 14.8 (one box = $\frac{1}{16}$). Looking closely at the larger Punnett square in Figure 14.8, you will see that 2 of the 16 boxes ($\frac{1}{8}$) correspond to the *YyRR* genotype.

Now let's see how we can combine the multiplication and addition rules to solve even more complex problems in Mendelian genetics. Imagine a cross of two pea varieties in which we track the inheritance of three characters. Let's cross a trihybrid with purple flowers and yellow, round seeds (heterozygous for all three genes) with a plant with purple flowers and green, wrinkled seeds (heterozygous for flower color but homozygous recessive for the other two characters). Using Mendelian symbols, our cross is *PpYyRr* $\times$ *Ppyyrr*. What fraction of offspring from this cross are predicted to exhibit the recessive phenotypes for *at least two* of the three characters?

To answer this question, we can start by listing all genotypes we could get that fulfill this condition: *ppyyRr*, *ppYyrr*, *Ppyyrr*, *PPyyrr*, and *ppyyrr*. (Because the condition is *at least two* recessive traits, it includes the last genotype, which shows all three recessive traits.) Next, we calculate the probability for each of these genotypes resulting from our *PpYyRr* $\times$ *Ppyyrr* cross by multiplying together the individual probabilities for the allele pairs, just as we did in our dihybrid example. Note that in a cross involving heterozygous and homozygous allele pairs (for example, *Yy* $\times$ *yy*), the probability of heterozygous offspring is $\frac{1}{2}$ and the probability of homozygous offspring is $\frac{1}{2}$. Finally, we use the addition rule to add the probabilities for all the different genotypes that fulfill the condition of at least two recessive traits, as shown below:

ppyyRr	$\frac{1}{4}$ (probability of *pp*) $\times$ $\frac{1}{2}$ (*yy*) $\times$ $\frac{1}{2}$(*Rr*)	= $\frac{1}{16}$
ppYyrr	$\frac{1}{4}$ $\times$ $\frac{1}{2}$ $\times$ $\frac{1}{2}$	= $\frac{1}{16}$
Ppyyrr	$\frac{1}{2}$ $\times$ $\frac{1}{2}$ $\times$ $\frac{1}{2}$	= $\frac{2}{16}$
PPyyrr	$\frac{1}{4}$ $\times$ $\frac{1}{2}$ $\times$ $\frac{1}{2}$	= $\frac{1}{16}$
ppyyrr	$\frac{1}{4}$ $\times$ $\frac{1}{2}$ $\times$ $\frac{1}{2}$	= $\frac{1}{16}$
Chance of *at least two* recessive traits		= $\frac{6}{16}$ or $\frac{3}{8}$

In time, you'll be able to solve genetics problems faster by using the rules of probability than by filling in Punnett squares.

We cannot predict with certainty the exact numbers of progeny of different genotypes resulting from a genetic cross. But the rules of probability give us the *chance* of various outcomes. Usually, the larger the sample size, the closer the results will conform to our predictions. Mendel understood this statistical feature of inheritance and had a keen sense of the rules of chance. It was for this reason that he set up his experiments so as to generate, and then count, large numbers of offspring from his crosses.

CONCEPT CHECK 14.2

1. For any gene with a dominant allele *A* and recessive allele *a*, what proportions of the offspring from an *AA* $\times$ *Aa* cross are expected to be homozygous dominant, homozygous recessive, and heterozygous?

2. Two organisms, with genotypes *BbDD* and *BBDd*, are mated. Assuming independent assortment of the *B/b* and *D/d* genes, write the genotypes of all possible offspring from this cross and use the rules of probability to calculate the chance of each genotype occurring.

3. **WHAT IF?** Three characters (flower color, seed color, and pod shape) are considered in a cross between two pea plants: *PpYyIi* $\times$ *ppYyii*. What fraction of offspring are predicted to be homozygous recessive for at least two of the three characters?

For suggested answers, see Appendix A.

CONCEPT 14.3

Inheritance patterns are often more complex than predicted by simple Mendelian genetics

In the 20th century, geneticists extended Mendelian principles not only to diverse organisms, but also to patterns of inheritance more complex than those described by Mendel. For the work that led to his two laws of inheritance, Mendel chose pea plant characters that turn out to have a relatively simple genetic basis: Each character is determined by one gene, for which there are only two alleles, one completely dominant and the other completely recessive. (There is one exception: Mendel's pod-shape character is actually determined by two genes.) Not all heritable characters are determined so simply, and the relationship between genotype and phenotype is rarely so straightforward. Mendel himself realized that he could not explain the more complicated patterns he observed in crosses involving other pea characters or other plant species. This does not diminish the utility of Mendelian genetics, however, because the basic principles of segregation and independent assortment apply even to more complex patterns of inheritance. In this section, we will extend Mendelian genetics to hereditary patterns that were not reported by Mendel.

Extending Mendelian Genetics for a Single Gene

The inheritance of characters determined by a single gene deviates from simple Mendelian patterns when alleles are not completely dominant or recessive, when a particular gene has more than two alleles, or when a single gene produces multiple phenotypes. We will describe examples of each of these situations in this section.

Degrees of Dominance

Alleles can show different degrees of dominance and recessiveness in relation to each other. In Mendel's classic pea crosses, the F_1 offspring always looked like one of the two parental varieties because one allele in a pair showed **complete dominance** over the other. In such situations, the phenotypes of the heterozygote and the dominant homozygote are indistinguishable.

For some genes, however, neither allele is completely dominant, and the F_1 hybrids have a phenotype somewhere between those of the two parental varieties. This phenomenon, called **incomplete dominance**, is seen when red snapdragons are crossed with white snapdragons: All the F_1 hybrids have pink flowers **(Figure 14.10)**. This third, intermediate phenotype results from flowers of the heterozygotes having less red pigment than the red homozygotes. (This is unlike the case of Mendel's pea plants, where the Pp heterozygotes make enough pigment for the flowers to be purple, indistinguishable from those of PP plants.)

At first glance, incomplete dominance of either allele seems to provide evidence for the blending hypothesis of inheritance, which would predict that the red or white trait could never reappear among offspring from the pink hybrids. In fact, interbreeding F_1 hybrids produces F_2 offspring with a phenotypic ratio of one red to two pink to one white. (Because heterozygotes have a separate phenotype, the genotypic and phenotypic ratios for the F_2 generation are the same, 1:2:1.) The segregation of the red-flower and white-flower alleles in the gametes produced by the pink-flowered plants confirms that the alleles for flower color are heritable factors that maintain their identity in the hybrids; that is, inheritance is particulate.

Another variation on dominance relationships between alleles is called **codominance**; in this variation, the two alleles each affect the phenotype in separate, distinguishable ways. For example, the human MN blood group is determined by codominant alleles for two specific molecules located on the surface of red blood cells, the M and N molecules. A single gene locus, at which two allelic variations are possible, determines the phenotype of this blood group. Individuals homozygous for the M allele (MM) have red blood cells with only M molecules; individuals homozygous for the N allele (NN) have red blood cells with only N

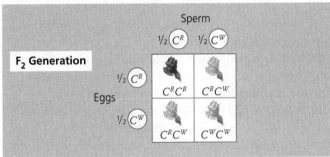

▲ **Figure 14.10 Incomplete dominance in snapdragon color.** When red snapdragons are crossed with white ones, the F_1 hybrids have pink flowers. Segregation of alleles into gametes of the F_1 plants results in an F_2 generation with a 1:2:1 ratio for both genotype and phenotype. Neither allele is dominant, so rather than using upper- and lowercase letters, we use the letter C with a superscript to indicate an allele for flower color: C^R for red and C^W for white.

? *Suppose a classmate argues that this figure supports the blending hypothesis for inheritance. What might your classmate say, and how would you respond?*

molecules. But *both* M and N molecules are present on the red blood cells of individuals heterozygous for the M and N alleles (MN). Note that the MN phenotype is *not* intermediate between the M and N phenotypes, which distinguishes codominance from incomplete dominance. Rather, *both* M and N phenotypes are exhibited by heterozygotes, since both molecules are present.

The Relationship Between Dominance and Phenotype We've now seen that the relative effects of two alleles range from complete dominance of one allele, through incomplete dominance of either allele, to codominance of both alleles. It is important to understand that an allele is called *dominant* because it is seen in the phenotype, not because it somehow subdues a recessive allele. Alleles are simply variations in a gene's nucleotide sequence (see Figure 14.4). When a dominant allele coexists with a recessive allele in a heterozygote, they do not actually interact at all. It is in the pathway from genotype to phenotype that dominance and recessiveness come into play.

To illustrate the relationship between dominance and phenotype, we can use one of the characters Mendel studied—round versus wrinkled pea seed shape. The dominant allele (round) codes for an enzyme that helps convert an unbranched form of starch to a branched form in the seed. The recessive allele (wrinkled) codes for a defective form of this enzyme, leading to an accumulation of unbranched starch, which causes excess water to enter the seed by osmosis. Later, when the seed dries, it wrinkles. If a dominant allele is present, no excess water enters the seed and it does not wrinkle when it dries. One dominant allele results in enough of the enzyme to synthesize adequate amounts of branched starch, which means that dominant homozygotes and heterozygotes have the same phenotype: round seeds.

A closer look at the relationship between dominance and phenotype reveals an intriguing fact: For any character, the observed dominant/recessive relationship of alleles depends on the level at which we examine phenotype. **Tay-Sachs disease**, an inherited disorder in humans, is an example. The brain cells of a child with Tay-Sachs disease cannot metabolize certain lipids because a crucial enzyme does not work properly. As these lipids accumulate in brain cells, the child begins to suffer seizures, blindness, and degeneration of motor and mental performance and dies within a few years.

Only children who inherit two copies of the Tay-Sachs allele (homozygotes) have the disease. Thus, at the *organismal* level, the Tay-Sachs allele qualifies as recessive. However, the activity level of the lipid-metabolizing enzyme in heterozygotes is intermediate between that in individuals homozygous for the normal allele and that in individuals with Tay-Sachs disease. The intermediate phenotype observed at the *biochemical* level is characteristic of incomplete dominance of either allele. Fortunately, the heterozygote condition does not lead to disease symptoms, apparently because half the normal enzyme activity is sufficient to prevent lipid accumulation in the brain. Extending our analysis to yet another level, we find that heterozygous individuals produce equal numbers of normal and dysfunctional enzyme molecules. Thus, at the *molecular* level, the normal allele and the Tay-Sachs allele are codominant. As you can see, whether alleles appear to be completely dominant, incompletely dominant, or codominant depends on the level at which the phenotype is analyzed.

Frequency of Dominant Alleles Although you might assume that the dominant allele for a particular character would be more common than the recessive allele, this is not a given. For example, about one baby out of 400 in the United States is born with extra fingers or toes, a condition known as

polydactyly. Some cases are caused by the presence of a dominant allele. The low frequency of polydactyly indicates that the recessive allele, which results in five digits per appendage, is far more prevalent than the dominant allele in the population. In Chapter 23, you will learn how relative frequencies of alleles in a population are affected by natural selection.

Multiple Alleles

Only two alleles exist for the pea characters that Mendel studied, but most genes exist in more than two allelic forms. The ABO blood groups in humans, for instance, are determined by three alleles of a single gene: I^A, I^B, and i. A person's blood group may be one of four types: A, B, AB, or O. These letters refer to two carbohydrates—A and B—that may be found on the surface of red blood cells. A person's blood cells may have carbohydrate A (type A blood), carbohydrate B (type B), both (type AB), or neither (type O), as shown in **Figure 14.11**. Matching compatible blood groups is critical for safe blood transfusions (see Chapter 43).

Pleiotropy

So far, we have treated Mendelian inheritance as though each gene affects only one phenotypic character. Most genes, however, have multiple phenotypic effects, a property called **pleiotropy** (from the Greek *pleion*, more). In humans, for example, pleiotropic alleles are responsible for the multiple symptoms associated with certain hereditary diseases, such as cystic fibrosis and sickle-cell disease, discussed later

(a) **The three alleles for the ABO blood groups and their carbohydrates.** Each allele codes for an enzyme that may add a specific carbohydrate (designated by the superscript on the allele and shown as a triangle or circle) to red blood cells.			
Allele	I^A	I^B	i
Carbohydrate	A △	B ○	none

(b) **Blood group genotypes and phenotypes.** There are six possible genotypes, resulting in four different phenotypes.				
Genotype	$I^A I^A$ or $I^A i$	$I^B I^B$ or $I^B i$	$I^A I^B$	ii
Red blood cell appearance				
Phenotype (blood group)	A	B	AB	O

▲ **Figure 14.11 Multiple alleles for the ABO blood groups.** The four blood groups result from different combinations of three alleles.

? *Based on the surface carbohydrate phenotype in (b), what are the dominance relationships among the alleles?*

in this chapter. In the garden pea, the gene that determines flower color also affects the color of the coating on the outer surface of the seed, which can be gray or white. Given the intricate molecular and cellular interactions responsible for an organism's development and physiology, it isn't surprising that a single gene can affect a number of characteristics.

Extending Mendelian Genetics for Two or More Genes

Dominance relationships, multiple alleles, and pleiotropy all have to do with the effects of the alleles of a single gene. We now consider two situations in which two or more genes are involved in determining a particular phenotype: epistasis, where one gene affects the phenotype of another because the two gene products interact; and polygenic inheritance, where multiple genes independently affect a single trait.

Epistasis

In **epistasis** (from the Greek for "standing upon"), the phenotypic expression of a gene at one locus alters that of a gene at a second locus. An example will help clarify this concept. In Labrador retrievers (commonly called "Labs"), black coat color is dominant to brown. Let's designate *B* and *b* as the two alleles for this character. For a Lab to have brown fur, its genotype must be *bb*; these dogs are called chocolate Labs. But there is more to the story. A second gene determines whether or not pigment will be deposited in the hair. The dominant allele, symbolized by *E*, results in the deposition of either black or brown pigment, depending on the genotype at the first locus. But if the Lab is homozygous recessive for the second locus (*ee*), then the coat is yellow, regardless of the genotype at the black/brown locus (so-called golden Labs). In this case, the gene for pigment deposition (*E/e*) is said to be epistatic to the gene that codes for black or brown pigment (*B/b*).

What happens if we mate black Labs that are heterozygous for both genes (*BbEe*)? Although the two genes affect the same phenotypic character (coat color), they follow the law of independent assortment. Thus, our breeding experiment represents an F_1 dihybrid cross, like those that produced a 9:3:3:1 ratio in Mendel's experiments. We can use a Punnett square to represent the genotypes of the F_2 offspring **(Figure 14.12)**. As a result of epistasis, the phenotypic ratio among the F_2 offspring is 9 black to 3 chocolate to 4 golden Labs. Other types of epistatic interactions produce different ratios, but all are modified versions of 9:3:3:1.

Polygenic Inheritance

Mendel studied characters that could be classified on an either-or basis, such as purple versus white flower color. But many characters, such as human skin color and height, are not one of two discrete characters, but instead vary in the

▲ **Figure 14.12 An example of epistasis.** This Punnett square illustrates the genotypes and phenotypes predicted for offspring of matings between two black Labrador retrievers of genotype *BbEe*. The *E/e* gene, which is epistatic to the *B/b* gene coding for hair pigment, controls whether or not pigment of any color will be deposited in the hair.

? *Explain the genetic basis for the difference between the ratio (9:3:4) of phenotypes seen in this cross and that seen in Figure 14.8.*

population in gradations along a continuum. These are called **quantitative characters**. Quantitative variation usually indicates **polygenic inheritance**, an additive effect of two or more genes on a single phenotypic character. (In a way, this is the converse of pleiotropy, where a single gene affects several phenotypic characters.) Height is a good example of polygenic inheritance: A recent study using genomic methods identified at least 180 genes that affect height.

Skin pigmentation in humans is also controlled by many separately inherited genes. Here, we'll simplify the story in order to understand the concept of polygenic inheritance. Let's consider three genes, with a dark-skin allele for each gene (*A*, *B*, or *C*) contributing one "unit" of darkness (also a simplification) to the phenotype and being incompletely dominant to the other allele (*a*, *b*, or *c*). In our model, an *AABBCC* person would be very dark, while an *aabbcc* individual would be very light. An *AaBbCc* person would have skin of an intermediate shade. Because the alleles have a cumulative effect, the genotypes *AaBbCc* and *AABbcc* would make the same genetic contribution (three units) to skin darkness. There are seven skin-color phenotypes that could result from a mating between *AaBbCc* heterozygotes, as shown in **Figure 14.13**. In a large number of such matings, the majority of offspring would be expected to have intermediate phenotypes (skin color in the middle range). You can graph the predictions from the Punnett square in the Scientific Skills Exercise. Environmental factors, such as exposure to the sun, also affect the skin-color phenotype.

Nature and Nurture: The Environmental Impact on Phenotype

Another departure from simple Mendelian genetics arises when the phenotype for a character depends on environment as well as genotype. A single tree, locked into its inherited genotype, has leaves that vary in size, shape, and greenness, depending on their exposure to wind and sun. For humans, nutrition influences height, exercise alters build, sun-tanning darkens the skin, and experience improves performance on intelligence tests. Even identical twins, who are genetic equals, accumulate phenotypic differences as a result of their unique experiences.

Phenotypes:

| 1/64 | 6/64 | 15/64 | 20/64 | 15/64 | 6/64 | 1/64 |

Number of
dark-skin alleles: 0   1   2   3   4   5   6

▲ **Figure 14.13 A simplified model for polygenic inheritance of skin color.** In this model, three separately inherited genes affect skin color. The heterozygous individuals (*AaBbCc*) represented by the two rectangles at the top of this figure each carry three dark-skin alleles (black circles, which represent *A*, *B*, or *C*) and three light-skin alleles (white circles, which represent *a*, *b*, or *c*). The Punnett square shows all the possible genetic combinations in gametes and offspring of many hypothetical matings between these heterozygotes. The results are summarized by the phenotypic frequencies (fractions) under the Punnett square. (The phenotypic ratio of the skin colors shown in the boxes is 1:6:15:20:15:6:1.)

▲ **Figure 14.14 The effect of environment on phenotype.** The outcome of a genotype lies within a phenotypic range that depends on the environment in which the genotype is expressed. For example, the acidity and free aluminum content of the soil affect the color range of hydrangea flowers of the same genetic variety. The color ranges from pink (basic soil) to blue-violet (acidic soil), and free aluminum is necessary for bluer colors.

Whether human characteristics are more influenced by genes or the environment—in everyday terms, nature versus nurture—is a debate that we will not attempt to settle here. We can say, however, that a genotype generally is not associated with a rigidly defined phenotype, but rather with a range of phenotypic possibilities due to environmental influences **(Figure 14.14)**. For some characters, such as the ABO blood group system, the phenotypic range has no breadth whatsoever; that is, a given genotype mandates a very specific phenotype. Other characteristics, such as a person's blood count of red and white cells, vary quite a bit, depending on such factors as the altitude, the customary level of physical activity, and the presence of infectious agents.

Generally, the phenotypic range is broadest for polygenic characters. Environment contributes to the quantitative nature of these characters, as we have seen in the continuous variation of skin color. Geneticists refer to such characters as **multifactorial**, meaning that many factors, both genetic and environmental, collectively influence phenotype.

A Mendelian View of Heredity and Variation

We have now broadened our view of Mendelian inheritance by exploring degrees of dominance as well as multiple alleles, pleiotropy, epistasis, polygenic inheritance, and the phenotypic impact of the environment. How can we integrate these refinements into a comprehensive theory of Mendelian genetics? The key is to make the transition from the reductionist emphasis on single genes and phenotypic characters to the emergent properties of the organism as a whole, one of the themes of this book.

The term *phenotype* can refer not only to specific characters, such as flower color and blood group, but also to an organism in its entirety—*all* aspects of its physical appearance, internal anatomy, physiology, and behavior. Similarly, the term *genotype* can refer to an organism's entire genetic makeup, not just its alleles for a single genetic locus. In most

Making a Histogram and Analyzing a Distribution Pattern

What Is the Distribution of Phenotypes Among Offspring of Two Parents Who Are Both Heterozygous for Three Additive Genes? Human skin color is a polygenic trait that is determined by the additive effects of many different genes. In this exercise, you will work with a simplified model of skin-color genetics where only three genes are assumed to affect the darkness of skin color and where each gene has two alleles—dark or light (see Figure 14.13). In this model, each dark allele contributes equally to the darkness of skin color, and each pair of alleles segregates independently of each other pair. Using a type of graph called a histogram, you will determine the distribution of phenotypes of offspring with different numbers of dark-skin alleles. (For additional information about graphs, see the Scientific Skills Review in Appendix F and in the Study Area in MasteringBiology.)

How This Model Is Analyzed To predict the phenotypes of the offspring of parents heterozygous for the three genes in our simplified model, we can use the Punnett square in Figure 14.13. The heterozygous individuals (*AaBbCc*) represented by the two rectangles at the top of this figure each carry three dark-skin alleles (black circles, which represent *A*, *B*, or *C*) and three light-skin alleles (white circles, which represent *a*, *b*, or *c*). The Punnett square shows all the possible genetic combinations in gametes and in offspring of a large number of hypothetical matings between these heterozygotes.

Predictions from the Punnett Square If we assume that each square in the Punnett square represents one offspring of the heterozygous *AaBbCc* parents, then the squares below show the frequencies of all seven possible phenotypes of offspring, with each phenotype having a specific number of dark-skin alleles.

Phenotypes:	$\frac{1}{64}$	$\frac{6}{64}$	$\frac{15}{64}$	$\frac{20}{64}$	$\frac{15}{64}$	$\frac{6}{64}$	$\frac{1}{64}$
Number of dark-skin alleles:	0	1	2	3	4	5	6

Interpret the Data

1. A histogram is a bar graph that shows the distribution of numeric data (here, the number of dark-skin alleles). To make a histogram of the allele distribution, put skin color (as the number of dark-skin alleles) along the x-axis and number of offspring (out of 64) with each phenotype on the y-axis. There are no gaps in our allele data, so draw the bars next to each other with no space in between.

2. You can see that the skin-color phenotypes are not distributed uniformly. (a) Which phenotype has the highest frequency? Draw a vertical dashed line through that bar. (b) Distributions of values like this one tend to show one of several common patterns. Sketch a rough curve that approximates the values and look at its shape. Is it symmetrically distributed around a central peak value (a "normal distribution," sometimes called a bell curve); is it skewed to one end of the x-axis or the other (a "skewed distribution"); or does it show two apparent groups of frequencies (a "bimodal distribution")? Explain the reason for the curve's shape. (It will help to read the text description that supports Figure 14.13.)

3. If one of the three genes were lethal when homozygous recessive, what would happen to the distribution of phenotype frequencies? To determine this, use *bb* as an example of a lethal genotype. Using Figure 14.13, identify offspring where the center circle (the *B/b* gene) in both the top and bottom rows of the square is white, representing the homozygous state *bb*. Because *bb* individuals would not survive, cross out those squares, then count the phenotype frequencies of the surviving offspring according to the number of dark-skin alleles (0–6) and graph the new data. What happens to the shape of the curve compared with the curve in question 2? What does this indicate about the distribution of phenotype frequencies?

MB A version of this Scientific Skills Exercise can be assigned in MasteringBiology.

Further Reading R. A. Sturm, A golden age of human pigmentation genetics, *Trends in Genetics* 22:464–468 (2006).

---

cases, a gene's impact on phenotype is affected by other genes and by the environment. In this integrated view of heredity and variation, an organism's phenotype reflects its overall genotype and unique environmental history.

Considering all that can occur in the pathway from genotype to phenotype, it is indeed impressive that Mendel could uncover the fundamental principles governing the transmission of individual genes from parents to offspring. Mendel's two laws, of segregation and of independent assortment, explain heritable variations in terms of alternative forms of genes (hereditary "particles," now known as the alleles of genes) that are passed along, generation after generation, according to simple rules of probability. This theory of inheritance is equally valid for peas, flies, fishes, birds, and human beings—indeed, for any organism with a sexual life cycle. Furthermore, by extending the principles of segregation and independent assortment to help explain such hereditary patterns as epistasis and quantitative characters, we begin to see how broadly Mendelian genetics applies. From Mendel's

abbey garden came a theory of particulate inheritance that anchors modern genetics. In the last section of this chapter, we will apply Mendelian genetics to human inheritance, with emphasis on the transmission of hereditary diseases.

CONCEPT CHECK 14.3

1. *Incomplete dominance* and *epistasis* are both terms that define genetic relationships. What is the most basic distinction between these terms?

2. If a man with type AB blood marries a woman with type O, what blood types would you expect in their children? What fraction would you expect of each type?

3. **WHAT IF?** A rooster with gray feathers and a hen of the same phenotype produce 15 gray, 6 black, and 8 white chicks. What is the simplest explanation for the inheritance of these colors in chickens? What phenotypes would you expect in the offspring of a cross between a gray rooster and a black hen?

For suggested answers, see Appendix A.

CONCEPT 14.4

Many human traits follow Mendelian patterns of inheritance

Peas are convenient subjects for genetic research, but humans are not. The human generation span is long—about 20 years—and human parents produce many fewer offspring than peas and most other species. Even more important, it wouldn't be ethical to ask pairs of humans to breed so that the phenotypes of their offspring could be analyzed! In spite of these constraints, the study of human genetics continues, spurred on by our desire to understand our own inheritance. New molecular biological techniques have led to many breakthrough discoveries, as we will see in Chapter 20, but basic Mendelian genetics endures as the foundation of human genetics.

Pedigree Analysis

Unable to manipulate the mating patterns of people, geneticists instead analyze the results of matings that have already occurred. They do so by collecting information about a family's history for a particular trait and assembling this information into a family tree describing the traits of parents and children across the generations—the family **pedigree**.

Figure 14.15a shows a three-generation pedigree that traces the occurrence of a pointed contour of the hairline on the forehead. This trait, called a widow's peak, is due to a dominant allele, *W*. Because the widow's-peak allele is dominant, all individuals who lack a widow's peak must be homozygous recessive (*ww*). The two grandparents with widow's peaks must have the *Ww* genotype, since some of their offspring are homozygous recessive. The offspring in the second generation who *do* have widow's peaks must also be heterozygous, because they are the products of *Ww* × *ww* matings. The third generation in this pedigree consists of two sisters. The one who has a widow's peak could be either homozygous (*WW*) or heterozygous (*Ww*), given what we know about the genotypes of her parents (both *Ww*).

Figure 14.15b is a pedigree of the same family, but this time we focus on a recessive trait, attached earlobes. We'll use *f* for the recessive allele and *F* for the dominant allele, which results in free earlobes. As you work your way through the pedigree, notice once again that you can apply what you have learned about Mendelian inheritance to understand the genotypes shown for the family members.

An important application of a pedigree is to help us calculate the probability that a future child will have a particular genotype and phenotype. Suppose that the couple represented in the second generation of Figure 14.15 decides to have one more child. What is the probability that the child will have a widow's peak? This is equivalent to a

Key

□ Male ■ Affected male □—○ Mating

○ Female ● Affected female Offspring, in birth order (first-born on left)

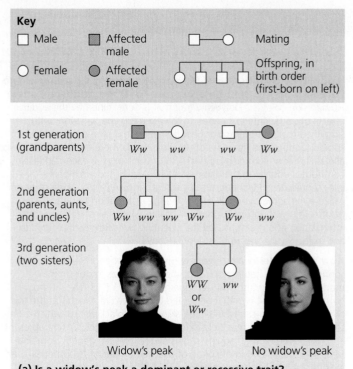

(a) Is a widow's peak a dominant or recessive trait?
Tips for pedigree analysis: Notice in the third generation that the second-born daughter lacks a widow's peak, although both of her parents had the trait. Such a pattern of inheritance supports the hypothesis that the trait is due to a dominant allele. If the trait were due to a *recessive* allele, and both parents had the recessive phenotype, then *all* of their offspring would also have the recessive phenotype.

(b) Is an attached earlobe a dominant or recessive trait?
Tips for pedigree analysis: Notice that the first-born daughter in the third generation has attached earlobes, although both of her parents lack that trait (they have free earlobes). Such a pattern is easily explained if the attached-lobe phenotype is due to a recessive allele. If it were due to a *dominant* allele, then at least one parent would also have had the trait.

▲ **Figure 14.15 Pedigree analysis.** Each of these pedigrees traces a trait through three generations of the same family. The two traits have different inheritance patterns, as shown by the pedigrees.

Mendelian F_1 monohybrid cross ($Ww \times Ww$), and thus the probability that a child will inherit a dominant allele and have a widow's peak is ¾ (¼ WW + ½ Ww). What is the probability that the child will have attached earlobes? Again, we can treat this as a monohybrid cross ($Ff \times Ff$), but this time we want to know the chance that the offspring will be homozygous recessive (ff). That probability is ¼. Finally, what is the chance that the child will have a widow's peak *and* attached earlobes? Assuming that the genes for these two characters are on different chromosomes, the two pairs of alleles will assort independently in this dihybrid cross ($WwFf \times WwFf$). Thus, we can use the multiplication rule: ¾ (chance of widow's peak) × ¼ (chance of attached earlobes) = 3/16 (chance of widow's peak and attached earlobes).

Pedigrees are a more serious matter when the alleles in question cause disabling or deadly diseases instead of innocuous human variations such as hairline or earlobe configuration. However, for disorders inherited as simple Mendelian traits, the same techniques of pedigree analysis apply.

Recessively Inherited Disorders

Thousands of genetic disorders are known to be inherited as simple recessive traits. These disorders range in severity from relatively mild, such as albinism (lack of pigmentation, which results in susceptibility to skin cancers and vision problems), to life-threatening, such as cystic fibrosis.

The Behavior of Recessive Alleles

How can we account for the behavior of alleles that cause recessively inherited disorders? Recall that genes code for proteins of specific function. An allele that causes a genetic disorder (let's call it allele *a*) codes for either a malfunctioning protein or no protein at all. In the case of disorders classified as recessive, heterozygotes (Aa) are typically normal in phenotype because one copy of the normal allele (A) produces a sufficient amount of the specific protein. Thus, a recessively inherited disorder shows up only in the homozygous individuals (aa) who inherit one recessive allele from each parent. Although phenotypically normal with regard to the disorder, heterozygotes may transmit the recessive allele to their offspring and thus are called **carriers**. **Figure 14.16** illustrates these ideas using albinism as an example.

Most people who have recessive disorders are born to parents who are carriers of the disorder but have a normal phenotype, as is the case shown in the Punnett square in Figure 14.16. A mating between two carriers corresponds to a Mendelian F_1 monohybrid cross, so the predicted genotypic ratio for the offspring is 1 AA : 2 Aa : 1 aa. Thus, each child has a ¼ chance of inheriting a double dose of the recessive allele; in the case of albinism, such a child will be albino. From the genotypic ratio, we also can see that out of three offspring with the *normal* phenotype (one AA plus

▲ **Figure 14.16 Albinism: a recessive trait.** One of the two sisters shown here has normal coloration; the other is albino. Most recessive homozygotes are born to parents who are carriers of the disorder but themselves have a normal phenotype, the case shown in the Punnett square.

? *What is the probability that the sister with normal coloration is a carrier of the albinism allele?*

two Aa), two are predicted to be heterozygous carriers, a ⅔ chance. Recessive homozygotes could also result from $Aa \times aa$ and $aa \times aa$ matings, but if the disorder is lethal before reproductive age or results in sterility (neither of which is true for albinism), no aa individuals will reproduce. Even if recessive homozygotes are able to reproduce, this will occur relatively rarely, since such individuals account for a much smaller percentage of the population than heterozygous carriers (for reasons we'll examine in Chapter 23).

In general, genetic disorders are not evenly distributed among all groups of people. For example, the incidence of Tay-Sachs disease, which we described earlier in this chapter, is disproportionately high among Ashkenazic Jews, Jewish people whose ancestors lived in central Europe. In that population, Tay-Sachs disease occurs in one out of 3,600 births, an incidence about 100 times greater than that among non-Jews or Mediterranean (Sephardic) Jews. This uneven distribution results from the different genetic histories of the world's peoples during less technological times, when populations were more geographically (and hence genetically) isolated.

When a disease-causing recessive allele is rare, it is relatively unlikely that two carriers of the same harmful allele will meet and mate. The probability of passing on recessive traits increases greatly, however, if the man and woman are close relatives (for example, siblings or first cousins). This is because people with recent common ancestors are more likely to carry the same recessive alleles than are unrelated people. Thus, these consanguineous ("same blood") matings, indicated in pedigrees by double lines, are more likely to produce offspring homozygous for recessive traits—including harmful ones. Such effects can be observed in many types of domesticated and zoo animals that have become inbred.

There is debate among geneticists about the extent to which human consanguinity increases the risk of inherited diseases. Many deleterious alleles have such severe effects that a homozygous embryo spontaneously aborts long before birth. Still, most societies and cultures have laws or taboos forbidding marriages between close relatives. These rules may have evolved out of empirical observation that in most populations, stillbirths and birth defects are more common when parents are closely related. Social and economic factors have also influenced the development of customs and laws against consanguineous marriages.

Cystic Fibrosis

The most common lethal genetic disease in the United States is **cystic fibrosis**, which strikes one out of every 2,500 people of European descent but is much rarer in other groups. Among people of European descent, one out of 25 (4%) are carriers of the cystic fibrosis allele. The normal allele for this gene codes for a membrane protein that functions in the transport of chloride ions between certain cells and the extracellular fluid. These chloride transport channels are defective or absent in the plasma membranes of children who inherit two recessive alleles for cystic fibrosis. The result is an abnormally high concentration of extracellular chloride, which causes the mucus that coats certain cells to become thicker and stickier than normal. The mucus builds up in the pancreas, lungs, digestive tract, and other organs, leading to multiple (pleiotropic) effects, including poor absorption of nutrients from the intestines, chronic bronchitis, and recurrent bacterial infections.

Untreated, cystic fibrosis can cause death by the age of 5. Daily doses of antibiotics to stop infection, gentle pounding on the chest to clear mucus from clogged airways, and other therapies can prolong life. In the United States, more than half of those with cystic fibrosis now survive into their 30s and beyond.

Sickle-Cell Disease: A Genetic Disorder with Evolutionary Implications

EVOLUTION The most common inherited disorder among people of African descent is **sickle-cell disease**, which affects one out of 400 African-Americans. Sickle-cell disease is caused by the substitution of a single amino acid in the hemoglobin protein of red blood cells; in homozygous individuals, all hemoglobin is of the sickle-cell (abnormal) variety. When the oxygen content of an affected individual's blood is low (at high altitudes or under physical stress, for instance), the sickle-cell hemoglobin proteins aggregate into long fibers that deform the red cells into a sickle shape (see Figure 5.19). Sickled cells may clump and clog small blood vessels, often leading to other symptoms throughout the body, including physical weakness, pain, organ damage, and even paralysis. Regular blood transfusions can ward off brain damage in children with sickle-cell disease, and new drugs can help prevent or treat other problems, but there is currently no widely available cure.

Although two sickle-cell alleles are necessary for an individual to manifest full-blown sickle-cell disease, the presence of one sickle-cell allele can affect the phenotype. Thus, at the organismal level, the normal allele is incompletely dominant to the sickle-cell allele **(Figure 14.17)**. At the molecular level, the two alleles are codominant; both normal and abnormal (sickle-cell) hemoglobins are made in heterozygotes (carriers), who are said to have *sickle-cell trait*. Heterozygotes are usually healthy but may suffer some symptoms during long periods of reduced blood oxygen.

About one out of ten African-Americans have sickle-cell trait, an unusually high frequency of heterozygotes for an allele with severe detrimental effects in homozygotes. Why haven't evolutionary processes resulted in the disappearance of this allele among this population? One explanation is that having a single copy of the sickle-cell allele reduces the frequency and severity of malaria attacks, especially among young children. The malaria parasite spends part of its life cycle in red blood cells (see Figure 28.16), and the presence of even heterozygous amounts of sickle-cell hemoglobin results in lower parasite densities and hence reduced malaria symptoms. Thus, in tropical Africa, where infection with the

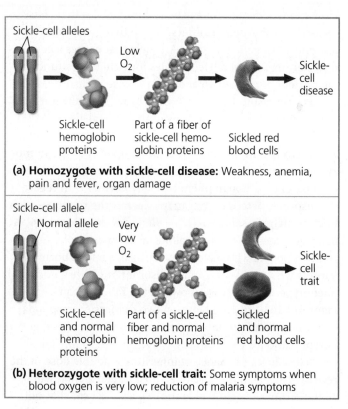

(a) Homozygote with sickle-cell disease: Weakness, anemia, pain and fever, organ damage

(b) Heterozygote with sickle-cell trait: Some symptoms when blood oxygen is very low; reduction of malaria symptoms

▲ **Figure 14.17 Sickle-cell disease and sickle-cell trait.**

malaria parasite is common, the sickle-cell allele confers an advantage to heterozygotes even though it is harmful in the homozygous state. (The balance between these two effects will be discussed in Chapter 23; see Figure 23.17.) The relatively high frequency of African-Americans with sickle-cell trait is a vestige of their African roots.

Dominantly Inherited Disorders

Although many harmful alleles are recessive, a number of human disorders are due to dominant alleles. One example is *achondroplasia*, a form of dwarfism that occurs in one of every 25,000 people. Heterozygous individuals have the dwarf phenotype **(Figure 14.18)**. Therefore, all people who are not achondroplastic dwarfs—99.99% of the population—are homozygous for the recessive allele. Like the presence of extra fingers or toes mentioned earlier, achondroplasia is a trait for which the recessive allele is much more prevalent than the corresponding dominant allele.

Dominant alleles that cause a lethal disease are much less common than recessive alleles that have lethal effects. All lethal alleles arise by mutations (changes to the DNA) in cells that produce sperm or eggs; presumably, such mutations are equally likely to be recessive or dominant. A lethal recessive allele can be passed from one generation to the next by heterozygous carriers because the carriers themselves have normal phenotypes. A lethal dominant allele, however, often causes the death of afflicted individuals before they can mature and reproduce, so the allele is not passed on to future generations.

In cases of late-onset diseases, however, a lethal dominant allele may be passed on. If symptoms first appear after reproductive age, the individual may already have transmitted the allele to his or her children. For example, a degenerative disease of the nervous system, called **Huntington's disease**, is caused by a lethal dominant allele that has no obvious phenotypic effect until the individual is about 35 to 45 years old. Once the deterioration of the nervous system begins, it is irreversible and inevitably fatal. As with other dominant traits, a child born to a parent with the Huntington's disease allele has a 50% chance of inheriting the allele and the disorder (see the Punnett square in Figure 14.18). In the United States, this disease afflicts about one in 10,000 people.

At one time, the onset of symptoms was the only way to know if a person had inherited the Huntington's allele, but this is no longer the case. By analyzing DNA samples from a large family with a high incidence of the disorder, geneticists tracked the Huntington's allele to a locus near the tip of chromosome 4, and the gene was sequenced in 1993. This information led to the development of a test that could detect the presence of the Huntington's allele in an individual's genome. (The methods that make such tests possible are discussed in Chapter 20.) The availability of this test poses an agonizing dilemma for those with a family history of Huntington's disease. Some individuals may want to be tested for this disease, whereas others may decide it would be too stressful to find out whether they carry the allele.

Multifactorial Disorders

The hereditary diseases we have discussed so far are sometimes described as simple Mendelian disorders because they result from abnormality of one or both alleles at a single genetic locus. Many more people are susceptible to diseases that have a multifactorial basis—a genetic component plus a significant environmental influence. Heart disease, diabetes, cancer, alcoholism, certain mental illnesses such as schizophrenia and bipolar disorder, and many other diseases are multifactorial. In these cases, the hereditary component is polygenic. For example, many genes affect cardiovascular health, making some of us more prone than others to heart attacks and strokes. No matter what our genotype, however, our lifestyle has a tremendous effect on phenotype for cardiovascular health and other multifactorial characters. Exercise, a healthful diet, abstinence from smoking, and an ability to handle stressful situations all reduce our risk of heart disease and some types of cancer.

Genetic Testing and Counseling

Avoiding simple Mendelian disorders is possible when the risk of a particular genetic disorder can be assessed before a child is conceived or during the early stages of the pregnancy. Many hospitals have genetic counselors who can provide information to prospective parents concerned about a family history for a specific disease. Fetal and newborn testing can also reveal genetic disorders.

▲ **Figure 14.18 Achondroplasia: a dominant trait.** Dr. Michael C. Ain has achondroplasia, a form of dwarfism caused by a dominant allele. This has inspired his work: He is a specialist in the repair of bone defects caused by achondroplasia and other disorders. The dominant allele (*D*) might have arisen as a mutation in the egg or sperm of a parent or could have been inherited from an affected parent, as shown for an affected father in the Punnett square.

Counseling Based on Mendelian Genetics and Probability Rules

Consider the case of a hypothetical couple, John and Carol. Each had a brother who died from the same recessively inherited lethal disease. Before conceiving their first child, John and Carol seek genetic counseling to determine the risk of having a child with the disease. From the information about their brothers, we know that both parents of John and both parents of Carol must have been carriers of the recessive allele. Thus, John and Carol are both products of $Aa \times Aa$ crosses, where a symbolizes the allele that causes this particular disease. We also know that John and Carol are not homozygous recessive (aa), because they do not have the disease. Therefore, their genotypes are either AA or Aa.

Given a genotypic ratio of 1 AA : 2 Aa : 1 aa for offspring of an $Aa \times Aa$ cross, John and Carol each have a ⅔ chance of being carriers (Aa). According to the rule of multiplication, the overall probability of their firstborn having the disorder is ⅔ (the chance that John is a carrier) times ⅔ (the chance that Carol is a carrier) times ¼ (the chance of two carriers having a child with the disease), which equals ⅑. Suppose that Carol and John decide to have a child—after all, there is an ⁸⁄₉ chance that their baby will not have the disorder. If, despite these odds, their child is born with the disease, then we would know that *both* John and Carol are, in fact, carriers (Aa genotype). If both John and Carol are carriers, there is a ¼ chance that any subsequent child this couple has will have the disease. The probability is higher for subsequent children because the diagnosis of the disease in the first child established that both parents are carriers, not because the genotype of the first child affects in any way that of future children.

When we use Mendel's laws to predict possible outcomes of matings, it is important to remember that each child represents an independent event in the sense that its genotype is unaffected by the genotypes of older siblings. Suppose that John and Carol have three more children, and *all three* have the hypothetical hereditary disease. There is only one chance in 64 (¼ × ¼ × ¼) that such an outcome will occur. Despite this run of misfortune, the chance that still another child of this couple will have the disease remains ¼.

Tests for Identifying Carriers

Most children with recessive disorders are born to parents with normal phenotypes. The key to accurately assessing the genetic risk for a particular disease is therefore to find out whether the prospective parents are heterozygous carriers of the recessive allele. For an increasing number of heritable disorders, tests are available that can distinguish individuals of normal phenotype who are dominant homozygotes from those who are heterozygous carriers. There are now tests that can identify carriers of the alleles for Tay-Sachs disease, sickle-cell disease, and the most common form of cystic fibrosis.

These tests for identifying carriers enable people with family histories of genetic disorders to make informed decisions about having children, but raise other issues. Could carriers be denied health or life insurance or lose the jobs providing those benefits, even though they themselves are healthy? The Genetic Information Nondiscrimination Act, signed into law in the United States in 2008, allays these concerns by prohibiting discrimination in employment or insurance coverage based on genetic test results. A question that remains is whether sufficient genetic counseling is available to help large numbers of individuals understand their genetic test results. Even when test results are clearly understood, affected individuals may still face difficult decisions. Advances in biotechnology offer the potential to reduce human suffering, but along with them come ethical issues that require conscientious deliberation.

Fetal Testing

Suppose a couple expecting a child learns that they are both carriers of the Tay-Sachs allele. In the 14th–16th week of pregnancy, tests performed along with a technique called **amniocentesis** can determine whether the developing fetus has Tay-Sachs disease **(Figure 14.19a)**. In this procedure, a physician inserts a needle into the uterus and extracts about 10 mL of amniotic fluid, the liquid that bathes the fetus. Some genetic disorders can be detected from the presence of certain molecules in the amniotic fluid itself. Tests for other disorders, including Tay-Sachs disease, are performed on the DNA of cells cultured in the laboratory, descendants of fetal cells sloughed off into the amniotic fluid. A karyotype of these cultured cells can also identify certain chromosomal defects (see Figure 13.3).

In an alternative technique called **chorionic villus sampling (CVS)**, a physician inserts a narrow tube through the cervix into the uterus and suctions out a tiny sample of tissue from the placenta, the organ that transmits nutrients and fetal wastes between the fetus and the mother **(Figure 14.19b)**. The cells of the chorionic villi of the placenta, the portion sampled, are derived from the fetus and have the same genotype and DNA sequence as the new individual. These cells are proliferating rapidly enough to allow karyotyping to be carried out immediately. This rapid analysis represents an advantage over amniocentesis, in which the cells must be cultured for several weeks before karyotyping. Another advantage of CVS is that it can be performed as early as the 8th–10th week of pregnancy.

Medical scientists have also developed methods for isolating fetal cells, or even fetal DNA, that have escaped into the mother's blood. Although very few are present,

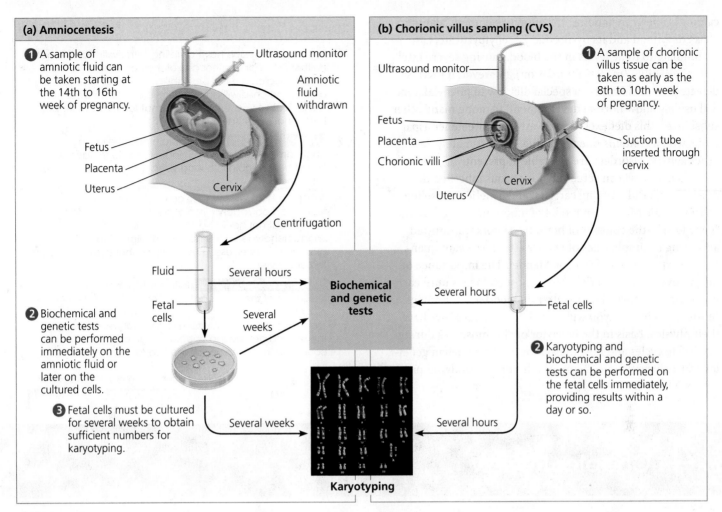

(a) Amniocentesis

1 A sample of amniotic fluid can be taken starting at the 14th to 16th week of pregnancy.

Ultrasound monitor

Amniotic fluid withdrawn

Fetus

Placenta

Uterus

Cervix

Centrifugation

Fluid

Several hours

Biochemical and genetic tests

Fetal cells

Several weeks

2 Biochemical and genetic tests can be performed immediately on the amniotic fluid or later on the cultured cells.

3 Fetal cells must be cultured for several weeks to obtain sufficient numbers for karyotyping.

Several weeks

(b) Chorionic villus sampling (CVS)

Ultrasound monitor

1 A sample of chorionic villus tissue can be taken as early as the 8th to 10th week of pregnancy.

Fetus

Placenta

Chorionic villi

Cervix

Uterus

Suction tube inserted through cervix

Several hours

Fetal cells

2 Karyotyping and biochemical and genetic tests can be performed on the fetal cells immediately, providing results within a day or so.

Several hours

Karyotyping

▲ **Figure 14.19 Testing a fetus for genetic disorders.** Biochemical tests may detect substances associated with particular disorders, and genetic testing can detect many genetic abnormalities. Karyotyping shows whether the chromosomes of the fetus are normal in number and appearance.

the cells can be cultured and tested, and the fetal DNA can be analyzed. In 2012, researchers were able to analyze the entire genome of a fetus, comparing sequences of samples obtained from both parents and fetal DNA found in the mother's blood. This noninvasive method will likely become the method of choice in diagnosing most genetically based disorders.

Imaging techniques allow a physician to examine a fetus directly for major anatomical abnormalities that might not show up in genetic tests. In the *ultrasound* technique, reflected sound waves are used to produce an image of the fetus by a simple noninvasive procedure. In *fetoscopy*, a needle-thin tube containing a viewing scope and fiber optics (to transmit light) is inserted into the uterus.

Ultrasound and isolation of fetal cells or DNA from maternal blood pose no known risk to either mother or fetus, while the other procedures can cause complications in a small percentage of cases. Amniocentesis or CVS for

diagnostic testing is generally offered to women over age 35, due to their increased risk of bearing a child with Down syndrome, and may also be offered to younger women if there are known concerns. If the fetal tests reveal a serious disorder like Tay-Sachs, the parents face the difficult choice of either terminating the pregnancy or preparing to care for a child with a genetic disorder, one that might even be fatal. Parental and fetal screening for Tay-Sachs alleles done since 1980 has reduced the number of children born with this incurable disease by 90%.

Newborn Screening

Some genetic disorders can be detected at birth by simple biochemical tests that are now routinely performed in most hospitals in the United States. One common screening program is for phenylketonuria (PKU), a recessively inherited disorder that occurs in about one out of every 10,000–15,000 births in the United States. Children with this disease cannot properly metabolize the amino acid phenylalanine. This compound and its by-product, phenylpyruvate, can accumulate to toxic levels in the blood, causing severe intellectual disability (mental retardation). However, if PKU is detected in the newborn, a special diet low in phenylalanine will usually allow normal development. (Among many other substances, this diet excludes the artificial sweetener aspartame, which contains phenylalanine.) Unfortunately, few other genetic disorders are treatable at present.

Fetal and newborn screening for serious inherited diseases, tests for identifying carriers, and genetic counseling all rely on the Mendelian model of inheritance. We owe the "gene idea"—the concept of heritable factors transmitted according to simple rules of chance—to the elegant quantitative experiments of Gregor Mendel. The importance of his discoveries was overlooked by most biologists until early in the 20th century, decades after he reported his findings. In the next chapter, you will learn how Mendel's laws have their physical basis in the behavior of chromosomes during sexual life cycles and how the synthesis of Mendelian genetics and a chromosome theory of inheritance catalyzed progress in genetics.

CONCEPT CHECK 14.4

1. Beth and Tom each have a sibling with cystic fibrosis, but neither Beth nor Tom nor any of their parents have the disease. Calculate the probability that if this couple has a child, the child will have cystic fibrosis. What would be the probability if a test revealed that Tom is a carrier but Beth is not? Explain your answers.

2. **MAKE CONNECTIONS** Explain how the change of a single amino acid in hemoglobin leads to the aggregation of hemoglobin into long fibers. (Review Figures 5.14, 5.18, and 5.19.)

3. Joan was born with six toes on each foot, a dominant trait called polydactyly. Two of her five siblings and her mother, but not her father, also have extra digits. What is Joan's genotype for the number-of-digits character? Explain your answer. Use D and d to symbolize the alleles for this character.

4. **MAKE CONNECTIONS** In Table 14.1, note the phenotypic ratio of the dominant to recessive trait in the F_2 generation for the monohybrid cross involving flower color. Then determine the phenotypic ratio for the offspring of the second-generation couple in Figure 14.15b. What accounts for the difference in the two ratios?

For suggested answers, see Appendix A.

14 Chapter Review

SUMMARY OF KEY CONCEPTS

CONCEPT 14.1

Mendel used the scientific approach to identify two laws of inheritance (pp. 268–274)

- Gregor Mendel formulated a theory of inheritance based on experiments with garden peas, proposing that parents pass on to their offspring discrete genes that retain their identity through generations. This theory includes two "laws."
- The **law of segregation** states that genes have alternative forms, or **alleles**. In a diploid organism, the two alleles of a gene segregate (separate) during meiosis and gamete formation; each sperm or egg carries only one allele of each pair. This law explains the 3:1 ratio of F_2 phenotypes observed when **monohybrids** self-pollinate. Each organism inherits one allele for each gene from each parent. In **heterozygotes**, the two alleles are different; expression of the **dominant allele** masks the phenotypic effect of the **recessive allele**. **Homozygotes** have identical alleles of a given gene and are **true-breeding**.
- The **law of independent assortment** states that the pair of alleles for a given gene segregates into gametes independently of the pair of alleles for any other gene. In a cross between **dihybrids** (individuals heterozygous for two genes), the offspring have four phenotypes in a 9:3:3:1 ratio.

? *When Mendel did crosses of true-breeding purple- and white-flowered pea plants, the white-flowered trait disappeared from the F_1 generation but reappeared in the F_2 generation. Use genetic terms to explain why that happened.*

CONCEPT 14.2

Probability laws govern Mendelian inheritance (pp. 274–276)

Rr
Segregation of alleles into sperm

Sperm

$^1/_2$ ▢ R $^1/_2$ ▢

- The **multiplication rule** states that the probability of two or more events occurring together is equal to the product of the individual probabilities of the independent single events. The **addition rule** states that the probability of an event that can occur in two or more independent, mutually exclusive ways is the sum of the individual probabilities.
- The rules of probability can be used to solve complex genetics problems. A dihybrid or other multicharacter cross is equivalent to two or more independent monohybrid crosses occurring simultaneously. In calculating the chances of the various offspring genotypes from such crosses, each character is first considered separately and then the individual probabilities are multiplied.

DRAW IT *Redraw the Punnett square on the right side of Figure 14.8 as two smaller monohybrid Punnett squares, one for each gene. Below each square, list the fractions of each phenotype produced. Use the rule of multiplication to compute the overall fraction of each possible dihybrid phenotype. What is the phenotypic ratio?*

Inheritance patterns are often more complex than predicted by simple Mendelian genetics (pp. 276–281)

- Extensions of Mendelian genetics for a single gene:

Relationship among alleles of a single gene	Description	Example
Complete dominance of one allele	Heterozygous phenotype same as that of homozygous dominant	PP Pp
Incomplete dominance of either allele	Heterozygous phenotype intermediate between the two homozygous phenotypes	$C^R C^R$ $C^R C^W$ $C^W C^W$
Codominance	Both phenotypes expressed in heterozygotes	$I^A I^B$
Multiple alleles	In the population, some genes have more than two alleles	ABO blood group alleles I^A, I^B, i
Pleiotropy	One gene affects multiple phenotypic characters	Sickle-cell disease

- Extensions of Mendelian genetics for two or more genes:

Relationship among two or more genes	Description	Example
Epistasis	The phenotypic expression of one gene affects the expression of another gene	$BbEe$ × $BbEe$ ... 9 : 3 : 4
Polygenic inheritance	A single phenotypic character is affected by two or more genes	$AaBbCc$ × $AaBbCc$

- The expression of a genotype can be affected by environmental influences, resulting in a range of phenotypes. Polygenic characters that are also influenced by the environment are called **multifactorial** characters.
- An organism's overall phenotype, including its physical appearance, internal anatomy, physiology, and behavior, reflects its overall genotype and unique environmental history. Even in more complex inheritance patterns, Mendel's fundamental laws of segregation and independent assortment still apply.

? *Which of the following are demonstrated by the inheritance patterns of the ABO blood group alleles: complete dominance, incomplete dominance, codominance, multiple alleles, pleiotropy, epistasis, and/or polygenic inheritance? Explain each of your answers.*

Many human traits follow Mendelian patterns of inheritance (pp. 282–288)

- Analysis of family **pedigrees** can be used to deduce the possible genotypes of individuals and make predictions about future offspring. Such predictions are statistical probabilities rather than certainties.

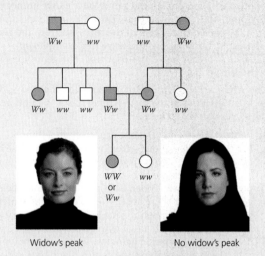

Widow's peak   No widow's peak

- Many genetic disorders are inherited as simple recessive traits. Most affected (homozygous recessive) individuals are children of phenotypically normal, heterozygous **carriers**.
- The sickle-cell allele has probably persisted for evolutionary reasons: Heterozygotes have an advantage because one copy of the sickle-cell allele reduces both the frequency and severity of malaria attacks.

- Lethal dominant alleles are eliminated from the population if affected people die before reproducing. Nonlethal dominant alleles and lethal ones that strike relatively late in life can be inherited in a Mendelian way.
- Many human diseases are multifactorial—that is, they have both genetic and environmental components and do not follow simple Mendelian inheritance patterns.
- Using family histories, genetic counselors help couples determine the probability that their children will have genetic disorders. Genetic testing of prospective parents to reveal whether they are carriers of recessive alleles associated with specific disorders has become widely available. **Amniocentesis** and **chorionic villus sampling** can indicate whether a suspected genetic disorder is present in a fetus. Other genetic tests can be performed after birth.

? *Both members of a couple know that they are carriers of the cystic fibrosis allele. None of their three children has cystic fibrosis, but any one of them might be a carrier. They would like to have a fourth child but are worried that he or she would very likely have the disease, since the first three do not. What would you tell the couple? Would it remove some uncertainty from their prediction if they could find out from genetic tests whether the three children are carriers?*

1. Write down symbols for the alleles. (These may be given in the problem.) When represented by single letters, the dominant allele is uppercase and the recessive is lowercase.

2. Write down the possible genotypes, as determined by the phenotype.
   a. If the phenotype is that of the dominant trait (for example, purple flowers), then the genotype is either homozygous dominant or heterozygous (*PP* or *Pp*, in this example).
   b. If the phenotype is that of the recessive trait, the genotype must be homozygous recessive (for example, *pp*).
   c. If the problem says "true-breeding," the genotype is homozygous.

3. Determine what the problem is asking for. If asked to do a cross, write it out in the form [Genotype] × [Genotype], using the alleles you've decided on.

4. To figure out the outcome of a cross, set up a Punnett square.
   a. Put the gametes of one parent at the top and those of the other on the left. To determine the allele(s) in each gamete for a given genotype, set up a systematic way to list all the possibilities. (Remember, each gamete has one allele of each gene.) Note that there are 2^n possible types of gametes, where *n* is the number of gene loci that are heterozygous. For example, an individual with genotype *AaBbCc* would produce $2^3 = 8$ types of gametes. Write the genotypes of the gametes in circles above the columns and to the left of the rows.
   b. Fill in the Punnett square as if each possible sperm were fertilizing each possible egg, making all of the possible offspring. In a cross of *AaBbCc* × *AaBbCc*, for example, the Punnett square would have 8 columns and 8 rows, so there are 64 different offspring; you would know the genotype of each and thus the phenotype. Count genotypes and phenotypes to obtain the genotypic and phenotypic ratios. Because the Punnett square is so large, this method is not the most efficient. See tip 5.

5. You can use the rules of probability if the Punnett square would be too big. (For example, see the question at the end of the summary for Concept 14.2 and question 7 below.) You can consider each gene separately (see Concept 14.2).

6. If, instead, the problem gives you the phenotypic ratios of offspring but not the genotypes of the parents in a given cross, the phenotypes can help you deduce the parents' unknown genotypes.
   a. For example, if ½ of the offspring have the recessive phenotype and ½ the dominant, you know that the cross was between a heterozygote and a homozygous recessive.
   b. If the ratio is 3:1, the cross was between two heterozygotes.
   c. If two genes are involved and you see a 9:3:3:1 ratio in the offspring, you know that each parent is heterozygous for both genes. Caution: Don't assume that the reported numbers will exactly equal the predicted ratios. For example, if there are 13 offspring with the dominant trait and 11 with the recessive, assume that the ratio is one dominant to one recessive.

7. For pedigree problems, use the tips in Figure 14.15 and below to determine what kind of trait is involved.
   a. If parents without the trait have offspring with the trait, the trait must be recessive and the parents both carriers.
   b. If the trait is seen in every generation, it is most likely dominant (see the next possibility, though).
   c. If both parents have the trait and the trait is recessive, all offspring will show the trait.
   d. To determine the likely genotype of a certain individual in a pedigree, first label the genotypes of all the family members you can. Even if some of the genotypes are incomplete, label what you do know. For example, if an individual has the dominant phenotype, the genotype must be *AA* or *Aa*; you can write this as *A*–. Try different possibilities to see which fits the results. Use the rules of probability to calculate the probability of each possible genotype being the correct one.

LEVEL 1: KNOWLEDGE/COMPREHENSION

1. **DRAW IT** Two pea plants heterozygous for the characters of pod color and pod shape are crossed. Draw a Punnett square to determine the phenotypic ratios of the offspring.

2. A man with type A blood marries a woman with type B blood. Their child has type O blood. What are the genotypes of these three individuals? What genotypes, and in what frequencies, would you expect in future offspring from this marriage?

3. A man has six fingers on each hand and six toes on each foot. His wife and their daughter have the normal number of digits. Remember that extra digits is a dominant trait. What fraction of this couple's children would be expected to have extra digits?

4. **DRAW IT** A pea plant heterozygous for inflated pods (*Ii*) is crossed with a plant homozygous for constricted pods (*ii*). Draw a Punnett square for this cross to predict genotypic and phenotypic ratios. Assume that pollen comes from the *ii* plant.

LEVEL 2: APPLICATION/ANALYSIS

5. Flower position, stem length, and seed shape are three characters that Mendel studied. Each is controlled by an independently assorting gene and has dominant and recessive expression as indicated in Table 14.1. If a plant that is heterozygous for all three characters is allowed to self-fertilize, what proportion of the offspring would you expect to be as follows? (*Note*: Use the rules of probability instead of a huge Punnett square.)
   (a) homozygous for the three dominant traits
   (b) homozygous for the three recessive traits
   (c) heterozygous for all three characters
   (d) homozygous for axial and tall, heterozygous for seed shape

6. Phenylketonuria (PKU) is an inherited disease caused by a recessive allele. If a woman and her husband, who are both carriers, have three children, what is the probability of each of the following?
   (a) All three children are of normal phenotype.
   (b) One or more of the three children have the disease.
   (c) All three children have the disease.
   (d) At least one child is phenotypically normal.

   (*Note:* It will help to remember that the probabilities of all possible outcomes always add up to 1.)

7. The genotype of F_1 individuals in a tetrahybrid cross is *AaBbCcDd*. Assuming independent assortment of these four genes, what are the probabilities that F_2 offspring will have the following genotypes?
   (a) *aabbccdd*   (d) *AaBBccDd*
   (b) *AaBbCcDd*   (e) *AaBBCCdd*
   (c) *AABBCCDD*

8. What is the probability that each of the following pairs of parents will produce the indicated offspring? (Assume independent assortment of all gene pairs.)
   (a) $AABBCC \times aabbcc \rightarrow AaBbCc$
   (b) $AABbCc \times AaBbCc \rightarrow AAbbCC$
   (c) $AaBbCc \times AaBbCc \rightarrow AaBbCc$
   (d) $aaBbCC \times AABbcc \rightarrow AaBbCc$

9. Karen and Steve each have a sibling with sickle-cell disease. Neither Karen nor Steve nor any of their parents have the disease, and none of them have been tested to see if they have the sickle-cell trait. Based on this incomplete information, calculate the probability that if this couple has a child, the child will have sickle-cell disease.

10. In 1981, a stray black cat with unusual rounded, curled-back ears was adopted by a family in California. Hundreds of descendants of the cat have since been born, and cat fanciers hope to develop the curl cat into a show breed. Suppose you owned the first curl cat and wanted to develop a true-breeding variety. How would you determine whether the curl allele is dominant or recessive? How would you obtain true-breeding curl cats? How could you be sure they are true-breeding?

11. In tigers, a recessive allele of a particular gene causes both an absence of fur pigmentation (a white tiger) and a cross-eyed condition. If two phenotypically normal tigers that are heterozygous at this locus are mated, what percentage of their offspring will be cross-eyed? What percentage of cross-eyed tigers will be white?

12. In maize (corn) plants, a dominant allele I inhibits kernel color, while the recessive allele i permits color when homozygous. At a different locus, the dominant allele P causes purple kernel color, while the homozygous recessive genotype pp causes red kernels. If plants heterozygous at both loci are crossed, what will be the phenotypic ratio of the offspring?

13. The pedigree below traces the inheritance of alkaptonuria, a biochemical disorder. Affected individuals, indicated here by the colored circles and squares, are unable to metabolize a substance called alkapton, which colors the urine and stains body tissues. Does alkaptonuria appear to be caused by a dominant allele or by a recessive allele? Fill in the genotypes of the individuals whose genotypes can be deduced. What genotypes are possible for each of the other individuals?

14. Imagine that you are a genetic counselor, and a couple planning to start a family comes to you for information. Charles was married once before, and he and his first wife had a child with cystic fibrosis. The brother of his current wife, Elaine, died of cystic fibrosis. What is the probability that Charles and Elaine will have a baby with cystic fibrosis? (Neither Charles, Elaine, nor their parents have cystic fibrosis.)

LEVEL 3: SYNTHESIS/EVALUATION

15. **EVOLUTION CONNECTION**
Over the past half century, there has been a trend in the United States and other developed countries for people to marry and start families later in life than did their parents and grandparents. What effects might this trend have on the incidence (frequency) of late-acting dominant lethal alleles in the population?

16. **SCIENTIFIC INQUIRY**
You are handed a mystery pea plant with tall stems and axial flowers and asked to determine its genotype as quickly as possible. You know that the allele for tall stems (T) is dominant to that for dwarf stems (t) and that the allele for axial flowers (A) is dominant to that for terminal flowers (a).
   (a) What are *all* the possible genotypes for your mystery plant?
   (b) Describe the *one* cross you would do, out in your garden, to determine the exact genotype of your mystery plant.
   (c) While waiting for the results of your cross, you predict the results for each possible genotype listed in part a. How do you do this? Why is this not called "performing a cross"?
   (d) Explain how the results of your cross and your predictions will help you learn the genotype of your mystery plant.

17. **WRITE ABOUT A THEME: INFORMATION**
The continuity of life is based on heritable information in the form of DNA. In a short essay (100–150 words), explain how the passage of genes from parents to offspring, in the form of particular alleles, ensures perpetuation of parental traits in offspring and, at the same time, genetic variation among offspring. Use genetic terms in your explanation.

18. **SYNTHESIZE YOUR KNOWLEDGE**

Just for fun, imagine that "shirt-striping" is a phenotypic character caused by a single gene. Make up a genetic explanation for the appearance of the family in the above photograph, consistent with their "shirt phenotypes." Include in your answer the presumed allele combinations for "shirt-striping" in each family member. What is the inheritance pattern shown by the child?

For selected answers, see Appendix A.

MasteringBiology®

15

The Chromosomal Basis of Inheritance

KEY CONCEPTS

15.1 Morgan showed that Mendelian inheritance has its physical basis in the behavior of chromosomes: *Scientific inquiry*

15.2 Sex-linked genes exhibit unique patterns of inheritance

15.3 Linked genes tend to be inherited together because they are located near each other on the same chromosome

15.4 Alterations of chromosome number or structure cause some genetic disorders

15.5 Some inheritance patterns are exceptions to standard Mendelian inheritance

▲ **Figure 15.1 Where are Mendel's hereditary factors located in the cell?**

Locating Genes Along Chromosomes

Today, we know that genes—Mendel's "factors"—are segments of DNA located along chromosomes. We can see the location of a particular gene by tagging chromosomes with a fluorescent dye that highlights that gene. For example, the two yellow spots in **Figure 15.1** mark a specific gene on human chromosome 6. (The chromosome has duplicated, so the allele on that chromosome is present as two copies, one per sister chromatid.) However, Gregor Mendel's "hereditary factors" were purely an abstract concept when he proposed their existence in 1860. At that time, no cellular structures had been identified that could house these imaginary units, and most biologists were skeptical about Mendel's proposed laws of inheritance.

Using improved techniques of microscopy, cytologists worked out the process of mitosis in 1875 (see the drawing at the lower left) and meiosis in the 1890s. Cytology and genetics converged as biologists began to see parallels between the behavior of Mendel's proposed hereditary factors during sexual life cycles and the behavior of chromosomes: As shown in **Figure 15.2**, chromosomes and genes are both present in pairs in diploid cells, and homologous chromosomes separate and alleles segregate during the process of meiosis. Furthermore, after meiosis, fertilization restores the paired condition for both chromosomes and genes.

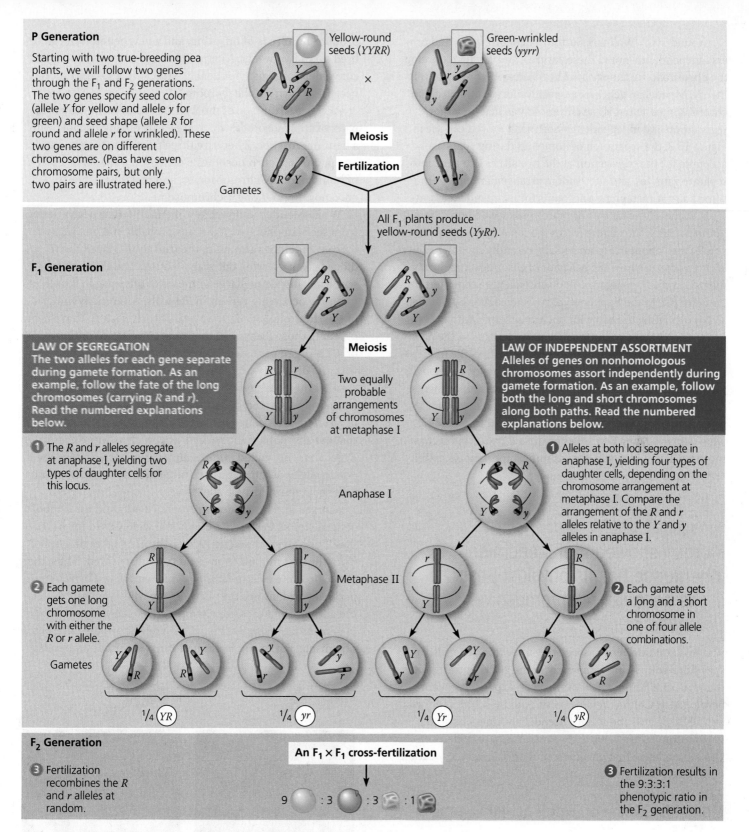

P Generation

Starting with two true-breeding pea plants, we will follow two genes through the F_1 and F_2 generations. The two genes specify seed color (allele Y for yellow and allele y for green) and seed shape (allele R for round and allele r for wrinkled). These two genes are on different chromosomes. (Peas have seven chromosome pairs, but only two pairs are illustrated here.)

Yellow-round seeds (*YYRR*)

Green-wrinkled seeds (*yyrr*)

×

Meiosis

Fertilization

Gametes

All F_1 plants produce yellow-round seeds (*YyRr*).

F_1 Generation

LAW OF SEGREGATION
The two alleles for each gene separate during gamete formation. As an example, follow the fate of the long chromosomes (carrying R and r). Read the numbered explanations below.

Meiosis

Two equally probable arrangements of chromosomes at metaphase I

LAW OF INDEPENDENT ASSORTMENT
Alleles of genes on nonhomologous chromosomes assort independently during gamete formation. As an example, follow both the long and short chromosomes along both paths. Read the numbered explanations below.

1 The R and r alleles segregate at anaphase I, yielding two types of daughter cells for this locus.

Anaphase I

1 Alleles at both loci segregate in anaphase I, yielding four types of daughter cells, depending on the chromosome arrangement at metaphase I. Compare the arrangement of the R and r alleles relative to the Y and y alleles in anaphase I.

Metaphase II

2 Each gamete gets one long chromosome with either the R or r allele.

Gametes

2 Each gamete gets a long and a short chromosome in one of four allele combinations.

¼ (*YR*)   ¼ (*yr*)   ¼ (*Yr*)   ¼ (*yR*)

F_2 Generation

3 Fertilization recombines the R and r alleles at random.

An F_1 × F_1 cross-fertilization

9 : 3 : 3 : 1

3 Fertilization results in the 9:3:3:1 phenotypic ratio in the F_2 generation.

▲ **Figure 15.2 The chromosomal basis of Mendel's laws.** Here we correlate the results of one of Mendel's dihybrid crosses (see Figure 14.8) with the behavior of chromosomes during meiosis (see Figure 13.8). The arrangement of chromosomes at metaphase I of meiosis and their movement during anaphase I account, respectively, for the independent assortment and segregation of the alleles for seed color and shape. Each cell that undergoes meiosis in an F_1 plant produces two kinds of gametes. If we count the results for all cells, however, each F_1 plant produces equal numbers of all four kinds of gametes because the alternative chromosome arrangements at metaphase I are equally likely.

? *If you crossed an F_1 plant with a plant that was homozygous recessive for both genes (yyrr), how would the phenotypic ratio of the offspring compare with the 9:3:3:1 ratio seen here?*

Around 1902, Walter S. Sutton, Theodor Boveri, and others independently noted these parallels and began to develop the **chromosome theory of inheritance**. According to this theory, Mendelian genes have specific loci (positions) along chromosomes, and it is the chromosomes that undergo segregation and independent assortment. As you can see in Figure 15.2, the separation of homologs during anaphase I accounts for the segregation of the two alleles of a gene into separate gametes, and the random arrangement of chromosome pairs at metaphase I accounts for independent assortment of the alleles for two or more genes located on different homolog pairs. This figure traces the same dihybrid pea cross you learned about in Figure 14.8. By carefully studying Figure 15.2, you can see how the behavior of chromosomes during meiosis in the F_1 generation and subsequent random fertilization give rise to the F_2 phenotypic ratio observed by Mendel.

In correlating the behavior of chromosomes with that of genes, this chapter will extend what you learned in the past two chapters. First, we'll describe evidence from the fruit fly that strongly supported the chromosome theory. (Although this theory made a lot of sense, it still required experimental evidence.) Next, we'll explore the chromosomal basis for the transmission of genes from parents to offspring, including what happens when two genes are linked on the same chromosome. Finally, we will discuss some important exceptions to the standard mode of inheritance.

CONCEPT 15.1

Morgan showed that Mendelian inheritance has its physical basis in the behavior of chromosomes: *Scientific inquiry*

The first solid evidence associating a specific gene with a specific chromosome came early in the 20th century from the work of Thomas Hunt Morgan, an experimental embryologist at Columbia University. Although Morgan was initially skeptical about both Mendelian genetics and the chromosome theory, his early experiments provided convincing evidence that chromosomes are indeed the location of Mendel's heritable factors.

Morgan's Choice of Experimental Organism

Many times in the history of biology, important discoveries have come to those insightful or lucky enough to choose an experimental organism suitable for the research problem being tackled. Mendel chose the garden pea because a number of distinct varieties were available. For his work, Morgan selected a species of fruit fly, *Drosophila melanogaster*, a common insect that feeds on the fungi growing on fruit. Fruit flies are prolific breeders; a single mating will produce hundreds of offspring, and a new generation can be bred every two weeks. Morgan's laboratory began using this convenient organism for genetic studies in 1907 and soon became known as "the fly room."

Another advantage of the fruit fly is that it has only four pairs of chromosomes, which are easily distinguishable with a light microscope. There are three pairs of autosomes and one pair of sex chromosomes. Female fruit flies have a pair of homologous X chromosomes, and males have one X chromosome and one Y chromosome.

While Mendel could readily obtain different pea varieties from seed suppliers, Morgan was probably the first person to want different varieties of the fruit fly. He faced the tedious task of carrying out many matings and then microscopically inspecting large numbers of offspring in search of naturally occurring variant individuals. After many months of this, he complained, "Two years' work wasted. I have been breeding those flies for all that time and I've got nothing out of it." Morgan persisted, however, and was finally rewarded with the discovery of a single male fly with white eyes instead of the usual red. The phenotype for a character most commonly observed in natural populations, such as red eyes in *Drosophila*, is called the **wild type (Figure 15.3)**. Traits that are alternatives to the wild type, such as white eyes in *Drosophila*, are called *mutant phenotypes* because they are due to alleles assumed to have originated as changes, or mutations, in the wild-type allele.

Morgan and his students invented a notation for symbolizing alleles in *Drosophila* that is still widely used for fruit flies. For a given character in flies, the gene takes its symbol from the first mutant (non–wild type) discovered. Thus, the allele for white eyes in *Drosophila* is symbolized by *w*. A superscript + identifies the allele for the wild-type trait: w^+ for the allele for red eyes, for example. Over the years, a variety of gene notation systems have been developed for different organisms. For example, human genes are usually written

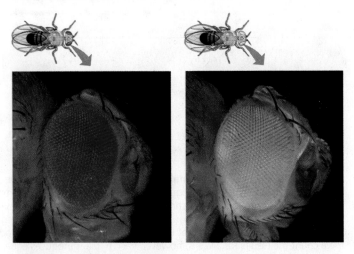

▲ **Figure 15.3 Morgan's first mutant.** Wild-type *Drosophila* flies have red eyes (left). Among his flies, Morgan discovered a mutant male with white eyes (right). This variation made it possible for Morgan to trace a gene for eye color to a specific chromosome (LMs).

in all capitals, such as *HD* for the allele for Huntington's disease.

Correlating Behavior of a Gene's Alleles with Behavior of a Chromosome Pair

Morgan mated his white-eyed male fly with a red-eyed female. All the F_1 offspring had red eyes, suggesting that the wild-type allele is dominant. When Morgan bred the F_1 flies to each other, he observed the classical 3:1 phenotypic ratio among the F_2 offspring. However, there was a surprising additional result: The white-eye trait showed up only in males. All the F_2 females had red eyes, while half the males had red eyes and half had white eyes. Therefore, Morgan concluded that somehow a fly's eye color was linked to its sex. (If the eye-color gene were unrelated to sex, half of the white-eyed flies would have been male and half female.)

Recall that a female fly has two X chromosomes (XX), while a male fly has an X and a Y (XY). The correlation between the trait of white eye color and the male sex of the affected F_2 flies suggested to Morgan that the gene involved in his white-eyed mutant was located exclusively on the X chromosome, with no corresponding allele present on the Y chromosome. His reasoning can be followed in **Figure 15.4**. For a male, a single copy of the mutant allele would confer white eyes; since a male has only one X chromosome, there can be no wild-type allele (w^+) present to mask the recessive allele. However, a female could have white eyes only if both her X chromosomes carried the recessive mutant allele (w). This was impossible for the F_2 females in Morgan's experiment because all the F_1 fathers had red eyes, so each F_2 female received a w^+ allele on the X chromosome inherited from her father.

Morgan's finding of the correlation between a particular trait and an individual's sex provided support for the chromosome theory of inheritance: namely, that a specific gene is carried on a specific chromosome (in this case, an eye-color gene on the X chromosome). In addition, Morgan's work indicated that genes located on a sex chromosome exhibit unique inheritance patterns, which we will discuss in the next section. Recognizing the importance of Morgan's early work, many bright students were attracted to his fly room.

CONCEPT CHECK 15.1

1. Which one of Mendel's laws relates to the inheritance of alleles for a single character? Which law relates to the inheritance of alleles for two characters in a dihybrid cross?

2. **MAKE CONNECTIONS** Review the description of meiosis (see Figure 13.8) and Mendel's laws of segregation and independent assortment (see Concept 14.1). What is the physical basis for each of Mendel's laws?

3. **WHAT IF?** Propose a possible reason that the first naturally occurring mutant fruit fly Morgan saw involved a gene on a sex chromosome.

For suggested answers, see Appendix A.

▼ **Figure 15.4** | Inquiry

In a cross between a wild-type female fruit fly and a mutant white-eyed male, what color eyes will the F_1 and F_2 offspring have?

Experiment Thomas Hunt Morgan wanted to analyze the behavior of two alleles of a fruit fly eye-color gene. In crosses similar to those done by Mendel with pea plants, Morgan and his colleagues mated a wild-type (red-eyed) female with a mutant white-eyed male.

Morgan then bred an F_1 red-eyed female to an F_1 red-eyed male to produce the F_2 generation.

Results The F_2 generation showed a typical Mendelian ratio of 3 red-eyed flies : 1 white-eyed fly. However, all white-eyed flies were males; no females displayed the white-eye trait.

Conclusion All F_1 offspring had red eyes, so the mutant white-eye trait (w) must be recessive to the wild-type red-eye trait (w^+). Since the recessive trait—white eyes—was expressed only in males in the F_2 generation, Morgan deduced that this eye-color gene is located on the X chromosome and that there is no corresponding locus on the Y chromosome.

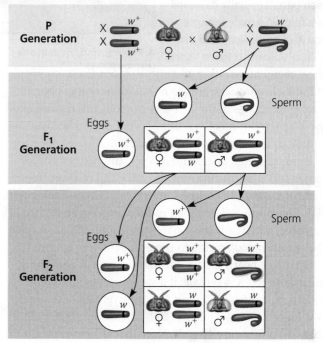

Source: T. H. Morgan, Sex-limited inheritance in *Drosophila*, *Science* 32:120–122 (1910).

(MB) A related Experimental Inquiry Tutorial can be assigned in MasteringBiology.

WHAT IF? *Suppose this eye-color gene were located on an autosome. Predict the phenotypes (including gender) of the F_2 flies in this hypothetical cross. (Hint: Draw a Punnett square.)*

CONCEPT 15.2

Sex-linked genes exhibit unique patterns of inheritance

As you just learned, Morgan's discovery of a trait (white eyes) that correlated with the sex of flies was a key episode in the development of the chromosome theory of inheritance. Because the identity of the sex chromosomes in an individual could be inferred by observing the sex of the fly, the behavior of the two members of the pair of sex chromosomes could be correlated with the behavior of the two alleles of the eye-color gene. In this section, we'll take a closer look at the role of sex chromosomes in inheritance.

The Chromosomal Basis of Sex

Although the anatomical and physiological differences between women and men are numerous, the chromosomal basis for determining sex is rather simple. Humans and other mammals have two types of sex chromosomes, designated X and Y. The Y chromosome is much smaller than the X chromosome (**Figure 15.5**). A person who inherits two X chromosomes, one from each parent, usually develops as a female; a male inherits one X chromosome and one Y chromosome (**Figure 15.6a**). Short segments at either end

▲ **Figure 15.5 Human sex chromosomes.**

of the Y chromosome are the only regions that are homologous with regions of the X. These homologous regions allow the X and Y chromosomes in males to pair and behave like homologs during meiosis in the testes.

In mammalian testes and ovaries, the two sex chromosomes segregate during meiosis. Each egg receives one X chromosome. In contrast, sperm fall into two categories: Half the sperm cells a male produces receive an X chromosome, and half receive a Y chromosome. We can trace the sex of each offspring to the events of conception: If a sperm cell bearing an X chromosome fertilizes an egg, the zygote is XX, a female; if a sperm cell containing a Y chromosome fertilizes an egg, the zygote is XY, a male (see Figure 15.6a). Thus, sex determination is a matter of chance—a fifty-fifty chance. Note that the mammalian X-Y system isn't the only chromosomal system for determining sex. **Figure 15.6b–d** illustrates three other systems.

In humans, the anatomical signs of sex begin to emerge when the embryo is about 2 months old. Before then, the rudiments of the gonads are generic—they can develop into either testes or ovaries, depending on whether or not a Y chromosome is present. In 1990, a British research team

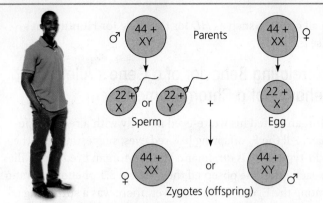

(a) The X-Y system. In mammals, the sex of an offspring depends on whether the sperm cell contains an X chromosome or a Y.

(b) The X-0 system. In grasshoppers, cockroaches, and some other insects, there is only one type of sex chromosome, the X. Females are XX; males have only one sex chromosome (X0). Sex of the offspring is determined by whether the sperm cell contains an X chromosome or no sex chromosome.

(c) The Z-W system. In birds, some fishes, and some insects, the sex chromosomes present in the egg (not the sperm) determine the sex of offspring. The sex chromosomes are designated Z and W. Females are ZW and males are ZZ.

(d) The haplo-diploid system. There are no sex chromosomes in most species of bees and ants. Females develop from fertilized eggs and are thus diploid. Males develop from unfertilized eggs and are haploid; they have no fathers.

▲ **Figure 15.6 Some chromosomal systems of sex determination.** Numerals indicate the number of autosomes in the species pictured. In *Drosophila*, males are XY, but sex depends on the ratio between the number of X chromosomes and the number of autosome sets, not simply on the presence of a Y chromosome.

identified a gene on the Y chromosome required for the development of testes. They named the gene *SRY*, for *s*ex-determining *r*egion of *Y*. In the absence of *SRY*, the gonads develop into ovaries. The biochemical, physiological, and anatomical features that distinguish males and females are complex, and many genes are involved in their development. In fact, *SRY* codes for a protein that regulates other genes.

Researchers have sequenced the human Y chromosome and have identified 78 genes that code for about 25 proteins (some genes are duplicates). About half of these genes are expressed only in the testis, and some are required for normal testicular functioning and the production of normal sperm. A gene located on either sex chromosome is called a **sex-linked gene**; those located on the Y chromosome are called *Y-linked genes*. The Y chromosome is passed along virtually intact from a father to all his sons. Because there are so few Y-linked genes, very few disorders are transferred from father to son on the Y chromosome. A rare example is that in the absence of certain Y-linked genes, an XY individual is male but does not produce normal sperm.

The human X chromosome contains approximately 1,100 genes, which are called **X-linked genes**. The fact that males and females inherit a different number of X chromosomes leads to a pattern of inheritance different from that produced by genes located on autosomes.

Inheritance of X-Linked Genes

While most Y-linked genes help determine sex, the X chromosomes have genes for many characters unrelated to sex. X-linked genes in humans follow the same pattern of inheritance that Morgan observed for the eye-color locus he studied in *Drosophila* (see Figure 15.4). Fathers pass X-linked alleles to all of their daughters but to none of their sons. In contrast, mothers can pass X-linked alleles to both sons and daughters, as shown in **Figure 15.7** for the inheritance of a mild X-linked disorder, red-green color blindness.

If an X-linked trait is due to a recessive allele, a female will express the phenotype only if she is homozygous for

that allele. Because males have only one locus, the terms *homozygous* and *heterozygous* lack meaning for describing their X-linked genes; the term *hemizygous* is used in such cases. Any male receiving the recessive allele from his mother will express the trait. For this reason, far more males than females have X-linked recessive disorders. However, even though the chance of a female inheriting a double dose of the mutant allele is much less than the probability of a male inheriting a single dose, there *are* females with X-linked disorders. For instance, color blindness is almost always inherited as an X-linked trait. A color-blind daughter may be born to a color-blind father whose mate is a carrier (see Figure 15.7c). Because the X-linked allele for color blindness is relatively rare, though, the probability that such a man and woman will mate is low.

A number of human X-linked disorders are much more serious than color blindness, such as **Duchenne muscular dystrophy**, which affects about one out of 3,500 males born in the United States. The disease is characterized by a progressive weakening of the muscles and loss of coordination. Affected individuals rarely live past their early 20s. Researchers have traced the disorder to the absence of a key muscle protein called dystrophin and have mapped the gene for this protein to a specific locus on the X chromosome.

Hemophilia is an X-linked recessive disorder defined by the absence of one or more of the proteins required for blood clotting. When a person with hemophilia is injured, bleeding is prolonged because a firm clot is slow to form. Small cuts in the skin are usually not a problem, but bleeding in the muscles or joints can be painful and can lead to serious damage. In the 1800s, hemophilia was widespread among the royal families of Europe. Queen Victoria of

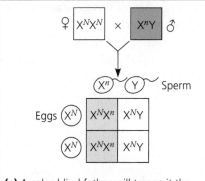

(a) A color-blind father will transmit the mutant allele to all daughters but to no sons. When the mother is a dominant homozygote, the daughters will have the normal phenotype but will be carriers of the mutation.

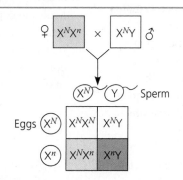

(b) If a carrier mates with a male who has normal color vision, there is a 50% chance that each daughter will be a carrier like her mother and a 50% chance that each son will have the disorder.

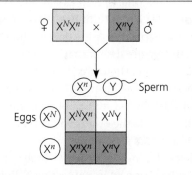

(c) If a carrier mates with a color-blind male, there is a 50% chance that each child born to them will have the disorder, regardless of sex. Daughters who have normal color vision will be carriers, whereas males who have normal color vision will be free of the recessive allele.

▲ **Figure 15.7 The transmission of X-linked recessive traits.** In this diagram, red-green color blindness is used as an example. The superscript N represents the dominant allele for normal color vision carried on the X chromosome, while n represents the recessive allele, which has a mutation for color blindness. White boxes indicate unaffected individuals, light orange boxes indicate carriers, and dark orange boxes indicate color-blind individuals.

? *If a color-blind woman married a man who had normal color vision, what would be the probable phenotypes of their children?*

England is known to have passed the allele to several of her descendants. Subsequent intermarriage with royal family members of other nations, such as Spain and Russia, further spread this X-linked trait, and its incidence is well documented in royal pedigrees. A few years ago, new genomic techniques allowed sequencing of DNA from tiny amounts isolated from the buried remains of royal family members. The genetic basis of the mutation, and how it resulted in a nonfunctional blood-clotting factor, is now understood. Today, people with hemophilia are treated as needed with intravenous injections of the protein that is missing.

X Inactivation in Female Mammals

Female mammals, including human females, inherit two X chromosomes—twice the number inherited by males—so you may wonder whether females make twice as much as males of the proteins encoded by X-linked genes. In fact, almost all of one X chromosome in each cell in female mammals becomes inactivated during early embryonic development. As a result, the cells of females and males have the same effective dose (one copy) of most X-linked genes. The inactive X in each cell of a female condenses into a compact object called a **Barr body** (discovered by Canadian anatomist Murray Barr), which lies along the inside of the nuclear envelope. Most of the genes of the X chromosome that forms the Barr body are not expressed. In the ovaries, however, Barr-body chromosomes are reactivated in the cells that give rise to eggs, such that following meiosis, every female gamete (egg) has an active X.

British geneticist Mary Lyon demonstrated that the selection of which X chromosome will form the Barr body occurs randomly and independently in each embryonic cell present at the time of X inactivation. As a consequence, females consist of a *mosaic* of two types of cells: those with the active X derived from the father and those with the active X derived from the mother. After an X chromosome is inactivated in a particular cell, all mitotic descendants of that cell have the same inactive X. Thus, if a female is heterozygous for a sex-linked trait, about half her cells will express one allele, while the others will express the alternate allele. **Figure 15.8** shows how this mosaicism results in the mottled coloration of a tortoiseshell cat. In humans, mosaicism can be observed in a recessive X-linked mutation that prevents the development of sweat glands. A woman who is heterozygous for this trait has patches of normal skin and patches of skin lacking sweat glands.

Inactivation of an X chromosome involves modification of the DNA and proteins bound to it, called histones, including attachment of methyl groups (—CH_3) to DNA nucleotides. (The regulatory role of DNA methylation is discussed in Chapter 18.) A particular region of each X chromosome contains several genes involved in the inactivation process. The two regions, one on each X chromosome,

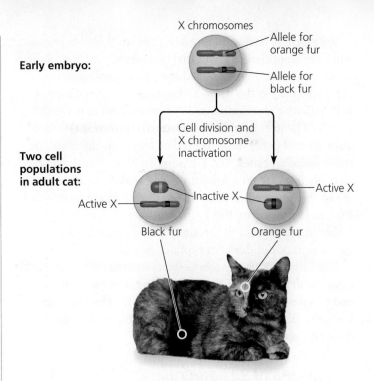

▲ **Figure 15.8 X inactivation and the tortoiseshell cat.** The tortoiseshell gene is on the X chromosome, and the tortoiseshell phenotype requires the presence of two different alleles, one for orange fur and one for black fur. Normally, only females can have both alleles, because only they have two X chromosomes. If a female cat is heterozygous for the tortoiseshell gene, she is tortoiseshell. Orange patches are formed by populations of cells in which the X chromosome with the orange allele is active; black patches have cells in which the X chromosome with the black allele is active. ("Calico" cats also have white areas, which are determined by another gene.)

associate briefly with each other in each cell at an early stage of embryonic development. Then one of the genes, called *XIST* (for <u>X</u>-<u>i</u>nactive <u>s</u>pecific <u>t</u>ranscript) becomes active *only* on the chromosome that will become the Barr body. Multiple copies of the RNA product of this gene apparently attach to the X chromosome on which they are made, eventually almost covering it. Interaction of this RNA with the chromosome initiates X inactivation, and the RNA products of other nearby genes help to regulate the process.

CONCEPT CHECK 15.2

1. A white-eyed female *Drosophila* is mated with a red-eyed (wild-type) male, the reciprocal cross of the one shown in Figure 15.4. What phenotypes and genotypes do you predict for the offspring?

2. Neither Tim nor Rhoda has Duchenne muscular dystrophy, but their firstborn son does. What is the probability that a second child will have the disease? What is the probability if the second child is a boy? A girl?

3. **MAKE CONNECTIONS** Consider what you learned about dominant and recessive alleles in Concept 14.1. If a disorder were caused by a dominant X-linked allele, how would the inheritance pattern differ from what we see for recessive X-linked disorders?

For suggested answers, see Appendix A.

Linked genes tend to be inherited together because they are located near each other on the same chromosome

The number of genes in a cell is far greater than the number of chromosomes; in fact, each chromosome (except the Y) has hundreds or thousands of genes. Genes located near each other on the same chromosome tend to be inherited together in genetic crosses; such genes are said to be genetically linked and are called **linked genes**. When geneticists follow linked genes in breeding experiments, the results deviate from those expected from Mendel's law of independent assortment.

How Linkage Affects Inheritance

To see how linkage between genes affects the inheritance of two different characters, let's examine another of Morgan's *Drosophila* experiments. In this case, the characters are body color and wing size, each with two different phenotypes. Wild-type flies have gray bodies and normal-sized wings. In addition to these flies, Morgan had managed to obtain, through breeding, doubly mutant flies with black bodies and wings much smaller than normal, called vestigial wings. The mutant alleles are recessive to the wild-type alleles, and neither gene is on a sex chromosome. In his investigation of these two genes, Morgan carried out the crosses shown in **Figure 15.9**. The first was a P generation cross to generate F_1 dihybrid flies, and the second was a testcross.

▼ **Figure 15.9** | Inquiry

How does linkage between two genes affect inheritance of characters?

Experiment Morgan wanted to know whether the genes for body color and wing size are genetically linked, and if so, how this affects their inheritance. The alleles for body color are b^+ (gray) and b (black), and those for wing size are vg^+ (normal) and vg (vestigial).

Morgan mated true-breeding P (parental) generation flies—wild-type flies with black, vestigial-winged flies—to produce heterozygous F_1 dihybrids ($b^+ b\ vg^+ vg$), all of which were wild-type in appearance.

He then mated wild-type F_1 dihybrid females with homozygous recessive males. This testcross will reveal the genotype of the eggs made by the dihybrid female.

The testcross male's sperm contributes only recessive alleles, so the phenotype of the offspring reflects the genotype of the female's eggs.

Note: Although only females (with pointed abdomens) are shown, half the offspring in each class would be males (with rounded abdomens).

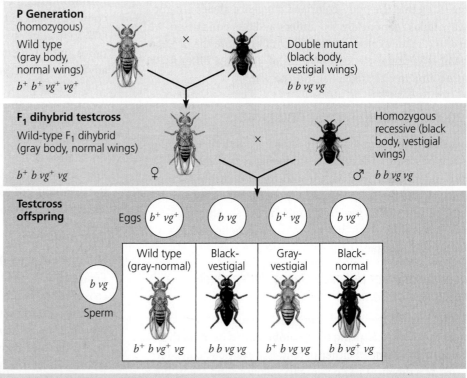

PREDICTED RATIOS

Predicted ratio if genes are located on different chromosomes:	1	:	1	:	1	:	1
Predicted ratio if genes are located on the same chromosome *and* parental alleles are always inherited together:	1	:	1	:	0	:	0
Results Data from Morgan's experiment:	965	:	944	:	206	:	185

Conclusion Since most offspring had a parental (P generation) phenotype, Morgan concluded that the genes for body color and wing size are genetically linked on the same chromosome. However, the production of a relatively small number of offspring with nonparental phenotypes indicated that some mechanism occasionally breaks the linkage between specific alleles of genes on the same chromosome.

Source: T. H. Morgan and C. J. Lynch, The linkage of two factors in *Drosophila* that are not sex-linked, *Biological Bulletin* 23:174–182 (1912).

WHAT IF? If the parental (P generation) flies had been true-breeding for gray body with vestigial wings and black body with normal wings, which phenotypic class(es) would be largest among the testcross offspring?

The resulting flies had a much higher proportion of the combinations of traits seen in the P generation flies (called parental phenotypes) than would be expected if the two genes assorted independently. Morgan thus concluded that body color and wing size are usually inherited together in specific (parental) combinations because the genes for these characters are near each other on the same chromosome:

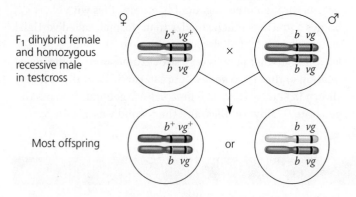

However, as Figure 15.9 shows, both of the combinations of traits not seen in the P generation (called nonparental phenotypes) were also produced in Morgan's experiments, suggesting that the body-color and wing-size alleles are not always linked genetically. To understand this conclusion, we need to further explore **genetic recombination**, the production of offspring with combinations of traits that differ from those found in either P generation parent.*

Genetic Recombination and Linkage

Meiosis and random fertilization generate genetic variation among offspring of sexually reproducing organisms due to independent assortment of chromosomes, crossing over in meiosis I, and the possibility of any sperm fertilizing any egg (see Concept 13.4). Here we'll examine the chromosomal basis of recombination in relation to the genetic findings of Mendel and Morgan.

Recombination of Unlinked Genes: Independent Assortment of Chromosomes

Mendel learned from crosses in which he followed two characters that some offspring have combinations of traits that do not match those of either parent. For example, consider a cross of a dihybrid pea plant with yellow-round seeds, heterozygous for both seed color and seed shape (*YyRr*), with a plant homozygous for both recessive alleles (with green-wrinkled seeds, *yyrr*). (This acts as a testcross because the results will reveal the genotype of the gametes made in the

dihybrid *YyRr* plant.) Let's represent the cross by the following Punnett square:

Notice in this Punnett square that one-half of the offspring are expected to inherit a phenotype that matches either of the phenotypes of the P (parental) generation originally crossed to produce the F₁ dihybrid (see Figure 15.2). These matching offspring are called **parental types**. But two nonparental phenotypes are also found among the offspring. Because these offspring have new combinations of seed shape and color, they are called **recombinant types**, or **recombinants** for short. When 50% of all offspring are recombinants, as in this example, geneticists say that there is a 50% frequency of recombination. The predicted phenotypic ratios among the offspring are similar to what Mendel actually found in his *YyRr* × *yyrr* crosses.

A 50% frequency of recombination in such testcrosses is observed for any two genes that are located on different chromosomes and thus cannot be linked. The physical basis of recombination between unlinked genes is the random orientation of homologous chromosomes at metaphase I of meiosis, which leads to the independent assortment of the two unlinked genes (see Figure 13.11 and the question in the Figure 15.2 legend).

Recombination of Linked Genes: Crossing Over

Now, let's explain the results of the *Drosophila* testcross in Figure 15.9. Recall that most of the offspring from the testcross for body color and wing size had parental phenotypes. That suggested that the two genes were on the same chromosome, since the occurrence of parental types with a frequency greater than 50% indicates that the genes are linked. About 17% of offspring, however, were recombinants.

Seeing these results, Morgan proposed that some process must occasionally break the physical connection between specific alleles of genes on the same chromosome. Later experiments showed that this process, now called **crossing over**, accounts for the recombination of linked genes. In crossing over, which occurs while replicated homologous chromosomes are paired during prophase of meiosis I, a set of proteins orchestrates an exchange of corresponding segments of one maternal and one paternal chromatid (see

---

* As you proceed, be sure to keep in mind the distinction between the terms *linked genes* (two or more genes on the same chromosome that tend to be inherited together) and *sex-linked gene* (a single gene on a sex chromosome).

▶ **Figure 15.10 Chromosomal basis for recombination of linked genes.** In these diagrams re-creating the testcross in Figure 15.9, we track chromosomes as well as genes. The maternal chromosomes (present in the wild-type F_1 dihybrid) are color-coded red and pink to distinguish one homolog from the other before any meiotic crossing over has occurred. Because crossing over between the b^+/b and vg^+/vg loci occurs in some, but not all, egg-producing cells, more eggs with parental-type chromosomes than with recombinant ones are produced in the mating females. Fertilization of the eggs by sperm of genotype $b\ vg$ gives rise to some recombinant offspring. The recombination frequency is the percentage of recombinant flies in the total pool of offspring.

DRAW IT *Suppose, as in the question at the bottom of Figure 15.9, the parental (P generation) flies were true-breeding for gray body with vestigial wings and black body with normal wings. Draw the chromosomes in each of the four possible kinds of eggs from an F_1 female, and label each chromosome as "parental" or "recombinant."*

$$\text{Recombination frequency} = \frac{391\ \text{recombinants}}{2{,}300\ \text{total offspring}} \times 100 = 17\%$$

Figure 13.9). In effect, when a single crossover occurs, end portions of two nonsister chromatids trade places.

Figure 15.10 shows how crossing over in a dihybrid female fly resulted in recombinant eggs and ultimately recombinant offspring in Morgan's testcross. Most eggs had a chromosome with either the $b^+\ vg^+$ or $b\ vg$ parental genotype, but some had a recombinant chromosome ($b^+\ vg$ or $b\ vg^+$). Fertilization of

all classes of eggs by homozygous recessive sperm ($b\ vg$) produced an offspring population in which 17% exhibited a nonparental, recombinant phenotype, reflecting combinations of alleles not seen before in either P generation parent. In the Scientific Skills Exercise, you can use a statistical test to analyze the results from an F_1 dihybrid testcross and see whether the two genes assort independently or are linked.

Using the Chi-Square (χ^2) Test

Are Two Genes Linked or Unlinked? Genes that are in close proximity on the same chromosome will result in the linked alleles being inherited together more often than not. But how can you tell if certain alleles are inherited together due to linkage or whether they just happen to assort together? In this exercise, you will use a simple statistical test, the chi-square (χ^2) test, to analyze phenotypes of F_1 testcross progeny in order to see whether two genes are linked or unlinked.

How These Experiments Are Done If genes are unlinked and assorting independently, the phenotypic ratio of offspring from an F_1 testcross is expected to be 1:1:1:1 (see Figure 15.9). If the two genes are linked, however, the observed phenotypic ratio of the offspring will not match that ratio. Given that random fluctuations in the data do occur, how much must the observed numbers deviate from the expected numbers for us to conclude that the genes are not assorting independently but may instead be linked? To answer this question, scientists use a statistical test. This test, called a chi-square (χ^2) test, compares an observed data set to an expected data set predicted by a hypothesis (here, that the genes are unlinked) and measures the discrepancy between the two, thus determining the "goodness of fit." If the discrepancy between the observed and expected data sets is so large that it is unlikely to have occurred by random fluctuation, we say there is statistically significant evidence against the hypothesis (or, more specifically, evidence for the genes being linked). If the discrepancy is small, then our observations are well explained by random variation alone. In this case, we say the observed data are consistent with our hypothesis, or that the discrepancy is statistically insignificant. Note, however, that consistency with our hypothesis is not the same as proof of our hypothesis. Also, the size of the experimental data set is important: With small data sets like this one, even if the genes are linked, discrepancies might be small by chance alone if the linkage is weak. For simplicity, we overlook the effect of sample size here.

Data from the Simulated Experiment In cosmos plants, purple stem (*A*) is dominant to green stem (*a*), and short petals (*B*) is dominant to long petals (*b*). In a simulated cross, *AABB* plants were crossed with *aabb* plants to generate F_1 dihybrids (*AaBb*), which were then testcrossed (*AaBb* × *aabb*). A total of 900 offspring plants were scored for stem color and flower petal length.

▲ **Cosmos plants**

the expected number of each phenotype out of the 900 total offspring, and enter the values in the data table.

2. The goodness of fit is measured by χ^2. This statistic measures the amounts by which the observed values differ from their respective predictions to indicate how closely the two sets of values match. The formula for calculating this value is

$$\chi^2 = \sum \frac{(o - e)^2}{e}$$

where o = observed and e = expected. Calculate the χ^2 value for the data using the table below. Fill out the table, carrying out the operations indicated in the top row. Then add up the entries in the last column to find the χ^2 value.

Testcross Offspring	Expected (e)	Observed (o)	Deviation (o − e)	(o − e)²	(o − e)²/e
(*A–B–*)		220			
(*aaB–*)		210			
(*A–bb*)		231			
(*aabb*)		239			
				χ^2 = Sum	

3. The χ^2 value means nothing on its own—it is used to find the probability that, assuming the hypothesis is true, the observed data set could have resulted from random fluctuations. A low probability suggests that the observed data are not consistent with the hypothesis, and thus the hypothesis should be rejected. A standard cutoff point used by biologists is a probability of 0.05 (5%). If the probability corresponding to the χ^2 value is 0.05 or less, the differences between observed and expected values are considered statistically significant and the hypothesis (that the genes are unlinked) should be rejected. If the probability is above 0.05, the results are not statistically significant; the observed data are consistent with the hypothesis. To find the probability, locate your χ^2 value in the χ^2 Distribution Table in Appendix F. The "degrees of freedom" (df) of your data set is the number of categories (here, 4 phenotypes) minus 1, so df = 3.
(a) Determine which values on the df = 3 line of the table your calculated χ^2 value lies between. (b) The column headings for these values show the probability range for your χ^2 number. Based on whether there are nonsignificant ($p > 0.05$) or significant ($p \leq 0.05$) differences between the observed and expected values, are the data consistent with the hypothesis that the two genes are unlinked and assorting independently, or is there enough evidence to reject this hypothesis?

(MB) A version of this Scientific Skills Exercise can be assigned in MasteringBiology.

Offspring from test-cross of *AaBb* (F_1) × *aabb*	Purple stem/short petals (*A–B–*)	Green stem/short petals (*aaB–*)	Purple stem/long petals (*A–bb*)	Green stem/long petals (*aabb*)
Expected ratio if the genes are unlinked	1	1	1	1
Expected number of offspring (of 900)				
Observed number of offspring (of 900)	220	210	231	239

Interpret the Data

1. The results in the data table are from a simulated F_1 dihybrid testcross. The hypothesis that the two genes are unlinked predicts the offspring phenotypic ratio will be 1:1:1:1. Using this ratio, calculate

New Combinations of Alleles: Variation for Natural Selection

EVOLUTION The physical behavior of chromosomes during meiosis contributes to the generation of variation in offspring (see Concept 13.4). Each pair of homologous chromosomes lines up independently of other pairs during metaphase I, and crossing over prior to that, during prophase I, can mix and match parts of maternal and paternal homologs. Mendel's elegant experiments show that the behavior of the abstract entities known as genes—or, more concretely, alleles of genes—also leads to variation in offspring (see Concept 14.1). Now, putting these different ideas together, you can see that the recombinant chromosomes resulting from crossing over may bring alleles together in new combinations, and the subsequent events of meiosis distribute to gametes the recombinant chromosomes in a multitude of combinations, such as the new variants seen in Figures 15.9 and 15.10. Random fertilization then increases even further the number of variant allele combinations that can be created.

This abundance of genetic variation provides the raw material on which natural selection works. If the traits conferred by particular combinations of alleles are better suited for a given environment, organisms possessing those genotypes will be expected to thrive and leave more offspring, ensuring the continuation of their genetic complement. In the next generation, of course, the alleles will be shuffled anew. Ultimately, the interplay between environment and genotype will determine which genetic combinations persist over time.

Mapping the Distance Between Genes Using Recombination Data: *Scientific Inquiry*

The discovery of linked genes and recombination due to crossing over motivated one of Morgan's students, Alfred H. Sturtevant, to work out a method for constructing a **genetic map**, an ordered list of the genetic loci along a particular chromosome.

Sturtevant hypothesized that the percentage of recombinant offspring, the *recombination frequency*, calculated from experiments like the one in Figures 15.9 and 15.10, depends on the distance between genes on a chromosome. He assumed that crossing over is a random event, with the chance of crossing over approximately equal at all points along a chromosome. Based on these assumptions, Sturtevant predicted that *the farther apart two genes are, the higher the probability that a crossover will occur between them and therefore the higher the recombination frequency.* His reasoning was simple: The greater the distance between two genes, the more points there are between them where crossing over can occur. Using recombination data from various fruit fly crosses, Sturtevant proceeded to assign relative positions to genes on the same chromosomes—that is, to *map* genes.

A genetic map based on recombination frequencies is called a **linkage map**. **Figure 15.11** shows Sturtevant's linkage map of three genes: the body-color (*b*) and wing-size (*vg*) genes depicted in Figure 15.10 and a third gene, called cinnabar (*cn*). Cinnabar is one of many *Drosophila* genes affecting eye color. Cinnabar eyes, a mutant phenotype, are a brighter red than the wild-type color. The recombination frequency between *cn* and *b* is 9%; that between *cn* and *vg*, 9.5%; and that between *b* and *vg*, 17%. In other words, crossovers between *cn* and *b* and between *cn* and *vg* are about half as frequent as crossovers between *b* and *vg*. Only a map that locates *cn* about midway between *b* and *vg* is consistent with these data, as you can prove to yourself by drawing alternative maps. Sturtevant expressed the distances between genes in **map units**, defining one map unit as equivalent to a 1% recombination frequency.

In practice, the interpretation of recombination data is more complicated than this example suggests. Some genes on a chromosome are so far from each other that a crossover between them is virtually certain. The observed frequency of recombination in crosses involving two such

---

▼ Figure 15.11 Research Method

Constructing a Linkage Map

Application A linkage map shows the relative locations of genes along a chromosome.

Technique A linkage map is based on the assumption that the probability of a crossover between two genetic loci is proportional to the distance separating the loci. The recombination frequencies used to construct a linkage map for a particular chromosome are obtained from experimental crosses, such as the cross depicted in Figures 15.9 and 15.10. The distances between genes are expressed as map units, with one map unit equivalent to a 1% recombination frequency. Genes are arranged on the chromosome in the order that best fits the data.

Results In this example, the observed recombination frequencies between three *Drosophila* gene pairs (*b–cn* 9%, *cn–vg* 9.5%, and *b–vg* 17%) best fit a linear order in which *cn* is positioned about halfway between the other two genes:

The *b–vg* recombination frequency (17%) is slightly less than the sum of the *b–cn* and *cn–vg* frequencies (9 + 9.5 = 18.5%) because of the few times that one crossover occurs between *b* and *cn* and another crossover occurs between *cn* and *vg*. The second crossover would "cancel out" the first, reducing the observed *b–vg* recombination frequency while contributing to the frequency between each of the closer pairs of genes. The value of 18.5% (18.5 map units) is closer to the actual distance between the genes. In practice, a geneticist would add the smaller distances in constructing a map.

genes can have a maximum value of 50%, a result indistinguishable from that for genes on different chromosomes. In this case, the physical connection between genes on the same chromosome is not reflected in the results of genetic crosses. Despite being on the same chromosome and thus being *physically connected*, the genes are *genetically unlinked*; alleles of such genes assort independently, as if they were on different chromosomes. In fact, at least two of the genes for pea characters that Mendel studied are now known to be on the same chromosome, but the distance between them is so great that linkage is not observed in genetic crosses. Consequently, the two genes behaved as if they were on different chromosomes in Mendel's experiments. Genes located far apart on a chromosome are mapped by adding the recombination frequencies from crosses involving closer pairs of genes lying between the two distant genes.

Using recombination data, Sturtevant and his colleagues were able to map numerous *Drosophila* genes in linear arrays. They found that the genes clustered into four groups of linked genes (*linkage groups*). Light microscopy had revealed four pairs of chromosomes in *Drosophila*, so the linkage map provided additional evidence that genes are located on chromosomes. Each chromosome has a linear array of specific genes, each gene with its own locus (**Figure 15.12**).

Because a linkage map is based strictly on recombination frequencies, it gives only an approximate picture of a chromosome. The frequency of crossing over is not actually uniform over the length of a chromosome, as Sturtevant assumed, and therefore map units do not correspond to actual physical distances (in nanometers, for instance). A linkage map does portray the order of genes along a chromosome, but it does not accurately portray the precise locations of those genes. Other methods enable geneticists to construct *cytogenetic maps* of chromosomes, which locate genes with respect to chromosomal features, such as stained bands, that can be seen in the microscope. Technical advances over the last two decades have enormously increased the rate and affordability of DNA sequencing. Today, most researchers sequence whole genomes to map the locations of genes of a given species. The entire nucleotide sequence is the ultimate physical map of a chromosome, revealing the physical distances between gene loci in DNA nucleotides (see Concept 21.1). Comparing a linkage map with such a physical map or with a cytogenetic map of the same chromosome, we find that the linear order of genes is identical in all the maps, but the spacing between genes is not.

CONCEPT 15.4

Alterations of chromosome number or structure cause some genetic disorders

As you have learned so far in this chapter, the phenotype of an organism can be affected by small-scale changes involving individual genes. Random mutations are the source of all new alleles, which can lead to new phenotypic traits.

Large-scale chromosomal changes can also affect an organism's phenotype. Physical and chemical disturbances, as well as errors during meiosis, can damage chromosomes in major ways or alter their number in a cell. Large-scale chromosomal alterations in humans and other mammals often lead to spontaneous abortion (miscarriage) of a fetus, and individuals born with these types of genetic defects commonly exhibit various developmental disorders. Plants may tolerate such genetic defects better than animals do.

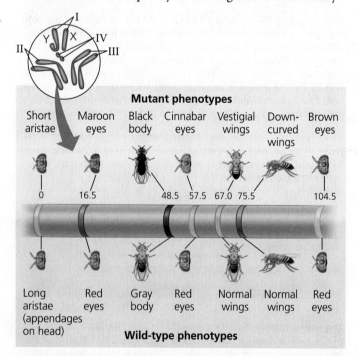

Mutant phenotypes

| Short aristae | Maroon eyes | Black body | Cinnabar eyes | Vestigial wings | Down-curved wings | Brown eyes |

0   16.5   48.5   57.5   67.0   75.5   104.5

| Long aristae (appendages on head) | Red eyes | Gray body | Red eyes | Normal wings | Normal wings | Red eyes |

Wild-type phenotypes

▲ **Figure 15.12 A partial genetic (linkage) map of a *Drosophila* chromosome.** This simplified map shows just seven of the genes that have been mapped on *Drosophila* chromosome II. (DNA sequencing has revealed over 9,000 genes on that chromosome.) The number at each gene locus indicates the number of map units between that locus and the locus for arista length (left). Notice that more than one gene can affect a given phenotypic characteristic, such as eye color.

Abnormal Chromosome Number

Ideally, the meiotic spindle distributes chromosomes to daughter cells without error. But there is an occasional mishap, called a **nondisjunction**, in which the members of a pair of homologous chromosomes do not move apart properly during meiosis I or sister chromatids fail to separate during meiosis II **(Figure 15.13)**. In nondisjunction, one gamete receives two of the same type of chromosome and another gamete receives no copy. The other chromosomes are usually distributed normally.

If either of the aberrant gametes unites with a normal one at fertilization, the zygote will also have an abnormal number of a particular chromosome, a condition known as **aneuploidy**. Fertilization involving a gamete that has no copy of a particular chromosome will lead to a missing chromosome in the zygote (so that the cell has $2n - 1$ chromosomes); the aneuploid zygote is said to be **monosomic** for that chromosome. If a chromosome is present in triplicate in the zygote (so that the cell has $2n + 1$ chromosomes), the aneuploid cell is **trisomic** for that chromosome. Mitosis will subsequently transmit the anomaly to all embryonic cells. Monosomy and trisomy are estimated to occur in between 10 and 25% of human conceptions, and is the main reason for pregnancy loss. If the organism survives, it usually has a set of traits caused by the abnormal dose of the genes associated with the extra or missing chromosome. Down syndrome is an example of trisomy in humans that

will be discussed later. Nondisjunction can also occur during mitosis. If such an error takes place early in embryonic development, then the aneuploid condition is passed along by mitosis to a large number of cells and is likely to have a substantial effect on the organism.

Some organisms have more than two complete chromosome sets in all somatic cells. The general term for this chromosomal alteration is **polyploidy**; the specific terms *triploidy* ($3n$) and *tetraploidy* ($4n$) indicate three or four chromosomal sets, respectively. One way a triploid cell may arise is by the fertilization of an abnormal diploid egg produced by nondisjunction of all its chromosomes. Tetraploidy could result from the failure of a $2n$ zygote to divide after replicating its chromosomes. Subsequent normal mitotic divisions would then produce a $4n$ embryo.

Polyploidy is fairly common in the plant kingdom. The spontaneous origin of polyploid individuals plays an important role in plant evolution (see Chapter 24). Many species we eat are polyploid: Bananas are triploid, wheat hexaploid ($6n$), and strawberries octoploid ($8n$). Polyploid animal species are much less common, but there are a few fishes and amphibians known to be polyploid. In general, polyploids are more nearly normal in appearance than aneuploids. One extra (or missing) chromosome apparently disrupts genetic balance more than does an entire extra set of chromosomes.

Alterations of Chromosome Structure

Errors in meiosis or damaging agents such as radiation can cause breakage of a chromosome, which can lead to four types of changes in chromosome structure **(Figure 15.14)**. A **deletion** occurs when a chromosomal fragment is lost. The affected chromosome is then missing certain genes. The "deleted" fragment may become attached as an extra segment to a sister chromatid, producing a **duplication**. Alternatively, a detached fragment could attach to a nonsister chromatid of a homologous chromosome. In that case, though, the "duplicated" segments might not be identical because the homologs could carry different alleles of certain genes. A chromosomal fragment may also reattach to the original chromosome but in the reverse orientation, producing an **inversion**. A fourth possible result of chromosomal breakage is for the fragment to join a nonhomologous chromosome, a rearrangement called a **translocation**.

Deletions and duplications are especially likely to occur during meiosis. In crossing over, nonsister chromatids sometimes exchange unequal-sized segments of DNA, so that one partner gives up more genes than it receives. The products of such an unequal crossover are one chromosome with a deletion and one chromosome with a duplication.

A diploid embryo that is homozygous for a large deletion (or has a single X chromosome with a large deletion, in a male) is usually missing a number of essential genes, a condition typically lethal. Duplications and translocations also tend

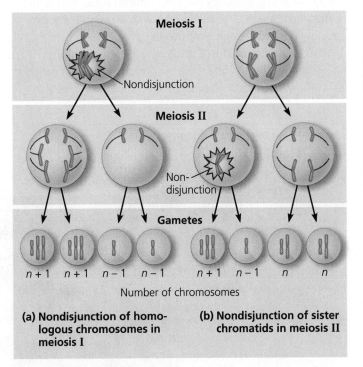

Meiosis I

Nondisjunction

Meiosis II

Non-disjunction

Gametes

$n + 1$ $\quad$ $n + 1$ $\quad$ $n - 1$ $\quad$ $n - 1$ $\qquad$ $n + 1$ $\quad$ $n - 1$ $\quad$ n $\quad$ n

Number of chromosomes

(a) Nondisjunction of homologous chromosomes in meiosis I

(b) Nondisjunction of sister chromatids in meiosis II

▲ **Figure 15.13 Meiotic nondisjunction.** Gametes with an abnormal chromosome number can arise by nondisjunction in either meiosis I or meiosis II. For simplicity, the figure does not show the spores formed by meiosis in plants. Ultimately, spores form gametes that have the defects shown. (See Figure 13.6.)

▼ Figure 15.14 Alterations of chromosome structure. Red arrows indicate breakage points. Dark purple highlights the chromosomal parts affected by the rearrangements.

(a) Deletion

A **deletion** removes a chromosomal segment.

(b) Duplication

A **duplication** repeats a segment.

(c) Inversion

An **inversion** reverses a segment within a chromosome.

(d) Translocation

A **translocation** moves a segment from one chromosome to a nonhomologous chromosome. In a reciprocal translocation, the most common type, nonhomologous chromosomes exchange fragments.

Less often, a nonreciprocal translocation occurs: A chromosome transfers a fragment but receives none in return (not shown).

to be harmful. In reciprocal translocations, in which segments are exchanged between nonhomologous chromosomes, and in inversions, the balance of genes is not abnormal—all genes are present in their normal doses. Nevertheless, translocations and inversions can alter phenotype because a gene's expression can be influenced by its location among neighboring genes, which can have devastating effects.

Human Disorders Due to Chromosomal Alterations

Alterations of chromosome number and structure are associated with a number of serious human disorders. As described earlier, nondisjunction in meiosis results in aneuploidy in gametes and any resulting zygotes. Although

the frequency of aneuploid zygotes may be quite high in humans, most of these chromosomal alterations are so disastrous to development that the affected embryos are spontaneously aborted long before birth. However, some types of aneuploidy appear to upset the genetic balance less than others, where individuals with certain aneuploid conditions can survive to birth and beyond. These individuals have a set of traits—a *syndrome*—characteristic of the type of aneuploidy. Genetic disorders caused by aneuploidy can be diagnosed before birth by fetal testing (see Figure 14.19).

Down Syndrome (Trisomy 21)

One aneuploid condition, **Down syndrome**, affects approximately one out of every 830 children born in the United States (**Figure 15.15**). Down syndrome is usually the result of an extra chromosome 21, so that each body cell has a total of 47 chromosomes. Because the cells are trisomic for chromosome 21, Down syndrome is often called *trisomy 21*. Down syndrome includes characteristic facial features, short stature, correctable heart defects, and developmental delays. Individuals with Down syndrome have an increased chance of developing leukemia and Alzheimer's disease but have a lower rate of high blood pressure, atherosclerosis (hardening of the arteries), stroke, and many types of solid tumors. Although people with Down syndrome, on average, have a life span shorter than normal, most, with proper medical treatment, live to middle age and beyond. Many live independently or at home with their families, are employed, and are valuable contributors to their communities. Almost all males and about half of females with Down syndrome are sexually underdeveloped and sterile.

The frequency of Down syndrome increases with the age of the mother. While the disorder occurs in just 0.04% of children born to women under age 30, the risk climbs

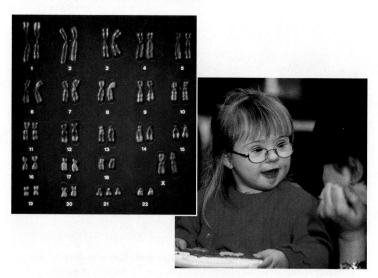

▲ **Figure 15.15 Down syndrome.** The karyotype shows trisomy 21, the most common cause of Down syndrome. The child exhibits the facial features characteristic of this disorder.

to 0.92% for mothers at age 40 and is even higher for older mothers. The correlation of Down syndrome with maternal age has not yet been explained. Most cases result from nondisjunction during meiosis I, and some research points to an age-dependent abnormality in meiosis. Trisomies of some other chromosomes also increase in incidence with maternal age, although infants with other autosomal trisomies rarely survive for long. Due to its low risk and its potential for providing useful information, prenatal screening for trisomies in the embryo is now offered to all pregnant women. In 2008, the Prenatally and Postnatally Diagnosed Conditions Awareness Act was signed into law in the United States. This law stipulates that medical practitioners give accurate, up-to-date information about any prenatal or postnatal diagnosis received by parents and that they connect parents with appropriate support services.

Aneuploidy of Sex Chromosomes

Aneuploid conditions involving sex chromosomes appear to upset the genetic balance less than those involving autosomes. This may be because the Y chromosome carries relatively few genes. Also, extra copies of the X chromosome simply become inactivated as Barr bodies.

An extra X chromosome in a male, producing XXY, occurs approximately once in every 500 to 1,000 live male births. People with this disorder, called *Klinefelter syndrome*, have male sex organs, but the testes are abnormally small and the man is sterile. Even though the extra X is inactivated, some breast enlargement and other female body characteristics are common. Affected individuals may have subnormal intelligence. About 1 of every 1,000 males is born with an extra Y chromosome (XYY). These males undergo normal sexual development and do not exhibit any well-defined syndrome, but tend to be taller than average.

Females with trisomy X (XXX), which occurs once in approximately 1,000 live female births, are healthy and have no unusual physical features other than being slightly taller than average. Triple-X females are at risk for learning disabilities but are fertile. Monosomy X, which is called *Turner syndrome*, occurs about once in every 2,500 female births and is the only known viable monosomy in humans. Although these X0 individuals are phenotypically female, they are sterile because their sex organs do not mature. When provided with estrogen replacement therapy, girls with Turner syndrome do develop secondary sex characteristics. Most have normal intelligence.

Disorders Caused by Structurally Altered Chromosomes

Many deletions in human chromosomes, even in a heterozygous state, cause severe problems. One such syndrome, known as *cri du chat* ("cry of the cat"), results from a specific deletion in chromosome 5. A child born with this deletion is severely intellectually disabled, has a small head with

▲ **Figure 15.16 Translocation associated with chronic myelogenous leukemia (CML).** The cancerous cells in nearly all CML patients contain an abnormally short chromosome 22, the so-called Philadelphia chromosome, and an abnormally long chromosome 9. These altered chromosomes result from the reciprocal translocation shown here, which presumably occurred in a single white blood cell precursor undergoing mitosis and was then passed along to all descendant cells.

unusual facial features, and has a cry that sounds like the mewing of a distressed cat. Such individuals usually die in infancy or early childhood.

Chromosomal translocations have been implicated in certain cancers, including *chronic myelogenous leukemia* (*CML*). This disease occurs when a reciprocal translocation happens during mitosis of cells that will become white blood cells. In these cells, the exchange of a large portion of chromosome 22 with a small fragment from a tip of chromosome 9 produces a much shortened, easily recognized chromosome 22, called the *Philadelphia chromosome* **(Figure 15.16)**. Such an exchange causes cancer by activating a gene that leads to uncontrolled cell cycle progression. (The mechanism of gene activation will be discussed in Chapter 18.)

CONCEPT CHECK 15.4

1. About 5% of individuals with Down syndrome have a chromosomal translocation in which a third copy of chromosome 21 is attached to chromosome 14. If this translocation occurred in a parent's gonad, how could it lead to Down syndrome in a child?

2. **WHAT IF?** The ABO blood type locus has been mapped on chromosome 9. A father who has type AB blood and a mother who has type O blood have a child with trisomy 9 and type A blood. Using this information, can you tell in which parent the nondisjunction occurred? Explain your answer. (See Figure 14.11.)

3. **MAKE CONNECTIONS** The gene that is activated on the Philadelphia chromosome codes for an intracellular tyrosine kinase. Review the discussion of cell cycle control in Concept 12.3, and explain how the activation of this gene could contribute to the development of cancer.

For suggested answers, see Appendix A.

CONCEPT 15.5

Some inheritance patterns are exceptions to standard Mendelian inheritance

In the previous section, you learned about deviations from the usual patterns of chromosomal inheritance due to abnormal events in meiosis and mitosis. We conclude this chapter by describing two normally occurring exceptions to Mendelian genetics, one involving genes located in the nucleus and the other involving genes located outside the nucleus. In both cases, the sex of the parent contributing an allele is a factor in the pattern of inheritance.

Genomic Imprinting

Throughout our discussions of Mendelian genetics and the chromosomal basis of inheritance, we have assumed that a given allele will have the same effect whether it was inherited from the mother or the father. This is probably a safe assumption most of the time. For example, when Mendel crossed purple-flowered pea plants with white-flowered pea plants, he observed the same results regardless of whether the purple-flowered parent supplied the eggs or the sperm. In recent years, however, geneticists have identified a number of traits in mammals that depend on which parent passed along the alleles for those traits. Such variation in phenotype depending on whether an allele is inherited from the male or female parent is called **genomic imprinting**. (Note that unlike sex-linked genes, most imprinted genes are on autosomes.) Using newer DNA sequence-based methods, over 60 imprinted genes have been identified, with hundreds more suspected.

Genomic imprinting occurs during gamete formation and results in the silencing of a particular allele of certain genes. Because these genes are imprinted differently in sperm and eggs, the offspring expresses only one allele of an imprinted gene, the one that has been inherited from either the female or the male parent. The imprints are then transmitted to all body cells during development. In each generation, the old imprints are "erased" in gamete-producing cells, and the chromosomes of the developing gametes are newly imprinted according to the sex of the individual forming the gametes. In a given species, the imprinted genes are always imprinted in the same way. For instance, a gene imprinted for maternal allele expression is always imprinted this way, generation after generation.

Consider, for example, the mouse gene for insulin-like growth factor 2 (*Igf2*), one of the first imprinted genes to be identified. Although this growth factor is required for normal prenatal growth, only the paternal allele is expressed **(Figure 15.17a)**. Evidence that the *Igf2* gene is imprinted

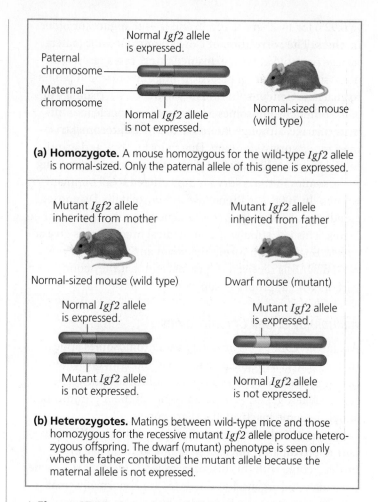

(a) Homozygote. A mouse homozygous for the wild-type *Igf2* allele is normal-sized. Only the paternal allele of this gene is expressed.

(b) Heterozygotes. Matings between wild-type mice and those homozygous for the recessive mutant *Igf2* allele produce heterozygous offspring. The dwarf (mutant) phenotype is seen only when the father contributed the mutant allele because the maternal allele is not expressed.

▲ **Figure 15.17** Genomic imprinting of the mouse *Igf2* gene.

came initially from crosses between normal-sized (wild-type) mice and dwarf (mutant) mice homozygous for a recessive mutation in the *Igf2* gene. The phenotypes of heterozygous offspring (with one normal allele and one mutant) differed depending on whether the mutant allele came from the mother or the father **(Figure 15.17b)**.

What exactly is a genomic imprint? In many cases, it seems to consist of methyl (—CH$_3$) groups that are added to cytosine nucleotides of one of the alleles. Such methylation may silence the allele, an effect consistent with evidence that heavily methylated genes are usually inactive (see Concept 18.2). However, for a few genes, methylation has been shown to *activate* expression of the allele. This is the case for the *Igf2* gene: Methylation of certain cytosines on the paternal chromosome leads to expression of the paternal *Igf2* allele, by an indirect mechanism involving chromatin condensation.

Genomic imprinting is thought to affect only a small fraction of the genes in mammalian genomes, but most of the known imprinted genes are critical for embryonic development. In experiments with mice, embryos engineered to inherit both copies of certain chromosomes from the same parent usually die before birth, whether that parent is male or female. A few years ago, however, scientists in Japan combined the genetic material from two eggs in a zygote while allowing expression of the *Igf2* gene from only one of the egg nuclei. The zygote developed into an apparently healthy mouse. Normal development seems to require that embryonic cells have exactly one active copy—not zero, not two—of certain genes. The association of improper imprinting with abnormal development and certain cancers has stimulated ongoing studies of how different genes are imprinted.

Inheritance of Organelle Genes

Although our focus in this chapter has been on the chromosomal basis of inheritance, we end with an important amendment: Not all of a eukaryotic cell's genes are located on nuclear chromosomes, or even in the nucleus; some genes are located in organelles in the cytoplasm. Because they are outside the nucleus, these genes are sometimes called *extranuclear genes* or *cytoplasmic genes*. Mitochondria, as well as chloroplasts and other plastids in plants, contain small circular DNA molecules that carry a number of genes. These organelles reproduce themselves and transmit their genes to daughter organelles. Organelle genes are not distributed to offspring according to the same rules that direct the distribution of nuclear chromosomes during meiosis, so they do not display Mendelian inheritance.

The first hint that extranuclear genes exist came from studies by the German scientist Carl Correns on the inheritance of yellow or white patches on the leaves of an otherwise green plant. In 1909, he observed that the coloration of the offspring was determined only by the maternal parent (the source of eggs) and not by the paternal parent (the source of sperm). Subsequent research showed that such coloration patterns, or variegation, are due to mutations in plastid genes that control pigmentation **(Figure 15.18)**. In most plants, a zygote receives all its plastids from the cytoplasm of the egg and none from the sperm, which contributes little more than a haploid set of chromosomes. An egg may contain plastids with different alleles for a pigmentation gene. As the zygote develops, plastids containing wild-type or mutant pigmentation genes are distributed randomly to

▼ **Figure 15.18 A painted nettle coleus plant.** The variegated (patterned) leaves on this coleus plant (*Solenostemon scutellarioides*) result from mutations that affect expression of pigment genes located in plastids, which generally are inherited from the maternal parent.

daughter cells. The pattern of leaf coloration exhibited by a plant depends on the ratio of wild-type to mutant plastids in its various tissues.

Similar maternal inheritance is also the rule for mitochondrial genes in most animals and plants, because almost all the mitochondria passed on to a zygote come from the cytoplasm of the egg. (The few mitochondria contributed by the sperm appear to be destroyed in the egg by autophagy; see Figure 6.13.) The products of most mitochondrial genes help make up the protein complexes of the electron transport chain and ATP synthase (see Figure 9.15). Defects in one or more of these proteins, therefore, reduce the amount of ATP the cell can make and have been shown to cause a number of rare human disorders. Because the parts of the body most susceptible to energy deprivation are the nervous system and the muscles, most mitochondrial diseases primarily affect these systems. For example, *mitochondrial myopathy* causes weakness, intolerance of exercise, and muscle deterioration. Another mitochondrial disorder is *Leber's hereditary optic neuropathy*, which can produce sudden blindness in people as young as their 20s or 30s. The four mutations found thus far to cause this disorder affect oxidative phosphorylation during cellular respiration, a crucial function for the cell (see Concept 9.4).

In addition to the rare diseases clearly caused by defects in mitochondrial DNA, mitochondrial mutations inherited from a person's mother may contribute to at least some types of diabetes and heart disease, as well as to other disorders that commonly debilitate the elderly, such as Alzheimer's disease. In the course of a lifetime, new mutations gradually accumulate in our mitochondrial DNA, and some researchers think that these mutations play a role in the normal aging process.

Wherever genes are located in the cell—in the nucleus or in cytoplasmic organelles—their inheritance depends on the precise replication of DNA. In the next chapter, you will learn how this molecular reproduction occurs.

CONCEPT CHECK 15.5

1. Gene dosage—the number of copies of a gene that are actively being expressed—is important to proper development. Identify and describe two processes that establish the proper dosage of certain genes.

2. Reciprocal crosses between two primrose varieties, A and B, produced the following results: A female × B male → offspring with all green (nonvariegated) leaves; B female × A male → offspring with patterned (variegated) leaves. Explain these results.

3. **WHAT IF?** Mitochondrial genes are critical to the energy metabolism of cells, but mitochondrial disorders caused by mutations in these genes are generally not lethal. Why not?

For suggested answers, see Appendix A.

SUMMARY OF KEY CONCEPTS

CONCEPT 15.1

Morgan showed that Mendelian inheritance has its physical basis in the behavior of chromosomes: *scientific inquiry* (pp. 294–295)

- Morgan's work with an eye color gene in *Drosophila* led to the **chromosome theory of inheritance**, which states that genes are located on chromosomes and that the behavior of chromosomes during meiosis accounts for Mendel's laws.

? *What characteristic of the sex chromosomes allowed Morgan to correlate their behavior with that of the alleles of the eye-color gene?*

CONCEPT 15.2

Sex-linked genes exhibit unique patterns of inheritance (pp. 296–298)

- Sex is often chromosomally based. Humans and other mammals have an X-Y system in which sex is determined by whether a Y chromosome is present. Other systems are found in birds, fishes, and insects.
- The sex chromosomes carry **sex-linked genes**, virtually all of which are on the X chromosome (X-linked). Any male who inherits a recessive X-linked allele (from his mother) will express the trait, such as color blindness.
- In mammalian females, one of the two X chromosomes in each cell is randomly inactivated during early embryonic development, becoming highly condensed into a **Barr body**.

? *Why are males affected much more often than females by X-linked disorders?*

CONCEPT 15.3

Linked genes tend to be inherited together because they are located near each other on the same chromosome (pp. 299–304)

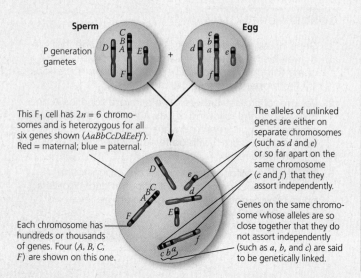

This F$_1$ cell has 2n = 6 chromosomes and is heterozygous for all six genes shown (*AaBbCcDdEeFf*). Red = maternal; blue = paternal.

Each chromosome has hundreds or thousands of genes. Four (*A, B, C, F*) are shown on this one.

The alleles of unlinked genes are either on separate chromosomes (such as *d* and *e*) or so far apart on the same chromosome (*c* and *f*) that they assort independently.

Genes on the same chromosome whose alleles are so close together that they do not assort independently (such as *a*, *b*, and *c*) are said to be genetically linked.

- Among offspring from an F$_1$ dihybrid testcross, **parental types** have the same combination of traits as those in the P generation parents. **Recombinant types** (**recombinants**) exhibit new combinations of traits not seen in either P generation parent. Because of the independent assortment of chromosomes, unlinked genes exhibit a 50% frequency of recombination in the gametes. For genetically **linked genes**, **crossing over** between nonsister chromatids during meiosis I accounts for the observed recombinants, always less than 50% of the total.
- The order of genes on a chromosome and the relative distances between them can be deduced from recombination frequencies observed in genetic crosses. These data allow construction of a **linkage map** (a type of **genetic map**). The farther apart genes are, the more likely their allele combinations will be recombined during crossing over.

? *Why are specific alleles of two distant genes more likely to show recombination than those of two closer genes?*

CONCEPT 15.4

Alterations of chromosome number or structure cause some genetic disorders (pp. 304–307)

- **Aneuploidy**, an abnormal chromosome number, can result from **nondisjunction** during meiosis. When a normal gamete unites with one containing two copies or no copies of a particular chromosome, the resulting zygote and its descendant cells either have one extra copy of that chromosome (**trisomy**, $2n + 1$) or are missing a copy (**monosomy**, $2n - 1$). **Polyploidy** (more than two complete sets of chromosomes) can result from complete nondisjunction during gamete formation.
- Chromosome breakage can result in alterations of chromosome structure: **deletions**, **duplications**, **inversions**, and **translocations**. Translocations can be reciprocal or nonreciprocal.
- Changes in the number of chromosomes per cell or in the structure of individual chromosomes can affect the phenotype and, in some cases, lead to disorders. Such alterations cause **Down syndrome** (usually due to trisomy of chromosome 21), certain cancers associated with chromosomal translocations, and various other human disorders.

? *Why are inversions and reciprocal translocations less likely to be lethal than are aneuploidy, duplications, deletions, and nonreciprocal translocations?*

CONCEPT 15.5

Some inheritance patterns are exceptions to standard Mendelian inheritance (pp. 308–309)

- In mammals, the phenotypic effects of a small number of particular genes depend on which allele is inherited from each parent, a phenomenon called **genomic imprinting**. Imprints are formed during gamete production, with the result that one allele (either maternal or paternal) is not expressed in offspring.
- The inheritance of traits controlled by the genes present in mitochondria and plastids depends solely on the maternal parent because the zygote's cytoplasm containing these organelles comes from the egg. Some diseases affecting the nervous and muscular systems are caused by defects in mitochondrial genes that prevent cells from making enough ATP.

? *Explain how genomic imprinting and inheritance of mitochondrial and chloroplast DNA are exceptions to standard Mendelian inheritance.*

LEVEL 1: KNOWLEDGE/COMPREHENSION

1. A man with hemophilia (a recessive, sex-linked condition) has a daughter of normal phenotype. She marries a man who is normal for the trait. What is the probability that a daughter of this mating will have hemophilia? That a son will have hemophilia? If the couple has four sons, what is the probability that all four will be born with hemophilia?

2. Pseudohypertrophic muscular dystrophy is an inherited disorder that causes gradual deterioration of the muscles. It is seen almost exclusively in boys born to apparently normal parents and usually results in death in the early teens. Is this disorder caused by a dominant or a recessive allele? Is its inheritance sex-linked or autosomal? How do you know? Explain why this disorder is almost never seen in girls.

3. A wild-type fruit fly (heterozygous for gray body color and normal wings) is mated with a black fly with vestigial wings. The offspring have the following phenotypic distribution: wild-type, 778; black-vestigial, 785; black-normal, 158; gray-vestigial, 162. What is the recombination frequency between these genes for body color and wing size? Is this consistent with the results of the experiment in Figure 15.9?

4. A planet is inhabited by creatures that reproduce with the same hereditary patterns seen in humans. Three phenotypic characters are height (T = tall, t = dwarf), head appendages (A = antennae, a = no antennae), and nose morphology (S = upturned snout, s = downturned snout). Since the creatures are not "intelligent," Earth scientists are able to do some controlled breeding experiments using various heterozygotes in testcrosses. For tall heterozygotes with antennae, the offspring are tall-antennae, 46; dwarf-antennae, 7; dwarf-no antennae, 42; tall-no antennae, 5. For heterozygotes with antennae and an upturned snout, the offspring are antennae-upturned snout, 47; antennae-downturned snout, 2; no antennae-downturned snout, 48; no antennae-upturned snout, 3. Calculate the recombination frequencies for both experiments.

LEVEL 2: APPLICATION/ANALYSIS

5. Using the information from problem 4, scientists do a further testcross using a heterozygote for height and nose morphology. The offspring are tall-upturned snout, 40; dwarf-upturned snout, 9; dwarf-downturned snout, 42; tall-downturned snout, 9. Calculate the recombination frequency from these data, and then use your answer from problem 4 to determine the correct order of the three linked genes.

6. A wild-type fruit fly (heterozygous for gray body color and red eyes) is mated with a black fruit fly with purple eyes. The offspring are wild-type, 721; black-purple, 751; gray-purple, 49; black-red, 45. What is the recombination frequency between these genes for body color and eye color? Using information from problem 3, what fruit flies (genotypes and phenotypes) would you mate to determine the order of the body-color, wing-size, and eye-color genes on the chromosome?

7. Assume that genes A and B are on the same chromosome and are 50 map units apart. An animal heterozygous at both loci is crossed with one that is homozygous recessive at both loci. What percentage of the offspring will show recombinant phenotypes resulting from crossovers? Without knowing these genes are on the same chromosome, how would you interpret the results of this cross?

8. Two genes of a flower, one controlling blue (B) versus white (b) petals and the other controlling round (R) versus oval (r) stamens, are linked and are 10 map units apart. You cross a homozygous blue-oval plant with a homozygous white-round plant. The resulting F_1 progeny are crossed with homozygous white-oval plants, and 1,000 F_2 progeny are obtained. How many F_2 plants of each of the four phenotypes do you expect?

9. You design *Drosophila* crosses to provide recombination data for gene *a*, which is located on the chromosome shown in Figure 15.12. Gene *a* has recombination frequencies of 14% with the vestigial-wing locus and 26% with the brown-eye locus. Approximately where is *a* located along the chromosome?

LEVEL 3: SYNTHESIS/EVALUATION

10. Banana plants, which are triploid, are seedless and therefore sterile. Propose a possible explanation.

11. **EVOLUTION CONNECTION**
Crossing over is thought to be evolutionarily advantageous because it continually shuffles genetic alleles into novel combinations. Until recently, it was thought that the genes on the Y chromosome might degenerate because they lack homologous genes on the X chromosome with which to pair up prior to crossing over. However, when the Y chromosome was sequenced, eight large regions were found to be internally homologous to each other, and quite a few of the 78 genes represent duplicates. (Y chromosome researcher David Page has called it a "hall of mirrors.") What might be a benefit of these regions?

12. **SCIENTIFIC INQUIRY**
DRAW IT Assume you are mapping genes A, B, C, and D in *Drosophila*. You know that these genes are linked on the same chromosome, and you determine the recombination frequencies between each pair of genes to be as follows: A–B, 8%; A–C, 28%; A–D, 25%; B–C, 20%; B–D, 33%.
(a) Describe how you determined the recombination frequencies for each pair of genes.
(b) Draw a chromosome map based on your data.

13. **WRITE ABOUT A THEME: INFORMATION**
The continuity of life is based on heritable information in the form of DNA. In a short essay (100–150 words), relate the structure and behavior of chromosomes to inheritance in both asexually and sexually reproducing species.

14. **SYNTHESIZE YOUR KNOWLEDGE**

Butterflies have an X-Y sex determination system that is different from that of flies or humans. Female butterflies may be either XY or XO, while butterflies with two or more X chromosomes are males. This photograph shows a tiger swallowtail *gynandromorph*, which is half male (left side) and half female (right side). Given that the first division of the zygote divides the embryo into the future right and left halves of the butterfly, propose a hypothesis that explains how nondisjunction during the first mitosis might have produced this unusual-looking butterfly.

For selected answers, see Appendix A.

MasteringBiology®

Students Go to **MasteringBiology** for assignments, the eText, and the Study Area with practice tests, animations, and activities.

Instructors Go to **MasteringBiology** for automatically graded tutorials and questions that you can assign to your students, plus Instructor Resources.

16

The Molecular Basis of Inheritance

▲ **Figure 16.1** **What is the structure of DNA?**

KEY CONCEPTS

16.1 DNA is the genetic material

16.2 Many proteins work together in DNA replication and repair

16.3 A chromosome consists of a DNA molecule packed together with proteins

▲ James Watson (left) and Francis Crick with their DNA model.

Life's Operating Instructions

In April 1953, James Watson and Francis Crick shook the scientific world by proposing an elegant double-helical model for the structure of deoxyribonucleic acid, or DNA **(Figure 16.1).** The photo at the lower left shows the DNA model they constructed from sheet metal and wire. Over the past 60 years, their model has become an icon of modern biology. Gregor Mendel's heritable factors and Thomas Hunt Morgan's genes on chromosomes are, in fact, composed of DNA. Chemically speaking, your genetic endowment is the DNA you inherited from your parents. DNA, the substance of inheritance, is the most celebrated molecule of our time.

Of all nature's molecules, nucleic acids are unique in their ability to direct their own replication from monomers. Indeed, the resemblance of offspring to their parents has its basis in the accurate replication of DNA and its transmission from one generation to the next. Hereditary information in DNA directs the development of your biochemical, anatomical, physiological, and, to some extent, behavioral traits. In this chapter, you will discover how biologists deduced that DNA is the genetic material and how Watson and Crick worked out its structure. You will also learn how a molecule of DNA is copied during **DNA replication** and how cells repair their DNA. Finally, you will explore how a molecule of DNA is packaged together with proteins in a chromosome.

CONCEPT 16.1

DNA is the genetic material

Today, even schoolchildren have heard of DNA, and scientists routinely manipulate DNA in the laboratory, often to change the heritable traits of cells in their experiments. Early in the 20th century, however, identifying the molecules of inheritance loomed as a major challenge to biologists.

The Search for the Genetic Material: *Scientific Inquiry*

Once T. H. Morgan's group showed that genes exist as parts of chromosomes (described in Chapter 15), the two chemical components of chromosomes—DNA and protein—emerged as the leading candidates for the genetic material. Until the 1940s, the case for proteins seemed stronger: Biochemists had identified proteins as a class of macromolecules with great heterogeneity and specificity of function, essential requirements for the hereditary material. Moreover, little was known about nucleic acids, whose physical and chemical properties seemed far too uniform to account for the multitude of specific inherited traits exhibited by every organism. This view gradually changed as the role of DNA in heredity was worked out in studies of bacteria and the viruses that infect them, systems far simpler than fruit flies or humans. Let's trace the search for the genetic material as a case study in scientific inquiry.

Evidence That DNA Can Transform Bacteria

In 1928, a British medical officer named Frederick Griffith was trying to develop a vaccine against pneumonia. He was studying *Streptococcus pneumoniae*, a bacterium that causes pneumonia in mammals. Griffith had two strains (varieties) of the bacterium, one pathogenic (disease-causing) and one nonpathogenic (harmless). He was surprised to find that when he killed the pathogenic bacteria with heat and then mixed the cell remains with living bacteria of the nonpathogenic strain, some of the living cells became pathogenic **(Figure 16.2)**. Furthermore, this newly acquired trait of pathogenicity was inherited by all the descendants of the transformed bacteria. Apparently, some chemical component of the dead pathogenic cells caused this heritable change, although the identity of the substance was not known. Griffith called the phenomenon **transformation**, now defined as a change in genotype and phenotype due to the assimilation of external DNA by a cell. Later work by Oswald Avery, Maclyn McCarty, and Colin MacLeod identified the transforming substance as DNA.

Scientists remained skeptical, however, many still viewing proteins as better candidates for the genetic material. Also, many biologists were not convinced that bacterial genes would be similar in composition and function to those of

▼ **Figure 16.2** **Inquiry**

Can a genetic trait be transferred between different bacterial strains?

Experiment Frederick Griffith studied two strains of the bacterium *Streptococcus pneumoniae*. The S (smooth) strain can cause pneumonia in mice; it is pathogenic because the cells have an outer capsule that protects them from an animal's immune system. Cells of the R (rough) strain lack a capsule and are nonpathogenic. To test for the trait of pathogenicity, Griffith injected mice with the two strains:

Living S cells (pathogenic control) | Living R cells (nonpathogenic control) | Heat-killed S cells (nonpathogenic control) | Mixture of heat-killed S cells and living R cells

Results

Mouse dies | **Mouse healthy** | **Mouse healthy** | **Mouse dies**

In blood sample, living S cells were found. They could reproduce, yielding more S cells.

Conclusion The living R bacteria had been transformed into pathogenic S bacteria by an unknown, heritable substance from the dead S cells that enabled the R cells to make capsules.

Source: F. Griffith, The significance of pneumococcal types, *Journal of Hygiene* 27:113–159 (1928).

WHAT IF? *How did this experiment rule out the possibility that the R cells simply used the dead S cells' capsules to become pathogenic?*

more complex organisms. But the major reason for the continued doubt was that so little was known about DNA.

Evidence That Viral DNA Can Program Cells

Additional evidence that DNA was the genetic material came from studies of viruses that infect bacteria **(Figure 16.3)**. These viruses are called **bacteriophages** (meaning "bacteria-eaters"), or **phages** for short. Viruses are much simpler than

▶ **Figure 16.3** **A virus infecting a bacterial cell.** A phage called T2 attaches to a host cell and injects its genetic material through the plasma membrane, while the head and tail parts remain on the outer bacterial surface (colorized TEM).

Phage head — DNA — Tail sheath — Tail fiber — Genetic material — Bacterial cell

100 nm

cells. A **virus** is little more than DNA (or sometimes RNA) enclosed by a protective coat, which is often simply protein. To produce more viruses, a virus must infect a cell and take over the cell's metabolic machinery.

Phages have been widely used as tools by researchers in molecular genetics. In 1952, Alfred Hershey and Martha Chase performed experiments showing that DNA is the genetic material of a phage known as T2. This is one of many phages that infect *Escherichia coli* (*E. coli*), a bacterium that normally lives in the intestines of mammals and is a model organism for molecular biologists. At that time,

biologists already knew that T2, like many other phages, was composed almost entirely of DNA and protein. They also knew that the T2 phage could quickly turn an *E. coli* cell into a T2-producing factory that released many copies of new phages when the cell ruptured. Somehow, T2 could reprogram its host cell to produce viruses. But which viral component—protein or DNA—was responsible?

Hershey and Chase answered this question by devising an experiment showing that only one of the two components of T2 actually enters the *E. coli* cell during infection **(Figure 16.4)**. In their experiment, they used a radioactive

---

▼ **Figure 16.4**   Inquiry

Is protein or DNA the genetic material of phage T2?

Experiment Alfred Hershey and Martha Chase used radioactive sulfur and phosphorus to trace the fates of protein and DNA, respectively, of T2 phages that infected bacterial cells. They wanted to see which of these molecules entered the cells and could reprogram them to make more phages.

Results When proteins were labeled (batch 1), radioactivity remained outside the cells, but when DNA was labeled (batch 2), radioactivity was found inside the cells. Bacterial cells containing radioactive phage DNA released new phages with some radioactive phosphorus.

Conclusion Phage DNA entered bacterial cells, but phage proteins did not. Hershey and Chase concluded that DNA, not protein, functions as the genetic material of phage T2.

Source: A. D. Hershey and M. Chase, Independent functions of viral protein and nucleic acid in growth of bacteriophage, *Journal of General Physiology* 36:39–56 (1952).

WHAT IF? *How would the results have differed if proteins carried the genetic information?*

---

isotope of sulfur to tag protein in one batch of T2 and a radioactive isotope of phosphorus to tag DNA in a second batch. Because protein, but not DNA, contains sulfur, radioactive sulfur atoms were incorporated only into the protein of the phage. In a similar way, the atoms of radioactive phosphorus labeled only the DNA, not the protein, because nearly all the phage's phosphorus is in its DNA. In the experiment, separate samples of nonradioactive *E. coli* cells were infected with the protein-labeled and DNA-labeled batches of T2. The researchers then tested the two samples shortly after the onset of infection to see which type of molecule—protein or DNA—had entered the bacterial cells and would therefore be capable of reprogramming them.

Hershey and Chase found that the phage DNA entered the host cells but the phage protein did not. Moreover, when these bacteria were returned to a culture medium, and the infection ran its course, the *E. coli* released phages that contained some radioactive phosphorus. This result further showed that the DNA inside the cell played an ongoing role during the infection process.

Hershey and Chase concluded that the DNA injected by the phage must be the molecule carrying the genetic information that makes the cells produce new viral DNA and proteins. The Hershey-Chase experiment was a landmark study because it provided powerful evidence that nucleic acids, rather than proteins, are the hereditary material, at least for certain viruses.

Additional Evidence That DNA Is the Genetic Material

Further evidence that DNA is the genetic material came from the laboratory of biochemist Erwin Chargaff. It was already known that DNA is a polymer of nucleotides, each consisting of three components: a nitrogenous (nitrogen-containing) base, a pentose sugar called deoxyribose, and a phosphate group (**Figure 16.5**). The base can be adenine (A), thymine (T), guanine (G), or cytosine (C). Chargaff analyzed the base composition of DNA from a number of different organisms. In 1950, he reported that the base composition of DNA varies from one species to another. For example, he found that 32.8% of sea urchin DNA nucleotides have the base A, whereas only 30.4% of human DNA nucleotides have the base A and only 24.7% of the DNA nucleotides from the bacterium *E. coli* have the base A. Chargaff's evidence of molecular diversity among species, which most scientists had presumed to be absent from DNA, made DNA a more credible candidate for the genetic material.

Chargaff also noticed a peculiar regularity in the ratios of nucleotide bases. In the DNA of each species he studied, the number of adenines approximately equaled the number

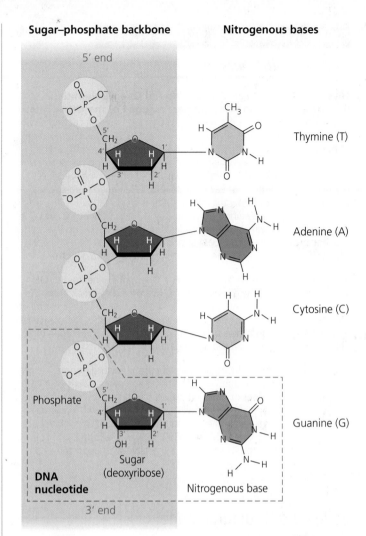

Sugar–phosphate backbone **Nitrogenous bases**

5′ end

Thymine (T)

Adenine (A)

Cytosine (C)

Phosphate

Guanine (G)

DNA nucleotide

Sugar (deoxyribose)

Nitrogenous base

3′ end

▲ **Figure 16.5 The structure of a DNA strand.** Each of the four DNA nucleotide monomers consists of a nitrogenous base (T, A, C, or G), the sugar deoxyribose (blue), and a phosphate group (yellow). The phosphate group of one nucleotide is attached to the sugar of the next, forming a "backbone" of alternating phosphates and sugars from which the bases project. The polynucleotide strand has directionality, from the 5′ end (with the phosphate group) to the 3′ end (with the —OH group of the sugar). 5′ and 3′ refer to the numbers assigned to the carbons in the sugar ring.

of thymines, and the number of guanines approximately equaled the number of cytosines. In sea urchin DNA, for example, Chargaff's analysis found the four bases in these percentages: A = 32.8% and T = 32.1%; G = 17.7% and C = 17.3%. (The percentages are not exactly the same because of limitations in Chargaff's techniques.)

These two findings became known as *Chargaff's rules*: (1) the base composition v of DNA aries between species, and (2) for each species, the percentages of A and T bases are roughly equal and the percentages of G and C bases are roughly equal. In the **Scientific Skills Exercise,** you can use Chargaff's rules to predict unknown percentages of nucleotide bases. The basis for these rules remained unexplained until the discovery of the double helix.

Working with Data in a Table

Given the Percentage Composition of One Nucleotide in a Genome, Can We Predict the Percentages of the Other Three Nucleotides? Even before the structure of DNA was elucidated, Erwin Chargaff and his coworkers noticed a pattern in the base composition of nucleotides from different organisms: The percentage of adenine (A) bases roughly equaled that of thymine (T) bases, and the percentage of cytosine (C) bases roughly equaled that of guanine (G) bases. Further, the percentage of each pair (A/T or C/G) varied from species to species. We now know that the 1:1 A/T and C/G ratios are due to complementary base pairing between A and T and between C and G in the DNA double helix, and interspecies differences are due to the unique sequences of bases along a DNA strand. In this exercise, you will apply Chargaff's rules to predict the composition of bases in a genome.

How the Experiments Were Done In Chargaff's experiments, DNA was extracted from the given organism, hydrolyzed to break apart the individual nucleotides, and then analyzed chemically. (These experiments provided approximate values for each type of nucleotide. Today, whole-genome sequencing allows base composition analysis to be done more precisely directly from the sequence data.)

Data from the Experiments Tables are useful for organizing sets of data representing a common set of values (here, percentages of A, G, C, and T) for a number of different samples (in this case, from different species). You can apply the patterns that you see in the known data to predict unknown values. In the table at the upper right, complete base distribution data are given for sea urchin DNA and salmon DNA; you will use Chargaff's rules to fill in the rest of the table with predicted values.

Source of DNA	Base Percentage			
	Adenine	Guanine	Cytosine	Thymine
Sea urchin	32.8	17.7	17.3	32.1
Salmon	29.7	20.8	20.4	29.1
Wheat	28.1	21.8	22.7	
E. coli	24.7	26.0		
Human	30.4			30.1
Ox	29.0			

Interpret the Data

1. Explain how the sea urchin and salmon data demonstrate both of Chargaff's rules.

2. Using Chargaff's rules, fill in the table with your predictions of the missing percentages of bases, starting with the wheat genome and proceeding through *E. coli*, human, and ox. Show how you arrived at your answers.

3. If Chargaff's rule—that the amount of A equals the amount of T and the amount of C equals the amount of G—is valid, then hypothetically we could extrapolate this to the combined DNA of all species on Earth (like one huge Earth genome). To see whether the data in the table support this hypothesis, calculate the average percentage for each base in your completed table by averaging the values in each column. Does Chargaff's equivalence rule still hold true?

(MB) A version of this Scientific Skills Exercise can be assigned in MasteringBiology.

Data from several papers by Chargaff: for example, E. Chargaff et al., Composition of the desoxypentose nucleic acids of four genera of sea-urchin, *Journal of Biological Chemistry* 195:155–160 (1952).

Building a Structural Model of DNA: *Scientific Inquiry*

Once most biologists were convinced that DNA was the genetic material, the challenge was to determine how the structure of DNA could account for its role in inheritance. By the early 1950s, the arrangement of covalent bonds in a nucleic acid polymer was well established (see Figure 16.5), and researchers focused on discovering the three-dimensional structure of DNA. Among the scientists working on the problem were Linus Pauling, at the California Institute of Technology, and Maurice Wilkins and Rosalind Franklin, at King's College in London. First to come up with the correct answer, however, were two scientists who were relatively unknown at the time—the American James Watson and the Englishman Francis Crick.

The brief but celebrated partnership that solved the puzzle of DNA structure began soon after Watson journeyed to Cambridge University, where Crick was studying protein structure with a technique called X-ray crystallography (see Figure 5.22). While visiting the laboratory of Maurice Wilkins, Watson saw an X-ray diffraction image of DNA produced by Wilkins's accomplished colleague Rosalind Franklin **(Figure 16.6a)**. Images produced by X-ray crystallography are not actually pictures of molecules. The spots and smudges in **Figure 16.6b** were produced by X-rays that were diffracted (deflected) as they passed through aligned fibers of purified DNA. Watson was familiar with the type of X-ray diffraction pattern that helical molecules produce, and an examination of the photo that Wilkins showed him confirmed that DNA was helical in shape. It also augmented earlier data obtained by Franklin and others suggesting the

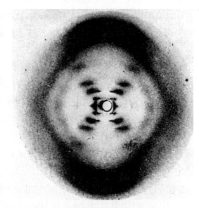

(a) Rosalind Franklin **(b) Franklin's X-ray diffraction photograph of DNA**

▲ **Figure 16.6 Rosalind Franklin and her X-ray diffraction photo of DNA.** Franklin, a very accomplished X-ray crystallographer, conducted critical experiments resulting in the photo that allowed Watson and Crick to deduce the double-helical structure of DNA.

width of the helix and the spacing of the nitrogenous bases along it. The pattern in this photo implied that the helix was made up of two strands, contrary to a three-stranded model that Linus Pauling had proposed a short time earlier. The presence of two strands accounts for the now-familiar term **double helix (Figure 16.7)**.

Watson and Crick began building models of a double helix that would conform to the X-ray measurements and what was then known about the chemistry of DNA, including Chargaff's rule of base equivalences. Having also read an unpublished annual report summarizing Franklin's work, they knew she had concluded that the sugar-phosphate backbones were on the outside of the DNA molecule, contrary to their working model. Franklin's arrangement was appealing because it put the relatively hydrophobic nitrogenous bases in the molecule's interior, away from the surrounding aqueous solution, and the negatively charged phosphate groups wouldn't be forced together in the interior. Watson constructed such a model, shown in the lower photo on the first page of this chapter.

In this model, the two sugar-phosphate backbones are **antiparallel**—that is, their subunits run in opposite directions (see Figure 16.7b). You can imagine the overall arrangement as a rope ladder with rigid rungs. The side ropes represent the sugar-phosphate backbones, and the rungs represent pairs of nitrogenous bases. Now imagine twisting the ladder to form a helix. Franklin's X-ray data indicated that the helix makes one full turn every 3.4 nm along its length. With the bases stacked just 0.34 nm apart, there are ten layers of base pairs, or rungs of the ladder, in each full turn of the helix.

The nitrogenous bases of the double helix are paired in specific combinations: adenine (A) with thymine (T), and guanine (G) with cytosine (C). It was mainly by trial and error that Watson and Crick arrived at this key feature of DNA. At first, Watson imagined that the bases paired like with like—for example, A with A and C with C. But this model did not fit the X-ray data, which suggested that the double helix had a uniform diameter. Why is this requirement inconsistent with like-with-like pairing of bases? Adenine and guanine are purines, nitrogenous bases with two organic rings, while cytosine and thymine are nitrogenous bases called pyrimidines, which have a single ring. Thus, purines (A and G) are about twice as wide as pyrimidines (C and T). A purine-purine pair is too wide and a pyrimidine-pyrimidine pair too narrow to account for the 2-nm

(a) Key features of DNA structure. The "ribbons" in this diagram represent the sugar-phosphate backbones of the two DNA strands. The helix is "right-handed," curving up to the right. The two strands are held together by hydrogen bonds (dotted lines) between the nitrogenous bases, which are paired in the interior of the double helix.

(b) Partial chemical structure. For clarity, the two DNA strands are shown untwisted in this partial chemical structure. Strong covalent bonds link the units of each strand, while weaker hydrogen bonds between the bases hold one strand to the other. Notice that the strands are antiparallel, meaning that they are oriented in opposite directions, like the lanes of a divided highway.

(c) Space-filling model. The tight stacking of the base pairs is clear in this computer-generated, space-filling model. Van der Waals interactions between the stacked pairs play a major role in holding the molecule together.

▲ **Figure 16.7 The structure of the double helix.**

diameter of the double helix. Always pairing a purine with a pyrimidine, however, results in a uniform diameter:

Purine + purine: too wide

Pyrimidine + pyrimidine: too narrow

Purine + pyrimidine: width consistent with X-ray data

Watson and Crick reasoned that there must be additional specificity of pairing dictated by the structure of the bases. Each base has chemical side groups that can form hydrogen bonds with its appropriate partner: Adenine can form two hydrogen bonds with thymine and only thymine; guanine forms three hydrogen bonds with cytosine and only cytosine. In shorthand, A pairs with T, and G pairs with C (Figure 16.8).

The Watson-Crick model took into account Chargaff's ratios and ultimately explained them. Wherever one strand of a DNA molecule has an A, the partner strand has a T. Similarly, a G in one strand is always paired with a C in the complementary strand. Therefore, in the DNA of any organism, the amount of adenine equals the amount of thymine, and the amount of guanine equals the amount of cytosine. (Modern DNA sequencing techniques have confirmed that the amounts are exactly equal.) Although the base-pairing rules dictate the combinations of nitrogenous bases that form the "rungs" of the double helix, they do not restrict the sequence of nucleotides *along* each DNA strand. The linear sequence of the four bases can be varied in countless ways, and each gene has a unique base sequence.

Adenine (A)   **Thymine (T)**

Guanine (G)   **Cytosine (C)**

▲ **Figure 16.8 Base pairing in DNA.** The pairs of nitrogenous bases in a DNA double helix are held together by hydrogen bonds, shown here as black dotted lines.

In April 1953, Watson and Crick surprised the scientific world with a succinct, one-page paper that reported their molecular model for DNA: the double helix, which has since become the symbol of molecular biology. Watson and Crick, along with Maurice Wilkins, were awarded the Nobel Prize in 1962 for this work. (Sadly, Rosalind Franklin had died at the age of 38 in 1958 and was thus ineligible for the prize.) The beauty of the double helix model was that the structure of DNA suggested the basic mechanism of its replication.

CONCEPT CHECK 16.1

1. Given a polynucleotide sequence such as GAATTC, can you tell which is the 5′ end? If not, what further information do you need to identify the ends? (See Figure 16.5.)

2. **WHAT IF?** Griffith did not expect transformation to occur in his experiment. What results was he expecting? Explain.

For suggested answers, see Appendix A.

CONCEPT 16.2

Many proteins work together in DNA replication and repair

The relationship between structure and function is manifest in the double helix. The idea that there is specific pairing of nitrogenous bases in DNA was the flash of inspiration that led Watson and Crick to the double helix. At the same time, they saw the functional significance of the base-pairing rules. They ended their classic paper with this wry statement: "It has not escaped our notice that the specific pairing we have postulated immediately suggests a possible copying mechanism for the genetic material."* In this section, you will learn about the basic principle of DNA replication, as well as some important details of the process.

The Basic Principle: Base Pairing to a Template Strand

In a second paper, Watson and Crick stated their hypothesis for how DNA replicates:

> Now our model for deoxyribonucleic acid is, in effect, a pair of templates, each of which is complementary to the other. We imagine that prior to duplication the hydrogen bonds are broken, and the two chains unwind and separate. Each chain then acts as a template for the formation on to itself of a new companion chain, so that eventually we shall have two pairs of chains, where we only had one before. Moreover, the sequence of the pairs of bases will have been duplicated exactly.†

*J. D. Watson and F. H. C. Crick, Molecular structure of nucleic acids: a structure for deoxyribose nucleic acids, *Nature* 171:737–738 (1953).

†J. D. Watson and F. H. C. Crick, Genetical implications of the structure of deoxyribonucleic acid, *Nature* 171:964–967 (1953).

(a) The parental molecule has two complementary strands of DNA. Each base is paired by hydrogen bonding with its specific partner, A with T and G with C.

(b) First, the two DNA strands are separated. Each parental strand can now serve as a template for a new, complementary strand.

(c) Nucleotides complementary to the parental (dark blue) strand are connected to form the sugar-phosphate backbones of the new "daughter" (light blue) strands.

▲ **Figure 16.9 A model for DNA replication: the basic concept.** In this simplified illustration, a short segment of DNA has been untwisted. Simple shapes symbolize the four kinds of bases. Dark blue represents DNA strands present in the parental molecule; light blue represents newly synthesized DNA.

Figure 16.9 illustrates Watson and Crick's basic idea. To make it easier to follow, we show only a short section of double helix in untwisted form. Notice that if you cover one of the two DNA strands of Figure 16.9a, you can still determine its linear sequence of nucleotides by referring to the uncovered strand and applying the base-pairing rules. The two strands are complementary; each stores the information necessary to reconstruct the other. When a cell copies a DNA molecule, each strand serves as a template for ordering nucleotides into a new, complementary strand. Nucleotides line up along the template strand according to the base-pairing rules and are linked to form the new strands. Where there was one double-stranded DNA molecule at the beginning of the process, there are soon two, each an exact replica of the "parental" molecule. The copying mechanism is analogous to using a photographic negative to make a positive image, which can in turn be used to make another negative, and so on.

This model of DNA replication remained untested for several years following publication of the DNA structure. The requisite experiments were simple in concept but difficult to perform. Watson and Crick's model predicts that when a double helix replicates, each of the two daughter molecules will have one old strand, from the parental molecule, and one newly made strand. This **semiconservative model** can be distinguished from a conservative model of replication, in which the two parental strands somehow come back together after the process (that is, the parental molecule is conserved). In yet a third model, called the dispersive model, all four strands of DNA following replication have a mixture of old and new DNA. These three models are shown in **Figure 16.10**. Although mechanisms for conservative or dispersive DNA replication are not easy to devise, these models remained possibilities until they could be

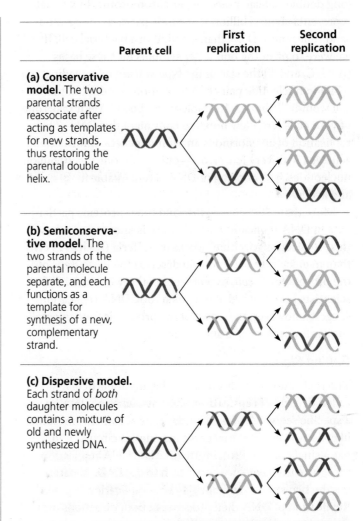

| Parent cell | First replication | Second replication |

(a) Conservative model. The two parental strands reassociate after acting as templates for new strands, thus restoring the parental double helix.

(b) Semiconservative model. The two strands of the parental molecule separate, and each functions as a template for synthesis of a new, complementary strand.

(c) Dispersive model. Each strand of *both* daughter molecules contains a mixture of old and newly synthesized DNA.

▲ **Figure 16.10 Three alternative models of DNA replication.** Each short segment of double helix symbolizes the DNA within a cell. Beginning with a parent cell, we follow the DNA for two more generations of cells—two rounds of DNA replication. Parental DNA is dark blue; newly made DNA is light blue.

ruled out. After two years of preliminary work at the California Institute of Technology in the late 1950s, Matthew Meselson and Franklin Stahl devised a clever experiment that distinguished between the three models, described in **Figure 16.11**. The results of their experiment supported the semiconservative model of DNA replication, as predicted by Watson and Crick, and is widely acknowledged among biologists to be a classic example of elegant experimental design.

The basic principle of DNA replication is conceptually simple. However, the actual process involves some complicated biochemical gymnastics, as we will now see.

DNA Replication: *A Closer Look*

The bacterium *E. coli* has a single chromosome of about 4.6 million nucleotide pairs. In a favorable environment, an *E. coli* cell can copy all this DNA and divide to form two genetically identical daughter cells in less than an hour. Each of *your* cells has 46 DNA molecules in its nucleus, one long double-helical molecule per chromosome. In all, that represents about 6 billion nucleotide pairs, or over a thousand times more DNA than is found in a bacterial cell. If we were to print the one-letter symbols for these bases (A, G, C, and T) the size of the type you are now reading, the 6 billion nucleotide pairs of information in a diploid human cell would fill about 1,400 biology textbooks. Yet it takes one of your cells just a few hours to copy all of this DNA. This replication of an enormous amount of genetic information is achieved with very few errors—only about one per 10 billion nucleotides. The copying of DNA is remarkable in its speed and accuracy.

More than a dozen enzymes and other proteins participate in DNA replication. Much more is known about how this "replication machine" works in bacteria (such as *E. coli*) than in eukaryotes, and we will describe the basic steps of the process for *E. coli*, except where otherwise noted. What scientists have learned about eukaryotic DNA replication suggests, however, that most of the process is fundamentally similar for prokaryotes and eukaryotes.

Getting Started

The replication of a chromosome begins at particular sites called **origins of replication**, short stretches of DNA having a specific sequence of nucleotides. The *E. coli* chromosome, like many other bacterial chromosomes, is circular and has a single origin. Proteins that initiate DNA replication recognize this sequence and attach to the DNA, separating the two strands and opening up a replication "bubble." Replication of DNA then proceeds in both directions until the entire molecule is copied (**Figure 16.12a**). In contrast to a bacterial chromosome, a eukaryotic chromosome may have hundreds or even a few thousand replication origins. Multiple replication bubbles form and eventually fuse, thus speeding up the copying of the very long DNA molecules

▼ Figure 16.11 | Inquiry

Does DNA replication follow the conservative, semiconservative, or dispersive model?

Experiment Matthew Meselson and Franklin Stahl cultured *E. coli* for several generations in a medium containing nucleotide precursors labeled with a heavy isotope of nitrogen, ^{15}N. They then transferred the bacteria to a medium with only ^{14}N, a lighter isotope. A sample was taken after the first DNA replication; another sample was taken after the second replication. They extracted DNA from the bacteria in the samples and then centrifuged each DNA sample to separate DNA of different densities.

1 Bacteria cultured in medium with ^{15}N (heavy isotope)

2 Bacteria transferred to medium with ^{14}N (lighter isotope)

Results

3 DNA sample centrifuged after first replication

4 DNA sample centrifuged after second replication

Less dense

More dense

Conclusion Meselson and Stahl compared their results to those predicted by each of the three models in Figure 16.10, as shown below. The first replication in the ^{14}N medium produced a band of hybrid (^{15}N-^{14}N) DNA. This result eliminated the conservative model. The second replication produced both light and hybrid DNA, a result that refuted the dispersive model and supported the semiconservative model. They therefore concluded that DNA replication is semiconservative.

Predictions:	First replication	Second replication
Conservative model		
Semiconservative model		
Dispersive model		

Source: M. Meselson and F. W. Stahl, The replication of DNA in *Escherichia coli*, *Proceedings of the National Academy of Sciences USA* 44:671–682 (1958).

Inquiry in Action Read and analyze the original paper in *Inquiry in Action: Interpreting Scientific Papers.*

(MB) A related Experimental Inquiry Tutorial can be assigned in MasteringBiology.

WHAT IF? *If Meselson and Stahl had first grown the cells in ^{14}N-containing medium and then moved them into ^{15}N-containing medium before taking samples, what would have been the result?*

Origin of replication

Parental (template) strand

Daughter (new) strand

Bacterial chromosome

Double-stranded DNA molecule

Replication bubble

Replication fork

Two daughter DNA molecules

0.5 μm

(a) Origin of replication in an *E. coli* cell. In the circular chromosome of *E. coli* and many other bacteria, only one origin of replication is present. The parental strands separate at the origin, forming a replication bubble with two forks (red arrows). Replication proceeds in both directions until the forks meet on the other side, resulting in two daughter DNA molecules. The TEM shows a bacterial chromosome with a large replication bubble. New and old strands cannot be seen individually in the TEM.

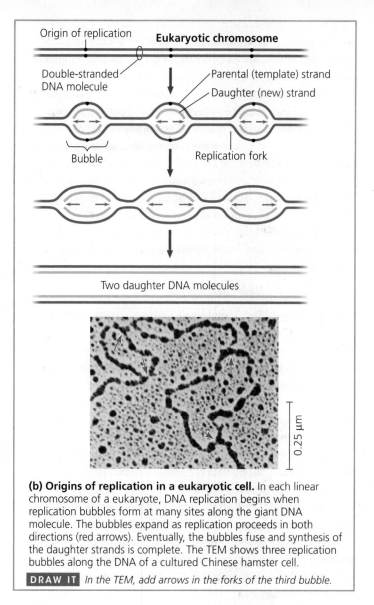

Origin of replication

Eukaryotic chromosome

Double-stranded DNA molecule

Parental (template) strand

Daughter (new) strand

Bubble

Replication fork

Two daughter DNA molecules

0.25 μm

(b) Origins of replication in a eukaryotic cell. In each linear chromosome of a eukaryote, DNA replication begins when replication bubbles form at many sites along the giant DNA molecule. The bubbles expand as replication proceeds in both directions (red arrows). Eventually, the bubbles fuse and synthesis of the daughter strands is complete. The TEM shows three replication bubbles along the DNA of a cultured Chinese hamster cell.

DRAW IT *In the TEM, add arrows in the forks of the third bubble.*

▲ **Figure 16.12 Origins of replication in *E. coli* and eukaryotes.** The red arrows indicate the movement of the replication forks and thus the overall directions of DNA replication within each bubble.

(Figure 16.12b). As in bacteria, eukaryotic DNA replication proceeds in both directions from each origin.

At each end of a replication bubble is a **replication fork**, a Y-shaped region where the parental strands of DNA are being unwound. Several kinds of proteins participate in the unwinding **(Figure 16.13)**. **Helicases** are enzymes that untwist the double helix at the replication forks, separating the two parental strands and making them available as template strands. After the parental strands separate, **single-strand binding proteins** bind to the unpaired DNA strands, keeping them from re-pairing. The untwisting of the double helix causes tighter twisting and strain ahead of the replication fork. **Topoisomerase** helps relieve this strain by breaking, swiveling, and rejoining DNA strands.

The unwound sections of parental DNA strands are now available to serve as templates for the synthesis of new

Topoisomerase breaks, swivels, and rejoins the parental DNA ahead of the replication fork, relieving the strain caused by unwinding.

Primase synthesizes RNA primers, using the parental DNA as a template.

3'

RNA primer

3'

5'

5'

3'

Replication fork

Helicase unwinds and separates the parental DNA strands.

Single-strand binding proteins stabilize the unwound parental strands.

5'

▲ **Figure 16.13 Some of the proteins involved in the initiation of DNA replication.** The same proteins function at both replication forks in a replication bubble. For simplicity, only the left-hand fork is shown, and the DNA bases are drawn much larger in relation to the proteins than they are in reality.

complementary DNA strands. However, the enzymes that synthesize DNA cannot *initiate* the synthesis of a polynucleotide; they can only add DNA nucleotides to the end of an already existing chain that is base-paired with the template strand. The initial nucleotide chain that is produced during DNA synthesis is actually a short stretch of RNA, not DNA. This RNA chain is called a **primer** and is synthesized by the enzyme **primase** (see Figure 16.13). Primase starts a complementary RNA chain from a single RNA nucleotide, adding more RNA nucleotides one at a time, using the parental DNA strand as a template. The completed primer, generally 5–10 nucleotides long, is thus base-paired to the template strand. The new DNA strand will start from the 3′ end of the RNA primer.

Synthesizing a New DNA Strand

Enzymes called **DNA polymerases** catalyze the synthesis of new DNA by adding nucleotides to a preexisting chain. In *E. coli*, there are several different DNA polymerases, but two appear to play the major roles in DNA replication: DNA polymerase III and DNA polymerase I. The situation in eukaryotes is more complicated, with at least 11 different DNA polymerases discovered so far; however, the general principles are the same.

Most DNA polymerases require a primer and a DNA template strand, along which complementary DNA nucleotides are lined up. In *E. coli*, DNA polymerase III (abbreviated DNA pol III) adds a DNA nucleotide to the RNA primer and then continues adding DNA nucleotides, complementary to the parental DNA template strand, to the growing end of the new DNA strand. The rate of elongation is about 500 nucleotides per second in bacteria and 50 per second in human cells.

Each nucleotide to be added to a growing DNA strand consists of a sugar attached to a base and to three phosphate groups. You have already encountered such a molecule—ATP (adenosine triphosphate; see Figure 8.9). The only difference between the ATP of energy metabolism and dATP, the adenine nucleotide used to make DNA, is the sugar component, which is deoxyribose in the building block of DNA but ribose in ATP. Like ATP, the nucleotides used for DNA synthesis are chemically reactive, partly because their triphosphate tails have an unstable cluster of negative charge. As each monomer joins the growing end of a DNA strand, two phosphate groups are lost as a molecule of pyrophosphate (P—P_i). Subsequent hydrolysis of the pyrophosphate to two molecules of inorganic phosphate (P_i) is a coupled exergonic reaction that helps drive the polymerization reaction **(Figure 16.14)**.

Antiparallel Elongation

As we have noted previously, the two ends of a DNA strand are different, giving each strand directionality, like a one-way street (see Figure 16.5). In addition, the two strands of

▲ **Figure 16.14 Incorporation of a nucleotide into a DNA strand.** DNA polymerase catalyzes the addition of a nucleotide to the 3′ end of a growing DNA strand, with the release of two phosphates.

? *Use this diagram to explain what we mean when we say that each DNA strand has directionality.*

DNA in a double helix are antiparallel, meaning that they are oriented in opposite directions to each other, like the lanes of a divided highway (see Figure 16.14). Therefore, the two new strands formed during DNA replication must also be antiparallel to their template strands.

How does the antiparallel arrangement of the double helix affect replication? Because of their structure, DNA polymerases can add nucleotides only to the free 3′ end of a primer or growing DNA strand, never to the 5′ end (see Figure 16.14). Thus, a new DNA strand can elongate only in the 5′ → 3′ direction. With this in mind, let's examine one of the two replication forks in a bubble **(Figure 16.15)**. Along one template strand, DNA polymerase III can synthesize a complementary strand continuously by elongating the new DNA in the mandatory 5′ → 3′ direction. DNA pol III remains in the replication fork on that template strand and continuously adds nucleotides to the new complementary strand as the fork progresses. The DNA strand made by this mechanism is called the **leading strand**. Only one primer is required for DNA pol III to synthesize the entire leading strand (see Figure 16.15).

To elongate the other new strand of DNA in the mandatory 5′ → 3′ direction, DNA pol III must work along the other template strand in the direction *away from* the replication fork. The DNA strand elongating in this direction is called the **lagging strand**.* In contrast to the leading strand,

---

*Synthesis of the leading strand and synthesis of the lagging strand occur concurrently and at the same rate. The lagging strand is so named because its synthesis is delayed slightly relative to synthesis of the leading strand; each new fragment of the lagging strand cannot be started until enough template has been exposed at the replication fork.

Overview

Leading strand — Origin of replication — Lagging strand

Primer

Lagging strand — Leading strand

Overall directions of replication

❶ After RNA primer is made, DNA pol III starts to synthesize the leading strand.

Origin of replication

3′
5′

RNA primer

Sliding clamp

DNA pol III

Parental DNA

3′
5′

5′
3′

3′

5′

5′
3′

3′

5′

❷ The leading strand is elongated continuously in the 5′→ 3′ direction as the fork progresses.

▲ **Figure 16.15 Synthesis of the leading strand during DNA replication.** This diagram focuses on the left replication fork shown in the overview box. DNA polymerase III (DNA pol III), shaped like a cupped hand, is shown closely associated with a protein called the "sliding clamp" that encircles the newly synthesized double helix like a doughnut. The sliding clamp moves DNA pol III along the DNA template strand.

which elongates continuously, the lagging strand is synthesized discontinuously, as a series of segments. These segments of the lagging strand are called **Okazaki fragments**, after the Japanese scientist who discovered them. The fragments are about 1,000–2,000 nucleotides long in *E. coli* and 100–200 nucleotides long in eukaryotes.

Figure 16.16 illustrates the steps in the synthesis of the lagging strand at one fork. Whereas only one primer is required on the leading strand, each Okazaki fragment on the lagging strand must be primed separately (steps and ❹). After DNA pol III forms an Okazaki fragment (steps ❷–❹), another DNA polymerase, DNA polymerase I (DNA pol I), replaces the RNA nucleotides of the adjacent primer with DNA nucleotides (step ❺). But DNA pol I cannot join the final nucleotide of this replacement DNA segment to the first DNA nucleotide of the adjacent Okazaki fragment. Another enzyme, **DNA ligase**, accomplishes this task, joining the sugar-phosphate backbones of all the Okazaki fragments into a continuous DNA strand (step ❻).

Overview

Leading strand — Origin of replication — Lagging strand

Lagging strand

Leading strand

Overall directions of replication

❶ Primase joins RNA nucleotides into a primer.

Template strand

Origin of replication

3′
5′

3′

5′
3′

❷ DNA pol III adds DNA nucleotides to the primer, forming Okazaki fragment 1.

RNA primer for fragment 1

3′
5′

❸ After reaching the next RNA primer to the right, DNA pol III detaches.

Okazaki fragment 1

3′
5′

RNA primer for fragment 2

Okazaki fragment 2

❹ Fragment 2 is primed. Then DNA pol III adds DNA nucleotides, detaching when it reaches the fragment 1 primer.

3′
5′

❺ DNA pol I replaces the RNA with DNA, adding nucleotides to the 3′ end of fragment 2 (and, earlier, of fragment 1).

3′
5′

❻ DNA ligase forms a bond between the newest DNA and the DNA of fragment 1.

❼ The lagging strand in this region is now complete.

3′
5′

Overall direction of replication

▲ **Figure 16.16 Synthesis of the lagging strand.**

Figure 16.17 and **Table 16.1** summarize DNA replication. Please study them carefully before proceeding.

The DNA Replication Complex

It is traditional—and convenient—to represent DNA polymerase molecules as locomotives moving along a DNA railroad track, but such a model is inaccurate in two important ways. First, the various proteins that participate in DNA replication actually form a single large complex, a "DNA replication machine." Many protein-protein interactions facilitate the efficiency of this complex. For example, by interacting with other proteins at the fork, primase apparently acts as a molecular brake, slowing progress of the replication fork and coordinating the placement of primers and

the rates of replication on the leading and lagging strands. Second, the DNA replication complex may not move along the DNA; rather, the DNA may move through the complex during the replication process. In eukaryotic cells, multiple copies of the complex, perhaps grouped into "factories," may be anchored to the nuclear matrix, a framework of fibers extending through the interior of the nucleus. Experimental evidence supports a model in which two DNA polymerase molecules, one on each template strand, "reel in" the parental DNA and extrude newly made daughter DNA molecules. In this so-called trombone model, the lagging strand is also looped back through the complex (**Figure 16.18**).

▲ **Figure 16.17 A summary of bacterial DNA replication.** The detailed diagram shows the left-hand replication fork of the replication bubble shown in the overview (upper right). Viewing each daughter strand in its entirety in the overview, you can see that half of it is made continuously as the leading strand, while the other half (on the other side of the origin) is synthesized in fragments as the lagging strand.

DRAW IT *Draw a similar diagram showing the right-hand fork of this bubble, numbering the Okazaki fragments appropriately. Label all 5' and 3' ends.*

Table 16.1 Bacterial DNA Replication Proteins and Their Functions

Protein	Function
Helicase	Unwinds parental double helix at replication forks
Single-strand binding protein	Binds to and stabilizes single-stranded DNA until it is used as a template
Topoisomerase	Relieves overwinding strain ahead of replication forks by breaking, swiveling, and rejoining DNA strands
Primase	Synthesizes an RNA primer at 5′ end of leading strand and at 5′ end of each Okazaki fragment of lagging strand
DNA pol III	Using parental DNA as a template, synthesizes new DNA strand by adding nucleotides to an RNA primer or a pre-existing DNA strand
DNA pol I	Removes RNA nucleotides of primer from 5′ end and replaces them with DNA nucleotides
DNA ligase	Joins Okazaki fragments of lagging strand; on leading strand, joins 3′ end of DNA that replaces primer to rest of leading strand DNA

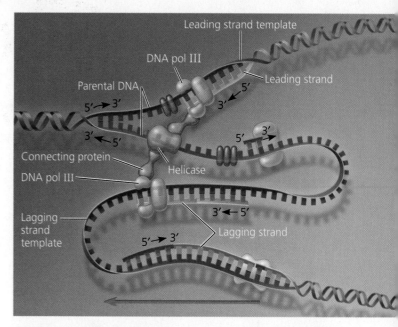

▲ **Figure 16.18 A current model of the DNA replication complex.** Two DNA polymerase III molecules work together in a complex with helicase and other proteins. One DNA polymerase acts on each template strand. The lagging strand template DNA loops through the complex, resembling the slide of a trombone. (This is often called the trombone model.)

DRAW IT *Draw a line tracing the lagging strand template along the entire stretch of DNA shown here.*

ANIMATION **BioFlix** Visit the Study Area in **MasteringBiology** for the BioFlix® 3-D Animation on DNA Replication. BioFlix Tutorials can also be assigned in MasteringBiology.

Proofreading and Repairing DNA

We cannot attribute the accuracy of DNA replication solely to the specificity of base pairing. Initial pairing errors between incoming nucleotides and those in the template strand occur at a rate of one in 10^5 nucleotides. However, errors in the completed DNA molecule amount to only one in 10^{10} (10 billion) nucleotides, an error rate that is 100,000 times lower. This is because during DNA replication, DNA polymerases proofread each nucleotide against its template as soon as it is covalently bonded to the growing strand. Upon finding an incorrectly paired nucleotide, the polymerase removes the nucleotide and then resumes synthesis. (This action is similar to fixing a word processing error by deleting the wrong letter and then entering the correct letter.)

Mismatched nucleotides sometimes evade proofreading by a DNA polymerase. In **mismatch repair**, other enzymes remove and replace incorrectly paired nucleotides that have resulted from replication errors. Researchers spotlighted the importance of such repair enzymes when they found that a hereditary defect in one of them is associated with a form of colon cancer. Apparently, this defect allows cancer-causing errors to accumulate in the DNA faster than normal.

Incorrectly paired or altered nucleotides can also arise after replication. In fact, maintenance of the genetic

information encoded in DNA requires frequent repair of various kinds of damage to existing DNA. DNA molecules are constantly subjected to potentially harmful chemical and physical agents, such as X-rays, as we'll discuss in Chapter 17. In addition, DNA bases often undergo spontaneous chemical changes under normal cellular conditions. However, these changes in DNA are usually corrected before they become permanent changes—*mutations*—perpetuated through successive replications. Each cell continuously monitors and repairs its genetic material. Because repair of damaged DNA is so important to the survival of an organism, it is no surprise that many different DNA repair enzymes have evolved. Almost 100 are known in *E. coli*, and about 130 have been identified so far in humans.

Most cellular systems for repairing incorrectly paired nucleotides, whether they are due to DNA damage or to replication errors, use a mechanism that takes advantage of the base-paired structure of DNA. In many cases, a segment of the strand containing the damage is cut out (excised) by a DNA-cutting enzyme—a **nuclease**—and the resulting gap is then filled in with nucleotides, using the undamaged strand as a template. The enzymes involved in filling the gap are

① Teams of enzymes detect and repair damaged DNA, such as this thymine dimer (often caused by ultraviolet radiation), which distorts the DNA molecule.

Nuclease

② A nuclease enzyme cuts the damaged DNA strand at two points, and the damaged section is removed.

DNA polymerase

③ Repair synthesis by a DNA polymerase fills in the missing nucleotides.

DNA ligase

④ DNA ligase seals the free end of the new DNA to the old DNA, making the strand complete.

▲ **Figure 16.19 Nucleotide excision repair of DNA damage.**

a DNA polymerase and DNA ligase. One such DNA repair system is called **nucleotide excision repair (Figure 16.19)**.

An important function of the DNA repair enzymes in our skin cells is to repair genetic damage caused by the ultraviolet rays of sunlight. One type of damage, shown in Figure 16.19, is the covalent linking of thymine bases that are adjacent on a DNA strand. Such *thymine dimers* cause the DNA to buckle and interfere with DNA replication. The importance of repairing this kind of damage is underscored by a disorder called xeroderma pigmentosum, which in most cases is caused by an inherited defect in a nucleotide excision repair enzyme. Individuals with this disorder are hypersensitive to sunlight; mutations in their skin cells caused by ultraviolet light are left uncorrected, resulting in skin cancer.

Evolutionary Significance of Altered DNA Nucleotides

EVOLUTION Faithful replication of the genome and repair of DNA damage are important for the functioning of the organism and for passing on a complete, accurate genome to the next generation. The error rate after proofreading and repair is extremely low, but rare mistakes do slip through. Once a mismatched nucleotide pair is replicated, the sequence change is permanent in the daughter molecule that has the incorrect nucleotide as well as in any subsequent copies. As we mentioned earlier, a permanent change in the DNA sequence is called a mutation.

Mutations can change the phenotype of an organism (as you'll learn in Chapter 17). And if they occur in germ cells, which give rise to gametes, mutations can be passed on from generation to generation. The vast majority of such changes either have no effect or are harmful, but a very small percentage can be beneficial. In either case, mutations are the original source of the variation on which natural selection operates during evolution and are ultimately responsible for the appearance of new species. (You'll learn more about this process in Unit Four.) The balance between complete fidelity of DNA replication or repair and a low mutation rate has, over long periods of time, allowed the evolution of the rich diversity of species we see on Earth today.

Replicating the Ends of DNA Molecules

For linear DNA, such as the DNA of eukaryotic chromosomes, the usual replication machinery cannot complete the 5′ ends of daughter DNA strands. This is a consequence of the fact that a DNA polymerase can add nucleotides only to the 3′ end of a preexisting polynucleotide. Even if an Okazaki fragment can be started with an RNA primer bound to the very end of the template strand, once that primer is removed, it cannot be replaced with DNA because there is no 3′ end available for nucleotide addition **(Figure 16.20)**. As a result, repeated rounds of replication produce shorter and shorter DNA molecules with uneven ("staggered") ends.

Most prokaryotes have a circular chromosome, with no ends, so the shortening of DNA does not occur. But what protects the genes of linear eukaryotic chromosomes from being eroded away during successive rounds of DNA replication? Eukaryotic chromosomal DNA molecules have special nucleotide sequences called **telomeres** at their ends **(Figure 16.21)**. Telomeres do not contain genes; instead, the DNA typically consists of multiple repetitions of one short nucleotide sequence. In each human telomere, for example, the six-nucleotide sequence TTAGGG is repeated between 100 and 1,000 times. Telomeres have two protective functions.

First, specific proteins associated with telomeric DNA prevent the staggered ends of the daughter molecule from activating the cell's systems for monitoring DNA damage. (Staggered ends of a DNA molecule, which often result from double-strand breaks, can trigger signal transduction pathways leading to cell cycle arrest or cell death.) Second, telomeric DNA acts as a kind of buffer zone that provides some protection against the organism's genes shortening, somewhat like how the plastic-wrapped ends of a shoelace slow its unraveling. However, telomeres do not prevent the erosion of genes near the ends of chromosomes; they merely postpone it.

As shown in Figure 16.20, telomeres become shorter during every round of replication. Thus, as expected, telomeric DNA tends to be shorter in dividing somatic cells of older

Ends of parental DNA strands

5′
3′

Leading strand
Lagging strand

Last fragment   Next-to-last fragment

Lagging strand
RNA primer

5′
3′

Parental strand

Primer removed but cannot be replaced with DNA because no 3′ end available for DNA polymerase

Removal of primers and replacement with DNA where a 3′ end is available

5′
3′

Second round of replication

New leading strand
5′
3′

New lagging strand
5′
3′

Further rounds of replication

Shorter and shorter daughter molecules

▲ **Figure 16.20 Shortening of the ends of linear DNA molecules.** Here we follow the end of one strand of a DNA molecule through two rounds of replication. After the first round, the new lagging strand is shorter than its template. After a second round, both the leading and lagging strands have become shorter than the original parental DNA. Although not shown here, the other ends of these DNA molecules also become shorter.

individuals and in cultured cells that have divided many times. It has been proposed that shortening of telomeres is somehow connected to the aging process of certain tissues and even to aging of the organism as a whole.

But what about cells whose genome must persist virtually unchanged from an organism to its offspring over many generations? If the chromosomes of germ cells became shorter in every cell cycle, essential genes would eventually be missing from the gametes they produce. However, this does not occur: An enzyme called *telomerase* catalyzes the lengthening of telomeres in eukaryotic germ cells, thus restoring their original length and compensating for the shortening that occurs during DNA replication. Telomerase is not active in most human somatic cells, but its activity varies from tissue to tissue. The activity of telomerase in germ cells results in telomeres of maximum length in the zygote.

⊢ 1 μm ⊣

▲ **Figure 16.21 Telomeres.** Eukaryotes have repetitive, noncoding sequences called telomeres at the ends of their DNA. Telomeres are stained orange in these mouse chromosomes (LM).

Normal shortening of telomeres may protect organisms from cancer by limiting the number of divisions that somatic cells can undergo. Cells from large tumors often have unusually short telomeres, as we would expect for cells that have undergone many cell divisions. Further shortening would presumably lead to self-destruction of the tumor cells. Telomerase activity is abnormally high in cancerous somatic cells, suggesting that its ability to stabilize telomere length may allow these cancer cells to persist. Many cancer cells do seem capable of unlimited cell division, as do immortal strains of cultured cells (see Chapter 12). For several years, researchers have studied inhibition of telomerase as a possible cancer therapy. Thus far, while studies that inhibited telomerase in mice with tumors have led to the death of cancer cells, eventually the cells have restored the length of their telomeres by an alternative pathway. This is an area of ongoing research that may eventually yield useful cancer treatments.

Thus far in this chapter, you have learned about the structure and replication of a DNA molecule. In the next section, we'll take a step back and examine how DNA is packaged into chromosomes, the structures that carry the genetic information.

CONCEPT CHECK 16.2

1. What role does complementary base pairing play in the replication of DNA?

2. Identify two major functions of DNA pol III in DNA replication.

3. **MAKE CONNECTIONS** What is the relationship between DNA replication and the S phase of the cell cycle? See Figure 12.6.

4. **WHAT IF?** If the DNA pol I in a given cell were nonfunctional, how would that affect the synthesis of a *leading* strand? In the overview box in Figure 16.17, point out where DNA pol I would normally function on the top leading strand.

For suggested answers, see Appendix A.

A chromosome consists of a DNA molecule packed together with proteins

The main component of the genome in most bacteria is one double-stranded, circular DNA molecule that is associated with a small amount of protein. Although we refer to this structure as the bacterial chromosome, it is very different from a eukaryotic chromosome, which consists of one linear DNA molecule associated with a large amount of protein. In *E. coli*, the chromosomal DNA consists of about 4.6 million nucleotide pairs, representing about 4,400 genes. This is 100 times more DNA than is found in a typical virus, but only about one-thousandth as much DNA as in a human somatic cell. Still, that is a tremendous amount of DNA to be packaged in such a small container.

Stretched out, the DNA of an *E. coli* cell would measure about a millimeter in length, which is 500 times longer than the cell. Within a bacterium, however, certain proteins

▼ Figure 16.22

Exploring Chromatin Packing in a Eukaryotic Chromosome

This series of diagrams and transmission electron micrographs depicts a current model for the progressive levels of DNA coiling and folding. The illustration zooms out from a single molecule of DNA to a metaphase chromosome, which is large enough to be seen with a light microscope.

Nucleosome
(10 nm in diameter)

DNA
double helix
(2 nm in diameter)

Histones

Histone tail

H1

DNA, the double helix

Shown here is a ribbon model of DNA, with each ribbon representing one of the sugar-phosphate backbones. Recall that the phosphate groups along the backbone contribute a negative charge along the outside of each strand. The TEM shows a molecule of naked (protein-free) DNA; the double helix alone is 2 nm across.

Histones

Proteins called **histones** are responsible for the first level of DNA packing in chromatin. Although each histone is small—containing only about 100 amino acids—the total mass of histone in chromatin roughly equals the mass of DNA. More than a fifth of a histone's amino acids are positively charged (lysine or arginine) and therefore bind tightly to the negatively charged DNA.

Four types of histones are most common in chromatin: H2A, H2B, H3, and H4. The histones are very similar among eukaryotes; for example, all but two of the amino acids in cow H4 are identical to those in pea H4. The apparent conservation of histone genes during evolution probably reflects the important role of histones in organizing DNA within cells.

These four types of histones are critical to the next level of DNA packing. (A fifth type of histone, called H1, is involved in a further stage of packing.)

Nucleosomes, or "beads on a string" (10-nm fiber)

In electron micrographs, unfolded chromatin is 10 nm in diameter (the *10-nm fiber*). Such chromatin resembles beads on a string (see the TEM). Each "bead" is a **nucleosome**, the basic unit of DNA packing; the "string" between beads is called *linker DNA*.

A nucleosome consists of DNA wound twice around a protein core of eight histones, two each of the main histone types (H2A, H2B, H3, and H4). The amino end (N-terminus) of each histone (the *histone tail*) extends outward from the nucleosome.

In the cell cycle, the histones leave the DNA only briefly during DNA replication. Generally, they do the same during transcription, another process that requires access to the DNA by the cell's molecular machinery. Nucleosomes, and in particular their histone tails, are involved in the regulation of gene expression.

cause the chromosome to coil and "supercoil," densely packing it so that it fills only part of the cell. Unlike the nucleus of a eukaryotic cell, this dense region of DNA in a bacterium, called the nucleoid, is not bounded by membrane (see Figure 6.5).

Each eukaryotic chromosome contains a single linear DNA double helix that, in humans, averages about 1.5×10^8 nucleotide pairs. This is an enormous amount of DNA relative to a chromosome's condensed length. If completely stretched out, such a DNA molecule would be about 4 cm long, thousands of times the diameter of a cell nucleus—and that's not even considering the DNA of the other 45 human chromosomes!

In the cell, eukaryotic DNA is precisely combined with a large amount of protein. Together, this complex of DNA and protein, called **chromatin**, fits into the nucleus through an elaborate, multilevel system of packing. Our current view of the successive levels of DNA packing in a chromosome is outlined in **Figure 16.22**. Study this figure carefully before reading further.

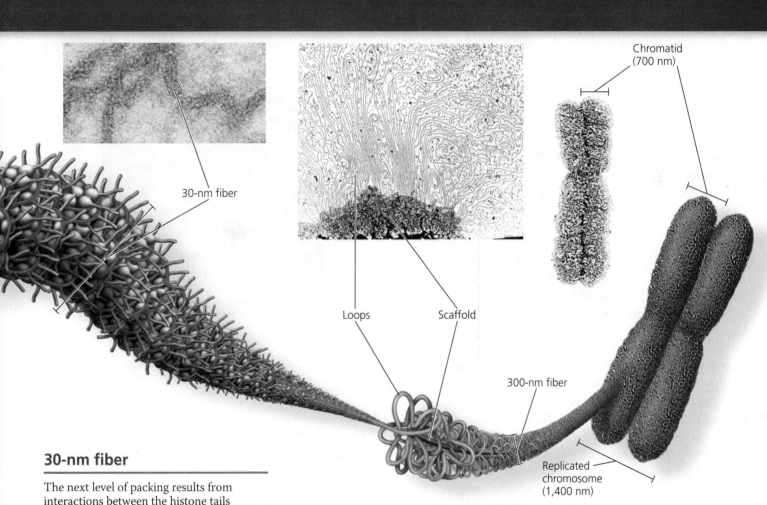

Chromatid (700 nm)

30-nm fiber

Loops   Scaffold

300-nm fiber

Replicated chromosome (1,400 nm)

30-nm fiber

The next level of packing results from interactions between the histone tails of one nucleosome and the linker DNA and nucleosomes on either side. The fifth histone, H1, is involved at this level. These interactions cause the extended 10-nm fiber to coil or fold, forming a chromatin fiber roughly 30 nm in thickness, the *30-nm fiber*. Although the 30-nm fiber is quite prevalent in the interphase nucleus, the packing arrangement of nucleosomes in this form of chromatin is still a matter of some debate.

Looped domains (300-nm fiber)

The 30-nm fiber, in turn, forms loops called *looped domains* attached to a chromosome scaffold composed of proteins, thus making up a *300-nm fiber*. The scaffold is rich in one type of topoisomerase, and H1 molecules also appear to be present.

Metaphase chromosome

In a mitotic chromosome, the looped domains themselves coil and fold in a manner not yet fully understood, further compacting all the chromatin to produce the characteristic metaphase chromosome (also shown in the micrograph above). The width of one chromatid is 700 nm. Particular genes always end up located at the same places in metaphase chromosomes, indicating that the packing steps are highly specific and precise.

Chromatin undergoes striking changes in its degree of packing during the course of the cell cycle (see Figure 12.7). In interphase cells stained for light microscopy, the chromatin usually appears as a diffuse mass within the nucleus, suggesting that the chromatin is highly extended. As a cell prepares for mitosis, its chromatin coils and folds up (condenses), eventually forming a characteristic number of short, thick metaphase chromosomes that are distinguishable from each other with the light microscope **(Figure 16.23a)**.

Though interphase chromatin is generally much less condensed than the chromatin of mitotic chromosomes, it shows several of the same levels of higher-order packing. Some of the chromatin comprising a chromosome seems to be present as a 10-nm fiber, but much is compacted into a 30-nm fiber, which in some regions is further folded into looped domains. Early on, biologists assumed that interphase chromatin was a tangled mass in the nucleus, like a bowl of spaghetti, but this is far from the case. Although an interphase chromosome lacks an obvious scaffold, its looped domains appear to be attached to the nuclear lamina, on the inside of the nuclear envelope, and perhaps also to fibers of the nuclear matrix. These attachments may help organize regions of chromatin where genes are active. The chromatin of each chromosome occupies a specific restricted area within the interphase nucleus, and the chromatin fibers of different chromosomes do not appear to be entangled **(Figure 16.23b)**.

Even during interphase, the centromeres and telomeres of chromosomes, as well as other chromosomal regions in some cells, exist in a highly condensed state similar to that seen in a metaphase chromosome. This type of interphase chromatin, visible as irregular clumps with a light microscope, is called **heterochromatin**, to distinguish it from the less compacted, more dispersed **euchromatin** ("true chromatin"). Because of its compaction, heterochromatic DNA is largely inaccessible to the machinery in the cell responsible for transcribing the genetic information coded in the DNA, a crucial early step in gene expression. In contrast, the looser packing of euchromatin makes its DNA accessible to this machinery, so the genes present in euchromatin can be transcribed. The chromosome is a dynamic structure that is condensed, loosened, modified, and remodeled as necessary for various cell processes, including mitosis, meiosis, and gene activity. Chemical modifications of histones affect the state of chromatin condensation and also have multiple effects on gene activity, as you'll see in Chapter 18.

In this chapter, you have learned how DNA molecules are arranged in chromosomes and how DNA replication provides the copies of genes that parents pass to offspring. However, it is not enough that genes be copied and transmitted; the information they carry must be used by the cell. In other words, genes must also be expressed. In the next chapter, we will examine how the cell expresses the genetic information encoded in DNA.

(a) These metaphase chromosomes have been "painted" so that the two homologs of a pair are the same color. Above is a spread of treated chromosomes; on the right, they have been organized into a karyotype.

5 μm

(b) The ability to visually distinguish among chromosomes makes it possible to see how the chromosomes are arranged in the interphase nucleus. Each chromosome appears to occupy a specific territory during interphase. In general, the two homologs of a pair are not located together.

▲ **Figure 16.23 "Painting" chromosomes.** Researchers can treat ("paint") human chromosomes with molecular tags that cause each chromosome pair to appear a different color.

MAKE CONNECTIONS *If you arrested a human cell in metaphase I of meiosis and applied this technique, what would you observe? How would this differ from what you would see in metaphase of mitosis? Review Figure 13.8 and Figure 12.7.*

CONCEPT CHECK 16.3

1. Describe the structure of a nucleosome, the basic unit of DNA packing in eukaryotic cells.
2. What two properties, one structural and one functional, distinguish heterochromatin from euchromatin?
3. **MAKE CONNECTIONS** Interphase chromosomes appear to be attached to the nuclear lamina and perhaps also the nuclear matrix. Describe these two structures. See Figure 6.9 and the associated text.

For suggested answers, see Appendix A.

16 Chapter Review

SUMMARY OF KEY CONCEPTS

CONCEPT 16.1

DNA is the genetic material (pp. 313–318)

- Experiments with bacteria and with **phages** provided the first strong evidence that the genetic material is DNA.
- Watson and Crick deduced that DNA is a **double helix** and built a structural model. Two **antiparallel** sugar-phosphate chains wind around the outside of the molecule; the nitrogenous bases project into the interior, where they hydrogen-bond in specific pairs, A with T, G with C.

Nitrogenous bases

Sugar-phosphate backbone

Hydrogen bond

? *What does it mean when we say that the two DNA strands in the double helix are antiparallel? What would an end of the double helix look like if the strands were parallel?*

CONCEPT 16.2

Many proteins work together in DNA replication and repair (pp. 318–327)

- The Meselson-Stahl experiment showed that **DNA replication** is **semiconservative**: The parental molecule unwinds, and each strand then serves as a template for the synthesis of a new strand according to base-pairing rules.
- DNA replication at one **replication fork** is summarized here:

DNA pol III synthesizes **leading strand** continuously

Parental DNA

5′
3′

Helicase

DNA pol III starts DNA synthesis at 3′ end of primer, continues in 5′ → 3′ direction

Primase synthesizes a short RNA **primer**

Lagging strand synthesized in short **Okazaki fragments**, later joined by **DNA ligase**

DNA pol I replaces the RNA primer with DNA nucleotides

Origin of replication

3′
5′

3′
5′

- DNA polymerases proofread new DNA, replacing incorrect nucleotides. In **mismatch repair**, enzymes correct errors that persist. **Nucleotide excision repair** is a process by which **nucleases** cut out and other enzymes replace damaged stretches of DNA.
- The ends of eukaryotic chromosomal DNA get shorter with each round of replication. The presence of **telomeres**, repetitive sequences at the ends of linear DNA molecules, postpones the erosion of genes. Telomerase catalyzes the lengthening of telomeres in germ cells.

? *Compare DNA replication on the leading and lagging strands, including both similarities and differences.*

CONCEPT 16.3

A chromosome consists of a DNA molecule packed together with proteins (pp. 328–330)

- The chromosome of most bacterial species is a circular DNA molecule with some associated proteins, making up the nucleoid. The **chromatin** making up a eukaryotic chromosome is composed of DNA, **histones**, and other proteins. The histones bind to each other and to the DNA to form **nucleosomes**, the most basic units of DNA packing. Histone tails extend outward from each bead-like nucleosome core. Additional coiling and folding lead ultimately to the highly condensed chromatin of the metaphase chromosome. Chromosomes occupy restricted areas in the interphase nucleus. In interphase cells, most chromatin is less compacted (**euchromatin**), but some remains highly condensed (**heterochromatin**). Euchromatin, but not heterochromatin, is generally accessible for transcription of genes.

? *Describe the levels of chromatin packing you'd expect to see in an interphase nucleus.*

TEST YOUR UNDERSTANDING

LEVEL 1: KNOWLEDGE/COMPREHENSION

1. In his work with pneumonia-causing bacteria and mice, Griffith found that
   a. the protein coat from pathogenic cells was able to transform nonpathogenic cells.
   b. heat-killed pathogenic cells caused pneumonia.
   c. some substance from pathogenic cells was transferred to nonpathogenic cells, making them pathogenic.
   d. the polysaccharide coat of bacteria caused pneumonia.

2. What is the basis for the difference in how the leading and lagging strands of DNA molecules are synthesized?
   a. The origins of replication occur only at the 5′ end.
   b. Helicases and single-strand binding proteins work at the 5′ end.
   c. DNA polymerase can join new nucleotides only to the 3′ end of a pre-existing strand.
   d. DNA ligase works only in the 3′ → 5′ direction.

3. In analyzing the number of different bases in a DNA sample, which result would be consistent with the base-pairing rules?
   a. $A = G$
   b. $A + G = C + T$
   c. $A + T = G + C$
   d. $A = C$

4. The elongation of the leading strand during DNA synthesis
   a. progresses away from the replication fork.
   b. occurs in the 3′ → 5′ direction.
   c. does not require a template strand.
   d. depends on the action of DNA polymerase.

5. In a nucleosome, the DNA is wrapped around
   a. histones.
   b. ribosomes.
   c. polymerase molecules.
   d. a thymine dimer.

This example illustrates the main point of this chapter: The DNA inherited by an organism leads to specific traits by dictating the synthesis of proteins and of RNA molecules involved in protein synthesis. In other words, proteins are the link between genotype and phenotype. **Gene expression** is the process by which DNA directs the synthesis of proteins (or, in some cases, just RNAs). The expression of genes that code for proteins includes two stages: transcription and translation. This chapter describes the flow of information from gene to protein and explains how genetic mutations affect organisms through their proteins. Understanding the processes of gene expression, which are similar in all three domains of life, will allow us to revisit the concept of the gene in more detail at the end of the chapter.

Genes specify proteins via transcription and translation

Before going into the details of how genes direct protein synthesis, let's step back and examine how the fundamental relationship between genes and proteins was discovered.

Evidence from the Study of Metabolic Defects

In 1902, British physician Archibald Garrod was the first to suggest that genes dictate phenotypes through enzymes that catalyze specific chemical reactions in the cell. Garrod postulated that the symptoms of an inherited disease reflect a person's inability to make a particular enzyme. He later referred to such diseases as "inborn errors of metabolism." Garrod gave as one example the hereditary condition called alkaptonuria. In this disorder, the urine is black because it contains the chemical alkapton, which darkens upon exposure to air. Garrod reasoned that most people have an enzyme that metabolizes alkapton, whereas people with alkaptonuria have inherited an inability to make that metabolic enzyme.

Garrod may have been the first to recognize that Mendel's principles of heredity apply to humans as well as peas. Garrod's realization was ahead of its time, but research several decades later supported his hypothesis that a gene dictates the production of a specific enzyme, later named the *one gene–one enzyme hypothesis*. Biochemists accumulated much evidence that cells synthesize and degrade most organic molecules via metabolic pathways, in which each chemical reaction in a sequence is catalyzed by a specific enzyme (see Concept 8.1). Such metabolic pathways lead, for instance, to the synthesis of the pigments that give the brown deer in Figure 17.1 their fur color or fruit flies (*Drosophila*) their eye color (see Figure 15.3). In the 1930s, the American biochemist and geneticist George Beadle and his French colleague Boris Ephrussi speculated that in *Drosophila*, each of the various mutations affecting eye color blocks pigment synthesis at a specific step by preventing production of the enzyme that catalyzes that step. But neither the chemical reactions nor the enzymes that catalyze them were known at the time.

Nutritional Mutants in Neurospora: Scientific Inquiry

A breakthrough in demonstrating the relationship between genes and enzymes came a few years later at Stanford University, where Beadle and Edward Tatum began working with a bread mold, *Neurospora crassa*. They bombarded *Neurospora* with X-rays, shown in the 1920s to cause genetic changes, and then looked among the survivors for mutants that differed in their nutritional needs from the wild-type bread mold. Wild-type *Neurospora* has modest food requirements. It can grow in the laboratory on a simple solution of inorganic salts, glucose, and the vitamin biotin, incorporated into agar, a support medium. From this minimal medium, the mold cells use their metabolic pathways to produce all the other molecules they need. Beadle and Tatum identified mutants that could not survive on minimal medium, apparently because they were unable to synthesize certain essential molecules from the minimal ingredients. To ensure survival of these nutritional mutants, Beadle and Tatum allowed them to grow on a complete growth medium, which consisted of minimal medium supplemented with all 20 amino acids and a few other nutrients. The complete growth medium could support any mutant that couldn't synthesize one of the supplements.

To characterize the metabolic defect in each nutritional mutant, Beadle and Tatum took samples from the mutant growing on complete medium and distributed them to a number of different vials. Each vial contained minimal medium plus a single additional nutrient. The particular supplement that allowed growth indicated the metabolic defect. For example, if the only supplemented vial that supported growth of the mutant was the one fortified with the amino acid arginine, the researchers could conclude that the mutant was defective in the biochemical pathway that wild-type cells use to synthesize arginine.

In fact, such arginine-requiring mutants were obtained and studied by two colleagues of Beadle and Tatum, Adrian Srb and Norman Horowitz, who wanted to investigate the biochemical pathway for arginine synthesis in *Neurospora* **(Figure 17.2)**. Srb and Horowitz pinned down each mutant's defect more specifically, using additional tests to distinguish among three classes of arginine-requiring mutants. Mutants in each class required a different set of compounds along the arginine-synthesizing pathway, which has three steps. These results, and those of many similar experiments done by Beadle and Tatum, suggested that each class was blocked at a different step in this pathway because mutants in that class lacked the enzyme that catalyzes the blocked step.

Inquiry

Do individual genes specify the enzymes that function in a biochemical pathway?

Experiment Working with the mold *Neurospora crassa*, Adrian Srb and Norman Horowitz, then at Stanford University, used Beadle and Tatum's experimental approach to isolate mutants that required arginine in their growth medium. The researchers showed that these mutants fell into three classes, each defective in a different gene. From studies by others on mammalian liver cells, they suspected that the metabolic pathway of arginine biosynthesis involved a precursor nutrient and the intermediate molecules ornithine and citrulline, as shown in the diagram on the right.

Their most famous experiment, shown here, tested both the *one gene–one enzyme hypothesis* and their postulated arginine-synthesizing pathway. In this experiment, they grew their three classes of mutants under the four different conditions shown in the Results Table below. They included minimal medium (MM) as a control, knowing that wild-type cells could grow on MM but mutant cells could not. (See test tubes below.)

Growth: Wild-type cells growing and dividing

No growth: Mutant cells cannot grow and divide

Control: Minimal medium

Results As shown in the table on the right, the wild-type strain was capable of growth under all experimental conditions, requiring only the minimal medium. The three classes of mutants each had a specific set of growth requirements. For example, class II mutants could not grow when ornithine alone was added but could grow when either citrulline or arginine was added.

Results Table	Classes of *Neurospora crassa*			
Condition	**Wild type**	**Class I mutants**	**Class II mutants**	**Class III mutants**
Minimal medium (MM) (control)				
MM + ornithine				
MM + citrulline				
MM + arginine (control)				
Summary of results	Can grow with or without any supplements	Can grow on ornithine, citrulline, or arginine	Can grow only on citrulline or arginine	Require arginine to grow

Conclusion From the growth requirements of the mutants, Srb and Horowitz deduced that each class of mutant was unable to carry out one step in the pathway for synthesizing arginine, presumably because it lacked the necessary enzyme, as shown in the table on the right. Because each of their mutants was mutated in a single gene, they concluded that each mutated gene must normally dictate the production of one enzyme. Their results supported the one gene–one enzyme hypothesis, proposed by Beadle and Tatum, and also confirmed that the arginine pathway described in the mammalian liver also operates in *Neurospora*. (Notice in the Results Table that a mutant can grow only if supplied with a compound made *after* the defective step because this bypasses the defect.)

Source: A. M. Srb and N. H. Horowitz, The ornithine cycle in *Neurospora* and its genetic control, *Journal of Biological Chemistry* 154:129–139 (1944).

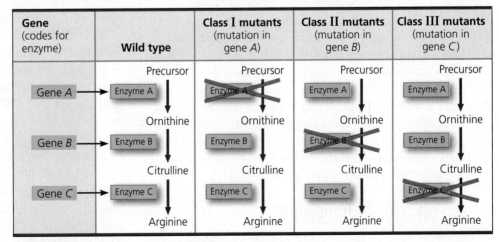

WHAT IF? *Suppose the experiment had shown that class I mutants could grow only in MM supplemented by ornithine or arginine and that class II mutants could grow in MM supplemented by citrulline, ornithine, or arginine. What conclusions would the researchers have drawn from those results regarding the biochemical pathway and the defect in class I and class II mutants?*

Because each mutant was defective in a single gene, Beadle and Tatum saw that, taken together, the collected results provided strong support for a working hypothesis they had proposed earlier. The one gene–one enzyme hypothesis, as they dubbed it, states that the function of a gene is to dictate the production of a specific enzyme. Further support for this hypothesis came from experiments that identified the specific enzymes lacking in the mutants. Beadle and Tatum shared a Nobel Prize in 1958 for "their discovery that genes act by regulating definite chemical events" (in the words of the Nobel committee).

Today, we know of countless examples in which a mutation in a gene causes a faulty enzyme that in turn leads to an identifiable condition. The albino deer in Figure 17.1 lacks a key enzyme called tyrosinase in the metabolic pathway that produces melanin, a dark pigment. The absence of melanin causes white fur and other effects throughout the deer's body. Its nose, ears, and hooves, as well as its eyes, are pink because no melanin is present to mask the reddish color of the blood vessels that run through those structures.

The Products of Gene Expression: A Developing Story

As researchers learned more about proteins, they made revisions to the one gene–one enzyme hypothesis. First of all, not all proteins are enzymes. Keratin, the structural protein of animal hair, and the hormone insulin are two examples of nonenzyme proteins. Because proteins that are not enzymes are nevertheless gene products, molecular biologists began to think in terms of one gene–one protein. However, many proteins are constructed from two or more different polypeptide chains, and each polypeptide is specified by its own gene. For example, hemoglobin, the oxygen-transporting protein of vertebrate red blood cells, contains two kinds of polypeptides, and thus two genes code for this protein (see Figure 5.18). Beadle and Tatum's idea was therefore restated as the *one gene–one polypeptide hypothesis*. Even this description is not entirely accurate, though. First, in many cases, a eukaryotic gene can code for a set of closely related polypeptides via a process called alternative splicing, which you will learn about later in this chapter. Second, quite a few genes code for RNA molecules that have important functions in cells even though they are never translated into protein. For now, we will focus on genes that do code for polypeptides. (Note that it is common to refer to these gene products as proteins—a practice you will encounter in this book—rather than more precisely as polypeptides.)

Basic Principles of Transcription and Translation

Genes provide the instructions for making specific proteins. But a gene does not build a protein directly. The bridge between DNA and protein synthesis is the nucleic acid RNA.

RNA is chemically similar to DNA except that it contains ribose instead of deoxyribose as its sugar and has the nitrogenous base uracil rather than thymine (see Figure 5.24). Thus, each nucleotide along a DNA strand has A, G, C, or T as its base, and each nucleotide along an RNA strand has A, G, C, or U as its base. An RNA molecule usually consists of a single strand.

It is customary to describe the flow of information from gene to protein in linguistic terms because both nucleic acids and proteins are polymers with specific sequences of monomers that convey information, much as specific sequences of letters communicate information in a language like English. In DNA or RNA, the monomers are the four types of nucleotides, which differ in their nitrogenous bases. Genes are typically hundreds or thousands of nucleotides long, each gene having a specific sequence of nucleotides. Each polypeptide of a protein also has monomers arranged in a particular linear order (the protein's primary structure), but its monomers are amino acids. Thus, nucleic acids and proteins contain information written in two different chemical languages. Getting from DNA to protein requires two major stages: transcription and translation.

Transcription is the synthesis of RNA using information in the DNA. The two nucleic acids are written in different forms of the same language, and the information is simply transcribed, or "rewritten," from DNA to RNA. Just as a DNA strand provides a template for making a new complementary strand during DNA replication, it also can serve as a template for assembling a complementary sequence of RNA nucleotides. For a protein-coding gene, the resulting RNA molecule is a faithful transcript of the gene's protein-building instructions. This type of RNA molecule is called **messenger RNA (mRNA)** because it carries a genetic message from the DNA to the protein-synthesizing machinery of the cell. (Transcription is the general term for the synthesis of *any* kind of RNA on a DNA template. Later, you will learn about some other types of RNA produced by transcription.)

Translation is the synthesis of a polypeptide using the information in the mRNA. During this stage, there is a change in language: The cell must translate the nucleotide sequence of an mRNA molecule into the amino acid sequence of a polypeptide. The sites of translation are **ribosomes**, molecular complexes that facilitate the orderly linking of amino acids into polypeptide chains.

Transcription and translation occur in all organisms—those that lack a membrane-bounded nucleus (bacteria and archaea) and those that have one (eukaryotes). Because most studies of transcription and translation have used bacteria and eukaryotic cells, they are our main focus in this chapter. Our understanding of transcription and translation in archaea lags behind, but we do know that archaeal cells share some features of gene expression with bacteria and others with eukaryotes.

The basic mechanics of transcription and translation are similar for bacteria and eukaryotes, but there is an important difference in the flow of genetic information within the cells. Because bacteria do not have nuclei, their DNA is not separated by nuclear membranes from ribosomes and the other protein-synthesizing equipment **(Figure 17.3a)**. As you will see later, this lack of compartmentalization allows translation of an mRNA to begin while its transcription is still in progress. In a eukaryotic cell, by contrast, the nuclear envelope separates transcription from translation in space and time **(Figure 17.3b)**. Transcription occurs in the nucleus, and mRNA is then transported to the cytoplasm, where translation occurs. But before eukaryotic RNA transcripts from protein-coding genes can leave the nucleus, they are modified in various ways to produce the final, functional mRNA. The transcription of a protein-coding eukaryotic gene results in *pre-mRNA*, and further processing yields the finished mRNA. The initial RNA transcript from any gene, including those specifying RNA that is not translated into protein, is more generally called a **primary transcript**.

To summarize: Genes program protein synthesis via genetic messages in the form of messenger RNA. Put another way, cells are governed by a molecular chain of command with a directional flow of genetic information, shown here by arrows:

This concept was dubbed the *central dogma* by Francis Crick in 1956. How has the concept held up over time? In the 1970s, scientists were surprised to discover that some enzymes exist that use RNA molecules as templates for DNA synthesis (a process you'll read about in Chapter 19). However, these exceptions do not invalidate the idea that, in general, genetic information flows from DNA to RNA to protein. In the next section, we discuss how the instructions for assembling amino acids into a specific order are encoded in nucleic acids.

The Genetic Code

When biologists began to suspect that the instructions for protein synthesis were encoded in DNA, they recognized a problem: There are only four nucleotide bases to specify 20 amino acids. Thus, the genetic code cannot be a language like Chinese, where each written symbol corresponds to a word. How many nucleotides, then, correspond to an amino acid?

Codons: Triplets of Nucleotides

If each kind of nucleotide base were translated into an amino acid, only four amino acids could be specified, one per nucleotide base. Would a language of two-letter code

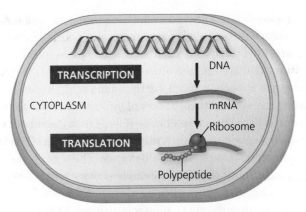

(a) Bacterial cell. In a bacterial cell, which lacks a nucleus, mRNA produced by transcription is immediately translated without additional processing.

(b) Eukaryotic cell. The nucleus provides a separate compartment for transcription. The original RNA transcript, called pre-mRNA, is processed in various ways before leaving the nucleus as mRNA.

▲ **Figure 17.3 Overview: the roles of transcription and translation in the flow of genetic information.** In a cell, inherited information flows from DNA to RNA to protein. The two main stages of information flow are transcription and translation. A miniature version of part (a) or (b) accompanies several figures later in the chapter as an orientation diagram to help you see where a particular figure fits into the overall scheme.

words suffice? The two-nucleotide sequence AG, for example, could specify one amino acid, and GT could specify another. Since there are four possible nucleotide bases in each position, this would give us 16 (that is, 4×4, or 4^2) possible arrangements—still not enough to code for all 20 amino acids.

Triplets of nucleotide bases are the smallest units of uniform length that can code for all the amino acids. If each arrangement of three consecutive nucleotide bases specifies an amino acid, there can be 64 (that is, 4^3) possible code words—more than enough to specify all the amino acids. Experiments have verified that the flow of information from gene to protein is based on a **triplet code**: The genetic instructions for a polypeptide chain are written in the DNA as a series of nonoverlapping, three-nucleotide words. The series of words in a gene is transcribed into a complementary series of nonoverlapping, three-nucleotide words in mRNA, which is then translated into a chain of amino acids **(Figure 17.4)**.

During transcription, the gene determines the sequence of nucleotide bases along the length of the RNA molecule that is being synthesized. For each gene, only one of the two DNA strands is transcribed. This strand is called the **template strand** because it provides the pattern, or template, for the sequence of nucleotides in an RNA transcript. For any given gene, the same strand is used as the template every time the gene is transcribed. For other genes on the same DNA molecule, however, the opposite strand may be the one that always functions as the template.

An mRNA molecule is complementary rather than identical to its DNA template because RNA nucleotides are assembled on the template according to base-pairing rules (see Figure 17.4). The pairs are similar to those that form during DNA replication, except that U (the RNA substitute for T) pairs with A and the mRNA nucleotides contain ribose instead of deoxyribose. Like a new strand of DNA, the RNA molecule is synthesized in an antiparallel direction to the template strand of DNA. (To review what is meant by "antiparallel" and the 5′ and 3′ ends of a nucleic acid chain, see Figure 16.7.) In the example in Figure 17.4, the nucleotide triplet ACC along the DNA (written as 3′-ACC-5′) provides a template for 5′-UGG-3′ in the mRNA molecule. The mRNA nucleotide triplets are called **codons**, and they are customarily written in the 5′ → 3′ direction. In our example, UGG is the codon for the amino acid tryptophan (abbreviated Trp). The term *codon* is also used for the DNA nucleotide triplets along the *nontemplate* strand. These codons are complementary to the template strand and thus identical in sequence to the mRNA, except that they have a T wherever there is a U in the mRNA. (For this reason, the nontemplate DNA strand is often called the *coding strand*.)

During translation, the sequence of codons along an mRNA molecule is decoded, or translated, into a sequence of amino acids making up a polypeptide chain. The codons are read by the translation machinery in the 5′ → 3′ direction along the mRNA. Each codon specifies which one of the 20 amino acids will be incorporated at the corresponding position along a polypeptide. Because codons are nucleotide triplets, the number of nucleotides making up a genetic message must be three times the number of amino acids in the protein product. For example, it takes 300 nucleotides along an mRNA strand to code for the amino acids in a polypeptide that is 100 amino acids long.

Cracking the Code

Molecular biologists cracked the genetic code of life in the early 1960s when a series of elegant experiments disclosed the amino acid translations of each of the RNA codons. The first codon was deciphered in 1961 by Marshall Nirenberg, of the National Institutes of Health, along with his colleagues. Nirenberg synthesized an artificial mRNA by linking identical RNA nucleotides containing uracil as their base. No matter where this message started or stopped, it could contain only one codon in repetition: UUU. Nirenberg added this "poly-U" to a test-tube mixture containing amino acids, ribosomes, and the other components required for protein synthesis. His artificial system translated the poly-U into a polypeptide containing many units of the amino acid phenylalanine (Phe), strung together as a long polyphenylalanine chain. Thus, Nirenberg determined that the mRNA codon UUU specifies the amino acid phenylalanine. Soon, the amino acids specified by the codons AAA, GGG, and CCC were also determined.

▲ **Figure 17.4 The triplet code.** For each gene, one DNA strand functions as a template for transcription of RNAs, such as mRNA. The base-pairing rules for DNA synthesis also guide transcription, except that uracil (U) takes the place of thymine (T) in RNA. During translation, the mRNA is read as a sequence of nucleotide triplets, called codons. Each codon specifies an amino acid to be added to the growing polypeptide chain. The mRNA is read in the 5′ → 3′ direction.

? *Write the sequence of the mRNA strand and the nontemplate DNA strand—in both cases reading from 5′ to 3′—and compare them.*

Although more elaborate techniques were required to decode mixed triplets such as AUA and CGA, all 64 codons were deciphered by the mid-1960s. As **Figure 17.5** shows, 61 of the 64 triplets code for amino acids. The three codons that do not designate amino acids are "stop" signals, or termination codons, marking the end of translation. Notice that the codon AUG has a dual function: It codes for the amino acid methionine (Met) and also functions as a "start" signal, or initiation codon. Genetic messages usually begin with the mRNA codon AUG, which signals the protein-synthesizing machinery to begin translating the mRNA at that location. (Because AUG also stands for methionine, polypeptide chains begin with methionine when they are synthesized. However, an enzyme may subsequently remove this starter amino acid from the chain.)

Notice in Figure 17.5 that there is redundancy in the genetic code, but no ambiguity. For example, although codons GAA and GAG both specify glutamic acid (redundancy), neither of them ever specifies any other amino acid (no ambiguity). The redundancy in the code is not altogether random. In many cases, codons that are synonyms for a particular amino acid differ only in the third nucleotide base of the triplet. We will consider the significance of this redundancy later in the chapter.

Our ability to extract the intended message from a written language depends on reading the symbols in the correct groupings—that is, in the correct **reading frame**. Consider this statement: "The red dog ate the bug." Group the letters incorrectly by starting at the wrong point, and the result will probably be gibberish: for example, "her edd oga tet heb ug." The reading frame is also important in the molecular language of cells. The short stretch of polypeptide shown in Figure 17.4, for instance, will be made correctly only if the mRNA nucleotides are read from left to right (5′ → 3′) in the groups of three shown in the figure: UGG UUU GGC UCA. Although a genetic message is written with no spaces between the codons, the cell's protein-synthesizing machinery reads the message as a series of nonoverlapping three-letter words. The message is *not* read as a series of overlapping words—UGGUUU, and so on—which would convey a very different message.

Evolution of the Genetic Code

EVOLUTION   The genetic code is nearly universal, shared by organisms from the simplest bacteria to the most complex plants and animals. The RNA codon CCG, for instance, is translated as the amino acid proline in all organisms whose genetic code has been examined. In laboratory experiments, genes can be transcribed and translated after being transplanted from one species to another, sometimes with quite striking results, as shown in **Figure 17.6**. Bacteria can

Second mRNA base

First mRNA base (5′ end of codon)	U	C	A	G	Third mRNA base (3′ end of codon)
U	UUU UUC Phe / UUA UUG Leu	UCU UCC UCA UCG Ser	UAU UAC Tyr / UAA Stop UAG Stop	UGU UGC Cys / UGA Stop / UGG Trp	U C A G
C	CUU CUC CUA CUG Leu	CCU CCC CCA CCG Pro	CAU CAC His / CAA CAG Gln	CGU CGC CGA CGG Arg	U C A G
A	AUU AUC Ile / AUA / AUG Met or start	ACU ACC ACA ACG Thr	AAU AAC Asn / AAA AAG Lys	AGU AGC Ser / AGA AGG Arg	U C A G
G	GUU GUC GUA GUG Val	GCU GCC GCA GCG Ala	GAU GAC Asp / GAA GAG Glu	GGU GGC GGA GGG Gly	U C A G

▲ **Figure 17.5 The codon table for mRNA.** The three nucleotide bases of an mRNA codon are designated here as the first, second, and third bases, reading in the 5′ → 3′ direction along the mRNA. (Practice using this table by finding the codons in Figure 17.4.) The codon AUG not only stands for the amino acid methionine (Met) but also functions as a "start" signal for ribosomes to begin translating the mRNA at that point. Three of the 64 codons function as "stop" signals, marking where ribosomes end translation. See Figure 5.14 for a list of the full names of all the amino acids.

(a) **Tobacco plant expressing a firefly gene.** The yellow glow is produced by a chemical reaction catalyzed by the protein product of the firefly gene.

(b) **Pig expressing a jellyfish gene.** Researchers injected a jellyfish gene for a fluorescent protein into fertilized pig eggs. One developed into this fluorescent pig.

▲ **Figure 17.6 Expression of genes from different species.** Because diverse forms of life share a common genetic code, one species can be programmed to produce proteins characteristic of a second species by introducing DNA from the second species into the first.

be programmed by the insertion of human genes to synthesize certain human proteins for medical use, such as insulin. Such applications have produced many exciting developments in the area of biotechnology (see Chapter 20).

Despite a small number of exceptions in which a few codons differ from the standard ones, the evolutionary significance of the code's near universality is clear. A language shared by all living things must have been operating very early in the history of life—early enough to be present in the common ancestor of all present-day organisms. A shared genetic vocabulary is a reminder of the kinship that bonds all life on Earth.

CONCEPT CHECK 17.1

1. **MAKE CONNECTIONS** In a research article about alkaptonuria published in 1902, Garrod suggested that humans inherit two "characters" (alleles) for a particular enzyme and that both parents must contribute a faulty version for the offspring to have the disorder. Today, would this disorder be called dominant or recessive? (See Concept 14.4.)

2. What polypeptide product would you expect from a poly-G mRNA that is 30 nucleotides long?

3. **DRAW IT** The template strand of a gene contains the sequence 3'-TTCAGTCGT-5'. Draw the nontemplate sequence and mRNA sequence, indicating the 5' and 3' ends of each. Compare the two sequences.

4. **DRAW IT** Imagine that the nontemplate sequence in question 3 had been transcribed instead of the template sequence. Draw the mRNA sequence and translate it using Figure 17.5. (Be sure to pay attention to the 5' and 3' ends.) Predict how well the protein synthesized from the nontemplate strand would function, if at all.

For suggested answers, see Appendix A.

CONCEPT 17.2

Transcription is the DNA-directed synthesis of RNA: *A closer look*

Now that we have considered the linguistic logic and evolutionary significance of the genetic code, we are ready to reexamine transcription, the first stage of gene expression, in more detail.

Molecular Components of Transcription

Messenger RNA, the carrier of information from DNA to the cell's protein-synthesizing machinery, is transcribed from the template strand of a gene. An enzyme called an **RNA polymerase** pries the two strands of DNA apart and joins together RNA nucleotides complementary to the DNA template strand, thus elongating the RNA polynucleotide **(Figure 17.7)**. Like the DNA polymerases that function in

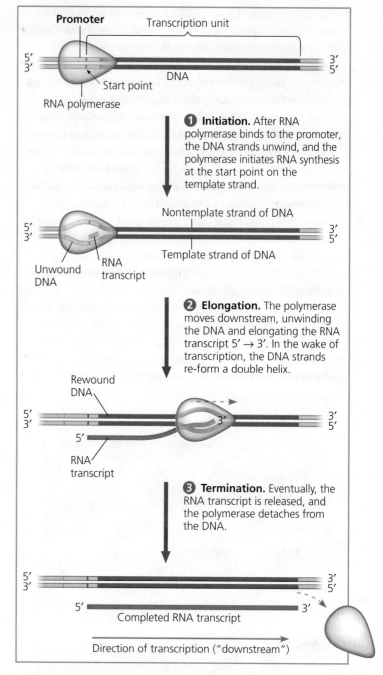

▲ **Figure 17.7 The stages of transcription: initiation, elongation, and termination.** This general depiction of transcription applies to both bacteria and eukaryotes, but the details of termination differ, as described in the text. Also, in a bacterium, the RNA transcript is immediately usable as mRNA; in a eukaryote, the RNA transcript must first undergo processing.

MAKE CONNECTIONS *Compare the use of a template strand during transcription and replication. See Figure 16.17.*

DNA replication, RNA polymerases can assemble a polynucleotide only in its 5' → 3' direction. Unlike DNA polymerases, however, RNA polymerases are able to start a chain from scratch; they don't need a primer.

Specific sequences of nucleotides along the DNA mark where transcription of a gene begins and ends. The DNA sequence where RNA polymerase attaches and initiates transcription is known as the **promoter**; in bacteria, the sequence that signals the end of transcription is called the **terminator**. (The termination mechanism is different in eukaryotes; we'll describe it later.) Molecular biologists refer to the direction of transcription as "downstream" and the other direction as "upstream." These terms are also used to describe the positions of nucleotide sequences within the DNA or RNA. Thus, the promoter sequence in DNA is said to be upstream from the terminator. The stretch of DNA downstream from the promoter that is transcribed into an RNA molecule is called a **transcription unit**.

Bacteria have a single type of RNA polymerase that synthesizes not only mRNA but also other types of RNA that function in protein synthesis, such as ribosomal RNA. In contrast, eukaryotes have at least three types of RNA polymerase in their nuclei; the one used for pre-mRNA synthesis is called RNA polymerase II. The other RNA polymerases transcribe RNA molecules that are not translated into protein. In the discussion that follows, we start with the features of mRNA synthesis common to both bacteria and eukaryotes and then describe some key differences.

Synthesis of an RNA Transcript

The three stages of transcription, as shown in Figure 17.7 and described next, are initiation, elongation, and termination of the RNA chain. Study Figure 17.7 to familiarize yourself with the stages and the terms used to describe them.

RNA Polymerase Binding and Initiation of Transcription

The promoter of a gene includes within it the transcription **start point** (the nucleotide where RNA synthesis actually begins) and typically extends several dozen or more nucleotide pairs upstream from the start point. RNA polymerase binds in a precise location and orientation on the promoter, therefore determining where transcription starts and which of the two strands of the DNA helix is used as the template.

Certain sections of a promoter are especially important for binding RNA polymerase. In bacteria, part of the RNA polymerase itself specifically recognizes and binds to the promoter. In eukaryotes, a collection of proteins called **transcription factors** mediate the binding of RNA polymerase and the initiation of transcription. Only after transcription factors are attached to the promoter does RNA polymerase II bind to it. The whole complex of transcription factors and RNA polymerase II bound to the promoter is called a **transcription initiation complex**. **Figure 17.8** shows the role of transcription factors and a crucial promoter DNA sequence called a **TATA box** in forming the initiation complex at a eukaryotic promoter.

The interaction between eukaryotic RNA polymerase II and transcription factors is an example of the importance

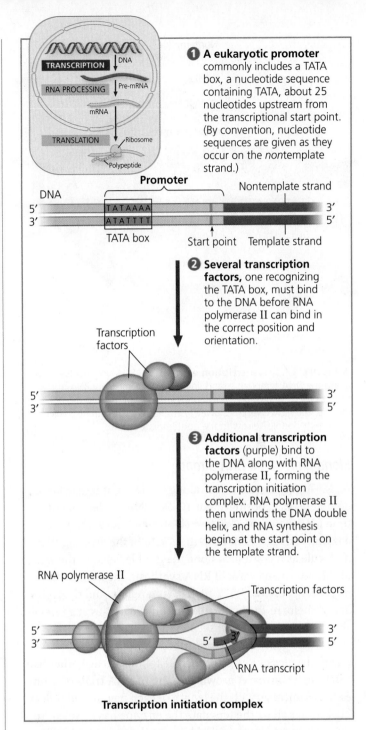

❶ **A eukaryotic promoter** commonly includes a TATA box, a nucleotide sequence containing TATA, about 25 nucleotides upstream from the transcriptional start point. (By convention, nucleotide sequences are given as they occur on the *non*template strand.)

❷ **Several transcription factors,** one recognizing the TATA box, must bind to the DNA before RNA polymerase II can bind in the correct position and orientation.

❸ **Additional transcription factors** (purple) bind to the DNA along with RNA polymerase II, forming the transcription initiation complex. RNA polymerase II then unwinds the DNA double helix, and RNA synthesis begins at the start point on the template strand.

Transcription initiation complex

▲ **Figure 17.8 The initiation of transcription at a eukaryotic promoter.** In eukaryotic cells, proteins called transcription factors mediate the initiation of transcription by RNA polymerase II.

? *Explain how the interaction of RNA polymerase with the promoter would differ if the figure showed transcription initiation for bacteria.*

of protein-protein interactions in controlling eukaryotic transcription. Once the appropriate transcription factors are firmly attached to the promoter DNA and the polymerase is bound in the correct orientation, the enzyme unwinds the two DNA strands and begins transcribing the template strand at the start point.

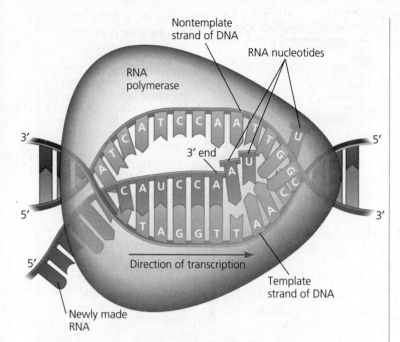

Nontemplate
strand of DNA

RNA
polymerase

RNA nucleotides

3′ end

Direction of transcription

Template
strand of DNA

Newly made
RNA

▲ **Figure 17.9 Transcription elongation.** RNA polymerase moves along the DNA template strand, joining complementary RNA nucleotides to the 3′ end of the growing RNA transcript. Behind the polymerase, the new RNA peels away from the template strand, which re-forms a double helix with the nontemplate strand.

Elongation of the RNA Strand

As RNA polymerase moves along the DNA, it untwists the double helix, exposing about 10–20 DNA nucleotides at a time for pairing with RNA nucleotides **(Figure 17.9)**. The enzyme adds nucleotides to the 3′ end of the growing RNA molecule as it continues along the double helix. In the wake of this advancing wave of RNA synthesis, the new RNA molecule peels away from its DNA template, and the DNA double helix re-forms. Transcription progresses at a rate of about 40 nucleotides per second in eukaryotes.

A single gene can be transcribed simultaneously by several molecules of RNA polymerase following each other like trucks in a convoy. A growing strand of RNA trails off from each polymerase, with the length of each new strand reflecting how far along the template the enzyme has traveled from the start point (see the mRNA molecules in Figure 17.22). The congregation of many polymerase molecules simultaneously transcribing a single gene increases the amount of mRNA transcribed from it, which helps the cell make the encoded protein in large amounts.

Termination of Transcription

The mechanism of termination differs between bacteria and eukaryotes. In bacteria, transcription proceeds through a terminator sequence in the DNA. The transcribed terminator (an RNA sequence) functions as the termination signal, causing the polymerase to detach from the DNA and release the transcript, which requires no further modification before translation. In eukaryotes, RNA polymerase II

transcribes a sequence on the DNA called the polyadenylation signal sequence, which specifies a polyadenylation signal (AAUAAA) in the pre-mRNA. This is called a "signal" because once this stretch of six RNA nucleotides appears, it is immediately bound by certain proteins in the nucleus. Then, at a point about 10–35 nucleotides downstream from the AAUAAA, these proteins cut it free from the polymerase, releasing the pre-mRNA. The pre-mRNA then undergoes processing, the topic of the next section. Although that cleavage marks the end of the mRNA, the RNA polymerase II continues to transcribe. Since the new 5′ end isn't protected by a cap, however, enzymes degrade the RNA from the 5′ end. The polymerase continues transcribing, pursued by the enzymes, until they catch up to the polymerase and it dissociates from the DNA.

CONCEPT CHECK **17.2**

1. What is a promoter? Is it located at the upstream or downstream end of a transcription unit?

2. What enables RNA polymerase to start transcribing a gene at the right place on the DNA in a bacterial cell? In a eukaryotic cell?

3. **WHAT IF?** Suppose X-rays caused a sequence change in the TATA box of a particular gene's promoter. How would that affect transcription of the gene? (See Figure 17.8.)

For suggested answers, see Appendix A.

CONCEPT **17.3**

Eukaryotic cells modify RNA after transcription

Enzymes in the eukaryotic nucleus modify pre-mRNA in specific ways before the genetic message is dispatched to the cytoplasm. During this **RNA processing**, both ends of the primary transcript are altered. Also, in most cases, certain interior sections of the RNA molecule are cut out and the remaining parts spliced together. These modifications produce an mRNA molecule ready for translation.

Alteration of mRNA Ends

Each end of a pre-mRNA molecule is modified in a particular way **(Figure 17.10)**. The 5′ end, which is synthesized first, receives a **5′ cap**, a modified form of a guanine (G) nucleotide added onto the 5′ end after transcription of the first 20–40 nucleotides. The 3′ end of the pre-mRNA molecule is also modified before the mRNA exits the nucleus. Recall that the pre-mRNA is released soon after the polyadenylation signal, AAUAAA, is transcribed. At the 3′ end, an enzyme then adds 50–250 more adenine (A) nucleotides, forming a **poly-A tail**. The 5′ cap and poly-A tail share several important functions. First, they seem to facilitate the

A modified guanine nucleotide added to the 5' end

50–250 adenine nucleotides added to the 3' end

Region that includes protein-coding segments

Polyadenylation signal

5'

3'

G—Ⓟ—Ⓟ—Ⓟ—   AAUAAA   AAA···AAA

5' Cap 5' UTR Start codon Stop codon 3' UTR **Poly-A tail**

▲ **Figure 17.10 RNA processing: Addition of the 5' cap and poly-A tail.** Enzymes modify the two ends of a eukaryotic pre-mRNA molecule. The modified ends may promote the export of mRNA from the nucleus, and they help protect the mRNA from degradation. When the mRNA reaches the cytoplasm, the modified ends, in conjunction with certain cytoplasmic proteins, facilitate ribosome attachment. The 5' cap and poly-A tail are not translated into protein, nor are the regions called the 5' untranslated region (5' UTR) and 3' untranslated region (3' UTR). The pink segments will be described shortly (see Figure 17.11).

export of the mature mRNA from the nucleus. Second, they help protect the mRNA from degradation by hydrolytic enzymes. And third, they help ribosomes attach to the 5' end of the mRNA once the mRNA reaches the cytoplasm. Figure 17.10 shows a diagram of a eukaryotic mRNA molecule with cap and tail. The figure also shows the untranslated regions (UTRs) at the 5' and 3' ends of the mRNA (referred to as the 5' UTR and 3' UTR). The UTRs are parts of the mRNA that will not be translated into protein, but they have other functions, such as ribosome binding.

Split Genes and RNA Splicing

A remarkable stage of RNA processing in the eukaryotic nucleus is the removal of large portions of the RNA molecule that is initially synthesized. This cut-and-paste job, called **RNA splicing**, is similar to editing a video **(Figure 17.11)**. The average length of a transcription unit along a human DNA molecule is about 27,000 nucleotide pairs, so the primary RNA transcript is also that long. However, the average-sized protein of 400 amino acids requires only 1,200 nucleotides in RNA to code for it. (Remember, each amino acid is encoded by a *triplet* of nucleotides.) This means that most eukaryotic genes and their RNA transcripts have long noncoding stretches of nucleotides, regions that are not translated. Even more surprising is that most of these noncoding sequences are interspersed between coding segments of the gene and thus between coding segments of the pre-mRNA. In other words, the sequence of DNA nucleotides that codes for a eukaryotic polypeptide is usually not continuous; it is split into segments. The noncoding segments of nucleic acid that lie between coding regions are called *int*ervening sequences, or **introns.** The other regions are called **exons**, because they are eventually *ex*pressed, usually by being translated into amino acid sequences. (Exceptions include the UTRs of the exons at the ends of the RNA, which make up part of the mRNA but are not translated into protein. Because of these exceptions, you may prefer to think of exons as sequences of RNA that *ex*it the nucleus.) The terms *intron* and *exon* are used for both RNA sequences and the DNA sequences that encode them.

In making a primary transcript from a gene, RNA polymerase II transcribes both introns and exons from the DNA, but the mRNA molecule that enters the cytoplasm is an abridged version. The introns are cut out from the molecule

Pre-mRNA

5' Exon Intron Exon Intron Exon 3'

5' Cap   Poly-A tail

Codon numbers: 1–30 31–104 105–146

Introns cut out and exons spliced together

mRNA

5' Cap   Poly-A tail

5' UTR 1–146 3' UTR

Coding segment

© Pearson Education, Inc.

▲ **Figure 17.11 RNA processing: RNA splicing.** The RNA molecule shown here codes for β-globin, one of the polypeptides of hemoglobin. The numbers under the RNA refer to codons; β-globin is 146 amino acids long. The β-globin gene and its pre-mRNA transcript have three exons, corresponding to sequences that will leave the nucleus as mRNA. (The 5' UTR and 3' UTR are parts of exons because they are included in the mRNA; however, they do not code for protein.) During RNA processing, the introns are cut out and the exons spliced together. In many genes, the introns are much longer than the exons.

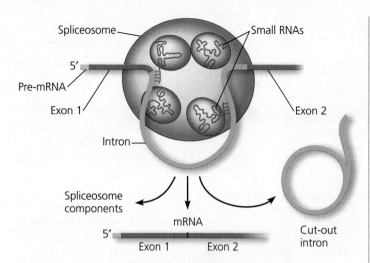

▲ Figure 17.12 A spliceosome splicing a pre-mRNA. The diagram shows a portion of a pre-mRNA transcript, with an intron (pink) flanked by two exons (red). Small RNAs within the spliceosome base-pair with nucleotides at specific sites along the intron. Next, the spliceosome catalyzes cutting of the pre-mRNA and the splicing together of the exons, releasing the intron for rapid degradation.

and the exons joined together, forming an mRNA molecule with a continuous coding sequence. This is the process of RNA splicing.

How is pre-mRNA splicing carried out? The removal of introns is accomplished by a large complex made of proteins and small RNAs called a **spliceosome**. This complex binds to several short nucleotide sequences along an intron, including key sequences at each end **(Figure 17.12)**. The intron is then released (and rapidly degraded), and the spliceosome joins together the two exons that flanked the intron. It turns out that the small RNAs in the spliceosome not only participate in spliceosome assembly and splice site recognition, but also catalyze the splicing reaction.

Ribozymes

The idea of a catalytic role for the RNAs in the spliceosome arose from the discovery of **ribozymes**, RNA molecules that function as enzymes. In some organisms, RNA splicing can occur without proteins or even additional RNA molecules: The intron RNA functions as a ribozyme and catalyzes its own excision! For example, in the ciliate protist *Tetrahymena*, self-splicing occurs in the production of ribosomal RNA (rRNA), a component of the organism's ribosomes. The pre-rRNA actually removes its own introns. The discovery of ribozymes rendered obsolete the idea that all biological catalysts are proteins.

Three properties of RNA enable some RNA molecules to function as enzymes. First, because RNA is single-stranded, a region of an RNA molecule may base-pair, in an antiparallel arrangement, with a complementary region elsewhere in the same molecule; this gives the molecule a particular three-dimensional structure. A specific structure is essential to the catalytic function of ribozymes, just as it is

for enzymatic proteins. Second, like certain amino acids in an enzymatic protein, some of the bases in RNA contain functional groups that can participate in catalysis. Third, the ability of RNA to hydrogen-bond with other nucleic acid molecules (either RNA or DNA) adds specificity to its catalytic activity. For example, complementary base pairing between the RNA of the spliceosome and the RNA of a primary RNA transcript precisely locates the region where the ribozyme catalyzes splicing. Later in this chapter, you will see how these properties of RNA also allow it to perform important noncatalytic roles in the cell, such as recognition of the three-nucleotide codons on mRNA.

The Functional and Evolutionary Importance of Introns

EVOLUTION Whether or not RNA splicing and the presence of introns have provided selective advantages during evolutionary history is a matter of some debate. In any case, it is informative to consider their possible adaptive benefits. Specific functions have not been identified for most introns, but at least some contain sequences that regulate gene expression, and many affect gene products.

One important consequence of the presence of introns in genes is that a single gene can encode more than one kind of polypeptide. Many genes are known to give rise to two or more different polypeptides, depending on which segments are treated as exons during RNA processing; this is called **alternative RNA splicing** (see Figure 18.13). For example, sex differences in fruit flies are largely due to differences in how males and females splice the RNA transcribed from certain genes. Results from the Human Genome Project (discussed in Concept 21.1) suggest that alternative RNA splicing is one reason humans can get along with about the same number of genes as a nematode (roundworm). Because of alternative splicing, the number of different protein products an organism produces can be much greater than its number of genes.

Proteins often have a modular architecture consisting of discrete structural and functional regions called **domains**. One domain of an enzyme, for example, might include the active site, while another might allow the enzyme to bind to a cellular membrane. In quite a few cases, different exons code for the different domains of a protein **(Figure 17.13)**.

The presence of introns in a gene may facilitate the evolution of new and potentially beneficial proteins as a result of a process known as *exon shuffling*. Introns increase the probability of crossing over between the exons of alleles of a gene—simply by providing more terrain for crossovers without interrupting coding sequences. This might result in new combinations of exons and proteins with altered structure and function. We can also imagine the occasional mixing and matching of exons between completely different (nonallelic) genes. Exon shuffling of either sort could lead to new proteins with novel combinations of functions. While most of the shuffling would result in nonbeneficial changes, occasionally a beneficial variant might arise.

© Pearson Education, Inc.

▲ **Figure 17.13 Correspondence between exons and protein domains.**

CONCEPT CHECK 17.3

1. There are fewer than 21,000 human genes. How, then, can human cells make 75,000–100,000 different proteins?

2. How is RNA splicing similar to how you would watch a television show recorded earlier using a DVR? What would introns correspond to in this analogy?

3. **WHAT IF?** What would be the effect of treating cells with an agent that removed the cap from mRNAs?

For suggested answers, see Appendix A.

CONCEPT 17.4

Translation is the RNA-directed synthesis of a polypeptide: *A closer look*

We will now examine in greater detail how genetic information flows from mRNA to protein—the process of translation. As we did for transcription, we'll concentrate on the basic steps of translation that occur in both bacteria and eukaryotes, while pointing out key differences.

Molecular Components of Translation

In the process of translation, a cell "reads" a genetic message and builds a polypeptide accordingly. The message is a series of codons along an mRNA molecule, and the translator is called **transfer RNA (tRNA)**. The function of tRNA is to transfer amino acids from the cytoplasmic pool of amino acids to a growing polypeptide in a ribosome. A cell keeps its cytoplasm stocked with all 20 amino acids, either by synthesizing them from other compounds or by taking them up from the surrounding solution. The ribosome, a structure

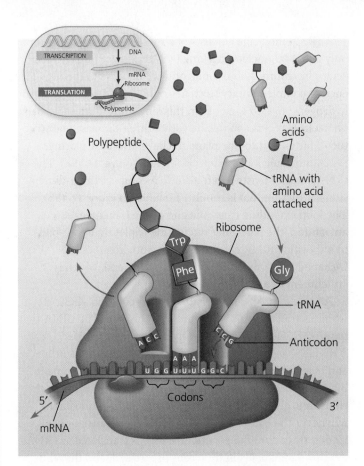

▲ **Figure 17.14 Translation: the basic concept.** As a molecule of mRNA is moved through a ribosome, codons are translated into amino acids, one by one. The interpreters are tRNA molecules, each type with a specific nucleotide triplet called an anticodon at one end and a corresponding amino acid at the other end. A tRNA adds its amino acid cargo to a growing polypeptide chain when the anticodon hydrogen-bonds to the complementary codon on the mRNA. The figures that follow show some of the details of translation in a bacterial cell.

 ANIMATION **BioFlix** Visit the Study Area in **MasteringBiology** for the BioFlix® 3-D Animation on Protein Synthesis. BioFlix Tutorials can also be assigned in MasteringBiology.

made of proteins and RNAs, adds each amino acid brought to it by tRNA to the growing end of a polypeptide chain **(Figure 17.14)**.

Translation is simple in principle but complex in its biochemistry and mechanics, especially in the eukaryotic cell. In dissecting translation, we'll focus on the slightly less complicated version of the process that occurs in bacteria. We'll first look at the major players in this process and then see how they act together in making a polypeptide.

The Structure and Function of Transfer RNA

The key to translating a genetic message into a specific amino acid sequence is the fact that each tRNA molecule translates a given mRNA codon into a certain amino acid. This is possible because a tRNA bears a specific amino acid at one end, while at the other end is a nucleotide triplet that can base-pair with the complementary codon on mRNA.

A tRNA molecule consists of a single RNA strand that is only about 80 nucleotides long (whereas most mRNA molecules have hundreds of nucleotides). Because of the presence of complementary stretches of nucleotide bases that can hydrogen-bond to each other, this single strand can fold back on itself and form a molecule with a three-dimensional structure. Flattened into one plane to clarify this base pairing, a tRNA molecule looks like a cloverleaf (**Figure 17.15a**). The tRNA actually twists and folds into a compact three-dimensional structure that is roughly L-shaped (**Figure 17.15b**). The loop extending from one end of the L includes the **anticodon**, the particular nucleotide triplet that base-pairs to a specific mRNA codon. From the other end of the L-shaped tRNA molecule protrudes its 3′ end, which is the attachment site for an amino acid.

As an example, consider the mRNA codon 5′-GGC-3′, which is translated as the amino acid glycine. The tRNA that base-pairs with this codon by hydrogen bonding has 3′-CCG-5′ as its anticodon and carries glycine at its other end (see the incoming tRNA approaching the ribosome in Figure 17.14). As an mRNA molecule is moved through a ribosome, glycine will be added to the polypeptide chain whenever the codon GGC is presented for translation. Codon by codon, the genetic message is translated as tRNAs deposit amino acids in the order prescribed, and the ribosome joins the amino acids into a chain. The tRNA molecule is a translator in the sense that it can read a nucleic acid word (the mRNA codon) and interpret it as a protein word (the amino acid).

Like mRNA and other types of cellular RNA, transfer RNA molecules are transcribed from DNA templates. In a eukaryotic cell, tRNA, like mRNA, is made in the nucleus and then travels from the nucleus to the cytoplasm, where it will participate in the process of translation. In both bacterial and eukaryotic cells, each tRNA molecule is used repeatedly, picking up its designated amino acid in the cytosol, depositing this cargo onto a polypeptide chain at the ribosome, and then leaving the ribosome, ready to pick up another of the same amino acid.

The accurate translation of a genetic message requires two instances of molecular recognition. First, a tRNA that binds to an mRNA codon specifying a particular amino acid must carry that amino acid, and no other, to the ribosome. The correct matching up of tRNA and amino acid is carried out by a family of related enzymes called **aminoacyl-tRNA synthetases (Figure 17.16)**. The active site of each type of aminoacyl-tRNA synthetase fits only a specific combination of amino acid and tRNA. There are 20 different synthetases, one for each amino acid; each synthetase is able to bind to all the different tRNAs that code for its particular amino acid. The synthetase catalyzes the covalent attachment of the amino acid to its tRNA in a process driven by the hydrolysis of ATP. The resulting aminoacyl tRNA, also called a charged tRNA, is released from the enzyme and is then

(a) Two-dimensional structure. The four base-paired regions and three loops are characteristic of all tRNAs, as is the base sequence of the amino acid attachment site at the 3′ end. The anticodon triplet is unique to each tRNA type, as are some sequences in the other two loops. (The asterisks mark bases that have been chemically modified, a characteristic of tRNA. The modified bases contribute to tRNA function in a way that is not yet understood.)

(b) Three-dimensional structure

(c) Symbol used in this book

▲ **Figure 17.15 The structure of transfer RNA (tRNA).** Anticodons are conventionally written 3′ → 5′ to align properly with codons written 5′ → 3′ (see Figure 17.14). For base pairing, RNA strands must be antiparallel, like DNA. For example, anticodon 3′-AAG-5′ pairs with mRNA codon 5′-UUC-3′.

available to deliver its amino acid to a growing polypeptide chain on a ribosome.

The second instance of molecular recognition is the pairing of the tRNA anticodon with the appropriate mRNA codon. If one tRNA variety existed for each mRNA codon specifying an amino acid, there would be 61 tRNAs (see Figure 17.5). In fact, there are only about 45, signifying that some tRNAs must be able to bind to more than one codon.

① The amino acid and the appropriate tRNA enter the active site of the specific synthetase.

Tyrosine (Tyr) (amino acid)

Tyrosyl-tRNA synthetase (enzyme), which can only bind tyrosine and Tyr-tRNA

Tyr-tRNA

A U A

Anticodon on tRNA complementary to the Tyr codon on mRNA

ATP

AMP + 2 ℗ᵢ

② Using ATP, the synthetase catalyzes the covalent bonding of the amino acid to its specific tRNA.

Aminoacyl-tRNA synthetase

tRNA

Amino acid

③ The tRNA, charged with its amino acid, is released by the synthetase.

Computer model

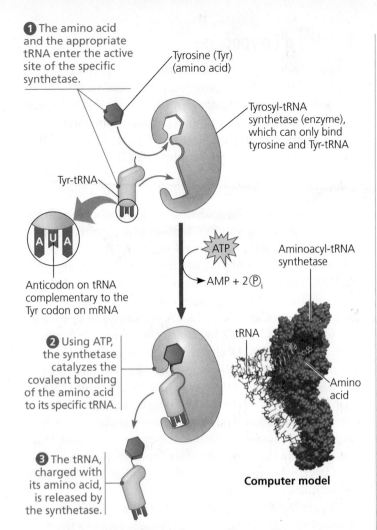

▲ **Figure 17.16 Aminoacyl-tRNA synthetases provide specificity in joining amino acids to their tRNAs.** Linkage of a tRNA to its amino acid is an endergonic process that occurs at the expense of ATP, which loses two phosphate groups, becoming AMP (adenosine monophosphate).

Such versatility is possible because the rules for base pairing between the third nucleotide base of a codon and the corresponding base of a tRNA anticodon are relaxed compared to those at other codon positions. For example, the nucleotide base U at the 5′ end of a tRNA anticodon can pair with either A or G in the third position (at the 3′ end) of an mRNA codon. The flexible base pairing at this codon position is called **wobble**. Wobble explains why the synonymous codons for a given amino acid most often differ in their third nucleotide base, but not in the other bases. A case in point is that a tRNA with the anticodon 3′-UCU-5′ can base-pair with either the mRNA codon 5′-AGA-3′ or 5′-AGG-3′, both of which code for arginine (see Figure 17.5).

Ribosomes

Ribosomes facilitate the specific coupling of tRNA anticodons with mRNA codons during protein synthesis. A ribosome consists of a large subunit and a small subunit, each made up of proteins and one or more **ribosomal RNAs (rRNAs) (Figure 17.17)**. In eukaryotes, the subunits are

(a) **Computer model of functioning ribosome.** This is a model of a bacterial ribosome, showing its overall shape. The eukaryotic ribosome is roughly similar. A ribosomal subunit is a complex of ribosomal RNA molecules and proteins.

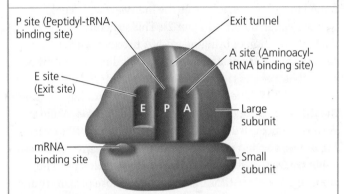

(b) **Schematic model showing binding sites.** A ribosome has an mRNA binding site and three tRNA binding sites, known as the A, P, and E sites. This schematic ribosome will appear in later diagrams.

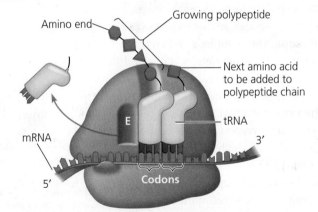

(c) **Schematic model with mRNA and tRNA.** A tRNA fits into a binding site when its anticodon base-pairs with an mRNA codon. The P site holds the tRNA attached to the growing polypeptide. The A site holds the tRNA carrying the next amino acid to be added to the polypeptide chain. Discharged tRNAs leave from the E site. The polypeptide grows at its carboxyl end.

▲ **Figure 17.17 The anatomy of a functioning ribosome.**

made in the nucleolus. Ribosomal RNA genes are transcribed, and the RNA is processed and assembled with proteins imported from the cytoplasm. Completed ribosomal subunits are then exported via nuclear pores to the cytoplasm. In both bacteria and eukaryotes, a large and a small subunit join to form a functional ribosome only when attached to an mRNA molecule. About one-third of the mass of a ribosome is made up of proteins; the rest consists of rRNAs, either three molecules (in bacteria) or four (in eukaryotes). Because most cells contain thousands of ribosomes, rRNA is the most abundant type of cellular RNA.

Although the ribosomes of bacteria and eukaryotes are very similar in structure and function, eukaryotic ribosomes are slightly larger, as well as differing somewhat from bacterial ribosomes in their molecular composition. The differences are medically significant. Certain antibiotic drugs can inactivate bacterial ribosomes without affecting eukaryotic ribosomes. These drugs, including tetracycline and streptomycin, are used to combat bacterial infections.

The structure of the bacterial ribosome has been determined to the atomic level (see the interview with Venki Ramakrishnan before Chapter 2). This structure clearly reflects its function of bringing mRNA together with tRNAs carrying amino acids. In addition to a binding site for mRNA, each ribosome has three binding sites for tRNA, as described in Figure 17.17. The **P site** (peptidyl-tRNA binding site) holds the tRNA carrying the growing polypeptide chain, while the **A site** (aminoacyl-tRNA binding site) holds the tRNA carrying the next amino acid to be added to the chain. Discharged tRNAs leave the ribosome from the **E site** (exit site). The ribosome holds the tRNA and mRNA in close proximity and positions the new amino acid so that it can be added to the carboxyl end of the growing polypeptide. It then catalyzes the formation of the peptide bond. As the polypeptide becomes longer, it passes through an *exit tunnel* in the ribosome's large subunit. When the polypeptide is complete, it is released through the exit tunnel.

There is strong evidence supporting the hypothesis that rRNA, not protein, is primarily responsible for both the structure and the function of the ribosome. The proteins, which are largely on the exterior, support the shape changes of the rRNA molecules as they carry out catalysis during translation. Ribosomal RNA is the main constituent of the A and P sites and of the interface between the two subunits; it also acts as the catalyst of peptide bond formation. Thus, a ribosome can be regarded as one colossal ribozyme!

Building a Polypeptide

We can divide translation, the synthesis of a polypeptide chain, into three stages: initiation, elongation, and termination. All three stages require protein "factors" that aid in the translation process. For certain aspects of chain initiation and elongation, energy is also required. It is provided by the hydrolysis of guanosine triphosphate (GTP).

Ribosome Association and Initiation of Translation

The initiation stage of translation brings together mRNA, a tRNA bearing the first amino acid of the polypeptide, and the two subunits of a ribosome (**Figure 17.18**). First, a small ribosomal subunit binds to both mRNA and a specific initiator tRNA, which carries the amino acid methionine. In bacteria, the small subunit can bind these two in either order; it binds the mRNA at a specific RNA sequence, just upstream of the start codon, AUG. In eukaryotes, the small subunit, with the initiator tRNA already bound, binds to the 5′ cap of the mRNA and then moves, or *scans*, downstream along the mRNA until it reaches the start codon; the initiator tRNA then hydrogen-bonds to the AUG start codon. In either case, the start codon signals the start of translation; this is important because it establishes the codon reading frame for the mRNA. In the Scientific Skills Exercise, you can work with DNA sequences encoding the ribosomal binding sites on the mRNAs of a group of *E. coli* genes.

The union of mRNA, initiator tRNA, and a small ribosomal subunit is followed by the attachment of a large ribosomal subunit, completing the *translation initiation complex*. Proteins called *initiation factors* are required to

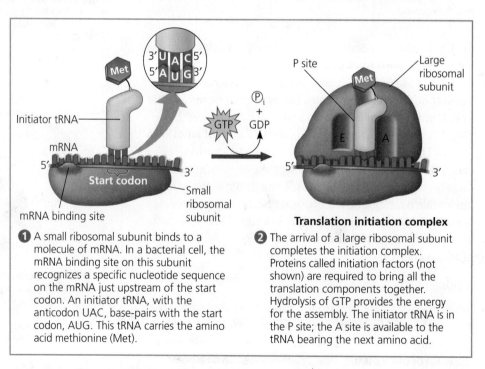

❶ A small ribosomal subunit binds to a molecule of mRNA. In a bacterial cell, the mRNA binding site on this subunit recognizes a specific nucleotide sequence on the mRNA just upstream of the start codon. An initiator tRNA, with the anticodon UAC, base-pairs with the start codon, AUG. This tRNA carries the amino acid methionine (Met).

❷ The arrival of a large ribosomal subunit completes the initiation complex. Proteins called initiation factors (not shown) are required to bring all the translation components together. Hydrolysis of GTP provides the energy for the assembly. The initiator tRNA is in the P site; the A site is available to the tRNA bearing the next amino acid.

▲ **Figure 17.18 The initiation of translation.**

Interpreting a Sequence Logo

How Can a Sequence Logo Be Used to Identify Ribosome Binding Sites? When initiating translation, ribosomes bind to an mRNA at a ribosome binding site upstream of the AUG start codon. Because mRNAs from different genes all bind to a ribosome, the genes encoding these mRNAs are likely to have a similar base sequence where the ribosomes bind. Therefore, candidate ribosome binding sites on mRNA can be identified by comparing DNA sequences (and thus the mRNA sequences) of multiple genes in a species, searching the region upstream of the start codon for shared ("conserved") stretches of bases. In this exercise, you will analyze DNA sequences from multiple such genes, represented by a visual graphic called a sequence logo.

How the Experiment Was Done The DNA sequences of 149 genes from the *E. coli* genome were aligned using computer software. The aim was to identify similar base sequences—at the appropriate location in each gene—as potential ribosome binding sites. Rather than presenting the data as a series of 149 sequences aligned in a column (a sequence alignment), the researchers used a sequence logo.

Data from the Experiment To show how sequence logos are made, the potential ribosome binding regions from 10 *E. coli* genes are shown in a sequence alignment, followed by the sequence logo derived from the aligned sequences. Note that the DNA shown is the nontemplate (coding) strand, which is how DNA sequences are typically presented.

thrA	GGTAACGAGGTAACAACCATGCGAGTG
lacA	CATAACGGAGTGATCGCATTGAACATG
lacY	CGCGTAAGGAAATCCATTATGTACTAT
lacZ	TTCACACAGGAAACAGCTATGACCATG
lacI	CAATTCAGGGTGGTGAATGTGAAACCA
recA	GGCATGACAGGAGTAAAAATGGCTATC
galR	ACCCACTAAGGTATTTTCATGGCGACC
metJ	AAGAGGATTAAGTATCTCATGGCTGAA
lexA	ATACACCCAGGGGGGCGGAATGAAAGCG
trpR	TAACAATGGCGACATATTATGGCCCAA

▲ **Sequence alignment**

▲ **Sequence logo**

Interpret the Data

1. In the sequence logo (bottom, left), the horizontal axis shows the primary sequence of the DNA by nucleotide position. Letters for each base are stacked on top of each other according to their relative frequency at that position among the aligned sequences, with the most common base as the largest letter at the top of the stack. The height of each letter represents the relative frequency of that base *at that position*. (a) In the sequence alignment, count the number of each base at position –9 and order them from most to least frequent. Compare this to the size and placement of each base at –9 in the logo. (b) Do the same for positions 0 and 1.

2. The height of a stack of letters in a logo indicates the predictive power of that stack (determined statistically). If the stack is tall, we can be more confident in predicting what base will be in that position if a new sequence is added to the logo. For example, at position 2, all 10 sequences have a G; the probability of finding a G there in a new sequence is very high, as is the stack. For short stacks, the bases all have about the same frequency, so it's hard to predict a base at those positions. (a) Which two positions have the most predictable bases? What bases do you predict would be at those positions in a newly sequenced gene? (b) Which 12 positions have the least predictable bases? How do you know? How does this reflect the relative frequencies of the bases shown in the 10 sequences? Use the two leftmost positions of the 12 as examples in your answer.

3. In the actual experiment, the researchers used 149 sequences to build their sequence logo, which is shown below. There is a stack at each position, even if short, because the sequence logo includes more data. (a) Which three positions in this sequence logo have the most predictable bases? Name the most frequent base at each. (b) Which positions have the least predictable bases? How can you tell?

4. A consensus sequence identifies the base occurring most often at each position in the set of sequences. (a) Write out the consensus sequence of this (the nontemplate) strand. In any position where the base can't be determined, put a dash. (b) Which provides more information—the consensus sequence or the sequence logo? What is lost in the less informative method?

5. (a) Based on the logo, what five adjacent base positions in the 5' UTR region are most likely to be involved in ribosome binding? Explain. (b) What is represented by the bases in positions 0–2?

MB A version of this Scientific Skills Exercise can be assigned in MasteringBiology.

Further Reading T. D. Schneider and R. M. Stephens, Sequence logos: A new way to display consensus sequences, *Nucleic Acids Research* 18:6097–6100 (1990).

bring all these components together. The cell also expends energy obtained by hydrolysis of a GTP molecule to form the initiation complex. At the completion of the initiation process, the initiator tRNA sits in the P site of the ribosome, and the vacant A site is ready for the next aminoacyl tRNA. Note that a polypeptide is always synthesized in one direction, from the initial methionine at the amino end, also called the N-terminus, toward the final amino acid at the carboxyl end, also called the C-terminus (see Figure 5.15).

Elongation of the Polypeptide Chain

In the elongation stage of translation, amino acids are added one by one to the previous amino acid at the C-terminus of the growing chain. Each addition involves the participation of several proteins called *elongation factors* and occurs in a three-step cycle described in **Figure 17.19**. Energy expenditure occurs in the first and third steps. Codon recognition requires hydrolysis of one molecule of GTP, which increases the accuracy and efficiency of this step. One more GTP is hydrolyzed to provide energy for the translocation step.

The mRNA is moved through the ribosome in one direction only, 5' end first; this is equivalent to the ribosome moving 5' → 3' on the mRNA. The important point is that the ribosome and the mRNA move relative to each other, unidirectionally, codon by codon. The elongation cycle takes less than a tenth of a second in bacteria and is repeated as each amino acid is added to the chain until the polypeptide is completed. The empty tRNAs that are released from the E site return to the cytoplasm, where they will be reloaded with the appropriate amino acid (see Figure 17.16).

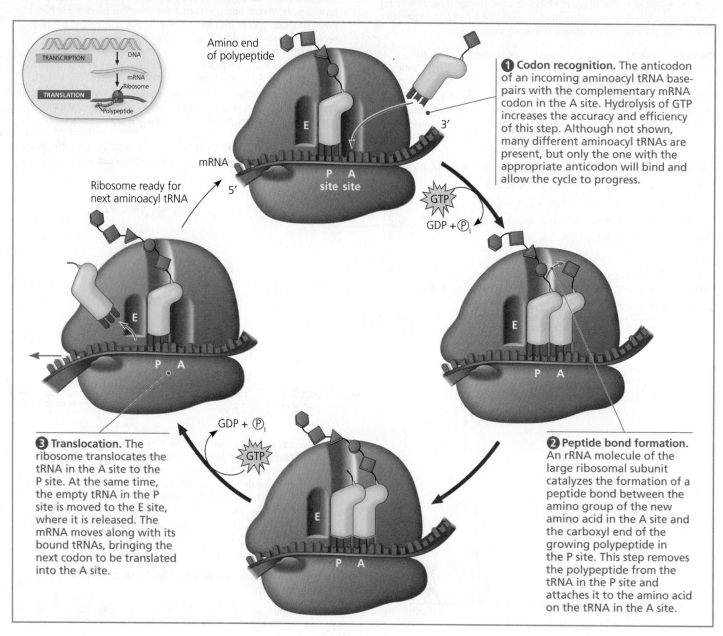

1 Codon recognition. The anticodon of an incoming aminoacyl tRNA base-pairs with the complementary mRNA codon in the A site. Hydrolysis of GTP increases the accuracy and efficiency of this step. Although not shown, many different aminoacyl tRNAs are present, but only the one with the appropriate anticodon will bind and allow the cycle to progress.

2 Peptide bond formation. An rRNA molecule of the large ribosomal subunit catalyzes the formation of a peptide bond between the amino group of the new amino acid in the A site and the carboxyl end of the growing polypeptide in the P site. This step removes the polypeptide from the tRNA in the P site and attaches it to the amino acid on the tRNA in the A site.

3 Translocation. The ribosome translocates the tRNA in the A site to the P site. At the same time, the empty tRNA in the P site is moved to the E site, where it is released. The mRNA moves along with its bound tRNAs, bringing the next codon to be translated into the A site.

▲ **Figure 17.19 The elongation cycle of translation.** The hydrolysis of GTP plays an important role in the elongation process. Not shown are the proteins called elongation factors.

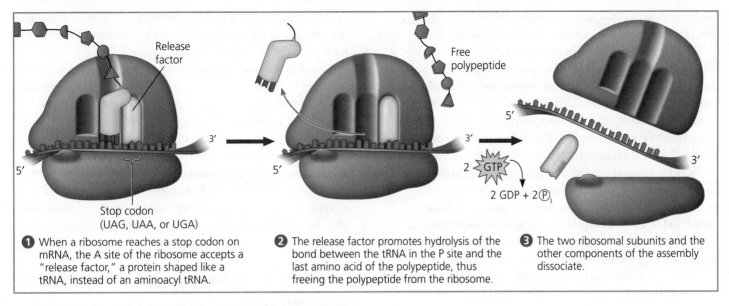

① When a ribosome reaches a stop codon on mRNA, the A site of the ribosome accepts a "release factor," a protein shaped like a tRNA, instead of an aminoacyl tRNA.

② The release factor promotes hydrolysis of the bond between the tRNA in the P site and the last amino acid of the polypeptide, thus freeing the polypeptide from the ribosome.

③ The two ribosomal subunits and the other components of the assembly dissociate.

▲ **Figure 17.20 The termination of translation.** Like elongation, termination requires GTP hydrolysis as well as additional protein factors, which are not shown here.

Termination of Translation

The final stage of translation is termination **(Figure 17.20)**. Elongation continues until a stop codon in the mRNA reaches the A site of the ribosome. The nucleotide base triplets UAG, UAA, and UGA do not code for amino acids but instead act as signals to stop translation. A *release factor*, a protein shaped like an aminoacyl tRNA, binds directly to the stop codon in the A site. The release factor causes the addition of a water molecule instead of an amino acid to the polypeptide chain. (There are plenty of water molecules available in the aqueous cellular environment.) This reaction breaks (hydrolyzes) the bond between the completed polypeptide and the tRNA in the P site, releasing the polypeptide through the exit tunnel of the ribosome's large subunit. The remainder of the translation assembly then comes apart in a multistep process, aided by other protein factors. Breakdown of the translation assembly requires the hydrolysis of two more GTP molecules.

Completing and Targeting the Functional Protein

The process of translation is often not sufficient to make a functional protein. In this section, you will learn about modifications that polypeptide chains undergo after the translation process as well as some of the mechanisms used to target completed proteins to specific sites in the cell.

Protein Folding and Post-Translational Modifications

During its synthesis, a polypeptide chain begins to coil and fold spontaneously as a consequence of its amino acid sequence (primary structure), forming a protein with a specific shape: a three-dimensional molecule with secondary and tertiary structure (see Figure 5.18). Thus, a gene determines primary structure, and primary structure in turn determines shape. In many cases, a chaperone protein (chaperonin) helps the polypeptide fold correctly (see Figure 5.21).

Additional steps—*post-translational modifications*—may be required before the protein can begin doing its particular job in the cell. Certain amino acids may be chemically modified by the attachment of sugars, lipids, phosphate groups, or other additions. Enzymes may remove one or more amino acids from the leading (amino) end of the polypeptide chain. In some cases, a polypeptide chain may be enzymatically cleaved into two or more pieces. For example, the protein insulin is first synthesized as a single polypeptide chain but becomes active only after an enzyme cuts out a central part of the chain, leaving a protein made up of two polypeptide chains connected by disulfide bridges. In other cases, two or more polypeptides that are synthesized separately may come together, becoming the subunits of a protein that has quaternary structure. A familiar example is hemoglobin (see Figure 5.18).

Targeting Polypeptides to Specific Locations

In electron micrographs of eukaryotic cells active in protein synthesis, two populations of ribosomes are evident: free and bound (see Figure 6.10). Free ribosomes are suspended in the cytosol and mostly synthesize proteins that stay in the cytosol and function there. In contrast, bound ribosomes are attached to the cytosolic side of the endoplasmic reticulum (ER) or to the nuclear envelope. Bound ribosomes make proteins of the endomembrane system (the nuclear envelope, ER, Golgi apparatus, lysosomes, vacuoles, and plasma membrane) as well as proteins secreted from the cell, such as insulin. It is important to note that the ribosomes themselves are identical and can alternate between being free one time they are used and bound the next.

What determines whether a ribosome is free in the cytosol or bound to rough ER? Polypeptide synthesis always begins in the cytosol as a free ribosome starts to translate an mRNA molecule. There the process continues to completion—*unless* the growing polypeptide itself cues the ribosome to attach to the ER. The polypeptides of proteins destined for the endomembrane system or for secretion are marked by a **signal peptide**, which targets the protein to the ER (**Figure 17.21**). The signal peptide, a sequence of about 20 amino acids at or near the leading end (N-terminus) of the polypeptide, is recognized as it emerges from the ribosome by a protein-RNA complex called a **signal-recognition particle (SRP)**. This particle functions as an escort that brings the ribosome to a receptor protein built into the ER membrane. The receptor is part of a multiprotein translocation complex. Polypeptide synthesis continues there, and the growing polypeptide snakes across the membrane into the ER lumen via a protein pore. The signal peptide is usually removed by an enzyme. The rest of the completed polypeptide, if it is to be secreted from the cell, is released into solution within the ER lumen (as in Figure 17.21). Alternatively, if the polypeptide is to be a membrane protein, it remains partially embedded in the ER membrane. In either case, it travels in a transport vesicle to its destination (see, for example, Figure 7.9).

Other kinds of signal peptides are used to target polypeptides to mitochondria, chloroplasts, the interior of the nucleus, and other organelles that are not part of the endomembrane system. The critical difference in these cases is that translation is completed in the cytosol before the polypeptide is imported into the organelle. Translocation mechanisms also vary, but in all cases studied to date, the "postal zip codes" that address proteins for secretion or to cellular locations are signal peptides of some sort. Bacteria also employ signal peptides to target proteins to the plasma membrane for secretion.

Making Multiple Polypeptides in Bacteria and Eukaryotes

In previous sections, you learned how a single polypeptide is synthesized using the information encoded in an mRNA molecule. When a polypeptide is required in a cell, though, the need is for many copies, not just one.

A single ribosome can make an average-sized polypeptide in less than a minute. In both bacteria and eukaryotes,

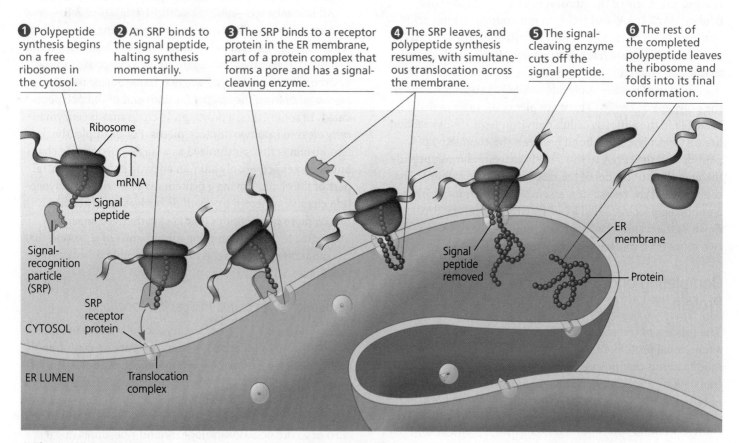

❶ Polypeptide synthesis begins on a free ribosome in the cytosol.

❷ An SRP binds to the signal peptide, halting synthesis momentarily.

❸ The SRP binds to a receptor protein in the ER membrane, part of a protein complex that forms a pore and has a signal-cleaving enzyme.

❹ The SRP leaves, and polypeptide synthesis resumes, with simultaneous translocation across the membrane.

❺ The signal-cleaving enzyme cuts off the signal peptide.

❻ The rest of the completed polypeptide leaves the ribosome and folds into its final conformation.

Ribosome
mRNA
Signal peptide
Signal-recognition particle (SRP)
SRP receptor protein
CYTOSOL
Translocation complex
ER LUMEN
Signal peptide removed
ER membrane
Protein

▲ **Figure 17.21** The signal mechanism for targeting proteins to the ER.

MAKE CONNECTIONS *If this protein were destined for secretion, what would happen to it after its synthesis was completed? See Figure 7.9.*

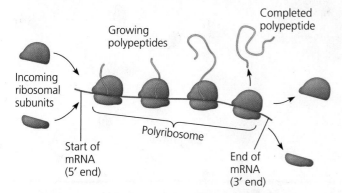

Completed polypeptide

Growing polypeptides

Incoming ribosomal subunits

Polyribosome

Start of mRNA (5′ end)

End of mRNA (3′ end)

(a) An mRNA molecule is generally translated simultaneously by several ribosomes in clusters called polyribosomes.

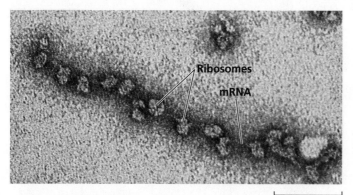

Ribosomes

mRNA

0.1 μm

(b) This micrograph shows a large polyribosome in a bacterial cell. Growing polypeptides are not visible here (TEM).

▲ **Figure 17.22 Polyribosomes.**

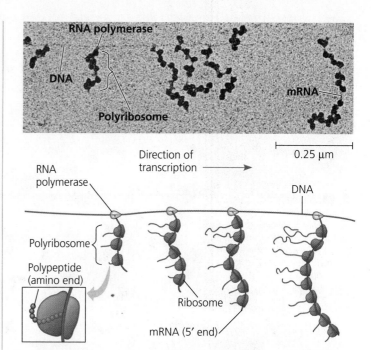

RNA polymerase

DNA

Polyribosome

mRNA

0.25 μm

RNA polymerase

Direction of transcription

DNA

Polyribosome

Polypeptide (amino end)

Ribosome

mRNA (5′ end)

▲ **Figure 17.23 Coupled transcription and translation in bacteria.** In bacterial cells, the translation of mRNA can begin as soon as the leading (5′) end of the mRNA molecule peels away from the DNA template. The micrograph (TEM) shows a strand of *E. coli* DNA being transcribed by RNA polymerase molecules. Attached to each RNA polymerase molecule is a growing strand of mRNA, which is already being translated by ribosomes. The newly synthesized polypeptides are not visible in the micrograph but are shown in the diagram.

? *Which one of the mRNA molecules started being transcribed first? On that mRNA, which ribosome started translating the mRNA first?*

however, multiple ribosomes translate an mRNA at the same time **(Figure 17.22)**; that is, a single mRNA is used to make many copies of a polypeptide simultaneously. Once a ribosome is far enough past the start codon, a second ribosome can attach to the mRNA, eventually resulting in a number of ribosomes trailing along the mRNA. Such strings of ribosomes, called **polyribosomes** (or **polysomes**), can be seen with an electron microscope (see Figure 17.22). They enable a cell to make many copies of a polypeptide very quickly.

Another way both bacteria and eukaryotes augment the number of copies of a polypeptide is by transcribing multiple mRNAs from the same gene, as we mentioned earlier. However, the coordination of the two processes—transcription and translation—differ in the two groups. The most important differences between bacteria and eukaryotes arise from the bacterial cell's lack of compartmental organization. Like a one-room workshop, a bacterial cell ensures a streamlined operation by coupling the two processes. In the absence of a nucleus, it can simultaneously transcribe and translate the same gene **(Figure 17.23)**, and the newly made protein can quickly diffuse to its site of function.

In contrast, the eukaryotic cell's nuclear envelope segregates transcription from translation and provides a compartment for extensive RNA processing. This processing stage includes additional steps, discussed earlier, the regulation of which can help coordinate the eukaryotic cell's elaborate activities. **Figure 17.24** summarizes the path from gene to polypeptide in a eukaryotic cell.

CONCEPT CHECK 17.4

1. What two processes ensure that the correct amino acid is added to a growing polypeptide chain?

2. Discuss the ways in which rRNA structure likely contributes to ribosomal function.

3. Describe how a polypeptide to be secreted reaches the endomembrane system.

4. **WHAT IF? DRAW IT** Draw a tRNA with the anticodon 3′-CGU-5′. What two different codons could it bind to? Draw each codon on an mRNA, labeling all 5′ and 3′ ends, the tRNA, and the amino acid it carries.

5. **WHAT IF?** In eukaryotic cells, mRNAs have been found to have a circular arrangement in which proteins hold the poly-A tail near the 5′ cap. How might this increase translation efficiency?

For suggested answers, see Appendix A.

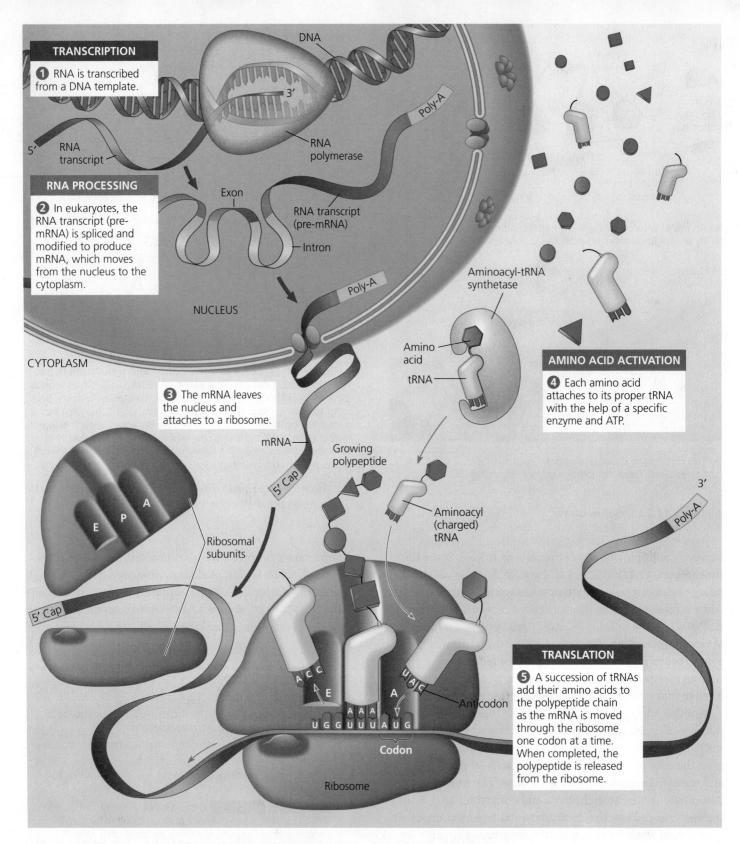

TRANSCRIPTION

1 RNA is transcribed from a DNA template.

DNA

RNA polymerase

3'

5'

RNA transcript

Poly-A

RNA PROCESSING

2 In eukaryotes, the RNA transcript (pre-mRNA) is spliced and modified to produce mRNA, which moves from the nucleus to the cytoplasm.

Exon

RNA transcript (pre-mRNA)

Intron

NUCLEUS

CYTOPLASM

Poly-A

3 The mRNA leaves the nucleus and attaches to a ribosome.

mRNA

5' Cap

Growing polypeptide

Aminoacyl-tRNA synthetase

Amino acid

tRNA

AMINO ACID ACTIVATION

4 Each amino acid attaches to its proper tRNA with the help of a specific enzyme and ATP.

3'

Poly-A

Aminoacyl (charged) tRNA

Ribosomal subunits

5' Cap

E P A

Anticodon

TRANSLATION

5 A succession of tRNAs add their amino acids to the polypeptide chain as the mRNA is moved through the ribosome one codon at a time. When completed, the polypeptide is released from the ribosome.

A C C

E

U A C

A

A A A

U G G U U U A U G

Codon

Ribosome

▲ **Figure 17.24 A summary of transcription and translation in a eukaryotic cell.** This diagram shows the path from one gene to one polypeptide. Keep in mind that each gene in the DNA can be transcribed repeatedly into many identical RNA molecules and that each mRNA can be translated repeatedly to yield many identical polypeptide molecules. (Also, remember that the final products of some genes are not polypeptides but RNA molecules, including tRNA and rRNA.) In general, the steps of transcription and translation are similar in bacterial, archaeal, and eukaryotic cells. The major difference is the occurrence of RNA processing in the eukaryotic nucleus. Other significant differences are found in the initiation stages of both transcription and translation and in the termination of transcription.

Mutations of one or a few nucleotides can affect protein structure and function

Now that you have explored the process of gene expression, you are ready to understand the effects of changes to the genetic information of a cell. These changes, called **mutations**, are responsible for the huge diversity of genes found among organisms because mutations are the ultimate source of new genes. Earlier, we considered chromosomal rearrangements that affect long segments of DNA (see Figure 15.14); these are considered large-scale mutations. Here we examine small-scale mutations of one or a few nucleotide pairs, including **point mutations**, changes in a single nucleotide pair of a gene.

If a point mutation occurs in a gamete or in a cell that gives rise to gametes, it may be transmitted to offspring and to future generations. If the mutation has an adverse effect on the phenotype of a person, the mutant condition is referred to as a genetic disorder or hereditary disease. For example, we can trace the genetic basis of sickle-cell disease to the mutation of a single nucleotide pair in the gene that encodes the β-globin polypeptide of hemoglobin. The change of a single nucleotide in the DNA's template strand leads to the production of an abnormal protein **(Figure 17.25**; also see Figure 5.19). In individuals who are homozygous for the mutant allele, the sickling of red blood cells caused by the altered hemoglobin produces the multiple symptoms associated with sickle-cell disease (see Concept 14.4 and Figure 23.17). Another disorder caused by a point mutation is a heart condition called familial cardiomyopathy that is responsible for some incidents of sudden death in young athletes. Point mutations in several genes that encode muscle proteins have been identified, any of which can lead to this disorder.

Types of Small-Scale Mutations

Let's now consider how small-scale mutations affect proteins. Point mutations within a gene can be divided into two general categories: (1) single nucleotide-pair substitutions and (2) nucleotide-pair insertions or deletions. Insertions and deletions can involve one or more nucleotide pairs.

Substitutions

A **nucleotide-pair substitution** is the replacement of one nucleotide and its partner with another pair of nucleotides **(Figure 17.26a)**. Some substitutions have no effect on the encoded protein, owing to the redundancy of the genetic code. For example, if 3′-CCG-5′ on the template strand mutated to 3′-CCA-5′, the mRNA codon that used to be GGC would become GGU, but a glycine would still be inserted at the proper location in the protein (see Figure 17.5). In other words, a change in a nucleotide pair may transform one codon into another that is translated into the same amino acid. Such a change is an example of a **silent mutation**, which has no observable effect on the phenotype. (Silent mutations can occur outside genes as well.) Substitutions that change one amino acid to another one are called **missense mutations**. Such a mutation may have little effect on the protein: The new amino acid may have properties similar to those of the amino acid it replaces, or it may be in a region of the protein where the exact sequence of amino acids is not essential to the protein's function.

However, the nucleotide-pair substitutions of greatest interest are those that cause a major change in a protein. The alteration of a single amino acid in a crucial area of a protein—such as in the part of the β-globin subunit of hemoglobin shown in Figure 17.25 or in the active site of an enzyme as shown in Figure 8.19—can significantly alter protein activity. Occasionally, such a mutation leads to an improved protein or one with novel capabilities, but much more often such mutations are neutral or detrimental, leading to a useless or less active protein that impairs cellular function.

Substitution mutations are usually missense mutations; that is, the altered codon still codes for an amino acid and thus makes sense, although not necessarily the *right* sense. But a point mutation can also change a codon for an amino acid into a stop codon. This is called a **nonsense mutation**,

Wild-type β-globin	Sickle-cell β-globin	
Wild-type β-globin DNA 3′ C T C 5′ 5′ G A G 3′	Mutant β-globin DNA 3′ C A C 5′ 5′ G T G 3′	In the DNA, the mutant (sickle-cell) template strand (top) has an A where the wild-type template has a T.
mRNA 5′ G A G 3′	mRNA 5′ G U G 3′	The mutant mRNA has a U instead of an A in one codon.
Normal hemoglobin Glu	Sickle-cell hemoglobin Val	The mutant β-globin has a valine (Val) instead of a glutamic acid (Glu).

▲ **Figure 17.25 The molecular basis of sickle-cell disease: a point mutation.** The allele that causes sickle-cell disease differs from the wild-type (normal) allele by a single DNA nucleotide pair. The micrographs are SEMs of a normal red blood cell (on the left) and a sickled red blood cell (right) from individuals homozygous for either wild-type or mutant alleles, respectively.

▼ **Figure 17.26 Types of small-scale mutations that affect mRNA sequence.** All but one of the types shown here also affect the amino acid sequence of the encoded polypeptide.

Wild type

DNA template strand 3′ T A C T T C A A A C C G A T T 5′
5′ A T G A A G T T T G G C T A A 3′
mRNA 5′ A U G A A G U U U G G C U A A 3′
Protein Met — Lys — Phe — Gly — Stop
Amino end / Carboxyl end

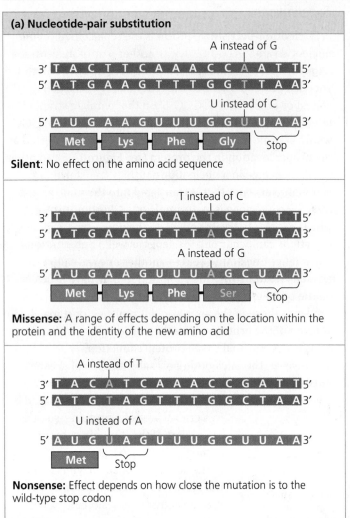

(a) Nucleotide-pair substitution

A instead of G
3′ T A C T T C A A A C C A T T 5′
5′ A T G A A G T T T G G T T A A 3′
U instead of C
5′ A U G A A G U U U G G U U A A 3′
Met — Lys — Phe — Gly — Stop

Silent: No effect on the amino acid sequence

T instead of C
3′ T A C T T C A A A T C G A T T 5′
5′ A T G A A G T T T A G C T A A 3′
A instead of G
5′ A U G A A G U U U A G C U A A 3′
Met — Lys — Phe — Ser — Stop

Missense: A range of effects depending on the location within the protein and the identity of the new amino acid

A instead of T
3′ T A C A T C A A A C C G A T T 5′
5′ A T G T A G T T T G G C T A A 3′
U instead of A
5′ A U G U A G U U U G G U U A A 3′
Met — Stop

Nonsense: Effect depends on how close the mutation is to the wild-type stop codon

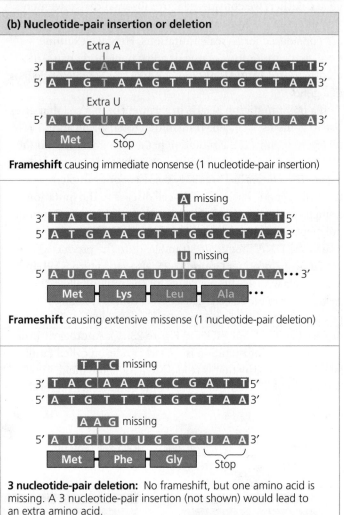

(b) Nucleotide-pair insertion or deletion

Extra A
3′ T A C A T T C A A A C C G A T T 5′
5′ A T G T A A G T T T G G C T A A 3′
Extra U
5′ A U G U A A G U U U G G C U A A 3′
Met — Stop

Frameshift causing immediate nonsense (1 nucleotide-pair insertion)

A missing
3′ T A C T T C A A C C G A T T 5′
5′ A T G A A G T T G G C T A A 3′
U missing
5′ A U G A A G U U G G C U A A ··· 3′
Met — Lys — Leu — Ala — ···

Frameshift causing extensive missense (1 nucleotide-pair deletion)

T T C missing
3′ T A C A A A C C G A T T 5′
5′ A T G T T T G G C T A A 3′
A A G missing
5′ A U G U U U G G C U A A 3′
Met — Phe — Gly — Stop

3 nucleotide-pair deletion: No frameshift, but one amino acid is missing. A 3 nucleotide-pair insertion (not shown) would lead to an extra amino acid.

and it causes translation to be terminated prematurely; the resulting polypeptide will be shorter than the polypeptide encoded by the normal gene. Nearly all nonsense mutations lead to nonfunctional proteins.

Insertions and Deletions

Insertions and **deletions** are additions or losses of nucleotide pairs in a gene **(Figure 17.26b)**. These mutations have a disastrous effect on the resulting protein more often than substitutions do. Insertion or deletion of nucleotides may

alter the reading frame of the genetic message, the triplet grouping of nucleotides on the mRNA that is read during translation. Such a mutation, called a **frameshift mutation**, occurs whenever the number of nucleotides inserted or deleted is not a multiple of three. All nucleotides downstream of the deletion or insertion will be improperly grouped into codons; the result will be extensive missense, usually ending sooner or later in nonsense and premature termination. Unless the frameshift is very near the end of the gene, the protein is almost certain to be nonfunctional.

New Mutations and Mutagens

Mutations can arise in a number of ways. Errors during DNA replication or recombination can lead to nucleotide-pair substitutions, insertions, or deletions, as well as to mutations affecting longer stretches of DNA. If an incorrect nucleotide is added to a growing chain during replication, for example, the base on that nucleotide will then be mismatched with the nucleotide base on the other strand. In many cases, the error will be corrected by DNA proofreading and repair systems (see Concept 16.2). Otherwise, the incorrect base will be used as a template in the next round of replication, resulting in a mutation. Such mutations are called *spontaneous mutations*. It is difficult to calculate the rate at which such mutations occur. Rough estimates have been made of the rate of mutation during DNA replication for both *E. coli* and eukaryotes, and the numbers are similar: About one nucleotide in every 10^{10} is altered, and the change is passed on to the next generation of cells.

A number of physical and chemical agents, called **mutagens**, interact with DNA in ways that cause mutations. In the 1920s, Hermann Muller discovered that X-rays caused genetic changes in fruit flies, and he used X-rays to make *Drosophila* mutants for his genetic studies. But he also recognized an alarming implication of his discovery: X-rays and other forms of high-energy radiation pose hazards to the genetic material of people as well as laboratory organisms. Mutagenic radiation, a physical mutagen, includes ultraviolet (UV) light, which can cause disruptive thymine dimers in DNA (see Figure 16.19).

Chemical mutagens fall into several categories. Nucleotide analogs are chemicals similar to normal DNA nucleotides but that pair incorrectly during DNA replication. Other chemical mutagens interfere with correct DNA replication by inserting themselves into the DNA and distorting the double helix. Still other mutagens cause chemical changes in bases that change their pairing properties.

Researchers have developed a variety of methods to test the mutagenic activity of chemicals. A major application of these tests is the preliminary screening of chemicals to identify those that may cause cancer. This approach makes sense because most carcinogens (cancer-causing chemicals) are mutagenic, and conversely, most mutagens are carcinogenic.

What Is a Gene? *Revisiting the Question*

Our definition of a gene has evolved over the past few chapters, as it has through the history of genetics. We began with the Mendelian concept of a gene as a discrete unit of inheritance that affects a phenotypic character (Chapter 14). We saw that Morgan and his colleagues assigned such genes to specific loci on chromosomes (Chapter 15). We went on to view a gene as a region of specific nucleotide sequence along the length of the DNA molecule of a chromosome (Chapter 16). Finally, in this chapter, we have considered a functional definition of a gene as a DNA sequence that codes for a specific polypeptide chain. All these definitions are useful, depending on the context in which genes are being studied.

We now realize that saying a gene codes for a polypeptide is an oversimplification. Most eukaryotic genes contain noncoding segments (such as introns), so large portions of these genes have no corresponding segments in polypeptides. Molecular biologists also often include promoters and certain other regulatory regions of DNA within the boundaries of a gene. These DNA sequences are not transcribed, but they can be considered part of the functional gene because they must be present for transcription to occur. Our definition of a gene must also be broad enough to include the DNA that is transcribed into rRNA, tRNA, and other RNAs that are not translated. These genes have no polypeptide products but play crucial roles in the cell. Thus, we arrive at the following definition: *A gene is a region of DNA that can be expressed to produce a final functional product that is either a polypeptide or an RNA molecule.*

When considering phenotypes, however, it is often useful to start by focusing on genes that code for polypeptides. In this chapter, you have learned in molecular terms how a typical gene is expressed—by transcription into RNA and then translation into a polypeptide that forms a protein of specific structure and function. Proteins, in turn, bring about an organism's observable phenotype.

A given type of cell expresses only a subset of its genes. This is an essential feature in multicellular organisms: You'd be in trouble if the lens cells in your eyes started expressing the genes for hair proteins, which are normally expressed only in hair follicle cells! Gene expression is precisely regulated, which we'll explore in the next chapter, beginning with the simpler case of bacteria and continuing with eukaryotes.

CONCEPT CHECK 17.5

1. What happens when one nucleotide pair is lost from the middle of the coding sequence of a gene?

2. **MAKE CONNECTIONS** Individuals heterozygous for the sickle-cell allele are generally healthy but show phenotypic effects of the allele under some circumstances (see Figure 14.17). Explain in terms of gene expression.

3. **WHAT IF?** **DRAW IT** The template strand of a gene includes this sequence:
   3'-TACTTGTCCGATATC-5'. It is mutated to
   3'-TACTTGTCCAATATC-5'. For both normal and mutant sequences, draw the double-stranded DNA, the resulting mRNA, and the amino acid sequence each encodes. What is the effect of the mutation on the amino acid sequence?

For suggested answers, see Appendix A.

SUMMARY OF KEY CONCEPTS

CONCEPT 17.1

Genes specify proteins via transcription and translation (pp. 334–340)

- Beadle and Tatum's studies of mutant strains of *Neurospora* led to the one gene–one polypeptide hypothesis. During **gene expression**, the information encoded in genes is used to make specific polypeptide chains (enzymes and other proteins) or RNA molecules.
- **Transcription** is the synthesis of RNA complementary to a **template strand** of DNA. **Translation** is the synthesis of a polypeptide whose amino acid sequence is specified by the nucleotide sequence in **mRNA**.
- Genetic information is encoded as a sequence of nonoverlapping nucleotide triplets, or **codons**. A codon in messenger RNA (mRNA) either is translated into an amino acid (61 of the 64 codons) or serves as a stop signal (3 codons). Codons must be read in the correct **reading frame**.

? *Describe the process of gene expression, by which a gene affects the phenotype of an organism.*

CONCEPT 17.2

Transcription is the DNA-directed synthesis of RNA: *A closer look* (pp. 340–342)

- RNA synthesis is catalyzed by **RNA polymerase**, which links together RNA nucleotides complementary to a DNA template strand. This process follows the same base-pairing rules as DNA replication, except that in RNA, uracil substitutes for thymine.

- The three stages of transcription are initiation, elongation, and termination. A **promoter**, often including a **TATA box** in eukaryotes, establishes where RNA synthesis is initiated. **Transcription factors** help eukaryotic RNA polymerase recognize promoter sequences, forming a **transcription initiation complex**. Termination differs in bacteria and eukaryotes.

? *What are the similarities and differences in the initiation of gene transcription in bacteria and eukaryotes?*

CONCEPT 17.3

Eukaryotic cells modify RNA after transcription (pp. 342–345)

- Eukaryotic mRNAs undergo **RNA processing**, which includes RNA splicing, the addition of a modified nucleotide **5′ cap** to the 5′ end, and the addition of a **poly-A tail** to the 3′ end.

- Most eukaryotic genes are split into segments: They have **introns** interspersed among the **exons** (the regions included in the mRNA). In **RNA splicing**, introns are removed and exons joined. RNA splicing is typically carried out by **spliceosomes**, but in some cases, RNA alone catalyzes its own splicing. The catalytic ability of some RNA molecules, called **ribozymes**, derives from the inherent properties of RNA. The presence of introns allows for **alternative RNA splicing**.

? *What function do the 5′ cap and the poly-A tail serve on a eukaryotic mRNA?*

CONCEPT 17.4

Translation is the RNA-directed synthesis of a polypeptide: *A closer look* (pp. 345–354)

- A cell translates an mRNA message into protein using **transfer RNAs (tRNAs)**. After being bound to a specific amino acid by an **aminoacyl-tRNA synthetase**, a tRNA lines up via its **anticodon** at the complementary codon on mRNA. A **ribosome**, made up of **ribosomal RNAs (rRNAs)** and proteins, facilitates this coupling with binding sites for mRNA and tRNA.
- Ribosomes coordinate the three stages of translation: initiation, elongation, and termination. The formation of peptide bonds between amino acids is catalyzed by rRNA as tRNAs move through the **A** and **P sites** and exit through the **E site**.

- After translation, modifications to proteins can affect their shape. Free ribosomes in the cytosol initiate synthesis of all proteins, but proteins with a **signal peptide** are synthesized on the ER.
- A gene can be transcribed by multiple RNA polymerases simultaneously. A single mRNA molecule can be translated simultaneously by a number of ribosomes, forming a **polyribosome**. In bacteria, these processes are coupled, but in eukaryotes they are separated in space and time by the nuclear membrane.

? *What function do tRNAs serve in the process of translation?*

CONCEPT 17.5

Mutations of one or a few nucleotides can affect protein structure and function (pp. 355–357)

- Small-scale **mutations** include **point mutations**, changes in one DNA nucleotide pair, which may lead to production of nonfunctional proteins. **Nucleotide-pair substitutions** can cause **missense** or **nonsense mutations**. Nucleotide-pair **insertions** or **deletions** may produce **frameshift mutations**.
- Spontaneous mutations can occur during DNA replication, recombination, or repair. Chemical and physical **mutagens** cause DNA damage that can alter genes.

? *What will be the results of chemically modifying one nucleotide base of a gene? What role is played by DNA repair systems in the cell?*

TEST YOUR UNDERSTANDING

LEVEL 1: KNOWLEDGE/COMPREHENSION

1. In eukaryotic cells, transcription cannot begin until
   a. the two DNA strands have completely separated and exposed the promoter.
   b. several transcription factors have bound to the promoter.
   c. the 5′ caps are removed from the mRNA.
   d. the DNA introns are removed from the template.

2. Which of the following is *not* true of a codon?
   a. It may code for the same amino acid as another codon.
   b. It never codes for more than one amino acid.
   c. It extends from one end of a tRNA molecule.
   d. It is the basic unit of the genetic code.

3. The anticodon of a particular tRNA molecule is
   a. complementary to the corresponding mRNA codon.
   b. complementary to the corresponding triplet in rRNA.
   c. the part of tRNA that bonds to a specific amino acid.
   d. catalytic, making the tRNA a ribozyme.

4. Which of the following is *not* true of RNA processing?
   a. Exons are cut out before mRNA leaves the nucleus.
   b. Nucleotides may be added at both ends of the RNA.
   c. Ribozymes may function in RNA splicing.
   d. RNA splicing can be catalyzed by spliceosomes.

5. Which component is *not* directly involved in translation?
   a. GTP
   b. DNA
   c. tRNA
   d. ribosomes

LEVEL 2: APPLICATION/ANALYSIS

6. Using Figure 17.5, identify a 5′ → 3′ sequence of nucleotides in the DNA template strand for an mRNA coding for the polypeptide sequence Phe-Pro-Lys.
   a. 5′-UUUGGGAAA-3′
   b. 5′-GAACCCCTT-3′
   c. 5′-CTTCGGGAA-3′
   d. 5′-AAACCCUUU-3′

7. Which of the following mutations would be *most* likely to have a harmful effect on an organism?
   a. a deletion of three nucleotides near the middle of a gene
   b. a single nucleotide deletion in the middle of an intron
   c. a single nucleotide deletion near the end of the coding sequence
   d. a single nucleotide insertion downstream of, and close to, the start of the coding sequence

8. Would the coupling of the processes shown in Figure 17.23 be found in a eukaryotic cell? Explain why or why not.

9. **DRAW IT** Fill in the following table:

Type of RNA	Functions
Messenger RNA (mRNA)	
Transfer RNA (tRNA)	
	Plays catalytic (ribozyme) roles and structural roles in ribosomes
Primary transcript	
Small RNAs in the spliceosome	

LEVEL 3: SYNTHESIS/EVALUATION

10. **EVOLUTION CONNECTION**
    Most amino acids are coded for by a set of similar codons (see Figure 17.5). What evolutionary explanations can you give for this pattern? (*Hint*: There is one explanation relating to ancestry, and some less obvious ones of a "form-fits-function" type.)

11. **SCIENTIFIC INQUIRY**
    Knowing that the genetic code is almost universal, a scientist uses molecular biological methods to insert the human β-globin gene (shown in Figure 17.11) into bacterial cells, hoping the cells will express it and synthesize functional β-globin protein. Instead, the protein produced is nonfunctional and is found to contain many fewer amino acids than does β-globin made by a eukaryotic cell. Explain why.

12. **WRITE ABOUT A THEME: INFORMATION**
    Evolution accounts for the unity and diversity of life, and the continuity of life is based on heritable information in the form of DNA. In a short essay (100–150 words), discuss how the fidelity with which DNA is inherited is related to the processes of evolution. (Review the discussion of proofreading and DNA repair in Concept 16.2.)

13. **SYNTHESIZE YOUR KNOWLEDGE**

Some mutations result in proteins that function well at one temperature but are nonfunctional at a different (usually higher) temperature. Siamese cats have such a "temperature-sensitive" mutation in a gene encoding an enzyme that makes dark pigment in the fur. The mutation results in the breed's distinctive point markings and lighter body color (see the photo). Using this information and what you learned in the chapter, explain the pattern of the cat's fur pigmentation.

For selected answers, see Appendix A.

MasteringBiology®

Students Go to **MasteringBiology** for assignments, the eText, and the Study Area with practice tests, animations, and activities.

Instructors Go to **MasteringBiology** for automatically graded tutorials and questions that you can assign to your students, plus Instructor Resources.

18

Regulation of Gene Expression

KEY CONCEPTS

18.1 Bacteria often respond to environmental change by regulating transcription

18.2 Eukaryotic gene expression is regulated at many stages

18.3 Noncoding RNAs play multiple roles in controlling gene expression

18.4 A program of differential gene expression leads to the different cell types in a multicellular organism

18.5 Cancer results from genetic changes that affect cell cycle control

▲ **Figure 18.1 How can this fish's eyes see equally well in both air and water?**

Differential Expression of Genes

The fish in **Figure 18.1** is keeping an eye out for predators above—or, more precisely, half of each eye! *Anableps anableps*, commonly known as "cuatro ojos" ("four eyes"), glides through freshwater lakes and ponds in Central and South America with the upper half of each eye protruding from the water. The eye's upper half is particularly well-suited for aerial vision and the lower half for aquatic vision. The molecular basis of this specialization has recently been revealed: The cells of the two parts of the eye express a slightly different set of genes involved in vision, even though these two groups of cells are quite similar and contain identical genomes. What is the biological mechanism underlying the difference in gene expression that makes this remarkable feat possible?

A hallmark of prokaryotic and eukaryotic cells alike—from a bacterium to the cells of a fish—is their intricate and precise regulation of gene expression. In this chapter, we first explore how bacteria regulate expression of their genes in response to different environmental conditions. We then examine how eukaryotes regulate gene expression to maintain different cell types, including the many roles played by RNA molecules. In the final two sections, we explore the role of gene regulation in both embryonic development, as the ultimate example of proper gene regulation, and cancer, as an illustration of what happens when regulation goes awry. Orchestrating proper gene expression by all cells is crucial to the functions of life.

Bacteria often respond to environmental change by regulating transcription

Bacterial cells that can conserve resources and energy have a selective advantage over cells that are unable to do so. Thus, natural selection has favored bacteria that express only the genes whose products are needed by the cell.

Consider, for instance, an individual *Escherichia coli* cell living in the erratic environment of a human colon, dependent for its nutrients on the whimsical eating habits of its host. If the environment is lacking in the amino acid tryptophan, which the bacterium needs to survive, the cell responds by activating a metabolic pathway that makes tryptophan from another compound. Later, if the human host eats a tryptophan-rich meal, the bacterial cell stops producing tryptophan, thus avoiding wasting resources to produce a substance readily available in prefabricated form from the surrounding solution. This is just one example of how bacteria tune their metabolism to changing environments.

Metabolic control occurs on two levels, as shown for the synthesis of tryptophan in **Figure 18.2**. First, cells can adjust the activity of enzymes already present. This is a fairly fast response, which relies on the sensitivity of many enzymes to chemical cues that increase or decrease their catalytic activity (see Concept 8.5). The activity of the first enzyme in the pathway is inhibited by the pathway's end product **(Figure 18.2a)**. Thus, if tryptophan accumulates in a cell, it shuts down the synthesis of more tryptophan by inhibiting enzyme activity. Such *feedback inhibition*, typical of anabolic (biosynthetic) pathways, allows a cell to adapt to short-term fluctuations in the supply of a substance it needs.

Second, cells can adjust the production level of certain enzymes; that is, they can regulate the expression of the genes encoding the enzymes. If, in our example, the environment provides all the tryptophan the cell needs, the cell stops making the enzymes that catalyze the synthesis of tryptophan **(Figure 18.2b)**. In this case, the control of enzyme production occurs at the level of transcription, the synthesis of messenger RNA coding for these enzymes. More generally, many genes of the bacterial genome are switched on or off by changes in the metabolic status of the cell. One basic mechanism for this control of gene expression in bacteria, described as the *operon model*, was discovered in 1961 by François Jacob and Jacques Monod at the Pasteur Institute in Paris. Let's see what an operon is and how it works.

Operons: The Basic Concept

E. coli synthesizes the amino acid tryptophan from a precursor molecule in the three-step pathway shown in Figure 18.2. Each reaction in the pathway is catalyzed by a specific enzyme, and the five genes that code for the

▲ **Figure 18.2 Regulation of a metabolic pathway.** In the pathway for tryptophan synthesis, an abundance of tryptophan can both **(a)** inhibit the activity of the first enzyme in the pathway (feedback inhibition), a rapid response, and **(b)** repress expression of the genes encoding all subunits of the enzymes in the pathway, a longer-term response. Genes *trpE* and *trpD* encode the two subunits of enzyme 1, and genes *trpB* and *trpA* encode the two subunits of enzyme 3. (The genes were named before the order in which they functioned in the pathway was determined.) The ⊖ symbol stands for inhibition.

subunits of these enzymes are clustered together on the bacterial chromosome. A single promoter serves all five genes, which together constitute a transcription unit. (Recall from Concept 17.2 that a promoter is a site where RNA polymerase can bind to DNA and begin transcription.) Thus, transcription gives rise to one long mRNA molecule that codes for the five polypeptides making up the enzymes in the tryptophan pathway **(Figure 18.3a)**. The cell can translate this one mRNA into five separate polypeptides because the mRNA is punctuated with start and stop codons that signal where the coding sequence for each polypeptide begins and ends.

A key advantage of grouping genes of related function into one transcription unit is that a single "on-off switch" can control the whole cluster of functionally related genes; in other words, these genes are *coordinately controlled*. When an *E. coli* cell must make tryptophan for itself because the nutrient medium lacks this amino acid, all the enzymes for the metabolic pathway are synthesized at one time. The switch is a segment of DNA called an **operator**. Both its location and name suit its function: Positioned within the promoter or, in some cases, between the promoter and the enzyme-coding genes, the operator controls the access of RNA polymerase to the genes. All together, the operator,

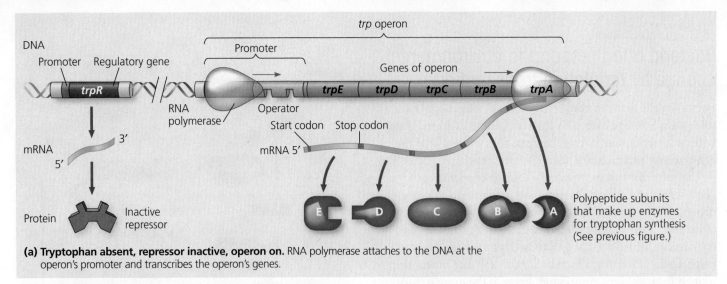

DNA

Promoter   Regulatory gene

trpR

RNA polymerase

Promoter

Operator

trp operon

Genes of operon

trpE | **trpD** | **trpC** | **trpB** | **trpA**

Start codon   Stop codon

mRNA 3′
5′

mRNA 5′

Protein   Inactive repressor

E   D   C   B   A

Polypeptide subunits that make up enzymes for tryptophan synthesis (See previous figure.)

(a) Tryptophan absent, repressor inactive, operon on. RNA polymerase attaches to the DNA at the operon's promoter and transcribes the operon's genes.

DNA

trpR   **trpE**

No RNA made

mRNA 3′
5′

Protein   Active repressor

Tryptophan (corepressor)

(b) Tryptophan present, repressor active, operon off. As tryptophan accumulates, it inhibits its own production by activating the repressor protein, which binds to the operator, blocking transcription.

▲ **Figure 18.3 The *trp* operon in *E. coli*: regulated synthesis of repressible enzymes.** Tryptophan is an amino acid produced by an anabolic pathway catalyzed by repressible enzymes. **(a)** The five genes encoding the polypeptide subunits of the enzymes in this pathway (see Figure 18.2) are grouped, along with a promoter, into the *trp* operon. The *trp* operator (the repressor binding site) is located within the *trp* promoter (the RNA polymerase binding site). **(b)** Accumulation of tryptophan, the end product of the pathway, represses transcription of the *trp* operon, thus blocking synthesis of all the enzymes in the pathway and shutting down tryptophan production.

? *Describe what happens to the* trp *operon as the cell uses up its store of tryptophan.*

the promoter, and the genes they control—the entire stretch of DNA required for enzyme production for the tryptophan pathway—constitute an **operon**. The *trp* operon (*trp* for tryptophan) is one of many operons in the *E. coli* genome (see Figure 18.3).

If the operator is the operon's switch for controlling transcription, how does this switch work? By itself, the *trp* operon is turned on; that is, RNA polymerase can bind to the promoter and transcribe the genes of the operon. The operon can be switched off by a protein that is called the *trp* **repressor**. The repressor binds to the operator and blocks attachment of RNA polymerase to the promoter, preventing transcription of the genes **(Figure 18.3b)**. A repressor protein is specific for the operator of a particular operon. For example, the repressor that switches off the *trp* operon by binding to the *trp* operator has no effect on other operons in the *E. coli* genome.

The *trp* repressor is the protein product of a **regulatory gene** called *trpR*, which is located some distance from the *trp* operon and has its own promoter. Regulatory genes are

expressed continuously, although at a low rate, and a few *trp* repressor molecules are always present in *E. coli* cells. Why, then, is the *trp* operon not switched off permanently? First, the binding of repressors to operators is reversible. An operator alternates between two states: one with the repressor bound and one without the repressor bound. The relative duration of the repressor-bound state increases when there are more active repressor molecules present. Second, the *trp* repressor, like most regulatory proteins, is an allosteric protein, with two alternative shapes—one active and the other inactive (see Figure 8.20). The *trp* repressor is synthesized in the inactive form, which has little affinity for the *trp* operator. Only when a tryptophan molecule binds to the *trp* repressor at an allosteric site does the repressor protein change its shape to the active form, which can attach to the operator, turning the operon off.

Tryptophan functions in this system as a **corepressor**, a small molecule that cooperates with a repressor protein to switch an operon off. As tryptophan accumulates, more tryptophan molecules associate with *trp* repressor molecules, which can then bind to the *trp* operator and shut down production of the tryptophan pathway enzymes. If the cell's tryptophan level drops, transcription of the operon's genes resumes. The *trp* operon is one example of how gene expression can respond to changes in the cell's internal and external environment.

Repressible and Inducible Operons: Two Types of Negative Gene Regulation

The *trp* operon is said to be a *repressible operon* because its transcription is usually on but can be inhibited (repressed) when a specific small molecule (in this case, tryptophan) binds allosterically to a regulatory protein. In contrast, an *inducible operon* is usually off but can be stimulated (induced) when a specific small molecule interacts with a regulatory protein. The classic example of an inducible operon is the *lac* operon (*lac* for lactose).

The disaccharide lactose (milk sugar) is available to *E. coli* in the human colon if the host drinks milk. Lactose metabolism begins with hydrolysis of the disaccharide into its component monosaccharides (glucose and galactose), a reaction catalyzed by the enzyme β-galactosidase. Only a few molecules of this enzyme are present in an *E. coli* cell growing in the absence of lactose. If lactose is added to the bacterium's environment, however, the number of β-galactosidase molecules in the cell can increase a thousandfold within about 15 minutes.

The gene for β-galactosidase (*lacZ*) is part of the *lac* operon **(Figure 18.4)**, which includes two other genes coding for enzymes that function in the use of lactose. The entire transcription unit is under the command of one main operator and promoter. The regulatory gene, *lacI*, located outside the operon, codes for an allosteric repressor protein that can switch off the *lac* operon by binding to the operator. So far, this sounds just like regulation of the *trp* operon, but there is one important difference. Recall that the *trp* repressor protein is inactive by itself and requires tryptophan as a co-repressor in order to bind to the operator. The *lac* repressor, in contrast, is active by itself, binding to the operator and switching the *lac* operon off. In this case, a specific small molecule, called an **inducer**, *inactivates* the repressor.

For the *lac* operon, the inducer is allolactose, an isomer of lactose formed in small amounts from lactose that enters the cell. In the absence of lactose (and hence allolactose), the *lac* repressor is in its active shape, and the genes of the *lac* operon are silenced **(Figure 18.4a)**. If lactose is present, allolactose binds to the *lac* repressor and alters its shape, nullifying the repressor's ability to attach to the operator. Without the repressor bound, the *lac* operon is transcribed into mRNA for the lactose-utilizing enzymes **(Figure 18.4b)**.

In the context of gene regulation, the enzymes of the lactose pathway are referred to as *inducible enzymes* because their synthesis is induced by a chemical signal (allolactose, in this case). Analogously, the enzymes for tryptophan synthesis are said to be repressible. *Repressible enzymes* generally function in anabolic pathways, which synthesize essential end products from raw materials (precursors). By

(a) Lactose absent, repressor active, operon off. The *lac* repressor is innately active, and in the absence of lactose it switches off the operon by binding to the operator.

(b) Lactose present, repressor inactive, operon on. Allolactose, an isomer of lactose, derepresses the operon by inactivating the repressor. In this way, the enzymes for lactose utilization are induced.

◀ **Figure 18.4 The *lac* operon in *E. coli*: regulated synthesis of inducible enzymes.** *E. coli* uses three enzymes to take up and metabolize lactose, the genes for which are clustered in the *lac* operon. The first gene, *lacZ*, codes for β-galactosidase, which hydrolyzes lactose to glucose and galactose. The second, *lacY*, codes for a permease, the membrane protein that transports lactose into the cell. The third, *lacA*, codes for transacetylase, whose function in lactose metabolism is unclear. Unusually, the gene for the *lac* repressor, *lacI*, is adjacent to the *lac* operon; the function of the teal region within the promoter will be revealed in Figure 18.5.

suspending production of an end product when it is already present in sufficient quantity, the cell can allocate its organic precursors and energy for other uses. In contrast, inducible enzymes usually function in catabolic pathways, which break down a nutrient to simpler molecules. By producing the appropriate enzymes only when the nutrient is available, the cell avoids wasting energy and precursors making proteins that are not needed.

Regulation of both the *trp* and *lac* operons involves the *negative* control of genes, because the operons are switched off by the active form of the repressor protein. It may be easier to see this for the *trp* operon, but it is also true for the *lac* operon. Allolactose induces enzyme synthesis not by directly activating the *lac* operon, but by freeing it from the negative effect of the repressor. Gene regulation is said to be *positive* only when a regulatory protein interacts directly with the genome to switch transcription on.

Positive Gene Regulation

When glucose and lactose are both present in its environment, *E. coli* preferentially uses glucose. The enzymes for glucose breakdown in glycolysis (see Figure 9.9) are continually present. Only when lactose is present *and* glucose is in short supply does *E. coli* use lactose as an energy source, and only then does it synthesize appreciable quantities of the enzymes for lactose breakdown.

How does the *E. coli* cell sense the glucose concentration and relay this information to the *lac* operon? Again, the mechanism depends on the interaction of an allosteric regulatory protein with a small organic molecule, in this case **cyclic AMP (cAMP)**, which accumulates when glucose is scarce (see Figure 11.11 for the structure of cAMP). The regulatory protein, called *catabolite activator protein (CAP)*, is an **activator**, a protein that binds to DNA and stimulates transcription of a gene. When cAMP binds to this regulatory protein, CAP assumes its active shape and can attach to a specific site at the upstream end of the *lac* promoter **(Figure 18.5a)**. This attachment increases the affinity of RNA polymerase for the promoter, which is actually rather low even when no repressor is bound to the operator. By facilitating the binding of RNA polymerase to the promoter and thereby increasing the rate of transcription, the attachment of CAP to the promoter directly stimulates gene expression. Therefore, this mechanism qualifies as positive regulation.

If the amount of glucose in the cell increases, the cAMP concentration falls, and without cAMP, CAP detaches from the operon. Because CAP is inactive, RNA polymerase binds less efficiently to the promoter, and transcription of the *lac* operon proceeds only at a low level, even when lactose is present **(Figure 18.5b)**. Thus, the *lac* operon is under dual control: negative control by the *lac* repressor and positive control by CAP. The state of the *lac* repressor (with or without bound allolactose) determines whether or not

transcription of the *lac* operon's genes occurs at all; the state of CAP (with or without bound cAMP) controls the *rate* of transcription if the operon is repressor-free. It is as though the operon has both an on-off switch and a volume control.

In addition to regulating the *lac* operon, CAP helps regulate other operons that encode enzymes used in catabolic pathways. All told, it may affect the expression of more than 100 genes in *E. coli*. When glucose is plentiful and CAP is inactive, the synthesis of enzymes that catabolize compounds other than glucose generally slows down. The ability to catabolize other compounds, such as lactose, enables a cell deprived of glucose to survive. The compounds present in the cell at the moment determine which operons are switched on—the result of simple interactions of activator and repressor proteins with the promoters of the genes in question.

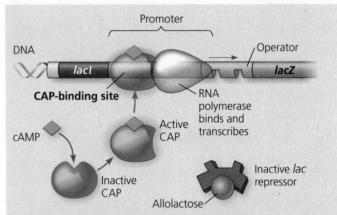

(a) Lactose present, glucose scarce (cAMP level high): abundant *lac* mRNA synthesized. If glucose is scarce, the high level of cAMP activates CAP, and the *lac* operon produces large amounts of mRNA coding for the enzymes in the lactose pathway.

(b) Lactose present, glucose present (cAMP level low): little *lac* mRNA synthesized. When glucose is present, cAMP is scarce, and CAP is unable to stimulate transcription at a significant rate, even though no repressor is bound.

▲ **Figure 18.5 Positive control of the lac operon by catabolite activator protein (CAP).** RNA polymerase has high affinity for the *lac* promoter only when CAP is bound to a DNA site at the upstream end of the promoter. CAP, in turn, attaches to its DNA site only when associated with cyclic AMP (cAMP), whose concentration in the cell rises when the glucose concentration falls. Thus, when glucose is present, even if lactose is also available, the cell preferentially catabolizes glucose and makes very little of the lactose-utilizing enzymes.

1. How does binding of the *trp* corepressor to its repressor alter repressor function and transcription? What about the binding of the *lac* inducer to its repressor?

2. Describe the binding of RNA polymerase, repressors, and activators to the *lac* operon when both lactose and glucose are scarce. What is the effect of these scarcities on transcription of the *lac* operon?

3. **WHAT IF?** A certain mutation in *E. coli* changes the *lac* operator so that the active repressor cannot bind. How would this affect the cell's production of β-galactosidase?

For suggested answers, see Appendix A.

CONCEPT 18.2

Eukaryotic gene expression is regulated at many stages

All organisms, whether prokaryotes or eukaryotes, must regulate which genes are expressed at any given time. Both unicellular organisms and the cells of multicellular organisms continually turn genes on and off in response to signals from their external and internal environments. Regulation of gene expression is also essential for cell specialization in multicellular organisms, which are made up of different types of cells. To perform its own distinct role, each cell type must maintain a specific program of gene expression in which certain genes are expressed and others are not.

Differential Gene Expression

A typical human cell might express about 20% of its protein-coding genes at any given time. Highly differentiated cells, such as muscle or nerve cells, express an even smaller fraction of their genes. Almost all the cells in a multicellular organism contain an identical genome. (Cells of the immune system are one exception, as you will see in Chapter 43.) However, the subset of genes expressed in the cells of each type is unique, allowing these cells to carry out their specific function. The differences between cell types, therefore, are due not to different genes being present, but to **differential gene expression**, the expression of different genes by cells with the same genome.

The function of any cell, whether a single-celled eukaryote or a particular cell type in a multicellular organism, depends on the appropriate set of genes being expressed. The transcription factors of a cell must locate the right genes at the right time, a task on a par with finding a needle in a haystack. When gene expression proceeds abnormally, serious imbalances and diseases, including cancer, can arise.

Figure 18.6 summarizes the process of gene expression in a eukaryotic cell, highlighting key stages in the expression of a protein-coding gene. Each stage depicted in Figure 18.6

▲ **Figure 18.6 Stages in gene expression that can be regulated in eukaryotic cells.** In this diagram, the colored boxes indicate the processes most often regulated; each color indicates the type of molecule that is affected (blue = DNA, red/orange = RNA, purple = protein). The nuclear envelope separating transcription from translation in eukaryotic cells offers an opportunity for post-transcriptional control in the form of RNA processing that is absent in prokaryotes. In addition, eukaryotes have a greater variety of control mechanisms operating before transcription and after translation. The expression of any given gene, however, does not necessarily involve every stage shown; for example, during processing, some but not all polypeptides are cleaved.

is a potential control point at which gene expression can be turned on or off, accelerated, or slowed down.

Fifty or so years ago, an understanding of the mechanisms that control gene expression in eukaryotes seemed almost hopelessly out of reach. Since then, new research methods, notably advances in DNA technology (see Chapter 20), have enabled molecular biologists to uncover many details of eukaryotic gene regulation. In all organisms, gene expression is commonly controlled at transcription; regulation at this stage often occurs in response to signals coming from outside the cell, such as hormones or other signaling molecules. For this reason, the term *gene expression* is often equated with transcription for both bacteria and eukaryotes. While this may most often be the case for bacteria, the greater complexity of eukaryotic cell structure and function provides opportunities for regulating gene expression at many additional stages (see Figure 18.6). In the remainder of this section, we'll examine some of the important control points of eukaryotic gene expression more closely.

Regulation of Chromatin Structure

Recall that the DNA of eukaryotic cells is packaged with proteins in an elaborate complex known as chromatin, the basic unit of which is the nucleosome (see Figure 16.22). The structural organization of chromatin not only packs a cell's DNA into a compact form that fits inside the nucleus, but also helps regulate gene expression in several ways. The location of a gene's promoter, relative to both placement of nucleosomes and the sites where the DNA attaches to the chromosome scaffold, can affect whether the gene is transcribed. In addition, genes within heterochromatin, which is highly condensed, are usually not expressed. Lastly, certain

chemical modifications to the histone proteins and to the DNA of chromatin can influence both chromatin structure and gene expression. Here we examine the effects of these modifications, which are catalyzed by specific enzymes.

Histone Modifications and DNA Methylation

There is abundant evidence that chemical modifications to histones, the proteins around which the DNA is wrapped in nucleosomes, play a direct role in the regulation of gene transcription. The N-terminus of each histone molecule in a nucleosome protrudes outward from the nucleosome **(Figure 18.7a)**. These histone tails are accessible to various modifying enzymes that catalyze the addition or removal of specific chemical groups, such as acetyl (—COCH$_3$), methyl, and phosphate groups. Generally, **histone acetylation** appears to promote transcription by opening up the chromatin structure **(Figure 18.7b)**, while addition of methyl groups can lead to the condensation of chromatin and reduced transcription.

While some enzymes methylate the tails of histone proteins, a different set of enzymes can methylate certain bases in the DNA itself, usually cytosine. Such **DNA methylation** occurs in most plants, animals, and fungi. Long stretches of inactive DNA, such as that of inactivated mammalian X chromosomes (see Figure 15.8), are generally more methylated than regions of actively transcribed DNA. On a smaller scale, individual genes are usually more heavily methylated in cells in which they are not expressed. Removal of the extra methyl groups can turn on some of these genes.

Once methylated, genes usually stay that way through successive cell divisions in a given individual. At DNA sites where one strand is already methylated, enzymes methylate the correct daughter strand after each round of DNA replication.

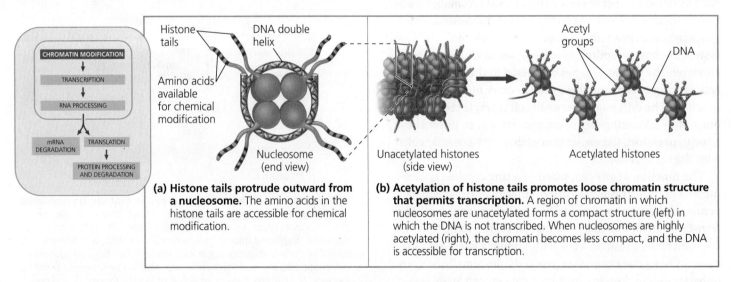

(a) **Histone tails protrude outward from a nucleosome.** The amino acids in the histone tails are accessible for chemical modification.

(b) **Acetylation of histone tails promotes loose chromatin structure that permits transcription.** A region of chromatin in which nucleosomes are unacetylated forms a compact structure (left) in which the DNA is not transcribed. When nucleosomes are highly acetylated (right), the chromatin becomes less compact, and the DNA is accessible for transcription.

▲ **Figure 18.7 A simple model of histone tails and the effect of histone acetylation.** In addition to acetylation, histones can undergo several other types of modifications that also help determine the chromatin configuration in a region.

Methylation patterns are thus passed on, and cells forming specialized tissues keep a chemical record of what occurred during embryonic development. A methylation pattern maintained in this way also accounts for *genomic imprinting* in mammals, where methylation permanently regulates expression of either the maternal or paternal allele of particular genes at the start of development (see Figure 15.17).

Epigenetic Inheritance

The chromatin modifications that we have just discussed do not entail a change in the DNA sequence, yet they still may be passed along to future generations of cells. Inheritance of traits transmitted by mechanisms not involving the nucleotide sequence itself is called **epigenetic inheritance**. Whereas mutations in the DNA are permanent changes, modifications to the chromatin can be reversed. For example, DNA methylation patterns are largely erased and reestablished during gamete formation.

Researchers are amassing more and more evidence for the importance of epigenetic information in the regulation of gene expression. Epigenetic variations might help explain why one identical twin acquires a genetically based disease, such as schizophrenia, but the other does not, despite their identical genomes. Alterations in normal patterns of DNA methylation are seen in some cancers, where they are associated with inappropriate gene expression. Evidently, enzymes that modify chromatin structure are integral parts of the eukaryotic cell's machinery for regulating transcription.

Regulation of Transcription Initiation

Chromatin-modifying enzymes provide initial control of gene expression by making a region of DNA either more or less able to bind the transcription machinery. Once the chromatin of a gene is optimally modified for expression, the initiation of transcription is the next major step at which gene expression is regulated. As in bacteria, the regulation of transcription initiation in eukaryotes involves proteins that bind to DNA and either facilitate or inhibit binding of RNA polymerase. The process is more complicated in eukaryotes, however. Before looking at how eukaryotic cells control their transcription, let's review the structure of a typical eukaryotic gene and its transcript.

Organization of a Typical Eukaryotic Gene

A eukaryotic gene and the DNA elements (segments) that control it are typically organized as shown in **Figure 18.8**, which extends what you learned about eukaryotic genes in Chapter 17. Recall that a cluster of proteins called a *transcription initiation complex* assembles on the promoter sequence at the "upstream" end of the gene. One of these proteins, RNA polymerase II, then proceeds to transcribe

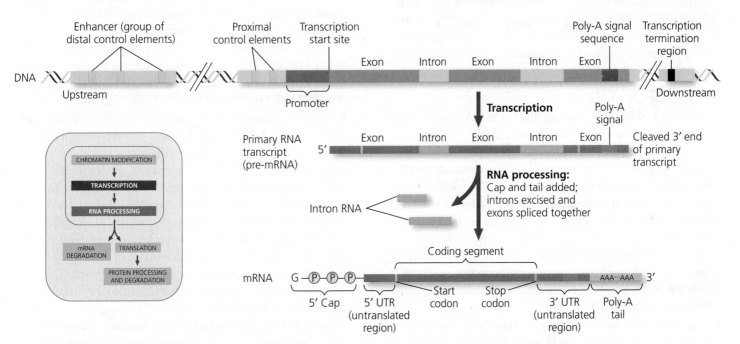

▲ **Figure 18.8 A eukaryotic gene and its transcript.** Each eukaryotic gene has a promoter, a DNA sequence where RNA polymerase binds and starts transcription, proceeding "downstream." A number of control elements (gold) are involved in regulating the initiation of transcription; these are DNA sequences located near (proximal to) or far from (distal to) the promoter. Distal control elements can be grouped together as enhancers, one of which is shown for this gene. A polyadenylation (poly-A) signal sequence in the last exon of the gene is transcribed into an RNA sequence that signals where the transcript is cleaved and the poly-A tail added. Transcription may continue for hundreds of nucleotides beyond the poly-A signal before terminating. RNA processing of the primary transcript into a functional mRNA involves three steps: addition of the 5′ cap, addition of the poly-A tail, and splicing. In the cell, the 5′ cap is added soon after transcription is initiated, and splicing occurs while transcription is still under way (see Figure 17.10).

the gene, synthesizing a primary RNA transcript (pre-mRNA). RNA processing includes enzymatic addition of a 5′ cap and a poly-A tail, as well as splicing out of introns, to yield a mature mRNA. Associated with most eukaryotic genes are multiple **control elements**, segments of noncoding DNA that serve as binding sites for the proteins called transcription factors, which in turn regulate transcription. Control elements and the transcription factors they bind are critical to the precise regulation of gene expression seen in different cell types.

The Roles of Transcription Factors

To initiate transcription, eukaryotic RNA polymerase requires the assistance of transcription factors. Some transcription factors (such as those illustrated in Figure 17.8) are essential for the transcription of *all* protein-coding genes; therefore, they are often called *general transcription factors*. A few general transcription factors bind to a DNA sequence such as the TATA box within the promoter, but most bind to proteins, including other transcription factors and RNA polymerase II. Protein-protein interactions are crucial to the initiation of eukaryotic transcription. Only when the complete initiation complex has assembled can the polymerase begin to move along the DNA template strand, producing a complementary strand of RNA.

The interaction of general transcription factors and RNA polymerase II with a promoter usually leads to a low rate of initiation and production of few RNA transcripts. In eukaryotes, high levels of transcription of particular genes at the appropriate time and place depend on the interaction of control elements with another set of proteins, which can be thought of as *specific transcription factors*.

Enhancers and Specific Transcription Factors As you can see in Figure 18.8, some control elements, named *proximal control elements*, are located close to the promoter. (Although some biologists consider proximal control elements part of the promoter, in this book we do not.) The more distant *distal control elements*, groupings of which are called **enhancers**, may be thousands of nucleotides upstream or downstream of a gene or even within an intron. A given gene may have multiple enhancers, each active at a different time or in a different cell type or location in the organism. Each enhancer, however, is generally associated with only that gene and no other.

In eukaryotes, the rate of gene expression can be strongly increased or decreased by the binding of specific transcription factors, either activators or repressors, to the control elements of enhancers. Hundreds of transcription activators have been discovered in eukaryotes; the structure of one example is shown in **Figure 18.9**. Researchers have identified two types of structural domains that are commonly found

▲ **Figure 18.9 The structure of MyoD, an activator.** The MyoD protein is made up of two subunits (purple and salmon) with extensive regions of α helix. Each subunit has one DNA-binding domain and one activation domain. The latter includes binding sites for the other subunit and for other proteins. MyoD is involved in muscle development in vertebrate embryos (see Concept 18.4).

in a large number of activator proteins. The first is a DNA-binding domain—a part of the protein's three-dimensional structure that binds to DNA—and the second is an activation domain. Activation domains bind other regulatory proteins or components of the transcription machinery, facilitating a series of protein-protein interactions that result in enhanced transcription of a given gene. A transcription factor can have one or more of either type of domain.

Figure 18.10 shows the currently accepted model for how binding of activators to an enhancer located far from the promoter can influence transcription. Protein-mediated bending of the DNA is thought to bring the bound activators into contact with a group of *mediator proteins*, which in turn interact with proteins at the promoter. These protein-protein interactions help assemble and position the initiation complex on the promoter. Many studies support this model, including one showing that the proteins regulating a mouse globin gene contact both the gene's promoter and an enhancer located about 50,000 nucleotides upstream. Protein interactions allow these two regions in the DNA to come together in a very specific fashion, in spite of the large number of nucleotide pairs between them. In the Scientific Skills Exercise, you can work with data from an experiment that identified the control elements in an enhancer of a particular human gene.

Specific transcription factors that function as repressors can inhibit gene expression in several different ways. Some repressors bind directly to control element DNA (in enhancers or elsewhere), blocking activator binding. Other repressors interfere with the activator itself so it can't bind the DNA.

In addition to influencing transcription directly, some activators and repressors act indirectly by affecting chromatin

① **Activator proteins bind to distal control elements grouped as an enhancer in the DNA. This enhancer has three binding sites, each called a distal control element.**

DNA

Activators

Enhancer

Distal control element

Promoter

TATA box

Gene

② **A DNA-bending protein brings the bound activators closer to the promoter. General transcription factors, mediator proteins, and RNA polymerase II are nearby.**

DNA-bending protein

General transcription factors

Group of mediator proteins

RNA polymerase II

③ **The activators bind to certain mediator proteins and general transcription factors, helping them form an active transcription initiation complex on the promoter.**

RNA polymerase II

Transcription initiation complex

RNA synthesis

CHROMATIN MODIFICATION

TRANSCRIPTION

RNA PROCESSING

mRNA DEGRADATION

TRANSLATION

PROTEIN PROCESSING AND DEGRADATION

▲ **Figure 18.10 A model for the action of enhancers and transcription activators.** Bending of the DNA by a protein enables enhancers to influence a promoter hundreds or even thousands of nucleotides away. Specific transcription factors called activators bind to the enhancer DNA sequences and then to a group of mediator proteins, which in turn bind to general transcription factors and ultimately RNA polymerase II, assembling the transcription initiation complex. These protein-protein interactions facilitate the correct positioning of the complex on the promoter and the initiation of RNA synthesis. Only one enhancer (with three gold control elements) is shown here, but a gene may have several enhancers that act at different times or in different cell types.

structure. Studies using yeast and mammalian cells show that some activators recruit proteins that acetylate histones near the promoters of specific genes, thus promoting transcription (see Figure 18.7). Similarly, some repressors recruit proteins that remove acetyl groups from histones, leading to reduced transcription, a phenomenon referred to as *silencing*. Indeed, recruitment of chromatin-modifying proteins seems to be the most common mechanism of repression in eukaryotic cells.

Combinatorial Control of Gene Activation In eukaryotes, the precise control of transcription depends largely on the binding of activators to DNA control elements. Considering the great number of genes that must be regulated in a typical animal or plant cell, the number of completely different nucleotide sequences found in control elements is surprisingly small. A dozen or so short nucleotide sequences appear again and again in the control elements for different genes. On average, each enhancer is composed of about ten control

Analyzing DNA Deletion Experiments

What Control Elements Regulate Expression of the *mPGES-1* Gene? The promoter of a gene includes the DNA immediately upstream of the transcription start site, but the control elements regulating the level at which the gene is transcribed may be thousands of base pairs upstream of the promoter, grouped in an enhancer. Because the distance and spacing of control elements make them difficult to identify, scientists begin by deleting possible control elements and measuring the effect on gene expression. In this exercise, you will analyze data obtained from DNA deletion experiments that tested possible control elements for the human gene *mPGES-1*. This gene codes for an enzyme that synthesizes a type of prostaglandin, a chemical made during inflammation.

How the Experiment Was Done The researchers hypothesized that there were three possible control elements in an enhancer region located 8–9 kilobases upstream of the *mPGES-1* gene. Control elements regulate whatever gene is in the appropriate downstream location. Thus, to test the activity of the possible elements, researchers first synthesized molecules of DNA ("constructs") with the intact enhancer region upstream of a "reporter gene," a gene whose mRNA product could be easily measured experimentally. Next, they synthesized three more DNA constructs but deleted one of the three proposed control elements in each (see left side of figure). The researchers then introduced each DNA construct into a separate human cell culture, where the cells took up the artificial DNA molecules. After 48 hours, the amount of reporter gene mRNA made by the cells was measured. Comparing these amounts allowed researchers to determine if any of the deletions had an effect on expression of the reporter gene, mimicking the effect that deletions would have had on *mPGES-1* gene expression. (The *mPGES-1* gene itself couldn't be used to measure expression levels because the cells express their own *mPGES-1* gene, mRNA from which would otherwise confuse the results.)

Data from the Experiment The diagrams on the left side of the figure show the intact DNA sequence (top) and the three experimental DNA constructs. A red X is located on the possible control element (1, 2, or 3) that was deleted in each experimental DNA construct. The area between the slashes represents the approximately 8 kilobases of DNA located between the promoter and the enhancer region. The horizontal bar graph on the right shows the amount of reporter gene mRNA that was present in each cell culture after 48 hours relative to the amount that was in the culture containing the intact enhancer region (top bar = 100%).

© 2012 The Biochemical Society

Interpret the Data

1. (a) What is the independent variable in the graph (that is, what variable was manipulated by the scientists)? (b) What is the dependent variable (that is, what variable responded to the changes in the independent variable)? (c) What was the control treatment in this experiment? Label it on the diagram.

2. Do the data suggest that any of these possible control elements are actual control elements? Explain.

3. (a) Did deletion of any of the possible control elements cause a *reduction* in reporter gene expression? If so, which one(s), and how can you tell? (b) If loss of a control element causes a reduction in gene expression, what must be the normal role of that control element? Provide a biological explanation for how the loss of such a control element could lead to a reduction in gene expression.

4. (a) Did deletion of any of the possible control elements cause an *increase* in reporter gene expression relative to the control? If so, which one(s), and how can you tell? (b) If loss of a control element causes an increase in gene expression, what must be the normal role of that control element? Propose a biological explanation for how the loss of such a control element could lead to an increase in gene expression.

(MB) A version of this Scientific Skills Exercise can be assigned in MasteringBiology.

Data from J. N. Walters et al., Regulation of human microsomal prostaglandin E synthase-1 by IL-1b requires a distal enhancer element with a unique role for C/EBPb, *Biochemical Journal* 443:561–571 (2012).

elements, each of which can bind only one or two specific transcription factors. It is the particular *combination* of control elements in an enhancer associated with a gene, rather than the presence of a single unique control element, that is important in regulating transcription of the gene.

Even with only a dozen control element sequences available, a very large number of combinations are possible. Each combination of control elements will be able to activate transcription only when the appropriate activator proteins are present, which may occur at a precise time during development or in a particular cell type. **Figure 18.11** illustrates how the use of different combinations of just a few control elements can allow differential regulation of transcription in two representative cell types—liver cells and lens cells. This can occur because each cell type contains a different group of activator proteins. Although the cells of an embryo all arise from one cell (the fertilized egg), diverse paths during embryonic development lead to different mixes of activator proteins in each type of cell. How cell types come to differ during this process will be explored in Concept 18.4.

► **Figure 18.11 Cell type–specific transcription.** Both liver cells and lens cells have the genes for making the proteins albumin and crystallin, but only liver cells make albumin (a blood protein) and only lens cells make crystallin (the main protein of the lens of the eye). The specific transcription factors made in a cell determine which genes are expressed. In this example, the genes for albumin and crystallin are shown at the top, each with an enhancer made up of three different control elements. Although the enhancers for the two genes both have a gray control element, each enhancer has a unique combination of elements. All the activator proteins required for high-level expression of the albumin gene are present only in liver cells **(a)**, whereas the activators needed for expression of the crystallin gene are present only in lens cells **(b)**. For simplicity, we consider only the role of specific transcription factors that are activators here, although repressors may also influence transcription in certain cell types.

? *Describe the enhancer for the albumin gene in each type of cell. How would the nucleotide sequence of this enhancer in the liver cell compare with that in the lens cell?*

(a) **Liver cell.** The albumin gene is expressed, and the crystallin gene is not.

(b) **Lens cell.** The crystallin gene is expressed, and the albumin gene is not.

Coordinately Controlled Genes in Eukaryotes

How does the eukaryotic cell deal with a group of genes of related function that need to be turned on or off at the same time? Earlier in this chapter, you learned that in bacteria, such coordinately controlled genes are often clustered into an operon, which is regulated by a single promoter and transcribed into a single mRNA molecule. Thus, the genes are expressed together, and the encoded proteins are produced concurrently. With a few exceptions, operons that work in this way have *not* been found in eukaryotic cells.

Co-expressed eukaryotic genes, such as genes coding for the enzymes of a metabolic pathway, are typically scattered over different chromosomes. Here, coordinate gene expression depends on the association of a specific combination of control elements with every gene of a dispersed group. Activator proteins in the nucleus that recognize the control elements bind to them, promoting simultaneous transcription of the genes, no matter where they are in the genome.

Coordinate control of dispersed genes in a eukaryotic cell often occurs in response to chemical signals from outside the cell. A steroid hormone, for example, enters a cell and binds to a specific intracellular receptor protein, forming a hormone-receptor complex that serves as a transcription activator (see Figure 11.9). Every gene whose transcription is stimulated by a particular steroid hormone, regardless of its chromosomal location, has a control element recognized by that hormone-receptor complex. This is how estrogen activates a group of genes that stimulate cell division in uterine cells, preparing the uterus for pregnancy.

Many signaling molecules, such as nonsteroid hormones and growth factors, bind to receptors on a cell's surface and never actually enter the cell. Such molecules can control gene expression indirectly by triggering signal transduction pathways that lead to activation of particular transcription activators or repressors (see Figure 11.15). Coordinate regulation in such pathways is the same as for steroid hormones: Genes with the same sets of control elements are activated by the same chemical signals. Because this system for coordinating gene regulation is so widespread, scientists think that it probably arose early in evolutionary history.

Nuclear Architecture and Gene Expression

You saw in Figure 16.23b that each chromosome in the interphase nucleus occupies a distinct territory. The chromosomes are not completely isolated, however. Recently, techniques have been developed that allow researchers to cross-link and identify regions of chromosomes that associate with each other during interphase. These studies reveal that loops of chromatin extend from individual chromosomal territories into specific sites in the nucleus (**Figure 18.12**). Different loops from the same chromosome and loops from other chromosomes may congregate in such sites, some of which are rich in RNA polymerases and other transcription-associated proteins. Like a recreation center that draws members from many different neighborhoods, these so-called *transcription factories* are thought to be areas specialized for a common function.

The old view that the nuclear contents are like a bowl of amorphous chromosomal spaghetti has given way to a new model of a nucleus with a defined architecture and regulated movements of chromatin. Relocation of particular genes from their chromosomal territories to transcription factories may be part of the process of readying genes for transcription. This is an exciting area of current research that raises many fascinating questions for consideration.

▲ **Figure 18.12 Chromosomal interactions in the interphase nucleus.** Although each chromosome has its own territory (see Figure 16.23b), loops of chromatin may extend into other sites in the nucleus. Some of these sites are transcription factories that are occupied by multiple chromatin loops from the same chromosome (blue loops) or other chromosomes (red and green loops).

Mechanisms of Post-Transcriptional Regulation

Transcription alone does not constitute gene expression. The expression of a protein-coding gene is ultimately measured by the amount of functional protein a cell makes, and much happens between the synthesis of the RNA transcript and the activity of the protein in the cell. Many regulatory mechanisms operate at the various stages after transcription (see Figure 18.6). These mechanisms allow a cell to fine-tune gene expression rapidly in response to environmental changes without altering its transcription patterns. Here we discuss how cells can regulate gene expression once a gene has been transcribed.

RNA Processing

RNA processing in the nucleus and the export of mature RNA to the cytoplasm provide several opportunities for regulating gene expression that are not available in prokaryotes. One example of regulation at the RNA-processing level is **alternative RNA splicing**, in which different mRNA molecules are produced from the same primary transcript, depending on which RNA segments are treated as exons and which as introns. Regulatory proteins specific to a cell type control intron-exon choices by binding to regulatory sequences within the primary transcript.

A simple example of alternative RNA splicing is shown in **Figure 18.13** for the troponin T gene, which encodes two different (though related) proteins. Other genes code

▼ **Figure 18.13 Alternative RNA splicing of the troponin T gene.** The primary transcript of this gene can be spliced in more than one way, generating different mRNA molecules. Notice that one mRNA molecule has ended up with exon 3 (green) and the other with exon 4 (purple). These two mRNAs are translated into different but related muscle proteins.

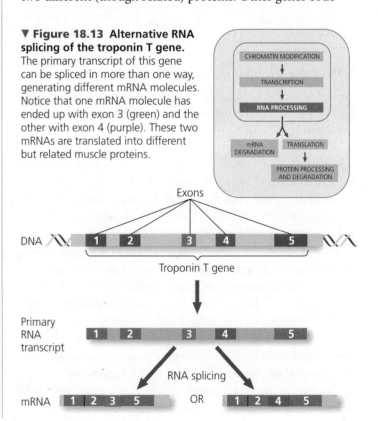

for many more possible products. For instance, researchers have found a *Drosophila* gene with enough alternatively spliced exons to generate about 19,000 membrane proteins that have different extracellular domains. At least 17,500 (94%) of the alternative mRNAs are actually synthesized. Each developing nerve cell in the fly appears to synthesize a unique form of the protein, which acts as an identification badge on the cell surface.

It is clear that alternative RNA splicing can significantly expand the repertoire of a eukaryotic genome. In fact, alternative splicing was proposed as one explanation for the surprisingly low number of human genes counted when the human genome was sequenced. The number of human genes was found to be similar to that of a soil worm (nematode), a mustard plant, or a sea anemone. This discovery prompted questions about what, if not the number of genes, accounts for the more complex morphology (external form) of humans. It turns out that 75–100% of human genes that have multiple exons probably undergo alternative splicing. Thus, the extent of alternative splicing greatly multiplies the number of possible human proteins, which may be better correlated with complexity of form.

Initiation of Translation and mRNA Degradation

Translation presents another opportunity for regulating gene expression; such regulation occurs most commonly at the initiation stage (see Figure 17.18). For some mRNAs, the initiation of translation can be blocked by regulatory proteins that bind to specific sequences or structures within the untranslated region (UTR) at the 5′ or 3′ end, preventing the attachment of ribosomes. (Recall from Chapter 17 that both the 5′ cap and the poly-A tail of an mRNA molecule are important for ribosome binding.)

Alternatively, translation of *all* the mRNAs in a cell may be regulated simultaneously. In a eukaryotic cell, such "global" control usually involves the activation or inactivation of one or more of the protein factors required to initiate translation. This mechanism plays a role in starting translation of mRNAs that are stored in eggs. Just after fertilization, translation is triggered by the sudden activation of translation initiation factors. The response is a burst of synthesis of the proteins encoded by the stored mRNAs. Some plants and algae store mRNAs during periods of darkness; light then triggers the reactivation of the translational apparatus.

The life span of mRNA molecules in the cytoplasm is important in determining the pattern of protein synthesis in a cell. Bacterial mRNA molecules typically are degraded by enzymes within a few minutes of their synthesis. This short life span of mRNAs is one reason bacteria can change their patterns of protein synthesis so quickly in response to environmental changes. In contrast, mRNAs in multicellular eukaryotes typically survive for hours, days, or even weeks. For instance, the mRNAs for the hemoglobin polypeptides (α-globin and β-globin) in developing red blood cells are unusually stable, and these long-lived mRNAs are translated repeatedly in red blood cells.

Nucleotide sequences that affect how long an mRNA remains intact are often found in the untranslated region (UTR) at the 3′ end of the molecule (see Figure 18.8). In one experiment, researchers transferred such a sequence from the short-lived mRNA for a growth factor to the 3′ end of a normally stable globin mRNA. The globin mRNA was quickly degraded.

During the past few years, other mechanisms that degrade or block expression of mRNA molecules have come to light. These mechanisms involve an important group of newly discovered RNA molecules that regulate gene expression at several levels, and we will discuss them later in this chapter.

Protein Processing and Degradation

The final opportunities for controlling gene expression occur after translation. Often, eukaryotic polypeptides must be processed to yield functional protein molecules. For instance, cleavage of the initial insulin polypeptide (proinsulin) forms the active hormone. In addition, many proteins undergo chemical modifications that make them functional. Regulatory proteins are commonly activated or inactivated by the reversible addition of phosphate groups, and proteins destined for the surface of animal cells acquire sugars. Cell-surface proteins and many others must also be transported to target destinations in the cell in order to function. Regulation might occur at any of the steps involved in modifying or transporting a protein.

Finally, the length of time each protein functions in the cell is strictly regulated by means of selective degradation. Many proteins, such as the cyclins involved in regulating the cell cycle, must be relatively short-lived if the cell is to function appropriately (see Figure 12.16). To mark a particular protein for destruction, the cell commonly attaches molecules of a small protein called ubiquitin to the protein. Giant protein complexes called proteasomes then recognize the ubiquitin-tagged proteins and degrade them.

CONCEPT CHECK 18.2

1. In general, what are the effects of histone acetylation and DNA methylation on gene expression?

2. Compare the roles of general and specific transcription factors in regulating gene expression.

3. **WHAT IF?** Suppose you compared the nucleotide sequences of the distal control elements in the enhancers of three genes that are expressed only in muscle cells. What would you expect to find? Why?

4. Once mRNA encoding a particular protein reaches the cytoplasm, what are four mechanisms that can regulate the amount of the protein that is active in the cell?

For suggested answers, see Appendix A.

Noncoding RNAs play multiple roles in controlling gene expression

Genome sequencing has revealed that protein-coding DNA accounts for only 1.5% of the human genome and a similarly small percentage of the genomes of many other multicellular eukaryotes. A very small fraction of the non-protein-coding DNA consists of genes for RNAs such as ribosomal RNA and transfer RNA. Until recently, most of the remaining DNA was assumed to be untranscribed. The idea was that since it didn't specify proteins or the few known types of RNA, such DNA didn't contain meaningful genetic information. However, a flood of recent data has contradicted this idea. For example, a massive study of the entire human genome completed in 2012 showed that roughly 75% of the genome is transcribed at some point in any given cell. Introns account for only a fraction of this transcribed, nontranslated RNA. These and other results suggest that a significant amount of the genome may be transcribed into non-protein-coding RNAs—also called *noncoding RNAs*, or *ncRNAs*—including a variety of small RNAs. While many questions about the functions of these RNAs remain unanswered, researchers are uncovering more evidence of their biological roles every day.

Biologists are excited about these recent discoveries, which hint at a large, diverse population of RNA molecules in the cell that play crucial roles in regulating gene expression—but have gone largely unnoticed until now. Subsequent research has impelled revision of the long-standing view that because mRNAs code for proteins, they are the most important RNAs functioning in the cell. This represents a major shift in the thinking of biologists, one that you are witnessing as students entering this field of study. It's as if our exclusive focus on a famous rock star has blinded us to the many backup musicians and songwriters working behind the scenes.

Effects on mRNAs by MicroRNAs and Small Interfering RNAs

Regulation by both small and large ncRNAs is known to occur at several points in the pathway of gene expression, including mRNA translation and chromatin modification. We will focus mainly on two types of small ncRNAs that have been extensively studied in the past few years. The importance of these RNAs was acknowledged when they were the focus of the 2006 Nobel Prize in Physiology or Medicine, which was awarded for work completed only 8 years earlier.

Since 1993, a number of research studies have uncovered small single-stranded RNA molecules, called **microRNAs**

(**miRNAs**), capable of binding to complementary sequences in mRNA molecules. A longer RNA precursor is processed by cellular enzymes into an miRNA, a single-stranded RNA of about 22 nucleotides that forms a complex with one or more proteins. The miRNA allows the complex to bind to any mRNA molecule with at least 7 or 8 nucleotides of complementary sequence. The miRNA-protein complex then either degrades the target mRNA or blocks its translation (**Figure 18.14**). It has been estimated that expression of at least one-half of all human genes may be regulated by miRNAs, a remarkable figure given that the existence of miRNAs was unknown a mere two decades ago.

Another class of small RNAs are called **small interfering RNAs (siRNAs)**. These are similar in size and function to miRNAs—both can associate with the same proteins, producing similar results. In fact, if siRNA precursor RNA molecules are injected into a cell, the cell's machinery can process them into siRNAs that turn off expression of genes with related sequences, similarly to how miRNAs function. The distinction between miRNAs and siRNAs is based on subtle differences in the structure of their precursors, which

1 The miRNA binds to a target mRNA with at least 7 complementary bases.

mRNA degraded   OR   Translation blocked

2 If miRNA and mRNA bases are complementary all along their length, the mRNA is degraded (left); if the match is less complete, translation is blocked (right).

▲ **Figure 18.14 Regulation of gene expression by miRNAs.** A 22-nucleotide miRNA, formed by enzymatic processing of an RNA precursor, associates with one or more proteins in a complex. The complex can then degrade or block translation of target mRNAs.

in both cases are RNA molecules that are mostly double-stranded. The blocking of gene expression by siRNAs is called **RNA interference (RNAi)**, and it is used in the laboratory as a means of disabling specific genes to investigate their function.

How did the RNAi pathway evolve? As you will learn in Chapter 19, some viruses have double-stranded RNA genomes. Given that the cellular RNAi pathway can process double-stranded RNAs into homing devices that lead to destruction of related RNAs, some scientists think that this pathway may have evolved as a natural defense against infection by such viruses. However, the fact that RNAi can also affect the expression of nonviral cellular genes may reflect a different evolutionary origin for the RNAi pathway. Moreover, many species, including mammals, apparently produce their own long, double-stranded RNA precursors to small RNAs such as siRNAs. Once produced, these RNAs can interfere with gene expression at stages other than translation, as we'll discuss next.

Chromatin Remodeling by ncRNAs

The pervasive function of noncoding RNAs in regulating gene expression is becoming increasingly obvious, and one more effect of ncRNAs is worth discussing here. In addition to regulating mRNAs, some ncRNAs act to bring about remodeling of chromatin structure. One example occurs during formation of heterochromatin at the centromere, as studied in a species of yeast.

In the S phase of the cell cycle, the centromeric regions of DNA must be loosened for chromosomal replication and then re-condensed into heterochromatin in preparation for mitosis. In some yeasts, siRNAs produced by the yeast cells themselves are required to re-form the heterochromatin at the centromeres. A model for how this happens is shown in **Figure 18.15**. Exactly how the process starts and the order of the steps are still being debated, but biologists all agree on the general idea: The siRNA system in yeast interacts with other noncoding RNAs and with chromatin-modifying enzymes to remodel chromatin structure at the centromere. In most mammalian cells, siRNAs are not known to occur, and the mechanism for centromere DNA condensation is not yet understood. However, it may turn out to involve other small ncRNAs.

A newly discovered class of small ncRNAs is called *piwi-interacting RNAs*, or *piRNAs*. (Dr. Haifan Lin, whose interview appears before Chapter 6, discovered and named piRNAs.) These RNAs also induce formation of heterochromatin, blocking expression of some parasitic DNA elements in the genome known as transposons. (Transposons are discussed in Chapter 21.) Usually 24–31 nucleotides in length, piRNAs are processed from a longer, single-stranded RNA

1 RNA transcripts (red) are produced from centromeric DNA.

2 Each RNA transcript is used as a template by a yeast enzyme that synthesizes the complementary strand, forming double-stranded RNA.

3 The double-stranded RNA is processed into short, single-stranded siRNAs that associate with proteins, forming siRNA-protein complexes.

4 The siRNA-protein complexes bind the RNA transcripts being produced from the centromeric DNA and, in this way, are tethered to the centromere region.

5 Proteins in the siRNA-protein complexes recruit enzymes (green) that chemically modify the histones within the chromatin and initiate chromatin condensation.

6 Ultimately, this process leads to formation of heterochromatin at the centromere.

▲ **Figure 18.15 Condensation of chromatin at the centromere.** In one type of yeast, siRNAs and longer noncoding RNAs cooperate in the pathway that leads to re-formation of highly condensed heterochromatin at the centromere of each chromatid after DNA replication.

precursor. They play an indispensable role in the germ cells of many animal species, where they appear to help reestablish appropriate methylation patterns in the genome during gamete formation.

Finally, ncRNAs are responsible for X chromosome inactivation, which, in most female mammals, prevents expression of genes located on one of the X chromosomes (see Figure 15.8). In this case, transcripts of the XIST gene located on the chromosome to be inactivated bind back to and coat that chromosome, and this binding leads to condensation of the entire chromosome into heterochromatin.

The cases we have just described involve chromatin remodeling in large regions of the chromosome. Because chromatin structure affects transcription and thus gene expression, RNA-based regulation of chromatin structure is likely to play an important role in gene regulation.

The Evolutionary Significance of Small ncRNAs

EVOLUTION Small ncRNAs can regulate gene expression at multiple steps and in many ways. In general, extra levels of gene regulation might allow evolution of a higher degree of complexity of form. The versatility of miRNA regulation has therefore led some biologists to hypothesize that an increase in the number of different miRNAs specified by the genome of a given species has allowed morphological complexity to increase over evolutionary time. While this hypothesis is still being evaluated, it is logical to expand the discussion to include all small ncRNAs. Exciting new techniques for rapidly sequencing genomes have allowed biologists to begin asking how many genes for ncRNAs are present in the genome of any given species. A survey of different species supports the notion that siRNAs evolved first, followed by miRNAs and later piRNAs, which are found only in animals. And while there are hundreds of types of miRNAs, there appear to be 60,000 or so types of piRNAs, allowing the potential for very sophisticated gene regulation by piRNAs.

Given the extensive functions of ncRNAs, it is not surprising that many of the ncRNAs characterized thus far play important roles in embryonic development—the topic we turn to in the next section. Embryonic development is perhaps the ultimate example of precisely regulated gene expression.

CONCEPT CHECK 18.3

1. Compare miRNAs and siRNAs, including their functions.
2. **WHAT IF?** Suppose the mRNA being degraded in Figure 18.14 coded for a protein that promotes cell division in a multicellular organism. What would happen if a mutation disabled the gene for the miRNA that triggers this degradation?

For suggested answers, see Appendix A.

A program of differential gene expression leads to the different cell types in a multicellular organism

In the embryonic development of multicellular organisms, a fertilized egg (a zygote) gives rise to cells of many different types, each with a different structure and corresponding function. Typically, cells are organized into tissues, tissues into organs, organs into organ systems, and organ systems into the whole organism. Thus, any developmental program must produce cells of different types that form higher-level structures arranged in a particular way in three dimensions. The processes that occur during development in plants and animals are detailed in Chapters 35 and 47, respectively. In this chapter, we focus on the program of regulation of gene expression that orchestrates development, using a few animal species as examples.

A Genetic Program for Embryonic Development

The photos in **Figure 18.16** illustrate the dramatic difference between a frog zygote and the tadpole it becomes. This remarkable transformation results from three interrelated processes: cell division, cell differentiation, and morphogenesis. Through a succession of mitotic cell divisions, the zygote gives rise to a large number of cells. Cell division alone, however, would merely produce a great ball of identical cells, nothing like a tadpole. During embryonic development, cells not only increase in number, but also undergo cell **differentiation**, the process by which cells become specialized in structure and function. Moreover, the different kinds of cells are not randomly distributed but are organized into tissues and organs in a particular three-dimensional

(a) Fertilized eggs of a frog **(b) Newly hatched tadpole**

▲ **Figure 18.16 From fertilized egg to animal: What a difference four days makes.** It takes just four days for cell division, differentiation, and morphogenesis to transform each of the fertilized frog eggs shown in **(a)** into a tadpole like the one in **(b)**.

arrangement. The physical processes that give an organism its shape constitute **morphogenesis**, the development of the form of an organism and its structures.

All three processes are rooted in cellular behavior. Even morphogenesis, the shaping of the organism, can be traced back to changes in the shape, motility, and other characteristics of the cells that make up various regions of the embryo. As you have seen, the activities of a cell depend on the genes it expresses and the proteins it produces. Almost all cells in an organism have the same genome; therefore, differential gene expression results from the genes being regulated differently in each cell type.

In Figure 18.11, you saw a simplified view of how differential gene expression occurs in two cell types, a liver cell and a lens cell. Each of these fully differentiated cells has a particular mix of specific activators that turn on the collection of genes whose products are required in the cell. The fact that both cells arose through a series of mitoses from a common fertilized egg inevitably leads to a question: How do different sets of activators come to be present in the two cells?

It turns out that materials placed into the egg by the mother set up a sequential program of gene regulation that is carried out as cells divide, and this program coordinates cell differentiation during embryonic development. To understand how this works, we will consider two basic developmental processes: First, we'll explore how cells that arise from early embryonic mitoses develop the differences that start each cell along its own differentiation pathway. Second, we'll see how cellular differentiation leads to one particular cell type, using muscle development as an example.

Cytoplasmic Determinants and Inductive Signals

What generates the first differences among cells in an early embryo? And what controls the differentiation of all the various cell types as development proceeds? By this point in the chapter, you can probably deduce the answer: The specific genes expressed in any particular cell of a developing organism determine its path. Two sources of information, used to varying extents in different species, "tell" a cell which genes to express at any given time during embryonic development.

One important source of information early in development is the egg's cytoplasm, which contains both RNA and proteins encoded by the mother's DNA. The cytoplasm of an unfertilized egg is not homogeneous. Messenger RNA, proteins, other substances, and organelles are distributed unevenly in the unfertilized egg, and this unevenness has a profound impact on the development of the future embryo in many species. Maternal substances in the egg that influence the course of early development are called **cytoplasmic determinants (Figure 18.17a)**. After fertilization, early mitotic divisions distribute the zygote's cytoplasm

▼ **Figure 18.17 Sources of developmental information for the early embryo.**

(a) Cytoplasmic determinants in the egg

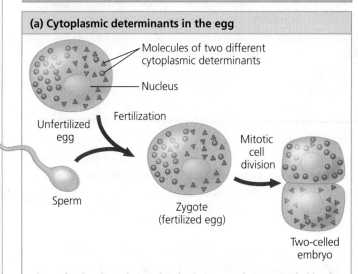

The unfertilized egg has molecules in its cytoplasm, encoded by the mother's genes, that influence development. Many of these cytoplasmic determinants, like the two shown here, are unevenly distributed in the egg. After fertilization and mitotic division, the cell nuclei of the embryo are exposed to different sets of cytoplasmic determinants and, as a result, express different genes.

(b) Induction by nearby cells

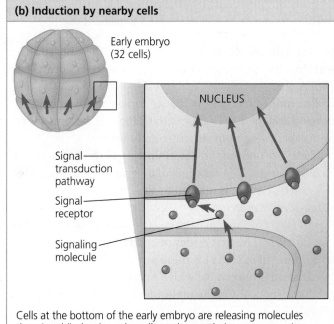

Cells at the bottom of the early embryo are releasing molecules that signal (induce) nearby cells to change their gene expression.

into separate cells. The nuclei of these cells may thus be exposed to different cytoplasmic determinants, depending on which portions of the zygotic cytoplasm a cell received. The combination of cytoplasmic determinants in a cell helps determine its developmental fate by regulating expression of the cell's genes during the course of cell differentiation.

The other major source of developmental information, which becomes increasingly important as the number of embryonic cells increases, is the environment around a particular cell. Most influential are the signals impinging on an embryonic cell from other embryonic cells in the vicinity, including contact with cell-surface molecules on neighboring cells and the binding of growth factors secreted by neighboring cells (see Chapter 11). Such signals cause changes in the target cells, a process called **induction** (**Figure 18.17b**). The molecules conveying these signals within the target cell are cell-surface receptors and other signaling pathway proteins. In general, the signaling molecules send a cell down a specific developmental path by causing changes in its gene expression that eventually result in observable cellular changes. Thus, interactions between embryonic cells help induce differentiation into the many specialized cell types making up a new organism.

Sequential Regulation of Gene Expression During Cellular Differentiation

The earliest changes that set a cell on its path to specialization are subtle ones, showing up only at the molecular level. Before biologists knew much about the molecular changes occurring in embryos, they coined the term **determination** to refer to the point at which an embryonic cell is irreversibly committed to becoming a particular cell type. Once it has undergone determination, an embryonic cell can be experimentally placed in another location in the embryo and it will still differentiate into the cell type that is its normal fate. Differentiation, then, is the process by which a cell attains its determined fate. As the tissues and organs of an embryo develop and their cells differentiate, the cells become more noticeably different in structure and function.

Today we understand determination in terms of molecular changes. The outcome of determination, observable cell differentiation, is marked by the expression of genes for *tissue-specific proteins*. These proteins are found only in a specific cell type and give the cell its characteristic structure and function. The first evidence of differentiation is the appearance of mRNAs for these proteins. Eventually, differentiation is observable with a microscope as changes in cellular structure. On the molecular level, different sets of genes are sequentially expressed in a regulated manner as new cells arise from division of their precursors. A number of the steps in gene expression may be regulated during differentiation, with transcription among the most common. In the fully differentiated cell, transcription remains the principal regulatory point for maintaining appropriate gene expression.

Differentiated cells are specialists at making tissue-specific proteins. For example, as a result of transcriptional regulation, liver cells specialize in making albumin, and lens cells specialize in making crystallin (see Figure 18.11). Skeletal muscle cells in vertebrates are another instructive example. Each of these cells is a long fiber containing many nuclei within a single plasma membrane. Skeletal muscle cells have high concentrations of muscle-specific versions of the contractile proteins myosin and actin, as well as membrane receptor proteins that detect signals from nerve cells.

Muscle cells develop from embryonic precursor cells that have the potential to develop into a number of cell types, including cartilage cells and fat cells, but particular conditions commit them to becoming muscle cells. Although the committed cells appear unchanged under the microscope, determination has occurred, and they are now *myoblasts*. Eventually, myoblasts start to churn out large amounts of muscle-specific proteins and fuse to form mature, elongated, multinucleate skeletal muscle cells.

Researchers have worked out what happens at the molecular level during muscle cell determination by growing myoblasts in culture and analyzing them using molecular techniques you will learn about in Chapter 20. In a series of experiments, they isolated different genes, caused each to be expressed in a separate embryonic precursor cell, and then looked for differentiation into myoblasts and muscle cells. In this way, they identified several so-called "master regulatory genes" whose protein products commit the cells to becoming skeletal muscle. Thus, in the case of muscle cells, the molecular basis of determination is the expression of one or more of these master regulatory genes.

To understand more about how determination occurs in muscle cell differentiation, let's focus on the master regulatory gene called *myoD* (**Figure 18.18**). This gene encodes MyoD protein, a transcription factor that binds to specific control elements in the enhancers of various target genes and stimulates their expression (see Figure 18.9). Some target genes for MyoD encode still other muscle-specific transcription factors. MyoD also stimulates expression of the *myoD* gene itself, an example of positive feedback that perpetuates MyoD's effect in maintaining the cell's differentiated state. Presumably, all the genes activated by MyoD have enhancer control elements recognized by MyoD and are thus coordinately controlled. Finally, the secondary transcription factors activate the genes for proteins such as myosin and actin that confer the unique properties of skeletal muscle cells.

The *myoD* gene deserves its designation as a master regulatory gene. Researchers have shown that MyoD is capable of changing some kinds of fully differentiated nonmuscle cells, such as fat cells and liver cells, into muscle cells. Why doesn't it work on *all* kinds of cells? One likely explanation is that activation of the muscle-specific genes is not solely dependent on MyoD but requires a particular *combination* of regulatory proteins, some of which are lacking in cells that do not respond to MyoD. The determination and differentiation of other kinds of tissues may play out in a similar fashion.

We have now seen how different programs of gene expression that are activated in the fertilized egg can result in differentiated cells and tissues. But for the tissues to function effectively in the organism as a whole, the organism's

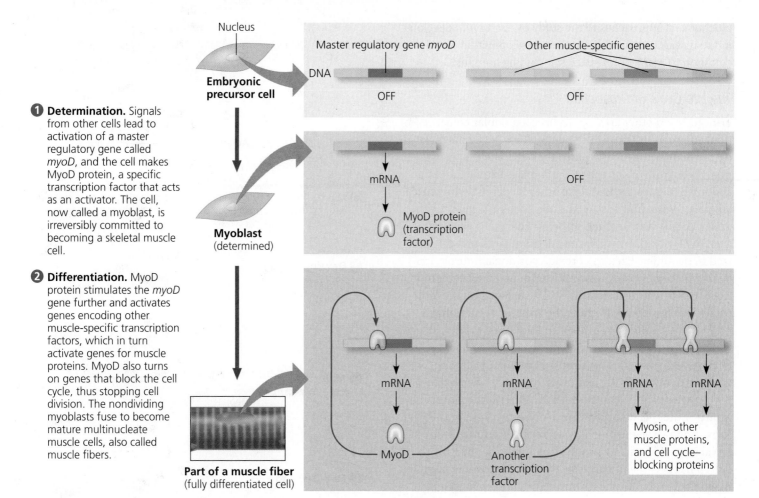

① Determination. Signals from other cells lead to activation of a master regulatory gene called *myoD*, and the cell makes MyoD protein, a specific transcription factor that acts as an activator. The cell, now called a myoblast, is irreversibly committed to becoming a skeletal muscle cell.

② Differentiation. MyoD protein stimulates the *myoD* gene further and activates genes encoding other muscle-specific transcription factors, which in turn activate genes for muscle proteins. MyoD also turns on genes that block the cell cycle, thus stopping cell division. The nondividing myoblasts fuse to become mature multinucleate muscle cells, also called muscle fibers.

Nucleus

Embryonic precursor cell

Myoblast (determined)

Part of a muscle fiber (fully differentiated cell)

Master regulatory gene *myoD*   Other muscle-specific genes

DNA   OFF   OFF

mRNA   OFF

MyoD protein (transcription factor)

mRNA   mRNA   mRNA   mRNA

MyoD   Another transcription factor

Myosin, other muscle proteins, and cell cycle–blocking proteins

▲ **Figure 18.18 Determination and differentiation of muscle cells.** Skeletal muscle cells arise from embryonic cells as a result of changes in gene expression. (In this depiction, the process of gene activation is greatly simplified.)

WHAT IF? *What would happen if a mutation in the* myoD *gene resulted in a MyoD protein that could not activate the* myoD *gene?*

body plan—its overall three-dimensional arrangement—must be established and superimposed on the differentiation process. Next we'll investigate the molecular basis for the establishment of the body plan, using the well-studied fruit fly *Drosophila melanogaster* as an example.

Pattern Formation: Setting Up the Body Plan

Cytoplasmic determinants and inductive signals both contribute to the development of a spatial organization in which the tissues and organs of an organism are all in their characteristic places. This process is called **pattern formation**.

Just as the locations of the front, back, and sides of a new building are determined before construction begins, pattern formation in animals begins in the early embryo, when the major axes of an animal are established. In a bilaterally symmetrical animal, the relative positions of head and tail, right and left sides, and back and front—the three major body axes—are set up before the organs appear. The molecular cues that control pattern formation, collectively called

positional information, are provided by cytoplasmic determinants and inductive signals (see Figure 18.17). These cues tell a cell its location relative to the body axes and to neighboring cells and determine how the cell and its progeny will respond to future molecular signals.

During the first half of the 20th century, classical embryologists made detailed anatomical observations of embryonic development in a number of species and performed experiments in which they manipulated embryonic tissues. Although this research laid the groundwork for understanding the mechanisms of development, it did not reveal the specific molecules that guide development or determine how patterns are established.

Then, in the 1940s, scientists began using the genetic approach—the study of mutants—to investigate *Drosophila* development. That approach has had spectacular success. These studies have established that genes control development and have led to an understanding of the key roles that specific molecules play in defining position and directing differentiation. By combining anatomical, genetic, and biochemical approaches to the study of *Drosophila* development, researchers have discovered developmental principles common to many other species, including humans.

The Life Cycle of Drosophila

Fruit flies and other arthropods have a modular construction, an ordered series of segments. These segments make up the body's three major parts: the head, the thorax (the mid-body, from which the wings and legs extend), and the abdomen **(Figure 18.19a)**. Like other bilaterally symmetrical animals, *Drosophila* has an anterior-posterior (head-to-tail) axis, a dorsal-ventral (back-to-belly) axis, and a right-left axis. In *Drosophila*, cytoplasmic determinants that are localized in the unfertilized egg provide positional information for the placement of anterior-posterior and dorsal-ventral axes even before fertilization. We'll focus here on the molecules involved in establishing the anterior-posterior axis.

The *Drosophila* egg develops in the female's ovary, surrounded by ovarian cells called nurse cells and follicle cells **(Figure 18.19b,** top). These support cells supply the egg with nutrients, mRNAs, and other substances needed for development and make the egg shell. After fertilization and laying of the egg, embryonic development results in the formation of a segmented larva, which goes through three larval stages. Then, in a process much like that by which a caterpillar becomes a butterfly, the fly larva forms a pupa in which it metamorphoses into the adult fly pictured in Figure 18.19a.

Genetic Analysis of Early Development: Scientific Inquiry

Edward B. Lewis was a visionary American biologist who, in the 1940s, first showed the value of the genetic approach to studying embryonic development in *Drosophila*. Lewis studied bizarre mutant flies with developmental defects that led to extra wings or legs in the wrong place **(Figure 18.20)**. He located the mutations on the fly's genetic map, thus connecting the developmental abnormalities to specific genes. This research supplied the first concrete evidence that genes somehow direct the developmental processes studied by embryologists. The genes Lewis discovered, called **homeotic genes**, control pattern formation in the late embryo, larva, and adult.

Further insight into pattern formation during early embryonic development did not come for another 30 years, when two researchers in Germany, Christiane Nüsslein-Volhard and Eric Wieschaus, set out to identify *all* the genes that affect segment formation in *Drosophila*. The project was daunting for three reasons. The first was the sheer number of *Drosophila* genes, now known to total about 14,000. The genes affecting segmentation might be just a few needles in a haystack or might be so numerous and varied that the scientists would be unable to make sense of them.

(a) Adult. The adult fly is segmented, and multiple segments make up each of the three main body parts—head, thorax, and abdomen. The body axes are shown by arrows.

❶ **Developing egg** within ovarian follicle

❷ **Mature, unfertilized egg**

❸ **Fertilized egg**

❹ **Segmented embryo**

❺ **Larva**

(b) Development from egg to larva. ❶ The egg (yellow) is surrounded by support cells (follicle cells) within one of the mother's ovaries. ❷ The developing egg enlarges as nutrients and mRNAs are supplied to it by other support cells (nurse cells), which shrink. Eventually, the mature egg fills the egg shell that is secreted by the follicle cells. ❸ The egg is fertilized within the mother and then laid. It develops into ❹ a segmented embryo and then ❺ a larva, which has three stages. The third stage forms a pupa (not shown), within which the larva metamorphoses into the adult shown in (a).

▲ **Figure 18.19 Key developmental events in the life cycle of *Drosophila*.**

Second, mutations affecting a process as fundamental as segmentation would surely be **embryonic lethals**, mutations with phenotypes causing death at the embryonic or larval stage. Because organisms with embryonic lethal mutations

▲ **Figure 18.20 Abnormal pattern formation in *Drosophila*.** Mutations in certain regulatory genes, called homeotic genes, cause abnormal placement of structures in an animal. These colorized scanning electron micrographs contrast the head of a wild-type fruit fly, bearing a pair of small antennae, with that of a homeotic mutant (a fly with a mutation in a single gene), bearing a pair of legs in place of antennae.

never reproduce, they cannot be bred for study. The researchers dealt with this problem by looking for recessive mutations, which can be propagated in heterozygous flies that act as genetic carriers. Third, cytoplasmic determinants in the egg were known to play a role in axis formation, so the researchers knew they would have to study the mother's genes as well as those of the embryo. It is the mother's genes that we will discuss further as we focus on how the anterior-posterior body axis is set up in the developing egg.

Nüsslein-Volhard and Wieschaus began their search for segmentation genes by exposing flies to a mutagenic chemical that affected the flies' gametes. They mated the mutagenized flies and then scanned their descendants for dead embryos or larvae with abnormal segmentation or other defects. For example, to find genes that might set up the anterior-posterior axis, they looked for embryos or larvae with abnormal ends, such as two heads or two tails, predicting that such abnormalities would arise from mutations in maternal genes required for correctly setting up the offspring's head or tail end.

Using this approach, Nüsslein-Volhard and Wieschaus eventually identified about 1,200 genes essential for pattern formation during embryonic development. Of these, about 120 were essential for normal segmentation. Over several years, the researchers were able to group these segmentation genes by general function, to map them, and to clone many of them for further study in the lab. The result was a detailed molecular understanding of the early steps in pattern formation in *Drosophila*.

When the results of Nüsslein-Volhard and Wieschaus were combined with Lewis's earlier work, a coherent picture of *Drosophila* development emerged. In recognition of their discoveries, the three researchers were awarded a Nobel Prize in 1995. Next, let's consider a specific example of the genes that Nüsslein-Volhard, Wieschaus, and co-workers found.

Axis Establishment

As we mentioned earlier, cytoplasmic determinants in the egg are the substances that initially establish the axes of the *Drosophila* body. These substances are encoded by genes of the mother, fittingly called maternal effect genes. A **maternal effect gene** is a gene that, when mutant in the mother, results in a mutant phenotype in the offspring, regardless of the offspring's own genotype. In fruit fly development, the mRNA or protein products of maternal effect genes are placed in the egg while it is still in the mother's ovary. When the mother has a mutation in such a gene, she makes a defective gene product (or none at all), and her eggs are defective; when these eggs are fertilized, they fail to develop properly.

Because they control the orientation (polarity) of the egg and consequently that of the fly, these maternal effect genes are also called **egg-polarity genes**. One group of these genes sets up the anterior-posterior axis of the embryo, while a second group establishes the dorsal-ventral axis. Like mutations in segmentation genes, mutations in maternal effect genes are generally embryonic lethals.

Bicoid: A Morphogen that Determines Head Structures To see how maternal effect genes determine the body axes of the offspring, we will focus on one such gene, called *bicoid*, a term meaning "two-tailed." An embryo or larva whose mother has two mutant *bicoid* alleles lacks the front half of its body and has posterior structures at both ends **(Figure 18.21)**. This phenotype suggested to Nüsslein-Volhard and her colleagues that the product of the mother's *bicoid* gene is essential for setting up the anterior end of the fly and might be concentrated at the future anterior end of

▲ **Figure 18.21 Effect of the *bicoid* gene on *Drosophila* development.** A wild-type fruit fly larva has a head, three thoracic (T) segments, eight abdominal (A) segments, and a tail. A larva whose mother has two mutant alleles of the *bicoid* gene has two tails and lacks all anterior structures (LMs).

the embryo. This hypothesis is an example of the *morphogen gradient hypothesis* first proposed by embryologists a century ago, where gradients of substances called **morphogens** establish an embryo's axes and other features of its form.

DNA technology and other modern biochemical methods enabled the researchers to test whether the *bicoid* product, a protein called Bicoid, is in fact a morphogen that determines the anterior end of the fly. The first question they asked was whether the mRNA and protein products of this gene are located in the egg in a position consistent with the hypothesis. They found that *bicoid* mRNA is highly concentrated at the extreme anterior end of the mature egg (**Figure 18.22**). After the egg is fertilized, the mRNA is translated into protein. The Bicoid protein then diffuses from the anterior end toward the posterior, resulting in a gradient of protein within the early embryo, with the highest concentration at the anterior end. These results are consistent with the hypothesis that Bicoid protein specifies the fly's anterior end. To test the hypothesis more specifically, scientists injected pure *bicoid* mRNA into various regions of early embryos. The protein that resulted from its translation caused anterior structures to form at the injection sites.

The *bicoid* research was groundbreaking for several reasons. First, it led to the identification of a specific protein required for some of the earliest steps in pattern formation. It thus helped us understand how different regions of the egg can give rise to cells that go down different developmental pathways. Second, it increased our understanding of the mother's critical role in the initial phases of embryonic development. Finally, the principle that a gradient of morphogens can determine polarity and position has proved to be a key developmental concept for a number of species, just as early embryologists had thought.

Maternal mRNAs are crucial during development of many species. In *Drosophila*, gradients of specific proteins encoded by maternal mRNAs not only determine the posterior and anterior ends but also establish the dorsal-ventral axis. As the fly embryo grows, it reaches a point when the embryonic program of gene expression takes over, and the maternal mRNAs must be destroyed. (This process involves miRNAs in *Drosophila* and other species.) Later, positional information encoded by the embryo's genes, operating on an ever finer scale, establishes a specific number of correctly oriented segments and triggers the formation of each segment's characteristic structures. When the genes operating in this final step are abnormal, the pattern of the adult is abnormal, as you saw in Figure 18.20.

Evolutionary Developmental Biology ("Evo-Devo")

EVOLUTION The fly with legs emerging from its head in Figure 18.20 is the result of a single mutation in one gene. The gene does not encode an antenna protein, however. Instead, it encodes a transcription factor that regulates other

▼ **Figure 18.22** | Inquiry

Could Bicoid be a morphogen that determines the anterior end of a fruit fly?

Experiment Using a genetic approach to study *Drosophila* development, Christiane Nüsslein-Volhard and colleagues at two research institutions in Germany analyzed expression of the *bicoid* gene. The researchers hypothesized that *bicoid* normally codes for a morphogen that specifies the head (anterior) end of the embryo. To begin to test this hypothesis, they used molecular techniques to determine whether the mRNA and protein encoded by this gene were found in the anterior end of the fertilized egg and early embryo of wild-type flies.

Results *Bicoid* mRNA (dark blue in the light micrographs and drawings) was confined to the anterior end of the unfertilized egg. Later in development, Bicoid protein (dark orange) was seen to be concentrated in cells at the anterior end of the embryo.

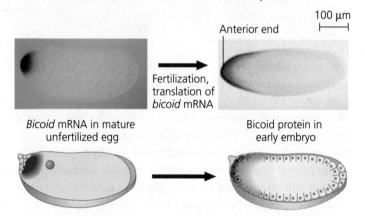

Bicoid mRNA in mature unfertilized egg

Bicoid protein in early embryo

Conclusion The location of *bicoid* mRNA and the diffuse gradient of Bicoid protein seen later are consistent with the hypothesis that Bicoid protein is a morphogen specifying formation of head-specific structures.

Source: C. Nüsslein-Volhard et al., Determination of anteroposterior polarity in *Drosophila, Science* 238:1675–1681 (1987); W. Driever and C. Nüsslein-Volhard, A gradient of *bicoid* protein in *Drosophila* embryos, *Cell* 54:83–93 (1988); T. Berleth et al., The role of localization of *bicoid* RNA in organizing the anterior pattern of the *Drosophila* embryo, *EMBO Journal* 7:1749–1756 (1988).

WHAT IF? *The researchers needed further evidence, so they injected* bicoid *mRNA into the anterior end of an egg from a female with a mutation disabling the* bicoid *gene. Given that the hypothesis was supported, what do you think were their results?*

genes, and its malfunction leads to misplaced structures, such as legs instead of antennae. The observation that a change in gene regulation during development could lead to such a fantastic change in body form prompted some scientists to consider whether these types of mutations could contribute to evolution by generating novel body shapes. Ultimately this line of inquiry gave rise to the field of evolutionary developmental biology, so-called "evo-devo," which will be further discussed in Chapter 21.

In this section, we have seen how a carefully orchestrated program of sequential gene regulation controls the transformation of a fertilized egg into a multicellular organism. The program is carefully balanced between turning on the genes for differentiation in the right place and turning off other genes. Even when an organism is fully developed, gene expression is regulated in a similarly fine-tuned manner. In the final section of the chapter, we'll consider how fine this tuning is by looking at how specific changes in expression of just a few genes can lead to the development of cancer.

CONCEPT CHECK 18.4

1. **MAKE CONNECTIONS** As you learned in Chapter 12, mitosis gives rise to two daughter cells that are genetically identical to the parent cell. Yet you, the product of many mitotic divisions, are not composed of identical cells. Why?

2. **MAKE CONNECTIONS** Explain how the signaling molecules released by an embryonic cell can induce changes in a neighboring cell without entering the cell. (See Figures 11.15 and 11.16.)

3. Why are fruit fly maternal effect genes also called egg-polarity genes?

4. **WHAT IF?** In Figure 18.17b, the lower cell is synthesizing signaling molecules, whereas the upper cell is expressing receptors for these molecules. In terms of gene regulation and cytoplasmic determinants, explain how these cells came to synthesize different molecules.

For suggested answers, see Appendix A.

CONCEPT 18.5

Cancer results from genetic changes that affect cell cycle control

In Chapter 12, we considered cancer as a type of disease in which cells escape from the control mechanisms that normally limit their growth. Now that we have discussed the molecular basis of gene expression and its regulation, we are ready to look at cancer more closely. The gene regulation systems that go wrong during cancer turn out to be the very same systems that play important roles in embryonic development, the immune response, and many other biological processes. Thus, research into the molecular basis of cancer has both benefited from and informed many other fields of biology.

Types of Genes Associated with Cancer

The genes that normally regulate cell growth and division during the cell cycle include genes for growth factors, their receptors, and the intracellular molecules of signaling pathways. (To review cell signaling, see Chapter 11; for the cell cycle, see Chapter 12.) Mutations that alter any of these genes in somatic cells can lead to cancer. The agent of such change can be random spontaneous mutation. However, it is also likely that many cancer-causing mutations result from environmental influences, such as chemical carcinogens, X-rays and other high-energy radiation, and some viruses.

Cancer research led to the discovery of cancer-causing genes called **oncogenes** (from the Greek *onco*, tumor) in certain types of viruses (see Chapter 19). Subsequently, close counterparts of viral oncogenes were found in the genomes of humans and other animals. The normal versions of the cellular genes, called **proto-oncogenes**, code for proteins that stimulate normal cell growth and division.

How might a proto-oncogene—a gene that has an essential function in normal cells—become an oncogene, a cancer-causing gene? In general, an oncogene arises from a genetic change that leads to an increase either in the amount of the proto-oncogene's protein product or in the intrinsic activity of each protein molecule. The genetic changes that convert proto-oncogenes to oncogenes fall into three main categories: movement of DNA within the genome, amplification of a proto-oncogene, and point mutations in a control element or in the proto-oncogene itself **(Figure 18.23)**.

▲ **Figure 18.23 Genetic changes that can turn proto-oncogenes into oncogenes.**

Cancer cells are frequently found to contain chromosomes that have broken and rejoined incorrectly, translocating fragments from one chromosome to another (see Figure 15.14). Having learned how gene expression is regulated, you can now see the possible consequences of such translocations. If a translocated proto-oncogene ends up near an especially active promoter (or other control element), its transcription may increase, making it an oncogene. The second main type of genetic change, amplification, increases the number of copies of the proto-oncogene in the cell through repeated gene duplication (discussed in Chapter 21). The third possibility is a point mutation either (1) in the promoter or an enhancer that controls a proto-oncogene, causing an increase in its expression, or (2) in the coding sequence of the proto-oncogene, changing the gene's product to a protein that is more active or more resistant to degradation than the normal protein. These mechanisms can lead to abnormal stimulation of the cell cycle and put the cell on the path to becoming a cancer cell.

Tumor-Suppressor Genes

In addition to genes whose products normally promote cell division, cells contain genes whose normal products *inhibit* cell division. Such genes are called **tumor-suppressor genes** because the proteins they encode help prevent uncontrolled cell growth. Any mutation that decreases the normal activity of a tumor-suppressor protein may contribute to the onset of cancer, in effect stimulating growth through the absence of suppression.

The protein products of tumor-suppressor genes have various functions. Some tumor-suppressor proteins repair damaged DNA, a function that prevents the cell from accumulating cancer-causing mutations. Other tumor-suppressor proteins control the adhesion of cells to each other or to the extracellular matrix; proper cell anchorage is crucial in normal tissues—and is often absent in cancers. Still other tumor-suppressor proteins are components of cell-signaling pathways that inhibit the cell cycle.

Interference with Normal Cell-Signaling Pathways

The proteins encoded by many proto-oncogenes and tumor-suppressor genes are components of cell-signaling pathways. Let's take a closer look at how such proteins function in normal cells and what goes wrong with their function in cancer cells. We will focus on the products of two key genes, the *ras* proto-oncogene and the *p53* tumor-suppressor gene. Mutations in *ras* occur in about 30% of human cancers, and mutations in *p53* in more than 50%.

The Ras protein, encoded by the **ras gene** (named for <u>ra</u>t <u>s</u>arcoma, a connective tissue cancer), is a G protein that relays a signal from a growth factor receptor on the plasma membrane to a cascade of protein kinases (see Figure 11.8). The cellular response at the end of the pathway is the synthesis of a protein that stimulates the cell cycle **(Figure 18.24a)**. Normally, such a pathway will not operate unless triggered by the appropriate growth factor. But certain mutations in the *ras* gene can lead to production of a hyperactive Ras protein that triggers the kinase cascade even in the absence of growth factor, resulting in increased cell division **(Figure 18.24b)**. In fact, hyperactive versions or excess amounts of any of the pathway's components can have the same outcome: excessive cell division.

Figure 18.25a shows a pathway in which an intracellular signal leads to the synthesis of a protein that suppresses the cell cycle. In this case, the signal is damage to the cell's DNA, perhaps as the result of exposure to ultraviolet light. Operation of this signaling pathway blocks the cell cycle until the damage has been repaired. Otherwise, the damage might contribute to tumor formation by causing mutations or chromosomal abnormalities. Thus, the genes for the components of the pathway act as tumor-suppressor genes. The **p53 gene**, named for the 53,000-dalton molecular weight of its protein product, is a tumor-suppressor gene. The protein it encodes is a specific transcription factor that promotes the synthesis of cell cycle–inhibiting proteins. That is why a mutation that knocks out the *p53* gene, like a mutation that leads to a hyperactive Ras protein, can lead to excessive cell growth and cancer **(Figure 18.25b)**.

The *p53* gene has been called the "guardian angel of the genome." Once the gene is activated—for example, by DNA damage—the p53 protein functions as an activator for several other genes. Often it activates a gene called *p21*, whose product halts the cell cycle by binding to cyclin-dependent kinases, allowing time for the cell to repair the DNA. Researchers recently showed that p53 also activates expression of a group of miRNAs, which in turn inhibit the cell cycle. In addition, the p53 protein can turn on genes directly involved in DNA repair. Finally, when DNA damage is irreparable, p53 activates "suicide" genes, whose protein products bring about programmed cell death (apoptosis; see Figure 11.20). Thus, p53 acts in several ways to prevent a cell from passing on mutations due to DNA damage. If mutations do accumulate and the cell survives through many divisions—as is more likely if the *p53* tumor-suppressor gene is defective or missing—cancer may ensue. The many functions of p53 suggest a complex picture of regulation in normal cells, one that we do not yet fully understand.

For the present, the diagrams in Figure 18.24 and Figure 18.25 are an accurate view of how mutations can contribute to cancer, but we still don't know exactly how a particular cell becomes a cancer cell. As we discover previously unknown aspects of gene regulation, it is informative

► **Figure 18.24 Normal and mutant cell cycle–stimulating pathway.**
(a) The normal pathway is triggered by ❶ a growth factor that binds to ❷ its receptor in the plasma membrane. The signal is relayed to ❸ a G protein called Ras. Like all G proteins, Ras is active when GTP is bound to it. Ras passes the signal to ❹ a series of protein kinases. The last kinase activates ❺ a transcription factor (activator) that turns on one or more genes for ❻ a protein that stimulates the cell cycle. **(b)** If a mutation makes Ras or any other pathway component abnormally active, excessive cell division and cancer may result.

(a) Normal cell cycle–stimulating pathway.

(b) Mutant cell cycle–stimulating pathway.

► **Figure 18.25 Normal and mutant cell cycle–inhibiting pathway. (a)** In the normal pathway, ❶ DNA damage is an intracellular signal that is passed via ❷ protein kinases, leading to activation of ❸ p53. Activated p53 promotes ❹ transcription of the gene for ❺ a protein that inhibits the cell cycle. The resulting suppression of cell division ensures that the damaged DNA is not replicated. If the DNA damage is irreparable, then the p53 signal leads to programmed cell death (apoptosis). **(b)** Mutations causing deficiencies in any pathway component can contribute to the development of cancer.

? *Explain whether a cancer-causing mutation in a tumor-suppressor gene, such as p53, is more likely to be a recessive or a dominant mutation.*

(a) Normal cell cycle–inhibiting pathway

(b) Mutant cell cycle–inhibiting pathway

to study their role in the onset of cancer. Such studies have shown, for instance, that DNA methylation and histone modification patterns differ in normal and cancer cells and that miRNAs probably participate in cancer development. While we've learned a lot about cancer by studying cell-signaling pathways, there is still a lot left to learn.

The Multistep Model of Cancer Development

More than one somatic mutation is generally needed to produce all the changes characteristic of a full-fledged cancer cell. This may help explain why the incidence of cancer increases greatly with age. If cancer results from an accumulation of mutations and if mutations occur throughout life, then the longer we live, the more likely we are to develop cancer.

The model of a multistep path to cancer is well supported by studies of one of the best-understood types of human cancer: colorectal cancer, which affects the colon and/or rectum. About 140,000 new cases of colorectal cancer are diagnosed each year in the United States, and the disease causes 50,000 deaths per year. Like most cancers, colorectal cancer develops gradually (**Figure 18.26**). The first sign is often a polyp, a small, benign growth in the colon lining. The cells of the polyp look normal, although they divide unusually frequently. The tumor grows and may eventually become malignant, invading other tissues. The development of a malignant tumor is paralleled by a gradual accumulation of mutations that convert proto-oncogenes to oncogenes and knock out tumor-suppressor genes. A *ras* oncogene and a mutated *p53* tumor-suppressor gene are often involved.

About half a dozen changes must occur at the DNA level for a cell to become fully cancerous. These changes usually include the appearance of at least one active oncogene and the mutation or loss of several tumor-suppressor genes. Furthermore, since mutant tumor-suppressor alleles are usually recessive, in most cases mutations must knock out *both* alleles in a cell's genome to block tumor suppression. (Most oncogenes, on the other hand, behave as dominant alleles.) The order in which these changes must occur is still under investigation, as is the relative importance of different mutations.

Since we understand the progression of this type of cancer, routine screenings are recommended to identify and remove any suspicious polyps. The colorectal cancer mortality rate has been declining for the past 20 years, due in part to increased screening and in part to improved treatments. Treatments for other cancers have improved as well. Dramatic technical advances in the sequencing of DNA and mRNA have allowed medical researchers to compare the genes expressed by different types of tumors and by the same type in different individuals. These comparisons have led to personalized cancer treatments based on the molecular characteristics of an individual's tumor.

Breast cancer is the second most common form of cancer in the United States, and the first among women. Each year, this cancer strikes over 230,000 women (and some men) in the United States and kills 40,000 (450,000 worldwide). A major problem with understanding breast cancer is its heterogeneity: Tumors differ in significant ways. Identifying differences between types of breast cancer is expected to improve treatment and decrease the mortality rate. In November of 2012, The Cancer Genome Atlas Network, sponsored by the National Institutes of Health, published the results of a multi-team effort that used a genomics approach to profile subtypes of breast cancer based on their molecular signatures. Four major types of breast cancer were identified (**Figure 18.27**).

▼ **Figure 18.26 A multistep model for the development of colorectal cancer.** This type of cancer is one of the best understood. Changes in a tumor parallel a series of genetic changes, including mutations affecting several tumor-suppressor genes (such as *p53*) and the *ras* proto-oncogene. Mutations of tumor-suppressor genes often entail loss (deletion) of the gene. *APC* stands for "adenomatous polyposis coli," and *SMAD4* is a gene involved in signaling that results in apoptosis. Other mutation sequences can also lead to colorectal cancer.

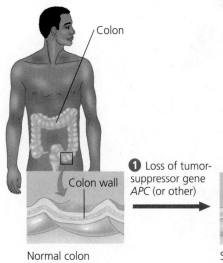

Colon

Colon wall

Normal colon epithelial cells

1 Loss of tumor-suppressor gene *APC* (or other)

Small benign growth (polyp)

2 Activation of *ras* oncogene

3 Loss of tumor-suppressor gene *SMAD4*

Larger benign growth (adenoma)

4 Loss of tumor-suppressor gene *p53*

5 Additional mutations

Malignant tumor (carcinoma)

© Pearson Education, Inc.

Genomics, Cell Signaling, and Cancer

Modern medicine that melds genome-wide molecular studies with cell-signaling research is transforming the treatment of many diseases, such as breast cancer. Using micro-array analysis (*see Figure 20.13*) and other techniques, researchers measured the relative levels of mRNA transcripts for every gene in many different breast cancer tumor samples. They identified four major subtypes of breast cancer, shown below, that differ in their expression of three signal receptors involved in regulating cell growth and division (*see Figures 11.8 and 11.9*). Normal levels of these signal receptors (indicated by +) are represented in a normal breast cell at the right. The absence (−) or excess expression (++ or +++) of these receptors can cause aberrant cell signaling, leading in some cases to inappropriate cell division, which may contribute to cancer (*see Figure 18.24*). Breast cancer treatments are becoming more effective because they can be tailored to the specific cancer subtype.

Normal Breast Cells in a Milk Duct

- ERα⁺
- PR⁺
- HER2⁺

Duct interior

Estrogen receptor alpha (ERα)

Progesterone receptor (PR)

HER2 (a receptor tyrosine kinase)

Support cell

Extracellular matrix

Breast Cancer Subtypes

Luminal A	Luminal B	HER2	Basal-like

Luminal A
- ERα⁺⁺⁺
- PR⁺⁺
- HER2⁻
- 40% of breast cancers
- Best prognosis

Luminal B
- ERα⁺⁺
- PR⁺⁺
- HER2⁻ (shown); some HER2⁺⁺
- 15–20% of breast cancers
- Poorer prognosis than luminal A subtype

HER2
- ERα⁻
- PR⁻
- HER2⁺⁺
- 10–15% of breast cancers
- Poorer prognosis than luminal A subtype

Basal-like
- ERα⁻
- PR⁻
- HER2⁻
- 15–20% of breast cancers
- More aggressive; poorer prognosis than other subtypes

Both luminal subtypes overexpress ERα (luminal A more than luminal B) and PR, and usually lack expression of HER2. Both can be treated with drugs that target ERα and inactivate it, the most well-known drug being Tamoxifen. These subtypes can also be treated with drugs that inhibit estrogen synthesis.

MAKE CONNECTIONS *When researchers compared gene expression in normal breast cells and cells from breast cancers, they found that the genes showing the most significant differences in expression encoded signal receptors, as shown here. Given what you learned in Chapters 11, 12, and this chapter, explain why this result is not surprising.*

The HER2 subtype overexpresses HER2. Because it does not express either ERα or PR at normal levels, the cells are unresponsive to therapies aimed against those two receptors. However, patients with the HER2 subtype can be treated with Herceptin, an antibody protein that inactivates the tyrosine kinase activity of HER2 (*see Concept 12.3*).

The basal-like subtype is "triple negative"—it does not express ERα, PR, or HER2. It often has a mutation in the tumor suppressor gene BRCA1 (*see Concept 18.5*). Treatments that target ER, PR, or HER2 are not effective, but new treatments are being developed. Currently, patients are treated with cytotoxic chemotherapy, which selectively kills fast-growing cells.

Inherited Predisposition and Environmental Factors Contributing to Cancer

The fact that multiple genetic changes are required to produce a cancer cell helps explain the observation that cancers can run in families. An individual inheriting an oncogene or a mutant allele of a tumor-suppressor gene is one step closer to accumulating the necessary mutations for cancer to develop than is an individual without any such mutations.

Geneticists are devoting significant effort to identifying inherited cancer alleles so that predisposition to certain cancers can be detected early in life. About 15% of colorectal cancers, for example, involve inherited mutations. Many of these affect the tumor-suppressor gene called *adenomatous polyposis coli*, or *APC* (see Figure 18.26). This gene has multiple functions in the cell, including regulation of cell migration and adhesion. Even in patients with no family history of the disease, the *APC* gene is mutated in 60% of colorectal cancers. In these individuals, new mutations must occur in both *APC* alleles before the gene's function is lost. Since only 15% of colorectal cancers are associated with known inherited mutations, researchers continue in their efforts to identify "markers" that could predict the risk of developing this type of cancer.

Given the prevalence and significance of breast cancer, it is not surprising that it was one of the first cancers for which the role of inheritance was investigated. It turns out that for 5–10% of patients with breast cancer, there is evidence of a strong inherited predisposition. Geneticist Mary-Claire King began working on this problem in the mid-1970s. After 16 years of research, she convincingly demonstrated that mutations in one gene—*BRCA1*—were associated with increased susceptibility to breast cancer, a finding that flew in the face of medical opinion at the time. (*BRCA* stands for <u>br</u>east <u>ca</u>ncer.) Mutations in that gene or a gene called *BRCA2* are found in at least half of inherited breast cancers, and tests using DNA sequencing can detect these mutations. A woman who inherits one mutant *BRCA1* allele has a 60% probability of developing breast cancer before the age of 50, compared with only a 2% probability for an individual homozygous for the normal allele.

BRCA1 and *BRCA2* are considered tumor-suppressor genes because their wild-type alleles protect against breast cancer and their mutant alleles are recessive. (Note that mutations in *BRCA1* are commonly found in the genomes of cells from basal-like breast cancers; see Figure 18.27.) The BRCA1 and BRCA2 proteins both appear to function in the cell's DNA damage repair pathway. More is known about BRCA2, which, in association with another protein, helps repair breaks that occur in both strands of DNA; this repair function is crucial for maintaining undamaged DNA in a cell's nucleus.

Because DNA breakage can contribute to cancer, it makes sense that the risk of cancer can be lowered by minimizing exposure to DNA-damaging agents, such as the ultraviolet radiation in sunlight and chemicals found in cigarette smoke. Novel genomics-based analyses of specific cancers, such as the approach described in Figure 18.27, are contributing to both early diagnosis and development of treatments that interfere with expression of key genes in tumors. Ultimately, such approaches are expected to lower the death rate from cancer.

The Role of Viruses in Cancer

The study of genes associated with cancer, inherited or not, increases our basic understanding of how disruption of normal gene regulation can result in this disease. In addition to the mutations and other genetic alterations described in this section, a number of *tumor viruses* can cause cancer in various animals, including humans. In fact, one of the earliest breakthroughs in understanding cancer came in 1911, when Peyton Rous, an American pathologist, discovered a virus that causes cancer in chickens. The Epstein-Barr virus, which causes infectious mononucleosis, has been linked to several types of cancer in humans, notably Burkitt's lymphoma. Papillomaviruses are associated with cancer of the cervix, and a virus called HTLV-1 causes a type of adult leukemia. Worldwide, viruses seem to play a role in about 15% of the cases of human cancer.

Viruses may at first seem very different from mutations as a cause of cancer. However, we now know that viruses can interfere with gene regulation in several ways if they integrate their genetic material into the DNA of a cell. Viral integration may donate an oncogene to the cell, disrupt a tumor-suppressor gene, or convert a proto-oncogene to an oncogene. In addition, some viruses produce proteins that inactivate p53 and other tumor-suppressor proteins, making the cell more prone to becoming cancerous. Viruses are powerful biological agents, and you'll learn more about their function in Chapter 19.

CONCEPT CHECK 18.5

1. **MAKE CONNECTIONS** The p53 protein can activate genes involved in apoptosis, or programmed cell death. Discuss how mutations in genes coding for proteins that function in apoptosis could contribute to cancer. (Review Concept 11.5.)

2. Under what circumstances is cancer considered to have a hereditary component?

3. **WHAT IF?** Cancer-promoting mutations are likely to have different effects on the activity of proteins encoded by proto-oncogenes than they do on proteins encoded by tumor-suppressor genes. Explain.

For suggested answers, see Appendix A.

SUMMARY OF KEY CONCEPTS

CONCEPT 18.1

Bacteria often respond to environmental change by regulating transcription (pp. 361–365)

- Cells control metabolism by regulating enzyme activity or the expression of genes coding for enzymes. In bacteria, genes are often clustered into operons, with one promoter serving several adjacent genes. An operator site on the DNA switches the operon on or off, resulting in coordinate regulation of the genes.

- Both repressible and inducible operons are examples of negative gene regulation. In either type of operon, binding of a specific **repressor** protein to the operator shuts off transcription. (The repressor is encoded by a separate **regulatory gene**.) In a repressible operon, the repressor is active when bound to a **corepressor**, usually the end product of an anabolic pathway.

Repressible operon:

In an inducible operon, binding of an **inducer** to an innately active repressor inactivates the repressor and turns on transcription. Inducible enzymes usually function in catabolic pathways.

Inducible operon:

- Some operons are also subject to positive gene regulation via a stimulatory **activator** protein, such as catabolite activator protein (CAP), which, when activated by **cyclic AMP**, binds to a site within the promoter and stimulates transcription.

? *Compare and contrast the roles of a corepressor and an inducer in negative regulation of an operon.*

CONCEPT 18.2

Eukaryotic gene expression is regulated at many stages (pp. 365–373)

? *Describe what must happen for a cell-type-specific gene to be transcribed in a cell of that type.*

CONCEPT 18.3

Noncoding RNAs play multiple roles in controlling gene expression (pp. 374–376)

? *Why are miRNAs called noncoding RNAs? Explain how they participate in gene regulation.*

CONCEPT 18.4

A program of differential gene expression leads to the different cell types in a multicellular organism (pp. 376–383)

- Embryonic cells become committed to a certain fate (**determination**), and undergo **differentiation**, becoming specialized in structure and function for their determined fate. Cells have different structures and functions not because they contain different genomes but because they express different genes. **Morphogenesis** encompasses the processes that give shape to the organism and its various structures.
- **Cytoplasmic determinants** in the unfertilized egg regulate the expression of genes in the zygote and embryo that affect the developmental fate of embryonic cells. In the process called **induction**, signaling molecules from embryonic cells cause transcriptional changes in nearby target cells.
- Differentiation is heralded by the appearance of tissue-specific proteins, which enable differentiated cells to carry out their specialized roles.
- In animals, **pattern formation**, the development of a spatial organization of tissues and organs, begins in the early embryo. **Positional information**, the molecular cues that control pattern formation, tells a cell its location relative to the body's axes and to other cells. In *Drosophila*, gradients of **morphogens** encoded by **maternal effect genes** determine the body axes. For example, the gradient of **Bicoid** protein determines the anterior-posterior axis.

? *Describe the two main processes that cause embryonic cells to head down different pathways to their final fates.*

CONCEPT 18.5

Cancer results from genetic changes that affect cell cycle control (pp. 383–388)

- The products of **proto-oncogenes** and **tumor-suppressor genes** control cell division. A DNA change that makes a proto-oncogene excessively active converts it to an **oncogene**, which may promote excessive cell division and cancer. A tumor-suppressor gene encodes a protein that inhibits abnormal cell division. A mutation in a tumor-suppressor gene that reduces the activity of its protein product may also lead to excessive cell division and possibly to cancer.
- Many proto-oncogenes and tumor-suppressor genes encode components of growth-stimulating and growth-inhibiting signaling pathways, respectively, and mutations in these genes can interfere with normal cell-signaling pathways. A hyperactive version of a protein in a stimulatory pathway, such as **Ras** (a G protein), functions as an oncogene protein. A defective version of a protein in an inhibitory pathway, such as **p53** (a transcription activator), fails to function as a tumor suppressor.

EFFECTS OF MUTATIONS

Protein overexpressed → Increased cell division ← Protein absent

Cell cycle overstimulated | Increased cell division | Cell cycle not inhibited

- In the multistep model of cancer development, normal cells are converted to cancer cells by the accumulation of mutations affecting proto-oncogenes and tumor-suppressor genes. Technical advances in DNA and mRNA sequencing are enabling cancer treatments that are more individually based.

- Genomics-based studies have resulted in researchers proposing four subtypes of breast cancer, based on expression of genes by tumor cells.
- Individuals who inherit a mutant allele of a proto-oncogene or tumor-suppressor gene have a predisposition to develop a particular cancer. Certain viruses promote cancer by integration of viral DNA into a cell's genome.

? *Compare the usual functions of proteins encoded by proto-oncogenes with those of proteins encoded by tumor-suppressor genes.*

TEST YOUR UNDERSTANDING

LEVEL 1: KNOWLEDGE/COMPREHENSION

1. If a particular operon encodes enzymes for making an essential amino acid and is regulated like the *trp* operon, then
   a. the amino acid inactivates the repressor.
   b. the repressor is active in the absence of the amino acid.
   c. the amino acid acts as a corepressor.
   d. the amino acid turns on transcription of the operon.

2. Muscle cells differ from nerve cells mainly because they
   a. express different genes.
   b. contain different genes.
   c. use different genetic codes.
   d. have unique ribosomes.

3. The functioning of enhancers is an example of
   a. a eukaryotic equivalent of prokaryotic promoter functioning.
   b. transcriptional control of gene expression.
   c. the stimulation of translation by initiation factors.
   d. post-translational control that activates certain proteins.

4. Cell differentiation always involves
   a. transcription of the *myoD* gene.
   b. the movement of cells.
   c. the production of tissue-specific proteins.
   d. the selective loss of certain genes from the genome.

5. Which of the following is an example of post-transcriptional control of gene expression?
   a. the addition of methyl groups to cytosine bases of DNA
   b. the binding of transcription factors to a promoter
   c. the removal of introns and alternative splicing of exons
   d. gene amplification contributing to cancer

LEVEL 2: APPLICATION/ANALYSIS

6. What would occur if the repressor of an inducible operon were mutated so it could not bind the operator?
   a. irreversible binding of the repressor to the promoter
   b. reduced transcription of the operon's genes
   c. buildup of a substrate for the pathway controlled by the operon
   d. continuous transcription of the operon's genes

7. Absence of *bicoid* mRNA from a *Drosophila* egg leads to the absence of anterior larval body parts and mirror-image duplication of posterior parts. This is evidence that the product of the *bicoid* gene
   a. normally leads to formation of head structures.
   b. normally leads to formation of tail structures.
   c. is transcribed in the early embryo.
   d. is a protein present in all head structures.

8. Which of the following statements about the DNA in one of your brain cells is true?
   a. Most of the DNA codes for protein.
   b. The majority of genes are likely to be transcribed.
   c. It is the same as the DNA in one of your liver cells.
   d. Each gene lies immediately adjacent to an enhancer.

9. Within a cell, the amount of protein made using a given mRNA molecule depends partly on
   a. the degree of DNA methylation.
   b. the rate at which the mRNA is degraded.
   c. the number of introns present in the mRNA.
   d. the types of ribosomes present in the cytoplasm.

10. Proto-oncogenes can change into oncogenes that cause cancer. Which of the following best explains the presence of these potential time bombs in eukaryotic cells?
    a. Proto-oncogenes first arose from viral infections.
    b. Proto-oncogenes are mutant versions of normal genes.
    c. Proto-oncogenes are genetic "junk."
    d. Proto-oncogenes normally help regulate cell division.

LEVEL 3: SYNTHESIS/EVALUATION

11. **DRAW IT** The diagram below shows five genes, including their enhancers, from the genome of a certain species. Imagine that orange, blue, green, black, red, and purple activator proteins exist that can bind to the appropriately color-coded control elements in the enhancers of these genes.

(a) Draw an X above enhancer elements (of all the genes) that would have activators bound in a cell in which only gene 5 is transcribed. Which colored activators would be present?

(b) Draw a dot above all enhancer elements that would have activators bound in a cell in which the green, blue, and orange activators are present. Which gene(s) would be transcribed?

(c) Imagine that genes 1, 2, and 4 code for nerve-specific proteins, and genes 3 and 5 are skin specific. Which activators would have to be present in each cell type to ensure transcription of the appropriate genes?

12. **EVOLUTION CONNECTION**
DNA sequences can act as "tape measures of evolution" (see Chapter 5). Scientists analyzing the human genome sequence were surprised to find that some of the regions of the human genome that are most highly conserved (similar to comparable regions in other species) don't code for proteins. Propose a possible explanation for this observation.

13. **SCIENTIFIC INQUIRY**
Prostate cells usually require testosterone and other androgens to survive. But some prostate cancer cells thrive despite treatments that eliminate androgens. One hypothesis is that estrogen, often considered a female hormone, may be activating genes normally controlled by an androgen in these cancer cells. Describe one or more experiments to test this hypothesis. (See Figure 11.9 to review the action of these steroid hormones.)

14. **SCIENCE, TECHNOLOGY, AND SOCIETY**
Trace amounts of dioxin were present in Agent Orange, a defoliant sprayed on vegetation during the Vietnam War. Animal tests suggest that dioxin can cause birth defects, cancer, liver and thymus damage, and immune system suppression, sometimes leading to death. But the animal tests are equivocal; a hamster is not affected by a dose that can kill a guinea pig. Dioxin acts like a steroid hormone, entering a cell and binding to a cytoplasmic receptor that then binds the cell's DNA. How might this mechanism help explain the variety of dioxin's effects on different body systems and in different animals? How might you determine whether a type of illness is related to dioxin exposure? How might you determine whether a particular individual became ill as a result of exposure to dioxin? Which would be more difficult to demonstrate? Why?

15. **WRITE ABOUT A THEME: INTERACTIONS**
In a short essay (100–150 words), discuss how the processes shown in Figure 18.2 are examples of feedback mechanisms regulating biological systems in bacterial cells.

16. **SYNTHESIZE YOUR KNOWLEDGE**

The flashlight fish has an organ under its eye that emits light, which serves to startle predators and attract prey, and allows the fish to communicate with other fish. Some species can rotate the organ inside and then out, so the light appears to flash on and off. The light is not actually emitted by the fish itself, however, but by bacteria that live in the organ in a mutualistic relationship with the fish. (While providing light for the fish, the bacteria receive nutrients from the fish and in fact are unable to survive anywhere else.) The bacteria must multiply until they reach a certain density in the organ (a "quorum"; see Concept 11.1), at which point they all begin emitting light at the same time. There is a group of six or so genes, called *lux* genes, whose gene products are necessary for light formation. Given that these bacterial genes are regulated together, propose a hypothesis for how the genes are organized and regulated.

For selected answers, see Appendix A.

MasteringBiology®

Students Go to **MasteringBiology** for assignments, the eText, and the Study Area with practice tests, animations, and activities.

Instructors Go to **MasteringBiology** for automatically graded tutorials and questions that you can assign to your students, plus Instructor Resources.

19

Viruses

KEY CONCEPTS

19.1 A virus consists of a nucleic acid surrounded by a protein coat

19.2 Viruses replicate only in host cells

19.3 Viruses, viroids, and prions are formidable pathogens in animals and plants

▲ **Figure 19.1 Are the viruses (red) budding from this cell alive?**

A Borrowed Life

The image in **Figure 19.1** shows a remarkable event: On the left is a human immune cell under siege, releasing scores more of its invaders, which will go on to infect other cells. The attackers (red) are human immunodeficiency viruses (HIV). (The same scenario is shown in the micrograph at the lower left.) By injecting its genetic information into a cell, a single virus hijacks a cell, recruiting cellular machinery to manufacture many new viruses and promote further infection. Left untreated, HIV causes acquired immunodeficiency syndrome (AIDS) by destroying vital immune system cells.

Compared to eukaryotic and even prokaryotic cells, viruses are much smaller and simpler in structure. Lacking the structures and metabolic machinery found in a cell, a **virus** is an infectious particle consisting of little more than genes packaged in a protein coat.

Are viruses living or nonliving? Because viruses are capable of causing many diseases, researchers in the late 1800s saw a parallel with bacteria and proposed that viruses were the simplest of living forms. However, viruses cannot reproduce or carry out metabolism outside of a host cell. Most biologists studying viruses today would likely agree that they are not alive but exist in a shady area between life-forms and chemicals. The simple phrase used recently by two researchers describes them aptly enough: Viruses lead "a kind of borrowed life."

To a large extent, molecular biology was born in the laboratories of biologists studying viruses that infect bacteria. Experiments with these viruses provided evidence that genes are made of nucleic acids, and they were critical in working out the molecular mechanisms of the fundamental processes of DNA replication, transcription, and translation.

Beyond their value as experimental systems, viruses have unique genetic mechanisms that are interesting in their own right and that also help us understand how viruses cause disease. In addition, the study of viruses has led to the development of techniques that enable scientists to manipulate genes and transfer them from one organism to another. These techniques play an important role in basic research, biotechnology, and medical applications. For instance, viruses are used as agents of gene transfer in gene therapy (see Concept 20.4).

In this chapter, we will explore the biology of viruses, beginning with their structure and then describing how they replicate. Next, we will discuss the role of viruses as disease-causing agents, or pathogens, and conclude by considering some even simpler infectious agents called viroids and prions.

CONCEPT 19.1

A virus consists of a nucleic acid surrounded by a protein coat

Scientists were able to detect viruses indirectly long before they were actually able to see them. The story of how viruses were discovered begins near the end of the 19th century.

The Discovery of Viruses: *Scientific Inquiry*

Tobacco mosaic disease stunts the growth of tobacco plants and gives their leaves a mottled, or mosaic, coloration. In 1883, Adolf Mayer, a German scientist, discovered that he could transmit the disease from plant to plant by rubbing sap extracted from diseased leaves onto healthy plants. After an unsuccessful search for an infectious microbe in the sap, Mayer suggested that the disease was caused by unusually small bacteria that were invisible under a microscope. This hypothesis was tested a decade later by Dimitri Ivanowsky, a Russian biologist who passed sap from infected tobacco leaves through a filter designed to remove bacteria. After filtration, the sap still produced mosaic disease.

But Ivanowsky clung to the hypothesis that bacteria caused tobacco mosaic disease. Perhaps, he reasoned, the bacteria were small enough to pass through the filter or made a toxin that could do so. The second possibility was ruled out when the Dutch botanist Martinus Beijerinck carried out a classic series of experiments that showed that the infectious agent in the filtered sap could replicate **(Figure 19.2)**.

In fact, the pathogen replicated only within the host it infected. In further experiments, Beijerinck showed that unlike

▼ **Figure 19.2** | **Inquiry**

What causes tobacco mosaic disease?

Experiment In the late 1800s, Martinus Beijerinck, of the Technical School in Delft, the Netherlands, investigated the properties of the agent that causes tobacco mosaic disease (then called spot disease).

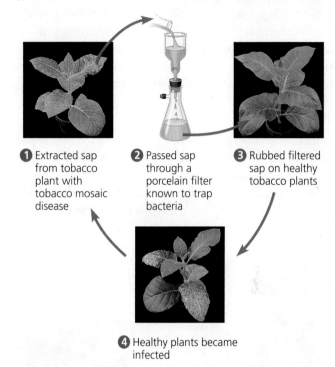

❶ Extracted sap from tobacco plant with tobacco mosaic disease

❷ Passed sap through a porcelain filter known to trap bacteria

❸ Rubbed filtered sap on healthy tobacco plants

❹ Healthy plants became infected

Results When the filtered sap was rubbed on healthy plants, they became infected. Their sap, extracted and filtered, could then act as a source of infection for another group of plants. Each successive group of plants developed the disease to the same extent as earlier groups.

Conclusion The infectious agent was apparently not a bacterium because it could pass through a bacterium-trapping filter. The pathogen must have been replicating in the plants because its ability to cause disease was undiluted after several transfers from plant to plant.

Source: M. J. Beijerinck, Concerning a *contagium vivum fluidum* as cause of the spot disease of tobacco leaves, *Verhandelingen der Koninkyke akademie Wettenschappen te Amsterdam* 65:3–21 (1898). Translation published in English as Phytopathological Classics Number 7 (1942), American Phytopathological Society Press, St. Paul, MN.

WHAT IF? *If Beijerinck had observed that the infection of each group was weaker than that of the previous group and that ultimately the sap could no longer cause disease, what might he have concluded?*

bacteria used in the lab at that time, the mysterious agent of mosaic disease could not be cultivated on nutrient media in test tubes or petri dishes. Beijerinck imagined a replicating particle much smaller and simpler than a bacterium, and he is generally credited with being the first scientist to voice the concept of a virus. His suspicions were confirmed in 1935 when the American scientist Wendell Stanley crystallized the infectious particle, now known as tobacco mosaic virus (TMV). Subsequently, TMV and many other viruses were actually seen with the help of the electron microscope.

Structure of Viruses

The tiniest viruses are only 20 nm in diameter—smaller than a ribosome. Millions could easily fit on a pinhead. Even the largest known virus, which has a diameter of several hundred nanometers, is barely visible under the light microscope. Stanley's discovery that some viruses could be crystallized was exciting and puzzling news. Not even the simplest of cells can aggregate into regular crystals. But if viruses are not cells, then what are they? Examining the structure of a virus more closely reveals that it is an infectious particle consisting of nucleic acid enclosed in a protein coat and, for some viruses, surrounded by a membranous envelope.

Viral Genomes

We usually think of genes as being made of double-stranded DNA, but many viruses defy this convention. Their genomes may consist of double-stranded DNA, single-stranded DNA, double-stranded RNA, or single-stranded RNA, depending on the type of virus. A virus is called a DNA virus or an RNA virus, based on the kind of nucleic acid that makes up its genome. In either case, the genome is usually organized as a single linear or circular molecule of nucleic acid, although the genomes of some viruses consist of multiple molecules of nucleic acid. The smallest viruses known have only three genes in their genome, while the largest have several hundred to a thousand. For comparison, bacterial genomes contain about 200 to a few thousand genes.

Capsids and Envelopes

The protein shell enclosing the viral genome is called a **capsid**. Depending on the type of virus, the capsid may be rod-shaped, polyhedral, or more complex in shape. Capsids are built from a large number of protein subunits called *capsomeres*, but the number of different *kinds* of proteins in a capsid is usually small. Tobacco mosaic virus has a rigid, rod-shaped capsid made from over a thousand molecules of a single type of protein arranged in a helix; rod-shaped viruses are commonly called *helical viruses* for this reason **(Figure 19.3a)**. Adenoviruses, which infect the respiratory

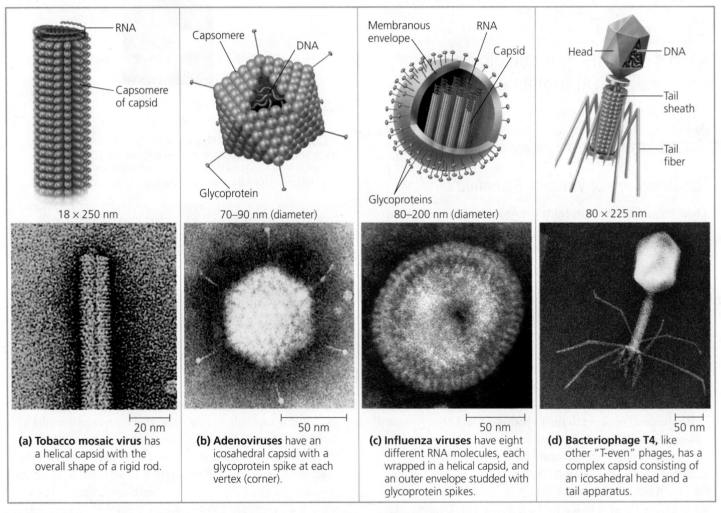

18 × 250 nm   70–90 nm (diameter)   80–200 nm (diameter)   80 × 225 nm

20 nm   50 nm   50 nm   50 nm

(a) Tobacco mosaic virus has a helical capsid with the overall shape of a rigid rod.

(b) Adenoviruses have an icosahedral capsid with a glycoprotein spike at each vertex (corner).

(c) Influenza viruses have eight different RNA molecules, each wrapped in a helical capsid, and an outer envelope studded with glycoprotein spikes.

(d) Bacteriophage T4, like other "T-even" phages, has a complex capsid consisting of an icosahedral head and a tail apparatus.

▲ **Figure 19.3 Viral structure.** Viruses are made up of nucleic acid (DNA or RNA) enclosed in a protein coat (the capsid) and sometimes further wrapped in a membranous envelope. The individual protein subunits making up the capsid are called capsomeres. Although diverse in size and shape, viruses have many common structural features. (All micrographs are colorized TEMs.)

tracts of animals, have 252 identical protein molecules arranged in a polyhedral capsid with 20 triangular facets—an icosahedron; thus, these and other similarly shaped viruses are referred to as *icosahedral viruses* (**Figure 19.3b**).

Some viruses have accessory structures that help them infect their hosts. For instance, a membranous envelope surrounds the capsids of influenza viruses and many other viruses found in animals (**Figure 19.3c**). These **viral envelopes**, which are derived from the membranes of the host cell, contain host cell phospholipids and membrane proteins. They also contain proteins and glycoproteins of viral origin. (Glycoproteins are proteins with carbohydrates covalently attached.) Some viruses carry a few viral enzyme molecules within their capsids.

Many of the most complex capsids are found among the viruses that infect bacteria, called **bacteriophages**, or simply **phages**. The first phages studied included seven that infect *Escherichia coli*. These seven phages were named type 1 (T1), type 2 (T2), and so forth, in the order of their discovery. The three T-even phages (T2, T4, and T6) turned out to be very similar in structure. Their capsids have elongated icosahedral heads enclosing their DNA. Attached to the head is a protein tail piece with fibers by which the phages attach to a bacterial cell (**Figure 19.3d**). In the next section, we'll examine how these few viral parts function together with cellular components to produce large numbers of viral progeny.

CONCEPT CHECK 19.1

1. Compare the structures of tobacco mosaic virus (TMV) and influenza virus (see Figure 19.3).

2. MAKE CONNECTIONS Bacteriophages were used to provide evidence that DNA carries genetic information (see Figure 16.4). Briefly describe the experiment carried out by Hershey and Chase, including in your description why the researchers chose to use phages.

For suggested answers, see Appendix A.

CONCEPT 19.2

Viruses replicate only in host cells

Viruses lack metabolic enzymes and equipment for making proteins, such as ribosomes. They are obligate intracellular parasites; in other words, they can replicate only within a host cell. It is fair to say that viruses in isolation are merely packaged sets of genes in transit from one host cell to another.

Each particular virus can infect cells of only a limited number of host species, called the **host range** of the virus. This host specificity results from the evolution of recognition systems by the virus. Viruses usually identify host cells by a "lock-and-key" fit between viral surface proteins and specific receptor molecules on the outside of cells. (According to one model, such receptor molecules originally carried out functions that benefited the host cell but were co-opted later by

viruses as portals of entry.) Some viruses have broad host ranges. For example, West Nile virus and equine encephalitis virus are distinctly different viruses that can each infect mosquitoes, birds, horses, and humans. Other viruses have host ranges so narrow that they infect only a single species. Measles virus, for instance, can infect only humans. Furthermore, viral infection of multicellular eukaryotes is usually limited to particular tissues. Human cold viruses infect only the cells lining the upper respiratory tract, and the AIDS virus binds to receptors present only on certain types of immune system cells.

General Features of Viral Replicative Cycles

A viral infection begins when a virus binds to a host cell and the viral genome makes its way inside (**Figure 19.4**). The

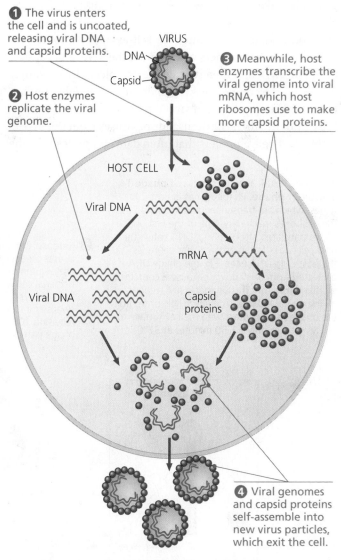

❶ The virus enters the cell and is uncoated, releasing viral DNA and capsid proteins.

VIRUS

DNA

Capsid

❷ Host enzymes replicate the viral genome.

❸ Meanwhile, host enzymes transcribe the viral genome into viral mRNA, which host ribosomes use to make more capsid proteins.

HOST CELL

Viral DNA

mRNA

Viral DNA

Capsid proteins

❹ Viral genomes and capsid proteins self-assemble into new virus particles, which exit the cell.

▲ **Figure 19.4 A simplified viral replicative cycle.** A virus is an intracellular parasite that uses the equipment and small molecules of its host cell to replicate. In this simplest of viral cycles, the parasite is a DNA virus with a capsid consisting of a single type of protein.

DRAW IT *Label each of the straight black arrows with one word representing the name of the process that is occurring. Review Figure 17.24.*

mechanism of genome entry depends on the type of virus and the type of host cell. For example, T-even phages use their elaborate tail apparatus to inject DNA into a bacterium (see Figure 19.3d). Other viruses are taken up by endocytosis or, in the case of enveloped viruses, by fusion of the viral envelope with the host's plasma membrane. Once the viral genome is inside, the proteins it encodes can commandeer the host, reprogramming the cell to copy the viral genome and manufacture viral proteins. The host provides the nucleotides for making viral nucleic acids, as well as enzymes, ribosomes, tRNAs, amino acids, ATP, and other components needed for making the viral proteins. Many DNA viruses use the DNA polymerases of the host cell to synthesize new genomes along the templates provided by the viral DNA. In contrast, to replicate their genomes, RNA viruses use virally encoded RNA polymerases that can use RNA as a template. (Uninfected cells generally make no enzymes for carrying out this process.)

After the viral nucleic acid molecules and capsomeres are produced, they spontaneously self-assemble into new viruses. In fact, researchers can separate the RNA and capsomeres of TMV and then reassemble complete viruses simply by mixing the components together under the right conditions. The simplest type of viral replicative cycle ends with the exit of hundreds or thousands of viruses from the infected host cell, a process that often damages or destroys the cell. Such cellular damage and death, as well as the body's responses to this destruction, cause many of the symptoms associated with viral infections. The viral progeny that exit a cell have the potential to infect additional cells, spreading the viral infection.

There are many variations on the simplified viral replicative cycle we have just described. We will now take a look at some of these variations in bacterial viruses (phages) and animal viruses; later in the chapter, we will consider plant viruses.

Replicative Cycles of Phages

Phages are the best understood of all viruses, although some of them are also among the most complex. Research on phages led to the discovery that some double-stranded DNA viruses can replicate by two alternative mechanisms: the lytic cycle and the lysogenic cycle.

The Lytic Cycle

A phage replicative cycle that culminates in death of the host cell is known as a **lytic cycle (Figure 19.5)**. The term refers to the last stage of infection, during which the bacterium lyses (breaks open) and releases the phages that were produced within the cell. Each of these phages can then infect a healthy cell, and a few successive lytic cycles can destroy an entire

▶ **Figure 19.5 The lytic cycle of phage T4, a virulent phage.** Phage T4 has almost 300 genes, which are transcribed and translated using the host cell's machinery. One of the first phage genes translated after the viral DNA enters the host cell codes for an enzyme that degrades the host cell's DNA (step ❷); the phage DNA is protected from breakdown because it contains a modified form of cytosine that is not recognized by the phage enzyme. The entire lytic cycle, from the phage's first contact with the cell surface to cell lysis, takes only 20–30 minutes at 37°C.

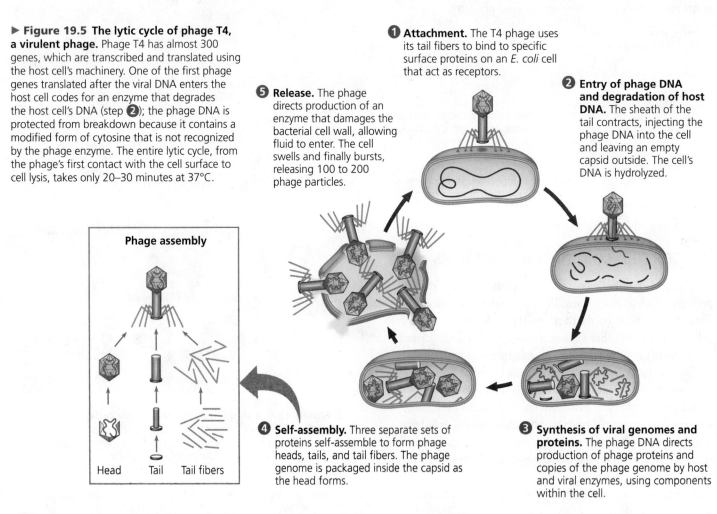

❶ **Attachment.** The T4 phage uses its tail fibers to bind to specific surface proteins on an *E. coli* cell that act as receptors.

❷ **Entry of phage DNA and degradation of host DNA.** The sheath of the tail contracts, injecting the phage DNA into the cell and leaving an empty capsid outside. The cell's DNA is hydrolyzed.

❸ **Synthesis of viral genomes and proteins.** The phage DNA directs production of phage proteins and copies of the phage genome by host and viral enzymes, using components within the cell.

❹ **Self-assembly.** Three separate sets of proteins self-assemble to form phage heads, tails, and tail fibers. The phage genome is packaged inside the capsid as the head forms.

❺ **Release.** The phage directs production of an enzyme that damages the bacterial cell wall, allowing fluid to enter. The cell swells and finally bursts, releasing 100 to 200 phage particles.

Phage assembly

Head   Tail   Tail fibers

bacterial population in just a few hours. A phage that replicates only by a lytic cycle is a **virulent phage**. Figure 19.5 illustrates the major steps in the lytic cycle of T4, a typical virulent phage. Study this figure before proceeding.

After reading about the lytic cycle, you may wonder why phages haven't exterminated all bacteria. The reason is that bacteria have their own defenses. First, natural selection favors bacterial mutants with surface proteins that are no longer recognized as receptors by a particular type of phage. Second, when phage DNA does enter a bacterium, the DNA often is identified as foreign and cut up by cellular enzymes called **restriction enzymes**, which are so named because their activity *restricts* the ability of the phage to replicate within the bacterium. The bacterial cell's own DNA is methylated in a way that prevents attack by its own restriction enzymes. But just as natural selection favors bacteria with receptors altered by mutation or efficient restriction enzymes, it also favors phage mutants that can bind the altered receptors or are resistant to particular restriction enzymes. Thus, the parasite-host relationship is in constant evolutionary flux.

There is yet a third important reason bacteria have been spared from extinction as a result of phage activity. Instead of lysing their host cells, many phages coexist with them in a state called lysogeny, which we'll now discuss.

The Lysogenic Cycle

In contrast to the lytic cycle, which kills the host cell, the **lysogenic cycle** allows replication of the phage genome without destroying the host. Phages capable of using both modes of replicating within a bacterium are called **temperate phages**. A temperate phage called lambda, written with the Greek letter λ, has been widely used in biological research. Phage λ resembles T4, but its tail has only one short tail fiber.

Infection of an *E. coli* cell by phage λ begins when the phage binds to the surface of the cell and injects its linear DNA genome **(Figure 19.6)**. Within the host, the λ DNA molecule forms a circle. What happens next depends on the replicative mode: lytic cycle or lysogenic cycle. During a lytic cycle, the viral genes immediately turn the host cell into a λ-producing factory, and the cell soon lyses and releases its virus progeny. During a lysogenic cycle, however, the λ DNA molecule is incorporated into a specific site on the *E. coli* chromosome by viral proteins that break both circular DNA molecules and join them to each other. When integrated into the bacterial chromosome in this way, the viral DNA is known as a **prophage**. One prophage gene codes for a protein that prevents transcription of most of the other prophage genes. Thus, the phage genome is mostly silent

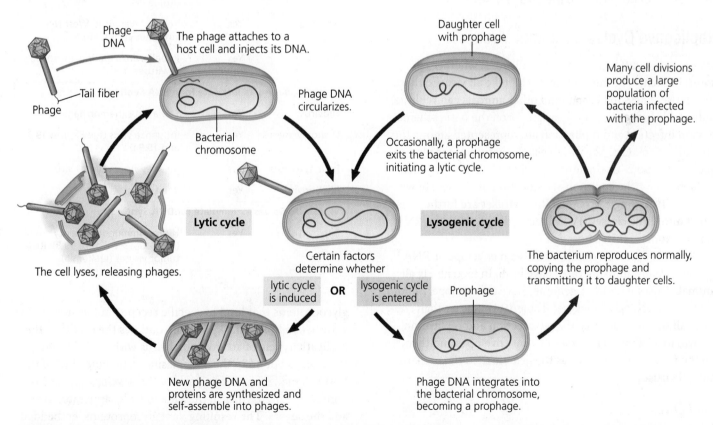

▲ **Figure 19.6 The lytic and lysogenic cycles of phage λ, a temperate phage.** After entering the bacterial cell and circularizing, the λ DNA can immediately initiate the production of a large number of progeny phages (lytic cycle) or integrate into the bacterial chromosome (lysogenic cycle). In most cases, phage λ follows the lytic pathway, which is similar to that detailed in Figure 19.5. However, once a lysogenic cycle begins, the prophage may be carried in the host cell's chromosome for many generations. Phage λ has one main tail fiber, which is short.

within the bacterium. Every time the *E. coli* cell prepares to divide, it replicates the phage DNA along with its own chromosome such that each daughter cell inherits a prophage. A single infected cell can quickly give rise to a large population of bacteria carrying the virus in prophage form. This mechanism enables viruses to propagate without killing the host cells on which they depend.

The term *lysogenic* signifiies that prophages are capable of generating active phages that lyse their host cells. This occurs when the λ genome (or that of another temperate phage) is induced to exit the bacterial chromosome and initiate a lytic cycle. An environmental signal, such as a certain chemical or high-energy radiation, usually triggers the switchover from the lysogenic to the lytic mode.

In addition to the gene for the viral protein that prevents transcription, a few other prophage genes may be expressed during lysogeny. Expression of these genes may alter the host's phenotype, a phenomenon that can have important medical significance. For example, the three species of bacteria that cause the human diseases diphtheria, botulism, and scarlet fever would not be so harmful to humans without certain prophage genes that cause the host bacteria to make toxins. And the difference between the *E. coli* strain in our intestines and the O157:H7 strain that has caused several deaths by food poisoning appears to be the presence of toxin genes of prophages in the O157:H7 strain.

Replicative Cycles of Animal Viruses

Everyone has suffered from viral infections, whether cold sores, influenza, or the common cold. Like all viruses, those that cause illness in humans and other animals can replicate only inside host cells. Many variations on the basic scheme of viral infection and replication are represented among the animal viruses. One key variable is the nature of the viral genome (double- or single-stranded DNA or RNA), which is the basis for the common classification of viruses shown in **Table 19.1**. Single-stranded RNA viruses are further classified into three classes (IV–VI) according to how the RNA genome functions in a host cell.

Whereas few bacteriophages have an envelope or RNA genome, many animal viruses have both. In fact, nearly all animal viruses with RNA genomes have an envelope, as do some with DNA genomes (see Table 19.1). Rather than consider all the mechanisms of viral infection and replication, we will focus first on the roles of viral envelopes and then on the functioning of RNA as the genetic material of many animal viruses.

Viral Envelopes

An animal virus equipped with an envelope—that is, an outer membrane—uses it to enter the host cell. Protruding from the outer surface of this envelope are viral

Table 19.1 Classes of Animal Viruses

Class/Family	Envelope?	Examples That Cause Human Diseases
I. Double-Stranded DNA (dsDNA)		
Adenovirus (see Figure 19.3b)	No	Respiratory viruses; tumor-causing viruses
Papillomavirus	No	Warts, cervical cancer
Polyomavirus	No	Tumors
Herpesvirus	Yes	Herpes simplex I and II (cold sores, genital sores); varicella zoster (shingles, chicken pox); Epstein-Barr virus (mononucleosis, Burkitt's lymphoma)
Poxvirus	Yes	Smallpox virus; cowpox virus
II. Single-Stranded DNA (ssDNA)		
Parvovirus	No	B19 parvovirus (mild rash)
III. Double-Stranded RNA (dsRNA)		
Reovirus	No	Rotavirus (diarrhea); Colorado tick fever virus
IV. Single-Stranded RNA (ssRNA); Serves as mRNA		
Picornavirus	No	Rhinovirus (common cold); poliovirus; hepatitis A virus; other intestinal viruses
Coronavirus	Yes	Severe acute respiratory syndrome (SARS)
Flavivirus	Yes	Yellow fever virus; West Nile virus; hepatitis C virus
Togavirus	Yes	Rubella virus; equine encephalitis viruses
V. ssRNA; Serves as Template for mRNA Synthesis		
Filovirus	Yes	Ebola virus (hemorrhagic fever)
Orthomyxovirus	Yes	Influenza virus (see Figures 19.3c and 19.9a)
Paramyxovirus	Yes	Measles virus; mumps virus
Rhabdovirus	Yes	Rabies virus
VI. ssRNA; Serves as Template for DNA Synthesis		
Retrovirus	Yes	Human immunodeficiency virus (HIV/AIDS; see Figure 19.8); RNA tumor viruses (leukemia)

glycoproteins that bind to specific receptor molecules on the surface of a host cell. **Figure 19.7** outlines the events in the replicative cycle of an enveloped virus with an RNA genome. Ribosomes bound to the endoplasmic reticulum (ER) of the host cell make the protein parts of the envelope glycoproteins; cellular enzymes in the ER and Golgi apparatus then add the sugars. The resulting viral glycoproteins, embedded in membrane derived from the host cell, are transported to the cell surface. In a process much like exocytosis, new viral capsids are wrapped in membrane as they bud from the cell.

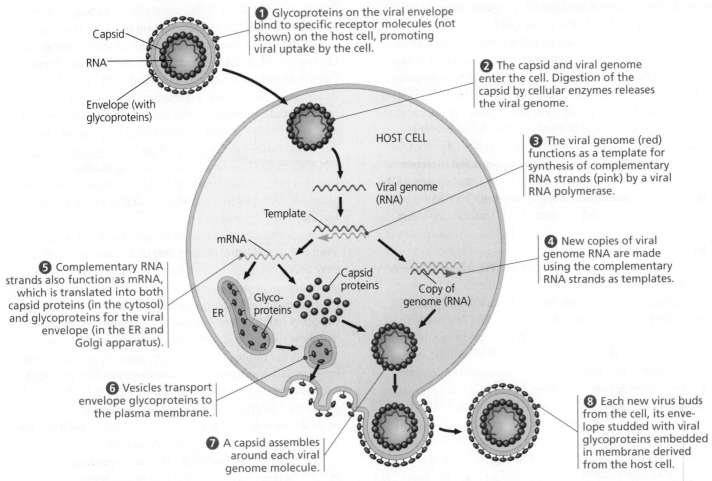

1 Glycoproteins on the viral envelope bind to specific receptor molecules (not shown) on the host cell, promoting viral uptake by the cell.

2 The capsid and viral genome enter the cell. Digestion of the capsid by cellular enzymes releases the viral genome.

3 The viral genome (red) functions as a template for synthesis of complementary RNA strands (pink) by a viral RNA polymerase.

4 New copies of viral genome RNA are made using the complementary RNA strands as templates.

5 Complementary RNA strands also function as mRNA, which is translated into both capsid proteins (in the cytosol) and glycoproteins for the viral envelope (in the ER and Golgi apparatus).

6 Vesicles transport envelope glycoproteins to the plasma membrane.

7 A capsid assembles around each viral genome molecule.

8 Each new virus buds from the cell, its envelope studded with viral glycoproteins embedded in membrane derived from the host cell.

Capsid

RNA

Envelope (with glycoproteins)

HOST CELL

Viral genome (RNA)

Template

mRNA

Capsid proteins

Glyco-proteins

ER

Copy of genome (RNA)

▲ **Figure 19.7 The replicative cycle of an enveloped RNA virus.** Shown here is a virus with a single-stranded RNA genome that functions as a template for synthesis of mRNA (class V of Table 19.1). Some enveloped viruses enter the host cell by fusion of the envelope with the cell's plasma membrane; others enter by endocytosis. For all enveloped RNA viruses, formation of new envelopes for progeny viruses occurs by the mechanism depicted in this figure.

? *Name a virus that has infected you and has a replicative cycle matching this one. (Hint: See Table 19.1.)*

In other words, the viral envelope is usually derived from the host cell's plasma membrane, although all or most of the molecules of this membrane are specified by viral genes. The enveloped viruses are now free to infect other cells. This replicative cycle does not necessarily kill the host cell, in contrast to the lytic cycles of phages.

Some viruses have envelopes that are not derived from plasma membrane. Herpesviruses, for example, are temporarily cloaked in membrane derived from the nuclear envelope of the host; they then shed this membrane in the cytoplasm and acquire a new envelope made from membrane of the Golgi apparatus. These viruses have a double-stranded DNA genome and replicate within the host cell nucleus, using a combination of viral and cellular enzymes to replicate and transcribe their DNA. In the case of herpesviruses, copies of the viral DNA can remain behind as mini-chromosomes in the nuclei of certain nerve cells. There they remain latent until some sort of physical or emotional stress triggers a new round of active virus production. The infection of other cells by these new viruses causes the blisters

characteristic of herpes, such as cold sores or genital sores. Once someone acquires a herpesvirus infection, flare-ups may recur throughout the person's life.

RNA as Viral Genetic Material

Although some phages and most plant viruses are RNA viruses, the broadest variety of RNA genomes is found among the viruses that infect animals. There are three types of single-stranded RNA genomes found in animal viruses. The genome of class IV viruses can directly serve as mRNA and thus can be translated into viral protein immediately after infection. Figure 19.7 shows a virus of class V, in which the RNA genome serves instead as a *template* for mRNA synthesis. The RNA genome is transcribed into complementary RNA strands, which function both as mRNA and as templates for the synthesis of additional copies of genomic RNA. All viruses that use an RNA genome as a template for mRNA transcription require RNA → RNA synthesis. These viruses use a viral enzyme capable of carrying out this process; there are no such enzymes in most cells. The enzyme used in this process is packaged during viral self-assembly with the genome inside the viral capsid.

The RNA animal viruses with the most complicated replicative cycles are the **retroviruses** (class VI). These viruses are equipped with an enzyme called **reverse transcriptase**, which transcribes an RNA template into DNA, providing an RNA → DNA information flow, the opposite of the usual direction. This unusual phenomenon is the source of the name retroviruses (*retro* means "backward"). Of particular medical importance is **HIV (human immunodeficiency virus)**, the retrovirus shown in Figure 19.1 that causes **AIDS (acquired immunodeficiency syndrome)**. HIV and other retroviruses are enveloped viruses that contain two identical molecules of single-stranded RNA and two molecules of reverse transcriptase.

The HIV replicative cycle (traced in **Figure 19.8**) is typical of a retrovirus. After HIV enters a host cell, its reverse transcriptase molecules are released into the cytoplasm, where they catalyze synthesis of viral DNA. The newly made viral DNA then enters the cell's nucleus and integrates into the DNA of a chromosome. The integrated viral DNA, called a **provirus**, never leaves the host's genome, remaining a permanent resident of the cell. (Recall that a prophage, in contrast, leaves the host's genome at the start of a lytic cycle.) The RNA polymerase of the host transcribes the proviral DNA into RNA molecules, which can function both as mRNA for the synthesis of viral proteins and as genomes for the new viruses that will be assembled and released from the cell. In Chapter 43, we describe how HIV causes the deterioration of the immune system that occurs in AIDS.

Evolution of Viruses

EVOLUTION We began this chapter by asking whether or not viruses are alive. Viruses do not really fit our definition of living organisms. An isolated virus is biologically inert, unable to replicate its genes or regenerate its own ATP. Yet it has a genetic program written in the universal language of life. Do we think of viruses as nature's most complex associations of molecules or as the simplest forms of life? Either way, we must bend our usual definitions. Although viruses cannot replicate or carry out metabolic activities independently, their use of the genetic code makes it hard to deny their evolutionary connection to the living world.

How did viruses originate? Viruses have been found that infect every form of life—not just bacteria, animals, and plants, but also archaea, fungi, and algae and other protists. Because they depend on cells for their own propagation, it seems likely that viruses are not the descendants of precellular forms of life but evolved—possibly multiple times—*after* the first cells appeared. Most molecular biologists favor the hypothesis that viruses originated from naked bits of cellular nucleic acids that moved from one cell to another, perhaps via injured cell surfaces. The evolution of genes coding for

capsid proteins may have allowed viruses to bind cell membranes, thus facilitating the infection of uninjured cells.

Candidates for the original sources of viral genomes include plasmids and transposons. *Plasmids* are small, circular DNA molecules found in bacteria and in the unicellular eukaryotes called yeasts. Plasmids exist apart from and can replicate independently of the bacterial chromosome, and are occasionally transferred between cells; plasmids are discussed further in Chapters 20 and 27. *Transposons* are DNA segments that can move from one location to another within a cell's genome, to be detailed in Chapter 21. Thus, plasmids, transposons, and viruses all share an important feature: They are *mobile genetic elements*.

Consistent with this notion of pieces of DNA shuttling from cell to cell is the observation that a viral genome can have more in common with the genome of its host than with the genomes of viruses that infect other hosts. Indeed, some viral genes are essentially identical to genes of the host. On the other hand, recent sequencing of many viral genomes has shown that the genetic sequences of some viruses are quite similar to those of seemingly distantly related viruses; for example, some animal viruses share similar sequences with plant viruses. This genetic similarity may reflect the persistence of groups of viral genes that were favored by natural selection during the early evolution of both viruses and the eukaryotic cells that served as their hosts.

The debate about the origin of viruses was reinvigorated in 2003 by reports of one of the largest viruses yet discovered: Mimivirus is a double-stranded DNA (dsDNA) virus with an icosahedral capsid that is 400 nm in diameter, the size of a small bacterium. Its genome contains 1.2 million bases (Mb)—about 100 times as many as the influenza virus genome—and an estimated 1,000 genes. Perhaps the most surprising aspect of mimivirus, however, was that its genome included genes previously found only in cellular genomes. Some of these genes code for proteins involved in translation, DNA repair, protein folding, and polysaccharide synthesis. Whether mimivirus evolved *before* the first cells and then developed an exploitative relationship with them, or evolved more recently and simply scavenged genes from its hosts is not yet settled. In 2013 an even larger virus was discovered that cannot be classified with any existing known virus. This virus is 1 μm (1,000 nm) in diameter, with a dsDNA genome of around 2–2.5 Mb, larger than that of some small eukaryotes. What's more, over 90% of its 2,000 or so genes are unrelated to cellular genes, inspiring the naming of this virus as pandoravirus. How these and all other viruses fit in the tree of life is an intriguing, unresolved question.

The ongoing evolutionary relationship between viruses and the genomes of their host cells is an association that continues to make viruses very useful experimental systems in molecular biology. Knowledge about viruses also allows many practical applications, since viruses have a tremendous impact on all organisms through their ability to cause disease.

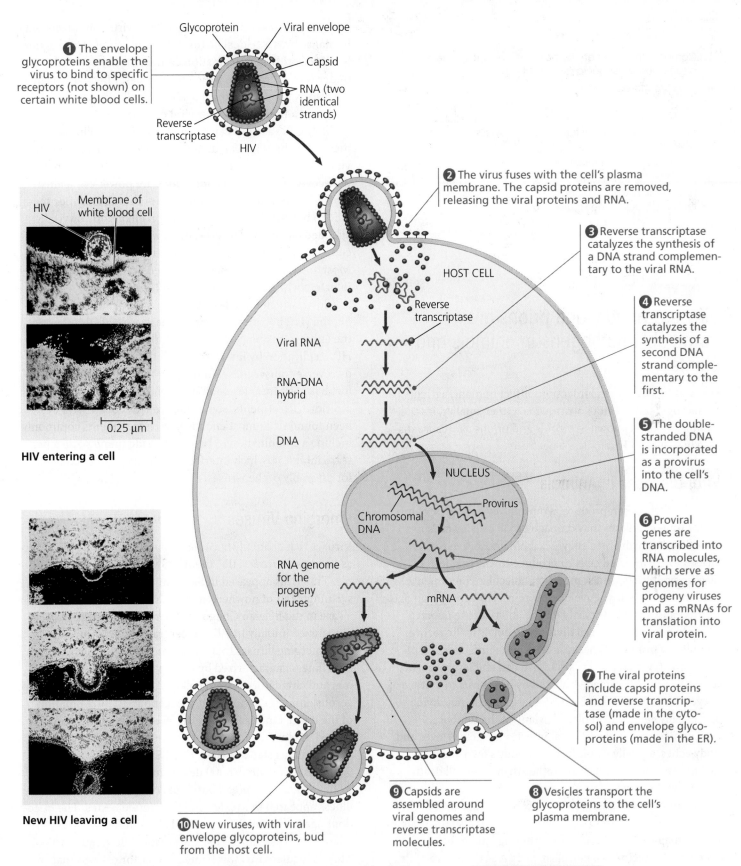

① The envelope glycoproteins enable the virus to bind to specific receptors (not shown) on certain white blood cells.

Glycoprotein   Viral envelope
Capsid
RNA (two identical strands)
Reverse transcriptase
HIV

HIV
Membrane of white blood cell

0.25 μm

HIV entering a cell

New HIV leaving a cell

② The virus fuses with the cell's plasma membrane. The capsid proteins are removed, releasing the viral proteins and RNA.

③ Reverse transcriptase catalyzes the synthesis of a DNA strand complementary to the viral RNA.

④ Reverse transcriptase catalyzes the synthesis of a second DNA strand complementary to the first.

HOST CELL

Reverse transcriptase

Viral RNA

RNA-DNA hybrid

DNA

⑤ The double-stranded DNA is incorporated as a provirus into the cell's DNA.

NUCLEUS

Provirus

Chromosomal DNA

⑥ Proviral genes are transcribed into RNA molecules, which serve as genomes for progeny viruses and as mRNAs for translation into viral protein.

RNA genome for the progeny viruses

mRNA

⑦ The viral proteins include capsid proteins and reverse transcriptase (made in the cytosol) and envelope glycoproteins (made in the ER).

⑨ Capsids are assembled around viral genomes and reverse transcriptase molecules.

⑧ Vesicles transport the glycoproteins to the cell's plasma membrane.

⑩ New viruses, with viral envelope glycoproteins, bud from the host cell.

▲ **Figure 19.8 The replicative cycle of HIV, the retrovirus that causes AIDS.** Note in step ⑤ that DNA synthesized from the viral RNA genome is integrated as a provirus into the host cell chromosomal DNA, a characteristic unique to retroviruses. For simplicity, the cell-surface proteins that act as receptors for HIV are not shown. The photos on the left (artificially colored TEMs) show HIV entering and leaving a human white blood cell.

MAKE CONNECTIONS *Describe what is known about binding of HIV to immune system cells. (See Figure 7.8.) How was this discovered?*

1. Compare the effect on the host cell of a lytic (virulent) phage and a lysogenic (temperate) phage.

2. MAKE CONNECTIONS The RNA virus in Figure 19.7 has a viral RNA polymerase that functions in step 3 of the virus's replicative cycle. Compare this with a cellular RNA polymerase in terms of template and overall function (see Figure 17.9).

3. Why is HIV called a retrovirus?

4. WHAT IF? If you were a researcher trying to combat HIV infection, what molecular processes could you attempt to block? (See Figure 19.8.)

For suggested answers, see Appendix A.

CONCEPT 19.3

Viruses, viroids, and prions are formidable pathogens in animals and plants

Diseases caused by viral infections afflict humans, agricultural crops, and livestock worldwide. Other smaller, less complex entities known as viroids and prions also cause disease in plants and animals, respectively.

Viral Diseases in Animals

A viral infection can produce symptoms by a number of different routes. Viruses may damage or kill cells by causing the release of hydrolytic enzymes from lysosomes. Some viruses cause infected cells to produce toxins that lead to disease symptoms, and some have molecular components that are toxic, such as envelope proteins. How much damage a virus causes depends partly on the ability of the infected tissue to regenerate by cell division. People usually recover completely from colds because the epithelium of the respiratory tract, which the viruses infect, can efficiently repair itself. In contrast, damage inflicted by poliovirus to mature nerve cells is permanent because these cells do not divide and usually cannot be replaced. Many of the temporary symptoms associated with viral infections, such as fever and body aches, actually result from the body's own efforts to defend itself against infection rather than from cell death caused by the virus.

The immune system is a complex and critical part of the body's natural defenses (see Chapter 43). It is also the basis for the major medical tool for preventing viral infections—vaccines. A **vaccine** is a harmless variant or derivative of a pathogen that stimulates the immune system to mount defenses against the harmful pathogen. Smallpox, a viral disease that was at one time a devastating scourge in many parts of the world, was eradicated by a vaccination program carried out by the World Health Organization (WHO). The

very narrow host range of the smallpox virus—it infects only humans—was a critical factor in the success of this program. Similar worldwide vaccination campaigns are currently under way to eradicate polio and measles. Effective vaccines are also available to protect against rubella, mumps, hepatitis B, and a number of other viral diseases.

Although vaccines can prevent certain viral illnesses, medical technology can do little, at present, to cure most viral infections once they occur. The antibiotics that help us recover from bacterial infections are powerless against viruses. Antibiotics kill bacteria by inhibiting enzymes specific to bacteria but have no effect on eukaryotic or virally encoded enzymes. However, the few enzymes that are encoded only by viruses have provided targets for other drugs. Most antiviral drugs resemble nucleosides and as a result interfere with viral nucleic acid synthesis. One such drug is acyclovir, which impedes herpesvirus replication by inhibiting the viral polymerase that synthesizes viral DNA but not the eukaryotic one. Similarly, azidothymidine (AZT) curbs HIV replication by interfering with the synthesis of DNA by reverse transcriptase. In the past two decades, much effort has gone into developing drugs against HIV. Currently, multidrug treatments, sometimes called "cocktails," have been found to be most effective. Such treatments commonly include a combination of two nucleoside mimics and a protease inhibitor, which interferes with an enzyme required for assembly of the viruses.

Emerging Viruses

Viruses that suddenly become apparent are often referred to as *emerging viruses*. HIV, the AIDS virus, is a classic example: This virus appeared in San Francisco in the early 1980s, seemingly out of nowhere, although later studies uncovered a case in the Belgian Congo in 1959. The deadly Ebola virus, recognized initially in 1976 in central Africa, is one of several emerging viruses that cause *hemorrhagic fever*, an often fatal illness characterized by fever, vomiting, massive bleeding, and circulatory system collapse. A number of other dangerous emerging viruses cause encephalitis, inflammation of the brain. One example is the West Nile virus, which appeared in North America in 1999 and has now spread to all 48 contiguous states in the United States, resulting in over 5,000 cases and almost 300 deaths in 2012.

In 2009, a widespread outbreak, or **epidemic**, of a flu-like illness appeared in Mexico and the United States. The infectious agent was quickly identified as an influenza virus related to viruses that cause the seasonal flu **(Figure 19.9a)**. This particular virus was named H1N1 for reasons that will be explained shortly. The illness spread rapidly, prompting WHO to declare a global epidemic, or **pandemic**, shortly thereafter. Half a year later, the disease had reached 207 countries, infecting over 600,000 people and killing almost 8,000. Public health agencies responded rapidly with

(a) 2009 pandemic H1N1 influenza A virus. Viruses (blue) are seen on an infected cell (green) in this colorized SEM.

(b) 2009 pandemic screening. At a South Korean airport, thermal scans were used to detect passengers with a fever who might have the H1N1 flu.

▲ **Figure 19.9 Influenza in humans.**

guidelines for shutting down schools and other public places, and vaccine development and screening efforts were accelerated **(Figure 19.9b)**.

How do such viruses burst on the human scene, giving rise to harmful diseases that were previously rare or even unknown? Three processes contribute to the emergence of viral diseases. The first, and perhaps most important, is the mutation of existing viruses. RNA viruses tend to have an unusually high rate of mutation because viral RNA polymerases do not proofread and correct errors in replicating their RNA genomes. Some mutations change existing viruses into new genetic varieties (strains) that can cause disease, even in individuals who are immune to the ancestral virus. For instance, seasonal flu epidemics are caused by new strains of influenza virus genetically different enough from earlier strains that people have little immunity to them. You'll see an example of this process in the Scientific Skills Exercise, where you'll analyze genetic changes in variants of the 2009 H1N1 flu virus and correlate them with spread of the disease.

A second process that can lead to the emergence of viral diseases is the dissemination of a viral disease from a small, isolated human population. For instance, AIDS went unnamed and virtually unnoticed for decades before it began to spread around the world. In this case, technological and social factors, including affordable international travel, blood transfusions, sexual promiscuity, and the abuse of intravenous drugs, allowed a previously rare human disease to become a global scourge.

A third source of new viral diseases in humans is the spread of existing viruses from other animals. Scientists estimate that about three-quarters of new human diseases originate in this way. Animals that harbor and can transmit a particular virus but are generally unaffected by it are said to act as a natural reservoir for that virus. For example, the H1N1 virus that caused the 2009 flu pandemic mentioned earlier was likely passed to humans from pigs; for this reason, the disease it caused was originally called "swine flu."

In general, flu epidemics provide an instructive example of the effects of viruses moving between species. There are three types of influenza virus: types B and C, which infect only humans and have never caused an epidemic, and type A, which infects a wide range of animals, including birds, pigs, horses, and humans. Influenza A strains have caused four major flu epidemics among humans in the last 100 years. The worst was the first one, the "Spanish flu" pandemic of 1918–1919, which killed 40–50 million people, including many World War I soldiers.

Different strains of influenza A are given standardized names; for example, both the strain that caused the 1918 flu and the one that caused the 2009 pandemic flu are called H1N1. The name identifies which forms of two viral surface proteins are present: hemagglutinin (H) and neuraminidase (N). There are 16 different types of hemagglutinin, a protein that helps the flu virus attach to host cells, and 9 types of neuraminidase, an enzyme that helps release new virus particles from infected cells. Waterbirds have been found that carry viruses with all possible combinations of H and N.

A likely scenario for the 1918 pandemic and others is that the virus mutated as it passed from one host species to another. When an animal like a pig or a bird is infected with more than one strain of flu virus, the different strains can undergo genetic recombination if the RNA molecules making up their genomes mix and match during viral assembly. Pigs were probably the main hosts for recombination that led to the 2009 flu virus, which turns out to contain sequences from bird, pig, and human flu viruses. Coupled with mutation, these reassortments can lead to the emergence of a viral strain capable of infecting human cells. People who have never been exposed to that particular strain before will lack immunity, and the recombinant virus has the potential to be highly pathogenic. If such a flu virus recombines with viruses that circulate widely among humans, it may acquire the ability to spread easily from person to person, dramatically increasing the potential for a major human outbreak.

One potential long-term threat is the avian flu caused by an H5N1 virus carried by wild and domestic birds. The first documented transmission from birds to humans occurred in Hong Kong in 1997. Since then, the overall mortality rate due to H5N1 has been greater than 50% of those infected—an alarming number. Also, the host range of H5N1 is expanding, which provides increasing chances for reassortment between different strains. If the H5N1 avian flu virus evolves so that it can spread easily from person to person, it could represent a major global health threat akin to that of the 1918 pandemic.

How easily could this happen? Recently, scientists working with ferrets, small mammals that are animal models

Analyzing a Sequence-Based Phylogenetic Tree to Understand Viral Evolution

How Can Sequence Data Be Used to Track Flu Virus Evolution During Pandemic Waves? In 2009, an influenza A H1N1 virus caused a pandemic, and the virus has continued to resurface in outbreaks across the world. Researchers in Taiwan were curious about why the virus kept appearing despite widespread flu vaccine initiatives. They hypothesized that newly evolved variant strains of the H1N1 virus were able to evade human immune system defenses. To test this hypothesis, they needed to determine if each wave of the flu outbreak was caused by a different H1N1 variant strain.

How the Experiment Was Done Scientists obtained the genome sequences for 4,703 virus isolates collected from patients with H1N1 flu in Taiwan. They compared the sequences in different strains for the viral hemagglutinin (HA) gene, and based on mutations that had occurred, arranged the isolates into a phylogenetic tree (see Figure 26.5 for information on how to read phylogenetic trees).

▲ H1N1 flu vaccination.

Data from the Experiment The figure at the upper left shows a phylogenetic tree; each branch tip is one variant strain of the H1N1 virus with a unique HA gene sequence. The tree is a way to visualize a working hypothesis about the evolutionary relationships between H1N1 variants.

Interpret the Data

1. The phylogenetic tree shows the hypothesized evolutionary relationship between the variant strains of H1N1 virus. The more closely connected two variants are, the more alike they are in terms of HA gene sequence. Each fork in a branch, called a node, shows where two lineages separate due to different accumulated mutations. The length of the branches is a measure of how many sequence differences there are between the variants, indicating how distantly related they are. Referring to the phylogenetic tree, which variants are more closely related to each other: A/Taiwan1018/2011 and A/Taiwan/552/2011 or A/Taiwan1018/2011 and A/Taiwan/8542/2009? Explain your answer.

2. The scientists arranged the branches into groups made up of one ancestral variant and all of its descendant, mutated variants. They are color-coded in the figure. Using Group 11 as an example, trace the lineage of its variants. (a) Do all of the nodes have the same number of branches or branch tips? (b) Are all of the branches in the group the same length? (c) What do these results indicate?

3. The graph at the lower left shows the number of isolates collected (each from an ill patient) on the y-axis and the month and year that the isolates were collected on the x-axis. Each group of variants is plotted separately with a line color that matches the tree diagram. (a) Which group of variants was the earliest to cause the first wave of H1N1 flu in over 100 patients in Taiwan? (b) Once a group of variants had a peak number of infections, did members of that same group cause another (later) wave of infection? (c) One variant in Group 1 (green, uppermost branch) was used to make a vaccine that was distributed very early in the pandemic. Based on the graphed data, does it look like the vaccine was effective?

4. Groups 9, 10, and 11 all had H1N1 variants that caused a large number of infections at the same time in Taiwan. Does this mean that the scientists' hypothesis, that new variants cause new waves of infection, was incorrect? Explain your answer.

(MB) A version of this Scientific Skills Exercise can be assigned in MasteringBiology.

Data from J.-R. Yang et al., New variants and age shift to high fatality groups contribute to severe successive waves in the 2009 influenza pandemic in Taiwan, *PLoS ONE* 6(11): e28288 (2011).

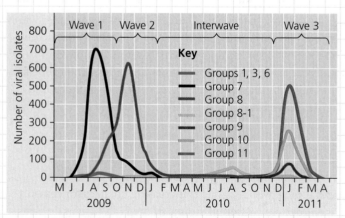

▲ Scientists graphed the number of isolates by the month and year of isolate collection to show the period in which each viral variant was actively causing illness in people.

for human flu, found out that only a few mutations of the avian flu virus would allow infection of cells in the human nasal cavity and windpipe. Furthermore, when the scientists transferred nasal swabs serially from ferret to ferret, the virus became transmissible through the air. Reports of this startling discovery at a scientific conference in 2011 ignited a firestorm of debate about whether to publish the results. Ultimately, the scientific community and various governmental groups decided the benefits of potentially understanding how to prevent pandemics would outweigh the risks of the information being used for harmful purposes, and the work was published in 2012.

As we have seen, emerging viruses are generally not new; rather, they are existing viruses that mutate, disseminate more widely in the current host species, or spread to new host species. Changes in host behavior or environmental changes can increase the viral traffic responsible for emerging diseases. For instance, new roads built through remote areas can allow viruses to spread between previously isolated human populations. Also, the destruction of forests to expand cropland can bring humans into contact with other animals that may host viruses capable of infecting humans.

Viral Diseases in Plants

More than 2,000 types of viral diseases of plants are known, and together they account for an estimated annual loss of $15 billion worldwide due to their destruction of agricultural and horticultural crops. Common signs of viral infection include bleached or brown spots on leaves and fruits (as on the squash shown below, right), stunted growth, and damaged flowers or roots, all of which can diminish the yield and quality of crops.

Plant viruses have the same basic structure and mode of replication as animal viruses. Most plant viruses discovered thus far, including tobacco mosaic virus (TMV), have an RNA genome. Many have a helical capsid, like TMV, while others have an icosahedral capsid (see Figure 19.3).

Viral diseases of plants spread by two major routes. In the first route, called *horizontal transmission*, a plant is infected from an external source of the virus. Because the invading virus must get past the plant's outer protective layer of cells (the epidermis), a plant becomes more susceptible to viral infections if it has been damaged by wind, injury, or herbivores. Herbivores, especially insects, pose a double threat because they can also act as carriers of viruses, transmitting disease from plant to plant. Moreover, farmers and gardeners may transmit plant viruses inadvertently on pruning shears and other tools. The other route of viral infection is *vertical transmission*, in which a plant inherits a viral infection from a parent. Vertical transmission can occur in asexual

propagation (for example, through cuttings) or in sexual reproduction via infected seeds.

Once a virus enters a plant cell and begins replicating, viral genomes and associated proteins can spread throughout the plant by means of plasmodesmata, the cytoplasmic connections that penetrate the walls between adjacent plant cells (see Figure 36.18). The passage of viral macromolecules from cell to cell is facilitated by virally encoded proteins that cause enlargement of plasmodesmata. Scientists have not yet devised cures for most viral plant diseases. Consequently, research efforts are focused largely on reducing the transmission of such diseases and on breeding resistant varieties of crop plants.

Viroids and Prions: The Simplest Infectious Agents

As small and simple as viruses are, they dwarf another class of pathogens: **viroids**. These are circular RNA molecules, only a few hundred nucleotides long, that infect plants. Viroids do not encode proteins but can replicate in host plant cells, apparently using host cell enzymes. These small RNA molecules seem to cause errors in the regulatory systems that control plant growth; the typical signs of viroid diseases are abnormal development and stunted growth. One viroid disease, called cadang-cadang, has killed more than 10 million coconut palms in the Philippines.

An important lesson from viroids is that a single molecule can be an infectious agent that spreads a disease. But viroids are nucleic acids, whose ability to be replicated is well known. Even more surprising is the evidence for infectious *proteins*, called **prions**, which appear to cause a number of degenerative brain diseases in various animal species. These diseases include scrapie in sheep; mad cow disease, which has plagued the European beef industry in recent years; and Creutzfeldt-Jakob disease in humans, which has caused the death of some 150 people in Great Britain. Prions can be transmitted in food, as may occur when people eat prion-laden beef from cattle with mad cow disease. Kuru, another human disease caused by prions, was identified in the early 1900s among the South Fore natives of New Guinea. A kuru epidemic peaked there in the 1960s, puzzling scientists, who at first thought the disease had a genetic basis. Eventually, however, anthropological investigations ferreted out how the disease was spread: ritual cannibalism, a widespread practice among South Fore natives at that time.

Two characteristics of prions are especially alarming. First, prions act very slowly, with an incubation period of at least ten years before symptoms develop. The lengthy incubation period prevents sources of infection from being identified until long after the first cases appear, allowing many

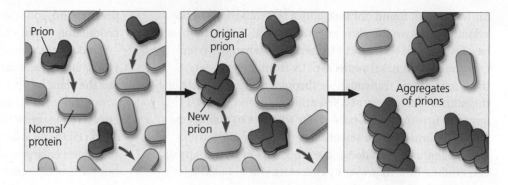

► **Figure 19.10 Model for how prions propagate.** Prions are misfolded versions of normal brain proteins. When a prion contacts a normally folded version of the same protein, it may induce the normal protein to assume the abnormal shape. The resulting chain reaction may continue until high levels of prion aggregation cause cellular malfunction and eventual degeneration of the brain.

Prion

Normal protein

Original prion

New prion

Aggregates of prions

more infections to occur. Second, prions are virtually indestructible; they are not destroyed or deactivated by heating to normal cooking temperatures. To date, there is no known cure for prion diseases, and the only hope for developing effective treatments lies in understanding the process of infection.

How can a protein, which cannot replicate itself, be a transmissible pathogen? According to the leading model, a prion is a misfolded form of a protein normally present in brain cells. When the prion gets into a cell containing the normal form of the protein, the prion somehow converts normal protein molecules to the misfolded prion versions. Several prions then aggregate into a complex that can convert other normal proteins to prions, which join the chain **(Figure 19.10)**. Prion aggregation interferes with normal cellular functions and causes disease symptoms. This model was greeted with much skepticism when it was first

proposed by Stanley Prusiner in the early 1980s, but it is now widely accepted. Prusiner was awarded the Nobel Prize in 1997 for his work on prions. He has recently proposed that prions are also involved in neurodegenerative diseases such as Alzheimer's and Parkinson disease. There are many outstanding questions about these small infectious agents.

CONCEPT CHECK 19.3

1. Describe two ways that a preexisting virus can become an emerging virus.
2. Contrast horizontal and vertical transmission of viruses in plants.
3. **WHAT IF?** TMV has been isolated from virtually all commercial tobacco products. Why, then, is TMV infection not an additional hazard for smokers?

For suggested answers, see Appendix A.

19 Chapter Review

SUMMARY OF KEY CONCEPTS

CONCEPT 19.1

A virus consists of a nucleic acid surrounded by a protein coat (pp. 393–395)

- Researchers discovered viruses in the late 1800s by studying a plant disease, tobacco mosaic disease.
- A **virus** is a small nucleic acid genome enclosed in a protein **capsid** and sometimes a membranous **viral envelope**. The genome may be single- or double-stranded DNA or RNA.

? *Are viruses generally considered living or nonliving? Explain.*

CONCEPT 19.2

Viruses replicate only in host cells (pp. 395–402)

- Viruses use enzymes, ribosomes, and small molecules of host cells to synthesize progeny viruses during replication. Each type of virus has a characteristic **host range**.
- **Phages** (viruses that infect bacteria) can replicate by two alternative mechanisms: the **lytic cycle** and the **lysogenic cycle**.

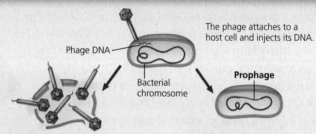

The phage attaches to a host cell and injects its DNA.

Phage DNA

Bacterial chromosome

Prophage

Lytic cycle
- **Virulent** or **temperate phage**
- Destruction of host DNA
- Production of new phages
- Lysis of host cell causes release of progeny phages

Lysogenic cycle
- **Temperate phage** only
- Genome integrates into bacterial chromosome as **prophage**, which (1) is replicated and passed on to daughter cells and (2) can be induced to leave the chromosome and initiate a lytic cycle

- Many animal viruses have an envelope. **Retroviruses** (such as **HIV**) use the enzyme **reverse transcriptase** to copy their RNA genome into DNA, which can be integrated into the host genome as a **provirus**.
- Since viruses can replicate only within cells, they probably evolved after the first cells appeared, perhaps as packaged fragments of cellular nucleic acid.

? *Describe enzymes that are not found in most cells but are necessary for the replication of viruses of certain types.*

CONCEPT 19.3

Viruses, viroids, and prions are formidable pathogens in animals and plants (pp. 402–406)

- Symptoms of viral diseases may be caused by direct viral harm to cells or by the body's immune response. **Vaccines** stimulate the immune system to defend the host against specific viruses.
- An **epidemic**, a widespread outbreak of a disease, can become a **pandemic**, a global epidemic.
- Outbreaks of emerging viral diseases in humans are usually not new, but rather are caused by existing viruses that expand their host territory. The H1N1 2009 flu virus was a new combination of pig, human, and avian viral genes that caused a pandemic. The H5N1 avian flu virus has the potential to cause a high-mortality flu pandemic.
- Viruses enter plant cells through damaged cell walls (horizontal transmission) or are inherited from a parent (vertical transmission).
- **Viroids** are naked RNA molecules that infect plants and disrupt their growth. **Prions** are slow-acting, virtually indestructible infectious proteins that cause brain diseases in mammals.

> **?** *What aspect of an RNA virus makes it more likely than a DNA virus to become an emerging virus?*

TEST YOUR UNDERSTANDING

LEVEL 1: KNOWLEDGE/COMPREHENSION

1. Which of the following characteristics, structures, or processes is common to both bacteria and viruses?
   a. metabolism
   b. ribosomes
   c. genetic material composed of nucleic acid
   d. cell division

2. Emerging viruses arise by
   a. mutation of existing viruses.
   b. the spread of existing viruses to new host species.
   c. the spread of existing viruses more widely within their host species.
   d. all of the above.

3. To cause a human pandemic, the H5N1 avian flu virus would have to
   a. spread to primates such as chimpanzees.
   b. develop into a virus with a different host range.
   c. become capable of human-to-human transmission.
   d. become much more pathogenic.

LEVEL 2: APPLICATION/ANALYSIS

4. A bacterium is infected with an experimentally constructed bacteriophage composed of the T2 phage protein coat and T4 phage DNA. The new phages produced would have
   a. T2 protein and T4 DNA.
   b. T2 protein and T2 DNA.
   c. T4 protein and T4 DNA.
   d. T4 protein and T2 DNA.

5. RNA viruses require their own supply of certain enzymes because
   a. host cells rapidly destroy the viruses.
   b. host cells lack enzymes that can replicate the viral genome.
   c. these enzymes translate viral mRNA into proteins.
   d. these enzymes penetrate host cell membranes.

6. **DRAW IT** Redraw Figure 19.7 to show the replicative cycle of a virus with a single-stranded genome that can function as mRNA (a class IV virus).

LEVEL 3: SYNTHESIS/EVALUATION

7. **EVOLUTION CONNECTION** The success of some viruses lies in their ability to evolve rapidly within the host. Such a virus evades the host's defenses by mutating and producing many altered progeny viruses before the body can mount an attack. Thus, the viruses present late in infection differ from those that initially infected the body. Discuss this as an example of evolution in microcosm. Which viral lineages tend to predominate?

8. **SCIENTIFIC INQUIRY** When bacteria infect an animal, the number of bacteria in the body increases in an exponential fashion (graph A). After infection by a virulent animal virus with a lytic replicative cycle, there is no evidence of infection for a while. Then the number of viruses rises suddenly and subsequently increases in a series of steps (graph B). Explain the difference in the curves.

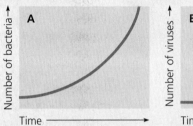

9. **WRITE ABOUT A THEME: ORGANIZATION**
   While viruses are considered by most scientists to be nonliving, they do show some characteristics of life, including the correlation of structure and function. In a short essay (100–150 words), discuss how the structure of a virus correlates with its function.

10. **SYNTHESIZE YOUR KNOWLEDGE**

Oseltamivir (Tamiflu)—an antiviral drug prescribed for influenza—acts to inhibit the enzyme neuraminidase. Explain how this drug could prevent infection in someone exposed to the flu or could shorten the course of flu in an infected patient (the two reasons for which it is prescribed).

For selected answers, see Appendix A.

MasteringBiology®

Students Go to **MasteringBiology** for assignments, the eText, and the Study Area with practice tests, animations, and activities.

Instructors Go to **MasteringBiology** for automatically graded tutorials and questions that you can assign to your students, plus Instructor Resources.

20

DNA Tools and Biotechnology

KEY CONCEPTS

20.1 DNA sequencing and DNA cloning are valuable tools for genetic engineering and biological inquiry

20.2 Biologists use DNA technology to study gene expression and function

20.3 Cloned organisms and stem cells are useful for basic research and other applications

20.4 The practical applications of DNA-based biotechnology affect our lives in many ways

▲ **Figure 20.1 How can the technique shown in this model speed up DNA sequencing?**

The DNA Toolbox

The last five to ten years have seen some extraordinary feats in biology, among them determination of the complete DNA sequences of several extinct species, including woolly mammoths (see below, left), Neanderthals, and a 700,000-year-old horse. Pivotal to those discoveries was the sequencing of the human genome, essentially completed in 2003. This endeavor marked a turning point in biology because it sparked remarkable technological advances in DNA sequencing.

The first human genome sequence took several years at a cost of 1 billion dollars; the time and cost of sequencing a genome have been in free fall since then. **Figure 20.1** shows a model of a sequencing technique in which the nucleotides of a single strand of DNA are passed one by one through a tiny pore in a membrane, and the resulting tiny changes in an electrical current are used to determine the nucleotide sequence. Developers of this technique, which you will learn more about later in the chapter, claim that ultimately we will be able to sequence a human genome in about 6 hours on a $900 device the size of a pack of gum.

In this chapter, we'll first describe the main techniques for sequencing and manipulating DNA—**DNA technology**—and for using these DNA tools to analyze gene expression. Next, we'll explore advances in cloning organisms and producing stem cells, techniques that have both expanded our basic understanding of biology and enhanced our ability to apply that understanding to global problems. In the last section, we'll survey the practical applications of DNA-based **biotechnology**, the manipulation of organisms or their components to make useful products. Today, the applications of DNA technology affect everything from agriculture to criminal law to medical research. We will end by considering some of the important social and ethical issues that arise as biotechnology becomes more pervasive in our lives.

CONCEPT 20.1

DNA sequencing and DNA cloning are valuable tools for genetic engineering and biological inquiry

The discovery of the structure of the DNA molecule, with its two complementary strands, opened the door for the development of DNA sequencing and many other techniques used in biological research today. Key to many of these techniques is **nucleic acid hybridization**, the base pairing of one strand of a nucleic acid to the complementary sequence on a strand from *another* nucleic acid molecule. In this section, we'll first describe DNA sequencing techniques. Then we'll explore other important methods used in **genetic engineering**, the direct manipulation of genes for practical purposes.

DNA Sequencing

Researchers can exploit the principle of complementary base pairing to determine the complete nucleotide sequence of a DNA molecule, a process called **DNA sequencing**. The DNA is first cut into fragments, and then each fragment is sequenced. Today, sequencing is carried out by machines **(Figure 20.2)**. The first automated procedure used a technique called *dideoxyribonucleotide* (or *dideoxy*) *chain termination sequencing*. In this technique, one strand of a DNA fragment is used as a template for synthesis of a nested set of complementary fragments; these are further analyzed to yield the sequence, as shown in detail in **Figure 20.3**. Biochemist Frederick Sanger received the Nobel Prize in 1980 for developing this method. Dideoxy sequencing is still widely used today for routine small-scale sequencing jobs, in machines like that shown in Figure 20.2a.

In the last ten years, "next-generation sequencing" techniques have been developed that do not rely on chain termination. Instead, DNA fragments are amplified (copied) to yield an enormous number of identical fragments **(Figure 20.4)**. A specific strand of each fragment is immobilized, and the complementary strand is synthesized, one nucleotide at a time. A chemical technique enables electronic monitors to identify in real time which of the four nucleotides is added; this method is thus called *sequencing by synthesis*. Thousands or hundreds of thousands of fragments, each about 400–1,000 nucleotides long, are sequenced in parallel in machines like those shown in Figure 20.2b, accounting for the high rate of nucleotides

(a) Standard sequencing machine

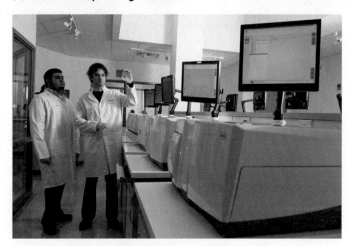

(b) Next-generation sequencing machines

▲ **Figure 20.2 DNA sequencing machines. (a)** This standard sequencing machine uses the dideoxy chain termination sequencing method (see Figure 20.3). It can sequence up to about 120,000 nucleotides in 10 hours and is used for sequencing small numbers of samples with shorter sequences. **(b)** Next-generation sequencing machines use "sequencing by synthesis" (see Figure 20.4). Today's machines can sequence 700–900 *million* nucleotides in 10 hours and are used for larger sequencing jobs.

sequenced per hour. This is an example of "high-throughput" DNA technology, and is currently the method of choice for studies where massive numbers of DNA samples—even representing an entire genome—are being sequenced.

Further technical developments have given rise to "third-generation sequencing," with each new technique being faster and less expensive than the previous. In these new methods, the DNA is neither cut into fragments nor amplified. Instead, a single, very long DNA molecule is sequenced on its own. Several groups have been working on the idea of moving a single strand of a DNA molecule through a very small pore (a *nanopore*) in a membrane, detecting the bases one by one by their interruption of an electrical current. One model of this concept is shown in Figure 20.1, in which the pore is a protein channel embedded in a lipid membrane. (Other researchers are using artificial membranes and nanopores.) The idea is that each type of base would interrupt the current for a slightly different length of time. This example is only one of many different approaches to further increase the rate and cut the cost of sequencing.

Research Method

Dideoxy Chain Termination Method for Sequencing DNA

Application The sequence of nucleotides in any DNA fragment of up to 800–1,000 base pairs in length can be determined rapidly with machines that carry out sequencing reactions and separate the labeled reaction products by length.

Technique This method is based on synthesis of a nested set of DNA strands complementary to one strand of a DNA fragment. Each new strand starts with the same primer and ends with a dideoxyribonucleotide (ddNTP), a modified deoxyribonucleotide (dNTP). Incorporation of a ddNTP terminates a growing DNA strand because it lacks a 3′ —OH group, the site for attachment of the next nucleotide (see Figure 16.14). In the set of new strands, each nucleotide position along the original sequence is represented by strands ending at that point with the complementary ddNTP. Because each type of ddNTP is tagged with a distinct fluorescent label, the identity of the ending nucleotides of the new strands, and ultimately the entire original sequence, can be determined.

1 The fragment of DNA to be sequenced is denatured into single strands and incubated in a test tube with the necessary ingredients for DNA synthesis: a primer designed to base-pair with the known 3′ end of the template strand, DNA polymerase, the four dNTPs, and the four ddNTPs, each tagged with a specific fluorescent molecule.

2 Synthesis of each new strand starts at the 3′ end of the primer and continues until a ddNTP happens to be inserted instead of the equivalent dNTP. The incorporated ddNTP prevents further elongation of the strand. Eventually, a set of labeled strands of every possible length is generated, with the color of the tag representing the last nucleotide in the sequence.

3 The labeled strands in the mixture are separated by passage through a gel that allows shorter strands to move through more quickly than longer ones. For DNA sequencing, the gel is in a capillary tube, and its small diameter allows a fluorescence detector to sense the color of each fluorescent tag as the strands come through. Strands differing in length by as little as one nucleotide can be distinguished from each other.

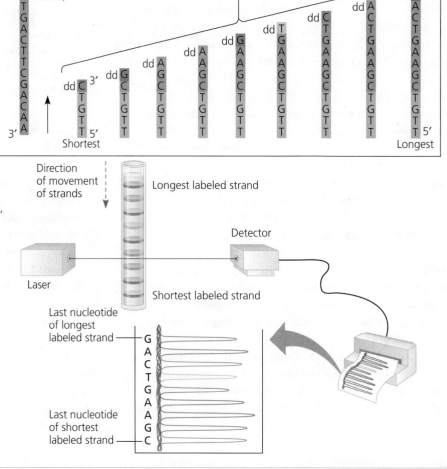

Results The color of the fluorescent tag on each strand indicates the identity of the nucleotide at its 3′-end. The results can be printed out as a spectrogram, and the sequence, which is complementary to the template strand, can then be read from bottom (shortest strand) to top (longest strand). (Notice that the sequence here begins after the primer.)

Research Method

Next-Generation Sequencing

Application In current next-generation sequencing techniques, each fragment is 400–1,000 nucleotides long; by sequencing the fragments in parallel, 700–900 million nucleotides can be sequenced in 10 hours.

Technique See numbered steps and diagrams.

Results Each of the 2,000,000 wells in the multiwell plate, which holds a different fragment, yields a different sequence. The results for one fragment are shown below as a "flow-gram." The sequences of the entire set of fragments are analyzed using computer software, which "stitches" them together into a whole sequence—here, an entire genome.

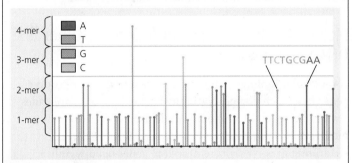

INTERPRET THE DATA *If the template strand has two or more identical nucleotides in a row, their complementary nucleotides will be added one after the other in the same flow step. How are two or more of the same nucleotide (in a row) detected in the flow-gram? (See sample on the right.) Write out the sequence of the first 25 nucleotides in the flow-gram above, starting from the left. (Ignore the very short lines.)*

1 Genomic DNA is fragmented, and fragments of 400 to 1,000 base pairs are selected.

2 Each fragment is isolated with a bead in a droplet of aqueous solution.

3 The fragment is copied over and over by a technique called PCR (to be described later). All the 5′ ends of one strand are specifically "captured" by the bead. Eventually, 10^6 identical copies of the same single strand, which will be used as a template strand, are attached to the bead.

4 The bead is placed into a small well along with DNA polymerases and primers that can hybridize to the 3′ end of the single (template) strand.

5 The well is one of 2 million on a multiwell plate, each containing a different DNA fragment to be sequenced. A solution of one of the four nucleotides is added to all wells and then washed off. This is done sequentially for all four nucleotides: dATP, dTTP, dGTP, and then dCTP. The entire process is then repeated.

6 In each well, if the next base on the template strand (T in this example) is complementary to the added nucleotide (A, here), the nucleotide is joined to the growing strand, releasing PP$_i$, which causes a flash of light that is recorded.

7 The nucleotide is washed off and a different nucleotide (dTTP, here) is added. If the nucleotide is not complementary to the next template base (G, here), it is not joined to the strand and there is no flash.

8 The process of adding and washing off the four nucleotides is repeated until every fragment has a complete complementary strand. The pattern of flashes reveals the sequence of the original fragment in each well.

Improved DNA sequencing techniques have transformed the way in which we can explore fundamental biological questions about evolution and how life works. Little more than a decade after the human genome sequence was announced, researchers had completed sequencing roughly 4,000 bacterial, 190 archaeal, and 180 eukaryotic genomes, with more than 17,000 additional species under way. Complete genome sequences have been determined for cells from several cancers, for ancient humans, and for the many bacteria that live in the human intestine. In Chapter 21, you'll learn more about how this new sequencing technology has informed us about the evolution of species and the evolution of the genome itself. Now, let's consider how individual genes are studied.

Making Multiple Copies of a Gene or Other DNA Segment

A molecular biologist studying a particular gene or group of genes faces a challenge. Naturally occurring DNA molecules are very long, and a single molecule usually carries many hundreds or even thousands of genes. Moreover, in many eukaryotic genomes, protein-coding genes occupy only a small proportion of the chromosomal DNA, the rest being noncoding nucleotide sequences. A single human gene, for example, might constitute only 1/100,000 of a chromosomal DNA molecule. As a further complication, the distinctions between a gene and the surrounding DNA are subtle, consisting only of differences in nucleotide sequence. To work directly with specific genes, scientists have developed methods for preparing well-defined segments of DNA in multiple identical copies, a process called **DNA cloning**.

Most methods for cloning pieces of DNA in the laboratory share certain general features. One common approach uses bacteria, most often *Escherichia coli*. Recall from Figure 16.12 that the *E. coli* chromosome is a large circular molecule of DNA. In addition to their bacterial chromosome, *E. coli* and many other bacteria also have **plasmids**, small, circular DNA molecules that are replicated separately. A plasmid has only a small number of genes; these genes may be useful when the bacterium is in a particular environment but may not be required for survival or reproduction under most conditions

To clone pieces of DNA using bacteria, researchers first obtain a plasmid (originally isolated from a bacterial cell and genetically engineered for efficient cloning) and insert DNA from another source ("foreign" DNA) into it **(Figure 20.5)**. The resulting plasmid is now a **recombinant DNA** molecule, a molecule containing DNA from two different sources, very often different species. The plasmid is then returned to a bacterial cell, producing a *recombinant bacterium*. This single cell reproduces through repeated cell divisions to form a clone of cells, a population of genetically identical cells. Because the dividing bacteria replicate the recombinant plasmid and pass it on to their descendants, the

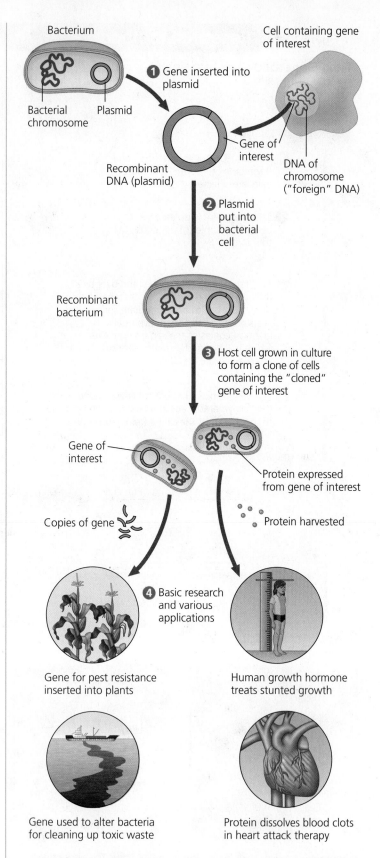

▲ **Figure 20.5 Gene cloning and some uses of cloned genes.** In this simplified diagram of gene cloning, we start with a plasmid (originally isolated from a bacterial cell) and a gene of interest from another organism. Only one plasmid and one copy of the gene of interest are shown at the top of the figure, but the starting materials would include many of each.

foreign DNA and any genes it carries are cloned at the same time. The production of multiple copies of a single gene is a type of DNA cloning called **gene cloning**.

In our example in Figure 20.5, the plasmid acts as a **cloning vector**, a DNA molecule that can carry foreign DNA into a host cell and replicate there. Bacterial plasmids are widely used as cloning vectors for several reasons: They can be readily obtained from commercial suppliers, manipulated to form recombinant plasmids by insertion of foreign DNA in a test tube (*in vitro*, from the Latin meaning "in glass"), and then easily introduced into bacterial cells. Moreover, recombinant bacterial plasmids (and the foreign DNA they carry) multiply rapidly owing to the high reproductive rate of their host (bacterial) cells. The foreign DNA in Figure 20.5 is a gene from a eukaryotic cell; we will describe in more detail how the foreign DNA segment was obtained later in this section.

Gene cloning is useful for two basic purposes: to make many copies of, or *amplify*, a particular gene and to produce a protein product (see Figure 20.5). Researchers can isolate copies of a cloned gene from bacteria for use in basic research or to endow another organism with a new metabolic capability, such as pest resistance. For example, a resistance gene present in one crop species might be cloned and transferred into plants of another species. Alternatively, a protein with medical uses, such as human growth hormone, can be harvested in large quantities from cultures of bacteria carrying a cloned gene for the protein. (We'll describe the techniques for expressing cloned genes later.) Since one gene is only a very small part of the total DNA in a cell, the ability to amplify such rare DNA fragments, by cloning or other means, is crucial for any application involving a single gene.

Using Restriction Enzymes to Make a Recombinant DNA Plasmid

Gene cloning and genetic engineering generally rely on the use of enzymes that cut DNA molecules at a limited number of specific locations. These enzymes, called restriction endonucleases, or **restriction enzymes**, were discovered in the late 1960s by biologists doing basic research on bacteria. Restriction enzymes protect the bacterial cell by cutting up foreign DNA from other organisms or phages (see Concept 19.2).

Hundreds of different restriction enzymes have been identified and isolated. Each restriction enzyme is very specific, recognizing a particular short DNA sequence, or **restriction site**, and cutting both DNA strands at precise points within this restriction site. The DNA of a bacterial cell is protected from the cell's own restriction enzymes by the addition of methyl groups (—CH$_3$) to adenines or cytosines within the sequences recognized by the enzymes.

Figure 20.6 shows how restriction enzymes are used during DNA cloning to join DNA fragments together. At the top is a bacterial plasmid (like the one in Figure 20.5) with

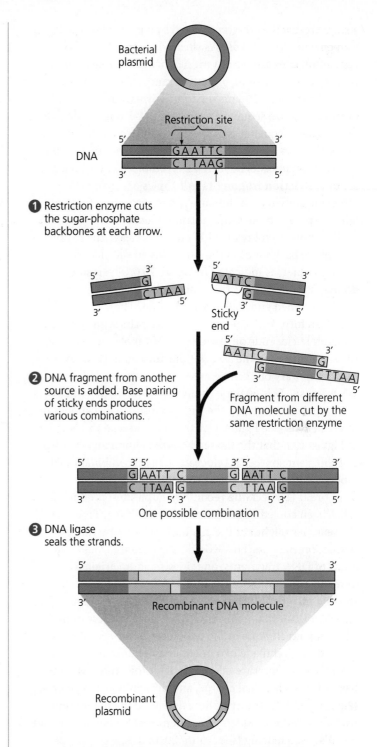

▲ **Figure 20.6 Using a restriction enzyme and DNA ligase to make a recombinant DNA plasmid.** The restriction enzyme in this example (called *Eco*RI) recognizes a specific six-base-pair sequence, the restriction site, present at one place in this plasmid. The enzyme makes staggered cuts in the sugar-phosphate backbones within this sequence, producing fragments with sticky ends. Foreign DNA fragments with complementary sticky ends can base-pair with the plasmid ends; the ligated product is a recombinant plasmid. (The two original sticky ends can also base-pair, forming a circle; ligation would result in the original non-recombinant plasmid.)

DRAW IT *The restriction enzyme* Hind*III recognizes the sequence 5'-AAGCTT-3', cutting between the two As. Draw the double-stranded sequence before and after the enzyme cuts it.*

a single restriction site recognized by a particular restriction enzyme from *E. coli*. As shown in Figure 20.6, most restriction sites are symmetrical. That is, the sequence of nucleotides is the same on both strands when read in the $5' \rightarrow 3'$ direction. The most commonly used restriction enzymes recognize sequences containing 4-8 nucleotide pairs. Because any sequence this short usually occurs (by chance) many times in a long DNA molecule, a restriction enzyme will make many cuts in such a DNA molecule, yielding a set of **restriction fragments**. All copies of a given DNA molecule always yield the same set of restriction fragments when exposed to the same restriction enzyme.

The most useful restriction enzymes cleave the sugar-phosphate backbones in the two DNA strands in a staggered manner, as indicated in Figure 20.6. The resulting double-stranded restriction fragments have at least one single-stranded end, called a **sticky end**. These short extensions can form hydrogen-bonded base pairs with complementary sticky ends on any other DNA molecules cut with the same enzyme. The associations formed in this way are only temporary but can be made permanent by the enzyme **DNA ligase**. This enzyme catalyzes the formation of covalent bonds that close up the sugar-phosphate backbones of DNA strands (see Figure 16.16). You can see at the bottom of Figure 20.6 that the ligase-catalyzed joining of DNA from two different sources produces a stable recombinant DNA molecule, in this example a recombinant plasmid.

In order to check the recombinant plasmid product after it has been copied many times in host cells (see Figure 20.5), a researcher might cut the products again using the same restriction enzyme. This would be expected to yield two kinds of DNA fragments, one the size of the original plasmid and one the size of the inserted DNA fragment, the two starting materials at the top of Figure 20.6. To separate and visualize DNA fragments of different lengths, researchers carry out a technique called **gel electrophoresis**. This technique uses a gel made of a polymer as a molecular sieve to separate out a mixture of nucleic acids (or proteins) on the basis of size, electrical charge, and other physical properties **(Figure 20.7)**. Gel electrophoresis is used in conjunction with many different techniques in molecular biology, including DNA sequencing (see Figure 20.3).

Now that we have discussed the cloning vector in some detail, let's consider the foreign DNA to be inserted. The most common way to obtain many copies of the gene to be cloned is by PCR, described next.

Amplifying DNA: The Polymerase Chain Reaction (PCR) and Its Use in DNA Cloning

Today, most researchers have some information about the sequence of the gene or other DNA segment they want to clone. Using this information, they can start with the entire

(a) Each sample, a mixture of different DNA molecules, is placed in a separate well near one end of a thin slab of agarose gel. The gel is set into a small plastic support and immersed in an aqueous, buffered solution in a tray with electrodes at each end. The current is then turned on, causing the negatively charged DNA molecules to move toward the positive electrode.

(b) Shorter molecules are slowed down less than longer ones, so they move faster through the gel. After the current is turned off, a DNA-binding dye is added that fluoresces pink in UV light. Each pink band corresponds to many thousands of DNA molecules of the same length. The horizontal ladder of bands at the bottom of the gel is a set of restriction fragments of known sizes for comparison with samples of unknown length.

▲ **Figure 20.7 Gel electrophoresis.** A gel made of a polymer acts as a molecular sieve to separate nucleic acids or proteins differing in size, electrical charge, or other physical properties as they move in an electric field. In the example shown here, DNA molecules are separated by length in a gel made of a polysaccharide called agarose.

collection of genomic DNA from the particular species of interest and obtain many copies of the desired gene by using a technique called the **polymerase chain reaction**, or **PCR**. **Figure 20.8** illustrates the steps in PCR. Within a few hours, this technique can make billions of copies of a specific target DNA segment in a sample, even if that segment makes up less than 0.001% of the total DNA in the sample.

In the PCR procedure, a three-step cycle brings about a chain reaction that produces an exponentially growing population of identical DNA molecules. During each cycle, the reaction mixture is heated to denature (separate) the strands of the double-stranded DNA and then cooled to allow annealing (hydrogen bonding) of short, single-stranded DNA primers complementary to sequences on opposite strands

The Polymerase Chain Reaction (PCR)

Application With PCR, any specific segment (the so-called target sequence) within a DNA sample can be copied many times (amplified), completely *in vitro*.

Technique PCR requires double-stranded DNA containing the target sequence, a heat-resistant DNA polymerase, all four nucleotides, and two 15- to 20-nucleotide DNA strands that serve as primers. One primer is complementary to one end of the target sequence on one strand; the second primer is complementary to the other end of the sequence on the other strand.

Genomic DNA

Target sequence

Cycle 1 yields 2 molecules

❶ Denaturation: Heat briefly to separate DNA strands.

❷ Annealing: Cool to allow primers to form hydrogen bonds with ends of target sequence.

Primers

❸ Extension: DNA polymerase adds nucleotides to the 3′ end of each primer.

New nucleotides

Cycle 2 yields 4 molecules

Cycle 3 yields 8 molecules; 2 molecules (in white boxes) match target sequence

© Pearson Education, Inc.

Results After 3 cycles, two molecules match the target sequence exactly. After 30 more cycles, over 1 billion (10^9) molecules match the target sequence.

at each end of the target sequence; finally, a heat-stable DNA polymerase extends the primers in the $5′ \rightarrow 3′$ direction. If a standard DNA polymerase were used, the protein would be denatured along with the DNA during the first heating step and would have to be replaced after each cycle. The key to automating PCR was the discovery of an unusual heat-stable DNA polymerase called Taq polymerase, named after the bacterial species from which it was first isolated. This bacterial species, *Thermus aquaticus*, lives in hot springs, and the stability of its DNA polymerase at high temperatures is an evolutionary adaptation that enables the bacterium to survive and reproduce at temperatures up to 95°C.

PCR is speedy and very specific. Only minuscule amounts of DNA need be present in the starting material, and this DNA can be partially degraded, as long as a few molecules contain the complete target sequence. The key to the high specificity is the pair of primers used for each PCR amplification. The primer sequences are chosen so they hybridize *only* to sequences at opposite ends of the target segment, one on the 3′ end of each strand. (For high specificity, the primers must be at least 15 or so nucleotides long.) By the end of the third cycle, one-fourth of the molecules are identical to the target segment, with both strands the appropriate length. With each successive cycle, the number of target segment molecules of the correct length doubles, so the number of molecules equals 2^n, where n is the number of cycles. After 30 more cycles, about a billion copies of the target sequence are present!

Despite its speed and specificity, PCR amplification cannot substitute for gene cloning in cells when large amounts of a gene are required. This is because occasional errors during PCR replication limit the number of good copies and the length of DNA fragments that can be copied. Instead, PCR is used to provide a supply of the specific DNA fragment for cloning. PCR primers are synthesized to include a restriction site at each end of the DNA fragment that matches the site in the cloning vector. Then the fragment and vector are cut, allowed to hybridize, and ligated

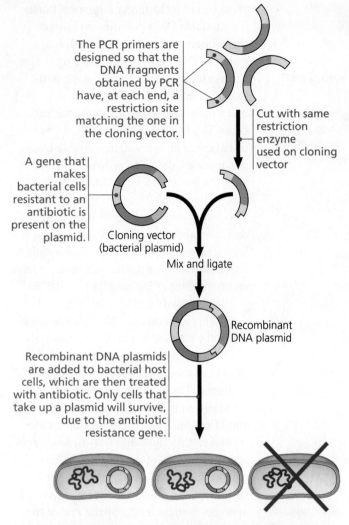

The PCR primers are designed so that the DNA fragments obtained by PCR have, at each end, a restriction site matching the one in the cloning vector.

Cut with same restriction enzyme used on cloning vector

A gene that makes bacterial cells resistant to an antibiotic is present on the plasmid.

Cloning vector (bacterial plasmid)

Mix and ligate

Recombinant DNA plasmid

Recombinant DNA plasmids are added to bacterial host cells, which are then treated with antibiotic. Only cells that take up a plasmid will survive, due to the antibiotic resistance gene.

▲ **Figure 20.9 Use of a restriction enzyme and PCR in gene cloning.** This figure takes a closer look at the process shown at the top of Figure 20.5. PCR is used to produce multiple copies of the DNA fragment or gene of interest. The ends of the fragments have the same restriction site as the cloning vector. The plasmid and the DNA fragments are cut with the same restriction enzyme, combined so the sticky ends can hybridize, ligated together, and introduced into bacterial host cells. The plasmid also contains an antibiotic resistance gene that allows only cells with a plasmid to survive when the antibiotic is present. Other genetic engineering techniques are used to ensure that cells with nonrecombinant plasmids can be eliminated.

together **(Figure 20.9)**. The plasmids from the resulting bacterial clones are sequenced so that clones carrying plasmids with error-free inserts can be selected.

Devised in 1985, PCR has had a major impact on biological research and genetic engineering. PCR has been used to amplify DNA from a wide variety of sources: a 40,000-year-old frozen woolly mammoth (see the photo on the first page of this chapter); fingerprints or tiny amounts of blood, tissue, or semen found at crime scenes; single embryonic cells for rapid prenatal diagnosis of genetic disorders (see Figure 14.19); and cells infected with viruses that are difficult to detect, such as HIV. (To test for HIV, viral genes are amplified.) We'll return to applications of PCR later.

Expressing Cloned Eukaryotic Genes

Once a gene has been cloned in host cells, its protein product can be expressed in large amounts for research or for practical applications, which we'll explore in Concept 20.4. Cloned genes can be expressed in either bacterial or eukaryotic cells; each option has advantages and disadvantages.

Bacterial Expression Systems

Getting a cloned eukaryotic gene to function in bacterial host cells can be difficult because certain aspects of gene expression are different in eukaryotes and bacteria. To overcome differences in promoters and other DNA control sequences, scientists usually employ an **expression vector**, a cloning vector that contains a highly active bacterial promoter just upstream of a restriction site where the eukaryotic gene can be inserted in the correct reading frame. The bacterial host cell will recognize the promoter and proceed to express the foreign gene now linked to that promoter. Such expression vectors allow the synthesis of many eukaryotic proteins in bacterial cells.

Another problem with expressing cloned eukaryotic genes in bacteria is the presence of noncoding regions (introns; see Concept 17.3) in most eukaryotic genes. Introns can make a eukaryotic gene very long and unwieldy, and they prevent correct expression of the gene by bacterial cells, which do not have RNA-splicing machinery. This problem can be surmounted by using a form of the gene that includes only the exons. (This is called *complementary DNA*, or *cDNA*; see Figure 20.11.)

Eukaryotic DNA Cloning and Expression Systems

Molecular biologists can avoid eukaryotic-bacterial incompatibility by using eukaryotic cells such as yeasts, rather than bacteria, as hosts for cloning and expressing eukaryotic genes of interest. Yeasts, single-celled fungi, offer two advantages: They are as easy to grow as bacteria, and they have plasmids, a rarity among eukaryotes. Scientists have even constructed recombinant plasmids that combine yeast and bacterial DNA and can replicate in either type of cell.

Another reason to use eukaryotic host cells for expressing a cloned eukaryotic gene is that many eukaryotic proteins will not function unless they are modified after translation—for example, by the addition of carbohydrate groups (glycosylation) or lipid groups. Bacterial cells cannot carry out these modifications, and if the gene product requiring such processing is from a mammal, even yeast cells may not be able to modify the protein correctly. Several cultured cell types have proved successful as host cells for this purpose, including some mammalian cell lines and an insect cell line that can be infected by a virus (called baculovirus) carrying recombinant DNA.

Besides using vectors, scientists have developed a variety of other methods for introducing recombinant DNA into eukaryotic cells. In **electroporation**, a brief electrical pulse applied to a solution containing cells creates temporary holes in their plasma membranes, through which DNA can enter. (This technique is now commonly used for bacteria as well.) Alternatively, scientists can inject DNA directly into single eukaryotic cells using microscopically thin needles. Another way to get DNA into plant cells is by using the soil bacterium *Agrobacterium tumefaciens*, as we'll discuss later. Whatever the method, if the introduced DNA is incorporated into a cell's genome by genetic recombination, then it can be expressed by the cell.

To study the function of a particular protein, researchers can introduce different mutant forms of the gene for that protein into eukaryotic cells. The cells express different versions of the protein, and the resulting phenotypes provide information about the normal protein's function. For this purpose, researchers may use a cloning vector with viral DNA sequences that allow the introduced DNA to integrate into a chromosome and be stably expressed. The same approach can be used to express noncoding RNAs in order to study their role as agents of gene regulation in the cell. (Noncoding RNAs are discussed in Concept 18.3.)

Cross-Species Gene Expression and Evolutionary Ancestry

EVOLUTION The ability to express eukaryotic proteins in bacteria (even if the proteins aren't modified properly) is quite remarkable when we consider how different eukaryotic and bacterial cells are. In fact, examples abound of genes that are taken from one species and function perfectly well when transferred into another very different species. These observations underscore the shared evolutionary ancestry of species living today.

One example involves a gene called *Pax-6*, which has been found in animals as diverse as vertebrates and fruit flies. The vertebrate *Pax-6* gene product (the PAX-6 protein) triggers a complex program of gene expression resulting in formation of the vertebrate eye, which has a single lens. Expression of the fly *Pax-6* gene leads to formation of the compound fly eye, which is quite different from the vertebrate eye. When the mouse *Pax-6* gene was cloned and introduced into a fly embryo so that it replaced the fly's own *Pax-6* gene, researchers were surprised to see that the mouse version of the gene led to formation of a compound fly eye (see Figure 50.16). Conversely, when the fly *Pax-6* gene was transferred into a vertebrate embryo—a frog, in this case—a frog eye formed. Although the genetic programs triggered in vertebrates and flies generate very different eyes, the two versions of the *Pax-6* gene can substitute for each other to trigger lens development, evidence of their evolution from a gene in a very ancient common ancestor.

Simpler examples are seen in Figure 17.6, where a firefly gene is expressed in a tobacco plant and a jellyfish gene in

a pig. Because of their ancient evolutionary roots, all living organisms share the same basic mechanisms of gene expression. This commonality is the basis of many recombinant DNA techniques described in this chapter.

CONCEPT CHECK 20.1

1. The restriction site for an enzyme called *Pvu*I is the following sequence:

    5'-C G A T C G-3'
    3'-G C T A G C-5'

    Staggered cuts are made between the T and C on each strand. What type of bonds are being cleaved?

2. **DRAW IT** One strand of a DNA molecule has the following sequence: 5'-CCTTGACGATCGTTACCG-3'. Draw the other strand. Will *Pvu*I cut this molecule? If so, draw the products.

3. What are some potential difficulties in using plasmid vectors and bacterial host cells to produce large quantities of proteins from cloned eukaryotic genes?

4. **MAKE CONNECTIONS** Compare Figure 20.8 with Figure 16.20. How does replication of DNA ends during PCR proceed without shortening the fragments each time?

For suggested answers, see Appendix A.

CONCEPT 20.2

Biologists use DNA technology to study gene expression and function

To see how a biological system works, scientists seek to understand the functioning of the system's component parts. Analysis of when and where a gene or group of genes is expressed can provide important clues about their function.

Analyzing Gene Expression

Biologists driven to understand the assorted cell types of a multicellular organism, cancer cells, or the developing tissues of an embryo first try to discover which genes are expressed by the cells of interest. The most straightforward way to do this is usually to identify the mRNAs being made. We'll first examine techniques that look for patterns of expression of specific individual genes. Next, we'll explore ways to characterize groups of genes being expressed by cells or tissues of interest. As you will see, all of these procedures depend in some way on base pairing between complementary nucleotide sequences.

Studying the Expression of Single Genes

Suppose we have cloned a gene that we suspect plays an important role in the embryonic development of *Drosophila melanogaster* (the fruit fly). The first thing we might want to know is which embryonic cells express the gene—in other words, where in the embryo is the corresponding mRNA found? We can detect the mRNA by nucleic acid hybridization with molecules of complementary sequence that we can follow in some way. The complementary molecule, a short, single-stranded nucleic acid that can be either RNA or DNA, is called a **nucleic acid probe**. Using our cloned gene as a template, we can synthesize a probe complementary to the mRNA. For example, if part of the sequence on the mRNA were

$5'$ ···CUCAUCACCGGC··· $3'$

then we would synthesize this single-stranded DNA probe:

$3'$ GAGTAGTGGCCG $5'$

Each probe molecule is labeled during synthesis with a fluorescent tag so we can follow it. A solution containing probe molecules is applied to *Drosophila* embryos, allowing the probe to hybridize specifically with any complementary sequences on the many mRNAs in embryonic cells that are transcribing the gene. Because this technique allows us to see the mRNA in place (or *in situ*, in Latin) in the intact organism, this technique is called *in situ* **hybridization**. Different probes can be labeled with different fluorescent dyes, sometimes with strikingly beautiful results **(Figure 20.10)**.

Other mRNA detection techniques may be preferable for comparing the amounts of a specific mRNA in several samples at the same time—for example, in different cell types or in embryos at different stages of development. One method that is widely used is called the **reverse transcriptase-polymerase chain reaction**, or **RT-PCR**.

RT-PCR begins by turning sample sets of mRNAs into double-stranded DNAs with the corresponding sequences. First, the enzyme reverse transcriptase (from a retrovirus; see Figure 19.8) is used *in vitro* to make a single-stranded DNA *reverse transcript* of each mRNA molecule **(Figure 20.11)**. Recall that the 3′ end of the mRNA has a stretch of adenine (A) nucleotides called a poly-A tail. This allows use of a short complementary strand of thymine deoxyribonucleotides (poly-dT) as a primer for synthesis of this DNA strand. Following enzymatic degradation of the mRNA, a second DNA strand, complementary to the first, is synthesized by DNA polymerase. The resulting double-stranded DNA is called **complementary DNA (cDNA)**. (Made from mRNA, cDNA lacks introns and can be used for protein expression in bacteria, as mentioned earlier.) To analyze the timing of expression of the *Drosophila* gene of interest, for example, we would first isolate all the mRNAs from different stages of *Drosophila* embryos and make cDNA from each stage **(Figure 20.12)**. Then we'd use PCR to find any cDNA derived from the gene of interest.

As you will recall from Figure 20.8, PCR is a way of rapidly making many copies of one specific stretch of double-stranded DNA, using primers that hybridize to the opposite ends of the segment of interest. In our case, we would add primers corresponding to a segment of our *Drosophila* gene,

The yellow probe hybridizes with mRNAs in cells that are expressing the *wingless* (*wg*) gene, which encodes a secreted signaling protein.

The blue probe hybridizes with mRNAs in cells that are expressing the *engrailed* (*en*) gene, which encodes a transcription factor.

▲ **Figure 20.10 Determining where genes are expressed by** *in situ* **hybridization analysis.** A *Drosophila* embryo was incubated in a solution containing probes for five different mRNAs, each probe labeled with a different fluorescently colored tag. The embryo was then viewed from the belly (ventral) side using fluorescence microscopy; the resulting fluorescent micrograph is shown in the middle, above. Each color marks where a specific gene is expressed as mRNA. The arrows from the groups of yellow and blue cells above the micrograph show a magnified view of nucleic acid hybridization of the appropriately colored probe to the mRNA. Yellow cells (expressing the *wg* gene) interact with blue cells (expressing the *en* gene); their interaction helps establish the pattern in a body segment. The diagram at the bottom clarifies the eight segments visible in this view.

using the cDNA from each embryonic stage as a template for PCR amplification in separate samples. When the products are analyzed on a gel, only samples that originally contained mRNA from the gene of interest will show bands containing copies of the amplified region. A recent enhancement involves using a fluorescent dye that fluoresces only when bound to a double-stranded PCR product. The newer PCR machines can detect the light and measure the PCR product, thus avoiding the need for electrophoresis while also

① Reverse transcriptase is added to a test tube containing mRNA isolated from a sample of cells.

② Reverse transcriptase makes the first DNA strand using the mRNA as a template and a short poly-dT as a DNA primer.

③ mRNA is degraded by another enzyme.

④ DNA polymerase synthesizes the second DNA strand, using a primer in the reaction mixture. (Several options exist for primers.)

⑤ The result is cDNA, which carries the complete coding sequence of the gene but no introns.

DNA in nucleus

mRNAs in cytoplasm

Reverse transcriptase

mRNA

Poly-A tail

A A A A A A 3'
T T T T 5'

DNA strand

Primer (poly-dT)

5' ▢▢▢▢▢▢▢ A A A A A A 3'
3' ━━━━━━━ T T T T T 5'

DNA polymerase

5'
3'   3'
                  5'

5' ━━━━━━━━━━━ 3'
3' ━━━━━━━━━━━ 5'

cDNA

▲ **Figure 20.11 Making complementary DNA (cDNA) from eukaryotic genes.** Complementary DNA is made *in vitro* using mRNA as a template for the first strand. The mRNA contains only exons, so the resulting double-stranded cDNA carries the continuous coding sequence of the gene. Only one mRNA is shown here, but the final collection of cDNAs would reflect all the mRNAs present in the cell sample. Figure 20.12 shows how the cDNA of interest is identified.

providing quantitative data, a distinct advantage. RT-PCR can also be carried out with mRNAs collected from different tissues at one time to discover which tissue is producing a specific mRNA.

In the Scientific Skills Exercise, you can work with data from an experiment that analyzed expression of a gene involved in paw formation in the mouse. The study investigated mRNA expression using two techniques. One of these methods was qualitative (*in situ* hybridization), whereas the other approach was quantitative (PCR).

Studying the Expression of Interacting Groups of Genes

A major goal of biologists is to learn how genes act together to produce and maintain a functioning organism. Now that the genomes of a number of species have been sequenced, it is possible to study the expression of large groups of genes—the so-called *systems approach*. Researchers use what is known about the whole genome to investigate which genes are transcribed in different tissues or at different stages of development. One aim is to identify networks of gene expression across an entire genome.

▼ **Figure 20.12** | Research Method

RT-PCR Analysis of the Expression of Single Genes

Application RT-PCR uses the enzyme reverse transcriptase (RT) in combination with PCR and gel electrophoresis. RT-PCR can be used to compare gene expression between samples—for instance, in different embryonic stages, in different tissues, or in the same type of cell under different conditions.

Technique In this example, samples containing mRNAs from six embryonic stages of *Drosophila* were analyzed for a specific mRNA as shown below. (In steps 1 and 2, the mRNA from only one stage is shown.)

① **cDNA synthesis** is carried out by incubating the mRNAs with reverse transcriptase and other necessary components.

② **PCR amplification** of the sample is performed using primers specific to the *Drosophila* gene of interest.

③ **Gel electrophoresis** will reveal amplified DNA products only in samples that contained mRNA transcribed from the specific *Drosophila* gene.

mRNAs

cDNAs

Primers

Specific gene

Embryonic stages
1 2 3 4 5 6

Results The mRNA for this gene first is expressed at stage 2 and continues to be expressed through stage 6. The size of the amplified fragment (shown by its position on the gel) depends on the distance between the primers that were used (not on the size of the mRNA).

Genome-wide expression studies can be carried out using **DNA microarray assays**. A DNA microarray consists of tiny amounts of a large number of single-stranded DNA fragments representing different genes fixed to a glass slide in a tightly spaced array, or grid. (The microarray is also called a *DNA chip* by analogy to a computer chip.) Ideally, these fragments represent all the genes of an organism.

The basic strategy in such studies is to isolate the mRNAs made in a cell of interest and use these molecules as templates for making the corresponding cDNAs by reverse transcription. In microarray assays, these cDNAs are labeled with fluorescent molecules and then allowed to hybridize to a DNA microarray. Most often, the cDNAs from two

Analyzing Quantitative and Spatial Gene Expression Data

How Is a Particular *Hox* Gene Regulated During Paw Development? *Hox* genes code for transcription factor proteins, which in turn control sets of genes important for animal development (see Concept 21.6 for more information on *Hox* genes). One group of *Hox* genes, the *Hoxd* genes, plays a role in establishing the pattern of the different digits (fingers and toes) at the end of a limb. Unlike the *mPGES-1* gene mentioned in the Chapter 18 Scientific Skills Exercise, *Hox* genes have very large, complicated regulatory regions, including control elements that may be hundreds of kilobases (kb; thousands of nucleotides) away from the gene.

In cases like this, how do biologists locate the DNA segments that contain important elements? They begin by removing (deleting) large segments of DNA and studying the effect on gene expression. In this exercise, you'll compare data from two different but complementary approaches that look at the expression of a specific *Hoxd* gene (*Hoxd13*). One approach quantifies overall expression; the other approach is less quantitative but gives important spatial localization information.

How the Experiment Was Done Researchers interested in the regulation of *Hoxd13* gene expression genetically engineered a set of mice (*transgenic* mice) that had different segments of DNA deleted upstream of the gene. They then compared levels and patterns of *Hoxd13* gene expression in the developing paws of 12.5-day-old transgenic mouse embryos (with the DNA deletions) with those seen in wild-type mouse embryos of the same age.

They used two different approaches: In some mice, they extracted the mRNA from the embryonic paws and quantified the overall level of *Hoxd13* mRNA in the whole paw using quantitative RT-PCR. In another set of the same transgenic mice, they used *in situ* hybridization to pinpoint exactly where in the paws the *Hoxd13* gene was expressed as mRNA. The particular technique that was used causes the *Hoxd13* mRNA to appear blue, or black for the highest mRNA levels.

Data from the Experiment The top-most diagram (upper right) depicts the very large regulatory region upstream of the *Hoxd13* gene. The area between the slashes represents the long stretch of DNA located between the promoter and the regulatory region.

The diagrams to the left of the bar graph show, first, the intact DNA (830 kb) and, next, the three altered DNA sequences. (Each is called a "deletion" because a particular section of DNA has been deleted from it.) A red X indicates the segment (A, B, and/or C) that was deleted in each experimental treatment.

The horizontal bar graph shows the amount of *Hoxd13* mRNA that was present in the digit-formation zone of each mutant 12.5-day-old embryo paw relative to the amount that was in the digit-formation zone of the mouse that had the intact regulatory region (top bar = 100%).

The images on the right are fluorescent micrographs of the embryo paws showing the location of the *Hoxd13* mRNA (stain appears blue or black). The white triangles show the location where the thumb will form.

Interpret the Data

1. The researchers hypothesized that all three regulatory segments (A, B, and C) were required for full expression of the *Hoxd13* gene. By measuring the amount of *Hoxd13* mRNA in the embryo paw zones where digits develop, they could measure the effect of the

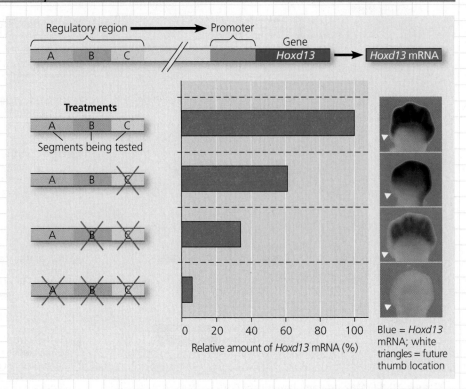

Blue = *Hoxd13* mRNA; white triangles = future thumb location

regulatory segments singly and in combination. Refer to the graph to answer these questions, noting that the segments being tested are shown on the vertical axis and the relative amount of *Hoxd13* mRNA is shown on the horizontal axis. (a) Which of the four treatments was used as a control for the experiment? (b) The hypothesis is that all three segments together are required for highest expression of the *Hoxd13* gene. Is this supported by the results? Explain your answer.

2. (a) What is the effect on the amount of *Hoxd13* mRNA when segments B and C are both deleted, compared with the control? (b) Is this effect visible in the blue-stained regions of the *in situ* hybridizations? How would you describe the spatial pattern of gene expression in the embryo paws that lack segments B and C? (You'll need to look carefully at different regions of each paw and how they differ.)

3. (a) What is the effect on the amount of *Hoxd13* mRNA when just segment C is deleted, compared with the control? (b) Is this effect visible in the *in situ* hybridizations? How would you describe the spatial pattern of gene expression in embryo paws that lack just segment C, compared with the control and with the paws that lack segments B and C?

4. If the researchers had only measured the amount of *Hoxd13* mRNA and not done the *in situ* hybridizations, what important information about the role of the regulatory segments in *Hoxd13* gene expression during paw development would have been missed? Conversely, if the researchers had only done the *in situ* hybridizations, what information would have been inaccessible?

(MB) A version of this Scientific Skills Exercise can be assigned in MasteringBiology.

Data from T. Montavon et al., A regulatory archipelago controls *Hox* genes transcription in digits, *Cell* 147:1132–1145 (2011).

Each dot is a well containing identical copies of DNA fragments that carry a specific gene.

The genes in the red wells are expressed in one tissue and bind the red cDNAs.

The genes in the green wells are expressed in the other tissue and bind the green cDNAs.

The genes in the yellow wells are expressed in both tissues and bind both red and green cDNAs, appearing yellow.

The genes in the black wells are not expressed in either tissue and do not bind either cDNA.

◄ DNA microarray (actual size)

▲ **Figure 20.13 DNA microarray assay of gene expression levels.** Researchers synthesized two sets of cDNAs, fluorescently labeled red or green, from mRNAs from two different human tissues. These cDNAs were hybridized with a microarray containing 5,760 human genes (about 25% of human genes), resulting in the pattern shown here. The intensity of fluorescence at each spot is a measure of the relative expression in the two samples of the gene represented by that spot: Red indicates expression in one sample, green in the other, yellow in both, and black in neither.

samples (for example, different tissues) are labeled with molecules that emit different colors and tested on the same microarray. **Figure 20.13** shows the result of such an experiment, identifying the subsets of genes in the genome that are being expressed in one tissue compared with another. DNA technology makes such studies possible; with automation, they are easily performed on a large scale. Scientists can now measure the expression of thousands of genes at one time.

Alternatively, with the advent of rapid, inexpensive DNA sequencing methods, researchers can now afford to simply sequence the cDNA samples from different tissues or different embryonic stages in order to discover which genes are expressed. This straightforward method is called *RNA sequencing* or *RNA-seq* (pronounced "RNA-seek"), even though it is the cDNA that is actually sequenced. As the price of DNA sequencing plummets, this method is becoming more widely used for many applications. In most cases, however, expression of individual genes would still need to be confirmed by RT-PCR.

By uncovering gene interactions and providing clues to gene function, DNA microarray assays and RNA-seq may contribute to a better understanding of diseases and suggest new diagnostic techniques or therapies. For instance, comparing patterns of gene expression in breast cancer tumors and noncancerous breast tissue has already resulted in more informed and effective treatment protocols (see Figure 18.27). Ultimately, information from these methods should provide a grander view of how ensembles of genes interact to form an organism and maintain its vital systems.

Determining Gene Function

Once they identify a gene of interest, how do scientists determine its function? A gene's sequence can be compared with sequences in other species. If the function of a similar gene in another species is known, one might suspect that the gene product in question performs a comparable task. Data about the location and timing of gene expression may reinforce the suggested function. To obtain stronger evidence, one approach is to disable the gene and then observe the consequences in the cell or organism. In one such technique, called *in vitro* **mutagenesis**, specific mutations are introduced into a cloned gene, and the mutated gene is returned to a cell in such a way that it disables ("knocks out") the normal cellular copies of the same gene. If the introduced mutations alter or destroy the function of the gene product, the phenotype of the mutant cell may help reveal the function of the missing normal protein. Using molecular and genetic techniques worked out in the 1980s, researchers can generate mice with any given gene disabled, in order to study the role of that gene in development and in the adult. Mario Capecchi, Martin Evans, and Oliver Smithies received the Nobel Prize in 2007 for developing this technique.

A newer method for silencing expression of selected genes exploits the phenomenon of **RNA interference (RNAi)**, described in Chapter 18. This experimental approach uses synthetic double-stranded RNA molecules matching the sequence of a particular gene to trigger breakdown of the gene's messenger RNA or to block its translation. In organisms such as the nematode and the fruit fly, RNAi has already proved valuable for analyzing the functions of genes on a large scale.

In humans, ethical considerations prohibit knocking out genes to determine their functions. An alternative approach is to analyze the genomes of large numbers of people with a certain phenotypic condition or disease, such as heart disease or diabetes, to try to find differences they all share compared with people without that condition. The assumption is that these differences may be associated with one or more malfunctioning genes, thus in a sense being naturally occurring gene knockouts. Such large-scale analyses, called **genome-wide association studies**, do not require complete sequencing of all the genomes in the two groups. Instead, researchers test for *genetic markers*, DNA sequences that vary in the population. In a gene, such sequence variation is the basis of different alleles, as we have seen for sickle-cell disease (see Figure 17.25). And just like the coding sequences of genes, noncoding DNA at a specific locus on a chromosome may exhibit small nucleotide differences among individuals. Variations in coding or noncoding DNA sequence among a population are called polymorphisms (from the Greek for "many forms").

Among the most useful genetic markers in tracking down genes that contribute to diseases and disorders are single base-pair variations in the genomes of the human population. A single base-pair site where variation is found in at least 1% of the population is called a **single nucleotide polymorphism** (**SNP**, pronounced "snip"). A few million SNPs occur in the human genome, about once in 100–300 base pairs of both coding and noncoding DNA sequences. It isn't necessary to sequence the DNA of multiple individuals to find SNPs; today they can be detected by very sensitive microarray analysis or by PCR.

Once a SNP is identified that is found in all affected people, researchers focus on that region and sequence it. In nearly all cases, the SNP itself does not contribute directly to the disease in question by altering the encoded protein; in fact, most SNPs are in noncoding regions. Instead, if the SNP and a disease-causing allele are close enough, scientists can take advantage of the fact that crossing over between the marker and the gene is very unlikely during gamete formation. Therefore, the marker and gene will almost always be inherited together, even though the marker is not part of the gene **(Figure 20.14)**. SNPs have been found that correlate with diabetes, heart disease, and several types of cancer, and the search is on for genes that might be involved.

The experimental approaches you have learned about thus far focused on working with molecules, mainly DNA and proteins. In a parallel line of inquiry, biologists have

DNA

SNP

Normal allele

Disease-causing allele

▲ **Figure 20.14 Single nucleotide polymorphisms (SNPs) as genetic markers for disease-causing alleles.** This diagram depicts homologous segments of DNA from two groups of individuals, those in one group having a particular disease or condition with a genetic basis. Unaffected people have an A/T pair at a particular SNP locus, while affected people have a C/G pair at that locus. A SNP that varies in this way is likely to be closely linked to one or more alleles of genes that contribute to the disease in question.

MAKE CONNECTIONS *What does it mean for a SNP to be "closely linked" to a disease-causing allele, and how does this allow the SNP to be used as a genetic marker? (See Concept 15.3.)*

been developing powerful techniques for cloning whole multicellular organisms. One aim of this work is to obtain special types of cells, called stem cells, that can give rise to all types of tissues. Being able to manipulate stem cells would allow scientists to use the DNA-based methods previously discussed to alter stem cells for the treatment of diseases. Methods involving the cloning of organisms and production of stem cells are the subject of the next section.

CONCEPT CHECK 20.2

1. Describe the role of complementary base pairing during RT-PCR and DNA microarray analysis.

2. **WHAT IF?** Consider the microarray in Figure 20.13. If a sample from normal tissue is labeled with a green fluorescent dye, and a sample from cancerous tissue is labeled red, what color spots would represent genes you would be interested in if you were studying cancer? Explain.

For suggested answers, see Appendix A.

CONCEPT 20.3

Cloned organisms and stem cells are useful for basic research and other applications

Along with advances in DNA technology, scientists have been developing and refining methods for cloning whole multicellular organisms from single cells. In this context, cloning produces one or more organisms that are genetically identical to the "parent" that donated the single cell. This is often called *organismal cloning* to differentiate it from gene cloning and, more significantly, from cell cloning—the division of an asexually reproducing cell into a group of genetically identical cells. (The common theme is that the product is genetically identical to the parent. In fact, the word *clone* comes from the Greek *klon*, meaning "twig.") The current interest in organismal cloning arises primarily from its ability to generate stem cells. A **stem cell** is a relatively unspecialized cell that can both reproduce itself indefinitely and, under appropriate conditions, differentiate into specialized cells of one or more types. Stem cells have great potential for regenerating damaged tissues.

The cloning of plants and animals was first attempted over 50 years ago in experiments designed to answer basic biological questions. For example, researchers wondered if all the cells of an organism have the same genes or whether cells lose genes during the process of differentiation (see Concept 18.4). One way to answer this question is to see whether a differentiated cell can generate a whole organism—in other words, whether cloning an organism is possible. Let's discuss these early experiments before we consider more recent progress in organismal cloning and procedures for producing stem cells.

▲ Figure 20.15 The cloning of a whole carrot plant from a single carrot cell.

Cross section of carrot root

Small fragments

Fragments were cultured in nutrient medium; stirring caused single cells to shear off into the liquid.

Single cells free in suspension began to divide.

Embryonic plant developed from a cultured single cell.

Plantlet was cultured on agar medium. Later it was planted in soil.

Adult plant

Cloning Plants: Single-Cell Cultures

The successful cloning of whole plants from single differentiated cells was accomplished during the 1950s by F. C. Steward and his students at Cornell University, who worked with carrot plants (**Figure 20.15**). They found that differentiated cells taken from the root (the carrot) and incubated in culture medium could grow into normal adult plants, each genetically identical to the parent plant. These results showed that differentiation does not necessarily involve irreversible changes in the DNA. In plants, at least, mature cells can "dedifferentiate" and then give rise to all the specialized cell types of the organism. Any cell with this potential is said to be **totipotent**.

Plant cloning is used extensively in agriculture. For plants such as orchids, cloning is the only commercially practical means of reproducing plants. In other cases, cloning has been used to reproduce a plant with valuable characteristics, such as resistance to plant pathogens. In fact, you yourself may be a plant cloner: If you have ever grown a new plant from a cutting, you have practiced cloning!

Cloning Animals: Nuclear Transplantation

Differentiated cells from animals generally do not divide in culture, much less develop into the multiple cell types of a new organism. Therefore, early researchers had to use a different approach to answer the question: Are differentiated animal cells totipotent? Their approach was to remove the nucleus of an unfertilized or fertilized egg and replace it

with the nucleus of a differentiated cell, a procedure called *nuclear transplantation*. If the nucleus from the differentiated donor cell retains its full genetic capability, then it should be able to direct development of the recipient cell into all the tissues and organs of an organism.

Such experiments were conducted on one species of frog (*Rana pipiens*) by Robert Briggs and Thomas King in the 1950s and on another (*Xenopus laevis*) by John Gurdon in the 1970s (**Figure 20.16**). These researchers transplanted a

▼ Figure 20.16 **Inquiry**

Can the nucleus from a differentiated animal cell direct development of an organism?

Experiment John Gurdon and colleagues at Oxford University, in England, destroyed the nuclei of frog (*Xenopus laevis*) eggs by exposing the eggs to ultraviolet light. They then transplanted nuclei from cells of frog embryos and tadpoles into the enucleated eggs.

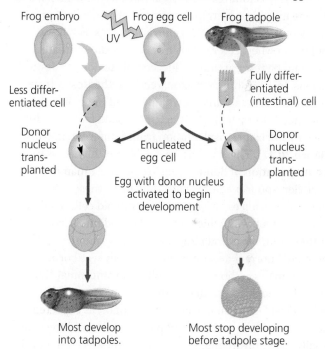

Frog embryo

Frog egg cell

Frog tadpole

UV

Less differentiated cell

Fully differentiated (intestinal) cell

Donor nucleus transplanted

Enucleated egg cell

Donor nucleus transplanted

Egg with donor nucleus activated to begin development

Most develop into tadpoles.

Most stop developing before tadpole stage.

Results When the transplanted nuclei came from an early embryo, the cells of which are relatively undifferentiated, most of the recipient eggs developed into tadpoles. But when the nuclei came from the fully differentiated intestinal cells of a tadpole, fewer than 2% of the eggs developed into normal tadpoles, and most of the embryos stopped developing at a much earlier stage.

Conclusion The nucleus from a differentiated frog cell can direct development of a tadpole. However, its ability to do so decreases as the donor cell becomes more differentiated, presumably because of changes in the nucleus.

Source: J. B. Gurdon et al., The developmental capacity of nuclei transplanted from keratinized cells of adult frogs, *Journal of Embryology and Experimental Morphology* 34:93–112 (1975).

WHAT IF? *If each cell in a four-cell embryo was already so specialized that it was not totipotent, what results would you predict for the experiment on the left side of the figure?*

nucleus from an embryonic or tadpole cell into an enucle-ated (nucleus-lacking) egg of the same species. In Gurdon's experiments, the transplanted nucleus was often able to support normal development of the egg into a tadpole. However, he found that the potential of a transplanted nucleus to direct normal development was inversely related to the age of the donor: the older the donor nucleus, the lower the percentage of normally developing tadpoles (see Figure 20.16).

From these results, Gurdon concluded that something in the nucleus *does* change as animal cells differentiate. In frogs and most other animals, nuclear potential tends to be restricted more and more as embryonic development and cell differentiation progress. These were foundational experiments that ultimately led to stem cell technology, and Gurdon received the 2012 Nobel Prize in Medicine for this work.

Reproductive Cloning of Mammals

In addition to cloning frogs, researchers have long been able to clone mammals by transplanting nuclei or cells from a variety of early embryos into enucleated eggs. But it was not known whether a nucleus from a fully differentiated cell could be reprogrammed successfully to act as a donor nucleus. In 1997, however, researchers at the Roslin Institute in Scotland captured newspaper headlines when they announced the birth of Dolly, a lamb cloned from an adult sheep by nuclear transplantation from a differentiated cell **(Figure 20.17)**. These researchers achieved the necessary dedifferentiation of donor nuclei by culturing mammary cells in nutrient-poor medium. They then fused these cells with enucleated sheep eggs. The resulting diploid cells divided to form early embryos, which were implanted into surrogate mothers. Out of several hundred embryos, one successfully completed normal development, and Dolly was born.

Later analyses showed that Dolly's chromosomal DNA was indeed identical to that of the nucleus donor. (Her mitochondrial DNA came from the egg donor, as expected.) At the age of 6, Dolly suffered complications from a lung disease usually seen only in much older sheep and was euthanized. Dolly's premature death, as well as an arthritic condition, led to speculation that her cells were in some way not quite as healthy as those of a normal sheep, possibly reflecting incomplete reprogramming of the original transplanted nucleus.

Since that time, researchers have cloned numerous other mammals, including mice, cats, cows, horses, pigs, dogs, and monkeys. In most cases, their goal has been the production of new individuals; this is known as *reproductive cloning*. We have already learned a lot from such experiments. For example, cloned animals of the same species do *not* always look or behave identically. In a herd of cows cloned from the same line of cultured cells, certain cows are dominant in behavior and others are more submissive. Another example of nonidentity in clones is the first cloned cat, named CC for

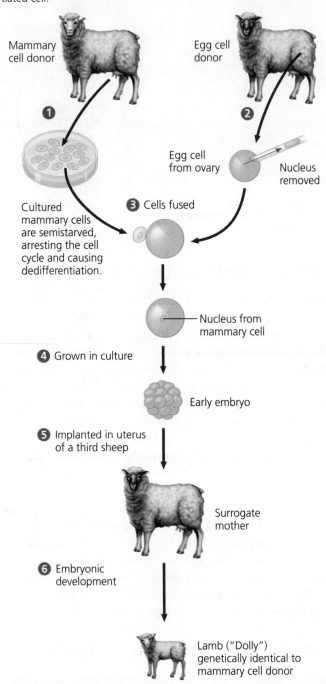

▼ Figure 20.17

Research Method

Reproductive Cloning of a Mammal by Nuclear Transplantation

Application This method produces cloned animals with nuclear genes identical to those of the animal supplying the nucleus.

Technique Shown here is the procedure used to produce Dolly, the first reported case of a mammal cloned using the nucleus of a differentiated cell.

Mammary cell donor

Egg cell donor

①

②

Egg cell from ovary

Nucleus removed

Cultured mammary cells are semistarved, arresting the cell cycle and causing dedifferentiation.

③ Cells fused

Nucleus from mammary cell

④ Grown in culture

Early embryo

⑤ Implanted in uterus of a third sheep

Surrogate mother

⑥ Embryonic development

Lamb ("Dolly") genetically identical to mammary cell donor

Results The genetic makeup of the cloned animal is identical to that of the animal supplying the nucleus but differs from that of the egg donor and surrogate mother. (The latter two are "Scottish blackface" sheep, with dark faces.)

▲ **Figure 20.18 CC, the first cloned cat, and her single parent.** Rainbow (left) donated the nucleus in a cloning procedure that resulted in CC (right). However, the two cats are not identical: Rainbow is a classic calico cat with orange patches on her fur and has a "reserved personality," while CC has a gray and white coat and is more playful.

Carbon Copy **(Figure 20.18)**. She has a calico coat, like her single female parent, but the color and pattern are different because of random X chromosome inactivation, which is a normal occurrence during embryonic development (see Figure 15.8). And identical human twins, which are naturally occurring "clones," are always slightly different. Clearly, environmental influences and random phenomena play a significant role during development.

Faulty Gene Regulation in Cloned Animals

In most nuclear transplantation studies thus far, only a small percentage of cloned embryos develop normally to birth. And like Dolly, many cloned animals exhibit defects. Cloned mice, for instance, are prone to obesity, pneumonia, liver failure, and premature death. Scientists assert that even cloned animals that appear normal are likely to have subtle defects.

In recent years, we have begun to uncover some reasons for the low efficiency of cloning and the high incidence of abnormalities. In the nuclei of fully differentiated cells, a small subset of genes is turned on and expression of the rest is repressed. This regulation often is the result of epigenetic changes in chromatin, such as acetylation of histones or methylation of DNA (see Figure 18.7). During the nuclear transfer procedure, many of these changes must be reversed in the later-stage nucleus from a donor animal for genes to be expressed or repressed appropriately in early stages of development. Researchers have found that the DNA in cells from cloned embryos, like that of differentiated cells, often has more methyl groups than does the DNA in equivalent cells from normal embryos of the same species. This finding suggests that the reprogramming of donor nuclei requires

more accurate and complete chromatin restructuring than occurs during cloning procedures. Because DNA methylation helps regulate gene expression, misplaced or extra methyl groups in the DNA of donor nuclei may interfere with the pattern of gene expression necessary for normal embryonic development. In fact, the success of a cloning attempt may depend in large part on whether or not the chromatin in the donor nucleus can be artificially modified to resemble that of a newly fertilized egg.

Stem Cells of Animals

Progress in cloning mammalian embryos, including primates, has heightened speculation about the cloning of humans, which has not yet been achieved. The main reason researchers are trying to clone human embryos is not for reproduction, but for the production of stem cells to treat human diseases. Recall that a stem cell is a relatively unspecialized cell that can both reproduce itself indefinitely and, under appropriate conditions, differentiate into specialized cells of one or more types **(Figure 20.19)**. Thus, stem cells are able both to replenish their own population and to generate cells that travel down specific differentiation pathways.

Embryonic and Adult Stem Cells

Many early animal embryos contain stem cells capable of giving rise to differentiated cells of any type. Stem cells can be isolated from early embryos at a stage called the blastula stage or its human equivalent, the blastocyst stage. In culture, these *embryonic stem (ES) cells* reproduce indefinitely; and depending on culture conditions, they can be made to differentiate

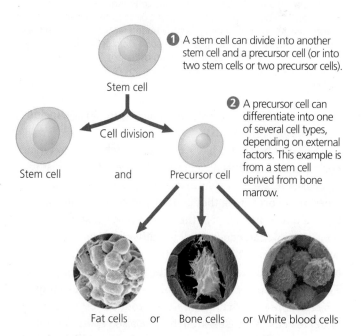

① A stem cell can divide into another stem cell and a precursor cell (or into two stem cells or two precursor cells).

② A precursor cell can differentiate into one of several cell types, depending on external factors. This example is from a stem cell derived from bone marrow.

Stem cell

Cell division

Stem cell and Precursor cell

Fat cells or Bone cells or White blood cells

▲ **Figure 20.19 How stem cells maintain their own population and generate differentiated cells.**

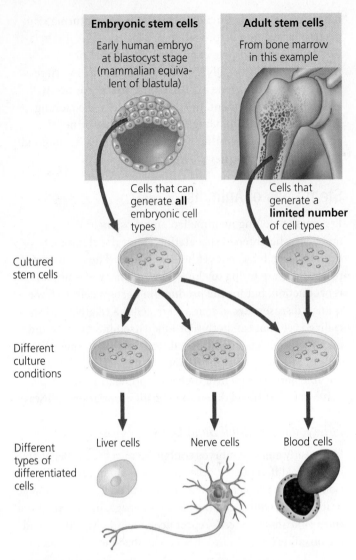

Embryonic stem cells

Early human embryo at blastocyst stage (mammalian equivalent of blastula)

Adult stem cells

From bone marrow in this example

Cells that can generate **all** embryonic cell types

Cells that generate a **limited number** of cell types

Cultured stem cells

Different culture conditions

Different types of differentiated cells

Liver cells

Nerve cells

Blood cells

▲ **Figure 20.20 Working with stem cells.** Animal stem cells, which can be isolated from early embryos or adult tissues and grown in culture, are self-perpetuating, relatively undifferentiated cells. Embryonic stem cells are easier to grow than adult stem cells and can theoretically give rise to *all* types of cells in an organism. The range of cell types that can arise from adult stem cells is not yet fully understood.

into a wide variety of specialized cells **(Figure 20.20)**, including even eggs and sperm.

The adult body also has stem cells, which serve to replace nonreproducing specialized cells as needed. In contrast to ES cells, *adult stem cells* are not able to give rise to all cell types in the organism, though they can generate multiple types. For example, one of the several types of stem cells in bone marrow can generate all the different kinds of blood cells (see Figure 20.20), and another can differentiate into bone, cartilage, fat, muscle, and the linings of blood vessels. To the surprise of many, the adult brain has been found to contain stem cells that continue to produce certain kinds of nerve cells there. Researchers have also reported finding stem cells in skin, hair, eyes, and dental pulp. Although adult animals have only tiny numbers of stem cells, scientists are

learning to identify and isolate these cells from various tissues and, in some cases, to grow them in culture. With the right culture conditions (for instance, the addition of specific growth factors), cultured stem cells from adult animals have been made to differentiate into multiple types of specialized cells, although none are as versatile as ES cells.

Research with embryonic or adult stem cells is a source of valuable data about differentiation and has enormous potential for medical applications. The ultimate aim is to supply cells for the repair of damaged or diseased organs: for example, insulin-producing pancreatic cells for people with type 1 diabetes or certain kinds of brain cells for people with Parkinson's disease or Huntington's disease. Adult stem cells from bone marrow have long been used as a source of immune system cells in patients whose own immune systems are nonfunctional because of genetic disorders or radiation treatments for cancer.

The developmental potential of adult stem cells is limited to certain tissues. ES cells hold more promise than adult stem cells for most medical applications because ES cells are **pluripotent**, capable of differentiating into many different cell types. The only way to obtain ES cells thus far, however, has been to harvest them from human embryos, which raises ethical and political issues.

ES cells are currently obtained from embryos donated by patients undergoing infertility treatments or from long-term cell cultures originally established with cells isolated from donated embryos. If scientists were able to clone human embryos to the blastocyst stage, they might be able to use such clones as the source of ES cells in the future. Furthermore, with a donor nucleus from a person with a particular disease, they might be able to produce ES cells that match the patient and are thus not rejected by his or her immune system when used for treatment. When the main aim of cloning is to produce ES cells to treat disease, the process is called *therapeutic cloning*. Although most people believe that reproductive cloning of humans is unethical, opinions vary about the morality of therapeutic cloning.

Induced Pluripotent Stem (iPS) Cells

Resolving the debate now seems less urgent because researchers have learned to turn back the clock in fully differentiated cells, reprogramming them to act like ES cells. The accomplishment of this feat, which posed formidable obstacles, was announced in 2007, first by labs using mouse skin cells and then by additional groups using cells from human skin and other organs or tissues. In all these cases, researchers transformed the differentiated cells into a type of ES cell by using a retrovirus to introduce extra, cloned copies of four "stem cell" master regulatory genes. The "deprogrammed" cells are known as *induced pluripotent stem* (*iPS*) cells because, in using this fairly simple laboratory technique to return them to their undifferentiated state, pluripotency has been restored. The experiments that first transformed human differentiated cells into iPS cells are described in **Figure 20.21**. Shinya Yamanaka received the 2012 Nobel Prize in Medicine for this work, shared with John Gurdon, whose work you read about in Figure 20.16.

By many criteria, iPS cells can perform most of the functions of ES cells, but there are some differences in gene expression and other cellular functions, such as cell division. At least until these differences are fully understood, the study of ES cells will continue to make important contributions to the development of stem cell therapies. (In fact, it is likely that ES cells will always be a focus of basic research as well.) In the meantime, work is proceeding using the iPS cells that have been experimentally produced.

There are two major potential uses for human iPS cells. First, cells from patients suffering from diseases can be reprogrammed to become iPS cells, which can act as model cells for studying the disease and potential treatments. Human iPS cell lines have already been developed from individuals with type 1 diabetes, Parkinson's disease, and at least a dozen other diseases. Second, in the field of regenerative medicine, a patient's own cells could be reprogrammed into iPS cells and then used to replace nonfunctional tissues, such as insulin-producing cells of the pancreas.

Recently, in another surprising development, researchers have been able to identify genes that can directly reprogram a differentiated cell into another type of differentiated cell without passing through a pluripotent state. In the first reported example, one type of cell in the pancreas was transformed into another type. However, the two types of cells do not need to be very closely related: Another research group has been able to directly reprogram a skin fibroblast into a nerve cell. Development techniques that direct iPS cells or even fully differentiated cells to become specific cell types for regenerative medicine is an area of intense research, one that has already seen some success. The iPS cells created in this way could eventually provide tailor-made "replacement" cells for patients without using any human eggs or embryos, thus circumventing most ethical objections.

CONCEPT CHECK 20.3

1. Based on current knowledge, how would you explain the difference in the percentage of tadpoles that developed from the two kinds of donor nuclei in Figure 20.16?

2. If you were to clone a carrot using the technique shown in Figure 20.15, would all the progeny plants ("clones") look identical? Why or why not?

3. **MAKE CONNECTIONS** Compare an individual carrot cell in Figure 20.15 with the fully differentiated muscle cell in Figure 18.18 in terms of their potential to develop into different cell types.

For suggested answers, see Appendix A.

▼ **Figure 20.21** **Inquiry**

Can a fully differentiated human cell be "deprogrammed" to become a stem cell?

Experiment Shinya Yamanaka and colleagues at Kyoto University, in Japan, used a retroviral vector to introduce four genes into fully differentiated human skin fibroblast cells. The cells were then cultured in a medium that would support growth of stem cells.

Stem cell

Precursor cell

Oct3/4

Sox2

Klf4

c-Myc

Skin fibroblast cell

Four "stem cell" master regulator genes were introduced, using the retroviral cloning vector.

Induced pluripotent stem (iPS) cell

Results Two weeks later, the cells resembled embryonic stem cells in appearance and were actively dividing. Their gene expression patterns, gene methylation patterns, and other characteristics were also consistent with those of embryonic stem cells. The iPS cells were able to differentiate into heart muscle cells, as well as other cell types.

Conclusion The four genes induced differentiated skin cells to become pluripotent stem cells, with characteristics of embryonic stem cells.

Source: K. Takahashi et al., Induction of pluripotent stem cells from adult human fibroblasts by defined factors, *Cell* 131:861–872 (2007).

WHAT IF? *Patients with diseases such as heart disease, diabetes, or Alzheimer's could have their own skin cells reprogrammed to become iPS cells. Once procedures have been developed for converting iPS cells into heart, pancreatic, or nervous system cells, the patients' own iPS cells might be used to treat their disease. When organs are transplanted from a donor to a diseased recipient, the recipient's immune system may reject the transplant, a condition with serious and often fatal consequences. Would using iPS cells be expected to carry the same risk? Why or why not? Given that these cells are actively dividing, undifferentiated cells, what risks might this procedure carry?*

The practical applications of DNA-based biotechnology affect our lives in many ways

DNA technology is in the news almost every day. Most often, the topic is a new and promising application in medicine, but this is just one of numerous fields benefiting from DNA technology and genetic engineering.

Medical Applications

One important use of DNA technology is the identification of human genes whose mutation plays a role in genetic diseases. These discoveries may lead to ways of diagnosing, treating, and even preventing such conditions. DNA technology is also contributing to our understanding of "nongenetic" diseases, from arthritis to AIDS, since a person's genes influence susceptibility to these diseases. Furthermore, diseases of all sorts involve changes in gene expression within the affected cells and often within the patient's immune system. By using DNA microarray assays (see Figure 20.13) or other techniques to compare gene expression in healthy and diseased tissues, researchers hope to find many of the genes that are turned on or off in particular diseases. These genes and their products are potential targets for prevention or therapy.

Diagnosis and Treatment of Diseases

A new chapter in the diagnosis of infectious diseases has been opened by DNA technology, in particular the use of PCR and labeled nucleic acid probes to track down pathogens. For example, because the sequence of the RNA genome of HIV is known, RT-PCR can be used to amplify, and thus detect, HIV RNA in blood or tissue samples (see Figure 20.12). RT-PCR is often the best way to detect an otherwise elusive infective agent.

Medical scientists can now diagnose hundreds of human genetic disorders by using PCR with primers that target the genes associated with these disorders. The amplified DNA product is then sequenced to reveal the presence or absence of the disease-causing mutation. Among the genes for human diseases that have been identified are those for sickle-cell disease, hemophilia, cystic fibrosis, Huntington's disease, and Duchenne muscular dystrophy. Individuals afflicted with such diseases can often be identified before the onset of symptoms, even before birth (see Figure 14.19). PCR can also be used to identify symptomless carriers of potentially harmful recessive alleles.

As you learned earlier, genome-wide association studies have pinpointed SNPs (single nucleotide polymorphisms) that are linked to disease-causing alleles (see Figure 20.13).

Individuals can be tested by PCR and sequencing for a SNP that is correlated with the abnormal allele. The presence of particular SNPs is correlated with increased risk for conditions such as heart disease, Alzheimer's, and some types of cancer. Companies that offer individual genetic testing for risk factors like these are looking for previously identified, linked SNPs. It may be helpful for individuals to learn about their health risks, with the understanding that such genetic tests merely reflect correlations and do not make predictions.

The techniques described in this chapter have also prompted improvements in disease treatments. By analyzing the expression of many genes in breast cancer patients, researchers have been able to refine their understanding of the different subtypes of breast cancer (see Figure 18.27). Knowing the expression levels of particular genes can help physicians determine the likelihood that the cancer will recur, thus helping them design an appropriate treatment. Given that some low-risk patients have a 96% survival rate over a ten-year period with no treatment, gene expression analysis allows doctors and patients access to valuable information when they are considering treatment options.

Many envision a future of "personalized medicine" where each person's genetic profile can inform them about diseases or conditions for which they are especially at risk and help them make treatment choices. As we will discuss later in the chapter, a *genetic profile* is currently taken to mean a set of genetic markers such as SNPs. Ultimately, however, it will likely mean the complete DNA sequence of an individual—once sequencing becomes inexpensive enough. (See the interview with Charles Rotimi before Chapter 13.) Our ability to sequence a person's genome rapidly and inexpensively is advancing faster than our development of appropriate treatments for the conditions we are characterizing. Still, the identification of genes involved in these conditions provides us with good targets for therapeutic interventions.

Human Gene Therapy

Gene therapy—the introduction of genes into an afflicted individual for therapeutic purposes—holds great potential for treating the relatively small number of disorders traceable to a single defective gene. In theory, a normal allele of the defective gene could be inserted into the somatic cells of the tissue affected by the disorder.

For gene therapy of somatic cells to be permanent, the cells that receive the normal allele must be cells that multiply throughout the patient's life. Bone marrow cells, which include the stem cells that give rise to all the cells of the blood and immune system, are prime candidates. **Figure 20.22** outlines one procedure for gene therapy of an individual whose bone marrow cells do not produce a vital enzyme because of a single defective gene. One type of severe combined immunodeficiency (SCID) is caused by this kind of defect. If the treatment is successful, the patient's bone marrow cells will begin producing the missing protein, and the patient may be cured.

① Insert RNA version of normal allele into retrovirus or other viral vector.

Cloned gene (normal allele, absent from patient's cells)

Viral RNA

Viral capsid

② Let virus infect bone marrow cells that have been removed from the patient and cultured.

③ Viral DNA carrying the normal allele inserts into chromosome.

Bone marrow cell from patient

④ Inject engineered cells into patient.

Bone marrow

▲ **Figure 20.22 Gene therapy using a retroviral vector.** A retrovirus that has been rendered harmless is used as a vector in this procedure, which exploits the ability of a retrovirus to insert a DNA transcript of its RNA genome into the chromosomal DNA of its host cell (see Figure 19.8). If the foreign gene carried by the retroviral vector is expressed, the cell and its descendants will possess the gene product. Cells that reproduce throughout life, such as bone marrow cells, are ideal candidates for gene therapy.

The procedure shown in Figure 20.22 has been used in gene therapy trials for SCID. In a trial begun in France in 2000, ten young children with SCID were treated by the same procedure. Nine of these patients showed significant, definitive improvement after two years, the first indisputable success of gene therapy. However, three of the patients subsequently developed leukemia, a type of blood cell cancer, and one of them died. Researchers have concluded it is likely that the insertion of the retroviral vector occurred near a gene that triggers the proliferation of blood cells. Using a viral vector that does not come from a retrovirus, clinical researchers have treated at least three other genetic diseases somewhat successfully with gene therapy: a type of progressive blindness (see Concept 50.3), a degenerative disease of the nervous system, and a blood disorder involving the β-globin gene. The successful trials involve very few patients but are still cause for cautious optimism.

Gene therapy raises many technical issues. For example, how can the activity of the transferred gene be controlled

so that cells make appropriate amounts of the gene product at the right time and in the right place? How can we be sure that the insertion of the therapeutic gene does not harm some other necessary cell function? As more is learned about DNA control elements and gene interactions, researchers may be able to answer such questions.

In addition to technical challenges, gene therapy provokes ethical questions. Some critics believe that tampering with human genes in any way is immoral or unethical. Other observers see no fundamental difference between the transplantation of genes into somatic cells and the transplantation of organs. You might wonder whether scientists are considering engineering human germ-line cells in the hope of correcting a defect in future generations. At present, no one in the mainstream scientific community is pursuing this goal—it is considered much too risky. Such genetic engineering is routinely done in laboratory mice, though, and the technical problems relating to similar genetic engineering in humans will eventually be solved. Under what circumstances, if any, should we alter the genomes of human germ lines? Would this inevitably lead to the practice of eugenics, a deliberate effort to control the genetic makeup of human populations? While we may not have to resolve these questions right now, considering them is worthwhile because they will probably arise at some point in the future.

Pharmaceutical Products

The pharmaceutical industry derives significant benefit from advances in DNA technology and genetic research, applying them to the development of useful drugs to treat diseases. Pharmaceutical products are synthesized using methods of either organic chemistry or biotechnology, depending on the nature of the product.

Synthesis of Small Molecules for Use as Drugs Determining the sequence and structure of proteins crucial for tumor cell survival has led to the identification of small molecules that combat certain cancers by blocking the function of these proteins. One drug, imatinib (trade name Gleevec), is a small molecule that inhibits a specific receptor tyrosine kinase (see Figure 11.8). The overexpression of this receptor, resulting from a chromosomal translocation, is instrumental in causing chronic myelogenous leukemia (CML; see Figure 15.16). Patients in the early stages of CML who are treated with imatinib have exhibited nearly complete, sustained remission from the cancer. Drugs that work in a similar way have also been used with success to treat a few types of lung and breast cancers. This approach is feasible only for cancers for which the molecular basis is fairly well understood.

In many cases of such drug-treated tumors, though, cells later arise that are resistant to the new drug. In one study, the whole genome of the tumor cells was sequenced both before and after the appearance of drug resistance. Comparison of the sequences showed genetic changes that allowed the tumor cells to "get around" the drug-inhibited protein. So we can see that cancer cells demonstrate the principles of evolution: Certain tumor cells have a random mutation that allows them to survive in the presence of a particular drug, and as a consequence of natural selection in the presence of the drug, these are the cells that survive and reproduce.

Protein Production in Cell Cultures Pharmaceutical products that are proteins are commonly synthesized on a large scale using cell cultures. You learned earlier in the chapter about DNA cloning and gene expression systems for producing large quantities of a chosen protein that is present naturally in only minute amounts. The host cells used in such expression systems can even be engineered to secrete a protein as it is made, thereby simplifying the task of purifying it by traditional biochemical methods.

Among the first pharmaceutical products manufactured in this way were human insulin and human growth hormone (HGH). Some 2 million people with diabetes in the United States depend on insulin treatment to control their disease. Human growth hormone has been a boon to children born with a form of dwarfism caused by inadequate amounts of HGH. Another important pharmaceutical product produced by genetic engineering is tissue plasminogen activator (TPA). If administered shortly after a heart attack, TPA helps dissolve blood clots and reduces the risk of subsequent heart attacks.

For the past 25 years, scientists have also been working on producing proteins in plant cell cultures. They have enjoyed recent success using carrot cells in culture to make an enzyme involved in fat breakdown that is used for treatment of a rare human disease. Plant cells are easily grown in culture (see Figure 20.15), requiring less precise conditions than animal cells. Also, they are unlikely to get contaminated by viruses that could infect animals, a situation that has on occasion held up production of the enzyme for some time. This successful accomplishment is likely to be further extended to other therapeutic proteins in the future.

Protein Production by "Pharm" Animals In some cases, instead of using cell systems to produce large quantities of protein products, pharmaceutical scientists can use whole animals. They can introduce a gene from an animal of one genotype into the genome of another individual, often of a different species. This individual is then called a **transgenic** animal. To do this, they first remove eggs from a female of the recipient species and fertilize them *in vitro*. Meanwhile, they have cloned the desired gene from the donor organism. They then inject the cloned DNA directly into the nuclei of the fertilized eggs. Some of the cells integrate the foreign DNA, the *transgene*, into their genome and are able to express the foreign gene. The engineered embryos that arise from these zygotes are then surgically implanted in a surrogate mother. If an embryo develops successfully, the result is a transgenic animal that expresses its new, "foreign" gene.

▲ **Figure 20.23 Goats as "pharm" animals.** This transgenic goat carries a gene for a human blood protein, antithrombin, which she secretes in her milk. Patients with a rare hereditary disorder in which this protein is lacking suffer from formation of blood clots in their blood vessels. Easily purified from the goat's milk, the protein is used to prevent blood clots in these patients during surgery or childbirth.

Assuming that the introduced gene encodes a protein desired in large quantities, these transgenic animals can act as pharmaceutical "factories." For example, a transgene for a human blood protein such as antithrombin, which prevents blood clots, can be inserted into the genome of a goat in such a way that the transgene's product is secreted in the animal's milk **(Figure 20.23)**. The protein is then purified from the milk (which is easier than purification from a cell culture).

Human proteins produced in transgenic farm animals for use in humans may differ in some ways from the naturally produced human proteins, possibly because of subtle differences in protein modification. Therefore, such proteins must be tested very carefully to ensure that they (or contaminants from the farm animals) will not cause allergic reactions or other adverse effects in patients who receive them.

Forensic Evidence and Genetic Profiles

In violent crimes, body fluids or small pieces of tissue may be left at the scene or on the clothes or other possessions of the victim or assailant. If enough blood, semen, or tissue is available, forensic laboratories can determine the blood type or tissue type by using antibodies to detect specific cell-surface proteins. However, such tests require fairly fresh samples in relatively large amounts. Also, because many people have the same blood or tissue type, this approach can only exclude a suspect; it cannot provide strong evidence of guilt.

DNA testing, on the other hand, can identify the guilty individual with a high degree of certainty, because the DNA sequence of every person is unique (except for identical twins). Genetic markers that vary in the population can be analyzed for a given person to determine that individual's unique set of genetic markers, or **genetic profile**. (This term is preferred over "DNA fingerprint" by forensic scientists, who want to emphasize the heritable aspect of these markers rather than the fact that they produce a pattern on a gel that, like a fingerprint, is visually recognizable.) The FBI started applying DNA technology to forensics in 1988, using a method involving gel electrophoresis and nucleic acid hybridization to detect similarities and differences in DNA samples. This method required much smaller samples of blood or tissue than earlier methods—only about 1,000 cells.

Today, forensic scientists use an even more sensitive method that takes advantage of variations in length of genetic markers called **short tandem repeats (STRs)**. These are tandemly repeated units of two- to five-nucleotide sequences in specific regions of the genome. The number of repeats present in these regions is highly variable from person to person (polymorphic), and even for a single individual, the two alleles of an STR may differ from each other. For example, one individual may have the sequence ACAT repeated 30 times at one genome locus and 15 times at the same locus on the other homolog, whereas another individual may have 18 repeats at this locus on each homolog. (These two genotypes can be expressed by the two repeat numbers: 30,15 and 18,18.) PCR is used to amplify particular STRs, using sets of primers that are labeled with different-colored fluorescent tags; the length of the region, and thus the number of repeats, can then be determined by electrophoresis. The PCR step allows use of this method even when the DNA is in poor condition or available only in minute quantities. A tissue sample containing as few as 20 cells can be sufficient for PCR amplification.

In a murder case, for example, this method can be used to compare DNA samples from the suspect, the victim, and a small amount of blood found at the crime scene. The forensic scientist tests only a few selected portions of the DNA—usually 13 STR markers. However, even this small set of markers can provide a forensically useful genetic profile because the probability that two people (who are not identical twins) would have exactly the same set of STR markers is vanishingly small. The Innocence Project, a nonprofit organization dedicated to overturning wrongful convictions, uses STR analysis of archived samples from crime scenes to revisit old cases. As of 2013, more than 300 innocent people have been released from prison as a result of forensic and legal work by this group **(Figure 20.24)**.

Genetic profiles can also be useful for other purposes. A comparison of the DNA of a mother, her child, and the purported father can conclusively settle a question of paternity. Sometimes paternity is of historical interest: Genetic profiles provided strong evidence that Thomas Jefferson or one of his close male relatives fathered at least one of the children of his slave Sally Hemings. Genetic profiles can also identify victims of mass casualties. The largest such effort occurred after the attack on the World Trade Center in 2001; more than 10,000 samples of victims' remains were compared with DNA samples from personal items, such as toothbrushes, provided by families. Ultimately, forensic scientists

(a) In 1984, Earl Washington was convicted and sentenced to death for the 1982 rape and murder of Rebecca Williams. His sentence was commuted to life in prison in 1993 due to new doubts about the evidence. In 2000, STR analysis by forensic scientists associated with the Innocence Project showed conclusively that he was innocent. This photo shows Washington just before his release in 2001, after 17 years in prison.

Source of sample	STR marker 1	STR marker 2	STR marker 3
Semen on victim	17,19	13,16	12,12
Earl Washington	16,18	14,15	11,12
Kenneth Tinsley	17,19	13,16	12,12

(b) In STR analysis, selected STR markers in a DNA sample are amplified by PCR, and the PCR products are separated by electrophoresis. The procedure reveals how many repeats are present for each STR locus in the sample. An individual has two alleles per STR locus, each with a certain number of repeats. This table shows the number of repeats for three STR markers in three samples: from semen found on the victim, from Washington, and from another man (Kenneth Tinsley), who was in prison because of an unrelated conviction. These and other STR data (not shown) exonerated Washington and led Tinsley to plead guilty to the murder.

▲ **Figure 20.24** STR analysis used to release an innocent man from prison.

succeeded in identifying almost 3,000 victims using these methods.

Just how reliable is a genetic profile? The greater the number of markers examined in a DNA sample, the more likely it is that the profile is unique to one individual. In forensic cases using STR analysis with 13 markers, the probability of two people having identical DNA profiles is somewhere between one chance in 10 billion and one in several trillion. (For comparison, the world's population is between 7 and 8 billion.) The exact probability depends on the frequency of those markers in the general population. Information on how common various markers are in different ethnic groups is critical because these marker frequencies may vary considerably among ethnic groups and between a particular ethnic group and the population as a whole. With the increasing availability of frequency data, forensic scientists can make extremely accurate statistical calculations. Thus, despite problems that can still arise from insufficient data, human error, or flawed evidence, genetic profiles are now accepted as compelling evidence by legal experts and scientists alike.

Environmental Cleanup

Increasingly, the remarkable ability of certain microorganisms to transform chemicals is being exploited for environmental cleanup. If the growth needs of such microbes make them unsuitable for direct use, scientists can now transfer the genes for their valuable metabolic capabilities into other microorganisms, which can then be used to treat environmental problems. For example, many bacteria can extract heavy metals, such as copper, lead, and nickel, from their environments and incorporate the metals into compounds such as copper sulfate or lead sulfate, which are readily recoverable. Genetically engineered microbes may become important in both mining (especially as ore reserves are depleted) and cleaning up highly toxic mining wastes. Biotechnologists are also trying to engineer microbes that can degrade chlorinated hydrocarbons and other harmful compounds. These microbes could be used in wastewater treatment plants or by manufacturers before the compounds are ever released into the environment.

Agricultural Applications

Scientists are working to learn more about the genomes of agriculturally important plants and animals. For a number of years, they have been using DNA technology in an effort to improve agricultural productivity. The selective breeding of both livestock (animal husbandry) and crops has exploited naturally occurring mutations and genetic recombination for thousands of years.

As we described earlier, DNA technology enables scientists to produce transgenic animals, which speeds up the selective breeding process. The goals of creating a transgenic animal are often the same as the goals of traditional breeding—for instance, to make a sheep with better quality wool, a pig with leaner meat, or a cow that will mature in a shorter time. Scientists might, for example, identify and clone a gene that causes the development of larger muscles (muscles make up most of the meat we eat) in one breed of cattle and transfer it to other cattle or even to sheep. However, problems such as low fertility or increased susceptibility to disease are not uncommon among farm animals carrying genes from other species. Animal health and welfare are important issues to consider when developing transgenic animals.

Agricultural scientists have already endowed a number of crop plants with genes for desirable traits, such as delayed ripening and resistance to spoilage and disease, as well as drought. The most commonly used vector for introducing new genes into plant cells is a plasmid, called the *Ti plasmid*, from the soil bacterium *Agrobacterium tumefaciens*. This plasmid integrates a segment of its DNA into the chromosomal DNA of its host plant cells (see Figure 35.25). To make transgenic plants, researchers engineer the plasmid to carry genes of interest and introduce it into cells. For many plant species, a single tissue cell grown in culture can give rise to an adult plant (see Figure 20.15). Thus, genetic manipulations can be performed on an ordinary somatic cell and the cell then used to generate an organism with new traits.

Genetic engineering is rapidly replacing traditional plant-breeding programs, especially for useful traits, such as herbicide or pest resistance, determined by one or a few genes. Crops engineered with a bacterial gene making the plants resistant to an herbicide can grow while weeds are destroyed, and genetically engineered crops that can resist destructive insects reduce the need for chemical insecticides. In India, the insertion of a salinity resistance gene from a coastal mangrove plant into the genomes of several rice varieties has resulted in rice plants that can grow in water three times as salty as seawater. The research foundation that carried out this feat of genetic engineering estimates that one-third of all irrigated land has high salinity owing to overirrigation and intensive use of chemical fertilizers, representing a serious threat to the food supply. Thus, salinity-resistant crop plants would be enormously valuable worldwide.

Safety and Ethical Questions Raised by DNA Technology

Early concerns about potential dangers associated with recombinant DNA technology focused on the possibility that hazardous new pathogens might be created. What might happen, for instance, if cancer cell genes were transferred into bacteria or viruses? To guard against such rogue microbes, scientists developed a set of guidelines that were adopted as formal government regulations in the United States and some other countries. One safety measure is a set of strict laboratory procedures designed to protect researchers from infection by engineered microbes and to prevent the microbes from accidentally leaving the laboratory. In addition, strains of microorganisms to be used in recombinant DNA experiments are genetically crippled to ensure that they cannot survive outside the laboratory. Finally, certain obviously dangerous experiments have been banned.

Today, most public concern about possible hazards centers not on recombinant microbes but on **genetically modified (GM) organisms** used as food. A GM organism is one that has acquired by artificial means one or more genes from another species or even from another variety of the same species. Some salmon, for example, have been genetically modified by addition of a more active salmon growth hormone gene. However, the majority of the GM organisms that contribute to our food supply are not animals, but crop plants.

GM crops are widespread in the United States, Argentina, and Brazil; together these countries account for over 80% of the world's acreage devoted to such crops. In the United States, most corn, soybean, and canola crops are genetically modified, and GM products are not required to be labeled at present. However, the same foods are an ongoing subject of controversy in Europe, where the GM revolution has met with strong opposition. Many Europeans are concerned about the safety of GM foods and the possible environmental consequences of growing GM plants. In the year 2000, negotiators from 130 countries agreed on a Biosafety Protocol that requires exporters to identify GM organisms present in bulk food shipments and allows importing countries to decide whether the products pose environmental or health risks. (Although the United States declined to sign the agreement, it went into effect anyway because the majority of countries were in favor of it.) Since then, European countries have, on occasion, refused crops from the United States and other countries, leading to trade disputes. Although a small number of GM crops have been grown on European soil, these products have generally failed in local markets, and the future of GM crops in Europe is uncertain.

Advocates of a cautious approach toward GM crops fear that transgenic plants might pass their new genes to close relatives in nearby wild areas. We know that lawn and crop grasses, for example, commonly exchange genes with wild relatives via pollen transfer. If crop plants carrying genes for resistance to herbicides, diseases, or insect pests pollinated wild ones, the offspring might become "super weeds" that are very difficult to control. Another worry concerns possible risks to human health from GM foods. Some people fear that the protein products of transgenes might lead to allergic reactions. Although there is some evidence that this could happen, advocates claim that these proteins could be tested in advance to avoid producing ones that cause allergic reactions. (For further discussion of plant biotechnology and GM crops, see Concept 38.3.)

Today, governments and regulatory agencies throughout the world are grappling with how to facilitate the use of biotechnology in agriculture, industry, and medicine while ensuring that new products and procedures are safe. In the United States, such applications of biotechnology are evaluated for potential risks by various regulatory agencies, including the Food and Drug Administration, the Environmental Protection Agency, the National Institutes of Health, and the Department of Agriculture. Meanwhile, these same agencies and the public must consider the ethical implications of biotechnology.

Advances in biotechnology have allowed us to obtain complete genome sequences for humans and many other species, providing a vast treasure trove of information about genes. We can ask how certain genes differ from species to species, as well as how genes and, ultimately, entire genomes have evolved. (These are the subjects of Chapter 21.) At the same time, the increasing speed and falling cost of sequencing the genomes of individuals are raising significant ethical questions. Who should have the right to examine someone else's genetic information? How should that information be used? Should a person's genome be a factor in determining eligibility for a job or insurance? Ethical considerations, as well as concerns about potential environmental and health hazards, will likely slow some applications of biotechnology. There is always a danger that too much regulation will stifle basic research and its potential benefits. However, the power of DNA technology and genetic engineering—our ability to profoundly and rapidly alter species that have been evolving for millennia—demands that we proceed with humility and caution.

CONCEPT CHECK 20.4

1. What is the advantage of using stem cells for gene therapy?
2. List at least three different properties that have been acquired by crop plants via genetic engineering.
3. **WHAT IF?** As a physician, you have a patient with symptoms that suggest a hepatitis A infection, but you have not been able to detect viral proteins in the blood. Knowing that hepatitis A is an RNA virus, what lab test could you perform to support your diagnosis? Explain the results that would support your hypothesis.

For suggested answers, see Appendix A.

---

20 Chapter Review

SUMMARY OF KEY CONCEPTS

CONCEPT 20.1

DNA sequencing and DNA cloning are valuable tools for genetic engineering and biological inquiry (pp. 409–417)

- **Nucleic acid hybridization**, the base pairing of one strand of a nucleic acid to the complementary sequence on a strand from another nucleic acid molecule, is widely used in DNA technology.

- **DNA sequencing** can be carried out using the *dideoxy chain termination* method in automated sequencing machines.
- Next-generation (high-throughput) techniques for sequencing DNA are based on *sequencing by synthesis*: DNA polymerase is used to synthesize a stretch of DNA from a single-stranded template, and the order in which nucleotides are added reveals the sequence.
- **Gene cloning** (or DNA cloning) produces multiple copies of a gene (or DNA fragment) that can be used in analyzing and manipulating DNA and can yield useful new products or organisms with beneficial traits.

- In **genetic engineering**, bacterial **restriction enzymes** are used to cut DNA molecules within short, specific nucleotide sequences (**restriction sites**), yielding a set of double-stranded **restriction fragments** with single-stranded **sticky ends**:

Sticky end

- The sticky ends on **restriction fragments** from one DNA source can base-pair with complementary sticky ends on fragments from other DNA molecules. Sealing the base-paired fragments with **DNA ligase** produces **recombinant DNA** molecules.
- DNA restriction fragments of different lengths can be separated by **gel electrophoresis**.
- The **polymerase chain reaction (PCR)** can produce many copies of (amplify) a specific target segment of DNA *in vitro*, using primers that bracket the desired sequence and a heat-resistant DNA polymerase.
- To clone a eukaryotic gene:

Cloning vector (often a bacterial plasmid)

DNA fragments obtained by PCR or from another source (cut by same restriction enzyme used on cloning vector)

Mix and ligate

Recombinant DNA plasmids

Recombinant plasmids are returned to host cells, each of which divides to form a clone of cells.
- Several technical difficulties hinder the expression of cloned eukaryotic genes in bacterial host cells. The use of cultured eukaryotic cells as host cells, coupled with appropriate **expression vectors**, helps avoid these problems.

?   *Describe how the process of gene cloning results in a cell clone containing a recombinant plasmid.*

CONCEPT 20.2

Biologists use DNA technology to study gene expression and function (pp. 417–422)

- Several techniques use hybridization of a **nucleic acid probe** to detect the presence of specific mRNAs.
- *In situ* hybridization and **RT-PCR** can detect the presence of a given mRNA in a tissue or an RNA sample, respectively.
- **DNA microarrays** are used to identify sets of genes co-expressed by a group of cells. Alternatively, their cDNAs can be sequenced (RNA-seq).
- For a gene of unknown function, experimental inactivation of the gene (a gene knockout) and observation of the resulting phenotypic effects can provide clues to its function. In humans, **genome-wide association studies** use **single nucleotide polymorphisms (SNPs)** as genetic markers for alleles that are associated with particular conditions.

?   *What useful information is obtained by detecting expression of specific genes?*

CONCEPT 20.3

Cloned organisms and stem cells are useful for basic research and other applications (pp. 422–427)

- The question of whether all the cells in an organism have the same genome prompted the first attempts at organismal cloning.
- Single differentiated cells from plants are often **totipotent**: capable of generating all the tissues of a complete new plant.
- Transplantation of the nucleus from a differentiated animal cell into an enucleated egg can sometimes give rise to a new animal.
- Certain embryonic **stem cells** (ES cells) from animal embryos and particular adult stem cells from adult tissues can reproduce and differentiate both in the lab and in the organism, offering the potential for medical use. ES cells are **pluripotent** but difficult to acquire. Induced pluripotent stem (iPS) cells, generated by reprogramming differentiated cells, resemble ES cells in their capacity to differentiate. Some differentiated cells have been directly reprogrammed to become different cell types. These cells and iPS cells hold promise for medical research and regenerative medicine.

?   *Describe how a researcher could carry out (1) organismal cloning, (2) production of ES cells, and (3) generation of iPS cells, focusing on how the cells are reprogrammed and using mice as an example. (The procedures are basically the same in humans and mice.)*

CONCEPT 20.4

The practical applications of DNA-based biotechnology affect our lives in many ways (pp. 428–433)

- DNA technology, including the analysis of genetic markers such as SNPs, is increasingly being used in the diagnosis of genetic and other diseases and offers potential for better treatment of genetic disorders (or even permanent cures through **gene therapy**), as well as more informed cancer therapies. DNA technology is used with cell cultures in the large-scale production of protein hormones and other proteins with therapeutic uses. Some therapeutic proteins are being produced in **transgenic** "pharm" animals.
- Analysis of genetic markers such as **short tandem repeats (STRs)** in DNA isolated from tissue or body fluids found at crime scenes leads to a **genetic profile**. Use of genetic profiles can provide definitive evidence that a suspect is innocent or strong evidence of guilt. Such analysis is also useful in parenthood disputes and in identifying the remains of crime victims.
- Genetically engineered microorganisms can be used to extract minerals from the environment or degrade various types of toxic waste materials.
- The aims of developing transgenic plants and animals are to improve agricultural productivity and food quality.
- The potential benefits of genetic engineering must be carefully weighed against the potential for harm to humans or the environment.

?   *What factors affect whether a given genetic disease would be a good candidate for successful gene therapy?*

TEST YOUR UNDERSTANDING

LEVEL 1: KNOWLEDGE/COMPREHENSION

1. In DNA technology, the term *vector* can refer to
   a. the enzyme that cuts DNA into restriction fragments.
   b. the sticky end of a DNA fragment.
   c. a SNP marker.
   d. a plasmid used to transfer DNA into a living cell.

2. Which of the following tools of DNA technology is incorrectly paired with its use?
   a. electrophoresis—separation of DNA fragments
   b. DNA ligase—cutting DNA, creating sticky ends of restriction fragments
   c. DNA polymerase—polymerase chain reaction to amplify sections of DNA
   d. reverse transcriptase—production of cDNA from mRNA

3. Plants are more readily manipulated by genetic engineering than are animals because
   a. plant genes do not contain introns.
   b. more vectors are available for transferring recombinant DNA into plant cells.
   c. a somatic plant cell can often give rise to a complete plant.
   d. plant cells have larger nuclei.

4. A paleontologist has recovered a bit of tissue from the 400-year-old preserved skin of an extinct dodo (a bird). To compare a specific region of the DNA from a sample with DNA from living birds, which of the following would be most useful for increasing the amount of dodo DNA available for testing?
   a. SNP analysis
   b. polymerase chain reaction (PCR)
   c. electroporation
   d. gel electrophoresis

5. DNA technology has many medical applications. Which of the following is *not* done routinely at present?
   a. production of hormones for treating diabetes and dwarfism
   b. production of microbes that can metabolize toxins
   c. introduction of genetically engineered genes into human gametes
   d. prenatal identification of genetic disease alleles

LEVEL 2: APPLICATION/ANALYSIS

6. Which of the following would *not* be true of cDNA produced using human brain tissue as the starting material?
   a. It could be amplified by the polymerase chain reaction.
   b. It was produced from pre-mRNA using reverse transcriptase.
   c. It could be labeled and used as a probe to detect genes expressed in the brain.
   d. It lacks the introns of the pre-mRNA.

7. Expression of a cloned eukaryotic gene in a bacterial cell involves many challenges. The use of mRNA and reverse transcriptase is part of a strategy to solve the problem of
   a. post-transcriptional processing.
   b. post-translational processing.
   c. nucleic acid hybridization.
   d. restriction fragment ligation.

8. Which of the following sequences in double-stranded DNA is most likely to be recognized as a cutting site for a restriction enzyme?
   a. AAGG   c. ACCA
      TTCC   TGGT
   b. GGCC   d. AAAA
      CCGG   TTTT

LEVEL 3: SYNTHESIS/EVALUATION

9. **MAKE CONNECTIONS** Imagine you want to study one of the human crystallins, proteins present in the lens of the eye (see Figure 1.8). To obtain a sufficient amount of the protein of interest, you decide to clone the gene that codes for it. Assume you know the sequence of this gene. How would you go about this?

10. **DRAW IT** You are cloning an aardvark gene, using a bacterial plasmid as a vector. The green diagram shows the plasmid, which contains the restriction site for the enzyme used in Figure 20.6. Above the plasmid is a segment of linear aardvark DNA that was synthesized using PCR. Diagram your cloning procedure, showing what would happen to these two molecules during each step. Use one color for the aardvark DNA and its bases and another color for those of the plasmid. Label each step and all 5′ and 3′ ends.

5′ GAATTCTAAAGCGCTTATGAATTC 3′
3′ CTTAAGATTTCGCGAATACTTAAG 5′
Aardvark DNA

Plasmid

11. **EVOLUTION CONNECTION**
    Ethical considerations aside, if DNA-based technologies became widely used, how might they change the way evolution proceeds, as compared with the natural evolutionary mechanisms that have operated for the past 4 billion years?

12. **SCIENTIFIC INQUIRY**
    You hope to study a gene that codes for a neurotransmitter protein produced in human brain cells. You know the amino acid sequence of the protein. Explain how you might (a) identify what genes are expressed in a specific type of brain cell, (b) identify (and isolate) the neurotransmitter gene, (c) produce multiple copies of the gene for study, and (d) produce large quantities of the neurotransmitter for evaluation as a potential medication.

13. **WRITE ABOUT A THEME: INFORMATION**
    In a short essay (100–150 words), discuss how the genetic basis of life plays a central role in biotechnology.

14. **SYNTHESIZE YOUR KNOWLEDGE**

The water in the Yellowstone National Park hot springs shown here is around 160°F (70°C). Biologists assumed that no species of organisms could live in water above about 130°F (55°C), so they were surprised to find several species of bacteria there, now called *thermophiles* ("heat-lovers"). You've learned in this chapter how an enzyme from one species, *Thermus aquaticus*, made feasible one of the most important DNA-based techniques used in labs today. What was the enzyme, and what was the value of its being isolated from a thermophile? Can you think of reasons other enzymes from this bacterium (or other thermophiles) might also be valuable?

For selected answers, see Appendix A.

MasteringBiology®

Students Go to **MasteringBiology** for assignments, the eText, and the Study Area with practice tests, animations, and activities.

Instructors Go to **MasteringBiology** for automatically graded tutorials and questions that you can assign to your students, plus Instructor Resources.

21
Genomes and Their Evolution

KEY CONCEPTS

21.1 The Human Genome Project fostered development of faster, less expensive sequencing techniques

21.2 Scientists use bioinformatics to analyze genomes and their functions

21.3 Genomes vary in size, number of genes, and gene density

21.4 Multicellular eukaryotes have much noncoding DNA and many multigene families

21.5 Duplication, rearrangement, and mutation of DNA contribute to genome evolution

21.6 Comparing genome sequences provides clues to evolution and development

▲ **Figure 21.1** What genomic information distinguishes a human from a chimpanzee?

Reading the Leaves from the Tree of Life

The chimpanzee (*Pan troglodytes*) is our closest living relative on the evolution-ary tree of life. The boy in **Figure 21.1** and his chimpanzee companion are intently studying the same leaf, but only one of them is able to talk about it. What accounts for this difference between two primates that share so much of their evolutionary history? With the advent of recent techniques for rapidly sequencing complete genomes, we have now started to address the genetic basis of intriguing questions like this.

The chimpanzee genome was sequenced two years after sequencing of the human genome was largely completed. Now that we can compare our genome, base by base, with that of the chimpanzee, we can tackle the more general issue of what differences in genetic information account for the distinct characteristics of these two species of primates.

In addition to determining the sequences of the human and chimpanzee ge-nomes, researchers have obtained complete genome sequences for *Escherichia coli* and numerous other prokaryotes, as well as many eukaryotes, including *Zea mays* (corn), *Drosophila melanogaster* (fruit fly), *Mus musculus* (house mouse), and *Pongo pygmaeus* (orangutan). In 2010, a draft sequence was announced for the genome of *Homo neanderthalensis,* an extinct species closely related to present-day humans. These whole and partial genomes are of great interest in their own right, but they

◀ House mouse (*Mus musculus*)

also provide important insights into evolution as well as other biological processes. Broadening the human-chimpanzee comparison to the genomes of other primates and more distantly related animals should reveal the sets of genes that control group-defining characteristics. Beyond that, comparisons with the genomes of bacteria, archaea, fungi, protists, and plants should enlighten us about the long evolutionary history of shared ancient genes and their products.

With the genomes of many species fully sequenced, scientists can study whole sets of genes and their interactions, an approach called **genomics**. The sequencing efforts that feed this approach have generated, and continue to generate, enormous volumes of data. The need to deal with this ever-increasing flood of information has spawned the field of **bioinformatics**, the application of computational methods to the storage and analysis of biological data.

We will begin this chapter by discussing two approaches to genome sequencing and some of the advances in bioinformatics and its applications. We will then summarize what has been learned from the genomes that have been sequenced thus far. Next, we will describe the composition of the human genome as a representative genome of a complex multicellular eukaryote. Finally, we will explore current ideas about how genomes evolve and about how the evolution of developmental mechanisms could have generated the great diversity of life on Earth today.

The Human Genome Project fostered development of faster, less expensive sequencing techniques

Sequencing of the human genome, an ambitious undertaking, officially began as the **Human Genome Project** in 1990. Organized by an international, publicly funded consortium of scientists at universities and research institutes, the project involved 20 large sequencing centers in six countries plus a host of other labs working on smaller parts of the project.

After the human genome sequence was largely completed in 2003, the sequence of each chromosome was analyzed and described in a series of papers, the last of which covered chromosome 1 and was published in 2006. With this refinement, researchers termed the sequencing "virtually complete."

The ultimate goal in mapping any genome is to determine the complete nucleotide sequence of each chromosome. For the human genome, this was accomplished by sequencing machines (see Figure 20.2), using the dideoxy chain termination method described in Figure 20.3. Even with automation, though, the sequencing of all 3 billion base pairs in a haploid set of human chromosomes presented a formidable challenge. In fact, a major thrust of the Human

Genome Project was the development of technology for faster sequencing, as described in Chapter 20. Improvements over the years chipped away at each time-consuming step, enabling the rate of sequencing to accelerate impressively: Whereas a productive lab could typically sequence 1,000 base pairs a day in the 1980s, by the year 2000 each research center working on the Human Genome Project was sequencing 1,000 base pairs *per second*, 24 hours a day, seven days a week. Methods like this that can analyze biological materials very rapidly and produce enormous volumes of data are said to be "high-throughput." Sequencing machines are an example of high-throughput devices.

Two approaches complemented each other in obtaining the complete sequence. The initial approach was a methodical one that built on an earlier storehouse of human genetic information. In 1998, however, molecular biologist J. Craig Venter set up a company (Celera Genomics) and declared his intention to sequence the entire human genome using an alternative strategy. The **whole-genome shotgun approach** starts with the cloning and sequencing of DNA fragments from randomly cut DNA. Powerful computer programs then assemble the resulting very large number of overlapping short sequences into a single continuous sequence **(Figure 21.2)**.

Today, the whole-genome shotgun approach is widely used, although other approaches are required for some

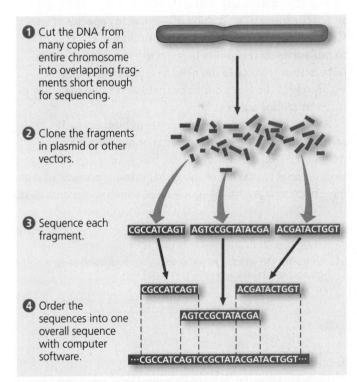

1 Cut the DNA from many copies of an entire chromosome into overlapping fragments short enough for sequencing.

2 Clone the fragments in plasmid or other vectors.

3 Sequence each fragment.

CGCCATCAGT   AGTCCGCTATACGA   ACGATACTGGT

4 Order the sequences into one overall sequence with computer software.

CGCCATCAGT   ACGATACTGGT
        AGTCCGCTATACGA
···CGCCATCAGTCCGCTATACGATACTGGT···

▲ **Figure 21.2 Whole-genome shotgun approach to sequencing.** In this approach, developed by J. Craig Venter and colleagues at Celera Genomics, random DNA fragments are cloned (see Figure 20.5), sequenced (see Figure 20.3), and then ordered relative to each other.

? *The fragments in stage 2 of this figure are depicted as scattered, rather than being in an ordered array. How does this depiction reflect the approach?*

regions of the genome that are difficult to sequence due to repetitive nucleotide sequences. Also, the development of newer sequencing techniques, generally called *sequencing by synthesis* (see Figure 20.4), has resulted in massive increases in speed and decreases in the cost of sequencing entire genomes. In these new techniques, many very small DNA fragments (each about 400–1,000 base pairs long) are sequenced at the same time, and computer software rapidly assembles the complete sequence. Because of the sensitivity of these techniques, the fragments can be sequenced directly; the cloning step (stage ❷ in Figure 21.2) is unnecessary. Whereas sequencing the first human genome took 13 years and cost $100 million, James Watson's genome was sequenced during four months in 2007 for about $1 million, and we are rapidly approaching the day when an individual's genome can be sequenced in a matter of hours for less than $1,000.

These technological advances have also facilitated an approach called **metagenomics** (from the Greek *meta*, beyond), in which DNA from an entire group of species (a *metagenome*) is collected from an environmental sample and sequenced. Again, computer software accomplishes the task of sorting out the partial sequences and assembling them into the individual specific genomes. So far, this approach has been applied to microbial communities found in environments as diverse as the Sargasso Sea and the human intestine. A 2012 study characterized the astounding diversity of the human "microbiome"—the many species of bacteria that coexist within and upon our bodies and contribute to our survival. The ability to sequence the DNA of mixed populations eliminates the need to culture each species separately in the lab, a difficulty that has limited the study of many microbial species.

At first glance, genome sequences of humans and other organisms are simply dry lists of nucleotide bases—millions of A's, T's, C's, and G's in mind-numbing succession. Crucial to making sense of this massive amount of data have been new analytical approaches, which we discuss next.

CONCEPT CHECK **21.1**

1. Describe the whole-genome shotgun approach to genome sequencing.

For suggested answers, see Appendix A.

CONCEPT 21.2

Scientists use bioinformatics to analyze genomes and their functions

Each of the 20 or so sequencing centers around the world working on the Human Genome Project churned out voluminous amounts of DNA sequence day after day. As the data began to accumulate, the need to coordinate efforts to keep track of all the sequences became clear. Thanks to the foresight of research scientists and government officials involved in the Human Genome Project, its goals included the establishment of banks of data, or databases, and the refining of analytical software. These databases and software programs would then be centralized and made readily accessible on the Internet. Accomplishing this aim has accelerated progress in DNA sequence analysis by making bioinformatics resources available to researchers worldwide and by speeding up the dissemination of information.

Centralized Resources for Analyzing Genome Sequences

Government-funded agencies carried out their mandate to establish databases and provide software with which scientists could analyze the sequence data. For example, in the United States, a joint endeavor between the National Library of Medicine and the National Institutes of Health (NIH) created the National Center for Biotechnology Information (NCBI), which maintains a website (www.ncbi.nlm.nih.gov) with extensive bioinformatics resources. On this site are links to databases, software, and a wealth of information about genomics and related topics. Similar websites have also been established by the European Molecular Biology Laboratory, the DNA Data Bank of Japan, and BGI (formerly known as the Beijing Genome Institute) in Shenzhen, China, three genome centers with which the NCBI collaborates. These large, comprehensive websites are complemented by others maintained by individual or small groups of laboratories. Smaller websites often provide databases and software designed for a narrower purpose, such as studying genetic and genomic changes in one particular type of cancer.

The NCBI database of sequences is called GenBank. As of July 2013, it included the sequences of 165 million fragments of genomic DNA, totaling 153 billion base pairs! GenBank is constantly updated, and the amount of data it contains is estimated to double approximately every 18 months. Any sequence in the database can be retrieved and analyzed using software from the NCBI website or elsewhere.

One software program available on the NCBI website, called BLAST, allows the visitor to compare a DNA sequence with every sequence in GenBank, base by base. A researcher might search for similar regions in other genes of the same species, or among the genes of other species. Another program allows comparison of predicted protein sequences. Yet a third can search any protein sequence for common stretches of amino acids (domains) for which a function is known or suspected, and it can show a three-dimensional model of the domain alongside other relevant information **(Figure 21.3)**. There is even a software program that can compare a collection of sequences, either nucleic acids or polypeptides, and diagram them in the form of an

① In this window, a partial amino acid sequence from an unknown muskmelon protein ("Query") is aligned with sequences from other proteins that the computer program found to be similar. Each sequence represents a domain called WD40.

② Four hallmarks of the WD40 domain are highlighted in yellow. (Sequence similarity is based on chemical aspects of the amino acids, so the amino acids in each hallmark region are not always identical.)

③ The Cn3D program displays a three-dimensional ribbon model of cow transducin (the protein highlighted in purple in the Sequence Alignment Viewer). This protein is the only one of those shown for which a structure has been determined. The sequence similarity of the other proteins to cow transducin suggests that their structures are likely to be similar.

④ Cow transducin contains seven WD40 domains, one of which is highlighted here in gray.

⑤ The yellow segments correspond to the WD40 hallmarks highlighted in yellow in the window above.

⑥ This window displays information about the WD40 domain from the Conserved Domain Database.

WD40 - Sequence Alignment Viewer

```
                              Query   ~~~ktGGIRL~RHfksVSAVEWHRk~~gDYLSTlvLreSRAVLIHQlsk
              Cow [transducin]   ~nvrvSRELA~GHtgyLSCCRFLDd~~nQIVTs~~Sg~DTTCALWDie~
     Mustard weed [transducin]   gtvpvSRMLT~GHrgyVSCCQYVPneda HLITS~~Sg~DQTCILWDvtt
             Corn [GNB protein]   gnmpvSRILT~GHkgyVSSCQYVPdgetRLITS~~Sg~DQTCVLWDvt~
            Human [PAFA protein]   ~~~ecIRTMH~GHdhnVSSVAIMPng~dHIVSA~~Sr~DKTIKMWEvg~
Nematode [unknown protein #1]   ~~~rcVKTLK~GHtnyVFCCCFNPs~~gTLIAS~~GsfDETIRIWCar~
Nematode [unknown protein #2]   ~~~rmTKTLK~GHnnyVFCCNFNPq~~sSLVVS~~GsfDESVRIWDvk~
       Fission yeast [FWDR protein]   ~~~seCISILhGHtdsVLCLTFDS~~~~TLLVS~~GsaDCTVKLWHfs~
```

WD40 - Cn3D 4.1

CDD Descriptive Items

Name: WD40

WD40 domain, found in a number of eukaryotic proteins that cover a wide variety of functions including adaptor/regulatory modules in signal transduction, pre-mRNA processing and cytoskeleton assembly; typically contains a GH dipeptide 11-24 residues from its N-terminus and the WD dipeptide at its C-terminus and is 40 residues long, hence the name WD40;

▲ **Figure 21.3 Bioinformatics tools that are available on the Internet.** A website maintained by the National Center for Biotechnology Information (NCBI) allows scientists and the public to access DNA and protein sequences and other stored data. The site includes a link to a protein structure database (Conserved Domain Database, CDD) that can find and describe similar domains in related proteins, as well as software (Cn3D, "See in 3D") that displays three-dimensional models of domains for which the structure has been determined. Some results are shown from a search for regions of proteins similar to an amino acid sequence in a muskmelon protein. The WD40 domain is one of the most abundant domains in proteins encoded by eukaryotic genomes. Within these proteins, it often plays a key role in molecular interactions during signal transduction in cells.

evolutionary tree based on the sequence relationships. (One such diagram is shown in Figure 21.17.)

Two research institutions, Rutgers University and the University of California, San Diego, also maintain a worldwide Protein Data Bank, a database of all three-dimensional protein structures that have been determined. (The database is accessible at www.wwpdb.org.) These structures can be rotated by the viewer to show all sides of the protein. Throughout this book, you'll find images of protein structures that have been obtained from the Protein Data Bank.

There is a vast array of resources available for researchers anywhere in the world to use free of charge. Let us now consider the types of questions scientists can address using these resources.

Identifying Protein-Coding Genes and Understanding Their Functions

Using available DNA sequences, geneticists can study genes directly, rather than taking the classical genetic approach, which requires determining the genotype from the phenotype. But this more recent approach poses a new challenge: What does the gene actually do? Given a long DNA sequence from a database such as GenBank, scientists aim to identify all protein-coding genes in the sequence and ultimately their functions. This process is called **gene annotation**.

In the past, gene annotation was carried out laboriously by individual scientists interested in particular genes, but the process has now been largely automated. The usual approach is to use software to scan the stored sequences for transcriptional and translational start and stop signals, for RNA-splicing sites, and for other telltale signs of protein-coding genes. The software also looks for certain short sequences that specify known mRNAs. Thousands of such sequences, called *expressed sequence tags*, or *ESTs*, have been collected from cDNA sequences and are cataloged in computer databases. This type of analysis identifies sequences that may turn out to be previously unknown protein-coding genes.

The identities of about half of the human genes were known before the Human Genome Project began. But what about the others, the previously unknown genes revealed by analysis of DNA sequences? Clues about their identities and functions come from comparing sequences that might be genes with those of known genes from other organisms, using the software described previously. Due to redundancy in the genetic code, the DNA sequence itself may vary more among species than the protein sequence does. Thus, scientists interested in proteins often compare the predicted amino acid sequence of a protein to that of other proteins.

Sometimes a newly identified sequence will match, at least partially, the sequence of a gene or protein in another species whose function is well known. For example, a plant researcher working on signaling pathways in the muskmelon would be excited to see that a partial amino acid sequence from a gene she had identified matched with sequences in other species encoding a so-called "WD40 domain" (see Figure 21.3). These WD40 domains are present in many eukaryotes and are known to function in signal transduction pathways. Alternatively, a new gene sequence might be similar to a previously encountered sequence whose function is still unknown. Another possibility is that the sequence is entirely unlike anything ever seen before. This was true for about a third of the genes of *E. coli* when its genome was sequenced. In the last case, protein function is usually deduced through a combination of biochemical and functional studies. The biochemical approach aims to determine the three-dimensional structure of the protein as well as other attributes, such as potential binding sites for other molecules. Functional studies usually involve blocking or disabling the gene in an organism to see how the phenotype is affected. RNAi, described in Concept 18.3, is an example of an experimental technique used to block gene function.

Understanding Genes and Gene Expression at the Systems Level

The impressive computational power provided by the tools of bioinformatics allows the study of whole sets of genes and their interactions, as well as the comparison of genomes from different species. Genomics is a rich source of new insights into fundamental questions about genome organization, regulation of gene expression, embryonic development, and evolution.

One informative approach has been taken by an ongoing research project called ENCODE (Encyclopedia of DNA Elements), which began in 2003. The aim of the project is to learn everything possible about the functionally important elements in the human genome using multiple experimental techniques. Investigators have sought to identify protein-coding genes and genes for noncoding RNAs, along with sequences that regulate gene expression, such as enhancers and promoters. In addition, they have extensively characterized DNA and histone modifications and chromatin structure. The second phase of the project, involving more than

440 scientists in 32 research groups, culminated with the simultaneous publication of 30 papers in 2012, describing over 1,600 large data sets. The power of this project is that it provides the opportunity to compare results from specific projects with each other, yielding a much richer picture of the whole genome.

Perhaps the most striking finding is that about 75% of the genome is transcribed at some point in at least one of the cell types studied, even though less than 2% codes for proteins. Furthermore, biochemical functions have been assigned to DNA elements making up at least 80% of the genome. To learn more about the different types of functional elements, parallel projects are analyzing in a similar way the genomes of two model organisms, the soil nematode *Caenorhabditis elegans* and the fruit fly *Drosophila melanogaster*. Because genetic and biochemical experiments using DNA technology can be performed on these species, testing the activities of potentially functional DNA elements in their genomes is expected to illuminate the workings of the human genome.

The scientific progress resulting from sequencing genomes and studying large sets of genes has encouraged scientists to attempt similar systematic studies of sets of proteins and their properties (such as their abundance, chemical modifications, and interactions), an approach called **proteomics**. (A *proteome* is the entire set of proteins expressed by a cell or group of cells.) Proteins, not the genes that encode them, carry out most of the activities of the cell. Therefore, we must study when and where proteins are produced in an organism, as well as how they interact in networks, if we are to understand the functioning of cells and organisms.

How Systems Are Studied: An Example

Genomics and proteomics are enabling molecular biologists to approach the study of life from an increasingly global perspective. Using the tools we have described, biologists have begun to compile catalogs of genes and proteins—listings of all the "parts" that contribute to the operation of cells, tissues, and organisms. With such catalogs in hand, researchers have shifted their attention from the individual parts to their functional integration in biological systems. As you may recall, in Chapter 1 we discussed this approach, called **systems biology**, which aims to model the dynamic behavior of whole biological systems based on the study of the interactions among the system's parts. Because of the vast amounts of data generated in these types of studies, advances in computer technology and bioinformatics have been crucial in making systems biology possible.

One important use of the systems biology approach is to define gene and protein interaction networks. To map the protein interaction network in the yeast *Saccharomyces cerevisiae*, for instance, researchers used sophisticated techniques to knock out (disable) pairs of genes, one pair at a time, creating doubly mutant cells. They then compared the fitness of each double mutant (based in part on the size of

Figure 21.4 The systems biology approach to protein interactions. This global protein interaction map shows the likely interactions (lines) among about 4,500 gene products (dots) in *Saccharomyces cerevisiae*, the budding yeast. Dots of the same color represent gene products involved in one of the 13 similarly colored cellular functions listed around the map. The white dots represent proteins that haven't been assigned to any color-coded function. The expanded area shows additional details of one map region where the gene products (blue dots) carry out amino acid biosynthesis, uptake, and related functions.

the cell colony it formed) to that predicted from the fitness of each of the two single mutants. The researchers reasoned that if the observed fitness matched the prediction, then the products of the two genes didn't interact with each other, but if the observed fitness was greater or less than predicted, then the gene products interacted in the cell. They then used computer software to build a graphic model by "mapping" the gene products to certain locations in the model, based on the similarity of their interactions. This resulted in the network-like "functional map" of protein interactions shown in **Figure 21.4**. Processing the vast number of protein-protein interactions generated by this experiment and integrating them into the completed map required powerful computers, mathematical tools, and newly developed software.

Application of Systems Biology to Medicine

The Cancer Genome Atlas is another example of systems biology in which a large group of interacting genes and gene products are analyzed together. This project, under the joint leadership of the National Cancer Institute and the NIH, aims to determine how changes in biological systems lead to cancer. A three-year pilot project ending in 2010 set out to find all the common mutations in three types of cancer— lung cancer, ovarian cancer, and glioblastoma of the brain— by comparing gene sequences and patterns of gene expression in cancer cells with those in normal cells. Work on glioblastoma confirmed the role of several suspected genes and identified a few previously unknown ones, suggesting possible new targets for therapies. The approach proved so fruitful for these three types of cancer that it has been extended to ten other types, chosen because they are common and often lethal in humans.

As high-throughput techniques become more rapid and less expensive, they are being increasingly applied to the problem of cancer. Rather than sequencing only protein-coding genes, sequencing the whole genomes of many tumors of a particular type allows scientists to uncover common chromosomal abnormalities, as well as any other consistent changes in these aberrant genomes.

In addition to whole-genome sequencing, silicon and glass "chips" that hold a microarray of most of the known human genes are now used to analyze gene expression patterns in patients suffering from various cancers and other diseases **(Figure 21.5)**. Analyzing which genes are over- or under-expressed in a particular cancer may allow physicians to tailor patients' treatment to their unique

◄ **Figure 21.5 A human gene microarray chip.** Tiny spots of DNA arranged in a grid on this silicon wafer represent almost all of the genes in the human genome. Using this chip, researchers can analyze expression patterns for all these genes at the same time.

genetic makeup and the specifics of their cancers. This approach has been used to begin to characterize subsets of particular cancers, enabling more refined treatments. Breast cancer is one example (see Figure 18.27).

Ultimately, medical records may include an individual's DNA sequence, a sort of genetic bar code, with regions highlighted that predispose the person to specific diseases. The use of such sequences for personalized medicine—disease prevention and treatment—has great potential. (See the interview with Charles Rotimi before Chapter 13.)

Systems biology is a very efficient way to study emergent properties at the molecular level. Recall from Chapter 1 that according to the theme of emergent properties, novel properties arise at each successive level of biological complexity as a result of the arrangement of building blocks at the underlying level. The more we can learn about the arrangement and interactions of the components of genetic systems, the deeper will be our understanding of whole organisms. The rest of this chapter will survey what we've learned from genomic studies thus far.

CONCEPT CHECK 21.2

1. What role does the Internet play in current genomics and proteomics research?

2. Explain the advantage of the systems biology approach to studying cancer versus the approach of studying a single gene at a time.

3. **MAKE CONNECTIONS** The ENCODE pilot project found that at least 75% of the genome is transcribed into RNAs, far more than could be accounted for by protein-coding genes. Review Concepts 17.3 and 18.3 and suggest some roles that these RNAs might play.

4. **MAKE CONNECTIONS** In Concept 20.2, you learned about genome-wide association studies. Explain how these studies use the systems biology approach.

For suggested answers, see Appendix A.

CONCEPT 21.3

Genomes vary in size, number of genes, and gene density

By April 2013, the sequencing of over 4,300 genomes had been completed and that of about 9,600 genomes and 370 metagenomes was in progress. In the completely sequenced group, about 4,000 are genomes of bacteria, and 186 are archaeal genomes. Among the 183 eukaryotic species in the group are vertebrates, invertebrates, protists, fungi, and plants. The accumulated genome sequences contain a wealth of information that we are now beginning to mine. What have we learned so far by comparing the genomes that have been sequenced? In this section, we will examine the characteristics of genome size, number of genes, and gene density.

Because these characteristics are so broad, we will focus on general trends, for which there are often exceptions.

Genome Size

Comparing the three domains (Bacteria, Archaea, and Eukarya), we find a general difference in genome size between prokaryotes and eukaryotes **(Table 21.1)**. While there are some exceptions, most bacterial genomes have between 1 and 6 million base pairs (Mb); the genome of *E. coli*, for instance, has 4.6 Mb. Genomes of archaea are, for the most part, within the size range of bacterial genomes. (Keep in mind, however, that many fewer archaeal genomes have been completely sequenced, so this picture may change.) Eukaryotic genomes tend to be larger: The genome of the single-celled yeast *Saccharomyces cerevisiae* (a fungus) has about 12 Mb, while most animals and plants, which are multicellular, have genomes of at least 100 Mb. There are 165 Mb in

Table 21.1	Genome Sizes and Estimated Numbers of Genes*		
Organism	Haploid Genome Size (Mb)	Number of Genes	Genes per Mb
Bacteria			
Haemophilus influenzae	1.8	1,700	940
Escherichia coli	4.6	4,400	950
Archaea			
Archaeoglobus fulgidus	2.2	2,500	1,130
Methanosarcina barkeri	4.8	3,600	750
Eukaryotes			
Saccharomyces cerevisiae (yeast, a fungus)	12	6,300	525
Caenorhabditis elegans (nematode)	100	20,100	200
Arabidopsis thaliana (mustard family plant)	120	27,000	225
Daphnia pulex (water flea)	200	31,000	155
Drosophila melanogaster (fruit fly)	165	14,000	85
Oryza sativa (rice)	430	42,000	98
Zea mays (corn)	2,300	32,000	14
Ailuropoda melanoleuca (giant panda)	2,400	21,000	9
Homo sapiens (human)	3,000	<21,000	7
Paris japonica (Japanese canopy plant)	149,000	ND	ND

*Some values given here are likely to be revised as genome analysis continues. Mb = million base pairs. ND = not determined.

the fruit fly genome, while humans have 3,000 Mb, about 500 to 3,000 times as many as a typical bacterium.

Aside from this general difference between prokaryotes and eukaryotes, a comparison of genome sizes among eukaryotes fails to reveal any systematic relationship between genome size and the organism's phenotype. For instance, the genome of *Paris japonica*, the Japanese canopy plant, contains 149 billion base pairs (149,000 Mb), about 50 times the size of the human genome. Even more striking, there is a single-celled amoeba, *Polychaos dubium*, whose genome size has been estimated at 670 billion base pairs (670,000 Mb). (This genome has not yet been sequenced.) On a finer scale, comparing two insect species, the cricket (*Anabrus simplex*) genome turns out to have 11 times as many base pairs as the *Drosophila melanogaster* genome. There is a wide range of genome sizes within the groups of unicellular eukaryotes, insects, amphibians, and plants and less of a range within mammals and reptiles.

Number of Genes

The number of genes also varies between prokaryotes and eukaryotes: Bacteria and archaea, in general, have fewer genes than eukaryotes. Free-living bacteria and archaea have from 1,500 to 7,500 genes, while the number of genes in eukaryotes ranges from about 5,000 for unicellular fungi (yeasts) to at least 40,000 for some multicellular eukaryotes.

Within the eukaryotes, the number of genes in a species is often lower than expected from considering simply the size of its genome. Looking at Table 21.1, you can see that the genome of the nematode *C. elegans* is 100 Mb in size and contains roughly 20,100 genes. The *Drosophila melanogaster* genome, in comparison, is much bigger (165 Mb) but has only about two-thirds the number of genes—14,000 genes.

Considering an example closer to home, we noted that the human genome contains 3,000 Mb, well over ten times the size of either the *D. melanogaster* or *C. elegans* genome. At the outset of the Human Genome Project, biologists expected somewhere between 50,000 and 100,000 genes to be identified in the completed sequence, based on the number of known human proteins. As the project progressed, the estimate was revised downward several times, and the ENCODE project discussed above has established the number to be fewer than 21,000. This relatively low number, similar to the number of genes in the nematode *C. elegans*, surprised biologists, who had been expecting many more human genes.

What genetic attributes allow humans (and other vertebrates) to get by with no more genes than nematodes? An important factor is that vertebrate genomes "get more bang for the buck" from their coding sequences because of extensive alternative splicing of RNA transcripts. Recall that this process generates more than one polypeptide from a single gene (see Figure 18.13). A typical human gene contains about ten exons, and an estimated 90% or more of these multi-exon genes are spliced in at least two different ways. Some genes are expressed in hundreds of alternatively spliced forms, others in just two. Scientists have not yet catalogued all of the different forms, but it is clear that the number of different proteins encoded in the human genome far exceeds the proposed number of genes.

Additional polypeptide diversity could result from post-translational modifications such as cleavage or the addition of carbohydrate groups in different cell types or at different developmental stages. Finally, the discovery of miRNAs and other small RNAs that play regulatory roles have added a new variable to the mix (see Concept 18.3). Some scientists think that this added level of regulation, when present, may contribute to greater organismal complexity for a given number of genes.

Gene Density and Noncoding DNA

We can take both genome size and number of genes into account by comparing gene density in different species. In other words, we can ask: How many genes are there in a given length of DNA? When we compare the genomes of bacteria, archaea, and eukaryotes, we see that eukaryotes generally have larger genomes but fewer genes in a given number of base pairs. Humans have hundreds or thousands of times as many base pairs in their genome as most bacteria, as we already noted, but only 5 to 15 times as many genes; thus, gene density is lower in humans (see Table 21.1). Even unicellular eukaryotes, such as yeasts, have fewer genes per million base pairs than bacteria and archaea. Among the genomes that have been sequenced completely thus far, humans and other mammals have the lowest gene density.

In all bacterial genomes studied so far, most of the DNA consists of genes for protein, tRNA, or rRNA; the small amount remaining consists mainly of nontranscribed regulatory sequences, such as promoters. The sequence of nucleotides along a bacterial protein-coding gene proceeds from start to finish without interruption by noncoding sequences (introns). In eukaryotic genomes, by contrast, most of the DNA neither encodes protein nor is transcribed into RNA molecules of known function, and the DNA includes more complex regulatory sequences. In fact, humans have 10,000 times as much noncoding DNA as bacteria. Some of this DNA in multicellular eukaryotes is present as introns within genes. Indeed, introns account for most of the difference in average length between human genes (27,000 base pairs) and bacterial genes (1,000 base pairs).

In addition to introns, multicellular eukaryotes have a vast amount of non-protein-coding DNA between genes. In the next section, we will describe the composition and arrangement of these great stretches of DNA in the human genome.

1. According to the best current estimate, the human genome contains fewer than 21,000 genes. However, there is evidence that human cells produce many more than 21,000 different polypeptides. What processes might account for this discrepancy?

2. The number of sequenced genomes is constantly being updated. Go to www.genomesonline.org to find the current number of completed genomes for each domain as well as the number of genomes whose sequencing is in progress. (*Hint*: Click on "Complete Projects" and, on the "Incomplete Projects" page, click on "In progress" to find the most up-to-date numbers.)

3. **WHAT IF?** What evolutionary processes might account for prokaryotes having smaller genomes than eukaryotes?

For suggested answers, see Appendix A.

CONCEPT 21.4

Multicellular eukaryotes have much noncoding DNA and many multigene families

We have spent most of this chapter, and indeed this unit, focusing on genes that code for proteins. Yet the coding regions of these genes and the genes for noncoding RNA products such as rRNA, tRNA, and miRNA make up only a small portion of the genomes of most multicellular eukaryotes. For example, once the sequencing of the human genome was completed, it became clear that only a tiny part—about 1.5%—codes for proteins or is transcribed into rRNAs or tRNAs. **Figure 21.6** shows what is known about the makeup of the remaining 98.5% of the genome.

Gene-related regulatory sequences and introns account, respectively, for 5% and about 20% of the human genome. The rest, located between functional genes, includes some unique (single-copy) noncoding DNA, such as gene fragments and **pseudogenes**, former genes that have accumulated mutations over a long time and no longer produce functional proteins. (The genes that produce small noncoding RNAs are a tiny percentage of the genome, distributed between the 20% introns and the 15% unique noncoding DNA.) Most intergenic DNA, however, is **repetitive DNA**, which consists of sequences that are present in multiple copies in the genome. Surprisingly, about 75% of this repetitive DNA (44% of the entire human genome) is made up of units called transposable elements and sequences related to them.

The bulk of many eukaryotic genomes consists of DNA sequences that neither code for proteins nor are transcribed to produce RNAs with known functions; this noncoding DNA was often described in the past as "junk DNA." However, genome comparisons over the past 10 years have revealed the persistence of this DNA in diverse genomes over

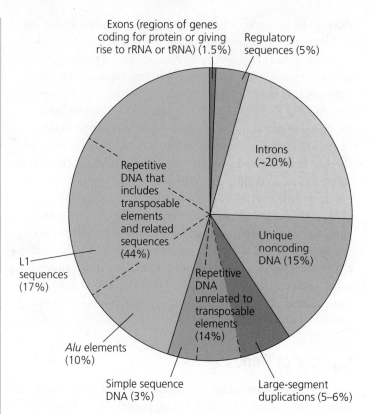

▲ **Figure 21.6 Types of DNA sequences in the human genome.** The gene sequences that code for proteins or are transcribed into rRNA or tRNA molecules make up only about 1.5% of the human genome (dark purple in the pie chart), while introns and regulatory sequences associated with genes (light purple) make up about a quarter. The vast majority of the human genome does not code for proteins or give rise to known RNAs, and much of it is repetitive DNA (dark and light green and teal). Because repetitive DNA is the most difficult to sequence and analyze, classification of some portions is tentative, and the percentages given here may shift slightly as genome analysis proceeds.

many hundreds of generations. For example, the genomes of humans, rats, and mice contain almost 500 regions of noncoding DNA that are *identical* in sequence in all three species. This is a higher level of sequence conservation than is seen for protein-coding regions in these species, strongly suggesting that the noncoding regions have important functions. The results of the ENCODE project discussed earlier have thoroughly underscored the key roles played in the cell by much of this noncoding DNA. In the next few pages, we examine how genes and noncoding DNA sequences are organized within genomes of multicellular eukaryotes, using the human genome as our main example. Genome organization tells us a lot about how genomes have evolved and continue to evolve, as we'll discuss in Concept 21.5.

Transposable Elements and Related Sequences

Both prokaryotes and eukaryotes have stretches of DNA that can move from one location to another within the genome. These stretches are known as *transposable genetic elements*, or simply **transposable elements**. During the process called

▲ **Figure 21.7 The effect of transposable elements on corn kernel color.** Barbara McClintock first proposed the idea of mobile genetic elements after observing variegations in the color of the kernels on a corn cob (right).

transposition, a transposable element moves from one site in a cell's DNA to a different target site by a type of recombination process. Transposable elements are sometimes called "jumping genes," but actually they never completely detach from the cell's DNA. Instead, the original and new DNA sites are brought very close together by enzymes and other proteins that bend the DNA.

The first evidence for wandering DNA segments came from American geneticist Barbara McClintock's breeding experiments with Indian corn (maize) in the 1940s and 1950s **(Figure 21.7)**. As she tracked corn plants through multiple generations, McClintock identified changes in the color of corn kernels that made sense only if she postulated the existence of genetic elements capable of moving from other locations in the genome into the genes for kernel color, disrupting the genes so that the kernel color was changed. McClintock's discovery was met with great skepticism and virtually discounted at the time. Her careful work and insightful ideas were finally validated many years later when transposable elements were found in bacteria. In 1983, at the age of 81, McClintock received the Nobel Prize for her pioneering research.

Movement of Transposons and Retrotransposons

Eukaryotic transposable elements are of two types. The first type are **transposons**, which move within a genome by means of a DNA intermediate. Transposons can move by a "cut-and-paste" mechanism, which removes the element from the original site, or by a "copy-and-paste" mechanism, which leaves a copy behind **(Figure 21.8)**. Both mechanisms require an enzyme called *transposase*, which is generally encoded by the transposon.

Most transposable elements in eukaryotic genomes are of the second type, **retrotransposons**, which move by

© Pearson Education, Inc.

▲ **Figure 21.8 Transposon movement.** Movement of transposons by either the copy-and-paste mechanism (shown here) or the cut-and-paste mechanism involves a double-stranded DNA intermediate that is inserted into the genome.

? *How would this figure differ if it showed the cut-and-paste mechanism?*

means of an RNA intermediate that is a transcript of the retrotransposon DNA. Thus, retrotransposons always leave a copy at the original site during transposition **(Figure 21.9)**. To insert at another site, the RNA intermediate is first converted back to DNA by reverse transcriptase, an enzyme encoded by the retrotransposon. (Reverse transcriptase is also encoded by retroviruses, as you learned in Concept 19.2. In fact, retroviruses may have evolved from retrotransposons.) Another cellular enzyme catalyzes insertion of the reverse-transcribed DNA at a new site.

Sequences Related to Transposable Elements

Multiple copies of transposable elements and sequences related to them are scattered throughout eukaryotic genomes. A single unit is usually hundreds to thousands of base pairs long, and the dispersed "copies" are similar but usually not identical to each other. Some of these are transposable

© Pearson Education, Inc.

▲ **Figure 21.9 Retrotransposon movement.** Movement begins with synthesis of a single-stranded RNA intermediate. The remaining steps are essentially identical to part of the retrovirus replicative cycle (see Figure 19.8).

elements that can move; the enzymes required for this movement may be encoded by any transposable element, including the one that is moving. Others are related sequences that have lost the ability to move altogether. Transposable elements and related sequences make up 25–50% of most mammalian genomes (see Figure 21.6) and even higher percentages in amphibians and many plants. In fact, the very large size of some plant genomes is accounted for not by extra genes, but by extra transposable elements. For example, sequences like these make up 85% of the corn genome!

In humans and other primates, a large portion of transposable element–related DNA consists of a family of similar sequences called *Alu elements*. These sequences alone account for approximately 10% of the human genome. *Alu* elements are about 300 nucleotides long, much shorter than most functional transposable elements, and they do not code for any protein. However, many *Alu* elements are transcribed into RNA, and at least some of these RNAs are thought to help regulate gene expression.

An even larger percentage (17%) of the human genome is made up of a type of retrotransposon called *LINE-1*, or *L1*. These sequences are much longer than *Alu* elements—about 6,500 base pairs—and typically have a very low rate of transposition. However, researchers working with rats have found L1 retrotransposons to be more active in cells of the developing brain. They have proposed that different effects on gene expression of L1 retrotransposition in developing neurons may contribute to the great diversity of neuronal cell types (see Concept 48.1).

Although many transposable elements encode proteins, these proteins do not carry out normal cellular functions. Therefore, transposable elements are usually included in the "noncoding" DNA category, along with other repetitive sequences.

Other Repetitive DNA, Including Simple Sequence DNA

Repetitive DNA that is not related to transposable elements has probably arisen from mistakes during DNA replication or recombination. Such DNA accounts for about 14% of the human genome (see Figure 21.6). About a third of this (5–6% of the human genome) consists of duplications of long stretches of DNA, with each unit ranging from 10,000 to 300,000 base pairs. These long segments seem to have been copied from one chromosomal location to another site on the same or a different chromosome and probably include some functional genes.

In contrast to scattered copies of long sequences, **simple sequence DNA** contains many copies of tandemly repeated short sequences, as in the following example (showing one DNA strand only):

... GTTACGTTACGTTACGTTACGTTACGTTAC ...

In this case, the repeated unit (GTTAC) consists of 5 nucleotides. Repeated units may contain as many as 500 nucleotides, but often contain fewer than 15 nucleotides, as in this example. When the unit contains 2–5 nucleotides, the series of repeats is called a **short tandem repeat**, or **STR**; we discussed the use of STR analysis in preparing genetic profiles in Concept 20.4. The number of copies of the repeated unit can vary from site to site within a given genome. There could be as many as several hundred thousand repetitions of the GTTAC unit at one site, but only half that number at another. STR analysis is performed on sites selected because they have relatively few repeats. The repeat number can vary from person to person, and since humans are diploid, each person has two alleles per site, which can differ. This diversity produces the variation represented in the genetic profiles that result from STR analysis. Altogether, simple sequence DNA makes up 3% of the human genome.

Much of a genome's simple sequence DNA is located at chromosomal telomeres and centromeres, suggesting that this DNA plays a structural role for chromosomes. The DNA at centromeres is essential for the separation of chromatids in cell division (see Concept 12.2). Centromeric DNA, along with simple sequence DNA located elsewhere, may also help organize the chromatin within the interphase nucleus. The simple sequence DNA located at telomeres, at the tips of chromosomes, prevents genes from being lost as the DNA shortens with each round of replication (see Concept 16.2). Telomeric DNA also binds proteins that protect the ends of a chromosome from degradation and from joining to other chromosomes.

Short repetitive sequences like those described here provide a challenge for whole-genome shotgun sequencing, because the presence of many short repeats hinders accurate reassembly of fragment sequences by computers. Regions of simple sequence DNA account for much of the uncertainty present in estimates of whole-genome sizes.

Genes and Multigene Families

We finish our discussion of the various types of DNA sequences in eukaryotic genomes with a closer look at genes. Recall that DNA sequences that code for proteins or give rise to tRNA or rRNA compose a mere 1.5% of the human genome (see Figure 21.6). If we include introns and regulatory sequences associated with genes, the total amount of DNA that is gene-related—coding and noncoding—constitutes about 25% of the human genome. Put another way, only about 6% (1.5% out of 25%) of the length of the average gene is represented in the final gene product.

Like the genes of bacteria, many eukaryotic genes are present as unique sequences, with only one copy per haploid set of chromosomes. But in the human genome and the genomes of many other animals and plants, solitary genes make up less than half of the total gene-related DNA. The rest occur in **multigene families**, collections of two or more identical or very similar genes.

In multigene families that consist of *identical* DNA sequences, those sequences are usually clustered tandemly and, with the notable exception of the genes for histone proteins, have RNAs as their final products. An example is the family of identical DNA sequences that are the genes for the three largest rRNA molecules **(Figure 21.10a)**. These rRNA molecules are transcribed from a single transcription unit that is repeated tandemly hundreds to thousands of times in one or several clusters in the genome of a multicellular eukaryote. The many copies of this rRNA transcription unit help cells to quickly make the millions of ribosomes needed for active protein synthesis. The primary transcript is cleaved to yield the three rRNA molecules, which combine with proteins and one other kind of rRNA (5S rRNA) to form ribosomal subunits.

The classic examples of multigene families of *nonidentical* genes are two related families of genes that encode globins, a group of proteins that include the α and β polypeptide subunits of hemoglobin. One family, located on chromosome 16 in humans, encodes various forms of α-globin; the other, on chromosome 11, encodes forms of β-globin **(Figure 21.10b)**. The different forms of each globin subunit are expressed at different times in development, allowing hemoglobin to function effectively in the changing environment of the developing animal. In humans, for example, the embryonic and fetal forms of hemoglobin have a higher affinity for oxygen than the adult forms, ensuring the efficient transfer of oxygen from mother to fetus. Also found in the globin gene family clusters are several pseudogenes. The evolution of these two globin gene families will be further discussed in Concept 21.5.

Analyzing the arrangement of the genes in gene families has given biologists insight into the evolution of genomes. We will consider some of the processes that have shaped the genomes of different species over evolutionary time in the next section.

CONCEPT CHECK 21.4

1. Discuss the characteristics of mammalian genomes that make them larger than prokaryotic genomes.

2. Which of the three mechanisms described in Figures 21.8 and 21.9 result(s) in a copy remaining at the original site as well as a copy appearing in a new location?

3. Contrast the organizations of the rRNA gene family and the globin gene families. For each, explain how the existence of a family of genes benefits the organism.

4. **MAKE CONNECTIONS** Assign each DNA segment at the top of Figure 18.8 to a sector in the pie chart in Figure 21.6.

For suggested answers, see Appendix A.

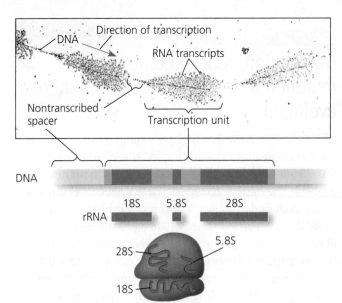

(a) Part of the ribosomal RNA gene family. The TEM at the top shows three of the hundreds of copies of rRNA transcription units in the rRNA gene family of a salamander genome. Each "feather" corresponds to a single unit being transcribed by about 100 molecules of RNA polymerase (dark dots along the DNA), moving left to right (red arrow). The growing RNA transcripts extend from the DNA. In the diagram of a transcription unit below the TEM, the genes for three types of rRNA (darker blue) are adjacent to regions that are transcribed but later removed (medium blue). A single transcript is processed to yield one of each of the three rRNAs (red), key components of the ribosome.

(b) The human α-globin and β-globin gene families. Adult hemoglobin is composed of two α-globin and two β-globin polypeptide subunits, as shown in the molecular model. The genes (darker blue) encoding α- and β-globins are found in two families, organized as shown here. The noncoding DNA (light blue) separating the functional genes within each family includes pseudogenes (ψ; gold), versions of the functional genes that no longer encode functional polypeptides. Genes and pseudogenes are named with Greek letters, as you have seen previously for the α- and β-globins. Some genes are expressed only in the embryo or fetus.

▲ **Figure 21.10 Gene families.**

? *In (a), how could you determine the direction of transcription if it weren't indicated by the red arrow?*

Duplication, rearrangement, and mutation of DNA contribute to genome evolution

EVOLUTION Now that we have explored the makeup of the human genome as an example, let's see what we can learn from the composition of the genome about how it evolved. The basis of change at the genomic level is mutation, which underlies much of genome evolution. It seems likely that the earliest forms of life had a minimal number of genes—those necessary for survival and reproduction. If this were indeed the case, one aspect of evolution must have been an increase in the size of the genome, with the extra genetic material providing the raw material for gene diversification. In this section, we will first describe how extra copies of all or part of a genome can arise and then consider subsequent processes that can lead to the evolution of proteins (or RNA products) with slightly different or entirely new functions.

Duplication of Entire Chromosome Sets

An accident in meiosis can result in one or more extra sets of chromosomes, a condition known as polyploidy. Although such accidents would most often be lethal, in rare cases they could facilitate the evolution of genes. In a polyploid organism, one set of genes can provide essential functions for the organism. The genes in the one or more extra sets can diverge by accumulating mutations; these variations may persist if the organism carrying them survives and reproduces. In this way, genes with novel functions can evolve. As long as one copy of an essential gene is expressed, the divergence of another copy can lead to its encoded protein acting in a novel way, thereby changing the organism's phenotype.

The outcome of this accumulation of mutations may be the branching off of a new species. While polyploidy is rare among animals, it is relatively common among plants, especially flowering plants. Some botanists estimate that as many as 80% of the plant species that are alive today show evidence of polyploidy having occurred among their ancestral species. You'll learn more about how polyploidy leads to plant speciation in Concept 24.2.

Alterations of Chromosome Structure

With the recent explosion in genomic sequence information, we can now compare the chromosomal organizations of many different species in detail. This information allows us to make inferences about the evolutionary processes that shape chromosomes and may drive speciation. For example, scientists have long known that sometime in the

▲ **Figure 21.11 Human and chimpanzee chromosomes.** The positions of telomere-like and centromere-like sequences on human chromosome 2 (left) match those of telomeres on chimp chromosomes 12 and 13 and the centromere on chimp chromosome 13 (right). This suggests that chromosomes 12 and 13 in a human ancestor fused end to end to form human chromosome 2. The centromere from ancestral chromosome 12 remained functional on human chromosome 2, while the one from ancestral chromosome 13 did not.

last 6 million years, when the ancestors of humans and chimpanzees diverged as species, the fusion of two ancestral chromosomes in the human line led to different haploid numbers for humans ($n = 23$) and chimpanzees ($n = 24$). The banding patterns in stained chromosomes suggested that the ancestral versions of current chimp chromosomes 12 and 13 fused end to end, forming chromosome 2 in an ancestor of the human lineage. Sequencing and analysis of human chromosome 2 during the Human Genome Project provided very strong supporting evidence for the model we have just described **(Figure 21.11)**.

In another study of broader scope, researchers compared the DNA sequence of each human chromosome with the whole-genome sequence of the mouse **(Figure 21.12)**.

▲ **Figure 21.12 Human and mouse chromosomes.** Here, we can see that DNA sequences very similar to large blocks of human chromosome 16 (colored areas in this diagram) are found on mouse chromosomes 7, 8, 16, and 17. This finding suggests that the DNA sequence in each block has stayed together in the mouse and human lineages since the time they diverged from a common ancestor.

One part of their study showed that large blocks of genes on human chromosome 16 are found on four mouse chromosomes, indicating that the genes in each block stayed together in both the mouse and the human lineages during their divergent evolution from a common ancestor.

Performing the same comparative analysis between chromosomes of humans and six other mammalian species allowed the researchers to reconstruct the evolutionary history of chromosomal rearrangements in these eight species. They found many duplications and inversions of large portions of chromosomes, the result of errors during meiotic recombination in which the DNA broke and was rejoined incorrectly. The rate of these events seems to have begun accelerating about 100 million years ago, around 35 million years before large dinosaurs became extinct and the number of mammalian species began rapidly increasing. The apparent coincidence is interesting because chromosomal rearrangements are thought to contribute to the generation of new species. Although two individuals with different arrangements could still mate and produce offspring, the offspring would have two nonequivalent sets of chromosomes, making meiosis inefficient or even impossible. Thus, chromosomal rearrangements would lead to two populations that could not successfully mate with each other, a step on the way to their becoming two separate species. (You'll learn more about this in Concept 24.2.)

The same study also unearthed a pattern with medical relevance. Analysis of the chromosomal breakage points associated with the rearrangements showed that specific sites were used over and over again. A number of these recombination "hot spots" correspond to locations of chromosomal rearrangements within the human genome that are associated with congenital diseases (see Concept 15.4).

Duplication and Divergence of Gene-Sized Regions of DNA

Errors during meiosis can also lead to the duplication of chromosomal regions that are smaller than the ones we've just discussed, including segments the length of individual genes. Unequal crossing over during prophase I of meiosis, for instance, can result in one chromosome with a deletion and another with a duplication of a particular gene. Transposable elements can provide homologous sites where nonsister chromatids can cross over, even when other chromatid regions are not correctly aligned **Figure 21.13**.

Also, slippage can occur during DNA replication, such that the template shifts with respect to the new complementary strand, and a part of the template strand is either skipped by the replication machinery or used twice as a template. As a result, a segment of DNA is deleted or duplicated. It is easy to imagine how such errors could occur in regions of repeats. The variable number of repeated units of

▲ **Figure 21.13 Gene duplication due to unequal crossing over.** One mechanism by which a gene (or other DNA segment) can be duplicated is recombination during meiosis between copies of a transposable element flanking the gene. Such recombination between misaligned nonsister chromatids of homologous chromosomes produces one chromatid with two copies of the gene and one chromatid with no copy.

MAKE CONNECTIONS *Examine how crossing over occurs in Figure 13.9. In the middle panel above, draw a line through the portions that result in the upper chromatid in the bottom panel. Use a different color to do the same for the other chromatid.*

simple sequence DNA at a given site, used for STR analysis, is probably due to errors like these. Evidence that unequal crossing over and template slippage during DNA replication lead to duplication of genes is found in the existence of multigene families, such as the globin family.

Evolution of Genes with Related Functions: The Human Globin Genes

Figure 21.10b diagrams the organization of the α-globin and β-globin gene families as they exist in the human genome today. Now, let's consider how events such as duplications can lead to the evolution of genes with related functions like the globin genes. A comparison of gene sequences within a multigene family can suggest the order in which the genes arose. Re-creating the evolutionary history of the globin genes using this approach indicates that they all evolved from one common ancestral globin gene that underwent duplication and divergence into the α-globin and β-globin ancestral genes about 450–500 million years ago. Each of these genes was later duplicated several times, and the copies then diverged from each other in sequence, yielding the current

Figure 21.14 A model for the evolution of the human α-globin and β-globin gene families from a single ancestral globin gene.

? *The gold elements are pseudogenes. Explain how they could have arisen after gene duplication.*

family members **(Figure 21.14)**. In fact, the common ancestral globin gene also gave rise to the oxygen-binding muscle protein myoglobin and to the plant protein leghemoglobin. The latter two proteins function as monomers, and their genes are included in a "globin superfamily."

After the duplication events, the differences between the genes in the globin families undoubtedly arose from mutations that accumulated in the gene copies over many generations. The current model is that the necessary function provided by an α-globin protein, for example, was fulfilled by one gene, while other copies of the α-globin gene accumulated random mutations. Many mutations may have had an adverse effect on the organism and others may have had no effect, but a few mutations must have altered the function of the protein product in a way that was advantageous to the organism at a particular life stage without substantially changing the protein's oxygen-carrying function. Presumably, natural selection acted on these altered genes, maintaining them in the population.

In the **Scientific Skills Exercise**, you can compare amino acid sequences of the globin family members and see how such comparisons were used to generate the model for globin gene evolution shown in Figure 21.14. The existence of several pseudogenes among the functional globin genes provides additional evidence for this model: Random mutations in these "genes" over evolutionary time have destroyed their function.

Evolution of Genes with Novel Functions

In the evolution of the globin gene families, gene duplication and subsequent divergence produced family members

whose protein products performed functions similar to each other (oxygen transport). However, an alternative scenario is that one copy of a duplicated gene can undergo alterations that lead to a completely new function for the protein product. The genes for lysozyme and α-lactalbumin are good examples of this type of situation.

Lysozyme is an enzyme that helps protect animals against bacterial infection by hydrolyzing bacterial cell walls (see Figure 5.16); α-lactalbumin is a nonenzymatic protein that plays a role in milk production in mammals. The two proteins are quite similar in their amino acid sequences and three-dimensional structures **(Figure 21.15)**. Both genes are found in mammals, whereas only the lysozyme gene is present in birds. These findings suggest that at some time after the lineages leading to mammals and birds had separated, the lysozyme gene was duplicated in the mammalian lineage but not in the avian lineage. Subsequently, one copy of the duplicated lysozyme gene evolved into a gene encoding α-lactalbumin, a protein with a completely different function. In a recent study, evolutionary biologists searched vertebrate genomes for genes with similar sequences. There appear to be at least eight members of the lysozyme family, with related genes found in other mammalian species as well. The functions of all the encoded gene products are not yet known, but it will be exciting to discover whether they are as different as the functions of lysozyme and α-lactalbumin.

Besides the duplication and divergence of whole genes, rearrangement of existing DNA sequences within genes has also contributed to genome evolution. The presence of introns may have promoted the evolution of new proteins by facilitating the duplication or shuffling of exons, as we'll discuss next.

Rearrangements of Parts of Genes: Exon Duplication and Exon Shuffling

Recall from Concept 17.3 that an exon often codes for a protein domain, a distinct structural and functional region of a protein molecule. We've already seen that unequal crossing over during meiosis can lead to duplication of a gene on one chromosome and its loss from the homologous chromosome (see Figure 21.13). By a similar process, a particular exon within a gene could be duplicated on one chromosome and deleted from the other. The gene with the duplicated exon would code for a protein containing

(a) Lysozyme　　　　　　　　　　**(b) α–lactalbumin**

Lysozyme	**1**	KVFERCELAR	TLKRLGMDGY	RGISLANWMC	LAKWESGYNT	RATNYNAGDR
α–lactalbumin	**1**	KQFTKCELSQ	LLK--DIDGY	GGIALPELIC	TMFHTSGYDT	QAIVENN--E
Lysozyme	**51**	STDYGIFQIN	SRYWCNDGKT	PGAVNACHLS	CSALLQDNIA	DAVACAKRVV
α–lactalbumin	**51**	STEYGLFQIS	NKLWCKSSQV	PQSRNICDIS	CDKFLDDDIT	DDIMCAKKIL
Lysozyme	**101**	RDPQGIRAWV	AWRNRCQ-NR	DVRQYVQGCG	V	
α–lactalbumin	**101**	D-IKGIDYWL	AHKALCT--E	KLEQWLCEKL	–	

(c) Amino acid sequence alignments of lysozyme and α–lactalbumin

▲ **Figure 21.15 Comparison of lysozyme and α-lactalbumin proteins.** Computer-generated ribbon models of the similar structures of **(a)** lysozyme and **(b)** α-lactalbumin are shown, along with a comparison of the amino acid sequences of the two proteins. The amino acids are arranged in groups of 10 for ease of reading, and single-letter amino acid codes are used (see Figure 5.14). Identical amino acids are highlighted in yellow, and dashes indicate gaps in one sequence that have been introduced by the software to optimize the alignment.

MAKE CONNECTIONS *Even though two amino acids are not identical, they may be structurally and chemically similar and therefore behave similarly. Using Figure 5.14 as a reference, examine the non-identical amino acids in positions 1-30 and note cases where the amino acids in the two sequences are similar.*

a second copy of the encoded domain. This change in the protein's structure might augment its function by increasing its stability, enhancing its ability to bind a particular ligand, or altering some other property. Quite a few protein-coding genes have multiple copies of related exons, which presumably arose by duplication and then diverged. The gene encoding the extracellular matrix protein collagen is a good example. Collagen is a structural protein with a highly repetitive amino acid sequence, which reflects the repetitive pattern of exons in the collagen gene.

Alternatively, we can imagine the occasional mixing and matching of different exons either within a gene or between two different (nonallelic) genes owing to errors in meiotic recombination. This process, termed *exon shuffling*, could lead to new proteins with novel combinations of functions. As an example, let's consider the gene for tissue plasminogen activator (TPA). The TPA protein is an extracellular protein that helps control blood clotting. It has four domains of three types, each encoded by an exon; one exon is present in two copies. Because each type of exon is also found in other proteins, the current version of the gene for TPA is thought to have arisen by several instances of exon shuffling and duplication **(Figure 21.16)**.

▲ **Figure 21.16 Evolution of a new gene by exon shuffling.** Exon shuffling could have moved exons, each encoding a particular domain, from ancestral forms of the genes for epidermal growth factor, fibronectin, and plasminogen (left) into the evolving gene for tissue plasminogen activator, TPA (right). Duplication of the "kringle" exon (K) from the plasminogen gene after its movement could account for the two copies of this exon in the TPA gene existing today.

? *How could the presence of transposable elements within introns have facilitated the exon shuffling shown here?*

Reading an Amino Acid Sequence Identity Table

How Have Amino Acid Sequences of Human Globin Genes Diverged During Their Evolution? To build a model of the evolutionary history of the globin genes (see Figure 21.14), researchers compared the amino acid sequences of the polypeptides they encode. In this exercise, you will analyze comparisons of the amino acid sequences of globin polypeptides to shed light on their evolutionary relationships.

How the Experiment Was Done Scientists obtained the DNA sequences for each of the eight globin genes and "translated" them into amino acid sequences. They then used a computer program to align the sequences (with dashes indicating gaps in one sequence) and calculate a percent identity value for each pair of globins. The percent identity reflects the number of positions with identical amino acids relative to the total number of amino acids in a globin polypeptide. The data were displayed in a table to show the pairwise comparisons.

Data from the Experiment The following table shows an example of a pairwise alignment—that of the α_1-globin (alpha-1 globin) and ζ-globin (zeta globin) amino acid sequences—using the standard single-letter symbols for amino acids. To the left of each line of amino acid sequence is the number of the first amino acid in that line. The percent identity value for the α_1- and ζ-globin amino acid sequences was calculated by counting the number of matching amino acids (87, highlighted

in yellow), dividing by the total number of amino acid positions (143), and then multiplying by 100. This resulted in a 61% identity value for the α_1-ζ pair, as shown in the amino acid identity table at the bottom of the page. The values for other globin pairs were calculated in the same way.

▲ Hemoglobin

Interpret the Data

1. Notice that in the alignment table, the data are arranged so each globin pair can be compared. (a) Notice that some cells in the table have dashed lines. Given the pairs that are being compared for these cells, what percent identity value is implied by the dashed lines? (b) Notice that the cells in the lower left half of the table are blank. Using the information already provided in the table, fill in the missing values. Why does it make sense that these cells were left blank?

2. The earlier that two genes arose from a duplicated gene, the more their nucleotide sequences can have diverged, which may result in amino acid differences in the protein products. (a) Based on that premise, identify which two genes are most divergent from each other. What is the percent amino acid identity between their polypeptides? (b) Using the same approach, identify which two globin genes are the most recently duplicated. What is the percent identity between them?

3. The model of globin gene evolution shown in Figure 21.14 suggests that an ancestral gene duplicated and mutated to become α- and β-globin genes, and then each one was further duplicated and mutated. What features of the data set support the model?

4. Make a list of all the percent identity values from the table, starting with 100% at the top. Next to each number write the globin pair(s) with that percent identity value. Use one color for the globins from the α family and a different color for the globins from the β family. (a) Compare the order of pairs on your list with their positions in the model shown in Figure 21.14. Does the order of pairs describe the same relative "closeness" of globin family members seen in the model? (b) Compare the percent identity values for pairs within the α or β group to the values for between-group pairs.

(MB) A version of this Scientific Skills Exercise can be assigned in MasteringBiology.

Data from NCBI database. **Further Reading** R. C. Hardison, Globin genes on the move, *Journal of Biology* 7:35.1–35.5 (2008).

Globin	Alignment of Globin Amino Acid Sequences
α_1	1 MVLSPADKTNVKAAWGKVGAHAGEYGAEAL
ζ	1 MSLTKTERTIIVSMWAKISTQADTIGTETL
α_1	31 ERMFLSFPTTKTYFPHFDLSH–GSAQVKGH
ζ	31 ERLFLSHPQTKTYFPHFDL–HPGSAQLRAH
α_1	61 GKKVADALTNAVAHVDDMPNALSALSDLHA
ζ	61 GSKVVAAVGDAVKSIDDIGGALSKLSELHA
α_1	91 HKLRVDPVNFKLLSHCLLVTLAAHLPAEFT
ζ	91 YILRVDPVNFKLLSHCLLVTLAARFPADFT
α_1	121 PAVHASLDKFLASVSTVLTSKYR
ζ	121 AEAHAAWDKFLSVVSSVLTEKYR

Amino Acid Identity Table								
		α Family			β Family			
		α_1 (alpha 1)	α_2 (alpha 2)	ζ (zeta)	β (beta)	δ (delta)	ϵ (epsilon)	A_γ (gamma A)	G_γ (gamma G)
α Family	α_1	-----	100	61	45	44	39	42	42
	α_2		-----	61	45	44	39	42	42
	ζ			-----	38	40	41	41	41
β Family	β				-----	93	76	73	73
	δ					-----	73	71	72
	ϵ						-----	80	80
	A_γ							-----	99
	G_γ								-----

How Transposable Elements Contribute to Genome Evolution

The persistence of transposable elements as a large fraction of some eukaryotic genomes is consistent with the idea that they play an important role in shaping a genome over evolutionary time. These elements can contribute to the evolution of the genome in several ways. They can promote recombination, disrupt cellular genes or control elements, and carry entire genes or individual exons to new locations.

Transposable elements of similar sequence scattered throughout the genome facilitate recombination between different chromosomes by providing homologous regions for crossing over. Most such recombination events are probably detrimental, causing chromosomal translocations and other changes in the genome that may be lethal to the organism. But over the course of evolutionary time, an occasional recombination event of this sort may be advantageous to the organism. (For the change to be heritable, of course, it must happen in a cell that will give rise to a gamete.)

The movement of a transposable element can have a variety of consequences. For instance, if a transposable element "jumps" into the middle of a protein-coding sequence, it will prevent the production of a normal transcript of the gene. If a transposable element inserts within a regulatory sequence, the transposition may lead to increased or decreased production of one or more proteins. Transposition caused both types of effects on the genes coding for pigment-synthesizing enzymes in McClintock's corn kernels. Again, while such changes are usually harmful, in the long run some may prove beneficial by providing a survival advantage.

During transposition, a transposable element may carry along a gene or even a group of genes to a new position in the genome. This mechanism probably accounts for the location of the α-globin and β-globin gene families on different human chromosomes, as well as the dispersion of the genes of certain other gene families. By a similar tag-along process, an exon from one gene may be inserted into another gene in a mechanism similar to that of exon shuffling during recombination. For example, an exon may be inserted by transposition into the intron of a protein-coding gene. If the inserted exon is retained in the RNA transcript during RNA splicing, the protein that is synthesized will have an additional domain, which may confer a new function on the protein.

All the processes discussed in this section most often produce either harmful effects, which may be lethal, or no effect at all. In a few cases, however, small heritable changes may occur that are beneficial. Over many generations, the resulting genetic diversity provides valuable raw material for natural selection. Diversification of genes and their products is an important factor in the evolution of new species. Thus, the accumulation of changes in the genome of each species provides a record of its evolutionary history. To read this record, we must be able to identify genomic changes. Comparing the genomes of different species allows us to do that and has increased our understanding of how genomes evolve. You will learn more about these topics next.

CONCEPT CHECK 21.5

1. Describe three examples of errors in cellular processes that lead to DNA duplications.

2. Explain how multiple exons might have arisen in the ancestral EGF and fibronectin genes shown on the left side of Figure 21.16.

3. What are three ways that transposable elements are thought to contribute to genome evolution?

4. **WHAT IF?** In 2005, Icelandic scientists reported finding a large chromosomal inversion present in 20% of northern Europeans, and they noted that Icelandic women with this inversion had significantly more children than women without it. What would you expect to happen to the frequency of this inversion in the Icelandic population in future generations?

For suggested answers, see Appendix A.

CONCEPT 21.6

Comparing genome sequences provides clues to evolution and development

EVOLUTION One researcher has likened the current state of biology to the Age of Exploration in the 15th century, which occurred soon after major improvements in navigation and ship design. In the last 25 years, we have seen rapid advances in genome sequencing and data collection, new techniques for assessing gene activity across the whole genome, and refined approaches for understanding how genes and their products work together in complex systems. We are truly poised on the brink of a new world.

Comparisons of genome sequences from different species reveal a lot about the evolutionary history of life, from very ancient to more recent. Similarly, comparative studies of the genetic programs that direct embryonic development in different species are beginning to clarify the mechanisms that generated the great diversity of life-forms present today. In this final section of the chapter, we will discuss what has been learned from these two approaches.

Comparing Genomes

The more similar in sequence the genes and genomes of two species are, the more closely related those species are in their evolutionary history. Comparing genomes of closely related species sheds light on more recent evolutionary events, whereas comparing genomes of very distantly related species helps us understand ancient evolutionary history. In

▲ **Figure 21.17 Evolutionary relationships of the three domains of life.** The tree diagram at the top shows the ancient divergence of bacteria, archaea, and eukaryotes. A portion of the eukaryote lineage is expanded in the inset to show the more recent divergence of three mammalian species discussed in this chapter.

either case, learning about characteristics that are shared or divergent between groups enhances our picture of the evolution of organisms and biological processes. As you learned in Chapter 1, the evolutionary relationships between species can be represented by a diagram in the form of a tree (often turned sideways), where each branch point marks the divergence of two lineages. **Figure 21.17** shows the evolutionary relationships of some groups and species we will discuss.

Comparing Distantly Related Species

Determining which genes have remained similar—that is, are *highly conserved*—in distantly related species can help clarify evolutionary relationships among species that diverged from each other long ago. Indeed, comparisons of the specific gene sequences of bacteria, archaea, and eukaryotes indicate that these three groups diverged between 2 and 4 billion years ago and strongly support the theory that they are the fundamental domains of life (see Figure 21.17).

In addition to their value in evolutionary biology, comparative genomic studies confirm the relevance of research on model organisms to our understanding of biology in general and human biology in particular. Very ancient genes can still be surprisingly similar in disparate species. As a case in point, several yeast genes are so similar to certain human disease genes (genes whose mutation causes disease) that researchers have deduced the functions of the human genes by studying their yeast counterparts. This striking result underscores the common origin of these two distantly related species.

Comparing Closely Related Species

The genomes of two closely related species are likely to be organized similarly because of their relatively recent divergence. In the past, this kind of similarity allowed the fully sequenced genome of one species to be used as a scaffold for assembling the genomic sequences of a closely related species, accelerating mapping of the second genome. For instance, using the human genome sequence as a guide, researchers were able to quickly sequence the chimpanzee genome. With the advent of new and faster sequencing techniques, most genomes are assembled individually, as has been done recently for the bonobo and gorilla genomes. (Along with chimpanzees, bonobos are the other African ape species that are the closest living relatives to humans.)

The recent divergence of two closely related species also underlies the small number of gene differences that are found when their genomes are compared. The particular genetic differences can therefore be more easily correlated with phenotypic differences between the two species. An exciting application of this type of analysis is seen as researchers compare the human genome with the genomes of the chimpanzee, mouse, rat, and other mammals. Identifying the genes shared by all of these species but not by nonmammals should give clues about what it takes to make a mammal, while finding the genes shared by chimpanzees and humans but not by rodents will tell us something about primates. And, of course, comparing the human genome with that of the chimpanzee will help us answer the tantalizing question we asked at the beginning of the chapter: What genomic information defines a human or a chimpanzee?

An analysis of the overall composition of the human and chimpanzee genomes, which are thought to have diverged only about 6 million years ago (see Figure 21.17), reveals some general differences. Considering single nucleotide substitutions, the two genomes differ by only 1.2%. When researchers looked at longer stretches of DNA, however, they were surprised to find a further 2.7% difference due to insertions or deletions of larger regions in the genome of one or the other species; many of the insertions were duplications or other repetitive DNA. In fact, a third of the human duplications are not present in the chimpanzee genome, and some of these duplications contain regions associated with human diseases. There are more *Alu* elements in the human genome than in the chimpanzee genome, and the latter contains many copies of a retroviral provirus not present in humans. All of these observations provide clues to the forces that might have swept the two genomes along different paths, but we don't have a complete picture yet.

The sequencing of the bonobo genome, completed in 2012, revealed that in some regions, human sequences were more closely related to either chimpanzee or bonobo sequences than chimpanzee or bonobo sequences were to each other. Such a fine-grained comparison of three closely related species allows even more detail to be worked out in reconstructing their related evolutionary history.

We also don't know how the genetic differences revealed by genome sequencing might account for the distinct characteristics of each species. To discover the basis for the phenotypic differences between chimpanzees and humans, biologists are studying specific genes and types of genes that differ between the two species and comparing them with their counterparts in other mammals. This approach has revealed a number of genes that are apparently changing (evolving) faster in the human than in either the chimpanzee or the mouse. Among them are genes involved in defense against malaria and tuberculosis as well as at least one gene that regulates brain size. When genes are classified by function, the genes that seem to be evolving the fastest are those that code for transcription factors. This discovery makes sense because transcription factors regulate gene expression and thus play a key role in orchestrating the overall genetic program.

One transcription factor whose gene shows evidence of rapid change in the human lineage is called FOXP2 (Figure 21.18). Several lines of evidence suggest that the

---

▼ Figure 21.18 | Inquiry

What is the function of a gene (*FOXP2*) that is rapidly evolving in the human lineage?

Experiment Several lines of evidence support a role for the *FOXP2* gene in the development of speech and language in humans and of vocalization in other vertebrates. In 2005, Joseph Buxbaum and collaborators at the Mount Sinai School of Medicine and several other institutions tested the function of *FOXP2*. They used the mouse, a model organism in which genes can be easily knocked out, as a representative vertebrate that vocalizes: Mice produce ultrasonic squeaks (whistles) to communicate stress. The researchers used genetic engineering to produce mice in which one or both copies of *FOXP2* were disrupted.

| **Wild type: two normal copies of FOXP2** | **Heterozygote: one copy of FOXP2 disrupted** | **Homozygote: both copies of FOXP2 disrupted** |

They then compared the phenotypes of these mice. Two of the characters they examined are included here: brain anatomy and vocalization.

Experiment 1: Researchers cut thin sections of brain and stained them with reagents that allow visualization of brain anatomy in a UV fluorescence microscope.

Experiment 2: Researchers separated each newborn pup from its mother and recorded the number of ultrasonic whistles produced by the pup.

Results

Experiment 1 Results: Disruption of both copies of *FOXP2* led to brain abnormalities in which the cells were disorganized. Phenotypic effects on the brain of heterozygotes, with one disrupted copy, were less severe. (Each color in the micrographs below reveals a different cell or tissue type.)

Experiment 2 Results: Disruption of both copies of *FOXP2* led to an absence of ultrasonic vocalization in response to stress. The effect on vocalization in the heterozygote was also extreme.

Wild type

Heterozygote

Homozygote

Conclusion *FOXP2* plays a significant role in the development of functional communication systems in mice. The results augment evidence from studies of birds and humans, supporting the hypothesis that *FOXP2* may act similarly in diverse organisms.

Source: W. Shu et al., Altered ultrasonic vocalization in mice with a disruption in the Foxp2 gene, Proceedings of the National Academy of Sciences 102:9643–9648 (2005).

WHAT IF? *Since the results support a role for mouse FOXP2 in vocalization, you might wonder whether the human FOXP2 protein is a key regulator of speech. If you were given the amino acid sequences of wild-type and mutant human FOXP2 proteins and the wild-type chimpanzee FOXP2 protein, how would you investigate this question? What further clues could you obtain by comparing these sequences to that of the mouse FOXP2 protein?*

FOXP2 gene functions in vocalization in vertebrates. For one thing, mutations in this gene can produce severe speech and language impairment in humans. Moreover, the *FOXP2* gene is expressed in the brains of zebra finches and canaries at the time when these songbirds are learning their songs. But perhaps the strongest evidence comes from a "knockout" experiment in which researchers disrupted the *FOXP2* gene in mice and analyzed the resulting phenotype (see Figure 21.18). The homozygous mutant mice had malformed brains and failed to emit normal ultrasonic vocalizations, and mice with one faulty copy of the gene also showed significant problems with vocalization. These results support the idea that the *FOXP2* gene product turns on genes involved in vocalization.

Expanding on this analysis, another research group more recently replaced the *FOXP2* gene in mice with a "humanized" copy coding for the human versions of two amino acids that differ between human and chimp; these are the changes potentially responsible for a human's ability to speak. Although the mice were generally healthy, they had subtly different vocalizations and showed changes in brain cells in circuits associated with speech in human brains.

In 2010, the Neanderthal genome was sequenced from a very small amount of preserved genomic DNA. Neanderthals (*Homo neanderthalensis*) are members of the same genus to which humans (*Homo sapiens*) belong (see Concept 34.7). A reconstruction of their evolutionary history based on genomic comparisons between the two species suggests that some groups of humans and Neanderthals co-existed and interbred for a period of time before Neanderthals went extinct about 30,000 years ago. While Neanderthals have sometimes been portrayed as primitive beings that could only grunt, their *FOXP2* gene sequence encodes an identical protein to that of humans. This suggests that Neanderthals may have been capable of speech of some type and, along with other observed genetic similarities, forces us to reevaluate our image of our recent extinct relatives.

The *FOXP2* story is an excellent example of how different approaches can complement each other in uncovering biological phenomena of widespread importance. The *FOXP2* experiments used mice as a model for humans because it would be unethical (as well as impractical) to carry out such experiments in humans. Mice and humans, which diverged about 65.5 million years ago (see Figure 21.17), share about 85% of their genes. This genetic similarity can be exploited in studying human genetic disorders. If researchers know the organ or tissue that is affected by a particular genetic disorder, they can look for genes that are expressed in these locations in mice.

Further research efforts are under way to extend genomic studies to many more species, including neglected species from diverse branches of the tree of life. These studies will advance our understanding of evolution, of course, as well as all aspects of biology, from human health to ecology.

Comparing Genomes Within a Species

Another exciting consequence of our ability to analyze genomes is our growing understanding of the spectrum of genetic variation in humans. Because the history of the human species is so short—probably about 200,000 years—the amount of DNA variation among humans is small compared to that of many other species. Much of our diversity seems to be in the form of single nucleotide polymorphisms (SNPs). SNPs are single base-pair sites where variation is found in at least 1% of the population (see Concept 20.2); they are usually detected by DNA sequencing. In the human genome, SNPs occur on average about once in 100–300 base pairs. Scientists have already identified the location of several million SNP sites in the human genome and continue to find more.

In the course of this search, they have also found other variations—including chromosomal regions with inversions, deletions, and duplications. The most surprising discovery has been the widespread occurrence of *copy-number variants* (*CNVs*), loci where some individuals have one or multiple copies of a particular gene or genetic region, rather than the standard two copies (one on each homolog). CNVs result from regions of the genome being duplicated or deleted inconsistently within the population. A recent study of 40 people found more than 8,000 CNVs involving 13% of the genes in the genome, and these CNVs probably represent just a small subset of the total. Since these variants encompass much longer stretches of DNA than the single nucleotides of SNPs, CNVs are more likely to have phenotypic consequences and to play a role in complex diseases and disorders. At the very least, the high incidence of copy-number variation casts doubt on the meaning of the phrase "a normal human genome."

Copy-number variants, SNPs, and variations in repetitive DNA such as short tandem repeats (STRs) are useful genetic markers for studying human evolution. In one study, the genomes of two Africans from different communities were sequenced: Archbishop Desmond Tutu, the South African civil rights advocate and a member of the Bantu tribe, the majority population in southern Africa; and !Gubi, a hunter-gatherer from the Khoisan community in Namibia, a minority African population that is probably the human group with the oldest known lineage. The comparison revealed many differences, as you might expect. The analysis was then broadened to compare the protein-coding regions of !Gubi's genome with those of three other Khoisan community members (self-identified Bushmen) living nearby. Remarkably, the four African genomes differed more from each other than a European would from an Asian. These data highlight the extensive diversity among African genomes. Extending this approach will help us answer important questions about the differences between human populations and the migratory routes of human populations throughout history.

Widespread Conservation of Developmental Genes Among Animals

Biologists in the field of evolutionary developmental biology, or **evo-devo** as it is often called, compare developmental processes of different multicellular organisms. Their aim is to understand how these processes have evolved and how changes in them can modify existing organismal features or lead to new ones. With the advent of molecular techniques and the recent flood of genomic information, we are beginning to realize that the genomes of related species with strikingly different forms may have only minor differences in gene sequence or, perhaps more importantly, in gene regulation. Discovering the molecular basis of these differences in turn helps us understand the origins of the myriad diverse forms that cohabit this planet, thus informing our study of evolution.

In Chapter 18, you learned about the homeotic genes in *Drosophila melanogaster*, which specify the identity of body segments in the fruit fly (see Figure 18.20). Molecular analysis of the homeotic genes in *Drosophila* has shown that they all include a 180-nucleotide sequence called a **homeobox**, which codes for a 60-amino-acid *homeodomain* in the encoded proteins. An identical or very similar nucleotide sequence has been discovered in the homeotic genes of many invertebrates and vertebrates. The sequences are so similar between humans and fruit flies, in fact, that one researcher has whimsically referred to flies as "little people with wings." The resemblance even extends to the organization of these genes: The vertebrate genes homologous to the homeotic genes of fruit flies have kept the same chromosomal arrangement **(Figure 21.19)**. Homeobox-containing sequences have also been found in regulatory genes of much more distantly related eukaryotes, including plants and yeasts. From these similarities, we can deduce that the homeobox DNA sequence evolved very early in the history of life and was sufficiently valuable to organisms to have been conserved in animals and plants virtually unchanged for hundreds of millions of years.

Homeotic genes in animals were named *Hox* genes, short for *homeobox*-containing genes, because homeotic genes were the first genes found to have this sequence. Other homeobox-containing genes were later found that do not act as homeotic genes; that is, they do not directly control the identity of body parts. However, most of these genes, in animals at least, are associated with development, suggesting their ancient and fundamental importance in that process. In *Drosophila*, for example, homeoboxes are present not only in the homeotic genes but also in the egg-polarity gene *bicoid* (see Figures 18.21 and 18.22), in several of the segmentation genes, and in a master regulatory gene for eye development.

Researchers have discovered that the homeobox-encoded homeodomain binds to DNA when the protein functions

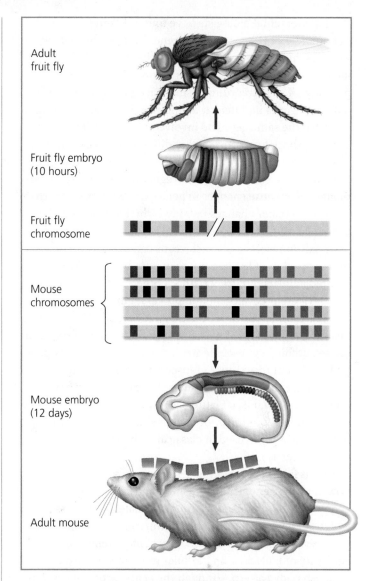

▲ **Figure 21.19 Conservation of homeotic genes in a fruit fly and a mouse.** Homeotic genes that control the form of anterior and posterior structures of the body occur in the same linear sequence on chromosomes in *Drosophila* and mice. Each colored band on the chromosomes shown here represents a homeotic gene. In fruit flies, all homeotic genes are found on one chromosome. The mouse and other mammals have the same or similar sets of genes on four chromosomes. The color code indicates the parts of the embryos in which these genes are expressed and the adult body regions that result. All of these genes are essentially identical in flies and mice, except for those represented by black bands, which are less similar in the two animals.

as a transcription factor. Elsewhere in the protein, domains that are more variable interact with other transcription factors, allowing the homeodomain-containing protein to recognize specific enhancers and regulate the associated genes. Proteins with homeodomains probably regulate development by coordinating the transcription of batteries of developmental genes, switching them on or off. In embryos of *Drosophila* and other animal species, different combinations of homeobox genes are active in different parts of the embryo. This selective expression of regulatory genes, varying over time and space, is central to pattern formation.

Developmental biologists have found that in addition to homeotic genes, many other genes involved in development are highly conserved from species to species. These include numerous genes encoding components of signaling pathways. The extraordinary similarity among some developmental genes in different animal species raises a question: How can the same genes be involved in the development of animals whose forms are so very different from each other?

Ongoing studies are suggesting answers to this question. In some cases, small changes in regulatory sequences of particular genes cause changes in gene expression patterns that can lead to major changes in body form. For example, the differing patterns of expression of the *Hox* genes along the body axis in insects and crustaceans can explain the variation in number of leg-bearing segments among these segmented animals **(Figure 21.20)**. In other cases, similar genes direct different developmental processes in various organisms, resulting in diverse body shapes. Several *Hox* genes, for instance, are expressed in the embryonic and larval stages of the sea urchin, a nonsegmented animal that has a body plan quite different from those of insects and mice. Sea urchin adults make the pincushion-shaped shells you may have seen on the beach (see Figure 8.4); two species of live sea urchins are shown in the photo below. Sea urchins are among the organisms long used in classical embryological studies (see Chapter 47).

In this final chapter of the genetics unit, you have learned how studying genomic composition and comparing the genomes of different species can illuminate the process by which genomes evolve. Further, comparing developmental programs, we can see that the unity of life is reflected in the similarity of molecular and cellular mechanisms used to establish body pattern, although the genes directing development may differ among organisms. The similarities between genomes reflect the common ancestry of life on Earth. But the differences are also crucial, for they have created the huge diversity of organisms that have evolved. In the remainder of the book, we expand our perspective beyond the level of molecules, cells, and genes to explore this diversity on the organismal level.

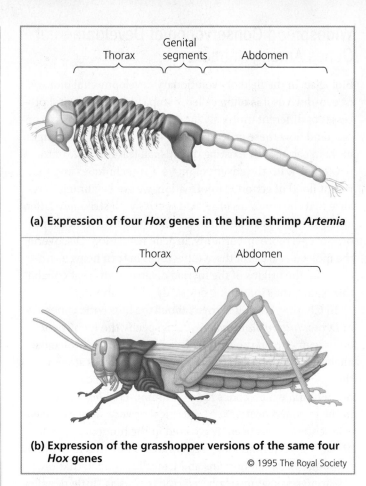

(a) Expression of four *Hox* genes in the brine shrimp *Artemia*

(b) Expression of the grasshopper versions of the same four *Hox* genes

© 1995 The Royal Society

▲ **Figure 21.20 Effect of differences in *Hox* gene expression in crustaceans and insects.** Changes in the expression patterns of *Hox* genes have occurred over evolutionary time. These changes account in part for the different body plans of the brine shrimp *Artemia*, a crustacean (top), and the grasshopper, an insect. Shown here are regions of the adult body color-coded for expression of four *Hox* genes that determine the formation of particular body parts during embryonic development. Each color represents a specific *Hox* gene. Colored stripes on the thorax of *Artemia* indicate co-expression of three *Hox* genes.

CONCEPT CHECK 21.6

1. Would you expect the genome of the macaque (a monkey) to be more similar to the mouse genome or the human genome? Why?

2. The DNA sequences called homeoboxes, which help homeotic genes in animals direct development, are common to flies and mice. Given this similarity, explain why these animals are so different.

3. **WHAT IF?** There are three times as many *Alu* elements in the human genome as in the chimpanzee genome. How do you think these extra *Alu* elements arose in the human genome? Propose a role they might have played in the divergence of these two species.

For suggested answers, see Appendix A.

SUMMARY OF KEY CONCEPTS

CONCEPT 21.1

The Human Genome Project fostered development of faster, less expensive sequencing techniques (pp. 437–438)

- The **Human Genome Project** was largely completed in 2003, aided by major advances in sequencing technology.
- In the **whole-genome shotgun** approach, the whole genome is cut into many small, overlapping fragments that are sequenced; computer software then assembles the genome sequence.

? *How did the Human Genome Project result in more rapid, less expensive DNA sequencing technology?*

CONCEPT 21.2

Scientists use bioinformatics to analyze genomes and their functions (pp. 438–442)

- Computer analysis of genome sequences aids **gene annotation**, the identification of protein-coding sequences. Methods to detemine gene function include comparing sequences of newly discovered genes with those of known genes in other species and observing the effects of experimentally inactivating the genes.
- In systems biology, scientists use the computer-based tools of **bioinformatics** to compare genomes and study sets of genes and proteins as whole systems (**genomics** and **proteomics**). Studies include large-scale analyses of protein interactions, functional DNA elements, and genes contributing to medical conditions.

? *What has been the most significant finding of the ENCODE project? Why was the project expanded to include non-human species?*

CONCEPT 21.3

Genomes vary in size, number of genes, and gene density (pp. 442–444)

	Bacteria	Archaea	Eukarya
Genome size	Most are 1–6 Mb		Most are 10–4,000 Mb, but a few are much larger
Number of genes	1,500–7,500		5,000–40,000
Gene density	Higher than in eukaryotes		Lower than in prokaryotes (Within eukaryotes, lower density is correlated with larger genomes.)
Introns	None in protein-coding genes	Present in some genes	Present in most genes of multicellular eukaryotes, but only in some genes of unicellular eukaryotes
Other noncoding DNA	Very little		Can exist in large amounts; generally more repetitive noncoding DNA in multicellular eukaryotes

? *Compare genome size, gene number, and gene density (a) in the three domains and (b) among eukaryotes.*

CONCEPT 21.4

Multicellular eukaryotes have much noncoding DNA and many multigene families (pp. 444–447)

- Only 1.5% of the human genome codes for proteins or gives rise to rRNAs or tRNAs; the rest is noncoding DNA, including **pseudogenes** and **repetitive DNA** of unknown function.
- The most abundant type of repetitive DNA in multicellular eukaryotes consists of **transposable elements** and related sequences. In eukaryotes, there are two types of transposable elements: **transposons**, which move via a DNA intermediate, and **retrotransposons**, which are more prevalent and move via an RNA intermediate.
- Other repetitive DNA includes short, noncoding sequences that are tandemly repeated thousands of times (**simple sequence DNA**, which includes **STRs**); these sequences are especially prominent in centromeres and telomeres, where they probably play structural roles in the chromosome.
- Though many eukaryotic genes are present in one copy per haploid chromosome set, others (most, in some species) are members of a gene family, such as the human globin gene families:

? *Explain how the function of transposable elements might account for their prevalence in human noncoding DNA.*

CONCEPT 21.5

Duplication, rearrangement, and mutation of DNA contribute to genome evolution (pp. 448–453)

- Errors in cell division can lead to extra copies of all or part of entire chromosome sets, which may then diverge if one set accumulates sequence changes. Polyploidy occurs more often among plants than animals, and contributes to speciation.
- The chromosomal organization of genomes can be compared among species, providing information about evolutionary relationships. Within a given species, rearrangements of chromosomes are thought to contribute to the emergence of new species.
- The genes encoding the various related but different globin proteins evolved from one common ancestral globin gene, which duplicated and diverged into α-globin and β-globin ancestral genes. Subsequent duplication and random mutation gave rise to the present globin genes, all of which code for oxygen-binding proteins. The copies of some duplicated genes have diverged so much that the functions of their encoded proteins (such as lysozyme and α-lactalbumin) are now substantially different.
- Rearrangement of exons within and between genes during evolution has led to genes containing multiple copies of similar exons and/or several different exons derived from other genes.
- Movement of transposable elements or recombination between copies of the same element can generate new sequence combinations that are beneficial to the organism. These may alter the functions of genes or their patterns of expression and regulation.

? *How could chromosomal rearrangements lead to the emergence of new species?*

Comparing genome sequences provides clues to evolution and development (pp. 453–458)

- Comparisons of genomes from widely divergent and closely related species provide valuable information about ancient and more recent evolutionary history, respectively. Analysis of single nucleotide polymorphisms (SNPs) and copy-number variants (CNVs) among individuals in a species can also shed light on the evolution of that species.
- Evolutionary developmental (**evo-devo**) biologists have shown that homeotic genes and some other genes associated with animal development contain a **homeobox** region whose sequence is highly conserved among diverse species. Related sequences are present in the genes of plants and yeasts.

? *What type of information can be obtained by comparing the genomes of closely related species? Of very distantly related species?*

TEST YOUR UNDERSTANDING

LEVEL 1: KNOWLEDGE/COMPREHENSION

1. Bioinformatics includes all of the following except
   a. using computer programs to align DNA sequences.
   b. using DNA technology to combine DNA from two different sources in a test tube.
   c. developing computer-based tools for genome analysis.
   d. using mathematical tools to make sense of biological systems.

2. Homeotic genes
   a. encode transcription factors that control the expression of genes responsible for specific anatomical structures.
   b. are found only in *Drosophila* and other arthropods.
   c. are the only genes that contain the homeobox domain.
   d. encode proteins that form anatomical structures in the fly.

LEVEL 2: APPLICATION/ANALYSIS

3. Two eukaryotic proteins have one domain in common but are otherwise very different. Which of the following processes is most likely to have contributed to this similarity?
   a. gene duplication
   b. RNA splicing
   c. exon shuffling
   d. random point mutations

4. **DRAW IT** Below are the amino acid sequences (using the single-letter code; see Figure 5.14) of four short segments of the FOXP2 protein from six species: chimpanzee (C), orangutan (O), gorilla (G), rhesus macaque (R), mouse (M), and human (H). These segments contain all of the amino acid differences between the FOXP2 proteins of these species.

   1. ATETI...PKSSD...TSSTT...NARRD

   2. ATETI...PKSSE...TSSTT...NARRD

   3. ATETI...PKSSD...TSSTT...NARRD

   4. ATETI...PKSSD...TSSNT...S ARRD

   5. ATETI...PKSSD...TSSTT...NARRD

   6. VTETI...PKSSD...TSSTT...NARRD

   Use a highlighter to color any amino acid that varies among the species. (Color that amino acid in all sequences.)
   (a) The C, G, R sequences are identical. Which lines correspond to those sequences?
   (b) The H sequence differs from that of the C, G, R species at two amino acids. Underline the two differences in the H sequence.

   (c) The O sequence differs from the C, G, R sequences at one amino acid (having V instead of A) and from the H sequence at three amino acids. Which line is the O sequence?
   (d) In the M sequence, circle the amino acid(s) that differ from the C, G, R sequences, and draw a square around those that differ from the H sequence.
   (e) Primates and rodents diverged between 60 and 100 million years ago, and chimpanzees and humans about 6 million years ago. What can you conclude by comparing the amino acid differences between the mouse and the C, G, R species with those between the human and the C, G, R species?

LEVEL 3: SYNTHESIS/EVALUATION

5. **EVOLUTION CONNECTION**
   Genes important in the embryonic development of animals, such as homeobox-containing genes, have been relatively well conserved during evolution; that is, they are more similar among different species than are many other genes. Why is this?

6. **SCIENTIFIC INQUIRY**
   The scientists mapping the SNPs in the human genome noticed that groups of SNPs tended to be inherited together, in blocks known as haplotypes, ranging in length from 5,000 to 200,000 base pairs. There are as few as four or five commonly occurring combinations of SNPs per haplotype. Integrating what you've learned throughout this chapter and this unit, propose an explanation for this observation.

7. **WRITE ABOUT A THEME: INFORMATION**
   The continuity of life is based on heritable information in the form of DNA. In a short essay (100–150 words), explain how mutations in protein-coding genes and regulatory DNA contribute to evolution.

8. **SYNTHESIZE YOUR KNOWLEDGE**

Insects have three thoracic (trunk) segments. While researchers have found insect fossils with pairs of wings on all three segments, modern insects have wings or related structures on only the second and third segment. It turns out that in modern insects, *Hox* gene products act to inhibit wing formation on the first segment. The treehopper insect (above) is somewhat of an exception. In addition to having wings on its second segment, the treehopper's first segment has an ornate helmet that resembles a set of thorns, which a recent study has found to be a modified, fused pair of "wings." The thorn-like structure helps to camouflage the treehopper in tree branches, thus reducing its risk of predation. Explain how changes in gene regulation could have led to the evolution of such a structure.

For selected answers, see Appendix A.

MasteringBiology®

Students Go to **MasteringBiology** for assignments, the eText, and the Study Area with practice tests, animations, and activities.

Instructors Go to **MasteringBiology** for automatically graded tutorials and questions that you can assign to your students, plus Instructor Resources.

7 ANIMAL FORM AND FUNCTION

AN INTERVIEW WITH

Ulrike Heberlein

Born in Chile, Ulrike Heberlein received her B.S. and M.S. degrees from the University of Concepción. At the University of California, Berkeley, she completed a Ph.D. in biochemistry as well as postdoctoral work in genetics. In 1993, she set up her own laboratory at the University of California, San Francisco, to study alcohol tolerance and addiction. Since 2012, Dr. Heberlein has been the Scientific Program Director at the Janelia Farm Research Campus of the Howard Hughes Medical Institute. She was elected in 2010 to the U.S. National Academy of Sciences as a foreign member.

What path led you to your current research?

In Chile, at the time I finished my studies, it wasn't clear that science was something a woman should be doing in a serious way. Instead, I came to the United States where I did a lot of river rafting, earning money part of the year as a lab technician. I was just about to move overseas to coordinate trips on the Zambesi River in Africa when I realized that rafting wasn't really going to be it for me in the long run. My lab supervisors told me, "You know, you really should go to grad school." I did, and I'm very grateful to them. In grad school I did biochemistry, then learned fly genetics as a postdoctoral fellow. Afterwards, I wrote a proposal to use flies as a model for studying alcohol use and addiction, which I've been doing ever since.

> " **That's the idea of the inebriometer—it really is chromatography of drunk flies.** "

◄ Inebriometer setups in Dr. Heberlein's lab.

How does one study the effects of alcohol on flies?

We use an "inebriometer," which is a column containing a set of partial separations called baffles. If you put flies in the column and put a light at the top, the flies have a natural tendency to walk up the sides against gravity toward the light. Then, if you circulate alcohol vapor through the column, the flies inhale the alcohol and start falling from one baffle to the next. They right themselves and then resume falling. The idea of the baffles is that you don't want them to fall once and go all the way to the bottom. You want it to be like chromatography in a biochemistry lab, where molecules bind and unbind, over and over, separating according to their properties. Once the flies are really drunk, they come out the bottom. So we measure the time it takes for them to reach the bottom. Instead of getting a peak of protein, you get a peak of drunk flies with a mean time to exit the column. That's the idea of the inebriometer—it really is chromatography of drunk flies.

Tell us about some of the things you've discovered.

Our goal is to identify mutations that cause altered responses to alcohol. For example, we can identify flies that are more sensitive to alcohol because they come out of the inebriometer at, say, 15 minutes instead of 20, or flies that are more resistant, because they come out at, for example, 30 minutes. The first two or three mutants that we isolated and analyzed turned out to be learning and memory mutants. That was a satisfying result, because addiction involves learning and remembering the association between a certain feeling (such as intoxication) and the environment (for example, a bar). We have also identified mutations that affect tolerance, the decrease in response to a given level of alcohol over time. What was really cool is that we were able to identify a mutation in the corresponding gene in mice and found that the mice with this mutation also have a defect in alcohol tolerance.

What do you most want to know about addiction?

The goal is to understand the biological mechanism that changes the way neurons talk to each other in addiction. If we can get at that core, we might be able to develop effective medications. Currently there are no good drugs that work for most alcohol addicts.

(MB) For an extended interview and video clip, go to the Study Area in MasteringBiology.

40

Basic Principles of Animal Form and Function

KEY CONCEPTS

40.1 Animal form and function are correlated at all levels of organization

40.2 Feedback control maintains the internal environment in many animals

40.3 Homeostatic processes for thermoregulation involve form, function, and behavior

40.4 Energy requirements are related to animal size, activity, and environment

▲ **Figure 40.1 How do long legs help this scavenger survive in the scorching desert heat?**

Diverse Forms, Common Challenges

The desert ant (genus *Cataglyphis*) in **Figure 40.1** is a scavenger, devouring insects that have succumbed to the daytime heat of the Sahara Desert. To gather corpses for feeding, the ant forages when surface temperatures on the sunbaked sand exceed 60°C (140°F), well above the thermal limit for virtually all animals. How, then, does the desert ant survive in these conditions? To answer this question, we need to look closely at the ant's **anatomy**, or biological form.

In studying the desert ant, researchers noted that its stilt-like legs are disproportionately long. Elevated 4 mm above the sand by these legs, the ant's body is exposed to a temperature 6°C lower than that at ground level. Researchers have also found that a desert ant can use its long legs to run as fast as 1 m/sec, close to the top speed recorded for any running arthropod. Speedy sprinting minimizes the time that the ant is out of its nest and exposed to the sun. Thus, having long legs allows the desert ant to be active during the heat of the day, when competition for food and the risk of predation are lowest.

Over the course of its life, an ant faces the same fundamental challenges as any other animal, whether hydra, hawk, or human. All animals must obtain nutrients and oxygen, fight off infection, and produce offspring. Given that they share these and other basic requirements, why do species vary so enormously in organization and appearance? The answer lies in natural selection and adaptation. Natural selection favors those variations in a population that increase relative fitness (see Chapter 23). The evolutionary adaptations that enable survival vary among environments and species but frequently result in a close match of form to function, as shown by the legs of the desert ant.

Because form and function are correlated, examining anatomy often provides clues to **physiology**—biological function. In this chapter, we'll begin our study of animal form and function by examining the levels of organization in the animal body and the systems for coordinating the activities of different body parts. Next, we'll use the example of body temperature regulation to illustrate how animals control their internal environment. Finally, we'll explore how anatomy and physiology relate to an animal's interactions with the environment and its management of energy use.

CONCEPT 40.1

Animal form and function are correlated at all levels of organization

An animal's size and shape are fundamental aspects of form that significantly affect the way the animal interacts with its environment. Although we may refer to size and shape as elements of a "body plan" or "design," this does not imply a process of conscious invention. The body plan of an animal is the result of a pattern of development programmed by the genome, itself the product of millions of years of evolution.

Evolution of Animal Size and Shape

EVOLUTION Many different body plans have arisen during the course of evolution, but these variations fall within certain bounds. Physical laws that govern strength, diffusion, movement, and heat exchange limit the range of animal forms.

As an example of how physical laws constrain evolution, let's consider how some properties of water limit the possible shapes for animals that are fast swimmers. Water is about a thousand times denser than air and also far more viscous. Therefore, any bump on an animal's body surface that causes drag impedes a swimmer more than it would a runner or flyer. Tuna and other fast ray-finned fishes can swim at speeds up to 80 km/hr (50 miles/hour). Sharks, penguins, dolphins, and seals are also relatively fast swimmers. As illustrated by the three examples in **Figure 40.2**, these animals all have a shape that is fusiform, meaning tapered on both ends. The similar streamlined shape found in these speedy

Seal

Penguin

Tuna

▲ **Figure 40.2 Convergent evolution in fast swimmers.**

vertebrates is an example of convergent evolution (see Chapter 22). Natural selection often results in similar adaptations when diverse organisms face the same environmental challenge, such as overcoming drag during swimming.

Physical laws also influence animal body plans with regard to maximum size. As body dimensions increase, thicker skeletons are required to maintain adequate support. This limitation affects internal skeletons, such as those of vertebrates, as well as external skeletons, such as those of insects and other arthropods. In addition, as bodies increase in size, the muscles required for locomotion must represent an ever-larger fraction of the total body mass. At some point, mobility becomes limited. By considering the fraction of body mass in leg muscles and the effective force such muscles generate, scientists can estimate maximum running speed for a wide range of body plans. Such calculations indicate that the dinosaur *Tyrannosaurus rex*, which stood more than 6 m tall, probably could run at 30 km/hr (19 miles/hour), about as fast as the fastest humans today can run.

Exchange with the Environment

Animals must exchange nutrients, waste products, and gases with their environment, and this requirement imposes an additional limitation on body plans. Exchange occurs as substances dissolved in an aqueous solution move across the plasma membrane of each cell. A single-celled organism, such as the amoeba in **Figure 40.3a**, has a sufficient membrane surface area in contact with its environment to carry out all necessary exchange. In contrast, an animal is composed of many cells, each with its own plasma membrane across which exchange must occur. The rate of exchange is proportional to membrane surface area involved in exchange, whereas the amount of material that must be exchanged is proportional to the body volume. A multicellular organization therefore works only if every cell has access to a suitable aqueous environment, either inside or outside the animal's body.

Many animals with a simple internal organization have body plans that enable direct exchange between almost all their cells and the external environment. For example, a pond-dwelling hydra, which has a saclike body plan, has a body wall only two cell layers thick **(Figure 40.3b)**. Because its gastrovascular cavity opens to the external environment, both the outer and inner layers of cells are constantly bathed by pond water. Another common body plan that maximizes exposure to the surrounding medium is a flat shape. Consider, for instance, a parasitic tapeworm,

▼ **Figure 40.3 Direct exchange with the environment.**

Mouth

Gastrovascular cavity

Exchange

Exchange

Exchange

Exchange

0.1 mm

1 mm

(a) An amoeba, a single-celled organism

(b) A hydra, an animal with two layers of cells

which can reach several meters in length (see Figure 33.12). A thin, flat shape places most cells of the worm in direct contact with its particular environment—the nutrient-rich intestinal fluid of a vertebrate host.

Our bodies and those of most other animals are composed of compact masses of cells, with an internal organization much more complex than that of a hydra or a tapeworm. For such a body plan, increasing the number

of cells decreases the ratio of outer surface area to total volume. As an extreme comparison, the ratio of outer surface area to volume for a whale is hundreds of thousands of times smaller than that for a water flea. Nevertheless, every cell in the whale must be bathed in fluid and have access to oxygen, nutrients, and other resources. How is this accomplished?

In whales and most other animals, the evolutionary adaptations that enable sufficient exchange with the environment are specialized surfaces that are extensively branched or folded **(Figure 40.4)**. In almost all cases, these exchange surfaces lie within the body, an arrangement that protects their delicate tissues from abrasion or dehydration and allows for streamlined body contours. The branching or folding greatly increases surface area: In humans, the internal exchange surfaces for digestion, respiration, and circulation each have an area more than 25 times that of the skin.

Internal body fluids link exchange surfaces to body cells. The spaces between cells are filled with fluid, in many animals called **interstitial fluid** (from the Latin for "stand between"). Complex body plans also include a circulatory fluid, such as blood. Exchange between the interstitial fluid and the circulatory fluid enables cells throughout the body to obtain nutrients and get rid of wastes (see Figure 40.4).

▶ **Figure 40.4 Internal exchange surfaces of complex animals.** Most animals have surfaces that are specialized for exchanging chemicals with the surroundings. These exchange surfaces are usually internal but are connected to the environment via openings on the body surface (the mouth, for example). The exchange surfaces are finely branched or folded, giving them a very large area. The digestive, respiratory, and excretory systems all have such exchange surfaces. The circulatory system carries chemicals transported across these surfaces throughout the body.

? *In what sense are exchange surfaces such as the lining of the digestive system both internal and external?*

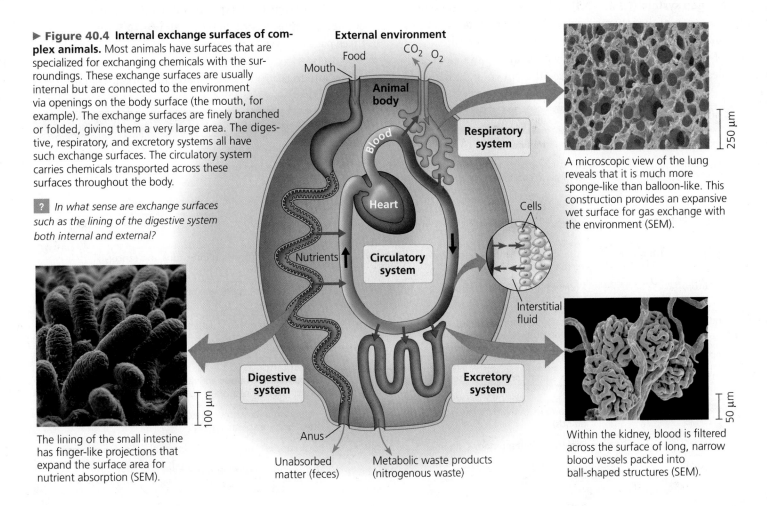

External environment

Food

CO_2 O_2

Mouth

Animal body

Respiratory system

Blood

Heart

Cells

Nutrients

Circulatory system

Interstitial fluid

Digestive system

Excretory system

Anus

Unabsorbed matter (feces)

Metabolic waste products (nitrogenous waste)

250 μm

A microscopic view of the lung reveals that it is much more sponge-like than balloon-like. This construction provides an expansive wet surface for gas exchange with the environment (SEM).

100 μm

The lining of the small intestine has finger-like projections that expand the surface area for nutrient absorption (SEM).

50 μm

Within the kidney, blood is filtered across the surface of long, narrow blood vessels packed into ball-shaped structures (SEM).

Despite the greater challenges of exchange with the environment, complex body plans have distinct benefits over simple ones. For example, an external skeleton can protect against predators, and sensory organs can provide detailed information on the animal's surroundings. Internal digestive organs can break down food gradually, controlling the release of stored energy. In addition, specialized filtration systems can adjust the composition of the internal fluid that bathes the animal's body cells. In this way, an animal can maintain a relatively stable internal environment while living in a changeable external environment. A complex body plan is especially advantageous for animals living on land, where the external environment may be highly variable.

Hierarchical Organization of Body Plans

Cells form a working animal body through their emergent properties, which arise from successive levels of structural and functional organization (see Chapter 1). Cells are organized into **tissues**, groups of cells with a similar appearance and a common function. Different types of tissues are further organized into functional units called **organs**. (The simplest animals, such as sponges, lack organs or even true tissues.) Groups of organs that work together, providing an additional level of organization and coordination, make up an **organ system (Table 40.1)**. Thus, for example, the skin is an organ of the integumentary system, which protects against infection and helps regulate body temperature.

Many organs contain tissues with distinct physiological roles. In some cases, the roles are different enough that we consider the organ to belong to more than one organ system. The pancreas, for instance, produces enzymes critical to the function of the digestive system and also regulates the level of sugar in the blood as a vital part of the endocrine system.

Just as viewing the body's organization from the "bottom up" (from cells to organ systems) reveals emergent properties, a "top-down" view of the hierarchy reveals the multilayered basis of specialization. Consider the human digestive system: the mouth, pharynx, esophagus, stomach, small and large intestines, accessory organs, and anus. Each organ has specific roles in digestion. One role of the stomach, for example, is to initiate the breakdown of proteins. This process requires a churning motion powered by stomach muscles, as well as digestive juices secreted by the stomach lining. Producing digestive juices, in turn, requires highly specialized cell types: One cell type secretes a protein-digesting enzyme, a second generates concentrated hydrochloric acid, and a third produces mucus, which protects the stomach lining.

The specialized and complex organ systems of animals are built from a limited set of cell and tissue types. For example, lungs and blood vessels have different functions but are lined by tissues that are of the same basic type and that therefore share many properties.

There are four main types of animal tissues: epithelial, connective, muscle, and nervous. **Figure 40.5**, on the next three pages, explores the structure and function of each type. In later chapters, we'll discuss how these tissue types contribute to the functions of particular organ systems.

Table 40.1   Organ Systems in Mammals

Organ System	Main Components	Main Functions
Digestive	Mouth, pharynx, esophagus, stomach, intestines, liver, pancreas, anus	Food processing (ingestion, digestion, absorption, elimination)
Circulatory	Heart, blood vessels, blood	Internal distribution of materials
Respiratory	Lungs, trachea, other breathing tubes	Gas exchange (uptake of oxygen; disposal of carbon dioxide)
Immune and lymphatic	Bone marrow, lymph nodes, thymus, spleen, lymph vessels	Body defense (fighting infections and cancer)
Excretory	Kidneys, ureters, urinary bladder, urethra	Disposal of metabolic wastes; regulation of osmotic balance of blood
Endocrine	Pituitary, thyroid, pancreas, adrenal, and other hormone-secreting glands	Coordination of body activities (such as digestion and metabolism)
Reproductive	Ovaries or testes and associated organs	Reproduction
Nervous	Brain, spinal cord, nerves, sensory organs	Coordination of body activities; detection of stimuli and formulation of responses to them
Integumentary	Skin and its derivatives (such as hair, claws, skin glands)	Protection against mechanical injury, infection, dehydration; thermoregulation
Skeletal	Skeleton (bones, tendons, ligaments, cartilage)	Body support, protection of internal organs, movement
Muscular	Skeletal muscles	Locomotion and other movement

Exploring Structure and Function in Animal Tissues

Epithelial Tissue

Occurring as sheets of cells, **epithelial tissues**, or **epithelia** (singular, *epithelium*), cover the outside of the body and line organs and cavities within the body. Because epithelial cells are closely packed, often with tight junctions, they function as a barrier against mechanical injury, pathogens, and fluid loss. Epithelia also form active interfaces with the environment. For example, the epithelium that lines the nasal passages is crucial for olfaction, the sense of smell. Note how different cell shapes and arrangements correlate with distinct functions.

Stratified squamous epithelium

Apical surface

Basal surface

A stratified squamous epithelium is multilayered and regenerates rapidly. New cells formed by division near the basal surface (see micrograph below) push outward, replacing cells that are sloughed off. This epithelium is commonly found on surfaces subject to abrasion, such as the outer skin and the linings of the mouth, anus, and vagina.

Cuboidal epithelium

A cuboidal epithelium, with dice-shaped cells specialized for secretion, makes up the epithelium of kidney tubules and many glands, including the thyroid gland and salivary glands.

Simple columnar epithelium

The large, brick-shaped cells of simple columnar epithelia are often found where secretion or active absorption is important. For example, a simple columnar epithelium lines the intestines, secreting digestive juices and absorbing nutrients.

Simple squamous epithelium

The single layer of platelike cells that form a simple squamous epithelium functions in the exchange of material by diffusion. This type of epithelium, which is thin and leaky, lines blood vessels and the air sacs of the lungs, where diffusion of nutrients and gases is critical.

Pseudostratified columnar epithelium

A pseudostratified epithelium consists of a single layer of cells varying in height and the position of their nuclei. In many vertebrates, a pseudostratified epithelium of ciliated cells forms a mucous membrane that lines portions of the respiratory tract. The beating cilia sweep the film of mucus along the surface.

Lumen

Apical surface

Basal surface

10 μm

Polarity of epithelia

All epithelia are polarized, meaning that they have two different sides. The *apical* surface faces the lumen (cavity) or outside of the organ and is therefore exposed to fluid or air. Specialized projections often cover this surface. For example, the apical surface of the epithelium lining the small intestine is covered with microvilli, projections that increase the surface area available for absorbing nutrients. The opposite side of each epithelium is the *basal* surface.

Continued on next page

Connective Tissue

Connective tissue, consisting of a sparse population of cells scattered through an extracellular matrix, holds many tissues and organs together and in place. The matrix generally consists of a web of fibers embedded in a liquid, jellylike, or solid foundation. Within the matrix are numerous cells called **fibroblasts**, which secrete fiber proteins, and **macrophages**, which engulf foreign particles and any cell debris by phagocytosis.

Connective tissue fibers are of three kinds: *Collagenous fibers* provide strength and flexibility,

reticular fibers join connective tissue to adjacent tissues, and *elastic fibers* make tissues elastic. If you pinch a fold of tissue on the back of your hand, the collagenous and reticular fibers prevent the skin from being pulled far from the bone, whereas the elastic fibers restore the skin to its original shape when you release your grip. Different mixtures of fibers and foundation form the major types of connective tissue shown below.

Loose connective tissue

The most widespread connective tissue in the vertebrate body is *loose connective tissue*, which binds epithelia to underlying tissues and holds organs in place. Loose connective tissue gets its name from the loose weave of its fibers, which include all three types. It is found in the skin and throughout the body.

Collagenous fiber

120 μm

Elastic fiber

Fibrous connective tissue

Fibrous connective tissue is dense with collagenous fibers. It is found in **tendons**, which attach muscles to bones, and in **ligaments**, which connect bones at joints.

30 μm

Nuclei

Bone

The skeleton of most vertebrates is made of **bone**, a mineralized connective tissue. Bone-forming cells called *osteoblasts* deposit a matrix of collagen. Calcium, magnesium, and phosphate ions combine into a hard mineral within the matrix. The microscopic structure of hard mammalian bone consists of repeating units called *osteons*. Each osteon has concentric layers of the mineralized matrix, which are deposited around a central canal containing blood vessels and nerves.

Central canal

700 μm

Osteon

Blood

Blood has a liquid extracellular matrix called plasma, which consists of water, salts, and dissolved proteins. Suspended in plasma are erythrocytes (red blood cells), leukocytes (white blood cells), and cell fragments called platelets. Red cells carry oxygen, white cells function in defense, and platelets aid in blood clotting.

Plasma

White blood cells

55 μm

Red blood cells

Adipose tissue

Adipose tissue is a specialized loose connective tissue that stores fat in adipose cells distributed throughout its matrix. Adipose tissue pads and insulates the body and stores fuel as fat molecules. Each adipose cell contains a large fat droplet that swells when fat is stored and shrinks when the body uses that fat as fuel.

Fat droplets

150 μm

Cartilage

Cartilage contains collagenous fibers embedded in a rubbery protein-carbohydrate complex called chondroitin sulfate. Cells called *chondrocytes* secrete the collagen and chondroitin sulfate, which together make cartilage a strong yet flexible support material. The skeletons of many vertebrate embryos contain cartilage that is replaced by bone as the embryo matures. Cartilage remains in some locations, such as the disks that act as cushions between vertebrae.

Chondrocytes

100 μm

Chondroitin sulfate

Muscle Tissue

The tissue responsible for nearly all types of body movement is **muscle tissue**. All muscle cells consist of filaments containing the proteins actin and myosin, which together enable muscles to contract. There are three types of muscle tissue in the vertebrate body: skeletal, smooth, and cardiac.

Skeletal muscle

Attached to bones by tendons, **skeletal muscle**, or *striated muscle*, is responsible for voluntary movements. Skeletal muscle consists of bundles of long cells called muscle fibers. During development, skeletal muscle fibers form by the fusion of many cells, resulting in multiple nuclei in each muscle fiber. The arrangement of contractile units, or sarcomeres, along the fibers gives the cells a striped (striated) appearance. In adult mammals, building muscle increases the size but not the number of muscle fibers.

Nuclei

Muscle fiber

Sarcomere

100 μm

Smooth muscle

Smooth muscle, which lacks striations, is found in the walls of the digestive tract, urinary bladder, arteries, and other internal organs. The cells are spindle-shaped. Smooth muscles are responsible for involuntary body activities, such as churning of the stomach and constriction of arteries.

Nucleus   Muscle fibers   25 μm

Cardiac muscle

Cardiac muscle forms the contractile wall of the heart. It is striated like skeletal muscle and has similar contractile properties. Unlike skeletal muscle, however, cardiac muscle has fibers that interconnect via intercalated disks, which relay signals from cell to cell and help synchronize heart contraction.

Nucleus   Intercalated disk   25 μm

Nervous Tissue

Nervous tissue functions in the receipt, processing, and transmission of information. Nervous tissue contains **neurons**, or nerve cells, which transmit nerve impulses, as well as support cells called **glial cells**, or simply **glia**. In many animals, a concentration of nervous tissue forms a brain, an information-processing center.

Neurons

Neurons are the basic units of the nervous system. A neuron receives nerve impulses from other neurons via its cell body and multiple extensions called dendrites. Neurons transmit impulses to neurons, muscles, or other cells via extensions called axons, which are often bundled together into nerves.

Neuron:

Dendrites

Cell body

Axon

40 μm

(Fluorescent LM)

Glia

The various types of glia help nourish, insulate, and replenish neurons, and in some cases, modulate neuron function.

Glia   15 μm

Axons of neurons

Blood vessel

(Confocal LM)

Coordination and Control

An animal's tissues, organs, and organ systems must act in concert with one another. For example, during long dives, the seal shown in Figure 40.2 slows its heart rate, collapses its lungs, and lowers its body temperature while propelling itself forward with its hind flippers. Coordinating activity across an animal's body in this way requires communication between different locations in the body. What signals are used to coordinate activity? How do the signals move within the body? There are two sets of answers to these questions, reflecting the two major systems for coordinating and controlling responses to stimuli: the endocrine and nervous systems (**Figure 40.6**).

In the **endocrine system**, signaling molecules released into the bloodstream by endocrine cells are carried to all locations in the body. In the **nervous system**, neurons transmit signals along dedicated routes connecting specific locations in the body. In each system, the type of pathway used is the same regardless of whether the signal's ultimate target is at the other end of the body or just a few cell diameters away.

The signaling molecules broadcast throughout the body by the endocrine system are called **hormones**. Different hormones cause distinct effects, and only cells that have receptors for a particular hormone respond (Figure 40.6a). Depending on which cells have receptors for that hormone, the hormone may have an effect in just a single location or in sites throughout the body. For example, thyroid-stimulating hormone (TSH), which acts solely on thyroid cells, stimulates release of thyroid hormone, which acts on nearly every body tissue to increase oxygen consumption and heat production. It takes seconds for hormones to be released into the bloodstream and carried throughout the body. The effects are often long-lasting, however, because hormones can remain in the bloodstream for minutes or even hours.

In the nervous system, signals called nerve impulses travel to specific target cells along communication lines consisting mainly of axons (Figure 40.6b). Nerve impulses can act on other neurons, on muscle cells, and on cells and glands that produce secretions. Unlike the endocrine system, the nervous system conveys information by the particular *pathway* the signal takes. For example, a person can distinguish different musical notes because within the ear, each note's frequency activates neurons that connect to slightly different regions of the brain.

Communication in the nervous system usually involves more than one type of signal. Nerve impulses travel along axons, sometimes over long distances, as changes in voltage. In contrast, passing information from one neuron to another often involves very short-range chemical signals. Overall, transmission in the nervous system is extremely fast; nerve impulses take only a fraction of a second to reach the target and last only a fraction of a second.

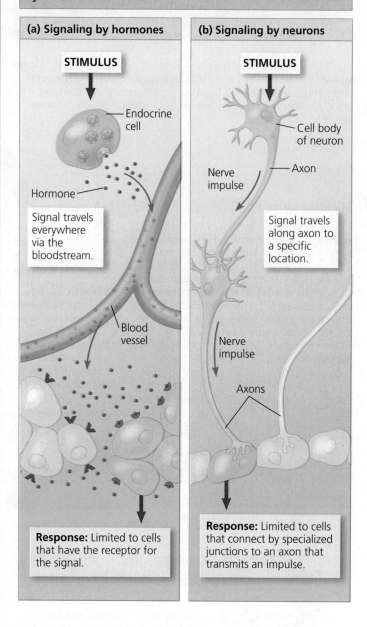

▼ **Figure 40.6 Signaling in the endocrine and nervous systems.**

(a) Signaling by hormones

STIMULUS

Endocrine cell

Hormone

Signal travels everywhere via the bloodstream.

Blood vessel

Response: Limited to cells that have the receptor for the signal.

(b) Signaling by neurons

STIMULUS

Cell body of neuron

Nerve impulse

Axon

Signal travels along axon to a specific location.

Nerve impulse

Axons

Response: Limited to cells that connect by specialized junctions to an axon that transmits an impulse.

Because the two major communication systems of the body differ in signal type, transmission, speed, and duration, it is not surprising that they are adapted to different functions. The endocrine system is especially well adapted for coordinating gradual changes that affect the entire body, such as growth, development, reproduction, metabolic processes, and digestion. The nervous system is well suited for directing immediate and rapid responses to the environment, such as reflexes and other rapid movements.

Although the functions of the endocrine and nervous systems are distinct, the two systems often work in close coordination. Both contribute to maintaining a stable internal environment, our next topic of discussion.

1. What properties do all types of epithelia share?

2. Consider the idealized animal in Figure 40.4. At which sites must oxygen cross a plasma membrane in traveling from the external environment to the cytoplasm of a body cell?

3. **WHAT IF?** Suppose you are standing at the edge of a cliff and suddenly slip—you barely manage to keep your balance and avoid falling. As your heart races, you feel a burst of energy, due in part to a surge of blood into dilated (widened) vessels in your muscles and an upward spike in the level of glucose in your blood. Why might you expect that this "fight-or-flight" response requires both the nervous and endocrine systems?

For suggested answers, see Appendix A.

CONCEPT 40.2

Feedback control maintains the internal environment in many animals

Many organ systems play a role in managing an animal's internal environment, a task that can present a major challenge. Imagine if your body temperature soared every time you took a hot shower or drank a freshly brewed cup of coffee. Faced with environmental fluctuations, animals manage their internal environment by either regulating or conforming.

Regulating and Conforming

An animal is a **regulator** for an environmental variable if it uses internal mechanisms to control internal change in the face of external fluctuation. The otter in **Figure 40.7** is a regulator for temperature, keeping its body at a temperature that is largely independent of that of the water in which it swims. In contrast, an animal is a **conformer** for a particular variable if it allows its internal condition to change in accordance with external changes in the variable. The bass in Figure 40.7 conforms to the temperature of the lake it inhabits. As the water warms or cools, so does the bass's body. Some animals conform to more constant environments. For example, many marine invertebrates, such as spider crabs of the genus *Libinia*, let their internal solute concentration conform to the relatively stable solute concentration (salinity) of their ocean environment.

Regulating and conforming represent extremes on a continuum. An animal may regulate some internal conditions while allowing others to conform to the environment. For instance, even though the bass conforms to the temperature of the surrounding water, it regulates the solute concentration in its blood and interstitial fluid. You'll learn more about the mechanisms of this regulation in Chapter 44.

Homeostasis

The steady body temperature of a river otter and the stable concentration of solutes in a freshwater bass are examples of **homeostasis**, which means "steady state," referring to the maintenance of internal balance. In achieving homeostasis, animals maintain a relatively constant internal environment even when the external environment changes significantly.

Many animals exhibit homeostasis for a range of physical and chemical properties. For example, humans maintain a fairly constant body temperature of about 37°C (98.6°F), a blood pH within 0.1 pH unit of 7.4, and a blood glucose concentration that is predominantly in the range of 70–110 mg of glucose per 100 mL of blood.

▶ **Figure 40.7 The relationship between body and environmental temperatures in an aquatic temperature regulator and an aquatic temperature conformer.** The river otter regulates its body temperature, keeping it stable across a wide range of environmental temperatures. The largemouth bass, meanwhile, allows its internal environment to conform to the water temperature.

Thermostat turns heater off.

Room temperature increases.

Room temperature decreases.

ROOM TEMPERATURE
AT 20°C
(set point)

Room temperature increases.

Room temperature decreases.

Thermostat turns heater on.

▲ **Figure 40.8 A nonliving example of temperature regulation: control of room temperature.** Regulating room temperature depends on a control center (a thermostat) that detects temperature change and activates mechanisms that reverse that change.

WHAT IF? *Label at least one stimulus, response, and sensor/control center in the above figure. How would adding an air conditioner to the system contribute to homeostasis?*

Mechanisms of Homeostasis

Before exploring homeostasis in animals, let's first consider a nonliving example: the regulation of room temperature **(Figure 40.8)**. Let's assume you want to keep a room at 20°C (68°F), a comfortable temperature for normal activity. You set a control device—the thermostat—to 20°C. A thermometer in the thermostat monitors the room temperature. If the temperature falls below 20°C, the thermostat responds by turning on a radiator, furnace, or other heater. Once the room temperature reaches 20°C, the thermostat switches off the heater. If the temperature then drifts below 20°C, the thermostat activates another heating cycle.

Like a home heating system, an animal achieves homeostasis by maintaining a variable, such as body temperature or solute concentration, at or near a particular value, or **set point**. A fluctuation in the variable above or below the set point serves as the **stimulus** detected by a **sensor**. Upon receiving a signal from the sensor, a *control center* generates output that triggers a **response**, a physiological activity that helps return the variable to the set point. In the home heating example, a drop in temperature below the set point acts as a stimulus, the thermostat serves as the sensor and control center, and the heater produces the response.

Feedback Control in Homeostasis

Just as in the circuit shown in Figure 40.8, homeostasis in animals relies largely on **negative feedback**, a control mechanism that reduces, or "damps," the stimulus. For example, when you exercise vigorously, you produce heat, which increases your body temperature. Your nervous system detects this increase and triggers sweating. As you sweat, the evaporation of moisture from your skin cools your body, helping return your body temperature to its set point and eliminating the stimulus.

Homeostasis is a dynamic equilibrium, an interplay between external factors that tend to change the internal environment and internal control mechanisms that oppose such changes. Note that physiological responses to stimuli are not instantaneous, just as switching on a furnace does not immediately warm a room. As a result, homeostasis moderates but doesn't eliminate changes in the internal environment. Additional fluctuation occurs if a variable has a *normal range*—an upper and lower limit—rather than a set point. This is equivalent to a thermostat that turns on a heater when the room temperature drops to 19°C (66°F) and turns off the heater when the temperature reaches 21°C (70°F). Regardless of whether there is a set point or a normal range, homeostasis is enhanced by adaptations that reduce fluctuations, such as insulation in the case of temperature and physiological buffers in the case of pH.

Unlike negative feedback, **positive feedback** is a control mechanism that amplifies rather than reduces the stimulus (see Figure 1.11). In animals, positive-feedback loops do not play a major role in homeostasis, but instead help drive processes to completion. During childbirth, for instance, the pressure of the baby's head against sensors near the opening of the mother's uterus stimulates the uterus to contract. These contractions result in greater pressure against the opening of the uterus, heightening the contractions and thereby causing even greater pressure, until the baby is born.

Alterations in Homeostasis

The set points and normal ranges for homeostasis can change under various circumstances. In fact, *regulated changes* in the internal environment are essential to normal body functions. Some regulated changes occur during a particular stage in life, such as the radical shift in hormone balance that occurs during puberty. Other regulated changes are cyclic, such as the variation in hormone levels responsible for a woman's menstrual cycle (see Figure 46.14).

In all animals (and plants, too), certain cyclic alterations in metabolism reflect a **circadian rhythm**, a set of physiological changes that occur roughly every 24 hours. One way to observe this rhythm is to monitor body temperature, which in humans typically undergoes a cyclic rise and fall

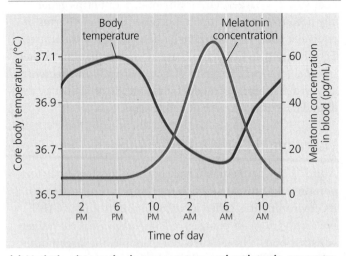

(a) **Variation in core body temperature and melatonin concentration in blood.** Researchers measured these two variables in resting but awake volunteers in an isolation chamber with constant temperature and low light. (Melatonin is a hormone that appears to be involved in sleep/wake cycles.)

(b) **The human circadian clock.** Metabolic activities undergo daily cycles in response to the circadian clock. As illustrated for a typical individual who rises early in the morning, eats lunch around noon, and sleeps at night, these cyclic changes occur throughout a 24-hour day.

▲ **Figure 40.9 Human circadian rhythm.**

of more than 0.6°C (1°F) in every 24-hour period. Remarkably, a biological clock maintains this rhythm even when variations in human activity, room temperature, and light levels are minimized **(Figure 40.9a)**. A circadian rhythm is thus intrinsic to the body, although the biological clock is normally coordinated with the cycle of light and darkness in the environment **(Figure 40.9b)**. For example, the hormone melatonin is secreted at night, and more is released during the longer nights of winter. External stimuli can reset the biological clock, but the effect is not immediate. That is why flying across several time zones results in jet lag, a mismatch between the circadian rhythm and local environment that persists until the clock fully resets.

▲ **Figure 40.10 Acclimitization by mountain climbers in the Himalayas.** To lessen the risk of altitude sickness when ascending a high peak, climbers acclimatize by camping partway up the mountain. Spending time at an intermediate altitude allows the circulatory and respiratory systems to become more efficient in capturing and distributing oxygen at a lower concentration.

One way in which homeostasis may be altered is through **acclimatization**, the gradual process by which an animal adjusts to changes in its external environment. For instance, when an elk moves up into the mountains from sea level, the lower oxygen concentration in the high mountain air stimulates the animal to breathe more rapidly and deeply. As a result, more CO_2 is lost through exhalation, raising blood pH above its normal range. As the animal acclimatizes over several days, changes in kidney function cause it to excrete more alkaline urine, returning blood pH to its normal range. Other mammals, including humans, are also capable of acclimitizing to dramatic altitude changes **(Figure 40.10)**.

Note that acclimatization, a temporary change during an animal's lifetime, should not be confused with adaptation, a process of change in a population brought about by natural selection acting over many generations.

CONCEPT CHECK 40.2

1. **MAKE CONNECTIONS** How does negative feedback in thermoregulation differ from feedback inhibition in an enzyme-catalyzed biosynthetic process (see Figure 8.21)?

2. If you were deciding where to put the thermostat in a house, what factors would govern your decision? How do these factors relate to the fact that many homeostatic control sensors in humans are located in the brain?

3. **MAKE CONNECTIONS** Like animals, cyanobacteria have a circadian rhythm. By analyzing the genes that maintain biological clocks, scientists concluded that the 24-hour rhythms of humans and cyanobacteria reflect convergent evolution (see Concept 26.2). What evidence would have supported this conclusion? Explain.

For suggested answers, see Appendix A.

Homeostatic processes for thermoregulation involve form, function, and behavior

In this section, we'll examine the regulation of body temperature as an example of how form and function work together in regulating an animal's internal environment. Later chapters in this unit will discuss other physiological systems involved in maintaining homeostasis.

Thermoregulation is the process by which animals maintain their body temperature within a normal range. Body temperatures outside the normal range can reduce the efficiency of enzymatic reactions, alter the fluidity of cellular membranes, and affect other temperature-sensitive biochemical processes, potentially with fatal results.

Endothermy and Ectothermy

Heat for thermoregulation can come from either internal metabolism or the external environment. Humans and other mammals, as well as birds, are **endothermic**, meaning that they are warmed mostly by heat generated by metabolism. A few nonavian reptiles, some fishes, and many insect species are also mainly endothermic. In contrast, many nonavian reptiles and fishes, amphibians, and most invertebrates are **ectothermic**, meaning that they gain most of their heat from external sources. Endothermy and ectothermy are not mutually exclusive, however. For example, a bird is mainly endothermic, but it may warm itself in the sun on a cold morning, much as an ectothermic lizard does.

Endotherms can maintain a stable body temperature even in the face of large fluctuations in the environmental temperature. In a cold environment, an endotherm generates enough heat to keep its body substantially warmer than its surroundings **(Figure 40.11a)**. In a hot environment, endothermic vertebrates have mechanisms for cooling their bodies, enabling them to withstand heat loads that are intolerable for most ectotherms.

Although ectotherms do not generate enough heat for thermoregulation, many adjust their body temperature by behavioral means, such as seeking out shade or basking in the sun **(Figure 40.11b)**. Because their

heat source is largely environmental, ectotherms generally need to consume much less food than endotherms of equivalent size—an advantage if food supplies are limited. Ectotherms also usually tolerate larger fluctuations in their internal temperature. Overall, ectothermy is an effective and successful strategy in most environments, as shown by the abundance and diversity of ectotherms.

Variation in Body Temperature

Animals can have either a variable or a constant body temperature. An animal whose body temperature varies with its environment is called a *poikilotherm* (from the Greek *poikilos*, varied). In contrast, a *homeotherm* has a relatively constant body temperature. For example, the largemouth bass is a poikilotherm, and the river otter is a homeotherm (see Figure 40.7).

From the descriptions of ectotherms and endotherms, it might seem that all ectotherms are poikilothermic and all endotherms are homeothermic. In fact, there is no fixed relationship between the source of heat and the stability of body temperature. Many ectothermic marine fishes and invertebrates inhabit waters with such stable temperatures that their body temperature varies less than that of mammals and other endotherms. Conversely, the body temperature of a few endotherms varies considerably. For example, bats and hummingbirds may periodically enter an inactive state in which they maintain a lower body temperature.

It is a common misconception that ectotherms are "cold-blooded" and endotherms are "warm-blooded." Ectotherms do not necessarily have low body temperatures. On the contrary, when sitting in the sun, many ectothermic lizards have higher body temperatures than mammals. Thus, the terms *cold-blooded* and *warm-blooded* are misleading and are avoided in scientific communication.

(a) A walrus, an endotherm

▲ **Figure 40.11 Thermoregulation by internal or external sources of heat.** Endotherms obtain heat from their internal metabolism, whereas ectotherms rely on heat from their external environment.

(b) A lizard, an ectotherm

Balancing Heat Loss and Gain

Thermoregulation depends on an animal's ability to control the exchange of heat with its environment. An organism, like any object, exchanges heat by radiation, evaporation, convection, and conduction (**Figure 40.12**). Note that heat is always transferred from an object of higher temperature to one of lower temperature.

The essence of thermoregulation is maintaining a rate of heat gain that equals the rate of heat loss. Animals do this through mechanisms that either reduce heat exchange overall or favor heat exchange in a particular direction. In mammals, several of these mechanisms involve the **integumentary system**, the outer covering of the body, consisting of the skin, hair, and nails (claws or hooves in some species).

Insulation

A major thermoregulatory adaptation in mammals and birds is insulation, which reduces the flow of heat between an animal's body and its environment. Such insulation may include hair or feathers as well as layers of fat formed by adipose tissue.

Many animals that rely on insulation to reduce overall heat exchange also adjust their insulating layers to help thermoregulate. Most land mammals and birds, for example, react to cold by raising their fur or feathers. This action traps a thicker layer of air, thereby increasing the effectiveness of the insulation. To repel water that would reduce the insulating capacity of feathers or fur, some animals secrete oily substances, such as the oils that birds apply to their feathers during preening. Lacking feathers or fur, humans must rely primarily on fat for insulation. We do, however, get "goose bumps," a vestige of hair raising inherited from our furry ancestors.

Insulation is particularly important for marine mammals, such as whales and walruses. These animals swim in water colder than their body core, and many species spend at least part of the year in nearly freezing polar seas. The problem of thermoregulation is made worse by the fact that the transfer of heat to water occurs 50 to 100 times more rapidly than heat transfer to air. Just under their skin, marine mammals have a very thick layer of insulating fat called blubber. The insulation that blubber provides is so effective that marine mammals can maintain body core temperatures of about 36–38°C (97–100°F) without

Radiation is the emission of electromagnetic waves by all objects warmer than absolute zero. Here, a lizard absorbs heat radiating from the distant sun and radiates a smaller amount of energy to the surrounding air.

Evaporation is the removal of heat from the surface of a liquid that is losing some of its molecules as gas. Evaporation of water from a lizard's moist surfaces that are exposed to the environment has a strong cooling effect.

Convection is the transfer of heat by the movement of air or liquid past a surface, as when a breeze contributes to heat loss from a lizard's dry skin or when blood moves heat from the body core to the extremities.

Conduction is the direct transfer of thermal motion (heat) between molecules of objects in contact with each other, as when a lizard sits on a hot rock.

▲ **Figure 40.12 Heat exchange between an organism and its environment.**

? *Which type or types of heat exchange occur when you fan yourself on a hot day?*

requiring much more energy from food than land mammals of similar size.

Circulatory Adaptations

Circulatory systems provide a major route for heat flow between the interior and exterior of the body. Adaptations that regulate the extent of blood flow near the body surface or that trap heat within the body core play a significant role in thermoregulation.

In response to changes in the temperature of their surroundings, many animals alter the amount of blood (and hence heat) flowing between their body core and their skin. Nerve signals that relax the muscles of the vessel walls result in *vasodilation*, a widening of superficial blood vessels (those near the body surface). As a consequence of the increase in vessel diameter, blood flow in the skin increases. In endotherms, vasodilation usually warms the skin and increases the transfer of body heat to the environment by radiation, conduction, and convection (see Figure 40.12). The reverse process, *vasoconstriction*, reduces blood flow and heat transfer by decreasing the diameter of superficial vessels.

Like endotherms, some ectotherms control heat exchange by regulating blood flow. For example, when the marine iguana of the Galápagos Islands swims in the cold ocean, its superficial blood vessels undergo vasoconstriction.

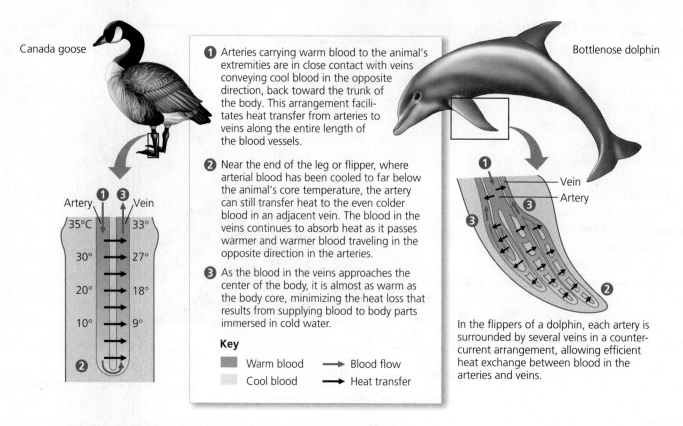

Canada goose

① Arteries carrying warm blood to the animal's extremities are in close contact with veins conveying cool blood in the opposite direction, back toward the trunk of the body. This arrangement facilitates heat transfer from arteries to veins along the entire length of the blood vessels.

② Near the end of the leg or flipper, where arterial blood has been cooled to far below the animal's core temperature, the artery can still transfer heat to the even colder blood in an adjacent vein. The blood in the veins continues to absorb heat as it passes warmer and warmer blood traveling in the opposite direction in the arteries.

③ As the blood in the veins approaches the center of the body, it is almost as warm as the body core, minimizing the heat loss that results from supplying blood to body parts immersed in cold water.

Key

■ Warm blood   → Blood flow

□ Cool blood   → Heat transfer

Bottlenose dolphin

Vein
Artery

In the flippers of a dolphin, each artery is surrounded by several veins in a counter-current arrangement, allowing efficient heat exchange between blood in the arteries and veins.

Artery Vein

35°C   33°
30°   27°
20°   18°
10°   9°

▲ **Figure 40.13 Countercurrent heat exchangers.** A countercurrent exchange system traps heat in the body core, thus reducing heat loss from the extremities, particularly when they are immersed in cold water or in contact with ice or snow. In essence, heat in the arterial blood emerging from the body core is transferred directly to the returning venous blood instead of being lost to the environment.

This process routes more blood to the core of the iguana's body, conserving body heat.

In many birds and mammals, reducing heat loss from the body relies on **countercurrent exchange**, the transfer of heat (or solutes) between fluids that are flowing in opposite directions. In a countercurrent heat exchanger, arteries and veins are located adjacent to each other **(Figure 40.13)**. Because blood flows through the arteries and veins in opposite directions, this arrangement allows heat exchange to be remarkably efficient. As warm blood moves from the body core in the arteries, it transfers heat to the colder blood returning from the extremities in the veins. Most importantly, heat is transferred along the entire length of the exchanger, maximizing the rate of heat exchange.

Certain sharks, fishes, and insects also use countercurrent heat exchange. Although most sharks and fishes are temperature conformers, countercurrent heat exchangers are found in some large, powerful swimmers, including great white sharks, bluefin tuna, and swordfish. By keeping the main swimming muscles several degrees warmer than tissues near the animal's surface, this adaptation enables the vigorous, sustained activity that is characteristic of these animals. Similarly, many endothermic insects (bumblebees, honeybees, and some moths) have a countercurrent exchanger that helps maintain a high temperature in their thorax, where flight muscles are located.

Cooling by Evaporative Heat Loss

Many mammals and birds live in places where thermoregulation requires cooling as well as warming. If the environmental temperature is above their body temperature, animals gain heat from the environment as well as from metabolism. In this situation, evaporation is the only way to keep body temperature from rising. Terrestrial animals lose water by evaporation from their skin and respiratory surfaces. Water absorbs considerable heat when it evaporates (see Chapter 3); this heat is carried away from the body surface with the water vapor.

Some animals exhibit adaptations that greatly facilitate evaporative cooling. Bathing or sweating moistens the skin; many terrestrial mammals have sweat glands controlled by the nervous system. Panting is also important in many mammals and in birds. Some birds have a pouch richly supplied with blood vessels in the floor of the mouth; fluttering the pouch increases evaporation. Pigeons, for example, can use this adaptation to keep their body temperature close to 40°C (104°F) in air temperatures as high as 60°C (140°F), as long as they have sufficient water.

Behavioral Responses

Both endotherms and ectotherms control body temperature through behavioral responses to changes in the environment. Many ectotherms maintain a nearly constant body temperature by engaging in relatively simple behaviors. When cold, they seek warm places, orienting themselves toward heat sources and expanding the portion of their body surface exposed to the heat source (see Figure 40.11b). When hot, they bathe, move to cool areas, or turn in another direction, minimizing their absorption of heat from the sun. For example, a dragonfly's "obelisk" posture is an adaptation that minimizes the amount of body surface exposed to the sun and thus to heating (Figure 40.14).

Honeybees use a thermoregulatory mechanism that depends on social behavior. In cold weather, they increase heat production and huddle together, thereby retaining heat. Individuals move between the cooler outer edges of the huddle and the warmer center, thus circulating and distributing the heat. Even when huddling, honeybees must expend considerable energy to keep warm during long periods of cold weather. (This is the main function of storing large quantities of fuel in the hive in the form of honey.) In hot weather, honeybees cool the hive by transporting water to the hive and fanning with their wings, promoting evaporation and convection. Thus, a honeybee colony uses many of the mechanisms of thermoregulation seen in individual animals.

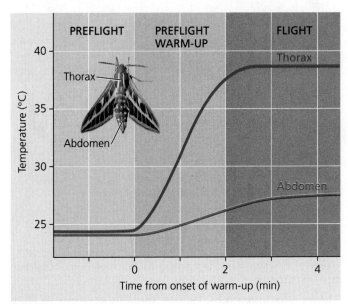

▲ **Figure 40.14 Thermoregulatory behavior in a dragonfly.** By orienting its body so that the narrow tip of its abdomen faces the sun, the dragonfly minimizes heating by solar radiation.

Adjusting Metabolic Heat Production

Because endotherms generally maintain a body temperature considerably higher than that of the environment, they must counteract continual heat loss. Endotherms can vary heat production—*thermogenesis*—to match changing rates of heat loss. Thermogenesis is increased by such muscle activity as moving or shivering. For example, shivering helps chickadees, birds with a body mass of only 20 g, remain active and hold their body temperature nearly constant at 40°C (104°F) in environmental temperatures as low as −40°C (−40°F), as long as they have adequate food.

The smallest endotherms—flying insects such as bees and moths—are also capable of varying heat production. Their capacity to elevate body temperature depends on powerful flight muscles, which generate large amounts of heat when contracting. Many endothermic insects warm up by shivering before taking off. As they contract their flight muscles in synchrony, only slight wing movements occur, but considerable heat is produced. Chemical reactions, and hence cellular respiration, accelerate in the warmed-up flight "motors," enabling these insects to fly even when the air is cold (Figure 40.15).

In some mammals, certain hormones can cause mitochondria to increase their metabolic activity and produce heat instead of ATP. This process, called *nonshivering thermogenesis*, takes place throughout the body. Some mammals also have a tissue called *brown fat* in their neck and between their shoulders that is specialized for rapid heat production. (The presence of many more mitochondria than in white adipose tissue is what gives brown fat its characteristic color.) Brown fat is found in the infants of many mammals, as well as in adult mammals that hibernate. In human infants, brown fat represents about 5% of total body weight. Brown fat has recently been detected in human adults; adults were observed to have larger amounts of brown fat in cooler conditions than in warmer ones. Together, nonshivering and shivering thermogenesis enable mammals and birds to increase their metabolic heat production by as much as five to ten times.

▲ **Figure 40.15 Preflight warm-up in the hawkmoth.** The hawkmoth (*Manduca sexta*) is one of many insect species that use a shivering-like mechanism for preflight warm-up of thoracic flight muscles. Warming up helps these muscles produce enough power to let the animal take off. Once the moth is airborne, flight muscle activity maintains a high thoracic temperature.

A few large reptiles become endothermic in particular circumstances. Researchers found that a female Burmese python (*Python molurus bivittatus*) maintained a body temperature roughly 6°C (11°F) above that of the surrounding air during the month when she was incubating eggs. Where did the heat come from? Further studies showed that some pythons, like mammals and birds, can raise their body temperature through shivering (**Figure 40.16**). These findings contributed to the idea, still under debate, that certain groups of Mesozoic dinosaurs were endothermic (see Chapter 34).

▼ **Figure 40.16** | Inquiry

How does a Burmese python generate heat while incubating eggs?

Experiment Herndon Dowling and colleagues at the Bronx Zoo in New York observed that when a female Burmese python incubated eggs by wrapping her body around them, she raised her body temperature and frequently contracted the muscles in her coils. To learn if the contractions were elevating her body temperature, they placed the python and her eggs in a chamber. As they varied the chamber's temperature, they monitored the python's muscle contractions as well as her oxygen uptake, a measure of her rate of cellular respiration.

Results The python's oxygen consumption increased when the temperature in the chamber decreased. Her oxygen consumption also increased with the rate of muscle contraction.

Conclusion Because oxygen consumption, which generates heat through cellular respiration, increased linearly with the rate of muscle contraction, the researchers concluded that the muscle contractions, a form of shivering, were the source of the Burmese python's elevated body temperature.

Source: V. H. Hutchison, H. G. Dowling, and A. Vinegar, Thermoregulation in a brooding female Indian python, *Python molurus bivittatus, Science* 151:694–696 (1966). Reprinted with permission of AAAS.

WHAT IF? *Suppose you varied air temperature and measured oxygen consumption for a female Burmese python without a clutch of eggs. Since she would not show shivering behavior, how would you expect the snake's oxygen consumption to vary with environmental temperature?*

Acclimatization in Thermoregulation

Acclimatization contributes to thermoregulation in many animal species. In birds and mammals, acclimatization to seasonal temperature changes often includes adjusting insulation—growing a thicker coat of fur in the winter and shedding it in the summer, for example. These changes help endotherms keep a constant body temperature year-round.

Acclimatization in ectotherms often includes adjustments at the cellular level. Cells may produce variants of enzymes that have the same function but different optimal temperatures. Also, the proportions of saturated and unsaturated lipids in membranes may change; unsaturated lipids help keep membranes fluid at lower temperatures (see Figure 7.5). Some ectotherms that experience subzero body temperatures protect themselves by producing "antifreeze" proteins that prevent ice formation in their cells. In the Arctic and Southern (Antarctic) Oceans, these proteins enable certain fishes to survive in water as cold as −2°C (28°F), below the freezing point of unprotected body fluids (about −1°C, or 30°F).

Physiological Thermostats and Fever

The regulation of body temperature in humans and other mammals is brought about by a complex system based on feedback mechanisms. The sensors for thermoregulation are concentrated in the **hypothalamus**, the brain region that also controls the circadian clock. Within the hypothalamus, a group of nerve cells functions as a thermostat, responding to body temperatures outside the normal range by activating mechanisms that promote heat loss or gain **(Figure 40.17)**.

Warm sensors signal the hypothalamic thermostat when the temperature of the blood increases; cold sensors signal when it decreases. (Because the same blood vessel supplies the hypothalamus and ears, an ear thermometer records the temperature detected by the hypothalamic thermostat.) At body temperatures below the normal range, the thermostat inhibits heat loss mechanisms while activating mechanisms that either save heat, including constriction of vessels in the skin, or generate heat, such as shivering. In response to elevated body temperature, the thermostat shuts down heat retention mechanisms and promotes cooling of the body by dilation of vessels in the skin, sweating, or panting.

In the course of certain bacterial and viral infections, mammals and birds develop *fever*, an elevated body temperature. A variety of experiments have shown that fever reflects an increase in the normal range for the biological thermostat. For example, artificially raising the temperature of the hypothalamus in an infected animal reduces fever in the rest of the body!

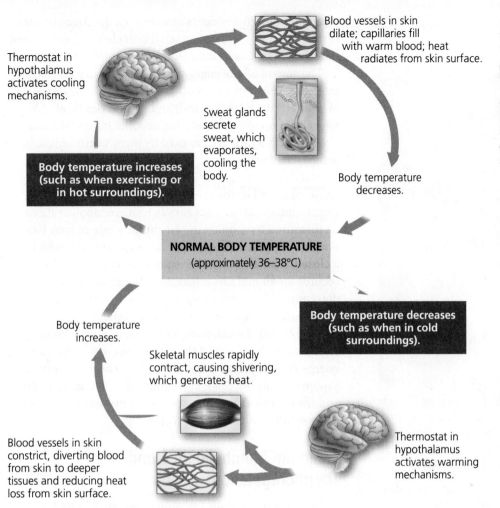

Blood vessels in skin dilate; capillaries fill with warm blood; heat radiates from skin surface.

Thermostat in hypothalamus activates cooling mechanisms.

Sweat glands secrete sweat, which evaporates, cooling the body.

Body temperature increases (such as when exercising or in hot surroundings).

Body temperature decreases.

NORMAL BODY TEMPERATURE (approximately 36–38°C)

Body temperature increases.

Body temperature decreases (such as when in cold surroundings).

Skeletal muscles rapidly contract, causing shivering, which generates heat.

Thermostat in hypothalamus activates warming mechanisms.

Blood vessels in skin constrict, diverting blood from skin to deeper tissues and reducing heat loss from skin surface.

◀ **Figure 40.17 The thermostatic function of the hypothalamus in human thermoregulation.**

WHAT IF? *Suppose at the end of a hard run on a hot day you find that there are no drinks left in the cooler. If, out of desperation, you dunk your head into the cooler, how might the ice-cold water affect the rate at which your body temperature returns to normal?*

Although only endotherms develop fever, lizards exhibit a related response. When infected with certain bacteria, the desert iguana (*Dipsosaurus dorsalis*) seeks a warmer environment and then maintains a body temperature that is elevated by 2–4°C (4–7°F). Similar observations in fishes, amphibians, and even cockroaches indicate that this response to certain infections is a common feature of many animal species.

Having explored thermoregulation in depth, we'll conclude our introduction to animal form and function by considering the different ways that animals allocate, use, and conserve energy.

CONCEPT CHECK 40.3

1. What mode of heat exchange is involved in "wind chill," when moving air feels colder than still air at the same temperature? Explain.

2. Flowers differ in how much sunlight they absorb. Why might this matter to a hummingbird seeking nectar on a cool morning?

3. **WHAT IF?** Why is shivering likely during the onset of a fever?

For suggested answers, see Appendix A.

CONCEPT 40.4

Energy requirements are related to animal size, activity, and environment

One of the unifying themes of biology introduced in Chapter 1 is that life requires energy transfer and transformation. Like other organisms, animals use chemical energy for growth, repair, activity, and reproduction. The overall flow and transformation of energy in an animal—its **bioenergetics**—determines nutritional needs and is related to the animal's size, activity, and environment.

Energy Allocation and Use

Organisms can be classified by how they obtain chemical energy. Most autotrophs, such as plants, harness light energy to build energy-rich organic molecules and then use those molecules for fuel. Most heterotrophs, such as animals, obtain their chemical energy from food, which contains organic molecules synthesized by other organisms.

Animals use chemical energy harvested from the food they eat to fuel metabolism and activity. Food is digested

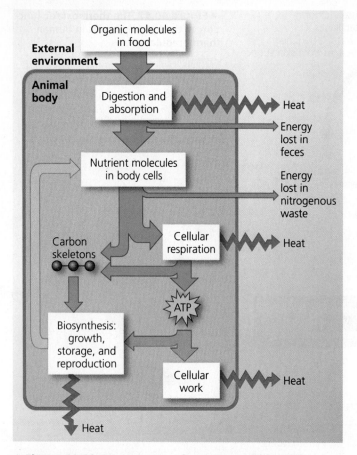

▲ **Figure 40.18 Bioenergetics of an animal: an overview.**

MAKE CONNECTIONS *Use the idea of energy coupling to explain why heat is produced in the absorption of nutrients, in cellular respiration, and in the synthesis of biopolymers (see Concept 8.3).*

by enzymatic hydrolysis (see Figure 5.2b), and nutrients are absorbed by body cells **(Figure 40.18)**. Most nutrient molecules are used to generate ATP. The ATP produced by cellular respiration and fermentation powers cellular work, enabling cells, organs, and organ systems to perform the functions that keep an animal alive. Energy in the form of ATP is also used in biosynthesis, which is needed for body growth and repair, synthesis of storage material such as fat, and production of gametes. The production and use of ATP generate heat, which the animal eventually gives off to its surroundings.

Quantifying Energy Use

How much of the total energy an animal obtains from food does it need just to stay alive? How much energy must be expended to walk, run, swim, or fly from one place to another? What fraction of the energy intake is used for

reproduction? Physiologists answer such questions by measuring the rate at which an animal uses chemical energy and how this rate changes in different circumstances.

The sum of all the energy an animal uses in a given time interval is called its **metabolic rate**. Energy is measured in joules (J) or in calories (cal) and kilocalories (kcal). (A kilocalorie equals 1,000 calories, or 4,184 joules. The unit Calorie, with a capital C, as used by many nutritionists, is actually a kilocalorie.)

Metabolic rate can be determined in several ways. Because nearly all of the chemical energy used in cellular respiration eventually appears as heat, metabolic rate can be measured by monitoring an animal's rate of heat loss. For this approach, researchers use a calorimeter, which is a closed, insulated chamber equipped with a device that records an animal's heat loss. Metabolic rate can also be determined from the amount of oxygen consumed or carbon dioxide produced by an animal's cellular respiration **(Figure 40.19)**. To calculate metabolic rate over longer periods, researchers record the rate of food consumption, the energy content of the food (about 4.5–5 kcal per gram of protein or carbohydrate and about 9 kcal per gram of fat), and the chemical energy lost in waste products (feces and urine or other nitrogenous wastes).

Minimum Metabolic Rate and Thermoregulation

Animals must maintain a minimum metabolic rate for basic functions such as cell maintenance, breathing, and heartbeat. Researchers measure this minimum metabolic rate differently for endotherms and ectotherms. The minimum metabolic rate of a nongrowing endotherm that is at rest, has an empty stomach, and is not experiencing stress is called the **basal metabolic rate (BMR)**. BMR is measured under a "comfortable" temperature range—a range

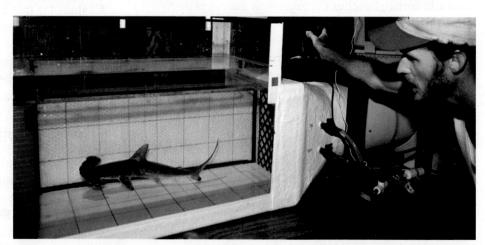

▲ **Figure 40.19 Measuring the rate of oxygen consumption by a swimming shark.** A researcher monitors the decrease in oxygen level over time in the recirculating water of a juvenile hammerhead's tank.

that requires no generation or shedding of heat above the minimum. The minimum metabolic rate of ectotherms is determined at a specific temperature because changes in the environmental temperature alter body temperature and therefore metabolic rate. The metabolic rate of a fasting, nonstressed ectotherm at rest at a particular temperature is called its **standard metabolic rate (SMR)**.

Comparisons of minimum metabolic rates reveal that endothermy and ectothermy have different energy costs. The BMR for humans averages 1,600–1,800 kcal per day for adult males and 1,300–1,500 kcal per day for adult females. These BMRs are about equivalent to the rate of energy use by a 75-watt lightbulb. In contrast, the SMR of an American alligator is only about 60 kcal per day at 20°C (68°F). Since this represents less than $\frac{1}{20}$ the energy used by a comparably sized adult human, the lower energetic requirement of ectothermy is readily apparent.

Influences on Metabolic Rate

Metabolic rate is affected by many factors besides whether the animal is an endotherm or an ectotherm. Some key factors are age, sex, size, activity, temperature, and nutrition. Here we'll examine the effects of size and activity.

Size and Metabolic Rate

Larger animals have more body mass and therefore require more chemical energy. Remarkably, the relationship between overall metabolic rate and body mass is constant across a wide range of sizes and forms, as illustrated for various mammals in **Figure 40.20a**. In fact, for even more varied organisms ranging in size from bacteria to blue whales, metabolic rate remains roughly proportional to body mass to the three-quarter power ($m^{3/4}$). Scientists are still researching the basis of this relationship, which applies to ectotherms as well as endotherms.

The relationship of metabolic rate to size profoundly affects energy consumption by body cells and tissues. As shown in **Figure 40.20b**, the energy it takes to maintain each gram of body mass is inversely related to body size. Each gram of a mouse, for instance, requires about 20 times as many calories as a gram of an elephant, even though the whole elephant uses far more calories than the whole mouse. The smaller animal's higher metabolic rate per gram demands a higher rate of oxygen delivery. To meet this demand, the smaller animal must have a higher breathing rate, blood volume (relative to its size), and heart rate.

Thinking about body size in bioenergetic terms reveals how trade-offs shape the evolution of body plans. As body size decreases, each gram of tissue increases in energy cost. As body size increases, energy costs per gram of tissue decrease, but an ever-larger fraction of body tissue is required for exchange, support, and locomotion.

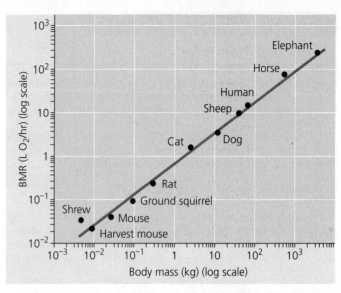

(a) Relationship of basal metabolic rate (BMR) to body size for various mammals. From shrew to elephant, size increases 1 millionfold.

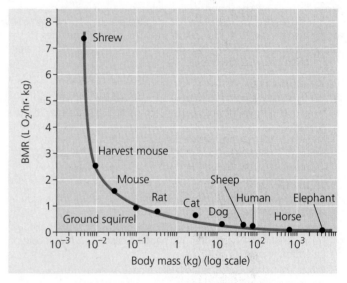

(b) Relationship of BMR per kilogram of body mass to body size for the same mammals as in (a).

▲ **Figure 40.20** **The relationship of metabolic rate to body size.**

INTERPRET THE DATA *Based on the graph in (a), one observer suggests that a group of 100 ground squirrels has the same basal metabolic rate as 1 dog. A second observer looking at the same graph disagrees. Who is correct?*

Activity and Metabolic Rate

For both ectotherms and endotherms, activity greatly affects metabolic rate. Even a person reading quietly at a desk or an insect twitching its wings consumes energy beyond the BMR or SMR. Maximum metabolic rates (the highest rates of ATP use) occur during peak activity, such as lifting heavy weights, sprinting, or high-speed swimming. In general, the maximum metabolic rate an animal can sustain is inversely related to the duration of activity.

Interpreting Pie Charts

How Do Energy Budgets Differ for Three Terrestrial Vertebrates?

To explore bioenergetics in animal bodies, let's consider typical annual energy budgets for three terrestrial vertebrates that vary in size and thermoregulatory strategy: a 4-kg male Adélie penguin, a 25-g (0.025-kg) female deer mouse, and a 4-kg female ball python. The penguin is well-insulated against his Antarctic environment but must expend energy in swimming to catch food, incubating eggs laid by his partner, and bringing food to his chicks. The tiny deer mouse lives in a temperate environment where food may be readily available, but her small size causes rapid loss of body heat. Unlike the penguin and mouse, the python is ectothermic and keeps growing throughout her life. She produces eggs but does not incubate them. In this exercise, we'll compare the energy expenditures of these animals for five important functions: basal (standard) metabolism, reproduction, thermoregulation, activity, and growth.

How the Data Were Obtained
Energy budgets were calculated for each of the animals based on measurements from field and laboratory studies.

Data from the Experiments
Pie charts are a good way to compare *relative* differences in a set of variables. In the pie charts here, the sizes of the wedges represent the relative annual energy expenditures for the functions shown in the key. The total annual expenditure for each animal is given below its pie chart.

Interpret the Data

1. You can estimate the contribution of each wedge in a pie chart by remembering that the entire circle represents 100%, half is 50%, and so on. What percent of the mouse's energy budget goes to basal metabolism? What percent of the penguin's budget is for activity?

2. Without considering the sizes of the wedges, how do the three pie charts differ in which functions they include? Explain these differences.

3. Does the penguin or the mouse expend a greater proportion of its energy budget on thermoregulation? Why?

4. Now look at the *total* annual energy expenditures for each animal. How much more energy does the penguin expend each year compared to the similarly sized python?

5. Which animal expends the most kilocalories per year on thermoregulation?

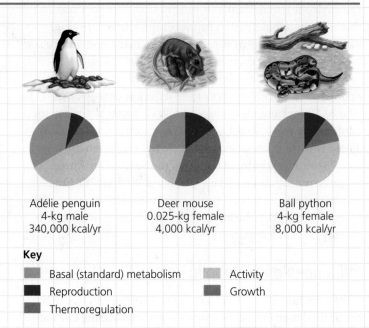

Adélie penguin
4-kg male
340,000 kcal/yr

Deer mouse
0.025-kg female
4,000 kcal/yr

Ball python
4-kg female
8,000 kcal/yr

Key

- Basal (standard) metabolism
- Reproduction
- Thermoregulation
- Activity
- Growth

6. If you monitored energy allocation in the penguin for just a few months instead of an entire year, you might find the growth category to be a significant part of the pie chart. Given that adult penguins don't grow from year to year, how would you explain this finding?

(MB) A version of this Scientific Skills Exercise can be assigned in MasteringBiology.

Data from M. A. Chappell et al., Energetics of foraging in breeding Adélie penguins, *Ecology* 74:2450–2461 (1993); M. A. Chappell et al., Voluntary running in deer mice: speed, distance, energy costs, and temperature effects, *Journal of Experimental Biology* 207:3839–3854 (2004); T. M. Ellis and M. A. Chappell, Metabolism, temperature relations, maternal behavior, and reproductive energetics in the ball python (*Python regius*), *Journal of Comparative Physiology B* 157:393–402 (1987).

For most terrestrial animals, the average daily rate of energy consumption is two to four times BMR (for endotherms) or SMR (for ectotherms). Humans in most developed countries have an unusually low average daily metabolic rate of about 1.5 times BMR—an indication of a relatively sedentary lifestyle.

The fraction of an animal's energy "budget" that is devoted to activity depends on many factors, including its environment, behavior, size, and thermoregulation. In the Scientific Skills Exercise, you'll interpret data on the annual energy budgets of three terrestrial vertebrates.

Torpor and Energy Conservation

Despite their many adaptations for homeostasis, animals may encounter conditions that severely challenge their abilities to balance their heat, energy, and materials budgets. For example, at certain times of the day or year, their surroundings may be extremely hot or cold, or food may be unavailable. **Torpor**, a physiological state of decreased activity and metabolism, is an adaptation that enables animals to save energy while avoiding difficult and dangerous conditions.

Many small mammals and birds exhibit a daily torpor that seems to be adapted to feeding patterns. For instance, some bats feed at night and go into torpor in daylight. Chickadees and hummingbirds feed during the day and often go into torpor on cold nights; the body temperature of chickadees drops as much as 10°C (18°F) at night, and the temperature of hummingbirds can fall 25°C (45°F) or more. All endotherms that exhibit daily torpor are relatively small; when active, they have high metabolic rates and thus very high rates of energy consumption.

Hibernation is long-term torpor that is an adaptation to winter cold and food scarcity. When a mammal enters hibernation, its body temperature declines as its body's thermostat is turned down. The temperature reduction may be dramatic: Some hibernating mammals cool to as low as 1–2°C (34–36°F),

▲ **Hibernating dormouse** (*Muscardinus avellanarius*)

and at least one, the Arctic ground squirrel (*Spermophilus parryii*), can enter a supercooled (unfrozen) state in which its body temperature dips below 0°C (32°F). Periodically, perhaps every two weeks or so, hibernating animals undergo arousal, raising their body temperature and becoming active briefly before resuming hibernation.

The energy savings from hibernation are huge: Metabolic rates during hibernation can be 20 times lower than if the animal attempted to maintain normal body temperatures of 36–38°C (97–100°F). As a result, hibernators such as the ground squirrel can survive through the winter on limited supplies of energy stored in the body tissues or as food cached in a burrow. Similarly, the slow metabolism and inactivity of *estivation*, or summer torpor, enables animals to survive long periods of high temperatures and scarce water.

What happens to the circadian rhythm in hibernating animals? In the past, researchers reported detecting daily biological rhythms in hibernating animals. However, in some cases the animals were probably in a state of torpor from which they could readily arouse, rather than "deep" hibernation. More recently, a group of researchers in France addressed this question in a different way, examining the machinery of the biological clock rather than the rhythms it controls **(Figure 40.21)**. Working with the European hamster, they found that molecular components of the clock stopped oscillating during hibernation. These findings support the hypothesis that the circadian clock ceases operation during hibernation, at least in this species.

From tissue types to homeostasis, this chapter has focused on the whole animal. We also investigated how animals exchange materials with the environment and how size and activity affect metabolic rate. For much of the rest of this unit, we'll explore how specialized organs and organ systems enable animals to meet the basic challenges of life. In Unit 6, we investigated how plants meet the same challenges. **Figure 40.22**, on the next two pages, highlights some fundamental similarities and differences in the evolutionary adaptations of plants and animals. This figure is thus a review of Unit 6, an introduction to Unit 7, and, most importantly, an illustration of the connections that unify the myriad forms of life.

▼ **Figure 40.21** | Inquiry

What happens to the circadian clock during hibernation?

Experiment To determine whether the 24-hour biological clock continues to run during hibernation, Paul Pévet and colleagues at the University of Louis Pasteur in Strasbourg, France, studied molecular components of the circadian clock in the European hamster (*Cricetus cricetus*). The researchers measured RNA levels for two clock genes—*Per2* and *Bmal1*—during normal activity (euthermia) and during hibernation in constant darkness. The RNA samples were obtained from the suprachiasmatic nuclei (SCN), a pair of structures in the mammalian brain that control circadian rhythms.

Results

Conclusion Hibernation disrupted circadian variation in the hamster's clock gene RNA levels. Further experiments demonstrated that this disruption was not simply due to the dark environment during hibernation, since for nonhibernating animals RNA levels during a darkened daytime were the same as in daylight. The researchers concluded that the biological clock stops running in hibernating European hamsters and, perhaps, in other hibernators as well.

Source: F. G. Revel et al., The circadian clock stops ticking during deep hibernation in the European hamster, *Proceedings of the National Academy of Sciences USA* 104:13816–13820 (2007).

WHAT IF? *Suppose you discovered a new hamster gene and found that the levels of RNA for this gene were constant during hibernation. What could you conclude about the day and night RNA levels for this gene during euthermia?*

CONCEPT CHECK 40.4

1. If a mouse and a small lizard of the same mass (both at rest) were placed in experimental chambers under identical environmental conditions, which animal would consume oxygen at a higher rate? Explain.

2. Which animal must eat a larger proportion of its weight in food each day: a house cat or an African lion caged in a zoo? Explain.

3. **WHAT IF?** Suppose the animals at a zoo were resting comfortably and remained at rest while the nighttime air temperature dropped. If the temperature change were sufficient to cause a change in metabolic rate, what changes would you expect for an alligator and a lion?

For suggested answers, see Appendix A.

MAKE CONNECTIONS

Life Challenges and Solutions in Plants and Animals

Multicellular organisms face a common set of challenges. Comparing the solutions that have evolved in plants and animals reveals both unity (shared elements) and diversity (distinct features) across these two lineages.

Nutritional Mode

All living things must obtain energy and carbon from the environment to grow, survive, and reproduce. Plants are autotrophs, obtaining their energy through photosynthesis and their carbon from inorganic sources, whereas animals are heterotrophs, obtaining their energy and carbon from food. Evolutionary adaptations in plants and animals support these different nutritional modes. The broad surface of many leaves (left) enhances light capture for photosynthesis. When hunting, a bobcat relies on stealth, speed, and sharp claws (right). *See Concepts 36.1 and 41.1.*

Growth and Regulation

The growth and development of both plants and animals are controlled by hormones. In plants, hormones may act in a local area or be transported in the body. They control growth patterns, flowering, fruit development, and more (left). In animals, hormones circulate throughout the body and act in specific target tissues, controlling homeostatic processes and developmental events such as molting (below). *See Concepts 39.2 and 45.3.*

Environmental Response

All forms of life must detect and respond appropriately to conditions in their environment. Specialized organs sense environmental signals. For example, the floral head of a sunflower (left) and an insect's eyes (right) both contain photoreceptors that detect light. Environmental signals activate specific receptor proteins, triggering signal transduction pathways that initiate cellular responses coordinated by chemical and electrical communication. *See Concepts 39.1 and 50.1.*

Transport

All but the simplest multicellular organisms must transport nutrients and waste products between locations in the body. A system of tubelike vessels is the common evolutionary solution, while the mechanism of circulation varies. Plants harness solar energy to transport water, minerals, and sugars through specialized tubes (left). In animals, a pump (heart) moves circulatory fluid through vessels (right). *See Concepts 35.1 and 42.3.*

Reproduction

In sexual reproduction, specialized tissues and structures produce and exchange gametes. Offspring are generally supplied with nutritional stores that facilitate rapid growth and development. For example, seeds (left) have stored food reserves that supply energy to the young seedling, while milk provides sustenance for juvenile mammals (right). *See Concepts 38.1 and 46.5.*

Absorption

Organisms need to absorb nutrients. The root hairs of plants (left) and the villi (projections) that line the intestines of vertebrates (right) increase the surface area available for absorption. *See Concepts 36.3 and 41.3.*

Gas Exchange

The exchange of certain gases with the environment is essential for life. Respiration by plants and animals requires taking up oxygen (O_2) and releasing carbon dioxide (CO_2). In photosynthesis, net exchange occurs in the opposite direction: CO_2 uptake and O_2 release. In both plants and animals, highly convoluted surfaces that increase the area available for gas exchange have evolved, such as the spongy mesophyll of leaves (left) and the alveoli of lungs (right). *See Concepts 35.3 and 42.5.*

MAKE CONNECTIONS *Compare the adaptations that enable plants and animals to respond to the challenges of living in hot and cold environments. See Concepts 39.4 and 40.3.*

ANIMATION Visit the Study Area in **MasteringBiology** for related BioFlix® 3-D Animations in Chapters 36, 42, and 45.

SUMMARY OF KEY CONCEPTS

CONCEPT 40.1

Animal form and function are correlated at all levels of organization (pp. 868–875)

- Physical laws constrain the evolution of an animal's size and shape. These constraints contribute to convergent evolution in animal body forms.
- Each animal cell must have access to an aqueous environment. Simple two-layered sacs and flat shapes maximize exposure to the surrounding medium. More complex body plans have highly folded internal surfaces specialized for exchanging materials.
- Animal bodies are based on a hierarchy of cells, **tissues, organs**, and **organ systems**. **Epithelial tissue** forms active interfaces on external and internal surfaces; **connective tissue** binds and supports other tissues; **muscle tissue** contracts, moving body parts; and **nervous tissue** transmits nerve impulses throughout the body.
- The endocrine and nervous systems are the two means of communication between different locations in the body. The endocrine system broadcasts signaling molecules called **hormones** everywhere via the bloodstream, but only certain cells are responsive to each hormone. The nervous system uses dedicated cellular circuits involving electrical and chemical signals to send information to specific locations.

? *For a large animal, what challenges would a spherical shape pose for carrying out exchange with the environment?*

CONCEPT 40.2

Feedback control maintains the internal environment in many animals (pp. 875–877)

- Animals *regulate* (control) certain internal variables while allowing other internal variables to *conform* to external changes. **Homeostasis** is the maintenance of a steady state despite internal and external changes.
- Homeostatic mechanisms are usually based on **negative feedback**, in which the **response** reduces the **stimulus**. In contrast, **positive feedback** involves amplification of a stimulus by the response and often brings about a change in state, such as the transition from pregnancy to childbirth.

NORMAL RANGE for internal variable

Response

Stimulus: change in internal variable

Control center

Sensor

- Regulated change in the internal environment is essential to normal function. **Circadian rhythms** are daily fluctuations in metabolism and behavior tuned to the cycles of light and dark in the environment. Other environmental changes may trigger **acclimatization**, a temporary shift in the steady state.

? *Is it accurate to define homeostasis as a constant internal environment? Explain.*

CONCEPT 40.3

Homeostatic processes for thermoregulation involve form, function, and behavior (pp. 878–883)

- An animal maintains its internal temperature within a tolerable range by **thermoregulation**. **Endotherms** are warmed mostly by heat generated by metabolism. **Ectotherms** get most of their heat from external sources. Endothermy requires a greater expenditure of energy. Body temperature may vary with environmental temperature, as in *poikilotherms*, or be relatively constant, as in *homeotherms*.
- In thermoregulation, physiological and behavioral adjustments balance heat gain and loss, which occur through **radiation**, **evaporation**, **convection**, and **conduction**. Insulation and **countercurrent exchange** reduce heat loss, whereas panting, sweating, and bathing increase evaporation, cooling the body. Many ectotherms and endotherms adjust their rate of heat exchange with their surroundings by vasodilation or vasoconstriction and by behavioral responses.
- Many mammals and birds adjust their amount of body insulation in response to changes in environmental temperature. Ectotherms undergo a variety of changes at the cellular level to acclimatize to shifts in temperature.
- The **hypothalamus** acts as the thermostat in mammalian regulation of body temperature. Fever reflects a resetting of this thermostat to a higher normal range in response to infection.

? *Given that humans thermoregulate, explain why your skin is cooler than your body core.*

CONCEPT 40.4

Energy requirements are related to animal size, activity, and environment (pp. 883–889)

- Animals obtain chemical energy from food, storing it for short-term use in ATP. The total amount of energy used in a unit of time defines an animal's **metabolic rate**.
- Under similar conditions and for animals of the same size, the **basal metabolic rate** of endotherms is substantially higher than the **standard metabolic rate** of ectotherms. Minimum metabolic rate per gram is inversely related to body size among similar animals. Animals allocate energy for basal (or standard) metabolism, activity, homeostasis, growth, and reproduction.
- **Torpor**, a state of decreased activity and metabolism, conserves energy during environmental extremes. Animals may enter torpor during sleep periods (daily torpor), in winter (**hibernation**), or in summer (estivation).

? *Why do small animals breathe more rapidly than large animals?*

TEST YOUR UNDERSTANDING

LEVEL 1: KNOWLEDGE/COMPREHENSION

1. The body tissue that consists largely of material located outside of cells is
   a. epithelial tissue.
   b. connective tissue.
   c. muscle tissue.
   d. nervous tissue.

2. Which of the following would increase the rate of heat exchange between an animal and its environment?
   a. feathers or fur
   b. vasoconstriction
   c. wind blowing across the body surface
   d. countercurrent heat exchanger

3. Consider the energy budgets for a human, an elephant, a penguin, a mouse, and a snake. The _____ would have the highest total annual energy expenditure, and the _____ would have the highest energy expenditure per unit mass.
   a. elephant; mouse
   b. elephant; human
   c. mouse; snake
   d. penguin; mouse

LEVEL 2: APPLICATION/ANALYSIS

4. Compared with a smaller cell, a larger cell of the same shape has
   a. less surface area.
   b. less surface area per unit of volume.
   c. the same surface area-to-volume ratio.
   d. a smaller cytoplasm-to-nucleus ratio.

5. An animal's inputs of energy and materials would exceed its outputs
   a. if the animal is an endotherm, which must always take in more energy because of its high metabolic rate.
   b. if it is actively foraging for food.
   c. if it is growing and increasing its mass.
   d. never; homeostasis makes these energy and material budgets always balance.

6. You are studying a large tropical reptile that has a high and relatively stable body temperature. How would you determine whether this animal is an endotherm or an ectotherm?
   a. You know from its high and stable body temperature that it must be an endotherm.
   b. You subject this reptile to various temperatures in the lab and find that its body temperature and metabolic rate change with the ambient temperature. You conclude that it is an ectotherm.
   c. You note that its environment has a high and stable temperature. Because its body temperature matches the environmental temperature, you conclude that it is an ectotherm.
   d. You measure the metabolic rate of the reptile, and because it is higher than that of a related species that lives in temperate forests, you conclude that this reptile is an endotherm and its relative is an ectotherm.

7. Which of the following animals uses the largest percentage of its energy budget for homeostatic regulation?
   a. a marine jelly (an invertebrate)
   b. a snake in a temperate forest
   c. a desert insect
   d. a desert bird

8. **DRAW IT** Draw a model of the control circuit(s) required for driving an automobile at a fairly constant speed over a hilly road. Indicate each feature that represents a sensor, stimulus, or response.

LEVEL 3: SYNTHESIS/EVALUATION

9. **EVOLUTION CONNECTION**
   In 1847, the German biologist Christian Bergmann noted that mammals and birds living at higher latitudes (farther from the equator) are on average larger and bulkier than related species found at lower latitudes. Suggest an evolutionary hypothesis to explain this observation.

10. **SCIENTIFIC INQUIRY**
    Eastern tent caterpillars (*Malacosoma americanum*) live in large groups in silk nests, resembling tents, which they build in trees. They are among the first insects to be active in early spring, when daily temperature fluctuates from freezing to very hot. Over the course of a day, they display striking differences in behavior: Early in the morning, they rest in a tightly packed group on the tent's east-facing surface. In midafternoon, they are on its undersurface, each caterpillar hanging by a few of its legs. Propose a hypothesis to explain this behavior. How could you test it?

11. **SCIENCE, TECHNOLOGY, AND SOCIETY**
    Medical researchers are investigating artificial substitutes for various human tissues. Why might artificial blood or skin be useful? What characteristics would these substitutes need in order to function well in the body? Why do real tissues work better? Why not use the real tissues if they work better? What other artificial tissues might be useful? What problems do you anticipate in developing and applying them?

12. **WRITE ABOUT A THEME: ENERGY AND MATTER**
    In a short essay (about 100–150 words) focusing on energy transfer and transformation, discuss the advantages and disadvantages of hibernation.

13. **SYNTHESIZE YOUR KNOWLEDGE**

These macaques (*Macaca fuscata*) are partially immersed in a hot spring in a snowy region of Japan. What are some ways that form, function, and behavior contribute to homeostasis for these animals?

For selected answers, see Appendix A.

MasteringBiology®

Students Go to **MasteringBiology** for assignments, the eText, and the Study Area with practice tests, animations, and activities.

Instructors Go to **MasteringBiology** for automatically graded tutorials and questions that you can assign to your students, plus Instructor Resources.

41
Animal Nutrition

KEY CONCEPTS

41.1 An animal's diet must supply chemical energy, organic molecules, and essential nutrients

41.2 The main stages of food processing are ingestion, digestion, absorption, and elimination

41.3 Organs specialized for sequential stages of food processing form the mammalian digestive system

41.4 Evolutionary adaptations of vertebrate digestive systems correlate with diet

41.5 Feedback circuits regulate digestion, energy storage, and appetite

▲ **Figure 41.1** How does a crab help an otter make fur?

The Need to Feed

Dinnertime has arrived for the sea otter in **Figure 41.1** (and for the crab, though in quite a different sense). The muscles and other organs of the crab will be chewed into pieces, broken down by acid and enzymes in the otter's digestive system, and finally absorbed as small molecules into the body of the otter. Such a process is what is meant by animal **nutrition**: food being taken in, taken apart, and taken up.

Although dining on fish, crabs, urchins, and abalone is the sea otter's specialty, all animals eat other organisms—dead or alive, piecemeal or whole. Unlike plants, animals must consume food for both energy and the organic molecules used to assemble new molecules, cells, and tissues. Despite this shared need, animals have diverse diets. **Herbivores**, such as cattle, sea slugs, and caterpillars, dine mainly on plants or algae. **Carnivores**, such as sea otters, hawks, and spiders, mostly eat other animals. Rats and other **omnivores** (from the Latin *omnis*, all) don't in fact eat everything, but they do regularly consume animals as well as plants or algae. We humans are typically omnivores, as are cockroaches and crows.

The terms *herbivore*, *carnivore*, and *omnivore* represent the kinds of food an animal usually eats. Keep in mind, however, that most animals are opportunistic feeders, eating foods outside their standard diet when their usual foods aren't available.

For example, deer are herbivores, but in addition to feeding on grass and other plants, they occasionally eat insects, worms, or bird eggs. Note as well that microorganisms are an unavoidable "supplement" in every animal's diet.

Animals must eat. But to survive and reproduce, they must also balance their consumption, storage, and use of food. Sea otters, for example, support a high rate of metabolism by eating up to 25% of their body mass each day. Eating too little food, too much food, or the wrong mixture of foods can endanger an animal's health. In this chapter, we'll survey the nutritional requirements of animals, explore diverse evolutionary adaptations for obtaining and processing food, and investigate the regulation of energy intake and expenditure.

CONCEPT 41.1

An animal's diet must supply chemical energy, organic molecules, and essential nutrients

Overall, an adequate diet must satisfy three nutritional needs: chemical energy for cellular processes, organic building blocks for macromolecules, and essential nutrients.

The activities of cells, tissues, organs, and whole animals depend on sources of chemical energy in the diet. This energy is used to produce ATP, which powers processes ranging from DNA replication and cell division to vision and flight. To meet the continuous requirement for ATP, animals ingest and digest nutrients, including carbohydrates, proteins, and lipids, for use in cellular respiration and energy storage.

In addition to providing fuel for ATP production, an animal's diet must supply the raw materials needed for biosynthesis. To build the complex molecules it needs to grow, maintain itself, and reproduce, an animal must obtain two types of organic precursors from its food. Animals need a source of organic carbon (such as sugar) and a source of organic nitrogen (such as protein). Starting with these materials, animals can construct a great variety of organic molecules.

Essential Nutrients

Some cellular processes require materials that an animal cannot assemble from simpler organic precursors. These materials—preassembled organic molecules and minerals—are called **essential nutrients**. Obtained from an animal's diet, essential nutrients include essential amino acids and fatty acids, vitamins, and minerals. Essential nutrients have key functions in cells, including serving as substrates of enzymes, as coenzymes, and as cofactors in biosynthetic reactions **(Figure 41.2)**. Needs for particular nutrients vary among species. For instance, ascorbic acid (vitamin C) is an essential nutrient for humans and other primates, as well as guinea pigs, but not for many other animals.

Essential Amino Acids

Animals require 20 amino acids to make proteins (see Figure 5.14). Most animal species have the enzymes to synthesize about half of these amino acids, as long as their diet includes sulfur and organic nitrogen. The remaining amino acids must be obtained from food in prefabricated form and are therefore called **essential amino acids**. Many animals, including adult humans, require eight amino acids in their diet: isoleucine, leucine, lysine, methionine, phenylalanine, threonine, tryptophan, and valine. (Human infants also need a ninth, histidine.)

The proteins in animal products such as meat, eggs, and cheese are "complete," which means that they provide all the essential amino acids in their proper proportions. In contrast, most plant proteins are "incomplete," being deficient in one or more essential amino acids. Corn (maize), for example, is deficient in tryptophan and lysine, whereas beans are lacking in methionine. However, vegetarians can easily obtain all of the essential amino acids by eating a varied diet of plant proteins.

▲ **Figure 41.2 Roles of essential nutrients.** Linoleic acid is converted by the enzyme fatty acid desaturase to γ-linoleic acid, a precursor for phospholipids and prostaglandins. This biosynthetic reaction illustrates common functions of the four classes of essential nutrients, labeled in blue. Note that nearly every enzyme or other protein in animal bodies contains some essential amino acids, as indicated in the partial sequence shown for fatty acid desaturase.

Essential Fatty Acids

Animals require fatty acids to synthesize a variety of cellular components, including membrane phospholipids, signaling molecules, and storage fats. Although animals can synthesize many fatty acids, they lack the enzymes to form the double bonds found in certain required fatty acids. Instead, these molecules must be obtained from the diet and are considered **essential fatty acids**. In mammals, they include linoleic acid (see Figure 41.2). Because seeds, grains, and vegetables generally furnish ample quantities of essential fatty acids, deficiencies in this class of nutrients are rare.

Vitamins

As Albert Szent-Györgyi, the discoverer of vitamin C, once quipped, "A vitamin is a substance that makes you ill if you *don't* eat it." **Vitamins** are organic molecules that are required in the diet in very small amounts. They have diverse functions. Vitamin B$_2$, for example, is converted in the body to FAD, a coenzyme used in many metabolic processes, including cellular respiration (see Figure 9.12). For humans, 13 vitamins have been identified. Depending on the vitamin, the required amount ranges from 0.01 to 100 mg per day.

Vitamins are classified as water-soluble or fat-soluble **(Table 41.1)**. B vitamins, which generally act as coenzymes, are water-soluble. So is vitamin C, which is required for the production of connective tissue. Fat-soluble vitamins include vitamin A, which is incorporated into visual pigments of the eye, and vitamin D, which aids in calcium absorption and bone formation. The dietary requirement for vitamin D is variable in humans because we can synthesize it from other molecules when our skin is exposed to sunlight.

For people with imbalanced diets, taking vitamin supplements that provide recommended daily levels is certainly reasonable. It is far less clear that massive doses of vitamins confer any health benefits or are even safe. Moderate overdoses of water-soluble vitamins are probably harmless because excesses are excreted in urine. However, excesses of fat-soluble vitamins are deposited in body fat, so overconsumption may cause them to accumulate to toxic levels.

Minerals

Dietary **minerals** are inorganic nutrients, such as iron and sulfur, that are usually required in small amounts—from less than 1 mg to about 2,500 mg per day. As shown in **Table 41.2**,

Table 41.1 Vitamin Requirements of Humans

Vitamin	Major Dietary Sources	Major Functions in the Body	Symptoms of Deficiency
Water-Soluble Vitamins			
B$_1$ (thiamine)	Pork, legumes, peanuts, whole grains	Coenzyme used in removing CO_2 from organic compounds	Beriberi (tingling, poor coordination, reduced heart function)
B$_2$ (riboflavin)	Dairy products, meats, enriched grains, vegetables	Component of coenzymes FAD and FMN	Skin lesions, such as cracks at corners of mouth
B$_3$ (niacin)	Nuts, meats, grains	Component of coenzymes NAD$^+$ and NADP$^+$	Skin and gastrointestinal lesions, delusions, confusion
B$_5$ (pantothenic acid)	Meats, dairy products, whole grains, fruits, vegetables	Component of coenzyme A	Fatigue, numbness, tingling of hands and feet
B$_6$ (pyridoxine)	Meats, vegetables, whole grains	Coenzyme used in amino acid metabolism	Irritability, convulsions, muscular twitching, anemia
B$_7$ (biotin)	Legumes, other vegetables, meats	Coenzyme in synthesis of fat, glycogen, and amino acids	Scaly skin inflammation, neuromuscular disorders
B$_9$ (folic acid)	Green vegetables, oranges, nuts, legumes, whole grains	Coenzyme in nucleic acid and amino acid metabolism	Anemia, birth defects
B$_{12}$ (cobalamin)	Meats, eggs, dairy products	Production of nucleic acids and red blood cells	Anemia, numbness, loss of balance
C (ascorbic acid)	Citrus fruits, broccoli, tomatoes	Used in collagen synthesis; antioxidant	Scurvy (degeneration of skin and teeth), delayed wound healing
Fat-Soluble Vitamins			
A (retinol)	Dark green and orange vegetables and fruits, dairy products	Component of visual pigments; maintenance of epithelial tissues	Blindness, skin disorders, impaired immunity
D	Dairy products, egg yolk	Aids in absorption and use of calcium and phosphorus	Rickets (bone deformities) in children, bone softening in adults
E (tocopherol)	Vegetable oils, nuts, seeds	Antioxidant; helps prevent damage to cell membranes	Nervous system degeneration
K (phylloquinone)	Green vegetables, tea; also made by colon bacteria	Important in blood clotting	Defective blood clotting

minerals have diverse functions in animal physiology. Some are assembled into the structure of proteins; iron, for example, is incorporated into the oxygen carrier hemoglobin as well as some enzymes (see Figure 41.2). In contrast, sodium, potassium, and chloride are important in the functioning of nerves and muscles and in maintaining osmotic balance between cells and the surrounding body fluid. In vertebrates, the mineral iodine is incorporated into thyroid hormone, which regulates metabolic rate. Vertebrates also require relatively large quantities of calcium and phosphorus for building and maintaining bone.

Ingesting large amounts of some minerals can upset homeostatic balance and impair health. For example, excess salt (sodium chloride) can contribute to high blood pressure. This is a particular problem in the United States, where the typical person consumes enough salt to provide about 20 times the required amount of sodium. Packaged (prepared) foods often contain large amounts of sodium chloride, even if they do not taste very salty.

Dietary Deficiencies

A diet that lacks one or more essential nutrients or consistently supplies less chemical energy than the body requires results in *malnutrition*, a failure to obtain adequate nutrition. Malnutrition resulting from either type of dietary deficiency can have negative impacts on health and survival and affects one out of four children worldwide.

Deficiencies in Essential Nutrients

Insufficient intake of essential nutrients can cause deformities, disease, and even death. For example, cattle, deer, and other herbivores may develop dangerously fragile bones if they graze on plants growing in soil that lacks phosphorus. In such environments, some grazing animals obtain missing nutrients by consuming concentrated sources of salt or other minerals (**Figure 41.3**). Similarly, some birds supplement their diet with snail shells, and certain tortoises ingest stones.

▲ **Figure 41.3 Obtaining essential nutrients from an unusual source.** A juvenile chamois (*Rupicapra rupicapra*), an herbivore, licks salts from exposed rocks in its alpine habitat. This behavior is common among herbivores that live where soils and plants provide insufficient amounts of minerals, such as sodium, calcium, phosphorus, and iron.

Table 41.2	Mineral Requirements of Humans*		
Mineral	**Major Dietary Sources**	**Major Functions in the Body**	**Symptoms of Deficiency**
Calcium (Ca)	Dairy products, dark green vegetables, legumes	Bone and tooth formation, blood clotting, nerve and muscle function	Impaired growth, loss of bone mass
Phosphorus (P)	Dairy products, meats, grains	Bone and tooth formation, acid-base balance, nucleotide synthesis	Weakness, loss of minerals from bone, calcium loss
Sulfur (S)	Proteins from many sources	Component of certain amino acids	Impaired growth, fatigue, swelling
Potassium (K)	Meats, dairy products, many fruits and vegetables, grains	Acid-base balance, water balance, nerve function	Muscular weakness, paralysis, nausea, heart failure
Chlorine (Cl)	Table salt	Acid-base balance, formation of gastric juice, nerve function, osmotic balance	Muscle cramps, reduced appetite
Sodium (Na)	Table salt	Acid-base balance, water balance, nerve function	Muscle cramps, reduced appetite
Magnesium (Mg)	Whole grains, green leafy vegetables	Enzyme cofactor; ATP bioenergetics	Nervous system disturbances
Iron (Fe)	Meats, eggs, legumes, whole grains, green leafy vegetables	Component of hemoglobin and of electron carriers; enzyme cofactor	Iron-deficiency anemia, weakness, impaired immunity
Fluorine (F)	Drinking water, tea, seafood	Maintenance of tooth structure	Higher frequency of tooth decay
Iodine (I)	Seafood, iodized salt	Component of thyroid hormones	Goiter (enlarged thyroid gland)

*Calcium through Magnesium are bracketed as "More than 200 mg per day required"

*Additional minerals required in trace amounts include cobalt (Co), copper (Cu), manganese (Mn), molybdenum (Mo), selenium (Se), and zinc (Zn). All of these minerals, as well as those in the table, can be harmful in excess.

Like other animals, humans sometimes suffer from diets lacking in essential nutrients. A diet that provides insufficient amounts of one or more essential amino acids causes protein deficiency, the most common type of malnutrition among humans. In children, protein deficiency may arise if their diet shifts from breast milk to foods that contain relatively little protein, such as rice. Such children, if they survive infancy, often have impaired physical and mental development.

In populations subsisting on simple rice diets, individuals are often deficient in vitamin A, which can result in blindness or death. To overcome this problem, scientists have engineered "Golden Rice," a strain of rice that synthesizes the orange-colored pigment beta-carotene, which the body converts to vitamin A (see Concept 38.3).

Undernutrition

A diet that fails to provide adequate sources of chemical energy results in *undernutrition*. When an animal is undernourished, a series of events unfold: The body uses up stored carbohydrates and fat and then begins breaking down its own proteins for fuel; muscles begin to decrease in size; and the brain may become protein-deficient. If energy intake remains less than energy expenditures, the animal will eventually die. Even if a seriously undernourished animal survives, some of the damage may be irreversible.

Human undernutrition is most common when drought, war, or another crisis severely disrupts the food supply. In sub-Saharan Africa, where the AIDS epidemic has crippled both rural and urban communities, approximately 200 million children and adults cannot obtain enough food.

Sometimes undernutrition occurs within well-fed human populations as a result of eating disorders. For example, anorexia nervosa leads individuals, usually female, to starve themselves compulsively.

Assessing Nutritional Needs

Determining the ideal diet for the human population is an important but difficult problem for scientists. As objects of study, people present many challenges. Unlike laboratory animals, humans are genetically diverse. They also live in settings far more varied than the stable and uniform environment that scientists use to facilitate comparisons in laboratory experiments. Ethical concerns present an additional barrier. For example, it is not acceptable to investigate the nutritional needs of children in a way that might harm a child's growth or development.

Many insights into human nutrition have come from *epidemiology*, the study of human health and disease at the population level. In the 1970s, for instance, researchers discovered that children born to women of low socioeconomic status were more likely to have neural tube defects, which occur when tissue fails to enclose the developing brain and

▼ **Figure 41.4** **Inquiry**

Can diet influence the frequency of birth defects?

Experiment Richard Smithells, of the University of Leeds, in England, examined the effect of vitamin supplementation on the risk of neural tube defects. Women who had had one or more babies with such a defect were put into two study groups. The experimental group consisted of those who were planning a pregnancy and began taking a multivitamin at least four weeks before attempting conception. The control group, who were not given vitamins, included women who declined them and women who were already pregnant. The numbers of neural tube defects resulting from the pregnancies were recorded for each group.

Results

Group	Number of Infants/Fetuses Studied	Infants/Fetuses with a Neural Tube Defect
Vitamin supplements (experimental group)	141	1
No vitamin supplements (control group)	204	12

Conclusion This controlled study provided evidence that vitamin supplementation protects against neural tube defects, at least after the first pregnancy. Follow-up trials demonstrated that folic acid alone provided an equivalent protective effect.

Source: R. W. Smithells et al., Possible prevention of neural-tube defects by periconceptional vitamin supplementation, *Lancet* 315:339–340 (1980).

Inquiry in Action Read and analyze the original paper in *Inquiry in Action: Interpreting Scientific Papers.*

INTERPRET THE DATA *After folic acid supplementation became standard in the U.S., the frequency of neural tube defects dropped to an average of just 1 in 5,000 live births. Propose two explanations why the observed frequency was much higher in the experimental group of the Smithells study.*

WHAT IF? *Subsequent studies were designed to learn if folic acid supplements prevent neural tube defects during first-time pregnancies. To determine the required number of subjects, what type of additional information did the researchers need?*

spinal cord (see Concept 47.2). The English scientist Richard Smithells thought that malnutrition among these women might be responsible. As described in **Figure 41.4**, he found that vitamin supplementation greatly reduced the risk of neural tube defects. In other studies, he obtained evidence that folic acid (vitamin B_9) was the specific vitamin responsible, a finding confirmed by other researchers. Based on this evidence, the United States in 1998 began to require that folic acid be added to enriched grain products used to make bread, cereals, and other foods. Follow-up studies have documented the effectiveness of this program in reducing the frequency of neural tube defects. Thus, at a time when microsurgery and sophisticated diagnostic imaging dominate the headlines, a simple dietary change such as folic acid supplementation may be among the greatest contributors to human health.

CONCEPT CHECK 41.1

1. All 20 amino acids are needed to make animal proteins. Why aren't they all essential to animal diets?

2. MAKE CONNECTIONS Considering the role of enzymes in metabolic reactions (see Concept 8.4), explain why vitamins are required in very small amounts in the diet.

3. WHAT IF? If a zoo animal eating ample food shows signs of malnutrition, how might a researcher determine which nutrient is lacking in its diet?

For suggested answers, see Appendix A.

CONCEPT 41.2

The main stages of food processing are ingestion, digestion, absorption, and elimination

In this section, we turn from nutritional requirements to the mechanisms by which animals process food. Food processing can be divided into four distinct stages: ingestion, digestion, absorption, and elimination (Figure 41.5).

The first stage, **ingestion**, is the act of eating or feeding. Given the variation in food sources among animal species, it is not surprising that strategies for extracting resources from food also differ widely. Figure 41.6, on the next page, surveys and classifies the principal feeding mechanisms

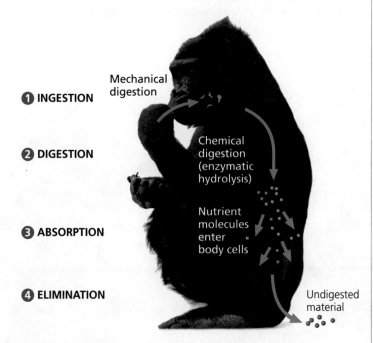

❶ INGESTION — Mechanical digestion

❷ DIGESTION — Chemical digestion (enzymatic hydrolysis)

Nutrient molecules enter body cells

❸ ABSORPTION

❹ ELIMINATION — Undigested material

▲ Figure 41.5 The stages of food processing.

that have evolved in animals. We will focus in this chapter on the shared aspects of food processing, pausing periodically to consider some adaptations to particular diets or environments.

During **digestion**, the second stage of food processing, food is broken down into molecules small enough for the body to absorb. Mechanical digestion, such as chewing, typically precedes chemical digestion. Mechanical digestion breaks food into smaller pieces, increasing the surface area available for chemical processes. Chemical digestion is necessary because animals cannot directly use the proteins, carbohydrates, nucleic acids, fats, and phospholipids in food. One problem is that these molecules are too large to pass through membranes and enter the cells of the animal. In addition, the large molecules in food are not all identical to those the animal needs for its particular tissues and functions. When large molecules in food are broken down into their components, however, the animal can use these smaller molecules to assemble the large molecules it needs. For example, although fruit flies and humans have very different diets, both convert proteins in their food to the same 20 amino acids from which they assemble all of the specific proteins in their bodies.

A cell makes a macromolecule or fat by linking together smaller components; it does so by removing a molecule of water for each new covalent bond formed. Chemical digestion by enzymes reverses this process by breaking bonds through the addition of water (see Figure 5.2). This splitting process is called *enzymatic hydrolysis*. A variety of enzymes catalyze the digestion of large molecules in food. Polysaccharides and disaccharides are split into simple sugars; proteins are broken down into amino acids; and nucleic acids are cleaved into nucleotides and their components. Enzymatic hydrolysis also releases fatty acids and other components from fats and phospholipids. In many animals, such as the gorilla in Figure 41.5, digestion of some materials is accomplished by bacteria living in the digestive system.

The last two stages of food processing occur after the food is digested. In the third stage, **absorption**, the animal's cells take up (absorb) small molecules such as amino acids and simple sugars. **Elimination** completes the process as undigested material passes out of the digestive system.

Digestive Compartments

In our overview of food processing, we have seen that digestive enzymes hydrolyze the same biological materials (such as proteins, fats, and carbohydrates) that make up the bodies of the animals themselves. How, then, are animals able to digest food without digesting their own cells and tissues? The evolutionary adaptation that allows animals to avoid self-digestion is the processing of food within specialized intracellular or extracellular compartments.

Exploring Four Main Feeding Mechanisms of Animals

Filter Feeding

Baleen

Many aquatic animals are **filter feeders**, which strain small organisms or food particles from the surrounding medium. The humpback whale, shown above, is one example. Attached to the whale's upper jaw are comblike plates called baleen, which remove small invertebrates and fish from enormous volumes of water and sometimes mud. Filter feeding in water is a type of suspension feeding, which also includes removing suspended food particles from the surrounding medium by capture or trapping mechanisms.

Substrate Feeding

Substrate feeders are animals that live in or on their food source. This leaf miner caterpillar, the larva of a moth, is eating through the soft tissue of an oak leaf, leaving a dark trail of feces in its wake. Other substrate feeders include maggots (fly larvae), which burrow into animal carcasses.

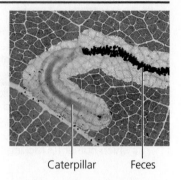

Caterpillar   Feces

Fluid Feeding

Fluid feeders suck nutrient-rich fluid from a living host. This mosquito has pierced the skin of its human host with hollow, needlelike mouthparts and is consuming a blood meal (colorized SEM). Similarly, aphids are fluid feeders that tap the phloem sap of plants. In contrast to such parasites, some fluid feeders actually benefit

their hosts. For example, hummingbirds and bees move pollen between flowers as they fluid-feed on nectar.

Bulk Feeding

Most animals, including humans, are **bulk feeders**, which eat relatively large pieces of food. Their adaptations include tentacles, pincers, claws, venomous fangs, jaws, and teeth that kill their prey or tear off pieces of meat or vegetation. In this amazing scene, a rock python is beginning to ingest a gazelle it has captured and killed. Snakes cannot chew their food into pieces and must swallow it whole—even if the prey is much bigger than the diameter of the snake. They can do so because the lower jaw is loosely hinged to the skull by an elastic ligament that permits the mouth and throat to open very wide. After swallowing its prey, which may take more than an hour, the python will spend two weeks or longer digesting its meal.

Intracellular Digestion

Food vacuoles—cellular organelles in which hydrolytic enzymes break down food—are the simplest digestive compartments. The hydrolysis of food inside vacuoles, called intracellular digestion, begins after a cell engulfs solid food by phagocytosis or liquid food by pinocytosis (see Figure 7.19). Newly formed food vacuoles fuse with lysosomes, organelles containing hydrolytic enzymes. This fusion of organelles brings food in contact with the enzymes, allowing digestion to occur safely within a compartment enclosed by a protective membrane. A few animals, such as sponges, digest their food entirely by this intracellular mechanism (see Figure 33.4).

Extracellular Digestion

In most animal species, hydrolysis occurs largely by extracellular digestion, the breakdown of food in compartments that are continuous with the outside of the animal's body. Having one or more extracellular compartments for digestion enables an animal to devour much larger pieces of food than can be ingested by phagocytosis.

Many animals with relatively simple body plans have a digestive compartment with a single opening **(Figure 41.7)**. This pouch, called a **gastrovascular cavity**, functions in digestion as well as in the distribution of nutrients throughout the body (hence the *vascular* part of the term). The cnidarians called hydras provide a good example of how a gastrovascular cavity works. A carnivore, the hydra uses its tentacles to stuff captured prey through its mouth into its gastrovascular cavity. Specialized gland cells of the hydra's gastrodermis, the tissue layer that lines the cavity, then secrete digestive enzymes that break the soft tissues of the prey into tiny pieces. Other cells of the gastrodermis engulf these

food particles, and most of the hydrolysis of macromolecules occurs intracellularly, as in sponges. After the hydra has digested its meal, undigested materials that remain in its gastrovascular cavity, such as exoskeletons of small crustaceans, are eliminated through its mouth. Many flatworms also have a gastrovascular cavity (see Figure 33.10).

In contrast with cnidarians and flatworms, most animals have a digestive tube extending between two openings, a mouth and an anus **(Figure 41.8)**. Such a tube is called a *complete digestive tract* or, more commonly, an **alimentary canal**. Because food moves along the alimentary canal in a

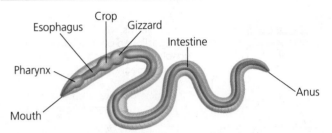

(a) Earthworm. The alimentary canal of an earthworm includes a muscular pharynx that sucks food in through the mouth. Food passes through the esophagus and is stored and moistened in the crop. Mechanical digestion occurs in the muscular gizzard, which pulverizes food with the aid of small bits of sand and gravel. Further digestion and absorption occur in the intestine.

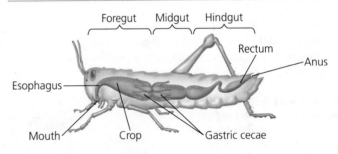

(b) Grasshopper. A grasshopper has several digestive chambers grouped into three main regions: a foregut, with an esophagus and crop; a midgut; and a hindgut. Food is moistened and stored in the crop, but most digestion occurs in the midgut. Pouches called gastric cecae (singular, *ceca*) extend from the beginning of the midgut and function in digestion and absorption.

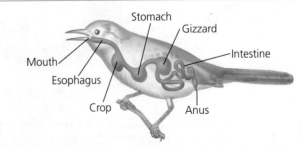

(c) Bird. Many birds have a crop for storing food and a stomach and gizzard for mechanically digesting it. Chemical digestion and absorption of nutrients occur in the intestine.

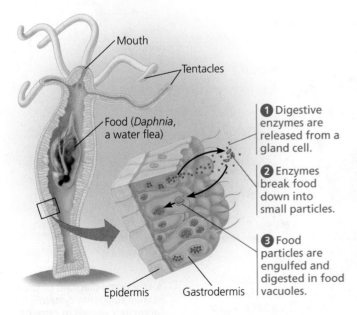

1 Digestive enzymes are released from a gland cell.

2 Enzymes break food down into small particles.

3 Food particles are engulfed and digested in food vacuoles.

▲ **Figure 41.7 Digestion in a hydra.** Digestion begins in the gastrovascular cavity and is completed intracellularly after small food particles are engulfed by specialized cells of the gastrodermis.

▲ **Figure 41.8 Alimentary canals.** These examples illustrate variation in the organization and structure of compartments that carry out stepwise digestion, storage, and absorption in different animals.

single direction, the tube can be organized into specialized compartments that carry out digestion and nutrient absorption in a stepwise fashion. An animal with an alimentary canal can ingest food while earlier meals are still being digested, a feat that is likely to be difficult or inefficient for an animal with a gastrovascular cavity. In the next section, we'll explore the organization of a mammalian alimentary canal.

CONCEPT CHECK 41.2

1. Distinguish the overall structure of a gastrovascular cavity from that of an alimentary canal.

2. In what sense are nutrients from a recently ingested meal not really "inside" your body prior to the absorption stage of food processing?

3. **WHAT IF?** Thinking in broad terms, what similarities can you identify between digestion in an animal body and the breakdown of gasoline in an automobile? (You don't have to know about auto mechanics.)

For suggested answers, see Appendix A.

CONCEPT 41.3

Organs specialized for sequential stages of food processing form the mammalian digestive system

Because most animals, including mammals, have an alimentary canal, the mammalian digestive system can serve to illustrate the general principles of food processing. In mammals, the digestive system consists of the alimentary canal and various accessory glands that secrete digestive juices through ducts into the canal **(Figure 41.9)**. The accessory glands of the mammalian digestive system are three pairs of salivary glands, the pancreas, the liver, and the gallbladder.

Food is pushed along the alimentary canal by **peristalsis**, alternating waves of contraction and relaxation in the smooth muscles lining the canal. At some of the junctions between specialized compartments, the muscular layer forms ringlike valves called **sphincters**. Acting like drawstrings to close off the alimentary canal, sphincters regulate the passage of material between compartments.

Using the human digestive system as a model, let's now follow a meal through the alimentary canal. As we do so, we'll examine in more detail what happens to the food in each digestive compartment along the way.

The Oral Cavity, Pharynx, and Esophagus

Ingestion and the initial steps of digestion occur in the mouth, or **oral cavity**. Mechanical digestion begins as teeth of various shapes cut, mash, and grind food, making the food easier to swallow and increasing its surface area. Meanwhile, the **salivary glands** deliver saliva through ducts to the oral cavity. The release of saliva when food enters the mouth is a reflex, an automatic reaction mediated by the nervous system. Saliva may also be released before food enters the mouth, triggered by a learned association between eating and the time of day, a cooking odor, or another stimulus.

▶ **Figure 41.9 The human digestive system.** After food is chewed and swallowed, it takes 5–10 seconds for it to pass down the esophagus and into the stomach, where it spends 2–6 hours being partially digested. Final digestion and nutrient absorption occur in the small intestine over a period of 5–6 hours. Within 12–24 hours, any undigested material passes through the large intestine, and feces are expelled through the anus.

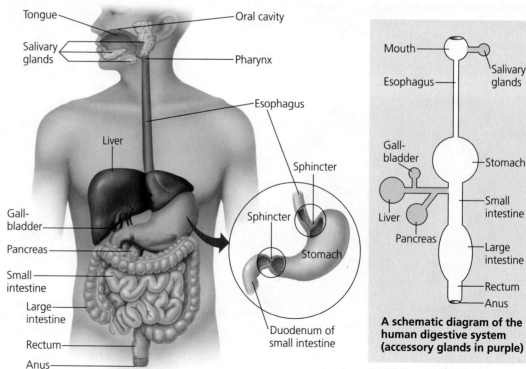

© Pearson Education, Inc.

A schematic diagram of the human digestive system (accessory glands in purple)

© 1996 Cengage Learning, Inc.

Saliva initiates chemical digestion while also protecting the oral cavity. The enzyme **amylase**, found in saliva, hydrolyzes starch (a glucose polymer from plants) and glycogen (a glucose polymer from animals) into smaller polysaccharides and the disaccharide maltose. Much of the protective effect of saliva is provided by **mucus**, a viscous mixture of water, salts, cells, and slippery glycoproteins (carbohydrate-protein complexes) called mucins. Mucus in saliva protects the lining of the mouth from abrasion and lubricates food for easier swallowing. Additional components of saliva include buffers, which help prevent tooth decay by neutralizing acid, and antimicrobial agents (such as lysozyme; see Figure 5.16), which protect against bacteria that enter the mouth with food.

Much as a doorman screens and assists people entering a fancy hotel, the tongue aids digestive processes by evaluating ingested material and then enabling its further passage. When food arrives at the oral cavity, the tongue plays a critical role in distinguishing which foods should be processed further. (See Chapter 50 for a discussion of the sense of taste.) After food is deemed acceptable and chewing commences, tongue movements manipulate the mixture of saliva and food, helping shape it into a ball called a **bolus**. During swallowing, the tongue provides further help, pushing the bolus to the back of the oral cavity and into the pharynx.

The **pharynx**, or throat region, opens to two passageways: the trachea (windpipe) and the esophagus **(Figure 41.10)**. The trachea leads to the lungs (see Figure 42.23), whereas the **esophagus** connects to the stomach. Once food enters the esophagus, peristaltic contractions of smooth muscle move each bolus to the stomach.

Swallowing must be carefully choreographed to keep food and liquids from entering the trachea and causing choking, a blockage of the trachea. The resulting lack of airflow into the lungs can be fatal if the material is not dislodged by vigorous coughing, a series of back slaps, or a forced upward thrust of the diaphragm (the Heimlich maneuver).

Digestion in the Stomach

The **stomach**, which is located just below the diaphragm, stores food and begins digestion of proteins. With accordion-like folds and a very elastic wall, this organ can stretch to accommodate about 2 L of food and fluid. The stomach secretes a digestive fluid called **gastric juice** and mixes it with the food through a churning action. This mixture of ingested food and gastric juice is called **chyme**.

Chemical Digestion in the Stomach

Two components of gastric juice carry out chemical digestion. One is hydrochloric acid (HCl), which disrupts the extracellular matrix that binds cells together in meat and plant material. The concentration of HCl is so high that the pH of gastric juice is about 2, acidic enough to dissolve iron nails (and to kill most bacteria). This low pH denatures (unfolds) proteins in food, increasing exposure of their peptide bonds. The exposed bonds are attacked by the second component of gastric juice—a **protease**, or protein-digesting enzyme, called **pepsin**. Unlike most enzymes, pepsin works best in a very acidic environment. By breaking peptide bonds, it cleaves proteins into smaller polypeptides. Further digestion to individual amino acids occurs in the small intestine.

Why doesn't gastric juice destroy the stomach cells that make it? The answer is that the ingredients of gastric juice are kept inactive until they are released into the lumen (cavity) of the stomach.

The components of gastric juice are produced by two types of cells in the gastric glands of the stomach. *Parietal cells* use an ATP-driven pump to expel hydrogen ions into the lumen. At the same time, chloride ions diffuse into the

▶ **Figure 41.10 Intersection of the human airway and digestive tract.** In humans, the pharynx connects to the trachea and the esophagus. **(a)** At most times, a contracted sphincter seals off the esophagus while the trachea remains open. **(b)** When a food bolus arrives at the pharynx, the swallowing reflex is triggered. Movement of the larynx, the upper part of the airway, tips a flap of tissue called the epiglottis down, preventing food from entering the trachea. At the same time, the esophageal sphincter relaxes, allowing the bolus to pass into the esophagus. The trachea then reopens, and peristaltic contractions of the esophagus move the bolus to the stomach.

(a) Trachea open

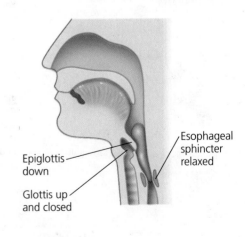

(b) Esophagus open

lumen through specific membrane channels of the parietal cells. It is therefore only within the lumen that hydrogen and chloride ions combine to form HCl (**Figure 41.11**). Meanwhile, *chief cells* release pepsin into the lumen in an inactive form called **pepsinogen**. HCl converts pepsinogen to active pepsin by clipping off a small portion of the molecule and exposing its active site. Through these processes, both HCl and pepsin form in the lumen of the stomach, not within the cells of the gastric glands.

Stomach

Interior surface of stomach. The interior surface of the stomach wall is highly folded and dotted with pits leading into tubular gastric glands.

Epithelium

Gastric gland. The gastric glands have three types of cells that secrete different components of the gastric juice: mucous cells, chief cells, and parietal cells.

Mucous cells secrete mucus, which lubricates and protects the cells lining the stomach.

Chief cells secrete pepsinogen, an inactive form of the digestive enzyme pepsin.

Parietal cells produce the components of hydrochloric acid (HCl).

The production of gastric juice

Pepsinogen → Pepsin (active enzyme)

HCl

Chief cell

H^+
Cl^-

Parietal cell

❶ Pepsinogen and HCl are introduced into the lumen of the stomach.

❷ HCl converts pepsinogen to pepsin.

❸ Pepsin then activates more pepsinogen, starting a chain reaction. Pepsin begins the chemical digestion of proteins.

▲ **Figure 41.11 The stomach and its secretions.**

After hydrochloric acid converts a small amount of pepsinogen to pepsin, pepsin itself helps activate the remaining pepsinogen. Pepsin, like HCl, can clip pepsinogen to expose the enzyme's active site. This generates more pepsin, which activates more pepsinogen. This series of events is an example of positive feedback (see Concept 40.2).

Why don't HCl and pepsin eat through the lining of the stomach? For one thing, mucus secreted by cells in gastric glands protects against self-digestion (see Figure 41.11). In addition, cell division adds a new epithelial layer every three days, replacing cells before they are fully eroded by digestive juices. Under certain circumstances, however, damaged areas of the stomach lining called gastric ulcers can appear. It had been thought that they were caused by psychological stress and resulting excess acid secretion. However, Australian researchers Barry Marshall and Robin Warren discovered that infection by the acid-tolerant bacterium *Helicobacter pylori* causes ulcers. They also demonstrated that an antibiotic could cure most gastric ulcers. For these findings, they were awarded the Nobel Prize in 2005.

Stomach Dynamics

Chemical digestion by gastric juice is facilitated by the churning action of the stomach. This coordinated series of muscle contractions and relaxations mixes the stomach contents about every 20 seconds. As a result of mixing and enzyme action, what begins as a recently swallowed meal becomes the acidic, nutrient-rich broth known as chyme. Most of the time, sphincters close off the stomach at both ends (see Figure 41.9). The sphincter between the esophagus and the stomach normally opens only when a bolus arrives. Occasionally, however, a person experiences acid reflux, a backflow of chyme from the stomach into the lower end of the esophagus. The resulting irritation of the esophagus is commonly called "heartburn."

Peristaltic contractions typically empty the contents of the stomach into the small intestine within 2–6 hours after a meal. The sphincter located where the stomach opens to the small intestine helps regulate passage into the small intestine, allowing only one squirt of chyme at a time.

Digestion in the Small Intestine

Although chemical digestion of some nutrients begins in the oral cavity or stomach, most enzymatic hydrolysis of the macromolecules from food occurs in the small intestine (**Figure 41.12**). The **small intestine** is the alimentary canal's longest compartment—over 6 m (20 feet) long in humans! Its name refers to its small diameter, compared with that of the large intestine. The first 25 cm (10 inches) or so of the small intestine forms the **duodenum**. It is here that chyme from the stomach mixes with digestive juices from the pancreas, liver, and gallbladder, as well as from gland cells of the intestinal wall itself. As you will see in Concept 41.5, hormones released by the stomach and duodenum control the digestive secretions into the alimentary canal.

Pancreatic Secretions

The **pancreas** aids chemical digestion by producing an alkaline solution rich in bicarbonate as well as several enzymes (see Figure 41.12). The bicarbonate neutralizes the acidity of chyme and acts as a buffer. Among the pancreatic enzymes are trypsin and chymotrypsin, proteases secreted into the duodenum in inactive forms. In a chain reaction similar to the activation of pepsin, they are activated when safely located in the lumen of the duodenum.

Bile Production by the Liver

Digestion of fats and other lipids begins in the small intestine and relies on the production of **bile**, a mixture of substances that is made in the **liver**. Bile contains bile salts, which act as emulsifiers (detergents) that aid in digestion and absorption of lipids. Bile is stored and concentrated in the **gallbladder**.

Bile production is integral to one of the other vital functions of the liver: the destruction of red blood cells that are no longer fully functional. In producing bile, the liver incorporates some pigments that are by-products of red blood cell disassembly. These bile pigments are then eliminated from the body with the feces. In some liver or blood disorders, bile pigments accumulate in the skin, resulting in a characteristic yellowing called jaundice.

Secretions of the Small Intestine

The epithelial lining of the duodenum is the source of several digestive enzymes (see Figure 41.12). Some are secreted into the lumen of the duodenum, whereas others are bound to the surface of epithelial cells.

▼ **Figure 41.12 Chemical digestion in the human digestive system.** The timing and location of chemical breakdown are specific to each class of nutrients.

? *Pepsin is resistant to the denaturing effect of the low pH environment of the stomach. Thinking about the different digestive processes that occur in the small intestine, describe an adaptation shared by the digestive enzymes in that compartment.*

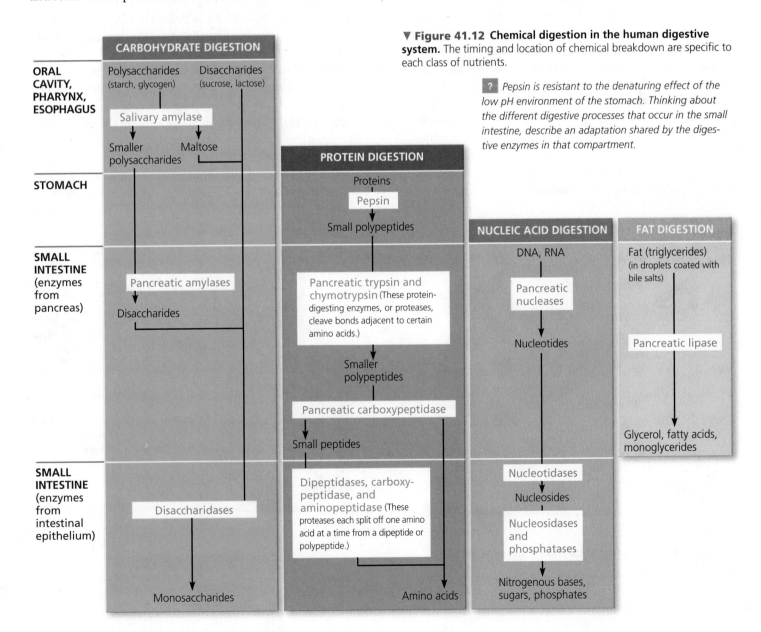

While enzymatic hydrolysis proceeds, peristalsis moves the mixture of chyme and digestive juices along the small intestine. Most digestion is completed in the duodenum. The remaining regions of the small intestine, called the *jejunum* and *ileum*, are the major sites for absorption of nutrients, as discussed next.

Absorption in the Small Intestine

To reach body tissues, nutrients in the lumen must first be absorbed across the lining of the alimentary canal. Most of this absorption occurs at the highly folded surface of the small intestine, as illustrated in **Figure 41.13**. Large folds in the lining encircle the intestine and are studded with finger-like projections called **villi**. In turn, each epithelial cell of a villus has on its apical surface many microscopic projections, or **microvilli**, that are exposed to the intestinal lumen. The many side-by-side microvilli give cells of the intestinal epithelium a brush-like appearance that is reflected in the name *brush border*. Together, the folds, villi, and microvilli of the small intestine have a surface area of 200–300 m^2, roughly the size of a tennis court. This enormous surface area is an evolutionary adaptation that greatly increases the rate of nutrient absorption (see Figure 33.9 for more discussion and examples of maximizing surface area in diverse organisms).

Depending on the nutrient, transport across the epithelial cells can be passive or active (see Chapter 7). The sugar fructose, for example, moves by facilitated diffusion down its concentration gradient from the lumen of the small intestine into the epithelial cells. From there, fructose exits the basal surface and is absorbed into microscopic blood vessels, or capillaries, at the core of each villus. Other nutrients, including amino acids, small peptides, vitamins, and most glucose molecules, are pumped against concentration gradients into the epithelial cells of the villus. This active transport allows much more absorption of those nutrients than would be possible with passive diffusion alone.

The capillaries and veins that carry nutrient-rich blood away from the villi converge into the **hepatic portal vein**, a blood vessel that leads directly to the liver. From the liver, blood travels to the heart and then to other tissues and organs. This arrangement serves two major functions. First, it allows the liver to regulate the distribution of nutrients to the rest of the body. Because the liver can interconvert many organic molecules, blood that leaves the liver may have a very different nutrient balance than the blood that entered. Second, the arrangement allows the liver to remove toxic substances before the blood circulates broadly. The liver is the primary site for the detoxification of many organic molecules, including drugs, that are foreign to the body.

Although many nutrients leave the small intestine through the bloodstream, some products of fat (triglyceride, also known as triacylglycerol) digestion take a different path **(Figure 41.14)**. Hydrolysis of fats by lipase in the small intestine generates fatty acids and monoglycerides. (A monoglyceride is a single fatty acid joined to glycerol.) These products are absorbed by epithelial cells and recombined into triglycerides. They are then coated with phospholipids, cholesterol,

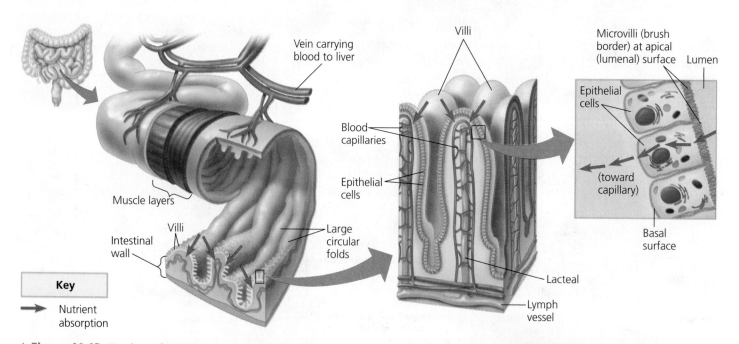

Key

→ Nutrient absorption

▲ **Figure 41.13** **Nutrient absorption in the small intestine.**

? *Tapeworms sometimes infect the human alimentary canal, anchoring themselves to the wall of the small intestine. Based on how digestion is compartmentalized along the mammalian alimentary canal, what digestive functions would you expect these parasites to have?*

ANIMATION

BioFlix Visit the Study Area in **MasteringBiology** for the BioFlix® 3-D Animation on Membrane Transport.

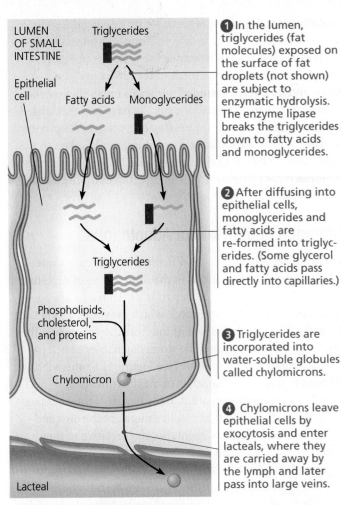

LUMEN OF SMALL INTESTINE

Triglycerides

Epithelial cell

Fatty acids   Monoglycerides

Triglycerides

Phospholipids, cholesterol, and proteins

Chylomicron

Lacteal

❶ In the lumen, triglycerides (fat molecules) exposed on the surface of fat droplets (not shown) are subject to enzymatic hydrolysis. The enzyme lipase breaks the triglycerides down to fatty acids and monoglycerides.

❷ After diffusing into epithelial cells, monoglycerides and fatty acids are re-formed into triglycerides. (Some glycerol and fatty acids pass directly into capillaries.)

❸ Triglycerides are incorporated into water-soluble globules called chylomicrons.

❹ Chylomicrons leave epithelial cells by exocytosis and enter lacteals, where they are carried away by the lymph and later pass into large veins.

▲ **Figure 41.14 Absorption of fats.** Because fats are insoluble in water, adaptations are needed to digest and absorb them. Bile salts (not shown) break up large fat droplets and maintain a small droplet size in the intestinal lumen, exposing more of the fat at the surface to enzymatic hydrolysis. The fatty acids and monoglycerides released by hydrolysis can diffuse into epithelial cells, where fats are reassembled and incorporated into water-soluble chylomicrons that enter the lymphatic system.

and proteins, forming globules called **chylomicrons**. Being water soluble, chylomicrons can dissolve in the blood and travel via the circulatory system.

Before reaching the bloodstream, chylomicrons are first transported from an epithelial cell in the intestine into a **lacteal**, a vessel at the core of each villus (see Figures 41.13 and 41.14). Lacteals are part of the vertebrate lymphatic system, which is a network of vessels filled with a clear fluid called lymph. Starting at the lacteals, lymph containing the chylomicrons passes into the larger vessels of the lymphatic system and eventually into large veins that return the blood to the heart.

In addition to absorbing nutrients, the small intestine has an important function in the recovery of water and ions. Each day we consume about 2 L of water and secrete another 7 L in digestive juices. Typically all but 0.1 L of the water is reabsorbed in the intestines, with most of the

recovery occurring in the small intestine. There is no mechanism for active transport of water. Instead, water is reabsorbed by osmosis when sodium and other ions are pumped out of the lumen of the intestine.

Processing in the Large Intestine

The alimentary canal ends with the **large intestine**, which includes the colon, cecum, and rectum. The small intestine connects to the large intestine at a T-shaped junction **(Figure 41.15)**. One arm of the T is the 1.5-m-long **colon**, which leads to the rectum and anus. The other arm is a pouch called the **cecum**. The cecum is important for fermenting ingested material, especially in animals that eat large amounts of plant material.

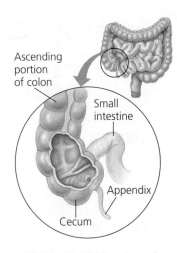

Ascending portion of colon

Small intestine

Appendix

Cecum

▲ **Figure 41.15 Junction of the small and large intestines.**

Compared with many other mammals, humans have a small cecum. The **appendix**, a finger-like extension of the human cecum, has a minor and dispensable role in immunity.

The colon completes the reabsorption of water that began in the small intestine. What remain are the **feces**, the wastes of the digestive system, which become increasingly solid as they are moved along the colon by peristalsis. It takes approximately 12–24 hours for material to travel the length of the colon. If the lining of the colon is irritated—by a viral or bacterial infection, for instance—less water than normal may be reabsorbed, resulting in diarrhea. The opposite problem, constipation, occurs when the feces move along the colon too slowly. Too much water is reabsorbed, and the feces become compacted.

The undigested material in feces includes cellulose fiber. Although it provides no caloric value (energy) to humans, fiber helps move food along the alimentary canal.

A rich community of mostly harmless bacteria lives on the unabsorbed organic material in the human colon, contributing approximately one-third of the dry weight of feces. As by-products of their metabolism, many colon bacteria generate gases, including methane and hydrogen sulfide, the latter of which has an offensive odor. These gases and ingested air are expelled through the anus.

The terminal portion of the large intestine is the **rectum**, where the feces are stored until they can be eliminated. Between the rectum and the anus are two sphincters, the inner one being involuntary and the outer one being voluntary. Periodically, strong contractions of the colon create an urge to defecate. Because filling of the stomach triggers a reflex that increases the rate of contractions in the colon, the urge to defecate often follows a meal.

We have followed a meal from one opening (the mouth) of the alimentary canal to the other (the anus). Next we'll look at some adaptations of this general digestive plan in different animals.

CONCEPT CHECK 41.3

1. Explain why a proton pump inhibitor, such as the drug Prilosec, relieves the symptoms of acid reflux.

2. Thinking about our nutritional needs and feeding behavior, propose an evolutionary explanation for why amylase, unlike other digestive enzymes, is secreted into the mouth.

3. **WHAT IF?** If you mixed gastric juice with crushed food in a test tube, what would happen?

For suggested answers, see Appendix A.

CONCEPT 41.4

Evolutionary adaptations of vertebrate digestive systems correlate with diet

EVOLUTION The digestive systems of mammals and other vertebrates are variations on a common plan, but there are many intriguing adaptations, often associated with the animal's diet. To highlight how form fits function, we'll examine a few of them.

Dental Adaptations

Dentition, an animal's assortment of teeth, is one example of structural variation reflecting diet **(Figure 41.16)**. The evolutionary adaptation of teeth for processing different kinds of food is one of the major reasons mammals have been so successful. For example, the sea otter in Figure 41.1 uses its sharp canine teeth to tear apart prey such as crabs and its slightly rounded molars to crush their shells. Nonmammalian vertebrates generally have less specialized dentition, but there are interesting exceptions. Venomous snakes, such as rattlesnakes, have fangs, modified teeth that inject venom into prey. Some fangs are hollow, like syringes, whereas others drip the toxin along grooves on the surfaces of the teeth.

Stomach and Intestinal Adaptations

Evolutionary adaptations to differences in diet are sometimes apparent as variations in the dimensions of digestive organs. For example, large, expandable stomachs are common in carnivorous vertebrates, which may wait a long time between meals and must eat as much as they can when they do catch prey. An expandable stomach enables a rock python to ingest a whole gazelle (see Figure 41.6) and a 200-kg African lion to consume 40 kg of meat in one meal!

Adaptation is also apparent in the length of the digestive system in different vertebrates. In general, herbivores and omnivores have longer alimentary canals relative to their body size than do carnivores. Plant matter is more difficult to digest than meat because it contains cell walls. A longer digestive tract furnishes more time for digestion and more surface area for the absorption of nutrients. As an example, consider the coyote and koala in **Figure 41.17**. Although these two mammals are about the same size, the koala's intestines are much longer, enhancing the processing of fibrous, protein-poor eucalyptus leaves from which the koala obtains nearly all of its nutrients and water.

▼ **Figure 41.16 Dentition and diet.**

Carnivore	Herbivore	Omnivore
Carnivores, such as members of the dog and cat families, generally have large, pointed incisors and canines that can be used to kill prey and rip or cut away pieces of flesh. The jagged premolars and molars crush and shred food.	Herbivores, such as horses and deer, usually have premolars and molars with broad, ridged surfaces that grind tough plant material. The incisors and canines are generally modified for biting off pieces of vegetation. In some herbivores, canines are absent.	As omnivores, humans are adapted to eating both plants and meat. Adults have 32 teeth. From front to back along either side of the mouth are four bladelike incisors for biting, a pair of pointed canines for tearing, four premolars for grinding, and six molars for crushing (see inset, top view).

Key ▪ Incisors ▪ Canines ▪ Premolars ▪ Molars

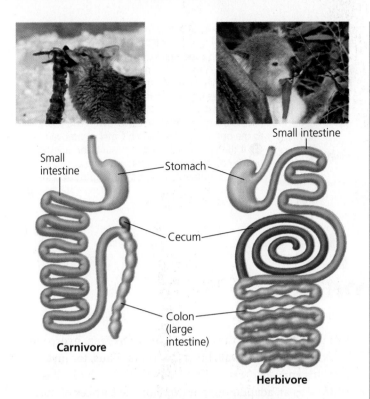

Small
intestine
— Stomach

— Cecum —

Small intestine

Colon
(large
intestine)

Carnivore

Herbivore

▲ **Figure 41.17 The alimentary canals of a carnivore (coyote) and herbivore (koala).** The relatively short digestive tract of the coyote is sufficient for digesting meat and absorbing its nutrients. In contrast, the koala's long alimentary canal is specialized for digesting eucalyptus leaves. Extensive chewing chops the leaves into tiny pieces, increasing exposure to digestive juices. In the long cecum and the upper portion of the colon, symbiotic bacteria further digest the shredded leaves, releasing nutrients that the koala can absorb.

Mutualistic Adaptations

An estimated 10–100 trillion bacteria live in the human digestive system. One bacterial inhabitant, *Escherichia coli,* is so common in the digestive system that its presence in lakes and streams is a useful indicator of contamination by untreated sewage.

The coexistence of humans and many of these bacteria involves mutualistic symbiosis, a mutually beneficial interaction between two species (see Concept 54.1). For example, some intestinal bacteria produce vitamins, such as vitamin K, biotin, and folic acid, that supplement our dietary intake when absorbed into the blood. Intestinal bacteria also regulate the development of the intestinal epithelium and the function of the innate immune system.

Recently, we have greatly expanded our knowledge of the collection of bacteria, called the *microbiome,* in the human digestive system. To identify these bacteria, both beneficial and harmful, scientists are using a DNA sequencing approach based on the polymerase chain reaction (see Figure 20.8). They have found more than 400 bacterial species in the human digestive tract, a far greater number than had been identified through approaches relying on laboratory culture and characterization.

H. pylori

▲ **Figure 41.18 The stomach microbiome.** By copying and sequencing bacterial DNA in samples obtained from human stomachs, researchers characterized the bacterial community that makes up the stomach microbiome. In samples from individuals infected with *Helicobacter pylori,* more than 95% of the sequences were from that species, which belongs to the phylum Proteobacteria. The stomach microbiome in uninfected individuals was much more diverse.

One recent microbiome study provided an important clue as to why the bacterium *H. pylori* disrupts stomach health, leading to ulcers. After collecting stomach tissue from uninfected and *H. pylori*-infected adults, researchers identified all the bacterial species in each sample. What they found was remarkable: *H. pylori* infection led to a near complete elimination from the stomach of all other bacterial species **(Figure 41.18)**. Such studies on differences in the microbiome as a result of particular diseases holds promise for the development of new and more effective therapies.

Mutualistic Adaptations in Herbivores

Mutualistic symbiosis is particularly important in herbivores. Much of the chemical energy in herbivore diets comes from the cellulose of plant cell walls, but animals do not produce enzymes that hydrolyze cellulose. Instead, many vertebrates (as well as termites, whose wooden diets consist largely of cellulose) host large populations of mutualistic bacteria and protists in fermentation chambers in their alimentary canals. These microorganisms have enzymes that can digest cellulose to simple sugars and other compounds that the animal can absorb. In many cases, the microorganisms also use the sugars from digested cellulose in the production of a variety of nutrients essential to the animal, such as vitamins and amino acids.

In horses, koalas, and elephants, mutualistic microorganisms are housed in a large cecum. In contrast, the hoatzin, an herbivorous bird found in South American rain forests,

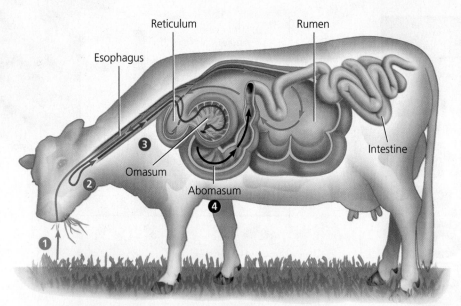

Reticulum

Esophagus

Rumen

Omasum

Abomasum

Intestine

3

2

4

1

◀ **Figure 41.19 Ruminant digestion.** The stomach of a cow, a ruminant, has four chambers. ❶ Chewed food first enters the rumen and reticulum, where mutualistic microorganisms digest cellulose in the plant material. ❷ Periodically, the cow regurgitates and rechews "cud" from the reticulum, further breaking down fibers and thereby enhancing microbial action. ❸ The reswallowed cud passes to the omasum, where some water is removed. ❹ It then passes to the abomasum, for digestion by the cow's enzymes. In this way, the cow obtains significant nutrients from both the grass and the mutualistic microorganisms, which maintain a stable population in the rumen.

hosts microorganisms in a large, muscular crop (an esophageal pouch; see Figure 41.8). Hard ridges in the wall of the crop grind plant leaves into small fragments, and the microorganisms break down cellulose.

In rabbits and some rodents, mutualistic bacteria live in the large intestine as well as in the cecum. Since most nutrients are absorbed in the small intestine, nourishing byproducts of fermentation by bacteria in the large intestine are initially lost with the feces. Rabbits and rodents recover these nutrients by *coprophagy* (from the Greek, meaning "dung eating"), feeding on some of their feces and then passing the food through the alimentary canal a second time. The familiar rabbit "pellets," which are not reingested, are the feces eliminated after food has passed through the digestive tract twice.

The most elaborate adaptations for an herbivorous diet have evolved in the animals called *ruminants*, the cud-chewing animals that include deer, sheep, and cattle **(Figure 41.19)**.

Although we have focused our discussion on vertebrates, adaptations related to digestion are also widespread among other animals. Some of the most remarkable examples are the giant tubeworms (over 3 m long) that live at pressures as high as 260 atmospheres around deep-sea hydrothermal vents (see Figure 52.14). These worms have no mouth or digestive system. Instead, they obtain all of their energy and nutrients from mutualistic bacteria that live within their bodies. The bacteria carry out chemoautotrophy (see

▲ **Giant tubeworm**

Concept 27.3) using the carbon dioxide, oxygen, hydrogen sulfide, and nitrate available at the vents. Thus, for invertebrates and vertebrates alike, mutualistic symbiosis has evolved as an adaptation that expands the sources of nutrition available to animals. Having examined how animals optimize their extraction of nutrients from food, we'll next turn to the challenge of balancing the use of these nutrients.

CONCEPT CHECK 41.4

1. What are two advantages of a longer alimentary canal for processing plant material that is difficult to digest?

2. What features of a mammal's digestive system make it an attractive habitat for mutualistic microorganisms?

3. **WHAT IF?** "Lactose-intolerant" people have a shortage of lactase, the enzyme that breaks down lactose in milk. As a result, they sometimes develop cramps, bloating, or diarrhea after consuming dairy products. Suppose such a person ate yogurt containing bacteria that produce lactase. Why would eating yogurt likely provide at best only temporary relief of the symptoms?

For suggested answers, see Appendix A.

CONCEPT 41.5

Feedback circuits regulate digestion, energy storage, and appetite

The processes that enable an animal to obtain nutrients are matched to the organism's circumstances and need for energy—an example of evolutionary adaptation.

Regulation of Digestion

Many animals have long intervals between meals and do not need their digestive systems to be active continuously.

Instead, each step in processing is activated as food reaches a new compartment in the alimentary canal. The arrival of food triggers the secretion of substances that promote the next stage of chemical digestion, as well as muscular contractions that propel food farther along the canal. For example, you learned earlier that nervous reflexes stimulate the release of saliva when food enters the oral cavity and orchestrate swallowing when a bolus of food reaches the pharynx. Similarly, the arrival of food in the stomach triggers churning and the release of gastric juices. A branch of the nervous system called the *enteric division*, which is dedicated to the digestive organs, regulates these events as well as peristalsis in the small and large intestines.

The endocrine system also plays a critical role in controlling digestion. As described in **Figure 41.20**, a series of hormones released by the stomach and duodenum help ensure that digestive secretions are present only when needed. Like all hormones, they are transported through the bloodstream. This is true even for the hormone gastrin, whose target (the stomach) is the same organ that secretes it.

Regulation of Energy Storage

When an animal takes in more energy-rich molecules than it needs for metabolism and activity, it stores the excess energy (see Concept 40.4). In concluding our overview of nutrition, we'll examine some ways in which animals manage their energy allocation.

In humans, the first sites used for energy storage are liver and muscle cells. In these cells, excess energy from the diet is stored in glycogen, a polymer made up of many glucose units (see Figure 5.6b). Once glycogen depots are full, any additional excess energy is usually stored in fat in adipose cells.

When fewer calories are taken in than are expended—perhaps because of sustained heavy exercise or lack of food—the human body generally expends liver glycogen first and then draws on muscle glycogen and fat. Fats are especially rich in energy; oxidizing a gram of fat liberates about twice the energy liberated from a gram of carbohydrate or protein. For this reason, adipose tissue provides the most space-efficient way for the body to store large amounts of energy. Most healthy people have enough stored fat to sustain them through several weeks without food.

Glucose Homeostasis

The synthesis and breakdown of glycogen are central not only to energy storage, but also to maintaining metabolic balance through glucose homeostasis. In humans, the normal range for the concentration of glucose in the blood is 70–110 mg/100 mL. Because glucose is a major fuel for cellular respiration and a key source of carbon skeletons for biosynthesis, maintaining blood glucose concentrations near this normal range is critical.

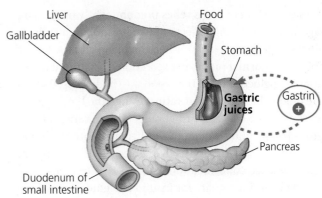

❶ As food arrives at the stomach, it stretches the stomach walls, triggering release of the hormone *gastrin*. Gastrin circulates via the bloodstream back to the stomach, where it stimulates production of gastric juices.

❷ Chyme—an acidic mixture of partially digested food—eventually passes from the stomach to the duodenum. The duodenum responds to amino acids or fatty acids in the chyme by releasing the digestive hormones cholecystokinin and secretin. *Cholecystokinin (CCK)* stimulates the release of digestive enzymes from the pancreas and of bile from the gallbladder. *Secretin* stimulates the pancreas to release bicarbonate (HCO_3^-), which neutralizes chyme.

❸ If the chyme is rich in fats, the high levels of secretin and CCK released act on the stomach to inhibit peristalsis and secretion of gastric juices, thereby slowing digestion.

Key ➕ Stimulation ➖ Inhibition

▲ **Figure 41.20 Hormonal control of digestion.**

Glucose homeostasis relies predominantly on the antagonistic (opposing) effects of two hormones, insulin and glucagon **(Figure 41.21)**. When the blood glucose level rises above the normal range, the secretion of **insulin** triggers the uptake of glucose from the blood into body cells, decreasing the blood glucose concentration. When the blood glucose level drops below the normal range, the secretion of **glucagon** promotes the release of glucose into the blood from energy stores, such as liver glycogen, increasing the blood glucose concentration.

The liver is a key site for insulin and glucagon action. After a carbohydrate-rich meal, for example, rising levels of insulin promote biosynthesis of glycogen from glucose entering the liver in the hepatic portal vein. Between meals, when blood in the hepatic portal vein has a much lower glucose concentration, glucagon stimulates the liver to break down glycogen, convert amino acids and glycerol to glucose, and release glucose into the blood.

Insulin also acts on nearly all body cells to stimulate glucose uptake from blood. A major exception is brain cells, which can take up glucose whether or not insulin is present. This evolutionary adaptation ensures that the brain almost always has access to circulating fuel, even if supplies are low.

Glucagon and insulin are both produced in the pancreas. Scattered throughout this organ are cell clusters called pancreatic islets. Each pancreatic islet has *alpha cells*, which make glucagon, and *beta cells*, which make insulin. Like all hormones, insulin and glucagon are secreted into the interstitial fluid and enter the circulatory system.

Overall, hormone-secreting cells make up only 1–2% of the mass of the pancreas. Other cells in the pancreas produce and secrete bicarbonate ions and the digestive enzymes active in the small intestine (see Figure 41.12). These secretions are released into small ducts that empty into the pancreatic duct, which leads to the small intestine. Thus, the pancreas has functions in both the endocrine and digestive systems.

Diabetes Mellitus

In discussing the role of insulin and glucagon in glucose homeostasis, we have focused exclusively on a healthy metabolic state. However, a number of disorders can disrupt glucose homeostasis with potentially serious consequences, especially for the heart, blood vessels, eyes, and kidneys. The best known and most prevalent of these disorders is diabetes mellitus.

The disease **diabetes mellitus** is caused by a deficiency of insulin or a decreased response to insulin in target tissues. Blood glucose levels rise, but cells are unable to take up enough glucose to meet metabolic needs. Instead, fat becomes the main substrate for cellular respiration. In severe

▶ **Figure 41.21 Homeostatic regulation of cellular fuel.** After a meal is digested, glucose and other monomers are absorbed into the blood from the digestive tract. The human body regulates the use and storage of glucose, a major cellular fuel.

MAKE CONNECTIONS *What form of feedback control does each of these regulatory circuits reflect (see Concept 40.2)?*

ANIMATION *BioFlix* Visit the Study Area in **MasteringBiology** for the BioFlix® 3-D Animation on Homeostasis: Regulating Blood Sugar.

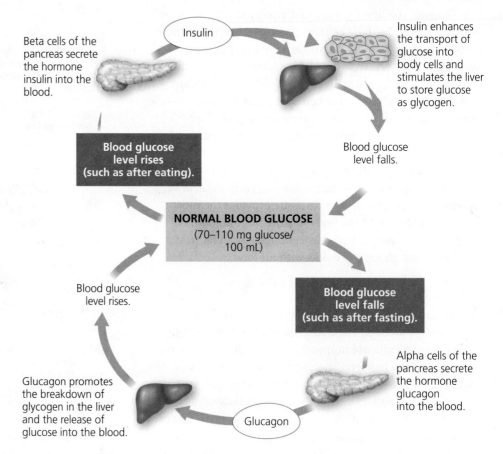

Beta cells of the pancreas secrete the hormone insulin into the blood.

Insulin

Insulin enhances the transport of glucose into body cells and stimulates the liver to store glucose as glycogen.

Blood glucose level falls.

Blood glucose level rises (such as after eating).

NORMAL BLOOD GLUCOSE (70–110 mg glucose/ 100 mL)

Blood glucose level falls (such as after fasting).

Alpha cells of the pancreas secrete the hormone glucagon into the blood.

Glucagon

Glucagon promotes the breakdown of glycogen in the liver and the release of glucose into the blood.

Blood glucose level rises.

cases, acidic metabolites formed during fat breakdown accumulate in the blood, threatening life by lowering blood pH and depleting sodium and potassium ions from the body.

In people with diabetes mellitus, the level of glucose in the blood may exceed the capacity of the kidneys to reabsorb this nutrient. Glucose that remains in the kidney filtrate is excreted. For this reason, the presence of sugar in urine is one test for this disorder. As glucose is concentrated in the urine, more water is excreted along with it, resulting in excessive volumes of urine. *Diabetes* (from the Greek *diabainein*, to pass through) refers to this copious urination, and *mellitus* (from the Greek *meli*, honey) refers to the presence of sugar in urine.

Type 1 Diabetes There are two main types of diabetes mellitus. Each is marked by high blood glucose levels, but with very different causes. *Type 1 diabetes*, or insulin-dependent diabetes, is an autoimmune disorder in which the immune system destroys the beta cells of the pancreas. Type 1 diabetes, which usually appears during childhood, destroys the person's ability to produce insulin. Treatment consists of insulin injections, typically given several times daily. In the past, insulin was extracted from animal pancreases, but now human insulin can be obtained from genetically engineered bacteria, a relatively inexpensive source (see Figure 20.2). Stem cell research may someday provide a cure for type 1 diabetes by generating replacement beta cells that restore insulin production by the pancreas.

Type 2 Diabetes Non-insulin-dependent diabetes, or *type 2 diabetes*, is characterized by a failure of target cells to respond normally to insulin. Insulin is produced, but target cells fail to take up glucose from the blood, and blood glucose levels remain elevated. Although heredity can play a role in type 2 diabetes, excess body weight and lack of exercise significantly increase the risk. This form of diabetes generally appears after age 40, but even children can develop the disease, particularly if they are overweight and sedentary. More than 90% of people with diabetes have type 2. Many can control their blood glucose levels with regular exercise and a healthy diet; some require medications. Nevertheless, type 2 diabetes is the seventh most common cause of death in the United States and a growing public health problem worldwide.

The resistance to insulin signaling in type 2 diabetes is sometimes due to a genetic defect in the insulin receptor or the insulin response pathway. In many cases, however, events in target cells suppress activity of an otherwise functional response pathway. One source of this suppression appears to be inflammatory signals generated by the innate immune system (see Chapter 43). How obesity and inactivity relate to this suppression is being studied in both humans and laboratory animals.

Regulation of Appetite and Consumption

Consuming more calories than the body needs for normal metabolism, or *overnourishment*, can lead to obesity, the excessive accumulation of fat. Obesity, in turn, contributes to a number of health problems, including type 2 diabetes, cancer of the colon and breast, and cardiovascular disease that can result in heart attacks and strokes. It is estimated that obesity is a factor in about 300,000 deaths per year in the United States alone.

Researchers have discovered several homeostatic mechanisms that operate as feedback circuits controlling the storage and metabolism of fat. A network of neurons relays and integrates information from the digestive system to regulate secretion of hormones that regulate long-term and short-term appetite. The target for these hormones is a "satiety center" in the brain **(Figure 41.22)**. For example, *ghrelin*, a hormone secreted by the stomach wall, triggers feelings of hunger before meals. In contrast, both insulin and *PYY*, a hormone secreted by the small intestine after meals,

Secreted by the stomach wall, **ghrelin** is one of the signals that triggers feelings of hunger as mealtimes approach. In dieters who lose weight, ghrelin levels increase, which may be one reason it's so hard to stay on a diet.

A rise in blood sugar level after a meal stimulates the pancreas to secrete **insulin**. In addition to its other functions, insulin suppresses appetite by acting on the brain.

Produced by adipose (fat) tissue, **leptin** suppresses appetite. When the amount of body fat decreases, leptin levels fall, and appetite increases.

The hormone **PYY**, secreted by the small intestine after meals, acts as an appetite suppressant that counters the appetite stimulant ghrelin.

© 2003 AAAS

▲ **Figure 41.22 A few of the appetite-regulating hormones.** Secreted by various organs and tissues, the hormones reach the brain via the bloodstream. These signals act on a region of the brain that in turn controls the "satiety center," which generates the nervous impulses that make us feel either hungry or satiated ("full"). The hormone ghrelin is an appetite stimulant; the other three hormones shown here are appetite suppressants.

Interpreting Data from Experiments with Genetic Mutants

What Are the Roles of the *ob* and *db* Genes in Appetite Regulation? A mutation that disrupts a physiological process is often used to study the normal function of the mutated gene. Ideally, researchers use a standard set of conditions and compare animals that differ genetically only in whether a particular gene is mutant (nonfunctional) or wild-type (normal). In this way, a difference in phenotype, the physiological property being measured, can be attributed to a difference in genotype, the presence or absence of the mutation. To study the role of specific genes in regulating appetite, researchers used laboratory animals with known mutations in those genes.

Mice in which recessive mutations inactivate both copies of either the *ob* gene or the *db* gene eat voraciously and grow much more massive than wild-type mice. In the photograph below, the mouse on the right is wild-type, whereas the obese mouse on the left has an inactivating mutation in both copies of the *ob* gene.

One hypothesis for the normal role of the *ob* and *db* genes is that they participate in a hormone pathway that suppresses appetite when caloric intake is sufficient. Before setting out to isolate the potential hormone, researchers explored this hypothesis genetically.

How the Experiment Was Done The researchers measured the mass of young subject mice of various genotypes and surgically linked the circulatory system of each one to that of another mouse. This procedure ensured that any factor circulating in the bloodstream of either mouse would be transferred to the other in the pair. After eight weeks, they again measured the mass of each subject mouse.

Data from the Experiment

	Genotype Pairing (red type indicates mutant genes)		Average Change in Body Mass of Subject (g)
	Subject	**Paired with**	
(a)	*ob⁺/ob⁺, db⁺/db⁺*	*ob⁺/ob⁺, db⁺/db⁺*	8.3
(b)	*ob/ob, db⁺/db⁺*	*ob/ob, db⁺/db⁺*	38.7
(c)	*ob/ob, db⁺/db⁺*	*ob⁺/ob⁺, db⁺/db⁺*	8.2
(d)	*ob/ob, db⁺/db⁺*	*ob⁺/ob⁺, db/db*	−14.9*

* Due to pronounced weight loss and weakening, subjects in this pairing were remeasured after less than eight weeks.

Interpret the Data

1. First, practice reading the genotype information given in the data table. For example, pairing (a) joined two mice that each had the wild-type version of both genes. Describe the two mice in pairing (b), pairing (c), and pairing (d). Explain how each pairing contributed to the experimental design.

2. Compare the results observed for pairing (a) and pairing (b) in terms of phenotype. If the results had been identical for these two pairings, what would that outcome have implied about the experimental design?

3. Compare the results observed for pairing (c) to those observed for pairing (b). Based on these results, does the *ob⁺* gene product appear to promote or suppress appetite? Explain your answer.

4. Describe the results observed for pairing (d). Note how these results differ from those for pairing (b). Suggest a hypothesis to explain this difference. How could you test your hypothesis using the kinds of mice in this study?

(MB) A version of this Scientific Skills Exercise can be assigned in MasteringBiology.

Data from D. L. Coleman, Effects of parabiosis of obese mice with diabetes and normal mice, *Diabetologia* 9:294–298 (1973).

---

suppress appetite. *Leptin*, a hormone produced by adipose (fat) tissue, also suppresses appetite and appears to play a major role in regulating body fat levels. In the Scientific Skills Exercise, you'll interpret data from an experiment studying genes that affect leptin production and function in mice.

Obtaining food, digesting it, and absorbing nutrients are part of the larger story of how animals fuel their activities. Provisioning the body also involves distributing nutrients (circulation), and using nutrients for metabolism requires exchanging respiratory gases with the environment. These processes and the adaptations that facilitate them are the focus of Chapter 42.

CONCEPT CHECK 41.5

1. Explain how people can become obese even if their intake of dietary fat is relatively low compared with carbohydrate intake.

2. **WHAT IF?** Suppose you were studying two groups of obese people with genetic abnormalities in the leptin pathway. In one group, the leptin levels are abnormally high; in the other group, they are abnormally low. How would each group's leptin levels change if they ate a low-calorie diet for an extended period? Explain.

3. **WHAT IF?** An insulinoma is a cancerous mass of pancreatic beta cells that secrete insulin but do not respond to feedback mechanisms. How you would expect an insulinoma to affect blood glucose levels and liver activity?

For suggested answers, see Appendix A.

- Animals have diverse diets. **Herbivores** mainly eat plants; **carnivores** mainly eat other animals; and **omnivores** eat both. In meeting their nutritional needs, animals must balance consumption, storage, and use of food.

CONCEPT 41.1

An animal's diet must supply chemical energy, organic molecules, and essential nutrients (pp. 893–897)

- Food provides animals with energy for ATP production, carbon skeletons for biosynthesis, and **essential nutrients**—nutrients that must be supplied in preassembled form. Essential nutrients include certain amino acids and fatty acids that animals cannot synthesize; **vitamins**, which are organic molecules; and **minerals**, which are inorganic substances.
- Animals can suffer from two types of malnutrition: an inadequate intake of essential nutrients and a deficiency in sources of chemical energy. Studies of disease at the population level help researchers determine human dietary requirements.

? *How can an enzyme cofactor needed for a process that is vital to all animals be an essential nutrient (vitamin) for only some?*

CONCEPT 41.2

The main stages of food processing are ingestion, digestion, absorption, and elimination (pp. 897–900)

Stages of food processing

1 **INGESTION** (eating)

2 **DIGESTION** (enzymatic breakdown of large molecules)

3 **ABSORPTION** (uptake of nutrients by cells)

4 **ELIMINATION** (passage of undigested materials out of the body in feces)

Undigested material

- Animals differ in the ways they obtain and ingest food. Many animals are **bulk feeders**, eating large pieces of food. Other strategies include filter feeding, suspension feeding, and fluid feeding.
- Compartmentalization is necessary to avoid self-digestion. In intracellular digestion, food particles are engulfed by endocytosis and digested within food vacuoles that have fused with lysosomes. In extracellular digestion, which is used by most animals, enzymatic hydrolysis occurs outside cells in a **gastrovascular cavity** or **alimentary canal**.

? *Propose an artificial diet that would eliminate the need for one of the first three steps in food processing.*

CONCEPT 41.3

Organs specialized for sequential stages of food processing form the mammalian digestive system (pp. 900–906)

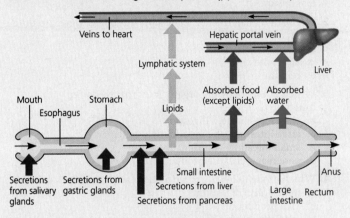

? *What structural feature of the small intestine makes it better suited for absorption of nutrients than the stomach?*

CONCEPT 41.4

Evolutionary adaptations of vertebrate digestive systems correlate with diet (pp. 906–908)

- Vertebrate digestive systems display many evolutionary adaptations associated with diet. For example, dentition, which is the assortment of teeth, generally correlates with diet. In a form of mutualism, many herbivores, including cows, have fermentation chambers where microorganisms digest cellulose. Herbivores also usually have longer alimentary canals than carnivores, reflecting the longer time needed to digest vegetation.

? *How does human anatomy indicate that our primate ancestors were not strict vegetarians?*

CONCEPT 41.5

Feedback circuits regulate digestion, energy storage, and appetite (pp. 908–912)

- **Nutrition** is regulated at multiple levels. Food in the alimentary canal triggers nervous and hormonal responses that control the secretion of digestive juices and that promote the movement of ingested material through the canal. The availability of glucose for energy production is regulated by the hormones **insulin** and **glucagon**, which control the synthesis and breakdown of glycogen.
- Vertebrates store excess calories in glycogen (in liver and muscle cells) and in fat (in adipose cells). These energy stores can be tapped when an animal expends more calories than it consumes. If, however, an animal consumes more calories than it needs for normal metabolism, the resulting overnourishment can lead to the serious health problem of obesity.
- Several hormones, including leptin and insulin, regulate appetite by affecting the brain's satiety center.

? *Explain why your stomach might make growling noises when you skip a meal.*

LEVEL 1: KNOWLEDGE/COMPREHENSION

1. Fat digestion yields fatty acids and glycerol, whereas protein digestion yields amino acids. Both digestive processes
   a. occur inside cells in most animals.
   b. add a water molecule to break bonds.
   c. require a low pH resulting from HCl production.
   d. consume ATP.

2. The mammalian trachea and esophagus both connect to the
   a. pharynx.
   b. stomach.
   c. large intestine.
   d. rectum.

3. Which of the following organs is *incorrectly* paired with its function?
   a. stomach—protein digestion
   b. large intestine—bile production
   c. small intestine—nutrient absorption
   d. pancreas—enzyme production

4. Which of the following is *not* a major activity of the stomach?
   a. mechanical digestion
   b. HCl production
   c. nutrient absorption
   d. enzyme secretion

LEVEL 2: APPLICATION/ANALYSIS

5. After surgical removal of an infected gallbladder, a person must be especially careful to restrict dietary intake of
   a. starch.
   b. protein.
   c. sugar.
   d. fat.

6. If you were to jog 1 km a few hours after lunch, which stored fuel would you probably tap?
   a. muscle proteins
   b. muscle and liver glycogen
   c. fat in the liver
   d. fat in adipose tissue

LEVEL 3: SYNTHESIS/EVALUATION

7. **DRAW IT** Make a flowchart of the events that occur after partially digested food leaves the stomach. Use the following terms: bicarbonate secretion, circulation, decrease in acidity, increase in acidity, secretin secretion, signal detection. Next to each term, indicate the compartment(s) involved. You may use terms more than once.

8. **EVOLUTION CONNECTION**
   The human esophagus and trachea share a passage leading from the mouth and nasal passages, which can cause problems. After reviewing vertebrate evolution (see Chapter 34), explain how the evolutionary concept of descent with modification explains this "imperfect" anatomy.

9. **SCIENTIFIC INQUIRY**
   In human populations of northern European origin, the disorder called hemochromatosis causes excess iron uptake from food and affects one in 200 adults. Among adults, men are ten times as likely as women to suffer from iron overload. Taking into account the existence of a menstrual cycle in humans, devise a hypothesis that explains this difference.

10. **WRITE ABOUT A THEME: ORGANIZATION**
    Hair is largely made up of the protein keratin. In a short essay (100–150 words), explain why a shampoo containing protein is not effective in replacing the protein in damaged hair.

11. SYNTHESIZE YOUR KNOWLEDGE

Hummingbirds are well adapted to obtain sugary nectar from flowers, but they use some of the energy obtained from nectar when they forage for insects and spiders. Explain why this foraging is necessary.

For selected answers, see Appendix A.

MasteringBiology®

Students Go to **MasteringBiology** for assignments, the eText, and the Study Area with practice tests, animations, and activities.

Instructors Go to **MasteringBiology** for automatically graded tutorials and questions that you can assign to your students, plus Instructor Resources.

42

Circulation and Gas Exchange

KEY CONCEPTS

42.1 Circulatory systems link exchange surfaces with cells throughout the body

42.2 Coordinated cycles of heart contraction drive double circulation in mammals

42.3 Patterns of blood pressure and flow reflect the structure and arrangement of blood vessels

42.4 Blood components function in exchange, transport, and defense

42.5 Gas exchange occurs across specialized respiratory surfaces

42.6 Breathing ventilates the lungs

42.7 Adaptations for gas exchange include pigments that bind and transport gases

▲ Figure 42.1 How does a feathery fringe help this animal survive?

Trading Places

The animal in **Figure 42.1** may look like a creature from a science fiction film, but it's actually an axolotl, a salamander native to shallow ponds in central Mexico. The feathery red appendages jutting out from the head of this albino adult are gills. Although external gills are uncommon in adult animals, they help the axolotl carry out a process common to all organisms—the exchange of substances between body cells and the environment.

The exchange of substances between an axolotl or any other animal and its surroundings ultimately occurs at the cellular level. The resources that an animal cell requires, such as nutrients and oxygen (O_2), enter the cytoplasm by crossing the plasma membrane. Metabolic by-products, such as carbon dioxide (CO_2), exit the cell by crossing the same membrane. In unicellular organisms, exchange occurs directly with the external environment. For most multicellular organisms, however, direct transfer of materials between every cell and the environment is not possible. Instead, these organisms rely on specialized systems that carry out exchange with the environment and that transport materials between sites of exchange and the rest of the body.

The reddish color and the branching structure of the axolotl's gills reflect the intimate association between exchange and transport. Tiny blood vessels lie close to the surface of each filament in the gills. Across this surface, there is a net diffusion of O_2 from the surrounding water into the blood and of CO_2 from the blood into the water. The short distances involved allow diffusion to be rapid. Pumping of the axolotl's heart propels the oxygen-rich blood from the gill filaments to all other tissues of the body. There, more short-range exchange occurs, involving nutrients and O_2 as well as CO_2 and other wastes.

Because internal transport and gas exchange are functionally related in most animals, not just axolotls, we'll discuss circulatory and respiratory systems together in this chapter. By considering examples of these systems from a range of species, we'll explore the common elements as well as the remarkable variation in form and organization. We'll also highlight the roles of circulatory and respiratory systems in maintaining homeostasis.

CONCEPT 42.1

Circulatory systems link exchange surfaces with cells throughout the body

The molecular trade that an animal carries out with its environment—gaining O_2 and nutrients while shedding CO_2 and other waste products—must ultimately involve every cell in the body. Small molecules, including O_2 and CO_2, can move between cells and their immediate surroundings by diffusion (see Chapter 7). When there is a difference in concentration, diffusion can result in net movement. But such movement is very slow for distances of more than a few millimeters. That's because the time it takes for a substance to diffuse from one place to another is proportional to the *square* of the distance. For example, a quantity of glucose that takes 1 second to diffuse 100 μm will take 100 seconds to diffuse 1 mm and almost 3 hours to diffuse 1 cm! This relationship between diffusion time and distance places a substantial constraint on the body plan of any animal.

Given that net movement by diffusion is rapid only over very small distances, how does each cell of an animal participate in exchange? Natural selection has resulted in two basic adaptations that permit effective exchange for all of an animal's cells. One adaptation is a body plan that places many or all cells in direct contact with the environment. Each cell can thus exchange materials directly with the surrounding medium. This type of body plan is found only in certain invertebrates, including cnidarians and flatworms. The other adaptation, found in all other animals, is a circulatory system. Such systems move fluid between each cell's immediate surroundings and the body tissues where exchange with the environment occurs.

Gastrovascular Cavities

Let's begin by looking at some animals whose body shapes put many of their cells into contact with their environment, enabling them to live without a distinct circulatory system. In hydras, jellies, and other cnidarians, a central **gastrovascular cavity** functions in the distribution of substances throughout the body, as well as in digestion (see Figure 41.7). An opening at one end connects the cavity to the surrounding water. In a hydra, thin branches of the gastrovascular cavity extend into the animal's tentacles. In jellies and some other cnidarians, the gastrovascular cavity has a much more elaborate branching pattern **(Figure 42.2a)**.

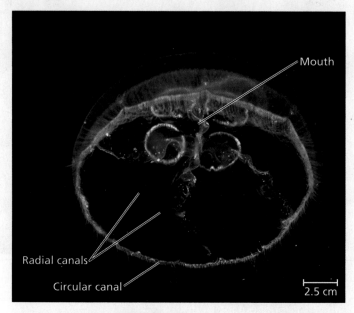

(a) The moon jelly *Aurelia*, a cnidarian. The jelly is viewed here from its underside (oral surface). The mouth leads to an elaborate gastrovascular cavity that consists of radial canals leading to and from a circular canal. Ciliated cells lining the canals circulate fluid within the cavity.

(b) The planarian *Dugesia*, a flatworm. The mouth and pharynx on the ventral side lead to the highly branched gastrovascular cavity, stained dark red in this specimen (LM).

▲ **Figure 42.2 Internal transport in gastrovascular cavities.**

WHAT IF? *Suppose a gastrovascular cavity were open at two ends, with fluid entering one end and leaving the other. How would this affect the cavity's functions in gas exchange and digestion?*

In animals with a gastrovascular cavity, fluid bathes both the inner and outer tissue layers, facilitating exchange of gases and cellular waste. Only the cells lining the cavity have direct access to nutrients released by digestion. However, because the body wall is a mere two cells thick, nutrients need diffuse only a short distance to reach the cells of the outer tissue layer.

Planarians and most other flatworms also survive without a circulatory system. Their combination of a gastrovascular cavity and a flat body is well suited for exchange with the environment **(Figure 42.2b)**. A flat body optimizes exchange by increasing surface area and minimizing diffusion distances.

Open and Closed Circulatory Systems

A circulatory system has three basic components: a circulatory fluid, a set of interconnecting vessels, and a muscular pump, the **heart**. The heart powers circulation by using metabolic energy to elevate the circulatory fluid's hydrostatic pressure, the pressure the fluid exerts on surrounding vessels. The fluid then flows through the vessels and back to the heart.

By transporting fluid throughout the body, the circulatory system functionally connects the aqueous environment of the body cells to the organs that exchange gases, absorb nutrients, and dispose of wastes. In mammals, for example, O_2 from inhaled air diffuses across only two layers of cells in the lungs before reaching the blood. The circulatory system then carries the oxygen-rich blood to all parts of the body. As the blood courses throughout the body tissues in tiny blood vessels, O_2 in the blood diffuses only a short distance before entering the fluid that directly bathes the cells.

Circulatory systems are either open or closed. In an **open circulatory system**, the circulatory fluid, called **hemolymph**, is also the *interstitial fluid* that bathes body cells. Arthropods, such as grasshoppers, and some molluscs, including clams, have open circulatory systems. Heart contraction pumps the hemolymph through the circulatory vessels into interconnected sinuses, spaces surrounding the organs **(Figure 42.3a)**. Within the sinuses, chemical exchange occurs between the hemolymph and body cells. Relaxation of the heart draws hemolymph back in through pores, which are equipped with valves that close when the heart contracts. Body movements periodically squeeze the sinuses, helping circulate the hemolymph. The open circulatory system of larger crustaceans, such as lobsters and crabs, includes a more extensive system of vessels as well as an accessory pump.

In a **closed circulatory system**, a circulatory fluid called **blood** is confined to vessels and is distinct from the interstitial fluid **(Figure 42.3b)**. One or more hearts pump blood into large vessels that branch into smaller ones that infiltrate the organs. Chemical exchange occurs between the blood

▼ **Figure 42.3 Open and closed circulatory systems.**

(a) An open circulatory system

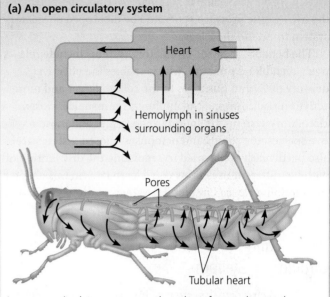

Heart

Hemolymph in sinuses surrounding organs

Pores

Tubular heart

In an open circulatory system, such as that of a grasshopper, hemolymph surrounding body tissues also acts as the circulatory fluid.

(b) A closed circulatory system

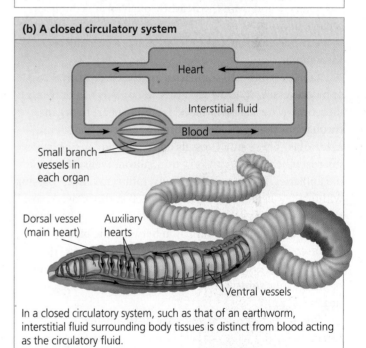

Heart

Interstitial fluid

Blood

Small branch vessels in each organ

Dorsal vessel (main heart)

Auxiliary hearts

Ventral vessels

In a closed circulatory system, such as that of an earthworm, interstitial fluid surrounding body tissues is distinct from blood acting as the circulatory fluid.

and the interstitial fluid, as well as between the interstitial fluid and body cells. Annelids (including earthworms), cephalopods (including squids and octopuses), and all vertebrates have closed circulatory systems.

The fact that both open and closed circulatory systems are widespread among animals suggests that each system offers evolutionary advantages. The lower hydrostatic pressures typically associated with open circulatory systems make them less costly than closed systems in terms of energy expenditure. In some invertebrates, open circulatory systems serve additional functions. For example, spiders use the hydrostatic pressure generated by their open circulatory system to extend their legs.

The benefits of closed circulatory systems include relatively high blood pressure, which enables the effective delivery of O_2 and nutrients to the cells of larger and more active animals. Among the molluscs, for instance, closed circulatory systems are found in the largest and most active species, the squids and octopuses. Closed systems are also particularly well suited to regulating the distribution of blood to different organs, as you'll learn later in this chapter. In examining closed circulatory systems in more detail, we'll focus on vertebrates.

Organization of Vertebrate Circulatory Systems

The closed circulatory system of humans and other vertebrates is often called the **cardiovascular system**. Blood circulates to and from the heart through an amazingly extensive network of vessels: The total length of blood vessels in an average human adult is twice Earth's circumference at the equator!

Arteries, veins, and capillaries are the three main types of blood vessels. Within each type, blood flows in only one direction. **Arteries** carry blood from the heart to organs throughout the body. Within organs, arteries branch into **arterioles**. These small vessels convey blood to **capillaries**, microscopic vessels with very thin, porous walls. Networks of capillaries, called **capillary beds**, infiltrate tissues, passing within a few cell diameters of every cell in the body. Across the thin walls of capillaries, chemicals, including dissolved gases, are exchanged by diffusion between the blood and the interstitial fluid around the tissue cells. At their "downstream" end, capillaries converge into **venules**, and venules converge into **veins**, the vessels that carry blood back to the heart.

Note that arteries and veins are distinguished by the *direction* in which they carry blood, not by the O_2 content or other characteristics of the blood they contain. Arteries carry blood *away* from the heart toward capillaries, and veins return blood *toward* the heart from capillaries. The only exceptions are the portal veins, which carry blood between pairs of capillary beds. The hepatic portal vein, for example, carries blood from capillary beds in the digestive system to capillary beds in the liver (see Chapter 41).

The hearts of all vertebrates contain two or more muscular chambers. The chambers that receive blood entering the heart are called **atria** (singular, *atrium*). The chambers responsible for pumping blood out of the heart are called **ventricles**. The number of chambers and the extent to which they are separated from one another differ substantially among groups of vertebrates, as we'll discuss next. These important differences reflect the close fit of form to function that arises from natural selection.

Single Circulation

In bony fishes, rays, and sharks, the heart consists of two chambers: an atrium and a ventricle (**Figure 42.4a**). The blood passes through the heart once in each complete circuit through the body, an arrangement called **single circulation**. Blood entering the heart collects in the atrium before transfer to the ventricle. Contraction of the ventricle pumps blood to a capillary bed in the gills, where there is a net diffusion of O_2 into the blood and of CO_2 out of the blood. As blood leaves the gills, the capillaries converge into a vessel that carries oxygen-rich blood to capillary beds throughout the body. Blood then returns to the heart.

In single circulation, blood that leaves the heart passes through two capillary beds before returning to the heart. When blood flows through a capillary bed, blood pressure drops substantially, for reasons we'll explain shortly. The drop in blood pressure in the gills limits the rate of blood flow in the rest of the animal's body. As the animal swims, however, the contraction and relaxation of its muscles help accelerate the relatively sluggish pace of circulation.

Double Circulation

The circulatory systems of amphibians, reptiles, and mammals have two circuits, an arrangement called **double circulation (Figure 42.4b and c)**. In animals with double circulation, the pumps for the two circuits are combined into a single organ, the heart. Having both pumps within a single heart simplifies coordination of the pumping cycles. One pump, the right side of the heart, delivers oxygen-poor blood to the capillary beds of the gas exchange tissues, where there is a net movement of O_2 into the blood and of CO_2 out of the blood. This part of the circulation is called a *pulmonary circuit* if the capillary beds involved are all in the lungs, as in reptiles and mammals. It is called a *pulmocutaneous circuit* if it includes capillaries in both the lungs and the skin, as in many amphibians.

After the oxygen-enriched blood leaves the gas exchange tissues, it enters the other pump, the left side of the heart. Contraction of the heart propels this blood to capillary beds in organs and tissues throughout the body. Following the exchange of O_2 and CO_2, as well as nutrients and waste products, the now oxygen-poor blood returns to the heart, completing the **systemic circuit**.

Double circulation provides a vigorous flow of blood to the brain, muscles, and other organs because the heart repressurizes the blood destined for these tissues after it passes through the capillary beds of the lungs or skin.

(a) Single circulation: fish

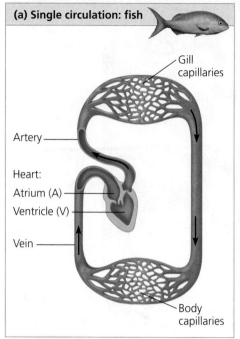

Gill capillaries

Artery

Heart:
Atrium (A)
Ventricle (V)

Vein

Body capillaries

(b) Double circulation: amphibian

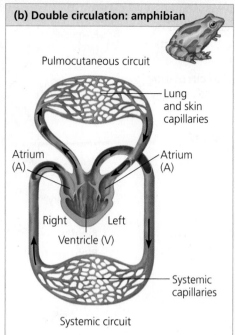

Pulmocutaneous circuit

Lung and skin capillaries

Atrium (A)

Atrium (A)

Right   Left

Ventricle (V)

Systemic capillaries

Systemic circuit

(c) Double circulation: mammal

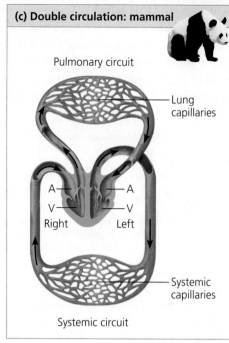

Pulmonary circuit

Lung capillaries

A   A
V   V
Right   Left

Systemic capillaries

Systemic circuit

Key
■ Oxygen-rich blood
■ Oxygen-poor blood

(Note that circulatory systems are shown as if the body were facing you: The right side of the heart is shown on the left, and vice versa.)

Indeed, blood pressure is often much higher in the systemic circuit than in the gas exchange circuit. In contrast, with single circulation blood flows under reduced pressure directly from the gas exchange organs to other organs.

Evolutionary Variation in Double Circulation

EVOLUTION Some vertebrates with double circulation are intermittent breathers. For example, amphibians and many reptiles fill their lungs with air periodically, passing long periods without gas exchange or relying on another gas exchange tissue, typically the skin. These animals have adaptations that enable the circulatory system to temporarily bypass the lungs in part or in whole:

- Frogs and other amphibians have a heart with three chambers—two atria and one ventricle (see Figure 42.4b). A ridge within the ventricle diverts most (about 90%) of the oxygen-rich blood from the left atrium into the systemic circuit and most of the oxygen-poor blood from the right atrium into the pulmocutaneous circuit. When a frog is underwater, the incomplete division of the ventricle allows the frog to adjust its circulation, shutting off most blood flow to its temporarily ineffective lungs. Blood flow continues to the skin, which acts as the sole site of gas exchange while the frog is submerged.
- In the three-chambered heart of turtles, snakes, and lizards, an incomplete septum partially divides the single

ventricle into separate right and left chambers. Two major arteries, called aortas, lead to the systemic circulation. As with amphibians, the circulatory system enables control of the relative amount of blood flowing to the lungs and the rest of the body.
- In alligators, caimans, and other crocodilians, the ventricles are divided by a complete septum, but the pulmonary and systemic circuits connect where the arteries exit the heart. This connection allows arterial valves to shunt blood flow away from the lungs temporarily, such as when the animal is underwater.

Double circulation in birds and mammals is quite different from that in other vertebrates. As shown for a panda in Figure 42.4c, the heart has two atria and two completely divided ventricles. The left side of the heart receives and pumps only oxygen-rich blood, while the right side receives and pumps only oxygen-poor blood. Unlike amphibians and many reptiles, birds and mammals cannot vary blood flow to the lungs without varying blood flow throughout the body in parallel.

How has natural selection shaped the double circulation of birds and mammals? As endotherms, birds and mammals use about ten times as much energy as equal-sized ectotherms. Their circulatory systems therefore need to deliver about ten times as much fuel and O_2 to their tissues and remove ten times as much CO_2 and other wastes. This large traffic of substances is made possible by the separate and independently powered systemic and pulmonary circuits and by large hearts that pump the necessary volume of blood. A powerful four-chambered heart arose independently in the distinct ancestors of birds and mammals and thus reflects convergent evolution (see Chapter 34).

In the next section, we'll restrict our focus to circulation in mammals and to the anatomy and physiology of the key circulatory organ—the heart.

CONCEPT CHECK 42.1

1. How is the flow of hemolymph through an open circulatory system similar to the flow of water through an outdoor fountain?

2. Three-chambered hearts with incomplete septa were once viewed as being less adapted to circulatory function than mammalian hearts. What advantage of such hearts did this viewpoint overlook?

3. **WHAT IF?** The heart of a normally developing human fetus has a hole between the left and right atria. In some cases, this hole does not close completely before birth. If the hole weren't surgically corrected, how would it affect the O_2 content of the blood entering the systemic circuit?

For suggested answers, see Appendix A.

CONCEPT 42.2

Coordinated cycles of heart contraction drive double circulation in mammals

The timely delivery of O_2 to the body's organs is critical: Some brain cells, for example, die if their O_2 supply is interrupted for as little as a few minutes. How does the mammalian cardiovascular system meet the body's continuous (although variable) demand for O_2? To answer this question, we must consider how the parts of the system are arranged and how each part functions.

Mammalian Circulation

Let's first examine the overall organization of the mammalian cardiovascular system, beginning with the pulmonary circuit. (The circled numbers refer to corresponding locations in **Figure 42.5**.) Contraction of ❶ the right ventricle pumps blood to the lungs via ❷ the pulmonary arteries. As the blood flows through ❸ capillary beds in the left and right lungs, it loads O_2 and unloads CO_2. Oxygen-rich blood returns from the lungs via the pulmonary veins to ❹ the left atrium of the heart. Next, the oxygen-rich blood flows into ❺ the heart's left ventricle, which pumps the oxygen-rich blood out to body tissues through the systemic circuit. Blood leaves the left ventricle via ❻ the aorta, which conveys blood to arteries leading throughout the body. The first

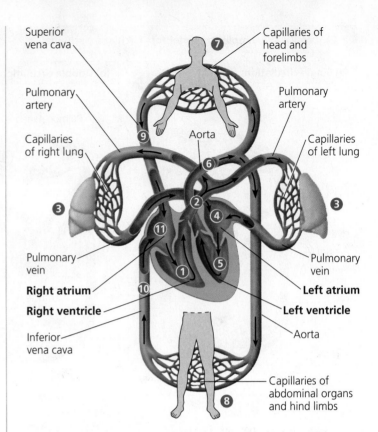

▲ **Figure 42.5 The mammalian cardiovascular system: an overview.** Note that the dual circuits operate simultaneously, not in the serial fashion that the numbering in the diagram suggests. The two ventricles pump in unison; while some blood is traveling in the pulmonary circuit, the rest of the blood is flowing in the systemic circuit.

branches leading from the aorta are the coronary arteries (not shown), which supply blood to the heart muscle itself. Then branches lead to ❼ capillary beds in the head and arms (forelimbs). The aorta then descends into the abdomen, supplying oxygen-rich blood to arteries leading to ❽ capillary beds in the abdominal organs and legs (hind limbs). Within the capillaries, there is a net diffusion of O_2 from the blood to the tissues and of CO_2 (produced by cellular respiration) into the blood. Capillaries rejoin, forming venules, which convey blood to veins. Oxygen-poor blood from the head, neck, and forelimbs is channeled into a large vein, ❾ the superior vena cava. Another large vein, ❿ the inferior vena cava, drains blood from the trunk and hind limbs. The two venae cavae empty their blood into ⓫ the right atrium, from which the oxygen-poor blood flows into the right ventricle.

The Mammalian Heart: *A Closer Look*

Using the human heart as an example, let's now take a closer look at how the mammalian heart works **(Figure 42.6)**. Located behind the sternum (breastbone), the human heart is about the size of a clenched fist and consists mostly of cardiac muscle (see Figure 40.5). The two atria have relatively

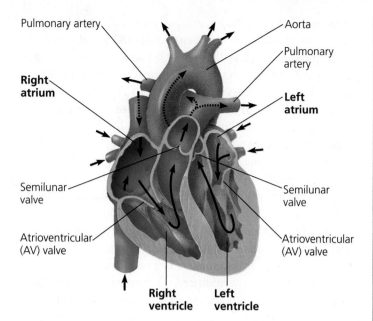

Pulmonary artery

Aorta

Pulmonary artery

Right atrium

Left atrium

Semilunar valve

Semilunar valve

Atrioventricular (AV) valve

Atrioventricular (AV) valve

Right ventricle

Left ventricle

▲ **Figure 42.6 The mammalian heart: a closer look.** Notice the locations of the valves, which prevent backflow of blood within the heart. Also notice how the atria and left and right ventricles differ in the thickness of their muscular walls.

thin walls and serve as collection chambers for blood returning to the heart from the lungs or other body tissues. Much of the blood that enters the atria flows into the ventricles while all heart chambers are relaxed. The remainder is transferred by contraction of the atria before the ventricles begin to contract. Compared to the atria, the ventricles have thicker walls and contract much more forcefully—especially the left ventricle, which pumps blood throughout the body via the systemic circuit. Although the left ventricle contracts with greater force than the right ventricle, it pumps the same volume of blood as the right ventricle during each contraction.

The heart contracts and relaxes in a rhythmic cycle. When it contracts, it pumps blood; when it relaxes, its chambers fill with blood. One complete sequence of pumping and filling is referred to as the **cardiac cycle**. The contraction phase of the cycle is called **systole**, and the relaxation phase is called **diastole (Figure 42.7)**.

The volume of blood each ventricle pumps per minute is the **cardiac output**. Two factors determine cardiac output: the rate of contraction, or **heart rate** (number of beats per minute), and the **stroke volume**, the amount of blood pumped by a ventricle in a single contraction. The average stroke volume in humans is about 70 mL. Multiplying this stroke volume by a resting heart rate of 72 beats per minute yields a cardiac output of 5 L/min—about equal to the total volume of blood in the human body. During heavy exercise, cardiac output increases as much as fivefold.

Four valves in the heart prevent backflow and keep blood moving in the correct direction (see Figures 42.6 and 42.7).

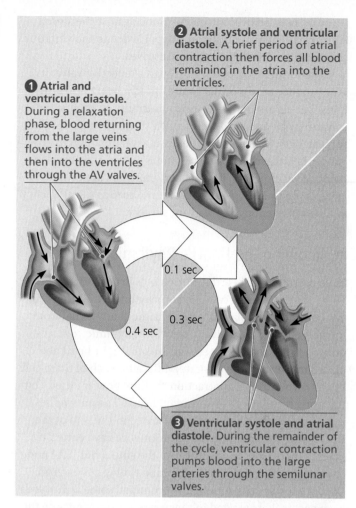

❶ **Atrial and ventricular diastole.** During a relaxation phase, blood returning from the large veins flows into the atria and then into the ventricles through the AV valves.

❷ **Atrial systole and ventricular diastole.** A brief period of atrial contraction then forces all blood remaining in the atria into the ventricles.

0.1 sec

0.3 sec

0.4 sec

❸ **Ventricular systole and atrial diastole.** During the remainder of the cycle, ventricular contraction pumps blood into the large arteries through the semilunar valves.

▲ **Figure 42.7 The cardiac cycle.** For an adult human at rest with a heart rate of about 72 beats per minute, one complete cardiac cycle takes about 0.8 second. Note that during all but 0.1 second of the cardiac cycle, the atria are relaxed and are filling with blood returning via the veins.

Made of flaps of connective tissue, the valves open when pushed from one side and close when pushed from the other. An **atrioventricular (AV) valve** lies between each atrium and ventricle. The AV valves are anchored by strong fibers that prevent them from turning inside out. Pressure generated by the powerful contraction of the ventricles closes the AV valves, keeping blood from flowing back into the atria. **Semilunar valves** are located at the two exits of the heart: where the aorta leaves the left ventricle and where the pulmonary artery leaves the right ventricle. These valves are pushed open by the pressure generated during contraction of the ventricles. When the ventricles relax, blood pressure built up in the aorta and pulmonary artery closes the semilunar valves and prevents significant backflow.

You can follow the closing of the two sets of heart valves either with a stethoscope or by pressing your ear tightly against the chest of a friend (or a friendly dog). The sound pattern is "lub-dup, lub-dup, lub-dup." The first heart sound ("lub") is created by the recoil of blood against the closed AV valves. The second sound ("dup") is due to the vibrations caused by closing of the semilunar valves.

If blood squirts backward through a defective valve, it may produce an abnormal sound called a **heart murmur**. Some people are born with heart murmurs; in others, the valves may be damaged by infection (from rheumatic fever, for instance). When a valve defect is severe enough to endanger health, surgeons may implant a mechanical replacement valve. However, not all heart murmurs are caused by a defect, and most valve defects do not reduce the efficiency of blood flow enough to warrant surgery.

Maintaining the Heart's Rhythmic Beat

In vertebrates, the heartbeat originates in the heart itself. Some cardiac muscle cells are autorhythmic, meaning they can contract and relax repeatedly without any signal from the nervous system. You can see these rhythmic contractions in tissue that has been removed from the heart and placed in a dish in the laboratory! Because each of these cells has its own intrinsic contraction rhythm, how are their contractions coordinated in the intact heart? The answer lies in a group of autorhythmic cells located in the wall of the right atrium, near where the superior vena cava enters the heart. This cluster of cells is called the **sinoatrial (SA) node**, or *pacemaker*, and it sets the rate and timing at which all cardiac muscle cells contract. (In contrast, some arthropods have pacemakers located in the nervous system, outside the heart.)

The SA node produces electrical impulses much like those produced by nerve cells. Because cardiac muscle cells are electrically coupled through gap junctions (see Figure 6.30), impulses from the SA node spread rapidly within heart tissue. In addition, these impulses generate currents that are conducted to the skin via body fluids. In an **electrocardiogram** (**ECG** or, often, **EKG**, from the German spelling), these currents are recorded by electrodes placed on the skin. The resulting graph of current against time has a characteristic shape that represents the stages in the cardiac cycle **(Figure 42.8)**.

Impulses from the SA node first spread rapidly through the walls of the atria, causing both atria to contract in unison. During atrial contraction, the impulses originating at the SA node reach other autorhythmic cells located

in the wall between the left and right atria. These cells form a relay point called the **atrioventricular (AV) node**. Here the impulses are delayed for about 0.1 second before spreading to the heart apex. This delay allows the atria to empty completely before the ventricles contract. Then the signals from the AV node are conducted to the heart apex and throughout the ventricular walls by specialized structures called bundle branches and Purkinje fibers.

Physiological cues alter heart tempo by regulating the pacemaker function of the SA node. Two portions of the nervous system, the sympathetic and parasympathetic divisions, are largely responsible for this regulation. They function like the accelerator and brake in a car: For example, when you stand up and start walking, the sympathetic division speeds up your pacemaker. The resulting increase in heart rate provides the additional O_2 needed by the muscles that are powering your activity. If you then sit down and relax, the parasympathetic division slows down your pacemaker, decreasing your heart rate and thus conserving energy. Hormones secreted into the blood also influence the pacemaker. For instance, epinephrine, the "fight-or-flight" hormone secreted by the adrenal glands, speeds up the pacemaker. A third type of input that affects the pacemaker is body temperature. An increase of only 1°C raises the heart rate by about 10 beats per minute. This is the reason your heart beats faster when you have a fever.

Having examined the operation of the circulatory pump, we turn in the next section to the forces and structures that influence blood flow in the vessels of each circuit.

❶ Signals (yellow) from SA node spread through atria.

❷ Signals are delayed at AV node.

❸ Bundle branches pass signals to heart apex.

❹ Signals spread throughout ventricles.

SA node (pacemaker)

AV node

Bundle branches   Heart apex

Purkinje fibers

ECG

▲ **Figure 42.8 The control of heart rhythm.** Electrical signals follow a set path through the heart in establishing the heart rhythm. The diagrams at the top trace the movement of these signals (yellow) during the cardiac cycle; specialized muscle cells involved in controlling of the rhythm are indicated in orange. Under each step, the corresponding portion of an electrocardiogram (ECG) is highlighted (yellow). In step 4, the portion of the ECG to the right of the "spike" represents electrical activity that reprimes the ventricles for the next round of contraction.

WHAT IF? *If your doctor gave you a copy of your ECG recording, how could you determine what your heart rate had been during the test?*

1. Explain why blood has a higher O_2 concentration in the pulmonary veins than in the venae cavae, which are also veins.

2. Why is it important that the AV node delay the electrical impulse moving from the SA node and the atria to the ventricles?

3. **WHAT IF?** After you exercise regularly for several months, your resting heart rate decreases, but your cardiac output at rest is unchanged. What other change in the function of your heart at rest could explain these findings?

For suggested answers, see Appendix A.

CONCEPT 42.3

Patterns of blood pressure and flow reflect the structure and arrangement of blood vessels

The vertebrate circulatory system enables blood to deliver oxygen and nutrients and remove wastes throughout the body. In doing so, the circulatory system relies on a branching network of vessels much like the plumbing system that delivers fresh water to a city and removes its wastes. In fact, the same physical principles that govern the operation of plumbing systems apply to the functioning of blood vessels.

Blood Vessel Structure and Function

Blood vessels contain a central lumen (cavity) lined with an **endothelium**, a single layer of flattened epithelial cells. The smooth surface of the endothelium minimizes resistance to the flow of blood. Surrounding the endothelium are layers of tissue that differ in capillaries, arteries, and veins, reflecting the specialized functions of these vessels.

Capillaries are the smallest blood vessels, having a diameter only slightly greater than that of a red blood cell **(Figure 42.9)**. Capillaries also have very thin walls, which consist of just an endothelium and a surrounding extracellular layer called the *basal lamina*. The exchange of substances between the blood and interstitial fluid occurs only in capillaries because only there are blood vessel walls thin enough to permit this exchange.

The walls of arteries and veins have a more complex organization than those of capillaries. Both arteries and veins have two layers of tissue surrounding the endothelium. The outer layer is formed by connective tissue that contains elastic fibers, which allow the vessel to stretch and recoil, and collagen, which provides strength. The layer next to the endothelium contains smooth muscle and more elastic fibers.

While similar in organization, the walls of arteries and veins differ, reflecting distinct adaptations to the particular functions of these vessels in circulation. The walls of arteries are thick and strong, accommodating blood pumped at high pressure by the heart. They are also elastic. When the heart relaxes between contractions, the arterial walls recoil, helping maintain blood pressure and flow to capillaries. Signals from the nervous system and hormones circulating in the blood act on the smooth muscle in arteries and arterioles, dilating or constricting these vessels and thus controlling blood flow to different parts of the body.

▲ **Figure 42.9 The structure of blood vessels.**

Because veins convey blood back to the heart at a lower pressure, they do not require thick walls. For a given blood vessel diameter, a vein has a wall only about a third as thick as that of an artery. Unlike arteries, veins contain valves, which maintain a unidirectional flow of blood despite the low blood pressure in these vessels.

We consider next how blood vessel diameter, vessel number, and blood pressure influence the speed at which blood flows in different locations within the body.

Blood Flow Velocity

To understand how blood vessel diameter influences blood flow, consider how water flows through a thick hose connected to a faucet. When the faucet is turned on, water flows at the same velocity at each point along the hose. However, if a narrow nozzle is attached to the end of the hose, the water will exit the nozzle at a much greater velocity. Because water doesn't compress under pressure, the volume of water moving through the nozzle in a given time must be the same as the volume moving through the rest of the hose. The cross-sectional area of the nozzle is smaller than that of the hose, so the water speeds up in the nozzle.

An analogous situation exists in the circulatory system, but blood *slows* as it moves from arteries to arterioles to the much narrower capillaries. Why? The reason is that the number of capillaries is enormous, roughly 7 billion in a human body. Each artery conveys blood to so many capillaries that the *total* cross-sectional area is much greater in capillary beds than in the arteries or any other part of the circulatory system **(Figure 42.10)**. The result is a dramatic decrease in velocity from the arteries to the capillaries: Blood travels 500 times more slowly in the capillaries (about 0.1 cm/sec) than in the aorta (about 48 cm/sec). After passing through the capillaries, the blood speeds up as it enters the venules and veins, which have smaller *total* cross-sectional areas than the capillaries.

Blood Pressure

Blood, like all fluids, flows from areas of higher pressure to areas of lower pressure. Contraction of a heart ventricle generates blood pressure, which exerts a force in all directions. The part of the force directed lengthwise in an artery causes the blood to flow away from the heart, the site of highest pressure. The part of the force exerted sideways stretches the wall of the artery. Following ventricular contraction, the recoil of the elastic arterial walls plays a critical role in maintaining blood pressure, and hence blood flow, throughout the cardiac cycle. Once the blood enters the millions of tiny arterioles and capillaries, the narrow diameter of these vessels generates substantial resistance to flow. By the time the blood enters the veins, this resistance has dissipated much of the pressure generated by the pumping heart.

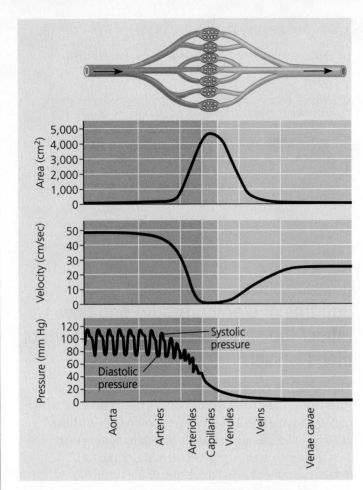

▲ **Figure 42.10 The interrelationship of cross-sectional area of blood vessels, blood flow velocity, and blood pressure.** As a result of an increase in total cross-sectional area, blood flow velocity decreases markedly in the arterioles and is lowest in the capillaries. Blood pressure, the main force driving blood from the heart to the capillaries, is highest in the aorta and other arteries.

Changes in Blood Pressure During the Cardiac Cycle

Arterial blood pressure is highest when the heart contracts during ventricular systole. The pressure at this time is called **systolic pressure** (see Figure 42.10). Each spike in blood pressure caused by ventricular contraction stretches the arteries. By placing your fingers on the inside of your wrist, you can feel a **pulse**—the rhythmic bulging of the artery walls with each heartbeat. The pressure surge is partly due to the narrow openings of arterioles impeding the exit of blood from the arteries. When the heart contracts, blood enters the arteries faster than it can leave, and the vessels stretch from the rise in pressure.

During diastole, the elastic walls of the arteries snap back. As a consequence, there is a lower but still substantial blood pressure when the ventricles are relaxed (**diastolic pressure**). Before enough blood has flowed into the arterioles to completely relieve pressure in the arteries, the heart contracts again. Because the arteries remain pressurized throughout the cardiac cycle (see Figure 42.10), blood continuously flows into arterioles and capillaries.

Regulation of Blood Pressure

Homeostatic mechanisms regulate arterial blood pressure by altering the diameter of arterioles. As the smooth muscles in arteriole walls contract, the arterioles narrow, a process called **vasoconstriction**. Narrowing of the arterioles increases blood pressure upstream in the arteries. When the smooth muscles relax, the arterioles undergo **vasodilation**, an increase in diameter that causes blood pressure in the arteries to fall.

Researchers have identified nitric oxide (NO), a gas, as a major inducer of vasodilation and endothelin, a peptide, as the most potent inducer of vasoconstriction. Cues from the nervous and endocrine systems regulate production of NO and endothelin in blood vessels, where their activities regulate blood pressure.

Vasoconstriction and vasodilation are often coupled to changes in cardiac output that also affect blood pressure. This coordination of regulatory mechanisms maintains adequate blood flow as the body's demands on the circulatory system change. During heavy exercise, for example, the arterioles in working muscles dilate, causing a greater flow of oxygen-rich blood to the muscles. By itself, this increased flow to the muscles would cause a drop in blood pressure (and therefore blood flow) in the body as a whole. However, cardiac output increases at the same time, maintaining blood pressure and supporting the necessary increase in blood flow.

Blood Pressure and Gravity

Blood pressure is generally measured for an artery in the arm at the same height as the heart **(Figure 42.11)**. For a healthy 20-year-old human at rest, arterial blood pressure in the systemic circuit is typically about 120 millimeters of mercury (mm Hg) at systole and 70 mm Hg at diastole, expressed as 120/70. (Arterial blood pressure in the pulmonary circuit is six to ten times lower.)

Gravity has a significant effect on blood pressure. When you are standing, for example, your head is roughly 0.35 m higher than your chest, and the arterial blood pressure in your brain is about 27 mm Hg less than that near your heart. If the blood pressure in your brain is too low to provide adequate

blood flow, you will likely faint. By causing your body to collapse to the ground, fainting effectively places your head at the level of your heart, quickly increasing blood flow to your brain.

For animals with very long necks, the blood pressure required to overcome gravity is particularly high. A giraffe, for example, requires a systolic pressure of more than 250 mm Hg near the heart to get blood to its head. When a giraffe lowers its head to drink, one-way valves and sinuses, along with feedback mechanisms that reduce cardiac output, prevent this high pressure from damaging its brain. We can calculate that a dinosaur with a neck nearly 10 m long would have required even greater systolic pressure—nearly 760 mm Hg—to pump blood to its brain when its head was fully raised. However, calculations based on anatomy and inferred metabolic rate suggest that dinosaurs did not have a heart powerful enough to generate such high pressure. Based on this evidence as well as studies of neck bone structure, some biologists have concluded that the long-necked dinosaurs fed close to the ground rather than on high foliage.

Gravity is also a consideration for blood flow in veins, especially those in the legs. When you stand or sit, gravity draws blood downward to your legs and feet and impedes its upward return to the heart. Although blood pressure in veins is relatively low, valves inside the veins help maintain

❶ A sphygmomanometer, an inflatable cuff attached to a pressure gauge, measures blood pressure in an artery. The cuff is inflated until the pressure closes the artery, so that no blood flows past the cuff. When this occurs, the pressure exerted by the cuff exceeds the pressure in the artery.

❷ The cuff is allowed to deflate gradually. When the pressure exerted by the cuff falls just below that in the artery, blood pulses into the forearm, generating sounds that can be heard with the stethoscope. The pressure measured at this point is the systolic pressure (120 mm Hg in this example).

❸ The cuff is allowed to deflate further, just until the blood flows freely through the artery and the sounds below the cuff disappear. The pressure at this point is the diastolic pressure (70 mm Hg in this example).

▲ **Figure 42.11 Measurement of blood pressure.** Blood pressure is recorded as two numbers separated by a slash. The first number is the systolic pressure; the second is the diastolic pressure.

▶ Figure 42.12 Blood flow in veins. Skeletal muscle contraction squeezes and constricts veins. Flaps of tissue within the veins act as one-way valves that keep blood moving only toward the heart. If you sit or stand too long, the lack of muscular activity may cause your feet to swell as blood pools in your veins.

Direction of blood flow in vein (toward heart)

Valve (open)

Skeletal muscle

Valve (closed)

the unidirectional flow of blood within these vessels. The return of blood to the heart is further enhanced by rhythmic contractions of smooth muscles in the walls of venules and veins and by the contraction of skeletal muscles during exercise **(Figure 42.12).**

In rare instances, runners and other athletes can suffer heart failure if they stop vigorous exercise abruptly. When the leg muscles suddenly cease contracting and relaxing, less blood returns to the heart, which continues to beat rapidly. If the heart is weak or damaged, this inadequate blood flow may cause the heart to malfunction. To reduce the risk of stressing the heart excessively, athletes are encouraged to follow hard exercise with moderate activity, such as walking, to "cool down" until their heart rate approaches its resting level.

Capillary Function

At any given time, only about 5–10% of the body's capillaries have blood flowing through them. However, each tissue has many capillaries, so every part of the body is supplied with blood at all times. Capillaries in the brain, heart, kidneys, and liver are usually filled to capacity, but at many other sites the blood supply varies over time as blood is diverted from one destination to another. For example, blood flow to the skin is regulated to help control body temperature, and blood supply to the digestive tract increases after a meal. In contrast, blood is diverted from the digestive tract and supplied more generously to skeletal muscles and skin during strenuous exercise.

Given that capillaries lack smooth muscle, how is blood flow in capillary beds altered? One mechanism is constriction or dilation of the arterioles that supply capillary beds. A second mechanism involves *precapillary sphincters*, rings of smooth muscle located at the entrance to capillary beds **(Figure 42.13).** Opening and closing these muscular rings

regulate and redirect the passage of blood into particular sets of capillaries. The signals regulating blood flow by these mechanisms include nerve impulses, hormones traveling throughout the bloodstream, and chemicals produced locally. For example, the chemical histamine released by cells at a wound site causes vasodilation. The result is increased blood flow and increased access of disease-fighting white blood cells to invading microorganisms.

As you have read, the critical exchange of substances between the blood and interstitial fluid takes place across the thin endothelial walls of the capillaries. Some substances are carried across the endothelium in vesicles that form on one side by endocytosis and release their contents on the opposite side by exocytosis. Small molecules, such as O_2 and CO_2, simply diffuse across the endothelial cells or, in some tissues, through microscopic pores in the capillary wall. These openings also provide the route for transport of small solutes such as sugars, salts, and urea, as well as for bulk flow of fluid into tissues driven by blood pressure within the capillary.

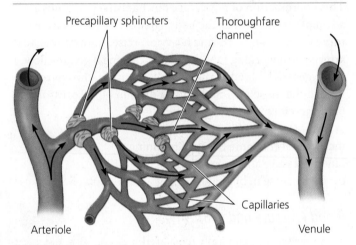

Precapillary sphincters

Thoroughfare channel

Capillaries

Arteriole

Venule

(a) Sphincters relaxed

Arteriole

Venule

(b) Sphincters contracted

▲ Figure 42.13 Blood flow in capillary beds. Precapillary sphincters regulate the passage of blood into capillary beds. Some blood flows directly from arterioles to venules through capillaries called thoroughfare channels, which are always open.

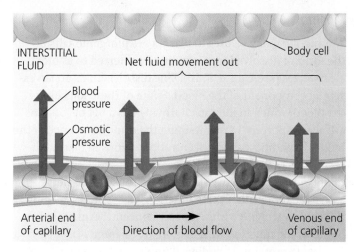

INTERSTITIAL FLUID

Net fluid movement out

Body cell

Blood pressure

Osmotic pressure

Arterial end of capillary

Direction of blood flow

Venous end of capillary

▲ **Figure 42.14 Fluid exchange between capillaries and the interstitial fluid.** This diagram shows a hypothetical capillary in which blood pressure exceeds osmotic pressure throughout the entire length of the capillary. In other capillaries, blood pressure may be lower than osmotic pressure along all or part of the capillary.

Two opposing forces control the movement of fluid between the capillaries and the surrounding tissues: Blood pressure tends to drive fluid out of the capillaries, and the presence of blood proteins tends to pull fluid back **(Figure 42.14)**. Many blood proteins (and all blood cells) are too large to pass readily through the endothelium, and they remain in the capillaries. These dissolved proteins are responsible for much of the blood's *osmotic pressure* (the pressure produced by the difference in solute concentration across a membrane). The difference in osmotic pressure between the blood and the interstitial fluid opposes fluid movement out of the capillaries. On average, blood pressure is greater than the opposing forces, leading to a net loss of fluid from capillaries. The net loss is generally greatest at the arterial end of these vessels, where blood pressure is highest.

Fluid Return by the Lymphatic System

The adult human body each day loses approximately 4–8 L of fluid from capillaries to the surrounding tissues. There is also some leakage of blood proteins, even though the capillary wall is not very permeable to large molecules. The lost fluid and proteins return to the blood via the **lymphatic system**, which includes a network of tiny vessels intermingled among capillaries of the cardiovascular system, as well as larger vessels into which small vessels empty.

After entering the lymphatic system by diffusion, the fluid lost by capillaries is called **lymph**; its composition is about the same as that of interstitial fluid. The lymphatic system drains into large veins of the cardiovascular system at the base of the neck (see Figure 43.7). This joining of the lymphatic and cardiovascular systems enables lipids to be transferred from the small intestine to the blood (see Chapter 41).

The movement of lymph from peripheral tissues to the heart relies on much the same mechanisms that assist blood

▶ **Figure 42.15 Human lymph nodes and vessels.** In this colorized X-ray image of the groin, lymph nodes and vessels are visible next to the upper thigh bone (femur).

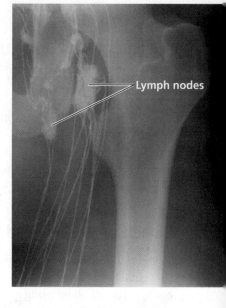

Lymph nodes

flow in veins. Lymph vessels, like veins, have valves that prevent the backflow of fluid. Rhythmic contractions of the vessel walls help draw fluid into the small lymphatic vessels. In addition, skeletal muscle contractions play a role in moving lymph.

Disruptions in lymph flow often result in fluid accumulation, or edema, in affected tissues. In some circumstances, the consequence is more severe. For example, certain species of parasitic worms that lodge in lymph vessels and thereby block lymph movement cause elephantiasis, a condition marked by extreme swelling in limbs or other body parts.

Along a lymph vessel are small, lymph-filtering organs called **lymph nodes**, which play an important role in the body's defense **(Figure 42.15)**. Inside each lymph node is a honeycomb of connective tissue with spaces filled by white blood cells, which function in defense. When the body is fighting an infection, the white blood cells multiply rapidly, and the lymph nodes become swollen and tender. This is why your doctor may check for swollen lymph nodes in your neck, armpits, or groin when you feel sick. Because lymph nodes also trap circulating cancer cells, doctors may examine the lymph nodes of cancer patients to detect the spread of the disease.

In recent years, evidence has surfaced demonstrating that the lymphatic system also plays a role in harmful immune responses, such as those responsible for asthma. Because of these and other findings, the lymphatic system, largely ignored until the 1990s, has become a very active and promising area of biomedical research.

CONCEPT CHECK 42.3

1. What is the primary cause of the low velocity of blood flow in capillaries?

2. What short-term changes in cardiovascular function might best enable skeletal muscles to help an animal escape from a dangerous situation?

3. **WHAT IF?** If you had additional hearts distributed throughout your body, what would be one likely advantage and one likely disadvantage?

For suggested answers, see Appendix A.

Blood components function in exchange, transport, and defense

As you read in Concept 42.1, the fluid transported by an open circulatory system is continuous with the fluid that surrounds all of the body cells and therefore has the same composition. In contrast, the fluid in a closed circulatory system can be much more highly specialized, as is the case for the blood of vertebrates.

Blood Composition and Function

Vertebrate blood is a connective tissue consisting of cells suspended in a liquid matrix called **plasma**. Separating the components of blood using a centrifuge reveals that cellular elements (cells and cell fragments) occupy about 45% of the volume of blood **(Figure 42.16)**. The remainder is plasma. Dissolved in the plasma are ions and proteins that, together with the blood cells, function in osmotic regulation, transport, and defense.

Plasma

Among the many solutes in plasma are inorganic salts in the form of dissolved ions, sometimes referred to as blood electrolytes (see Figure 42.16). The dissolved ions are an essential component of the blood. Some of these ions buffer the blood, which in humans normally has a pH of 7.4. Ions are also important in maintaining the osmotic balance of the blood. In addition, the concentration of ions in plasma directly affects the composition of the interstitial fluid, where many of these ions have a vital role in muscle and nerve activity. Serving all of these functions necessitates keeping plasma electrolytes within narrow concentration ranges (a homeostatic function we'll explore in Chapter 44).

Plasma proteins, including albumins, act as buffers against pH changes and help maintain the osmotic balance between blood and interstitial fluid. Certain plasma proteins have additional functions. Immunoglobulins, or antibodies, combat viruses and other foreign agents that invade the body (see Figure 43.10). Apolipoproteins escort lipids, which are insoluble in water and can travel in blood only when bound to proteins. Plasma also contains fibrinogens, which are clotting factors that help plug leaks when blood vessels are injured. (The term *serum* refers to blood plasma from which these clotting factors have been removed.)

Plasma also contains a wide variety of other substances in transit from one part of the body to another, including

Plasma 55%	
Constituent	**Major functions**
Water	Solvent
Ions (blood electrolytes) Sodium Potassium Calcium Magnesium Chloride Bicarbonate	Osmotic balance, pH buffering, and regulation of membrane permeability
Plasma proteins Albumin	Osmotic balance, pH buffering
Immunoglobulins (antibodies)	Defense
Apolipoproteins	Lipid transport
Fibrinogen	Clotting
Substances transported by blood Nutrients (such as glucose, fatty acids, vitamins) Waste products of metabolism Respiratory gases (O_2 and CO_2) Hormones	

Separated blood elements

Cellular elements 45%		
Cell type	**Number per µL (mm³) of blood**	**Functions**
Leukocytes (white blood cells) Basophils Lymphocytes Eosinophils Neutrophils Monocytes	5,000–10,000	Defense and immunity
Platelets	250,000–400,000	Blood clotting
Erythrocytes (red blood cells)	5,000,000–6,000,000	Transport of O_2 and some CO_2

▲ **Figure 42.16 The composition of mammalian blood.**

nutrients, metabolic wastes, respiratory gases, and hormones. Plasma has a much higher protein concentration than interstitial fluid, although the two fluids are otherwise similar. (Capillary walls, remember, are not very permeable to proteins.)

Cellular Elements

Blood contains two classes of cells: red blood cells, which transport O_2, and white blood cells, which function in defense (see Figure 42.16). Also suspended in blood plasma are **platelets**, cell fragments that are involved in the clotting process.

Erythrocytes Red blood cells, or **erythrocytes**, are by far the most numerous blood cells. Each microliter (μL, or mm^3) of human blood contains 5–6 million red cells, and there are about 25 trillion of these cells in the body's 5 L of blood. Their main function is O_2 transport, and their structure is closely related to this function. Human erythrocytes are small disks (7–8 μm in diameter) that are biconcave—thinner in the center than at the edges. This shape increases surface area, enhancing the rate of diffusion of O_2 across the plasma membrane. Mature mammalian erythrocytes lack nuclei. This unusual characteristic leaves more space in these tiny cells for **hemoglobin**, the iron-containing protein that transports O_2 (see Figure 5.18). Erythrocytes also lack mitochondria and generate their ATP exclusively by anaerobic metabolism. Oxygen transport would be less efficient if erythrocytes were aerobic and consumed some of the O_2 they carry.

Despite its small size, an erythrocyte contains about 250 million molecules of hemoglobin (Hb). Because each molecule of hemoglobin binds up to four molecules of O_2, one erythrocyte can transport about 1 billion O_2 molecules. As erythrocytes pass through the capillary beds of lungs, gills, or other respiratory organs, O_2 diffuses into the erythrocytes and binds to hemoglobin. In the systemic capillaries, O_2 dissociates from hemoglobin and diffuses into body cells.

In **sickle-cell disease**, an abnormal form of hemoglobin (Hb^S) polymerizes into aggregates. Because the concentration of hemoglobin in erythrocytes is so high, these aggregates are large enough to distort the erythrocyte into an elongated, curved shape that resembles a sickle. This abnormality results from an alteration in the amino acid sequence of hemoglobin at a single position (see Figure 5.19).

Sickle-cell disease significantly impairs the function of the circulatory system. Sickled cells often lodge in arterioles and capillaries, preventing delivery of O_2 and nutrients and removal of CO_2 and wastes. Blood vessel blockage and resulting organ swelling often result in severe pain. In addition, sickled cells frequently rupture, reducing the number of red blood cells available for transporting O_2. The average life span of a sickled erythrocyte is only 20 days—one-sixth

that of a normal erythrocyte. The rate of erythrocyte loss outstrips their production rate. Short-term therapy includes replacement of erythrocytes by blood transfusion; long-term treatments are generally aimed at inhibiting aggregation of Hb^S.

Leukocytes The blood contains five major types of white blood cells, or **leukocytes**. Their function is to fight infections. Some are phagocytic, engulfing and digesting microorganisms as well as debris from the body's own dead cells. Other leukocytes, called lymphocytes, develop into B cells and T cells that mount immune responses against foreign substances (as we'll discuss in Concepts 43.2 and 43.3). Normally, 1 μL of human blood contains about 5,000–10,000 leukocytes; their numbers increase temporarily whenever the body is fighting an infection. Unlike erythrocytes, leukocytes are also found outside the circulatory system, patrolling both interstitial fluid and the lymphatic system.

Platelets Platelets are pinched-off cytoplasmic fragments of specialized bone marrow cells. They are about 2–3 μm in diameter and have no nuclei. Platelets serve both structural and molecular functions in blood clotting.

Stem Cells and the Replacement of Cellular Elements

Erythrocytes, leukocytes, and platelets all develop from a common source: multipotent **stem cells** that are dedicated to replenishing the body's blood cell populations **(Figure 42.17)**.

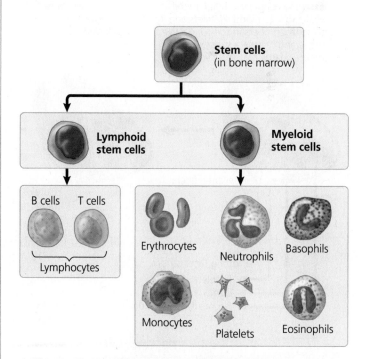

▲ **Figure 42.17 Differentiation of blood cells.** Multipotent stem cells in bone marrow give rise to two specialized sets of stem cells. One set, the lymphoid stem cells, produces B and T cells (lymphocytes), which function in immunity (see Figures 43.9 and 43.11). The other set, the myeloid stem cells, produces all other blood cells, as well as platelets.

The stem cells that produce blood cells are located in the red marrow inside bones, particularly the ribs, vertebrae, sternum, and pelvis. Multipotent stem cells are so named because they have the ability to form multiple types of cells—in this case, the myeloid and lymphoid cell lineages. When a stem cell divides, one daughter cell remains a stem cell while the other takes on a specialized function.

Throughout a person's life, stem cells replace the worn-out cellular elements of blood. Erythrocytes are the shortest-lived, circulating for only 120 days on average before being replaced. A negative-feedback mechanism, sensitive to the amount of O_2 reaching the body's tissues via the blood, controls erythrocyte production. If the tissues do not receive enough O_2, the kidneys synthesize and secrete a hormone called **erythropoietin (EPO)** that stimulates the generation of more erythrocytes. If the blood is delivering more O_2 than the tissues can use, the level of EPO falls and erythrocyte production slows.

Recombinant DNA technology is now used to synthesize EPO in cultured cells. Physicians use recombinant EPO to treat people with health problems such as *anemia*, a condition of lower-than-normal erythrocyte or hemoglobin levels that lowers the oxygen-carrying capacity of the blood. Some athletes inject themselves with EPO to increase their erythrocyte levels, although this practice, a form of blood doping, has been banned by major sports organizations. In recent years, a number of well-known runners and cyclists have been found to have used EPO-related drugs and have forfeited both their records and their right to participate in future competitions.

Blood Clotting

The occasional cut or scrape is not life-threatening because blood components seal the broken blood vessels. A break in a blood vessel wall exposes proteins that attract platelets and initiate coagulation, the conversion of liquid components of blood to a solid clot. The coagulant, or sealant, circulates in an inactive form called fibrinogen. In response to a broken blood vessel, platelets release clotting factors that trigger reactions leading to the formation of thrombin, an enzyme that converts fibrinogen to fibrin. Newly formed fibrin aggregates into threads that form the framework of the clot. Thrombin also activates a factor that catalyzes the formation of more thrombin, driving clotting to completion through positive feedback (see Chapter 40). The steps in the production of a blood clot are diagrammed in **Figure 42.18**. Any genetic mutation that blocks a step in the clotting

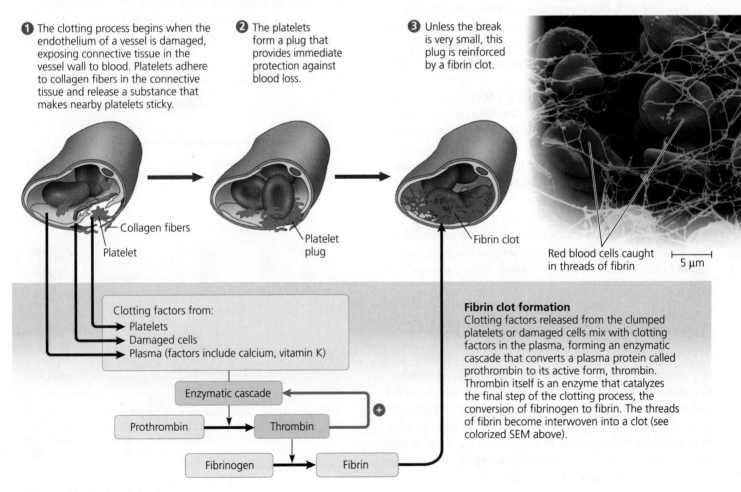

❶ The clotting process begins when the endothelium of a vessel is damaged, exposing connective tissue in the vessel wall to blood. Platelets adhere to collagen fibers in the connective tissue and release a substance that makes nearby platelets sticky.

❷ The platelets form a plug that provides immediate protection against blood loss.

❸ Unless the break is very small, this plug is reinforced by a fibrin clot.

Collagen fibers

Platelet

Platelet plug

Fibrin clot

Red blood cells caught in threads of fibrin

5 μm

Clotting factors from:
- Platelets
- Damaged cells
- Plasma (factors include calcium, vitamin K)

Enzymatic cascade

Prothrombin → Thrombin

Fibrinogen → Fibrin

Fibrin clot formation
Clotting factors released from the clumped platelets or damaged cells mix with clotting factors in the plasma, forming an enzymatic cascade that converts a plasma protein called prothrombin to its active form, thrombin. Thrombin itself is an enzyme that catalyzes the final step of the clotting process, the conversion of fibrinogen to fibrin. The threads of fibrin become interwoven into a clot (see colorized SEM above).

▲ **Figure 42.18 Blood clotting.**

process can cause hemophilia, a disease characterized by excessive bleeding and bruising from even minor cuts and bumps (see Chapter 15).

Anticlotting factors in the blood normally prevent spontaneous clotting in the absence of injury. Sometimes, however, clots form within a blood vessel, blocking the flow of blood. Such a clot is called a **thrombus** (plural, *thrombi*). We'll explore how thrombi form and the dangers that they pose shortly.

Cardiovascular Disease

Each year, cardiovascular diseases—disorders of the heart and blood vessels—kill more than 750,000 people in the United States. These diseases range from minor disturbances of vein or heart valve function to life-threatening disruptions of blood flow to the heart or brain.

Atherosclerosis, Heart Attacks, and Stroke

Healthy arteries have a smooth inner lining that reduces resistance to blood flow. However, damage or infection can roughen the lining and lead to **atherosclerosis**, the hardening of the arteries by accumulation of fatty deposits. A key player in the development of atherosclerosis is cholesterol, a steroid that is important for maintaining normal membrane fluidity in animal cells (see Chapter 7). Cholesterol travels in blood plasma mainly in particles that consist of thousands of cholesterol molecules and other lipids bound to a protein. One type of particle—**low-density lipoprotein (LDL)**—delivers cholesterol to cells for membrane production. Another type—**high-density lipoprotein (HDL)**—scavenges excess cholesterol for return to the liver. Individuals with a high ratio of LDL to HDL are at substantially increased risk for atherosclerosis.

In atherosclerosis, damage to the arterial lining results in *inflammation*, the body's reaction to injury. Leukocytes are attracted to the inflamed area and begin to take up lipids, including cholesterol. A fatty deposit, called a plaque, grows steadily, incorporating fibrous connective tissue and additional cholesterol. As the plaque grows, the walls of the artery become thick and stiff, and the obstruction of the artery increases. If the plaque ruptures, a thrombus can form in the artery **(Figure 42.19)**.

The result of untreated atherosclerosis is often a heart attack or a stroke. A **heart attack**, also called a *myocardial infarction*, is the damage or death of cardiac muscle tissue resulting from blockage of one or more coronary arteries, which supply oxygen-rich blood to the heart muscle. Because the coronary arteries are small in diameter, they are especially vulnerable to obstruction by atherosclerotic plaques or thrombi. Such blockage can destroy cardiac muscle quickly because the constantly beating heart muscle cannot survive long without O_2. If a large enough portion of the heart is affected, the heart will stop beating, and the victim will die

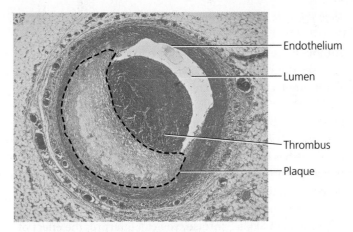

▲ **Figure 42.19 Atherosclerosis.** In atherosclerosis, thickening of an arterial wall by plaque formation can restrict blood flow through the artery. If a plaque ruptures, a thrombus can form, further restricting blood flow. Fragments of a ruptured plaque can also travel via the bloodstream and become lodged in other arteries. If the blockage is in an artery that supplies the heart or brain, the result could be a heart attack or stroke, respectively.

within a few minutes unless a heartbeat is restored by cardiopulmonary resuscitation (CPR) or some other emergency procedure. A **stroke** is the death of nervous tissue in the brain due to a lack of O_2. Strokes usually result from rupture or blockage of arteries in the head. The effects of a stroke and the individual's chance of survival depend on the extent and location of the damaged brain tissue. If a stroke results from arterial blockage by a thrombus, rapid administration of a clot-dissolving drug may help limit the damage.

Although atherosclerosis often isn't detected until critical blood flow is disrupted, there can be warning signs. Partial blockage of the coronary arteries may cause occasional chest pain, a condition known as angina pectoris. The pain is most likely to be felt when the heart is laboring under stress, and it signals that part of the heart is not receiving enough O_2. An obstructed artery may be treated surgically, either by inserting a mesh tube called a stent to expand the artery **(Figure 42.20)** or by transplanting a healthy blood vessel from the chest or a limb to bypass the blockage.

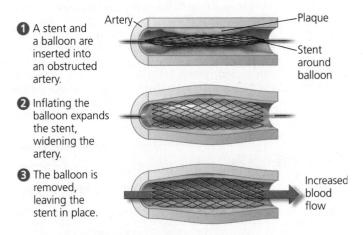

❶ A stent and a balloon are inserted into an obstructed artery.

❷ Inflating the balloon expands the stent, widening the artery.

❸ The balloon is removed, leaving the stent in place.

Artery — Plaque — Stent around balloon

Increased blood flow

▲ **Figure 42.20 Inserting a stent to widen an obstructed artery.**

Risk Factors and Treatment of Cardiovascular Disease

Although the tendency to develop particular cardiovascular diseases is inherited, it is also strongly influenced by lifestyle. For example, exercise decreases the LDL/HDL ratio, reducing the risk of cardiovascular disease. In contrast, smoking and consumption of certain processed vegetable oils called *trans fats* (see Chapter 5) increase the LDL/HDL ratio.

There has been considerable progress in the last decade in preventing cardiovascular disease. For many individuals at high risk, treatment with drugs called statins can lower LDL levels and thereby reduce the risk of heart attacks In the Scientific Skills Exercise, you can interpret the effect of a genetic mutation on blood LDL levels.

The recognition that inflammation plays a central role in atherosclerosis and thrombus formation is also influencing the treatment of cardiovascular disease. For example, aspirin, which inhibits the inflammatory response, has been found to help prevent the recurrence of heart attacks and stroke. Researchers have also focused on C-reactive protein (CRP), which is produced by the liver and found in the blood during episodes of acute inflammation. Like a high level of LDL cholesterol, the presence of significant amounts of CRP in blood is a useful risk indicator for cardiovascular disease.

Hypertension (high blood pressure) is yet another contributor to heart attack and stroke. According to one hypothesis, chronic high blood pressure damages the endothelium that lines the arteries, promoting plaque formation. The usual definition of hypertension in adults is a systolic pressure above 140 mm Hg or a diastolic pressure above 90 mm Hg. Fortunately, hypertension is simple to diagnose and can usually be controlled by dietary changes, exercise, medication, or a combination of these approaches.

SCIENTIFIC SKILLS EXERCISE

Making and Interpreting Histograms

Does Inactivating the PCSK9 Enzyme Lower LDL Levels?
Researchers interested in genetic factors affecting susceptibility to cardiovascular disease examined the DNA of 15,000 individuals. They found that 3% of the individuals had a mutation that inactivates one copy of the gene for PCSK9, a liver enzyme. Because mutations that *increase* the activity of PCSK9 are known to *increase* levels of LDL cholesterol in the blood, the researchers hypothesized that *inactivating* mutations in this gene would *lower* LDL levels. In this exercise, you will interpret the results of an experiment they carried out to test this hypothesis.

How the Experiment Was Done Researchers measured LDL cholesterol levels in blood plasma from 85 individuals with one copy of the *PCSK9* gene inactivated (the study group) and from 3,278 individuals with two functional copies of the gene (the control group).

Data from the Experiment
The plasma LDL cholesterol levels for the control group and study group are shown in the table at the bottom.

Interpret the Data
1. Graphing often facilitates data interpretation. For this exercise, graph the data in each row of the table as a *histogram* (a type of bar graph). Label the *y*-axis as *Percent of Individuals* and the *x*-axis as *Plasma LDL cholesterol (mg/dl)*. Divide the *x*-axis into twelve equal divisions, one for each range of values (0–25, 26–50, etc). Moving along the *x*-axis, draw a series of twelve vertical bars, with the height of each bar indicating the percentage of samples that fall into the specified range. Note that some bars will be of zero height, such as for a plasma LDL cholesterol level in the 0–25 mg/dL (milligram/deciliter) range. Add the percentages for the relevant bars to calculate the percentage of individuals in the study and control groups that had an LDL cholesterol level of 100 mg/dL or less. (For additional information

about histograms, see the Scientific Skills Review in Appendix F and the Study Area in MasteringBiology.)

2. Comparing the two histograms you drew, do you find support for the researchers' hypothesis? Explain.

3. What if instead of graphing the data you had compared the range of concentrations for plasma LDL cholesterol (low to high) in the control and study groups? How would the conclusions you could draw have differed?

4. Propose an explanation for the fact that the two histograms overlap as much as they do.

5. Consider two individuals with a plasma LDL cholesterol level of 160 mg/dL, one from the study group and one from the control group. What do you predict regarding their relative risk of developing cardiovascular disease? Explain how you arrived at your prediction. What role did the histograms play in helping you make your prediction?

(MB) A version of this Scientific Skills Exercise can be assigned in MasteringBiology.

Data from J. C. Cohen et al., Sequence variations in *PCSK9*, low LDL, and protection against coronary heart disease, *New England Journal of Medicine* 354:1264–1272 (2006).

Plasma LDL Cholesterol (milligrams/deciliter)

	0–25	26–50	51–75	76–100	101–125	126–150	151–175	176–200	201–225	226–250	251–275	276–300
Control Group	0%	1%	4%	13%	23%	23%	18%	10%	5%	2%	1%	0%
Study Group	0%	4%	31%	23%	21%	13%	2%	1%	2%	0%	2%	0%

1. Explain why a physician might order a white cell count for a patient with symptoms of an infection.

2. Clots in arteries can cause heart attacks and strokes. Why, then, does it make sense to treat people with hemophilia by introducing clotting factors into their blood?

3. **WHAT IF?** Nitroglycerin (the key ingredient in dynamite) is sometimes prescribed for heart disease patients. Within the body, the nitroglycerin is converted to nitric oxide. Why would you expect nitroglycerin to relieve chest pain in these patients?

4. **MAKE CONNECTIONS** The allele that encodes Hb^S is codominant with the allele encoding normal hemoglobin (Hb) (see Concept 14.4). What can you deduce about the properties of Hb and Hb^S with regard to aggregate formation and sickling?

5. **MAKE CONNECTIONS** How do stem cells from the bone marrow of an adult differ from embryonic stem cells (see Concept 20.3)?

For suggested answers, see Appendix A.

CONCEPT 42.5

Gas exchange occurs across specialized respiratory surfaces

In the remainder of this chapter, we will focus on the process of **gas exchange**. Although this process is often called respiratory exchange or respiration, it should not be confused with the energy transformations of cellular respiration. Gas exchange is the uptake of molecular O_2 from the environment and the discharge of CO_2 to the environment.

Partial Pressure Gradients in Gas Exchange

To understand the driving forces for gas exchange, we must consider **partial pressure**, which is simply the pressure exerted by a particular gas in a mixture of gases. Once we know partial pressures, we can predict the net movement of a gas at an exchange surface: A gas always undergoes net diffusion from a region of higher partial pressure to a region of lower partial pressure.

To calculate partial pressures, we need to know the pressure that a gas mixture exerts and the fraction of the mixture represented by a particular gas. Let's consider O_2 as an example. At sea level, the atmosphere exerts a downward force equal to that of a column of mercury (Hg) 760 mm high. Atmospheric pressure at sea level is thus 760 mm Hg. Since the atmosphere is 21% O_2 by volume, the partial pressure of O_2 is 0.21×760, or about 160 mm Hg. This value is called the *partial pressure* of O_2 (abbreviated P_{O_2}) because it is the part of atmospheric pressure contributed by O_2. The partial pressure of CO_2 (abbreviated P_{CO_2}) is much less, only 0.29 mm Hg at sea level.

Table 42.1 Comparing Air and Water as Respiratory Media

	Air (Sea Level)	Water (20°C)	Air to Water Ratio
O_2 Partial Pressure	160 mm	160 mm	1 : 1
O_2 Concentration	210 ml/L	7 ml/L	30 : 1
Density	0.0013 kg/L	1 kg/L	1 : 770
Viscosity	0.02 cP	1 cP	1 : 50

Partial pressures also apply to gases dissolved in a liquid, such as water. When water is exposed to air, an equilibrium is reached in which the partial pressure of each gas in the water equals the partial pressure of that gas in the air. Thus, water exposed to air at sea level has a P_{O_2} of 160 mm Hg, the same as in the atmosphere. However, O_2 is much less soluble in water than in air. As a result, air contains much more O_2 than water at the same P_{O_2} **(Table 42.1)**.

Respiratory Media

The conditions for gas exchange vary considerably, depending on whether the respiratory medium—the source of O_2—is air or water. As already noted, O_2 is plentiful in air, making up about 21% of Earth's atmosphere by volume. As shown in Table 42.1, air is much less dense and less viscous than water, so it is easier to move and to force through small passageways. As a result, breathing air is relatively easy and need not be particularly efficient. Humans, for example, extract only about 25% of the O_2 in inhaled air.

Gas exchange with water as the respiratory medium is much more demanding. The amount of O_2 dissolved in a given volume of water varies but is always less than in an equivalent volume of air: Water in many freshwater habitats contains only about 7 mL of dissolved O_2 per liter, a concentration roughly 30 times less than in air. Furthermore, the warmer and saltier the water is, the less dissolved O_2 it can hold. Water's lower O_2 content, greater density, and greater viscosity mean that aquatic animals such as fishes and lobsters must expend considerable energy to carry out gas exchange. In the context of these challenges, adaptations have evolved that enable most aquatic animals to be very efficient in gas exchange. Many of these adaptations involve the organization of the surfaces dedicated to exchange.

Respiratory Surfaces

Specialization for gas exchange is apparent in the structure of the respiratory surface, the part of an animal's body where gas exchange occurs. Like all living cells, the cells that carry out gas exchange have a plasma membrane that must be in contact with an aqueous solution. Respiratory surfaces are therefore always moist.

The movement of O_2 and CO_2 across respiratory surfaces takes place by diffusion. The rate of diffusion is proportional to the surface area across which it occurs and inversely proportional to the square of the distance through which molecules must move. In other words, gas exchange is fast when the area for diffusion is large and the path for diffusion is short. As a result, respiratory surfaces tend to be large and thin.

In some relatively simple animals, such as sponges, cnidarians, and flatworms, every cell in the body is close enough to the external environment that gases can diffuse quickly between any cell and the environment. In many animals, however, the bulk of the body's cells lack immediate access to the environment. The respiratory surface in these animals is a thin, moist epithelium that constitutes a respiratory organ.

In some animals, including earthworms and some amphibians, the skin serves as a respiratory organ. A dense network of capillaries just below the skin facilitates the exchange of gases between the circulatory system and the environment. For most animals, however, the general body surface lacks sufficient area to exchange gases for the whole organism. The evolutionary solution to this limitation is a respiratory organ that is extensively folded or branched, thereby enlarging the available surface area for gas exchange. Gills, tracheae, and lungs are three such organs.

Gills in Aquatic Animals

Gills are outfoldings of the body surface that are suspended in the water. As illustrated in **Figure 42.21**, the distribution of gills over the body can vary considerably. Regardless of

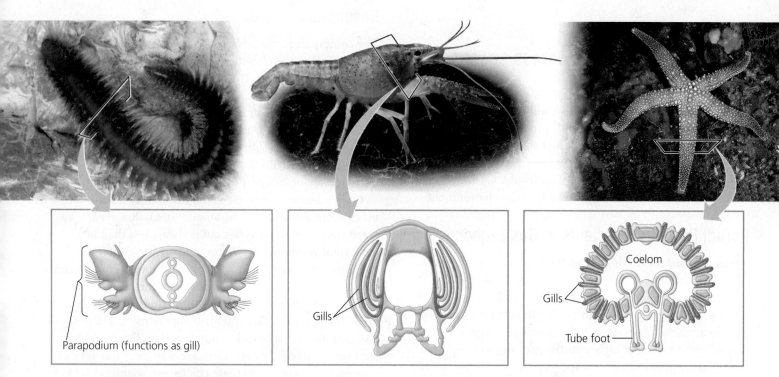

(a) Marine worm. Many polychaetes (marine worms of the phylum Annelida) have a pair of flattened appendages called parapodia on each body segment. The parapodia serve as gills and also function in crawling and swimming.

(b) Crayfish. Crayfish and other crustaceans have long, feathery gills covered by the exoskeleton. Specialized body appendages drive water over the gill surfaces.

(c) Sea star. The gills of a sea star are simple tubular projections of the skin. The hollow core of each gill is an extension of the coelom (body cavity). Gas exchange occurs by diffusion across the gill surfaces, and fluid in the coelom circulates in and out of the gills, aiding gas transport. The tube feet surfaces also function in gas exchange.

▲ **Figure 42.21 Diversity in the structure of gills, external body surfaces that function in gas exchange.**

MAKE CONNECTIONS *Animals with bilateral symmetry are divided into three main lineages (see Figure 32.11). What are those lineages? How many are represented by the animals shown above?*

their distribution, gills often have a total surface area much greater than that of the rest of the body's exterior.

Movement of the respiratory medium over the respiratory surface, a process called **ventilation**, maintains the partial pressure gradients of O_2 and CO_2 across the gill that are necessary for gas exchange. To promote ventilation, most gill-bearing animals either move their gills through the water or move water over their gills. For example, crayfish and lobsters have paddle-like appendages that drive a current of water over the gills, whereas mussels and clams move water with cilia. Octopuses and squids ventilate their gills by taking in and ejecting water, with the side benefit of locomotion by jet propulsion. Fishes use the motion of swimming or coordinated movements of the mouth and gill covers to ventilate their gills. In both cases, a current of water enters the mouth of the fish, passes through slits in the pharynx, flows over the gills, and then exits the body **(Figure 42.22)**.

In fishes, the efficiency of gas exchange is maximized by **countercurrent exchange**, the exchange of a substance or heat between two fluids flowing in opposite directions. In a fish gill, the two fluids are blood and water. Because blood flows in the direction opposite to that of water passing over the gills, at each point in its travel blood is less saturated with O_2 than the water it meets (see Figure 42.22). As blood enters a gill capillary, it encounters water that is completing its passage through the gill. Depleted of much of its dissolved O_2, this water nevertheless has a higher P_{O_2} than the incoming blood, and O_2 transfer takes place. As the blood continues its passage, its P_{O_2} steadily increases, but so does that of the water it encounters, since each successive position in the blood's travel corresponds to an earlier position in the water's passage over the gills. Thus, a partial pressure gradient favoring the diffusion of O_2 from water to blood exists along the entire length of the capillary.

Countercurrent exchange mechanisms are remarkably efficient. In the fish gill, more than 80% of the O_2 dissolved in the water is removed as the water passes over the respiratory surface. In other settings, countercurrent exchange contributes to temperature regulation (see Chapter 40) and to the functioning of the mammalian kidney (see Chapter 44).

Tracheal Systems in Insects

In most terrestrial animals, respiratory surfaces are enclosed within the body, exposed to the atmosphere only through narrow tubes. Although the most familiar example of such an arrangement is the lung, the most common is the insect **tracheal system**, a network of air tubes that branch throughout the body. The largest tubes, called tracheae, open to the outside. The finest branches extend close to the surface of nearly every cell, where gas is exchanged by diffusion across the moist epithelium that lines the tips of the tracheal branches. Because the tracheal system brings air within a very short distance of virtually every body cell in an

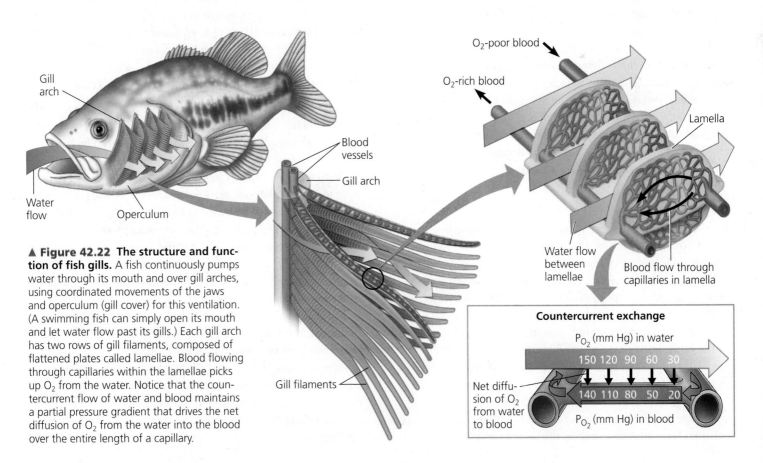

▲ **Figure 42.22 The structure and function of fish gills.** A fish continuously pumps water through its mouth and over gill arches, using coordinated movements of the jaws and operculum (gill cover) for this ventilation. (A swimming fish can simply open its mouth and let water flow past its gills.) Each gill arch has two rows of gill filaments, composed of flattened plates called lamellae. Blood flowing through capillaries within the lamellae picks up O_2 from the water. Notice that the countercurrent flow of water and blood maintains a partial pressure gradient that drives the net diffusion of O_2 from the water into the blood over the entire length of a capillary.

(a) The respiratory system of an insect consists of branched internal tubes. The largest tubes, called tracheae, connect to external openings spaced along the insect's body surface. Air sacs formed from enlarged portions of the tracheae are found near organs that require a large supply of oxygen.

(b) Rings of chitin keep the tracheae open, allowing air to enter and pass into smaller tubes called tracheoles. The branched tracheoles deliver air directly to cells throughout the body. Tracheoles have closed ends filled with fluid (blue-gray). When the animal is active and using more O_2, most of the fluid is withdrawn into the body. This increases the surface area of air-filled tracheoles in contact with cells.

(c) The TEM above shows cross sections of tracheoles in a tiny piece of insect flight muscle. Each of the numerous mitochondria in the muscle cells lies within about 5 μm of a tracheole.

▲ **Figure 42.23 A tracheal system.**

insect, it can transport O_2 and CO_2 without the participation of the animal's open circulatory system.

For small insects, diffusion through the tracheae brings in enough O_2 and removes enough CO_2 to support cellular respiration. Larger insects meet their higher energy demands by ventilating their tracheal systems with rhythmic body movements that compress and expand the air tubes like bellows. For example, consider an insect in flight, which has a very high metabolic rate, consuming 10 to 200 times more O_2 than it does at rest. In many flying insects, alternating contraction and relaxation of the flight muscles pump air rapidly through the tracheal system. The flight muscle cells are packed with mitochondria that support the high metabolic rate, and the tracheal tubes supply these ATP-generating organelles with ample O_2. Thus, adaptations of tracheal systems are directly related to bioenergetics **(Figure 42.23)**.

Lungs

Unlike tracheal systems, which branch throughout the insect body, **lungs** are localized respiratory organs. Representing an infolding of the body surface, they are typically subdivided into numerous pockets. Because the respiratory surface of a lung is not in direct contact with all other parts of the body, the gap must be bridged by the circulatory system, which transports gases between the lungs and the rest of the body. Lungs have evolved in organisms with open circulatory systems, such as spiders and land snails, as well as in vertebrates.

Among vertebrates that lack gills, the use of lungs for gas exchange varies. Amphibians rely heavily on diffusion across external body surfaces, such as the skin, to carry out gas

exchange; lungs, if present, are relatively small. In contrast, most reptiles (including all birds) and all mammals depend entirely on lungs for gas exchange. Turtles are an exception; they supplement lung breathing with gas exchange across moist epithelial surfaces continuous with their mouth or anus. Lungs and air breathing have evolved in a few aquatic vertebrates as adaptations to living in oxygen-poor water or to spending part of their time exposed to air (for instance, when the water level of a pond recedes).

Mammalian Respiratory Systems: A Closer Look

In mammals, a system of branching ducts conveys air to the lungs, which are located in the thoracic cavity **(Figure 42.24)**. Air enters through the nostrils and is then filtered by hairs, warmed, humidified, and sampled for odors as it flows through a maze of spaces in the nasal cavity. The nasal cavity leads to the pharynx, an intersection where the paths for air and food cross. When food is swallowed, the **larynx** (the upper part of the respiratory tract) moves upward and tips the epiglottis over the glottis, which is the opening of the **trachea**, or windpipe. This allows food to go down the esophagus to the stomach (see Figure 41.10). The rest of the time, the glottis is open, enabling breathing.

From the larynx, air passes into the trachea. The cartilage that reinforces the walls of both the larynx and the trachea keeps this part of the airway open. Within the larynx of most mammals, the exhaled air rushes by a pair of elastic bands of muscle called vocal folds, or, in humans, vocal cords. Sounds are produced when muscles in the larynx are tensed, stretching the cords so that they vibrate. High-pitched sounds result from tightly stretched cords vibrating rapidly; low-pitched sounds come from looser cords vibrating slowly.

The trachea branches into two **bronchi** (singular, *bronchus*), one leading to each lung. Within the lung, the bronchi branch repeatedly into finer and finer tubes called **bronchioles**. The entire system of air ducts has the appearance of an inverted tree, the trunk being the trachea. The epithelium lining the major branches of this respiratory tree is covered by cilia and a thin film of mucus. The mucus traps dust, pollen, and other particulate contaminants, and the beating cilia move the mucus upward to the pharynx, where it can be swallowed into the esophagus. This process, sometimes referred to as the "mucus escalator," plays a crucial role in cleansing the respiratory system.

Gas exchange in mammals occurs in **alveoli** (singular, *alveolus*; see Figure 42.24), air sacs clustered at the tips of the tiniest bronchioles. Human lungs contain millions of alveoli, which together have a surface area of about 100 m²—50 times that of the skin. Oxygen in the air entering the alveoli dissolves in the moist film lining their inner surfaces and rapidly diffuses across the epithelium into a web of capillaries that surrounds each alveolus. Net diffusion of carbon dioxide occurs in the opposite direction, from the capillaries across the epithelium of the alveolus and into the air space.

Lacking cilia or significant air currents to remove particles from their surface, alveoli are highly susceptible to contamination. White blood cells patrol the alveoli, engulfing foreign particles. However, if too much particulate matter reaches the alveoli, the defenses can be overwhelmed, leading to inflammation and irreversible damage. For example, particulates from cigarette smoke that enter alveoli can cause a permanent reduction in lung capacity. For coal miners, inhalation of large amounts of coal dust can lead to silicosis, a disabling, irreversible, and sometimes fatal lung disease.

The film of liquid that lines alveoli is subject to surface tension, an attractive force that has the effect of minimizing a liquid's surface area (see Chapter 3). Given their tiny diameter (about 0.25 mm), why don't alveoli collapse under high surface tension? It turns out that alveoli produce a mixture of phospholipids and proteins called **surfactant**, for *surf*ace-*act*ive agent, which coats the alveoli and reduces surface tension.

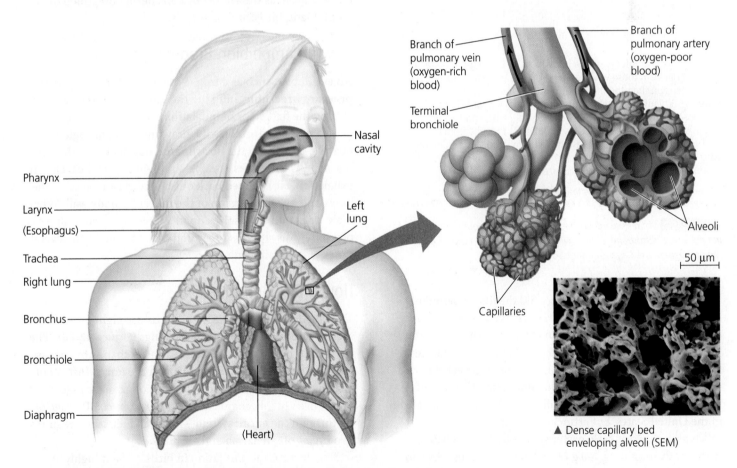

Pharynx

Larynx

(Esophagus)

Trachea

Right lung

Bronchus

Bronchiole

Diaphragm

(Heart)

Nasal cavity

Left lung

Branch of pulmonary vein (oxygen-rich blood)

Branch of pulmonary artery (oxygen-poor blood)

Terminal bronchiole

Alveoli

Capillaries

50 μm

▲ Dense capillary bed enveloping alveoli (SEM)

▲ **Figure 42.24 The mammalian respiratory system.** From the nasal cavity and pharynx, inhaled air passes through the larynx, trachea, and bronchi to the bronchioles, which end in microscopic alveoli lined by a thin, moist epithelium. Branches of the pulmonary arteries convey oxygen-poor blood to the alveoli; branches of the pulmonary veins transport oxygen-rich blood from the alveoli back to the heart.

What causes respiratory distress syndrome?

Experiment Mary Ellen Avery, a research fellow at Harvard University, hypothesized that a lack of surfactant caused respiratory distress syndrome (RDS) in preterm infants. To test this hypothesis, she obtained autopsy samples of lungs from infants who had died of RDS or from other causes. She extracted material from the samples and let it form a film on water. Avery then measured the tension (in dynes per centimeter) across the water surface and recorded the lowest surface tension observed for each sample.

Results Avery noted a pattern when she grouped the samples based on the body mass of the infant: less than 1,200 g (2.7 pounds) and 1,200 g or greater.

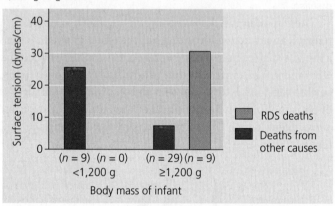

Conclusion For infants with a body mass of 1,200 g or greater, the material from those who had died of RDS exhibited much higher surface tension than the material from those who had died from other causes. Avery inferred that infants' lungs normally contain a surface-tension-reducing substance (now called surfactant) and that a lack of this substance was a likely cause of RDS. The results from infants with a body mass less than 1,200 g were similar to those from infants who had died from RDS, suggesting that surfactant is not normally produced until a fetus reaches this size.

Source: M. E. Avery and J. Mead, Surface properties in relation to atelectasis and hyaline membrane disease, *American Journal of Diseases of Children* 97:517–523 (1959).

WHAT IF? *If the researchers had measured the amount of surfactant in lung samples from the infants, what graph would you expect if the surfactant were plotted against infant body mass?*

In the 1950s, Mary Ellen Avery did the first experiment linking surfactant deficiency to *respiratory distress syndrome (RDS)*, a disease common in infants born 6 weeks or more before their due dates **(Figure 42.25)**. (The average full-term human pregnancy is 38 weeks.) Later studies revealed that surfactant typically appears in the lungs after 33 weeks of development. In the 1950s, RDS killed 10,000 infants annually in the United States, but artificial surfactants are now used successfully to treat early preterm infants. Treated babies with a body mass over 900 g (2 pounds) at birth usually survive without long-term health problems. For her contributions, Avery received the National Medal of Science in 1991.

Having surveyed the route that air follows when we breathe, we'll turn next to the process of breathing itself.

1. Why is the position of lung tissues *within* the body an advantage for terrestrial animals?
2. After a heavy rain, earthworms come to the surface. How would you explain this behavior in terms of an earthworm's requirements for gas exchange?
3. **MAKE CONNECTIONS** Describe the role of countercurrent exchange in facilitating both respiration and thermoregulation (see Concept 40.3).

For suggested answers, see Appendix A.

CONCEPT 42.6

Breathing ventilates the lungs

Like fishes, terrestrial vertebrates rely on ventilation to maintain high O_2 and low CO_2 concentrations at the gas exchange surface. The process that ventilates lungs is **breathing**, the alternating inhalation and exhalation of air. A variety of mechanisms for moving air in and out of lungs have evolved, as we will see by considering breathing in amphibians, birds, and mammals.

How an Amphibian Breathes

An amphibian such as a frog ventilates its lungs by **positive pressure breathing**, inflating the lungs with forced airflow. During the first stage of inhalation, muscles lower the floor of an amphibian's oral cavity, drawing in air through its nostrils. Next, with the nostrils and mouth closed, the floor of the oral cavity rises, forcing air down the trachea. During exhalation, air is forced back out by the elastic recoil of the lungs and by compression of the muscular body wall. When male frogs puff themselves up in aggressive or courtship displays, they disrupt this breathing cycle, taking in air several times without allowing any release.

How a Bird Breathes

To bring fresh air to their lungs, birds use eight or nine air sacs situated on either side of the lungs **(Figure 42.26)**. The air sacs do not function directly in gas exchange but act as bellows that keep air flowing through the lungs. Instead of alveoli, which are dead ends, the sites of gas exchange in bird lungs are tiny channels called *parabronchi*. Passage of air through the entire system—lungs and air sacs—requires two cycles of inhalation and exhalation.

Two features of ventilation in birds make it highly efficient. First, when birds breathe, they pass air over the gas exchange surface in only one direction. Second, incoming fresh air does not mix with air that has already carried out gas exchange.

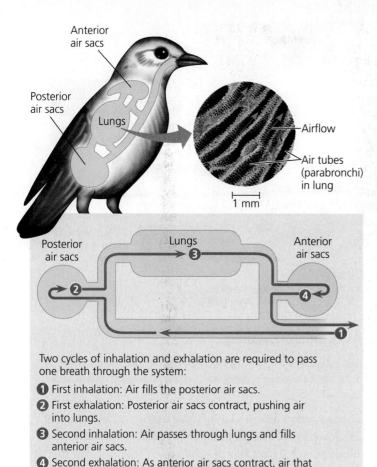

Two cycles of inhalation and exhalation are required to pass one breath through the system:

1 First inhalation: Air fills the posterior air sacs.

2 First exhalation: Posterior air sacs contract, pushing air into lungs.

3 Second inhalation: Air passes through lungs and fills anterior air sacs.

4 Second exhalation: As anterior air sacs contract, air that entered body at first inhalation is pushed out of body.

▲ **Figure 42.26 The avian respiratory system.** This diagram traces a breath of air through the respiratory system of a bird. As shown, two cycles of inhalation and exhalation are required for the air to pass all the way through the system and out of the bird.

How a Mammal Breathes

Unlike amphibians and birds, mammals employ **negative pressure breathing**—pulling, rather than pushing, air into their lungs **(Figure 42.27)**. Using muscle contraction to actively expand the thoracic cavity, mammals lower air pressure in their lungs below that of the air outside their body. Because gas flows from a region of higher pressure to a region of lower pressure, air rushes through the nostrils and mouth and down the breathing tubes to the alveoli. During exhalation, the muscles controlling the thoracic cavity relax, and the volume of the cavity is reduced. The increased air pressure in the alveoli forces air up the breathing tubes and out of the body. Thus, inhalation is always active and requires work, whereas exhalation is usually passive.

Expanding the thoracic cavity during inhalation involves the animal's rib muscles and the **diaphragm**, a sheet of skeletal muscle that forms the bottom wall of the cavity. Contracting one set of rib muscles expands the rib cage, the front wall of the thoracic cavity, by pulling the ribs upward and the sternum outward. At the same time, the diaphragm

contracts, expanding the thoracic cavity downward. The effect of the descending diaphragm is similar to that of a plunger being drawn out of a syringe.

Within the thoracic cavity, a double membrane surrounds the lungs. The inner layer of this membrane adheres to the outside of the lungs, and the outer layer adheres to the wall of the thoracic cavity. A thin space filled with fluid separates the two layers. Surface tension in the fluid causes the two layers to stick together like two plates of glass separated by a film of water: The layers can slide smoothly past each other, but they cannot be pulled apart easily. Consequently, the volume of the thoracic cavity and the volume of the lungs change in unison.

Depending on activity level, additional muscles may be recruited to aid breathing. The rib muscles and diaphragm are sufficient to change lung volume when a mammal is at rest. During exercise, other muscles of the neck, back, and chest increase the volume of the thoracic cavity by raising the rib cage. In kangaroos and some other mammals, locomotion causes a rhythmic movement of organs in the abdomen, including the stomach and liver. The result is a piston-like pumping motion that pushes and pulls on the diaphragm, further increasing the volume of air moved in and out of the lungs.

The volume of air inhaled and exhaled with each breath is called **tidal volume**. It averages about 500 mL in resting humans. The tidal volume during maximal inhalation and exhalation is the **vital capacity**, which is about 3.4 L and 4.8 L for college-age women and men, respectively. The air that remains after a forced exhalation is called the **residual volume**. With age, the lungs lose their resilience, and residual volume increases at the expense of vital capacity.

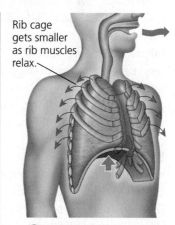

1 INHALATION: Diaphragm contracts (moves down).

2 EXHALATION: Diaphragm relaxes (moves up).

▲ **Figure 42.27 Negative pressure breathing.** A mammal breathes by changing the air pressure within its lungs relative to the pressure of the outside atmosphere.

WHAT IF? *The walls of alveoli contain elastic fibers that allow the alveoli to expand and contract with each breath. If the alveoli lost their elasticity, how would that affect gas exchange in the lungs?*

Because the lungs in mammals do not completely empty with each breath, and because inhalation occurs through the same airways as exhalation, each inhalation mixes fresh air with oxygen-depleted residual air. As a result, the maximum P_{O_2} in alveoli is always considerably less than in the atmosphere. The maximum P_{O_2} in lungs is also less for mammals than for birds, which have a unidirectional flow of air through the lungs. This is one reason mammals function less well than birds at high altitude. For example, humans have great difficulty obtaining enough O_2 when climbing at high elevations, such as those in the Himalayas. However, bar-headed geese and several other bird species easily fly through high Himalayan passes during their migrations.

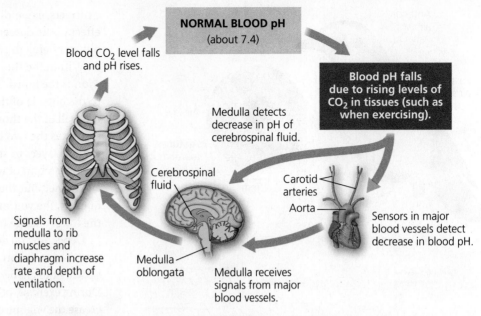

▲ Figure 42.28 Homeostatic control of breathing.

WHAT IF? *Suppose a person began breathing very rapidly while resting. Describe the effect on blood CO_2 levels and the steps by which the negative-feedback circuit would restore homeostasis.*

Control of Breathing in Humans

Although you can voluntarily hold your breath or breathe faster and deeper, most of the time your breathing is regulated by involuntary mechanisms. These control mechanisms ensure that gas exchange is coordinated with blood circulation and with metabolic demand.

The neurons mainly responsible for regulating breathing are in the medulla oblongata, near the base of the brain (**Figure 42.28**). Neural circuits in the medulla form a pair of *breathing control centers* that establish the breathing rhythm. When you breathe deeply, a negative-feedback mechanism prevents the lungs from overexpanding: During inhalation, sensors that detect stretching of the lung tissue send nerve impulses to the control circuits in the medulla, inhibiting further inhalation.

In regulating breathing, the medulla uses the pH of the surrounding tissue fluid as an indicator of blood CO_2 concentration. The reason pH can be used in this way is that blood CO_2 is the main determinant of the pH of cerebrospinal fluid, the fluid surrounding the brain and spinal cord. Carbon dioxide diffuses from the blood to the cerebrospinal fluid, where it reacts with water and forms carbonic acid (H_2CO_3). The H_2CO_3 can then dissociate into a bicarbonate ion (HCO_3^-) and a hydrogen ion (H^+):

$$CO_2 + H_2O \rightleftharpoons H_2CO_3 \rightleftharpoons HCO_3^- + H^+$$

Consider what happens if metabolic activity increases, such as occurs during exercise. Increased metabolism raises the concentration of CO_2 in the blood and cerebrospinal fluid. Through the reactions shown above, the higher CO_2 concentration leads to an increase in the concentration of H^+, lowering pH. Sensors in the medulla as well as in major blood vessels detect this pH change. In response, the medulla's control circuits increase the depth and rate of breathing (see Figure 42.28). Both remain high until the excess CO_2 is eliminated in exhaled air and pH returns to a normal value.

The blood O_2 level usually has little effect on the breathing control centers. However, when the O_2 level drops very low (at high altitudes, for instance), O_2 sensors in the aorta and the carotid arteries in the neck send signals to the breathing control centers, which respond by increasing the breathing rate. The regulation of breathing is modulated by additional neural circuits, primarily in the pons, a part of the brain next to the medulla.

Breathing control is effective only if ventilation is matched to blood flow through alveolar capillaries. During exercise, for instance, such coordination couples an increased breathing rate, which enhances O_2 uptake and CO_2 removal, with an increase in cardiac output.

CONCEPT CHECK 42.6

1. How does an increase in the CO_2 concentration in the blood affect the pH of cerebrospinal fluid?

2. A drop in blood pH causes an increase in heart rate. What is the function of this control mechanism?

3. **WHAT IF?** If an injury tore a small hole in the membranes surrounding your lungs, what effect on lung function would you expect?

For suggested answers, see Appendix A.

CONCEPT 42.7

Adaptations for gas exchange include pigments that bind and transport gases

The high metabolic demands of many animals necessitate the exchange of large quantities of O_2 and CO_2. Here we'll examine how blood molecules called respiratory pigments facilitate this exchange through their interaction with O_2 and CO_2. We'll also investigate physiological adaptations that enable animals to be active under conditions of high metabolic load or very limiting P_{O_2}. As a basis for exploring these topics, let's summarize the basic gas exchange circuit in humans.

Coordination of Circulation and Gas Exchange

The partial pressures of O_2 and CO_2 in the blood vary as the gases move between air, blood, and other body tissues, as shown in **Figure 42.29**. ❶ During inhalation, fresh air mixes with air remaining in the lungs. ❷ The resulting mixture formed in the alveoli has a higher P_{O_2} and a lower P_{CO_2} than the blood flowing through the alveolar capillaries. Consequently, there is a net diffusion of O_2 down its partial pressure gradient from the air in the alveoli to the blood. Meanwhile, CO_2 in the blood undergoes net diffusion into the air in the alveoli. ❸ By the time the blood leaves the lungs in the pulmonary veins, its P_{O_2} and P_{CO_2} match the values for those gases in the alveoli. After returning to the heart, this blood is pumped through the systemic circuit.

❹ In the systemic capillaries, gradients of partial pressure favor the net diffusion of O_2 out of the blood and CO_2 into the blood. These gradients exist because cellular respiration in the mitochondria of cells near each capillary removes O_2 from and adds CO_2 to the surrounding interstitial fluid. ❺ After the blood unloads O_2 and loads CO_2, it is returned to the heart and pumped to the lungs again. ❻ There, exchange occurs across the alveolar capillaries, resulting in exhaled air enriched in CO_2 and partially depleted of O_2.

Respiratory Pigments

The low solubility of O_2 in water (and thus in blood) poses a problem for animals that rely on the circulatory system to deliver O_2. For example, a person

requires almost 2 L of O_2 per minute during intense exercise, and all of it must be carried in the blood from the lungs to the active tissues. At normal body temperature and air pressure, however, only 4.5 mL of O_2 can dissolve into a liter of blood in the lungs. Even if 80% of the dissolved O_2 were delivered to the tissues, the heart would still need to pump 555 L of blood per minute!

In fact, animals transport most of their O_2 bound to proteins called **respiratory pigments**. Respiratory pigments circulate with the blood or hemolymph and are often contained within specialized cells. The pigments greatly increase the amount of O_2 that can be carried in the circulatory fluid (from 4.5 to about 200 mL of O_2 per liter in mammalian blood). In our example of an exercising human with an O_2 delivery rate of 80%, the presence of a respiratory pigment reduces the cardiac output necessary for O_2 transport to a manageable 12.5 L of blood per minute.

A variety of respiratory pigments have evolved in animals. With a few exceptions, these molecules have a distinctive color (hence the term *pigment*) and consist of a metal bound to a protein. One example is the blue pigment *hemocyanin*, which has copper as its oxygen-binding component and is found in arthropods and many molluscs.

The respiratory pigment of almost all vertebrates and many invertebrates is hemoglobin. In vertebrates, it is

© Pearson Education, Inc.

▲ **Figure 42.29 Loading and unloading of respiratory gases.**

WHAT IF? *If you consciously forced more air out of your lungs each time you exhaled, how would that affect the values shown in the figure?*

BioFlix Visit the Study Area in **MasteringBiology** for the BioFlix® 3-D Animation on Gas Exchange. BioFlix Tutorials can also be assigned in MasteringBiology.

contained in erythrocytes and has four subunits (polypeptide chains), each with a cofactor called a heme group that has an iron atom at its center. Each iron atom binds one molecule of O_2, so a hemoglobin molecule can carry four

Hemoglobin

molecules of O_2. Like all respiratory pigments, hemoglobin binds O_2 reversibly, loading O_2 in the lungs or gills and unloading it elsewhere in the body. This process is enhanced by cooperativity between the hemoglobin subunits (see Concept 8.5). When O_2 binds to one subunit, the others change shape slightly, increasing affinity for O_2. When four O_2 molecules are bound and one subunit unloads its O_2, the other three subunits more readily unload O_2, as an associated shape change lowers their affinity for O_2.

Cooperativity in O_2 binding and release is evident in the dissociation curve for hemoglobin **(Figure 42.30a)**. Over the range of P_{O_2} where the dissociation curve has a steep slope, even a slight change in P_{O_2} causes hemoglobin to load or unload a substantial amount of O_2. The steep part of the curve corresponds to the range of P_{O_2} found in body tissues. When cells in a particular location begin working harder—during exercise, for instance—P_{O_2} dips in their vicinity as the O_2 is consumed in cellular respiration. Because of subunit cooperativity, a slight drop in P_{O_2} causes a relatively large increase in the amount of O_2 the blood unloads.

The production of CO_2 during cellular respiration promotes the unloading of O_2 by hemoglobin in active tissues. As we have seen, CO_2 reacts with water, forming carbonic acid, which lowers the pH of its surroundings. Low pH, in turn, decreases the affinity of hemoglobin for O_2, an effect called the **Bohr shift (Figure 42.30b)**. Thus, where CO_2 production is greater, hemoglobin releases more O_2, which can then be used to support more cellular respiration.

Hemoglobin also assists in buffering the blood—that is, preventing harmful changes in pH. And it has a minor role in CO_2 transport, the topic we'll explore next.

Carbon Dioxide Transport

Only about 7% of the CO_2 released by respiring cells is transported in solution in blood plasma. The rest diffuses from plasma into erythrocytes and reacts with water (assisted by the enzyme carbonic anhydrase), forming H_2CO_3. The H_2CO_3 readily dissociates into H^+ and HCO_3^-. Most H^+ binds to hemoglobin and other proteins, minimizing change in blood pH. Most HCO_3^- diffuses out of the erythrocytes and is transported to the lungs in the plasma. The remaining HCO_3^-, representing about 5% of the CO_2, binds to hemoglobin and is transported in erythrocytes.

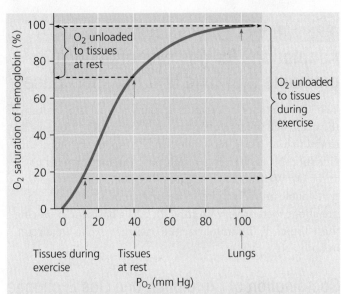

(a) P_{O_2} and hemoglobin dissociation at pH 7.4. The curve shows the relative amounts of O_2 bound to hemoglobin exposed to solutions with different P_{O_2}. At a P_{O_2} of 100 mm Hg, typical in the lungs, hemoglobin is about 98% saturated with O_2. At a P_{O_2} of 40 mm Hg, common in resting tissues, hemoglobin is about 70% saturated, having unloaded nearly a third of its O_2. As shown in the above graph, hemoglobin can release much more O_2 to metabolically very active tissues, such as muscle tissue during exercise.

(b) pH and hemoglobin dissociation. In very active tissues, CO_2 from cellular respiration reacts with water to form carbonic acid, decreasing pH. Because hydrogen ions affect hemoglobin shape, a drop in pH shifts the O_2 dissociation curve toward the right (the Bohr shift). For a given P_{O_2}, hemoglobin releases more O_2 at a lower pH, supporting increased cellular respiration.

▲ **Figure 42.30 Dissociation curves for hemoglobin at 37°C.**

When blood flows through the lungs, the relative partial pressures of CO_2 favor the net diffusion of CO_2 out of the blood. As CO_2 diffuses into alveoli, the amount of CO_2 in the blood decreases. This decrease shifts the chemical equilibrium in favor of the conversion of HCO_3^- to CO_2, enabling further net diffusion of CO_2 into alveoli. Overall, the P_{CO_2} gradient is sufficient to reduce P_{CO_2} by about 15% during passage of blood through the lungs.

Respiratory Adaptations of Diving Mammals

EVOLUTION Animals vary greatly in their ability to spend time in environments in which there is no access to their normal respiratory medium—for example, when an air-breathing mammal swims underwater. Whereas most humans, even expert divers, cannot hold their breath longer than 2 or 3 minutes or swim deeper than 20 m, the Weddell seal of Antarctica routinely plunges to 200–500 m and remains there for 20 minutes to more than an hour. (Humans can remain submerged for comparable periods, but only with specialized gear and compressed air tanks.) Another diving mammal, the elephant seal, can reach depths of 1,500 m—almost a mile—and stay submerged for as long as 2 hours! One elephant seal carrying a recording device spent 40 days at sea, diving almost continuously with no surface period longer than 6 minutes.

The ability of seals and other marine mammals to power their bodies during long dives showcases two related phenomena—the response to environmental challenges over the short term by physiological adjustments and adaptation over the long term as a result of natural selection. We'll use the Weddell seal to explore both phenomena.

One adaptation of diving mammals to prolonged stays underwater is a capacity to store large amounts of O_2 in their bodies. Although the Weddell seal has relatively small lungs compared with humans, it has about twice the volume of blood per kilogram of body mass as a human. Furthermore, seals and other diving mammals have a high concentration of an oxygen-storing protein called **myoglobin** in their muscles. As a result, the Weddell seal can store about twice as much O_2 per kilogram of body mass as can a human.

▲ Weddell seal

Diving mammals not only have a relatively large O_2 stockpile but also have adaptations that conserve O_2. They swim with little muscular effort and glide passively for prolonged periods. During a dive, their heart rate and O_2 consumption rate decrease, and most blood is routed to the brain, spinal cord, eyes, adrenal glands, and, in pregnant seals, the placenta. Blood supply to the muscles is restricted or, during the longest dives, shut off altogether. During dives of more than about 20 minutes, a Weddell seal's muscles deplete the O_2 stored in myoglobin and then derive their ATP from fermentation instead of respiration (see Chapter 9).

How did these adaptations arise over the course of evolution? All mammals, including humans, have a diving reflex triggered by a plunge or fall into water: When the face contacts cold water, the heart rate immediately decreases and blood flow to body extremities is reduced. Genetic changes that strengthened this reflex would have provided a selective advantage to seal ancestors foraging underwater. Also, genetic variations that increased traits such as blood volume or myoglobin concentration would have improved diving ability and therefore been favored during selection over many generations.

CONCEPT CHECK 42.7

1. What determines whether the net diffusion of O_2 and CO_2 is into or out of the capillaries in the tissues and near the alveoli? Explain.

2. How does the Bohr shift help deliver O_2 to very active tissues?

3. **WHAT IF?** A doctor might give bicarbonate (HCO_3^-) to a patient who is breathing very rapidly. What is the doctor assuming about the patient's blood chemistry?

For suggested answers, see Appendix A.

---

42 Chapter Review

SUMMARY OF KEY CONCEPTS

CONCEPT 42.1

Circulatory systems link exchange surfaces with cells throughout the body (pp. 916–920)

- In animals with simple body plans, a gastrovascular cavity mediates exchange between the environment and cells that can be reached by diffusion. Because diffusion is slow over long distances, most complex animals have a circulatory system that moves fluid between cells and the organs that carry out exchange with the environment. Arthropods and most molluscs have an **open circulatory system**, in which **hemolymph** bathes organs directly. Vertebrates have a **closed circulatory system**, in which **blood** circulates in a closed network of pumps and vessels.

- The closed circulatory system of vertebrates consists of blood, **blood vessels**, and a two- to four-chambered **heart**. Blood pumped by a heart **ventricle** passes to **arteries** and then to the **capillaries**, sites of chemical exchange between blood and interstitial fluid. **Veins** return blood from capillaries to an **atrium**, which passes blood to a ventricle. Fishes, rays, and sharks have a single pump in their circulation. Air-breathing vertebrates have two pumps combined in a single heart. Variations in ventricle number and separation reflect adaptations to different environments and metabolic needs.

? *How does the flow of a fluid in a closed circulatory system differ from the movement of molecules between cells and their environment with regard to distance traveled, direction traveled, and driving force?*

CONCEPT 42.2

Coordinated cycles of heart contraction drive double circulation in mammals (pp. 920–923)

- The right ventricle pumps blood to the lungs, where it loads O_2 and unloads CO_2. Oxygen-rich blood from the lungs enters the heart at the left atrium and is pumped to the body tissues by the left ventricle. Blood returns to the heart through the right atrium.

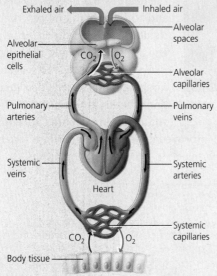

© Pearson Education, Inc.

- The **cardiac cycle**, a complete sequence of the heart's pumping and filling, consists of a period of contraction, called **systole**, and a period of relaxation, called **diastole**. Heart function can be assessed by measuring the **pulse** (number of times the heart beats each minute) and **cardiac output** (volume of blood pumped by each ventricle per minute).
- The heartbeat originates with impulses at the **sinoatrial (SA) node** (pacemaker) of the right atrium. They trigger atrial contraction, are delayed at the **atrioventricular (AV) node**, and are then conducted along the bundle branches and Purkinje fibers, triggering ventricular contraction. The nervous system, hormones, and body temperature affect pacemaker activity.

? *What changes in cardiac function might you expect after surgical replacement of a defective heart valve?*

CONCEPT 42.3

Patterns of blood pressure and flow reflect the structure and arrangement of blood vessels (pp. 923–927)

- Blood vessels have structures well adapted to function. Capillaries have narrow diameters and thin walls that facilitate exchange. The velocity of blood flow is lowest in the capillary beds as a result of their large total cross-sectional area. Arteries

contain thick elastic walls that maintain blood pressure. Veins contain one-way valves that contribute to the return of blood to the heart. Blood pressure is altered by changes in cardiac output and by variable constriction of arterioles.
- Fluid leaks out of capillaries and is returned to blood by the **lymphatic system**, which also defends against infection.

? *If you placed your forearm on your head, how, if at all, would the blood pressure in that arm change? Explain.*

CONCEPT 42.4

Blood components function in exchange, transport, and defense (pp. 928–933)

- Whole blood consists of cells and cell fragments (**platelets**) suspended in a liquid matrix called **plasma**. Plasma proteins influence blood pH, osmotic pressure, and viscosity, and they function in lipid transport, immunity (antibodies), and blood clotting (fibrinogen). Red blood cells, or **erythrocytes**, transport O_2. Five types of white blood cells, or **leukocytes**, function in defense against microorganisms and foreign substances in the blood. Platelets function in blood clotting, a cascade of reactions that converts plasma fibrinogen to fibrin.
- A variety of diseases impair function of the circulatory system. In **sickle-cell disease**, an aberrant form of **hemoglobin** disrupts erythrocyte shape and function, leading to blockage of small blood vessels and a decrease in the oxygen-carrying capacity of the blood. In cardiovascular disease, inflammation of the arterial lining enhances deposition of lipids and cells, resulting in the potential for life-threatening damage to the heart or brain.

? *In the absence of infection, what percentage of cells in human blood are leukocytes?*

CONCEPT 42.5

Gas exchange occurs across specialized respiratory surfaces (pp. 933–938)

- At all sites of **gas exchange**, a gas undergoes net diffusion from where its **partial pressure** is higher to where it is lower. Air is more conducive to gas exchange than water because air has a higher O_2 content, lower density, and lower viscosity.
- The structure and organization of respiratory surfaces differ among animal species. Gills are outfoldings of the body surface specialized for gas exchange in water. The effectiveness of gas exchange in some gills, including those of fishes, is increased by **ventilation** and **countercurrent exchange** between blood and water. Gas exchange in insects relies on a **tracheal system**, a branched network of tubes that bring O_2 directly to cells. Spiders, land snails, and most terrestrial vertebrates have internal **lungs**. In mammals, air inhaled through the nostrils passes through the pharynx into the **trachea, bronchi, bronchioles**, and dead-end **alveoli**, where gas exchange occurs.

? *Why does altitude have almost no effect on an animal's ability to rid itself of CO_2 through gas exchange?*

CONCEPT 42.6

Breathing ventilates the lungs (pp. 938–940)

- Breathing mechanisms vary substantially among vertebrates. An amphibian ventilates its lungs by **positive pressure breathing**, which forces air down the trachea. Birds use a system of air sacs as bellows to keep air flowing through the lungs in one direction only, preventing the mixing of incoming and outgoing air. Mammals ventilate their lungs by **negative pressure breathing**, which pulls air into the lungs when the rib muscles and

diaphragm contract. Incoming and outgoing air mix, decreasing the efficiency of ventilation.

- Sensors detect the pH of cerebrospinal fluid (reflecting CO_2 concentration in the blood), and a control center in the medulla oblongata adjusts breathing rate and depth to match metabolic demands. Additional input to the control center is provided by sensors in the aorta and carotid arteries that monitor blood levels of O_2 as well as CO_2 (via blood pH).

? *How does air in the lungs differ from the fresh air that enters the body during inspiration?*

CONCEPT 42.7

Adaptations for gas exchange include pigments that bind and transport gases (pp. 941–943)

- In the lungs, gradients of partial pressure favor the net diffusion of O_2 into the blood and CO_2 out of the blood. The opposite situation exists in the rest of the body. **Respiratory pigments** such as hemocyanin and hemoglobin bind O_2, greatly increasing the amount of O_2 transported by the circulatory system.
- Evolutionary adaptations enable some animals to satisfy extraordinary O_2 demands. Deep-diving mammals stockpile O_2 in blood and other tissues and deplete it slowly.

? *How is the role of a respiratory pigment like that of an enzyme?*

TEST YOUR UNDERSTANDING

LEVEL 1: KNOWLEDGE/COMPREHENSION

1. Which of the following respiratory systems is not closely associated with a blood supply?
   a. the lungs of a vertebrate
   b. the gills of a fish
   c. the tracheal system of an insect
   d. the skin of an earthworm

2. Blood returning to the mammalian heart in a pulmonary vein drains first into the
   a. left atrium.   c. left ventricle.
   b. right atrium.   d. right ventricle.

3. Pulse is a direct measure of
   a. blood pressure.   c. cardiac output.
   b. stroke volume.   d. heart rate.

4. When you hold your breath, which of the following blood gas changes first leads to the urge to breathe?
   a. rising O_2 c. rising CO_2
   b. falling O_2 d. falling CO_2

5. One feature that amphibians and humans have in common is
   a. the number of heart chambers.
   b. a complete separation of circuits for circulation.
   c. the number of circuits for circulation.
   d. a low blood pressure in the systemic circuit.

LEVEL 2: APPLICATION/ANALYSIS

6. If a molecule of CO_2 released into the blood in your left toe is exhaled from your nose, it must pass through all of the following except
   a. the pulmonary vein.   c. the right atrium.
   b. the trachea.   d. the right ventricle.

7. Compared with the interstitial fluid that bathes active muscle cells, blood reaching these cells in arterioles has a
   a. higher P_{O_2}.
   b. higher P_{CO_2}.
   c. greater bicarbonate concentration.
   d. lower pH.

LEVEL 3: SYNTHESIS/EVALUATION

8. **DRAW IT** Plot blood pressure against time for one cardiac cycle in humans, drawing separate lines for the pressure in the aorta, the left ventricle, and the right ventricle. Below the time axis, add a vertical arrow pointing to the time when you expect a peak in atrial blood pressure.

9. **EVOLUTION CONNECTION**
   One of the opponents of the movie monster Godzilla is Mothra, a giant mothlike creature with a wingspan of several dozen meters. The largest known insects were Paleozoic dragonflies with half-meter wingspans. Focusing on respiration and gas exchange, explain why giant insects are improbable.

10. **SCIENTIFIC INQUIRY**
    INTERPRET THE DATA
    The hemoglobin of a human fetus differs from adult hemoglobin. Compare the dissociation curves of the two hemoglobins in the graph at right. Describe how they differ, and propose a hypothesis to explain the benefit of this difference.

11. **SCIENCE, TECHNOLOGY, AND SOCIETY**
    Hundreds of studies have linked smoking with cardiovascular and lung disease. According to most health authorities, smoking is the leading cause of preventable, premature death in the United States. What are some arguments in favor of a total ban on cigarette advertising? What are arguments in opposition? Do you favor or oppose such a ban? Explain.

12. **WRITE ABOUT A THEME: INTERACTIONS**
    Some athletes prepare for competition at sea level by sleeping in a tent in which P_{O_2} is kept low. When climbing high peaks, some mountaineers breathe from bottles of pure O_2. In a short essay (100–150 words), relate these behaviors to the mechanism of O_2 transport in the human body and to physiological interactions with our gaseous environment.

13. **SYNTHESIZE YOUR KNOWLEDGE**

The diving bell spider (*Argyroneta aquatica*) stores air underwater in a net of silk. Explain why this adaptation could be more advantageous than having gills, taking into account differences in gas exchange media and gas exchange organs among animals.

For selected answers, see Appendix A.

MasteringBiology®

43

The Immune System

KEY CONCEPTS

43.1 In innate immunity, recognition and response rely on traits common to groups of pathogens

43.2 In adaptive immunity, receptors provide pathogen-specific recognition

43.3 Adaptive immunity defends against infection of body fluids and body cells

43.4 Disruptions in immune system function can elicit or exacerbate disease

▲ **Figure 43.1** What triggered this attack by an immune cell on a clump of bacteria?

Recognition and Response

For a **pathogen**—a bacterium, fungus, virus, or other disease-causing agent—the internal environment of an animal is a nearly ideal habitat. The animal body offers a ready source of nutrients, a protected setting, and a means of transport to new environments. From the perspective of a cold or flu virus, we are wonderful hosts. From our vantage point, the situation is not so ideal. Fortunately, adaptations have arisen over the course of evolution that protect animals against many pathogens.

Dedicated immune cells in the body fluids and tissues of most animals specifically interact with and destroy pathogens. For example, **Figure 43.1** shows an immune cell called a macrophage (brown) engulfing rod-shaped bacteria (green). Some immune cells are types of white blood cells called lymphocytes (such as the one shown at left with bacteria). Most lymphocytes recognize and respond to specific types of pathogens. Together, the body's defenses make up the **immune system**, which enables an animal to avoid or limit many infections. A foreign molecule or cell doesn't have to be pathogenic to elicit an immune response, but we'll focus in this chapter on the immune system's role in defending against pathogens.

The first lines of defense offered by immune systems help prevent pathogens from gaining entrance to the body. For example, an outer covering, such as a skin

946

or shell, blocks entry by many pathogens. Sealing off the entire body surface is impossible, however, because gas exchange, nutrition, and reproduction require openings to the environment. Secretions that trap or kill microbes guard the body's entrances and exits, while the linings of the digestive tract, airway, and other exchange surfaces provide additional barriers to infection.

If a pathogen breaches barrier defenses and enters the body, the problem of how to fend off attack changes substantially. Housed within body fluids and tissues, the invader is no longer an outsider. To fight infections, an animal's immune system must detect foreign particles and cells within the body. In other words, a properly functioning immune system distinguishes nonself from self. How is this accomplished? Immune cells produce receptor molecules that bind specifically to molecules from foreign cells or viruses and activate defense responses. The specific binding of immune receptors to foreign molecules is a type of *molecular recognition* and is the central event in identifying nonself particles and cells.

Two types of molecular recognition provide the basis for the two types of immune defense found among animals: innate immunity, which is common to all animals, and adaptive immunity, which is found only in vertebrates. **Figure 43.2** summarizes these two types of immunity, highlighting fundamental similarities and differences.

In **innate immunity**, which includes barrier defenses, molecular recognition relies on a small set of receptor proteins that bind to molecules or structures that are absent from animal bodies but common to a group of viruses, bacteria, or other microbes. Binding of an innate immune receptor to a foreign molecule activates internal defenses, enabling responses to a very broad range of pathogens.

In **adaptive immunity**, molecular recognition relies on a vast arsenal of receptors, each of which recognizes a feature typically found only on a particular part of a particular molecule in a particular pathogen. As a result, recognition and response in adaptive immunity occur with tremendous specificity.

The adaptive immune response, also known as the acquired immune response, is activated after the innate immune response and develops more slowly. The names *adaptive* and *acquired* reflect the fact that this immune response is enhanced by previous exposure to the infecting pathogen. Examples of adaptive responses include the synthesis of proteins that inactivate a bacterial toxin and the targeted killing of a virus-infected body cell.

In this chapter, we'll examine how each type of immunity protects animals from disease. We'll also investigate how pathogens can avoid or overwhelm the immune system and how defects in the immune system can imperil health.

CONCEPT 43.1

In innate immunity, recognition and response rely on traits common to groups of pathogens

Innate immunity is found in all animals (as well as in plants). In exploring innate immunity, we'll begin with invertebrates, which repel and fight infection with only this type of immunity. We'll then turn to vertebrates, in which innate immunity serves both as an immediate defense against infection and as the foundation for adaptive immune defenses.

Innate Immunity of Invertebrates

The great success of insects in terrestrial and freshwater habitats teeming with diverse pathogens highlights the effectiveness of invertebrate innate immunity. In each of these environments, insects rely on their exoskeleton as a first line of defense against infection. Composed largely of the polysaccharide chitin, the exoskeleton provides an effective barrier defense against most pathogens. Chitin also lines the insect intestine, where it blocks infection by many pathogens ingested with food. **Lysozyme**, an enzyme that breaks down bacterial cell walls, further protects the insect digestive system.

Any pathogen that breaches an insect's barrier defenses encounters a number of internal immune defenses. Immune cells called *hemocytes* travel throughout the body in the hemolymph, the insect circulatory fluid. Some hemocytes

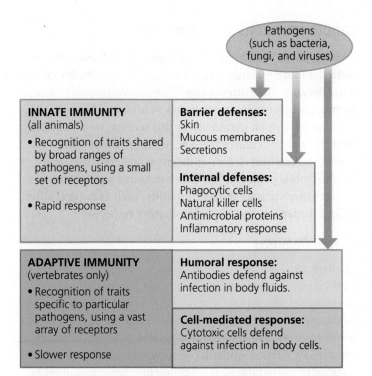

▲ **Figure 43.2 Overview of animal immunity.** Immune responses in animals can be divided into innate and adaptive immunity. Some components of innate immunity contribute to activation of adaptive immune defenses.

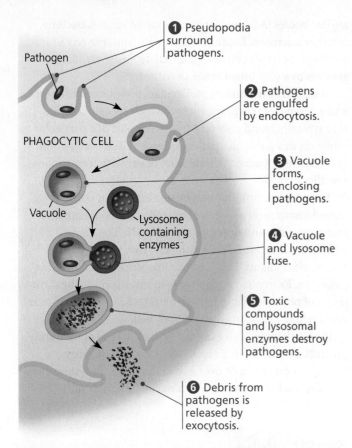

① Pseudopodia surround pathogens.

Pathogen

② Pathogens are engulfed by endocytosis.

PHAGOCYTIC CELL

③ Vacuole forms, enclosing pathogens.

Vacuole

Lysosome containing enzymes

④ Vacuole and lysosome fuse.

⑤ Toxic compounds and lysosomal enzymes destroy pathogens.

⑥ Debris from pathogens is released by exocytosis.

▲ **Figure 43.3 Phagocytosis.** This diagram depicts events in the ingestion and destruction of pathogens by a typical phagocytic cell.

ingest and break down bacteria and other foreign substances, a process known as **phagocytosis (Figure 43.3).** Other hemocytes release chemicals that kill pathogens and help entrap large parasites, such as *Plasmodium*, the parasite of mosquitoes that causes malaria. In addition, encounters with pathogens in the hemolymph cause hemocytes and certain other cells to secrete *antimicrobial peptides*, which are short chains of amino acids. These peptides circulate throughout the body of the insect **(Figure 43.4)** and inactivate or kill fungi and bacteria by disrupting their plasma membranes.

◄ **Figure 43.4 An inducible innate immune response.** These fruit flies were engineered to express the green fluorescent protein (GFP) gene upon activation of the innate immune response. The fly on the top was injected with bacteria; the fly on the bottom was not. Only the injected fly activates antimicrobial peptide genes, produces GFP, and glows bright green under fluorescent light.

Immune cells of insects bind to molecules found only in the outer layers of fungi or bacteria. Fungal cell walls contain certain unique polysaccharides, whereas bacterial cell walls have polymers containing combinations of sugars and amino acids not found in animal cells. Such macromolecules serve as identity tags in the process of pathogen recognition. Insect immune cells secrete recognition proteins, each of which binds specifically to a macromolecule characteristic of a broad class of bacteria or fungi.

Innate immune responses are distinct for different classes of pathogens. For example, when the fungus *Neurospora crassa* infects a fruit fly, pieces of the fungal cell wall bind to a recognition protein. Together, the complex activates the protein Toll, a receptor on the surface of hemocytes. Signal transduction from the Toll receptor to the cell nucleus leads to synthesis of a set of antimicrobial peptides active against fungi. If the fly is instead infected by the bacterium *Micrococcus luteus*, a different recognition protein is activated, and the fly produces a different set of antimicrobial peptides effective against *M. luteus* and many related bacteria.

Because fruit flies secrete many distinct antimicrobial peptides in response to a single infection, it is difficult to study the activity of any one peptide. To get around this problem, Bruno Lemaitre and fellow researchers used modern genetic techniques to reprogram the fly immune system **(Figure 43.5).** They found that the synthesis of a single type of antimicrobial peptide in the fly's body could provide an effective and specific immune defense.

Innate Immunity of Vertebrates

Among jawed vertebrates, innate immune defenses coexist with the more recently evolved system of adaptive immunity. Because most discoveries regarding vertebrate innate immunity have come from studies of mice and humans, we'll focus here on mammals. In this section, we'll consider first the innate defenses that are similar to those found among invertebrates: barrier defenses, phagocytosis, and antimicrobial peptides. We'll then examine some unique aspects of vertebrate innate immunity, such as natural killer cells, interferons, and the inflammatory response.

Barrier Defenses

In mammals, barrier defenses block the entry of many pathogens. These defenses include the skin and the mucous membranes lining the digestive, respiratory, urinary, and reproductive tracts. The mucous membranes produce *mucus*, a viscous fluid that traps pathogens and other particles. In the airway, ciliated epithelial cells sweep mucus and any entrapped material upward, helping prevent infection of the lungs. Saliva, tears, and mucous secretions that bathe various exposed epithelia provide a washing action that also inhibits colonization by fungi and bacteria.

Inquiry

Can a single antimicrobial peptide protect fruit flies against infection?

Experiment In 2002, Bruno Lemaitre and colleagues in France devised a novel strategy to test the function of a single antimicrobial peptide. They began with a mutant fruit fly strain in which pathogens are recognized but the signaling that would normally trigger innate immune responses is blocked. As a result, the mutant flies do not make any antimicrobial peptides. The researchers then genetically engineered some of the mutant flies to express significant amounts of a single antimicrobial peptide, either drosomycin or defensin. The scientists infected the various flies with the fungus *Neurospora crassa* and monitored survival over a five-day period. They repeated the procedure for infection by the bacterium *Micrococcus luteus*.

Results

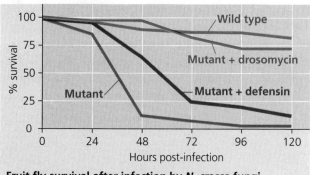

Fruit fly survival after infection by *N. crassa* fungi

Fruit fly survival after infection by *M. luteus* bacteria

Conclusion Each of the two antimicrobial peptides provided a protective immune response. Furthermore, the different peptides defended against different pathogens. Drosomycin was effective against *N. crassa*, and defensin was effective against *M. luteus*.

Source: P. Tzou, J. Reichhart, and B. Lemaitre, Constitutive expression of a single antimicrobial peptide can restore wild-type resistance to infection in immunodeficient *Drosophila* mutants, *Proceedings of the National Academy of Sciences USA* 99:2152–2157 (2002).

WHAT IF? *Even if a particular antimicrobial peptide showed no beneficial effect in such an experiment, why might it still be beneficial to flies?*

Beyond their physical role in inhibiting microbial entry, body secretions create an environment that is hostile to many pathogens. Lysozyme in tears, saliva, and mucous secretions destroys the cell walls of susceptible bacteria as they enter the openings around the eyes or the upper respiratory tract. Microbes in food or water and those in swallowed mucus must also contend with the acidic environment of the stomach, which kills most of them before they can enter the intestines. Similarly, secretions from oil and sweat glands give human skin a pH ranging from 3 to 5, acidic enough to prevent the growth of many bacteria.

Cellular Innate Defenses

Many pathogens that defeat the barrier defenses of mammals are engulfed by phagocytic cells that use several types of receptors to detect viral, fungal, or bacterial components. Some mammalian receptors are very similar to the Toll receptor of insects, a remarkable discovery that was recognized with the Nobel Prize in medicine or physiology in 2011. Each mammalian **Toll-like receptor (TLR)** binds to fragments of molecules normally absent from the vertebrate body but characteristic of a set of pathogens **(Figure 43.6)**. For example, TLR3, on the inner surface of vesicles formed by endocytosis, binds to double-stranded RNA, a form

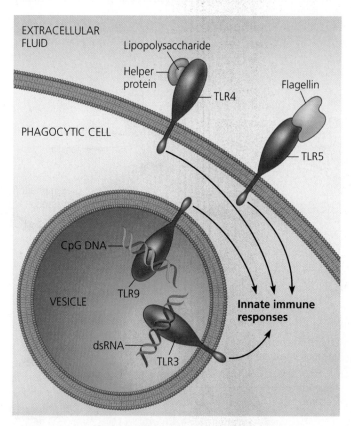

▲ **Figure 43.6 TLR signaling.** Each mammalian Toll-like receptor (TLR) recognizes a molecular pattern characteristic of a group of pathogens. Lipopolysaccharide, flagellin, CpG DNA (DNA containing unmethylated CG sequences), and double-stranded (ds) RNA are all found in bacteria, fungi, or viruses but not in animal cells. Together with other recognition and response factors, TLR proteins trigger internal innate immune defenses.

? *Some TLR proteins are on the cell surface, whereas others are inside vesicles. Suggest a possible benefit of this distribution.*

of nucleic acid characteristic of certain viruses. Similarly, TLR4, located on immune cell plasma membranes, recognizes lipopolysaccharide, a type of molecule found on the surface of many bacteria, and TLR5 recognizes flagellin, the main protein of bacterial flagella.

As in invertebrates, detection of invading pathogens in mammals triggers phagocytosis and destruction. The two main types of phagocytic cells in the mammalian body are neutrophils and macrophages. **Neutrophils**, which circulate in the blood, are attracted by signals from infected tissues and then engulf and destroy the infecting pathogens. **Macrophages** ("big eaters"), like the one shown in Figure 43.1, are larger phagocytic cells. Some migrate throughout the body, whereas others reside permanently in organs and tissues where they are likely to encounter pathogens. For example, some macrophages are located in the spleen, where pathogens in the blood are often trapped.

Two other types of phagocytic cells—dendritic cells and eosinophils—provide additional functions in innate defense. **Dendritic cells** mainly populate tissues, such as skin, that contact the environment. They stimulate adaptive immunity

against pathogens they encounter and engulf, as we'll explore shortly. *Eosinophils*, often found beneath mucosal surfaces, are important in defending against multicellular invaders, such as parasitic worms. Upon encountering such parasites, eosinophils discharge destructive enzymes.

Cellular innate defenses in vertebrates also involve **natural killer cells**. These cells circulate through the body and detect the abnormal array of surface proteins characteristic of some virus-infected and cancerous cells. Natural killer cells do not engulf stricken cells. Instead, they release chemicals that lead to cell death, inhibiting further spread of the virus or cancer.

Many cellular innate defenses in vertebrates involve the lymphatic system, a network that distributes the fluid called lymph throughout the body **(Figure 43.7)**. Some macrophages reside in lymph nodes, where they engulf pathogens that have entered the lymph from the interstitial fluid. Dendritic cells reside outside the lymphatic system but migrate to the lymph nodes after interacting with pathogens. Within the lymph nodes, dendritic cells interact with other immune cells, stimulating adaptive immunity.

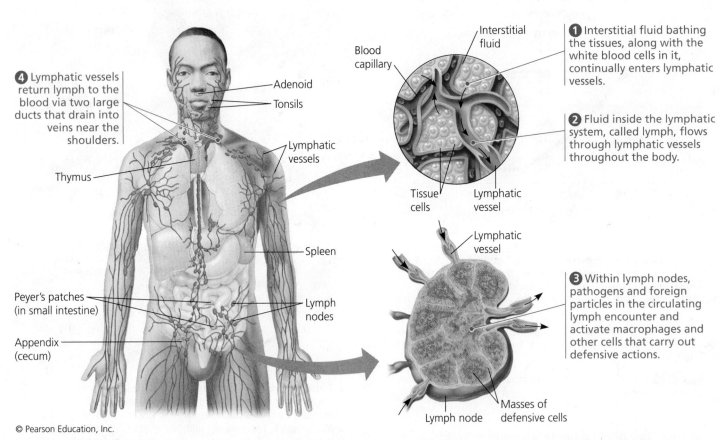

© Pearson Education, Inc.

▲ Figure 43.7 The human lymphatic system. The lymphatic system consists of lymphatic vessels (shown in green), through which lymph travels, and structures that trap foreign substances. These structures include lymph nodes (orange) and lymphoid organs (yellow): the adenoids, tonsils, spleen, Peyer's patches, and appendix. Steps 1–4 trace the flow of lymph and illustrate the role of lymph nodes in activating adaptive immunity. (Concept 42.3 will describe the relationship between the lymphatic and circulatory systems.)

Antimicrobial Peptides and Proteins

In mammals, pathogen recognition triggers the production and release of a variety of peptides and proteins that attack pathogens or impede their reproduction. Some of these defense molecules function like the antimicrobial peptides of insects, damaging broad groups of pathogens by disrupting membrane integrity. Others, including the interferons and complement proteins, are unique to vertebrate immune systems.

Interferons are proteins that provide innate defense by interfering with viral infections. Virus-infected body cells secrete interferons, which induce nearby uninfected cells to produce substances that inhibit viral replication. In this way, interferons limit the cell-to-cell spread of viruses in the body, helping control viral infections such as colds and influenza. Some white blood cells secrete a different type of interferon that helps activate macrophages, enhancing their phagocytic ability. Pharmaceutical companies now use recombinant DNA technology to mass-produce interferons to help treat certain viral infections, such as hepatitis C.

The infection-fighting **complement system** consists of roughly 30 proteins in blood plasma. These proteins circulate in an inactive state and are activated by substances on the surface of many microbes. Activation results in a cascade of biochemical reactions that can lead to lysis (bursting) of invading cells. The complement system also functions in the inflammatory response, our next topic, as well as in the adaptive defenses discussed later in the chapter.

Inflammatory Response

The pain and swelling that alert you to a splinter under your skin are the result of a local **inflammatory response**, the changes brought about by signaling molecules released upon injury or infection **(Figure 43.8)**. One important inflammatory signaling molecule is **histamine**, which is stored in densely packed vesicles of **mast cells**, found in connective tissue. Histamine released at sites of damage triggers nearby blood vessels to dilate and become more permeable. The dilated capillaries leak fluid into neighboring tissues, causing localized swelling.

Macrophages and neutrophils also participate in the inflammatory response. Once activated, these cells discharge *cytokines*, signaling molecules that modulate immune responses. The cytokines released by macrophages and neutrophils promote blood flow to the site of injury or infection. The increase in local blood supply produces the redness and increased skin temperature typical of the inflammatory response (from the Latin *inflammare*, to set on fire).

During inflammation, cycles of signaling and response transform the site. Activated complement proteins promote further release of histamine, attracting more phagocytic cells that enter injured tissues (see Figure 43.8) and carry out additional phagocytosis. At the same time, enhanced blood flow to the site helps deliver antimicrobial peptides. The result is an accumulation of *pus*, a fluid rich in white blood cells, dead pathogens, and cell debris from damaged tissue.

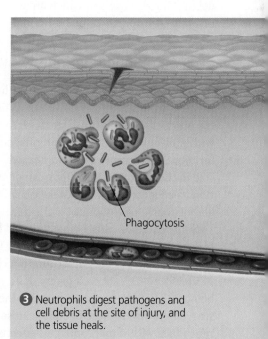

© Pearson Education, Inc.

❶ At the injury site, mast cells release histamines, which cause nearby capillaries to dilate. Macrophages release other signaling molecules that increase local blood flow.

❷ Capillaries widen and become more permeable, allowing fluid containing antimicrobial peptides to enter the tissue. Signals released by immune cells attract neutrophils.

❸ Neutrophils digest pathogens and cell debris at the site of injury, and the tissue heals.

▲ **Figure 43.8 Major events in a local inflammatory response.**

A minor injury or infection causes a local inflammatory response, but severe tissue damage or infection may lead to a response that is systemic (throughout the body). Cells in injured or infected tissue often secrete molecules that stimulate the release of additional neutrophils from the bone marrow. In the case of a severe infection, such as meningitis or appendicitis, the number of white blood cells in the bloodstream may increase several-fold within only a few hours.

Another systemic inflammatory response is fever. In response to certain pathogens, substances released by activated macrophages cause the body's thermostat to reset to a higher temperature (see Chapter 40). There is good evidence that fever can be beneficial in fighting certain infections, although the underlying mechanism is still a subject of debate. One hypothesis is that an elevated body temperature may enhance phagocytosis and, by speeding up chemical reactions, accelerate tissue repair.

Certain bacterial infections can induce an overwhelming systemic inflammatory response, leading to a life-threatening condition that is known as *septic shock*. Characterized by very high fever, low blood pressure, and poor blood flow through capillaries, septic shock occurs most often in the very old and the very young. It is fatal in roughly one-third of cases and contributes to the death of more than 200,000 people each year in the United States alone.

Chronic (ongoing) inflammation can also threaten human health. For example, millions of individuals worldwide suffer from Crohn's disease and ulcerative colitis, often debilitating disorders in which an unregulated inflammatory response disrupts intestinal function.

Evasion of Innate Immunity by Pathogens

Adaptations have evolved in some pathogens that enable them to avoid destruction by phagocytic cells. For example, the outer capsule that surrounds certain bacteria interferes with molecular recognition and phagocytosis. One such bacterium, *Streptococcus pneumoniae*, which played a critical role in the discovery that DNA can convey genetic information (see Figure 16.2), can cause ear infections, meningitis, and of course pneumonia.

Some bacteria, after being engulfed by a host cell, resist breakdown within lysosomes. An example is *Mycobacterium tuberculosis*, the bacterium that causes tuberculosis (TB). Figure 43.1 shows a group of *M. tuberculosis* bacteria being engulfed by a macrophage. Rather than being destroyed, however, these bacteria can sometimes grow and reproduce within macrophages, effectively hidden from the body's innate immune defenses. These and other mechanisms that prevent destruction by the innate immune system make certain fungi and bacteria substantial pathogenic threats. Indeed, TB kills more than a million people a year worldwide.

CONCEPT CHECK 43.1

1. Although pus is often seen simply as a sign of infection, it is also an indicator of immune defenses in action. Explain.

2. **MAKE CONNECTIONS** How do the molecules that activate the vertebrate TLR signal transduction pathway differ from the ligands in most other signaling pathways (see Concept 11.2)?

3. **WHAT IF?** Suppose humans were the major host for a bacterial species. What temperature would you predict would be optimal for growth of this species? Explain.

For suggested answers, see Appendix A.

CONCEPT 43.2

In adaptive immunity, receptors provide pathogen-specific recognition

Vertebrates are unique in having both adaptive and innate immunity. The adaptive response relies on T cells and B cells, which are types of white blood cells called **lymphocytes**. Like all blood cells, lymphocytes originate from

Mature B cell   Mature T cell

stem cells in the bone marrow. Some migrate from the bone marrow to the **thymus**, an organ in the thoracic cavity above the heart (see Figure 43.7). These lymphocytes mature into **T cells**. Lymphocytes that remain and mature in the bone marrow develop as **B cells**. (Lymphocytes of a third type remain in the blood and become the natural killer cells active in innate immunity.)

Any substance that elicits a B or T cell response is called an **antigen**. In adaptive immunity, recognition occurs when a B cell or T cell binds to an antigen, such as a bacterial or viral protein, via a protein called an **antigen receptor**. Each antigen receptor binds to just one part of one molecule from a particular pathogen, such as a species of bacteria or strain of virus. Although the cells of the immune system produce millions of different antigen receptors, all of the antigen receptors made by a single B or T cell are identical. Infection by a virus, bacterium, or other pathogen triggers activation of B and T cells with antigen receptors specific for parts of that pathogen. B and T cells are shown in this text with only a few antigen receptors, but there are actually about 100,000 antigen receptors on the surface of a single B or T cell.

Antigens are usually foreign and are typically large molecules, either proteins or polysaccharides. Many antigens protrude from the surface of foreign cells or viruses. Other antigens, such as toxins secreted by bacteria, are released into the extracellular fluid.

The small, accessible portion of an antigen that binds to an antigen receptor is called an **epitope**. An example is a group of amino acids in a particular protein. A single antigen usually has several epitopes, each binding a receptor with a different specificity. Because all antigen receptors produced by a single B cell or T cell are identical, they bind to the same epitope. Each B or T cell thus displays *specificity* for a particular epitope, enabling it to respond to any pathogen that produces molecules containing that epitope.

The antigen receptors of B cells and T cells have similar components, but they encounter antigens in different ways. We'll consider the two processes in turn.

Antigen Recognition by B Cells and Antibodies

Each B cell antigen receptor is a Y-shaped molecule consisting of four polypeptide chains: two identical **heavy chains** and two identical **light chains**, with disulfide bridges linking the chains together **(Figure 43.9)**. A transmembrane region near one end of each heavy chain anchors the receptor in the cell's plasma membrane. A short tail region at the end of the heavy chain extends into the cytoplasm.

The light and heavy chains each have a *constant (C) region*, where amino acid sequences vary little among the receptors on different B cells. The C region includes the cytoplasmic tail and transmembrane region of the heavy chain and all of the disulfide bridges. Within the two tips of the Y shape (see Figure 43.9), each chain has a *variable (V) region*, so named because its amino acid sequence varies extensively from one B cell to another. Together, parts of a heavy-chain V region and a light-chain V region form an asymmetric binding site for an antigen. As shown in Figure 43.9, each B cell antigen receptor has two identical antigen-binding sites.

Binding of a B cell antigen receptor to an antigen is an early step in B cell activation, leading to formation of cells that secrete a soluble form of the receptor **(Figure 43.10a)**.

This secreted protein is called an **antibody**, also known as an **immunoglobulin (Ig)**. Antibodies have the same Y-shaped structure as B cell antigen receptors but are secreted rather than membrane bound. It is antibodies, rather than B cells themselves, that actually help defend against pathogens.

The antigen-binding site of a membrane-bound receptor or antibody has a unique shape that provides a lock-and-key fit for a particular epitope. Many noncovalent bonds between an epitope and the surface of the binding site provide a stable and specific interaction. Differences in the amino acid sequences of variable regions provide the variation in binding surfaces that enables this highly specific binding.

B cell antigen receptors and antibodies bind to intact antigens in the blood and lymph. As illustrated in **Figure 43.10b** for antibodies, they can bind to antigens on the surface of pathogens or free in body fluids. The antigen receptors of T cells function quite differently, as we'll see next.

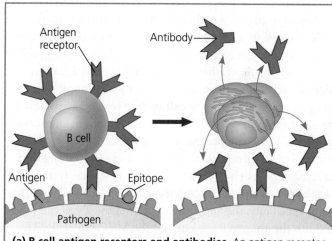

(a) B cell antigen receptors and antibodies. An antigen receptor of a B cell binds to an epitope, a particular part of an antigen. Following binding, the B cell gives rise to cells that secrete a soluble form of the antigen receptor. This soluble receptor, called an antibody, is specific for the same epitope as the original B cell.

(b) Antigen receptor specificity. Different antibodies can recognize distinct epitopes on the same antigen. Furthermore, antibodies can recognize free antigens as well as antigens on a pathogen's surface.

▲ **Figure 43.10 Antigen recognition by B cells and antibodies.**

MAKE CONNECTIONS *The interactions depicted here involve a highly specific binding between antigen and receptor (see Figure 5.17). How is this similar to an enzyme-substrate interaction (see Figure 8.15)?*

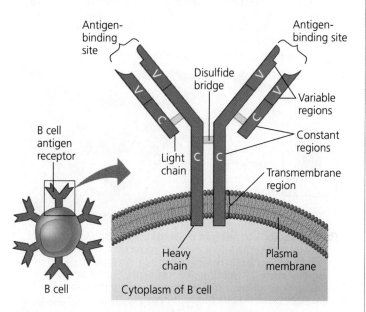

▲ **Figure 43.9 The structure of a B cell antigen receptor.**

Antigen Recognition by T Cells

For a T cell, the antigen receptor consists of two different polypeptide chains, an *α chain* and a *β chain*, linked by a disulfide bridge **(Figure 43.11)**. Near the base of the T cell antigen receptor (often called simply a T cell receptor) is a transmembrane region that anchors the molecule in the cell's plasma membrane. At the outer tip of the molecule, the variable (V) regions of the α and β chains together form a single antigen-binding site. The remainder of the molecule is made up of the constant (C) regions.

Whereas the antigen receptors of B cells bind to epitopes of *intact* antigens on pathogens or circulating free in body fluids, those of T cells bind only to fragments of antigens that are displayed, or presented, on the surface of host cells. The host protein that displays the antigen fragment on the cell surface is called a **major histocompatibility complex (MHC) molecule**.

Recognition of protein antigens by T cells begins when a pathogen or part of a pathogen either infects or is taken in by a host cell **(Figure 43.12a)**. Inside the host cell, enzymes cleave the antigen into smaller peptides. Each peptide, called an *antigen fragment*, then binds to an MHC molecule inside the cell. Movement of the MHC molecule and bound antigen fragment up to the cell surface results in **antigen presentation**, display of the antigen fragment in an exposed groove of the MHC protein. **Figure 43.12b** shows a close-up view of antigen presentation, a process advertising the fact that a host cell contains a foreign substance. If the cell displaying an antigen fragment encounters a T cell with the right specificity, the antigen receptor on the T cell can bind to both the antigen fragment and the MHC molecule. This interaction of an MHC molecule, an antigen fragment, and an antigen receptor is necessary for a T cell to participate in an adaptive immune response, as you'll see later.

B Cell and T Cell Development

Now that you know how B cells and T cells recognize antigens, let's consider four major characteristics of adaptive immunity. First, there is an immense diversity of lymphocytes and receptors, enabling the immune system to detect pathogens never before encountered. Second, adaptive immunity normally has self-tolerance, the lack of reactivity against an animal's own molecules and cells. Third, cell proliferation triggered by activation greatly increases the number of B and T cells specific for an antigen. Fourth, there is a stronger and more rapid response to an antigen encountered previously, due to a feature known as *immunological memory*, which we'll discuss later in the chapter.

Receptor diversity and self-tolerance arise as a lymphocyte matures. Proliferation of cells and the formation of immunological memory occur later, after a mature lymphocyte encounters and binds to a specific antigen. We'll consider these four characteristics in the order in which they develop.

▲ **Figure 43.11 The structure of a T cell antigen receptor.**

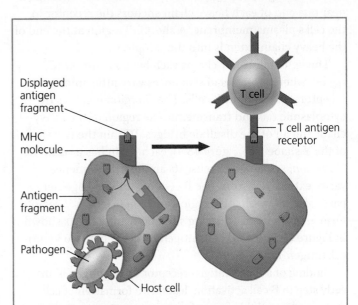

(a) Antigen recognition by a T cell. Inside the host cell, an antigen fragment from a pathogen binds to an MHC molecule and is brought up to the cell surface, where it is displayed. The combination of MHC molecule and antigen fragment is recognized by a T cell.

(b) A closer look at antigen presentation. As shown in this ribbon model, the top of the MHC molecule cradles an antigen fragment, like a bun holding a hot dog. An MHC molecule can display many different antigen fragments, but the antigen receptor of a T cell is specific for a single antigen fragment.

▲ **Figure 43.12 Antigen recognition by T cells.**

Generation of B Cell and T Cell Diversity

Each person makes more than 1 million different B cell antigen receptors and 10 million different T cell antigen receptors. Yet there are only about 20,000 protein-coding genes in the human genome. How, then, do we generate such remarkable diversity in antigen receptors? The answer lies in combinations. Think of selecting a car with a choice of three interior colors and six exterior colors. There are 18 (3×6) color combinations to consider. Similarly, by combining variable elements, the immune system assembles many different receptors from a much smaller collection of parts.

To understand the origin of receptor diversity, let's consider an immunoglobulin (Ig) gene that encodes the light chain of both membrane-bound B cell antigen receptors and secreted antibodies (immunoglobulins). Although we'll analyze only a single Ig light-chain gene, all B and T cell antigen receptor genes undergo very similar transformations.

The capacity to generate diversity is built into the structure of Ig genes. A receptor light chain is encoded by three gene segments: a variable (V) segment, a joining (J) segment, and a constant (C) segment. The V and J segments together encode the variable region of the receptor chain, while the C segment encodes the constant region. The light-chain gene contains a single C segment, 40 different V segments, and 5 different J segments. These alternative copies of the V and J segments are arranged within the gene in a series **(Figure 43.13)**. Because a functional gene is built from one copy of each type of segment, the pieces can be combined in 200 different ways (40 $V \times$ 5 $J \times$ 1 C). The number of different heavy-chain combinations is even greater, resulting in even more diversity.

Assembling a functional Ig gene requires rearranging the DNA. Early in B cell development, an enzyme complex called *recombinase* links one light-chain V gene segment to one J gene segment. This recombination event eliminates the long stretch of DNA between the segments, forming a single exon that is part V and part J. Because there is only an intron between the J and C DNA segments, no further rearrangement of DNA is required. Instead, the J and C

▲ **Figure 43.13** **Immunoglobulin (antibody) gene rearrangement.** The joining of randomly selected V and J gene segments (V_{39} and J_5 in the example shown) results in a functional gene that encodes the light-chain polypeptide of a B cell antigen receptor. Transcription, splicing, and translation result in a light chain that combines with a polypeptide produced from an independently rearranged heavy-chain gene to form a functional receptor. Mature B cells (and T cells) are exceptions to the generalization that all nucleated cells in the body have exactly the same DNA.

MAKE CONNECTIONS *Both alternative splicing and joining of* V *and* J *segments by recombination generate diverse gene products from a limited set of gene segments (see Figure 18.13). How do these processes differ?*

segments of the RNA transcript will be joined when splicing removes the intervening RNA. (See Figure 17.11 to review RNA splicing.)

Recombinase acts randomly, linking any one of the 40 *V* gene segments to any one of the 5 *J* gene segments. Heavy-chain genes undergo a similar rearrangement. In any given cell, however, only one allele of a light-chain gene and one allele of a heavy-chain gene are rearranged. Furthermore, the rearrangements are permanent and are passed on to the daughter cells when the lymphocyte divides.

After both a light-chain and a heavy-chain gene have been rearranged, antigen receptors can be synthesized. The rearranged genes are transcribed, and the transcripts are processed for translation. Following translation, the light chain and heavy chain assemble together, forming an antigen receptor (see Figure 43.13). Each pair of randomly rearranged heavy and light chains results in a different antigen-binding site. For the total population of B cells in a human body, the number of such combinations has been calculated as 3.5×10^6. Furthermore, mutations introduced during *VJ* recombination add additional variation, making the number of possible antigen-binding specificities even greater.

Origin of Self-Tolerance

In adaptive immunity, how does the body distinguish self from nonself? Because antigen receptor genes are randomly rearranged, some immature lymphocytes produce receptors specific for epitopes on the organism's own molecules. If these self-reactive lymphocytes were not eliminated or inactivated, the immune system could not distinguish self from nonself and would attack body proteins, cells, and tissues. Instead, as lymphocytes mature in the bone marrow or thymus, their antigen receptors are tested for self-reactivity. Some B and T cells with receptors specific for the body's own molecules are destroyed by *apoptosis*, which is a programmed cell death (see Chapter 11). The remaining self-reactive lymphocytes are typically rendered nonfunctional, leaving only those that react to foreign molecules. Since the body normally lacks mature lymphocytes that can react against its own components, the immune system is said to exhibit *self-tolerance*.

Proliferation of B Cells and T Cells

Despite the enormous variety of antigen receptors, only a tiny fraction are specific for a given epitope. How then does an effective adaptive response develop? To begin with, an antigen is presented to a steady stream of lymphocytes in the lymph nodes (see Figure 43.7) until a match is made. A successful match between an antigen receptor and an epitope initiates events that activate the lymphocyte bearing the receptor.

Once activated, a B cell or T cell undergoes multiple cell divisions. For each activated cell, the result of this proliferation is a clone, a population of cells that are identical to the original cell. Some cells from this clone become **effector cells**, short-lived cells that take effect immediately against the antigen and any pathogens producing that antigen. The effector forms of B cells are **plasma cells**, which secrete antibodies. The effector forms of T cells are helper T cells and cytotoxic T cells, whose roles we'll explore in Concept 43.3. The remaining cells in the clone become **memory cells**, long-lived cells that can give rise to effector cells if the same antigen is encountered later in the animal's life.

The proliferation of a B cell or T cell into a clone of cells occurs in response to a specific antigen and to immune cell signals. The process is called **clonal selection** because an encounter with an antigen *selects* which lymphocyte will divide to produce a *clonal* population of thousands of cells specific for a particular epitope. Cells that have antigen receptors specific for other antigens do not respond.

Figure 43.14 summarizes the process of clonal selection, using the example of B cells, which generate memory cells and plasma cells. When T cells undergo clonal selection, they generate memory T cells and effector T cells (cytotoxic T cells and helper T cells).

Immunological Memory

Immunological memory is responsible for the long-term protection that a prior infection provides against many diseases, such as chicken pox. This type of protection was noted almost 2,400 years ago by the Greek historian Thucydides. He observed that individuals who had recovered from the plague could safely care for those who were sick or dying, "for the same man was never attacked twice—never at least fatally."

Prior exposure to an antigen alters the speed, strength, and duration of the immune response. The production of effector cells from a clone of lymphocytes during the first exposure to an antigen is the basis for the **primary immune response**. The primary response peaks about 10–17 days after the initial exposure. During this time, selected B cells and T cells give rise to their effector forms. If an individual is exposed again to the same antigen, the response is faster (typically peaking only 2–7 days after exposure), of greater magnitude, and more prolonged. This is the **secondary immune response**, a hallmark of adaptive, or acquired, immunity. Because selected B cells give rise to antibody-secreting effector cells, measuring the concentrations of specific antibodies in blood over time distinguishes the primary and secondary immune responses (**Figure 43.15**).

The secondary immune response relies on the reservoir of T and B memory cells generated following initial exposure to an antigen. Because these cells are long-lived, they provide the basis for immunological memory, which

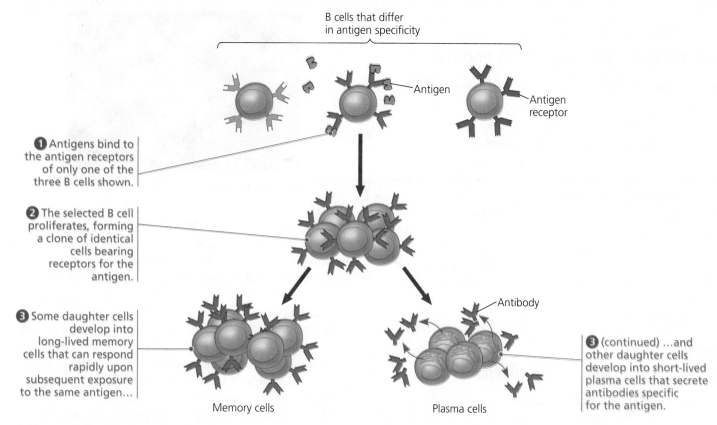

① Antigens bind to the antigen receptors of only one of the three B cells shown.

② The selected B cell proliferates, forming a clone of identical cells bearing receptors for the antigen.

③ Some daughter cells develop into long-lived memory cells that can respond rapidly upon subsequent exposure to the same antigen…

B cells that differ in antigen specificity

Antigen

Antigen receptor

Antibody

③ (continued) …and other daughter cells develop into short-lived plasma cells that secrete antibodies specific for the antigen.

Memory cells

Plasma cells

▲ **Figure 43.14** Clonal selection of B cells.

Primary immune response to antigen A produces antibodies to A.

Secondary immune response to antigen A produces antibodies to A; **primary immune response** to antigen B produces antibodies to B.

Antibodies to A

Antibodies to B

Exposure to antigen A

Exposure to antigens A and B

Time (days)

▲ **Figure 43.15** **The specificity of immunological memory.** Long-lived memory cells generated in the primary response to antigen A give rise to a heightened secondary response to the same antigen, but they do not affect the primary response to a different antigen (B).

INTERPRET THE DATA *Assume that on average one out of every 10^5 B cells in the body is specific for antigen A on day 16 and that the number of B cells producing a specific antibody is proportional to the concentration of that antibody. What would you predict is the frequency of B cells specific for antigen A on day 36?*

can span many decades. (Effector cells have much shorter life spans, which is why the immune response diminishes after an infection is overcome.) If an antigen is encountered again, memory cells specific for that antigen enable the rapid formation of clones of thousands of effector cells also specific for that antigen, thus generating a greatly enhanced immune defense.

Although the processes for antigen recognition, clonal selection, and immunological memory are similar for B cells and T cells, these two classes of lymphocytes fight infection in different ways and in different settings, as we'll explore in Concept 43.3.

CONCEPT CHECK **43.2**

1. **DRAW IT** Sketch a B cell antigen receptor. Label the V and C regions of the light and heavy chains. Label the antigen-binding sites, disulfide bridges, and transmembrane region. Where are these features located relative to the V and C regions?

2. Explain two advantages of having memory cells when a pathogen is encountered for a second time.

3. **WHAT IF?** If both copies of a light-chain gene and a heavy-chain gene recombined in each (diploid) B cell, how would this affect B cell development and function?

For suggested answers, see Appendix A.

CONCEPT 43.3

Adaptive immunity defends against infection of body fluids and body cells

Having considered how clones of lymphocytes arise, we now explore how these cells help fight infections and minimize damage by pathogens. The defenses provided by B and T lymphocytes can be divided into a humoral immune response and a cell-mediated immune response. The **humoral immune response** occurs in the blood and lymph, which were once called body humors (fluids). In the humoral response, antibodies help neutralize or eliminate toxins and pathogens in the blood and lymph. In the **cell-mediated immune response**, specialized T cells destroy infected host cells. Both responses can include both a primary immune response and a secondary immune response, with memory cells enabling the secondary response.

Helper T Cells: A Response to Nearly All Antigens

A type of T cell called a **helper T cell** triggers both the humoral and cell-mediated immune responses. Helper T cells themselves do not carry out those responses. Instead, signals from helper T cells initiate production of antibodies that neutralize pathogens and activate T cells that will kill the infected cells.

▲ **A dendritic cell** (colorized SEM).

Two requirements must be met for a helper T cell to activate adaptive immune responses. First, a foreign molecule must be present that can bind specifically to the antigen receptor of the T cell. Second, this antigen must be displayed on the surface of an **antigen-presenting cell**. The antigen-presenting cell can be a dendritic cell, macrophage, or B cell.

When host cells are infected, they too display antigens on their surface. What then distinguishes an antigen-presenting cell? The answer lies in the existence of two classes of MHC molecules. Most body cells have only the class I MHC molecules, but antigen-presenting cells have class I and class II MHC molecules. Class II molecules provide a molecular signature by which an antigen-presenting cell is recognized.

A helper T cell and the antigen-presenting cell displaying its specific epitope have a complex interaction **(Figure 43.16)**. The antigen receptors on the surface of the helper T cell

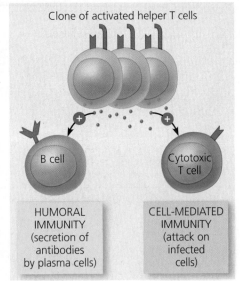

❶ An antigen-presenting cell engulfs a pathogen, degrades it, and displays antigen fragments complexed with class II MHC molecules on the cell surface. A specific helper T cell binds to this complex via its antigen receptor and an accessory protein (called CD4).

❷ Binding of the helper T cell promotes secretion of cytokines by the antigen-presenting cell. These cytokines, along with cytokines from the helper T cell itself, activate the helper T cell and stimulate its proliferation.

❸ Cell proliferation produces a clone of activated helper T cells. All cells in the clone have receptors for the same antigen fragment complex with the same antigen specificity. These cells secrete other cytokines, which help activate B cells and cytotoxic T cells.

▲ **Figure 43.16 The central role of helper T cells in humoral and cell-mediated immune responses.** In this example, a helper T cell responds to a dendritic cell displaying a microbial antigen.

bind to the antigen fragment and to the class II MHC molecule displaying that fragment on the antigen-presenting cell. At the same time, an accessory protein called CD4 on the helper T cell surface binds to the class II MHC molecule, helping keep the cells joined. As the two cells interact, signals in the form of cytokines are exchanged. For example, the cytokines secreted from a dendritic cell act in combination with the antigen to stimulate the helper T cell, causing it to produce its own set of cytokines. Also, extensive contact between the cell surfaces enables further information exchange.

Antigen-presenting cells interact with helper T cells in several contexts. Antigen presentation by a dendritic cell or macrophage activates a helper T cell, which proliferates, forming a clone of activated cells. In contrast, B cells present antigens to *already* activated helper T cells, which in turn activate the B cells themselves. Activated helper T cells also help stimulate cytotoxic T cells, as we'll discuss next.

Cytotoxic T Cells: A Response to Infected Cells

In the absence of an immune response, pathogens can reproduce in and kill infected cells, as shown at the upper right. In the cell-mediated immune response, **cytotoxic T cells** use toxic proteins to kill cells infected by viruses or other intracellular pathogens before pathogens fully mature. To become active, cytotoxic T cells require signals from helper T cells and interaction with an antigen-presenting cell. Fragments of foreign proteins produced in infected host

▲ **A dying infected cell** (colorized SEM).

cells associate with class I MHC molecules and are displayed on the cell surface, where they can be recognized by cytotoxic T cells **(Figure 43.17)**. As with helper T cells, cytotoxic T cells have an accessory protein that binds to the MHC molecule. This accessory protein, called CD8, helps keep the two cells in contact while the cytotoxic T cell is activated.

The targeted destruction of an infected host cell by a cytotoxic T cell involves the secretion of proteins that disrupt membrane integrity and trigger cell death (apoptosis; see Figure 43.17). The death of the infected cell not only deprives the pathogen of a place to multiply, but also exposes cell contents to circulating antibodies, which mark released antigens for disposal.

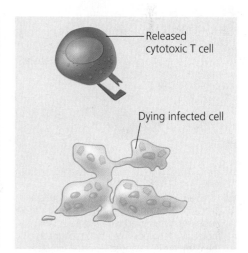

❶ An activated cytotoxic T cell binds to a class I MHC–antigen fragment complex on an infected cell via its antigen receptor and an accessory protein (called CD8).

❷ The T cell releases perforin molecules, which form pores in the infected cell membrane, and granzymes, enzymes that break down proteins. Granzymes enter the infected cell by endocytosis.

❸ The granzymes initiate apoptosis within the infected cell, leading to fragmentation of the nucleus and cytoplasm and eventual cell death. The released cytotoxic T cell can attack other infected cells.

▲ **Figure 43.17 The killing action of cytotoxic T cells on an infected host cell.** An activated cytotoxic T cell releases molecules that make pores in an infected cell's membrane and enzymes that break down proteins, promoting the cell's death.

B Cells and Antibodies: A Response to Extracellular Pathogens

The secretion of antibodies by B cells is the hallmark of the humoral immune response. It begins with activation of the B cells.

Activation of B Cells

As illustrated in **Figure 43.18**, activation of B cells involves both helper T cells and proteins on the surface of pathogens. Stimulated by both an antigen and cytokines, the B cell proliferates and differentiates into memory B cells and antibody-secreting plasma cells.

The pathway for antigen processing and display in B cells differs from that in other antigen-presenting cells. A macrophage or dendritic cell can present fragments from a wide variety of protein antigens, whereas a B cell presents only the antigen to which it specifically binds. When an antigen first binds to receptors on the surface of a B cell, the cell takes in a few foreign molecules by receptor-mediated endocytosis (see Figure 7.19). The class II MHC protein of the B cell then presents an antigen fragment to a helper T cell. This direct cell-to-cell contact is usually critical to B cell activation (see step 2 in Figure 43.18).

B cell activation leads to a robust humoral immune response: A single activated B cell gives rise to thousands of identical plasma cells. These plasma cells stop expressing a membrane-bound antigen receptor and begin producing and secreting antibodies (see step 3 in Figure 43.18). Each plasma cell secretes approximately 2,000 antibodies every second during its 4- to 5-day life span, nearly a trillion antibody molecules in total. Furthermore, most antigens recognized by B cells contain multiple epitopes. An exposure to a single antigen therefore normally activates a variety of B cells, which give rise to different plasma cells producing antibodies directed against different epitopes on the common antigen.

Antibody Function

Antibodies do not actually kill pathogens, but by binding to antigens, they interfere with pathogen activity or mark pathogens in various ways for inactivation or destruction. Consider, for example, *neutralization*, a process in which antibodies bind to proteins on the surface of a virus **(Figure 43.19a)**. The bound antibodies prevent infection of a host cell, thus neutralizing the virus. Similarly, antibodies sometimes bind to toxins released in body fluids, preventing the toxins from entering body cells.

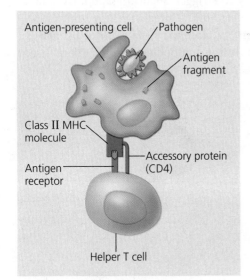

① After an antigen-presenting cell engulfs and degrades a pathogen, it displays an antigen fragment complexed with a class II MHC molecule. A helper T cell that recognizes the complex is activated with the aid of cytokines secreted from the antigen-presenting cell.

② When a B cell with receptors for the same epitope internalizes the antigen, it displays an antigen fragment on the cell surface in a complex with a class II MHC molecule. An activated helper T cell bearing receptors specific for the displayed fragment binds to and activates the B cell.

③ The activated B cell proliferates and differentiates into memory B cells and antibody-secreting plasma cells. The secreted antibodies are specific for the same antigen that initiated the response.

▲ **Figure 43.18 Activation of a B cell in the humoral immune response.** Most protein antigens require activated helper T cells to trigger a humoral response. A macrophage (shown here) or a dendritic cell can activate a helper T cell, which in turn can activate a B cell to give rise to antibody-secreting plasma cells.

? *What function do cell-surface antigen receptors play for memory B cells?*

(a) Neutralization

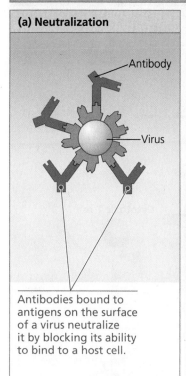

Antibodies bound to antigens on the surface of a virus neutralize it by blocking its ability to bind to a host cell.

(b) Opsonization

Binding of antibodies to antigens on the surface of bacteria promotes phagocytosis by macrophages and neutrophils.

(c) Activation of complement system and pore formation

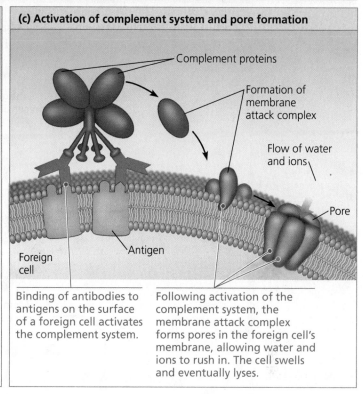

Binding of antibodies to antigens on the surface of a foreign cell activates the complement system.

Following activation of the complement system, the membrane attack complex forms pores in the foreign cell's membrane, allowing water and ions to rush in. The cell swells and eventually lyses.

In *opsonization*, antibodies bound to antigens on bacteria do not block infection, but instead present a readily recognized structure for macrophages or neutrophils, thereby promoting phagocytosis **(Figure 43.19b)**. Because each antibody has two antigen-binding sites, antibodies can also facilitate phagocytosis by linking bacterial cells, viruses, or other foreign substances into aggregates.

When antibodies facilitate phagocytosis, as in opsonization, they also help fine-tune the humoral immune response. Recall that phagocytosis enables macrophages and dendritic cells to present antigens to and stimulate helper T cells, which in turn stimulate the very B cells whose antibodies contribute to phagocytosis. This positive feedback between innate and adaptive immunity contributes to a coordinated, effective response to infection.

Antibodies sometimes work together with the proteins of the complement system. (The name *complement* reflects the fact that these proteins increase the effectiveness of antibody-directed attacks on bacteria.) Binding of a complement protein to an antigen-antibody complex on a foreign cell triggers the generation of a *membrane attack complex* that forms a pore in the membrane of the cell. Ions and water rush into the cell, causing it to swell and lyse **(Figure 43.19c)**. Whether activated as part of innate or adaptive defenses, this cascade of complement protein activity results in the lysis of foreign cells and produces factors that promote inflammation or stimulate phagocytosis.

Although antibodies are the cornerstones of the response in body fluids, there is also a mechanism by which they can bring about the death of infected body cells. When a virus uses a cell's biosynthetic machinery to produce viral proteins, these viral products can appear on the cell surface. If antibodies specific for epitopes on these viral proteins bind to the exposed proteins, the presence of bound antibody at the cell surface can recruit a natural killer cell. The natural killer cell then releases proteins that cause the infected cell to undergo apoptosis. Thus the activities of the innate and adaptive immune systems are once again closely linked.

B cells can express five types, or *classes*, of immunoglobulin (IgA, IgD, IgE, IgG, and IgM). For a given B cell, each class has an identical antigen-binding specificity but a distinct heavy-chain C region. The B cell antigen receptor, known as IgD, is membrane bound. The other four classes consist of soluble antibodies, including those found in blood, tears, saliva, and breast milk.

Summary of the Humoral and Cell-Mediated Immune Responses

As noted earlier, both the humoral and cell-mediated responses can include primary and secondary immune responses. Memory cells of each type—helper T cell, B cell, and cytotoxic T cell—enable the secondary response. For example, when body fluids are reinfected by a pathogen

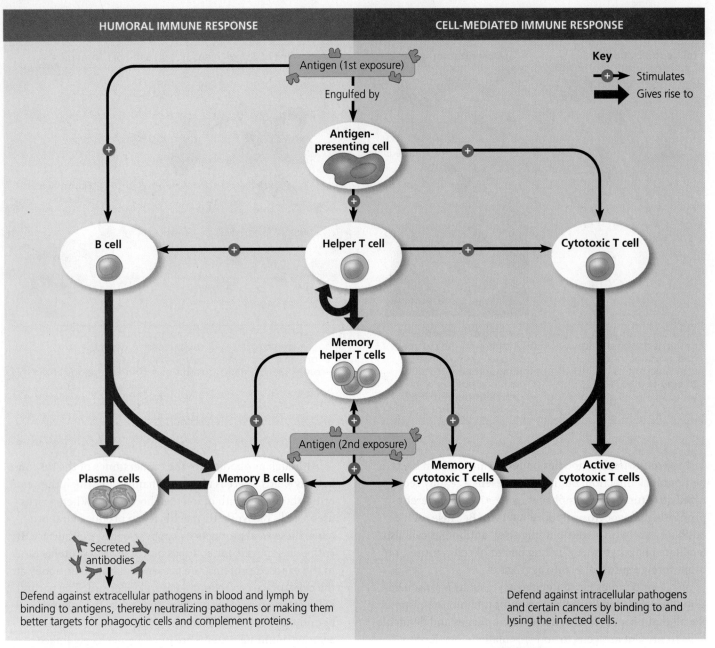

HUMORAL IMMUNE RESPONSE

CELL-MEDIATED IMMUNE RESPONSE

Antigen (1st exposure)

Engulfed by

Antigen-
presenting cell

B cell

Helper T cell

Cytotoxic T cell

Memory
helper T cells

Antigen (2nd exposure)

Plasma cells

Memory B cells

Memory
cytotoxic T cells

Active
cytotoxic T cells

Secreted
antibodies

Key

+ → Stimulates

→ Gives rise to

Defend against extracellular pathogens in blood and lymph by binding to antigens, thereby neutralizing pathogens or making them better targets for phagocytic cells and complement proteins.

Defend against intracellular pathogens and certain cancers by binding to and lysing the infected cells.

▲ **Figure 43.20 An overview of the adaptive immune response.**

? *Identify each arrow as representing part of the primary or secondary response.*

ANIMATION **BioFlix** Visit the Study Area in **MasteringBiology** for the BioFlix® 3-D Animation on Immunology.

encountered previously, memory B cells and memory helper T cells initiate a secondary humoral response. **Figure 43.20** summarizes adaptive immunity, reviews the events that initiate humoral and cell-mediated immune responses, and highlights the central role of the helper T cell.

Active and Passive Immunity

Our discussion of adaptive immunity has to this point focused on **active immunity**, the defenses that arise when a pathogen infects the body and prompts a primary or

secondary immune response. A different type of immunity results when the IgG antibodies in the blood of a pregnant female cross the placenta to her fetus. This protection is called **passive immunity** because the antibodies in the recipient (in this case, the fetus) are produced by another individual (the mother). IgA antibodies present in breast milk provide additional passive immunity to the infant's digestive tract while the infant's immune system develops. Because passive immunity does not involve the recipient's B and T cells, it persists only as long as the transferred antibodies last (a few weeks to a few months).

Both active immunity and passive immunity can be induced artificially. Active immunity can develop from the introduction of antigens into the body through **immunization**. In 1796, Edward Jenner noted that milkmaids who had cowpox, a mild disease usually seen only in cows, did not contract smallpox, a far more dangerous disease. In the first documented immunization (or *vaccination*, from the Latin *vacca*, cow), Jenner used the cowpox virus to induce adaptive immunity against the closely related smallpox virus. Today, immunizations are carried out with preparations of antigen (vaccines) obtained from many sources, including inactivated bacterial toxins, killed or weakened pathogens, and even genes encoding microbial proteins. Because all of these agents induce a primary immune response and immunological memory, an encounter with the pathogen from which the vaccine was derived triggers a rapid and strong secondary immune response (see Figure 43.15).

Vaccination programs have been successful against many infectious diseases that once killed or incapacitated large numbers of people. A worldwide vaccination campaign led to eradication of smallpox in the late 1970s. In industrialized nations, routine immunization of infants and children has dramatically reduced the incidence of sometimes devastating diseases, such as polio, measles, and whooping cough. Unfortunately, not all pathogens are easily managed by vaccination. Furthermore, some vaccines are not readily available in impoverished areas of the globe.

Misinformation about vaccine safety and disease risk has led to a substantial and growing public health problem. Consider measles as just one example. Side effects of immunization are remarkably rare, with fewer than one in a million children suffering a significant allergic reaction to the measles vaccine. The disease, however, is quite dangerous, killing more than 200,000 people each year. Declines in measles vaccination rates in parts of the United Kingdom, Russia, and the United States have resulted in a number of recent measles outbreaks and many preventable deaths.

In artificial passive immunization, antibodies from an immune animal are injected into a nonimmune animal. For example, humans bitten by venomous snakes are sometimes treated with antivenin, serum from sheep or horses that have been immunized against a snake venom. When injected immediately after a snakebite, the antibodies in antivenin can neutralize toxins in the venom before the toxins do massive damage.

Antibodies as Tools

Antibodies that an animal produces after exposure to an antigen are the products of many different clones of plasma cells **(Figure 43.21)**, each specific for a different epitope. However, antibodies can also be prepared from a single clone of B cells grown in culture. The **monoclonal antibodies**

Endoplasmic reticulum of plasma cell

2 μm

▲ **Figure 43.21 A plasma cell.** A plasma cell contains abundant endoplasmic reticulum, a common feature of cells dedicated to making proteins for secretion (TEM).

produced by such a culture are identical and specific for the same epitope on an antigen.

Monoclonal antibodies have provided the basis for many recent advances in medical diagnosis and treatment. For example, home pregnancy test kits use monoclonal antibodies to detect human chorionic gonadotropin (hCG). Because hCG is produced as soon as an embryo implants in the uterus (see Chapter 46), the presence of this hormone in a woman's urine is a reliable indicator for a very early stage of pregnancy. Monoclonal antibodies are also produced in large amounts and injected as a therapy for a number of human diseases, including certain cancers.

Immune Rejection

Like pathogens, cells from another person can be recognized as foreign and attacked by immune defenses. For example, skin transplanted from one person to a genetically nonidentical person will look healthy for a week or so but will then be destroyed (rejected) by the recipient's immune response. Keep in mind that the body's rejection of transplanted tissues or organs or of an incompatible blood transfusion is the expected reaction of a healthy immune system exposed to foreign antigens. (It remains a largely unanswered question why a pregnant woman does not reject her fetus as nonself tissue.)

Blood Groups

To avoid a blood transfusion being recognized as foreign by the recipient's immune system, doctors must take into account a property of the donor and recipient known as the ABO blood group. Red blood cells are designated as type A if they have the A carbohydrate on their surface. Similarly, the B carbohydrate is found on the surface of type B red blood cells; both A and B carbohydrates are found on type AB red blood cells; and neither carbohydrate is found on type O red blood cells (see Figure 14.11).

Why does the immune system recognize particular sugars on red blood cells? It turns out that certain bacteria normally present in the body have epitopes very similar to the A and B carbohydrates. Responding to the bacterial epitope similar to the B carbohydrate, a person with type A blood makes antibodies that will react with the B carbohydrate. That same person doesn't make antibodies against the bacterial epitope similar to the A carbohydrate because lymphocytes reactive with the body's own molecules are inactivated or eliminated during development.

To understand how ABO blood groups affect transfusions, let's consider the immune response of someone with type A blood. If a person with type A blood receives a transfusion of type B blood, the anti-B antibodies in the type A blood cause an immediate and devastating transfusion reaction. The transfused red blood cells undergo lysis, which can lead to chills, fever, shock, and kidney malfunction. By the same token, anti-A antibodies in the donated type B blood will act against the recipient's type A red blood cells. Although such interactions prevent type O individuals from receiving transfusions of any other blood type, the discovery of enzymes that can cleave the A and B carbohydrates from red blood cells may eliminate this problem.

Tissue and Organ Transplants

Each of us expresses MHC proteins from more than a dozen different genes. Furthermore, more than 100 different versions, or alleles, of these genes exist among humans. In transplants or grafts of an organ or a piece of tissue between individuals, these different forms of MHC molecules can act as antigens, stimulating an immune response that leads to rejection. Note that the diversity of MHC molecules almost guarantees that no two people, except identical twins, will have exactly the same set. As a result, some MHC molecules on the donated tissue are foreign to the recipient in the vast majority of grafts and transplants.

To minimize rejection in a graft or transplant operation, physicians use donor tissue bearing MHC molecules that match those of the recipient as closely as possible. In addition, the recipient takes medicines that suppress immune responses (but as a result leave the recipient more susceptible to infections).

Transplants of bone marrow from one person to another can also cause an immune reaction, but for a different reason. Bone marrow transplants are used to treat leukemia and other cancers as well as various hematological (blood cell) diseases. Prior to receiving transplanted bone marrow, the recipient is typically treated with radiation to eliminate his or her own bone marrow cells, thus

destroying the source of abnormal cells. This treatment effectively obliterates the recipient's immune system, leaving little chance of graft rejection. However, lymphocytes in the donated marrow may react against the recipient. This *graft-versus-host reaction* is limited if the MHC molecules of the donor and recipient are well matched. Bone marrow donor programs continually seek volunteers because the great variability of MHC molecules makes a diverse pool of donors essential.

CONCEPT 43.4

Disruptions in immune system function can elicit or exacerbate disease

Although adaptive immunity offers significant protection against a wide range of pathogens, it is not fail-safe. Here we'll first examine the disorders and diseases that arise when adaptive immunity is blocked or misregulated. We'll then turn to some of the evolutionary adaptations of pathogens that diminish the effectiveness of adaptive immune responses in the host.

Exaggerated, Self-Directed, and Diminished Immune Responses

The highly regulated interplay among lymphocytes, other body cells, and foreign substances generates an immune response that provides extraordinary protection against many pathogens. When allergic, autoimmune, or immunodeficiency disorders disrupt this delicate balance, the effects are frequently severe.

Allergies

Allergies are exaggerated (hypersensitive) responses to certain antigens called *allergens*. The most common allergies involve antibodies of the IgE class. Hay fever, for instance, occurs when plasma cells secrete IgE antibodies specific for antigens on the surface of pollen grains (**Figure 43.22**). Some IgE antibodies attach by their base to mast cells in connective tissues. Pollen grains that enter the body later attach to the antigen-binding sites of these IgE antibodies. Such attachment links adjacent IgE molecules, inducing the mast cell to release histamine and other inflammatory chemicals. Acting on a variety of cell types, these chemicals bring about the typical allergy symptoms: sneezing, runny nose, teary eyes, and smooth muscle contractions in the lungs that can inhibit effective breathing. Drugs known as antihistamines block receptors for histamine, diminishing allergy symptoms (and inflammation).

An acute allergic response sometimes leads to a life-threatening reaction called *anaphylactic shock*. Inflammatory chemicals released from mast cells trigger constriction of bronchioles and sudden dilation of peripheral blood vessels, which causes a precipitous drop in blood pressure. Death may occur within minutes due to the inability to breathe and lack of blood flow. Substances that can cause anaphylactic shock in allergic individuals include bee venom, penicillin, peanuts, and shellfish. People with severe hypersensitivities often carry syringes containing the hormone epinephrine. An injection of epinephrine rapidly counteracts this allergic response, constricting peripheral blood vessels, reducing swelling in the throat, and relaxing muscles in the lungs to help breathing (see Figure 45.8).

IgE

Mast cell

Allergen (second exposure)

1 IgE antibodies produced in response to initial exposure to an allergen bind to receptors on mast cells.

2 On subsequent exposure to the same allergen, IgE molecules attached to a mast cell recognize and bind the allergen.

Vesicle
Histamine

3 Cross-linking of adjacent IgE molecules triggers release of histamine and other chemicals, leading to allergy symptoms.

▲ **Figure 43.22 Mast cells, IgE, and the allergic response.** In this example, pollen grains act as the allergen.

Autoimmune Diseases

In some people, the immune system is active against particular molecules of the body, causing an **autoimmune disease**. Such a loss of self-tolerance has many forms. In systemic lupus erythematosus, commonly called *lupus*, the immune system generates antibodies against histones and DNA released by the normal breakdown of body cells. These self-reactive antibodies cause skin rashes, fever, arthritis, and kidney dysfunction. Other targets of autoimmunity include the insulin-producing beta cells of the pancreas (in type 1 diabetes) and the myelin sheaths that encase many neurons (in multiple sclerosis).

Heredity, gender, and environment all influence susceptibility to autoimmune disorders. For example, members of certain families show an increased susceptibility to particular autoimmune disorders. In addition, many autoimmune diseases afflict females more often than males. Women are nine times as likely as men to suffer from lupus and two to three times as likely to develop *rheumatoid arthritis*, a damaging and painful inflammation of the cartilage and bone in joints (**Figure 43.23**). The cause of this sex bias, as well as the rise in autoimmune disease frequency in industrialized countries, is an area of active research and debate.

▲ **Figure 43.23** X-ray of hands that are deformed by rheumatoid arthritis.

Exertion, Stress, and the Immune System

Many forms of exertion and stress influence immune system function. For example, moderate exercise improves immune system function and significantly reduces susceptibility to the common cold and other infections of the upper respiratory tract. In contrast, exercise to the point of exhaustion leads to more frequent infections and more severe symptoms. Studies of marathon runners support the conclusion that exercise intensity is the critical variable. On average, such runners get sick less often than their more sedentary peers during training, a time of moderate exertion, but markedly more often in the period immediately following the grueling race itself. Similarly, psychological stress has been shown to disrupt immune system regulation by altering the interplay of the hormonal, nervous, and immune systems (see Figure 45.20). Research also confirms that rest is important for immunity: Adults who averaged fewer than 7 hours of sleep got sick three times as often when exposed to a cold virus as those who averaged at least 8 hours.

Immunodeficiency Diseases

A disorder in which an immune system response to antigens is defective or absent is called an immunodeficiency. Whatever its cause and nature, an immunodeficiency can lead to frequent and recurrent infections and increased susceptibility to certain cancers.

An *inborn immunodeficiency* results from a genetic or developmental defect in the production of immune system cells or of specific proteins, such as antibodies or the proteins of the complement system. Depending on the specific defect, either innate or adaptive defenses—or both—may be impaired. In severe combined immunodeficiency (SCID), functional lymphocytes are rare or absent. Lacking an adaptive immune response, SCID patients are susceptible to infections, such as pneumonia and meningitis, that can cause death in infancy. Treatments include bone marrow and stem cell transplantation.

Later in life, exposure to chemicals or biological agents can cause an *acquired immunodeficiency*. Drugs used to fight autoimmune diseases or prevent transplant rejection suppress the immune system, leading to an immunodeficient state. Certain cancers also suppress the immune system, especially Hodgkin's disease, which damages the lymphatic system. Acquired immunodeficiencies range from temporary states that may arise from physiological stress to the devastating disease AIDS (acquired immune deficiency syndrome), which we'll discuss in the next section.

Evolutionary Adaptations of Pathogens That Underlie Immune System Avoidance

EVOLUTION Just as immune systems that ward off pathogens have evolved in animals, mechanisms that thwart immune responses have evolved in pathogens. Using human pathogens as examples, we'll examine some common mechanisms: antigenic variation, latency, and direct attack on the immune system.

Antigenic Variation

One mechanism for escaping the body's defenses is for a pathogen to alter how it appears to the immune system. Immunological memory is a record of the foreign epitopes an animal has encountered. If the pathogen that expressed those epitopes no longer does so, it can reinfect or remain in a host without triggering the rapid and robust response that memory cells provide. Such changes in epitope expression are called *antigenic variation*. The parasite that causes sleeping sickness (trypanosomiasis) provides an extreme example, periodically switching at random among 1,000 different versions of the protein found over its entire surface. In the Scientific Skills Exercise, you'll interpret data on this form of antigenic variation and the body's response.

Antigenic variation is the main reason the influenza, or "flu," virus remains a major public health problem. As it replicates in one human host after another, the virus undergoes frequent mutations. Because any change that lessens recognition by the immune system provides a selective advantage, the virus steadily accumulates mutations that change its surface proteins, reducing the effectiveness of the host immune response. As a result, a new flu vaccine must be developed, produced, and distributed each year. In addition, the human influenza virus occasionally forms new strains by exchanging genes with influenza viruses that infect domesticated animals, such as pigs or chickens. When this occurs, the new strain may not be recognized by any of the memory cells in the human population. The resulting outbreak can be deadly: The 1918–1919 influenza outbreak killed more than 20 million people.

In 2009, an influenza virus called H1N1 appeared that contained a novel combination of genes from flu viruses that normally circulate in pigs, birds, and humans. The rapid spread of this flu across the human population caused a *pandemic*, an outbreak of worldwide proportions. Fortunately, a rapidly developed H1N1 vaccine soon provided public health officials with an excellent means of slowing the spread of this virus and reducing the impact of the outbreak.

Latency

Some viruses avoid an immune response by infecting cells and then entering a largely inactive state called *latency*. Because production of most viral proteins and free viruses ceases, latent viruses do not trigger an adaptive immune response. Nevertheless, the viral genome persists in the nuclei of infected cells, either as a separate DNA molecule or as a copy integrated into the host genome. Latency typically persists until conditions arise that are favorable for viral transmission or unfavorable for host survival, such as when the host is infected by another pathogen. Such circumstances trigger the synthesis and release of free viruses that can infect new hosts.

Herpes simplex viruses, which establish themselves in human sensory neurons, provide a good example of latency. The type 1 virus causes most oral herpes infections, whereas the type 2 virus is responsible for most cases of genital herpes. Because sensory neurons express relatively few MHC I molecules, the infected cells are inefficient at presenting viral antigens to circulating lymphocytes. Stimuli such as fever, emotional stress, or menstruation reactivate the virus to replicate and infect surrounding epithelial tissues. Activation of the type 1 virus can result in blisters around the mouth that are inaccurately called "cold" sores. The type 2 virus can cause genital sores, but people infected with either the type 1 or type 2 virus often lack any symptoms. Infections of the type 2 virus, which is sexually transmitted, pose

Comparing Two Variables on a Common x-Axis

How Does the Immune System Respond to a Changing Pathogen? Natural selection favors parasites that are able to maintain a low-level infection in a host for a long time. *Trypanosoma*, the unicellular parasite that causes sleeping sickness, is one example. The glycoproteins covering a trypanosome's surface are encoded by a gene that is duplicated more than a thousand times in the organism's genome. Each copy is slightly different. By periodically switching among these genes, the trypanosome can display a series of surface glycoproteins with different molecular structures. In this exercise, you will interpret two data sets to explore hypotheses about the benefits of the trypanosome's ever-shifting surface glycoproteins and the host's immune response.

▲ Trypanosomes (yellow) and red blood cells

Part A: Data from a Study of Parasite Levels This study measured the abundance of parasites in the blood of one human patient during the first few weeks of a chronic infection.

Day	Number of Parasites (in millions) per mL of Blood
4	0.1
6	0.3
8	1.2
10	0.2
12	0.2
14	0.9
16	0.6
18	0.1
20	0.7
22	1.2
24	0.2

Part A: Interpret the Data

1. Plot the data in the above table as a line graph. Which column is the independent variable, and which is the dependent variable? Put the independent variable on the *x*-axis. (For additional information about graphs, see the Scientific Skills Review in Appendix F and the Study Area in MasteringBiology.)

2. Visually displaying data in a graph can help make patterns in the data more noticeable. Describe any patterns revealed by your graph.

3. Assume that a drop in parasite abundance reflects an effective immune response by the host. Formulate a hypothesis to explain the pattern you described in question 2.

Part B: Data from a Study of Antibody Levels Many decades after scientists first observed the pattern of *Trypanosoma* abundance over the course of infection, researchers identified antibodies specific to different forms of the parasite's surface glycoprotein. The table below lists the relative abundance of two such antibodies during the early period of chronic infection, using an index ranging from 0 (absent) to 1.

Day	Antibody Specific to Glycoprotein Variant A	Antibody Specific to Glycoprotein Variant B
4	0	0
6	0	0
8	0.2	0
10	0.5	0
12	1	0
14	1	0.1
16	1	0.3
18	1	0.9
20	1	1
22	1	1
24	1	1

Part B: Interpret the Data

4. Note that these data were collected over the same period of infection (days 4–24) as the parasite abundance data you graphed in part A. Therefore, you can incorporate these new data into your first graph, using the same *x*-axis. However, since the antibody level data are measured in a different way than the parasite abundance data, add a second set of *y*-axis labels on the right side of your graph. Then, using different colors or sets of symbols, add the data for the two antibody types. Labeling the *y*-axis two different ways enables you to compare how two dependent variables change relative to a shared independent variable.

5. Describe any patterns you observe by comparing the two data sets over the same period. Do these patterns support your hypothesis from part A? Do they prove that hypothesis? Explain.

6. Scientists can now also distinguish the abundance of trypanosomes recognized specifically by antibodies type A and type B. How would incorporating such information change your graph?

(MB) A version of this Scientific Skills Exercise can be assigned in MasteringBiology.

Data from L. J. Morrison, et al., Probabilistic order in antigenic variation of Trypanosoma brucei, *International Journal for Parasitology* 35:961-972 (2005) and L. J. Morrison, et al.,Antigenic variation in the African trypanosome: molecular mechanisms and phenotypic complexity, *Cellular Microbiology* 1: 1724-1734 (2009).

a serious threat to the babies of infected mothers and can increase transmission of the virus that causes AIDS.

Attack on the Immune System: HIV

The **human immunodeficiency virus (HIV)**, the pathogen that causes AIDS, both escapes and attacks the adaptive immune response. Once introduced into the body, HIV infects helper T cells with high efficiency by binding specifically to the CD4 accessory protein (see Figure 43.16). HIV also infects some cell types that have low levels of CD4, such as macrophages and brain cells. Inside cells, the HIV RNA genome is reverse-transcribed, and the product DNA is integrated into the host cell's genome (see Figure 19.8). In this form, the viral genome can direct the production of new viruses.

Although the body responds to HIV with an immune response sufficient to eliminate most viral infections, some HIV invariably escapes. One reason HIV persists is that it has a very high mutation rate. Altered proteins on the surface of some mutated viruses reduce interaction with antibodies and cytotoxic T cells. Such viruses replicate and mutate further. HIV thus evolves within the body. The continued presence of HIV is also helped by latency while the viral DNA is integrated in the host cell's genome. This latent DNA is shielded from the immune system as well as from antiviral agents currently used against HIV, which attack only actively replicating viruses.

Over time, an untreated HIV infection not only avoids the adaptive immune response but also abolishes it **(Figure 43.24)**. Viral replication and cell death triggered by the virus lead to loss of helper T cells, impairing both humoral and cell-mediated immune responses. The eventual result is **acquired immunodeficiency syndrome (AIDS)**, an impairment in immune responses that leaves the body susceptible to infections and cancers that a healthy immune system would usually defeat. For example, *Pneumocystis carinii*, a common fungus that does not cause disease in healthy individuals, can result in severe pneumonia in people with AIDS. Such opportunistic diseases, as well as nerve damage and body wasting, are the primary causes of death in AIDS patients, not HIV itself.

Transmission of HIV requires the transfer of virus particles or infected cells from person to person via body fluids such as semen, blood, or breast milk. Unprotected sex (that is, without using a condom) and transmission via HIV-contaminated needles (typically among intravenous drug users) cause the vast majority of HIV infections. The virus can enter the body through mucosal linings of the vagina, vulva, penis, or rectum during intercourse or via the mouth during oral sex. People infected with HIV can transmit the disease in the first few weeks of infection, *before* they produce HIV-specific antibodies that can be detected in a blood test. Currently, 10–50% of all new HIV infections appear to be caused by recently infected individuals. Although HIV infection cannot be cured, drugs have been developed that can significantly slow HIV replication and the progression to AIDS.

Cancer and Immunity

When adaptive immunity is inactivated, the frequency of certain cancers increases dramatically. For example, the risk of developing Kaposi's sarcoma is 20,000 times greater for untreated AIDS patients than for healthy people. This observation was unanticipated. If the immune system recognizes only nonself, it should fail to recognize the uncontrolled growth of self cells that is the hallmark of cancer. It turns out, however, that viruses are involved in about 15–20% of all human cancers. Because the immune system can recognize viral proteins as foreign, it can act as a defense against viruses that can cause cancer and against cancer cells that harbor viruses.

Scientists have identified six viruses that can cause cancer in humans. The Kaposi's sarcoma herpesvirus is one such virus. Hepatitis B virus, which can trigger liver cancer, is another. A vaccine introduced in 1986 for hepatitis B virus was the first vaccine shown to help prevent a specific human cancer. Rapid progress on virus-induced cancers continues. In 2006, the release of a vaccine that is derived from human papillomavirus (HPV) marked a major victory against cervical cancer, as well as other cancers that can affect sexually active men or women.

▲ **Human papillomavirus**

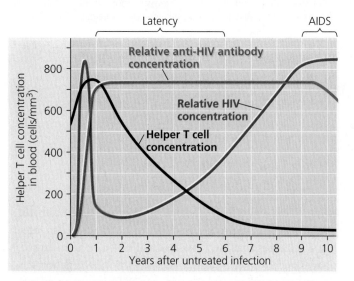

▲ **Figure 43.24 The progress of an untreated HIV infection.**

CONCEPT CHECK 43.4

1. In the muscular disease myasthenia gravis, antibodies bind to and block certain receptors on muscle cells, preventing muscle contraction. Is this disease best classified as an immunodeficiency disease, an autoimmune disease, or an allergic reaction? Explain.

2. People with herpes simplex type 1 viruses often get mouth sores when they have a cold or similar infection. How might this location benefit the virus?

3. **WHAT IF?** How would a macrophage deficiency likely affect a person's innate and adaptive defenses?

For suggested answers, see Appendix A.

SUMMARY OF KEY CONCEPTS

CONCEPT 43.1

In innate immunity, recognition and response rely on traits common to groups of pathogens (pp. 947–952)

- In both invertebrates and vertebrates, innate immunity is mediated by physical and chemical barriers as well as cell-based defenses. Activation of innate immune responses relies on recognition proteins specific for broad classes of pathogens. Microbes that penetrate barrier defenses are ingested by phagocytic cells, which in vertebrates include **macrophages** and **dendritic cells**. Additional cellular defenses include **natural killer cells**, which can induce the death of virus-infected cells. **Complement system** proteins, **interferons**, and other antimicrobial peptides also act against pathogens. In the **inflammatory response**, **histamine** and other chemicals that are released at the injury site promote changes in blood vessels that enhance immune cell access.

- Pathogens sometimes evade innate immune defenses. For example, some bacteria have an outer capsule that prevents recognition, while others are resistant to breakdown within lysosomes.

? *In what ways does innate immunity protect the mammalian digestive tract?*

CONCEPT 43.2

In adaptive immunity, receptors provide pathogen-specific recognition (pp. 952–957)

- **Adaptive immunity** relies on two types of **lymphocytes** that arise from stem cells in the bone marrow: **B cells** and **T cells**. Lymphocytes have cell-surface **antigen receptors** for foreign molecules (**antigens**). All receptor proteins on a single B or T cell are the same, but there are millions of B and T cells in the body that differ in the foreign molecules that their receptors recognize. Upon infection, B and T cells specific for the pathogen are activated. Some T cells help other lymphocytes; others kill infected host cells. B cells called **plasma cells** produce soluble proteins called **antibodies**, which bind to foreign molecules and cells. Activated B and T cells called **memory cells** defend against future infections by the same pathogen.

- Recognition of foreign molecules by B cells and T cells involves the binding of variable regions of receptors to an **epitope**, a small region of an antigen. B cells and antibodies recognize epitopes on the surface of antigens circulating in the blood or lymph. T cells recognize epitopes in small antigen fragments (peptides) that are presented on the surface of host cells by proteins called **major histocompatibility complex (MHC) molecules** This interaction activates a T cell, enabling it to participate in adaptive immunity.

- The four major characteristics of B and T cell development are the generation of cell diversity, self-tolerance, proliferation, and immunological memory. Proliferation and memory are both based on **clonal selection**, illustrated here for B cells:

? *Why is the adaptive immune response to an initial infection slower than the innate response?*

CONCEPT 43.3

Adaptive immunity defends against infection of body fluids and body cells (pp. 958–964)

- **Helper T cells** interact with antigen fragments displayed by class II MHC molecules on the surface of **antigen-presenting cells**: dendritic cells, macrophages, and B cells. Activated helper T cells secrete **cytokines** that stimulate other lymphocytes. In the **cell-mediated immune response**, activated **cytotoxic T cells** trigger destruction of infected cells. In the **humoral immune response**, antibodies help eliminate antigens by promoting phagocytosis and complement-mediated lysis.

- **Active immunity** develops in response to infection or to immunization. The transfer of antibodies in **passive immunity** provides immediate, short-term protection.

- Tissues or cells transferred from one person to another are subject to immune rejection. In tissue grafts and organ transplants, MHC molecules stimulate rejection. Lymphocytes in bone marrow transplants may cause a graft-versus-host reaction.

? *Is immunological memory after a natural infection fundamentally different from immunological memory after vaccination? Explain.*

Disruptions in immune system function can elicit or exacerbate disease (pp. 964–968)

- In allergies, such as hay fever, the interaction of antibodies and allergens triggers immune cells to release histamine and other mediators that cause vascular changes and allergic symptoms. Loss of self-tolerance can lead to **autoimmune diseases**, such as multiple sclerosis. Inborn immunodeficiencies result from defects that interfere with innate, humoral, or cell-mediated defenses. **AIDS** is an acquired immunodeficiency caused by **HIV**.

- Antigenic variation, latency, and direct assault on the immune system allow some pathogens to thwart immune responses. HIV infection destroys helper T cells, leaving the patient prone to disease. Immune defense against cancer appears to primarily involve action against viruses that can cause cancer and cancer cells that harbor viruses.

? *Is being infected with HIV the same as having AIDS? Explain.*

TEST YOUR UNDERSTANDING

LEVEL 1: KNOWLEDGE/COMPREHENSION

1. Which of these is *not* part of insect immunity?
   a. enzyme activation of pathogen-killing chemicals
   b. activation of natural killer cells
   c. phagocytosis by hemocytes
   d. production of antimicrobial peptides

2. An epitope associates with which part of an antigen receptor or antibody?
   a. the tail
   b. the heavy-chain constant regions only
   c. variable regions of a heavy chain and light chain combined
   d. the light-chain constant regions only

3. Which statement best describes the difference in responses of effector B cells (plasma cells) and cytotoxic T cells?
   a. B cells confer active immunity; cytotoxic T cells confer passive immunity.
   b. B cells respond the first time a pathogen is present; cytotoxic T cells respond subsequent times.
   c. B cells secrete antibodies against a pathogen; cytotoxic T cells kill pathogen-infected host cells.
   d. B cells carry out the cell-mediated response; cytotoxic T cells carry out the humoral response.

LEVEL 2: APPLICATION/ANALYSIS

4. Which of the following statements is *not* true?
   a. An antibody has more than one antigen-binding site.
   b. A lymphocyte has receptors for multiple different antigens.
   c. An antigen can have different epitopes.
   d. A liver cell makes one class of MHC molecule.

5. Which of the following should be the same in identical twins?
   a. the set of antibodies produced
   b. the set of MHC molecules produced
   c. the set of T cell antigen receptors produced
   d. the set of immune cells eliminated as self-reactive

LEVEL 3: SYNTHESIS/EVALUATION

6. Vaccination increases the number of
   a. different receptors that recognize a pathogen.
   b. lymphocytes with receptors that can bind to the pathogen.
   c. epitopes that the immune system can recognize.
   d. MHC molecules that can present an antigen.

7. Which of the following would *not* help a virus avoid triggering an adaptive immune response?
   a. having frequent mutations in genes for surface proteins
   b. infecting cells that produce very few MHC molecules
   c. producing proteins very similar to those of other viruses
   d. infecting and killing helper T cells

8. **DRAW IT** Consider a pencil-shaped protein with two epitopes, Y (the "eraser" end) and Z (the "point" end). They are recognized by antibodies A1 and A2, respectively. Draw and label a picture showing the antibodies linking proteins into a complex that could trigger endocytosis by a macrophage.

9. **MAKE CONNECTIONS** Contrast clonal selection with Lamarck's idea for the inheritance of acquired characteristics (see Concept 22.1).

10. **EVOLUTION CONNECTION**
    Describe one invertebrate mechanism of defense against pathogens and discuss how it is an evolutionary adaptation retained in vertebrates.

11. **SCIENTIFIC INQUIRY**
    The presence of bacterial lipopolysaccharide (LPS) in the blood is a major cause of septic shock. Suppose you have available purified LPS and several strains of mice, each with a mutation that inactivates a particular TLR gene. How might you use these mice to test the feasibility of treating septic shock with a drug that blocks TLR signaling?

12. **WRITE ABOUT A THEME: INFORMATION**
    Among all nucleated body cells, only B and T cells lose DNA during their development and maturation. In a short essay (100–150 words), discuss the relationship between this loss and DNA as heritable biological information, focusing on similarities between cellular and organismal generations.

13. **SYNTHESIZE YOUR KNOWLEDGE**

This photo shows a child receiving an oral vaccine against polio, a disease caused by a virus that infects neurons. Given that the body cannot readily replace most neurons, why is it important that a polio vaccine stimulate not only a cell-mediated response but also a humoral response?

For suggested answers, see Appendix A.

MasteringBiology®

Students Go to **MasteringBiology** for assignments, the eText, and the Study Area with practice tests, animations, and activities.

Instructors Go to **MasteringBiology** for automatically graded tutorials and questions that you can assign to your students, plus Instructor Resources.

44

Osmoregulation and Excretion

KEY CONCEPTS

44.1 Osmoregulation balances the uptake and loss of water and solutes

44.2 An animal's nitrogenous wastes reflect its phylogeny and habitat

44.3 Diverse excretory systems are variations on a tubular theme

44.4 The nephron is organized for stepwise processing of blood filtrate

44.5 Hormonal circuits link kidney function, water balance, and blood pressure

▲ **Figure 44.1 How does an albatross drink salt water without ill effect?**

A Balancing Act

At 3.5 m, the wingspan of a wandering albatross (*Diomedea exulans*) is the largest of any living bird. But the albatross commands attention for more than just its size. This massive bird remains at sea day and night throughout the year, returning to land only to reproduce. A human with only seawater to drink would die of dehydration, but faced with the same conditions, the albatross thrives (**Figure 44.1**).

For both albatross and human, maintaining the fluid balance of their tissues requires that the relative concentrations of water and solutes be kept within fairly narrow limits. In addition, ions such as sodium and calcium must be maintained at concentrations that permit normal activity of muscles, neurons, and other body cells. Homeostasis thus requires **osmoregulation**, the general term for the processes by which animals control solute concentrations and balance water gain and loss.

A number of mechanisms for water and solute control have arisen during evolution, reflecting the varied and often severe osmoregulatory challenges presented by an animal's surroundings. The arid conditions of a desert, for instance, can quickly deplete an animal of body water. Despite a quite different environment, albatrosses and other marine animals also face potential dehydration. The success of these animals depends on conserving

971

water and, for marine birds and fishes, eliminating excess salts. Freshwater animals face a distinct challenge: an environment that threatens to dilute their body fluids. These organisms survive by conserving solutes and absorbing salts from their surroundings.

In safeguarding their internal fluids, animals must deal with ammonia, a toxic metabolite produced by the dismantling of *nitrogenous* (nitrogen-containing) molecules, chiefly proteins and nucleic acids. Several different mechanisms have evolved for **excretion**, the process that rids the body of nitrogenous metabolites and other metabolic waste products. Because systems for excretion and osmoregulation are structurally and functionally linked in many animals, we'll consider both of these processes in this chapter.

CONCEPT 44.1

Osmoregulation balances the uptake and loss of water and solutes

Just as thermoregulation depends on balancing heat loss and gain (see Concept 40.3), regulating the chemical composition of body fluids depends on balancing the uptake and loss of water and solutes. If water uptake is excessive, animal cells swell and burst; if water loss is substantial, they shrivel and die. Ultimately, the driving force for the movement of both water and solutes—in animals as in all other organisms—is a concentration gradient of one or more solutes across the plasma membrane.

Osmosis and Osmolarity

Water enters and leaves cells by osmosis, which occurs when two solutions separated by a membrane differ in total solute concentration **(Figure 44.2)**. The unit of measurement for solute concentration is **osmolarity**, the number of moles of solute per liter of solution. The osmolarity of human blood is about 300 milliosmoles per liter (mOsm/L), whereas that of seawater is about 1,000 mOsm/L.

Two solutions with the same osmolarity are said to be *isoosmotic*. If a selectively permeable membrane separates the solutions, water molecules will continually cross the membrane at equal rates in both directions. Thus, there is no *net* movement of water by osmosis between isoosmotic solutions. When two solutions differ in osmolarity, the solution with the higher concentration of solutes is said to be *hyperosmotic*, and the more dilute solution is said to be *hypoosmotic*. Water flows by osmosis from a hypoosmotic solution to a hyperosmotic one (see Figure 44.2).*

Osmoregulatory Challenges and Mechanisms

An animal can maintain water balance in two ways. One is to be an **osmoconformer**: to be isoosmotic with its surroundings. The second is to be an **osmoregulator**: to control internal osmolarity independent of that of the external environment.

All osmoconformers are marine animals. Because an osmoconformer's internal osmolarity is the same as that of its environment, there is no tendency to gain or lose water. Many osmoconformers live in water that has a stable composition and hence have a constant internal osmolarity.

Osmoregulation enables animals to live in environments that are uninhabitable for osmoconformers, such as fresh water and terrestrial habitats, or to move between marine and freshwater environments **(Figure 44.3)**. To survive in a hypoosmotic environment, an osmoregulator must discharge excess water. In a hyperosmotic environment, an osmoregulator must instead take in water to offset osmotic loss. Osmoregulation also allows many marine animals

▲ **Figure 44.3 Sockeye salmon (*Oncorhynchus nerka*), osmoregulators that migrate between rivers and the ocean.**

Selectively permeable membrane

Solutes   Water

Hyperosmotic side:
• Higher solute concentration
• Lower free H_2O concentration

Hypoosmotic side:
• Lower solute concentration
• Higher free H_2O concentration

Net water flow

▲ **Figure 44.2 Solute concentration and osmosis.**

---

*In this chapter, we use the terms *isoosmotic*, *hypoosmotic*, and *hyperosmotic*, which refer specifically to osmolarity, instead of *isotonic*, *hypotonic*, and *hypertonic*. The latter set of terms applies to the response of animal cells—whether they swell or shrink—in solutions of known solute concentrations.

to maintain an internal osmolarity different from that of seawater.

Most animals, whether osmoconformers or osmoregulators, cannot tolerate substantial changes in external osmolarity and are said to be *stenohaline* (from the Greek *stenos*, narrow, and *halos*, salt). In contrast, *euryhaline* animals (from the Greek *eurys*, broad) can survive large fluctuations in external osmolarity. Euryhaline osmoconformers include many barnacles and mussels, which are alternately submerged and exposed by tides; euryhaline osmoregulators include striped bass and the various species of salmon (see Figure 44.3).

Next we'll examine some adaptations for osmoregulation that have evolved in marine, freshwater, and terrestrial animals.

Marine Animals

Most marine invertebrates are osmoconformers. Their osmolarity is the same as that of seawater. They therefore face no substantial challenges in water balance. However, because these animals differ considerably from seawater in the concentrations of *specific* solutes, they must actively transport these solutes to maintain homeostasis. For example, although the concentration of magnesium ions (Mg^{2+}) in seawater is 50 mM (millimolar, or 10^{-3} mol/L), homeostatic mechanisms in the Atlantic lobster (*Homarus americanus*) result in a Mg^{2+} concentration of less than 9 mM in its hemolymph (circulatory fluid).

Many marine vertebrates and some marine invertebrates are osmoregulators. For most of these animals, the ocean is a strongly dehydrating environment. For example, marine fishes, such as the cod in **Figure 44.4a**, constantly lose water by osmosis. Such fishes balance the water loss by drinking large amounts of seawater, and they eliminate the ingested salts through their gills and kidneys.

A distinct osmoregulatory strategy evolved in marine sharks and most other chondrichthyans (cartilaginous animals; see Chapter 34). Like "bony fishes" (as we'll refer collectively to ray-finned and lobe-finned fishes in this chapter), sharks have an internal salt concentration much lower than that of seawater. Thus, salt tends to diffuse into their bodies from the water, especially across their gills. Unlike bony fishes, however, marine sharks are not hypoosmotic to seawater. The explanation is that shark tissue contains high concentrations of urea, a nitrogenous waste product of protein and nucleic acid metabolism (see Figure 44.7). A shark's body fluids also contain trimethylamine oxide (TMAO), an organic molecule that protects proteins from damage by urea. Together, the salts, urea, TMAO, and other compounds maintained in the body fluids of sharks result in an osmolarity very close to that of seawater. For this reason, sharks are often considered osmoconformers. However, because the solute concentration in their body fluids is actually somewhat higher than 1,000 mOsm/L, water slowly *enters* the shark's body by osmosis and in food (sharks do not drink). This small influx of water is disposed of in urine produced by the shark's kidneys. The urine also removes some of the salt that diffuses into the shark's body; the rest is lost in feces or is secreted from a specialized gland.

Freshwater Animals

The osmoregulatory problems of freshwater animals are the opposite of those of marine animals. The body fluids of freshwater animals must be hyperosmotic because animal cells cannot tolerate salt concentrations as low as that of lake or river water. Having internal fluids with an osmolarity higher than that of their surroundings, freshwater animals face the problem of gaining water by osmosis and losing salts by diffusion. Many freshwater animals, including bony fishes such as the perch in **Figure 44.4b**, solve the

▼ **Figure 44.4 Osmoregulation in marine and freshwater bony fishes: a comparison.**

(a) Osmoregulation in a marine fish

Gain of water and salt ions from food

Excretion of salt ions from gills

Osmotic water **loss** through gills and other parts of body surface

SALT WATER

Gain of water and salt ions from drinking seawater

Excretion of salt ions and small amounts of water in scanty urine from kidneys

Key
Water
Salt

(b) Osmoregulation in a freshwater fish

Gain of water and some ions in food

Uptake of salt ions by gills

Osmotic water **gain** through gills and other parts of body surface

FRESH WATER

Excretion of salt ions and large amounts of water in dilute urine from kidneys problem of water balance by drinking almost no water and excreting large amounts of very dilute urine. At the same time, salts lost by diffusion and in the urine are replenished by eating. Freshwater fishes also replenish salts by uptake across their gills.

Salmon and other euryhaline fishes that migrate between fresh water and seawater undergo dramatic changes in osmoregulatory status. When living in rivers and streams, salmon osmoregulate like other freshwater fishes, producing large amounts of dilute urine and taking up salt from the dilute environment through their gills. When they migrate to the ocean, salmon acclimatize. They produce more of the steroid hormone cortisol, which increases the number and size of salt-secreting chloride cells. As a result of these and other physiological changes, salmon in salt water excrete excess salt from their gills and produce only small amounts of urine—just like bony fishes that spend their entire lives in salt water.

Animals That Live in Temporary Waters

Extreme dehydration, or *desiccation*, is fatal for most animals. However, a few aquatic invertebrates that live in temporary ponds and in films of water around soil particles can lose almost all their body water and survive. These animals enter a dormant state when their habitats dry up, an adaptation called **anhydrobiosis** ("life without water"). Among the most striking examples are the tardigrades, or water bears, tiny invertebrates less than 1 mm long **(Figure 44.5)**. In their active, hydrated state, they contain about 85% water by weight, but they can dehydrate to less than 2% water and survive in an inactive state, dry as dust, for a decade or more. Just add water, and within hours the rehydrated tardigrades are moving about and feeding.

Anhydrobiosis requires adaptations that keep cell membranes intact. Researchers are just beginning to learn how

(a) Hydrated tardigrade

(b) Dehydrated tardigrade

▲ **Figure 44.5 Anhydrobiosis.** Tardigrades (SEM images) inhabit temporary ponds as well as droplets of water in soil and on moist plants.

tardigrades survive drying out, but studies of anhydrobiotic roundworms (phylum Nematoda; see Chapter 33) show that desiccated individuals contain large amounts of sugars. In particular, a disaccharide called trehalose seems to protect the cells by replacing the water that is normally associated with proteins and membrane lipids. Many insects that survive freezing in the winter also use trehalose as a membrane protectant, as do some plants resistant to desiccation.

Recently, scientists began applying lessons learned from the study of anhydrobiosis to the preservation of biological materials. Traditionally, samples of protein, DNA, and cells have been kept in ultracold freezers (−80°C), consuming large amounts of energy and space. Now, however, the manufacture of materials modeled after the protectants found in anhydrobiotic species has enabled such samples to be stored in compact chambers at room temperature.

Land Animals

The threat of dehydration is a major regulatory problem for terrestrial plants and animals. Adaptations that reduce water loss are key to survival on land. Much as a waxy cuticle contributes to the success of land plants, the body coverings of most terrestrial animals help prevent dehydration. Examples are the waxy layers of insect exoskeletons, the shells of land snails, and the layers of dead, keratinized skin cells covering most terrestrial vertebrates, including humans. Many terrestrial animals, especially desert-dwellers, are nocturnal, which reduces evaporative water loss because of the lower temperature and higher humidity of night air.

Despite these and other adaptations, most terrestrial animals lose water through many routes: in urine and feces, across their skin, and from the surfaces of gas exchange organs. Land animals maintain water balance by drinking and eating moist foods and by producing water metabolically through cellular respiration.

A number of desert animals are well enough adapted for minimizing water loss that they can survive for long periods of time without drinking. Camels, for example, can lose 25% of their body water and survive. (In contrast, a human who loses half this amount of body water will die from heart failure.) In the Scientific Skills Exercise, you can examine water balance in another desert species, the sandy inland mouse.

Energetics of Osmoregulation

Maintaining an osmolarity difference between an animal's body and its external environment carries an energy cost. Because diffusion tends to equalize concentrations in a system, osmoregulators must expend energy to maintain the osmotic gradients that cause water to move in or out. They do so by using active transport to manipulate solute concentrations in their body fluids.

SCIENTIFIC SKILLS EXERCISE

Describing and Interpreting Quantitative Data

How Do Desert Mice Maintain Osmotic Homeostasis? The sandy inland mouse, recently reclassified as *Pseudomys hermannsburgensis*, is an Australian desert mammal that can survive indefinitely on a diet of dried seeds without drinking water. To study this species' adaptations to its arid environment, researchers conducted a laboratory experiment in which they controlled access to water. In this exercise, you will analyze some of the data from the experiment.

How the Experiment Was Done Nine captured mice were kept in an environmentally controlled room and given birdseed (10% water by weight) to eat. In part A of the study, the mice had unlimited access to tap water for drinking; in part B of the study, the mice were not given any drinking water for 35 days, similar to conditions in their natural habitat. At the end of parts A and B, the researchers measured the osmolarity and urea concentration of the urine and blood of each mouse. The mice were also weighed three times a week.

Data from the Experiment

Access to Water	Mean Osmolarity (mOsm/L)		Mean Urea Concentration (mM)	
	Urine	Blood	Urine	Blood
Part A: Unlimited	490	350	330	7.6
Part B: None	4,700	320	2,700	11

In part A, the mice drank about 33% of their body weight each day. The change in body weight during the study was negligible for all mice.

Interpret the Data

1. In words, describe how the data differ between the unlimited water and no-water conditions for the following: (a) osmolarity of urine; (b) osmolarity of blood; (c) urea concentration in urine; (d) urea concentration in blood. (e) Does this data set provide evidence of homeostatic regulation? Explain.

2. (a) Calculate the ratio of urine osmolarity to blood osmolarity for mice with unlimited access to water. (b) Calculate this ratio for mice with no access to water. (c) What conclusion would you draw from these ratios?

3. If the amount of urine produced were different in the two conditions, how would that affect your calculation? Explain.

(MB) A version of this Scientific Skills Exercise can be assigned in MasteringBiology.

Data from R. E. MacMillen et al., Water economy and energy metabolism of the sandy inland mouse, *Leggadina hermannsburgensis*, *Journal of Mammalogy* 53:529–539 (1972).

The energy cost of osmoregulation depends on how different an animal's osmolarity is from its surroundings, how easily water and solutes can move across the animal's surface, and how much work is required to pump solutes across the membrane. Osmoregulation accounts for 5% or more of the resting metabolic rate of many fishes. For brine shrimp, small crustaceans that live in extremely salty lakes, the gradient between internal and external osmolarity is very large, and the cost of osmoregulation is correspondingly high—as much as 30% of the resting metabolic rate.

The energy cost to an animal of maintaining water and salt balance is minimized by having body fluids that are adapted to the salinity of the animal's habitat. Thus, the body fluids of most animals that live in fresh water (which has an osmolarity of 0.5–15 mOsm/L) have lower solute concentrations than the body fluids of their closest relatives that live in seawater (1,000 mOsm/L). For instance, whereas marine molluscs have body fluids with solute concentrations of approximately 1,000 mOsm/L, some freshwater molluscs maintain the osmolarity of their body fluids at just 40 mOsm/L. In each case, minimizing the osmotic difference between body fluids and the surrounding environment decreases the energy cost of osmoregulation.

Transport Epithelia in Osmoregulation

The ultimate function of osmoregulation is to control solute concentrations in cells, but most animals do this indirectly by managing the solute content of an internal body fluid that bathes the cells. In insects and other animals with an open circulatory system, the fluid surrounding cells is hemolymph. In vertebrates and other animals with a closed circulatory system, the cells are bathed in an interstitial fluid that contains a mixture of solutes controlled indirectly by the blood. Maintaining the composition of such fluids depends on structures ranging from individual cells that regulate solute movement to complex organs such as the vertebrate kidney.

In most animals, osmoregulation and metabolic waste disposal rely on **transport epithelia**—one or more layers of epithelial cells specialized for moving particular solutes in controlled amounts in specific directions. Transport epithelia are typically arranged into complex tubular networks with extensive surface areas. Some transport epithelia face the outside environment directly, while others line channels connected to the outside by an opening on the body surface.

The transport epithelium that enables the albatross and other marine birds to survive on seawater remained undiscovered for many years. To explore this question, researchers gave captive marine birds only seawater to drink. Although very little salt appeared in the birds' urine, fluid dripping from the tip of their beaks was a concentrated solution of salt (NaCl). The source of this solution was a pair of nasal salt glands (**Figure 44.6**). Salt glands, which are also found in sea turtles and marine iguanas, use active transport of ions to secrete a fluid much saltier than the ocean. Even though drinking seawater brings in a lot of salt, the salt gland enables these marine vertebrates to achieve a net gain of water. By contrast, humans who drink a given volume of seawater must use a *greater* volume of water to excrete the salt load, with the result that they become dehydrated.

Transport epithelia that function in maintaining water balance also often function in disposal of metabolic wastes. We'll see examples of this coordinated function in our upcoming consideration of earthworm and insect excretory systems as well as the vertebrate kidney.

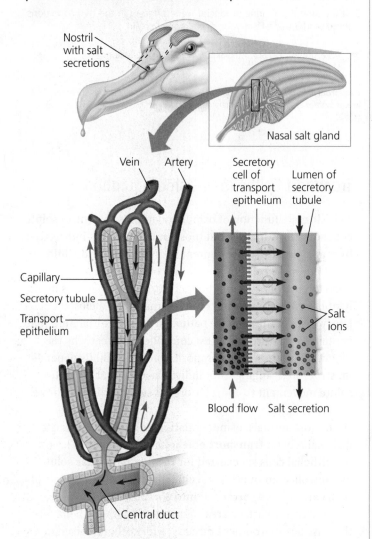

▲ **Figure 44.6 Salt secretion in the nasal glands of a marine bird.** Salt is transported from the blood into secretory tubules, which drain into central ducts leading to the nostrils.

1. The movement of salt from the surrounding water to the blood of a freshwater fish requires the expenditure of energy in the form of ATP. Why?

2. Why aren't any freshwater animals osmoconformers?

3. **WHAT IF?** Researchers found that a camel in the sun required much more water when its fur was shaved off, although its body temperature was the same. What can you conclude about the relationship between osmoregulation and the insulation provided by fur?

For suggested answers, see Appendix A.

CONCEPT 44.2

An animal's nitrogenous wastes reflect its phylogeny and habitat

Because most metabolic wastes must be dissolved in water to be excreted from the body, the type and quantity of an animal's waste products may have a large impact on its water balance. In this regard, some of the most significant waste products are the nitrogenous breakdown products of proteins and nucleic acids. When proteins and nucleic acids are broken apart for energy or converted to carbohydrates or fats, enzymes remove nitrogen in the form of **ammonia** (NH_3). Ammonia is very toxic, in part because its ion, ammonium (NH_4^+), can interfere with oxidative phosphorylation. Although some animals excrete ammonia directly, many species expend energy to convert it to less toxic compounds prior to excretion.

Forms of Nitrogenous Waste

Animals excrete nitrogenous wastes as ammonia, urea, or uric acid (**Figure 44.7**). These different forms vary significantly in their toxicity and the energy costs of producing them.

Ammonia

Animals that excrete nitrogenous wastes as ammonia need access to lots of water because ammonia can be tolerated only at very low concentrations. Therefore, ammonia excretion is most common in aquatic species. In many invertebrates, ammonia release occurs across the whole body surface.

Urea

Although ammonia excretion works well in many aquatic species, it is much less suitable for land animals. Ammonia is so toxic that it can be transported and excreted only in large volumes of very dilute solutions. Most terrestrial animals and many marine species simply do not have access to sufficient water to routinely excrete ammonia. Instead, they mainly excrete a different nitrogenous waste, **urea**. In

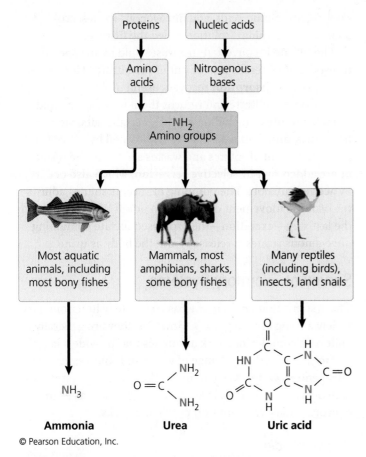

▲ Figure 44.7 Forms of nitrogenous waste.

© Pearson Education, Inc.

vertebrates, urea is the product of a metabolic cycle that combines ammonia with carbon dioxide in the liver.

The main advantage of urea is its very low toxicity. The main disadvantage is its energy cost: Animals must expend energy to produce urea from ammonia. From a bioenergetic standpoint, we would predict that animals that spend part of their lives in water and part on land would switch between excreting ammonia (thereby saving energy) and excreting urea (reducing excretory water loss). Indeed, many amphibians excrete mainly ammonia when they are aquatic tadpoles and switch largely to urea excretion when they become land-dwelling adults.

Uric Acid

Insects, land snails, and many reptiles, including birds, excrete **uric acid** as their primary nitrogenous waste. (Bird droppings, or *guano*, are a mixture of white uric acid and brown feces.) Uric acid is relatively nontoxic and does not readily dissolve in water. It therefore can be excreted as a semisolid paste with very little water loss. However, uric acid is even more energetically expensive than urea, requiring considerable ATP for synthesis from ammonia.

While not primarily uric acid producers, humans and some other animals generate a small amount of uric acid from purine breakdown. Diseases that alter this process reflect problems that can arise when a metabolic product is

insoluble. For example, a genetic defect in purine metabolism predisposes Dalmatian dogs to form uric acid stones in their bladder. In humans, adult males are particularly susceptible to *gout*, a painful joint inflammation caused by deposits of uric acid crystals. Meals containing purine-rich animal tissues can increase the inflammation. Some dinosaurs appear to have been similarly affected: Fossilized bones of *Tyrannosaurus rex* exhibit joint damage characteristic of gout.

The Influence of Evolution and Environment on Nitrogenous Wastes

EVOLUTION In general, the kind of nitrogenous wastes an animal excretes depends on both the species' evolutionary history (phylogeny) and its habitat, especially the availability of water. For example, terrestrial turtles (which often live in dry areas) excrete mainly uric acid, whereas aquatic turtles excrete both urea and ammonia. Another factor affecting the primary type of nitrogenous waste produced by a particular group of animals is the immediate environment of the animal egg. For example, soluble wastes can diffuse out of a shell-less amphibian egg or be carried away from a mammalian embryo by the mother's blood. However, the shelled eggs produced by birds and other reptiles (see Figure 34.25) are permeable to gases but not to liquids, which means that soluble nitrogenous wastes released by an embryo would be trapped within the egg and could accumulate to dangerous levels. (Although urea is much less harmful than ammonia, it is toxic at very high concentrations.) Using uric acid as a waste product conveys a selective advantage because it precipitates out of solution and can be stored within the egg as a harmless solid left behind when the animal hatches.

Regardless of the type of nitrogenous waste, the amount produced is coupled to the animal's energy budget. Endotherms, which use energy at high rates, eat more food and produce more nitrogenous waste than ectotherms. The amount of nitrogenous waste is also linked to diet. Predators, which derive much of their energy from protein, excrete more nitrogen than animals that rely mainly on lipids or carbohydrates as energy sources.

Having surveyed the forms of nitrogenous waste and their interrelationship with evolutionary lineage, habitat, and energy consumption, we'll turn next to the processes and systems animals use to excrete these and other wastes.

CONCEPT CHECK **44.2**

1. What advantage does uric acid offer as a nitrogenous waste in arid environments?

2. **WHAT IF?** Suppose a bird and a human both have gout. Why might reducing purine in their diets help the human much more than the bird?

For suggested answers, see Appendix A.

Diverse excretory systems are variations on a tubular theme

Whether an animal lives on land, in salt water, or in fresh water, water balance depends on the regulation of solute movement between internal fluids and the external environment. Much of this movement is handled by excretory systems. These systems are central to homeostasis because they dispose of metabolic wastes and control body fluid composition.

Excretory Processes

Animals across a wide range of species produce a fluid waste called urine through the basic steps shown in **Figure 44.8**. In the first step, body fluid (blood, coelomic fluid, or hemolymph) is brought in contact with the selectively permeable membrane of a transport epithelium. In most cases, hydrostatic pressure (blood pressure in many animals) drives a process of **filtration**. Cells, as well as proteins and other large molecules, cannot cross the epithelial membrane and remain in the body fluid. In contrast, water and small solutes, such as

salts, sugars, amino acids, and nitrogenous wastes, cross the membrane, forming a solution called the **filtrate**.

The filtrate is converted to a waste fluid by the specific transport of materials into or out of the filtrate. The process of selective **reabsorption** recovers useful molecules and water from the filtrate and returns them to the body fluid. Valuable solutes—including glucose, certain salts, vitamins, hormones, and amino acids—are reabsorbed by active transport. Nonessential solutes and wastes are left in the filtrate or are added to it by selective **secretion**, which also occurs by active transport. The pumping of various solutes adjusts the osmotic movement of water into or out of the filtrate. In the last step—excretion—the processed filtrate containing nitrogenous wastes is released from the body as urine.

Survey of Excretory Systems

The systems that perform the basic excretory functions vary widely among animal groups. However, they are generally built on a complex network of tubules that provide a large surface area for the exchange of water and solutes, including nitrogenous wastes. We'll examine the excretory systems of flatworms, earthworms, insects, and vertebrates as examples of evolutionary variations on tubule networks.

Protonephridia

As illustrated in **Figure 44.9**, the excretory systems of flatworms (phylum Platyhelminthes) consist of units called

Capillary

Filtrate

1 Filtration. The excretory tubule collects a filtrate from the blood. Water and solutes are forced by blood pressure across the selectively permeable membranes of a cluster of capillaries and into the excretory tubule.

Excretory tubule

2 Reabsorption. The transport epithelium reclaims valuable substances from the filtrate and returns them to the body fluids.

3 Secretion. Other substances, such as toxins and excess ions, are extracted from body fluids and added to the contents of the excretory tubule.

Urine

4 Excretion. The altered filtrate (urine) leaves the system and the body.

▲ **Figure 44.8 Key steps of excretory system function: an overview.** Most excretory systems produce a filtrate by pressure-filtering body fluids and then modify the filtrate's contents. This diagram is modeled after the vertebrate excretory system.

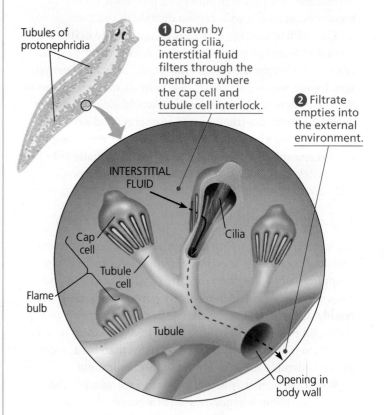

Tubules of protonephridia

1 Drawn by beating cilia, interstitial fluid filters through the membrane where the cap cell and tubule cell interlock.

2 Filtrate empties into the external environment.

INTERSTITIAL FLUID

Cilia

Cap cell

Tubule cell

Flame bulb

Tubule

Opening in body wall

▲ **Figure 44.9 Protonephridia in a planarian.**

protonephridia (singular, *protonephridium*), which form a network of dead-end tubules. The tubules, which are connected to external openings, branch throughout the flatworm body, which lacks a coelom (body cavity). Cellular units called flame bulbs cap the branches of each protonephridium. Consisting of a tubule cell and a cap cell, each flame bulb has a tuft of cilia projecting into the tubule. During filtration, the beating of the cilia draws water and solutes from the interstitial fluid through the flame bulb, releasing filtrate into the tubule network. (The name *flame bulb* derives from the moving cilia's resemblance to a flickering flame.) The processed filtrate moves outward through the tubules and empties as urine into the environment. The urine of freshwater flatworms is low in solutes, helping balance the osmotic uptake of water from the environment.

Protonephridia are also found in rotifers, some annelids, mollusc larvae, and lancelets (see Figure 34.4). Among these animals, the function of the protonephridia varies. In the freshwater flatworms, protonephridia serve chiefly in osmoregulation. Most metabolic wastes diffuse out of the animal across the body surface or are excreted into the gastrovascular cavity and eliminated through the mouth (see Figure 33.10). However, in some parasitic flatworms, which are isoosmotic to the surrounding fluids of their host organisms, the main function of protonephridia is the disposal of nitrogenous wastes. Natural selection has thus adapted protonephridia to different tasks in different environments.

Metanephridia

Most annelids, such as earthworms, have **metanephridia** (singular, *metanephridium*), excretory organs that collect fluid directly from the coelom **(Figure 44.10)**. Each segment

of an annelid has a pair of metanephridia, which are immersed in coelomic fluid and enveloped by a capillary network. A ciliated funnel surrounds the internal opening of each metanephridium. As the cilia beat, fluid is drawn into a collecting tubule, which includes a storage bladder that opens to the outside.

The metanephridia of an earthworm have both excretory and osmoregulatory functions. As urine moves along the tubule, the transport epithelium bordering the lumen reabsorbs most solutes and returns them to the blood in the capillaries. Nitrogenous wastes remain in the tubule and are excreted to the environment. Earthworms inhabit damp soil and therefore usually experience a net uptake of water by osmosis through their skin. Their metanephridia balance the water influx by producing urine that is dilute (hypoosmotic to body fluids).

Malpighian Tubules

Insects and other terrestrial arthropods have organs called **Malpighian tubules** that remove nitrogenous wastes and that also function in osmoregulation **(Figure 44.11)**. The Malpighian tubules extend from dead-end tips immersed in hemolymph to openings into the digestive tract. The filtration step common to other excretory systems is absent. Instead, the transport epithelium that lines the tubules secretes certain solutes, including nitrogenous wastes, from the hemolymph into the lumen of the tubule. Water follows the solutes into the tubule by osmosis, and the fluid then

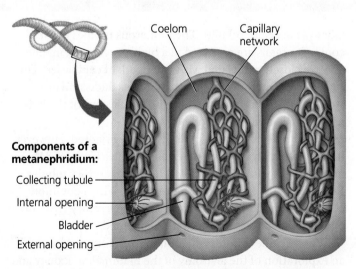

▲ Figure 44.10 Metanephridia of an earthworm. Each segment of the worm contains a pair of metanephridia, which collect coelomic fluid from the adjacent anterior segment. The region highlighted in yellow illustrates the organization of one metanephridium of a pair; the other would be behind it.

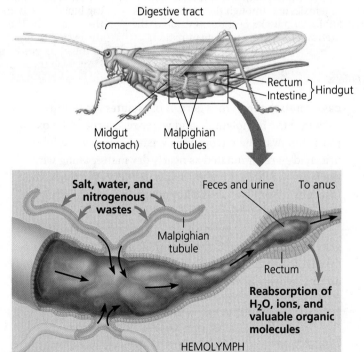

▲ Figure 44.11 Malpighian tubules of insects. Malpighian tubules are outpocketings of the digestive tract that remove nitrogenous wastes and function in osmoregulation.

Exploring The Mammalian Excretory System

Excretory Organs

Posterior vena cava
Renal artery and vein
Aorta
Kidney
Ureter
Urinary bladder
Urethra

In humans, the excretory system consists of **kidneys**, a pair of organs each about 10 cm in length, as well as organs for transporting and storing urine. Urine produced by each kidney exits through a duct called the **ureter**; the two ureters drain into a common sac called the **urinary bladder**. During urination, urine is expelled from the bladder through a tube called the **urethra**, which empties to the outside near the vagina in females and through the penis in males. Sphincter muscles near the junction of the urethra and bladder regulate urination.

Kidney Structure

Renal cortex
Renal medulla
Renal artery
Renal vein
Ureter
© Pearson Education, Inc.
Renal pelvis

Each kidney has an outer **renal cortex** and an inner **renal medulla**. Both regions are supplied with blood by a renal artery and drained by a renal vein. Within the cortex and medulla lie tightly packed excretory tubules and associated blood vessels. The excretory tubules carry and process a filtrate produced from the blood entering the kidney. Nearly all of the fluid in the filtrate is reabsorbed into the surrounding blood vessels and exits the kidney in the renal vein. The remaining fluid leaves the excretory tubules as urine, is collected in the inner **renal pelvis**, and exits the kidney via the ureter.

Nephron Types

Cortical nephron
Juxtamedullary nephron
Renal cortex
Renal medulla

Weaving back and forth across the renal cortex and medulla are the **nephrons**, the functional units of the vertebrate kidney. Of the roughly 1 million nephrons in a human kidney, 85% are **cortical nephrons**, which reach only a short distance into the medulla. The remainder, the **juxtamedullary nephrons**, extend deep into the medulla. Juxtamedullary nephrons are essential for production of urine that is hyperosmotic to body fluids, a key adaptation for water conservation in mammals.

---

passes into the rectum. There, most solutes are pumped back into the hemolymph, and water reabsorption by osmosis follows. The nitrogenous wastes—mainly insoluble uric acid—are eliminated as nearly dry matter along with the feces. Capable of conserving water very effectively, the insect excretory system is a key adaptation contributing to these animals' tremendous success on land.

Some terrestrial insects have an additional adaptation for water balance: The rectal end of their gut enables water uptake from the air. Although some species absorb water from air only when it is very humid, others, such as fleas (genus *Xenopsylla*), can capture water from the atmosphere when relative humidity is as low as 50%.

Kidneys

In vertebrates and some other chordates, a specialized organ called the kidney functions in both osmoregulation and excretion. Like the excretory organs of most animal phyla,

kidneys consist of tubules. The numerous tubules of these compact organs are arranged in a highly organized manner and are closely associated with a network of capillaries. The vertebrate excretory system also includes ducts and other structures that carry urine from the tubules out of the kidney and, eventually, the body.

Vertebrate kidneys are typically nonsegmented. However, hagfishes, which are jawless vertebrates (see Chapter 34), have kidneys with segmentally arranged excretory tubules. Because hagfishes and other vertebrates share a common chordate ancestor, it is possible that the excretory structures of vertebrate ancestors also were segmented.

We conclude this introduction to excretory systems with an exploration of the anatomy of the mammalian kidney and associated structures (**Figure 44.12**). Familiarizing yourself with the terms and diagrams in this figure will provide you with a solid foundation for learning about filtrate processing in the kidney, our focus in the next concept.

Nephron Organization

Afferent arteriole
from renal artery   Glomerulus

Bowman's
capsule

**Proximal
tubule**

**Distal
tubule**

Peritubular
capillaries

Efferent
arteriole from
glomerulus

Branch of
renal vein

Descending
limb

Vasa
recta

**Loop of
Henle**

Collecting
duct

Ascending
limb

Each nephron consists of a single long tubule as well as a ball of capillaries called the **glomerulus**. The blind end of the tubule forms a cup-shaped swelling, called **Bowman's capsule**, which surrounds the glomerulus. Filtrate is formed when blood pressure forces fluid from the blood in the glomerulus into the lumen of Bowman's capsule. Processing occurs as the filtrate passes through three major regions of the nephron: the **proximal tubule**, the **loop of Henle** (a hairpin turn with a descending limb and an ascending limb), and the **distal tubule**. A **collecting duct** receives processed filtrate from many nephrons and transports it to the renal pelvis.

Each nephron is supplied with blood by an *afferent arteriole*, an offshoot of the renal artery that branches and forms the capillaries of the glomerulus. The capillaries converge as they leave the glomerulus, forming an *efferent arteriole*. Branches of this vessel form the **peritubular capillaries**, which surround the proximal and distal tubules. Other branches extend downward and form the **vasa recta**, hairpin-shaped capillaries that serve the renal medulla, including the long loop of Henle of juxtamedullary nephrons.

▶ In this SEM of densely packed blood vessels from a human kidney, arterioles and peritubular capillaries appear pink; the glomeruli appear yellow.

200 μm

CONCEPT CHECK 44.3

1. Compare and contrast the ways that metabolic waste products enter the excretory systems of flatworms, earthworms, and insects.

2. What is the function of the filtration step in excretory systems?

3. Where and how does filtrate originate in the vertebrate kidney, and by what two routes do the components of the filtrate exit the kidney?

4. **WHAT IF?** Kidney failure is often treated by hemodialysis, in which blood diverted out of the body is filtered and then allowed to flow on one side of a semipermeable membrane. Fluid called dialysate flows in the opposite direction on the other side of the membrane. In replacing the reabsorption and secretion of solutes in a functional kidney, the makeup of the starting dialysate is critical. What initial solute composition would work well?

For suggested answers, see Appendix A.

CONCEPT 44.4

The nephron is organized for stepwise processing of blood filtrate

We'll continue our exploration of the nephron with a discussion of filtrate processing. We'll then focus on how tubules, capillaries, and surrounding tissue function together.

The porous capillaries and specialized cells of Bowman's capsule are permeable to water and small solutes, but not blood cells or large molecules, such as plasma proteins. Thus, the filtrate produced in the capsule contains salts, glucose, amino acids, vitamins, nitrogenous wastes, and other small molecules. Because such molecules pass freely between glomerular capillaries and Bowman's capsule, the concentrations of these substances in the initial filtrate are the same as those in blood plasma.

From Blood Filtrate to Urine: *A Closer Look*

In this section, we'll follow filtrate along its path in the nephron and collecting duct, examining how each region contributes to the stepwise processing of filtrate into urine. The circled numbers correspond to the numbers in **Figure 44.13**.

❶ Proximal tubule. Reabsorption in the proximal tubule is critical for the recapture of ions, water, and valuable nutrients from the huge volume of initial filtrate. NaCl (salt) in the filtrate enters the cells of the transport epithelium by facilitated diffusion and cotransport mechanisms (see Figures 7.14 and 7.18). The epithelial cells actively transport Na^+ into the interstitial fluid, and this transfer of positive charge out of the tubule drives the passive transport of Cl^-.

As salt moves from the filtrate to the interstitial fluid, water follows by osmosis. The salt and water then diffuse from the interstitial fluid into the peritubular capillaries. Glucose, amino acids, potassium ions (K^+), and other essential substances are also actively or passively transported from the filtrate to the interstitial fluid and then into the peritubular capillaries.

Processing of filtrate in the proximal tubule helps maintain a relatively constant pH in body fluids. Cells of the transport epithelium secrete H^+ into the lumen of the tubule but also synthesize and secrete ammonia, which acts as a buffer to trap H^+ in the form of ammonium ions (NH_4^+). The more acidic the filtrate is, the more ammonia the cells produce and secrete, and a mammal's urine usually contains some ammonia from this source (even though most nitrogenous waste is excreted as urea). The proximal tubules also reabsorb about 90% of the buffer bicarbonate (HCO_3^-) from the filtrate, contributing further to pH balance in body fluids.

As the filtrate passes through the proximal tubule, materials to be excreted become concentrated. Many wastes leave the body fluids during the nonselective filtration process and remain in the filtrate while water and salts are reabsorbed. Urea, for example, is reabsorbed at a much lower rate than are salt and water. In addition, some materials are actively secreted into the filtrate from surrounding tissues. For example, drugs and toxins that have been processed in the liver pass from the peritubular capillaries into the interstitial fluid. These molecules are then actively secreted by the transport epithelium into the lumen of the proximal tubule.

❷ Descending limb of the loop of Henle. Reabsorption of water continues as the filtrate moves into the descending limb of the loop of Henle. Here numerous water channels formed by **aquaporin** proteins make the transport epithelium freely permeable to water. In contrast, there are almost no channels for salt and other small solutes, resulting in very low permeability for these substances.

For water to move out of the tubule by osmosis, the interstitial fluid bathing the tubule must be hyperosmotic to the filtrate. This condition is met along the entire length of the descending limb, because the osmolarity of the interstitial fluid increases progressively from the outer cortex to the inner medulla of the kidney. As a result, the filtrate loses water and increases in solute concentration all along its journey down the descending limb.

❸ Ascending limb of the loop of Henle. The filtrate reaches the tip of the loop and then returns to the cortex in the ascending limb. Unlike the descending limb, the ascending limb has a transport epithelium that lacks water channels. Consequently, the epithelial membrane that faces the filtrate in the ascending limb is impermeable to water.

The ascending limb has two specialized regions: a thin segment near the loop tip and a thick segment adjacent to the distal tubule. As filtrate ascends in the thin segment, NaCl, which became concentrated in the descending limb, diffuses out of the permeable tubule into the interstitial fluid. This movement of NaCl out of the tubule helps maintain the osmolarity of the interstitial fluid in the medulla. In the thick segment of the ascending limb, the movement of NaCl out of the filtrate continues. Here, however, the epithelium actively transports NaCl into the interstitial fluid. As a result of losing salt but not water, the filtrate becomes progressively more dilute as it moves up to the cortex in the ascending limb of the loop.

❹ Distal tubule. The distal tubule plays a key role in regulating the K^+ and NaCl concentration of body fluids. This regulation involves variation in the amount of K^+ secreted into the filtrate as well as the amount of NaCl reabsorbed from the filtrate. Like the proximal tubule, the distal tubule contributes to pH regulation by the controlled secretion of H^+ and reabsorption of HCO_3^-.

❺ Collecting duct. The collecting duct carries the filtrate through the medulla to the renal pelvis. Final processing of the filtrate by the transport epithelium of the collecting duct forms the urine.

Under normal conditions, approximately 1,600 L of blood flows through a pair of human kidneys each day. Processing of this enormous traffic of blood by the nephrons and collecting ducts yields about 180 L of initial filtrate. Of this, about 99% of the water and nearly all of the sugars, amino acids, vitamins, and other organic nutrients are reabsorbed into the blood, leaving only about 1.5 L of urine to be transported to the bladder.

As filtrate passes along the transport epithelium of the collecting duct, hormonal control of permeability and transport determines the extent to which the urine becomes concentrated.

When the kidneys are conserving water, aquaporin channels in the collecting duct allow water molecules to cross the epithelium. At the same time, the epithelium remains impermeable to salt and, in the renal cortex, to urea. As the collecting duct traverses the gradient of osmolarity in the

© Pearson Education, Inc.

Filtrate

H₂O
Salts (NaCl and others)
HCO₃⁻
H⁺
Urea
Glucose, amino acids
Some drugs

Key

→ Active transport

→ Passive transport

▲ **Figure 44.13 The nephron and collecting duct: regional functions of the transport epithelium.** The numbered regions in this diagram are keyed to the circled numbers in the text discussion of kidney function.

? *Some cells lining tubules in the kidney maintain normal cell volume by synthesizing organic solutes. Where in the kidney would you expect to find these cells? Explain.*

kidney, the filtrate becomes increasingly concentrated, losing more and more water by osmosis to the hyperosmotic interstitial fluid. In the inner medulla, the duct becomes permeable to urea. Because of the high urea concentration in the filtrate at this point, some urea diffuses out of the duct and into the interstitial fluid. Along with NaCl, this urea contributes to the high osmolarity of the interstitial fluid in the medulla. The net result is urine that is hyperosmotic to the general body fluids.

When producing dilute rather than concentrated urine, the kidney actively reabsorbs salts without allowing water to follow by osmosis. At these times, the epithelium lacks aquaporin channels, and NaCl is actively transported out of filtrate. As we'll see shortly, the state of the collecting duct epithelium is controlled by hormones that together maintain homeostasis for osmolarity, blood pressure, and blood volume.

Solute Gradients and Water Conservation

The mammalian kidney's ability to conserve water is a key terrestrial adaptation. In humans, the osmolarity of blood is about 300 mOsm/L, but the kidney can excrete urine up to four times as concentrated—about 1,200 mOsm/L. Some mammals can do even better: Australian hopping mice, small marsupials that live in dry desert regions, can produce urine with an osmolarity of 9,300 mOsm/L, 25 times as concentrated as the animal's blood.

In a mammalian kidney, the production of hyperosmotic urine is possible only because considerable energy is expended for the active transport of solutes against concentration gradients. The nephrons—particularly the loops of Henle—can be thought of as energy-consuming machines that produce an osmolarity gradient suitable for extracting water from the filtrate in the collecting duct. The primary solutes affecting osmolarity are NaCl, which is concentrated in the renal medulla by the loop of Henle, and urea, which passes across the epithelium of the collecting duct in the inner medulla.

Concentrating Urine in the Mammalian Kidney

To better understand the physiology of the mammalian kidney as a water-conserving organ, let's retrace the flow of filtrate through the excretory tubule. This time, let's focus on how the juxtamedullary nephrons maintain an osmolarity gradient in the tissues that surround the loop of Henle and how they use that gradient to excrete a hyperosmotic urine **(Figure 44.14)**. Filtrate passing from Bowman's capsule to the proximal tubule has about the same osmolarity as blood. A large amount of water *and* salt is reabsorbed from the filtrate as it flows through the proximal tubule in the renal cortex. As a result, the filtrate's volume decreases substantially, but its osmolarity remains about the same.

As the filtrate flows from cortex to medulla in the descending limb of the loop of Henle, water leaves the tubule by osmosis. Solutes, including NaCl, become more concentrated, increasing the osmolarity of the filtrate. The highest osmolarity (about 1,200 mOsm/L) occurs at the elbow of the loop of Henle. This maximizes the diffusion of salt out of the tubule as the filtrate rounds the curve and enters the ascending limb, which is permeable to salt but not to water. NaCl diffusing from the ascending limb helps maintain a high osmolarity in the interstitial fluid of the renal medulla.

Notice that the loop of Henle has several qualities of a countercurrent system, such as the systems that maximize oxygen absorption by fish gills (see Figure 42.21) or reduce heat loss in endotherms (see Figure 40.13). In those cases, the countercurrent mechanisms involve passive movement along either an oxygen concentration gradient or a heat gradient. In contrast, the countercurrent system involving the loop of Henle expends energy to actively transport NaCl from the filtrate in the upper part of the ascending limb of the loop. Such countercurrent systems, which expend energy to create concentration gradients, are called **countercurrent multiplier systems**. The countercurrent multiplier system involving the loop of Henle maintains a high salt concentration in the interior of the kidney, enabling the kidney to form concentrated urine.

What prevents the capillaries of the vasa recta from dissipating the gradient by carrying away the high concentration of NaCl in the medulla's interstitial fluid? As shown in Figure 44.12, the descending and ascending vessels of the vasa recta carry blood in opposite directions through the kidney's osmolarity gradient. As the descending vessel conveys blood toward the inner medulla, water is lost from the blood and NaCl is gained by diffusion. These net fluxes are reversed as blood flows back toward the cortex in the ascending vessel,

▶ **Figure 44.14 How the human kidney concentrates urine: the two-solute model.** Two solutes contribute to the osmolarity of the interstitial fluid: NaCl (used as shorthand here to refer collectively to Na^+ and Cl^-) and urea. The loop of Henle maintains the interstitial gradient of NaCl, which increases continuously in concentration from the cortex to the inner medulla. Urea diffuses into the interstitial fluid of the medulla from the collecting duct (although most of the urea in the filtrate remains in the collecting duct and is excreted). The filtrate makes three trips between the cortex and medulla: first down, then up, and then down again in the collecting duct. As the filtrate flows in the collecting duct past interstitial fluid of increasing osmolarity, more water moves out of the duct by osmosis. The loss of water concentrates the solutes, including urea, that will be excreted in the urine.

WHAT IF? *The drug furosemide blocks the cotransporters for Na^+ and Cl^- in the ascending limb of the loop of Henle. What effect would you expect this drug to have on urine volume?*

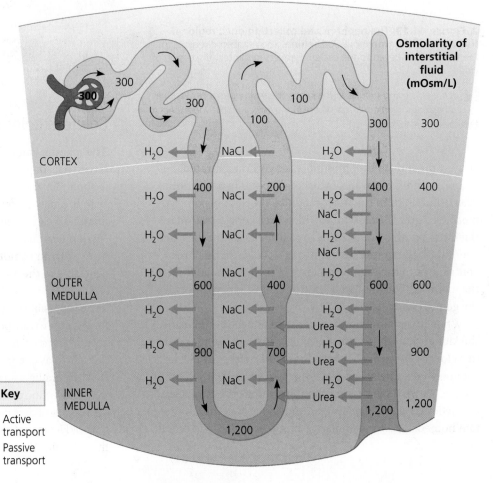

Osmolarity of interstitial fluid (mOsm/L)

CORTEX

OUTER MEDULLA

INNER MEDULLA

Key

→ Active transport
→ Passive transport

with water reentering the blood and salt diffusing out. Thus, the vasa recta can supply the kidney with nutrients and other important substances carried by the blood without interfering with the osmolarity gradient in the inner and outer medulla.

The countercurrent-like characteristics of the loop of Henle and the vasa recta help to generate the steep osmotic gradient between the medulla and cortex. However, diffusion will eventually eliminate any osmotic gradient within animal tissue unless gradient formation is supported by an expenditure of energy. In the kidney, this expenditure largely occurs in the thick segment of the ascending limb of the loop of Henle, where NaCl is actively transported out of the tubule. Even with the benefits of countercurrent exchange, this process—along with other renal active transport systems—consumes considerable ATP. Thus, for its size, the kidney has one of the highest metabolic rates of any organ.

As a result of active transport of NaCl out of the thick segment of the ascending limb, the filtrate is actually hypoosmotic to body fluids by the time it reaches the distal tubule. Next the filtrate descends again toward the medulla, this time in the collecting duct, which is permeable to water but not to salt. Therefore, osmosis extracts water from the filtrate as it passes from cortex to medulla and encounters interstitial fluid of increasing osmolarity. This process concentrates salt, urea, and other solutes in the filtrate. Some urea passes out of the lower portion of the collecting duct and contributes to the high interstitial osmolarity of the inner medulla. (This urea is recycled by diffusion into the loop of Henle, but continual leakage from the collecting duct maintains a high interstitial urea concentration.) When the kidney concentrates urine maximally, the urine reaches 1,200 mOsm/L, the osmolarity of the interstitial fluid in the inner medulla. Although *isoosmotic* to the inner medulla's interstitial fluid, the urine is *hyperosmotic* to blood and interstitial fluid elsewhere in the body. This high osmolarity allows the solutes remaining in the urine to be excreted from the body with minimal water loss.

Adaptations of the Vertebrate Kidney to Diverse Environments

EVOLUTION Vertebrates occupy habitats ranging from rain forests to deserts and from some of the saltiest bodies of water to the nearly pure waters of high mountain lakes. Variations in nephron structure and function equip the kidneys of different vertebrates for osmoregulation in their various habitats. Of particular importance are the relative numbers of juxtamedullary and cortical nephrons (see Figure 44.12) and the length of the loop of Henle in the juxtamedullary nephrons. The adaptive importance of these variations is made apparent by comparing species that inhabit a wide range of environments or by comparing the responses of different vertebrate groups to similar environmental conditions.

Mammals

The juxtamedullary nephron, with its urine-concentrating features, is a key adaptation to terrestrial life, enabling mammals to get rid of salts and nitrogenous wastes without squandering water. As we have seen, the remarkable ability of the mammalian kidney to produce hyperosmotic urine depends on the precise arrangement of the tubules and collecting ducts in the renal cortex and medulla. In this respect, the kidney is one of the clearest examples of how natural selection links the function of an organ to its structure.

Mammals that excrete the most hyperosmotic urine, such as Australian hopping mice, North American kangaroo rats, and other desert mammals, have many juxtamedullary nephrons with loops of Henle that extend deep into the medulla. Long loops maintain steep osmotic gradients in the kidney, resulting in urine becoming very concentrated as it passes from cortex to medulla in the collecting ducts.

In contrast, beavers, muskrats, and other aquatic mammals that spend much of their time in fresh water and rarely face problems of dehydration have mostly cortical nephrons, resulting in a much lower ability to concentrate urine. Terrestrial mammals living in moist conditions have loops of Henle of intermediate length and the capacity to produce urine intermediate in concentration to that produced by freshwater and desert mammals.

Case Study: *Kidney Function in the Vampire Bat*

The South American vampire bat shown in **Figure 44.15** illustrates the versatility of the mammalian kidney. This species feeds at night on the blood of large birds and mammals. The bat uses its sharp teeth to make a small incision in the prey's skin and then laps up blood from the wound (the prey

▲ **Figure 44.15** A vampire bat (*Desmodus rotundas*), a mammal with unique excretory challenges.

is typically not seriously harmed). Anticoagulants in the bat's saliva prevent the blood from clotting.

A vampire bat may search for hours and fly long distances to locate a suitable victim. When it does find prey, it benefits from consuming as much blood as possible. Often drinking more than half its body mass, the bat is at risk of becoming too heavy to fly. As it feeds, however, the bat's kidneys excrete large volumes of dilute urine, up to 24% of body mass per hour. Having lost enough weight to take off, the bat can fly back to its roost in a cave or hollow tree, where it spends the day.

In the roost, the vampire bat faces a different regulatory problem. Most of the nutrition it derives from blood comes in the form of protein. Digesting proteins generates large quantities of urea, but roosting bats lack access to the drinking water necessary to dilute it. Instead, their kidneys shift to producing small quantities of highly concentrated urine (up to 4,600 mOsm/L), an adjustment that disposes of the urea load while conserving as much water as possible. The vampire bat's ability to alternate rapidly between producing large amounts of dilute urine and small amounts of very hyperosmotic urine is an essential part of its adaptation to an unusual food source.

Birds and Other Reptiles

Most birds, including the albatross (see Figure 44.1) and the ostrich **(Figure 44.16)**, live in environments that are dehydrating. Like mammals, birds have kidneys with juxtamedullary nephrons that specialize in conserving water. However, the nephrons of birds have loops of Henle that extend less far into the medulla than those of mammals. Thus, bird kidneys cannot concentrate urine to the high osmolarities achieved by mammalian kidneys.

▲ **Figure 44.16 An ostrich (*Struthio camelus*), an animal well adapted to its dry environment.**

Although birds can produce hyperosmotic urine, their main water conservation adaptation is having uric acid as the nitrogenous waste molecule.

Other reptiles' kidneys have only cortical nephrons and produce urine that is isoosmotic or hypoosmotic to body fluids. However, the epithelium of the cloaca from which urine and feces leave the body conserves fluid by reabsorbing water from these wastes. Also like birds, most other reptiles excrete their nitrogenous wastes as uric acid.

Freshwater Fishes and Amphibians

Freshwater fishes are hyperosmotic to their surroundings, so they must excrete excess water continuously. In contrast to mammals and birds, freshwater fishes produce large volumes of very dilute urine. Their kidneys, which contain many nephrons, produce filtrate at a high rate. Freshwater fishes conserve salts by reabsorbing ions from the filtrate in their distal tubules, leaving water behind.

Amphibian kidneys function much like those of freshwater fishes. When frogs are in fresh water, their kidneys excrete dilute urine while their skin accumulates certain salts from the water by active transport. On land, where dehydration is the most pressing problem of osmoregulation, frogs conserve body fluid by reabsorbing water across the epithelium of the urinary bladder.

Marine Bony Fishes

The tissues of marine bony fishes gain excess salts from their surroundings and lose water. These environmental challenges are opposite to those faced by their freshwater relatives. Compared with freshwater fishes, marine fishes have fewer and smaller nephrons, and their nephrons lack a distal tubule. In addition, their kidneys have small glomeruli or lack glomeruli entirely. In keeping with these features, filtration rates are low and very little urine is excreted.

The main function of kidneys in marine bony fishes is to get rid of divalent ions (those with a charge of 2+ or 2−) such as calcium (Ca^{2+}), magnesium (Mg^{2+}), and sulfate (SO_4^{2-}). Marine fishes take in divalent ions by incessantly drinking seawater. They rid themselves of these ions by secreting them into the proximal tubules of the nephrons and excreting them in urine. Osmoregulation in marine bony fishes also relies on specialized *chloride cells* in the gills. By establishing ion gradients that enable secretion of salt (NaCl) into seawater, the chloride cells maintain proper levels of monovalent ions (charge of 1+ or 1−) such as Na^+ and Cl^-.

The generation of ion gradients and the movement of ions across membranes is central to salt and water balance in marine bony fishes. These events, however, are by no means unique to these organisms nor to homeostasis. As illustrated by the examples in **Figure 44.17**, osmoregulation by chloride cells is but one of many diverse physiological processes that are driven by the movement of ions across a membrane.

MAKE CONNECTIONS

Ion Movement and Gradients

The transport of ions across the plasma membrane of a cell is a fundamental activity of all animals, and indeed of all living things. By generating ion gradients, ion transport provides the potential energy that powers processes ranging from an organism's regulation of salts and gases in internal fluids to its perception of and locomotion through its environment.

Information Processing

In neurons, the opening and closing of channels selective for sodium or other ions underlies the transmission of information as nerve impulses. These signals enable nervous systems to receive and process input and to direct appropriate output, such as this leap of a frog capturing prey. *See Concept 48.3.*

Osmoregulation

In marine bony fishes, ion gradients drive secretion of salt (NaCl), a process essential to avoid dehydration. Within gills, the pumps, cotransporters, and channels of specialized chloride cells function together to drive salt from the blood across the gill epithelium and into the surrounding salt water. *See Concept 44.1.*

Locomotion

A gradient of H^+ ions powers the bacterial flagellum. An electron transport chain generates this gradient, establishing a higher concentration of H^+ outside the bacterial cell. Protons reentering the cell provide a force that causes the flagellar motor to rotate. The rotating motor turns the curved hook, causing the attached filament to propel the cell. *See Concepts 9.4 and 27.1.*

Gas Exchange

Ion gradients provide the basis for the opening of plant stomata by surrounding guard cells. Active transport of H^+ out of a guard cell generates a voltage (membrane potential) that drives inward movement of K^+ ions. This uptake of K^+ by guard cells triggers an osmotic influx of water that changes cell shape, bowing the guard cells outward and thereby opening the stoma. *See Concept 36.4.*

MAKE CONNECTIONS *Explain why the set of forces driving ion movement across the plasma membrane of a cell are described as an electrochemical (electrical and chemical) gradient (see Concept 7.4).*

ANIMATION *BioFlix* Visit the Study Area in **MasteringBiology** for the BioFlix 3-D Animation on Membrane Transport (Chapter 7). BioFlix Tutorials can also be assigned in

1. What do the number and length of nephrons in a fish's kidney indicate about the fish's habitat? How do they correlate with urine production?

2. Many medications make the epithelium of the collecting duct less permeable to water. How would taking such a medication affect kidney output?

3. **WHAT IF?** If blood pressure in the afferent arteriole leading to a glomerulus decreased, how would the rate of blood filtration within Bowman's capsule be affected? Explain.

For suggested answers, see Appendix A.

CONCEPT 44.5

Hormonal circuits link kidney function, water balance, and blood pressure

In mammals, both the volume and osmolarity of urine are adjusted according to an animal's water and salt balance and its rate of urea production. In situations of high salt intake and low water availability, a mammal can excrete urea and salt in small volumes of hyperosmotic urine with minimal water loss. If salt is scarce and fluid intake is high, the kidney can instead get rid of the excess water with little salt loss by producing large volumes of hypoosmotic urine. At such times, the urine can be as dilute as 70 mOsm/L, less than one fourth the osmolarity of human blood.

How are urine volume and osmolarity regulated so effectively? As we'll explore in this final portion of the chapter, two major control circuits that respond to different stimuli together restore and maintain normal water and salt balance.

Homeostatic Regulation of the Kidney

A combination of nervous and hormonal controls manages the osmoregulatory function of the mammalian kidney. Through their effects on the amount and osmolarity of urine, these controls contribute to homeostasis for both blood pressure and blood volume.

Antidiuretic Hormone

One key hormone in the regulatory circuitry of the kidney is antidiuretic hormone (ADH), also called *vasopressin*. Osmoreceptor cells in the hypothalamus monitor the osmolarity of blood and regulate the release of ADH from the posterior pituitary.

To understand the role of ADH, let's consider first what occurs when blood osmolarity rises, such as after eating salty food or losing water through sweating **(Figure 44.18)**. When osmolarity rises above the set point of 300 mOsm/L, ADH release into the bloodstream increases. Within the kidney, the main targets of ADH are the collecting ducts. There, ADH brings about changes that make the epithelium more permeable to water. The resulting increase in water reabsorption concentrates urine, reduces urine volume, and lowers blood osmolarity back toward the set point. As the osmolarity of the blood falls, a negative-feedback mechanism reduces the activity of osmoreceptor cells in the hypothalamus, and ADH secretion is reduced.

What happens if, instead of ingesting salt or sweating profusely, you drink a large amount of water? The resulting reduction in blood osmolarity below the set point causes a drop in ADH secretion to a very low level. The resulting decrease in permeability of the collecting ducts reduces water reabsorption, resulting in discharge of large volumes

▶ **Figure 44.18 Regulation of fluid retention in the kidney by antidiuretic hormone (ADH).** Osmoreceptors in the hypothalamus monitor blood osmolarity via its effect on the net diffusion of water into or out of the receptor cells. When blood osmolarity increases, signals from the osmoreceptors trigger a release of ADH from the posterior pituitary, as well as thirst. Drinking water reduces blood osmolarity, inhibiting further ADH secretion and thereby completing the feedback circuit.

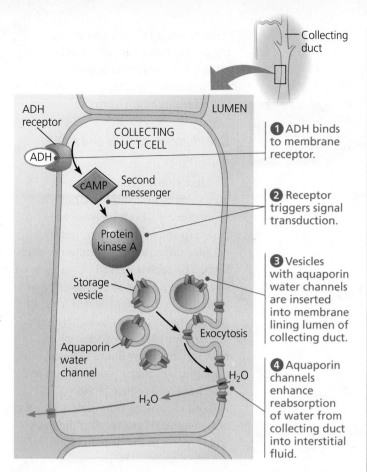

Collecting duct

ADH receptor

LUMEN

COLLECTING DUCT CELL

ADH

cAMP — Second messenger

Protein kinase A

Storage vesicle

Exocytosis

Aquaporin water channel

H_2O

H_2O

❶ ADH binds to membrane receptor.

❷ Receptor triggers signal transduction.

❸ Vesicles with aquaporin water channels are inserted into membrane lining lumen of collecting duct.

❹ Aquaporin channels enhance reabsorption of water from collecting duct into interstitial fluid.

▲ **Figure 44.19 ADH response pathway in the collecting duct.**

of dilute urine. (A high level of urine production is called diuresis; ADH is therefore called *anti*diuretic hormone.)

How does ADH influence water uptake in the kidney's collecting ducts? Binding of ADH to receptor molecules leads to a temporary increase in the number of aquaporin proteins inserted in the membranes of collecting duct cells **(Figure 44.19)**. Additional aquaporin channels recapture more water, reducing urine volume.

Blood osmolarity, ADH release, and water reabsorption in the kidney are normally linked in a feedback circuit that contributes to homeostasis. Anything that disrupts this circuit can interfere with water balance. For example, alcohol inhibits ADH release, leading to excessive urinary water loss and dehydration (which may cause some of the symptoms of a hangover).

Mutations that prevent ADH production or that inactivate the ADH receptor gene disrupt homeostasis by blocking the insertion of additional aquaporin channels in the collecting duct membrane. The resulting disorder can cause severe dehydration and solute imbalance due to production of copious, dilute urine. These symptoms give the disorder its name: *diabetes insipidus* (from the Greek for "to pass through" and "having no flavor"). Could mutations in an aquaporin gene have a similar effect? **Figure 44.20** describes an experimental approach that addressed this question.

▼ **Figure 44.20** | **Inquiry**

Can aquaporin mutations cause diabetes?

Experiment Researchers studied a diabetes insipidus patient with a normal ADH receptor gene but two mutant alleles (A and B) of the aquaporin-2 gene. The resulting changes are shown below in an alignment of protein sequences that includes other species.

Source of Aquaporin-2 Gene Sequence	Amino Acids 183–191* in Encoded Protein	Amino Acids 212–220* in Encoded Protein
Frog (*Xenopus laevis*)	MNPARSFAP	GIFASLIYN
Lizard (*Anolis carolinensis*)	MNPARSFGP	AVVASLLYN
Chicken (*Gallus gallus*)	MNPARSFAP	AAAASIIYN
Human (*Homo sapiens*)	MNPARSLAP	AILGSLLYN
Conserved residues	MNPARSxxP	xxxxSxxYN
Patient's gene: allele A	MNPACSLAP	AILGSLLYN
Patient's gene: allele B	MNPARSLAP	AILGPLLYN

*The numbering is based on the human aquaporin-2 protein sequence.

Each mutation changed the protein sequence at a highly conserved position. To test the hypothesis that the changes affect function, researchers used frog oocytes, cells that will express foreign messenger RNA and can be readily collected from adult female frogs.

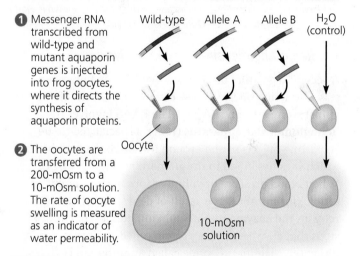

❶ Messenger RNA transcribed from wild-type and mutant aquaporin genes is injected into frog oocytes, where it directs the synthesis of aquaporin proteins.

Wild-type   Allele A   Allele B H_2O (control)

Oocyte

❷ The oocytes are transferred from a 200-mOsm to a 10-mOsm solution. The rate of oocyte swelling is measured as an indicator of water permeability.

10-mOsm solution

Results

Source of Injected mRNA	Rate of Swelling (μm/sec)
Human wild type	196
Patient's allele A	17
Patient's allele B	18
None	20

Conclusion Because each mutation inactivates aquaporin as a water channel, the patient's disorder can be attributed to these mutations.

Source: P. M. Deen et al., Requirement of human renal water channel aquaporin-2 for vasopressin-dependent concentration of urine, *Science* 264:92–95 (1994). Reprinted with permission from AAAS.

WHAT IF? *If you measured ADH levels in patients with ADH receptor mutations and in patients with aquaporin mutations, what would you expect to find, compared with wild-type subjects?*

More Na$^+$ and H$_2$O are reabsorbed in distal tubules, increasing blood volume.

NORMAL BLOOD PRESSURE AND VOLUME

Aldosterone

Adrenal gland

Arterioles constrict, increasing blood pressure.

Angiotensin II

ACE

Angiotensin I

Renin

Angiotensinogen

Liver

Blood pressure or blood volume drops (for example, due to dehydration or blood loss).

Distal tubule

JGA releases renin.

Sensors in JGA detect decrease in pressure or volume.

Juxtaglomerular apparatus (JGA)

▲ **Figure 44.21 Regulation of blood volume and blood pressure by the renin-angiotensin-aldosterone system (RAAS).**

MAKE CONNECTIONS *Compare the activity of renin and ACE in the RAAS with that of the protein kinases in a phosphorylation cascade (such as the one shown in Figure 11.10). How are the roles of these enzymes similar and different in the two regulated response pathways?*

The Renin-Angiotensin-Aldosterone System

A second regulatory mechanism that helps maintain homeostasis by acting on the kidney is the **renin-angiotensin-aldosterone system (RAAS)**. The RAAS involves the **juxtaglomerular apparatus (JGA)**, a specialized tissue consisting of cells of and around the afferent arteriole, which supplies blood to the glomerulus **(Figure 44.21)**. When blood pressure or volume drops in the afferent arteriole (for instance, as a result of dehydration), the JGA releases the enzyme renin. Renin initiates a sequence of steps that cleave a plasma protein called angiotensinogen, ultimately yielding a peptide called **angiotensin II**.

Functioning as a hormone, angiotensin II raises blood pressure by constricting arterioles, which decreases blood flow to capillaries in the kidney (and elsewhere). Angiotensin II also stimulates the adrenal glands to release a hormone called **aldosterone**. Aldosterone causes the nephrons' distal tubules and collecting duct to reabsorb more Na$^+$ and water, increasing blood volume and pressure.

Because angiotensin II acts in several ways that increase blood pressure, drugs that block angiotensin II production are widely used to treat hypertension (chronic high blood pressure). Many of these drugs are specific inhibitors of angiotensin converting enzyme (ACE), which catalyzes one of the steps in the production of angiotensin II.

The renin-angiotensin-aldosterone system operates as a feedback circuit. A drop in blood pressure and blood volume triggers renin release. The resulting production of angiotensin II and release of aldosterone cause a rise in blood pressure and volume, reducing the release of renin from the JGA.

Coordination of ADH and RAAS Activity

The functions of ADH and the RAAS may seem to be redundant, but this is not the case. Both increase water reabsorption in the kidney, but they counter different osmoregulatory problems. The release of ADH is a response to an increase in blood osmolarity, as when the body is dehydrated from excessive water loss or inadequate water intake. However, an excessive loss of both salt and body fluids—caused, for example, by a major wound or severe diarrhea—will reduce blood volume *without* increasing osmolarity. This will not affect ADH release, but the RAAS will respond to the drop in blood volume and pressure by increasing water and Na$^+$ reabsorption. Thus, ADH and the RAAS are partners in homeostasis. ADH alone would lower blood Na$^+$ concentration via water reabsorption in the kidney, but the RAAS helps maintain body fluid osmolarity at the set point by stimulating Na$^+$ reabsorption.

Another hormone, **atrial natriuretic peptide (ANP)**, opposes the RAAS. The walls of the atria of the heart release ANP in response to an increase in blood volume and pressure. ANP inhibits the release of renin from the JGA, inhibits NaCl reabsorption by the collecting ducts, and reduces aldosterone release from the adrenal glands. These actions lower blood volume and pressure. Thus, ADH, the RAAS, and ANP provide an elaborate system of checks and balances that regulate the kidney's ability to control the osmolarity, salt concentration, volume, and pressure of blood. The precise regulatory role of ANP is an area of active research.

CONCEPT CHECK 44.5

1. How does alcohol affect regulation of water balance in the body?

2. Why could it be dangerous to drink a very large amount of water in a short period of time?

3. **WHAT IF?** Conn's syndrome is a condition caused by tumors of the adrenal cortex that secrete high amounts of aldosterone in an unregulated manner. What would you expect to be the major symptom of this disorder?

For suggested answers, see Appendix A.

SUMMARY OF KEY CONCEPTS

CONCEPT 44.1

Osmoregulation balances the uptake and loss of water and solutes (pp. 972–976)

Animal	Inflow/Outflow	Urine
Freshwater fish. Lives in water less concentrated than body fluids; fish tends to gain water, lose salt	Does not drink water. Salt in (active transport by gills), H_2O in. Salt out	▶ Large volume of urine ▶ Urine is less concentrated than body fluids
Marine bony fish. Lives in water more concentrated than body fluids; fish tends to lose water, gain salt	Drinks water. Salt in, H_2O out. Salt out (active transport by gills)	▶ Small volume of urine ▶ Urine is slightly less concentrated than body fluids
Terrestrial vertebrate. Terrestrial environment; tends to lose body water to air	Drinks water. Salt in (by mouth). H_2O and salt out	▶ Moderate volume of urine ▶ Urine is more concentrated than body fluids

© Pearson Education, Inc.

- Cells balance water gain and loss through **osmoregulation**, a process based on the controlled movement of solutes between internal fluids and the external environment and on the movement of water, which follows by osmosis.
- **Osmoconformers** are isoosmotic with their marine environment and do not regulate their **osmolarity**. In contrast, **osmoregulators** control water uptake and loss in a hypoosmotic or hyperosmotic environment, respectively. Water-conserving excretory organs help terrestrial animals avoid desiccation, which can be life-threatening. Animals that live in temporary waters may enter a dormant state called **anhydrobiosis** when their habitats dry up.
- Transport epithelia contain specialized epithelial cells that control the solute movements required for waste disposal and osmoregulation.

? *Under what environmental conditions does water move into a cell by osmosis?*

CONCEPT 44.2

An animal's nitrogenous wastes reflect its phylogeny and habitat (pp. 976–977)

- Protein and nucleic acid metabolism generates **ammonia**. Most aquatic animals excrete ammonia. Mammals and most adult amphibians convert ammonia to the less toxic **urea**, which is excreted with a minimal loss of water. Insects and many reptiles, including birds, convert ammonia to **uric acid**, a mostly insoluble waste excreted in a paste-like urine.
- The kind of nitrogenous waste excreted depends on an animal's evolutionary history and habitat. The amount excreted is coupled to the animal's energy budget and dietary protein intake.

DRAW IT *Construct a table summarizing the three major types of nitrogenous wastes and their relative toxicity, energy cost to produce, and associated water loss during excretion.*

CONCEPT 44.3

Diverse excretory systems are variations on a tubular theme (pp. 978–981)

- Most excretory systems carry out **filtration**, **reabsorption**, **secretion**, and **excretion**. Invertebrate excretory systems include the **protonephridia** of flatworms, the **metanephridia** of earthworms, and the **Malpighian tubules** of insects. **Kidneys** function in both excretion and osmoregulation in vertebrates.
- Excretory tubules (consisting of **nephrons** and **collecting ducts**) and blood vessels pack the mammalian kidney. Blood pressure forces fluid from blood in the **glomerulus** into the lumen of **Bowman's capsule**. Following reabsorption and secretion, filtrate flows into a collecting duct. The **ureter** conveys urine from the **renal pelvis** to the **urinary bladder**.

? *Given that a typical excretory system selectively absorbs and secretes materials, what function does filtration serve?*

CONCEPT 44.4

The nephron is organized for stepwise processing of blood filtrate (pp. 981–988)

- Within the nephron, selective secretion and reabsorption in the **proximal tubule** alter filtrate volume and composition. The *descending limb* of the **loop of Henle** is permeable to water but not salt; water moves by osmosis into the interstitial fluid. The *ascending limb* is permeable to salt but not water; salt leaves by diffusion and by active transport. The **distal tubule** and collecting duct regulate K^+ and NaCl levels in body fluids.
- In mammals, **a countercurrent multiplier system** involving the loop of Henle maintains the gradient of salt concentration in the kidney interior. Urea exiting the collecting duct contributes to the osmotic gradient of the kidney.
- Natural selection has shaped the form and function of nephrons in various vertebrates to the osmoregulatory challenges of the animals' habitats. For example, desert mammals, which excrete the most hyperosmotic urine, have loops of Henle that extend deep into the **renal medulla**, whereas mammals in moist habitats have shorter loops and excrete more dilute urine.

? *How do cortical and juxtamedullary nephrons differ with respect to reabsorbing nutrients and concentrating urine?*

Hormonal circuits link kidney function, water balance, and blood pressure (pp. 988–990)

- The posterior pituitary gland releases antidiuretic hormone (ADH) when blood osmolarity rises above a set point, such as when water intake is inadequate. ADH increases the permeability to water of the collecting ducts by increasing the number of epithelial **aquaporin** channels.
- When blood pressure or blood volume in the afferent arteriole drops, the **juxtaglomerular apparatus** releases renin. **Angiotensin II** formed in response to renin constricts arterioles and triggers release of the hormone **aldosterone**, raising blood pressure and reducing the release of renin. This **renin-angiotensin-aldosterone system** has functions that overlap with those of ADH and are opposed by **atrial natriuretic peptide**.

? *Why can only some patients with diabetes insipidus be treated effectively with ADH?*

TEST YOUR UNDERSTANDING

LEVEL 1: KNOWLEDGE/COMPREHENSION

1. *Unlike* an earthworm's metanephridia, a mammalian nephron
    a. is intimately associated with a capillary network.
    b. functions in both osmoregulation and excretion.
    c. receives filtrate from blood instead of coelomic fluid.
    d. has a transport epithelium.

2. Which process in the nephron is *least* selective?
    a. filtration
    b. reabsorption
    c. active transport
    d. secretion

3. Which of the following animals generally has the lowest volume of urine production?
    a. vampire bat
    b. salmon in fresh water
    c. marine bony fish
    d. freshwater bony fish

LEVEL 2: APPLICATION/ANALYSIS

4. The high osmolarity of the renal medulla is maintained by all of the following *except*
    a. active transport of salt from the upper region of the ascending limb.
    b. the spatial arrangement of juxtamedullary nephrons.
    c. diffusion of urea from the collecting duct.
    d. diffusion of salt from the descending limb of the loop of Henle.

5. Natural selection should favor the highest proportion of juxtamedullary nephrons in which of the following species?
    a. river otter
    b. mouse living in a temperate broadleaf forest
    c. mouse living in a desert
    d. beaver

6. African lungfish, which are often found in small stagnant pools of fresh water, produce urea as a nitrogenous waste. What is the advantage of this adaptation?
    a. Urea takes less energy to synthesize than ammonia.
    b. Small stagnant pools do not provide enough water to dilute ammonia, which is toxic.
    c. Urea forms an insoluble precipitate.
    d. Urea makes lungfish tissue hypoosmotic to the pool.

LEVEL 3: SYNTHESIS/EVALUATION

7. **INTERPRET THE DATA** Use the data below to draw four pie charts for water gain and loss in a kangaroo rat and a human.

	Kangaroo Rat	Human
Water Gain (mL)		
Ingested in food	0.2	750
Ingested in liquid	0	1,500
Derived from metabolism	1.8	250
Water Loss (mL)		
Urine	0.45	1,500
Feces	0.09	100
Evaporation	1.46	900

Which routes of water gain and loss make up a much larger share of the total in a kangaroo rat than in a human?

8. **EVOLUTION CONNECTION**
Merriam's kangaroo rats (*Dipodomys merriami*) live in North American habitats ranging from moist, cool woodlands to hot deserts. Assuming that natural selection has resulted in differences in water conservation between *D. merriami* populations, propose a hypothesis concerning the relative rates of evaporative water loss by populations that live in moist versus dry environments. Using a humidity sensor to detect this evaporative water loss, how could you test your hypothesis?

9. **SCIENTIFIC INQUIRY**
You are exploring kidney function in kangaroo rats. You measure urine volume and osmolarity, as well as the amount of chloride (Cl^-) and urea in the urine. If the water source provided to the animals were switched from tap water to a 2% NaCl solution, what change in urine osmolarity would you expect? How would you determine if this change was more likely due to a change in the excretion of Cl^- or urea?

10. **WRITE ABOUT A THEME: ORGANIZATION**
In a short essay (100–150 words), compare how membrane structures in the loop of Henle and collecting duct of the mammalian kidney enable water to be recovered from filtrate in the process of osmoregulation.

11. **SYNTHESIZE YOUR KNOWLEDGE**

The marine iguana (*Amblyrhynchus cristatus*), which spends long periods under water feeding on seaweed, relies on both salt glands and kidneys for homeostasis of its internal fluids. Describe how these organs together meet the particular osmoregulatory challenges of this animal's environment.

For selected answers, see Appendix A.

MasteringBiology®

Students Go to **MasteringBiology** for assignments, the eText, and the Study Area with practice tests, animations, and activities.

Instructors Go to **MasteringBiology** for automatically graded tutorials and questions that you can assign to your students, plus Instructor Resources.

45

Hormones and the Endocrine System

KEY CONCEPTS

45.1 Hormones and other signaling molecules bind to target receptors, triggering specific response pathways

45.2 Feedback regulation and coordination with the nervous system are common in endocrine signaling

45.3 Endocrine glands respond to diverse stimuli in regulating homeostasis, development, and behavior

▲ **Figure 45.1 What makes male and female elephant seals look so different?**

The Body's Long-Distance Regulators

Although we often distinguish animals of different species by their appearance, in many species the females and males look quite different from each other. Such is the case for the elephant seals (*Mirounga angustirostris*) shown in **Figure 45.1**. The male is much larger than the female, and only he has the prominent proboscis for which the species is named. Males are also far more territorial and aggressive than females. A sex-determining gene on the Y chromosome makes a seal embryo male. But how does the presence of this gene lead to male size, shape, and behavior? The answer to this and many other questions about biological processes involves signaling molecules called **hormones** (from the Greek *horman*, to excite).

In animals, hormones are secreted into the extracellular fluid, circulate in the blood (or hemolymph), and communicate regulatory messages throughout the body. In the case of the elephant seal, increased secretion of particular hormones at puberty triggers sexual maturation, as well as the accompanying changes that distinguish adult females and males. Hormones influence much more than sex and reproduction, however. For example, when seals, humans, and other mammals are stressed, are dehydrated, or have low blood sugar levels, hormones coordinate the physiological responses that restore balance in our bodies.

◀ **Male elephant seals sparring**

Each hormone binds to specific receptors in the body. Although a given hormone can reach all cells of the body, only some cells have receptors for that hormone. A hormone elicits a response—such as a change in metabolism—in specific *target cells*, those that have the matching receptor. Cells lacking a receptor for that hormone are unaffected.

Chemical signaling by hormones is the function of the **endocrine system**, one of the two basic systems for communication and regulation in the animal body. The other major communication and control system is the **nervous system**, a network of specialized cells—neurons—that transmit signals along dedicated pathways. These signals in turn regulate neurons, muscle cells, and endocrine cells. Because signaling by neurons can regulate the release of hormones, the nervous and endocrine systems often overlap in function.

In this chapter, we'll begin with an overview of the different types of chemical signaling in animals. We'll then explore how hormones regulate target cells, how hormone secretion is regulated, and how hormones help maintain homeostasis. We'll also consider the ways in which endocrine and nervous system activities are coordinated and examine the role of hormones in regulating growth and development.

CONCEPT 45.1

Hormones and other signaling molecules bind to target receptors, triggering specific response pathways

We'll begin our consideration of the endocrine system by examining the diverse ways that animal cells use chemical signals to communicate.

Intercellular Communication

Communication between animal cells via secreted signals is often classified by two criteria: the type of secreting cell and the route taken by the signal in reaching its target. **Figure 45.2** illustrates five forms of signaling distinguished in this manner. We'll explore these forms in turn.

Endocrine Signaling

In endocrine signaling (see Figure 45.2a), hormones secreted into extracellular fluid by endocrine cells reach target cells via the bloodstream (or hemolymph). One function of endocrine signaling is to maintain homeostasis. Hormones regulate properties that include blood pressure and volume, energy metabolism and allocation, and solute concentrations in body fluids. Endocrine signaling also mediates responses to environmental stimuli, regulates growth and development, and, as discussed above, triggers physical and behavioral changes underlying sexual maturity and reproduction.

(a) In **endocrine signaling**, secreted molecules diffuse into the bloodstream and trigger responses in target cells anywhere in the body.

(b) In **paracrine signaling**, secreted molecules diffuse locally and trigger a response in neighboring cells.

(c) In **autocrine signaling**, secreted molecules diffuse locally and trigger a response in the cells that secrete them.

(d) In **synaptic signaling**, neurotransmitters diffuse across synapses and trigger responses in cells of target tissues (neurons, muscles, or glands).

(e) In **neuroendocrine signaling**, neurohormones diffuse into the bloodstream and trigger responses in target cells anywhere in the body.

▲ **Figure 45.2 Intercellular communication by secreted molecules.** In each type of signaling, secreted molecules (•) bind to a specific receptor protein (⌣) expressed by target cells. Some receptors are located inside cells, but for simplicity, here all are drawn on the cell surface.

Paracrine and Autocrine Signaling

Many types of cells produce and secrete **local regulators**, molecules that act over short distances and reach their target cells solely by diffusion. Once secreted, local regulators act on their target cells within seconds or even milliseconds. Local regulators include cytokines, which enable communication between immune cells (see Figure 43.16 and Figure 43.18), and growth factors, which promote the growth, division, and development of many types of cells.

Depending on the target cell, signaling by local regulators can be either paracrine or autocrine. In **paracrine** signaling (from the Greek *para*, to one side of), target cells lie near the secreting cell (see Figure 45.2b). In **autocrine** signaling (from the Greek *auto*, self), the secreting cells themselves are the target cells (see Figure 45.2c).

Paracrine and autocrine signaling play roles in many physiological processes, including blood pressure regulation, nervous system function, and reproduction. Local regulators that mediate such signaling include the **prostaglandins**, so named because they were first discovered in prostate gland secretions that contribute to semen. In the reproductive tract of a female, prostaglandins introduced in semen stimulate the smooth muscles of the uterine wall to contract, helping sperm reach an egg. At the onset of childbirth, prostaglandins produced by the placenta cause the uterine muscles to become more excitable, helping to induce labor (see Figure 46.18).

Prostaglandins also act in the immune system, promoting inflammation and the sensation of pain in response to injury. That is why drugs that block prostaglandin synthesis, such as aspirin and ibuprofen, have both anti-inflammatory and pain-relieving effects. Prostaglandins also help regulate the aggregation of platelets, one step in the formation of blood clots. Because blood clots in vessels that supply the heart can block blood flow, causing a heart attack (see Concept 42.4), some physicians recommend that people at risk for a heart attack take aspirin on a regular basis.

Synaptic and Neuroendocrine Signaling

Secreted molecules are crucial for two types of signaling by neurons. In *synaptic signaling*, neurons form specialized junctions called synapses with target cells, such as other neurons and muscle cells. At most synapses, neurons secrete molecules called **neurotransmitters** that diffuse a very short distance and bind to receptors on the target cells (see Figure 45.2d). Neurotransmitters are central to sensation, memory, cognition, and movement (as we'll explore in Chapters 48–50).

In *neuroendocrine signaling*, specialized neurons called neurosecretory cells secrete **neurohormones**, which diffuse from nerve cell endings into the bloodstream (see Figure 45.2e). One example of a neurohormone is antidiuretic hormone, which is essential to kidney function and water balance (see Concept 44.5). Many neurohormones function in the regulation of endocrine signaling, as we'll discuss later in this chapter.

Signaling by Pheromones

Not all secreted signaling molecules act within the body. Members of a particular animal species sometimes

▲ **Figure 45.3 Signaling by pheromones.** Using their lowered antennae, these Asian army ants (*Leptogenys distinguenda*) follow a pheromone-marked trail as they carry pupae and larvae to a new nest site.

communicate with each other via **pheromones**, chemicals that are released into the external environment. For example, when a foraging ant discovers a new food source, it marks its path back to the nest with a pheromone. Ants also use pheromones for guidance when a colony migrates to a new location **(Figure 45.3)**.

Pheromones serve a wide range of functions that include defining territories, warning of predators, and attracting potential mates. The polyphemus moth (*Antheraea polyphemus*) provides a noteworthy example: The sex pheromone released into the air by a female enables her to attract a male of the species from up to 4.5 km away. You'll read more about pheromone function when we take up the topic of animal behavior in Chapter 51.

Chemical Classes of Local Regulators and Hormones

Molecules used in intercellular signaling vary substantially in size and chemical properties. Let's take a look at some of the most common classes of local regulators and hormones.

Classes of Local Regulators

One group of local regulators, the prostaglandins, are modified fatty acids. Many other local regulators, including cytokines and growth factors, are polypeptides, and some are gases.

Nitric oxide (NO), a gas, functions in the body as both a local regulator and a neurotransmitter. When the level of oxygen in the blood falls, endothelial cells in blood vessel walls synthesize and release NO. After diffusing into the surrounding smooth muscle cells, NO activates an enzyme that relaxes the cells. The result is vasodilation, which increases blood flow to tissues.

In human males, NO's ability to promote vasodilation enables sexual function by increasing blood flow into the penis, producing an erection. The drug Viagra (sildenafil citrate), a

Water-soluble (hydrophilic)	Lipid-soluble (hydrophobic)
Polypeptides	**Steroids**
Insulin	Cortisol

0.8 nm

Amines

Epinephrine

Thyroxine

▲ **Figure 45.4 Differences in hormone solubility and structure.**

MAKE CONNECTIONS *Cells synthesize epinephrine from the amino acid tyrosine (see Figure 5.14). On the structure of epinephrine shown above, draw an arrow pointing to the position corresponding to the α carbon of tyrosine.*

treatment for male erectile dysfunction, sustains an erection by prolonging activity of the NO response pathway.

Classes of Hormones

Hormones fall into three major chemical classes: polypeptides, steroids, and amines **(Figure 45.4)**. The hormone insulin, for example, is a polypeptide that contains two chains in its active form. Steroid hormones, such as cortisol, are lipids that contain four fused carbon rings. All are derived from the steroid cholesterol (see Figure 5.12). Epinephrine and thyroxine are amine hormones, each synthesized from a single amino acid, either tyrosine or tryptophan.

As Figure 45.4 indicates, hormones vary in their solubility in aqueous and lipid-rich environments. Polypeptides and most amine hormones are water-soluble, whereas steroid hormones and other largely nonpolar (hydrophobic) hormones, such as thyroxine, are lipid-soluble.

Cellular Response Pathways

There are several differences between the response pathways for water-soluble and lipid-soluble signaling molecules.

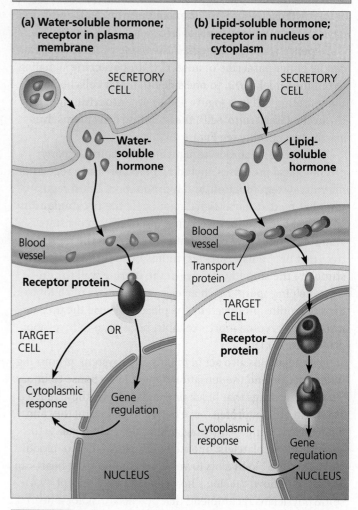

▼ **Figure 45.5 Variation in hormone receptor location.**

(a) Water-soluble hormone; receptor in plasma membrane

SECRETORY CELL

Water-soluble hormone

Blood vessel

Receptor protein

TARGET CELL

OR

Cytoplasmic response

Gene regulation

NUCLEUS

(b) Lipid-soluble hormone; receptor in nucleus or cytoplasm

SECRETORY CELL

Lipid-soluble hormone

Blood vessel

Transport protein

TARGET CELL

Receptor protein

Cytoplasmic response

Gene regulation

NUCLEUS

WHAT IF? *Suppose you are studying a cell's response to a particular hormone. You observe that the cell produces the same response to the hormone whether or not the cell is treated with a chemical that blocks transcription. What can you surmise about the hormone and its receptor?*

To focus this and subsequent discussions, we'll restrict our presentation to endocrine signaling.

One difference in cellular hormone response pathways is the location of the target cells' receptor proteins. Water-soluble hormones are secreted by exocytosis and travel freely in the bloodstream. Being insoluble in lipids, they cannot diffuse through the plasma membranes of target cells. Instead, these hormones bind to cell-surface receptors, inducing changes in cytoplasmic molecules and sometimes altering gene transcription **(Figure 45.5a)**. In contrast, lipid-soluble hormones diffuse out across the membranes of endocrine cells. Outside the cell, they bind to transport proteins that keep them soluble in the aqueous environment of the blood. Upon leaving the blood, they diffuse into target cells and typically bind to receptors in the cytoplasm or nucleus **(Figure 45.5b)**. The hormone-bound receptor then triggers changes in gene transcription.

To follow the distinct cellular responses to water-soluble and lipid-soluble hormones, we'll examine the two response pathways in turn.

Pathway for Water-Soluble Hormones

The binding of a water-soluble hormone to a receptor protein triggers events at the plasma membrane that result in a cellular response. The response may be the activation of an enzyme, a change in the uptake or secretion of specific molecules, or a rearrangement of the cytoskeleton. In addition, some cell-surface receptors cause proteins in the cytoplasm to move into the nucleus and alter the transcription of specific genes.

The series of changes in cellular proteins that converts the extracellular chemical signal to a specific intracellular response is called **signal transduction**. A signal transduction pathway typically involves multiple steps, each involving specific molecular interactions (see Chapter 11).

To explore the role of signal transduction in hormone signaling, consider one response to short-term stress. When you are in a stressful situation, perhaps running to catch a bus, the adrenal glands that lie atop your kidneys secrete the hormone **epinephrine**, also known as *adrenaline*. Upon reaching the liver, epinephrine binds to a G protein-coupled receptor in the plasma membrane of target cells **(Figure 45.6)**. The binding of hormone to receptor triggers a cascade of events in liver cells involving synthesis of cyclic AMP (cAMP) as a short-lived *second messenger*. Activation of protein kinase A by cAMP leads to activation of an enzyme required for glycogen breakdown and inactivation of an enzyme needed for glycogen synthesis. The net result is

that the liver releases glucose into the bloodstream, providing the fuel you need to chase the departing bus.

Pathway for Lipid-Soluble Hormones

Intracellular receptors for lipid-soluble hormones perform the entire task of transducing a signal within a target cell. The hormone activates the receptor, which then directly triggers the cell's response. In most cases, the response to a lipid-soluble hormone is a change in gene expression.

Most steroid hormone receptors are predominantly located in the cytosol prior to binding to a hormone. When a steroid hormone binds to its cytosolic receptor, a hormone-receptor complex forms, which moves into the nucleus (see Figure 18.9). There, the receptor portion of the complex alters transcription of particular genes by interacting with a specific DNA-binding protein or response element in the DNA. (In some cell types, steroid hormones trigger additional responses by interacting with other kinds of receptor proteins located at the cell surface).

Among the best-characterized steroid hormone receptors are those that bind to estrogens, steroid hormones necessary for female reproductive function in vertebrates. For example, in female birds and frogs, estradiol, a form of estrogen, binds to a specific cytoplasmic receptor in liver cells. Binding of estradiol to this receptor activates transcription of the gene for the protein vitellogenin **(Figure 45.7)**. Following translation of the messenger RNA, vitellogenin is secreted

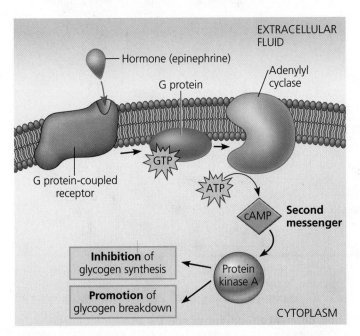

▲ **Figure 45.6 Signal transduction triggered by a cell-surface hormone receptor.**

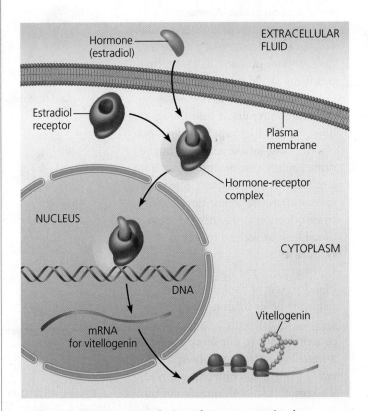

▲ **Figure 45.7 Direct regulation of gene expression by a steroid hormone receptor.**

and transported in the blood to the reproductive system, where it is used to produce egg yolk.

Thyroxine, vitamin D, and other lipid-soluble hormones that are not steroids have receptors that are typically located in the nucleus. These receptors bind to hormone molecules that diffuse from the bloodstream across both the plasma membrane and nuclear envelope. Once bound to a hormone, the receptor binds to specific sites in the cell's DNA and stimulates the transcription of specific genes.

Multiple Effects of Hormones

Many hormones elicit more than one type of response in the body. Consider, for example, epinephrine. As we noted earlier, this hormone triggers glycogen breakdown in the liver. However, epinephrine also *increases* blood flow to major skeletal muscles and *decreases* blood flow to the digestive tract. These varied responses enhance the rapid reactions of the body in emergencies.

How can a hormone such as epinephrine have such widely varying effects? A single hormone can elicit multiple responses if its target cells differ in their receptor type or in the molecules that produce the response. Consider the target cells for epinephrine:

- In liver cells, epinephrine binds to a β-type receptor in the plasma membrane. This receptor activates the enzyme protein kinase A, which in turn regulates enzymes of glycogen metabolism, causing release of glucose into the blood **(Figure 45.8a)**. (Note that this is the signal transduction pathway illustrated in Figure 45.6.)
- In the smooth muscle cells lining blood vessels that supply skeletal muscle, the same kinase activated by the same epinephrine receptor inactivates a muscle-specific enzyme. The result is smooth muscle relaxation, leading to vasodilation and hence increased blood flow to skeletal muscles **(Figure 45.8b)**.
- In the smooth muscle cells lining blood vessels of the intestines, epinephrine binds to an α-type receptor **(Figure 45.8c)**. Rather than activating protein kinase A, this receptor triggers a signaling pathway involving a different G protein and different enzymes. The result is smooth muscle contraction that brings about vasoconstriction, restricting blood flow to the intestines.

Lipid-soluble hormones also exert different effects on different target cells. For example, estradiol, which stimulates a bird's liver to synthesize the yolk protein vitellogenin, stimulates the reproductive system to synthesize proteins that form the egg white.

Endocrine Tissues and Organs

Some endocrine cells are found in organs that are part of other organ systems. For example, the stomach contains isolated endocrine cells that help regulate digestive processes by secreting the hormone gastrin. More often, endocrine cells are grouped in ductless organs called **endocrine glands**, such as the thyroid and parathyroid glands and the gonads, either testes in males or ovaries in females. The endocrine glands of humans are illustrated in **Figure 45.9**. This overview of endocrine glands and the hormones that they produce will serve as a useful point of reference as you move through the chapter.

Note that endocrine glands secrete hormones directly into the surrounding fluid. In contrast, *exocrine glands*,

▲ **Figure 45.8 One hormone, different effects.** Epinephrine, the primary "fight-or-flight" hormone, produces different responses in different target cells. Target cells with the same receptor exhibit different responses if they have different signal transduction pathways or effector proteins; compare (a) with (b). Target cells with different receptors for the hormone may also exhibit different responses; compare (b) with (c).

Endocrine gland	Hormones
Pineal gland	• **Melatonin:** Participates in regulation of biological rhythms.
Hypothalamus	• **Hormones released from posterior pituitary (oxytocin and vasopressin)** • **Releasing and inhibiting hormones:** Regulate anterior pituitary
Pituitary gland	
Anterior pituitary	• **Follicle-stimulating hormone (FSH)** and **luteinizing hormone (LH):** Stimulate ovaries and testes • **Thyroid-stimulating hormone (TSH):** Stimulates thyroid gland • **Adrenocorticotropic hormone (ACTH):** Stimulates adrenal cortex • **Prolactin:** Stimulates mammary gland cells • **Growth hormone (GH):** Stimulates growth and metabolic functions
Posterior pituitary	• **Oxytocin:** Stimulates contraction of smooth muscle cells in uterus and mammary glands • **Vasopressin:** (also called **antidiuretic hormone, ADH**): Promotes retention of water by kidneys; influences social behavior and bonding
Thyroid gland	• **Thyroid hormone (T_3 and T_4):** Stimulates and maintains metabolic processes • **Calcitonin:** Lowers blood calcium level
Parathyroid glands	• **Parathyroid hormone (PTH):** Raises blood calcium level
Adrenal glands	
Adrenal medulla	• **Epinephrine** and **norepinephrine:** Raise blood glucose level; increase metabolic activities; constrict certain blood vessels.
Adrenal cortex	• **Glucocorticoids:** Raise blood glucose level • **Mineralocorticoids:** Promote reabsorption of Na^+ and excretion of K^+ in kidneys
Pancreas	• **Insulin:** Lowers blood glucose level • **Glucagon:** Raises blood glucose level
Ovaries (female)	• **Estrogens*:** Stimulate uterine lining growth; promote development and maintenance of female secondary sex characteristics • **Progestins*:** Promote uterine lining growth
Testes (male)	• **Androgens*:** Support sperm formation; promote development and maintenance of male secondary sex characteristics

*Found in both males and females, but with a major role in one sex

such as salivary glands, have ducts that carry secreted substances onto body surfaces or into body cavities. This distinction is reflected in the glands' names: The Greek *endo* (within) and *exo* (out of) refer to secretion into or out of body fluids, while *crine* (from the Greek word meaning "separate") refers to movement away from the secreting cell. In the case of the pancreas, endocrine and exocrine tissues are found in the same gland: Ductless tissues secrete hormones, whereas tissues with ducts secrete enzymes and bicarbonate.

CONCEPT CHECK 45.1

1. How do response mechanisms in target cells differ for water-soluble and lipid-soluble hormones?

2. In what way does one activity described for prostaglandins resemble that of a pheromone?

3. **MAKE CONNECTIONS** How is the action of epinephrine on blood flow to muscles in the fight-or-flight response similar to the action of the plant hormone auxin in apical dominance (see Concept 39.2)?

For suggested answers, see Appendix A.

Feedback regulation and coordination with the nervous system are common in endocrine signaling

So far, we have explored forms of intercellular signaling as well as hormone structure, recognition, and response. We turn now to considering how regulatory pathways that control hormone secretion are organized.

Simple Hormone Pathways

In examining the regulation of hormone secretion, we begin with two basic types of organization—simple endocrine and simple neuroendocrine pathways. In a *simple endocrine pathway*, endocrine cells respond directly to an internal or environmental stimulus by secreting a particular hormone **(Figure 45.10)**. The hormone travels in the bloodstream to target cells, where it interacts with its specific receptors. Signal transduction within target cells brings about a physiological response.

As an example of a simple endocrine pathway, we'll consider the control of pH in the duodenum, the first part of the small intestine. The digestive juices of the stomach are extremely acidic and must be neutralized before further digestion can occur. As the stomach contents enter the duodenum, their low pH stimulates endocrine cells in the lining of the duodenum to secrete the hormone *secretin* into the extracellular fluid (see Figure 45.10). From there, secretin diffuses into the blood. Circulating secretin reaches target cells in the pancreas, which respond by releasing bicarbonate into ducts leading to the duodenum. This response—the release of bicarbonate—raises the pH in the duodenum, neutralizing the stomach acid.

Neuroendocrine pathways include additional steps and involve more than one cell type. In a *simple neuroendocrine pathway*, the stimulus is received by a sensory neuron, which stimulates a neurosecretory cell **(Figure 45.11)**. The neurosecretory cell then secretes a neurohormone, which diffuses into the bloodstream and travels to target cells.

As an example of a simple neuroendocrine pathway, consider the regulation of milk release during nursing in mammals. Suckling by an infant stimulates sensory

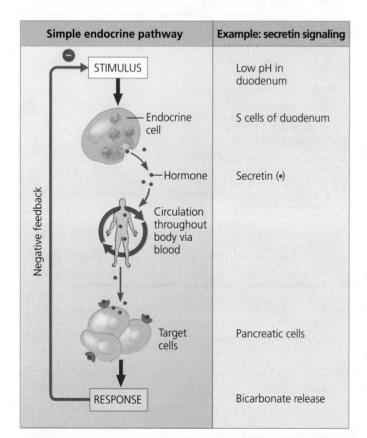

▲ **Figure 45.10 A simple endocrine pathway.** Endocrine cells respond to a change in some internal or external variable—the stimulus—by secreting hormone molecules that trigger a specific response by target cells. In the case of secretin signaling, the simple endocrine pathway is self-limiting because the response to secretin (bicarbonate release) reduces the stimulus (low pH) through negative feedback.

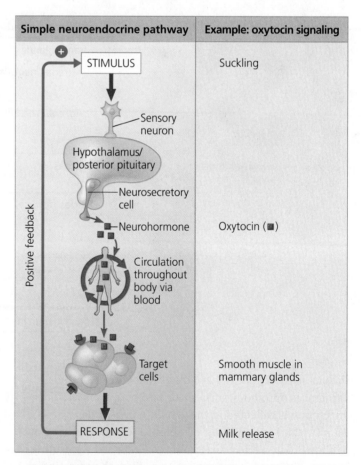

▲ **Figure 45.11 A simple neuroendocrine pathway.** Sensory neurons respond to a stimulus by sending nerve impulses to a neurosecretory cell, triggering secretion of a neurohormone. Upon reaching its target cells, the neurohormone binds to its receptor, triggering a specific response. In oxytocin signaling, the response increases the stimulus, forming a positive-feedback loop that amplifies signaling.

neurons in the nipples, generating signals in the nervous system that reach the hypothalamus. Nerve impulses from the hypothalamus then trigger the release of the neurohormone **oxytocin** from the posterior pituitary gland (see Figure 45.11). In response to circulating oxytocin, the mammary glands secrete milk.

Feedback Regulation

A feedback loop linking the response back to the initial stimulus is characteristic of control pathways. Often, regulation involves **negative feedback**, in which the response reduces the initial stimulus. For instance, bicarbonate release in response to secretin increases pH in the intestine, eliminating the stimulus and thereby shutting off secretin release (see Figure 45.10). By decreasing hormone signaling, negative-feedback regulation prevents excessive pathway activity.

Whereas negative feedback dampens a stimulus, **positive feedback** reinforces a stimulus, leading to an even greater response. For example, in the oxytocin pathway outlined in Figure 45.11, the mammary glands secrete milk in response to circulating oxytocin. Milk released in response to the oxytocin leads to more suckling and therefore more stimulation. Activation of the pathway is sustained until the baby stops suckling. When mammals give birth, oxytocin induces target cells in the uterine muscles to contract. This pathway is also characterized by positive-feedback regulation, such that it drives the birth process to completion.

While positive feedback amplifies both stimulus and response, negative feedback helps restore a preexisting state. It is not surprising, therefore, that hormone pathways involved in homeostasis typically involve negative feedback. Often such pathways are paired, providing even more balanced control. For example, the regulation of blood glucose levels relies on the antagonistic effects of insulin and glucagon (see Figure 41.21).

Coordination of Endocrine and Nervous Systems

In a wide range of animals, endocrine organs in the brain integrate function of the endocrine system with that of the nervous system. We'll explore the basic principles of such integration in invertebrates and vertebrates.

Invertebrates

The control of development in a moth illustrates neuroendocrine coordination in invertebrates. A moth larva, such as this colorful caterpillar of the giant silk moth (*Hyalophora cecropia*), grows in stages. Because its exoskeleton cannot stretch, the larva must periodically molt, shedding the old exoskeleton and secreting a new one. The endocrine pathway that controls molting originates in the larval brain **(Figure 45.12)**. There, neurosecretory cells

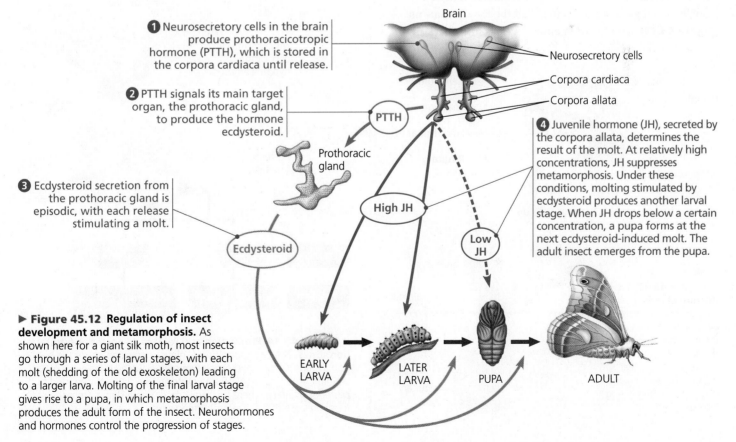

❶ Neurosecretory cells in the brain produce prothoracicotropic hormone (PTTH), which is stored in the corpora cardiaca until release.

❷ PTTH signals its main target organ, the prothoracic gland, to produce the hormone ecdysteroid.

❸ Ecdysteroid secretion from the prothoracic gland is episodic, with each release stimulating a molt.

❹ Juvenile hormone (JH), secreted by the corpora allata, determines the result of the molt. At relatively high concentrations, JH suppresses metamorphosis. Under these conditions, molting stimulated by ecdysteroid produces another larval stage. When JH drops below a certain concentration, a pupa forms at the next ecdysteroid-induced molt. The adult insect emerges from the pupa.

Brain
Neurosecretory cells
Corpora cardiaca
Corpora allata
PTTH
Prothoracic gland
High JH
Low JH
Ecdysteroid
EARLY LARVA
LATER LARVA
PUPA
ADULT

▶ **Figure 45.12 Regulation of insect development and metamorphosis.** As shown here for a giant silk moth, most insects go through a series of larval stages, with each molt (shedding of the old exoskeleton) leading to a larger larva. Molting of the final larval stage gives rise to a pupa, in which metamorphosis produces the adult form of the insect. Neurohormones and hormones control the progression of stages.

produce PTTH, a polypeptide neurohormone. When PTTH reaches an endocrine organ called the prothoracic gland, it directs release of a second hormone, *ecdysteroid*. Bursts of ecdysteroid trigger each successive molt.

Ecdysteroid also controls a remarkable change in form called metamorphosis. Within the larva lie islands of tissues that will become the eyes, wings, brain, and other structures of the adult. Once the plump, crawling larva becomes a stationary pupa, these islands of cells take over. They complete their program of development, while many larval tissues undergo programmed cell death. The end result is the transformation of the crawling caterpillar into a free-flying moth.

Given that ecdysteroid can cause molting or metamorphosis, what determines which process takes place? The answer is another signal, juvenile hormone (JH), secreted by a pair of endocrine glands behind the brain. JH modulates the activity of ecdysteroid. As long as the level of JH is high, ecdysteroid stimulates molting (and thus maintains the "juvenile" larval state). When the JH level drops, ecdysteroid induces formation of a pupa, within which metamorphosis occurs.

Understanding the coordination between the nervous system and endocrine system in insects has led to advancements in agricultural pest control. For example, one type of chemical developed to control insect pests is a compound that binds to the ecdysteroid receptor, causing insect larvae to molt prematurely and die.

Vertebrates

In vertebrates, coordination of endocrine signaling relies heavily on a region of the brain called the **hypothalamus** (**Figure 45.13**). The hypothalamus receives information from nerves throughout the body and, in response, initiates endocrine signaling appropriate to environmental conditions. In many vertebrates, for example, nerve signals from the brain pass sensory information to the hypothalamus about seasonal changes. The hypothalamus, in turn, regulates the release of reproductive hormones required during the breeding season.

Signals from the hypothalamus travel to the **pituitary gland**, a gland located at the base of the hypothalamus (see Figure 45.13). Roughly the size and shape of a lima bean, the pituitary has discrete posterior and anterior parts, or lobes, which are actually two fused glands that perform very different functions. The **posterior pituitary** is an extension of the hypothalamus. Hypothalamic axons that reach into the posterior pituitary secrete neurohormones synthesized in the hypothalamus. In contrast, the **anterior pituitary** is an endocrine gland that synthesizes and secretes hormones in response to hormones from the hypothalamus.

Posterior Pituitary Hormones

Neurosecretory cells of the hypothalamus synthesize the two posterior pituitary hormones: antidiuretic hormone and oxytocin. After traveling to the posterior pituitary within the long axons of the neurosecretory cells, these neurohormones are stored, to be released in response to nerve impulses transmitted by the hypothalamus (**Figure 45.14**).

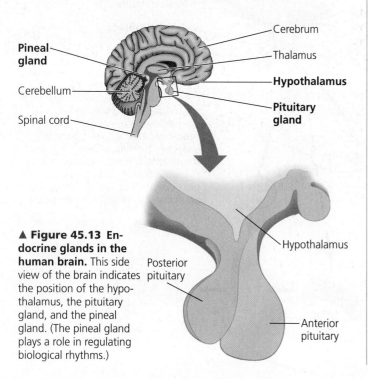

▲ **Figure 45.13 Endocrine glands in the human brain.** This side view of the brain indicates the position of the hypothalamus, the pituitary gland, and the pineal gland. (The pineal gland plays a role in regulating biological rhythms.)

▲ **Figure 45.14 Production and release of posterior pituitary hormones.** The posterior pituitary gland is an extension of the hypothalamus. Certain neurosecretory cells in the hypothalamus make antidiuretic hormone (ADH) and oxytocin, which are transported to the posterior pituitary, where they are stored. Nerve signals from the brain trigger release of these neurohormones.

Antidiuretic hormone (ADH), or *vasopressin*, regulates kidney function. Secretion of ADH increases water retention in the kidneys, helping maintain normal blood osmolarity (see Concept 44.5). ADH also has an important role in social behavior (see Concept 51.4).

Oxytocin has multiple functions related to reproduction. As we have seen, in female mammals oxytocin controls milk secretion by the mammary glands and regulates uterine contractions during birthing. In addition, oxytocin has targets in the brain, where it influences behaviors related to maternal care, pair bonding, and sexual activity.

Anterior Pituitary Hormones

Hormones secreted by the anterior pituitary control a diverse set of processes in the human body, including metabolism, osmoregulation, and reproduction. As illustrated in **Figure 45.15**, many anterior pituitary hormones, but not all, regulate the activity of other endocrine glands or tissues.

Hormones secreted by the hypothalamus control the release of all anterior pituitary hormones. Each hypothalamic hormone is either a *releasing hormone* or an *inhibiting hormone*, reflecting its role in promoting or inhibiting release of one or more specific hormones by the anterior pituitary. *Prolactin-releasing hormone*, for example, is a hypothalamic hormone that stimulates the anterior pituitary to secrete **prolactin**, which has activities that include stimulating milk production. Every anterior pituitary hormone is controlled by at least one releasing hormone. Some, such as prolactin, have both a releasing hormone and an inhibiting hormone.

The hypothalamic releasing and inhibiting hormones are secreted near capillaries at the base of the hypothalamus. The capillaries drain into short blood vessels, called portal vessels, which subdivide into a second capillary bed within the anterior pituitary. Releasing and inhibiting hormones thus have direct access to the gland they control.

Sets of hormones from the hypothalamus, the anterior pituitary, and a target endocrine gland are often organized into a *hormone cascade pathway*. Signals to the brain stimulate the hypothalamus to secrete a hormone that stimulates or inhibits release of an anterior pituitary hormone. The anterior pituitary hormone in turn acts on another endocrine organ, stimulating secretion of yet another hormone, which exerts effects on specific target tissues.

In a sense, hormone cascade pathways redirect signals from the hypothalamus to other endocrine glands. For this reason, the anterior pituitary hormones in these pathways are called **tropic hormones** or *tropins*, from the Greek word for bending or turning. For example, the hormones FSH and LH secreted by the anterior pituitary are called gonadotropins because they convey signals from the hypothalamus to the gonads (testes or ovaries). To learn more about tropic hormones and hormone cascade pathways, we'll turn next to thyroid gland function and regulation.

▶ **Figure 45.15 Production and release of anterior pituitary hormones.** The release of hormones synthesized in the anterior pituitary gland is controlled by hypothalamic releasing and inhibiting hormones. The hypothalamic hormones are secreted by neurosecretory cells and enter a capillary network within the hypothalamus. These capillaries drain into portal vessels that connect with a second capillary network in the anterior pituitary.

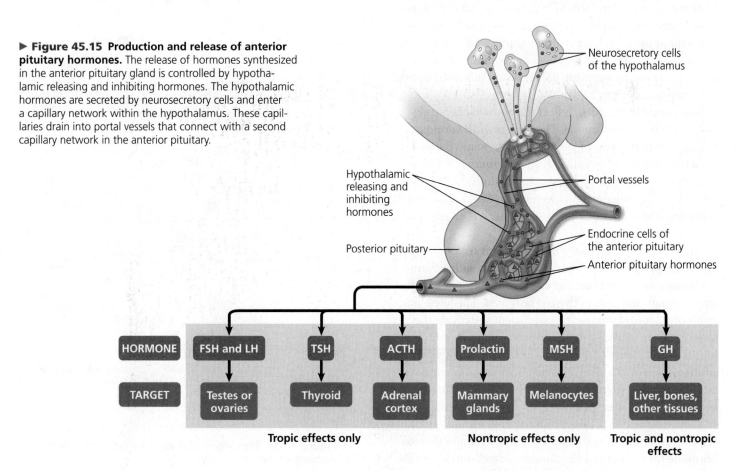

Thyroid Regulation: A Hormone Cascade Pathway

In humans and other mammals, **thyroid hormone** regulates bioenergetics; helps maintain normal blood pressure, heart rate, and muscle tone; and regulates digestive and reproductive functions. If the level of thyroid hormone in the blood drops, the hypothalamus responds by initiating a hormone cascade pathway **(Figure 45.16)**. The hypothalamus secretes thyrotropin-releasing hormone (TRH), causing the anterior pituitary to secrete a tropic hormone known as either thyroid-stimulating hormone (TSH) or thyrotropin. TSH stimulates release of thyroid hormone by the **thyroid gland**, an organ in the neck consisting of two lobes on the ventral surface of the trachea. As thyroid hormone accumulates, it increases metabolic rate, while also initiating negative feedback that prevents its overproduction.

Disorders of Thyroid Function and Regulation

Disruption of thyroid hormone production and regulation can result in serious disorders. Hypothyroidism, the secretion of too little thyroid hormone, can cause weight gain, lethargy, and intolerance to cold in adults. In contrast, excessive secretion of thyroid hormone, known as hyperthyroidism, can lead to high body temperature, profuse sweating, weight loss, irritability, and high blood pressure.

The most common form of hyperthyroidism in humans is Graves' disease. Protruding eyes, caused by fluid accumulation behind the eyes, are a typical symptom. In this autoimmune disorder, the body produces antibodies that bind to and activate the receptor for TSH, causing sustained thyroid hormone production.

Some thyroid disorders reflect the unusual chemical makeup of thyroid hormone. The term *thyroid hormone* actually refers to a pair of very similar hormones derived from the amino acid tyrosine. *Triiodothyronine* (T_3) contains three iodine atoms, whereas tetraiodothyronine, or *thyroxine* (T_4), contains four (see Figure 45.4). Because thyroid hormone production requires iodine, it is an essential mineral.

Although iodine is readily obtained from seafood or iodized salt, people in many parts of the world suffer from inadequate iodine in their diet and therefore cannot synthesize adequate amounts of thyroid hormone. The low blood levels of thyroid hormone are insufficient to provide the usual negative feedback on the hypothalamus and anterior pituitary (see Figure 45.16). As a consequence, the pituitary continues to secrete TSH. Elevated TSH levels cause an enlargement of the thyroid gland, resulting in a swelling of the neck known as goiter.

Proper thyroid function is also required for normal development. Humans and other vertebrates require thyroid hormone for the normal functioning of bone-forming cells,

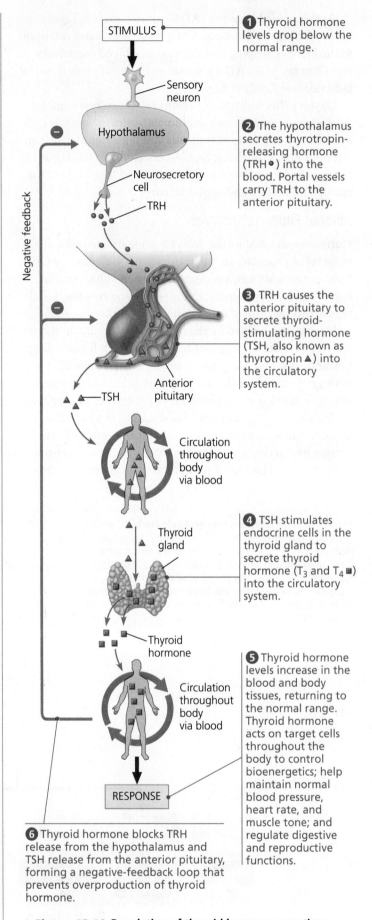

① Thyroid hormone levels drop below the normal range.

② The hypothalamus secretes thyrotropin-releasing hormone (TRH●) into the blood. Portal vessels carry TRH to the anterior pituitary.

③ TRH causes the anterior pituitary to secrete thyroid-stimulating hormone (TSH, also known as thyrotropin▲) into the circulatory system.

④ TSH stimulates endocrine cells in the thyroid gland to secrete thyroid hormone (T_3 and T_4■) into the circulatory system.

⑤ Thyroid hormone levels increase in the blood and body tissues, returning to the normal range. Thyroid hormone acts on target cells throughout the body to control bioenergetics; help maintain normal blood pressure, heart rate, and muscle tone; and regulate digestive and reproductive functions.

⑥ Thyroid hormone blocks TRH release from the hypothalamus and TSH release from the anterior pituitary, forming a negative-feedback loop that prevents overproduction of thyroid hormone.

▲ **Figure 45.16 Regulation of thyroid hormone secretion: a hormone cascade pathway.**

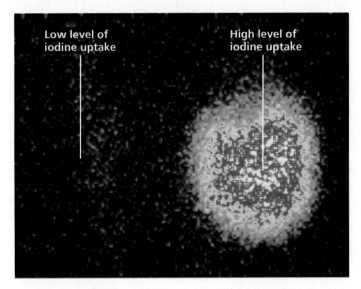

▲ **Figure 45.17 Thyroid scan.** Physicians can use a radioactive isotope of iodine to detect abnormal patterns of iodine uptake that could indicate a thyroid disorder.

as well as for the branching of nerve cells during embryonic development of the brain. In humans, congenital hypothyroidism, an inherited condition of thyroid deficiency, results in markedly retarded skeletal growth and poor mental development. These defects can often be avoided, at least partially, if treatment with thyroid hormone begins early in life. Iodine deficiency in childhood causes the same defects, but it is fully preventable if iodized salt is used in food preparation.

The fact that iodine in the body is dedicated to the production of thyroid hormone provides a novel diagnostic tool for disorders of thyroid function: Radioactive forms of iodine enable specific imaging of the thyroid gland **(Figure 45.17)**.

Hormonal Regulation of Growth

Growth hormone (GH), which is secreted by the anterior pituitary, stimulates growth through both tropic and nontropic effects. A major target, the liver, responds to GH by releasing *insulin-like growth factors* (IGFs), which circulate in the blood and directly stimulate bone and cartilage growth. (IGFs also appear to play a key role in aging in many animal species.) In the absence of GH, the skeleton of an immature animal stops growing. GH also exerts diverse metabolic effects that tend to raise blood glucose levels, thus opposing the effects of insulin.

Abnormal production of GH in humans can result in several disorders, depending on when the problem occurs and whether it involves hypersecretion (too much) or hyposecretion (too little). Hypersecretion of GH during childhood can lead to gigantism, in which the person grows unusually tall but retains relatively normal body proportions **(Figure 45.18)**. Excessive GH production in adulthood stimulates bony growth in the few body parts that are still responsive to the hormone—predominantly the face, hands, and feet. The result

▲ **Figure 45.18 Effect of growth hormone overproduction.** Shown here surrounded by his family, Robert Wadlow grew to a height of 2.7 m (8 feet 11 inches) by age 22, making him the tallest man in history. His height was due to excess secretion of growth hormone by his pituitary gland.

is an overgrowth of the extremities called acromegaly (from the Greek *acros*, extreme, and *mega*, large).

Hyposecretion of GH in childhood retards long-bone growth and can lead to pituitary dwarfism. Individuals with this disorder are for the most part properly proportioned but generally reach a height of only about 1.2 m (4 feet). If diagnosed before puberty, pituitary dwarfism can be treated successfully with human GH (also called HGH). Since the mid-1980s, recombinant DNA technology has been used to produce HGH in bacteria (see Concept 20.4). Treatment of affected children with recombinant HGH is now fairly routine.

CONCEPT CHECK **45.2**

1. What are the roles of oxytocin and prolactin in regulating the mammary glands?

2. How do the two fused glands of the pituitary gland differ in function?

3. **WHAT IF?** Propose an explanation for why people with defects in specific endocrine pathways typically have defects in the final gland in the pathway rather than in the hypothalamus or pituitary.

4. **WHAT IF?** Lab tests of two patients, each diagnosed with excessive thyroid hormone production, revealed elevated levels of TSH in one but not the other. Was the diagnosis of one patient necessarily incorrect? Explain.

For suggested answers, see Appendix A.

Endocrine glands respond to diverse stimuli in regulating homeostasis, development, and behavior

In the remainder of this chapter, we'll focus on endocrine function in homeostasis, development, and behavior. We'll begin with another example of a simple hormone pathway, the regulation of calcium ion concentration in the circulatory system.

Parathyroid Hormone and Vitamin D: Control of Blood Calcium

Because calcium ions (Ca^{2+}) are essential to the normal functioning of all cells, homeostatic control of blood calcium level is vital. If the blood Ca^{2+} level falls substantially, skeletal muscles begin to contract convulsively, a potentially fatal condition. If the blood Ca^{2+} level rises substantially, precipitates of calcium phosphate can form in body tissues, leading to widespread organ damage.

In mammals, the **parathyroid glands**, a set of four small structures embedded in the posterior surface of the thyroid (see Figure 45.9), play a major role in blood Ca^{2+} regulation. When the blood Ca^{2+} level falls below a set point of about 10 mg/100 mL, these glands release **parathyroid hormone (PTH)**.

PTH raises the level of blood Ca^{2+} through direct effects in bones and the kidneys and an indirect effect on the intestines **(Figure 45.19)**. In bones, PTH causes the mineralized matrix to break down, releasing Ca^{2+} into the blood. In the kidneys, PTH directly stimulates reabsorption of Ca^{2+} through the renal tubules. In addition, PTH indirectly raises blood Ca^{2+} levels by promoting production of vitamin D. A precursor form of vitamin D is obtained from food or synthesized by skin exposed to sunlight. Conversion of this precursor to active vitamin D begins in the liver. PTH acts in the kidney to stimulate completion of the conversion process. Vitamin D in turn acts on the intestines, stimulating the uptake of Ca^{2+} from food. As the blood Ca^{2+} level rises, a negative-feedback loop inhibits further release of PTH from the parathyroid glands (not shown in Figure 45.19).

The thyroid gland can also contribute to calcium homeostasis. If the blood Ca^{2+} level rises above the set point, the thyroid gland releases **calcitonin**, a hormone that inhibits bone breakdown and enhances Ca^{2+} excretion by the kidneys. In fishes, rodents, and some other animals, calcitonin is required for Ca^{2+} homeostasis. In humans, however, calcitonin is apparently needed only during the extensive bone growth of childhood.

Adrenal Hormones: Response to Stress

The **adrenal glands** of vertebrates are located atop the kidneys (the *renal* organs). In mammals, each adrenal gland is actually made up of two glands with different cell types, functions, and embryonic origins: the adrenal *cortex*, the outer portion, and the adrenal *medulla*, the central portion. The adrenal cortex consists of true endocrine cells, whereas the secretory cells of the adrenal medulla develop from neural tissue. Thus, like the pituitary gland, each adrenal gland is a fused endocrine and neuroendocrine gland.

Catecholamines from the Adrenal Medulla

Imagine that while walking in the woods at night you hear a growling noise nearby. "A bear?" you wonder. Your heart beats faster, your breathing quickens, your muscles tense, and your thoughts speed up. These and other rapid responses to perceived danger comprise the "fight-or-flight" response. This coordinated set of physiological changes is triggered by two hormones of the adrenal medulla, epinephrine (adrenaline) and **norepinephrine** (also known as noradrenaline). Both are **catecholamines**, a class of amine hormones synthesized from the amino acid tyrosine.

The adrenal medulla secretes epinephrine and norepinephrine in response to short-term stress—whether extreme

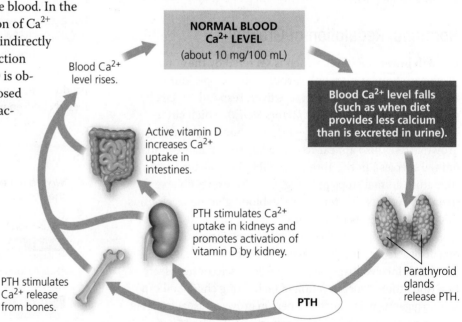

Blood Ca^{2+} level rises.

NORMAL BLOOD Ca^{2+} LEVEL (about 10 mg/100 mL)

Blood Ca^{2+} level falls (such as when diet provides less calcium than is excreted in urine).

Active vitamin D increases Ca^{2+} uptake in intestines.

PTH stimulates Ca^{2+} uptake in kidneys and promotes activation of vitamin D by kidney.

PTH stimulates Ca^{2+} release from bones.

PTH

Parathyroid glands release PTH.

▲ **Figure 45.19 The roles of parathyroid hormone (PTH) in regulating blood calcium levels in mammals.**

▼ Figure 45.20 Stress and the adrenal gland.

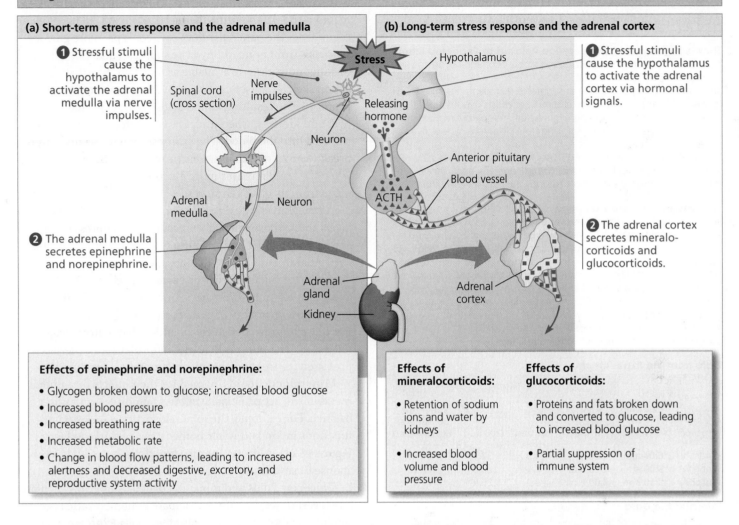

(a) Short-term stress response and the adrenal medulla

❶ Stressful stimuli cause the hypothalamus to activate the adrenal medulla via nerve impulses.

Spinal cord (cross section)

Stress

Nerve impulses

Neuron

Adrenal medulla

Neuron

❷ The adrenal medulla secretes epinephrine and norepinephrine.

Adrenal gland

Kidney

Effects of epinephrine and norepinephrine:

- Glycogen broken down to glucose; increased blood glucose
- Increased blood pressure
- Increased breathing rate
- Increased metabolic rate
- Change in blood flow patterns, leading to increased alertness and decreased digestive, excretory, and reproductive system activity

(b) Long-term stress response and the adrenal cortex

Hypothalamus

Releasing hormone

Anterior pituitary

Blood vessel

ACTH

❶ Stressful stimuli cause the hypothalamus to activate the adrenal cortex via hormonal signals.

❷ The adrenal cortex secretes mineralo-corticoids and glucocorticoids.

Adrenal cortex

Effects of mineralocorticoids:

- Retention of sodium ions and water by kidneys
- Increased blood volume and blood pressure

Effects of glucocorticoids:

- Proteins and fats broken down and converted to glucose, leading to increased blood glucose
- Partial suppression of immune system

pleasure or life-threatening danger. A major activity of these hormones is to increase the amount of chemical energy available for immediate use **(Figure 45.20a)**. Both epinephrine and norepinephrine increase the rate of glycogen breakdown in the liver and skeletal muscles, and both promote the release of glucose by liver cells and of fatty acids from fat cells. The released glucose and fatty acids circulate in the blood and can be used by body cells as fuel.

In addition to increasing the availability of energy sources, epinephrine and norepinephrine exert profound effects on the cardiovascular and respiratory systems. For example, they increase heart rate and stroke volume and dilate the bronchioles in the lungs, actions that raise the rate of oxygen delivery to body cells. For this reason, doctors may prescribe epinephrine as a heart stimulant or to open the airways during an asthma attack. These catecholamines also alter blood flow, causing constriction of some blood vessels and dilation of others (see Figure 45.8). The overall effect is to shunt blood away from the skin, digestive organs, and kidneys, while increasing the blood supply to the heart, brain, and skeletal muscles. Epinephrine generally has a

stronger effect on heart and metabolic rates, while norepinephrine primarily modulates blood pressure.

Note that epinephrine and norepinephrine are produced not only in the adrenal medulla, but also in the nervous system. In the latter location they function as neurotransmitters, as you'll read in Chapter 48.

Steroid Hormones from the Adrenal Cortex

Whereas the adrenal medulla responds to short-term stress, the adrenal cortex functions in the body's response to long-term stress **(Figure 45.20b)**. In contrast to the adrenal medulla, which reacts to nervous input, the adrenal cortex responds to endocrine signals. Stressful stimuli cause the hypothalamus to secrete a releasing hormone that stimulates the anterior pituitary to release adrenocorticotropic hormone (ACTH), a tropic hormone. When ACTH reaches the adrenal cortex via the bloodstream, it stimulates the endocrine cells to synthesize and secrete a family of steroids called *corticosteroids*. The two main types of corticosteroids in humans are glucocorticoids and mineralocorticoids.

Designing a Controlled Experiment

How is Nighttime ACTH Secretion Related to Expected Sleep Duration? Humans secrete increasing amounts of adrenocorticotropic hormone (ACTH) during the late stages of normal sleep, with the peak secretion occurring at the time of spontaneous waking. Because ACTH is released in response to stressful stimuli, scientists hypothesized that ACTH secretion prior to waking might be an anticipatory response to the stress associated with transitioning from sleep to a more active state. If so, an individual's expectation of waking at a particular time might influence the timing of ACTH secretion. How can such a hypothesis be tested? In this exercise, you will examine how researchers designed a controlled experiment to study the role of expectation.

How the Experiment Was Done Researchers studied 15 healthy volunteers in their mid-twenties over three nights. Each night each subject was told when he or she would be awakened: 6:00 or 9:00 a.m. The subjects went to sleep at midnight. Subjects in the "short" or "long" protocol group were awakened at the expected time (6:00 or 9:00 a.m., respectively). Subjects in the "surprise" protocol group were told they would be awakened at 9:00 a.m., but were actually awakened three hours early, at 6:00 a.m. At set times, blood samples were drawn to determine plasma levels of ACTH. To determine the change (Δ) in ACTH concentration post-waking, the researchers compared samples drawn at waking and 30 minutes later.

Data from the Experiment

Sleep Protocol	Expected Wake Time	Actual Wake Time	Mean Plasma ACTH Level (pg/mL)		
			1:00 a.m.	6:00 a.m.	Δ in the 30 Minutes Post-waking
Short	6:00 a.m.	6:00 a.m.	9.9	37.3	10.6
Long	9:00 a.m.	9:00 a.m.	8.1	26.5	12.2
Surprise	9:00 a.m.	6:00 a.m.	8.0	25.5	22.1

Interpret the Data

1. Describe the role of the "surprise" protocol in the experimental design.

2. Each subject was given a different protocol on each of the three nights, and the order of the protocols was varied among the subjects that so that one third had each protocol each night. What factors were the researchers attempting to control for with this approach?

3. For subjects in the short protocol, what was the mean ACTH level at waking? Using the data in the last two columns, calculate the mean level 30 minutes later. Was the rate of change faster or slower in that 30-minute period than during the interval from 1:00 to 6:00 a.m.?

4. How does the change in ACTH levels between 1:00 and 6:00 a.m. for the surprise protocol compare to that for the short and long protocols? Does this result support the hypothesis being tested? Explain.

5. Using the data in the last two columns, calculate the mean ACTH concentration 30 minutes post-waking for the surprise protocol and compare to your answer for Question 3. What do your results suggest about a person's physiological response immediately after waking?

6. What are some variables that weren't controlled for in this experiment that could be explored in a follow-up study?

(MB) A version of this Scientific Skills Exercise can be assigned in MasteringBiology.

Data from J. Born, et al., Timing the end of nocturnal sleep, *Nature* 397:29-30 (1999).

As reflected in their name, **glucocorticoids**, such as cortisol (see Figure 45.4), have a primary effect on glucose metabolism. Augmenting the fuel-mobilizing effects of glucagon from the pancreas, glucocorticoids promote glucose synthesis from noncarbohydrate sources, such as proteins, making more glucose available as fuel. Glucocorticoids also act on skeletal muscle, causing the breakdown of muscle proteins. The resulting amino acids are transported to the liver and kidneys, where they are converted to glucose and released into the blood. The synthesis of glucose upon the breakdown of muscle proteins provides circulating fuel when the body requires more glucose than the liver can mobilize from its glycogen stores.

When glucocorticoids are introduced into the body at levels above those normally present, they suppress certain components of the body's immune system. Because of this anti-inflammatory effect, glucocorticoids are sometimes used to treat inflammatory diseases such as arthritis. However, long-term use can have serious side effects, reflecting the potent activity of glucocorticoids on metabolism. For these reasons, nonsteroidal anti-inflammatory drugs (NSAIDs), including aspirin and ibuprofen, are generally preferred for treating chronic inflammatory conditions.

Mineralocorticoids, named for their effects on mineral metabolism, act principally in maintaining salt and water balance. For example, the mineralocorticoid *aldosterone* functions in ion and water homeostasis of the blood (see Figure 44.21). Aldosterone also functions in the body's response to severe stress.

Glucocorticoids and mineralocorticoids not only mediate stress responses, but also participate in homeostatic regulation of metabolism. In the Scientific Skills Exercise, you can explore an experiment investigating changes in ACTH secretion as humans awaken from sleep.

Sex Hormones

Sex hormones affect growth, development, reproductive cycles, and sexual behavior. Whereas the adrenal glands secrete small quantities of these hormones, the gonads (testes of males and ovaries of females) are their principal sources. The gonads produce and secrete three major types of steroid sex hormones: androgens, estrogens, and progestins. All three types are found in both males and females but in different proportions.

The testes primarily synthesize **androgens**, the main one being **testosterone**. In humans, testosterone first functions before birth, promoting development of male reproductive structures **(Figure 45.21)**. Androgens play a major role again at puberty, when they are responsible for the development of male secondary sex characteristics. High concentrations of androgen lead to a low voice and male patterns of hair growth, as well as increases in muscle and bone mass. The

Bipotential gonad

Male duct (Wolffian)

Female duct (Müllerian)

Embryo (XY or XX)

Testosterone

AMH

Absence of male hormones

Testis

Ovary

Vas deferens

Uterus

Bladder

Seminal vesicle

Oviduct

Bladder

Male (XY) fetus

Female (XX) fetus

▲ **Figure 45.21 Sex hormones regulate formation of internal reproductive structures in human development.** In a male (XY) embryo, the bipotential gonads become the testes, which secrete testosterone and anti-Müllerian hormone (AMH). Testosterone directs formation of sperm-carrying ducts (vas deferens and seminal vesicles), while AMH causes the female ducts to degenerate. In the absence of these testis hormones, the male ducts degenerate and female structures form, including the oviduct, uterus, and vagina.

muscle-building, or anabolic, action of testosterone and related steroids has enticed some athletes to take them as supplements, despite prohibitions against their use in nearly all sports. Use of anabolic steroids, while effective in increasing muscle mass, can cause severe acne outbreaks and liver damage, as well as significant decreases in sperm count and testicular size.

Estrogens, of which the most important is **estradiol**, are responsible for the maintenance of the female reproductive system and for the development of female secondary sex characteristics. In mammals, **progestins**, which include **progesterone**, are primarily involved in preparing and maintaining tissues of the uterus required to support the growth and development of an embryo.

Estrogens and other gonadal sex hormones are components of hormone cascade pathways. Synthesis of these hormones is controlled by two gonadotropins from the anterior pituitary gland, follicle-stimulating hormone and luteinizing hormone (see Figure 45.15). Gonadotropin secretion is in turn controlled by GnRH (gonadotropin-releasing hormone), from the hypothalamus. We'll examine the feedback

relationships that regulate gonadal hormone secretion in detail when we discuss animal reproduction in Chapter 46.

Endocrine Disruptors

Between 1938 and 1971, some pregnant women at risk for pregnancy complications were prescribed a synthetic estrogen called diethylstilbestrol (DES). What was not known until 1971 was that exposure to DES can alter reproductive system development in the fetus. Daughters of women who took DES are more frequently afflicted with certain reproductive abnormalities, including vaginal and cervical cancer, structural changes in the reproductive organs, and increased risk of miscarriage (spontaneous abortion). DES is now recognized as an *endocrine disruptor*, a foreign molecule that interrupts the normal function of a hormone pathway.

In recent years, some scientists have hypothesized that molecules in the environment also act as endocrine disruptors. For example, bisphenol A, a chemical used in making some plastics, has been studied for potential interference with normal reproduction and development. In addition, it has been suggested that some estrogen-like molecules, such as those present in soybeans and other edible plant products, have the beneficial effect of lowering breast cancer risk. Sorting out such effects, whether harmful or beneficial, has proven quite difficult, in part because enzymes in the liver change the properties of any such molecules entering the body through the digestive system.

Hormones and Biological Rhythms

There is still much to be learned about the hormone **melatonin**, a modified amino acid that regulates functions related to light and the seasons. Melatonin is produced by the **pineal gland**, a small mass of tissue near the center of the mammalian brain (see Figure 45.13).

Although melatonin affects skin pigmentation in many vertebrates, its primary effects relate to biological rhythms associated with reproduction and with daily activity levels (see Figure 40.9). Melatonin is secreted at night, and the amount released depends on the length of the night. In winter, for example, when days are short and nights are long, more melatonin is secreted. There is also good evidence that nightly increases in the levels of melatonin play a significant role in promoting sleep.

The release of melatonin by the pineal gland is controlled by a group of neurons in the hypothalamus called the suprachiasmatic nucleus (SCN). The SCN functions as a biological clock and receives input from specialized light-sensitive neurons in the retina of the eye. Although the SCN regulates melatonin production during the 24-hour light/dark cycle, melatonin also influences SCN activity. We'll consider biological rhythms further in Chapter 49, where we analyze experiments on SCN function.

Evolution of Hormone Function

EVOLUTION Many of the hormones described in this chapter are found in a broad range of animal species. Over the course of evolution, however, the functions of particular hormones have diverged. Thyroid hormone, which regulates metabolism in a number of animals, provides one example. In frogs, thyroid hormone (thyroxine) has taken on an apparently unique function: stimulating tail resorption during metamorphosis, the change in form from tadpole to adult frog **(Figure 45.22)**.

▲ **Tadpole**

▲ **Adult frog**

◀ **Figure 45.22 Specialized role of a hormone in frog metamorphosis.** The hormone thyroxine is responsible for the resorption of the tadpole's tail as the frog develops into its adult form.

Diverse functions have also evolved for many other vertebrate hormones. Prolactin, a product of the anterior pituitary, has an especially broad range of activities: It stimulates mammary gland growth and milk synthesis in mammals, regulates fat metabolism and reproduction in birds, delays metamorphosis in amphibians, and regulates salt and water balance in freshwater fishes. These varied activities suggest that prolactin is an ancient hormone with functions that have diversified during the evolution of vertebrate groups.

Melanocyte-stimulating hormone (MSH), secreted by the anterior pituitary, provides another example of a hormone with distinct functions in different evolutionary lineages. In amphibians, fishes, and reptiles, MSH regulates skin color by controlling pigment distribution in skin cells called melanocytes. In mammals, MSH functions in hunger and metabolism in addition to skin coloration.

The specialized action of MSH that has evolved in the mammalian brain may prove to be of particular medical importance. Many patients with late-stage cancer, AIDS, tuberculosis, and certain aging disorders suffer from a devastating wasting condition called cachexia. Characterized by weight loss, muscle atrophy, and loss of appetite, cachexia responds poorly to existing therapies. However, it turns out that activation of a brain receptor for MSH produces some of the same changes seen in cachexia. Moreover, in experiments on mice with mutations that cause cancer and consequently cachexia, treatment with drugs that blocked the brain MSH receptor prevented cachexia. Whether such drugs can be used to treat cachexia in humans is an area of active study.

CONCEPT CHECK 45.3

1. If a hormone pathway produces a transient response to a stimulus, how would shortening the stimulus duration affect the need for negative feedback?

2. How would a decrease in the number of corticosteroid receptors in the hypothalamus affect levels of corticosteroids in the blood?

3. **WHAT IF?** Suppose you receive an injection of cortisone, a glucocorticoid, in an inflamed joint. What aspect of glucocorticoid activity would you be exploiting? If a glucocorticoid pill were also effective at treating the inflammation, why would it still be preferable to introduce the drug locally?

For suggested answers, see Appendix A.

---

45 Chapter Review

SUMMARY OF KEY CONCEPTS

CONCEPT 45.1

Hormones and other signaling molecules bind to target receptors, triggering specific response pathways (pp. 994–999)

- The forms of signaling between animal cells differ in the type of secreting cell and the route taken by the signal to its target.

Endocrine signals, or **hormones**, are secreted into the extracellular fluid by endocrine cells or ductless glands and reach target cells via circulatory fluids. **Paracrine** signals act on neighboring cells, whereas **autocrine** signals act on the secreting cell itself. **Neurotransmitters** also act locally, but **neurohormones** can act throughout the body. **Pheromones** are released into the environment for communication between animals of the same species.

- **Local regulators**, which carry out paracrine and autocrine signaling, include cytokines and growth factors (polypeptides), **prostaglandins** (modified fatty acids), and **nitric oxide** (a gas).

- Polypeptides, steroids, and amines comprise the major classes of animal hormones. Depending on whether they are water-soluble or lipid-soluble, hormones activate different response pathways.

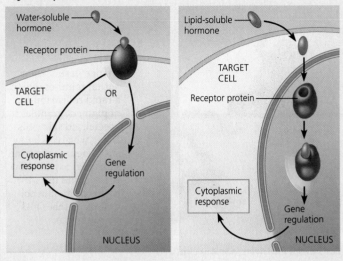

? *Predict what would happen if you injected a water-soluble hormone directly into the cytosol of a target cell.*

CONCEPT 45.2

Feedback regulation and coordination with the nervous system are common in endocrine signaling (pp. 1000–1005)

- Hormone pathways may be regulated by **negative feedback**, which dampens the stimulus, or **positive feedback**, which amplifies the stimulus and drives the response to completion.
- In insects, molting and development are controlled by three hormones: PTTH; ecdysteroid, whose release is triggered by PTTH; and juvenile hormone. Coordination of signals from the nervous and endocrine systems and modulation of one hormone activity by another bring about the sequence of developmental stages that lead to an adult form.
- In vertebrates, neurosecretory cells in the **hypothalamus** produce two hormones that are secreted by the **posterior pituitary** and that act directly on nonendocrine tissues: **oxytocin**, which induces uterine contractions and release of milk from mammary glands, and **antidiuretic hormone (ADH)**, which enhances water reabsorption in the kidneys.
- Other hypothalamic cells produce hormones that are transported to the **anterior pituitary**, where they stimulate or inhibit the release of particular hormones.
- Often, anterior pituitary hormones act in a cascade. For example, the secretion of thyroid-stimulating hormone (TSH) is regulated by thyrotropin-releasing hormone (TRH). TSH in turn induces the **thyroid gland** to secrete **thyroid hormone**, a combination of the iodine-containing hormones T_3 and T_4. Thyroid hormone stimulates metabolism and influences development and maturation.
- Most anterior pituitary hormones are **tropic hormones**, acting on endocrine tissues or glands to regulate hormone secretion. Tropic hormones of the anterior pituitary include TSH, follicle-stimulating hormone (FSH), luteinizing hormone (LH), and adrenocorticotropic hormone (ACTH). **Growth hormone** (GH) has both tropic and nontropic effects. It promotes growth directly, affects metabolism, and stimulates the production of growth factors by other tissues.

? *Which major endocrine organs described in Figure 45.9 are regulated independently of the hypothalamus and pituitary?*

CONCEPT 45.3

Endocrine glands respond to diverse stimuli in regulating homeostasis, development, and behavior (pp. 1006–1010)

- **Parathyroid hormone** (PTH), secreted by the **parathyroid glands**, causes bone to release Ca^{2+} into the blood and stimulates reabsorption of Ca^{2+} in the kidneys. PTH also stimulates the kidneys to activate vitamin D, which promotes intestinal uptake of Ca^{2+} from food. **Calcitonin**, secreted by the thyroid, has the opposite effects in bones and kidneys as PTH. Calcitonin is important for calcium homeostasis in adults of some vertebrates, but not humans.
- In response to stress, neurosecretory cells in the adrenal medulla release **epinephrine** and **norepinephrine**, which mediate various fight-or-flight responses. The adrenal cortex releases **glucocorticoids**, such as cortisol, which influence glucose metabolism and the immune system. It also releases **mineralocorticoids**, primarily aldosterone, which help regulate salt and water balance.
- Sex hormones regulate growth, development, reproduction, and sexual behavior. Although the adrenal cortex produces small amounts of these hormones, the gonads (testes and ovaries) serve as the major source. All three types—**androgens**, **estrogens**, and **progestins**—are produced in males and females, but in different proportions.
- The **pineal gland**, located within the brain, secretes **melatonin**, which functions in biological rhythms related to reproduction and sleep. Release of melatonin is controlled by the SCN, the region of the brain that functions as a biological clock.
- Hormones have acquired distinct roles in different species over the course of evolution. **Prolactin** stimulates milk production in mammals but has diverse effects in other vertebrates. **Melanocyte-stimulating hormone** (MSH) influences fat metabolism in mammals and skin pigmentation in other vertebrates.

? *ADH and epinephrine act as hormones when released into the bloodstream and as neurotransmitters when released in synapses between neurons. What is similar about the endocrine glands that produce these two molecules?*

TEST YOUR UNDERSTANDING

LEVEL 1: KNOWLEDGE/COMPREHENSION

1. Which of the following is *not* an accurate statement?
   a. Hormones are chemical messengers that travel to target cells through the circulatory system.
   b. Hormones often regulate homeostasis through antagonistic functions.
   c. Hormones of the same chemical class usually have the same function.
   d. Hormones are often regulated through feedback loops.

2. The hypothalamus
   a. synthesizes all of the hormones produced by the pituitary gland.
   b. influences the function of only one lobe of the pituitary gland.
   c. produces only inhibitory hormones.
   d. regulates both reproduction and body temperature.

3. Growth factors are local regulators that
   a. are produced by the anterior pituitary.
   b. are modified fatty acids that stimulate bone and cartilage growth.
   c. are found on the surface of cancer cells and stimulate abnormal cell division.
   d. bind to cell-surface receptors and stimulate growth and development of target cells.

4. Which hormone is *incorrectly* paired with its action?
   a. oxytocin—stimulates uterine contractions during childbirth
   b. thyroxine—inhibits metabolic processes
   c. ACTH—stimulates the release of glucocorticoids by the adrenal cortex
   d. melatonin—affects biological rhythms and seasonal reproduction

LEVEL 2: APPLICATION/ANALYSIS

5. Steroid and peptide hormones typically have in common
   a. their solubility in cell membranes.
   b. their requirement for travel through the bloodstream.
   c. the location of their receptors.
   d. their reliance on signal transduction in the cell.

6. Which of the following is the most likely explanation for hypothyroidism in a patient whose iodine level is normal?
   a. greater production of T_3 than of T_4
   b. hyposecretion of TSH
   c. hypersecretion of MSH
   d. a decrease in the thyroid secretion of calcitonin

7. The relationship between the insect hormones ecdysteroid and PTTH is an example of
   a. an interaction of the endocrine and nervous systems.
   b. homeostasis achieved by positive feedback.
   c. homeostasis maintained by antagonistic hormones.
   d. competitive inhibition of a hormone receptor.

8. **DRAW IT** In mammals, milk production by mammary glands is controlled by prolactin and prolactin-releasing hormone. Draw a simple sketch of this pathway, including glands, tissues, hormones, routes for hormone movement, and effects.

LEVEL 3: SYNTHESIS/EVALUATION

9. **EVOLUTION CONNECTION**
   The intracellular receptors used by all the steroid and thyroid hormones are similar enough in structure that they are all considered members of one "superfamily" of proteins. Propose a hypothesis for how the genes encoding these receptors may have evolved. (*Hint*: See Figure 21.13.) How could you test your hypothesis using DNA sequence data?

10. **SCIENTIFIC INQUIRY**
    INTERPRET THE DATA Chronically high levels of glucocorticoids can result in obesity, muscle weakness, and depression, a combination of symptoms called Cushing's syndrome. Excessive activity of either the pituitary or the adrenal gland can be the cause. To determine which gland has abnormal activity in a particular patient, doctors use the drug dexamethasone, a synthetic glucocorticoid that blocks ACTH release. Based on the graph, which gland is affected in patient X?

11. **WRITE ABOUT A THEME: INTERACTIONS**
    In a short essay (100–150 words), use specific examples to discuss the role of hormones in an animal's responses to changes in its environment.

12. **SYNTHESIZE YOUR KNOWLEDGE**

The frog on the left was injected with MSH, causing a change in skin color within minutes due to a rapid redistribution of pigment granules in specialized skin cells. Using what you know about neuroendocrine signaling, explain how a frog could use MSH to match its skin coloration to that of its surroundings.

For selected answers, see Appendix A.

MasteringBiology®

Students Go to **MasteringBiology** for assignments, the eText, and the Study Area with practice tests, animations, and activities.

Instructors Go to **MasteringBiology** for automatically graded tutorials and questions that you can assign to your students, plus Instructor Resources.

46

Animal Reproduction

KEY CONCEPTS

46.1 Both asexual and sexual reproduction occur in the animal kingdom

46.2 Fertilization depends on mechanisms that bring together sperm and eggs of the same species

46.3 Reproductive organs produce and transport gametes

46.4 The interplay of tropic and sex hormones regulates mammalian reproduction

46.5 In placental mammals, an embryo develops fully within the mother's uterus

▲ **Figure 46.1 How can each of these sea slugs be both male and female?**

Pairing Up for Sexual Reproduction

The sea slugs, or nudibranchs (*Nembrotha chamberlaini*), in **Figure 46.1** are mating. If not disturbed, these marine molluscs may remain joined for hours. Sperm will be transferred and will fertilize eggs. A few weeks later, sexual reproduction will be complete. New individuals will hatch, but which parent is the mother? The answer is simple yet probably unexpected: both. In fact, each sea slug produces eggs *and* sperm.

As humans, we tend to think of reproduction in terms of the mating of males and females and the fusion of sperm and eggs. Animal reproduction, however, takes many forms. In some species, individuals change their sex during their lifetime; in other species, such as sea slugs, an individual is both male and female. There are animals that can fertilize their own eggs, as well as others that can reproduce without any form of sex. For certain species, such as honeybees, only a few individuals within a large population reproduce.

A population outlives its members only by reproduction, the generation of new individuals from existing ones. In this chapter, we'll compare the diverse reproductive mechanisms that have evolved among animals. We'll then examine details of mammalian reproduction, with emphasis on the well-studied example of humans. We'll focus on reproduction mostly from the parents' perspective, deferring the details of embryonic development until the next chapter.

Both asexual and sexual reproduction occur in the animal kingdom

There are two modes of animal reproduction—sexual and asexual. In **sexual reproduction**, the fusion of haploid gametes forms a diploid cell, the **zygote**. The animal that develops from a zygote can in turn give rise to gametes by meiosis (see Figure 13.8). The female gamete, the **egg**, is large and nonmotile, whereas the male gamete, the **sperm**, is generally much smaller and motile. In **asexual reproduction**, new individuals are generated without the fusion of egg and sperm. For most asexual animals, reproduction relies entirely on mitotic cell division.

For the vast majority of animals, reproduction is primarily or exclusively sexual. However, there are species that have a primarily asexual mode of reproduction, and in a few all-female species reproduction is exclusively asexual. These include the microscopic bdelloid rotifer (see Figure 13.13), as well as certain species of whiptail lizards, which we'll discuss shortly.

Mechanisms of Asexual Reproduction

Several simple forms of asexual reproduction are found only among invertebrates. One of these is *budding*, in which new individuals arise from outgrowths of existing ones (see Figure 13.2). In stony corals, for example, buds form and remain attached to the parent. The eventual result is a colony more than 1 m across, consisting of thousands of connected individuals. Also common among invertebrates is **fission**, the separation of a parent organism into two individuals of approximately equal size (**Figure 46.2**).

Asexual reproduction can be a two-step process: *fragmentation*, the breaking of the body into several pieces, followed by *regeneration*, regrowth of lost body parts. If more than one piece grows and develops into a complete animal, the effect is reproduction. For example, certain annelid worms can split into several fragments, each regenerating a complete worm in less than a week. Numerous sponges, cnidarians, and tunicates also reproduce by fragmentation and regeneration.

A particularly intriguing form of asexual reproduction is **parthenogenesis**, in which an egg develops without being

▲ **Figure 46.2 Asexual reproduction of a sea anemone (*Anthopleura elegantissima*).** The large individual in the center is undergoing fission, dividing into two approximately equal-sized offspring, each a genetic copy of the parent.

fertilized. Among invertebrates, parthenogenesis occurs in certain species of bees, wasps, and ants. The progeny can be either haploid or diploid. In the case of honeybees, males (drones) are fertile haploid adults that arise by parthenogenesis. In contrast, female honeybees, including both the sterile workers and the fertile queens, are diploid adults that develop from fertilized eggs. Among vertebrates, parthenogenesis has been observed quite rarely (in about one in every thousand species). Zookeepers have discovered parthenogenesis in the Komodo dragon and in a species of hammerhead shark: In both cases, females had been kept isolated from males but nevertheless produced offspring.

Sexual Reproduction: An Evolutionary Enigma

EVOLUTION Sex must enhance reproductive success or survival because it would otherwise rapidly disappear. To see why, consider an animal population in which half the females reproduce sexually and half reproduce asexually (**Figure 46.3**). We'll assume that the number of offspring per female is a constant, two in this case. The two offspring of an asexual female will both be daughters that will each give birth to two more reproductive daughters. In contrast, half of a sexual female's offspring will be male. The number of sexual offspring will remain the same at each generation, because both a male and a female are required to reproduce. Thus, the asexual condition will increase in frequency at each generation. Yet despite this "twofold cost," sex is maintained even in animal species that can also reproduce asexually.

What advantage does sex provide? The answer remains elusive. Most hypotheses focus on the unique combinations of parental genes formed during meiotic recombination and fertilization. By producing offspring of varied genotypes, sexual reproduction may enhance the reproductive success of parents when environmental factors, such as pathogens, change relatively rapidly. In contrast, asexual reproduction is expected to be most advantageous in stable, favorable environments because it perpetuates successful genotypes precisely.

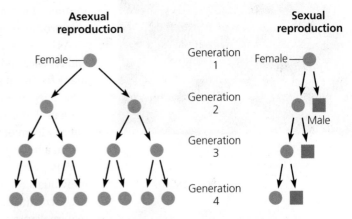

▲ **Figure 46.3 The "reproductive handicap" of sex.** These diagrams contrast asexual versus sexual reproduction over four generations, assuming two surviving offspring per female.

There are a number of reasons why the unique gene combinations formed during sexual reproduction might be advantageous. One is that beneficial gene combinations arising through recombination might speed up adaptation. Although this idea appears straightforward, the theoretical advantage is significant only when the rate of beneficial mutations is high and population size is small. Another idea is that the shuffling of genes during sexual reproduction might allow a population to rid itself of sets of harmful genes more readily.

Reproductive Cycles

Most animals exhibit cycles in reproductive activity, often related to changing seasons. These cycles are controlled by hormones, whose secretion in turn is regulated by environmental cues. In this way, animals conserve resources, reproducing only when sufficient energy sources are available and when environmental conditions favor the survival of offspring. For example, ewes (female sheep) have a reproductive cycle lasting 15–17 days. **Ovulation**, the release of mature eggs, occurs at the midpoint of each cycle. For ewes, reproductive cycles generally occur only during fall and early winter, and the length of any pregnancy is five months. Thus, most lambs are born in the early spring, when their chances of survival are optimal.

Because seasonal changes are often important cues for reproduction, global climate change can decrease reproductive success. Danish researchers have demonstrated just such an effect on caribou (wild reindeer) in Greenland. In spring, caribou migrate to calving grounds to eat sprouting plants, give birth, and care for their new calves. Prior to 1993, the arrival of the caribou at the calving grounds coincided with the brief period during which the plants were nutritious and digestible. Since 1993, however, average spring temperatures in the calving grounds have increased by more than 4°C, and the plants now sprout two weeks earlier. Because caribou migration is triggered by day length, not temperature, there is a mismatch between the timing of new plant growth and caribou birthing. Without adequate nutrition for the nursing females, the number of caribou offspring produced each year declined by 75% in just 14 years.

Reproductive cycles are also found among animals that can reproduce both sexually and asexually. Consider, for instance, the water flea (genus *Daphnia*). A *Daphnia* female can produce eggs of two types. One type of egg requires fertilization to develop, but the other type does not and develops instead by parthenogenesis. Asexual reproduction occurs when environmental conditions are favorable, whereas sexual reproduction occurs during times of environmental stress. As a result, the switch between sexual and asexual reproduction is roughly linked to season.

Some species of whiptail lizards in the genus *Aspidoscelis* exhibit a very different type of reproductive cycle: Reproduction is exclusively asexual, and there are no males.

Nevertheless, these lizards have courtship and mating behaviors very similar to those of sexual species of *Aspidoscelis*. During the breeding season, one female of each mating pair mimics a male **(Figure 46.4a)**. Members of the pair alternate roles two or three times during the season. An individual adopts female behavior when the level of the hormone estradiol is high, and it switches to male-like behavior when the level of the hormone progesterone is high **(Figure 46.4b)**. A female is more likely to ovulate if she is mounted at a critical time of the hormone cycle; isolated lizards lay fewer eggs than those that go through the motions of sex. These findings support the hypothesis that these parthenogenetic lizards evolved from species having two sexes and still require certain sexual stimuli for maximum reproductive success.

(a) Both lizards in this photograph are *A. uniparens* females. The one on top is playing the role of a male. Individuals switch sex roles two or three times during the breeding season.

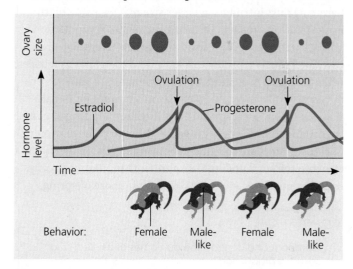

(b) The changes in sexual behavior of *A. uniparens* individuals are correlated with the cycles of ovulation and changing levels of the sex hormones estradiol and progesterone. These drawings track the changes in ovary size, hormone levels, and sexual behavior of one female lizard (shown in brown).

▲ **Figure 46.4 Sexual behavior in parthenogenetic lizards.** The desert-grassland whiptail lizard (*Aspidoscelis uniparens*) is an all-female species. These reptiles reproduce by parthenogenesis, the development of an unfertilized egg, but ovulation is stimulated by mating behavior.

INTERPRET THE DATA *If you plotted hormone levels for the lizard shown in gray, how would your graph differ from the graph in (b)?*

Variation in Patterns of Sexual Reproduction

For many animals, finding a partner for sexual reproduction can be challenging. Adaptations that arose during the evolution of some species meet this challenge in a novel way—by blurring the distinction between male and female. One such adaptation arose among sessile (stationary) animals, such as barnacles; burrowing animals, such as clams; and some parasites, including tapeworms. These animals have a very limited opportunity to find a mate. The evolutionary solution in this case is **hermaphroditism**, in which each individual has both male and female reproductive systems (the term *hermaphrodite* merges the names Hermes and Aphrodite, a Greek god and goddess). Because each hermaphrodite reproduces as both a male and a female, *any* two individuals can mate. Each animal donates and receives sperm during mating, as the sea slugs in Figure 46.1 are doing. In some species, hermaphrodites can also self-fertilize, allowing a form of sexual reproduction that doesn't require any partner.

The bluehead wrasse (*Thalassoma bifasciatum*) provides an example of a quite different variation in sexual reproduction. These coral reef fish live in harems, each consisting of a single male and several females. When the lone male dies, the opportunity for sexual reproduction would appear lost. Instead, the largest female in the harem transforms into a male and within a week begins to produce sperm instead of eggs. What selective pressure in the evolution of the bluehead wrasse resulted in sex reversal for the female with the largest body? Because it is the male wrasse that defends a harem against intruders, a larger size may be particularly important for a male in ensuring successful reproduction.

Certain oyster species also undergo sex reversal. In this case, individuals reproduce as males and then later as females, when their size is greatest. Since the number of gametes produced generally increases with size much more for females than for males, sex reversal in this direction maximizes gamete production. The result is enhanced reproductive success: Because oysters are sedentary animals and release their gametes into the surrounding water rather than mating directly, releasing more gametes tends to result in more offspring.

CONCEPT CHECK 46.1

1. Compare and contrast the outcomes of asexual and sexual reproduction.

2. Parthenogenesis is the most common form of asexual reproduction in animals that at other times reproduce sexually. What characteristic of parthenogenesis might explain this observation?

3. **WHAT IF?** If a hermaphrodite self-fertilizes, will the offspring be identical to the parent? Explain.

4. **MAKE CONNECTIONS** What examples of plant reproduction are most similar to asexual reproduction in animals? (See Concept 38.2.)

For suggested answers, see Appendix A.

Fertilization depends on mechanisms that bring together sperm and eggs of the same species

The union of sperm and egg—**fertilization**—can be either external or internal. In species with *external fertilization*, the female releases eggs into the environment, where the male then fertilizes them **(Figure 46.5)**. Other species have *internal fertilization*: Sperm are deposited in or near the female reproductive tract, and fertilization occurs within the tract. (We'll discuss the cellular and molecular details of fertilization in Chapter 47.)

A moist habitat is almost always required for external fertilization, both to prevent the gametes from drying out and to allow the sperm to swim to the eggs. Many aquatic invertebrates simply shed their eggs and sperm into the surroundings, and fertilization occurs without the parents making physical contact. However, timing is crucial to ensure that mature sperm and eggs encounter one another.

Among some species with external fertilization, individuals clustered in the same area release their gametes into the water at the same time, a process known as *spawning*. In some cases, chemical signals that one individual generates in releasing gametes trigger others to release gametes. In other cases, environmental cues, such as temperature or day length, cause a whole population to release gametes at one time. For example, the palolo worm, native to coral reefs of the South Pacific, times its spawning to both the season and

▲ **Figure 46.5 External fertilization.** Many species of amphibians reproduce by external fertilization. In most of these species, behavioral adaptations ensure that a male is present when the female releases eggs. Here, a female frog (on bottom) has released a mass of eggs in response to being clasped by a male. The male released sperm (not visible) at the same time, and external fertilization has already occurred in the water.

the lunar cycle. In spring, when the moon is in its last quarter, palolo worms break in half, releasing tail segments engorged with sperm or eggs. These packets rise to the ocean surface and burst in such vast numbers that the sea appears milky with gametes. The sperm quickly fertilize the floating eggs, and within hours, the palolo's once-a-year reproductive frenzy is complete.

When external fertilization is not synchronous across a population, individuals may exhibit specific "courtship" behaviors leading to the fertilization of the eggs of one female by one male (see Figure 46.5). By triggering the release of both sperm and eggs, these behaviors increase the probability of successful fertilization.

Internal fertilization is an adaptation that enables sperm to reach an egg even when the environment is dry. It typically requires cooperative behavior that leads to copulation, as well as sophisticated and compatible reproductive systems. The male copulatory organ delivers sperm, and the female reproductive tract often has receptacles for storage and delivery of sperm to mature eggs.

No matter how fertilization occurs, the mating animals may make use of *pheromones*, chemicals released by one organism that can influence the physiology and behavior of other individuals of the same species. Pheromones are small, volatile or water-soluble molecules that disperse into the environment and, like hormones, are active at very low concentrations (see Chapter 45). Many pheromones function as mate attractants, enabling some female insects to be detected by males more than a kilometer away.

There is as yet no good evidence for human pheromones. It was once postulated that female roommates produce pheromones that trigger synchrony in reproductive (menstrual) cycles, but further statistical analyses failed to support this idea.

Ensuring the Survival of Offspring

Internal fertilization is typically associated with the production of fewer gametes than external fertilization but results in the survival of a higher fraction of zygotes. Better zygote survival is due in part to the fact that eggs fertilized internally are sheltered from potential predators. However, internal fertilization is also more often associated with mechanisms that provide greater protection of the embryos and parental care of the young. For example, the internally fertilized eggs of birds and other reptiles have shells and internal membranes that protect against water loss and physical damage during the eggs' external development (see Figure 34.25). In contrast, the eggs of fishes and amphibians have only a gelatinous coat and lack internal membranes.

Rather than secreting a protective eggshell, some animals retain the embryo for a portion of its development within the female's reproductive tract. The offspring of marsupial mammals, such as kangaroos and opossums, spend only a short

◄ **Figure 46.6 Parental care in an invertebrate.** Compared with many other insects, giant water bugs of the genus *Belostoma* produce relatively few offspring but offer much greater parental protection. Following internal fertilization, the female glues her fertilized eggs to the back of the male (shown here). The male carries them for days, frequently fanning water over them to keep the eggs moist, aerated, and free of parasites.

period in the uterus as embryos; they then crawl out and complete development attached to a mammary gland in the mother's pouch. Embryos of eutherian (placental) mammals, such as humans, remain in the uterus throughout fetal development. There they are nourished by the mother's blood supply through a temporary organ, the placenta. The embryos of some fishes and sharks also complete development internally.

When a caribou or kangaroo is born or when a baby eagle hatches out of an egg, the newborn is not yet capable of independent existence. Instead, mammals nurse their offspring and adult birds feed their young. Parental care is in fact widespread among animals, including invertebrates **(Figure 46.6)**.

Gamete Production and Delivery

Sexual reproduction in animals relies on sets of cells that are precursors for eggs and sperm. Cells dedicated to this function are often established early in the formation of the embryo and remain inactive while the body plan takes shape. Cycles of growth and mitosis then increase, or *amplify*, the number of cells available for making eggs or sperm.

In producing gametes from the amplified precursor cells and making them available for fertilization, animals employ a variety of reproductive systems. **Gonads**, organs that produce gametes, are found in many but not all animals. Exceptions include the palolo, discussed above. The palolo and most other polychaete worms (phylum Annelida) have separate sexes but lack distinct gonads; rather, the eggs and sperm develop from undifferentiated cells lining the coelom (body cavity). As the gametes mature, they are released from the body wall and fill the coelom. Depending on the species, mature gametes in these worms may be shed through the excretory opening, or the swelling mass of eggs may split a portion of the body open, spilling the eggs into the environment.

More elaborate reproductive systems include sets of accessory tubes and glands that carry, nourish, and protect the gametes and sometimes the developing embryos. Most insects, for example, have separate sexes with complex reproductive systems **(Figure 46.7)**. In many insect species, the female reproductive system includes one or more **spermathecae** (singular, *spermatheca*), sacs in which sperm may be stored for extended periods, a year or more in some species. Because the female releases male gametes from the spermathecae only in response to the appropriate stimuli, fertilization occurs under conditions likely to be well suited to embryonic development.

Vertebrate reproductive systems display limited but significant variations. In some vertebrates, the uterus is divided into two chambers; in others, including humans and birds, it is a single structure. In many nonmammalian vertebrates, the digestive, excretory, and reproductive systems have a common opening to the outside, the **cloaca**, a structure probably present in the ancestors of all vertebrates. Males of these species lack a well-developed penis and instead release sperm by turning the cloaca inside out. In contrast, mammals generally lack a cloaca and have a separate opening for the digestive tract. In addition, most female mammals have separate openings for the excretory and reproductive systems.

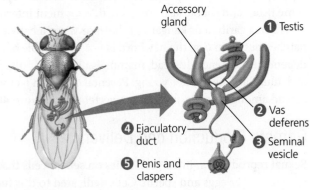

(a) Male fruit fly. Sperm form in the testes, pass through a sperm duct (vas deferens), and are stored in the seminal vesicles. The male ejaculates sperm along with fluid from the accessory glands. (Males of some species of insects and other arthropods have appendages called claspers that grasp the female during copulation.)

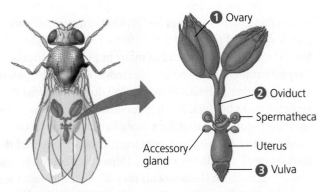

(b) Female fruit fly. Eggs develop in the ovaries and then travel through the oviducts to the uterus. After mating, sperm are stored in the spermathecae, which are connected to the uterus by short ducts. The female uses a stored sperm to fertilize each egg as it enters the uterus before she passes the egg out through the vulva.

▲ **Figure 46.7** **Insect reproductive anatomy.** Circled numbers indicate sequences of sperm and egg movement.

Although fertilization involves the union of a single egg and sperm, animals often mate with more than one member of the other sex. Monogamy, the sustained sexual partnership of two individuals, is rare among animals, including most mammals. Mechanisms have evolved, however, that enhance the reproductive success of a male with a particular female and diminish the chance of that female mating successfully with another partner. For example, some male insects transfer secretions that make a female less receptive to courtship, reducing the likelihood of her mating again.

Can females also influence the relative reproductive success of their mates? This question intrigued two scientific collaborators working in Europe. Studying female fruit flies that copulated with one male and then another, the researchers traced the fate of sperm transferred in the first mating. As shown in **Figure 46.8**, females play a major role in determining the outcome of multiple matings. The processes by which gametes and individuals compete during reproduction remain a vibrant research area.

▼ **Figure 46.8** | Inquiry

Why is sperm usage biased when female fruit flies mate twice?

Experiment When a female fruit fly mates twice, 80% of the offspring result from the second mating. Scientists had hypothesized that ejaculate from the second mating displaces sperm from the first mating. To test this hypothesis, Rhonda Snook, at the University of Sheffield, and David Hosken, at the University of Zurich, used mutant males with altered reproductive systems. "No-ejaculate" males mate but do not transfer sperm or fluid to females. "No-sperm" males mate and ejaculate but make no sperm. The researchers allowed females to mate first with wild-type males and then with wild-type males, no-sperm males, or no-ejaculate males. As a control, some females were mated only once (to wild-type males). The scientists then dissected each female under a microscope and recorded whether sperm were absent from the spermathecae, the major sperm storage organs.

Results

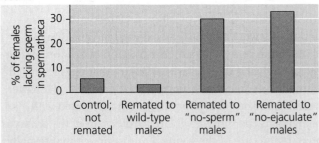

Conclusion Because remating reduces sperm storage when no sperm or fluids are transferred, the hypothesis that ejaculate from a second mating displaces stored sperm is incorrect. Instead, it appears females may get rid of stored sperm in response to remating, perhaps allowing for replacing stored sperm, possibly of diminished fitness, with fresh sperm.

Source: R. R. Snook and D. J. Hosken, Sperm death and dumping in *Drosophila*, *Nature* 428:939–941 (2004).

WHAT IF? *Suppose males in the first mating had a mutant allele for the dominant trait of smaller eyes. What fraction of the females would produce some offspring with smaller eyes?*

1. How does internal fertilization facilitate life on land?

2. What mechanisms have evolved in animals with (a) external fertilization and (b) internal fertilization that help ensure that offspring survive to adulthood?

3. **MAKE CONNECTIONS** What are the shared and distinct functions of the uterus of an insect and the ovary of a flowering plant? (See Figure 38.4.)

For suggested answers, see Appendix A.

CONCEPT 46.3

Reproductive organs produce and transport gametes

Having surveyed some of the general features of animal reproduction, we'll focus in the rest of the chapter on humans, beginning with the reproductive anatomy of each sex.

Human Male Reproductive Anatomy

The human male's external reproductive organs are the scrotum and penis. The internal reproductive organs consist of gonads that produce both sperm and reproductive hormones, accessory glands that secrete products essential to sperm movement, and ducts that carry the sperm and glandular secretions **(Figure 46.9)**.

Testes

The male gonads, or **testes** (singular, *testis*), produce sperm in highly coiled tubes called **seminiferous tubules**. Most mammals produce sperm properly only when the testes are cooler than the rest of the body. In humans and many other mammals, testis temperature is maintained about 2°C below the core body temperature by the **scrotum**, a fold of the body wall.

The testes develop in the abdominal cavity and descend into the scrotum just before birth (a testis within a scrotum is a *testicle*). In many rodents, the testes are drawn back into the cavity between breeding seasons, interrupting sperm maturation. Some mammals whose body temperature is low enough to allow sperm maturation—such as whales and elephants—retain the testes in the abdominal cavity at all times.

Ducts

From the seminiferous tubules of a testis, the sperm pass into the coiled duct of an **epididymis**. In humans, it takes 3 weeks for sperm to travel the 6-m length of this duct, during which time the sperm complete maturation and become motile. During **ejaculation**, the sperm are propelled from each epididymis through a muscular duct, the **vas deferens**. Each vas deferens (one from each epididymis) extends around and behind the urinary bladder, where it joins a duct from the seminal vesicle, forming a short *ejaculatory duct*. The ejaculatory ducts open into the **urethra**, the outlet tube for both the excretory system and the reproductive system.

▲ **Figure 46.9 Reproductive anatomy of the human male.** Some nonreproductive structures are labeled in parentheses for orientation purposes.

The urethra runs through the penis and opens to the outside at the tip of the penis.

Accessory Glands

Three sets of accessory glands—the seminal vesicles, the prostate gland, and the bulbourethral glands—produce secretions that combine with sperm to form **semen**, the fluid that is ejaculated. Two **seminal vesicles** contribute about 60% of the volume of semen. The fluid from the seminal vesicles is thick, yellowish, and alkaline. It contains mucus, the sugar fructose (which provides most of the sperm's energy), a coagulating enzyme, ascorbic acid, and local regulators called prostaglandins (see Chapter 45).

The **prostate gland** secretes its products directly into the urethra through small ducts. Thin and milky, the fluid from this gland contains anticoagulant enzymes and citrate (a sperm nutrient). The prostate undergoes benign (noncancerous) enlargement in more than half of all men over age 40 and in almost all men over 70. In addition, prostate cancer, which most often afflicts men 65 and older, is one of the most common human cancers.

The *bulbourethral glands* are a pair of small glands along the urethra below the prostate. Before ejaculation, they secrete clear mucus that neutralizes any acidic urine remaining in the urethra. There is evidence that bulbourethral fluid carries some sperm released before ejaculation, which may contribute to the high failure rate of the withdrawal method of birth control (coitus interruptus).

Penis

The human **penis** contains the urethra as well as three cylinders of spongy erectile tissue. During sexual arousal, the erectile tissue fills with blood from the arteries. As this tissue fills, the increasing pressure seals off the veins that drain the penis, causing it to engorge with blood. The resulting erection enables the penis to be inserted into the vagina. Alcohol consumption, certain drugs, emotional issues, and aging all can cause an inability to achieve an erection (erectile dysfunction). For individuals with long-term erectile dysfunction, drugs such as Viagra promote the vasodilating action of the local regulator nitric oxide (NO; see Chapter 45); the resulting relaxation of smooth muscles in the blood vessels of the penis enhances blood flow into the erectile tissues. Although all mammals rely on penile erection for mating, the penis of raccoons, walruses, whales, and several other mammals also contains a bone, the baculum, which is thought to further stiffen the penis for mating.

The main shaft of the penis is covered by relatively thick skin. The head, or **glans**, of the penis has a much thinner outer layer and is consequently more sensitive to stimulation. The human glans is surrounded by a fold of skin called the **prepuce**, or foreskin, which is removed if a male is circumcised.

Human Female Reproductive Anatomy

The human female's external reproductive structures are the clitoris and two sets of labia, which surround the clitoris and vaginal opening. The internal organs consist of gonads, which produce eggs and reproductive hormones, and a system of ducts and chambers, which receive and carry gametes and house the embryo and fetus (**Figure 46.10**).

Ovaries

The female gonads are a pair of **ovaries** that flank the uterus and are held in place in the abdominal cavity by ligaments. The outer layer of each ovary is packed with **follicles**, each consisting of an **oocyte**, a partially developed egg, surrounded by support cells. The surrounding cells nourish and protect the oocyte during much of its formation and development.

Oviducts and Uterus

An **oviduct**, or fallopian tube, extends from the uterus toward a funnel-like opening at each ovary. The dimensions of this tube vary along its length, with the inside diameter near the uterus being as narrow as a human hair. Upon ovulation, cilia on the epithelial lining of the oviduct help collect the egg by drawing fluid from the body cavity into the oviduct. Together with wavelike contractions of the oviduct, the cilia convey the egg down the duct to the **uterus**, also known as the womb. The uterus is a thick, muscular organ that can expand during pregnancy to accommodate a 4-kg fetus. The inner lining of the uterus, the **endometrium**, is richly supplied with blood vessels. The neck of the uterus, called the **cervix**, opens into the vagina.

Vagina and Vulva

The **vagina** is a muscular but elastic chamber that is the site for insertion of the penis and deposition of sperm during copulation. The vagina, which also serves as the birth canal through which a baby is born, opens to the outside at the **vulva**, the collective term for the external female genitalia.

A pair of thick, fatty ridges, the **labia majora**, encloses and protects the rest of the vulva. The vaginal opening and the separate opening of the urethra are located within a cavity bordered by a pair of slender skin folds, the **labia minora**. A thin piece of tissue called the *hymen* partly covers the vaginal opening in humans at birth and usually until sexual intercourse or vigorous physical activity ruptures it. Located at the top of the labia minora, the **clitoris** consists of erectile tissue supporting a rounded glans, or head, covered by a small hood of skin, the prepuce. During sexual arousal, the clitoris, vagina, and labia minora all engorge with blood and enlarge. Richly supplied with nerve endings, the clitoris is one of the most sensitive points of sexual stimulation.

connective and fatty (adipose) tissue in addition to the mammary glands. Because the low level of estradiol in males limits the development of the fat deposits, male breasts usually remain small.

Gametogenesis

With this overview of anatomy in mind, we turn to **gametogenesis**, which is the production of gametes. **Figure 46.11** explores this process in human males and females, highlighting the close relationship between gonadal structure and function.

Spermatogenesis, the formation and development of sperm, is continuous and prolific in adult human males. Cell division and maturation occur throughout the seminiferous tubules coiled within the two testes, producing hundreds of millions of sperm each day. For a single sperm, the process takes about 7 weeks from start to finish.

Oogenesis, the development of mature oocytes (eggs), is a prolonged process in the human female. Immature eggs form in the ovary of the female embryo but do not complete their development until years, and often decades, later.

Spermatogenesis differs from the process of oogenesis in three significant ways:

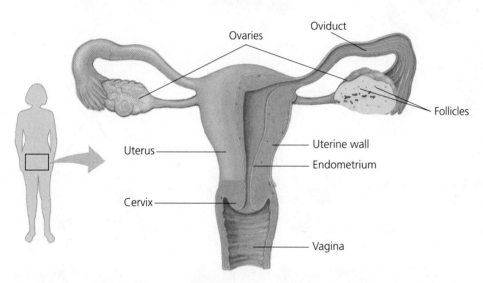

▲ **Figure 46.10 Reproductive anatomy of the human female.** Some nonreproductive structures are labeled in parentheses for orientation purposes.

- Only in spermatogenesis do all four products of meiosis develop into mature gametes. In oogenesis, cytokinesis during meiosis is unequal, with almost all the cytoplasm segregated to a single daughter cell. This large cell is destined to become the egg; the other products of meiosis, smaller cells known as polar bodies, degenerate.
- Spermatogenesis occurs throughout adolescence and adulthood. In contrast, the mitotic divisions that occur in oogenesis in human females are thought to be complete before birth, and the production of mature gametes ceases at about age 50.
- Spermatogenesis produces mature sperm from precursor cells in a continuous sequence, whereas there are long interruptions in oogenesis.

Sexual arousal also induces the vestibular glands near the vaginal opening to secrete lubricating mucus, thereby facilitating intercourse.

Mammary Glands

The **mammary glands** are present in both sexes, but they normally produce milk only in females. Though not part of the reproductive system, the female mammary glands are important to reproduction. Within the glands, small sacs of epithelial tissue secrete milk, which drains into a series of ducts that open at the nipple. The breasts contain

Spermatogenesis

Stem cells that give rise to sperm are situated near the outer edge of the seminiferous tubules. Their progeny move inward as they pass through the spermatocyte and spermatid stages, and sperm are released into the lumen (fluid-filled cavity) of the tubule. The sperm travel along the tubule into the epididymis, where they become motile.

The stem cells arise from division and differentiation of primordial germ cells in the embryonic testes. In mature testes, they divide mitotically to form **spermatogonia**, which in turn generate spermatocytes by mitosis. Each spermatocyte gives rise to four spermatids through meiosis, reducing the chromosome number from diploid ($2n = 46$ in humans) to haploid ($n = 23$). Spermatids undergo extensive changes in differentiating into sperm.

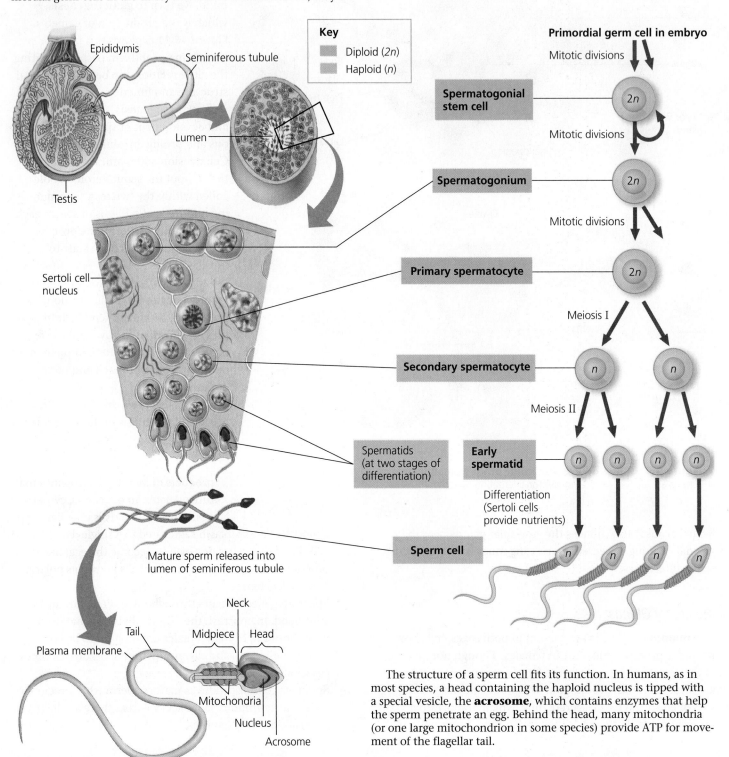

Key
- Diploid ($2n$)
- Haploid (n)

Epididymis
Seminiferous tubule
Lumen
Testis
Sertoli cell nucleus
Spermatids (at two stages of differentiation)
Mature sperm released into lumen of seminiferous tubule
Tail — Midpiece — Head
Neck
Plasma membrane
Mitochondria
Nucleus
Acrosome

Primordial germ cell in embryo
Mitotic divisions
Spermatogonial stem cell — $2n$
Mitotic divisions
Spermatogonium — $2n$
Mitotic divisions
Primary spermatocyte — $2n$
Meiosis I
Secondary spermatocyte — n n
Meiosis II
Early spermatid — n n n n
Differentiation (Sertoli cells provide nutrients)
Sperm cell — n n n n

The structure of a sperm cell fits its function. In humans, as in most species, a head containing the haploid nucleus is tipped with a special vesicle, the **acrosome**, which contains enzymes that help the sperm penetrate an egg. Behind the head, many mitochondria (or one large mitochondrion in some species) provide ATP for movement of the flagellar tail.

Oogenesis

Oogenesis begins in the female embryo with the production of **oogonia** from primordial germ cells. The oogonia divide by mitosis to form cells that begin meiosis, but stop the process at prophase I before birth. These developmentally arrested cells, which are **primary oocytes**, each reside within a small follicle, a cavity lined with protective cells. At birth, the ovaries together contain about 1–2 million primary oocytes, of which about 500 fully mature between puberty and menopause.

To the best of our current knowledge, women are born with all the primary oocytes they will ever have. It is worth noting, however, that a similar conclusion regarding most other mammals was overturned in 2004 when researchers discovered that the ovaries of adult mice contain multiplying oogonia that develop into oocytes. If the same turned out to be true of humans, it might be that the marked decline in fertility that occurs as women age results from both a depletion of oogonia and the degeneration of aging oocytes.

Beginning at puberty, follicle-stimulating hormone (FSH) periodically stimulates a small group of follicles to resume growth and development. Typically, only one follicle fully matures each month, with its primary oocyte completing meiosis I. The second meiotic division begins, but stops at metaphase. Thus arrested in meiosis II, **the secondary oocyte** is released at ovulation, when its follicle breaks open. Only if a sperm penetrates the oocyte does meiosis II resume. (In other animal species, the sperm may enter the oocyte at the same stage, earlier, or later.) Each of the two meiotic divisions involves unequal cytokinesis, with the smaller cells becoming polar bodies that eventually degenerate (the first polar body may or may not divide again). As a result, the functional product of complete oogenesis is a single mature egg containing a sperm head. Fertilization is defined strictly as the fusion of the haploid nuclei of the sperm and secondary oocyte, although the term is often used loosely to mean the entry of the sperm head into the egg.

The ruptured follicle left behind after ovulation develops into the corpus luteum. The corpus luteum secretes estradiol as well as progesterone, a hormone that helps maintain the uterine lining during pregnancy. If the egg is not fertilized, the corpus luteum degenerates, and a new follicle matures during the next cycle.

WHAT IF? *Suppose you are analyzing the DNA from the polar bodies formed during human oogenesis. If the woman who produced the oocyte has a mutation in a known disease gene, would analyzing the polar body DNA allow you to infer whether the mutation is present in the mature oocyte? Explain.*

1. Why might frequent use of a hot tub make it harder for a couple to conceive a child?

2. The process of oogenesis is often described as the production of a haploid egg by meiosis, but in some animals, including humans, this is not an entirely accurate description. Explain.

3. **WHAT IF?** If each vas deferens in a male was surgically sealed off, what changes would you expect in sexual response and ejaculate composition?

For suggested answers, see Appendix A.

CONCEPT 46.4

The interplay of tropic and sex hormones regulates mammalian reproduction

In both male and female humans, the coordinated actions of hormones from the hypothalamus, anterior pituitary, and gonads govern reproduction. The hypothalamus secretes *gonadotropin-releasing hormone* (GnRH), which then directs the anterior pituitary to secrete the gonadotropins, **follicle-stimulating hormone (FSH)** and **luteinizing hormone (LH)** (see Figure 45.15). FSH and LH are tropic hormones, meaning that they regulate the activity of endocrine cells or glands. They are called *gonadotropins* because they act on the male and female gonads, and they support gametogenesis, in part by stimulating sex hormone production.

The main sex hormones are steroid hormones. They consist of *androgens*, principally **testosterone**; *estrogens*, principally **estradiol**; and **progesterone**. Males and females differ in their blood concentrations of particular hormones. Testosterone levels are roughly ten times higher in males than in females. In contrast, estradiol levels are about ten times higher in females than in males; females also produce more progesterone. The gonads are the major source of sex hormones, with much smaller amounts being produced by the adrenal glands.

Like gonadotropins, sex hormones regulate gametogenesis both directly and indirectly, but they have other actions as well. For example, androgens are responsible for the territorial songs of male birds and the courtship displays of male lizards **(Figure 46.12)**. In human embryos, androgens promote the appearance of the primary sex characteristics of males, the structures directly involved in reproduction. These include the seminal vesicles and associated ducts, as well as external reproductive structures. In the Scientific Skills Exercise, you can interpret the results of an experiment investigating the development of reproductive structures in mammals.

▲ **Figure 46.12 Androgen-dependent male anatomy and behavior in a lizard.** A male anole (*Norops ortoni*) extends his dewlap, a brightly colored skin flap beneath the throat. Testosterone is required for the dewlap to develop and for the male to display this skin flap when attracting mates and guarding territory.

At puberty, sex hormones in human males and females induce formation of secondary sex characteristics, the physical and behavioral differences between males and females that are not directly related to the reproductive system. In males, androgens cause the voice to deepen, facial and pubic hair to develop, and muscles to grow (by stimulating protein synthesis). Androgens also promote specific sexual behaviors and sex drive, as well as an increase in general aggressiveness. Estrogens similarly have multiple effects in females. At puberty, estradiol stimulates breast and pubic hair development. Estradiol also influences female sexual behavior, induces fat deposition in the breasts and hips, increases water retention, and alters calcium metabolism.

We now turn to the roles of gonadotropins and sex hormones in gametogenesis, beginning with males.

Hormonal Control of the Male Reproductive System

FSH and LH, released by the anterior pituitary in response to GnRH from the hypothalamus, direct spermatogenesis by acting on different types of cells in the testis **(Figure 46.13)**. FSH stimulates *Sertoli cells*, located within the seminiferous tubules, to nourish developing sperm (see Figure 46.11). LH causes *Leydig cells*, scattered in connective tissue between the tubules, to produce testosterone and other androgens, which promote spermatogenesis in the tubules.

Two negative-feedback mechanisms control sex hormone production in males (see Figure 46.13). Testosterone regulates blood levels of GnRH, FSH, and LH through inhibitory effects on the hypothalamus and anterior pituitary. In addition, *inhibin*, a hormone that in males is produced by Sertoli cells, acts on the anterior pituitary gland to reduce FSH secretion. Together, these negative-feedback circuits maintain androgen levels in the normal range.

Making Inferences and Designing an Experiment

What Role Do Hormones Play in Making a Mammal Male or Female? In non-egg-laying mammals, females have two X chromosomes, whereas males have one X chromosome and one Y chromosome. In the 1940s, French physiologist Alfred Jost wondered whether development of mammalian embryos as female or male in accord with their chromosome set requires instructions in the form of hormones produced by the gonads. In this exercise, you will interpret the results of an experiment that Jost performed to answer this question.

How the Experiment Was Done Working with rabbit embryos still in the mother's uterus at a stage before sex differences are observable, Jost surgically removed the portion of each embryo that would form the ovaries or testes. When the baby rabbits were born, he made note of their chromosomal sex and whether their genital structures were male or female.

Data from the Experiment

	Appearance of Genitalia	
Chromosome Set	No Surgery	Embryonic Gonad Removed
XY (male)	Male	Female
XX (female)	Female	Female

Interpret the Data

1. This experiment is an example of a research approach in which scientists infer how something works normally based on what happens when the normal process is blocked. What normal process was blocked in Jost's experiment? From the results, what inference can you make about the role of the gonads in controlling the development of mammalian genitalia?

2. The data in Jost's experiment could be explained if some aspect of the surgery other than gonad removal caused female genitalia to develop. If you were to repeat Jost's experiment, how might you test the validity of such an explanation?

3. What result would Jost have obtained if female development also required a signal from the gonad?

4. Design another experiment to determine whether the signal that controls male development is a hormone. Make sure to identify your hypothesis, prediction, data collection plan, and controls.

(MB) A version of this Scientific Skills Exercise can be assigned in MasteringBiology.

Data from A. Jost, Recherches sur la differenciation sexuelle de l'embryon de lapin (Studies on the sexual differentiation of the rabbit embryo), *Archives d'Anatomie Microscopique et de Morphologie Experimentale* 36:271–316 (1947).

Leydig cells have other roles besides producing testosterone. They in fact secrete small quantities of many other hormones and local regulators, including oxytocin, renin, angiotensin, corticotropin-releasing factor, growth factors, and prostaglandins. These signals coordinate the activity of reproduction with growth, metabolism, homeostasis, and behavior.

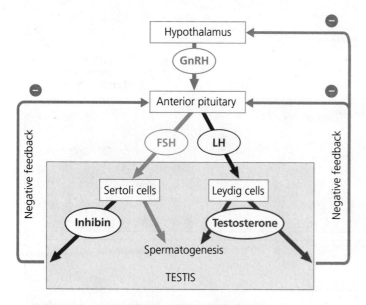

▲ **Figure 46.13 Hormonal control of the testes.**

Hormonal Control of Female Reproductive Cycles

Whereas human males produce sperm continuously, human females produce eggs in cycles. Ovulation occurs only after the endometrium (lining of the uterus) has started to thicken and develop a rich blood supply, preparing the uterus for the possible implantation of an embryo. If pregnancy does not occur, the uterine lining is sloughed off, and another cycle begins. The cyclic shedding of the blood-rich endometrium from the uterus, a process that occurs in a flow through the cervix and vagina, is called **menstruation**.

There are two closely linked reproductive cycles in human females. The term *menstrual cycle* refers specifically to the changes that occur about once a month in the uterus; therefore it is also called the **uterine cycle**. The cyclic changes in the uterus are controlled by the **ovarian cycle**, cyclic events that occur in the ovaries. Thus, the female reproductive cycle is actually one integrated cycle involving two organs, the uterus and the ovaries.

Menstrual cycles average 28 days (although cycles vary, ranging from about 20 to 40 days). Hormone activity links the two cycles, synchronizing ovarian follicle growth and ovulation with the establishment of a uterine lining that can support embryonic development.

Figure 46.14 outlines the major events of the female reproductive cycles, illustrating the close coordination across different tissues in the body.

The Ovarian Cycle

The ovarian cycle begins ❶ with the release from the hypothalamus of GnRH, which stimulates the anterior pituitary to ❷ secrete small amounts of FSH and LH. ❸ Follicle-stimulating hormone (as its name implies) stimulates follicle growth, aided by LH, and ❹ the cells of the growing follicles start to make estradiol. There is a slow rise in estradiol concentration during most of the *follicular phase*, the part of the ovarian cycle during which follicles grow and oocytes mature. (Several follicles begin to grow with each cycle, but usually only one matures; the others disintegrate.) The low levels of estradiol inhibit secretion of the pituitary hormones, keeping the levels of FSH and LH relatively low. During this portion of the cycle, regulation of the hormones controlling reproduction closely parallels the regulation observed in males.

❺ When estradiol secretion by the growing follicle begins to rise steeply, ❻ the FSH and LH levels increase markedly. Why? Whereas a low level of estradiol inhibits the secretion of pituitary gonadotropins, a high concentration has the opposite effect: It stimulates gonadotropin secretion by causing the hypothalamus to increase its output of GnRH. A high estradiol concentration also increases the GnRH sensitivity of LH-releasing cells in the pituitary, resulting in a further increase in LH levels.

❼ The maturing follicle, containing a fluid-filled cavity, enlarges, forming a bulge at the surface of the ovary. The follicular phase ends at ovulation, about a day after the LH surge. In response to both FSH and the peak in LH level, the follicle and adjacent wall of the ovary rupture, releasing the secondary oocyte. At or near the time of ovulation, women sometimes feel a

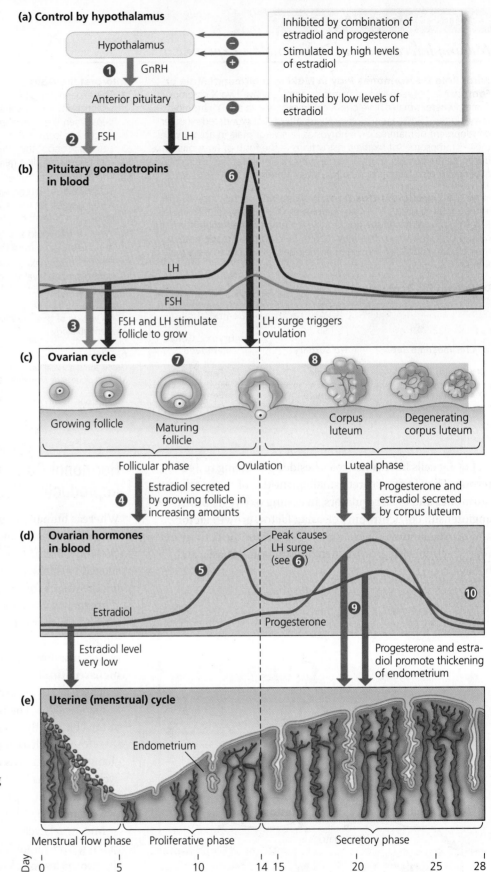

▲ **Figure 46.14 The reproductive cycles of the human female.** This figure shows how **(c)** the ovarian cycle and **(e)** the uterine (menstrual) cycle are regulated by changing hormone levels in the blood, depicted in parts **(a)**, **(b)**, and **(d)**. The time scale at the bottom of the figure applies to parts **(b)–(e)**.

distinctive pain in the lower abdomen, on the same side as the ovary in which the oocyte was released.

The *luteal phase* of the ovarian cycle follows ovulation. ❽ Luteinizing hormone stimulates the follicular tissue left behind in the ovary to transform into a corpus luteum, a glandular structure. Under continued stimulation by LH, the corpus luteum secretes progesterone and estradiol, which in combination exert negative feedback on the hypothalamus and pituitary. This feedback reduces the secretion of LH and FSH to very low levels, preventing another egg from maturing when a pregnancy may already be under way.

If pregnancy does not occur, low gonadotropin levels at the end of the luteal phase cause the corpus luteum to disintegrate, triggering a sharp decline in estradiol and progesterone concentrations. The decreasing levels of ovarian steroid hormones liberate the hypothalamus and pituitary from the negative-feedback effect of these hormones. The pituitary can then begin to secrete enough FSH to stimulate the growth of new follicles in the ovary, initiating the next ovarian cycle.

The Uterine (Menstrual) Cycle

Prior to ovulation, ovarian steroid hormones stimulate the uterus to prepare for support of an embryo. Estradiol secreted in increasing amounts by growing follicles signals the endometrium to thicken. In this way, the follicular phase of the ovarian cycle is coordinated with the *proliferative phase* of the uterine cycle. After ovulation, ❾ the estradiol and progesterone secreted by the corpus luteum stimulate maintenance and further development of the uterine lining, including enlargement of arteries and growth of endometrial glands. These glands secrete a nutrient fluid that can sustain an early embryo even before it implants in the uterine lining. Thus, the luteal phase of the ovarian cycle is coordinated with the *secretory phase* of the uterine cycle.

If an embryo has not implanted in the endometrium by the end of the secretory phase, the corpus luteum disintegrates. The resulting drop ❿ in ovarian hormone levels causes arteries in the endometrium to constrict. Deprived of its circulation, the uterine lining largely disintegrates, releasing blood that is shed along with endometrial tissue and fluid. The result is menstruation—the *menstrual flow phase* of the uterine cycle. During this phase, which usually lasts a few days, a new group of ovarian follicles begin to grow. By convention, the first day of flow is designated day 1 of the new uterine (and ovarian) cycle.

About 7% of women of reproductive age suffer from a disorder called **endometriosis**, in which some cells of the uterine lining migrate to an abdominal location that is abnormal, or **ectopic** (from the Greek *ektopos*, away from a place). Having migrated to a location such as an oviduct, ovary, or large intestine, the ectopic tissue responds to hormones in the bloodstream. Like the uterine endometrium, the ectopic tissue swells and breaks down during each ovarian cycle, resulting in

pelvic pain and bleeding into the abdomen. Researchers have not yet determined why endometriosis occurs, but hormonal therapy or surgery can be used to lessen discomfort.

Menopause

After about 500 cycles, a woman undergoes **menopause**, the cessation of ovulation and menstruation. Menopause usually occurs between the ages of 46 and 54. During this interval, the ovaries lose their responsiveness to FSH and LH, resulting in a decline in estradiol production.

Menopause is an unusual phenomenon. In most other species, females and males can reproduce throughout life. Is there an evolutionary explanation for menopause? One intriguing hypothesis proposes that during early human evolution, undergoing menopause after bearing several children allowed a mother to provide better care for her children and grandchildren, thereby increasing the chances for survival of individuals who share much of her genetic makeup.

Menstrual Versus Estrous Cycles

In all female mammals, the endometrium thickens before ovulation, but only humans and some other primates have menstrual cycles. Other mammals have **estrous cycles**, in which in the absence of a pregnancy, the uterus reabsorbs the endometrium and no extensive fluid flow occurs. Whereas human females may engage in sexual activity throughout the menstrual cycle, mammals with estrous cycles usually copulate only during the period surrounding ovulation. This period, called estrus (from the Latin *oestrus*, frenzy, passion), is the only time the female is receptive to mating. It is often called "heat," and the female's temperature does increase slightly.

The length and frequency of estrous cycles vary widely among mammals. Bears and wolves have one estrous cycle per year; elephants have several. Rats have estrous cycles throughout the year, each lasting just five days.

Human Sexual Response

The arousal of sexual interest in humans is complex, involving a variety of psychological as well as physical factors. Although reproductive structures in the male and female differ in appearance, a number serve similar functions in arousal, reflecting their shared developmental origin. For example, the same embryonic tissues give rise to the scrotum and the labia majora, to the skin on the penis and the labia minora, and to the glans of the penis and the clitoris. Furthermore, the general pattern of human sexual response is similar in males and females. Two types of physiological reactions predominate in both sexes: *vasocongestion*, the filling of a tissue with blood, and *myotonia*, increased muscle tension.

The sexual response cycle can be divided into four phases: excitement, plateau, orgasm, and resolution. An important function of the excitement phase is to prepare the vagina and penis for *coitus* (sexual intercourse). During this phase, vaso-congestion is particularly evident in erection of the penis and clitoris and in enlargement of the testicles, labia, and breasts. The vagina becomes lubricated, and myotonia may occur, as evident in nipple erection or tension of the limbs.

In the plateau phase, sexual responses continue as a result of direct stimulation of the genitalia. In females, the outer third of the vagina becomes vasocongested, while the inner two-thirds slightly expands. This change, coupled with the elevation of the uterus, forms a depression for receiving sperm at the back of the vagina. Breathing quickens and heart rate rises, sometimes to 150 beats per minute—not only in response to the physical effort of sexual activity, but also as an involuntary reaction to stimulation by the autonomic nervous system (see Figure 49.9).

Orgasm is characterized by rhythmic, involuntary contractions of the reproductive structures in both sexes. Male orgasm has two stages. The first, emission, occurs when the glands and ducts of the reproductive tract contract, forcing semen into the urethra. Expulsion, or ejaculation, occurs when the urethra contracts and the semen is expelled. During female orgasm, the uterus and outer vagina contract, but the inner two-thirds of the vagina does not. Orgasm is the shortest phase of the sexual response cycle, usually lasting only a few seconds. In both sexes, contractions occur at about 0.8-second intervals and may also involve the anal sphincter and several abdominal muscles.

The resolution phase completes the cycle and reverses the responses of the earlier stages. Vasocongested organs return to normal size and color, and muscles relax. Most of these changes are completed within 5 minutes, but some may take as long as an hour. Following orgasm, the male typically enters a refractory period, lasting from a few minutes to hours, when erection and orgasm cannot be achieved. Females do not have a refractory period, making possible multiple orgasms within a short period of time.

CONCEPT 46.5

In placental mammals, an embryo develops fully within the mother's uterus

Having surveyed the ovarian and uterine cycles of human females, we turn now to reproduction itself, beginning with the events that transform an egg into a developing embryo.

Conception, Embryonic Development, and Birth

During human copulation, the male delivers 2–5 mL of semen containing hundreds of millions of sperm. When first ejaculated, the semen coagulates, which likely keeps the ejaculate in place until sperm reach the cervix. Soon after, anticoagulants liquefy the semen, and the sperm swim through the uterus and oviducts. Fertilization—also called **conception** in humans—occurs when a sperm fuses with an egg (mature oocyte) in an oviduct (**Figure 46.15**).

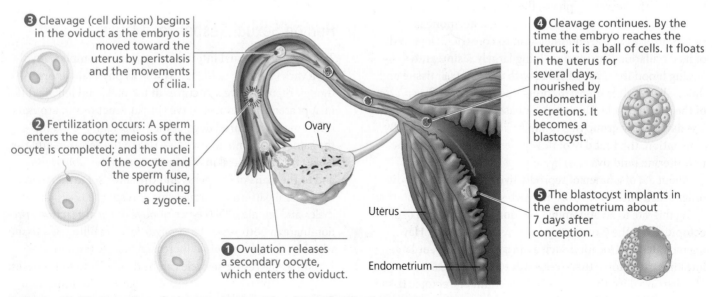

❸ Cleavage (cell division) begins in the oviduct as the embryo is moved toward the uterus by peristalsis and the movements of cilia.

❷ Fertilization occurs: A sperm enters the oocyte; meiosis of the oocyte is completed; and the nuclei of the oocyte and the sperm fuse, producing a zygote.

Ovary

❶ Ovulation releases a secondary oocyte, which enters the oviduct.

Uterus

Endometrium

❹ Cleavage continues. By the time the embryo reaches the uterus, it is a ball of cells. It floats in the uterus for several days, nourished by endometrial secretions. It becomes a blastocyst.

❺ The blastocyst implants in the endometrium about 7 days after conception.

▲ **Figure 46.15 Formation of a human zygote and early postfertilization events.**

The zygote begins a series of cell divisions called cleavage about 24 hours after fertilization and after an additional 4 days produces a **blastocyst**, a sphere of cells surrounding a central cavity. A few days later, the embryo implants into the endometrium of the uterus. The condition of carrying one or more embryos in the uterus is called **pregnancy**, or **gestation**. Human pregnancy averages 266 days (38 weeks) from fertilization of the egg, or 40 weeks from the start of the last menstrual cycle. In comparison, gestation averages 21 days in many rodents, 270 days in cows, and more than 600 days in elephants. The roughly nine months of human gestation are divided into three *trimesters* of equal length.

First Trimester

During the first trimester, the implanted embryo secretes hormones that signal its presence and regulate the mother's reproductive system. One embryonic hormone, *human chorionic gonadotropin (hCG)*, acts like pituitary LH in maintaining secretion of progesterone and estrogens by the corpus luteum through the first few months of pregnancy. Some hCG passes from the maternal blood to the urine, where it can be detected by the most common early pregnancy tests.

Not all embryos are capable of completing development. Many spontaneously stop developing as a result of chromosomal or developmental abnormalities. Much less often, a fertilized egg lodges in an oviduct (fallopian tube), resulting in a tubal, or ectopic, pregnancy. Such pregnancies cannot be sustained and may rupture the oviduct, resulting in serious internal bleeding. The risk of ectopic pregnancy increases if the oviduct is scarred by bacterial infections arising during childbirth, by medical procedures, or by a sexually transmitted disease.

During its first 2–4 weeks of development, the embryo obtains nutrients directly from the endometrium. Meanwhile, the outer layer of the blastocyst, which is called the **trophoblast**, grows outward and mingles with the endometrium, eventually helping form the **placenta**. This disk-shaped organ, containing both embryonic and maternal blood vessels, can weigh close to 1 kg at birth. Diffusion of material between the maternal and embryonic circulatory systems supplies nutrients, provides immune protection, exchanges respiratory gases, and disposes of metabolic wastes for the embryo. Blood from the embryo travels to the placenta through the arteries of the umbilical cord and returns via the umbilical vein **(Figure 46.16)**.

▲ **Figure 46.16 Placental circulation.**
From the 4th week of development until birth, the placenta, a combination of maternal and embryonic tissues, transports nutrients, respiratory gases, and wastes between the embryo or fetus and the mother. Maternal blood enters the placenta in arteries, flows through blood pools in the endometrium, and leaves via veins. Embryonic or fetal blood, which remains in vessels, enters the placenta through arteries and passes through capillaries in finger-like chorionic villi, where oxygen and nutrients are acquired. Fetal blood leaves the placenta through veins leading back to the fetus. Materials are exchanged by diffusion, active transport, and selective absorption between the fetal capillary bed and the maternal blood pools.

? *In a rare genetic disorder, the absence of a particular enzyme leads to increased testosterone production. When the fetus has this disorder, the mother develops a male-like pattern of body hair during the pregnancy. Explain why.*

Occasionally, an embryo splits during the first month of development, resulting in identical, or *monozygotic* (one-egg), twins. Fraternal, or *dizygotic*, twins arise in a very different way: Two follicles mature in a single cycle, followed by independent fertilization and implantation of two genetically distinct embryos.

The first trimester is the main period of **organogenesis**, the development of the body organs **(Figure 46.17a)**. During organogenesis, the embryo is particularly susceptible to damage. For example, alcohol that passes through the placenta and reaches the developing central nervous system of the embryo can cause fetal alcohol syndrome, a disorder that can result in mental retardation and other serious birth defects. The heart begins beating by the 4th week; a heartbeat can be detected at 8–10 weeks. At 8 weeks, all the major structures of the adult are present in rudimentary form, and the embryo is called a **fetus**. At the end of the first trimester, the fetus, although well differentiated, is only 5 cm long.

Meanwhile, high levels of progesterone bring about rapid changes in the mother: Mucus in the cervix forms a plug that protects against infection, the maternal part of the placenta grows, the breasts and uterus get larger, and both ovulation and menstrual cycling stop. About three-fourths of all pregnant women experience nausea, misleadingly called "morning sickness," during the first trimester.

Second and Third Trimesters

During the second trimester, the fetus grows to about 30 cm in length and is very active **(Figure 46.17b and c)**. The mother may feel fetal movements as early as one month into the second trimester, and fetal activity is typically visible through the abdominal wall one to two months later. Hormone levels stabilize as hCG secretion declines; the corpus luteum deteriorates; and the placenta completely takes over the production of progesterone, the hormone that maintains the pregnancy.

During the third trimester, the fetus grows to about 3–4 kg in weight and 50 cm in length. Fetal activity may decrease as the fetus fills the available space. As the fetus grows and the uterus expands around it, the mother's abdominal organs become compressed and displaced, leading to digestive blockages and a need for frequent urination.

Childbirth begins with *labor*, a series of strong, rhythmic uterine contractions that push the fetus and placenta out of

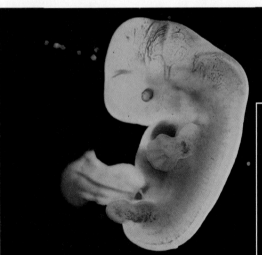

(a) 5 weeks. Limb buds, eyes, the heart, the liver, and rudiments of all other organs have started to develop in the embryo, which is only about 1 cm long.

(b) 14 weeks. Growth and development of the offspring, now called a fetus, continue during the second trimester. This fetus is about 6 cm long.

(c) 20 weeks. Growth to nearly 20 cm in length requires adoption of the fetal position (head at knees) due to the limited space available.

▲ **Figure 46.17 Some stages of human development during the first and second trimesters.**

▲ **Figure 46.18 Positive feedback in labor.**

? *Predict the effect of a single dose of oxytocin on a pregnant woman at the end of 39 weeks gestation.*

the body. Once labor begins, local regulators (prostaglandins) and hormones (chiefly estradiol and oxytocin) induce and regulate further contractions of the uterus **(Figure 46.18)**. Central to this regulation is a positive-feedback loop (see Concept 45.2) in which uterine contractions stimulate secretion of oxytocin, which in turn stimulates further contractions.

Labor is typically described as having three stages **(Figure 46.19)**. The first stage is the thinning and opening up (dilation) of the cervix. The second stage is the expulsion, or delivery, of the baby. Continuous strong contractions force the fetus out of the uterus and through the vagina. The final stage of labor is the delivery of the placenta.

One aspect of postnatal care unique to mammals is *lactation*, the production of mother's milk. In response to suckling by the newborn and changes in estradiol levels after birth, the hypothalamus signals the anterior pituitary to secrete prolactin, which stimulates the mammary glands to produce milk. Suckling also stimulates the secretion of oxytocin from the posterior pituitary, which triggers release of milk from the mammary glands (see Figure 45.14).

Maternal Immune Tolerance of the Embryo and Fetus

Pregnancy is an immunological puzzle. Because half of the embryo's genes are inherited from the father, many of the chemical markers present on the surface of the embryo are foreign to the mother. Why, then, does the mother not reject the embryo as a foreign body, as she would a tissue or organ graft from another person? One intriguing clue comes

1 Dilation of the cervix

2 Expulsion: delivery of the infant

3 Delivery of the placenta

▲ **Figure 46.19 The three stages of labor.**

from the relationship between certain autoimmune disorders and pregnancy. For example, the symptoms of rheumatoid arthritis, an autoimmune disease of the joints, become less severe during pregnancy. Such observations suggest that the overall regulation of the immune system changes during pregnancy. Sorting out these changes and how they might protect the developing fetus is an active area of research for immunologists.

Contraception and Abortion

Contraception, the deliberate prevention of pregnancy, can be achieved in a number of ways. Some contraceptive methods prevent gamete development or release from female or male gonads; others prevent fertilization by keeping sperm and egg apart; and still others prevent implantation of an embryo. For complete information on contraceptive methods, you should consult a health-care provider. The following brief introduction to the biology of the most common methods and the corresponding diagram in **Figure 46.20** make no pretense of being a contraception manual.

Fertilization can be prevented by abstinence from sexual intercourse or by any of several kinds of barriers that keep live sperm from contacting the egg. Temporary abstinence, sometimes called *natural family planning*, depends on refraining from intercourse when conception is most likely. Because the egg can survive in the oviduct for 24–48 hours and sperm for up to 5 days, a couple practicing temporary abstinence should not engage in intercourse for a significant number of days before and after ovulation. Contraceptive methods based on fertility awareness require knowledge of physiological indicators associated with ovulation, such as changes in cervical mucus. Note also that a pregnancy rate of 10–20% is typically reported for couples practicing natural family planning. (In this context, pregnancy rate is the percentage of women who become pregnant in one year while using a particular pregnancy prevention method.)

As a method of preventing fertilization, *coitus interruptus*, or withdrawal (removal of the penis from the vagina before ejaculation), is unreliable. Sperm from a previous ejaculate may be transferred in secretions that precede ejaculation. Furthermore, a split-second lapse in timing or willpower can result in tens of millions of sperm being transferred before withdrawal.

Used properly, several methods of contraception that block sperm from meeting the egg have pregnancy rates of less than 10%. The *condom* is a thin, latex rubber or natural membrane sheath that fits over the penis to collect the semen. For sexually active individuals, latex condoms are the only contraceptives that are highly effective in preventing the spread of AIDS and other *sexually transmitted diseases* (*STDs*), also known as *sexually transmitted infections* (*STIs*). This protection is not absolute, however. Another common barrier device is the *diaphragm*, a dome-shaped rubber cap inserted into the upper portion of the vagina before intercourse. Both of these devices have lower pregnancy rates when used in conjunction with a spermicidal (sperm-killing) foam or jelly. Other barrier devices include the vaginal pouch, or "female condom."

Except for complete abstinence from sexual intercourse or sterilization (discussed later), the most effective means

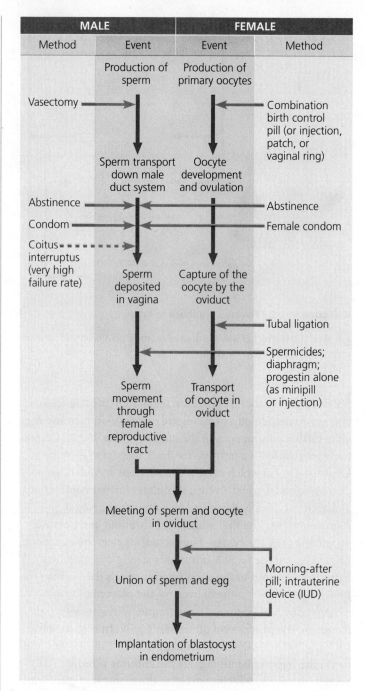

▲ **Figure 46.20 Mechanisms of several contraceptive methods.** Red arrows indicate where these methods, devices, or products interfere with events from the production of sperm and primary oocytes to implantation of a developing embryo.

of birth control are the intrauterine device (IUD) and hormonal contraceptives. The IUD has a pregnancy rate of 1% or less and is the most commonly used reversible method of birth control outside the United States. Placed in the uterus by a doctor, the IUD interferes with fertilization and implantation. Hormonal contraceptives, most often in the form of **birth control pills**, also have pregnancy rates of 1% or less.

The most commonly prescribed hormonal contraceptives combine a synthetic estrogen and a synthetic progestin (progesterone-like hormone). This combination mimics negative feedback in the ovarian cycle, stopping the release of GnRH by the hypothalamus and thus of FSH and LH by the pituitary. The prevention of LH release blocks ovulation. In addition, the inhibition of FSH secretion by the low dose of estrogens in the pills prevents follicles from developing.

Another hormonal contraceptive with a very low pregnancy rate contains only progestin. Progestin causes thickening of a woman's cervical mucus so that it blocks sperm from entering the uterus. Progestin also decreases the frequency of ovulation and causes changes in the endometrium that may interfere with implantation if fertilization occurs. This contraceptive can be administered as injections that last for three months or as a tablet ("minipill") taken daily.

Hormonal contraceptives have both harmful and beneficial side effects. They increase the risk of some cardiovascular disorders slightly for nonsmokers and quite substantially (3- to 10-fold) for women who smoke regularly. At the same time, oral contraceptives eliminate the dangers of pregnancy; women on birth control pills have mortality rates about one-half those of pregnant women. Birth control pills also decrease the risk of ovarian and endometrial cancers. No hormonal contraceptives are available for men.

Sterilization is the permanent prevention of gamete production or release. **Tubal ligation** in women usually involves sealing shut or tying off (ligating) a section of each oviduct to prevent eggs from traveling into the uterus. Similarly, **vasectomy** in men is the cutting and tying off of each vas deferens to prevent sperm from entering the urethra. Sex hormone secretion and sexual function are unaffected by both procedures, with no change in menstrual cycles in females or ejaculate volume in males. Although tubal ligation and vasectomy are considered permanent, both procedures can in many cases be reversed by microsurgery.

The termination of a pregnancy in progress is called **abortion**. Spontaneous abortion, or *miscarriage*, is very common; it occurs in as many as one-third of all pregnancies, often before the woman is even aware she is pregnant. In addition, each year about 850,000 women in the United States choose to have an abortion performed by a physician.

A drug called mifepristone, or RU486, can terminate a pregnancy nonsurgically within the first 7 weeks. RU486 blocks progesterone receptors in the uterus, thus preventing progesterone from maintaining the pregnancy. It is taken with a small amount of prostaglandin to induce uterine contractions.

Modern Reproductive Technologies

Recent scientific and technological advances have made it possible to address many reproductive problems, including genetic diseases and infertility.

Detecting Disorders During Pregnancy

Many developmental problems and genetic diseases can now be diagnosed while the fetus is in the uterus. Ultrasound imaging, which generates images using sound frequencies above the normal hearing range, is commonly used to analyze the fetus's size and condition. In amniocentesis and chorionic villus sampling, a needle is used to obtain fetal cells from fluid or tissue surrounding the embryo; these cells then provide the basis for genetic analysis (see Figure 14.19).

In the newest reproductive technology, a pregnant mother's blood is used to analyze the genome of her fetus. As discussed in Chapter 14, a pregnant woman's blood contains DNA from the growing embryo. How does it get there? The mother's blood reaches the embryo through the placenta. When cells produced by the embryo grow old, die, and break open within the placenta, the released DNA enters the mother's circulation. Although the blood also contains pieces of DNA from the mother, about 10-15% of the DNA circulating in the blood is from the fetus. Both the polymerase chain reaction (PCR) and high throughput sequencing can convert the bits of fetal DNA into useful information.

Unfortunately, almost all detectable disorders remain untreatable in the uterus, and many cannot be corrected even after birth. Genetic testing may leave parents faced with difficult decisions about whether to terminate a pregnancy or to raise a child who may have profound defects and a short life expectancy. These are complex issues that demand careful, informed thought and competent genetic counseling.

Parents will be receiving even more genetic information and confronting further questions in the near future. Indeed, in 2012 we learned of the first infant whose entire genome was known before birth. Nevertheless, completing a genome sequence does not ensure complete information. Consider, for example, Klinefelter syndrome, in which males have an extra X chromosome. This disorder is quite common, affecting 1 in 1,000 men, and can cause reduced testosterone, a feminized appearance, and infertility. However, while some men with an extra X chromosome have a debilitating disorder, others have symptoms so mild that they are unaware of the condition. For other disorders, such as diabetes, heart disease, or cancer, a genome sequence may only indicate the degree of risk. How parents will use this and other information in having and raising children is a question with no clear answers.

Infertility and In Vitro Fertilization

Infertility—an inability to conceive offspring—is quite common, affecting about one in ten couples in the United States and worldwide. The causes of infertility are varied, and the likelihood of a reproductive defect is nearly the same for men and women. For women, however, the risk of reproductive difficulties, as well as genetic abnormalities of the fetus, increases steadily past age 35. Evidence suggests that the prolonged period of time oocytes spend in meiosis is largely responsible for this increased risk.

Among preventable causes of infertility, STDs are the most significant. In women 15–24 years old, approximately 700,000 cases of chlamydia and gonorrhea are reported annually in the United States. The actual number of women infected with the chlamydia or gonorrhea bacterium is considerably higher because most women with these infections have no symptoms and are therefore unaware of their infection. Up to 40% of women who remain untreated for either chlamydia or gonorrhea develop an inflammatory disorder that can lead to infertility or to potentially fatal complications during pregnancy.

Some forms of infertility are treatable. Hormone therapy can sometimes increase sperm or egg production, and surgery can often correct ducts that formed improperly or have become blocked. In some cases, doctors recommend *in vitro* fertilization (IVF), which involves combining oocytes and sperm in the laboratory. Fertilized eggs are incubated until they have formed at least eight cells and are then transferred to the woman's uterus for implantation. If mature sperm are defective or low in number, a whole sperm or a spermatid nucleus is injected directly into an oocyte (Figure 46.21). Though costly, IVF procedures have enabled more than a million couples to conceive children.

By whatever means fertilization occurs, a developmental program follows that transforms the single-celled zygote into a multicellular organism. The mechanisms of this remarkable program of development in humans and other animals are the subject of Chapter 47.

▲ **Figure 46.21 *In vitro* fertilization (IVF).** In this form of IVF, a technician holds the egg in place with a pipette (left) and uses a very fine needle to inject one sperm into the egg cytoplasm (colorized LM).

CONCEPT CHECK 46.5

1. Why does testing for hCG (human chorionic gonadotropin) work as a pregnancy test early in pregnancy but not late in pregnancy? What is the function of hCG in pregnancy?

2. In what ways are tubal ligation and vasectomy similar?

3. **WHAT IF?** If a sperm nucleus is injected into an oocyte, what steps of gametogenesis and conception are bypassed?

For suggested answers, see Appendix A.

46 Chapter Review

SUMMARY OF KEY CONCEPTS

CONCEPT 46.1

Both asexual and sexual reproduction occur in the animal kingdom (pp. 1014–1016)

- **Sexual reproduction** requires the fusion of male and female gametes, forming a diploid **zygote**. **Asexual reproduction** is the production of offspring without gamete fusion. Mechanisms of asexual reproduction include budding, **fission**, and fragmentation with regeneration. Variations on the mode of reproduction are achieved through **parthenogenesis**, **hermaphroditism**, and sex reversal. Hormones and environmental cues control reproductive cycles.

? *Would a pair of haploid offspring produced by parthenogenesis be genetically identical? Explain.*

CONCEPT 46.2

Fertilization depends on mechanisms that bring together sperm and eggs of the same species (pp. 1016–1019)

- **Fertilization** occurs externally, when sperm and eggs are both released outside the body, or internally, when sperm deposited by the male fertilize an egg in the female reproductive system. In either case, fertilization requires coordinated timing, which may be mediated by environmental cues, pheromones, or courtship behavior. Internal fertilization is often associated with relatively fewer offspring and greater protection of offspring by the parents. Systems for gamete production and delivery range from undifferentiated cells in the body cavity to complex systems that include **gonads**, which produce gametes, and accessory tubes and glands that protect or transport gametes and embryos. Although sexual reproduction involves a partnership, it also provides an opportunity for competition between individuals and between gametes.

Complex reproductive systems in fruit flies

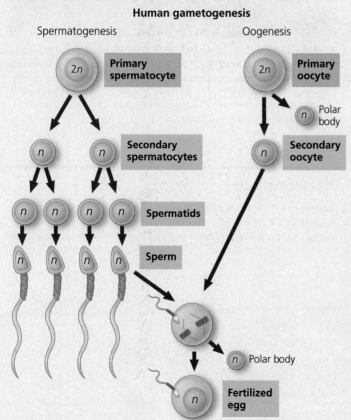

Male fruit fly

- Testis
- Vas deferens
- Ejaculatory duct
- Seminal vesicle
- Penis and claspers

Female fruit fly

- Ovary
- Oviduct
- Spermatheca
- Accessory gland
- Uterus
- Vulva

Key to labels:
Gamete production
Gamete protection and transport

> **?** *Identify which of the following, if any, are unique to mammals: a female uterus, a male vas deferens, extended internal development, and parental care of newborns.*

CONCEPT 46.3

Reproductive organs produce and transport gametes (pp. 1019–1024)

- In human males, **sperm** are produced in **testes**, which are suspended outside the body in the **scrotum**. Ducts connect the testes to internal accessory glands and to the **penis**. The reproductive system of the human female consists principally of the **labia** and the **glans** of the **clitoris** externally and the **vagina**, **uterus**, **oviducts**, and **ovaries** internally. **Eggs** are produced in the ovaries and upon fertilization develop in the uterus.
- **Gametogenesis**, or gamete production, consists of the processes of **spermatogenesis** in males and **oogenesis** in females. Human spermatogenesis is continuous and produces four sperm per meiosis. Human oogenesis is discontinuous and cyclic, generating one egg per meiosis.

Human gametogenesis

Spermatogenesis

- 2n **Primary spermatocyte**
- n / n **Secondary spermatocytes**
- n n n n **Spermatids**
- n n n n **Sperm**

Oogenesis

- 2n **Primary oocyte**
- n Polar body
- n **Secondary oocyte**
- n Polar body
- n **Fertilized egg**

> **?** *How does the difference in size and cellular contents between sperm and eggs relate to their specific functions in reproduction?*

CONCEPT 46.4

The interplay of tropic and sex hormones regulates mammalian reproduction (pp. 1024–1028)

- In mammals, GnRH from the hypothalamus regulates the release of two hormones, **FSH** and **LH**, from the anterior pituitary. In males, FSH and LH control the secretion of androgens (chiefly **testosterone**) and sperm production. In females, cyclic secretion of FSH and LH orchestrates the **ovarian** and **uterine cycles** via estrogens (primarily **estradiol**) and **progesterone**. The developing **follicle** and the **corpus luteum** also secrete hormones, which help coordinate the uterine and ovarian cycles through positive and negative feedback.

Ovarian cycle

- Growing follicle
- Maturing follicle
- Corpus luteum
- Degenerating corpus luteum

Follicular phase | Ovulation | Luteal phase

Uterine (menstrual) cycle

- Endometrium

Menstrual flow phase | Proliferative phase | Secretory phase

Day: 0 | 5 | 10 | 14 15 | 20 | 25 | 28

- In **estrous cycles**, the lining of the **endometrium** is reabsorbed, and sexual receptivity is limited to a heat period. Reproductive structures with a shared origin in development underlie many features of human sexual arousal and orgasm common to males and females.

> **?** *Why do anabolic steroids lead to reduced sperm counts?*

CONCEPT 46.5

In placental mammals, an embryo develops fully within the mother's uterus (pp. 1028–1034)

- After fertilization and the completion of meiosis in the oviduct, the zygote undergoes a series of cell divisions and develops into a **blastocyst** before implantation in the endometrium. All major organs start developing by 8 weeks. A pregnant woman's acceptance of her "foreign" offspring likely reflects partial suppression of the maternal immune response.
- **Contraception** may prevent release of mature gametes from the gonads, fertilization, or embryo implantation. **Abortion** is the termination of a pregnancy in progress.
- Reproductive technologies can help detect problems before birth and can assist infertile couples. Infertility may be treated through hormone therapy or *in vitro* fertilization.

> **?** *What route would oxygen in the mother's blood follow to arrive at a body cell of the fetus?*

LEVEL 1: KNOWLEDGE/COMPREHENSION

1. Which of the following characterizes parthenogenesis?
   a. An individual may change its sex during its lifetime.
   b. Specialized groups of cells grow into new individuals.
   c. An organism is first a male and then a female.
   d. An egg develops without being fertilized.

2. In male mammals, excretory and reproductive systems share
   a. the vas deferens.
   b. the urethra.
   c. the seminal vesicle.
   d. the prostate.

3. Which of the following is *not* properly paired?
   a. seminiferous tubule—cervix
   b. vas deferens—oviduct
   c. testosterone—estradiol
   d. scrotum—labia majora

4. Peaks of LH and FSH production occur during
   a. the menstrual flow phase of the uterine cycle.
   b. the beginning of the follicular phase of the ovarian cycle.
   c. the period just before ovulation.
   d. the secretory phase of the menstrual cycle.

5. During human gestation, rudiments of all organs develop
   a. in the first trimester.
   b. in the second trimester.
   c. in the third trimester.
   d. during the blastocyst stage.

LEVEL 2: APPLICATION/ANALYSIS

6. Which of the following is a true statement?
   a. All mammals have menstrual cycles.
   b. The endometrial lining is shed in menstrual cycles but reabsorbed in estrous cycles.
   c. Estrous cycles are more frequent than menstrual cycles.
   d. Ovulation occurs before the endometrium thickens in estrous cycles.

7. For which of the following is the number the same in human males and females?
   a. interruptions in meiotic divisions
   b. functional gametes produced by meiosis
   c. meiotic divisions required to produce each gamete
   d. different cell types produced by meiosis

8. Which statement about human reproduction is false?
   a. Fertilization occurs in the oviduct.
   b. Spermatogenesis and oogenesis require different temperatures.
   c. An oocyte completes meiosis after a sperm penetrates it.
   d. The earliest stages of spermatogenesis occur closest to the lumen of the seminiferous tubules.

LEVEL 3: SYNTHESIS/EVALUATION

9. **DRAW IT** In human spermatogenesis, mitosis of a stem cell gives rise to one cell that remains a stem cell and one cell that becomes a spermatogonium. (a) Draw four rounds of mitosis for a stem cell, and label the daughter cells. (b) For one spermatogonium, draw the cells it would produce from one round of mitosis followed by meiosis. Label the cells, and label mitosis and meiosis. (c) What would happen if stem cells divided like spermatogonia?

10. **EVOLUTION CONNECTION**
    Hermaphroditism is often found in animals that are fixed to a surface. Motile species are less often hermaphroditic. Why?

11. **SCIENTIFIC INQUIRY**
    You discover a new egg-laying worm species. You dissect four adults and find both oocytes and sperm in each. Cells outside the gonad contain five chromosome pairs. Lacking genetic variants, how would you determine whether the worms can self-fertilize?

12. **WRITE ABOUT A THEME: ENERGY AND MATTER**
    In a short essay (100–150 words), discuss how different types of energy investment by females contribute to the reproductive success of a frog, a chicken, and a human.

13. **SYNTHESIZE YOUR KNOWLEDGE**

A female Komodo dragon (*Varanus komodoensis*) kept in isolation in a zoo had progeny. Each of the offspring had two identical copies of every gene in its genome. However, the offspring were not identical to one another. Based on your understanding of parthenogenesis and meiosis, generate a hypothesis to explain these observations.

For selected answers, see Appendix A.

MasteringBiology®

Students Go to **MasteringBiology** for assignments, the eText, and the Study Area with practice tests, animations, and activities.

Instructors Go to **MasteringBiology** for automatically graded tutorials and questions that you can assign to your students, plus Instructor Resources.

KEY CONCEPTS

47.1 Fertilization and cleavage initiate embryonic development

47.2 Morphogenesis in animals involves specific changes in cell shape, position, and survival

47.3 Cytoplasmic determinants and inductive signals contribute to cell fate specification

▲ **Figure 47.1 How did a single cell develop into this intricately detailed embryo?**

A Body-Building Plan

The 7-week-old human embryo in **Figure 47.1** has already achieved a remarkable number of milestones in its development. Its heart—the red spot in the center—is beating, and a digestive tract traverses the length of its body. Its brain is forming (at the upper left in the photo), while the blocks of tissue that will give rise to the vertebrae are lined up along its back.

By combining molecular genetics with classical embryology, developmental biologists have learned a great deal about the transformation of a fertilized egg into an adult. Examining embryos from a range of species, such as the chick embryo shown at the left, biologists have long noted common features of early stages, as evident by comparing the human and chick embryos shown on this page. More recently, researchers have demonstrated that specific patterns of gene expression in a developing embryo direct cells to adopt distinct fates. Furthermore, even animals that display widely differing body plans share many basic mechanisms of development and often use a common set of regulatory genes. For example, the gene that specifies heart location in a human embryo (such as the one in Figure 47.1) has a close counterpart with a nearly identical function in the fruit fly *Drosophila melanogaster*. Researchers dubbed the fly gene *tinman*. Why? Embryos in which this gene is defective lack a heart, much like the Tin Man in *The Wizard of Oz*.

1037

In studying development, biologists frequently make use of **model organisms**, species chosen for the ease with which they can be studied in the laboratory. *Drosophila melanogaster*, for example, is a useful model organism: Its life cycle is short, and mutants can be readily identified and studied (see Chapters 15 and 18). In this chapter, we will concentrate on four other model organisms: the sea urchin, the frog, the chick, and the nematode (roundworm). We will also explore some aspects of human embryonic development. Even though humans are not model organisms, we are, of course, intensely interested in our own species.

Development occurs at many points in the life cycle of an animal (**Figure 47.2**). In a frog, for example, a major developmental period is metamorphosis, when the larva (tadpole) undergoes sweeping changes in anatomy in becoming an adult. Development occurs in the adult too, as when stem cells in the gonads produce sperm and eggs (gametes). In this chapter, our focus is on embryonic development.

Across a range of animal species, embryonic development involves common stages that occur in a set order. The first is fertilization, the fusion of sperm and egg. Development proceeds with the cleavage stage, during which a series of cell divisions divide, or cleave, the embryo into many cells. These cleavage divisions, which typically are rapid and lack accompanying cell growth, generate a hollow ball of cells called a blastula. Next, the blastula folds in on itself, rearranging into a multilayered embryo, the gastrula, in a process called gastrulation. During organogenesis, the last major stage of embryonic development, local changes in cell shape and large-scale changes in cell location generate the rudimentary organs from which adult structures grow.

Our exploration of embryonic development will begin with a description of the basic stages common to most animals. We will then look at some of the cellular mechanisms that generate body form. Finally, we will consider how a cell becomes committed to a particular specialized role.

Fertilization and cleavage initiate embryonic development

In considering the initiation of embryonic development, we'll begin with the events surrounding **fertilization**, the formation of a diploid zygote from a haploid egg and sperm.

Fertilization

Molecules and events at the egg surface play a crucial role in each step of fertilization. First, sperm dissolve or penetrate any protective layer surrounding the egg to reach the plasma membrane. Next, molecules on the sperm surface bind to receptors on the egg surface, helping ensure that fertilization involves a sperm and egg of the same species. Finally, changes at the surface of the egg prevent *polyspermy*, a condition in which multiple sperm nuclei enter the egg, fatally disrupting development.

The cell surface events that take place during fertilization have been studied most extensively in sea urchins, members of the phylum Echinodermata (see Figure 33.45). Sea urchin gametes are easy to collect, and fertilization is external. As a result, researchers can observe fertilization and subsequent development simply by combining eggs and sperm in seawater in the laboratory. Furthermore, fertilization in sea urchins provides a good general model for the same process in vertebrates.

The Acrosomal Reaction

When sea urchins release their gametes into the water, the jelly coat that surrounds the egg exudes soluble molecules that attract the sperm, which swim toward the egg. As soon as a sperm head contacts the jelly coat of an egg, molecules in the jelly coat trigger the **acrosomal reaction** in the sperm. As detailed in **Figure 47.3**, this reaction begins with the discharge of hydrolytic enzymes from the **acrosome**, a specialized vesicle at the tip of the sperm. These enzymes partially digest the jelly coat, enabling a sperm structure called the *acrosomal process* to elongate and penetrate the coat. Protein molecules on the tip of the extended acrosomal process bind to specific receptor proteins that jut out from the plasma membrane of the egg. This "lock-and-key" recognition is especially important for sea urchins and other species with external fertilization because the water into

▲ **Figure 47.2 Developmental events in the life cycle of a frog.**

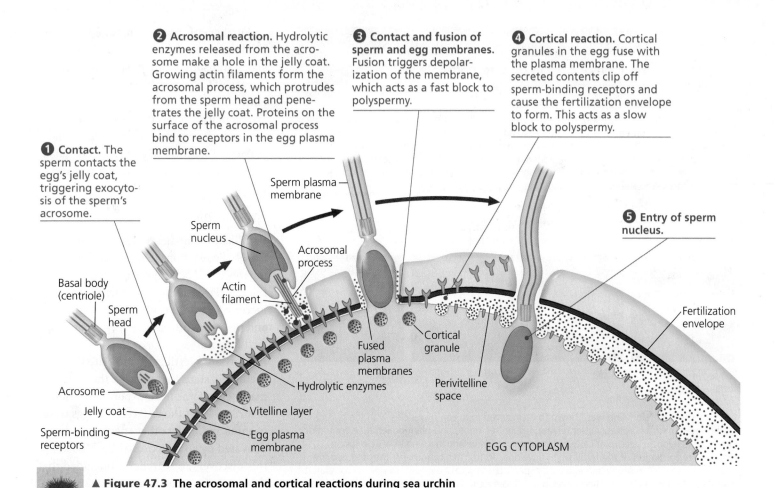

① Contact. The sperm contacts the egg's jelly coat, triggering exocytosis of the sperm's acrosome.

② Acrosomal reaction. Hydrolytic enzymes released from the acrosome make a hole in the jelly coat. Growing actin filaments form the acrosomal process, which protrudes from the sperm head and penetrates the jelly coat. Proteins on the surface of the acrosomal process bind to receptors in the egg plasma membrane.

③ Contact and fusion of sperm and egg membranes. Fusion triggers depolarization of the membrane, which acts as a fast block to polyspermy.

④ Cortical reaction. Cortical granules in the egg fuse with the plasma membrane. The secreted contents clip off sperm-binding receptors and cause the fertilization envelope to form. This acts as a slow block to polyspermy.

⑤ Entry of sperm nucleus.

Basal body (centriole)
Sperm head
Sperm nucleus
Sperm plasma membrane
Acrosomal process
Actin filament
Acrosome
Jelly coat
Hydrolytic enzymes
Sperm-binding receptors
Vitelline layer
Egg plasma membrane
Fused plasma membranes
Cortical granule
Perivitelline space
EGG CYTOPLASM
Fertilization envelope

▲ **Figure 47.3 The acrosomal and cortical reactions during sea urchin fertilization.** The events following contact of a single sperm and egg ensure that the nucleus of only one sperm enters the egg cytoplasm.

The icon above is a simplified drawing of an adult sea urchin. Throughout the chapter, this icon and others representing an adult frog, chicken, nematode, and human indicate the animals whose embryos are featured in certain figures.

which sperm and eggs are released may contain gametes of other species.

The recognition event between the sperm and egg triggers fusion of their plasma membranes. The sperm nucleus then enters the egg cytoplasm as ion channels open in the egg's plasma membrane. Sodium ions diffuse into the egg and cause *depolarization*, a decrease in the membrane potential, the charge difference across the plasma membrane (see Chapter 7). The depolarization occurs within about 1–3 seconds after a sperm binds to an egg. By preventing additional sperm from fusing with the egg's plasma membrane, this depolarization acts as the **fast block to polyspermy**.

The Cortical Reaction

Although membrane depolarization in sea urchins lasts for only a minute or so, there is a longer-lasting change that prevents polyspermy. This **slow block to polyspermy** is established by vesicles that lie just beneath the egg plasma membrane, in the rim of cytoplasm known as the cortex.

Within seconds after a sperm binds to the egg, these vesicles, called cortical granules, fuse with the egg plasma membrane (see Figure 47.3, step 4). Contents of the cortical granules are released into the space between the plasma membrane and the surrounding vitelline layer, a structure formed by the egg's extracellular matrix. Enzymes and other macromolecules from the granules then trigger a *cortical reaction*, which lifts the vitelline layer away from the egg and hardens the layer into a protective fertilization envelope. Additional enzymes clip off and release the external portions of the remaining receptor proteins, along with any attached sperm.

Formation of the fertilization envelope requires a high concentration of calcium ions (Ca^{2+}) in the egg. Does a change in the Ca^{2+} concentration trigger the cortical reaction? To answer this question, researchers used a calcium-sensitive dye to assess how Ca^{2+} is distributed in the egg before and during fertilization. As described in **Figure 47.4**, they found that Ca^{2+} spread across the egg in a wave that correlated with the appearance of the fertilization envelope.

Does the distribution of Ca²⁺ in an egg correlate with formation of the fertilization envelope?

Experiment During fertilization, fusion of cortical granules with the egg plasma membrane causes the fertilization envelope to rise and spread around the egg from the point of sperm binding. To produce this series of images, investigators mixed sea urchin eggs with sperm, waited for 10 to 60 seconds, and then added a chemical fixative, freezing cellular structures in place. The researchers then took photomicrographs of each sample. When these images are ordered according to the time of fixation, they illustrate the stages in fertilization membrane formation for a single egg.

Calcium ion (Ca^{2+}) signaling was known to be involved in fusion of vesicles with the plasma membrane during neurotransmitter release, insulin secretion, and plant pollen tube formation. Researchers hypothesized that calcium ion signaling is similarly involved in vesicle fusion required for formation of the fertilization envelope. To test this hypothesis, they tracked the release of free Ca^{2+} in sea urchin eggs after sperm binding to see if calcium release correlated with formation of the fertilization envelope. A fluorescent dye that glows when it binds free Ca^{2+} was injected into unfertilized eggs. The scientists then added sea urchin sperm and observed the eggs with a fluorescence microscope as fertilization took place, producing the results shown here.

Results A rise in cytosolic Ca^{2+} concentration began on the side of the egg where the sperm had entered and spread in a wave to the other side of the egg. Soon after the wave passed, the fertilization envelope rose.

Conclusion The researchers concluded that Ca^{2+} release is correlated with the cortical reaction and formation of the fertilization envelope, supporting their hypothesis that an increase in Ca^{2+} levels triggers cortical granule fusion.

Sources: R. Steinhardt et al., Intracellular calcium release at fertilization in the sea urchin egg, *Developmental Biology* 58:185–197 (1977). M. Hafner et al., Wave of free calcium at fertilization in the sea urchin egg visualized with Fura-2, *Cell Motility and the Cytoskeleton* 9:271–277 (1988).

(MB) See the related Experimental Inquiry Tutorial in MasteringBiology.

WHAT IF? *Suppose you were given a chemical compound that could enter the egg and bind to Ca^{2+}, blocking its function. How would you use this compound to further test the hypothesis that a rise in Ca^{2+} level triggers cortical granule fusion?*

Further studies demonstrated that the binding of sperm to the egg activates a signal transduction pathway that triggers release of Ca^{2+} into the cytosol from the endoplasmic reticulum. The resulting increase in Ca^{2+} levels causes cortical granules to fuse with the plasma membrane. A cortical reaction triggered by Ca^{2+} also occurs in vertebrates such as fishes and mammals.

Egg Activation

Fertilization initiates and speeds up metabolic reactions that trigger the onset of embryonic development, "activating" the egg. There is, for example, a marked increase in the rates of cellular respiration and protein synthesis in the egg following fertilization.

How does fertilization initiate the metabolic steps that activate the egg? A major clue came from experiments demonstrating that the unfertilized eggs of sea urchins and many other species can be activated by an injection of Ca^{2+}. Based on this discovery, researchers concluded that the rise in Ca^{2+} concentration that causes the cortical reaction also causes egg activation. Subsequent experiments revealed that artificial activation is possible even if the nucleus has been removed from the egg. This further finding indicates that the proteins and mRNAs required for activation are already present in the cytoplasm of the unfertilized egg.

Not until about 20 minutes after the sperm nucleus enters the sea urchin egg do the sperm and egg nuclei fuse. DNA synthesis then begins. The first cell division, which occurs after about 90 minutes, marks the end of the fertilization stage.

Fertilization in other species shares many features with the process in sea urchins. However, there are differences, such as the stage of meiosis the egg has reached by the time it is fertilized. Sea urchin eggs have already completed meiosis when they are released from the female. In other species, eggs are arrested at a specific stage of meiosis and do not complete the meiotic divisions until a sperm head enters. Human eggs, for example, are arrested at metaphase of meiosis II prior to sperm entry (see Figure 46.11).

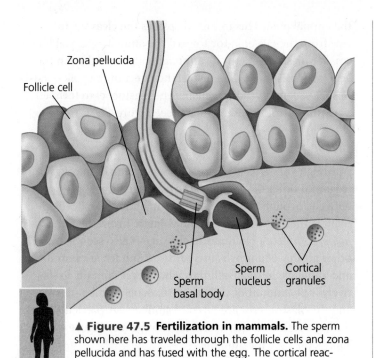

Zona pellucida

Follicle cell

Sperm basal body

Sperm nucleus

Cortical granules

▲ **Figure 47.5 Fertilization in mammals.** The sperm shown here has traveled through the follicle cells and zona pellucida and has fused with the egg. The cortical reaction has begun, initiating events that ensure that only one sperm nucleus enters the egg.

Fertilization in Mammals

Unlike sea urchins and most other marine invertebrates, terrestrial animals, including mammals, fertilize eggs internally. Support cells of the developing follicle surround the mammalian egg before and after ovulation. As shown in **Figure 47.5**, a sperm must travel through this layer of follicle cells before it reaches the **zona pellucida**, the extracellular matrix of the egg. There, the binding of a sperm to a sperm receptor induces an acrosomal reaction, facilitating sperm entry.

As in sea urchin fertilization, sperm binding triggers a cortical reaction, the release of enzymes from cortical granules to the outside of the cell. These enzymes catalyze changes in the zona pellucida, which then functions as the slow block to polyspermy. (No fast block to polyspermy has been identified in mammals.)

Overall, the process of fertilization is much slower in mammals than in sea urchins: The first cell division occurs within 12–36 hours after sperm binding in mammals, compared with about 90 minutes in sea urchins. This cell division marks the end of fertilization and the beginning of the next stage of development, cleavage.

Cleavage

Once fertilization is complete, the zygotes of many animal species undergo a succession of rapid cell divisions that characterize the **cleavage** stage of early development. During cleavage, the cell cycle consists primarily of the S (DNA synthesis) and M (mitosis) phases. The G_1 and G_2 (gap) phases are essentially skipped, and little or no protein synthesis occurs (see Figure 12.6 for a review of the cell cycle). As a result, there is no increase in mass. Instead, cleavage partitions the cytoplasm of the large fertilized egg into many smaller cells called **blastomeres**. The first five to seven cleavage divisions produce a hollow ball of cells, the **blastula**, surrounding a fluid-filled cavity called the **blastocoel** (**Figure 47.6**).

The pattern of cleavage divisions differs among species. In some cases, as in sand dollars and sea urchins, the division pattern is uniform across the embryo (see Figure 47.6). In others, including frogs, the pattern is asymmetric, with regions of the embryo differing in both the number and size of newly formed cells.

(a) Fertilized egg. Shown here is the zygote shortly before the first cleavage division, surrounded by the fertilization envelope.

(b) Four-cell stage. Remnants of the mitotic spindle can be seen between the two pairs of cells that have just completed the second cleavage division.

(c) Early blastula. After further cleavage divisions, the embryo is a multicellular ball that is still surrounded by the fertilization envelope. The blastocoel has begun to form in the center.

50 µm

(d) Later blastula. A single layer of cells surrounds a large blastocoel. (Although not visible here, the fertilization envelope is still present at this stage.)

▲ **Figure 47.6 Cleavage in an echinoderm embryo.** Cleavage is a series of mitotic cell divisions that transform the fertilized egg into a blastula, a hollow ball composed of cells called blastomeres. These light micrographs show the cleavage stages of a sand dollar embryo, which are virtually identical to those of a sea urchin.

Cleavage Pattern in Frogs

In frogs (and many other animals), cleavage is asymmetric (**Figure 47.7**), reflecting the asymmetric distribution of **yolk** (stored nutrients) across the egg. Yolk is often concentrated toward one pole, called the **vegetal pole**, and away from the opposite or **animal pole**. As a result, the two halves of the egg, called the animal and vegetal hemispheres, differ in color. As we will see shortly, the yolk greatly affects the pattern of cleavage.

When an animal cell divides, an indentation called a *cleavage furrow* forms in the cell surface as cytokinesis divides the cell in half. As shown in Figure 47.7, the first two cleavage furrows in the frog embryo form parallel to the line (or meridian) connecting the two poles. During these divisions, the main effect of yolk is to slow completion of cytokinesis. As a result, the first cleavage furrow is still dividing the yolky cytoplasm in the vegetal hemisphere when the second cell division begins. Eventually, four blastomeres of equal size extend from the animal pole to the vegetal pole.

During the third division, the yolk begins to affect the relative size of cells produced in the two hemispheres. This division is equatorial (perpendicular to the line connecting the poles) and produces an eight-celled embryo. However, as each of the four blastomeres begins this division, yolk near the vegetal pole displaces the mitotic apparatus toward the animal pole. This in turn displaces the cleavage furrow from the egg equator toward the animal pole, yielding smaller blastomeres in the animal hemisphere than in the vegetal hemisphere. The displacing effect of the yolk persists in subsequent divisions, causing the blastocoel to form entirely in the animal hemisphere (see Figure 47.7).

Cleavage Patterns in Other Animals

Although yolk affects where division occurs in the eggs of frogs and other amphibians, the cleavage furrow still passes entirely through the egg. Cleavage in amphibian development is therefore said to be **holoblastic** (from the Greek *holos*, complete). Holoblastic cleavage is also seen in many other groups of animals, including echinoderms, mammals, and annelids. In those animals whose eggs contain a relatively little amount of yolk, the blastocoel forms centrally and the blastomeres are often of similar size, particularly during the first few divisions of cleavage (see Figure 47.6). This is the case for humans.

Yolk is most plentiful and has its most pronounced effect on cleavage in the eggs of birds, other reptiles, many fishes, and insects. In these animals, the volume of yolk is so great that cleavage furrows cannot pass through it, and only the region of the egg lacking yolk undergoes cleavage. This incomplete cleavage of a yolk-rich egg is said to be **meroblastic** (from the Greek *meros*, partial).

▶ **Figure 47.7 Cleavage in a frog embryo.** The cleavage planes in the first and second divisions extend from the animal pole to the vegetal pole, but the third cleavage is perpendicular to the polar axis. In some species, the first division bisects the gray crescent, a lighter-colored region that appears opposite the site of sperm entry.

Zygote

Animal hemisphere

Cleavage furrow

Vegetal hemisphere

Gray crescent

2-cell stage forming

4-cell stage forming

Animal pole

8-cell stage

Blastocoel

Blastula (cross section)

0.25 mm

8-cell stage (viewed from the animal pole). The large amount of yolk displaces the third cleavage toward the animal pole, forming two tiers of cells. The four cells near the animal pole (closer, in this view) are smaller than the other four cells (colorized SEM).

0.25 mm

Blastula (at least 128 cells). As cleavage continues, a fluid-filled cavity, the blastocoel, forms within the embryo. Because of unequal cell division, the blastocoel is located in the animal hemisphere. Both the drawing and the micrograph (assembled from fluorescence images) show cross sections of a blastula with about 4,000 cells.

Interpreting a Change in Slope

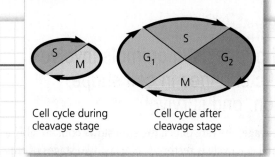

Cell cycle during
cleavage stage

Cell cycle after
cleavage stage

What Causes the End of Cleavage in a Frog Embryo? During cleavage in a frog embryo, as in many other animals, the cell cycle consists mainly of the S (DNA synthesis) and M (mitosis) phases, and there are no G_1 and G_2 phases. However, after the 12th cell division, G_1 and G_2 phases appear, and the cells grow, producing proteins and cytoplasmic organelles. These and other changes in activity mark the end of cleavage. But what triggers the change in the cell cycle?

How the Experiments Were Done Researchers tested the hypothesis that a mechanism for counting cell divisions determines when cleavage ends. They allowed frog embryos to take up radioactively labeled nucleosides, in one experiment labeling thymidine to measure DNA synthesis and in another experiment labeling uridine to measure RNA synthesis. They then repeated these two experiments in the presence of a toxin that prevents cell division by blocking cleavage furrow formation and cytokinesis.

Data from the Experiments

	Nucleic Acid Synthesis (on scale of 0–100)										
DNA Toxin added	35	48	54	71	83	85	88	87	100	96	
DNA No toxin	10	24	28	31	47	49	49	53	55	55	55
RNA Toxin added			0		6		25	27			33
RNA No toxin			0		3		14	22			27
Time Point (every 35 min)	1	2	3	4	5	6	7	8	9	10	11

Interpret the Data

1. How were the researchers able to independently measure DNA synthesis and RNA synthesis?

2. Use the data in the table to create a graph showing DNA synthesis and RNA synthesis with and without the toxin that prevents cell division. Note that time point 5 corresponds to cell division 12. For the DNA data, draw a straight line to represent the general trend for time points 1–5 and another straight line for time points 5 and later. For RNA, connect each data point with the next. Describe the changes in synthesis that occur at the end of cleavage.

3. The researchers hypothesized that the toxin increases diffusion of thymidine into the embryos. Explain their logic.

4. Do the data support the hypothesis that the timing of the end of cleavage depends on counting cell divisions? Explain.

5. In a separate experiment, researchers disrupted the block to polyspermy, generating embryos with 7 to 10 sperm nuclei. At the end of cleavage, these embryos had the same nucleus-to-cytoplasm ratio as the wild-type embryos, but cleavage ended at the 10th cell division rather than the 12th cell division. What do these results indicate about the timing of the end of cleavage?

(MB) A version of this Scientific Skills Exercise can be assigned in MasteringBiology.

Data from J. Newport and M. Kirschner, A major developmental transition in early *Xenopus* embryos: I. Characterization and timing of cellular changes at the midblastula stage, *Cell* 30:675–686 (1982).

For chickens and other birds, the part of the egg that we commonly call the yolk is actually the entire egg cell. Cell divisions are limited to a small whitish area at the animal pole. These divisions produce a cap of cells that sort into upper and lower layers. The cavity between these two layers is the avian version of the blastocoel.

In *Drosophila* and most other insects, yolk is found throughout the egg. Early in development, multiple rounds of mitosis occur without cytokinesis. In other words, no cell membranes form around the early nuclei. The first several hundred nuclei spread throughout the yolk and later migrate to the outer edge of the embryo. After several more rounds of mitosis, a plasma membrane forms around each nucleus, and the embryo, now the equivalent of a blastula, consists of a single layer of about 6,000 cells surrounding a mass of yolk (see Figure 18.22).

Regulation of Cleavage

The single nucleus in a newly fertilized egg has too little DNA to produce the amount of messenger RNA required to meet the cell's need for new proteins. Instead, initial development is carried out by RNA and proteins deposited in the egg during oogenesis. After cleavage, the egg cytoplasm has been divided among the many blastomeres, each with its own nucleus. Because each blastomere is much smaller than the entire egg, its nucleus can make enough RNA to program the cell's metabolism and further development.

Given that the number of cleavage divisions varies among animals, what mechanism determines the end of the cleavage stage? The Scientific Skills Exercise explores one of the landmark studies that addressed this question.

CONCEPT CHECK 47.1

1. How does the fertilization envelope form in sea urchins? What is its function?

2. **WHAT IF?** Predict what would happen if Ca^{2+} was injected into an unfertilized sea urchin egg.

3. **MAKE CONNECTIONS** Thinking about cell cycle control, would you expect MPF activity to remain steady during cleavage (see Figure 12.16)? Explain your logic.

For suggested answers, see Appendix A.

Morphogenesis in animals involves specific changes in cell shape, position, and survival

After cleavage, the rate of cell division slows considerably as the normal cell cycle is restored. The last two stages of embryonic development are responsible for **morphogenesis**, the cellular and tissue-based processes by which the animal body takes shape. During **gastrulation**, a set of cells at or near the surface of the blastula moves to an interior location, cell layers are established, and a primitive digestive tube is formed. Further transformation occurs during **organogenesis**, the formation of organs. We will discuss these two stages in turn, focusing in each case on the development of a few model organisms.

Gastrulation

Gastrulation is a dramatic reorganization of the hollow blastula into a two-layered or three-layered embryo called a **gastrula**. The cell layers produced are collectively called the embryonic **germ layers** (from the Latin *germen*, to sprout or germinate). In the late gastrula, **ectoderm** forms the outer layer and **endoderm** lines the embryonic digestive compartment or tract. In cnidarians and a few other radially symmetrical animals, only these two germ layers form during gastrulation. Such animals are called diploblasts (see Chapter 32). In contrast, vertebrates and other animals with bilateral symmetry are triploblasts, in which a third germ layer, the **mesoderm**, forms between the ectoderm and the endoderm.

Gastrulation in Sea Urchins

As illustrated in **Figure 47.8**, gastrulation in the sea urchin involves cell migration as well as *invagination*, the infolding of a sheet of cells into the embryo. Extensive rearrangement of cells transforms the shallow depression into a deeper, narrower, blind-ended tube called the **archenteron**. The open end of the archenteron, which will become the anus, is called the **blastopore**. A second opening,

which will become the mouth, forms later. Sea urchins and other animals in which the mouth develops from the second opening of the embryo are called *deuterostomes* (from the Greek, meaning "second mouth"). All chordates, including ourselves and other vertebrates, fall in this grouping (see Chapter 32). In contrast, mollusks, annelids, and arthropods are *protostomes*, animals in which the mouth develops from the first opening formed during gastrulation.

Gastrulation in Frogs

Each germ layer contributes to a distinct set of structures in the adult animal, as shown for vertebrates in **Figure 47.9**. Some organs and many organ systems of the adult derive from more than one germ layer. For example, the adrenal glands have both ectodermal and mesoderm tissue, and many other endocrine glands contain endodermal tissue.

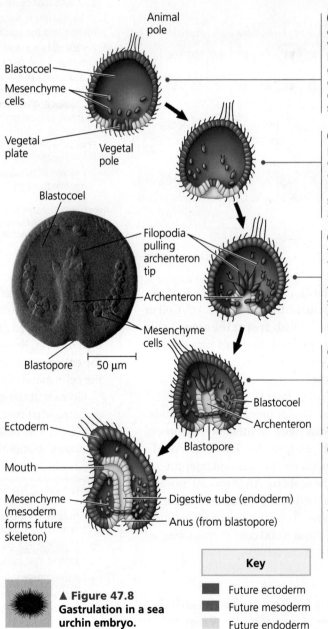

❶ A group of *mesenchyme* cells migrates from the vegetal pole of the blastula into the blastocoel. Some of these cells will eventually secrete calcium carbonate and form a simple internal skeleton.

❷ Cells at the vegetal plate flatten slightly, causing the vegetal pole of the embryo to buckle inward. This infolding of a sheet of cells is called *invagination*.

❸ Endoderm cells form the archenteron, the future digestive tube. New mesenchyme cells at the tip of the archenteron send out thin extensions (filopodia) toward the blastocoel wall (left, LM).

❹ The filopodia contract, dragging the archenteron across the blastocoel. The open end of the archenteron, which will become the anus, is called the blastospore.

❺ Fusion of the archenteron with the blastocoel wall forms the digestive tube, which now has a mouth and an anus. The gastrula has three germ layers and is covered with cilia, which will function in feeding and movement.

▲ **Figure 47.8 Gastrulation in a sea urchin embryo.**

Key
- Future ectoderm
- Future mesoderm
- Future endoderm

Frogs and other bilaterally symmetrical animals have a dorsal (top) side and a ventral (bottom) side, a left side and a right side, and an anterior (front) end and a posterior (back) end. The cell movements that begin gastrulation occur on the dorsal side of the blastula, opposite where the sperm entered the egg **(Figure 47.10)**. As in the sea urchin, the frog's anus develops from the blastopore, and the mouth eventually breaks through at the opposite end of the archenteron.

▼ **Figure 47.9 Major derivatives of the three embryonic germ layers in vertebrates.**

ECTODERM (outer layer of embryo)	MESODERM (middle layer of embryo)	ENDODERM (inner layer of embryo)
• Epidermis of skin and its derivatives (including sweat glands, hair follicles) • Nervous and sensory systems • Pituitary gland, adrenal medulla • Jaws and teeth • Germ cells	• Skeletal and muscular systems • Circulatory and lymphatic systems • Excretory and reproductive systems (except germ cells) • Dermis of skin • Adrenal cortex	• Epithelial lining of digestive tract and associated organs (liver, pancreas) • Epithelial lining of respiratory, excretory, and reproductive tracts and ducts • Thymus, thyroid, and parathyroid glands

▼ **Figure 47.10 Gastrulation in a frog embryo.** In the frog blastula, the blastocoel is displaced toward the animal pole and is surrounded by a wall several cells thick.

❶ Gastrulation begins when cells on the dorsal side invaginate to form a small indented crease, the blastopore. The part above the crease is called the **dorsal lip**. As the blastopore is forming, a sheet of cells begins to spread out of the animal hemisphere, rolls inward over the dorsal lip (involution), and moves into the interior (shown by the dashed arrow). In the interior, these cells will form endoderm and mesoderm, with the endodermal layer on the inside. Meanwhile, cells at the animal pole change shape and begin spreading over the outer surface.

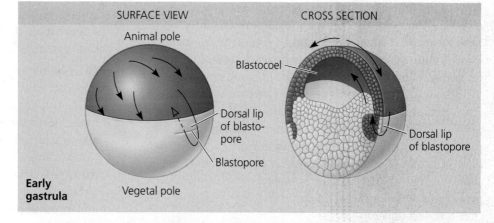

❷ The blastopore extends around both sides of the embryo as more cells invaginate. When the ends meet, the blastopore forms a circle that becomes smaller as ectoderm spreads downward over the surface. Internally, continued involution expands the endoderm and mesoderm; an archenteron forms and grows as the blastocoel shrinks and eventually disappears.

❸ Late in gastrulation, the cells remaining on the surface make up the ectoderm. The endoderm is the innermost layer, and the mesoderm lies between the ectoderm and endoderm. The circular blastopore surrounds a plug of yolk-filled cells.

Key

- Future ectoderm
- Future mesoderm
- Future endoderm

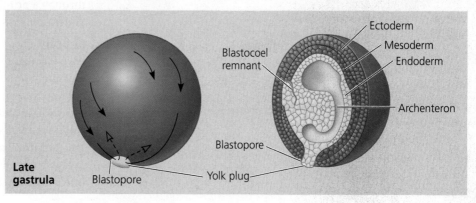

Gastrulation in Chicks

The starting point for gastrulation in chicks is an embryo consisting of upper and lower layers—known as the *epiblast* and *hypoblast*—lying atop a yolk mass. All the cells that will form the embryo come from the epiblast. During gastrulation, some epiblast cells move toward the midline of the blastoderm, detach, and move inward toward the yolk **(Figure 47.11)**. The pileup of cells moving inward at the blastoderm's midline produces a thickening called the **primitive streak**. Some of these cells move downward and form endoderm, pushing aside the hypoblast cells, while others migrate laterally (sideways) and form mesoderm. The cells left behind on the surface of the embryo at the end of gastrulation will become ectoderm. The hypoblast cells later segregate from the endoderm and eventually form part of the sac that surrounds the yolk and also part of the stalk that connects the yolk mass to the embryo.

Over the course of chick gastrulation, the primitive streak lengthens and narrows. This shape change results from a movement and sorting of cells called convergent extension. We'll explore the mechanism of this process shortly, when we examine how form and shape arise in development.

Although different terms describe gastrulation in different vertebrate species, the rearrangements and movements of cells exhibit a number of fundamental similarities. In particular, the primitive streak, shown in Figure 47.11 for the chick embryo, is the counterpart of the blastopore lip, shown in Figure 47.10 for the frog embryo. Formation of a primitive streak is also central to human embryo gastrulation, our next topic.

▲ **Figure 47.11 Gastrulation in a chick embryo.** This is a cross section of a gastrulating embryo, looking toward the anterior end.

Gastrulation in Humans

Unlike the large, yolky eggs of many vertebrates, human eggs are quite small, storing little in the way of food reserves. Fertilization takes place in the oviduct, and development begins while the embryo completes its journey down the oviduct to the uterus (see Figure 46.15).

Figure 47.12 outlines development of the human embryo, starting about 6 days after fertilization. This depiction is largely based on observations of embryos from other mammals, such as the mouse, and of very early human embryos following *in vitro* fertilization.

❶ At the end of cleavage, the embryo has more than 100 cells arranged around a central cavity and has reached the uterus. At this stage, the embryo is called a **blastocyst**, the mammalian version of a blastula. Clustered at one end of the blastocyst cavity is a group of cells called the **inner cell mass**, which will develop into the embryo proper. It is the cells of the very early blastocyst stage that are the source of embryonic stem cell lines (see Concept 20.3).

❷ Embryo implantation is initiated by the **trophoblast**, the outer epithelium of the blastocyst. Enzymes secreted by the trophoblast during implantation break down molecules of the endometrium, the lining of the uterus, allowing invasion by the blastocyst. The trophoblast also extends finger-like projections that cause capillaries in the endometrium to spill out blood that can be captured by trophoblast tissues. Around the time the embryo undergoes implantation, the inner cell mass of the blastocyst forms a flat disk with an inner layer of cells, the *epiblast*, and an outer layer, the *hypoblast*. As is true for a bird embryo, the human embryo develops almost entirely from epiblast cells.

❸ Following implantation, the trophoblast continues to expand into the endometrium, and four new membranes appear. Although these **extraembryonic membranes** arise from the embryo, they enclose specialized structures located outside the embryo. As implantation is completed, gastrulation begins. Some epiblast cells remain as ectoderm on the surface, while others move inward through a primitive streak and form mesoderm and endoderm, just as in the chick (see Figure 47.11).

❹ By the end of gastrulation, the embryonic germ layers have formed. Extraembryonic mesoderm and four distinct extraembryonic membranes now surround the embryo. As development proceeds, cells of the invading trophoblast, the epiblast, and the adjacent endometrial tissue all contribute to the formation of the placenta. This vital organ mediates the exchange of nutrients, gases, and nitrogenous wastes between the developing embryo and the mother (see Figure 46.16).

1 Blastocyst reaches uterus.

- Endometrial epithelium (uterine lining)
- Inner cell mass
- Trophoblast
- Blastocoel
- Uterus

2 Blastocyst implants (7 days after fertilization).

- Maternal blood vessel
- Expanding region of trophoblast
- Epiblast
- Hypoblast
- Trophoblast

3 Extraembryonic membranes start to form (10–11 days), and gastrulation begins (13 days).

- Expanding region of trophoblast
- Amniotic cavity
- Epiblast
- Hypoblast
- Yolk sac (from hypoblast)
- Extraembryonic mesoderm cells (from epiblast)
- Chorion (from trophoblast)

4 Gastrulation has produced a three-layered embryo with four extraembryonic membranes: the amnion, chorion, yolk sac, and allantois.

- Amnion
- Chorion
- Ectoderm
- Mesoderm
- Endoderm
- Yolk sac
- Extraembryonic mesoderm
- Allantois

▲ **Figure 47.12 Four stages in the early embryonic development of a human.** The names of the tissues that develop into the embryo proper are printed in blue.

Developmental Adaptations of Amniotes

EVOLUTION Mammals and reptiles (including birds) form four extraembryonic membranes: the chorion, allantois, amnion, and yolk sac (**Figure 47.13**; see also Figure 34.25). In all these groups, such membranes provide a "life-support system" for further embryonic development. Why did this adaptation appear in the evolutionary history of reptiles and mammals,

- Chorion
- Allantois
- Amnion
- Yolk sac

▲ **Figure 47.13 The four extra-embryonic membranes in the shelled egg of a reptile.**

but not other vertebrates, such as fishes and amphibians? We can formulate a reasonable hypothesis by considering a few basic facts about embryonic development. All vertebrate embryos require an aqueous environment for their development. The embryos of fishes and amphibians usually develop in the surrounding sea or pond and need no specialized water-filled enclosure. However, the extensive colonization of land by vertebrates was possible only after the evolution of structures that would allow reproduction in dry environments. Two such structures exist today: (1) the shelled egg of birds and other reptiles as well as a few mammals (the monotremes) and (2) the uterus of marsupial and eutherian mammals. Inside the shell or uterus, the embryos of these animals are surrounded by fluid within a sac formed by one of the extraembryonic membranes, the amnion. Mammals and reptiles, including birds, are therefore called **amniotes** (see Concept 34.5).

For the most part, the extraembryonic membranes have similar functions in mammals and reptiles, consistent with a common evolutionary origin. The chorion is the site of gas exchange, and the fluid within the amnion physically protects the developing embryo. (This amniotic fluid is released from the vagina when a pregnant woman's "water breaks" before childbirth.) The allantois, which disposes of wastes in the reptilian egg, is incorporated into the umbilical cord in mammals. There it forms blood vessels that transport oxygen and nutrients from the placenta to the embryo and rid the embryo of carbon dioxide and nitrogenous wastes. The fourth extraembryonic membrane, the yolk sac, encloses yolk in the eggs of reptiles. In mammals it is a site of early formation of blood cells, which later migrate into the embryo proper. Thus, the extraembryonic membranes common to reptiles and mammals exhibit adaptations specific to development within a shelled egg or a uterus.

After gastrulation is complete and any extraembryonic membranes are formed, the next stage of embryonic development begins: organogenesis, the formation of organs.

Organogenesis

During organogenesis, regions of the three embryonic germ layers develop into the rudiments of organs. Often, cells from two or three germ layers participate in formation of a single organ, with interactions between cells of different germ layers helping to specify cell fates. Adoption of particular developmental fates may in turn cause cells to change shape or, in certain circumstances, migrate to another location in the body. To see how these processes contribute to organogenesis, we'll consider *neurulation*, the early steps in the formation of the brain and spinal cord in vertebrates.

Neurulation

Neurulation begins as cells from the dorsal mesoderm form the **notochord**, a rod that extends along the dorsal side of the chordate embryo, as seen for the frog in **Figure 47.14a**.

Signaling molecules secreted by these mesodermal cells and other tissues cause the ectoderm above the notochord to become the *neural plate*. Formation of the neural plate is thus an example of **induction**, a process in which a group of cells or tissues influences the development of another group through close-range interactions (see Figure 18.17b).

After the neural plate is formed, its cells change shape, curving the structure inward. In this way, the neural plate rolls itself into the **neural tube**, which runs along the anterior-posterior axis of the embryo **(Figure 47.14b)**. The neural tube will become the brain in the head and the spinal cord along the rest of the body. In contrast, the notochord disappears before birth, although parts persist as the inner portions of the disks in the adult spine. (These are the disks that can herniate or rupture, causing back pain.)

Neurulation, like other stages of development, is sometimes imperfect. In humans, an error in neural tube

(a) Neural plate formation. By this stage, the notochord has developed from dorsal mesoderm, and the dorsal ectoderm has thickened, forming the neural plate, in response to signals from other embryonic tissues. The neural folds are the two ridges that form the lateral edges of the neural plate. These folds are visible in the micrograph (LM) of a whole embryo.

(b) Neural tube formation. Infolding and pinching off of the neural plate generates the neural tube. Note the neural crest cells, which will migrate and form nerves, teeth, and other structures.

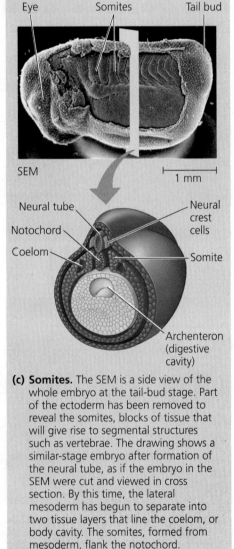

(c) Somites. The SEM is a side view of the whole embryo at the tail-bud stage. Part of the ectoderm has been removed to reveal the somites, blocks of tissue that will give rise to segmental structures such as vertebrae. The drawing shows a similar-stage embryo after formation of the neural tube, as if the embryo in the SEM were cut and viewed in cross section. By this time, the lateral mesoderm has begun to separate into two tissue layers that line the coelom, or body cavity. The somites, formed from mesoderm, flank the notochord.

▲ **Figure 47.14 Neurulation in a frog embryo.**

formation results in *spina bifida*, the most common disabling birth defect in the United States. In spina bifida, a portion of the neural tube fails to develop or close properly, leaving an opening in the spinal column and causing nerve damage. Although the opening can be surgically repaired shortly after birth, the nerve damage is permanent, resulting in varying degrees of leg paralysis.

Cell Migration in Organogenesis

Although organogenesis requires local cellular interactions and activities, some cells undergo long-range migration. For example, two sets of cells that develop near the neural tube of vertebrate embryos migrate in the body before assuming their developmental fate. The first set is a band of cells called the **neural crest**, which develops along the borders where the neural tube pinches off from the ectoderm (see Figure 47.14b). Neural crest cells subsequently migrate to many parts of the embryo, forming a variety of tissues that include peripheral nerves as well as parts of the teeth and skull bones.

A second set of migratory cells is formed when groups of cells located in strips of mesoderm lateral to the notochord separate into blocks called **somites (Figure 47.14c)**. The somites are arranged serially on both sides along the length of the notochord. Somites play a significant role in organizing the segmented structure of the vertebrate body. Parts of the somites dissociate into mesenchyme cells, which migrate individually to new locations. Some of these cells form the vertebrae. Somite cells that become mesenchymal also form the muscles associated with the vertebral column and the ribs.

By contributing to formation of vertebrae, ribs, and associated muscles, serially repeating structures of the embryo (somites) form repeated structures in the adult. Chordates, including ourselves, are thus segmented, although in the adult form the segmentation is much less obvious than in shrimp and many other segmented invertebrates.

Organogenesis in Chicks and Insects

Early organogenesis in the chick is quite similar to that in the frog. For example, the borders of the chick blastoderm fold downward and come together, pinching the embryo into a three-layered tube joined under the middle of the body to the yolk **(Figure 47.15a)**. By the time the chick embryo is 3 days old, rudiments of the major organs, including the brain, eyes, and heart, are readily apparent **(Figure 47.15b)**.

In invertebrates, organogenesis is somewhat different, which is not surprising, given that their body plans diverge significantly from those of vertebrates. In insects, for example, tissues of the nervous system form on the ventral side of the insect embryo rather than the dorsal side, as in vertebrates. The mechanism, however, is quite similar to vertebrate neurulation: Ectoderm along the anterior-posterior axis rolls into a tube inside the embryo. Furthermore, the molecular signaling pathways that bring about the events in different locations in the two groups are remarkably similar, underscoring a shared evolutionary history. Likewise, formation of other organs in invertebrates involves many of the same cellular activities observed in vertebrates: inductive interactions, cell shape changes, and cell migration.

As we have seen in our consideration of gastrulation and organogenesis, changes in cell shape and location are essential to early development. We turn now to an exploration of how these changes take place.

▶ **Figure 47.15 Organogenesis in a chick embryo.**

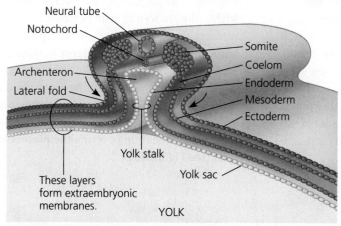

Neural tube
Notochord
Somite
Coelom
Archenteron
Endoderm
Lateral fold
Mesoderm
Ectoderm
Yolk stalk
Yolk sac
These layers form extraembryonic membranes.
YOLK

(a) Early organogenesis. The archenteron forms when lateral folds pinch the embryo away from the yolk. The embryo remains open to the yolk, attached by the yolk stalk, about midway along its length, as shown in this cross section. The notochord, neural tube, and somites subsequently develop much as they do in the frog. The germ layers lateral to the embryo itself form extraembryonic membranes.

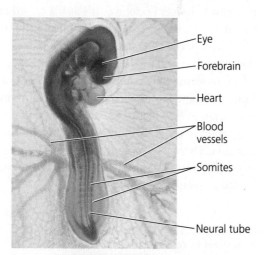

Eye
Forebrain
Heart
Blood vessels
Somites
Neural tube

(b) Late organogenesis. Rudiments of most major organs have already formed in this chick embryo, which is 3 days old and about 2–3 mm long. The extraembryonic membranes eventually are supplied by blood vessels extending from the embryo; several major blood vessels are seen here in this light micrograph (LM).

Mechanisms of Morphogenesis

Morphogenesis is a major stage of development in both animals and plants, but only in animals does it involve the *movement* of cells. The rigid cell wall that surrounds plant cells prevents complex movements like those that occur during gastrulation and organogenesis. In animals, movement of parts of a cell can bring about changes in cell shape or enable a cell to migrate from one place to another within the embryo. One set of cellular components essential to these events is the collection of microtubules and microfilaments that make up the cytoskeleton (see Table 6.1).

The Cytoskeleton in Morphogenesis

Reorganization of the cytoskeleton is a major force in changing cell shape during development. As an example, let's return to the topic of neurulation. At the onset of neural tube formation, microtubules oriented from dorsal to ventral in a sheet of ectodermal cells help lengthen the cells along that axis **(Figure 47.16)**. At the dorsal end of each cell is a bundle of actin filaments (microfilaments) oriented crosswise. These actin filaments contract, giving the cells a wedge shape that bends the ectoderm layer inward. Similar changes in cell shape occur at the hinge regions where the neural tube is pinching off from the ectoderm. However, the generation of wedge-shaped cells is not limited to neurulation or even to vertebrates. In *Drosophila* gastrulation, for instance, the formation of wedge-shaped cells along the ventral surface is responsible for invagination of a tube of cells that form the mesoderm.

The cytoskeleton also directs a morphogenetic movement called **convergent extension**, a rearrangement that causes a sheet of cells to become narrower (converge) while it becomes longer (extends). It's as if a crowd of people waiting to enter a theater for a concert begin to form a single-file line. The cells elongate, with their ends pointing in the direction they will move, and they then wedge between each other to form fewer columns of cells **(Figure 47.17)**. This is how, for example, the archenteron elongates in the sea urchin embryo (see Figure 47.8). Convergent extension is also important in other settings, such as involution in the frog gastrula. There, convergent extension changes the gastrulating embryo from a spherical shape to the rounded rectangular shape seen in Figure 47.14c.

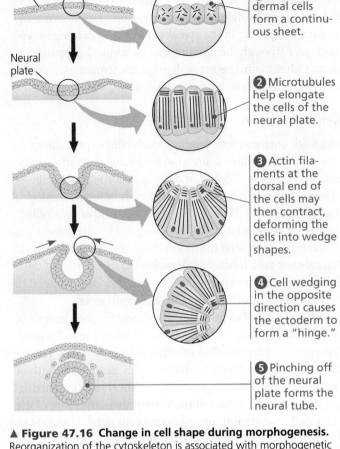

▲ **Figure 47.16 Change in cell shape during morphogenesis.** Reorganization of the cytoskeleton is associated with morphogenetic changes in embryonic tissues, as shown here for the formation of the neural tube in vertebrates.

1. Cuboidal ectodermal cells form a continuous sheet.
2. Microtubules help elongate the cells of the neural plate.
3. Actin filaments at the dorsal end of the cells may then contract, deforming the cells into wedge shapes.
4. Cell wedging in the opposite direction causes the ectoderm to form a "hinge."
5. Pinching off of the neural plate forms the neural tube.

The cytoskeleton is responsible not only for cell shape changes but also for cell migration. During organogenesis in vertebrates, cells from the neural crest and from somites migrate to locations throughout the embryo. Cells "crawl" within the embryo by using cytoskeletal fibers to extend and retract cellular protrusions. This type of motility is akin to amoeboid movement (see Figure 6.26b). Transmembrane glycoproteins called *cell adhesion molecules* play a key role in cell migration by promoting interaction between pairs of cells. Cell migration also involves the *extracellular matrix* (*ECM*), the meshwork of secreted glycoproteins and other macromolecules lying outside the plasma membranes of cells (see Figure 6.28).

▶ **Figure 47.17 Convergent extension of a sheet of cells.** In this simplified diagram, the cells elongate coordinately in a particular direction and crawl between each other (convergence) as the sheet becomes longer and narrower (extension).

Convergence
Cells elongate and crawl between each other.

Extension
The sheet of cells becomes longer and narrower.

The ECM helps to guide cells in many types of movements, such as migration of individual cells and shape changes of cell sheets. Cells that line migration pathways regulate movement of migrating cells by secreting specific molecules into the ECM. For these reasons, there is a substantial effort underway to generate an artificial ECM that can serve as a scaffold for the repair or replacement of damaged tissues or organs. One promising approach involves the use of nanofiber fabrication to produce materials that mimic the essential properties of the natural ECM.

Programmed Cell Death

Just as certain cells of the embryo are programmed to change shape or location, others are programmed to die. A type of *programmed cell death* called **apoptosis** is in fact a common feature of animal development. At various times in development, individual cells, sets of cells, or whole tissues cease to develop, die, and are engulfed by neighboring cells. In some cases, a structure functions in a larval or other immature form of the organism and then is eliminated during later development. One familiar example is provided by the cells in the tail of a tadpole, which undergo apoptosis during frog metamorphosis (see Figure 45.22).

In both nervous and immune system development, large numbers of cells undergo apoptosis. In the vertebrate nervous system, for instance, many more neurons are produced during development than exist in the adult. In general, neurons survive if they make functional connections with other neurons and die if they do not (see Concept 49.4). In the adaptive immune system, cells that are self-reactive are often eliminated by apoptosis, as are effector cells that arise after encountering a pathogen but are no longer required after the infection has been eliminated.

Some cells that undergo apoptosis don't seem to have any function in the developing embryo. Why do such cells form? The answer can be found by considering the evolution of amphibians, birds, and mammals. When these groups began to diverge during evolution, the developmental program for making a vertebrate body was already in place. The differences in present-day body forms arose through modification of that common developmental program (which is why the early embryos of all vertebrates look so similar). As these groups evolved, many structures produced by the ancestral program that no longer offered a selective advantage were targeted for cell death. For example, the shared developmental program generates webbing between the embryonic digits, but in many birds and mammals, including humans, the webbing is eliminated by apoptosis (see Figure 11.21).

As you have seen, cell behavior and the molecular mechanisms underlying it are crucial to the morphogenesis of the embryo. In the next section, you'll learn that a shared set of cellular and genetic processes ensure that the various types of cells end up in the right places in each embryo.

CONCEPT CHECK 47.2

1. In the frog embryo, convergent extension elongates the notochord. Explain how the words *convergent* and *extension* apply to this process.

2. **WHAT IF?** Predict what would happen if, just before neural tube formation, you treated frog embryos with a drug that enters all the cells of the embryo and blocks the function of microfilaments.

3. **MAKE CONNECTIONS** Unlike some other types of birth defects, neural tube defects are largely preventable. Explain (see Figure 41.4).

For suggested answers, see Appendix A.

CONCEPT 47.3

Cytoplasmic determinants and inductive signals contribute to cell fate specification

During embryonic development, cells arise by division, take up particular locations in the body, and become specialized in structure and function. Where a cell resides, how it appears, and what it does define its development fate. Developmental biologists use the terms **determination** to refer to the process by which a cell or group of cells becomes committed to a particular fate and **differentiation** to refer to the resulting specialization in structure and function. You may find it a useful analogy to think about determination being equivalent to declaring a major in college and differentiation being comparable to taking the courses required by your major.

Every diploid cell formed during an animal's development has the same genome. With the exception of certain mature immune cells, the collection of genes present in a given cell is the same throughout the cell's life. How, then, do cells acquire different fates? As discussed in Concept 18.4, particular tissues, and often cells within a tissue, differ from one another by expressing distinct sets of genes from their shared genome.

A major focus of developmental biology is to uncover the mechanisms that direct the differences in gene expression underlying developmental fates. As one step toward this goal, scientists often seek to trace tissues and cell types back to their origins in the early embryo.

Fate Mapping

One way to trace the ancestry of embryonic cells is direct observation through the microscope. Such studies produced the first **fate maps**, diagrams showing the structures arising from each region of an embryo. In the 1920s, German embryologist Walther Vogt used this approach to

(a) Fate map of a frog embryo. The fates of groups of cells in a frog blastula (left) were determined in part by marking different regions of the blastula surface with nontoxic dyes of various colors. The embryos were sectioned at later stages of development, such as the neural tube stage shown on the right, and the locations of the dyed cells determined. The two embryonic stages shown here represent the result of numerous such experiments.

(b) Cell lineage analysis in a tunicate. In lineage analysis, an individual blastomere is injected with a dye during cleavage, as indicated in the drawings of 64-cell embryos of a tunicate, an invertebrate chordate (top). The dark regions in the light micrographs of larvae (bottom) correspond to the cells that developed from the two different blastomeres indicated in the drawings.

▲ **Figure 47.18 Fate mapping for two chordates.**

determine where groups of cells from the blastula end up in the gastrula **(Figure 47.18a)**. Later researchers developed techniques that allowed them to mark an individual blastomere during cleavage and then follow the marker as it was distributed to all the mitotic descendants of that cell **(Figure 47.18b)**.

A much more comprehensive approach to fate mapping has been carried out on the soil-dwelling nematode *Caenorhabditis elegans*. This roundworm is about 1 mm long, has a simple, transparent body with only a few types of cells, and develops into a mature adult hermaphrodite in only 3½ days in the laboratory. These attributes allowed Sydney Brenner, Robert Horvitz, and John Sulston to determine the complete developmental history, or *lineage*, of every cell in *C. elegans*. They found that every adult hermaphrodite has exactly 959 somatic cells, which arise from the fertilized egg in virtually the same way for every individual. Careful microscopic observations of worms at all stages of development, coupled with experiments in which particular cells or groups of cells were destroyed by a laser beam or through mutations, resulted in the cell lineage diagram shown in **Figure 47.19**. Using this cell lineage

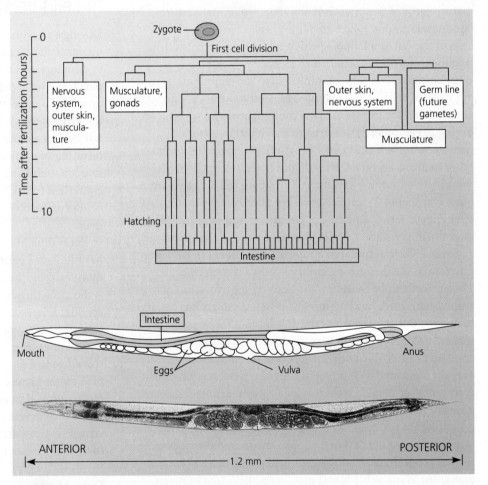

▲ **Figure 47.19 Cell lineage in *Caenorhabditis elegans*.** The *C. elegans* embryo is transparent, making it possible for researchers to trace the lineage of every cell, from the zygote to the adult worm (LM). The diagram shows a detailed lineage only for the intestine, which is derived exclusively from one of the first four cells formed from the zygote.

INTERPRET THE DATA *The pattern of divisions that produces cells of the C. elegans intestine is always the same. Is the number of divisions that gives rise to a mature cell always the same?*

diagram, you can identify all of the progeny of a single cell, just as you would use a family history to trace the descendants of one great-great-grandparent.

As an example of a particular cell fate let's consider *germ cells*, the specialized cells that give rise to eggs or sperm. In all animals studied, complexes of RNA and protein are involved in the specification of germ cell fate. In *C. elegans*, such complexes, called *P granules*, can be detected in four cells of the newly hatched larva **(Figure 47.20)** and, later, in the cells of the adult gonad that produce sperm or eggs.

Tracing the position of the P granules provides a dramatic illustration of cell fate specification during development. As shown in **Figure 47.21** ❶ and ❷, the P granules are distributed throughout the newly fertilized egg but move to the posterior end of the zygote before the first cleavage division. ❸ As a result, only the posterior of the two cells formed by the first division contains P granules. ❹ The P granules continue to be asymmetrically partitioned during subsequent divisions. Thus, the P granules act as cytoplasmic determinants (see Concept 18.4), fixing germ cell fate at the earliest stage of *C. elegans* development.

Fate mapping in *C. elegans* paved the way for major discoveries about programmed cell death. Lineage analysis demonstrated that exactly 131 cells die during normal *C. elegans* development. In the 1980s, researchers found that a mutation inactivating a single gene allows all 131 cells to live. Further research revealed that this gene is part of a pathway that controls and carries out apoptosis in a wide range of animals, including humans. In 2002, Brenner, Horvitz, and Sulston shared a Nobel Prize for their use of the *C. elegans* fate map in studies of programmed cell death and organogenesis.

Having established fate maps for early development, scientists were positioned to answer questions about underlying mechanisms, such as how the basic axes of the embryo are established, a process known as axis formation.

100 µm

Cells with P granules

▲ **Figure 47.20 Determination of germ cell fate in *C. elegans*.** Labeling with a fluorescent antibody that is specific for a *C. elegans* P granule protein (green) reveals the incorporation of P granules into four cells of the newly hatched larva (two of the four cells are visible in this view).

20 µm

❶ Newly fertilized egg

❷ Zygote prior to first division

❸ Two-cell embryo

❹ Four-cell embryo

▶ **Figure 47.21 Partitioning of P granules during *C. elegans* development.** The differential interference contrast micrographs (left) highlight the boundaries of nuclei and cells through the first two cell divisions. The fluorescence micrographs (right) show identically staged embryos labeled with a fluorescent antibody specific for a P granule protein.

Axis Formation

A body plan with bilateral symmetry is found across a range of animals, including nematodes, echinoderms, and vertebrates (see Chapter 32). As shown for a frog tadpole in **Figure 47.22a**, this body plan exhibits asymmetry along the dorsal-ventral and anterior-posterior axes. The right-left axis is largely symmetrical, as the two sides are roughly mirror images. When and how are the three axes established?

In the frog, the future position of the anterior-posterior axis is determined during oogenesis. Asymmetry in the egg is apparent in the formation of two distinct hemispheres: Dark melanin granules are embedded in the cortex of the animal hemisphere, whereas a yellow yolk fills the vegetal hemisphere. This animal-vegetal asymmetry dictates where the anterior-posterior axis forms in the embryo. Note, however, that the anterior-posterior and animal-vegetal axes are not the same; that is, the head of the embryo does not coincide with the animal pole.

Surprisingly, the dorsal-ventral axis of the frog embryo is determined at random. Once the sperm and egg fuse, the egg surface—the plasma membrane and associated cortex—rotates with respect to the inner cytoplasm, a movement called *cortical rotation*. From the perspective of the animal pole, this rotation is always toward the point of sperm entry, wherever in the animal hemisphere it occurs **(Figure 47.22b)**.

How does cortical rotation establish the dorsal-ventral axis? Cortical rotation allows molecules in one portion of the vegetal cortex to interact with molecules in the inner cytoplasm of the animal hemisphere. These inductive interactions activate regulatory proteins in specific portions of the vegetal cortex, leading to expression of different sets of genes in dorsal and ventral regions of the embryo.

In chicks, gravity is apparently involved in establishing the anterior-posterior axis as the egg travels down the hen's oviduct before being laid. Later, pH differences between the two sides of the blastoderm cells establish the dorsal-ventral axis. If the pH is artificially reversed above and below the blastoderm, the cells' fates will be reversed: The side facing the egg white will become the ventral part of the embryo, whereas the side facing the yolk will become the dorsal part.

In mammals, no polarity is obvious until after cleavage. However, the results of recent experiments suggest that the orientation of the egg and sperm nuclei before they fuse influences the location of the first cleavage plane and thus may play a role in establishing the embryonic axes. In insects, morphogen gradients establish both the anterior-posterior and dorsal-ventral axes (see Chapter 18).

Once the anterior-posterior and dorsal-ventral axes are established, the position of the left-right axis is fixed. Nevertheless, specific molecular mechanisms must establish which side is left and which is right. In vertebrates, there are marked left-right differences in the location of internal organs as well as in the organization and structure of the heart and brain.

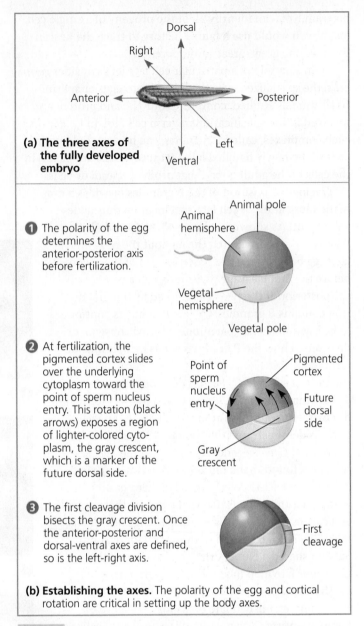

(a) The three axes of the fully developed embryo

① The polarity of the egg determines the anterior-posterior axis before fertilization.

② At fertilization, the pigmented cortex slides over the underlying cytoplasm toward the point of sperm nucleus entry. This rotation (black arrows) exposes a region of lighter-colored cytoplasm, the gray crescent, which is a marker of the future dorsal side.

③ The first cleavage division bisects the gray crescent. Once the anterior-posterior and dorsal-ventral axes are defined, so is the left-right axis.

(b) Establishing the axes. The polarity of the egg and cortical rotation are critical in setting up the body axes.

▲ **Figure 47.22 The body axes and their establishment in an amphibian.** All three axes are established before the zygote begins to undergo cleavage.

WHAT IF? *When researchers allowed normal cortical rotation to occur, and then forced the opposite rotation, the result was a two-headed embryo. How might you explain this finding, thinking about how cortical rotation influences body axis formation?*

Recent research has revealed that cilia are involved in setting up this left-right asymmetry. We will discuss this and other developmental roles of cilia at the end of this chapter.

Restricting Developmental Potential

Earlier we described determination in terms of commitment to a particular cell fate. The fertilized egg gives rise to all cell fates. How long during development do cells retain this ability? The German zoologist Hans Spemann addressed this question in 1938. By manipulating embryos to perturb normal development and then examining cell fate after the manipulation, he was able to assay a cell's *developmental potential*, the range of structures to which it can give rise **(Figure 47.23)**. The work of Spemann and others demonstrated that the first two blastomeres of the frog embryo are **totipotent**, meaning that they can each develop into all the different cell types of that species.

In mammals, embryonic cells remain totipotent through the eight-cell stage, much longer than in many other animals. Recent work, however, indicates that the very early cells (even the first two) are not actually equivalent in a normal embryo.

Rather, their totipotency when isolated likely means that the cells can regulate their fate in response to their embryonic environment. Once the 16-cell stage is reached, mammalian cells are determined to form the trophoblast or the inner cell mass. Although the cells have a limited developmental potential from this point onward, their nuclei remain totipotent, as demonstrated in transplantation and cloning experiments (see Figures 20.16 and 20.17).

The totipotency of cells early in human embryogenesis is the reason why you or a classmate may have an identical twin. Identical (monozygotic) twins result when cells or groups of cells from a single embryo become separated. If the separation occurs before the trophoblast and inner cell mass become differentiated, two embryos grow, each with its own chorion and amnion. This is the case for about a third of identical twins. For the rest, the two embryos that develop share a chorion and, in very rare cases where separation is particularly late, an amnion as well.

Regardless of how uniform or varied early embryonic cells are in a particular species, the progressive restriction of developmental potential is a general feature of development in all animals. In general, the tissue-specific fates of cells are fixed in a late gastrula, but not always so in an early gastrula. For example, if the dorsal ectoderm of an early amphibian gastrula is experimentally replaced with ectoderm from some other location in the same gastrula, the transplanted tissue forms a neural plate. But if the same experiment is performed on a late-stage gastrula, the transplanted ectoderm does not respond to its new environment and does not form a neural plate.

Cell Fate Determination and Pattern Formation by Inductive Signals

As embryonic development continues, cells influence each other's fates by induction. At the molecular level, the response to an inductive signal is usually to switch on a set of genes that make the receiving cells differentiate into a specific cell type or tissue. Here we will examine examples of this important developmental process in organizing the basic body plan of an embryo and in directing development of a vertebrate limb.

▼ **Figure 47.23** | Inquiry

How does distribution of the gray crescent affect the developmental potential of the first two daughter cells?

Experiment Hans Spemann, at the University of Freiburg-im-Breisgau, in Germany, carried out the following experiment in 1938 to test whether substances were located asymmetrically in the gray crescent.

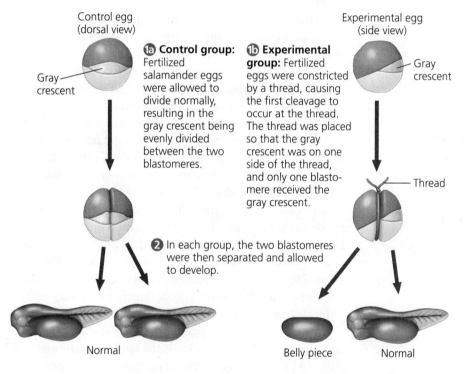

1a Control group: Fertilized salamander eggs were allowed to divide normally, resulting in the gray crescent being evenly divided between the two blastomeres.

1b Experimental group: Fertilized eggs were constricted by a thread, causing the first cleavage to occur at the thread. The thread was placed so that the gray crescent was on one side of the thread, and only one blastomere received the gray crescent.

2 In each group, the two blastomeres were then separated and allowed to develop.

Results Blastomeres that received half or all of the material in the gray crescent developed into normal embryos, but a blastomere that received none of the gray crescent gave rise to an abnormal embryo without dorsal structures. Spemann called it a "belly piece."

Conclusion The developmental potential of the two blastomeres normally formed during the first cleavage division depends on their acquisition of cytoplasmic determinants localized in the gray crescent.

Source: H. Spemann, *Embryonic Development and Induction*, Yale University Press, New Haven, CT (1938).

WHAT IF? *In a similar experiment 40 years earlier, embryologist Hans Roux allowed the first cleavage to occur and then used a needle to kill just one blastomere. The embryo that developed from the remaining blastomere (plus remnants of the dead cell) was abnormal, resembling a half-embryo. How might the presence of molecules in the dead cell explain why Roux's result differed from the control result in Spemann's experiment?*

The "Organizer" of Spemann and Mangold

Before his studies of totipotency in the fertilized frog egg, Spemann had investigated cell fate determination during gastrulation. In these experiments, he and his student Hilde Mangold transplanted tissues between early gastrulas. In their most famous such experiment, summarized in **Figure 47.24**, they made a remarkable discovery. Not only

▼ **Figure 47.24** | Inquiry

Can the dorsal lip of the blastopore induce cells in another part of the amphibian embryo to change their developmental fate?

Experiment In 1924, Hans Spemann and Hilde Mangold, at the University of Freiburg-im-Breisgau in Germany, investigated the inductive ability of the dorsal lip. Using newts, they transplanted a piece of the dorsal lip from a pigmented gastrula to the ventral side of a nonpigmented gastrula; cross sections are shown here.

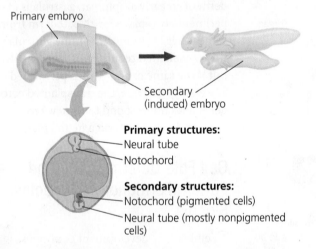

Results The recipient embryo formed a second notochord and neural tube in the region of the transplant, and eventually most of a second embryo developed. In the interior of the double embryo, secondary structures were formed partly from recipient tissue.

Primary embryo

Secondary (induced) embryo

Primary structures:
— Neural tube
— Notochord

Secondary structures:
— Notochord (pigmented cells)
— Neural tube (mostly nonpigmented cells)

Conclusion The transplanted dorsal lip was able to induce cells in a different region of the recipient to form structures different from their normal fate. In effect, the transplanted dorsal lip "organized" the later development of an entire extra embryo.

Source: H. Spemann and H. Mangold, Induction of embryonic primordia by implantation of organizers from a different species, Trans. V. Hamburger (1924). Reprinted in *International Journal of Developmental Biology* 45:13–38 (2001).

WHAT IF? *Because the transplant caused the recipient tissue to become something it would not have otherwise, a signal must have passed from the dorsal lip. If you identified a protein candidate for the signaling molecule, how would injecting it into ventral cells of a gastrula test its function?*

did a transplanted dorsal lip of the blastopore continue to be a blastopore lip, but it also triggered gastrulation of the surrounding tissue. They concluded that the dorsal lip of the blastopore in the early gastrula functions as an "organizer" of the embryo's body plan, inducing changes in surrounding tissue that direct formation of the notochord, the neural tube, and other organs.

Nearly a century later, developmental biologists are still studying the basis of induction by what is now called *Spemann's organizer*. An important clue has come from studies of a growth factor called bone morphogenetic protein 4 (BMP-4). One major function of the organizer seems to be to inactivate BMP-4 on the dorsal side of the embryo. Inactivation of BMP-4 allows cells on the dorsal side to make dorsal structures, such as the notochord and neural tube. Proteins related to BMP-4 and its inhibitors are found as well in invertebrates such as the fruit fly, where they also function in regulating the dorsal-ventral axis.

Formation of the Vertebrate Limb

Inductive signals play a major role in **pattern formation**, the process governing the arrangement of organs and tissues in their characteristic places in three-dimensional space. The molecular cues that control pattern formation, called **positional information**, tell a cell where it is with respect to the animal's body axes and help to determine how the cell and its descendants will respond to molecular signaling.

In Chapter 18, we discussed pattern formation in the development of *Drosophila*. For the study of pattern formation in vertebrates, a classic model system has been limb development in the chick. The wings and legs of chicks, like all vertebrate limbs, begin as limb buds, bumps of mesodermal tissue covered by a layer of ectoderm **(Figure 47.25a)**. Each component of a chick limb, such as a specific bone or muscle, develops with a precise location and orientation relative to three axes: proximal-distal (shoulder to fingertip), anterior-posterior (thumb to little finger), and dorsal-ventral (knuckle to palm), as shown in **Figure 47.25b**.

Two regions in a limb bud have profound effects on its development. One such region is the **apical ectodermal ridge (AER)**, a thickened area of ectoderm at the tip of the bud (see Figure 47.25a). Surgically removing the AER blocks outgrowth of the limb along the proximal-distal axis. Why? The AER secretes a protein signal called fibroblast growth factor (FGF) that promotes limb-bud outgrowth. If the AER is replaced with beads soaked with FGF, a nearly normal limb develops.

The second major limb-bud regulatory region is the **zone of polarizing activity (ZPA)**, a specialized block of mesodermal tissue (see Figure 47.25a). The ZPA regulates development along the anterior-posterior axis of the limb. Cells nearest the ZPA form posterior structures, such as the most posterior of the chick's digits (equivalent to our little finger);

cells farthest from the ZPA form anterior structures, including the most anterior digit (like our thumb). This model is based on several lines of experiments, including the tissue transplantations outlined in **Figure 47.26**.

Like the AER, the ZPA influences development by secreting a protein signal. The signal secreted by the ZPA is called Sonic hedgehog, named after both a video game character and a similar protein in *Drosophila* that also regulates

(a) Organizer regions.
Vertebrate limbs develop from protrusions called limb buds, each consisting of mesoderm cells covered by a layer of ectoderm. Two regions in each limb bud, the apical ectodermal ridge (AER, shown in this SEM) and the zone of polarizing activity (ZPA), play key roles as organizers in limb pattern formation.

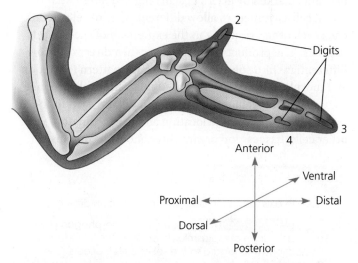

(b) Wing of chick embryo. As the bud develops into a limb, a specific pattern of tissues emerges. In the chick wing, for example, the digits are always present in the arrangement shown here. Pattern formation requires each embryonic cell to receive some kind of positional information indicating location along the three axes of the limb. The AER and ZPA secrete molecules that help provide this information. (Numbers are assigned to the digits based on a convention established for vertebrate limbs. The chicken wing has only four digits; the first digit points backward and is not shown in the diagram.)

▲ **Figure 47.25 Vertebrate limb development.**

development. Implanting cells genetically engineered to produce Sonic hedgehog into the anterior region of a normal limb bud causes formation of a mirror-image limb—just as if a ZPA had been grafted there. Furthermore, experiments with mice reveal that production of Sonic hedgehog in part of the limb bud where it is normally absent can result in extra toes.

The AER and ZPA regulate the axes of a limb bud, but what determines whether the bud develops into a forelimb or hind limb? That information is provided by spatial

▼ **Figure 47.26** Inquiry

What role does the zone of polarizing activity (ZPA) play in limb pattern formation in vertebrates?

Experiment In 1985, researchers were eager to investigate the nature of the zone of polarizing activity. They transplanted ZPA tissue from a donor chick embryo under the ectoderm in the anterior margin of a limb bud in another chick (the host).

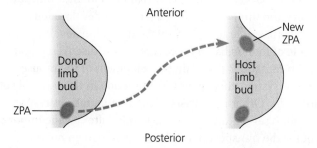

Results The host limb bud developed extra digits from host tissue in a mirror-image arrangement to the normal digits, which also formed (compare with Figure 47.24b, which shows a normal chick wing).

Conclusion The mirror-image duplication observed in this experiment suggests that ZPA cells secrete a signal that diffuses from its source and conveys positional information indicating "posterior." As the distance from the ZPA increases, the signal concentration decreases, and hence more anterior digits develop.

Source: L. S. Honig and D. Summerbell, Maps of strength of positional signaling activity in the developing chick wing bud, *Journal of Embryology and Experimental Morphology* 87:163–174 (1985).

WHAT IF? *Suppose you learned that the ZPA forms after the AER, leading you to develop the hypothesis that the AER is necessary for formation of the ZPA. If you removed the AER and looked for expression of Sonic hedgehog, how would that test your hypothesis?*

patterns of *Hox* genes, which specify different developmental fates in particular body regions (see Figure 21.18).

BMP-4, FGF, hedgehog, and Hox proteins are examples of a much larger set of molecules that govern cell fates in animals. Having mapped out many of the basic functions of these molecules in embryonic development, researchers are now addressing their role in organogenesis, focusing in particular on the development of the brain.

Cilia and Cell Fate

For many years, biologists studying organogenesis largely ignored the cellular organelles known as cilia. That is no longer the case. There is now good evidence that cilia are essential for specifying cell fate in human embryos.

Like other mammals, humans have stationary and motile cilia (see Figure 6.24). Stationary primary cilia, or *monocilia*, jut from the surface of nearly all cells, one per cell. In contrast, motile cilia are restricted to cells that propel fluid over their surface, such as the epithelial cells of airways, and on sperm (as flagella that propel sperm movement). Both stationary and motile cilia play vital roles in development.

Genetic studies provided vital clues to the developmental role of monocilia. In 2003, researchers discovered that certain mutations disrupting development of the mouse nervous system affect genes that function in the assembly of monocilia. Other geneticists found that mutations responsible for a severe kidney disease in mice alter a gene important for the transport of materials up and down monocilia. In addition, mutations in humans that block the function of monocilia were linked to cystic kidney disease.

Given that monocilia are stationary, how do they function in development? The answer is that monocilia act as antennae on the cell surface, receiving signals from multiple signaling proteins, including Sonic hedgehog. Mechanisms that regulate the set of receptor proteins that are present tune the cilium to particular signals. When the monocilia are defective, signaling is disrupted.

Insight into the role of motile cilia in development grew from the identification of Kartagener's syndrome, a particular set of medical conditions that often appear together. These conditions include male infertility due to immotile sperm and infections of the nasal sinuses and bronchi in both males and females. However, by far the most intriguing feature of Kartagener's syndrome is *situs inversus*, a reversal of the normal left-right asymmetry of the organs in the chest and abdomen **(Figure 47.27)**. The heart, for example, is on the right side rather than the left. (By itself, situs inversus causes no significant medical problems.)

Scientists studying Kartagener's syndrome came to realize that all of the associated conditions result from a defect that makes cilia immotile. Without motility, sperm tails cannot beat and airway cells cannot sweep mucus and microbes

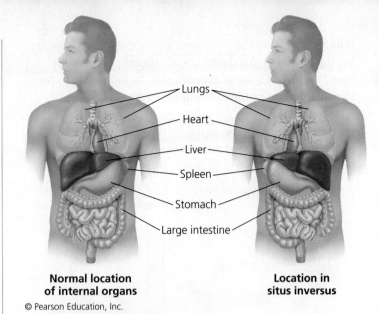

| Normal location of internal organs | Location in situs inversus |

© Pearson Education, Inc.

▲ **Figure 47.27 Situs inversus, a reversal of normal left-right asymmetry in the chest and abdomen.**

out of the airway. But what causes situs inversus in these individuals? The current model proposes that ciliary motion in a particular part of the embryo is essential for normal development. Evidence indicates that movement of the cilia generates a leftward fluid flow, breaking the symmetry between left and right sides. Without that flow, asymmetry along the left-right axis arises randomly, and half of the affected embryos develop situs inversus.

If we step back from the specification of particular cell fates to consider development as a whole, we see a sequence of events marked by cycles of signaling and differentiation. Initial cell asymmetries allow different types of cells to influence each other, resulting in the expression of specific sets of genes. The products of these genes then direct cells to differentiate into specific types. Through pattern formation and morphogenesis, differentiated cells ultimately produce a complex arrangement of tissues and organs, each functioning in its appropriate location and in coordination with other cells, tissues, and organs throughout the organism.

CONCEPT CHECK 47.3

1. How do axis formation and pattern formation differ?

2. **MAKE CONNECTIONS** How does a morphogen gradient differ from cytoplasmic determinants and inductive interactions with regard to the set of cells it affects (see Concept 18.4)?

3. **WHAT IF?** If the ventral cells of an early frog gastrula are experimentally induced to express large amounts of a protein that inhibits BMP-4, could a second embryo develop? Explain.

4. **WHAT IF?** If you removed the ZPA from a limb bud and then placed a bead soaked in Sonic hedgehog in the middle of the bud, what would be the most likely result?

For suggested answers, see Appendix A.

CONCEPT 47.1

Fertilization and cleavage initiate embryonic development (pp. 1038–1043)

- **Fertilization** forms a diploid zygote and initiates embryonic development. The **acrosomal reaction** releases hydrolytic enzymes from the sperm head that digest material surrounding the egg.

Sperm-egg fusion and depolarization of egg membrane (fast block to polyspermy)

Cortical granule release (cortical reaction)

Formation of fertilization envelope (slow block to polyspermy)

In mammalian fertilization, the cortical reaction modifies the zona pellucida as a **slow block to polyspermy**.

- Fertilization is followed by **cleavage**, a period of rapid cell division without growth, producing a large number of cells called **blastomeres**. The amount and distribution of **yolk** strongly influence the pattern of cleavage. The midblastula transition marks the end of cleavage, which in many species generates a **blastula** containing a fluid-filled cavity, the **blastocoel**.

2-cell stage forming

Animal pole

8-cell stage

Vegetal pole

Blastula

Blastocoel

? *What cell-surface event would likely fail if a sperm contacted an egg of another species?*

CONCEPT 47.2

Morphogenesis in animals involves specific changes in cell shape, position, and survival (pp. 1044–1051)

- **Gastrulation** converts the blastula to a **gastrula**, which has a primitive digestive cavity and three **germ layers: ectoderm** (blue), which forms the outer layer of the embryo, **mesoderm** (red), which forms the middle layer, and **endoderm** (yellow), which gives rise to the innermost tissues.

- Gastrulation and organogenesis in mammals resemble the processes in birds and other reptiles. After fertilization and early cleavage in the oviduct, the **blastocyst** implants in the uterus. The **trophoblast** initiates formation of the fetal portion of the placenta, and the embryo proper develops from a cell layer, the epiblast, within the blastocyst.

- The embryos of birds, other reptiles, and mammals develop within a fluid-filled sac that is contained within a shell or the uterus. In these organisms, the three germ layers produce four **extraembryonic membranes**: the amnion, chorion, yolk sac, and allantois.

- The organs of the animal body develop from specific portions of the three embryonic germ layers. Early events in **organogenesis** in vertebrates include neurulation: formation of the **notochord** by cells of the dorsal mesoderm and development of the **neural tube** from infolding of the ectodermal neural plate.

Neural tube

Notochord

Coelom

Neural tube

Notochord

Coelom

- Cytoskeletal rearrangements cause changes in the shape of cells that underlie cell movements in gastrulation and organogenesis, including invaginations and **convergent extension**. The cytoskeleton is also involved in cell migration, which relies on cell adhesion molecules and the extracellular matrix to help cells reach specific destinations. Migratory cells arise both from the neural crest and from somites.

? *How does the neural tube form? How do neural crest cells arise?*

CONCEPT 47.3

Cytoplasmic determinants and inductive signals contribute to cell fate specification (pp. 1051–1058)

- Experimentally derived **fate maps** of embryos show that specific regions of the zygote or blastula develop into specific parts of older embryos. The complete cell lineage has been worked out for *C. elegans*, revealing that programmed cell death contributes to animal development. In all species, the developmental potential of cells becomes progressively more limited as embryonic development proceeds.

- Cells in a developing embryo receive and respond to **positional information** that varies with location. This information is often in the form of signaling molecules secreted by cells in specific regions of the embryo, such as the dorsal lip of the blastopore in the amphibian gastrula and the **apical ectodermal ridge** and **zone of polarizing activity** of the vertebrate limb bud.

? *Suppose you found two classes of mouse mutations, one that affected limb development only and one that affected both limb and kidney development. Which class would be more likely to alter the function of monocilia? Explain.*

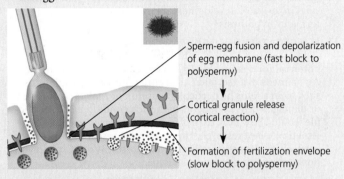

LEVEL 1: KNOWLEDGE/COMPREHENSION

1. The cortical reaction of sea urchin eggs functions directly in
   a. the formation of a fertilization envelope.
   b. the production of a fast block to polyspermy.
   c. the generation of an electrical impulse by the egg.
   d. the fusion of egg and sperm nuclei.

2. Which of the following is common to the development of both birds and mammals?
   a. holoblastic cleavage
   b. epiblast and hypoblast
   c. trophoblast
   d. gray crescent

3. The archenteron develops into
   a. the mesoderm.
   b. the endoderm.
   c. the placenta.
   d. the lumen of the digestive tract.

4. What structural adaptation in chickens allows them to lay their eggs in arid environments rather than in water?
   a. extraembryonic membranes
   b. yolk
   c. cleavage
   d. gastrulation

LEVEL 2: APPLICATION/ANALYSIS

5. If an egg cell were treated with EDTA, a chemical that binds calcium and magnesium ions,
   a. the acrosomal reaction would be blocked.
   b. the fusion of sperm and egg nuclei would be blocked.
   c. the fast block to polyspermy would not occur.
   d. the fertilization envelope would not form.

6. In humans, identical twins are possible because
   a. extraembryonic cells interact with the zygote nucleus.
   b. convergent extension occurs.
   c. early blastomeres can form a complete embryo if isolated.
   d. the gray crescent divides the dorsal-ventral axis into new cells.

7. Cells transplanted from the neural tube of a frog embryo to the ventral part of another embryo develop into nervous system tissues. This result indicates that the transplanted cells were
   a. totipotent.
   b. determined.
   c. differentiated.
   d. mesenchymal.

8. **DRAW IT** Each blue sphere in the figure below represents a cell in a cell lineage. Draw two modified versions of the cell lineage so that each version produces three cells. Use apoptosis in one of the versions, marking any dead cells with an X.

LEVEL 3: SYNTHESIS/EVALUATION

9. **EVOLUTION CONNECTION**
   Evolution in insects and vertebrates has involved the repeated duplication of body segments, followed by fusion of some segments and specialization of their structure and function. What parts of vertebrate anatomy reflect the vertebrate segmentation pattern?

10. **SCIENTIFIC INQUIRY**
    The "snout" of a frog tadpole bears a sucker. A salamander tadpole has a mustache-shaped structure called a balancer in the same area. Suppose that you perform an experiment in which you transplant ectoderm from the side of a young salamander embryo to the snout of a frog embryo. The tadpole that develops has a balancer. When you transplant ectoderm from the side of a slightly older salamander embryo to the snout of a frog embryo, the frog tadpole ends up with a patch of salamander skin on its snout. Suggest a hypothesis to explain these results in terms of developmental mechanisms. How might you test your hypothesis?

11. **SCIENCE, TECHNOLOGY, AND SOCIETY**
    Many scientists think that fetal tissue transplants offer great potential for treating Parkinson's disease, epilepsy, diabetes, Alzheimer's disease, and spinal cord injuries. Why might tissues from a fetus be particularly useful for replacing diseased or damaged cells in patients with such conditions? Some people would allow only tissues from miscarriages to be used in fetal transplant research. However, most researchers prefer to use tissues from surgically aborted fetuses. Why? Explain your position on this controversial issue.

12. **WRITE ABOUT A THEME: ORGANIZATION**
    In a short essay (100–150 words), describe how the emergent properties of the cells of the gastrula direct embryonic development.

13. **SYNTHESIZE YOUR KNOWLEDGE**

Occasionally, two-headed animals are born, such as this turtle. Thinking about the occurrence of identical twins and the property of totipotency, explain how this might occur.

For selected answers, see Appendix A.

MasteringBiology®

Students Go to **MasteringBiology** for assignments, the eText, and the Study Area with practice tests, animations, and activities.

Instructors Go to **MasteringBiology** for automatically graded tutorials and questions that you can assign to your students, plus Instructor Resources.

48

Neurons, Synapses, and Signaling

KEY CONCEPTS

48.1 Neuron structure and organization reflect function in information transfer

48.2 Ion pumps and ion channels establish the resting potential of a neuron

48.3 Action potentials are the signals conducted by axons

48.4 Neurons communicate with other cells at synapses

▲ Ribbon model of one example of a toxic peptide from cone snail venom

▲ **Figure 48.1 What makes this snail such a deadly predator?**

Lines of Communication

The tropical cone snail (*Conus geographus*) in **Figure 48.1** is small and slow-moving, yet it is a dangerous hunter. A carnivore, this marine snail hunts, kills, and dines on fish. Injecting venom with a hollow, harpoon-like tooth, the cone snail paralyzes its free-swimming prey in seconds. The venom is so deadly that unlucky scuba divers have died from just a single injection. What makes cone snail venom so fast acting and lethal? The answer is its mixture of toxin molecules, each with a specific mechanism of disabling **neurons**, the nerve cells that transfer information within the body. Because the venom almost instantaneously disrupts neuronal control of locomotion and respiration, an animal attacked by the cone snail cannot escape, defend itself, or otherwise survive.

Communication by neurons largely consists of long-distance electrical signals and short-distance chemical signals. The specialized structure of neurons allows them to use pulses of electrical current to receive, transmit, and regulate the flow of information over long distances within the body. In transferring information from one cell to another, neurons often rely on chemical signals that act over very short distances. The mixture of molecules in a cone snail's venom is particularly potent because it interferes with both electrical and chemical signaling by neurons.

All neurons transmit electrical signals within the cell in an identical manner. Thus a neuron transmitting sensory input encodes information in the same way as a neuron processing information or triggering movement. The particular connections made by the active neuron are what distinguishes the type of information being transmitted. Interpreting nerve impulses therefore involves sorting neuronal paths and connections. In more complex animals, this processing is carried out largely in groups of neurons organized into a **brain** or into simpler clusters called **ganglia**.

In this chapter, we look closely at the structure of a neuron and explore the molecules and physical principles that govern signaling by neurons. In the remaining chapters in this unit, we will examine nervous systems, information processing, and the systems that detect stimuli and that carry out responses to those stimuli. The unit concludes by looking at how these functions are integrated in producing behavior.

CONCEPT 48.1

Neuron structure and organization reflect function in information transfer

Our starting point for exploring the nervous system is the neuron, a cell type exemplifying the close fit of form and function that often arises over the course of evolution.

Neuron Structure and Function

The ability of a neuron to receive and transmit information is based on a highly specialized cellular organization **(Figure 48.2)**. Most of a neuron's organelles, including its nucleus, are located in the **cell body**. A typical neuron has numerous highly branched extensions called **dendrites** (from the Greek *dendron*, tree). Together with the cell body, the dendrites *receive* signals from other neurons. A neuron also has a single **axon**, an extension that *transmits* signals to other cells. Axons are often much longer than dendrites, and some, such as those that reach from the spinal cord of a giraffe to the muscle cells in its feet, are over a meter long. The cone-shaped base of an axon, called the axon hillock, is typically where signals that travel down the axon are generated. Near its other end, an axon usually divides into many branches.

Each branched end of an axon transmits information to another cell at a junction called a **synapse** (see Figure 48.2). The part of each axon branch that forms this specialized junction is a *synaptic terminal*. At most synapses, chemical messengers called **neurotransmitters** pass information from the transmitting neuron to the receiving cell. In describing a synapse, we refer to the transmitting neuron as the *presynaptic cell* and the neuron, muscle, or gland cell that receives the signal as the *postsynaptic cell*.

The neurons of vertebrates and most invertebrates require supporting cells called **glial cells**, or **glia** (from a Greek word meaning "glue") **(Figure 48.3)**. Glia nourish neurons, insulate the axons of neurons, and regulate the extracellular fluid surrounding neurons. In addition, glia sometimes function in replenishing certain groups of neurons and in transmitting information (as we'll discuss later in this chapter and in Chapter 49). Overall, glia outnumber neurons in the mammalian brain 10- to 50-fold.

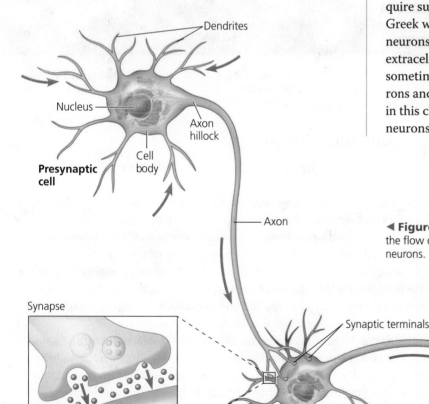

◀ **Figure 48.2 Neuron structure.** Arrows illustrate the flow of signals into, along, between, and out of neurons.

80 μm

Glia   Cell bodies of neurons

▲ **Figure 48.3 Glia in the mammalian brain.** This micrograph (a fluorescently labeled laser confocal image) shows a region of the rat brain packed with glia and interneurons. The glia are labeled red, the DNA in nuclei is labeled blue, and the dendrites of neurons are labeled green.

Introduction to Information Processing

Information processing by a nervous system occurs in three stages: sensory input, integration, and motor output. As an example, let's consider the cone snail discussed earlier, focusing on the steps involved in identifying and attacking its prey **(Figure 48.4)**. To generate sensory input to the nervous system, the snail surveys its environment with its tubelike siphon, sampling scents that might reveal a nearby fish. During the integration stage, the nervous system processes input to determine if a fish is in fact present and, if so, where the fish is located. Motor output from the processing center then initiates attack, activating neurons that trigger release of the harpoon-like tooth toward the prey.

▲ **Figure 48.4 Summary of information processing.** The cone snail's siphon acts as a sensor, transferring information to the neuronal circuits in the snail's head. If prey is detected, these circuits issue motor commands, triggering release of a harpoon-like tooth from the proboscis.

In all but the simplest animals, specialized populations of neurons handle each stage of information processing.

- **Sensory neurons**, like those in the snail's siphon, transmit information about external stimuli such as light, touch, or smell, or internal conditions such as blood pressure or muscle tension.
- Neurons in the brain or ganglia integrate (analyze and interpret) the sensory input, taking into account the immediate context and the animal's experience. The vast majority of neurons in the brain are **interneurons**, which form the local circuits connecting neurons in the brain.
- Neurons that extend out of the processing centers trigger output in the form of muscle or gland activity. For example, **motor neurons** transmit signals to muscle cells, causing them to contract.

In many animals, the neurons that carry out integration are organized in a **central nervous system (CNS)**. The neurons that carry information into and out of the CNS constitute the **peripheral nervous system (PNS)**. When bundled together, the axons of neurons form **nerves**.

Depending on its role in information processing, the shape of a neuron can vary from simple to quite complex **(Figure 48.5)**. Neurons that transmit information to many target cells do so through highly branched axons. Similarly, neurons that have highly branched dendrites can receive input through tens of thousands of synapses in some interneurons.

▲ **Figure 48.5 Structural diversity of neurons.** In these drawings of neurons, cell bodies and dendrites are black and axons are red.

1. Compare and contrast the structure and function of axons and dendrites.

2. Describe the basic pathway of information flow through neurons that causes you to turn your head when someone calls your name.

3. **WHAT IF?** How might increased branching of an axon help coordinate responses to signals communicated by the nervous system?

For suggested answers, see Appendix A.

CONCEPT 48.2

Ion pumps and ion channels establish the resting potential of a neuron

We turn now to the essential role of ions in neuronal signaling. In neurons, as in other cells, ions are unequally distributed between the interior of cells and the surrounding fluid (see Chapter 7). As a result, the inside of a cell is negatively charged relative to the outside. Because the attraction of opposite charges across the plasma membrane is a source of potential energy, this charge difference, or voltage, is called the **membrane potential**. For a resting neuron—one that is not sending a signal—the membrane potential is called the **resting potential** and is typically between −60 and −80 mV (millivolts).

Inputs from other neurons or specific stimuli cause changes in the neuron's membrane potential that act as signals, transmitting information. Fundamentally, rapid changes in membrane potential are what enable us to see the intricate structure of a spiderweb, hear a song, or ride a bicycle. Thus, to understand how neurons function, we need to examine how chemical and electrical forces form, maintain, and alter membrane potentials.

Formation of the Resting Potential

Potassium ions (K^+) and sodium ions (Na^+) play an essential role in the formation of the resting potential. These ions each have a concentration gradient across the plasma membrane of a neuron **(Table 48.1)**. In most neurons, the concentration of K^+ is higher inside the cell, while the concentration of Na^+ is higher outside. The Na^+ and K^+ gradients are maintained by the **sodium-potassium pump** (see Chapter 7). This pump uses the energy of ATP hydrolysis to actively transport Na^+ out of the cell and K^+ into the cell **(Figure 48.6)**. (There are also concentration gradients for chloride ions (Cl^-) and other anions, as shown in Table 48.1, but we can ignore these for now.)

The sodium-potassium pump transports three Na^+ out of the cell for every two K^+ that it transports in. Although this pumping generates a net export of positive charge, the resulting voltage difference is only a few millivolts. Why, then, is there a voltage difference of 60 to 80 mV in a resting neuron? The answer lies in ion movement through **ion channels**, pores formed by clusters of specialized proteins that span the membrane. Ion channels allow ions to diffuse back and forth across the membrane. As ions diffuse through channels, they carry with them units of electrical

OUTSIDE OF CELL

INSIDE OF CELL

Key

 Na^+

K^+

 Sodium-potassium pump

 Potassium channel

 Sodium channel

▲ **Figure 48.6 The basis of the membrane potential.** The sodium-potassium pump generates and maintains the ionic gradients of Na^+ and K^+ shown in Table 48.1. (Many such pump molecules are located in the plasma membrane of each cell.) Although there is a substantial concentration gradient of sodium across the membrane, very little net diffusion of Na^+ occurs because there are very few open sodium channels. In contrast, the many open potassium channels allow a significant net outflow of K^+. Because the membrane is only weakly permeable to chloride and other anions, this outflow of K^+ results in a net negative charge inside the cell.

Table 48.1	Ion Concentrations Inside and Outside of Mammalian Neurons	
Ion	**Intracellular Concentration (m*M*)**	**Extracellular Concentration (m*M*)**
Potassium (K^+)	140	5
Sodium (Na^+)	15	150
Chloride (Cl^-)	10	120
Large anions (A^-), such as proteins, inside cell	100	(not applicable)

charge. Any resulting *net* movement of positive or negative charge will generate a membrane potential, or voltage across the membrane.

The concentration gradients of ions across the plasma membrane represent a chemical form of potential energy that can be harnessed for cellular processes (see Figure 44.17). Ion channels that convert this chemical potential energy to electrical potential energy can do so because they have *selective permeability*, allowing only certain ions to pass. For example, a potassium channel allows K^+ to diffuse freely across the membrane, but not other ions, such as Na^+ or Cl^-.

Diffusion of K^+ through potassium channels that are always open (sometimes called leak channels) is critical for establishing the resting potential. The K^+ concentration is 140 mM inside the cell, but only 5 mM outside. The chemical concentration gradient thus favors a net outflow of K^+. Furthermore, a resting neuron has many open potassium channels, but very few open sodium channels (see Figure 48.6). Because Na^+ and other ions can't readily cross the membrane, K^+ outflow leads to a net negative charge inside the cell. This buildup of negative charge within the neuron is the major source of the membrane potential.

What stops the buildup of negative charge? The excess negative charges inside the cell exert an attractive force that opposes the flow of additional positively charged potassium ions out of the cell. The separation of charge (voltage) thus results in an electrical gradient that counterbalances the chemical concentration gradient of K^+.

Modeling the Resting Potential

The net flow of K^+ out of a neuron proceeds until the chemical and electrical forces are in balance. How well do these two forces account for the resting potential in a mammalian neuron? Consider a simple model consisting of two chambers separated by an artificial membrane (**Figure 48.7a**). To begin, imagine that the membrane contains many open ion channels, all of which allow only K^+ to diffuse across. To produce a K^+ concentration gradient like that of a mammalian neuron, we place a solution of 140 mM potassium chloride (KCl) in the inner chamber and 5 mM KCl in the outer chamber. The K^+ will diffuse down its concentration gradient into the outer chamber. But because the chloride ions (Cl^-) lack a means of crossing the membrane, there will be an excess of negative charge in the inner chamber.

When our model neuron reaches equilibrium, the electrical gradient will exactly balance the chemical gradient, so that no further net diffusion of K^+ occurs across the membrane. The magnitude of the membrane voltage at equilibrium for a particular ion is called that ion's **equilibrium potential** (E_{ion}). For a membrane permeable to a single type of ion, E_{ion} can be calculated using a formula called the Nernst equation. At human body temperature (37°C) and for an ion with a net charge of 1+, such as K^+ or Na^+, the Nernst equation is

$$E_{ion} = 62mV\left(\log\frac{[ion]_{outside}}{[ion]_{inside}}\right)$$

Plugging the K^+ concentrations into the Nernst equation reveals that the equilibrium potential for K^+ (E_K) is −90 mV (see Figure 48.7a). The minus sign indicates that K^+ is at equilibrium when the inside of the membrane is 90 mV more negative than the outside.

While the equilibrium potential for K^+ is −90 mV, the resting potential of a mammalian neuron is somewhat less negative. This difference reflects the small but steady movement of Na^+ across the few open sodium channels in a resting neuron. The concentration gradient of Na^+ has a direction opposite

▶ **Figure 48.7 Modeling a mammalian neuron.** Each container is divided into two chambers by an artificial membrane. Ion channels allow free diffusion for particular ions, resulting in the net ion flow represented by arrows. **(a)** The presence of open potassium channels makes the membrane selectively permeable to K^+, and the inner chamber contains a 28-fold higher concentration of K^+ than the outer chamber; at equilibrium, the inside of the membrane is −90 mV relative to the outside. **(b)** The membrane is selectively permeable to Na^+, and the inner chamber contains a tenfold lower concentration of Na^+ than the outer chamber; at equilibrium, the inside of the membrane is +62 mV relative to the outside.

WHAT IF? *Consider the effect of adding potassium or chloride channels to the membrane in (b). How would the membrane potential be affected in each case?*

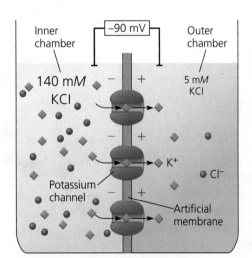

(a) Membrane selectively permeable to K^+

Nernst equation for K^+ equilibrium potential at 37°C:

$$E_K = 62\ mV\left(\log\frac{5\ mM}{140\ mM}\right) = -90\ mV$$

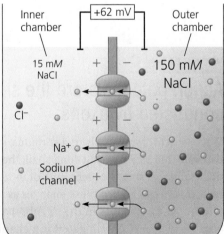

(b) Membrane selectively permeable to Na^+

Nernst equation for Na^+ equilibrium potential at 37°C:

$$E_{Na} = 62\ mV\left(\log\frac{150\ mM}{15\ mM}\right) = +62\ mV$$

to that of K$^+$ (see Table 48.1). Na$^+$ therefore diffuses into the cell, making the inside of the cell less negative. If we model a membrane in which the only open channels are selectively permeable to Na$^+$, we find that a tenfold higher concentration of Na$^+$ in the outer chamber results in an equilibrium potential (E_{Na}) of +62 mV **(Figure 48.7b)**. In an actual neuron, the resting potential (−60 to −80 mV) is much closer to E_K than to E_{Na} because there are many open potassium channels but only a small number of open sodium channels.

Because neither K$^+$ nor Na$^+$ is at equilibrium in a resting neuron, there is a net flow of each ion (a current) across the membrane. The resting potential remains steady, which means that the K$^+$ and Na$^+$ currents are equal and opposite. Ion concentrations on either side of the membrane also remain steady. Why? The resting potential arises from the net movement of far fewer ions than would be required to alter the concentration gradients.

Under conditions that allow Na$^+$ to cross the membrane more readily, the membrane potential will move toward E_{Na} and away from E_K. As you'll see in the next section, this is precisely what happens during the generation of a nerve impulse.

CONCEPT CHECK 48.2

1. Under what circumstances could ions flow through an ion channel from a region of lower ion concentration to a region of higher ion concentration?

2. **WHAT IF?** Suppose a cell's membrane potential shifts from −70 mV to −50 mV. What changes in the cell's permeability to K$^+$ or Na$^+$ could cause such a shift?

3. **MAKE CONNECTIONS** Review Figure 7.10, which illustrates the diffusion of dye molecules across a membrane. Could diffusion eliminate the concentration gradient of a dye that has a net charge? Explain.

For suggested answers, see Appendix A.

CONCEPT 48.3

Action potentials are the signals conducted by axons

When a neuron responds to a stimulus, such as the scent of fish detected by a hunting cone snail, the membrane potential changes. Using the technique of intracellular recording, researchers can record these changes as a function of time **(Figure 48.8)**. Changes in the membrane potential occur because neurons contain **gated ion channels**, ion channels that open or close in response to stimuli. The opening or closing of gated ion channels alters the membrane's permeability to particular ions, which in turn alters the membrane potential.

Intracellular Recording

Application Electrophysiologists use intracellular recording to measure the membrane potential of neurons and other cells.

Technique A microelectrode is made from a glass capillary tube filled with an electrically conductive salt solution. One end of the tube tapers to an extremely fine tip (diameter < 1 μm). While looking through a microscope, the experimenter uses a micropositioner to insert the tip of the microelectrode into a cell. A voltage recorder (usually an oscilloscope or a computer-based system) measures the voltage between the microelectrode tip inside the cell and a reference electrode placed in the solution outside the cell.

Hyperpolarization and Depolarization

When gated ion channels are stimulated to open, ions flow across the membrane, changing the membrane potential **(Figure 48.9)**. For example, opening gated potassium channels in a resting neuron increases the membrane's permeability to K$^+$. Net diffusion of K$^+$ out of the neuron increases, shifting the membrane potential toward E_K (−90 mV at 37°C). This increase in the magnitude of the membrane potential, called a **hyperpolarization**, makes the inside of the membrane more negative **(Figure 48.10a)**. In a resting neuron, hyperpolarization results from any stimulus that increases the outflow of positive ions or the inflow of negative ions.

Gate closed: No ions flow across membrane.

Gate open: Ions flow through channel.

▲ **Figure 48.9 Voltage-gated ion channel.** A change in the membrane potential in one direction (indicated by the right-pointing arrow) opens the voltage-gated channel. The opposite change (left-pointing arrow) closes the channel.

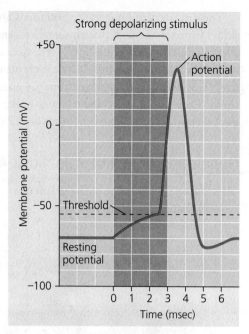

(a) Graded hyperpolarizations produced by two stimuli that increase membrane permeability to K⁺. The larger stimulus produces a larger hyperpolarization.

(b) Graded depolarizations produced by two stimuli that increase membrane permeability to Na⁺. The larger stimulus produces a larger depolarization.

(c) Action potential triggered by a depolarization that reaches the threshold.

▲ **Figure 48.10 Graded potentials and an action potential in a neuron.**

DRAW IT *Redraw the graph in (c), extending the y-axis. Then label the positions of* E_K *and* E_{Na}.

Although opening potassium channels in a resting neuron causes hyperpolarization, opening some other types of ion channels has an opposite effect, making the inside of the membrane less negative **(Figure 48.10b)**. A reduction in the magnitude of the membrane potential is a **depolarization**. In neurons, depolarization often involves gated sodium channels. If a stimulus causes gated sodium channels to open, the membrane's permeability to Na⁺ increases. Na⁺ diffuses into the cell along its concentration gradient, causing a depolarization as the membrane potential shifts toward E_{Na} (+62 mV at 37°C).

Graded Potentials and Action Potentials

Sometimes, the response to hyperpolarization or depolarization is simply a shift in the membrane potential. This shift, called a **graded potential**, has a magnitude that varies with the strength of the stimulus: A larger stimulus causes a greater change in the membrane potential (see Figure 48.10a and b). Graded potentials induce a small electrical current that leaks out of the neuron as it flows along the membrane. Graded potentials thus decay with time and with distance from their source.

If a depolarization shifts the membrane potential sufficiently, the result is a massive change in membrane voltage called an **action potential**. Unlike graded potentials, action potentials have a constant magnitude and can regenerate in adjacent regions of the membrane. Action potentials can

therefore spread along axons, making them well suited for transmitting a signal over long distances.

Action potentials arise because some of the ion channels in neurons are **voltage-gated ion channels**, opening or closing when the membrane potential passes a particular level (see Figure 48.9). If a depolarization opens voltage-gated sodium channels, the resulting flow of Na⁺ into the neuron results in further depolarization. Because the sodium channels are voltage gated, the increased depolarization causes more sodium channels to open, leading to an even greater flow of current. The result is a process of positive feedback that triggers a very rapid opening of many voltage-gated sodium channels and the marked temporary change in membrane potential that defines an action potential **(Figure 48.10c)**.

Action potentials occur whenever a depolarization increases the membrane voltage to a particular value, called the **threshold**. For many mammalian neurons, the threshold is a membrane potential of about −55 mV. Once initiated, the action potential has a magnitude that is independent of the strength of the triggering stimulus. Because action potentials either occur fully or do not occur at all, they represent an *all-or-none* response to stimuli. This all-or-none property reflects the fact that depolarization opens voltage-gated sodium channels, causing further depolarization. The positive-feedback loop of channel opening and depolarization triggers an action potential whenever the membrane potential reaches threshold.

The discovery of how action potentials are generated resulted from the work of British scientists Andrew Huxley and Alan Hodgkin in the 1940s and 1950s. Because no techniques were available for studying electrical events in small cells, they took electrical recordings from the giant neurons of the squid. Their experiments led to the model presented in the next section, which earned them a Nobel Prize.

Generation of Action Potentials: *A Closer Look*

The characteristic shape of the graph of an action potential reflects changes in membrane potential resulting from ion movement through voltage-gated sodium and potassium channels **(Figure 48.11)**. Depolarization opens both types of channels, but they respond independently and sequentially. Sodium channels open first, initiating the action potential. As the action potential proceeds, sodium channels become *inactivated*: A loop of the channel protein moves, blocking ion flow through the opening. Sodium channels remain inactivated until after the membrane returns to the resting potential and the channels close. In contrast, potassium channels open more slowly than sodium channels, but remain open and functional until the end of the action potential.

Key
- Na$^+$
- K$^+$

❸ Rising phase of the action potential
Depolarization opens most sodium channels, while the potassium channels remain closed. Na$^+$ influx makes the inside of the membrane positive with respect to the outside.

❹ Falling phase of the action potential
Most sodium channels become inactivated, blocking Na$^+$ inflow. Most potassium channels open, permitting K$^+$ outflow, which makes the inside of the cell negative again.

❷ Depolarization A stimulus opens some sodium channels. Na$^+$ inflow through those channels depolarizes the membrane. If the depolarization reaches the threshold, it triggers an action potential.

OUTSIDE OF CELL
Sodium channel
Potassium channel
INSIDE OF CELL
Inactivation loop

❶ Resting state The gated Na$^+$ and K$^+$ channels are closed. Ungated channels (not shown) maintain the resting potential.

❺ Undershoot The sodium channels close, but some potassium channels are still open. As these potassium channels close and the sodium channels become unblocked (though still closed), the membrane returns to its resting state.

▲ Figure 48.11 The role of voltage-gated ion channels in the generation of an action potential. The circled numbers on the graph in the center and the colors of the action potential phases correspond to the five diagrams showing voltage-gated sodium and potassium channels in a neuron's plasma membrane. (Ungated ion channels are not illustrated.)

ANIMATION **BioFlix** Visit the Study Area in **MasteringBiology** for the BioFlix® 3-D Animation on How Neurons Work.

To understand further how voltage-gated channels shape the action potential, consider the process as a series of stages, as depicted in Figure 48.11. ❶ When the membrane of the axon is at the resting potential, most voltage-gated sodium channels are closed. Some potassium channels are open, but most voltage-gated potassium channels are closed. ❷ When a stimulus depolarizes the membrane, some gated sodium channels open, allowing more Na^+ to diffuse into the cell. The Na^+ inflow causes further depolarization, which opens still more gated sodium channels, allowing even more Na^+ to diffuse into the cell. ❸ Once the threshold is crossed, the positive-feedback cycle rapidly brings the membrane potential close to E_{Na}. This stage of the action potential is called the *rising phase*. ❹ Two events prevent the membrane potential from actually reaching E_{Na}: Voltage-gated sodium channels inactivate soon after opening, halting Na^+ inflow; and most voltage-gated potassium channels open, causing a rapid outflow of K^+. Both events quickly bring the membrane potential back toward E_K. This stage is called the *falling phase*. ❺ In the final phase of an action potential, called the *undershoot*, the membrane's permeability to K^+ is higher than at rest, so the membrane potential is closer to E_K than it is at the resting potential. The gated potassium channels eventually close, and the membrane potential returns to the resting potential.

The sodium channels remain inactivated during the falling phase and the early part of the undershoot. As a result, if a second depolarizing stimulus occurs during this period, it will be unable to trigger an action potential. The "downtime" when a second action potential cannot be initiated is called the **refractory period**. One consequence of the refractory period is to limit the maximum frequency at which action potentials can be generated. As we will discuss shortly, the refractory period also ensures that all signals in an axon travel in one direction, from the cell body to the axon terminals.

Note that the refractory period is due to the inactivation of sodium channels, not to a change in the ion gradients across the plasma membrane. The flow of charged particles during an action potential involves far too few ions to change the concentration on either side of the membrane significantly.

Conduction of Action Potentials

Having described the events of a single action potential, we'll explore next how a series of action potentials moves a signal along an axon. At the site where an action potential is initiated (usually the axon hillock), Na^+ inflow during the rising phase creates an electrical current that depolarizes the neighboring region of the axon membrane **(Figure 48.12)**. The depolarization is large enough to reach threshold, causing an action potential in the neighboring region. This process is repeated many times along the length of the axon. Because an

An action potential is generated as Na^+ flows inward across the membrane at one location.

The depolarization of the action potential spreads to the neighboring region of the membrane, reinitiating the action potential there. To the left of this region, the membrane is repolarizing as K^+ flows outward.

The depolarization-repolarization process is repeated in the next region of the membrane. In this way, local currents of ions *across* the plasma membrane cause the action potential to be propagated *along* the length of the axon.

▲ **Figure 48.12 Conduction of an action potential.** This figure shows events at three successive times as an action potential passes from left to right. At each point along the axon, voltage-gated ion channels go through the sequence of changes shown in Figure 48.11. Membrane colors correspond to the action potential phases in Figure 48.11.

DRAW IT *For the axon segment shown, consider a point at the left end, a point in the middle, and a point at the right end. Draw a graph for each point showing the change in membrane potential over time at that point as a single nerve impulse moves from left to right across the segment.*

action potential is an all-or-none event, the magnitude and duration of the action potential are the same at each position along the axon. The net result is the movement of a nerve impulse from the cell body to the synaptic terminals, much like the cascade of events triggered by knocking over the first domino in a line.

An action potential that starts at the axon hillock moves along the axon only toward the synaptic terminals. Why? Immediately behind the traveling zone of depolarization caused by Na⁺ inflow is a zone of repolarization caused by K⁺ outflow. In the repolarized zone, the sodium channels remain inactivated. Consequently, the inward current that depolarizes the axon membrane *ahead* of the action potential cannot produce another action potential *behind* it. This prevents action potentials from traveling back toward the cell body.

For most neurons, the interval between the onset of an action potential and the beginning of the undershoot is only 1–2 milliseconds (msec). Because action potentials are so brief, a neuron can produce them as often as hundreds per second. Furthermore, the rate at which action potentials are produced conveys information about the strength of the input signal. In hearing, for example, louder sounds result in more frequent action potentials in neurons connecting the ear to the brain. Similarly, increased frequency of action potentials in a neuron that stimulates skeletal muscle tissue will increase the tension in the contracting muscle. Differences in the number of action potentials in a given time are in fact the only variable in how information is encoded and transmitted along an axon.

Gated ion channels and action potentials have a central role in nervous system activity. As a consequence, mutations in genes that encode ion channel proteins can cause disorders affecting the nerves or brain—or the muscles or heart, depending largely on where in the body the gene for the ion channel protein is expressed. For example, mutations affecting voltage-gated sodium channels in skeletal muscle cells can cause myotonia, a periodic spasming of those muscles. Mutations affecting sodium channels in the brain can cause epilepsy, in which groups of nerve cells fire simultaneously and excessively, producing seizures.

Evolutionary Adaptations of Axon Structure

EVOLUTION The rate at which the axons within nerves conduct action potentials governs how rapidly an animal can react to danger or opportunity. As a consequence, natural selection often results in anatomical adaptations that increase conduction speed. One such adaptation is a wider axon. Axon width matters because resistance to electrical current flow is inversely proportional to the cross-sectional area of a conductor (such as a wire or an axon). In the same way that a wide hose offers less resistance to the flow of water than does a narrow hose, a wide axon provides less resistance to the current associated with an action potential than does a narrow axon.

In invertebrates, conduction speed varies from several centimeters per second in very narrow axons to approximately 30 m/sec in the giant axons of some arthropods and molluscs. These giant axons (up to 1 mm wide) function in rapid behavioral responses, such as the muscle contraction that propels a hunting squid toward its prey.

Vertebrate axons have narrow diameters but can still conduct action potentials at high speed. How is this possible? The evolutionary adaptation that enables fast conduction in vertebrate axons is electrical insulation, analogous to the plastic insulation that encases many electrical wires. Insulation causes the depolarizing current associated with an action potential to travel farther along the axon interior, bringing more distant regions to the threshold sooner.

The electrical insulation that surrounds vertebrate axons is called a **myelin sheath (Figure 48.13)**. Myelin sheaths are produced by two types of glia: **oligodendrocytes** in the CNS and **Schwann cells** in the PNS. During development, these specialized glia wrap axons in many layers of membrane. The membranes forming these layers are mostly lipid, which is a poor conductor of electrical current and thus a good insulator.

0.1 μm

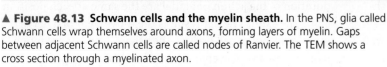

▲ **Figure 48.13 Schwann cells and the myelin sheath.** In the PNS, glia called Schwann cells wrap themselves around axons, forming layers of myelin. Gaps between adjacent Schwann cells are called nodes of Ranvier. The TEM shows a cross section through a myelinated axon.

▶ **Figure 48.14 Saltatory conduction.** In a myelinated axon, the depolarizing current during an action potential at one node of Ranvier spreads along the interior of the axon to the next node (blue arrows), where voltage-gated sodium channels enable reinitiation. Thus, the action potential appears to jump from node to node as it travels along the axon (red arrows).

Schwann cell

Depolarized region (node of Ranvier)

Cell body

Myelin sheath

Axon

In myelinated axons, voltage-gated sodium channels are restricted to gaps in the myelin sheath called **nodes of Ranvier** (see Figure 48.13). Furthermore, the extracellular fluid is in contact with the axon membrane only at the nodes. As a result, action potentials are not generated in the regions between the nodes. Rather, the inward current produced during the rising phase of the action potential at a node travels within the axon all the way to the next node. There, the current depolarizes the membrane and regenerates the action potential **(Figure 48.14)**.

Action potentials propagate more rapidly in myelinated axons because the time-consuming process of opening and closing of ion channels occurs at only a limited number of positions along the axon. This mechanism for propagating action potentials is called **saltatory conduction** (from the Latin *saltare*, to leap) because the action potential appears to jump along the axon from node to node.

The major selective advantage of myelination is its space efficiency. A myelinated axon 20 μm in diameter has a conduction speed faster than that of a squid giant axon with a diameter 40 times greater. Consequently, more than 2,000 of those myelinated axons can be packed into the space occupied by just one giant axon.

For any axon, myelinated or not, the conduction of an action potential to the end of the axon sets the stage for the next step in neuronal signaling—the transfer of information to another cell. This information handoff occurs at synapses, our next topic.

CONCEPT 48.4

Neurons communicate with other cells at synapses

In most cases, action potentials are not transmitted from neurons to other cells. However, information is transmitted, and this transmission occurs at synaptic terminals, such as those shown in **Figure 48.15**. Some synapses, called electrical synapses, contain gap junctions (see Figure 6.30), which *do* allow electrical current to flow directly from one neuron to another. In both vertebrates and invertebrates, electrical synapses synchronize the activity of neurons responsible for certain rapid, unvarying behaviors. For example, electrical synapses associated with the giant axons of squids and lobsters facilitate swift escapes from danger. There are also many electrical synapses in the vertebrate brain.

The majority of synapses are chemical synapses, which involve the release of a chemical neurotransmitter by the presynaptic neuron. At each terminal, the presynaptic neuron synthesizes the neurotransmitter and packages it in multiple membrane-enclosed compartments called *synaptic vesicles*. The arrival of an action potential at a synaptic terminal depolarizes the plasma membrane, opening voltage-gated channels that allow Ca^{2+} to diffuse into

Postsynaptic neuron

Synaptic terminals of presynaptic neurons

5 μm

▲ **Figure 48.15 Synaptic terminals on the cell body of a postsynaptic neuron (colorized SEM).**

the terminal **(Figure 48.16)**. The resulting rise in Ca^{2+} concentration in the terminal causes some of the synaptic vesicles to fuse with the terminal membrane, releasing the neurotransmitter.

Once released, the neurotransmitter diffuses across the *synaptic cleft*, the gap that separates the presynaptic neuron from the postsynaptic cell. Diffusion time is very short because the gap is less than 50 nm across. Upon reaching the postsynaptic membrane, the neurotransmitter binds to and activates a specific receptor in the membrane.

Information transfer is much more readily modified at chemical synapses than at electrical synapses. A variety of factors can affect the amount of neurotransmitter that is released or the responsiveness of the postsynaptic cell. Such modifications underlie an animal's ability to alter its

behavior in response to change and form the basis for learning and memory (as you will read in Chapter 49).

Generation of Postsynaptic Potentials

At many chemical synapses, the receptor protein that binds and responds to neurotransmitters is a **ligand-gated ion channel**, often called an *ionotropic receptor*. These receptors are clustered in the membrane of the postsynaptic cell, directly opposite the synaptic terminal. Binding of the neurotransmitter (the receptor's ligand) to a particular part of the receptor opens the channel and allows specific ions to diffuse across the postsynaptic membrane. The result is a *postsynaptic potential*, a graded potential in the postsynaptic cell.

At some synapses, the ligand-gated ion channel is permeable to both K^+ and Na^+ (see Figure 48.16). When this channel opens, the membrane potential depolarizes toward a value roughly midway between E_K and E_{Na}. Because such a depolarization brings the membrane potential

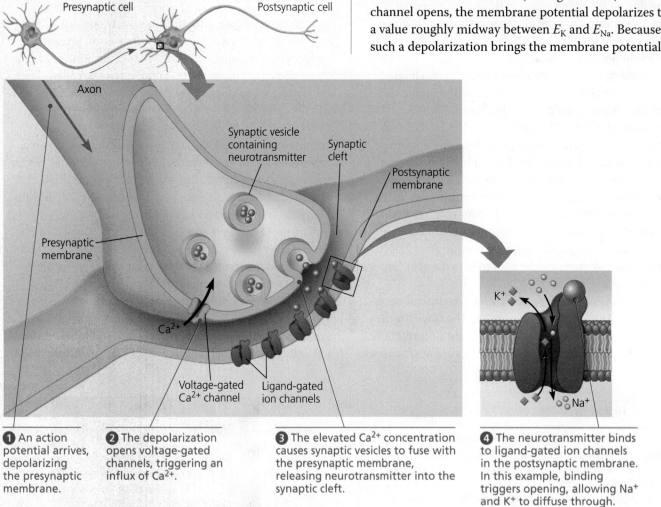

① An action potential arrives, depolarizing the presynaptic membrane.

② The depolarization opens voltage-gated channels, triggering an influx of Ca^{2+}.

③ The elevated Ca^{2+} concentration causes synaptic vesicles to fuse with the presynaptic membrane, releasing neurotransmitter into the synaptic cleft.

④ The neurotransmitter binds to ligand-gated ion channels in the postsynaptic membrane. In this example, binding triggers opening, allowing Na^+ and K^+ to diffuse through.

▲ **Figure 48.16 A chemical synapse.** This figure illustrates the sequence of events that transmits a signal across a chemical synapse. In response to binding of neurotransmitter, ligand-gated ion channels in the postsynaptic membrane open (as shown here) or, less commonly, close. Synaptic transmission ends when the neurotransmitter diffuses out of the synaptic cleft, is taken up by the synaptic terminal or by another cell, or is degraded by an enzyme.

WHAT IF? *If all the Ca^{2+} in the fluid surrounding a neuron were removed, how would this affect the transmission of information within and between neurons?*

ANIMATION ***BioFlix*** Visit the Study Area in MasteringBiology for the BioFlix® 3-D Animation on How Synapses Work.

toward threshold, it is called an **excitatory postsynaptic potential (EPSP)**.

At other synapses, the ligand-gated ion channel is selectively permeable for only K^+ or Cl^-. When such a channel opens, the postsynaptic membrane hyperpolarizes. A hyperpolarization produced in this manner is an **inhibitory postsynaptic potential (IPSP)** because it moves the membrane potential further from threshold.

Summation of Postsynaptic Potentials

The cell body and dendrites of a postsynaptic neuron may receive inputs from chemical synapses formed with hundreds or even thousands of synaptic terminals (see Figure 48.15). Often, some of these are excitatory and others inhibitory.

The magnitude of the postsynaptic potential at any one synapse varies with a number of factors, including the amount of neurotransmitter released by the presynaptic neuron. As a graded potential, a postsynaptic potential becomes smaller with distance from the synapse. Therefore, by the time a single EPSP reaches the axon hillock, it is usually too small to trigger an action potential **(Figure 48.17a)**.

On some occasions, two EPSPs occur at a single synapse in such rapid succession that the postsynaptic neuron's membrane potential has not returned to the resting potential before the arrival of the second EPSP. When that happens, the EPSPs add together, an effect called **temporal summation (Figure 48.17b)**. Moreover, EPSPs produced nearly simultaneously by *different* synapses on the same

postsynaptic neuron can also add together, an effect called **spatial summation (Figure 48.17c)**. Through spatial and temporal summation, several EPSPs can combine to depolarize the membrane at the axon hillock to threshold, causing the postsynaptic neuron to produce an action potential. Summation applies as well to IPSPs: Two or more IPSPs occurring nearly simultaneously at synapses in the same region or in rapid succession at the same synapse have a larger effect than a single IPSP. Through summation, an IPSP can also counter the effect of an EPSP **(Figure 48.17d)**.

The interplay between multiple excitatory and inhibitory inputs is the essence of integration in the nervous system. The axon hillock is the neuron's integrating center, the region where the membrane potential at any instant represents the summed effect of all EPSPs and IPSPs. Whenever the membrane potential at the axon hillock reaches threshold, an action potential is generated and travels along the axon to its synaptic terminals. After the refractory period, the neuron may produce another action potential, provided the membrane potential at the axon hillock once again reaches threshold.

Modulated Signaling at Synapses

So far, we have focused on synapses where a neurotransmitter binds directly to an ion channel, causing the channel to open. However, there are also synapses in which the receptor for the neurotransmitter is *not* part of an ion channel. At these synapses, the neurotransmitter binds

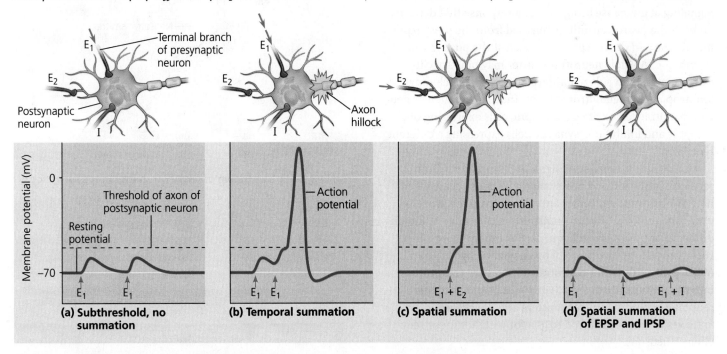

▲ **Figure 48.17 Summation of postsynaptic potentials.** These graphs trace changes in the membrane potential at a postsynaptic neuron's axon hillock. The arrows indicate times when postsynaptic potentials occur at two excitatory synapses (E_1 and E_2, green in the diagrams above the graphs) and at one inhibitory synapse (I, red). Like most EPSPs, those produced at E_1 or E_2 do not reach the threshold at the axon hillock without summation.

to a *metabotropic receptor*, so called because the resulting opening or closing of ion channels depends on one or more metabolic steps. Binding of a neurotransmitter to a metabotropic receptor activates a signal transduction pathway in the postsynaptic cell involving a second messenger (see Chapter 11). Compared with the postsynaptic potentials produced by ligand-gated channels, the effects of these second-messenger systems have a slower onset but last longer (minutes or even hours). Second messengers modulate the responsiveness of postsynaptic neurons to inputs in diverse ways, such as by altering the number of open potassium channels.

A variety of signal transduction pathways play a role in modulating synaptic transmission. One of the best-studied pathways involves cyclic AMP (cAMP) as a second messenger. For example, when the neurotransmitter norepinephrine binds to its metabotropic receptor, the neurotransmitter–receptor complex activates a G protein, which in turn activates adenylyl cyclase, the enzyme that converts ATP to cAMP (see Figure 11.11). Cyclic AMP activates protein kinase A, which phosphorylates specific ion channel proteins in the postsynaptic membrane, causing them to open or close. Because of the amplifying effect of the signal transduction pathway, the binding of a neurotransmitter molecule to a metabotropic receptor can open or close many channels.

Neurotransmitters

Signaling at a synapse brings about a response that depends on both the neurotransmitter released from the presynaptic membrane and the receptor produced at the postsynaptic membrane. A single neurotransmitter may bind specifically to more than a dozen different receptors, including ionotropic and metabotropic types. Indeed, a particular neurotransmitter can excite postsynaptic cells expressing one receptor and inhibit postsynaptic cells expressing a different receptor.

How is neurotransmitter signaling terminated? Both receptor activation and postsynaptic response cease when neurotransmitter molecules are cleared from the synaptic cleft. The removal of neurotransmitters can occur by simple diffusion or by other mechanisms. For example, some neurotransmitters are inactivated by enzymatic hydrolysis **(Figure 48.18a)**. Other neurotransmitters are recaptured into the presynaptic neuron **(Figure 48.18b)**. Once this reuptake occurs, neurotransmitters are repackaged in synaptic vesicles or transferred to glia for metabolism or recycling to neurons.

With these basic properties of neurotransmitters in mind, let's now examine some specific examples, beginning with **acetylcholine**, a common neurotransmitter in both invertebrates and vertebrates.

Acetylcholine

Acetylcholine is vital for nervous system functions that include muscle stimulation, memory formation, and learning. In vertebrates, there are two major classes of acetylcholine receptor. One is a ligand-gated ion channel, which functions at the vertebrate *neuromuscular junction*, the site where a motor neuron forms a synapse with a skeletal muscle cell. When acetylcholine released by motor neurons binds this receptor, the ion channel opens, producing an EPSP. This excitatory activity is soon terminated by acetylcholinesterase, an enzyme in the synaptic cleft that hydrolyzes the neurotransmitter.

The acetylcholine receptor active at the neuromuscular junction is also found elsewhere in the PNS, as well as in the CNS. There this ionotropic receptor can bind nicotine, a chemical found in tobacco and tobacco smoke. Nicotine's effects as a physiological and psychological stimulant result from its binding to this receptor.

A metabotropic acetylcholine receptor is found at locations that include the vertebrate CNS and heart. In heart muscle, acetylcholine released by neurons activates a signal transduction pathway. The G proteins in the pathway inhibit adenylyl cyclase and open potassium channels in the muscle cell membrane. Both effects reduce the rate at which the heart pumps. Thus, the effect of acetylcholine in heart muscle is inhibitory rather than excitatory.

(a) Enzymatic breakdown of neurotransmitter in the synaptic cleft

(b) Reuptake of neurotransmitter by presynaptic neuron

▲ **Figure 48.18 Two mechanisms of terminating neurotransmission.**

A number of toxins disrupt neurotransmission by acetylcholine. For example, the nerve gas sarin inhibits acetylcholinesterase, causing a buildup of acetylcholine to levels that trigger paralysis and typically death. In contrast, certain bacteria produce a toxin that inhibits presynaptic release of acetylcholine. This toxin causes a rare but often fatal form of food poisoning called botulism. Untreated botulism is typically fatal because muscles required for breathing fail to contract when acetylcholine release is blocked. Today, injections of the botulinum toxin, known by the trade name Botox, are used cosmetically to minimize wrinkles around the eyes or mouth by blocking transmission at synapses that control particular facial muscles.

Although acetylcholine has many roles, it is just one of more than 100 known neurotransmitters. As shown by the examples in **Table 48.2**, the rest fall into four classes: amino acids, biogenic amines, neuropeptides, and gases.

Amino Acids

Glutamate is one of several amino acids that can act as a neurotransmitter. In invertebrates, glutamate, rather than acetylcholine, is the neurotransmitter at the neuromuscular junction. In vertebrates, glutamate is the most common neurotransmitter in the CNS. Synapses at which glutamate is the neurotransmitter have a key role in the formation of long-term memory (as we will discuss in Chapter 49).

The amino acid **gamma-aminobutyric acid (GABA)** is the neurotransmitter at most inhibitory synapses in the brain. Binding of GABA to receptors in postsynaptic cells increases membrane permeability to Cl^-, resulting in an IPSP. The widely prescribed drug diazepam (Valium) reduces anxiety through binding to a site on a GABA receptor.

A third amino acid, glycine, acts at inhibitory synapses in parts of the CNS that lie outside of the brain. There, glycine binds to an ionotropic receptor that is inhibited by strychnine, a chemical often used as a rat poison.

Biogenic Amines

The neurotransmitters grouped as **biogenic amines** are synthesized from amino acids and include **norepinephrine**, which is made from tyrosine. Norepinephrine is an excitatory neurotransmitter in the autonomic nervous system, a branch of the PNS. Outside the nervous system, norepinephrine has distinct but related functions as a hormone, as does the chemically similar biogenic amine *epinephrine* (see Chapter 45).

The biogenic amines **dopamine**, made from tyrosine, and **serotonin**, made from tryptophan, are released at many sites in the brain and affect sleep, mood, attention, and learning. Some psychoactive drugs, including LSD and mescaline, apparently produce their hallucinatory effects by binding to brain receptors for these neurotransmitters.

Biogenic amines have a central role in a number of nervous system disorders and treatments (see Chapter 49). The degenerative illness Parkinson's disease is associated with a lack of dopamine in the brain. In addition, depression is often treated with drugs that increase the brain concentrations of biogenic amines. Prozac, for instance, enhances the effect of serotonin by inhibiting its reuptake after release.

Neuropeptides

Several **neuropeptides**, relatively short chains of amino acids, serve as neurotransmitters that operate via metabotropic receptors. Such peptides are typically produced by cleavage of much larger protein precursors. The neuropeptide *substance P* is a key excitatory neurotransmitter that mediates our perception of pain, while other neuropeptides, called **endorphins**, function as natural analgesics, decreasing pain perception.

Endorphins are produced in the brain during times of physical or emotional stress, such as childbirth. In addition to relieving pain, they reduce urine output, decrease respiration, and produce euphoria, as well as other emotional effects. Because opiates (drugs such as morphine and heroin) bind to the same receptor proteins as endorphins, opiates mimic endorphins and produce many of the same

Table 48.2 Major Neurotransmitters

Neurotransmitter	Structure
Acetylcholine	
Amino Acids	
Glutamate	
GABA (gamma-aminobutyric acid)	
Glycine	
Biogenic Amines	
Norepinephrine	
Dopamine	
Serotonin	
Neuropeptides (a very diverse group, only two of which are shown)	
Substance P	Arg—Pro—Lys—Pro—Gln—Gln—Phe—Phe—Gly—Leu—Met
Met-enkephalin (an endorphin)	Tyr—Gly—Gly—Phe—Met
Gases	
Nitric oxide	N=O

Interpreting Data Values Expressed in Scientific Notation

Does the Brain Have Specific Protein Receptors for Opiates?
A team of researchers were looking for opiate receptors in the mammalian brain. Knowing that the drug naloxone blocks the analgesic effect of opiates, they hypothesized that naloxone acts by binding tightly to brain opiate receptors without activating them. In this exercise, you will interpret the results of an experiment that the researchers conducted to test their hypothesis.

How the Experiment Was Done The researchers added radioactive naloxone to a protein mixture prepared from rodent brains. If the mixture contained opiate receptors or other proteins that could bind naloxone, the radioactivity would stably associate with the mixture. To determine whether the binding was due to specific opiate receptors, they tested other drugs, opiate and non-opiate, for their ability to block naloxone binding.

Radioactive naloxone

① Radioactive naloxone and a test drug are incubated with a protein mixture.

Drug

② Proteins are trapped on a filter. Bound naloxone is detected by measuring radioactivity.

Data from the Experiment

Drug	Opiate	Lowest Concentration That Blocked Naloxone Binding
Morphine	Yes	6×10^{-9} M
Methadone	Yes	2×10^{-8} M
Levorphanol	Yes	2×10^{-9} M
Phenobarbital	No	No effect at 10^{-4} M
Atropine	No	No effect at 10^{-4} M
Serotonin	No	No effect at 10^{-4} M

Interpret the Data

1. The data above are expressed in scientific notation: a numerical factor times a power of 10. Remember that a negative power of 10 means a number less than 1. For example, 10^{-1} M (molar) can also be written as 0.1 M. Write the concentrations in the table above for morphine and atropine in this alternative format.

2. Compare the concentrations listed in the table for methadone and phenobarbital. Which concentration is higher? By how much?

3. Would phenobarbital, atropine, or serotonin have blocked naloxone binding at a concentration of 10^{-5} M? Explain why or why not.

4. Which drugs blocked naloxone binding in this experiment? What do these results indicate about the brain receptors for naloxone?

5. If researchers instead used tissue from intestinal muscles rather than brains, they found no naloxone binding. What does that suggest about opiate receptors in mammalian muscle?

(MB) A version of this Scientific Skills Exercise can be assigned in MasteringBiology.

Data from C. B. Pert and S. H. Snyder, Opiate receptor: demonstration in nervous tissue, *Science* 179:1011–1014 (1973).

---

physiological effects (see Figure 2.16). In the Scientific Skills Exercise, you can interpret data from an experiment designed to search for opiate receptors in the brain.

Gases

Some vertebrate neurons release dissolved gases as neurotransmitters. In human males, for example, certain neurons release nitric oxide (NO) into the erectile tissue of the penis during sexual arousal. The resulting relaxation of smooth muscle in the blood vessel walls of the spongy erectile tissue allows the tissue to fill with blood, producing an erection. The erectile dysfunction drug Viagra works by inhibiting an enzyme that terminates the action of NO.

Unlike most neurotransmitters, NO is not stored in cytoplasmic vesicles but is instead synthesized on demand. NO diffuses into neighboring target cells, produces a change, and is broken down—all within a few seconds. In many of its targets, including smooth muscle cells, NO works like many hormones, stimulating an enzyme to synthesize a second messenger that directly affects cellular metabolism.

Although inhaling the gas carbon monoxide (CO) can be deadly, the vertebrate body uses the enzyme heme oxygenase to produce small amounts of CO, some of which acts as a neurotransmitter. In the brain, CO regulates the release of hypothalamic hormones. In the PNS, it acts as an inhibitory neurotransmitter that hyperpolarizes the plasma membrane of intestinal smooth muscle cells.

In the next chapter, we'll consider how the cellular and biochemical mechanisms we have discussed contribute to nervous system function on the system level.

CONCEPT CHECK 48.4

1. How is it possible for a particular neurotransmitter to produce opposite effects in different tissues?

2. Organophosphate pesticides work by inhibiting acetylcholinesterase, the enzyme that breaks down the neurotransmitter acetylcholine. Explain how these toxins would affect EPSPs produced by acetylcholine.

3. MAKE CONNECTIONS Name one or more membrane activities that occur both in fertilization of an egg and in neurotransmission across a synapse (see Figure 47.3).

For suggested answers, see Appendix A.

CONCEPT 48.1

Neuron structure and organization reflect function in information transfer (pp. 1062–1064)

- Most neurons have branched **dendrites** that receive signals from other neurons and an **axon** that transmits signals to other cells at **synapses**. Neurons rely on **glia** for functions that include nourishment, insulation, and regulation.

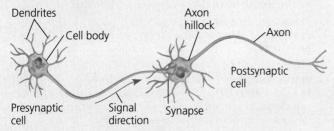

Dendrites
Cell body
Axon hillock
Axon
Postsynaptic cell
Presynaptic cell
Signal direction
Synapse

- A **central nervous system (CNS)** and a **peripheral nervous system (PNS)** process information in three stages: sensory input, integration, and motor output to effector cells.

  ? *How would severing an axon affect the flow of information in a neuron?*

CONCEPT 48.2

Ion pumps and ion channels establish the resting potential of a neuron (pp. 1064–1066)

- Ionic gradients generate a voltage difference, or **membrane potential**, across the plasma membrane of cells. The concentration of Na^+ is higher outside than inside; the reverse is true for K^+. In resting neurons, the plasma membrane has many open potassium channels but few open sodium channels. Diffusion of ions, principally K^+, through channels generates a **resting potential**, with the inside more negative than the outside.

  ? *Suppose you placed an isolated neuron in a solution similar to extracellular fluid and later transferred the neuron to a solution lacking any sodium ions. What change would you expect in the resting potential?*

CONCEPT 48.3

Action potentials are the signals conducted by axons (pp. 1066–1071)

- Neurons have gated ion channels that open or close in response to stimuli, leading to changes in the membrane potential. An increase in the magnitude of the membrane potential is a **hyperpolarization**; a decrease is a **depolarization**. Changes in membrane potential that vary continuously with the strength of a stimulus are known as **graded potentials**.
- An **action potential** is a brief, all-or-none depolarization of a neuron's plasma membrane. When a graded depolarization brings the membrane potential to **threshold**, many **voltage-gated ion channels** open, triggering an inflow of Na^+ that rapidly brings the membrane potential to a positive value. A

negative membrane potential is restored by the inactivation of sodium channels and by the opening of many voltage-gated potassium channels, which increases K^+ outflow. A **refractory period** follows, corresponding to the interval when the sodium channels are inactivated.

Action potential

Membrane potential (mV)

+50
0
−50
−100

Rising phase
Falling phase
Threshold (−55)
Resting potential
−70
Depolarization
Undershoot

Time (msec)
0 1 2 3 4 5 6

- A nerve impulse travels from the axon hillock to the synaptic terminals by propagating a series of action potentials along the axon. The speed of conduction increases with the diameter of the axon and, in many vertebrate axons, with **myelination**. Action potentials in axons insulated by myelination appear to jump from one **node of Ranvier** to the next, a process called **saltatory conduction**.

  INTERPRET THE DATA *Assuming a refractory period equal in length to the action potential (see graph above), what is the maximum frequency per unit time at which a neuron could fire action potentials?*

CONCEPT 48.4

Neurons communicate with other cells at synapses (pp. 1071–1076)

- In an electrical **synapse**, electrical current flows directly from one cell to another. In a chemical synapse, depolarization causes synaptic vesicles to fuse with the terminal membrane and release **neurotransmitter** into the synaptic cleft.
- At many synapses, the neurotransmitter binds to **ligand-gated ion channels** in the postsynaptic membrane, producing an **excitatory** or **inhibitory postsynaptic potential** (EPSP or IPSP). The neurotransmitter then diffuses out of the cleft, is taken up by surrounding cells, or is degraded by enzymes. A single neuron has many synapses on its dendrites and cell body. **Temporal** and **spatial summation** of EPSPs and IPSPs at the axon hillock determine whether a neuron generates an action potential.
- Different receptors for the same neurotransmitter produce different effects. Some neurotransmitter receptors activate signal transduction pathways, which can produce long-lasting changes in postsynaptic cells. Major neurotransmitters include acetylcholine; the amino acids GABA, glutamate, and glycine; biogenic amines; neuropeptides; and gases such as NO.

  ? *Why are many drugs that are used to treat nervous system diseases or to affect brain function targeted to specific receptors rather than particular neurotransmitters?*

LEVEL 1: KNOWLEDGE/COMPREHENSION

1. What happens when a resting neuron's membrane depolarizes?
   a. There is a net diffusion of Na^+ out of the cell.
   b. The equilibrium potential for K^+ (E_K) becomes more positive.
   c. The neuron's membrane voltage becomes more positive.
   d. The cell's inside is more negative than the outside.

2. A common feature of action potentials is that they
   a. cause the membrane to hyperpolarize and then depolarize.
   b. can undergo temporal and spatial summation.
   c. are triggered by a depolarization that reaches threshold.
   d. move at the same speed along all axons.

3. Where are neurotransmitter receptors located?
   a. the nuclear membrane
   b. the nodes of Ranvier
   c. the postsynaptic membrane
   d. synaptic vesicle membranes

LEVEL 2: APPLICATION/ANALYSIS

4. Why are action potentials usually conducted in one direction?
   a. Ions can flow along the axon in only one direction.
   b. The brief refractory period prevents reopening of voltage-gated Na^+ channels.
   c. The axon hillock has a higher membrane potential than the terminals of the axon.
   d. Voltage-gated channels for both Na^+ and K^+ open in only one direction.

5. Which of the following is the most *direct* result of depolarizing the presynaptic membrane of an axon terminal?
   a. Voltage-gated calcium channels in the membrane open.
   b. Synaptic vesicles fuse with the membrane.
   c. Ligand-gated channels open, allowing neurotransmitters to enter the synaptic cleft.
   d. An EPSP or IPSP is generated in the postsynaptic cell.

6. Suppose a particular neurotransmitter causes an IPSP in postsynaptic cell X and an EPSP in postsynaptic cell Y. A likely explanation is that
   a. the threshold value in the postsynaptic membrane is different for cell X and cell Y.
   b. the axon of cell X is myelinated, but that of cell Y is not.
   c. only cell Y produces an enzyme that terminates the activity of the neurotransmitter.
   d. cells X and Y express different receptor molecules for this particular neurotransmitter.

LEVEL 3: SYNTHESIS/EVALUATION

7. **WHAT IF?** Ouabain, a plant substance used in some cultures to poison hunting arrows, disables the sodium-potassium pump. What change in the resting potential would you expect to see if you treated a neuron with ouabain? Explain.

8. **WHAT IF?** If a drug mimicked the activity of GABA in the CNS, what general effect on behavior might you expect? Explain.

9. **DRAW IT** Suppose a researcher inserts a pair of electrodes at two different positions along the middle of an axon dissected out of a squid. By applying a depolarizing stimulus, the researcher brings the plasma membrane at both positions to threshold. Using the drawing below as a model, create one or more drawings that illustrate where each action potential would terminate.

Electrode

Squid axon

10. **EVOLUTION CONNECTION**
    An action potential is an all-or-none event. This on/off signaling is an evolutionary adaptation of animals that must sense and act in a complex environment. It is possible to imagine a nervous system in which the action potentials are graded, with the amplitude depending on the size of the stimulus. What evolutionary advantage might on/off signaling have over a graded (continuously variable) kind of signaling?

11. **SCIENTIFIC INQUIRY**
    From what you know about action potentials and synapses, propose two or three hypotheses for how various anesthetics might block pain.

12. **WRITE ABOUT A THEME: ORGANIZATION**
    In a short essay (100–150 words), describe how the structure and electrical properties of vertebrate neurons reflect similarities and differences with other animal cells.

13. **SYNTHESIZE YOUR KNOWLEDGE**

The rattlesnake alerts enemies to its presence with a rattle—a set of modified scales at the tip of its tail. Describe the distinct roles of gated ion channels in initiating and moving a signal along the nerve from the snake's head to its tail and then from that nerve to the muscle that shakes the rattle.

For selected answers, see Appendix A.

MasteringBiology®

Students Go to **MasteringBiology** for assignments, the eText, and the Study Area with practice tests, animations, and activities.

Instructors Go to **MasteringBiology** for automatically graded tutorials and questions that you can assign to your students, plus Instructor Resources.

49

Nervous Systems

KEY CONCEPTS

49.1 Nervous systems consist of circuits of neurons and supporting cells

49.2 The vertebrate brain is regionally specialized

49.3 The cerebral cortex controls voluntary movement and cognitive functions

49.4 Changes in synaptic connections underlie memory and learning

49.5 Many nervous system disorders can be explained in molecular terms

▲ **Figure 49.1 How do scientists identify individual neurons in the brain?**

Command and Control Center

What happens in your brain when you solve a math problem or listen to music? Answering such a question was for a long time nearly unimaginable. The human brain contains an estimated 10^{11} (100 billion) neurons. Interconnecting these brain cells are circuits more complex than those of even the most powerful supercomputers. However, thanks in part to several exciting new technologies, scientists have begun to explore the cellular mechanisms that underlie thought and emotion.

One breakthrough came with the development of powerful imaging techniques that reveal activity in the working brain. Researchers can monitor multiple areas of the human brain while a subject is performing various tasks, such as speaking, looking at pictures, or forming a mental image of a person's face. They can use these techniques to look for a correlation between a particular task and activity in specific brain areas.

A more recent advance in exploring the brain relies on a method for expressing random combinations of colored proteins in brain cells—such that each cell shows up in a different color. The result is a "brainbow" like the one in **Figure 49.1**, which highlights neurons in the brain of a mouse. In this image, each neuron expresses one of more than 90 different color combinations of four fluorescent proteins.

Using the brainbow technology, neuroscientists hope to develop detailed maps of the connections that transfer information between particular regions of the brain.

In this chapter, we'll discuss the organization and evolution of animal nervous systems, exploring how groups of neurons function in specialized circuits dedicated to specific tasks. Next we'll focus on specialization in regions of the vertebrate brain. We'll then turn to the ways in which brain activity makes information storage and organization possible. Finally, we'll consider several disorders of the nervous system that are the subject of intense research today.

CONCEPT 49.1

Nervous systems consist of circuits of neurons and supporting cells

The ability to sense and react originated billions of years ago in prokaryotes, enhancing survival and reproductive success in changing environments. Later in evolution, modification of simple recognition and response processes provided a basis for communication between cells in an animal body. By the time of the Cambrian explosion more than 500 million years ago (see Chapter 32), specialized systems of neurons had appeared that enable animals to sense their surroundings and respond rapidly.

Hydras, jellies, and other cnidarians are the simplest animals with nervous systems. In most cnidarians, interconnected neurons form a diffuse *nerve net* (**Figure 49.2a**), which controls the contraction and expansion of the gastrovascular cavity. In more complex animals, the axons of multiple neurons are often bundled together, forming **nerves**. These fibrous structures channel and organize information flow along specific routes through the nervous system. For example, sea stars have a set of radial nerves connecting to a central nerve ring (**Figure 49.2b**). Within each arm of a sea star, the radial nerve is linked to a nerve net from which it receives input and to which it sends signals that control muscle contraction.

Animals that have elongated, bilaterally symmetrical bodies have even more specialized nervous systems. The organization of neurons in such animals reflects *cephalization*, an evolutionary trend toward a clustering of sensory neurons and interneurons at the anterior (front) end of the body. These anterior neurons communicate with cells elsewhere in the body, including neurons located in one or more nerve cords extending toward the posterior (rear) end.

As you learned in Concept 48.1, in many animals neurons that carry out integration form a **central nervous system (CNS)**, and neurons that carry information into and out of the CNS form a **peripheral nervous system (PNS)**. In nonsegmented worms, such as the planarian in **Figure 49.2c**, a small brain and longitudinal nerve cords constitute the simplest

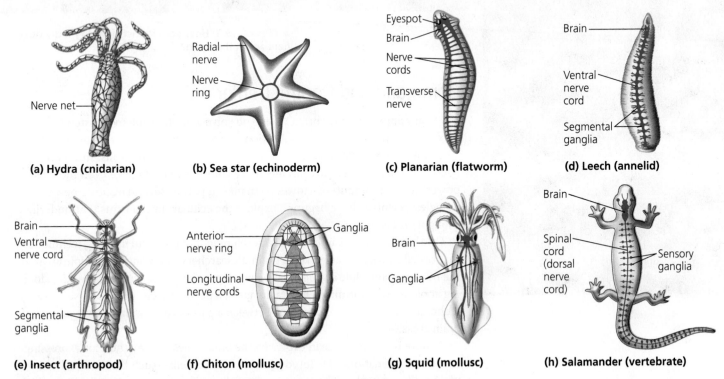

(a) Hydra (cnidarian)　(b) Sea star (echinoderm)　(c) Planarian (flatworm)　(d) Leech (annelid)

(e) Insect (arthropod)　(f) Chiton (mollusc)　(g) Squid (mollusc)　(h) Salamander (vertebrate)

▲ **Figure 49.2 Nervous system organization. (a)** A hydra contains individual neurons (purple) organized in a diffuse nerve net. **(b–h)** Animals with more sophisticated nervous systems contain groups of neurons (blue) organized into nerves and often ganglia and a brain.

clearly defined CNS. In some nonsegmented worms, the entire nervous system is constructed from only a small number of cells, as in the case of the nematode *Caenorhabditis elegans*. In this species, an adult worm (hermaphrodite) has exactly 302 neurons, no more and no fewer. More complex invertebrates, such as segmented worms (annelids; **Figure 49.2d**) and arthropods **(Figure 49.2e)**, have many more neurons. Their behavior is regulated by more complicated brains and by ventral nerve cords containing **ganglia**, segmentally arranged clusters of neurons.

Within an animal group, nervous system organization often correlates with lifestyle. Among the molluscs, for example, sessile and slow-moving species, such as clams and chitons, have relatively simple sense organs and little or no cephalization **(Figure 49.2f)**. In contrast, active predatory molluscs, such as octopuses and squids **(Figure 49.2g)**, have the most sophisticated nervous systems of any invertebrates, rivaling those of some vertebrates. With their large, image-forming eyes and a brain containing millions of neurons, octopuses can learn to discriminate between visual patterns and to perform complex tasks.

In vertebrates **(Figure 49.2h)**, the brain and the spinal cord form the CNS; nerves and ganglia are the key components of the PNS. Regional specialization is a hallmark of both systems, as we will see throughout this chapter.

Glia

As discussed in Chapter 48, the nervous systems of vertebrates and most invertebrates include not only neurons but also **glial cells**, or **glia**. Some examples of glia are the Schwann cells that produce the myelin sheaths surrounding axons in the PNS and oligodendrocytes, their counterparts in the CNS. **Figure 49.3** illustrates the major types of glia in the adult vertebrate and provides an overview of the ways in which they nourish, support, and regulate the functioning of neurons.

One of the essential roles of glia is in nervous system development. In embryos, cells called *radial glia* form tracks along which newly formed neurons migrate from the neural tube, the structure that gives rise to the CNS (see Figure 47.14). Later, glia called **astrocytes** participate in formation of the *blood-brain barrier*, a specialization of the walls of brain capillaries that restricts the entry of most substances from the blood into the CNS.

Both radial glia and astrocytes can act as stem cells, which retain the ability to divide indefinitely. While some of their progeny remain undifferentiated, others differentiate into specialized cells. Studies with mice reveal that stem cells in the brain give rise to neurons that mature, migrate to particular locations, and become incorporated into the

Ependymal cells line the ventricles of the brain (see Figure 49.5) and have cilia that promote circulation of the cerebrospinal fluid.

Astrocytes (from the Greek *astron*, star), found in the CNS, facilitate information transfer at synapses and in some instances release neurotransmitters. Astrocytes next to active neurons cause nearby blood vessels to dilate, increasing blood flow and enabling the neurons to obtain oxygen and glucose more quickly. Astrocytes also regulate extracellular concentrations of ions and neurotransmitters.

Oligodendrocytes myelinate axons in the CNS. Myelination greatly increases the conduction speed of action potentials.

Microglia are immune cells in the CNS that protect against pathogens.

Schwann cells myelinate axons in the PNS.

▲ **Figure 49.3 Glia in the vertebrate nervous system.**

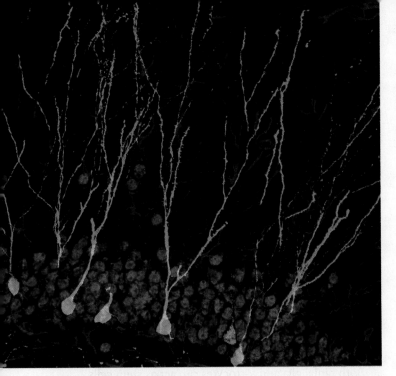

▲ Figure 49.4 Newly born neurons in the brain of an adult mouse. In this light micrograph, new neurons derived from adult stem cells are labeled with green fluorescent protein (GFP), and all neurons are labeled with a DNA-binding dye, colored red in this image.

circuitry of the adult nervous system **(Figure 49.4)**. Researchers are now tackling the challenge of finding a way to use neural stem cells as a means of replacing brain tissue that has ceased to function properly.

Organization of the Vertebrate Nervous System

During embryonic development in vertebrates, the central nervous system develops from the hollow dorsal nerve cord— a hallmark of chordates (see Figure 34.3). The cavity of the nerve cord gives rise to the narrow **central canal** of the spinal cord as well as the *ventricles* of the brain **(Figure 49.5)**. Both

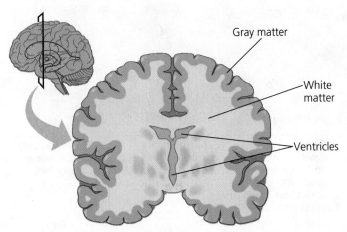

▲ Figure 49.5 Ventricles, gray matter, and white matter. Ventricles deep in the brain's interior contain cerebrospinal fluid. Most of the gray matter is on the brain surface, surrounding the white matter.

the canal and ventricles fill with *cerebrospinal fluid,* which is formed in the brain by filtration of arterial blood. The cerebrospinal fluid circulates slowly through the ventricles and central canal and then drains into the veins, supplying the CNS with nutrients and hormones and carrying away wastes.

In addition to these fluid-filled spaces, the brain and spinal cord contain gray matter and white matter (see Figure 49.5). **Gray matter** is primarily made up of neuron cell bodies. **White matter** consists mainly of bundled axons. In the spinal cord, white matter makes up the outer layer, consistent with its function in linking the CNS to sensory and motor neurons of the PNS. In the brain, white matter is predominantly in the interior, where signaling between neurons functions in learning, feeling emotions, processing sensory information, and generating commands.

In vertebrates, the spinal cord runs lengthwise inside the vertebral column, known as the spine **(Figure 49.6)**. The spinal cord conveys information to and from the brain and generates basic patterns of locomotion. It also acts independently of the brain as part of the simple nerve circuits that produce **reflexes**, the body's automatic responses to certain stimuli.

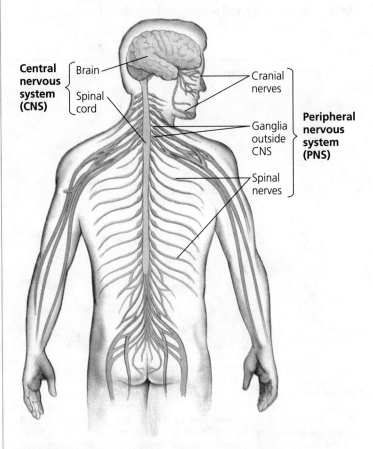

▲ Figure 49.6 The vertebrate nervous system. The central nervous system consists of the brain and spinal cord (yellow). Left-right pairs of cranial nerves, spinal nerves, and ganglia make up most of the peripheral nervous system (dark gold).

► **Figure 49.7 The knee-jerk reflex.** Many neurons are involved in this reflex, but for simplicity, only a few neurons are shown.

MAKE CONNECTIONS *Using the nerve signals to the hamstring and quadriceps in this reflex as an example, propose a model for regulation of smooth muscle activity in the esophagus during the swallowing reflex (see Figure 41.10).*

❶ The reflex is initiated artificially by tapping the tendon connected to the quadriceps muscle.

❷ Sensors detect a sudden stretch in the quadriceps, and **sensory neurons** convey the information to the spinal cord.

❸ In response to signals from the sensory neurons, **motor neurons** convey signals to the quadriceps, causing it to contract and jerking the lower leg forward.

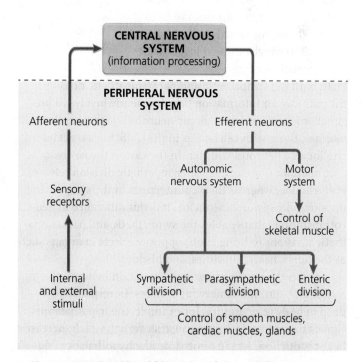

Cell body of sensory neuron in dorsal root ganglion

Gray matter White matter

Quadriceps muscle

Spinal cord (cross section)

Hamstring muscle

❺ Motor neurons that lead to the hamstring muscle are inhibited by the interneurons. This inhibition prevents contraction of the hamstring, which would resist the action of the quadriceps.

❹ **Interneurons** in the spinal cord also receive signals from sensory neurons.

Key ● Sensory neuron ● Motor neuron ● Interneuron

A reflex protects the body by providing a rapid, involuntary response to a particular stimulus. For example, if you accidentally put your hand on a hot burner, your hand begins to jerk back before your brain processes pain. Similarly, the knee-jerk reflex protects you when you pick up an unexpectedly heavy object. If your legs buckle, the tension across your knees triggers contraction of your thigh muscle (quadriceps), helping you stay upright and support the load. During a physical exam, your doctor may trigger the knee-jerk reflex with a triangular mallet to help assess nervous system function **(Figure 49.7)**.

The Peripheral Nervous System

The PNS transmits information to and from the CNS and plays a large role in regulating both an animal's movement and its internal environment **(Figure 49.8)**. Sensory information reaches the CNS along PNS neurons designated as *afferent* (from the Latin, meaning "to carry toward"). Following information processing within the CNS, instructions then travel to muscles, glands, and endocrine cells along PNS neurons designated as *efferent* (from the Latin, meaning "to carry away"). Most nerves contain both afferent and efferent neurons.

The PNS has two efferent components: the motor system and the autonomic nervous system (see Figure 49.8). The **motor system** consists of neurons that carry signals to skeletal muscles. Motor control can be voluntary, as when you raise your hand to ask a question, or involuntary, as in the knee-jerk reflex controlled by the spinal cord. In contrast, regulation of smooth and cardiac muscles by the **autonomic nervous system** is generally involuntary. The three divisions of the autonomic nervous system—sympathetic, parasympathetic, and enteric—together control the organs of the digestive, cardiovascular, excretory, and endocrine systems. For example, networks of neurons that form the **enteric division** of the autonomic nervous system are active in the digestive tract, pancreas, and gallbladder.

CENTRAL NERVOUS SYSTEM (information processing)

PERIPHERAL NERVOUS SYSTEM

Afferent neurons

Efferent neurons

Sensory receptors

Autonomic nervous system

Motor system

Control of skeletal muscle

Internal and external stimuli

Sympathetic division

Parasympathetic division

Enteric division

Control of smooth muscles, cardiac muscles, glands

▲ **Figure 49.8 Functional hierarchy of the vertebrate peripheral nervous system.**

The sympathetic and parasympathetic divisions of the autonomic nervous system have largely antagonistic (opposite) functions in regulating organ function **(Figure 49.9)**. Activation of the **sympathetic division** corresponds to arousal and energy generation (the "fight-or-flight" response). For example, the heart beats faster, digestion is inhibited, the liver converts glycogen to glucose, and the adrenal medulla increases secretion of epinephrine (adrenaline). Activation of the **parasympathetic division** generally causes opposite responses that promote calming and a return to self-maintenance functions ("rest and digest"). Thus, heart rate decreases, digestion is enhanced, and glycogen production increases. However, in regulating reproductive activity, a function that is not homeostatic, the parasympathetic division complements rather than antagonizes the sympathetic division (see Figure 49.9).

The two divisions differ not only in overall function but also in organization and signals released. Parasympathetic nerves exit the CNS at the base of the brain or spinal cord and form synapses in ganglia near or within an internal organ (see Figure 49.9). In contrast, sympathetic nerves typically exit the CNS midway along the spinal cord and form synapses in ganglia located just outside of the spinal cord.

In both the sympathetic and parasympathetic divisions, the pathway for information flow frequently involves a preganglionic and a postganglionic neuron. The *preganglionic neurons*, those with cell bodies in the CNS, release acetylcholine as a neurotransmitter. In the case of the *postganglionic neurons*, those of the parasympathetic division release acetycholine, whereas their counterparts in the sympathetic division release norepinephrine. It is this difference in neurotransmitters that enables the sympathetic and parasympathetic divisions to bring about opposite effects in organs such as the lungs, heart, intestines, and bladder.

Homeostasis often relies on cooperation between the motor and autonomic nervous systems. In response to a drop in body temperature, for example, the hypothalamus signals the motor system to cause shivering, which increases heat production. At the same time, the hypothalamus signals the autonomic nervous system to constrict surface blood vessels, reducing heat loss.

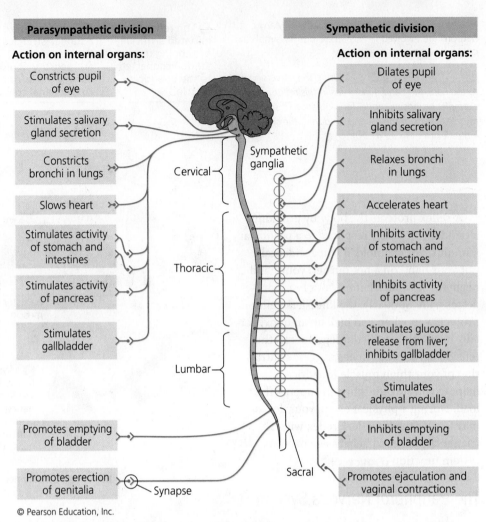

© Pearson Education, Inc.

▲ **Figure 49.9 The parasympathetic and sympathetic divisions of the autonomic nervous system.** Most pathways in each division involve two neurons. The axon of the first neuron extends from a cell body in the CNS to a set of PNS neurons whose cell bodies are clustered into a ganglion (plural, *ganglia*). The axons of these PNS neurons transmit instructions to internal organs, where they form synapses with smooth muscle, cardiac muscle, or gland cells.

CONCEPT CHECK 49.1

1. Which division of the autonomic nervous system would likely be activated if a student learned that an exam she had forgotten about would start in 5 minutes? Explain your answer.

2. **WHAT IF?** Suppose a person had an accident that severed a small nerve required to move some of the fingers of the right hand. Would you also expect an effect on sensation from those fingers?

3. **MAKE CONNECTIONS** Most tissues regulated by the autonomic nervous system receive both sympathetic and parasympathetic input from postganglionic neurons. Responses are typically local. In contrast, the adrenal medulla receives input only from the sympathetic division and only from preganglionic neurons, yet responses are observed throughout the body. Explain why (see Figure 45.20).

For suggested answers, see Appendix A.

The vertebrate brain is regionally specialized

We turn now to the vertebrate brain, which has three major regions: the forebrain, midbrain, and hindbrain (shown here for a ray-finned fish).

Each region is specialized in function. The **forebrain**, which contains the *olfactory bulb* and *cerebrum*, has activities that include processing of olfactory input (smells), regulation of sleep, learning, and any complex processing. The **midbrain**, located centrally in the brain, coordinates routing of sensory input. The **hindbrain**, part of which forms the *cerebellum*, controls involuntary activities, such as blood circulation, and coordinates motor activities, such as locomotion.

EVOLUTION Comparing vertebrates across a phylogenetic tree, we see that the relative sizes of particular brain regions vary **(Figure 49.10)**. Furthermore, these size differences reflect differences in the importance of particular brain functions. Consider, for example, ray-finned fishes, which explore their environment using olfaction, vision,

and a lateral line system that detects water currents, electrical stimuli, and body position. The olfactory bulb, which detects scents in the water, is relatively large in these fishes. So is the midbrain, which processes input from the visual and lateral line systems. In contrast, the cerebrum, required for complex processing and learning, is relatively small. Evolution has thus resulted in a close match of structure to function, with the size of particular brain regions correlating with their importance for that species in nervous system function and, hence, species survival and reproduction.

The correlation between the size and function of brain regions can also be observed by considering the cerebellum. Free swimming ray-finned fishes, such as the tuna, control movement in three dimensions in the open water and have a relatively large cerebellum. In comparison, the cerebellum is much smaller in species that don't swim actively, such as the lamprey.

If one compares birds and mammals with groups that diverged from the common vertebrate ancestor earlier in evolution, two trends are apparent. First, the forebrain of birds and mammals occupies a larger fraction of the brain than it does in amphibians, fishes, and other vertebrates. Second, birds and mammals have much larger brains relative to body size than do other groups. Indeed, the ratio of brain size to body weight is ten times as large for birds and mammals as for their evolutionary ancestors. These differences in both overall brain size and the relative size of the forebrain reflect the greater capacity of birds and mammals for cognition and higher-order reasoning, traits we will return to later in this chapter.

In the case of humans, it is estimated that the brain contains 100 billion neurons. How are so many cells organized into circuits and networks that can perform highly sophisticated information processing, storage, and retrieval? In addressing this question, let's begin with **Figure 49.11**, which explores the overall architecture of the human brain. You can use this figure to trace how brain structures arise during embryonic development; as a reference for their size, shape, and location in the adult brain; and as an introduction to their best-understood functions.

To learn more about how particular brain structure and brain organization overall relate to brain function in humans, we'll first consider activity cycles of the brain and the physiological basis of emotion. Then, in Concept 49.3, we'll shift our attention to regional specialization within the cerebrum.

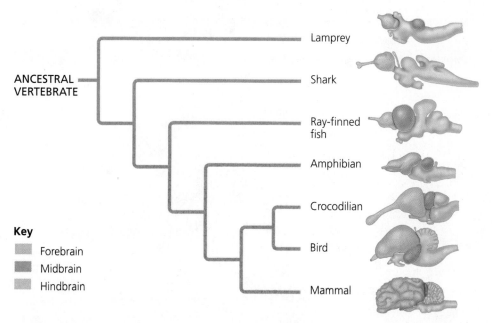

▲ **Figure 49.10 Vertebrate brain structure and evolution.** During evolution, differences arose in the relative size of the major structures common to vertebrate brains. As discussed in the text, size differences correlate with the importance of particular brain functions for particular vertebrate groups.

Exploring The Organization of the Human Brain

The brain is the most complex organ in the human body. Surrounded by the thick bones of the skull, the brain is divided into a set of distinctive structures, some of which are visible in the magnetic resonance image (MRI) of an adult's head shown at right. The diagram below traces the development of these structures in the embryo. Their major functions are explained on the facing page.

Human Brain Development

As a human embryo develops, the neural tube forms three anterior bulges—the forebrain, midbrain, and hindbrain—that together produce the adult brain. The midbrain and portions of the hindbrain give rise to the **brainstem**, a stalk that joins with the spinal cord at the base of the brain. The rest of the hindbrain gives rise to the **cerebellum**, which lies behind the brainstem. The third anterior bulge, the forebrain, develops into the diencephalon, including the neuroendocrine tissues of the brain, and the telencephalon, which becomes the **cerebrum**. Rapid, expansive growth of the telencephalon during the second and third months causes the outer portion, or cortex, of the cerebrum to extend over and around much of the rest of the brain.

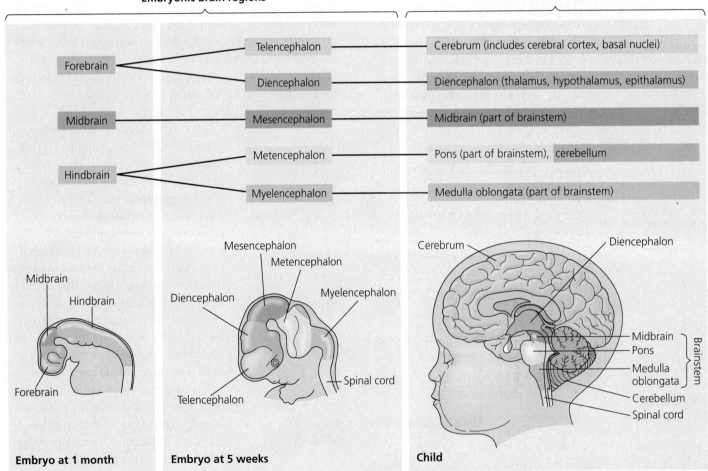

Embryonic brain regions

Brain structures in child and adult

Forebrain	Telencephalon	Cerebrum (includes cerebral cortex, basal nuclei)
	Diencephalon	Diencephalon (thalamus, hypothalamus, epithalamus)
Midbrain	Mesencephalon	Midbrain (part of brainstem)
Hindbrain	Metencephalon	Pons (part of brainstem), cerebellum
	Myelencephalon	Medulla oblongata (part of brainstem)

Embryo at 1 month

Midbrain
Hindbrain
Forebrain

Embryo at 5 weeks

Mesencephalon
Metencephalon
Diencephalon
Myelencephalon
Telencephalon
Spinal cord

Child

Cerebrum
Diencephalon
Midbrain
Pons
Medulla oblongata
Cerebellum
Spinal cord
Brainstem

The Cerebrum

The cerebrum controls skeletal muscle contraction and is the center for learning, emotion, memory, and perception. It is divided into right and left **cerebral hemispheres**. The outer layer of the cerebrum is called the **cerebral cortex** and is vital for perception, voluntary movement, and learning. The left side of the cerebral cortex receives information from, and controls the movement of, the right side of the body, and vice versa. A thick band of axons known as the **corpus callosum** enables the right and left cerebral cortices to communicate. Deep within the white matter, clusters of neurons called *basal nuclei* serve as centers for planning and learning movement sequences. Damage to these sites during fetal development can result in cerebral palsy, a disorder resulting from a disruption in the transmission of motor commands to the muscles.

The Cerebellum

The cerebellum coordinates movement and balance and helps in learning and remembering motor skills. The cerebellum receives sensory information about the positions of the joints and the lengths of the muscles, as well as input from the auditory (hearing) and visual systems. It also monitors motor commands issued by the cerebrum. The cerebellum integrates this information as it carries out coordination and error checking during motor and perceptual functions. Hand-eye coordination is an example of cerebellar control; if the cerebellum is damaged, the eyes can follow a moving object, but they will not stop at the same place as the object. Hand movement toward the object will also be erratic.

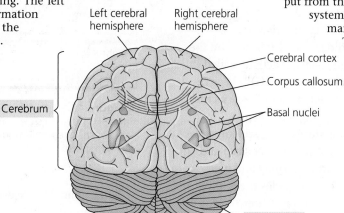

Left cerebral hemisphere
Right cerebral hemisphere
Cerebral cortex
Corpus callosum
Basal nuclei
Cerebrum
Cerebellum

Adult brain viewed from the rear

The Diencephalon

The diencephalon gives rise to the thalamus, hypothalamus, and epithalamus. The **thalamus** is the main input center for sensory information going to the cerebrum. Incoming information from all the senses, as well as from the cerebral cortex, is sorted in the thalamus and sent to the appropriate cerebral centers for further processing. The thalamus is formed by two masses, each roughly the size and shape of a walnut. A much smaller structure, the **hypothalamus**, constitutes a control center that includes the body's thermostat as well as the central biological clock. Through its regulation of the pituitary gland, the hypothalamus regulates hunger and thirst, plays a role in sexual and mating behaviors, and initiates the fight-or-flight response. The hypothalamus is also the source of posterior pituitary hormones and of releasing hormones that act on the anterior pituitary (see Figures 45.14 and 45.16). The *epithalamus* includes the pineal gland, the source of melatonin. It also contains one of several clusters of capillaries that generate cerebrospinal fluid from blood.

Diencephalon
Thalamus
Pineal gland
Hypothalamus
Pituitary gland
Spinal cord

The Brainstem

The brainstem consists of the midbrain, the **pons**, and the **medulla oblongata** (commonly called the *medulla*). The midbrain receives and integrates several types of sensory information and sends it to specific regions of the forebrain. All sensory axons involved in hearing either terminate in the midbrain or pass through it on their way to the cerebrum. In addition, the midbrain coordinates visual reflexes, such as the peripheral vision reflex: The head turns toward an object approaching from the side without the brain having formed an image of the object.

A major function of the pons and medulla is to transfer information between the PNS and the midbrain and forebrain. The pons and medulla also help coordinate large-scale body movements, such as running and climbing. Most axons that carry instructions about these movements cross from one side of the CNS to the other in the medulla. As a result, the right side of the brain controls much of the movement of the left side of the body, and vice versa. An additional function of the medulla is the control of several automatic, homeostatic functions, including breathing, heart and blood vessel activity, swallowing, vomiting, and digestion. The pons also participates in some of these activities; for example, it regulates the breathing centers in the medulla.

Midbrain
Pons
Medulla oblongata

Arousal and Sleep

If you've ever drifted off to sleep while listening to a lecture (or reading a book), you know that your attentiveness and mental alertness can change rapidly. Such transitions are regulated by the brainstem and cerebrum, which control arousal and sleep. Arousal is a state of awareness of the external world. Sleep is a state in which external stimuli are received but not consciously perceived.

Contrary to appearances, sleep is an active state, at least for the brain. By placing electrodes at multiple sites on the scalp, we can record patterns of electrical activity called brain waves in an electroencephalogram (EEG). These recordings reveal that brain wave frequencies change as the brain progresses through distinct stages of sleep.

Although sleep is essential for survival, we still know very little about its function. One hypothesis is that sleep and dreams are involved in consolidating learning and memory. Evidence supporting this hypothesis includes the finding that test subjects who are kept awake for 36 hours have a reduced ability to remember when particular events occurred, even if they first "perk up" with caffeine. Other experiments show that regions of the brain that are activated during a learning task can become active again during sleep.

Arousal and sleep are controlled in part by the *reticular formation*, a diffuse network formed primarily by neurons in the midbrain and pons **(Figure 49.12)**. These neurons control the timing of sleep periods characterized by rapid eye movements (REMs) and by vivid dreams. Sleep is also regulated by the biological clock and by regions of the forebrain that regulate sleep intensity and duration.

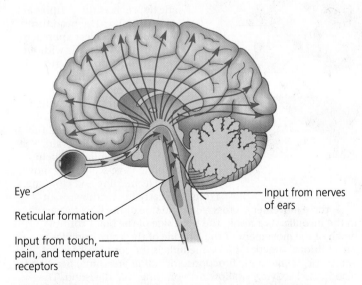

Eye

Reticular formation

Input from touch, pain, and temperature receptors

Input from nerves of ears

▲ **Figure 49.12 The reticular formation.** Once thought to consist of a single diffuse network of neurons, the reticular formation is now recognized as many distinct clusters of neurons. These clusters function in part to filter sensory input (blue arrows), blocking familiar and repetitive information that constantly enters the nervous system before sending the filtered input to the cerebral cortex (green arrows).

Key

⋀⋀ Low-frequency waves characteristic of sleep

⋁⋁ High-frequency waves characteristic of wakefulness

Location	Time: 0 hours	Time: 1 hour
Left hemisphere	⋀⋀⋀⋀	⋁⋁⋁
Right hemisphere	⋁⋁⋁	⋀⋀⋀⋀

▲ **Figure 49.13 Dolphins can be asleep and awake at the same time.** EEG recordings were made separately for the two sides of a dolphin's brain. At each time point, low-frequency activity was recorded in one hemisphere while higher-frequency activity typical of being awake was recorded in the other hemisphere.

Some animals have evolutionary adaptations that allow for substantial activity during sleep. Bottlenose dolphins, for example, swim while sleeping, rising to the surface to breathe air on a regular basis. How do they manage this feat? As in other mammals, the forebrain is physically and functionally divided into two halves, the right and left hemispheres. Noting that dolphins sleep with one eye open and one closed, researchers hypothesized that only one side of the brain is asleep at a time. EEG recordings from each hemisphere of sleeping dolphins support this hypothesis **(Figure 49.13)**.

Biological Clock Regulation

Cycles of sleep and wakefulness are an example of a circadian rhythm, a daily cycle of biological activity. Such cycles, which occur in organisms ranging from bacteria to humans, rely on a **biological clock**, a molecular mechanism that directs periodic gene expression and cellular activity. Although biological clocks are typically synchronized to the cycles of light and dark in the environment, they can maintain a roughly 24-hour cycle even in the absence of environmental cues (see Figure 40.9). For example, in a constant environment humans exhibit a sleep/wake cycle of 24.2 hours, with very little variation among individuals.

What normally links an animal's biological clock to environmental cycles of light and dark? In mammals, circadian rhythms are coordinated by a group of neurons in the hypothalamus called the **suprachiasmatic nucleus**, or **SCN**. (Certain clusters of neurons in the CNS are referred to as "nuclei.") In response to sensory information from the eyes, the SCN acts as a pacemaker, synchronizing the biological clock in cells throughout the body to the natural cycles of day length. In the Scientific Skills Exercise, you can interpret data from an experiment and propose experiments to test the role of the SCN in hamster circadian rhythms.

Designing an Experiment Using Genetic Mutants

Does the SCN Control the Circadian Rhythm in Hamsters?
By surgically removing the SCN from laboratory mammals, scientists demonstrated that the SCN is required for circadian rhythms. Those experiments did not, however, reveal whether circadian rhythms originate in the SCN. To answer this question, researchers performed an SCN transplant experiment on wild-type and mutant hamsters (*Mesocricetus auratus*). Whereas wild-type hamsters have a circadian cycle lasting about 24 hours in the absence of external cues, hamsters homozygous for the τ (tau) mutation have a cycle lasting only about 20 hours. In this exercise, you will evaluate the design of this experiment and propose additional experiments to gain further insight.

How the Experiment Was Done The researchers surgically removed the SCN from wild-type and τ hamsters. Several weeks later, each of these hamsters received a transplant of an SCN from a hamster of the opposite genotype. To determine the periodicity of rhythmic activity for the hamsters before the surgery and after the transplants, the researchers measured activity levels over a three-week period. They plotted the data collected for each day in the manner shown in Figure 40.9a and then calculated the circadian cycle period.

Data from the Experiment In 80% of the hamsters in which the SCN had been removed, transplanting an SCN from another hamster restored rhythmic activity. For hamsters in which an SCN transplant restored a circadian rhythm, the net effect of the two procedures (SCN removal and replacement) on the circadian cycle period is graphed at the upper right. Each red line connects the two data points for an individual hamster.

Interpret the Data

1. In a controlled experiment, researchers manipulate one variable at a time. What was the variable manipulated in this study? Why did the researchers use more than one hamster for each procedure? What traits of the individual hamsters would likely have been held constant among the treatment groups?

2. For the wild-type hamsters that received τ SCN transplants, what would have been an appropriate experimental control?

3. What general trends does the graph above reveal about the circadian cycle period of the transplant recipients? Do the trends differ for the wild-type and τ recipients? Based on these data, what can you conclude about the role of the SCN in determining the period of the circadian rhythm?

4. In 20% of the hamsters, there was no restoration of rhythmic activity following the SCN transplant. What are some possible reasons for this finding? Do you think you can be confident of your conclusion about the role of the SCN based on data from 80% of the hamsters?

5. Suppose that researchers identified a mutant hamster that lacked rhythmic activity; that is, its circadian activity cycle had no regular pattern. Propose SCN transplant experiments using such a mutant along with (a) wild-type and (b) τ hamsters. Predict the results of those experiments in light of your conclusion in question 3.

(MB) A version of this Scientific Skills Exercise can be assigned in MasteringBiology.

Data from M. R. Ralph et al., Transplanted suprachiasmatic nucleus determines circadian period, *Science* 247:975–978 (1990). Reprinted with permission from AAAS.

Emotions

Whereas a single structure in the brain controls the biological clock, the generation and experience of emotions depend on many brain structures, including the amygdala, hippocampus, and parts of the thalamus. As shown in **Figure 49.14**, these structures border the brainstem in mammals and are therefore called the *limbic system* (from the Latin *limbus*, border).

Generating emotion and experiencing emotion often require interactions between different regions of the brain. For example, laughing and crying both involve the limbic system interacting with sensory areas of the forebrain. Similarly, structures in the forebrain attach emotional "feelings" to survival-related functions controlled by the brainstem, including aggression, feeding, and sexuality.

Emotional experiences are often stored as memories that can be recalled by similar circumstances. For example, a situation that causes you to remember a frightening event

▲ **Figure 49.14 The limbic system in the human brain.**

can trigger a faster heart rate, sweating, and mental state of fear, even if there is currently nothing scary or threatening in your surroundings. The brain structure that is most important for this emotional memory is the **amygdala**, an almond-shaped mass of nuclei (clusters of neurons) located near the base of the cerebrum.

To study the function of the human amygdala, researchers sometimes present adult subjects with an image followed by an unpleasant experience, such as a mild electrical shock. After several trials, study participants experience *autonomic arousal*—as measured by increased heart rate or sweating—if they see the image again. Subjects with brain damage confined to the amygdala can recall the image because their explicit memory is intact. However, they do not exhibit autonomic arousal, indicating that damage to the amygdala has resulted in a reduced capacity for emotional memory.

Functional Imaging of the Brain

Today, the amygdala and other brain structures are being probed and analyzed with functional imaging methods. The first widely used technique was positron-emission tomography (PET), in which injection of radioactive glucose enables a display of metabolic activity. Today, many studies rely on functional magnetic resonance imaging (fMRI). In fMRI, a subject lies with his or her head in the center of a large, doughnut-shaped magnet. Brain activity in a region is detected by changes in the local oxygen concentration. By scanning the brain while the subject performs a task, such as forming a mental image of a person's face, researchers can correlate particular tasks with activity in specific brain areas.

In one experiment using fMRI, researchers mapped brain activity while subjects listened to music that they described as happy or sad **(Figure 49.15)**. Listening to happy music led to increased activity in the nucleus accumbens, a brain

Nucleus accumbens   Amygdala

Happy music   **Sad music**

▲ **Figure 49.15 Functional imaging in the working brain.** Functional magnetic resonance imaging (fMRI) was used to reveal brain activity associated with music that listeners described as happy or sad.

WHAT IF? *In the experiment that produced the images shown above, some regions of the brain were active under both conditions. What function might such regions carry out?*

structure important for the perception of pleasure. In contrast, subjects who heard sad music had increased activity in the amygdala.

The range of applications of fMRI includes monitoring recovery from stroke, mapping abnormalities in migraine headaches, and increasing the effectiveness of brain surgery. This technique has even been used to explore sex-based differences in the CNS, demonstrating, for instance, that cerebral blood flow is higher on average in women than in men.

CONCEPT CHECK 49.2

1. When you wave your right hand, what part of your brain initiates the action?

2. People who are inebriated have difficulty touching their nose with their eyes closed. Which brain region does this observation indicate is one of those impaired by alcohol?

3. **WHAT IF?** Suppose you examine two groups of individuals with CNS damage. In one group, the damage has resulted in a coma (a prolonged state of unconsciousness). In the other group, it has caused paralysis (a loss of skeletal muscle function throughout the body). Relative to the position of the midbrain and pons, where is the likely site of damage in each group? Explain.

For suggested answers, see Appendix A.

CONCEPT 49.3

The cerebral cortex controls voluntary movement and cognitive functions

We turn now to the cerebrum, the part of the brain essential for language, cognition, memory, consciousness, and awareness of our surroundings. As shown in Figure 49.11, the cerebrum is the largest structure in the human brain. Like the brain overall, it exhibits regional specialization. For the most part, cognitive functions reside in the cortex, the outer layer of the cerebrum. Within the cortex, *sensory areas* receive and process sensory information, *association areas* integrate the information, and *motor areas* transmit instructions to other parts of the body.

In discussing the location of particular functions in the cerebral cortex, neurobiologists often use four regions, or *lobes*, as physical landmarks. As shown in **Figure 49.16**, each side of the cerebral cortex has a frontal, temporal, occipital, and parietal lobe (each is named for a nearby bone of the skull).

Information Processing

Broadly speaking, there are two sources of sensory input to the human cerebral cortex. Some sensory input comes from groups of receptors clustered in dedicated sensory organs, such as the eyes and nose. Other sensory input originates

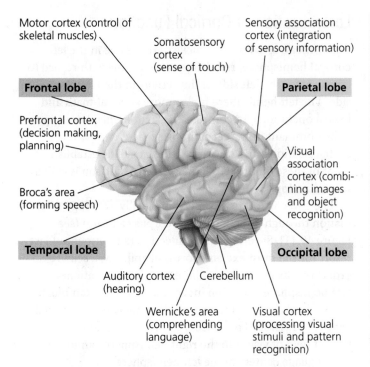

Motor cortex (control of skeletal muscles)

Somatosensory cortex (sense of touch)

Sensory association cortex (integration of sensory information)

Frontal lobe

Parietal lobe

Prefrontal cortex (decision making, planning)

Visual association cortex (combining images and object recognition)

Broca's area (forming speech)

Temporal lobe

Occipital lobe

Auditory cortex (hearing)

Cerebellum

Wernicke's area (comprehending language)

Visual cortex (processing visual stimuli and pattern recognition)

▲ **Figure 49.16 The human cerebral cortex.** Each side of the cerebral cortex is divided into four lobes, and each lobe has specialized functions, some of which are listed here. Some areas on the left side of the brain (shown here) have different functions from those on the right side (not shown).

in individual receptors in the hands, scalp, and elsewhere in the body. These somatic sensory, or *somatosensory*, receptors (from the Greek *soma*, body) provide information about touch, pain, pressure, temperature, and the position of muscles and limbs.

Most sensory information coming into the cortex is directed via the thalamus to primary sensory areas within the brain lobes. Information received at the primary sensory areas is passed along to nearby association areas, which process particular features in the sensory input. In the occipital lobe, for instance, some groups of neurons in the primary visual area are specifically sensitive to rays of light oriented in a particular direction. In the visual association area, information related to such features is combined in a region dedicated to recognizing complex images, such as faces.

Once processed, sensory information passes to the prefrontal cortex, which helps plan actions and movement. The cerebral cortex may then generate motor commands that cause particular behaviors—moving a limb or saying hello, for example. These commands consist of action potentials produced by neurons in the motor cortex, which lies at the rear of the frontal lobe (see Figure 49.16). The action potentials travel along axons to the brainstem and spinal cord, where they excite motor neurons, which in turn excite skeletal muscle cells.

In the somatosensory cortex and motor cortex, neurons are arranged according to the part of the body that generates the sensory input or receives the motor commands **(Figure 49.17)**. For example, neurons that process sensory information from the legs and feet lie in the region of the somatosensory cortex closest to the midline. Neurons that control muscles in the legs and feet are located in the corresponding region of the motor cortex. Notice in Figure 49.17 that the cortical surface area devoted to each body part is not proportional to the size of the part. Instead, surface area correlates with the extent of neuronal control needed

▶ **Figure 49.17 Body part representation in the primary motor and primary somatosensory cortices.** In these cross-sectional maps of the cortices, the cortical surface area devoted to each body part is represented by the relative size of that part in the cartoons.

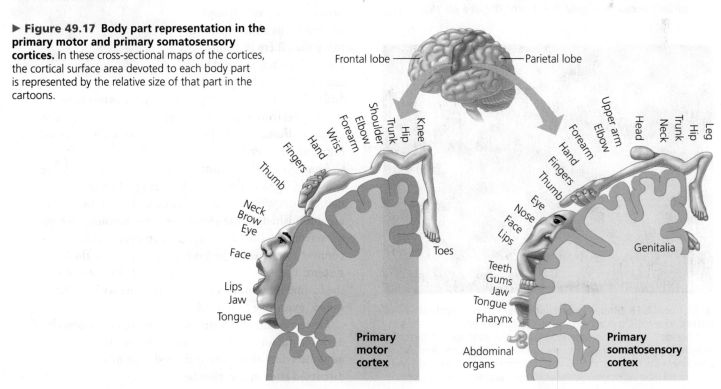

Frontal lobe

Parietal lobe

Shoulder, Trunk, Hip, Knee, Elbow, Forearm, Wrist, Hand, Fingers, Thumb, Neck, Brow, Eye, Face, Lips, Jaw, Tongue, Toes

Primary motor cortex

Upper arm, Elbow, Forearm, Hand, Fingers, Thumb, Eye, Nose, Face, Lips, Head, Neck, Trunk, Hip, Leg, Genitalia, Teeth, Gums, Jaw, Tongue, Pharynx, Abdominal organs

Primary somatosensory cortex

(for the motor cortex) or with the number of sensory neurons that extend axons to that part (for the somatosensory cortex). Thus, the surface area of the motor cortex devoted to the face is much larger than that devoted to the trunk, reflecting the extensive involvement of facial muscles in communication.

Although our focus here is on humans, it is worth noting that the processing sites for sensory information vary among vertebrates. In ray-finned fishes, for example, the relatively large midbrain (see Figure 49.10) serves as the primary center for processing and responding to visual stimuli. Such differences reflect a recognizable evolutionary trend: Following the vertebrate phylogenetic tree from sharks to ray-finned fishes, amphibians, reptiles, and finally mammals, one observes a steadily increasing role for the forebrain in processing sensory information.

Language and Speech

The mapping of cognitive functions within the cortex began in the 1800s when physicians studied the effects of damage to particular regions of the cortex by injuries, strokes, or tumors. Pierre Broca conducted postmortem (after death) examinations of patients who had been able to understand language but unable to speak. He discovered that many had defects in a small region of the left frontal lobe, now known as *Broca's area*. Karl Wernicke found that damage to a posterior portion of the left temporal lobe, now called *Wernicke's area*, abolished the ability to comprehend speech but not the ability to speak. PET studies have now confirmed activity in Broca's area during speech generation and Wernicke's area when speech is heard **(Figure 49.18)**.

▲ **Figure 49.18 Mapping language areas in the cerebral cortex.** These PET images show regions with different activity levels in one person's brain during four activities, all related to speech. Increases in activity are seen in Wernicke's area when hearing words, Broca's area when speaking words, the visual cortex when seeing words, and the frontal lobe when generating words (without reading them).

Lateralization of Cortical Function

Both Broca's area and Wernicke's area reside in the left cortical hemisphere, reflecting a greater role with regard to language for the left side of the cerebrum than for the right side. The left hemisphere is also more adept at math and logical operations. In contrast, the right hemisphere appears to be dominant in the recognition of faces and patterns, spatial relations, and nonverbal thinking. The establishment of these differences in hemisphere function is called **lateralization**.

The two cortical hemispheres normally exchange information through the fibers of the corpus callosum (see Figure 49.11). Severing this connection (a treatment of last resort for the most extreme forms of epilepsy, a seizure disorder) results in a "split-brain" effect. In such patients, the two hemispheres function independently. For example, they cannot read even a familiar word that appears only in their left field of vision: The sensory information that travels from the left field of vision to the right hemisphere cannot reach the language centers in the left hemisphere.

Frontal Lobe Function

In 1848, a horrific accident pointed to the role of the prefrontal cortex in temperament and decision making. Phineas Gage was the foreman of a railroad construction crew when an explosion drove an iron rod through his head. The rod, which was more than 3 cm in diameter at one end, entered his skull just below his left eye

and exited through the top of his head, damaging large portions of his frontal lobe. Gage recovered, but his personality changed dramatically. He became emotionally detached, impatient, and erratic in his behavior.

Some frontal lobe tumors cause symptoms similar to those of Gage's brain injury. Intellect and memory seem intact, but decision making is flawed and emotional responses are diminished. In the 1900s, the same problems resulted from frontal lobotomy, a surgical procedure that severs the connection between the prefrontal cortex and the limbic system. Together, these observations provide evidence that the frontal lobes have a substantial influence on what are called "executive functions."

Once a common treatment for severe behavioral disorders, frontal lobotomy is no longer in use. Instead, behavioral disorders are typically treated with medications, as discussed later in this chapter.

Evolution of Cognition in Vertebrates

EVOLUTION In nearly all vertebrates, the brain has the same basic structures (see Figure 49.10). Given this uniform organization, how did a capacity for advanced cognition, the perception and reasoning that constitute knowledge, evolve in certain species? One hypothesis is that higher-order reasoning required evolution of an extensively convoluted cerebral cortex, as is found in humans, other primates, and cetaceans (whales, dolphins, and porpoises). Indeed, in humans the cerebral cortex accounts for about 80% of total brain mass.

Birds, on the other hand, lack a convoluted cerebral cortex and were therefore thought to have much lower intellectual capacity than primates and cetaceans. However, experiments in recent years have refuted this idea. Western scrub jays (*Aphelocoma californica*) can remember which food items they hid first. New Caledonian crows (*Corvus moneduloides*) are highly skilled at making and using tools, an ability otherwise well documented only for humans and some other apes. Furthermore, African gray parrots (*Psittacus erithacus*) understand numerical and abstract concepts, such as "same" and "different" and "none."

The anatomical basis for sophisticated information processing in birds appears to be a clustered organization of neurons within the *pallium*, the top or outer portion of the brain **(Figure 49.19a)**. This arrangement is different from

(a) Songbird brain

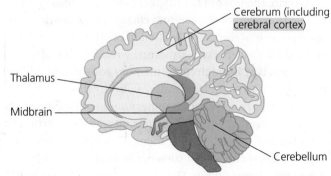

(b) Human brain

▲ **Figure 49.19 Comparison of regions for higher cognition in avian and human brains.** Although structurally different, the pallium of a songbird brain (a) and the cerebral cortex of the human brain (b) play similar roles in higher cognitive activities and make many similar connections with other brain structures.

that in the human cerebral cortex, where six parallel layers of neurons are arranged tangential to the brain surface **(Figure 49.19b)**. Thus, evolution has resulted in two types of outer brain organization in vertebrates that support complex and flexible brain function.

How did the bird pallium and human cerebral cortex arise during evolution? The current consensus is that the common ancestor of birds and mammals had a pallium in which neurons were organized into nuclei, as is still found in birds. Early in mammalian evolution, this clustered organization was transformed into a layered one. However, connectivity was maintained such that, for example, the thalamus relays sensory input relating to sights, sounds, and touch to the pallium in birds and the cerebral cortex in mammals.

Sophisticated information processing depends not only on the overall organization of a brain but also on the very small-scale changes that enable learning and encode memory. We'll turn to these changes in the context of humans in the next section.

CONCEPT CHECK 49.3

1. How can studying individuals with damage to a particular brain region provide insight into the normal function of that region?

2. How do the functions of Broca's area and Wernicke's area each relate to the activity of the surrounding cortex?

3. **WHAT IF?** If a woman with a severed corpus callosum viewed a photograph of a familiar face, first in her left field of vision and then in her right field, why would she find it difficult to put a name to the face?

For suggested answers, see Appendix A.

CONCEPT 49.4

Changes in synaptic connections underlie memory and learning

During embryonic development, regulated gene expression and signal transduction establish the overall structure of the nervous system (see Chapter 47). Two processes then dominate the remaining development and remodeling of the nervous system. The first is a competition among neurons for survival. Neurons compete for growth-supporting factors, which are produced in limited quantities by tissues that direct neuron growth. Cells that don't reach the proper locations fail to receive such factors and undergo programmed cell death. The competition is so severe that half of the neurons formed in the embryo are eliminated. The net effect is the preferential survival of neurons that are located properly within the nervous system.

Synapse elimination is the second major process that shapes the nervous system. A developing neuron forms numerous synapses, more than are required for its proper function. The activity of that neuron then stabilizes some synapses and destabilizes others. By the end of embryonic development, more than half of all synapses have been eliminated.

Together, neuron death and synapse elimination set up the basic network of cells and connections within the nervous system required throughout life.

Neuronal Plasticity

Although the overall organization of the CNS is established during embryonic development, the connections between neurons can be modified. This capacity for the nervous system to be remodeled, especially in response to its own activity, is called **neuronal plasticity**.

Much of the reshaping of the nervous system occurs at synapses. When the activity of a synapse coincides with that of other synapses, changes may occur that reinforce that synaptic connection. Conversely, when the activity of a synapse fails to correlate in this way with that of other synapses, the synaptic connection sometimes becomes weaker. In this way, synapses belonging to circuits that link information in useful ways are maintained, whereas those that convey bits of information lacking any context are lost.

Figure 49.20a illustrates how activity-dependent events can result in either the addition or loss of a synapse. If you think of signals in the nervous system as traffic on a highway, such changes are comparable to adding or removing an entrance ramp. The net effect is to increase signaling between particular pairs of neurons and decrease signaling between other pairs. As shown in **Figure 49.20b**, changes can also strengthen or weaken signaling at a synapse. In our traffic analogy, this would be equivalent to widening or narrowing an entrance ramp.

Research indicates that *autism*, a developmental disorder that first appears early in childhood, involves a disruption of activity-dependent remodeling at synapses. Children affected with autism display impaired communication and social interaction, as well as stereotyped and repetitive behaviors.

Although the underlying causes of autism are unknown, there is a strong genetic contribution to this and related disorders. Extensive research has ruled out a link to vaccine preservatives, once proposed as a potential risk factor. Further understanding of the autism-associated disruption in synaptic plasticity may help efforts to better understand and treat this disorder.

Memory and Learning

Neuronal plasticity is essential to the formation of memories. We are constantly checking what is happening against what just happened. We hold information for a time in **short-term**

(a) Connections between neurons are strengthened or weakened in response to activity. High-level activity at the synapse of the postsynaptic neuron with presynaptic neuron N_1 leads to recruitment of additional axon terminals from that neuron. Lack of activity at the synapse with presynaptic neuron N_2 leads to loss of functional connections with that neuron.

(b) If two synapses on the same postsynaptic cell are often active at the same time, the strength of the postsynaptic response may increase at both synapses.

▲ **Figure 49.20 Neuronal plasticity.** Synaptic connections can change over time, depending on the activity level at the synapse.

memory and then release it if it becomes irrelevant. If we wish to retain knowledge of a name, phone number, or other fact, the mechanisms of **long-term memory** are activated. If we later need to recall the name or number, we fetch it from long-term memory and return it to short-term memory.

Both short-term and long-term memory involve the storage of information in the cerebral cortex. In short-term memory, this information is accessed via temporary links formed in the hippocampus. When memories are made long-term, the links in the hippocampus are replaced by connections within the cerebral cortex itself. As discussed earlier, some of this consolidation of memory is thought to occur during sleep. Furthermore, the reactivation of the hippocampus that is required for memory consolidation likely forms the basis for at least some of our dreams.

According to our current understanding of memory, the hippocampus is essential for acquiring new long-term memories but not for maintaining them. This hypothesis readily explains the symptoms of some individuals who suffer damage to the hippocampus: They cannot form any new lasting memories but can freely recall events from before their injury. In effect, their lack of normal hippocampal function traps them in their past.

What evolutionary advantage might be offered by organizing short-term and long-term memories differently? One hypothesis is that the delay in forming connections in the cerebral cortex allows long-term memories to be integrated gradually into the existing store of knowledge and experience, providing a basis for more meaningful associations. Consistent with this hypothesis, the transfer of information from short-term to long-term memory is enhanced by the association of new data with data previously learned and stored in long-term memory. For example, it's easier to learn a new card game if you already have "card sense" from playing other card games.

Motor skills, such as tying your shoes or writing, are usually learned by repetition. You can perform these skills without consciously recalling the individual steps required to do these tasks correctly. Learning skills and procedures, such as those required to ride a bicycle, appears to involve cellular mechanisms very similar to those responsible for brain growth and development. In such cases, neurons actually make new connections. In contrast, memorizing phone numbers, facts, and places—which can be very rapid and may require only one exposure to the relevant item—may rely mainly on changes in the strength of existing neuronal connections. Next we will consider one way that such changes in strength can take place.

Long-Term Potentiation

In searching for the physiological basis of memory, researchers have concentrated their attention on processes that can alter a synaptic connection, making the flow of communication either more efficient or less efficient. We will focus here on **long-term potentiation (LTP)**, a lasting increase in the strength of synaptic transmission.

First characterized in tissue slices from the hippocampus, LTP involves a presynaptic neuron that releases the excitatory neurotransmitter glutamate. For LTP to occur, there must be a high-frequency series of action potentials in this presynaptic neuron. In addition, these action potentials must arrive at the synaptic terminal at the same time that the postsynaptic cell receives a depolarizing stimulus at another synapse. The net effect is to strengthen a synapse whose activity coincides with that of another input (see Figure 48.17a).

LTP involves two types of glutamate receptors, each named for a molecule—NMDA or AMPA—that can be used to artificially activate that particular receptor. As shown in **Figure 49.21**, the set of receptors present on the postsynaptic membrane changes in response to an active synapse and a depolarizing stimulus. The result is LTP—a stable increase in the size of the postsynaptic potentials at the synapse. Because LTP can last for days or weeks in dissected tissue, it is thought to represent one of the fundamental processes by which memories are stored and learning takes place.

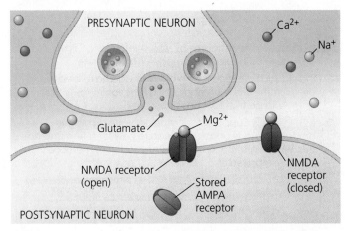

(a) Synapse prior to long-term potentiation (LTP). The NMDA glutamate receptors open in response to glutamate but are blocked by Mg^{2+}.

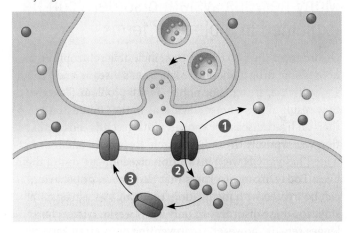

(b) Establishing LTP. Activity at nearby synapses (not shown) depolarizes the postsynaptic membrane, causing ❶ Mg^{2+} release from NMDA receptors. The unblocked receptors respond to glutamate by allowing ❷ an influx of Na^+ and Ca^{2+}. The Ca^{2+} influx triggers ❸ insertion of stored AMPA glutamate receptors into the postsynaptic membrane.

(c) Synapse exhibiting LTP. Glutamate release activates ❶ AMPA receptors that trigger ❷ depolarization. The depolarization unblocks ❸ NMDA receptors. Together, the AMPA and NMDA receptors trigger postsynaptic potentials strong enough to initiate ❹ action potentials without input from other synapses. Additional mechanisms (not shown) contribute to LTP, including receptor modification by protein kinases.

▲ **Figure 49.21 Long-term potentiation in the brain.**

1. Outline two mechanisms by which information flow between two neurons in an adult can increase.

2. Individuals with localized brain damage have been very useful in the study of many brain functions. Why is this unlikely to be true for consciousness?

3. **WHAT IF?** Suppose that a person with damage to the hippocampus is unable to acquire new long-term memories. Why might the acquisition of short-term memories also be impaired?

For suggested answers, see Appendix A.

CONCEPT 49.5

Many nervous system disorders can be explained in molecular terms

Disorders of the nervous system, including schizophrenia, depression, drug addiction, Alzheimer's disease, and Parkinson's disease, are a major public health problem. Together, they result in more hospitalizations in the United States than do heart disease or cancer. Until recently, hospitalization was typically the only available treatment, and many affected individuals were institutionalized for the rest of their lives. Today, many disorders that alter mood or behavior can be treated with medication, reducing average hospital stays for these disorders to only a few weeks. Many challenges remain, however, to preventing or treating nervous system disorders, especially for Alzheimer's and other diseases that lead to nervous system degeneration.

Major research efforts are under way to identify genes that cause or contribute to disorders of the nervous system. Identifying such genes offers hope for identifying causes, predicting outcomes, and developing effective treatments. For most nervous system disorders, however, genetic contributions only partially account for which individuals are affected. The other significant contribution to disease comes from environmental factors. Unfortunately, environmental contributions are typically very difficult to identify.

To distinguish between genetic and environmental variables, scientists often carry out family studies. In such studies, researchers track how family members are related genetically, which individuals are affected, and which family members grew up in the same household. These studies are especially informative when one of the affected individuals has either an identical twin or an adopted sibling who is genetically unrelated. The results of family studies indicate that certain nervous system disorders, such as schizophrenia, have a very strong genetic component. However, as shown in **Figure 49.22**, the disease is also subject to environmental influences, since an individual who shares 100% of his or her genes with a schizophrenic twin has only a 48% chance of developing the disorder.

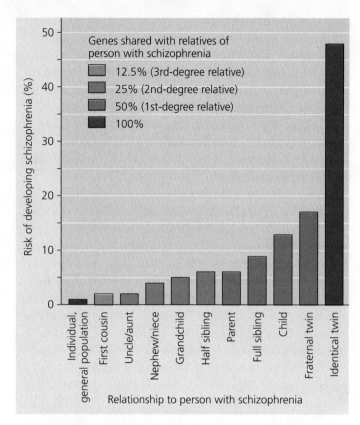

▲ **Figure 49.22 Genetic contribution to schizophrenia.** First cousins, uncles, and aunts of a person with schizophrenia have twice the risk of unrelated members of the population of developing the disease. The risks for closer relatives are many times greater.

INTERPRET THE DATA *What is the likelihood of a person developing schizophrenia if the disorder affects his or her fraternal twin? How would the likelihood change if DNA sequencing revealed that the twins shared the genetic variants that contribute to the disorder?*

Schizophrenia

Approximately 1% of the world's population suffers from **schizophrenia**, a severe mental disturbance characterized by psychotic episodes in which patients have a distorted perception of reality. People with schizophrenia typically experience hallucinations (such as "voices" that only they can hear) and delusions (for example, the idea that others are plotting to harm them). Despite the commonly held notion, schizophrenia does not necessarily result in multiple personalities. Rather, the name *schizophrenia* (from the Greek *schizo*, split, and *phren*, mind) refers to the fragmentation of what are normally integrated brain functions.

Two lines of evidence suggest that schizophrenia affects neuronal pathways that use dopamine as a neurotransmitter. First, the drug amphetamine ("speed"), which stimulates dopamine release, can produce the same set of symptoms as schizophrenia. Second, many of the drugs that alleviate the symptoms of schizophrenia block dopamine receptors. Schizophrenia may also alter glutamate signaling: The street drug "angel dust," or PCP, blocks glutamate receptors and induces strong schizophrenia-like symptoms.

Depression

Depression is a disorder characterized by depressed mood, as well as abnormalities in sleep, appetite, and energy level. Two broad forms of depressive illness are known: major depressive disorder and bipolar disorder. Individuals affected by **major depressive disorder** undergo periods—often lasting many months—during which once enjoyable activities provide no pleasure and provoke no interest. One of the most common nervous system disorders, major depression affects about one in every seven adults at some point, and twice as many women as men.

Bipolar disorder, or manic-depressive disorder, involves extreme swings of mood and affects about 1% of the world's population. The manic phase is characterized by high self-esteem, increased energy, a flow of ideas, overtalkativeness, and increased risk taking. In its milder forms, this phase is sometimes associated with great creativity, and some well-known artists, musicians, and literary figures (Vincent Van Gogh, Robert Schumann, Virginia Woolf, and Ernest Hemingway, to name a few) have had very productive periods during manic phases. The depressive phase comes with lowered ability to feel pleasure, loss of motivation, sleep disturbances, and feelings of worthlessness. These symptoms can be so severe that affected individuals attempt suicide.

Major depressive and bipolar disorders are among the nervous system disorders for which effective therapies are available. Many drugs used to treat depressive illness, including fluoxetine (Prozac), increase the activity of biogenic amines in the brain.

The Brain's Reward System and Drug Addiction

Emotions are strongly influenced by a neuronal circuit in the brain called the *reward system*. The reward system provides motivation for activities that enhance survival and reproduction, such as eating in response to hunger, drinking when thirsty, and engaging in sexual activity when aroused. As shown in **Figure 49.23**, inputs to the reward system are received by neurons in a region near the base of the brain called the *ventral tegmental area (VTA)*. When activated, these neurons release dopamine from their synaptic terminals in specific regions of the cerebrum, including the *nucleus accumbens* (see Figure 49.15).

The brain's reward system is dramatically affected by drug addiction, a disorder characterized by compulsive consumption of a drug and loss of control in limiting intake. Addictive drugs, which range from sedatives to stimulants and include alcohol, cocaine, nicotine, and heroin, enhance the activity of the dopamine pathway (see Figure 49.23). As addiction develops, there are also long-lasting changes in the reward circuitry. The result is a craving for the drug independent of any pleasure associated with consumption.

▲ Figure 49.23 Effects of addictive drugs on the reward system of the mammalian brain. Addictive drugs alter the transmission of signals in the pathway formed by neurons of the ventral tegmental area (VTA), a region near the base of the brain.

MAKE CONNECTIONS *What effect would you expect if you depolarized the neurons in the VTA (see Concept 48.3)? Explain.*

Laboratory animals are highly valuable in exploring how the reward system works and how addictive drugs affect its function. For example, Ulrike Heberlein, interviewed at the start of Unit Seven, has shown that the response of fruit flies to alcohol resembles that of humans in several ways, including a loss of coordination and eventually consciousness upon inebriation and a change in responsiveness to alcohol over time. Using fly genetics, she is discovering genes that carry out or control these responses. To study the effects of cocaine or amphetamine in rats, researchers outfit a cage with a dispensing system linked to a lever. In such circumstances, rats exhibit addictive behavior, continuing to self-administer the drug rather than seek food, even to the point of starvation.

As scientists expand their knowledge about the brain's reward system and the various forms of addiction, there is hope that the insights will lead to more effective prevention and treatment.

Alzheimer's Disease

Alzheimer's disease is a mental deterioration, or dementia, characterized by confusion and memory loss. Its incidence

Amyloid plaque   Neurofibrillary tangle   20 μm

▲ **Figure 49.24 Microscopic signs of Alzheimer's disease.** A hallmark of Alzheimer's disease is the presence in brain tissue of neurofibrillary tangles surrounding plaques made of β-amyloid (LM).

is age related, rising from about 10% at age 65 to about 35% at age 85. The disease is progressive, with patients gradually becoming less able to function and eventually needing to be dressed, bathed, and fed by others. Moreover, patients with Alzheimer's disease often lose their ability to recognize people, including their immediate family, and may treat them with suspicion and hostility.

As shown in **Figure 49.24**, examining the brains of individuals who have died of Alzheimer's disease reveals two characteristic features: amyloid plaques and neurofibrillary tangles. There is also often massive shrinkage of brain tissue, reflecting the death of neurons in many areas of the brain, including the hippocampus and cerebral cortex.

The plaques are aggregates of β-amyloid, an insoluble peptide that is cleaved from the extracellular portion of a membrane protein found in neurons. Membrane enzymes, called secretases, catalyze the cleavage, causing β-amyloid to accumulate in plaques outside the neurons. It is these plaques that appear to trigger the death of surrounding neurons.

The neurofibrillary tangles observed in Alzheimer's disease are primarily made up of the tau protein. (This protein is unrelated to the tau mutation that affects circadian rhythm in hamsters.) The tau protein normally helps assemble and maintain microtubules that transport nutrients along axons. In Alzheimer's disease, tau undergoes changes that cause it to bind to itself, resulting in neurofibrillary tangles. There is evidence that changes in tau are associated with the appearance of early-onset Alzheimer's disease, a much less common disorder that affects relatively young individuals.

There is currently no cure for Alzheimer's disease, but an enormous effort has led to the recent development of drugs that are partially effective in relieving some symptoms. Doctors are also beginning to use functional brain imaging to diagnose Alzheimer's disease in patients exhibiting early signs of dementia.

Parkinson's Disease

Symptoms of **Parkinson's disease**, a motor disorder, include muscle tremors, poor balance, a flexed posture, and a shuffling gait. Facial muscles become rigid, limiting the ability of patients to vary their expressions. Cognitive defects may also develop. Like Alzheimer's disease, Parkinson's disease is a progressive brain illness and is more common with advancing age. The incidence of Parkinson's disease is about 1% at age 65 and about 5% at age 85. In the U.S. population, approximately 1 million people are afflicted.

Parkinson's disease involves the death of neurons in the midbrain that normally release dopamine at synapses in the basal nuclei. As with Alzheimer's disease, protein aggregates accumulate. Most cases of Parkinson's disease lack an identifiable cause; however, a rare form of the disease that appears in relatively young adults has a clear genetic basis. Molecular studies of mutations linked to this early-onset Parkinson's disease reveal disruption of genes required for certain mitochondrial functions. Researchers are investigating whether mitochondrial defects also contribute to the more common and later-onset form of the disease.

At present Parkinson's disease can be treated, but not cured. Approaches used to manage the symptoms include brain surgery, deep-brain stimulation, and a dopamine-related drug, L-dopa. Unlike dopamine, L-dopa crosses the blood-brain barrier. Within the brain, the enzyme dopa decarboxylase converts the drug to dopamine, reducing the severity of Parkinson's disease symptoms:

$$HO-\bigcirc-CH_2-CH(NH_2)-CO_2H \xrightarrow{\text{Dopa decarboxylase}} HO-\bigcirc-CH_2-CH_2-NH_2$$

L-dopa   →   Dopamine

One potential cure is to implant dopamine-secreting neurons, either in the midbrain or in the basal nuclei. Laboratory studies of this strategy show promise: In rats with an experimentally induced condition that mimics Parkinson's disease, implanting dopamine-secreting neurons can lead to a recovery of motor control. Whether this regenerative approach can also work in humans is one of many important questions in modern brain research.

CONCEPT CHECK 49.5

1. Compare Alzheimer's disease and Parkinson's disease.
2. How is dopamine activity related to schizophrenia, drug addiction, and Parkinson's disease?
3. **WHAT IF?** If you could detect early-stage Alzheimer's disease, would you expect to see brain changes that were similar to, although less extensive than, those seen in patients who have died of this disease? Explain.

For suggested answers, see Appendix A.

CONCEPT 49.1

Nervous systems consist of circuits of neurons and supporting cells (pp. 1080–1084)

- Invertebrate nervous systems range in complexity from simple nerve nets to highly centralized nervous systems having complicated brains and ventral nerve cords.

Hydra (cnidarian)   **Salamander (vertebrate)**

- In vertebrates, the **central nervous system (CNS)**, consisting of the brain and the spinal cord, integrates information, while the **nerves** of the **peripheral nervous system (PNS)** transmit sensory and motor signals between the CNS and the rest of the body. The simplest circuits control **reflex** responses, in which sensory input is linked to motor output without involvement of the brain.

- Afferent neurons carry sensory signals to the CNS. Efferent neurons function in either the **motor system**, which carries signals to skeletal muscles, or the **autonomic nervous system**, which regulates smooth and cardiac muscles. The **sympathetic** and **parasympathetic divisions** of the autonomic nervous system have antagonistic effects on a diverse set of target organs, while the **enteric division** controls the activity of many digestive organs.
- Vertebrate neurons are supported by **glia**, including **astrocytes**, oligodendrocytes, and Schwann cells. Some glia serve as stem cells that can differentiate into mature neurons.

? *How does the circuitry of a reflex facilitate a rapid response?*

CONCEPT 49.2

The vertebrate brain is regionally specialized (pp. 1085–1090)

- The cerebrum has two hemispheres, each of which consists of cortical **gray matter** overlying **white matter** and basal nuclei. The basal nuclei are important in planning and learning movements. The **pons** and **medulla oblongata** are relay stations for information traveling between the PNS and the cerebrum. The reticular formation, a network of neurons within the **brainstem**, regulates sleep and arousal. The **cerebellum** helps coordinate motor, perceptual, and cognitive functions. The **thalamus** is the main center through which sensory information passes to the **cerebrum**. The **hypothalamus** regulates homeostasis and basic survival behaviors. Within the hypothalamus, a group of neurons called the **suprachiasmatic nucleus (SCN)** acts as the pacemaker for circadian rhythms. The **amygdala** plays a key role in recognizing and recalling a number of emotions.

? *What roles do the midbrain, cerebellum, thalamus, and cerebrum play in vision and responses to visual input?*

CONCEPT 49.3

The cerebral cortex controls voluntary movement and cognitive functions (pp. 1090–1093)

- Each side of the **cerebral cortex** has four lobes—frontal, temporal, occipital, and parietal—that contain primary sensory areas and association areas. Association areas integrate information from different sensory areas. Broca's area and Wernicke's area are essential for generating and understanding language. These functions are concentrated in the left **cerebral hemisphere**, as are math and logic operations. The right hemisphere appears to be stronger at pattern recognition and nonverbal thinking.
- In the somatosensory cortex and the motor cortex, neurons are distributed according to the part of the body that generates sensory input or receives motor commands.
- Primates and cetaceans, which are capable of higher cognition, have an extensively convoluted cerebral cortex. In birds, a brain region called the pallium contains clustered nuclei that carry out functions similar to those performed by the cerebral cortex of mammals. Some birds can solve problems and understand abstractions in a manner indicative of higher cognition.

? *A patient has trouble with language and has paralysis on one side of the body. Which side would you expect to be paralyzed? Why?*

CONCEPT 49.4

Changes in synaptic connections underlie memory and learning (pp. 1093–1096)

- During development, more neurons and synapses form than will exist in the adult. The programmed death of neurons and elimination of synapses in embryos establish the basic structure of the nervous system. In the adult, reshaping of the nervous system can involve the loss or addition of synapses or the strengthening or weakening of signaling at synapses. This capacity for remodeling is termed **neuronal plasticity**. **Short-term memory** relies on temporary links in the hippocampus. In **long-term memory**, these temporary links are replaced by connections within the cerebral cortex.

? *Learning multiple languages is typically easier early in childhood than later in life. How does this fit with our understanding of neural development?*

CONCEPT 49.5

Many nervous system disorders can be explained in molecular terms (pp. 1096–1098)

- **Schizophrenia**, which is characterized by hallucinations, delusions, and other symptoms, affects neuronal pathways that use dopamine as a neurotransmitter. Drugs that increase the activity of biogenic amines in the brain can be used to treat **bipolar disorder** and **major depressive disorder**. The compulsive drug use that characterizes addiction reflects altered activity of the brain's reward system, which normally provides motivation for actions that enhance survival or reproduction.
- **Alzheimer's disease** and **Parkinson's disease** are neurodegenerative and typically age related. Alzheimer's disease is a dementia in which neurofibrillary tangles and amyloid plaques form in the brain. Parkinson's disease is a motor disorder caused by the death of dopamine-secreting neurons and associated with the presence of protein aggregates.

? *The fact that both amphetamine and PCP have effects similar to the symptoms of schizophrenia suggests a potentially complex basis for this disease. Explain.*

TEST YOUR UNDERSTANDING

LEVEL 1: KNOWLEDGE/COMPREHENSION

1. Wakefulness is regulated by the reticular formation, which is present in the
   a. basal nuclei.
   b. brainstem.
   c. limbic system.
   d. spinal cord.

2. Which of the following structures or regions is *incorrectly* paired with its function?
   a. limbic system—motor control of speech
   b. medulla oblongata—homeostatic control
   c. cerebellum—coordination of movement and balance
   d. amygdala—emotional memory

3. Patients with damage to Wernicke's area have difficulty
   a. coordinating limb movement.
   b. generating speech.
   c. recognizing faces.
   d. understanding language.

4. The cerebral cortex does *not* play a major role in
   a. short-term memory.   c. circadian rhythm.
   b. long-term memory.   d. breath holding.

LEVEL 2: APPLICATION/ANALYSIS

5. After suffering a stroke, a patient can see objects anywhere in front of him but pays attention only to objects in his right field of vision. When asked to describe these objects, he has difficulty judging their size and distance. What part of the brain was likely damaged by the stroke?
   a. the left frontal lobe   c. the right parietal lobe
   b. the right frontal lobe   d. the corpus callosum

6. Injury localized to the hypothalamus would most likely disrupt
   a. regulation of body temperature.
   b. short-term memory.
   c. executive functions, such as decision making.
   d. sorting of sensory information.

7. **DRAW IT** The reflex that pulls your hand away when you prick your finger on a sharp object relies on a neuronal circuit with two synapses in the spinal cord. (a) Using a circle to represent a cross section of the spinal cord, draw the circuit, labeling the types of neurons, the direction of information flow in each, and the locations of synapses. (b) Draw a simple diagram of the brain indicating where pain would eventually be perceived.

LEVEL 3: SYNTHESIS/EVALUATION

8. **EVOLUTION CONNECTION**
   Scientists often use measures of "higher-order thinking" to assess intelligence in other animals. For example, birds are judged to have sophisticated thought processes because they can use tools and make use of abstract concepts. What problems do you see in defining intelligence in these ways?

9. **SCIENTIFIC INQUIRY**
   Consider an individual who had been fluent in American Sign Language before suffering an injury to his left cerebral hemisphere. After the injury, he could still understand that sign language but could not readily generate sign language that represented his thoughts. What two hypotheses could explain this finding? How might you distinguish between them?

10. **SCIENCE, TECHNOLOGY, AND SOCIETY**
    With increasingly sophisticated methods for scanning brain activity, scientists are developing the ability to detect an individual's particular emotions and thought processes from outside the body. What benefits and problems do you envision when such technology becomes readily available?

11. **WRITE ABOUT A THEME: INFORMATION**
    In a short essay (100–150 words), explain how specification of the adult nervous system by the genome is incomplete.

12. **SYNTHESIZE YOUR KNOWLEDGE**

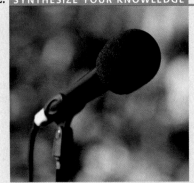

Imagine you are standing at a microphone in front of a crowd. Checking your notes, you begin speaking. Using the information in this chapter, describe the series of events in particular regions of the brain that enabled you to say the very first word.

MasteringBiology®

Students Go to **MasteringBiology** for assignments, the eText, and the Study Area with practice tests, animations, and activities.

Instructors Go to **MasteringBiology** for automatically graded tutorials and questions that you can assign to your students, plus Instructor Resources.

50

Sensory and Motor Mechanisms

KEY CONCEPTS

50.1 Sensory receptors transduce
stimulus energy and transmit
signals to the central nervous
system

50.2 The mechanoreceptors
responsible for hearing and
equilibrium detect moving fluid
or settling particles

50.3 The diverse visual receptors
of animals depend on light-
absorbing pigments

50.4 The senses of taste and smell
rely on similar sets of sensory
receptors

50.5 The physical interaction of
protein filaments is required for
muscle function

50.6 Skeletal systems transform
muscle contraction into
locomotion

▲ **Figure 50.1 Of what use is a star-shaped nose?**

Sense and Sensibility

Tunneling beneath the wetlands of eastern North America, the star-nosed mole (*Condylura cristata*) lives in almost total darkness. Virtually blind, the mole is nonetheless a remarkably deft predator, capable of detecting and eating its prey in as little as 120 milliseconds. Central to this hunting prowess are 11 pairs of appendages that protrude from its nose, forming a prominent pink star **(Figure 50.1)**. Although they look a bit like fingers, these appendages are not used in grasping. Nor are they used to detect odors. Instead, they are highly specialized to detect touch. Just below their surface lie 25,000 touch-sensitive receptors, more than are found in your whole hand. Over 100,000 neurons relay tactile information from these receptors to the mole's brain.

Detecting and processing sensory information and generating motor responses provide the physiological basis for all animal behavior. In this chapter, we'll explore the processes of sensing and acting in both vertebrates and invertebrates. We'll start with sensory processes that convey information about an animal's external and internal environment to its brain. We'll then consider the structure and function of muscles and skeletons that carry out movements as instructed by the brain. Finally, we'll investigate various mechanisms of animal movement. These topics will lead us naturally to our discussion of animal behavior in Chapter 51.

CONCEPT 50.1

Sensory receptors transduce stimulus energy and transmit signals to the central nervous system

All sensory processes begin with stimuli, and all stimuli represent forms of energy. A sensory receptor converts stimulus energy to a change in membrane potential, thereby regulating the output of action potentials to the central nervous system (CNS). Decoding of this information within the CNS results in sensation.

When a stimulus is received and processed by the nervous system, a motor response may be generated. One of the simplest stimulus-response circuits is a reflex, such as the knee-jerk reflex shown in Figure 49.7. Many other behaviors rely on more elaborate processing of sensory input. As an example, consider how the star-nosed mole forages **(Figure 50.2)**. When the mole's nose contacts an object in its tunnel, touch receptors in the nose are activated. These receptors transmit sensory information about the object to the mole's brain. Circuits in the brain integrate the input and initiate one of two response pathways, depending on whether food was detected. Motor output commands sent from the brain to skeletal muscles cause the mole to either bite down with its teeth or continue moving along the tunnel.

With this overview in mind, let's examine the general organization and activity of animal sensory systems. We'll focus on four basic functions common to sensory pathways: sensory reception, transduction, transmission, and perception.

Sensory Reception and Transduction

A sensory pathway begins with **sensory reception**, the detection of a stimulus by sensory cells. Some sensory cells are themselves specialized neurons, whereas others are non-neuronal cells that regulate neurons **(Figure 50.3)**. Some exist singly; others are collected in sensory organs, such as the star-shaped nose of the mole in Figure 50.1.

The term **sensory receptor** is used to describe a sensory cell or organ, as well as the subcellular structure that detects stimuli. Many sensory receptors detect stimuli from outside the body, such as heat, light, pressure, or chemicals. However, there are also receptors for stimuli from within the body, such as blood pressure and body position. Activating a sensory receptor does not necessarily require a large amount of stimulus energy. Indeed, some sensory receptors can detect the smallest possible unit of stimulus. Most light receptors, for example, can detect a single quantum (photon) of light.

Although animals use a range of sensory receptors to detect widely varying stimuli, the effect in all cases is to open or close ion channels. Thus, for example, ion channels either

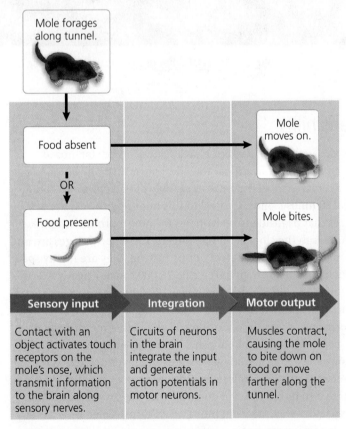

▲ **Figure 50.2 A simple response pathway: foraging by a star-nosed mole.**

▼ **Figure 50.3 Categories of sensory receptors.**

Neuronal receptors: Receptor *is* afferent neuron.	Non-neuronal receptors: Receptor *regulates* afferent neuron.

open or close when a substance outside the cell binds to a chemical receptor in the plasma membrane. The resulting flow of ions across the membrane changes the membrane potential.

The conversion of a physical or chemical stimulus to a change in the membrane potential of a sensory receptor is called **sensory transduction**, and the change in membrane potential itself is known as a **receptor potential**. Receptor potentials are graded potentials; their magnitude varies with the strength of the stimulus.

Transmission

Sensory information travels through the nervous system as nerve impulses, or action potentials. For many sensory receptors, transducing the energy in a stimulus into a receptor potential initiates action potentials that are transmitted to the CNS.

Neurons that act directly as sensory receptors produce action potentials and have an axon that extends into the CNS (see Figure 50.3). Non-neuronal sensory receptor cells form chemical synapses with sensory (afferent) neurons and typically respond to stimuli by increasing the rate at which the afferent neurons produce action potentials. (One exception is in the vertebrate visual system, discussed in Concept 50.3.)

The size of a receptor potential increases with the intensity of the stimulus. If the receptor is a sensory neuron, a larger receptor potential results in more frequent action potentials **(Figure 50.4)**. If the receptor is not a sensory neuron, a larger receptor potential usually causes more neurotransmitter to be released.

Many sensory neurons spontaneously generate action potentials at a low rate. In these neurons, a stimulus does not switch the production of action potentials on or off, but it does change *how often* an action potential is produced. In this manner, such neurons are also able to alert the nervous system to changes in stimulus intensity.

▲ **Figure 50.4 Coding of stimulus intensity by a single sensory receptor.**

Processing of sensory information can occur before, during, and after transmission of action potentials to the CNS. In many cases, the *integration* of sensory information begins as soon as the information is received. Receptor potentials produced by stimuli delivered to different parts of a sensory receptor cell are integrated through summation, as are postsynaptic potentials in sensory neurons that form synapses with multiple receptors (see Figure 48.15). As we will discuss shortly, sensory structures such as eyes also provide higher levels of integration, and the brain further processes all incoming signals.

Perception

When action potentials reach the brain via sensory neurons, circuits of neurons process this input, generating the **perception** of the stimuli. Perceptions—such as colors, smells, sounds, and tastes—are constructions formed in the brain and do not exist outside it. So, if a tree falls and no animal is present to hear it, is there a sound? The falling tree certainly produces pressure waves in the air, but if sound is defined as a perception, then there is none unless an animal senses the waves and its brain perceives them.

An action potential triggered by light striking the eye has the same properties as an action potential triggered by air vibrating in the ear. How, then, do we distinguish sights, sounds, and other stimuli? The answer lies in the connections that link sensory receptors to the brain. Action potentials from sensory receptors travel along neurons that are dedicated to a particular stimulus; these dedicated neurons synapse with particular neurons in the brain or spinal cord. As a result, the brain distinguishes stimuli such as sight or sound solely by the path along which the action potentials have arrived.

Amplification and Adaptation

The transduction of stimuli by sensory receptors is subject to two types of modification—amplification and adaptation. **Amplification** refers to the strengthening of a sensory signal during transduction. The effect can be considerable. For example, an action potential conducted from the eye to the human brain has about 100,000 times as much energy as the few photons of light that triggered it.

Amplification that occurs in sensory receptor cells often requires signal transduction pathways involving second messengers. Because these pathways include enzyme-catalyzed reactions, they amplify signal strength through the formation of many product molecules by a single enzyme molecule. Amplification may also take place in accessory structures of a complex sense organ, as when the pressure associated with sound waves is enhanced more than 20-fold before reaching receptors in the innermost part of the ear.

Upon continued stimulation, many receptors undergo a decrease in responsiveness termed **sensory adaptation** (not to be confused with the evolutionary term *adaptation*). Without sensory adaptation, you would be constantly aware of feeling every beat of your heart and every bit of clothing on your body. Adaptation also enables you to see, hear, and smell changes in the environment that vary widely in stimulus intensity.

Types of Sensory Receptors

We can classify sensory receptors into five categories based on the nature of the stimuli they transduce: mechanoreceptors, chemoreceptors, electromagnetic receptors, thermoreceptors, and pain receptors.

Mechanoreceptors

Mechanoreceptors sense physical deformation caused by forms of mechanical energy such as pressure, touch, stretch, motion, and sound. Mechanoreceptors typically consist of ion channels that are linked to structures that extend outside the cell, such as "hairs" (cilia), as well as internal cell structures, such as the cytoskeleton. Bending or stretching of the external structure generates tension that alters the permeability of the ion channels. This change in ion permeability alters the membrane potential, resulting in a depolarization or hyperpolarization (see Chapter 48).

The vertebrate stretch receptor, a mechanoreceptor that detects muscle movement, triggers the familiar knee-jerk reflex (see Figure 49.7). Vertebrate stretch receptors are dendrites of sensory neurons that spiral around the middle of certain small skeletal muscle fibers. When the muscle fibers are stretched, the sensory neurons depolarize, triggering nerve impulses that reach the spinal cord, activate motor neurons, and generate a reflex response.

Mechanoreceptors that are the dendrites of sensory neurons are also responsible for the mammalian sense of touch. Touch receptors are often embedded in layers of connective tissue. The structure of the connective tissue and the location of the receptors dramatically affect the type of mechanical energy (light touch, vibration, or strong pressure) that best stimulates them **(Figure 50.5)**. Receptors that detect a light touch or vibration are close to the surface of the skin; they transduce very slight inputs of mechanical energy into receptor potentials. Receptors that respond to stronger pressure and vibrations are in deep skin layers.

Some animals use mechanoreceptors to literally get a feel for their environment. For example, cats as well as many rodents have extremely sensitive mechanoreceptors at the base of their whiskers. Because deflection of different whiskers triggers action potentials that reach different cells in the brain, an animal's whiskers provide detailed information about nearby objects.

▲ **Figure 50.5 Sensory receptors in human skin.** Most receptors in the dermis are encapsulated by connective tissue. Receptors in the epidermis are naked dendrites, as are hair movement receptors that wind around the base of hairs in the dermis.

Chemoreceptors

Chemoreceptors include both general receptors—those that transmit information about total solute concentration—and specific receptors—those that respond to individual kinds of molecules. Osmoreceptors in the mammalian brain, for example, detect changes in the total solute concentration of the blood and stimulate thirst when osmolarity increases (see Figure 44.18). Most animals also have receptors for specific molecules, including glucose, oxygen, carbon dioxide, and amino acids.

Two of the most sensitive and specific chemoreceptors known are found in the antennae of the male silkworm moth **(Figure 50.6)**; they detect the two chemical components of the female moth sex pheromone. For pheromones and other molecules detected by chemoreceptors, the stimulus molecule binds to the specific receptor on the membrane of the sensory cell and initiates changes in ion permeability.

Electromagnetic Receptors

Electromagnetic receptors detect forms of electromagnetic energy, such as light, electricity, and magnetism. For example, the platypus has electroreceptors on its bill that are

▲ **Figure 50.6 Chemoreceptors in an insect.** The antennae of the male silkworm moth *Bombyx mori* are covered with sensory hairs, visible in the SEM enlargement. The hairs have chemoreceptors that are highly sensitive to the sex pheromone released by the female.

(a) Some migrating animals, such as these beluga whales, apparently sense Earth's magnetic field and use the information, along with other cues, for orientation.

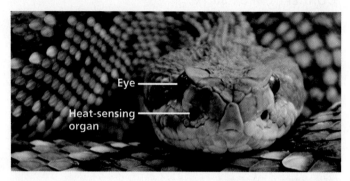

(b) This rattlesnake and other pit vipers have a pair of heat-sensing pit organs, one anterior to and just below each eye. These organs are sensitive enough to detect the infrared radiation emitted by a warm prey a meter away. The snake moves its head from side to side until the radiation is detected equally by the two pit organs, indicating that the prey is straight ahead.

▲ **Figure 50.7 Examples of electromagnetic reception and thermoreception.**

thought to detect the electric field generated by the muscles of crustaceans, small fish, and other prey. In a few cases, the animal detecting the stimulus is also its source: Some fishes generate electric currents and then use electroreceptors to locate prey or other objects that disturb those currents.

Many animals appear to use Earth's magnetic field lines to orient themselves as they migrate **(Figure 50.7a)**, and the iron-containing mineral magnetite may be responsible for this ability. Once collected by sailors to make compasses for navigation, magnetite is found in many vertebrates (including salmon, pigeons, sea turtles, and humans), in bees, in some molluscs, and in certain protists and prokaryotes that orient to Earth's magnetic field.

Thermoreceptors

Thermoreceptors detect heat and cold. For example, certain venomous snakes rely on thermoreceptors to detect the infrared radiation emitted by warm prey. These thermoreceptors are located in a pair of pit organs on the snake's head **(Figure 50.7b)**. Human thermoreceptors, which are located in the skin and in the anterior hypothalamus, send information to the body's thermostat in the posterior hypothalamus. Recently, our understanding of thermoreception has increased substantially, thanks to scientists with an appreciation for fiery foods. Jalapeno and cayenne peppers that we describe as "hot" contain a substance called capsaicin. Applying capsaicin to a sensory neuron causes an influx of calcium ions. When scientists identified the receptor protein

in neurons that binds capsaicin, they made a fascinating discovery: The receptor opens a calcium channel in response not only to capsaicin, but also to high temperatures (42°C or higher). In essence, spicy foods taste "hot" because they activate the same receptors as hot soup and coffee.

Mammals have a variety of thermoreceptors, each specific for a particular temperature range. The capsaicin receptor and at least five other types of thermoreceptors belong to the TRP (transient receptor potential) family of ion channel proteins. Just as the TRP-type receptor specific for high temperature is sensitive to capsaicin, the receptor for temperatures below 28°C can be activated by menthol, a plant product that we perceive to have a "cool" flavor.

Pain Receptors

Extreme pressure or temperature, as well as certain chemicals, can damage animal tissues. To detect stimuli that reflect such noxious (harmful) conditions, animals rely on **nociceptors** (from the Latin *nocere*, to hurt), also called **pain receptors**. By triggering defensive reactions, such as withdrawal from danger, the perception of pain serves an important function.

Chemicals produced in an animal's body sometimes enhance the perception of pain. For example, damaged tissues produce prostaglandins, which act as local regulators of inflammation (see Chapter 45). Prostaglandins worsen pain by increasing nociceptor sensitivity to noxious stimuli. Aspirin and ibuprofen reduce pain by inhibiting the synthesis of prostaglandins.

Next we'll turn our focus to sensory systems, beginning with systems for maintaining balance and detecting sound.

CONCEPT CHECK 50.1

1. Which one of the five categories of sensory receptors is primarily dedicated to external stimuli?

2. Why can eating "hot" peppers cause a person to sweat?

3. **WHAT IF?** If you stimulated a sensory neuron electrically, how would that stimulation be perceived?

For suggested answers, see Appendix A.

CONCEPT 50.2

The mechanoreceptors responsible for hearing and equilibrium detect moving fluid or settling particles

Hearing and the perception of body equilibrium, or balance, are related in most animals. For both senses, mechanoreceptor cells produce receptor potentials in response to deflection of cell-surface structures by settling particles or moving fluid.

Sensing of Gravity and Sound in Invertebrates

To sense gravity and maintain equilibrium, most invertebrates rely on mechanoreceptors located in organs called **statocysts (Figure 50.8)**. In a typical statocyst, **statoliths,**

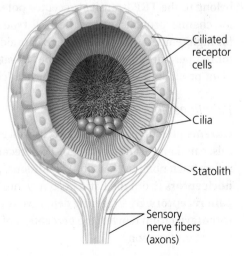

▶ **Figure 50.8 The statocyst of an invertebrate.** The settling of granules called statoliths to the low point in the chamber bends cilia on receptor cells in that location, providing the brain with information about the orientation of the body with respect to gravity.

Ciliated receptor cells

Cilia

Statolith

Sensory nerve fibers (axons)

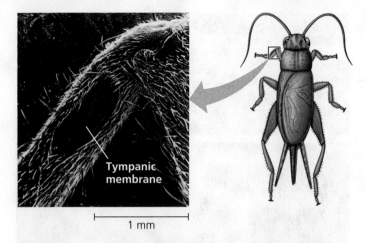

▲ **Figure 50.9 An insect's "ear"—on its leg.** The tympanic membrane, visible in this SEM of a cricket's front leg, vibrates in response to sound waves. The vibrations stimulate mechanoreceptors attached to the inside of the tympanic membrane.

Tympanic membrane

1 mm

granules formed by grains of sand or other dense materials, sit freely in a chamber lined with ciliated cells. Each time an animal repositions itself, the statoliths resettle, stimulating mechanoreceptors at the low point in the chamber.

How did researchers test the hypothesis that resettling of statoliths informs an invertebrate about its position relative to Earth's gravity? In one key experiment, statoliths were replaced with metal shavings. Researchers then "tricked" crayfish into swimming upside down by using magnets to pull the shavings to the upper end of statocysts at the base of their antennae.

Many (perhaps most) insects have body hairs that vibrate in response to sound waves. Hairs of different stiffnesses and lengths vibrate at different frequencies. For example, fine hairs on the antennae of a male mosquito vibrate in a specific way in response to the hum produced by the beating wings of flying females. The importance of this sensory system in the attraction of males to a potential mate can be demonstrated very simply: A tuning fork vibrating at the same frequency as that of a female's wings will by itself attract males.

Many insects also detect sound by means of vibration-sensitive organs, which consist in some species of a tympanic membrane (eardrum) stretched over an internal air chamber **(Figure 50.9)**. Cockroaches lack such a tympanic membrane, but instead have vibration-sensitive organs that sense air movement, such as that caused by a descending human foot.

Hearing and Equilibrium in Mammals

In mammals, as in most other terrestrial vertebrates, the sensory organs for hearing and equilibrium are closely associated. **Figure 50.10** explores the structure and function of these organs in the human ear.

Exploring The Structure of the Human Ear

1 Overview of Ear Structure

The **outer ear** consists of the external pinna and the auditory canal, which collect sound waves and channel them to the **tympanic membrane** (eardrum), which separates the outer ear from the middle ear. In the **middle ear**, three small bones—the malleus (hammer), incus (anvil), and stapes (stirrup)—transmit vibrations to the **oval window**, which is a membrane beneath the stapes. The middle ear also opens into the **Eustachian tube**, which connects to the pharynx and equalizes pressure between the middle ear and the atmosphere. The **inner ear** consists of fluid-filled chambers, including the **semicircular canals**, which function in equilibrium, and the coiled **cochlea** (from the Latin meaning "snail"), a bony chamber that is involved in hearing.

2 The Cochlea

The cochlea has two large canals—an upper vestibular canal and a lower tympanic canal—separated by a smaller cochlear duct. Both canals are filled with fluid.

▲ Bundled hairs projecting from a single mammalian hair cell (SEM). Two shorter rows of hairs lie behind the tall hairs in the foreground.

4 Hair Cell

Projecting from each hair cell is a bundle of rod-shaped "hairs," each containing a core of actin filaments. Vibration of the basilar membrane in response to sound raises and lowers the hair cells, bending the hairs against the surrounding fluid and the tectorial membrane. When the hairs within the bundle are displaced, mechanoreceptors are activated, changing the membrane potential of the hair cell.

3 The Organ of Corti

The floor of the cochlear duct, the basilar membrane, bears the **organ of Corti**, which contains the mechanoreceptors of the ear, hair cells with hairs projecting into the cochlear duct. Many of the hairs are attached to the tectorial membrane, which hangs over the organ of Corti like an awning. Sound waves make the basilar membrane vibrate, which results in bending of the hairs and depolarization of the hair cells.

Hearing

Vibrating objects, such as a plucked guitar string or the vocal cords of a person who is talking, create pressure waves in the surrounding air. In *hearing*, the ear transduces this mechanical stimulus (pressure waves) into nerve impulses that the brain perceives as sound. To hear music, speech, or other sounds in our environment, we rely on **hair cells**, sensory cells with hairlike projections that detect motion.

Before vibration waves reach hair cells, they are amplified and transformed by several accessory structures. The first steps involve structures in the ear that convert the vibrations of moving air to pressure waves in fluid. Moving air that reaches the outer ear causes the tympanic membrane to vibrate. The three bones of the middle ear transmit these vibrations to the oval window, a membrane on the cochlea's surface. When one of those bones, the stapes, vibrates against the oval window, it creates pressure waves in the fluid (called perilymph) inside the cochlea.

Upon entering the vestibular canal, fluid pressure waves push down on the cochlear duct and basilar membrane. In response, the basilar membrane and attached hair cells vibrate up and down. The hairs projecting from the hair cells are deflected by the fixed tectorial membrane, which lies above (see Figure 50.10). With each vibration, the hairs bend first in one direction and then the other, causing ion channels in the hair cells to open or close. Bending in one direction depolarizes hair cells, increasing neurotransmitter release and the frequency of action potentials directed to the brain along the auditory nerve **(Figure 50.11)**. Bending the hairs in the other direction hyperpolarizes hair cells, reducing neurotransmitter release and the frequency of auditory nerve sensations.

What prevents pressure waves from reverberating within the ear and causing prolonged sensation? After propagating through the vestibular canal, pressure waves pass around the apex (tip) of the cochlea and dissipate as they strike the **round window (Figure 50.12a)**. This damping of sound waves resets the apparatus for the next vibrations that arrive.

The ear captures information about two important sound variables: volume and pitch. *Volume* (loudness) is determined by the amplitude, or height, of the sound wave. A large-amplitude wave causes more vigorous vibration of the basilar membrane, greater bending of the hairs on hair cells, and more action potentials in the sensory neurons. *Pitch* is determined by a sound wave's frequency, the number of vibrations per unit time. The detection of sound wave frequency takes place in the cochlea and relies on the asymmetric structure of that organ.

The cochlea can distinguish pitch because the basilar membrane is not uniform along its length: It is relatively narrow and stiff at the base of the cochlea near the oval window and wider and more flexible at the apex. Each region of the basilar membrane is tuned to a different vibration frequency **(Figure 50.12b)**. Furthermore, each region is connected by axons to a different location in the cerebral cortex. Consequently, when a sound wave causes vibration of a particular region of the basilar membrane, a specific site in our cortex is stimulated and we perceive sound of a particular pitch.

(a) No bending of hairs

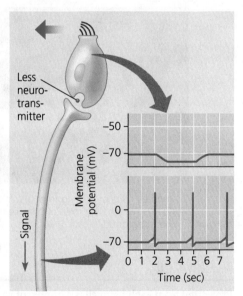

(b) Bending of hairs in one direction

(c) Bending of hairs in other direction

▲ **Figure 50.11 Sensory reception by hair cells.** Vertebrate hair cells required for hearing and balance have "hairs" formed into a bundle that bends when surrounding fluid moves. Each hair cell releases an excitatory neurotransmitter at a synapse with a sensory neuron, which conducts action potentials to the CNS. Bending of the bundle in one direction depolarizes the hair cell, causing it to release more neurotransmitter and increasing the frequency of action potentials in the sensory neuron. Bending in the other direction has the opposite effect.

(a) Vibrations of the stapes against the oval window produce pressure waves (black arrows) in the fluid (perilymph; blue) of the cochlea. (For purposes of illustration, the cochlea on the right is drawn partially uncoiled.) The waves travel to the apex via the vestibular canal and back towards the base via the tympanic canal. The energy in the waves causes the basilar membrane (pink) to vibrate, stimulating hair cells (not shown). Because the basilar membrane varies in stiffness along its length, each point along the membrane vibrates maximally in response to waves of a particular frequency.

(b) These graphs show the patterns of vibration along the basilar membrane for three different frequencies, high (top), medium (middle), and low (bottom). The higher the frequency, the closer the vibration to the oval window.

▲ **Figure 50.12 Transduction in the cochlea.**

INTERPRET THE DATA *A musical chord consists of several notes, each formed by a sound wave of different frequency. If a chord had notes with frequencies of 100, 1,000, and 6,000 Hz, what would happen to the basilar membrane? How would this result in your hearing a chord?*

Equilibrium

Several organs in the inner ear of humans and most other mammals detect body movement, position, and balance. For example, the chambers called the **utricle** and **saccule** allow us to perceive position with respect to gravity or linear movement **(Figure 50.13)**. Each of these chambers, which are situated in a vestibule behind the oval window, contains

hair cells that project into a gelatinous material. Embedded in this gel are small calcium carbonate particles called *otoliths* ("ear stones"). When you tilt your head, the otoliths press on the hairs protruding into the gel. The hair cell receptors transform this deflection into a change in the output of sensory neurons, signaling the brain that your head is at an angle. The otoliths are also responsible for your ability to

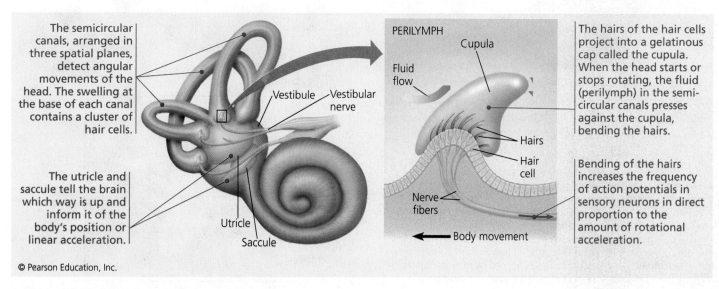

▲ **Figure 50.13 Organs of equilibrium in the inner ear.**

perceive acceleration, as, for example, when a stationary car in which you are sitting pulls forward.

Three fluid-filled semicircular canals connected to the utricle detect turning of the head and other rotational acceleration. Within each canal, the hair cells form a cluster, with the hairs projecting into a gelatinous cap called a cupula (see Figure 50.13). Because the three canals are arranged in the three spatial planes, they can detect angular motion of the head in any direction. If you spin in place, the fluid in each canal eventually comes to equilibrium and remains in that state until you stop. At that point, the moving fluid encounters a stationary cupula, triggering the false sensation of angular motion that we call dizziness.

Hearing and Equilibrium in Other Vertebrates

Fishes rely on several systems for detecting movement and vibrations in their aquatic environment. One system involves a pair of inner ears that contain otoliths and hair cells. Unlike mammals, fishes have no eardrum, cochlea, or opening to the outside of the body. Instead, the vibrations of the water caused by sound waves are conducted to the inner ear through the skeleton of the head. Some fishes also have a series of bones that conduct vibrations to the inner ear from the swim bladder (see Figure 34.15).

Most fishes and aquatic amphibians are able to detect low-frequency waves by means of a **lateral line system** along both sides of their body **(Figure 50.14)**. As in our semicircular canals, receptors are formed from a cluster of hair cells whose hairs are embedded in a cupula. Water entering the lateral line system through numerous pores bends the cupula, leading to depolarization of the hair cells and production of action potentials. In this way, the fish perceives its movement through water or the direction and velocity of water currents flowing over its body. The lateral line system also detects water movements or vibrations generated by prey, predators, and other moving objects.

In the ear of a frog or toad, sound vibrations in the air are conducted to the inner ear by a tympanic membrane on the body surface and a single middle ear bone. The same is true in birds and other reptiles, although they, like mammals, have a cochlea.

CONCEPT CHECK 50.2

1. How are otoliths adaptive for burrowing mammals, such as the star-nosed mole?

2. **WHAT IF?** Suppose a series of pressure waves in your cochlea caused a vibration of the basilar membrane that moves gradually from the apex toward the base. How would your brain interpret this stimulus?

3. **WHAT IF?** If the stapes became fused to the other middle ear bones or to the oval window, how would this condition affect hearing? Explain.

4. **MAKE CONNECTIONS** Plants use statoliths to detect gravity (see Figure 39.22). How do plants and animals differ with regard to the type of compartment in which statoliths are found and the physiological mechanism for detecting their response to gravity?

For suggested answers, see Appendix A.

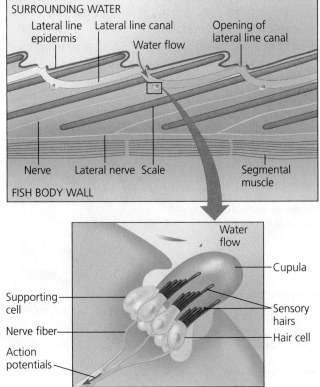

▲ **Figure 50.14 The lateral line system in a fish.** The sensory organs of the lateral line stretch from head to tail along each side of the fish. Water movement into and through the lateral line canals pushes on the gelatinous cupula, bending the hair cells within. In response, the hair cells generate receptor potentials, triggering action potentials that are conveyed to the brain. This information enables a fish to monitor water currents, any pressure waves produced by moving objects, and any low frequency sounds conducted through the water.

The diverse visual receptors of animals depend on light-absorbing pigments

The ability to detect light has a central role in the interaction of nearly all animals with their environment. Although the organs used for vision vary considerably among animals, the underlying mechanism for capturing light is the same, suggesting a common evolutionary origin.

Evolution of Visual Perception

EVOLUTION Light detectors in the animal kingdom range from simple clusters of cells that detect only the direction and intensity of light to complex organs that form images. These diverse light detectors all contain **photoreceptors**, sensory cells that contain light-absorbing pigment molecules. Furthermore, the genes that specify where and when photoreceptors arise during embryonic development are shared among flatworms, annelids, arthropods, and vertebrates. It is thus very probable that the genetic underpinnings of all photoreceptors were already present in the earliest bilaterian animals.

Light-Detecting Organs

Most invertebrates have some kind of light-detecting organ. One of the simplest is that of planarians (**Figure 50.15**). A pair of ocelli (singular, *ocellus*), which are sometimes called

(a) The planarian's brain directs the body to turn until the sensations from the two ocelli are equal and minimal, causing the animal to move away from light.

(b) Whereas light striking the front of an ocellus excites the photoreceptors, light striking the back is blocked by the screening pigment. In this way, the ocelli indicate the direction of a light source, triggering the light avoidance behavior.

▲ **Figure 50.15 Ocelli and orientation behavior of a planarian.**

eyespots, are located in the head region. Photoreceptors in each ocellus receive light only through an opening where there are no pigmented cells. By comparing the rate of action potentials coming from the two ocelli, the planarian is able to move away from a light source until it reaches a shaded location, where a rock or other object is likely to hide it from predators.

Compound Eyes

Insects and crustaceans have compound eyes, as do some polychaete worms. A **compound eye** consists of up to several thousand light detectors called **ommatidia** (the "facets" of the eye), each with its own light-focusing lens (**Figure 50.16**). Each ommatidium detects light from a tiny portion of the visual field (the area seen when the eyes point forward). A compound eye is very effective at detecting movement, an important adaptation for flying insects and small animals constantly threatened with predation. Many compound eyes, including those of the fly in Figure 50.16, offer a very wide field of view.

Insects have excellent color vision, and some (including bees) can see into the ultraviolet (UV) range of the electromagnetic spectrum. Because UV light is invisible to humans, we miss seeing differences in the environment that bees and

(a) The faceted eyes on the head of a fly form a repeating pattern visible in this photomicrograph.

2 mm

(b) The cornea and crystalline cone of each ommatidium together function as a lens that focuses light on the rhabdom, an organelle formed by and extending inward from a circle of photoreceptors. The rhabdom traps light, serving as the photosensitive part of the ommatidium. Information gathered from different intensities of light entering the many ommatidia from different angles is used to form a visual image.

▲ **Figure 50.16 Compound eyes.**

other insects detect. In studying animal behavior, we cannot simply extrapolate our sensory world to other species; different animals have different sensitivities and different brain organizations.

Single-Lens Eyes

Among invertebrates, **single-lens eyes** are found in some jellies and polychaete worms, as well as in spiders and many molluscs. A single-lens eye works somewhat like a camera. The eye of an octopus or squid, for example, has a small opening, the **pupil**, through which light enters. Like a camera's adjustable aperture, the **iris** contracts or expands, changing the diameter of the pupil to let in more or less light. Behind the pupil, a single lens directs light on a layer of photoreceptors. Similar to a camera's focusing action, muscles in an invertebrate's single-lens eye move the lens forward or backward, focusing on objects at different distances.

▼ Figure 50.17
Exploring The Structure of the Human Eye

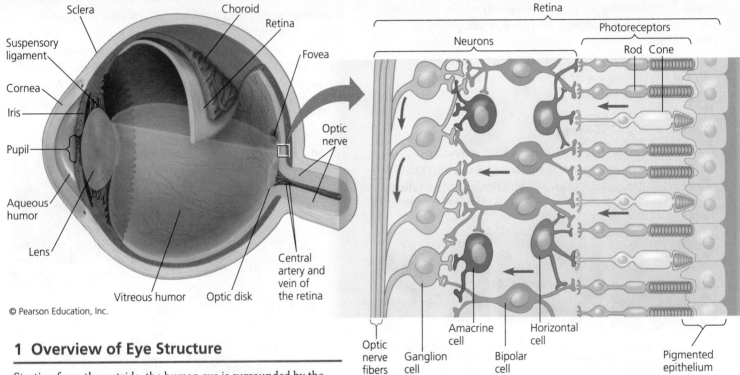

© Pearson Education, Inc.

1 Overview of Eye Structure

Starting from the outside, the human eye is surrounded by the conjunctiva, a mucous membrane (not shown); the sclera, a connective tissue; and the choroid, a thin, pigmented layer. At the front, the sclera forms the transparent *cornea* and the choroid forms the colored *iris*. By changing size, the iris regulates the amount of light entering the pupil, the hole in the center of the iris. Just inside the choroid, the neurons and photoreceptors of the **retina** form the innermost layer of the eyeball. The optic nerve exits the eye at the optic disk.

The **lens**, a transparent disk of protein, divides the eye into two cavities. In front of the lens lies the *aqueous humor,* a clear watery substance. Blockage of ducts that drain this fluid can produce glaucoma, a condition in which increased pressure in the eye damages the optic nerve, causing vision loss. Behind the lens lies the jellylike *vitreous humor* (illustrated here in the lower portion of the eyeball).

2 The Retina

Light (coming from left in the above view) strikes the retina, passing through largely transparent layers of neurons before reaching the rods and cones, two types of photoreceptors that differ in shape and in function. The neurons of the retina then relay visual information captured by the photoreceptors to the optic nerve and brain along the pathways shown with red arrows. Each *bipolar cell* receives information from several rods or cones, and each *ganglion cell* gathers input from several bipolar cells. *Horizontal* and *amacrine cells* integrate information across the retina.

One region of the retina, the optic disk, lacks photoreceptors. As a result, this region forms a "blind spot" where light is not detected.

The eyes of all vertebrates have a single lens. In fishes, focusing occurs as in invertebrates, with the lens moving forward or backward. In other species, including mammals, focusing is achieved by changing the shape of the lens.

The Vertebrate Visual System

The human eye will serve as our model of vision in vertebrates. As described in **Figure 50.17**, vision begins when photons of light enter the eye and strike the rods and cones. There the energy of each photon is captured by a shift in configuration of a single chemical bond in retinal.

Although light detection in the eye is the first stage in vision, remember that it is actually the brain that "sees." Thus, to understand vision, we must examine how the capture of light by retinal changes the production of action potentials and then follow these signals to the visual centers of the brain, where images are perceived.

Rod
Synaptic terminal · Cell body · Outer segment · Disks
Cone

Rod
Cone

© Pearson Education, Inc.

3 Photoreceptor Cells

Humans have two main types of photoreceptor cells: rods and cones. Within the outer segment of a rod or cone is a stack of membranous disks in which *visual pigments* are embedded. **Rods** are more sensitive to light but do not distinguish colors; they enable us to see at night, but only in black and white. **Cones** provide color vision, but, being less sensitive, contribute very little to night vision. There are three types of cones. Each has a different sensitivity across the visible spectrum, providing an optimal response to red, green, or blue light.

In the colorized SEM shown above, cones (green), rods (light tan), and adjacent neurons (purple) are visible. The pigmented epithelium, which was removed in this preparation, would be to the right.

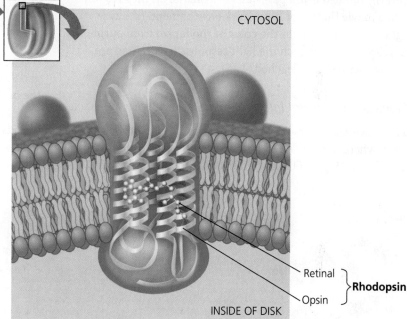

CYTOSOL

Retinal ⎫
Opsin ⎬ **Rhodopsin**

INSIDE OF DISK

© Pearson Education, Inc.

Retinal: *cis* isomer

Light   Enzymes

Retinal: *trans* isomer

4 Visual Pigments

Vertebrate visual pigments consist of a light-absorbing molecule called **retinal** (a derivative of vitamin A) bound to a membrane protein called an **opsin**. Seven α helices of each opsin molecule span the disk membrane. The visual pigment of rods, shown here, is called **rhodopsin**.

Retinal exists as two isomers. Absorption of light shifts one bond in retinal from a *cis* to a *trans* arrangement, converting the molecule from an angled shape to a straight shape. This change in configuration destabilizes and activates the opsin protein to which retinal is bound.

Sensory Transduction in the Eye

The transduction of visual information to the nervous system begins with the light-induced conversion of *cis*-retinal to *trans*-retinal. As shown in **Figure 50.18**, this conversion activates rhodopsin, which activates a G protein, which in turn activates an enzyme called phosphodiesterase. The substrate for this enzyme is cyclic GMP, which in the dark binds to sodium ion (Na^+) channels and keeps them open. When phosphodiesterase hydrolyzes cyclic GMP, Na^+ channels close, and the cell becomes hyperpolarized.

The signal transduction pathway in photoreceptor cells normally shuts off as enzymes convert retinal back to the *cis* form, returning rhodopsin to its inactive state. In very bright light, however, rhodopsin remains active, and the response in the rods becomes saturated. If the amount of light entering the eyes decreases abruptly, the rods do not regain full responsiveness for several minutes. This is why you are temporarily blinded if you pass quickly from the bright sunshine into a movie theater or other dark environment. (Because light activation changes the color of rhodopsin from purple to yellow, rods in which the light response is saturated are often described as "bleached.")

Processing of Visual Information in the Retina

The processing of visual information begins in the retina itself, where both rods and cones form synapses with bipolar cells (see Figure 50.17). In the dark, rods and cones are depolarized and continually release the neurotransmitter glutamate at these synapses **(Figure 50.19)**. Some bipolar cells depolarize in response to glutamate, whereas others hyperpolarize. When light strikes the rods and cones, they hyperpolarize, shutting off their release of glutamate. In response, the bipolar cells that are depolarized by glutamate hyperpolarize, and those that are hyperpolarized by glutamate depolarize.

Signals from rods and cones can follow several different pathways in the retina. Some information passes directly from photoreceptors to bipolar cells to ganglion cells. In other cases, horizontal cells carry signals from one rod or cone to other photoreceptors and to several bipolar cells. When an illuminated rod or cone stimulates a horizontal cell, the horizontal cell inhibits more distant photoreceptors and bipolar cells that are not illuminated. The result is that the region receiving light appears lighter and the dark surroundings even darker. This form of integration, called *lateral inhibition*, sharpens edges and enhances contrast in the image. Amacrine cells distribute some information from one bipolar cell to several ganglion cells. Lateral inhibition is repeated by the interactions of the amacrine cells with the ganglion cells and occurs at all levels of visual processing in the brain.

A single ganglion cell receives information from an array of rods and cones, each of which responds to light coming from a particular location. Together, the rods and cones that are feeding information to one ganglion cell define

1 Light converts *cis*-retinal to *trans*-retinal, activating rhodopsin.

2 Active rhodopsin in turn activates a G protein called transducin.

3 Transducin activates the enzyme phosphodiesterase.

4 Activated phosphodiesterase detaches cGMP from Na^+ channels in the plasma membrane by hydrolyzing cGMP to GMP.

5 The Na^+ channels close when cGMP detaches. The membrane's permeability to Na^+ decreases, and the rod hyperpolarizes.

▲ **Figure 50.18 Production of the receptor potential in a rod cell.** In rods (and cones), the receptor potential triggered by light is a hyperpolarization, not a depolarization.

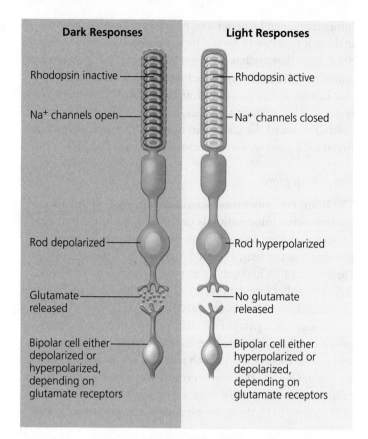

Dark Responses | **Light Responses**

Rhodopsin inactive — Rhodopsin active

Na⁺ channels open — Na⁺ channels closed

Rod depolarized — Rod hyperpolarized

Glutamate released — No glutamate released

Bipolar cell either depolarized or hyperpolarized, depending on glutamate receptors — Bipolar cell either hyperpolarized or depolarized, depending on glutamate receptors

▲ **Figure 50.19 Synaptic activity of rod cells in light and dark.**

? *Like rods, cone cells are depolarized when their opsin molecules are inactive. In the case of a cone, why might it be misleading to call this a dark response?*

a *receptive field*—the part of the visual field to which that ganglion cell can respond. The fewer rods or cones that supply a single ganglion cell, the smaller the receptive field is. A smaller receptive field typically results in a sharper image because the information about where light has struck the retina is more precise.

Processing of Visual Information in the Brain

Axons of ganglion cells form the optic nerves that transmit sensations from the eyes to the brain **(Figure 50.20)**. The two optic nerves meet at the *optic chiasm* near the center of the base of the cerebral cortex. Axons in the optic nerves are routed at the optic chiasm such that sensations from the left visual field of both eyes are transmitted to the right side of the brain, and sensations from the right visual field are transmitted to the left side of the brain. (Note that each visual field, whether right or left, involves input from both eyes.)

Within the brain, most ganglion cell axons lead to the *lateral geniculate nuclei*, which have axons that reach the *primary visual cortex* in the cerebrum. Additional neurons carry the information to higher-order visual processing and

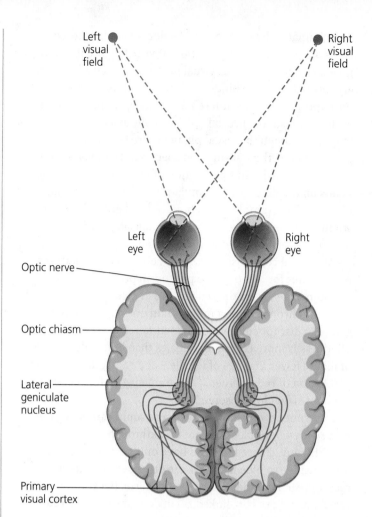

▲ **Figure 50.20 Neural pathways for vision.** Each optic nerve contains about a million axons that synapse with interneurons in the lateral geniculate nuclei. The nuclei relay sensations to the primary visual cortex, one of many brain centers that cooperate in constructing our visual perceptions.

integrating centers elsewhere in the cortex. Researchers estimate that at least 30% of the cerebral cortex, comprising hundreds of millions of neurons in perhaps dozens of integrating centers, takes part in formulating what we actually "see." Determining how these centers integrate such components of our vision as color, motion, depth, shape, and detail is the focus of much exciting research.

Color Vision

Among vertebrates, most fishes, amphibians, and reptiles, including birds, have very good color vision. Humans and other primates also see color well, but are among the minority of mammals with this ability. Many mammals are nocturnal, and having a high proportion of rods in the retina is an adaptation that gives these animals keen night vision. Cats, for instance, are usually most active at night; they have limited color vision and probably see a pastel world during the day.

In humans, the perception of color is based on three types of cones, each with a different visual pigment—red, green, or blue. The three visual pigments, called *photopsins*, are formed from the binding of retinal to three distinct opsin proteins. Slight differences in the opsin proteins cause each photopsin to absorb light optimally at a different wavelength. Although the visual pigments are designated as red, green, or blue, their absorption spectra in fact overlap. For this reason, the brain's perception of intermediate hues depends on the differential stimulation of two or more classes of cones. For example, when both red and green cones are stimulated, we may see yellow or orange, depending on which class is more strongly stimulated.

Abnormal color vision typically results from mutations in the genes for one or more photopsin proteins. Because the human genes for the red and green pigments are located on the X chromosome, a mutation in one copy of either gene can disrupt color vision in males. For this reason, color blindness is more common in males than in females (5–8% of males, fewer than 1% of females) and nearly always affects perception of red or green. (The human gene for the blue pigment is on chromosome 7.)

Experiments on color vision in the squirrel monkey (*Saimiri sciureus*) enabled a recent breakthrough in the field of gene therapy. These monkeys have only two opsin genes, one sensitive to blue light and the other sensitive to either red or green light, depending on the allele. Because the red/green opsin gene is X-linked, all males have only the red- or green-sensitive version and are red-green color-blind. When researchers injected a virus containing the gene for the missing version into the retina of adult male monkeys, evidence of full color vision was apparent after 20 weeks **(Figure 50.21)**.

The squirrel monkey gene therapy studies demonstrate that the neural circuits required to process visual information can be generated or activated even in adults, making it possible to treat a range of vision disorders. Indeed, gene therapy has been used to treat Leber's congenital amaurosis (LCA), an inherited retinal degenerative disease that causes severe loss of vision. After using gene therapy to restore vision in dogs and mice with LCA, researchers successfully treated the disease in humans by injecting the functional LCA gene in a viral vector (see Figure 20.22).

The Visual Field

The brain not only processes visual information but also controls what information is captured. One important type of control is focusing, which in humans occurs by changing the shape of the lens, as noted earlier and illustrated in **Figure 50.22**. When you focus your eyes on a close object, your lenses become almost spherical. When you view a distant object, your lenses are flattened.

Although our peripheral vision allows us to see objects over a nearly 180° range, the distribution of photoreceptors across the eye limits both what we see and how well we see it. Overall, the human retina contains about 125 million rods and 6 million cones. At the **fovea**, the center of the visual field, there are no rods but a very high density

▲ **Figure 50.21 Gene therapy for vision.** Once color-blind, this adult male monkey treated with gene therapy demonstrates his ability to distinguish red from green.

MAKE CONNECTIONS *Red-green color blindness is X-linked in squirrel monkeys and humans (see Figure 15.7). Why is the inheritance pattern in humans not apparent in squirrel monkeys?*

▼ **Figure 50.22 Focusing in the mammalian eye.** Ciliary muscles control the shape of the lens, which bends light and focuses it on the retina. The thicker the lens, the more sharply the light is bent.

(a) Near vision (accommodation)

Ciliary muscles contract, pulling border of choroid toward lens.

Suspensory ligaments relax.

Lens becomes thicker and rounder, focusing on nearby objects.

Choroid

Retina

(b) Distance vision

Ciliary muscles relax, and border of choroid moves away from lens.

Suspensory ligaments pull against lens.

Lens becomes flatter, focusing on distant objects.

of cones—about 150,000 cones per square millimeter. The ratio of cones to rods falls with distance from the fovea, with the peripheral regions having only rods. In daylight, you achieve your sharpest vision by looking directly at an object, such that light shines on the tightly packed cones in your fovea. At night, looking directly at a dimly lit object is ineffective, since the rods—the more sensitive light receptors—are absent from the fovea. For this reason you see a dim star best by focusing on a point just to one side of it.

CONCEPT CHECK 50.3

1. Contrast the light-detecting organs of planarians and flies. How is each organ adaptive for the lifestyle of the animal?

2. In a condition called presbyopia, the eyes' lenses lose much of their elasticity and maintain a flat shape. Explain how this condition affects a person's vision.

3. **WHAT IF?** Our brain receives more action potentials when our eyes are exposed to light even though our photoreceptors release more neurotransmitter in the dark. Propose an explanation.

4. **MAKE CONNECTIONS** Compare the function of retinal in the eye with that of the pigment chlorophyll in a plant photosystem (see Concept 10.2).

For suggested answers, see Appendix A.

CONCEPT 50.4

The senses of taste and smell rely on similar sets of sensory receptors

Animals use their chemical senses for a wide range of purposes, such as to find mates, to recognize marked territories, and to help navigate during migration. Animals such as ants and bees that live in large social groups rely extensively on chemical "conversation." In all animals, chemical senses are important in feeding behavior. For example, a hydra retracts its tentacles toward its mouth when it detects the compound glutathione, which is released from prey captured by the tentacles.

The perceptions of **gustation** (taste) and **olfaction** (smell) both depend on chemoreceptors. In the case of terrestrial animals, taste is the detection of chemicals called **tastants** that are present in a solution, and smell is the detection of **odorants** that are carried through the air. There is no distinction between taste and smell in aquatic animals.

In insects, taste receptors are located within sensory hairs located on the feet and in mouthparts, where they are used to select food. A tasting hair contains several chemoreceptors, each especially responsive to a particular class of tastant, such as sugar or salt. Insects are also capable of smelling airborne odorants using olfactory hairs, usually located on their antennae (see Figure 50.6). The chemical DEET (*N,N*-diethyl-meta-toluamide), sold as an insect "repellant," actually protects against bites by blocking the olfactory receptor in mosquitoes that detects human scent.

Taste in Mammals

Humans and other mammals perceive five tastes: sweet, sour, salty, bitter, and umami. Umami (Japanese for "delicious") is elicited by the amino acid glutamate. Used as a flavor enhancer, monosodium glutamate (MSG) occurs naturally in foods such as meat and aged cheese. Researchers have identified the receptor proteins for all five tastes.

For decades, many researchers assumed that a taste cell could have more than one type of receptor. An alternative idea is that each taste cell has a single receptor type, programming the cell to recognize only one of the five tastes. Which hypothesis is correct? In 2005, scientists at the University of California, San Diego, used a cloned bitter taste receptor to genetically reprogram gustation in a mouse **(Figure 50.23)**.

▼ **Figure 50.23** | Inquiry

How do mammals detect different tastes?

Experiment To investigate the basis of mammalian taste perception, researchers used a chemical called phenyl-β-D-glucopyranoside (PBDG). Humans find PBDG extremely bitter. Mice, however, lack a receptor for PBDG. Mice avoid drinking water containing other bitter tastants but show no aversion to water that contains PBDG.

Using a molecular cloning strategy, Mueller generated mice that made the human PBDG receptor in cells that normally make either a sweet receptor or a bitter receptor. The mice were given a choice of two bottles, one filled with pure water and one filled with water containing PBDG at varying concentrations. The researchers then observed whether the mice had an attraction or an aversion to PBDG.

Results

Relative consumption = (Fluid intake from bottle containing PBDG ÷ Total fluid intake) × 100%

Conclusion The researchers found that the presence of a bitter receptor in sweet taste cells is sufficient to cause mice to be attracted to a bitter chemical. They concluded that the mammalian brain must therefore perceive sweet or bitter taste solely on the basis of which sensory neurons are activated.

Source: K. L. Mueller et al., The receptors and coding logic for bitter taste, *Nature* 434:225–229 (2005).

WHAT IF? *Suppose instead of the PBDG receptor the researchers had used a receptor specific for a sweetener that humans crave but mice ignore. How would the results of the experiment have differed?*

Based on these and other studies, the researchers concluded that an individual taste cell expresses a single receptor type and detects tastants representing only one of the five tastes.

The receptor cells for taste in mammals are modified epithelial cells organized into **taste buds**, which are scattered in several areas of the tongue and mouth (**Figure 50.24**). Most taste buds on the tongue are associated with nipple-shaped projections called papillae. Any region of the tongue with taste buds can detect any of the five types of taste. (The frequently reproduced "taste maps" of the tongue are thus not accurate.)

The sensation of sweet, umami, and bitter tastes requires a G protein-coupled receptor, or GPCR (see Figure 11.7).

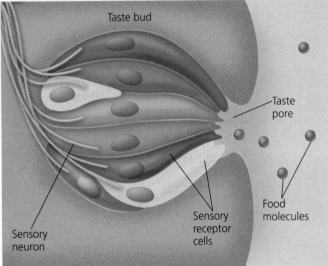

(a) **The tongue**. Small raised structures called papillae cover the tongue surface. The enlarged cross section shows the side walls of a papilla lined with taste buds.

Key

Sweet   Bitter
Salty   Umami
Sour

(b) **A taste bud**. Taste buds in all regions of the tongue contain sensory receptor cells specific for each of the five taste types.
© Pearson Education, Inc.

▲ **Figure 50.24 Human taste receptors.**

In humans, there are more than 30 different receptors for bitter taste, and each receptor is able to recognize multiple bitter tastants. In contrast, humans have one type of sweet receptor and one type of umami receptor, each assembled from a different pair of GPCR proteins. Other GPCR proteins are critical for the sense of smell, as we will discuss shortly.

The receptor for sour tastants belongs to the TRP family and is similar to the capsaicin receptor and other thermoreceptor proteins. In taste buds, the TRP proteins of the sour receptor assemble into an ion channel in the plasma membrane of the taste cell. Binding of an acid or other sour-tasting substance to the receptor triggers a change in the ion channel. Depolarization occurs, activating a sensory neuron.

The taste receptor for salt turns out to be a sodium channel. Not surprisingly, it specifically detects sodium salts, such as the NaCl that we use in cooking and flavoring.

Smell in Humans

In olfaction, unlike gustation, the sensory cells are neurons. Olfactory receptor cells line the upper portion of the nasal cavity and send impulses along their axons to the olfactory bulb of the brain (**Figure 50.25**). The receptive ends of the cells contain cilia that extend into the layer of mucus coating the nasal cavity. When an odorant diffuses into this region, it binds to a specific GPCR protein called an odorant receptor (OR) on the plasma membrane of the olfactory cilia. These events trigger signal transduction leading to the production of cyclic AMP. In olfactory cells, cyclic AMP opens channels in the plasma membrane that are permeable to both Na^+ and Ca^{2+}. The flow of these ions into the receptor cell leads to depolarization of the membrane, generating action potentials.

Humans can distinguish thousands of different odors, each caused by a structurally distinct odorant. This level of sensory discrimination requires many different ORs. In 1991, Richard Axel and Linda Buck, working at Columbia University, discovered a family of more than 1,000 OR genes—about 3% of all human genes. Each olfactory receptor cell appears to express one OR gene. Cells selective for different odorants are interspersed in the nasal cavity. Those cells that express the same OR gene transmit action potentials to the same small region of the olfactory bulb. In 2004, Axel and Buck shared a Nobel Prize for their studies of the gene family and receptors that function in olfaction.

After odorants are detected, information from olfactory receptors is collected and integrated. Genetic studies on mice, worms, and flies have shown that signals from the nervous system regulate this process, dialing the response to particular odorants up or down. As a result, animals can detect the location of food sources even if the concentration of a key odorant is particularly low or high.

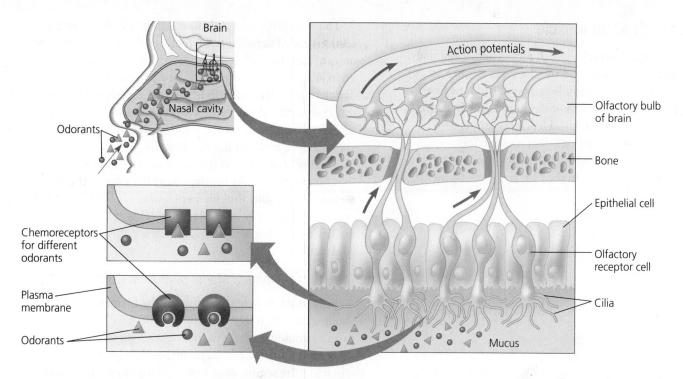

▲ Figure 50.25 Smell in humans. Odorant molecules bind to specific chemoreceptor proteins in the plasma membrane of olfactory receptor cells, triggering action potentials. Each olfactory receptor cell has just one type of chemoreceptor. As shown, cells that express different chemoreceptors detect different odorants.

WHAT IF? *If you spray an "air freshener" in a musty room, would you be affecting detection, transmission, or perception of the odorants responsible for the musty smell?*

Studies of model organisms also reveal that complex mixtures of odorants are not processed as the simple sum of each input. Rather, the brain integrates olfactory information from different receptors into single sensations. These sensations contribute to the perception of the environment in the present and to the memory of events and emotions.

Although the receptors and neuronal pathways for taste and smell are independent, the two senses do interact. Indeed, much of the complex flavor humans experience when eating is due to our sense of smell. If the olfactory system is blocked, as occurs when you have a head cold, the perception of taste is sharply reduced.

CONCEPT CHECK 50.4

1. Explain why some taste receptor cells and all olfactory receptor cells use G protein-coupled receptors, yet only olfactory receptor cells produce action potentials.

2. Pathways involving G proteins provide an opportunity for an increase in signal strength in the course of signal transduction, a change referred to as amplification. How might this be beneficial in olfaction?

3. **WHAT IF?** If you discovered a mutation in mice that disrupted the ability to taste sweet, bitter, and umami, but not sour or salty, what might you predict about where this mutation acts in the signaling pathways used by these receptors?

For suggested answers, see Appendix A.

CONCEPT 50.5

The physical interaction of protein filaments is required for muscle function

In discussing sensory mechanisms, we have seen some examples of how sensory inputs to the nervous system result in specific behaviors: the touch-guided foraging of a star-nosed mole, the upside-down swimming of a crayfish with manipulated statocysts, and the light-avoiding maneuvers of planarians. Underlying these diverse behaviors are common fundamental mechanisms: Feeding, swimming, and crawling all require muscle activity in response to nervous system motor output.

Muscle cell contraction relies on the interaction between protein structures called thin and thick filaments. The major component of **thin filaments** is the globular protein actin. In thin filaments, two strands of polymerized actin are coiled around one another; similar actin structures called microfilaments function in cell motility. The **thick filaments** are staggered arrays of myosin molecules. Muscle contraction is the product of filament movement powered by chemical energy; muscle extension occurs only passively. To understand how filaments contribute to muscle contraction, we will begin by examining vertebrate skeletal muscle.

Vertebrate Skeletal Muscle

Vertebrate **skeletal muscle**, which moves bones and body, has a hierarchy of smaller and smaller units **(Figure 50.26)**. Within a typical skeletal muscle is a bundle of long fibers running parallel to the length of the muscle. Each fiber is a single cell with multiple nuclei (each nucleus is derived from one of the embryonic cells that fused to form the muscle cell). Inside a muscle cell lies a longitudinal bundle of **myofibrils**, which contain the thin and thick filaments.

© Pearson Education, Inc.

▲ **Figure 50.26 The structure of skeletal muscle.**

The myofibrils in muscle fibers are made up of repeating sections called **sarcomeres**, which are the basic contractile units of skeletal muscle. The borders of the sarcomere line up in adjacent myofibrils, forming a pattern of light and dark bands (striations) visible with a light microscope. For this reason, skeletal muscle is also called *striated muscle*. Thin filaments attach at the Z lines, while thick filaments are anchored at the M lines centered in the sarcomere (see Figure 50.26). In a resting (relaxed) myofibril, thick and thin filaments partially overlap. Near the edge of the sarcomere there are only thin filaments, whereas the zone in the center contains only thick filaments. This arrangement is the key to how the sarcomere, and hence the whole muscle, contracts.

The Sliding-Filament Model of Muscle Contraction

A contracting muscle shortens, but the filaments that bring about contraction stay the same length. To explain this apparent paradox, we'll focus first on a single sarcomere. As shown in **Figure 50.27**, the filaments slide past each other, much like the segments of a telescoping support pole. According to the well-accepted **sliding-filament model**, the thin and thick filaments ratchet past each other, powered by myosin molecules.

Figure 50.28 illustrates the cycles of change in the myosin molecule that form the basis for the longitudinal sliding of the thick and thin filaments. Each myosin molecule has a long "tail" region and a globular "head" region. The tail adheres to the tails of other myosin molecules, binding together the thick filament. The head, which extends to the side, can bind ATP. Hydrolysis of bound ATP converts myosin to a high-energy form that binds to actin, forming a cross-bridge. The myosin head then returns to its low-energy form as it pulls the thin filament toward the center of the sarcomere. When a new molecule of ATP binds to the myosin head, the cross-bridge is broken.

Muscle contraction requires repeated cycles of binding and release. In each cycle, the myosin head freed from a cross-bridge cleaves the newly bound ATP and binds again to actin. Because the thin filament moved toward the center of the sarcomere in the previous cycle, the myosin head now attaches to a new binding site farther along the thin filament. A thick filament contains approximately 350 heads, each of which forms and re-forms about five cross-bridges per second, driving the thick and thin filaments past each other.

At rest, most muscle fibers contain only enough ATP for a few contractions. Powering repetitive contractions requires two other storage compounds: creatine phosphate and glycogen. Transfer of a phosphate group from creatine phosphate to ADP in an enzyme-catalyzed reaction synthesizes additional ATP. In this way, the resting supply of creatine phosphate can sustain contractions for about 15

► **Figure 50.27 The sliding-filament model of muscle contraction.** The drawings on the left show that the lengths of the thick (myosin) filaments (purple) and thin (actin) filaments (orange) remain the same as a muscle fiber contracts.

① Starting here, the myosin head is bound to ATP and is in its low-energy configuration.

② The myosin head hydrolyzes ATP to ADP and phosphate (Ⓟ) and is in its high-energy configuration.

⑤ Binding of a new molecule of ATP releases the myosin head from actin, and a new cycle begins.

③ The myosin head binds to actin, forming a cross-bridge.

④ Releasing ADP and inorganic phosphate (Ⓟᵢ), myosin returns to its low-energy configuration, sliding the thin filament.

Thin filament moves toward center of sarcomere.

▲ **Figure 50.28 Myosin-actin interactions underlying muscle fiber contraction.**

? *When ATP binds, what prevents the filaments from sliding back into their original positions?*

ANIMATION **BioFlix** Visit the Study Area at **MasteringBiology** for the BioFlix® 3-D Animation on Muscle Contraction. BioFlix Tutorials can also be assigned in MasteringBiology.

seconds. ATP stores are also replenished when glycogen is broken down to glucose. During light or moderate muscle activity, this glucose is metabolized by aerobic respiration. This highly efficient metabolic process yields enough power to sustain contractions for nearly an hour. During intense muscle activity, oxygen becomes limiting and ATP is instead generated by lactic acid fermentation (see Chapter 9). This anaerobic pathway, although very rapid, generates much less ATP per glucose molecule and can sustain contraction for only about 1 minute.

The Role of Calcium and Regulatory Proteins

Calcium ions (Ca^{2+}) and proteins bound to actin play crucial roles in muscle contraction and relaxation. **Tropomyosin**, a regulatory protein, and the **troponin complex**, a set of additional regulatory proteins, are bound to the actin strands of thin filaments. In a muscle fiber at rest, tropomyosin covers the myosin-binding sites along the thin filament, preventing actin and myosin from interacting **(Figure 50.29a)**. When Ca^{2+} accumulates in the cytosol, it binds to the troponin complex, causing tropomyosin bound along the actin strands to shift position and expose the myosin-binding sites on the thin filament **(Figure 50.29b)**. Thus, when the Ca^{2+} concentration rises in the cytosol, the thin and thick filaments slide past each other, and the muscle fiber contracts. When the Ca^{2+} concentration falls, the binding sites are covered, and contraction stops.

Motor neurons cause muscle contraction by triggering the release of Ca^{2+} into the cytosol of muscle cells with

(a) Myosin-binding sites blocked

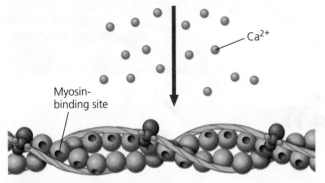

(b) Myosin-binding sites exposed

▲ **Figure 50.29 The role of regulatory proteins and calcium in muscle fiber contraction.** Each thin filament consists of two strands of actin, two long molecules of tropomyosin, and multiple copies of the troponin complex.

which they form synapses. This regulation of Ca^{2+} concentration is a multistep process involving a network of membranes and compartments within the muscle cell. As you read the following description, refer to the overview and diagram in **Figure 50.30**.

The arrival of an action potential at the synaptic terminal of a motor neuron causes release of the neurotransmitter acetylcholine. Binding of acetylcholine to receptors on the muscle fiber leads to a depolarization, triggering an action potential. Within the muscle fiber, the action potential spreads deep into the interior, following infoldings of the plasma membrane called **transverse (T) tubules**. These make close contact with the **sarcoplasmic reticulum (SR)**, a specialized endoplasmic reticulum. As the action potential spreads along the T tubules, it triggers changes in the SR, opening Ca^{2+} channels. Calcium ions stored in the interior of the SR flow through open channels into the cytosol and bind to the troponin complex, initiating the muscle fiber contraction.

When motor neuron input stops, the filaments slide back to their starting position. Relaxation begins as transport proteins in the SR pump Ca^{2+} in from the cytosol. When the Ca^{2+} concentration in the cytosol drops to a low level, the regulatory proteins bound to the thin filament shift back to their starting position, once again blocking the myosin-binding sites. At the same time, the Ca^{2+} pumped from the cytosol accumulates in the SR, providing the stores needed to respond to the next action potential.

Several diseases cause paralysis by interfering with the excitation of skeletal muscle fibers by motor neurons. In amyotrophic lateral sclerosis (ALS), motor neurons in the spinal cord and brainstem degenerate, and muscle fibers atrophy. ALS is progressive and usually fatal within five years after symptoms appear. In myasthenia gravis, a person produces antibodies to the acetylcholine receptors of skeletal muscle. As the disease progresses and the number of receptors decreases, transmission between motor neurons and muscle fibers declines. Myasthenia gravis can generally be controlled with drugs that inhibit acetylcholinesterase or suppress the immune system.

Nervous Control of Muscle Tension

Whereas contraction of a single skeletal muscle fiber is a brief all-or-none twitch, contraction of a whole muscle, such as the biceps in your upper arm, is graded; you can voluntarily alter the extent and strength of its contraction. The nervous system produces graded contractions of whole muscles by varying (1) the number of muscle fibers that contract and (2) the rate at which muscle fibers are stimulated. Let's consider each mechanism in turn.

In vertebrates, each branched motor neuron may synapse with many muscle fibers, although each fiber is controlled by only one motor neuron. A **motor unit** consists of a single motor neuron and all the muscle fibers it controls

Exploring The Regulation of Skeletal Muscle Contraction

The electrical, chemical, and molecular events regulating skeletal muscle contraction are shown in a cutaway view of a muscle cell and in the enlarged diagram below. Action potentials (red arrows) triggered by the motor neuron sweep across the muscle fiber and into it along the transverse (T) tubules, initiating the movements of calcium (green dots) that regulate muscle activity.

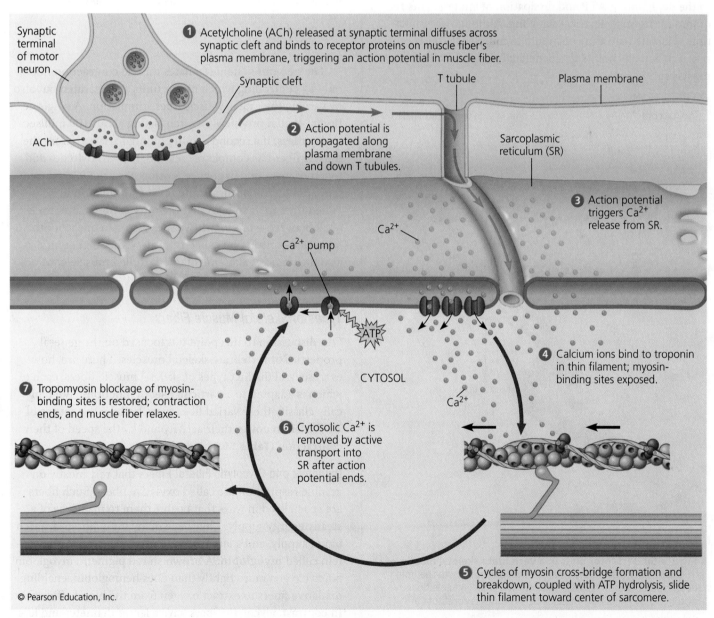

1 Acetylcholine (ACh) released at synaptic terminal diffuses across synaptic cleft and binds to receptor proteins on muscle fiber's plasma membrane, triggering an action potential in muscle fiber.

2 Action potential is propagated along plasma membrane and down T tubules.

3 Action potential triggers Ca^{2+} release from SR.

4 Calcium ions bind to troponin in thin filament; myosin-binding sites exposed.

5 Cycles of myosin cross-bridge formation and breakdown, coupled with ATP hydrolysis, slide thin filament toward center of sarcomere.

6 Cytosolic Ca^{2+} is removed by active transport into SR after action potential ends.

7 Tropomyosin blockage of myosin-binding sites is restored; contraction ends, and muscle fiber relaxes.

© Pearson Education, Inc.

(Figure 50.31). When a motor neuron produces an action potential, all the muscle fibers in its motor unit contract as a group. The strength of the resulting contraction depends on how many muscle fibers the motor neuron controls. In the whole muscle, there may be hundreds of motor units.

As more and more of the motor neurons controlling the muscle are activated, a process called *recruitment*, the force (tension) developed by a muscle progressively increases Depending on the number of motor neurons your brain recruits and the size of their motor units, you can lift a fork or something much heavier, like your biology textbook. Some muscles, especially those that hold up the body and maintain posture, are almost always partially contracted. In such muscles, the nervous system may alternate activation among the motor units, reducing the length of time any one set of fibers is contracted.

Prolonged contraction can result in muscle fatigue due to the depletion of ATP and dissipation of ion gradients required for normal electrical signaling. Although accumulation of lactate may also contribute to muscle fatigue, recent research actually points to a beneficial effect of lactate on muscle function.

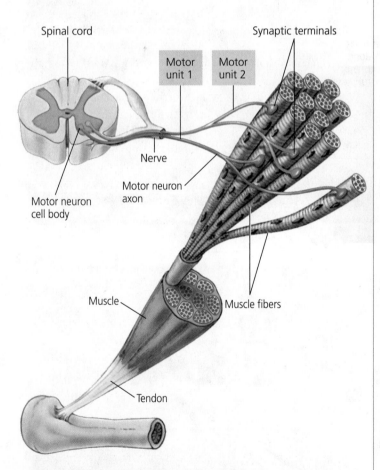

▲ **Figure 50.31 Motor units in a vertebrate skeletal muscle.** Each muscle fiber (cell) forms synapses with only one motor neuron, but each motor neuron typically synapses with many muscle fibers. A motor neuron and all the muscle fibers it controls constitute a motor unit.

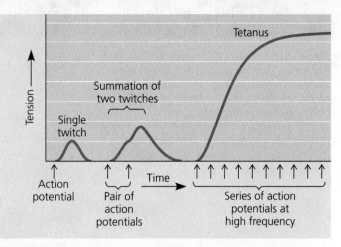

▲ **Figure 50.32 Summation of twitches.** This graph illustrates how the number of action potentials during a short period of time influences the tension developed in a muscle fiber.

? *How could the nervous system cause a skeletal muscle to produce the most forceful contraction it is capable of?*

The nervous system regulates muscle contraction not only by controlling which motor units are activated but also by varying the rate of muscle fiber stimulation. A single action potential produces a twitch lasting about 100 milliseconds or less. If a second action potential arrives before the muscle fiber has completely relaxed, the two twitches add together, resulting in greater tension **(Figure 50.32)**. Further summation occurs as the rate of stimulation increases. When the rate is so high that the muscle fiber cannot relax at all between stimuli, the twitches fuse into one smooth, sustained contraction called **tetanus**. (Note that tetanus is also the name of a disease of uncontrolled muscle contraction caused by a bacterial toxin.)

Types of Skeletal Muscle Fibers

Our discussion to this point has focused on the general properties of vertebrate skeletal muscles. There are, however, several distinct types of skeletal muscle fibers, each of which is adapted to a particular set of functions. We typically classify these varied fiber types both by the source of ATP used to power their activity and by the speed of their contraction **(Table 50.1)**.

Oxidative and Glycolytic Fibers Fibers that rely mostly on aerobic respiration are called oxidative fibers. Such fibers are specialized in ways that enable them to make use of a steady energy supply: They have many mitochondria, a rich blood supply, and a large amount of an oxygen-storing protein called **myoglobin**. A brownish red pigment, myoglobin binds oxygen more tightly than does hemoglobin, enabling oxidative fibers to extract oxygen from the blood efficiently. In contrast, glycolytic fibers have a larger diameter and less

Table 50.1 Types of Skeletal Muscle Fibers

	Slow Oxidative	Fast Oxidative	Fast Glycolytic
Contraction speed	Slow	Fast	Fast
Major ATP source	Aerobic respiration	Aerobic respiration	Glycolysis
Rate of fatigue	Slow	Intermediate	Fast
Mitochondria	Many	Many	Few
Myoglobin content	High (red muscle)	High (red muscle)	Low (white muscle)

myoglobin. Also, glycolytic fibers use glycolysis as their primary source of ATP and fatigue more readily than oxidative fibers. These two fiber types are readily apparent in the muscle of poultry and fish: The dark meat is made up of oxidative fibers rich in myoglobin, and the light meat is composed of glycolytic fibers.

Fast-Twitch and Slow-Twitch Fibers Muscle fibers vary in the speed with which they contract: **Fast-twitch fibers** develop tension two to three times faster than **slow-twitch fibers**. Fast fibers enable brief, rapid, powerful contractions. Compared with a fast fiber, a slow fiber has less sarcoplasmic reticulum and pumps Ca^{2+} more slowly. Because Ca^{2+} remains in the cytosol longer, a muscle twitch in a slow fiber lasts about five times as long as one in a fast fiber.

The difference in contraction speed between slow-twitch and fast-twitch fibers mainly reflects the rate at which their myosin heads hydrolyze ATP. However, there isn't a one-to-one relationship between contraction speed and ATP source. Whereas all slow-twitch fibers are oxidative, fast-twitch fibers can be either glycolytic or oxidative.

Most human skeletal muscles contain both fast-twitch and slow-twitch fibers, although the muscles of the eye and hand are exclusively fast-twitch. In a muscle that has a mixture of fast and slow fibers, the relative proportions of each are genetically determined. However, if such a muscle is used repeatedly for activities requiring high endurance, some fast glycolytic fibers can develop into fast oxidative fibers. Because fast oxidative fibers fatigue more slowly than fast glycolytic fibers, the result will be a muscle that is more resistant to fatigue.

Some vertebrates have skeletal muscle fibers that twitch at rates far faster than any human muscle. For example, super-fast muscles produce a rattlesnake's rattle and a dove's coo. Even faster are the muscles surrounding the gas-filled swim bladder of the male toadfish **(Figure 50.33)**. In producing its "boat whistle" mating call, the toadfish can contract and relax these muscles more than 200 times per second!

▲ **Figure 50.33 Specialization of skeletal muscles.** The male toadfish (*Opsanus tau*) uses superfast muscles to produce its mating call.

Other Types of Muscle

Although all muscles share the same fundamental mechanism of contraction—actin and myosin filaments sliding past each other—there are many different types of muscle. Vertebrates, for example, have cardiac muscle and smooth muscle in addition to skeletal muscle (see Figure 40.5).

Vertebrate **cardiac muscle** is found only in the heart. Like skeletal muscle, cardiac muscle is striated. However, skeletal and cardiac muscle fibers differ in their electrical and membrane properties. Whereas skeletal muscle fibers require motor neuron input to produce action potentials, ion channels in the plasma membrane of cardiac muscle cells cause rhythmic depolarizations that trigger action potentials without nervous system input. Furthermore, these action potentials last up to 20 times longer than those of the skeletal muscle fibers.

Adjacent cardiac muscles cells are electrically coupled by specialized regions called **intercalated disks**. This coupling enables the action potential generated by specialized cells in one part of the heart to spread, causing the whole heart to contract. A long refractory period prevents summation and tetanus.

Smooth muscle in vertebrates is found mainly in the walls of hollow organs, such as blood vessels and organs of the digestive tract. Smooth muscle cells lack striations because their actin and myosin filaments are not regularly arrayed along the length of the cell. Instead, the thick filaments are scattered throughout the cytoplasm, and the thin filaments are attached to structures called dense bodies, some of which are tethered to the plasma membrane. There is less myosin than in striated muscle fibers, and the myosin is not associated with specific actin strands. Some smooth muscle cells contract only when stimulated by neurons of the autonomic nervous system. Others are electrically coupled to one another and can generate action potentials without input from neurons. Smooth muscles contract and relax more slowly than striated muscles.

Although Ca^{2+} regulates smooth muscle contraction, the mechanism for regulation is different from that in skeletal and cardiac muscle. Smooth muscle cells have no troponin complex or T tubules, and their sarcoplasmic reticulum is not well developed. During an action potential, Ca^{2+} enters the cytosol mainly through the plasma membrane. Calcium ions cause contraction by binding to the protein calmodulin, which activates an enzyme that phosphorylates the myosin head, enabling cross-bridge activity.

Invertebrates have muscle cells similar to vertebrate skeletal and smooth muscle cells, and arthropod skeletal muscles are nearly identical to those of vertebrates. However, because the flight muscles of insects are capable of independent, rhythmic contraction, the wings of some insects can actually beat faster than action potentials can arrive from the central nervous system. Another interesting evolutionary adaptation has been discovered in the muscles that hold a clam's shell closed. The thick filaments in these muscles contain a protein called paramyosin that enables the muscles to remain contracted for as long as a month with only a low rate of energy consumption.

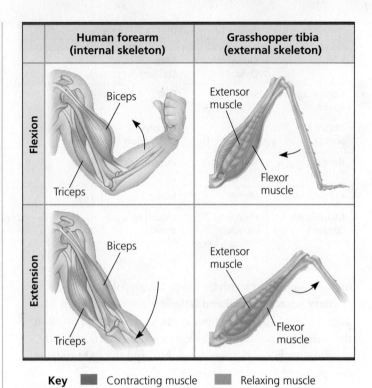

Human forearm (internal skeleton)	Grasshopper tibia (external skeleton)

Flexion — Biceps, Triceps / Extensor muscle, Flexor muscle

Extension — Biceps, Triceps / Extensor muscle, Flexor muscle

Key ▪ Contracting muscle ▪ Relaxing muscle

▲ **Figure 50.34 The interaction of muscles and skeletons in movement.** Back-and-forth movement of a body part is generally accomplished by antagonistic muscles. This arrangement works with either an internal skeleton, as in mammals, or an external skeleton, as in insects.

CONCEPT CHECK 50.5

1. Contrast the role of Ca^{2+} in the contraction of a skeletal muscle fiber and a smooth muscle cell.
2. **WHAT IF?** Why are the muscles of an animal that has recently died likely to be stiff?
3. **MAKE CONNECTIONS** How does the activity of tropomyosin and troponin in muscle contraction compare with the activity of a competitive inhibitor in enzyme action? (See Figure 8.18b.)

For suggested answers, see Appendix A.

CONCEPT 50.6

Skeletal systems transform muscle contraction into locomotion

Converting muscle contraction to movement requires a skeleton—a rigid structure to which muscles can attach. An animal changes its shape or location by contracting muscles connecting two parts of its skeleton. Often muscles are anchored to bone indirectly via connective tissue formed into a tendon.

Because muscles exert force only during contraction, moving a body part back and forth typically requires two muscles attached to the same section of the skeleton. We can see such an arrangement of muscles in the upper portion of a human arm or grasshopper leg **(Figure 50.34)**. Although we call such muscles an antagonistic pair, their function is actually cooperative, coordinated by the nervous system. For example, when you extend your arm, motor neurons trigger your triceps muscle to contract while the absence of neuronal input allows your biceps to relax.

Vital for movement, the skeletons of animals also function in support and protection. Most land animals would collapse if they had no skeleton to support their mass. Even an animal living in water would be formless without a framework to maintain its shape. In many animals, a hard skeleton also protects soft tissues. For example, the vertebrate skull protects the brain, and the ribs of terrestrial vertebrates form a cage around the heart, lungs, and other internal organs.

Types of Skeletal Systems

Although we tend to think of skeletons only as interconnected sets of bones, skeletons come in many different forms. Hardened support structures can be external (as in exoskeletons), internal (as in endoskeletons), or even absent (as in fluid-based, or hydrostatic, skeletons).

Hydrostatic Skeletons

A **hydrostatic skeleton** consists of fluid held under pressure in a closed body compartment. This is the main type of skeleton in most cnidarians, flatworms, nematodes, and annelids (see Chapter 33). These animals control their form and movement by using muscles to change the shape of fluid-filled compartments. Among the cnidarians, for example, a hydra elongates by closing its mouth and constricting its central gastrovascular cavity using contractile cells in its body wall. Because water maintains its volume under pressure, the cavity must elongate when its diameter is decreased.

Worms carry out locomotion in a variety of ways. In planarians and other flatworms, movement results mainly from muscles in the body wall exerting localized forces against the interstitial fluid. In nematodes (roundworms), longitudinal muscles contracting around the fluid-filled body cavity move the animal forward by wavelike motions called undulations. In earthworms and many other annelids, circular and longitudinal muscles act together to change the shape of individual fluid-filled segments, which are divided by septa. These shape changes bring about **peristalsis**, a movement produced by rhythmic waves of muscle contractions passing from front to back **(Figure 50.35)**.

Hydrostatic skeletons are well suited for life in aquatic environments. On land, they provide support for crawling and burrowing and may cushion internal organs from shocks. However, a hydrostatic skeleton cannot support walking or running, in which an animal's body is held off the ground.

Exoskeletons

The clam shell you find on a beach once served as an **exoskeleton**, a hard covering deposited on an animal's surface. The shells of clams and most other molluscs are made of calcium carbonate secreted by the mantle, a sheetlike extension of the body wall (see Figure 33.15). Clams and other bivalves close their hinged shell using muscles attached to the inside of this exoskeleton. As the animal grows, it enlarges its shell by adding to the outer edge.

Insects and other arthropods have a jointed exoskeleton called a *cuticle*, a nonliving coat secreted by the epidermis. About 30–50% of the arthropod cuticle consists of **chitin**, a polysaccharide similar to cellulose (see Figure 5.8). Fibrils of chitin are embedded in a protein matrix, forming a composite material that combines strength and flexibility. The cuticle may be hardened with organic compounds and, in some cases, calcium salts. In body parts that must be flexible, such as leg joints, the cuticle remains unhardened. Muscles are attached to knobs and plates of the cuticle that extend into the interior of the body. With each growth

1 At the moment depicted, body segments at the earthworm's head end and just in front of the rear end are short and thick (longitudinal muscles contracted; circular muscles relaxed) and are anchored to the ground by bristles. The other segments are thin and elongated (circular muscles contracted; longitudinal muscles relaxed).

2 The head has moved forward because circular muscles in the head segments have contracted. Segments behind the head and at the rear are now thick and anchored, thus preventing the worm from slipping backward.

3 The head segments are thick again and anchored in their new positions. The rear segments have released their hold on the ground and have been pulled forward.

▲ **Figure 50.35 Crawling by peristalsis.** Contraction of the longitudinal muscles thickens and shortens the earthworm; contraction of the circular muscles constricts and elongates it.

spurt, an arthropod must shed its exoskeleton (molt) and produce a larger one.

Endoskeletons

Animals ranging from sponges to mammals have a hardened internal skeleton, or **endoskeleton**, buried within their soft tissues. In sponges, the endoskeleton consists of hard needle-like structures of inorganic material or fibers made of protein. Echinoderms' bodies are reinforced by ossicles, hard plates composed of magnesium carbonate and calcium carbonate crystals. Whereas the ossicles of sea urchins are tightly bound, the ossicles of sea stars are more loosely linked, allowing a sea star to change the shape of its arms.

Chordates have an endoskeleton consisting of cartilage, bone, or some combination of these materials (see

Figure 40.5). The mammalian skeleton contains more than 200 bones, some fused together and others connected at joints by ligaments that allow freedom of movement **(Figures 50.36** and **50.37).** Cells called *osteoblasts* secrete bone matrix and thereby build and repair bone (see Figure 40.5). *Osteoclasts* have an opposite function, resorbing bone components in remodeling of the skeleton.

How thick does an endoskeleton need to be? We can begin to answer this question by applying ideas from civil engineering. The weight of a building increases with the cube of its dimensions. However, the strength of a support depends on its cross-sectional area, which only increases with the square of its diameter. We can thus predict that if we scaled up a mouse

to the size of an elephant, the legs of the giant mouse would be too thin to support its weight. Indeed, large animals have very different body proportions from small ones.

In applying the building analogy, we might also predict that the size of leg bones should be directly proportional to the strain imposed by body weight. Animal bodies, however, are complex and nonrigid. In supporting body weight, it turns out that body posture—the position of the legs relative to the main body—is more important than leg size, at least in mammals and birds. In addition, muscles and tendons, which hold the legs of large mammals relatively straight and positioned under the body, actually bear most of the load.

▼ **Figure 50.36** Bones and joints of the human skeleton.

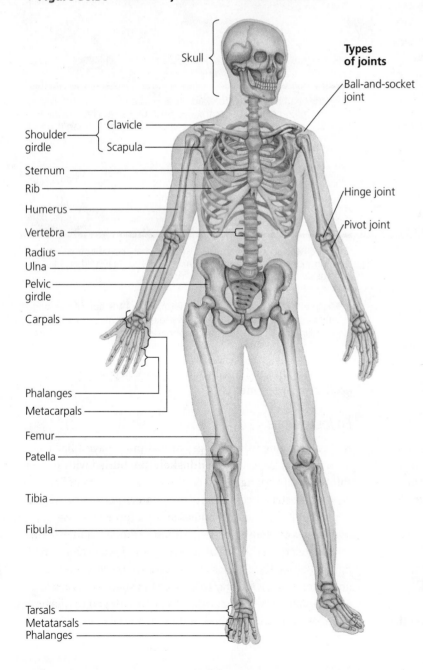

▼ **Figure 50.37** Types of joints.

Ball-and-socket joint

Ball-and-socket joints are found where the humerus contacts the shoulder girdle and where the femur contacts the pelvic girdle. These joints enable the arms and legs to rotate and move in several planes.

Hinge joint

Hinge joints, such as between the humerus and the head of the ulna, restrict movement to a single plane.

Pivot joint

Pivot joints enable rotating the forearm at the elbow and turning the head from side to side.

Types of Locomotion

Movement is a hallmark of animals. Even animals fixed to a surface move their body parts: Sponges use beating flagella to generate water currents that draw and trap small food particles, and sessile cnidarians wave tentacles that capture prey (see Chapter 33). Most animals, however, are mobile and spend a considerable portion of their time and energy actively searching for food, escaping from danger, and seeking mates. These activities involve **locomotion**—active travel from place to place.

Friction and gravity tend to keep an animal stationary and therefore oppose locomotion. To move, an animal must expend energy to overcome these two forces. As we will see next, the amount of energy required to oppose friction or gravity is often reduced by an animal body plan adapted for movement in a particular environment.

▲ **Figure 50.38 Energy-efficient locomotion on land.** Members of the kangaroo family travel from place to place mainly by leaping on their large hind legs. Kinetic energy momentarily stored in tendons after each leap provides a boost for the next leap. In fact, a large kangaroo hopping at 30 km/hr uses no more energy per minute than it does at 6 km/hr. The large tail helps to balance the kangaroo when it leaps as well as when it sits.

Locomotion on Land

On land, a walking, running, hopping, or crawling animal must be able to support itself and move against gravity, but air poses relatively little resistance, at least at moderate speeds. When a land animal walks, runs, or hops, its leg muscles expend energy both to propel it and to keep it from falling down. With each step, the animal's leg muscles must overcome inertia by accelerating a leg from a standing start. For moving on land, powerful muscles and strong skeletal support are therefore more important than a streamlined shape.

Diverse adaptations for traveling on land have evolved in various vertebrates. For example, kangaroos have large, powerful muscles in their hind legs, suitable for locomotion by hopping **(Figure 50.38)**. As a kangaroo lands after each leap, tendons in its hind legs momentarily store energy. The farther the animal hops, the more energy its tendons store. Analogous to the energy in a compressed spring, the energy stored in the tendons is available for the next jump and reduces the total amount of energy the animal must expend to travel. The legs of an insect, dog, or human also retain some energy during walking or running, although a considerably smaller share than those of a kangaroo.

Maintaining balance is another prerequisite for walking, running, or hopping. A kangaroo's large tail helps balance its body during leaps and also forms a stable tripod with its hind legs when the animal sits or moves slowly. Illustrating the same principle, a walking cat, dog, or horse keeps three feet on the ground. Bipedal animals, such as humans and birds, keep part of at least one foot on the ground when walking. When an animal runs, all four feet (or both feet for bipeds) may be off the ground briefly, but at running speeds it is momentum more than foot contact that keeps the body upright.

Crawling poses a very different challenge. Having much of its body in contact with the ground, a crawling animal must exert considerable effort to overcome friction. As you have read, earthworms crawl by peristalsis. In contrast, many snakes crawl by undulating their entire body from side to side. Assisted by large, movable scales on its underside, a snake's body pushes against the ground, propelling the animal forward. Some snakes, such as boa constrictors and pythons, creep straight forward, driven by muscles that lift belly scales off the ground, tilt the scales forward, and then push them backward against the ground.

Swimming

Because most animals are reasonably buoyant in water, overcoming gravity is less of a problem for swimming animals than for species that move on land or through the air. On the other hand, water is a much denser and more viscous medium than air, and thus drag (friction) is a major problem for aquatic animals. A sleek, fusiform (torpedo-like) shape is a common adaptation of fast swimmers (see Figure 40.2).

Most animal phyla include species that swim, but swimming occurs in diverse ways. Many insects and four-legged vertebrates use their legs as oars to push against the water. Squids, scallops, and some cnidarians are jet-propelled, taking in water and squirting it out in bursts. Sharks and bony fishes swim by moving their body and tail from side to side, while whales and dolphins move by undulating their body and tail up and down.

Interpreting a Graph with Log Scales

What Are the Energy Costs of Locomotion? In the 1960s, animal physiologist Knut Schmidt-Nielsen, at Duke University, wondered whether general principles govern the energy costs of different forms of locomotion among diverse animal species. To answer this question, he drew on his own experiments as well as those of other researchers. In this exercise you will analyze the combined results of these studies and evaluate the rationale for plotting the experimental data on a graph with logarithmic scales.

How the Experiments Were Done Researchers measured the rate of oxygen consumption or carbon dioxide production in animals that ran on treadmills, swam in water flumes, or flew in wind tunnels. For example, a tube connected to a plastic face mask collected gases exhaled by a parakeet during flight (see photo at upper right). From these measurements, Schmidt-Nielsen calculated the amount of energy each animal used to transport a given amount of body mass over a given distance (calories/kilogram · meter).

Data from the Experiments Schmidt-Nielsen plotted the cost of running, flying, and swimming versus body mass on a single graph with logarithmic (log) scales for the axes. He then drew a best-fit straight line through the data points for each form of locomotion. (On the graph below, the individual data points are not shown.)

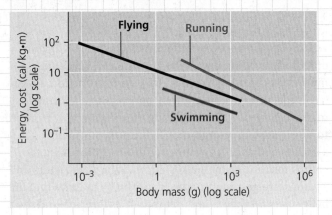

Interpret the Data

1. The body masses of the animals used in these experiments ranged from about 0.001 g to 1,000,000 g, and their rates of energy use ranged from about 0.1 cal/kg · m to 100 cal/kg · m. If you were to plot these data on a graph with linear instead of log scales for the axes, how would you draw the axes so that all of the data would be visible? What is the advantage of using log scales for plotting data with a wide range of values? (For additional information about graphs, see the Scientific Skills Review in Appendix F and in the Study Area in MasteringBiology.)

2. Based on the graph, how much greater is the energy cost of flying for an animal that weighs 10^{-3} g than for an animal that weighs 1 g? For any given form of locomotion, which travels more efficiently, a larger animal or smaller animal?

3. The slopes of the flying and swimming lines are very similar. Based on your answer to question 2, if the energy cost of a 2-g swimming animal is 1.2 cal/kg · m, what is the estimated energy cost of a 2-kg swimming animal?

4. Considering animals with a body mass of about 100 g, rank the three forms of locomotion from highest energy cost to lowest energy cost. Were these the results you expected, based on your own experience? What could explain the energy cost of running compared to that of flying or swimming?

5. Schmidt-Nielson calculated the swimming cost in a mallard duck and found that it was nearly 20 times as high as the swimming cost in a salmon of the same body mass. What could explain the greater swimming efficiency of salmon?

(MB) A version of this Scientific Skills Exercise can be assigned in MasteringBiology.

Data from K. Schmidt-Nielsen, Locomotion: Energy cost of swimming, flying, and running, *Science* 177:222–228 (1972). Reprinted with permission from AAAS.

Flying

Active flight (in contrast to gliding downward from a tree) has evolved in only a few animal groups: insects, reptiles (including birds), and, among the mammals, bats. One group of flying reptiles, the pterosaurs, died out millions of years ago, leaving birds and bats as the only flying vertebrates.

Gravity poses a major problem for a flying animal because its wings must develop enough lift to overcome gravity's downward force. The key to flight is wing shape. All wings act as airfoils—structures whose shape alters air currents in a way that helps animals or airplanes stay aloft. As for the body to which the wings attach, a fusiform shape helps reduce drag in air as it does in water.

Flying animals are relatively light, with body masses ranging from less than a gram for some insects to about 20 kg for the largest flying birds. Many flying animals have structural adaptations that contribute to low body mass. Birds, for example, have no urinary bladder or teeth and have relatively large bones with air-filled regions that help lessen the bird's weight (see Chapter 34).

Flying, running, and swimming each impose different energetic demands on animals. In the Scientific Skills Exercise, you can interpret a graph that compares the relative energy costs of these three forms of locomotion.

CONCEPT CHECK 50.6

1. In what way are septa an important feature of the earthworm skeleton?

2. Contrast swimming and flying in terms of the main problems they pose and the adaptations that allow animals to overcome those problems.

3. **WHAT IF?** When using your arms to lower yourself into a chair, you bend your arms without using your biceps. Explain how this is possible. (*Hint:* Think about gravity as an antagonistic force.)

For suggested answers, see Appendix A.

CONCEPT 50.1

Sensory receptors transduce stimulus energy and transmit signals to the central nervous system (pp. 1102–1106)

- The detection of a stimulus precedes **sensory transduction**, the change in the membrane potential of a **sensory receptor** in response to a stimulus. The resulting receptor potential controls **transmission** of action potentials to the CNS, where sensory information is integrated to generate **perceptions**. The frequency of action potentials in an axon and the number of axons activated determine stimulus strength. The identity of the axon carrying the signal encodes the nature or quality of the stimulus.
- **Mechanoreceptors** respond to stimuli such as pressure, touch, stretch, motion, and sound. **Chemoreceptors** detect either total solute concentrations or specific molecules. **Electromagnetic receptors** detect different forms of electromagnetic radiation. **Thermoreceptors** signal surface and core temperatures of the body. Pain is detected by a group of **nociceptors** that respond to excess heat, pressure, or specific classes of chemicals.

? *To simplify sensory receptor classification, why might it make sense to eliminate nociceptors as a distinct class?*

CONCEPT 50.2

The mechanoreceptors responsible for hearing and equilibrium detect moving fluid or settling particles (pp. 1106–1100)

- Most invertebrates sense their orientation with respect to gravity by means of **statocysts**. Specialized **hair cells** form the basis for hearing and balance in mammals and for detection of water movement in fishes and aquatic amphibians. In mammals, the **tympanic membrane** (eardrum) transmits sound waves to bones of the middle ear, which transmit the waves through the oval window to the fluid in the coiled **cochlea** of the inner ear. Pressure waves in the fluid vibrate the basilar membrane, depolarizing hair cells and triggering action potentials that travel via the auditory nerve to the brain. Receptors in the inner ear function in balance and equilibrium.

? *How are music volume and pitch encoded in signals to the brain?*

CONCEPT 50.3

The diverse visual receptors of animals depend on light-absorbing pigments (pp. 1111–1117)

- Invertebrates have varied light detectors, including simple light-sensitive eyespots, image-forming compound eyes, and single-lens eyes. In the vertebrate eye, a single lens is used to focus light on **photoreceptors** in the **retina**. Both **rods** and **cones** contain a pigment, **retinal**, bonded to a protein (opsin). Absorption of light by retinal triggers a signal transduction pathway that hyperpolarizes the photoreceptors, causing them to release less neurotransmitter. Synapses transmit information from photoreceptors to cells that integrate information and convey it to the brain along axons that form the optic nerve.

? *How does processing of sensory information sent to the vertebrate brain in vision differ from that in hearing or olfaction?*

CONCEPT 50.4

The senses of taste and smell rely on similar sets of sensory receptors (pp. 1117–1119)

- Taste (**gustation**) and smell (**olfaction**) depend on stimulation of chemoreceptors by small dissolved molecules. In humans, sensory cells in taste buds express a receptor type specific for one of the five taste perceptions: sweet, sour, salty, bitter, and umami (elicited by glutamate). Olfactory receptor cells line the upper part of the nasal cavity. More than 1,000 genes code for membrane proteins that bind to specific classes of odorants, and each receptor cell appears to express only one of those genes.

? *Why do foods taste bland when you have a head cold?*

CONCEPT 50.5

The physical interaction of protein filaments is required for muscle function (pp. 1119–1126)

- The muscle cells (fibers) of vertebrate skeletal muscle contain myofibrils composed of **thin filaments** of (mostly) actin and **thick filaments** of myosin. These filaments are organized into repeating units called **sarcomeres**. Myosin heads, energized by the hydrolysis of ATP, bind to the thin filaments, form cross-bridges, and then release upon binding ATP anew. As this cycle repeats, the thick and thin filaments slide past each other, shortening the sarcomere and contracting the muscle fiber.

- Motor neurons release acetylcholine, triggering action potentials in muscle fibers that stimulate the release of Ca^{2+} from the **sarcoplasmic reticulum**. When the Ca^{2+} binds the **troponin complex**, **tropomyosin** moves, exposing the myosin-binding sites on actin and thus initiating cross-bridge formation. A **motor unit** consists of a motor neuron and the muscle fibers it controls. A twitch results from one action potential. Skeletal muscle fibers are slow-twitch or fast-twitch and oxidative or glycolytic.
- Cardiac muscle, found in the heart, consists of striated cells electrically connected by intercalated disks and generate action potentials without input from neurons. In smooth muscles, contractions are initiated by the muscles or by stimulation from neurons in the autonomic nervous system.

? *What are two major functions of ATP hydrolysis in skeletal muscle activity?*

CONCEPT 50.6

Skeletal systems transform muscle contraction into locomotion (pp. 1126–1130)

- Skeletal muscles, often in antagonistic pairs, contract and pull against the skeleton. Skeletons may be **hydrostatic** and maintained by fluid pressure, as in worms; hardened into **exoskeletons**, as in insects; or in the form of **endoskeletons**, as in vertebrates.
- Each form of **locomotion**—swimming, movement on land, or flying—presents a particular challenge. For example, swimmers need to overcome friction, but face less of a challenge from gravity than do animals that move on land or fly.

? *Explain how microscopic and macroscopic anchoring of muscle filaments enables you to bend your elbow.*

TEST YOUR UNDERSTANDING

LEVEL 1: KNOWLEDGE/COMPREHENSION

1. Which of the following sensory receptors is *incorrectly* paired with its category?
   a. hair cell—mechanoreceptor
   b. muscle spindle—mechanoreceptor
   c. taste receptor—chemoreceptor
   d. olfactory receptor—electromagnetic receptor

2. The middle ear converts
   a. air pressure waves to fluid pressure waves.
   b. air pressure waves to nerve impulses.
   c. fluid pressure waves to nerve impulses.
   d. pressure waves to hair cell movements.

3. During the contraction of a vertebrate skeletal muscle fiber, calcium ions
   a. break cross-bridges by acting as a cofactor in the hydrolysis of ATP.
   b. bind with troponin, changing its shape so that the myosin-binding sites on actin are exposed.
   c. transmit action potentials from the motor neuron to the muscle fiber.
   d. spread action potentials through the T tubules.

LEVEL 2: APPLICATION/ANALYSIS

4. Which sensory distinction is *not* encoded by a difference in neuron identity?
   a. white and red
   b. red and green
   c. loud and faint
   d. salty and sweet

5. The transduction of sound waves into action potentials occurs
   a. within the tectorial membrane as it is stimulated by the hair cells.
   b. when hair cells are bent against the tectorial membrane, causing them to depolarize and release neurotransmitter that stimulates sensory neurons.
   c. as the basilar membrane vibrates at different frequencies in response to the varying volume of sounds.
   d. within the middle ear as the vibrations are amplified by the malleus, incus, and stapes.

LEVEL 3: SYNTHESIS/EVALUATION

6. Although some sharks close their eyes just before they bite, their bites are on target. Researchers have noted that sharks often misdirect their bites at metal objects and that they can find batteries buried under sand. This evidence suggests that sharks keep track of their prey during the split second before they bite, in the same way that
   a. a rattlesnake finds a mouse in its burrow.
   b. an insect avoids being stepped on.
   c. a star-nosed mole locates its prey in tunnels.
   d. a platypus locates its prey in a muddy river.

7. **DRAW IT** Based on the information in the text, fill in the following graph. Use one line for rods and another line for cones.

8. **EVOLUTION CONNECTION**
   In general, locomotion on land will require more energy than locomotion in water. By integrating what you learned about animal form and function in Unit 7, discuss some of the evolutionary adaptations of mammals that support the high energy requirements for moving on land.

9. **SCIENTIFIC INQUIRY**
   Although skeletal muscles generally fatigue fairly rapidly, clam shell muscles have a protein called paramyosin that allows them to sustain contraction for up to a month. From your knowledge of the cellular mechanism of contraction, propose a hypothesis to explain how paramyosin might work. How would you test your hypothesis experimentally?

10. **WRITE ABOUT A THEME: ORGANIZATION**
    In a short essay (100–150 words), describe at least three ways in which the structure of the lens of the human eye is well adapted to its function in vision.

11. **SYNTHESIZE YOUR KNOWLEDGE**

Bloodhounds, which are adept at following a scent trail even days old, have 1,000 times as many olfactory receptor cells as we have. How might this difference contribute to the tracking ability of these dogs? What differences in brain organization would you expect in comparing a bloodhound and a human?

For selected answers, see Appendix A.

MasteringBiology®

Students Go to **MasteringBiology** for assignments, the eText, and the Study Area with practice tests, animations, and activities.

Instructors Go to **MasteringBiology** for automatically graded tutorials and questions that you can assign to your students, plus Instructor Resources.

51

Animal Behavior

KEY CONCEPTS

51.1 Discrete sensory inputs can stimulate both simple and complex behaviors

51.2 Learning establishes specific links between experience and behavior

51.3 Selection for individual survival and reproductive success can explain diverse behaviors

51.4 Genetic analyses and the concept of inclusive fitness provide a basis for studying the evolution of behavior

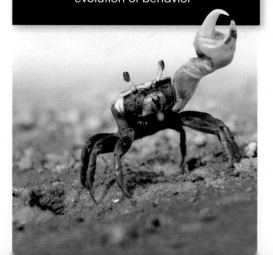

▲ **Figure 51.1 What prompts a male fiddler crab to display his giant claw?**

The How and Why of Animal Activity

Unlike most animals, male fiddler crabs (genus *Uca*) are highly asymmetrical: One claw grows to giant proportions, up to half the mass of the entire body **(Figure 51.1)**. The name *fiddler* comes from the crab's behavior as it feeds on algae from the mudflats where it lives: The smaller of the front claws moves to and from the mouth in front of the enlarged claw. At other times the male waves his large claw in the air. What triggers this behavior? What purpose does it serve?

Claw waving by a male fiddler crab has two functions. Waving the claw, which can be used as a weapon, helps the crab *repel* other males wandering too close to his burrow. Vigorous claw waving also helps him *attract* females, who wander through the crab colony in search of a mate. After the male fiddler crab lures a female to his burrow, he seals her in with mud or sand in preparation for mating.

Animal behavior, be it solitary or social, fixed or variable, is based on physiological systems and processes. An individual **behavior** is an action carried out by muscles under control of the nervous system. Examples include an animal using its throat muscles to produce a song, releasing a scent to mark its territory, or simply waving a claw. Behavior is an essential part of acquiring nutrients and finding a partner for sexual reproduction. Behavior also contributes to homeostasis, as when honeybees huddle to conserve heat (see Concept 40.3). In short, all of animal physiology contributes to behavior, and behavior influences all of physiology.

Being essential for survival and reproduction, behavior is subject to substantial natural selection over time. This evolutionary process of selection also affects anatomy because the recognition and communication that underlie many behaviors depend on body form and appearance. Thus, the enlarged claw of the male fiddler crab is an adaptation that enables the display essential for recognition by other members of the species. Similarly, the positioning of the eyes on stalks held well above the crab's head enables him to see intruders from far off.

In this chapter, we'll examine how behavior is controlled, how it develops during an animal's life, and how it is influenced by genes and the environment. We'll also explore the ways in which behavior evolves over many generations. Shifting our focus from an animal's inner workings to its interactions with the outside world will set the stage for exploring ecology, the subject of Unit Eight.

CONCEPT 51.1

Discrete sensory inputs can stimulate both simple and complex behaviors

What approach do biologists use to determine how behaviors arise and what functions they serve? The Dutch scientist Niko Tinbergen, a pioneer in the study of animal behavior, suggested that understanding any behavior requires answering four questions, which can be summarized as follows:

1. What stimulus elicits the behavior, and what physiological mechanisms mediate the response?
2. How does the animal's experience during growth and development influence the response?
3. How does the behavior aid survival and reproduction?
4. What is the behavior's evolutionary history?

Tinbergen's first two questions ask about *proximate causation*: "how" a behavior occurs or is modified. The last two questions ask about *ultimate causation*: "why" a behavior occurs in the context of natural selection. Thus any given behavior has both proximate and ultimate causes.

Studies on proximate causation by Tinbergen and two other early researchers—Karl von Frisch and Konrad Lorenz—earned the three scientists a Nobel Prize in 1973. We'll consider those experiments in the early part of the chapter. The concept of ultimate causation is central to **behavioral ecology**, the study of the ecological and evolutionary basis for animal behavior. We'll explore this vibrant area of modern biological research in the rest of the chapter.

Fixed Action Patterns

In addressing Tinbergen's first question, the nature of the stimuli that trigger behavior, we'll begin with behavioral

responses to well-defined stimuli, starting with an example from Tinbergen's own experiments.

As part of his research, Tinbergen kept fish tanks containing three-spined sticklebacks (*Gasterosteus aculeatus*). Male sticklebacks, which have red bellies, attack other males that invade their nesting territories. Tinbergen noticed that his male sticklebacks also behaved aggressively when a red truck passed within view of their tank. Inspired by this chance observation, he carried out experiments showing that the red color of an intruder's underside is the proximate cause of the attack behavior. A male stickleback will not attack a fish lacking red coloration (note that female sticklebacks never have red bellies), but will attack even unrealistic models if they contain areas of red color **(Figure 51.2)**.

The territorial response of male sticklebacks is an example of a **fixed action pattern**, a sequence of unlearned acts directly linked to a simple stimulus. Fixed action patterns are essentially unchangeable and, once initiated, usually carried to completion. The trigger for the behavior is an

(a) A male stickleback fish attacks other male sticklebacks that invade its nesting territory. The red belly of the intruding male (left) acts as the sign stimulus that releases the aggressive behavior.

(b) The realistic model at the top, without a red underside, produces no aggressive response in a male three-spined stickleback. The other models, with red undersides, produce strong responses.

▲ **Figure 51.2 Sign stimuli in a classic fixed action pattern.**

? *Suggest an explanation for why this behavior evolved (its ultimate causation).*

external cue called a **sign stimulus**, such as a red object that prompts the male stickleback's aggressive behavior.

Migration

Environmental stimuli not only trigger behaviors but also provide cues that animals use to carry out those behaviors. For example, a wide variety of birds, fishes, and other animals use environmental cues to guide **migration**—a regular, long-distance change in location **(Figure 51.3)**. In the course of migration, many animals pass through environments they have not previously encountered. How, then, do they find their way in these foreign settings?

Some migrating animals track their position relative to the sun, even though the sun's position relative to Earth changes throughout the day. Animals can adjust for these changes by means of a *circadian clock*, an internal mechanism that maintains a 24-hour activity rhythm or cycle (see Concept 49.2). For example, experiments have shown that migrating birds orient differently relative to the sun at distinct times of the day. Nocturnal animals can instead use the North Star, which has a constant position in the night sky.

Although the sun and stars can provide useful clues for navigation, these landmarks can be obscured by clouds. How do migrating animals overcome this problem? A simple experiment with homing pigeons provides one answer. On an overcast day, placing a small magnet on the head of a homing pigeon prevents it from returning efficiently to its roost. Researchers concluded that pigeons sense their position relative to Earth's magnetic field and can thereby navigate without solar or celestial cues.

The way in which animals detect Earth's magnetic field remains a matter of investigation. It is known that the heads of migrating birds (and fishes) contain bits of magnetite, a magnetic iron mineral. There is also evidence that cells in the pigeon's brainstem encode information about magnetic field direction, intensity, and polarity. The search continues for magnetoreceptors, which in migrating birds appear to be located in the eye, beak, and perhaps inner ear.

Behavioral Rhythms

Although the circadian clock plays a small but significant role in navigation by some migrating species, it has a major role in the daily activity of all animals. As discussed in Chapters 40 and 49, the clock is responsible for a circadian rhythm, a daily cycle of rest and activity. The clock is normally synchronized with the light and dark cycles of the environment but can maintain rhythmic activity even under constant environmental conditions, such as during hibernation.

Some behaviors, such as migration and reproduction, reflect biological rhythms with a longer cycle, or period, than the circadian rhythm. Behavioral rhythms linked to the yearly cycle of seasons are called *circannual rhythms*. Although migration and reproduction typically correlate with food availability, these behaviors are not a direct response to changes in food intake. Instead, circannual rhythms, like circadian rhythms, are influenced by the periods of daylight and darkness in the environment. For example, studies with several bird species have shown that an artificial environment with extended daylight can induce out-of-season migratory behavior.

Not all biological rhythms are linked to the light and dark cycles in the environment. Consider, for instance, the fiddler crab shown in Figure 51.1. The male's claw-waving courtship behavior is linked to the timing of the new and full moon. Why? Fiddler crabs begin their lives as plankton, settling in the mudflats after several larval stages. By courting at the time of the new or full moon, crabs link their reproduction to the times of greatest tidal movement. The tides disperse larvae to deeper waters, where they complete early development in relative safety before returning to the tidal flats.

▼ **Figure 51.3 Migration.** Wildebeest herds migrate long distances twice each year, changing their feeding grounds in coordination with the dry and rainy seasons.

Animal Signals and Communication

Claw waving by fiddler crabs during courtship is an example of one animal (the male crab) generating the stimulus that guides the behavior of another animal (the female crab). A stimulus transmitted from one organism to another is called a **signal**. The transmission and reception of signals between animals constitute **communication**, which often has a role in the proximate causation of behavior.

Forms of Animal Communication

Let's consider the courtship behavior of the fruit fly, *Drosophila melanogaster*, as an introduction to the four common modes of animal communication: visual, chemical, tactile, and auditory.

Fruit fly courtship constitutes a *stimulus-response chain*, in which the response to each stimulus is itself the stimulus for the next behavior **(Figure 51.4)**. In the first step, a male detects a female in his field of vision and orients his body toward hers. To confirm she belongs to his species, he uses his olfactory system to detect chemicals she releases into the air. The male then approaches and touches the female with a foreleg. This touching, or tactile communication, alerts the female to the male's presence. In the third stage of courtship, the male extends and vibrates one of his wings, producing a courtship song. This auditory communication informs the female whether the male is of the same species. Only if all of these forms of communication are successful will the female allow the male to attempt copulation.

In general, the form of communication that evolves is closely related to an animal's lifestyle and environment. For example, most terrestrial mammals are nocturnal, which makes visual displays relatively ineffective. Instead, these species use olfactory and auditory signals, which work as well in the dark as in the light. In contrast, most birds are diurnal (active mainly in daytime) and communicate primarily by visual and auditory signals. Humans are also diurnal and, like birds, use primarily visual and auditory communication.

We can thus detect and appreciate the songs and bright colors used by birds to communicate but miss many chemical cues on which other mammals base their behavior.

The information content of animal communication varies considerably. One of the most remarkable examples is the symbolic language of the European honeybee (*Apis mellifera*), discovered in the early 1900s by Austrian researcher Karl von Frisch. Using glass-walled observation hives, he and his students spent several decades observing honeybees. Methodical recordings of bee movements enabled von Frisch to decipher a "dance language" that returning foragers use to inform other bees about the distance and direction of travel to food sources.

A returning bee quickly becomes the center of attention for other bees, called followers **(Figure 51.5a)**. If the food source is close to the hive (less than 50 m away), the returning bee moves in tight circles while moving its abdomen from side to side **(Figure 51.5b)**. This behavior, called the "round dance," motivates the follower bees to leave the hive and search for nearby food.

When the food source is farther from the nest, the returning bee instead performs a "waggle dance." This dance, consisting of a half-circle swing in one direction, a straight run during which the bee waggles its abdomen, and a half-circle swing in the other direction, communicates to the follower bees both the direction and distance of the food source in relation to the hive **(Figure 51.5c)**. The angle of the straight run relative to the hive's vertical surface is the same as the horizontal angle of the food in relation to the sun. For example, if the returning bee runs at a 30° angle to the right of vertical, the follower bees leaving the hive fly 30° to the right of the horizontal direction of the sun. A dance with a longer straight run, and therefore more abdominal waggles per run, indicates a greater distance to the food source. As follower bees exit the hive, they fly almost directly to the area indicated by the waggle dance. By using flower odor and other clues, they locate the food source within this area.

▶ **Figure 51.4 Courtship behavior of the fruit fly.** Fruit fly courtship involves a fixed set of behaviors that follow one another in a rigid order.

Male visually recognizes female.

Female releases chemicals detected by the male's sense of smell.

❶ Orienting

Male taps female's abdomen with a foreleg.

❷ Tapping

Male extends and vibrates wing, producing a courtship song.

❸ "Singing"

(a) Worker bees cluster around a recently returned bee.

(b) The round dance indicates that food is near.

Beehive

Location **A**:
Food source is in same direction as sun.

Location **B**:
Food source is in direction opposite sun.

Location **C**:
Food source is 30° to right of sun.

(c) The waggle dance is performed when food is distant. The waggle dance resembles a figure eight. Distance is indicated by the number of abdominal waggles performed in the straight-run part of the dance. Direction is indicated by the angle (in relation to the vertical surface of the hive) of the straight run.

▲ **Figure 51.5 Honeybee dance language.** Honeybees returning to the hive communicate the location of food sources through the symbolic language of a dance.

Pheromones

Animals that communicate through odors or tastes emit chemical substances called **pheromones**. Pheromones are especially common among mammals and insects and often relate to reproductive behavior. For example, pheromones are the basis for the chemical communication in fruit fly courtship (see Figure 51.4). Pheromones are not limited to short-distance signaling, however. Male silkworm moths have receptors that can detect the pheromone from a female moth from several kilometers away (see Figure 50.6).

In a honeybee colony, pheromones produced by the queen and her daughters, the workers, maintain the hive's complex social order. One pheromone (once called the queen substance) has a particularly wide range of effects. It attracts workers to the queen, inhibits development of ovaries in workers, and attracts males (drones) to the queen during her mating flights out of the hive.

Pheromones can also serve as alarm signals. For example, when a minnow or catfish is injured, a substance released from the fish's skin disperses in the water, inducing a fright response in other fish. These nearby fish become more vigilant and often form tightly packed schools near the river or lake bottom, where they are safer from attack (**Figure 51.6**). Pheromones can be very effective at remarkably low concentrations. For instance, just 1 cm^2 of skin from a fathead minnow contains sufficient alarm substance to induce a reaction in 58,000 L of water.

So far in this chapter, we have explored the types of stimuli that elicit behaviors—the first part of Tinbergen's first question. The second part of that question—the physiological mechanisms that mediate responses—involves the nervous, muscular, and skeletal systems: Stimuli activate sensory systems, are processed in the central nervous system, and result in motor outputs that constitute behavior. Thus, we are ready to focus on Tinbergen's second question—how experience influences behavior.

❶ Minnows are widely dispersed in an aquarium before an alarm substance is introduced.

❷ Within seconds of the alarm substance being introduced, minnows aggregate near the bottom of the aquarium and reduce their movement.

▲ **Figure 51.6 Minnows responding to the presence of an alarm substance.**

1. If an egg rolls out of the nest, a mother graylag goose will retrieve it by nudging it with her beak and head. If researchers remove the egg or substitute a ball during this process, the goose continues to bob her beak and head while she moves back to the nest. Explain how and why this behavior occurs.

2. **WHAT IF?** Suppose you exposed various fish species from the minnows' environment to the alarm substance from minnows. Thinking about natural selection, suggest why some species might respond like minnows, some might increase their activity, and some might show no change.

3. **MAKE CONNECTIONS** How is the lunar-linked rhythm of fiddler crab courtship similar in mechanism and function to the seasonal timing of plant flowering? (See Concept 39.3.)

For suggested answers, see Appendix A.

CONCEPT 51.2

Learning establishes specific links between experience and behavior

For some behaviors—such as a fixed action pattern, a courtship stimulus-response chain, and pheromone signaling—nearly all individuals in a population behave alike. Behavior that is developmentally fixed in this way is known as **innate behavior**. Other behaviors, however, vary with experience and thus differ between individuals.

Experience and Behavior

Tinbergen's second question asks how an animal's experiences during growth and development influence the response to stimuli. One informative approach to this question is a **cross-fostering study**, in which the young of one species are placed in the care of adults from another species. The extent to which the offspring's behavior changes in such a situation provides a measure of how the social and physical environment influences behavior.

Certain mouse species have behaviors well suited for cross-fostering studies. Male California mice (*Peromyscus californicus*) are highly aggressive toward other mice and provide extensive parental care. In contrast, male white-footed mice (*Peromyscus leucopus*) are less aggressive and engage in little parental care. When the pups of each species were placed in the nests of the other species, the cross-fostering altered some behaviors of both species **(Table 51.1)**. For instance, male California mice raised by white-footed mice were less aggressive toward intruders. Thus, experience during development can strongly influence aggressive behavior in these rodents.

One of the most important findings of the cross-fostering experiments with mice was that the influence of experience

Table 51.1 Influence of Cross-Fostering on Male Mice*

Species	Aggression Toward an Intruder	Aggression In Neutral Situation	Paternal Behavior
California mice fostered by white-footed mice	Reduced	No difference	Reduced
White-footed mice fostered by California mice	No difference	Increased	No difference

*Comparisons are with mice raised by parents of their own species.

on behavior can be passed on to progeny: When the cross-fostered California mice became parents, they spent less time retrieving offspring who wandered off than did California mice raised by their own species. Thus, experience during development can modify physiology in a way that alters parental behavior, extending the influence of environment to a subsequent generation.

For humans, the influence of genetics and environment on behavior can be explored by a **twin study**, in which researchers compare the behavior of identical twins raised apart with the behavior of those raised in the same household. Twin studies have been instrumental in studying disorders, such as schizophrenia, anxiety disorders, and alcoholism, that alter human behavior.

Learning

One powerful way that an animal's environment can influence its behavior is through **learning**, the modification of behavior as a result of specific experiences. The capacity for learning depends on nervous system organization established during development following instructions encoded in the genome. Learning itself involves the formation of memories by specific changes in neuronal connectivity (see Concept 49.4). Therefore, the essential challenge for research into learning is not to decide between nature (genes) and nurture (environment), but rather to explore the contributions of *both* nature and nurture in shaping learning and, more generally, behavior.

Imprinting

In some species, the ability of offspring to recognize and be recognized by a parent is essential for survival. In the young, this learning often takes the form of **imprinting**, the establishment of a long-lasting behavioral response to a particular individual or object. Imprinting can take place only during a specific time period in development, called the **sensitive period**. Among gulls, for instance, the sensitive period for a parent to bond with its young lasts one to two days. During the sensitive period, the young imprint on their parent and learn basic behaviors, while the parent learns to recognize its offspring. If bonding does not occur, the parent will not care for the offspring, leading to the death of the offspring and a decrease in the reproductive success of the parent.

How do the young know on whom—or what—to imprint? Experiments with many species of waterfowl indicate that young birds have no innate recognition of "mother." Rather, they identify with the first object they encounter that has certain key characteristics. In the 1930s, the Austrian researcher Konrad Lorenz showed that the principal imprinting stimulus in graylag geese (*Anser anser*) is a nearby object that is moving away from the young. When incubator-hatched goslings spent their first few hours with Lorenz rather than with a goose, they imprinted on him and steadfastly followed him from then on **(Figure 51.7a)**. Furthermore, they showed no recognition of their biological mother.

Imprinting has become an important component of efforts to save endangered species, such as the whooping crane (*Grus americana*). Scientists tried raising whooping cranes in captivity by using sandhill cranes (*Grus canadensis*) as foster parents. However, because the whooping cranes imprinted on their foster parents, none formed a *pair-bond* (strong attachment) with a whooping crane mate. To avoid such problems, captive breeding programs now isolate young cranes, exposing them to the sights and sounds of members of their own species.

Scientists have made further use of imprinting to teach cranes born in captivity to migrate along safe routes. Young whooping cranes are imprinted on humans in "crane suits" and then allowed to follow these "parents" as they fly ultralight aircraft along selected migration routes **(Figure 51.7b)**. Importantly, these cranes still pair-bond with other whooping cranes, indicating that the crane costumes have the features required to direct "normal" imprinting.

Spatial Learning and Cognitive Maps

Every natural environment has spatial variation, as in locations of nest sites, hazards, food, and prospective mates. Therefore, an organism's fitness may be enhanced by the capacity for **spatial learning**, the establishment of a memory that reflects the environment's spatial structure.

The idea of spatial learning intrigued Tinbergen while he was a graduate student in the Netherlands. At that time, he was studying the female digger wasp (*Philanthus triangulum*), which nests in small burrows dug into sand dunes. When a wasp leaves her nest to go hunting, she hides the entrance from potential intruders by covering it with sand. When she returns, however, she flies directly to her hidden

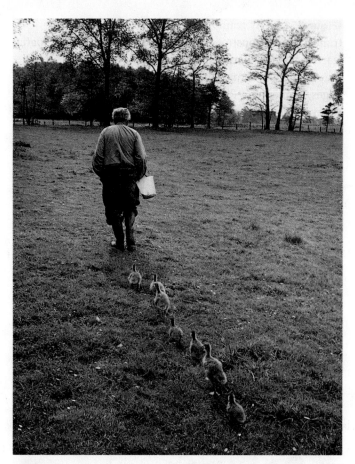

(a) These young greylag geese imprinted on ethologist Konrad Lorenz.

(b) A pilot wearing a crane suit and flying an ultralight plane acts as a surrogate parent to direct the migration of whooping cranes.

▲ **Figure 51.7 Imprinting.** Imprinting can be altered to **(a)** investigate animal behavior or **(b)** direct animal behavior.

WHAT IF? *Suppose the geese following Lorenz were bred to each other. How might their imprinting on Lorenz affect their offspring? Explain.*

nest, despite the presence of hundreds of other burrows in the area. How does she accomplish this feat? Tinbergen hypothesized that a wasp locates her nest by learning its position relative to visible landmarks. To test his hypothesis, he carried out an experiment in the wasps' natural habitat

(Figure 51.8). By manipulating objects around nest entrances, he demonstrated that digger wasps engage in spatial learning. This experiment was so simple and informative that it could be summarized very concisely. In fact, at 32 pages, Tinbergen's Ph.D. thesis from 1932 is still the shortest ever approved at Leiden University.

▼ **Figure 51.8** | Inquiry

Does a digger wasp use landmarks to find her nest?

Experiment A female digger wasp covers the entrance to her nest while foraging for food, but finds the correct wasp nest reliably upon her return 30 minutes or more later. Niko Tinbergen wanted to test the hypothesis that a wasp learns visual landmarks that mark her nest before she leaves on hunting trips. First, he marked one nest with a ring of pinecones while the wasp was in the burrow. After leaving the nest to forage, the wasp returned to the nest successfully.

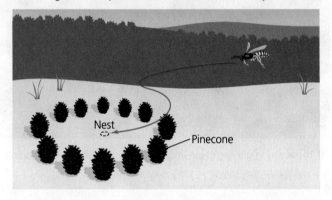

Two days later, after the wasp had again left, Tinbergen shifted the ring of pinecones away from the nest. Then he waited to observe the wasp's behavior.

Results When the wasp returned, she flew to the center of the pinecone circle instead of to the nearby nest. Repeating the experiment with many wasps, Tinbergen obtained the same results.

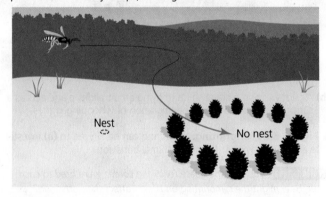

Conclusion The experiment supported the hypothesis that digger wasps use visual landmarks to keep track of their nests.

Source: N. Tinbergen, *The Study of Instinct*, Clarendon Press, Oxford (1951).

WHAT IF? *Suppose the digger wasp had returned to her original nest site, despite the pinecones having been moved. What alternative hypotheses might you propose regarding how the wasp finds her nest and why the pinecones didn't misdirect the wasp?*

In some animals, spatial learning involves formulating a **cognitive map**, a representation in an animal's nervous system of the spatial relationships between objects in its surroundings. One striking example is found in the Clark's nutcracker (*Nucifraga columbiana*), a relative of ravens, crows, and jays. In the fall, nutcrackers hide pine seeds for retrieval during the winter. By experimentally varying the distance between landmarks in the birds' environment, researchers discovered that the birds kept track of the halfway point between landmarks, rather than a fixed distance, to find their hidden food stores.

Associative Learning

Learning often involves making associations between experiences. Consider, for example, a blue jay (*Cyanocitta cristata*) that ingests a brightly colored monarch butterfly (*Danaus plexippus*). Substances that the monarch accumulates from milkweed plants cause the blue jay to vomit almost immediately **(Figure 51.9)**. Following such experiences, blue jays avoid attacking monarchs and similar-looking butterflies. The ability to associate one environmental feature (such as a color) with another (such as a foul taste) is called **associative learning**.

Associative learning is well suited to study in the laboratory. Such studies typically involve either classical conditioning or operant conditioning. In *classical conditioning*, an arbitrary stimulus becomes associated with a particular outcome. Russian physiologist Ivan Pavlov carried out early experiments in classical conditioning, demonstrating that if he always rang a bell just before feeding a dog, the dog would eventually salivate when the bell sounded, anticipating food. In *operant conditioning*, also called trial-and-error learning, an animal first learns to associate one of its behaviors with a reward or punishment and then tends to repeat or avoid that behavior (see Figure 51.9). B. F. Skinner, an

▲ **Figure 51.9 Associative learning.** Having ingested and vomited a monarch butterfly, a blue jay has probably learned to avoid this species.

American pioneer in the study of operant conditioning, explored this process in the laboratory by, for example, having a rat learn through trial and error to obtain food by pressing a lever.

Studies reveal that animals can learn to link many pairs of features of their environment, but not all. For example, pigeons can learn to associate danger with a sound but not with a color. However, they can learn to associate a color with food. What does this mean? The development and organization of the pigeon's nervous system apparently restrict the associations that can be formed. Moreover, such restrictions are not limited to birds. Rats, for example, can learn to avoid illness-inducing foods on the basis of smells, but not on the basis of sights or sounds.

If we consider how behavior evolves, the fact that some animals can't learn to make particular associations appears logical. The associations an animal can readily form typically reflect relationships likely to occur in nature. Conversely, associations that can't be formed are those unlikely to be of selective advantage in a native environment. In the case of a rat's diet in the wild, for example, a harmful food is far more likely to have a certain odor than to be associated with a particular sound.

Cognition and Problem Solving

The most complex forms of learning involve **cognition**—the process of knowing that involves awareness, reasoning, recollection, and judgment. Although it was once argued that only primates and certain marine mammals have high-level thought processes, many other groups of animals, including insects, appear to exhibit cognition in controlled laboratory studies. For example, an experiment using Y-shaped mazes provided evidence for abstract thinking in honeybees. One maze had different colors, and one had different black-and-white striped patterns, either vertical or horizontal bars. Two groups of honeybees were trained in the color maze. Upon entering, a bee would see a sample color and could then choose between an arm of the maze with the same color or an arm with a different color. Only one arm contained a food reward. The first group of bees were rewarded for flying into the arm with the *same* color as the sample (**Figure 51.10❶**); the second group were rewarded for choosing the arm with the *different* color. Next, bees from

each group were tested in the bar maze, which had no food reward. After encountering a sample black-and-white pattern of bars, a bee could choose an arm with the same pattern or an arm with a different pattern. The bees in the first group most often chose the arm with the same pattern (**Figure 51.10❷**), whereas those in the second group typically chose the arm with the different pattern.

The maze experiments provide strong experimental support for the hypothesis that honeybees can distinguish on the basis of "same" and "different." Remarkably, research published in 2010 indicates that honeybees can also learn to distinguish between human faces.

The information-processing ability of a nervous system can also be revealed in **problem solving**, the cognitive activity of devising a method to proceed from one state to another in the face of real or apparent obstacles. For example, if a chimpanzee is placed in a room with several boxes on the floor and a banana hung high out of reach, the chimp can assess the situation and stack the boxes, enabling it to reach the food. Problem-solving behavior is highly developed in some mammals, especially primates and dolphins. Notable examples have also been observed in some bird species, especially corvids. In one study, ravens were confronted with food hanging from a branch by a string. After failing to grab the food in flight, one raven flew to the branch and alternately pulled up and stepped on the string until the food was within reach. A number of other ravens eventually arrived at similar solutions. Nevertheless, some ravens failed to solve the problem, indicating that problem-solving success in this species, as in others, varies with individual experience and abilities.

❶ **Bees were trained in a color maze**. As shown here, one group were rewarded for choosing the same color as the stimulus.

❷ **Bees were tested in a pattern maze**. If previously rewarded for choosing the same color, bees most often chose lines oriented the same way as the stimulus.

▲ **Figure 51.10 A maze test of abstract thinking by honeybees**. These mazes are designed to test whether honeybees can distinguish "same" from "different."

Development of Learned Behaviors

Most of the learned behaviors we have discussed develop over a relatively short time. Some behaviors develop more gradually. For example, some bird species learn songs in stages.

In the case of the white-crowned sparrow (*Zonotrichia leucophrys*), the first stage of song learning takes place early in life, when the fledgling sparrow first hears the song. If a fledgling is prevented from hearing real sparrows or recordings of sparrow songs during the first 50 days of its life, it fails to develop the adult song of its species. Although the young bird does not sing during the sensitive period, it memorizes the song of its species by listening to other white-crowned sparrows sing. During the sensitive period, fledglings chirp more in response to songs of their own species than to songs of other species. Thus, although young white-crowned sparrows learn the songs they will sing later on, learning appears to be bounded by genetically controlled preferences.

The sensitive period when a white-crowned sparrow memorizes its species' song is followed by a second learning phase when the juvenile bird sings tentative notes called a subsong. The juvenile bird hears its own singing and compares it with the song memorized during the sensitive period. Once a sparrow's own song matches the one it memorized, the song "crystallizes" as the final song, and the bird sings only this adult song for the rest of its life.

The song-learning process can be quite different in other bird species. Canaries, for example, do not have a single sensitive period for song learning. A young canary begins with a subsong, but the full song does not crystallize in the same way as in white-crowned sparrows. Between breeding seasons, the song becomes flexible again, and an adult male may learn new song "syllables" each year, adding to the song it already sings.

Song learning is one of many examples of how animals learn from other members of their species. In finishing our exploration of learning, we'll look at several more examples that reflect the more general phenomenon of social learning.

Social Learning

Many animals learn to solve problems by observing the behavior of other individuals. Young wild chimpanzees, for example, learn how to crack open oil palm nuts with two stones by copying experienced chimpanzees **(Figure 51.11)**. This type of learning through observing others is called **social learning**.

Another example of how social learning can modify behavior comes from studies of the vervet monkeys (*Cercopithecus aethiops*) in Amboseli National Park, Kenya. Vervet monkeys, which are about the size of a domestic cat, produce a complex set of alarm calls. Amboseli vervets give

▲ **Figure 51.11 A young chimpanzee learning to crack oil palm nuts by observing an experienced elder.**

distinct alarm calls for leopards, eagles, and snakes, all of which prey on vervets. When a vervet sees a leopard, it gives a loud barking sound; when it sees an eagle, it gives a short double-syllable cough; and the snake alarm call is a "chutter." Upon hearing a particular alarm call, other vervets in the group behave in an appropriate way: They run up a tree on hearing the alarm for a leopard (vervets are nimbler than leopards in the trees); look up on hearing the alarm for an eagle; and look down on hearing the alarm for a snake **(Figure 51.12)**.

Infant vervet monkeys give alarm calls, but in a relatively undiscriminating way. For example, they give the "eagle" alarm on seeing any bird, including harmless birds such as

▲ **Figure 51.12 Vervet monkeys learning correct use of alarm calls.** On seeing a python (foreground), vervet monkeys give a distinct "snake" alarm call (inset), and the members of the group stand upright and look down.

bee-eaters. With age, the monkeys improve their accuracy. In fact, adult vervet monkeys give the eagle alarm only on seeing an eagle belonging to either of the two species that eat vervets. Infants probably learn how to give the right call by observing other members of the group and receiving social confirmation. For instance, if the infant gives the call on the right occasion—say, an eagle alarm when there is an eagle overhead—another member of the group will also give the eagle call. But if the infant gives the call when a bee-eater flies by, the adults in the group are silent. Thus, vervet monkeys have an initial, unlearned tendency to give calls upon seeing potentially threatening objects in the environment. Learning fine-tunes the call so that adult vervets give calls only in response to genuine danger and can fine-tune the alarm calls of the next generation.

Social learning forms the roots of **culture**, which can be defined as a system of information transfer through social learning or teaching that influences the behavior of individuals in a population. Cultural transfer of information can alter behavioral phenotypes and thereby influence the fitness of individuals.

Changes in behavior that result from natural selection occur on a much longer time scale than does learning. In Concept 51.3, we'll examine the relationship between particular behaviors and the processes of selection related to survival and reproduction.

CONCEPT CHECK 51.2

1. How might associative learning explain why different species of distasteful or stinging insects have similar colors?

2. **WHAT IF?** How might you position and manipulate a few objects in a lab to test whether an animal can use a cognitive map to remember the location of a food source?

3. **MAKE CONNECTIONS** How might a learned behavior contribute to speciation? (See Concept 24.1.)

For suggested answers, see Appendix A.

CONCEPT 51.3

Selection for individual survival and reproductive success can explain diverse behaviors

EVOLUTION We turn now to Tinbergen's third question—how behavior enhances survival and reproduction in a population. The focus thus shifts from proximate causation—the "how" questions—to ultimate causation—the "why" questions. We'll begin by considering the activity of gathering food. Food-obtaining behavior, or **foraging**, includes not only eating but also any activities an animal uses to search for, recognize, and capture food items.

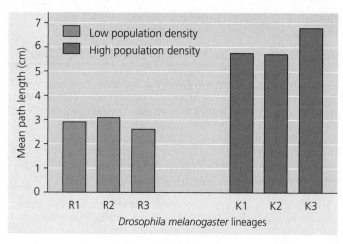

▲ **Figure 51.13 Evolution of foraging behavior by laboratory populations of *Drosophila melanogaster*.** After 74 generations of living at low population density, *D. melanogaster* larvae (populations R1–R3) followed foraging paths significantly shorter than those of *D. melanogaster* larvae that had lived at high density (populations K1–K3).

INTERPRET THE DATA *What alternative hypothesis is ruled out by having three R and K lines, rather than one of each?*

Evolution of Foraging Behavior

The fruit fly allows us to examine one way that foraging behavior might have evolved. Variation in a gene called *forager* (*for*) dictates how far *Drosophila* larvae travel when foraging. On average, larvae carrying the *for*^{R} ("Rover") allele travel nearly twice as far while foraging as do larvae with the *for*^{s} ("sitter") allele.

Both the *for*^{R} and *for*^{s} alleles are present in natural populations. What circumstances might favor one or the other allele? The answer became apparent in experiments that maintained flies at either low or high population densities for many generations. Larvae in populations kept at a low density foraged over shorter distances than those in populations kept at high density (**Figure 51.13**). Furthermore, the *for*^{s} allele increased in frequency in the low-density populations, whereas the *for*^{R} allele increased in frequency in the high-density group. These changes make sense. At a low population density, short-distance foraging yields sufficient food, while long-distance foraging would result in unnecessary energy expenditure. Under crowded conditions, long-distance foraging could enable larvae to move beyond areas depleted of food. Thus, an interpretable evolutionary change in behavior occurred in the course of the experiment.

Optimal Foraging Model

To study the ultimate causation of foraging strategies, biologists sometimes apply a type of cost-benefit analysis used in economics. This idea proposes that foraging behavior is a compromise between the benefits of nutrition and the costs of obtaining food. These costs might include the energy

Testing a Hypothesis with a Quantitative Model

Do Crows Display Optimal Foraging Behavior? On islands off British Columbia, Canada, Northwestern crows (*Corvus caurinus*) search rocky tide pools for sea snails called whelks. After spotting a whelk, the crow picks it up in its beak, flies upward, and drops the whelk onto the rocks. If the drop is successful, the shell breaks and the crow can dine on the whelk's soft parts. If not, the crow flies up and drops the whelk again and again until the shell breaks. What determines how high the crow flies? If energetic considerations dominated selection for the crow's foraging behavior, the average drop height might reflect a trade-off between the cost of flying higher and the benefit of more frequent success. In this exercise you'll test how well this optimal foraging model predicts the average drop height observed in nature.

How the Experiments Were Done The height of drops made by crows in the wild was measured by referring to a marked pole erected nearby. In the test, the crow's behavior was simulated using a device that dropped a whelk onto the rocks from a fixed platform. The average number of drops required to break whelks from various platform heights was recorded and averaged over many trials with the device. Combining the data for each platform height, total "flight" height was calculated by multiplying the height times the average number of drops required.

Data from the Experiment

Interpret the Data

1. How does the average number of drops required to break open a whelk depend on platform height for a drop of 5 meters or less? For drops of more than 5 meters?
2. Total flight height can be considered to be a measure of the total energy required to break open a whelk. Why is this value lower for a platform set at 5 meters than for one at 2 or 15 meters?
3. Compare the drop height preferred by crows with the graph of total flight height for the platform drops. Are the data consistent with the hypothesis of optimal foraging? Explain.
4. In testing the optimal foraging model, it was assumed that changing the height of the drop only changed the total energy required. Do you think this is a realistic limitation, or might other factors than total energy be affected by height?
5. Researchers observed that the crows only gather and drop the largest whelks. What are some reasons crows might favor larger whelks?
6. It turned out that the probability of a whelk breaking was the same for a whelk dropped for the first time as for an unbroken whelk dropped several times previously. If the probability of breaking instead increased, what change might you predict in the crow's behavior?

(MB) A version of this Scientific Skills Exercise can be assigned in MasteringBiology.

Data from R. Zach, Shell-dropping: Decision-making and optimal foraging in northwestern crows, *Behavior* 68:106–117 (1979).

expenditure of foraging as well as the risk of being eaten while foraging. According to this **optimal foraging model**, natural selection should favor a foraging behavior that minimizes the costs of foraging and maximizes the benefits. The Scientific Skills Exercise provides an example of how this model can be applied to animals in the wild.

Balancing Risk and Reward

One of the most significant potential costs to a forager is risk of predation. Maximizing energy gain and minimizing energy costs are of little benefit if the behavior makes the forager a likely meal for a predator. It seems logical,

therefore, that predation risk would influence foraging behavior. Such appears to be the case for the mule deer (*Odocoileus hemionus*), which lives in the mountains of western North America. Researchers found that the food available for mule deer was fairly uniform across the potential foraging areas, although somewhat lower in open, nonforested areas. In contrast, the risk of predation differed greatly; mountain lions (*Puma concolor*), the major predator, killed large numbers of mule deer at forest edges and only a small number in open areas and forest interiors.

How does mule deer foraging behavior reflect the differences in predation risk in particular areas? Mule deer feed predominantly in open areas. Thus, it appears that mule deer foraging behavior reflects the large variation in predation risk and not the smaller variation in food availability. This result underscores the point that behavior typically reflects a compromise between competing selective pressures.

Mating Behavior and Mate Choice

Just as foraging is crucial for individual survival, mating behavior and mate choice play a major role in determining reproductive success. These behaviors include seeking or attracting mates, choosing among potential mates, competing for mates, and caring for offspring.

Mating Systems and Sexual Dimorphism

Although we tend to think of mating simply as the union of a male and female, species vary greatly with regard to *mating systems*, the length and number of relationships between males and females. In some animal species, mating is *promiscuous*, with no strong pair-bonds. In others, mates form a relationship of some duration that is **monogamous** (one male mating with one female) or **polygamous** (an individual of one sex mating with several of the other). Polygamous relationships involve *polygyny*, a single male and many females, or *polyandry*, a single female and multiple males.

The extent to which males and females differ in appearance, a characteristic known as *sexual dimorphism*, typically varies with the type of mating system **(Figure 51.14)**. Among monogamous species, males and females often look very similar. In contrast, among polygamous species, the sex that attracts multiple mating partners is typically showier and larger than the opposite sex. We'll discuss the evolutionary basis of these differences shortly.

Mating Systems and Parental Care

The needs of the young are an important factor constraining the evolution of mating systems. Most newly hatched birds, for instance, cannot care for themselves. Rather, they require a large, continuous food supply, a need that is difficult for a single parent to meet. In such cases, a male that stays with and helps a single mate may ultimately have more viable offspring than it would by going off to seek additional mates. This may explain why many birds are monogamous. In contrast, for birds with young that can feed and care for themselves almost immediately after hatching, the males derive less benefit from staying with their partner. Males of these species, such as pheasants and quail, can maximize their reproductive success by seeking other mates, and polygyny is relatively common in such birds. In the case of mammals, the lactating female is often the only food source for the young, and males usually play no role in raising the young. In mammalian species where males protect the females and young, such as lions, a male or small group of males typically cares for a harem of many females.

▼ **Figure 51.14 Relationship between mating system and male and female forms.**

(a) Monogamy

In monogamous species, such as these western gulls (*Larus occidentalis*), males and females are difficult to distinguish using external characteristics only.

(b) Polygyny

Among polygynous species, such as elk (*Cervus canadensis*), the male (right) is often highly ornamented.

(c) Polyandry

In polyandrous species, such as these red-necked phalaropes (*Phalaropus lobatus*), females (right) are generally more ornamented than males.

▲ **Figure 51.15 Paternal care by a male jawfish.** The male jaw-fish, which lives in tropical marine environments, holds the eggs it has fertilized in its mouth, keeping them aerated and protecting them from egg predators until the young hatch.

Another factor influencing mating behavior and parental care is *certainty of paternity.* Young born to or eggs laid by a female definitely contain that female's genes. However, even within a normally monogamous relationship, a male other than the female's usual mate may have fathered that female's offspring. The certainty of paternity is relatively low in most species with internal fertilization because the acts of mating and birth (or mating and egg laying) are separated over time. This could explain why exclusively male parental care is rare in bird and mammal species. However, the males of many species with internal fertilization engage in behaviors that appear to increase their certainty of paternity. These behaviors include guarding females, removing any sperm from the female reproductive tract before copulation, and introducing large quantities of sperm that displace the sperm of other males.

Certainty of paternity is high when egg laying and mating occur together, as in external fertilization. This may explain why parental care in aquatic invertebrates, fishes, and amphibians, when it occurs at all, is at least as likely to be by males as by females (**Figure 51.15**; see also Figure 46.6). Among fishes and amphibians, parental care occurs in fewer than 10% of species with internal fertilization but in more than half of species with external fertilization.

It is important to point out that certainty of paternity does not mean that animals are aware of those factors when they behave a certain way. Parental behavior correlated with certainty of paternity exists because it has been reinforced over generations by natural selection. The intriguing relationship between certainty of paternity and male parental care remains an area of active research.

Sexual Selection and Mate Choice

Sexual dimorphism results from sexual selection, a form of natural selection in which differences in reproductive success among individuals are a consequence of differences in mating success (see Concept 23.4). Sexual selection can take the form of *intersexual selection,* in which members of one sex choose mates on the basis of characteristics of the other sex, such as courtship songs, or *intrasexual selection,* which involves competition between members of one sex for mates.

Mate Choice by Females Mate preferences of females may play a central role in the evolution of male behavior and anatomy through intersexual selection. Consider, for example, the courtship behavior of stalk-eyed flies. The eyes of these insects are at the tips of stalks, which are longer in males than in females. During courtship, a male approaches the female headfirst. Researchers have shown that females are more likely to mate with males that have relatively long eyestalks. Why would females favor this seemingly arbitrary trait? Ornaments such as long eyestalks in these flies and bright coloration in birds correlate in general with health and vitality. A female whose mate choice is a healthy male is likely to produce more offspring that survive to reproduce. As a result, males may compete with each other in ritualized contests to attract female attention (**Figure 51.16**).

▲ **Figure 51.16 Male stalk-eyed flies face off for female attention.** In such ritual showdowns, the male whose eyestalk length is smaller usually retreats peacefully.

Mate choice can also be influenced by imprinting, as revealed by experiments carried out with zebra finches. Both male and female zebra finches normally lack any feather crest on their head (**Figure 51.17**). To explore whether parental

▶ **Figure 51.17 Appearance of zebra finches in nature.** The male zebra finch (left) is more highly patterned and colorful than the female zebra finch.

appearance affects mate preference in offspring independent of any genetic influence, researchers provided zebra finches with artificial ornamentation. A 2.5-cm-long red feather was taped to the forehead feathers of either or both zebra finch parents when their chicks were 8 days old, approximately 2 days before they opened their eyes. A control group of zebra finches were raised by unadorned parents. When the chicks matured, they were presented with prospective mates that were either artificially ornamented with a red feather or non-ornamented **(Figure 51.18)**. Males showed no preference. Females raised by a male parent that was not ornamented also showed no preference. However, females raised by an ornamented male parent preferred ornamented males as their own mates. Thus, female finches apparently take cues from their fathers in choosing mates.

Mate-choice copying, a behavior in which individuals in a population copy the mate choice of others, has been studied in the guppy *Poecilia reticulata*. When a female guppy chooses between males with no other females present, the female almost always chooses the male with more orange coloration. To explore if the behavior of other females could influence this preference, an experiment was set up using both living females and artificial model females **(Figure 51.19)**. If a female guppy observed the model "courting" a male with less extensive orange markings, she often copied the preference of the model

female. That is, the female chose the male that had been presented in association with a model female rather than a more orange alternative. The exceptions were also informative. Mate-choice behavior typically did not change when the difference in coloration was particularly large. Mate-choice copying can thus mask genetically controlled female preference below a certain threshold of difference, in this case for male color.

▲ **Figure 51.18 Sexual selection influenced by imprinting.** Experiments demonstrated that female zebra finch chicks that had imprinted on artificially ornamented fathers preferred ornamented males as adult mates. For all experimental groups, male offspring showed no preference for either ornamented or non-ornamented female mates.

▲ **Figure 51.19 Mate choice copying by female guppies (*Poecilia reticulata*).** In the absence of other females (control group), female guppies generally choose males with more orange coloration. However, when a female model is placed near one of the males (experimental group), female guppies often copy the apparent mate choice of the model, even if the male is less colorful than others. Guppy females ignored the mate choice of the model only if an alternative male had much more orange coloration.

Mate-choice copying, a form of social learning, has also been observed in several other fish and bird species. What is the selective pressure for such a mechanism? One possibility is that a female that mates with males that are attractive to other females increases the probability that her male offspring will also be attractive and have high reproductive success.

Male Competition for Mates The previous examples show how female choice can select for one best type of male in a given situation, resulting in low variation among males. Similarly, male competition for mates can reduce variation among males. Such competition may involve *agonistic behavior*, an often-ritualized contest that determines which competitor gains access to a resource, such as food or mates (**Figure 51.20**; see also Figure 51.16).

Despite the potential for male competition to select for reduced variation, behavioral and morphological variation in males is extremely high in some vertebrate species, including species of fish and deer, as well as in a wide variety of invertebrates. In some species, sexual selection has led to the evolution of alternative male mating behavior and morphology. How do scientists analyze situations where more than one mating behavior can result in successful reproduction? One approach relies on the rules that govern games.

▲ **Figure 51.20 Agonistic interaction.** Male eastern grey kangaroos (*Macropus giganteus*) often "box" in contests that determine which male is most likely to mate with an available female. Typically, one male snorts loudly and strikes the other with his forelimbs. If the male under attack does not retreat, the fight may escalate into grappling or the two males balancing on their tails while attempting to kick each other with the sharp toenails of their hind feet.

Applying Game Theory

Often, the fitness of a particular behavioral phenotype is influenced by other behavioral phenotypes in the population. In studying such situations, behavioral ecologists use a range of tools, including game theory. Developed by American mathematician John Nash and others to model human economic behavior, **game theory** evaluates alternative strategies in situations where the outcome depends on the strategies of all the individuals involved.

As an example of applying game theory to mating behavior, let's consider the side-blotched lizard (*Uta stansburiana*) of California. Genetic variations give rise to males with orange, blue, or yellow throats (**Figure 51.21**). One would expect that natural selection would favor one of the three color types, yet all three persist. Why? The answer appears to lie in the fact that each throat color is associated with a different pattern of behavior: Orange-throat males are the most aggressive and defend large territories that contain many females. Blue-throat males are also territorial but defend smaller

▲ **Figure 51.21 Male polymorphism in the side-blotched lizard (*Uta stansburiana*).** An orange-throat male, left; a blue-throat male, center; a yellow-throat male, right.

territories and fewer females. Yellow-throats are nonterritorial males that mimic females and use "sneaky" tactics to gain the chance to mate.

Evidence indicates that the mating success of each male lizard type is influenced by the relative abundance of the other types, an example of frequency-dependent selection. In one study population, the most frequent throat coloration changed over a period of several years from blue to orange to yellow and back to blue.

By comparing the competition between side-blotched lizard males to the children's game of rock-paper-scissors, scientists devised an explanation for the cycles of variation in the lizard population. In the game, paper defeats rock, rock defeats scissors, and scissors defeats paper. Each hand symbol thus wins one matchup but loses the other. Similarly, each type of male lizard has an advantage over one of the other two types. When blue-throats are abundant, they can defend the few females in their territories from the advances of the sneaky yellow-throat males. However, blue-throats cannot defend their territories against the hyperaggressive orange-throats. Once the orange-throats become the most abundant, the larger number of females in each territory provides the opportunity for the yellow-throats to have greater mating success. The yellow-throats become more frequent, but then give way to the blue-throats, whose tactic of guarding small territories once again allows them the most success. Thus, following the population over time, one sees a persistence of all three color types and a periodic shift in which type is most prevalent.

Game theory provides a way to think about complex evolutionary problems in which relative performance (reproductive success relative to other phenotypes), not absolute performance, is the key to understanding the evolution of behavior. This makes game theory an important tool because the relative performance of one phenotype compared with others is a measure of Darwinian fitness.

CONCEPT CHECK 51.3

1. Why does the mode of fertilization correlate with the presence or absence of male parental care?

2. **MAKE CONNECTIONS** Balancing selection can maintain variation at a locus (see Concept 23.4). Based on the foraging experiments described in this chapter, devise a simple hypothesis to explain the presence of both for^R and for^s alleles in natural fly populations.

3. **WHAT IF?** Suppose an infection in a side-blotched lizard population killed many more males than females. What would be the immediate effect on male competition for reproductive success?

For suggested answers, see Appendix A.

CONCEPT 51.4

Genetic analyses and the concept of inclusive fitness provide a basis for studying the evolution of behavior

EVOLUTION We'll now explore issues related to Tinbergen's fourth question—the evolutionary history of behaviors. We will first look at the genetic control of a behavior. Next, we will examine the genetic variation underlying the evolution of particular behaviors. Finally, we will see how expanding the definition of fitness beyond individual survival can help explain "selfless" behavior.

Genetic Basis of Behavior

In exploring the genetic basis of behavior, we'll begin with the courtship behavior of the male fruit fly, diagrammed in Figure 51.4. During courtship, the male fly carries out a complex series of actions in response to multiple sensory stimuli. Genetic studies have revealed that a single gene called *fru* controls this entire courtship ritual. If the *fru* gene is mutated to an inactive form, males do not court or mate with females. (The name *fru* is short for *fruitless*, reflecting the absence of offspring from the mutant males.) Normal male and female

flies express distinct forms of the *fru* gene. When females are genetically manipulated to express the male form of *fru*, they court other females, performing the role normally played by the male. How can a single gene control so many different actions? Experiments carried out cooperatively in several laboratories demonstrated that *fru* is a master regulatory gene that directs the expression and activity of many genes with narrower functions. Together, genes that are controlled by the *fru* gene bring about sex-specific development of the fly nervous system. In effect, *fru* programs the fly for male courtship behavior by overseeing a male-specific wiring of the central nervous system.

In many cases, differences in behavior arise not from gene inactivation, but from variation in the activity or amount of a gene product. One striking example comes from the study of two related species of voles, which are small, mouse-like rodents. Male meadow voles (*Microtus pennsylvanicus*) are solitary and do not form lasting relationships with mates. Following mating, they pay little attention to their pups. In contrast, male prairie voles (*Microtus ochrogaster*) form a pair-bond with a single female after they mate (**Figure 51.22**). Male prairie voles hover over their young pups, licking them and carrying them, while acting aggressively toward intruders.

A peptide neurotransmitter is critical for the partnering and parental behavior of male voles. Known as ADH or vasopressin (see Chapter 44), this peptide is released during mating and binds to a specific receptor in the central nervous system. When male prairie voles are given a drug that inhibits the brain receptor for vasopressin, they fail to form pair-bonds after mating.

◄ **Figure 51.22 A pair of prairie voles (*Microtus ochrogaster*) huddling.** Male North American prairie voles associate closely with their mates, as shown here, and contribute substantially to the care of young.

The vasopressin receptor gene is much more highly expressed in the brain of prairie voles than in the brain of meadow voles. Testing the hypothesis that vasopressin receptor levels in the brain regulate postmating behavior, researchers inserted the vasopressin receptor gene from prairie voles into meadow voles. The male meadow voles carrying this gene not only developed brains with higher levels of the vasopressin receptor but also showed many of the same mating behaviors as male prairie voles, such as pair-bonding. Thus, although many genes influence pair-bonding and parenting in voles, a change in vasopressin receptor levels is sufficient to alter the development of these behaviors.

Genetic Variation and the Evolution of Behavior

Behavioral differences between closely related species, such as meadow and prairie voles, are common. Significant differences in behavior can also be found *within* a species but are often less obvious. When behavioral variation between populations of a species correlates with variation in environmental conditions, it may reflect natural selection.

Case Study: *Variation in Prey Selection*

An example of genetically based behavioral variation within a species involves prey selection by the western garter snake (*Thamnophis elegans*). The natural diet of this species differs widely across its range in California. Coastal populations feed predominantly on banana slugs (*Ariolimax californicus*) **(Figure 51.23)**. Inland populations feed on frogs, leeches, and fish, but not banana slugs. In fact, banana slugs are rare or absent in the inland habitats.

When researchers offered banana slugs to snakes from each wild population, most coastal snakes readily ate them, whereas inland snakes tended to refuse. To what extent does genetic variation contribute to a fondness for banana slugs? To answer this question, researchers collected pregnant snakes from each wild population and housed them in separate cages in the laboratory. While still very young, the offspring were offered a small piece of banana slug on each of ten days. More than 60% of the young snakes from coastal mothers ate banana slugs on eight or more of the ten days. In contrast, fewer than 20% of the young snakes from inland mothers ate a piece of banana slug even once. Perhaps not surprisingly, banana slugs thus appear to be a genetically acquired taste.

How did a genetically determined difference in feeding preference come to match the snakes' habitats so well? It turns out that the coastal and inland populations also vary with respect to their ability to recognize and respond to odor molecules produced by banana slugs. Researchers hypothesize that when inland snakes colonized coastal habitats more than 10,000 years ago, some of them could recognize banana slugs by scent. Because these snakes took advantage

▲ **Figure 51.23 Western garter snake from a coastal habitat eating a banana slug.** Experiments indicate that the preference of these snakes for banana slugs may be influenced more by genetics than by environment.

of this food source, they had higher fitness than snakes in the population that ignored the slugs. Over hundreds or thousands of generations, the capacity to recognize the slugs as prey increased in frequency in the coastal population. The marked variation in behavior observed today between the coastal and inland populations may be evidence of this past evolutionary change.

Case Study: *Variation in Migratory Patterns*

Another species suited to the study of behavioral variation is the blackcap (*Sylvia atricapilla*), a small migratory warbler. Blackcaps that breed in Germany generally migrate southwest to Spain and then south to Africa for the winter. In the 1950s, a few blackcaps began to spend their winters in Britain, and over time the population of blackcaps wintering in Britain grew to many thousands. Leg bands showed that some of these birds had migrated westward from central Germany. Was this change in the pattern of migration the outcome of natural selection? If so, the birds wintering in Britain must have a heritable difference in migratory behavior. To test this hypothesis, researchers at the Max Planck Research Center in Radolfzell, Germany, devised a strategy to study migratory orientation in the laboratory **(Figure 51.24)**. The results demonstrated that the two patterns of migration—to the west and to the southwest—do in fact reflect genetic differences between the two populations.

The study of western European blackcaps indicated that the change in their migratory behavior occurred both recently and rapidly. Before the year 1950, there were no known westward-migrating blackcaps in Germany. By the 1990s, westward migrants made up 7–11% of the blackcap populations of Germany. Once westward migration began,

Are differences in migratory orientation within a species genetically determined?

Experiment Peter Berthold and colleagues in southern Germany raised two sets of young birds called blackcaps for their study. One group consisted of the offspring of blackcaps captured while wintering in Britain and then bred in Germany in an outdoor cage. The other group consisted of young birds collected from nests near the laboratory and then raised in cages. In the autumn, Berthold's team placed the blackcaps captured in Britain and the young birds raised in cages in large, glass-covered funnel cages lined with carbon-coated paper for 1.5–2 hours. When the funnels were placed outside at night, the birds moved around, making marks on the paper that indicated the direction in which they were trying to "migrate."

Scratch marks

Results The wintering adult birds captured in Britain and their laboratory-raised offspring both attempted to migrate to the west. In contrast, the young birds collected from nests in southern Germany attempted to migrate to the southwest.

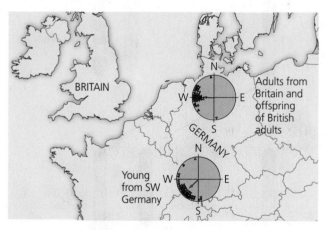

BRITAIN

GERMANY

Adults from Britain and offspring of British adults

Young from SW Germany

Conclusion The young of the British blackcaps and the young birds from Germany (the control group) were raised under similar conditions but showed very different migratory orientations, indicating that their migratory orientation has a genetic basis.

Source: P. Berthold et al., Rapid microevolution of migratory behavior in a wild bird species, *Nature* 360:668–690 (1992).

WHAT IF? *Suppose the birds had not shown a difference in orientation in these experiments. Could you conclude that the behavior was not genetically based? Explain.*

it persisted and increased in frequency, perhaps due to the widespread use of winter bird feeders in Britain, as well as shorter migration distances.

Altruism

We typically assume that behaviors are selfish; that is, they benefit the individual at the expense of others, especially competitors. For example, superior foraging ability by one individual may leave less food for others. The problem comes with "unselfish" behaviors. How can such behaviors arise through natural selection? To answer this question, let's look more closely at some examples of unselfish behavior and consider how they might arise.

In discussing selflessness, we will use the term **altruism** to describe a behavior that reduces an animal's individual fitness but increases the fitness of other individuals in the population. Consider, for example, the Belding's ground squirrel, which lives in the western United States and is vulnerable to predators such as coyotes and hawks. A squirrel that sees a predator approach often gives a high-pitched alarm call that alerts unaware individuals to retreat to their burrows. Note that for the squirrel that warns others, the conspicuous alarm behavior increases the risk of being killed because it brings attention to the caller's location.

Another example of altruistic behavior occurs in honey-bee societies, in which the workers are sterile. The workers themselves never reproduce, but they labor on behalf of a single fertile queen. Furthermore, the workers sting intruders, a behavior that helps defend the hive but results in the death of those workers.

Altruism is also observed in naked mole rats (*Heterocephalus glaber*), highly social rodents that live in underground chambers and tunnels in southern and northeastern Africa. The naked mole rat, which is almost hairless and nearly blind, lives in colonies of 75 to 250 or more individuals **(Figure 51.25)**. Each colony has only one reproducing female, the queen, who mates with one to three males, called

▲ **Figure 51.25 Naked mole rats, a species of colonial mammal that exhibits altruistic behavior.** Pictured here is a queen nursing offspring while surrounded by other members of the colony.

kings. The rest of the colony consists of nonreproductive females and males who at times sacrifice themselves to protect the queen or kings from snakes or other predators that invade the colony.

Inclusive Fitness

With these examples from ground squirrels, honeybees, and mole rats in mind, let's return to the question of how altruistic behavior arises during evolution. The easiest case to consider is that of parents sacrificing for their offspring. When parents sacrifice their own well-being to produce and aid offspring, this act actually increases the fitness of the parents because it maximizes their genetic representation in the population. By this logic, altruistic behavior can be maintained by evolution even though it does not enhance the survival and reproductive success of the self-sacrificing individuals.

What about circumstances when individuals help others who are not their offspring? By considering a broader group of relatives than just parents and offspring, Biologist William Hamilton found an answer. He began by proposing that an animal could increase its genetic representation in the next generation by helping close relatives other than its own offspring. Like parents and offspring, full siblings have half their genes in common. Therefore, selection might also favor helping siblings or helping one's parents produce more siblings. This thinking led Hamilton to the idea of **inclusive fitness**, the total effect an individual has on proliferating its genes by producing its own offspring *and* by providing aid that enables other close relatives to produce offspring.

Hamilton's Rule and Kin Selection

The power of Hamilton's hypothesis was that it provided a way to measure, or quantify, the effect of altruism on fitness. According to Hamilton, the three key variables in an act of altruism are the benefit to the recipient, the cost to the altruist, and the coefficient of relatedness. The benefit, B, is the average number of *extra* offspring that the recipient of an altruistic act produces. The cost, C, is how many *fewer* offspring the altruist produces. The **coefficient of relatedness**, r, equals the fraction of genes that, on average, are shared. Natural selection favors altruism when the benefit to the recipient multiplied by the coefficient of relatedness exceeds the cost to the altruist—in other words, when $rB > C$. This statement is called **Hamilton's rule**.

To better understand Hamilton's rule, let's apply it to a human population in which the average individual has two children. We'll imagine that a young man is close to drowning in heavy surf, and his sister risks her life to swim out and pull her sibling to safety. If the young man had drowned, his reproductive output would have been zero; but now, if we use the average, he can father two children. The benefit to the man is thus two offspring ($B = 2$). What cost is incurred by his sister? Let's say that she has a 25% chance of

drowning in attempting the rescue. The cost of the altruistic act to the sister is then 0.25 times 2, the number of offspring she would be expected to have if she had stayed on shore ($C = 0.25 \times 2 = 0.5$). Finally, we note that a brother and sister share half their genes on average ($r = 0.5$). One way to see this is in terms of the segregation of homologous chromosomes that occurs during meiosis of gametes (**Figure 51.26**; see also Chapter 13).

We can now use our values of B, C, and r to evaluate whether natural selection would favor the altruistic act in our imaginary scenario. For the surf rescue, $rB = 0.5 \times 2 = 1$, whereas $C = 0.5$. Because rB is greater than C, Hamilton's rule is satisfied; thus, natural selection would favor this altruistic act.

Averaging over many individuals and generations, any particular gene in a sister faced with the situation described will be passed on to more offspring if she risks the rescue than if she does not. Among the genes propagated in this way may be some that contribute to altruistic behavior. Natural selection that thus favors altruism by enhancing the reproductive success of relatives is called **kin selection**.

Kin selection weakens with hereditary distance. Siblings have an r of 0.5, but between an aunt and her niece, $r = 0.25$ (¼), and between first cousins, $r = 0.125$ (⅛). Notice that as the degree of relatedness decreases, the rB term in the Hamilton inequality also decreases. Would natural selection favor rescuing a cousin? Not unless the surf were less treacherous. For the original conditions, $rB = 0.125 \times 2 = 0.25$, which is only half the value of C (0.5). British geneticist J. B. S. Haldane

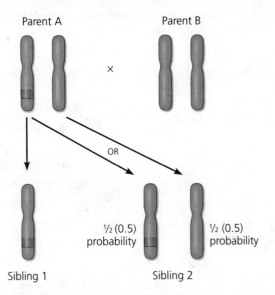

▲ **Figure 51.26 The coefficient of relatedness between siblings.** The red band indicates a particular allele (version of a gene) present on one chromosome, but not its homolog, in parent A. Sibling 1 has inherited the allele from parent A. There is a probability of ½ that sibling 2 will also inherit this allele from parent A. Any allele present on one chromosome of either parent will behave similarly. The coefficient of relatedness between the two siblings is thus ½, or 0.5.

WHAT IF? *The coefficient of relatedness of an individual to a full (nontwin) sibling or to either parent is the same: 0.5. Does this value also hold true in cases of polyandry and polygyny?*

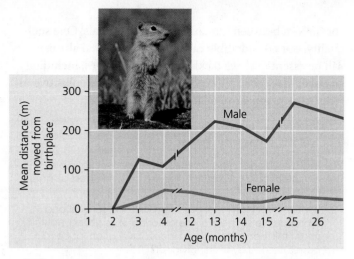

Figure with y-axis labeled "Mean distance (m) moved from birthplace" showing values 0, 100, 200, 300 and x-axis labeled "Age (months)" with values 1, 2, 3, 4, 12, 13, 14, 15, 25, 26. Two curves labeled "Male" and "Female."

▲ **Figure 51.27 Kin selection and altruism in Belding's ground squirrels.** This graph helps explain the male-female difference in altruistic behavior of ground squirrels. Once weaned (pups are nursed for about one month), females are more likely than males to live near close relatives. Alarm calls that warn these relatives increase the inclusive fitness of the female altruist.

appears to have anticipated these ideas when he jokingly stated that he would not lay down his life for one brother, but would do so for two brothers or eight cousins.

If kin selection explains altruism, then the examples of unselfish behavior we observe among diverse animal species should involve close relatives. This is apparently the case, but often in complex ways. Like most mammals, female Belding's ground squirrels settle close to their site of birth, whereas males settle at distant sites (**Figure 51.27**). Since nearly all alarm calls are given by females, they are most likely aiding close relatives. In the case of worker bees, who are all sterile, anything they do to help the entire hive benefits the only permanent member who is reproductively active—the queen, who is their mother.

In the case of naked mole rats, DNA analyses have shown that all the individuals in a colony are closely related. Genetically, the queen appears to be a sibling, daughter, or mother of the kings, and the nonreproductive mole rats are the queen's direct descendants or her siblings. Therefore, when a nonreproductive individual enhances a queen's or king's chances of reproducing, the altruist increases the chance that some genes identical to its own will be passed to the next generation.

Reciprocal Altruism

Some animals occasionally behave altruistically toward others who are not relatives. A baboon may help an unrelated companion in a fight, or a wolf may offer food to another wolf even though they share no kinship. Such behavior can be adaptive if the aided individual returns the favor in the future. This sort of exchange of aid, called **reciprocal altruism**, is commonly invoked to explain altruism that occurs between unrelated humans. Reciprocal altruism is rare in other animals; it is limited largely to species (such as chimpanzees)

with social groups stable enough that individuals have many chances to exchange aid. It is generally thought to occur when individuals are likely to meet again and when there would be negative consequences associated with not returning favors to individuals who had been helpful in the past, a pattern of behavior that behavioral ecologists refer to as "cheating."

Since cheating may benefit the cheater substantially, how could reciprocal altruism evolve? Game theory provides a possible answer in the form of a behavioral strategy called *tit for tat*. In the tit-for-tat strategy, an individual treats another in the same way it was treated the last time they met. Individuals adopting this behavior are always altruistic, or cooperative, on the first encounter with another individual and will remain so as long as their altruism is reciprocated. When their cooperation is not reciprocated, however, individuals employing tit for tat will retaliate immediately but return to cooperative behavior as soon as the other individual becomes cooperative. The tit-for-tat strategy has been used to explain the few apparently reciprocal altruistic interactions observed in animals—ranging from blood sharing between nonrelated vampire bats to social grooming in primates.

Evolution and Human Culture

As animals, humans behave (and, sometimes, misbehave). Just as humans vary extensively in anatomical features, we display substantial variations in behavior. Environment intervenes in the path from genotype to phenotype for physical traits, but does so much more profoundly for behavioral traits. Furthermore, as a consequence of our marked capacity for learning, humans are probably more able than any other animal to acquire new behaviors and skills (**Figure 51.28**).

Some human activities have a less easily defined function in survival and reproduction than do, for example, foraging or courtship. One of these activities is play, which is sometimes defined as behavior that appears purposeless. We recognize play in children and what we think is play in the young of other vertebrates. Behavioral biologists describe "object play," such as chimps playing with leaves, locomotor play, such as the acrobatics of an antelope, and "social play," such as the interactions and antics of lion cubs. These categories, however, do little to inform us about the function of play. One idea is that, rather than generating specific skills or experience, play serves as preparation

▲ **Figure 51.28 Learning a new behavior.**

for unexpected events and for circumstances that cannot be controlled.

Human behavior and culture are related to evolutionary theory in the discipline of **sociobiology**. The main premise of sociobiology is that certain behavioral characteristics exist because they are expressions of genes that have been perpetuated by natural selection. In his seminal 1975 book *Sociobiology: The New Synthesis*, E. O. Wilson speculated about the evolutionary basis of certain kinds of social behavior. By including a few examples from human culture, he sparked a debate that continues today.

Over our recent evolutionary history, we have built up structured societies with governments, laws, cultural values, and religions that define what is acceptable behavior and what is not, even when unacceptable behavior might enhance an individual's Darwinian fitness. Perhaps it is our social and cultural institutions that make us distinct and that provide those qualities that at times make less apparent the

continuum between humans and other animals. One such quality, our considerable capacity for reciprocal altruism, will be essential as we tackle current challenges, including global climate change, in which individual and collective interests often appear to be in conflict.

CONCEPT CHECK 51.4

1. Explain why geographic variation in garter snake prey choice might indicate that the behavior evolved by natural selection.

2. Suppose an individual organism aids the survival and reproductive success of the offspring of its sibling. How might this behavior result in indirect selection for certain genes carried by that individual?

3. **WHAT IF?** Suppose you applied Hamilton's logic to a situation in which one individual is past reproductive age. Could there still be selection for an altruistic act?

For suggested answers, see Appendix A.

51 Chapter Review

SUMMARY OF KEY CONCEPTS

CONCEPT 51.1

Discrete sensory inputs can stimulate both simple and complex behaviors (pp. 1134–1138)

- **Behavior** is the sum of an animal's responses to external and internal stimuli. In behavior studies, proximate, or "how," questions focus on the stimuli that trigger a behavior and on genetic, physiological, and anatomical mechanisms underlying a behavioral act. Ultimate, or "why," questions address evolutionary significance.
- A **fixed action pattern** is a largely invariant behavior triggered by a simple cue known as a **sign stimulus**. Migratory movements involve navigation, which can be based on orientation relative to the sun, the stars, or Earth's magnetic field. Animal behavior is often synchronized to the circadian cycle of light and dark in the environment or to cues that cycle over the seasons.
- The transmission and reception of signals constitute animal **communication**. Animals use visual, auditory, chemical, and tactile signals. Chemical substances called pheromones transmit species-specific information between members of a species in behaviors ranging from foraging to courtship.

? *How is migration based on circannual rhythms poorly suited for adaptation to global climate change?*

CONCEPT 51.2

Learning establishes specific links between experience and behavior (pp. 1138–1143)

- Cross-fostering studies can be used to measure the influence of social environment and experience on behavior.

- **Learning**, the modification of behavior as a result of experience, can take many forms:

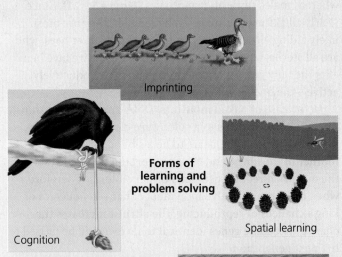

Imprinting

Cognition

Forms of learning and problem solving

Spatial learning

Associative learning

Social learning

? *How do imprinting in geese and song development in sparrows differ with regard to the resulting behavior?*

CONCEPT 51.3

Selection for individual survival and reproductive success can explain diverse behaviors (pp. 1143–1149)

- Controlled experiments in the laboratory can give rise to interpretable evolutionary changes in behavior.
- An **optimal foraging model** is based on the idea that natural selection should favor foraging behavior that minimizes the costs of foraging and maximizes the benefits.
- Sexual dimorphism correlates with the type of mating relationship between males and females. These include **monogamous** and **polygamous** mating systems. Variations in mating system and mode of fertilization affect certainty of paternity, which in turn has a significant influence on mating behavior and parental care.
- Game theory provides a way of thinking about evolution in situations where the fitness of a particular behavioral phenotype is influenced by other behavioral phenotypes in the population.

? *In some spider species, the female eats the male immediately after copulation. How might you explain this behavior from an evolutionary perspective?*

CONCEPT 51.4

Genetic analyses and the concept of inclusive fitness provide a basis for studying the evolution of behavior (pp. 1149–1154)

- Genetic studies in insects have revealed the existence of master regulatory genes that control complex behaviors. Within the underlying hierarchy, multiple genes influence specific behaviors, such as a courtship song. Research on voles has revealed that variation in a single gene can determine differences in complex behaviors involved in both mating and parenting.
- When behavioral variation within a species correlates with variation in environmental conditions, it may be evidence of past evolution. Field and laboratory studies have documented the genetic basis for a change in migratory behavior of certain birds and revealed behavioral differences in snakes that correlate with geographic variation in prey availability.
- **Altruism** can be explained by the concept of **inclusive fitness**, the total effect an individual has on proliferating its genes by producing its own offspring *and* by providing aid that enables close relatives to produce offspring. The **coefficient of relatedness** and **Hamilton's rule** provide a way of measuring the strength of the selective forces favoring altruism against the potential cost of the "selfless" behavior. Kin selection favors altruistic behavior by enhancing the reproductive success of relatives.

? *What insight about the genetic basis of behavior emerges from studying the effects of courtship mutations in fruit flies and of pair-bonding in voles?*

TEST YOUR UNDERSTANDING

LEVEL 1: KNOWLEDGE/COMPREHENSION

1. Which of the following is true of innate behaviors?
   a. Their expression is only weakly influenced by genes.
   b. They occur with or without environmental stimuli.
   c. They are expressed in most individuals in a population.
   d. They occur in invertebrates and some vertebrates but not mammals.

2. According to Hamilton's rule,
   a. natural selection does not favor altruistic behavior that causes the death of the altruist.
   b. natural selection favors altruistic acts when the resulting benefit to the recipient, corrected for relatedness, exceeds the cost to the altruist.
   c. natural selection is more likely to favor altruistic behavior that benefits an offspring than altruistic behavior that benefits a sibling.
   d. the effects of kin selection are larger than the effects of direct natural selection on individuals.

3. Female spotted sandpipers aggressively court males and, after mating, leave the clutch of young for the male to incubate. This sequence may be repeated several times with different males until no available males remain, forcing the female to incubate her last clutch. Which of the following terms best describes this behavior?
   a. polygyny
   b. polyandry
   c. promiscuity
   d. certainty of paternity

LEVEL 2: APPLICATION/ANALYSIS

4. A region of the canary forebrain shrinks during the nonbreeding season and enlarges when breeding season begins. This change is probably associated with the annual
   a. addition of new syllables to a canary's song repertoire.
   b. crystallization of subsong into adult songs.
   c. sensitive period in which canary parents imprint on new offspring.
   d. elimination of the memorized template for songs sung the previous year.

5. Although many chimpanzees live in environments containing oil palm nuts, members of only a few populations use stones to crack open the nuts. The likely explanation is that
   a. the behavioral difference is caused by genetic differences between populations.
   b. members of different populations have different nutritional requirements.
   c. the cultural tradition of using stones to crack nuts has arisen in only some populations.
   d. members of different populations differ in learning ability.

6. Which of the following is *not* required for a behavioral trait to evolve by natural selection?
   a. In each individual, the form of the behavior is determined entirely by genes.
   b. The behavior varies among individuals.
   c. An individual's reproductive success depends in part on how the behavior is performed.
   d. Some component of the behavior is genetically inherited.

LEVEL 3: SYNTHESIS/EVALUATION

7. **DRAW IT** You are considering two optimal foraging models for the behavior of a mussel-feeding shorebird, the oystercatcher. In model A, the energetic reward increases solely with mussel size. In model B, you take into consideration that larger mussels are more difficult to open. Draw a graph of reward (energy benefit on a scale of 0–10) versus mussel length (scale of 0–70 mm) for each model. Assume that mussels under 10 mm provide no benefit and are ignored by the birds. Also assume that mussels start becoming difficult to open when they reach 40 mm in length and impossible to open when 70 mm long. Considering the graphs you have drawn, what observations and measurements would you make in this shorebird's habitat to help determine which model is more accurate?

8. EVOLUTION CONNECTION
We often explain our behavior in terms of subjective feelings, motives, or reasons, but evolutionary explanations are based on reproductive fitness. What is the relationship between the two kinds of explanation? For instance, is a human explanation for behavior, such as "falling in love," incompatible with an evolutionary explanation?

9. SCIENTIFIC INQUIRY
Scientists studying scrub jays found that "helpers" often assist mated pairs of birds in raising their young. The helpers lack territories and mates of their own. Instead, they help the territory owners gather food for their offspring. Propose a hypothesis to explain what advantage there might be for the helpers to engage in this behavior instead of seeking their own territories and mates. How would you test your hypothesis? If it is correct, what results would you expect your tests to yield?

10. SCIENCE, TECHNOLOGY, AND SOCIETY
Researchers are very interested in studying identical twins separated at birth and raised apart. So far, the data reveal that such twins frequently have similar personalities, mannerisms, habits, and interests. What general question do you think researchers hope to answer by studying such twins? Why do identical twins make good subjects for this research? What are the potential pitfalls of this research? What abuses might occur if the studies are not evaluated critically?

11. WRITE ABOUT A THEME: INFORMATION
Learning is defined as a change in behavior as a result of experience. In a short essay (100–150 words), describe the role of heritable information in the acquisition of learning, using some examples from imprinting and associative learning.

12. SYNTHESIZE YOUR KNOWLEDGE

Acorn woodpeckers (*Melanerpes formicivorus*) stash acorns in storage holes they drill in trees. When these woodpeckers breed, the offspring from previous years often help with parental duties. Activities of these nonbreeding helpers include incubating eggs and defending stashed acorns. What are some questions about the proximate and ultimate causation of these behaviors that a behavioral biologist might ask?

For selected answers, see Appendix A.

MasteringBiology®

Students Go to **MasteringBiology** for assignments, the eText, and the Study Area with practice tests, animations, and activities.

Instructors Go to **MasteringBiology** for automatically graded tutorials and questions that you can assign to your students, plus Instructor Resources.

Chapter 1

Concept Check 1.1

1. Examples: A molecule consists of *atoms* bonded together. Each organelle has an orderly arrangement of *molecules*. Photosynthetic plant cells contain *organelles* called chloroplasts. A tissue consists of a group of similar *cells*. Organs such as the heart are constructed from several *tissues*. A complex multicellular organism, such as a plant, has several types of *organs*, such as leaves and roots. A population is a set of *organisms* of the same species. A community consists of *populations* of the various species inhabiting a specific area. An ecosystem consists of a biological *community* along with the nonliving factors important to life, such as air, soil, and water. The biosphere is made up of all of Earth's *ecosystems*.   **2.** (a) New properties emerge at successive levels of biological organization: Structure and function are correlated. (b) Life's processes involve the expression and transmission of genetic information. (c) Life requires the transfer and transformation of energy and matter.   **3.** Some possible answers: *Organization (Emergent properties):* The ability of a human heart to pump blood requires an intact heart; it is not a capability of any of the heart's tissues or cells working alone. *Organization (Structure and function):* The strong, sharp teeth of a wolf are well suited to grasping and dismembering its prey. *Information:* Human eye color is determined by the combination of genes inherited from the two parents. *Energy and Matter:* A plant, such as a grass, absorbs energy from the sun and transforms it into molecules that act as stored fuel. Animals can eat parts of the plant and use the food for energy to carry out their activities. *Interactions (Ecosystems):* A mouse eats food, such as nuts or grasses, and deposits some of the food material as wastes (feces and urine). Construction of a nest rearranges the physical environment and may hasten degradation of some of its components. The mouse may also act as food for a predator. *Interactions (Molecules):* When your stomach is full, it signals your brain to decrease your appetite. *Evolution:* All plants have chloroplasts, indicating their descent from a common ancestor.

Concept Check 1.2

1. An address pinpoints a location by tracking from broader to narrower categories—a state, city, zip, street, and building number. This is analogous to the groups-subordinate-to-groups structure of biological taxonomy.   **2.** The naturally occurring heritable variation in a population is "edited" by natural selection because individuals with heritable traits better suited to the environment survive and reproduce more successfully than others. Over time, better-suited individuals persist and their percentage in the population increases, while less well-suited individuals become less prevalent—a type of population editing.
3.

Ancestral eukaryotes
- Plants
- Fungi
- Animals

Concept Check 1.3

1. Inductive reasoning derives generalizations from specific cases; deductive reasoning predicts specific outcomes from general premises.   **2.** The fur coat color of the mouse models is the independent variable because this is the variable that was changed intentionally by the researchers. Predation is the dependent variable, measured by the investigators and recorded as the proportion of the total number of attacked models.   **3.** Compared to a hypothesis, a scientific theory is usually more general and substantiated by a much greater amount of evidence. Natural selection is an explanatory idea that applies to all kinds of organisms and is supported by vast amounts of evidence of various kinds.   **4.** Based on the mouse coloration in Figure 1.25, you might expect that the mice that live on the sandy soil would be lighter in color and those that live on the lava rock would be much darker. And in fact, that is what researchers have found. You would predict that each color of mouse would be less preyed upon in its native habitat than it would be in the other habitat. (Research results also support this prediction.) You could repeat the Hoekstra experiment with colored models, painted to resemble these two types of mouse. Or you could try transplanting some of each population to its non-native habitat and counting how many you can recapture over the next few days, then comparing the four samples as was done in Hoekstra's experiment. (The painted models are easier to recapture, of course!) In the live mouse transplantation experiment, you would have to do controls to eliminate the variable represented by the transplanted mice being in a new, unknown territory. You could control for the transplantation process by transplanting some dark mice from one area of lava rock to one far distant, and some light mice from one area of sandy soil to a distant area.

Concept Check 1.4

1. Science aims to understand natural phenomena and how they work, while technology involves application of scientific discoveries for a particular purpose or to solve a specific problem.   **2.** Natural selection could be operating. Malaria is present in sub-Saharan Africa, so there might be an advantage to people with the sickle-cell disease form of the gene that makes them more able to survive and pass on their genes to offspring. Among those of African descent living in the United States, where malaria is absent, there would be no advantage, so they would be selected against more strongly, resulting in fewer individuals with the sickle-cell disease form of the gene.

Summary of Key Concepts Questions

1.1 Evolution explains the most fundamental aspects of all life on Earth. It accounts for the common features shared by all forms of life due to descent from a common ancestor, while also providing an explanation for how the great diversity of living organisms on the planet has arisen.   **1.2** Ancestors of the dandelion plant may have exhibited variation in how well their seeds spread to fertile soil for rooting. The variant plants that produced seeds that could travel farther may have had less competition upon reaching fertile soil. They may therefore have survived better and been able to produce more offspring. Over time, a higher and higher proportion of individuals in the population would have had the adaptation of parachute-like structures attached to seeds for seed dispersal.   **1.3** Gathering and interpreting data are core activities in the scientific process, and they are affected by, and affect in turn, three other arenas of the scientific process: exploration and discovery, community analysis and feedback, and societal benefits and outcomes.   **1.4** Different approaches taken by scientists studying natural phenomena at different levels complement each other, so more is learned about each problem being studied. A diversity of backgrounds among scientists may lead to fruitful ideas in the same way that important innovations have often arisen where a mix of cultures coexist, due to multiple different viewpoints.

Test Your Understanding

1. b **2.** d **3.** a **4.** c **5.** c **6.** c **7.** b **8.** c **9.** a **10.** d
11. Your figure should show: (1) For the biosphere, the Earth with an arrow coming out of a tropical ocean; (2) for the ecosystem, a distant view of a coral reef; (3) for the community, a collection of reef animals and algae, with corals, fishes, some seaweed, and any other organisms you can think of; (4) for the population, a group of fish of the same species; (5) for the organism, one fish from your population; (6) for the organ, the fish's stomach, and for the organ system, the whole digestive tract (see Chapter 41 for help); (7) for a tissue, a group of similar cells from the stomach; (8) for a cell, one cell from the tissue, showing its nucleus and a few other organelles; (9) for an organelle, the nucleus, where most of the cell's DNA is located; and (10) for a molecule, a DNA double helix. Your sketches can be very rough!

Chapter 2

Figure Questions

Figure 2.7 Atomic number = 12; 12 protons, 12 electrons; 3 electron shells; 2 valence electrons   **Figure 2.14** One possible answer:

Figure 2.17 The plant is submerged in water (H_2O), in which the CO_2 is dissolved. The sun's energy is used to make sugar, which is found in the plant and can act as food for the plant itself, as well as for animals that eat the plant. The oxygen (O_2) is present in the bubbles.

Concept Check 2.1

1. Table salt (sodium chloride) is made up of sodium and chlorine. We are able to eat the compound, showing that it has different properties from those of a metal (sodium) and a poisonous gas (chlorine).   **2.** Yes, because an organism requires trace elements, even though only in small amounts   **3.** A person with an iron deficiency will probably show fatigue and other effects of a low oxygen level in the blood. (The condition is called anemia and can also result from too few red blood cells or abnormal hemoglobin.)   **4.** Variant ancestral plants that could tolerate elevated levels of the elements in serpentine soils could grow and reproduce there. (Plants that were well adapted to nonserpentine soils would not be expected to survive in serpentine areas.) The offspring of the variants would also vary, with those most capable of thriving under serpentine conditions growing best and reproducing most. Over many generations, this probably led to the serpentine-adapted species we see today.

Concept Check 2.2

1. 7   **2.** $^{15}_{7}N$ **3.** 9 electrons; two electron shells; $1s$, $2s$, $2p$ (three orbitals); 1 electron is needed to fill the valence shell.   **4.** The elements in a row all have the same number of electron shells. In a column, all the elements have the same number of electrons in their valence shells.

Concept Check 2.3

1. Each carbon atom has only three covalent bonds instead of the required four.   **2.** The attraction between oppositely charged ions, forming ionic bonds   **3.** If you could synthesize molecules that mimic these shapes, you might be able to treat diseases or conditions caused by the inability of affected individuals to synthesize such molecules.

Concept Check 2.4

1.

2. At equilibrium, the forward and reverse reactions occur at the same rate.
3. $C_6H_{12}O_6 + 6\,O_2 \rightarrow 6\,CO_2 + 6\,H_2O + $ Energy. Glucose and oxygen react to form carbon dioxide and water, releasing energy. We breathe in oxygen because we need it for this reaction to occur, and we breathe out carbon dioxide because it is a by-product of this reaction. (This reaction is called cellular respiration, and you will learn more about it in Chapter 9.)

Summary of Key Concepts Questions

2.1 Iodine (part of a thyroid hormone) and iron (part of hemoglobin in blood) are both trace elements, required in minute quantities. Calcium and phosphorus (components of bones and teeth) are needed by the body in much greater quantities.
2.2

Both neon and argon have completed valence shells, containing 8 electrons. They do not have unpaired electrons that could participate in chemical bonds.   **2.3** Electrons are shared equally between the two atoms in a nonpolar covalent bond. In a polar covalent bond, the electrons are drawn closer to the more electronegative atom. In the formation of ions, an electron is completely transferred from one atom to a much more electronegative atom.   **2.4** The concentration of products would increase as the added reactants were converted to products. Eventually, an equilibrium would again be reached in which the forward and reverse reactions were proceeding at the same rate and the relative concentrations of reactants and products returned to where they were before the addition of more reactants.

Test Your Understanding

1. a   **2.** d   **3.** b   **4.** a   **5.** d   **6.** b   **7.** c   **8.** d
9.

a.   This structure makes sense because all valence shells are complete, and all bonds have the correct number of electrons.

b.   This structure doesn't make sense because H has only 1 electron to share, so it cannot form bonds with 2 atoms.

Chapter 3

Figure Questions

Figure 3.2 One possible answer:

Figure 3.6 Without hydrogen bonds, water would behave like other small molecules, and the solid phase (ice) would be denser than liquid water. The ice would sink to the bottom and would no longer insulate the whole body of water, which would eventually freeze because the average annual temperature at the South Pole is −50°C. The krill could not survive.   **Figure 3.7** Heating the solution would cause the water to evaporate faster than it is evaporating at room temperature. At a certain point, there wouldn't be enough water molecules to dissolve the salt ions. The salt would start coming out of solution and re-forming crystals. Eventually, all the water would evaporate, leaving behind a pile of salt like the original pile.

Concept Check 3.1

1. Electronegativity is the attraction of an atom for the electrons of a covalent bond. Because oxygen is more electronegative than hydrogen, the oxygen atom in H_2O pulls electrons toward itself, resulting in a partial negative charge on the oxygen atom and partial positive charges on the hydrogen atoms. Atoms in neighboring water molecules with opposite partial charges are attracted to each other, forming a hydrogen bond.   **2.** The hydrogen atoms of one molecule, with their partial positive charges, would repel the hydrogen atoms of the adjacent molecule.   **3.** The covalent bonds of water molecules would not be polar, and water molecules would not form hydrogen bonds with each other.

Concept Check 3.2

1. Hydrogen bonds hold neighboring water molecules together. This cohesion helps chains of water molecules move upward against gravity in water-conducting cells as water evaporates from the leaves. Adhesion between water molecules and the walls of the water-conducting cells also helps counter gravity.   **2.** High humidity hampers cooling by suppressing the evaporation of sweat.   **3.** As water freezes, it expands because water molecules move farther apart in forming ice crystals. When there is water in a crevice of a boulder, expansion due to freezing may crack the boulder.   **4.** The hydrophobic substance repels water, perhaps helping to keep the ends of the legs from becoming coated with water and breaking through the surface. If the legs were coated with a hydrophilic substance, water would be drawn up them, possibly making it more difficult for the water strider to walk on water.

Concept Check 3.3

1. 10^5, or 100,000   **2.** $[H^+] = 0.01\,M = 10^{-2}\,M$, so pH = 2.   **3.** $CH_3COOH \rightarrow CH_3COO^- + H^+$. CH_3COOH is the acid (the H^+ donor), and CH_3COO^- is the base (the H^+ acceptor).   **4.** The pH of the water should decrease from 7 to about 2; the pH of the acetic acid solution will decrease only a small amount, because as a weak acid, it acts as a buffer. The reaction shown for question 3 will shift to the left, with CH_3COO^- accepting the influx of H^+ and becoming CH_3COOH molecules.

Summary of Key Concepts Questions
3.1

No. A covalent bond is a strong bond in which electrons are shared between two atoms. A hydrogen bond is a weak bond, which does not involve electron sharing, but is simply an attraction between two partial charges on neighboring atoms. **3.2** Ions dissolve in water when polar water molecules form a hydration shell around them. Polar molecules dissolve as water molecules form hydrogen bonds with them and surround them. Solutions are homogeneous mixtures of solute and solvent. **3.3** CO_2 reacts with H_2O to form carbonic acid (H_2CO_3), which dissociates into H^+ and bicarbonate (HCO_3^-). Although the carbonic acid–bicarbonate reaction is a buffering system, adding CO_2 drives the reaction to the right, releasing more H^+ and lowering pH. The excess protons combine with CO_3^{2-} to form bicarbonate ions, lowering the concentration of carbonate ions available for the formation of calcium carbonate (calcification) by corals.

Test Your Understanding

1. c **2.** d **3.** c **4.** a **5.** d

6.

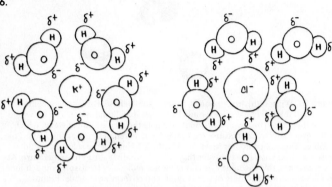

7. Due to intermolecular hydrogen bonds, water has a high specific heat (the amount of heat required to increase the temperature of water by 1°C). When water is heated, much of the heat is absorbed in breaking hydrogen bonds before the water molecules increase their motion and the temperature increases. Conversely, when water is cooled, many H bonds are formed, which releases a significant amount of heat. This release of heat can provide some protection against freezing of the plants' leaves, thus protecting the cells from damage.

Chapter 4

Figure Questions

Figure 4.2 Because the concentration of the reactants influences the equilibrium (as discussed in Chapter 2), there might have been more HCN relative to CH_2O, since there would have been a higher concentration of the reactant gas containing nitrogen.

Figure 4.4

Na·   ·P̈·   ·S̈:   ·C̈l:

Figure 4.6 The tails of fats contain only carbon-hydrogen bonds, which are relatively nonpolar. Because the tails occupy the bulk of a fat molecule, they make the molecule as a whole nonpolar and therefore incapable of forming hydrogen bonds with water.

Figure 4.7

```
          H
          |
      H - C - H
      H   |   H
      |   |   |
  H - C - C - C - H
      H   |   H
      |   |
      H - C - H
          |
          H
```

Concept Check 4.1

1. Prior to Wöhler's experiment, the prevailing view was that only living organisms could synthesize "organic" compounds. Wöhler made urea, an organic compound, without the involvement of living organisms. **2.** The spark provided energy needed for the inorganic molecules in the atmosphere to react with each other. (You'll learn more about energy and chemical reactions in Chapter 8.)

Concept Check 4.2

1.

a. H and H on one carbon, H and H on the other, C=C
b. H and Cl on one carbon, Cl and H on the other, C=C

2. The forms of C_4H_{10} in (b) are structural isomers, as are the butenes in (c). **3.** Both consist largely of hydrocarbon chains. **4.** No. There is not enough diversity in the atoms. It can't form structural isomers because there is only one way for three carbons to attach to each other (in a line). There are no double bonds, so *cis-trans* isomers are not possible. Each carbon has at least two hydrogens attached to it, so the molecule is symmetrical and cannot have enantiomers.

Concept Check 4.3

1. It has both an amino group (—NH₂), which makes it an amine, and a carboxyl group (—COOH), which makes it a carboxylic acid. **2.** The ATP molecule loses

a phosphate, becoming ADP. **3.** A chemical group that can act as a base has been replaced with a group that can act as an acid, increasing the acidic properties of the molecule. The shape of the molecule would also change, likely changing the molecules with which it can interact. The original cysteine molecule has an asymmetric carbon in the center. After replacement of the amino group with a carboxyl group, this carbon is no longer asymmetric.

Summary of Key Concepts Questions

4.1 Miller showed that organic molecules could form under the physical and chemical conditions estimated to have been present on early Earth. This abiotic synthesis of organic molecules would have been a first step in the origin of life. **4.2** Acetone and propanal are structural isomers. Acetic acid and glycine have no asymmetric carbons, whereas glycerol phosphate has one. Therefore, glycerol phosphate can exist as forms that are enantiomers, but acetic acid and glycine cannot. **4.3** The methyl group is nonpolar and not reactive. The other six groups are called functional groups because they can participate in chemical reactions. Also, all except the sulfhydryl group are hydrophilic, increasing the solubility of organic compounds in water.

Test Your Understanding

1. b **2.** b **3.** c **4.** c **5.** a **6.** b **7.** a
8. The molecule on the right; the middle carbon is asymmetric.
9. ·Si· Si has 4 valence electrons, the same number as carbon. Therefore, silicon would be able to form long chains, including branches, that could act as skeletons for large molecules. It would clearly do this much better than neon (with no valence electrons) or aluminum (with 3 valence electrons).

Chapter 5

Figure Questions

Figure 5.3 Glucose and fructose are structural isomers.

Figure 5.4

Note that the oxygen on carbon 5 lost its proton and that the oxygen on carbon 2, which used to be the carbonyl oxygen, gained a proton. Four carbons are in the fructose ring, and two are not. (The latter two carbons are attached to carbons 2 and 5, which are in the ring.) The fructose ring differs from the glucose ring, which has five carbons in the ring and one that is not. (Note that the orientation of this fructose molecule is flipped horizontally relative to that of the one in Figure 5.5b.)

Figure 5.5

(Note that fructose is oriented differently from glucose in Figure 5.5b, and from the fructose shown in the answer for Figure 5.4, above.)

Figure 5.11

Figure 5.12

Figure 5.15

Figure 5.19 The R group on glutamic acid is acidic and hydrophilic, whereas that on valine is nonpolar and hydrophobic. Therefore, it is unlikely that valine and glutamic acid participate in the same intramolecular interactions. A change in these interactions could (and does) cause a disruption of molecular structure.

Figure 5.22 The helical stretches are α helices; these can be seen clearly in many places in the RNA polymerase II model, such as the bottom middle, the upper right, and the lower right areas. Although β pleated sheets may be present, they are not as easy to see.

Figure 5.26 Using a genomics approach allows us to use gene sequences to identify species, and to learn about evolutionary relationships among any two species. This is because all species are related by their evolutionary history, and the evidence is in the DNA sequences. Proteomics—looking at proteins that are expressed—allows us to learn about how organisms or cells are functioning at a given time, or in an association with another species.

Concept Check 5.1
1. The four main classes are proteins, carbohydrates, lipids, and nucleic acids. Lipids are not polymers. **2.** Nine, with one water molecule required to hydrolyze each connection between adjacent monomers **3.** The amino acids in the fish protein must be released in hydrolysis reactions and incorporated into other proteins in dehydration reactions.

Concept Check 5.2
1. $C_3H_6O_3$ **2.** $C_{12}H_{22}O_{11}$ **3.** The antibiotic treatment is likely to have killed the cellulose-digesting prokaryotes in the cow's gut. The absence of these prokaryotes would hamper the cow's ability to obtain energy from food and could lead to weight loss and possibly death. Thus, prokaryotic species are reintroduced, in appropriate combinations, in the gut culture given to treated cows.

Concept Check 5.3
1. Both have a glycerol molecule attached to fatty acids. The glycerol of a fat has three fatty acids attached, whereas the glycerol of a phospholipid is attached to two fatty acids and one phosphate group. **2.** Human sex hormones are steroids, a type of compound that is hydrophobic and thus classified as a lipid. **3.** The oil droplet membrane could consist of a single layer of phospholipids rather than a bilayer, because an arrangement in which the hydrophobic tails of the membrane phospholipids were in contact with the hydrocarbon regions of the oil molecules would be more stable.

Concept Check 5.4
1. Secondary structure involves hydrogen bonds between atoms of the polypeptide backbone. Tertiary structure involves interactions between atoms of the side chains of the amino acid subunits. **2.** The two ring forms of glucose are called α and β, depending on how the glycosidic bond dictates the position of a hydroxyl group. Proteins have α helices and β pleated sheets, two types of repeating structures found in polypeptides due to interactions between the repeating constituents of the chain (not the side chains). The hemoglobin molecule is made up of two types of polypeptides, containing two molecules each of α-globin and β-globin. **3.** These are all nonpolar, hydrophobic amino acids, so you would expect this region to be located in the interior of the folded polypeptide, where it would not contact the aqueous environment inside the cell.

Concept Check 5.5
1.

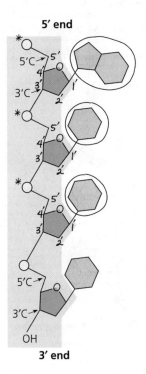

2.

5′–T A G G C C T–3′
3′–A T C C G G A–5′

Concept Check 5.6
1. The DNA of an organism encodes all of its proteins, and proteins are the molecules that carry out the work of cells, whether an organism is unicellular or multicellular. By knowing the DNA sequence of an organism, scientists would be able to catalog the protein sequences as well. **2.** Ultimately, the DNA sequence carries the information necessary to make the proteins that determine the traits of a particular species. Because the traits of the two species are similar, you would expect the proteins to be similar as well, and therefore the gene sequences should also have a high degree of similarity.

Summary of Key Concepts Questions
Concept 5.1 The polymers of large carbohydrates (polysaccharides), proteins, and nucleic acids are built from three different types of monomers (monosaccharides, amino acids, and nucleotides, respectively). **Concept 5.2** Both starch and cellulose are polymers of glucose, but the glucose monomers are in the α configuration in starch and the β configuration in cellulose. The glycosidic linkages thus have different geometries, giving the polymers different shapes and thus different properties. Starch is an energy-storage compound in plants; cellulose is a structural component of plant cell walls. Humans can hydrolyze starch to provide energy but cannot hydrolyze cellulose. Cellulose aids in the passage of food through the digestive tract. **Concept 5.3** Lipids are not polymers because they do not exist as a chain of linked monomers. They are not considered macromolecules because they do not reach the giant size of many polysaccharides, proteins, and nucleic acids. **Concept 5.4** A polypeptide, which may consist of hundreds of amino acids in a specific sequence (primary structure), has regions of coils and pleats (secondary structure), which are then folded into irregular contortions (tertiary structure) and may be noncovalently associated with other polypeptides (quaternary structure). The linear order of amino acids, with the varying properties of their side chains (R groups), determines what secondary and tertiary structures will form to produce a protein. The resulting unique three-dimensional shapes of proteins are key to their specific and diverse functions. **Concept 5.5** The complementary base pairing of the two strands of DNA makes possible the precise replication of DNA every time a cell divides, ensuring that genetic information is faithfully transmitted. In some types of RNA, complementary base pairing enables RNA molecules to assume specific three-dimensional shapes that facilitate diverse

functions.   **Concept 5.6** You would expect the human gene sequence to be most similar to that of the mouse (another mammal), then to that of the fish (another vertebrate), and least similar to that of the fruit fly (an invertebrate).

Test Your Understanding
1. d   **2.** a   **3.** b   **4.** a   **5.** b   **6.** b   **7.** c
8.

	Monomers or Components	Polymer or larger molecule	Type of linkage
Carbohydrates	Monosaccharides	Polysaccharides	Glycosidic linkages
Lipids	Fatty acids	Triacylglycerols	Ester linkages
Proteins	Amino acids	Polypeptides	Peptide bonds
Nucleic acids	Nucleotides	Polynucleotides	Phosphodiester linkages

9.

Original Strand   Complementary strand

Chapter 6

Figure Questions

Figure 6.6 A phospholipid is a lipid consisting of a glycerol molecule joined to two fatty acids and one phosphate group. Together, the glycerol and phosphate end of the phospholipid form the "head," which is hydrophilic, while the hydrocarbon chains on the fatty acids form hydrophobic "tails." The presence in a single molecule of both a hydrophilic and a hydrophobic region makes the molecule ideal as the main building block of a cell or organelle membrane, which is a phospholipid bilayer. In this bilayer, the hydrophobic regions can associate with each other on the inside of the membrane, while the hydrophilic region of each can be in contact with the aqueous solution on either side.   **Figure 6.9** The DNA in a chromosome dictates synthesis of a messenger RNA (mRNA) molecule, which then moves out to the cytoplasm. There, the information is used for the production, on ribosomes, of proteins that carry out cellular functions. **Figure 6.22** Each centriole has 9 sets of 3 microtubules, so the entire centrosome (two centrioles) has 54 microtubules. Each microtubule consists of a helical array of tubulin dimers (as shown in Table 6.1).

1 microtubule

Triplet of microtubules

Figure 6.24

Central pair of microtubules

←They terminate here

The two central microtubules terminate above the basal body, so they aren't present at the level of the cross section through the basal body, indicated by the lower red rectangle in (a).

Concept Check 6.1
1. Stains used for light microscopy are colored molecules that bind to cell components, affecting the light passing through, while stains used for electron microscopy involve heavy metals that affect the beams of electrons.   **2.** (a) Light microscope, (b) scanning electron microscope

Concept Check 6.2
1. See Figure 6.8.
2.

125

1

This cell would have the same volume as the cells in columns 2 and 3 but proportionally more surface area than that in column 2 and less than that in column 3. Thus, the surface-to-volume ratio should be greater than 1.2 but less than 6. To obtain the surface area, you would add the area of the six sides (the top, bottom, sides, and ends): $125 + 125 + 125 + 125 + 1 + 1 = 502$. The surface-to-volume ratio equals 502 divided by a volume of 125, or 4.0.

Concept Check 6.3
1. Ribosomes in the cytoplasm translate the genetic message, carried from the DNA in the nucleus by mRNA, into a polypeptide chain.   **2.** Nucleoli consist of DNA and the ribosomal RNA (rRNA) made according to its instructions, as well as proteins imported from the cytoplasm. Together, the rRNA and proteins are assembled into large and small ribosomal subunits. (These are exported through nuclear pores to the cytoplasm, where they will participate in polypeptide synthesis.)   **3.** Each chromosome consists of one long DNA molecule attached to numerous protein molecules, a combination called chromatin. As a cell begins division, each chromosome becomes "condensed" as its diffuse mass of chromatin coils up.

Concept Check 6.4
1. The primary distinction between rough and smooth ER is the presence of bound ribosomes on the rough ER. Both types of ER make phospholipids, but membrane proteins and secretory proteins are all produced by the ribosomes on the rough ER. The smooth ER also functions in detoxification, carbohydrate metabolism, and storage of calcium ions.   **2.** Transport vesicles move membranes and substances they enclose between other components of the endomembrane system.   **3.** The mRNA is synthesized in the nucleus and then passes out through a nuclear pore to be translated on a bound ribosome, attached to the rough ER. The protein is synthesized into the lumen of the ER and perhaps modified there. A transport vesicle carries the protein to the Golgi apparatus. After further modification in the Golgi, another transport vesicle carries it back to the ER, where it will perform its cellular function.

Concept Check 6.5
1. Both organelles are involved in energy transformation, mitochondria in cellular respiration and chloroplasts in photosynthesis. They both have multiple membranes that separate their interiors into compartments. In both organelles, the innermost membranes—cristae, or infoldings of the inner membrane, in mitochondria, and the thylakoid membranes in chloroplasts—have large surface areas with embedded enzymes that carry out their main functions.   **2.** Yes. Plant cells are able to make their own sugar by photosynthesis, but mitochondria in these eukaryotic cells are the organelles that are able to generate energy from sugars, a function required in all cells.   **3.** Mitochondria and chloroplasts are not derived from the ER, nor are they connected physically or via transport vesicles to organelles of the endomembrane system. Mitochondria and chloroplasts are structurally quite different from vesicles derived from the ER, which are bounded by a single membrane.

Concept Check 6.6

1. Both systems of movement involve long filaments that are moved in relation to each other by motor proteins that grip, release, and grip again adjacent polymers. **2.** Such individuals have defects in the microtubule-based movement of cilia and flagella. Thus, the sperm can't move because of malfunctioning or nonexistent flagella, and the airways are compromised because cilia that line the trachea malfunction or don't exist, and so mucus cannot be cleared from the lungs.

Concept Check 6.7

1. The most obvious difference is the presence of direct cytoplasmic connections between cells of plants (plasmodesmata) and animals (gap junctions). These connections result in the cytoplasm being continuous between adjacent cells. **2.** The cell would not be able to function properly and would probably soon die, as the cell wall or ECM must be permeable to allow the exchange of matter between the cell and its external environment. Molecules involved in energy production and use must be allowed entry, as well as those that provide information about the cell's environment. Other molecules, such as products synthesized by the cell for export and the by-products of cellular respiration, must be allowed to exit. **3.** The parts of the protein that face aqueous regions would be expected to have polar or charged (hydrophilic) amino acids, while the parts that go through the membrane would be expected to have nonpolar (hydrophobic) amino acids. You would predict polar or charged amino acids at each end (tail), in the region of the cytoplasmic loop, and in the regions of the two extracellular loops. You would predict nonpolar amino acids in the four regions that go through the membrane between the tails and loops.

Summary of Key Concepts Questions

6.1 Both light and electron microscopy allow cells to be studied visually, thus helping us understand internal cellular structure and the arrangement of cell components. Cell fractionation techniques separate out different groups of cell components, which can then be analyzed biochemically to determine their function. Performing microscopy on the same cell fraction helps to correlate the biochemical function of the cell with the cell component responsible. **6.2** The separation of different functions in different organelles has several advantages. Reactants and enzymes can be concentrated in one area instead of spread throughout the cell. Reactions that require specific conditions, such as a lower pH, can be compartmentalized. And enzymes for specific reactions are often embedded in the membranes that enclose or partition an organelle. **6.3** The nucleus contains the genetic material of the cell in the form of DNA, which codes for messenger RNA, which in turn provides instructions for the synthesis of proteins (including the proteins that make up part of the ribosomes). DNA also codes for ribosomal RNA, which is combined with proteins in the nucleolus into the subunits of ribosomes. Within the cytoplasm, ribosomes join with mRNA to build polypeptides, using the genetic information in the mRNA. **6.4** Transport vesicles move proteins and membranes synthesized by the rough ER to the Golgi for further processing and then to the plasma membrane, lysosomes, or other locations in the cell, including back to the ER. **6.5** According to the endosymbiont theory, mitochondria originated from an oxygen-using prokaryotic cell that was engulfed by an ancestral eukaryotic cell. Over time, the host and endosymbiont evolved into a single organism. Chloroplasts originated when at least one of these eukaryotic cells containing mitochondria engulfed and then retained a photosynthetic prokaryote. **6.6** Inside the cell, motor proteins interact with components of the cytoskeleton to move cellular parts. Motor proteins "walk" vesicles along microtubules. The movement of cytoplasm within a cell involves interactions of the motor protein myosin and microfilaments (actin filaments). Whole cells can be moved by the rapid bending of flagella or cilia, which is caused by the motor-protein-powered sliding of microtubules within these structures. Cell movement can also occur when pseudopodia form at one end of a cell (caused by actin polymerization into a filamentous network), followed by contraction of the cell toward that end; this is powered by interactions of microfilaments with myosin. Interactions of motor proteins and microfilaments in muscle cells can cause muscle contraction that can propel whole organisms (for example, by walking or swimming). **6.7** A plant cell wall is primarily composed of microfibrils of cellulose embedded in other polysaccharides and proteins. The ECM of animal cells is primarily composed of collagen and other protein fibers, such as fibronectins and other glycoproteins. These fibers are embedded in a network of carbohydrate-rich proteoglycans. A plant cell wall provides structural support for the cell and, collectively, for the plant body. In addition to giving support, the ECM of an animal cell allows for communication of environmental changes into the cell.

Test Your Understanding

1. b **2.** c **3.** b **4.** a **5.** a **6.** c **7.** c **8.** See Figure 6.8.

Chapter 7

Figure Questions
Figure 7.2

Hydrophilic portion

Hydrophobic portion

The hydrophilic portion is in contact with an aqueous environment (cytosol or extracellular fluid), and the hydrophobic portion is in contact with the hydrophobic portions of other phospholipids in the interior of the bilayer. **Figure 7.4** You couldn't rule out movement of proteins within membranes of the same species. You might propose that the membrane lipids and proteins from one species weren't able to mingle with those from the other species because of some incompatibility. **Figure 7.7** A transmembrane protein like the dimer in (f) might change its shape upon binding to a particular ECM molecule. The new shape might enable the interior portion of the protein to bind to a second, cytoplasmic protein that would relay the message to the inside of the cell, as shown in (c). **Figure 7.8** The shape of a protein on the HIV surface is likely to be complementary to the shape of the receptor (CD4) and also to that of the co-receptor (CCR5). A molecule that was a similar shape to the HIV surface protein could bind CCR5, blocking HIV binding. (Another answer would be a molecule that bound to CCR5 and changed the shape of CCR5 so it could no longer bind HIV.) **Figure 7.9**

The protein would contact the extracellular fluid. The protein extends into the ER lumen. Once the vesicle fuses with the plasma membrane, the "inside" of the ER membrane, facing the lumen, will become the "outside" of the plasma membrane, facing the extracellular fluid. **Figure 7.11** The orange dye would be evenly distributed throughout the solution on both sides of the membrane. The solution levels would not be affected because the orange dye can diffuse through the membrane and equalize its concentration. Thus, no additional osmosis would take place in either direction. **Figure 7.16** The diamond solutes are moving into the cell (down), and the round solutes are moving out of the cell (up); both are moving against their concentration gradient.

Concept Check 7.1

1. They are on the inner side of the transport vesicle membrane. **2.** The grasses living in the cooler region would be expected to have more unsaturated fatty acids in their membranes because those fatty acids remain fluid at lower temperatures. The grasses living immediately adjacent to the hot springs would be expected to have more saturated fatty acids, which would allow the fatty acids to "stack" more closely, making the membranes less fluid and therefore helping them to stay intact at higher temperatures. (Cholesterol could not be used to moderate the effects of temperature on membrane fluidity because it is not found within plant cell membranes.)

Concept Check 7.2

1. O_2 and CO_2 are both nonpolar molecules that can easily pass through the hydrophobic interior of a membrane. **2.** Water is a polar molecule, so it cannot pass very rapidly through the hydrophobic region in the middle of a phospholipid bilayer. **3.** The hydronium ion is charged, while glycerol is not. Charge is probably more significant than size as a basis for exclusion by the aquaporin channel.

Concept Check 7.3

1. CO_2 is a nonpolar molecule that can diffuse through the plasma membrane. As long as it diffuses away so that the concentration remains low outside the cell, it will continue to exit the cell in this way. (This is the opposite of the case for O_2, described in this section.) **2.** The activity of *Paramecium caudatum*'s contractile vacuole will decrease. The vacuole pumps out excess water that accumulates in the cell; this accumulation occurs only in a hypotonic environment.

Concept Check 7.4

1. The pump uses ATP. To establish a voltage, ions have to be pumped against their gradients, which requires energy. **2.** Each ion is being transported against its electrochemical gradient. If either ion were transported down its electrochemical gradient, this *would* be considered cotransport. **3.** The internal environment of a lysosome is acidic, so it has a higher concentration of H^+ than does the cytoplasm. Therefore, you might expect the membrane of the lysosome to have a proton pump such as that shown in Figure 7.17 to pump H^+ into the lysosome.

Concept Check 7.5

1. Exocytosis. When a transport vesicle fuses with the plasma membrane, the vesicle membrane becomes part of the plasma membrane.

2.

3. The glycoprotein would be synthesized in the ER lumen, move through the Golgi apparatus, and then travel in a vesicle to the plasma membrane, where it would undergo exocytosis and become part of the ECM.

Summary of Key Concepts Questions

7.1 Plasma membranes define the cell by separating the cellular components from the external environment. This allows conditions inside cells to be controlled by membrane proteins, which regulate entry and exit of molecules and even cell function (see Figure 7.7). The processes of life can be carried out inside the controlled environment of the cell, so membranes are crucial. In eukaryotes, membranes also function to subdivide the cytoplasm into different compartments where distinct processes can occur, even under differing conditions such as pH.   **7.2** Aquaporins are channel proteins that greatly increase the permeability of a membrane to water molecules, which are polar and therefore do not readily diffuse through the hydrophobic interior of the membrane.   **7.3** There will be a net diffusion of water out of a cell into a hypertonic solution. The free water concentration is higher inside the cell than in the solution (where water molecules are not free, but are clustered around the higher concentration of solute particles).   **7.4** One of the solutes moved by the cotransporter is actively transported against its concentration gradient. The energy for this transport comes from the concentration gradient of the other solute, which was established by an electrogenic pump that used energy to transport the other solute across the membrane.   **7.5** In receptor-mediated endocytosis, specific molecules act as ligands when they bind to receptors on the plasma membrane. The cell can acquire bulk quantities of those molecules when a coated pit forms a vesicle and carries the bound molecules into the cell.

Test Your Understanding

1. b   **2.** c   **3.** a   **4.** c   **5.** b
6. (a)

(b) The solution outside is hypotonic. It has less sucrose, which is a nonpenetrating solute. (c) See answer for (a). (d) The artificial cell will become more turgid. (e) Eventually, the two solutions will have the same solute concentrations. Even though sucrose can't move through the membrane, water flow (osmosis) will lead to isotonic conditions.

Chapter 8

Figure Questions

Figure 8.5 With a proton pump (Figure 7.17), the energy stored in ATP is used to pump protons across the membrane and build up a higher (nonrandom) concentration outside of the cell, so this process results in higher free energy. When solute molecules (analogous to H^+ ions) are uniformly distributed, similar to the random distribution in the bottom of (b), the system has less free energy than it does in the top of (b). The system in the bottom can do no work. Because the concentration gradient created by a proton pump (Figure 7.17) represents higher free energy, this system has the potential to do work (as you will see in Chapter 9).
Figure 8.10 Glutamic acid has a carboxyl group at the end of its R group. Glutamine has exactly the same structure as glutamic acid, except that there is an amino group in place of the —OH on the R group. (The O atom on the R group leaves during the synthesis reaction.)

Figure 8.13

Figure 8.16

Figure 8.17

Concept Check 8.1

1. The second law is the trend toward randomization, or increasing entropy. When the concentrations of a substance on both sides of a membrane are equal, the distribution is more random than when they are unequal. Diffusion of a substance to a region where it is initially less concentrated increases entropy, making it an energetically favorable (spontaneous) process as described by the second law. This explains the process seen in Figure 7.10.   **2.** The apple has potential energy in its position hanging on the tree, and the sugars and other nutrients it contains have chemical energy. The apple has kinetic energy as it falls from the tree to the ground. Finally, when the apple is digested and its molecules broken down, some of the chemical energy is used to do work, and the rest is lost as thermal energy.   **3.** The sugar crystals become less ordered (entropy increases) as they dissolve and become randomly spread out in the water. Over time, the water evaporates, and the crystals form again because the water volume is insufficient to keep them in solution. While the reappearance of sugar crystals may represent a "spontaneous" increase in order (decrease in entropy), it is balanced by the decrease in order (increase in entropy) of the water molecules, which changed from a relatively compact arrangement as liquid water to a much more dispersed and disordered form as water vapor.

Concept Check 8.2

1. Cellular respiration is a spontaneous and exergonic process. The energy released from glucose is used to do work in the cell or is lost as heat.   **2.** Catabolism breaks down organic molecules, releasing their chemical energy and resulting in smaller products with more entropy, as when moving from the top to the bottom of part (c). Anabolism consumes energy to synthesize larger molecules from simpler ones, as when moving from the bottom to the top of part (c).   **3.** The reaction is exergonic because it releases energy—in this case, in the form of light. (This is a nonbiological version of the bioluminescence seen in Figure 8.1.)

Concept Check 8.3

1. ATP usually transfers energy to endergonic processes by phosphorylating (adding phosphate groups to) other molecules. (Exergonic processes phosphorylate ADP to regenerate ATP.)   **2.** A set of coupled reactions can transform the first combination into the second. Since this is an exergonic process overall, ΔG is negative and the first combination must have more free energy (see Figure 8.10).
3. Active transport: The solute is being transported against its concentration gradient, which requires energy, provided by ATP hydrolysis.

Concept Check 8.4

1. A spontaneous reaction is a reaction that is exergonic. However, if it has a high activation energy that is rarely attained, the rate of the reaction may be low.
2. Only the specific substrate(s) will fit properly into the active site of an enzyme,

the part of the enzyme that carries out catalysis. **3.** In the presence of malonate, increase the concentration of the normal substrate (succinate) and see whether the rate of reaction increases. If it does, malonate is a competitive inhibitor. **4.** If lactose weren't present in the environment as a source of food and the fucose-containing disaccharide were available, bacteria that could digest the latter would be better able to grow and multiply than those that could not.

Concept Check 8.5

1. The activator binds in such a way that it stabilizes the active form of an enzyme, whereas the inhibitor stabilizes the inactive form. **2.** A catabolic pathway breaks down organic molecules, generating energy that is stored in ATP molecules. In feedback inhibition of such a pathway, ATP (one product) would act as an allosteric inhibitor of an enzyme catalyzing an early step in the catabolic process. When ATP is plentiful, the pathway would be turned off and no more would be made.

Summary of Key Concepts Questions

8.1 The process of "ordering" a cell's structure is accompanied by an increase in the entropy or disorder of the universe. For example, an animal cell takes in highly ordered organic molecules as the source of matter and energy used to build and maintain its structures. In the same process, however, the cell releases heat and the simple molecules of carbon dioxide and water to the surroundings. The increase in entropy of the latter process offsets the entropy decrease in the former. **8.2** A spontaneous reaction has a negative ΔG and is exergonic. For a chemical reaction to proceed with a net release of free energy $(-\Delta G)$, the enthalpy or total energy of the system must decrease $(-\Delta H)$, and/or the entropy or disorder must increase (yielding a more negative term, $-T\Delta S$). Spontaneous reactions supply the energy to perform cellular work. **8.3** The free energy released from the hydrolysis of ATP may drive endergonic reactions through the transfer of a phosphate group to a reactant molecule, forming a more reactive phosphorylated intermediate. ATP hydrolysis also powers the mechanical and transport work of a cell, often by powering shape changes in the relevant motor proteins. Cellular respiration, the catabolic breakdown of glucose, provides the energy for the endergonic regeneration of ATP from ADP and $\circledP_i$. **8.4** Activation energy barriers prevent the complex molecules of the cell, which are rich in free energy, from spontaneously breaking down to less ordered, more stable molecules. Enzymes permit a regulated metabolism by binding to specific substrates and forming enzyme-substrate complexes that selectively lower the E_A for the chemical reactions in a cell. **8.5** A cell tightly regulates its metabolic pathways in response to fluctuating needs for energy and materials. The binding of activators or inhibitors to regulatory sites on allosteric enzymes stabilizes either the active or inactive form of the subunits. For example, the binding of ATP to a catabolic enzyme in a cell with excess ATP would inhibit that pathway. Such types of feedback inhibition preserve chemical resources within a cell. If ATP supplies are depleted, binding of ADP to the regulatory site of catabolic enzymes would activate that pathway, generating more ATP.

Test Your Understanding

1. b **2.** c **3.** b **4.** a **5.** c **6.** d **7.** c

9.

A. The substrate molecules are entering the cells, so no product is made yet.
B. There is sufficient substrate, so the reaction is proceeding at a maximum rate.
C. As the substrate is used up, the rate decreases (the slope is less steep).
D. The line is flat because no new substrate remains and thus no new product appears.

Chapter 9

Figure Questions

Figure 9.4 The reduced form has an extra hydrogen, along with 2 electrons, bound to the carbon shown at the top of the nicotinamide (opposite the N). There are different numbers and positions of double bonds in the two forms: The oxidized form has three double bonds in the ring, while the reduced form has only two. (In organic chemistry you may learn, or will learn, that three double bonds in a ring are able to "resonate," or act as a ring of electrons.) In the oxidized form there is a $+$ charge on the N (because it is sharing 4 electron pairs), whereas in the reduced form it is only sharing 3 electron pairs (having a pair of electrons to itself). **Figure 9.7** Because there is no external source of energy for the reaction, it must be exergonic, and the reactants must be at a higher energy level than the products. **Figure 9.9** The removal would probably stop glycolysis, or at least slow it down, since it would push the equilibrium for step 5 toward the bottom (toward DHAP). If less (or no) glyceraldehyde 3-phosphate were available, step 6 would slow down (or be unable to occur). **Figure 9.15** At first, some ATP could be made, since electron transport could proceed as far as complex III, and a small H^+ gradient could be built up. Soon, however, no more electrons could be passed to complex III because it could not be reoxidized by passing its electrons to complex IV. **Figure 9.16** First, there are 2 NADH from the oxidation of pyruvate plus 6 NADH from the citric acid cycle (CAC); 8 NADH $\times$ 2.5 ATP/NADH = 20 ATP. Second, there are 2 FADH$_2$ from the CAC; 2 FADH$_2$ $\times$ 1.5 ATP/FADH$_2$ = 3 ATP. Third, the 2 NADH from glycolysis enter the mitochondrion through one of two

types of shuttle. They pass their electrons either to 2 FAD, which become FADH$_2$ and result in 3 ATP, or to 2 NAD$^+$, which become NADH and result in 5 ATP. Thus, $20 + 3 + 3 = 26$ ATP, or $20 + 3 + 5 = 28$ ATP from all NADH and FADH$_2$.

Concept Check 9.1

1. Both processes include glycolysis, the citric acid cycle, and oxidative phosphorylation. In aerobic respiration, the final electron acceptor is molecular oxygen (O_2); in anaerobic respiration, the final electron acceptor is a different substance. **2.** $C_4H_6O_5$ would be oxidized and NAD$^+$ would be reduced.

Concept Check 9.2

1. NAD$^+$ acts as the oxidizing agent in step 6, accepting electrons from glyceraldehyde 3-phosphate, which thus acts as the reducing agent.

Concept Check 9.3

1. NADH and FADH$_2$; they will donate electrons to the electron transport chain. **2.** CO_2 is released from the pyruvate that is the end product of glycolysis, and CO_2 is also released during the citric acid cycle. **3.** In both cases, the precursor molecule loses a CO_2 molecule and then donates electrons to an electron carrier in an oxidation step. Also, the product has been activated due to the attachment of a CoA group.

Concept Check 9.4

1. Oxidative phosphorylation would eventually stop entirely, resulting in no ATP production by this process. Without oxygen to "pull" electrons down the electron transport chain, H^+ would not be pumped into the mitochondrion's intermembrane space and chemiosmosis would not occur. **2.** Decreasing the pH means addition of H^+. This would establish a proton gradient even without the function of the electron transport chain, and we would expect ATP synthase to function and synthesize ATP. (In fact, it was experiments like this that provided support for chemiosmosis as an energy-coupling mechanism.) **3.** One of the components of the electron transport chain, ubiquinone (Q), must be able to diffuse within the membrane. It could not do so if the membrane were locked rigidly into place.

Concept Check 9.5

1. A derivative of pyruvate, such as acetaldehyde during alcohol fermentation, or pyruvate itself during lactic acid fermentation; oxygen **2.** The cell would need to consume glucose at a rate about 16 times the consumption rate in the aerobic environment (2 ATP are generated by fermentation versus up to 32 ATP by cellular respiration).

Concept Check 9.6

1. The fat is much more reduced; it has many —CH$_2$— units, and in all these bonds the electrons are equally shared. The electrons present in a carbohydrate molecule are already somewhat oxidized (shared unequally in bonds), as quite a few of them are bound to oxygen. Electrons that are equally shared, as in fat, have a higher energy level than electrons that are unequally shared, as in carbohydrates. Thus, fat is a much better fuel than carbohydrate. **2.** When we consume more food than necessary for metabolic processes, our body synthesizes fat as a way of storing energy for later use. **3.** AMP will accumulate, stimulating phosphofructokinase, and thus increasing the rate of glycolysis. Since oxygen is not present, the cell will convert pyruvate to lactate in lactic acid fermentation, providing a supply of ATP. **4.** When oxygen is present, the fatty acid chains containing most of the energy of a fat are oxidized and fed into the citric acid cycle and the electron transport chain. During intense exercise, however, oxygen is scarce in muscle cells, so ATP must be generated by glycolysis alone. A very small part of the fat molecule, the glycerol backbone, can be oxidized via glycolysis, but the amount of energy released by this portion is insignificant compared to that released by the fatty acid chains. (This is why moderate exercise, staying below 70% maximum heart rate, is better for burning fat—because enough oxygen remains available to the muscles.)

Summary of Key Concepts Questions

9.1 Most of the ATP produced in cellular respiration comes from oxidative phosphorylation, in which the energy released from redox reactions in an electron transport chain is used to produce ATP. In substrate-level phosphorylation, an enzyme directly transfers a phosphate group to ADP from an intermediate substrate. All ATP production in glycolysis occurs by substrate-level phosphorylation; this form of ATP production also occurs at one step in the citric acid cycle. **9.2** The oxidation of the three-carbon sugar, glyceraldehyde 3-phosphate, yields energy. In this oxidation, electrons and H^+ are transferred to NAD$^+$, forming NADH, and a phosphate group is attached to the oxidized substrate. ATP is then formed by substrate-level phosphorylation when this phosphate group is transferred to ADP. **9.3** The release of six molecules of CO_2 represents the complete oxidation of glucose. During the processing of two pyruvates to acetyl CoA, the fully oxidized carboxyl groups (—COO$^-$) are given off as 2 CO_2. The remaining four carbons are released as CO_2 in the citric acid cycle as citrate is oxidized back to oxaloacetate. **9.4** The flow of H^+ through the ATP synthase complex causes the rotor and attached rod to rotate, exposing catalytic sites in the knob portion that produce ATP from ADP and $\circledP_i$. ATP synthases are found in the inner mitochondrial membrane, the plasma membrane of prokaryotes, and membranes within chloroplasts. **9.5** Aerobic respiration yields more ATP. The 2 ATP produced by substrate-level phosphorylation in glycolysis represent the total energy yield of fermentation. NADH passes its "high-energy" electrons to pyruvate or a derivative of pyruvate, recycling NAD$^+$ and allowing glycolysis to continue. In anaerobic respiration, the NADH produced during glycolysis, as well as additional molecules of NADH produced as pyruvate is oxidized, are used to generate ATP molecules. An electron transport chain captures the energy of the electrons in NADH via a series of redox reactions; ultimately, the electrons are transferred to an electronegative molecule other than oxygen.   **9.6** The ATP produced by catabolic pathways is used to drive anabolic pathways. Also, many of the intermediates of glycolysis and the citric acid cycle are used in the biosynthesis of a cell's molecules.

Test Your Understanding
1. c   **2.** c   **3.** a   **4.** b   **5.** d   **6.** a   **7.** b
8. Since the overall process of glycolysis results in net production of ATP, it would make sense for the process to slow down when ATP levels have increased substantially. Thus, we would expect ATP to allosterically inhibit phosphofructokinase.   **9.** The proton pump in Figure 7.17 is carrying out active transport, using ATP hydrolysis to pump protons against their concentration gradient. Because ATP is required, this is active transport of protons. The ATP synthase in Figure 9.14 is using the flow of protons down their concentration gradient to power ATP synthesis. Because the protons are moving down their concentration gradient, no energy is required, and this is passive transport.
11.

H^+ would continue to be pumped across the membrane into the intermembrane space, increasing the difference between the matrix pH and the intermembrane space pH. H^+ would not be able to flow back through ATP synthase, since the enzyme is inhibited by the poison, so rather than maintaining a constant difference across the membrane, the difference would continue to increase. (Ultimately, the H^+ concentration in the intermembrane space would be so high that no more H^+ would be able to be pumped against the gradient, but this isn't shown in the graph.)

Chapter 10

Figure Questions
Figure 10.3 Situating containers of algae near sources of CO_2 emissions makes sense because algae need CO_2 to carry out photosynthesis. The higher their rate of photosynthesis, the more plant oil they will produce. At the same time, algae would be absorbing the CO_2 emitted from industrial plants or from car engines, reducing the amount of CO_2 entering the atmosphere.   **Figure 10.12** In the leaf, most of the chlorophyll electrons excited by photon absorption are used to power the reactions of photosynthesis.   **Figure 10.16** The person at the top of the photosystem I tower would not turn to his left and throw his electron into the bucket. Instead, he would throw it onto the top of the ramp at his right, next to the photosystem II tower. The electron would then roll down the ramp, get energized by a photon, and return to him. This cycle would continue as long as light was available. (This is why it's called cyclic electron flow.)   **Figure 10.22** Yes, plants can break down the sugar (in the form of glucose) by cellular respiration, producing ATPs for various cellular processes such as endergonic chemical reactions, transport of substances across membranes, and movement of molecules in the cell. ATPs are also used for the movement of chloroplasts during cellular streaming in some plant cells (see Figure 6.26).   **Figure 10.23** The gene encoding hexokinase is part of the DNA of a chromosome in the nucleus. There, the gene is transcribed into mRNA, which is transported to the cytoplasm where it is translated on a free ribosome into a polypeptide. The polypeptide folds into a functional protein with secondary and tertiary structure. Once functional, it carries out the first reaction of glycolysis in the cytoplasm.

Concept Check 10.1
1. CO_2 enters the leaves via stomata, and water enters via roots and is carried to the leaves through veins.   **2.** Using ^{18}O, a heavy isotope of oxygen, as a label, researchers were able to confirm van Niel's hypothesis that the oxygen produced during photosynthesis comes from water, not from carbon dioxide.   **3.** The light reactions could *not* keep producing NADPH and ATP without the $NADP^+$, ADP, and ℗ᵢ that the Calvin cycle generates. The two cycles are interdependent.

Concept Check 10.2
1. Green, because green light is mostly transmitted and reflected—not absorbed—by photosynthetic pigments   **2.** Water (H_2O) is the initial electron donor; $NADP^+$ accepts electrons at the end of the electron transport chain, becoming reduced to NADPH.   **3.** In this experiment, the rate of ATP synthesis would slow and eventually stop. Because the added compound would not allow a proton gradient to build up across the membrane, ATP synthase could not catalyze ATP production.

Concept Check 10.3
1. 6, 18, 12   **2.** The more potential energy a molecule stores, the more energy and reducing power are required for the formation of that molecule. Glucose is a valuable energy source because it is highly reduced, storing lots of potential energy in its electrons. To reduce CO_2 to glucose, much energy and reducing power are required in the form of large numbers of ATP and NADPH molecules, respectively.   **3.** The light reactions require ADP and $NADP^+$, which would not be formed in sufficient quantities from ATP and NADPH if the Calvin cycle stopped.

4.

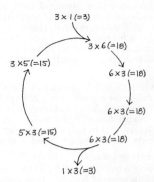

Three carbon atoms enter the cycle, one by one, as individual CO_2 molecules, and leave the cycle in one three-carbon molecule (G3P) per three turns of the cycle.
5. In glycolysis, G3P acts as an intermediate. The 6-carbon sugar fructose 1,6-bisphosphate is cleaved into two 3-carbon sugars, one of which is G3P. The other is an isomer called dihydroxyacetone phosphate (DHAP), which can be converted to G3P by an isomerase. Because G3P is the substrate for the next enzyme, it is constantly removed, and the reaction equilibrium is pulled in the direction of conversion of DHAP to more G3P. In the Calvin cycle, G3P acts as both an intermediate and a product. For every three CO_2 molecules that enter the cycle, six G3P molecules are formed, five of which must remain in the cycle and become rearranged to regenerate three 5-carbon RuBP molecules. The one remaining G3P is a product, which can be thought of as the result of "reducing" the three CO_2 molecules that entered the cycle into a 3-carbon sugar that can later be used to generate energy.

Concept Check 10.4
1. Photorespiration decreases photosynthetic output by adding oxygen, instead of carbon dioxide, to the Calvin cycle. As a result, no sugar is generated (no carbon is fixed), and O_2 is used rather than generated.   **2.** Without PS II, no O_2 is generated in bundle-sheath cells. This avoids the problem of O_2 competing with CO_2 for binding to rubisco in these cells.   **3.** Both problems are caused by a drastic change in Earth's atmosphere due to burning of fossil fuels. The increase in CO_2 concentration affects ocean chemistry by decreasing pH, thus affecting calcification by marine organisms. On land, CO_2 concentration and air temperature are conditions that plants have become adapted to, and changes in these characteristics have a strong effect on photosynthesis by plants. Thus, alteration of these two fundamental factors could have critical effects on organisms all around the planet, in all different habitats.   **4.** C_4 and CAM species would replace many of the C_3 species.

Summary of Key Concepts Questions
10.1 CO_2 and H_2O are the products of respiration; they are the reactants in photosynthesis. In respiration, glucose is oxidized to CO_2 and electrons are passed through an electron transfer chain from glucose to O_2, producing H_2O. In photosynthesis, H_2O is the source of electrons, which are energized by light, temporarily stored in NADPH, and used to reduce CO_2 to carbohydrate.
10.2 The action spectrum of photosynthesis shows that some wavelengths of light that are not absorbed by chlorophyll *a* are still effective at promoting photosynthesis. The light-harvesting complexes of photosystems contain accessory pigments such as chlorophyll *b* and carotenoids, which absorb different wavelengths and pass the energy to chlorophyll *a*, broadening the spectrum of light usable for photosynthesis.
10.3

In the reduction phase of the Calvin cycle, ATP phosphorylates a three-carbon compound, and NADPH then reduces this compound to G3P. ATP is also used in the regeneration phase, when five molecules of G3P are converted to three molecules of the five-carbon compound RuBP. Rubisco catalyzes the first step of carbon fixation—the addition of CO_2 to RuBP.   **10.4** Both C_4 photosynthesis and CAM photosynthesis involve initial fixation of CO_2 to produce a four-carbon compound (in mesophyll cells in C_4 plants and at night in CAM plants). These compounds are then broken down to release CO_2 (in the bundle-sheath cells in C_4 plants and during the day in CAM plants). ATP is required for recycling the molecule that is used initially to combine with CO_2. These pathways avoid the photorespiration that consumes ATP and reduces the photosynthetic output of C_3 plants when they close stomata on hot, dry, bright days. Thus, hot, arid climates would favor C_4 and CAM plants.

Test Your Understanding
1. d **2.** b **3.** c **4.** a **5.** c **6.** b **7.** c
10.

The ATP would end up outside the thylakoid. The thylakoids were able to make ATP in the dark because the researchers set up an artificial proton concentration gradient across the thylakoid membrane; thus, the light reactions were not necessary to establish the H^+ gradient required for ATP synthesis by ATP synthase.

Chapter 11

Figure Questions
Figure 11.6 Epinephrine is a signaling molecule; presumably, it binds to a cell-surface receptor protein. **Figure 11.8** This is an example of passive transport. The ion is moving down its concentration gradient, and no energy is required. **Figure 11.9** The aldosterone molecule is hydrophobic and can therefore pass directly through the lipid bilayer of the plasma membrane into the cell. (Hydrophilic molecules cannot do this.) **Figure 11.10** The entire phosphorylation cascade wouldn't operate. Regardless of whether or not the signaling molecule was bound, protein kinase 3 would always be inactive and would not be able to activate the purple-colored protein leading to the cellular response. **Figure 11.11** The signaling molecule (cAMP) would remain in its active form and would continue to signal. **Figure 11.16** 100,000,000 (one hundred million or 10^8) glucose molecules are released. The first step results in $100\times$ amplification (one epinephrine activates 100 G proteins); the next step does not amplify the response; the next step is a $100\times$ amplification (10^2 active adenylyl cyclase molecules to 10^4 cyclic AMPs); the next step does not amplify; the next two steps are each $10\times$ amplifications, and the final step is a $100\times$ amplification. **Figure 11.17** The signaling pathway shown in Figure 11.14 leads to the splitting of PIP_2 into the second messengers DAG and IP_3, which produce different responses. (The response elicited by DAG is mentioned but not shown.) The pathway shown for cell B is similar in that it branches and leads to two responses.

Concept Check 11.1
1. The two cells of opposite mating type (**a** and **α**) each secrete a certain signaling molecule, which can only be bound by receptors carried on cells of the opposite mating type. Thus, the **a** mating factor cannot bind to another **a** cell and cause it to grow toward the first **a** cell. Only an **α** cell can "receive" the signaling molecule and respond by directed growth (see the Scientific Skills Exercise). **2.** Glycogen phosphorylase acts in the third stage, the response to epinephrine signaling. **3.** Glucose 1-phosphate is not generated, because the activation of the enzyme requires an intact cell, with an intact receptor in the membrane and an intact signal transduction pathway. The enzyme cannot be activated directly by interaction with the signaling molecule in the test tube.

Concept Check 11.2
1. NGF is water-soluble (hydrophilic), so it cannot pass through the lipid membrane to reach intracellular receptors, as steroid hormones can. Therefore, you'd expect the NGF receptor to be in the plasma membrane—which is, in fact, the case. **2.** The cell with the faulty receptor would not be able to respond appropriately to the signaling molecule when it was present. This would most likely have dire consequences for the cell, since regulation of the cell's activities by this receptor would not occur appropriately. **3.** Binding of a ligand to a receptor changes the shape of the receptor, altering the ability of the receptor to transmit a signal. Binding of an allosteric regulator to an enzyme changes the shape of the enzyme, either promoting or inhibiting enzyme activity. **4.** When the receptor is actively transmitting a signal to the inside of the cell, it is bound to a G protein. To determine a structure corresponding to that state, it might be useful to crystallize the receptor in the presence of many copies of the G protein. (In fact, a research group used this approach successfully with a G protein-coupled receptor related to the one shown in Figure 11.8.)

Concept Check 11.3
1. A protein kinase is an enzyme that transfers a phosphate group from ATP to a protein, usually activating that protein (often a second type of protein kinase). Many signal transduction pathways include a series of such interactions, in which each phosphorylated protein kinase in turn phosphorylates the next protein kinase in the series. Such phosphorylation cascades carry a signal from outside the cell to

the cellular protein(s) that will carry out the response. **2.** Protein phosphatases reverse the effects of the kinases, and unless the signaling molecule is at a high enough concentration that it is continuously rebinding the receptor, the kinase molecules will all be returned to their inactive states by phosphatases. **3.** The signal that is being transduced is the *information* that a signaling molecule is bound to the cell-surface receptor. Information is transduced by way of sequential protein-protein interactions that change protein shapes, causing them to function in a way that passes the signal (the information) along. **4.** The IP_3-gated channel opens, allowing calcium ions to flow out of the ER and into the cytoplasm, which raises the cytosolic Ca^{2+} concentration.

Concept Check 11.4
1. At each step in a cascade of sequential activations, one molecule or ion may activate numerous molecules functioning in the next step. This causes the response to be amplified at each such step and overall results in a large amplification of the original signal. **2.** Scaffolding proteins hold molecular components of signaling pathways in a complex with each other. Different scaffolding proteins would assemble different collections of proteins, leading to different cellular responses in the two cells. **3.** A malfunctioning protein phosphatase would not be able to dephosphorylate a particular receptor or relay protein. As a result, the signaling pathway, once activated, would not be able to be terminated. (In fact, one study found altered protein phosphatases in cells from 25% of colorectal tumors.)

Concept Check 11.5
1. In formation of the hand or paw in mammals, cells in the regions between the digits are programmed to undergo apoptosis. This serves to shape the digits of the hand or paw so that they are not webbed. (A lack of apoptosis in these regions in water birds results in webbed feet.) **2.** If a receptor protein for a death-signaling molecule were defective such that it was activated even in the absence of the death signal, this would lead to apoptosis when it wouldn't normally occur. Similar defects in any of the proteins in the signaling pathway would have the same effect if the defective proteins activated relay or response proteins in the absence of interaction with the previous protein or second messenger in the pathway. Conversely, if any protein in the pathway were defective in its ability to respond to an interaction with an early protein or other molecule or ion, apoptosis would not occur when it normally should. For example, a receptor protein for a death-signaling ligand might not be able to be activated, even when ligand was bound. This would stop the signal from being transduced into the cell.

Summary of Key Concepts Questions
11.1 A cell is able to respond to a hormone only if it has a receptor protein on the cell surface or inside the cell that can bind to the hormone. The response to a hormone depends on the specific signal transduction pathway within the cell, which will lead to the specific cellular response. The response can vary for different types of cells. **11.2** Both GPCRs and RTKs have an extracellular binding site for a signaling molecule (ligand) and one or more α helical regions of the polypeptide that spans the membrane. A GPCR functions singly, while RTKs tend to dimerize or form larger groups of RTKs. GPCRs usually trigger a single transduction pathway, whereas the multiple activated tyrosines on an RTK dimer may trigger several different transduction pathways at the same time. **11.3** A protein kinase is an enzyme that adds a phosphate group to another protein. Protein kinases are often part of a phosphorylation cascade that transduces a signal. A second messenger is a small, nonprotein molecule or ion that rapidly diffuses and relays a signal throughout a cell. Both protein kinases and second messengers can operate in the same pathway. For example, the second messenger cAMP often activates protein kinase A, which then phosphorylates other proteins. **11.4** In G protein-coupled pathways, the GTPase portion of a G protein converts GTP to GDP and inactivates the G protein. Protein phosphatases remove phosphate groups from activated proteins, thus stopping a phosphorylation cascade of protein kinases. Phosphodiesterase converts cAMP to AMP, thus reducing the effect of cAMP in a signal transduction pathway. **11.5** The basic mechanism of controlled cell suicide evolved early in eukaryotic evolution, and the genetic basis for these pathways has been conserved during animal evolution. Such a mechanism is essential to the development and maintenance of all animals.

Test Your Understanding
1. d **2.** a **3.** b **4.** a **5.** c **6.** c **7.** c
8. This is one possible drawing of the pathway. (Similar drawings would also be correct.)

Chapter 12

Figure Questions
Figure 12.4

One sister chromatid

Circling the other chromatid instead would also be correct.   **Figure 12.5** The chromosome has four arms.   **Figure 12.7** 12; 2; 2; 1

Figure 12.8

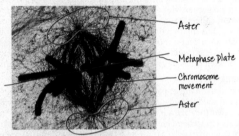

Aster

Metaphase plate

Chromosome movement

Aster

Figure 12.9 The mark would have moved toward the nearer pole. The lengths of fluorescent microtubules between that pole and the mark would have decreased, while the lengths between the chromosomes and the mark would have remained the same.   **Figure 12.14** In both cases, the G_1 nucleus would have remained in G_1 until the time it normally would have entered the S phase. Chromosome condensation and spindle formation would not have occurred until the S and G_2 phases had been completed.   **Figure 12.16** Passing the G_2 checkpoint in the diagram corresponds to the beginning of the "Time" axis of the graph, and entry into the mitotic phase (yellow background on the diagram) corresponds to the peaks of MPF activity and cyclin concentration on the graph (see the yellow M banner over the peaks). During G_1 and S phase in the diagram, Cdk is present without cyclin, so on the graph both cyclin concentration and MPF activity are low. The curved purple arrow in the diagram shows increasing cyclin concentration, seen on the graph during the end of S phase and throughout G_2 phase. Then the cell cycle begins again.   **Figure 12.17** The cell would divide under conditions where it was inappropriate to do so. If the daughter cells and their descendants also ignored either of the checkpoints and divided, there would soon be an abnormal mass of cells. (This type of inappropriate cell division can contribute to the development of cancer.)   **Figure 12.18** The cells in the vessel with PDGF would not be able to respond to the growth factor signal and thus would not divide. The culture would resemble that without the added PDGF.

Concept Check 12.1
1. 1; 1; 2   **2.** 39; 39; 78

Concept Check 12.2
1. 6 chromosomes, duplicated; 12 chromatids   **2.** Following mitosis, cytokinesis results in two genetically identical daughter cells in both plant cells and animal cells. However, the mechanism of dividing the cytoplasm is different in animals and plants. In an animal cell, cytokinesis occurs by cleavage, which divides the parent cell in two with a contractile ring of actin filaments. In a plant cell, a cell plate forms in the middle of the cell and grows until its membrane fuses with the plasma membrane of the parent cell. A new cell wall grows inside the cell plate.   **3.** From the end of S phase in interphase through the end of metaphase in mitosis   **4.** During eukaryotic cell division, tubulin is involved in spindle formation and chromosome movement, while actin functions during cytokinesis. In bacterial binary fission, it's the opposite: Tubulin-like molecules are thought to act in daughter cell separation, and actin-like molecules are thought to move the daughter bacterial chromosomes to opposite ends of the cell.   **5.** A kinetochore connects the spindle (a motor; note that it has motor proteins) to a chromosome (the cargo it will move).   **6.** Microtubules made up of tubulin in the cell provide "rails" along which vesicles and other organelles can travel, based on interactions of motor proteins with tubulin in the microtubules. In muscle cells, actin in microfilaments interacts with myosin filaments to cause muscle contraction.

Concept Check 12.3
1. The nucleus on the right was originally in the G_1 phase; therefore, it had not yet duplicated its chromosomes. The nucleus on the left was in the M phase, so it had already duplicated its chromosomes.   **2.** A sufficient amount of MPF has to exist for a cell to pass the G_2 checkpoint; this occurs through the accumulation of cyclin proteins, which combine with Cdk to form (active) MPF.   **3.** The intracellular estrogen receptor, once activated, would be able to act as a transcription factor in the nucleus, turning on genes that may cause the cell to pass a checkpoint and divide. The HER2 receptor, when activated by a ligand, would form a dimer, and each subunit of the dimer would phosphorylate the other. This would lead to a series of signal transduction steps, ultimately turning on genes in the nucleus. As in the case of the estrogen receptor, the genes would code for proteins necessary to commit the cell to divide.

Summary of Key Concepts Questions
12.1 The DNA of a eukaryotic cell is packaged into structures called *chromosomes*. Each chromosome is a long molecule of DNA, which carries hundreds to thousands of genes, with associated proteins that maintain chromosome structure and help control gene activity. This DNA-protein complex is called *chromatin*. The chromatin of each chromosome is long and thin when the cell is not dividing. Prior to cell division, each chromosome is duplicated, and the resulting sister *chromatids* are attached to each other by proteins at the centromeres and, for many species, all along their lengths (a phenomenon called sister chromatid cohesion).   **12.2** Chromosomes exist as single DNA molecules in G_1 of interphase and in anaphase and telophase of mitosis. During S phase, DNA replication produces sister chromatids, which persist during G_2 of interphase and through prophase, prometaphase, and metaphase of mitosis.   **12.3** Checkpoints allow cellular surveillance mechanisms to determine whether the cell is prepared to go to the next stage. Internal and external signals move a cell past these checkpoints. The G_1 checkpoint, called the "restriction point" in mammalian cells, determines whether a cell will complete the cell cycle and divide or switch into the G_0 phase. The signals to pass this checkpoint often are external—such as growth factors. Passing the G_2 checkpoint requires sufficient numbers of active MPF complexes, which in turn orchestrate several mitotic events. MPF also initiates degradation of its cyclin component, terminating the M phase. The M phase will not begin again until sufficient cyclin is produced during the next S and G_2 phases. The signal to pass the M phase checkpoint is not activated until all chromosomes are attached to kinetochore fibers and are aligned at the metaphase plate. Only then will sister chromatid separation occur.

Test Your Understanding
1. b   **2.** a   **3.** c   **4.** c   **5.** a   **6.** b   **7.** a   **8.** d
9. See Figure 12.7 for a description of major events.

Prometaphase   Prophase   Telophase

Metaphase   Anaphase

Only one cell is indicated for each stage, but other correct answers are also present in this micrograph.

10.

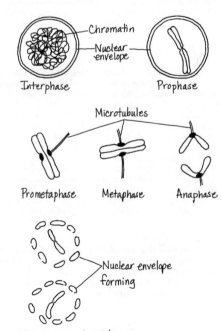

Chromatin

Nuclear envelope

Interphase   Prophase

Microtubules

Prometaphase   Metaphase   Anaphase

Nuclear envelope forming

Telophase and cytokinesis

Chapter 13

Figure Questions

Figure 13.4 Two sets of chromosomes are present. Three pairs of homologous chromosomes are present. **Figure 13.7**

(A short strand of DNA is shown here for simplicity, but each chromosome or chromatid contains a very long coiled and folded DNA molecule.)

Figure 13.8 If a cell with six chromosomes undergoes two rounds of mitosis, each of the four resulting cells will have six chromosomes, while the four cells resulting from meiosis in Figure 13.8 each have three chromosomes. In mitosis, DNA replication (and thus chromosome duplication) precedes each prophase, ensuring that daughter cells have the same number of chromosomes as the parent cell. In meiosis, in contrast, DNA replication occurs only before prophase I (not prophase II). Thus, in two rounds of mitosis, the chromosomes duplicate twice and divide twice, while in meiosis, the chromosomes duplicate once and divide twice. **Figure 13.10** Yes. Each of the six chromosomes (three per cell) shown in telophase I has one nonrecombinant chromatid and one recombinant chromatid. Therefore, eight possible sets of chromosomes can be generated for the cell on the left and eight for the cell on the right.

Concept Check 13.1

1. Parents pass genes to their offspring; by dictating the production of messenger RNAs (mRNAs), the genes program cells to make specific enzymes and other proteins, whose cumulative action produces an individual's inherited traits. **2.** Such organisms reproduce by mitosis, which generates offspring whose genomes are exact copies of the parent's genome (in the absence of mutation). **3.** She should clone it. Cross-breeding it with another plant would generate offspring that have additional variation, which she no longer desires now that she has obtained her ideal orchid.

Concept Check 13.2

1. Each of the six chromosomes is duplicated, so each contains two DNA double helices. Therefore, there are 12 DNA molecules in the cell. The haploid number, n, is 3. One set is always haploid. **2.** 23; 2. **3.** This organism has the life cycle shown in Figure 13.6c. Therefore, it must be a fungus or a protist, perhaps an alga.

Concept Check 13.3

1. The chromosomes are similar in that each is composed of two sister chromatids, and the individual chromosomes are positioned similarly at the metaphase plate. The chromosomes differ in that in a mitotically dividing cell, sister chromatids of each chromosome are genetically identical, but in a meiotically dividing cell, sister chromatids are genetically distinct because of crossing over in meiosis I. Moreover, the chromosomes in metaphase of mitosis can be a diploid set or a haploid set, but the chromosomes in metaphase of meiosis II always consist of a haploid set. **2.** If crossing over did not occur, the two homologs would not be associated in any way. This might result in incorrect arrangement of homologs during metaphase I and ultimately in formation of gametes with an abnormal number of chromosomes.

Concept Check 13.4

1. Mutations in a gene lead to the different versions (alleles) of that gene. **2.** Without crossing over, independent assortment of chromosomes during meiosis I theoretically can generate 2^n possible haploid gametes, and random fertilization can produce $2^n \times 2^n$ possible diploid zygotes. Because the haploid number (n) of grasshoppers is 23 and that of fruit flies is 4, two grasshoppers would be expected to produce a greater variety of zygotes than would two fruit flies. **3.** If the segments of the maternal and paternal chromatids that undergo crossing over are genetically identical and thus have the same two alleles for every gene, then the recombinant chromosomes will be genetically equivalent to the parental chromosomes. Crossing over contributes to genetic variation only when it involves the rearrangement of different alleles.

Summary of Key Concepts Questions

13.1 Genes program specific traits, and offspring inherit their genes from each parent, accounting for similarities in their appearance to one or the other parent. Humans reproduce sexually, which ensures new combinations of genes (and thus traits) in the offspring. Consequently, the offspring are not clones of their parents (which would be the case if humans reproduced asexually). **13.2** Animals and plants both reproduce sexually, alternating meiosis with fertilization. Both have haploid gametes that unite to form a diploid zygote, which then goes on to divide mitotically, forming a diploid multicellular organism. In animals, haploid cells become gametes and don't undergo mitosis, while in plants, the haploid cells resulting from meiosis undergo mitosis to form a haploid multicellular organism, the gametophyte. This organism then goes on to generate haploid gametes. (In plants such as trees, the gametophyte is quite reduced in size and not obvious to the casual observer.) **13.3** At the end of meiosis I, the two members of a homologous pair end up in different cells, so they cannot pair up and undergo crossing over. **13.4** First, during independent assortment in metaphase I, each pair of homologous chromosomes lines up independent of each other pair at the metaphase plate, so a daughter cell of meiosis I randomly inherits either a maternal or paternal chromosome. Second, due to crossing over, each chromosome is not exclusively maternal or paternal, but includes regions at the ends of the chromatid from a nonsister chromatid (a chromatid of the other homolog). (The nonsister segment can also be in an internal region of the chromatid if a second crossover occurs beyond the first one before the end of the chromatid.) This provides much additional diversity in the form of new combinations of alleles. Third, random fertilization ensures even more variation, since any sperm of a large number containing many possible genetic combinations can fertilize any egg of a similarly large number of possible combinations.

Test Your Understanding

1. a **2.** b **3.** a **4.** d **5.** c
6. (a)

(b) A haploid set is made up of one long, one medium, and one short chromosome. For example, the chromosomes of one color make up a haploid set. (In cases where crossovers have occurred, a haploid set of one color may include segments of chromatids of the other color.) All red and blue chromosomes together make up a diploid set. (c) Metaphase I **7.** This cell must be undergoing meiosis because homologous chromosomes are associated with each other at the metaphase plate; this does not occur in mitosis.

Chapter 14

Figure Questions

Figure 14.3 All offspring would have purple flowers. (The ratio would be 1 purple : 0 white.) The P generation plants are true-breeding, so mating two purple-flowered plants produces the same result as self-pollination: All the offspring have the same trait.

Figure 14.8

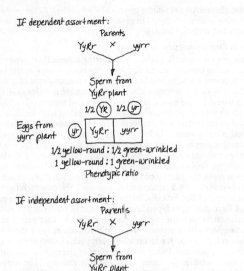

If dependent assortment:

Parents

YyRr × yyrr

Sperm from YyRr plant

1/2 YR   1/2 yr

Eggs from yyrr plant   yr | YyRr | yyrr |

1/2 yellow-round : 1/2 green-wrinkled
1 yellow-round : 1 green-wrinkled
Phenotypic ratio

If independent assortment:

Parents

YyRr × yyrr

Sperm from YyRr plant

Eggs from yyrr plant   1/4 YR 1/4 Yr 1/4 yR 1/4 yr

yr | YyRr | Yyrr | yyRr | yyrr |

1/4 yellow-round : 1/4 yellow-wrinkled :
1/4 green-round : 1/4 green-wrinkled
1 yellow-round : 1 yellow-wrinkled : 1 green-round : 1 green-wrinkled
Phenotypic ratio

Yes, this cross would also have allowed Mendel to make different predictions for the two hypotheses, thereby allowing him to distinguish the correct one. **Figure 14.10** Your classmate would probably point out that the F₁ generation hybrids show an intermediate phenotype between those of the homozygous parents, which supports the blending hypothesis. You could respond that crossing the F₁ hybrids results in the reappearance of the white phenotype, rather than identical pink offspring, which fails to support the idea of traits blending during inheritance. **Figure 14.11** Both the I^A and I^B alleles are dominant to the i allele, which results in no attached carbohydrate. The I^A and I^B alleles are codominant; both are expressed in the phenotype of I^AI^B heterozygotes, who have type AB blood. **Figure 14.12** In this cross the final "3" and "1" of a standard cross are lumped together as a single phenotype. This occurs because in dogs that are ee, no pigment is deposited, thus the three dogs that have a B in their genotype (normally black) can no longer be distinguished from the dog who is bb (normally brown). **Figure 14.16** In the Punnett square, two of the three individuals with normal coloration are carriers, so the probability is ⅔. (Note that you must take into account everything you know when you calculate probability: You know she is not aa, so there are only three possible genotypes to consider.)

Concept Check 14.1

1. According to the law of independent assortment, 25 plants (¹⁄₁₆ of the offspring) are predicted to be aatt, or recessive for both characters. The actual result is likely to differ slightly from this value.

Parents

AaTt × AaTt

Sperm from AaTt plant

AT   At   aT   at

Eggs from AaTt plant

AT | AATT | AATt | AaTT | AaTt |
At | AATt | AAtt | AaTt | Aatt |
aT | AaTT | AaTt | aaTT | aaTt |
at | AaTt | Aatt | aaTt | aatt |

2. The plant could make eight different gametes (YRI, YRi, YrI, Yri, yRI, yRi, yrI, and yri). To fit all the possible gametes in a self-pollination, a Punnett square would need 8 rows and 8 columns. It would have spaces for the 64 possible unions of gametes in the offspring. **3.** Self-pollination is sexual reproduction because meiosis is involved in forming gametes, which unite during fertilization. As a result, the offspring in self-pollination are genetically different from the parent. (As mentioned in the footnote near the beginning of Concept 14.1, we have simplified the explanation in referring to the single pea plant as a parent. Technically, the gametophytes in the flower are the two "parents.")

Concept Check 14.2

1. ½ homozygous dominant (AA), 0 homozygous recessive (aa), and ½ heterozygous (Aa) **2.** ¼ BBDD; ¼ BbDD; ¼ BBDd; ¼ BbDd **3.** The genotypes that fulfill this condition are ppyyIi, ppYyii, Ppyyii, ppYYii, and ppyyii. Use the multiplication rule to find the probability of getting each genotype, and then use the addition rule to find the overall probability of meeting the conditions of this problem:

ppyy Ii   ½ (probability of pp) × ¼ (yy) × ½ (Ii) = 1/16
ppYy ii   ½ (pp) × ½ (Yy) × ½ (ii) = 2/16
Ppyy ii   ½ (Pp) × ¼ (yy) × ½ (ii) = 1/16
ppYY ii   ½ (pp) × ¼ (YY) × ½ (ii) = 1/16
ppyy ii   ½ (pp) × ¼ (yy) × ½ (ii) = 1/16

Fraction predicted to have at least two recessive traits = 6/16 or 3/8

Concept Check 14.3

1. Incomplete dominance describes the relationship between two alleles of a single gene, whereas epistasis relates to the genetic relationship between two genes (and the respective alleles of each). **2.** Half of the children would be expected to have type A blood and half type B blood. **3.** The black and white alleles are incompletely dominant, with heterozygotes being gray in color. A cross between a gray rooster and a black hen should yield approximately equal numbers of gray and black offspring.

Concept Check 14.4

1. ⅑ (Since cystic fibrosis is caused by a recessive allele, Beth and Tom's siblings who have CF must be homozygous recessive. Therefore, each parent must be a carrier of the recessive allele. Since neither Beth nor Tom has CF, this means they each have a ⅔ chance of being a carrier. If they are both carriers, there is a ¼ chance that they will have a child with CF. ⅔ × ⅔ × ¼ = ⅑); 0 (Both Beth and Tom would have to be carriers to produce a child with the disease.) **2.** In normal hemoglobin, the sixth amino acid is glutamic acid (Glu), which is acidic (has a negative charge on its side chain). In sickle-cell hemoglobin, Glu is replaced by valine (Val), which is a nonpolar amino acid, very different from Glu. The primary structure of a protein (its amino acid sequence) ultimately determines the shape of the protein and thus its function. The substitution of Val for Glu enables the hemoglobin molecules to interact with each other and form long fibers, leading to the protein's deficient function and the deformation of the red blood cell. **3.** Joan's genotype is Dd. Because the allele for polydactyly (D) is dominant to the allele for five digits per appendage (d), the trait is expressed in people with either the DD or Dd genotype. But because Joan's father does not have polydactyly, his genotype must be dd, which means that Joan inherited a d allele from him. Therefore Joan, who does have the trait, must be heterozygous. **4.** In the monohybrid cross involving flower color, the ratio is 3.15 purple : 1 white, while in the human family in the pedigree, the ratio in the third generation is 1 free : 1 attached earlobe. The difference is due to the small sample size (two offspring) in the human family. If the second-generation couple in this pedigree were able to have 929 offspring as in the pea plant cross, the ratio would likely be closer to 3:1. (Note that none of the pea plant crosses in Table 14.1 yielded exactly a 3:1 ratio.)

Summary of Key Concepts Questions

14.1 Alternative versions of genes, called alleles, are passed from parent to offspring during sexual reproduction. In a cross between purple- and white-flowered homozygous parents, the F₁ offspring are all heterozygous, each inheriting a purple allele from one parent and a white allele from the other. Because the purple allele is dominant, it determines the phenotype of the F₁ offspring to be purple, and the expression of the white allele is masked. Only in the F₂ generation is it possible for a white allele to exist in a homozygous state, which causes the white trait to be expressed.

14.2

Sperm
½ Y   ½ y

Eggs
½ Y | YY | Yy |
½ y | Yy | yy |

¾ yellow
¼ green

Sperm
½ R   ½ r

Eggs
½ R | RR | Rr |
½ r | Rr | rr |

¾ round
¼ wrinkled

¾ yellow × ¾ round = 9/16 yellow-round
¾ yellow × ¼ wrinkled = 3/16 yellow-wrinkled
¼ green × ¾ round = 3/16 green-round
¼ green × ¼ wrinkled = 1/16 green-wrinkled

= 9 yellow-round : 3 yellow-wrinkled : 3 green-round : 1 green-wrinkled

14.3 The ABO blood group is an example of multiple alleles because this single gene has more than two alleles (I^A, I^B, and i). Two of the alleles, I^A and I^B, exhibit codominance, since both carbohydrates (A and B) are present when these two alleles exist together in a genotype. I^A and I^B each exhibit complete dominance over the i allele. This situation is not an example of incomplete dominance because each allele affects the phenotype in a distinguishable way, so the result is not intermediate between the two phenotypes. Because this situation involves a single gene, it is not an example of epistasis or polygenic inheritance. **14.4** The chance of the fourth child having cystic fibrosis is ¼, as it was for each of the other children, because each birth is an independent event. We already know both parents are carriers, so whether their first three children are carriers or not has no bearing on the probability that their next child will have the disease. The parents' genotypes provide the only relevant information.

Test Your Understanding

1.

9 green-inflated : 3 green-constricted : 3 yellow-inflated : 1 yellow-constricted

2. Man $I^A i$; woman $I^B i$; child ii. Genotypes for future children are predicted to be $\frac{1}{4}\,I^A I^B$, $\frac{1}{4}\,I^A i$, $\frac{1}{4}\,I^B i$, $\frac{1}{4}\,ii$. **3.** $\frac{1}{2}$ **4.** A cross of $Ii \times ii$ would yield offspring with a genotypic ratio of 1 Ii : 1 ii (2:2 is an equivalent answer) and a phenotypic ratio of 1 inflated : 1 constricted (2:2 is equivalent).

Parents

$Ii \times ii$

Genotypic ratio 1 Ii : 1 ii (2:2 is equivalent)

Phenotypic ratio 1 inflated : 1 constricted (2:2 is equivalent)

5. (a) $\frac{1}{64}$; (b) $\frac{1}{64}$; (c) $\frac{1}{8}$; (d) $\frac{1}{32}$ **6.** (a) $\frac{3}{4} \times \frac{3}{4} \times \frac{3}{4} = \frac{27}{64}$; (b) $1 - \frac{27}{64} = \frac{37}{64}$; (c) $\frac{1}{4} \times \frac{1}{4} \times \frac{1}{4} = \frac{1}{64}$; (d) $1 - \frac{1}{64} = \frac{63}{64}$ **7.** (a) $\frac{1}{256}$; (b) $\frac{1}{16}$; (c) $\frac{1}{256}$; (d) $\frac{1}{64}$; (e) $\frac{1}{128}$ **8.** (a) 1; (b) $\frac{1}{32}$; (c) $\frac{1}{8}$; (d) $\frac{1}{2}$ **9.** $\frac{1}{9}$ **10.** Matings of the original mutant cat with true-breeding noncurl cats will produce both curl and noncurl F_1 offspring if the curl allele is dominant, but only noncurl offspring if the curl allele is recessive. You would obtain some true-breeding offspring homozygous for the curl allele from matings between the F_1 cats resulting from the original curl $\times$ noncurl crosses whether the curl trait is dominant or recessive. You know that cats are true-breeding when curl $\times$ curl matings produce only curl offspring. As it turns out, the allele that causes curled ears is dominant. **11.** 25%, or $\frac{1}{4}$, will be cross-eyed; all (100%) of the cross-eyed offspring will also be white. **12.** The dominant allele I is epistatic to the P/p locus, and thus the genotypic ratio for the F_1 generation will be 9 I–P– (colorless) : 3 I–pp (colorless) : 3 iiP– (purple) : 1 $iipp$ (red). Overall, the phenotypic ratio is 12 colorless : 3 purple : 1 red. **13.** Recessive. All affected individuals (Arlene, Tom, Wilma, and Carla) are homozygous recessive aa. George is Aa, since some of his children with Arlene are affected. Sam, Ann, Daniel, and Alan are each Aa, since they are all unaffected children with one affected parent. Michael also is Aa, since he has an affected child (Carla) with his heterozygous wife Ann. Sandra, Tina, and Christopher can each have either the AA or Aa genotype. **14.** $\frac{1}{6}$

Chapter 15

Figure Questions

Figure 15.2 The ratio would be 1 yellow-round : 1 green-round : 1 yellow-wrinkled : 1 green-wrinkled. **Figure 15.4** About $\frac{3}{4}$ of the F_2 offspring would have red eyes and about $\frac{1}{4}$ would have white eyes. About half of the white-eyed flies would be female and half would be male; similarly, about half of the red-eyed flies would be female and half would be male. (Note that the homologs with the eye color alleles would be the same shape in the Punnett square, and each offspring would inherit two alleles. The sex of the flies would be determined separately by inheritance of the sex chromosomes. Thus your Punnett square would have four possible combinations in sperm and four in eggs; it would be 16 squares altogether.) **Figure 15.7** All the males would be color-blind, and all the females would be carriers. (Another way to say this is that $\frac{1}{2}$ the offspring would be color-blind males, and $\frac{1}{2}$ the offspring would be carrier females.) **Figure 15.9** The two largest classes would still be the parental-type offspring (offspring with the phenotypes of the true-breeding P generation flies), but now they would be gray-vestigial

and black-normal because those were the specific allele combinations in the P generation. **Figure 15.10** The two chromosomes below, left, are like the two chromosomes inherited by the F_1 female, one from each P generation fly. They are passed by the F_1 female intact to the offspring and thus could be called "parental" chromosomes. The other two chromosomes result from crossing over during meiosis in the F_1 female. Because they have combinations of alleles not seen in either of the F_1 female's chromosomes, they can be called "recombinant" chromosomes. (Note that in this example, the alleles on the recombinant chromosomes, b^+vg^+ and $b\,vg$, are the allele combinations that were on the parental chromosomes in the cross shown in Figures 15.9 and 15.10. The basis for calling them parental chromosomes is that they have the combination of alleles that was present on the P generation chromosomes.)

Parental chromosomes   Recombinant chromosomes

Concept Check 15.1

1. The law of segregation relates to the inheritance of alleles for a single character. The law of independent assortment of alleles relates to the inheritance of alleles for two characters. **2.** The physical basis for the law of segregation is the separation of homologs in anaphase I. The physical basis for the law of independent assortment is the alternative arrangements of different homologous chromosome pairs in metaphase I. **3.** To show the mutant phenotype, a male needs to possess only one mutant allele. If this gene had been on a pair of autosomes, *two* mutant alleles would have had to be present for an individual to show the recessive mutant phenotype, a much less probable situation.

Concept Check 15.2

1. Because the gene for this eye-color character is located on the X chromosome, all female offspring will be red-eyed and heterozygous ($X^{w^+}X^w$); all male offspring will inherit a Y chromosome from the father and be white-eyed (X^wY). (Another way to say this is that $\frac{1}{2}$ the offspring will be red-eyed, heterozygous [carrier] females, and $\frac{1}{2}$ will be white-eyed males.) **2.** $\frac{1}{4}$ ($\frac{1}{2}$ chance that the child will inherit a Y chromosome from the father and be male $\times$ $\frac{1}{2}$ chance that he will inherit the X carrying the disease allele from his mother). If the child is a boy, there is a $\frac{1}{2}$ chance he will have the disease; a female would have zero chance (but $\frac{1}{2}$ chance of being a carrier). **3.** With a disorder caused by a dominant allele, there is no such thing as a "carrier," since those with the allele have the disorder. Because the allele is dominant, the females lose any "advantage" in having two X chromosomes, since one disorder-associated allele is sufficient to result in the disorder. All fathers who have the dominant allele will pass it along to *all* their daughters, who will also have the disorder. A mother who has the allele (and thus the disorder) will pass it to half of her sons and half of her daughters.

Concept Check 15.3

1. Crossing over during meiosis I in the heterozygous parent produces some gametes with recombinant genotypes for the two genes. Offspring with a recombinant phenotype arise from fertilization of the recombinant gametes by homozygous recessive gametes from the double-mutant parent. **2.** In each case, the alleles contributed by the female parent (in the egg) determine the phenotype of the offspring because the male in this cross contributes only recessive alleles. Thus, identifying the phenotype of the offspring tells you what alleles were in the egg. **3.** No. The order could be A-C-B or C-A-B. To determine which possibility is correct, you need to know the recombination frequency between B and C.

Concept Check 15.4

1. In meiosis, a combined 14-21 chromosome will behave as one chromosome. If a gamete receives the combined 14-21 chromosome and a normal copy of chromosome 21, trisomy 21 will result when this gamete combines with a normal gamete during fertilization. **2.** No. The child can be either $I^A I^A i$ or $I^A ii$. A sperm of genotype $I^A I^A$ could result from nondisjunction in the father during meiosis II, while an egg with the genotype ii could result from nondisjunction in the mother during either meiosis I or meiosis II. **3.** Activation of this gene could lead to the production of too much of this kinase. If the kinase is involved in a signaling pathway that triggers cell division, too much of it could trigger unrestricted cell division, which in turn could contribute to the development of a cancer (in this case, a cancer of one type of white blood cell).

Concept Check 15.5

1. Inactivation of an X chromosome in females and genomic imprinting. Because of X inactivation, the effective dose of genes on the X chromosome is the same in males and females. As a result of genomic imprinting, only one allele of certain genes is phenotypically expressed. **2.** The genes for leaf coloration are located in plastids within the cytoplasm. Normally, only the maternal parent transmits plastid genes to offspring. Since variegated offspring are produced only when the female parent is of the B variety, we can conclude that variety B contains both the wild-type and mutant alleles of pigment genes, producing variegated leaves. (Variety A must contain only the wild-type allele of pigment genes.) **3.** Each cell contains numerous mitochondria, and in affected individuals, most cells contain a variable mixture of normal and mutant mitochondria. The normal mitochondria carry out enough cellular respiration for survival. (The situation is similar for chloroplasts.)

Summary of Key Concepts Questions

15.1 Because the sex chromosomes are different from each other and because they determine the sex of the offspring, Morgan could use the sex of the offspring as a phenotypic characteristic to follow the parental chromosomes. (He could also have followed them under a microscope, as the X and Y chromosomes look different.) At the same time, he could record eye color to follow the eye-color alleles. **15.2** Males have only one X chromosome, along with a Y chromosome, while females have two X chromosomes. The Y chromosome has very few genes on it, while the X has about 1,000. When a recessive X-linked allele that causes a disorder is inherited by a male on the X from his mother, there isn't a second allele present on the Y (males are hemizygous), so the male has the disorder. Because females have two X chromosomes, they must inherit two recessive alleles in order to have the disorder, a rarer occurrence. **15.3** Crossing over results in new combinations of alleles. Crossing over is a random occurrence, and the more distance there is between two genes, the more chances there are for crossing over to occur, leading to a new allele combination. **15.4** In inversions and reciprocal translocations, the same genetic material is present in the same relative amount but just organized differently. In aneuploidy, duplications, deletions, and nonreciprocal translocations, the balance of genetic material is upset, as large segments are either missing or present in more than one copy. Apparently, this type of imbalance is very damaging to the organism. (Although it isn't lethal in the developing embryo, the reciprocal translocation that produces the Philadelphia chromosome can lead to a serious condition, cancer, by altering the expression of important genes.) **15.5** In these cases, the sex of the parent contributing an allele affects the inheritance pattern. For imprinted genes, either the paternal or the maternal allele is expressed, depending on the imprint. For mitochondrial and chloroplast genes, only the maternal contribution will affect offspring phenotype because the offspring inherit these organelles from the mother, via the egg cytoplasm.

Test Your Understanding

1. 0; ½; $\frac{1}{16}$ **2.** Recessive; if the disorder were dominant, it would affect at least one parent of a child born with the disorder. The disorder's inheritance is sex-linked because it is seen only in boys. For a girl to have the disorder, she would have to inherit recessive alleles from *both* parents. This would be very rare, since males with the recessive allele on their X chromosome die in their early teens. **3.** 17%; yes, it is consistent. In Figure 15.9, the recombination frequency was also 17%. (You'd expect this to be the case since these are the very same two genes, and their distance from each other wouldn't change from one experiment to another.) **4.** Between *T* and *A*, 12%; between *A* and *S*, 5% **5.** Between *T* and *S*, 18%; sequence of genes is *T–A–S* **6.** 6%; wild-type heterozygous for normal wings and red eyes × recessive homozygous for vestigial wings and purple eyes **7.** Fifty percent of the offspring will show phenotypes resulting from crossovers. These results would be the same as those from a cross where *A* and *B* were *not* on the same chromosome, and you would interpret the results to mean that the genes are unlinked. (Further crosses involving other genes on the same chromosome would reveal the genetic linkage and map distances.) **8.** 450 each of blue-oval and white-round (parentals) and 50 each of blue-round and white-oval (recombinants) **9.** About one-third of the distance from the vestigial-wing locus to the brown-eye locus **10.** Because bananas are triploid, homologous pairs cannot line up during meiosis. Therefore, it is not possible to generate gametes that can fuse to produce a zygote with the triploid number of chromosomes. **12.** (a) For each pair of genes, you had to generate an F_1 dihybrid fly; let's use the *A* and *B* genes as an example. You obtained homozygous parental flies, either the first with dominant alleles of the two genes (*AABB*) and the second with recessive alleles (*aabb*), or the first with dominant alleles of gene *A* and recessive alleles of gene *B* (*AAbb*) and the second with recessive alleles of gene *A* and dominant alleles of gene *B* (*aaBB*). Breeding either of these pairs of P generation flies gave you an F_1 dihybrid, which you then testcrossed with a doubly homozygous recessive fly (*aabb*). You classed the offspring as parental or recombinant, based on the genotypes of the P generation parents (either of the two pairs described above). You added up the number of recombinant types and then divided by the total number of offspring. This gave you the recombination percentage (in this case, 8%), which you can translate into map units (8 map units) to construct your map.

(b)

Chapter 16

Figure Questions

Figure 16.2 The living S cells found in the blood sample were able to reproduce to yield more S cells, indicating that the S trait is a permanent, heritable change, rather than just a one-time use of the dead S cells' capsules. **Figure 16.4** The radioactivity would have been found in the pellet when proteins were labeled (batch 1) because proteins would have had to enter the bacterial cells to program them with genetic instructions. It's hard for us to imagine now, but the DNA might have played a structural role that allowed some of the proteins to be injected while it remained outside the bacterial cell (thus no radioactivity in the pellet in batch 2). **Figure 16.11** The tube from the first replication would look the same, with a middle band of hybrid ^{15}N-^{14}N DNA, but the second tube would not have the upper band of two light blue strands. Instead, it would have a bottom band of two dark blue strands, like the bottom band in the result predicted after one replication

in the conservative model. **Figure 16.12** In the bubble at the top in (b), arrows should be drawn pointing left and right to indicate the two replication forks. **Figure 16.14** Looking at any of the DNA strands, we see that one end is called the 5′ end and the other the 3′ end. If we proceed from the 5′ end to the 3′ end on the left-most strand, for example, we list the components in this order: phosphate group → 5′ C of the sugar → 3′ C → phosphate → 5′ C → 3′ C. Going in the opposite direction on the same strand, the components proceed in the reverse order: 3′ C → 5′ C → phosphate. Thus, the two directions are distinguishable, which is what we mean when we say that the strands have directionality. (Review Figure 16.5 if necessary.)

Figure 16.17

Figure 16.18

Figure 16.23 The two members of a homologous pair (which would be the same color) would be associated tightly together at the metaphase plate. In metaphase of mitosis, however, each chromosome would be lined up individually, so the two chromosomes of the same color would be in different places at the metaphase plate.

Concept Check 16.1

1. You can't tell which end is the 5′ end. You need to know which end has a phosphate group on the 5′ carbon (the 5′ end) or which end has an —OH group on the 3′ carbon (the 3′ end). **2.** He expected that the mouse injected with the mixture of heat-killed S cells and living R cells would survive, since neither type of cell alone would kill the mouse.

Concept Check 16.2

1. Complementary base pairing ensures that the two daughter molecules are exact copies of the parental molecule. When the two strands of the parental molecule separate, each serves as a template on which nucleotides are arranged, by the base-pairing rules, into new complementary strands. **2.** DNA pol III covalently adds nucleotides to new DNA strands and proofreads each added nucleotide for correct base pairing. **3.** In the cell cycle, DNA synthesis occurs during the S phase, between the G_1 and G_2 phases of interphase. DNA replication is therefore complete before the mitotic phase begins. **4.** Synthesis of the leading strand is initiated by an RNA primer, which must be removed and replaced with DNA, a task that could not be performed if the cell's DNA pol I were nonfunctional. In the overview box in Figure 16.17, just to the left of the top origin of replication, a functional DNA pol I would replace the RNA primer of the leading strand (shown in red) with DNA nucleotides (blue). The nucleotides would be added onto the 3′ end of the final Okazaki fragment of the upper lagging strand (the right half of the replication bubble).

Concept Check 16.3

1. A nucleosome is made up of eight histone proteins, two each of four different types, around which DNA is wound. Linker DNA runs from one nucleosome to the next. **2.** Euchromatin is chromatin that becomes less compacted during interphase and is accessible to the cellular machinery responsible for gene activity. Heterochromatin, on the other hand, remains quite condensed during interphase and contains genes that are largely inaccessible to this machinery.   **3.** The nuclear lamina is a netlike array of protein filaments that provides mechanical support just inside the nuclear envelope and thus maintains the shape of the nucleus. Considerable evidence also supports the existence of a nuclear matrix, a framework of protein fibers extending throughout the nuclear interior.

Summary of Key Concepts Questions

16.1 Each strand in the double helix has polarity; the end with a phosphate group on the 5′ carbon of the sugar is called the 5′ end, and the end with an —OH group on the 3′ carbon of the sugar is called the 3′ end. The two strands run in opposite directions, one running 5′ → 3′ and the other alongside it running 3′ → 5′. Thus, each end of the molecule has both a 5′ and a 3′ end. This arrangement is called "antiparallel." If the strands were parallel, they would both run 5′ → 3′ in the same direction, so an end of the molecule would have either two 5′ ends or two 3′ ends.   **16.2** On both the leading and lagging strands, DNA polymerase adds onto the 3′ end of an RNA primer synthesized by primase, synthesizing DNA in the 5′ → 3′ direction. Because the parental strands are antiparallel, however, only on the leading strand does synthesis proceed continuously into the replication fork. The lagging strand is synthesized bit by bit in the direction away from the fork as a series of shorter Okazaki fragments, which are later joined together by DNA ligase. Each fragment is initiated by synthesis of an RNA primer by primase as soon as a given stretch of single-stranded template strand is opened up. Although both strands are synthesized at the same rate, synthesis of the lagging strand is delayed because initiation of each fragment begins only when sufficient template strand is available.   **16.3** Most of the chromatin in an interphase nucleus is fairly uncondensed. Much is present as the 30-nm fiber, with some in the form of the 10-nm fiber and some as looped domains of the 30-nm fiber. (These different levels of chromatin packing may reflect differences in gene expression occurring in these regions.) Also, a small percentage of the chromatin, such as that at the centromeres and telomeres, is highly condensed heterochromatin.

Test Your Understanding

1. c   **2.** c   **3.** b   **4.** d   **5.** a   **6.** d   **7.** b   **8.** a
9. Like histones, the *E. coli* proteins would be expected to contain many basic (positively charged) amino acids, such as lysine and arginine, which can form weak bonds with the negatively charged phosphate groups on the sugar-phosphate backbone of the DNA molecule.

11.

Chapter 17

Figure Questions

Figure 17.2 The previously presumed pathway would have been wrong. The new results would support this pathway: precursor → citrulline → ornithine → arginine. They would also indicate that class I mutants have a defect in the second step and class II mutants have a defect in the first step.   **Figure 17.4** The mRNA sequence (5′-UGGUUUGGCUCA-3′) is the same as the nontemplate DNA strand sequence (5′-TGGTTTGGCTCA-3′), except there is a U in the mRNA wherever there is a T in the DNA.   **Figure 17.7** The processes are similar in that polymerases form polynucleotides complementary to an antiparallel DNA template strand. In replication, however, both strands act as templates, whereas in transcription, only one DNA strand acts as a template.   **Figure 17.8** The RNA polymerase would bind directly to the promoter, rather than depending on the previous binding of other factors.   **Figure 17.21** It would be packaged in a vesicle, transported to the Golgi apparatus for further processing, and then transported via a vesicle to the plasma membrane. The vesicle would fuse with the membrane, releasing the protein outside the cell.   **Figure 17.23** The mRNA farthest to the right (the longest one) started transcription first. The ribosome at the top, closest to the DNA, started translating first and thus has the longest polypeptide.

Concept Check 17.1

1. Recessive   **2.** A polypeptide made up of 10 Gly (glycine) amino acids
3.

Template sequence
(from problem):   3′-TTCAGTCGT-5′

Nontemplate sequence: 5′-AAGTCAGCA-3′

mRNA sequence: 5′-AAGUCAGCA-3′

The nontemplate and mRNA nucleotide sequences are the same except that there is a T in the nontemplate strand of DNA wherever there is a U in the mRNA.
4.

"Template sequence" (from nontemplate sequence in problem, written 3′ → 5′):   3′-ACGACTGAA-5′

mRNA sequence: 5′-UGCUGACUU-3′

Translated: Cys-STOP-Leu

(Remember that the mRNA is antiparallel to the DNA strand.) A protein translated from the nontemplate sequence would have a completely different amino acid sequence and would most likely be nonfunctional. (It would also be shorter because of the stop signal shown in the mRNA sequence above—and possibly others earlier in the mRNA sequence.)

Concept Check 17.2

1. A promoter is the region of DNA to which RNA polymerase binds to begin transcription. It is at the upstream end of the gene (transcription unit).   **2.** In a bacterial cell, part of the RNA polymerase recognizes the gene's promoter and binds to it. In a eukaryotic cell, transcription factors mediate the binding of RNA polymerase to the promoter. In both cases, sequences in the promoter bind precisely to the RNA polymerase, so the enzyme is in the right location and orientation.   **3.** The transcription factor that recognizes the TATA sequence would be unable to bind, so RNA polymerase could not bind and transcription of that gene probably would not occur.

Concept Check 17.3

1. Due to alternative splicing of exons, each gene can result in multiple different mRNAs and can thus direct synthesis of multiple different proteins.   **2.** In watching a show recorded with a DVR, you watch segments of the show itself (exons) and fast-forward through the commercials, which are thus like introns.   **3.** Once the mRNA has exited the nucleus, the cap prevents it from being degraded by hydrolytic enzymes and facilitates its attachment to ribosomes. If the cap were removed from all mRNAs, the cell would no longer be able to synthesize any proteins and would probably die.

Concept Check 17.4

1. First, each aminoacyl-tRNA synthetase specifically recognizes a single amino acid and attaches it only to an appropriate tRNA. Second, a tRNA charged with its specific amino acid binds only to an mRNA codon for that amino acid.   **2.** The structure and function of the ribosome seem to depend more on the rRNAs than on the ribosomal proteins. Because it is single-stranded, an RNA molecule can hydrogen-bond with itself and with other RNA molecules. RNA molecules make up the interface between the two ribosomal subunits, so presumably RNA-RNA binding helps hold the ribosome together. The binding site for mRNA in the ribosome includes rRNA that can bind the mRNA. Also, complementary hydrogen bonding within an RNA molecule allows it to assume a particular three-dimensional shape and, along with the RNA's functional groups, enables rRNA to catalyze peptide bond formation during translation.   **3.** A signal peptide on the leading end of the polypeptide being synthesized is recognized by a signal-recognition particle that brings the ribosome to the ER membrane. There the ribosome attaches and continues to synthesize the polypeptide, depositing it in the ER lumen.   **4.** Because of wobble, the tRNA could bind to either 5′-GCA-3′ or 5′-GCG-3′, both of which code for alanine (Ala). Alanine would be attached to the tRNA.

5. When one ribosome terminates translation and dissociates, the two subunits would be very close to the cap. This could facilitate their rebinding and initiating synthesis of a new polypeptide, thus increasing the efficiency of translation.

Concept Check 17.5

1. In the mRNA, the reading frame downstream from the deletion is shifted, leading to a long string of incorrect amino acids in the polypeptide, and in most cases, a stop codon will arise, leading to premature termination. The polypeptide will most likely be nonfunctional.   **2.** Heterozygous individuals, said to have sickle-cell trait, have a copy each of the wild-type allele and the sickle-cell allele. Both alleles will be expressed, so these individuals will have both normal and sickle-cell hemoglobin molecules. Apparently, having a mix of the two forms of β-globin has no effect under most conditions, but during prolonged periods of low blood oxygen (such as at higher altitudes), these individuals can show some signs of sickle-cell disease.

3.

Normal DNA sequence
(template strand is on top):
  3′–TACTTGTCCGATATC–5′
  5′–ATGAACAGGCTATAG–3′

mRNA sequence: 5′–AUGAACAGGCUAUAG–3′

Amino acid sequence: Met-Asn-Arg-Leu-STOP

Mutated DNA sequence
(template strand is on top):
  3′–TACTTGTCCAATATC–5′
  5′–ATGAACAGGTTATAG–3′

mRNA sequence: 5′–AUGAACAGGUUAUAG–3′

Amino acid sequence: Met-Asn-Arg-Leu-STOP

No effect: The amino acid sequence is Met-Asn-Arg-Leu both before and after the mutation because the mRNA codons 5′-CUA-3′ and 5′-UUA-3′ both code for Leu. (The fifth codon is a stop codon.)

Summary of Key Concepts Questions

17.1 A gene contains genetic information in the form of a nucleotide sequence. The gene is first transcribed into an RNA molecule, and a messenger RNA molecule is ultimately translated into a polypeptide. The polypeptide makes up part or all of a protein, which performs a function in the cell and contributes to the phenotype of the organism. **17.2** Both bacterial and eukaryotic genes have promoters, regions where RNA polymerase ultimately binds and begins transcription. In bacteria, RNA polymerase binds directly to the promoter; in eukaryotes, transcription factors bind first to the promoter, and then RNA polymerase binds to the transcription factors and promoter together. **17.3** Both the 5′ cap and the poly-A tail help the mRNA exit from the nucleus and then, in the cytoplasm, help ensure mRNA stability and allow it to bind to ribosomes. **17.4** tRNAs function as translators between the nucleotide-based language of mRNA and the amino-acid-based language of polypeptides. A tRNA carries a specific amino acid, and the anticodon on the tRNA is complementary to the codon on the mRNA that codes for that amino acid. In the ribosome, the tRNA binds to the A site. Then, the polypeptide being synthesized (currently on the tRNA in the P site) is joined to the new amino acid, which becomes the new (C-terminal) end of the polypeptide. Next, the tRNA in the A site moves to the P site. When the polypeptide is transferred to the new tRNA, thus adding the new amino acid, the now empty tRNA moves from the P site to the E site, where it exits the ribosome. **17.5** When a nucleotide base is altered chemically, its base-pairing characteristics may be changed. When that happens, an incorrect nucleotide is likely to be incorporated into the complementary strand during the next replication of the DNA, and successive rounds of replication will perpetuate the mutation. Once the gene is transcribed, the mutated codon may code for a different amino acid that inhibits or changes the function of a protein. If the chemical change in the base is detected and repaired by the DNA repair system before the next replication, no mutation will result.

Test Your Understanding

1. b **2.** c **3.** a **4.** a **5.** b **6.** c **7.** d
8. No, transcription and translation are separated in space and time in a eukaryotic cell, as a result of the eukaryotyic cell's nuclear membrane.

9.

Type of RNA	Functions
Messenger RNA (mRNA)	Carries information specifying amino acid sequences of proteins from DNA to ribosomes
Transfer RNA (tRNA)	Serves as translator molecule in protein synthesis; translates mRNA codons into amino acids
Ribosomal RNA (rRNA)	Plays catalytic (ribozyme) roles and structural roles in ribosomes
Primary transcript	Is a precursor to mRNA, rRNA, or tRNA, before being processed; also, some of the RNA in introns acts as a ribozyme, catalyzing its own splicing
Small RNAs in the ribosome	Plays structural and catalytic roles in spliceosomes, the complexes of protein and RNA that splice pre-mRNA

Chapter 18

Figure Questions

Figure 18.3 As the concentration of tryptophan in the cell falls, eventually there will be none bound to repressor molecules. These will then change into their inactive shapes and dissociate from the operator, allowing transcription of the operon to resume. The enzymes for tryptophan synthesis will be made, and they will again begin to synthesize tryptophan in the cell. **Figure 18.11** In both types of cell, the albumin gene enhancer has the three control elements colored yellow, gray, and red. The sequences in the liver and lens cells would be identical, since the cells are in the same organism. **Figure 18.18** Even if the mutant MyoD protein couldn't activate the *myoD* gene, it could still turn on genes for the other proteins in the pathway (other transcription factors, which would turn on the genes for muscle-specific proteins, for example). Therefore, some differentiation would occur. But unless there were other activators that could compensate for the loss of the MyoD protein's activation of the *myoD* gene, the cell would not be able to maintain its differentiated state. **Figure 18.22** Normal Bicoid protein would be made in the anterior end and compensate for the presence of mutant *bicoid* mRNA put into the egg by the mother. Development should be normal, with a head present. **Figure 18.25** The mutation is likely to be recessive because it is more likely to have an effect if both copies of the gene are mutated and code for nonfunctional proteins. If one normal copy of the gene is present, its product could inhibit the cell cycle. (However, there are also known cases of dominant *p53* mutations.) **Figure 18.27** Cancer is a disease in which cell division occurs without its usual regulation. Cell division can be stimulated by growth factors (see Figure 12.18), which bind to cell-surface receptors (see Figure 11.8). Cancer cells evade these normal controls and can often divide in the absence of growth factors (see Figure 12.19). This suggests that the receptor proteins or some other components in a signaling pathway are abnormal in some way (see, for example, the mutant Ras protein in Figure 18.24) or are expressed at abnormal levels, as seen for the receptors in this figure. Under some circumstances in the mammalian body, steroid hormones such as estrogen and progesterone can also promote cell division. These molecules also use cell-signaling pathways, as described in Chapter 11 (see Figure 11.9). Because signaling receptors are involved in triggering cells to undergo cell division, it is not surprising that altered genes encoding these proteins might play a significant role in the development of cancer. Genes might be altered either through a mutation that changes the function of the protein product or a mutation that causes the gene to be expressed at abnormal levels that disrupt the overall regulation of the signaling pathway.

Concept Check 18.1

1. Binding by the *trp* corepressor (tryptophan) activates the *trp* repressor, shutting off transcription of the *trp* operon; binding by the *lac* inducer (allolactose) inactivates the *lac* repressor, leading to transcription of the *lac* operon. **2.** When glucose is scarce, cAMP is bound to CAP and CAP is bound to the promoter, favoring the binding of RNA polymerase. However, in the absence of lactose, the repressor is bound to the operator, blocking RNA polymerase binding to the promoter. Therefore, the operon genes are not transcribed. **3.** The cell would continuously produce β-galactosidase and the two other enzymes for lactose utilization, even in the absence of lactose, thus wasting cell resources.

Concept Check 18.2

1. Histone acetylation is generally associated with gene expression, while DNA methylation is generally associated with lack of expression. **2.** General transcription factors function in assembling the transcription initiation complex at the promoters for all genes. Specific transcription factors bind to control elements associated with a particular gene and, once bound, either increase (activators) or decrease (repressors) transcription of that gene. **3.** The three genes should have some similar or identical sequences in the control elements of their enhancers. Because of this similarity, the same specific transcription factors in muscle cells could bind to the enhancers of all three genes and stimulate their expression coordinately. **4.** Regulation of translation initiation, degradation of the mRNA, activation of the protein (by chemical modification, for example), and protein degradation

Concept Check 18.3

1. Both miRNAs and siRNAs are small, single-stranded RNAs that associate with a complex of proteins and then can base-pair with mRNAs that have a complementary sequence. This base pairing leads to either degradation of the mRNA or blockage of its translation. In some yeasts, siRNAs associated with proteins in a different complex can bind back to centromeric chromatin, recruiting enzymes that cause condensation of that chromatin into heterochromatin. Both miRNAs and siRNAs are processed from double-stranded RNA precursors, but have subtle variations in the structure of those precursors. **2.** The mRNA would persist and be translated into the cell division-promoting protein, and the cell would probably divide. If the intact miRNA is necessary for inhibition of cell division, then division of this cell might be inappropriate. Uncontrolled cell division could lead to formation of a mass of cells (tumor) that prevents proper functioning of the organism and could contribute to the development of cancer.

Concept Check 18.4

1. Cells undergo differentiation during embryonic development, becoming different from each other. Therefore, the adult organism is made up of many highly specialized cell types. **2.** By binding to a receptor on the receiving cell's surface and triggering a signal transduction pathway, involving intracellular molecules such as second messengers and transcription factors that affect gene expression **3.** Because their products, made and deposited into the egg by the mother, determine the head and tail ends, as well as the back and belly, of the embryo (and eventually the adult fly) **4.** The lower cell is synthesizing signaling molecules because the gene encoding them is activated, meaning that the appropriate specific transcription factors are binding to the gene's enhancer. The genes encoding these specific transcription factors are also being expressed in this cell because the transcriptional activators that can turn them on were expressed in the precursor to this cell. A similar explanation also applies to the cells expressing the receptor proteins. This scenario began with specific cytoplasmic determinants localized in specific regions of the egg. These cytoplasmic determinants were distributed unevenly to daughter cells, resulting in cells going down different developmental pathways.

Concept Check 18.5

1. Apoptosis is signaled by p53 protein when a cell has extensive DNA damage, so apoptosis plays a protective role in eliminating a cell that might contribute to cancer. If mutations in the genes in the apoptotic pathway blocked apoptosis, a cell with such damage could continue to divide and might lead to tumor formation. **2.** When an individual has inherited an oncogene or a mutant allele of a tumor-suppressor gene **3.** A cancer-causing mutation in a proto-oncogene usually makes the gene product overactive, whereas a cancer-causing mutation in a tumor-suppressor gene usually makes the gene product nonfunctional.

Summary of Key Concepts Questions

18.1 A corepressor and an inducer are both small molecules that bind to the repressor protein in an operon, causing the repressor to change shape. In the case of a corepressor (like tryptophan), this shape change allows the repressor to bind to the operator, blocking transcription. In contrast, an inducer causes the repressor to dissociate from the operator, allowing transcription to begin. **18.2** The chromatin must not be tightly condensed because it must be accessible to transcription factors. The appropriate specific transcription factors (activators) must bind to the control elements in the enhancer of the gene, while repressors must not be bound. The DNA must be bent by a bending protein so the activators can contact the mediator proteins and form a complex with general transcription factors at the promoter. Then RNA polymerase must bind and begin transcription. **18.3** miRNAs do not "code" for the amino acids of a protein—they are never translated. Each miRNA associates with a group of proteins to form a complex. Binding of the complex to an mRNA with a complementary sequence causes that mRNA to be degraded or blocks its translation. This is considered gene regulation because it controls the amount of a particular mRNA that can be translated into a functional protein. **18.4** The first process involves cytoplasmic determinants, including mRNAs and proteins, placed into specific locations in the egg by the mother. The cells that are formed from different regions in the egg during early cell divisions will have different proteins in them, which will direct different programs of gene expression. The second process involves the cell in question responding to signaling molecules secreted by neighboring cells. The signaling pathway in the responding cell also leads to a different pattern of gene expression. The coordination of these two processes results in each cell following a unique pathway in the developing embryo. **18.5** The protein product of a proto-oncogene is usually involved in a pathway that stimulates cell division. The protein product of a tumor-suppressor gene is usually involved in a pathway that inhibits cell division.

Test Your Understanding

1. c **2.** a **3.** b **4.** c **5.** c **6.** d **7.** a **8.** c **9.** b **10.** d
11. (a)

The purple, blue, and red activator proteins would be present.
(b)

Only gene 4 would be transcribed.
(c) In nerve cells, the orange, blue, green, and black activators would have to be present, thus activating transcription of genes 1, 2, and 4. In skin cells, the red, black, purple, and blue activators would have to be present, thus activating genes 3 and 5.

Chapter 19

Figure Questions

Figure 19.2 Beijerinck might have concluded that the agent was a toxin produced by the plant that was able to pass through a filter but that became more and more

dilute. In this case, he would have concluded that the infectious agent could not replicate.
Figure 19.4

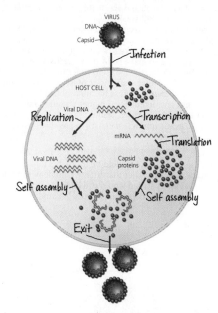

Figure 19.7 Any class V virus, including the viruses that cause influenza (flu), measles, and mumps **Figure 19.8** The main protein on the cell surface that HIV binds to is called CD4. However, HIV also requires a "co-receptor," which in many cases is a protein called CCR5. HIV binds to both of these proteins together and then is taken into the cell. Researchers discovered this requirement by studying individuals who seemed to be resistant to HIV infection, despite multiple exposures. These individuals turned out to have mutations in the gene that encodes CCR5 such that the protein apparently cannot act as a co-receptor, and so HIV can't enter and infect cells.

Concept Check 19.1

1. TMV consists of one molecule of RNA surrounded by a helical array of proteins. The influenza virus has eight molecules of RNA, each surrounded by a helical array of proteins, similar to the arrangement of the single RNA molecule in TMV. Another difference between the viruses is that the influenza virus has an outer envelope and TMV does not. **2.** The T2 phages were an excellent choice for use in the Hershey-Chase experiment because they consist of only DNA surrounded by a protein coat, and DNA and protein were the two candidates for macromolecules that carried genetic information. Hershey and Chase were able to radioactively label each type of molecule alone and follow it during separate infections of *E. coli* cells with T2. Only the DNA entered the bacterial cell during infection, and only labeled DNA showed up in some of the progeny phage. Hershey and Chase concluded that the DNA must carry the genetic information necessary for the phage to reprogram the cell and produce progeny phages.

Concept Check 19.2

1. Lytic phages can only carry out lysis of the host cell, whereas lysogenic phages may either lyse the host cell or integrate into the host chromosome. In the latter case, the viral DNA (prophage) is simply replicated along with the host chromosome. Under certain conditions, a prophage may exit the host chromosome and initiate a lytic cycle. **2.** Both the viral RNA polymerase and the RNA polymerase in Figure 17.9 synthesize an RNA molecule complementary to a template strand. However, the RNA polymerase in Figure 17.9 uses one of the strands of the DNA double helix as a template, whereas the viral RNA polymerase uses the RNA of the viral genome as a template. **3.** HIV is called a retrovirus because it synthesizes DNA using its RNA genome as a template. This is the reverse ("retro") of the usual DNA → RNA information flow. **4.** There are many steps that could be interfered with: binding of the virus to the cell, reverse transcriptase function, integration into the host cell chromosome, genome synthesis (in this case, transcription of RNA from the integrated provirus), assembly of the virus inside the cell, and budding of the virus. (Many of these, if not all, are targets of actual medical strategies to block progress of the infection in HIV-infected people.)

Concept Check 19.3

1. Mutations can lead to a new strain of a virus that can no longer be effectively fought by the immune system, even if an animal had been exposed to the original strain; a virus can jump from one species to a new host; and a rare virus can spread if a host population becomes less isolated. **2.** In horizontal transmission, a plant is infected from an external source of virus, which could enter through a break in the plant's epidermis due to damage by herbivores or other agents. In vertical transmission, a plant inherits viruses from its parent either via infected seeds (sexual reproduction) or via an infected cutting (asexual reproduction). **3.** Humans are not within the host range of TMV, so they can't be infected by the virus. (TMV can't bind human cells and infect them.)

Summary of Key Concepts Questions

19.1 Viruses are generally considered nonliving, because they are not capable of replicating outside of a host cell and are unable to carry out the energy-transforming reactions of metabolism. To replicate and carry out metabolism, they depend completely on host enzymes and resources. **19.2** Single-stranded RNA viruses require an RNA polymerase that can make RNA using an RNA template. (Cellular RNA polymerases make RNA using a DNA template.) Retroviruses require reverse transcriptases to make DNA using an RNA template. (Once the first DNA strand has been made, the same enzyme can promote synthesis of the second DNA strand.) **19.3** The mutation rate of RNA viruses is higher than that of DNA viruses because RNA polymerase has no proofreading function, so errors in replication are not corrected. Their higher mutation rate means that RNA viruses change faster than DNA viruses, leading to their being able to have an altered host range and to evade immune defenses in possible hosts.

Test Your Understanding

1. c **2.** d **3.** c **4.** c **5.** b
6. As shown below, the viral genome would be translated into capsid proteins and envelope glycoproteins directly, rather than after a complementary RNA copy was made. A complementary RNA strand would still be made, however, that could be used as a template for many new copies of the viral genome.

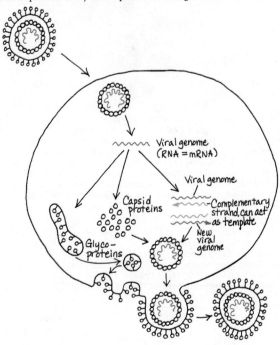

Chapter 20

Figure Questions
Figure 20.6

Figure 20.14 Crossing over, which causes recombination, is a random event. The chance of crossing over occurring between two loci increases as the distance between them increases. The SNP is located very close to an unknown disease-causing allele, and therefore crossing over rarely occurs between the SNP and the allele, so the SNP is a genetic marker indicating the presence of the particular allele. **Figure 20.16** None of the eggs with the transplanted nuclei from the four-cell embryo at the upper left would have developed into a tadpole. Also, the result might include only some of the tissues of a tadpole, which might differ, depending on which nucleus was transplanted. (This assumes that there was some way to tell the four cells apart, as one can in some frog species.) **Figure 20.21** Using converted iPS cells would not carry the same risk, which is its major advantage. Because the donor cells would come from the patient, they would be perfectly matched. The patient's immune system would recognize them as "self" cells and would not mount an attack (which is what leads to rejection). On the other hand, cells that are rapidly dividing might carry a risk of inducing some type of tumor or contributing to development of cancer.

Concept Check 20.1

1. The covalent sugar-phosphate bonds of the DNA strands **2.** Yes, *Pvu*I will cut the molecule.

3. Some human genes are too large to be incorporated into bacterial plasmids. Bacterial cells lack the means to process RNA transcripts into mRNA, and even if the need for RNA processing is avoided by using cDNA, bacteria lack enzymes to catalyze the post-translational processing that many human proteins require to function properly. **4.** During the replication of the ends of linear DNA molecules (see Figure 16.20), an RNA primer is used at the 5′ end of each new strand. The RNA must be replaced by DNA nucleotides, but DNA polymerase is incapable of starting from scratch at the 5′ end of a new DNA strand. During PCR, the primers are made of DNA nucleotides already, so they don't need to be replaced—they just remain as part of each new strand. Therefore, there is no problem with end replication during PCR, and the fragments don't shorten with each replication.

Concept Check 20.2

1. In RT-PCR, the primers must base-pair with their target sequences in the DNA mixture, locating one specific region among many. In DNA microarray analysis, the labeled probe binds only to the specific target sequence due to complementary nucleic acid hybridization (DNA-DNA hybridization). **2.** As a researcher interested in cancer development, you would want to study genes represented by spots that are green or red because these are genes for which the expression level differs between the two types of tissues. Some of these genes may be expressed differently as a result of cancer, while others might play a role in causing cancer, so both would be of interest.

Concept Check 20.3

1. The state of chromatin modification in the nucleus from the intestinal cell was undoubtedly less similar to that of a nucleus from a fertilized egg, explaining why many fewer of these nuclei were able to be reprogrammed. In contrast, the chromatin in a nucleus from a cell at the four-cell stage would have been much more like that of a nucleus in a fertilized egg and therefore much more easily programmed to direct development. **2.** No, primarily because of subtle (and perhaps not so subtle) differences in their environments **3.** The carrot cell has much more potential. The cloning experiment shows that an individual carrot cell can generate all the tissues of an adult plant. The muscle cell, on the other hand, will always remain a muscle cell because of its genetic program (it expresses the *myoD* gene, which ensures continued differentiation). The muscle cell is like other fully differentiated animal cells: It will remain fully differentiated on its own unless it is reprogrammed into an iPS cell using the new techniques described here. (This would be quite difficult to accomplish because a muscle cell has multiple nuclei.)

Concept Check 20.4

1. Stem cells continue to reproduce themselves, ensuring that the corrective gene product will continue to be made. **2.** Herbicide resistance, pest resistance, disease resistance, salinity resistance, drought resistance, and delayed ripening
3. Because hepatitis A is an RNA virus, you could isolate RNA from the blood and try to detect copies of hepatitis A RNA by RT-PCR. You would first reverse-transcribe the blood mRNA into cDNA and then use PCR to amplify the cDNA, using primers specific to hepatitis A sequences. If you then ran the products on an electrophoretic gel, the presence of a band of the appropriate size would support your hypothesis.

Summary of Key Concepts Questions

20.1 A plasmid vector and a source of foreign DNA to be cloned are both cut with the same restriction enzyme, generating restriction fragments with sticky ends. These fragments are mixed together, ligated, and reintroduced into bacterial cells. The plasmid has a gene for resistance to an antibiotic. That antibiotic is added to the host cells, and only cells that have taken up a plasmid will grow. (Another technique allows researchers to select only the cells that have a recombinant plasmid, rather than the original plasmid without an inserted gene.) **20.2** The genes that are expressed in a given tissue or cell type determine the proteins (and noncoding RNAs) that are the basis of the structure and functions of that tissue or cell type. Understanding which groups of interacting genes establish particular structures and allow certain functions will help us learn how the parts of an organism work together and help us treat diseases that occur when faulty gene expression leads to malfunctioning tissues. **20.3** Cloning a mouse involves transplanting a nucleus from a differentiated mouse cell into a mouse egg cell that has had its own nucleus removed. Fertilizing the egg cell and promoting its development into an embryo in a surrogate mother results in a mouse that is genetically identical to the mouse that donated the nucleus. In this case, the differentiated nucleus has been reprogrammed by factors in the egg cytoplasm. Mouse ES cells are generated from inner cells in mouse blastocysts, so in this case the cells are "naturally" reprogrammed by the process of reproduction and development. (Cloned mouse embryos can also be used as a source of ES cells.) iPS cells can be generated without the use of embryos from a differentiated adult mouse cell, by adding certain transcription factors into the cell. In this case, the transcription factors are reprogramming the cells to become pluripotent. **20.4** First, the disease must be caused by a single gene, and the molecular basis of the problem must be understood. Second, the cells that are going to be introduced into the patient must be cells that will integrate into body tissues and continue to multiply (and provide the needed gene product). Third, the gene must be able to be introduced into the cells in question in a safe way, as there have been instances of cancer resulting from some gene therapy trials. (Note that this will require testing the procedure in mice; moreover, the factors that determine a safe vector are not yet well understood. Maybe one of you will go on to solve this problem!)

Test Your Understanding

1. d **2.** b **3.** c **4.** b **5.** c **6.** b **7.** a **8.** b
9. You would use PCR to amplify the gene. This could be done from genomic DNA. Alternatively, mRNA could be isolated from lens cells and reverse-transcribed by reverse transcriptase to make cDNA. This cDNA could then be used for PCR.
10.

Chapter 21

Figure Questions

Figure 21.2 In stage 2 of this figure, the order of the fragments relative to each other is not known and will be determined later by computer. **Figure 21.8** The transposon would be cut out of the DNA at the original site rather than copied, so the figure would show the original stretch of DNA without the transposon after the mobile transposon had been cut out. **Figure 21.10** The RNA transcripts extending from the DNA in each transcription unit are shorter on the left and longer on the right. This means that RNA polymerase must be starting on the left end of the unit and moving toward the right.
Figure 21.13

Crossover point

Figure 21.14 Pseudogenes are nonfunctional. They could have arisen by any mutations in the second copy that made the gene product unable to function. Examples would be base changes that introduce stop codons in the sequence, alter amino acids, or change a region of the gene promoter so that the gene can no longer be expressed. **Figure 21.15** At position 5, there is an R (arginine) in lysozyme and a K (lysine) in α-lactalbumin; both of these are basic amino acids.

At position 16, there is a G (glutamic acid) in lysozyme and a D (aspartic acid) in α-lactalbumin; both of these are acidic. **Figure 21.16** Let's say a transposable element (TE) existed in the intron to the left of the indicated EGF exon in the EGF gene, and the same TE was present in the intron to the right of the indicated F exon in the fibronectin gene. During meiotic recombination, these TEs could cause nonsister chromatids on homologous chromosomes to pair up incorrectly, as seen in Figure 21.13. One gene might end up with an F exon next to an EGF exon. Further mistakes in pairing over many generations might result in these two exons being separated from the rest of the gene and placed next to a single or duplicated K exon. In general, the presence of repeated sequences in introns and between genes facilitates these processes because it allows incorrect pairing of nonsister chromatids, leading to novel exon combinations. **Figure 21.18** Since you know that chimpanzees do not speak but humans do, you'd probably want to know how many amino acid differences there are between the human wild-type FOXP2 protein and that of the chimpanzee and whether these changes affect the function of the protein. (As we explain later in the text, there are two amino acid differences.) You know that humans with mutations in this gene have severe language impairment. You would want to learn more about the human mutations by checking whether they affect the same amino acids in the gene product that the chimpanzee sequence differences affect. If so, those amino acids might play an important role in the function of the protein in language. Going further, you could analyze the differences between the chimpanzee and mouse FOXP2 proteins. You might ask: Are they more similar than the chimpanzee and human proteins? (It turns out that the chimpanzee and mouse proteins have only one amino acid difference and thus are more similar than the chimpanzee and human proteins, which have two differences, and also more similar than the human and mouse proteins, which have three differences.)

Concept Check 21.1

1. In the whole-genome shotgun approach, short fragments are generated by cutting the genome with multiple restriction enzymes. These fragments are cloned and sequenced and then ordered by computer programs that identify overlapping regions (see Figure 21.2).

Concept Check 21.2

1. The Internet allows centralization of databases such as GenBank and software resources such as BLAST, making them freely accessible. Having all the data in a central database, easily accessible on the Internet, minimizes the possibility of errors and of researchers working with different data. It streamlines the process of science, since all researchers are able to use the same software programs, rather than each having to obtain their own, possibly different, software. It speeds up dissemination of data and ensures as much as possible that errors are corrected in a timely fashion. These are just a few answers; you can probably think of more.
2. Cancer is a disease caused by multiple factors. To focus on a single gene or a single defect would ignore other factors that may influence the cancer and even the behavior of the single gene being studied. The systems approach, because it takes into account many factors at the same time, is more likely to lead to an understanding of the causes and most useful treatments for cancer. **3.** Some of the transcribed region is accounted for by introns. The rest is transcribed into noncoding RNAs, including small RNAs, such as microRNAs (miRNAs) or siRNAs. These RNAs help regulate gene expression by blocking translation, causing degradation of mRNA, binding to the promoter and repressing transcription, or causing remodeling of chromatin structure. The longer noncoding RNAs may also contribute to gene regulation or to chromatin remodeling. **4.** Genome-wide association studies use the systems biology approach in that they consider the correlation of many single nucleotide polymorphisms (SNPs) with particular diseases, such as heart disease and diabetes, in an attempt to find patterns of SNPs that correlate with each disease.

Concept Check 21.3

1. Alternative splicing of RNA transcripts from a gene and post-translational processing of polypeptides **2.** The total number of completed genomes is found by clicking on "Complete Projects"; the number of completed genomes for each domain is indicated at the top of this page. The number of genomes "In Progress" is included under "Incomplete Projects"; click that link to see the number of incomplete genomes, broken down by domain. You can also see the breakdown for genomes "In Progress." (*Note*: You can click on the "Size" column and the table will be re-sorted by genome size. Scroll down to get an idea of relative sizes of genomes in the three domains. Remember, though, that most of the sequenced genomes are bacterial.) **3.** Prokaryotes are generally smaller cells than eukaryotic cells, and they reproduce by binary fission. The evolutionary process involved is natural selection for more quickly reproducing cells: The faster they can replicate their DNA and divide, the more likely they will be able to dominate a population of prokaryotes. The less DNA they have to replicate, then, the faster they will reproduce.

Concept Check 21.4

1. The number of genes is higher in mammals, and the amount of noncoding DNA is greater. Also, the presence of introns in mammalian genes makes them larger, on average, than prokaryotic genes. **2.** In the copy-and-paste transposon mechanism and in retrotransposition **3.** In the rRNA gene family, identical transcription units for all three different RNA products are present in long arrays, repeated one after the other. The large number of copies of the rRNA genes enable organisms to produce the rRNA for enough ribosomes to carry out active protein synthesis, and the single transcription unit for the three rRNAs ensures that the relative amounts of the different rRNA molecules produced are correct—every time one rRNA is made, a copy of each of the other two is made as well. Rather than numerous identical units, each globin gene family consists of a relatively small number of nonidentical genes. The differences in the globin proteins encoded by these genes result in production of hemoglobin molecules adapted to particular developmental stages of the organism. **4.** The exons would be classified as exons (1.5%); the enhancer region containing the distal control elements, the region closer to the promoter containing the proximal control elements, and the promoter itself would be classified as regulatory sequences (5%); and the introns would be classified as introns (20%).

Concept Check 21.5

1. If meiosis is faulty, two copies of the entire genome can end up in a single cell. Errors in crossing over during meiosis can lead to one segment being duplicated while another is deleted. During DNA replication, slippage backward along the template strand can result in segment duplication. **2.** For either gene, a mistake in crossing over during meiosis could have occurred between the two copies of that gene, such that one copy ended up with a duplicated exon. (The other copy would have ended up with a deleted exon.) This could have happened several times, resulting in the multiple copies of a particular exon in each gene. **3.** Homologous transposable elements scattered throughout the genome provide sites where recombination can occur between different chromosomes. Movement of these elements into coding or regulatory sequences may change expression of genes. Transposable elements also can carry genes with them, leading to dispersion of genes and in some cases different patterns of expression. Transport of an exon during transposition and its insertion into a gene may add a new functional domain to the originally encoded protein, a type of exon shuffling. (For any of these changes to be heritable, they must happen in germ cells, cells that will give rise to gametes.) **4.** Because more offspring are born to women who have this inversion, it must provide some advantage during the process of reproduction and development. Because proportionally more offspring have this inversion, we would expect it to persist and spread in the population. (In fact, evidence in the study allowed the researchers to conclude that it has been increasing in proportion in the population. You'll learn more about population genetics in the next unit.)

Concept Check 21.6

1. Because both humans and macaques are primates, their genomes are expected to be more similar than the macaque and mouse genomes are. The mouse lineage diverged from the primate lineage before the human and macaque lineages diverged. **2.** Homeotic genes differ in their *non*homeobox sequences, which determine the interactions of homeotic gene products with other transcription factors and hence which genes are regulated by the homeotic genes. These nonhomeobox sequences differ in the two organisms, as do the expression patterns of the homeobox genes. **3.** *Alu* elements must have undergone transposition more actively in the human genome for some reason. Their increased numbers may have then allowed more recombination errors in the human genome, resulting in more or different duplications. The divergence of the organization and content of the two genomes presumably made the chromosomes of each genome less homologous to those of the other, thus accelerating divergence of the two species by making matings less and less likely to result in fertile offspring.

Summary of Key Concepts Questions

21.1 One focus of the Human Genome Project was to improve sequencing technology in order to speed up the process. During the project, many advances in sequencing technology allowed faster reactions, which were therefore less expensive. **21.2** The most significant finding is that more than 75% of the human genome appears to be transcribed at some point in at least one of the cell types studied. Also, at least 80% of the genome contains an element that is functional, participating in gene regulation or maintaining chromatin structure in some way. The project was expanded to include other species to further investigate the functions of these transcribed DNA elements. It is necessary to carry out this type of analysis on the genomes of species that can be used in laboratory experiments. **21.3** (a) In general, bacteria and archaea have smaller genomes, lower numbers of genes, and higher gene density than eukaryotes. (b) Among eukaryotes, there is no apparent systematic relationship between genome size and phenotype. The number of genes is often lower than would be expected from the size of the genome—in other words, the gene density is often lower in larger genomes. (Humans are an example.) **21.4** Transposable element–related sequences can move from place to place in the genome, and a subset of these sequences make a new copy of themselves when they do so. Thus, it is not surprising that they make up a significant percentage of the genome, and this percentage might be expected to increase over evolutionary time. **21.5** Chromosomal rearrangements within a species lead to some individuals having different chromosomal arrangements. Each of these individuals could still undergo meiosis and produce gametes, and fertilization involving gametes with different chromosomal arrangements could result in viable offspring. However, during meiosis in the offspring, the maternal and paternal chromosomes might not be able to pair up, causing gametes with incomplete sets of chromosomes to form. Most often, when zygotes are produced from such gametes, they do not survive. Ultimately, a new species could form if two different chromosomal arrangements became prevalent within a population and individuals could mate successfully only with other individuals having the same arrangement. **21.6** Comparing the genomes of two closely related species can reveal information about more recent evolutionary events, perhaps events that resulted in the distinguishing characteristics of the two species. Comparing the genomes of very distantly related species can tell us about evolutionary events that occurred a very long time ago. For example, genes that are shared between two distantly related species must have arisen before the two species diverged.

Test Your Understanding

1. b **2.** a **3.** c

4.

1. ATETI...PKSSD...TSSTT...NARRD
2. ATETI...PKSS E ...TSSTT... NARRD
3. ATETI...PKSSD...TSSTT...NARRD
4. ATETI...PKSSD...TSS NT... S ARRD
5. ATETI...PKSSD...TSSTT...NARRD
6. VTETI...PKSSD...TSSTT...NARRD

(a) Lines 1, 3, and 5 are the C, G, R species. (b) Line 4 is the human sequence. See the above figure for the differences between the human and C, G, R sequences— the underlined amino acids at which the human sequence has an N where the C, G, R sequences have a T, and an S where C, G, R have an N. (c) Line 6 is the orangutan sequence. (d) See the above figure. There is one amino acid difference between the mouse (the circled E on line 2) and the C, G, R species (which have a D in that position). There are three amino acid differences between the mouse and the human. (The boxed E, T, and N in the mouse sequence are instead D, N, and S, respectively, in the human sequence.) (e) Because only one amino acid difference arose during the 60–100 million years since the mouse and C, G, R species diverged, it is somewhat surprising that two additional amino acid differences resulted during the 6 million years since chimpanzees and humans diverged. This indicates that the *FOXP2* gene has been evolving faster in the human lineage than in the lineages of other primates.

Chapter 40

Figure Questions

Figure 40.4 Such exchange surfaces are internal in the sense that they are inside the body. However, they are also continuous with openings on the external body surface that contact the environment. **Figure 40.8** The stimuli (gray boxes) are the room temperature increasing in the top loop or decreasing in the bottom loop. The responses could include the heater turning off and the temperature decreasing in the top loop and the heater turning on and the temperature increasing in the bottom loop. The sensor/control center is the thermostat. The air conditioner would form a second control circuit, cooling the house when air temperature exceeded the set point. Such opposing, or antagonistic, pairs of control circuits increase the effectiveness of a homeostatic mechanism. **Figure 40.12** Convection is occurring as the movement of the fan passes air over your skin. Evaporation may also be occurring if your skin is damp with sweat. You also radiate a small amount of heat to the surrounding air at all times. **Figure 40.16** If a female Burmese python were not incubating eggs, her oxygen consumption would decrease with decreasing temperature, as for any other ectotherm. **Figure 40.17** The ice water would cool tissues in your head, including blood that would then circulate throughout your body. This effect would accelerate the return to a normal body temperature. If, however, the ice water reached the eardrum and cooled the blood vessel that supplies the hypothalamus, the hypothalamic thermostat would respond by inhibiting sweating and constricting blood vessels in the skin, slowing cooling elsewhere in the body. **Figure 40.18** The transport of nutrients across membranes and the synthesis of RNA and protein are coupled to ATP hydrolysis. These processes proceed spontaneously because there is an overall drop in free energy, with the excess energy given off as heat. Similarly, less than half of the free energy in glucose is captured in the coupled reactions of cellular respiration. The remainder of the energy is released as heat. **Figure 40.21** Nothing. Although genes that show a circadian variation in expression during euthermia exhibit constant RNA levels during hibernation, a gene that shows constant expression during hibernation might also show constant expression during euthermia.

Concept Check 40.1

1. All types of epithelia consist of cells that line a surface, are tightly packed, are situated on top of a basal lamina, and form an active and protective interface with the external environment. **2.** An oxygen molecule must cross a plasma membrane when entering the body at an exchange surface in the respiratory system, in both entering and exiting the circulatory system, and in moving from the interstitial fluid to the cytoplasm of the body cell. **3.** You need the nervous system to perceive the danger and provoke a split-second muscular response to keep from falling. The nervous system, however, does not make a direct connection with blood vessels or glucose-storing cells in the liver. Instead, the nervous system triggers the release of a hormone (called epinephrine, or adrenaline) by the endocrine system, bringing about a change in these tissues in just a few seconds.

Concept Check 40.2

1. In thermoregulation, the product of the pathway (a change in temperature) decreases pathway activity by reducing the stimulus. In an enzyme-catalyzed biosynthetic process, the product of the pathway (in this case, isoleucine) inhibits the pathway that generated it. **2.** You would want to put the thermostat close to where you would be spending time, where it would be protected from environmental perturbations, such as direct sunshine, and not right in the path of the output of the heating system. Similarly, the sensors for homeostasis located in the human brain are separated from environmental influences and can monitor conditions in a vital and sensitive tissue. **3.** In convergent evolution, the same biological trait arises independently in two or more species. Gene analysis can provide evidence for an independent origin. In particular, if the genes responsible for the trait in one species lack significant sequence similarity to the corresponding genes in another species, scientists conclude that there is a separate genetic basis for the trait in the two species and thus an independent origin. In the case of circadian rhythms, the clock genes in cyanobacteria appear unrelated to those in humans.

Concept Check 40.3

1. "Wind chill" involves heat loss through convection, as the moving air contributes to heat loss from the skin surface. **2.** The hummingbird, being a very small endotherm, has a very high metabolic rate. If by absorbing sunlight certain flowers warm their nectar, a hummingbird feeding on these flowers is saved the metabolic expense of warming the nectar to its body temperature. **3.** To raise body temperature to the higher range of fever, the hypothalamus triggers heat generation by muscular contractions, or shivering. The person with a fever may in fact say that they feel cold, even though their body temperature is above normal.

Concept Check 40.4

1. The mouse would consume oxygen at a higher rate because it is an endotherm, so its basal metabolic rate is higher than the ectothermic lizard's standard metabolic rate. **2.** The house cat; smaller animals have a higher metabolic rate per unit body mass and a greater demand for food per unit body mass. **3.** The alligator's body temperature would decrease along with the air temperature. Its metabolic rate would therefore also decrease as chemical reactions slowed. In contrast, the lion's body temperature would not change. Its metabolic rate would increase as it shivered and produced heat to keep its body temperature constant.

Summary of Key Concepts Questions

40.1 Animals exchange materials with their environment across their body surface, and a spherical shape has the minimum surface area per unit volume. As body size increases, the ratio of surface area to body volume decreases. **40.2** No; an animal's internal environment fluctuates slightly around set points or within normal ranges. Homeostasis is a dynamic state. Furthermore, there are sometimes programmed changes in set points, such as those resulting in radical increases in hormone levels at particular times in development. **40.3** Heat exchange across the skin is a primary mechanism for the regulation of body core temperature, with the result that the skin is cooler than the body core. **40.4** Small animals have a higher BMR per unit mass and therefore consume more oxygen per unit mass than large animals. A higher breathing rate is required to support this increased oxygen consumption.

Test Your Understanding

1. b **2.** c **3.** a **4.** b **5.** c **6.** b **7.** d
8.

Chapter 41

Figure Questions

Figure 41.4 What if? As in the described study, the researchers needed a sample size large enough that they could expect a significant number of neural tube defects in the control group. The information needed to determine the appropriate sample size was the frequency of neural tube defects in first-time pregnancies in the general population. **Figure 41.12** Since enzymes are proteins, and proteins are hydrolyzed in the small intestine, the digestive enzymes in that compartment need to be resistant to enzymatic cleavage other than the cleavage required to activate them. **Figure 41.13** None. Since digestion is completed in the small intestine, tapeworms simply absorb predigested nutrients through their large body surface. **Figure 41.21** Both insulin and glucagon are involved in negative feedback circuits.

Concept Check 41.1

1. The only essential amino acids are those that an animal cannot synthesize from other molecules. **2.** Many vitamins serve as enzyme cofactors, which, like enzymes themselves, are unchanged by the chemical reactions in which they participate. Therefore, only very small amounts of vitamins are needed. **3.** To identify the essential nutrient missing from an animal's diet, a researcher could supplement the diet with individual nutrients and determine which nutrient eliminates the signs of malnutrition.

Concept Check 41.2

1. A gastrovascular cavity is a digestive pouch with a single opening that functions in both ingestion and elimination; an alimentary canal is a digestive tube with a separate mouth and anus at opposite ends. **2.** As long as nutrients are within the cavity of the alimentary canal, they are in a compartment that is continuous with the outside environment via the mouth and anus and have not yet crossed a membrane to enter the body. **3.** Just as food remains outside the body in a digestive tract, gasoline moves from the fuel tank to the engine, and waste products exit through the exhaust without ever entering the passenger compartment of the automobile. In addition, gasoline, like food, is broken down in a specialized compartment, so that the rest of the automobile (or body) is protected from disassembly. In both cases, high-energy fuels are consumed, complex molecules are broken down into simpler ones, and waste products are eliminated.

Concept Check 41.3

1. Because parietal cells in the stomach pump hydrogen ions into the stomach lumen where they combine with chloride ions to form HCl, a proton pump inhibitor reduces the acidity of chyme and thus the irritation that occurs when chyme enters the esophagus. **2.** By releasing sugars from starch or glycogen in the mouth, amylase might allow us to recognize foods that provide a ready source of energy. **3.** Proteins would be denatured and digested into peptides. Further digestion, to individual amino acids, would require enzymatic secretions found in the small intestine. No digestion of carbohydrates or lipids would occur.

Concept Check 41.4

1. The increased time for transit through the alimentary canal allows for more extensive processing, and the increased surface area of the canal provides greater opportunity for absorption. **2.** A mammal's digestive system provides mutualistic microbes with an environment that is protected against other microbes by saliva and gastric juice, that is held at a constant temperature conducive to enzyme action, and that provides a steady source of nutrients. **3.** For the yogurt treatment to be effective, the bacteria from yogurt would have to establish a mutualistic relationship with the small intestine, where disaccharides are broken down and sugars are absorbed. Conditions in the small intestine are likely to be very different from those in a yogurt culture. The bacteria might be killed before they reach the small intestine, or they might not be able to grow there in sufficient numbers to aid in digestion.

Concept Check 41.5

1. Over the long term, the body stores excess calories in fat, whether those calories come from fat, carbohydrate, or protein in food. **2.** In normal individuals, leptin levels decline during fasting. Individuals in the group with low levels of leptin are likely to be defective in leptin production, so leptin levels would remain low regardless of food intake. Individuals in the group with high leptin levels are likely to be defective in responding to leptin, but they still should shut off leptin production as fat stores are used up. **3.** The excess production of insulin will cause blood glucose levels to decrease below normal physiological levels. It will also trigger glycogen synthesis in the liver, further decreasing blood glucose levels. However, low blood glucose levels will stimulate the release of glucagon from alpha cells in the pancreas, which will trigger glycogen breakdown. Thus, there will be antagonistic effects in the liver.

Summary of Key Concepts Questions

41.1 Since the cofactor is necessary in all animals, those animals that do not require it in their diet must be able to synthesize it from other organic molecules. **41.2** A liquid diet containing glucose, amino acids, and other building blocks could be ingested and absorbed without the need for mechanical or chemical digestion. **41.3** The small intestine has a much larger surface area than the stomach. **41.4** The assortment of teeth in our mouth and the short length of our cecum suggest that our ancestors' digestive systems were not specialized for digesting plant material. **41.5** When mealtime arrives, nervous inputs from the brain signal the stomach to prepare to digest food through secretions and churning.

Test Your Understanding

1. b **2.** a **3.** b **4.** c **5.** d **6.** b
7.

Chapter 42

Figure Questions

Figure 42.2 Although gas exchange might be improved by a steady, one-way flow of fluid, there would likely be inadequate time for food to be digested and nutrients absorbed if fluid flowed through the cavity in this manner.   **Figure 42.8** Each feature of the ECG recording, such as the sharp upward spike, occurs once per cardiac cycle. Using the x-axis to measure the time in seconds between successive spikes and dividing that number into 60 would yield the heart rate as the number of cycles per minute.   **Figure 42.20** The three main lineages are Deuterostomia, Lophotrochozoa, and Ecdysozoa. All three are represented by the animals shown in Figure 42.22: Polychaetes (phylum Annelida) are lophotrochozoans, crayfish (phylum Arthropoda) are ecdysozoans, and sea stars (phylum Echinodermata) are deuterostomes.   **Figure 42.24** The reduction in surface tension results from the presence of surfactant. Therefore, for all the infants who had died of RDS, you would expect the amount of surfactant to be near zero. For infants who had died of other causes, you would expect the amount of surfactant to be near zero for body masses less than 1,200 g but much greater than zero for body masses above 1,200 g.   **Figure 42.27** Since exhalation is largely passive, the recoil of the elastic fibers in alveoli helps force air out of the lungs. When alveoli lose their elasticity, as occurs in the disease emphysema, less air is exhaled. Because more air is left in the lungs, less fresh air can be inhaled. With a smaller volume of air exchanged, there is a decrease in the partial pressure gradient that drives gas exchange.
Figure 42.28 Breathing at a rate greater than that needed to meet metabolic demand (hyperventilation) would lower blood CO_2 levels. Sensors in major blood vessels and the medulla would signal the breathing control center to decrease the rate of contraction of the diaphragm and rib muscles, decreasing the breathing rate and restoring normal CO_2 levels in the blood and other tissues.   **Figure 42.29** The resulting increase in tidal volume would enhance ventilation within the lungs, increasing P_{O_2} and decreasing P_{CO_2} in the alveoli.

Concept Check 42.1

1. In both an open circulatory system and a fountain, fluid is pumped through a tube and then returns to the pump after collecting in a pool.   **2.** The ability to shut off blood supply to the lungs when the animal is submerged   **3.** The O_2 content would be abnormally low because some oxygen-depleted blood returned to the right atrium from the systemic circuit would mix with the oxygen-rich blood in the left atrium.

Concept Check 42.2

1. The pulmonary veins carry blood that has just passed through capillary beds in the lungs, where it accumulated O_2. The venae cavae carry blood that has just passed through capillary beds in the rest of the body, where it lost O_2 to the tissues.   **2.** The delay allows the atria to empty completely, filling ventricles fully before they contract.   **3.** The heart, like any other muscle, becomes stronger through regular exercise. You would expect a stronger heart to have a greater stroke volume, which would allow for the decrease in heart rate.

Concept Check 42.3

1. The large total cross-sectional area of the capillaries   **2.** An increase in blood pressure and cardiac output combined with the diversion of more blood to the skeletal muscles would increase the capacity for action by increasing the rate of blood circulation and delivering more O_2 and nutrients to the skeletal muscles.   **3.** Additional hearts could be used to improve blood return from the legs. However, it might be difficult to coordinate the activity of multiple hearts and to maintain adequate blood flow to hearts far from the gas exchange organs.

Concept Check 42.4

1. An increase in the number of white blood cells (leukocytes) may indicate that the person is combating an infection.   **2.** Clotting factors do not initiate clotting but are essential steps in the clotting process.   **3.** The chest pain results from inadequate blood flow in coronary arteries. Vasodilation promoted by nitric oxide from nitroglycerin increases blood flow, providing the heart muscle with additional oxygen and thus relieving the pain.   **4.** When a mutant allele is codominant with the wild-type allele, the phenotype of heterozygotes is intermediate between that of wild-type and mutant homozygotes. Therefore, in the presence of wild-type Hb, the aggregation of Hb^S that causes sickling must be significantly reduced. Based on this fact, some therapies for sickle-cell disease are aimed at boosting adult expression of another hemoglobin gene in the body, such as that normally expressed only in the fetus.   **5.** Embryonic stem cells are pluripotent rather than multipotent, meaning that they can give rise to many rather than a few different cell types.

Concept Check 42.5

1. Their interior position helps them stay moist. If the respiratory surfaces of lungs extended out into the terrestrial environment, they would quickly dry out, and diffusion of O_2 and CO_2 across these surfaces would stop.   **2.** Earthworms need to keep their skin moist for gas exchange, but they need air outside this moist layer. If they stay in their waterlogged tunnels after a heavy rain, they will suffocate because they cannot get as much O_2 from water as from air.   **3.** In the gills of fishes, water passes over the gills in the direction opposite to that of blood flowing through the gill capillaries, maximizing the extraction of oxygen from the water along the length of the exchange surface. Similarly, in the extremities of some vertebrates, blood flows in opposite directions in neighboring veins and arteries; this countercurrent arrangement maximizes the recapture of heat from blood leaving the body core in arteries, which is important for thermoregulation in cold environments.

Concept Check 42.6

1. An increase in blood CO_2 concentration causes an increase in the rate of CO_2 diffusion into the cerebrospinal fluid, where the CO_2 combines with water to form carbonic acid. Dissociation of carbonic acid releases hydrogen ions, decreasing the pH of the cerebrospinal fluid.   **2.** Increased heart rate increases the rate at which CO_2-rich blood is delivered to the lungs, where CO_2 is removed.   **3.** A hole would allow air to enter the space between the inner and outer layers of the double membrane, resulting in a condition called a pneumothorax. The two layers would no longer stick together, and the lung on the side with the hole would collapse and cease functioning.

Concept Check 42.7

1. Differences in partial pressure; the net diffusion of gases occurs from a region of higher partial pressure to a region of lower partial pressure.   **2.** The Bohr shift causes hemoglobin to release more O_2 at a lower pH, such as found in the vicinity of tissues with high rates of cellular respiration and CO_2 release.   **3.** The doctor is assuming that the rapid breathing is the body's response to low blood pH. Metabolic acidosis, the lowering of blood pH as a result of metabolism, can have many causes, including complications of certain types of diabetes, shock (extremely low blood pressure), and poisoning.

Summary of Key Concepts Questions

42.1 In a closed circulatory system, an ATP-driven muscular pump generally moves fluids in one direction on a scale of millimeters to meters. Exchange between cells and their environment relies on diffusion, which involves random movements of molecules. Concentration gradients of molecules across exchange surfaces can drive rapid net diffusion on a scale of 1 mm or less.   **42.2** Replacement of a defective valve should increase stroke volume. A lower heart rate would therefore be sufficient to maintain the same cardiac output.   **42.3** Blood pressure in the arm would fall by 25–30 mm Hg, the same difference as is normally seen between your heart and your brain.   **42.4** One microliter of blood contains about 5 million erythrocytes and 5,000 leukocytes, so leukocytes make up only about 0.1% of the cells in the absence of infection.   **42.5** Because CO_2 is such a small fraction of atmospheric gas (0.29 mm Hg/760 mm Hg, or less than 0.04%), the partial pressure gradient of CO_2 between the respiratory surface and the environment always strongly favors the release of CO_2 to the atmosphere.   **42.6** Because the lungs do not empty completely with each breath, incoming and outgoing air mix, so the air in lungs represents a mixture of fresh and stale air.   **42.7** An enzyme speeds up a reaction without changing the equilibrium and without being consumed. Similarly, a respiratory pigment speeds up the exchange of gases between the body and the external environment without changing the equilibrium and without being consumed.

Test Your Understanding

1. c   **2.** a   **3.** d   **4.** c   **5.** c   **6.** a   **7.** a
8.

Chapter 43

Figure Questions

Figure 43.5 The seemingly inactive peptides might offer protection against pathogens other than those studied. Also, some antimicrobial peptides might work best in combination.   **Figure 43.6** Cell-surface TLRs recognize molecules on the surface of pathogens, whereas TLRs in vesicles recognize internal molecules of pathogens after the pathogens are broken down.   **Figure 43.10** Part of the enzyme or antigen receptor provides a structural "backbone" that maintains overall shape, while interaction occurs at a surface with a close fit to the substrate or antigen. The combined effect of multiple noncovalent interactions at the active site or binding site is a high-affinity interaction of tremendous specificity.   **Figure 43.13** After gene rearrangement, a lymphocyte and its daughter cells make a single version of the antigen receptor. In contrast, alternative splicing is not heritable and can give rise to diverse gene products in a single cell.   **Figure 43.18** These receptors enable memory cells to present antigen on their cell surface to a helper T cell. This presentation of antigen is required to activate memory cells in a secondary immune response.   **Figure 43.20** Primary response: arrows extending from Antigen (1st exposure), Antigen-presenting cell, Helper T cell, B cell, Plasma cells, Cytotoxic T cell, and Active cytotoxic T cells; secondary response: arrows extending from Antigen (2nd exposure), Memory helper T cells, Memory B cells, Memory cytotoxic T cells, Plasma cells, and Active cytotoxic T cells.

Concept Check 43.1

1. Because pus contains white blood cells, fluid, and cell debris, it indicates an active and at least partially successful inflammatory response against invading pathogens. **2.** Whereas the ligand for the TLR receptor is a foreign molecule, the ligand for many signal transduction pathways is a molecule produced by the organism itself. **3.** Bacteria with a human host would likely grow optimally at normal human body temperature or, if fever were often induced, at a temperature a few degrees higher.

Concept Check 43.2

1. See Figure 43.9. The transmembrane regions lie within the C regions, which also form the disulfide bridges. In contrast, the antigen-binding sites are in the V regions. **2.** Generating memory cells ensures both that a receptor specific for a particular epitope will be present and that there will be more lymphocytes with this specificity than in a host that had never encountered the antigen. **3.** If each B cell produced two different light and heavy chains for its antigen receptor, different combinations would make four different receptors. If any one were self-reactive, the lymphocyte would be eliminated in the generation of self-tolerance. For this reason, many more B cells would be eliminated, and those that could respond to a foreign antigen would be less effective at doing so due to the variety of receptors (and antibodies) they express.

Concept Check 43.3

1. A child lacking a thymus would have no functional T cells. Without helper T cells to help activate B cells, the child would be unable to produce antibodies against extracellular bacteria. Furthermore, without cytotoxic T cells or helper T cells, the child's immune system would be unable to kill virus-infected cells. **2.** Since the antigen-binding site is intact, the antibody fragments could neutralize viruses and opsonize bacteria. **3.** If the handler developed immunity to proteins in the antivenin, another injection could provoke a severe immune response. The handler's immune system might also now produce antibodies that could neutralize the venom.

Concept Check 43.4

1. Myasthenia gravis is considered an autoimmune disease because the immune system produces antibodies against self molecules (certain receptors on muscle cells). **2.** A person with a cold is likely to produce oral and nasal secretions that facilitate viral transfer. In addition, since sickness can cause incapacitation or death, a virus that is programmed to exit the host when there is a physiological stress has the opportunity to find a new host at a time when the current host may cease to function. **3.** A person with a macrophage deficiency would have frequent infections. The causes would be poor innate responses, due to diminished phagocytosis and inflammation, and poor adaptive responses, due to the lack of macrophages to present antigens to helper T cells.

Summary of Key Concepts Questions

43.1 Lysozyme in saliva destroys bacterial cell walls; the viscosity of mucus helps trap bacteria; acidic pH in the stomach kills many bacteria; and the tight packing of cells lining the gut provides a physical barrier to infection. **43.2** Sufficient numbers of cells to mediate an innate immune response are always present, whereas an adaptive response requires selection and proliferation of an initially very small cell population specific for the infecting pathogen. **43.3** No. Immunological memory after a natural infection and that after vaccination are very similar. There may be minor differences in the particular antigens that can be recognized in a subsequent infection. **43.4** No. AIDS refers to a loss of immune function that can occur over time in an individual infected with HIV. However, certain multidrug combinations ("cocktails") or rare genetic variations usually prevent progression to AIDS in HIV-infected individuals.

Test Your Understanding

1. b **2.** c **3.** c **4.** b **5.** b **6.** b **7.** c
8. One possible answer:

Chapter 44

Figure Questions

Figure 44.13 You would expect to find these cells lining tubules where they pass through the renal medulla. Because the extracellular fluid of the renal medulla has a very high osmolarity, production of organic solutes by tubule cells in this region keeps intracellular osmolarity high, with the result that these cells maintain normal volume. **Figure 44.14** Furosemide increases urine volume. The absence of ion transport in the ascending limb leaves the filtrate too concentrated for substantial volume reduction in the distal tubule and collecting duct. **Figure 44.17** When the concentration of an ion differs across a plasma membrane, the difference in the concentration of ions inside and outside represents chemical potential energy, while the resulting difference in charge inside and outside represents electrical potential energy. **Figure 44.20** The ADH levels would likely be elevated in both sets of patients with mutations because either defect prevents the recapture of water that restores blood osmolarity to normal levels. **Figure 44.21** Each molecule of

renin or ACE activates multiple molecules of the next protein in the pathway. The same is true for the protein kinases. The proteases differ from the protein kinases in at least two ways. First, whereas phosphatases can remove the phosphates added to proteins by kinases, cells lack enzymes that can rejoin polypeptides separated by proteases. Second, proteases of this type do not require activation by another enzyme molecule.

Concept Check 44.1

1. Because the salt is moved against its concentration gradient, from low concentration (fresh water) to high concentration (blood) **2.** A freshwater osmoconformer would have body fluids too dilute to carry out life's processes. **3.** Without a layer of insulating fur, the camel must use the cooling effect of evaporative water loss to maintain body temperature, thus linking thermoregulation and osmoregulation.

Concept Check 44.2

1. Because uric acid is largely insoluble in water, it can be excreted as a semisolid paste, thereby reducing an animal's water loss. **2.** Humans produce uric acid from purine breakdown, and reducing purines in the diet often lessens the severity of gout. Birds, however, produce uric acid as a waste product of general nitrogen metabolism. They would therefore need a diet low in all nitrogen-containing compounds, not just purines.

Concept Check 44.3

1. In flatworms, ciliated cells draw interstitial fluids containing waste products into protonephridia. In earthworms, waste products pass from interstitial fluids into the coelom. From there, cilia move the wastes into metanephridia via a funnel surrounding an internal opening to the metanephridia. In insects, the Malpighian tubules pump fluids from the hemolymph, which receives waste products during exchange with cells in the course of circulation. **2.** Filtration produces a fluid for exchange processes that is free of cells and large molecules, which are of benefit to the animal and could not readily be reabsorbed. **3.** Filtrate is formed when the glomerulus filters blood from the renal artery within Bowman's capsule. Some of the filtrate contents are recovered, enter capillaries, and exit in the renal vein; the rest remain in the filtrate and pass out of the kidney in the ureter. **4.** The presence of Na⁺ and other ions (electrolytes) in the dialysate would limit the extent to which they would be removed from the filtrate during dialysis. Adjusting the electrolytes in the starting dialysate can thus lead to the restoration of proper electrolyte concentrations in the plasma. Similarly, the absence of urea and other waste products in the starting dialysate facilitates their removal from the filtrate.

Concept Check 44.4

1. The numerous nephrons and well-developed glomeruli of freshwater fishes produce urine at a high rate, while the small numbers of nephrons and smaller glomeruli of marine fishes produce urine at a low rate. **2.** The kidney medulla would absorb less water; thus, the drug would increase the amount of water lost in the urine. **3.** A decline in blood pressure in the afferent arteriole would reduce the rate of filtration by moving less material through the vessels.

Concept Check 44.5

1. Alcohol inhibits the release of ADH, causing an increase in urinary water loss and increasing the chance of dehydration. **2.** The consumption of a very large amount of water in a short period of time, coupled with an absence of solute intake, can reduce sodium levels in the blood below tolerable levels. This condition, called hyponatremia, leads to disorientation and, sometimes, respiratory distress. It has occurred in some marathon runners who drink water rather than sports drinks. (It has also caused the death of a fraternity pledge as a consequence of a water hazing ritual and the death of a contestant in a water-drinking competition.) **3.** High blood pressure

Summary of Key Concepts Questions

44.1 Water moves into a cell by osmosis when the fluid outside the cells is hypoosmotic (has a lower solute concentration than the cytosol).
44.2

Waste Attribute	Ammonia	Urea	Uric Acid
Toxicity	High	Very low	Low
Energy cost to produce	Low	Moderate	High
Water loss to excretion	High	Moderate	Low

44.3 Filtration retains large molecules that would be difficult to transport across membranes. **44.4** Both types of nephrons have proximal tubules that can reabsorb nutrients, but only juxtamedullary nephrons have loops of Henle that extend deep into the renal medulla. Thus, only kidneys containing juxtamedullary nephrons can produce urine that is more concentrated than the blood. **44.5** Patients who don't produce ADH have symptoms relieved by treatment with the hormone, but many patients with diabetes insipidus lack functional receptors for ADH.

Test Your Understanding

1. c **2.** a **3.** c **4.** d **5.** c **6.** b

Chapter 45

HO—CH—CH₂—NH—CH₃ ... OH ... HO
Epinephrine

Figure 45.5 The hormone is water-soluble and has a cell-surface receptor. Such receptors, unlike those for lipid-soluble hormones, can cause observable changes in cells without hormone-dependent gene transcription.

Concept Check 45.1

1. Water-soluble hormones, which cannot penetrate the plasma membrane, bind to cell-surface receptors. This interaction triggers an intracellular signal transduction pathway that ultimately alters the activity of a preexisting protein in the cytoplasm and/or changes transcription of specific genes in the nucleus. Steroid hormones are lipid-soluble and can cross the plasma membrane into the cell interior, where they bind to receptors located in the cytosol or nucleus. The hormone-receptor complex then functions directly as a transcription factor that changes transcription of specific genes. **2.** Prostaglandins in semen that induce contractions in the uterus are acting as signaling molecules that are transferred from one individual to another of the same species (like pheromones), thus aiding in reproduction. **3.** Both hormones produce opposite effects in different target tissues. In the fight-or-flight response, epinephrine increases blood flow to skeletal muscles and reduces blood flow to smooth muscles in the digestive system. In establishing apical dominance, auxin promotes the growth of apical buds and inhibits the growth of lateral buds.

Concept Check 45.2

1. Prolactin regulates milk production, whereas oxytocin regulates milk release. **2.** The posterior pituitary, an extension of the hypothalamus that contains the axons of neurosecretory cells, is the storage and release site for two neurohormones, oxytocin and antidiuretic hormone (ADH). The anterior pituitary contains endocrine cells that make at least six different hormones. Secretion of anterior pituitary hormones is controlled by hypothalamic hormones that travel via blood vessels to the anterior pituitary. **3.** The hypothalamus and pituitary glands function in many different endocrine pathways. Many defects in these glands, such as those affecting growth or organization, would therefore disrupt many hormone pathways. Only a very specific defect, such as a mutation affecting a particular hormone receptor, would alter just one endocrine pathway. The situation is quite different for the final gland in a pathway, such as the thyroid gland. In this case, a wide range of defects that disrupt gland function would disrupt only the one pathway or small set of pathways in which that gland functions. **4.** Both diagnoses could be correct. In one case, the thyroid gland may produce excess thyroid hormone despite normal hormonal input from the hypothalamus and anterior pituitary. In the other, abnormally elevated hormonal input (elevated TSH levels) may be the cause of the overactive thyroid gland.

Concept Check 45.3

1. If the function of the pathway is to provide a transient response, a short-lived stimulus would be less dependent on negative feedback. **2.** The levels of these hormones in the blood would become very high. This would be due to the diminished negative feedback on the hypothalamic neurons that secrete the releasing hormone that stimulates the secretion of ACTH by the anterior pituitary. **3.** You would be exploiting the anti-inflammatory activity of glucocorticoids. Local injection avoids the effects on glucose metabolism that would occur if glucocorticoids were taken orally and transported throughout the body in the bloodstream.

Summary of Key Concepts Questions

45.1 Because receptors for water-soluble hormones are located on the cell surface, facing the extracellular space, injecting the hormone into the cytosol would not trigger a response. **45.2** The pancreas, parathyroid glands, and pineal gland **45.3** Both the pituitary and the adrenal glands are formed by fusion of neural and nonneural tissue. ADH is secreted by the neurosecretory portion of the pituitary gland, and epinephrine is secreted by the neurosecretory portion of the adrenal gland.

Test Your Understanding

1. c **2.** d **3.** d **4.** b **5.** b **6.** b **7.** a

8.

Prolactin-releasing hormone circulates in body via blood
↓
Anterior pituitary secretes prolactin (o)
Prolactin circulates in body via blood
↓
Mammary glands
↓
Milk production

Chapter 46

Figure 46.8 When successfully courted by a second male, regardless of his genotype, about one-third of the females rid themselves of all sperm from the first mating. Thus, two-thirds retained some sperm from the first mating. We would therefore predict that two-thirds of those females would have some offspring exhibiting the small-eye phenotype of the dominant mutation carried by the males with which the females mated first. **Figure 46.11** The analysis would be informative because the polar bodies contain all of the maternal chromosomes that don't end up in the mature egg. For example, finding two copies of the disease gene in the polar bodies would indicate its absence in the egg. This method of genetic testing is sometimes carried out when oocytes collected from a female are fertilized with sperm in a laboratory dish. **Figure 46.16** Testosterone can pass from fetal blood to maternal blood via the placental circulation, temporarily upsetting the hormonal balance in the mother. **Figure 46.18** Oxytocin would most likely induce labor, starting a positive-feedback loop that would direct labor to completion. Synthetic oxytocin is in fact frequently used to induce labor when prolonged pregnancy might endanger the mother or fetus.

Concept Check 46.1

1. The offspring of sexual reproduction are more genetically diverse. However, asexual reproduction can produce more offspring over multiple generations. **2.** Unlike other forms of asexual reproduction, parthenogenesis involves gamete production. By controlling whether or not haploid eggs are fertilized, species such as honeybees can readily switch between asexual and sexual reproduction. **3.** No. Owing to random assortment of chromosomes during meiosis, the offspring may receive the same copy or different copies of a particular parental chromosome from the sperm and the egg. Furthermore, genetic recombination during meiosis will result in reassortment of genes between pairs of parental chromosomes. **4.** Both fragmentation and budding in animals have direct counterparts in the asexual reproduction of plants.

Concept Check 46.2

1. Internal fertilization allows sperm to reach the egg without either gamete drying out. **2.** (a) Animals with external fertilization tend to release many gametes at once, resulting in the production of enormous numbers of zygotes. This increases the chances that some will survive to adulthood. (b) Animals with internal fertilization produce fewer offspring but generally exhibit greater care of the embryos and the young. **3.** Like the uterus of an insect, the ovary of a plant is the site of fertilization. Unlike the plant ovary, the uterus is not the site of egg production, which occurs in the insect ovary. In addition, the fertilized insect egg is expelled from the uterus, whereas the plant embryo develops within a seed in the ovary.

Concept Check 46.3

1. Spermatogenesis occurs normally only when the testicles are cooler than normal body temperature. Extensive use of a hot tub (or of very tight-fitting underwear) can cause a decrease in sperm quality and number. **2.** In humans, the secondary oocyte combines with a sperm before it finishes the second meiotic division. Thus, oogenesis is completed after, not before, fertilization. **3.** The only effect of sealing off each vas deferens is an absence of sperm in the ejaculate. Sexual response and ejaculate volume are unchanged. The cutting and sealing off of these ducts, a *vasectomy*, is a common surgical procedure for men who do not wish to produce any (more) offspring.

Concept Check 46.4

1. In the testis, FSH stimulates the Sertoli cells, which nourish developing sperm. LH stimulates the production of androgens (mainly testosterone), which in turn stimulate sperm production. In both females and males, FSH encourages the growth of cells that support and nourish developing gametes (follicle cells in females and Sertoli cells in males), and LH stimulates the production of sex hormones that promote gametogenesis (estrogens, primarily estradiol, in females and androgens, especially testosterone, in males). **2.** In estrous cycles, which occur in most female mammals, the endometrium is reabsorbed (rather than shed) if fertilization does not occur. Estrous cycles often occur just once or a few times a year, and the female is usually receptive to copulation only during the period around ovulation. Menstrual cycles are found only in humans and some other primates. **3.** The combination of estradiol and progesterone would have a negative-feedback effect on the hypothalamus, blocking release of GnRH. This would interfere with LH secretion by the pituitary, thus preventing ovulation. This is in fact one basis of action of the most common hormonal contraceptives. **4.** In the viral replicative cycle, the production of new viral genomes is coordinated with capsid protein expression and with the production of phospholipids for viral coats. In the reproductive cycle of a human female, there is hormonally based coordination of egg maturation with the development of support tissues of the uterus.

Concept Check 46.5

1. The secretion of hCG by the early embryo stimulates the corpus luteum to make progesterone, which helps maintain the pregnancy. During the second trimester, however, hCG production drops, the corpus luteum disintegrates, and the placenta completely takes over progesterone production. **2.** Both tubal ligation and vasectomy block the movement of gametes from the gonads to a site where fertilization could take place. **3.** The introduction of a sperm nucleus directly into an oocyte bypasses the sperm's acquisition of motility in the epididymis, its swimming to meet the egg in the oviduct, and its fusion with the egg.

Summary of Key Concepts Questions

46.1 No. Because parthenogenesis involves meiosis, the mother would pass on to each offspring a random and therefore typically distinct combination of the chromosomes she inherited from her mother and father. **46.2** None **46.3** The small size and lack of cytoplasm characteristic of a sperm are adaptations well suited to its function as a delivery vehicle for DNA. The large size and rich cytoplasmic contents of eggs support the growth and development of the embryo. **46.4** Circulating anabolic steroids mimic the feedback regulation of testosterone, turning off pituitary signaling to the testes and thereby blocking the release of signals required for spermatogenesis. **46.5** Oxygen in maternal blood diffuses from pools in the endometrium into fetal capillaries in the chorionic villi of the placenta, and from there travels throughout the circulatory system of the fetus.

Test Your Understanding

1. d **2.** b **3.** a **4.** c **5.** a **6.** b **7.** c **8.** d
9.

(c) The supply of stem cells would be used up, and spermatogenesis would not be able to continue.

Chapter 47

Figure Questions

Figure 47.4 You could inject the compound into an unfertilized egg, expose the egg to sperm, and see whether the fertilization envelope forms. **Figure 47.22** When the researchers allowed normal cortical rotation to occur, the "back-forming" determinants were activated. When they then forced the opposite rotation to occur, the back was established on the opposite side as well. Because the molecules on the normal side were already activated, forcing the opposite rotation apparently did not "cancel out" the establishment of the back side by the first rotation. **Figure 47.23** In Spemann's control, the two blastomeres were physically separated, and each grew into a whole embryo. In Roux's experiment, remnants of the dead blastomere were still contacting the live blastomere, which developed into a half-embryo. Therefore, molecules present in the dead cell's remnants may have been signaling to the live cell, inhibiting it from making all the embryonic structures. **Figure 47.24** You could inject the isolated protein (or an mRNA encoding it) into ventral cells of an earlier gastrula. If dorsal structures form on the ventral side, that would support the idea that the protein is the signaling molecule secreted or presented by the dorsal lip. You should also do a control experiment to make sure the injection process alone did not cause dorsal structures to form. **Figure 47.26** Either Sonic hedgehog mRNA or protein can serve as a marker of the ZPA. If either was absent after removal of the AER, that would support your hypothesis. You could also block FGF function and see whether the ZPA formed (by looking for Sonic hedgehog).

Concept Check 47.1

1. The fertilization envelope forms after cortical granules release their contents outside the egg, causing the vitelline membrane to rise and harden. The fertilization envelope serves as a barrier to fertilization by more than one sperm. **2.** The increased Ca^{2+} concentration in the egg would cause the cortical granules to fuse with the plasma membrane, releasing their contents and causing a fertilization envelope to form, even though no sperm had entered. This would prevent fertilization. **3.** You would expect it to fluctuate. The fluctuation of MPF drives the transition between DNA replication (S phase) and mitosis (M phase), which is still required in the abbreviated cleavage cell cycle.

Concept Check 47.2

1. The cells of the notochord migrate toward the midline of the embryo (converge), rearranging themselves so there are fewer cells across the notochord, which thus becomes longer overall (extends; see Figure 47.17). **2.** Because microfilaments would not be able to contract and decrease the size of one end of the cell, both the inward bending in the middle of the neural tube and the outward bending of the hinge regions at the edges would be blocked. Therefore, the neural tube probably would not form. **3.** Dietary intake of the vitamin folic acid dramatically reduces the frequency of neural tube defects.

Concept Check 47.3

1. Axis formation establishes the location and polarity of the three axes that provide the coordinates for development. Pattern formation positions particular tissues and organs in the three-dimensional space defined by those coordinates. **2.** Morphogen gradients act by specifying cell fates across a field of cells through variation in the level of a determinant. Morphogen gradients thus act more globally than cytoplasmic determinants or inductive interactions between pairs of cells. **3.** Yes, a second embryo could develop because inhibiting BMP-4 activity would have the same effect as transplanting an organizer. **4.** The limb that developed probably would have a mirror-image duplication, with the most posterior digits in the middle and the most anterior digits at either end.

Summary of Key Concepts Questions

47.1 The binding of a sperm to a receptor on the egg surface is very specific and likely would not occur if the two gametes were from different species. Without sperm binding, the sperm and egg membranes would not fuse. **47.2** The neural tube forms when the neural plate, a band of ectodermal tissue oriented along the anterior-posterior axis on the dorsal side of the embryo, rolls into a tube and pinches off from the rest of the ectoderm. Neural crest cells arise as groups of cells in the regions between the edges of the neural tube and the surrounding ectoderm migrate away from the neural tube. **47.3** Mutations that affected both limb and kidney development would be more likely to alter the function of monocilia because these organelles are important in several signaling pathways. Mutations that affected limb development but not kidney development would more likely alter a single pathway, such as Hedgehog signaling.

Test Your Understanding

1. a **2.** b **3.** d **4.** a **5.** d **6.** c **7.** b
8.

Chapter 48

Figure Questions

Figure 48.7 Adding chloride channels would make the membrane potential less positive. Adding sodium or potassium channels would have no effect, because sodium ions are already at equilibrium and there are no potassium ions present.
Figure 48.10

Figure 48.12

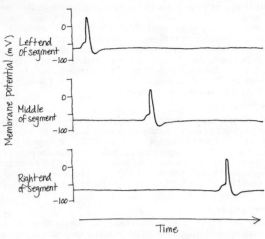

Figure 48.16 The production and transmission of action potentials would be unaffected. However, action potentials arriving at chemical synapses would be unable to trigger release of neurotransmitter. Signaling at such synapses would thus be blocked.

Concept Check 48.1

1. Axons and dendrites extend from the cell body and function in information flow. Dendrites transfer information to the cell body, whereas axons transmit information from the cell body. A typical neuron has multiple dendrites and one axon.　**2.** Sensors in your ear transmit information to your brain. There the activity of interneurons in processing centers enables you to recognize your name. In response, signals transmitted via motor neurons cause contraction of muscles that turn your neck.　**3.** Increased branching would allow control of a greater number of postsynaptic cells, enhancing coordination of responses to nervous system signals.

Concept Check 48.2

1. Ions can flow against a chemical concentration gradient if there is an opposing electrical gradient of greater magnitude.　**2.** A decrease in permeability to K^+, an increase in permeability to Na^+, or both　**3.** Charged dye molecules could equilibrate only if other charged molecules could also cross the membrane. If not, a membrane potential would develop that would counterbalance the chemical gradient.

Concept Check 48.3

1. A graded potential has a magnitude that varies with stimulus strength, whereas an action potential has an all-or-none magnitude that is independent of stimulus strength.　**2.** Loss of the insulation provided by myelin sheaths leads to a disruption of action potential propagation along axons. Voltage-gated sodium channels are restricted to the nodes of Ranvier, and without the insulating effect of myelin, the inward current produced at one node during an action potential cannot depolarize the membrane to the threshold at the next node.　**3.** Positive feedback is responsible for the rapid opening of many voltage-gated sodium channels, causing the rapid outflow of sodium ions responsible for the rising phase of the action potential. As the membrane potential becomes positive, voltage-gated potassium channels open in a form of negative feedback that helps bring about the falling phase of the action potential.　**4.** The maximum frequency would decrease because the refractory period would be extended.

Concept Check 48.4

1. It can bind to different types of receptors, each triggering a specific response in postsynaptic cells.　**2.** These toxins would prolong the EPSPs that acetylcholine produces because the neurotransmitter would remain longer in the synaptic cleft.　**3.** Membrane depolarization, exocytosis, and membrane fusion each occur in fertilization and in neurotransmission.

Summary of Key Concepts Questions

48.1 It would prevent information from being transmitted away from the cell body along the axon.　**48.2** There are very few open sodium channels in a resting neuron, so the resting potential either would not change or would become slightly more negative (hyperpolarization).　**48.4** A given neurotransmitter can have many receptors that differ in their location and activity. Drugs that target receptor activity rather than neurotransmitter release or stability are therefore likely to exhibit greater specificity and potentially have fewer undesirable side effects.

Test Your Understanding

1. c　**2.** c　**3.** c　**4.** b　**5.** a　**6.** d
7. The activity of the sodium-potassium pump is essential to maintain the resting potential. With the pump inactivated, the sodium and potassium concentration gradients would gradually disappear, resulting in a greatly reduced resting potential.　**8.** Since GABA is an inhibitory neurotransmitter in the CNS, this drug would be expected to decrease brain activity. A decrease in brain activity might be expected to slow down or reduce behavioral activity. Many sedative drugs act

in this fashion.　**9.** As shown in this pair of drawings, a pair of action potentials would move outward in both directions from each electrode. (Action potentials are unidirectional only if they begin at one end of an axon.) However, because of the refractory period, the two action potentials between the electrodes both stop where they meet. Thus, only one action potential reaches the synaptic terminals.

Chapter 49

Figure Questions

Figure 49.7 During swallowing, muscles along the esophagus alternately contract and relax, resulting in peristalsis. One model to explain this alternation is that each section of muscle receives nerve impulses that alternate between excitation and inhibition, just as the quadriceps and hamstring receive opposing signals in the knee-jerk reflex.　**Figure 49.15** Regions you would expect to be active regardless of the type of music played would include ones that are important for processing and interpreting sounds.　**Figure 49.23** If the depolarization brings the membrane potential to or past threshold, it should initiate action potentials that cause dopamine release from the VTA neurons. This should mimic natural stimulation of the brain reward system, resulting in positive and perhaps pleasurable sensations.

Concept Check 49.1

1. The sympathetic division would likely be activated. It mediates the "fight-or-flight" response in stressful situations.　**2.** Nerves contain bundles of axons, some that belong to motor neurons, which send signals outward from the CNS, and some that belong to sensory neurons, which bring signals into the CNS. Therefore, you would expect effects on both motor control and sensation.　**3.** Neurosecretory cells of the adrenal medulla secrete the hormones epinephrine and norepinephrine in response to preganglionic input from sympathetic neurons. These hormones travel in the circulation throughout the body, triggering responses in many tissues.

Concept Check 49.2

1. The cerebral cortex on the left side of the brain initiates voluntary movement of the right side of the body.　**2.** Alcohol diminishes function of the cerebellum.
3. A coma reflects a disruption in the cycles of sleep and arousal regulated by communication between the midbrain and pons (reticular formation) and the cerebrum. You would expect this group to have damage to the midbrain, the pons, the cerebrum, or any part of the brain between these structures. Paralysis reflects an inability to carry out motor commands transmitted from the cerebrum to the spinal cord. You would expect this group to have damage to the portion of the CNS extending from the spinal cord up to but not including the midbrain and pons.

Concept Check 49.3

1. Brain damage that disrupts behavior, cognition, memory, or other functions provides evidence that the portion of the brain affected by the damage is important for the normal activity that is blocked or altered.　**2.** Broca's area, which is active during the generation of speech, is located near the motor cortex, which controls skeletal muscles, including those in the face. Wernicke's area, which is active when speech is heard, is located in the posterior part of the temporal lobe, which is involved in hearing.　**3.** Each cerebral hemisphere is specialized for different parts of this task—the right for face recognition and the left for language. Without an intact corpus callosum, neither hemisphere can take advantage of the other's processing abilities.

Concept Check 49.4

1. There can be an increase in the number of synapses between the neurons or an increase in the strength of existing synaptic connections.　**2.** If consciousness is an emergent property resulting from the interaction of many different regions of the brain, then it is unlikely that localized brain damage will have a discrete effect on consciousness.　**3.** The hippocampus is responsible for organizing newly acquired information. Without hippocampal function, the links necessary to retrieve information from the cerebral cortex will be lacking, and no functional memory, short- or long-term, will be formed.

Concept Check 49.5

1. Both are progressive brain diseases whose risk increases with advancing age. Both result from the death of brain neurons and are associated with the accumulation of peptide or protein aggregates.　**2.** The symptoms of schizophrenia can be mimicked by a drug that stimulates dopamine-releasing neurons. The brain's reward system, which is involved in drug addiction, is composed of dopamine-releasing neurons that connect the ventral tegmental area to regions in the cerebrum. Parkinson's disease results from the death of dopamine-releasing neurons.   **3.** Not necessarily. It might be that the plaques, tangles, and missing regions of the brain seen at death reflect secondary effects, the consequence of other unseen changes that are actually responsible for the alterations in brain function.

Summary of Key Concepts Questions

49.1 Because reflex circuits involve only a few neurons—the simplest consist of a sensory neuron and a motor neuron—the path for information transfer is short and simple, increasing the speed of the response.   **49.2** The midbrain coordinates visual reflexes; the cerebellum controls coordination of movement that depends on visual input; the thalamus serves as a routing center for visual information; and the cerebrum is essential for converting visual input to a visual image.   **49.3** You would expect the right side of the body to be paralyzed because it is controlled by the left cerebral hemisphere, where language generation and interpretation are localized.   **49.4** Learning a new language likely requires the maintenance of synapses that are formed during early development but are otherwise lost prior to adulthood.   **49.5** Whereas amphetamine stimulates dopamine release, PCP blocks glutamate receptors, suggesting that schizophrenia does not reflect a defect in the function of just one neurotransmitter.

Test Your Understanding

1. b   **2.** a   **3.** d   **4.** c   **5.** c   **6.** a
7.

Chapter 50

Figure Questions

Figure 50.19 Each of the three types of cones is most sensitive to a different wavelength of light. A cone might be fully depolarized when there is light present if the light is at a wavelength far from its optimum.   **Figure 50.21** In humans, an X chromosome with a defect in the red or green opsin gene is much less common than a wild-type X chromosome. Color blindness therefore typically skips a generation as the defective allele passes from an affected male to a carrier daughter and back to an affected grandson. In squirrel monkeys, no X chromosome can confer full color vision. As a result, all males are color-blind and no unusual inheritance pattern is observed.   **Figure 50.23** The results of the experiment would have been identical. What matters is the activation of particular sets of neurons, not the manner in which they are activated. Any signal from a bitter cell will be interpreted by the brain as a bitter taste, regardless of the nature of the compound and the receptor involved.   **Figure 50.25** Only perception. Binding of an odorant to its receptor will cause action potentials to be sent to the brain. Although an excess of that odorant might cause a diminished response through adaptation, another odorant can mask the first only at the level of perception in the brain.   **Figure 50.28** Hundreds of myosin heads participate in sliding each pair of thick and thin filaments past each other. Because cross-bridge formation and breakdown are not synchronized, many myosin heads are exerting force on the thin filaments at all times during muscle contraction.   **Figure 50.32** By causing all of the motor neurons that control the muscle to generate action potentials at a rate high enough to produce tetanus in all of the muscle fibers

Concept Check 50.1

1. Electromagnetic receptors in general detect only external stimuli. Nonelectromagnetic receptors, such as chemoreceptors or mechanoreceptors, can act as either internal or external sensors.   **2.** The capsaicin present in the peppers activates the thermoreceptor for high temperatures. In response to the perceived high temperature, the nervous system triggers sweating to achieve evaporative cooling.   **3.** You would perceive the electrical stimulus as if the sensory receptors that regulate that neuron had been activated. For example, electrical stimulation of the sensory neuron controlled by the thermoreceptor activated by menthol would likely be perceived as a local cooling.

Concept Check 50.2

1. Otoliths detect the animal's orientation with respect to gravity, providing information that is essential in environments such as the tunnel habitat of the star-nosed mole, where light cues are absent.   **2.** As a sound that changes gradually from a very low to a very high pitch   **3.** The stapes and the other middle ear bones transmit vibrations from the tympanic membrane to the oval window. Fusion of these bones (as occurs in a disease called otosclerosis) would block this transmission and result in hearing loss.   **4.** In animals, the statoliths are extracellular. In contrast, the statoliths of plants are found within an intracellular organelle. The methods for detecting their location also differ. In animals, detection is by means of mechanoreceptors on ciliated cells. In plants, the mechanism appears to involve calcium signaling.

Concept Check 50.3

1. Planarians have ocelli that cannot form images but can sense the intensity and direction of light, providing enough information to enable the animals to find protection in shaded places. Flies have compound eyes that form images and excel at detecting movement.   **2.** The person can focus on distant objects but not close objects (without glasses) because close focusing requires the lens to become almost spherical. This problem is common after age 50.   **3.** The signal produced by rod and cone cells is glutamate, and their release of glutamate decreases upon exposure to light. However, a decrease in glutamate production causes other retinal cells to increase the rate at which action potentials are sent to the brain, so that the brain receives more action potentials in light than in dark.   **4.** Absorption of light by retinal converts retinal from its *cis* isomer to its *trans* isomer, initiating the process of light detection. In contrast, a photon absorbed by chlorophyll does not bring about isomerization, but instead boosts an electron to a higher energy orbital, initiating the electron flow that generates ATP and NADPH.

Concept Check 50.4

1. Both taste cells and olfactory cells have receptor proteins in their plasma membrane that bind certain substances, leading to membrane depolarization through a signal transduction pathway involving a G protein. However, olfactory cells are sensory neurons, whereas taste cells are not.   **2.** Since animals rely on chemical signals for behaviors that include finding mates, marking territories, and avoiding dangerous substances, it is adaptive for the olfactory system to have a robust response to a very small number of molecules of a particular odorant.   **3.** Because the sweet, bitter, and umami tastes involve GPCR proteins but the sour taste does not, you might predict that the mutation is in a molecule that acts in the signal transduction pathway common to the different GPCRs.

Concept Check 50.5

1. In a skeletal muscle fiber, Ca^{2+} binds to the troponin complex, which moves tropomyosin away from the myosin-binding sites on actin and allows cross-bridges to form. In a smooth muscle cell, Ca^{2+} binds to calmodulin, which activates an enzyme that phosphorylates the myosin head and thus enables cross-bridge formation.   **2.** *Rigor mortis*, a Latin phrase meaning "stiffness of death," results from the complete depletion of ATP in skeletal muscle. Since ATP is required to release myosin from actin and to pump Ca^{2+} out of the cytosol, muscles become chronically contracted beginning about 3–4 hours after death.   **3.** A competitive inhibitor binds to the same site as the substrate for the enzyme. In contrast, the troponin and tropomyosin complex masks, but does not bind to, the myosin-binding sites on actin.

Concept Check 50.6

1. Septa provide the divisions of the coelom that allow for peristalsis, a form of locomotion requiring independent control of different body segments.   **2.** The main problem in swimming is drag; a fusiform body minimizes drag. The main problem in flying is overcoming gravity; wings shaped like airfoils provide lift, and adaptations such as air-filled bones reduce body mass.   **3.** When you grasp the sides of the chair, you are using a contraction of the triceps to keep your arms extended against the pull of gravity on your body. As you lower yourself slowly into the chair, you gradually decrease the number of motor units in the triceps that are contracted. Contracting your biceps would jerk you down, since you would no longer be opposing gravity.

Summary of Key Concepts Questions

50.1 Nociceptors overlap with other classes of receptors in the type of stimulus they detect. They differ from other receptors only in how a particular stimulus is perceived.   **50.2** Volume is encoded by the frequency of action potentials transmitted to the brain; pitch is encoded by which axons are transmitting action potentials.   **50.3** The major difference is that neurons in the retina integrate information from multiple sensory receptors (photoreceptors) before transmitting information to the central nervous system.   **50.4** Our olfactory sense is responsible for most of what we describe as distinct tastes. A head cold or other source of congestion blocks odorant access to receptors lining portions of the nasal cavity.
50.5 Hydrolysis of ATP is required to convert myosin to a high-energy configuration for binding to actin and to power the Ca^{2+} pump that removes cytosolic Ca^{2+} during muscle relaxation.   **50.6** Human body movements rely on the contraction of muscles anchored to a rigid endoskeleton. Tendons attach muscles to bones, which in turn are composed of fibers built up from a basic organizational unit, the sarcomere. The thin and thick filaments have separate points of attachment within the sarcomere. In response to nervous system motor output, the formation and breakdown of cross-bridges between myosin heads and actin ratchet the thin and thick filaments past each other. Because the filaments are anchored, this sliding

movement shortens the muscle fibers. Furthermore, because the fibers themselves are part of the muscles attached at each end to bones, muscle contraction moves bones of the body relative to each other. In this way, the structural anchoring of muscles and filaments enables muscle function, such as the bending of an elbow by contraction of the biceps.

Test Your Understanding
1. d **2.** a **3.** b **4.** c **5.** b **6.** d
7.

Position along retina (in degrees away from fovea)

The answer shows the actual distribution of rods and cones in the human eye. Your graph may differ, but should have the following properties: Only cones at the fovea; fewer cones and more rods at both ends of the *x*-axis; no photoreceptors in the optic disk.

Chapter 51

Figure Questions

Figure 51.2 The fixed action pattern based on the sign stimulus of a red belly ensures that the male will chase away any invading males of his species. By chasing away such males, the defender decreases the chance that another male will fertilize eggs laid in his nesting territory. **Figure 51.7** There should be no effect. Imprinting is an innate behavior that is carried out anew in each generation. Assuming the nest was not disturbed, the offspring of the Lorenz followers would imprint on the mother goose. **Figure 51.8** Perhaps the wasp doesn't use visual cues. It might also be that wasps recognize objects native to their environment, but not foreign objects, such as the pinecones. Tinbergen addressed these ideas before carrying out the pinecone study. When he swept away the pebbles and sticks around the nest, the wasps could no longer find their nests. If he shifted the natural objects in their natural arrangement, the shift in the landmarks caused a shift in the site to which the wasps returned. Finally, if natural objects around the nest site were replaced with pinecones while the wasp was in the burrow, the wasp nevertheless found her way back to the nest site. **Figure 51.24** It might be that the birds require stimuli during flight to exhibit their migratory preference. If this were true, the birds would show the same orientation in the funnel experiment despite their distinct genetic programming. **Figure 51.26** It holds true for some, but not all individuals. If a parent has more than one reproductive partner, the offspring of different partners will have a coefficient of relatedness less than 0.5.

Concept Check 51.1

1. The proximate explanation for this fixed action pattern might be that nudging and rolling are released by the sign stimulus of an object outside the nest, and the behavior is carried to completion once initiated. The ultimate explanation might be that ensuring that eggs remain in the nest increases the chance of producing healthy offspring. **2.** There might be selective pressure for other prey fish to detect an injured fish because the source of the injury might threaten them as well. Among predators, there might be selection for those that are attracted to the alarm substance because they would be more likely to encounter crippled prey. Fish with adequate defenses might show no change because they have a selective advantage if they do not waste energy responding to the alarm substance. **3.** In both cases, the detection of periodic variation in the environment results in a reproductive cycle timed to environmental conditions that optimize the opportunity for success.

Concept Check 51.2

1. Natural selection would tend to favor convergence in color pattern because a predator learning to associate a pattern with a sting or bad taste would avoid all other individuals with that same color pattern, regardless of species. **2.** You might move objects around to establish an abstract rule, such as "past landmark A, the same distance as A is from the starting point," while maintaining a minimum of fixed metric relationships, that is, avoiding having the food directly adjacent to or a set distance from a landmark. As you might surmise, designing an informative experiment of this kind is not easy. **3.** Learned behavior, just like innate behavior, can contribute to reproductive isolation and thus to speciation. For example, learned bird songs contribute to species recognition during courtship, thereby helping ensure that only members of the same species mate.

Concept Check 51.3

1. Certainty of paternity is higher with external fertilization. **2.** Balancing selection could maintain the two alleles at the *forager* locus if population density fluctuated from one generation to another. At times of low population density, the energy-conserving sitter larvae (carrying the *for^s* allele) would be favored, while at higher population density, the more mobile Rover larvae (*for^R* allele) would have a selective advantage. **3.** Because females would now be present in much larger numbers than males, all three types of males should have some reproductive success. Nevertheless, since the advantage that the blue-throats rely on—a limited number of females in their territory—will be absent, the yellow-throats are likely to increase in frequency in the short term.

Concept Check 51.4

1. Because this geographic variation corresponds to differences in prey availability between two garter snake habitats, it seems likely that snakes with characteristics enabling them to feed on the abundant prey in their locale would have had increased survival and reproductive success. In this way, natural selection would have resulted in the divergent foraging behaviors. **2.** The fact that the individual shares some genes with the offspring of its sibling (in the case of humans, with the individual's niece or nephew) means that the reproductive success of that niece or nephew increases the representation of those genes in the population (selects for them). **3.** The older individual cannot be the beneficiary because he or she cannot have extra offspring. However, the cost is low for an older individual performing the altruistic act because that individual has already reproduced (but perhaps is still caring for a child or grandchild). There can therefore be selection for an altruistic act by a postreproductive individual that benefits a young relative.

Summary of Key Concepts Questions

51.1 Circannual rhythms are typically based on the cycles of light and dark in the environment. As the global climate changes, animals that migrate in response to these rhythms may shift to a location before or after local environmental conditions are optimal for reproduction and survival. **51.2** For the goose, all that is acquired is an object at which the behavior is directed. In the case of the sparrow, learning takes place that will give shape to the behavior itself. **51.3** Because feeding the female is likely to improve her reproductive success, the genes from the sacrificed male are likely to appear in a greater number of progeny. **51.4** Studying the genetic basis of these behaviors reveals that changes in a single gene can have large-scale effects on even complex behaviors.

Test Your Understanding

1. c **2.** b **3.** b **4.** a **5.** c **6.** a
7.

You could measure the size of mussels that oystercatchers successfully open and compare that with the size distribution in the habitat.

Atomic number (number of protons)
Element symbol
Atomic mass (number of protons plus number of neutrons averaged over all isotopes)

Metals | Metalloids | Nonmetals

Representative elements

Groups: Elements in a vertical column have the same number of electrons in their valence (outer) shell and thus have similar chemical properties.

Periods: Each horizontal row contains elements with the same total number of electron shells. Across each period, elements are ordered by increasing atomic number.

Halogens | Noble gases

Name (Symbol)	Atomic Number	Name (Symbol)	Atomic Number	Name (Symbol)	Atomic Number	Name (Symbol)	Atomic Number	Name (Symbol)	Atomic Number
Actinium (Ac)	89	Copernicium (Cn)	112	Iodine (I)	53	Osmium (Os)	76	Silicon (Si)	14
Aluminum (Al)	13	Copper (Cu)	29	Iridium (Ir)	77	Oxygen (O)	8	Silver (Ag)	47
Americium (Am)	95	Curium (Cm)	96	Iron (Fe)	26	Palladium (Pd)	46	Sodium (Na)	11
Antimony (Sb)	51	Darmstadtium (Ds)	110	Krypton (Kr)	36	Phosphorus (P)	15	Strontium (Sr)	38
Argon (Ar)	18	Dubnium (Db)	105	Lanthanum (La)	57	Platinum (Pt)	78	Sulfur (S)	16
Arsenic (As)	33	Dysprosium (Dy)	66	Lawrencium (Lr)	103	Plutonium (Pu)	94	Tantalum (Ta)	73
Astatine (At)	85	Einsteinium (Es)	99	Lead (Pb)	82	Polonium (Po)	84	Technetium (Tc)	43
Barium (Ba)	56	Erbium (Er)	68	Lithium (Li)	3	Potassium (K)	19	Tellurium (Te)	52
Berkelium (Bk)	97	Europium (Eu)	63	Livermorium (Lv)	116	Praseodymium (Pr)	59	Terbium (Tb)	65
Beryllium (Be)	4	Fermium (Fm)	100	Lutetium (Lu)	71	Promethium (Pm)	61	Thallium (Tl)	81
Bismuth (Bi)	83	Flerovium (Fl)	114	Magnesium (Mg)	12	Protactinium (Pa)	91	Thorium (Th)	90
Bohrium (Bh)	107	Fluorine (F)	9	Manganese (Mn)	25	Radium (Ra)	88	Thulium (Tm)	69
Boron (B)	5	Francium (Fr)	87	Meitnerium (Mt)	109	Radon (Rn)	86	Tin (Sn)	50
Bromine (Br)	35	Gadolinium (Gd)	64	Mendelevium (Md)	101	Rhenium (Re)	75	Titanium (Ti)	22
Cadmium (Cd)	48	Gallium (Ga)	31	Mercury (Hg)	80	Rhodium (Rh)	45	Tungsten (W)	74
Calcium (Ca)	20	Germanium (Ge)	32	Molybdenum (Mo)	42	Roentgenium (Rg)	111	Uranium (U)	92
Californium (Cf)	98	Gold (Au)	79	Neodymium (Nd)	60	Rubidium (Rb)	37	Vanadium (V)	23
Carbon (C)	6	Hafnium (Hf)	72	Neon (Ne)	10	Ruthenium (Ru)	44	Xenon (Xe)	54
Cerium (Ce)	58	Hassium (Hs)	108	Neptunium (Np)	93	Rutherfordium (Rf)	104	Ytterbium (Yb)	70
Cesium (Cs)	55	Helium (He)	2	Nickel (Ni)	28	Samarium (Sm)	62	Yttrium (Y)	39
Chlorine (Cl)	17	Holmium (Ho)	67	Niobium (Nb)	41	Scandium (Sc)	21	Zinc (Zn)	30
Chromium (Cr)	24	Hydrogen (H)	1	Nitrogen (N)	7	Seaborgium (Sg)	106	Zirconium (Zr)	40
Cobalt (Co)	27	Indium (In)	49	Nobelium (No)	102	Selenium (Se)	34		

Metric Prefixes:
10^9 = giga (G) 10^{-2} = centi (c) 10^{-9} = nano (n)
10^6 = mega (M) 10^{-3} = milli (m) 10^{-12} = pico (p)
10^3 = kilo (k) 10^{-6} = micro (μ) 10^{-15} = femto (f)

Measurement	Unit and Abbreviation	Metric Equivalent	Metric-to-English Conversion Factor	English-to-Metric Conversion Factor
Length	1 kilometer (km)	= 1,000 (10^3) meters	1 km = 0.62 mile	1 mile = 1.61 km
	1 meter (m)	= 100 (10^2) centimeters = 1,000 millimeters	1 m = 1.09 yards 1 m = 3.28 feet 1 m = 39.37 inches	1 yard = 0.914 m 1 foot = 0.305 m
	1 centimeter (cm)	= 0.01 (10^{-2}) meter	1 cm = 0.394 inch	1 foot = 30.5 cm 1 inch = 2.54 cm
	1 millimeter (mm)	= 0.001 (10^{-3}) meter	1 mm = 0.039 inch	
	1 micrometer (μm) (formerly micron, μ)	= 10^{-6} meter (10^{-3} mm)		
	1 nanometer (nm) (formerly millimicron, mμ)	= 10^{-9} meter (10^{-3} μm)		
	1 angstrom (Å)	= 10^{-10} meter (10^{-4} μm)		
Area	1 hectare (ha)	= 10,000 square meters	1 ha = 2.47 acres	1 acre = 0.405 ha
	1 square meter (m^2)	= 10,000 square centimeters	1 m^2 = 1.196 square yards 1 m^2 = 10.764 square feet	1 square yard = 0.8361 m^2 1 square foot = 0.0929 m^2
	1 square centimeter (cm^2)	= 100 square millimeters	1 cm^2 = 0.155 square inch	1 square inch = 6.4516 cm^2
Mass	1 metric ton (t)	= 1,000 kilograms	1 t = 1.103 tons	1 ton = 0.907 t
	1 kilogram (kg)	= 1,000 grams	1 kg = 2.205 pounds	1 pound = 0.4536 kg
	1 gram (g)	= 1,000 milligrams	1 g = 0.0353 ounce 1 g = 15.432 grains	1 ounce = 28.35 g
	1 milligram (mg)	= 10^{-3} gram	1 mg = approx. 0.015 grain	
	1 microgram (μg)	= 10^{-6} gram		
Volume (solids)	1 cubic meter (m^3)	= 1,000,000 cubic centimeters	1 m^3 = 1.308 cubic yards 1 m^3 = 35.315 cubic feet	1 cubic yard = 0.7646 m^3 1 cubic foot = 0.0283 m^3
	1 cubic centimeter (cm^3 or cc)	= 10^{-6} cubic meter	1 cm^3 = 0.061 cubic inch	1 cubic inch = 16.387 cm^3
	1 cubic millimeter (mm^3)	= 10^{-9} cubic meter = 10^{-3} cubic centimeter		
Volume (liquids and gases)	1 kiloliter (kL or kl)	= 1,000 liters	1 kL = 264.17 gallons	
	1 liter (L or l)	= 1,000 milliliters	1 L = 0.264 gallon 1 L = 1.057 quarts	1 gallon = 3.785 L 1 quart = 0.946 L
	1 milliliter (mL or ml)	= 10^{-3} liter = 1 cubic centimeter	1 mL = 0.034 fluid ounce 1 mL = approx. ¼ teaspoon 1 mL = approx. 15–16 drops (gtt.)	1 quart = 946 mL 1 pint = 473 mL 1 fluid ounce = 29.57 mL 1 teaspoon = approx. 5 mL
	1 microliter (μL or μl)	= 10^{-6} liter (10^{-3} milliliter)		
Pressure	1 megapascal (MPa)	= 1,000 kilopascals	1 MPa = 10 bars	1 bar = 0.1 MPa
	1 kilopascal (kPa)	= 1,000 pascals	1 kPa = 0.01 bar	1 bar = 100 kPa
	1 pascal (Pa)	= 1 newton/m^2 (N/m^2)	1 Pa = 1.0×10^{-5} bar	1 bar = 1.0×10^5 Pa
Time	1 second (s or sec)	= 1/60 minute		
	1 millisecond (ms or msec)	= 10^{-3} second		
Temperature	Degrees Celsius (°C) (0 K [Kelvin] = −273.15°C)		°F = 9/5°C + 32	°C = 5/9 (°F − 32)

Eye

Ocular lens

Objective lens

Specimen

Condenser lens

Light source

Electron source

Condenser lens

Specimen

Objective lens

Intermediate image

Projector lens

Eye

Binoculars

Final image on digital detector, fluorescent screen, or photographic film

Light Microscope

In light microscopy, light is focused on a specimen by a glass condenser lens; the image is then magnified by an objective lens and an ocular lens for projection on the eye, digital camera, digital video camera, or photographic film.

Electron Microscope

In electron microscopy, a beam of electrons (top of the microscope) is used instead of light, and electromagnets are used instead of glass lenses. The electron beam is focused on the specimen by a condenser lens; the image is magnified by an objective lens and a projector lens for projection on a digital detector, fluorescent screen, or photographic film.

Appendix D Microscopes

This appendix presents a taxonomic classification for the major extant groups of organisms discussed in this text; not all phyla are included. The classification presented here is based on the three-domain system, which assigns the two major groups of prokaryotes, bacteria and archaea, to separate domains (with eukaryotes making up the third domain).

Various alternative classification schemes are discussed in Unit Five of the text. The taxonomic turmoil includes debates about the number and boundaries of kingdoms and about the alignment of the Linnaean classification hierarchy with the findings of modern cladistic analysis. In this review, asterisks (*) indicate currently recognized phyla thought by some systematists to be paraphyletic.

DOMAIN BACTERIA

- **Proteobacteria**
- **Chlamydia**
- **Spirochetes**
- **Gram-Positive Bacteria**
- **Cyanobacteria**

DOMAIN ARCHAEA

- **Korarchaeota**
- **Euryarchaeota**
- **Crenarchaeota**
- **Nanoarchaeota**

DOMAIN EUKARYA

In the phylogenetic hypothesis we present in Chapter 28, major clades of eukaryotes are grouped together in the four "supergroups" listed in bold type below and on the facing page. Formerly, all the eukaryotes generally called protists were assigned to a single kingdom, Protista. However, advances in systematics have made it clear that some protists are more closely related to plants, fungi, or animals than they are to other protists. As a result, the kingdom Protista has been abandoned.

Excavata
- Diplomonadida (diplomonads)
- Parabasala (parabasalids)
- Euglenozoa (euglenozoans)
    Kinetoplastida (kinetoplastids)
    Euglenophyta (euglenids)

"SAR" Clade
- Stramenopila (stramenopiles)
    Chrysophyta (golden algae)
    Phaeophyta (brown algae)
    Bacillariophyta (diatoms)

- Alveolata (alveolates)
    Dinoflagellata (dinoflagellates)
    Apicomplexa (apicomplexans)
    Ciliophora (ciliates)
- Rhizaria (rhizarians)
    Radiolaria (radiolarians)
    Foraminifera (forams)
    Cercozoa (cercozoans)

Archaeplastida
- Rhodophyta (red algae)
- Chlorophyta (green algae: chlorophytes)
- Charophyta (green algae: charophytes)
- Plantae
    Phylum Hepatophyta (liverworts) ⎫
    Phylum Bryophyta (mosses)   ⎬ Nonvascular plants (bryophytes)
    Phylum Anthocerophyta (hornworts) ⎭
    Phylum Lycophyta (lycophytes)   ⎫
    Phylum Monilophyta (ferns, horsetails, whisk ferns) ⎬ Seedless vascular plants
    Phylum Ginkgophyta (ginkgo)   ⎫
    Phylum Cycadophyta (cycads)   ⎬ Gymnosperms ⎫
    Phylum Gnetophyta (gnetophytes)   ⎪   ⎬ Seed plants
    Phylum Coniferophyta (conifers)   ⎭   ⎪
    Phylum Anthophyta (flowering plants) ⎬ Angiosperms ⎭

Unikonta

- Amoebozoa (amoebozoans)
    - Myxogastrida (plasmodial slime molds)
    - Dictyostelida (cellular slime molds)
    - Tubulinea (tubulinids)
    - Entamoeba (entamoebas)
- Nucleariida (nucleariids)
- Fungi
    - *Phylum Chytridiomycota (chytrids)
    - *Phylum Zygomycota (zygomycetes)
    - Phylum Glomeromycota (glomeromycetes)
    - Phylum Ascomycota (ascomycetes)
    - Phylum Basidiomycota (basidiomycetes)

- Choanoflagellata (choanoflagellates)
- Animalia
    - Phylum Porifera (sponges)
    - Phylum Ctenophora (comb jellies)
    - Phylum Cnidaria (cnidarians)
        - Medusozoa (hydrozoans, jellies, box jellies)
        - Anthozoa (sea anemones and most corals)
    - Phylum Acoela (acoel flatworms)
    - Phylum Placozoa (placozoans)
    - Lophotrochozoa (lophotrochozoans)
    - Phylum Platyhelminthes (flatworms)
        - Catenulida (chain worms)
        - Rhabditophora (planarians, flukes, tapeworms)
    - Phylum Nemertea (proboscis worms)
    - Phylum Ectoprocta (ectoprocts)
    - Phylum Brachiopoda (brachiopods)
    - Phylum Rotifera (rotifers)
    - Phylum Cycliophora (cycliophorans)
    - Phylum Mollusca (molluscs)
        - Polyplacophora (chitons)
        - Gastropoda (gastropods)
        - Bivalvia (bivalves)
        - Cephalopoda (cephalopods)
    - Phylum Annelida (segmented worms)
        - Errantia (errantians)
        - Sedentaria (sedentarians)
    - Phylum Acanthocephala (spiny-headed worms)

Ecdysozoa (ecdysozoans)
- Phylum Loricifera (loriciferans)
- Phylum Priapula (priapulans)
- Phylum Nematoda (roundworms)
- Phylum Arthropoda (This survey groups arthropods into a single phylum, but some zoologists now split the arthropods into multiple phyla.)
    - Chelicerata (horseshoe crabs, arachnids)
    - Myriapoda (millipedes, centipedes)
    - Pancrustacea (crustaceans, insects)
- Phylum Tardigrada (tardigrades)
- Phylum Onychophora (velvet worms)

Deuterostomia (deuterostomes)
- Phylum Hemichordata (hemichordates)
- Phylum Echinodermata (echinoderms)
    - Asteroidea (sea stars, sea daisies)
    - Ophiuroidea (brittle stars)
    - Echinoides (sea urchins, sand dollars)
    - Crinoidea (sea lilies)
    - Holothuroidea (sea cucumbers)
- Phylum Chordata (chordates)
    - Cephalochordata (cephalochordates: lancelets)
    - Urochordata (urochordates: tunicates)
    - Cyclostomata (cyclostomes)
        - Myxini (hagfishes)
        - Petromyzontida (lampreys)
    - Gnathostomata (gnathostomes)
        - Chondrichthyes (sharks, rays, chimaeras)
        - Actinopterygii (ray-finned fishes)
        - Actinistia (coelacanths)
        - Dipnoi (lungfishes)
        - Amphibia (amphibians: frogs, salamanders, caecilians)
        - Reptilia (reptiles: tuataras, lizards, snakes, turtles, crocodilians, birds)
        - Mammalia (mammals)

} Vertebrates

Appendix E Classification of Life

Graphs

Graphs provide a visual representation of numerical data. They may reveal patterns or trends in the data that are not easy to recognize in a table. A graph is a diagram that shows how one variable in a data set is related (or perhaps not related) to another variable. If one variable is dependent on the other, the dependent variable is typically plotted on the *y*-axis and the independent variable on the *x*-axis. Types of graphs that are frequently used in biology include scatter plots, line graphs, bar graphs, and histograms.

▶ A **scatter plot** is used when the data for all variables are numerical and continuous. Each piece of data is represented by a point. In a **line graph**, each data point is connected to the next point in the data set with a straight line, as in the graph to the right. (To practice making and interpreting scatter plots and line graphs, see the Scientific Skills Exercises in Chapters 2, 3, 7, 8, 10, 13, 19, 24, 34, 43, 47, 49, 50, 52, 54, and 56.)

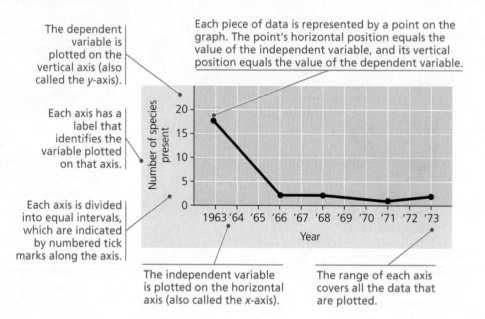

The dependent variable is plotted on the vertical axis (also called the *y*-axis).

Each axis has a label that identifies the variable plotted on that axis.

Each axis is divided into equal intervals, which are indicated by numbered tick marks along the axis.

Each piece of data is represented by a point on the graph. The point's horizontal position equals the value of the independent variable, and its vertical position equals the value of the dependent variable.

The independent variable is plotted on the horizontal axis (also called the *x*-axis).

The range of each axis covers all the data that are plotted.

▼ Two or more data sets can be plotted on the same line graph to show how two dependent variables are related to the same independent variable. (To practice making and interpreting line graphs with two or more data sets, see the Scientific Skills Exercises in Chapters 7, 43, 47, 49, 50, 52, and 56.)

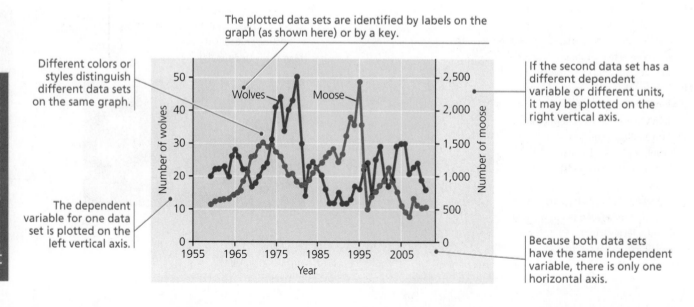

The plotted data sets are identified by labels on the graph (as shown here) or by a key.

Different colors or styles distinguish different data sets on the same graph.

The dependent variable for one data set is plotted on the left vertical axis.

If the second data set has a different dependent variable or different units, it may be plotted on the right vertical axis.

Because both data sets have the same independent variable, there is only one horizontal axis.

▼ In some scatter-plot graphs, a straight or curved line is drawn through the entire data set to show the general trend in the data. A straight line that mathematically fits the data best is called a *regression line*. Alternatively, a mathematical function that best fits the data may describe a curved line, often termed a *best-fit curve*. (To practice making and interpreting regression lines, see the Scientific Skills Exercises in Chapters 3, 10, and 34.)

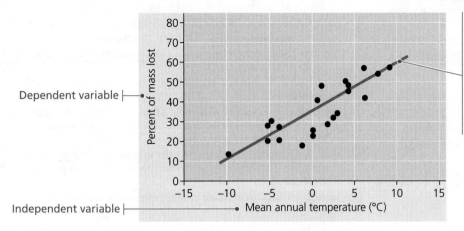

Dependent variable ⊢

Independent variable ⊢

The regression line can be expressed as a mathematical equation. It allows you to predict the value of the dependent variable for any value of the independent variable within the range of the data set and, less commonly, beyond the range of the data.

▼ A **bar graph** is a kind of graph in which the independent variable represents groups or non-numerical categories and the values of the dependent variable(s) are shown by bars. (To practice making and interpreting bar graphs, see the Scientific Skills Exercises in Chapters 1, 9, 18, 20, 22, 25, 27, 29, 33, 35, 39, 51, 52, and 54.)

As in a line graph or scatter plot, the vertical axis is usually used for the dependent variable.

The axis for the dependent variable is labeled and divided into equal intervals indicated by numbered tick marks.

Each piece of data is represented by a bar on the graph. The top of the bar aligns with the value of the dependent variable.

If multiple data sets are plotted on the same bar graph, they are distinguished by bars of different colors or styles and identified by labels or a key.

The groups or categories of the independent variable are usually spaced equally along the horizontal axis. (In some bar graphs, the horizontal axis is used for the dependent variable and the vertical axis for the independent variable.)

▶ A variant of a bar graph called a **histogram** can be made for numeric data by first grouping, or "binning," the variable plotted on the *x*-axis into intervals of equal width. The "bins" may be integers or ranges of numbers. In the histogram at right, the intervals are 25 mg/dL wide. The height of each bar shows the percent (or alternatively, the number) of experimental subjects whose characteristics can be described by one of the intervals plotted on the *x*-axis. (To practice making and interpreting histograms, see the Scientific Skills Exercises in Chapters 12, 14, and 42.)

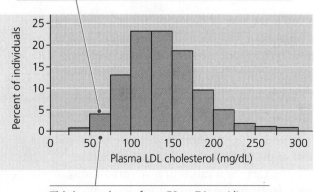

The height of this bar shows the percent of individuals (about 4%) whose plasma LDL cholesterol levels are in the range indicated on the *x*-axis.

This interval runs from 50 to 74 mg/dL.

Glossary of Scientific Inquiry Terms

See Concept 1.3 for more discussion of the process of scientific inquiry.

control group In a controlled experiment, a set of subjects that lacks (or does not receive) the specific factor being tested. Ideally, the control group should be identical to the experimental group in other respects.

controlled experiment An experiment in which an experimental group is compared with a control group that varies only in the factor being tested.

data Recorded observations.

deductive reasoning A type of logic in which specific results are predicted from a general premise.

dependent variable A variable whose value is measured during an experiment or other test to see whether it is influenced by changes in another variable (the independent variable).

experiment A scientific test, carried out under controlled conditions, involving manipulation of one or more factors in a system in order to see the effects of those changes.

experimental group A set of subjects that has (or receives) the specific factor being tested in a controlled experiment.

hypothesis A testable explanation for a set of observations based on the available data and guided by inductive reasoning. A hypothesis is narrower in scope than a theory.

independent variable A variable whose value is manipulated or changed during an experiment or other test to reveal possible effects on another variable (the dependent variable).

inductive reasoning A type of logic in which generalizations are based on a large number of specific observations.

inquiry The search for information and explanation, often focusing on specific questions.

model A physical or conceptual representation of a natural phenomenon.

prediction In deductive reasoning, a forecast that follows logically from a hypothesis. By testing predictions, experiments may allow certain hypotheses to be rejected.

theory An explanation that is broader in scope than a hypothesis, generates new hypotheses, and is supported by a large body of evidence.

variable A factor that varies in an experiment or other test.

Chi-Square (χ^2) Distribution Table

To use the table, find the row that corresponds to the degrees of freedom in your data set. (The degrees of freedom is the number of categories of data minus 1.) Move along that row to the pair of values that your calculated χ^2 value lies between. Move up from those numbers to the probabilities at the top of the columns to find the probability range for your χ^2 value. A probability of 0.05 or less is generally considered significant. (To practice using the chi-square test, see the Scientific Skills Exercise in Chapter 15.)

Degrees of Freedom (df)	Probability										
	0.95	0.90	0.80	0.70	0.50	0.30	0.20	0.10	0.05	0.01	0.001
1	0.004	0.02	0.06	0.15	0.45	1.07	1.64	2.71	3.84	6.64	10.83
2	0.10	0.21	0.45	0.71	1.39	2.41	3.22	4.61	5.99	9.21	13.82
3	0.35	0.58	1.01	1.42	2.37	3.66	4.64	6.25	7.82	11.34	16.27
4	0.71	1.06	1.65	2.19	3.36	4.88	5.99	7.78	9.49	13.28	18.47
5	1.15	1.61	2.34	3.00	4.35	6.06	7.29	9.24	11.07	15.09	20.52
6	1.64	2.20	3.07	3.83	5.35	7.23	8.56	10.64	12.59	16.81	22.46
7	2.17	2.83	3.82	4.67	6.35	8.38	9.80	12.02	14.07	18.48	24.32
8	2.73	3.49	4.59	5.53	7.34	9.52	11.03	13.36	15.51	20.09	26.12
9	3.33	4.17	5.38	6.39	8.34	10.66	12.24	14.68	16.92	21.67	27.88
10	3.94	4.87	6.18	7.27	9.34	11.78	13.44	15.99	18.31	23.21	29.59

Mean and Standard Deviation

The **mean** is the sum of all data points in a data set divided by the number of data points. The mean (or average) represents a "typical" or central value around which the data points are clustered. The mean of a variable x (denoted by $\bar{x}$) is calculated from the following equation:

$$\bar{x} = \frac{1}{n}\sum_{i=1}^{n} x_i$$

In this formula, n is the number of observations, and x_i is the value of the ith observation of variable x; the "$\sum$" symbol indicates that the n values of x_i are to be summed. (To practice calculating the mean, see the Scientific Skills Exercises in Chapters 32 and 34.)

The **standard deviation** provides a measure of the variation found in a set of data points. The standard deviation of a variable x (denoted s_x) is calculated from the following equation:

$$s = \sqrt{\frac{\sum_{i=1}^{n}(x_i - \bar{x})^2}{n-1}}$$

In this formula, n is the number of observations, x_i is the value of the ith observation of variable x, and $\bar{x}$ is the mean of x; the "$\sum$" symbol indicates that the n values of $(x_i - \bar{x})^2$ are to be summed. (To practice calculating standard deviation, see the Scientific Skills Exercises in Chapters 32 and 34.)

CREDITS

Photo Credits

Cover Image Martin Turner/Flickr/Getty Images

New Content Unit I Mark J. Winter/Science Source; **Unit II** Thomas Deerinck and Mark Ellisman, NCMIR; **Unit III** Andrey Prokhorov/E+/Getty Images; **Unit IV** Richard Bizley/Science Source; **Unit V** DOE Photo; **Unit VI** Giuseppe Mazza; **Unit VII** Matthias Wittlinger; **Unit VIII** Jordi Bas Casas/NHPA/Photoshot.

Detailed Contents p xxxii dandelions Carola Koserowsky/AGE Fotostock; **gecko** Martin Harvey/Peter Arnold/Getty Images; **p. xxxiii cell** Thomas Deerinck and Mark Ellisman, NCMIR; **ribbon model** Mark J. Winter/Science Source; **p. xxxiv giraffe** Uryadnikov/Shutterstock; **tree** Aflo/Nature Picture Library; **p. xxxv mitosis** George von Dassow; **flower** John Swithinbank/Garden World Images/AGE Fotostock; **p. xxxvi DNA** Andrey Prokhorov/E+/Getty Images; **ribosome** Venki Ramakirshnan; **p. xxxvii viruses** Richard Bizley/Science Source; **membrane model** Dr. Ian Derrington; **pxxxviii caterpillar** Robert Sisson/National Geographic Stock; **tortoise** Pete Oxford/Nature Picture Library; **p. xxxix hot spring** Shaeri Mukherjee; **stentors** Eric V. Grave/Science Source; **p. xl fireweed** Lyn Topinka/USGS; **lizard** Stephen Dalton/ Nature Picture Library; **p. xli coral reef** Image Quest Marine; **p. xlii bee** GFC Collection/Alamy; **snowflake plant** Giuseppe Mazza; **p. xliii otter** Jeff Foott/Discovery Channel Images/Getty Images; **p. xliv macrophage** O.Bellini/Shutterstock; **elephant seals** Phillip Colla/Oceanlight.com; **p. xlv lizard** Pete Oxford/Nature Picture Library; **synapses** Image by Sebastian Jessberger, Fred H. Gage, Laboratory of Genetics LOG-G, The Salk Institute for Biological Studies; **p. xlvi turtles** Harpe/Robert Harding World Imagery; **p. xlvii fox** Jordi Bas Casas/NHPA/Photoshot.

Unit Opening Interviews UNIT I p. 27 portrait Courtesy of Venki Ramakrishnan; **ribosome model** Courtesy of Venki Ramakrishnan. From V. Ramakrishnan, What we have learned from ribosome structures (The Heatley Medal Lecture), *Biochem. Soc. Trans.* 2008 Aug;36(4):567–574 (2008). **UNIT II p. 92 portrait** Haifan Lin; **Piwi protein** Haifan Lin; **UNIT III p. 251 portrait** National Human Genome Research Institute; **villagers** Nigel Pavitt/John Warburton-Lee Photography/Alamy; **UNIT IV p. 461 portrait** Josh Frost, Pearson Education; **mouse** J. B. Miller/Florida Park Service; **UNIT V p. 546 portrait** Josh Frost, Pearson Education; **choanoflagellates** Nicole King; **UNIT VI p. 751 portrait** Jeff Dangl Lab; *Arabidopsis* Daniel Aviv, Jeff Dangl Lab; **UNIT VII p. 866 portrait** Ulrike Heberlein; **laboratory setup** Ulrike Heberlein; **UNIT VIII p. 1157 portrait** Josh Frost, Pearson Education; **recovery after fire** Courtesy of Monica Turner.

Chapter 1 Carola Koserowsky/AGE Fotostock; **p. xlviii** Steve Bloom Images/Alamy; **1.2 sunflower** ImageState Media Partners Limited; **seahorse** R. Dirscherl/FLPA; **rabbit** Joe McDonald/Corbis; **butterfly** Toshiaki Ono/amana images/Alamy; **plant** Frederic Didillon/Garden Picture Library/Getty Images; **Venus flytrap** Kim Taylor and Jane Burton/DK Images; **giraffes** Malcolm Schuyl/FLPA; **1.3.1** WorldSat International/Science Source; **1.3.2** Bill Brooks/Alamy; **1.3.3** Linda Freshwaters/ Alamy; **1.3.4** Michael Orton/Photographer's Choice/Getty Images; **1.3.5** Ross M. Horowitz/Iconica/Getty Images; **1.3.6** Photodisc/Getty Images; **1.3.7** Jeremy Burgess/Science Source; **1.3.8** Texas A and M University; **1.3.9** E.H. Newcomb and W.P. Wergin/Biological Photo Service; **p. 4** Jim Zipp/Science Source; **1.4 eukaryotic** Steve Gschmeissner/Science Source; **1.4 prokaryotic** S. C. Holt/Biological Photo Service; **1.5** Conly L. Rieder, Ph.D.; **1.6** Camille Tokerud/Getty Images; **1.8a left** Carol Yepes/Flickr RF/Getty Images; **right** Ralf Dahm, Max Planck Institute for Developmental Biology, Tübingen, Germany; **1.10** James Balog/Getty Images; **1.13a** Oliver Meckes, Nicole Ottawa/Science Source; **1.13b** Eye of Science/Science Source; **1.13c left to right** Kunst and Scheidulin/AGE Fotostock; daksel/Fotolia; Anup Shah/Nature Picture Library; D.P. Wilson/Science Source; **1.14 pond** basel101658/Shutterstock; **paramecium** VVG/SPL/Science Source; **cross section** W. L. Dentler/Biological Photo Service; **cilia** OMIKRON/Science Source; **1.15** Dede Randrianarisata, Macalester College; **1.16 left** American Museum of Natural History; **right** ARCHIV/ Science Source; **1.17 left to right** zhaoyan/Shutterstock; Sebastian Knight/ Shutterstock; Volodymyr Goinyk/Shutterstock; **1.19** Frank Greenaway/DK Images; **1.21** Karl Ammann/Corbis Images; **inset** Tim Ridley/DK Images; **1.23 girl** Martin Shields/Alamy; **woman** EightFish/The Image Bank/Getty Images; **canoe** Rolf Hicker Photography/All Canada Photos/Alamy; **group** Seelevel.com; **1.24 white mouse** Courtesy of Hopi Hoekstra, Harvard University; **sand dunes** From Darwin to DNA: The genetic basis of color adaptations. In *In the Light of Evolution: Essays from the Laboratory and Field* ed. J. Losos, Roberts and Co. Photo by Sacha Vignieri; **field** Sacha Vignieri; **brown mouse** Shawn P. Carey, Migration Productions; **1.25** From S. N. Vignieri, J. Larson, and H. E. Hoekstra, The selective advantage of cryptic coloration in mice. *Evolution* 64:2153–2158 (2010). Fig. 1; **p. 22** Imagebroker/FLPA; **1.26** Jay Janner/Austin American-Statesman/AP Photo; **p. 26** Chris Mattison/Alamy.

Chapter 2 2.1 Kim Taylor/Nature Picture Library; **p. 28** Kim Taylor/Nature Picture Library; **2.2 sodium** Chip Clark; **chlorine, sodium chloride** Pearson Education; **2.3 landscape** Michael C. Hogan; **flower** CNPS California Native Plant Society; **rock** Andrew Alden; **2.5** National Library of Medicine; **p. 33** Pascal Goetgheluck/Science Source; **2.13** Pearson Education; **p. 39** Martin Harvey/Peter Arnold/Getty Images; **2.17** Nigel Cattlin/Science Source; **p. 43 top** Rolf Nussbaumer/Nature Picture Library; **bottom** Thomas Eisner.

Chapter 3 3.1 Teiji Saga/Science Source; **p. 44** Datacraft/UIG. Collection: Universal Images Group/AGE Fotostock; **3.4** iStockphoto; **3.6** Jan van Franeker/Alfred-Wegener-Institut fur Polar-und Meeresforschung; **3.9** NASA/JPL-Caltech/University of Arizona; **3.10 top to bottom** Jakub Semeniuk/iStockphoto; Feng Yu/iStockphoto; Monika Wisniewska/iStockphoto; Beth Van Trees/Shutterstock; **p. 54** The University of Queensland; **p. 56** Eric Guilloret/Biosphoto/Science Source.

Chapter 4 4.1 Florian Möllers/Nature Picture Library; **p. 58 notes** The Register of Stanley Miller Papers 1952 to 2010 in the Mandeville Special Collection Library, Laboratory Notebook 2, page 114, Serial number 655, MSS642, Box 25, Mandeville Collections, Geisel Library; **vials** Robert Benson, courtesy of Jeffrey Bada; **4.6** David M. Phillips/Science Source; **p. 65** George Sanker/Nature Picture Library.

Chapter 5 5.1 Mark J. Winter/Science Source; **p. 66** T. Naeser/Ludwig-Maximilians-Universitat Munchen; **5.6 potatoes** Dougal Waters/Getty Images; **plant cell** John Durham/Science Source; **starch** John N. A. Lott/Biological Photo Service; **glycogen** Dr. Paul B. Lazarow, Ph.D. Professor and Chairman; **cellulose** Biophoto Associates/ Science Source; **5.8 top** F. Collet/Science Source; **bottom** Corbis; **5.10a** DK Images; **5.10b** David Murray/DK Images; **5.13 eggs** Andrey Stratilatov/Shutterstock; **muscle tissue** Nina Zanetti; **connective tissue** Nina Zanetti; **5.16c** Clive Freeman/ Science Source; **5.17** Peter M. Colman; **5.18** Dieter Hopf/AGE Fotostock; **5.19** Eye of Science/Science Source; **5.21** Reprinted by permission from Nature. P. B. Sigler from Z. Xu, A. L. Horwich, and P. B. Sigler. 388:741–750 Copyright © 1997 Macmillan Magazines Limited; **5.22** Dave Bushnell; **5.26 DNA** Alfred Pasieka/Science Source; **Neanderthal** Viktor Deak; **doctor** CHASSENET/BSIP SA/Alamy; **hippo** Frontline Photography/Alamy; **whale** WaterFrame/Alamy; **elephants** ImageBroker/FLPA; **plant** David Read, Department of Animal and Plant Sciences, University of Sheffield; **p. 89 human** Ianych/Shutterstock; **monkey** David Bagnall/Alamy; **gibbon** Eric Isselee/Shutterstock; **p. 91 chick** Africa Studio/Shutterstock.

Chapter 6 6.1 Don W. Fawcett/Science Source; **6.3 brightfield, phase-contrast, DIC** Elisabeth Pierson, FNWI-Radboud University Nijmegen, Pearson Education; **6.3 fluorescence** Michael W. Davidson, The Florida State University Research Foundation/Molecular Expressions; **confocal** Karl Garsha, Beckman Institute for Advanced Science and Technology, University of Illinois; **deconvolution** Dr. James G. Evans, Whitehead Institute, MIT, Boston, MA, USA; **super-resolution** From K. I. Willig et al., STED microscopy reveals that synaptotagmin remains clustered after synaptic vesicle exocytosis, *Nature* 440(13) (2006), doi:10.1038/nature04592, Letters; **SEM** From A. S. Shah et al., Motile cilia of human airway epithelia are chemosensory, Science Express, 23 July 2009, *Science* 325(5944):1131–1134 (2009). Pseudocolored scanning electron micrograph by Tom Moninger (epithelia generated by Phil Karp); **TEM** William Dentler, Biological Photo Service; **6.5b** S. C. Holt, University of Texas Health Center/Biological Photo Service; **6.6** Daniel S. Friend; **p. 99** Kelly Tatchell; **6.8 p. 100 left to right** S. Cinti/Science Source; SPL/Science Source; A. Barry Dowsett/Science Source; **6.8 p. 101 left to right** Biophoto Associates/Science Source; SPL/Science Source; William Dentler, Center for Bioinformatics, University of Kansas: From W. L. Dentler and C. Adams, Flagellar microtubule dynamics in chlamydomonas: cytochalasin d induces periods of microtubule shortening and elongation; and colchicine induces disassembly of the distal, but not proximal, half of the flagellum, *The Journal of Cell Biology* 117(6):1289–1298, Copyright © 1992 by The Rockefeller University Press; **p. 102** Thomas Deerinck and Mark Ellisman, NCMIR; **6.9 top left** Reproduced by permission from L. Orci and A. Perelet, *Freeze-Etch Histology*, Springer-Verlag, Heidelberg (1975). Copyright ©1975 by Springer-Verlag GmbH & Co KG; **6.9 lower left** Reproduced by permission from A. C. Faberge, *Cell Tiss. Res.* 151 Copyright © 1974 by Springer-Verlag GmbH & Co KG; **6.9 lower right** Reprinted by permission from U. Aebi et al., *Nature* 323:560–564 (1996), Copyright © 1996, figure 1a. Used with permission. Macmillan Magazines Limited; **6.10 left** D. W. Fawcett/ Science Source; **6.10 right** Courtesy Harry Noller, UCSC; **6.11** R. Bolender, Don Fawcett/Science Source; **6.12** D. W. Fawcett/Science Source; **6.13** Daniel S. Friend; **6.14** Eldon H. Newcomb; **6.17a** Daniel S. Friend; **6.17b** From Y. Hayashi and K. Ueda, The shape of mitochondria and the number of mitochondrial nucleoids during the cell cycle of *Euglena gracilis*, *Journal of Cell Science* 93:565–570 (1989), Copyright © 1989 by Company of Biologists; **6.18a** Courtesy of W. P. Wergin and E. H. Newcomb, University of Wisconsin/Biological Photo Service; **6.18b** Franz Grolig, Philipps-University Marburg, Germany. Image acquired with the confocal microscope Leica TCS SP2; From S. E. Fredrick and E. H. Newcomb, *The Journal of Cell Biology* 43:343 (1969). Provided by E. H. Newcomb; **6.20** Albert Tousson, High Resolution Imaging Facility, University of Alabama at Birmingham; **6.21** Bruce J. Schnapp; **Table 6.1 left** Mary Osborn; **middle** Frank Solomon; **right** Mark S. Ladinsky and J. Richard McIntosh, University of Colorado; **6.22** Kent L. McDonald; **6.23a** Biophoto Associates/Science Source; **6.23b** Oliver Meckes and Nicole Ottawa/ Science Source; **6.24a** OMIKRON/Science Source; **6.24b** W. L. Dentler/Biological Photo Service; **6.24c** R. W. Linck and R. E. Stephens, Functional protofilament numbering of ciliary, flagellar, and centriolar microtubules, *Cell Motil. Cytoskeleton* 64(7):489–495 (2007); cover. Micrograph by D. Woodrum Hensley; **6.25** From H. Nobutaka, *The Journal of Cell Biology* 94:425 (1982) by copyright permission of The Rockefeller University Press; **6.26a** Clara Franzini-Armstrong, University of Pennsylvania; **6.26b** M. I. Walker/Photo Researchers; **6.26c** Michael Clayton, University of Wisconsin-Madison; **6.27** G. F. Leedale/Science Source; **6.29** Micrograph by W. P. Wergin, provided by E. H. Newcomb; **6.30 top** From D. J. Kelly, *The Journal of Cell Biology* 28:51 (1966), Fig.17. Reproduced by copyright permission of The Rockefeller University Press; **6.30 center** Reproduced by permission from L. Orci and A. Perelet, *Freeze-Etch Histology*, Springer-Verlag, Heidelberg (1975). Copyright © 1975 by Springer-Verlag GmbH & Co KG; **6.30 bottom** From C. Peracchia and A. F. Dulhunty, *The Journal of Cell Biology* 70:419 (1976) by copyright permission of The Rockefeller University Press; **6.31** Lennart Nilsson/Scanpix Sweden AB; **p. 123** Susumu Nishinaga/Science Source.

Chapter 7 7.1 B. L. de Groot; **p. 124** Roderick Mackinnon; **7.13** Michael Abbey/ Science Source; **7.19 left** H. S. Pankratz, T. C. Beaman, and P. Gerhardt/Biological Photo Service; **7.19 center** D. W. Fawcett/Photo Researchers; **7.19 right** M. M. Perry

Chapter 47 **47.1** Scanpix Sweden AB; **p. 1037** Oxford Scientific/Getty Images; **47.4 top** From V. D. Vacquier and J. E. Payne, Methods for quantitating sea urchin sperm-egg binding, *Exp. Cell Res.* 82(1):227–235 (1973); **bottom** From M. Hafner et al., Wave of free calcium at fertilization in the sea urchin egg visualized with Fura-2, *Cell Motil. Cytoskel.* 9:271–277 (1988); **47.6** George von Dassow; **47.7a** Jurgen Berger, SpemanMax Planck Campus Tubingen; **47.7b** Andrew J. Ewald, Johns Hopkins Medical School; **47.8** Charles A. Ettensohn; **47.14a** Huw Williams; **47.14c** Thomas Poole, SUNY Health Science Center; **47.15b** Dr. Keith Wheeler/Science Source; **47.18b** From H. Nishida, *Developmental Biology* 121: 526 (1987). Reprinted by permission of Academic Press; **47.20** Adapted from Strome, *International Review of Cytology* 114:81–123 (1989); **47.21** Adapted from Strome, *International Review of Cytology* 114:81–123 (1989); **47.25** Kathryn W. Tosney, University of Michigan; **47.26** Dennis Summerbell; **p. 1060** James Gerholdt/Peter Arnold/Getty Images.

Chapter 48 **48.1** Franco Banfi/Science Source; **48.3** Thomas Deerinck; **48.13** From Bear, Connors, and Paradiso, *Neuroscience: Exploring the Brain* © 1996, p. 43; **48.15** Edwin R. Lewis, Professor Emeritus, University of California-Berkeley; **p. 1078** B.A.E./Alamy.

Chapter 49 **49.1** Image by Tamily Weissman, Harvard University. The Brainbow mouse was produced by J. Livet et al., *Nature* 450:56–62 (2007); **49.4** Image by Sebastian Jessberger. Fred H. Gage, Laboratory of Genetics LOG-G, The Salk Institute for Biological Studies; **49.11** Larry Mulvehill/Corbis; **49.15** From M. T. Mitterschiffthaler et al., A functional MRI study of happy and sad affective states induced by classical music, *Hum. Brain Mapp.* 28(11):1150–1162 (2007); **49.18** Marcus E. Raichle, M.D., Washington University Medical Center; **p. 1092** From H. Bigelow, Dr. Harlow's Case of recovery from the passage of an iron bar through the head, *Am. Journal of the Med. Sci.* July 1850, XXXIX. Images from the History of Medicine (NLM); **49.24** Martin M. Rotker/Science Source; **p. 1100** Eric Delmar/E+/Getty Images.

Chapter 50 **50.1** Kenneth Catania; **50.6 top** R. A. Steinbrecht; **bottom** CSIRO; **50.7a** Michael Nolan/Robert Harding World Imagery; **50.7b** Grischa Georgiew/ AGE Fotostock; **50.9** From R. Elzinga, *Fundamentals of Entomology*, 3rd ed., Prentice-Hall, Upper Saddle River, NJ (1987) ©1987, p. 185. Reprinted by permission of Prentice-Hall, Upper Saddle River, NJ; **50.10** SPL/Science Source; **50.16a** USDA/ APHIS Animal and Plant Health Inspection Service; **50.17** Steve Gschmeissner/ Science Source; **50.21** From K. Mancuso et al., Gene therapy for red-green colour blindness in adult primates, *Nature* 461(7265):784–787 (2009). Photo: Neitz Laboratory; **50.26** Professor Clara Franzini-Armstrong, University of Pennsylvania; **50.28** Dr. H. E. Huxley; **50.33** George Cathcart Photography; **50.38** Dave Watts/NHPA/ Science Source; **p. 1130** Vance A. Tucker; **p. 1132** Dogs/Fotolia.

Chapter 51 **51.1** Manamana/Shutterstock; **p. 1133** Ivan Kuzmin/Alamy; **51.3** Denis-Huot/Hemis/Alamy; **51.5** Kenneth Lorenzen, UC Davis; **51.7a** Thomas D. McAvoy/Getty Images; **51.7b** Operation Migration – USA; **51.9** Lincoln Brower, Sweet Briar College; **51.11** Clive Bromhall/Oxford Scientific/Getty Images; **51.12** Richard Wrangham, **inset** Alissa Crandall/Corbis Images; **p. 1144** Matt Goff; **51.14a** Matt T. Lee; **51.14b** David Osborn/Alamy; **51.14c** David Tipling/Frank Lane Picture Agency Limited; **51.15** James D. Watt/Image Quest Marine; **51.16** Courtesy of Gerald S. Wilkinson; from G. S. Wilkinson and G. N. Dodson, In *The Evolution of Mating Systems in Insects and Arachnids*, eds. J. Choe and B. Crespi, Cambridge University Press, Cambridge, pp. 310–328 (1997); **51.17** Cyril Laubscher/DK Images; **51.20** Martin Harvey/Peter Arnold/Getty Images; **51.21** Erik Svensson, Lund University, Sweden; **51.22** Lowell Getz and Lisa Davis; **51.23** Rory Doolin; **51.25** Jennifer Jarvis; **51.27** Marie Read/NHPA/Photoshot; **51.28** Creatas/JupiterImages/Thinkstock/Getty Images; **p. 1156** William Leaman/Alamy.

Appendix A **p. A-5 left** OMIKRON/Science Source; **right** W. L. Dentler/Biological Photo Service; **p. A-11 top left** Biophoto/Science Source; **bottom left** J. Richard McIntosh, University of Colorado at Boulder; **right** J. L. Carson/Custom Medical Stock Photo; **p. A-34** Peter Kitin.

Appendix E **p. E-1 top left** Oliver Meckes/Nicole Ottawa/Science Source; **bottom left** Eye of Science/Science Source; **middle** M. I. Walker/NHPA/Photoshot; **right** Howard Rice/DK Images; **p. E-2 left** Phil Dotson/Science Source; **right** Oliver Wien/ epa European Pressphoto Agency creative account/Alamy.

Illustration and Text Credits

Chapter 1 **1.23** Adaptation of figure from "The real process of science," from Understanding Science website. Copyright © 2013 by The University of California Museum of Paleontology, Berkeley, and the Regents of the University of California. Material used courtesy of the UC Museum of Paleontology. ucmp.berkeley.edu; **1.25** Adaptation of figure 3 from "From Darwin to DNA: The Genetic Basis of Color Adaptations" by Hopi E. Hoekstra, edited by Jonathan Losos, from *In The Light of Evolution: Essays from the Laboratory and Field.* Copyright © 2011 by Roberts Company Publishers, Inc. Reprinted with permission. Adaptation of Figure 1b from "The Selective Advantage of Crypsis in Mice" by Sacha N. Vignieri et al., from *Evolution*, July 2010, Volume 64(7). Copyright © 2010 by Society for the Study of Evolution. Reprinted with permission of John Wiley & Sons Ltd.; **p. 21 Quote** Source: Isaac Newton quoted in *Never at Rest: A Biography of Isaac Newton* by Richard Westfall. Cambridge University Press, 1983; **1 SSE** Source: Data from "Adaptive Coloration in *Peromyscus polionotus*: Experimental Selection by Owls" by Donald W. Kaufman, from *Journal of Mammology*, May 1974, Volume 55(2).

Chapter 2 **2 SSE** Source: Data from "Revised Age of Late Neanderthal Occupation and the End of the Middle Paleolithic in the Northern Caucasus" by Ron Pinhasi et al., *Proceedings of the National Academy of Sciences of the United States of America*, 2011, Volume 108(21).

Chapter 3 **3.8** Source: Based on "Stimulating Water and the Molecules of Life" by Mark Gerstein and Michael Levitt, from *Scientific American*, November 1998; **03. Un04** Adaptation of figure 5 from "Effect of Calcium Carbonate Saturation State on the Calcification Rate of an Experimental Coral Reef" by C. Langdon et al., from *Global Biogeochemical Cycles*, June 2000, Volume 14(2). Copyright © 2000 by American Geophysical Union. Reprinted with permission of Wiley Inc.; **3 SSE** Source: Data from "Effect of Calcium Carbonate Saturation State on the Calcification Rate of an Experimental Coral Reef" by Chris Langdon, et al., from *Global Biogeochemical Cycles*, June 2000, Volume 14(2).

Chapter 4 **4.2** Source: Based on "A Production of Amino Acids under Possible Primitive Earth Conditions" by Stanley L. Miller, from *Science*, New Series, May 15, 1953, Volume 117(3046); **4 SSE** Source: Data from "Primordial Synthesis of Amines and Amino Acids in a 1958 Miller H$_2$S-rich Spark Discharge Experiment" by Eric T. Parker et al., from PNAS, March 22, 2012, Volume 108(12); **4.6b** Figure adapted from *Biochemistry*, 2nd Edition, by Christopher K. Mathews and Kensal E. Van Holde. Copyright © 1996 by Pearson Education, Inc. Adapted and electronically reproduced by permission of Pearson Education, Inc., Upper Saddle River, New Jersey; **4.7** Figure adapted from *The World Of The Cell*, 3rd Edition, by Wayne M. Becker, Jane B. Reece, and Martin F. Poenie. Copyright © 1996 by Pearson Education, Inc. Adapted and electronically reproduced by permission of Pearson Education, Inc., Upper Saddle River, New Jersey.

Chapter 5 **5.11** Figure adapted from *Biology: The Science of Life*, 3rd Edition, by Robert Wallace, Gerald Sanders, and Robert Ferl. Copyright © 1991 by Pearson Education, Inc. Adapted and electronically reproduced by permission of Pearson Education, Inc., Upper Saddle River, New Jersey; **5.13h, 5.18f** Source: Protein Data Bank ID 1CGD: "Hydration Structure of a Collagen Peptide" by Jordi Bella et al., from *Structure*, September 1995, Volume 3(9); **5.16a, b** Figure adapted from "How Amino-Acid Insertions Are Allowed in an Alpha-helix of T4 Lysozyme" by D. W. Heinz et al., from *Nature*, February 1993, Volume 362(6412). Copyright © 1993 by Macmillan Publishers Ltd. Reprinted with permission; **5.18d** Source: Protein Data Bank ID 3GS0: "Novel Transthyretin Amyloid Fibril Formation Inhibitors: Synthesis, Biological Evaluation, and X-ray Structural Analysis" by Satheesh K. Palaninathan et al., from PLOS ONE, July 21, 2009, Volume 4(7); **5.18g** Source: Protein Data Bank ID 2HHB: "The Crystal Structure of Human Deoxyhaemoglobin at 1.74 A Resolution" by G. Fermi et al., from *Journal of Molecular Biology*, May 1984, Volume 175(2); **5.22b** Adaptation of figure 2c from "Structural Basis of Transcription: An RNA Polymerase II Elongation Complex at 3.3 Resolution" by Averell L. Gnatt et al., from *Science*, June 2001, Volume 292(5523). Copyright © 2001 by AAAS. Reprinted with permission; **5 SSE** Source: Data for human from "Molecular and Population Genetic Analysis of Allelic Sequence Diversity at the Human Beta-globin Locus" by S. M. Fullerton et al., from *Proceedings of the National Academy of Sciences USA*, March 1994, Volume 91(5); Data for three species from "The Primary Structure of the Alpha and Beta Polypeptide Chains of Adult Hemoglobin of the Rhesus Monkey (*Macaca mulafta*). Biochemical Studies on Hemoglobins and Myoglobins. IV" by Genji Matsuda et al., from *International Journal of Protein Research*, December 1970, Volume 2(1–4); data for gibbon from "Primate Hemoglobins: Some Sequences and Some Proposals Concerning the Character of Evolution and Mutation" by Samuel H. Boyer et al., from *Biochemical Genetics*, October 1971, Volume 5(5).

Chapter 6 **6.6b** Figure adapted from *The World of the Cell*, 3rd Edition, by Wayne M. Becker, Jane B. Reece, and Martin F. Poenie. Copyright © 1996 by Pearson Education, Inc. Adapted and electronically reproduced by permission of Pearson Education, Inc., Upper Saddle River, New Jersey; **6.8** Adaptation of figure 3.2 from *Human Anatomy and Physiology*, 8th Edition, by Elaine N. Marieb and Katja N. Hoehn, 2010. Copyright © 2010 by Pearson Education, Inc. Reprinted and electronically reproduced by permission of Pearson Education, Inc. Upper Saddle River, New Jersey; **6.9** Adaptation of figure 3.29 from *Human Anatomy and Physiology*, 8th Edition, by Elaine N. Marieb and Katja N. Hoehn, 2010. Copyright © 2010 by Pearson Education, Inc. Reprinted and electronically reproduced by permission of Pearson Education, Inc. Upper Saddle River, New Jersey; **6.10** Adaptation of figure 3.2 from *Human Anatomy and Physiology*, 8th Edition, by Elaine N. Marieb and Katja N. Hoehn, 2010. Copyright © 2010 by Pearson Education, Inc. Reprinted and electronically reproduced by permission of Pearson Education, Inc. Upper Saddle River, New Jersey; **6.11** Adaptation of figure 3.18 from *Human Anatomy and Physiology*, 8th Edition, by Elaine N. Marieb and Katja N. Hoehn, 2010. Copyright © 2010 by Pearson Education, Inc. Reprinted and electronically reproduced by permission of Pearson Education, Inc. Upper Saddle River, New Jersey; **6.12** Adaptation of figure 3.19 from *Human Anatomy and Physiology*, 8th Edition, by Elaine N. Marieb and Katja N. Hoehn, 2010. Copyright © 2010 by Pearson Education, Inc. Reprinted and electronically reproduced by permission of Pearson Education, Inc. Upper Saddle River, New Jersey; **6.13a** Adaptation of figure 3.2 from *Human Anatomy and Physiology*, 8th Edition, by Elaine N. Marieb and Katja N. Hoehn, 2010. Copyright © 2010 by Pearson Education, Inc. Reprinted and electronically reproduced by permission of Pearson Education, Inc. Upper Saddle River, New Jersey; **6.15** Adaptation of figure 3.20 from *Human Anatomy and Physiology*, 8th Edition, by Elaine N. Marieb and Katja N. Hoehn, 2010. Copyright © 2010 by Pearson Education, Inc. Reprinted and electronically reproduced by permission of Pearson Education, Inc. Upper Saddle River, New Jersey; **6.17** Adaptation of figure 3.17 from *Human Anatomy and Physiology*, 8th Edition, by Elaine N. Marieb and Katja N. Hoehn, 2010. Copyright © 2010 by Pearson Education, Inc. Reprinted and electronically reproduced by permission of Pearson Education, Inc. Upper Saddle River, New Jersey; **Table 6.1** Adaptation of table 15.1 from *Becker's World of the Cell*, 8th Edition, by Jeff Hardin et al. Copyright © 1996 by Pearson Education, Inc. Reprinted and electronically reproduced by permission of Pearson Education, Inc. Upper Saddle River, New Jersey; **6.22** Adaptation of figure 3.25 from *Human Anatomy and Physiology*, 8th Edition, by Elaine N. Marieb and Katja N. Hoehn, 2010. Copyright © 2010 by Pearson Education, Inc. Reprinted and electronically reproduced by permission of Pearson Education, Inc. Upper Saddle River, New Jersey; **6.24** Adaptation of figures 3.2 and 3.26 from *Human Anatomy and Physiology*, 8th Edition, by Elaine N. Marieb and Katja N. Hoehn, 2010. Copyright © 2010 by Pearson Education, Inc. Reprinted and electronically reproduced by permission of Pearson Education, Inc. Upper Saddle River, New Jersey; **6.EOC01, 6.EOC03, 6.EOC04** Adaptation of figure 3.2 from *Human Anatomy and Physiology*, 8th Edition, by Elaine N. Marieb and Katja N. Hoehn, 2010. Copyright © 2010 by Pearson Education, Inc. Reprinted and electronically reproduced by permission of Pearson Education, Inc. Upper Saddle River, New Jersey.

Chapter 7 **7.4** Source: Based on "The Rapid Intermixing of Cell Surface Antigens After Formation of Mouse-Human Heterokaryons" by L. D. Frye and M. Edidin, from *Journal of Cell Science*, September 1970, Volume 7; **7.6** Source: Protein Data Bank ID 3HAO: "Similar Energetic Contributions of Packing in the Core of Membrane and Water-Soluble Proteins" by Nathan H. Joh et al., from *Journal of the American Chemical Society*, Volume 131(31); **7 SSE** Adaptation of Figure 1 from "Developmental Changes in Glucose Transport of Guinea Pig Erythrocytes" by Takahito Kondo and Ernest Beutler, from *Journal of Clinical Investigation*, January 1980, Volume 65(1). Copyright © by American Society for Clinical Investigation. Permission to reprint conveyed through Copyright Clearance Center, Inc.

Chapter 8 **8 SSE** Source: Data from "Diets Enriched in Sucrose or Fat Increase Gluconeogenesis and G-6-Pase but Not Basal Glucose Production in Rats" by S. R. Commerford et al., from *American Journal of Physiology–Endocrinology and Metabolism*, September 2002, Volume 283(3); **8.19** Source: Protein Data Bank ID 3e1f: "Direct and Indirect Roles of His-418 in Metal Binding and in the Activity of Beta-Galactosidase (*E. coli*)" by Douglas H. Juers et al., from *Protein Science*, June 2009, Volume 18(6); **8.20** Source: Protein Data Bank ID 1MDYO: "Crystal Structure of MyoD bHLH Domain-DNA Complex: Perspectives on DNA Recognition and Implications for Transcriptional Activation" from *Cell*, May 1994, Volume 77(3); **8.22** Adaptation of figure 3.2 from *Human Anatomy and Physiology*, 8th Edition, by Elaine N. Marieb and Katja N. Hoehn, 2010. Copyright © 2010 by Pearson Education, Inc. Reprinted and electronically reproduced by permission of Pearson Education, Inc. Upper Saddle River, New Jersey.

Chapter 9 **9.5** Adaptation of figure 2.69 from *Molecular Biology of the Cell*, 4th Edition, by Bruce Alberts et al. Copyright © 2002 by Garland Science/Taylor & Francis LLC. Reprinted with permission; **9.9** Figure adapted from *Biochemistry*, 4th Edition, by Christopher K. Mathews et al. Copyright 2013 by Pearson Education, Inc. Adapted and electronically reproduced by permission of Pearson Education, Inc., Upper Saddle River, New Jersey; **9 SSE** Source: Data from "The Quantitative Contributions of Mitochondrial Proton Leak and ATP Turnover Reactions to the Changed Respiration Rates of Hepatocytes from Rats of Different Thyroid Status" by Mary-Ellen Harper and Martin D. Brand, from *Journal of Biological Chemistry*, July 1993, Volume 268(20); **p. 184 Quote** Source: Pharmavite LLC., 2012.

Chapter 10 **10.10** Source: Based on "*Bacterium photometricum. Ein Beitrag zur vergteiehenden Physiologie des Licht- und Farbensinnes*" by Theodore W. Engelmann, from *Archive Für Die Gesamte Physiologie Des Menschen Und Der Tiere*, 1883, Volume 30(1); **10.13b** Adaptation of figure 1a from "Architecture of the Photosynthetic Oxygen-Evolving Center" by Kristina N. Ferreira et al., from *Science*, March 2004, Volume 303(5665). Copyright © 2004 by AAAS. Reprinted with permission; **10.15** Adaptation of Figure 4.1 from *Energy, Plants, and Man*, by Richard Walker and David Alan Walker. Copyright © 1992 by Richard Walker and David Alan Walker. Reprinted with permission of Richard Walker; **10 SSE** Source: Data from "Potential Effects of Global Atmospheric CO_2 Enrichment on the Growth and Competitiveness of C_3 and C_4 Weed and Crop Plants" by D. T. Patterson and E. P. Flint, from *Weed Science*, 1980, Volume 28.

Chapter 11 **11.8** *The World of the Cell*, 3rd Edition, by Wayne M. Becker, Jane B. Reece, and Martin F. Poenie. Copyright © 1996 by Pearson Education. Reprinted and electronically reproduced by permission of Pearson Education, Inc., Upper Saddle River, New Jersey; **11.12** Figure adapted from *The World of the Cell*, 3rd Edition, by Wayne M. Becker, Jane B. Reece, and Martin F. Poenie. Copyright © 1996 by Pearson Education, Inc. Adapted and electronically reproduced by permission of Pearson Education, Inc., Upper Saddle River, New Jersey; **p. 232 Quote** Source: Rudolf Virchow.

Chapter 12 **12.9** Source: Based on "Chromosomes Move Poleward in Anaphase along Stationary Microtubules That Coordinately Disassemble from Their Kinetochore Ends" by Gary J. Gorbsky et al., from *Journal of Cell Biology*, January 1987, Volume 104(1); **12.13** Adaptation of figure 18.41 from *Molecular Biology of the Cell*, 4th Edition, by Bruce Alberts et al. Copyright © 2002 by Garland Science/Taylor & Francis LLC. Reprinted with permission; **12.14** Source: Based on "Mammalian Cell Fusion: Induction of Premature Chromosome Condensation in Interphase Nuclei" by R. T. Johnson and P. N. Rao, from *Nature*, May 1970, Volume 226(5247); **12 SSE** Adaptation of Figure 3A from "Regulation of Glioblastoma Progression by Cord Blood Stem Cells Is Mediated by Downregulation of Cyclin D1" by Kiran K. Velpula et al., from PLoS ONE, March 24, 2011, Volume 6(3). Copyright © 2011 by Kiran K. Velpula et al. Article is open-access and distributed under the terms of the Creative Commons Attribution License, which permits unrestricted use, distribution, and reproduction in any medium, provided the original author and source are credited.

Chapter 14 **14.3** Source: Based on "Experiments in Plant Hybridization" by Gregor Mendel, from *Proceedings of the Natural History Society of Brunn*, 1866, Volume 4; **14.8** Source: Based on "Experiments in Plant Hybridization" by Gregor Mendel, from *Proceedings of the Natural History Society of Brunn*, 1866, Volume 4; **p. 294 Quote** Source: Thomas Hunt Morgan quoted in "Embryology and Its Relations" by Ross G. Harrison, from *Science*, April 16, 1937, Volume 85(2207).

Chapter 15 **15.4** Source: Based on "Sex Limited Inheritance in *Drosophila*" by Thomas Hunt Morgan, from *Science*, New Series, July 1910, Volume 32(812); **15.9** Source: Based on "The Linkage of Two Factors in *Drosophila* That Are Not Sex-Linked" by Thomas Hunt Morgan and Clara J. Lynch, from *Biological Bulletin*, August 1912, Volume 23(3).

Chapter 16 **16.2** Source: Based on "The Significance of Pneumococcal Types" by Fred Griffith, from *Journal of Hygiene*, January 1928, Volume 27(2); **16.4** Source: Based on "Independent Functions of Viral Protein and Nucleic Acid in Growth of Bacteriophage" by Alfred D. Hershey and Martha Chase, from *Journal of General Physiology*, May 1952, Volume 36(1); **16 SSE** Source: Data from "Composition of the Desoxypentose Nucleic Acids of Four Genera of Sea-urchin" by Erwin Chargaff et al., from *Biochemistry*, 1952, Volume 195; **p. 318 Quote** Source: "Molecular Structure of Nucleic Acids: A Structure for Deoxyribose Nucleic Acid" by James D. Watson and Francis H. Crick, from *Nature*, April 1953, Volume 171(4356); **p. 318 Quote** Source:

J. D. Watson and F. H. C. Crick, Genetical implications of the structure of deoxyribonucleic acid, *Nature* 171:964–967 (1953); **16.11** Source: Based on "The Replication of DNA in *Escherichia coli*" by Matthew Meselson and Franklin W. Stahl, from PNAS, July 1958, Volume 44(7).

Chapter 17 **17.2** Source: Based on "The Ornithine Cycle in Neurospora and Its Genetic Control" by Adrian M. Srb and N. H. Horowitz, from *Biochemistry*, June 1944, Volume 154(1); **17.11** *The World of the Cell*, 3rd Edition, by Wayne M. Becker, Jane B. Reece, and Martin F. Poenie. Copyright © 1996 by Pearson Education. Reprinted and electronically reproduced by permission of Pearson Education, Inc., Upper Saddle River, New Jersey; **17.13** *Principles of Cell and Molecular Biology*, 2nd Edition, by Lewis J. Kleinsmith and Valerie M. Kish. Copyright © 1995 by Pearson Education. Reprinted and electronically reproduced by permission of Pearson Education, Inc., Upper Saddle River, New Jersey; **17 SSE** Material provided courtesy of Dr. Thomas Schneider, National Cancer Institute, National Institutes of Health, 2012.

Chapter 18 **18 SSE** Source: Based on "Regulation of Human Microsomal Prostaglandin E Synthase-1 by IL-1b Requires a Distal Enhancer Element with a Unique Role for C/EBPb" by Jewell N. Walters et al., from *Biochemical Journal*, April 15, 2012, Volume 443(2); **18.26** Figure adapted from *The World of the Cell*, 3rd Edition, by Wayne M. Becker, Jane B. Reece, and Martin F. Poenie. Copyright © 1996 by Pearson Education, Inc. Adapted and electronically reproduced by permission of Pearson Education, Inc., Upper Saddle River, New Jersey.

Chapter 19 **19.2** Source: Based on "Concerning a Contagium Vivum Fluidum as Cause of the Spot Disease of Tobacco Leaves" by M. W. Beijerinck, from *Verhandelingen Der Koninkyke Akademie Wetschappen Te Amsterdam*, 1898, Volume 65. Translation published in English as *Phytopathological Classics*, Number 7. American Phytopathological Society Press, 1942; **19 SSE 01** Adaptation of Figure 2B from "New Variants and Age Shift to High Fatality Groups Contribute to Severe Successive Waves in the 2009 Influenza Pandemic in Taiwan" by Ji-Rong Yang et al., from PLOS ONE, November 30, 2011, Volume 6(11). Copyright © 2011 Yang et al. This is an open-access article distributed under the terms of the Creative Commons Attribution License, which permits unrestricted use, distribution, and reproduction in any medium, provided the original author and source are credited; **19 SSE 02** Adaptation of Figure 3A from "New Variants and Age Shift to High Fatality Groups Contribute to Severe Successive Waves in the 2009 Influenza Pandemic in Taiwan" by Ji-Rong Yang et al., from PLOS ONE, November 30, 2011, Volume 6(11). Copyright © 2011 Yang et al. This is an open-access article distributed under the terms of the Creative Commons Attribution License, which permits unrestricted use, distribution, and reproduction in any medium, provided the original author and source are credited.

Chapter 20 **20.8** Figure adapted from *The World of the Cell*, 3rd Edition, by Wayne M. Becker, Jane B. Reece, and Martin F. Poenie. Copyright © 1996 by Pearson Education, Inc. Adapted and electronically reproduced by permission of Pearson Education, Inc., Upper Saddle River, New Jersey; **20 SSE** Source: Data from "A Regulatory Archipelago Controls Hox Genes Transcription in Digits" by Thomas Montavon et al., from CELL, November 23, 2011, Volume 147(5); **20.16** Source: Based on "The Developmental Capacity of Nuclei Transplanted from Keratinized Skin Cells of Adult Frogs" by John B. Gurdon et al., from *Journal of Embryology and Experimental Morphology*, August 1975, Volume 34(1).

Chapter 21 **21.3** Source: Simulated screen shots based on Mac OS X and from data found at NCBI, U.S. National Library of Medicine using Conserved Domain Database, Sequence Alignment Viewer, and Cn3D; **21.8** Figure adapted from *The World of the Cell*, 3rd Edition, by Wayne M. Becker, Jane B. Reece, and Martin F. Poenie. Copyright © 1996 by Pearson Education, Inc. Adapted and electronically reproduced by permission of Pearson Education, Inc., Upper Saddle River, New Jersey; **21.9** Figure adapted from *The World of the Cell*, 3rd Edition, by Wayne M. Becker, Jane B. Reece, and Martin F. Poenie. Copyright © 1996 by Pearson Education, Inc. Adapted and electronically reproduced by permission of Pearson Education, Inc., Upper Saddle River, New Jersey; **21 SSE and 21.Un01** Source: Data from the NCBI database; **21.18b** Adapted from figure 4(c) in "Altered Ultrasonic Vocalization in Mice with a Disruption in the *Foxp2* Gene" by Weiguo Shu et al., from PNAS, July 2005, Volume 102(27). Copyright © 2005 by National Academy of Sciences, U.S.A. Reprinted with permission; **21.20** Adaptation of figure 3 from "Hox Genes and the Evolution of Diverse Body Plans" by Michael Akam, from *Philosophical Transactions of the Royal Society B: Biological Sciences*, September 29, 1995, Volume 349(1329): 313–319. Copyright © 1995 by the Royal Society. Reprinted with permission.

Chapter 40 **40.15** Adaptation of figure 7 from "Thermoregulation in Endothermic Insects" by Bernd Heinrich from *Science*, August 1974, Volume 185(4153). Copyright © 1974 by AAAS. Reprinted with permission; **40.16** Adaptation of Figure 2 from "Thermoregulation in a Brooding Female Indian Python, *Python molurus bivittatus*" by Victor H. Hutchison, Herndon G. Dowling, and Allen Vinegar from *Science*, February 1966, Volume 151(3711). Copyright © 1966 by AAAS. Reprinted with permission; **40 SSE** Sources: Data from "Energetics of Foraging in Breeding Adélie Penguins" by Mark A. Chappell et al., from *Ecology*, December 1993, Volume 74(8); "Voluntary Running in Deer Mice: Speed, Distance, Energy Costs, and Temperature Effects" by Mark A. Chappell et al., from *Journal of Experimental Biology*, October 2004, Volume 207(22); and "Metabolism, Temperature Relations, Maternal Behavior, and Reproductive Energetics in the Ball Python (*Python regius*)" by Tamir M. Ellis and Mark A. Chappell, from *Journal of Comparative Physiology B*, 1987, Volume 157(3); **40.21** Adaptation of Figures 2b and 2c from "The Circadian Clock Stops Ticking During Deep Hibernation in the European Hamster" by Florent G. Revel et al., from PNAS, August 2007, Volume 104(24). Copyright © 2007 by National Academy of Sciences. Reprinted with permission.

Chapter 41 **41.4** Source: Based on "Possible Prevention of Neural-Tube Defects by Periconceptional Vitamin Supplementation" by Richard Smithells et al., *Lancet*, February 1980, Volume 315(8164); **41.9** *Human Anatomy and Physiology*, 8th Edition, by

Elaine N. Marieb and Katja Hoehn. Copyright © 2010 by Pearson Education. Reprinted and electronically reproduced by permission of Pearson Education, Inc., Upper Saddle River, New Jersey; **41.9b** Figure adapted from *Human Physiology*, 3rd Edition, by R. A. Rhodes. Copyright © 1996 by Brooks/Cole, a part of Cengage Learning, Inc. Reprinted with permission. www.cengage.com/permissions; **41.22** Adaptation of illustration "Appetite Controllers" from "Cellular Warriors at the Battle of the Bulge" by Kathleen Sutliff and Jean Marx, from *Science*, February 2003, Volume 299(5608). Copyright © 2003 by AAAS; **41 SSE** Source: Data from "Effects of Parabiosis of Obese with Diabetes and Normal Mice" by D. L. Coleman, from *Diabetologia*, 1973, Volume 9(4).

Chapter 42 42 SSE Source: Based on Figure 1A from "Sequence Variations in PCSK9, Low LDL, and Protection against Coronary Heart Disease" by Jonathan C. Cohen et al., from *New England Journal of Medicine*, March 2006, Volume 354(12); **42.25** Source: Data from "Surface Properties in Relation to Atelectasis and 106 Hyaline Membrane Disease" by M. E. Avery and J. Mead, from *American Journal of Diseases of Children*, May 1959, Volume 97(5, part 1); **42.29, 42.EOC01** Figure adapted from *Human Anatomy and Physiology*, 8th Edition, by Elaine N. Marieb and Katja Hoehn. Copyright © 2010 by Pearson Education, Inc. Adapted and electronically reproduced by permission of Pearson Education, Inc., Upper Saddle River, New Jersey.

Chapter 43 43.5a Adaptation of figure 4a from "Constitutive Expression of a Single Antimicrobial Peptide Can Restore Wild-Type Resistance to Infection in Immunodeficient *Drosophila* Mutants" by Phoebe Tzou et al., from PNAS, February 2002, Volume 99(4). Copyright © 2002 by National Academy of Sciences. Reprinted with permission; **43.5b** Adaptation of figure 2a from "Constitutive Expression of a Single Antimicrobial Peptide Can Restore Wild-Type Resistance to Infection in Immunodeficient *Drosophila* Mutants" by Phoebe Tzou et al., from PNAS, February 2002, Volume 99(4). Copyright © 2002 by National Academy of Sciences. Reprinted with permission; **43.7a** Figure adapted from *Human Anatomy and Physiology*, 8th Edition, by Elaine N. Marieb and Katja Hoehn. Copyright © 2010 by Pearson Education, Inc. Adapted and electronically reproduced by permission of Pearson Education, Inc., Upper Saddle River, New Jersey; **43.7b** Figure adapted from *Human Anatomy and Physiology*, 8th Edition, by Elaine N. Marieb and Katja Hoehn. Copyright © 2010 by Pearson Education, Inc. Adapted and electronically reproduced by permission of Pearson Education, Inc., Upper Saddle River, New Jersey; **43.8** Figure adapted from *Microbiology*: *An Introduction*, 11th Edition, by Gerard J. Tortora, Berdell R. Funke, and Christine L. Case. Copyright © 2012 Pearson Education Inc. Adapted and electronically reproduced by permission of Pearson Education, Inc., Upper Saddle River, New Jersey.

Chapter 44 44 SSE Source: Data from "Water Economy and Energy Metabolism of the Sandy Inland Mouse, *Leggadina hermannsburgensis*" by Richard E. MacMillen et al., from *Journal of Mammalogy*, August 1972, Volume 53(3); **44.7** Figure adapted from *Zoology*, 1st Edition, by Lawrence G. Mitchell. Copyright © 1988 by Pearson Education Inc. Adapted and electronically reproduced by permission of Pearson Education, Inc., Upper Saddle River, New Jersey; **44.12b, 44.13** Figure adapted from *Human Anatomy and Physiology*, 8th Edition, by Elaine N. Marieb and Katja Hoehn. Copyright © 2010 by Pearson Education, Inc. Adapted and electronically reproduced by permission of Pearson Education, Inc., Upper Saddle River, New Jersey; **44.20** "Requirement of Human Renal Water Channel Aquaporin-2 for Vasopressin-Dependent Concentration in Urine" by P. M. Deen et al., from *Science*, April 1994, Volume 264(5155). Copyright © 1994 by AAAS. Reprinted with permission; **44.EOC01** Figure adapted from *Life: An Introduction to Biology*, 3rd Edition, by William Samson Beck. Copyright © 1991 by Pearson Education, Inc. Adapted and electronically reproduced by permission of Pearson Education, Inc., Upper Saddle River, New Jersey; **44.Ans01** Source: Data for kangaroo rat from *Animal Physiology: Adaptation and Environment* by Knut Schmidt-Nielsen. Cambridge University Press, 1991.

Chapter 45 45 SSE Data from J. Born, et al., "Timing the end of nocturnal sleep," *Nature*, 397:29-30 (1999).

Chapter 46 46.8 Adaptation of Figure 2 from "Sperm Death and Dumping in *Drosophila*" by Rhonda R. Snook and David J. Hosken, from *Nature*, April 29, 2004, Volume 428(6986). Copyright © 2004 by Macmillan Publishers Ltd. Reprinted with permission; **46 SSE** Source: Data from "*Recherches sur la Différenciation Sexuelle de L'embryon de Lapin* (Studies on the Sexual Differentiation of the Rabbit Embryo)" by Alfred Jost, from *Archives D'anatomie Microscopique Et De Morphologie Experimentale*, 1947, Volume 36; **46.16** Figure adapted from *Human Anatomy and Physiology*, 8th Edition, by Elaine N. Marieb and Katja Hoehn. Copyright © 2010 by Pearson Education, Inc. Adapted and electronically reproduced by permission of Pearson Education, Inc., Upper Saddle River, New Jersey.

Chapter 47 47.4 Source: Based on "Intracellular Calcium Release at Fertilization in the Sea Urchin Egg" by R. Steinhardt et al., from *Developmental Biology*, July 1977, Volume 58(1); **47.10(b) and 47.14** Figures adapted from "Cell Commitment and Gene Expression in the Axolotl Embryo" by T. J. Mohun, et al., from *Cell*, November 1980, Volume 22(1); **47.17** Adaptation from figure 1.9 and Box 8c from *Principles of Development*, 4th Edition, by Lewis Wolpert. Copyright © 2011 by Oxford University Press. Reprinted with permission; **47.19** Adaptation of figure 21.17 from *Molecular Biology of the Cell*, 4th Edition, by Bruce Alberts et al. Copyright © 2002 by Garland Science/Taylor & Francis LLC. Reprinted with permission; **47.23** Source: Based on *Embryonic Development and Induction* by Hans Spemann. Yale University Press, 1938; **47.24a, b** Adaptation from figure 1.9 and Box 8c from *Principles of Development*, 4th Edition, by Lewis Wolpert. Copyright © 2011 by Oxford University Press. Reprinted with permission; **47.24b** Adaptation of Figure 15.12 from *Developmental Biology* by Scott F. Gilbert. Copyright © 1997 by Sinauer Associates, Inc. Reprinted with permission; **47.26** Source: Based on "Maps of Strength of Positional Signalling Activity in

the Developing Chick Wing Bud" by Lawrence S. Honig and Dennis Summerbell, from *Journal of Embryology and Experimental Morphology*, June 1985, Volume 87(1); **47.27** Figure adapted from *Human Anatomy and Physiology*, 8th Edition, by Elaine N. Marieb and Katja Hoehn. Copyright © 2010 by Pearson Education, Inc. Adapted and electronically reproduced by permission of Pearson Education, Inc., Upper Saddle River, New Jersey.

Chapter 48 48.11f Source: Based on figure 6-2d from *Cellular Physiology of Nerve and Muscle*, 4th Edition, by Gary G. Matthews. Wiley-Blackwell, 2003; **48 SSE** Source: Data from "Opiate Receptor: Demonstration in Nervous Tissue" by Candace B. Pert and Solomon H. Snyder, from *Science*, March 1973, Volume 179(4077).

Chapter 49 49.9 *Human Anatomy and Physiology*, 8th Edition, by Elaine N. Marieb and Katja Hoehn. Copyright © 2010 by Pearson Education. Reprinted and electronically reproduced by permission of Pearson Education, Inc., Upper Saddle River, New Jersey; **49.13** Source: Based on "Sleep in Marine Mammals" by L. M. Mukhametov, from *Sleep Mechanisms*, edited by Alexander A. Borberly and J. L. Valatx. Springer, 1984; **49 SSE** Adaptation of Figure 2a from "Transplanted Suprachiasmatic Nucleus Determines Circadian Period" by Martin R. Ralph et al., from *Science*, February 1990, Volume 247(4945). Copyright © 1990 by AAAS. Reprinted with permission; **49.19** Adaptation of figure 1c from "Avian Brains and a New Understanding of Vertebrate Brain Evolution" by Erich D. Jarvis et al., from *Nature Reviews Neuroscience*, February 2005, Volume 6(2). Copyright © 2005 by Macmillan Publishers Ltd. Reprinted with permission; **49.22** Adaptation of figure 10 from *Schizophrenia Genesis: The Origins of Madness* by Irving I. Gottesman. Copyright © 1991 by Irving I. Gottesman. Reprinted by permission of Worth Publishers.

Chapter 50 50.12 *Human Anatomy and Physiology*, 8th Edition, by Elaine N. Marieb and Katja Hoehn. Copyright © 2010 by Pearson Education. Reprinted and electronically reproduced by permission of Pearson Education, Inc., Upper Saddle River, New Jersey; **50.13** *Human Anatomy and Physiology*, 8th Edition, by Elaine N. Marieb and Katja Hoehn. Copyright © 2010 by Pearson Education. Reprinted and electronically reproduced by permission of Pearson Education, Inc., Upper Saddle River, New Jersey; **50.17a** Figure adapted from *Human Anatomy and Physiology*, 8th Edition, by Elaine N. Marieb and Katja Hoehn. Copyright © 2010 by Pearson Education, Inc. Adapted and electronically reproduced by permission of Pearson Education, Inc., Upper Saddle River, New Jersey; **50.17b** Figure adapted from *Human Anatomy and Physiology*, 8th Edition, by Elaine N. Marieb and Katja Hoehn. Copyright © 2010 by Pearson Education, Inc. Adapted and electronically reproduced by permission of Pearson Education, Inc., Upper Saddle River, New Jersey; **50.23a** Adaptation of figure 4b from "The Receptors and Coding Logic for Bitter Taste" by Ken L. Muller et al., from *Nature*, March 10, 2005, Volume 434(7030). Copyright © 2005 by Macmillan Publishers Ltd. Reprinted with permission; **50.24a** Adaptation of figure 15.23(a) from *Human Anatomy and Physiology*, 8th Edition, by Elaine N. Marieb and Katja Hoehn. Copyright © 2010 by Pearson Education, Inc. Adapted and electronically reproduced by permission of Pearson Education, Inc., Upper Saddle River, New Jersey. Adaptation of figure 15.23(b) from *Human Anatomy and Physiology*, 8th Edition, by Elaine N. Marieb and Katja Hoehn. Copyright © 2010 by Pearson Education, Inc. Adapted and electronically reproduced by permission of Pearson Education, Inc., Upper Saddle River, New Jersey; **50.26** Figure adapted from *Human Anatomy and Physiology*, 8th Edition, by Elaine N. Marieb and Katja Hoehn. Copyright © 2010 by Pearson Education, Inc. Adapted and electronically reproduced by permission of Pearson Education, Inc., Upper Saddle River, New Jersey; **50.30** Figure adapted from *Human Anatomy and Physiology*, 8th Edition, by Elaine N. Marieb and Katja Hoehn. Copyright © 2010 by Pearson Education, Inc. Adapted and electronically reproduced by permission of Pearson Education, Inc., Upper Saddle River, New Jersey; **50 SSE** Adaptation of figure 4 from "Locomotion: Energy Cost of Swimming, Flying, and Running" by Knut Schmidt-Nielsen, from *Science*, July 1972, Volume 177(4045). Copyright © 1972 by AAAS. Reprinted with permission.

Chapter 51 51.2b Adaptation of figure 20 from *The Study of Instincts* by Nikolaas Tinbergen. Copyright © 1989 by Oxford University Press. Reprinted with permission. Adaptation of figures 65 and 66 in *Inleiding tot de Diersociologie*, by Nikolaas Tinbergen, © 1946. Reprinted by permission of E. Barendrecht-Tinbergen. **51.4** Adaptation of figure 1 from "*Drosophila*: Genetics Meets Behavior" by Marla B. Sokolowski, from *Nature Reviews: Genetics*, November 2001, Volume 2(11). Copyright © 2001 by Macmillan Publishers Ltd. Reprinted with permission; **51.24b** Adaptation of figure 1 from "Rapid Microevolution of Migratory Behaviour in a Wild Bird Species" by P. Berthold et al., from *Nature*, December 1992, Volume 360(6405). Copyright © 1992 by Macmillan Publishers Ltd. Reprinted with permission; **51.8, 51.EOC** Figure adapted from *Zoology*, 1st Edition, by Lawrence G. Mitchell et al. Pearson Education Inc., 1988; **51.10** Adaptation of figure 3a from "Prospective and Retrospective Learning in Honeybees" by Martin Giurfa and Julie Bernard, from *International Journal of Comparative Psychology*, 2006, Volume 19(3). Copyright © 2006 by International Society for Comparative Psychology. Reprinted with permission; **51.13** Adaptation of figure 2a from "Evolution of Foraging Behavior in *Drosophila* by Density-Dependent Selection" by Maria B. Sokolowski et al., from PNAS, July 8, 1997, Volume 94(14). Copyright © 1997 by National Academy of Sciences, U.S.A. Reprinted with permission; **51 SSE** Source: Data from "Shell Dropping: Decision-Making and Optimal Foraging in Northwestern Crows" by Reto Zach, from *Behaviour*, 1979, Volume 68(1–2); **51.18** Reprinted with the permission of Dr. Klaudia White; **51.24a** Adaptations of photograph by Jonathan Blair from *Animal Behavior: An Evolutionary Approach*, 7th Edition, by John Alcock. Copyright © 2002 by Sinauer Associates, Inc. Reprinted with permission.

GLOSSARY

Pronunciation Key

ā	ace
a/ah	ash
ch	chose
ē	meet
e/eh	bet
g	game
ī	ice
i	hit
ks	box
kw	quick
ng	song
ō	robe
o	ox
oy	boy
s	say
sh	shell
th	thin
ū	boot
u/uh	up
z	zoo

′ = primary accent
′ = secondary accent

5′ cap A modified form of guanine nucleotide added onto the 5′ end of a pre-mRNA molecule.

ABC hypothesis A model of flower formation identifying three classes of organ identity genes that direct formation of the four types of floral organs.

abiotic (ā′-bī-ot′-ik) Nonliving; referring to the physical and chemical properties of an environment.

abortion The termination of a pregnancy in progress.

abscisic acid (ABA) (ab-sis′-ik) A plant hormone that slows growth, often antagonizing the actions of growth hormones. Two of its many effects are to promote seed dormancy and facilitate drought tolerance.

absorption The third stage of food processing in animals: the uptake of small nutrient molecules by an organism's body.

absorption spectrum The range of a pigment's ability to absorb various wavelengths of light; also a graph of such a range.

abyssal zone (uh-bis′-ul) The part of the ocean's benthic zone between 2,000 and 6,000 m deep.

acanthodian (ak′-an-thō′-dē-un) Any of a group of ancient jawed aquatic vertebrates from the Silurian and Devonian periods.

accessory fruit A fruit, or assemblage of fruits, in which the fleshy parts are derived largely or entirely from tissues other than the ovary.

acclimatization (uh-klī′-muh-tī -zā′-shun) Physiological adjustment to a change in an environmental factor.

acetyl CoA Acetyl coenzyme A; the entry compound for the citric acid cycle in cellular respiration, formed from a two-carbon fragment of pyruvate attached to a coenzyme.

acetylcholine (as′-uh-til-kō′-lēn) One of the most common neurotransmitters; functions by binding to receptors and altering the permeability of the postsynaptic membrane to specific ions, either depolarizing or hyperpolarizing the membrane.

acid A substance that increases the hydrogen ion concentration of a solution.

acoelomate (uh-sē′-lō-māt) A solid-bodied animal lacking a cavity between the gut and outer body wall.

acquired immunodeficiency syndrome (AIDS) The symptoms and signs present during the late stages of HIV infection, defined by a specified reduction in the number of T cells and the appearance of characteristic secondary infections.

acrosomal reaction (ak′-ruh-sōm′-ul) The discharge of hydrolytic enzymes from the acrosome, a vesicle in the tip of a sperm, when the sperm approaches or contacts an egg.

acrosome (ak′-ruh-sōm) A vesicle in the tip of a sperm containing hydrolytic enzymes and other proteins that help the sperm reach the egg.

actin (ak′-tin) A globular protein that links into chains, two of which twist helically about each other, forming microfilaments (actin filaments) in muscle and other kinds of cells.

action potential An electrical signal that propagates (travels) along the membrane of a neuron or other excitable cell as a nongraded (all-or-none) depolarization.

action spectrum A graph that profiles the relative effectiveness of different wavelengths of radiation in driving a particular process.

activation energy The amount of energy that reactants must absorb before a chemical reaction will start; also called free energy of activation.

activator A protein that binds to DNA and stimulates gene transcription. In prokaryotes, activators bind in or near the promoter; in eukaryotes, activators generally bind to control elements in enhancers.

active immunity Long-lasting immunity conferred by the action of B cells and T cells and the resulting B and T memory cells specific for a pathogen. Active immunity can develop as a result of natural infection or immunization.

active site The specific region of an enzyme that binds the substrate and that forms the pocket in which catalysis occurs.

active transport The movement of a substance across a cell membrane against its concentration or electrochemical gradient, mediated by specific transport proteins and requiring an expenditure of energy.

adaptation Inherited characteristic of an organism that enhances its survival and reproduction in a specific environment.

adaptive evolution Evolution that results in a better match between organisms and their environment.

adaptive immunity A vertebrate-specific defense that is mediated by B lymphocytes (B cells) and T lymphocytes (T cells) and that exhibits specificity, memory, and self-nonself recognition; also called acquired immunity.

adaptive radiation Period of evolutionary change in which groups of organisms form many new species whose adaptations allow them to fill different ecological roles in their communities.

addition rule A rule of probability stating that the probability of any one of two or more mutually exclusive events occurring can be determined by adding their individual probabilities.

adenosine triphosphate See ATP (adenosine triphosphate).

adenylyl cyclase (uh-den′-uh-lil) An enzyme that converts ATP to cyclic AMP in response to an extracellular signal.

adhesion The clinging of one substance to another, such as water to plant cell walls by means of hydrogen bonds.

adipose tissue A connective tissue that insulates the body and serves as a fuel reserve; contains fat-storing cells called adipose cells.

adrenal gland (uh-drē′-nul) One of two endocrine glands located adjacent to the kidneys in mammals. Endocrine cells in the outer portion (cortex) respond to adrenocorticotropic hormone (ACTH) by secreting steroid hormones that help maintain homeostasis during long-term stress. Neurosecretory cells in the central portion (medulla) secrete epinephrine and norepinephrine in response to nerve signals triggered by short-term stress.

aerobic respiration A catabolic pathway for organic molecules, using oxygen (O_2) as the final electron acceptor in an electron transport chain and ultimately producing ATP. This is the most efficient catabolic pathway and is carried out in most eukaryotic cells and many prokaryotic organisms.

age structure The relative number of individuals of each age in a population.

aggregate fruit A fruit derived from a single flower that has more than one carpel.

AIDS (acquired immunodeficiency syndrome) The symptoms and signs present during the late stages of HIV infection, defined by a specified reduction in the number of T cells and the appearance of characteristic secondary infections.

alcohol fermentation Glycolysis followed by the reduction of pyruvate to ethyl alcohol, regenerating NAD$^+$ and releasing carbon dioxide.

aldosterone (al-dos′-tuh-rōn) A steroid hormone that acts on tubules of the kidney to regulate the transport of sodium ions (Na$^+$) and potassium ions (K$^+$).

alga (plural, **algae**) A member of a diverse collection of photosynthetic protists that includes both unicellular and multicellular forms. Algal species are included in three eukaryote supergroups (Excavata, "SAR" clade, and Archaeplastida).

alimentary canal (al′-uh-men′-tuh-rē) A complete digestive tract, consisting of a tube running between a mouth and an anus.

alkaline vent A deep-sea hydrothermal vent that releases water that is warm (40–90°C) rather than hot and that has a high pH (is basic). These vents consist of tiny pores lined with iron and other catalytic minerals that some scientists hypothesize might have been the location of the earliest abiotic synthesis of organic compounds.

allele (uh-lē′-ul) Any of the alternative versions of a gene that may produce distinguishable phenotypic effects.

allopatric speciation (al′-uh-pat′-rik) The formation of new species in populations that are geographically isolated from one another.

allopolyploid (al′-ō-pol′-ē-ployd) A fertile individual that has more than two chromosome sets as a result of two different species interbreeding and combining their chromosomes.

allosteric regulation The binding of a regulatory molecule to a protein at one site that affects the function of the protein at a different site.

alpha (α) helix (al′-fuh hē′-liks) A coiled region constituting one form of the secondary structure of proteins, arising from a specific pattern of hydrogen bonding between atoms of the polypeptide backbone (not the side chains).

alternation of generations A life cycle in which there is both a multicellular diploid form, the sporophyte, and a multicellular haploid form, the gametophyte; characteristic of plants and some algae.

alternative RNA splicing A type of eukaryotic gene regulation at the RNA-processing level in which different mRNA molecules are produced from the same primary transcript, depending on which RNA segments are treated as exons and which as introns.

altruism (al′-trū-iz-um) Selflessness; behavior that reduces an individual's fitness while increasing the fitness of another individual.

alveolates (al-vē′-uh-lets) One of the three major subgroups for which the "SAR" eukaryotic supergroup is named. This clade arose by secondary endosymbiosis; alveolate protists have membrane-enclosed sacs (alveoli) located just under the plasma membrane.

alveolus (al-vē′-uh-lus) (plural, **alveoli**) One of the dead-end air sacs where gas exchange occurs in a mammalian lung.

Alzheimer's disease (alts′-hī-merz) An age-related dementia (mental deterioration) characterized by confusion and memory loss.

amino acid (uh-mēn′-ō) An organic molecule possessing both a carboxyl and an amino group. Amino acids serve as the monomers of polypeptides.

amino group (uh-mēn′-ō) A chemical group consisting of a nitrogen atom bonded to two hydrogen atoms; can act as a base in solution, accepting a hydrogen ion and acquiring a charge of 1+.

aminoacyl-tRNA synthetase An enzyme that joins each amino acid to the appropriate tRNA.

ammonia A small, toxic molecule (NH_3) produced by nitrogen fixation or as a metabolic waste product of protein and nucleic acid metabolism.

ammonite A member of a group of shelled cephalopods that were important marine predators for hundreds of millions of years until their extinction at the end of the Cretaceous period (65.5 million years ago).

amniocentesis (am′-nē-ō-sen-tē′-sis) A technique associated with prenatal diagnosis in which amniotic fluid is obtained by aspiration from a needle inserted into the uterus. The fluid and the fetal cells it contains are analyzed to detect certain genetic and congenital defects in the fetus.

amniote (am′-nē-ōt) A member of a clade of tetrapods named for a key derived character, the amniotic egg, which contains specialized membranes, including the fluid-filled amnion, that protect the embryo. Amniotes include mammals as well as birds and other reptiles.

amniotic egg An egg that contains specialized membranes that function in protection, nourishment, and gas exchange. The amniotic egg was a major evolutionary innovation, allowing embryos to develop on land in a fluid-filled sac, thus reducing the dependence of tetrapods on water for reproduction.

amoeba (uh-mē′-buh) A protist characterized by the presence of pseudopodia.

amoebocyte (uh-mē′-buh-sīt′) An amoeba-like cell that moves by pseudopodia and is found in most animals. Depending on the species, it may digest and distribute food, dispose of wastes, form skeletal fibers, fight infections, or change into other cell types.

amoebozoan (uh-mē′-buh-zō′-an) A protist in a clade that includes many species with lobe- or tube-shaped pseudopodia.

amphibian A member of the clade of tetrapods that includes salamanders, frogs, and caecilians.

amphipathic (am′-fē-path′-ik) Having both a hydrophilic region and a hydrophobic region.

amplification The strengthening of stimulus energy during transduction.

amygdala (uh-mig′-duh-luh) A structure in the temporal lobe of the vertebrate brain that has a major role in the processing of emotions.

amylase (am′-uh-lās′) An enzyme that hydrolyzes starch (a glucose polymer from plants) and glycogen (a glucose polymer from animals) into smaller polysaccharides and the disaccharide maltose.

anabolic pathway (an′-uh-bol′-ik) A metabolic pathway that consumes energy to synthesize a complex molecule from simpler molecules.

anaerobic respiration (an-er-ō′-bik) A catabolic pathway in which inorganic molecules other than oxygen accept electrons at the "downhill" end of electron transport chains.

analogous Having characteristics that are similar because of convergent evolution, not homology.

analogy (an-al′-uh-jē) Similarity between two species that is due to convergent evolution rather than to descent from a common ancestor with the same trait.

anaphase The fourth stage of mitosis, in which the chromatids of each chromosome have separated and the daughter chromosomes are moving to the poles of the cell.

anatomy The structure of an organism.

anchorage dependence The requirement that a cell must be attached to a substratum in order to initiate cell division.

androgen (an′-drō-jen) Any steroid hormone, such as testosterone, that stimulates the development and maintenance of the male reproductive system and secondary sex characteristics.

aneuploidy (an′-yū-ploy′-dē) A chromosomal aberration in which one or more chromosomes are present in extra copies or are deficient in number.

angiosperm (an′-jē-ō-sperm) A flowering plant, which forms seeds inside a protective chamber called an ovary.

angiotensin II A peptide hormone that stimulates constriction of precapillary arterioles and increases reabsorption of NaCl and water by the proximal tubules of the kidney, increasing blood pressure and volume.

anhydrobiosis (an-hī′-drō-bī-ō′-sis) A dormant state involving loss of almost all body water.

animal pole The point at the end of an egg in the hemisphere where the least yolk is concentrated; opposite of vegetal pole.

anion (an′-ī-on) A negatively charged ion.

anterior Pertaining to the front, or head, of a bilaterally symmetrical animal.

anterior pituitary A portion of the pituitary gland that develops from nonneural tissue; consists of endocrine cells that synthesize and secrete several tropic and nontropic hormones.

anther In an angiosperm, the terminal pollen sac of a stamen, where pollen grains containing sperm-producing male gametophytes form.

antheridium (an-thuh-rid′-ē-um) (plural, **antheridia**) In plants, the male gametangium, a moist chamber in which gametes develop.

anthropoid (an′-thruh-poyd) A member of a primate group made up of the monkeys and the apes (gibbons, orangutans, gorillas, chimpanzees, bonobos, and humans).

antibody A protein secreted by plasma cells (differentiated B cells) that binds to a particular antigen; also called immunoglobulin. All antibodies have the same Y-shaped structure and in their monomer form consist of two identical heavy chains and two identical light chains.

anticodon (an′-tī-kō′-don) A nucleotide triplet at one end of a tRNA molecule that base-pairs with a particular complementary codon on an mRNA molecule.

antidiuretic hormone (ADH) (an'-tī-dī-yū-ret'-ik) A peptide hormone, also called vasopressin, that promotes water retention by the kidneys. Produced in the hypothalamus and released from the posterior pituitary, ADH also functions in the brain.

antigen (an'-ti-jen) A substance that elicits an immune response by binding to receptors of B or T cells.

antigen presentation (an'-ti-jen) The process by which an MHC molecule binds to a fragment of an intracellular protein antigen and carries it to the cell surface, where it is displayed and can be recognized by a T cell.

antigen-presenting cell (an'-ti-jen) A cell that upon ingesting pathogens or internalizing pathogen proteins generates peptide fragments that are bound by class II MHC molecules and subsequently displayed on the cell surface to T cells. Macrophages, dendritic cells, and B cells are the primary antigen-presenting cells.

antigen receptor (an'-ti-jen) The general term for a surface protein, located on B cells and T cells, that binds to antigens, initiating adaptive immune responses. The antigen receptors on B cells are called B cell receptors, and the antigen receptors on T cells are called T cell receptors.

antiparallel Referring to the arrangement of the sugar-phosphate backbones in a DNA double helix (they run in opposite $5' \rightarrow 3'$ directions).

aphotic zone (ā'-fō'-tik) The part of an ocean or lake beneath the photic zone, where light does not penetrate sufficiently for photosynthesis to occur.

apical bud (ā'-pik-ul) A bud at the tip of a plant stem; also called a terminal bud.

apical dominance (ā'-pik-ul) Tendency for growth to be concentrated at the tip of a plant shoot, because the apical bud partially inhibits axillary bud growth.

apical ectodermal ridge (AER) (ā'-pik-ul) A thickened area of ectoderm at the tip of a limb bud that promotes outgrowth of the limb bud.

apical meristem (ā'-pik-ul măr'-uh-stem) Embryonic plant tissue in the tips of roots and buds of shoots. The dividing cells of an apical meristem enable the plant to grow in length.

apicomplexan (ap'-ē-kom-pleks'-un) A protist in a clade that includes many species that parasitize animals. Some apicomplexans cause human disease.

apomixis (ap'-uh-mik'-sis) The ability of some plant species to reproduce asexually through seeds without fertilization by a male gamete.

apoplast (ap'-ō-plast) Everything external to the plasma membrane of a plant cell, including cell walls, intercellular spaces, and the space within dead structures such as xylem vessels and tracheids.

apoptosis (ā-puh-tō'-sus) A type of programmed cell death, which is brought about by activation of enzymes that break down many chemical components in the cell.

aposematic coloration (ap'-ō-si-mat'-ik) The bright warning coloration of many animals with effective physical or chemical defenses.

appendix A small, finger-like extension of the vertebrate cecum; contains a mass of white blood cells that contribute to immunity.

aquaporin A channel protein in a cellular membrane that specifically facilitates osmosis, the diffusion of free water across the membrane.

aqueous solution (ā'-kwē-us) A solution in which water is the solvent.

arachnid A member of a subgroup of the major arthropod clade Chelicerata. Arachnids have six pairs of appendages, including four pairs of walking legs, and include spiders, scorpions, ticks, and mites.

arbuscular mycorrhiza (ar-bus'-kyū-lur mī'-kō-rī'-zuh) Association of a fungus with a plant root system in which the fungus causes the invagination of the host (plant) cells' plasma membranes.

arbuscular mycorrhizal fungus (ar-bus'-kyū-lur) A symbiotic fungus whose hyphae grow through the cell wall of plant roots and extend into the root cell (enclosed in tubes formed by invagination of the root cell plasma membrane).

Archaea (ar'-kē'-uh) One of two prokaryotic domains, the other being Bacteria.

Archaeplastida (ar'-kē-plas'-tid-uh) One of four supergroups of eukaryotes proposed in a current hypothesis of the evolutionary history of eukaryotes. This monophyletic group, which includes red algae, green algae, and land plants, descended from an ancient protist ancestor that engulfed a cyanobacterium. *See also* Excavata, "SAR" clade, and Unikonta.

archegonium (ar-ki-gō'-nē-um) (plural, **archegonia**) In plants, the female gametangium, a moist chamber in which gametes develop.

archenteron (ar-ken'-tuh-ron) The endoderm-lined cavity, formed during gastrulation, that develops into the digestive tract of an animal.

archosaur (ar'-kō-sōr) A member of the reptilian group that includes crocodiles, alligators and dinosaurs, including birds.

arteriole (ar-ter'-ē-ōl) A vessel that conveys blood between an artery and a capillary bed.

artery A vessel that carries blood away from the heart to organs throughout the body.

arthropod A segmented ecdysozoan with a hard exoskeleton and jointed appendages. Familiar examples include insects, spiders, millipedes, and crabs.

artificial selection The selective breeding of domesticated plants and animals to encourage the occurrence of desirable traits.

ascocarp The fruiting body of a sac fungus (ascomycete).

ascomycete (as'-kuh-mī'-sēt) A member of the fungal phylum Ascomycota, commonly called sac fungus. The name comes from the saclike structure in which the spores develop.

ascus (plural, **asci**) A saclike spore capsule located at the tip of a dikaryotic hypha of a sac fungus.

asexual reproduction The generation of offspring from a single parent that occurs without the fusion of gametes (by budding, division of a single cell, or division of the entire organism into two or more parts). In most cases, the offspring are genetically identical to the parent.

A site One of a ribosome's three binding sites for tRNA during translation. The A site holds the tRNA carrying the next amino acid to be added to the polypeptide chain. (A stands for aminoacyl tRNA.)

assisted migration The translocation of a species to a favorable habitat beyond its native range for the purpose of protecting the species from human-caused threats.

associative learning The acquired ability to associate one environmental feature (such as a color) with another (such as danger).

aster A radial array of short microtubules that extends from each centrosome toward the plasma membrane in an animal cell undergoing mitosis.

astrocyte A glial cell with diverse functions, including providing structural support for neurons, regulating the interstitial environment, facilitating synaptic transmission, and assisting in regulating the blood supply to the brain.

atherosclerosis A cardiovascular disease in which fatty deposits called plaques develop in the inner walls of the arteries, obstructing the arteries and causing them to harden.

atom The smallest unit of matter that retains the properties of an element.

atomic mass The total mass of an atom, numerically equivalent to the mass in grams of 1 mole of the atom. (For an element with more than one isotope, the atomic mass is the average mass of the naturally occurring isotopes, weighted by their abundance.)

atomic nucleus An atom's dense central core, containing protons and neutrons.

atomic number The number of protons in the nucleus of an atom, unique for each element and designated by a subscript.

ATP (adenosine triphosphate) (a-den'-ō-sēn trī-fos'-fāt) An adenine-containing nucleoside triphosphate that releases free energy when its phosphate bonds are hydrolyzed. This energy is used to drive endergonic reactions in cells.

ATP synthase A complex of several membrane proteins that functions in chemiosmosis with adjacent electron transport chains, using the energy of a hydrogen ion (proton) concentration gradient to make ATP. ATP synthases are found in the inner mitochondrial membranes of eukaryotic cells and in the plasma membranes of prokaryotes.

atrial natriuretic peptide (ANP) (ā'-trē-ul na'-trē-yū-ret'-ik) A peptide hormone secreted by cells of the atria of the heart in response to high blood pressure. ANP's effects on the kidney alter ion and water movement and reduce blood pressure.

atrioventricular (AV) node A region of specialized heart muscle tissue between the left and right atria where electrical impulses are delayed for about 0.1 second before spreading to both ventricles and causing them to contract.

atrioventricular (AV) valve A heart valve located between each atrium and ventricle that prevents a backflow of blood when the ventricle contracts.

atrium (ā′-trē-um) (plural, **atria**) A chamber of the vertebrate heart that receives blood from the veins and transfers blood to a ventricle.

autocrine Referring to a secreted molecule that acts on the cell that secreted it.

autoimmune disease An immunological disorder in which the immune system turns against self.

autonomic nervous system (ot′-ō-nom′-ik) An efferent branch of the vertebrate peripheral nervous system that regulates the internal environment; consists of the sympathetic, parasympathetic, and enteric divisions.

autopolyploid (ot′-ō-pol′-ē-ployd) An individual that has more than two chromosome sets that are all derived from a single species.

autosome (ot′-ō-sōm) A chromosome that is not directly involved in determining sex; not a sex chromosome.

autotroph (ot′-ō-trōf) An organism that obtains organic food molecules without eating other organisms or substances derived from other organisms. Autotrophs use energy from the sun or from oxidation of inorganic substances to make organic molecules from inorganic ones.

auxin (ôk′-sin) A term that primarily refers to indoleacetic acid (IAA), a natural plant hormone that has a variety of effects, including cell elongation, root formation, secondary growth, and fruit growth.

axillary bud (ak′-sil-ār-ē) A structure that has the potential to form a lateral shoot, or branch. The bud appears in the angle formed between a leaf and a stem.

axon (ak′-son) A typically long extension, or process, of a neuron that carries nerve impulses away from the cell body toward target cells.

B cells The lymphocytes that complete their development in the bone marrow and become effector cells for the humoral immune response.

Bacteria One of two prokaryotic domains, the other being Archaea.

bacteriophage (bak-tēr′-ē-ō-fāj) A virus that infects bacteria; also called a phage.

bacteroid A form of the bacterium *Rhizobium* contained within the vesicles formed by the root cells of a root nodule.

balancing selection Natural selection that maintains two or more phenotypic forms in a population.

bar graph A graph in which the independent variable represents groups or nonnumerical categories and the values of the dependent variable(s) are shown by bars.

bark All tissues external to the vascular cambium, consisting mainly of the secondary phloem and layers of periderm.

Barr body A dense object lying along the inside of the nuclear envelope in cells of female mammals, representing a highly condensed, inactivated X chromosome.

basal angiosperm A member of one of three clades of early-diverging lineages of extant flowering plants. Examples are *Amborella*, water lilies, and star anise and its relatives.

basal body (bā′-sul) A eukaryotic cell structure consisting of a "9 + 0" arrangement of microtubule triplets. The basal body may organize the microtubule assembly of a cilium or flagellum and is structurally very similar to a centriole.

basal metabolic rate (BMR) The metabolic rate of a resting, fasting, and nonstressed endotherm at a comfortable temperature.

basal taxon In a specified group of organisms, a taxon whose evolutionary lineage diverged early in the history of the group.

base A substance that reduces the hydrogen ion concentration of a solution.

basidiocarp Elaborate fruiting body of a dikaryotic mycelium of a club fungus.

basidiomycete (buh-sid′-ē-ō-mī′-sēt) A member of the fungal phylum Basidiomycota, commonly called club fungus. The name comes from the club-like shape of the basidium.

basidium (plural, **basidia**) (buh-sid′-ē-um, buh-sid′-ē-ah) A reproductive appendage that produces sexual spores on the gills of mushrooms (club fungi).

Batesian mimicry (bāt′-zē-un mim′-uh-krē) A type of mimicry in which a harmless species looks like a species that is poisonous or otherwise harmful to predators.

behavior Individually, an action carried out by muscles or glands under control of the nervous system in response to a stimulus; collectively, the sum of an animal's responses to external and internal stimuli.

behavioral ecology The study of the evolution of and ecological basis for animal behavior.

benign tumor A mass of abnormal cells with specific genetic and cellular changes such that the cells are not capable of surviving at a new site and generally remain at the site of the tumor's origin.

benthic zone The bottom surface of an aquatic environment.

benthos (ben′-thōz) The communities of organisms living in the benthic zone of an aquatic biome.

beta (β) pleated sheet One form of the secondary structure of proteins in which the polypeptide chain folds back and forth. Two regions of the chain lie parallel to each other and are held together by hydrogen bonds between atoms of the polypeptide backbone (not the side chains).

beta oxidation A metabolic sequence that breaks fatty acids down to two-carbon fragments that enter the citric acid cycle as acetyl CoA.

bicoid A maternal effect gene that codes for a protein responsible for specifying the anterior end in *Drosophila melanogaster*.

bilateral symmetry Body symmetry in which a central longitudinal plane divides the body into two equal but opposite halves.

bilaterian (bī′-luh-ter′-ē-uhn) A member of a clade of animals with bilateral symmetry and three germ layers.

bile A mixture of substances that is produced in the liver and stored in the gallbladder; enables formation of fat droplets in water as an aid in the digestion and absorption of fats.

binary fission A method of asexual reproduction by "division in half." In prokaryotes, binary fission does not involve mitosis, but in single-celled eukaryotes that undergo binary fission, mitosis is part of the process.

binomial A common term for the two-part, latinized format for naming a species, consisting of the genus and specific epithet; also called a binomen.

biodiversity hot spot A relatively small area with numerous endemic species and a large number of endangered and threatened species.

bioenergetics (1) The overall flow and transformation of energy in an organism. (2) The study of how energy flows through organisms.

biofilm A surface-coating colony of one or more species of prokaryotes that engage in metabolic cooperation.

biofuel A fuel produced from biomass.

biogenic amine A neurotransmitter derived from an amino acid.

biogeochemical cycle Any of the various chemical cycles, which involve both biotic and abiotic components of ecosystems.

biogeography The scientific study of the past and present geographic distributions of species.

bioinformatics The use of computers, software, and mathematical models to process and integrate biological information from large data sets.

biological augmentation An approach to restoration ecology that uses organisms to add essential materials to a degraded ecosystem.

biological clock An internal timekeeper that controls an organism's biological rhythms. The biological clock marks time with or without environmental cues but often requires signals from the environment to remain tuned to an appropriate period. *See also* circadian rhythm.

biological magnification A process in which retained substances become more concentrated at each higher trophic level in a food chain.

biological species concept Definition of a species as a group of populations whose members have the potential to interbreed in nature and produce viable, fertile offspring but do not produce viable, fertile offspring with members of other such groups.

biology The scientific study of life.

biomanipulation An approach that applies the top-down model of community organization to alter ecosystem characteristics. For example, ecologists can prevent algal blooms and eutrophication by altering the density of higher-level consumers in lakes instead of by using chemical treatments.

biomass The total mass of organic matter comprising a group of organisms in a particular habitat.

biome (bī′-ōm) Any of the world's major ecosystem types, often classified according to the predominant vegetation for terrestrial biomes and the physical environment for aquatic biomes and characterized by adaptations of organisms to that particular environment.

bioremediation The use of organisms to detoxify and restore polluted and degraded ecosystems.

biosphere The entire portion of Earth inhabited by life; the sum of all the planet's ecosystems.

biotechnology The manipulation of organisms or their components to produce useful products.

biotic (bī-ot′-ik) Pertaining to the living factors—the organisms—in an environment.

bipolar disorder A depressive mental illness characterized by swings of mood from high to low; also called manic-depressive disorder.

birth control pill A hormonal contraceptive that inhibits ovulation, retards follicular development, or alters a woman's cervical mucus to prevent sperm from entering the uterus.

blade (1) A leaflike structure of a seaweed that provides most of the surface area for photosynthesis. (2) The flattened portion of a typical leaf.

blastocoel (blas′-tuh-sēl) The fluid-filled cavity that forms in the center of a blastula.

blastocyst (blas′-tuh-sist) The blastula stage of mammalian embryonic development, consisting of an inner cell mass, a cavity, and an outer layer, the trophoblast. In humans, the blastocyst forms 1 week after fertilization.

blastomere An early embryonic cell arising during the cleavage stage of an early embryo.

blastopore (blas′-tō-pōr) In a gastrula, the opening of the archenteron that typically develops into the anus in deuterostomes and the mouth in protostomes.

blastula (blas′-tyū-luh) A hollow ball of cells that marks the end of the cleavage stage during early embryonic development in animals.

blood A connective tissue with a fluid matrix called plasma in which red blood cells, white blood cells, and cell fragments called platelets are suspended.

blue-light photoreceptor A type of light receptor in plants that initiates a variety of responses, such as phototropism and slowing of hypocotyl elongation.

body cavity A fluid- or air-filled space between the digestive tract and the body wall.

body plan In multicellular eukaryotes, a set of morphological and developmental traits that are integrated into a functional whole—the living organism.

Bohr shift A lowering of the affinity of hemoglobin for oxygen, caused by a drop in pH. It facilitates the release of oxygen from hemoglobin in the vicinity of active tissues.

bolus A lubricated ball of chewed food.

bone A connective tissue consisting of living cells held in a rigid matrix of collagen fibers embedded in calcium salts.

book lung An organ of gas exchange in spiders, consisting of stacked plates contained in an internal chamber.

bottleneck effect Genetic drift that occurs when the size of a population is reduced, as by a natural disaster or human actions. Typically, the surviving population is no longer genetically representative of the original population.

bottom-up model A model of community organization in which mineral nutrients influence community organization by controlling plant or phytoplankton numbers, which in turn control herbivore numbers, which in turn control predator numbers.

Bowman's capsule (bō′-munz) A cup-shaped receptacle in the vertebrate kidney that is the initial, expanded segment of the nephron, where filtrate enters from the blood.

brachiopod (bra′-kē-uh-pod′) A marine lophophorate with a shell divided into dorsal and ventral halves; also called lamp shells.

brain Organ of the central nervous system where information is processed and integrated.

brainstem A collection of structures in the vertebrate brain, including the midbrain, the pons, and the medulla oblongata; functions in homeostasis, coordination of movement, and conduction of information to higher brain centers.

branch point The representation on a phylogenetic tree of the divergence of two or more taxa from a common ancestor. A branch point is usually shown as a dichotomy in which a branch representing the ancestral lineage splits (at the branch point) into two branches, one for each of the two descendant lineages.

brassinosteroid A steroid hormone in plants that has a variety of effects, including inducing cell elongation, retarding leaf abscission, and promoting xylem differentiation.

breathing Ventilation of the lungs through alternating inhalation and exhalation.

bronchiole (brong′-kē-ōl′) A fine branch of the bronchi that transports air to alveoli.

bronchus (brong′-kus) (plural, **bronchi**) One of a pair of breathing tubes that branch from the trachea into the lungs.

brown alga A multicellular, photosynthetic protist with a characteristic brown or olive color that results from carotenoids in its plastids. Most brown algae are marine, and some have a plantlike body.

bryophyte (brī′-uh-fīt) An informal name for a moss, liverwort, or hornwort; a nonvascular plant that lives on land but lacks some of the terrestrial adaptations of vascular plants.

buffer A solution that contains a weak acid and its corresponding base. A buffer minimizes changes in pH when acids or bases are added to the solution.

bulk feeder An animal that eats relatively large pieces of food.

bulk flow The movement of a fluid due to a difference in pressure between two locations.

bundle-sheath cell In C_4 plants, a type of photosynthetic cell arranged into tightly packed sheaths around the veins of a leaf.

C_3 plant A plant that uses the Calvin cycle for the initial steps that incorporate CO_2 into organic material, forming a three-carbon compound as the first stable intermediate.

C_4 plant A plant in which the Calvin cycle is preceded by reactions that incorporate CO_2 into a four-carbon compound, the end product of which supplies CO_2 for the Calvin cycle.

calcitonin (kal′-si-tō′-nin) A hormone secreted by the thyroid gland that lowers blood calcium levels by promoting calcium deposition in bone and calcium excretion from the kidneys; nonessential in adult humans.

callus A mass of dividing, undifferentiated cells growing in culture.

calorie (cal) The amount of heat energy required to raise the temperature of 1 g of water by 1°C; also the amount of heat energy that 1 g of water releases when it cools by 1°C. The Calorie (with a capital C), usually used to indicate the energy content of food, is a kilocalorie.

Calvin cycle The second of two major stages in photosynthesis (following the light reactions), involving fixation of atmospheric CO_2 and reduction of the fixed carbon into carbohydrate.

Cambrian explosion A relatively brief time in geologic history when many present-day phyla of animals first appeared in the fossil record. This burst of evolutionary change occurred about 535–525 million years ago and saw the emergence of the first large, hard-bodied animals.

CAM plant A plant that uses crassulacean acid metabolism, an adaptation for photosynthesis in arid conditions. In this process, CO_2 entering open stomata during the night is converted to organic acids, which release CO_2 for the Calvin cycle during the day, when stomata are closed.

canopy The uppermost layer of vegetation in a terrestrial biome.

capillary (kap′-il-ār′-ē) A microscopic blood vessel that penetrates the tissues and consists of a single layer of endothelial cells that allows exchange between the blood and interstitial fluid.

capillary bed (kap′-il-ār′-ē) A network of capillaries in a tissue or organ.

capsid The protein shell that encloses a viral genome. It may be rod-shaped, polyhedral, or more complex in shape.

capsule (1) In many prokaryotes, a dense and well-defined layer of polysaccharide or protein that surrounds the cell wall and is sticky, protecting the cell and enabling it to adhere to substrates or other cells. (2) The sporangium of a bryophyte (moss, liverwort, or hornwort).

carbohydrate (kar′-bō-hī′-drāt) A sugar (monosaccharide) or one of its dimers (disaccharides) or polymers (polysaccharides).

carbon fixation The initial incorporation of carbon from CO_2 into an organic compound by an autotrophic organism (a plant, another photosynthetic organism, or a chemoautotrophic prokaryote).

carbonyl group (kar-buh-nēl′) A chemical group present in aldehydes and ketones and consisting of a carbon atom double-bonded to an oxygen atom.

carboxyl group (kar-bok′-sil) A chemical group present in organic acids and consisting of a single carbon atom double-bonded to an oxygen atom and also bonded to a hydroxyl group.

cardiac cycle (kar′-dē-ak) The alternating contractions and relaxations of the heart.

cardiac muscle (kar'-dē-ak) A type of striated muscle that forms the contractile wall of the heart. Its cells are joined by intercalated disks that relay the electrical signals underlying each heartbeat.

cardiac output (kar'-dē-ak) The volume of blood pumped per minute by each ventricle of the heart.

cardiovascular system A closed circulatory system with a heart and branching network of arteries, capillaries, and veins. The system is characteristic of vertebrates.

carnivore An animal that mainly eats other animals.

carotenoid (kuh-rot'-uh-noyd') An accessory pigment, either yellow or orange, in the chloroplasts of plants and in some prokaryotes. By absorbing wavelengths of light that chlorophyll cannot, carotenoids broaden the spectrum of colors that can drive photosynthesis.

carpel (kar'-pul) The ovule-producing reproductive organ of a flower, consisting of the stigma, style, and ovary.

carrier In genetics, an individual who is heterozygous at a given genetic locus for a recessively inherited disorder. The heterozygote is generally phenotypically normal for the disorder but can pass on the recessive allele to offspring.

carrying capacity The maximum population size that can be supported by the available resources, symbolized as K.

cartilage (kar'-til-ij) A flexible connective tissue with an abundance of collagenous fibers embedded in chondroitin sulfate.

Casparian strip (ka-spär'-ē-un) A water-impermeable ring of wax in the endodermal cells of plants that blocks the passive flow of water and solutes into the stele by way of cell walls.

catabolic pathway (kat'-uh-bol'-ik) A metabolic pathway that releases energy by breaking down complex molecules to simpler molecules.

catalyst (kat'-uh-list) A chemical agent that selectively increases the rate of a reaction without being consumed by the reaction.

catecholamine (kat'-uh-kōl'-uh-mēn) Any of a class of neurotransmitters and hormones, including the hormones epinephrine and norepinephrine, that are synthesized from the amino acid tyrosine.

cation (cat'-ī'-on) A positively charged ion.

cation exchange (cat'-ī'-on) A process in which positively charged minerals are made available to a plant when hydrogen ions in the soil displace mineral ions from the clay particles.

cecum (sē'-kum) (plural, **ceca**) The blind pouch forming one branch of the large intestine.

cell body The part of a neuron that houses the nucleus and most other organelles.

cell cycle An ordered sequence of events in the life of a cell, from its origin in the division of a parent cell until its own division into two. The eukaryotic cell cycle is composed of interphase (including G_1, S, and G_2 subphases) and M phase (including mitosis and cytokinesis).

cell cycle control system A cyclically operating set of molecules in the eukaryotic cell that

both triggers and coordinates key events in the cell cycle.

cell division The reproduction of cells.

cell fractionation The disruption of a cell and separation of its parts by centrifugation at successively higher speeds.

cell-mediated immune response The branch of adaptive immunity that involves the activation of cytotoxic T cells, which defend against infected cells.

cell plate A membrane-bounded, flattened sac located at the midline of a dividing plant cell, inside which the new cell wall forms during cytokinesis.

cellular respiration The catabolic pathways of aerobic and anaerobic respiration, which break down organic molecules and use an electron transport chain for the production of ATP.

cellulose (sel'-yū-lōs) A structural polysaccharide of plant cell walls, consisting of glucose monomers joined by β glycosidic linkages.

cell wall A protective layer external to the plasma membrane in the cells of plants, prokaryotes, fungi, and some protists. Polysaccharides such as cellulose (in plants and some protists), chitin (in fungi), and peptidoglycan (in bacteria) are important structural components of cell walls.

central nervous system (CNS) The portion of the nervous system where signal integration occurs; in vertebrate animals, the brain and spinal cord.

central vacuole In a mature plant cell, a large membranous sac with diverse roles in growth, storage, and sequestration of toxic substances.

centriole (sen'-trē-ōl) A structure in the centrosome of an animal cell composed of a cylinder of microtubule triplets arranged in a "9 + 0" pattern. A centrosome has a pair of centrioles.

centromere (sen'-trō-mēr) In a duplicated chromosome, the region on each sister chromatid where it is most closely attached to the other chromatid by proteins that bind to the centromeric DNA. Other proteins condense the chromatin in that region, so it appears as a narrow "waist" on the duplicated chromosome. (An unduplicated chromosome has a single centromere, identified by the proteins bound there.)

centrosome (sen'-trō-sōm) A structure present in the cytoplasm of animal cells that functions as a microtubule-organizing center and is important during cell division. A centrosome has two centrioles.

cercozoan An amoeboid or flagellated protist that feeds with threadlike pseudopodia.

cerebellum (sãr'-ruh-bel'-um) Part of the vertebrate hindbrain located dorsally; functions in unconscious coordination of movement and balance.

cerebral cortex (suh-rē'-brul) The surface of the cerebrum; the largest and most complex part of the mammalian brain, containing nerve cell bodies of the cerebrum; the part of the vertebrate brain most changed through evolution.

cerebral hemisphere (suh-rē'-brul) The right or left side of the cerebrum.

cerebrum (suh-rē'-brum) The dorsal portion of the vertebrate forebrain, composed of right and left hemispheres; the integrating center for memory, learning, emotions, and other highly complex functions of the central nervous system.

cervix (ser'-viks) The neck of the uterus, which opens into the vagina.

chaparral A scrubland biome of dense, spiny evergreen shrubs found at midlatitudes along coasts where cold ocean currents circulate offshore; characterized by mild, rainy winters and long, hot, dry summers.

chaperonin (shap'-er-ō'-nin) A protein complex that assists in the proper folding of other proteins.

character An observable heritable feature that may vary among individuals.

character displacement The tendency for characteristics to be more divergent in sympatric populations of two species than in allopatric populations of the same two species.

checkpoint A control point in the cell cycle where stop and go-ahead signals can regulate the cycle.

chelicera (kē-lih'-suh-ruh) (plural, **chelicerae**) One of a pair of clawlike feeding appendages characteristic of chelicerates.

chelicerate (kē-lih-suh'-rāte) An arthropod that has chelicerae and a body divided into a cephalothorax and an abdomen. Living chelicerates include sea spiders, horseshoe crabs, scorpions, ticks, and spiders.

chemical bond An attraction between two atoms, resulting from a sharing of outer-shell electrons or the presence of opposite charges on the atoms. The bonded atoms gain complete outer electron shells.

chemical energy Energy available in molecules for release in a chemical reaction; a form of potential energy.

chemical equilibrium In a chemical reaction, the state in which the rate of the forward reaction equals the rate of the reverse reaction, so that the relative concentrations of the reactants and products do not change with time.

chemical reaction The making and breaking of chemical bonds, leading to changes in the composition of matter.

chemiosmosis (kem'-ē-oz-mō'-sis) An energy-coupling mechanism that uses energy stored in the form of a hydrogen ion gradient across a membrane to drive cellular work, such as the synthesis of ATP. Under aerobic conditions, most ATP synthesis in cells occurs by chemiosmosis.

chemoautotroph (kē'-mō-ot'-ō-trōf) An organism that obtains energy by oxidizing inorganic substances and needs only carbon dioxide as a carbon source.

chemoheterotroph (kē'-mō-het'-er-ō-trōf) An organism that requires organic molecules for both energy and carbon.

chemoreceptor A sensory receptor that responds to a chemical stimulus, such as a solute or an odorant.

chiasma (plural, **chiasmata**) (kī-az'-muh, kī-az'-muh-tuh) The X-shaped, microscopically visible region where crossing over has occurred earlier in prophase I between homologous nonsister chromatids. Chiasmata become visible after synapsis ends, with the two homologs remaining associated due to sister chromatid cohesion.

chitin (kī'-tin) A structural polysaccharide, consisting of amino sugar monomers, found in many fungal cell walls and in the exoskeletons of all arthropods.

chlorophyll (klōr'-ō-fil) A green pigment located in membranes within the chloroplasts of plants and algae and in the membranes of certain prokaryotes. Chlorophyll *a* participates directly in the light reactions, which convert solar energy to chemical energy.

chlorophyll *a* (klōr'-ō-fil) A photosynthetic pigment that participates directly in the light reactions, which convert solar energy to chemical energy.

chlorophyll *b* (klōr'-ō-fil) An accessory photosynthetic pigment that transfers energy to chlorophyll *a*.

chloroplast (klōr'-ō-plast) An organelle found in plants and photosynthetic protists that absorbs sunlight and uses it to drive the synthesis of organic compounds from carbon dioxide and water.

choanocyte (kō-an'-uh-sīt) A flagellated feeding cell found in sponges. Also called a collar cell, it has a collar-like ring that traps food particles around the base of its flagellum.

cholesterol (kō-les'-tuh-rol) A steroid that forms an essential component of animal cell membranes and acts as a precursor molecule for the synthesis of other biologically important steroids, such as many hormones.

chondrichthyan (kon-drik'-thē-an) A member of the clade Chondrichthyes, vertebrates with skeletons made mostly of cartilage, such as sharks and rays.

chordate A member of the phylum Chordata, animals that at some point during their development have a notochord; a dorsal, hollow nerve cord; pharyngeal slits or clefts; and a muscular, post-anal tail.

chorionic villus sampling (CVS) (kōr'-ē-on'-ik vil'-us) A technique associated with prenatal diagnosis in which a small sample of the fetal portion of the placenta is removed for analysis to detect certain genetic and congenital defects in the fetus.

chromatin (krō'-muh-tin) The complex of DNA and proteins that makes up eukaryotic chromosomes. When the cell is not dividing, chromatin exists in its dispersed form, as a mass of very long, thin fibers that are not visible with a light microscope.

chromosome (krō'-muh-sōm) A cellular structure consisting of one DNA molecule and associated protein molecules. (In some contexts, such as genome sequencing, the term may refer to the DNA alone.) A eukaryotic cell typically has multiple, linear chromosomes, which are located in the nucleus. A prokaryotic cell often has a single, circular chromosome, which is found in the nucleoid, a region that is not enclosed by a membrane. *See also* chromatin.

chromosome theory of inheritance (krō'-muh-sōm) A basic principle in biology stating that genes are located at specific positions (loci) on chromosomes and that the behavior of chromosomes during meiosis accounts for inheritance patterns.

chylomicron (kī'-lō-mī'-kron) A lipid transport globule composed of fats mixed with cholesterol and coated with proteins.

chyme (kīm) The mixture of partially digested food and digestive juices formed in the stomach.

chytrid (kī'-trid) A member of the fungal phylum Chytridiomycota, mostly aquatic fungi with flagellated zoospores that represent an early-diverging fungal lineage.

ciliate (sil'-ē-it) A type of protist that moves by means of cilia.

cilium (sil'-ē-um) (plural, **cilia**) A short appendage containing microtubules in eukaryotic cells. A motile cilium is specialized for locomotion or moving fluid past the cell; it is formed from a core of nine outer doublet microtubules and two inner single microtubules (the "9 + 2" arrangement) ensheathed in an extension of the plasma membrane. A primary cilium is usually nonmotile and plays a sensory and signaling role; it lacks the two inner microtubules (the "9 + 0" arrangement).

circadian rhythm (ser-kā'-dē-un) A physiological cycle of about 24 hours that persists even in the absence of external cues.

***cis-trans* isomer** One of several compounds that have the same molecular formula and covalent bonds between atoms but differ in the spatial arrangements of their atoms owing to the inflexibility of double bonds; formerly called a geometric isomer.

citric acid cycle A chemical cycle involving eight steps that completes the metabolic breakdown of glucose molecules begun in glycolysis by oxidizing acetyl CoA (derived from pyruvate) to carbon dioxide; occurs within the mitochondrion in eukaryotic cells and in the cytosol of prokaryotes; together with pyruvate oxidation, the second major stage in cellular respiration.

clade (klayd) A group of species that includes an ancestral species and all of its descendants. A clade is equivalent to a monophyletic group.

cladistics (kluh-dis'-tiks) An approach to systematics in which organisms are placed into groups called clades based primarily on common descent.

class In Linnaean classification, the taxonomic category above the level of order.

cleavage (1) The process of cytokinesis in animal cells, characterized by pinching of the plasma membrane. (2) The succession of rapid cell divisions without significant growth during early embryonic development that converts the zygote to a ball of cells.

cleavage furrow The first sign of cleavage in an animal cell; a shallow groove around the cell in the cell surface near the old metaphase plate.

climate The long-term prevailing weather conditions at a given place.

climograph A plot of the temperature and precipitation in a particular region.

clitoris (klit'-uh-ris) An organ at the upper intersection of the labia minora that engorges with blood and becomes erect during sexual arousal.

cloaca (klō-ā'-kuh) A common opening for the digestive, urinary, and reproductive tracts found in many nonmammalian vertebrates but in few mammals.

clonal selection The process by which an antigen selectively binds to and activates only those lymphocytes bearing receptors specific for the antigen. The selected lymphocytes proliferate and differentiate into a clone of effector cells and a clone of memory cells specific for the stimulating antigen.

clone (1) A lineage of genetically identical individuals or cells. (2) In popular usage, an individual that is genetically identical to another individual. (3) As a verb, to make one or more genetic replicas of an individual or cell. *See also* gene cloning.

cloning vector In genetic engineering, a DNA molecule that can carry foreign DNA into a host cell and replicate there. Cloning vectors include plasmids and bacterial artificial chromosomes (BACs), which move recombinant DNA from a test tube back into a cell, and viruses that transfer recombinant DNA by infection.

closed circulatory system A circulatory system in which blood is confined to vessels and is kept separate from the interstitial fluid.

cnidocyte (nī'-duh-sīt) A specialized cell unique to the phylum Cnidaria; contains a capsule-like organelle housing a coiled thread that, when discharged, explodes outward and functions in prey capture or defense.

cochlea (kok'-lē-uh) The complex, coiled organ of hearing that contains the organ of Corti.

codominance The situation in which the phenotypes of both alleles are exhibited in the heterozygote because both alleles affect the phenotype in separate, distinguishable ways.

codon (kō'-don) A three-nucleotide sequence of DNA or mRNA that specifies a particular amino acid or termination signal; the basic unit of the genetic code.

coefficient of relatedness The fraction of genes that, on average, are shared by two individuals.

coelom (sē'-lōm) A body cavity lined by tissue derived only from mesoderm.

coelomate (sē'-lō-māt) An animal that possesses a true coelom (a body cavity lined by tissue completely derived from mesoderm).

coenocytic fungus (sē'-no-si'-tic) A fungus that lacks septa and hence whose body is made up of a continuous cytoplasmic mass that may contain hundreds or thousands of nuclei.

coenzyme (kō-en'-zīm) An organic molecule serving as a cofactor. Most vitamins function as coenzymes in metabolic reactions.

coevolution The joint evolution of two interacting species, each in response to selection imposed by the other.

cofactor Any nonprotein molecule or ion that is required for the proper functioning of an enzyme. Cofactors can be permanently bound to the active site or may bind loosely and reversibly, along with the substrate, during catalysis.

cognition The process of knowing that may include awareness, reasoning, recollection, and judgment.

cognitive map A neural representation of the abstract spatial relationships between objects in an animal's surroundings.

cohesion The linking together of like molecules, often by hydrogen bonds.

cohesion-tension hypothesis The leading explanation of the ascent of xylem sap. It states that transpiration exerts pull on xylem sap, putting the sap under negative pressure, or tension, and that the cohesion of water molecules transmits this pull along the entire length of the xylem from shoots to roots.

cohort A group of individuals of the same age in a population.

coleoptile (kō′-lē-op′-tul) The covering of the young shoot of the embryo of a grass seed.

coleorhiza (kō′-lē-uh-rī′-zuh) The covering of the young root of the embryo of a grass seed.

collagen A glycoprotein in the extracellular matrix of animal cells that forms strong fibers, found extensively in connective tissue and bone; the most abundant protein in the animal kingdom.

collecting duct The location in the kidney where processed filtrate, called urine, is collected from the renal tubules.

collenchyma cell (kō-len′-kim-uh) A flexible plant cell type that occurs in strands or cylinders that support young parts of the plant without restraining growth.

colon (kō′-len) The largest section of the vertebrate large intestine; functions in water absorption and formation of feces.

commensalism (kuh-men′-suh-lizm) A symbiotic relationship in which one organism benefits but the other is neither helped nor harmed.

communication In animal behavior, a process involving transmission of, reception of, and response to signals. The term is also used in connection with other organisms, as well as individual cells of multicellular organisms.

community All the organisms that inhabit a particular area; an assemblage of populations of different species living close enough together for potential interaction.

community ecology The study of how interactions between species affect community structure and organization.

companion cell A type of plant cell that is connected to a sieve-tube element by many plasmodesmata and whose nucleus and ribosomes may serve one or more adjacent sieve-tube elements.

competitive exclusion The concept that when populations of two similar species compete for the same limited resources, one population will use the resources more efficiently and have a reproductive advantage that will eventually lead to the elimination of the other population.

competitive inhibitor A substance that reduces the activity of an enzyme by entering the active site in place of the substrate, whose structure it mimics.

complement system A group of about 30 blood proteins that may amplify the inflammatory response, enhance phagocytosis, or directly lyse extracellular pathogens.

complementary DNA (cDNA) A double-stranded DNA molecule made *in vitro* using mRNA as a template and the enzymes reverse transcriptase and DNA polymerase. A cDNA molecule corresponds to the exons of a gene.

complete dominance The situation in which the phenotypes of the heterozygote and dominant homozygote are indistinguishable.

complete flower A flower that has all four basic floral organs: sepals, petals, stamens, and carpels.

complete metamorphosis The transformation of a larva into an adult that looks very different, and often functions very differently in its environment, than the larva.

compound A substance consisting of two or more different elements combined in a fixed ratio.

compound eye A type of multifaceted eye in insects and crustaceans consisting of up to several thousand light-detecting, focusing ommatidia.

concentration gradient A region along which the density of a chemical substance increases or decreases.

conception The fertilization of an egg by a sperm in humans.

cone A cone-shaped cell in the retina of the vertebrate eye, sensitive to color.

conformer An animal for which an internal condition conforms to (changes in accordance with) changes in an environmental variable.

conidium (plural, **conidia**) A haploid spore produced at the tip of a specialized hypha in ascomycetes during asexual reproduction.

conifer A member of the largest gymnosperm phylum. Most conifers are cone-bearing trees, such as pines and firs.

conjugation (kon′-jū-gā′-shun) (1) In prokaryotes, the direct transfer of DNA between two cells that are temporarily joined. When the two cells are members of different species, conjugation results in horizontal gene transfer. (2) In ciliates, a sexual process in which two cells exchange haploid micronuclei but do not reproduce.

connective tissue Animal tissue that functions mainly to bind and support other tissues, having a sparse population of cells scattered through an extracellular matrix.

conodont An early, soft-bodied vertebrate with prominent eyes and dental elements.

conservation biology The integrated study of ecology, evolutionary biology, physiology, molecular biology, and genetics to sustain biological diversity at all levels.

consumer An organism that feeds on producers, other consumers, or nonliving organic material.

contraception The deliberate prevention of pregnancy.

contractile vacuole A membranous sac that helps move excess water out of certain freshwater protists.

control element A segment of noncoding DNA that helps regulate transcription of a gene by serving as a binding site for a transcription factor. Multiple control elements are present in a eukaryotic gene's enhancer.

control group In a controlled experiment, a set of subjects that lacks (or does not receive) the specific factor being tested. Ideally, the control group should be identical to the experimental group in other respects.

controlled experiment An experiment in which an experimental group is compared with a control group that varies only in the factor being tested.

convergent evolution The evolution of similar features in independent evolutionary lineages.

convergent extension A process in which the cells of a tissue layer rearrange themselves in such a way that the sheet of cells becomes narrower (converges) and longer (extends).

cooperativity A kind of allosteric regulation whereby a shape change in one subunit of a protein caused by substrate binding is transmitted to all the other subunits, facilitating binding of additional substrate molecules to those subunits.

coral reef Typically a warm-water, tropical ecosystem dominated by the hard skeletal structures secreted primarily by corals. Some coral reefs also exist in cold, deep waters.

corepressor A small molecule that binds to a bacterial repressor protein and changes the protein's shape, allowing it to bind to the operator and switch an operon off.

cork cambium (kam′-bē-um) A cylinder of meristematic tissue in woody plants that replaces the epidermis with thicker, tougher cork cells.

corpus callosum (kor′-pus kuh-lō′-sum) The thick band of nerve fibers that connects the right and left cerebral hemispheres in mammals, enabling the hemispheres to process information together.

corpus luteum (kor′-pus lū′-tē-um) A secreting tissue in the ovary that forms from the collapsed follicle after ovulation and produces progesterone.

cortex (1) The outer region of cytoplasm in a eukaryotic cell, lying just under the plasma membrane, that has a more gel-like consistency than the inner regions due to the presence of multiple microfilaments. (2) In plants, ground tissue that is between the vascular tissue and dermal tissue in a root or eudicot stem.

cortical nephron In mammals and birds, a nephron with a loop of Henle located almost entirely in the renal cortex.

cotransport The coupling of the "downhill" diffusion of one substance to the "uphill" transport of another against its own concentration gradient.

cotyledon (kot′-uh-lē′-dun) A seed leaf of an angiosperm embryo. Some species have one cotyledon, others two.

countercurrent exchange The exchange of a substance or heat between two fluids flowing in opposite directions. For example, blood in a fish gill flows in the opposite direction of water passing over the gill, maximizing diffusion of oxygen into and carbon dioxide out of the blood.

countercurrent multiplier system A countercurrent system in which energy is expended in active transport to facilitate exchange of materials and generate concentration gradients.

covalent bond (kō-vā′-lent) A type of strong chemical bond in which two atoms share one or more pairs of valence electrons.

crassulacean acid metabolism (CAM) An adaptation for photosynthesis in arid conditions, first discovered in the family Crassulaceae. In this process, a plant takes up CO_2 and incorporates it into a variety of organic acids at night; during the day, CO_2 is released from organic acids for use in the Calvin cycle.

crista (plural, **cristae**) (kris′-tuh, kris′-tē) An infolding of the inner membrane of a mitochondrion. The inner membrane houses electron transport chains and molecules of the enzyme catalyzing the synthesis of ATP (ATP synthase).

critical load The amount of added nutrient, usually nitrogen or phosphorus, that can be absorbed by plants without damaging ecosystem integrity.

crop rotation The practice of growing different crops in succession on the same land chiefly to preserve the productive capacity of the soil.

cross-fostering study A behavioral study in which the young of one species are placed in the care of adults from another species.

crossing over The reciprocal exchange of genetic material between nonsister chromatids during prophase I of meiosis.

cross-pollination In angiosperms, the transfer of pollen from an anther of a flower on one plant to the stigma of a flower on another plant of the same species.

cryptic coloration Camouflage that makes a potential prey difficult to spot against its background.

culture A system of information transfer through social learning or teaching that influences the behavior of individuals in a population.

cuticle (kyū′-tuh-kul) (1) A waxy covering on the surface of stems and leaves that prevents desiccation in terrestrial plants. (2) The exoskeleton of an arthropod, consisting of layers of protein and chitin that are variously modified for different functions. (3) A tough coat that covers the body of a nematode.

cyclic AMP (cAMP) Cyclic adenosine monophosphate, a ring-shaped molecule made from ATP that is a common intracellular signaling molecule (second messenger) in eukaryotic cells. It is also a regulator of some bacterial operons.

cyclic electron flow A route of electron flow during the light reactions of photosynthesis that involves only one photosystem and that produces ATP but not NADPH or O_2.

cyclin (sī′-klin) A cellular protein that occurs in a cyclically fluctuating concentration and that plays an important role in regulating the cell cycle.

cyclin-dependent kinase (Cdk) (sī′-klin) A protein kinase that is active only when attached to a particular cyclin.

cyclostome A member of the vertebrate subgroup lacking jaws. Cyclostomes include hagfishes and lampreys.

cystic fibrosis (sis′-tik fī-brō′-sis) A human genetic disorder caused by a recessive allele for a chloride channel protein; characterized by an excessive secretion of mucus and consequent vulnerability to infection; fatal if untreated.

cytochrome (sī′-tō-krōm) An iron-containing protein that is a component of electron transport chains in the mitochondria and chloroplasts of eukaryotic cells and the plasma membranes of prokaryotic cells.

cytokinesis (sī′-tō-kuh-nē′-sis) The division of the cytoplasm to form two separate daughter cells immediately after mitosis, meiosis I, or meiosis II.

cytokinin (sī′-tō-kī′-nin) Any of a class of related plant hormones that retard aging and act in concert with auxin to stimulate cell division, influence the pathway of differentiation, and control apical dominance.

cytoplasm (sī′-tō-plaz-um) The contents of the cell bounded by the plasma membrane; in eukaryotes, the portion exclusive of the nucleus.

cytoplasmic determinant A maternal substance, such as a protein or RNA, that when placed into an egg influences the course of early development by regulating the expression of genes that affect the developmental fate of cells.

cytoplasmic streaming A circular flow of cytoplasm, involving interactions of myosin and actin filaments, that speeds the distribution of materials within cells.

cytoskeleton A network of microtubules, microfilaments, and intermediate filaments that extend throughout the cytoplasm and serve a variety of mechanical, transport, and signaling functions.

cytosol (sī′-tō-sol) The semifluid portion of the cytoplasm.

cytotoxic T cell A type of lymphocyte that, when activated, kills infected cells as well as certain cancer cells and transplanted cells.

dalton A measure of mass for atoms and subatomic particles; the same as the atomic mass unit, or amu.

data Recorded observations.

day-neutral plant A plant in which flower formation is not controlled by photoperiod or day length.

decomposer An organism that absorbs nutrients from nonliving organic material such as corpses, fallen plant material, and the wastes of living organisms and converts them to inorganic forms; a detritivore.

deductive reasoning A type of logic in which specific results are predicted from a general premise.

deep-sea hydrothermal vent A dark, hot, oxygen-deficient environment associated with volcanic activity on or near the seafloor. The producers in a vent community are chemoautotrophic prokaryotes.

de-etiolation The changes a plant shoot undergoes in response to sunlight; also known informally as greening.

dehydration reaction A chemical reaction in which two molecules become covalently bonded to each other with the removal of a water molecule.

deletion (1) A deficiency in a chromosome resulting from the loss of a fragment through breakage. (2) A mutational loss of one or more nucleotide pairs from a gene.

demographic transition In a stable population, a shift from high birth and death rates to low birth and death rates.

demography The study of changes over time in the vital statistics of populations, especially birth rates and death rates.

denaturation (dē-nā′-chur-ā′-shun) In proteins, a process in which a protein loses its native shape due to the disruption of weak chemical bonds and interactions, thereby becoming biologically inactive; in DNA, the separation of the two strands of the double helix. Denaturation occurs under extreme (noncellular) conditions of pH, salt concentration, or temperature.

dendrite (den′-drīt) One of usually numerous, short, highly branched extensions of a neuron that receive signals from other neurons.

dendritic cell An antigen-presenting cell, located mainly in lymphatic tissues and skin, that is particularly efficient in presenting antigens to helper T cells, thereby initiating a primary immune response.

density The number of individuals per unit area or volume.

density dependent Referring to any characteristic that varies with population density.

density-dependent inhibition The phenomenon observed in normal animal cells that causes them to stop dividing when they come into contact with one another.

density independent Referring to any characteristic that is not affected by population density.

deoxyribonucleic acid (DNA) (dē-ok′-sē-rī′-bō-nū-klā′-ik) A nucleic acid molecule, usually a double-stranded helix, in which each polynucleotide strand consists of nucleotide monomers with a deoxyribose sugar and the nitrogenous bases adenine (A), cytosine (C), guanine (G), and thymine (T); capable of being replicated and determining the inherited structure of a cell's proteins.

deoxyribose (dē-ok′-si-rī′-bōs) The sugar component of DNA nucleotides, having one fewer hydroxyl group than ribose, the sugar component of RNA nucleotides.

dependent variable A variable whose value is measured during an experiment or other test to see whether it is influenced by changes in another variable (the independent variable).

depolarization A change in a cell's membrane potential such that the inside of the membrane is made less negative relative to the outside. For example, a neuron membrane is depolarized if a stimulus decreases its voltage from the resting potential of −70 mV in the direction of zero voltage.

dermal tissue system The outer protective covering of plants.

desert A terrestrial biome characterized by very low precipitation.

desmosome A type of intercellular junction in animal cells that functions as a rivet, fastening cells together.

determinate cleavage A type of embryonic development in protostomes that rigidly casts the developmental fate of each embryonic cell very early.

determinate growth A type of growth characteristic of most animals and some plant organs, in which growth stops after a certain size is reached.

determination The progressive restriction of developmental potential in which the possible fate of each cell becomes more limited as an embryo develops. At the end of determination, a cell is committed to its fate.

detritivore (deh-trī′-tuh-vōr) A consumer that derives its energy and nutrients from nonliving organic material such as corpses, fallen plant material, and the wastes of living organisms; a decomposer.

detritus (di-trī′-tus) Dead organic matter.

deuteromycete (dū′-tuh-rō-mī′-sēt) Traditional classification for a fungus with no known sexual stage.

deuterostome development (dū′-tuh-rō-stōm′) In animals, a developmental mode distinguished by the development of the anus from the blastopore; often also characterized by radial cleavage and by the body cavity forming as outpockets of mesodermal tissue.

Deuterostomia (dū′-tuh-rō-stōm′-ē-uh) One of the three main lineages of bilaterian animals. *See also* Ecdysozoa and Lophotrochozoa.

development The events involved in an organism's changing gradually from a simple to a more complex or specialized form.

diabetes mellitus (dī′-uh-bē′-tis mel′-uh-tus) An endocrine disorder marked by an inability to maintain glucose homeostasis. The type 1 form results from autoimmune destruction of insulin-secreting cells; treatment usually requires daily insulin injections. The type 2 form most commonly results from reduced responsiveness of target cells to insulin; obesity and lack of exercise are risk factors.

diacylglycerol (DAG) (dī-a′-sil-glis′-er-ol) A second messenger produced by the cleavage of the phospholipid PIP_2 in the plasma membrane.

diaphragm (dī′-uh-fram′) (1) A sheet of muscle that forms the bottom wall of the thoracic cavity in mammals. Contraction of the diaphragm pulls air into the lungs. (2) A dome-shaped rubber cup fitted into the upper portion of the vagina before sexual intercourse. It serves as a physical barrier to the passage of sperm into the uterus.

diapsid (dī-ap′-sid) A member of an amniote clade distinguished by a pair of holes on each side of the skull. Diapsids include the lepidosaurs and archosaurs.

diastole (dī-as′-tō-lē) The stage of the cardiac cycle in which a heart chamber is relaxed and fills with blood.

diastolic pressure Blood pressure in the arteries when the ventricles are relaxed.

diatom Photosynthetic protist in the stramenopile clade; diatoms have a unique glass-like wall made of silicon dioxide embedded in an organic matrix.

dicot A term traditionally used to refer to flowering plants that have two embryonic seed leaves, or cotyledons. Recent molecular evidence indicates that dicots do not form a clade; species once classified as dicots are now grouped into eudicots, magnoliids, and several lineages of basal angiosperms.

differential gene expression The expression of different sets of genes by cells with the same genome.

differentiation The process by which a cell or group of cells becomes specialized in structure and function.

diffusion The random thermal motion of particles of liquids, gases, or solids. In the presence of a concentration or electrochemical gradient, diffusion results in the net movement of a substance from a region where it is more concentrated to a region where it is less concentrated.

digestion The second stage of food processing in animals: the breaking down of food into molecules small enough for the body to absorb.

dihybrid (dī′-hī′-brid) An organism that is heterozygous with respect to two genes of interest. All the offspring from a cross between parents doubly homozygous for different alleles are dihybrids. For example, parents of genotypes *AABB* and *aabb* produce a dihybrid of genotype *AaBb*.

dihybrid cross (dī′-hī′-brid) A cross between two organisms that are each heterozygous for both of the characters being followed (or the self-pollination of a plant that is heterozygous for both characters).

dikaryotic (dī′-kār-ē-ot′-ik) Referring to a fungal mycelium with two haploid nuclei per cell, one from each parent.

dinoflagellate (dī′-nō-flaj′-uh-let) A member of a group of mostly unicellular photosynthetic algae with two flagella situated in perpendicular grooves in cellulose plates covering the cell.

dinosaur A member of an extremely diverse clade of reptiles varying in body shape, size, and habitat. Birds are the only extant dinosaurs.

dioecious (dī-ē′-shus) In plant biology, having the male and female reproductive parts on different individuals of the same species.

diploblastic Having two germ layers.

diploid cell (dip′-loyd) A cell containing two sets of chromosomes (2*n*), one set inherited from each parent.

diplomonad A protist that has modified mitochondria, two equal-sized nuclei, and multiple flagella.

directional selection Natural selection in which individuals at one end of the phenotypic range survive or reproduce more successfully than do other individuals.

disaccharide (dī-sak′-uh-rīd) A double sugar, consisting of two monosaccharides joined by a glycosidic linkage formed by a dehydration reaction.

dispersal The movement of individuals or gametes away from their parent location. This movement sometimes expands the geographic range of a population or species.

dispersion The pattern of spacing among individuals within the boundaries of a population.

disruptive selection Natural selection in which individuals on both extremes of a phenotypic range survive or reproduce more successfully than do individuals with intermediate phenotypes.

distal tubule In the vertebrate kidney, the portion of a nephron that helps refine filtrate and empties it into a collecting duct.

disturbance A natural or human-caused event that changes a biological community and usually removes organisms from it. Disturbances, such as fires and storms, play a pivotal role in structuring many communities.

disulfide bridge A strong covalent bond formed when the sulfur of one cysteine monomer bonds to the sulfur of another cysteine monomer.

DNA (deoxyribonucleic acid) (dē-ok′-sē-rī′-bō-nū-klā′-ik) A nucleic acid molecule, usually a double-stranded helix, in which each polynucleotide strand consists of nucleotide monomers with a deoxyribose sugar and the nitrogenous bases adenine (A), cytosine (C), guanine (G), and thymine (T); capable of being replicated and determining the inherited structure of a cell's proteins.

DNA cloning The production of multiple copies of a specific DNA segment.

DNA ligase (lī′-gās) A linking enzyme essential for DNA replication; catalyzes the covalent bonding of the 3′ end of one DNA fragment (such as an Okazaki fragment) to the 5′ end of another DNA fragment (such as a growing DNA chain).

DNA methylation The presence of methyl groups on the DNA bases (usually cytosine) of plants, animals, and fungi. (The term also refers to the process of adding methyl groups to DNA bases.)

DNA microarray assay A method to detect and measure the expression of thousands of genes at one time. Tiny amounts of a large number of single-stranded DNA fragments representing different genes are fixed to a glass slide and tested for hybridization with samples of labeled cDNA.

DNA polymerase (puh-lim′-er-ās) An enzyme that catalyzes the elongation of new DNA (for example, at a replication fork) by the addition of nucleotides to the 3′ end of an existing chain. There are several different DNA polymerases; DNA polymerase III and DNA polymerase I play major roles in DNA replication in *E. coli*.

DNA replication The process by which a DNA molecule is copied; also called DNA synthesis.

DNA sequencing Determining the complete nucleotide sequence of a gene or DNA segment.

DNA technology Techniques for sequencing and manipulating DNA.

domain (1) A taxonomic category above the kingdom level. The three domains are

Archaea, Bacteria, and Eukarya. (2) A discrete structural and functional region of a protein.

dominant allele An allele that is fully expressed in the phenotype of a heterozygote.

dominant species A species with substantially higher abundance or biomass than other species in a community. Dominant species exert a powerful control over the occurrence and distribution of other species.

dopamine A neurotransmitter that is a catecholamine, like epinephrine and norepinephrine.

dormancy A condition typified by extremely low metabolic rate and a suspension of growth and development.

dorsal Pertaining to the top of an animal with radial or bilateral symmetry.

dorsal lip The region above the blastopore on the dorsal side of the amphibian embryo.

double bond A double covalent bond; the sharing of two pairs of valence electrons by two atoms.

double circulation A circulatory system consisting of separate pulmonary and systemic circuits, in which blood passes through the heart after completing each circuit.

double fertilization A mechanism of fertilization in angiosperms in which two sperm cells unite with two cells in the female gametophyte (embryo sac) to form the zygote and endosperm.

double helix The form of native DNA, referring to its two adjacent antiparallel polynucleotide strands wound around an imaginary axis into a spiral shape.

Down syndrome A human genetic disease usually caused by the presence of an extra chromosome 21; characterized by developmental delays and heart and other defects that are generally treatable or non-life-threatening.

Duchenne muscular dystrophy (duh-shen´) A human genetic disease caused by a sex-linked recessive allele; characterized by progressive weakening and a loss of muscle tissue.

duodenum (dū´-uh-dēn´-um) The first section of the small intestine, where chyme from the stomach mixes with digestive juices from the pancreas, liver, and gallbladder as well as from gland cells of the intestinal wall.

duplication An aberration in chromosome structure due to fusion with a fragment from a homologous chromosome, such that a portion of a chromosome is duplicated.

dynein (dī´-nē-un) In cilia and flagella, a large motor protein extending from one microtubule doublet to the adjacent doublet. ATP hydrolysis drives changes in dynein shape that lead to bending of cilia and flagella.

E site One of a ribosome's three binding sites for tRNA during translation. The E site is the place where discharged tRNAs leave the ribosome. (E stands for exit.)

Ecdysozoa (ek´-dē-sō-zō´-uh) One of the three main lineages of bilaterian animals; many ecdysozoans are molting animals. *See also* Deuterostomia and Lophotrochozoa.

echinoderm (i-kī´-nō-derm) A slow-moving or sessile marine deuterostome with a water vascular system and, in larvae, bilateral symmetry. Echinoderms include sea stars, brittle stars, sea urchins, feather stars, and sea cucumbers.

ecological footprint The aggregate land and water area required by a person, city, or nation to produce all of the resources it consumes and to absorb all of the wastes it generates.

ecological niche (nich) The sum of a species' use of the biotic and abiotic resources in its environment.

ecological species concept Definition of a species in terms of ecological niche, the sum of how members of the species interact with the nonliving and living parts of their environment.

ecological succession Transition in the species composition of a community following a disturbance; establishment of a community in an area virtually barren of life.

ecology The study of how organisms interact with each other and their environment.

ecosystem All the organisms in a given area as well as the abiotic factors with which they interact; one or more communities and the physical environment around them.

ecosystem ecology The study of energy flow and the cycling of chemicals among the various biotic and abiotic components in an ecosystem.

ecosystem engineer An organism that influences community structure by causing physical changes in the environment.

ecosystem service A function performed by an ecosystem that directly or indirectly benefits humans.

ecotone The transition from one type of habitat or ecosystem to another, such as the transition from a forest to a grassland.

ectoderm (ek´-tō-durm) The outermost of the three primary germ layers in animal embryos; gives rise to the outer covering and, in some phyla, the nervous system, inner ear, and lens of the eye.

ectomycorrhiza (plural, **ectomycorrhizae**) (ek´-tō-mī´-kō-rī´-zuh, ek´-tō-mī´-kō-rī´-zē) Association of a fungus with a plant root system in which the fungus surrounds the roots but does not cause invagination of the host (plant) cell's plasma membrane.

ectomycorrhizal fungus A symbiotic fungus that forms sheaths of hyphae over the surface of plant roots and also grows into extracellular spaces of the root cortex.

ectoparasite A parasite that feeds on the external surface of a host.

ectopic Occurring in an abnormal location.

ectoproct A sessile, colonial lophophorate; also called a bryozoan.

ectothermic Referring to organisms for which external sources provide most of the heat for temperature regulation.

Ediacaran biota (ē´-dē-uh-keh´-run bī-ō´-tuh) An early group of macroscopic, soft-bodied, multicellular eukaryotes known from fossils that range in age from 635 million to 535 million years old.

effective population size An estimate of the size of a population based on the numbers of females and males that successfully breed; generally smaller than the total population.

effector Pathogen-encoded protein that cripples the host's innate immune system.

effector cell (1) A muscle cell or gland cell that carries out the body's response to stimuli as directed by signals from the brain or other processing center of the nervous system. (2) A lymphocyte that has undergone clonal selection and is capable of mediating an adaptive immune response.

egg The female gamete.

egg-polarity gene A gene that helps control the orientation (polarity) of the egg; also called a maternal effect gene.

ejaculation The propulsion of sperm from the epididymis through the muscular vas deferens, ejaculatory duct, and urethra.

electrocardiogram (ECG or EKG) A record of the electrical impulses that travel through heart muscle during the cardiac cycle.

electrochemical gradient The diffusion gradient of an ion, which is affected by both the concentration difference of an ion across a membrane (a chemical force) and the ion's tendency to move relative to the membrane potential (an electrical force).

electrogenic pump An active transport protein that generates voltage across a membrane while pumping ions.

electromagnetic receptor A receptor of electromagnetic energy, such as visible light, electricity, or magnetism.

electromagnetic spectrum The entire spectrum of electromagnetic radiation, ranging in wavelength from less than a nanometer to more than a kilometer.

electron A subatomic particle with a single negative electrical charge and a mass about 1/2,000 that of a neutron or proton. One or more electrons move around the nucleus of an atom.

electron microscope (EM) A microscope that uses magnets to focus an electron beam on or through a specimen, resulting in a practical resolution that is 100-fold greater than that of a light microscope using standard techniques. A transmission electron microscope (TEM) is used to study the internal structure of thin sections of cells. A scanning electron microscope (SEM) is used to study the fine details of cell surfaces.

electron shell An energy level of electrons at a characteristic average distance from the nucleus of an atom.

electron transport chain A sequence of electron carrier molecules (membrane proteins) that shuttle electrons down a series of redox reactions that release energy used to make ATP.

electronegativity The attraction of a given atom for the electrons of a covalent bond.

electroporation A technique to introduce recombinant DNA into cells by applying a brief electrical pulse to a solution containing the cells. The pulse creates temporary holes in the cells' plasma membranes, through which DNA can enter.

element Any substance that cannot be broken down to any other substance by chemical reactions.

elimination The fourth and final stage of food processing in animals: the passing of undigested material out of the body.

embryo sac (em'-brē-ō) The female gametophyte of angiosperms, formed from the growth and division of the megaspore into a multicellular structure that typically has eight haploid nuclei.

embryonic lethal A mutation with a phenotype leading to death of an embryo or larva.

embryophyte Alternate name for land plants that refers to their shared derived trait of multicellular, dependent embryos.

emergent properties New properties that arise with each step upward in the hierarchy of life, owing to the arrangement and interactions of parts as complexity increases.

emigration The movement of individuals out of a population.

enantiomer (en-an'-tē-ō-mer) One of two compounds that are mirror images of each other and that differ in shape due to the presence of an asymmetric carbon.

endangered species A species that is in danger of extinction throughout all or a significant portion of its range.

endemic (en-dem'-ik) Referring to a species that is confined to a specific geographic area.

endergonic reaction (en'-der-gon'-ik) A nonspontaneous chemical reaction in which free energy is absorbed from the surroundings.

endocrine gland (en'-dō-krin) A ductless gland that secretes hormones directly into the interstitial fluid, from which they diffuse into the bloodstream.

endocrine system (en'-dō-krin) In animals, the internal system of communication involving hormones, the ductless glands that secrete hormones, and the molecular receptors on or in target cells that respond to hormones; functions in concert with the nervous system to effect internal regulation and maintain homeostasis.

endocytosis (en'-dō-sī-tō'-sis) Cellular uptake of biological molecules and particulate matter via formation of vesicles from the plasma membrane.

endoderm (en'-dō-durm) The innermost of the three primary germ layers in animal embryos; lines the archenteron and gives rise to the liver, pancreas, lungs, and the lining of the digestive tract in species that have these structures.

endodermis In plant roots, the innermost layer of the cortex that surrounds the vascular cylinder.

endomembrane system The collection of membranes inside and surrounding a eukaryotic cell, related either through direct physical contact or by the transfer of membranous vesicles; includes the plasma membrane, the nuclear envelope, the smooth and rough endoplasmic reticulum, the Golgi apparatus, lysosomes, vesicles, and vacuoles.

endometriosis (en'-dō-mē-trē-ō'-sis) The condition resulting from the presence of endometrial tissue outside of the uterus.

endometrium (en'-dō-mē'-trē-um) The inner lining of the uterus, which is richly supplied with blood vessels.

endoparasite A parasite that lives within a host.

endophyte A harmless fungus, or occasionally another organism, that lives between cells of a plant part or multicellular alga.

endoplasmic reticulum (ER) (en'-dō-plaz'-mik ruh-tik'-yū-lum) An extensive membranous network in eukaryotic cells, continuous with the outer nuclear membrane and composed of ribosome-studded (rough) and ribosome-free (smooth) regions.

endorphin (en-dōr'-fin) Any of several hormones produced in the brain and anterior pituitary that inhibit pain perception.

endoskeleton A hard skeleton buried within the soft tissues of an animal.

endosperm In angiosperms, a nutrient-rich tissue formed by the union of a sperm with two polar nuclei during double fertilization. The endosperm provides nourishment to the developing embryo in angiosperm seeds.

endospore A thick-coated, resistant cell produced by some bacterial cells when they are exposed to harsh conditions.

endosymbiont theory The theory that mitochondria and plastids, including chloroplasts, originated as prokaryotic cells engulfed by a host cell. The engulfed cell and its host cell then evolved into a single organism. *See also* endosymbiosis.

endosymbiosis A relationship between two species in which one organism lives inside the cell or cells of another organism. *See also* endosymbiont theory.

endothelium (en'-dō-thē'-lē-um) The simple squamous layer of cells lining the lumen of blood vessels.

endothermic Referring to organisms that are warmed by heat generated by their own metabolism. This heat usually maintains a relatively stable body temperature higher than that of the external environment.

endotoxin A toxic component of the outer membrane of certain gram-negative bacteria that is released only when the bacteria die.

energetic hypothesis The concept that the length of a food chain is limited by the inefficiency of energy transfer along the chain.

energy The capacity to cause change, especially to do work (to move matter against an opposing force).

energy coupling In cellular metabolism, the use of energy released from an exergonic reaction to drive an endergonic reaction.

enhancer A segment of eukaryotic DNA containing multiple control elements, usually located far from the gene whose transcription it regulates.

enteric division One of three divisions of the autonomic nervous system; consists of networks of neurons in the digestive tract, pancreas, and gallbladder; normally regulated by the sympathetic and parasympathetic divisions of the autonomic nervous system.

entropy A measure of disorder, or randomness.

enzyme (en'-zīm) A macromolecule serving as a catalyst, a chemical agent that increases the rate of a reaction without being consumed by the reaction. Most enzymes are proteins.

enzyme-substrate complex (en'-zīm) A temporary complex formed when an enzyme binds to its substrate molecule(s).

epicotyl (ep'-uh-kot'-ul) In an angiosperm embryo, the embryonic axis above the point of attachment of the cotyledon(s) and below the first pair of miniature leaves.

epidemic A widespread outbreak of a disease.

epidermis (1) The dermal tissue system of nonwoody plants, usually consisting of a single layer of tightly packed cells. (2) The outermost layer of cells in an animal.

epididymis (ep'-uh-did'-uh-mus) A coiled tubule located adjacent to the mammalian testis where sperm are stored.

epigenetic inheritance Inheritance of traits transmitted by mechanisms that do not involve the nucleotide sequence.

epinephrine (ep'-i-nef'-rin) A catecholamine that, when secreted as a hormone by the adrenal medulla, mediates "fight-or-flight" responses to short-term stresses; also released by some neurons as a neurotransmitter; also called adrenaline.

epiphyte (ep'-uh-fīt) A plant that nourishes itself but grows on the surface of another plant for support, usually on the branches or trunks of trees.

epistasis (ep'-i-stā'-sis) A type of gene interaction in which the phenotypic expression of one gene alters that of another independently inherited gene.

epithelial tissue (ep'-uh-thē'-lē-ul) Sheets of tightly packed cells that line organs and body cavities as well as external surfaces.

epithelium An epithelial tissue.

epitope A small, accessible region of an antigen to which an antigen receptor or antibody binds.

equilibrium potential (E_{ion}) The magnitude of a cell's membrane voltage at equilibrium; calculated using the Nernst equation.

erythrocyte (eh-rith'-ruh-sīt) A blood cell that contains hemoglobin, which transports oxygen; also called a red blood cell.

erythropoietin (EPO) (eh-rith'-rō-poy'-uh-tin) A hormone that stimulates the production of erythrocytes. It is secreted by the kidney when body tissues do not receive enough oxygen.

esophagus (eh-sof'-uh-gus) A muscular tube that conducts food, by peristalsis, from the pharynx to the stomach.

essential amino acid An amino acid that an animal cannot synthesize itself and must be obtained from food in prefabricated form.

essential element A chemical element required for an organism to survive, grow, and reproduce.

essential fatty acid An unsaturated fatty acid that an animal needs but cannot make.

essential nutrient A substance that an organism cannot synthesize from any other material and therefore must absorb in preassembled form.

estradiol (es'-truh-dī'-ol) A steroid hormone that stimulates the development and maintenance of the female reproductive system and secondary sex characteristics; the major estrogen in mammals.

estrogen (es'-trō-jen) Any steroid hormone, such as estradiol, that stimulates the development and maintenance of the female reproductive system and secondary sex characteristics.

estrous cycle (es'-trus) A reproductive cycle characteristic of female mammals except humans and certain other primates, in which the nonpregnant endometrium is reabsorbed rather than shed, and sexual response occurs only during mid-cycle at estrus.

estuary The area where a freshwater stream or river merges with the ocean.

ethylene (eth'-uh-lēn) A gaseous plant hormone involved in responses to mechanical stress, programmed cell death, leaf abscission, and fruit ripening.

etiolation Plant morphological adaptations for growing in darkness.

euchromatin (yū-krō'-muh-tin) The less condensed form of eukaryotic chromatin that is available for transcription.

eudicot (yū-dī'-kot) A member of a clade that contains the vast majority of flowering plants that have two embryonic seed leaves, or cotyledons.

euglenid (yū'-glen-id) A protist, such as *Euglena* or its relatives, characterized by an anterior pocket from which one or two flagella emerge.

euglenozoan A member of a diverse clade of flagellated protists that includes predatory heterotrophs, photosynthetic autotrophs, and pathogenic parasites.

Eukarya (yū-kar'-ē-uh) The domain that includes all eukaryotic organisms.

eukaryotic cell (yū'-ker-ē-ot'-ik) A type of cell with a membrane-enclosed nucleus and membrane-enclosed organelles. Organisms with eukaryotic cells (protists, plants, fungi, and animals) are called eukaryotes.

eumetazoan (yū'-met-uh-zō'-un) A member of a clade of animals with true tissues. All animals except sponges and a few other groups are eumetazoans.

eurypterid (yur-ip'-tuh-rid) An extinct carnivorous chelicerate; also called a water scorpion.

Eustachian tube (yū-stā'-shun) The tube that connects the middle ear to the pharynx.

eutherian (yū-thēr'-ē-un) Placental mammal; mammal whose young complete their embryonic development within the uterus, joined to the mother by the placenta.

eutrophic lake (yū-trōf'-ik) A lake that has a high rate of biological productivity supported by a high rate of nutrient cycling.

eutrophication A process by which nutrients, particularly phosphorus and nitrogen, become highly concentrated in a body of water, leading to increased growth of organisms such as algae or cyanobacteria.

evaporative cooling The process in which the surface of an object becomes cooler during evaporation, a result of the molecules with the greatest kinetic energy changing from the liquid to the gaseous state.

evapotranspiration The total evaporation of water from an ecosystem, including water transpired by plants and evaporated from a landscape, usually measured in millimeters and estimated for a year.

evo-devo Evolutionary developmental biology; a field of biology that compares developmental processes of different multicellular organisms to understand how these processes have evolved and how changes can modify existing organismal features or lead to new ones.

evolution Descent with modification; the idea that living species are descendants of ancestral species that were different from the present-day ones; also defined more narrowly as the change in the genetic composition of a population from generation to generation.

evolutionary tree A branching diagram that reflects a hypothesis about evolutionary relationships among groups of organisms.

Excavata (ex'-kuh-vah'-tuh) One of four supergroups of eukaryotes proposed in a current hypothesis of the evolutionary history of eukaryotes. Excavates have unique cytoskeletal features, and some species have an "excavated" feeding groove on one side of the cell body. *See also* "SAR" clade, Archaeplastida, and Unikonta.

excitatory postsynaptic potential (EPSP) An electrical change (depolarization) in the membrane of a postsynaptic cell caused by the binding of an excitatory neurotransmitter from a presynaptic cell to a postsynaptic receptor; makes it more likely for a postsynaptic cell to generate an action potential.

excretion The disposal of nitrogen-containing metabolites and other waste products.

exergonic reaction (ek'-ser-gon'-ik) A spontaneous chemical reaction in which there is a net release of free energy.

exocytosis (ek'-sō-sī-tō'-sis) The cellular secretion of biological molecules by the fusion of vesicles containing them with the plasma membrane.

exon A sequence within a primary transcript that remains in the RNA after RNA processing; also refers to the region of DNA from which this sequence was transcribed.

exoskeleton A hard encasement on the surface of an animal, such as the shell of a mollusc or the cuticle of an arthropod, that provides protection and points of attachment for muscles.

exotoxin (ek'-sō-tok'-sin) A toxic protein that is secreted by a prokaryote or other pathogen and that produces specific symptoms, even if the pathogen is no longer present.

expansin Plant enzyme that breaks the cross-links (hydrogen bonds) between cellulose microfibrils and other cell wall constituents, loosening the wall's fabric.

experiment A scientific test, carried out under controlled conditions, involving manipulation of one or more factors in a system in order to see the effects of those changes.

experimental group A set of subjects that has (or receives) the specific factor being tested in a controlled experiment.

exponential population growth Growth of a population in an ideal, unlimited environment, represented by a J-shaped curve when population size is plotted over time.

expression vector A cloning vector that contains a highly active bacterial promoter just upstream of a restriction site where a eukaryotic gene can be inserted, allowing the gene to be expressed in a bacterial cell. Expression vectors are also available that have been genetically engineered for use in specific types of eukaryotic cells.

extinction vortex A downward population spiral in which inbreeding and genetic drift combine to cause a small population to shrink and, unless the spiral is reversed, become extinct.

extracellular matrix (ECM) The meshwork surrounding animal cells, consisting of glycoproteins, polysaccharides, and proteoglycans synthesized and secreted by cells.

extraembryonic membrane One of four membranes (yolk sac, amnion, chorion, and allantois) located outside the embryo that support the developing embryo in reptiles and mammals.

extreme halophile An organism that lives in a highly saline environment, such as the Great Salt Lake or the Dead Sea.

extreme thermophile An organism that thrives in hot environments (often 60–80°C or hotter).

extremophile An organism that lives in environmental conditions so extreme that few other species can survive there. Extremophiles include extreme halophiles ("salt lovers") and extreme thermophiles ("heat lovers").

F_1 generation The first filial, hybrid (heterozygous) offspring arising from a parental (P generation) cross.

F_2 generation The offspring resulting from interbreeding (or self-pollination) of the hybrid F_1 generation.

facilitated diffusion The passage of molecules or ions down their electrochemical gradient across a biological membrane with the assistance of specific transmembrane transport proteins, requiring no energy expenditure.

facilitation An interaction in which one species has a positive effect on the survival and reproduction of another species without the intimate association of a symbiosis.

facultative anaerobe (fak'-ul-tā'-tiv an'-uh-rōb) An organism that makes ATP by aerobic respiration if oxygen is present but that switches to anaerobic respiration or fermentation if oxygen is not present.

family In Linnaean classification, the taxonomic category above genus.

fast block to polyspermy The depolarization of the egg plasma membrane that begins within 1–3 seconds after a sperm binds to an egg membrane protein. The depolarization lasts about 1 minute and prevents additional sperm from fusing with the egg during that time.

fast-twitch fiber A muscle fiber used for rapid, powerful contractions.

fat A lipid consisting of three fatty acids linked to one glycerol molecule; also called a triacylglycerol or triglyceride.

fate map A territorial diagram of embryonic development that displays the future derivatives of individual cells and tissues.

fatty acid A carboxylic acid with a long carbon chain. Fatty acids vary in length and in the number and location of double bonds; three fatty acids linked to a glycerol molecule form a fat molecule, also called triacylglycerol or triglyceride.

feces (fē'-sēz) The wastes of the digestive tract.

feedback inhibition A method of metabolic control in which the end product of a metabolic pathway acts as an inhibitor of an enzyme within that pathway.

feedback regulation The regulation of a process by its output or end product.

fermentation A catabolic process that makes a limited amount of ATP from glucose (or other organic molecules) without an electron transport chain and that produces a characteristic end product, such as ethyl alcohol or lactic acid.

fertilization (1) The union of haploid gametes to produce a diploid zygote. (2) The addition of mineral nutrients to the soil.

fetus (fē'-tus) A developing mammal that has all the major structures of an adult. In humans, the fetal stage lasts from the 9th week of gestation until birth.

F factor In bacteria, the DNA segment that confers the ability to form pili for conjugation and associated functions required for the transfer of DNA from donor to recipient. The F factor may exist as a plasmid or be integrated into the bacterial chromosome.

fiber A lignified cell type that reinforces the xylem of angiosperms and functions in mechanical support; a slender, tapered sclerenchyma cell that usually occurs in bundles.

fibroblast (fī'-brō-blast) A type of cell in loose connective tissue that secretes the protein ingredients of the extracellular fibers.

fibronectin An extracellular glycoprotein secreted by animal cells that helps them attach to the extracellular matrix.

filament In an angiosperm, the stalk portion of the stamen, the pollen-producing reproductive organ of a flower.

filter feeder An animal that feeds by using a filtration mechanism to strain small organisms or food particles from its surroundings.

filtrate Cell-free fluid extracted from the body fluid by the excretory system.

filtration In excretory systems, the extraction of water and small solutes, including metabolic wastes, from the body fluid.

fimbria (plural, **fimbriae**) A short, hairlike appendage of a prokaryotic cell that helps it adhere to the substrate or to other cells.

first law of thermodynamics The principle of conservation of energy: Energy can be transferred and transformed, but it cannot be created or destroyed.

fission The separation of an organism into two or more individuals of approximately equal size.

fixed action pattern In animal behavior, a sequence of unlearned acts that is essentially unchangeable and, once initiated, usually carried to completion.

flaccid (flas'-id) Limp. Lacking turgor (stiffness or firmness), as in a plant cell in surroundings where there is a tendency for water to leave the cell. (A walled cell becomes flaccid if it has a higher water potential than its surroundings, resulting in the loss of water.)

flagellum (fluh-jel'-um) (plural, **flagella**) A long cellular appendage specialized for locomotion. Like motile cilia, eukaryotic flagella have a core with nine outer doublet microtubules and two inner single microtubules (the "9 + 2" arrangement) ensheathed in an extension of the plasma membrane. Prokaryotic flagella have a different structure.

florigen A flowering signal, probably a protein, that is made in leaves under certain conditions and that travels to the shoot apical meristems, inducing them to switch from vegetative to reproductive growth.

flower In an angiosperm, a specialized shoot with up to four sets of modified leaves, bearing structures that function in sexual reproduction.

fluid feeder An animal that lives by sucking nutrient-rich fluids from another living organism.

fluid mosaic model The currently accepted model of cell membrane structure, which envisions the membrane as a mosaic of protein molecules drifting laterally in a fluid bilayer of phospholipids.

follicle (fol'-uh-kul) A microscopic structure in the ovary that contains the developing oocyte and secretes estrogens.

follicle-stimulating hormone (FSH) (fol'-uh-kul) A tropic hormone that is produced and secreted by the anterior pituitary and that stimulates the production of eggs by the ovaries and sperm by the testes.

food chain The pathway along which food energy is transferred from trophic level to trophic level, beginning with producers.

food vacuole A membranous sac formed by phagocytosis of microorganisms or particles to be used as food by the cell.

food web The interconnected feeding relationships in an ecosystem.

foot (1) The portion of a bryophyte sporophyte that gathers sugars, amino acids, water, and minerals from the parent gametophyte via transfer cells. (2) One of the three main parts of a mollusc; a muscular structure usually used for movement. *See also* mantle and visceral mass.

foraging The seeking and obtaining of food.

foram (foraminiferan) An aquatic protist that secretes a hardened shell containing calcium carbonate and extends pseudopodia through pores in the shell.

forebrain One of three ancestral and embryonic regions of the vertebrate brain; develops into the thalamus, hypothalamus, and cerebrum.

fossil A preserved remnant or impression of an organism that lived in the past.

founder effect Genetic drift that occurs when a few individuals become isolated from a larger population and form a new population whose gene pool composition is not reflective of that of the original population.

fovea (fō'-vē-uh) The place on the retina at the eye's center of focus, where cones are highly concentrated.

F plasmid The plasmid form of the F factor.

fragmentation A means of asexual reproduction whereby a single parent breaks into parts that regenerate into whole new individuals.

frameshift mutation A mutation occurring when nucleotides are inserted in or deleted from a gene and the number inserted or deleted is not a multiple of three, resulting in the improper grouping of the subsequent nucleotides into codons.

free energy The portion of a biological system's energy that can perform work when temperature and pressure are uniform throughout the system. The change in free energy of a system (ΔG) is calculated by the equation $\Delta G = \Delta H - T\Delta S$, where ΔH is the change in enthalpy (in biological systems, equivalent to total energy), ΔT is the absolute temperature, and ΔS is the change in entropy.

frequency-dependent selection Selection in which the fitness of a phenotype depends on how common the phenotype is in a population.

fruit A mature ovary of a flower. The fruit protects dormant seeds and often functions in their dispersal.

functional group A specific configuration of atoms commonly attached to the carbon skeletons of organic molecules and involved in chemical reactions.

G_0 phase A nondividing state occupied by cells that have left the cell cycle, sometimes reversibly.

G_1 phase The first gap, or growth phase, of the cell cycle, consisting of the portion of interphase before DNA synthesis begins.

G_2 phase The second gap, or growth phase, of the cell cycle, consisting of the portion of interphase after DNA synthesis occurs.

gallbladder An organ that stores bile and releases it as needed into the small intestine.

game theory An approach to evaluating alternative strategies in situations where the outcome of a particular strategy depends on the strategies used by other individuals.

gametangium (gam'-uh-tan'-jē-um) (plural, **gametangia**) Multicellular plant structure in which gametes are formed. Female gametangia are called archegonia, and male gametangia are called antheridia.

gamete (gam'-ēt) A haploid reproductive cell, such as an egg or sperm. Gametes unite during sexual reproduction to produce a diploid zygote.

gametogenesis (guh-mē'-tō-gen'-uh-sis) The process by which gametes are produced.

gametophore (guh-mē'-tō-fōr) The mature gamete-producing structure of a moss gametophyte.

gametophyte (guh-mē'-tō-fīt) In organisms (plants and some algae) that have alternation of generations, the multicellular haploid form that produces haploid gametes by mitosis. The haploid gametes unite and develop into sporophytes.

gamma-aminobutyric acid (GABA) An amino acid that functions as a CNS neurotransmitter in the central nervous system of vertebrates.

ganglion (gang'-glē-uhn) (plural, **ganglia**) A cluster (functional group) of nerve cell bodies in a centralized nervous system.

gap junction A type of intercellular junction in animal cells, consisting of proteins surrounding a pore that allows the passage of materials between cells.

gas exchange The uptake of molecular oxygen from the environment and the discharge of carbon dioxide to the environment.

gastric juice A digestive fluid secreted by the stomach.

gastrovascular cavity A central cavity with a single opening in the body of certain animals, including cnidarians and flatworms, that functions in both the digestion and distribution of nutrients.

gastrula (gas'-trū-luh) An embryonic stage in animal development encompassing the formation of three layers: ectoderm, mesoderm, and endoderm.

gastrulation (gas'-trū-lā'-shun) In animal development, a series of cell and tissue movements in which the blastula-stage embryo folds inward, producing a three-layered embryo, the gastrula.

gated channel A transmembrane protein channel that opens or closes in response to a particular stimulus.

gated ion channel A gated channel for a specific ion. The opening or closing of such channels may alter a cell's membrane potential.

gel electrophoresis (ē-lek'-trō-fōr-ē'-sis) A technique for separating nucleic acids or proteins on the basis of their size and electrical charge, both of which affect their rate of movement through an electric field in a gel made of agarose or another polymer.

gene A discrete unit of hereditary information consisting of a specific nucleotide sequence in DNA (or RNA, in some viruses).

gene annotation Analysis of genomic sequences to identify protein-coding genes and determine the function of their products.

gene cloning The production of multiple copies of a gene.

gene expression The process by which information encoded in DNA directs the synthesis of proteins or, in some cases, RNAs that are not translated into proteins and instead function as RNAs.

gene flow The transfer of alleles from one population to another, resulting from the movement of fertile individuals or their gametes.

gene pool The aggregate of all copies of every type of allele at all loci in every individual in a population. The term is also used in a more restricted sense as the aggregate of alleles for just one or a few loci in a population.

gene therapy The introduction of genes into an afflicted individual for therapeutic purposes.

genetic drift A process in which chance events cause unpredictable fluctuations in allele frequencies from one generation to the next. Effects of genetic drift are most pronounced in small populations.

genetic engineering The direct manipulation of genes for practical purposes.

genetic map An ordered list of genetic loci (genes or other genetic markers) along a chromosome.

genetic profile An individual's unique set of genetic markers, detected most often today by PCR or, previously, by electrophoresis and nucleic acid probes.

genetic recombination General term for the production of offspring with combinations of traits that differ from those found in either parent.

genetic variation Differences among individuals in the composition of their genes or other DNA segments.

genetically modified (GM) organism An organism that has acquired one or more genes by artificial means; also called a transgenic organism.

genetics The scientific study of heredity and hereditary variation.

genome (jē'-nōm) The genetic material of an organism or virus; the complete complement of an organism's or virus's genes along with its noncoding nucleic acid sequences.

genome-wide association study (jē'-nōm) A large-scale analysis of the genomes of many people having a certain phenotype or disease, with the aim of finding genetic markers that correlate with that phenotype or disease.

genomic imprinting (juh-nō'-mik) A phenomenon in which expression of an allele in offspring depends on whether the allele is inherited from the male or female parent.

genomics (juh-nō'-miks) The systematic study of whole sets of genes (or other DNA) and their interactions within a species, as well as genome comparisons between species.

genotype (jē'-nō-tīp) The genetic makeup, or set of alleles, of an organism.

genus (jē'-nus) (plural, **genera**) A taxonomic category above the species level, designated by the first word of a species' two-part scientific name.

geologic record A standard time scale dividing Earth's history into time periods, grouped into four eons—Hadean, Archaean, Proterozoic, and Phanerozoic—and further subdivided into eras, periods, and epochs.

germ layer One of the three main layers in a gastrula that will form the various tissues and organs of an animal body.

gestation (jes-tā'-shun) *See* pregnancy.

gibberellin (jib'-uh-rel'-in) Any of a class of related plant hormones that stimulate growth in the stem and leaves, trigger the germination of seeds and breaking of bud dormancy, and (with auxin) stimulate fruit development.

glans The rounded structure at the tip of the clitoris or penis that is involved in sexual arousal.

glia (glial cells) Cells of the nervous system that support, regulate, and augment the functions of neurons.

global ecology The study of the functioning and distribution of organisms across the biosphere and how the regional exchange of energy and materials affects them.

glomeromycete (glō'-mer-ō-mī'-sēt) A member of the fungal phylum Glomeromycota, characterized by a distinct branching form of mycorrhizae called arbuscular mycorrhizae.

glomerulus (glō-mār'-yū-lus) A ball of capillaries surrounded by Bowman's capsule in the nephron and serving as the site of filtration in the vertebrate kidney.

glucocorticoid A steroid hormone that is secreted by the adrenal cortex and that influences glucose metabolism and immune function.

glucagon (glū'-kuh-gon) A hormone secreted by pancreatic alpha cells that raises blood glucose levels. It promotes glycogen breakdown and release of glucose by the liver.

glutamate An amino acid that functions as a neurotransmitter in the central nervous system.

glyceraldehyde 3-phosphate (G3P) (glis'-er-al'-de-hīd) A three-carbon carbohydrate that is the direct product of the Calvin cycle; it is also an intermediate in glycolysis.

glycogen (glī'-kō-jen) An extensively branched glucose storage polysaccharide found in the liver and muscle of animals; the animal equivalent of starch.

glycolipid A lipid with one or more covalently attached carbohydrates.

glycolysis (glī-kol'-uh-sis) A series of reactions that ultimately splits glucose into pyruvate. Glycolysis occurs in almost all living cells, serving as the starting point for fermentation or cellular respiration.

glycoprotein A protein with one or more covalently attached carbohydrates.

glycosidic linkage A covalent bond formed between two monosaccharides by a dehydration reaction.

gnathostome (na'-thu-stōm) A member of the vertebrate subgroup possessing jaws. The gnathostomes include sharks and rays, ray-finned fishes, coelacanths, lungfishes, amphibians, reptiles, and mammals.

golden alga A biflagellated, photosynthetic protist named for its color, which results from its yellow and brown carotenoids.

Golgi apparatus (gol'-jē) An organelle in eukaryotic cells consisting of stacks of flat membranous sacs that modify, store, and route products of the endoplasmic reticulum and synthesize some products, notably noncellulose carbohydrates.

gonad (gō'-nad) A male or female gamete-producing organ.

G protein A GTP-binding protein that relays signals from a plasma membrane signal receptor, known as a G protein-coupled receptor, to other signal transduction proteins inside the cell.

G protein-coupled receptor (GPCR) A signal receptor protein in the plasma membrane that responds to the binding of a signaling molecule by activating a G protein. Also called a G protein-linked receptor.

graded potential In a neuron, a shift in the membrane potential that has an amplitude proportional to signal strength and that decays as it spreads.

Gram stain A staining method that distinguishes between two different kinds of bacterial cell walls; may be used to help determine medical response to an infection.

gram-negative Describing the group of bacteria that have a cell wall that is structurally more complex and contains less peptidoglycan than the cell wall of gram-positive bacteria. Gram-negative bacteria are often more toxic than gram-positive bacteria.

gram-positive Describing the group of bacteria that have a cell wall that is structurally less complex and contains more peptidoglycan than the cell wall of gram-negative bacteria. Gram-positive bacteria are usually less toxic than gram-negative bacteria.

granum (gran'-um) (plural, **grana**) A stack of membrane-bounded thylakoids in the chloroplast. Grana function in the light reactions of photosynthesis.

gravitropism (grav'-uh-trō'-pizm) A response of a plant or animal to gravity.

gray matter Regions of clustered neuron cell bodies within the CNS.

green alga A photosynthetic protist, named for green chloroplasts that are similar in structure and pigment composition to the chloroplasts of land plants. Green algae are a paraphyletic group; some members are more closely related to land plants than they are to other green algae.

greenhouse effect The warming of Earth due to the atmospheric accumulation of carbon dioxide and certain other gases, which absorb reflected infrared radiation and reradiate some of it back toward Earth.

gross primary production (GPP) The total primary production of an ecosystem.

ground tissue system Plant tissues that are neither vascular nor dermal, fulfilling a variety of functions, such as storage, photosynthesis, and support.

growth factor (1) A protein that must be present in the extracellular environment (culture medium or animal body) for the growth and normal development of certain types of cells. (2) A local regulator that acts on nearby cells to stimulate cell proliferation and differentiation.

growth hormone (GH) A hormone that is produced and secreted by the anterior pituitary and that has both direct (nontropic) and tropic effects on a wide variety of tissues.

guard cells The two cells that flank the stomatal pore and regulate the opening and closing of the pore.

gustation The sense of taste.

guttation The exudation of water droplets from leaves, caused by root pressure in certain plants.

gymnosperm (jim'-nō-sperm) A vascular plant that bears naked seeds—seeds not enclosed in protective chambers.

hair cell A mechanosensory cell that alters output to the nervous system when hairlike projections on the cell surface are displaced.

half-life The amount of time it takes for 50% of a sample of a radioactive isotope to decay.

halophile *See* extreme halophile.

Hamilton's rule The principle that for natural selection to favor an altruistic act, the benefit

to the recipient, devalued by the coefficient of relatedness, must exceed the cost to the altruist.

haploid cell (hap'-loyd) A cell containing only one set of chromosomes (*n*).

Hardy-Weinberg equilibrium The state of a population in which frequencies of alleles and genotypes remain constant from generation to generation, provided that only Mendelian segregation and recombination of alleles are at work.

haustorium (plural, **haustoria**) (ho-stōr'-ē-um, ho-stōr'-ē-uh) In certain symbiotic fungi, a specialized hypha that can penetrate the tissues of host organisms.

heart A muscular pump that uses metabolic energy to elevate the hydrostatic pressure of the circulatory fluid (blood or hemolymph). The fluid then flows down a pressure gradient through the body and eventually returns to the heart.

heart attack The damage or death of cardiac muscle tissue resulting from prolonged blockage of one or more coronary arteries.

heart murmur A hissing sound that most often results from blood squirting backward through a leaky valve in the heart.

heart rate The frequency of heart contraction (in beats per minute).

heat Thermal energy in transfer from one body of matter to another.

heat of vaporization The quantity of heat a liquid must absorb for 1 g of it to be converted from the liquid to the gaseous state.

heat-shock protein A protein that helps protect other proteins during heat stress. Heat-shock proteins are found in plants, animals, and microorganisms.

heavy chain One of the two types of polypeptide chains that make up an antibody molecule and B cell receptor; consists of a variable region, which contributes to the antigen-binding site, and a constant region.

helicase An enzyme that untwists the double helix of DNA at replication forks, separating the two strands and making them available as template strands.

helper T cell A type of T cell that, when activated, secretes cytokines that promote the response of B cells (humoral response) and cytotoxic T cells (cell-mediated response) to antigens.

hemoglobin (hē'-mō-glō'-bin) An iron-containing protein in red blood cells that reversibly binds oxygen.

hemolymph (hē'-mō-limf') In invertebrates with an open circulatory system, the body fluid that bathes tissues.

hemophilia (hē'-muh-fil'-ē-uh) A human genetic disease caused by a sex-linked recessive allele resulting in the absence of one or more blood-clotting proteins; characterized by excessive bleeding following injury.

hepatic portal vein A large vessel that conveys nutrient-laden blood from the small intestine to the liver, which regulates the blood's nutrient content.

herbivore (hur'-bi-vōr') An animal that mainly eats plants or algae.

herbivory An interaction in which an organism eats part of a plant or alga.

heredity The transmission of traits from one generation to the next.

hermaphrodite (hur-maf'-ruh-dīt') An individual that functions as both male and female in sexual reproduction by producing both sperm and eggs.

hermaphroditism (hur-maf'-rō-dī-tizm) A condition in which an individual has both female and male gonads and functions as both a male and a female in sexual reproduction by producing both sperm and eggs.

heterochromatin (het'-er-ō-krō'-muh-tin) Eukaryotic chromatin that remains highly compacted during interphase and is generally not transcribed.

heterochrony (het'-uh-rok'-ruh-nē) Evolutionary change in the timing or rate of an organism's development.

heterocyst (het'-er-ō-sist) A specialized cell that engages in nitrogen fixation in some filamentous cyanobacteria; also called a heterocyte.

heterokaryon (het'-er-ō-kār'-ē-un) A fungal mycelium that contains two or more haploid nuclei per cell.

heteromorphic (het'-er-ō-mōr'-fik) Referring to a condition in the life cycle of plants and certain algae in which the sporophyte and gametophyte generations differ in morphology.

heterosporous (het-er-os'-pōr-us) Referring to a plant species that has two kinds of spores: microspores, which develop into male gametophytes, and megaspores, which develop into female gametophytes.

heterotroph (het'-er-ō-trōf) An organism that obtains organic food molecules by eating other organisms or substances derived from them.

heterozygote advantage Greater reproductive success of heterozygous individuals compared with homozygotes; tends to preserve variation in a gene pool.

heterozygous (het'-er-ō-zī'-gus) Having two different alleles for a given gene.

hibernation A long-term physiological state in which metabolism decreases, the heart and respiratory system slow down, and body temperature is maintained at a lower level than normal.

high-density lipoprotein (HDL) A particle in the blood made up of thousands of cholesterol molecules and other lipids bound to a protein. HDL scavenges excess cholesterol.

hindbrain One of three ancestral and embryonic regions of the vertebrate brain; develops into the medulla oblongata, pons, and cerebellum.

histamine (his'-tuh-mēn) A substance released by mast cells that causes blood vessels to dilate and become more permeable in inflammatory and allergic responses.

histogram A variant of a bar graph that is made for numeric data by first grouping, or "binning," the variable plotted on the *x*-axis into intervals of equal width. The "bins" may be integers or ranges of numbers. The height of each bar shows the percent or number of experimental subjects whose characteristics can be described by one of the intervals plotted on the *x*-axis.

histone (his'-tōn) A small protein with a high proportion of positively charged amino acids that binds to the negatively charged DNA and plays a key role in chromatin structure.

histone acetylation (his'-tōn) The attachment of acetyl groups to certain amino acids of histone proteins.

HIV (human immunodeficiency virus) The infectious agent that causes AIDS. HIV is a retrovirus.

holdfast A rootlike structure that anchors a seaweed.

holoblastic (hō'-lō-blas'-tik) Referring to a type of cleavage in which there is complete division of the egg; occurs in eggs that have little yolk (such as those of the sea urchin) or a moderate amount of yolk (such as those of the frog).

homeobox (hō'-mē-ō-boks') A 180-nucleotide sequence within homeotic genes and some other developmental genes that is widely conserved in animals. Related sequences occur in plants and yeasts.

homeostasis (hō'-mē-ō-stā'-sis) The steady-state physiological condition of the body.

homeotic gene (hō-mē-o'-tik) Any of the master regulatory genes that control placement and spatial organization of body parts in animals, plants, and fungi by controlling the developmental fate of groups of cells.

hominin (hō'-mi-nin) A member of the human branch of the evolutionary tree. Hominins include *Homo sapiens* and our ancestors, a group of extinct species that are more closely related to us than to chimpanzees.

homologous chromosomes (or homologs) (hō-mol'-uh-gus) A pair of chromosomes of the same length, centromere position, and staining pattern that possess genes for the same characters at corresponding loci. One homologous chromosome is inherited from the organism's father, the other from the mother. Also called a homologous pair.

homologous structures (hō-mol'-uh-gus) Structures in different species that are similar because of common ancestry.

homology (hō-mol'-ō-jē) Similarity in characteristics resulting from a shared ancestry.

homoplasy (hō'-muh-play'-zē) A similar (analogous) structure or molecular sequence that has evolved independently in two species.

homosporous (hō-mos'-puh-rus) Referring to a plant species that has a single kind of spore, which typically develops into a bisexual gametophyte.

homozygous (hō'-mō-zī'-gus) Having two identical alleles for a given gene.

horizontal gene transfer The transfer of genes from one genome to another through mechanisms such as transposable elements, plasmid exchange, viral activity, and perhaps fusions of different organisms.

hormone In multicellular organisms, one of many types of secreted chemicals that are formed in specialized cells, travel in body fluids, and act on specific target cells in other parts of the organism, changing the target cells' functioning.

hornwort A small, herbaceous, nonvascular plant that is a member of the phylum Anthocerophyta.

host The larger participant in a symbiotic relationship, often providing a home and food source for the smaller symbiont.

host range The limited number of species whose cells can be infected by a particular virus.

Human Genome Project An international collaborative effort to map and sequence the DNA of the entire human genome.

human immunodeficiency virus (HIV) The infectious agent that causes AIDS (acquired immunodeficiency syndrome). HIV is a retrovirus.

humoral immune response (hyū'-mer-ul) The branch of adaptive immunity that involves the activation of B cells and that leads to the production of antibodies, which defend against bacteria and viruses in body fluids.

humus (hyū'-mus) Decomposing organic material that is a component of topsoil.

Huntington's disease A human genetic disease caused by a dominant allele; characterized by uncontrollable body movements and degeneration of the nervous system; usually fatal 10 to 20 years after the onset of symptoms.

hybrid Offspring that results from the mating of individuals from two different species or from two true-breeding varieties of the same species.

hybrid zone A geographic region in which members of different species meet and mate, producing at least some offspring of mixed ancestry.

hybridization In genetics, the mating, or crossing, of two true-breeding varieties.

hydration shell The sphere of water molecules around a dissolved ion.

hydrocarbon An organic molecule consisting only of carbon and hydrogen.

hydrogen bond A type of weak chemical bond that is formed when the slightly positive hydrogen atom of a polar covalent bond in one molecule is attracted to the slightly negative atom of a polar covalent bond in another molecule or in another region of the same molecule.

hydrogen ion A single proton with a charge of $1+$. The dissociation of a water molecule (H_2O) leads to the generation of a hydroxide ion (OH^-) and a hydrogen ion (H^+); in water, H^+ is not found alone but associates with a water molecule to form a hydronium ion.

hydrolysis (hī-drol'-uh-sis) A chemical reaction that breaks bonds between two molecules by the addition of water; functions in disassembly of polymers to monomers.

hydronium ion A water molecule that has an extra proton bound to it; H_3O^+, commonly represented as H^+.

hydrophilic (hī'-drō-fil'-ik) Having an affinity for water.

hydrophobic (hī'-drō-fō'-bik) Having no affinity for water; tending to coalesce and form droplets in water.

hydrophobic interaction (hī'-drō-fō'-bik) A type of weak chemical interaction caused when molecules that do not mix with water coalesce to exclude water.

hydroponic culture A method in which plants are grown in mineral solutions rather than in soil.

hydrostatic skeleton A skeletal system composed of fluid held under pressure in a closed body compartment; the main skeleton of most cnidarians, flatworms, nematodes, and annelids.

hydrothermal vent An area on the deep sea-floor where heated water and minerals from Earth's interior gush into the seawater.

hydroxide ion A water molecule that has lost a proton; OH^-.

hydroxyl group (hī-drok'-sil) A chemical group consisting of an oxygen atom joined to a hydrogen atom. Molecules possessing this group are soluble in water and are called alcohols.

hyperpolarization A change in a cell's membrane potential such that the inside of the membrane becomes more negative relative to the outside. Hyperpolarization reduces the chance that a neuron will transmit a nerve impulse.

hypersensitive response A plant's localized defense response to a pathogen, involving the death of cells around the site of infection.

hypertension A disorder in which blood pressure remains abnormally high.

hypertonic Referring to a solution that, when surrounding a cell, will cause the cell to lose water.

hypha (plural, **hyphae**) (hī'-fuh, hī'-fē) One of many connected filaments that collectively make up the mycelium of a fungus.

hypocotyl (hī'-puh-cot'-ul) In an angiosperm embryo, the embryonic axis below the point of attachment of the cotyledon(s) and above the radicle.

hypothalamus (hī'-pō-thal'-uh-mus) The ventral part of the vertebrate forebrain; functions in maintaining homeostasis, especially in coordinating the endocrine and nervous systems; secretes hormones of the posterior pituitary and releasing factors that regulate the anterior pituitary.

hypothesis (hī-poth'-uh-sis) A testable explanation for a set of observations based on the available data and guided by inductive reasoning. A hypothesis is narrower in scope than a theory.

hypotonic Referring to a solution that, when surrounding a cell, will cause the cell to take up water.

imbibition The physical adsorption of water onto the internal surfaces of structures.

immigration The influx of new individuals into a population from other areas.

immune system An organism's system of defenses against agents that cause disease.

immunization The process of generating a state of immunity by artificial means. In vaccination, an inactive or weakened form of a pathogen is administered, inducing B and T cell responses and immunological memory. In passive immunization, antibodies specific for a particular pathogen are administered, conferring immediate but temporary protection.

immunoglobulin (Ig) (im'-yŭ-nō-glob'-yŭ-lin) *See* antibody.

imprinting In animal behavior, the formation at a specific stage in life of a long-lasting behavioral response to a specific individual or object. *See also* genomic imprinting.

inclusive fitness The total effect an individual has on proliferating its genes by producing its own offspring and by providing aid that enables other close relatives to increase production of their offspring.

incomplete dominance The situation in which the phenotype of heterozygotes is intermediate between the phenotypes of individuals homozygous for either allele.

incomplete flower A flower in which one or more of the four basic floral organs (sepals, petals, stamens, or carpels) are either absent or nonfunctional.

incomplete metamorphosis A type of development in certain insects, such as grasshoppers, in which the young (called nymphs) resemble adults but are smaller and have different body proportions. The nymph goes through a series of molts, each time looking more like an adult, until it reaches full size.

independent variable A variable whose value is manipulated or changed during an experiment or other test to reveal possible effects on another variable (the dependent variable).

indeterminate cleavage A type of embryonic development in deuterostomes in which each cell produced by early cleavage divisions retains the capacity to develop into a complete embryo.

indeterminate growth A type of growth characteristic of plants, in which the organism continues to grow as long as it lives.

induced fit Caused by entry of the substrate, the change in shape of the active site of an enzyme so that it binds more snugly to the substrate.

inducer A specific small molecule that binds to a bacterial repressor protein and changes the repressor's shape so that it cannot bind to an operator, thus switching an operon on.

induction A process in which a group of cells or tissues influences the development of another group through close-range interactions.

inductive reasoning A type of logic in which generalizations are based on a large number of specific observations.

inflammatory response An innate immune defense triggered by physical injury or infection of tissue involving the release of substances that promote swelling, enhance the infiltration of white blood cells, and aid in tissue repair and destruction of invading pathogens.

inflorescence A group of flowers tightly clustered together.

ingestion The first stage of food processing in animals: the act of eating.

ingroup A species or group of species whose evolutionary relationships are being examined in a given analysis.

inhibitory postsynaptic potential (IPSP) An electrical change (usually hyperpolarization) in the membrane of a postsynaptic neuron caused by the binding of an inhibitory neurotransmitter from a presynaptic cell to a postsynaptic receptor; makes it more difficult for a postsynaptic neuron to generate an action potential.

innate behavior Animal behavior that is developmentally fixed and under strong genetic control. Innate behavior is exhibited in virtually the same form by all individuals in a population despite internal and external environmental differences during development and throughout their lifetimes.

innate immunity A form of defense common to all animals that is active immediately upon exposure to a pathogen and that is the same whether or not the pathogen has been encountered previously.

inner cell mass An inner cluster of cells at one end of a mammalian blastocyst that subsequently develops into the embryo proper and some of the extraembryonic membranes.

inositol trisphosphate (IP₃) (in-ō'-suh-tol) A second messenger that functions as an intermediate between certain signaling molecules and a subsequent second messenger, Ca^{2+}, by causing a rise in cytoplasmic Ca^{2+} concentration.

inquiry The search for information and explanation, often focusing on specific questions.

insertion A mutation involving the addition of one or more nucleotide pairs to a gene.

***in situ* hybridization** A technique using nucleic acid hybridization with a labeled probe to detect the location of a specific mRNA in an intact organism.

insulin (in'-suh-lin) A hormone secreted by pancreatic beta cells that lowers blood glucose levels. It promotes the uptake of glucose by most body cells and the synthesis and storage of glycogen in the liver and also stimulates protein and fat synthesis.

integral protein A transmembrane protein with hydrophobic regions that extend into and often completely span the hydrophobic interior of the membrane and with hydrophilic regions in contact with the aqueous solution on one or both sides of the membrane (or lining the channel in the case of a channel protein).

integrin (in'-tuh-grin) In animal cells, a transmembrane receptor protein with two subunits that interconnects the extracellular matrix and the cytoskeleton.

integument (in-teg'-yŭ-ment) Layer of sporophyte tissue that contributes to the structure of an ovule of a seed plant.

integumentary system The outer covering of a mammal's body, including skin, hair, and nails, claws, or hooves.

intercalated disk (in-ter'-kuh-lā'-ted) A specialized junction between cardiac muscle cells that provides direct electrical coupling between the cells.

interferon (in'-ter-fēr'-on) A protein that has antiviral or immune regulatory functions. Interferon-α and interferon-β, secreted by virus-infected cells, help nearby cells resist viral infection; interferon-γ, secreted by T cells, helps activate macrophages.

intermediate disturbance hypothesis The concept that moderate levels of disturbance can foster greater species diversity than low or high levels of disturbance.

intermediate filament A component of the cytoskeleton that includes filaments intermediate in size between microtubules and microfilaments.

interneuron An association neuron; a nerve cell within the central nervous system that forms synapses with sensory and/or motor neurons and integrates sensory input and motor output.

internode A segment of a plant stem between the points where leaves are attached.

interphase The period in the cell cycle when the cell is not dividing. During interphase, cellular metabolic activity is high, chromosomes and organelles are duplicated, and cell size may increase. Interphase often accounts for about 90% of the cell cycle.

intersexual selection A form of natural selection in which individuals of one sex (usually the females) are choosy in selecting their mates from the other sex; also called mate choice.

interspecific competition Competition for resources between individuals of two or more species when resources are in short supply.

interspecific interaction A relationship between individuals of two or more species in a community.

interstitial fluid The fluid filling the spaces between cells in most animals.

intertidal zone The shallow zone of the ocean adjacent to land and between the high- and low-tide lines.

intrasexual selection A form of natural selection in which there is direct competition among individuals of one sex for mates of the opposite sex.

introduced species A species moved by humans, either intentionally or accidentally, from its native location to a new geographic region; also called non-native or exotic species.

intron (in'-tron) A noncoding, intervening sequence within a primary transcript that is removed from the transcript during RNA processing; also refers to the region of DNA from which this sequence was transcribed.

invasive species A species, often introduced by humans, that takes hold outside its native range.

inversion An aberration in chromosome structure resulting from reattachment of a chromosomal fragment in a reverse orientation to the chromosome from which it originated.

invertebrate An animal without a backbone. Invertebrates make up 95% of animal species.

***in vitro* fertilization (IVF)** (vē'-trō) Fertilization of oocytes in laboratory containers followed by artificial implantation of the early embryo in the mother's uterus.

***in vitro* mutagenesis** A technique used to discover the function of a gene by cloning it, introducing specific changes into the cloned gene's sequence, reinserting the mutated gene into a cell, and studying the phenotype of the mutant.

ion (ī′-on) An atom or group of atoms that has gained or lost one or more electrons, thus acquiring a charge.

ion channel (ī′-on) A transmembrane protein channel that allows a specific ion to diffuse across the membrane down its concentration or electrochemical gradient.

ionic bond (ī-on′-ik) A chemical bond resulting from the attraction between oppositely charged ions.

ionic compound (ī-on′-ik) A compound resulting from the formation of an ionic bond; also called a salt.

iris The colored part of the vertebrate eye, formed by the anterior portion of the choroid.

isomer (ī′-sō-mer) One of several compounds with the same molecular formula but different structures and therefore different properties. The three types of isomers are structural isomers, *cis-trans* isomers, and enantiomers.

isomorphic Referring to alternating generations in plants and certain algae in which the sporophytes and gametophytes look alike, although they differ in chromosome number.

isotonic (ī′-sō-ton′-ik) Referring to a solution that, when surrounding a cell, causes no net movement of water into or out of the cell.

isotope (ī′-sō-tōp′) One of several atomic forms of an element, each with the same number of protons but a different number of neutrons, thus differing in atomic mass.

iteroparity Reproduction in which adults produce offspring over many years; also called repeated reproduction.

jasmonate Any of a class of plant hormones that regulate a wide range of developmental processes in plants and play a key role in plant defense against herbivores.

joule (J) A unit of energy: 1 J = 0.239 cal; 1 cal = 4.184 J.

juxtaglomerular apparatus (JGA) (juks′-tuh-gluh-mār′-yū-ler) A specialized tissue in nephrons that releases the enzyme renin in response to a drop in blood pressure or volume.

juxtamedullary nephron In mammals and birds, a nephron with a loop of Henle that extends far into the renal medulla.

karyogamy (kār′-ē-og′-uh-mē) In fungi, the fusion of haploid nuclei contributed by the two parents; occurs as one stage of sexual reproduction, preceded by plasmogamy.

karyotype (kār′-ē-ō-tīp) A display of the chromosome pairs of a cell arranged by size and shape.

keystone species A species that is not necessarily abundant in a community yet exerts strong control on community structure by the nature of its ecological role or niche.

kidney In vertebrates, one of a pair of excretory organs where blood filtrate is formed and processed into urine.

kilocalorie (kcal) A thousand calories; the amount of heat energy required to raise the temperature of 1 kg of water by 1°C.

kinetic energy (kuh-net′-ik) The energy associated with the relative motion of objects.

Moving matter can perform work by imparting motion to other matter.

kinetic energy (kuh-net′-ik) The energy associated with the relative motion of objects. Moving matter can perform work by imparting motion to other matter.

kinetochore (kuh-net′-uh-kōr) A structure of proteins attached to the centromere that links each sister chromatid to the mitotic spindle.

kinetoplastid A protist, such as a trypanosome, that has a single large mitochondrion that houses an organized mass of DNA.

kingdom A taxonomic category, the second broadest after domain.

kin selection Natural selection that favors altruistic behavior by enhancing the reproductive success of relatives.

K-selection Selection for life history traits that are sensitive to population density; also called density-dependent selection.

labia majora A pair of thick, fatty ridges that encloses and protects the rest of the vulva.

labia minora A pair of slender skin folds that surrounds the openings of the vagina and urethra.

lacteal (lak′-tē-ul) A tiny lymph vessel extending into the core of an intestinal villus and serving as the destination for absorbed chylomicrons.

lactic acid fermentation Glycolysis followed by the reduction of pyruvate to lactate, regenerating NAD^+ with no release of carbon dioxide.

lagging strand A discontinuously synthesized DNA strand that elongates by means of Okazaki fragments, each synthesized in a $5' \rightarrow 3'$ direction away from the replication fork.

lancelet A member of the clade Cephalochordata, small blade-shaped marine chordates that lack a backbone.

landscape An area containing several different ecosystems linked by exchanges of energy, materials, and organisms.

landscape ecology The study of how the spatial arrangement of habitat types affects the distribution and abundance of organisms and ecosystem processes.

large intestine The portion of the vertebrate alimentary canal between the small intestine and the anus; functions mainly in water absorption and the formation of feces.

larva (lar′-vuh) (plural, **larvae**) A free-living, sexually immature form in some animal life cycles that may differ from the adult animal in morphology, nutrition, and habitat.

larynx (lār′-inks) The portion of the respiratory tract containing the vocal cords; also called the voice box.

lateralization Segregation of functions in the cortex of the left and right cerebral hemispheres.

lateral line system A mechanoreceptor system consisting of a series of pores and receptor units along the sides of the body in fishes and aquatic amphibians; detects water movements made by the animal itself and by other moving objects.

lateral meristem (mār′-uh-stem) A meristem that thickens the roots and shoots of woody

plants. The vascular cambium and cork cambium are lateral meristems.

lateral root A root that arises from the pericycle of an established root.

law of conservation of mass A physical law stating that matter can change form but cannot be created or destroyed. In a closed system, the mass of the system is constant.

law of independent assortment Mendel's second law, stating that each pair of alleles segregates, or assorts, independently of each other pair during gamete formation; applies when genes for two characters are located on different pairs of homologous chromosomes or when they are far enough apart on the same chromosome to behave as though they are on different chromosomes.

law of segregation Mendel's first law, stating that the two alleles in a pair segregate (separate from each other) into different gametes during gamete formation.

leading strand The new complementary DNA strand synthesized continuously along the template strand toward the replication fork in the mandatory $5' \rightarrow 3'$ direction.

leaf The main photosynthetic organ of vascular plants.

leaf primordium (plural, **primordia**) A finger-like projection along the flank of a shoot apical meristem, from which a leaf arises.

learning The modification of behavior as a result of specific experiences.

lens The structure in an eye that focuses light rays onto the photoreceptors.

lenticel (len′-ti-sel) A small raised area in the bark of stems and roots that enables gas exchange between living cells and the outside air.

lepidosaur (leh-pid′-uh-sōr) A member of the reptilian group that includes lizards, snakes, and two species of New Zealand animals called tuataras.

leukocyte (lū′-kō-sīt′) A blood cell that functions in fighting infections; also called a white blood cell.

lichen The mutualistic association between a fungus and a photosynthetic alga or cyanobacterium.

life cycle The generation-to-generation sequence of stages in the reproductive history of an organism.

life history The traits that affect an organism's schedule of reproduction and survival.

life table An age-specific summary of the survival pattern of a population.

ligament A fibrous connective tissue that joins bones together at joints.

ligand (lig′-und) A molecule that binds specifically to another molecule, usually a larger one.

ligand-gated ion channel (lig′-und) A transmembrane protein containing a pore that opens or closes as it changes shape in response to a signaling molecule (ligand), allowing or blocking the flow of specific ions; also called an ionotropic receptor.

light chain One of the two types of polypeptide chains that make up an antibody molecule and B cell receptor; consists of a variable region, which contributes to the antigen-binding site, and a constant region.

light-harvesting complex A complex of proteins associated with pigment molecules (including chlorophyll *a*, chlorophyll *b*, and carotenoids) that captures light energy and transfers it to reaction-center pigments in a photosystem.

light microscope (LM) An optical instrument with lenses that refract (bend) visible light to magnify images of specimens.

light reactions The first of two major stages in photosynthesis (preceding the Calvin cycle). These reactions, which occur on the thylakoid membranes of the chloroplast or on membranes of certain prokaryotes, convert solar energy to the chemical energy of ATP and NADPH, releasing oxygen in the process.

lignin (lig'-nin) A strong polymer embedded in the cellulose matrix of the secondary cell walls of vascular plants that provides structural support in terrestrial species.

limiting nutrient An element that must be added for production to increase in a particular area.

limnetic zone In a lake, the well-lit, open surface waters far from shore.

linear electron flow A route of electron flow during the light reactions of photosynthesis that involves both photosystems (I and II) and produces ATP, NADPH, and O_2. The net electron flow is from H_2O to $NADP^+$.

line graph A graph in which each data point is connected to the next point in the data set with a straight line.

linkage map A genetic map based on the frequencies of recombination between markers during crossing over of homologous chromosomes.

linked genes Genes located close enough together on a chromosome that they tend to be inherited together.

lipid (lip'-id) Any of a group of large biological molecules, including fats, phospholipids, and steroids, that mix poorly, if at all, with water.

littoral zone In a lake, the shallow, well-lit waters close to shore.

liver A large internal organ in vertebrates that performs diverse functions, such as producing bile, maintaining blood glucose level, and detoxifying poisonous chemicals in the blood.

liverwort A small, herbaceous, nonvascular plant that is a member of the phylum Hepatophyta.

loam The most fertile soil type, made up of roughly equal amounts of sand, silt, and clay.

lobe-fin A member of the vertebrate clade Sarcopterygii, osteichthyans with rod-shaped muscular fins, including coelacanths, lungfishes, and tetrapods.

local regulator A secreted molecule that influences cells near where it is secreted.

locomotion Active motion from place to place.

locus (lō'-kus) (plural, **loci**) (lō'-sī) A specific place along the length of a chromosome where a given gene is located.

logistic population growth Population growth that levels off as population size approaches carrying capacity.

long-day plant A plant that flowers (usually in late spring or early summer) only when the light period is longer than a critical length.

long-term memory The ability to hold, associate, and recall information over one's lifetime.

long-term potentiation (LTP) An enhanced responsiveness to an action potential (nerve signal) by a receiving neuron.

loop of Henle (hen'-lē) The hairpin turn, with a descending and ascending limb, between the proximal and distal tubules of the vertebrate kidney; functions in water and salt reabsorption.

lophophore (lof'-uh-fōr) In some lophotrochozoan animals, including brachiopods, a crown of ciliated tentacles that surround the mouth and function in feeding.

Lophotrochozoa (lo-phah'-truh-kō-zō'-uh) One of the three main lineages of bilaterian animals; lophotrochozoans include organisms that have lophophores or trochophore larvae. *See also* Deuterostomia and Ecdysozoa.

low-density lipoprotein (LDL) A particle in the blood made up of thousands of cholesterol molecules and other lipids bound to a protein. LDL transports cholesterol from the liver for incorporation into cell membranes.

lung An infolded respiratory surface of a terrestrial vertebrate, land snail, or spider that connects to the atmosphere by narrow tubes.

luteinizing hormone (LH) (lū'-tē-uh-nī'-zing) A tropic hormone that is produced and secreted by the anterior pituitary and that stimulates ovulation in females and androgen production in males.

lycophyte (lī'-kuh-fīt) An informal name for a member of the phylum Lycophyta, which includes club mosses, spike mosses, and quillworts.

lymph The colorless fluid, derived from interstitial fluid, in the lymphatic system of vertebrates.

lymph node An organ located along a lymph vessel. Lymph nodes filter lymph and contain cells that attack viruses and bacteria.

lymphatic system A system of vessels and nodes, separate from the circulatory system, that returns fluid, proteins, and cells to the blood.

lymphocyte A type of white blood cell that mediates immune responses. The two main classes are B cells and T cells.

lysogenic cycle (lī'-sō-jen'-ik) A type of phage replicative cycle in which the viral genome becomes incorporated into the bacterial host chromosome as a prophage, is replicated along with the chromosome, and does not kill the host.

lysosome (lī'-suh-sōm) A membrane-enclosed sac of hydrolytic enzymes found in the cytoplasm of animal cells and some protists.

lysozyme (lī'-sō-zīm) An enzyme that destroys bacterial cell walls; in mammals, it is found in sweat, tears, and saliva.

lytic cycle (lit'-ik) A type of phage replicative cycle resulting in the release of new phages by lysis (and death) of the host cell.

macroclimate Large-scale patterns in climate; the climate of an entire region.

macroevolution Evolutionary change above the species level. Examples of macroevolutionary change include the origin of a new group of organisms through a series of speciation events and the impact of mass extinctions on the diversity of life and its subsequent recovery.

macromolecule A giant molecule formed by the joining of smaller molecules, usually by a dehydration reaction. Polysaccharides, proteins, and nucleic acids are macromolecules.

macronutrient An essential element that an organism must obtain in relatively large amounts. *See also* micronutrient.

macrophage (mak'-rō-fāj) A phagocytic cell present in many tissues that functions in innate immunity by destroying microbes and in acquired immunity as an antigen-presenting cell.

magnoliid A member of the angiosperm clade that is most closely related to the combined eudicot and monocot clades. Extant examples are magnolias, laurels, and black pepper plants.

major depressive disorder A mood disorder characterized by feelings of sadness, lack of self-worth, emptiness, or loss of interest in nearly all things.

major histocompatibility complex (MHC) molecule A host protein that functions in antigen presentation. Foreign MHC molecules on transplanted tissue can trigger T cell responses that may lead to rejection of the transplant.

malignant tumor A cancerous tumor containing cells that have significant genetic and cellular changes and are capable of invading and surviving in new sites. Malignant tumors can impair the functions of one or more organs.

Malpighian tubule (mal-pig'-ē-un) A unique excretory organ of insects that empties into the digestive tract, removes nitrogenous wastes from the hemolymph, and functions in osmoregulation.

mammal A member of the clade Mammalia, amniotes that have hair and mammary glands (glands that produce milk).

mammary gland An exocrine gland that secretes milk for nourishing the young. Mammary glands are characteristic of mammals.

mantle One of the three main parts of a mollusc; a fold of tissue that drapes over the mollusc's visceral mass and may secrete a shell. *See also* foot and visceral mass.

mantle cavity A water-filled chamber that houses the gills, anus, and excretory pores of a mollusc.

map unit A unit of measurement of the distance between genes. One map unit is equivalent to a 1% recombination frequency.

marine benthic zone The ocean floor.

mark-recapture method A sampling technique used to estimate the size of animal populations.

marsupial (mar-sū'-pē-ul) A mammal, such as a koala, kangaroo, or opossum, whose young complete their embryonic development inside a maternal pouch called the marsupium.

mass extinction The elimination of a large number of species throughout Earth, the result of global environmental changes.

mass number The sum of the number of protons and neutrons in an atom's nucleus.

mast cell A vertebrate body cell that produces histamine and other molecules that trigger inflammation in response to infection and in allergic reactions.

mate-choice copying Behavior in which individuals in a population copy the mate choice of others, apparently as a result of social learning.

maternal effect gene A gene that, when mutant in the mother, results in a mutant phenotype in the offspring, regardless of the offspring's genotype. Maternal effect genes, also called egg-polarity genes, were first identified in *Drosophila melanogaster*.

matter Anything that takes up space and has mass.

maximum likelihood As applied to DNA sequence data, a principle that states that when considering multiple phylogenetic hypotheses, one should take into account the hypothesis that reflects the most likely sequence of evolutionary events, given certain rules about how DNA changes over time.

maximum parsimony A principle that states that when considering multiple explanations for an observation, one should first investigate the simplest explanation that is consistent with the facts.

mean The sum of all data points in a data set divided by the number of data points.

mechanoreceptor A sensory receptor that detects physical deformation in the body's environment associated with pressure, touch, stretch, motion, or sound.

medulla oblongata (meh-dul'-uh ŏb'-long-gō'-tuh) The lowest part of the vertebrate brain, commonly called the medulla; a swelling of the hindbrain anterior to the spinal cord that controls autonomic, homeostatic functions, including breathing, heart and blood vessel activity, swallowing, digestion, and vomiting.

medusa (plural, **medusae**) (muh-dū'-suh) The floating, flattened, mouth-down version of the cnidarian body plan. The alternate form is the polyp.

megapascal (MPa) (meg'-uh-pas-kal') A unit of pressure equivalent to about 10 atmospheres of pressure.

megaphyll (meh'-guh-fil) A leaf with a highly branched vascular system, characteristic of the vast majority of vascular plants. *See also* microphyll.

megaspore A spore from a heterosporous plant species that develops into a female gametophyte.

meiosis (mī-ō'-sis) A modified type of cell division in sexually reproducing organisms consisting of two rounds of cell division but only one round of DNA replication. It results in cells with half the number of chromosome sets as the original cell.

meiosis I (mī-ō'-sis) The first division of a two-stage process of cell division in sexually reproducing organisms that results in cells with half the number of chromosome sets as the original cell.

meiosis II (mī-ō'-sis) The second division of a two-stage process of cell division in sexually reproducing organisms that results in cells with half the number of chromosome sets as the original cell.

melanocyte-stimulating hormone (MSH) A hormone produced and secreted by the anterior pituitary with multiple activities, including regulating the behavior of pigment-containing cells in the skin of some vertebrates.

melatonin A hormone that is secreted by the pineal gland and that is involved in the regulation of biological rhythms and sleep.

membrane potential The difference in electrical charge (voltage) across a cell's plasma membrane due to the differential distribution of ions. Membrane potential affects the activity of excitable cells and the transmembrane movement of all charged substances.

memory cell One of a clone of long-lived lymphocytes, formed during the primary immune response, that remains in a lymphoid organ until activated by exposure to the same antigen that triggered its formation. Activated memory cells mount the secondary immune response.

menopause The cessation of ovulation and menstruation marking the end of a human female's reproductive years.

menstrual cycle (men'-strū-ul) *See* uterine cycle.

menstruation The shedding of portions of the endometrium during a uterine (menstrual) cycle.

meristem (mār'-uh-stem) Plant tissue that remains embryonic as long as the plant lives, allowing for indeterminate growth.

meristem identity gene (mār'-uh-stem) A plant gene that promotes the switch from vegetative growth to flowering.

meroblastic (mār'-ō-blas'-tik) Referring to a type of cleavage in which there is incomplete division of a yolk-rich egg, characteristic of avian development.

mesoderm (mez'-ō-derm) The middle primary germ layer in a triploblastic animal embryo; develops into the notochord, the lining of the coelom, muscles, skeleton, gonads, kidneys, and most of the circulatory system in species that have these structures.

mesohyl (mez'-ō-hīl) A gelatinous region between the two layers of cells of a sponge.

mesophyll (mez'-ō-fil) Leaf cells specialized for photosynthesis. In C_3 and CAM plants, mesophyll cells are located between the upper and lower epidermis; in C_4 plants, they are located between the bundle-sheath cells and the epidermis.

messenger RNA (mRNA) A type of RNA, synthesized using a DNA template, that attaches to ribosomes in the cytoplasm and specifies the primary structure of a protein. (In eukaryotes, the primary RNA transcript must undergo RNA processing to become mRNA.)

metabolic pathway A series of chemical reactions that either builds a complex molecule (anabolic pathway) or breaks down a complex molecule to simpler molecules (catabolic pathway).

metabolic rate The total amount of energy an animal uses in a unit of time.

metabolism (muh-tab'-uh-lizm) The totality of an organism's chemical reactions, consisting of catabolic and anabolic pathways, which manage the material and energy resources of the organism.

metagenomics The collection and sequencing of DNA from a group of species, usually an environmental sample of microorganisms. Computer software sorts partial sequences and assembles them into genome sequences of individual species making up the sample.

metamorphosis (met'-uh-mōr'-fuh-sis) A developmental transformation that turns an animal larva into either an adult or an adult-like stage that is not yet sexually mature.

metanephridium (met'-uh-nuh-frid'-ē-um) (plural, **metanephridia**) An excretory organ found in many invertebrates that typically consists of tubules connecting ciliated internal openings to external openings.

metaphase The third stage of mitosis, in which the spindle is complete and the chromosomes, attached to microtubules at their kinetochores, are all aligned at the metaphase plate.

metaphase plate An imaginary structure located at a plane midway between the two poles of a cell in metaphase on which the centromeres of all the duplicated chromosomes are located.

metapopulation A group of spatially separated populations of one species that interact through immigration and emigration.

metastasis (muh-tas'-tuh-sis) The spread of cancer cells to locations distant from their original site.

methanogen (meth-an'-ō-jen) An organism that produces methane as a waste product of the way it obtains energy. All known methanogens are in domain Archaea.

methyl group A chemical group consisting of a carbon bonded to three hydrogen atoms. The methyl group may be attached to a carbon or to a different atom.

microclimate Climate patterns on a very fine scale, such as the specific climatic conditions underneath a log.

microevolution Evolutionary change below the species level; change in the allele frequencies in a population over generations.

microfilament A cable composed of actin proteins in the cytoplasm of almost every eukaryotic cell, making up part of the cytoskeleton and acting alone or with myosin to cause cell contraction; also called an actin filament.

micronutrient An essential element that an organism needs in very small amounts. *See also* macronutrient.

microphyll (mī'-krō-fil) In lycophytes, a small leaf with a single unbranched vein. *See also* megaphyll.

micropyle A pore in the integuments of an ovule.

microRNA (miRNA) A small, single-stranded RNA molecule, generated from a double-stranded RNA precursor. The miRNA associates with one or more proteins in a complex that can degrade or prevent translation of an mRNA with a complementary sequence.

microspore A spore from a heterosporous plant species that develops into a male gametophyte.

microtubule A hollow rod composed of tubulin proteins that makes up part of the cytoskeleton in all eukaryotic cells and is found in cilia and flagella.

microvillus (plural, **microvilli**) One of many fine, finger-like projections of the epithelial cells in the lumen of the small intestine that increase its surface area.

midbrain One of three ancestral and embryonic regions of the vertebrate brain; develops into sensory integrating and relay centers that send sensory information to the cerebrum.

middle lamella (luh-mel'-uh) In plants, a thin layer of adhesive extracellular material, primarily pectins, found between the primary walls of adjacent young cells.

migration A regular, long-distance change in location.

mineral In nutrition, a simple nutrient that is inorganic and therefore cannot be synthesized in the body.

mineralocorticoid A steroid hormone secreted by the adrenal cortex that regulates salt and water homeostasis.

minimum viable population (MVP) The smallest population size at which a species is able to sustain its numbers and survive.

mismatch repair The cellular process that uses specific enzymes to remove and replace incorrectly paired nucleotides.

missense mutation A nucleotide-pair substitution that results in a codon that codes for a different amino acid.

mitochondrial matrix The compartment of the mitochondrion enclosed by the inner membrane and containing enzymes and substrates for the citric acid cycle, as well as ribosomes and DNA.

mitochondrion (mī'-tō-kon'-drē-un) (plural, **mitochondria**) An organelle in eukaryotic cells that serves as the site of cellular respiration; uses oxygen to break down organic molecules and synthesize ATP.

mitosis (mī-tō'-sis) A process of nuclear division in eukaryotic cells conventionally divided into five stages: prophase, prometaphase, metaphase, anaphase, and telophase. Mitosis conserves chromosome number by allocating replicated chromosomes equally to each of the daughter nuclei.

mitotic (M) phase The phase of the cell cycle that includes mitosis and cytokinesis.

mitotic spindle An assemblage of microtubules and associated proteins that is involved in the movement of chromosomes during mitosis.

mixotroph An organism that is capable of both photosynthesis and heterotrophy.

model A physical or conceptual representation of a natural phenomenon.

model organism A particular species chosen for research into broad biological principles because it is representative of a larger group and usually easy to grow in a lab.

molarity A common measure of solute concentration, referring to the number of moles of solute per liter of solution.

mold Informal term for a fungus that grows as a filamentous fungus, producing haploid spores by mitosis and forming a visible mycelium.

mole (mol) The number of grams of a substance that equals its molecular or atomic mass in daltons; a mole contains Avogadro's number of the molecules or atoms in question.

molecular clock A method for estimating the time required for a given amount of evolutionary change, based on the observation that some regions of genomes evolve at constant rates.

molecular mass The sum of the masses of all the atoms in a molecule; sometimes called molecular weight.

molecule Two or more atoms held together by covalent bonds.

molting A process in ecdysozoans in which the exoskeleton is shed at intervals, allowing growth by the production of a larger exoskeleton.

monilophyte An informal name for a member of the phylum Monilophyta, which includes ferns, horsetails, and whisk ferns and their relatives.

monoclonal antibody (mon'-ō-klōn'-ul) Any of a preparation of antibodies that have been produced by a single clone of cultured cells and thus are all specific for the same epitope.

monocot A member of a clade consisting of flowering plants that have one embryonic seed leaf, or cotyledon.

monogamous (muh-nog'-uh-mus) Referring to a type of relationship in which one male mates with just one female.

monohybrid An organism that is heterozygous with respect to a single gene of interest. All the offspring from a cross between parents homozygous for different alleles are monohybrids. For example, parents of genotypes *AA* and *aa* produce a monohybrid of genotype *Aa*.

monohybrid cross A cross between two organisms that are heterozygous for the character being followed (or the self-pollination of a heterozygous plant).

monomer (mon'-uh-mer) The subunit that serves as the building block of a polymer.

monophyletic (mon'-ō-fī-let'-ik) Pertaining to a group of taxa that consists of a common ancestor and all of its descendants. A monophyletic taxon is equivalent to a clade.

monosaccharide (mon'-ō-sak'-uh-rīd) The simplest carbohydrate, active alone or serving as a monomer for disaccharides and polysaccharides. Also called simple sugars, monosaccharides have molecular formulas that are generally some multiple of CH_2O.

monosomic Referring to a diploid cell that has only one copy of a particular chromosome instead of the normal two.

monotreme An egg-laying mammal, such as a platypus or echidna. Like all mammals, monotremes have hair and produce milk, but they lack nipples.

morphogen A substance, such as Bicoid protein in *Drosophila*, that provides positional information in the form of a concentration gradient along an embryonic axis.

morphogenesis (mōr'-fō-jen'-uh-sis) The development of the form of an organism and its structures.

morphological species concept Definition of a species in terms of measurable anatomical criteria.

moss A small, herbaceous, nonvascular plant that is a member of the phylum Bryophyta.

motor neuron A nerve cell that transmits signals from the brain or spinal cord to muscles or glands.

motor protein A protein that interacts with cytoskeletal elements and other cell components, producing movement of the whole cell or parts of the cell.

motor system An efferent branch of the vertebrate peripheral nervous system composed of motor neurons that carry signals to skeletal muscles in response to external stimuli.

motor unit A single motor neuron and all the muscle fibers it controls.

movement corridor A series of small clumps or a narrow strip of quality habitat (usable by organisms) that connects otherwise isolated patches of quality habitat.

MPF Maturation-promoting factor (or M-phase-promoting factor); a protein complex required for a cell to progress from late interphase to mitosis. The active form consists of cyclin and a protein kinase.

mucus A viscous and slippery mixture of glycoproteins, cells, salts, and water that moistens and protects the membranes lining body cavities that open to the exterior.

Müllerian mimicry (myū-lār'-ē-un mim'-uh-krē) Reciprocal mimicry by two unpalatable species.

multifactorial Referring to a phenotypic character that is influenced by multiple genes and environmental factors.

multigene family A collection of genes with similar or identical sequences, presumably of common origin.

multiple fruit A fruit derived from an entire inflorescence.

multiplication rule A rule of probability stating that the probability of two or more independent events occurring together can be determined by multiplying their individual probabilities.

muscle tissue Tissue consisting of long muscle cells that can contract, either on its own or when stimulated by nerve impulses.

mutagen (myū'-tuh-jen) A chemical or physical agent that interacts with DNA and can cause a mutation.

mutation (myū-tā'-shun) A change in the nucleotide sequence of an organism's DNA or in the DNA or RNA of a virus.

mutualism (myū'-chū-ul-izm) A symbiotic relationship in which both participants benefit.

mycelium (mī-sē'-lē-um) The densely branched network of hyphae in a fungus.

mycorrhiza (plural, **mycorrhizae**) (mī′-kō-rī′-zuh, mī′-kō-rī′-zē) A mutualistic association of plant roots and fungus.

mycosis (mī-kō′-sis) General term for a fungal infection.

myelin sheath (mī′-uh-lin) Wrapped around the axon of a neuron, an insulating coat of cell membranes from Schwann cells or oligodendrocytes. It is interrupted by nodes of Ranvier, where action potentials are generated.

myofibril (mī′-ō-fī′-bril) A longitudinal bundle in a muscle cell (fiber) that contains thin filaments of actin and regulatory proteins and thick filaments of myosin.

myoglobin (mī′-uh-glō′-bin) An oxygen-storing, pigmented protein in muscle cells.

myosin (mī′-uh-sin) A type of motor protein that associates into filaments that interact with actin filaments to cause cell contraction.

myriapod (mir′-ē-uh-pod′) A terrestrial arthropod with many body segments and one or two pairs of legs per segment. Millipedes and centipedes are the two major groups of living myriapods.

NAD⁺ Nicotinamide adenine dinucleotide, a coenzyme that cycles easily between oxidized (NAD^+) and reduced (NADH) states, thus acting as an electron carrier.

NADP⁺ Nicotinamide adenine dinucleotide phosphate, an electron acceptor that, as NADPH, temporarily stores energized electrons produced during the light reactions.

natural killer cell A type of white blood cell that can kill tumor cells and virus-infected cells as part of innate immunity.

natural selection A process in which individuals that have certain inherited traits tend to survive and reproduce at higher rates than other individuals because of those traits.

negative feedback A form of regulation in which accumulation of an end product of a process slows the process; in physiology, a primary mechanism of homeostasis, whereby a change in a variable triggers a response that counteracts the initial change.

negative pressure breathing A breathing system in which air is pulled into the lungs.

nematocyst (nem′-uh-tuh-sist′) In a cnidocyte of a cnidarian, a capsule-like organelle containing a coiled thread that when discharged can penetrate the body wall of the prey.

nephron (nef′-ron) The tubular excretory unit of the vertebrate kidney.

neritic zone The shallow region of the ocean overlying the continental shelf.

nerve A fiber composed primarily of the bundled axons of neurons.

nervous system In animals, the fast-acting internal system of communication involving sensory receptors, networks of nerve cells, and connections to muscles and glands that respond to nerve signals; functions in concert with the endocrine system to effect internal regulation and maintain homeostasis.

nervous tissue Tissue made up of neurons and supportive cells.

net ecosystem production (NEP) The gross primary production of an ecosystem minus the energy used by all autotrophs and heterotrophs for respiration.

net primary production (NPP) The gross primary production of an ecosystem minus the energy used by the producers for respiration.

neural crest In vertebrates, a region located along the sides of the neural tube where it pinches off from the ectoderm. Neural crest cells migrate to various parts of the embryo and form pigment cells in the skin and parts of the skull, teeth, adrenal glands, and peripheral nervous system.

neural tube A tube of infolded ectodermal cells that runs along the anterior-posterior axis of a vertebrate, just dorsal to the notochord. It will give rise to the central nervous system.

neurohormone A molecule that is secreted by a neuron, travels in body fluids, and acts on specific target cells, changing their functioning.

neuron (nyūr′-on) A nerve cell; the fundamental unit of the nervous system, having structure and properties that allow it to conduct signals by taking advantage of the electrical charge across its plasma membrane.

neuronal plasticity The capacity of a nervous system to change with experience.

neuropeptide A relatively short chain of amino acids that serves as a neurotransmitter.

neurotransmitter A molecule that is released from the synaptic terminal of a neuron at a chemical synapse, diffuses across the synaptic cleft, and binds to the postsynaptic cell, triggering a response.

neutral variation Genetic variation that does not provide a selective advantage or disadvantage.

neutron A subatomic particle having no electrical charge (electrically neutral), with a mass of about 1.7×10^{-24} g, found in the nucleus of an atom.

neutrophil The most abundant type of white blood cell. Neutrophils are phagocytic and tend to self-destruct as they destroy foreign invaders, limiting their life span to a few days.

nitric oxide (NO) A gas produced by many types of cells that functions as a local regulator and as a neurotransmitter.

nitrogen cycle The natural process by which nitrogen, either from the atmosphere or from decomposed organic material, is converted by soil bacteria to compounds assimilated by plants. This incorporated nitrogen is then taken in by other organisms and subsequently released, acted on by bacteria, and made available again to the nonliving environment.

nitrogen fixation The conversion of atmospheric nitrogen (N_2) to ammonia (NH_3). Biological nitrogen fixation is carried out by certain prokaryotes, some of which have mutualistic relationships with plants.

nociceptor (nō′-si-sep′-tur) A sensory receptor that responds to noxious or painful stimuli; also called a pain receptor.

node A point along the stem of a plant at which leaves are attached.

node of Ranvier (ron′-vē-ā′) Gap in the myelin sheath of certain axons where an action potential may be generated. In saltatory conduction, an action potential is regenerated at each node, appearing to "jump" along the axon from node to node.

nodule A swelling on the root of a legume. Nodules are composed of plant cells that contain nitrogen-fixing bacteria of the genus *Rhizobium*.

noncompetitive inhibitor A substance that reduces the activity of an enzyme by binding to a location remote from the active site, changing the enzyme's shape so that the active site no longer effectively catalyzes the conversion of substrate to product.

nondisjunction An error in meiosis or mitosis in which members of a pair of homologous chromosomes or a pair of sister chromatids fail to separate properly from each other.

nonequilibrium model A model that maintains that communities change constantly after being buffeted by disturbances.

nonpolar covalent bond A type of covalent bond in which electrons are shared equally between two atoms of similar electronegativity.

nonsense mutation A mutation that changes an amino acid codon to one of the three stop codons, resulting in a shorter and usually nonfunctional protein.

norepinephrine A catecholamine that is chemically and functionally similar to epinephrine and acts as a hormone or neurotransmitter; also called noradrenaline.

northern coniferous forest A terrestrial biome characterized by long, cold winters and dominated by cone-bearing trees.

no-till agriculture A plowing technique that minimally disturbs the soil, thereby reducing soil loss.

notochord (nō′-tuh-kord′) A longitudinal, flexible rod made of tightly packed mesodermal cells that runs along the anterior-posterior axis of a chordate in the dorsal part of the body.

nuclear envelope In a eukaryotic cell, the double membrane that surrounds the nucleus, perforated with pores that regulate traffic with the cytoplasm. The outer membrane is continuous with the endoplasmic reticulum.

nuclear lamina A netlike array of protein filaments that lines the inner surface of the nuclear envelope and helps maintain the shape of the nucleus.

nucleariid A member of a group of unicellular, amoeboid protists that are more closely related to fungi than they are to other protists.

nuclease An enzyme that cuts DNA or RNA, either removing one or a few bases or hydrolyzing the DNA or RNA completely into its component nucleotides.

nucleic acid (nū-klā′-ik) A polymer (polynucleotide) consisting of many nucleotide monomers; serves as a blueprint for proteins and, through the actions of proteins, for all cellular activities. The two types are DNA and RNA.

nucleic acid hybridization (nū-klā′-ik) The base pairing of one strand of a nucleic acid to the complementary sequence on a strand from *another* nucleic acid molecule.

nucleic acid probe (nū-klā′-ik) In DNA technology, a labeled single-stranded nucleic acid molecule used to locate a specific nucleotide sequence in a nucleic acid sample. Molecules of the probe hydrogen-bond to the complementary sequence wherever it occurs; radioactive, fluorescent, or other labeling of the probe allows its location to be detected.

nucleoid (nū′-klē-oyd) A non-membrane-enclosed region in a prokaryotic cell where its chromosome is located.

nucleolus (nū-klē′-ō-lus) (plural, **nucleoli**) A specialized structure in the nucleus, consisting of chromosomal regions containing ribosomal RNA (rRNA) genes along with ribosomal proteins imported from the cytoplasm; site of rRNA synthesis and ribosomal subunit assembly. *See also* ribosome.

nucleosome (nū′-klē-ō-sōm′) The basic, bead-like unit of DNA packing in eukaryotes, consisting of a segment of DNA wound around a protein core composed of two copies of each of four types of histone.

nucleotide (nū′-klē-ō-tīd′) The building block of a nucleic acid, consisting of a five-carbon sugar covalently bonded to a nitrogenous base and one or more phosphate groups.

nucleotide excision repair (nū′-klē-ō-tīd′) A repair system that removes and then correctly replaces a damaged segment of DNA using the undamaged strand as a guide.

nucleotide-pair substitution (nū′-klē-ō-tīd′) A type of point mutation in which one nucleotide in a DNA strand and its partner in the complementary strand are replaced by another pair of nucleotides.

nucleus (1) An atom's central core, containing protons and neutrons. (2) The organelle of a eukaryotic cell that contains the genetic material in the form of chromosomes, made up of chromatin. (3) A cluster of neurons.

nutrition The process by which an organism takes in and makes use of food substances.

obligate aerobe (ob′-lig-et ār′-ōb) An organism that requires oxygen for cellular respiration and cannot live without it.

obligate anaerobe (ob′-lig-et an′-uh-rōb) An organism that carries out only fermentation or anaerobic respiration. Such organisms cannot use oxygen and in fact may be poisoned by it.

ocean acidification Decreasing pH of ocean waters due to absorption of excess atmospheric CO_2 from the burning of fossil fuels.

oceanic pelagic zone Most of the ocean's waters far from shore, constantly mixed by ocean currents.

odorant A molecule that can be detected by sensory receptors of the olfactory system.

Okazaki fragment (ō′-kah-zah′-kē) A short segment of DNA synthesized away from the replication fork on a template strand during DNA replication. Many such segments are joined together to make up the lagging strand of newly synthesized DNA.

olfaction The sense of smell.

oligodendrocyte A type of glial cell that forms insulating myelin sheaths around the axons of neurons in the central nervous system.

oligotrophic lake A nutrient-poor, clear lake with few phytoplankton.

ommatidium (ōm′-uh-tid′-ē-um) (plural, **ommatidia**) One of the facets of the compound eye of arthropods and some polychaete worms.

omnivore An animal that regularly eats animals as well as plants or algae.

oncogene (on′-kō-jēn) A gene found in viral or cellular genomes that is involved in triggering molecular events that can lead to cancer.

oocyte (ō′-uh-sīt) A cell in the female reproductive system that differentiates to form an egg.

oogenesis (ō′-uh-jen′-uh-sis) The process in the ovary that results in the production of female gametes.

oogonium (ō′-uh-gō′-nē-em) (plural, **oogonia**) A cell that divides mitotically to form oocytes.

open circulatory system A circulatory system in which fluid called hemolymph bathes the tissues and organs directly and there is no distinction between the circulating fluid and the interstitial fluid.

operator In bacterial and phage DNA, a sequence of nucleotides near the start of an operon to which an active repressor can attach. The binding of the repressor prevents RNA polymerase from attaching to the promoter and transcribing the genes of the operon.

operculum (ō-per′-kyuh-lum) In aquatic osteichthyans, a protective bony flap that covers and protects the gills.

operon (op′-er-on) A unit of genetic function found in bacteria and phages, consisting of a promoter, an operator, and a coordinately regulated cluster of genes whose products function in a common pathway.

opisthokont (uh-pis′-thuh-kont′) A member of an extremely diverse clade of eukaryotes that includes fungi, animals, and several closely-related groups of protists.

opposable thumb A thumb that can touch the ventral surface of the fingertips of all four fingers.

opsin A membrane protein bound to a light-absorbing pigment molecule.

optimal foraging model The basis for analyzing behavior as a compromise between feeding costs and feeding benefits.

oral cavity The mouth of an animal.

orbital The three-dimensional space where an electron is found 90% of the time.

order In Linnaean classification, the taxonomic category above the level of family.

organ A specialized center of body function composed of several different types of tissues.

organ identity gene A plant homeotic gene that uses positional information to determine which emerging leaves develop into which types of floral organs.

organ of Corti (kor′-tē) The actual hearing organ of the vertebrate ear, located in the floor of the cochlear duct in the inner ear; contains the receptor cells (hair cells) of the ear.

organ system A group of organs that work together in performing vital body functions.

organelle (ōr-guh-nel′) Any of several membrane-enclosed structures with specialized functions, suspended in the cytosol of eukaryotic cells.

organic chemistry The study of carbon compounds (organic compounds).

organismal ecology The branch of ecology concerned with the morphological,

physiological, and behavioral ways in which individual organisms meet the challenges posed by their biotic and abiotic environments.

organogenesis (ōr-gan′-ō-jen′-uh-sis) The process in which organ rudiments develop from the three germ layers after gastrulation.

origin of replication Site where the replication of a DNA molecule begins, consisting of a specific sequence of nucleotides.

orthologous genes Homologous genes that are found in different species because of speciation.

osculum (os′-kyuh-lum) A large opening in a sponge that connects the spongocoel to the environment.

osmoconformer An animal that is isoosmotic with its environment.

osmolarity (oz′-mō-lār′-uh-tē) Solute concentration expressed as molarity.

osmoregulation Regulation of solute concentrations and water balance by a cell or organism.

osmoregulator An animal that controls its internal osmolarity independent of the external environment.

osmosis (oz-mō′-sis) The diffusion of free water across a selectively permeable membrane.

osteichthyan (os′-tē-ik′-thē-an) A member of a vertebrate clade with jaws and mostly bony skeletons.

outgroup A species or group of species from an evolutionary lineage that is known to have diverged before the lineage that contains the group of species being studied. An outgroup is selected so that its members are closely related to the group of species being studied, but not as closely related as any study-group members are to each other.

oval window In the vertebrate ear, a membrane-covered gap in the skull bone, through which sound waves pass from the middle ear to the inner ear.

ovarian cycle (ō-vār′-ē-un) The cyclic recurrence of the follicular phase, ovulation, and the luteal phase in the mammalian ovary, regulated by hormones.

ovary (ō′-vuh-rē) (1) In flowers, the portion of a carpel in which the egg-containing ovules develop. (2) In animals, the structure that produces female gametes and reproductive hormones.

oviduct (ō′-vuh-duct) A tube passing from the ovary to the vagina in invertebrates or to the uterus in vertebrates, where it is also called a fallopian tube.

oviparous (ō-vip′-uh-rus) Referring to a type of development in which young hatch from eggs laid outside the mother's body.

ovoviviparous (ō′-vō-vī-vip′-uh-rus) Referring to a type of development in which young hatch from eggs that are retained in the mother's uterus.

ovulation The release of an egg from an ovary. In humans, an ovarian follicle releases an egg during each uterine (menstrual) cycle.

ovule (o′-vyūl) A structure that develops within the ovary of a seed plant and contains the female gametophyte.

oxidation The complete or partial loss of electrons from a substance involved in a redox reaction.

oxidative phosphorylation (fos'-fôr-uh-lā'-shun) The production of ATP using energy derived from the redox reactions of an electron transport chain; the third major stage of cellular respiration.

oxidizing agent The electron acceptor in a redox reaction.

oxytocin (ok'-si-tō'-sen) A hormone produced by the hypothalamus and released from the posterior pituitary. It induces contractions of the uterine muscles during labor and causes the mammary glands to eject milk during nursing.

p53 gene A tumor-suppressor gene that codes for a specific transcription factor that promotes the synthesis of proteins that inhibit the cell cycle.

paedomorphosis (pē'-duh-môr'-fuh-sis) The retention in an adult organism of the juvenile features of its evolutionary ancestors.

pain receptor A sensory receptor that responds to noxious or painful stimuli; also called a nociceptor.

paleoanthropology The study of human origins and evolution.

paleontology (pā'-lē-un-tol'-ō-jē) The scientific study of fossils.

pancreas (pan'-krē-us) A gland with exocrine and endocrine tissues. The exocrine portion functions in digestion, secreting enzymes and an alkaline solution into the small intestine via a duct; the ductless endocrine portion functions in homeostasis, secreting the hormones insulin and glucagon into the blood.

pancrustacean A member of a diverse arthropod clade that includes lobsters, crabs, barnacles and other crustaceans, as well as insects and their six-legged terrestrial relatives.

pandemic A global epidemic.

Pangaea (pan-jē'-uh) The supercontinent that formed near the end of the Paleozoic era, when plate movements brought all the landmasses of Earth together.

parabasalid A protist, such as a trichomonad, with modified mitochondria.

paracrine Referring to a secreted molecule that acts on a neighboring cell.

paralogous genes Homologous genes that are found in the same genome as a result of gene duplication.

paraphyletic (pār'-uh-fī-let'-ik) Pertaining to a group of taxa that consists of a common ancestor and some, but not all, of its descendants.

parareptile A basal group of reptiles, consisting mostly of large, stocky quadrupedal herbivores. Parareptiles died out in the late Triassic period.

parasite (pār'-uh-sīt) An organism that feeds on the cell contents, tissues, or body fluids of another species (the host) while in or on the host organism. Parasites harm but usually do not kill their host.

parasitism (pār'-uh-sit-izm) A symbiotic relationship in which one organism, the parasite, benefits at the expense of another, the host, by living either within or on the host.

parasympathetic division One of three divisions of the autonomic nervous system; generally enhances body activities that gain and conserve energy, such as digestion and reduced heart rate.

parathyroid gland One of four small endocrine glands, embedded in the surface of the thyroid gland, that secrete parathyroid hormone.

parathyroid hormone (PTH) A hormone secreted by the parathyroid glands that raises blood calcium level by promoting calcium release from bone and calcium retention by the kidneys.

parenchyma cell (puh-ren'-ki-muh) A relatively unspecialized plant cell type that carries out most of the metabolism, synthesizes and stores organic products, and develops into a more differentiated cell type.

parental type An offspring with a phenotype that matches one of the true-breeding parental (P generation) phenotypes; also refers to the phenotype itself.

Parkinson's disease A progressive brain disease characterized by difficulty in initiating movements, slowness of movement, and rigidity.

parthenogenesis (par'-thuh-nō'-jen'-uh-sis) A form of asexual reproduction in which females produce offspring from unfertilized eggs.

partial pressure The pressure exerted by a particular gas in a mixture of gases (for instance, the pressure exerted by oxygen in air).

passive immunity Short-term immunity conferred by the transfer of antibodies, as occurs in the transfer of maternal antibodies to a fetus or nursing infant.

passive transport The diffusion of a substance across a biological membrane with no expenditure of energy.

pathogen An organism or virus that causes disease.

pathogen-associated molecular patterns (PAMPs) Short molecular sequences that typify certain groups of pathogens and that are recognized by cells of the innate immune system.

pattern formation The development of a multicellular organism's spatial organization, the arrangement of organs and tissues in their characteristic places in three-dimensional space.

peat Extensive deposits of partially decayed organic material often formed primarily from the wetland moss *Sphagnum*.

pedigree A diagram of a family tree with conventional symbols, showing the occurrence of heritable characters in parents and offspring over multiple generations.

pelagic zone The open-water component of aquatic biomes.

penis The copulatory structure of male mammals.

PEP carboxylase An enzyme that adds CO_2 to phosphoenolpyruvate (PEP) to form oxaloacetate in mesophyll cells of C_4 plants. It acts prior to photosynthesis.

pepsin An enzyme present in gastric juice that begins the hydrolysis of proteins.

pepsinogen The inactive form of pepsin secreted by chief cells located in gastric pits of the stomach.

peptide bond The covalent bond between the carboxyl group on one amino acid and the amino group on another, formed by a dehydration reaction.

peptidoglycan (pep'-tid-ō-glī'-kan) A type of polymer in bacterial cell walls consisting of modified sugars cross-linked by short polypeptides.

perception The interpretation of sensory system input by the brain.

pericycle The outermost layer in the vascular cylinder, from which lateral roots arise.

periderm (pār'-uh-derm') The protective coat that replaces the epidermis in woody plants during secondary growth, formed of the cork and cork cambium.

peripheral nervous system (PNS) The sensory and motor neurons that connect to the central nervous system.

peripheral protein A protein loosely bound to the surface of a membrane or to part of an integral protein and not embedded in the lipid bilayer.

peristalsis (pār'-uh-stal'-sis) (1) Alternating waves of contraction and relaxation in the smooth muscles lining the alimentary canal that push food along the canal. (2) A type of movement on land produced by rhythmic waves of muscle contractions passing from front to back, as in many annelids.

peristome (pār'-uh-stōme') A ring of interlocking, tooth-like structures on the upper part of a moss capsule (sporangium), often specialized for gradual spore discharge.

peritubular capillary One of the tiny blood vessels that form a network surrounding the proximal and distal tubules in the kidney.

peroxisome (puh-rok'-suh-sōm') An organelle containing enzymes that transfer hydrogen atoms from various substrates to oxygen (O_2), producing and then degrading hydrogen peroxide (H_2O_2).

petal A modified leaf of a flowering plant. Petals are the often colorful parts of a flower that advertise it to insects and other pollinators.

petiole (pet'-ē-ōl) The stalk of a leaf, which joins the leaf to a node of the stem.

P generation The true-breeding (homozygous) parent individuals from which F_1 hybrid offspring are derived in studies of inheritance; P stands for "parental."

pH A measure of hydrogen ion concentration equal to $-\log [H^+]$ and ranging in value from 0 to 14.

phage (fāj) A virus that infects bacteria; also called a bacteriophage.

phagocytosis (fag'-ō-sī-tō'-sis) A type of endocytosis in which large particulate substances or small organisms are taken up by a cell. It is carried out by some protists and by certain immune cells of animals (in mammals, mainly macrophages, neutrophils, and dendritic cells).

pharyngeal cleft (fuh-rin′-jē-ul) In chordate embryos, one of the grooves that separate a series of arches along the outer surface of the pharynx and may develop into a pharyngeal slit.

pharyngeal slit (fuh-rin′-jē-ul) In chordate embryos, one of the slits that form from the pharyngeal clefts and open into the pharynx, later developing into gill slits in many vertebrates.

pharynx (făr′-inks) (1) An area in the vertebrate throat where air and food passages cross. (2) In flatworms, the muscular tube that protrudes from the ventral side of the worm and ends in the mouth.

phase change (1) A shift from one developmental phase to another. (2) In plants, a morphological change that arises from a transition in shoot apical meristem activity.

phenotype (fē′-nō-tīp) The observable physical and physiological traits of an organism, which are determined by its genetic makeup.

pheromone (făr′-uh-mōn) In animals and fungi, a small molecule released into the environment that functions in communication between members of the same species. In animals, it acts much like a hormone in influencing physiology and behavior.

phloem (flō′-em) Vascular plant tissue consisting of living cells arranged into elongated tubes that transport sugar and other organic nutrients throughout the plant.

phloem sap (flō′-em) The sugar-rich solution carried through a plant's sieve tubes.

phosphate group A chemical group consisting of a phosphorus atom bonded to four oxygen atoms; important in energy transfer.

phospholipid (fos′-fō-lip′-id) A lipid made up of glycerol joined to two fatty acids and a phosphate group. The hydrocarbon chains of the fatty acids act as nonpolar, hydrophobic tails, while the rest of the molecule acts as a polar, hydrophilic head. Phospholipids form bilayers that function as biological membranes.

phosphorylated intermediate (fos′-fōr-uh-lā′-ted) A molecule (often a reactant) with a phosphate group covalently bound to it, making it more reactive (less stable) than the unphosphorylated molecule.

phosphorylation cascade (fos′-fōr-uh-lā′-shun) A series of protein phosphorylations occurring sequentially in which each protein kinase phosphorylates the next, activating it; often found in signaling pathways.

photic zone (fō′-tic) The narrow top layer of an ocean or lake, where light penetrates sufficiently for photosynthesis to occur.

photoautotroph (fō′-tō-ot′-ō-trōf) An organism that harnesses light energy to drive the synthesis of organic compounds from carbon dioxide.

photoheterotroph (fō′-tō-het′-er-ō-trōf) An organism that uses light to generate ATP but must obtain carbon in organic form.

photomorphogenesis Effects of light on plant morphology.

photon (fō′-ton) A quantum, or discrete quantity, of light energy that behaves as if it were a particle.

photoperiodism (fō′-tō-pĕr′-ē-ō-dizm) A physiological response to photoperiod, the interval in a 24-hour period during which an organism is exposed to light. An example of photoperiodism is flowering.

photophosphorylation (fō′-tō-fos′-fōr-uh-lā′-shun) The process of generating ATP from ADP and phosphate by means of chemiosmosis, using a proton-motive force generated across the thylakoid membrane of the chloroplast or the membrane of certain prokaryotes during the light reactions of photosynthesis.

photoreceptor An electromagnetic receptor that detects the radiation known as visible light.

photorespiration A metabolic pathway that consumes oxygen and ATP, releases carbon dioxide, and decreases photosynthetic output. Photorespiration generally occurs on hot, dry, bright days, when stomata close and the O_2/CO_2 ratio in the leaf increases, favoring the binding of O_2 rather than CO_2 by rubisco.

photosynthesis (fō′-tō-sin′-thi-sis) The conversion of light energy to chemical energy that is stored in sugars or other organic compounds; occurs in plants, algae, and certain prokaryotes.

photosystem A light-capturing unit located in the thylakoid membrane of the chloroplast or in the membrane of some prokaryotes, consisting of a reaction-center complex surrounded by numerous light-harvesting complexes. There are two types of photosystems, I and II; they absorb light best at different wavelengths.

photosystem I (PS I) A light-capturing unit in a chloroplast's thylakoid membrane or in the membrane of some prokaryotes; it has two molecules of P700 chlorophyll *a* at its reaction center.

photosystem II (PS II) One of two light-capturing units in a chloroplast's thylakoid membrane or in the membrane of some prokaryotes; it has two molecules of P680 chlorophyll *a* at its reaction center.

phototropism (fō′-tō-trō′-pizm) Growth of a plant shoot toward or away from light.

phyllotaxy (fil′-uh-tak′-sē) The pattern of leaf attachment to the stem of a plant.

phylogenetic species concept Definition of a species as the smallest group of individuals that share a common ancestor, forming one branch on the tree of life.

phylogenetic tree A branching diagram that represents a hypothesis about the evolutionary history of a group of organisms.

phylogeny (fī-loj′-uh-nē) The evolutionary history of a species or group of related species.

phylum (fī′-lum) (plural, **phyla**) In Linnaean classification, the taxonomic category above class.

physiology The processes and functions of an organism.

phytochrome (fī′-tuh-krōm) A type of light receptor in plants that mostly absorbs red light and regulates many plant responses, such as seed germination and shade avoidance.

phytoremediation An emerging technology that seeks to reclaim contaminated areas by taking advantage of some plant species' ability to extract heavy metals and other pollutants from the soil and to concentrate them in easily harvested portions of the plant.

pilus (plural, **pili**) (pī′-lus, pī′-lī) In bacteria, a structure that links one cell to another at the start of conjugation; also called a sex pilus or conjugation pilus.

pineal gland (pī′-nē-ul) A small gland on the dorsal surface of the vertebrate forebrain that secretes the hormone melatonin.

pinocytosis (pī′-nō-sī-tō′-sis) A type of endocytosis in which the cell ingests extracellular fluid and its dissolved solutes.

pistil A single carpel or a group of fused carpels.

pith Ground tissue that is internal to the vascular tissue in a stem; in many monocot roots, parenchyma cells that form the central core of the vascular cylinder.

pituitary gland (puh-tū′-uh-tār′-ē) An endocrine gland at the base of the hypothalamus; consists of a posterior lobe, which stores and releases two hormones produced by the hypothalamus, and an anterior lobe, which produces and secretes many hormones that regulate diverse body functions.

placenta (pluh-sen′-tuh) A structure in the uterus of a pregnant eutherian mammal that nourishes the fetus with the mother's blood supply; formed from the uterine lining and embryonic membranes.

placoderm A member of an extinct group of fishlike vertebrates that had jaws and were enclosed in a tough outer armor.

planarian A free-living flatworm found in ponds and streams.

plasma (plaz′-muh) The liquid matrix of blood in which the blood cells are suspended.

plasma cell (plaz′-muh) The antibody-secreting effector cell of humoral immunity. Plasma cells arise from antigen-stimulated B cells.

plasma membrane (plaz′-muh) The membrane at the boundary of every cell that acts as a selective barrier, regulating the cell's chemical composition.

plasmid (plaz′-mid) A small, circular, double-stranded DNA molecule that carries accessory genes separate from those of a bacterial chromosome; in DNA cloning, plasmids are used as vectors carrying up to about 10,000 base pairs (10 kb) of DNA. Plasmids are also found in some eukaryotes, such as yeasts.

plasmodesma (plaz′-mō-dez′-muh) (plural, **plasmodesmata**) An open channel through the cell wall that connects the cytoplasm of adjacent plant cells, allowing water, small solutes, and some larger molecules to pass between the cells.

plasmogamy (plaz-moh′-guh-mē) In fungi, the fusion of the cytoplasm of cells from two individuals; occurs as one stage of sexual reproduction, followed later by karyogamy.

plasmolysis (plaz-mol′-uh-sis) A phenomenon in walled cells in which the cytoplasm shrivels and the plasma membrane pulls away from the cell wall; occurs when the cell loses water to a hypertonic environment.

plastid One of a family of closely related organelles that includes chloroplasts, chromoplasts, and amyloplasts. Plastids are found in cells of photosynthetic eukaryotes.

plate tectonics The theory that the continents are part of great plates of Earth's crust that float on the hot, underlying portion of the mantle. Movements in the mantle cause the continents to move slowly over time.

platelet A pinched-off cytoplasmic fragment of a specialized bone marrow cell. Platelets circulate in the blood and are important in blood clotting.

pleiotropy (plī'-o-truh-pē) The ability of a single gene to have multiple effects.

pluripotent Describing a cell that can give rise to many, but not all, parts of an organism.

point mutation A change in a single nucleotide pair of a gene.

polar covalent bond A covalent bond between atoms that differ in electronegativity. The shared electrons are pulled closer to the more electronegative atom, making it slightly negative and the other atom slightly positive.

polar molecule A molecule (such as water) with an uneven distribution of charges in different regions of the molecule.

polarity A lack of symmetry; structural differences in opposite ends of an organism or structure, such as the root end and shoot end of a plant.

pollen grain In seed plants, a structure consisting of the male gametophyte enclosed within a pollen wall.

pollen tube A tube that forms after germination of the pollen grain and that functions in the delivery of sperm to the ovule.

pollination (pol'-uh-nā'-shun) The transfer of pollen to the part of a seed plant containing the ovules, a process required for fertilization.

poly-A tail A sequence of 50–250 adenine nucleotides added onto the 3′ end of a pre-mRNA molecule.

polygamous Referring to a type of relationship in which an individual of one sex mates with several of the other.

polygenic inheritance (pol'-ē-jen'-ik) An additive effect of two or more genes on a single phenotypic character.

polymer (pol'-uh-mer) A long molecule consisting of many similar or identical monomers linked together by covalent bonds.

polymerase chain reaction (PCR) (puh-lim'-uh-rās) A technique for amplifying DNA *in vitro* by incubating it with specific primers, a heat-resistant DNA polymerase, and nucleotides.

polynucleotide (pol'-ē-nū'-klē-ō-tīd) A polymer consisting of many nucleotide monomers in a chain. The nucleotides can be those of DNA or RNA.

polyp The sessile variant of the cnidarian body plan. The alternate form is the medusa.

polypeptide (pol'-ē-pep'-tīd) A polymer of many amino acids linked together by peptide bonds.

polyphyletic (pol'-ē-fī-let'-ik) Pertaining to a group of taxa that includes distantly related organisms but does not include their most recent common ancestor.

polyploidy (pol'-ē-ploy'-dē) A chromosomal alteration in which the organism possesses more than two complete chromosome sets. It is the result of an accident of cell division.

polyribosome (polysome) (pol'-ē-rī'-buh-sōm') A group of several ribosomes attached to, and translating, the same messenger RNA molecule.

polysaccharide (pol'-ē-sak'-uh-rīd) A polymer of many monosaccharides, formed by dehydration reactions.

polytomy (puh-lit'-uh-mē) In a phylogenetic tree, a branch point from which more than two descendant taxa emerge. A polytomy indicates that the evolutionary relationships between the descendant taxa are not yet clear.

pons A portion of the brain that participates in certain automatic, homeostatic functions, such as regulating the breathing centers in the medulla.

population A group of individuals of the same species that live in the same area and interbreed, producing fertile offspring.

population dynamics The study of how complex interactions between biotic and abiotic factors influence variations in population size.

population ecology The study of populations in relation to their environment, including environmental influences on population density and distribution, age structure, and variations in population size.

positional information Molecular cues that control pattern formation in an animal or plant embryonic structure by indicating a cell's location relative to the organism's body axes. These cues elicit a response by genes that regulate development.

positive feedback A form of regulation in which an end product of a process speeds up that process; in physiology, a control mechanism in which a change in a variable triggers a response that reinforces or amplifies the change.

positive pressure breathing A breathing system in which air is forced into the lungs.

posterior Pertaining to the rear, or tail end, of a bilaterally symmetrical animal.

posterior pituitary An extension of the hypothalamus composed of nervous tissue that secretes oxytocin and antidiuretic hormone made in the hypothalamus; a temporary storage site for these hormones.

postzygotic barrier (pōst'-zī-got'-ik) A reproductive barrier that prevents hybrid zygotes produced by two different species from developing into viable, fertile adults.

potential energy The energy that matter possesses as a result of its location or spatial arrangement (structure).

predation An interaction between species in which one species, the predator, eats the other, the prey.

prediction In deductive reasoning, a forecast that follows logically from a hypothesis. By testing predictions, experiments may allow certain hypotheses to be rejected.

pregnancy The condition of carrying one or more embryos in the uterus; also called gestation.

prepuce (prē'-pyūs) A fold of skin covering the head of the clitoris or penis.

pressure potential (Ψ_P) A component of water potential that consists of the physical pressure on a solution, which can be positive, zero, or negative.

prezygotic barrier (prē'-zī-got'-ik) A reproductive barrier that impedes mating between species or hinders fertilization if interspecific mating is attempted.

primary cell wall In plants, a relatively thin and flexible layer that surrounds the plasma membrane of a young cell.

primary consumer An herbivore; an organism that eats plants or other autotrophs.

primary electron acceptor In the thylakoid membrane of a chloroplast or in the membrane of some prokaryotes, a specialized molecule that shares the reaction-center complex with a pair of chlorophyll *a* molecules and that accepts an electron from them.

primary growth Growth produced by apical meristems, lengthening stems and roots.

primary immune response The initial adaptive immune response to an antigen, which appears after a lag of about 10–17 days.

primary oocyte (ō'-uh-sīt) An oocyte prior to completion of meiosis I.

primary producer An autotroph, usually a photosynthetic organism. Collectively, autotrophs make up the trophic level of an ecosystem that ultimately supports all other levels.

primary production The amount of light energy converted to chemical energy (organic compounds) by the autotrophs in an ecosystem during a given time period.

primary structure The level of protein structure referring to the specific linear sequence of amino acids.

primary succession A type of ecological succession that occurs in an area where there were originally no organisms present and where soil has not yet formed.

primary transcript An initial RNA transcript from any gene; also called pre-mRNA when transcribed from a protein-coding gene.

primase An enzyme that joins RNA nucleotides to make a primer during DNA replication, using the parental DNA strand as a template.

primer A short stretch of RNA with a free 3′ end, bound by complementary base pairing to the template strand and elongated with DNA nucleotides during DNA replication.

primitive streak A thickening along the future anterior-posterior axis on the surface of an early avian or mammalian embryo, caused by a piling up of cells as they congregate at the midline before moving into the embryo.

prion An infectious agent that is a misfolded version of a normal cellular protein. Prions appear to increase in number by converting correctly folded versions of the protein to more prions.

problem solving The cognitive activity of devising a method to proceed from one state to another in the face of real or apparent obstacles.

producer An organism that produces organic compounds from CO_2 by harnessing light energy (in photosynthesis) or by oxidizing inorganic chemicals (in chemosynthetic reactions carried out by some prokaryotes).

product A material resulting from a chemical reaction.

production efficiency The percentage of energy stored in assimilated food that is not used for respiration or eliminated as waste.

progesterone A steroid hormone that prepares the uterus for pregnancy; the major progestin in mammals.

progestin Any steroid hormone with progesterone-like activity.

prokaryotic cell (prō′-kār′-ē-ot′-ik) A type of cell lacking a membrane-enclosed nucleus and membrane-enclosed organelles. Organisms with prokaryotic cells (bacteria and archaea) are called prokaryotes.

prolactin A hormone produced and secreted by the anterior pituitary with a great diversity of effects in different vertebrate species. In mammals, it stimulates growth of and milk production by the mammary glands.

prometaphase The second stage of mitosis, in which the nuclear envelope fragments and the spindle microtubules attach to the kinetochores of the chromosomes.

promoter A specific nucleotide sequence in the DNA of a gene that binds RNA polymerase, positioning it to start transcribing RNA at the appropriate place.

prophage (prō′-fāj) A phage genome that has been inserted into a specific site on a bacterial chromosome.

prophase The first stage of mitosis, in which the chromatin condenses into discrete chromosomes visible with a light microscope, the mitotic spindle begins to form, and the nucleolus disappears but the nucleus remains intact.

prostaglandin (pros′-tuh-glan′-din) One of a group of modified fatty acids that are secreted by virtually all tissues and that perform a wide variety of functions as local regulators.

prostate gland (pros′-tāt) A gland in human males that secretes an acid-neutralizing component of semen.

protease (prō′-tē-āz) An enzyme that digests proteins by hydrolysis.

protein (prō′-tēn) A biologically functional molecule consisting of one or more polypeptides folded and coiled into a specific three-dimensional structure.

protein kinase (prō′-tēn) An enzyme that transfers phosphate groups from ATP to a protein, thus phosphorylating the protein.

protein phosphatase (prō′-tēn) An enzyme that removes phosphate groups from (dephosphorylates) proteins, often functioning to reverse the effect of a protein kinase.

proteoglycan (prō′-tē-ō-glī′-kan) A large molecule consisting of a small core protein with many carbohydrate chains attached, found in the extracellular matrix of animal cells. A proteoglycan may consist of up to 95% carbohydrate.

proteome The entire set of proteins expressed by a given cell or group of cells.

proteomics (prō′-tē-ō′-miks) The systematic study of sets of proteins and their properties, including their abundance, chemical modifications, and interactions.

protist An informal term applied to any eukaryote that is not a plant, animal, or fungus. Most protists are unicellular, though some are colonial or multicellular.

protocell An abiotic precursor of a living cell that had a membrane-like structure and that maintained an internal chemistry different from that of its surroundings.

proton (prō′-ton) A subatomic particle with a single positive electrical charge, with a mass of about 1.7×10^{-24} g, found in the nucleus of an atom.

protonema (prō′-tuh-nē′-muh) (plural, **protonemata**) A mass of green, branched, one-cell-thick filaments produced by germinating moss spores.

protonephridium (prō′-tō-nuh-frid′-ē-um) (plural, **protonephridia**) An excretory system, such as the flame bulb system of flatworms, consisting of a network of tubules lacking internal openings.

proton-motive force (prō′-ton) The potential energy stored in the form of a proton electrochemical gradient, generated by the pumping of hydrogen ions (H^+) across a biological membrane during chemiosmosis.

proton pump (prō′-ton) An active transport protein in a cell membrane that uses ATP to transport hydrogen ions out of a cell against their concentration gradient, generating a membrane potential in the process.

proto-oncogene (prō′-tō-on′-kō-jēn) A normal cellular gene that has the potential to become an oncogene.

protoplast The living part of a plant cell, which also includes the plasma membrane.

protostome development In animals, a developmental mode distinguished by the development of the mouth from the blastopore; often also characterized by spiral cleavage and by the body cavity forming when solid masses of mesoderm split.

provirus A viral genome that is permanently inserted into a host genome.

proximal tubule In the vertebrate kidney, the portion of a nephron immediately downstream from Bowman's capsule that conveys and helps refine filtrate.

pseudocoelomate (sū′-dō-sē′-lō-māt) An animal whose body cavity is lined by tissue derived from mesoderm and endoderm.

pseudogene (sū′-dō-jēn) A DNA segment that is very similar to a real gene but does not yield a functional product; a DNA segment that formerly functioned as a gene but has become inactivated in a particular species because of mutation.

pseudopodium (sū′-dō-pō′-dē-um) (plural, **pseudopodia**) A cellular extension of amoeboid cells used in moving and feeding.

P site One of a ribosome's three binding sites for tRNA during translation. The P site holds the tRNA carrying the growing polypeptide chain. (P stands for peptidyl tRNA.)

pterosaur Winged reptile that lived during the Mesozoic era.

pulse The rhythmic bulging of the artery walls with each heartbeat.

punctuated equilibria In the fossil record, long periods of apparent stasis, in which a species undergoes little or no morphological change, interrupted by relatively brief periods of sudden change.

Punnett square A diagram used in the study of inheritance to show the predicted genotypic results of random fertilization in genetic crosses between individuals of known genotype.

pupil The opening in the iris, which admits light into the interior of the vertebrate eye. Muscles in the iris regulate its size.

purine (pyū′-rēn) One of two types of nitrogenous bases found in nucleotides, characterized by a six-membered ring fused to a five-membered ring. Adenine (A) and guanine (G) are purines.

pyrimidine (puh-rim′-uh-dēn) One of two types of nitrogenous bases found in nucleotides, characterized by a six-membered ring. Cytosine (C), thymine (T), and uracil (U) are pyrimidines.

quantitative character A heritable feature that varies continuously over a range rather than in an either-or fashion.

quaternary structure (kwot′-er-nār′-ē) The particular shape of a complex, aggregate protein, defined by the characteristic three-dimensional arrangement of its constituent subunits, each a polypeptide.

radial cleavage A type of embryonic development in deuterostomes in which the planes of cell division that transform the zygote into a ball of cells are either parallel or perpendicular to the vertical axis of the embryo, thereby aligning tiers of cells one above the other.

radial symmetry Symmetry in which the body is shaped like a pie or barrel (lacking a left side and a right side) and can be divided into mirror-imaged halves by any plane through its central axis.

radicle An embryonic root of a plant.

radioactive isotope An isotope (an atomic form of a chemical element) that is unstable; the nucleus decays spontaneously, giving off detectable particles and energy.

radiolarian A protist, usually marine, with a shell generally made of silica and pseudopodia that radiate from the central body.

radiometric dating A method for determining the absolute age of rocks and fossils, based on the half-life of radioactive isotopes.

radula A straplike scraping organ used by many molluscs during feeding.

ras **gene** A gene that codes for Ras, a G protein that relays a growth signal from a growth factor receptor on the plasma membrane to a cascade of protein kinases, ultimately resulting in stimulation of the cell cycle.

ratite (rat′-īt) A member of the group of flightless birds.

ray-finned fish A member of the clade Actinopterygii, aquatic osteichthyans with fins supported by long, flexible rays, including tuna, bass, and herring.

reabsorption In excretory systems, the recovery of solutes and water from filtrate.

reactant A starting material in a chemical reaction.

reaction-center complex A complex of proteins associated with a special pair of chlorophyll *a* molecules and a primary electron acceptor. Located centrally in a photosystem, this complex triggers the light reactions of photosynthesis. Excited by light energy, the pair of chlorophylls donates an electron to the primary electron acceptor, which passes an electron to an electron transport chain.

reading frame On an mRNA, the triplet grouping of ribonucleotides used by the translation machinery during polypeptide synthesis.

receptacle The base of a flower; the part of the stem that is the site of attachment of the floral organs.

reception In cellular communication, the first step of a signaling pathway in which a signaling molecule is detected by a receptor molecule on or in the cell.

receptor-mediated endocytosis (en′-dō-sī-tō′-sis) The movement of specific molecules into a cell by the infolding of vesicles containing proteins with receptor sites specific to the molecules being taken in; enables a cell to acquire bulk quantities of specific substances.

receptor potential An initial response of a receptor cell to a stimulus, consisting of a change in voltage across the receptor membrane proportional to the stimulus strength.

receptor tyrosine kinase (RTK) A receptor protein spanning the plasma membrane, the cytoplasmic (intracellular) part of which can catalyze the transfer of a phosphate group from ATP to a tyrosine on another protein. Receptor tyrosine kinases often respond to the binding of a signaling molecule by dimerizing and then phosphorylating a tyrosine on the cytoplasmic portion of the other receptor in the dimer.

recessive allele An allele whose phenotypic effect is not observed in a heterozygote.

reciprocal altruism Altruistic behavior between unrelated individuals, whereby the altruistic individual benefits in the future when the beneficiary reciprocates.

recombinant chromosome A chromosome created when crossing over combines DNA from two parents into a single chromosome.

recombinant DNA A DNA molecule made *in vitro* with segments from different sources.

recombinant type (recombinant) An offspring whose phenotype differs from that of the true-breeding P generation parents; also refers to the phenotype itself.

rectum The terminal portion of the large intestine, where the feces are stored prior to elimination.

red alga A photosynthetic protist, named for its color, which results from a red pigment that masks the green of chlorophyll. Most red algae are multicellular and marine.

redox reaction (rē′-doks) A chemical reaction involving the complete or partial transfer of one or more electrons from one reactant to another; short for **red**uction-**ox**idation reaction.

reducing agent The electron donor in a redox reaction.

reduction The complete or partial addition of electrons to a substance involved in a redox reaction.

reflex An automatic reaction to a stimulus, mediated by the spinal cord or lower brain.

refractory period (rē-frakt′-ōr-ē) The short time immediately after an action potential in which the neuron cannot respond to another stimulus, owing to the inactivation of voltage-gated sodium channels.

regulator An animal for which mechanisms of homeostasis moderate internal changes in a particular variable in the face of external fluctuation of that variable.

regulatory gene A gene that codes for a protein, such as a repressor, that controls the transcription of another gene or group of genes.

reinforcement In evolutionary biology, a process in which natural selection strengthens prezygotic barriers to reproduction, thus reducing the chances of hybrid formation. Such a process is likely to occur only if hybrid offspring are less fit than members of the parent species.

relative abundance The proportional abundance of different species in a community.

relative fitness The contribution an individual makes to the gene pool of the next generation, relative to the contributions of other individuals in the population.

renal cortex The outer portion of the vertebrate kidney.

renal medulla The inner portion of the vertebrate kidney, beneath the renal cortex.

renal pelvis The funnel-shaped chamber that receives processed filtrate from the vertebrate kidney's collecting ducts and is drained by the ureter.

renin-angiotensin-aldosterone system (RAAS) A hormone cascade pathway that helps regulate blood pressure and blood volume.

repetitive DNA Nucleotide sequences, usually noncoding, that are present in many copies in a eukaryotic genome. The repeated units may be short and arranged tandemly (in series) or long and dispersed in the genome.

replication fork A Y-shaped region on a replicating DNA molecule where the parental strands are being unwound and new strands are being synthesized.

repressor A protein that inhibits gene transcription. In prokaryotes, repressors bind to the DNA in or near the promoter. In eukaryotes, repressors may bind to control elements within enhancers, to activators, or to other proteins in a way that blocks activators from binding to DNA.

reproductive isolation The existence of biological factors (barriers) that impede members of two species from producing viable, fertile offspring.

reproductive table An age-specific summary of the reproductive rates in a population.

reptile A member of the clade of amniotes that includes tuataras, lizards, snakes, turtles, crocodilians, and birds.

residual volume The amount of air that remains in the lungs after forceful exhalation.

resource partitioning The division of environmental resources by coexisting species such that the niche of each species differs by one or more significant factors from the niches of all coexisting species.

respiratory pigment A protein that transports oxygen in blood or hemolymph.

response (1) In cellular communication, the change in a specific cellular activity brought about by a transduced signal from outside the cell. (2) In feedback regulation, a physiological activity triggered by a change in a variable.

resting potential The membrane potential characteristic of a nonconducting excitable cell, with the inside of the cell more negative than the outside.

restriction enzyme An endonuclease (type of enzyme) that recognizes and cuts DNA molecules foreign to a bacterium (such as phage genomes). The enzyme cuts at specific nucleotide sequences (restriction sites).

restriction fragment A DNA segment that results from the cutting of DNA by a restriction enzyme.

restriction site A specific sequence on a DNA strand that is recognized and cut by a restriction enzyme.

retina (ret′-i-nuh) The innermost layer of the vertebrate eye, containing photoreceptor cells (rods and cones) and neurons; transmits images formed by the lens to the brain via the optic nerve.

retinal The light-absorbing pigment in rods and cones of the vertebrate eye.

retrotransposon (re′-trō-trans-pō′-zon) A transposable element that moves within a genome by means of an RNA intermediate, a transcript of the retrotransposon DNA.

retrovirus (re′-trō-vī′-rus) An RNA virus that replicates by transcribing its RNA into DNA and then inserting the DNA into a cellular chromosome; an important class of cancer-causing viruses.

reverse transcriptase (tran-skrip′-tās) An enzyme encoded by certain viruses (retroviruses) that uses RNA as a template for DNA synthesis.

reverse transcriptase–polymerase chain reaction (RT-PCR) A technique for determining expression of a particular gene. It uses reverse transcriptase and DNA polymerase to synthesize cDNA from all the mRNA in a sample and then subjects the cDNA to PCR amplification using primers specific for the gene of interest.

Rhizaria (rī-za′-rē-uh) One of the three major subgroups for which the "SAR" eukaryotic supergroup is named. Many species in this clade are amoebas characterized by threadlike pseudopodia.

rhizobacterium A soil bacterium whose population size is much enhanced in the rhizosphere, the soil region close to a plant's roots.

rhizoid (rī'-zoyd) A long, tubular single cell or filament of cells that anchors bryophytes to the ground. Unlike roots, rhizoids are not composed of tissues, lack specialized conducting cells, and do not play a primary role in water and mineral absorption.

rhizosphere The soil region close to plant roots and characterized by a high level of microbiological activity.

rhodopsin (rō-dop'-sin) A visual pigment consisting of retinal and opsin. Upon absorbing light, the retinal changes shape and dissociates from the opsin.

ribonucleic acid (RNA) (rī'-bō-nū-klā'-ik) A type of nucleic acid consisting of a polynucleotide made up of nucleotide monomers with a ribose sugar and the nitrogenous bases adenine (A), cytosine (C), guanine (G), and uracil (U); usually single-stranded; functions in protein synthesis, in gene regulation, and as the genome of some viruses.

ribose The sugar component of RNA nucleotides.

ribosomal RNA (rRNA) (rī'-buh-sō'-mul) RNA molecules that, together with proteins, make up ribosomes; the most abundant type of RNA.

ribosome (rī'-buh-sōm) A complex of rRNA and protein molecules that functions as a site of protein synthesis in the cytoplasm; consists of a large and a small subunit. In eukaryotic cells, each subunit is assembled in the nucleolus. *See also* nucleolus.

ribozyme (rī'-buh-zīm) An RNA molecule that functions as an enzyme, such as an intron that catalyzes its own removal during RNA splicing.

RNA interference (RNAi) A mechanism for silencing the expression of specific genes. In RNAi, double-stranded RNA molecules that match the sequence of a particular gene are processed into siRNAs that either block translation or trigger the degradation of the gene's messenger RNA. This happens naturally in some cells, and can be carried out in laboratory experiments as well.

RNA polymerase An enzyme that links ribonucleotides into a growing RNA chain during transcription, based on complementary binding to nucleotides on a DNA template strand.

RNA processing Modification of RNA primary transcripts, including splicing out of introns, joining together of exons, and alteration of the 5' and 3' ends.

RNA splicing After synthesis of a eukaryotic primary RNA transcript, the removal of portions of the transcript (introns) that will not be included in the mRNA and the joining together of the remaining portions (exons).

rod A rodlike cell in the retina of the vertebrate eye, sensitive to low light intensity.

root An organ in vascular plants that anchors the plant and enables it to absorb water and minerals from the soil.

root cap A cone of cells at the tip of a plant root that protects the apical meristem.

root hair A tiny extension of a root epidermal cell, growing just behind the root tip and increasing surface area for absorption of water and minerals.

root pressure Pressure exerted in the roots of plants as the result of osmosis, causing exudation from cut stems and guttation of water from leaves.

root system All of a plant's roots, which anchor it in the soil, absorb and transport minerals and water, and store food.

rooted Describing a phylogenetic tree that contains a branch point (often, the one farthest to the left) representing the most recent common ancestor of all taxa in the tree.

rough ER That portion of the endoplasmic reticulum with ribosomes attached.

round window In the mammalian ear, the point of contact where vibrations of the stapes create a traveling series of pressure waves in the fluid of the cochlea.

R plasmid A bacterial plasmid carrying genes that confer resistance to certain antibiotics.

r-selection Selection for life history traits that maximize reproductive success in uncrowded environments; also called density-independent selection.

rubisco (rū-bis'-kō) Ribulose bisphosphate (RuBP) carboxylase-oxygenase, the enzyme that normally catalyzes the first step of the Calvin cycle (the addition of CO_2 to RuBP). When excess O_2 is present or CO_2 levels are low, rubisco can bind oxygen, resulting in photorespiration.

saccule In the vertebrate ear, a chamber in the vestibule behind the oval window that participates in the sense of balance.

salicylic acid (sal'-i-sil'-ik) A signaling molecule in plants that may be partially responsible for activating systemic acquired resistance to pathogens.

salivary gland A gland associated with the oral cavity that secretes substances that lubricate food and begin the process of chemical digestion.

salt A compound resulting from the formation of an ionic bond; also called an ionic compound.

saltatory conduction (sol'-tuh-tōr'-ē) Rapid transmission of a nerve impulse along an axon, resulting from the action potential jumping from one node of Ranvier to another, skipping the myelin-sheathed regions of membrane.

"SAR" clade One of four supergroups of eukaryotes proposed in a current hypothesis of the evolutionary history of eukaryotes. This supergroup contains a large, extremely diverse collection of protists from three major subgroups: stramenopiles, alveolates, and rhizarians. *See also* Excavata, Archaeplastida, and Unikonta.

sarcomere (sar'-kō-mēr) The fundamental, repeating unit of striated muscle, delimited by the Z lines.

sarcoplasmic reticulum (SR) (sar'-kō-plaz'-mik ruh-tik'-yū-lum) A specialized endoplasmic reticulum that regulates the calcium concentration in the cytosol of muscle cells.

saturated fatty acid A fatty acid in which all carbons in the hydrocarbon tail are connected by single bonds, thus maximizing the number of hydrogen atoms that are attached to the carbon skeleton.

savanna A tropical grassland biome with scattered individual trees and large herbivores and maintained by occasional fires and drought.

scaffolding protein A type of large relay protein to which several other relay proteins are simultaneously attached, increasing the efficiency of signal transduction.

scanning electron microscope (SEM) A microscope that uses an electron beam to scan the surface of a sample, coated with metal atoms, to study details of its topography.

scatter plot A graph in which each piece of data is represented by a point. A scatter plot is used when the data for all variables are numerical and continuous.

schizophrenia (skit'-suh-frē'-nē-uh) A severe mental disturbance characterized by psychotic episodes in which patients have a distorted perception of reality.

Schwann cell A type of glial cell that forms insulating myelin sheaths around the axons of neurons in the peripheral nervous system.

science An approach to understanding the natural world.

scion (sī'-un) The twig grafted onto the stock when making a graft.

sclereid (sklār'-ē-id) A short, irregular sclerenchyma cell in nutshells and seed coats. Sclereids are scattered throughout the parenchyma of some plants.

sclerenchyma cell (skluh-ren'-kim-uh) A rigid, supportive plant cell type usually lacking a protoplast and possessing thick secondary walls strengthened by lignin at maturity.

scrotum A pouch of skin outside the abdomen that houses the testes; functions in maintaining the testes at the lower temperature required for spermatogenesis.

second law of thermodynamics The principle stating that every energy transfer or transformation increases the entropy of the universe. Usable forms of energy are at least partly converted to heat.

second messenger A small, nonprotein, water-soluble molecule or ion, such as a calcium ion (Ca^{2+}) or cyclic AMP, that relays a signal to a cell's interior in response to a signaling molecule bound by a signal receptor protein.

secondary cell wall In plant cells, a strong and durable matrix that is often deposited in several laminated layers around the plasma membrane and provides protection and support.

secondary consumer A carnivore that eats herbivores.

secondary endosymbiosis A process in eukaryotic evolution in which a heterotrophic eukaryotic cell engulfed a photosynthetic eukaryotic cell, which survived in a symbiotic relationship inside the heterotrophic cell.

secondary growth Growth produced by lateral meristems, thickening the roots and shoots of woody plants.

secondary immune response The adaptive immune response elicited on second or subsequent exposures to a particular antigen. The secondary immune response is more rapid, of greater magnitude, and of longer duration than the primary immune response.

secondary oocyte (ō´-uh-sīt) An oocyte that has completed meiosis I.

secondary production The amount of chemical energy in consumers' food that is converted to their own new biomass during a given time period.

secondary structure Regions of repetitive coiling or folding of the polypeptide backbone of a protein due to hydrogen bonding between constituents of the backbone (not the side chains).

secondary succession A type of succession that occurs where an existing community has been cleared by some disturbance that leaves the soil or substrate intact.

secretion (1) The discharge of molecules synthesized by a cell. (2) The active transport of wastes and certain other solutes from the body fluid into the filtrate in an excretory system.

seed An adaptation of some terrestrial plants consisting of an embryo packaged along with a store of food within a protective coat.

seed coat A tough outer covering of a seed, formed from the outer coat of an ovule. In a flowering plant, the seed coat encloses and protects the embryo and endosperm.

seedless vascular plant An informal name for a plant that has vascular tissue but lacks seeds. Seedless vascular plants form a paraphyletic group that includes the phyla Lycophyta (club mosses and their relatives) and Monilophyta (ferns and their relatives).

selective permeability A property of biological membranes that allows them to regulate the passage of substances across them.

self-incompatibility The ability of a seed plant to reject its own pollen and sometimes the pollen of closely related individuals.

semelparity (seh´-mel-pār´-i-tē) Reproduction in which an organism produces all of its offspring in a single event; also called big-bang reproduction.

semen (sē´-mun) The fluid that is ejaculated by the male during orgasm; contains sperm and secretions from several glands of the male reproductive tract.

semicircular canals A three-part chamber of the inner ear that functions in maintaining equilibrium.

semiconservative model Type of DNA replication in which the replicated double helix consists of one old strand, derived from the parental molecule, and one newly made strand.

semilunar valve A valve located at each exit of the heart, where the aorta leaves the left ventricle and the pulmonary artery leaves the right ventricle.

seminal vesicle (sem´-i-nul ves´-i-kul) A gland in males that secretes a fluid component of semen that lubricates and nourishes sperm.

seminiferous tubule (sem´-i-nif´-er-us) A highly coiled tube in the testis in which sperm are produced.

senescence (se-nes´-ens) The growth phase in a plant or plant part (as a leaf) from full maturity to death.

sensitive period A limited phase in an animal's development when learning of particular behaviors can take place; also called a critical period.

sensor In homeostasis, a receptor that detects a stimulus.

sensory adaptation The tendency of sensory neurons to become less sensitive when they are stimulated repeatedly.

sensory neuron A nerve cell that receives information from the internal or external environment and transmits signals to the central nervous system.

sensory reception The detection of a stimulus by sensory cells.

sensory receptor A specialized structure or cell that responds to a stimulus from an animal's internal or external environment.

sensory transduction The conversion of stimulus energy to a change in the membrane potential of a sensory receptor cell.

sepal (sē´-pul) A modified leaf in angiosperms that helps enclose and protect a flower bud before it opens.

septum (plural, **septa**) One of the cross-walls that divide a fungal hypha into cells. Septa generally have pores large enough to allow ribosomes, mitochondria, and even nuclei to flow from cell to cell.

serial endosymbiosis A hypothesis for the origin of eukaryotes consisting of a sequence of endosymbiotic events in which mitochondria, chloroplasts, and perhaps other cellular structures were derived from small prokaryotes that had been engulfed by larger cells.

serotonin (ser´-uh-tō´-nin) A neurotransmitter, synthesized from the amino acid tryptophan, that functions in the central nervous system.

set point In homeostasis in animals, a value maintained for a particular variable, such as body temperature or solute concentration.

seta (sē´-tuh) (plural, **setae**) The elongated stalk of a bryophyte sporophyte.

sex chromosome A chromosome responsible for determining the sex of an individual.

sex-linked gene A gene located on either sex chromosome. Most sex-linked genes are on the X chromosome and show distinctive patterns of inheritance; there are very few genes on the Y chromosome.

sexual dimorphism (dī-mōr´-fizm) Differences between the secondary sex characteristics of males and females of the same species.

sexual reproduction A type of reproduction in which two parents give rise to offspring that have unique combinations of genes inherited from both parents via the gametes.

sexual selection A form of natural selection in which individuals with certain inherited characteristics are more likely than other individuals to obtain mates.

Shannon diversity An index of community diversity symbolized by H and represented by the equation $H = -(p_A \ln p_A + p_B \ln p_B + p_C \ln p_C + \ldots)$, where A, B, C . . . are species,

p is the relative abundance of each species, and ln is the natural logarithm.

shared ancestral character A character, shared by members of a particular clade, that originated in an ancestor that is not a member of that clade.

shared derived character An evolutionary novelty that is unique to a particular clade.

shoot system The aerial portion of a plant body, consisting of stems, leaves, and (in angiosperms) flowers.

short tandem repeat (STR) Simple sequence DNA containing multiple tandemly repeated units of two to five nucleotides. Variations in STRs act as genetic markers in STR analysis, used to prepare genetic profiles.

short-day plant A plant that flowers (usually in late summer, fall, or winter) only when the light period is shorter than a critical length.

short-term memory The ability to hold information, anticipations, or goals for a time and then release them if they become irrelevant.

sickle-cell disease A recessively inherited human blood disorder in which a single nucleotide change in the β-globin gene causes hemoglobin to aggregate, changing red blood cell shape and causing multiple symptoms in afflicted individuals.

sieve plate An end wall in a sieve-tube element, which facilitates the flow of phloem sap in angiosperm sieve tubes.

sieve-tube element A living cell that conducts sugars and other organic nutrients in the phloem of angiosperms; also called a sieve-tube member. Connected end to end, they form sieve tubes.

sign stimulus An external sensory cue that triggers a fixed action pattern by an animal.

signal In animal behavior, transmission of a stimulus from one animal to another. The term is also used in the context of communication in other kinds of organisms and in cell-to-cell communication in all multicellular organisms.

signal peptide A sequence of about 20 amino acids at or near the leading (amino) end of a polypeptide that targets it to the endoplasmic reticulum or other organelles in a eukaryotic cell.

signal-recognition particle (SRP) A protein-RNA complex that recognizes a signal peptide as it emerges from a ribosome and helps direct the ribosome to the endoplasmic reticulum (ER) by binding to a receptor protein on the ER.

signal transduction The linkage of a mechanical, chemical, or electromagnetic stimulus to a specific cellular response.

signal transduction pathway A series of steps linking a mechanical, chemical, or electrical stimulus to a specific cellular response.

silent mutation A nucleotide-pair substitution that has no observable effect on the phenotype; for example, within a gene, a mutation that results in a codon that codes for the same amino acid.

simple fruit A fruit derived from a single carpel or several fused carpels.

simple sequence DNA A DNA sequence that contains many copies of tandemly repeated short sequences.

single bond A single covalent bond; the sharing of a pair of valence electrons by two atoms.

single circulation A circulatory system consisting of a single pump and circuit, in which blood passes from the sites of gas exchange to the rest of the body before returning to the heart.

single-lens eye The camera-like eye found in some jellies, polychaete worms, spiders, and many molluscs.

single nucleotide polymorphism (SNP) A single base-pair site in a genome where nucleotide variation is found in at least 1% of the population.

single-strand binding protein A protein that binds to the unpaired DNA strands during DNA replication, stabilizing them and holding them apart while they serve as templates for the synthesis of complementary strands of DNA.

sinoatrial (sī′-nō-ā′-trē-uhl) **(SA) node** A region in the right atrium of the heart that sets the rate and timing at which all cardiac muscle cells contract; the pacemaker.

sister chromatids Two copies of a duplicated chromosome attached to each other by proteins at the centromere and, sometimes, along the arms. While joined, two sister chromatids make up one chromosome. Chromatids are eventually separated during mitosis or meiosis II.

sister taxa Groups of organisms that share an immediate common ancestor and hence are each other's closest relatives.

skeletal muscle A type of striated muscle that is generally responsible for the voluntary movements of the body.

sliding-filament model The idea that muscle contraction is based on the movement of thin (actin) filaments along thick (myosin) filaments, shortening the sarcomere, the basic unit of muscle organization.

slow block to polyspermy The formation of the fertilization envelope and other changes in an egg's surface that prevent fusion of the egg with more than one sperm. The slow block begins about 1 minute after fertilization.

slow-twitch fiber A muscle fiber that can sustain long contractions.

small interfering RNA (siRNA) One of multiple small, single-stranded RNA molecules generated by cellular machinery from a long, linear, double-stranded RNA molecule. The siRNA associates with one or more proteins in a complex that can degrade or prevent translation of an mRNA with a complementary sequence.

small intestine The longest section of the alimentary canal, so named because of its small diameter compared with that of the large intestine; the principal site of the enzymatic hydrolysis of food macromolecules and the absorption of nutrients.

smooth ER That portion of the endoplasmic reticulum that is free of ribosomes.

smooth muscle A type of muscle lacking the striations of skeletal and cardiac muscle because of the uniform distribution of myosin filaments in the cells; responsible for involuntary body activities.

social learning Modification of behavior through the observation of other individuals.

sociobiology The study of social behavior based on evolutionary theory.

sodium-potassium pump A transport protein in the plasma membrane of animal cells that actively transports sodium out of the cell and potassium into the cell.

soil horizon A soil layer with physical characteristics that differ from those of the layers above or beneath.

solute (sol′-yūt) A substance that is dissolved in a solution.

solute potential (Ψ_S) A component of water potential that is proportional to the molarity of a solution and that measures the effect of solutes on the direction of water movement; also called osmotic potential, it can be either zero or negative.

solution A liquid that is a homogeneous mixture of two or more substances.

solvent The dissolving agent of a solution. Water is the most versatile solvent known.

somatic cell (sō-mat′-ik) Any cell in a multicellular organism except a sperm or egg or their precursors.

somite One of a series of blocks of mesoderm that exist in pairs just lateral to the notochord in a vertebrate embryo.

soredium (suh-rē′-dē-um) (plural, **soredia**) In lichens, a small cluster of fungal hyphae with embedded algae.

sorus (plural, **sori**) A cluster of sporangia on a fern sporophyll. Sori may be arranged in various patterns, such as parallel lines or dots, which are useful in fern identification.

spatial learning The establishment of a memory that reflects the environment's spatial structure.

spatial summation A phenomenon of neural integration in which the membrane potential of the postsynaptic cell is determined by the combined effect of EPSPs or IPSPs produced nearly simultaneously by different synapses.

speciation (spē-sē-ā′-shun) An evolutionary process in which one species splits into two or more species.

species (spē′-sēz) A population or group of populations whose members have the potential to interbreed in nature and produce viable, fertile offspring but do not produce viable, fertile offspring with members of other such groups.

species-area curve (spē′-sēz) The biodiversity pattern that shows that the larger the geographic area of a community is, the more species it has.

species diversity (spē′-sēz) The number and relative abundance of species in a biological community.

species richness (spē′-sēz) The number of species in a biological community.

specific heat The amount of heat that must be absorbed or lost for 1 g of a substance to change its temperature by 1°C.

spectrophotometer An instrument that measures the proportions of light of different wavelengths absorbed and transmitted by a pigment solution.

sperm The male gamete.

spermatheca (sper′-muh-thē′-kuh) (plural, **spermathecae**) In many insects, a sac in the female reproductive system where sperm are stored.

spermatogenesis (sper-ma′-tō-gen′-uh-sis) The continuous and prolific production of mature sperm in the testis.

spermatogonium (sper-ma′-tō-gō′-nē-um) (plural, **spermatogonia**) A cell that divides mitotically to form spermatocytes.

S phase The synthesis phase of the cell cycle; the portion of interphase during which DNA is replicated.

sphincter (sfink′-ter) A ringlike band of muscle fibers that controls the size of an opening in the body, such as the passage between the esophagus and the stomach.

spiral cleavage A type of embryonic development in protostomes in which the planes of cell division that transform the zygote into a ball of cells are diagonal to the vertical axis of the embryo. As a result, the cells of each tier sit in the grooves between cells of adjacent tiers.

spliceosome (spli′-sō-sōm) A large complex made up of proteins and RNA molecules that splices RNA by interacting with the ends of an RNA intron, releasing the intron and joining the two adjacent exons.

spongocoel (spon′-jō-sēl) The central cavity of a sponge.

spontaneous process A process that occurs without an overall input of energy; a process that is energetically favorable.

sporangium (spōr-an′-jē-um) (plural, **sporangia**) A multicellular organ in fungi and plants in which meiosis occurs and haploid cells develop.

spore (1) In the life cycle of a plant or alga undergoing alternation of generations, a haploid cell produced in the sporophyte by meiosis. A spore can divide by mitosis to develop into a multicellular haploid individual, the gametophyte, without fusing with another cell. (2) In fungi, a haploid cell, produced either sexually or asexually, that produces a mycelium after germination.

sporophyll (spō′-ruh-fil) A modified leaf that bears sporangia and hence is specialized for reproduction.

sporophyte (spō-ruh-fīt′) In organisms (plants and some algae) that have alternation of generations, the multicellular diploid form that results from the union of gametes. The sporophyte produces haploid spores by meiosis that develop into gametophytes.

sporopollenin (spōr-uh-pol′-eh-nin) A durable polymer that covers exposed zygotes of charophyte algae and forms the walls of plant spores, preventing them from drying out.

stabilizing selection Natural selection in which intermediate phenotypes survive or reproduce more successfully than do extreme phenotypes.

stamen (stā'-men) The pollen-producing reproductive organ of a flower, consisting of an anther and a filament.

standard deviation A measure of the variation found in a set of data points.

standard metabolic rate (SMR) Metabolic rate of a resting, fasting, and nonstressed ectotherm at a particular temperature.

starch A storage polysaccharide in plants, consisting entirely of glucose monomers joined by α glycosidic linkages.

start point In transcription, the nucleotide position on the promoter where RNA polymerase begins synthesis of RNA.

statocyst (stat'-uh-sist') A type of mechanoreceptor that functions in equilibrium in invertebrates by use of statoliths, which stimulate hair cells in relation to gravity.

statolith (stat'-uh-lith') (1) In plants, a specialized plastid that contains dense starch grains and may play a role in detecting gravity. (2) In invertebrates, a dense particle that settles in response to gravity and is found in sensory organs that function in equilibrium.

stele (stēl) The vascular tissue of a stem or root.

stem A vascular plant organ consisting of an alternating system of nodes and internodes that support the leaves and reproductive structures.

stem cell Any relatively unspecialized cell that can produce, during a single division, one identical daughter cell and one more specialized daughter cell that can undergo further differentiation.

steroid A type of lipid characterized by a carbon skeleton consisting of four fused rings with various chemical groups attached.

sticky end A single-stranded end of a double-stranded restriction fragment.

stigma (plural, **stigmata**) The sticky part of a flower's carpel, which receives pollen grains.

stimulus In feedback regulation, a fluctuation in a variable that triggers a response.

stipe A stemlike structure of a seaweed.

stock The plant that provides the root system when making a graft.

stoma (stō'-muh) (plural, **stomata**) A microscopic pore surrounded by guard cells in the epidermis of leaves and stems that allows gas exchange between the environment and the interior of the plant.

stomach An organ of the digestive system that stores food and performs preliminary steps of digestion.

Stramenopila (strah'-men-ō'-pē-lah) One of the three major subgroups for which the "SAR" eukaryotic supergroup is named. This clade arose by secondary endosymbiosis and includes diatoms and brown algae.

stratum (strah'-tum) (plural, **strata**) A rock layer formed when new layers of sediment cover older ones and compress them.

strigolactone Any of a class of plant hormones that inhibit shoot branching, trigger the germination of parasitic plant seeds, and stimulate the association of plant roots with mycorrhizal fungi.

strobilus (strō-bi'-lus) (plural, **strobili**) The technical term for a cluster of sporophylls known commonly as a cone, found in most gymnosperms and some seedless vascular plants.

stroke The death of nervous tissue in the brain, usually resulting from rupture or blockage of arteries in the head.

stroke volume The volume of blood pumped by a heart ventricle in a single contraction.

stroma (strō'-muh) The dense fluid within the chloroplast surrounding the thylakoid membrane and containing ribosomes and DNA; involved in the synthesis of organic molecules from carbon dioxide and water.

stromatolite Layered rock that results from the activities of prokaryotes that bind thin films of sediment together.

structural isomer One of several compounds that have the same molecular formula but differ in the covalent arrangements of their atoms.

style The stalk of a flower's carpel, with the ovary at the base and the stigma at the top.

substrate The reactant on which an enzyme works.

substrate feeder An animal that lives in or on its food source, eating its way through the food.

substrate-level phosphorylation The enzyme-catalyzed formation of ATP by direct transfer of a phosphate group to ADP from an intermediate substrate in catabolism.

sugar sink A plant organ that is a net consumer or storer of sugar. Growing roots, shoot tips, stems, and fruits are examples of sugar sinks supplied by phloem.

sugar source A plant organ in which sugar is being produced by either photosynthesis or the breakdown of starch. Mature leaves are the primary sugar sources of plants.

sulfhydryl group A chemical group consisting of a sulfur atom bonded to a hydrogen atom.

suprachiasmatic nucleus (SCN) (sūp'-ruh-kē'-as-ma-tik) A group of neurons in the hypothalamus of mammals that functions as a biological clock.

surface tension A measure of how difficult it is to stretch or break the surface of a liquid. Water has a high surface tension because of the hydrogen bonding of surface molecules.

surfactant A substance secreted by alveoli that decreases surface tension in the fluid that coats the alveoli.

survivorship curve A plot of the number of members of a cohort that are still alive at each age; one way to represent age-specific mortality.

suspension feeder An animal that feeds by removing suspended food particles from the surrounding medium by a capture, trapping, or filtration mechanism.

sustainable agriculture Long-term productive farming methods that are environmentally safe.

sustainable development Development that meets the needs of people today without limiting the ability of future generations to meet their needs.

swim bladder In aquatic osteichthyans, an air sac that enables the animal to control its buoyancy in the water.

symbiont (sim'-bē-ont) The smaller participant in a symbiotic relationship, living in or on the host.

symbiosis An ecological relationship between organisms of two different species that live together in direct and intimate contact.

sympathetic division One of three divisions of the autonomic nervous system; generally increases energy expenditure and prepares the body for action.

sympatric speciation (sim-pat'-rik) The formation of new species in populations that live in the same geographic area.

symplast In plants, the continuum of cytoplasm connected by plasmodesmata between cells.

synapse (sin'-aps) The junction where a neuron communicates with another cell across a narrow gap via a neurotransmitter or an electrical coupling.

synapsid (si-nap'-sid) A member of an amniote clade distinguished by a single hole on each side of the skull. Synapsids include the mammals.

synapsis (si-nap'-sis) The pairing and physical connection of duplicated homologous chromosomes during prophase I of meiosis.

synaptonemal (si-nap'-tuh-nē'-muhl) **complex** A zipper-like structure composed of proteins, which connects two homologous chromosomes tightly along their lengths.

systematics A scientific discipline focused on classifying organisms and determining their evolutionary relationships.

systemic acquired resistance A defensive response in infected plants that helps protect healthy tissue from pathogenic invasion.

systemic circuit The branch of the circulatory system that supplies oxygenated blood to and carries deoxygenated blood away from organs and tissues throughout the body.

systems biology An approach to studying biology that aims to model the dynamic behavior of whole biological systems based on a study of the interactions among the system's parts.

systole (sis'-tō-lē) The stage of the cardiac cycle in which a heart chamber contracts and pumps blood.

systolic pressure Blood pressure in the arteries during contraction of the ventricles.

taproot A main vertical root that develops from an embryonic root and gives rise to lateral (branch) roots.

tastant Any chemical that stimulates the sensory receptors in a taste bud.

taste bud A collection of modified epithelial cells on the tongue or in the mouth that are receptors for taste in mammals.

TATA box A DNA sequence in eukaryotic promoters crucial in forming the transcription initiation complex.

taxis (tak'-sis) An oriented movement toward or away from a stimulus.

taxon (plural, **taxa**) A named taxonomic unit at any given level of classification.

taxonomy (tak-son'-uh-mē) A scientific discipline concerned with naming and classifying the diverse forms of life.

Tay-Sachs disease A human genetic disease caused by a recessive allele for a dysfunctional enzyme, leading to accumulation of certain lipids in the brain. Seizures, blindness, and degeneration of motor and mental performance usually become manifest a few months after birth, followed by death within a few years.

T cells The class of lymphocytes that mature in the thymus; they include both effector cells for the cell-mediated immune response and helper cells required for both branches of adaptive immunity.

technology The application of scientific knowledge for a specific purpose, often involving industry or commerce but also including uses in basic research.

telomere (tel'-uh-mēr) The tandemly repetitive DNA at the end of a eukaryotic chromosome's DNA molecule. Telomeres protect the organism's genes from being eroded during successive rounds of replication. See also repetitive DNA.

telophase The fifth and final stage of mitosis, in which daughter nuclei are forming and cytokinesis has typically begun.

temperate broadleaf forest A biome located throughout midlatitude regions where there is sufficient moisture to support the growth of large, broadleaf deciduous trees.

temperate grassland A terrestrial biome that exists at midlatitude regions and is dominated by grasses and forbs.

temperate phage A phage that is capable of replicating by either a lytic or lysogenic cycle.

temperature A measure in degrees of the average kinetic energy (thermal energy) of the atoms and molecules in a body of matter.

template strand The DNA strand that provides the pattern, or template, for ordering, by complementary base pairing, the sequence of nucleotides in an RNA transcript.

temporal summation A phenomenon of neural integration in which the membrane potential of the postsynaptic cell in a chemical synapse is determined by the combined effect of EPSPs or IPSPs produced in rapid succession.

tendon A fibrous connective tissue that attaches muscle to bone.

terminator In bacteria, a sequence of nucleotides in DNA that marks the end of a gene and signals RNA polymerase to release the newly made RNA molecule and detach from the DNA.

territoriality A behavior in which an animal defends a bounded physical space against encroachment by other individuals, usually of its own species.

tertiary consumer (ter'-shē-ār'-ē) A carnivore that eats other carnivores.

tertiary structure (ter'-shē-ār'-ē) The overall shape of a protein molecule due to interactions of amino acid side chains, including hydrophobic interactions, ionic bonds, hydrogen bonds, and disulfide bridges.

test In foram protists, a porous shell that consists of a single piece of organic material hardened with calcium carbonate.

testcross Breeding an organism of unknown genotype with a homozygous recessive individual to determine the unknown genotype. The ratio of phenotypes in the offspring reveals the unknown genotype.

testis (plural, **testes**) The male reproductive organ, or gonad, in which sperm and reproductive hormones are produced.

testosterone A steroid hormone required for development of the male reproductive system, spermatogenesis, and male secondary sex characteristics; the major androgen in mammals.

tetanus (tet'-uh-nus) The maximal, sustained contraction of a skeletal muscle, caused by a very high frequency of action potentials elicited by continual stimulation.

tetrapod A vertebrate clade whose members have limbs with digits. Tetrapods include mammals, amphibians, and birds and other reptiles.

thalamus (thal'-uh-mus) An integrating center of the vertebrate forebrain. Neurons with cell bodies in the thalamus relay neural input to specific areas in the cerebral cortex and regulate what information goes to the cerebral cortex.

theory An explanation that is broader in scope than a hypothesis, generates new hypotheses, and is supported by a large body of evidence.

thermal energy Kinetic energy due to the random motion of atoms and molecules; energy in its most random form. See also heat.

thermocline A narrow stratum of abrupt temperature change in the ocean and in many temperate-zone lakes.

thermodynamics (ther'-mō-dī-nam'-iks) The study of energy transformations that occur in a collection of matter. See also first law of thermodynamics and second law of thermodynamics.

thermophile See extreme thermophile.

thermoreceptor A receptor stimulated by either heat or cold.

thermoregulation The maintenance of internal body temperature within a tolerable range.

theropod A member of a group of dinosaurs that were bipedal carnivores.

thick filament A filament composed of staggered arrays of myosin molecules; a component of myofibrils in muscle fibers.

thigmomorphogenesis (thig'-mō-mor'-phō-gen'-uh-sis) A response in plants to chronic mechanical stimulation, resulting from increased ethylene production. An example is thickening stems in response to strong winds.

thigmotropism (thig-mō'-truh-pizm) A directional growth of a plant in response to touch.

thin filament A filament consisting of two strands of actin and two strands of regulatory protein coiled around one another; a component of myofibrils in muscle fibers.

threatened species A species that is considered likely to become endangered in the foreseeable future.

threshold The potential that an excitable cell membrane must reach for an action potential to be initiated.

thrombus A fibrin-containing clot that forms in a blood vessel and blocks the flow of blood.

thylakoid (thī'-luh-koyd) A flattened, membranous sac inside a chloroplast. Thylakoids often exist in stacks called grana that are interconnected; their membranes contain molecular "machinery" used to convert light energy to chemical energy.

thymus (thī'-mus) A small organ in the thoracic cavity of vertebrates where maturation of T cells is completed.

thyroid gland An endocrine gland, located on the ventral surface of the trachea, that secretes two iodine-containing hormones, triiodothyronine (T_3) and thyroxine (T_4), as well as calcitonin.

thyroid hormone Either of two iodine-containing hormones (triiodothyronine and thyroxine) that are secreted by the thyroid gland and that help regulate metabolism, development, and maturation in vertebrates.

thyroxine (T_4) One of two iodine-containing hormones that are secreted by the thyroid gland and that help regulate metabolism, development, and maturation in vertebrates.

tidal volume The volume of air a mammal inhales and exhales with each breath.

tight junction A type of intercellular junction between animal cells that prevents the leakage of material through the space between cells.

tissue An integrated group of cells with a common structure, function, or both.

tissue system One or more tissues organized into a functional unit connecting the organs of a plant.

Toll-like receptor (TLR) A membrane receptor on a phagocytic white blood cell that recognizes fragments of molecules common to a set of pathogens.

tonicity The ability of a solution surrounding a cell to cause that cell to gain or lose water.

top-down model A model of community organization in which predation influences community organization by controlling herbivore numbers, which in turn control plant or phytoplankton numbers, which in turn control nutrient levels; also called the trophic cascade model.

topoisomerase A protein that breaks, swivels, and rejoins DNA strands. During DNA replication, topoisomerase helps to relieve strain in the double helix ahead of the replication fork.

topsoil A mixture of particles derived from rock, living organisms, and decaying organic material (humus).

torpor A physiological state in which activity is low and metabolism decreases.

totipotent (tō'-tuh-pōt'-ent) Describing a cell that can give rise to all parts of the embryo and adult, as well as extraembryonic membranes in species that have them.

trace element An element indispensable for life but required in extremely minute amounts.

trachea (trā'-kē-uh) The portion of the respiratory tract that passes from the larynx to the bronchi; also called the windpipe.

tracheal system In insects, a system of branched, air-filled tubes that extends throughout the body and carries oxygen directly to cells.

tracheid (trā'-kē-id) A long, tapered water-conducting cell found in the xylem of nearly all vascular plants. Functioning tracheids are no longer living.

trait One of two or more detectable variants in a genetic character.

trans fat An unsaturated fat, formed artificially during hydrogenation of oils, containing one or more *trans* double bonds.

transcription The synthesis of RNA using a DNA template.

transcription factor A regulatory protein that binds to DNA and affects transcription of specific genes.

transcription initiation complex The completed assembly of transcription factors and RNA polymerase bound to a promoter.

transcription unit A region of DNA that is transcribed into an RNA molecule.

transduction (1) A process in which phages (viruses) carry bacterial DNA from one bacterial cell to another. When these two cells are members of different species, transduction results in horizontal gene transfer. (2) In cellular communication, the conversion of a signal from outside the cell to a form that can bring about a specific cellular response; also called signal transduction.

transfer RNA (tRNA) An RNA molecule that functions as a translator between nucleic acid and protein languages by carrying specific amino acids to the ribosome, where they recognize the appropriate codons in the mRNA.

transformation (1) The conversion of a normal cell into a cell that is able to divide indefinitely in culture, thus behaving like a cancer cell. (Malignant transformation may also describe the series of changes in a normal cell in an organism that change it into a malignant (cancerous) cell.) (2) A change in genotype and phenotype due to the assimilation of external DNA by a cell. When the external DNA is from a member of a different species, transformation results in horizontal gene transfer.

transgenic Pertaining to an organism whose genome contains a gene introduced from another organism of the same or a different species.

translation The synthesis of a polypeptide using the genetic information encoded in an mRNA molecule. There is a change of "language" from nucleotides to amino acids.

translocation (1) An aberration in chromosome structure resulting from attachment of a chromosomal fragment to a nonhomologous chromosome. (2) During protein synthesis, the third stage in the elongation cycle, when the RNA carrying the growing polypeptide moves from the A site to the P site on the ribosome. (3) The transport of organic nutrients in the phloem of vascular plants.

transmission The passage of a nerve impulse along axons.

transmission electron microscope (TEM) A microscope that passes an electron beam through very thin sections stained with metal atoms and is primarily used to study the internal ultrastructure of cells.

transpiration The evaporative loss of water from a plant.

transport epithelium One or more layers of specialized epithelial cells that carry out and regulate solute movement.

transport protein A transmembrane protein that helps a certain substance or class of closely related substances to cross the membrane.

transport vesicle A small membranous sac in a eukaryotic cell's cytoplasm carrying molecules produced by the cell.

transposable element A segment of DNA that can move within the genome of a cell by means of a DNA or RNA intermediate; also called a transposable genetic element.

transposon A transposable element that moves within a genome by means of a DNA intermediate.

transverse (T) tubule An infolding of the plasma membrane of skeletal muscle cells.

triacylglycerol (trī-as'-ul-glis'-uh-rol) A lipid consisting of three fatty acids linked to one glycerol molecule; also called a fat or triglyceride.

triple response A plant growth maneuver in response to mechanical stress, involving slowing of stem elongation, thickening of the stem, and a curvature that causes the stem to start growing horizontally.

triplet code A genetic information system in which sets of three-nucleotide-long words specify the amino acids for polypeptide chains.

triploblastic Possessing three germ layers: the endoderm, mesoderm, and ectoderm. All bilaterian animals are triploblastic.

trisomic Referring to a diploid cell that has three copies of a particular chromosome instead of the normal two.

trochophore larva (trō'-kuh-fōr) Distinctive larval stage observed in some lophotrochozoan animals, including some annelids and molluscs.

trophic efficiency The percentage of production transferred from one trophic level to the next higher trophic level.

trophic structure The different feeding relationships in an ecosystem, which determine the route of energy flow and the pattern of chemical cycling.

trophoblast The outer epithelium of a mammalian blastocyst. It forms the fetal part of the placenta, supporting embryonic development but not forming part of the embryo proper.

tropic hormone A hormone that has an endocrine gland or endocrine cells as a target.

tropical dry forest A terrestrial biome characterized by relatively high temperatures and precipitation overall but with a pronounced dry season.

tropical rain forest A terrestrial biome characterized by relatively high precipitation and temperatures year-round.

tropics Latitudes between 23.5° north and south.

tropism A growth response that results in the curvature of whole plant organs toward or away from stimuli due to differential rates of cell elongation.

tropomyosin The regulatory protein that blocks the myosin-binding sites on actin molecules.

troponin complex The regulatory proteins that control the position of tropomyosin on the thin filament.

true-breeding Referring to organisms that produce offspring of the same variety over many generations of self-pollination.

tubal ligation A means of sterilization in which a woman's two oviducts (fallopian tubes) are tied closed and a segment of each is removed to prevent eggs from reaching the uterus.

tube foot One of numerous extensions of an echinoderm's water vascular system. Tube feet function in locomotion and feeding.

tumor-suppressor gene A gene whose protein product inhibits cell division, thereby preventing the uncontrolled cell growth that contributes to cancer.

tundra A terrestrial biome at the extreme limits of plant growth. At the northernmost limits, it is called arctic tundra, and at high altitudes, where plant forms are limited to low shrubby or matlike vegetation, it is called alpine tundra.

tunicate A member of the clade Urochordata, sessile marine chordates that lack a backbone.

turgid (ter'-jid) Swollen or distended, as in plant cells. (A walled cell becomes turgid if it has a lower water potential than its surroundings, resulting in entry of water.)

turgor pressure The force directed against a plant cell wall after the influx of water and swelling of the cell due to osmosis.

turnover The mixing of waters as a result of changing water-temperature profiles in a lake.

turnover time The time required to replace the standing crop of a population or group of populations (for example, of phytoplankton), calculated as the ratio of standing crop to production.

twin study A behavioral study in which researchers compare the behavior of identical twins raised apart with that of identical twins raised in the same household.

tympanic membrane Another name for the eardrum, the membrane between the outer and middle ear.

Unikonta (yū'-ni-kon'-tuh) One of four supergroups of eukaryotes proposed in a current hypothesis of the evolutionary history of eukaryotes. This clade, which is supported by studies of myosin proteins and DNA, consists of amoebozoans and opisthokonts. *See also* Excavata, "SAR" clade, and Archaeplastida.

unsaturated fatty acid A fatty acid that has one or more double bonds between carbons in the hydrocarbon tail. Such bonding reduces the number of hydrogen atoms attached to the carbon skeleton.

urban ecology The study of organisms and their environment in urban and suburban settings.

urea A soluble nitrogenous waste produced in the liver by a metabolic cycle that combines ammonia with carbon dioxide.

ureter (yū-rē´-ter) A duct leading from the kidney to the urinary bladder.

urethra (yū-rē´-thruh) A tube that releases urine from the mammalian body near the vagina in females and through the penis in males; also serves in males as the exit tube for the reproductive system.

uric acid A product of protein and purine metabolism and the major nitrogenous waste product of insects, land snails, and many reptiles. Uric acid is relatively nontoxic and largely insoluble in water.

urinary bladder The pouch where urine is stored prior to elimination.

uterine cycle In humans and certain other primates, a type of reproductive cycle in which the nonpregnant endometrium is shed through the cervix into the vagina; also called the menstrual cycle.

uterus A female organ where eggs are fertilized and/or development of the young occurs.

utricle (yū´-trih-kuhl) In the vertebrate ear, a chamber in the vestibule behind the oval window that opens into the three semicircular canals.

vaccine A harmless variant or derivative of a pathogen that stimulates a host's immune system to mount defenses against the pathogen.

vacuole (vak´-yū-ōl´) A membrane-bounded vesicle whose specialized function varies in different kinds of cells.

vagina Part of the female reproductive system between the uterus and the outside opening; the birth canal in mammals. During copulation, the vagina accommodates the male's penis and receives sperm.

valence The bonding capacity of a given atom; usually equals the number of unpaired electrons required to complete the atom's outermost (valence) shell.

valence electron An electron in the outermost electron shell.

valence shell The outermost energy shell of an atom, containing the valence electrons involved in the chemical reactions of that atom.

van der Waals interactions Weak attractions between molecules or parts of molecules that result from transient local partial charges.

variable A factor that varies in an experiment or other test.

variation Differences between members of the same species.

vas deferens In mammals, the tube in the male reproductive system in which sperm travel from the epididymis to the urethra.

vasa recta The capillary system in the kidney that serves the loop of Henle.

vascular cambium A cylinder of meristematic tissue in woody plants that adds layers of secondary vascular tissue called secondary xylem (wood) and secondary phloem.

vascular plant A plant with vascular tissue. Vascular plants include all living plant species except liverworts, mosses, and hornworts.

vascular tissue Plant tissue consisting of cells joined into tubes that transport water and nutrients throughout the plant body.

vascular tissue system A transport system formed by xylem and phloem throughout a vascular plant. Xylem transports water and minerals; phloem transports sugars, the products of photosynthesis.

vasectomy The cutting and sealing of each vas deferens to prevent sperm from entering the urethra.

vasoconstriction A decrease in the diameter of blood vessels caused by contraction of smooth muscles in the vessel walls.

vasodilation An increase in the diameter of blood vessels caused by relaxation of smooth muscles in the vessel walls.

vector An organism that transmits pathogens from one host to another.

vegetal pole The point at the end of an egg in the hemisphere where most yolk is concentrated; opposite of animal pole.

vegetative propagation Asexual reproduction in plants that is facilitated or induced by humans.

vegetative reproduction Asexual reproduction in plants.

vein (1) In animals, a vessel that carries blood toward the heart. (2) In plants, a vascular bundle in a leaf.

ventilation The flow of air or water over a respiratory surface.

ventral Pertaining to the underside, or bottom, of an animal with radial or bilateral symmetry.

ventricle (ven´-tri-kul) (1) A heart chamber that pumps blood out of the heart. (2) A space in the vertebrate brain, filled with cerebrospinal fluid.

venule (ven´-yūl) A vessel that conveys blood between a capillary bed and a vein.

vernalization The use of cold treatment to induce a plant to flower.

vertebrate A chordate animal with vertebrae, the series of bones that make up the backbone.

vesicle (ves´-i-kul) A membranous sac in the cytoplasm of a eukaryotic cell.

vessel A continuous water-conducting micropipe found in most angiosperms and a few nonflowering vascular plants.

vessel element A short, wide water-conducting cell found in the xylem of most angiosperms and a few nonflowering vascular plants. Dead at maturity, vessel elements are aligned end to end to form micropipes called vessels.

vestigial structure A feature of an organism that is a historical remnant of a structure that served a function in the organism's ancestors.

villus (plural, **villi**) (1) A finger-like projection of the inner surface of the small intestine. (2) A finger-like projection of the chorion of the mammalian placenta. Large numbers of villi increase the surface areas of these organs.

viral envelope A membrane, derived from membranes of the host cell, that cloaks the capsid, which in turn encloses a viral genome.

viroid (vī´-royd) A plant pathogen consisting of a molecule of naked, circular RNA a few hundred nucleotides long.

virulent phage A phage that replicates only by a lytic cycle.

virus An infectious particle incapable of replicating outside of a cell, consisting of an RNA or DNA genome surrounded by a protein coat (capsid) and, for some viruses, a membranous envelope.

visceral mass One of the three main parts of a mollusc; the part containing most of the internal organs. *See also* foot and mantle.

visible light That portion of the electromagnetic spectrum that can be detected as various colors by the human eye, ranging in wavelength from about 380 nm to about 750 nm.

vital capacity The maximum volume of air that a mammal can inhale and exhale with each breath.

vitamin An organic molecule required in the diet in very small amounts. Many vitamins serve as coenzymes or parts of coenzymes.

viviparous (vī-vip´-uh-rus) Referring to a type of development in which the young are born alive after having been nourished in the uterus by blood from the placenta.

voltage-gated ion channel A specialized ion channel that opens or closes in response to changes in membrane potential.

vulva Collective term for the female external genitalia.

water potential (Ψ) The physical property predicting the direction in which water will flow, governed by solute concentration and applied pressure.

water vascular system A network of hydraulic canals unique to echinoderms that branches into extensions called tube feet, which function in locomotion and feeding.

wavelength The distance between crests of waves, such as those of the electromagnetic spectrum.

wetland A habitat that is inundated by water at least some of the time and that supports plants adapted to water-saturated soil.

white matter Tracts of axons within the CNS.

whole-genome shotgun approach Procedure for genome sequencing in which the genome is randomly cut into many overlapping short segments that are sequenced; computer software then assembles the complete sequence.

wild type The phenotype most commonly observed in natural populations; also refers to the individual with that phenotype.

wilting The drooping of leaves and stems as a result of plant cells becoming flaccid.

wobble Flexibility in the base-pairing rules in which the nucleotide at the 5′ end of a tRNA anticodon can form hydrogen bonds with more than one kind of base in the third position (3′ end) of a codon.

xerophyte (zir´-ō-fīt´) A plant adapted to an arid climate.

X-linked gene A gene located on the X chromosome; such genes show a distinctive pattern of inheritance.

X-ray crystallography A technique used to study the three-dimensional structure of molecules. It depends on the diffraction of an X-ray beam by the individual atoms of a crystallized molecule.

xylem (zī'-lum) Vascular plant tissue consisting mainly of tubular dead cells that conduct most of the water and minerals upward from the roots to the rest of the plant.

xylem sap (zī'-lum) The dilute solution of water and minerals carried through vessels and tracheids.

yeast Single-celled fungus. Yeasts reproduce asexually by binary fission or by the pinching of small buds off a parent cell. Many fungal species can grow both as yeasts and as a network of filaments; relatively few species grow only as yeasts.

yolk Nutrients stored in an egg.

zero population growth (ZPG) A period of stability in population size, when additions to the population through births and immigration are balanced by subtractions through deaths and emigration.

zona pellucida The extracellular matrix surrounding a mammalian egg.

zoned reserve An extensive region that includes areas relatively undisturbed by humans surrounded by areas that have been changed by human activity and are used for economic gain.

zone of polarizing activity (ZPA) A block of mesoderm located just under the ectoderm where the posterior side of a limb bud is attached to the body; required for proper pattern formation along the anterior-posterior axis of the limb.

zoonotic pathogen A disease-causing agent that is transmitted to humans from other animals.

zoospore Flagellated spore found in chytrid fungi and some protists.

zygomycete (zī'-guh-mī'-sēt) A member of the fungal phylum Zygomycota, characterized by the formation of a sturdy structure called a zygosporangium during sexual reproduction.

zygosporangium (zī'-guh-spōr-an'-jē-um) (plural, **zygosporangia**) In zygomycete fungi, a sturdy multinucleate structure in which karyogamy and meiosis occur.

zygote (zī'-gōt) The diploid cell produced by the union of haploid gametes during fertilization; a fertilized egg.

NOTE: A page number in regular type indicates where a topic is discussed in the text; a **bold** page number indicates where a term is bold and defined; an *f* following a page number indicates a figure (the topic may also be discussed in the text on that page); a *t* following a page number indicates a table (the topic may also be discussed in the text on that page).

A

a (yeast mating type), **211***f*, 214
ABC hypothesis, flower formation, 775*f*
abd-A gene, 701*f*
Abdomen, insect, 704*f*
Abiotic factors, **1163**
　microclimate and, 1163
　in pollination, 820*f*
　in species distributions, 1177*f*, 1179–1180*f*, 1181
Abiotic stresses, plant, **857***f*–858, 859
Abiotic synthesis, organic molecule, 57*f*–58, 520*f*–521*f*
Abnormal chromosome number disorders, 305*f*
ABO blood groups, 278*f*, 963–964
Abomasum, 908*f*
Abortion, 1032*f*–10**33**
　spontaneous, 304
Abscisic acid (ABA), **792**, 840*t*, **846***f*, 857
Abscission, leaf, 846, 848
Absorption, **897**
　in animal food processing, 897*f*
　in large intestine, 905*f*–906
　plant and animal, 889*f*
　in small intestine, 904*f*–905*f*
　of water and mineral by root cells, 786
Absorption spectrum, **191***f*
Abstinence, 1032*f*
Abyssal zone, **1171***f*
Acacia trees, 1214*f*
Acanthocephala, 682*f*
Acanthodians, **720**
Accessory fruits, **825***f*
Accessory glands, male reproductive, 1019*f*–1020
Acclimatization, **877***f*, 882
Accommodation, visual, 1116*f*
Acetic acid, 63*f*
Acetone, 63*f*
Acetylation, histone, 366*f*
Acetylcholine, **1074***f*–1075*t*, 1122–1123*f*, 1124
Acetylcholinesterase, 1075
Acetyl CoA (acetyl coenzyme A), **169***f*–171*f*
Acetylsalicylic acid, 645
Achondroplasia, 285*f*
Acid growth hypothesis, 842*f*–843*f*
Acidification, ocean, 53*f*–54
Acid precipitation, 1260*f*
Acid reflux, 902
Acids, **51**
　acid precipitation and, 1260
　amino acids as, 76–77*f*
　buffers and, 52–53
　hydrogen ions, bases, and, 51
　ocean acidification and, 53*f*–54, 1260
　pH scale and, 51–52*f*
Acoela, 681*f*
Acoelomates, **674***f*
Acorn worms, 683*f*
Acquired immunodeficiency, 966. *See also* AIDS (acquired immunodeficiency syndrome)

Acquired traits, noninheritance of, 465*f*
Acrosomal reactions, 1038–1039*f*
Acrosomes, **1022***f*, **1038**–1039*f*
Actin, 76*f*, **115**, 239, 873*f*
Actin filaments, 113*t*, 1050*f*, 1119–1120*f*, 1121*f*. *See also* Microfilaments
Actinistia, 723*f*
Actinopterygii (ray-finned fishes), 722*f*–723*f*
Action potentials, neuron, **1067**
　adaptations of axon structure for, 1070–1071*f*
　conduction of, 1069*f*–1070
　generation of, 1068*f*–1069
　graded potentials, voltage-gated ion channels, and, 1067*f*–1068
　hyperpolarization and depolarization of membrane potentials and, 1066*f*–1067*f*
　in long-term potentiation, 1095*f*
　in sensory systems, 1103
Action potentials, plant, **856**
Action spectrum, 191–192*f*, **849**
Activation, allosteric, 158*f*–159
Activation, egg, 1040
Activation energy, 151–**152**, 153*f*
Activators, 158*f*, **364***f*, 368*f*–369*f*
Active immunity, **962**–963
Active sites, enzyme, **153**–154*f*
Active transport, **134**
　ATP as energy for, 134–135*f*
　cotransport in, 136*f*–137
　maintenance of membrane potential by ion pumps in, 135–136*f*
　passive transport vs., 135*f*
　in plant cells, 207*f*
　of solutes across plant plasma membranes, 782, 783*f*
Activity, animal metabolic rate and, 885–886
Actual range, 1178
Acyclovir, 402
Adaptation, sensory, 1104
Adaptations, **466**. *See also* Evolution; Natural selection
　in amniote development, 1047
　axon width and myelination as, 1070*f*–1071*f*
　evolution and, 1*f* (facing page), 13*f*–15*f*, 466–467*f*, 468–470*f*
　as evolutionary compromises, 495
　floral, to prevent self-fertilization, 828–829*f*
　gas exchange, 941*f*–943*f*
　for heat exchange in animals, 879*f*–883*f*
　herbivory, 1213*f*
　mycorrhizae as plant, 810
　of native predator species to introduced prey species, 1211
　of pathogens to evade immune systems, 966–968*f*
　of plants and animals to life challenges, 888*f*–889*f*
　of plants to global climate change, 202–203
　of plants to terrestrial life, 201
　of plants to toxic elements, 30
　prokaryotic, 567*f*, 568*f*–572*f*, 575–576*f*, 577
　as property of life, 1*f*
　to reduce terrestrial nutrient limitations, 1239
　sexual reproduction patterns as, 1016
　of smooth muscles, 1126
　terrestrial, of fungi and land plants, 613, 654
　terrestrial, of seed plants, 631*f*–632*f*, 633
　of vertebrate digestive systems, 906*f*–908*f*
Adaptive evolution, **488**, 493*f*. *See also* Evolution; Natural selection
Adaptive immunity, **947**
　active and passive immunity of, and immunization, 962–963
　antibodies of, as medical tools, 963
　antigen recognition by B cells and antibodies of, 953*f*
　B cell and T cell development of, 954–955*f*, 956–957*f*
　B cells and antibodies in responses of, to extracellular pathogens, 960*f*–961*f*

　cytotoxic T cells in responses of, to infected cells, 959*f*
　helper T cells in responses of, to all antigens, 958*f*–959
　immune rejection and, 963–964
　immunological memory of, 956–957*f*
　molecular recognition by, 947*f*
　overview of, 952–53, 958, 961–962*f*
Adaptive radiations, 14*f*–15*f*, **536**–537*f*, 538, 730, 1178
Addition rule, **275**–276
Adenine, 85*f*–86, 315*f*–316, 844
Adenomatous polyposis coli (APC), 386*f*, 388
Adenoviruses, 394*f*–395
Adenylyl cyclase, **220**–221*f*
Adhesion, **45**–46*f*, 789–790
Adhesive chemicals, echinoderm, 708–709
Adipose tissue, **872***f*, 909
ADP (adenosine diphosphate)
　as enzyme activator, 158
　hydrolysis of ATP to, 148–149
　in sliding-filament model of muscle contraction, 1120–1121*f*
　synthesis of ATP from, 151*f*, 167, 173–174*f*, 175–176
Adrenal cortex, 999*f*, 1006, 1007*f*–1008
Adrenal glands, **1006**
　epinephrine and (*see* Epinephrine (adrenaline))
　in human endocrine system, 999*f*
　responses of, to stress, 1006–1007*f*, 1008
　rough ER and, 105
Adrenaline. *See* Epinephrine (adrenaline)
Adrenal medulla, 999*f*, 1006–1007*f*
Adrenocorticotropic hormone (ACTH), 999*f*, 1003*f*, 1007*f*–1008
Adult stem cells, 426*f*
Adventitious roots, 754, 771
Adventitious shoots, 771, 827*f*
Aerial roots, 754*f*
Aerobic prokaryotes, 571*f*
Aerobic respiration, **163**, 177–179
Afferent neurons, 1083*f*, 1102*f*
Afghanistan, age-structure pyramid for, 1203*f*
Africa, human population in, 1203, 1204
African-Americans
　health disparities in, 251
　sickle-cell disease in, 284*f*–285
African buffalo, 1215*f*
African elephants, 468*f*, 1191*f*, 1259
Africans
　genomes of, 251, 456
　sickle-cell disease in, 284*f*–285
African sleeping sickness, 707
Agave, 1195*f*
Age structure, human population, **1203***f*
Aggregate fruits, **825***f*
Aging, telomeric DNA and, 327
Aglaophyton major, 623*f*, 654
Agonistic behavior, 1148*f*
Agriculture. *See also* Crop plants
　allopolyploidy in, 508*f*–509*f*
　biotechnology in, 432–433
　C₃ plants in, 201
　community disturbances by, 1225
　effects of atmospheric carbon dioxide on productivity of, 203
　fertilizing in (*see* Fertilization, soil)
　fungal food products of, 664
　global human population size and, 1204–1205
　importance of insects to, 707
　importance of mycorrhizae to, 811
　nematode pests in, 699*f*
　nitrogen fixation and, 810
　nutrient pollution from, 1270*f*
　plant biotechnology and genetic engineering in, 830*f*–831, 832*f*–834
　plant breeding in, 816, 829, 830–831

3′ end (sugar-phosphate backbone), 86, 342–343*f*, 346*f*
3-phosphoglycerate, 199–200*f*
5′ cap, **342**–343*f*, 346*f*
5′ end (sugar-phosphate backbone), 86
5-methyl cytidine, **63***f*
10-nm fibers, DNA, 328*f*
30-nm fibers, DNA, 329*f*, 330
300-nm fibers, DNA, 329*f*

plant cloning in, 423f
seed plants in, 645f–646
soil conservation and sustainable, 801f–803f, 1269
vegetative propagation of plants in, 829
Agrobacterium tumefaciens, 417, 432, 578f, 584, 589, 770f
AIDS (acquired immunodeficiency syndrome), **400**, **968**. *See also* HIV (human immunodeficiency virus)
  cell-surface proteins and blocking HIV to prevent, 128f
  drug cocktails in treatment of, 483
  fungal mycoses and, 664
  HIV and, 392f, 400–401f
  host range of, 395
  immune system response to, 967–968f
Ain, Michael C., 285f
Air circulation patterns, global, 1160f
Air roots, 754f
Air sacs, 938–939f
Alanine, 77f
Alarm calls, 1142f–1143
Albatross, 971f, 976f
Albinism, 283f, 333f, 336
Albumin, 371f, 729f, 928f
Albuterol, 62f
Alcohol addiction, 866
Alcohol fermentation, **178**f
Alcoholic beverages, 664
Alder, 1224f
Aldoses, 68f
Aldosterone, 217–218f, **990**, 1008
Algae, **592**
  alternation of generations in, 256f
  biofuels from, 186f
  blooms of, 1221, 1238
  brown, 596f–597f, 598
  chloroplasts in, 110–111f
  as earliest multicellular eukaryotes, 529
  evolution of land plants from green, 612f–613
  evolution of photosynthetic, 592f–693f
  fossils of, 523f
  fungi and, as lichens, 658, 662f–663f
  golden, 596f
  green, 592f–593f, 603f–604f
  photosynthesis in, 185–186f
  as protists, 591f
  red, 592f–593f, 602f–603f
  structure and organelles of cells of, 101f
Algin, 597
Alimentary canals, 681f, **691**f, 697, **899**f–900, 906–907f
Alkaline vents, **520**–521f
Alkaloids, 862f
Alkaptonuria, 334
Allantois, 729f, 1047f
Allee, W. C., 1194
Allee effect, 1194
Alleles, **270**. *See also* Gene(s)
  correlating behavior of chromosome pairs with, 295f
  degrees of dominance of, and phenotypes, 277f–278
  dominant, in genetic disorders, 285f
  dominant vs. recessive, in Mendelian inheritance, 270–271f, 272f–274f
  frequencies of, in gene pools of populations, 484f
  genetic markers for disease-causing, 422f, 428
  genetic variation from recombination of, 303 (*see also* Recombination)
  genetic variation preserved in recessive, 494
  genomic imprinting of maternal or paternal, 367
  microevolution as alteration in frequencies of, in populations, 481f, 487–488f, 489f–490, 491f
  multiple, and pleiotropy, 278f–279
  mutations as sources of, 263, 482–483
  recessive, in genetic disorders, 283f–284f, 285
  in sexual life cycles, 257
  sickle-cell, 496f–497f
  testing populations for frequencies of, 484–485f, 486–487
Allergens, 833, 964–965

Allergies, 433, 964–965f
Alligators, 731f, 732
Allolactose, 363f
Allopatric populations, character displacement in, 1210–1211f
Allopatric speciation, **505**f–507f, 533
Allopolyploids, **508**f–509f
All-or-none responses, 1067
Allosteric regulation, 157–**158**f, 159
α (yeast mating type), **211**f, 214
Alpha cells, 910f
α chain, 954f
α-globin gene family, 447f
α-helix, **80**f
α-lactalbumin, 450, 451f
Alpha proteobacteria, 578f, 592
Alpine pennycress, 803
Alpine tundra, 1170f
Alpine woodsorrel, 829f
Alternate phyllotaxy, 780
Alternation of generations, **256**f, **597**f–598, **614**
Alternative fuels, 1274
Alternative RNA splicing, **344**–345f, 372f–373, 443
Alu elements, 446
Aluminum, bioremediation of, 1249
Aluminum toxicity, plant, 803, 805
Alveolates, 591f, **598**f–600f, 601
Alveoli, 598, **937**f
Alzheimer's disease, 83, 229, 406, **1097**–1098f
Amacrine cells, 1112f, 1114–1115f
Amazon rain forest, 1266f
Amborella trichopoda, 642f, 644f
Amebic dysentery, 607
American alligator, 731f
American beech trees, 1164f
American black bears, 10f
American chestnut trees, 1220
American Dust Bowl, 801f
American flamingo, 13f
American pokeweed, 825f
Amines, 996f
Amino acids, **75**
  abiotic synthesis of, 520f–521f
  activation of, in eukaryotic cells, 354f
  deamination of, for catabolism, 180
  in enzymatic catalysis, 154
  essential, 893
  in evolution of enzymes, 157f
  in genetic code, 337–338f, 339f–340
  human dietary deficiencies in, 896
  in polypeptides and proteins, 67, 75–77f, 78f (*see also* Polypeptides; Proteins)
  sequences of, 438–439f, 440, 452
  sickle-cell disease and, 82f
  specified by nucleotide triplets in translation, 345f–347f
  twenty, of proteins, 77f
  using sequences of, to test hypothesis on horizontal gene transfer, 564
Amino acid sequence identity tables, reading, in Scientific Skills Exercise, 452
Amino acid sequences, 438–439f, 440, 452
Aminoacyl-tRNA synthetases, **346**–347f
Amino group, **63**f
Aminooacyl tRNA, 346–347f
Amitochondriate protists, 588
Ammonia, **976**
  as base, 51
  hydrogen bonds and, 39f
  as nitrogenous waste, 976–977f, 982–983f
Ammonites, **695**f–696
Amniocentesis, **286**–287f, 1033
Amnion, 474, 729f, 1047f
Amniotes, **727**, **1047**
  derived characters of, 728–729f
  developmental adaptations of, 1047
  evolution of, 672
  fossils and early evolution of, 729f
  mammals as, 735
  phylogeny of, 727–28f
  reptiles, 729f–734f
Amniotic egg, **728**–729f

Amoebas, 117f, 232–233f, 443, 591f, **601**
Amoebocytes, **684**f–685
Amoeboid movement, 117f
Amoebozoans, **605**f–607f
AMP (adenosine monophosphate), 181f–182, 346–347f
AMPA receptors, 1095f
Amphetamines, 1096, 1097f
Amphibians, **726**
  adaptations of kidneys of, 986
  axis formation in, 1054f
  breathing in, 938
  cell developmental potential in, 1054–1055f
  cell fate and pattern formation by inductive signals in, 1056f
  cleavage in, 1042f–1043
  diversity of, 726f–727f
  double circulation in, 919f
  evolution of, 672
  external fertilization in, 1016f
  fungal parasites of, 663–664f
  gastrulation in, 1044–1045f
  hearing and equilibrium in, 1110f
  parental care in, 1146
  species distributions of, 1158f, 1180
Amphipathic molecules, **124**
Amplification, cancer gene, 383f–384
Amplification, sensory, **1103**–1104
Amplification, signal, 218, 224
Ampulla, sea star, 708f
Amygdala, 1089f–**1090**
Amylase, **901**
Amyloid plaques, 1098f
Amyloplasts, 111
Amylose, 70f, 111
Amytrophic lateral sclerosis (ALS), 1122
Anableps anableps, 360f
Anabolic pathways, **142**, 181
Anabolic steroids, 1009
Anaerobic respiration, 163, 177–179, **575**–576
Analogies, **551**f–552
Analogous structures, **475**
Anaphase, 235, 237f, 239f, 241f, 245, 261f
Anaphase I, 258f, 261f
Anaphase II, 259f
Anaphylactic shock, 965
Anatomical homologies, 473f–474
Anatomy, **867**f. *See also* Animal form and function; Morphology; Plant structure
Ancestral characters, shared, **554**f–555
Ancestry, common, 14f–15f, 473f–475f, 549–550f, 553–554, 642
Anchorage dependence, 246f
Anchoring junctions, 120f
Androgens, 999f, **1008**–1009f, 1024–1025f
Anemia, 930
Aneuploidies, **305**, 306f–307
Angiosperm reproduction
  asexual, 827f–828, 829f–830f
  breeding and genetic engineering in, 830f–831, 832f–834
  flower pollination in, 820f–821f
  flower structure and function in, 816f–817f, 825
  fruit structure and function in, 825f–826f
  life cycle of, 640f–641, 818–819f
  mutualisms in, 815f–816, 821f
  seed and fruit dispersal in, 827f
  seeds in, 822f–824f
Angiosperms, **617**
  bulk flow in sugar translocation in, 794–795f
  characteristics of, 638f–641f
  evolutionary mystery of, for C. Darwin, 471
  evolution of, 641f–643f
  evolution of seeds in, 632–633
  flowers of, 638f
  fruits of, 638, 639f
  gametophyte-sporophyte relationships in, 631f
  life cycle of, 640f–641, 818–819f
  G. Mendel's techniques of crossing, 268f–269f
  phylogeny of, 617t, 642f, 643f–644f
  reproduction of (*see* Angiosperm reproduction)
Angiotensin II, **990**

Anhydrobiosis, **974**f
Animal(s). *See also* Animal behavior; Animal
    development; Animal form and function;
    Animal hormones; Animal nutrition; Animal
    reproduction
  aquatic (*see* Aquatic animals)
  carbon in organic compounds of, 56
  catabolic pathways in, 180f–181
  cells of, 4f–5 (*see also* Animal cells)
  cell structure and specialization of tissues of, 668
  cellular respiration in hibernating, 176
  circulatory and gas exchange systems of (*see*
    Cardiovascular systems; Circulatory systems;
    Gas exchange systems)
  cloning of, 423f–425f
  as consumers and predators, 667f
  correlation of diversity of miRNAs with
    complexity of, 672
  defense mechanisms of, 28f
  endangered or threatened, 1256f
  in energy flow and chemical cycling, 7f
  in domain Eukarya, 11f
  evolutionary history of, 669f–671f, 672–673
  evolutionary links between plants and, 642–643f
  extinctions of, 696f
  flower pollination by, 820f–821f
  fruit and seed dispersal by, 826f
  fungal mutualisms with, 662f
  fungal parasites of, 663f–664f
  glycogen as storage polysaccharide for, 70f–71
  herbivore adaptations in, 471f–472
  immune systems of (*see* Immune systems)
  land colonization by, 530f–531f
  life challenges and solutions for, 888f–889f
  maximizing body surface area of, 689f
  microevolution of populations of (*see*
    Microevolution)
  neurons and nervous systems of (*see* Nervous
    systems; Neurons)
  as opisthokonts, 607
  osmoregulation and excretion of (*see* Excretory
    systems; Osmoregulation)
  phylogeny of, 676–677f, 678, 680f
  plant recruitment of, as herbivore defense, 863f
  production efficiency of, 1240
  protein production by "pharm" transgenic, 430f
  relationship of, to unikont protists, 604–605
  reproduction and development of, 668f–669
  seed dispersal by, 639f
  sensory and motor systems of (*see* Motor systems;
    Sensory systems)
  tropical deforestation and extinctions of, 645f–646
  zoonotic pathogens and, 1228–1229f
Animal behavior, **1133**
  cerebral cortex information processing and,
    1091f–1092
  genetics, altruism, and inclusive fitness in
    evolution of, 1149f–1153f, 1154
  hormones and, 993f
  learning and, 1138t–1142f, 1143
  species distributions and habitat selection,
    1178–1179
  stimuli for simple and complex, 1134f–1137f
  survival and reproductive success in evolution of,
    1143f–1144, 1145f–1148f, 1149
  in thermoregulation, 881f
Animal cells. *See also* Eukaryotic cells
  apoptosis in, 228f–229f
  cell junctions of, 120f
  cellular respiration in (*see* Cellular respiration)
  cytokinesis in, 239–240f
  endocytosis in, 138f
  extracellular matrix of, 118–119f
  local and long-distance cell signaling in, 212f, 213f
  meiosis in, 258f–259f
  nuclear transplantation of differentiated,
    423f–425f
  stem cells, 425f–427f
  structure and organelles of, 100f
  structure and specialization of, 668
  water balance of, 132f–133f
Animal development. *See also* Human embryonic
    development

  adaptations of, 888f
  animal phylogeny and, 676–677f
  cell fate specification in, 1051–1052f, 1053f–1058f
  comparing processes of, 457f–458f
  developmental biology and, 1037f–1038f
  fertilization and cleavage in, 1038–1039f,
    1040f–1042
  morphogenesis in, 1044f–1050f, 1051
  protostome vs. deuterostome, 675f–676
  reproduction and embryonic, 668f–669
Animal form and function
  anatomy and physiology as, 867f–868
  bioenergetics of, 883–884f, 885f–886, 887f
  body plans, 673f–675f, 676
  correlation of, at all levels of organization,
    868f–874f
  evolution of body size and shape in, 868f
  exchange with environment in, 868–869f, 870
  feedback regulation of homeostasis in, 875f–877f
  hierarchical organization of body plans in, 870t,
    871f–873f
  mammalian organ systems in, 870t
  regulation of, by endocrine and nervous systems,
    874f
  thermoregulation in, 878f–883f
Animal hormones, **874**, **993**. *See also* Endocrine
    systems; Hormones
  birth control, 1032f–1033
  in cell signaling pathways, 994f–995f
  chemical classes of, 995f–996f
  as chemical signals of endocrine systems and
    nervous systems, 993f–994
  in childbirth and labor, 1031f
  embryonic, 1029
  endocrine signaling pathways of, 996f–998f
  endocrine system glands and, 998f–999f
  endocrine systems and, in cell signaling, 874f
  erythropoietin (EPO), 930
  evolution of, 1010f
  in fight-or-flight responses, 210
  multiple effects of single, 998f
  in neuroendocrine signaling, 994f, 995, 1000f–
    1005f (*see also* Neuroendocrine signaling)
  plant hormones vs., 212, 888f
  regulation of appetite and consumption by,
    911f–912
  in regulation of digestive systems, 909f
  in regulation of mammalian reproduction,
    1024f–1026f, 1027
  in regulatory functions of endocrine glands,
    1006f–1009f
  in sex determination, 1025
Animalia, kingdom, 11f, 562, 563f
Animal nutrition, **892**. *See also* Human nutrition
  adaptations of vertebrate digestive systems for
    diets in, 906f–908f
  diets and requirements for, 892f–896f, 897
  digestive systems and, 900f–905f, 906
  feedback regulation of digestion, energy storage,
    and appetite in, 908–909f, 910–911f, 912
  feeding mechanisms in, 898f
  food processing stages in, 897f–899f, 900
  nutritional modes in, 667f–668, 888f
  prokaryotes in, 581
Animal pole, **1042**f
Animal reproduction. *See also* Human reproduction
  amphibian, 727
  asexual, 264–265f, 1014f
  development and, 668f–669
  fertilization mechanisms in, 1016f–1018f
  of fish, 722
  hormonal regulation of mammalian, 1024f–1026f,
    1027
  reproductive cycles in, 1015f
  sexual, as evolutionary enigma, 1014–1015f
  sexual life cycles in, 256f (*see also* Sexual life
    cycles)
  of sharks and rays, 722
  variations in patterns of, 1013f, 1016
Animal viruses
  classes of, 398t
  as pathogens, 401f, 402–403f, 404–405, 406f
  replicative cycles of, 398–399f, 400

Anions, 37–38f, 801, 1064t
Ankle bones, 475f–476f
Annelids, 682f, 696–697f, 698f, 917f, 979f, 1080f
Annual human population growth rates, 1202f
Annuals, 761
Antagonistic functions, autonomic nervous system,
    1084f
Antagonistic muscle pairs, 1126
Antarctica, 519f, 1218f, 1274f
Antennae, 1104, 1105f, 1117
Anterior pituitary gland, 999f, **1002**f–1005f, 1010,
    1024f–1026f, 1027
Anterior-posterior axis, 1054f
Anterior sides, **673**–674
Antheridia, 615f
Anthers, **638**f, 816
Anthocerophyta (hornworts), **618**, 620f
Anthophyta. *See* Angiosperms
Anthozoans, 686f, 687
Anthrax, 569f, 579f, 583
Anthropoids, **740**f–741, 742
Anti-aging effects, 844
Antibiotic drugs
  bacteria and, 568–569
  bacterial resistance to, 575, 583
  for cystic fibrosis, 284
  as enzyme inhibitors, 157
  evolution of resistance to, 472f–473
  fungal, 664
  gram-positive bacteria and, 579f
  prokaryotic ribosomes and, 571
  sponges and, 685
  viruses and, 402
Antibodies, **953**f
  antigen recognition by, 953f
  gene rearrangement by, 955f–960
  in humoral immune response, 958, 960f–961f
  as medical tools, 963
  as proteins, 76f, 79f
  role of, in adaptive immunity, 962–963
Anticodons, **346**f–347f
Antidiuretic hormone (ADH), 988f–989f, 999f,
    1002f–**1003**, 1150f–1151
Antifreeze proteins, 859, 882
Antigenic variation, 966, 967
Antigen fragments, 954
Antigen presentation, **954**f
Antigen-presenting cells, **958**f–959
Antigen receptors, **952**–953f, 954f
Antigens, **952**–953f, 958f–959
Antihistamines, 965
Anti-inflammatory drugs, 1008
Antimicrobial peptides, 948f, 949f, 951
Antioxidant properties, 193
Antiparallel DNA sugar-phosphate backbones,
    86–87f, 315f–316, **317**f–319f, 322–323f,
    324f–325f
Antithrombin, 430f
Antivenom, 963
Antiviral drugs, 402
Ants, 28f, 296f, 662f, 706f, 826f, 867f–868, 1214f
Anurans, 726f
Anus, 905–906
Aorta, 924f
Apes, 740–741f, 742
Aphids, 564, 795f
Aphotic zone, **1171**f
Apical buds, **755**
Apical dominance, **763**, 844f
Apical ectodermal ridge (AER), **1056**f–1057f, 1058
Apical meristems, 615f, **760**f–761f
Apical surface, epithelial, 871f
Apicomplexans, **598**–599f
Apicoplasts, 599f
Apodans, 726f
Apomixis, **827**
Apoplast, **781**–782f
Apoplastic route, 782f, 787f
Apoptosis, **228**, **1051**
  cell signaling pathways of, 228f–229f
  cytotoxic T cell response and, 959f
  ethylene in response to senescence and, 847–848
  molecular mechanisms of, 228f

in morphogenesis, 1051
  p53 gene and, 384
  plant response to flooding with, 857*f*
  as programmed cell death, 210, 227*f*–228
  self-tolerance vs., 955
Aposematic coloration, **1212***f*
Appendages, arthropod, 700–701
Appendix, **905***f*
Appetite regulation, 911*f*–912
Apple fruit, 825*f*
Apple maggot flies, 510
Aquaporins, **131**, **785**, **982**
  cellular membrane selective permeability and, 130
  facilitated diffusion and, 133*f*
  in kidney regulation, 988*f*–989*f*
  mutations in, as causes of diabetes insipidus, 989*f*
  in nephron processes, 982*f*–983*f*
  selective permeability of, 124*f*
  water diffusion and role of, 784–785
Aquatic animals
  adaptations of kidneys of, 986–987*f*
  gills for gas exchange in, 934*f*–935*f*
  nitrogenous wastes of, 976–977*f*
  osmoregulation in, 973*f*–974*f*
Aquatic biomes
  acid precipitation in, 1260
  biodiversity hot spots in, 1267*f*
  coral reefs, 1176*f*
  estuaries, 1174*f*
  habitat loss in, 1258
  intertidal zones, 1175*f*
  lakes, 1173*f*
  locomotion in, 1129
  marine benthic zones, 1176*f*
  net ecosystem production in, 1236–1237*f*
  nutrient cycling in, 1247
  oceanic pelagic zones, 1175*f*
  primary production in, 1237*f*–1238*f*
  protists as producers in, 608–609*f*
  streams and rivers, 1174*f*
  thermoregulation in, 875*f*
  wetlands, 1173*f*
  zonation in, 1171*f*–1172*f*
Aqueous humor, 1112*f*
Aqueous solutions, **48**
  acidic and basic conditions of, 51–52*f*, 53*f*–54
  solvents, solutes, and, 48–49*f*, 50
Aquifers, 802
Arabidopsis thaliana (mustard plant)
  altering gene expression of, with touch, 856*f*
  genome size of, 442*t*
  infected leaves, 751*f*
  as model organism, 23, 768–770*f*
  triple response in, 847*f*
Arachnids, 683*f*, **702***f*
Arbuscular mycorrhizae, **650**, 655*f*, 657*f*, **810**–811
Arbuscule, 531
Archaea
  domain, **11***f*, 562–563*f*, 580*t*–581
  genome sizes and number of genes for, 442*t*–443
  as prokaryotes, 97 (*see also* Prokaryotes)
  prokaryotic cells of, 4*f*–5 (*see also* Prokaryotic cells)
Archaea, domain, **11***f*, 562–563*f*, 580*t*–581
Archaean eon, 526*f*, 527*t*
Archaeognatha (bristletails), 706*f*
Archaeology, peat moss and, 622*f*
Archaeopteryx, 635*f*, 733*f*
Archaeplastida, **602**–603*f*, 604*f*
Archegonia, **615***f*
Archenterons, 675*f*, **676**, **1044***f*
Archosaurs, **730**
Arctic, 48, 1274
Arctic fox, 1232*f*
Arctic ground squirrel, 887
Arctic tundra ecosystem, 1242*f*–1243*f*
Ardipithecus ramidus, 742*f*–743*f*
Area effects, community diversity and, 1226*f*–1227*f*
Arginine, 77*f*, 334–335*f*, 336
Arid conditions, plants and, 201–202*f*, 203–204*f*
Aristotle, 464
Arms, chromatid, 234
Arnold, A. Elizabeth, 661*f*

Arousal
  autonomic, 1090
  brain functions in sleep and, 1088*f*
  human sexual, 1027–1028, 1076
Arsenic, 29–30
Art, humans and, 748*f*
Arteries, **918**–19*f*, 923*f*–924*f*, 925, 931*f*–932
Arterioles, **918**, 923*f*–924*f*, 925
Arthrophytes, 626*f*
Arthropods, **700**. *See also* Ecdysozoans
  chelicerates, 701–702*f*
  chitin as structural polysaccharide for, 72*f*
  compound eyes of, 1111*f*–1112
  crustaceans and insects as pancrustaceans, 703*f*–706*f*, 707
  evolution of, 672
  exoskeletons of, 1127
  general characteristics of, 701*f*
  Hox genes and body plan of, 700*f*
  land colonization by, 531
  Malpighian tubules of, 979*f*–980
  myriapods, 702–703*f*
  nervous systems of, 1080*f*
  origins of, 700–701
  phylogeny of, 683*f*, 703*f*
Artificial corridors, 1266*f*–1267
Artificial selection, 468–**469***f*, 470*f*, 645, 816, 830*f*–831
Artiodactyls, 739*f*
Ascending limb, loop of Henle, 982*f*–983*f*
Asci, **657**
Ascocarps, 655*f*, **657***f*
Ascomycetes, 655*f*, **657***f*–659*t*, 665*f*
Asexual reproduction, **253**, **827**, **1014**
  in angiosperms, 827*f*–828, 829*f*–830*f*
  in bryophytes, 621
  evolution of, in animals, 264–265*f*
  in fungi, 652*f*–653*f*
  inheritance in, 253*f*
  in lichens, 662*f*–663*f*
  mechanisms of, 1013*f*, 1014*f*
  in protists, 588
  in rotifers, 691–692
  sexual reproduction vs., 253*f*, 827–828, 1014*f*–1015 (*see also* Sexual reproduction)
Asian elephant, 468*f*
Asian ladybird beetles, 469*f*
A site (aminoacyl-tRNA binding site), 347*f*–348, 350*f*
Asparagine, 77*f*
Aspartic acid, 77*f*
Aspen trees, 778*f*, 827*f*
Aspirin, 645, 1008, 1106
Assassin bugs, 706*f*
Assembly stage, phage lytic cycle, 396*f*
Assisted migration, **1274**
Association areas, cerebral cortex, 1090
Associative learning, **1140***f*–1141
Asteroidea, 707–708*f*
Asters, 236*f*, **238***f*
Asthma, 62, 214, 927, 1007
Astragalus bones, 475*f*
Astrobiologists, 50
Astrocytes, **1081***f*–1082*f*
Asymmetrical cell division, 771*f*
Asymmetric carbon, 61*f*–62*f*, 68, 75
Asymmetry, body, 1054, 1058*f*
Atherosclerosis, 74, 75, 137, **931***f*–932
Athletes
  abuse of anabolic steroids by, 1009
  blood doping by, 930
Athlete's foot, 664
Atmosphere
  animal evolution and oxygen in, 671
  Earth's early, 520*f*–521*f*
  global climate change and carbon dioxide in, 1272–1273*f*
  ozone in, 1274*f*–1275*f*
  photosynthesis and oxygen in, 528*f*
Atomic mass, **31**
Atomic mass unit (amu), 31
Atomic nucleus, **30**–31
Atomic number, **31**
Atoms, **30***f*–31, 32*f*–35*f*, 188*f*–189

ATP (adenosine triphosphate), **64**, **149**
  in bioenergetics, 884*f*
  conversion of, to cyclic AMP, 220*f*–221*f*
  in DNA replication, 322
  energy coupling and, 148–151
  as energy for active transport, 134–135*f*
  as energy source for cellular processes, 64
  in feedback regulation of cellular respiration, 181*f*–182
  in muscle fiber contraction speed, 1125
  in photosynthesis, 189*f*–190, 195*f*–198*f*, 199, 204–205*f*
  regeneration of, in ATP cycle, 151*f*
  regulation of regeneration of, 158
  in sliding-filament model of muscle contraction, 1120–1121*f*, 1122*f*
  synthesis of, by cellular respiration, 162–163*f* (*see also* Cellular respiration)
  synthesis of, by fermentation and anaerobic respiration, 177–178*f*, 179
  in translation, 346–347*f*
  work as hydrolysis of, 149*f*–150
  yield of, at each stage of cellular respiration, 175*f*–176
ATP synthase, **173***f*–174*f*, 175
Atria, heart, **918**–919*f*, 920*f*–921*f*
Atrial natriuretic peptide (ANP), **990**
Atrioventricular (AV) nodes, **922***f*
Atrioventricular (AV) valves, **921***f*–922*f*
Attached earlobes pedigree analysis case, 282*f*–283
Attachment function, membrane protein, 128*f*
Attachment stage, phage lytic cycle, 396*f*
Auditory communication, 1136*f*
Aurea mutant tomato, 838*f*
Australia, 475*f*, 534, 598*f*, 736–737*f*
Australian moles, 551*f*–552
Australian thorny devil lizard, 731*f*
Australopiths, 743*f*–744*f*, 745–746
Autism, 1094
Autocrine signaling, 994*f*–**995**, 996
Autoimmune diseases, **965***f*
Autonomic arousal, 1090
Autonomic nervous system, **1083***f*–1084*f*
Autophagy, 107*f*–108
Autopolyploids, **508**
Autosomes, **255**
Autotrophs, **185**–186*f*, 575, 576*f*, 581, 888*f*, 1233
Auxin, 839–840*t*, 841*f*–**842***f*, 843–844, 848, 855
Avery, Mary Ellen, 938*f*
Avery, Oswald, 313
Avian flu, 403, 405, 1229*f*
Avogadro's number, 50
Axel, Richard, 1118
Axial polarity, 772*f*
Axillary buds, **755**
Axis formation, 381*f*–382*f*
Axolotls, 539*f*, 915*f*
Axons, 873*f*, **1062***f*, 1070*f*–1071*f*, 1082
Azidothymidine (AZT), 402

B
Bacillus anthracis, 569*f*
Bacillus coagulans, 97*f*
Bacillus thuringiensis, 831–832*f*
Backbone, nucleic acid, 86–87*f*
Backbone, polypeptide, 78*f*
Bacteria
  alcohol fermentation by, 178
  anaerobic respiration in, 177–178
  antibiotic drugs and, 348
  antibiotic resistance in, 472*f*–473, 575
  Bacteria, domain, **11***f*, 562–563*f*, 577*f*–579*f*, 580*t*
  binary fission in, 240–241*f*
  bioremediation using, 1249*f*
  cell signaling in, 211*f*–212
  cell structure of, 97*f*
  cellular integration and, 121*f*
  cholera and, 221
  conjugation in, 574*f*–575
  as detritivores, 1234*f*
  in digestive systems, 905, 907*f*–908*f*
  as DNA cloning vectors, 412*f*–413
  DNA packing in chromosomes of, 328–329

DNA replication in, 320–325f
evidence for DNA in research on, 313f–314f, 315
evolution of cell division in, 241–242f
evolution of glycolysis in, 179–180
expressing cloned eukaryotic genes in, 416, 417
flagellum, movement of, 987f
genome sizes and number of genes for, 442t–443
G proteins and infections by, 215f
Gram staining of, 568–569f
land colonization by, 530
as model organism (*see Escherichia coli* (*E. coli*) bacteria)
mutualistic and pathogenic, 582–583f
nitrogen-fixing, and plants, 807f–809f, 810
origin of photosynthesis in, 528
origins of mitochondria and chloroplasts, 109–110f
in Permian mass extinction, 534–535
photosynthesis of, 186f, 187, 197
phylogeny of, 577f–579f, 580
plant defenses against, 860
in polymerase chain reaction, 415–416f
as prokaryotes, 97 (*see also* Prokaryotes)
prokaryotic cells of, 4f–5 (*see also* Prokaryotic cells)
protecting fruit flies from infection by, 948f, 949f
regulation of transcription in, 361f–364f
relatedness of, to mitochondria, 589
soil, 801, 1217f
transcription and translation in, 336–337f, 353f
transcription in, 340f–342f
translation in (*see* Translation)
viral infections of (*see* Phages)
Bacteria, domain, 11f, 562–563f, 577f–579f, 580t
Bacteriophages (phages), **313**, **395**
capsids of, 394–395
in DNA research, 313f–314f, 315
prophages and temperate, 397f–398
replicative cycles of, 396f–397f, 398
in transduction, 573f
virulent, 396f–397f
Bacteriorhodopsin, 127f
Bacteroides thetaiotaomicron, 582–583
Bacteroids, **809**f–810
Bada, Jeffrey, 58
Bait-and-switch defense, 594
Baker, C. S., 551f
Baker's yeast. *See Saccharomyces cerevisiae* (yeast)
Balance, body, 1106f–1110f, 1129
Balancing selection, **494**–495f, 496f–497f
Baleen, 898f
Ball-and-socket joints, 1128f
Ball-and-stick models, 39f, 59f
Ballooning, spider, 702
Ball pythons, 886
Barbiturates, 104–105
Barbs, 639f
Bar graphs in Scientific Skills Exercises, 22, 177, 370, 420, 477, 584, 623, 694, 756, 858, 1144, 1181, 1211
Bark, **768**
Barley, 644f, 845f
Barnacles, 704f, 1210f
Barr, Murray, 298
Barr body, **298**f
Barrier contraceptives, 1032f
Barrier defenses, 946f–947f, 948–949
Barrier reefs, 1176f
Basal angiosperms, 642, **643**f–644f
Basal animals, 676–677f, 684
Basal body, **115**, 116f
Basal cells, 822f
Basal lamina, 923
Basal-like breast cancer, 387f
Basal metabolic rate (BMR), **884**f–885f, 886
Basal nuclei, 1087f
Basal surface, epithelial, 871f
Basal taxon, **550**f
Base pairing, DNA and RNA, 86–87f, 317–318f, 319f–320f
Bases, **51**–52f, 53, 76–77f
Basidiocarps, **660**f
Basidiomycetes, 651, 655f, **659**f–661f

Basidiospores, 660f
Basidium, **659**
Basilar membrane, 1107f
Basin wetlands, 1173f
Basking, reptilian, 729–730
Basophils, 928f, 930f
Bass fishes, 875f
Bassham, James, 189
Batesian mimicry, 1212f–**1213**
Batrachochytrium dendrobatidis, 663–664f
Bats, 14f, 552, 821f, 985f–986, 1256f
B cells, **952**–953f, 954f–955f, 956–957f, 960f
Bdelloid rotifers, 264–265f, 692
Beach mouse (*Peromyscus polionotus*), 19f, 20f, 461f
Beadle, George, 334–335f, 336
Beagle, Charles Darwin's voyage on H.M.S., 465–466f
Beaks
    finch, 466–467f, 480f–481f
    shapes of bird, 734f
    soapberry bug, 471f–472
Beans, 823f–824f, 851–852f, 893
Bears, 10f, 143f, 504f, 1263f, 1268
Beavers, 1220f
Bed bugs, 706f
Beech trees, 1164f
Bees, 296f, 706f, 815f–816f, 820f, 881
Beetles, 469f, 706f
Behavior, **1133**. *See also* Animal behavior
Behavioral ecology, **1134**
Behavioral isolation, 502f
Beijerinck, Martinus, 393
Belding's ground squirrels, 1151–1152, 1153f, 1187t–1188f, 1189t–1190
Beluga whales, 1105f
Benign tumors, **247**
Benson, Andrew, 189
Benthic zone, **1171**f
Benthos, **1171**
Berthold, Peter, 1151f
β2-adrenergic receptor, 214f, 217
β-amyloid, 1098
Beta-carotene, 832f, 896
Beta cells, 910f
β chain, 954f
β-galactosidase, 157f, 363f
β-globin, 89
β-globin gene family, 447f
β-keratin, bird feathers and, 732f
Beta oxidation, **181**
β pleated sheat, **80**f
Beta proteobacteria, 578f
BGI (formerly Beijing Genome Institute), 438
bicoid gene, **381**f–382f, 457
Biennials, 761
Big-bang reproduction, 1195
Bilateral symmetry, **673**
    animal, 673f–674, 676
    axis formation and, 1054
    flower, 638f, 643f, 817f
Bilaterians, **671**
    chordates, 713f
    invertebrates, 680f
    Lophotrochozoans, 688
    origin of, 671
    phylogeny of, 676–677f
Bilayers, phospholipid. *See* Phospholipid bilayers
Bile, **903**
Binary fission, **240**–241f, 571–572, 600f–601
Binding sites, ribosome, 347f–348
Binomials (nomenclature), 464, **548**–549f
Biochemical pathways. *See* Metabolic pathways
Biochemistry, 96
Biodiesel, 186f
Biodiversity
    angiosperm, 643f–644f (*see also* Angiosperms)
    animal (*see* Animal(s))
    of bacteria and archaea (*see* Archaea; Bacteria)
    classification of, 464
    conservation biology and, 1255 (*see also* Conservation biology)
    effects of mass extinctions on, 534f–536f
    evolution and, 12f–15f, 462f, 467 (*see also* Evolution)

of fungi (*see* Fungi)
gymnosperm, 635, 636f–637f
habitat loss and fragmentation and, 1257–1258
human welfare and, 1257f
invertebrate (*see* Invertebrates)
landscape ecology and regional conservation to sustain, 1265–1266f, 1267f–1269f
levels of, 1255f–1256f
plant (*see* Plant(s))
potential resurrection of extinct species for, 1260–1261f
protist (*see* Protists)
within species, 501f
taxonomy and classification of, 10f–11f
threats to, 1254f–1255f, 1258f–1260f
tree of life and, 14f–15f (*see also* Phylogenetic trees; Phylogenies; Tree of life)
tropical deforestation as threat to, 645f–646
unity in, 12f, 13f, 462f, 467
vertebrate (*see* Vertebrates)
Biodiversity hot spots, **1267**f
Bioenergetics, **142**, **883**. *See also* Metabolism
    energy allocation and use in, 883–884f
    energy budgets in, 886
    energy costs of foraging in, 1143–1144
    influences on metabolic rate in, 885f–886
    of locomotion, 1130
    metabolic rates and thermoregulation in, 884–885
    of osmoregulation, 974–975
    thyroid regulation of, 1004f–1005f
    torpor, hibernation, and energy conservation in, 886–887f
    of urea and uric acid wastes, 977
Biofilms, 212, **576**
Biofuels, 186f, 665f, **832**
Biogenic amines, **1075**t
Biogeochemical cycles, **1244**f–1245f, 1246–1247f, 1248f. *See also* Energy flow and chemical cycling
Biogeographic factors, community diversity and, 1225–1226f, 1227f–1228
Biogeography, **476**–477
Bioinformatics, **7**, **437**
    in analysis of protein structure, 83
    centralized resources of, for genome analysis, 438–439f
    genome analysis using genomics and, 437
    genomics, proteomics, and, 87–88f
    identifying protein-coding genes using gene annotation in, 439–440
    in study of genomes, 7
    systems biology and proteomics in study of genes and gene expression in, 440–441f, 442
Biological augmentation, **1250**
Biological clocks, 851–852f, 853f–854f, 855, **1088**–1089. *See also* Circadian rhythms
Biological Dynamics of Forest Fragments Project, 1266
Biological magnification, **1271**f–1272
Biological molecules. *See also* Organic compounds
    analyzing polypeptide sequence data of, 89
    carbohydrates as (*see* Carbohydrates)
    four classes of, 66
    genomics and proteomics in study of, 87–88f
    lipids as, 72–73f, 74f–75f
    macromolecules as polymers of monomers and, 66f–67f
    as measures of evolution, 89
    nucleic acids as, 84–85f, 86–87f
    proteins as (*see* Proteins)
Biological species concept, **501**f–504f
Biology, **1** (facing page)
    astrobiology in, 50f
    biodiversity in (*see* Animal(s); Biodiversity; Plant(s))
    biophilia and, 1277f
    cells in (*see* Cell(s))
    classification in (*see* Cladistics; Phylogenies; Systematics; Taxonomy)
    common unifying themes of, 2f–9f
    connection of, to chemistry, 28 (*see also* Chemistry)
    conservation biology in (*see* Conservation biology)

developmental biology in, 1037*f*–1038*f*
ecology in (*see* Ecology)
emergent properties at levels of biological organization in, 2*f*–4*f*, 5
evolutionary developmental (evo-devo) biology in, 382–383, 457, 463, 538
evolution as core theme of, 1 (facing page), 2, 9–10*f*, 11*f*–15*f* (*see also* Evolution)
expression and transmission of genetic information in, 5*f*–6*f*, 7 (*see also* Genetics)
genomics and proteomics in, 88*f*
interactions in biological systems in, 8*f*–9*f* (*see also* Interactions)
molecular biology in (*see* Molecular biology)
science of, 1 (with facing page), 16*f*–20*f*, 21–23*f*, 24 (*see also* Case studies; Inquiry Figures; Research Method Figures; Scientific Skills Exercises)
sociobiology in, 1154
systems biology in, 4, 440–441*f*, 442
transfer and transformation of energy and matter in, 7*f* (*see also* Energy)
Bioluminescence, 141*f*
Biomanipulation, **1221**
Biomass, **832**, **1217**, 1235–1236
Biomes, **1164**–1165*f*. See also Aquatic biomes; Biosphere; Global ecology; Terrestrial biomes
Biophilia, 1257, 1277*f*
Bioremediation, **584***f*, 803, **1250***f*
Biorhythms, melatonin and, 1009
Biosphere, **1159**. See also Earth
  biomes of, 1164–1165*f* (*see also* Aquatic biomes; Terrestrial biomes)
  biophilia and future of, 1277*f*
  ecological role of prokaryotes in, 581*f*–582
  global climate change of (*see* Global climate change)
  global ecology of, 1159*f* (*see also* Global ecology)
  as global ecosystem, 1233
  human population, and carrying capacity of, 1201*f*–1204*f*, 1205
  importance of seedless vascular plants to, 627–628
  as level of biological organization, 2*f*
  photosynthesis as process that feeds, 185*f*–186*f* (*see also* Photosynthesis)
Biosynthetic pathways, 142, 181
Biotechnology, **409**
  DNA sequencing, 6*f*–7
  as DNA technology, 409 (*see also* DNA technology)
  genetic code and, 340
  genetic engineering of plants, 831–832*f*, 833–834
  in genetic testing, 286–287*f*
  phytoremediation, 803
  practical applications of, 428–429*f*, 430*f*–431*f*, 432–433
  prokaryotes in, 583–584*f*, 585
  science, society, and, 23*f*
Biotic factors, **1163**
  microclimate and, 1163
  in pollination, 820*f*–821*f*
  in species distributions, 1177*f*, 1179*f*
Biotic stresses, plant, **857**, 859–860, 861*f*–863*f*
Bipedal animals, 744*f*–745, 1129
Bipolar cells, 1112*f*, 1114–1115*f*
Bipolar disorder, **1097**
Birds
  adaptations of kidneys of, 986
  alimentary canals in, 899*f*
  avian flu in, 1229*f*
  brains of, 1085*f*
  breathing by, 938–939*f*
  cleavage in, 1042–1043
  DDT and, 1271*f*
  derived characters of, 732*f*–733
  as descended from dinosaurs, 558*f*
  endangered or threatened, 1256*f*
  evolution of, 673
  evolution of cognition and brains of, 1093*f*
  evolution of finches, 466–467*f*, 480*f*–481*f*
  evolution of genes in, 450
  flight adaptations of, 1130
  flower pollination by, 821*f*

gastrulation in, 1046*f*
gene flow in great tits, 490–491*f*
genetic variation in migration patterns of, 1150–1151*f*
greater prairie chicken, 489*f*–490, 1262*f*–1263
hearing and equilibrium in, 1110*f*
limb formation in, 1056–1057*f*, 1058
living, 733*f*–734*f*
migration behaviors of, 1135
migration genetics of, 976–977*f*
nitrogenous wastes of, 976–977*f*
organogenesis in, 1049*f*
origin of, 733*f*
as pollinators, 516
problem solving of, 1141
red-cockaded woodpecker decline, 1264*f*–1265
salt excretion in marine, 976*f*
sex determination of, 296*f*
species-area curves for, 1227*f*
thermoregulation in, 880*f*
unity in diversity of, 13*f*
wings of, 552, 734*f*
Birth control, human, 1032–1033
Birth control pills, **1032***f*–1033
Birth defects, human, 896*f*, 1030
Births, human
  birth defects in, 896*f*, 1030
  demographics of, 1186–1187*f*, 1188*f*–1189*f*, 1190
  in density-dependent population growth, 1197*f*–1199*f*
  effects of vitamin supplementation on neural tube defects in, 896*f*
  in exponential population growth, 1190–1191*f*
  life-expectancy at birth, 1203
  newborn screening and, 287–288
  in population dynamics, 1186*f*
  stages of labor in, 1030–1031*f*
  zero population growth and human, 1202
Bisphenol A, 1009
Bitter tastes, 1117*f*–1118*f*
Bivalves, 694*f*–695*f*, 696*f*
Black bears, 10*f*
Black-bellied seedcracker finches, 492
Black bread mold, 656*f*–657
Blackcap warblers, 1150–1151*f*
Black rush plants, 1215*f*
Blacktip reef sharks, 721*f*
Blades, **596**, **755**
Blastocoel, **1041***f*
Blastocysts, 425–426*f*, 1028*f*, **1029**, **1046***f*–1047*f*
Blastomeres, **1041***f*
Blastopores, 675*f*, **676**, **1044***f*, 1056*f*
BLAST program, 438–439*f*
Blastula, 1038, **1041***f*
Blebbing, 227*f*–228
Blending hypothesis on inheritance, 267–268
Blindness, 309, 489, 579*f*, 896, 1116
Blind spot, eye, 1112*f*
Blood, **872***f*, **917**. *See also* Blood pressure; Blood vessels
  ABO blood groups for human, 278*f*
  animal thermoregulation and, 879*f*–880*f*
  apoptosis of human white blood cells, 227*f*
  blood groups of, 964
  cell division of bone marrow cells and, 232–233*f*
  cholesterol in, and atherosclerosis, 75
  in closed circulatory systems, 701, 917*f*–918 (*see also* Cardiovascular systems; Closed circulatory systems)
  clotting of, 9, 297–298, 412*f*, 430, 697*f*–698, 930*f*–931*f*, 998
  components of, 928*f*–929*f*, 930
  diffusion from, to interstitial fluid across capillary walls, 926–927*f*
  enzymes and glucose levels in, 156
  filtration of, by nephrons, 981*f*–983*f*
  flow of, in mammalian excretory system, 981*f*
  flow velocity of, 924*f*
  gas exchange systems and components of, 941*f*–943*f*
  glycoproteins and types of human, 129
  hormonal regulation of volume and pressure of, 990*f*
  hormones in, 993

immune system rejection of transfusions of, 963–964
melatonin concentrations in human, 877*f*
pH of human, 52–53
regulation of calcium levels in, by parathyroid glands, 1006*f*
regulation of glucose levels in, 8–9*f*
sickle-cell disease and (*see* Sickle-cell disease)
vampire bat digestion of, 985*f*–986
Blood-brain barrier, 1081
Blood doping, 930
Blood flow velocity, 924*f*
Blood flukes, 690*f*, 1214
Blood groups, 278*f*, 963–964
Bloodletting, 697–698
Blood poisoning, 578*f*
Blood pressure
  cardiac cycle of, and regulation of, 924*f*–925*f*, 926*f*
  in closed circulatory systems, 918
  hypertension and, 932
Blood vessels
  blood flow velocity in, 924*f*
  blood pressure in, 924*f*–925*f*, 926
  capillary function, 926*f*–927*f*
  lymphatic systems and, 927*f*
  of mammalian excretory system, 981*f*
  structure and function of, 923*f*–924
  Viagra and, 221
Blooms
  algal, 1221, 1237
  diatom, 596
  dinoflagellate, 598*f*
  nitrogen pollution and phytoplankton, 1270*f*
Blowfly, 821*f*
Bluefin tuna, 1259
Blue-footed boobies, 502*f*
Bluehead wrasse, 1016
Blue jays, 1140*f*
Blue-light photoreceptors, **849**–850*f*, 852
Bobcat, 888*f*
Body axes, 1054*f*
Body cavities, **674***f*–675
Body hairs, insect, 1106*f*
Body plans, **673**
  angiosperm, 642*f*
  animal, 673*f*–675*f*, 676
  arthropod, 700*f*–701*f*
  cell fate and (*see* Cell fate)
  correlation of diversity of miRNAs with complexity of animal, 672
  fungal, 649*f*–650*f*
  hierarchical organization of animal, 870*t*, 871*f*–873*f* (*see also* Animal form and function)
  homeotic genes and, 457*f*–458*f*
  human (*see* Human body)
  lichen, 662*f*–63*f*
  macroevolution of, 538*f*–540*f*, 541
  maximizing body surface area in animal, 689*f*
  mollusc, 692–693*f*
  morphogenesis and (*see* Morphogenesis)
  pattern formation of, 379–380*f*, 381*f*–382*f*, 383
  plant, as herbivore defense, 862*f*
Body size, metabolic rate and animal, 885*f*
Body temperature regulation. *See* Thermoregulation
Bog mummy, 622*f*
Bohr shift, 942*f*
Bolting, 845
Bolus, **901***f*
Bombina toads, 510–511*f*, 513
Bonds, chemical. *See* Chemical bonds
Bone, 719, **872***f*
Bone marrow, 232–233*f*, 428–429*f*, 964
Bone morphogenetic protein 4 (BMP-4), 1056
Bones
  of human skeleton, 1128*f*
  of mammalian ear, 735*f*
Bonobos, 454–455, 741*f*
Bony fishes, 973*f*–974
Book lungs, **702**
Boom-and-bust population cycles, 1200*f*
Borisy, Gary, 239*f*
Botox, 1075
Bottleneck effect, **489**

Bottlenose dolphins, 880*f*, 1088
Bottom-up model, trophic control, **1221**
Botulism, 215*f*, 398, 579*f*, 583, 1075
Boundaries
    community, 1208
    ecosystem, 1233, 1265–1266*f*
Bound ribosomes, 103*f*–104, 351–352
Boveri, Theodor, 294
Bowden, Richard, 621*f*
Bowman's capsule, **981***f*
Boysen-Jensen, Peter, 841*f*
Brachiopods, 681*f*, **692***f*
Brainbow technology, 1079*f*–1080
Brain cancer, 248
Brain(s), **1061**. *See also* Nervous systems
    arousal and sleep functions of, 1088*f*
    biological clock regulation by, 1088–1089
    breathing control centers in human, 940*f*
    in central nervous systems, 1080*f*–1081
    cerebral cortex and cognitive functions of,
        1090–1091*f*, 1092*f*–1093*f*
    development, 1086*f*, 1093–1094
    disorders of, 1097–1098*f*
    drug addiction and reward system of, 1097*f*
    emotional functions of, 1089*f*–1090
    evolution of chordate and vertebrate, 716*f*
    evolution of cognition in avian pallium and
        human, 1093*f*
    evolution of vertebrate, 1085*f*
    frontal lobe function of, 1092
    glia in mammalian, 1063*f*
    glioblastoma cancer of, 441
    human, 742, 1086*f*–1087*f*, 1089*f*, 1090–1098
    hypothalamus of human, in thermoregulation,
        882–883*f*
    imaging of, 1079*f*, 1090*f*
    information processing by, 1090–1091*f*, 1092*f*
    language and speech functions of, 1092*f*
    lateralization of cortical function of, 1092
    mammalian, 735
    Neanderthal, 746
    nervous tissue of, 873*f*
    in neuroendocrine signaling, 1002*f*–1005*f*
    neurons in, 1062, 1079*f*, 1085 (*see also* Neurons)
    opiate receptors in mammalian, 1076
    regions of, 1085*f*, 1088*f*–1090*f*
    in sensory systems, 1103
    strokes in, 931
    visual information processing in, 1115*f*
Brainstem, **1086***f*–1087*f*, 1088, 1089
Brain waves, 1088*f*
Branching, body surface area and, 689*f*
Branching, carbon skeleton, 60*f*
Branching, plant, 763
Branching evolution, 542–543
Branch length, phylogenetic tree, 555*f*–556*f*
Branch points, **549**–550*f*
Brassinosteroids, 839, 840*t*, **849**
Brawn, Jeffrey, 1262*f*
Brazil nut tree, 1196*f*
BRCA1 and *BRCA2* genes, 387*f*–388
Bread mold. *See Neurospora crassa* (bread mold)
Breakdown pathways, 142
Breast cancer, 217, 247*f*, 386–387*f*, 388, 428
Breasts, 1021
Breathing, **938**–939*f*, 940*f*
Breathing control centers, 940*f*
Breeding
    as artificial selection, 468–469*f*
    plant, 816, 829, 830–831
Brenner, Sydney, 1052
Brewer's yeast. *See Saccharomyces cerevisiae* (yeast)
Briggs, Robert, 423
Brightfield microscopy, **95***f*
Brine shrimp, 458*f*, 539*f*–540
Bristlecone pine tree, 637*f*
Bristletails, 706*f*
Brittle stars, 708*f*–709
Broca, Pierre, 1092
Broca's area, 1092*f*
Bronchi, **937***f*
Bronchioles, **937***f*
Brood bodies, 621

Brooding, 558*f*
Brown algae, 591*f*, **596***f*–597*f*, 598
Brown bears, 143*f*
Brown fat, 176, 881
Brown-headed cowbird, 1266
Brown tree snake, 1258
Brundtland, G. H., 1257
Brush border, 904*f*, 905
Brushtail possum, 736*f*
Bryophytes, **616**, **618**
    ecological and economic importance of, 621*f*–622*f*
    gametangia of, 615*f*
    gametophytes of, 618–619*f*, 621
    gametophyte-sporophyte relationships in, 631*f*
    mosses, liverworts, and hornworts as, 618, 620*f*
    as nonvascular plants, 616–617*t*
    phylogeny of, 617*f*
    sporophytes of, 621
Bryozoans, 681*f*, 692*f*
B soil horizon, 800*f*
Bt toxin, 831–832*f*, 833
Buck, Linda, 1118
Budding, 100*f*, 253*f*, 653*f*, 1014
Buffers, **52**–53
Bugs, 706*f*
Bulbourethral glands, 1019*f*–1020
Bulk feeders, **898***f*
Bulk flow, **785**
    as long-distance transport, 785
    as translocation mechanism in angiosperms,
        794–795*f*
    of water and minerals from roots to shoots,
        786–787*f*, 788*f*–789*f*, 790
Bumble bees, 516
Bundle sheath, 765*f*
Bundle-sheath cells, **201**–202*f*
Burgess Shale fossil bed, 523*f*
Burkholderia glathei, 581*f*
Burkitt's lymphoma, 388
Burmese pythons, 882*f*
Bush babies, 740
Bushmaster snakes, 729*f*
Buttercups, 705*f*, 706*f*, 820*f*, 833, 1001*f*–1002
Buttress roots, 754*f*
Buxbaum, Joseph, 454*f*

C

C$_3$ plants, **201**, 203
C$_4$ plants, **201**–202*f*, 203, 204*f*
Cacao tree, 661*f*
Cachexia, 1010
Cactus, 793*f*, 821*f*, 1166*f*
Cadang-cadang, 405
Cadherin proteins, 670*f*
Caecilians, 726*f*
Caenorhabditis elegans (soil worm)
    apoptosis in, 228*f*
    fate mapping for, 1052*f*–1053*f*
    genome size and number of genes of, 442*t*–443
    as model organism, 23, 699*f*
    nervous system of, 1080*f*–1081
Calcitonin, 999*f*, **1006***f*
Calcium, 29*t*
Calcium homeostasis, 1006*f*
Calcium ions
    diffusion of, across synapses, 1071–1072*f*
    in formation of fertilization envelope, 1039–1040*f*
    in regulation of muscle contraction, 1122–1123*f*,
        1124, 1126
    in signal transduction pathways, 221–222*f*,
        838*f*–839
California Current, 1162*f*
Callus, **829**
Calmodulin, 1126
Calorie (cal), **46**, 884
Calories, food, 46, 884
Calorimeters, 884
Calvin, Melvin, 189
Calvin cycle, 189*f*–190, 199–200*f*, 204–205*f*
Cambrian explosion, **530***f*, **671***f*–672
Cambrian period, 712*f*
Camels, 974

Camouflage, 19*f*–20*f*, 21–22, 462*f*, 470*f*, 1211
CAM (crassulacean acid metabolism) plants,
    203–**204***f*, 792–793*f*
Canada goose, 880*f*
Cancer
    abnormal cell cycle control systems in, 246*f*–247*f*,
        248
    abnormal protein kinases in, 220
    biotechnology in treatment of, 428–430
    carcinogen screening and, 357
    chromosomal translocations and, 307
    DNA microarray detection of, 421
    endocrine disruptors and, 1009
    faulty apoptosis in, 229
    faulty cell-surface receptors in, 214, 217
    faulty growth factors in, 223
    genetic markers for, 422
    genomics, cell signaling, and breast, 386–387*f*
    genomics and proteomics in study and treatment
        of, 88*f*
    HIV and, 968
    immunity against, 968
    immunodeficiency and, 966
    inherited disposition and environmental factors
        in, 388
    interferences with normal cell-signaling pathways
        in development of, 384–385*f*, 386
    lymph nodes and, 927
    mismatch repair and colon, 325
    multistep model of development of, 386*f*
    ozone depletion, UV radiation, and, 1275
    PET scanners and, 31–32*f*
    skin, 326, 1275
    species and genetic diversity and treatments for,
        1257*f*
    stem cells and, 426
    systems biology approach to, 441*f*–442
    telomeres and prevention of, 327
    treatment of, with cell cycle inhibitor, 248
    tumor-suppressor genes and, 384
    types of genes associated with, 383*f*–384
    viruses in, 388
Cancer Genome Atlas, 386–387*f*, 441
Candida albicans, 664
Cane toads, 1211
Cannibalism, 405
Canopy, **780**, **1166**
Canyon tree frog, 1212*f*
Capecchi, Mario, 421
Capillaries, **918**–919*f*, 923*f*–924*f*, 926*f*–927*f*
Capillary beds, **918**, 926*f*–927*f*
Capsaicin, 1105
Capsids, **394***f*–395*f*, 396
Capsomeres, 394*f*, 396
Capsule, 97*f*, **569***f*
Capsule, sporangium, **621**
Carbohydrates, **68**
    cell-cell recognition role of membrane, 128–129
    digestion of, 903*f*, 904–905*f*
    as fuel for catabolism, 180*f*–181
    glycoproteins and, 395 (*see also* Glycoproteins)
    as macromolecules, 66
    monosaccharides and disaccharides, 68*f*–69*f*
    oxidation of, during cellular respiration, 164–165
    in plant composition, 803
    polysaccharides, 70*f*–71*f*, 72*f*
    as product of photosynthesis, 204–205*f*
Carbon
    in amino acids, 75
    as essential element, 29*t*, 56, 64
    isotopes of, 31–33
    net ecosystem production and, 1236–1237*f*
    in organic compounds, 58–59*f*, 60 (*see also*
        Organic compounds)
    in peatlands, 622
    in plant composition, 803
Carbon-12, 524
Carbon-14, 524
Carbonate ions, 53*f*–54
Carbon cycle, 1245*f*
Carbon dioxide
    atmospheric, 203, 1272–1273*f*, 1274

in carbon fixation, 189*f*–190, 199–200*f*, 201–202*f*, 203–204*f*
covalent bonding of carbon atoms in, 60
diatom capture of, 596
diffusion of, across capillary walls, 926–927
fossil fuels, ocean acidification, and, 53*f*–54
in gas exchange, 933*t*–934, 941*f*–943*f*
in global climate change, 202–203
global climate change and, 48, 1163
inhibition of fruit ripening with, 848
in mammalian circulation, 920
metabolic rate and, 884
net ecosystem production and, 1236–1237*f*
nonvascular plants and, in Ordovician Period climate change, 623
in Permian mass extinction, 534–535
in photosynthesis, 41*f*
photosynthetic processing of, by marine protists, 609*f*
in plant cells, 207*f*
prokaryotic chemical recycling of, 581
in regulation of human breathing, 940*f*
rubisco as acceptor for, 199–200*f*
seedless vascular plants and, 627
in *Sphagnum* peat moss, 622
as stimulus for stomatal opening and closing, 791–792
tropical rain forest deforestation and, 645*f*–646
Carbon fixation, **189***f*–190, 199–200*f*, 201–202*f*, 203–204*f*
Carbonic acid, 51, 53*f*–54, 940
Carbon monoxide, 1076
Carbon skeletons, 60*f*–61*f*, 62*f*
Carbonyl group, **63***f*
Carboxyl group, **63***f*
Carcinogens, 357, 383. *See also* Cancer
Cardiac cycle, **921***f*, 924–925
Cardiac muscle, 873*f*, **1126**
Cardiac output, **921**
Cardiomyopathy, familial, 355*f*
Cardiovascular diseases, 74, 931*f*–932
Cardiovascular systems, **918**
   blood composition and function in, 928*f*–930, 931
   as closed circulatory systems, 918 (*see also* Circulatory systems)
   coordination of gas exchange systems and, 941*f*–943*f* (*see also* Gas exchange systems)
   diseases of, 74, 931*f*–932
   effects of adrenal hormones on, 1007
   evolutionary variations in double circulation of, 919–920
   hearts and blood vessels in single and double circulation of, 918–919*f*
   hearts in mammalian, 920*f*–922*f*
   lymphatic systems and, 927*f*
   patterns of blood pressure and flow in blood vessels of, 923*f*–927*f*
   single and double circulation in, 918–919*f*
Caribou, 484*f*, 1015
Carnivores, **892**
   alimentary canals of, 906–907*f*
   dentition and diet in, 906*f*
   diets of, 892
   energetic hypothesis and biomass of, 1219*f*
   phylogenetic tree of, 549*f*
   trophic efficiency of, 1241*f*
Carnivorous plants, 799*f*, 812*f*–813
Carotenoids, **193**, 564, 598
Carpellate flowers, 828
Carpels, 268–269, **638***f*, **816**
Carrier crabs, 1208*f*
Carrier proteins, 130, 133*f*, 134–135*f*
Carriers, genetic disorder, **283**–284, 286
Carrion flower, 821*f*
Carroll, Scott, 471*f*
Carroll, Sean, 700*f*
Carrots, 423*f*, 430
Carrying capacity (*K*), **1192**
   global, for human population, 1204*f*–1205
   in logistic population growth model, 1192*t*–1194*f*
Carson, Rachel, 1271*f*
Cartilage, **872***f*
Cartilage skeleton, 718, 720
Casein, 76*f*

Case studies
   on decline of red-cockaded woodpecker, 1264*f*–1265
   on evolution of tolerance to toxic elements, 30*f*
   on greater prairie chicken extinction vortex, 1262*f*
   on grizzly bear populations, 1263*f*
   on kidney function in vampire bats, 985*f*–986
   on nutrient cycling in Hubbard Brook Experimental Forest, 1247–1248*f*
   on predation and mouse coat coloration, 19*f*–20*f*
   on variation in migratory patterns, 1150–1151*f*
   on variation in prey selection, 1150*f*
Casparian strip, **786**, 787*f*
Caspases, 228
Cassava, 645, 832*f*
Castor beans, 823*f*
Catabolic pathways, 142, **142**
   cellular respiration as, 163
   redox reactions in, 163–164*f*, 165*f*–166*f*
   regulation of, 181*f*–182
   versatility of, 180–181
Catabolite activator protein (CAP), 364*f*
Catalysts, **75**, **151**. *See also* Enzymatic catalysis
Catalytic cycle, 154*f*
Cataracts, 1275
Catecholamines, **1006**–1007*f*
Catenulida, 688
Caterpillars, 462*f*, 482*f*, 898*f*, 1001*f*–1002, 1239*f*–1240
Cation exchange, **800**–801*f*
Cations, 37–38*f*
Cats, 298*f*, 424*f*–425
Cattails, 1180
Cattle, 908*f*
Cattle egrets, 1178*f*, 1215*f*
Causation, behavioral, 1134
Cavalier-Smith, Thomas, 605*f*
CC (Carbon Copy, cloned cat), 424*f*–425
CCR5 protein, 128*f*
Cecum, 905*f*
Cedar Creek Ecosystem Science Reserve, 1217*f*
Celera Genomics, 437*f*–438
Cell(s)
   animal (*see* Animal cells)
   in animal morphogenesis, 1050*f*–1051
   auxin in differentiation of, 844
   auxin in elongation of, 842–843*f*
   blood, 928*f*–929*f*
   calculating volume and surface area of, 99
   cell fractionation in study of, 96*f*–97
   cellular integration of, 121*f*
   cellular membranes of (*see* Cellular membranes)
   cellular respiration and (*see* Cellular respiration)
   communication between (*see* Cell signaling)
   cytokinins in division and differentiation of, 844
   differentiation of (*see* Differentiation, cell)
   division of, as fundamental to life, 232 (*see also* Cell cycle; Cell division)
   eukaryotic vs. prokaryotic, 97*f*–98*f*, 99 (*see also* Eukaryotic cells; Prokaryotic cells)
   as fundamental units of life, 3*f*, 4*f*–5, 93*f*
   locations of enzymes in, 159*f*
   metabolism of (*see* Metabolism)
   microscopy in study of, 94*f*–95*f*, 96
   photosynthesis and (*see* Photosynthesis)
   plant (*see* Plant cells)
   programmed death of (*see* Apoptosis)
   programming of, by viral DNA, 313*f*–314*f*, 315
   protein folding in, 83*f*–84*f*
   protocells as first, 521*f*–522
   sequential gene regulation in differentiation of, 378–379*f*
   in sickle-cell disease, 496*f*
   size range of, 94*f*
   stem cells (*see* Stem cells)
   transcription specific to type of, 370–371*f*
Cell adhesion molecules, 1050
Cell body, 873*f*, **1062***f*, 1073, 1082
Cell-cell recognition
   by cellular membranes, 128*f*–129
   in local cell signaling, 212*f*
Cell cycle, **233**. *See also* Cell cycle control system; Cell division
   binary fission in bacterial, 240–241*f*

cell division roles in, 232*f*–233*f*
cellular organization of chromosomes in, 233*f*–234
cytokinesis in, 239–240*f*, 241*f*
distribution of chromosomes during eukaryotic, 234*f*–235
evolution of mitosis of, 241–242*f*
interpreting histograms on, 248
mitosis stages of, in animal cells, 236*f*–237*f*
mitotic phases and interphases of, 235*f*
mitotic spindle in mitotic phase of, 235, 238*f*–239*f*
regulation of eukaryotic, by cell cycle control system, 242–243*f*, 244*f*–247*f*, 248
treating cancer by inhibiting, 248
Cell cycle control system, **243**. *See also* Cell cycle
   in cancer development, 246–247*f*, 248, 383*f*–384, 385*f*–387*f*, 388
   checkpoints in, 242–243*f*
   cyclins and cyclin-dependent kinases in, 243–244*f*
   cytoplasmic signals in, 243*f*
   internal and external signals at checkpoints of, as stop and go signs, 244–245*f*, 246*f*
   interpreting histograms on, 248
Cell cycle–inhibiting pathway, 385*f*
Cell cycle–stimulating pathway, 385*f*
Cell differentiation. *See* Differentiation, cell
Cell division, **232**
   bacterial, 240–241*f*
   cancer and interference with cell-signaling pathways of, 384–385*f*
   in cell cycle, 232*f*–233*f* (*see also* Cell cycle)
   cytokinins in, 844
   cytoplasmic determinants and induction in, 377*f*–378
   distribution of chromosomes during eukaryotic, 233*f*–234*f*, 235
   as embryonic development process, 376*f*–377 (*see also* Embryonic development)
   evolution of, 241–242*f*
   in meiosis, 257*f*–260*f* (*see also* Meiosis)
   in mitosis vs. in meiosis, 260–261*f*, 262
   newt lung cell, 5*f*
   in plant growth, 770*f*–772*f*
   prokaryotic, 571–572
Cell fate
   cilia and, 1058
   determination, differentiation, and, 1051
   fate mapping and, 1051–1052*f*, 1053*f*–1055*f*
   inductive signals in pattern formation and determination of, 1055–1056*f*, 1057*f*–1058
Cell fractionation, **96**–97
Cell junctions
   in local cell signaling, 212*f*
   plasmodesmata in plants, 119*f*–120
   tight junctions, desmosomes, and gap junctions in animals, 120*f*
Cell-mediated immune response, 947*f*, **958***f*–959*f*
Cell motility, 113*t*–114, 115*f*–117*f*, 1050*f*–1051
Cell plate, **240***f*, 241*f*
Cell signaling. *See also* Signal transduction pathways
   by animal endocrine and nervous systems, 874*f*
   in apoptosis, 210, 227*f*–229*f*
   cancer and interference with normal, 384–385*f*, 386
   in cell cycle control system, 243*f*–246*f* (*see also* Cell cycle control system)
   cellular membrane selective permeability and, 124*f*
   cilia in, 114–115
   evolution of, 211–212*f*
   feedback regulation of, 1000*f*–1001
   fight-or-flight responses in, 210*f*
   local and long-distance, 212*f*–213*f*
   mechanical, 119
   pathways of, 994*f*–995*f*, 1000*f*–1001 (*see also* Endocrine signaling; Neuroendocrine signaling)
   reception stage of, 214*f*–218*f*
   response stage of, 223*f*–225*f*, 226–227
   symplastic, 795–796
   three stages of, 212–213*f*, 214
   transduction stage of, 218, 219*f*–222*f*
   using experiments to test models of, 226
Cell-surface proteins, 119*f*, 128*f*
Cell-surface receptor tyrosine kinases (RTKs), 248
Cell-surface transmembrane receptors, 214, 215*f*–217*f*

Cellular hormone response pathways, 996*f*–998*f*, 1000*f*
Cellular innate immune defenses, 949*f*–950*f*
Cellular-level herbivore defenses, plant, 862*f*
Cellular membranes. *See also* Plasma membranes
    active transport across, 134–135*f*, 136*f*–137
    animal, 668
    bulk transport across, by exocytosis and endocytosis, 137–138*f*
    evolution of differences in lipid composition of, 127
    fluidity of, 126*f*–127
    as fluid mosaics of lipids and proteins, 125*f*–126
    interpreting scatter plots on glucose uptake across, 134
    membrane carbohydrates in cell-cell recognition by, 128–129
    membrane proteins of, 127*f*–128*f*, 130
    of mitochondria, 110, 111*f*
    movement across plant cell, 207*f*
    nuclear envelopes, 102, 103*f*
    organelles and internal, 98–99
    passive transport as diffusion across, 130–131*f*, 132*f*–133*f*
    phospholipids in, 74*f*–75
    in plant response to cold stress, 859
    selective permeability of, 124*f*, 129–130
    specialized prokaryotic, 571*f*
    synthesis and sidedness of, 129*f*
Cellular respiration, 163
    ATP production by catabolic pathways and, 163
    ATP yield at each stage of, 175*f*–176
    bar graphs of, 177
    biosynthesis in anabolic pathways and, 181
    as catabolic, 142, 163
    in energy flow and chemical cycling, 7*f*, 162*f*–163*f*
    enzymes for, in mitochondria, 159*f*
    evolutionary significance of glycolysis in, 179–180
    fermentation vs., 163, 177–178*f*, 179*f*
    glycolysis in, 168*f*–169*f*
    metabolic rate and, 884
    mitochondria in, 109–110*f*, 111*f*
    monosaccharides in, 69
    origin of, 528–529*f*
    overall reaction for, 147
    oxidative phosphorylation in, 172*f*–173*f*, 174*f*–175
    oxygen diffusion and, 131
    photosynthesis vs., 189 (*see also* Photosynthesis)
    in plant cells, 207*f*
    pyruvate oxidation and citric acid cycle in, 169*f*–171*f*
    redox reactions and, 163–164*f*, 165*f*–166*f*
    regulation of, via feedback mechanisms, 181*f*–182
    stages of, 166*f*–167*f*
    using cell fractionation to study, 97
    versatility of catabolic pathways and, 180*f*–181
Cellular slime molds, 606, 607*f*
Cellulose, 71
    fiber, 905
    microfibrils, 772*f*
    in plant cell walls, 71*f*–72, 118
    as product of photosynthesis, 204–205*f*
    proteins synthesizing, 613
Cellulose synthase, 118
Cell walls, 118
    cellulose in land plant, 613
    fungal cell, 100*f*
    osmosis, water balance, and, 132*f*–133*f*
    plant cell, 101*f*, 118*f*
    prokaryotic, 97*f*, 568–569*f*
Cenozoic era, 526*f*, 527*t*, 533*f*, 673
Center for Plant Conservation, 1256
Centipedes, 702–703*f*
Central canal, 1082*f*
Central disk, sea star, 708*f*
Central dogma, DNA, 337
Central nervous system (CNS), **1063**, **1080**. *See also* Brains
    neuronal plasticity of, 1093–1094*f*
    neurons of, 1063
    neurotransmitters and, 1075
    peripheral nervous system and, 1080–1081, 1084*f*
    in sensory systems, 1102, 1103
    structure and function of vertebrate, 1082*f*–1083*f*

Central vacuoles, 101*f*, **108**
Centrifuge, 96*f*, 97
Centrioles, **114**
Centromeres, **234***f*
Centromeric DNA, 446
Centrosomes, 100*f*, **114**, 238*f*
Century plants, 1195*f*
Cephalization, 1080–1081
Cephalochordata (lancelets), 713*f*, 714–715*f*, 716*f*
Cephalopods, 695*f*–696
Cercozoans, **601**–602*f*
Cerebellum, 1085*f*, **1086***f*–1087*f*
Cerebral cortex, **1087***f*, 1090–1091*f*, 1092*f*–1093*f*, 1094, 1108
Cerebral ganglia
    earthworm, 698*f*
    insect, 704*f*
Cerebral hemispheres, **1087***f*
Cerebrospinal fluid, 940, 1082
Cerebrum, 1085*f*, **1086***f*–1087*f*, 1088
Certainty of paternity, 1145–1146
Cervical cancer, 968
Cervix, **1020**–1021*f*
Cetaceans, 475*f*–476*f*, 739*f*
Cetartiodactyla, 739*f*
Chaetae, 696, 698*f*
Chagas' disease, 594
Chambered nautilus, 695*f*
Chameleons, 667*f*
Chamois, 895*f*
Change, global. *See* Global change
Change, spontaneous, 146*f*
Channel proteins, 130, 133*f*, 134
Chaparral biomes, **1168***f*
Chaperonins, 83*f*, 858
Character displacement, 1210–**1211***f*
Characters, **268**
    dominant vs. recessive traits and, 269–270*t*
    multifactorial, 280*f*
    shared ancestral and shared derived, 555*f*–556*f*
    taxonomy and, 548–549
    traits and, 268–269
Character tables, 554*f*, 555
Chargaff, Edwin, 315*f*–316
Chargaff's rules, 315*f*–316, 318
Charged tRNA, 346–347*f*
Charophytes, 603, 613, 613*f*
Chase, Martha, 314*f*–315
Cheating behavior, 1153
Checkpoints, cell cycle control system, **243***f*–245*f*
Cheetahs, 1199*f*
Chelicerae, **701**
Chelicerates, **701**
Chemical bonds, 36*f*–41*f*, 58–59*f*, 60
Chemical cycling, energy flow and. *See* Biogeochemical cycles; Energy flow and chemical cycling
Chemical defense, prey, 1212*f*
Chemical digestion, 901–902*f*
Chemical energy, **142**, 883–884*f*. *See also* Cellular respiration; Photosynthesis
Chemical equilibrium, **41**
    buffers and, 52–53
    in chemical reactions, 41
    free energy change and, 145–146*f*
    metabolism and, 147*f*–148*f*
Chemical mutagens, 357
Chemical reactions, **40**
    activation energy barrier of, 151–152
    chemical energy in, 142–143
    enzymatic catalysis of (*see* Enzymatic catalysis)
    free energy change and, 145–146*f*
    making and breaking of chemical bonds by, 40–41*f*
    metabolism and, 141 (*see also* Metabolism)
    in photosynthesis, 188*f*–189 (*see also* Light reactions)
Chemical signals, 1061–1062. *See also* Animal hormones; Hormones; Plant hormones
Chemical structure, DNA, 317*f*
Chemical synapses, 1071*f*–1072*f*. *See also* Synapses
Chemical work, 148–149, 150*f*
Chemiosmosis, 173–**174***f*, 175*f*, 189*f*, 197*f*–198*f*
Chemistry
    atoms in, 30*f*–31, 32*f*–35*f*, 188*f*–189

biological molecules in (*see* Biological molecules)
    calculating standard radioactive isotope decay curves in, 33
    chemical bonding between atoms in, 36*f*–41*f*, 58–59*f*, 60
    connection to biology, 28 (*see also* Biology)
    matter as elements and compounds in, 29*f*–30*f* (*see also* Compounds; Molecules)
    organic, as study of carbon compounds, 57–58 (*see also* Organic compounds)
    of water (*see* Water)
Chemoautotrophs, 576*f*
Chemoheterotrophs, 576*f*
Chemoreceptors, **1104**–1105*f*, 1117*f*–1119*f*
Chemosynthetic organisms, 1233
Chemotaxis, 570
Chemotherapy, 247, 387*f*
Chemotrophs, 575, 576*f*
Chesapeake Bay estuary food web, 1219*f*
Chestnut blight, 663, 860, 1220, 1228
Chiasmata, **258***f*, 260*f*–261*f*, 262
Chicken pox, 956
Chicks
    embryo image, 1037*f*
    gastrulation in, 1046*f*
    limb formation in, 1056–1057*f*, 1058
    organogenesis in, 1049*f*
Chicxulub crater, 535*f*
Chief cells, 902*f*
Childbirth, human, 1030–1031*f*. *See also* Births, human
Chimpanzees
    comparison of human genome with genome of, 89, 448*f*–449, 454*f*
    complete genome sequence for, 436*f*
    J. Goodall's research on, 16*f*
    heterochrony and differential growth rates in skulls of, 538*f*
    humans vs., 742
    as primates, 741*f*
    problem solving of, 1141
    skulls of humans and, 552
    social learning in, 1142*f*
    tool use by, 745
China, 1202
Chips, human gene microarray, 441*f*–442
Chi-square (χ^2) test in Scientific Skills Exercise, 302
Chitin, **72***f*, **649**–650, 701, **1127**
Chitons, 693*f*, 1080*f*
Chlamydia, 1034
Chlamydias, 579*f*
Chlamydomonas, 101*f*, 603–604*f*
Chlorarachniophytes, 593, 602
Chloride cells, 974, 986–987*f*
Chloride ions, 1064*t*–1065*f*
Chloride transport channels, 284
Chlorinated hydrocarbons, 1271*f*
Chlorine, 29*t*, 1275*f*
Chlorofluorocarbons (CFCs), 1274*f*–1275*f*
Chlorophyll, 187*f*–188, 192*f*–198*f*, 199
Chlorophyll *a*, **191**–192*f*, 194–196
Chlorophyll *b*, **191**–192*f*, 194
Chlorophytes, 603*f*–604*f*
Chloroplasts, **109**
    chemiosmosis in, 175
    chemiosmosis in mitochondria vs. in, 197*f*–198*f*, 199
    evolutionary origins of, 109–110*f*
    folding of, 689*f*
    light reactions in (*see* Light reactions)
    as organelles, 3*f*, 4–5
    photosynthesis by, 109–110*f*, 111*f*
    in plant cells, 101*f*, 207*f*
    as sites of photosynthesis, 187*f*–188, 204–205*f*
    transgenic crops and DNA in, 834
Chlorosis, 804, 806*f*
Choanocytes, **684***f*
Choanoflagellates, 546*f*, 607, 669*f*–670*f*
Cholecystokinin (CCK), 909*f*
Cholera, 215*f*, 221, 578*f*, 583
Cholesterol, **75***f*
    in cellular membranes, 126*f*

G protein-coupled receptors and, 214*f*
   receptor-mediated endocytosis and, 137
   types of, in blood, 931–932
Chondrichthyans, **720**–721*f*
Chondrocytes, 872*f*
Chondroitin sulfate, 872*f*
Chordates, **713**
   endoskeletons of, 1127–1128*f*
   evolution of, 716
   hagfishes and lampreys, 717*f*–718
   invertebrate, 683*f*, 709, 713*f*–716*f*
   lancelets, 714–715*f*
   phylogeny and derived characters of, 713*f*–714*f*
   phylogeny of, 676–677*f*
   tunicates, 715*f*–716*f*
   vertebrates as, 716
Chorion, 729*f*, 1047*f*
Chorionic villus sampling (CVS), **286**–287*f*, 1033
Choroid, 1112*f*
Chorophyll, 3*f*
Christmas tree worm, 697*f*
Chromatin, **102, 233, 329**
   animal cell, 100*f*
   in cell division, 233*f*–234*f*, 235
   in eukaryotic cell nucleus, 102, 103*f*
   in eukaryotic chromosomes, 328*f*–**329***f*, 330*f*
   plant cell, 101*f*
   regulation of structure of eukaryotic, 366*f*–367
   remodeling of, by siRNAs, 375*f*–376
Chromoplasts, 111
Chromosomal basis of inheritance
   as basis for Mendelian inheritance, 292*f*–293*f*, 294
   chromosomal alterations and genetic disorders in, 304–305*f*, 306*f*–307*f*
   evolution of gene concept from, 357
   exceptions to Mendelian inheritance in, 308*f*–309*f*
   genomic imprinting in, 308*f*–309
   inheritance of organelle genes in, 309*f*
   linked genes and linkage in, 299*f*–301*f*, 302–303*f*, 304*f*
   sex-linked genes in, 296*f*–298*f*
   T. H. Morgan's experimental discovery of, 294*f*–295*f*
Chromosomal breakage points, 449
Chromosomes, **102, 233.** *See also* DNA (deoxyribonucleic acid); Gene(s)
   alleles on, 270 (*see also* Alleles)
   alterations of, 304–305*f*, 306*f*–307*f*, 448*f*–449
   bacterial, 240–241*f*
   in cancer cells, 247–248
   in cell division, 232*f*–233*f*, 242*f*
   in chromosomal basis of Mendelian inheritance, 292*f*–293*f*, 294 (*see also* Chromosomal basis of inheritance)
   correlating behavior of alleles with pairs of, 295*f*
   crossing over and recombinant, 263–264*f*
   distribution of, during eukaryotic cell division, 233*f*–234*f*, 235
   DNA, genes, and, 5*f*–6*f*
   DNA and chromatin packing in, 328*f*–330*f*
   in eukaryotic cell nucleus, 102
   evidence in, for evolution of land plants from green algae, 613
   gene expression and interaction of, in interphase nucleus, 372*f*
   genetic variation due to mutations in, 482–483
   in genome evolution, 448*f*–449
   homologous, 254*f*–255*f*
   human, 254*f*–255*f*, 256
   independent assortment of, 263*f*
   inheritance of genes and, 253
   karyotypes of, 254*f*
   locating genes along, 292*f*–293*f*, 294
   mapping distance between genes on, 303*f*–304*f*
   in meiosis, 257*f*–261*f*, 262
   molecular tags and karyotypes of human, 330*f*
   movement of, on kinetochore microtubules, 238–239*f*
   in prokaryotic and eukaryotic cells, 97*f*–98, 571*f*
   prokaryotic conjugation and gene transfer between, 574*f*–575
Chromosome theory of inheritance, **294**
Chronic inflammation, 952

Chronic myelogenous leukemia (CML), 307*f*, 429–430
Chrysanthemums, 854
Chylomicrons, **905***f*
Chyme, **901,** 909*f*
Chytrids, **654,** 655*f*–656*f*, 663–664*f*, 727
Cichlid fish, 509*f*, 513*f*
Cigarette smoke, cancer and, 388
Cilia, **114**
   architecture of eukaryotic, and unity, 12*f*
   bronchial, 937
   cell fate and, 1058
   ciliate, 600
   flagella vs., 115*f*
   as microtubules, 114–115*f*, 116*f*
Ciliates, **600***f*–601
Cilium-based signaling, 114–115
Circadian rhythms, **792, 852, 876.** *See also* Biological clocks
   in animal behavior, 1135
   in animal homeostasis, 876–877*f*
   brain regulation of, 1088–1089
   hibernation and, 887*f*
   melatonin and, 1009
   in plant responses to light, 851–**852***f*, 853–854*f*, 855
   in stomatal opening and closing, 792
Circannual rhythms, 1135
Circulatory systems
   cardiovascular systems as closed, 918 (*see also* Cardiovascular systems)
   gas exchange systems and, 915*f*–916 (*see also* Gas exchange systems)
   gastrovascular cavities as, 916*f*–917
   internal exchange surfaces and, 869*f*
   invertebrate, 693*f*, 695, 698*f*
   open and closed, 917*f*–918
   thermoregulatory adaptations of animal, 879–980*f*
cis face, Golgi apparatus, 106*f*–107
cis isomers, 61
Cisternae, 104, 106*f*–107
Cisternal maturation model, 106
Cisternal space, 104
cis-trans isomers, **61***f*
Citric acid cycle, **166**–167*f*, 170*f*–171*f*, 175*f*
Citrulline, 335*f*
Clades, **553**–554*f*, 555, 617, 675
Cladistics, **553***f*–554*f*, 555. *See also* Systematics; Taxonomy
Clams, 692, 694*f*–695*f*
Classes, taxonomy, **548**–549*f*
Classical conditioning, 1140
Claw waving behavior of male fiddler crab, 1133*f*, 1135
Cleanup, environmental, 412*f*, 432
Cleavage, **239, 668, 1041**
   in animal embryonic development, 668, 1038, 1041*f*–1042*f*, 1043
   in cell cycle, 239–240*f*, 241*f*
   in human embryonic development, 1028*f*–1029
   in protostome and deuterostome development, 675*f*–676
Cleavage furrows, 237*f*, **239**–240*f*, 1042*f*
Clements, F. E., 1222
Climate, **1161.** *See also* Global climate change
   continental drift and changes in, 533
   effect of large bodies of water on, 47*f*
   global patterns of, 1160*f*
   greenhouse gases and, 1272–1273*f*, 1274
   latitudinal gradients and, affecting community diversity, 1226*f*
   macroclimate, microclimate, and, 1161, 1163
   nonvascular plants in Ordovician Period changes of, 623
   Permian mass extinction and changes in, 534–535
   regional and local effects on, 1161*f*–1163*f*
   seedless vascular plants and ancient, 627
   terrestrial biomes and, 1164–1165*f*
   using dendrochronology to study, 767*f*
Climate change, global. *See* Global climate change
Climax communities, 1222
Climographs, **1164**–1165*f*
Clitoris, **1020**–1021*f*
Cloaca, **721, 1018***f*
Clock, cell-cycle, 243–244*f*

Clock genes, 852
Clonal selection, **956**–957*f*
Clone (term), 422. *See also* Organismal cloning
Cloned genes. *See also* DNA cloning; Gene cloning
   expressing eukaryotic, 416–417
   in gene therapy, 428–429*f*
   uses for, 412*f*
Clones, **253.** *See also* Organismal cloning
   asexual reproduction of, 253*f*
   fragmentation and, 827*f*
   from plant cuttings, 829
   test-tube or *in vitro*, 830*f*
Cloning vectors, **413.** *See also* Recombinant DNA
Closed circulatory systems, 695, 698*f*, **917**–918, 975. *See also* Cardiovascular systems
Clostridium botulinum, 583
Clotting, blood, 9, 297–298, 412*f*, 430, 697*f*–698, 930*f*–931, 998
Club fungi, 659*f*–661*f*
Club mosses, 625–626*f*, 627
Clumped dispersion, 1186, 1187*f*
Clutch size, 1195*f*–1196*f*, 1197
Cnidarians, 681*f*, 685*f*–687*f*, 1080*f*
Cnidocytes, **685**–686*f*
Coal, 627–28
Coal gas, 846
Coastal Japan restoration project, 1251*f*
Coat coloration case studies, 19*f*–20*f*, 21–22
Cocaine, 1097*f*
Coccidioidomycosis, 664
Cochlea, **1107***f*, 1108–1109*f*
Cocklebur, 853
Cocktails, drug, 402, 483
Cod, 722
Coding DNA strands, 338
Codominance, **277**
Codon recognition, 350*f*
Codons, **338**
   in genetic code, 337–338*f*, 339*f*–340
   in translation, 345*f*–347*f*, 350*f*
Coefficient of relatedness (*r*), **1152***f*–1153
Coefficients, correlation, 672, 745
Coelacanths, 723*f*
Coelom, 674*f*–675, 698*f*
Coelomates, **674***f*–675
Coenocytic fungi, **650**
Coenzymes, **156**
Coevolution, **821***f*
Cofactors, **156**
Coffee, 645
Cognition, 1090, 1093, **1141***f*
Cognitive maps, **1140**
Cohesins, 234, 238, 261*f*
Cohesion, **45**–46*f*, 789–790
Cohesion-tension hypothesis, **788***f*–789*f*, 790
Cohorts, **1187**
Coho salmon, 1195
Coitus, human, 1027–1028, 1032–1033
Coitus interruptus, 1032*f*
Cold
   plant response to stress of, 859
   thermoreceptors and, 1105
Cold viruses, 395
Coleoptera (beetles), 706*f*
Coleoptiles, **823***f*–824*f*, 841*f*
Coleorhiza, **823***f*
Collagen, 76*f*, 81*f*, **118**–119, 668
Collagenous fibers, 872*f*
Collar cells, 669*f*
Collared flycatchers, 512*f*–513
Collared lemmings, 1198*f*
Collecting duct, **981***f*, 982–983*f*
Collenchyma cells, **758***f*, 764
Colon, **905***f*
Colon cancer, 325
Colonial algae, 603
Coloration
   case studies on mouse, 19*f*–20*f*, 21–22
   chromosome, 330*f*
   as prey defensive adaptation, 1212*f*–1213*f*
   skin, 1010
Color blindness, 297*f*, 1116*f*
Colorectal cancer, 386*f*, 388

Color vision, 1111, 1115–1116f
Columbine flowers, 821f
Columnar cells, 871f
Columnar epithelium, 871f
Combinatorial control elements, 369–370, 371f
Comb jellies, 681f
Comet collision, mass extinction by, 535f
Commensalism, **582**, 655f, 656, **1214f**–1215f
Commercial value
    of fungi, 664–665
    of mosses, 622f
Common arrowhead flower, 829f
Common juniper, 637f
Communicating junctions, 120f
Communication, animal, 874f, **1136f**–1137f
Communication, cellular. *See* Cell signaling
Communities, **1159, 1208**
    biogeographic factors affecting, 1225–1226f,
        1227f–1228
    disturbances of, 1222f–1225f
    diversity in, 1255f–1256f
    interspecific interactions in, 1209f–1215f
    as level of biological organization, 2f
    pathogen alteration of structure of, 1228–1229f
    scientific, 18f–19, 23–24
    species diversity and stability of, 1216f–1217f (*see
        also* Species diversity)
    study of, by community ecology, 1159f, 1208f–
        1209 (*see also* Community ecology)
    trophic structure of, 1217–1218f, 1219f–1220f,
        1221 (*see also* Trophic structure)
Community diversity, 1255f–1256f
Community ecology, **1159**f. *See also* Ecology
    biogeographic factors in, 1225–1226f, 1227f–1228
    community boundaries in, 1208f–1209 (*see also*
        Communities)
    disturbances in, 1222f–1225f
    interspecific interactions in, 1209f–1215f
    pathogens in, 1228–1229f
    species diversity and trophic structure in,
        1216f–1220f, 1221 (*see also* Species diversity;
        Trophic structure)
    zoonotic diseases in, 1228–1229f
Community-level herbivore defenses, plant, 863f
Companion cells, **759**f
Competition
    density-dependent population regulation by, 1198f
    interspecific, 1209–1210f, 1211f
    sexual, 493f–494f, 1148f
    in species distributions of plants, 1180
Competitive exclusion, **1209**
Competitive inhibitors, **156**f–157
Complementary base pairing, DNA and RNA, 86–87f
Complementary DNA (cDNA), **418**–419f, 421
Complement systems, 951, 961f
Complete digestive tracts, 899f–900
Complete dominance, **277**
Complete flowers, **638**f, **816**
Complete growth medium, 334–335f
Complete metamorphosis, **705**f, 706f
Complex eyes, 541–542f
Compound eyes, 706f, 888f, **1111f**–1112
Compound leaves, 755f
Compounds, **29**. *See also* Molecules
    biological (*see* Biological molecules)
    elements and, 29f–30f
    ionic, 38
    organic (*see* Organic compounds)
    pure elements vs., 37
Compromises, evolutionary, 495
Computational tools, 7, 438–439f, 440–441f, 442, 770.
        See also Bioinformatics
Concentration gradients, **131**f, 134–135f, 136f–137
Concentrations, chemical reactions and, 41
Conception, human, 1028f
Condoms, 1032f
Conduction, animal heat exchange and, **879**f
Conduction, neuron action potential, 1069–1070
Cones (photoreceptor), **1113**f, 1114–1115f,
        1116–1117
Cones, gymnosperm, 633, 637f
Cone snails, 1061f, 1063f
Confocal microscopy, **95**f, 96

Conformer animals, **875**f
Congenital disorders, 254f
Conidia, **658**f
Conifers, 617, **633**–634f, 635, 637f
Conjugation, 574f–575, **600**f–601
Connective tissue, animal, 76f, **872**f
Connell, Joseph, 1210f
Conodonts, **718**f–719
Consanguineous mating, human, 283–284
Conservation Areas, Costa Rican, 1268f
Conservation biology, **1254**. *See also* Ecology
    biodiversity and, 1254f–1261f
    conservation of mollusc species, 696f
    genomics and proteomics in, 88f
    global change and, 1269–1270f, 1271f–1275f
    landscape and regional conservation in, 1265–
        1266f, 1267f–1269f
    logistic population growth model in, 1194
    population conservation in, 1261f–1264f, 1265
    species-area curves of species richness in,
        1226f–1227f
    sustainable development in, 1276f–1277f
Conservation of energy, 143–144
Conservation of mass, law of, 1234
Conservative model, DNA replication, 319f–320f
Conserved Domain Database (CDD), 439f
Constant (C) region, light and heavy chain, 953f
Constipation, 905
Consumers, 7, 186, 667f, 668
Consumption, regulation of animal, 911f–912
Continental drift, 476–477, 532f–533f, 534
Contour tillage, 803f
Contraception, 1032f–1033, 1202
Contractile proteins, 76f
Contractile vacuoles, **108**, 133f
Contraction, muscle, 1120–1121f, 1122. *See also*
        Muscle
Contrast, 94
Control center, homeostatic, 876
Control elements, **368**f–369f, 370–371f
Control groups, 20
Controlled experiments, **20**f–21
    designing, in Scientific Skills Exercise, 1008
Convection, animal heat exchange and, **879**f
Convergent evolution, **475**
    analogies and, 551f–552
    of cactus and euphorbs, 1166f
    of fast swimmers, 868f
    of homologies, 475f
    of marsupials, 737f
    in phylogenies, 547f–548f
Convergent extension, 1050f
Conversion, data, 262
Cooksonia, 616
Cooling, evaporative, 47–48, 880
Cooper, Vaughn, 572f
Cooperativity, **158**
    in allosteric activation, 158f
    prokaryotic metabolic, 576f–577
    science and, 21–23
Coordinately controlled genes, 361, 371
Coordination, cell-signaling response, 224–225f
Copepods, 703–704f
Coprophagy, 908
Copy-number variants (CNVs), 456
CoQ (coenzyme Q), 173
Coral atolls, 1176f
Coral reefs, 54, 608, **1176**f, 1228
Corals, 686f–687f
Corepressors, **362**f
Cork cambium, **760**f, 768
Cork cells, 768
Cormorant, flightless, 500f, 505
Corn. *See* Maize (corn); *Zea mays* (corn)
Cornea, 1112f
Corn smut, 663f
Corpus callosum, **1087**f, 1092
Corpus luteum, 1021f, 1027
Correlation coefficients in Scientific Skills Exercise,
        672, 745
Correlations, positive and negative, in Scientific Skills
        Exercise, 828
Correns, Karl, 309f

Corridors, movement, 1266f–1267
Cortex, **116, 757**, 764f
Cortical microfilaments, 116
Cortical nephrons, 980f, 985
Cortical reactions, 1039f–1040
Cortical rotation, 1054f
Cortisol, 996f
Corvids, 1141
Costanza, Robert, 1257
Costa Rica
    sustainable development in, 1276f
    tropical dry forest restoration project in, 1250f
    zoned reserves in, 1268f
Cost-benefit behavior analysis, 1143–1144
Cotransport, **136**f–137
Cotyledons, **641**, 822f–824f
Countercurrent exchange, **880**f, **935**f
Countercurrent multiplier systems, 984–985
Courtship rituals. *See also* Mating behavior
    behavioral isolation and, 502f
    external fertilization and, 1017
    forms of animal communication in, 1136f
    genetic basis of, 1149
    reproductive cycles and, 1015f
    sexual selection and, 493f–494f, 1146f–1147f, 1148
Covalent bonds, **36**
    of disaccharides, 69f
    in organic compounds, 58–59f, 60, 64
    in protein tertiary structure, 81f
    types of, 36f–37f
Cowbirds, 1215
Coyotes, 906–907f
Crabs, 703, 892f, 1208f
"Crank" drug, 62
Crassulacean acid metabolism (CAM) plants,
        203–**204**f, 792–793f
Crawling, 1127f, 1129
Crayfish, 934f, 1106
C-reactive protein (CRP), 932
Creatin phosphate, 1120, 1122
Crenarchaeota clade, 581
Cretaceous mass extinction, 535f
Creutzfeldt-Jakob disease, 405
Crick, Francis
    central dogma of, 337
    discovery of DNA molecular structure by, 3, 23,
        312f, 316f–318f
    model of DNA replication by, 318f–319f
Crickets, 443, 706f, 1106f
Cri du chat, 307
Crinoidea, 709f
Cristae, **110**
Critical habitat, population conservation and,
        1264f–1265
Critical load, **1270**
Crocodiles, 558f, 732
Crop (esophageal pouch), 899f, 908
Crop plants. *See also* Agriculture; Plant(s)
    artificial selection and breeding of, 829, 830–831
    biotechnology and genetic engineering of,
        831–832f, 833–834
    effects of atmospheric carbon dioxide on, 203
    as polyploids, 509
    seed plants as, 645
    transgenic and genetically modified, 432–433
Crop rotation, **810**
Cross-fostering studies, **1138**t
Crossing over, **258, 300**
    chromosomal alterations during, 305–306f
    gene duplication due to unequal, 449f
    genetic variation from, 263–264f
    in meiosis, 258f, 260f
    recombination of linked genes in, 300–301f
Cross-pollination, **640**
    angiosperm, 640f–641
    G. Mendel's techniques of, 268f–269f
    of plants, 831
Cross-talk, cell-signaling, 225f
Crows, 1144
Crustaceans, 458f, 539f–540, 683f, 703f–704f
Crustose lichens, 662f
Cryolophosaurus, 519f–520

Cryptic coloration, 1212*f*
Cryptochromes, 850
Cryptomycota, 654
Crypts, 793*f*
Crystallin, 6*f*, 371*f*
Crystals, ice, 48*f*
C soil horizon, 800*f*
Ctenophora, 681*f*
C-terminus, 78*f*, 350
Cuatro ojos fish, 360*f*
Cuboidal epithelium, 871*f*
Cubozoans, 686*f*–687*f*
Cuckoo bee, 1212*f*
Cud, 908*f*
Culex pipiens (mosquito), 491
Culture, 1143, 1153*f*–54
Cupula, 1110*f*
Cuticle, ecdysozoan, 699, 701
Cuticle, exoskeleton, 1127
Cuticle, leaf, 757
Cuticle, plant, 616
Cuttings, plant, 423, 829, 843
Cutworms, 699
Cuvier, Georges, 463*f*, 464
Cyanobacteria
    blooms of, 1221
    bryophyte symbiosis with, 620*f*, 621
    chemical recycling by, 581
    evolution of glycolysis in, 179–180
    fungi and, as lichens, 658, 662*f*–663*f*
    land colonization by, 530
    metabolic cooperation in, 576*f*–577
    origin of photosynthesis in, 528
    photosynthesis by, 186*f*, 197, 579*f*
    protist endosymbiosis and photosynthetic, 592*f*–593*f*, 602*f*
    terrestrial, 612*f*
Cycads, 636*f*
Cyclic AMP (cyclic adenosine monophosphate, cAMP), 220*f*–221*f*, 364*f*, 997*f*, 1074
Cyclic data, graphing, in Scientific Skills Exercise, 1273
Cyclic electron flow, 196*f*–197
Cyclic GMP (cGMP), 221, 838*f*–839
Cyclin, 243–244*f*
Cyclin-dependent kinases (Cdks), 243–244*f*
Cycliophora, 682*f*
Cyclosporine, 664
Cyclostomes, 717
Cynodonts, 525*f*
Cysteine, 63*f*, 77*f*
Cystic fibrosis, 278–279, 284
Cystic kidney disease, 1058
Cytochromes, 173, 197, 229, 560
Cytogenetic maps, 304
Cytokines, 951, 994–995, 998
Cytokinesis, 234, 237*f*, 239–240*f*, 241*f*, 258*f*–259*f*
Cytokinins, 840*t*, 843–844*f*
Cytology, 96, 292
Cytoplasm, 98
    cell cycle control signals in, 243*f*
    cell-signaling responses in, 223*f*
    cytokinesis and division of, 234, 237*f*, 239–240*f*, 241*f*
    of prokaryotic and eukaryotic cells, 98–99
Cytoplasmic determinants, 377*f*
Cytoplasmic genes, 309
Cytoplasmic responses, cell-signaling, 223*f*
Cytoplasmic streaming, 117, 601
Cytosine, 85*f*–86, 315*f*–316
Cytoskeletons, 112
    actin microfilaments of, 113*t*, 115–116*f*, 117*f*
    animal cell, 100*f*
    ATP in mechanical work of, 150
    intermediate filaments of, 113*t*, 117
    membrane proteins and attachment to, 128*f*
    microtubules of, 113*t*, 114*f*–115*f*, 116*f*
    in morphogenesis, 1050*f*–1051
    plant cell, 101*f*
    structure and function of, 113*t*
    support and motility roles of, 112*f*–113*f*
Cytosol, 97
Cytosolic calcium ions, 838*f*–839

Cytotoxic chemotherapy, 387*f*
Cytotoxic T cells, 959*f*

D

dalton (atomic mass unit), 31, 50
Dalton, John, 31
Dance language, honeybee, 1136–1137*f*
Dandelions, 1*f* (facing page), 820*f*, 826*f*, 1187*f*, 1196*f*
Dangl, Jeffery, 751*f*, 807*f*
Danio rerio (zebrafish) model organism, 23
Daphnia (water flea), 442*t*, 1015, 1193*f*–1194
Darkness
    flowering in long-night plants and, 853*f*–854
    plant etiolation response to, 837*f*
Dark responses, rod cell, 1115*f*
D'Arrigo, Rosanne, 767*f*
Darwin, Charles. *See also* Evolution
    on barnacles, 704
    Beagle voyage and field research of, 465–466*f*, 467*f*
    on coevolution of flower-pollinator mutualism, 821
    on earthworms, 698
    evidence supporting theory of, 471*f*–476*f*, 477
    on grandeur of evolutionary process, 478
    historical context of life and ideas of, 463*f*–465*f*
    on island species, 477
    on lung evolution from swim bladders, 722
    on mystery of flowering plants, 471, 641, 817*f*
    on mystery of speciation, 500
    on natural selection, 264–265*f*, 481
    On the Origin of Species by Means of Natural Selection by, 463, 467, 477, 478
    speciation theory of, 467–468*f*, 469*f*–470*f*
    on species diversity of tropics, 1226
    study by, of phototropism in grass coleoptiles, 841*f*
    theory of descent with modification by, 12*f*–15*f*
    timeline of work of, 463*f*
Darwin, Francis, 841*f*
Data, 16, 16*f*, 18*f*, 21
Databases
    in estimating reproductive rates, 1188–1189*f*
    genome-sequence, 438–439*f*
Dating, radiometric, 32, 33, 524*f*
dATP, 322
Daughter cells, 232*f*–233, 234*f*–235
Day-neutral plants, 853*f*
db gene, 912
DDT pesticide, 157, 1271*f*
Dead zone, 1270*f*
Deamination, amino acid, 180
Deaths
    demographics of, 1186–1187*f*, 1188*f*–1189*f*, 1190
    in density-dependent population growth, 1197*f*–1199*f*
    in exponential population growth, 1190–1191*f*
    in human population dynamics, 1202–1203
    in population dynamics, 1186*f*
Death signals, apoptosis, 228*f*–229. *See also* Apoptosis
Decapods, 703*f*
Decay curves, radioactive isotope, 33
December solstice, 1161*f*
Deciduous forest, nutrient cycling in, 1247–1248*f*
Declining-population approach, population conservation, 1264*f*–1265
Decomposers, 581, 1234
    in energy flow and chemical recycling, 7*f*, 1234*f*–1235*f*
    fungi as, 649, 652*f*, 655*f*, 658–661
    lichens as, 663
    prokaryotic, 580–581
Decomposition, biogeochemical cycle, 1244, 1246–1247*f*
Deconvolution microscopy, 95*f*, 96
Deductive reasoning, 17
Deep-sea hydrothermal vents, 520–521*f*, 1176*f*
Deer, 333*f*, 336, 1144–1145
Deer mice, 492*f*, 886
DEET insect repellant, 1117
De-etiolation (greening), 837*f*–838*f*, 839
Defensive adaptations, prey, 28*f*, 1211–1212*f*, 1213*f*
Defensive proteins, 76*f*
Deficiencies, plant, 804, 806*f*, 811

Deforestation
    experimental, and nutrient cycling, 1247–1248*f*
    greenhouse gases and, 1274
    as human community disturbance, 1225
    loss of species from, 1254–1255*f*
    rising atmospheric carbon dioxide levels from, 1272–1273*f*, 1274
    threats to biodiversity from, 1255*f*
    of tropical rain forests, 645*f*–646
Degradation, protein, 373
Dehydration
    animal, 974
    plant, 201–202*f*, 203–204*f*, 530
Dehydration reactions, 67*f*
Dehydrogenases, 165, 167
Delayed reproduction, 1202
Deletions (mutations), 356*f*
Deletions, chromosome, 305–306*f*, 307
Delta proteobacteria, 578*f*
Dementia, 1097–1098*f*
Demographics, population, 1186–1187*f*, 1188*f*–1189, 1190
Demographic transition, 1202
Demography, 1186. *See also* Demographics, population
Denaturation, 82*f*–83
Dendrites, 873*f*, 1062*f*, 1073, 1104*f*
Dendritic cells, 950
Dendrobates pumilio, 518
Dendrochronology, 767*f*
Density, population, 1185–1186*f*, 1196*f*–1199*f*
Density-dependent inhibition, 245–246*f*
Density-dependent population change, 1197*f*–1199*f*
Density-dependent selection (*K*-selection), 1196*f*–1197
Density-independent population change, 1197
Density-independent selection (*R*-selection), 1196*f*–1197
Dentition, 524–525*f*, 526, 906*f*
Deoxyribose, 85*f*–86, 315*f*, 322
Dephosphorylation, protein, 220
Depolarization, 1039, 1066*f*–1067*f*, 1068*f*
Depolymerization, protein, 238
Depression, 1075, 1097
Derivatives, cell, 760
Derived characters, shared, 554*f*–555
Derived traits, land plant, 613–614*f*, 615–616
Dermal tissue system, plant, 756–757*f*
DES (diethylstilbestrol), 1009
Descent with modification theory, 12*f*–15*f*, 463, 466–467*f*, 477–478. *See also* Evolution
Desert ant, 867*f*–868
Desert camels, 974
Desert iguana, 883
Desert mice, 975
Deserts, 792–793*f*, 1163*f*, 1167*f*, 1233*f*
Desiccation, 974, 1180
Desmosomes, 120*f*
Desynchronization, 852–853
Determinate cleavage, 675*f*
Determinate growth, 760*f*–761*f*
Determination, 378–379*f*, 1051
Detoxification, 104–105, 111, 803
Detritivores, 1234*f*–1235*f*
Detritus, 1171, 1234–1235*f*
Deuteromycetes, 653
Deuterostome development, 675*f*–676
Deuterostomes, 676–677*f*, 683*f*, 707–708*f*, 709*f*, 713*f*, 1044. *See also* Chordates; Echinoderms
Development, 769
    as cell division function, 232–233*f*
    brain, 716*f*, 1086*f*, 1093–1094
    embryonic (*see* Embryonic development)
    in human life cycle, 255*f*–256 (*see also* Human embryonic development)
    macroevolution of, 539*f*–540*f*, 541
    plant and animal, 888*f* (*see also* Animal development; Plant development)
    at points in life cycles, 1038*f*
    postzygotic barriers and, 503*f*, 504
    as property of life, 1*f*
    sustainable (*see* Sustainable development)

Developmental biology, 1037*f*–1038*f*
Developmental genes. *See* Homeotic genes; *Hox* genes
Developmental plasticity, 769*f*
Developmental potential, cell fate and, 1054–1055*f*
Diabetes
    aquaporin mutations as causes of diabetes insipidus, 989*f*
    autoimmunity and, 965
    disruption of glucose homeostasis in, 910–911
    genetic engineering of insulin to treat, 430
Diabetes mellitus, **910**–911
Diacodexis, 476
Diacylglycerol (DAG), **222***f*
Diagnosis
    antibodies as tools in, 963
    biotechnology in, 428
Diaphragm, birth control, 1032*f*
Diaphragm, breathing and, **939***f*
Diapsids, **730**
Diarrhea, 136–137, 221, 583, 590*f*, 905
Diastole phase, **921***f*
Diastolic pressure, **924**–925*f*
Diatomaceous earth, 596
Diatoms, 242*f*, 591*f*, **595***f*–596, 1164
Diazepam, 1075
Dicots, **643***f*–644*f*
Dictyostelium discoideum, 606, 607*f*
Dideoxy (dideoxyribonucleotide) chain termination DNA sequencing, 409*f*–410*f*, 437
Diencephalon, 1087*f*
Diets. *See also* Food
    adaptations of vertebrate digestive systems for, 906*f*–908*f*
    assessing nutritional needs in, 896–897
    catabolism and human, 180*f*–181
    deficiencies in, 895*f*–896*f*
    essential nutrients for, 893*f*, 894*t*–895*t*
    genetic variation in prey selection and, 1150*f*
    nonheritable variation and, 482*f*
    phenylketonuria and, 486
    typical and opportunistic, 892*f*–893
Differential centrifugation, 96*f*
Differential gene expression, **365**. *See also* Gene regulation
    cytoplasmic determinants and induction in, 377*f*–378
    in eukaryotic gene regulation, 365*f*–366
    in gene regulation, 360*f*
    in pattern formation of body plans, 379–380*f*, 381*f*–382*f*, 383
    in processes of embryonic development, 376*f*–377 (*see also* Embryonic development)
    sequential regulation of, during cellular differentiation, 378–379*f*
Differential-interference microscopy, **95***f*
Differential reproductive success, 264–265*f*
Differential speciation success, 542–543
Differentiation, cell, **376**
    cytokinins in, 844
    as embryonic development process, 376*f*–377 (*see also* Embryonic development)
    plant development and, 757, 769, 773*f*
    sequential gene regulation in, 378–379*f*
    stem cells and, 425*f* (*see also* Stem cells)
Differentiation, determination vs., **1051**
Diffusion, **131**
    body surface area and, 689*f*
    effects on water balance of osmosis as, 131*f*–133*f*
    free energy change and, 146*f*
    interpreting scatter plots on glucose uptake as, 134
    as passive transport, 130–131*f*
    in plant cells, 207*f*
    proteins and facilitated, 133*f*
    of water across plant plasma membranes, 782–784, 785*f*
    of water and minerals into root cells, 786
Digestion, **897**
    in animal food processing, 897*f*
    digestive compartments in, 897*f*–899*f*, 900
    digestive systems and, 869*f*
    extracellular, 899*f*–900
    feeding mechanisms and, 898*f*
    fungal, 649, 662

hydrolysis in, 67
    intracellular, 899
    lysosomes in intracellular, 107*f*–108
    regulation of animal, 908–909*f*
    sea star, 707–708*f*
    in small intestine, 902–903*f*, 904*f*–905*f*
    in stomach, 901–902*f*
    vertebrate adaptations for, 906*f*–908*f*
Digestive enzymes, 76*f*
Digestive systems
    adaptations of, 906*f*–908*f*
    alimentary canal of, 900*f*
    feedback regulation of, 908–909*f*
    internal exchange surfaces and, 869*f*
    large intestine in, 905*f*–906
    oral cavity, pharynx, and esophagus in, 900–901*f*
    small intestine in, 902–903*f*, 904*f*–905*f*
    stomach in, 901–902*f*
Digger wasps, 1140*f*
Dihybrid crosses, **273**–274*f*
Dihybrids, **273**–274*f*
Dihydrofolate reductase (DHFR), 605*f*
Dihydroxyacetone, 68*f*
Dijkstra, Cor, 1196*f*
Dikaryotic mycelia, **651**
Dimetrodon fossil, 523*f*
Dimers, tubulin, 114
Dimorphism, sexual, 1145*f*
Dinoflagellates, 141*f*, 242*f*, **598***f*
Dinosaurs, **730**
    blood pressure of, 925
    C. Darwin and, 12*f*
    disappearance of, 673
    as early reptiles, 730
    flying, 1130
    in fossil record, 519*f*–520, 523*f*, 558*f*
    mass extinction of, 535*f*, 536
    in Mesozoic era, 526
Dioecious species, **828**–829*f*
Diphtheria, 398
Diploblastic animals, **674**
Diploid cells, **255**
    genetic variation preserved in recessive alleles of, 494
    haploid cells vs., 255
    mitosis vs. meiosis in, 260–261*f*, 262
    in sexual life cycles, 256*f*–257
Diplomonads, **593**
Dipnoi (lungfishes), 723–724
Diptera, 706*f*
Direct contact, cell signaling by, 212*f*
Direct inhibition hypothesis, 844
Directionality, DNA replication, 322–323*f*, 324*f*
Directional selection, **492***f*
Disaccharides, 69*f*
Diseases, animal
    density-dependent population regulation by, 1198*f*
    movement corridors and spread of, 1267
    viral, 394*f*, 401*f*, 402–403*f*, 404–405, 406*f*
Diseases, plant
    community structure and pathogens in, 1228
    density-dependent population regulation by, 1198*f*
    disease-resistant genes and, 860
    disease-suppressive soil and, 584
    prokaryotes in protection against, 584
    viral, 393*f*, 394*f*, 405
Diseases and disorders, human
    adenoviruses and, 394*f*–395
    alkaptonuria, 334
    allergies, 964–965*f*
    Alzheimer's disease, 406, 1097–1098*f*
    amebic dysentery, 607
    amytrophic lateral sclerosis (ALS), 1122
    antibiotic resistance and, 472*f*–473
    asthma, 62
    atherosclerosis, 74, 75, 137, 931*f*–932
    autism, 1094
    autoimmune, 965*f*
    bacterial, 398, 568–569*f*, 570, 583*f*
    biotechnology in diagnosis and treatment of, 428–429*f*, 430*f*
    cachexia, 1010
    cancer (*see* Cancer)

    cardiovascular diseases, 74, 931*f*–932
    cholera, 221
    color blindness, 297*f*, 1116*f*
    community ecology, pathogens, and, 1228–1229*f*
    cri du chat and chronic myelogenous leukemia (CML), 307*f*
    cystic fibrosis, 284
    cystic kidney disease, 1058
    density-dependent population regulation by, 1198*f*
    detecting fetal, during pregnancy, 1033
    diabetes (*see* Diabetes)
    diarrhea, 136–137
    dominantly inherited, 285*f*
    Down syndrome, 305, 306*f*–307
    drug addiction, 1097*f*
    Duchenne muscular dystrophy, 297
    due to chromosomal alterations, 304–305*f*, 306*f*–307*f*
    emerging viruses and, 402–403, 404–405, 406*f*
    endocrine disruptors and, 1009
    endometriosis, 1027
    epilepsy, 1092
    erectile dysfunction, 1076
    familial cardiomyopathy, 355*f*
    faulty apoptosis in nervous system and, 229
    faulty cell-surface receptors and, 214, 215*f*, 217
    flatworm parasites and, 690*f*–691*f*
    flesh-eating disease, 472*f*–473
    fungal, 664
    gastric ulcers and acid reflux, 902
    genetic (*see* Genetic disorders)
    genomics and proteomics in, 88*f*, 251
    gonorrhea, 570
    gout, 977
    growth-related, 1005*f*
    heart murmurs, 922
    hemophilia, 297–298, 931
    HIV/AIDS (*see* AIDS (acquired immunodeficiency syndrome); HIV (human immunodeficiency virus))
    Hodgkin's disease, 966
    Huntington's disease, 285
    hypercholesterolemia, 137
    hypertension, 932
    immune system disruptions and, 964–965*f*, 966–968*f*
    immunization against, 963
    immunodeficiency, 966
    influenza, 394*f*–395, 402–403*f*, 404–405
    insects as carriers of, 707
    iodine deficiency and goiter, 29
    Kartagener's syndrome, 1058*f*
    karyotypes and, 254*f*
    Klinefelter syndrome, 307
    Leber's congenital amaurosis (LCA), 1116
    lymphatic system and, 927
    major depressive disorder and bipolar disorder, 1097
    malaria (*see* Malaria)
    mitochondrial, 309
    mosaicism, 298
    multifactorial, 285
    mutations and, 355*f*–356*f*, 357
    myasthenia gravis, 1122
    myotonia and epilepsy, 1070
    nematode parasites and trichinosis, 699*f*–700
    of nervous system, 1096–1099
    neurodegenerative, 406
    neurotransmitters and, 1074–1076
    from ozone depletion, 1275
    parasitic (*see* Parasites)
    Parkinson's disease, 406, 1075, 1098
    phenylketonuria, 486–487
    pleiotropy and inherited, 278–279
    pneumonia, 313*f*, 573
    polydactyly, 278
    protein misfolding and, 83
    protists and, 590*f*–591*f*
    recessively inherited, 283*f*–284*f*, 285
    respiratory distress syndrome (RDS), 938*f*
    retinitis pigmentosa, 489
    schizophrenia, 1096*f*
    sexually transmitted diseases (STDs) (*see* Sexually transmitted diseases (STDs))

sickle-cell disease (see Sickle-cell disease)
sleeping sickness, 594f
spina bifida, 1048–1049
Tay-Sachs disease and lysosomal storage, 108, 278, 283–284, 286–287f
testing genetic markers for, 421–422f
thyroid, 1004f–1005f
Turner syndrome, 307
Vitamin A deficiency, 896
Wiskott-Aldrich syndrome (WAS), 227
xeroderma pigmentosum, 326
X-linked disorders, 297f–298
Disease-suppressive soil, 584
Disorder, entropy and, 144
Disparity, vertebrate, 713
Dispersal, **1178**
  fruit and seed, 826f
  movement corridors and, 1266f–1267
  seed, 639f
  in species distributions, 1178
Dispersion, population, **1185**, 1186–1187f
Dispersive model, DNA replication, 319f–320f
Disruptive selection, **492f**
Dissociation, water, 51
Distal control elements, 368
Distal tubule, **981f**, 982–983f
Distance vision, 1116f
Distribution patterns, analyzing, 281
Distributions, species. See Species distributions
Disturbances, **1166**, **1222f**–1225f
Disulfide bridges, **81f**
Divergence
  allopatric speciation and, 505f–507f
  of angiosperms, 641f–642
  of closely related species, 454f–455, 456
  of fungi, 653f–654
  in phylogenetic trees, 549–550f, 551
  of unikonts from other eukaryotes, 605f
Diversity
  B cell and T cell, 955f–960
  biological (see Biodiversity)
  evolution and, 462f, 467
  scientific, 23–24
  within a species, 501f
Diving mammals, respiratory adaptations of, 943f
Division, cell. See Cell division
Dixon, Henry, 788
Dizygotic twins, 1030
Dizziness, 1110
DNA (deoxyribonucleic acid), **5**, **84**. See also
    Chromosomes; Gene(s); Genetics; Nucleic acids
  analysis of Neanderthal, 747f
  analyzing DNA deletion experiments, 370
  in bacterial binary fission, 240–241f
  "barcode," 1216
  bending of, 368–369f
  in cancer cells, 247–248
  changes of, in meiosis of yeast cells, 262
  Chargaff's rules on structure of, 315f–316
  complementary DNA (see Complementary DNA
    (cDNA))
  components of, 85f–86
  discovery of structure of, 3, 23, 312f, 316f–318f
  diseases of mitochondrial, 309f
  distribution of, during eukaryotic cell division, 233f–234f, 235
  in ecological forensics, 1259
  elevation and UV damage to, affecting species
    distributions, 1180f
  eukaryotic, 4f–5, 97f–98, 102, 103f
  evidence for, as genetic material, 313f–315f, 316
  evolutionary significance of mutations of, 326
  evolution of genomes from changes in, 448f–451f, 452
  in expression and transmission of genetic
    information, 5f–6f, 7
  gene density and noncoding, 444
  genetic code for, 337–338f, 339f–340
  genetic variation due to mutations in, 482–483
  genomics, bioinformatics, and proteomics in study
    of, 6f–7
  genomics and proteomics in study of, 87–88f
  homeoboxes in, 457f–458f

human gene microarray chips containing, 441f–442
  inheritance of, in chromosomes and genes, 253
  as measure of evolution, 89
  methylation of, 366–367, 386
  molecular homologies and, 474, 551f–553f
  ozone depletion and damage to, 1275
  p53 gene and repair of, 384
  packing of proteins and, into chromosomes, 328f–330f
  phylogenies based on, 547f
  in plant cells, 206f
  programming of cells by viral, 313f–314f, 315
  prokaryotic, 4f–5, 97f–98, 571f, 573f–574f, 575, 577
  proofreading and repairing of, 325–326f
  recombinant (see Recombinant DNA)
  repetitive noncoding, 444f–445f, 446
  replication of (see DNA replication)
  roles of, in gene expression, 84f–85
  sequencing of (see DNA sequencing)
  simple sequence and short-tandem repeat (STR), 446
  species identity in mitochondrial, 551f
  structure of, 86–87f
  technology of (see DNA technology)
  testing of, in forensic science, 430–431f
  in transcription, 336–337f
  viral, 394f–397f, 398t–400 (see also DNA viruses)
  in vitro amplification of, using polymerase chain
    reaction, 414–415f
DNA "barcode," 1216
DNA bending, 445
DNA chips, 419, 421
DNA cloning, **412**
  copying DNA with gene cloning and, 412f–413
  expressing cloned eukaryotic genes in, 416–417
  in gene therapy, 428–429f
  using restriction enzymes to make recombinant
    DNA plasmids for, 413f–414
  in vitro amplification of DNA using polymerase
    chain reaction in, 414–415f
DNA Data Bank of Japan, 438
DNA deletion experiments in Scientific Skills
    Exercise, 370
DNA ligases, **323f**, 324f, 325t, 326f, 413f–**414**
DNA methylation, **366f**–367, 386, 425
DNA microarray assays, **419**, 421
DNA pol I and pol III, 324f, 325t
DNA polymerases, **322f**
DNA profiles, 1217
DNA replication, **312**
  base pairing to template strands in
    semiconservative model of, 318f–319f, 320f
  errors in, and genome evolution, 449f–451f
  evolutionary significance of mutations during, 326
  inheritance and, 5f–6f
  in molecular basis of inheritance, 312 (see also
    Molecular basis of inheritance)
  proofreading and repairing of DNA during, 325–326f
  steps of, 320f–325f
  of telomeres, 326–327f
DNA replication complex, 324f–325f
DNA sequences
  analyzing phylogenetic trees based on, to
    understand viral evolution, 404
  animal phylogeny and, 676–677f, 678
  constructing phylogenetic trees using, 556–557f, 558
  evaluating molecular homologies in, 552f–553f
  exon and intron, 343f–344f, 345f
  genes as, 357
  interpreting sequence logos for, 349
  noncoding, 443
  promoter and terminator, 340–341
  types of, in human genome, 444f
DNA sequencing, **409**
  of complementary DNA, 421
  in genetic testing for cancer predisposition, 388
  genome sequencing and, 437f–438
  genomics, bioinformatics, proteomics, and, 6f–7, 87–88f
  human genome sequencing by, 408f, 412

standard vs. next-generation techniques for, 409f–411f, 412
  systems biology, medicine, and, 441f–442
  three-domain taxonomy system and, 11f
DNA strands, 5f–6f, 316f–318f, 338, 413f–414. See
    also DNA replication
DNA technology, **408**
  amplifying DNA with polymerase chain reaction
    (PCR) in, 414–415f, 416
  in analyzing gene expression and function,
    417–418f, 419f–420, 421f–422f
  bioinformatics and, 438–439f, 440–441f, 442
  in biotechnology applications, 409, 428–429f,
    430–431f, 432–433 (see also Biotechnology)
  in breast cancer treatment, 248
  creating recombinant DNA plasmids using
    restriction enzymes and gel electrophoresis
    in, 413f–414f
  DNA cloning and gene cloning in, 412f–413
  DNA sequencing in, 408–411f, 412
  in ecological forensics, 1259f
  in eukaryotic gene regulation, 366
  in expressing cloned eukaryotic genes, 416–417
  genetic code and gene transplantation in, 339f
  organismal cloning in, 422–423f, 424f–427f
  science, society, and, 23f
DNA testing, forensic, 430–431f
DNA viruses, 394f–397, 398t–399, 400
Dobzhansky, Theodosius, 10
Dodder, 836f–837
Dog rose, 644f
Dolly (cloned lamb), 424f–425, 1260
Dolphins, 475f–476f, 880f, 1088, 1185f–1186, 1256f
Domains, protein, **344**–345f, 438–439f, 440, 670
Domains, taxonomy, 11f, 454f, **548**–549f, 562–563f,
    580t. See also Archaea, domain; Bacteria,
    domain; Eukarya, domain
Domestication, plant, 645
Dominance, degrees of, 277f–278
Dominant alleles, **270**–271f, 277f–278, 285f. See also
    Alleles
Dominantly inherited disorders, human, 285f
Dominant species, **1220**
Dominant traits, 269–270t
Dopamine, **1075t**, 1096, 1097f, 1098
Doppler, Christian, 268
Dormancy, endospore, 570f–571
Dormancy, seed, 633, **822**–823, 827–828, 846
Dormouse, 887
Dorsal lips, blastopore, **1045f**, 1056f
Dorsal sides, **673**
Dorsal-ventral axis, 1054f
Double bonds, **36**–37, 60f
Double circulation, **918**–919f, 920
Double fertilization, 640f–**641**, **818**–819f
Double helix, DNA, 5f–6, **86**–87f, 312f, 316f,
    317–318f, 328f
Double-stranded DNA (dsDNA) viruses, 398t, 400
Double-stranded RNA (dsRNA) viruses, 398t
Douglas fir, 637f
Dowling, Herndon, 882f
Down syndrome, 254f, 305, **306f**–307
Dragonflies, 881f
Drip irrigation, 802
Drosophila melanogaster (fruit fly). See also Fruit flies
  alternative RNA splicing in, 373
  analyzing single-gene expression in, 417–418f, 419f
  changes in developmental genes of, 539f–540
  complete genome sequence for, 436f
  courtship behaviors of, 1136f
  diploid and haploid numbers of, 255
  female bias in sperm usage of, 1018f
  foraging genes of, 1143f
  gene density of fungi vs., 659t
  genetic basis of behavior in, 1149
  genetic variation of, 481f–82f
  genome size and number of genes of, 442t–443
  homeotic genes in, 457f–458f
  inducible innate immune response in, 948f, 949f
  linkage maps of, 303f–304f
  linked genes and, 299f–301f
  as model organism, 23, 294f–295f, 1037–1038
  natural selection and adaptive evolution of, 488

one gene-one enzyme hypothesis on, 334
pattern formation of body plan of, 379–380f, 381f–382f
phylogenetic trees of, 555f–56f
protecting, against infection using antimicrobial peptide, 948f, 949f
Drosophila species (fruit flies), 506f, 516, 561
Drought
    abscisic acid in plant tolerance to, 846
    American Dust Bowl and, 801f
    plant responses to, 857
Drugs, 472f–473. *See also* Medicine; Pharmaceutical products
    addiction to, 1097f
    antibiotic (*see* Antibiotic drugs)
    antiviral, 402
    biotechnology in production of, 429–430f
    cocktails of, in AIDS treatment, 483
    enantiomers in, 62f
    as environmental toxins, 1271–1272f
    fungi and, 664–665
    molecular shape and, 40f, 79
    plant-derived, 645t–646
    species and genetic diversity and, 1257
    from sponges, 685
    tolerance of, 104–105
Dryas, 1224f
Dry fruits, 639f
Duchenne muscular dystrophy, **297**
Duckweed, 101f
Ducts, male reproductive, 1019f
Dulse, 603f
Dune fescue grass, 1197f
Dunstan, William, 1237f
Duodenum, **902**–3
Duplications, chromosome, **305**–306f, 448f–450f
Duplications, gene, 483, 559f–560
Dusky salamanders, 507
Dust Bowl, American, 801f
Dust mites, 702f
Dwarfism, 285f, 430, 1005
Dynamics, population, 1186f, 1198–1199f, 1200f–1201f. *See also* Population growth
Dyneins, **115**
Dysentery, 575, 607

E
Eagles, 1256f
Ear bones, mammalian, 524, 735f
Eardrum, 1106, **1107**f
Ears. *See also* Hearing
    bones of mammalian, 524, 735f
    human, 1107f
    insect, 1106f
Earth. *See also* Biosphere; Global ecology
    development of photosynthesis and atmospheric oxygen on, 528f
    importance of seed plants to ecosystems of, 630f
    importance of water on, 44
    mass extinctions of life on, 534f–536f
    origins of life on, 57f–58, 520f–521f, 522
    plate tectonics of, 532f–533f, 534
Earthworms, 698f, 801, 899f, 917f, 979f
Eastern box turtle, 730f
Eastern glass lizard, 547f–548f
Ebola virus, 402
Ecdysis. *See* Molting (ecdysis)
Ecdysozoans, **677**f
    arthropods, 700f–706f, 707 (*see also* Arthropods)
    nematodes, 699f–700
    phylogeny of, 682f–683f
Ecdysteroid, 1001f–1002
Echidnas, 736f
Echinoderms, 683f, **707**–708f, 709f, 1039f, 1041f, 1080f, 1127
Echinoidea, 709f
Ecological footprint, **1204**f–1205
Ecological forensics, 1259f
Ecological niches, **1209**–1210f
Ecological species concept, **504**
Ecological succession, **1223**–1224f, 1225f

Ecological time, 1172
Ecology, **1158**. *See also* Community ecology; Conservation biology; Ecosystem ecology; Global ecology; Landscape ecology; Organismal ecology; Population ecology
    biogeochemical cycles in, 1246
    factors of, in evolutionary rates, 532
    genomics and proteomics in, 88f
    as interactions between organisms and environment, 1158f
    mosses in, 621f–622f
    prokaryotes in, 581f–582, 583–584f, 585f
    roles of fungi in, 661f–664f
    scope and fields of, 1159f
    seedless vascular plants in, 627–628
    urban, 1269
Ecosystem diversity, 1255f–1256f
Ecosystem ecology, **1159**f, 1246. *See also* Ecology; Ecosystems
Ecosystem engineers, **1220**f
Ecosystems, **1159**f, **1232**, 1242f–1243f
    biogeochemical cycles in, 1244f–1248f
    characteristics and dynamics of, 1232f–1233f
    diversity of, 1255f–1256f
    edges between, 1265f–1266f
    effects of mass extinctions on, 536f
    energy flow and chemical cycling in, 7f, 162–163f, 1233–1234f
    fungi in, 661f–664f
    importance of mosses to, 621f–622f
    importance of seedless vascular plants to, 627–628
    importance of seed plants to, 630f
    interactions in, 8f
    as level of biological organization, 2f
    metagenomics and genome sequencing of species in, 438
    primary production in, 1235f–1238f, 1239
    prokaryotes in, 581f–582
    protists in, 608f–609f
    restoration ecology and restoration of degraded, 1248f–1251f
    secondary production in, 1239f–1240f, 1241f
Ecosystem services, **1257**
Ecotones, **1166**
Ectoderm, **674**, **1044**f, 1045f
Ectomycorrhizae, **810**–811
Ectomycorrhizal fungi, **650**, 655f
Ectoparasites, **1214**
Ectopic cells and tissue, **1027**
Ectopic pregnancies, 1029
Ectoprocts, 681f, **692**f
Ectothermic organisms, **730**, **878**f, 881f–882, 884–885
Edema, 927
Edges, ecosystem, 1265f–1266f
Ediacaran biota, 523f, 529, **670**f–671
Edidin, Michael, 126f
Effective population size, 63
Effector cells, **956**
Effectors, **860**
Effector-triggered immunity, 860
Efferent neurons, 1083f
Efficiency, cell-signaling, 225f–227
Egg-polarity genes, **381**
Eggs, **1014**
    amniotic, 728–729f
    amphibian, 727
    of birds and dinosaurs, 558f
    Burmese python thermogenesis for incubating, 882f
    in embryonic development, 376f–377
    as female gametes, 1014, 1017–1018f
    in fertilization, 1039f–1040f
    human, 234–235, 1021, 1028f
    human oogenesis and, 1023f
    nitrogenous wastes and, 977
    ovules and production of, in seed plants, 632f
Ejaculation, **1019**
Ejaculatory duct, 1019f
Elastic fibers, 872f
Elastin, 76f
Eldredge, Niles, 514
Electrically charged side chains, 76–77f

Electrical signals
    neuron, 874f, 1061–1062 (*see also* Neurons)
    phloem and symplastic, 796f
Electrical synapses, 1071. *See also* Synapses
Electric eels, 1105
Electrocardiogram (ECG or EKG), **922**f
Electrochemical gradients, **135**–136f
Electroencephalogram (EEG), 1088f
Electrogenic pump, **136**f
Electrolytes, blood plasma, 928f
Electromagnetic receptors, **1104**–1105f
Electromagnetic spectrum, **190**f
Electron distribution diagrams, 34f, 35f, 37f
Electronegativity, 37
Electron microscope (EM), **94**, 95f
Electrons, **30**
    chemical properties and distribution of, 34f–35
    cyclic flow of, in light reactions of photosynthesis, 196f–197
    in electron transport chains, 165f–166f
    energy levels of, 32f–34
    linear flow of, in light reactions of photosynthesis, 195f–196f
    orbitals of, 35f
    in organic compounds, 58–59f, 60
    in redox reactions, 163–164f
    as subatomic particles, 30f–31
Electron shells, 32f–**33**, 34f–35f
Electron transport chains, **166**
    in anaerobic respiration and fermentation, 177–178
    in cellular respiration, 165f–166f
    in chemiosmosis, 173–174f, 175
    in oxidative phosphorylation, 172f–173
Electrophysiologists, 1066f
Electroporation, **417**
Elements, **29**t–**34**f, 35, 803
Elephantiasis, 927
Elephants, 88f, 468f, 1191f, 1259
Elephant seals, 943f, 993f, 1261
Elevation
    climate and, 1163f
    ultraviolet (UV) light damage at, 1180f
Elicitors, 860
Elimination, **897**f, 905f–906
Elk, 1145f
Elkhorn coral, 1228
Elongation, antiparallel DNA strand, 322–323f, 324f–325f
Elongation factors, 350
Elongation stage
    transcription, 340f, 342f
    translation, 350f
Elton, Charles, 1218
Elvis monkey, 1254f
Embryo(s). *See also* Embryonic development
    anatomical homologies of vertebrate, 473f–474
    ensuring survival of, 1017f
    land plant, 614f
    maternal immune tolerance of, 1031
    monocot vs. eudicot, 643f
Embryo development, plant, 822f–823f
Embryology, 1037
Embryonic development. *See also* Differential gene expression
    analyzing single-gene expression in, 417f–418f, 419f
    animal, 668f–669 (*see also* Animal development)
    cell division, cell differentiation, and morphogenesis in, 376f–377
    cytoplasmic determinants and induction in, 377f–378
    genomic imprinting and, 308f–309
    human (*see* Human embryonic development)
    pattern formation of body plans in, 379–380f, 381f–382f, 383
    sequential gene regulation in, 378–379f
Embryonic lethals, **380**–381f
Embryonic stem (ES) cells, 425f–426f
Embryophytes, 613f, **614**f
Embryo sacs, 640f, **818**–819f
Emergent properties, **4**
    of compounds, 29f

integration of Mendelian inheritance with, 280–281
levels of biological organization and, 2f–3f, 4
of water (see Water)
weak chemical bonds and, 38
Emerging diseases, human, 1228
Emerging viruses, 402–403f, 404–405
Emigration, population dynamics of, **1186**f, 1190–1191f, 1200–1201f
Emotions, 1089f–1090
Emu, 733f
Enantiomers, **61**f–62f
Encephalitis, 402
ENCODE (Encyclopedia of DNA Elements), 440, 444
Endangered species, 1194f, **1256**f, 1267
Endangered Species Act (ESA), 1256
Endemic species, **477**
Endergonic reactions, 146–**147**f
Endocarp, 826f
Endocrine disruptors, 1009, 1271f
Endocrine glands, **998**
  adrenal gland, 1006–1007f, 1008
  gonads, 1008–1009f
  of human endocrine system, 998–999f
  in neuroendocrine signaling, 1002f–1005f
  parathyroid glands, 1006f
  pineal gland, 1009
  thyroid gland, 1004f–1005f
Endocrine signaling. See also Endocrine systems
  in cell signaling, 212–213f
  cellular response pathways for, 996f–998f, 1000f
  feedback regulation of, 1000f–1001
  hormones in, 993f–994f
Endocrine systems, **874**, **994**. See also Animal hormones
  cell signaling pathways of hormones and signaling molecules in, 993f–998f, 1000f
  coordination of nervous systems and, 994f, 995, 1000f–1005f (see also Neuroendocrine signaling)
  disruption of, 1009, 1271f
  endocrine glands and hormones of human, 998–999f
  evolution of hormone function in, 1010f
  feedback regulation of, 1000f–1001f, 1004f–1005f
  hormones and cell signaling in, 874f
  in regulation of blood pressure, 925
  in regulation of digestive systems, 909f
  regulatory functions of endocrine glands in, 1006f–1009f
Endocytosis, **137**–138f, 206f–207f
Endoderm, **674**, **1044**f, 1045f
Endodermis, **763**, **786**, 787f
Endomembrane system, **104**
  bound ribosomes and, 351–352
  elements of, 104–105f, 106f–109f
  signal mechanism for targeting polypeptides to, 352f
Endometriosis, **1027**
Endometrium, **1020**–1021f
Endoparasites, **1214**
Endophytes, **661**f–662, **807**
Endoplasmic reticulum (ER), **104**
  animal cell, 100f
  as biosynthetic factory, 104–105f
  cellular membrane synthesis and, 129f
  ribosomes and, 103f–104
  targeting polypeptides to, 351–352f
Endorphins, 40f, 79, **1075**t–1076
Endoskeletons, 1126f, **1127**–1128
Endosperm, **641**, **818**–819f, 822f–823f
Endospores, **569**f
Endosymbiont theory, **109**–110f, 187, **528**–529f
Endosymbiosis, 109–110f, 528–529f, **589**, 592f–593f, 602f
Endothelin, 925
Endothelium, blood vessel, **923**f, 926–927f
Endothermic organisms, **730**, **878**f, 881f–883f, 884–885
Endotoxins, **583**
Energetic hypothesis on food chain length, **1219**f
Energy, **32**, **142**
  animal (see Bioenergetics)

in Arctic tundra ecosystem, 1242f–1243f
ATP energy coupling and, 148–149f, 150f–151f
biofuel technology to reduce dependence on fossil fuels for, 832
chemiosmosis as energy-coupling mechanism, 173–174f, 175
conservation of, 1233
electrons and levels of, 32f–34
in energy flow and chemical cycling, 162–163f, 1233–1234f, 1235f, 1242f–1243f
enzymatic catalysis and (see Enzymatic catalysis)
forms of, 142–143f
free-energy change and (see Free-energy change)
global human use of, 1204f–1205
heat as, 46
laws of transformation of, 143f–144f, 145
life and transformations of, 141f
locomotion and, 1129–1131
metabolism and, 141 (see also Metabolism)
in photosynthesis, 41f
primary production of, in ecosystems, 1235–1236f, 1237f–1238f, 1239
regulation of storage of, in animal nutrition, 909–910f, 911f–912
secondary production of, in ecosystems, 1239f–1240f, 1241f
storage of, in fats, 74
transfer and transformation of, as theme of biology, 1f, 2, 7f
transformation of, by mitochondria and chloroplasts in eukaryotic cells, 109–110f, 111f
transformations of, in plant cells, 207f
Energy budgets
  animal, 886
  ecosystem, 1235–1236f, 1237f
Energy conservation, animal, 886–887f
Energy coupling, **148**–149f, 150f–151
Energy flow and chemical cycling, 7f, 162–163f, 1233–1234f, 1235f, 1242f–1243f. See also Biogeochemical cycles; Primary production; Secondary production
Engelmann, Theodor W., 192f
Enhancers, **368**f–369f
Entamoebas, 607
Enteric division, peripheral nervous system, 909, **1083**f–1084f
Enthalpy, 145
Entropy, **144**–145
Entry stage, phage lytic cycle, 396f
Enveloped viruses, 396, 398–399f
Environment
  adaptive evolution as fitness to, through natural selection, 488, 493f (see also Adaptive evolution)
  animal and plant responses to, 888f
  aquatic biomes and physical, 1164, 1171
  behavior and stimuli from, 1134f–1135f
  biotechnology in cleanup of, 412f, 432
  bottleneck effect from changes in, 489f–490
  cancer and factors of, 388
  cell cycle control system and factors of, 245–246f
  cellular membranes and factors of, 126f–127
  C. Darwin on natural selection and adaptations to, 13f–15f (see also Adaptations; Evolution; Natural selection)
  Earth's early, and origin of life, 520f–521f, 522
  ecology as interactions between organisms and, 1158f (see also Ecology)
  enzymatic catalysis and factors of, 155–156f, 157
  exchanges with, in animals, 868–869f, 870
  as factor in red maple leaf structure, 756
  gene regulation in response to, 372
  heat exchange with, in animals, 879f–883f
  human impacts on (see Human environmental impacts)
  impact of, on phenotypes, 280f
  induction in differential gene expression as response to, 377–378
  influence of evolution and, on nitrogenous wastes, 977
  interaction with, as theme of biology, 8f

metagenomics and genome sequencing of groups of species in, 438
nervous system disorders and, 1096f
as organisms and their surroundings, 462
plant responses to abiotic stresses from, 791–792, 856–857f, 858
population ecology as study of populations in, 1184f–1185 (see also Population ecology)
prokaryotic adaptations to extreme conditions in, 567f–568
protein structure and factors of, 82f–83
reproductive cycles and cues from, 1015
response to, as property of life, 1f
strength of ionic bonds and factors in, 38
vertebrate kidney adaptations to diverse, 985f–987f
Environmental issues. See also Ecology
  decline in amphibian populations, 727
  density-dependent population regulation by toxic waste, 1199f
  invasive exotic plants, 811
  prokaryotes, biotechnology, and, 583–584f, 585f
  threats to biodiversity, 1254f–1255f, 1258f–1260f
  threats to seed plant diversity, 645–646
Enzymatic catalysis. See also Enzymes
  activation energy barrier and, 151–152f
  allosteric regulation of, 157–158f, 159
  of cellular respiration, 181f–182
  cofactors and, 156
  effects of temperature and pH on, 155–156f
  in enzyme active sites, 154f
  enzyme inhibitors and, 156f–157
  evolution of enzymes and, 157f
  graphing, for blood glucose levels, 156
  lowering of activation energy by enzymes in, 152–153f
  in plant cells, 206f
  regulation of, 361f–364f
  in regulation of molecular interactions, 8–9f
  by ribozymes, 344
  substrate specificity of enzymes in, 153f–154
Enzymatic hydrolysis, 897, 903f
Enzymatic hydrolysis, neurotransmission and, 1074f
Enzymatic proteins, 76f
Enzymes, **67**, **151**. See also Enzymatic catalysis
  active sites of, 154f
  as catalysts, 151
  in cell-signaling nuclear responses, 223f
  in chemical digestion, 903f–904
  evolution of, 157f
  facilitation of synthesis and breakdown of polymers by, 67f
  fungal, 649
  in gastric juice, 901–902f
  gene relationship with, in protein synthesis, 334–335f, 336
  inducible and repressible, 363f–364
  locations of, in cells, 159f
  lowering plasma LDL levels by inactivating liver, 932
  lysosomes and, 107f–108
  as proteins, 75–76f, 128f
  in regulation of molecular interactions, 8–9f
  restriction (see Restriction enzymes)
  ribozymes as, 344
  in saliva, 901
  shape and function of RNA polymerases and, 83–84f
  smooth ER and rough ER, 104–105
  substrate specificity of, 153f–154
Enzyme-substrate complexes, **153**f–154
Eosinophils, 928f, 930f, 950
Ependymal cells, 1081f
Ephedrine, 636f
Ephrussi, Boris, 334
Epiblast cells, 1046f–1047f
Epicotyl, **822**–823f, 824f
Epidemics, **402**
  emerging viruses and, 402–403f, 404–405
  plant disease, 860–861
Epidemiology, 896
Epidermis, **756**f–757
Epididymis, **1019**f

Epigenetic inheritance, **367**
Epigenetics, 425
Epiglottis, 901*f*
Epilepsy, 1070, 1092
Epinephrine (adrenaline), **997**
    adrenal glands and, 999*f*, 1006–1007*f*
    as biogenic amine, 1075*t*
    in fight-or-flight responses, 210*f*, 922
    multiple effects of, 998*f*
    second messenger of, 220*f*–221*f*
    signal transduction pathway of, 212–214, 223, 224*f*
    as water-soluble hormone, 997*f*
Epiphytes, 626*f*, **812***f*–813
Epistasis, **279***f*
Epithalamus, 1087*f*
Epithelial tissue, **871***f*
    as barrier defense, 948
    cell junctions in, 120*f*
    in small intestine, 904*f*
    transport, in osmoregulation, 975–976*f*
Epitopes, **952**–953*f*, 963
Epsilon proteobacteria, 578*f*
Epstein-Barr virus, 388
Equational division, 262
Equilibrium
    chemical (*see* Chemical equilibrium)
    mechanoreceptors for sensing, 1106*f*–1110*f*
    population, 1197*f*
Equilibrium potential (E_{ion}), **1065***f*–1066
Equisetum, 626*f*, 627
Equus, 542–543*f*
Erectile dysfunction, 1020, 1076
Erection, penile, 995–996
Ergots, 663*f*
ER lumen, 104
Erosion, soil, 803*f*
Errantians, 697*f*
Errors, DNA replication, 325–326*f*
Erythrocytes (red blood cells), 82*f*, 494–495, 496*f*–497*f*, 872*f*, 928*f*–**929***f*
Erythropoietin (EPO), **930**
Escherichia coli (E. coli) bacteria, 589
    binary fission in, 240–241*f*
    complete genome sequence for, 436*f*
    DNA cloning and gene cloning of, 412*f*–413
    DNA replication and repair in, 320*f*–325*f*
    in gene cloning, 584
    genetic recombination and conjugation in, 574*f*–575
    genome size and number of genes of, 442*t*
    in human digestive system, 907*f*
    as model organism, 23
    pathogenic strains of, 583
    rapid adaptive evolution of, 572*f*–573
    regulation of gene expression in, 361*f*–364*f*
    viral infection of, 394*f*–395, 396*f*–397*f*, 398
    viral phages in DNA research on, 314*f*–315
E site (exit site), 347*f*–**348**
Esophagus, **901***f*, 902
Essential amino acids, **893**
Essential elements, **29***t*–30, 56, 64, **803**–804*f*, 805*t*
Essential fatty acids, **894**
Essential nutrients, animal, **893**, 894*t*–895*t*, 896–897
Estivation, 887
Estradiol, 62, 997*f*–998, 999*f*, **1009**, 1024, 1031*f*
Estrogens, 62, 371, 997*f*–998, 999*f*, **1009**, 1024, 1032*f*–1033, 1272*f*
Estrous cycles, **1027**
Estuaries, **1174***f*, 1180
Ethane, 59*f*
Ethanol, **63***f*, 178*f*, 585*f*, 1199*f*
Ethene (ethylene), 59*f*
Ethical issues
    on biotechnology, 432–433, 832–834
    on diagnosing fetal genetic diseases, 1033
    on DNA technology, 23*f*
    on gene therapy, 429
    on seed plant extinctions, 646
    on silencing gene expression in humans, 421
Ethylene, 212, 840*t*, **846**–848*f*, 857*f*
Etiolation, **837**
Euchromatin, **330**
Eudicots, **643***f*–644*f*, 762*f*, 764*f*, 822*f*–824*f*

Eugenics, 429
Euglenids, **594***f*–595
Euglenozoans, **594***f*–595
Euhadra species, 514–515
Eukarya, domain, **11***f*, 562–563*f*, 580*t*, 588
Eukaryotes. *See also* Animal(s); Fungi; Plant(s)
    cells of (*see* Eukaryotic cells)
    chemiosmosis in, 173–174*f*, 175
    cilia in, 12*f*
    electron transport chains in, 166–167
    endosymbiosis in evolution of, 589, 592*f*–593*f*
    Eukarya, domain, 11*f*, 562–563*f*, 580*t*, 588
    genome sizes and number of genes for, 442*t*–443
    origins of multicellular, 529–530*f*
    origins of single-celled, 528–529*f*
    photosynthesis of unicellular, 186*f*
    phylogenetic tree of, 605*f*
    protists as single-celled, 588 (*see also* Protists)
    taxonomy of, 562, 563*f*
    unikonts as first to diverge, 605*f*
Eukaryotic cells, **4**, **97**. *See also* Cell(s)
    animal and plant, 100*f*–101*f* (*see also* Animal cells; Plant cells)
    cellular integration of, 121*f*
    chromatin packing in chromosomes of, 328*f*–330*f*
    combinatorial transcription control for types of, 370–371*f*
    cytoskeletons of, 112*f*–117*f*
    distribution of chromosomes in cell division of, 233*f*–234*f*, 235
    DNA replication in, 320, 321*f*
    in embryonic development, 376*f*–377
    endomembrane system of, 104, 105*f*–109*f*
    evolution of cell division of, 241*f*–242*f*
    expressing cloned eukaryotic genes in, 416–417
    extracellular components and connections between, 118*f*–120*f*
    genetic instructions in nucleus of, 102, 103*f*
    internal membranes and organelles of, 99, 100*f*–101*f*
    mitochondria, chloroplasts, and peroxisomes of, 109, 110*f*–112*f*
    organization of typical genes in, 367*f*–368
    origins of, 528–529*f*
    plasma membranes of, 98*f*
    prokaryotic cells vs., 4*f*–5, 97*f*–98*f*, 99 (*see also* Prokaryotic cells)
    regulation of gene expression in (*see* Eukaryotic gene regulation)
    replication of DNA telomeres of, 326–327*f*
    ribosomes as protein factories of, 102–103*f*, 104
    RNA processing in, 342, 343*f*–345*f*
    transcription and translation in, 336–337*f*, 354*f*
    transcription in, 340*f*–342*f*
    translation in (*see* Translation)
    volume and surface area of, 98*f*–99
Eukaryotic gene regulation. *See also* Gene regulation
    analyzing DNA deletion experiments on, 370
    differential gene expression in, 360*f*, 365–366 (*see also* Differential gene expression)
    post-transcriptional regulation in, 372*f*–373
    regulation of chromatin structure in, 366*f*–367
    regulation of transcription initiation in, 367*f*–369*f*, 370–371*f*, 372*f*
Eukaryotic genomes
    evolution of, from DNA changes, 448*f*–451*f*, 452
    genes and multigene families in, 446–447*f*
    horizontal gene transfer in, 563
    noncoding repetitive DNA sequences in, 444*f*–445*f*, 446
    sizes and number of genes for, 442*t*–443
Eulipotyphla, 739*f*
Eumetazoans, **676**–677*f*, 680*f*, 685
Euphorbs, 1166*f*
Europe, 1251*f*
European flycatchers, 512*f*–513
European hamsters, 887*f*
European honeybees, 1136–1137*f*
European kestrels, 1196*f*–1197
European larch, 637*f*
European Molecular Biology Laboratory, 438
European robin, 13*f*
European starling, 1258

Euryarchaeota clade, 581
Euryhaline animals, 972
Eurypterids, **702***f*
Eustachian tube, **1107***f*
Eutherians (placental mammals), 475*f*, **737***f*–741*f*, 742. *See also* Primates
Eutrophication, 1221, **1238**, 1270*f*
Eutrophic lakes, **1173***f*
Evans, Martin, 421
Evaporation, 45–46*f*, **879***f*, 880
Evaporative cooling, 47–48
Evapotranspiration, **1226***f*, 1238*f*
Even-toed ungulates, 475*f*–476*f*
Evergreen trees, 637*f*
Evidence
    fossils as, for evolution, 12*f*
    scientific data as, 16*f*, 18*f*
    theories and, 21
Evo-devo. *See* Evolutionary developmental biology (evo-devo)
Evolution, **1** (facing page), **462**. *See also* Adaptations; Natural selection
    abiotic synthesis of organic molecules as origin of life on Earth, 57*f*–58
    altered DNA nucleotides as mutations in, 326
    of alternative carbon fixation mechanisms in plants, 201
    of amniotes, 729*f*
    of angiosperms, 641*f*–643*f*
    of animals, 669*f*–671*f*, 672–673
    of animal size and shape, 868*f*
    of antifreeze proteins, 859
    of arthropods, 700*f*–701*f*
    of axon width and myelination, 1070*f*–1071*f*
    of behaviors by associative learning, 1141
    of biological diversity (*see* Biodiversity)
    of biological order, 145
    of cell signaling, 211*f*–212
    of chordates, 716
    classification of diversity of life and, 10*f*–11*f*
    coevolution of flowers and pollinators in, 821*f*
    comparing genome sequences to study, 453*f*–454*f*, 455*f*–456, 457*f*–458*f*
    convergent (*see* Convergent evolution)
    as core theme of biology, 1 (facing page), 2, 9–10*f*
    cross-species gene expression in, 417
    Darwinian theory of, as descent with modification by natural selection, 12*f*–14*f*, 467–468*f*, 469*f*–470*f*
    of differences in cellular membrane lipid composition, 127
    divergence of human globin genes during, 452
    DNA and proteins as measures of, 89
    of drug resistance, 429–430
    early vertebrate, 718*f*–719*f*
    of ecological niches, 1209–1210*f*
    endosymbiosis in eukaryotic, 589, 592*f*–593*f*, 602*f*
    of enzymes, 157*f*
    evidence supporting Darwinian theory of, 471*f*–476*f*, 477
    evolutionary developmental biology "evo-devo" in study of, 382–383
    of extraembryonic membranes in amniote development, 1047
    field research by C. Darwin on, 465–466*f*, 467
    of fishes, 723–724
    of flowers, 817*f*
    of foraging behaviors, 1143*f*–1144, 1145
    of fungi, 653*f*–654
    of gas exchange, 941*f*–943*f*
    of genes and genomes, 559*f*–560
    of genetic code, 339*f*–340
    genetic variation and, of behavior, 1150*f*–1151*f*
    of genetic variation in populations, 264–265*f*
    of genomes from DNA changes, 448*f*–451*f*, 452
    genomics and proteomics in study of, 88*f*
    of glycolysis, 179–180
    of gnathostomes and jaws, 719*f*–720
    of gymnosperms, 635*f*
    historical context of Darwinian theory of, 463*f*–465*f*
    hominin and human, 742*f*–744*f*, 745–746*f*, 747*f*–748*f*

of hormone function, 1010f
of human genome, 560
influence of environment and, on nitrogenous wastes, 977
of introns, 344–345f
of land plants, 612f–613, 616–617t
of life history traits, 1195f–1196f, 1197
making and testing predictions of Darwinian, 477
of mammals, 735f–736
of mitochondria and chloroplasts, 109–110f
of mitosis, 241–242f
molecular clocks and rates of, 560–561f, 562f
of mycorrhizae in plants, 810
natural selection and genetic variation from recombination of alleles in, 303
of ncRNAs, 376
of pathogen detection by plants, 860
of pathogens that evade immune systems, 966–968f
pattern and process aspects of, 463, 477
of patterns of sexual reproduction, 1016
phylogenies as history of, 547–548, 549f–550f (see also Phylogenies)
of plant secondary growth, 768–769
of populations, 1184–1185
possible, of life on planets with water, 50f
of prokaryotic flagella, 570–571
radiometric dating and, 32
rapid prokaryotic, 572f–573
of reptiles, 730
of resource acquisition adaptations in vascular plants, 778f–781f
of seeds in seed plant, 632–633
sexual reproduction as enigma of, 1014f–1015
of short-term and long-term memory, 1094–1095
small population size and extinction vortex in, 1261f
of smooth muscles, 1126
speciation as conceptual bridge between macroevolution and microevolution, 501, 516 (see also Macroevolution; Microevolution; Speciation)
species dispersal and, 1178
theme of unity in diversity of life in, 462f, 467
theoretical aspects of Darwinian, 477–478
of tolerance to toxic elements, 30f
tree of life and, 14f–15f
unity in diversity in, 12f
using protein data to test hypotheses on horizontal gene transfer in, 564
of vascular plants, 622–623f, 624f–625f
of vertebrate brain structure, 1085f
of viruses, 400, 404
of visual perception, 1111f–1113f
Evolutionary developmental biology (evo-devo), 382–383, **457**, 463, 538
Evolutionary time, 1172
Evolutionary trees, 468f, **474**f–475. *See also* Phylogenetic trees
Exaptations, 542, 571
Excavates, 590f, **593**f–594f, 595
Exchange surfaces, animal, 868f–869f, 870
Excitatory postsynaptic potential (EPSP), 1072–**1073**
Excitement phase, sexual, 1027–1028
Excretion, **972**, 978f. *See also* Excretory systems; Osmoregulation
Excretory systems
    excretory processes of, 978f
    hormonal regulation of, 988f–990
    internal exchange surfaces and, 869f
    kidneys in mammalian and human, 980f–981f
    Malpighian tubules in, 979f–980
    metanephridia in, 979f
    nitrogenous wastes and, 972, 976–977f
    osmoregulation, excretion, and, 971f–974f, 975–976f
    processing of blood filtrate by nephrons in, 981–983f, 984f–987f
    protonephridia in, 978f–979
Executive functions, brain, 1092
Exercise, immune systems and, 965
Exercises, Scientific Skills. *See* Scientific Skills Exercises

Exergonic reactions, **146**–147f, 152f, 163
Exhalation, 938–939f, 940f
Exit tunnel, ribosome, 348
Exocrine glands, 999
Exocytosis, **137**, 206f–207f
Exons, **343**f–345f, 443, 450–451f, 481–482f
Exon shuffling, 344–345f, 451f
Exoskeletons, **687**, **1127**
    animal, 677
    anthozoan, 687
    arthropod, 701f
    chitin as structural polysaccharide in, 72f
    ectoproct, 692
    in locomotion, 1126f, **1127**
Exotic species, 1258–1259f
Exotoxins, **583**
Expansins, 842–843f
Experimental design, 16–21. *See also* Scientific Skills Exercises
Experiments, **20**, 16–21. *See also* Case studies; Inquiry Figures; Research Method Figures; Scientific Skills Exercises
Explosive seed dispersal, 639f
Exponential population growth model, 1190–**1191**f, 1192, 1201f–1202f
Expressed sequence tags (ESTs), 439–440
Expression vectors, **416**
Extension, muscle, 1126f
External factors, cell cycle control system, 245–246f
External fertilization, 1016f–1017, 1146
Extinctions
    of amphibians, 727
    current rate of, 1256
    ecological factors affecting rates of, 532
    extinction vortex and, 1261f
    in fossil record, 475, 522–523f
    global and local, 1256
    global temperature and, 535f–536
    human impacts on, 1255
    introduced species and, 1258
    island equilibrium model and, 1227
    mass, 534f–536f
    of molluscs, 696f
    resurrection of species after, 1260–1261f
    of seed plant species, 645f–646
    speciation and, 514, 515, 516
Extinction vortex, **1261**f
Extracellular digestion, 899f–900
Extracellular matrix (ECM), **118**–119, 128f, 1050–1051
Extraembryonic membranes, 728–729f, **1046**f–1047f
Extranuclear genes, 309
Extreme halophiles, **580**
Extreme thermophiles, **580**f–581
Extremophiles, **580**f–581
Eyes. *See also* Visual systems
    euglenid eyespot as, 594f
    evolution of, 541–542f
    evolution of light detecting organs and, 1111f–1113f
    insect compound, 706f, 888f
    vertebrate, 1112f–1116f, 1117
Eyespots, 594f, 1111f

F

F₁ (first filial) generations, **269**
F₂ (second filial) generations, **269**
Faceted eyes, arthropod, 1111f–1112
Facilitated diffusion, **133**f–134, 207f
Facilitation, **1215**f
Facultative anaerobes, **179**, **576**
Facultative mutualism, 1214
FAD (flavin adenine dinucleotide), 170f–171f, 176
FADH₂, 170f–171f, 173
Fairy ring, mushroom, 660–661f
Falling phase, action potential, 1068–1069
Familial cardiomyopathy, 355f
Families, taxonomy, 548–549f
Family planning, 1202
Family resemblance, genetics and, 252f
Family studies, 1096
Family trees, 282f–283
Fanwort, 769f

Far-red light, plant response to, 851f
Fast block to polyspermy, **1039**
Fast-twitch fibers, **1125**
Fate maps, **1051**–1052f, 1053f–1055f
Fathead minnows, 1272
Fatigue, muscle, 1124
Fats, **72**
    absorption of, in small intestine, 904–905f
    animal heat exchange and, 879
    blood cholesterol and, 932
    digestion of, 903f
    as fuel for catabolism, 180f–181
    hydrocarbons in, 60–61f
    as lipids, 72–73f, 74
    oxidation of, during cellular respiration, 164–165
    trans fats, 61
Fat-soluble vitamins, 894t
Fatty acids, **72**
    beta oxidation of, for catabolism, 180f–181
    essential, 894
    fats and, 72–73f, 74
Feathers, 732f–733
Feather stars, 709f
Feces, 691, 826f, **905**–906, 1239f–1240
Feedback inhibition, **159**f, 181f–182, 361f
Feedback regulation, **9**. *See also* Regulation
    of animal digestion, energy storage, and appetite, 908–909f, 910f–911f, 912
    of animal homeostasis, 875f–877f
    in density-dependent population growth, 1198
    of endocrine systems, 1001
    of molecular interactions, 8–9f
Feedback, scientific, 18f–19
Feeding mechanisms, 648f–650f, 651, **898**f
Feet, bird adaptation to perching, 734f
Female condoms, 1032
Female gametophytes, angiosperm, 818–819f
Females
    autoimmune diseases in human, 965
    fruit fly bias in sperm usage by, 1018f
    hormonal regulation of reproductive systems of human, 1025–1026f, 1027
    hormones of, 993f, 999f, 1000f–1001, 1002f–1003, 1009f
    inactivation of X-linked genes in mammalian, 298f
    mate choice by, 493f–494f, 1146–1147f, 1148
    maternal immune tolerance of embryo and fetus during pregnancy, 1031
    oogenesis in human, 1021, 1023f
    parental care by, 1145–1146
    parthenogenesis by, 691–692
    reproductive anatomy of human, 1020–1021f
    reproductive rates and, 1188–1189t, 1190, 1199f, 1202
    sex chromosomes of, 296f–297
Fermentation, **163**
    anaerobic and aerobic respiration vs., 177–178
    cellular respiration vs., 163, 179f
    types of, 178–179
Fern galls, 672
Ferns, 624f, 625–626f, 627, 631f
Ferrodoxin, 196f
Fertility schedules, 1189t
Fertilization, reproductive, **255**, **818**, **1016**, **1038**. *See also* Reproductive isolation
    angiosperm double, 640f–641, 818–819f (see also Pollination)
    in animal embryonic development, 1038–1039f, 1040f–1041f
    ensuring offspring survival following, 1017f
    external versus internal, 1016f–1017
    gamete production and delivery in, 1017–1018f
    genetic variation from random, 264, 303
    in human life cycle, 255f–256, 1028f
    mechanisms preventing angiosperm self-fertilization, 828–829f
    meiosis and, 235
    G. Mendel's techniques of plant, 268f–269f
    parental care and internal vs. external, 1146
    parthenogenic self-fertilization, 1014, 1015f
    prezygotic barriers and, 502f–503f, 504
    in varieties of sexual life cycles, 256f–257
    in vitro fertilization (IVF), 1034f

Fertilization, soil, **802**, 977, 1198f, 1239, 1270f
Fertilization envelope, 1039f–1040f
Fescue grass, 1197f
Fetal alcohol syndrome, 1030
Fetal testing, 286–287f
Fetoscopy, 287
Fetus, **1030**
    detecting disorders of, during pregnancy, 1033
    gestation and birth of, 1029f–1031f
    maternal immune tolerance of, 1031
Fever, 882–883f, 952
F factor, **574f**–575
Fiber cells, **758f**
Fibers, muscle, 1124–1125t
Fibrin, 930f
Fibrinogen, 930f
Fibroblast growth factor (FGF), 1056
Fibroblasts, 113t, 245, **872f**
Fibronectin, **119**
Fibrous connective tissue, 872f
Fibrous proteins, 78
Fibrous root systems, 754
Fiddler crabs, 1133f, 1135
Fierer, Noah, 1217f
Fight-or-flight responses, 210f, 922, 1084
Filamentous fungi, 653
Filaments, 873f
Filaments, flagellum, 570f–571
Filaments, flower, 638f
Filter feeders, **684f**, **898f**
Filtrates, **978f**, 981–983f
Filtration, **978f**
Fimbriae, 97f, 569f, **570**
Finches, 14–15f, 18, 466–467f, 480f–481f, 492, 1172
Fingerprints, DNA, 416, 430–431
Finland, 1221f
Fire, 1166, 1222–1223f
Firefly gene, 339f
Fireweed, 630f
First law of thermodynamics, **143f**
Fishapod discovery, 724f, 725
Fishes
    adaptations of kidneys of, 986–987f
    allopatric speciation in, 505f–506
    in biomanipulation, 1221
    changes in gene regulation of, 540f–541
    differential gene expression in, 360f
    discovery of "fishapod" *Tiktaalik*, 724f, 725
    endangered or threatened, 1256
    frequency-dependent selection in, 495f
    gills for gas exchange in, 934f–935f
    hearing and equilibrium in, 1110f
    hybrid zones of, 509f, 513f
    osmoregulation in, 973f–974
    parental care in, 1146f
    protists as pathogens of, 608
    ray-finned, and lobe-finned, 722f–723f, 724
    sex determination of, 296f
    sex reversal in, 1016
    single circulation in, 919f
    thermoregulation in, 875f
Fission, **1014f**
Fitness, relative, 491–492
FitzRoy, Robert, 465–466
Fixed action patterns, **1134f**–1135
Fixed alleles, 484, 490
Flaccid cells, **133**, 784, 785f, 791f
Flagella, **114**
    in animal cell, 100f
    bacterial, movement of, 987f
    cilia vs., 115f
    dinoflagellate, 598f
    euglenozoan, 594f
    flagellated sperm, 613
    as microtubules, 114–115f, 116f
    in prokaryotic cell, 97f, 570f–571
    in protistan cell, 101f
    stramenopile, 595f
Flagellated sperm, 613
Flagellin, 860
Flame bulbs, 688, 979
Flamingo, 13f, 734f

Flashlight fish, 582f
Flattening, body surface area and, 689f
Flatworms
    characteristics of, 681f, 688–689f, 690f–691f
    gastrovascular cavities of, 916f–917
    hydrostatic skeletons of, 1127f
    nervous systems of, 1080f
    protonephridia of, 978f–979
Flavin mononucleotide (FMN), 173
Flavoproteins, 173
Fleas, 980
Flemming, Walther, 235
Flesh-eating disease, 472f–473
Fleshy fruits, 639f
Fletcher, W. J., 1179f
Flexion, muscle, 1126f
Flies, 706f, 821f
Flight, 704–705f, 732f–733, 1130
Flightless birds, 500f, 505, 734f
Floating of ice, 48f
Flooding, 1222
Flooding, plant responses to, 857f
Floral meristems, 825
Florida, 1250f
Florida Keys mangrove islands, 1227f–1228
Florida Keys National Marine Sanctuary, 1269f
Florigen, **854f**–855
Flowering, 825
FLOWERING LOCUS T (FT) gene, 854f–855
Flowers, **638**
    adaptations of, that prevent self-fertilization,
        828–829f
    coevolution of pollinators and, 821f
    genetic control of formation and flowering of,
        774–775f
    hormonal control of flowering of, 854f–855
    monocot vs. eudicot, and pollination of, 643f
    photoperiodism and flowering of, 853f–854f
    pollination of, 815f–816, 820f–821f
    preventing transgene escape with genetically-
        engineered, 834
    structure and function of, 638f, 816f–817f
    trends in evolution of, 817f
Flu. *See* Influenza viruses
Fluctuation, population, 1199f–1200
Fluid feeders, **898f**
Fluid mosaic model, **124f**
Fluorescence, 193f, 248
Fluorescence microscopy, **95f**, 96
Fluoxetine, 1097
Fly agaric, 655f
Flycatchers, European, 512f–513
Flying fox bats, 1256f
Flying squirrels, 475f
Focusing, visual, 1116f–1117
Folding, body surface area and, 689f
Folding, protein, 83f–84f
Foliose lichens, 662f
Follicles, **1020**–1021f
Follicle-stimulating hormone (FSH), 999f, 1003f,
        1024–1025f, 1026f–1027
Follicular phase, 1026
Food. *See also* Animal nutrition; Trophic structure
    animal processing of, 897f–899f, 900
    in bioenergetics and metabolic rates, 883–884f
    brown algae as human, 597
    calories of, 46
    digestion of (*see* Digestion; Digestive systems)
    as fuel for catabolism, 180f–181
    as fuel for cellular respiration, 162–163
    fungi as human, 664
    genetically modified organisms (GMOs) as,
        432–433, 831–832f, 833–834
    land plants as, for animals, 612f
    as limiting factor for human population size,
        1204–1205
    population cycles and shortages of, 1200f
    ray-finned fishes as human, 722
    red algae as human, 602–603f
    seed plants as human, 645
Food chains, 1217–1218f, 1219f
Food poisoning, 398, 578f, 579f, 583, 1075
Food vacuoles, 107f–108, 600f, 899

Food webs, 608–609f, 1218f–1219f
Foolish seedling disease, 845
Foot, mollusc, **692**–693f
Foot, sporophyte, **621**
Foraging behaviors, **1143f**–1145
Foraminiferans (forams), 591f, **601f**
Forebrain, **1085f**
Forelimbs, mammalian, 473f
Forensic ecology, 1259f
Forensic science, 23f, 416, 430–431f
Foreskin, penile, 1020
Forest fires, 1222–1223f
Forests
    northern coniferous, 1169f
    temperate broadleaf, 1170f
    tropical, 1167f
Formic acid, 28
Fossil fuels
    biofuels as alternatives to, 186f
    biofuel technology to reduce dependence on, 832
    ecological footprints and, 1204f–1205
    global climate change and, 202–203, 1272–1273f,
        1274
    hydrocarbons as, 60
    ocean acidification and, 53f–54
    photosynthesis as source of, 186
    seedless vascular plants and, 627–628
Fossil record. *See also* Fossils
    angiosperms in, 641f–642
    animals in, 669f–671f, 672–673
    arthropods in, 700–701, 704
    colonization of land in, 530–531f
    dinosaurs in, 519f–520
    ecological factors affecting evolutionary rates in,
        532
    evidence in, for dinosaurs as ancestors of birds,
        558f
    evidence in, for evolutionary change, 12f
    evolutionary trends in, 542–543f
    forams in, 601
    fungi in, 653f–654
    geologic record and, 526, 527f
    gymnosperms in, 635f
    as history of life, 522–523f, 524
    land plant origin and diversification in, 616
    molecular clocks and, 561
    origin of mammals in, 524–525f, 526
    origin of multicellular organisms in, 529–530f
    origin of single-celled organisms in, 526, 528f–529f
    seedless vascular plants in, 622, 623f
Fossils, **464**. *See also* Fossil record
    amniote, 729f
    biogeography and, 476–477
    bird, 733f
    dating of, 524f
    of early vertebrates, 718f–719f
    as evidence for Darwinian evolution, 475f–476f
    evolutionary theories and, 464f
    of gnathostomes, 720f
    hominin, 742f–743f, 744
    Homo sapiens, 747–748f
    horseshoe crabs as living, 702f
    radiometric dating of, 32
    reptile and dinosaur, 730
    speciation patterns of, 514f
    tetrapod, 724f, 725f
    whisk ferns as living, 627
Foundation species, 1220f
Founder effect, **489**
Fovea, **1116f**–1117
Fox, 1232f
FOXP2 gene, 454f–455
F plasmids, 574f–**575**
Fractals, 752f
Fragmentation, habitat, 1258f, 1266f–1267
Fragmentation, reproductive, 827, 1014
Frameshift mutations, **356f**
Franklin, Rosalind, 316f–317, 318
Fraternal twins, 1030
Free energy, **145**
Free-energy change
    in coupled reactions, 150f
    free energy and, 145

metabolism and, 146–147*f*, 148*f*
stability, equilibrium, and, 145–146*f*
Free energy of activation (activation energy), 151–152
Free ribosomes, 103*f*–104, 351–352
Freezing, 859, 1222
Frequency-dependent selection, **495***f*
Freshwater animals, 973*f*–974, 986
Freshwater biomes, 1171*f*–1172*f*, 1256*f*
Freshwater marshes, 1180
Friction, locomotion and, 1129
Fringe wetlands, 1173*f*
Fringing reefs, 1176*f*
Fritillaries, 1200–1201*f*
Frogs
    as amphibians, 726*f*–727*f*
    axis formation in, 1054*f*
    cell developmental potential in, 1054–1055*f*
    cell fate and pattern formation by inductive signals
        in, 1056*f*
    cleavage in, 1042*f*–1043
    coloration of, 1212*f*
    discovery of new species of, 1158*f*, 1180
    embryonic development of, 376*f*
    external fertilization of, 1016*f*
    fate mapping for, 1052*f*
    fungal parasites of, 663–664*f*
    gastrulation in, 1044–1045*f*
    mate choice among tree, 494*f*
    metamorphosis of, 1010*f*
    neurulation in, 1048*f*
    nuclear transplantation in, 423*f*–424
    polyploidy in, 508
Fronds, 626*f*
Frontal lobe, 1091*f*, 1092
Frontal lobotomy, 1092
Frost-tolerant plants, 859
Fructose, 68*f*, 151, 153
Fruit flies
    hybrid sterility of, 516
    model organism (*see Drosophila melanogaster*
        (fruit fly))
    molecular clock of, 561
    reproductive isolation of allopatric populations
        of, 506*f*
Fruiting bodies, 211*f*, 606–607*f*, 655*f*, 657*f*–659*t*
Fruitlets, 825
Fruits, **639**, **825**
    angiosperm seeds as, 638, 639*f*
    auxin in growth of, 843
    dispersal of, 826*f*
    ethylene in ripening of, 848
    gibberellins in growth of, 845*f*
    structure and function of, 825*f*–826*f*
Fruticose lichens, 662*f*
Frye, Larry, 126*f*
Fuels
    alternative, 186*f*, 1274
    bacteria in production of ethanol, 585*f*
    fossil (*see* Fossil fuels)
    genetic engineering of, using fungi, 665*f*
    peat and coal, 622*f*, 627–628
    seed plants as, 645
Fumonisin, 833
Function, structure and, 4
Functional groups, **62**–63*f*
Functional magnetic resonance imaging (fMRI), 1090*f*
Fundamental niches, 1210
Fungi
    amphibian population declines due to, 727
    ascomycetes, 655*f*, 657*f*–659*t*
    basidiomycetes, 655*f*, 659*f*–661*f*
    biological augmentation using, 1249
    body structure of, 649–650*f*
    cells of, 100*f*
    chytrids, 654, 655*f*–656*f*
    as detritivores, 1234*f*
    in domain Eukarya, 11*f*
    expressing cloned eukaryotic genes in, 416–417
    fungal plant toxin, 833
    glomeromycetes, 655*f*, 657*f*
    land colonization by, 530–531*f*
    maximizing surface area by, 689*f*
    mycorrhizal, 616, 650*f*–651, 781, 810–811*f*

nutrient limitations and, 1239
nutritional and ecological roles of, 648*f*–649,
    661*f*–664*f*
as opisthokonts, 607
origin and evolution of, 653*f*–654
phylogeny and diversity of, 654, 655*f*–661
practical uses of, for humans, 664–665*f*
relationship of, to unikont protists, 604–605
sexual and asexual life cycles of, 256*f*–257,
    651–652*f*, 653*f*
terrestrial adaptations of, 654
zygomycetes, 655*f*, 656*f*–657*f*
Fungi, kingdom, 562, 563*f*
Fusarium, 833
Fusion, floral, 817*f*
Fusion, hybrid zone, 512*f*, 513*f*
Fynbos, 1168*f*

G

G$_0$ phase, **244**–245*f*
G$_1$ checkpoint, 243*f*–245*f*
G$_1$ phase, **235***f*
G$_2$ checkpoint, 243*f*–245*f*
G$_2$ phase, **235***f*, 236*f*
Gage, Phineas, 1092
Galactose, 68*f*, 363*f*
Galápagos Islands, 14–15*f*, 18, 466*f*–467*f*, 500*f*, 1172
Gallbladders, **903**
Gälweiler, Leo, 842*f*
Gametangia, **615***f*, 619–620
Gametes, **234**, **253**
    human gametogenesis and, 1021, 1022*f*–1023*f*
    production and delivery of, in animal
        reproduction, 1017–1018*f*
    production of, by meiosis, 234–235
    in sexual life cycles, 253, 255
Game theory, **1148***f*–1149, 1153
Gametic isolation, 503*f*
Gametogenesis, human, **1021**, 1022*f*–1023*f*
Gametophores, **618**–619*f*
Gametophytes, **614***f*
    in alternation of generations, 256*f*
    angiosperm, 818–19*f*
    brown algae, 598
    of land plants, 614*f*, 618–619*f*, 621
    in G. Mendel's experiments, 268*f*–269*f*
    sporophyte relationships with, in plants, 631*f*
Gamma-aminobutyric acid (GABA), **1075***t*
Gamma proteobacteria, 578*f*
Ganglia, **1061**, 1062, 1080*f*–1081
Ganglia, planarian, 690*f*. *See also* Cerebral ganglia
Ganglion cells, 1112*f*, 1114–1115*f*
Gap junctions, **120***f*, 212*f*
Garden peas, G. Mendel's experiments with,
    267*f*–274*f*
Garigue, 1168*f*
Garlic, 830*f*
Garlic mustard, 811
Garrod, Archibald, 334
Garter snakes, 502*f*, 1150*f*
Gas chromatography, 846
Gases
    greenhouse, 48, 53*f*
    water vapor, 44
Gas exchange
    arthropod, 701–702, 704*f*
    chordate, 714
    fish, 722
    ion movements and gradients and, 987*f*
    plant and animal, 889*f*
    shark, 720
Gas exchange systems, **933**
    circulatory systems and, 915*f*–916 (*see also*
        Circulatory systems)
    coordination of cardiovascular systems and,
        941*f*–943*f* (*see also* Cardiovascular systems)
    gills for, in aquatic animals, 934*f*–935*f*
    mammalian respiratory systems, 936–937*f*,
        938*f*–940*f* (*see also* Respiratory systems)
    partial pressure gradients in, 933
    respiratory media in, 933*f*
    respiratory surfaces in, 933–934
    tracheal systems for, in insects, 935–936*f*

Gasterosteus aculeatus, 540*f*–541
Gastric glands, 901–902*f*
Gastric juices, **901**–902*f*, 909*f*
Gastric ulcers, 902, 907*f*
Gastrin, 909*f*
Gastrodermis, 685*f*
Gastropods, 536, 693*f*–694, 696*f*
Gastrovascular cavities, 685*f*, **916***f*–917
Gastrovascular cavity, 690*f*, **899***f*
Gastrula, 668*f*, 1038, **1044***f*
Gastrulation, 668*f*, 674*f*–675, 1038, **1044***f*–1047*f*
Gated channels, **133**
Gated ion channels, **1066***f*–1071*f*
Gause, G. F., 1209
Geckos, 39, 563*f*, 1254*f*
Geckskin adhesive, 39
Geese, 880*f*
Gel electrophoresis, **414***f*
Genbank, 438–439*f*
Gene(s), **5**, **84**, **253**. *See also* Chromosomes; DNA
    (deoxyribonucleic acid); Genetics; Genomes
    alleles as alternative versions of, 270 (*see also*
        Alleles)
    animal developmental (*see Hox* genes)
    apoptosis, 228*f*
    appetite regulation, 912
    associated with cancer, 383*f*–384
    B cell and T cell diversity and rearrangement of,
        955*f*–960
    calibrating molecular clocks of, 560–561*f*
    for color vision, 1116*f*
    coordinately controlled, 361, 371
    density of, in genomes, 443
    divergence of human globin, during evolution, 452
    DNA technology in determining functions of,
        421–422*f*
    duplication of, due to unequal crossing over, 449*f*
    effects of developmental, 538*f*–539*f*
    enzyme relationship with, in protein synthesis,
        334–335*f*, 336
    evolution of, with novel functions, 450, 451*f*
    evolution of *FOXP2*, 454*f*–455
    evolution of homologous, 559*f*–560
    evolution of related-function, 449–450*f*
    extending Mendelian inheritance for, 277*f*–280*f*
        (*see also* Mendelian inheritance)
    flower formation, 774–775*f*
    foraging, 1143
    gene expression and, 5*f*–6*f*, 357 (*see also* Gene
        expression)
    genetic diversity and, 1257
    genetic variation due to alterations of number or
        position of, 483
    genomic imprinting and, 308*f*–309
    genomics, bioinformatics, and proteomics in study
        of, 6*f*–7, 87–88*f*
    as hereditary units, 253
    homeotic and *Hox*, 380*f*–381*f*, 457*f*–458*f*, 539
    homologous, 474
    horizontal gene transfer of, 562–563*f*, 564*f*
    Hox genes, 1058
    identifying linked or unlinked, 302
    identifying protein-coding, 439*f*–440
    inheritance of organelle, 309*f*
    jumping (*see* Transposable elements)
    linked, 299*f*–300, 301*f*
    locating, along chromosomes, 292*f*–293*f*, 294
    in macroevolution of development, 539*f*–540*f*, 541
    mapping distance between, on chromosomes,
        303*f*–304*f*
    maternal effect, egg-polarity, and morphogen,
        381*f*–382*f*
    G. Mendel's hereditary factors as, 267–268
    meristem identity and organ identity, 774*f*
    molecular homologies and, 551*f*–553*f*
    multigene families and, in eukaryotic genomes,
        446–447*f*
    notation system for, 294–295
    nucleic acids and, 84 (*see also* DNA
        (deoxyribonucleic acid); Nucleic acids; RNA
        (ribonucleic acid))
    number of, in genomes, 442*t*–443
    olfactory, 1118

organization of typical eukaryotic, 367*f*–368
pseudogenes, 444
rearrangement of parts of, 450–451*f*
regulation of (*see* Gene regulation)
regulatory, 362*f*
sex-linked, 296*f*–298*f*
speciation and, 515–516*f*
split, 343*f*–344*f*
study of, by systems biology, 440–441*f*, 442
transcription factors for, 218
transcription of, during cell-signal response stage, 223*f*
transgenes, 430*f*
transplanting, into different species, 339*f*
types of, associated with cancer, 385*f*
variability of, in genetic variation, 481
Genealogy, molecular, 89
Gene annotation, **439**–440
Gene cloning, **413***f*–414, 415–416*f*
Gene expression, **6**, **84**, **334**. *See also* Gene(s); Genetics
analyzing quantitative and spatial data on, 420
auxin and, 842
basic principles of transcription and translation in, 336–337*f*
of brain development genes in lancelets and vertebrates, 716*f*
changes in, in macroevolution, 539*f*–540*f*, 541
of cloned eukaryotic genes, 416–417
control of plant cell differentiation and, 773*f*
differential (*see* Differential gene expression)
DNA, RNA, and genes in, 6*f*
DNA technology in analysis of, 417–418*f*, 419*f*–420, 421*f*, 423*f*
DNA technology in silencing, 421–422*f*
evidence for, in study of metabolic defects, 334–335*f*, 336
evolutionary significance of cross-species, 417
experiment on, for red maple leaf structure, 756
flowering and, 854*f*–855
as flow of genetic information, 333*f*–334
gene concept and, 357
genetic code in, 337–338*f*, 339*f*–340
interpreting sequence logos to identify ribosome binding sites in, 349
mutations in, 355*f*–356*f*, 357
nematode parasite control of host, 700
nucleic acids in, 84*f*–85
polypeptide synthesis via RNA-directed translation in, 345*f*–348*f*, 349–350*f*, 351*f*–354*f*
regulation of (*see* Gene regulation)
RNA modification after transcription by eukaryotic cells in, 342–343*f*, 344*f*–345*f*
RNA synthesis via DNA-directed transcription in, 340*f*–342*f*
stages of, that can be regulated, 365*f*
study of, by systems biology, 440–441*f*, 442
summary of eukaryotic transcription and translation in, 354*f*
as transcription, 366 (*see also* Transcription)
Gene families, 559*f*–560
Gene flow, **490**
biological species concept and, 501, 504*f*
as cause of microevolution, 490–491*f*
Hardy-Weinberg equilibrium and, 486
between Neanderthals and humans, 747*f*
speciation and, 515
Gene pools, **484***f*
General transcription factors, 368
Generative cells, 640*f*, 818
Gene regulation
analyzing DNA deletion experiments on, 370
in bacterial transcription, 361*f*–364*f*
cancer due to faulty cell cycle control in, 383*f*–384, 385*f*–387*f*, 388 (*see also* Cancer)
changes in, in macroevolution, 540*f*–541
differential gene expression and, 360*f* (*see also* Differential gene expression)
in eukaryotic cells (*see* Eukaryotic gene regulation)
faulty, in cloned animals, 425
noncoding RNAs in, 374*f*–375*f*, 376
of plant cell differentiation, 773*f*
in plant signal transduction pathways, 839
steroid hormones and, 997*f*

Gene therapy, 393, **428**–429*f*, 1116*f*
Genetically modified (GM) organisms, **432**. *See also* Transgenic animals; Transgenic plants
fungi as, 665
issues about, 432–433, 832–834
plant biotechnology and genetic engineering of, 831–832*f*
Genetic code
codons and triplet code of nucleotides as, 337–338*f*
cracking of, 338–339*f*
of DNA, 5*f*–6*f*
evolution of, 339*f*–340
as molecular homology, 474
in mutations, 355*f*–356*f*
neutral variation and redundancy of, 482
as sequence of nitrogenous bases, 86
universality of, 15
Genetic counseling, 285–286
Genetic disorders
alkaptonuria, 334
biotechnology in diagnosis and treatment of, 416, 428–429*f*, 430*f*
from chromosomal alterations, 304–305*f*, 306*f*–307*f*
counseling for, 285–286
diagnosing fetal, 1033
dominantly inherited, 285*f*
multifactorial, 285
mutations in, 355*f*–356*f*, 357
recessively inherited, 283*f*–284*f*, 285
sickle-cell disease (*see* Sickle-cell disease)
testing for, 286–287*f*, 288
Genetic diversity. *See also* Genetic variation
in biodiversity, 1255*f*–1256
as factor in extinction vortex, 1261*f*
in human welfare, 1257
prokaryotic, 572*f*–574*f*, 575, 577
in small-population approach to population conservation, 1261*f*–1263*f*
Genetic drift, **488***f*–489*f*, 490
Genetic engineering, **409**
of antifreeze proteins, 859
DNA technology tools for, 409, 412*f*–416*f*, 417
of ethylene signal transduction pathways, 848
of fruit flies to express infection, 948*f*, 949*f*
fungi in, 665
of genetically modified (GM) organisms, 432–433, 832 (*see also* Genetically modified (GM) organisms)
of "pharm" animals, 430*f*
of plants (*see* Transgenic plants)
plant tissue culture and, 830
prokaryotes in, 583–584*f*, 585
Genetic Information Nondiscrimination Act, 286
Genetic maps, 303*f*–304*f*
Genetic markers
in diagnosing diseases, 428
in forensic evidence and genetic profiles, 430–431*f*
in genome-wide association studies, 421–422*f*
Genetic mutants in Scientific Skills Exercises, 912, 1089
Genetic profiles, 428, **430**–431, 1188–1189*f*
Genetic prospecting, 577
Genetic recombination, **300**
identifying linked genes for, 302
of linked genes in crossing over, 300–301*f*
natural selection and genetic variation from, 303
in prokaryotes, 573*f*–574*f*, 575
transposable elements and, 453
of unlinked genes in independent assortment of chromosomes, 300
Genetics, **252**. *See also* Genetic variation; Inheritance; Mendelian inheritance
of blood cholesterol levels, 932
cytology and, 292
designing experiments using genetic mutants, 1089
of drug addiction, 1097
in ecological forensics, 1259*f*
in estimating reproductive rates, 1188–1189*f*
flow of genetic information in plant cells, 206*f*

of foraging behaviors, 1143*f*
genetic basis of animal behavior, 1149*f*–1150
genomics and proteomics in, 87–88*f*
inheritance of chromosomes and genes in, 253
interpreting data from experiments with genetic mutants, 912
of nervous system disorders, 1096*f*
Punnett square as tool in, 271
of sickle-cell disease, 496*f*
solving complex problems of, with rules of probability, 275–276
of speciation, 515–516*f*
as study of heredity and hereditary variation, 252
vocabulary of, 272*f*
Genetic sequences in Scientific Skills Exercise, 589
Genetic testing
biotechnology in, 428
for breast cancer predisposition, 388
fetal, 286–287*f*, 1033
identifying carriers, 286
newborn, 287–288
Genetic variation, **252**, **481**
from crossing over and recombinant chromosomes, 263–264*f*
evolutionary significance of, within populations, 264–265*f*
extinction vortex and loss of, 1261–1263
in genetic diversity, 1256 (*see also* Genetic diversity)
genetics as study of, 252 (*see also* Genetics)
from independent assortment of chromosomes, 263*f*
microevolution of populations and sources of, 481*f*–482*f*, 483
in migratory patterns, 1150–1151*f*
molecular clocks and rates of, 560–561*f*
natural selection and, from recombinant chromosomes, 303
phylogenetic tree branch lengths and, 555*f*
preservation of, 494
in prey selection, 1150*f*
from random fertilization, 264
in sexual reproduction, 253
in small-population approach to population conservation, 1261*f*–1263*f*
Gene trees, 551*f*
Genomes, **6**, **233**. *See also* Gene(s)
analyzing phylogenetic trees based on, to understand viral evolution, 404
animal phylogeny and, 676–677*f*, 678
bioinformatics in analysis of, 438–439*f*, 440–441*f*, 442
in cell division, 233
comparing, 251, 453–454*f*, 455*f*–456, 670*f*
comparison of Neanderthal and human, 747*f*
complete, 659, 716, 769
differential gene expression for identical, 365*f*–366 (*see also* Differential gene expression)
evolutionary history in, 559*f*–560
evolution of, from DNA duplication, rearrangement, and mutation, 448*f*–451*f*, 452–453
gene density of, 659*t*
genetic testing of fetal, 1033
genome-wide association studies of, 421–422, 428
genomics, proteomics, and bioinformatics in study of, 6*f*–7, 87–88*f*, 251, 437
horizontal gene transfer between, 562–563*f*, 564*f*
Human Genome Project and development of DNA sequencing techniques for, 437*f*–438
interpreting data from, and generating hypotheses, 651
noncoding DNA and multigene families in eukaryotic, 444*f*–445*f*, 446–447*f*
p53 gene as guardian angel of, 384
prokaryotic, 571*f*
species with complete sequences of, 436*f*, 442*t*
variations in size, number of genes, gene density, and noncoding DNA of, 442*t*–443
viral, 394, 395*f*–397*f*, 398*t*
widespread conservation of developmental genes in animal, 457*f*–458*f*
Genome sequencing, 437*f*–438, 441*f*–442, 651

Genome-wide association studies, **421**–422, 428
Genomic data in Scientific Skills Exercise, 651
Genomic imprinting, **308**f–309, 367
Genomics, 6f–7, 87–88f, 251, 386–387f, **437**-438, 577
Genotypes, **272**
    DNA transformation and, 313
    gene expression as link between phenotypes and, 334
    genetic variation and, 481–482f
    heterozygote advantage and, 494–495
    phenotypes vs., 271f–272f, 280f–281
    relative fitness of, 492
Gentoo penguin, 13f
Genus, **548**–549f
Geographical barriers, allopatric speciation and, 505f–507f
Geographic species distributions. *See* Species distributions
Geologic record, **526**, 527t
Geometric isomers, 61
Geospiza fortis, 480f–481f
Germ cells
    fate maps and, 1053f
    human, 256, 1023f
    telomerase and telomeres in, 327
Germination
    gibberellins in, 845f
    phytochromes in, 850–851f
    seedling development after, 823–824f
    strigolactones in, 849
Germ layers, 674, **1044**f, 1045f
Gestation, **1029**f–1031f
Ghost crabs, 703f
Ghrelin, 911f
Giant panda, 442t
Giant sequoia tree, 768f
Giant squids, 695–696
Giardia intestinalis, 590f, 593
Gibberellins, 840t, 844–845f
Gibbons, 89, 741f
Gibbs, J. Willard, 145
Gibbs free energy, 145. *See also* Free-energy change
Gigantism, 1005f
Gills
    annelid, 697
    arthropod, 701
    of axolotls, 915f
    crustacean, 703
    of fishes, 722f
    for gas exchange in aquatic animals, 934f–935f
    mollusc, 693f
    osmoregulation by, 973f–974
Gill slits, 714f
Ginkgos, 636f
Giraffes, 162f, 925
Glabra-2 gene, 773f
Glaciation
    ecological succession after, 1224f–1225f
    seedless vascular plants and, 627
Glacier Bay, Alaska, 1224f–1225f
Glands, endocrine system. *See* Endocrine glands
Glans, 1019f–1020f
Glanville fritillaries, 1200–1201f
Glass lizard, 547f–548f
Gleason, H. A., 1222
Glia (glial cells), **873**, **1062**f–1063f, 1070f–1071f, **1081**f–1082f
Glioblastoma, 248, 441
Global biogeochemical cycles, 1244
Global carrying capacity, human population, 1204f–1205
Global change
    biodiversity hot spots and, 1267
    depletion of atmospheric ozone in, 1274f–1275f
    environmental toxins in, 1271f–1272f
    greenhouse gases and climate change in, 1272–1273f, 1274
    human impacts on, 1269
    nutrient enrichment in, 1270f
    sustainable development and, 1276f
    as threat to biodiversity, 1260
Global climate change
    coral reefs and, 687
    ecological footprints, fossil fuels, and, 1204f–1205

effects of, on photosynthetic marine protists, 609f
extinction rates and, 535f–536
greenhouse gases and, 1272–1273f, 1274
habitat loss from, 1258
melting of Arctic sea ice and, 48
nonvascular plants in Ordovician Period, 623
ocean acidification and, 53f–54
overharvesting of peat moss and, 622
in Permian mass extinction, 534–535
plant adaptations to, 202–203
seedless vascular plants and, 627–628
solutions for, 1274
species distributions and, 1163–1164f
tropical rain forest deforestation and, 645f–646
using dendrochronology to study, 767f
Global climate patterns, 1160f
Global cooling, 627
Global ecology, **1159**f. *See also* Ecology
    aquatic biomes in, 1171f–1172f, 1173f–1176f
    of biosphere, 1159f (*see also* Biosphere)
    effects of mass extinctions on, 536f
    global climate in, 1160f–1164f
    global human population size issues in, 1201f–1204f, 1205
    human environmental impacts in (*see* Human environmental impacts)
    importance of mycorrhizae to, 811
    ocean acidification in, 53f–54
    species distributions in, 1172, 1178f–1180f, 1181
    terrestrial biomes in, 1164–1165f, 1166f–1170f
Global ecosystem, biosphere as, 1233
Global energy budget, 1235
Global extinctions, 1256
Global human population, 1201f–1202f
Global net primary production, 1236f
Global temperatures, extinction rates and, 535f–536
Globigerina, 591f
Globin genes, human, 447f, 449–450f, 452
Globular proteins, 78
Glomeromycetes, 655f, **657**f
Glomerulus, **981**f
Glottis, 901f
Glucagon, 910f, **910**f, 999f
Glucocorticoids, 999f, 1007f, **1008**
Glucose
    enzymatic catalysis and, 151, 153
    enzymes and levels of, in blood, 156
    epinephrine and metabolism of, 998f
    as fuel for cellular respiration, 164–165
    glucocorticoids and metabolism of, 1007f–1008
    homeostasis of, 909–910f
    as monosaccharide, 68f–69f
    oxidation of, to pyruvate by glycolysis, 168f–169f
    in photosynthesis, 41, 188f, 204–205f
    in positive gene regulation, 364f
    regulation of blood, 8–9f
    in signal transduction pathways, 212–213
    transport of, 130, 134
Glucose-6-phosphatase, 156
Glutamate, **1075**t, 1095f–1096, 1114–1115f
Glutamic acid, 77f, 150f, 339
Glutamine, 77f, 150f
Glyceraldehyde, 68f
Glyceraldehyde 3-phosphate (G3P), **199**–200f, 204–205f
Glycerol phosphate, **63**f
Glycine, **63**f, 77f, 1075
Glycogen, **71**
    in cell signaling, 212–213, 223–224f
    in glucose metabolism, 8–9f, 909–910f
    in muscle contraction, 1120, 1122
    as storage polysaccharide, 70f–71
Glycogen phosphorylase, 213–214
Glycolipids, **129**
Glycolysis, **166**
    ATP yield in, 175f
    evolutionary significance of, 179–180
    fermentation and, 178f
    oxidation of glucose to pyruvate by, 168f–169f
    as stage of cellular respiration, 166–167f
Glycoproteins, **105**, **129**
    in animal morphogenesis, 1050
    in cellular membranes, 125f–126, 129

in extracellular matrix, 118–119f
genetic engineering of, using fungi, 665f
rough ER and, 105
viruses and, 394–395, 399f, 401f
Glycosidic linkages, **69**
Glyoxysomes, 111
Gnathostomes, **719**
    derived characters of, 719f–720
    fossil, 720f
    ray-finned fishes and lobe-fins as osteichthyans, 722f–723f, 724
    sharks and rays as chondrichthyans, 720–721f
    tetrapods as, 724
Gnetophytes, 636f, 641
Gnetum, 636f
Goats, 430f
Goatsbeard plants, 508–509f
Goiter, 29, 1004
Golden algae, **596**f
Golden Rice, 832, 896
Golgi apparatus, 100f, **105**–106f, 107, 129f, 206f
Gonadotropin-releasing hormone (GnRH), 1009, 1024–1025f, 1026f
Gonadotropins, 1003, 1008–1009f, 1024f–1026f, 1027
Gonads, 235, 256, 999f, 1008–1009f, **1017**
Gonorrhea, 570, 578f, 1034
Goodall, Jane, 16f
Gorillas, 89, 741f
Gormley, Andrew, 1185f
Gould, Stephen Jay, 514
Gout, 977
G protein-coupled receptors (GPCRs), 214f–215f, 216f–217, 221f, 1118
G proteins, 215f, 221f
Graded potentials, **1067**f–1068, 1073
Grades, taxonomy, 617, 675
Gradients, solute, 983–984f, 985
Grafting, plant, 829
Graft versus host reaction, 964
Gram (unit), 50
Gram, Hans Christian, 568
Gram-negative bacteria, **568**–569f, 578f
Gram-positive bacteria, **568**–569f, 579f
Gram stain technique, **568**–569f
Grant, Peter and Rosemary, 21, 480
Granum, **110**–111, 187f
Grapefruit, 639f
Grapes, 845f
Grapes of Wrath, The (book), 801f
Graphs in Scientific Skills Exercises
    bar, 22, 177, 370, 420, 477, 584, 623, 694, 756, 858, 1181, 1211
    comparing two variables on a common *x*-axis of, 967
    cyclic data, 1273
    estimating quantitative data from, 532
    histograms, 248, 281, 932
    interpreting changes in slope in, 1043
    line, 33, 155, 262, 404, 967, 1043, 1089, 1130, 1181, 1273
    with log scales, 1130
    pie charts, 886
    scatter plots, 54, 134, 203, 507, 745, 1211
    sequence logos, 349
Grass, phototropism in coleoptiles of, 841f
Grasshoppers, 458f, 704f, 706f, 899f, 917f, 936f, 1126f
Grasslands, 1169f, 1232f
Grassy stunt virus, 1257
Graves' disease, 1004
Gravitational motion, free energy and, 146f
Gravitropism, **855**f
Gravity
    axis formation and, 1054
    blood pressure and, 925–926f
    locomotion and, 1129
    mechanoreceptors for sensing, 1106, 1108
    plant responses to, 855f
Gray matter, **1082**f
Gray tree frogs, 494f, 508
Greater bilby, 736f–737
Greater prairie chickens, 489f–490, 1262f–1263
Great Salt Lake, 580
Great tits (*Parus major*), 490–491f, 734f
Green, Richard, 747f

Green algae, 101*f*, 591*f*, 592*f*–593*f*, **603***f*–4*f*, 612*f*–613, 658, 662*f*–663*f*
Greenhouse effect, **1272**–1273*f*, 1274
Greenhouse gases, 48, 53*f*, 1163, 1272–1273*f*, 1274
Greening, plant, 837*f*–838*f*, 839
Green manure, 810
Green parrot snake, 1212*f*
Griffith, Frederick, 313*f*
Grizzly bears, 504*f*, 1263*f*, 1268
Grolar bears, 504*f*
Gross primary production (GPP), **1235**–1236*f*
Ground squirrels, 887, 1187*f*–1188*f*, 1189*t*–1190
Ground tissue system, plant, **757**, 757*f*
Groups, control and experimental, 20*f*
Growth, 769. *See also* Plant growth
    as cell division function, 232–233*f*
    heterochrony and differential rates of, 538*f*–539*f*
    hormonal regulation of, 999*f*, 1003*f*, 1005*f*
    plant and animal, 888*f*
    as property of life, 1*f*
Growth, population. *See* Population growth
Growth factors, **245**
    in cell cycle control system, 245–246*f*
    cell fate and, 1056–1058
    in cell-signaling nuclear responses, 223*f*
    induction and, 378
    as local regulators in cell signaling, 212
Growth hormone (GH), 999*f*, 1003*f*, **1005***f*
Growth rings, tree, 767*f*
Grundler, Michael, 1158*f*
GTP (guanosine triphosphate), 170*f*–171*f*, 215*f*, 350*f*, 351*f*
GTPase, 227
Guanine, 85*f*–86, 315*f*–316
Guano, 977
Guard cells, **764**–765*f*, 791*f*–792
Guichon Creek project, 1269
Gulf of Carpentaria, 598*f*
Gulf of Mexico dead zone, 1270*f*
Gulf Stream, 1162*f*
Gulls, 1145*f*
Guppies, 477, 1147*f*
Gurdon, John, 423*f*
Gustation, **1117***f*–1118*f*
Gutenberg, Johannes, 23–24
Guttation, **787***f*–788
Gymnosperms, **617***t*
    evolution of, 635*f*
    evolution of seeds in, 632–633
    gametophyte-sporophyte relationships in, 631*f*
    life cycle of pine and, 634*f*–635
    ovules and production of seeds in, 632*f*
    phylogeny of, 617*f*, 635–636*f*, 637*f*
Gyres, ocean, 1162*f*

H
H1N1 virus, 403*f*–404, 966, 1228
H5N1 virus, 403, 405, 1229*f*
Habitat
    carrying capacity of, 1192*t*–1194*f*
    destruction of, in tropical rain forests, 645*f*–646
    fragmented, 1258*f*, 1266*f*–1267
    island habitat, 1226–1227*f*, 1228
    loss of, as threat to biodiversity, 1258
    nitrogenous wastes and, 977
    population conservation and critical, 1264*f*–1265
    requirements for red-cockaded woodpecker, 1264*f*–1265
    sympatric speciation and differentiation of, 510
Habitat corridors, 1249
Habitat isolation, 502*f*
Habitat selection behavior, 1178–1179
Hadean eon, 526*f*, 527*f*
Haemophilus influenzae, 442*t*
Hagfishes, **717***f*–718
Haikouella, 718*f*
Hair, mammalian, 735
Hair cells, 1106–1107*f*, **1108***f*
Hairy-cap moss, 620*f*
Haldane, J. B. S., 520
Hallucigenia, 523*f*, 700
Halobacterium, 567*f*, 580
Hamilton, William, 1152

Hamilton's rule, **1152***f*–1153
Hamsters, 887*f*, 1089
Haplo-diploid sex determination system, 296*f*
Haploid cells, **255**, 256*f*–257
Hardy-Weinberg equation, 484–487
    in Scientific Skills Exercise, 487
Hardy-Weinberg equilibrium, **484**–485*f*, 486–487
Hares, 1200*f*
Harper, John, 1197*f*
Haustoria, **650***f*
Hawaiian Islands, 506, 537*f*–538
Hawaiian silversword plants, 537*f*–538, 551, 1178*f*
Hawkmoth, 821*f*, 881*f*, 1212*f*
Hazel, 820*f*
Hazelnut, 639*f*
Head, insect, 704*f*
Head structure morphogen, 381*f*–382*f*
Hearing, 1106*f*–1110*f*
Heart attacks, 412*f*, 430, **931**–932
Heartbeat rhythm, 921–922*f*
Heartburn, 902
Heart disease, 214, 412*f*, 422, 430
Heart murmurs, **922**
Heart rate, **921**, 922
Hearts, **917**
    atrial natriuretic peptide hormone released by, 990*f*
    blood pressure and cardiac cycle of, 924–925
    in circulatory systems, 917*f*–918
    effects of adrenal hormones on, 1007
    insect, 704*f*
    location of, for human embryo, 1037
    mammalian, in cardiovascular systems, 920*f*–922*f*
    mollusc, 693*f*
    regulation of rhythmic beating of, 921–922*f*
Heartwood, 768
Heat, **46**, **142**
    as byproduct of cellular respiration, 176
    diffusion and, 130
    metabolic rate and loss of, 884
    plant response to stress of, 857–858
    temperature vs., 46
    thermophiles and, 580*f*–581
    thermoreceptors and, 1105
Heat exchange adaptations, animal, 879*f*–882*f*
Heat of vaporization, **47**
Heat-shock proteins, **858**
Heavy chains, 953*f*
Heberlein, Ulrike, 866*f*, 1097
Hector's dolphins, 1185*f*–1186
Hedgehog growth factor, 1057–1058
Heimlich maneuver, 901
HeLa cancer cells, 247
Helianthus species, 514–515*f*
Helical viruses, 394*f*
Helicases, 321*f*, 324*f*, 325*t*
Helicobacter pylori, 902, 907*f*
Helium, 30*f*
Helper T cells, **958***f*–959
Hemagglutinin gene, 404
Heme group, 173
Heme oxygenase, 1076
Hemichordata, 683*f*
Hemidactylus turcicus, 563*f*
Hemings, Sally, 431
Hemiptera, 706*f*
Hemispheres, brain, 1087*f*, 1092
Hemizygous organisms, 297
Hemocoel, 701
Hemocyanin, 941
Hemocytes, 947–948*f*
Hemoglobin, **929**
    α-globin and β-globin gene families and, 447*f*, 449–450*f*
    in circulation and gas exchange, 941*f*–942*f*
    cooperativity as allosteric regulation in, 158–159
    in erythrocytes, 929
    as measure of evolution, 89
    polypeptides in, 336
    as protein, 76*f*
    protein quaternary structure and, 81*f*
    sickle-cell disease and, 82*f*, 284*f*–285, 494–495, 496*f*–497*f*
Hemolymph, 701, **917***f*, 975, 979*f*–980

Hemophilia, **297**–298, 931
Hemorrhagic fever, 402
Henslow, John, 465
Hepatic portal veins, **904**
Hepatitis B virus, 402, 968
Hepatophyta (liverworts), 614*f*–615*f*, **618**, 620*f*
HER2 breast cancer, 217, 248, 387*f*
Herbicide resistance, 432
Herbicides
    auxin in, 843
    transgenic, 832
Herbivores, **892**
    alimentary canals of, 906–907*f*
    animals as, 667
    as biotic factors limiting species distributions, 1179*f*
    dentition and diet in, 906*f*
    energetic hypothesis and biomass of, 1219*f*
    evolutionary links between plants and, 642–643*f*
    insects as, 707
    mutualistic digestive adaptations of, 907–908*f*
    plant defenses against, 861, 862*f*–863*f*
Herbivory, **861**, 862*f*–863*f*, **1213***f*
Herceptin, 217, 248, 387*f*
Hereditary factors, genes as, 267–268, 292*f*. *See also* Gene(s)
Hereditary variation, 252*f*. *See also* Genetic variation
Heredity, 252*f*, 267–268. *See also* Inheritance; Mendelian inheritance
Hermaphrodites, **685**, 698
Hermaphroditism, **1016**
Heroin, 40, 79, 1097*f*
Herpes simplex viruses, 966–967
Herpesviruses, 399, 402, 966–967
Hershey, Alfred, 314*f*–315
Heterochromatin, **330**, 366, 376
Heterochrony, **538***f*–539*f*
Heterocysts (heterocytes), **576**
Heterokaryon mycelia, 651
Heteromorphic generations, 598
Heterosporous species, **625**, 632
Heterotrophs, **186**, 575, 576*f*, 588, 649, 668, 888*f*, 1233
Heterozygote advantage, **494**–495*f*, 496*f*–497*f*
Heterozygote protection, 482
Heterozygous organisms, **272**
Hexapoda. *See* Insects
Hexoses, 68*f*
Hfr cells, 574*f*–575
Hibernation, 176, **887***f*
Hierarchical classification, 548–549*f*
High-density lipoproteins (HDLs), **931**–932
Highly conserved genes, 454
High-resolution oxygen sensors, 1237*f*
High-throughput DNA technology, 7, 408*f*, 409*f*, 411*f*–412, 437*f*–438, 441
Hindbrain, **1085***f*
Hinge joints, 1128*f*
Hippocampus, 1089*f*, 1094–1095*f*
Hippopotamus, 88*f*
Hirudin, 697
Hirudinea, 696–697
Histamine, 951*f*, 965
Histidine, 77*f*
Histograms in Scientific Skills Exercises, 248, 281, 932
Histone acetylation, 366*f*
Histone modifications, 366*f*–367, 386
Histones, **328***f*
Hitchhiking commensalism, 1215
HIV (human immunodeficiency virus), **400**, **967**. *See also* AIDS (acquired immunodeficiency syndrome)
    AIDS and, 392*f*
    antiviral drugs and, as emerging virus, 402
    applying molecular clock to origin of, 561–562*f*
    attacks on immune system by, 967–968*f*
    biotechnology in diagnosis of, 428
    cell-surface proteins and blocking entry of, into cells, 128*f*
    host range of, 395
    rapid reproduction of, 483
    replicative cycle of, 401*f*
    as retrovirus, 398*t*, 400
HIV-1 M strain, 561–562*f*
Hodgkin, Alan, 1068

Hodgkin's disease, 966, 1257f
Hoekstra, Hopi, 20f, 21, 23, 461f, 476
Holdfasts, **596**
Holoblastic cleavage, **1042**
Holothuroidea, 709f
Homeoboxes, **457**–458f, 668–669
Homeodomains, 457
Homeostasis, **875**
  of blood calcium levels, 1006f
  as feedback regulation of animal internal
    environment, 875f–877f
  of glucose, 909–910f, 998f, 1007f–1008
  hormonal regulation of kidneys for, 988f–990f
  of human breathing, 940f
  osmoregulation for, 971f–972, 975
  peripheral nervous system in, 1084
  in plants and animals, 212
  thyroid, 1004f–1005f
Homeotherms, 878
Homeotic genes, **380**–381f, 457f–458f, **539f**–540f,
    541. See also Hox genes
Hominins, **742**
  Australopiths, 743–744f
  bipedalism in, 744f–745
  derived characters of, 742
  earliest, 742f–743f
  early Homo genus, 746f
  Homo sapiens, 747f–748f
  Neanderthals, 746–747f
  tool use in, 745–746
Homo erectus, 746
Homo ergaster, 746f
Homo floresiensis, 748f
Homogenization, 96f
Homo genus, 741–742, 746f–748f
Homo habilis, 746
Homologies, 473f–475f, 551f–553f
Homologous chromosomes (homologs), **254**
  alleles in, 257
  in chromosomal basis of Mendelian inheritance,
    292f–293f, 294
  human, 254f–255f
  in meiosis, 258f
  in mitosis vs. in meiosis, 260–261f, 262
Homologous genes, 559f–560
Homologous structures, 473f–475f
Homo neanderthalensis. See Neanderthals
Homoplasies, **552**, 553f
Homo sapiens, 33, 501f, 548, 659t, 743f, 747–748f. See
    also Human(s)
Homosporous species, **625**, 632
Homozygous organisms, **272**
Honeybees, 820f, 881, 1136f–1137f, 1141f, 1151
Honey mushrooms, 648f–650
Hook, flagellum, 570f–571
Hooke, Robert, 94
Hookworms, 699
Horizontal cells, 1112f, 1114–1115f
Horizontal gene transfer, 562–563f, 564, 573f–574f,
    575, 577, 583
Horizontal transmission, viral, 405
Hormonal proteins, 76f
Hormone cascade pathways, 1003, 1004f–1005f, 1009
Hormones, **212**
  animal vs. plant, 212, 888f (see also Animal
    hormones; Plant hormones)
  coordinate control of genes by, 371
  in fight-or-flight responses, 210
  as intracellular chemical signals, 217–218f
  kidney regulation by, 988f–990f
  in long-distance cell signaling, 212, 213f
  specificity of, 224–225
Hornworts, 618, 620f. See also Bryophytes
Horowitz, Norman, 334–335f
Horses, 408, 542–543f
Horseshoe crabs, 702f
Horsetails, 624f, 625–626f, 627
Horvitz, Robert, 1052
Hosken, David, 1018f
Host cells, endosymbiont, 528–529f
Host ranges, viral, **395f**–396
Hosts, parasite, **1214**, 1229f

Hosts, symbiont, **582**
Hot spots, biodiversity, 1267f
Hot springs, 580f–581
House gecko, 563f
House mouse (Mus musculus), 23, 436f. See also Mice
Hox genes. See also Homeotic genes
  analyzing quantitative and spatial gene expression
    data on, 420
  as animal development genes, 457f–458f, 668–669
  arthropod body plan and, 700f–701
  cell fate and, 1058
  jaws and, 719f–720
  lancelet, tunicate, and vertebrate, 715–716f
  in macroevolution of development, 539f–540f, 541
  origin of, 671
  in plants, 773f
HTLV-1 virus, 388
Hubbard Brook Experimental Forest, 1247–1248f,
    1260f
Human(s). See also Human body; Human embryonic
    development; Human environmental
    impacts; Human genetics; Human genome;
    Human nutrition; Human population;
    Human reproduction
  analyzing polypeptide sequence data for monkeys
    and, 89
  as anthropoid apes, 741–742
  apoptosis of white blood cells of, 227f
  biodiversity and welfare of, 1257f
  biological species concept and, 501f
  blood pH of, 52–53
  blood pressure of, 925f
  brown algae as food for, 597
  catabolism and diets of, 180f–181
  cells of, 93f
  chromosomes of, 102, 233–234f, 235, 254f–255f,
    256
  cilia in windpipes of, 12f
  circulatory systems of (see Cardiovascular
    systems)
  cloning of, 425
  derived characters of, 742
  determining gene function by analyzing genomes
    of, 421–422, 428
  digestive system of (see Digestive systems)
  DNA microarray assays on tissue of, 421f
  DNA sequencing of genome of, 408f, 412
  essential elements and trace elements for, 29t–30
  ethical issues on silencing gene expression in, 421
  evolution of culture in, 1153f–1154
  genomics and proteomics in study of, 87–88f
  glycoproteins and blood types of, 129
  as Homo sapiens, 743f, 747–748f
  importance of insects to, 707
  importance of seed plants to welfare of, 645f–646f
  inactivated olfactory receptor genes of, 483
  lymphatic systems of, 927
  origin of, 531
  overlap of Neanderthals and modern, 33
  practical uses of fungi for, 664–665f
  primate phylogenetic tree and, 740f
  prokaryotic impacts on, 582–583f, 584f–585f
  red algae as food for, 602–603f
  reducing hunger and malnutrition in, with
    transgenic crops, 831–832f
  regulation of breathing in, 940f
  regulation of molecular interactions in, 8–9f
  relationship of Neanderthals and, 746–747f
  sex chromosomes of, 296f–297
  skulls of chimpanzees and, 552
  small intestine surface area for, 689f
  sustainable development in Costa Rica and living
    conditions of, 1276f
  transgenic crops and health of, 833
  urban, 1269
Human body
  bacteria in, 582–583
  brain in nervous system of, 1079f–1080, 1085f–
    1090f (see also Brains; Nervous systems)
  circadian rhythms in thermoregulation of,
    876–877f
  digestive systems (see Digestive systems)

  ears of, 1107f
  endocrine glands and hormones of, 998–999f,
    1002f, 1003f (see also Animal hormones;
    Endocrine systems; Nervous systems)
  evolution of human eye, 541–542f
  excretory systems of, 980f–981f
  eyes of, 1112f–1113
  glucose homeostasis in, 909–910f
  heterochrony and differential growth rates in
    skulls of, 538f
  hypothalamus in thermoregulation of, 882–883f
  locomotion by interaction of muscles and
    skeletons of, 1126f
  lymphatic system of, 950f
  mechanoreceptors in skin of, 1104f
  metabolic rates of, 886
  osmoregulation of, 974
  overnourishment, obesity, and, 911f–912
  regulation of growth of, 1005f
  skeleton of, 1128f
  two-solute model of kidney function, 983–984f,
    985
Human chorionic gonadotropin (hCG), 963, 1029
Human embryonic development. See also Animal
    development
  brains in, 1086f
  cilia and cell fate in, 1058f
  conception, pregnancy, and birth in, 1028f–1231f
  embryo image, 1037f
  gastrulation in, 1046f–1047f
  maternal immune tolerance of embryo and fetus
    in, 1031
  neuron competition in, 1093–1094
Human environmental impacts
  on biodiversity, 1255f
  biodiversity crisis, 1254f–1255f (see also
    Biodiversity)
  biome disturbances, 1166
  community disturbances, 1225f
  global change, 1260f, 1269–1270f, 1271f–1275f
  habitat loss and fragmentation, 1258f
  introduced species, 1258–1259f
  melting of Arctic sea ice, 48
  ocean acidification, 53f–54
  overharvesting, 1259f
  spread of pathogens, 1228
  threats to biodiversity from, 1258f–1260f
Human genetics
  dominantly inherited disorders in, 285f
  genetic testing and counseling in, 285–286,
    287f–288
  molecular tags and karyotypes of chromosomes
    in, 330f
  multifactorial disorders in, 285
  pedigree analysis in, 282f–283
  recessively inherited disorders in, 283f–284f, 285
  skin pigmentation and, 279–280f
Human genome
  α-globin and β-globin gene families in, 447f,
    449–450f
  comparing genomes of other species with, 448f,
    453–454f, 455f–456
  complete sequence for, 436f
  evolution of, 560
  function of FOXP2 gene in, 454f–455
  gene density of fungal vs., 659t
  microarray chips containing, 441f
  sequencing of, 437f–438, 441f–442
  size, number of genes, gene density, and
    noncoding DNA of, 442t–443
  types of DNA sequences in, 444f
Human Genome Project, 87, 344, **437f**–438
Human growth hormone (HGH), 412f–413, 430, 1005
Human immunodeficiency virus (HIV). See HIV
    (human immunodeficiency virus)
Human nutrition. See also Animal nutrition
  assessing nutritional needs for, 896–897
  bacteria in, 582–583
  dietary deficiencies in, 896f
  essential nutrients for, 893f, 894t–895t
  transgenic crops and, 432–433
Human papillomavirus (HPV), 968

Human population
    biosphere carrying capacity for global, 1201f–1204f, 1205
    density-dependent population regulation of, by diseases, 1198f
    survivorship curves for, 1188f
Human reproduction. *See also* Animal reproduction
    conception, embryonic development, and birth in, 1028f–1031f
    contraception and abortion in, 1032f–1033
    endocrine disruptors and, 1009
    female reproductive organs of, 1020–1021f
    hormonal regulation of, 1024f–1027f
    as iteroparity, 1195f
    male reproductive organs of, 1019f–1020
    maternal immune tolerance of embryo and fetus in, 1031
    oogenesis in, 1023f
    prostaglandins and, 999
    reproductive technologies and, 1033–1034f
    sexual response in, 1027–1028
    spermatogenesis in, 1022f
Hummingbird hawkmoth, 706f
Hummingbirds, 4, 516, 734f, 821f
Humoral immune response, 947f, 958f–959f
Humpback whales, 898f
Humus, 800, 801
Hundred Heartbeat Club species, 1256f
Hunger, transgenic crops and reducing human, 831–832f
Huntington's disease, 285, 426
Hurricane Katrina, 1166
Hutton, James, 463f, 464
Huxley, Andrew, 1068
Hybrid breakdown, 503f
Hybridization, 269, 831, 833–834
Hybrid orbitals, 39f–40
Hybrids, 501
    bears, 504f
    reproductive barriers and sterility of, 503f
    speciation rates and, 514–515f
    sterility of, 516
Hybrid zones, 510–511f, 512f–513f
Hydrangea, 280f
Hydras, 253f, 685–686f, 687f, 899f, 1080f
Hydration shells, 49
Hydrocarbons, 60–61f, 665f
Hydrocarbon tail, chlorophyll, 192f
Hydrochloric acid, 51, 901–902f
Hydrogen
    covalent bonding and, 36f–37f
    as essential element, 29t, 56, 64
    in organic compounds, 59f
    oxidation of organic molecules containing, 164–165f
    in plant composition, 803
    in saturated and unsaturated fats, 73f–74
Hydrogen bonds, 39f
    in DNA structure, 86–87f
    floating of ice and, 48
    in water molecules, 45f
    as weak chemical bonds, 39f
Hydrogen ions, 51–52f, 53
Hydrogenosomes, 593
Hydrogen peroxide, 111
Hydrogen sulfide gas, 534–535
Hydrolysis, 67
    of ATP, 149f–151f
    disassembling of polymers to monomers by, 67f
    enzymatic, 897
    by lysosomes, 107f–108
Hydrolytic enzymes, fungal, 649
Hydronium ions, 51–52f, 53
Hydrophilic substances, 49, 76–77f, 125f–126
Hydrophobic interaction, 81f
Hydrophobic substances, 49, 76–77f, 125f–126
Hydroponic culture, 804f
Hydrostatic skeletons, 1127f
Hydrothermal vents, 520–21f, 580, 582, 908f
Hydroxide ions, 51–52f, 53
Hydroxyl group, 63f
Hydrozoans, 686f–687f
Hymen, 1020
Hymenoptera, 706f

Hypercholesterolemia, 137
Hypermastigote, 608f
Hyperosmotic solutions, 972f, 985
Hyperpolarization, 1066f–1067f
Hypersensitive response, plant, 860, 861
Hypertension, 932
Hypertonic solutions, 132f
Hyphae, fungal, 649f–650f, 651, 811
Hypoblast cells, 1046f–1047f
Hypocotyl, 822–823f, 824f
Hypoosmotic solutions, 972f
Hypothalamus, 882, 1002, 1087
    in homeostasis, 1084
    in human brain, 1087f
    in human endocrine system, 999f
    in kidney regulation, 988f–989f
    in neuroendocrine signaling, 1002f–1005f
    in regulation of mammalian reproduction, 1024f–1026f, 1027
    in sex hormone cascades, 1009
    in stress responses, 1007f
    suprachiasmatic nucleus (SCN) in, 1088–1089
    in thermoregulation, 882–883f
Hypotheses, 16. *See also* Inquiry Figures; Scientific Skills Exercises
    forming and testing of, in science, 16–17f, 18f–19
    phylogenetic trees as, 558f
    theories and, 21, 477–478
Hypothyroidism, 1004
Hypotonic solutions, 132f
Hyracoidea, 739f
Hyracotherium, 542–543f

I

Ibex, 1260–1261
Ibuprofen, 62f, 1008, 1106
Ice
    floating of, on liquid water, 48f
    on Mars, 50f
    as solid water, 44
Icosahedral viruses, 394f–395
Identical DNA sequences, 447f
Identical twins, 1030, 1055
Idioblasts, 862f
IgE antibodies, 964
Iguanas, 883
Ileum, 904
Imaging, brain, 1079f–1080, 1090f
Imaging techniques, fetal testing, 287
Imatinib, 429–430
Imbibition, 823
Immigration, population dynamics of, 1186f, 1190–1191f, 1200–1201f, 1227
Immune defenses, plant, 751, 859–860
Immune response
    primary and secondary, 956–957f
    trypanosome evasion of, 594
Immune systems, 946
    adaptations of pathogens to evade, 965–968f
    diseases of, 227
    disruptions of, 964–965f, 966
    HIV/AIDS and, 392f, 400 (*see also* AIDS (acquired immunodeficiency syndrome); HIV (human immunodeficiency virus))
    immune rejection by, 962–963
    immune responses by adaptive immunity in, 958f–963f, 964
    immune responses by innate immunity in, 947f–948f, 949f–951f, 952
    immunization and, 961–962, 967f
    leukocytes in, 929
    lymphatic systems and, 927f
    maternal immune tolerance of embryo and fetus during pregnancy, 1031
    membrane carbohydrate cell-cell recognition in, 128–129
    pathogen-specific recognition by adaptive immunity in, 952–953f, 954f–955f, 956–957f
    in plants, 751, 859–860
    prostaglandins in, 995
    recognition and response functions of innate and adaptive immunity in, 946f–947f
    stem cells and, 426
    trematode camouflage and, 690f

Immunity
    active and passive, and immunization, 962–963
    maternal immune tolerance of embryo and fetus during pregnancy, 1031
Immunization, 963
Immunodeficiency diseases, 966
Immunoglobulin (Ig), 953f, 955f–956, 961
Immunological memory, 954, 956–957f
Impala, 219f
Imprinting, 1138–1139f, 1146f–1147f
Inactivation, cell-signaling, 227
Inborn immunodeficiency, 966
Inclusive fitness, 1152f–1153f
Incomplete dominance, 277f
Incomplete flowers, 638f, 816
Incomplete metamorphosis, 705, 706f
Independent assortment, law of, 272–273, 274f, 293f–294, 300
Independent assortment of chromosomes, 263f
Independent variables, 21, 507
Indeterminate cleavage, 675f–676
Indeterminate growth, 760f–761f
Indian corn, 445f
Indian Ocean Subtropical Gyre, 1162f
Indian pipe, 812f
Indian rice, 1257
Indoleacetic acid (IAA), 842. *See also* Auxin
Indolebutyric acid (IBA), 843
Induced fit, 153f–154
Induced pluripotent stem cells, 426–427f
Inducers, 363f–364
Inducible enzymes, 363f–364
Inducible innate immune response, 948f, 949f
Inducible operons, 363f–364
Induction, 377f–378, 1048
Inductive reasoning, 16
Inductive signals, cell fate determination and pattern formation by, 1055–1056f, 1057f–1058
Industrialization, human population growth and, 1201f–1202
Inert elements, 35
Infant mortality, 1203, 1276f
Infection
    bacterial, 215f
    cytotoxic T cell response to, 959f
    fungal, 664
    inflammatory response and, 951–952
Infection thread, bacterial, 809f
Inferences, 1025
Infertility, 1033–1034f
Inflammation, 578f, 931f–932, 1008, 1106
Inflammatory response, 951f–952
Inflorescences, 816
Influenza viruses
    antibody proteins and, 79f
    antigenic variation of, 966
    in density-dependent population regulation, 1198f
    as emerging viruses, 402–403f, 404–405
    structure of, 394f–395
    as zoonotic, 1228–1229f
Information, as theme of biology, 2, 5f–6f, 7
Information processing
    cerebral cortex in, 1090–1091f
    ion movements and gradients and, 987f
    neuron, 1061–1062, 1063f
    problem solving and, 1141f
Infrared receptors, 1104–1105f
Ingestion, 897f
Ingroups, 555
Inhalation, 938–939f, 940f
Inheritance. *See also* Mendelian inheritance; Sexual life cycles
    blending hypothesis vs. particulate hypothesis on, 267–68
    of cancer predisposition, 388
    chromosomal basis of (*see* Chromosomal basis of inheritance)
    of chromosomes and genes, 253
    C. Darwin on, 13f–15f
    Darwinian theory on, 469f–470
    epigenetic, 367
    expression and transmission of genetic information in, 5f–6f, 7

genetics as study of, 252 (*see also* Genetics)
genetic variation and, 481
genomic imprinting and, 308*f*–309
Lamarck's theory on, 465
molecular basis of (*see* Molecular basis of inheritance)
of organelle genes, 309*f*
of X-linked genes, 297*f*–98
Inheritance of acquired characteristics principle, 465
Inhibin, 1024–1025*f*
Inhibiting hormones, 999*f*, 1003
Inhibition
    allosteric, 158*f*–159
    enzyme inhibitors and, 156*f*–157
    feedback, 159*f*
Inhibitory postsynaptic potential (IPSP), **1073**
Initials, cell, 760
Initiation factors, 348*f*, 350
Initiation stage
    regulation of transcription, 367*f*–369*f*, 370–371*f*, 372*f*
    regulation of translation, 373
    transcription, 340*f*, 341*f*
    translation, 348*f*, 350
Innate behavior, **1138**
Innate immunity, **947***f*
    antimicrobial peptides and proteins in, 948*f*, 949*f*, 951
    barrier defenses of, 948–949
    cellular innate defenses of, 949*f*–950*f*
    evasion of, by pathogens, 952
    inflammatory response of, 951*f*–952
    invertebrate, 947–948*f*, 949*f*
    molecular recognition by, 947*f*
    vertebrate, 948–949*f*, 950*f*–951*f*, 952
Inner cell mass, **1046***f*–1047*f*
Inner ear, **1107***f*
Innocence Project, 431*f*
Inorganic components, topsoil, 800–801*f*
Inositol trisphosphate (IP$_3$), 221–**222***f*
Inquiry Figures
    on abiotic synthesis of organic molecules as origin of life on Earth, 57*f*
    on aquaporin mutations as causes of diabetes insipidus, 989*f*
    on benefits of endophytes to woody plants, 661*f*
    on *bicoid* gene and body plan determination in fruit flies, 382*f*
    on bryophyte reduction of nitrogen leaching from soil, 621*f*
    on calcium ions in formation of fertilization envelope, 1040*f*
    on causes of greater prairie chicken decline, 1262*f*
    on cell cycle regulation by cytoplasmic signals, 243*f*
    on cell developmental potential, 1055*f*
    on cell fate and pattern formation by inductive signals from blastopore dorsal lip, 1056*f*
    on changes in gene regulation of stickleback fish, 540*f*
    on circadian clocks during hibernation, 887*f*
    on compositions of bacterial communities of roots, 807*f*
    on determining root of eukaryotic phylogenetic tree, 605*f*
    on digger wasp spatial learning, 1140*f*
    on discovery of virus causing tobacco mosaic disease, 393*f*
    on DNA replication models, 320*f*
    on dominant vs. recessive traits, 269*f*
    on effects of red light and far-red light on seed germination, 851*f*
    on effects of temperature on litter decomposition, 1247*f*
    on evolution by natural selection due to food source changes, 471*f*
    on eye color after crosses of wild-type and mutant fruit flies, 295*f*
    on female fruit fly bias in sperm usage, 1018*f*
    on function of *FOXP2* gene in human genome, 454*f*
    on gene-enzyme relationship in protein synthesis, 335*f*

on gene flow between Neanderthals and humans, 747*f*
on genetic basis of migratory orientation, 1151*f*
on *Hox* genes and arthropod body plan, 700*f*
on hypothesis of independent assortment, 273*f*
on inducing pluripotent stem cells, 427*f*
on interspecific competition and niches, 1210*f*
on linkage between genes and inheritance of characters, 299*f*
on mammalian taste detection, 1117*f*
on mate choice in tree frogs, 494*f*
on membrane protein movement, 126*f*
on most effective light wavelengths for photosynthesis, 192*f*
on nitrogen limitation of phytoplankton production, 1237*f*
on nuclear transplantation of differentiated animal cells, 423*f*
on phototropism in grass coleoptiles, 841*f*
on polar movement of auxin in plant shoots, 842*f*
on pressure-flow hypothesis about phloem sap sugar content near sources, 795*f*
on protecting fruit flies against infection with antimicrobial peptides, 949*f*
on protein vs. DNA as genetic material, 314*f*
on rapid prokaryotic evolution, 572*f*
on reproductive isolation from divergence of allopatric populations, 506*f*
on role of zone of polarizing activity (ZPA) in vertebrate limb formation, 1057*f*
on sea stars as keystone predators, 1220*f*
on sea urchin feeding as limiting seaweed distributions, 1179*f*
on sexual selection and reproductive isolation, 509*f*
on shape and function of RNA polymerase II, 84*f*
on shivering thermogenesis by Burmese pythons, 882*f*
on shortening of kinetochore microtubules during anaphase, 239*f*
on speciation from hybridization, 515*f*
on surfactants in respiratory distress syndrome, 938*f*
on survival costs of parental care in kestrels, 1196*f*
on transfer of genetic trait between bacterial strains, 313*f*
on using phylogenetic gene tree to identify species identity of whale meat, 551*f*
on vitamin supplementation and human neural tube birth defects, 896*f*
Inquiry, scientific, **16**, 16-24. *See also* Case studies; Inquiry Figures; Research Method Figures; Scientific Skills Exercises
Insecticide resistance, 491
Insects
    anatomy and features of, 704*f*–705*f*
    body plans of, 539*f*–540
    camouflage of, 462*f*, 470*f*
    cleavage in, 1042–1043
    compound eyes of, 1111*f*–1112
    defense mechanisms of, 28*f*
    evolution by natural selection in, due to food source changes, 471*f*–472
    exoskeletons of, 1127
    eyes of, 888*f*
    flower pollination by, 643*f*, 815*f*–816, 820*f*–821*f*
    gamete production and delivery in, 1018*f*
    Hox genes in, 457*f*–458*f*
    importance of, for humans, 707
    insecticide resistance in, 491
    malaria and, 599*f*
    Malpighian tubules of, 979*f*–980
    mechanoreceptors and hearing in, 1106*f*
    nervous systems of, 1080*f*
    neuroendocrine coordination in, 1001*f*–1002
    nonheritable variation in, 482*f*
    open circulatory systems of, 917*f*
    parasitic, 1214
    phylogeny and diversity of, 683*f*, 703*f*, 706*f*
    plant defenses against, 861, 862*f*–863*f*
    pollination by, 635*f*
    as pollinators, 516

sex chromosomes of, 296*f*
sex determination of, 296*f*
taste and smell in, 1117
thermoregulation in, 881*f*
tracheal systems for gas exchange in, 935–936*f*
Insertions (mutations), **356***f*
In situ hybridization, **418***f*, 420
Instability, free-energy change and, 145–146*f*
Instantaneous population growth rate, 1191
Insulation, animal thermoregulation and, 879
Insulin, **910**
    in diabetes mellitus, 910–911
    discovery of amino acid sequence of, 78
    exocytosis and, 137
    in glucose homeostasis, 910*f*
    in glucose metabolism, 8–9*f*, 212
    pancreas and, 999*f*
    as polypeptide, 996*f*
    production of, by biotechnology, 430
    as protein, 76*f*
    in regulation of appetite and consumption, 911*f*
    rough ER and, 105
    stem cells and, 426
Insulin-dependent diabetes, 911
Insulin-like growth factors (IGFs), 1005
Integral proteins, **127**
Integration
    cellular, 121*f*
    sensory, 1063*f*, 1102*f*, 1103
Integrins, **119**, 127
Integument, **632**, 818
Integumentary systems, **879**
Interactions
    as theme of biology, 2, 8*f*–9*f*
    interspecific (*see* Interspecific interactions)
    mycorrhizal, 651
    plant and animal, 642–643*f*
    prokaryotic ecological, 581*f*–582
Intercalary meristems, 763
Intercalated disks, 873*f*, **1126**
Intercellular communication. *See* Cell signaling
Intercellular joining function, membrane protein, 128*f*
Interdisciplinary research teams, 7
Interferons, **951**
Intermediate disturbance hypothesis, **1222***f*
Intermediate filaments, 100*f*, 101*f*, 113*t*, **117**
Intermembrane space, 110
Internal environments, animal, 868–869*f*, 870, 875*f*–877*f*
Internal factors, cell cycle control system, 245–46*f*
Internal fertilization, 1016–1017, 1146. *See also* Fertilization, reproductive
International Union for Conservation of Nature and Natural Resources (IUCN), 1256
Internet resources, genome-sequence, 438–439*f*, 440
Interneurons, **1063***f*, 1083*f*
Internodes, **755**
Interphase, **235***f*, 236*f*
Interphase nucleus transcription factories, 372*f*
Intersexual selection, **493***f*–494*f*, 1146
Interspecific competition, **1209**–1210*f*, 1211*f*
Interspecific interactions, **1209**
    competition, 1209–1210*f*, 1211*f*
    facilitation, 1215*f*
    genomics and proteomics in, 88*f*
    herbivory, 1213*f*
    predation, 1211–1212*f*, 1213*f*
    symbiosis, 1214*f*–1215*f*
    symbols of, 1208–1209
Interspecific mating, 501*f*. *See also* Mating
Interstitial fluid, **869***f*, 917, 926–927*f*, 975, 984–985
Intertidal zones, **1175***f*
Interviews
    Dangl, Jeffery, 751*f*
    Heberlein, Ulrike, 866*f*
    Hoekstra, Hopi, 461*f*
    King, Nicole, 546*f*
    Lin, Haifan, 92*f*
    Ramakrishnan, Venki, 27*f*
    Rotimi, Charles, 251*f*
    Turner, Monica, 1157*f*
Intestinal bacteria, 907*f*
Intestines, 582–583, 689*f*

Intracellular digestion, 899
Intracellular receptors, cell-signaling, 217–218*f*
Intracellular recording, 1066*f*
Intrasexual selection, **493***f*, 1146
Intrauterine devices (IUDs), 1032*f*
Intrinsic (physiological) factors, density-dependent population regulation by, 1199*f*
Introduced species, **1258–1259***f*
Introns, 343*f*–345*f*, 443, 481–482*f*
Invagination, 1044*f*
Invasive species, 811, **1217**
Inversions, chromosome, 305–306*f*
Invertebrate(s), **676, 680**
    action potential conduction speed in, 1070
    chordates, 713*f*–716*f*
    cnidarians, 681*f*, 685*f*–687*f*
    deuterostomes, echinoderms, and chordates, 683*f*, 707–708*f*, 709*f*
    ecdysozoans and arthropods, 682*f*–683*f*, 699*f*–706*f*, 707 (*see also* Arthropods; Ecdysozoans)
    gamete production and delivery in, 1018*f*
    hydrostatic skeletons of, 1127*f*
    innate immunity in, 947–948*f*, 949*f*
    lophotrochozoans, 681*f*–682*f*, 688–689*f*, 690*f*–698*f* (*see also* Lophotrochozoans)
    mechanoreceptors in, to sense gravity, 1106
    nervous systems of, 1080*f*–1081
    neuroendocrine signaling in, 1001*f*–1002
    organogenesis in, 1049
    osmoregulation in, 974*f*
    parental care in, 1017*f*
    phylogeny and diversity of, 680*f*–683*f*
    sponges, 681*f*, 684*f*–685
In vitro culturing, angiosperm, 830
In vitro DNA amplification, 414–415*f*
In vitro fertilization (IVF), 430, **1034**
In vitro mutagenesis, **421**
Iodine, 29
Iodine deficiencies, 1004–1005
Ion channel proteins, 1070
Ion channel receptors, 217*f*
Ion channels, **133, 1064**
    action potentials and gated, 1066*f*–1071*f*
    in mechanoreceptors, 1104
    neuron resting potential and, 1064*f*–1065*f*, 1066
Ion movements and gradients, in life processes, 987*f*
Ionic bonds, **37–38***f*
Ionic compounds (salts), 38*f*
Ionotropic receptors, 1072–1074
Ion pumps, 135–136*f*, 1064*f*–1065*f*, 1066
Ions, 37–38*f*, 928*f*, 987*f*, 1064*t*
Iridium, 535
Iris, **1112**
Iron
    in nutrient enrichment of oceans, 1238*t*
    plant deficiency in, 804
Iron oxide, 528
Irrigation, 802
Island ecosystems, 1232*f*–1233*f*
Island equilibrium model, 1226–1227*f*, 1228
Island species, 477
Isolated systems, 143, 147*f*
Isoleucine, 77*f*
Isoleucine synthesis, 159*f*
Isomers, 61*f*–62*f*
Isomorphic generations, **598**
Isoosmotic solutions, 972
Isopods, 703
Isotonic solutions, **132***f*
Isotopes, **31–32***f*, 33, 188, 1246
Israel, 580
Italy, age-structure pyramid for, 1203*f*
Iteroparity, **1195***f*
Ivanowsky, Dmitri, 393
Ivory, 1259

J

Jackson, Rob, 1217*f*
Jacob, François, 361, 541
Jacoby, Gordon C., 767*f*
Japan, 1203, 1251*f*
Japanese canopy plant, 442*t*–443
Japanese snails, 515–516
Jasmine, 849

Jasmonates, 840*t*, **849**
Jawfish, 1146*f*
Jawless vertebrates, 717*f*–719*f*
Jaws
    mammalian, 524–525*f*, 526
    snake, 493*f*
    vertebrate, 717, 719*f*–720
Jefferson, Thomas, 431
Jejunum, 904
Jellies (jellyfish), 681*f*, 685–686*f*, 916*f*
Jellyfish gene, 339*f*
Jenner, Edward, 963
Joints, human, 1128*f*
Joly, John, 788
Jost, Alfred, 1025
Joule (J), 46, 884
J-shaped exponential growth curve, 1191*f*–1192
Jumping genes. *See* Transposable elements
June solstice, 1161*f*
Juniper, 637*f*
Junk DNA. *See* Noncoding DNA
Juvenile hormone (JH), 1001*f*–1002
Juxtaglomerular apparatus (JGA), **990**
Juxtamedullary nephrons, **980***f*, 985

K

Kangaroos, 736–737*f*, 1129*f*, 1148*f*
Kaposi's sarcoma herpesvirus, 968
Kartagener's syndrome, 1058*f*
Karyogamy, **651***f*
Karyotypes, **254***f*, 286–287*f*, 306*f*, 330*f*
Katydids, 706*f*
Kaufman, D. W., 21–22*f*
Kelps, 597
Keratin, 76*f*, 336, 729
Kestrels, 1196*f*–1197
Ketoses, 68*f*
Keystone species, **1220**, 1265
Kidneys, **980**
    adaptations of vertebrate, to diverse environments, 985*f*–987*f*
    homeostatic regulation of, 988*f*–990*f*
    hormonal regulation of, 1002*f*–1003
    human cystic kidney disease, 1058
    osmoregulation in aquatic animals, 973*f*–974
    processing of blood filtrate in nephrons of, 981–983*f*
    solute gradients and water conservation by, 983–984*f*, 985
    structure of, in mammalian excretory systems, 980*f*–981*f*
Killifish, 477
Kilocalorie (kcal), 46, 884
Kimberella, 688
Kinases, 216*f*
Kinetic energy, **46, 142–143***f*
Kinetochore microtubules, 236*f*, 238–239*f*, 242*f*
Kinetochores, 236*f*, **238***f*–239*f*
Kinetoplastids, **594***f*
Kinetoplasts, 594
King, Mary-Claire, 388
King, Nicole, 546*f*, *670*
King, Thomas, 423
Kingdoms, taxonomy, 11*f*, **548–549***f*, 562
King penguins, 734*f*, 1187*f*
Kingsley, David, 540*f*
Kin selection, **1152–1153***f*
Kissimmee River restoration project, 1250*f*
Klinefelter syndrome, 307, 1033
Knee-jerk reflex, 1083*f*
Knob, ATP synthase, **173***f*
KNOTTED-1 gene, 773*f*
Koalas, 736, 906–907*f*
Kombu, 597
Korarchaeota clade, 581
Kornberg, Roger, 83–84*f*
Krebs, Hans, 170
Krebs cycle. *See* Citric acid cycle
Krill, 48*f*, 703–704*f*
K-selection (density-dependent selection), **1196***f*–1197
Kudzu, 1258–1259*f*
Kuru, 405

L

Labeling, GM products, 432–433
Labia majora, **1020**–1021*f*
Labia minora, **1020**–1021*f*
Labor, childbirth and, 1030–1031*f*
Labrador Current, 1162*f*
Lacks, Henrietta, 247
Lac operon, 363*f*–364
Lactate, 178*f*–179, 1124
Lactation, 1031
Lacteals, 904*f*–905
Lactic acid fermentation, **178***f*–179
Lactose, 69*f*, 363*f*–364
Lagging strand, DNA, **322–323***f*
Lagomorpha, 739*f*
Laguna Salada de Torrevieja, 567*f*
Lakes, 1171*f*–1172*f*, 1173*f*, 1238, 1270*f*
Lake Vesijärvi, 1221
Lake Victoria, 509*f*, 513*f*
Lamarck, Jean-Baptiste de, 463*f*, 465
λ (lambda) phage, 397*f*–398
Lampreys, **717***f*–718
Lamp shells, 681*f*, 692*f*
Lancelets, 709, 713*f*, **714**–715*f*, 716*f*
Land
    colonization of, 530–531*f*
    global human use of, 1204
    locomotion on, 1129*f*
    subsidence of, 802
Land plants. *See also* Plant(s)
    adaptive radiations of, 537*f*–538
    as Archaeplastida protists, 591*f*, 602
    derived traits of, 613–614*f*, 615*f*–616
    evolution of, from green algae, 612*f*–613*f*, 617*f*
    nonvascular bryophytes, 618–619*f*, 620*f*–622*f*
    origin, diversification, and phylogeny of, 613*f*, 616*f*–617*f*
    seedless vascular, 622–623*f*, 624*f*–627*f*, 628
    seed plants as (*see* Seed plants)
    ten phyla of extant, 617*t*
    terrestrial adaptations of, 613*f*
    terrestrial adaptations of fungi and, 654
Landscape ecology, 1159*f*. *See also* Ecology
    biodiversity hot spots in, 1267*f*
    landscape fragmentation and edges in, 1265–1266*f*
    movement corridors in, 1266*f*–1267
    philosophy of nature reserves in, 1267–1268
    urban ecology and, 1269
    zoned reserves in, 1268*f*–1269*f*
Landscapes, 1159*f*
Land snails, 693*f*, 696*f*
Language
    brain function and, 1092*f*
    FOXP2 gene and, 454*f*–455
Larch, 637*f*
Large intestine, 905*f*–906
Largemouth bass, 875*f*
Large-scale disturbances, 1223*f*
Larva, **668***f*, 705*f*
Larval dispersal, 532
Larynx, 901*f*, **936**–37*f*
Latency, viral, 966–967
Lateral geniculate nuclei, 1115*f*
Lateral inhibition, 1114
Lateralization, **1092**
Lateral line system, **720**, 722*f*, **1110***f*
Lateral meristems, **760***f*
Lateral roots, 753*f*, 763*f*
Latitude, sunlight intensity and, 1160*f*
Latitudinal gradients, community diversity and, 1226*f*
Law of conservation of mass, **1234**
Law of independent assortment, 272–**273**, 274*f*, 293*f*–294, 300
Law of segregation, 269*f*–**270***f*, 271*f*–273*f*, 293*f*–294
Laws of probability, 274–275*f*, 276
L-dopa, 1098
Leaching, 800
Leading strand, DNA, **322–323***f*
Leaf area index, 780–781*f*
Leaf-cutter ants, 662*f*
Leaf primordia, **763***f*
Leafy liverworts, 620*f*
Learned behaviors, 1142

Learning, **1138**
  associative, 1140*f*–1141
  cognition, problem solving, and, 1141*f*
  development of learned behaviors, 1142
  neuronal plasticity and, 1094–1095*f*
  sleep and, 1088
  social, 1142*f*–1143
Leaves (leaf), **625, 755**
  abscisic acid in abscission of, 846
  anatomy of, in C₄ plants, 202*f*
  auxin in pattern formation of, 843
  effects of transpiration on wilting and temperature of, 792
  ethylene in abscission of, 848*f*
  evolution of, in vascular plants, 625*f*
  green color of, 191*f*
  Hox genes in formation of, 773*f*
  leaf area index and arrangements of, 780–781*f*
  monocot vs. eudicot, 643*f*
  photosynthesis in, 187*f*–188
  structure of, 755*f*–756*f*
  tissue organization of, 764*f*–765*f*
Leber's congenital amaurosis (LCA), 1116
Leber's hereditary neuropathy, 309
Leeches, 697*f*–698, 1080*f*
Leeuwenhoek, Anton von, 1204
Left atrium, 920*f*–921*f*
Left-right axis, 1054*f*, 1058*f*
Left ventricle, 920*f*–921*f*
Leghemobloblin, 809
Legionnaires' disease, 578*f*
Legless lizards, 547*f*–548*f*
Legumes, 808*f*–809*f*, 810
Lemaitre, Bruno, 948, 949*f*
Lemmings, 1198*f*
Lemurs, 740*f*
Length, carbon skeleton, 60*f*
Lens, **1112***f*
Lenski, Richard, 572*f*
Lenticels, **768**
Leopards, 548–549*f*
Lepidopterans, 462*f*, 706*f*
Lepidosaurs, **730**, 731*f*–732
Leprosy, 579*f*
Leptin, 911*f*–912
Lettuce seed germination, 851*f*
Leucine, 77*f*
Leukemia, 307*f*, 388, 429, 964, 1257*f*
Leukocytes (white blood cells), 227*f*, 872*f*, 928*f*–**929***f*
Lewis, Edward B., 380–381
Lewis dot structures, 36, 37*f*
Leydig cells, 1024–1025*f*
Lichens, 658, **662***f*–663*f*, 1249
Life. *See also* Animal(s); Organisms; Plant(s)
  abiotic synthesis of organic molecules as origin of, 57*f*–58
  biological molecules of, 66 (*see also* Biological molecules)
  biology as scientific study of, 1 (facing page) (*see also* Biology; Science)
  carbon in organic compounds of, 56, 64
  cell division as fundamental to, 232
  cells as fundamental units of, 3*f*, 4*f*–5, 93*f* (*see also* Cell(s); Eukaryotic cells; Prokaryotic cells)
  cellular respiration and energy for, 162–163*f* (*see also* Cellular respiration)
  classification of diversity of, 10*f*–11*f*
  colonization of land by, 530–531*f*
  common biological themes in, 2*f*–9*f*
  conditions on early Earth and origin of, 519*f*–521*f*, 522
  diversity of (*see* Biodiversity)
  effects of speciation and extinction on, 531*f*–537*f*, 538
  energy conversion for, 141*f*
  essential elements and trace elements for, 29*t*–30
  evolution of, as core theme of biology, 1*f* (facing page), 9 (*see also* Evolution)
  fossil record as history of, 522–523*f*, 524 (*see also* Fossil record)
  geologic record and, 526*f*, 527*t*
  history of, as limitation of natural selection, 495
  importance of water for, 44 (*see also* Water)

levels of biological organization of, 2*f*–3*f*
  order as property of, 144*f*–145
  origin of multicellular, 529–530*f*
  origin of single-celled, 526, 528*f*–529*f*
  photosynthesis as process that feeds, 185*f*–186*f* (*see also* Photosynthesis)
  phylogenies as evolutionary history of, 547–548 (*see also* Phylogenies)
  possible evolution of, on planets with water, 50*f*
  properties of, 1*f*
  tree of, 14*f*–15*f* (*see also* Tree of life)
  unity in diversity of, 12*f*, 462*f*, 467
  viruses and characteristics of, 392*f*–393, 400
  web of, 564*f*
Life cycles, **254**. *See also* Sexual life cycles
  of angiosperms, 640*f*–641, 818–819*f*
  of apicomplexan *Plasmodium*, 599*f*
  of blood fluke *Schistosoma mansoni*, 690*f*
  of brown alga *Laminaria*, 597*f*
  of cellular slime mold *Dictyostelium*, 607*f*
  of ciliate *Paramecium caudatum*, 600*f*
  developmental events in, 1038*f*
  of *Drosophila melanogaster* (fruit fly), 380*f*
  of fern as seedless vascular plant, 624*f*
  of frog, 1038*f*
  of fungi, 651–652*f*, 653*f*, 656*f*, 658*f*, 660*f*
  of green algal chlorophyte *Chlamydomonas*, 604*f*
  of humans, 255*f*–256
  of hydrozoan *Obelia*, 687*f*
  of moss, 619*f*
  of pine tree and gymnosperms, 634*f*
  of plasmodial slime mold, 606*f*
  reproduction and, 254
Life expectancy at birth, 1203, 1276*f*
Life histories, population, **1195***f*–1196*f*, 1197
Life tables, population, **1187***t*
Ligaments, **872***f*
Ligand binding, 214
Ligand-gated ion channels, **217***f*, 1072*f*–1074
Ligands, **137, 214**, 220
Light chains, **953***f*
Light-detecting organs, 1111*f*
Light detector, euglenid, 594*f*
Light energy
  in energy flow and chemical cycling, 7*f*, 162–163*f*, 1233
  excitation of chlorophyll by, 193*f*
  in photosynthesis, 185*f*, 204–205*f* (*see also* Light reactions)
  primary production in aquatic ecosystems and limitations of, 1237
  properties of, 190*f*
  sunlight as, 142, 148
Light energy, plant responses to
  biological clocks and circadian rhythms in, 851*f*–852*f*, 853
  blue-light photoreceptors in, 849–850*f*
  de-etiolation signal transduction pathway for, 837*f*–838*f*, 839
  photomorphogenesis and action spectrum of, 849
  photoperiodism and seasonal responses in, 853–854*f*, 855
  phototropism and, 840–841
  phytochromes as photoreceptors in, 850–851*f*
  plant shoot architecture and, 780*f*–781*f*
  stomatal opening and closing as, 792
Light-harvesting complexes, **194***f*
Light microscope (LM), **94**
Light microscopy (LM), 95*f*
Light reactions, **189**. *See also* Photosynthesis
  chemiosmosis of, in chloroplasts vs. in mitochondria, 197–198*f*, 199
  cyclic electron flow in, 196*f*–197
  determination of absorption spectrum for, 191*f*
  excitation of chlorophyll by light energy in, 193*f*
  linear electron flow in, 195*f*–196*f*
  most effective wavelengths for, 192*f*
  nature of sunlight and, 190*f*
  photosynthetic pigments as light receptors in, 191*f*–192*f*, 193
  photosystems of, 193–194*f*, 195*f*–196*f*, 197
  as stage of photosynthesis, 189*f*–190, 204–205*f*
Light responses, rod cell, 1115*f*

Lignin, **624**, 659, **758***f*
Likens, Eugene, 1247–1248*f*
Lily, 644*f*
Limbic system, 1089*f*–1090
Limbs
  genes for formation of, 539*f*–540
  as homologous structures, 473*f*–474
  tetrapod, 724–725*f*
  vertebrate formation of, 1056–1057*f*, 1058*f*
Limiting nutrients, **1237***f*–1239*t*
Limnetic zone, **1173***f*
Limp cells, 784, 785*f*, 791*f*
Limpets, 541*f*–542*f*, 1179*f*
Lin, Haifan, 92*f*, 94, 375
LINE-1 retrotransposons, 446
Lineage-based mechanisms, 772
Linear electron flow, **195***f*–196*f*
Line graphs in Scientific Skills Exercises, 33, 155, 262, 404, 967, 1043, 1089, 1130, 1181, 1273
Linkage groups, 304*f*
Linkage maps, **303***f*–304*f*
Linked genes, **299**
  genetic recombination and, 300–301*f*
  identifying, 302
  inheritance of, 299*f*–300
  mapping of, 303*f*–304*f*
  natural selection and genetic variation from recombination of, 303
Linker DNA, 328*f*
Linnaean classification, 10*f*, 548–549*f*
Linnaeus, Carolus, 464, 548
Lionfish, 723*f*
Lipid bilayers. See Phospholipid bilayers
Lipids, **72**
  in cellular membranes, 102, 110, 125*f*–126
  evolution of differences in cellular membrane composition of, 127
  fats as, 72–73*f*, 74
  phospholipids as, 74*f*–75
  in plasma membranes, 98*f*–99
  smooth ER synthesis of, 104–105
  steroids as, 75*f*
  Tay-Sachs disease and, 278
Lipid-soluble hormones, 996*f*, 997*f*–998
Lipopolysaccharides, 568
Literacy rate, Costa Rican, 1276*f*
Litter decomposition, 1247*f*
Litter size, 1195*f*–1196*f*, 1197
Littoral zone, **1173***f*
Liver, **903**
  bile production by, 903
  blood flow through, 904
  in energy storage, 909–910*f*
  lowering plasma LDL levels by inactivating enzyme of, 932
Liver cells, epinephrine in, 998*f*
Liverworts, 614*f*–615*f*, **618**, 620*f*. See also Bryophytes
Living fossils, 627, 702*f*
Lizards, 547*f*–548*f*, 731*f*–732, 878*f*, 883, 1015*f*, 1148*f*, 1210*f*, 1254*f*
Loams, **800**
Lobe-fins, 722, **723***f*–724
Lobes, brain, 1089–1090*f*, 1091*f*, 1092
Lobopods, 700
Lobotomy, 1092
Lobsters, 701*f*, 703
Local biogeochemical cycles, 1244
Local cell signaling, 212*f*, 213*f*
Local extinctions, 1256
Local inflammatory response, 952
Local regulators, **994***f*–996
Lock-and-key specificity, viral, 395
Locomotion, 987*f*, 1126*f*, **1129***f*–1130
Locus, gene, **253**, 270
Lodgepole pines, 1223*f*
Logarithms, natural, 633
Loggerhead turtles, 1184*f*, 1188–1189*f*
Logistic equation in Scientific Skills Exercise, 1194
Logistic population growth model, **1192***t*–1194*f*
Logos, DNA sequence, 349
Log scales in Scientific Skills Exercise, 1130
Long-day plants, **853***f*
Long-distance cell signaling, 212*f*, 213*f*

Long-night plants, 853f–854
Long-term memory, **1094**–1095f
Long-term potentiation (LTP), **1095**f
Looped domains, DNA, 329f, 330
Loop of Henle, **981**f, 982–983f, 984
Loose connective tissue, 872f
Lophophorates, 692f
Lophophores, **677**f, 688, 692f
Lophotrochozoans, **677**f
　annelids, 696f–698f
　characteristics of, 688
　ectoproct and brachiopod lophophorates, 692f
　flatworms, 688–689f, 690f–691f
　molluscs, 692–693f, 694f–696f
　phylogeny of, 681f–682f
　rotifers, 691f–692
Lorenz, Konrad, 1134
Loricifera, 682f
Lorises, 740
"Lost City" vent field, 521
Low-density lipoproteins (LDLs), 137, **931**–932
LSD, 1075
Luminal A and Luminal B breast cancer, 387f
Lung cancer, 441
Lung cells, newt, 5f, 236f–237f
Lungfishes, 474f, 723–724
Lungs, **936**–937f, 938f–940f
Lupines, 1249
Lupus, 965
Luteal phase, 1027
Luteinizing hormone (LH), 999f, 1003f, **1024**–1025f, 1026f–1027
Lycophytes, **616**–617t, 625f–626f, 627
Lyell, Charles, 463f, 464, 466
Lyme disease, 579f, 583f, 1229f
Lymph, **927**f, 950f
Lymphatic systems, 905, **927**f, 950f
Lymph nodes, **927**f
Lymphocytes, 928f, 930f, 946f, **952**. See also B cells; T cells
Lymphoid stem cells, 929f
Lymph vessels, **927**f
Lynx, 1200f
Lyon, Mary, 298f
Lysine, 77f
Lysogenic cycle, **397**f–398
Lysosomal storage diseases, 108
Lysosomes, 100f, **107**–108
Lysozymes, 49f, 79f, 450, 451f, **947**–948f, 949
Lytic cycle, **396**f–397f

M

MacArthur, Robert, 1226–1227f
McCarty, Maclyn, 313
McClintock, Barbara, 445f
MacLeod, Colin, 313
Macroclimate, **1161**f–1163f
Macroevolution, **501**, **519**. See also Evolution
　adaptive radiations in, 536–537f, 538
　colonization of land in, 530–531f
　of development, 538f–540f, 541
　early Earth conditions for origin of life in, 520f–521f, 522
　fossil evidence for, 519f–520, 522–523f, 524f–525f, 526
　geologic record of key events in, 526f, 527t
　mass extinctions in, 534f–536f
　novelties and trends in, 541f–543f
　origin of multicellular organisms in, 529f–530f
　origin of single-celled organisms in, 526, 528f–529f
　plate tectonics and, 532f–533f, 534
　speciation and extinction rates of organisms in, 531f–537f, 538
　speciation as conceptual bridge between microevolution and, 501, 516 (see also Microevolution)
Macromolecules, **66**f–67f, 107f–108, 520f–521f, 796
Macronuclei, ciliate, 600f–601
Macronutrients, plant, **804**–805t
Macrophages, 107f–108, 121f, **872**f, 946f, **950**, 951f
Madagascar orchids, 821f
Mad cow disease, 83, 405
Madreporite, sea star, 708f

Mads-box genes, 539, 773, 774
Maggot flies, 510, 898f
Magnesium, 29t, 804
Magnetic field, Earth's, 1105f, 1135
Magnetite, 1105, 1135
Magnification, 94
Magnolia tree, 644f
Magnoliids, **643**f–644f
Maiden veil fungus, 659f
Maize (corn), 445f, 645, 771f
　artificial selection of, 830f
　health of transgenic *Bt*, 833
　precocious germination in, 846f
　proteins in, 893
　seeds, 823f–824f
Major depressive disorder, **1097**
Major histocompatibility complex (MHC) molecule, **954**f, 964
Make Connections Figures
　contributions of genomics and proteomics to biology, 88f
　genomics, cell-signaling, and cancer, 387f
　ion movement and gradients, 987f
　levels of plant defenses against herbivores, 862–863f
　life challenges and solutions in plants and animals, 888-889f
　maximizing surface area, 689f
　sickle-cell allele, 496-497f
　working cell, 206-207f
　working ecosystem, 1242-1243f
Malaria, 284f–285, 495, 497f, 591f, 599f, 608, 707
Malaysia, 1226–1227f
Male gametophytes, angiosperm, 818–819f
Males
　competition between, for mates, 1148f
　female mate choice and, 1146f–1147f, 1148
　hormonal regulation of reproductive systems of, 1024f–1025f
　hormones of, 993f, 1008–1009f
　parental care by, 1145–1146f
　reproductive anatomy of human, 1019f–1020
　sex chromosomes of, 296f–297
　sexual competition between, 493f–494f
　spermatogenesis in human, 1021–1022f
Malignant tumors, **247**f
Malnutrition, 831–832f, 895
Malpighian tubules, 704f, 979f–980
Malthus, Thomas, 463f
Maltose, 69f
Mammals, **735**
　adaptations of kidneys of, 985f–986
　adaptive radiation of, 536–537f
　amniotic eggs of, 728–729f
　bats as, 14f
　brains in nervous systems of, 1085f (see also Nervous systems)
　breathing in, 939f–940f
　cardiovascular systems of (see Cardiovascular systems)
　cellular respiration in hibernating, 176
　circadian clocks in hibernating, 887f
　comparing genomes of, 448f, 453–454f, 455f–456
　control of circadian rhythms in, 1088
　convergent evolution of, 475f, 737f
　derived characters of, 735
　digestive systems of (see Digestive systems)
　early evolution of, 735f–736
　endangered or threatened, 1256f
　eutherians and primates as placental, 737, 738f–741f, 742
　evolution of, 673
　evolution of melanocyte-stimulating hormone (MSH) in, 1010
　extraembryonic membranes of, 1047f
　fertilization in, 1041f
　gas exchange adaptations of, 941f–943f
　genomic imprinting in, 308f–309
　glia in brains of, 1063f
　hominins and humans as, 743–748
　homologous structures in, 473f
　hormonal regulation of reproduction in, 1024f–1026f, 1027 (see also Animal reproduction; Human reproduction)

inactivation of X-linked genes in female, 298f
ion concentrations inside and outside of neurons of, 1064t
kidneys in excretory systems of, 980f–981f (see also Excretory systems; Kidneys)
marsupials, 736f–737f
mechanoreceptors for hearing and equilibrium in, 1106f–1110f
modeling neurons of, 1065f
molecular clock for, 561f
monotremes, 736f
nitrogenous wastes of, 976–977f
opiate receptors in brains of, 1076
organ systems of, 870f
origination of cetaceans as terrestrial, 475f–476f
origin of, 524–525f, 526
osmoregulation in, 974, 975
phylogeny of, 738f–739f
reproductive cloning of, 424f–425f
respiratory systems of, 936–937f, 938f–940f
sex chromosomes of, 296f–297
taste in, 1117f–1118f
thermoregulation in, 875f
Mammary glands, 735, 1001, 1003, 1010, **1021**
Mammoths, 408f, 416, 1260–1261f
Manatee, 1213f
Mandibles, 702, 704f
Mangold, Hilda, 1056f
Mantids, 470f
Mantle, **692**–693f
Mantle cavity, **692**–693f
Maple tree leaves, 756
Mapping
　of brain activity, 1090f
　linkage, 303f–304f
Map units, **303**f
Maquis, 1168f
Marchantia, 614f–615f, 620f
March equinox, 1161f
Marine animals
　adaptations of kidneys of, 986–987f
　mass extinctions and, 536
　osmoregulation in, 973f
Marine benthic zones, **1176**f
Marine biomes, 1171f–1172, 1218f
Marine birds, 976f
Marine reserves, 1268–1269f
Marine snails, 532
Marine worm, 934f
Mark-recapture method, **1185**f
Mars, 50f
Marshall, Barry, 902
Marshes, 1180
Marsh gas, 580
Marsupials, 475f, 534, **736**f–737f, 739f
Marsupium, 736f–737
Mass, 29n, 31
Mass, law of conservation of, 1234
Mass extinctions, **534**f–536f
　of dinosaurs, 730
　possibility of current sixth, 696f
　speciation and, 514–516
　tropical deforestation and potential, 645f–646
Mass number, **31**
Mast cells, **951**f, 964
Master regulatory genes, 539f–540f, 541. See also Homeotic genes; *Hox* genes
Masting, 863f
Mate choice, 493f–494f, 509f, 512f–513, 1146f–1147f, 1148
Mate-choice copying, **1147**f
Mate recognition, 502f
Maternal age, Down syndrome and, 306–307
Maternal alleles, 367
Maternal chromosomes, 263
Maternal effect genes, **381**
Maternal inheritance, 309
Mating. See also Reproduction
　animal reproduction and, 1013f
　cell signaling in yeast, 211f–212, 226
　clumped dispersion and, 1185
　earthworm, 698
　external fertilization and, 1017

genetic disorders from human, 283–284
Hardy-Weinberg equilibrium and random, 486
human, 1027–1028, 1032–1033
human sexual arousal and, 1076
hybrid zones and, 510–511f
insect, 705
interspecific, and hybrids, 501f
of pea plants, 268f–269
reproductive barriers to, 501–502f, 503f–504
reproductive cycles and, 1015f
sexual selection and, 493f–494f
Mating behavior. *See also* Courtship rituals
applying game theory to, 1148f–1149
mating systems and parental care in, 1145–1146f
mating systems and sexual dimorphism in, 1145f
sexual selection and mate choice in, 1146f–1147f, 1148
Mating systems, 1145f
Matorral, 1168f
Matter, 2, 7, **29–30**. *See also* Energy
Maungatautari restoration project, 1251f
Maximum likelihood, **556**
Maximum parsimony, **556–557f**, 558
Mayer, Adolf, 393
Maze experiments, 1141f
M checkpoint, 244–245f
Meadowlarks, 501f
Meadow voles, 1150f–1151
Mean annual precipitation, 1238f
Measles, 395, 402
Measles virus, 963
Mechanical defense, prey, 1212f
Mechanical isolation, 502f
Mechanical signaling, 119
Mechanical stimuli, plant responses to, 855–856f
Mechanical stress, plant responses to, 847f
Mechanical work, 148, 150f
Mechanoreceptors, **1104f**, 1106f–1110f
Mediator proteins, 368–369f
Medicine. *See also* Drugs; Pharmaceutical products
antibodies as tools in, 963
application of systems biology to, 441–442
biotechnology in, 428–429f, 430f
blocking HIV entry into cells in, 128f
fungi in, 664
genomics and proteomics in, 88f
medical leeches in, 697f–698
plant-derived medicines in, 645t–646
radioactive tracers in, 31–32
stem cells in, 426–427
treatments of nervous system disorders in, 1096
Mediterranean climate, 1162
Mediterranean house gecko, 563f
Medulla oblongata (medulla), 940f, **1087f**
Medusa, **685f**, 686
Medusozoans, 686f–687f
Megapascal (MPa), **783**
Megaphylls, **625**, 625f
Megasporangia, 632f
Megaspores, **625**, 632f, **818–819f**
Megasporocytes, 818
Meiosis, **256**
in animal cells, 258f–259f
crossing over and synapsis during, 258f, 260f
DNA changes of yeast cells in, 262
errors in, 304–305f, 306f–307f
gamete formation by, in sexual life cycles, 256
genetic variation from gene alteration during, 483
genome evolution and errors in, 449f–451f
human gametogenesis and, 1021
in human life cycle, 255–256
microscopy of, 292f
mitosis vs., 260–261f, 262
production of gametes by, 234–235
stages of, 257f–260f
in varieties of sexual life cycles, 256f–257
Meiosis I, **257f**–258f, 260f–261f, 262
Meiosis II, **257f**, 259f, 261f–262
Melanin, 336
Melanocyte-stimulating hormone (MSH), 1003f, **1010**
Melatonin, 877f, 999f, **1009**, 1088
Membrane attack complex, 961f

Membrane potentials, 135–136f, **1064f**–1066f. *See also* Action potentials, neuron; Resting potentials, neuron
Membrane proteins, 105, 125f–128f, 150f
Membranes, amniotic egg extraembryonic, 728–729f
Membranes, cellular. *See* Cellular membranes
Memory
emotion and, 1090
neuronal plasticity and, 1094–1095f
sleep and, 1088
Memory cells, **956**
Mendel, Gregor
experimental, quantitative approach of, 268f–269
genes as hereditary factors of, 292f
law of independent assortment of, 272–274f
law of segregation of, 269f–273f
particulate hypothesis of, on inheritance, 267f–268
particulate model of inheritance of, 481
Mendelian inheritance
chromosomal basis of, 292f–293f, 294
environmental impacts on phenotypes and, 280f
evolution of gene concept from, 357
exceptions to, 308–309f
extending, for multiple genes, 279f–280f
extending, for single gene, 277f–278f, 279
genetic variation and, 481
human patterns of inheritance and, 282f–285f, 286–287f, 288
integrating, with emergent properties, 280–281
law of independent assortment of, 272–274f
law of segregation of, 269f–273t
laws of probability governing, 274–275f, 276
limitations of, 276
making histograms and analyzing distribution patterns for, 281
G. Mendel's experimental quantitative approach, 268f–269
G. Mendel's particulate hypothesis of inheritance as, 267f–268
Menopause, **1027**
Menstrual cycle, 1025, 1027
Menstrual flow phase, 1027
Menstruation, **1025**
Mercury pollution, 1272
Meristem identity genes, **774f**
Meristems, **760f**–761, 825, 843
Meroblastic cleavage, **1042**
Merozoites, 599f
Meselson, Matthew, 320f
Mesenchyme cells, 1044f
Mesoderm, **674**, 1044f, 1045f
Mesoglea, 685f
Mesohyl, **684f**–685
Mesonychoteuthis hamiltoni, 695–696
Mesophyll, 187f, 201–202f, 204, **764–765f**
Mesozoic era, 526f, 527t, 533f, 673
Messenger molecules, 212, 213f
Messenger RNA (mRNA), **336**. *See also* RNA (ribonucleic acid)
alteration of ends of, 342–343f
in analyzing gene expression, 417–418f, 419f, 420–421
in breast cancer, 387f
effects of miRNAs and siRNAs on, 374f–375
in gene expression, 6f, 84f–85
genetic code and, 338
mutations affecting, 355f–356f, 357
in plant cells, 206f
polyribosomes and, 352–353f
regulation of degradation of, 373
synthesis of, in cell signaling, 223f
synthesis of, in eukaryotic cell nucleus, 102
synthesis of, in transcription, 340f–342f
in transcription and translation, 336–337f
in translation, 345f–348f, 350
viral, 395f–396f, 398t, 399f–400
Metabolic defects, 334–335f, 336
Metabolic pathways, **142**. *See also* Metabolism
metabolic defects in, 334–335, 336
regulation of bacterial, 361f
Metabolic rates, 884f–885f, 886–887f
Metabolism, **142**. *See also* Bioenergetics
ATP energy coupling of exergonic and endergonic reactions in, 148–149f, 150f–151f

bioenergetics and metabolic rates of animal, 883–884f, 885f–886, 887f
catabolism and, 180f–181f
effects of adrenal hormones on, 1006–1007f, 1008
as energy conversion for life, 141f
enzymatic catalysis of reactions in (*see* Enzymatic catalysis)
evolution of hormones regulating, 1010
forms of energy for, 142–143f
free-energy change, equilibrium, and, 145–146f, 147f–148f
graphing reactions of, 155
laws of thermodynamics in, and 143f–144f, 145
metabolic pathways of, 142
nitrogenous wastes and, 977
osmoregulation and, 974–975
prokaryotic, 575–576f, 582, 585
protocell, 521f–522
radioactive tracers in research on, 31–32
regulation of cellular respiration and, 181f–182
role of enzymes as catalysts in, 75–76f
thermogenesis in animal, 881f–882f
thyroid regulation of, 1004f–1005f, 1010f
Metabotropic receptors, 1073–1074
Metagenomics, **438**, 577
Metamorphosis, **668**
amphibian, 726–727f
frog, 668f–669, 1010f
insect, 705f, 1001f–1002
lancelet, 714
tunicate, 715
Metanephridia, **979f**
Metanephridium, 693f, 698f
Metaphase, **235**, 237f–238f, 241f, 261f
Metaphase chromosomes, 329f–330f
Metaphase I, 258f, 261f
Metaphase II, 259f
Metaphase plate, 237f, **238f**, 260
Metapopulations, **1200–1201f**
Metastasis, 247f
Metazoans (Metazoa), 676–677f
Meteorites, 520–521f
Methamphetamine, 62
Methane
carbon and bonds in, 59f
combustion of, as redox reaction, 164f
covalent bonding and, 37f
molecular shape of, 39f–40
Methanogens, **580–581**
Methicillin, 472f–473
Methicillin-resistant *S. aureus* (MRSA), 472f–473
Methionine, 77f, 339
Methods, research. *See* Research methods
Methylation, DNA, 366–367, 386, 425
Methyl group, **63f**
Methyl jasmonate, 849
Methylmercury, 1272
Methylsalicylic acid, 860
Mexico, 1202
MHC (major histocompatibility complex) molecule, 964
Mice
appetite regulation in, 912
brains of, 1082f
camouflage case studies with, 19f–20f, 21–22
comparing human genome with genome of, 448f–449, 454f–455, 456
complete genome sequence for, 436f
energy budgets of, 886
FOXP2 gene evolution in, 454f–455
genomic imprinting of insulin-like growth factor gene of, 308f
homeotic genes in, 457f
Hox genes in paw development of, 420
as model organisms (*see Mus musculus* (house mouse))
modes of natural selection in, 492f
osmotic homeostasis in desert, 975
paw development of, 229f
transfer of genetic trait between bacterial strains in, 313f
Microarray analysis, 387f
Microarray chips, human genome, 441f

Microbial diversity, 1217f
Microbiomes, 907f
Microclimate, **1161**, 1163
Microevolution, **481**, **501**. *See also* Evolution
    adaptive evolution by natural selection in, 491–492f, 493f–497f, 498
    alteration of allele frequencies by natural selection, genetic drift, and gene flow in, 487–488f, 489f–490, 491f
    genetic variation and, 481f–482f, 483
    populations as smallest units of, 480f–481f
    of sickle-cell disease, 497f
    speciation as conceptual bridge between macroevolution and, 501, 516 (*see also* Macroevolution)
    using Hardy-Weinberg equation to test, 483–484f, 485f–486f, 487
Microfibrils
    cellulose, 772f
    in plant cell walls, 118
    in structural polysaccharides, 70f
Microfilaments, **115**
    animal cell, 100f
    in animal cytokinesis, 239–240f
    cytoskeleton structure and function and, 113t
    in morphogenesis, 1050f
    plant cell, 101f
    structure and function of, 115–116f, 117f
Microglia, 1081f
Micronuclei, ciliate, 600f–601
Micronutrients, plant, 804–805t
Microphylls, **625**, 625f
Micropyles, **641**, 818
MicroRNAs (miRNAs), **374**f, 376, 386, 672
Microscopy, 94f–95f, 96, 292f, 587f–588
Microsporangia, 632f, 818
Microspores, **625**, 632f, 818–819f
Microsporocytes, 818
Microtubule-organizing center, 238
Microtubules, **114**
    in animal cell, 100f
    in cell division, 235, 238f–239f, 242f
    centrosomes, centrioles, and, 114f
    cilia, flagella, and, 114–115f, 116f
    cytoskeleton structure and function and, 113t
    phragmoplasts, 613
    in plant cell, 101f
    plant cell walls and, 118
    structure and function of, 114f–115f, 116f
Microvilli, 98, 100f, 116f, 689f, **904**f, 904f
Midbrain, **1085**f
Middle ear, **1107**f
Middle lamella, **118**
Mifepristone (RU486), 1033
Migration, **1135**
    assisted, 1274
    electromagnetic receptors and, 1105f
    as fixed action pattern, 1135f
    genetic variation in patterns of, 1150–1151f
    movement corridors and, 1266f–1267
Milk, mammalian, 1001, 1003, 1010
Milkweed, 639f
Miller, Stanley, 57f–58, 520f
Millipedes, 702–703f
Mimic octopus, 1213f
Mimicry
    endorphin, 1075–1076
    molecular, 40f, 79
    as prey defensive adaptation, 862f, 1211–1212f, 1213f
Mimivirus, 400
Mimosa pudica, 796, 856f
Mimulus species, 516f
Mineralized dental elements, 718f
Mineralocorticoids, 999f, 1007f, **1008**
Minerals
    deficiencies of, in plants, 804, 806f
    mineralocorticoids and metabolism of, 1008
    mycorrhizae and plant deficiencies of, 811
    root architecture and acquisition of, 781
    transpiration of, from roots to shoots via xylem, 786–787f, 788f–789f, 790
    vascular plant transport of, 781–782f, 783f–784, 785f

Minerals, essential, **894**–895t
Miniaturization, gametophyte, 631f
Minimal medium, 334–335f
Minimum viable population (MVP), **1262**, 1268
Minnows, 1272
Miscarriages, 304, 1033
Misfolding, protein, 83
Mismatch repairs, **325**
Missense mutations, **355**–356f
Mistletoe, 812f
Mitchell, Peter, 175
Mites, 702f
Mitochondria, **109**
    animal cell, 100f
    animal hibernation and, 176
    in apoptosis, 228f–229
    chemical energy conversion by, 109–110f, 111f
    chemiosmosis in, 173–174f, 175
    chemiosmosis in chloroplasts vs. in, 197f–198f, 199
    electron transport chains in, 166–167
    endosymbiotic origin of, 528–529f
    enzymes in, 159f
    evolutionary origins of, 109–110f
    fungal cell, 100f
    inheritance of genes of, 309
    origin of, in endosymbiosis, 589, 592f–593f
    plant cell, 101f, 207f
    protist, 588
    pyruvate in, 169f
    using cell fractionation to study, 97
Mitochondria DNA (mtDNA)
    evolutionary rate of, 559
    species identity in, 551f
Mitochondrial matrix, **110**
Mitochondrial myopathy, 309
Mitosis, **234**. *See also* Cell cycle; Cell division
    in animal cells, 236f–237f
    in chromatin packing, 330f
    evolution of, 241–242f
    in human life cycle, 255f–256
    meiosis vs., 260–261f, 262
    microscopy of, 292f
    origin of term for, 235
    in plant cells, 241f
    in varieties of sexual life cycles, 256f–257
Mitosomes, 593
Mitotic (M) phase, **235**f
Mitotic spindles, **235**, 238f–239f
Mixotrophs, **588**
Mobile genetic elements, evolution of viruses and, 400
Model organisms, 22, **1038**
    Arabidopsis thaliana, 769–770f
    bread mold (*see Neurospora crassa* (bread mold))
    Caenorhabditis elegans, 699
    in developmental biology, 1038
    for DNA research, 314f–315 (*see also Escherichia coli (E. coli)* bacteria)
    house mouse (*Mus musculus*), 23, 436f (*see also* Mice)
    for T. Morgan's experiments, 294f–295f (*see also Drosophila melanogaster* (fruit fly))
    Neurospora crassa, 658f–659t
    scientific cooperation and, 22–23
Models
    atomic, 30f
    community disturbance, 1222f–1223f
    of covalent bonds, 36, 37f
    electron orbital, 35f
    exponential population growth, 1190–1191f, 1192
    island equilibrium, 1226–1227f, 1228
    logistic population growth, 1192t–1194f
    molecular-shape, 39f
    process of science, 18f
    testing hypotheses with quantitative in Scientific Skills Exercise, 1144
    using experiments to test in Scientific Skills Exercise, 226
Modified leaves, 756f
Modified roots, 754f
Modified stems, 755f
Molarity, **50**
Molar mass, 50

Molar ratios in Scientific Skills Exercise, 58
Mold model organism. *See Neurospora crassa* (bread mold)
Molds, **652**f–653f, 655f, 656f–657
Mole (mol), **50**
    in Scientific Skills Exercise, 58
Molecular basis of inheritance
    chromatin packing of DNA and proteins in eukaryotic chromosomes, 328f–330f
    discovery of double helix structure of DNA in, 312f, 316f–318f
    DNA as life's operating system in, 312f
    DNA replication and repair in (*see* DNA replication)
    evidence for DNA as genetic material in, 313f–315f, 316
    evolution of gene concept from, 357
Molecular biology
    Arabidopsis thaliana as model organism for, 769–770f
    importance of viruses to, 393
    measures of evolution in, 89
    molecular systematics and, 559
    mutants in, 839
    of plant development, 769f–775f
Molecular clocks, **560**–561f, 562f, 653f–654
Molecular formulas, 36, 37f, 59f
Molecular genetics
    in developmental biology, 1037
    in ecological forensics, 1259f
Molecular genetic variation, 481–482f
Molecular homologies, 474, 551f–553f
Molecular homoplasies, 553f
Molecular identification tags, 106–107
Molecular-level herbivore defenses, plant, 862f
Molecular mass, **50**
Molecular recognition, immune system, 947
Molecular systematics, 557f, 559f–560, 577f, 676f–677f, 678. *See also* Cladistics; Systematics; Taxonomy
Molecular tags, 330f
Molecules, **36**. *See also* Compounds
    biological (*see* Biological molecules)
    chemical bonds and formation of (*see* Chemical bonds)
    as level of biological organization, 3f
    organic (*see* Organic compounds)
    origin of self-replicating, 520f–521f, 522
    regulation of interactions of, 8–9f
    shape and function of, 39f–40, 59f
    structure of DNA and RNA, 5f–6f
Moles, 58, 551f–552f, 1101f
Molluscs, 682f
    bivalves, 694f–695f
    body plan of, 692–693f
    cephalopods, 695f–696
    chitons, 693f
    eye complexity in, 541f–542f
    gastropods, 693f–694
    nervous systems of, 1080f
    protecting freshwater and terrestrial, from extinction, 696f
Molting (ecdysis), 677, **699**, 701, 888f
Monarch butterflies, 833, 1140f
Monera, kingdom, 562
Monilophytes, **616**–617t
Monkey flowers, 516f, 828
Monkeys, 56f, 89, 740–741f, 742, 1116. *See also* Chimpanzees
Monocilia, 1058
Monoclonal antibodies, **963**
Monocots, **643**f–644f, 762f, 764f, 822–824f
Monocytes, 928f, 930f
Monod, Jacques, 361
Monogamous mating, 1018, **1145**f
Monoglycerides, 904–905f
Monohybrid crosses, **272**
Monohybrids, **272**
Monomers, **67**
Monophyletic groups, **553**f
Monosaccharides, **68**f–69f
Monosodium glutamate, 1117
Monosomic cells, **305**

Monosomy X, 307
Monotremes, **736**f, 739f
Monozygotic twins, 1030, 1055
Monterey County, California, 608
Montmorillonite clay, 521f–522
Montreal Protocol, 1275
Moon jelly, 916f
Moose, 1199f–1200
Moray eel, 723f
Morels, 657f, 664
Morgan, Thomas Hunt, 294f–295f, 299f–301f, 313
Mormon tea, 636f
"Morning-after" birth control pills, 1032f–1033
Morning sickness, 1030
Morphine, 40f, 79
Morphogenesis, **377**, **1044**. See also Embryonic
    development; Pattern formation
    apoptosis in, 1051
    cytoskeletons in, 1049–1050
    developmental adaptations of amniotes in, 1047
    gastrulation in, 1044f–1047f
    mechanisms of, 1050f–1051
    organogenesis in, 1048f–1049f
    plant development and, 769, 772–773f
Morphogen gradients, 382
Morphogens, 381f–**382**f
Morphological homologies, 551
Morphological isolation, 502f
Morphological species concept, **504**
Morphology
    animal phylogeny and, 676–677f
    fungal, 649f–650f
    macroevolution of, 538f–540f, 541
    species concepts and, 501
Mortality rates. See Deaths
Morton, Michael, 23f
Mosaicism, 298f
Mosquitoes, 491, 497f, 599f, 706f, 707, 898f
Mosquitofish, 505f–506
Mosses, 615f, **618**–619f, 620f–622f, 631f. See also
    Bryophytes
Moths, 462f, 706f, 820f, 1001f–1002
Motile cilia, 1058
Motility, prokaryotic, 570f–571
Motor, flagellum, 570f–571
Motor areas, cerebral cortex, 1090
Motor cortex, 1091f–1092
Motor neurons, **1063**f, **1083**f, 1122–1123f, 1124
Motor output stage, 1063f
Motor proteins, 76f, **113**f, 115, 116f, 150f, 238–239f
Motor systems, **1083**
    cardiac and smooth muscle in, 1125–1126
    muscle function in, 1119–1120f, 1121f–1125f,
        1126
    sensory systems and, 1101f, 1102f (see also Sensory
        systems)
    skeletal muscle contraction in, 119–120f,
        1121f–1125f
    skeletal systems and locomotion in, 1126f–1129f,
        1130
Motor unit, **1122**
Mountain lions, 1144–1145
Mountains, 1163f
Mount St. Helens, 630f
Mouse. See Mice
Mouse model organism. See Mus musculus (house
    mouse)
Mouth formation, 1044
Movement, prokaryotic, 570f–571
Movement corridors, **1266**f–1267
MPF (maturation-promoting factor), **243**–244f
mPGES-1 gene, 370
Mucous cells, 902f
Mucus, **901**, 902f, 948
Mucus escalator, 937
Mueller, Ken, 1117f
Mule deer, 1144–1145
Mules, 503f
Muller, Hermann, 357
Müllerian mimicry, 1212f–**1213**
Multicellular asexual reproduction, 253f
Multicellular organisms, 529–530f, 669f–670f
Multienzyme complexes, 159
Multifactorial characters, **280**

Multifactorial disorders, human, 285
Multigene families, 446–**447**f
Multiple fruits, **825**f
Multiple sclerosis, 965
Multiplication rule, **275**f–276
Multiprotein complexes, 172f–173
Mumps, 402
Murchison meteorite, 520–521
Muscle
    cardiac and smooth, 1125–1126
    contraction of, 1120–1121f, 1122
    regulation of contraction of, 1122–1123f, 1124f
    skeletal (see Skeletal muscle)
Muscle cells, 93f, 117, 378–379f, 909, 998f
Muscle fibers, 873f
Muscle tissue, **873**f
Muscular dystrophy, 297
Mushrooms, 648f–650, 655f, 657f, 659f–660f, 664. See
    also Fungi
Mus musculus (house mouse), 23, 436f. See also Mice
Mussels, 694f–695f, 696f
Mustard plant model organism. See Arabidopsis
    thaliana (mustard plant)
Mutagens, **357**
Mutant phenotypes, 294f–295f
Mutants
    designing experiments using genetic, 1089
    interpreting data from experiments with genetic,
        912
    in molecular biology, 839
    nutritional, in gene-enzyme relationship
        experiment, 334–335f, 336
Mutations, **355**f
    in alterations of chromosome structure, 448f–449
    in aquaporins causing diabetes insipidus, 989f
    in cancer development, 386f
    cancer genes and, 383f–384
    cellular slime mold, 606
    creating plant, in molecular biology, 770
    of developmental genes, 539f–540f
    in duplication and divergence of gene-sized
        regions, 449f–451f
    in duplication of entire chromosome sets, 448
    effects of, during cell division, 384–385f
    as embryonic lethals, 380–381f
    as errors in proofreading, 325
    evolution of enzymes by, 157f
    in exon duplication and exon shuffling, 450–451f
    in flowering, 774–75f
    genetic variation from, 303
    genome evolution and, 448f–451f, 452
    Hardy-Weinberg equilibrium and, 486
    of ion channel protein genes, 1070
    in mitochondrial DNA, 309
    molecular clock speed and, 561
    mutagens as cause of, 357
    natural selection and, 326
    nucleotide-pair substitutions, insertions, and
        deletions, 355–356f
    phenotypes and, 294f–295f, 304
    point mutations, 355f
    in prokaryotes, 572–573
    as source of alleles, 263
    as sources of genetic variation, 482–483
    transposable elements and, 453
Mutualism, **582**, **1214**
    bacterial, 582–583
    in flower pollination, 815f–816, 821f
    fungal, 649, 661f–663f (see also Mycorrhizae)
    as interspecific interaction, 1214f
    mycorrhizae as plant-fungi, 781, 810–811f
    nutrient limitations and, 1239
    plant-bacteria, 807f–809f, 810
    symbols for, 1209
    in vertebrate digestive systems, 907f–908f
Myasthenia gravis, 1122
Mycelium (mycelia), 649f–**650**, 651–652f, 653f
Mycobacterium tuberculosis, 583
Mycoplasmas, 579f
Mycorrhizae, **650**, **781**, **810**
    basidiomycetes in, 659
    biological augmentation using, 1249
    in colonization of land by plants, 530–531f
    evolution of, 654

genomic analysis of interactions of, 651
    as mutualism, 1214
    nutrient limitations and, 1239
    plant nutrition and, 810–811f
    plant roots and, 754
    as root-fungi mutualism, 781
    specialized hyphae in, 650f–651
    strigolactones and, 849
    terrestrial plants and, 616
Mycorrhizal associations, 754
Mycosis, **664**
Myelination, 1070f–1071f
Myelin sheath, **1070**f–1071f
Myeloid stem cells, 929f
Myllokunmingia fengjiaoa, 712f, 718
Myoblasts, 378–379f
Myocardial infarctions, 931f
MyoD activator, 368f
myoD gene, 378–379f
Myofibrils, **1120**f
Myoglobin, **943**, **1124**–1125t
Myopathy, 309
Myosin, 76f, **117**, 239, 379f, 873f
Myosin filaments, 1119–1120f, 1121f
Myotonia, 1027–1028, 1070
Myriapods, **701**, 702–703f
Myxini (hagfishes), 717f–718
Myxobacteria, 211f, 578f
Myxococcus xanthus, 211f

N

NAD⁺ (nicotinamide adenine dinucleotide), **165**f–
    166f, 170f–171f, 176, 178f–179
NADH, 170f–171f, 176, 178f–179
NADP⁺ (nicotinamide adenine dinucleotide
    phosphate), **189**f–190, 204–205f
NADPH, 189f–190, 195f–196f, 204–205f
Naked mole rats, 1151f–1152, 1153
Naloxone, 1076
Nanoarchaeota clade, 581
Nanopores, 409
Nasal glands, marine bird, 976f
Nash, John, 1148
National Cancer Institute, 441
National Center for Biotechnology Information
    (NCBI), 438–439f
National Institutes of Health (NIH), 438, 441
National Library of Medicine, 438
National Medal of Science, 938
Native Americans, 559
Natural family planning, 1032f
Natural killer (NK) cells, **950**
Natural logarithms in Scientific Skills Exercise, 633
Natural plastics, 584f
Natural range expansions, 1178
Natural selection, **13**, **467**. See also Adaptations;
    Evolution
    adaptations and, 466–467
    adaptive evolution and, 488
    Darwinian theory of descent with modification by,
        12f–15f, 466–467f, 477–478
    of developmental genes, 539
    directional, disruptive, and stabilizing selection
        in, 492f
    of ecological niches, 1209–1210f
    evolution of drug resistance by, 472f–473
    evolution of enzymes by, 157f
    in evolution of life history traits, 1195f–1196f,
        1197
    in evolution of populations, 1184–1185
    genetic variation for, from genetic recombination,
        303
    Hardy-Weinberg equilibrium and, 486
    insect evolution by, due to food source changes,
        471f–472
    key role of, in adaptive evolution, 493f
    limitations of, in creating perfect organisms, 495
    mutations and, 326
    relative fitness and, 491–492
    of ribozymes, 522
    sexual reproduction, genetic variation, and,
        264–265f
    species selection as, 542–543
Natural vs. supernatural explanations, 17–18

Nature reserves, philosophy of, 1267–1268
Nature vs. nurture, 280*f*, 756
Navigation, migration and, 1135*f*
Neanderthals, 33, 88*f*, 408, 436*f*, 456, 746–747*f*
Near vision, 1116*f*
Nectarine, 639*f*
Negative and positive correlations, 828
Negative feedback, **876**, **1001**
    in density-dependent population growth, 1198
    in endocrine system feedback regulation, 1001
    in feedback regulation, 9*f*
    in homeostasis, 876
Negative gene regulation, bacterial, 364
Negative gravitropism, 855
Negative pressure breathing, 939*f*–940
Neisseria gonorrhoeae, 578*f*
Nematocysts, **686***f*
Nematode model organism. *See Caenorhabditis elegans* (soil worm)
Nematodes, 683*f*, 699*f*–700, 1052*f*–1053*f*, 1127*f*
Nemertea, 682*f*
Neodenticula seminae (diatom), 1164
Neoproterozoic era, 670*f*–671*f*
Neornithes, 733
Nephrons, **980**
    Bowman's capsule in, 981
    evolution adaptations of, 985*f*–986*f*
    processing of blood filtrate to urine by, 982–983*f*
    structure of mammalian kidneys and, 980*f*–981*f*
Neritic zones, **1176***f*
Nernst equation, 1065
Nerve cells, 93*f*
Nerve cord, 704*f*, 714*f*, 716*f*
Nerve gas, 1075
Nerve nets, **1080**
Nerves, **1080**
Nervous systems, **874**, **994**
    cerebral cortex control of voluntary movement and cognitive functions in, 1090–1091*f*, 1092*f*–1093*f*
    disorders of, 1096*f*–1098*f*
    faulty apoptosis in diseases of human, 229
    Huntington's disease and, 285
    long-distance cell signaling in, 212, 213*f*
    memory, learning, and changes of synaptic connections in, 1093–1094*f*, 1095*f*
    neurons and cell signaling in, 874*f* (*see also* Neurons)
    regulation of blood pressure by, 925
    regulation of digestion by, 909
    regulation of heart rhythm by, 922*f*
    regulation of human breathing by, 940*f*
    regulation of skeletal muscle contraction by, 1122–1123*f*, 1124
    research methods for studying brains and, 1079*f*–1080
    synaptic and neuroendocrine signaling of, 994*f*, 995–996 (*see also* Neuroendocrine signaling)
    vertebrate brain in, 1085*f*–1090*f*
Nervous tissue, 873*f*
Nests
    of birds and dinosaurs, 558*f*
    red-cockaded woodpecker, 1264*f*–1265
Net ecosystem production (NEP), **1236**–1237*f*, 1238*f*
Net flux flow, 1236–1237
Net primary production (NPP), **1235**–1236*f*
Neural crest, 1048*f*–1049
Neural pathways, 1115*f*
Neural plate, 1048
Neural tube birth defects, human, 896*f*
Neural tubes, **1048***f*–1049
Neurodegenerative diseases, 406
Neuroendocrine signaling. *See also* Endocrine systems; Nervous systems
    endocrine glands and hormones for, 998–999*f*
    feedback regulation in pathways of, 1000*f*–1001
    hormone cascade pathway of thyroid regulation as, 1004*f*–1005*f*
    invertebrate, 1001*f*–1002
    neurohormones in, 994*f*, 995
    regulation of growth by, 1005*f*
    vertebrate hypothalamus and pituitary gland in, 1002*f*–1003*f*
Neurofibrillary tangles, 1098*f*
Neurohormones, **995**, 1002*f*–1003

Neuromuscular junctions, 1074
Neuronal plasticity, **1094***f*
Neurons, **873**, **1061**
    action potentials of, as signals conducted by axons, 1066*f*–1071*f*
    in cell signaling by animal nervous systems, 874*f*
    chemical and electrical signals of, 1061*f*–1062
    communication between cells and, at synapses, 1071*f*–1075*f*, 1076
    exocytosis and, 137
    in human eye, 1112*f*
    ion pumps, ion channels, and resting potential of, 1064*f*–1065*f*, 1066
    in nervous systems, 1079*f*–1080, 1083*f*–1084 (*see also* Nervous systems)
    as nervous tissue, 873*f*
    in neuroendocrine signaling, 995–996, 1000–1001
    neurotransmitters, neurohormones, and, 995
    olfactory, 1118–1119*f*
    plasticity of, in memory and learning, 1093–1094*f*, 1095*f*
    in sensory reception, 1102*f*–1103*f*
    structure and function of, in information transfer, 1062*f*–1063*f*
Neuropathy, 309
Neuropeptides, **1075***t*–1076
Neurosecretory cells, 1001*f*–1003*f*
Neurospora crassa (bread mold), 334–335*f*, 336, 658*f*–659*t*, 948
Neurotransmitters, **995**, **1062**
    as chemical messengers of neurons, 1062
    exocytosis and, 137
    major, 1075*t*
    mechanisms of terminating, 1074
    nitric oxide, 995–996
    properties of types of, 1074–1076
    synaptic signaling by, 1071*f*–1073*f*, 1074
Neurulation, 1048*f*–1049
Neutralization, 960–961*f*
Neutral mutations, 561
Neutral variation, **483**
Neutrons, 30–31
Neutrophils, 928*f*, 930*f*, **950**, 951–952
Nevada, 1250*f*
Newborn screening, 287–288
New Guinea, 736
Newton, Isaac, 21
Newts, 5*f*, 236*f*–237*f*
New World monkeys, 741*f*
New Zealand, 1251*f*
Next-generation DNA sequencing, 408*f*, 409*f*, 411*f*–412
Nicotine, 1074, 1097*f*, 1213
Night length, flowering and, 853*f*–854
Nirenberg, Marshall, 338
Nitrates, 1270*f*
Nitric oxide, 217, 925, **995**–996, 1020, 1076
Nitrification, 808
Nitrifying bacteria, 808
Nitrogen
    bacteria in plant acquisition of, 807*f*–809*f*, 810
    bryophyte reduction of leaching of, from soil, 621*f*
    as essential element, 29*t*, 56, 64
    as limiting nutrient in aquatic biomes, 1237*f*–1238
    nutrient enrichment and pollution by, 1270*f*
    in organic compounds, 59*f*
    prokaryotic chemical recycling of, 578*f*, 581*f*
    soil fertilization and, 802
Nitrogen cycle, 808, 1246*f*
Nitrogen fixation, **576**, **808**
    bacterial, 807*f*–809*f*, 810
    biological augmentation using plants for, 1249
    bryophyte, 620*f*, 621, 622
    lichens and, 663
    as mutualism, 1214
    nitrogen cycle and, 1246*f*
    prokaryotic, 576, 579*f*
Nitrogenous bases, 85*f*–86, 315*f*–316. *See also* Nucleotides
Nitrogenous wastes, 972, 976–977*f*
NMDA receptors, 1095*f*
Nobel Prize winners
    R. Axel and L. Buck, 1118

    G. Beadle and E. Tatum, 336
    M. Capecchi, M. Evans, and O. Smithies, 421
    for discovery of ncRNAs, 375
    for discovery of Toll receptor in insects, 949
    J. Gurdon, 424
    A. Huxley and A. Hodgkin, 1068
    F. Jacob, 541
    R. Kornberg, 84*f*
    B. Marshall and R. Warren, 902
    B. McClintock, 445
    P. Mitchell, 175
    C. Nüsslein-Volhard, E. Wieschaus, and E. Lewis, 381
    S. Prusiner, 406
    V. Ramakrishnan, 27
    F. Sanger, 409
    E. Sutherland, 212
    N. Tinbergen, K. von Frisch, and K. Lorenz, 1134
    J. Watson, F. Crick, and M. Wilkins, 318
Nociceptors, **1105**–1106
Nodes, lymph, 927*f*
Nodes, plant stem, **755**
Nodes of Ranvier, 1070*f*–**1071***f*
Nodules, 808–809*f*, 810
Nomarski microscopy, **95***f*
Nonbreeding adults, territoriality and, 1198*f*
Noncoding DNA, 443, 444*f*–445*f*, 446
Noncoding RNAs (ncRNAs), 374*f*–375*f*, 376
Noncompetitive inhibitors, **156***f*–157
Nondisjunction, **305***f*, 307
Nonequilibrium model, community, **1222**
Nonheritable variation, 482*f*
Nonidentical DNA sequences, 447*f*
Non-insulin-dependent diabetes, 911
Nonkinetochore microtubules, 236*f*, 238–239
Non-native species, 1258–59*f*
Nonpolar covalent bonds, **37**
Nonpolar side chains, 76–77*f*
Nonrenewable resources, human population size and, 1204*f*–1205
Nonsense mutations, **355**–356*f*
Nonshivering thermogenesis, 881
Nonsister chromatids, 255*f*, 260, 262, 264*f*
Nonspontaneous processes, 144
Nonsteroidal anti-inflammatory drugs (NSAIDs), 1008
Nonsteroid hormones, 371
Nontemplate DNA strand, 338
Nonvascular plants. *See* Bryophytes
Norepinephrine (noradrenaline), 999*f*, **1006**–1007*f*, **1075***t*
Nori, 602–603*f*
North Atlantic Subtropical Gyre, 1162*f*
Northern coniferous forests, **1169***f*
Northern red maple tree leaves, 756
North Pacific Subtropical Gyre, 1162*f*
Notation system, gene, 294–295
Notochords, **714***f*, **1048***f*–1049
Novelties, evolutionary, 541–542*f*
N-terminus, 78*f*, 328*f*, 350, 366*f*
Nuclear envelopes, 100*f*–101*f*, **102**–103*f*, 330, 337*f*, 353
Nucleariids, 607, **653**
Nuclear lamina, **102**, 103*f*, 117, 330
Nuclear magnetic resonance (NMR) spectroscopy, 83
Nuclear matrix, 102, 324*f*–325*f*, 330
Nuclear responses, cell-signaling, 223*f*
Nuclear transplantation, animal cloning and, 423*f*–425*f*
Nucleases, **325**
Nucleic acid hybridization, **409**
Nucleic acid probes, **418**, 428
Nucleic acids, **84**. *See also* DNA (deoxyribonucleic acid); RNA (ribonucleic acid)
    components of, 85*f*–86
    digestion of, 903*f*
    genes, nucleotides, and, 84 (*see also* Gene(s))
    as genetic material, 313 (*see also* DNA (deoxyribonucleic acid))
    as macromolecules, 66
    as nucleotide polymers, 86
    roles of, in gene expression, 84*f*–85 (*see also* Gene expression)

separating, with gel electrophoresis, 414*f*
structures of molecules of, 86–87*f*
viral, 394, 395*f*–397*f*, 398*t*
viroids as, 405
Nucleoids, 97, **571**
Nucleolus, 100*f*, 101*f*, **102**
Nucleomorphs, 593
Nucleosides, 85*f*
Nucleoside triphosphates, 322
Nucleosomes, 328*f*
Nucleotide excision repairs, **326***f*
Nucleotide-pair insertions and deletions, 356*f*
Nucleotide-pair substitutions, 355–356*f*
Nucleotides, **85**. *See also* Nucleic acids
coding and noncoding, 343*f*–345*f*
as components of nucleic acids, 84–85*f*, 86
in DNA sequencing techniques, 408*f*, 409*f*–411*f*, 412
DNA vs. RNA, 336
evolutionary significance of altered DNA, 326
in genetic code, 5*f*–6*f*
genetic code as triplet code of, 337–338*f*
genomics and proteomics in study of, 87–88*f*
mutations as base-pair substitutions, insertions, and deletions of, 355–356*f*
ratios of, 315*f*–316
in telomeres, 326–327*f*
variability of, in genetic variation, 481–482*f*
Nucleus, atomic, 30–31
Nucleus, cell, **102**
animal cell, 100*f*
cell division of, 234, 241–242*f* (*see also* Cell cycle; Cell division)
cell-signaling responses in, 223*f*
ciliate types of, 600*f*–601
DNA in eukaryotic cell, 97, 102, 103*f*
fungal cell, 100*f*
hormone receptors in, 998
plant cell, 101*f*
regulation of gene expression and architecture of, 372*f*
reproductive cloning by transplantation of eukaryotic, 423*f*–425*f*
Nucleus accumbens, 1090*f*, 1097*f*
Nudibranchs, 693*f*, 1013*f*
Number, offspring, 1195*f*–1196*f*, 1197
Nursing, 1001
Nurture vs. nature, 280*f*, 756
Nüsslein-Volhard, Chistiane, 380–382
Nutrient enrichment, global, 1270*f*
Nutrients
cycling of, 1244*f*–1245*f*, 1246–1247*f*, 1248*f* (*see also* Energy flow and chemical cycling)
nutrient enrichment experiments with, 1237*f*–1238
plant and animal absorption of, 889*f*
primary production in aquatic ecosystems and limitations of, 1237*f*–1238*f*
primary production in terrestrial ecosystems and limitations of, 1238*f*–1239
prokaryotic recycling of, 581*f*–582
Nutrition. *See also* Animal nutrition; Plant nutrition
essential elements and trace elements for, 29*t*–30
fungal, 648*f*–650*f*, 651
prokaryotic, 575–576*f*, 585
protist, 588
Nymphs, 705

O

Oak Ridge National Laboratory, bioremediation of, 1249*f*
Oak trees, 608*f*, 644*f*
Obelia, 686*f*–687*f*
Obesity, 911*f*–912
ob gene, 912
Obligate aerobes, **575**
Obligate anaerobes, **179**, **575**
Obligate mutualism, 1214
Observations
of evolutionary change, 471*f*–472*f*, 473
scientific, 16*f*, 18*f*
in Scientific Skills Exercise, 806
Occam's razor, 556

Occipital lobe, 1091*f*
Ocean acidification, 53*f*–54
Ocean currents, climate and, 1162*f*–1163*f*
Oceanic pelagic zone, **1175***f*, 1176*f*
Oceans
acidification of, 53*f*–54
climate and currents of, 1162*f*–1163*f*
marine benthic zones of, 1176*f*
as marine biome, 1171*f*–1172
moderation of climate by, 47*f*
net ecosystem production for, 1236–37*f*
nutrient enrichment of, 1238*t*
pelagic zones of, 1175*f*
tides of, 1175*f*
trawling of, as community disturbance, 1225*f*
Ocelli, 1111*f*
Ocotillo, 793*f*
Octopus, 692, 695*f*–696, 1213*f*
Odorant receptors (ORs), 1118–1119*f*
Odorants, **1117**, 1118–1119*f*
Odum, Eugene, 1209
Offspring
ensuring survival of, 1017*f*
life history traits in survival of, 1195*f*–1196*f*, 1197
Oil, conodonts and, 719
Oil spills, 584*f*. *See also* Fossil fuels
Okazaki fragments, **323**
Old World monkeys, 741*f*
Oleander, 793*f*
Olfaction, **1117**, 1118–1119*f*
Olfactory bulb, 1085*f*, 1118–1119*f*
Olfactory receptor genes, human, 483, 560
Oligochaetes, 696–697
Oligodendrocytes, **1070***f*–1071*f*, 1081*f*
Oligotropic lakes, **1173***f*
Omasum, 908*f*
Ommatidia, **1111***f*
Omnivores, **892**, 906*f*
Oncogenes, **383***f*–384, 386*f*
One gene–one enzyme hypothesis, 334–335*f*, 336, 659
One gene–one polypeptide hypothesis, 336
One gene–one protein hypothesis, 336
One-shot reproduction, 1195
On the Origin of Species by Means of Natural Selection (book), 12–13*f*, 463, 467, 477, 478, 481
Onychophorans, 683*f*
Oocytes, **1020**–1021*f*, 1023*f*
Oogenesis, **1021**, 1023*f*
Oogonia, 1023*f*, **1023***f*
Oparin, A. I., 520
Oparin-Haldane hypothesis, 520
Open circulatory systems, 693*f*, **701**, **917***f*–918
Open systems, 143, 148*f*
Operant conditioning, 1140–1141
Operators, 361–362*f*
Operculum, **722***f*
Operon model, 361
Operons, **361**
basic concept of, 361–362*f*
inducible, 363*f*–364
positive gene regulation and, 364*f*
repressible, 362*f*–363, 364
Ophiuroidea, 708*f*–709
Opiates, 40*f*, 79, 1075–1076
Opium, 1097*f*
Opium poppy, 862*f*
Opossums, 736
Opposable thumb, **740**
Opposite phyllotaxy, 780
Opsin, 1113*f*, 1116
Opsonization, 961*f*
Optic chiasm, 1115*f*
Optic disk, 1112*f*
Optic nerves, 1115*f*
Optimal conditions, enzymatic catalysis, 155–156*f*
Optimal foraging model, 1143*f*–**1144**
Oral cavity, **900**–901*f*
Orangutans, 436*f*, 741*f*, 745
Orbitals, electron, **35***f*, 39–40
Orchids, 644*f*, 815*f*–816, 821*f*
Order, as property of life, 1*f*, 144*f*–145

Orders, taxonomy, **548–549***f*
Ordovician Period global climate change, 623
Organelles, **94**
as enzyme locations, 159*f*
of eukaryotic cells, 98–99, 100*f*–101*f*
inheritance of genes in, 309*f*
as level of biological organization, 3*f*
lysosomal digestion of, 107*f*–108
plastids in plant cells, 111
of prokaryotic cells, 97*f*
using electron microscopy to study, 94
Organic chemistry, **57–58**
Organic compounds. *See also* Biological molecules
abiotic synthesis of, 520–521*f*
abiotic synthesis of, as origin of life on Earth, 57*f*, 58
ATP as, 64
bonding of carbon atoms in, 58–59*f*, 60*f*–62*f*
carbon in, as backbone of life, 56, 64
chemical functional groups and, 62–63*f*
organic chemistry as study of, 57–58
in plant cells, 207*f*
working with moles and molar ratios of, 58
Organic fertilizers, 802, 977
Organ identity genes, **774***f*
Organismal cloning
of animals, 423*f*–425*f*
of animal stem cells, 422, 425*f*–427*f*
of extinct species, 1260–1261*f*
of plants, 423*f*
Organismal ecology, **1159***f*. *See also* Ecology; Organisms
Organismal-level herbivore defenses, plant, 863*f*
Organisms. *See also* Animal(s); Fungi; Life; Plant(s)
acidic and basic conditions affecting, 51–52*f*, 53*f*–54
adaptations of, to environments, 462*f* (*see also* Adaptations)
Cambrian explosion in numbers of, 530*f*
carbon in organic compounds of, 56, 64
cells as fundamental units of, 4*f*–5, 93*f* (*see also* Cell(s))
cloning of (*see* Organismal cloning)
differential gene expression in multicellular (*see* Differential gene expression)
DNA in development of, 5*f*–6*f*
ecology as interactions between environment and, 1158*f* (*see also* Ecology)
effects of continental drift on, 533–534
effects of sickle-cell disease on, 497*f*
effects of speciation and extinctions on diversity of, 531*f*
genomics, bioinformatics, and proteomics in study of genomes of, 6*f*–7
geographic distributions of, 533–534
importance of water for, 44
inherited DNA and development of, 5*f*–6*f*
interactions of, as theme in biology, 8*f*
as level of biological organization, 2*f*
model (*see* Model organisms)
as open systems, 143
origin of mammalian, 524–525*f*, 526
origin of multicellular, 529–530*f*
origin of single-celled, 526, 528*f*–529*f*
possible effects of transgenic crops on nontarget, 833
regulation of molecular interactions within, 8–9*f*
single-celled, 3*f*
in topsoil, 801
transgenic (*see* Transgenic animals; Transgenic plants)
Organization, as theme of biology, 2*f*–4*f*, 5
Organizer, Spemann's, 1056*f*
Organ-level herbivore defenses, plant, 862*f*
Organ of Corti, **1107***f*
Organogenesis, **1030***f*, 1038, **1044***f*, 1048*f*–1049*f*
Organs, **753**, **870***t*
embryonic germ layers and, 1044*f*
endocrine system, 998–999*f* (*see also* Endocrine glands)
excretory, 980*f*–981*f*
eyes and light-detecting, 1111*f*–1113*f*
floral, 816*f*–817*f*

human reproductive, 1019f–1020, 1021f
immune system rejection of transplanted, 964
as level of biological organization, 3f
organogenesis of, 1038, 1044f, 1048f–1049f
plant roots, stems, and leaves as, 753f–756f
reverse positioning of human, in *situs inversus*, 1058f
smooth muscle in vertebrate, 1125–1126
Organs, digestive. See Digestive systems
Organ systems, **870**
internal exchange surfaces of, 869f
as level of biological organization, 3f
mammalian, 870t
Orgasm, 1028
Orientation
leaf, 780–781f
plant cell expansion, 772f
Orienting, 1136f
Origin-of-life studies, 57f–58
Origin of Species, The (book), 12–13f, 463, 467, 477–478, 481
Origins of replication, **240**–41f, **320**–321f
Ornithine, 335f
Orthologous genes, **559**f–560
Orthoptera, 706f
Oryza sativa (rice), 442t
Osculum, **684**f
Osmoconformers, **972**
Osmolarity, 972f, 983–984f, 985
Osmoreceptors, 1104
Osmoregulation, **132**, **971**
challenges and mechanisms of, for aquatic and terrestrial animals, 972f–974f, 975
energetics of, 974–975
excretion and, 972 (*see also* Excretory systems)
homeostasis by, 971f–972
ion movement and gradients and, 987f
osmosis and, 132f–133f
osmosis and osmolarity in, 972f
salinity and, 1180
transport epithelia in, 975–976f
Osmoregulators, **972**f
Osmosis, **132**, **782**
diffusion of water by, across plant plasma membranes, 782–784, 785f
effects of, on water balance, 131f–133f
osmolarity and, 972f
Osmotic pressure, blood, 927
Osteichthyans, **722**f–723f, 724
Osteoblasts, 872f, 1128
Osteoclasts, 1128
Osteons, 872f
Ostriches, 986f
Otoliths, 1108f–1109
Otters, 892f
Outer ear, **1107**f
Outgroups, **555**
Oval window, **1107**f
Ovarian cancer, 441
Ovarian cycle, **1025**–1026f, 1027
Ovaries, angiosperm, 617, **638**f–639f, 640f–641, **816**–817f, 825–826. See also Fruits
Ovaries, human, 256, 999f, 1008–1009f, **1020**–1021f
Overgrazing, 1225
Overharvesting, 696, 722, 1259f
Overnourishment, 911–912
Overproduction, offspring, 469f–470
Oviducts, **1020**–1021f
Oviparous organisms, **721**
Oviraptor dinosaurs, 558f
Ovoviviparous organisms, **721**
Ovulation, **1015**, 1028f
Ovules, **632**f, **816**
Owl-mouse predation study, 21–22
Oxidation, 111, 163–**164**f
Oxidative phosphorylation, 166–**167**f, 172f–175f
Oxidizing agents, 163–**164**f
Oxygen
atmospheric, in animal evolution, 671
catabolic pathways and, 163
in circulation and gas exchange, 941f–943f
covalent bonding and, 36f–37f
development of photosynthesis and atmospheric, 528f

diffusion of, across capillary walls, 926–927
in double circulation, 918–919f
electronegativity of, 37
as essential element, 29t, 56, 64
in gas exchange, 933t–934
in human breathing, 940
land plants production of, 612f
metabolic rate and, 884f
in net ecosystem production, 1236–1237f
in organic compounds, 59f
Permian mass extinction and low levels of, 534–535
in photosynthesis, 41f
in plant cells, 207f
in plant composition, 803
as product of photosynthesis, 186, 204–205f
prokaryotic chemical recycling of, 581
role of, in prokaryotic metabolism, 575
species distributions and availability of, 1180
Oxytocin, 999f, 1000f–**1001**, 1002f–1003, 1031f
Oyster drills, 536
Oysters, 692, 694f–695f
Ozone depletion, 1274f–1275f

P

p21 gene, 384
p53 gene, **384**–385f, 386f
P680 chlorophyll *a*, 194–196
P700 chlorophyll *a*, 194–196
Paabo, Svante, 747f
Pacemaker, heart, 922f
Pacific Island land snails, 696f
Pacman mechanism, 239
Paedomorphosis, 538–**539**f
Paine, Robert, 1220f
Pain receptors, **1105**–1106
Pair bonding, 1150f–1151
Pakicetus, 476
Paleoanthropology, **742**
Paleogene period, 532
Paleontology, 12f, 88f, **464**f
Paleozoic era, 526f, 527t, 533f, 671f–672
Palisade mesophyll, 764f–765f
Pallium, avian, 1093f
Palumbi, S. R., 551f
Pampas, 1169f
PAMP-triggered immunity, 860
Pancreas, **903**, 999f
in digestion, 903
exocytosis and, 137
in glucose homeostasis, 910f
rough ER and, 105
Pancrustaceans, **701**
Pandemics, **402**–403f, 404–405, 1228
Pandoravirus, 400
Pangaea, **476**–477, **533**f–534
Pan genus, 741f. See also Chimpanzees
Paper, 645
Paper wasps, 706f
Papillae, 1118f
Papillomaviruses, 388
Papua New Guinea, 1158f
Parabasalids, **593**f
Parabronchi, 938f–939f
Parachutes, seed and fruit, 826f
Paracrine signaling, 212, 213f, 994f–**995**, 996
Parahippus, 542–543f
Parakeets, 1130
Paralogous genes, 559f–**560**
Paramecium, 12f, 132, 133f, 600f, 1193f, 1209
Paramyosin, 1126
Paraphyletic groups, **553**f–554f
Parapodia, 696, 697
Parareptiles, **730**
Parasites, 579f, **582**, **1214**
animals as, 667
antigenic variation and, 967
apicomplexans, 598–599f
arachnids, 702f
cercozoans, 602
entamoebas, 607
flatworms, 690f–691f
fungi as, 649, 654, 659, 663f–664f

lampreys as, 717f–718
nematodes, 699f–700
plants as, 812f–813
protist, 590f, 593f, 608
in symbiosis, 1214
in zoonotic diseases, 1229
Parasitism, **582**, **1214**
Parasitoid wasps, 863f
Parasympathetic division, peripheral nervous system, 922f, 1083–**1084**
Parathion, 157
Parathyroid glands, 999f, **1006**f
Parathyroid hormone (PTH), 999f, **1006**f
Parenchyma cells, **758**f, 762f, 764
Parental alleles, genomic imprinting and, 308f–309
Parental care, 1017f, 1145–1146f, 1196f–1197
Parental types, **300**
Parietal cells, 901–902f
Parietal lobe, 1091f
Parkinson's disease, 83, 229, 406, 426–427, 665, 1075, **1098**
Parsimony, 556–557f, 558
Parthenogenesis, 691–692, **1014**, 1015f
Partial pressure, **933**
Particulate hypothesis on inheritance, 267–268
Particulate model of inheritance, 481
Parus major (great tit), 490–491f, 734f
Passeriformes, 734f
Passive immunity, **962**–963
Passive transport, **131**
active transport vs., 135f
diffusion as, 130–131f
facilitated diffusion as, 133f
interpreting scatter plots on glucose uptake as facilitated, 134
in plant cells, 207f
of water across plant plasma membranes, 782–784, 785f
water balance and osmosis as, 131f–133f
Patella vulgata, 541f–542f
Paternal alleles, 367
Paternal chromosomes, 263
Paternity
certainty of, 1145–1146
tests for, 431
Pathogen-associated molecular patterns (PAMPs), **860**
Pathogenicity trait, bacterial, 313f
Pathogens, **582**, **946**f
adaptations of, in immune system evasion, 966f–968f
alteration of community structure by, 1228–1229f
bacterial, 313f, 577f–579f, 580, 583f
B cells and antibodies as responses to extracellular, 960f–961f
cytotoxic T cell response to cells infected by, 959f
evasion of innate immunity by, 952
fungi as, 649, 658–659, 663f–664f
immune system recognition and response to, 946f–947f
plant defenses against, 859–861f
prokaryotic, 582, 583f
viruses as, 394f–395, 400, 401f, 402–403f, 404–405, 406f
Pathways, sensory, 1102f–1103f, 1104
Pattern
evolutionary, 463, 477, 547
taxonomy based on, 464
Pattern formation, **379**–380f, 381f–382f, 383, **772**–773f, 843, **1056**f–1058f. See also Morphogenesis
Pauling, Linus, 316–317
Pavlov, Ivan, 1140
Paw development, *Hox* genes in mouse, 420
Pax-6 gene, 417
PCBs (polychlorinated biphenyls), 1271f
PCSK9 enzyme, 932
Pea aphids, 564
Peacocks, 493f
Pea fruit, 825f
Pea plants, G. Mendel's experiments with, 267f–274f
Pearl mussels, 696f
Peat, **622**f, 627–628

Pectin, 118
Pedigrees, **282**f–283
Pedipalps, 702
Pelagic zone, **1171**f
Pellicle, 594f
Penguins, 13f, 734f, 868f, 886, 1187f
Penicillin, 157, 472, 664
Penicillium, 652f
Penis, 995–996, 1019f–**1020**, 1027–1028, 1076
Pentoses, 68f
PEP carboxylase, **202**f
Pepsin, 156, **901**–902f
Pepsinogen, **902**f
Peptide bonds, 78f, 350f
Peptides, antimicrobial, 948f–949f, 951
Peptidoglycan, 568–569f
Per capita birth rate, 1190–1192
Per capita death rate, 1190–1192
Per capita rate of increase, 1190–1192
Perception, **1103**, 1115f
Perch, 973f–974
Perennials, 761
Pericarp, 825–826
Pericycle, **763**f
Periderm, **757**, 768
Perilymph, 1108
Periodic table of elements, 34f
Peripheral nervous system (PNS), **1063**, 1075–1076,
     1080
     central nervous system and, 1080–1081, 1082f,
        1084f
     structure and function of vertebrate, 1083f–1084f
Peripheral proteins, **127**
Peripheral vision, 1116f–1117
Perissodactyla, 739f
Peristalsis, **900**–901f, **1127**f, 1129
Peristome, **621**
Peritubular capillaries, **981**f
Periwinkles, 1257f
Permafrost, 1170f
Permian mass extinction, 534f–535
Peromyscus polionotus, 19f–20f, 21–22
Peroxisomes, 100f, 101f, **112**
Personalized medicine, 88f, 428
Pertussis, 215f
Pesticides
     DDT, 157, 1271f
     transgenic, 831–832
Pest outbreaks, 1166
Pest resistance, plant, 412f, 432
Petals, **638**f, **816**
Petioles, 755
Petromyzontida (lampreys), 717f–718
PET scanners, 31–32f
Pévet, Paul, 887f
P (parental) generations, **269**
P granules, 1053f
pH, **52**
     acid precipitation and, 1260
     adjusting soil, 802–803
     buffers and, 52–53
     enzymatic catalysis and, 155–156f
     and hemoglobin dissociation, 942f
     of human cerebrospinal fluid, 940
     pH scale and, 51–52f
     prokaryotes and, 567
     protein denaturation and, 82f–83
     soil, in ecological succession, 1225f
     species distributions and soil, 1180–1181
PHA (polyhydroxyalkanoate), 584
Phages, **313**, **395**
     capsids of, 394f–395
     in DNA research, 313f–314f, 315
     prophages and temperate, 397–398
     replicative cycles of, 396f–397f, 398
     in transduction, 573f
     virulent, 396f–397f
Phagocytic cells, 949f–950f
Phagocytosis, **107**, **138**f, 947–**948**f
     cellular integration of, 121f
     as endocytosis, 137f–138f
     immune systems and, 949f–950f, 961f
     lysosomes and, 107f–108

Phalacrocorax harrisi, 500f, 505
Phanerozoic eon, 526f, 527t, 533f
Pharmaceutical products
     biotechnology in production of, 429–430f (*see also*
        Drugs; Medicine)
     as environmental toxins, 1271–1272f
     fungal, 664
     species and genetic diversity and, 1257
Pharyngeal clefts, **714**f
Pharyngeal slits, **714**f, 715f
Pharynx, 690f, **901**f
Phase changes, plant development, 773–774f
Phase-contrast microscopy, **95**f
Phenobarbital, 104
Phenolics, 862f
Phenotypes, **272**
     DNA transformation and, 313
     dominant alleles and, 277–278
     gene concept and, 357
     gene expression as link between genotypes and,
        334
     genetic mapping and, 303f
     genetic variation and, 481f–482
     genotypes vs., 271f–272f, 280f–281
     impact of environment on, 280f
     making histograms and analyzing distribution
        patterns of, 281
     mutant, 294f–295f, 326
     relative fitness and, 492
Phenylalanine, 77f, 287–288, 338, 486–487
Phenylketonuria (PKU), 287–288, 486–487
Pheromones, 651, 664, **995**f, 1017, **1137**f
Philadelphia chromosome, 307f
Philippine eagle, 1256f
Phloem, **624**, **757**, **779**
     primary growth and, 762f
     resource acquisition and, 779f
     sugar-conducting cells of, 759f
     sugar transport from sources to sinks via,
        793–794f, 795f
     symplastic communication through, 796
     vascular plant, 624
     in vascular tissue systems, 757
Phloem sap, **793**–794f, 795f
Phosphate group, **63**f
Phosphates, algal blooms and, 1237
Phosphodiesterase, 227
Phosphofructokinase, 181f–182
Phospholipid bilayers, 74f–75, 98f–99, 102, 110,
     125f–126, 130
Phospholipids, **74**
     in cellular membranes, 74f–75, 102, 110, 125f–126,
        130
     Golgi apparatus and, 106
     movement of, in cellular membranes, 126f–127
     in plasma membranes, 98f–99
Phosphorus
     as essential element, 29t, 56, 64
     as limiting nutrient in aquatic biomes, 1237f–1238
     plant deficiency in, 811
     soil fertilization and, 802
Phosphorus cycle, 1245f
Phosphorylated intermediates, 149–150f
Phosphorylation
     in cell-signal responses, 223f
     in cell-signal transduction, 219f–220
     in light reactions of photosynthesis, 189f
Photic zone, **1171**f
Photoautotrophs, 185f–186f, 576f, 588
Photoheterotrophs, 576f
Photomorphogenesis, **849**
Photons, **190**f, 193f
Photoperiodism, 853f–854f, 855
Photophosphorylation, **189**
Photoprotection, 193, 196
Photopsins, 1116
Photoreceptors, **1111**f–1113f
Photorespiration, **201**
Photosynthates, 753
Photosynthesis, **185**
     alternative mechanisms of carbon fixation in,
        201–202f, 203–204f
     biofuels from, 186f

Calvin cycle of, 199–200f
cellular respiration vs., 189 (*see also* Cellular
     respiration)
cercozoan, 602
chemical reactions in, 41f
chloroplasts in, 3f, 109–110f, 111f
conversion of light energy to chemical energy of
     food by, 187f–189f
cyanobacteria and, 579f
determining rate of, with satellites, 1236f
development of, and atmospheric oxygen, 528f
in energy flow and chemical cycling, 7f, 162–163f,
     1233
evolution of adaptations for resource acquisition
     and, 778f–781f
as gas exchange, 889f
importance of, 204–205f
lichens in, 662f–663f
light reactions of (*see* Light reactions)
maximizing surface area for, 689f
as plant nutritional mode, 888f
as process that feeds biosphere, 185f–186f
prokaryotic, 571f
protist, 588, 591f, 592f–593f, 608–609f
red and green algae, 602–603f, 604f
scatter plots with regression lines on atmospheric
     carbon dioxide and, 203
stramenopile, 596
sunlight availability and, 1180
two stages of, 189f–190
in vascular plants, 625
in working plant cells, 207f
zonation of aquatic biomes and, 1171
Photosystem I (PS I), **194**–195f, 196f
Photosystem II (PS II), **194**–195f, 196f
Photosystems, **194**–195f, 196f–197f
Phototrophs, 575, 576t
Phototropin, 850
Phototropism, **841**f–842f
Phragmoplasts, 613
pH scale, 51–52f
Phycoerythrin, 602
Phyla, taxonomy and, **548**–549f
     angiosperm, 642f
     bryophyte, 620f
     gymnosperm, 636f–637f
     land plant, 617t
Phyllotaxy, **780**f, 843
Phylogenetic bracketing, 558f
Phylogenetic species concept, **504**
Phylogenetic trees, **549**f. *See also* Evolutionary trees;
        Phylogenies
     analyzing sequence-based, to understand viral
        evolution, 404
     of animals, 677f
     applying, 550–551f
     of chordates, 713f
     cladistics in construction of, 553f–554f, 555
     of eukaryotes, 605f
     as hypotheses, 558f
     linking classification and phylogeny with,
        549f–550f
     of mammals, 738f–739f
     maximum parsimony and maximum likelihood in,
        556–557f, 558
     of primates, 740f
     of prokaryotes, 577f
     proportional branch lengths in, 555f–556f
     of protists, 590f
     of tetrapods, 725f
     tree of life and, 14f–15f
Phylogenies, **547**
     of amniotes, 728f
     of angiosperms, 642f, 643f–644f
     of animals, 676–677f, 678
     of chordates, 713f
     constructing phylogenetic trees for, 553f–558f (*see
        also* Phylogenetic trees)
     documentation of, in genomes, 559f–560
     of eukaryotes, 605f
     of fungi, 654, 655f–661
     gymnosperm, 635, 636f–637f
     as hypotheses, 558f
     inferring, from morphological and molecular data,
        551f–553f

investigating tree of life with, 547*f*–548*f*, 562–563*f*, 564*f*
of land plants, 617*f*
of mammals, 738*f*–739*f*
molecular clocks and evolutionary time in, 560–561*f*, 562*f*
practical applications of, 550–551*f*
of primates, 740*f*
of prokaryotes, 577*f*
of protists, 588–589, 590*f*–591*f*
systematics and, 548
taxonomy and evolutionary relationships in, 548–549*f*, 550*f*, 562, 563*f*
of tetrapods, 725*f*
Physical reconstruction, ecosystem, 1248–1249
Physiological thermostats, 882–883*f*
Physiology, 867*f*–**868**
Phytoalexins, 860
Phytochemicals, 193
Phytochromes, **849**
in circadian rhythms, 852
in plant signal transduction pathways, 838*f*
in seed germination, 850–851*f*
in shade avoidance in plants, 851
Phytophthora species, 608*f*, 1228
Phytoplankton. *See also* Plankton
dinoflagellate, 598*f*
green algae, 603
net ecosystem production of, in oceans, 1237*f*
nitrogen pollution and blooms of, 1270*f*
seasonality and, 1162
Phytoremediation, **803**
Pie charts in Scientific Skills Exercise, 886
Pied flycatchers, 512*f*–513
Pig, 339*f*
Pigmentation
gene expression and, 333*f*, 334
plant, 309*f*
skin, 279–280*f*
Pigments
as photosynthetic light receptors, 191*f*–912*f*, 193
in photosystems, 194*f*–198*f*, 199
respiratory, 941*f*–942*f*
visual, 1116
Pili, **570**, 574*f*–575
Pill bugs, 703
Pilobolus, 657*f*
Pineal gland, 999*f*, 1002*f*, **1009**, 1087*f*
Pineapple, 204*f*, 825*f*
Pine trees, 634*f*, 637*f*
Pin flower, 829*f*
Pinocytosis, **138***f*
Pinworms, 699
Pistils, **816**
Pitch, 1108
Pitcher plants, 812*f*
Pitch pine canker, 663
Pith, **757**, 764*f*
Pituitary dwarfism, 1005
Pituitary gland, **1002**, 1024, 1087*f*
in human endocrine system, 999*f*
in kidney regulation, 988*f*–989*f*
in neuroendocrine signaling, 1002*f*–1005*f*
Pit vipers, 731*f*, 732, 1104–1105*f*
Pivot joints, 1128*f*
Piwi-interacting RNAs (piRNAs), 92, 375–376
Piwi protein, 92*f*
Placenta, **736**, **1029***f*
Placental mammals. *See* Eutherians (placental mammals)
Placental transfer cells, 614*f*
Placoderm fossil, 523*f*
Placoderms, **720***f*
Placozoans, 681*f*
Plains, 1169*f*
Planarians, **688**–689*f*, 690*f*. *See also* Flatworms
Planes, plant cell division, 770*f*–772*f*
Planets, possible evolution of life on other, 50*f*
Plankton, 598, 601, 703. *See also* Phytoplankton
Plant(s). *See also* Angiosperms; Land plants; Plant development; Plant growth; Plant hormones; Plant nutrition; Plant responses; Plant structure; Seed plants
adaptations of, that reduce terrestrial nutrient limitations, 1239

adaptations of, to toxic elements, 30*f*
adaptive radiations of, 537*f*–538
alternation of generations in life cycles of, 256*f*, 614*f*
in Archaeplastida supergroup, 591*f*, 602
biofuels from, 186*f*
bioremediation using, 1249
carbon in organic compounds of, 56
cells of, 4*f*–5, 206*f*–207*f* (*see also* Plant cells)
cellulose as structural polysaccharide for, 71*f*–72
cloning of, 423*f*
community stability and diversity of, 1217*f*
crop (*see* Crop plants)
elements in composition of, 803
endangered or threatened, 1256
essential elements and trace elements for, 29–30
in domain Eukarya, 11*f*
evolutionary mystery of flowering, for C. Darwin, 471
facilitation in, 1215*f*
fungal mutualisms with, 659, 661*f*–662*f* (*see also* Mycorrhizae)
fungal pathogens of, 658–659, 663*f*
gametophyte-sporophyte relationships in, 631*f*
genetic engineering of transgenic, 412*f*, 432, 805–806*f*
genomics and proteomics in study of, 88*f*
global climate change and species distributions of, 1163–1164*f*
habitat loss and, 1258
immune response in, 751, 859–860
importance of insects to, 707
inheritance of organelle genes in, 309*f*
invasive exotic, 811
land colonization by, 530–531*f*
life challenges and solutions for, 888*f*–889*f*
nematode parasites of, 699
nonvascular, 618–619*f*, 620*f*–621
pathogens of, 751*f*, 1228
as photoautotrophs, 185*f*–186*f*
photosynthesis of (*see* Photosynthesis)
polyploidy in, 305
prey, defensive adaptations against, 1213
producing transgenic, using Ti plasmid, 770*f*
prokaryotic protection against diseases for, 584
protists as pathogens of, 608*f*
reproduction of (*see* Angiosperm reproduction)
resource acquisition for vascular, 778*f*–781*f*
rising atmospheric carbon dioxide levels and, 1274
salinity and species distributions of, 1180
starch as storage polysaccharide for, 70*f*–71
sympatric speciation in, 508*f*–509*f*
transgenic, 584
vascular (*see* Transport in vascular plants; Vascular plants)
water balance of cells of, 132*f*–133
water transport in, 45–46*f*
Plantae, kingdom, 11*f*, 562, 563*f*, 591*f*, 602, 613*f*
Plant cells. *See also* Eukaryotic cells
cell fate in pattern formation, 772–773
cell signaling in, 212
cellular activities of, 206*f*–207*f*
cell walls of, 118*f*
chloroplasts in, 109–110*f*, 111*f*
common types of, 757, 758*f*–759*f*
cytoplasmic streaming in, 117*f*
division and expansion of, in growth, 770*f*–772*f*
as eukaryotic cells, 101*f*
gene expression and control of differentiation of, 773*f*
in genetic engineering of protein products, 430
mitosis and cytokinesis in, 239–240*f*, 241*f*
photosynthesis in (*see* Photosynthesis)
plant cloning from single, 423*f* (*see also* Transgenic plants)
plasmodesmata as cell junctions in, 119*f*–120
Plant development
adaptations of, 888*f*
auxin in, 843
cell division and cell expansion in growth and, 770–771*f*, 772
gene expression and control of cell differentiation in, 773*f*
genetic control of flowering in, 774*f*–775*f*

growth, morphogenesis, and cell differentiation in, 769*f*
model organisms in the study of, 769–770*f*
morphogenesis and pattern formation in, 772–773*f*
phase changes in, 773–774*f*
Plant growth
adaptations of, 888*f*
cell division and cell expansion in, 770*f*–772*f*
meristem generation of cells for, 760*f*–761*f*
plant development and, 769
primary, 761*f*–765*f*
regulators of (*see* Plant hormones)
secondary, 765–766*f*, 767*f*–768*f*, 769
Plant hormones, **840**. *See also* Hormones
abscisic acid, 840*t*, 846*f*
animal hormones vs., 212, 888*f*
auxin, 840*t*, 841*f*–843*f*
brassinosteroids, 840*t*, 849
cytokinins, 840*t*, 843–844*f*
in de-etiolation (greening) responses, 839
ethylene, 840*t*, 846–847*f*, 848*f*
florigen, 854*f*–855
gibberellins, 840*t*, 844–845*f*
jasmonates, 840*t*, 849
in long-distance cell signaling, 212
overview of, 840*t*
as plant growth regulators, 840–841*f*
strigolactones, 840*t*
Plant nutrition
essential elements for, 803–804*f*, 805*t*–806*f*
mutualisms for, 806–807*f*, 808*f*–809*f*, 810–811*f*
nutritional modes in, 888*f*
photosynthesis and modes of, 185–186*f*
soil as complex ecosystem for, 799*f*–803*f*
unusual adaptations for, 799*f*–800, 812*f*–813
vascular plant acquisition of water and minerals, 781
vascular plant transport of water and minerals, 781–782*f*, 783*f*–784, 785*f*
Plant responses
to attacks by pathogens and herbivores, 751, 859–860, 861*f*–863*f*
to environmental stresses, 856–857*f*, 858–859
to gravity, 855*f*
to light, 849–850*f*, 851*f*–854*f*, 855
to mechanical stimuli, 855–856*f*
of parasitic dodder plant, 836*f*–837
plant hormones and, 840*t*–848*f*, 849
signal-transduction pathways linking signal reception to, 837*f*–838*f*, 839
Plant structure
cells in, 757, 758*f*–759*f*
diversity in, 752*f*–753
hierarchy of organs, tissues, and cells in, 752*f*–759*f*
meristem generation of cells for growth of, 760*f*–761*f*
plant development and, 769*f*–775*f*
primary growth of roots and shoots of, 761*f*–765*f*
secondary growth of stems and roots in woody plants, 765–766*f*, 767*f*–768*f*, 769
Plaque, arterial, 932
Plasma, **928***f*–929
Plasma cells, **956**, 963*f*
Plasma membranes, **98**. *See also* Cellular membranes
animal cell, 100*f*
chemiosmosis in prokaryotic, 173–174*f*, 175
electron transport chains in prokaryotic, 166
hormone receptors in, 997*f*
ion gradients and transport of ions across, 987*f*
microfilaments in, 116*f*
movement across plant cell, 207*f*
nuclear envelopes as, 102
plant cell, 101*f*
of prokaryotic and eukaryotic cells, 98*f*–99
prokaryotic cell, 97*f*
receptor proteins in, 214, 215*f*–217*f*
short-distance and long-distance transport across, 781–782*f*, 783*f*–784, 785*f*
Plasmids, **412**, **571**
in antibiotic resistance of bacteria, 575
in bacterial conjugation, 574*f*–575
evolution of viruses and, 400
producing transgenic plants using Ti, 432

prokaryotic, 571*f*
  as recombinant DNA, 412*f*–413*f*, 414
Plasmodesmata, **119**
  as cell junctions in plants, 119*f*–120
  in plant cells, 101*f*
  plant cell walls and, 118
  in plant local cell signaling, 212*f*
  in symplastic communication, 796*f*
Plasmodial slime molds, 606*f*
Plasmodium (protist), 591*f*, 599*f*, 608, 707
Plasmogamy, **651***f*
Plasmolysis, **133**, **784**
Plasticity, neuronal, 1093–1094*f*, 1095*f*
Plastics, natural, 584*f*
Plastids, **111**
  endosymbiontic origin of, 528–529*f*
  eukaryotic endosymbiosis and evolution of,
    592*f*–593*f*
Plastocyanin, 196*f*
Plastoquinone, 196*f*
Plateau phase, sexual, 1028
Platelet-derived growth factor (PDGF), 245–246*f*
Platelets, 9, 872*f*, 928*f*–929*f*
Plate tectonics, 532*f*–533*f*, 534
Platyhelminthes (flatworms). *See* Flatworms
Platypus, 736, 1105
Pleasure, brain activity and, 1090*f*, 1097*f*
Pleiotropy, **278**–279
Plesiosaur fossil, 523*f*
Plumule, 822*f*–823*f*
Pluripotent cells, **426**
Pneumatophores, 754*f*
Pneumonia, 313*f*, 573
Poaching, elephant, 1259
Podium, sea star, 708*f*
Poecilia reticulata (guppies), 477
Poikilotherms, 878
Point mutations, 355*f*–356*f*, 383*f*–384, 482–483
Poison dart frog, 1212*f*
Pokeweed, 825*f*
Polar bears, 504*f*
Polar covalent bonds, **37***f*, **45***f*
Polarity, **771**, 871*f*
Polar molecules, **45**
Polar side chains, 76–77*f*
Polar transport, auxin, 842*f*
Polio, 402
Pollen cones, 634*f*–635
Pollen grains, **632***f*, 640*f*–641, 643*f*, **818**–819*f*
Pollen tubes, **818**–819*f*, 821*f*
Pollination, **632**, **818**
  angiosperm cross-pollination, 640*f*–641
  asexual reproduction vs., 827
  coevolution of flowers and pollinators in, 821*f*
  cross-pollination in breeding plants, 831
  flowers and angiosperm, 638*f*
  flower shape and insect, 643*f*
  genetic engineering of flowers to force self-
    pollination, 834
  by insects, 635*f*
  insects in, 707
  mechanisms for preventing self-, 828*f*–829*f*
  mechanisms of, 820*f*–821*f*
  G. Mendel's techniques of, 268*f*–269*f*
  mutualistic relationships in, 815*f*–816
  seed plant, 632*f*
Pollinators
  coevolution of flowers and, 821*f*
  endangered or threatened, 1256*f*
  reproductive isolation and choice of, 516*f*
Pollution
  biomanipulation and, 1221
  coral reefs and, 687
  molluscs and water, 696
  nutrient, 1270*f*
  ocean acidification and, 53–54
  prokaryotes and bioremediation of, 584*f*
  toxin, 1271*f*–1272*f*
Polyadenylation signal sequence, 342
Polyandry, 1145*f*
Poly-A tail, **342**–343*f*
Polychaetes, 696–697*f*
Polychaos dubium (amoeba), 443

Polydactyly, 278
Polygamous mating, **1145***f*
Polygenic inheritance, **279**–80*f*, 284
Polygyny, 1145*f*
Polymerase chain reaction (PCR), **414**
  diagnosing diseases with, 428
  in estimating reproductive rates, 1188–1189*f*
  extreme thermophile archaea in, 580, 1257
  in forensic science, 430–431*f*
  in genomic analysis of fetuses, 1033
  in prokaryotic analysis, 577
  in RT-PCR analysis, 418*f*–419*f*
  in sequencing human digestive system
    microbiome, 907*f*
  in vitro amplification of DNA using, 414–415*f*,
    416*f*
Polymerases, 396
Polymerization, protein, 238
Polymers, 67*f*
Polymorphisms, 422, 428
Polynucleotides, 85*f*–86
Polypeptides, **75**, 996*f*
  amino acid monomers of, 75–76*f*, 77*f*
  as amino acid polymers, 78*f*
  analyzing sequence data of in Scientific Skills
    Exercise, 89
  mutations affecting, 355*f*–356*f*, 357
  one gene–one polypeptide hypethesis on, 336
  proteins as composed of, 78*f*
  synthesis of, in translation, 336–337*f*
  synthesizing multiple, with polyribosomes in
    translation, 352–353*f*
  targeting, to specific locations, 351–352*f*
  translation stages in synthesis of, 348*f*–349,
    350*f*–351*f*
Polyphyletic groups, **553***f*–554*f*
Polyplacophora (chitons), 693*f*
Polyploidy, 305, 508*f*–509*f*
Polyps, 386*f*, **685***f*
Polyribosomes (polysomes), 352–**353***f*
Polysaccharides, 70*f*–71*f*, 72*f*, 106
Polyspermy, 1038
Polytomies, 550*f*
Polytrichum, 620*f*, 621*f*
Pongo species, 436*f*, 741
Pons, 940, **1087***f*
Poplar trees, 769, 832
Population(s), **484**, **1159***f*, **1185**
  C. Darwin on natural selection and, 13*f*–15*f*
  density and dispersion of, 1185*f*–1187*f*
  determining size of, using mark-recapture
    method, 1185*f*
  diffusion of, of molecules, 130
  dynamics of, 1186*f*, 1198–1199*f*, 1200*f*–1201*f*
  effective size for, 1262–1263
  evolution of genetic variation in, 264–265*f*
  gene pools of, 484*f*
  genetic diversity of, 1256
  growth of (*see* Population growth)
  Hardy-Weinberg equilibrium and size of, 486
  human, 1201*f*–1204*f*, 1205
  as level of biological organization, 2*f*
  life histories of, 1195*f*–1196*f*, 1197
  minimum viable size for, 1262
  natural selection and evolution of, 469*f*–470
  population ecology as study of, 1184*f*–1185 (*see
    also* Population ecology)
  using Hardy-Weinberg principle to test
    microevolution in, 484–485*f*, 486–487
  vital statistics of, 1186–1187*f*, 1188*f*–1189*f*, 1190
Population conservation
  declining-population approach to, 1264*f*–1265
  small-population approach to, 1261*f*–1263*f*
  weighing conflicting demands in, 1265
Population cycles, 1200*f*
Population dynamics, 1186*f*, **1198**–1199*f*, 1200*f*–
  1201*f*. *See also* Population growth
Population ecology, **1159***f*. *See also* Ecology
  demography of population vital statistics in,
    1186–1187*f*, 1188*f*–1189*f*, 1190
  determining population size using mark-recapture
    method in, 1185*f*

human population in, 1201*f*–1204*f*, 1205
  population density and dispersion in, 1185*f*–1187*f*
  population dynamics in, 1198–1199*f*, 1200*f*–1201*f*
  population growth models in, 1190–1191*f*,
    1192*f*–1194*f* (*see also* Population growth)
  population growth regulation in, 1197–1199*f*
  as study of populations in environments, 1184*f*–
    1185 (*see also* Population(s))
Population growth. *See also* Population(s)
  density-dependent regulation of, 1197*t*–1199*f*
  exponential model of, 1190–1191*f*, 1192
  of human population, 1201*f*–1204*f*, 1205
  logistic model of, 1192*t*–1194*f*
  population dynamics and, 1186*f*, 1198–1199*f*,
    1200*f*–1201*f*
  using logistic equation to model, 1194
Population-level herbivore defenses, plant, 863*f*
Porcupine, 1212*f*
Pore complexes, 102, 103*f*
Pores, nuclear, 102, 103*f*
Pores, plasmodesmatal, 796
Porifera (sponges). *See* Sponges
Porphyra, 602–603*f*
Porphyrin ring, 192*f*
Porpoises, 475*f*–476*f*
Portal vessels, 1003*f*
Positional information, **379**, 1056*f*–1057*f*
Position-based mechanisms, plant, 772
Positive and negative correlations, 828
Positive feedback, **876**, **1001**
  in endocrine system feedback regulation, 1001
  in feedback regulation, 9
  in homeostasis, 876
Positive gene regulation, bacterial, 364*f*
Positive gravitropism, 855*f*
Positive pressure breathing, **938**
Positron-emission tomography (PET), 31–32*f*, 1090*f*
Possum, 736*f*
Posterior pituitary gland, 999*f*, **1002***f*–1003*f*
Posterior end, **674**
Postganglionic neurons, 1084
Postsynaptic cells, 1062
Postsynaptic neurons, 1073, 1095*f*
Postsynaptic potentials, 1072–1073*f*
Post-translational protein modifications, 351–352*f*
Postzygotic barriers, 503*f*, **504**
Potassium, 29*t*, 802
Potassium ions, 791*f*, 1064*t*–1065*f*, 1066
Potato blight, 860
Potatoes, 645, 837*f*–838*f*
Potential, cell developmental, 1054–1055*f*
Potential energy, **32**, 142–143*f*
Potential evapotranspiration, 1226
Potential range, 1178
Prairie chickens, 489*f*–490
Prairies, 1169*f*
Prairie voles, 1150*f*–1151
Precapillary sphincters, 926*f*
Precipitation
  climographs of, 1165*f*
  global patterns of, 1160*f*
  mountains, rain shadow, and, 1163*f*
  primary production in terrestrial biomes and,
    1238*f*
  water vapor and, 47
Precocious germination, 846*f*
Predation, **1211**
  allopatric speciation and, 505*f*–506
  camouflage and, 462*f*
  camouflage case studies and, 19*f*–20*f*, 21–22
  density-dependent population regulation by, 1198*f*
  genetic variation in, 1150*f*
  as interspecific interaction, 1211–1212*f*, 1213*f*
  population cycles and, 1200*f*
  as risk, 1144–1145
  symbols for, 1209
  top-down model of trophic control and, 1221
Predators
  adaptations of native, to introduced prey, 1211
  animals as, 667*f*, 668
  as biotic factors limiting species distributions,
    1179*f*
  cephalopods as, 695–696

evolution of animal, 671*f*
    insects as, 707
    mass extinctions and, 536
    plant recruitment of, as herbivore defense, 863*f*
Predictions, scientific, 16–17*f*, 18*f*, 487
Predisposition, cancer and inherited, 388
Preganglionic neurons, 1084
Pregnancy, human, **1029**
    conception and trimesters of, 1028*f*–1031*f*
    detecting disorders during, 1033
    detecting human, 963
    endocrine disruptors and, 1009
    prevention of, 1032*f*–1033
Pre-mRNA, 337*f*, 343*f*–344*f*, 367*f*
Prenatally and Postnatally Diagnosed Conditions
        Awareness Act, 307
Preprophase band, 770–771*f*
Prepuce, 1019*f*–**1020**
Pressure
    hearing and, 1108
    receptors for, 1104*f*
    root, 787–788*f*
    water potential and, 782–784
Pressure-flow hypothesis, 794–795*f*
Pressure potential, **783**
Presynaptic cells, 1062
Presynaptic neurons, 1073, 1074*f*, 1095*f*
Prey
    adaptations of native predators to introduced,
        1211
    defensive adaptations of, 1211–1212*f*, 1213*f*
    genetic variation in selection of, 1150*f*
Prezygotic barriers, 502*f*–503*f*, **504**
Priapula, 682*f*
Primary cell walls, **118**
Primary cilium, 114
Primary consumers, **1234**–1235*f*
Primary electron acceptors, **194**
Primary growth, plant, **760**
    meristem generation of cells for, 760*f*–761*f*
    of roots, 761*f*–763*f*
    of woody stems, 766*f*
Primary immune response, **956**–957*f*
Primary motor cortex, 1091*f*
Primary oocytes, **1023***f*
Primary producers, **1234**–1235*f*
Primary production, **1235**
    in aquatic ecosystems, 1237*f*–1238*f*
    in Arctic tundra ecosystem, 1242*f*–1243*f*
    determining, for oceans, 1237*f*
    determining, with satellites, 1236*f*
    ecosystem energy budgets in, 1235–1236*f*, 1237*f*
    in terrestrial ecosystems, 1238*f*–1239
Primary roots, 753
Primary somatosensory cortex, 1091*f*
Primary structure, protein, **80***f*
Primary succession, **1223**–1224*f*
Primary transcripts, **337**
Primary visual cortex, 1115*f*
Primases, 321*f*–322, 324*f*, 325*t*
Primates. *See also* Human(s)
    cloning of, 425
    derived characters of, 740
    HIV in, 561
    living, 740*f*–741*f*, 742
    in mammalian phylogeny, 739*f*
    phylogenetic tree of, 740*f*
Primers, 321*f*–**322**
Primitive streak, **1046***f*
Primordial germ cells, 1023*f*
Principle of conservation of energy, 143*f*–144
Printing press, 23–24
Prions, **405**–406*f*
Probability
    laws of, 274–275*f*, 276
    principle of maximum likelihood and, 556
Problem solving, **1141***f*
Proboscidea, 739*f*
Proboscis, 682*f*, 706*f*, 821
Process, evolutionary, 463, 477, 547
Producers, 7, 185*f*–186*f*, **608**–609*f*
Production efficiency, 1239*f*–**1240**
Products, **41**, 645

Progesterone, **1009***f*, **1024**
Progestins, 999*f*, 1008–**1009***f*, 1032*f*–1033
Proglottids, 691*f*
Programmed cell death. *See* Apoptosis
Projections, body surface area and, 689*f*
Prokaryotes
    adaptive abilities of, 567*f*–568
    archaea as, 580*f*–581
    bacteria as, 577–578*f*, 579*f*–580
    beneficial and harmful impacts of, on humans,
        582–583*f*, 584*f*–585*f*
    bioremediation using, 1249*f*
    cell signaling in, 211*f*–212
    cells of (*see* Prokaryotic cells)
    chemiosmosis in, 173–174*f*, 175
    ecological roles of, in biosphere, 581*f*–582*f*
    electron transport chains in, 166
    as endosymbionts, 528–529*f*
    evolution of glycolysis in, 179–180
    fossils of, 523*f*
    genetic diversity in, 572–573*f*, 574*f*–575
    genome sizes and number of genes for, 442*t*–443
    horizontal gene transfer in genomes of, 563
    land colonization by, 530
    nutritional and metabolic adaptations of,
        575–576*f*, 577
    origin of, 526, 528*f*
    photosynthesis in, 185–186*f*
    phylogeny of, 577*f*
    in protection of plants from diseases, 584
    structural and functional adaptations of, 568*f*–572*f*
    taxonomy of, 562, 563*f*
Prokaryotic cells, **5**, **97**. *See also* Cell(s)
    cell-surface structures of, 568–569*f*, 570*f*
    DNA replication in, 320*f*–325*f*
    eukaryotic cells vs., 4*f*–5, 97*f*–98*f*, 99 (*see also*
        Eukaryotic cells)
    evolution of cell division of, 241–242*f*
    programming of, by viral DNA, 313*f*–314*f*, 315
    regulation of transcription in, 361*f*–364*f*
    structure of, 97*f*
    transcription and translation in, 336–337*f*, 353*f*
    transcription in, 340*f*–342*f*
    translation in (*see* Translation)
Prolactin, 999*f*, **1003**, 1010*f*
Prolactin-releasing hormone, 1003
Proliferative phase, 1027
Proline, 77*f*, 339
Prometaphase, **235**, 236*f*, 241*f*
Promiscuous mating, 1145
Promoters, 340*f*–**341***f*, 806
Proof, hypotheses and, 17
Proofreading, DNA, 325–326*f*
Propanal, **63***f*
Properties, chemical, 34*f*–35
Properties, emergent. *See* Emergent properties
Prophages, **397***f*–398
Prophase, **235**, 236*f*, 241*f*, 261*f*
Prophase I, 258*f*, 260*f*–261*f*, 264*f*
Prophase II, 259*f*
Propithecus verreauxi, 740*f*
Prop roots, 754*f*
Prostaglandins, **995**, 1031*f*, 1106
Prostate glands, 999, 1019*f*–**1020**
Prosthetic groups, 173
Proteases, **901**
Proteasomes, 373
Protected areas, 1267*f*–1269*f*
Protein Data Bank, 439
Protein interaction networks, 440–441*f*
Protein kinases, **219***f*–220, 221*f*, 225–227
Protein phosphatases, **220**
Proteins, **75**. *See also* Amino acids
    amino acids of, 67, 75–77*f* (*see also* Amino acids)
    antibiotics and prokaryotic synthesis of, 571
    antifreeze, 882
    in bacterial binary fission, 240–241*f*
    biotechnology in production of, 430*f*
    blood plasma, 928*f*–929
    cadherin in choanoflagellates and animals, 670*f*
    in cell-signaling nuclear responses, 223*f*
    cell-signaling receptor, 214, 215*f*–217*f*
    in cellular membranes, 125*f*–128*f*

cellulose-synthesizing, 613
    as composed of polypeptides, 78*f* (*see also*
        Polypeptides)
    Conserved Domain Database (CDD) of structures
        of, 438–439*f*
    denaturation and renaturation of, 82*f*–83
    digestion of, 903*f*
    in DNA replication, 324*f*–325*t*
    DNA vs., as genetic material, 313, 314*f*–315
    domains of, 344–345*f*
    in electron transport chains, 172*f*–173
    enzymes as, 8–9*f*, 75–76*f*, 151, 157*f*
    essential amino acids in, 893
    evolution of genes for, with novel functions, 450,
        451*f*
    expressing cloned genes for, 417
    facilitated diffusion and, 133*f*
    florigen as, 855
    folding and post-translational modifications of,
        351–352*f*
    folding of, in cells, 83*f*–84*f*
    four levels of structure of, 79, 80*f*–81*f*
    as fuel for catabolism, 180*f*
    functions of types of, 76*f*
    human dietary deficiencies in, 896
    identifying genes coding for, 439*f*–440
    innate immune reponse and, 951
    as macromolecules, 66
    as measures of evolution, 89
    mediator, 368–369*f*
    motor (*see* Motor proteins)
    nonenzyme, 336
    nucleic acids in gene expression and synthesis of,
        84*f*–85
    packing of DNA and, into chromosomes,
        328*f*–330*f*
    phosphorylation of, in cell-signal transduction,
        219*f*–220
    in photosystems, 194*f*–198*f*, 199
    plant antifreeze, 859
    plant heat-shock, 858
    post-translational modification of, in plant
        responses, 839
    prions as infectious, 405–406*f*
    producing, with gene cloning, 412*f*–413
    in prokaryotic flagella, 570*f*–571
    proteomics in study of, 7, 87–88*f*, 440
    regulation of eukaryotic processing and
        degradation of, 373
    regulatory, 373, 378–379*f*
    in replication of DNA telomeres, 326
    repressor, 362*f*
    scaffolding, 225*f*–227
    separating, with gel electrophoresis, 414*f*
    synthesis of (*see* Protein synthesis)
    synthesis of, in expression and transmission of
        genetic information, 5*f*–6*f*, 7
    synthesis of, in plant cells, 206*f*
    systems biology in studying networks of, 440–441*f*
    transcription factors, 341*f*
    translation elongation factors, 350
    translation initiation factors, 348*f*, 350
    translation release factors, 351*f*
    transport (*see* Transport proteins)
    in transport and mechanical work, 150*f*
    using data on, to test hypotheses on horizontal
        gene transfer, 564
    viral movement, 796
    viruses and, 394–395, 396*f*–397*f*
    water-soluble, 49*f*
Protein sequences, 438–439*f*, 440
    in Scientific Skills Exercise, 564
Protein synthesis. *See also* Gene expression
    evidence for, in study of metabolic defects,
        334–335*f*, 336
    gene concept and, 357
    genetic code in, 337–338*f*, 339*f*–340
    mutations during, 355*f*–356*f*, 357
    by ribosomes, 102, 103*f*–104
    summary of, 354*f*
    via transcription, RNA processssing, and
        translation, 336–337*f* (*see also* RNA
        processing; Transcription; Translation)

Proteobacteria, 578*f*
Proteoglycans, **118–119**
Proteomes, 7, 440
Proteomics, 7, **87–88***f*, **440**
Proterozoic eon, 526*f*, 527*t*
Prothoracicotropic hormone (PTTH), 1001*f*–1002
Protista, kingdom, 562, 588
Protists, **587**
    cells of, 101*f*
    contractile vacuoles of, 108
    in domain Eukarya, 11*f*
    ecological roles of symbiotic and photosynthetic, 608*f*–609*f*
    endosymbiosis in evolution of, 589, 592*f*–593*f*, 602*f*
    excavates, 590*f*, 593*f*–594*f*, 595
    land plants, 591*f*, 602 (*see also* Land plants)
    microscopy in study of, 587*f*–588
    origin of fungi in, 653*f*–654
    photosynthesis in, 185–186*f*
    phylogeny of, 588–589, 590*f*–591*f*
    red and green algae, 591*f*, 602–603*f*, 604*f*
    SAR clade, 591*f*, 595–602*f*
    sexual life cycles of, 256*f*–257
    as single-celled eukaryotes, 588
    structural and functional diversity of, 588
    unikonts, 591*f*, 604–605*f*, 606*f*–607*f*
Protonema, **618**–619*f*
Protonephridia, **688**, 978*f*–**979**
Proton gradients, 174*f*–175
Proton-motive force, 174*f*–**175**
Proton pumps, **136***f*, 782, 783*f*, 842
Protons, **30**–31
Proto-oncogenes, **383***f*–384, 386*f*
Protoplasts, **783**
Protostome development, **675***f*–676
Protostomes, 1044
Proviruses, **400**, 401*f*
Proximal control elements, 368
Proximal tubule, **981***f*, 982–983*f*
Proximate causation, 1134
Prozac, 1075, 1097
Prusiner, Stanley, 406
Pseudocoelomates, **674***f*–675
Pseudogenes, **444**, 474
Pseudopodia, **117**, 138*f*, 591*f*, **601**–602
Pseudostratified columnar epithelium, 871*f*
Psilotum, 626*f*, 627
P site (peptidyl-tRNA binding site), 347*f*–**348**
Psychedelic rock gecko, 1254*f*
Psychoactive drugs, 1075
Pteraspis, 719*f*
Pterophytes, 624*f*, 625–626*f*, 627
Pterosaurs, **730**, 1130
Puberty, human, 1024
Puffballs, 659*f*
Pulmocutaneous circuit, 918–919*f*, 920
Pulmonary circuit, 918–919*f*, 920
Pulp, fruit, 825
Pulse, **924**
Punctuated equilibria, **514***f*
Puncture vine, 826*f*
Pundamilia species, 509*f*, 513*f*
Punnett squares, **271***f*–272, 279*f*, 280*f*
Pupa, 705*f*
Pupil, **1112**
Pure elements, 37
Purines, 85*f*–**86**, 317–318*f*, 977
Purple sulfur bacteria, 186*f*
Pus, 951
Puszta, 1169*f*
Pygmy date palm, 644*f*
Pyramids, age-structure, 1203*f*
Pyrenean ibex, 1260–1261
Pyrenean oak, 644*f*
Pyrimidines, 85*f*–**86**, 317–318*f*
Pyruvate
    ATP yield in oxidation of, 175*f*
    in fermentation, 179*f*
    oxidation of, as stage of cellular respiration, 166–167*f*
    oxidation of, to acetyl CoA, 169*f*–170*f*
    oxidation of glucose to, by glycolysis, 168*f*–169*f*

Pythons, 882*f*, 886
PYY hormone, 911*f*

Q

Qinling golden snub-nosed monkeys, 56*f*
Qualitative data, 16*f*
Quantitative approach, G. Mendel's, 268*f*–269
Quantitative characters, 279–280*f*
Quantitative data, 16. *See also* Scientific Skills Exercises
Quaternary structure, protein, 81*f*
Quillworts, 625–626*f*, 627
Quorum sensing, 211–212

R

RAAS (renin-angiotensin-aldosterone system), 990
Rabbits, 908
Raccoon, 333*f*
Radial canal, sea star, 708*f*
Radial cleavage, 675*f*
Radial glia, 1081
Radial symmetry, 638*f*, 643, 673*f*–674
Radiation
    alterations of chromosome structure by, 305
    animal heat exchange and, **879***f*
    cancer and, 383
    as cancer treatment, 247
    DNA damage from, 326
    mutagenic, 357
    prokaryotes and, 567
Radicle, **822**–823*f*
Radioactive isotopes, **31**–33, 314*f*–315, 524*f*, 1246
Radioactive isotope decay curve in Scientific Skills Exercise, 33
Radioactive tracers, 31–32*f*
Radiolarians, **601***f*
Radiometric dating, 32, 33, **524***f*
Radula, **692**–693*f*
Rain shadow, 1163*f*
Ramakrishnan, Venki, 27*f*, 85, 348
Random dispersion, 1186, 1187*f*
Random fertilization, 264, 303
Random mating, 486
Random mutations. *See* Mutations
Randomness, entropy and, 144
Range expansions, species, 1178
Ranges, actual and potential, 1178
Rapetosaurus krausei, 12*f*
Raphides, 862*f*
Rapid eye movements (REMs), 1088
ras gene, **384**–385*f*, 386*f*
Raspberry fruit, 825*f*
Ras protein, 384–385*f*
Rates, speciation, 514*f*–515*f*
Ratfish, 721*f*
Ratites, **733**–734*f*
Rattlesnakes, 1104–1105*f*
Ray-finned fishes, **722***f*–723*f*
Rays, 720–721*f*
Reabsorption, **978***f*
Reactants, 41
Reaction-center complexes, **194***f*
Reading frame, **339**, 356*f*
Realized niches, 1210*f*
Reasoning
    deductive, 17
    inductive, 16
Receptacle, flower, **816**, 817*f*
Reception, sensory, 1102*f*–1103
Reception stage, cell-signaling, **213**
    cell-surface transmembrane receptors in, 215*f*–217*f*
    intracellular receptors in, 217–218*f*
    ligands, ligand binding, and receptor proteins in, 214
    overview of, 213*f*
    in plant signal transduction pathways, 838*f*
    plasma membrane proteins as receptors in, 214*f*–217*f*
Receptive fields, 1114–1115
Receptor-mediated endocytosis, 138*f*
Receptor potential, **1103**
Receptor proteins, 76*f*

Receptors
    cellular innate immunity and, 949*f*–950*f*
    dendrites as, 1062
    glutamate, 1095*f*, 1096
    hormone, 994*f*, 996*f*, 997*f*–998
    opiate, 1076
    sensory, 1102*f*–1105*f*, 1106
    somatosensory, 1091*f*–1092
Receptor tyrosine kinases (RTKs), **216***f*–217, 219*f*–220, 248
Recessive alleles, **270**–271*f*, 278, 283*f*–284*f*, 285, 494. *See also* Alleles
Recessively inherited human disorders, 283*f*–284*f*, 285
Recessive traits, 269–270*t*, 283*f*, 297*f*–298
Reciprocal altruism, **1153**
Recombinant bacteria, 412*f*–413
Recombinant chromosomes, **264***f*
Recombinant DNA, **412**
    in DNA cloning and gene cloning, 412*f*–413
    ethical issues on, 432–433
    hirudin from leeches and, 697*f*–698
    producing transgenic plants using, 770*f*
    using restriction enzymes to make, 413*f*–414
Recombinants (recombinant types), **300**
Recombinase, 955*f*–956
Recombination. *See also* Recombinant DNA
    linkage maps based on frequency of, 303*f*–304*f*
    of linked genes, 300–301*f*
    natural selection and genetic variation from, 303
    of unlinked genes, 300
Recombination frequencies, 303*f*–304*f*
Reconstruction, ecosystem physical, 1248–1249
Recovery, seed plants and, 630*f*
Recruitment, motor neuron, 1124
Recruitment of predatory animals, plant, 863*f*
Rectum, **905**
Red algae, 591*f*, 592*f*–593*f*, 602–603*f*
Red blood cells. *See* Erythrocytes (red blood cells)
Red-cockaded woodpecker, 1264*f*–1265
Red light, plant responses to, 850–851*f*, 853–854*f*
Red mangrove, 846*f*
Red maple tree leaves, 756
Red-necked phalaropes, 1145*f*
Redox (oxidation-reduction) reactions, 163–**164***f*, 165*f*–166*f*, 189
Red tide, 598*f*
Reduced hybrid fertility, 503*f*
Reduced hybrid viability, 503*f*
Reducing agents, 163–**164***f*
Reduction, 163–**164***f*, 199–200*f*
Reductional division, 262
Reductionism, 3–4
Redundancy, genetic code, 339, 355, 482
Redwood trees, 253*f*
Reefs, ectoproct, 692
Reflexes, 901, 909, **1082***f*–1083*f*
Refractory period, **1069**
Regeneration, 698, 708, 1014
Regenerative medicine, 427
Regional adaptive radiations, 537*f*–538
Regional human population patterns, 1202
Regression lines in Scientific Skills Exercises, 54, 203, 745
Regulation. *See also* Osmoregulation
    of animal digestion, energy storage, and appetite, 908–909*f*, 910*f*–911*f*, 912
    by animal endocrine and nervous systems, 874*f*
    of biological clocks, 1088
    of biological rhythms, 1009
    of blood pressure, 925
    of cell-signaling responses, 223–225*f*, 226–227
    of cellular respiration via feedback mechanisms, 181*f*–182
    of cleavage, 1043
    by endocrine glands, 1006*f*–1009*f*
    of enzymatic catalysis, 157–158*f*, 159*f*
    extracellular matrix role in, 119
    feedback, of endocrine systems, 1000*f*
    feedback in, of molecular interactions, 8–9*f*
    of gene expression (*see* Gene regulation)
    of growth, 999*f*, 1003*f*, 1005*f*
    of heart rhythm, 922*f*
    homeostatic feedback, 875*f*–877*f*

hormonal, of mammalian sexual reproduction, 1024*f*–1026*f*, 1027
of human breathing, 940*f*
of muscle contraction, 1122–1123*f*, 1124
of neurons in sensory reception, 1102*f*
plant and animal, 888*f*
of population growth, 1197*f*–1201*f*
as property of life, 1*f*
Regulator animals, **875***f*
Regulatory genes, 362*f*
Regulatory proteins, 373, 378–379*f*, 1122–1123*f*, 1124
Reinforcement, hybrid zone, **512***f*–513
Rejection, immune system, 963–964
Relatedness, altruism and, 1152*f*–1153*f*
Relative abundance, species, **1216**. *See also* Species diversity
Relative fitness, 491–**492**
Relay proteins, 225*f*–227
Release factors, 351*f*
Release stage, phage lytic cycle, 396*f*
Releasing hormones, 999*f*, 1003
Renal cortex, **980***f*
Renal medulla, **980***f*
Renal pelvis, **980***f*
Renaturation, protein, 82*f*–83
Renin-angiotensin-aldosterone system (RAAS), **990**
Repair, DNA, 325–326*f*
Repetitive DNA, **444***f*
Replication fork, DNA, **321***f*
Replicative cycles, viral
of animal viruses, 398–399*f*, 400, 401*f*
general features of, 395*f*–396
of phages, 396*f*–397*f*, 398
Repolarization, 1070
Repressible enzymes, 363*f*–364
Repressible operons, 362*f*–363, 364
Repressors, **362***f*
Reproduction. *See also* Life cycles; Mating; Sexual life cycles
as cell division function, 232–233*f*
crustacean, 703
C. Darwin on natural selection and, 13*f*–15*f*
delayed human, in population growth, 1202
density-dependent population regulation by rates of, 1199*f*
effective population size and, 1263
evolution and differential success in, 264–265*f*
fungal, 651–652*f*, 653*f*
genetic disorders from human, 283–284
heterochrony and differential reproductive development, 538–539*f*
insect, 705
iteroparity vs. semelparity in, 1195*f*
life history traits in, 1195*f*–1196*f*, 1197
overreproduction of offspring and natural selection, 469*f*–470
plant and animal, 889*f* (*see also* Angiosperm reproduction; Animal reproduction)
prokaryotic binary fission, 571–572
as property of life, 1*f*
protist, 588
protocell, 521*f*–522
rapid, as source of genetic variation in viruses, 483
rapid prokaryotic, and mutation, 572*f*–573
rates of, 1188–1189*t*, 1190, 1199*f*, 1202
sexual, as source of genetic variation, 483
sexual vs. asexual, 253
Reproduction, plant. *See* Angiosperm reproduction
Reproductive barriers
in hybrid zones, 511–512*f*, 513*f*
reproductive isolation and types of, 501–502*f*, 503*f*–504
Reproductive cloning, 424*f*–425*f*
Reproductive cycles, animal, 1015*f*
Reproductive cycles, human, 1025–1026*f*, 1027
Reproductive isolation, **501**
allopatric speciation and, 505*f*–507*f*
hybrid zones and, 510–511*f*, 512*f*–513*f*
pollinator choice and, 516
reproductive barriers in, 501–502*f*, 503*f*–504
sexual selection and, 509*f*
Reproductive leaves, 756*f*

Reproductive organs, human
female, 1020–1021*f*
gametogenesis in, 1021, 1022*f*–1023*f*
male, 1019*f*–1020
Reproductive rates, 1188–1189*t*, 1190, 1199*f*, 1202
Reproductive success, 1018*f*
Reproductive tables, **1189***t*
Reptiles, **729**
adaptations of kidneys of, 986
amniotic eggs of, 728–729*f*
birds, 732*f*–734*f*
characteristics of, 729*f*–730
crocodilians, 731*f*, 732
evolution of, 673
extraembryonic membranes of, 1047*f*
hearing and equilibrium in, 1110*f*
lepidosaurs, 731*f*–732
in Mesozoic era, 526
nitrogenous wastes of, 976–977*f*
origin and evolutionary radiation of, 730
thermoregulation in, 882*f*
turtles, 730*f*–731
Research Method Figures
applying parsimony in molecular systematics, 557*f*
cell fractionation, 96*f*
constructing linkage maps, 303*f*
crossing pea plants, 268*f*
determining absorption spectra using spectrophotometers, 191*f*
determining population size using mark-recapture method, 1185*f*
determining primary production with satellites, 1236*f*
dideoxy chain termination method for DNA sequencing, 410*f*
hydroponic culture, 804*f*
intracellular recording, 1066*f*
G. Mendel's, 267*f*–274*f*
molecular tools for determining microbial diversity, 1217*f*
next-generation DNA sequencing, 411*f*
polymerase chain reaction, 415*f*
preparing karyotypes of chromosomes, 254*f*
producing transgenic plants using Ti plasmid, 770*f*
reproductive cloning of mammal by nuclear transplantation, 424*f*
RT-PCR (reverse transcriptase-polymerase chain reaction) analysis of single-gene expression, 419*f*
testcrosses, 273*f*
using dendrochronology to study climate, 767*f*
Residual volume, **939**
Resistance genes, 575
Resolution, 94
Resolution phase, sexual, 1028
Resource acquisition, vascular plant, 778*f*–781*f*. *See also* Transport in vascular plants; Vascular plants
Resource competition, density-dependent population regulation by, 1198*f*
Resource partitioning, 1209–**1210***f*
Respiration, cellular. *See* Cellular respiration
Respiration, plant and animal, 889*f*
Respiratory diseases, human, 1198*f*
Respiratory distress syndrome (RDS), 938*f*
Respiratory media, 933
Respiratory pigments, **941**–942*f*
Respiratory surfaces, 933–934
Respiratory systems. *See also* Gas exchange systems
breathing to ventilate lungs in, 938–939*f*, 940*f*
effects of adrenal hormones on, 1007
internal exchange surfaces and, 869*f*
lungs and components of, 936–937*f*
respiratory distress syndrome of, 938*f*
Response, homeostatic, **876**
Response pathways, hormone, 996*f*–998*f*, 1000*f*
Response stage, cell-signaling, **214**
cell-signaling specificity and coordination of responses in, 224–225*f*
increasing signaling efficiency in, 225*f*–227
nuclear and cytoplasmic responses in, 223*f*, 224*f*
overview of, 213*f*–214
regulation of responses in, 223–225*f*, 226–227

signal amplification in, 224
signal termination in, 227
Response to environment, 1*f*, 888*f*. *See also* Environment
Rest-and-digest responses, 1084
Resting potentials, neuron, **1064**
formation of, 1064*f*–1065
modeling of, 1065*f*–1066
Resting potential state, action potential, 1068*f*–1069
Restoration ecology
biological augmentation in, 1249
biomanipulation of trophic levels in, 1221
bioremediation in, 1249*f*
physical reconstruction in, 1248*f*–1249
worldwide projects of, 1250*f*–1251*f*
Restriction enzymes, **397**, **413**
making recombinant DNA plasmids using, 413*f*–414
polymerase chain reaction and, in gene cloning, 415–416*f*
Restriction fragments, **414**
Restriction sites, 413*f*–414
Resurrection, extinct species, 1260–1261*f*
Reticular fibers, 872*f*
Reticular formation, 1088*f*
Reticulum, 908*f*
Retina, **1112***f*, 1116
Retinal, **1113***f*, 1114*f*
Retinitis pigmentosa, 489
Retrotransposons, **445***f*
Retroviral vectors, gene therapy using, 429*f*
Retroviruses, **400**, 401*f*
Reverse transcriptase, **400**, 401*f*, 419*f*
Reverse transcriptase-polymerase chain reaction (RT-PCR), **418**
in analyzing single-gene expression, 418–419*f*, 420
diagnosing diseases with, 428
Reward system, brain, 1097*f*
Reward vs. risk, foraging behavior and, 1144–1145
R groups, amino acid, 75–77*f*
Rhabditophora, 688–689*f*, 690*f*–691*f*
Rhesus monkeys, 89
Rheumatoid arthritis, 965*f*
Rhine River restoration project, 1251*f*
Rhinoceros, 1194*f*
Rhizarians, 591*f*, **601***f*–602*f*
Rhizobacteria, **807***f*–809*f*, 810
Rhizobium bacteria, 807*f*–809*f*, 810
Rhizoids, **618**
Rhizomes, 755*f*
Rhizopus stolonifer, 656*f*–657
Rhizosphere, 584, **807***f*
Rhodopsin, **1113***f*, 1114*f*–1115*f*
Rhomaleosaurus victor, 523*f*
Ribbon model, 79*f*
Ribbon worms, 682*f*
Riboflavin, 170
Ribose, **86**
in ATP, 149
as monosaccharide, 68*f*
in nucleic acids, 85*f*–86
Ribosomal RNA (rRNA), 347*f*–348
in eukaryotic cell nucleus, 102
evolutionary rate of, 559
gene family of, 447*f*
interpreting comparisons of sequences of, 589
in molecular systematics, 577
Ribosomes, **102**, **336**
animal cell, 100*f*
identifying binding sites on, with sequence logos, 349
plant cell, 101*f*
in plant cells, 206*f*
polyribosomes and, 352–353*f*
prokaryotic, 571
in prokaryotic and eukaryotic cells, 97*f*–98
in protein synthesis, 102–103*f*, 104
protein synthesis in, 85
rough ER and, 105
structure of, 27*f*, 103*f*, 347*f*
in translation, 336–337*f*, 347*f*–349, 350*f*–351*f*
Ribozymes, 151, **344**, **522**
Ribulose, 68*f*

Rice, 442t, 503f, 645, 810, 832, 845, 1257
Rieseberg, Loren, 515f
Right atrium, 920f–921f
Right-left axis, 1054f, 1058f
Right ventricle, 920f–921f
Ring structures
    of carbon skeletons, 60f
    of cellulose-synthesizing proteins, 613
    of glucose, 69f
Ringworm, 664
Rising phase, action potential, 1068f–1069
Risk factors, cardiovascular disease, 932
Risk vs. reward, foraging behavior and, 1144–1145
Riverine wetlands, 1173f
River otters, 875f
Rivers, 1174f, 1180
RNA (ribonucleic acid), 84. See also Messenger RNA
    (mRNA); Nucleic acids; RNA processing;
    Transfer RNA (tRNA)
    ATP in, 149
    in circadian clock genes during hibernation, 887f
    components of, 85f–86
    development of self-replicating, 522
    in DNA replication, 321f–322
    elongation of strands of, 342f
    in eukaryotic cells, 102
    expressing noncoding, 417
    gene density in genomes and, 443
    in gene expression, 6f
    interpreting sequences of, 589
    as molecular homology, 474
    noncoding, in gene regulation, 374f–375f, 376
    in plant cells, 206f
    post-transcriptional modification of, 342,
        343f–345f
    in regulation of cleavage, 1043
    ribosomal RNA gene family, 447f
    roles of, in gene expression, 84f–85
    sequencing of, 421
    structure of, 86–87f
    synthesis of, in transcription, 336–337f, 340f–342f
    viral (see RNA viruses)
RNA enzymes. See Ribozymes
RNA interference (RNAi), 375, 421
RNA polymerases, 83–84f, 340f–342f, 367f–368
RNA processing, 342
    alteration of mRNA ends in, 342–343f
    eukaryotic transcription and, 367f–368
    evolutionary importance of introns in, 344–345f
    in gene expression and protein synthesis, 337–338f
    regulation of eukaryotic, 372f–373
    ribozymes in, 344
    split genes and RNA splicing in, 343f–344f
    summary of eukaryotic, 354f
RNA sequencing, 421
RNA splicing, 343f–345f, 372f–373
RNA viruses
    classes of, 398t
    HIV as, 400, 401f (see also HIV (human
        immunodeficiency virus))
    pandemics of, 403
    replicative cycles of, 395f–396, 398–399f
    retroviruses as, 399–400
    structure of, 394f–395
    viroids as, 405
Robin, European, 13f
Rock python, 898f
Rocks
    dating of, 524f
    nonvascular plants and weathering of, in
        Ordovician Period climate change, 623
    species distributions and, 1180–1181
Rod, ATP synthase, 173f
Rodents, 739f, 908
Rods (photoreceptor), 1113f, 1114–1115f, 1116–1117
Rod-shaped prokaryotes, 568f
Rolling circle replication, 574f
Romanesco, 752f–753
Root caps, 761f
Rooted phylogenetic trees, 550f
Root hairs, 753f–754f, 786
Root pressure, 787–788

Roots, 625, 753
    apical meristems of land plant, 615f
    architecture of, and acquisition of water and
        minerals, 781
    compositions of bacterial communities of, 807f
    drought responses of, 857
    evolution of, in vascular plants, 625
    fungal mycorrhizae and, 781
    gravitropism in, 855
    monocot vs. eudicot, 643f
    mycorrhizae and plant, 650f–651
    nitrogen-fixing bacteria and legume, 808f–809f,
        810
    primary growth of, 761f–763f
    rhizoids vs., 618
    secondary growth of, 765f–766f, 767f–768f
    seedling, 824f
    soil texture and, 800
    structure of, 753f–754f
    transport of water and minerals from, to shoots
        via xylem, 786–787f, 788f–789f, 790
Root systems, 753f–754f
Rosy periwinkle, 1257f
Rotifers, 681f, 691f–692
Rotimi, Charles, 251f, 428, 442
Rotor, ATP synthase, 173f
Rough ER, 100f, 101f, 104–105f
Round dance, honeybee, 1136–1137f
Round window, 1108–1109f
Roundworms, 683f, 699f–700, 1052f–1053f, 1127f
Rous, Peyton, 388
Rozella, 654
R plasmids, 575
R-selection (density-independent selection),
    1196f–1197
RU486 (mifepristone), 1033
Rubella, 402
Rubisco (RuBP carboxylase), 199–200f
Rubrivivax, 578f
Ruffed grouse, 1266
Rule of multiplication, 485
Rumen, 908f
Ruminants, 908f
Running, 1130
Rusts, 659
Ryther, John, 1237f

S

Saccharomyces cerevisiae (yeast)
    budding of, 653f
    cell signaling in, 211f–212
    directional cell growth during mating of, 226
    DNA changes in cells of, in meiosis, 262
    genome size and number of genes of, 442t–443
    human uses of, 664–665
    protein interaction network of, 440–441f
    toxic wastes of, in winemaking, 1199f
Saccule, 1109f
Sac fungi, 655f, 657f–659t
Safety issues
    on biotechnology, 432–433
    on plant biotechnology and genetic engineering,
        832–834
Saguaro cactus, 1177f
Sahara Desert, 867f
Sahelanthropus tchadensis, 742–743f
Salamanders, 503f, 507, 539f, 726f, 915f, 1080f
Salicylic acid, 861
Salinity
    aquatic biome, 1171
    extreme halophiles and, 567f, 580
    osmosis, water balance, and, 132
    plant responses to, 432, 857
    soil salinization and, 802
    species distributions and, 1180
Saliva, 900–901f
Salivary glands, 900f–901
Salmon, 974, 1180, 1195
Salmonella species, 583
Saltatory conduction, 1071f
Salt marshes, 1180, 1215f, 1240
Salt marsh hay, 1180
Salts (ionic compounds), 38f
    in blood plasma, 928f

diffusion of, across capillary walls, 926–927f
    ion gradients and transport of, 987f
    osmoregulation of, 972f–974f, 975–976f
Salt stress, plant responses to, 857
Saltwater, 971f, 973f, 976f
Salty tastes, 1117f–1118f
Sampling techniques, population, 1185f
San Andreas fault, 533
Sand dollars, 233f, 709
Sanger, Frederick, 78, 409
Sapwood, 768
"SAR" clade, 591f, 595f–602f
Sarcomeres, 873f, 1120f
Sarcoplasmic reticulum (SR), 1122f–1123f
Sarcopterygii (lobe-fins), 722, 723f–724
Sargasso Sea nutrient enrichment experiment, 1238t
Sarin, 157, 1075
Satellites, determining primary production with, 1236f
Satiety center, 911f
Saturated enzymes, 154
Saturated fats, 73f–74, 126f
Saturated fatty acids, 73f–74
Savannas, 744, 1168f
Savory tastes, 1117f–1118f
Scaffolding proteins, 225f–227
Scala naturae (scale of nature), Aristotle's, 464
Scale bar in Scientific Skills Exercise, 99
Scale-eating fish, 495f
Scales
    fish, 722
    reptile, 729
Scallops, 694f–695
Scanning electron microscope (SEM), 94–95f, 96
Scanning electron microscopy (SEM), 95f
Scarlet fever, 398
Scatter plots in Scientific Skills Exercises, 54, 134, 203,
    507, 745, 1211
Schistosoma mansoni, 690f
Schistosomiasis, 690f
Schizophrenia, 1096f
Schmidt-Nielsen, Knut, 1130
Schwann cells, 1070f–1071f, 1081f
Science, 16
    biology as study of life by, 1(facing page) (see also
        Biology)
    cooperative approach and model organisms in,
        21–23 (see also Model organisms)
    diverse viewpoints in, 23–24
    inquiry process of, 16f–20f, 21 (see also Case
        studies; Inquiry Figures)
    medical (see Medicine)
    methods (see Research Method Figures)
    skills (see Scientific Skills Exercises)
    society, technology, and, 23f
Scientific inquiry, 16, 16–24. See also Case studies;
    Inquiry Figures; Research Method Figures;
    Scientific Skills Exercises
Scientific method, 16–24, 17f, 18f. See also Case
    studies; Inquiry Figures; Research Method
    Figures; Scientific Skills Exercises
Scientific notation in Scientific Skills Exercise, 1076
Scientific Skills Exercises
    amino acid sequence identity tables, reading, 452
    bar graphs and line graphs, making and
        interpreting, 1181
    bar graphs and scatter plots, making and
        interpreting, 1211
    bar graphs, interpreting, 22, 370, 477, 756, 858
    bar graphs, making and interpreting, 177, 584, 623
    chi-square (χ^2) test, using, 302
    controlled experiment, designing, 1008
    correlation coefficients, calculating and
        interpreting, 672
    correlations, positive and negative, using to
        interpret data, 828
    cyclic data, graphing, 1273
    DNA deletion experiments, analysis of, 370
    experimental design, understanding, and
        interpreting data, 694
    experiments, using to test models, 226
    gene expression data, analysis of, 420
    genetic mutants, designing experiments using,
        1089

genetic mutants, interpreting data from experiments with, 912

genetic sequences, interpreting comparisons of, 589

genomic data, interpreting and generating hypotheses, 651

Hardy-Weinberg equation, using to interpret data and make predictions, 487

histograms, interpreting, 248

histograms, making and interpreting, 281, 932

hypotheses with quantitative models, testing, 1144

inferences, making, and designing experiments, 1025

line graphs and bar graphs, making and interpreting, 1181

line graphs, comparing two variables on a common *x*-axis, 967

line graphs, making, and calculating slopes, 155

line graphs, making, and converting between units of data, 262

logistic equation, using to model population growth, 1194

log scales, interpreting graphs with, 1130

moles and molar ratios of organic compounds, working with, 58

natural logarithms, using to interpret data, 633

observations, making, 806

pie charts, interpreting, 886

polypeptide sequence data, analysis of, 89

protein sequence data, using to test evolutionary hypotheses, 564

quantitative data, describing and interpreting, 975

quantitative data, estimating from graphs and developing hypotheses, 532

radioactive isotope decay curve, calculating, 33

regression line, determining equation of, 745

regression line, interpreting, 54

regression line, making, 203

scale bar, using to calculate cell volume and surface area, 99

scatter plots and bar graphs, making and interpreting, 1211

scatter plots, making, and interpreting data, 507

scatter plots with regression lines, interpreting, 54

scatter plots with regression lines, making, 203

scatter plots with two sets of data, interpreting, 134

scientific notation, interpreting data values expressed in, 1076

sequence-based phylogenetic trees, analysis of, 404

sequence logos, interpreting 349

slope, interpreting changes in, 1043

tables, working with data in, 58, 89, 155, 177, 203, 262, 302, 316, 452, 487, 507, 564, 584, 589, 623, 633, 651, 672, 745, 756, 784, 828, 912, 932, 967, 975, 1008, 1025, 1043, 1076, 1181, 1211, 1240, 1273

temperature coefficients, calculating and interpreting, 784

Scion, **829**

Sclera, 1112*f*

Sclereids, **758***f*

Sclerenchyma cells, **758***f*, 764

Sclerenchyma tissue, 862*f*

Scolex, 691*f*

Scorpions, 683*f*, 702*f*

Scrapie, 405

Scr gene, 539

Scrotum, **1019***f*

Scutellum, 823*f*

Scyphozoans, 686*f*

Sea anemones, 686*f*, 1014*f*

Seabirds, 1232*f*

Sea cucumbers, 709*f*

Sea daisies, 708*f*

Sea grasses, 612

Sea horse, 723*f*

Sea lampreys, 717*f*–718

Sea lettuce, 603*f*

Sea lilies, 709

Seals, 868*f*, 943*f*

Sea slugs, 693*f*, 1013*f*

Seasonality, 1161*f*–1162

Seasonal turnover, lake, 1171–1172*f*

Sea squirts, 716

Sea stars, 707–708*f*, 934*f*, 1080*f*, 1186, 1187*f*, 1220*f*

Sea urchins, 144*f*, 503*f*, 683*f*, 709*f*, 1039*f*, 1044*f*, 1179*f*, 1208*f*

Sea wasps, 686*f*–687*f*

Seawater, 971*f*, 973*f*, 976*f*

Seaweed, 591*f*, 596*f*–597*f*, 598, 602–603*f*, 1179*f*

Secondary cell walls, **118**

Secondary consumers, **1234**–1235*f*

Secondary endosymbiosis, 592*f*–593*f*

Secondary growth, plant, **760**

 cork cambium and periderm production in, 768

 evolution of, 768–769

 meristem generation of cells for, 760*f*–761*f*

 vascular cambium and secondary vascular tissue for, 765–766*f*, 767*f*–768*f*

Secondary immune response, **956**–957*f*

Secondary oocytes, **1023***f*

Secondary production, **1239**

 in Arctic tundra ecosystem, 1242*f*–1243*f*

 production efficiency in, 1239*f*–1240

 in salt marsh ecosystem, 1240

 trophic efficiency and ecological pyramids in, 1240–1241*f*

Secondary structure, protein, 80*f*

Secondary succession, **1224**–1225*f*

Secondary vascular tissue, 765–766*f*, 767*f*–768*f*

Second law of thermodynamics, 143*f*–**144**, 1233

Second messengers, **220**, **838**

 calcium ions, inositol trisphosphate (IP_3), and diacylglycerol (DAG) as, 221–222*f*

 cyclic AMP as, 220*f*–221*f*

 in hormone pathways, 997*f*

 in plant signal transduction, 838*f*–839

Secretin, 909*f*, 1000*f*–1001

Secretion, excretory system, 978*f*

Secretions

 cell signaling and, 994*f*–995*f* (see also Animal hormones; Neurohormones)

 digestive, 901–902*f*, 903–904

Secretory phase, 1027

Secretory proteins, 105

Secretory systems, prokaryotic, 571

Secretory tubules, marine bird, 976*f*

Sedentarians, 697*f*–698*f*

Sedimentary strata, 464*f*

Seed coat, 822*f*–823*f*

Seed germination, 850-851*f*

Seedless vascular plants, **616**

 gametophyte-sporophyte relationships in, 631*f*

 importance of, 627*f*–628

 life cycles of, 624*f*

 origin and traits of, 622–623*f*, 624*f*–625*f*

 phylogeny of, 616–617*t*, 625–626*f*, 627

Seedling development, 823–824*f*

Seed plants. *See also* Angiosperms; Gymnosperms; Land plants; Plant(s)

 angiosperms, 631*f*, 638–644*f* (see also Angiosperms)

 gymnosperms, 631*f*, 632*f*, 633–634*f*, 635*f*–637*f*

 importance of, to Earth's ecosystems, 630*f*

 importance of, to human welfare, 645*f*–646

 phylogeny of, 617*f*

 seeds and pollen grains as terrestrial adaptations of, 631*f*–632*f*, 633

 threats to biodiversity of, 645*f*–646

Seeds, **617**, **630**

 abscisic acid in dormancy of, 846

 development of plant seedlings from, 822*f*–824*f*

 dispersal of, 826*f*

 dormancy of, 633

 evolutionary advantage of, 632–633

 fruits and angiosperm, 639*f*

 gibberellins in germination of, 845*f*

 glyoxysomes in, 111

 phytochromes in germination of, 850–851*f*

 strigolactones in germination of, 849

Segmented worms, 682*f*

Segregation, law of, 269*f*–**270***f*, 271*f*–273*f*, 293*f*–294

Seizures, 1070

Selective breeding, 468–469*f*

Selective permeability, **124**, 129–130, 1065*f*

Self-assembly, protocell, 521*f*–522

Self-assembly stage, phage lytic cycle, 396*f*

Self-fertilization, 828–829*f*, 834

Self-incompatibility, **828**–829*f*, 834

Selfing, 828–829*f*, 834

Self-pollination, 269*f*

Self-pruning, 780

Self-replicating molecules, 520*f*–521*f*, 522

Self-thinning, 795

Self-tolerance, 955

Semelparity, **1195***f*

Semen, **1020**, 1028

Semicircular canals, **1107***f*, 1109*f*–1110

Semiconservative model, DNA replication, **319***f*–320*f*

Semilunar valves, 921*f*–922*f*

Seminal vesicles, 1019*f*–**1020**

Seminiferous tubules, **1019***f*, 1022*f*

Senescence, **847**–848

Senile dementia, 83

Sensitive period, 1138–**1139***f*

Sensitive plants, 796, 856*f*

Sensors, homeostatic, **876**

Sensory adaptation, **1104**

Sensory areas, cerebral cortex, 1090

Sensory input, 1063*f*, 1090–1091*f*, 1092*f*

Sensory neurons, **1063***f*, **1083***f*

Sensory pathways, 1102*f*–1103*f*, 1104

Sensory reception, **1102***f*–1103

Sensory receptors, 1102*f*–1105*f*, 1106

Sensory systems

 animal and plant, 888*f*

 arthropod, 701

 mechanoreceptors for hearing and equilibrium in, 1106*f*–1110*f*

 motor systems and, 1101*f*, 1102*f* (*see also* Motor systems)

 muscle function and, 1119–1120*f*, 1121*f*–1125*f*, 1126

 sensory receptors in, 1102*f*–1105*f*, 1106

 shark, 721

 skeletal systems, locomotion, and, 1126*f*–1129*f*, 1130

 snake, 732

 taste and smell receptors in, 1117*f*–1119*f*

 visual receptors in, 1111*f*–1116*f*, 1117

Sensory transduction, **1103**, 1114*f*

Sepals, **638***f*, **816**

Separase, 238

Separate electron orbitals model, 35*f*

Septa, **650***f*

September equinox, 1161*f*

Septic shock, 952

Sequence-based phylogenetic tree in Scientific Skills Exercise, 404

Sequence logo in Scientific Skills Exercise, 349

Sequencing by synthesis, 408*f*, 409*f*, 411*f*–412, 438. *See also* DNA sequencing

Sequoiadendron giganteum, 768*f*

Sequoia trees, 637*f*, 768*f*

Serial endosymbiosis, **528**–529*f*

Serine, 77*f*, 219

Serotonin, **1075***t*

Serpentine plant communities, 30*f*

Sertoli cells, 1024–1025*f*

Serum, 928

Seta, **621**

Set point, homeostatic, **876**

Severe combined immunodeficiency (SCID), 428–429*f*, 966

Sewage treatment, 584

Sex

 chromosomal basis of, 296*f*–297

 genomic imprinting and, 308*f*–309

Sex chromosomes, **255**

 human, 254–255*f*, 256

 patterns of inheritance of, 296*f*–298*f*

Sex determination, 1025

Sex hormones

 endocrine disruptors and, 1009

 as environmental toxins, 1272*f*

 functional groups and, 62

 in regulation of mammalian reproduction, 1024*f*–1026*f*, 1027

in sex determination, 1025
smooth ER synthesis of, 104–105
as steroids, 75*f*, 1008–1009*f*
Sex-linked genes, 296*f*, **297**–298*f*
Sex pili, 570, 574*f*–575
Sex reversal, 1016
Sexual dimorphism, **493***f*, 1145*f*
Sexual intercourse, human, 1027–1028, 1032–1033, 1076
Sexual life cycles. *See also* Life cycles
    alternation of fertilization and meiosis in, 254*f*–256*f*, 257
    angiosperm, 818–819*f*
    asexual reproduction vs., 253*f*
    chromosomal basis of Mendelian inheritance in, 292*f*–293*f*, 294 (*see also* Chromosomal basis of inheritance)
    evolution from genetic variation produced in, 263*f*–265*f*
    genetics of heredity and genetic variation in, 252*f*
    graphing DNA changes in meiosis of, 262
    human chromosome sets in, 254*f*–255*f*, 256
    inheritance of chromosomes and genes in, 253
    karyotypes of chromosomes in, 254*f*
    mitosis vs. meiosis in, 260–261*f*, 262
    protist, 588
    stages of meiosis in, 257*f*–260*f*
    varieties of, 256*f*–257
Sexually transmitted diseases (STDs), 579*f*, 593*f*, 1029, 1032*f*, 1034. *See also* AIDS (acquired immunodeficiency syndrome); HIV (human immunodeficiency virus)
Sexually transmitted infections (STIs), 1032
Sexual reproduction, **253**. *See also* Sexual life cycles
    in angiosperms (*see* Angiosperm reproduction)
    in animals, 668*f*–669 (*see also* Animal reproduction)
    asexual reproduction vs., 253*f*, 827–828
    in bryophytes, 618–619*f*, 620*f*–621
    flowers and angiosperm, 638*f*
    in fungi, 652*f*
    microevolution from sexual selection in, 493*f*–494*f*
    as source of genetic variation, 483
Sexual reproduction, animal, **1014**. *See also* Animal reproduction; Human reproduction
    asexual reproduction vs., 1014*f*–1015
    as evolutionary enigma, 1014*f*–1015
    fertilization mechanisms in, 1016*f*–1018*f*
    reproductive cycles in, 1015*f*
    variations in patterns of, 1016
Sexual response, human, 1027–1028
Sexual selection, **493***f*–494*f*, 509*f*, 1146*f*–1147*f*, 1148
S genes, 829
Shade avoidance, plant, 851
Shaffer, Mark, 1263*f*
Shannon diversity, **1216***f*
Shapes
    cell, 116, 117
    enzyme, 153*f*–154, 158*f*–159*f*, 220
    insect pollinators and flower, 643*f*
    molecular, 39*f*–40
    morphogenesis and cell, 1050*f*–1051
    of organic compounds, 59*f*
    prokaryotic, 568*f*
Shapiro, Michael, 540*f*
Shared ancestral characters, **554***f*–555
Shared derived characters, **554***f*–555
Sharks, 720–721*f*, 973
Shelf fungi, 659*f*
Shell drilling adaptation, 536
Shells, electron, 32*f*–35*f*
Shigella bacteria, 575
Shivering thermogenesis, 882*f*
Shoots, 842*f*
    apical meristems of land plant, 615*f*
    light capture and architecture of, 780*f*–781*f*
    primary growth of, 763*f*–765*f*
    transport of water and minerals from roots to, via xylem, 786–787*f*, 788*f*–789*f*, 790
Shoot systems, **753***f*
Short-day plants, **853***f*
Short tandem repeats (STRs), **431**, **446**

Short-term memory, **1094**–1095
Shrimp, 458*f*, 506–507*f*, 703
Sickle-cell disease, **82**, **284**, **929**
    abnormal hemoglobin in, 929
    evolution of, 497*f*
    heterozygote advantage in, 494–495
    pleiotropy and, 278–279
    point mutations and, 355*f*, 482, 496*f*
    protein primary structure changes and, 82*f*
    as recessively inherited, 284*f*–285
Side-blotched lizards, 1148*f*
Side chains, amino acid, 75–77*f*
Sidedness, cellular membrane, 129*f*
Sieve plates, **759***f*, 793–794
Sieve-tube elements, **759***f*
Sieve tubes, 793–794, 795*f*
Signaling molecules, 994*f*–995*f*. *See also* Animal hormones; Neurohormones; Neurotransmitters
Signal peptides, **351***f*
Signal-recognition particles (SRPs), **351***f*
Signals, animal, **1136***f*–1137*f*
Signal transduction, **997**
    in hormone pathways, 997*f*
    membrane proteins and, 128*f*
Signal transduction pathways, **214**
    cancer and interference with normal, 384–385*f*, 386
    in cell signaling, 210, 213*f*–214, 218–219
    coordinate control of, 371
    differential gene expression and induction in, 377–378
    evolution of, 211
    linking signal reception to plant responses, 837*f*–838*f*, 840
    neurotransmitters and, 1074
    second messengers in, 220*f*–221*f*, 222*f*
    in sensory amplification, 1103–1104
    in visual sensory transduction, 1114*f*
Sign stimulus, 1134*f*–**1135**
Silencing, gene expression, 421–422*f*
Silencing, transcription, 369
Silent mutations, 355*f*–356*f*
Silent Spring (book), 1271*f*
Silk, 80*f*, 702
Silk moth, 1001*f*–1002
Silkworm moths, 1104, 1105*f*
Silverfish, 706*f*
Silversword plants, 537*f*–538, 551
Simberloff, Dan, 1227*f*–1228
Simple columnar epithelium, 871*f*
Simple endocrine pathway, 1000*f*
Simple fruits, 825*f*
Simple leaves, 755*f*
Simple neuroendocrine pathway, 1000*f*–1001
Simple sequence DNA, **446**
Simple squamous epithelium, 871*f*
Singing, fruit fly, 1136*f*
Single bonds, **36**–37
Single-celled organisms, 526, 528*f*–529*f*, 588. *See also* Protists
Single circulation, **918**, 919*f*
Single-lens eyes, **1112***f*–1113
Single nucleotide polymorphisms (SNPs), **422***f*, 428, 456
Single-strand binding proteins, 321*f*, 325*t*
Single-stranded DNA (ssDNA) viruses, 398*t*
Single-stranded RNA (ssRNA) viruses, 398*t*, 399*f*–400
Sinoatrial (SA) node, **922***f*
Sirenia, 739*f*
Sister cells, 233
Sister chromatid cohesion, 234, 257
Sister chromatids, **234***f*–235, 255*f*, 258*f*–261*f*, 262, 264*f*
Sister species, 506
Sister taxa, **550***f*
Situs inversus, 1058*f*
Sixth mass extinction, 535*f*–536
Size
    brain, 1085*f*
    carrying capacity and population, 1192*t*–1194*f*
    determining population, using mark-recapture method, 1185*f*
    ecosystem, 1232–1233

evolution of axon, 1070*f*–1071*f*
    of genomes, 442*t*–443
    of global human population, 1201*f*–1204*f*, 1205
    Hardy-Weinberg equilibrium and population, 486
    Homo floresiensis, 748
    of hormones, 212
    individual survival and population, 1194
    locomotion costs and, 1130
    metabolic rate and animal body, 885*f*
    of offspring litter or clutch as life history trait, 1195*f*–1196*f*, 1197
    of plasmodesmatal pores, 796
    prokaryotic cell, 568
    of prokaryotic vs. eukaryotic cells, 4*f*–5, 98
    protist, 587
    of skeletons, 1128
Skeletal muscle, **873***f*, **1120**. *See also* Muscle
    in human breathing, 939*f*–940*f*
    locomotion from contraction of, in skeletal systems, 1126*f*–1129*f*, 1130
    muscle fibers of, 1124–1125*t*
    regulation of contraction of, 1122*f*–1124*f*
    sliding-filament model of contraction of, 1120–1121*f*, 1122
    structure of, 1119, 1120*f*
Skeletal systems
    bones and joints of human, 1128*f*
    cartilage, 718, 720
    energy costs of locomotion by, 1130
    locomotion from interaction of muscles and skeletons in, 1126*f*, 1129*f*–1130
    origins of, 719
    types of, 1126*f*–1127*f*
Skeletons, carbon, 60*f*–61*f*, 62*f*
Skills, scientific. *See* Scientific Skills Exercises
Skin
    cancer of, 326, 1275
    coloration, 1010
    heat exchange and, in animals, 879
    mechanoreceptors in human, 1104*f*
    pigmentation of human, 279–280*f*
Skinner, B. F., 1140–1141
Skulls, human vs. chimpanzee, 538*f*, 552
Skunks, 502*f*, 1212*f*
Sleep, ACTH secretion during, 1008
Sleep, brain functions and, 1088*f*
Sleeping sickness, 594*f*, 707, 967
Sleep movements, plant, 851–852*f*
Sliding-filament model, **1120**–1121*f*, 1122*f*
Slime, hagfish, 717
Slime bacteria, 211*f*
Slime layer, 569
Slime molds, 605–606*f*, 607*f*
Slope in Scientific Skills Exercises, 155, 1043
Slow block to polyspermy, **1039**
Slow-twitch fibers, **1125**
Slugs, 692
Small interfering RNAs (siRNAs), 374–375*f*, 376
Small intestine, 689*f*, **902**
    absorption in, 904*f*–905*f*
    adaptations of, 906*f*–907*f*
    digestion in, 902–903*f*, 904
Small-population approach, population conservation, 1261*f*–1263*f*
Smallpox, 402, 963
Smart plants, 806*f*
Smithells, Richard, 896*f*
Smithies, Oliver, 421
Smooth ER, 100*f*, 101*f*, **104**–105*f*
Smooth muscle, **873***f*, **1126**–1127
Smuts, 659
Snails, 502*f*, 515–516, 532, 692, 696*f*, 1061*f*, 1063*f*
Snakes, 493*f*, 729*f*, 731*f*–732, 963, 1104–1105*f*, 1150*f*, 1258
Snapdragons, 277*f*
Snapping shrimp, 506–507*f*
Snook, Rhonda, 1018*f*
Snow pea, 644*f*
Snowshoe hares, 1200*f*
Snowy owls, 1198*f*
Soapberry bugs, 471*f*–472
Social behavior, 1153*f*–1154
Social learning, **1142***f*–1143, 1148

Society
    plant biotechnology and, 834
    population age structure and, 1203
Society, science and, 18f–19, 23f
Sociobiology, **1154**
Sociobiology: The New Synthesis (book), 1154
Sodium, 29t
Sodium chloride
    elimination of excess, by marine birds, 976f
    human diets and, 895
    kidney processing of, 983–984f, 985
    nephron processing of, 982–983f
    osmoregulation of, 986–987f
    plant responses to excessive, 857
    as table salt, 29f, 38f, 48–49f
    in treating diarrhea, 136–137
Sodium ions, 1064t–1065f, 1066
Sodium-potassium pump, **135**, **1064**
    as active transport, 134–135f
    neuron resting potential and, 1064f–1065f, 1066
Software, bioinformatics, 438–439f, 440–441f, 442
Soil
    bacteria in, 578f, 581f–582, 807f–809f, 810
    bryophyte reduction of nitrogen leaching from,
        621f
    determining diversity of bacteria in, 1217f
    fungi in, 650f
    plant resource acquisition from, 781
    plant response to excessive salt in, 857
    prokaryotes in, as protection against plant
        diseases, 584
    species distributions and, 1180–1181
    sustainable agriculture and conservation of,
        801f–803f
    texture and composition of, 800f–801f
Soil conservation, 801f–803f
Soil horizons, **800f**
Soil worm model organism. *See Caenorhabditis
    elegans* (soil worm)
Solar energy
    in energy flow and chemical cycling, 7f, 1233
    global energy budget and, 1235
    in photosynthesis, 41f, 185f
    primary production in aquatic ecosystems and
        limitations of, 1237
Solute potential, **783**
Solutes, **48**–49f, 50
    animal osmoregulation of, 975–976f
    diffusion of, 130–131f
    diffusion of, across capillary walls, 926–927f
    effects of, on water potential, 783–784
    ion gradients and transport of, 987f
    osmoregulation of, 972f–974f
    short-distance transport of, across plant plasma
        membranes, 782, 783f
    transport of, from roots to shoots via xylem,
        786–787f, 788f–789f, 790
    transport of, from sources to sinks via phloem,
        793–794f, 795f
    two-solute model of kidney water conservation,
        983–984f, 985
Solutions, **48**–49f, 50
Solvents, **48**–49f, 50
Somatic cells, **233**, **253**
Somatosensory cortex, 1091f–1092
Somites, 714–715, 1048f–**1049**
Songs, bird learning of, 1142
Sonic hedgehog growth factor, 1057–1058
Soredia, **662**–663f
Sori, **625**
Sound receptors, 1104–1105f, 1106f–1110f
Sour tastes, 1117f–1118f
South Africa, 1251f
South American vampire bats, 985f–986
South Atlantic Subtropical Gyre, 1162f
South Pacific Subtropical Gyre, 1162f
Soybeans, 487, 808f–809f, 810, 1009
Space-filling models, 36, 37f, 39f, 59f, 74f, 79f, 317f
Spain, 567f
Spanish flu pandemic, 403
Spatial data, analyzing, 420
Spatial learning, **1139**–1140f
Spatial summation, **1073f**

Spawning, 1016–1017
Speciation, **500**
    allopatric, 505f–507f
    allopatric vs. sympatric, 505f, 510
    as conceptual bridge between microevolution and
        macroevolution, 501, 516
    Darwinian theory of, 467–468f, 469f–470f
    genetics of, 515–516f
    hybrid zones and reproductive isolation in,
        510–511f, 512f–513f
    as origin of species in Darwinian evolution, 500f
    orthologous genes and, 560
    reproductive isolation and biological species
        concept in, 501f–504f, 505
    species selection and differential, 542–543
    sympatric, 507–508f, 509f–510
    time course of, 514f–515f
Species, **501**
    biological concept of, 501f–504f
    classification of, 10f–11f, 464, 548–549f
    communities and, 2f (see also Communities)
    communities of (see Communities)
    comparing developmental processes of, 457f–458f
    comparing genomes of, 453–454f, 455f–456
    complete genome sequences for, 436f–437f, 442t
    cross-species gene expression in evolution of, 417
    C. Darwin's theory of origin and evolution of,
        12f–14f, 467–468f, 469f–470f (see also
        Evolution; Speciation)
    discovery of new, 1158f, 1254f
    distributions of (see Species distributions)
    diversity of (see Species diversity)
    dominant, keystone, and foundation, 1220f
    edge, 1266
    endangered or threatened, 1256f, 1267
    endemic, 477
    extinction of mollusc, 696f
    fusion of, 513f
    genome size, number of genes, gene density, and
        noncoding DNA for, 442t–443
    geographic distribution of, 476–477
    homologous genes in, 559f–560
    interactions between (see Interspecific
        interactions)
    introduced, 1258–1259f
    keystone, 1265
    loss of amphibian, 727
    metagenomics and genome sequencing of groups
        of, 438
    morphological, ecological, and phylogenetic
        concepts of, 504
    morphology and concepts of, 501
    number of named, 1254
    phylogenies as history of, for species, 547–548 (see
        also Phylogenies)
    populations of (see Population(s))
    resurrection of extinct, 1260–1261f
    sequenced genomes of, 412
    in tree of life, 14f–15f
    tropical deforestation and extinctions of, 645f–646
    using phylogenetic gene trees to identify, of whale
        meat, 550f–551
    vertebrate, 713
Species-area curve, **1226**–1227f
Species distributions
    abiotic factors in, 1179–1180f, 1181
    in aquatic biomes, 1172
    biotic factors in, 1179f
    combined biotic and abiotic factors in, 1177f
    dispersal factors in, 1178f
    ecological time vs. evolutionary time in, 1172
    global climate change and, 1163–1164f
    habitat selection behavior in, 1178–1179
Species diversity, **1216**
    benefits of, to humans, 1257f
    biodiversity crisis and, 1254f–1255f
    biogeographical factors affecting, 1225–1226f,
        1227f–1228
    community stability and, 1217f
    disturbances influencing, 1222f–1225f
    human impacts on, 1225f
    as level of biodiversity, 1255f–1256f
    species richness and relative abundance in, 1216f

threats to, 1256f
    trophic structure and, 1217–1218f, 1219f–1220f,
        1221 (see also Trophic structure)
Species richness, **1216**
    biogeographic factors affecting, 1226f–1227f, 1228
    species-area curves of, 1226f–1227f
    in species diversity, 1216 (see also Species
        diversity)
Species selection, 542–543
Species transplants, 1178
Specific heat, **46**–47f
Specificity
    cell-signaling, 224–225f
    enzyme substrate, 153f–154
    PCR, 415–416f
    viral, 395
Specific transcription factors, 368f–369f, 839
Spectrophotometer, **191f**
Speech
    brain function and, 1092f
    FOXP2 gene and, 454f–455
Spemann, Hans, 1054–1055f, 1056f
Spemann's organizer, 1056f
Sperm, **1014**
    biased usage of, in female fruit flies, 1018f
    chromosomes in human, 234–235
    conception and, 1028f
    in fertilization, 1038–1039f, 1040
    flagellated, in land plants, 613
    human spermatogenesis and, 1021–1022f
    as male gametes, 1014, 1017–1018f
    mammalian sex determination and, 296f
    seed plant (see Pollen grains)
Spermathecae, 705, **1018f**
Spermatids, 1022f
Spermatocytes, 1022f
Spermatogenesis, **1021**–1022f, 1025f
Spermatogonia, **1022f**
Spermicidal foam or jelly, 1032
Sphagnum moss, 615f, 622f
S phase, **235f**
Sphenisciformes (penguins), 734f
Spherical prokaryotes, 568f
Sphincters, **900f**–901f
Sphincters, precapillary, 926f
Sphygmomanometer, 925f
Spiders, 702f
Spike mosses, 625–626f, 627
Spina bifida, 1048–1049
Spinal cord, 1080f–1081, 1082f
Spines, 756f
Spines, sea star, 708f
Spinnerets, 702
Spiny-headed worms, 682f
Spiny mouse, 1210
Spiral cleavage, **675f**
Spiral phyllotaxy, 780
Spiral prokaryotes, 568f
Spiral valve, shark, 721
Spirobranchus giganteus, 697f
Spirochetes, 579f
Spirodela oligorrhiza, 101f
Spliceosomes, **344f**
Split-brain effect, 1092
Sponges
    Hox genes in, 669
    phylogeny of, 676–677f, 681f, 684f–685
Spongocoel, **684f**
Spongy mesophyll, 764–765f
Spontaneous abortions, 304, 1033
Spontaneous change, **146f**
Spontaneous mutations, 357, 383
Spontaneous processes, **144**
Sporangia, **615f**, 621, 625, 634f–635, 657f
Spores, **614f**, **650**
    in alternation of generations, 256f
    brown algae, 598
    cell signaling and bacterial, 211f
    fossilized land plant, 616f
    fungal, 649f, 650–651, 652f–653f
    of land plants, 614f–615f
    meiosis and production of, 269
    seeds vs., 632–633
    variations of, in vascular plants, 625

Sporocytes, **615f**
Sporophylls, **625**
Sporophytes, **614**
in alternation of generations, 256f
of bryophytes, 620f, 621
gametophyte relationships with, in plants, 631f
of land plants, 614f–615f
in pine tree life cycle, 634f–635
of seedless vascular plants, 623f–624f
Sporopollenin, **613**, 615f, 632
Sporozoites, 598–599f
Spotted ratfish, 721f
Spotted skunks, 502f
Spruce, 1224f
Squamous epithelium, 871f
Squids, 692, 695f–696, 1080f
Squirrel monkeys, 1116f
Srb, Adrian, 334–335f
S-shaped logistic growth curve, 1192–1193f
Stability, community, 1217f, 1222
Stability, equilibrium as, 145–146f
Stability, hybrid zone, 512f, 513
Stability, population, 1199f–1200, 1202
Stabilizing selection, **492f**
Stable isotopes, 31
Staghorn coral, 1228
Staghorn fern, 812f
Stahl, Franklin, 320f
Stalk-eyed flies, 1146f
Stamens, 268–269, **638f**, **816**
Staminate flowers, 828
Standard metabolic rate (SMR), **885f**–886
Standing crop, 1235–1236
Stanley, Wendell, 393–394
Staphylococcus aureus, 472f–473
Star anise, 644f
Starches, **70**
as fuel for catabolism, 180f
as product of photosynthesis, 204–205f
as storage polysaccharides, 70f–71
Starfish. *See* Sea stars
Starling, European, 1258
Star-nosed moles, 1101f
Start codons, 339f
Start point, transcription, **341f**
Statins, 932
Stationary cilia, 1058
Statistics, 16
Statocysts, **1106f**
Statoliths, **855f**, **1106f**
Stator, ATP synthase, **173f**
Stechmann, Alexandra, 605f
Steinbeck, John, 801f
Stele, **757**, 762f
Stem cells, **422**, **929**
animal embryonic and adult, 425–426f
animal induced pluripotent (iPS), 426–427f
generation of differentiated cells from, 425f
glia as, 1081–1082f
plant, 760
potential of, 422
in replacement of blood components, 929f–930
Stems, **755**
ethylene in triple response of, to mechanical
stress, 847f
gibberellins in elongation of, 845f
monocot vs. eudicot, 643f
primary and secondary growth of, 760f–761f
primary and secondary growth of woody, 766f
primary growth of, 763f–765f
secondary growth of, 765–766f, 767f–768f
structure of, 755f
Stenohaline animals, 972
Stents, 931f
Steppes, 1169f
Sterility
hybrid, 503f, 516
transgenic plant, 834
Sterilization, human, 1033
Steroid hormones, **75**
coordinate control of genes by, 371
functional groups and, 62

as intracellular chemical signals, 217–218f
as lipids, 75f
smooth ER synthesis of, 104–105
Steroids
adrenal gland and, 1007f–1008
brassinosteroids as, 849
as environmental toxins, 1272f
in human endocrine system, 999f
as lipid-soluble hormones, 996f
receptors for, 997f
sex hormones as, 1008–1009f
Steward, F. C., 423
Stickleback fish, 475, 540f–541, 1134f–1135
Sticky end, DNA, **414**
Stigma, **638f**
Stigma, angiosperm, **816**
Stimulus
environmental, 1134f–1135f
homeostatic, **876**
sensory, 1102f, 1103f
in stimulus-response chains, 1136f
Stingrays, 720–721f
Stink bugs, 706f
Stipes, **596**
Stock, **829**
Stolons, 755f
Stomach, **901**
adaptations of, 906–907f
chemical digestion in, 901–902f
Stomach ulcers, 578f
Stomata, **187**, **616**, **764**–765f, **771f**
of CAM plants, 203–204f
ion gradients and, 987f
land plant, 616
in photosynthesis, 187f
regulation of transpiration by opening and closing
of, 790–791f, 792
sporophyte, 621
transpiration and, 201
Stop codons, 339f, 351f
Storage leaves, 756f
Storage polysaccharides, 70f–71
Storage proteins, 76f
Storage roots, 754f
Storms, 1166, 1222
Stramenopiles, 591f, **595f**–597f, 598
Strangling aerial roots, 754f
Strasburger, Eduard, 788
Strata, **464f**, 522–523f
Stratified squamous epithelium, 871f
Streams, 1174f, 1269
Streptococcus, 313f, 569f, 573, 952
Stress
adrenal gland response to, 997f, 1006–1007f, 1008
ethylene in plant responses to, 847f
immune systems and, 965
Stretch receptors, 1104
Striated muscle, 1120. *See also* Skeletal muscle
Striga, 849
Strigolactones, 840t, 844, **849**
Strobili, **625**
Strobili, gymnosperm, 633
Strokes, 931f–932
Stroke volume, **921**
Stroma, **110**–111, **187f**, 189f–190, 197–198f, 199
Stromatolites, 523f, **526**
Structural formulas, 36, 37f, 59f, 74f
Structural isomers, **61f**
Structural polysaccharides, 71f–72f
Structural proteins, 76f
Structure, function and, 4
Struthioniformes (ratites), 733f–734f
Strychnine, 1075, 1213
Studies. *See* Inquiry experiments
Sturtevant, Alfred H., 303f–304f
Styles, flower, **638f**, **816**
Subatomic particles, 30–31
Suberin, 768
Subsidence, land, 802f
Substance P, 1075
Substrate feeders, **898f**
Substrate-level phosphorylation, 166–**167f**
Substrates, **153f**–154, 158f–159f

Succulent Karoo restoration project, 1251f
Succulent plants, 203–204f
Suckling, 1031
Sucrase, 151, 153
Sucrose
as disaccharide, 69f
enzymatic catalysis and, 151, 153
molecular mass of, 50
as product of photosynthesis, 204–205f
transport of, in vascular plants, 793–794f, 795f
Sudden oak death (SOD), 608f, 1228
Sugarcane, 204f
Sugar gliders, 475f
Sugar-phosphate backbone, DNA, 315f–316,
317f–319f, 322–323f, 324f–325f
Sugars. *See also* Carbohydrates
as components of nucleic acids, 85f–86
conduction of, in plant cells, 759f
monosaccharides and disaccharides, 68f–69f
polysaccharides, 70f–71f, 72f
as products of photosynthesis, 189f–190,
199–200f, 204–205f
translocation of, from sources to sinks via phloem,
793–794f, 795f
Sugar sinks, **794**
Sugar sources, **794**
Suicide genes, 384
Sulfhydryl group, **63f**
Sulfur, 29t, 56, 64
Sulfur bacteria, 578f
Sulfur dioxide emissions, 1260
Sulston, John, 1052
Sumner, Francis Bertody, 20
Sundews, 812f
Sunflowers, 514–515f, 888f
Sunlight
aquatic biomes and, 1171
cancer and, 388
DNA damage from, 326
in energy flow and chemical cycling, 7f, 162–163f,
1233
as energy for life, 142, 148
latitudinal variation in intensity of, 1160f
in photosynthesis, 185f, 204–205f
primary production in aquatic ecosystems and
limitations of, 1237
properties of, 190f
species distributions and availability of, 1180f
Supercontinent, 532, 533f
Supergroups, protist, 588–589, 590f–591f
Superimposed electron orbitals model, 35f
Supernatural vs. natural explanations, 17–18
Super-resolution microscopy, 95f, 96
Super weeds, 433
Suprachiasmatic nucleus (SCN), 887f, 1009,
1088–1089
Surface area
calculating cell volume and, 99
leaf, 625f
maximizing, by animals, 689f
Surface area-volume relationships, 98f
Surface tension, **46f**
Surfactants, **937**
Surroundings, systems and, 143
Survival
adaptations, natural selection, and, 469f–470
life histories and, 1195f–1196f, 1197
Survivorship curves, **1188f**
Suspension feeding, 715f, 721, 898f
Suspensor cells, 822f
Sustainability, 1276f
Sustainable agriculture, **802**
in Costa Rica zoned reserves, 1269
soil conservation in, 801f–803f
Sustainable development, **1276f**
Sutherland, Earl W., 212–213f, 214, 220–221
Sutton, Walter S., 294
Swallowing reflex, 901f
Swans, whooper, 44f
Sweden, 1202
Sweet potatoes, 645
Sweet tastes, 1117f–1118f
Swim bladders, 722

Swimming, 1129
Swine flu, 1228
Switchgrass, 832
Symbionts, **582**
Symbiosis, **582, 1214**. *See also* Commensalism;
    Mutualism; Parasitism
    in flower pollination, 815*f*–816
    fungal, 655*f*–656, 661*f*–663*f*
    in interspecific interactions, 1214*f*–1215*f*
    protist, 608*f*
sym genes, 654
Symmetry
    animal body, 673*f*–674
    body, 1054, 1058*f*
    flower, 638*f*, 643*f*
    plant cell division, 770*f*–772*f*
Sympathetic division, peripheral nervous system, 922*f*,
    1083–**1084**
Sympatric populations, character displacement in,
    1210–1211*f*
Sympatric speciation, **507**–508*f*, 509*f*–510
Symplast, **781**–782*f*
Symplastic communication, 795–796*f*
Symplastic domains, 796
Symplastic route, 782*f*, 787*f*
Synapses, **1062**
    electrical and chemical, 1071*f*–1072*f*
    generation of postsynaptic potentials and,
        1072–1073
    in memory and learning, 1093–1094*f*, 1095*f*
    modulated signaling at, 1073–1074
    neurotransmitters and, 1071–1072*f*, 1074*f*–1075*t*,
        1076
    in regulation of muscle contraction, 1122–1123*f*,
        1124
    scaffolding proteins and, 225*f*–227
    summation of postsynaptic potentials and, 1073*f*
Synapsids, 525*f*, **735***f*–736
Synapsis, 260*f*
Synaptic cleft, 1072
Synaptic signaling, 212, 213*f*, 994*f*, 995–996
Synaptic terminals, 1062
Synaptic vesicles, 1071
Synaptonemal complex, **260***f*
Syndromes, 306
Synthesis stage, phage lytic cycle, 396*f*
Synthetases, 346–347*f*
Syphilis, 579*f*
Systematics, **548**, 676–677*f*, 678. *See also* Cladistics;
    Molecular systematics; Taxonomy
Systemic acquired resistance, **860**–861*f*
Systemic circuit, **918**–919*f*, 920
Systemic inflammatory response, 952
Systemic lupus erythematosus, 965
Systemic mycoses, 664
Systems
    systems biology and biological, 3
    thermodynamics and isolated vs. open, 143,
        147*f*–148*f*
Systems biology, 4, **440**–441*f*, 442
Systole phase, **921***f*
Systolic pressure, **924**–925*f*

T

T2 phage, 314*f*–315
Table salt. *See* Sodium chloride
Tables in Scientific Skills Exercises, 58, 89, 155, 177,
        203, 262, 302, 316, 452, 487, 507, 564, 584,
        589, 623, 633, 651, 672, 745, 756, 784, 828,
        912, 932, 967, 975, 1008, 1025, 1043, 1076,
        1181, 1211, 1240, 1273
Tactile communication, 1136*f*
Tadpoles, 376*f*, 727*f*
Taiga, 1169*f*
Tail, muscular post-anal, 714*f*
Tails, histone, 328*f*, 366*f*
Takahe bird, 1251*f*
Tamoxifen, 387*f*
tangled-1 mutant, 771
Tannins, 1213
Tansley, A. G., 1222
Tapeworms, 681*f*, 691*f*
Tapping, in fruit fly courtship, 1136*f*
Taproots, **753***f*–754*f*

Taproot systems, 753*f*–754
Taq polymerase, 415, 1257
Tardigrades, 683*f*, 974*f*
Target cells, hormone, 994, 996*f*, 997*f*–998
Tarsiers, 740
Tar spot fungus, 663*f*
Tastants, **1117***f*–1118*f*
Taste, 1117*f*–1118*f*
Taste buds, **1118***f*
TATA boxes, **341***f*, 368
Tatum, Edward, 334–335*f*, 336
Tau protein, 1098
Taxis, **570**
Taxol, 247
Taxon, **548**–549*f*, 550*f*, 553
Taxonomy, **548**. *See also* Cladistics; Phylogenies;
    Systematics
    early schemes of, 464
    grouping of species in, 10*f*–11*f*
    mammalian, 738*f*–739*f*
    phylogenies and, 548–549*f*, 550*f*
    possible plant kingdoms, 613*f*
    ten phyla of extant land plants, 617*t*
    three-domain system of, 11*f*, 562, 563*f*
    tree of life of, 14*f*–15*f*
Tay-Sachs disease, **278**
    allele dominance and, 278
    fetal testing for, 286–287*f*
    as lysosomal storage disease, 108
    recessive alleles in, 283–284
T cells, **952**
    antigen recognition by, 954*f*
    cell-mediated immune response and, 958
    clonal selection of, 956, 957*f*
    development of, 954–955*f*, 956–957*f*
    diversity of, 955*f*–960
Tea, 645
Teal, John, 1240
Technology, **23***f*
    DNA (*see* Biotechnology; DNA technology)
    global carrying capacity and, 1205
    prokaryotes in research and, 583–584*f*, 585
Tectonic plates, 532*f*–533*f*
Teeth
    conodont mineralized dental elements, 718*f*
    diet and adaptations of, 906*f*
    mammalian, 524–525*f*, 526, 735
    origins of, 719
Telomerase, 327
Telomeres, **326**–327*f*
Telomeric DNA, 446
Telophase, **235**, 237*f*, 241*f*, 261*f*
Telophase I, 258*f*, 261*f*
Telophase II, 259*f*
Temperate broadleaf forests, **1170***f*, 1247–1248*f*
Temperate grasslands, **1169***f*
Temperate phages, **397***f*–398
Temperature, **46**
    aquatic biomes and, 1171–1172*f*
    climographs of, 1165*f*
    coefficients in Scientific Skills Exercise, 784
    correlation of atmospheric carbon dioxide with
        global, 1272–1273*f*, 1274
    effects of, on litter decomposition in ecosystems,
        1247*f*
    effects of transpiration on leaf, 792
    enzymatic catalysis and, 155–156*f*
    global, and extinction rates, 535*f*–536
    heat vs., 46
    membrane proteins and, 126*f*
    moderation of, by water, 46–47*f*, 48
    plant response to stress of, 857–859
    protein denaturation and, 82*f*–83
    regulation of body (*see* Thermoregulation)
    species distributions and, 1179
Templates, viral DNA and RNA, 398*t*, 399*f*–400
Template strands, DNA, 318–319*f*, 320*f*, 322*f*–325*f*,
    338
Tempo, speciation, 514*f*–515*f*
Temporal fenestra, 525*f*, 735
Temporal isolation, 502*f*
Temporal lobe, 1091*f*
Temporal summation, **1073***f*
Tendons, 872*f*

Tendrils, 756*f*
Tentacles, invertebrate, 680, 685, 695, 697*f*
Terminal cells, 822*f*
Termination, neurotransmission, 1074*f*
Termination codons, 339*f*
Termination stage
    transcription, 340*f*, 342
    translation, 351*f*
Terminators, 340*f*–**341**
Termites, 608*f*, 649
Terpenoids, 862*f*
Terrestrial adaptations
    mycorrhizae as plant, 810
    seed plant, 631*f*–632*f*, 633
Terrestrial biomes
    animal osmoregulation in, 974, 975
    biodiversity hot spots in, 1267*f*
    chaparral, 1168*f*
    climate and, 1164–1165*f*
    deserts, 1167*f*
    disturbance in, 1166
    food chains in, 1218*f*
    general features of, 1165–1166*f*
    global distribution of, 1165*f*
    locomotion in, 1129
    northern coniferous forests, 1169*f*
    nutrient cycling in, 1246–1247*f*, 1248*f*
    plant adaptations to, 201
    primary production in, 1238*f*–1239
    savannas, 1168*f*
    temperate broadleaf forests, 1170*f*
    temperate grasslands, 1169*f*
    tropical forests, 1167*f*
    tundra, 1170*f*, 1242*f*–1243*f*
Territoriality, **1186**, 1187*f*, 1199*f*
Tertiary consumers, **1234**–1235*f*
Tertiary structure, protein, 81*f*
Testcrosses, **272**, 273*f*, 299*f*–300*f*
Testes, 256, 999*f*, 1008–1009*f*, **1019***f*, 1025*f*
Testicles, 1019*f*
Testing, genetic. *See* Genetic testing
Testing, hypothesis, 16–17*f*, 18*f*–19
Testosterone, 62*f*, 1008–1009*f*, 1024–1025*f*
Tests, foraminiferan, **601**
Test-tube cloning, 830*f*
Tetanus, **1124**
Tetraploids, 508
Tetraploidy, 305
Tetrapods, **724**
    amniotes, 727
    amphibians, 726*f*–727*f*
    derived characters of, 724–725
    evolution of, 672
    homologous characteristics of, 474*f*–475
    land colonization by, 531
    as lobe-fins, 724
    origin and phylogeny of, 724*f*, 725*f*
    origin of, 524–525*f*, 526
Texture, soil, 800
Thalamus, **1087***f*, 1089*f*, 1091
Thalloid liverworts, 620*f*
Themes of biology, 2*f*–15*f*
Theobroma cacao, 661*f*–662
Theories, **21**, 477–478
Therapeutic cloning, 426
Therapsids, 525*f*
Thermal energy, **46**, 130, **142**
Thermocline, **1171***f*–1172
Thermodynamics, laws of, **143***f*–144, 1233
Thermogenesis, 881*f*–882*f*
Thermophiles, 580*f*–581
Thermoreceptors, **1105**
Thermoregulation, **878**
    acclimatization in, 882
    aquatic animal feedback regulation in, 875*f*
    balancing heat loss and gain in, 879*f*–882*f*
    circadian rhythms in human, 876–877*f*
    desert ant form and function for, 867*f*–868
    in endothermic and ectothermic animals, 878*f*
    physiological thermostats and fever in, 882–883*f*
    variation in animal body temperatures and, 878
Thermostatic thermoregulation, 882–883*f*
Thermus aquaticus, 415

Theropods, **730**
Thick filaments, **1119**–1120f, 1121f, 1125–1126
Thigmomorphogenesis, 855–**856**f
Thigmotropism, **856**f
Thin filaments, **1119**–1120f, 1121f, 1125–1126
Thiomargarita namibiensis, 568
Thirst, 1104
Thompson seedless grapes, 845f
Thoracic cavity, 939
Thorax, insect, 704f
Threatened species, **1256**f, 1267
Threonine, 77f, 219
Threshold, **1067**
Thrombin, 930f
Thrombus, **931**–932
Thrum flower, 829f
Thucydides, 956
Thumbs, opposable, 740
Thylakoid membranes, 187f–188, 194f–198f, 199
Thylakoids, **110**, **187**
    in chloroplasts, 110–111f
    light reactions in, 189f–190
    as sites of photosynthesis in chloroplasts,
        187f–188
Thylakoid space, 187f
Thymidylate synthase (TS), 605f
Thymine, 85f–86, 315f–316, 336, 338f
Thymine dimers, 326
Thymus, **952**
Thyroid gland, 999f, **1004**f–1005f
Thyroid hormone (T₃ and T₄), 999f, **1004**f–1005f,
    1010f
Thyroid hormones, 217
Thyroid-stimulating hormone (TSH), 999f, 1003f,
    1004f
Thyrotropin-releasing hormone (TRH), 1004f
Thyroxine (T₄), 996f, 1004, 1010f
Ticks, 583f, 702, 1229f
Tidal rhythms, 1135
Tidal volume, **939**
Tight junctions, **120**f
Tiktaalik fossil, 523f, 724f, 725
Time
    ecological and evolutionary, in species
        distributions, 1172
    phylogenetic tree branch lengths and, 555–556f
    required for human cell division, 235
Tinbergen, Niko, 1134, 1140f
tinman gene, 1037
Ti plasmid, 432, 770f
Tissue culture, plant, 830f
Tissue-level herbivore defenses, plant, 862f
Tissue plasminogen activator (TPA), 430, 451f
Tissues, **668**, **753**, **870**
    animal, 668, 870, 871f–873f
    animal body plan and, 674
    culturing plant, 830f
    of human endocrine system, 998f–999f
    immune system rejection of transplanted, 964
    as level of biological organization, 3f
    plant, 753, 756–757f
    proteins specific to, in cell differentiation, 378
    renewal of, as cell division function, 232–233f
Tissue-specific proteins, 378
Tissue systems, plant, **756**
    in leaves, 764f–765f
    in primary growth of roots, 761f–762f
    in primary growth of shoots, 763f–765f
    types of, 756–757f
Tit-for-tat strategy, 1153
Tmesipteris, 626f–627
Toadfish, 1125f
Toads, 510–511f, 513, 726
Tobacco mosaic virus (TMV), 393f, 394f, 405
Tobacco plant, 339f
Toll-like receptors (TLRs), 949f–950f
Tollund man, 622f
Tomatoes, 639f, 843
Tongue, 900f, 901f, 1118f
Tonicity, **132**f–133f
Tools, hominin use of, 745–746
Tooth cavities, 212
Top-down model, trophic control, **1221**
Topoisomerases, **321**f, 325f, 329f

Topsoil, **800**–801f
Torpor, **886**–887f
Torreya taxifolia tree transplantation, 1274
Tortoiseshell cats, 298f
Total biomass accumulation, 1236
Totipotent amoebocytes, 685
Totipotent cells, **423**, **1055**f
Totipotent plants, 829
Touch, plant response to, 855–856f
Touch receptors, 1104f
Tourism, zoned reserves and, 1269
Toxic waste
    bioremediation of, 1249f
    biotechnology in cleanup of, 412f, 432
    density-dependent population regulation by, 1199f
Toxins
    acetylcholine and, 1075
    detoxification and, 104–105, 111
    dinoflagellate, 598
    environmental, 1271f–1272f
    enzymatic catalysis and, 157
    evolution of tolerance to, 30
    fungal, 663f
    as prey defensive adapations, 1211
    soil, 803, 805
T phages, 394f–395, 396f–397
Trace elements, **29**f–30
Tracers, radioactive, 31–32f, 188
Trachea, 901f, **936**–937f
Tracheal systems, insect, 701, 704f, **935**–936f
Tracheids, **624**, **759**f
Tragopogon species, 508–509f
Traits, **268**. *See also* Alleles
    characters and, 268–269
    C. Darwin on natural selection and, 13f–15f
    dominant vs. recessive, 269–270t, 283f
    inheritance of, in Darwinian evolution, 469f–470
    inheritance of X-linked genes and recessive,
        297f–298
    land plant derived, 613–614f, 615f–616
    life history, 1195f–1196f, 1197
    noninheritance of acquired, 465f
    seedless vascular plant, 622–623f, 624f–625f
Transacetylase, 363f
Transcription, **336**
    effects of ncRNAs on, 375f–376
    eukaryotic gene regulation after, 372f–373
    in gene expression and protein synthesis, 334,
        336–337f
    molecular components and stages of, 340f–341
    regulation of, in plant responses, 839
    regulation of bacterial, 361f–364f
    regulation of eukaryotic initiation of, 367f–369f,
        370–371f, 372f
    RNA processing after, 342, 343f–345f
    summary of eukaryotic, 354f
    synthesis of RNA transcript during, 341f–342f
    template strands in, 338
Transcription factories, 372f
Transcription factors, **341**f
    in cell signaling, 218f, 223f
    in eukaryotic gene regulation, 368f–369f, 370–371f
Transcription initiation complex, **341**f, 367f–368, 369f
Transcription units, **341**
Transduction, genetic, **573**f
Transduction, sensory, 1103, 1108–1109f, 1114f
Transduction stage, cell-signaling, **214**
    multistep pathways and signal amplification in,
        218
    overview of, 213f–214
    in plant signal transduction pathways, 838f–839
    protein phosphorylation and dephosphorylation
        in, 219f–220
    signal transduction pathways and, 218–219
    small molecules and ions as second messengers in,
        220f–221f, 222f
    in yeast-cell mating, 211
trans face, Golgi apparatus, 106f–107
Trans fats, 61, **74**, 932
Transfer RNA (tRNA), **345**. *See also* RNA (ribonucleic
    acid)
    structure of, 86–87f
    in translation, 345f–348f, 350

Transformation, cancer and cellular, **247**f
Transformation, energy, 141f, 142–143f, 144f–145,
    207f. *See also* Metabolism
Transformation, genetic, **313**f, **573**, 770
Transfusions, blood, 963–964
Transgene escape issue, 833–834
Transgenes, 430f
Transgenic animals, **430**
Transgenic plants, **831**. *See also* Genetically modified
    (GM) organisms
    biotechnology and genetic engineering of,
        831–832f
    Golden Rice, 896
    improving plant nutrition with, 805–806f
    issues about agricultural crops as, 432–433,
        832–834
    producing, using Ti plasmid, 770f
    prokaryotes in genetic engineering of, 584
trans isomers, 61
Transitional ER, 105f
Transition state, 152
Translation, **336**
    basic concept of, 345f
    building polypeptides in, 348f–349, 350f–351f
    completing and targeting functional proteins in,
        351–352f
    in eukaryotic cells, 354f
    in gene expression and protein synthesis, 334,
        336–337f
    identifying ribosome binding sites with sequence
        logos in, 349
    molecular components of, 345f–347f, 348
    post-translational protein modification in plant
        responses, 839
    regulation of eukaryotic initiation of, 373
    ribosomes in, 347f–348
    summary of eukaryotic, 354f
    synthesizing multiple polypeptides with
        polyribosomes in, 352–353f
    transfer RNA in, 345f–347f
Translation initiation complex, 348f, 350
Translation initiation factors, 373
Translocation, 350f, 352
Translocation, cancer gene, 383f–384
Translocation, plant transport, **793**–794f, 795f
Translocations, chromosome, 305–306f, 307f
Transmembrane proteins, 127f–128f, 214, 215f–217f
Transmembrane route, 782f, 787f
Transmission, sensory, 1103
Transmission electron microscope (TEM), **96**
Transmission electron microscopy (TEM), **95**f
Transmission rate, disease, 1198f
Transpiration, **786**
    effects of, on plant wilting and leaf temperature,
        792
    plant adaptations for reducing evaporative water
        loss by, 792–793f
    regulation of, by opening and closing stomata,
        790–791f, 792
    in water and mineral transport from roots to
        shoots via xylem, 786–787f, 788f–789f, 790
Transpirational pull, 788f–789f
Transplants
    immune system rejection of organ, 964
    species, 1178
Transport, plant and animal, 889f. *See also* Circulatory
    systems; Transport in vascular plants
Transport epithelia, **975**–976f, 982–983f
Transport function, membrane protein, 128f
Transport in vascular plants, 624. *See also* Vascular
    plants
    regulation of transpiration rate by stomata in,
        790–791f, 792–793f
    resource acquisition adaptations and, 778f–781f
    short-distance and long-distance mechanisms of,
        781–782f, 783f–784, 785f
    sugar transport from sources to sinks via phloem
        in, 793–794f, 795f
    symplastic communication in, 795–796f
    of water and minerals from roots to shoots via
        xylem, 786–787f, 788f–789f, 790
    xylem and phloem in, 759f
Transport proteins, 76f, **130**
    in active transport, 134–135f

aquaporins, 784–785
  cellular membrane selective permeability and, 130
  as cotransporters, 136*f*–137
  facilitated diffusion and, 133*f*
  ion pumps and, 136
  plant solute transport and, 782, 783*f*
  water diffusion and, 784–785
Transport vesicles, **105**, 137–138*f*
Transport work, 148, 150*f*
Transposable elements, **444***f*–445*f*, 446, 453
Transposition process, 444*f*–445*f*, 446, 453
Transposons, 375–376, 400, **445***f*
Transthyretin protein, 80*f*–81*f*
Transverse (T) tubules, **1122***f*–1123*f*
Tree frogs, 494*f*
Tree of life
  Darwinian evolution and, 14*f*–15*f*, 468*f* (*see also* Evolutionary trees)
  phylogenies in investigation of, 547*f*–548*f*, 562–563*f*, 564
  three-domain taxonomy of, 562, 563*f*
Tree rings, 767*f*
Trees, photosynthesis in, 185*f*
Tree trunks, 768*f*
Trematodes, 690*f*
Trends, evolutionary, 542–543*f*
Triacylglycerols, **72**–73*f*, 74
Trial-and-error learning, 1140*f*–1141
Tricarboxylic acid cycle. *See* Citric acid cycle
Trichinosis, 699*f*–700
Trichomes, 757*f*, 793*f*, 862*f*
Trichomonas vaginalis, 593*f*
Triglycerides, **72**–73*f*, 74, 904–905*f*
Triiodothyronine (T₃), 1004
Trilobites, 700*f*
Trimesters, human pregnancy, 1029*f*–1031*f*
Trimethylamine oxide (TMAO), 973
Triple response, plant, **847***f*
Triplet code, 337–338*f*. *See also* Genetic code
Triploblastic animals, **674**
Triploidy, 305
Trisomic cells, **305**
Trisomy 21. *See* Down syndrome
Trisomy X, 307
Tristan da Cunha, 489
Triticum aestivum, 509
Trochophore larva, **677***f*, 688
Trophic cascade model, 1221
Trophic efficiency, **1240**–1241*f*
Trophic structure, **1217**
  bottom-up and top-down controls on, and biomanipulation of, 1221
  in ecosystem energy flow and chemical cycling, 1234*f*–1235*f*
  energetic hypothesis on restriction of food chain length, 1219*f*
  food webs of food chains in, 1217–1218*f*, 1219*f*
  species with large impacts on, 1219–1220*f*
  trophic efficiency of, 1240–1241*f*
Trophoblasts, **1029**, **1046***f*–1047*f*
Tropical cone snails, 1061*f*, 1063*f*
Tropical dry forests, **1167***f*
Tropical rain forests, **1167***f*
  biogeochemical cycles in, 1246–1247
  deforestation of, as threat to biodiversity, 645*f*–646
  fragmentation of, 1266*f*
  primary production in, 1238
Tropic hormones, **1003***f*
Tropic of Cancer, 1160*f*
Tropic of Capricorn, 1160*f*
Tropics, **1160***f*, 1226
Tropisms, **841**
Tropomyosin, **1122***f*–1123*f*
Troponin complex, **1122***f*
Troponin T, 372*f*
Trout, 722*f*
trp operon, 362*f*–363, 364
TRP (transient receptor potential) proteins, 1105, 1118
trp repressor, **362***f*
Truckee River restoration project, 1250*f*
True-breeding organisms, **269**
True bugs, 706*f*

Truffles, 657*f*, 664
Trypanosoma, 594*f*, 707, 967
Trypsin, 156
Tryptophan, 77*f*, 361*f*–362*f*, 1075
Tsetse flies, 707
Tuataras, 731*f*
Tubal ligation, 1032*f*–**1033**
Tubal pregnancies, 1029
Tube cells, 640*f*, 818
Tube feet, **707**–708*f*
Tuberculosis, 579*f*, 583, 952, 1198*f*
Tubers, 755*f*
Tubeworms, 908*f*
Tubules, kidney, 980
Tubulidentata, 739*f*
Tubulin, 114, 238
Tumbleweeds, 826*f*
Tumors, 429–430
Tumors, cancer, 247*f*–248
Tumor-suppressor genes, **384**, 386*f*, 388
Tumor viruses, 388
Tuna, 723*f*, 868*f*
Tundra, **1170***f*, 1232*f*
Tunicates, 709, 713*f*, **715***f*–716, 1052*f*
Turgid cells, 132–**133**, **784**, 785*f*, 791*f*
Turgor movements, plant, 856*f*
Turgor pressure, 132*f*–133, **783**
Turner, Monica, 1157*f*, 1223
Turner syndrome, 307
Turnover, 1171–**1172**
Turnover time, **1241***f*
Turtles, 730*f*–731, 1184*f*, 1188–1189*f*
Tutu, Desmond, 456
Twins, 1030, 1055
Twin studies, **1138**
Tympanic membrane, 1106, **1107***f*
Type 1 diabetes, 911
Type 2 diabetes, 911
Typhoid fever, 583
Tyrannosaurus rex, 730
Tyrosinase, 336
Tyrosine, 77*f*, 1004, 1075

U

Ubiquinone (Q), 173
Ubiquitin, 373
Ubx gene, 539*f*–540, 701*f*
Ulcers, 902, 907*f*
Ultimate causation, 1134
Ultrasound fetal testing, 287
Ultrasound imaging, 1033
Ultraviolet (UV) radiation
  cancer and, 388
  DNA damage from, 326
  elevation and, affecting species distributions, 1180*f*
  in insect vision, 1111–1112
  mutations from, 357
  ozone depletion and, 1274*f*–1275*f*
Ulva, 603*f*
Umami tastes, 1117*f*–1118*f*
Undernutrition, 896
Undershoot phase, action potential, 1068*f*–1069
Unger, Franz, 268
Ungulates, 475*f*–476*f*
Unicellular organisms, 526, 528*f*–529*f*
Uniform dispersion, 1186, 1187*f*
Unikonts, 591*f*, **604**–605*f*, 606*f*–607*f*
Unisexual flowers, 816
United States
  age-structure pyramid for, 1203*f*
  Endangered Species Act (ESA), 1256
Unity
  in biodiversity, 12*f*, 13*f*
  evolution and, 462*f*, 467
  in universality of genetic code, 339*f*–340
Unlinked genes
  identifying, 302
  mapping, 303*f*–304*f*
  recombination of, 300
Unsaturated fats, 73*f*–74, 126*f*
Unsaturated fatty acids, **73***f*–74
Unselfish behavior, 1151*f*–1153*f*
Untranslated regions (UTRs), 343*f*, 373
Upright posture, hominin, 742

Uracil, 85*f*–86, 336, 338*f*
Uranium, bioremediation of, 1249*f*
Uranium, half-life of, 32
Uranium-238, 524
Urban ecology, **1269**
Urea, 57, 60, 973, **976**–977*f*, 983–984*f*, 985
Ureter, **980***f*
Urethra, **980***f*, **1019***f*
Urey, Harold, 57, 520
Uric acid, **977***f*
Urinary bladder, **980***f*
Urine
  hyperosmotic, 985
  nephron processing of blood filtrate to, 982–983*f*
  two-solute model of concentration of, 983–984*f*, 985
Urochordata (tunicates), 713*f*, 715*f*–716
Urodela, 726*f*
USA300 bacteria, 472*f*
Use and disuse principle, Lamarck's, 465
Uterine cycle, **1025**, 1027
Uterus, **1020**–1021*f*
Utricle, **1109***f*

V

Vaccination, 963
Vaccines, **402**
Vacuolar sap, 772
Vacuoles, 100*f*, 101*f*, **108**
Vagina, **1020**–1021*f*, 1028
Vaginal pouch, 1032
Valence, **36**, 59*f*
Valence electrons, **35**, 36
Valence shells, **35**
Valine, 77*f*
Valium, 1075
Vampire bats, 985*f*–986
van der Waals interactions, **39**, 81*f*
van Leeuwenhoek, Antoni, 94, 587
van Niel, C. B., 188
Variable (V) region, light and heavy chain, 953*f*
Variables, **20**–21
  comparing two, 967
  identifying dependent and independent, 507
Variation, genetic. *See* Genetic variation
Variegation, 309*f*
Vasa recta, **981***f*
Vascular bundles, 757, 764*f*
Vascular cambium, **760***f*, 765–766*f*, 767*f*–768*f*, 843
Vascular cylinder, 757
Vascular plants, **616**. *See also* Seedless vascular plants; Seed plants
  origin and traits of, 622–623*f*, 624*f*–625*f*
  phylogeny of, 617*t*
  resource acquisition for, 778*f*–781*f*
  seedless (*see* Seedless vascular plants)
  transport in (*see* Transport in vascular plants)
Vascular rays, 767
Vascular tissue, **616**, 779*f*
Vascular tissue system, plant, **757***f*, 759*f*
Vascular transport, 530, 624
Vas deferens, **1019***f*
Vasectomy, 1032*f*–**1033**
Vasocongestion, 1027–1028
Vasoconstriction, 879, **925**
Vasodilation, 879, **925**, 995–996, 998, 1020
Vasopressin. *See* Antidiuretic hormone (ADH)
Vectors, zoonotic disease, **1229***f*
Vegetal pole, **1042***f*
Vegetarian diets, 893
Vegetation, terrestrial biomes and, 1164, 1165–1166*f*
Vegetative propagation, **829**, 843
Vegetative reproduction, **827**–828
Veins, blood, **918**–919*f*, 923*f*–924*f*, 925–926*f*
Veins, leaf, 187*f*, **755**, 764, 843
Veldts, 1169*f*
Velvetleaf plants, 203
Velvet worms, 683*f*
Venae cavae, 920, 924*f*
Venom, snail, 1061*f*
Venomous snakes, 732
Venter, Craig, 437*f*–438
Ventilation, **935**. *See also* Breathing

Ventral nerve cords
    earthworm, 698*f*
    planarian, 690*f*
Ventral side, **673**
Ventral tegmental area (VTA), 1097*f*
Ventricles, brain, 1082*f*
Ventricles, heart, **918**–919*f*, 920*f*–921*f*
Venules, **918**, 923*f*–924*f*
Venus flytrap, 796, 812*f*, 856
Vernalization, **854**
Verreaux's sifaka, 740*f*
Vertebrates, **676, 712**
    action potential conduction speed in, 1070
    adaptations of digestive systems of, 906*f*–908*f* (*see also* Digestive systems)
    amniotes and development of terrestrially adapted eggs in, 727–728*f*, 729*f*–734*f* (*see also* Amniotes)
    anatomical homologies in embryos of, 473*f*–474
    brains of, 1085*f*–1090*f*, 1093*f* (*see also* Nervous systems)
    cardiovascular systems of (*see* Cardiovascular systems)
    as chordates, 709, 713*f*–719*f* (*see also* Chordates)
    derived characters of, 716–717
    embryonic germ layers of, 1045*f*
    energy budgets for terrrestrial, 886
    evolution of, 672
    evolution of backbones and diversity vs. disparity in, 712*f*–713
    fossils and early evolution of, 718*f*–719*f*
    gamete production and delivery in, 1018
    gas exchange systems of (*see* Gas exchange systems)
    gnathostomes and development of jaws in, 719*f*–723*f*, 724
    hominins and humans, 742*f*–744*f*, 745–746*f*, 747*f*–748*f*
    innate immunity in, 948–949*f*, 950–951*f*, 952
    kidneys in excretory systems of, 980*f*–981*f*, 985–987*f* (*see also* Excretory systems; Kidneys)
    limb formation in, 1056–1057*f*, 1058*f*
    mammals, 735*f*–741*f*, 742
    mechanoreceptors for hearing and equilibrium in, 1106*f*–1110*f* (*see also* Sensory systems)
    neuroendocrine signaling in, 1002*f*–1005*f*
    organogenesis in, 1049*f*
    origins of bone and teeth in, 719
    phylogeny of, 676–677*f*
    small intestine surface area in, 689*f*
    tetrapods and development of limbs in, 724*f*–727*f*
    visual systems of, 1112*f*–1116*f*, 1117
Vertical layering, terrestrial biome, 1166
Vertical transmission, viral, 405
Vervet monkeys, 1142*f*
Vesicles, **104**
    abiotically produced, as protocells, 521*f*–522
    in endomembrane system, 104
    in exocytosis and endocytosis, 137–138*f*
    in plant cytokinesis, 239–240*f*
    self-replicating RNA in, 522
    transport, 105–106*f*, 107
Vessel elements, 642, **759***f*
Vessels, **759***f*
Vessels, blood. *See* Blood vessels
Vessels, lymph, 927*f*
Vestibular glands, 1021*f*
Vestigial structures, **474**
Viagra, 221, 995–996, 998, 1020, 1076
Vibrio cholerae, 221, 583
Vietnam, 1254*f*–1255*f*
Viewpoints, science and diverse, 23–24
Villi, 689*f*, **904***f*
Viral envelopes, 394*f*–**395**, 398–399*f*
Viral integration, 388
Viral movement proteins, 796*f*
Virchow, Rudolf, 232
Viroids, **405**
Virtual plants, computer-generated, 770
Virulent phages, 396*f*–**397***f*
Viruses, **314, 392**
    analyzing sequence-based phylogenetic trees to understand evolution of, 404

cancer-causing, 968
    in cancer development, 388
    cellular RNAi pathway and, 375
    classes of animal, 398*t*
    discovery of, 393*f*
    emerging, 402–403*f*, 404–405, 406*f*
    evolution of, 400
    features of replicative cycles of, 395*f*–396
    host range of, 395
    importance of, 392*f*–393
    infection of bacterial cells by, 313–314*f*, 315
    influenza (*see* Influenza viruses)
    latency of, 966–967
    as pathogens, 392*f*–393, 394*f*, 401*f*, 402–403*f*, 404–405, 406*f*
    rapid reproduction of, as source of genetic variation, 483
    replicative cycles of animal, 398–399*f*, 400, 401*f*
    replicative cycles of phages as, 396*f*–397*f*, 398
    structure of, 394*f*–395
    viral movement proteins of plant, 796
Visceral mass, **692**–693*f*
Visible light, **190***f*
Visual communication, 1136*f*
Visual cortex, 1115*f*
Visual pigments, 1113*f*, 1116
Visual systems
    color vision in, 1115–1116*f*
    compound eyes in, 1111*f*–1112
    evolution of light detectors in, 1111*f*–1113*f*
    gene therapy for vision in, 1116*f*
    light-detecting organs in, 1111*f*
    sensory transduction in, 1114*f*
    single-lens eyes in, 1112–1113
    structure of human eyes in, 1112*f*–1113*f*
    visual fields and focusing in, 1116*f*–1117
    visual information processing in brain in, 1115*f*
    visual information processing in retina in, 1114–1115*f*
Vital capacity, **939**
Vital statistics, population, 1186–1187*f*, 1188*f*–1189, 1190
Vitamin A deficiencies, 832, 896
Vitamin C, 894
Vitamin D, 998, 1006*f*
Vitamins, 156, **894**
    deficiencies of, 896
    effects of supplementation of, on neural tube defects in, 896*f*
    essential, 894*t*
    as lipid-soluble hormones, 998
    parathyroid hormone and, 1006*f*
Vitelline layer, 1039*f*
Vitellogenin, 997*f*–998
Vitreous humor, 1112*f*
Viviparous organisms, **721**
Vocal cords, 936–937
Vocal folds, 936–937
Vocalization, *FOXP2* gene and, 454*f*–455
Vogt, Walther, 1051–1052*f*
Volcanic springs, 580*f*
Volcanism, 630*f*
Volcanoes, 57, 58, 520*f*, 534–535
Voles, 1150*f*–1151
Voltage-gated ion channels, 217*f*, 1066*f*–**1067***f*, 1068*f*–1071*f*
Volume, 99, 1108
Volume–surface area relationships, 98*f*
Voluntary contraception, population growth and, 1202
Volutidae family, 532
Volvox, 591*f*, 603*f*
von Frisch, Karl, 1134, 1136
von Humboldt, Alexander, 1226
Vulva, **1020**–1021*f*

W

Waggle dance, honeybee, 1136–1137*f*
Wagler's pit viper, 731*f*
Waists, chromatid, 234
Walking, 1129
Wallace, Alfred Russel, 463*f*, 467, 1226
Walrus, 878*f*
Warming, global. *See* Global climate change

Warren, Robin, 902
Washington, Earl, 431*f*
Wasps, 706*f*, 863*f*, 1140*f*
Waste, toxic. *See* Toxic waste
Wastes, nitrogenous. *See* Nitrogenous wastes
Water
    acidic and basic conditions of, and living organisms, 51–52*f*, 53
    acidification as threat to quality of, 53*f*–54
    albatross drinking of salty, 971*f*
    biomanipulation and quality of, 1221
    in blood plasma, 928*f*
    cohesion of molecules and transport of, in plants, 45–46*f*
    conduction of, in plant cells, 759*f*
    conservation of, by kidneys, 983–984*f*, 985*f*–986*f*
    covalent bonding of, 36*f*–37*f*, 45*f*
    evolution of life on planets with, 50*f*
    floating of ice on liquid, 48*f*
    forms of, and importance of, to life on Earth, 44
    fruit and seed dispersal by, 826*f*
    hydrogen bonds and, 39*f*
    imbibition of, by seeds, 823
    ions in, 38
    irrigation with, 802
    latitudinal gradients and evapotranspiration of, 1226*f*
    as limiting factor on human population size, 1205
    maximizing body surface area and uptake of, 689*f*
    moderation of temperature by, 46–47*f*, 48
    molecular shape of, 39*f*
    molluscs and pollution of, 696
    plant adaptations for reducing evaporative loss of, 792–793*f*
    in plant composition, 803
    plant response to submergence in, 857
    regulation of transpiration and plant loss of, 790–791*f*, 792
    root architecture and acquisition of, 781
    seed dispersal by, 639*f*
    as solvent of life, 48–49*f*, 50
    species distributions and availability of, 1180
    splitting of, in photosynthesis, 188*f*
    transport of, across plant plasma membranes, 782–84, 785*f*
    transport of, from roots to shoots via xylem, 786–787*f*, 788*f*–789*f*, 790
Water balance
    effects of osmosis on, 131*f*–133*f*
    hormonal regulation of, 988*f*–990*f*
    in insects, 979*f*–980
    nitrogenous wastes and, 976
    osmoregulation of, 972*f*–974*f*, 975–976*f*
Water bears, 683*f*
Water bodies, climate and, 1162*f*–1163*f*
Water bugs, 1017*f*
Water conservation
    kidney adaptations for, 985*f*–986*f*
    kidney role in, 983–984*f*, 985
Water cycle, 1244*f*
Water fleas, 442*t*, 1015, 1193*f*–1194
Water lily, 644*f*
Water potential, **782**–783*f*, 784–785*f*
Water scorpions, 702*f*
Water vascular system, **707**–708*f*
Water-soluble hormones, 996*f*, 997*f*
Water-soluble vitamins, 894*t*
Water vapor, 44
Water vascular system, **707**–708*f*
Watkinson, Andrew, 1197*f*
Watson, James, 3, 23, 312*f*, 316*f*–318*f*, 319*f*
Wavelengths, electromagnetic, **190***f*–192*f*
Wawona Sequoia, 768*f*
WD40 domains, 439*f*–440
Weak acids, 51
Weather, population fluctuations and, 1199*f*–1200. *See also* Climate
Weathering, rock, 623
Web of life, 564*f*
Weddell seals, 943*f*
Weeds, transgene escape and, 833
Weevils, 706*f*
Weight, mass vs., 29*n*
Welch, Allison, 494*f*

Welwitschia, 636*f*
Wernicke, Karl, 1092
Wernicke's area, 1092*f*
Westemeier, Ronald, 1262*f*
Western garter snakes, 1150*f*
West Indian manatee, 1213*f*
West Nile virus, 395, 402
Wetlands, **1173***f*, 1256
Whales, 88*f*, 475*f*–476*f*, 550–551*f*, 704, 1259
Wheat, 509, 589, 645, 1198*f*
Whisk ferns, 625–626*f*, 627
White-band disease, 1228
White blood cells. *See* Leukocytes (white blood cells)
White-crowned sparrows, 1142
White matter, **1082***f*
White rhinoceros, 1194*f*
White-tailed deer, 1266
Whole-genome shotgun approach, DNA sequencing, 437*f*–438, 441*f*–442, 446, 651
Whooper swans, 44*f*
Whooping cough, 215*f*
Whorled phyllotaxy, 780
Widow's peak pedigree analysis case, 282*f*–283
Wieschaus, Eric, 380–381
Wildebeest, 1135*f*
Wildfires, 1166
Wild mustard, artificial selection and, 469*f*
Wild tobacco plants, 863*f*
Wild types, **294***f*
Wilkins, Maurice, 316, 318
Wilson, E. O., 1154, 1226–1227*f*, 1256*f*, 1257, 1277
Wilting, **784**, 792, 846, 857
Wind
    dispersal of mosses by, 621
    flower pollination by, 820*f*
    fruit and seed dispersal by, 826*f*
    global patterns of, 1160*f*
    seed dispersal by, 639*f*
Windpipes, 12*f*
Winged fruits and seeds, 826*f*
Wings
    bat, as evolutionary adaptation, 14*f*
    bat vs. bird, 552
    bird, 732*f*–733
    evolution of, 673
    flight muscles and, 1130
    insect, 704–705*f*, 706*f*

muscle contraction and insect, 1126
    pterosaur, 730
    seed, 639*f*
Wireframe models, 79*f*
Wiskott-Aldrich syndrome (WAS), 227
Witchweed, 849
Wobble, **347**
Wöhler, Friedrich, 57
Wollemi pine, 637*f*
Wolves, 1199*f*–1200, 1265
Wood, 645
Wood ants, 28*f*
Woolly mammoths, 408*f*, 416, 1260–1261*f*
Work, cellular, 146*f*–150*f*
World Trade Center attack, 431
Worldwide adaptive radiations, 536–537*f*
Worms, 1127*f*

X

X chromosomes, 254–255, 296*f*–298*f*, 376, 1025, 1033
Xenarthra, 739*f*
Xeroderma pigmentosum, 326
Xerophytes, **792**–793*f*
X-linked genes, **297***f*–298
X-O sex determination system, 296*f*
X-ray crystallography, **83**–84*f*, 217, 316*f*–317
X-rays
    cancer and, 383
    mutations from, 357
Xylem, **624**, **757**, **779**
    primary growth and, 762*f*
    resource acquisition and, 779*f*
    transport of water and minerals from roots to shoots via, 786–787*f*, 788*f*–789*f*, 790
    vascular plant, 624
    in vascular tissue systems, 757
    water-conducting cells of, 759*f*
Xylem sap, **786**–787*f*, 788*f*–789*f*, 790
X-Y sex determination system, 296*f*

Y

Yamanaka, Shinya, 427*f*
Yangtze River dolphin, 1256*f*
Y chromosomes, 254–255, 296*f*–297, 993*f*, 1025
Yeast cells, 100*f*
Yeast infections, 664

Yeasts, **649**
    alcohol fermentation by, 178
    asexual reproduction in, 653*f*
    cell division in, 242*f*
    cell signaling in, 211*f*–212, 226
    expressing cloned eukaryotic genes in, 416–417
    fungi as, 649, 664
    human uses of, 664–665
    model organism (*see Saccharomyces cerevisiae* (yeast))
Yellowfin tuna, 723*f*
Yellow jackets, 1212*f*
Yellowstone National Park
    ecosystem edges in, 1266*f*
    extreme thermophiles in, 580*f*–581
    forest fire disturbance of, 1157*f*, 1223*f*
    grizzly bear population in, 1263*f*, 1268
    Taq polymerase from bacterium in, 1257
Y-linked genes, 297
Yolk, **1042***f*–1043
Yolk sac, 729*f*, 1047*f*
Yucca, 820*f*

Z

Zambia, 1259
Zea mays (corn), 436*f*, 442*t*, 645, 771*f*
Zeatin, 844
Zeaxanthin, 851
Zebra finches, 1146*f*–1147*f*
Zebrafish model organism, 23
Zebra mussels, 1258
Zero population growth (ZPG), **1191**, 1202, 1205
Zona pellucida, **1041***f*
Zonation, aquatic, 1171*f*–1172*f*
Zoned reserves, **1268***f*–1269
Zone of cell division, 761*f*–762
Zone of differentiation, 761*f*–762
Zone of elongation, 761*f*–762
Zone of polarizing activity (ZPA), **1056***f*–1057*f*, 1058
Zoonotic pathogens, **1228**–1229*f*
Zoospores, 598, **656***f*
Z-W sex determination system, 296*f*
Zygentoma (silverfish), 706*f*
Zygomycetes, 655*f*, **656***f*–657*f*
Zygosporangium, **657***f*
Zygotes, **255***f*–256, **1014**, 1028*f*